# Weiss Ratings' Guide to Health Insurers

# Weiss Ratings' Guide to Health Insurers

A Quarterly Compilation of Health
Insurance Company Ratings and Analyses

**Summer 2018**



**GREY HOUSE PUBLISHING**

Weiss Ratings
4400 Northcorp Parkway
Palm Beach Gardens, FL 33410
561-627-3300



WeissRatings
Independent. Unbiased. Accurate. Trusted.

Published by Grey House Publishing, Inc., located at 4919 Route 22, Amenia, NY 12501; telephone 518-789-8700. Grey House Publishing neither guarantees the accuracy of the data contained herein nor assumes any responsibility for errors, omissions or discrepancies. Grey House Publishing accepts no payment for listing; inclusion in the publication of any organization, agency, institution, publication, service or individual does not imply endorsement of the publisher.

Grey House Publishing
4919 Route 22
PO Box 56
Amenia, NY 12501-0056

Edition No. 93, Summer 2018

ISBN: 978-1-68217-798-3
ISSN: 2158-5938

# Contents

# Terms and Conditions

This document is prepared strictly for the confidential use of our customer(s). It has been provided to you at your specific request. It is not directed to, or intended for distribution to or use by, any person or entity who is a citizen or resident of or located in any locality, state, country or other jurisdiction where such distribution, publication, availability or use would be contrary to law or regulation or which would subject Weiss Ratings or its affiliates to any registration or licensing requirement within such jurisdiction.

No part of the analysts' compensation was, is, or will be, directly or indirectly, related to the specific recommendations or views expressed in this research report.

This document is not intended for the direct or indirect solicitation of business. Weiss Ratings, LLC and its affiliates disclaims any and all liability to any person or entity for any loss or damage caused, in whole or in part, by any error (negligent or otherwise) or other circumstances involved in, resulting from or relating to the procurement, compilation, analysis, interpretation, editing, transcribing, publishing and/or dissemination or transmittal of any information contained herein.

Weiss Ratings has not taken any steps to ensure that the securities or investment vehicle referred to in this report are suitable for any particular investor. The investment or services contained or referred to in this report may not be suitable for you and it is recommended that you consult an independent investment advisor if you are in doubt about such investments or investment services. Nothing in this report constitutes investment, legal, accounting or tax advice or a representation that any investment or strategy is suitable or appropriate to your individual circumstances or otherwise constitutes a personal recommendation to you.

The ratings and other opinions contained in this document must be construed solely as statements of opinion from Weiss Ratings, LLC, and not statements of fact. Each rating or opinion must be weighed solely as a factor in your choice of an institution and should not be construed as a recommendation to buy, sell or otherwise act with respect to the particular product or company involved.

Past performance should not be taken as an indication or guarantee of future performance, and no representation or warranty, expressed or implied, is made regarding future performance. Information, opinions and estimates contained in this report reflect a judgment at its original date of publication and are subject to change without notice. Weiss Ratings offers a notification service for rating changes on companies you specify. For more information visit WeissRatings.com or call 1-877-934-7778. The price, value and income from any of the securities or financial instruments mentioned in this report can fall as well as rise.



**Message To Insurers**

All data on insurers filing a Health financial statement received on or before March 15, 2018 has been considered or incorporated into this edition of the Directory. If there are particular circumstances which you believe could affect your rating, please use the online survey (http://weissratings.com/survey/) or e-mail Weiss Ratings (insurancesurvey@weissinc.com) with documentation to support your request. If warranted, we will make every effort to incorporate the changes in our next edition.

# Welcome to Weiss Ratings'
# *Guide to Health Insurers*

Most people automatically assume their insurance company will survive, year after year. However, prudent consumers and professionals realize that in this world of shifting risks, the solvency of insurance companies can't be taken for granted.

If you are looking for accurate, unbiased ratings and data to help you choose health insurance for yourself, your family, your company, or your clients, *Weiss Ratings Guide to Health Insurers* gives you precisely what you need.

In fact, it's the only source that currently provides ratings and analyses on over 1,000 health insurers.

## Weiss Ratings' Mission Statement

Weiss Ratings' mission is to empower consumers, professionals, and institutions with high quality advisory information for selecting or monitoring a financial services company or financial investment.

In doing so, Weiss Ratings will adhere to the highest ethical standards by maintaining our independent, unbiased outlook and approach to advising our customers.

## Why rely on Weiss Ratings?

Weiss Ratings provides fair, objective ratings to help professionals and consumers alike make educated purchasing decisions.

At Weiss Ratings, integrity is number one. Weiss Ratings never takes a penny from insurance companies for its ratings. And, we publish Weiss Safety Ratings without regard for insurers' preferences. However, other rating agencies like A.M. Best, Fitch, Moody's, and Standard & Poor's are paid by insurance companies for their ratings and may even suppress unfavorable ratings at an insurer's request.

Our ratings are more frequently reviewed and updated than any other ratings. You can be sure that the information you receive is accurate and current – providing you with advance warning of financial vulnerability early enough to do something about it.

Other rating agencies focus primarily on a company's current claims paying ability and consider only mild economic adversity. Weiss Ratings also considers these issues, but in addition, our analysis covers a company's ability to deal with severe economic adversity and a sharp increase in claims.

Our use of more rigorous standards stems from the viewpoint that an insurance company's obligations to its policyholders should not depend on favorable business conditions. An insurer must be able to honor its policy commitments in bad times as well as good.

Our rating scale, from A to F, is easy to understand. Only a few outstanding companies receive an A (Excellent) rating, although there are many to choose from within the B (Good) category. An even larger group falls into the broad average range which receives C (Fair) ratings. Companies that demonstrate marked vulnerabilities receive either D (Weak) or E (Very Weak) ratings.

# How to Use This Guide

The purpose of the *Guide to Health Insurers* is to provide policyholders and prospective policy purchasers with a reliable source of insurance company ratings and analyses on a timely basis. We realize that the financial strength of an insurer is an important factor to consider when making the decision to purchase a policy or change companies. The ratings and analyses in this Guide can make that evaluation easier when you are considering:

- Medical reimbursement insurance
- Managed health care (PPOs and HMOs)
- Disability income
- Long-term care (nursing home) insurance

This Guide includes ratings for health insurers such as commercial for-profit insurers, mutual insurers, Blue Cross/Blue Shield plans, and for-profit and not-for-profit insurers. This is the only source of ratings on many of these companies.

In addition, many companies that offer health insurance also offer life, property or liability insurance. If you are shopping for any of those types of coverage, please refer to either our *Guide to Life and Annuity Insurers* or our *Guide to Property and Casualty Insurers.*

The rating for a particular company indicates our opinion regarding that company's ability to meet its commitments to the policyholder – not only under current economic conditions, but also during a declining economy or in the event of a sharp increase in claims. Such an increase in claims and related expenses may be triggered by any number of occurrences including rising medical costs, malpractice lawsuits, out-of-control administrative expenses, or the unexpected spread of a disease such as AIDS. The safest companies, however, should be prepared to deal with harsh and unforeseen circumstances.

To use this Guide most effectively, we recommend you follow the steps outlined below:

**Step 1** To ensure you evaluate the correct company, verify the company's exact name and state of domicile as it was given to you or appears on your policy. Many companies have similar names but are not related to one another, so you want to make sure the company you look up is really the one you are interested in evaluating.

**Step 2** Turn to Section I, the Index of Companies, and locate the company you are evaluating. This section contains all health insurance companies analyzed by Weiss Ratings including those that did not receive a Safety Rating. It is sorted alphabetically by the name of the company and shows the state of domicile following the name for additional verification.

**Step 3** Once you have located your specific company, the first column after the state of domicile shows its Weiss Safety Rating. See *About Weiss Safety Ratings* for information about what this rating means. If the rating has changed since the last issue of this Guide, a downgrade will be indicated with a down triangle ▼ to the left of the company name; an upgrade will be indicated with an up triangle ▲.

**Step 4** Following Weiss Safety Rating is some additional information about the company such as its type, size and capital level. Refer to the introduction of Section I, to see what each of these factors measures.

**Step 5** Some insurers have a bullet • following the domicile state in Section I. This means that more detailed information about the company is available in Section II.

If the company you are evaluating is identified with a bullet, turn to Section II, the Analysis of Largest Companies , and locate it there (otherwise skip to step 9). Section II contains all health insurers and Blue Cross/Blue Shield plans plus the largest property & casualty and life & annutiy insurers offering health insurance rated by Weiss, regardless of rating. It too is sorted alphabetically by the name of the company.

**Step 6** Once you have identified your company in Section II, you will find its Safety Rating and a description of the rating immediately to the right of the company name. Then, below the company name is a description of the various rating factors that were considered in assigning the company's rating. These factors and the information below them are designed to give you a better feel for the company and its strengths and weaknesses. Refer to the introduction of Section II to get a better understanding of what each of these factors means.

**Step 7** To the right, you will find a five-year summary of the company's Safety Rating, capitalization and income. Look for positive or negative trends in these data. Below the five-year summary, we have included a graphic illustration of the most crucial factor or factors impacting the company's rating. Again, the Section II introduction provides an overview of the content of each graph or table.

**Step 8** If the company you are evaluating is a Medicare HMO, you can also look it up in Section VII to get some idea of the quality of service being offered. Here you can see the number of complaints against a company that have reached the federal review level based on the most recent data available.

**Step 9** If you are interested in long-term care insurance, you can turn to Section V and get a listing of long-term care insurers. To compare long-term care policies see the Long-Term Care Insurance Planner within the Appendix.

**Step 10** If the company you are evaluating is not highly rated and you want to find an insurer with a higher rating, turn to the page in Section IV that has your state's name at the top. This section contains those Recommended Companies (rating of A+, A, A- or B+) that are licensed to underwrite health insurance in your state, sorted by rating. From here you can select a company and then refer back to Sections I and II to analyze it.

**Step 11** If you decide that you would like to contact one of Weiss Recommended Companies about obtaining a policy or for additional information, refer to Section III where you will find all of Weiss recommended companies listed alphabetically by name. Following each company's name is its address and phone number to assist you in making contact.

**Step 12** Many consumers have reported to us the difficulties they have encountered in finding a Recommended Company that offers the best pricing and benefits. Therefore, when considering medical reimbursement or managed care coverage, you may want to consider other companies that have received a good (B or B-) rating even though they did not make Weiss Recommended List. However, for long-term policies such as nursing home care or disability income, we recommend sticking to companies with a rating of B+ or higher.

**Step 13** In order to use Weiss Safety Ratings most effectively, we strongly recommend you consult the Important Warnings and Cautions. These are more than just "standard disclaimers." They are very important factors you should be aware of before using this Guide. If you have any questions regarding the precise meaning of specific terms used in the Guide, refer to the Glossary.

**Step 14** Make sure you stay up to date with the latest information available since the publication of this Guide. For information on how to set up a rating change notification service, acquire follow-up reports, or receive a more in-depth analysis of an individual company, visit www.weissratings.com or call 1-877-934-7778.

Data Sources: Annual and quarterly statutory statements filed with state insurance commissioners and data provided by the insurance companies being rated. Medicare HMO complaint data were provided by the Centers for Medicare and Medicaid Services: The Center for Health Dispute Resolution, (formerly known as Health Care Financing Administration), and is reprinted here. The National Association of Insurance Commissioners has provided some of the raw data. Any analyses or conclusions are not provided or endorsed by the NAIC.

Date of data analyzed: September 30, 2017 unless otherwise noted

# About Weiss Safety Ratings

The Weiss Ratings of insurers are based upon the annual and quarterly financial statements filed with state insurance commissioners. This data may be supplemented by information that we request from the insurance companies themselves. However, if a company chooses not to provide supplemental data, we reserve the right to rate the company based exclusively on publicly available data.

The Weiss Ratings are based on a complex analysis of hundreds of factors that are synthesized into a series of indexes: capitalization, investment safety (life, health and annuity companies only), reserve adequacy (property and casualty companies only), profitability, liquidity, and stability. These indexes are then used to arrive at a letter grade rating. A weak score on any one index can result in a low rating, as financial problems can be caused by any one of a number of factors, such as inadequate capital, unpredictable claims experience, poor liquidity, speculative investments, inadequate reserving, or consistent operating losses.

Our **Capital Index** gauges capital adequacy in terms of each insurer's ability to handle a variety of business and economic scenarios as they may impact investment performance, claims experience, persistency, and market position. The index combines two Risk-Adjusted Capital ratios as well as a leverage test that examines pricing risk.

Our **Investment Safety Index** measures the exposure of the company's investment portfolio to loss of principal and/or income due to default and market risks. Each investment area is rated by a factor that takes into consideration both quality and liquidity. (This factor is measured as a separate index only for life, health, and annuity insurers.)

Our **Reserve Adequacy Index** measures the adequacy of the company's reserves and its ability to accurately anticipate the level of claims it will receive. (This factor is measured as a separate index only for property and casualty insurers.)

Our **Profitability Index** measures the soundness of the company's operations and the contribution of profits to the company's financial strength. The profitability index is a composite of five sub-factors: 1) gain or loss on operations; 2) consistency of operating results; 3) impact of operating results on surplus; 4) adequacy of investment income as compared to the needs of policy reserves (life, health and annuity companies only); and 5) expenses in relation to industry norms for the types of policies that the company offers.

Our **Liquidity Index** evaluates a company's ability to raise the necessary cash to settle claims and honor cash withdrawal obligations. We model various cash flow scenarios, applying liquidity tests to determine how the company might fare in the event of an unexpected spike in claims and/or a run on policy surrenders.

Our **Stability Index** integrates a number of sub-factors that affect consistency (or lack thereof) in maintaining financial strength over time. These sub-factors will vary depending on the type of insurance company being evaluated but may include such things as 1) risk diversification in terms of company size, group size, number of policies in force, types of policies written, and use of reinsurance; 2) deterioration of operations as reported in critical asset, liability, income and expense items, such as surrender rates and premium volume; 3) years in operation; 4) former problem areas where, despite recent improvement, the company has yet to establish a record of stable performance over a suitable period of time; 5) a substantial shift in the company's operations; 6) potential instabilities such as reinsurance quality, asset/liability matching, and sources of capital; and 7) relationships with holding companies and affiliates.

In order to help guarantee our objectivity, we reserve the right to publish ratings expressing our opinion of a company's financial stability based exclusively on publicly available data and our own proprietary standards for safety.

Each of these indexes is measured according to the following range of values.

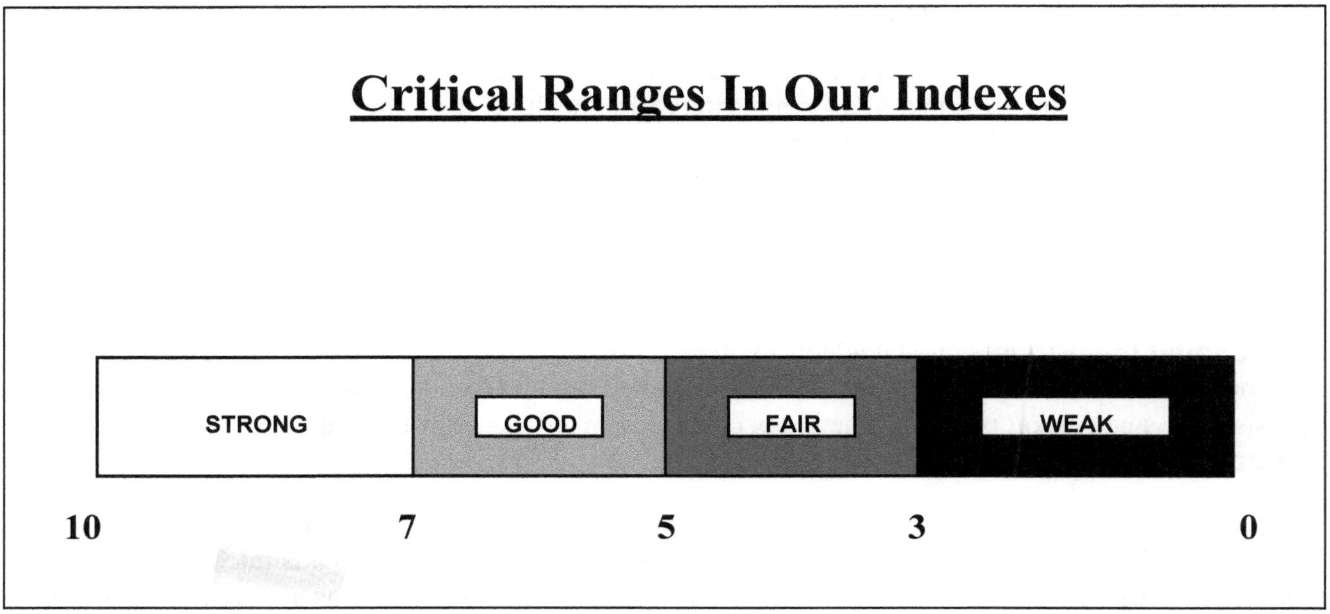

# What Our Ratings Mean

A **Excellent.** The company offers excellent financial security. It has maintained a conservative stance in its investment strategies, business operations and underwriting commitments. While the financial position of any company is subject to change, we believe that this company has the resources necessary to deal with severe economic conditions.

B **Good.** The company offers good financial security and has the resources to deal with a variety of adverse economic conditions. It comfortably exceeds the minimum levels for all of our rating criteria, and is likely to remain healthy for the near future. However, in the event of a severe recession or major financial crisis, we feel that this assessment should be reviewed to make sure that the firm is still maintaining adequate financial strength.

C **Fair.** The company offers fair financial security and is currently stable. But during an economic downturn or other financial pressures, we feel it may encounter difficulties in maintaining its financial stability.

D **Weak.** The company currently demonstrates what, in our opinion, we consider to be significant weaknesses which could negatively impact policyholders. In an unfavorable economic environment, these weaknesses could be magnified.

E **Very Weak.** The company currently demonstrates what we consider to be significant weaknesses and has also failed some of the basic tests that we use to identify fiscal stability. Therefore, even in a favorable economic environment, it is our opinion that policyholders could incur significant risks.

F **Failed.** The company is deemed failed if it is either 1) under supervision of an insurance regulatory authority; 2) in the process of rehabilitation; 3) in the process of liquidation; or 4) voluntarily dissolved after disciplinary or other regulatory action by an insurance regulatory authority.

\+ The **plus sign** is an indication that the company is in the upper third of the letter grade.

\- The **minus sign** is an indication that the company is in the lower third of the letter grade.

U **Unrated.** The company is unrated for one or more of the following reasons: (1) total assets are less than $1 million; (2) premium income for the current year was less than $100,000; (3) the company functions almost exclusively as a holding company rather than as an underwriter; (4) in our opinion, we do not have enough information to reliably issue a rating.

# How Our Ratings Differ From Those of Other Services

Weiss Safety Ratings are conservative and consumer oriented. We use tougher standards than other rating agencies because our system is specifically designed to inform risk-averse consumers about the financial strength of health insurers.

Our rating scale (A to F) is easy to understand by the general public. Users can intuitively understand that an A+ rating is at the top of the scale rather than in the middle like some of the other rating agencies.

Other rating agencies give top ratings more generously so that most companies receive excellent ratings.

More importantly, other rating agencies focus primarily on a company's *current* claims paying ability or consider only relatively mild economic adversity. We also consider these scenarios but extend our analysis to cover a company's ability to deal with severe economic adversity and potential liquidity problems. This stems from the viewpoint that an insurance company's obligations to its policyholders should not be contingent upon a healthy economy. The company must be capable of honoring its policy commitments in bad times as well.

Looking at the insurance industry as a whole, we note that several major rating firms have poor historical track records in identifying troubled companies. The 1980s saw a persistent decline in capital ratios, increased holdings of risky investments in the life and health industry as well as recurring long-term claims liabilities in the property and casualty industry. The insurance industry experienced similar issues before and during the Great Recession of 2007-2009. Despite these clear signs that insolvency risk was rising, other rating firms failed to downgrade at-risk insurance companies. Instead, they often rated companies by shades of excellence, understating the gravity of potential problems.

Other ratings agencies have not issued clear warnings that the ordinary consumer can understand. Few, if any, companies receive "weak" or "poor" ratings. Surely, weak companies do exist. However, the other rating agencies apparently do not view themselves as consumer advocates with the responsibility of warning the public about the risks involved in doing business with such companies.

Additionally, these firms will at times agree *not* to issue a rating if a company denies them permission to do so. In short, too often insurance rating agencies work hand-in-glove with the companies they rate.

At Weiss Ratings, although we seek to maintain good relationships with the firms, we owe our primary obligation to the consumer, not the industry. We reserve the right to rate companies based on publicly-available data and make the necessary conservative assumptions when companies choose not to provide additional data we might request.

| Comparison of Insurance Company Rating Agency Scales | | | | |
|---|---|---|---|---|
| **Weiss Ratings [a]** | **Best [a]** | **S&P** | **Moody's** | **Fitch** |
| A+, A, A- | A++, A+ | AAA | Aaa | AAA |
| B+, B, B- | A, A- | AA+, AA AA- | Aa1, Aa2, Aa3 | AA+, AA, AA- |
| C+, C, C- | B++, B+, | A+, A, A-,<br>BBB+, BBB, BBB- | A1, A2, A3,<br>Baa1, Baa2, Baa3 | A+, A, A-,<br>BBB+, BBB, BBB- |
| D+, D, D- | B, B-<br>C++, C+, C, C- | BB+, BB, BB-,<br>B+, B, B- | Ba1, Ba2, Ba3,<br>B1, B2, B3 | BB+, BB, BB-,<br>B+, B, B- |
| E+, E, E-<br>F | D<br>E, F | CCC<br>R | Caa, Ca, C | CCC+, CCC, CCC-<br>DD |

[a] Weiss Ratings and Best use additional symbols to designate that they recognize an insurer's existence but do not provide a rating. These symbols are not included in this table.

# Rate of Insurance Company Failures

Weiss Ratings provides quarterly safety ratings for thousands of insurance companies each year. Weiss Ratings strives for fairness and objectivity in its ratings and analyses, ensuring that each company receives the rating that most accurately depicts its current financial status, and more importantly, its ability to deal with severe economic adversity and a sharp increase in claims. Weiss Ratings has every confidence that its safety ratings provide an accurate representation of a company's stability.

In order for these ratings to be of any true value, it is important that they prove accurate over time. One way to determine the accuracy of a rating is to examine those insurance companies that have failed, and their respective Safety Ratings. A high percentage of failed companies with "A" ratings would indicate that Weiss Ratings is not being conservative enough with its "secure" ratings, while conversely, a low percentage of failures with "vulnerable" ratings would show that Weiss Ratings is overly conservative.

Over the past 28 years (1989–2016) Weiss Ratings has rated 627 insurance companies, for all industries, that subsequently failed. The chart below shows the number of failed companies in each rating category, the average number of companies rated in each category per year, and the percentage of annual failures for each letter grade.

| | Safety Rating | Number of Failed Companies | Average Number of Companies Rated per year | Percentage of Failed companies per year (by ratings category)* |
|---|---|---|---|---|
| Secure | A | 1 | 154 | 0.02% |
| | B | 6 | 1,105 | 0.02% |
| | C | 70 | 1,613 | 0.16% |
| Vulnerable | D | 276 | 751 | 1.31% |
| | E | 274 | 217 | 4.50% |

A=Excellent, B=Good, C=Fair, D=Weak, E=Very Weak

On average, only 0.10% of the companies Weiss rates as "secure" fail each year. On the other hand, an average of 2.03% of the companies Weiss rates as "vulnerable" fail annually. That means that a company rated by Weiss Ratings as "Vulnerable" is almost 21.2 times more likely to fail than a company rated as "Secure".

When considering a Weiss Safety Rating, one can be sure that they are getting the most fair, objective, and accurate financial rating available anywhere.

*Percentage of Failed companies per year = (Number of Failed Companies) / [(Average Number of Companies Rated per year) x (years in study)]

# What Does Average Mean?

At Weiss Ratings, we consider the words average and fair to mean just that – average and fair. So when we assign our ratings to insurers, a large percentage of companies receive an average C rating. That way, you can be sure that a company receiving Weiss B or A rating is truly above average. Likewise, you can feel confident that companies with D or E ratings are truly below average.

**Current Weiss Ratings Distribution for Health Insurers**

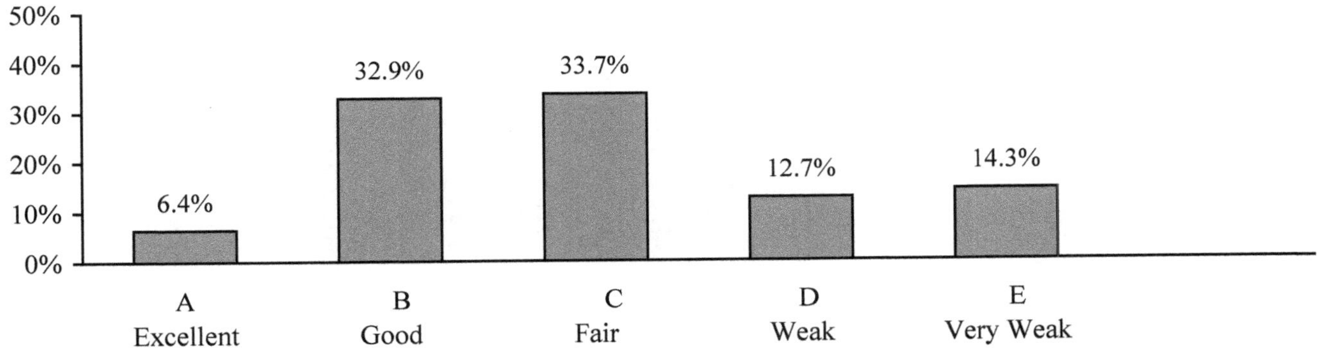

# Important Warnings and Cautions

1. A rating alone cannot tell the whole story. Please read the explanatory information contained in this publication. It is provided in order to give you an understanding of our rating philosophy, as well as paint a more complete picture of how we arrive at our opinion of a company's strengths and weaknesses.

2. Weiss Safety Ratings represent our opinion of a company's insolvency risk. As such, a high rating means we feel that the company has less chance of running into financial difficulties. A high rating is not a guarantee of solvency nor is a low rating a prediction of insolvency. Weiss Safety Ratings are not deemed to be a recommendation concerning the purchase or sale of the securities of any insurance company that is publicly owned.

3. Company performance is only one factor in determining a rating. Conditions in the marketplace and overall economic conditions are additional factors that may affect the company's financial strength. Therefore, a rating upgrade or downgrade does not necessarily reflect changes in the company's profits, capital or other financial measures, but may be due to external factors. Likewise, changes in Weiss indexes may reflect changes in our risk assessment of business or economic conditions as well as changes in company performance.

4. All firms that have the same Safety Rating should be considered to be essentially equal in strength. This is true regardless of any differences in the underlying numbers which might appear to indicate greater strengths. Weiss Safety Rating already takes into account a number of lesser factors which, due to space limitations, cannot be included in this publication.

5. A good rating requires consistency. If a company is excellent on four indicators and fair on one, the company may receive a fair rating. This requirement is necessary due to the fact that fiscal problems can arise from any *one* of several causes including speculative investments, inadequate capital resources or operating losses.

6. We are an independent rating agency and do not depend on the cooperation of the companies we rate. Our data are derived from annual and quarterly financial statements that we obtain from federal regulators and filings with state insurance commissioners. The latter may be supplemented by information insurance companies voluntarily provide upon request. Although we seek to maintain an open line of communication with the companies, we do not grant them the right to stop or influence publication of the ratings. This policy stems from the fact that this publication is designed for the protection of the consumer.

7. Affiliated companies do not automatically receive the same rating. We recognize that a troubled company may expect financial support from its parent or affiliates. Weiss Safety Ratings reflect our opinion of the measure of support that may become available to a subsidiary , if the subsidiary were to experience serious financial difficulties. In the case of a strong parent and a weaker subsidiary, the affiliate relationship will generally result in a higher rating for the subsidiary than it would have on a stand-alone basis. Seldom, however, would the rating be brought up to the level of the parent. This treatment is appropriate because we do not assume the parent would have either the resources or the will to "bail out" a troubled subsidiary during a severe economic crisis. Even when there is a binding legal obligation for a parent corporation to honor the policy obligations of its subsidiaries, the possibility exists that the subsidiary could be sold and lose its parental support. Therefore, it is quite common for one affiliate to have a higher rating than another. This is another reason why it is especially important that you have the precise name of the company you are evaluating.

# Section I

# Index of Companies

An analysis of over 1,439 rated and unrated

**U.S. Health Insurers**

Companies are listed in alphabetical order.

# Section I Contents

This section contains the information about company type, size and capital level for all rated and unrated health insurers analyzed by Weiss Ratings.

1. **Insurance Company Name** The legally-registered name, which can sometimes differ from the name that the company uses for advertising. If you cannot find the company you are interested in, or if you have any doubts regarding the precise name, verify the information with the company before looking the name up in this Guide. Also, determine the domicile state for confirmation. (See column 2.)

2. **Domicile State** The state which has primary regulatory responsibility for the company. It may differ from the location of the company's corporate headquarters. You do not have to be living in the domicile state to purchase insurance from this firm, provided it is licensed to do business in your state.

   Also use this column to confirm that you have located the correct company. It is possible for two unrelated companies to have the same name if they are domiciled in different states.

3. **Safety Rating** Our rating is measured on a scale from A to F and considers a wide range of factors. Please see *What Our Ratings Mean* for specific descriptions of each letter grade and the following pages for information on how our ratings differ from those of other rating agencies. Most important, when using this rating, please be sure to consider the Important Warnings and Cautions regarding the ratings' limitations and the underlying assumptions.

4. **Data Date** The latest quarter-end for which we have received the company's financial statement.

5. **Total Assets** All assets admitted by state insurance regulators in millions of dollars as of the most recent quarter end. This includes investments and current business assets such as receivables from agents, reinsurers and subscribers.

   The overall size is an important factor which affects the ability of a company to manage risk. Mortality, morbidity (sickness) and investment risks can be more effectively diversified by large companies. Because the insurance business is based on probability, the number of policies must be large enough so that actuarial statistics are valid. The larger the number of policyholders, the more reliable the actuarial projections will be. A large company with a correspondingly large policy base can spread its risk and minimize the effects of claims experience that exceeds actuarial expectations.

6. **Total Premiums** The amount of insurance premiums received from policyholders as of the most recent year end. If the company issues life insurance or property insurance, those premiums are included in this figure as well.

   Generally speaking, companies with large premium volume generally have more predictable claims experience.

**7. Health Premiums**

The amount of insurance premiums received from policyholders for health policies only as of the most recent year end.

Compare this figure with Total Premiums in the previous column to see how much of the company's business relates to health coverage.

**8. Capital and Surplus**

The company's statutory net worth in millions of dollars as of the most recent quarter end. Consumers may wish to limit the size of any policy so that the policyholder's maximum benefits do not exceed approximately 1% of the company's capital and surplus. For example, when buying a policy from a company with capital and surplus of $10,000,000, the 1% limit would be $100,000. (When performing this calculation, do not forget that figures in this column are expressed in millions of dollars.)

## Critical Ranges In Our Ratios

| *Indicators* | *Strong* | *Good* | *Fair* | *Weak* |
|---|---|---|---|---|
| **Risk-Adjusted Capital Ratio #1** | — | 1.0 or more | 0.75 - 0.99 | 0.74 or less |
| **Risk-Adjusted Capital Ratio #2** | 1.0 or more | 0.75 - 0.99 | 0.5 - 0.74 | 0.49 or less |

**9. Risk-Adjusted Capital Ratio #1**

This ratio examines the adequacy of the company's capital base and whether the company has sufficient capital resources to cover potential losses which might occur in an average recession or other moderate loss scenario. Specifically, the figure cited in this column answers the question: For every dollar of capital that we feel would be needed, how many dollars in capital resources does the company actually have? (See the table above for the levels which we believe are critical.) You may find that some companies have unusually high levels of capital. This often reflects special circumstances related to the small size or unusual operations of the company.

**10. Risk-Adjusted Capital Ratio #2**

This is similar to item 9. But in this case, the question relates to whether the company has enough capital cushion to withstand a *severe* recession or other severe loss scenario. For more details on risk-adjusted capital, see the Appendix.

| INSURANCE COMPANY NAME | DOM. STATE | RATING | DATA DATE | TOTAL ASSETS ($MIL) | TOTAL PREMIUMS ($MIL) | HEALTH PREMIUMS ($MIL) | CAPITAL & SURPLUS ($MIL) | RISK ADJUSTED CAPITAL RATIO 1 | RISK ADJUSTED CAPITAL RATIO 2 |
|---|---|---|---|---|---|---|---|---|---|
| 21ST CENTURY CENTENNIAL INS CO | PA | B | 3q 2017 | 598.7 | 349.6 | 0.0 | 598.6 | 1.88 | 1.87 |
| 21ST CENTURY PREMIER INS CO | PA | B- | 3q 2017 | 287.6 | 22.9 | 0.3 | 288.1 | 4.64 | 4.55 |
| 4 EVER LIFE INS CO | IL | • B | 3q 2017 | 217.2 | 175.5 | 167.7 | 86.6 | 5.46 | 3.55 |
| AAA LIFE INS CO | MI | B | 3q 2017 | 652.5 | 812.1 | 70.6 | 157.6 | 3.15 | 1.82 |
| ABILITY INS CO | NE | D- | 3q 2017 | 1,184.4 | 75.5 | 74.9 | 20.0 | 0.64 | 0.31 |
| ABSOLUTE TOTAL CARE INC | SC | • C- | 3q 2017 | 122.2 | 492.5 | 492.5 | 62.7 | 2.32 | 1.93 |
| ACCENDO INS CO | UT | U | | -- | -- | -- | -- | -- | -- |
| ACCESS INS CO | TX | C | 3q 2017 | 214.1 | 311.3 | 0.0 | 30.6 | 0.90 | 0.78 |
| ACE AMERICAN INS CO | PA | B- | 3q 2017 | 14,088.8 | 4,345.8 | 525.6 | 2,586.3 | 1.32 | 1.02 |
| ADVANCE INS CO OF KANSAS | KS | • B+ | 3q 2017 | 58.6 | 11.6 | 3.8 | 48.5 | 3.89 | 2.56 |
| ADVANTAGE HEALTH SOLUTIONS INC | IN | F | 1q 2017 | 13.7 | 72.1 | 72.1 | 9.7 | 1.37 | 1.14 |
| ADVENTIST HEALTH PLAN INC | CA | • D | 3q 2017 | 4.4 | 26.2 | 26.2 | 2.5 | 0.85 | 0.54 |
| ADVICARE CORP | SC | • C+ | 1q 2017 | 38.0 | 77.9 | 77.9 | 35.5 | 3.32 | 2.77 |
| ▼ AEGIS SECURITY INS CO | PA | C+ | 3q 2017 | 138.4 | 137.7 | 11.8 | 55.4 | 0.78 | 0.56 |
| ▲ AETNA BETTER HEALTH (AN OHIO CORP) | OH | • B | 3q 2017 | 391.2 | 858.2 | 858.2 | 172.2 | 4.14 | 3.45 |
| AETNA BETTER HEALTH INC | IL | • B- | 3q 2017 | 984.5 | 1,539.8 | 1,539.8 | 196.3 | 2.04 | 1.70 |
| AETNA BETTER HEALTH INC (A CT CORP) | CT | U | | -- | -- | -- | -- | -- | -- |
| AETNA BETTER HEALTH INC (A LA CORP) | LA | • C+ | 3q 2017 | 213.6 | 421.9 | 421.9 | 90.8 | 3.92 | 3.27 |
| AETNA BETTER HEALTH INC (A NJ CORP) | NJ | • B+ | 3q 2017 | 136.9 | 138.0 | 138.0 | 47.9 | 9.00 | 7.50 |
| AETNA BETTER HEALTH INC (A PA CORP) | PA | • D- | 3q 2017 | 480.4 | 867.8 | 867.8 | 125.2 | 3.38 | 2.81 |
| AETNA BETTER HEALTH OF KS INC | KS | U | | -- | -- | -- | -- | -- | -- |
| AETNA BETTER HEALTH OF MICHIGAN INC | MI | • B | 3q 2017 | 120.1 | 340.2 | 340.2 | 28.2 | 1.89 | 1.58 |
| AETNA BETTER HEALTH OF MISSOURI LLC | MO | • B- | 2q 2017 | 198.5 | 780.7 | 780.7 | 111.1 | 3.30 | 2.75 |
| AETNA BETTER HEALTH OF NV INC | NV | U | | -- | -- | -- | -- | -- | -- |
| ▲ AETNA BETTER HEALTH OF TEXAS INC | TX | • B+ | 3q 2017 | 120.2 | 251.1 | 251.1 | 48.6 | 3.54 | 2.95 |
| AETNA BETTER HLTH OF KY INS CO | KY | • B+ | 3q 2017 | 489.7 | 1,111.9 | 1,111.9 | 241.3 | 3.72 | 3.10 |
| AETNA HEALTH & LIFE INS CO | CT | • B+ | 3q 2017 | 2,403.1 | 181.1 | 181.1 | 262.1 | 1.88 | 1.17 |
| AETNA HEALTH INC (A CT CORP) | CT | • C | 3q 2017 | 149.2 | 245.6 | 245.6 | 83.4 | 6.19 | 5.16 |
| AETNA HEALTH INC (A FLORIDA CORP) | FL | • B+ | 3q 2017 | 590.4 | 1,982.9 | 1,982.9 | 269.1 | 2.76 | 2.30 |
| AETNA HEALTH INC (A GEORGIA CORP) | GA | • B | 3q 2017 | 280.3 | 605.1 | 605.1 | 114.9 | 3.23 | 2.69 |
| AETNA HEALTH INC (A MAINE CORP) | ME | • B- | 3q 2017 | 36.1 | 75.3 | 75.3 | 19.7 | 3.93 | 3.27 |
| AETNA HEALTH INC (A NEW JERSEY CORP) | NJ | • B | 3q 2017 | 315.9 | 887.0 | 887.0 | 188.0 | 3.87 | 3.23 |
| AETNA HEALTH INC (A NEW YORK CORP) | NY | • C+ | 3q 2017 | 282.3 | 172.3 | 172.3 | 227.3 | 19.40 | 16.17 |
| AETNA HEALTH INC (A PA CORP) | PA | • C+ | 3q 2017 | 1,372.7 | 3,951.7 | 3,951.7 | 596.0 | 3.41 | 2.84 |
| AETNA HEALTH INC (A TEXAS CORP) | TX | • C+ | 3q 2017 | 159.1 | 430.1 | 430.1 | 77.1 | 3.13 | 2.60 |
| AETNA HEALTH INC (LA) | LA | • B- | 3q 2017 | 45.1 | 111.1 | 111.1 | 28.8 | 5.24 | 4.36 |
| AETNA HEALTH INS CO | PA | • B- | 3q 2017 | 40.4 | 34.8 | 34.8 | 34.9 | 10.00 | 8.33 |
| AETNA HEALTH INS CO OF NY | NY | • C+ | 2q 2017 | 10.3 | 0.2 | 0.2 | 10.3 | 7.74 | 6.45 |
| ▼ AETNA HEALTH OF CALIFORNIA INC | CA | • C+ | 3q 2017 | 432.6 | 1,775.7 | 1,775.7 | 109.2 | 0.97 | 0.66 |
| AETNA HEALTH OF IOWA INC | IA | • C+ | 3q 2017 | 108.3 | 240.4 | 240.4 | 40.1 | 2.64 | 2.20 |
| ▼ AETNA HEALTH OF UTAH INC | UT | • C+ | 3q 2017 | 92.5 | 293.5 | 293.5 | 41.8 | 3.55 | 2.96 |
| ▼ AETNA HEALTHASSURANCE PA INC | PA | • D | 3q 2017 | 60.5 | 71.6 | 71.6 | 9.9 | 1.89 | 1.57 |
| AETNA LIFE INS CO | CT | • B | 3q 2017 | 22,767.9 | 27,375.9 | 26,305.9 | 3,979.7 | 1.53 | 1.14 |
| AHF MCO OF GEORGIA INC | GA | U | | -- | -- | -- | -- | -- | -- |
| AIDS HEALTHCARE FOUNDATION MCO OF FL | FL | • E- | 3q 2017 | 56.5 | 121.8 | 121.8 | 5.2 | 0.31 | 0.26 |
| AIG INS CO - PR | PR | B- | 3q 2017 | 150.1 | 64.3 | 0.3 | 86.7 | 9.65 | 5.83 |
| AIG SPECIALTY INS CO | IL | C+ | 3q 2017 | 114.7 | 724.6 | 1.2 | 58.2 | 9.83 | 8.85 |
| ALAMEDA ALLIANCE FOR HEALTH | CA | F | 3q 2017 | 824.6 | 820.9 | 820.9 | 192.2 | 3.45 | 2.11 |
| ALFA LIFE INS CORP | AL | B- | 3q 2017 | 1,422.9 | 158.3 | 0.7 | 264.0 | 2.97 | 1.66 |
| ALIGNMENT HEALTH PLAN | CA | • E | 3q 2017 | 100.4 | 227.8 | 227.8 | 14.4 | 0.15 | 0.09 |
| ALL SAVERS INS CO | IN | • C | 3q 2017 | 1,368.8 | 1,615.9 | 1,615.9 | 1,240.2 | 11.79 | 8.41 |
| ALL SAVERS LIFE INS CO OF CA | CA | C+ | 3q 2017 | 6.3 | 0.2 | 0.2 | 6.2 | 3.49 | 3.14 |

| INSURANCE COMPANY NAME | DOM. STATE | RATING | DATA DATE | TOTAL ASSETS ($MIL) | TOTAL PREMIUMS ($MIL) | HEALTH PREMIUMS ($MIL) | CAPITAL & SURPLUS ($MIL) | RISK ADJUSTED CAPITAL RATIO 1 | RATIO 2 |
|---|---|---|---|---|---|---|---|---|---|
| ALLCARE HEALTH PLAN INC | OR | • E | 3q 2017 | 14.7 | 33.5 | 33.5 | 7.6 | 1.11 | 0.93 |
| ALLEGIAN INS CO | TX | • C | 2q 2017 | 45.1 | 89.3 | 89.3 | 21.3 | 2.04 | 1.70 |
| ALLEGIANCE L&H INS CO | MT | • C | 3q 2017 | 14.4 | 13.6 | 13.6 | 12.2 | 11.31 | 9.42 |
| ALLIANCE HEALTH & LIFE INS CO | MI | • C | 3q 2017 | 109.7 | 399.0 | 399.0 | 24.8 | 0.85 | 0.71 |
| ALLIANT HEALTH PLANS INC | GA | • D- | 3q 2017 | 58.8 | 114.3 | 114.3 | 17.3 | 1.42 | 1.19 |
| ALLIANZ GLOBAL RISKS US INS CO | IL | C | 3q 2017 | 7,793.5 | 1,009.2 | 15.5 | 1,874.5 | 0.89 | 0.70 |
| ALLIANZ LIFE INS CO OF NORTH AMERICA | MN | B | 3q 2017 | 136,207.0 | 12,854.5 | 181.5 | 6,031.4 | 2.86 | 1.61 |
| ALLIANZ LIFE INS CO OF NY | NY | A | 3q 2017 | 3,347.7 | 248.7 | 3.5 | 184.6 | 5.26 | 3.46 |
| ALLSTATE LIFE INS CO | IL | B | 3q 2017 | 31,602.0 | 479.6 | 22.5 | 3,373.3 | 2.00 | 1.16 |
| ALLSTATE LIFE INS CO OF NEW YORK | NY | C+ | 3q 2017 | 6,325.8 | 187.2 | 17.4 | 605.4 | 2.45 | 1.28 |
| ALOHACARE | HI | • C+ | 3q 2017 | 149.8 | 317.3 | 317.3 | 66.9 | 2.26 | 1.88 |
| ALPHACARE OF NEW YORK INC | NY | • C- | 3q 2017 | 36.8 | 138.5 | 138.5 | 18.7 | 1.88 | 1.57 |
| AMALGAMATED CASUALTY INS CO | DC | B- | 3q 2017 | 57.7 | 12.1 | 0.0 | 42.2 | 6.91 | 4.18 |
| AMALGAMATED LIFE & HEALTH INS CO | IL | C | 3q 2017 | 5.7 | 4.6 | 4.6 | 3.9 | 2.23 | 2.01 |
| AMALGAMATED LIFE INS CO | NY | • A- | 3q 2017 | 124.9 | 51.2 | 22.3 | 61.4 | 5.10 | 3.93 |
| AMBETTER OF MAGNOLIA INC | MS | • C+ | 3q 2017 | 77.0 | 126.1 | 126.1 | 26.1 | 3.80 | 3.17 |
| AMBETTER OF PEACH STATE INC | GA | • C+ | 3q 2017 | 199.9 | 197.2 | 197.2 | 36.0 | 5.84 | 4.87 |
| AMERICAN ALTERNATIVE INS CORP | DE | C | 3q 2017 | 582.3 | 827.8 | 153.7 | 196.5 | 16.98 | 11.30 |
| AMERICAN BANKERS INS CO OF FL | FL | B | 3q 2017 | 2,202.0 | 3,787.0 | 145.5 | 521.2 | 2.36 | 1.44 |
| AMERICAN BANKERS LIFE ASR CO OF FL | FL | • C+ | 3q 2017 | 368.2 | 262.4 | 112.0 | 66.9 | 6.56 | 3.47 |
| AMERICAN BENEFIT LIFE INS CO | OK | C | 4q 2016 | 124.4 | 5.3 | 0.0 | 17.3 | 2.36 | 2.12 |
| AMERICAN CASUALTY CO OF READING | PA | C | 3q 2017 | 143.2 | 533.6 | 0.0 | 143.2 | 2.20 | 2.13 |
| AMERICAN COMMERCE INS CO | OH | B- | 3q 2017 | 356.6 | 392.0 | 0.1 | 109.6 | 2.46 | 1.98 |
| AMERICAN CONTINENTAL INS CO | TN | • B- | 3q 2017 | 253.8 | 472.9 | 422.9 | 100.7 | 1.62 | 1.22 |
| AMERICAN FAMILY INS CO | WI | B | 3q 2017 | 27.2 | 771.5 | 0.4 | 24.1 | 23.66 | 21.30 |
| AMERICAN FAMILY LIFE ASR CO OF COLUM | NE | • B+ | 3q 2017 | 113,507.0 | 19,346.7 | 14,111.4 | 11,350.2 | 1.81 | 1.41 |
| AMERICAN FAMILY LIFE ASR CO OF NY | NY | • A- | 3q 2017 | 945.4 | 315.9 | 304.1 | 298.3 | 5.56 | 3.70 |
| AMERICAN FAMILY MUTL INS CO SI | WI | B+ | 3q 2017 | 17,048.2 | 5,238.1 | 31.7 | 6,684.8 | 2.03 | 1.59 |
| AMERICAN FEDERATED LIFE INS CO | MS | B | 3q 2017 | 32.9 | 14.9 | 7.0 | 14.0 | 2.80 | 2.52 |
| AMERICAN FIDELITY ASR CO | OK | • B+ | 3q 2017 | 5,772.7 | 1,071.5 | 754.0 | 434.5 | 1.93 | 1.10 |
| AMERICAN FINANCIAL SECURITY L I C | MO | D | 3q 2017 | 9.4 | 2.5 | 2.5 | 6.4 | 3.12 | 2.80 |
| AMERICAN GENERAL LIFE INS CO | TX | B | 3q 2017 | 175,213.0 | 13,556.3 | 194.4 | 7,597.1 | 2.87 | 1.35 |
| AMERICAN GUARANTEE & LIABILITY INS | NY | C+ | 3q 2017 | 270.6 | 935.8 | 0.0 | 183.9 | 21.88 | 19.69 |
| AMERICAN HALLMARK INS CO OF TX | TX | B | 3q 2017 | 433.0 | 155.8 | 5.3 | 137.5 | 1.75 | 1.47 |
| AMERICAN HEALTH & LIFE INS CO | TX | • A- | 3q 2017 | 840.1 | 121.3 | 60.6 | 142.1 | 3.54 | 2.13 |
| AMERICAN HEALTH PLAN INC | TN | U | | -- | -- | -- | -- | -- | -- |
| AMERICAN HERITAGE LIFE INS CO | FL | • B | 3q 2017 | 1,915.6 | 999.5 | 841.8 | 323.1 | 1.10 | 0.85 |
| AMERICAN HOME ASR CO | NY | C | 3q 2017 | 25,901.9 | 714.8 | 14.1 | 6,120.0 | 2.17 | 1.42 |
| AMERICAN HOME LIFE INS CO | KS | C- | 3q 2017 | 259.2 | 26.3 | 0.0 | 21.6 | 2.17 | 1.18 |
| AMERICAN INCOME LIFE INS CO | IN | B- | 3q 2017 | 3,911.1 | 965.6 | 78.1 | 285.7 | 1.45 | 0.86 |
| AMERICAN INDEPENDENT NETWORK INS CO | NY | E- | 3q 2016 | 24.2 | 2.7 | 2.7 | -19.2 | -2.28 | -2.05 |
| AMERICAN INTEGRITY LIFE INS CO | AR | C- | 3q 2017 | 1.2 | 0.3 | 0.0 | 0.9 | 2.02 | 1.81 |
| AMERICAN LABOR LIFE INS CO | AZ | D | 3q 2017 | 9.7 | 1.1 | 1.1 | 7.6 | 3.31 | 2.98 |
| AMERICAN LIFE & SECURITY CORP | NE | E+ | 3q 2017 | 23.9 | 6.7 | 0.0 | 3.6 | 0.74 | 0.66 |
| AMERICAN LIFE INS CO | DE | • C | 3q 2017 | 12,555.4 | 1,283.7 | 517.2 | 6,472.0 | 1.30 | 1.24 |
| AMERICAN MEMORIAL LIFE INS CO | SD | B- | 3q 2017 | 3,127.0 | 530.7 | 0.0 | 140.9 | 1.51 | 0.76 |
| AMERICAN MODERN HOME INS CO | OH | C+ | 3q 2017 | 953.5 | 627.0 | 1.6 | 402.8 | 1.92 | 1.53 |
| AMERICAN MODERN LIFE INS CO | OH | • B | 3q 2017 | 40.2 | 9.0 | 3.9 | 31.7 | 2.45 | 2.33 |
| AMERICAN NATIONAL INS CO | TX | B | 3q 2017 | 19,479.5 | 1,819.1 | 67.5 | 3,070.7 | 1.23 | 1.00 |
| AMERICAN NATIONAL LIFE INS CO OF TX | TX | • B- | 3q 2017 | 121.7 | 45.2 | 41.3 | 33.5 | 3.77 | 3.19 |
| AMERICAN NATL LIFE INS CO OF NY | NY | B | 3q 2017 | 771.2 | 213.9 | 0.4 | 45.7 | 2.16 | 1.05 |
| AMERICAN PROGRESSIVE L&H I C OF NY | NY | • C | 3q 2017 | 269.8 | 526.0 | 514.9 | 104.2 | 1.09 | 0.89 |

| INSURANCE COMPANY NAME | DOM. STATE | RATING | DATA DATE | TOTAL ASSETS ($MIL) | TOTAL PREMIUMS ($MIL) | HEALTH PREMIUMS ($MIL) | CAPITAL & SURPLUS ($MIL) | RISK ADJUSTED CAPITAL RATIO 1 | RISK ADJUSTED CAPITAL RATIO 2 |
|---|---|---|---|---|---|---|---|---|---|
| AMERICAN PUBLIC LIFE INS CO | OK | • B | 3q 2017 | 98.4 | 72.9 | 72.0 | 29.9 | 1.95 | 1.47 |
| AMERICAN REPUBLIC CORP INS CO | IA | B | 3q 2017 | 22.9 | 52.0 | 51.8 | 8.3 | 2.11 | 1.90 |
| AMERICAN REPUBLIC INS CO | IA | • A- | 3q 2017 | 933.1 | 153.2 | 138.6 | 502.9 | 4.74 | 3.38 |
| AMERICAN RETIREMENT LIFE INS CO | OH | • C+ | 3q 2017 | 104.3 | 255.5 | 255.3 | 55.1 | 0.99 | 0.80 |
| AMERICAN SECURITY INS CO | DE | B- | 3q 2017 | 1,494.3 | 936.4 | 1.1 | 471.1 | 1.50 | 1.15 |
| AMERICAN SENTINEL INS CO | PA | C- | 3q 2017 | 47.8 | 0.7 | 0.2 | 17.0 | 0.57 | 0.41 |
| AMERICAN SPECIALTY HEALTH INS CO | IN | • B- | 3q 2017 | 9.1 | 1.8 | 1.8 | 8.3 | 34.13 | 28.44 |
| AMERICAN SPECIALTY HEALTH ODS OF NJ | NJ | • C | 4q 2016 | 2.7 | 10.1 | 10.1 | 2.1 | 1.26 | 1.05 |
| AMERICAN STATES INS CO | IN | B- | 3q 2017 | 145.2 | 463.8 | 0.2 | 134.4 | 66.26 | 59.64 |
| AMERICAN UNDERWRITERS LIFE INS CO | AZ | D | 3q 2017 | 65.3 | 7.4 | 1.0 | 7.9 | 0.56 | 0.42 |
| AMERICAN UNITED LIFE INS CO | IN | B+ | 3q 2017 | 27,567.2 | 3,617.8 | 97.5 | 1,008.2 | 2.66 | 1.33 |
| AMERICAS 1ST CHOICE HEALTH PLANS INC | SC | • E+ | 4q 2016 | 11.8 | 30.6 | 30.6 | 5.6 | 0.89 | 0.74 |
| AMERICAS 1ST CHOICE SOUTH CAROLINA | SC | • E- | 3q 2017 | 3.9 | 1.9 | 1.9 | 1.3 | 3.01 | 2.51 |
| ▼ AMERICASHEALTH PLAN INC | CA | • E+ | 3q 2017 | 3.5 | 0.9 | 0.9 | 0.6 | 5.55 | 3.66 |
| AMERICHOICE OF NEW JERSEY INC | NJ | • B | 3q 2017 | 592.3 | 2,549.2 | 2,549.2 | 309.8 | 2.31 | 1.92 |
| AMERICO FINANCIAL LIFE & ANNUITY INS | TX | B- | 3q 2017 | 4,411.2 | 417.1 | 1.1 | 485.1 | 1.84 | 1.07 |
| AMERIGROUP COMMUNITY CARE NM | NM | • B- | 2q 2017 | 70.5 | 18.8 | 18.8 | 64.0 | 33.54 | 27.95 |
| AMERIGROUP DISTRICT | DC | U | | -- | -- | -- | -- | -- | -- |
| AMERIGROUP INS CO | TX | • B | 3q 2017 | 260.0 | 624.2 | 624.2 | 135.5 | 3.85 | 3.20 |
| AMERIGROUP IOWA INC | IA | • C | 3q 2017 | 323.7 | 788.0 | 788.0 | 101.9 | 1.33 | 1.11 |
| AMERIGROUP KANSAS INC | KS | • B- | 3q 2017 | 294.4 | 997.7 | 997.7 | 168.4 | 3.10 | 2.58 |
| AMERIGROUP MARYLAND INC | MD | • B | 3q 2017 | 351.8 | 1,088.1 | 1,088.1 | 140.3 | 2.32 | 1.94 |
| AMERIGROUP MISSISSIPPI INC | MS | U | | -- | -- | -- | -- | -- | -- |
| AMERIGROUP NEVADA INC | NV | • B | 3q 2017 | 129.0 | 635.1 | 635.1 | 71.3 | 2.09 | 1.74 |
| AMERIGROUP NEW JERSEY INC | NJ | • B+ | 3q 2017 | 329.0 | 1,304.3 | 1,304.3 | 146.6 | 2.21 | 1.84 |
| AMERIGROUP OHIO INC | OH | U | | -- | -- | -- | -- | -- | -- |
| AMERIGROUP TENNESSEE INC | TN | • B- | 3q 2017 | 524.5 | 1,905.9 | 1,905.9 | 195.4 | 1.92 | 1.60 |
| AMERIGROUP TEXAS INC | TX | • A- | 3q 2017 | 1,042.5 | 3,861.6 | 3,861.6 | 477.2 | 2.42 | 2.01 |
| AMERIGROUP WASHINGTON INC | WA | • A- | 3q 2017 | 267.7 | 570.7 | 570.7 | 146.2 | 4.73 | 3.94 |
| AMERIHEALTH CARITAS IOWA INC | IA | • C- | 3q 2017 | 417.9 | 1,398.0 | 1,398.0 | 159.9 | 1.35 | 1.13 |
| AMERIHEALTH CARITAS OF LOUISIANA INC | LA | • C | 3q 2017 | 257.9 | 908.3 | 908.3 | 92.7 | 2.10 | 1.75 |
| AMERIHEALTH DISTRICT OF COLUMBIA INC | DC | • B- | 3q 2017 | 132.2 | 493.9 | 493.9 | 57.5 | 2.40 | 2.00 |
| AMERIHEALTH HMO INC | PA | • C | 3q 2017 | 106.0 | 14.9 | 14.9 | 18.1 | 8.86 | 7.39 |
| AMERIHEALTH INSURANCE CO OF NJ | NJ | • C- | 4q 2016 | 421.3 | 1,356.1 | 1,356.1 | 126.6 | 1.59 | 1.32 |
| AMERIHEALTH MICHIGAN INC | MI | • C- | 3q 2017 | 31.9 | 78.1 | 78.1 | 12.4 | 2.12 | 1.77 |
| AMERIHEALTH NEBRASKA INC | NE | • E- | 2q 2017 | 14.2 | 85.6 | 85.6 | 9.0 | 1.25 | 1.04 |
| AMERITAS LIFE INS CORP | NE | • B | 3q 2017 | 19,676.1 | 2,414.8 | 832.8 | 1,575.8 | 2.39 | 1.42 |
| AMERITAS LIFE INS CORP OF NY | NY | • B- | 3q 2017 | 1,249.8 | 139.9 | 39.1 | 100.8 | 2.20 | 1.18 |
| AMEX ASSURANCE CO | IL | • B | 3q 2017 | 239.1 | 180.1 | 69.0 | 198.7 | 11.32 | 6.57 |
| AMFIRST INS CO | OK | • B+ | 3q 2017 | 57.6 | 53.3 | 53.3 | 50.0 | 3.61 | 3.00 |
| AMGP GEORGIA MANAGED CARE CO INC | GA | • A- | 3q 2017 | 295.6 | 1,228.3 | 1,228.3 | 160.6 | 2.56 | 2.14 |
| AMGUARD INS CO | PA | C | 3q 2017 | 847.5 | 525.3 | 6.2 | 160.8 | 0.88 | 0.71 |
| ANTHEM BLUE CROSS LIFE & HEALTH INS | CA | • B- | 3q 2017 | 2,337.2 | 2,238.9 | 2,238.9 | 1,371.3 | 7.66 | 6.38 |
| ANTHEM HEALTH PLANS INC | CT | • B- | 3q 2017 | 718.5 | 1,663.8 | 1,663.8 | 281.0 | 2.91 | 2.43 |
| ANTHEM HEALTH PLANS OF KENTUCKY INC | KY | • B+ | 3q 2017 | 1,046.0 | 2,285.7 | 2,285.7 | 401.6 | 3.40 | 2.83 |
| ANTHEM HEALTH PLANS OF MAINE INC | ME | • B+ | 3q 2017 | 489.5 | 1,062.9 | 1,062.9 | 182.6 | 3.75 | 3.13 |
| ANTHEM HEALTH PLANS OF NEW HAMPSHIRE | NH | • B | 3q 2017 | 347.4 | 488.2 | 488.2 | 182.1 | 3.76 | 3.13 |
| ANTHEM HEALTH PLANS OF VIRGINIA | VA | • B- | 3q 2017 | 2,166.2 | 3,825.9 | 3,825.9 | 619.8 | 3.34 | 2.78 |
| ANTHEM INS COMPANIES INC | IN | • B- | 3q 2017 | 3,613.9 | 6,126.1 | 6,126.1 | 1,187.4 | 2.94 | 2.45 |
| ANTHEM KENTUCKY MANAGED CARE PLAN | KY | • A- | 3q 2017 | 237.7 | 588.9 | 588.9 | 143.3 | 4.22 | 3.52 |
| ANTHEM LIFE & DISABILITY INS CO | NY | B | 3q 2017 | 24.8 | 7.3 | 2.6 | 18.7 | 4.46 | 3.25 |
| ANTHEM LIFE INS CO | IN | • A- | 3q 2017 | 738.1 | 221.0 | 95.7 | 118.5 | 2.26 | 1.55 |

| INSURANCE COMPANY NAME | DOM. STATE | RATING | DATA DATE | TOTAL ASSETS ($MIL) | TOTAL PREMIUMS ($MIL) | HEALTH PREMIUMS ($MIL) | CAPITAL & SURPLUS ($MIL) | RISK ADJUSTED CAPITAL RATIO 1 | RATIO 2 |
|---|---|---|---|---|---|---|---|---|---|
| ANTILLES INS CO | PR | C | 3q 2017 | 69.9 | 21.5 | 0.0 | 39.3 | 2.42 | 1.54 |
| AR HEALTH & WELLNESS HLTH PLAN | AR | U | | -- | -- | -- | -- | -- | -- |
| ARCADIAN HEALTH PLAN INC | WA | • B- | 3q 2017 | 417.7 | 812.9 | 812.9 | 227.0 | 6.42 | 5.35 |
| ARCH INS CO | MO | C | 3q 2017 | 4,041.8 | 1,849.6 | 71.9 | 860.8 | 1.55 | 1.25 |
| ARKANSAS BANKERS LIFE INS CO | AR | D | 3q 2017 | 2.8 | 0.9 | 0.1 | 1.5 | 1.53 | 1.38 |
| ARKANSAS SUPERIOR SELECT INC | AR | • E | 3q 2017 | 6.9 | 5.1 | 5.1 | 2.3 | 2.08 | 1.73 |
| ARROWOOD INDEMNITY CO | DE | D | 3q 2017 | 1,235.9 | 0.0 | 0.0 | 183.3 | 0.26 | 0.15 |
| ASPIRE HEALTH PLAN | CA | • E- | 3q 2017 | 7.2 | 13.7 | 13.7 | -20.0 | 0.00 | 0.00 |
| ASSOCIATED MUTUAL | MI | D | 3q 2016 | 8.6 | 1.3 | 1.2 | 7.6 | 2.36 | 2.12 |
| ASSURANCEAMERICA INS CO | NE | D+ | 3q 2017 | 77.3 | 78.6 | 1.0 | 16.8 | 1.15 | 1.00 |
| ASSURITY LIFE INS CO | NE | • B+ | 3q 2017 | 2,726.8 | 266.3 | 109.3 | 332.2 | 2.76 | 1.54 |
| ASURIS NORTHWEST HEALTH | WA | • B- | 3q 2017 | 106.0 | 141.6 | 141.6 | 67.6 | 7.12 | 5.93 |
| ATHENE ANNUITY & LIFE ASR CO | DE | C | 3q 2017 | 13,029.6 | 143.4 | 20.4 | 1,320.0 | 0.94 | 0.72 |
| ATHENE ANNUITY & LIFE ASR CO OF NY | NY | C | 3q 2017 | 3,191.0 | 186.2 | 0.3 | 257.2 | 1.78 | 0.95 |
| ATHENE ANNUITY & LIFE CO | IA | C | 3q 2017 | 51,730.6 | 5,470.1 | 1.9 | 1,142.7 | 0.84 | 0.44 |
| ATHENE LIFE INS CO OF NEW YORK | NY | C | 3q 2017 | 974.8 | 45.6 | 0.7 | 81.2 | 2.77 | 1.31 |
| ATLANTA LIFE INS CO | GA | D+ | 3q 2017 | 43.0 | 1.5 | 0.1 | 12.7 | 1.74 | 1.22 |
| ATLANTIC COAST LIFE INS CO | SC | B- | 3q 2017 | 408.8 | 101.5 | 0.1 | 18.3 | 1.19 | 0.56 |
| ▼ ATLANTIC SPECIALTY INS CO | NY | C+ | 3q 2017 | 2,287.1 | 951.7 | 110.8 | 488.7 | 1.45 | 1.10 |
| ATLANTIS HEALTH PLAN | NY | U | | -- | -- | -- | -- | -- | -- |
| ATRIO HEALTH PLANS INC | OR | • C- | 3q 2017 | 82.9 | 203.3 | 203.3 | 19.6 | 1.28 | 1.07 |
| AULTCARE HEALTH INSURING CORP | OH | • B | 3q 2017 | 126.9 | 245.0 | 245.0 | 87.0 | 2.18 | 1.81 |
| AULTCARE INS CO | OH | • C+ | 3q 2017 | 100.7 | 259.3 | 259.3 | 48.7 | 2.29 | 1.91 |
| AUTO CLUB LIFE INS CO | MI | C+ | 3q 2017 | 774.8 | 8.5 | 0.7 | 79.5 | 1.05 | 0.75 |
| AUTO-OWNERS LIFE INS CO | MI | A- | 3q 2017 | 4,021.4 | 267.6 | 17.0 | 446.6 | 2.85 | 1.52 |
| AVALON INS CO | PA | • C | 3q 2017 | 33.2 | 63.8 | 63.8 | 11.4 | 1.52 | 1.27 |
| AVEMCO INS CO | MD | B- | 3q 2017 | 86.3 | 28.3 | 0.8 | 55.6 | 3.13 | 2.95 |
| AVERA HEALTH PLANS INC | SD | • C | 2q 2017 | 74.5 | 185.5 | 185.5 | 34.8 | 1.47 | 1.22 |
| AVMED INC | FL | • C | 3q 2017 | 359.1 | 964.8 | 964.8 | 95.4 | 1.19 | 0.99 |
| AXA EQUITABLE LIFE INS CO | NY | B+ | 3q 2017 | 187,479.0 | 13,476.5 | 61.1 | 5,790.3 | 2.03 | 1.27 |
| AXIS INS CO | IL | B | 3q 2017 | 1,514.1 | 804.4 | 62.5 | 516.6 | 1.80 | 1.37 |
| BALTIMORE LIFE INS CO | MD | B | 3q 2017 | 1,263.8 | 134.3 | 0.8 | 83.2 | 1.74 | 0.90 |
| BANKERS CONSECO LIFE INS CO | NY | D | 3q 2017 | 475.5 | 57.8 | 13.9 | 57.4 | 3.77 | 1.80 |
| BANKERS FIDELITY ASR CO | GA | B- | 3q 2017 | 10.2 | 7.4 | 7.4 | 9.3 | 3.86 | 3.47 |
| BANKERS FIDELITY LIFE INS CO | GA | • B | 3q 2017 | 140.6 | 97.7 | 87.7 | 29.7 | 1.07 | 0.82 |
| BANKERS LIFE & CAS CO | IL | • D+ | 3q 2017 | 18,092.1 | 2,276.3 | 855.7 | 1,326.1 | 2.32 | 1.20 |
| BANKERS LIFE INS CO | FL | C- | 3q 2017 | 283.9 | 57.5 | 0.0 | 35.1 | 2.84 | 1.48 |
| BANKERS LIFE OF LOUISIANA | LA | C | 3q 2017 | 17.1 | 33.6 | 21.8 | 5.4 | 1.74 | 1.56 |
| BANKERS RESERVE LIFE INS CO OF WI | WI | • C- | 3q 2017 | 368.2 | 1,958.6 | 1,958.6 | 192.3 | 1.87 | 1.55 |
| BANNER HEALTH & AETNA HLTH INS | AZ | U | | -- | -- | -- | -- | -- | -- |
| BANNER HLTH & AETNA HLTH PLAN | AZ | U | | -- | -- | -- | -- | -- | -- |
| BANNER LIFE INS CO | MD | C+ | 3q 2017 | 3,034.8 | 1,444.3 | 0.0 | 354.4 | 1.74 | 1.26 |
| BAPTIST HEALTH PLAN INC | KY | • D | 3q 2017 | 50.1 | 153.7 | 153.7 | 17.8 | 0.48 | 0.40 |
| BAY AREA ACCOUNTABLE CARE | CA | • D+ | 3q 2017 | 19.9 | 31.5 | 31.5 | 8.1 | 1.92 | 1.21 |
| BCBSIL GP HMO NFP | IL | U | | -- | -- | -- | -- | -- | -- |
| BCS INS CO | OH | • B | 3q 2017 | 273.3 | 348.7 | 198.9 | 160.3 | 9.90 | 5.63 |
| BEAZLEY INS CO | CT | B- | 3q 2017 | 309.2 | 268.1 | 18.9 | 121.9 | 3.59 | 2.44 |
| BEHEALTHY FLORIDA INC | FL | • D+ | 3q 2017 | 37.8 | 23.3 | 23.3 | 9.8 | 6.25 | 5.21 |
| BENCHMARK INS CO | KS | B- | 3q 2017 | 338.7 | 224.2 | 22.8 | 95.8 | 3.33 | 2.45 |
| BENEFICIAL LIFE INS CO | UT | B | 3q 2017 | 2,243.8 | 68.5 | 0.0 | 199.1 | 1.99 | 1.12 |
| BERKLEY INS CO | DE | B | 3q 2017 | 18,553.2 | 495.4 | 24.3 | 5,533.3 | 1.44 | 1.20 |
| BERKLEY LIFE & HEALTH INS CO | IA | • A | 3q 2017 | 286.6 | 295.7 | 295.5 | 148.9 | 4.66 | 3.48 |

| INSURANCE COMPANY NAME | DOM. STATE | RATING | DATA DATE | TOTAL ASSETS ($MIL) | TOTAL PREMIUMS ($MIL) | HEALTH PREMIUMS ($MIL) | CAPITAL & SURPLUS ($MIL) | RISK ADJUSTED CAPITAL RATIO 1 | RISK ADJUSTED CAPITAL RATIO 2 |
|---|---|---|---|---|---|---|---|---|---|
| BERKSHIRE HATHAWAY SPECIALTY INS CO | NE | C+ | 3q 2017 | 4,736.2 | 414.4 | 2.9 | 3,479.1 | 4.35 | 2.61 |
| BERKSHIRE LIFE INS CO OF AMERICA | MA | • B | 3q 2017 | 3,685.6 | 549.5 | 539.5 | 209.8 | 2.88 | 1.34 |
| BEST LIFE & HEALTH INS CO | TX | B+ | 3q 2017 | 20.9 | 33.9 | 33.3 | 16.2 | 1.97 | 1.59 |
| BEST MERIDIAN INS CO | FL | B- | 3q 2017 | 334.7 | 36.2 | 6.4 | 58.6 | 1.88 | 1.20 |
| BLUE ADVANTAGE PLUS OF KANSAS CITY | MO | • C | 3q 2017 | 40.0 | 29.3 | 29.3 | 14.8 | 1.68 | 1.40 |
| BLUE CARE NETWORK OF MICHIGAN | MI | • B+ | 3q 2017 | 2,177.8 | 3,399.3 | 3,399.3 | 1,290.0 | 6.95 | 5.79 |
| BLUE CARE OF MICHIGAN INC | MI | • C | 3q 2017 | 6.2 | 0.7 | 0.7 | 6.1 | 22.75 | 18.96 |
| ▲ BLUE CROSS & BLUE SHIELD MA HMO BLUE | MA | • A- | 3q 2017 | 2,283.0 | 4,596.5 | 4,596.5 | 1,376.9 | 4.41 | 3.67 |
| BLUE CROSS & BLUE SHIELD OF FLORIDA | FL | • B- | 3q 2017 | 5,938.0 | 9,387.5 | 9,387.5 | 1,767.5 | 4.27 | 3.56 |
| BLUE CROSS BLUE SHIELD HEALTHCARE GA | GA | • A- | 3q 2017 | 1,109.3 | 2,134.3 | 2,134.3 | 419.4 | 3.35 | 2.79 |
| BLUE CROSS BLUE SHIELD OF ALABAMA | AL | • B | 3q 2017 | 3,656.3 | 5,155.8 | 5,155.8 | 1,640.0 | 6.07 | 5.06 |
| BLUE CROSS BLUE SHIELD OF ARIZONA | AZ | • A+ | 3q 2017 | 2,020.4 | 2,048.1 | 2,048.1 | 1,274.4 | 7.07 | 5.89 |
| BLUE CROSS BLUE SHIELD OF GEORGIA | GA | • B- | 3q 2017 | 1,240.9 | 1,847.1 | 1,847.1 | 441.1 | 5.15 | 4.29 |
| BLUE CROSS BLUE SHIELD OF KANSAS INC | KS | • B | 3q 2017 | 1,571.6 | 1,931.4 | 1,931.4 | 821.1 | 2.00 | 1.54 |
| BLUE CROSS BLUE SHIELD OF KC | MO | • C+ | 3q 2017 | 1,343.9 | 1,718.1 | 1,718.1 | 723.3 | 5.30 | 4.42 |
| BLUE CROSS BLUE SHIELD OF MA | MA | • B- | 3q 2017 | 2,238.0 | 2,522.4 | 2,522.4 | 781.3 | 3.25 | 2.71 |
| BLUE CROSS BLUE SHIELD OF MICHIGAN | MI | • C | 3q 2017 | 8,404.4 | 7,899.3 | 7,899.3 | 4,057.7 | 3.74 | 3.12 |
| BLUE CROSS BLUE SHIELD OF MINNESOTA | MN | • C | 3q 2017 | 2,540.3 | 3,938.7 | 3,938.7 | 1,128.5 | 2.93 | 2.44 |
| BLUE CROSS BLUE SHIELD OF MS, MUTUAL | MS | • B | 2q 2017 | 946.4 | 1,334.1 | 1,334.1 | 634.1 | 7.92 | 6.60 |
| BLUE CROSS BLUE SHIELD OF NC | NC | • B | 3q 2017 | 5,341.5 | 7,178.1 | 7,178.1 | 2,988.8 | 6.53 | 5.44 |
| BLUE CROSS BLUE SHIELD OF NEBRASKA | NE | • C | 3q 2017 | 934.5 | 1,744.1 | 1,744.1 | 407.4 | 4.17 | 3.47 |
| BLUE CROSS BLUE SHIELD OF RI | RI | • C | 3q 2017 | 673.7 | 1,714.1 | 1,714.1 | 303.2 | 2.31 | 1.92 |
| BLUE CROSS BLUE SHIELD OF SC INC | SC | • A- | 3q 2017 | 4,019.7 | 2,639.2 | 2,639.2 | 2,580.5 | 5.93 | 4.95 |
| BLUE CROSS BLUE SHIELD OF VERMONT | VT | • B | 3q 2017 | 278.5 | 547.3 | 547.3 | 148.6 | 2.77 | 2.31 |
| BLUE CROSS BLUE SHIELD OF WISCONSIN | WI | • B- | 3q 2017 | 563.8 | 758.6 | 758.6 | 260.3 | 3.00 | 2.50 |
| BLUE CROSS BLUE SHIELD OF WYOMING | WY | • B- | 3q 2017 | 518.7 | 467.8 | 467.8 | 314.6 | 5.65 | 4.71 |
| BLUE CROSS COMPLETE OF MICHIGAN | MI | • E | 3q 2017 | 189.8 | 709.4 | 709.4 | 56.9 | 1.72 | 1.43 |
| BLUE CROSS OF CALIFORNIA | CA | • A+ | 3q 2017 | 7,951.3 | 16,650.0 | 16,650.0 | 2,554.1 | 3.06 | 1.94 |
| BLUE CROSS OF IDAHO CARE PLUS INC | ID | • C | 3q 2017 | 171.8 | 320.4 | 320.4 | 78.6 | 2.35 | 1.96 |
| BLUE CROSS OF IDAHO HEALTH SERVICE | ID | • B | 3q 2017 | 841.5 | 1,173.5 | 1,173.5 | 581.4 | 6.80 | 5.67 |
| BLUE SHIELD OF CALIFORNIA | CA | • A+ | 3q 2017 | 8,119.3 | 14,290.2 | 14,290.2 | 4,669.3 | 3.34 | 2.25 |
| BLUE SHIELD OF CALIFORNIA L&H INS CO | CA | • B | 3q 2017 | 338.4 | 314.7 | 303.8 | 164.0 | 3.14 | 2.43 |
| BLUEBONNET LIFE INS CO | MS | B+ | 3q 2017 | 62.2 | 5.3 | 0.0 | 57.4 | 8.02 | 7.22 |
| BLUECHOICE HEALTHPLAN OF SC INC | SC | • B | 3q 2017 | 352.1 | 969.9 | 969.9 | 227.9 | 3.85 | 3.21 |
| BLUECROSS BLUESHIELD KANSAS SOLUTION | KS | • C+ | 3q 2017 | 142.3 | 157.8 | 157.8 | 40.3 | 2.39 | 1.99 |
| BLUECROSS BLUESHIELD OF TENNESSEE | TN | • B | 3q 2017 | 3,018.0 | 4,739.9 | 4,739.9 | 2,090.7 | 7.61 | 6.35 |
| BOSTON MEDICAL CENTER HEALTH PLAN | MA | • B- | 3q 2017 | 457.9 | 1,574.5 | 1,574.5 | 236.1 | 1.91 | 1.59 |
| BOSTON MUTUAL LIFE INS CO | MA | • B+ | 3q 2017 | 1,424.8 | 227.8 | 57.1 | 209.6 | 2.31 | 1.51 |
| BRAVO HEALTH MID-ATLANTIC INC | MD | • C+ | 3q 2017 | 90.2 | 279.3 | 279.3 | 35.5 | 2.18 | 1.82 |
| BRAVO HEALTH PENNSYLVANIA INC | PA | • B | 3q 2017 | 304.4 | 721.7 | 721.7 | 154.7 | 3.92 | 3.26 |
| BRIDGESPAN HEALTH CO | UT | • E | 3q 2017 | 74.8 | 61.3 | 61.3 | 26.4 | 6.30 | 5.25 |
| BRIGHT HEALTH CO OF ARIZONA | AZ | U |  | -- | -- | -- | -- | -- | -- |
| BRIGHT HLTH INS CO OF AL INC | AL | U |  | -- | -- | -- | -- | -- | -- |
| BRIGHTHOUSE LIFE INSURANCE CO | DE | B | 3q 2017 | 175,382.0 | 7,640.9 | 225.7 | 5,510.3 | 3.38 | 1.65 |
| BROWN & TOLAND HEALTH SERVICES | CA | • E- | 3q 2017 | 24.8 | 82.2 | 82.2 | 0.6 | 0.07 | 0.04 |
| BUCKEYE COMMUNITY HEALTH PLAN INC | OH | • C+ | 3q 2017 | 494.4 | 2,048.4 | 2,048.4 | 245.9 | 2.60 | 2.16 |
| BUCKEYE HEALTH PLAN COMMUNITY | OH | U |  | -- | -- | -- | -- | -- | -- |
| BUPA INS CO | FL | • B | 3q 2017 | 303.2 | 315.4 | 315.4 | 143.3 | 3.40 | 2.83 |
| ▼ CALIFORNIA HEALTH & WELLNESS PLAN | CA | • C | 3q 2017 | 373.5 | 610.6 | 610.6 | 68.3 | 0.91 | 0.64 |
| CANADA LIFE ASSURANCE CO-US BRANCH | MI | C | 3q 2017 | 4,554.4 | 97.0 | 2.9 | 157.7 | 0.89 | 0.52 |
| CAPITAL ADVANTAGE ASR CO | PA | • C- | 3q 2017 | 605.0 | 1,218.0 | 1,218.0 | 264.0 | 3.20 | 2.67 |
| CAPITAL ADVANTAGE INS CO | PA | • C | 3q 2017 | 604.4 | 219.2 | 219.2 | 381.5 | 2.98 | 2.48 |



Arrows denote recent upgrades ▲ or downgrades ▼

• Bullets denote a more detailed analysis is available in Section II.

| INSURANCE COMPANY NAME | DOM. STATE | RATING | DATA DATE | TOTAL ASSETS ($MIL) | TOTAL PREMIUMS ($MIL) | HEALTH PREMIUMS ($MIL) | CAPITAL & SURPLUS ($MIL) | RISK ADJUSTED CAPITAL RATIO 1 | RISK ADJUSTED CAPITAL RATIO 2 |
|---|---|---|---|---|---|---|---|---|---|
| CAPITAL BLUE CROSS | PA | • B- | 3q 2017 | 1,138.4 | 297.5 | 297.5 | 737.6 | 4.33 | 3.60 |
| CAPITAL DISTRICT PHYSICIANS HEALTH P | NY | • B | 3q 2017 | 576.7 | 1,444.6 | 1,444.6 | 350.8 | 2.85 | 2.38 |
| CAPITAL HEALTH PLAN INC | FL | • B | 3q 2017 | 534.9 | 766.3 | 766.3 | 390.6 | 7.70 | 6.42 |
| CAPITAL RESERVE LIFE INS CO | MO | E+ | 3q 2017 | 1.3 | 0.1 | 0.0 | 1.3 | 2.44 | 2.20 |
| CAPITOL INDEMNITY CORP | WI | C | 3q 2017 | 576.1 | 62.3 | 0.4 | 259.7 | 1.80 | 1.35 |
| CARE 1ST HEALTH PLAN | CA | U | | -- | -- | -- | -- | -- | -- |
| CARE 1ST HEALTH PLAN INC | CA | • A+ | 3q 2017 | 1,094.9 | 2,137.1 | 2,137.1 | 430.7 | 3.06 | 2.55 |
| CARE IMPROVEMENT PLUS OF TEXAS INS | TX | • C | 3q 2017 | 632.1 | 1,155.1 | 1,155.1 | 172.7 | 3.00 | 2.50 |
| CARE IMPROVEMENT PLUS SOUTH CENTRAL | AR | • C | 3q 2017 | 761.0 | 3,705.3 | 3,705.3 | 384.0 | 1.97 | 1.64 |
| CARE IMPROVEMENT PLUS WI INS | WI | • C | 3q 2017 | 56.9 | 79.1 | 79.1 | 20.3 | 3.63 | 3.02 |
| ▲ CARE N CARE INS CO | TX | • C | 3q 2017 | 49.0 | 109.8 | 109.8 | 16.0 | 1.29 | 1.08 |
| CARE N CARE INS CO OF NORTH CAROLINA | NC | • D+ | 3q 2017 | 49.5 | 56.8 | 56.8 | 9.3 | 1.05 | 0.87 |
| CARE WISCONSIN HEALTH PLAN INC | WI | • B | 3q 2017 | 56.8 | 124.7 | 124.7 | 34.1 | 2.55 | 2.13 |
| CARECENTRIX OF NEW JERSEY INC | NJ | • D- | 4q 2016 | 30.9 | 18.0 | 18.0 | 3.4 | 0.66 | 0.55 |
| CARECONNECT INS CO | NY | • E- | 3q 2017 | 256.0 | 361.1 | 361.1 | 29.2 | 0.53 | 0.44 |
| CARECORE NJ LLC | NJ | • D- | 4q 2016 | 21.3 | 148.4 | 148.4 | 6.3 | 1.77 | 1.48 |
| CAREFIRST BLUECHOICE INC | DC | • A- | 3q 2017 | 1,137.7 | 3,102.9 | 3,102.9 | 694.0 | 4.70 | 3.91 |
| CAREFIRST OF MARYLAND INC | MD | • C+ | 3q 2017 | 1,419.7 | 1,946.6 | 1,946.6 | 563.1 | 3.69 | 3.07 |
| CAREMORE HEALTH PLAN | CA | • B+ | 3q 2017 | 317.1 | 949.8 | 949.8 | 94.8 | 3.17 | 1.99 |
| CAREMORE HEALTH PLAN OF ARIZONA INC | AZ | • B- | 3q 2017 | 65.8 | 134.8 | 134.8 | 29.6 | 4.88 | 4.06 |
| CAREMORE HEALTH PLAN OF NEVADA | NV | • D | 3q 2017 | 40.9 | 89.4 | 89.4 | 15.5 | 3.34 | 2.78 |
| CAREPLUS HEALTH PLANS INC | FL | • B- | 3q 2017 | 597.0 | 1,721.4 | 1,721.4 | 132.0 | 2.89 | 2.41 |
| CARESOURCE | OH | • B- | 3q 2017 | 1,692.5 | 7,030.7 | 7,030.7 | 725.8 | 1.68 | 1.40 |
| CARESOURCE INDIANA INC | IN | • D+ | 3q 2017 | 163.5 | 92.4 | 92.4 | 40.7 | 5.39 | 4.49 |
| CARESOURCE KENTUCKY CO | KY | • C | 3q 2017 | 48.3 | 31.3 | 31.3 | 14.2 | 3.64 | 3.03 |
| ▼ CARESOURCE WEST VIRGINIA CO | WV | • C | 3q 2017 | 22.6 | 5.2 | 5.2 | 5.2 | 4.32 | 3.60 |
| CARIBBEAN AMERICAN LIFE ASR CO | PR | B | 3q 2017 | 38.8 | 25.8 | 11.0 | 11.1 | 2.28 | 1.97 |
| CARIBBEAN AMERICAN PROPERTY INS CO | PR | C | 3q 2017 | 44.7 | 50.5 | 0.0 | 16.9 | 0.49 | 0.32 |
| CARILION CLINIC MEDICARE RESOURCES | VA | U | | -- | -- | -- | -- | -- | -- |
| CARITEN HEALTH PLAN INC | TN | • B | 3q 2017 | 527.1 | 1,283.3 | 1,283.3 | 203.5 | 3.52 | 2.93 |
| CATHOLIC SPECIAL NEEDS PLAN LLC | NY | • C | 3q 2017 | 18.1 | 48.3 | 48.3 | 5.9 | 0.75 | 0.62 |
| CATLIN INS CO | TX | C | 3q 2017 | 159.3 | 125.4 | 27.5 | 60.8 | 1.16 | 0.73 |
| CBHNP SERVICES INC | PA | U | | -- | -- | -- | -- | -- | -- |
| CDPHP UNIVERSAL BENEFITS INC | NY | • E+ | 3q 2017 | 188.0 | 703.4 | 703.4 | 126.2 | 2.53 | 2.11 |
| CELTIC INS CO | IL | • C+ | 3q 2017 | 1,115.4 | 781.9 | 781.9 | 179.4 | 4.01 | 3.34 |
| CELTICARE HEALTH PLAN OF MA INC | MA | • C | 3q 2017 | 67.8 | 174.2 | 174.2 | 33.6 | 3.46 | 2.88 |
| CENPATICO OF ARIZONA INC | AZ | • C+ | 3q 2017 | 128.2 | 655.7 | 655.7 | 60.3 | 1.97 | 1.64 |
| CENTENNIAL CASUALTY CO | AL | B- | 3q 2017 | 120.8 | 18.1 | 2.4 | 75.8 | 3.14 | 1.84 |
| CENTRAL HEALTH PLAN OF CALIFORNIA | CA | • E+ | 3q 2017 | 101.1 | 351.5 | 351.5 | 16.7 | 0.39 | 0.24 |
| CENTRAL RESERVE LIFE INS CO | OH | C+ | 3q 2017 | 22.2 | 6.3 | 5.6 | 21.2 | 1.10 | 1.07 |
| CENTRAL SECURITY LIFE INS CO | TX | D | 3q 2017 | 89.5 | 3.2 | 0.2 | 5.0 | 0.54 | 0.49 |
| CENTRAL STATES H & L CO OF OMAHA | NE | • A- | 3q 2017 | 411.0 | 105.6 | 46.8 | 146.7 | 4.51 | 3.21 |
| CENTRAL STATES INDEMNITY CO OF OMAHA | NE | • C+ | 3q 2017 | 498.9 | 137.6 | 87.1 | 411.0 | 3.87 | 2.43 |
| CENTRE LIFE INS CO | MA | • B- | 3q 2017 | 1,834.2 | 20.1 | 20.1 | 93.3 | 4.01 | 2.49 |
| CENTURION LIFE INS CO | IA | • D+ | 3q 2017 | 1,267.7 | 0.3 | 0.1 | 368.1 | 4.40 | 2.57 |
| CENTURY CASUALTY CO | GA | E- | 3q 2017 | 1.2 | 0.2 | 0.2 | 1.1 | 2.07 | 1.96 |
| CENTURY INS CO GUAM LTD | GU | D | 3q 2017 | 26.4 | 14.6 | 0.0 | 16.0 | 3.06 | 1.83 |
| CENTURY LIFE ASR CO | OK | D | 3q 2017 | 11.8 | 1.3 | 0.3 | 5.9 | 2.37 | 2.13 |
| CHA HMO INC | KY | • C+ | 3q 2017 | 59.2 | 128.3 | 128.3 | 23.5 | 3.83 | 3.19 |
| CHEROKEE INS CO | MI | B- | 3q 2017 | 531.8 | 206.1 | 46.1 | 188.8 | 2.82 | 1.62 |
| ▲ CHESAPEAKE LIFE INS CO | OK | • B | 3q 2017 | 157.9 | 221.9 | 178.4 | 91.0 | 2.28 | 1.81 |
| CHILDRENS COMMUNITY HEALTH PLAN INC | WI | • B | 3q 2017 | 79.4 | 235.8 | 235.8 | 40.9 | 1.80 | 1.50 |

| INSURANCE COMPANY NAME | DOM. STATE | RATING | DATA DATE | TOTAL ASSETS ($MIL) | TOTAL PREMIUMS ($MIL) | HEALTH PREMIUMS ($MIL) | CAPITAL & SURPLUS ($MIL) | RISK ADJUSTED CAPITAL RATIO 1 | RATIO 2 |
|---|---|---|---|---|---|---|---|---|---|
| CHILDRENS MEDICAL CENTER HEALTH PLAN | TX | • E- | 3q 2017 | 54.8 | 38.2 | 38.2 | 21.5 | 2.48 | 2.07 |
| CHOICE PHYSICIANS NETWORK | CA | • E+ | 3q 2017 | 20.8 | 105.6 | 105.6 | 4.6 | 0.37 | 0.22 |
| CHRISTIAN FIDELITY LIFE INS CO | TX | • B | 3q 2017 | 67.6 | 34.6 | 33.3 | 34.0 | 3.53 | 2.58 |
| CHRISTUS HEALTH PLAN | TX | • C- | 3q 2017 | 48.9 | 64.7 | 64.7 | 12.5 | 1.14 | 0.95 |
| CHUBB INS CO OF PR | PR | B | 2q 2017 | 146.4 | 58.5 | 11.9 | 49.3 | 1.47 | 1.15 |
| CICA LIFE INS CO OF AMERICA | CO | D | 3q 2017 | 989.6 | 159.0 | 0.9 | 46.7 | 0.76 | 0.55 |
| CIGNA HEALTH & LIFE INS CO | CT | • B | 3q 2017 | 8,705.3 | 12,338.5 | 12,338.1 | 3,606.0 | 1.82 | 1.40 |
| CIGNA HEALTHCARE OF ARIZONA INC | AZ | • E- | 3q 2017 | 161.2 | 566.0 | 566.0 | 58.0 | 1.80 | 1.50 |
| CIGNA HEALTHCARE OF CALIFORNIA INC | CA | • C | 3q 2017 | 146.6 | 915.6 | 915.6 | 36.1 | 1.16 | 0.71 |
| CIGNA HEALTHCARE OF COLORADO INC | CO | • C | 3q 2017 | 5.8 | 4.8 | 4.8 | 3.8 | 6.68 | 5.57 |
| CIGNA HEALTHCARE OF FLORIDA INC | FL | • C | 3q 2017 | 4.2 | 1.0 | 1.0 | 3.8 | 6.94 | 5.78 |
| CIGNA HEALTHCARE OF GEORGIA INC | GA | • E | 3q 2017 | 119.2 | 383.6 | 383.6 | 50.7 | 1.72 | 1.43 |
| CIGNA HEALTHCARE OF ILLINOIS INC | IL | • C- | 3q 2017 | 70.0 | 0.5 | 0.5 | 10.9 | 18.09 | 15.07 |
| CIGNA HEALTHCARE OF INDIANA INC | IN | • C+ | 3q 2017 | 1.8 | 1.1 | 1.1 | 1.4 | 2.58 | 2.15 |
| CIGNA HEALTHCARE OF NEW JERSEY INC | NJ | • E | 3q 2017 | 9.0 | 3.9 | 3.9 | 5.1 | 9.14 | 7.61 |
| CIGNA HEALTHCARE OF NORTH CAROLINA | NC | • C | 3q 2017 | 93.0 | 88.9 | 88.9 | 22.8 | 3.14 | 2.61 |
| CIGNA HEALTHCARE OF SOUTH CAROLINA | SC | • D- | 3q 2017 | 32.5 | 95.4 | 95.4 | 17.6 | 2.35 | 1.96 |
| CIGNA HEALTHCARE OF ST LOUIS | MO | • D+ | 3q 2017 | 14.0 | 22.2 | 22.2 | 6.9 | 2.54 | 2.12 |
| CIGNA HEALTHCARE OF TENNESSEE INC | TN | • C | 3q 2017 | 7.1 | 16.5 | 16.5 | 3.2 | 2.73 | 2.28 |
| CIGNA HEALTHCARE OF TEXAS INC | TX | • C- | 3q 2017 | 32.3 | 110.8 | 110.8 | 19.7 | 2.96 | 2.46 |
| CIGNA LIFE INS CO OF NEW YORK | NY | • A- | 3q 2017 | 403.0 | 167.0 | 113.1 | 95.7 | 2.47 | 1.61 |
| CIGNA WORLDWIDE INS CO | DE | B | 3q 2017 | 54.8 | 11.5 | 0.0 | 10.5 | 1.70 | 1.53 |
| CINCINNATI EQUITABLE LIFE INS CO | OH | C- | 3q 2017 | 135.9 | 36.6 | 0.1 | 7.4 | 0.95 | 0.61 |
| CINCINNATI LIFE INS CO | OH | B | 3q 2017 | 4,387.5 | 338.8 | 6.9 | 209.7 | 1.42 | 0.76 |
| CITIZENS FIDELITY INS CO | AR | C+ | 3q 2017 | 70.2 | 3.8 | 0.0 | 12.5 | 1.85 | 1.26 |
| CITIZENS NATIONAL LIFE INS CO | TX | C | 3q 2017 | 12.1 | 1.1 | 0.0 | 1.9 | 2.96 | 2.66 |
| CITIZENS SECURITY LIFE INS CO | KY | C | 3q 2017 | 26.3 | 49.3 | 43.2 | 15.0 | 0.85 | 0.75 |
| CLEARRIVER HEALTH | TN | • D | 2q 2017 | 6.1 | 4.3 | 4.3 | 5.2 | 6.59 | 5.49 |
| CLOISTER MUTL CAS INS CO | PA | C | 3q 2017 | 9.8 | 0.0 | 0.0 | 9.8 | 16.02 | 7.08 |
| CLOVER INSURANCE COMPANY | NJ | • C+ | 3q 2017 | 110.3 | 46.0 | 46.0 | 53.9 | 4.39 | 3.66 |
| CMFG LIFE INS CO | IA | B- | 3q 2017 | 17,660.7 | 2,492.0 | 572.2 | 2,154.5 | 1.64 | 1.27 |
| CMNTY CARE HLTH PLAN INC (WI) | WI | • C | 3q 2017 | 24.0 | 94.6 | 94.6 | 12.8 | 1.35 | 1.12 |
| CMNTY CARE HLTH PLAN OF LA INC | LA | • B | 3q 2017 | 293.1 | 785.3 | 785.3 | 105.6 | 2.41 | 2.01 |
| COLONIAL LIFE & ACCIDENT INS CO | SC | • C+ | 3q 2017 | 3,274.2 | 1,420.9 | 1,105.7 | 580.7 | 2.54 | 1.59 |
| COLONIAL LIFE INS CO OF TX | TX | C- | 3q 2017 | 19.2 | 1.1 | 0.3 | 14.3 | 4.46 | 3.14 |
| COLONIAL PENN LIFE INS CO | PA | • D+ | 3q 2017 | 860.4 | 680.2 | 419.8 | 97.4 | 1.27 | 0.73 |
| COLORADO ACCESS | CO | • E | 3q 2017 | 72.2 | 244.1 | 244.1 | 23.6 | 0.36 | 0.30 |
| ▼ COLORADO BANKERS LIFE INS CO | NC | B- | 3q 2017 | 946.9 | 96.5 | 3.7 | 110.5 | 4.69 | 2.57 |
| COLUMBIAN LIFE INS CO | IL | C | 3q 2017 | 324.4 | 227.5 | 0.1 | 24.4 | 1.32 | 0.86 |
| COLUMBIAN MUTUAL LIFE INS CO | NY | B | 3q 2017 | 1,445.0 | 77.2 | 2.2 | 102.6 | 1.62 | 1.04 |
| COLUMBUS LIFE INS CO | OH | C+ | 3q 2017 | 4,095.0 | 320.5 | 0.1 | 290.7 | 1.97 | 1.03 |
| COMBINED INS CO OF AMERICA | IL | • C+ | 3q 2017 | 1,507.0 | 904.9 | 812.0 | 159.5 | 1.30 | 0.90 |
| COMBINED LIFE INS CO OF NEW YORK | NY | • C+ | 3q 2017 | 442.6 | 137.4 | 118.4 | 42.8 | 1.16 | 0.82 |
| COMM TRAVELERS LIFE INS CO | NY | D | 3q 2017 | 23.1 | 4.2 | 4.2 | 12.6 | 4.05 | 3.64 |
| COMMON GROUND HEALTHCARE COOPERATIVE | WI | • D | 3q 2017 | 60.2 | 88.8 | 88.8 | 27.1 | 1.22 | 1.02 |
| COMMONWEALTH ANNUITY & LIFE INS CO | MA | B- | 3q 2017 | 10,828.2 | 104.6 | 0.3 | 2,156.7 | 0.79 | 0.73 |
| ▲ COMMUNITY CARE ALLIANCE OF ILLINOIS | IL | • C- | 3q 2017 | 20.3 | 42.7 | 42.7 | 4.7 | 0.64 | 0.53 |
| COMMUNITY CARE BEHAVIORAL HEALTH | PA | • B | 3q 2017 | 326.3 | 883.7 | 883.7 | 199.6 | 4.02 | 3.35 |
| COMMUNITY CARE HEALTH PLAN | CA | • C- | 3q 2017 | 9.3 | 20.8 | 20.8 | 6.7 | 2.66 | 1.69 |
| COMMUNITY FIRST GROUP HOSPITAL SERVI | TX | U | | -- | -- | -- | -- | -- | -- |
| COMMUNITY FIRST HEALTH PLANS INC | TX | • A | 3q 2017 | 151.9 | 424.2 | 424.2 | 99.9 | 3.06 | 2.55 |
| ▼ COMMUNITY HEALTH CHOICE INC | TX | • D | 3q 2017 | 160.6 | 1,121.5 | 1,121.5 | 8.8 | 0.08 | 0.07 |

| INSURANCE COMPANY NAME | DOM. STATE | RATING | DATA DATE | TOTAL ASSETS ($MIL) | TOTAL PREMIUMS ($MIL) | HEALTH PREMIUMS ($MIL) | CAPITAL & SURPLUS ($MIL) | RISK ADJUSTED CAPITAL RATIO 1 | RISK ADJUSTED CAPITAL RATIO 2 |
|---|---|---|---|---|---|---|---|---|---|
| COMMUNITY HEALTH CHOICE TX INC | TX | U | | -- | -- | -- | -- | -- | -- |
| COMMUNITY HEALTH GROUP | CA | • B | 3q 2017 | 928.8 | 1,184.5 | 1,184.5 | 527.7 | 8.21 | 4.97 |
| COMMUNITY HEALTH PLAN INS CO | MO | U | | -- | -- | -- | -- | -- | -- |
| COMMUNITY HEALTH PLAN OF WASHINGTON | WA | • B | 3q 2017 | 453.9 | 1,070.9 | 1,070.9 | 180.1 | 2.13 | 1.78 |
| COMMUNITY INS CO (OH) | OH | • B+ | 3q 2017 | 2,274.1 | 5,297.0 | 5,297.0 | 877.6 | 2.85 | 2.38 |
| COMMUNITYCARE GOVERNMENT PROGRAMS | OK | • D+ | 3q 2017 | 6.0 | 5.6 | 5.6 | 3.0 | 0.94 | 0.78 |
| COMMUNITYCARE HMO INC | OK | • B+ | 3q 2017 | 231.6 | 592.3 | 592.3 | 118.0 | 3.30 | 2.75 |
| COMMUNITYCARE L&H INS CO | OK | • B- | 3q 2017 | 17.9 | 54.0 | 54.0 | 8.8 | 1.79 | 1.49 |
| COMPANION LIFE INS CO | NY | B- | 3q 2017 | 1,084.6 | 139.4 | 0.0 | 53.8 | 1.58 | 0.83 |
| COMPANION LIFE INS CO | SC | • B+ | 3q 2017 | 359.8 | 725.3 | 693.7 | 206.2 | 2.68 | 2.07 |
| COMPCARE HEALTH SERVICES INS CORP | WI | • A- | 3q 2017 | 314.8 | 769.1 | 769.1 | 152.5 | 3.49 | 2.91 |
| COMPREHENSIVE MOBILE INS CO | AZ | • B | 3q 2017 | 2.4 | 2.9 | 2.9 | 2.0 | 5.34 | 4.45 |
| COMPREHENSIVE MOBILE PLAN UTAH INC | UT | U | | -- | -- | -- | -- | -- | -- |
| CONNECTICARE BENEFITS INC | CT | • D+ | 3q 2017 | 107.9 | 272.1 | 272.1 | 28.9 | 1.85 | 1.55 |
| CONNECTICARE INC | CT | • C | 3q 2017 | 236.1 | 793.8 | 793.8 | 90.4 | 2.08 | 1.73 |
| CONNECTICARE INS CO | CT | • C | 3q 2017 | 198.0 | 765.3 | 765.3 | 90.9 | 1.33 | 1.11 |
| CONNECTICARE OF MASSACHUSETTS INC | MA | • E- | 3q 2017 | 2.6 | 4.8 | 4.8 | 1.6 | 1.31 | 1.09 |
| CONNECTICUT GENERAL LIFE INS CO | CT | • B- | 3q 2017 | 18,077.3 | 743.6 | 244.2 | 4,307.1 | 1.33 | 1.21 |
| CONSTELLATION HEALTH LLC | PR | • E- | 3q 2017 | 41.1 | 169.8 | 169.8 | -10.3 | 0.00 | 0.00 |
| CONSTITUTION LIFE INS CO | TX | • D | 3q 2017 | 438.3 | 107.2 | 93.2 | 45.7 | 2.74 | 1.59 |
| CONSUMERS LIFE INS CO | OH | • B | 3q 2017 | 47.3 | 35.7 | 11.3 | 27.4 | 2.20 | 1.70 |
| CONTINENTAL AMERICAN INS CO | SC | • B | 3q 2017 | 671.3 | 456.1 | 441.7 | 173.3 | 1.94 | 1.40 |
| CONTINENTAL CASUALTY CO | IL | C+ | 3q 2017 | 43,789.2 | 6,766.2 | 494.9 | 10,805.4 | 1.99 | 1.50 |
| CONTINENTAL GENERAL INS CO | OH | • C+ | 3q 2017 | 1,372.6 | 228.3 | 212.0 | 73.5 | 0.99 | 0.65 |
| CONTINENTAL LIFE INS CO | PA | D+ | 3q 2017 | 27.1 | 4.7 | 0.0 | 2.6 | 0.68 | 0.61 |
| CONTINENTAL LIFE INS CO OF BRENTWOOD | TN | • C+ | 3q 2017 | 336.0 | 428.0 | 423.6 | 190.1 | 1.21 | 1.07 |
| CONTRA COSTA COUNTY MED SVCS | CA | • C | 3q 2017 | 379.8 | 692.0 | 692.0 | 53.9 | 1.19 | 0.75 |
| COOK CHILDRENS HEALTH PLAN | TX | • E+ | 3q 2017 | 121.5 | 345.7 | 345.7 | 63.5 | 2.10 | 1.75 |
| COOPERATIVA DE SEGUROS DE VIDA DE PR | PR | C- | 3q 2017 | 511.4 | 71.7 | 19.0 | 23.0 | 1.15 | 0.53 |
| COORDINATED CARE CORP | IN | • C+ | 3q 2017 | 392.7 | 1,091.2 | 1,091.2 | 147.2 | 2.96 | 2.47 |
| COORDINATED CARE OF WASHINGTON INC | WA | • D+ | 3q 2017 | 245.1 | 680.3 | 680.3 | 89.7 | 2.63 | 2.19 |
| COPIC INS CO | CO | A- | 3q 2017 | 765.4 | 84.7 | 1.1 | 428.4 | 5.76 | 3.74 |
| CORVESTA LIFE INS CO | AZ | U | | -- | -- | -- | -- | -- | -- |
| COUNTRY LIFE INS CO | IL | A+ | 3q 2017 | 9,441.1 | 534.8 | 107.6 | 1,171.1 | 2.08 | 1.37 |
| COUNTRYWAY INS CO | NY | C | 3q 2017 | 28.0 | 36.4 | 0.0 | 23.8 | 17.90 | 16.11 |
| COUNTY OF LOS ANGELES DEPT HEALTH | CA | U | | -- | -- | -- | -- | -- | -- |
| COVENTRY HEALTH & LIFE INS CO | MO | • B | 3q 2017 | 1,487.5 | 2,484.5 | 2,484.5 | 1,083.8 | 7.15 | 5.96 |
| COVENTRY HEALTH CARE OF FLORIDA INC | FL | • C+ | 3q 2017 | 351.7 | 1,368.1 | 1,368.1 | 194.1 | 3.03 | 2.53 |
| COVENTRY HEALTH CARE OF ILLINOIS INC | IL | • C | 3q 2017 | 174.7 | 481.2 | 481.2 | 90.0 | 3.39 | 2.82 |
| COVENTRY HEALTH CARE OF KANSAS INC | KS | • C+ | 3q 2017 | 68.0 | 367.9 | 367.9 | 48.5 | 3.06 | 2.55 |
| COVENTRY HEALTH CARE OF MISSOURI INC | MO | • C+ | 3q 2017 | 401.3 | 588.3 | 588.3 | 155.5 | 5.75 | 4.80 |
| COVENTRY HEALTH CARE OF NEBRASKA INC | NE | • B | 3q 2017 | 162.7 | 567.0 | 567.0 | 90.9 | 3.08 | 2.57 |
| COVENTRY HEALTH CARE OF VIRGINIA INC | VA | • C+ | 3q 2017 | 104.3 | 348.4 | 348.4 | 51.2 | 2.36 | 1.97 |
| COVENTRY HEALTH CARE OF WEST VA INC | WV | • B+ | 3q 2017 | 152.7 | 546.4 | 546.4 | 64.8 | 2.18 | 1.82 |
| COVENTRY HEALTH PLAN OF FLORIDA INC | FL | U | | -- | -- | -- | -- | -- | -- |
| COX HEALTH SYSTEMS HMO INC | MO | U | | -- | -- | -- | -- | -- | -- |
| ▼ COX HEALTH SYSTEMS INS CO | MO | • D+ | 3q 2017 | 37.1 | 131.8 | 131.8 | 10.0 | 0.50 | 0.41 |
| CRESTPOINT HEALTH INS CO | TN | • D | 1q 2017 | 12.0 | 21.8 | 21.8 | 8.6 | 2.08 | 1.74 |
| CRYSTAL RUN HEALTH INS CO INC | NY | • E- | 3q 2017 | 8.3 | 9.4 | 9.4 | 2.4 | 0.73 | 0.61 |
| CRYSTAL RUN HEALTH PLAN LLC | NY | • D- | 3q 2017 | 10.0 | 13.2 | 13.2 | 4.6 | 1.67 | 1.39 |
| CSI LIFE INS CO | NE | B- | 3q 2017 | 20.7 | 16.4 | 16.1 | 13.0 | 1.61 | 1.26 |
| DAILY UNDERWRITERS OF AMERICA | PA | C+ | 3q 2017 | 47.1 | 12.7 | 0.0 | 35.4 | 3.56 | 2.49 |

| INSURANCE COMPANY NAME | DOM. STATE | RATING | DATA DATE | TOTAL ASSETS ($MIL) | TOTAL PREMIUMS ($MIL) | HEALTH PREMIUMS ($MIL) | CAPITAL & SURPLUS ($MIL) | RISK ADJUSTED CAPITAL RATIO 1 | RISK ADJUSTED CAPITAL RATIO 2 |
|---|---|---|---|---|---|---|---|---|---|
| DAKOTA CAPITAL LIFE INS CO | ND | D | 3q 2017 | 6.5 | 1.2 | 0.0 | 1.4 | 1.09 | 0.98 |
| DAVITA HEALTH PLAN OF CA INC | CA | • D+ | 3q 2017 | 174.9 | 1,462.1 | 1,462.1 | 54.4 | 0.64 | 0.39 |
| DC CHARTERED HEALTH PLAN INC | DC | F | 4q 2012 | 56.1 | 0.0 | 0.0 | -9.6 | 0.00 | 0.00 |
| DEAN HEALTH INS INC | WI | U | | -- | -- | -- | -- | -- | -- |
| DEAN HEALTH PLAN INC | WI | • B+ | 3q 2017 | 225.0 | 1,250.9 | 1,250.9 | 128.2 | 2.11 | 1.76 |
| DEARBORN NATIONAL LIFE INS CO | IL | • B+ | 3q 2017 | 1,849.7 | 442.1 | 149.0 | 510.9 | 3.42 | 2.15 |
| DEARBORN NATIONAL LIFE INS CO OF NY | NY | B+ | 3q 2017 | 37.5 | 1.8 | 0.8 | 24.6 | 4.51 | 4.06 |
| DELAWARE AMERICAN LIFE INS CO | DE | • B+ | 3q 2017 | 137.9 | 80.3 | 68.3 | 76.3 | 4.69 | 3.47 |
| DELAWARE LIFE INS CO OF NEW YORK | NY | C+ | 3q 2017 | 2,573.8 | 36.3 | 0.2 | 418.7 | 8.97 | 4.27 |
| DELTA LIFE INS CO | GA | E+ | 3q 2017 | 65.9 | 14.4 | 1.2 | 9.3 | 0.60 | 0.36 |
| DENTAL NETWORK INC | MD | U | | -- | -- | -- | -- | -- | -- |
| DENTISTS BENEFITS INS CO | OR | C | 3q 2017 | 18.7 | 5.1 | 0.6 | 12.8 | 4.61 | 2.83 |
| DENVER HEALTH MEDICAL PLAN INC | CO | • B | 3q 2017 | 60.0 | 137.6 | 137.6 | 31.3 | 2.23 | 1.86 |
| DESERET MUTUAL INS CO | UT | B | 3q 2017 | 40.7 | 14.6 | 14.3 | 12.8 | 2.76 | 1.90 |
| DIGNITY HEALTH PROVIDER RESOURCES | CA | U | | -- | -- | -- | -- | -- | -- |
| DOMINION NATIONAL INSURANCE CO | NJ | U | | -- | -- | -- | -- | -- | -- |
| DONGBU INS CO LTD US GUAM BRANCH | GU | B- | 3q 2017 | 64.4 | 37.2 | 0.0 | 44.4 | 7.29 | 4.40 |
| ▲ DRISCOLL CHILDRENS HEALTH PLAN | TX | • C+ | 3q 2017 | 142.2 | 522.6 | 522.6 | 81.5 | 1.66 | 1.39 |
| EASY CHOICE HEALTH PLAN | CA | • C- | 3q 2017 | 155.8 | 382.1 | 382.1 | 31.4 | 1.06 | 0.66 |
| EDUCATORS HEALTH PLANS LIFE ACCIDENT | UT | • B | 3q 2017 | 40.8 | 39.3 | 39.3 | 20.4 | 2.84 | 2.37 |
| EL PASO HEALTH | TX | • A- | 3q 2017 | 64.2 | 199.7 | 199.7 | 43.1 | 2.23 | 1.86 |
| ELDERPLAN INC | NY | • C | 3q 2017 | 236.3 | 843.5 | 843.5 | 78.2 | 1.02 | 0.85 |
| EMC NATIONAL LIFE CO | IA | B | 3q 2017 | 940.0 | 74.1 | 1.6 | 106.7 | 2.58 | 1.46 |
| EMI HEALTH | UT | • A | 3q 2017 | 107.5 | 31.8 | 31.8 | 81.2 | 5.05 | 4.21 |
| EMPHESYS INS CO | TX | U | | -- | -- | -- | -- | -- | -- |
| EMPIRE FIRE & MARINE INS CO | NE | C+ | 3q 2017 | 58.2 | 368.4 | 14.8 | 39.3 | 11.58 | 10.42 |
| EMPIRE HEALTHCHOICE ASSURANCE INC | NY | • B- | 3q 2017 | 2,273.8 | 2,228.7 | 2,228.7 | 941.5 | 4.86 | 4.05 |
| EMPIRE HEALTHCHOICE HMO INC | NY | • C+ | 3q 2017 | 589.2 | 1,381.4 | 1,381.4 | 196.6 | 2.64 | 2.20 |
| EMPLOYERS INS OF WAUSAU | WI | B- | 3q 2017 | 6,149.7 | 186.8 | 0.0 | 1,536.0 | 2.28 | 1.58 |
| ENTERPRISE LIFE INS CO | TX | • B- | 3q 2017 | 50.0 | 1.0 | 1.0 | 32.2 | 1.16 | 1.03 |
| ENVISION INS CO | OH | U | | -- | -- | -- | -- | -- | -- |
| ENVOLVE DENTAL OF TEXAS INC | TX | U | | -- | -- | -- | -- | -- | -- |
| EON HEALTH INC (GA) | GA | U | | -- | -- | -- | -- | -- | -- |
| EPIC HEALTH PLAN | CA | • D- | 3q 2017 | 34.1 | 343.1 | 343.1 | 13.9 | 0.03 | 0.02 |
| EPIC LIFE INSURANCE CO | WI | C | 3q 2017 | 31.9 | 26.2 | 19.1 | 16.4 | 1.70 | 1.16 |
| ▼ EQUITABLE LIFE & CASUALTY INS CO | UT | • B- | 3q 2017 | 328.0 | 213.0 | 199.5 | 49.8 | 1.91 | 1.20 |
| ERIE FAMILY LIFE INS CO | PA | A- | 3q 2017 | 2,448.7 | 201.6 | 0.2 | 315.7 | 3.17 | 1.73 |
| ESSENCE HEALTHCARE INC | MO | • B+ | 3q 2017 | 288.5 | 657.2 | 657.2 | 86.8 | 1.65 | 1.38 |
| EVANSTON INS CO | IL | C | 3q 2017 | 4,762.4 | 1,233.7 | 0.7 | 1,454.0 | 1.90 | 1.28 |
| EVERENCE INS CO | IN | U | | -- | -- | -- | -- | -- | -- |
| EVEREST REINS CO | DE | B- | 3q 2017 | 11,011.8 | 200.0 | 24.8 | 3,355.6 | 2.79 | 1.76 |
| EVERGREEN HEALTH INC | MD | F | 1q 2017 | 32.6 | 134.4 | 134.4 | -11.7 | 0.00 | 0.00 |
| EXCELLUS HEALTH PLAN INC | NY | • B+ | 3q 2017 | 3,365.4 | 5,983.7 | 5,983.7 | 1,424.5 | 3.84 | 3.20 |
| FALLON COMMUNITY HEALTH PLAN | MA | • B- | 3q 2017 | 394.2 | 1,149.0 | 1,149.0 | 158.0 | 1.72 | 1.44 |
| FALLON HEALTH & LIFE ASR CO | MA | • E | 3q 2017 | 22.5 | 30.1 | 30.1 | 5.1 | 1.27 | 1.06 |
| FAMILY BENEFIT LIFE INS CO | MO | C | 3q 2017 | 150.4 | 37.4 | 0.0 | 9.4 | 1.08 | 0.77 |
| FAMILY HEALTH NETWORK INC | IL | • C | 3q 2017 | 278.6 | 504.1 | 504.1 | 62.4 | 0.87 | 0.73 |
| FAMILY HERITAGE LIFE INS CO OF AMER | OH | • B+ | 3q 2017 | 1,249.5 | 242.3 | 239.1 | 103.8 | 1.82 | 1.15 |
| FAMILY LIFE INS CO | TX | • C | 3q 2017 | 153.4 | 80.9 | 52.8 | 32.2 | 3.43 | 2.86 |
| FAMILYCARE HEALTH PLANS INC | OR | • E- | 3q 2017 | 29.2 | 47.3 | 47.3 | 14.9 | 1.77 | 1.47 |
| FARM BUREAU LIFE INS CO | IA | B+ | 3q 2017 | 8,948.8 | 713.0 | 7.0 | 645.4 | 2.24 | 1.16 |
| FARM BUREAU LIFE INS CO OF MISSOURI | MO | A- | 3q 2017 | 582.3 | 47.5 | 0.3 | 66.2 | 1.66 | 1.10 |

| INSURANCE COMPANY NAME | DOM. STATE | RATING | DATA DATE | TOTAL ASSETS ($MIL) | TOTAL PREMIUMS ($MIL) | HEALTH PREMIUMS ($MIL) | CAPITAL & SURPLUS ($MIL) | RISK ADJUSTED CAPITAL RATIO 1 | RISK ADJUSTED CAPITAL RATIO 2 |
|---|---|---|---|---|---|---|---|---|---|
| FARM BUREAU MUTUAL INS CO OF AR | AR | B | 3q 2017 | 412.6 | 237.1 | 0.1 | 247.9 | 6.31 | 4.41 |
| FARM BUREAU MUTUAL INS CO OF MI | MI | B | 3q 2017 | 772.1 | 167.9 | 0.0 | 393.0 | 4.75 | 3.12 |
| FARM FAMILY LIFE INS CO | NY | B | 3q 2017 | 1,359.1 | 75.2 | 5.1 | 192.5 | 2.61 | 1.47 |
| FARMERS MUTUAL HAIL INS CO OF IA | IA | B- | 3q 2017 | 1,056.2 | 486.5 | 0.0 | 459.8 | 1.43 | 1.00 |
| FARMERS NEW WORLD LIFE INS CO | WA | B- | 3q 2017 | 5,171.5 | 1,008.7 | 17.8 | 563.4 | 2.39 | 1.27 |
| FARMLAND MUTUAL INS CO | IA | B | 3q 2017 | 576.7 | 218.5 | 0.0 | 170.4 | 3.90 | 2.78 |
| FEDERAL INS CO | IN | B- | 3q 2017 | 27,298.2 | 5,824.1 | 225.1 | 11,843.0 | 1.32 | 1.19 |
| FEDERAL LIFE INS CO | IL | C- | 3q 2017 | 238.0 | 21.7 | 0.1 | 14.4 | 1.77 | 0.99 |
| FEDERATED LIFE INS CO | MN | A | 3q 2017 | 1,849.9 | 207.1 | 26.8 | 381.0 | 4.59 | 2.45 |
| FEDERATED MUTUAL INS CO | MN | • B | 3q 2017 | 5,784.4 | 1,453.8 | 486.5 | 3,296.2 | 3.52 | 2.80 |
| FIDELITY LIFE ASSN A LEGAL RESERVE | IL | C+ | 3q 2017 | 400.7 | 138.9 | 1.3 | 123.6 | 6.55 | 3.41 |
| FIDELITY SECURITY LIFE INS CO | MO | • B | 3q 2017 | 930.2 | 834.0 | 802.1 | 201.8 | 3.66 | 2.18 |
| FIDELITY SECURITY LIFE INS CO OF NY | NY | B | 3q 2017 | 41.1 | 22.5 | 22.5 | 11.0 | 2.35 | 2.04 |
| FINANCIAL AMERICAN LIFE INS CO | KS | E+ | 3q 2017 | 4.3 | -0.5 | 0.0 | 1.9 | 1.10 | 0.99 |
| FIRST ALLMERICA FINANCIAL LIFE INS | MA | B- | 3q 2017 | 3,380.8 | 62.9 | 0.1 | 199.2 | 4.34 | 2.03 |
| FIRST ASR LIFE OF AMERICA | LA | B | 3q 2017 | 40.7 | 12.2 | 2.3 | 35.1 | 3.31 | 3.07 |
| ▼ FIRST CARE INC | MD | • C+ | 3q 2017 | 7.4 | 0.6 | 0.6 | 6.5 | 111.68 | 93.07 |
| FIRST CHICAGO INS CO | IL | D | 3q 2017 | 85.4 | 55.0 | 0.0 | 16.5 | 1.05 | 0.68 |
| FIRST COMMUNITY HEALTH PLAN INC | AL | • B | 3q 2017 | 7.8 | 7.7 | 7.7 | 6.3 | 9.09 | 7.57 |
| FIRST CONTINENTAL LIFE & ACC INS CO | TX | D | 3q 2017 | 3.7 | 12.0 | 12.0 | 2.2 | 1.26 | 0.95 |
| FIRST HEALTH LIFE & HEALTH INS CO | TX | • B- | 3q 2017 | 515.7 | 799.0 | 798.3 | 207.8 | 1.49 | 1.22 |
| FIRST INS CO OF HI LTD | HI | C | 3q 2017 | 669.4 | 82.0 | 1.1 | 286.1 | 4.88 | 3.39 |
| ▲ FIRST MEDICAL HEALTH PLAN INC | PR | • E | 3q 2017 | 195.6 | 1,048.9 | 1,048.9 | 43.1 | 0.42 | 0.35 |
| FIRST NATIONAL LIFE INS CO | NE | C- | 3q 2017 | 5.9 | 0.9 | 0.4 | 1.9 | 0.90 | 0.60 |
| FIRST NET INS CO | GU | C- | 3q 2017 | 17.8 | 11.4 | 0.4 | 11.9 | 2.41 | 1.74 |
| FIRST PENN-PACIFIC LIFE INS CO | IN | B | 3q 2017 | 1,487.9 | 120.0 | 0.0 | 162.8 | 2.44 | 1.32 |
| FIRST PRIORITY LIFE INS CO | PA | U | | -- | -- | -- | -- | -- | -- |
| FIRST RELIANCE STANDARD LIFE INS CO | NY | • A | 3q 2017 | 197.5 | 85.2 | 50.7 | 66.7 | 5.84 | 3.71 |
| FIRST SYMETRA NATL LIFE INS CO OF NY | NY | B+ | 3q 2017 | 1,776.8 | 396.4 | 16.6 | 116.9 | 2.47 | 1.19 |
| FIRST UNUM LIFE INS CO | NY | • C+ | 3q 2017 | 3,352.5 | 430.1 | 343.4 | 306.9 | 2.76 | 1.39 |
| FIRSTCAROLINACARE INS CO | NC | • D | 3q 2017 | 35.1 | 117.7 | 117.7 | 12.1 | 0.76 | 0.63 |
| FIVE STAR LIFE INS CO | LA | C+ | 3q 2017 | 290.7 | 139.9 | 0.1 | 30.9 | 2.16 | 1.34 |
| FLORIDA COMBINED LIFE INS CO INC | FL | • C | 3q 2017 | 52.4 | 124.8 | 100.9 | 31.0 | 5.24 | 3.24 |
| FLORIDA HEALTH CARE PLAN INC | FL | • B+ | 3q 2017 | 204.7 | 428.0 | 428.0 | 90.4 | 5.68 | 4.74 |
| FLORIDA HLTH SOLUTION HMO CO | FL | U | | -- | -- | -- | -- | -- | -- |
| FLORIDA MHS INC | FL | • D | 3q 2017 | 237.3 | 549.1 | 549.1 | 107.6 | 2.51 | 2.09 |
| FLORIDA TRUE HEALTH INC | FL | • E | 3q 2017 | 222.2 | 1,102.8 | 1,102.8 | 86.6 | 1.53 | 1.28 |
| FORESTERS LIFE INS & ANNUITY CO | NY | C+ | 3q 2017 | 2,360.8 | 223.9 | 0.0 | 65.5 | 1.67 | 0.88 |
| FORETHOUGHT LIFE INS CO | IN | B | 3q 2017 | 30,543.9 | 5,896.9 | 71.7 | 1,683.7 | 1.31 | 0.72 |
| FOUNDATION LIFE INS CO OF AR | AR | D | 3q 2017 | 5.2 | 1.2 | 0.2 | 1.2 | 1.06 | 0.95 |
| ▲ FREEDOM HEALTH INC | FL | • D- | 3q 2017 | 282.0 | 871.2 | 871.2 | 41.7 | 0.45 | 0.38 |
| FREEDOM LIFE INS CO OF AMERICA | TX | • C+ | 3q 2017 | 132.9 | 271.7 | 242.9 | 71.1 | 0.95 | 0.79 |
| FREELANCERS INS CO | NY | U | | -- | -- | -- | -- | -- | -- |
| FRESENIUS HEALTH PLANS INS CO | IN | • D | 3q 2017 | 38.2 | 20.8 | 20.8 | 15.1 | 3.35 | 2.79 |
| FRESENIUS HEALTH PLANS OF NC INC | NC | • D+ | 3q 2017 | 14.3 | 7.0 | 7.0 | 2.9 | 1.11 | 0.92 |
| FRESENIUS HEALTH PLANS OF TEXAS INC | TX | U | | -- | -- | -- | -- | -- | -- |
| ▲ FRESNO-KINGS-MADERA REGIONAL HEALTH | CA | • D+ | 3q 2017 | 346.0 | 1,092.6 | 1,092.6 | 52.8 | 0.82 | 0.50 |
| FRIDAY HEALTH PLANS OF CO INC | CO | • E- | 3q 2017 | 22.3 | 92.5 | 92.5 | 3.3 | 0.12 | 0.10 |
| GARDEN STATE LIFE INS CO | TX | A- | 3q 2017 | 131.8 | 26.6 | 0.0 | 73.8 | 8.09 | 7.28 |
| GATEWAY HEALTH PLAN INC | PA | • B- | 3q 2017 | 829.4 | 2,380.6 | 2,380.6 | 359.7 | 2.79 | 2.32 |
| GATEWAY HEALTH PLAN OF OHIO INC | OH | • C | 3q 2017 | 46.3 | 78.5 | 78.5 | 13.3 | 2.81 | 2.35 |
| GEISINGER HEALTH PLAN | PA | • B+ | 3q 2017 | 688.5 | 2,132.4 | 2,132.4 | 313.5 | 1.97 | 1.64 |

| INSURANCE COMPANY NAME | DOM. STATE | RATING | DATA DATE | TOTAL ASSETS ($MIL) | TOTAL PREMIUMS ($MIL) | HEALTH PREMIUMS ($MIL) | CAPITAL & SURPLUS ($MIL) | RISK ADJUSTED CAPITAL RATIO 1 | RISK ADJUSTED CAPITAL RATIO 2 |
|---|---|---|---|---|---|---|---|---|---|
| GEISINGER INDEMNITY INS CO | PA | • C+ | 3q 2017 | 79.8 | 138.8 | 138.8 | 17.5 | 1.02 | 0.85 |
| GEISINGER QUALITY OPTIONS INC | PA | • C+ | 3q 2017 | 73.7 | 265.0 | 265.0 | 36.6 | 1.54 | 1.29 |
| GENERAL AMERICAN LIFE INS CO | MO | B | 3q 2017 | 13,263.1 | 459.1 | 6.3 | 1,008.6 | 3.23 | 1.45 |
| GENESIS INS CO | DE | C | 3q 2017 | 192.7 | 17.7 | 0.2 | 128.1 | 6.59 | 4.64 |
| GENWORTH LIFE & ANNUITY INS CO | VA | B- | 3q 2017 | 22,616.8 | 1,464.2 | 51.1 | 1,586.6 | 2.13 | 1.27 |
| GENWORTH LIFE INS CO | DE | • C+ | 3q 2017 | 40,425.9 | 2,884.4 | 2,482.0 | 3,257.4 | 1.36 | 1.00 |
| GENWORTH LIFE INS CO OF NEW YORK | NY | • C | 3q 2017 | 8,167.4 | 343.7 | 252.7 | 473.5 | 2.17 | 1.10 |
| GERBER LIFE INS CO | NY | • B+ | 3q 2017 | 3,650.7 | 907.7 | 471.7 | 311.4 | 1.74 | 1.04 |
| GERMANIA LIFE INS CO | TX | C+ | 3q 2017 | 88.7 | 10.3 | 0.0 | 8.3 | 1.06 | 0.95 |
| GHS HEALTH MAINTENANCE ORGANIZATION | OK | • B- | 3q 2017 | 62.3 | 38.7 | 38.7 | 19.7 | 2.47 | 2.05 |
| ▼ GHS INS CO | OK | • E- | 3q 2017 | 35.5 | 26.5 | 26.5 | 4.2 | 2.73 | 2.28 |
| GHS MANAGED HEALTH CARE PLANS INC | OK | • E | 2q 2017 | 27.7 | 35.3 | 35.3 | 11.2 | 2.75 | 2.29 |
| GLOBALHEALTH INC | OK | • D | 3q 2017 | 49.3 | 256.4 | 256.4 | 19.3 | 1.09 | 0.91 |
| GLOBE LIFE & ACCIDENT INS CO | NE | B- | 3q 2017 | 4,416.0 | 825.3 | 32.0 | 223.8 | 1.28 | 0.68 |
| GLOBE LIFE INSURANCE CO OF NY | NY | • B+ | 3q 2017 | 237.8 | 71.8 | 41.1 | 36.3 | 2.17 | 1.36 |
| GOLDEN RULE INS CO | IN | • B | 3q 2017 | 508.5 | 1,386.1 | 1,352.9 | 222.7 | 1.28 | 1.01 |
| GOLDEN SECURITY INS CO | TN | • B | 3q 2017 | 44.2 | 56.6 | 56.6 | 31.3 | 2.62 | 2.19 |
| GOLDEN STATE MEDICARE HEALTH PLAN | CA | • E+ | 3q 2017 | 6.5 | 66.0 | 66.0 | 1.3 | 0.19 | 0.12 |
| GOOD HEALTH HMO INC | MO | • C | 3q 2017 | 78.4 | 189.5 | 189.5 | 56.1 | 4.24 | 3.53 |
| GOOD SAMARITAN INS PLAN OF ND | ND | U | | -- | -- | -- | -- | -- | -- |
| GOOD SAMARITAN INS PLAN OF NE | NE | U | | -- | -- | -- | -- | -- | -- |
| GOOD SAMARITAN INS PLAN OF SD | SD | U | | -- | -- | -- | -- | -- | -- |
| GOVERNMENT EMPLOYEES INS CO | MD | B | 3q 2017 | 32,071.6 | 5,379.6 | 0.1 | 18,404.3 | 3.04 | 1.88 |
| GOVERNMENT PERSONNEL MUTUAL L I C | TX | • B+ | 3q 2017 | 832.3 | 80.8 | 32.6 | 122.3 | 2.50 | 1.62 |
| GPM HEALTH & LIFE INS CO | WA | B | 3q 2017 | 141.1 | 4.5 | 0.0 | 12.6 | 1.44 | 1.29 |
| GRAND VALLEY HEALTH PLAN INC | MI | • E- | 2q 2017 | 1.2 | 17.0 | 17.0 | 0.4 | 0.06 | 0.05 |
| GRANGE LIFE INS CO | OH | C | 3q 2017 | 406.6 | 102.4 | 0.2 | 73.1 | 2.50 | 1.69 |
| GRANITE STATE HEALTH PLAN INC | NH | • D+ | 3q 2017 | 92.3 | 280.8 | 280.8 | 22.8 | 6.53 | 5.44 |
| GREAT AMERICAN INS CO | OH | B | 3q 2017 | 7,086.1 | 2,021.8 | 47.4 | 1,480.2 | 1.41 | 1.08 |
| GREAT AMERICAN LIFE INS CO | OH | B- | 3q 2017 | 32,146.2 | 4,269.0 | 7.6 | 2,128.1 | 1.79 | 0.99 |
| GREAT CENTRAL LIFE INS CO | LA | C+ | 4q 2016 | 23.6 | 2.2 | 0.3 | 7.8 | 1.43 | 0.95 |
| GREAT FIDELITY LIFE INS CO | IN | D | 3q 2017 | 3.0 | 0.6 | 0.6 | 2.6 | 2.20 | 1.98 |
| GREAT MIDWEST INS CO | TX | • B | 3q 2017 | 206.6 | 151.2 | 71.4 | 103.4 | 2.67 | 1.74 |
| GREAT PLAINS CASUALTY INC | IA | C+ | 3q 2017 | 22.3 | 5.3 | 0.0 | 19.8 | 5.87 | 3.47 |
| GREAT SOUTHERN LIFE INS CO | TX | B | 3q 2017 | 215.2 | 55.9 | 1.7 | 49.6 | 5.39 | 2.79 |
| GREAT WEST LIFE ASR CO | MI | C+ | 3q 2017 | 75.8 | 11.8 | 1.5 | 24.9 | 3.17 | 2.69 |
| GREAT-WEST LIFE & ANNUITY INS CO | CO | B- | 3q 2017 | 59,394.3 | 6,056.6 | 59.0 | 1,054.9 | 1.24 | 0.67 |
| GREAT-WEST LIFE & ANNUITY INS OF NY | NY | B | 3q 2017 | 2,173.4 | 379.3 | 0.0 | 85.3 | 2.24 | 1.20 |
| GREATER GEORGIA LIFE INS CO | GA | B | 3q 2017 | 57.8 | 33.3 | 14.5 | 19.5 | 1.26 | 0.94 |
| GREENVILLE CASUALTY INS CO INC | SC | C- | 3q 2017 | 9.5 | 8.4 | 1.4 | 5.6 | 1.93 | 1.73 |
| GREENWICH INS CO | DE | C | 3q 2017 | 1,177.9 | 583.2 | 11.0 | 338.6 | 1.65 | 1.41 |
| GROUP HEALTH COOP OF EAU CLAIRE | WI | • E+ | 3q 2017 | 51.1 | 174.1 | 174.1 | 22.3 | 1.17 | 0.97 |
| GROUP HEALTH COOP OF S CENTRAL WI | WI | • D | 3q 2017 | 91.8 | 364.9 | 364.9 | 48.3 | 1.57 | 1.31 |
| GROUP HEALTH INCORPORATED | NY | • E | 3q 2017 | 652.7 | 908.8 | 908.8 | 229.6 | 3.10 | 2.58 |
| GROUP HEALTH PLAN INC | MN | • A- | 3q 2017 | 902.1 | 1,262.9 | 1,262.9 | 165.3 | 2.80 | 2.33 |
| GROUP HOSP & MEDICAL SERVICES INC | DC | • B- | 3q 2017 | 2,297.6 | 3,495.4 | 3,495.4 | 1,016.8 | 5.16 | 4.30 |
| GUARANTEE TRUST LIFE INS CO | IL | • B | 3q 2017 | 592.0 | 245.6 | 227.2 | 79.6 | 1.83 | 1.20 |
| GUARANTY ASSURANCE CO | LA | U | | -- | -- | -- | -- | -- | -- |
| GUARANTY INCOME LIFE INS CO | LA | C+ | 3q 2017 | 610.3 | 46.9 | 3.7 | 55.2 | 3.34 | 1.58 |
| GUARDIAN INS CO | VI | C | 3q 2017 | 49.6 | 25.6 | 0.0 | 13.8 | 1.73 | 1.36 |
| GUARDIAN LIFE INS CO OF AMERICA | NY | • A | 3q 2017 | 55,226.5 | 7,731.4 | 3,119.1 | 6,864.6 | 2.87 | 1.84 |
| GUGGENHEIM LIFE & ANNUITY CO | DE | B- | 3q 2017 | 13,970.4 | 818.0 | 0.0 | 553.0 | 1.06 | 0.62 |

| INSURANCE COMPANY NAME | DOM. STATE | RATING | DATA DATE | TOTAL ASSETS ($MIL) | TOTAL PREMIUMS ($MIL) | HEALTH PREMIUMS ($MIL) | CAPITAL & SURPLUS ($MIL) | RISK ADJUSTED CAPITAL RATIO 1 | RISK ADJUSTED CAPITAL RATIO 2 |
|---|---|---|---|---|---|---|---|---|---|
| GULF GUARANTY LIFE INS CO | MS | C | 3q 2017 | 18.4 | 6.5 | 3.3 | 10.5 | 1.55 | 1.17 |
| GUNDERSEN HEALTH PLAN INC | WI | • C- | 3q 2017 | 53.9 | 301.4 | 301.4 | 23.3 | 1.38 | 1.15 |
| GUNDERSEN HLTH PLAN MN INC | MN | • C | 3q 2017 | 3.0 | 6.4 | 6.4 | 2.1 | 1.23 | 1.02 |
| HAP MIDWEST HEALTH PLAN INC | MI | • C | 3q 2017 | 62.4 | 122.4 | 122.4 | 24.8 | 2.79 | 2.32 |
| ▲ HARBOR HEALTH PLAN INC | MI | • E | 3q 2017 | 17.1 | 51.8 | 51.8 | 7.0 | 1.42 | 1.19 |
| HARKEN HEALTH INS CO | WI | • C | 3q 2017 | 62.9 | 147.2 | 147.2 | 54.1 | 2.67 | 2.22 |
| HARLEYSVILLE LIFE INS CO | PA | B | 3q 2017 | 406.1 | 34.0 | 0.0 | 47.0 | 2.99 | 1.61 |
| HARMONY HEALTH PLAN INC | IL | • C | 3q 2017 | 514.9 | 1,069.7 | 1,069.7 | 158.6 | 3.20 | 2.67 |
| HARTFORD FIRE INS CO | CT | B | 3q 2017 | 25,552.7 | 1,700.9 | 0.0 | 12,463.4 | 2.01 | 1.55 |
| HARTFORD LIFE & ACCIDENT INS CO | CT | • B- | 3q 2017 | 9,168.5 | 2,978.8 | 1,699.7 | 1,624.3 | 4.00 | 2.53 |
| HARTFORD LIFE & ANNUITY INS CO | CT | B- | 3q 2017 | 36,874.4 | 1,248.2 | 0.2 | 1,456.7 | 4.16 | 2.08 |
| HARTFORD LIFE INS CO | CT | C+ | 3q 2017 | 110,132.0 | 2,272.6 | 101.0 | 4,100.6 | 1.60 | 1.20 |
| HARVARD PILGRIM HC OF NEW ENGLAND | MA | • C | 3q 2017 | 142.9 | 482.2 | 482.2 | 63.0 | 2.74 | 2.29 |
| HARVARD PILGRIM HEALTH CARE INC | MA | • C+ | 3q 2017 | 923.5 | 1,782.3 | 1,782.3 | 478.7 | 2.44 | 2.03 |
| ▼ HARVARD PILGRIM HEALTH CARE OF CT | CT | • D+ | 3q 2017 | 14.9 | 4.0 | 4.0 | 14.5 | 9.33 | 7.77 |
| HARVESTPLAINS HEALTH OF IOWA | IA | • C- | 2q 2017 | 3.2 | 2.7 | 2.7 | 3.0 | 6.40 | 5.33 |
| HAWAII MANAGEMENT ALLIANCE ASSOC | HI | • C- | 3q 2017 | 43.3 | 131.2 | 131.2 | 16.8 | 0.96 | 0.80 |
| HAWAII MEDICAL SERVICE ASSOCIATION | HI | • B- | 3q 2017 | 1,155.2 | 3,158.0 | 3,158.0 | 462.1 | 2.15 | 1.79 |
| HCC LIFE INS CO | IN | • B | 3q 2017 | 1,058.7 | 1,068.7 | 1,065.7 | 689.6 | 5.38 | 4.15 |
| HCC SPECIALTY INS CO | OK | B- | 3q 2017 | 19.9 | 23.6 | 0.1 | 16.8 | 16.91 | 15.22 |
| HCSC INS SERVICES CO | IL | • D- | 3q 2017 | 788.7 | 1,391.7 | 1,391.7 | 218.0 | 2.51 | 2.09 |
| HEALTH ADVANTAGE FLORIDA INC | FL | U | | -- | -- | -- | -- | -- | -- |
| HEALTH ALLIANCE CONNECT INC | IL | • C | 3q 2017 | 130.2 | 647.4 | 647.4 | 69.4 | 0.99 | 0.82 |
| HEALTH ALLIANCE MEDICAL PLANS | IL | • B- | 3q 2017 | 645.7 | 1,133.1 | 1,133.1 | 213.8 | 2.75 | 2.30 |
| ▲ HEALTH ALLIANCE NORTHWEST HEALTH PL | WA | • B- | 3q 2017 | 23.8 | 44.5 | 44.5 | 9.6 | 3.43 | 2.86 |
| HEALTH ALLIANCE PLAN OF MICHIGAN | MI | • C+ | 3q 2017 | 587.2 | 1,924.3 | 1,924.3 | 214.7 | 1.25 | 1.04 |
| HEALTH ALLIANCE-MIDWEST INC | IL | • E | 3q 2017 | 21.0 | 18.8 | 18.8 | 7.6 | 2.36 | 1.97 |
| HEALTH CARE SVC CORP A MUT LEG RES | IL | • B | 3q 2017 | 21,258.2 | 30,335.8 | 30,335.8 | 11,588.1 | 5.73 | 4.77 |
| HEALTH CHOICE INS CO | AZ | • E- | 1q 2017 | 22.8 | 26.9 | 26.9 | 4.4 | 0.49 | 0.41 |
| HEALTH CHOICE UTAH INC | UT | • E- | 3q 2017 | 21.7 | 55.6 | 55.6 | 13.9 | 1.59 | 1.33 |
| HEALTH FIRST COMMERCIAL PLANS INC | FL | • B- | 3q 2017 | 74.3 | 72.6 | 72.6 | 40.5 | 5.72 | 4.76 |
| ▲ HEALTH FIRST HEALTH PLANS INC | FL | • B | 3q 2017 | 157.3 | 443.3 | 443.3 | 69.2 | 2.01 | 1.68 |
| ▲ HEALTH FIRST INS INC | FL | • D | 3q 2017 | 5.6 | 0.3 | 0.3 | 4.6 | 4.13 | 3.44 |
| HEALTH INS CO OF AM INC | NY | • D | 3q 2017 | 1.5 | 0.6 | 0.6 | 0.5 | 7.67 | 6.39 |
| HEALTH INSURANCE PLAN OF GREATER NY | NY | • C- | 3q 2017 | 1,413.4 | 4,855.3 | 4,855.3 | 470.7 | 1.14 | 0.95 |
| HEALTH NET COMMUNITY SOLUTIONS INC | CA | • B | 3q 2017 | 3,147.0 | 7,482.8 | 7,482.8 | 944.7 | 2.02 | 1.37 |
| HEALTH NET HEALTH PLAN OF OREGON INC | OR | • E- | 3q 2017 | 210.2 | 506.2 | 506.2 | 101.5 | 2.58 | 2.15 |
| HEALTH NET LIFE INS CO | CA | • C | 3q 2017 | 748.6 | 1,499.3 | 1,497.5 | 423.9 | 3.78 | 3.10 |
| HEALTH NET OF ARIZONA INC | AZ | • C | 3q 2017 | 415.0 | 360.9 | 360.9 | 171.9 | 3.47 | 2.89 |
| HEALTH NET OF CALIFORNIA INC | CA | • C | 3q 2017 | 2,341.4 | 6,751.6 | 6,751.6 | 987.9 | 1.80 | 1.20 |
| HEALTH NEW ENGLAND INC | MA | • C- | 3q 2017 | 204.3 | 930.1 | 930.1 | 69.6 | 0.72 | 0.60 |
| ▲ HEALTH OPTIONS INC | FL | • B+ | 3q 2017 | 1,453.7 | 2,585.6 | 2,585.6 | 568.9 | 4.33 | 3.61 |
| HEALTH PARTNERS PLANS INC | PA | • B- | 3q 2017 | 681.2 | 1,917.0 | 1,917.0 | 134.5 | 0.96 | 0.80 |
| HEALTH PLAN OF CAREOREGON INC | OR | • C | 3q 2017 | 73.8 | 163.3 | 163.3 | 20.3 | 1.06 | 0.88 |
| HEALTH PLAN OF NEVADA INC | NV | • B | 3q 2017 | 690.0 | 2,569.9 | 2,569.9 | 299.0 | 2.64 | 2.20 |
| HEALTH PLAN OF WV INC | WV | • C | 3q 2017 | 260.8 | 566.7 | 566.7 | 148.3 | 2.35 | 1.96 |
| HEALTH REPUBLIC INS CO | OR | • E | 3q 2016 | 8.8 | 46.2 | 46.2 | 4.1 | 0.29 | 0.24 |
| HEALTH TRADITION HEALTH PLAN | WI | • B | 3q 2017 | 47.7 | 142.2 | 142.2 | 12.2 | 1.21 | 1.01 |
| HEALTHASSURANCE PENNSYLVANIA INC | PA | • B- | 3q 2017 | 417.8 | 1,015.7 | 1,015.7 | 170.2 | 3.37 | 2.81 |
| HEALTHFIRST HEALTH PLAN INC | NY | • C+ | 3q 2017 | 993.2 | 2,238.2 | 2,238.2 | 286.7 | 1.53 | 1.27 |
| HEALTHFIRST HEALTH PLAN NEW JERSEY | NJ | U | | -- | -- | -- | -- | -- | -- |
| HEALTHFIRST INSURANCE CO | NY | U | | -- | -- | -- | -- | -- | -- |



Arrows denote recent upgrades ▲ or downgrades▼

• Bullets denote a more detailed analysis is available in Section II.

| | INSURANCE COMPANY NAME | DOM. STATE | RATING | DATA DATE | TOTAL ASSETS ($MIL) | TOTAL PREMIUMS ($MIL) | HEALTH PREMIUMS ($MIL) | CAPITAL & SURPLUS ($MIL) | RISK ADJUSTED CAPITAL RATIO 1 | RISK ADJUSTED CAPITAL RATIO 2 |
|---|---|---|---|---|---|---|---|---|---|---|
| | HEALTHKEEPERS INC | VA | • B+ | 3q 2017 | 1,218.8 | 3,120.5 | 3,120.5 | 643.9 | 3.51 | 2.93 |
| | HEALTHLINK HMO INC | MO | U | | -- | -- | -- | -- | -- | -- |
| | HEALTHNOW NY INC | NY | • C+ | 3q 2017 | 1,140.1 | 2,311.2 | 2,311.2 | 609.2 | 3.87 | 3.23 |
| | HEALTHPARTNERS | MN | • A+ | 3q 2017 | 1,213.6 | 1,371.7 | 1,371.7 | 953.4 | 3.55 | 2.96 |
| | HEALTHPARTNERS INS CO | MN | • B | 3q 2017 | 386.9 | 1,053.8 | 1,053.8 | 193.5 | 2.80 | 2.33 |
| | HEALTHPLEX OF NJ INC | NJ | • D+ | 4q 2016 | 6.0 | 29.7 | 29.7 | 4.2 | 1.09 | 0.91 |
| | HEALTHPLUS INS CO TRUST | MI | U | | -- | -- | -- | -- | -- | -- |
| | HEALTHPLUS PARTNERS INC TRUST | MI | U | | -- | -- | -- | -- | -- | -- |
| | HEALTHSPAN LLC | OH | U | | -- | -- | -- | -- | -- | -- |
| ▼ | HEALTHSPRING L&H INS CO | TX | • C+ | 3q 2017 | 643.1 | 2,367.0 | 2,367.0 | 252.6 | 1.96 | 1.63 |
| | HEALTHSPRING OF ALABAMA INC | AL | • B | 3q 2017 | 213.1 | 694.8 | 694.8 | 77.6 | 2.32 | 1.93 |
| | HEALTHSPRING OF FLORIDA INC | FL | • B+ | 3q 2017 | 233.5 | 866.7 | 866.7 | 93.1 | 2.52 | 2.10 |
| | HEALTHSPRING OF TENNESSEE INC | TN | • B+ | 3q 2017 | 460.4 | 1,667.7 | 1,667.7 | 198.8 | 2.06 | 1.72 |
| | HEALTHY ALLIANCE LIFE INS CO | MO | • A- | 3q 2017 | 1,295.0 | 1,942.0 | 1,942.0 | 467.9 | 4.58 | 3.81 |
| | HEALTHY PALM BEACHES INC | FL | U | | -- | -- | -- | -- | -- | -- |
| | HEARTLAND NATIONAL LIFE INS CO | IN | B- | 3q 2017 | 12.9 | 30.6 | 30.5 | 7.9 | 2.96 | 2.67 |
| | HEARTLANDPLAINS HEALTH | NE | • E- | 3q 2017 | 5.0 | 6.3 | 6.3 | 2.0 | 1.88 | 1.56 |
| | HENNEPIN HEALTH | MN | • C | 3q 2017 | 88.9 | 127.0 | 127.0 | 37.0 | 2.79 | 2.32 |
| | HERITAGE PROVIDER NETWORK INC | CA | • D | 3q 2017 | 544.2 | 2,432.2 | 2,432.2 | 120.1 | 0.60 | 0.37 |
| | HIGHMARK BCBSD INC | DE | • B- | 3q 2017 | 407.7 | 705.8 | 705.8 | 210.1 | 5.07 | 4.22 |
| | HIGHMARK BENEFITS GROUP INC | PA | U | | -- | -- | -- | -- | -- | -- |
| | HIGHMARK CASUALTY INS CO | PA | • C | 3q 2017 | 282.1 | 138.7 | 116.2 | 185.5 | 4.91 | 3.22 |
| | HIGHMARK CHOICE CO | PA | U | | -- | -- | -- | -- | -- | -- |
| | HIGHMARK COVERAGE ADVANTAGE INC | PA | U | | -- | -- | -- | -- | -- | -- |
| | HIGHMARK INC | PA | • C | 3q 2017 | 7,778.7 | 8,742.8 | 8,742.8 | 4,327.3 | 3.61 | 3.01 |
| | HIGHMARK SELECT RESOURCES INC | PA | U | | -- | -- | -- | -- | -- | -- |
| | HIGHMARK SENIOR HEALTH CO | PA | U | | -- | -- | -- | -- | -- | -- |
| | HIGHMARK SENIOR SOLUTIONS CO | WV | U | | -- | -- | -- | -- | -- | -- |
| | HIGHMARK WEST VIRGINIA INC | WV | • B | 3q 2017 | 730.0 | 1,192.5 | 1,192.5 | 383.3 | 5.65 | 4.71 |
| | HIP INS CO OF NEW YORK | NY | • D- | 3q 2017 | 55.2 | 8.3 | 8.3 | 40.3 | 36.66 | 30.55 |
| | HM HEALTH INS CO | PA | U | | -- | -- | -- | -- | -- | -- |
| | HM LIFE INS CO | PA | • B- | 3q 2017 | 687.4 | 754.5 | 754.4 | 377.1 | 3.33 | 2.39 |
| | HM LIFE INS CO OF NEW YORK | NY | • B | 3q 2017 | 69.1 | 70.0 | 70.0 | 45.2 | 3.53 | 2.81 |
| | HMO COLORADO | CO | • B- | 3q 2017 | 216.9 | 285.2 | 285.2 | 83.0 | 4.58 | 3.82 |
| | HMO LOUISIANA INC | LA | • A+ | 3q 2017 | 669.8 | 719.2 | 719.2 | 388.5 | 8.41 | 7.01 |
| | HMO MINNESOTA | MN | • C | 3q 2017 | 851.4 | 1,816.2 | 1,816.2 | 458.9 | 3.71 | 3.09 |
| | HMO MISSOURI INC | MO | • B | 3q 2017 | 96.5 | 149.5 | 149.5 | 50.9 | 7.58 | 6.31 |
| | HMO OF NORTHEASTERN PENNSYLVANIA INC | PA | U | | -- | -- | -- | -- | -- | -- |
| | HMO PARTNERS INC | AR | • A+ | 3q 2017 | 135.4 | 191.1 | 191.1 | 66.5 | 5.59 | 4.66 |
| | HN1 THERAPY NETWORK NEW JERSEY LLC | NJ | • C- | 4q 2016 | 2.8 | 3.0 | 3.0 | 2.3 | 0.86 | 0.71 |
| | HNE INS CO | MA | • C | 3q 2017 | 5.1 | 0.5 | 0.5 | 5.0 | 71.70 | 59.75 |
| | HNE OF CONNECTICUT INC | CT | • D | 3q 2017 | 4.5 | 1.1 | 1.1 | 3.8 | 1.90 | 1.58 |
| | HOME STATE HEALTH PLAN INC | MO | • C- | 3q 2017 | 186.7 | 344.4 | 344.4 | 44.5 | 2.26 | 1.88 |
| | HOMELAND INS CO OF NY | NY | C | 3q 2017 | 117.8 | 197.1 | 3.4 | 115.5 | 2.27 | 2.23 |
| | HOMETOWN HEALTH PLAN INC | NV | • C- | 3q 2017 | 121.1 | 266.5 | 266.5 | 41.2 | 1.37 | 1.14 |
| | HOMETOWN HEALTH PROVIDERS INS CO | NV | • B- | 3q 2017 | 57.0 | 97.4 | 97.4 | 29.8 | 2.71 | 2.26 |
| ▲ | HOOSIER MOTOR MUTUAL INS CO | IN | • B | 3q 2017 | 12.0 | 0.6 | 0.6 | 11.5 | 11.15 | 9.29 |
| | HOPKINS HEALTH ADV INC | MD | • E | 3q 2017 | 27.1 | 42.7 | 42.7 | 2.4 | 0.25 | 0.21 |
| | HORACE MANN INS CO | IL | B | 3q 2017 | 484.3 | 227.1 | 0.0 | 186.1 | 2.99 | 1.96 |
| | HORACE MANN LIFE INS CO | IL | B | 3q 2017 | 9,154.5 | 633.7 | 3.1 | 455.3 | 1.73 | 0.87 |
| | HORIZON HEALTHCARE OF NEW JERSEY INC | NJ | • A- | 3q 2017 | 1,358.6 | 4,868.0 | 4,868.0 | 988.6 | 3.55 | 2.96 |
| | HORIZON HEALTHCARE SERVICES INC | NJ | • B | 4q 2016 | 4,257.6 | 6,692.7 | 6,692.7 | 2,385.9 | 3.59 | 3.00 |

| INSURANCE COMPANY NAME | DOM. STATE | RATING | DATA DATE | TOTAL ASSETS ($MIL) | TOTAL PREMIUMS ($MIL) | HEALTH PREMIUMS ($MIL) | CAPITAL & SURPLUS ($MIL) | RISK ADJUSTED CAPITAL RATIO 1 | RISK ADJUSTED CAPITAL RATIO 2 |
|---|---|---|---|---|---|---|---|---|---|
| HORIZON INS CO | NJ | • B- | 4q 2016 | 123.8 | 64.1 | 64.1 | 27.3 | 8.75 | 7.29 |
| HOUSTON CASUALTY CO | TX | B- | 3q 2017 | 3,966.7 | 390.4 | 26.2 | 2,075.4 | 1.76 | 1.53 |
| HPHC INS CO | MA | • D- | 3q 2017 | 283.2 | 774.5 | 774.5 | 79.1 | 1.61 | 1.34 |
| HSA HEALTH INS CO | UT | • D | 3q 2017 | 6.1 | 4.8 | 4.8 | 2.1 | 1.27 | 1.06 |
| HUMANA BENEFIT PLAN OF ILLINOIS | IL | • A- | 3q 2017 | 394.7 | 969.5 | 969.5 | 196.5 | 3.79 | 3.16 |
| HUMANA EMPLOYERS HEALTH PLAN OF GA | GA | • C | 3q 2017 | 755.0 | 1,903.8 | 1,903.8 | 531.0 | 4.03 | 3.36 |
| HUMANA HEALTH BENEFIT PLAN LA | LA | • B | 3q 2017 | 744.0 | 2,031.7 | 2,031.7 | 285.6 | 3.07 | 2.55 |
| HUMANA HEALTH CO OF NEW YORK INC | NY | • D- | 3q 2017 | 53.1 | 108.1 | 108.1 | 17.1 | 2.49 | 2.07 |
| HUMANA HEALTH INS CO OF FL INC | FL | • B- | 3q 2017 | 293.5 | 206.5 | 206.5 | 58.8 | 4.48 | 3.73 |
| HUMANA HEALTH PLAN INC | KY | • B- | 3q 2017 | 2,619.9 | 7,278.9 | 7,278.9 | 1,039.6 | 3.17 | 2.64 |
| HUMANA HEALTH PLAN OF CALIFORNIA INC | CA | U | | -- | -- | -- | -- | -- | -- |
| HUMANA HEALTH PLAN OF OHIO INC | OH | • B- | 3q 2017 | 153.8 | 728.8 | 728.8 | 118.7 | 3.10 | 2.58 |
| HUMANA HEALTH PLAN OF TEXAS INC | TX | • C | 3q 2017 | 253.1 | 805.9 | 805.9 | 139.1 | 2.82 | 2.35 |
| HUMANA HEALTH PLANS OF PUERTO RICO | PR | • C+ | 3q 2017 | 145.5 | 312.2 | 312.2 | 32.1 | 2.51 | 2.09 |
| HUMANA INS CO (WI) | WI | • A- | 3q 2017 | 10,120.6 | 22,960.9 | 22,960.9 | 4,043.5 | 2.76 | 2.30 |
| HUMANA INS CO OF KENTUCKY | KY | • C | 3q 2017 | 214.6 | 52.2 | 32.6 | 169.2 | 6.51 | 4.69 |
| HUMANA INS CO OF NY | NY | • B- | 3q 2017 | 198.9 | 291.8 | 291.8 | 68.8 | 4.53 | 3.78 |
| HUMANA INS CO OF PUERTO RICO INC | PR | • B- | 3q 2017 | 73.9 | 111.0 | 110.6 | 50.9 | 2.28 | 1.82 |
| HUMANA MEDICAL PLAN INC | FL | • B | 3q 2017 | 2,681.0 | 9,065.9 | 9,065.9 | 882.7 | 2.64 | 2.20 |
| HUMANA MEDICAL PLAN OF MICHIGAN INC | MI | • C+ | 3q 2017 | 50.2 | 115.1 | 115.1 | 30.1 | 4.11 | 3.43 |
| HUMANA MEDICAL PLAN OF PENNSYLVANIA | PA | • B | 3q 2017 | 46.0 | 56.1 | 56.1 | 21.7 | 5.65 | 4.71 |
| HUMANA MEDICAL PLAN OF UTAH INC | UT | • C+ | 3q 2017 | 30.9 | 46.0 | 46.0 | 17.6 | 4.53 | 3.77 |
| HUMANA REGIONAL HEALTH PLAN INC | AR | • B- | 3q 2017 | 22.1 | 30.6 | 30.6 | 14.1 | 6.21 | 5.18 |
| HUMANA WISCONSIN HEALTH ORGANIZATION | WI | • B- | 3q 2017 | 440.4 | 614.4 | 614.4 | 144.6 | 4.18 | 3.48 |
| IA AMERICAN LIFE INS CO | TX | C+ | 3q 2017 | 159.9 | 17.9 | 0.4 | 62.9 | 1.06 | 0.97 |
| IDEALIFE INS CO | CT | B- | 3q 2017 | 20.3 | 2.2 | 1.1 | 15.2 | 4.23 | 3.80 |
| ILLINICARE HEALTH PLAN INC | IL | • C- | 3q 2017 | 697.8 | 1,201.2 | 1,201.2 | 124.9 | 1.86 | 1.55 |
| ILLINOIS MUTUAL LIFE INS CO | IL | • B | 3q 2017 | 1,444.5 | 117.2 | 59.6 | 232.7 | 3.77 | 2.13 |
| ILLINOIS UNION INS CO | IL | C | 3q 2017 | 408.4 | 590.6 | 0.9 | 127.2 | 11.97 | 7.29 |
| IMPERIAL HEALTH PLAN OF CALIFORNIA | CA | • C- | 3q 2017 | 2.7 | 5.1 | 5.1 | 1.5 | 2.71 | 1.79 |
| IN UNIVERSITY HLTH PLANS INS | IN | U | | -- | -- | -- | -- | -- | -- |
| INDEMNITY INS CO OF NORTH AMERICA | PA | C | 3q 2017 | 488.1 | 905.4 | 0.9 | 131.7 | 2.77 | 1.84 |
| INDEPENDENCE AMERICAN INS CO | DE | • B- | 3q 2017 | 112.7 | 71.9 | 31.0 | 70.8 | 4.42 | 2.56 |
| INDEPENDENCE ASSURANCE CO | PA | U | | -- | -- | -- | -- | -- | -- |
| INDEPENDENCE BLUE CROSS | PA | • C- | 3q 2017 | 259.0 | 391.8 | 391.8 | 71.5 | 6.96 | 5.80 |
| INDEPENDENT CARE HEALTH PLAN | WI | • A- | 3q 2017 | 89.0 | 215.1 | 215.1 | 30.2 | 2.90 | 2.42 |
| INDEPENDENT HEALTH ASSOC INC | NY | • B- | 3q 2017 | 689.3 | 1,511.3 | 1,511.3 | 376.9 | 3.44 | 2.86 |
| INDEPENDENT HEALTH BENEFITS CORP | NY | • C | 3q 2017 | 227.8 | 606.8 | 606.8 | 90.3 | 1.91 | 1.59 |
| INDIANA UNIVERSITY HEALTH PLANS INC | IN | • E- | 3q 2017 | 21.6 | 75.1 | 75.1 | 8.5 | 1.99 | 1.66 |
| INDIANA UNIVERSITY HEALTH PLANS NFP | IN | • C+ | 3q 2017 | 46.6 | 180.0 | 180.0 | 15.6 | 1.54 | 1.28 |
| INDIVIDUAL ASR CO LIFE HEALTH & ACC | OK | D | 4q 2016 | 26.2 | 64.8 | 48.6 | 9.3 | 2.25 | 1.51 |
| INLAND EMPIRE HEALTH PLAN | CA | • A | 3q 2017 | 1,779.5 | 4,298.5 | 4,298.5 | 831.9 | 3.77 | 2.43 |
| INNOVATION HEALTH INS CO | VA | • C- | 3q 2017 | 206.6 | 244.0 | 244.0 | 38.9 | 1.76 | 1.47 |
| INNOVATION HEALTH PLAN INC | VA | • C- | 3q 2017 | 42.7 | 95.7 | 95.7 | 22.3 | 3.29 | 2.74 |
| INS CO OF NORTH AMERICA | PA | • C | 3q 2017 | 1,007.3 | 118.8 | 40.4 | 252.6 | 2.10 | 1.40 |
| INS CO OF SCOTT & WHITE | TX | • E- | 3q 2016 | 67.9 | 40.5 | 40.5 | 4.3 | 0.82 | 0.68 |
| INS CO OF THE SOUTH | GA | D+ | 3q 2017 | 45.0 | 97.9 | 0.1 | 15.0 | 0.51 | 0.45 |
| INS CO OF THE STATE OF PA | IL | C | 3q 2017 | 253.1 | 1,024.7 | 7.0 | 145.1 | 12.43 | 11.19 |
| INSTIL HEALTH INS CO | SC | U | | -- | -- | -- | -- | -- | -- |
| INSUREMAX INS CO | IN | E | 3q 2017 | 4.3 | -0.2 | 0.0 | 2.5 | 3.59 | 3.23 |
| INTEGON INDEMNITY CORP | NC | C | 3q 2017 | 178.8 | 172.2 | 8.3 | 23.0 | 1.64 | 1.48 |
| INTEGON NATIONAL INS CO | NC | C+ | 3q 2017 | 3,983.3 | 939.0 | 19.7 | 971.8 | 1.77 | 1.30 |

| INSURANCE COMPANY NAME | DOM. STATE | RATING | DATA DATE | TOTAL ASSETS ($MIL) | TOTAL PREMIUMS ($MIL) | HEALTH PREMIUMS ($MIL) | CAPITAL & SURPLUS ($MIL) | RISK ADJUSTED CAPITAL RATIO 1 | RISK ADJUSTED CAPITAL RATIO 2 |
|---|---|---|---|---|---|---|---|---|---|
| INTEGRAND ASR CO | PR | C | 3q 2017 | 126.9 | 66.0 | 1.5 | 56.7 | 2.19 | 1.51 |
| INTER-COUNTY HEALTH PLAN INC | PA | U | | -- | -- | -- | -- | -- | -- |
| INTER-COUNTY HOSPITALIZATION PLAN | PA | U | | -- | -- | -- | -- | -- | -- |
| INTERBORO INS CO | NY | C- | 3q 2017 | 78.8 | 44.6 | 0.2 | 40.8 | 2.93 | 2.39 |
| INTERVALLEY HEALTH PLAN | CA | • D | 3q 2017 | 64.0 | 289.7 | 289.7 | 22.4 | 0.85 | 0.54 |
| INTRAMERICA LIFE INS CO | NY | B | 3q 2017 | 34.1 | 0.7 | 0.0 | 10.1 | 2.14 | 1.92 |
| INVESTORS HERITAGE LIFE INS CO | KY | C | 3q 2017 | 453.0 | 55.3 | 3.4 | 26.7 | 1.35 | 0.78 |
| INVESTORS LIFE INS CO NORTH AMERICA | TX | B | 3q 2017 | 606.7 | 18.8 | 0.0 | 56.7 | 2.97 | 1.62 |
| INVOVA HEALH PLAN LLC | VA | • C | 3q 2017 | 61.3 | 196.3 | 196.3 | 23.9 | 2.50 | 2.09 |
| IRONSHORE INDEMNITY INC | MN | B- | 3q 2017 | 352.6 | 286.0 | 50.6 | 133.9 | 13.38 | 12.04 |
| ISLAND HOME INS CO | GU | D | 3q 2017 | 23.9 | 32.2 | 30.7 | 12.1 | 2.36 | 1.29 |
| JACKSON NATIONAL LIFE INS CO | MI | B+ | 3q 2017 | 222,617.0 | 18,340.2 | 54.9 | 4,304.2 | 1.76 | 0.97 |
| JEFFERSON INS CO | NY | C | 3q 2017 | 120.6 | 483.6 | 15.8 | 62.8 | 1.68 | 1.41 |
| JEFFERSON LIFE INS CO | TX | D | 3q 2017 | 2.2 | 0.4 | 0.4 | 1.4 | 1.75 | 1.57 |
| JEFFERSON NATIONAL LIFE INS CO | TX | C | 3q 2017 | 5,474.3 | 735.2 | 2.1 | 38.2 | 1.08 | 0.58 |
| JOHN ALDEN LIFE INS CO | WI | B- | 3q 2017 | 213.8 | 33.8 | 23.5 | 15.2 | 4.09 | 3.38 |
| JOHN HANCOCK LIFE & HEALTH INS CO | MA | • B | 3q 2017 | 12,953.4 | 630.4 | 629.4 | 805.5 | 2.90 | 1.65 |
| JOHN HANCOCK LIFE INS CO (USA) | MI | B | 3q 2017 | 240,367.0 | 19,808.6 | 1,522.9 | 7,581.6 | 1.33 | 0.85 |
| JOHN HANCOCK LIFE INS CO OF NY | NY | B | 3q 2017 | 17,497.1 | 1,102.0 | 3.1 | 1,479.9 | 3.51 | 1.89 |
| K S PLAN ADMINISTRATORS LLC | TX | • B+ | 3q 2017 | 116.8 | 334.8 | 334.8 | 60.0 | 1.96 | 1.64 |
| ▼ KAISER FNDTN HLTH PLAN OF WA | WA | • B+ | 3q 2017 | 1,673.0 | 2,449.0 | 2,449.0 | 925.1 | 4.48 | 3.73 |
| KAISER FNDTN HLTH PLAN WA OPTN | WA | • B | 3q 2017 | 298.9 | 903.9 | 903.9 | 148.9 | 2.93 | 2.44 |
| KAISER FOUNDATION HEALTH PLAN INC | CA | • A | 3q 2017 | 72,940.0 | 60,874.0 | 60,874.0 | 32,223.2 | 3.87 | 2.80 |
| KAISER FOUNDATION HP INC HI | HI | • C | 3q 2017 | 439.3 | 1,369.0 | 1,369.0 | 89.5 | 2.28 | 1.90 |
| KAISER FOUNDATION HP MID-ATL STATES | MD | • B | 3q 2017 | 1,213.6 | 3,264.8 | 3,264.8 | 219.0 | 1.06 | 0.88 |
| KAISER FOUNDATION HP NORTHWEST | OR | • B | 3q 2017 | 1,440.8 | 3,558.6 | 3,558.6 | 567.4 | 5.18 | 4.32 |
| KAISER FOUNDATION HP OF CO | CO | • B | 3q 2017 | 1,262.9 | 3,507.4 | 3,507.4 | 338.5 | 2.28 | 1.90 |
| KAISER FOUNDATION HP OF GA | GA | • C- | 3q 2017 | 491.3 | 1,458.6 | 1,458.6 | 164.8 | 1.42 | 1.18 |
| KAISER PERMANENTE INS CO | CA | • B | 3q 2017 | 195.9 | 123.1 | 123.1 | 117.0 | 14.17 | 11.81 |
| KANAWHA INS CO | SC | • B- | 3q 2017 | 2,383.6 | 178.2 | 149.1 | 148.2 | 2.59 | 1.38 |
| KANSAS CITY LIFE INS CO | MO | B | 3q 2017 | 3,415.5 | 303.0 | 55.1 | 323.1 | 1.44 | 0.88 |
| KANSAS SUPERIOR SELECT INC | KS | U | | -- | -- | -- | -- | -- | -- |
| ▲ KENTUCKY HOME LIFE INS CO | KY | C- | 3q 2017 | 5.6 | 2.4 | 0.8 | 3.6 | 3.00 | 2.70 |
| KENTUCKY SPIRIT HEALTH PLAN INC | KY | U | | -- | -- | -- | -- | -- | -- |
| KERN HEALTH SYSTEMS | CA | • B- | 3q 2017 | 425.6 | 671.5 | 671.5 | 194.4 | 5.34 | 3.25 |
| KEYSTONE HEALTH PLAN CENTRAL INC | PA | • C+ | 3q 2017 | 87.1 | 307.9 | 307.9 | 53.8 | 2.74 | 2.28 |
| KEYSTONE HEALTH PLAN EAST INC | PA | • C+ | 3q 2017 | 1,299.3 | 3,072.9 | 3,072.9 | 528.8 | 3.43 | 2.85 |
| KILPATRICK LIFE INS CO | LA | E+ | 3q 2017 | 192.2 | 17.0 | 0.3 | 7.8 | 0.67 | 0.38 |
| LA HEALTH SERVICE & INDEMNITY CO | LA | • B | 3q 2017 | 1,988.3 | 2,526.0 | 2,526.0 | 1,267.7 | 6.31 | 5.26 |
| LAFAYETTE LIFE INS CO | OH | B | 3q 2017 | 5,367.2 | 606.3 | 0.3 | 303.4 | 1.88 | 0.94 |
| LAMORAK INS CO | PA | U | | -- | -- | -- | -- | -- | -- |
| LANDCAR LIFE INS CO | UT | U | | -- | -- | -- | -- | -- | -- |
| LEADERS LIFE INS CO | OK | C | 3q 2017 | 6.8 | 10.0 | 0.8 | 3.6 | 2.01 | 1.74 |
| LEGAL SERVICE PLANS OF VIRGINIA INC | VA | • B | 3q 2017 | 2.4 | 9.1 | 9.1 | 1.2 | 1.84 | 1.53 |
| LEXINGTON INS CO | DE | C | 3q 2017 | 21,996.4 | 3,072.0 | 0.0 | 5,438.8 | 2.07 | 1.38 |
| LIBERTY ADVANTAGE LLC | NC | U | | -- | -- | -- | -- | -- | -- |
| LIBERTY BANKERS LIFE INS CO | OK | D+ | 3q 2017 | 1,678.4 | 280.3 | 0.2 | 203.1 | 1.20 | 0.79 |
| LIBERTY INS UNDERWRITERS INC | IL | C | 3q 2017 | 267.7 | 2,997.4 | 0.1 | 128.9 | 13.72 | 12.35 |
| LIBERTY LIFE ASR CO OF BOSTON | NH | • B | 3q 2017 | 18,681.2 | 2,825.2 | 962.1 | 1,174.7 | 1.88 | 1.09 |
| LIBERTY MUTUAL INS CO | MA | B | 3q 2017 | 46,757.0 | 2,158.1 | 1.2 | 14,998.1 | 1.37 | 1.17 |
| LIBERTY NATIONAL LIFE INS CO | NE | B | 3q 2017 | 7,474.5 | 560.6 | 132.5 | 551.7 | 1.89 | 0.98 |
| ▲ LIBERTY UNION LIFE ASR CO | MI | • C | 3q 2017 | 15.9 | 21.8 | 21.8 | 3.9 | 3.60 | 3.00 |



Arrows denote recent upgrades ▲ or downgrades▼

• Bullets denote a more detailed analysis is available in Section II.

| INSURANCE COMPANY NAME | DOM. STATE | RATING | DATA DATE | TOTAL ASSETS ($MIL) | TOTAL PREMIUMS ($MIL) | HEALTH PREMIUMS ($MIL) | CAPITAL & SURPLUS ($MIL) | RISK ADJUSTED CAPITAL RATIO 1 | RISK ADJUSTED CAPITAL RATIO 2 |
|---|---|---|---|---|---|---|---|---|---|
| LIFE ASSURANCE CO INC | OK | C- | 3q 2017 | 4.5 | 2.1 | 0.4 | 2.5 | 1.76 | 1.58 |
| LIFE INS CO OF ALABAMA | AL | • B | 3q 2017 | 126.5 | 36.8 | 30.0 | 41.9 | 3.56 | 2.22 |
| LIFE INS CO OF BOSTON & NEW YORK | NY | • A- | 3q 2017 | 148.4 | 27.9 | 11.7 | 30.3 | 3.33 | 2.50 |
| LIFE INS CO OF LOUISIANA | LA | D | 4q 2016 | 8.5 | 0.3 | 0.0 | 4.1 | 2.20 | 1.44 |
| LIFE INS CO OF NORTH AMERICA | PA | • B | 3q 2017 | 8,856.7 | 3,706.5 | 2,141.7 | 1,728.4 | 2.52 | 1.62 |
| LIFE INS CO OF THE SOUTHWEST | TX | B | 3q 2017 | 18,030.6 | 1,867.0 | 0.1 | 1,168.7 | 2.20 | 1.08 |
| LIFE OF AMERICA INS CO | TX | C | 3q 2017 | 12.0 | 0.1 | 0.1 | 2.2 | 0.74 | 0.56 |
| LIFE OF THE SOUTH INS CO | GA | C | 3q 2017 | 102.5 | 135.0 | 87.7 | 20.2 | 0.71 | 0.54 |
| LIFEMAP ASR CO | OR | • B- | 3q 2017 | 97.5 | 113.9 | 82.6 | 45.7 | 1.72 | 1.26 |
| LIFESECURE INS CO | MI | • D | 3q 2017 | 353.9 | 47.4 | 40.3 | 31.1 | 1.82 | 1.20 |
| LIFESHIELD NATIONAL INS CO | OK | B- | 3q 2017 | 73.7 | 4.4 | 1.0 | 24.9 | 2.08 | 1.25 |
| LIFEWISE ASR CO | WA | • A | 3q 2017 | 166.6 | 121.7 | 121.7 | 123.1 | 7.11 | 5.27 |
| LIFEWISE HEALTH PLAN OF OREGON | OR | • C | 3q 2017 | 18.0 | 135.9 | 135.9 | 14.0 | 1.81 | 1.51 |
| LIFEWISE HEALTH PLAN OF WASHINGTON | WA | • B | 3q 2017 | 123.5 | 176.0 | 176.0 | 77.5 | 7.40 | 6.17 |
| LINCOLN BENEFIT LIFE CO | NE | C+ | 3q 2017 | 11,535.0 | 1,438.8 | 58.1 | 499.9 | 1.48 | 0.74 |
| LINCOLN HERITAGE LIFE INS CO | IL | B- | 3q 2017 | 981.3 | 472.4 | 5.1 | 114.4 | 3.13 | 1.70 |
| LINCOLN LIFE & ANNUITY CO OF NY | NY | B | 3q 2017 | 14,347.2 | 1,113.4 | 49.3 | 1,215.2 | 4.79 | 2.36 |
| LINCOLN NATIONAL LIFE INS CO | IN | B | 3q 2017 | 235,288.0 | 19,548.7 | 1,238.0 | 7,707.3 | 1.47 | 0.99 |
| LOCAL INITIATIVE HEALTH AUTH LA | CA | • C | 3q 2017 | 5,958.0 | 7,755.3 | 7,755.3 | 677.0 | 1.16 | 0.70 |
| LONDON LIFE REINSURANCE CO | PA | • C+ | 3q 2017 | 201.2 | 0.0 | 0.0 | 58.5 | 5.82 | 3.59 |
| LONGEVITY INS CO | TX | B | 3q 2017 | 7.8 | 0.4 | 0.1 | 7.8 | 3.81 | 3.43 |
| LOUISIANA FARM BUREAU MUTUAL INS CO | LA | B | 3q 2017 | 229.4 | 145.7 | 0.1 | 142.7 | 5.82 | 5.14 |
| LOUISIANA HEALTHCARE CONNECTIONS INC | LA | • E | 3q 2017 | 440.3 | 1,740.3 | 1,740.3 | 99.8 | 1.45 | 1.21 |
| LOVELACE HEALTH SYSTEMS INC | NM | U | | -- | -- | -- | -- | -- | -- |
| ▲ LOYAL AMERICAN LIFE INS CO | OH | • B- | 3q 2017 | 304.3 | 192.2 | 186.0 | 104.9 | 1.20 | 0.99 |
| LYNDON SOUTHERN INS CO | DE | B | 3q 2017 | 180.7 | 395.5 | 1.6 | 52.8 | 3.41 | 1.90 |
| MADISON NATIONAL LIFE INS CO INC | WI | • C+ | 3q 2017 | 335.6 | 140.5 | 86.2 | 185.8 | 1.53 | 1.46 |
| MAGELLAN BEHAVIORAL HEALTH OF NE | NE | • B- | 1q 2017 | 39.4 | 115.4 | 115.4 | 14.9 | 7.97 | 6.64 |
| MAGELLAN BEHAVIORAL HEALTH OF NJ LLC | MD | • D+ | 4q 2016 | 2.5 | 0.1 | 0.1 | 2.3 | 88.03 | 73.36 |
| MAGELLAN BEHAVIORAL HEALTH OF PA INC | PA | • C+ | 3q 2017 | 109.6 | 460.3 | 460.3 | 51.7 | 1.41 | 1.18 |
| MAGELLAN COMPLETE CARE OF VA | VA | U | | -- | -- | -- | -- | -- | -- |
| MAGELLAN LIFE INS CO | DE | • B- | 3q 2017 | 22.6 | 61.3 | 61.3 | 12.8 | 1.81 | 1.51 |
| MAGNA INS CO | MS | • C- | 2q 2017 | 2.6 | 0.4 | 0.4 | 2.2 | 13.58 | 11.31 |
| MAGNOLIA GUARANTY LIFE INS CO | MS | C | 3q 2017 | 10.3 | 2.0 | 0.0 | 1.7 | 0.75 | 0.67 |
| MAGNOLIA HEALTH PLAN INC | MS | • D | 3q 2017 | 200.2 | 1,248.5 | 1,248.5 | 86.8 | 1.24 | 1.03 |
| MAINE COMMUNITY HEALTH OPTIONS | ME | • D | 3q 2017 | 86.4 | 377.8 | 377.8 | 46.8 | 0.52 | 0.43 |
| MAMSI L&H INS CO | MD | • C+ | 3q 2017 | 25.9 | 61.6 | 61.6 | 13.4 | 4.19 | 3.49 |
| MANHATTAN LIFE INS CO | NY | • B | 3q 2017 | 577.7 | 215.4 | 97.3 | 53.0 | 1.28 | 0.93 |
| MANHATTAN NATIONAL LIFE INS CO | OH | B- | 3q 2017 | 157.9 | 19.4 | 0.1 | 11.3 | 1.33 | 1.19 |
| MANHATTANLIFE ASSR CO OF AM | AR | • C | 3q 2017 | 390.7 | 78.7 | 75.7 | 102.0 | 0.64 | 0.58 |
| MAPFRE LIFE INS CO | DE | C | 3q 2017 | 20.3 | 0.3 | 0.1 | 17.5 | 4.77 | 4.29 |
| MAPFRE LIFE INS CO OF PR | PR | C- | 3q 2017 | 58.5 | 119.3 | 113.0 | 23.0 | 1.19 | 0.96 |
| MAPFRE PAN AMERICAN INS CO | PR | C | 3q 2017 | 38.3 | 29.3 | 0.0 | 13.2 | 0.90 | 0.59 |
| MAPFRE PRAICO INS CO | PR | C | 3q 2017 | 435.2 | 247.5 | 0.0 | 128.7 | 1.15 | 0.77 |
| MARKEL INS CO | IL | C | 3q 2017 | 1,744.5 | 555.3 | 19.8 | 440.2 | 1.90 | 1.01 |
| MARQUETTE INDEMNITY & LIFE INS CO | AZ | D+ | 3q 2017 | 5.8 | 1.0 | 0.7 | 2.0 | 1.25 | 1.13 |
| MARTINS POINT GENERATIONS ADVANTAGE | ME | • C- | 3q 2017 | 129.6 | 329.3 | 329.3 | 49.4 | 1.47 | 1.23 |
| MARTINS POINT GENERATIONS LLC | ME | U | | -- | -- | -- | -- | -- | -- |
| MASSACHUSETTS MUTUAL LIFE INS CO | MA | A- | 3q 2017 | 235,570.0 | 21,295.9 | 709.7 | 16,152.4 | 1.45 | 1.09 |
| MATTHEW THORNTON HEALTH PLAN | NH | • B | 3q 2017 | 232.5 | 508.0 | 508.0 | 117.3 | 4.08 | 3.40 |
| ▲ MCLAREN HEALTH PLAN COMMUNITY | MI | • B- | 3q 2017 | 35.2 | 61.0 | 61.0 | 18.0 | 2.31 | 1.92 |
| ▲ MCLAREN HEALTH PLAN INC | MI | • A- | 3q 2017 | 239.2 | 929.6 | 929.6 | 102.8 | 1.50 | 1.25 |



Arrows denote recent upgrades ▲ or downgrades▼

• Bullets denote a more detailed analysis is available in Section II.

| INSURANCE COMPANY NAME | DOM. STATE | RATING | DATA DATE | TOTAL ASSETS ($MIL) | TOTAL PREMIUMS ($MIL) | HEALTH PREMIUMS ($MIL) | CAPITAL & SURPLUS ($MIL) | RISK ADJUSTED CAPITAL RATIO 1 | RATIO 2 |
|---|---|---|---|---|---|---|---|---|---|
| MCS ADVANTAGE INC | PR | • E+ | 3q 2017 | 469.1 | 1,756.1 | 1,756.1 | 83.6 | 0.73 | 0.61 |
| MCS LIFE INS CO | PR | • D- | 3q 2017 | 83.9 | 309.8 | 307.3 | 30.3 | 0.56 | 0.49 |
| MD INDIVIDUAL PRACTICE ASSOC INC | MD | • B- | 3q 2017 | 79.8 | 307.8 | 307.8 | 46.1 | 11.24 | 9.36 |
| MDWISE INC | IN | • B | 3q 2017 | 207.9 | 1,433.7 | 1,433.7 | 96.4 | 1.35 | 1.13 |
| MDWISE MARKETPLACE INC | IN | • C | 3q 2017 | 51.4 | 136.8 | 136.8 | 9.8 | 1.46 | 1.22 |
| MEDAMERICA INS CO | PA | • C | 3q 2017 | 939.5 | 90.2 | 90.2 | 28.0 | 0.99 | 0.54 |
| MEDAMERICA INS CO OF FL | FL | B | 3q 2017 | 39.3 | 4.1 | 4.1 | 3.6 | 0.69 | 0.62 |
| MEDAMERICA INS CO OF NEW YORK | NY | D- | 3q 2017 | 763.0 | 47.7 | 47.7 | 9.9 | 0.77 | 0.45 |
| MEDCO CONTAINMENT INS CO OF NY | NY | • B | 3q 2017 | 124.1 | 123.8 | 123.8 | 50.2 | 5.03 | 4.19 |
| MEDCO CONTAINMENT LIFE INS CO | PA | • A- | 3q 2017 | 1,113.2 | 672.2 | 672.2 | 406.5 | 5.63 | 4.69 |
| MEDICA HEALTH PLANS | MN | • C | 3q 2017 | 535.5 | 2,327.5 | 2,327.5 | 353.9 | 2.12 | 1.76 |
| MEDICA HEALTH PLANS OF FLORIDA INC | FL | U | | -- | -- | -- | -- | -- | -- |
| MEDICA HEALTH PLANS OF WI | WI | • C | 3q 2017 | 116.1 | 221.6 | 221.6 | 58.3 | 2.37 | 1.98 |
| MEDICA HEALTHCARE PLANS INC | FL | • E | 3q 2017 | 222.9 | 533.9 | 533.9 | 69.2 | 2.60 | 2.17 |
| MEDICA INS CO | MN | • B | 3q 2017 | 809.4 | 1,967.7 | 1,967.7 | 349.8 | 3.01 | 2.51 |
| MEDICAL ASSOC CLINIC HEALTH PLAN | WI | • C+ | 3q 2017 | 3.8 | 25.5 | 25.5 | 3.1 | 1.39 | 1.16 |
| MEDICAL ASSOCIATES HEALTH PLAN INC | IA | • B- | 3q 2017 | 38.5 | 82.5 | 82.5 | 20.5 | 2.71 | 2.26 |
| MEDICAL BENEFITS MUTUAL LIFE INS CO | OH | D | 3q 2017 | 15.7 | 2.3 | 2.1 | 11.0 | 2.44 | 1.75 |
| MEDICAL HEALTH INS CORP OF OHIO | OH | • B+ | 3q 2017 | 138.6 | 328.2 | 328.2 | 60.7 | 3.20 | 2.67 |
| MEDICAL MUTUAL OF OHIO | OH | • A | 3q 2017 | 2,136.4 | 2,368.3 | 2,368.3 | 1,525.3 | 7.06 | 5.89 |
| MEDICO CORP LIFE INS CO | NE | A- | 3q 2017 | 63.9 | 82.3 | 82.3 | 22.8 | 3.32 | 2.99 |
| MEDICO INS CO | NE | • B | 3q 2017 | 82.1 | 136.9 | 135.3 | 34.6 | 4.13 | 3.72 |
| MEDICO LIFE & HEALTH INS CO | IA | B | 3q 2017 | 14.0 | 0.9 | 0.1 | 13.4 | 4.52 | 4.06 |
| MEDISUN INC | AZ | • B- | 3q 2017 | 168.8 | 590.9 | 590.9 | 55.2 | 1.09 | 0.91 |
| MEDSTAR FAMILY CHOICE INC | MD | • C | 3q 2017 | 263.1 | 749.3 | 749.3 | 78.9 | 1.08 | 0.90 |
| MEMBERS HEALTH INS CO | AZ | • C | 3q 2017 | 34.2 | 2.5 | 2.5 | 30.7 | 16.99 | 14.16 |
| MEMBERS LIFE INS CO | IA | C | 3q 2017 | 111.1 | 656.8 | 0.0 | 24.4 | 3.12 | 2.81 |
| MEMORIAL HERMANN HEALTH INS CO | TX | • C- | 3q 2017 | 47.1 | 92.8 | 92.8 | 22.5 | 1.56 | 1.30 |
| MEMORIAL HERMANN HEALTH PLAN INC | TX | • D+ | 3q 2017 | 35.5 | 55.7 | 55.7 | 10.2 | 1.06 | 0.89 |
| MERCHANTS MUTUAL INS CO | NY | B- | 3q 2017 | 525.1 | 196.5 | 0.0 | 203.4 | 2.90 | 2.38 |
| MERCY MARICOPA INTEGRATED CARE | AZ | U | | -- | -- | -- | -- | -- | -- |
| MERCYCARE HMO | WI | • C | 3q 2017 | 38.1 | 82.0 | 82.0 | 18.3 | 1.81 | 1.50 |
| MERCYCARE INS CO | WI | • D+ | 3q 2017 | 20.5 | 0.6 | 0.6 | 17.6 | 1.50 | 1.25 |
| MERIDIAN HEALTH PLAN OF ILLINOIS INC | IL | • C+ | 3q 2017 | 747.8 | 1,125.7 | 1,125.7 | 85.6 | 0.82 | 0.68 |
| MERIDIAN HEALTH PLAN OF IOWA INC | IA | • E+ | 1q 2017 | 8.9 | 0.3 | 0.3 | 7.2 | 4.63 | 3.86 |
| MERIDIAN HEALTH PLAN OF MICHIGAN INC | MI | • B | 3q 2017 | 515.8 | 2,420.8 | 2,420.8 | 177.0 | 1.10 | 0.92 |
| MERIT HEALTH INS CO | IL | • C | 3q 2017 | 182.1 | 59.8 | 59.8 | 50.4 | 4.82 | 4.01 |
| MERIT LIFE INS CO | IN | • B | 3q 2017 | 560.7 | 127.3 | 61.4 | 155.6 | 6.19 | 3.63 |
| METROPOLITAN LIFE INS CO | NY | B- | 3q 2017 | 401,351.0 | 34,110.3 | 7,737.7 | 10,422.8 | 1.31 | 0.83 |
| METROPOLITAN P&C INS CO | RI | B- | 3q 2017 | 5,874.3 | 1,431.6 | 20.0 | 2,404.5 | 2.07 | 1.67 |
| MHNET L&H INS CO | TX | U | | -- | -- | -- | -- | -- | -- |
| MHS HEALTH WISCONSIN | WI | • C+ | 3q 2017 | 71.0 | 183.6 | 183.6 | 48.5 | 4.65 | 3.88 |
| MICHIGAN COMPLETE HEALTH INC | MI | • C- | 3q 2017 | 16.6 | 46.9 | 46.9 | 7.4 | 2.65 | 2.20 |
| MID-WEST NATIONAL LIFE INS CO OF TN | TX | C | 3q 2017 | 63.6 | 20.2 | 8.9 | 18.6 | 2.34 | 2.11 |
| MIDLAND NATIONAL LIFE INS CO | IA | B+ | 3q 2017 | 55,140.0 | 6,648.7 | 0.1 | 3,549.7 | 2.29 | 1.17 |
| MIDWESTERN UNITED LIFE INS CO | IN | A | 3q 2017 | 233.4 | 3.2 | 0.0 | 133.9 | 13.49 | 12.14 |
| MII LIFE INC | MN | • B- | 3q 2017 | 952.4 | 0.6 | 0.6 | 46.1 | 3.36 | 2.80 |
| MINNESOTA LIFE INS CO | MN | B+ | 3q 2017 | 44,369.0 | 6,498.7 | 352.9 | 3,045.1 | 2.40 | 1.51 |
| MINUTEMAN HEALTH INC | MA | F | 1q 2017 | 117.5 | 61.2 | 61.2 | 5.7 | 0.26 | 0.21 |
| MISSISSIPPI TRUE | MS | U | | -- | -- | -- | -- | -- | -- |
| MISSOURI CARE INC | MO | • E | 3q 2017 | 191.1 | 349.5 | 349.5 | 71.9 | 4.33 | 3.61 |
| MISSOURI MEDICARE SELECT LLC | MO | • C- | 3q 2017 | 2.1 | 6.1 | 6.1 | 0.8 | 0.60 | 0.50 |



Arrows denote recent upgrades ▲ or downgrades▼

• Bullets denote a more detailed analysis is available in Section II.

| INSURANCE COMPANY NAME | DOM. STATE | RATING | DATA DATE | TOTAL ASSETS ($MIL) | TOTAL PREMIUMS ($MIL) | HEALTH PREMIUMS ($MIL) | CAPITAL & SURPLUS ($MIL) | RISK ADJUSTED CAPITAL RATIO 1 | RISK ADJUSTED CAPITAL RATIO 2 |
|---|---|---|---|---|---|---|---|---|---|
| ▲ MISSOURI VALLEY LIFE AND HLTH INS CO | MO | C+ | 3q 2017 | 18.9 | 16.7 | 16.2 | 11.2 | 2.36 | 1.80 |
| MMM HEALTHCARE LLC | PR | • E- | 3q 2017 | 490.8 | 1,593.6 | 1,593.6 | 137.3 | 1.20 | 1.00 |
| MMM MULTI HEALTH LLC | PR | • D | 3q 2017 | 151.2 | 249.6 | 249.6 | 53.0 | 2.74 | 2.28 |
| MODA HEALTH PLAN INC | OR | • E | 3q 2017 | 291.8 | 903.9 | 903.9 | 94.1 | 0.65 | 0.54 |
| MOLINA HEALTHCARE OF CALIFORNIA | CA | • C- | 3q 2017 | 1,139.4 | 2,470.4 | 2,470.4 | 152.4 | 1.18 | 0.73 |
| MOLINA HEALTHCARE OF FLORIDA INC | FL | • E | 3q 2017 | 1,058.3 | 1,961.9 | 1,961.9 | 198.4 | 1.82 | 1.51 |
| MOLINA HEALTHCARE OF ILLINOIS INC | IL | • E | 3q 2017 | 258.3 | 796.9 | 796.9 | 70.8 | 1.92 | 1.60 |
| MOLINA HEALTHCARE OF MICHIGAN INC | MI | • B- | 3q 2017 | 569.7 | 2,104.8 | 2,104.8 | 200.8 | 2.34 | 1.95 |
| MOLINA HEALTHCARE OF NEW MEXICO | NM | • C | 3q 2017 | 383.1 | 1,386.6 | 1,386.6 | 111.4 | 1.54 | 1.28 |
| MOLINA HEALTHCARE OF OHIO INC | OH | • B- | 3q 2017 | 548.1 | 2,198.5 | 2,198.5 | 257.2 | 2.50 | 2.08 |
| MOLINA HEALTHCARE OF PUERTO RICO INC | PR | • C- | 3q 2017 | 166.7 | 746.3 | 746.3 | 74.2 | 1.97 | 1.64 |
| MOLINA HEALTHCARE OF SOUTH CAROLINA | SC | • C | 3q 2017 | 117.0 | 411.8 | 411.8 | 48.9 | 2.50 | 2.09 |
| MOLINA HEALTHCARE OF TEXAS INC | TX | • B- | 3q 2017 | 891.1 | 2,606.1 | 2,606.1 | 281.5 | 2.07 | 1.72 |
| MOLINA HEALTHCARE OF TEXAS INS CO | TX | C | 3q 2017 | 8.7 | 49.5 | 49.5 | 8.6 | 3.85 | 2.56 |
| MOLINA HEALTHCARE OF UTAH INC | UT | • C- | 3q 2017 | 238.2 | 453.9 | 453.9 | 64.9 | 2.33 | 1.95 |
| MOLINA HEALTHCARE OF WASHINGTON INC | WA | • B | 3q 2017 | 852.4 | 2,307.8 | 2,307.8 | 293.0 | 2.19 | 1.83 |
| MOLINA HEALTHCARE OF WISCONSIN INC | WI | • E+ | 3q 2017 | 169.6 | 403.1 | 403.1 | 60.1 | 2.34 | 1.95 |
| MONARCH HEALTH PLAN | CA | • E- | 3q 2017 | 113.5 | 359.8 | 359.8 | 38.2 | 0.29 | 0.17 |
| MONARCH LIFE INS CO | MA | F | 4q 2016 | 667.1 | 13.7 | 12.5 | 4.7 | 0.46 | 0.23 |
| MONITOR LIFE INS CO OF NEW YORK | NY | B | 3q 2017 | 21.5 | 10.5 | 10.0 | 11.4 | 3.08 | 2.25 |
| MONTANA HEALTH COOPERATIVE | MT | • D | 3q 2017 | 79.9 | 123.0 | 123.0 | 42.0 | 1.19 | 0.99 |
| MONY LIFE INS CO | NY | B- | 3q 2017 | 7,266.9 | 286.5 | 29.1 | 454.8 | 2.49 | 1.32 |
| MONY LIFE INS CO OF AMERICA | AZ | B | 3q 2017 | 3,638.0 | 601.0 | 0.9 | 316.7 | 2.76 | 1.85 |
| MOTORISTS COMMERCIAL MUTUAL INS CO | OH | A- | 3q 2017 | 393.5 | 33.0 | 0.0 | 150.5 | 2.99 | 2.12 |
| MOUNT CARMEL HEALTH INS CO | OH | • D | 3q 2017 | 8.7 | 24.8 | 24.8 | 6.3 | 1.67 | 1.39 |
| MOUNT CARMEL HEALTH PLAN INC | OH | • C | 3q 2017 | 356.2 | 566.2 | 566.2 | 184.0 | 3.45 | 2.87 |
| MOUNTAIN LIFE INS CO | TN | C- | 3q 2017 | 10.3 | 3.5 | 0.9 | 5.4 | 2.11 | 1.90 |
| MULTINATIONAL LIFE INS CO | PR | C- | 3q 2017 | 114.0 | 51.1 | 30.6 | 17.9 | 1.87 | 1.06 |
| MUTUAL BENEFIT ASSN OF HAWAII | HI | U | | -- | -- | -- | -- | -- | -- |
| MUTUAL OF AMERICA LIFE INS CO | NY | A- | 3q 2017 | 20,499.3 | 2,264.8 | 3.2 | 986.1 | 3.07 | 1.45 |
| MUTUAL OF OMAHA INS CO | NE | • B+ | 3q 2017 | 7,661.2 | 1,317.5 | 1,317.5 | 3,083.3 | 1.07 | 0.99 |
| MUTUAL SAVINGS LIFE INS CO | AL | B | 3q 2017 | 468.6 | 37.9 | 4.7 | 42.3 | 2.36 | 1.42 |
| MUTUAL TRUST LIFE INS CO | IL | B | 3q 2017 | 1,998.7 | 202.0 | 0.3 | 150.6 | 2.28 | 1.16 |
| MVP HEALTH INS CO | NY | • E+ | 3q 2017 | 29.1 | 69.4 | 69.4 | 25.1 | 4.96 | 4.14 |
| MVP HEALTH PLAN INC | NY | • B- | 3q 2017 | 741.8 | 2,501.8 | 2,501.8 | 407.1 | 2.30 | 1.92 |
| MVP HEALTH SERVICES CORP | NY | • C | 3q 2017 | 134.5 | 491.4 | 491.4 | 52.8 | 0.70 | 0.58 |
| NATIONAL BENEFIT LIFE INS CO | NY | B+ | 3q 2017 | 537.3 | 161.2 | 0.8 | 156.7 | 6.96 | 3.70 |
| NATIONAL CASUALTY CO | OH | B+ | 3q 2017 | 406.6 | 867.7 | 1.9 | 139.0 | 13.22 | 11.90 |
| NATIONAL FAMILY CARE LIFE INS CO | TX | C | 3q 2017 | 16.5 | 6.8 | 5.7 | 9.6 | 3.08 | 2.77 |
| NATIONAL FOUNDATION LIFE INS CO | TX | B | 3q 2017 | 39.6 | 36.1 | 34.3 | 23.8 | 2.09 | 1.64 |
| NATIONAL GUARDIAN LIFE INS CO | WI | • B- | 3q 2017 | 3,859.7 | 907.8 | 379.6 | 336.0 | 1.67 | 1.04 |
| NATIONAL HEALTH INS CO | TX | C | 3q 2017 | 39.4 | 129.4 | 129.4 | 15.0 | 3.59 | 1.56 |
| NATIONAL INCOME LIFE INS CO | NY | B+ | 3q 2017 | 223.3 | 73.3 | 6.5 | 37.4 | 3.26 | 1.98 |
| NATIONAL INDEMNITY CO | NE | B | 3q 2017 | 204,745.0 | 212.2 | 0.0 | 105,559.0 | 1.81 | 1.49 |
| NATIONAL INS CO OF WI INC | WI | C | 3q 2017 | 13.6 | 0.3 | 0.3 | 11.9 | 7.39 | 6.02 |
| NATIONAL INTERSTATE INS CO | OH | C+ | 3q 2017 | 1,360.9 | 435.9 | 0.0 | 375.0 | 1.63 | 1.32 |
| NATIONAL LIABILITY & FIRE INS CO | CT | C+ | 3q 2017 | 2,502.4 | 585.6 | 0.0 | 1,026.7 | 2.38 | 1.52 |
| NATIONAL LIFE INS CO | VT | B | 3q 2017 | 9,442.4 | 511.9 | 23.4 | 1,986.3 | 1.56 | 1.30 |
| NATIONAL LLOYDS INS CO | TX | B- | 3q 2017 | 190.9 | 127.5 | 0.1 | 86.9 | 3.16 | 2.60 |
| NATIONAL SECURITY INS CO | AL | B | 3q 2017 | 56.7 | 6.3 | 1.9 | 15.0 | 2.30 | 1.63 |
| NATIONAL TEACHERS ASSOCIATES L I C | TX | • B | 3q 2017 | 535.3 | 129.6 | 126.7 | 110.4 | 3.03 | 2.03 |
| NATIONAL UNION FIRE INS CO | PA | C | 3q 2017 | 26,157.5 | 5,237.4 | 792.6 | 6,272.4 | 2.19 | 1.44 |



Arrows denote recent upgrades ▲ or downgrades▼

• Bullets denote a more detailed analysis is available in Section II.

| | INSURANCE COMPANY NAME | DOM. STATE | RATING | DATA DATE | TOTAL ASSETS ($MIL) | TOTAL PREMIUMS ($MIL) | HEALTH PREMIUMS ($MIL) | CAPITAL & SURPLUS ($MIL) | RISK ADJUSTED CAPITAL RATIO 1 | RISK ADJUSTED CAPITAL RATIO 2 |
|---|---|---|---|---|---|---|---|---|---|---|
| | NATIONAL WESTERN LIFE INS CO | CO | A | 3q 2017 | 11,058.8 | 999.9 | 2.7 | 1,341.4 | 4.32 | 2.24 |
| | NATIONWIDE LIFE & ANNUITY INS CO | OH | C | 3q 2017 | 18,807.0 | 3,808.2 | 1.3 | 1,147.9 | 2.97 | 1.42 |
| | NATIONWIDE LIFE INS CO | OH | B- | 3q 2017 | 141,988.0 | 10,694.4 | 275.3 | 5,682.6 | 2.51 | 1.53 |
| | NATIONWIDE MUTUAL INS CO | OH | B | 3q 2017 | 35,739.8 | 2,669.7 | 4.3 | 12,875.6 | 1.51 | 1.33 |
| | NATL PREVENTIVE SOLUTIONS CORP | IL | U | | -- | -- | -- | -- | -- | -- |
| | NEIGHBORHOOD HEALTH PARTNERSHIP INC | FL | • B | 3q 2017 | 162.6 | 578.0 | 578.0 | 70.6 | 2.46 | 2.05 |
| | NEIGHBORHOOD HEALTH PLAN | MA | • D | 3q 2017 | 556.1 | 2,560.0 | 2,560.0 | 296.1 | 1.54 | 1.28 |
| | NEIGHBORHOOD HEALTH PLAN OF RI INC | RI | • B | 3q 2017 | 422.9 | 1,121.9 | 1,121.9 | 102.9 | 1.09 | 0.91 |
| | NETCARE LIFE & HEALTH INS CO | GU | E+ | 3q 2017 | 29.0 | 22.9 | 17.7 | 4.4 | 0.74 | 0.56 |
| | NETWORK HEALTH INS CORP | WI | • C | 3q 2017 | 231.6 | 550.6 | 550.6 | 79.9 | 1.62 | 1.35 |
| | NETWORK HEALTH PLAN | WI | • B- | 3q 2017 | 90.1 | 370.9 | 370.9 | 51.8 | 1.89 | 1.57 |
| | NEW ENGLAND LIFE INS CO | MA | B | 3q 2017 | 10,196.3 | 277.9 | 7.3 | 572.5 | 4.91 | 2.47 |
| | NEW ERA LIFE INS CO | TX | • C | 3q 2017 | 533.5 | 202.7 | 104.2 | 79.9 | 0.99 | 0.75 |
| ▲ | NEW ERA LIFE INS CO OF THE MIDWEST | TX | C+ | 3q 2017 | 128.6 | 74.1 | 46.4 | 12.8 | 1.28 | 0.81 |
| | NEW HAMPSHIRE INS CO | IL | C | 3q 2017 | 213.7 | 1,375.0 | 2.6 | 184.7 | 34.06 | 26.51 |
| | NEW HEALTH VENTURES INC | CO | U | | -- | -- | -- | -- | -- | -- |
| | NEW MEXICO HEALTH CONNECTIONS | NM | • E- | 3q 2017 | 43.3 | 153.0 | 153.0 | 3.5 | 0.16 | 0.13 |
| | NEW WEST HEALTH SERVICES | MT | • E- | 1q 2017 | 8.7 | 121.2 | 121.2 | 4.9 | 0.13 | 0.11 |
| | NEW YORK LIFE INS CO | NY | A- | 3q 2017 | 176,417.0 | 14,971.5 | 473.9 | 21,012.4 | 1.80 | 1.37 |
| | NIAGARA LIFE & HEALTH INS CO | NY | B | 3q 2017 | 17.3 | 22.4 | 22.4 | 8.7 | 2.66 | 2.39 |
| | NIPPON LIFE INS CO OF AMERICA | IA | • A- | 3q 2017 | 219.6 | 287.2 | 285.8 | 141.7 | 3.78 | 2.99 |
| | NORIDIAN MUTUAL INS CO | ND | • B | 3q 2017 | 719.6 | 1,080.4 | 1,080.4 | 477.3 | 4.47 | 3.73 |
| | NORTH AMERICAN CAPACITY INS CO | NH | C | 3q 2017 | 159.3 | 159.4 | 0.4 | 51.7 | 5.70 | 5.13 |
| | NORTH AMERICAN CO FOR LIFE & H INS | IA | B | 3q 2017 | 24,509.7 | 3,830.8 | 0.0 | 1,645.6 | 2.42 | 1.16 |
| ▲ | NORTH AMERICAN INS CO | WI | B | 3q 2017 | 20.4 | 16.0 | 16.0 | 13.8 | 2.91 | 2.21 |
| | NORTH CAROLINA FARM BU MUTUAL INS CO | NC | B | 3q 2017 | 2,017.4 | 1,020.6 | 0.1 | 1,175.4 | 6.69 | 4.40 |
| | NORTH CAROLINA MUTUAL LIFE INS CO | NC | E- | 3q 2017 | 30.8 | 11.2 | 0.7 | -20.4 | -1.59 | -0.97 |
| | NORTH RIVER INS CO | NJ | C- | 3q 2017 | 1,076.9 | 231.3 | 2.5 | 298.2 | 1.19 | 0.87 |
| | NORTHWESTERN LONG TERM CARE INS CO | WI | • B | 3q 2017 | 196.0 | 601.4 | 601.4 | 104.8 | 7.89 | 3.17 |
| | NORTHWESTERN MUTUAL LIFE INS CO | WI | A- | 3q 2017 | 264,165.0 | 17,982.4 | 1,265.6 | 22,027.5 | 3.47 | 1.75 |
| | NORTHWESTERN NATL INS CO SEG ACCNT | WI | E- | 3q 2017 | 20.8 | 0.4 | 0.4 | 1.2 | 0.09 | 0.08 |
| | NOVA CASUALTY CO | NY | C+ | 3q 2017 | 92.3 | 216.4 | 0.0 | 90.7 | 2.09 | 2.07 |
| | NTA LIFE INS CO OF NEW YORK | NY | B | 3q 2017 | 7.5 | 0.9 | 0.9 | 7.0 | 3.64 | 3.27 |
| | OBI NATIONAL INS CO | PA | C+ | 3q 2017 | 13.3 | 18.7 | 0.0 | 13.2 | 148.50 | 71.71 |
| | OCCIDENTAL LIFE INS CO OF NC | TX | C | 3q 2017 | 256.3 | 52.5 | 0.1 | 27.7 | 2.78 | 1.71 |
| | OHIO CASUALTY INS CO | NH | C | 3q 2017 | 6,154.4 | 665.3 | 0.0 | 1,721.6 | 2.76 | 1.85 |
| | OHIO MOTORISTS LIFE INSURANCE CO | OH | B | 2q 2017 | 10.7 | 0.2 | 0.1 | 10.5 | 4.24 | 3.82 |
| | OHIO NATIONAL LIFE ASR CORP | OH | B+ | 3q 2017 | 4,048.6 | 605.7 | 20.9 | 292.7 | 2.23 | 1.15 |
| | OHIO NATIONAL LIFE INS CO | OH | B | 3q 2017 | 31,141.3 | 2,365.4 | 13.5 | 1,053.0 | 1.40 | 0.92 |
| | OHIO STATE LIFE INS CO | TX | B- | 3q 2017 | 12.7 | 31.7 | 0.0 | 10.4 | 19.67 | 10.31 |
| | OKLAHOMA FARM BUREAU MUTUAL INS CO | OK | B- | 3q 2017 | 297.5 | 211.4 | 0.0 | 106.4 | 1.96 | 1.46 |
| | OKLAHOMA SUPERIOR SELECT INC | OK | • E | 3q 2017 | 3.5 | 4.0 | 4.0 | 1.5 | 1.10 | 0.92 |
| | OLD AMERICAN INS CO | MO | B- | 3q 2017 | 264.1 | 83.0 | 0.5 | 26.3 | 2.69 | 1.64 |
| | OLD REPUB INS CO | PA | B | 3q 2017 | 2,981.2 | 1,274.1 | 0.0 | 1,120.5 | 3.94 | 2.42 |
| | OLD REPUBLIC LIFE INS CO | IL | • B- | 3q 2017 | 120.8 | 33.8 | 21.6 | 33.1 | 3.52 | 2.19 |
| | OLD SPARTAN LIFE INS CO INC | SC | C | 3q 2017 | 22.8 | 5.2 | 4.2 | 14.6 | 1.94 | 1.20 |
| | OLD SURETY LIFE INS CO | OK | C | 3q 2017 | 28.4 | 51.6 | 51.4 | 11.8 | 0.73 | 0.55 |
| | OLD UNITED LIFE INS CO | AZ | • B | 3q 2017 | 83.3 | 9.4 | 4.7 | 46.6 | 6.41 | 4.32 |
| | OMAHA HEALTH INS CO | NE | U | | -- | -- | -- | -- | -- | -- |
| | OMAHA INS CO | NE | • B- | 3q 2017 | 95.3 | 444.2 | 444.2 | 48.4 | 2.10 | 1.11 |
| | ON LOK SENIOR HEALTH SERVICES | CA | • B | 3q 2017 | 176.3 | 133.2 | 133.2 | 133.4 | 4.84 | 3.51 |
| | OPTIMA HEALTH INS CO | VA | • C | 3q 2017 | 33.6 | 51.6 | 51.6 | 14.5 | 2.88 | 2.40 |

| | INSURANCE COMPANY NAME | DOM. STATE | RATING | DATA DATE | TOTAL ASSETS ($MIL) | TOTAL PREMIUMS ($MIL) | HEALTH PREMIUMS ($MIL) | CAPITAL & SURPLUS ($MIL) | RISK ADJUSTED CAPITAL RATIO 1 | RISK ADJUSTED CAPITAL RATIO 2 |
|---|---|---|---|---|---|---|---|---|---|---|
| ▲ | OPTIMA HEALTH PLAN | VA | • A- | 3q 2017 | 445.1 | 1,423.6 | 1,423.6 | 251.4 | 2.19 | 1.82 |
| | OPTIMUM CHOICE INC | MD | • C+ | 3q 2017 | 62.9 | 182.8 | 182.8 | 21.7 | 4.76 | 3.97 |
| ▲ | OPTIMUM HEALTHCARE INC | FL | • E | 3q 2017 | 189.9 | 529.9 | 529.9 | 35.0 | 0.88 | 0.74 |
| | OPTUM INS OF OH INC | OH | B | 3q 2017 | 159.9 | 0.8 | 0.0 | 44.7 | 5.38 | 4.84 |
| | ORANGE PREVENTION & TREATMENT INTEGR | CA | • A- | 3q 2017 | 2,819.9 | 3,163.8 | 3,163.8 | 724.8 | 2.77 | 1.82 |
| | ORISKA INS CO | NY | E | 3q 2017 | 42.4 | 17.2 | 0.2 | 13.1 | 0.11 | 0.10 |
| | ORTHONET OF THE MID-ATLANTIC | NJ | • C | 4q 2016 | 16.5 | 4.2 | 4.2 | 11.4 | 45.60 | 38.00 |
| | OSCAR GARDEN STATE INSURANCE | NJ | U | | -- | -- | -- | -- | -- | -- |
| | OSCAR HEALTH PLAN OF CALIFORNIA | CA | • E- | 3q 2017 | 15.7 | 9.1 | 9.1 | -41.4 | 0.00 | 0.00 |
| | OSCAR INS CO OF TEXAS | TX | • D- | 3q 2017 | 51.3 | 88.6 | 88.6 | 15.1 | 0.84 | 0.70 |
| | OSCAR INS CORP | NY | • E- | 3q 2017 | 109.6 | 246.3 | 246.3 | 25.7 | 0.83 | 0.69 |
| | OSCAR INS CORP OF NEW JERSEY | NJ | • D | 4q 2016 | 70.4 | 82.1 | 82.1 | 10.2 | 1.09 | 0.91 |
| | OSCAR INSURANCE CORP OF OHIO | OH | U | | -- | -- | -- | -- | -- | -- |
| | OXFORD HEALTH INS INC | NY | • B | 3q 2017 | 2,629.9 | 6,431.1 | 6,431.1 | 1,502.5 | 4.82 | 4.02 |
| | OXFORD HEALTH PLANS (CT) INC | CT | • B- | 3q 2017 | 595.4 | 476.1 | 476.1 | 128.2 | 5.07 | 4.22 |
| | OXFORD HEALTH PLANS (NJ) INC | NJ | • B | 3q 2017 | 311.7 | 1,057.0 | 1,057.0 | 129.0 | 2.41 | 2.01 |
| | OXFORD HEALTH PLANS (NY) INC | NY | • B+ | 3q 2017 | 646.3 | 1,707.7 | 1,707.7 | 293.7 | 3.12 | 2.60 |
| | OXFORD LIFE INS CO | AZ | B | 3q 2017 | 1,907.3 | 301.4 | 49.6 | 197.9 | 1.71 | 1.15 |
| | OZARK NATIONAL LIFE INS CO | MO | B- | 3q 2017 | 816.3 | 85.9 | 0.3 | 139.4 | 4.91 | 2.75 |
| | PA HEALTH & WELLNESS INC | PA | U | | -- | -- | -- | -- | -- | -- |
| | PACIFIC CENTURY LIFE INS CORP | AZ | • B | 3q 2017 | 362.5 | 0.0 | 0.0 | 360.5 | 31.95 | 25.36 |
| | PACIFIC GUARDIAN LIFE INS CO LTD | HI | • A- | 3q 2017 | 552.3 | 81.7 | 41.8 | 103.7 | 4.03 | 2.33 |
| | PACIFICARE LIFE & HEALTH INS CO | IN | • C+ | 3q 2017 | 187.0 | 14.3 | 14.3 | 180.4 | 18.46 | 16.62 |
| | PACIFICARE LIFE ASR CO | CO | U | | -- | -- | -- | -- | -- | -- |
| | PACIFICARE OF ARIZONA INC | AZ | U | | -- | -- | -- | -- | -- | -- |
| | PACIFICARE OF COLORADO INC | CO | • B | 3q 2017 | 813.9 | 2,469.4 | 2,469.4 | 246.7 | 2.37 | 1.97 |
| | PACIFICARE OF NEVADA INC | NV | • E | 3q 2016 | 16.1 | 128.6 | 128.6 | 7.6 | 1.95 | 1.62 |
| | PACIFICSOURCE COMMUNITY HEALTH PLANS | OR | • B- | 3q 2017 | 171.4 | 345.1 | 345.1 | 78.3 | 2.31 | 1.92 |
| | PACIFICSOURCE HEALTH PLANS | OR | • C | 3q 2017 | 304.0 | 547.9 | 547.9 | 192.0 | 2.28 | 1.90 |
| | PAN AMERICAN LIFE INS CO OF PR | PR | B | 3q 2017 | 9.6 | 15.8 | 15.4 | 6.2 | 1.90 | 1.46 |
| | PAN-AMERICAN LIFE INS CO | LA | • B | 3q 2017 | 1,249.1 | 277.7 | 239.3 | 261.0 | 2.73 | 1.74 |
| | PARAMOUNT ADVANTAGE | OH | • A- | 3q 2017 | 305.9 | 1,000.4 | 1,000.4 | 168.1 | 2.25 | 1.88 |
| | PARAMOUNT CARE INC | OH | • C+ | 3q 2017 | 139.4 | 173.5 | 173.5 | 79.5 | 5.34 | 4.45 |
| | PARAMOUNT CARE OF MI INC | MI | • B | 3q 2017 | 15.8 | 21.9 | 21.9 | 12.3 | 4.88 | 4.07 |
| | PARAMOUNT INS CO (OH) | OH | • A- | 3q 2017 | 88.2 | 158.0 | 158.0 | 37.3 | 2.57 | 2.15 |
| | PARKLAND COMMUNITY HEALTH PLAN INC | TX | • B- | 3q 2017 | 152.0 | 520.7 | 520.7 | 88.8 | 2.10 | 1.75 |
| | PARTNERRE AMERICA INS CO | DE | • C+ | 3q 2017 | 374.8 | 91.6 | 42.6 | 114.4 | 8.77 | 5.34 |
| ▲ | PARTNERRE LIFE RE CO OF AM | AR | C | 3q 2017 | 53.1 | 0.0 | 0.0 | 23.2 | 1.80 | 1.22 |
| ▼ | PARTNERSHIP HEALTHPLAN OF CALIFORNIA | CA | • A- | 3q 2017 | 1,697.8 | 2,436.1 | 2,436.1 | 814.8 | 9.06 | 5.54 |
| | PATRIOT INS CO | ME | C | 3q 2017 | 132.0 | 49.8 | 0.0 | 51.8 | 5.68 | 3.93 |
| | PAUL REVERE LIFE INS CO | MA | • C+ | 3q 2017 | 3,653.7 | 268.5 | 255.3 | 213.5 | 1.49 | 0.90 |
| | PAVONIA LIFE INS CO OF MICHIGAN | MI | C | 3q 2017 | 1,039.7 | 45.8 | 6.8 | 70.5 | 1.30 | 0.78 |
| | PAVONIA LIFE INS CO OF NEW YORK | NY | C | 3q 2017 | 30.3 | 5.7 | 0.1 | 10.4 | 2.16 | 1.95 |
| | PEACH STATE HEALTH PLAN INC | GA | • C+ | 3q 2017 | 310.0 | 1,207.0 | 1,207.0 | 184.7 | 3.14 | 2.62 |
| | PEKIN LIFE INS CO | IL | • B | 3q 2017 | 1,465.6 | 230.9 | 77.9 | 129.3 | 2.09 | 1.24 |
| | PENN MUTUAL LIFE INS CO | PA | B | 3q 2017 | 20,377.0 | 1,872.0 | 9.8 | 1,734.7 | 1.87 | 1.25 |
| | PENNSYLVANIA LIFE INS CO | PA | U | | -- | -- | -- | -- | -- | -- |
| | PEOPLES HEALTH INC | LA | • D | 3q 2017 | 151.6 | 736.6 | 736.6 | 35.9 | 0.75 | 0.63 |
| | PHILADELPHIA AMERICAN LIFE INS CO | TX | • B | 3q 2017 | 290.6 | 182.2 | 150.9 | 35.5 | 1.59 | 1.02 |
| | PHILADELPHIA INDEMNITY INS CO | PA | B- | 3q 2017 | 8,820.6 | 3,009.1 | 1.5 | 2,491.9 | 2.55 | 1.89 |
| | PHOENIX HEALTH PLANS INC | AZ | • E | 3q 2017 | 43.1 | 167.9 | 167.9 | 34.6 | 1.61 | 1.34 |
| | PHOENIX LIFE INS CO | NY | E | 3q 2017 | 12,519.3 | 432.4 | 1.1 | 449.7 | 1.53 | 0.77 |

| INSURANCE COMPANY NAME | DOM. STATE | RATING | DATA DATE | TOTAL ASSETS ($MIL) | TOTAL PREMIUMS ($MIL) | HEALTH PREMIUMS ($MIL) | CAPITAL & SURPLUS ($MIL) | RISK ADJUSTED CAPITAL RATIO 1 | RISK ADJUSTED CAPITAL RATIO 2 |
|---|---|---|---|---|---|---|---|---|---|
| PHP INS CO | MI | • B | 3q 2017 | 16.5 | 35.7 | 35.7 | 12.8 | 3.21 | 2.68 |
| PHP INS CO OF IN INC | IN | U | | -- | -- | -- | -- | -- | -- |
| PHYSICIANS BENEFITS TRUST LIFE INS | IL | C | 3q 2017 | 8.1 | 5.8 | 5.8 | 5.1 | 2.37 | 2.13 |
| PHYSICIANS HEALTH CHOICE OF TEXAS | TX | • C | 3q 2017 | 212.8 | 417.5 | 417.5 | 14.7 | 1.08 | 0.90 |
| PHYSICIANS HEALTH PLAN OF NO IN | IN | • B | 3q 2017 | 86.3 | 179.9 | 179.9 | 59.9 | 2.90 | 2.42 |
| PHYSICIANS HP OF MID-MICHIGAN | MI | • B | 3q 2017 | 81.5 | 177.4 | 177.4 | 49.7 | 1.70 | 1.41 |
| PHYSICIANS LIFE INS CO | NE | A- | 3q 2017 | 1,625.7 | 364.6 | 68.6 | 160.2 | 3.21 | 1.65 |
| PHYSICIANS MUTUAL INS CO | NE | • A+ | 3q 2017 | 2,289.0 | 342.0 | 342.0 | 957.4 | 3.48 | 2.62 |
| PHYSICIANS PLUS INS CORP | WI | • D+ | 3q 2017 | 128.7 | 244.1 | 244.1 | 87.4 | 4.05 | 3.37 |
| PICA HEALTH INC | PR | U | | -- | -- | -- | -- | -- | -- |
| PIEDMONT COMMUNITY HEALTHCARE | VA | • D+ | 3q 2017 | 27.8 | 94.3 | 94.3 | 12.0 | 0.92 | 0.76 |
| PIEDMONT COMMUNITY HEALTHCARE HMO | VA | • C- | 3q 2017 | 5.0 | 10.7 | 10.7 | 3.1 | 1.28 | 1.06 |
| PIEDMONT WELLSTAR HEALTHPLANS INC | GA | • E | 1q 2017 | 17.6 | 1.6 | 1.6 | 8.2 | 6.32 | 5.26 |
| PIONEER EDUCATORS HEALTH TRUST | OR | • E | 3q 2017 | 3.8 | 17.4 | 17.4 | 1.2 | 0.28 | 0.23 |
| PIONEER MUTUAL LIFE INS CO | ND | B | 3q 2017 | 519.7 | 28.9 | 0.0 | 50.9 | 3.38 | 1.83 |
| PL MEDICO SERV DE SALUD BELLA VISTA | PR | • C- | 3q 2017 | 2.8 | 6.0 | 6.0 | 1.1 | 0.69 | 0.57 |
| PLAN DE SALUD MENONITA | PR | • C- | 3q 2017 | 6.5 | 14.0 | 14.0 | 3.5 | 1.27 | 1.06 |
| PLATEAU INS CO | TN | C | 3q 2017 | 26.7 | 49.1 | 24.3 | 13.2 | 3.02 | 2.23 |
| PLATTE RIVER INS CO | NE | C | 3q 2017 | 149.1 | 42.7 | 0.0 | 46.9 | 3.11 | 1.80 |
| PMC MEDICARE CHOICE LLC | PR | • D | 1q 2017 | 44.4 | 456.4 | 456.4 | 35.3 | 0.90 | 0.75 |
| PREFERRED CARE PARTNERS INC | FL | • E | 3q 2017 | 600.4 | 1,484.4 | 1,484.4 | 92.7 | 1.49 | 1.24 |
| PREFERREDONE COMMUNITY HEALTH PLAN | MN | • D | 3q 2017 | 3.8 | 10.3 | 10.3 | 2.8 | 1.90 | 1.58 |
| PREFERREDONE INS CO | MN | • D+ | 3q 2017 | 101.7 | 178.2 | 178.2 | 50.6 | 1.85 | 1.55 |
| PREMERA BLUE CROSS | WA | • B+ | 3q 2017 | 2,574.6 | 3,780.1 | 3,780.1 | 1,653.9 | 5.78 | 4.82 |
| PREMIER CHOICE DENTAL INC | AZ | U | | -- | -- | -- | -- | -- | -- |
| PREMIER HEALTH INSURING CORP | OH | • E | 3q 2017 | 38.4 | 77.0 | 77.0 | 12.6 | 1.17 | 0.98 |
| PREMIER HEALTH PLAN INC | OH | • D- | 3q 2017 | 14.8 | 20.7 | 20.7 | 6.7 | 1.46 | 1.22 |
| ▼ PREMIER HEALTH PLAN SERVICES INC | CA | • D | 3q 2017 | 21.8 | 99.6 | 99.6 | 5.2 | 0.60 | 0.38 |
| PRESBYTERIAN HEALTH PLAN INC | NM | • B | 3q 2017 | 539.5 | 1,838.9 | 1,838.9 | 239.3 | 1.96 | 1.63 |
| PRESBYTERIAN INS CO | NM | • B- | 3q 2017 | 54.8 | 177.6 | 177.6 | 29.0 | 1.54 | 1.29 |
| PRESIDENTIAL LIFE INS CO | TX | C | 3q 2017 | 4.3 | 0.1 | 0.0 | 2.8 | 2.40 | 2.16 |
| PRIMECARE MEDICAL NETWORK INC | CA | • B | 3q 2017 | 238.0 | 846.4 | 846.4 | 66.6 | 2.10 | 1.30 |
| PRIMERICA LIFE INS CO | MA | B | 3q 2017 | 1,457.4 | 2,068.4 | 0.5 | 586.2 | 1.34 | 1.13 |
| PRINCIPAL LIFE INS CO | IA | B+ | 3q 2017 | 185,959.0 | 8,070.9 | 1,607.4 | 5,318.8 | 2.22 | 1.22 |
| ▲ PRIORITY HEALTH | MI | • A | 3q 2017 | 1,290.9 | 2,663.2 | 2,663.2 | 685.4 | 3.13 | 2.61 |
| PRIORITY HEALTH CHOICE INC | MI | • B+ | 3q 2017 | 143.4 | 484.5 | 484.5 | 58.2 | 2.41 | 2.01 |
| ▲ PRIORITY HEALTH INS CO | MI | • B | 3q 2017 | 122.8 | 259.2 | 259.2 | 51.8 | 2.63 | 2.19 |
| PROFESSIONAL INS CO | TX | • D | 3q 2017 | 111.4 | 24.5 | 22.9 | 46.7 | 5.21 | 4.69 |
| PROMINENCE HEALTHFIRST | NV | • E | 3q 2017 | 93.3 | 169.5 | 169.5 | 48.5 | 2.12 | 1.77 |
| PROMINENCE HEALTHFIRST OF TEXAS INC | TX | • D+ | 3q 2017 | 23.1 | 23.1 | 23.1 | 10.7 | 2.73 | 2.28 |
| PROMINENCE PREFERRED HEALTH INS CO | NV | • E | 3q 2017 | 37.3 | 44.4 | 44.4 | 33.2 | 5.94 | 4.95 |
| ▲ PROSPECT HEALTH PLAN | CA | • E+ | 3q 2017 | 10.5 | 58.1 | 58.1 | 4.5 | 0.57 | 0.36 |
| PROTEC INS CO | IL | C+ | 3q 2017 | 4.4 | 3.8 | 0.1 | 3.9 | 3.02 | 2.72 |
| PROTECTIVE INS CO | IN | A- | 3q 2017 | 848.6 | 367.2 | 14.5 | 398.2 | 1.46 | 1.11 |
| PROTECTIVE LIFE & ANNUITY INS CO | AL | B | 3q 2017 | 2,028.3 | 68.7 | 0.2 | 162.1 | 2.46 | 1.24 |
| PROTECTIVE LIFE INS CO | TN | B | 3q 2017 | 47,125.6 | 2,970.2 | 25.4 | 4,451.2 | 1.78 | 1.28 |
| PROVIDENCE HEALTH ASR | OR | • B | 3q 2017 | 489.9 | 670.1 | 670.1 | 250.8 | 5.01 | 4.17 |
| PROVIDENCE HEALTH NETWORK | CA | • E- | 3q 2017 | 21.5 | 89.7 | 89.7 | 4.0 | 0.32 | 0.19 |
| PROVIDENCE HEALTH PLAN | OR | • A+ | 3q 2017 | 910.5 | 1,107.6 | 1,107.6 | 507.1 | 4.01 | 3.34 |
| PROVIDENT AMER LIFE & HEALTH INS CO | OH | B | 3q 2017 | 10.7 | 10.4 | 9.6 | 9.4 | 1.75 | 1.55 |
| PROVIDENT AMERICAN INS CO | TX | C- | 3q 2017 | 19.3 | 1.0 | 0.6 | 11.5 | 0.70 | 0.62 |
| PROVIDENT LIFE & ACCIDENT INS CO | TN | • C+ | 3q 2017 | 8,207.4 | 1,053.8 | 735.4 | 738.0 | 2.81 | 1.41 |

| INSURANCE COMPANY NAME | DOM. STATE | RATING | DATA DATE | TOTAL ASSETS ($MIL) | TOTAL PREMIUMS ($MIL) | HEALTH PREMIUMS ($MIL) | CAPITAL & SURPLUS ($MIL) | RISK ADJUSTED CAPITAL RATIO 1 | RISK ADJUSTED CAPITAL RATIO 2 |
|---|---|---|---|---|---|---|---|---|---|
| PROVIDENT LIFE & CAS INS CO | TN | • B- | 3q 2017 | 760.2 | 89.2 | 87.0 | 165.3 | 4.96 | 2.72 |
| PROVIDER PARTNERS HEALTH PLAN INC | MD | • E- | 3q 2017 | 3.3 | 0.7 | 0.7 | 0.8 | 0.29 | 0.24 |
| PRUDENTIAL INS CO OF AMERICA | NJ | B | 3q 2017 | 263,146.0 | 22,278.9 | 1,343.7 | 11,589.0 | 1.76 | 1.26 |
| PUBLIC SERVICE INS CO | IL | F | 4q 2016 | 295.1 | 53.0 | 0.0 | 28.3 | 0.13 | 0.07 |
| PUPIL BENEFITS PLAN INC | NE | • C- | 3q 2017 | 16.6 | 9.6 | 9.6 | 6.1 | 4.52 | 3.77 |
| PURITAN LIFE INS CO OF AMERICA | TX | C- | 3q 2017 | 54.9 | 8.2 | 5.4 | 17.8 | 3.78 | 3.37 |
| PYRAMID LIFE INS CO | KS | D- | 3q 2017 | 73.3 | 25.3 | 20.4 | 14.8 | 1.98 | 1.66 |
| QBE INS CORP | PA | B | 3q 2017 | 2,665.6 | 1,190.7 | 211.7 | 735.9 | 2.30 | 1.53 |
| QBE SEGUROS | PR | D | 3q 2017 | 103.8 | 65.8 | 0.4 | 15.3 | 0.61 | 0.39 |
| QBE SPECIALTY INS CO | ND | C- | 3q 2017 | 452.4 | 613.7 | 4.5 | 122.4 | 2.47 | 1.59 |
| QCA HEALTH PLAN INC | AR | • C- | 3q 2017 | 72.5 | 214.8 | 214.8 | 40.4 | 1.85 | 1.54 |
| QCC INS CO | PA | • C | 3q 2017 | 1,160.7 | 2,248.6 | 2,248.6 | 473.9 | 3.44 | 2.87 |
| QUALCHOICE ADVANTAGE INC | AR | • C- | 3q 2017 | 6.7 | 12.0 | 12.0 | 3.7 | 1.96 | 1.63 |
| QUALCHOICE L&H INS CO | AR | • D | 3q 2017 | 50.0 | 129.2 | 129.2 | 28.1 | 1.83 | 1.53 |
| REGAL LIFE OF AMERICA INS CO | TX | D- | 3q 2017 | 7.2 | 1.8 | 1.4 | 4.5 | 1.03 | 0.99 |
| REGENCE BL CROSS BL SHIELD OREGON | OR | • B+ | 3q 2017 | 1,253.4 | 1,780.8 | 1,780.8 | 730.8 | 7.24 | 6.04 |
| REGENCE BLUE CROSS BLUE SHIELD OF UT | UT | • B- | 3q 2017 | 622.8 | 1,020.1 | 1,020.1 | 323.9 | 6.63 | 5.52 |
| REGENCE BLUESHIELD | WA | • B | 3q 2017 | 1,806.9 | 1,673.9 | 1,673.9 | 1,181.5 | 9.01 | 7.51 |
| REGENCE BLUESHIELD OF IDAHO INC | ID | • B | 3q 2017 | 302.1 | 418.7 | 418.7 | 173.5 | 7.17 | 5.98 |
| RELIABLE LIFE INS CO | MO | B- | 3q 2017 | 22.7 | 110.1 | 9.1 | 11.9 | 2.07 | 1.03 |
| RELIANCE STANDARD LIFE INS CO | IL | • B | 3q 2017 | 11,909.1 | 2,079.4 | 814.1 | 1,089.1 | 1.84 | 0.99 |
| RELIASTAR LIFE INS CO | MN | • C+ | 3q 2017 | 20,125.4 | 2,902.0 | 1,001.4 | 1,547.1 | 1.96 | 1.18 |
| RELIASTAR LIFE INS CO OF NEW YORK | NY | B | 3q 2017 | 2,999.8 | 292.6 | 58.1 | 314.9 | 3.51 | 1.89 |
| RESERVE NATIONAL INS CO | OK | • B- | 3q 2017 | 118.6 | 138.9 | 117.1 | 31.6 | 1.41 | 1.06 |
| RESPONSE INDEMNITY CO OF CA | CA | C- | 3q 2017 | 8.0 | 13.4 | 0.0 | 5.3 | 5.72 | 4.47 |
| RETAILERS INS CO | MI | C- | 3q 2017 | 22.8 | 8.9 | 0.5 | 10.5 | 1.66 | 1.33 |
| RGA REINSURANCE CO | MO | • B- | 3q 2017 | 29,084.7 | 29.1 | 10.7 | 1,535.8 | 1.50 | 0.83 |
| RIVERLINK HEALTH | OH | • E+ | 3q 2017 | 6.2 | 9.3 | 9.3 | 2.9 | 1.97 | 1.64 |
| RIVERLINK HEALTH OF KENTUCKY INC | KY | • D- | 3q 2017 | 6.8 | 8.5 | 8.5 | 3.7 | 2.62 | 2.18 |
| RIVERSOURCE LIFE INS CO | MN | C | 3q 2017 | 104,669.0 | 5,946.9 | 345.6 | 2,657.8 | 1.49 | 0.92 |
| RIVERSOURCE LIFE INS CO OF NY | NY | C | 3q 2017 | 6,767.0 | 374.9 | 17.7 | 305.3 | 3.20 | 1.61 |
| ROCKY MOUNTAIN HEALTH MAINT ORG | CO | • C | 3q 2017 | 137.6 | 448.2 | 448.2 | 47.6 | 1.76 | 1.47 |
| ROCKY MOUNTAIN HEALTHCARE OPTIONS | CO | • D | 3q 2017 | 21.2 | 73.7 | 73.7 | 10.8 | 0.98 | 0.81 |
| ROCKY MOUNTAIN HOSPITAL & MEDICAL | CO | • B | 3q 2017 | 1,040.9 | 2,337.6 | 2,337.6 | 468.2 | 3.10 | 2.59 |
| ROYAL STATE NATIONAL INS CO LTD | HI | • C | 3q 2017 | 46.1 | 5.6 | 3.0 | 29.5 | 4.95 | 3.30 |
| RURAL MUTUAL INS CO | WI | B- | 3q 2017 | 496.1 | 194.0 | 0.7 | 259.4 | 6.44 | 4.37 |
| ▲ RYDER HEALTH PLAN INC | PR | • C | 3q 2017 | 1.6 | 2.6 | 2.6 | 0.6 | 1.54 | 1.28 |
| S USA LIFE INS CO INC | AZ | B | 3q 2017 | 13.5 | 1.4 | 0.1 | 6.9 | 2.52 | 2.27 |
| SAFEGUARD HEALTH PLANS INC A NV CORP | NV | U | | -- | -- | -- | -- | -- | -- |
| SAGICOR LIFE INS CO | TX | C- | 3q 2017 | 1,129.7 | 168.6 | 0.1 | 72.9 | 1.15 | 0.59 |
| SAMARITAN HEALTH PLANS INC | OR | • B | 3q 2017 | 35.8 | 73.4 | 73.4 | 12.4 | 1.28 | 1.06 |
| SAN FRANCISCO HEALTH AUTHORITY | CA | • B | 3q 2017 | 742.2 | 572.8 | 572.8 | 123.5 | 3.17 | 1.98 |
| SAN JOAQUIN CNTY HEALTH | CA | • C+ | 3q 2017 | 847.4 | 920.6 | 920.6 | 282.9 | 4.62 | 2.81 |
| SAN MATEO HEALTH COMMISSION | CA | • B+ | 3q 2017 | 657.3 | 792.3 | 792.3 | 301.9 | 5.66 | 3.48 |
| SANFORD HEALTH PLAN | SD | • C | 3q 2017 | 263.9 | 823.7 | 823.7 | 125.2 | 1.43 | 1.20 |
| SANFORD HEALTH PLAN OF MINNESOTA | MN | • E+ | 3q 2017 | 2.0 | 2.4 | 2.4 | 1.6 | 2.05 | 1.71 |
| SANFORD HEART OF AMERICA HEALTH PLAN | ND | • D+ | 3q 2017 | 3.5 | 3.4 | 3.4 | 2.6 | 2.76 | 2.30 |
| SANTA BARBARA SAN LUIS OBISPO REGION | CA | • B | 3q 2017 | 518.2 | 658.3 | 658.3 | 211.5 | 4.64 | 2.79 |
| SANTA CLARA COUNTY | CA | • D | 3q 2017 | 152.5 | 514.9 | 514.9 | 28.2 | 0.70 | 0.43 |
| SANTA CLARA COUNTY HEALTH AUTHORITY | CA | • C | 3q 2017 | 993.8 | 1,259.2 | 1,259.2 | 166.3 | 2.73 | 1.65 |
| SANTA CRUZ-MONTEREY-MERCED MGD MED | CA | • B- | 3q 2017 | 1,450.9 | 1,075.9 | 1,075.9 | 642.3 | 12.87 | 7.88 |
| SATELLITE HEALTH PLAN INC | CA | U | | -- | -- | -- | -- | -- | -- |

| INSURANCE COMPANY NAME | DOM. STATE | RATING | DATA DATE | TOTAL ASSETS ($MIL) | TOTAL PREMIUMS ($MIL) | HEALTH PREMIUMS ($MIL) | CAPITAL & SURPLUS ($MIL) | RISK ADJUSTED CAPITAL RATIO 1 | RISK ADJUSTED CAPITAL RATIO 2 |
|---|---|---|---|---|---|---|---|---|---|
| SB MUTL LIFE INS CO OF MA | MA | B+ | 3q 2017 | 3,015.1 | 368.7 | 0.0 | 202.3 | 1.57 | 0.98 |
| SBLI USA MUT LIFE INS CO INC | NY | B | 3q 2017 | 1,473.5 | 62.5 | 0.5 | 98.6 | 1.77 | 1.02 |
| SC FARM BUREAU MUTUAL INS CO | SC | C+ | 3q 2017 | 110.0 | 75.6 | 0.1 | 54.1 | 2.74 | 2.40 |
| SCAN HEALTH PLAN | CA | • C | 3q 2017 | 829.1 | 2,251.5 | 2,251.5 | 359.9 | 3.23 | 2.01 |
| SCOTT & WHITE HEALTH PLAN | TX | • C- | 3q 2017 | 287.2 | 670.1 | 670.1 | 100.8 | 0.70 | 0.58 |
| SCRIPPS HEALTH PLAN SERVICES INC | CA | • C- | 3q 2017 | 125.3 | 515.3 | 515.3 | 33.3 | 0.88 | 0.54 |
| SD STATE MEDICAL HOLDING CO | SD | • D | 3q 2017 | 23.4 | 79.2 | 79.2 | 12.7 | 0.63 | 0.52 |
| SEASIDE HEALTH PLAN | CA | • D- | 3q 2017 | 14.5 | 31.4 | 31.4 | 8.0 | 0.34 | 0.22 |
| SECURIAN LIFE INS CO | MN | B | 3q 2017 | 735.1 | 725.6 | 58.2 | 258.6 | 5.50 | 3.63 |
| SECURITY HEALTH PLAN OF WI INC | WI | • A- | 3q 2017 | 427.3 | 1,178.1 | 1,178.1 | 207.9 | 2.07 | 1.73 |
| SECURITY LIFE OF DENVER INS CO | CO | C+ | 3q 2017 | 14,202.1 | 836.1 | 0.0 | 979.0 | 1.70 | 0.99 |
| SECURITY MUTUAL LIFE INS CO OF NY | NY | B- | 3q 2017 | 2,737.7 | 376.3 | 14.2 | 158.1 | 1.66 | 0.89 |
| SECURITY NATIONAL LIFE INS CO | UT | D- | 3q 2017 | 580.3 | 72.8 | 0.1 | 34.2 | 0.50 | 0.33 |
| SECURITY PLAN LIFE INS CO | LA | C- | 3q 2017 | 310.3 | 42.3 | 0.6 | 26.4 | 1.17 | 0.78 |
| SECURITYCARE OF TENNESSEE INC | TN | • B | 3q 2017 | 11.5 | 21.7 | 21.7 | 6.8 | 2.98 | 2.49 |
| SELECT HEALTH OF SOUTH CAROLINA INC | SC | • B- | 3q 2017 | 340.4 | 1,337.3 | 1,337.3 | 170.4 | 2.38 | 1.98 |
| ▲ SELECTCARE HEALTH PLANS INC | TX | • C+ | 3q 2017 | 22.7 | 33.7 | 33.7 | 15.6 | 3.96 | 3.30 |
| SELECTCARE OF TEXAS INC | TX | • B | 3q 2017 | 278.3 | 833.8 | 833.8 | 73.2 | 1.41 | 1.17 |
| SELECTHEALTH BENEFIT ASR CO INC | UT | • C | 3q 2017 | 28.6 | 34.4 | 34.4 | 17.0 | 3.69 | 3.08 |
| SELECTHEALTH INC | UT | • C | 3q 2017 | 1,078.3 | 2,607.9 | 2,607.9 | 446.0 | 2.05 | 1.71 |
| SELECTIVE INS CO OF AM | NJ | B | 3q 2017 | 2,426.7 | 487.7 | 0.0 | 608.9 | 2.82 | 1.82 |
| SENDERO HEALTH PLANS INC | TX | • E- | 3q 2017 | 58.7 | 85.1 | 85.1 | 12.4 | 0.79 | 0.66 |
| SENIOR HEALTH INS CO OF PENNSYLVANIA | PA | • E- | 4q 2016 | 2,736.1 | 110.6 | 110.6 | 28.3 | 1.42 | 1.27 |
| SENIOR LIFE INS CO | GA | D+ | 3q 2017 | 58.0 | 49.0 | 0.0 | 12.4 | 2.00 | 0.99 |
| SENIOR WHOLE HEALTH OF NEW YORK INC | NY | • E | 3q 2017 | 90.2 | 245.7 | 245.7 | 32.5 | 1.13 | 0.94 |
| SENTINEL SECURITY LIFE INS CO | UT | C- | 3q 2017 | 705.2 | 209.1 | 37.1 | 45.8 | 0.98 | 0.48 |
| SENTRY INS A MUTUAL CO | WI | A | 3q 2017 | 8,232.3 | 510.0 | 2.8 | 5,018.5 | 2.70 | 2.22 |
| SENTRY LIFE INS CO | WI | A | 3q 2017 | 6,735.9 | 710.1 | 6.4 | 280.2 | 3.39 | 1.98 |
| SENTRY LIFE INS CO OF NEW YORK | NY | B | 3q 2017 | 107.6 | 14.2 | 0.1 | 10.0 | 1.23 | 1.11 |
| SENTRY SELECT INS CO | WI | B+ | 3q 2017 | 810.3 | 516.2 | 6.4 | 238.2 | 3.51 | 2.22 |
| SERVICE LIFE & CAS INS CO | TX | U | | -- | -- | -- | -- | -- | -- |
| SETON HEALTH PLAN INC | TX | • B- | 3q 2017 | 53.3 | 58.3 | 58.3 | 23.7 | 2.52 | 2.10 |
| SETTLERS LIFE INS CO | WI | B | 3q 2017 | 413.7 | 52.5 | 0.3 | 43.9 | 2.71 | 1.47 |
| SHA LLC | TX | • E | 3q 2017 | 101.4 | 614.6 | 614.6 | 56.4 | 0.92 | 0.77 |
| SHARP HEALTH PLAN | CA | • B | 3q 2017 | 136.6 | 612.1 | 612.1 | 82.7 | 1.63 | 1.06 |
| SHELTER LIFE INS CO | MO | B+ | 3q 2017 | 1,238.3 | 142.2 | 11.2 | 211.2 | 3.67 | 2.41 |
| SHELTERPOINT INS CO | FL | B | 3q 2017 | 8.6 | 0.4 | 0.4 | 8.1 | 4.17 | 3.76 |
| SHELTERPOINT LIFE INS CO | NY | • A | 3q 2017 | 110.1 | 91.9 | 90.3 | 62.2 | 2.51 | 2.11 |
| SHENANDOAH LIFE INS CO | VA | B- | 3q 2017 | 1,055.1 | 59.6 | 7.9 | 94.8 | 2.39 | 1.28 |
| SHERIDAN LIFE INS CO | OK | U | | -- | -- | -- | -- | -- | -- |
| SIERRA HEALTH AND LIFE INS CO INC | NV | • B | 3q 2017 | 4,140.2 | 8,918.3 | 8,918.3 | 1,490.2 | 3.11 | 2.59 |
| SIGNATURE ADVANTAGE LLC | KY | • D+ | 3q 2017 | 2.5 | 4.1 | 4.1 | 1.3 | 1.10 | 0.92 |
| SILVERSCRIPT INS CO | TN | • D | 3q 2017 | 4,421.7 | 2,483.6 | 2,483.6 | 793.6 | 6.77 | 5.64 |
| SILVERSUMMIT HEALTHPLAN INC | NV | U | | -- | -- | -- | -- | -- | -- |
| SIMPLY HEALTHCARE PLANS INC | FL | • A- | 3q 2017 | 434.0 | 1,213.9 | 1,213.9 | 149.2 | 2.31 | 1.92 |
| SIMPRA ADVANTAGE INC | AL | U | | -- | -- | -- | -- | -- | -- |
| SIRIUS AMERICA INS CO | NY | • B- | 3q 2017 | 1,364.8 | 140.4 | 139.1 | 544.0 | 1.11 | 0.79 |
| SISTEMAS MEDICOS NACIONALES SA DE CV | CA | • C+ | 3q 2017 | 52.2 | 78.6 | 78.6 | 32.7 | 4.10 | 2.71 |
| ▼ SOUNDPATH HEALTH | WA | • E- | 3q 2017 | 64.4 | 198.1 | 198.1 | 14.5 | 0.44 | 0.37 |
| SOUTHEASTERN INDIANA HEALTH ORG INC | IN | • C | 3q 2017 | 15.1 | 33.7 | 33.7 | 8.7 | 1.72 | 1.43 |
| SOUTHERN FARM BUREAU LIFE INS CO | MS | A | 3q 2017 | 14,163.7 | 1,010.9 | 32.2 | 2,573.4 | 4.56 | 2.44 |
| SOUTHERN FINANCIAL LIFE INS CO | KY | C | 3q 2017 | 8.3 | 12.0 | 5.6 | 3.2 | 1.66 | 1.50 |

| INSURANCE COMPANY NAME | DOM. STATE | RATING | DATA DATE | TOTAL ASSETS ($MIL) | TOTAL PREMIUMS ($MIL) | HEALTH PREMIUMS ($MIL) | CAPITAL & SURPLUS ($MIL) | RISK ADJUSTED CAPITAL RATIO 1 | RISK ADJUSTED CAPITAL RATIO 2 |
|---|---|---|---|---|---|---|---|---|---|
| SOUTHERN NATL LIFE INS CO INC | LA | B | 3q 2017 | 16.5 | 11.0 | 2.9 | 12.7 | 2.28 | 1.80 |
| SOUTHERN PIONEER LIFE INS CO | AR | B+ | 3q 2017 | 15.7 | 2.7 | 0.7 | 12.5 | 4.13 | 3.72 |
| SOUTHLAND NATIONAL INS CORP | NC | • C- | 1q 2017 | 381.0 | 7.8 | 5.8 | 35.4 | 1.42 | 0.86 |
| SOUTHWEST L&H INS CO | TX | • C- | 3q 2017 | 11.7 | 11.1 | 11.1 | 10.2 | 4.48 | 3.73 |
| SOUTHWEST SERVICE LIFE INS CO | TX | D- | 3q 2017 | 11.5 | 8.8 | 7.1 | 4.0 | 0.66 | 0.59 |
| SPARTAN PLAN IL INC | IL | U | | -- | -- | -- | -- | -- | -- |
| SPARTAN PLAN NY INC | NY | U | | -- | -- | -- | -- | -- | -- |
| SPARTAN PLAN PA INC | PA | U | | -- | -- | -- | -- | -- | -- |
| SPARTAN PLAN VA INC | VA | U | | -- | -- | -- | -- | -- | -- |
| STABLEVIEW HEALTH INC | KY | • D+ | 1q 2017 | 5.2 | 1.6 | 1.6 | 5.2 | 12.15 | 10.13 |
| STANDARD GUARANTY INS CO | DE | B- | 3q 2017 | 325.9 | 410.5 | 0.1 | 153.5 | 2.68 | 2.05 |
| STANDARD INS CO | OR | • B+ | 3q 2017 | 23,414.5 | 4,874.3 | 1,432.7 | 1,091.1 | 2.10 | 1.09 |
| STANDARD LIFE & ACCIDENT INS CO | TX | • A- | 3q 2017 | 516.7 | 124.5 | 111.8 | 287.7 | 6.18 | 3.79 |
| STANDARD LIFE & CAS INS CO | UT | D | 3q 2017 | 28.6 | 13.9 | 5.3 | 4.5 | 1.03 | 0.71 |
| STANDARD LIFE INS CO OF NY | NY | • A- | 3q 2017 | 292.4 | 91.5 | 54.5 | 96.3 | 4.68 | 3.05 |
| STANDARD SECURITY LIFE INS CO OF NY | NY | • B | 3q 2017 | 133.1 | 345.0 | 342.7 | 66.5 | 6.62 | 5.11 |
| STANFORD HEALTH CARE ADVANTAGE | CA | • E- | 3q 2017 | 6.5 | 6.7 | 6.7 | 2.2 | 1.33 | 0.91 |
| STARMOUNT LIFE INS CO | LA | • B | 3q 2017 | 76.4 | 101.9 | 93.4 | 34.8 | 1.11 | 0.86 |
| STARNET INS CO | DE | C | 3q 2017 | 238.3 | 387.6 | 3.2 | 118.2 | 12.87 | 11.58 |
| STARR INDEMNITY & LIABILITY CO | TX | B | 3q 2017 | 4,753.8 | 1,710.1 | 27.9 | 2,004.2 | 1.39 | 1.12 |
| STARR SURPLUS LINES INS CO | IL | B- | 3q 2017 | 376.5 | 442.7 | 0.0 | 131.9 | 2.15 | 1.29 |
| STATE AUTOMOBILE MUTUAL INS CO | OH | C+ | 3q 2017 | 2,446.7 | 410.9 | 0.0 | 786.3 | 1.09 | 0.96 |
| STATE FARM FIRE & CAS CO | IL | B+ | 3q 2017 | 39,417.8 | 19,397.5 | 1.1 | 16,699.7 | 2.74 | 1.71 |
| STATE FARM MUTUAL AUTOMOBILE INS CO | IL | B+ | 3q 2017 | 154,684.0 | 37,093.6 | 963.0 | 91,953.4 | 2.02 | 1.74 |
| STATE LIFE INS CO | IN | B | 3q 2017 | 7,619.4 | 792.5 | 21.3 | 472.4 | 2.01 | 1.04 |
| STATE MUTUAL INS CO | GA | • C- | 3q 2017 | 274.1 | 45.8 | 25.5 | 29.9 | 1.21 | 0.80 |
| STERLING INVESTORS LIFE INS CO | IN | D+ | 3q 2017 | 49.8 | 27.5 | 10.9 | 9.6 | 2.04 | 1.60 |
| STERLING LIFE INS CO | IL | B- | 3q 2017 | 41.2 | 76.5 | 74.9 | 18.4 | 1.00 | 0.77 |
| SUMMA INS CO | OH | • C- | 3q 2017 | 53.7 | 190.6 | 190.6 | 27.2 | 1.63 | 1.36 |
| SUMMACARE INC | OH | • C+ | 3q 2017 | 113.4 | 252.6 | 252.6 | 49.5 | 1.63 | 1.36 |
| SUN LIFE & HEALTH INS CO | MI | • D | 3q 2017 | 504.8 | 255.6 | 174.4 | 205.6 | 5.37 | 3.36 |
| ▲ SUN LIFE ASR CO OF CANADA | MI | • D- | 3q 2017 | 20,032.5 | 2,834.2 | 1,737.6 | 1,142.6 | 0.64 | 0.38 |
| SUNFLOWER STATE HEALTH PLAN INC | KS | • C- | 3q 2017 | 238.0 | 1,106.7 | 1,106.7 | 131.5 | 2.33 | 1.94 |
| SUNSET LIFE INS CO OF AMERICA | MO | B | 3q 2017 | 323.5 | 16.9 | 0.0 | 35.0 | 3.30 | 1.73 |
| SUNSHINE HEALTH | FL | • E | 3q 2017 | 724.8 | 3,627.5 | 3,627.5 | 363.5 | 1.84 | 1.53 |
| SUPERIOR HEALTHPLAN INC | TX | • C+ | 3q 2017 | 708.3 | 3,522.0 | 3,522.0 | 355.8 | 1.88 | 1.56 |
| SURENCY LIFE & HEALTH INS CO | KS | C | 3q 2017 | 10.4 | 12.6 | 12.4 | 8.1 | 2.74 | 2.09 |
| SURETY LIFE & CASUALTY INS CO | ND | C- | 3q 2017 | 12.1 | 1.4 | 0.6 | 4.8 | 1.97 | 1.77 |
| SURETY LIFE INS CO | NE | D | 3q 2017 | 19.3 | 35.3 | 0.0 | 18.8 | 3.15 | 1.53 |
| SUTTER HEALTH PLAN | CA | • D- | 3q 2017 | 91.1 | 188.2 | 188.2 | 22.2 | 1.23 | 0.78 |
| SWBC LIFE INS CO | TX | B | 3q 2017 | 28.3 | 12.4 | 7.4 | 18.2 | 3.05 | 2.05 |
| SWISS RE LIFE & HEALTH AMER INC | MO | • C | 3q 2017 | 14,355.3 | 0.4 | 0.4 | 1,457.4 | 1.74 | 1.09 |
| SYMETRA LIFE INS CO | IA | B+ | 3q 2017 | 36,133.8 | 4,486.8 | 666.5 | 2,198.7 | 2.05 | 1.10 |
| SYMPHONIX HEALTH INS INC | IL | • E+ | 3q 2017 | 293.4 | 357.9 | 357.9 | 32.6 | 2.73 | 2.27 |
| TAKECARE INS CO | GU | • D+ | 3q 2017 | 32.5 | 101.0 | 101.0 | 8.3 | 0.58 | 0.48 |
| TEACHERS INS & ANNUITY ASN OF AM | NY | A+ | 3q 2017 | 293,835.0 | 15,197.7 | 13.3 | 37,068.0 | 4.73 | 2.54 |
| TEXAS CHILDRENS HEALTH PLAN INC | TX | • D+ | 3q 2017 | 221.9 | 1,066.3 | 1,066.3 | 80.3 | 0.79 | 0.66 |
| TEXAS FARM BUREAU MUTUAL INS CO | TX | C | 3q 2017 | 738.6 | 563.3 | 0.7 | 299.9 | 2.47 | 2.25 |
| TEXAS HLTH + AETNA HLTH INS CO | TX | U | | -- | -- | -- | -- | -- | -- |
| TEXAS HLTH + AETNA HLTH PLAN | TX | U | | -- | -- | -- | -- | -- | -- |
| TEXAS LIFE INS CO | TX | B | 3q 2017 | 1,158.0 | 242.5 | 0.0 | 98.1 | 2.01 | 1.11 |
| THP INS CO | WV | • D | 3q 2017 | 48.8 | 71.7 | 71.7 | 27.2 | 3.40 | 2.83 |


Arrows denote recent upgrades ▲ or downgrades▼
• Bullets denote a more detailed analysis is available in Section II.

| | INSURANCE COMPANY NAME | DOM. STATE | RATING | DATA DATE | TOTAL ASSETS ($MIL) | TOTAL PREMIUMS ($MIL) | HEALTH PREMIUMS ($MIL) | CAPITAL & SURPLUS ($MIL) | RISK ADJUSTED CAPITAL RATIO 1 | RISK ADJUSTED CAPITAL RATIO 2 |
|---|---|---|---|---|---|---|---|---|---|---|
| | THRIVENT LIFE INS CO | WI | B | 3q 2017 | 3,809.6 | 154.2 | 0.0 | 161.2 | 1.89 | 0.93 |
| | TIAA-CREF LIFE INS CO | NY | B | 3q 2017 | 13,026.7 | 812.2 | 6.7 | 413.2 | 2.02 | 1.06 |
| | TIG INS CO | CA | C | 3q 2017 | 2,524.6 | 0.9 | 0.0 | 714.7 | 1.16 | 0.77 |
| ▲ | TIMBER PRODUCTS MANUFACTURERS TRUST | WA | • D- | 3q 2017 | 10.7 | 57.7 | 57.7 | 6.1 | 0.66 | 0.55 |
| | TIME INS CO | WI | • C+ | 3q 2017 | 108.9 | 289.3 | 249.6 | 50.1 | 5.57 | 4.84 |
| | TODAYS OPTIONS OF TEXAS INC | TX | • C | 3q 2017 | 10.2 | 3.5 | 3.5 | 6.9 | 7.90 | 6.58 |
| | TOKIO MARINE PACIFIC INS LTD | GU | • C | 3q 2017 | 116.6 | 147.8 | 132.9 | 78.4 | 4.66 | 2.50 |
| ▼ | TOTAL HEALTH CARE INC | MI | • C+ | 3q 2017 | 81.5 | 284.1 | 284.1 | 48.9 | 1.60 | 1.33 |
| | TOTAL HEALTH CARE USA INC | MI | • B+ | 3q 2017 | 68.3 | 139.3 | 139.3 | 39.9 | 3.47 | 2.89 |
| | TOUCHSTONE HEALTH HMO INC | NY | • E+ | 1q 2017 | 12.5 | 0.3 | 0.3 | 2.6 | 0.42 | 0.35 |
| | TOWN & COUNTRY LIFE INS CO | UT | C- | 3q 2017 | 7.8 | 4.5 | 4.4 | 4.6 | 2.49 | 1.99 |
| | TPM LIFE INS CO | PA | B | 3q 2017 | 19.6 | 6.5 | 6.3 | 4.7 | 1.46 | 1.07 |
| | TRANS CITY LIFE INS CO | AZ | C- | 3q 2017 | 19.9 | 2.0 | 0.5 | 9.9 | 3.44 | 3.10 |
| | TRANS OCEANIC LIFE INS CO | PR | • A- | 3q 2017 | 71.4 | 31.0 | 28.7 | 32.7 | 2.45 | 1.55 |
| | TRANSAMERICA CASUALTY INS CO | OH | B- | 3q 2017 | 370.7 | 390.6 | 0.5 | 187.4 | 2.65 | 1.85 |
| | TRANSAMERICA FINANCIAL LIFE INS CO | NY | B | 3q 2017 | 33,707.4 | 5,780.3 | 129.8 | 1,114.6 | 3.05 | 1.50 |
| | TRANSAMERICA LIFE INS CO | IA | B | 3q 2017 | 129,680.0 | 14,001.9 | 1,142.2 | 5,065.4 | 1.40 | 0.97 |
| | TRANSAMERICA PREMIER LIFE INS CO | IA | C+ | 3q 2017 | 41,444.3 | 3,323.5 | 808.2 | 1,494.5 | 2.03 | 1.05 |
| | TRAVELERS PROPERTY CAS OF AMERICA | CT | B | 3q 2017 | 882.5 | 4,856.6 | 0.0 | 446.9 | 13.77 | 8.82 |
| ▼ | TRH HEALTH INS CO | TN | • C | 3q 2017 | 127.7 | 296.7 | 296.7 | 66.0 | 2.21 | 1.85 |
| | TRILLIUM COMMUNITY HEALTH PLAN INC | OR | • C+ | 3q 2017 | 175.8 | 519.7 | 519.7 | 67.2 | 2.59 | 2.16 |
| | TRILOGY HEALTH INS INC | WI | • C | 3q 2017 | 6.1 | 20.4 | 20.4 | 3.2 | 0.90 | 0.75 |
| | TRINITY LIFE INS CO | OK | D- | 3q 2017 | 207.2 | 30.6 | 0.0 | 11.3 | 0.66 | 0.46 |
| | TRIPLE S VIDA INC | PR | • B- | 3q 2017 | 637.5 | 173.6 | 63.9 | 59.6 | 1.14 | 0.75 |
| | TRIPLE-S ADVANTAGE INC | PR | • C | 3q 2017 | 379.8 | 1,023.9 | 1,023.9 | 67.9 | 0.43 | 0.36 |
| | TRIPLE-S BLUE II | PR | D- | 4q 2016 | 13.4 | 8.4 | 8.3 | 2.8 | 1.03 | 0.92 |
| ▼ | TRIPLE-S SALUD INC | PR | • B- | 3q 2017 | 619.9 | 1,626.3 | 1,626.3 | 261.8 | 2.13 | 1.77 |
| | TRITON INS CO | TX | • C+ | 3q 2017 | 440.5 | 70.5 | 23.7 | 168.1 | 5.77 | 3.94 |
| ▲ | TRUSTED HEALTH PLAN INC | DC | • C+ | 3q 2017 | 56.5 | 147.4 | 147.4 | 17.3 | 1.02 | 0.85 |
| | TRUSTMARK INS CO | IL | • B+ | 3q 2017 | 1,532.5 | 359.3 | 168.8 | 317.5 | 2.83 | 1.60 |
| | TRUSTMARK LIFE INS CO | IL | • B+ | 3q 2017 | 320.1 | 146.5 | 143.5 | 178.0 | 7.86 | 5.00 |
| | TUFTS ASSOCIATED HEALTH MAINT ORG | MA | • B | 3q 2017 | 1,517.3 | 2,553.4 | 2,553.4 | 937.0 | 3.49 | 2.91 |
| | TUFTS HEALTH FREEDOM INS CO | NH | • C | 3q 2017 | 26.2 | 5.3 | 5.3 | 12.6 | 8.15 | 6.79 |
| | TUFTS HEALTH PUBLIC PLANS INC | MA | • C+ | 3q 2017 | 559.0 | 1,528.3 | 1,528.3 | 231.9 | 2.35 | 1.96 |
| | TUFTS INS CO | MA | • C- | 3q 2017 | 100.1 | 258.4 | 258.4 | 52.4 | 3.10 | 2.59 |
| | U S HEALTH & LIFE INS CO | MI | • B | 3q 2017 | 25.7 | 33.3 | 33.3 | 14.2 | 2.98 | 2.49 |
| | UCARE HEALTH INC | WI | • E | 2q 2017 | 19.5 | 1.6 | 1.6 | 18.4 | 7.86 | 6.55 |
| | UCARE MINNESOTA | MN | • B | 3q 2017 | 1,170.5 | 1,686.2 | 1,686.2 | 575.1 | 4.70 | 3.92 |
| | UHC OF CALIFORNIA INC | CA | • C | 3q 2017 | 1,242.4 | 6,668.2 | 6,668.2 | 224.6 | 0.71 | 0.44 |
| | ULTIMATE HEALTH PLANS INC | FL | • E | 3q 2017 | 22.4 | 52.0 | 52.0 | 5.8 | 0.74 | 0.62 |
| | UNDERWRITERS AT LLOYDS (KY) | KY | D | 3q 2017 | 193.2 | 37.4 | 1.2 | 33.4 | 0.64 | 0.40 |
| | UNDERWRITERS AT LLOYDS (VI) | VI | C- | 3q 2017 | 82.8 | 62.7 | 0.1 | 25.0 | 0.16 | 0.13 |
| ▲ | UNICARE HEALTH PLAN OF WEST VIRGINIA | WV | • A- | 3q 2017 | 110.0 | 484.5 | 484.5 | 69.6 | 2.45 | 2.04 |
| | UNICARE LIFE & HEALTH INS CO | IN | • B- | 3q 2017 | 305.5 | 245.1 | 84.0 | 70.8 | 1.82 | 1.37 |
| | UNIFIED LIFE INS CO | TX | • B | 3q 2017 | 213.5 | 99.9 | 94.3 | 25.3 | 1.94 | 1.17 |
| | UNIMERICA INS CO | WI | • B | 3q 2017 | 473.4 | 349.1 | 335.8 | 169.9 | 1.67 | 1.35 |
| | UNIMERICA LIFE INS CO OF NY | NY | B | 3q 2017 | 39.0 | 6.3 | 4.9 | 20.8 | 4.01 | 3.61 |
| | UNION FIDELITY LIFE INS CO | KS | • C | 3q 2017 | 19,526.8 | 29.5 | 16.4 | 748.4 | 1.58 | 0.79 |
| | UNION HEALTH SERVICE INC | IL | • B | 3q 2017 | 26.7 | 73.7 | 73.7 | 16.8 | 1.13 | 0.94 |
| | UNION LABOR LIFE INS CO | MD | • B | 3q 2017 | 3,544.9 | 167.3 | 104.2 | 93.9 | 2.01 | 1.30 |
| | UNION NATIONAL LIFE INS CO | LA | B | 3q 2017 | 20.9 | 82.6 | 6.2 | 16.0 | 4.96 | 2.48 |
| | UNION SECURITY INS CO | KS | • B | 3q 2017 | 2,690.2 | 1,013.0 | 743.0 | 129.1 | 2.61 | 1.37 |

| INSURANCE COMPANY NAME | DOM. STATE | RATING | DATA DATE | TOTAL ASSETS ($MIL) | TOTAL PREMIUMS ($MIL) | HEALTH PREMIUMS ($MIL) | CAPITAL & SURPLUS ($MIL) | RISK ADJUSTED CAPITAL RATIO 1 | RISK ADJUSTED CAPITAL RATIO 2 |
|---|---|---|---|---|---|---|---|---|---|
| UNION SECURITY LIFE INS CO OF NY | NY | • C+ | 3q 2017 | 74.4 | 24.0 | 20.0 | 52.8 | 6.51 | 5.86 |
| UNITED AMERICAN INS CO | NE | • B- | 3q 2017 | 1,006.6 | 614.1 | 573.1 | 206.2 | 1.65 | 1.23 |
| UNITED FARM FAMILY LIFE INS CO | IN | A | 3q 2017 | 2,312.3 | 144.9 | 0.7 | 327.8 | 3.32 | 1.98 |
| UNITED FIDELITY LIFE INS CO | TX | C | 3q 2017 | 791.2 | 7.1 | 0.2 | 505.2 | 0.79 | 0.77 |
| UNITED HEALTHCARE INS CO | CT | • C | 3q 2017 | 20,075.9 | 43,200.7 | 43,081.0 | 5,039.7 | 0.85 | 0.72 |
| UNITED HEALTHCARE INS CO OF IL | IL | • B | 3q 2017 | 336.3 | 1,065.1 | 1,065.1 | 156.9 | 2.77 | 2.31 |
| UNITED HEALTHCARE INS CO OF NY | NY | • B- | 3q 2017 | 1,497.9 | 1,664.4 | 1,664.4 | 498.2 | 21.78 | 18.15 |
| ▼ UNITED HEALTHCARE OF ALABAMA INC | AL | • B- | 3q 2017 | 78.0 | 559.7 | 559.7 | 39.4 | 1.79 | 1.49 |
| UNITED HEALTHCARE OF ARIZONA INC | AZ | • C | 3q 2017 | 49.2 | 111.4 | 111.4 | 21.8 | 5.32 | 4.43 |
| UNITED HEALTHCARE OF ARKANSAS INC | AR | • D- | 3q 2017 | 25.2 | 41.1 | 41.1 | 21.6 | 5.14 | 4.28 |
| UNITED HEALTHCARE OF COLORADO INC | CO | • D- | 3q 2017 | 32.6 | 87.9 | 87.9 | 13.3 | 2.32 | 1.93 |
| UNITED HEALTHCARE OF FLORIDA INC | FL | • D+ | 3q 2017 | 632.5 | 3,000.4 | 3,000.4 | 300.2 | 1.87 | 1.56 |
| UNITED HEALTHCARE OF GEORGIA INC | GA | • B | 3q 2017 | 112.2 | 287.3 | 287.3 | 58.2 | 3.24 | 2.70 |
| UNITED HEALTHCARE OF ILLINOIS INC | IL | • B- | 3q 2017 | 51.6 | 135.1 | 135.1 | 25.3 | 3.65 | 3.04 |
| UNITED HEALTHCARE OF KENTUCKY LTD | KY | • C | 3q 2017 | 31.2 | 105.1 | 105.1 | 14.2 | 2.13 | 1.78 |
| UNITED HEALTHCARE OF LOUISIANA INC | LA | • D | 3q 2017 | 557.7 | 1,644.8 | 1,644.8 | 180.5 | 2.21 | 1.84 |
| UNITED HEALTHCARE OF MID-ATLANTIC | MD | • B | 3q 2017 | 306.4 | 896.7 | 896.7 | 141.7 | 3.06 | 2.55 |
| UNITED HEALTHCARE OF MISSISSIPPI INC | MS | • C | 3q 2017 | 284.9 | 1,233.0 | 1,233.0 | 137.6 | 1.89 | 1.57 |
| UNITED HEALTHCARE OF NC INC | NC | • B | 3q 2017 | 218.4 | 931.0 | 931.0 | 151.4 | 3.30 | 2.75 |
| UNITED HEALTHCARE OF NEW ENGLAND INC | RI | • B- | 3q 2017 | 390.3 | 866.6 | 866.6 | 129.1 | 2.99 | 2.49 |
| UNITED HEALTHCARE OF NY INC | NY | • B+ | 3q 2017 | 1,277.0 | 3,870.2 | 3,870.2 | 574.0 | 2.57 | 2.15 |
| UNITED HEALTHCARE OF OHIO INC | OH | • C | 3q 2017 | 79.3 | 81.6 | 81.6 | 68.7 | 19.25 | 16.04 |
| UNITED HEALTHCARE OF THE MIDLANDS | NE | • B | 3q 2017 | 790.1 | 573.2 | 573.2 | 152.9 | 4.59 | 3.83 |
| UNITED HEALTHCARE OF THE MIDWEST INC | MO | • C+ | 3q 2017 | 417.1 | 1,275.7 | 1,275.7 | 178.1 | 2.80 | 2.33 |
| UNITED HEALTHCARE OF TX INC | TX | • B- | 3q 2017 | 39.8 | 80.2 | 80.2 | 15.9 | 3.26 | 2.72 |
| UNITED HEALTHCARE OF UTAH | UT | • B | 3q 2017 | 195.6 | 514.7 | 514.7 | 56.8 | 2.77 | 2.31 |
| UNITED HEALTHCARE OF WISCONSIN INC | WI | • B | 3q 2017 | 2,191.8 | 4,484.3 | 4,484.3 | 656.2 | 3.26 | 2.72 |
| UNITED HERITAGE LIFE INS CO | ID | B | 3q 2017 | 570.9 | 75.7 | 3.6 | 63.3 | 2.63 | 1.30 |
| UNITED HOME LIFE INS CO | IN | B | 3q 2017 | 92.9 | 42.5 | 0.0 | 20.5 | 2.53 | 2.28 |
| UNITED INS CO OF AMERICA | IL | B- | 3q 2017 | 3,823.5 | 170.5 | 8.6 | 430.4 | 1.76 | 1.04 |
| UNITED LIFE INS CO | IA | B | 3q 2017 | 1,502.8 | 138.7 | 1.6 | 145.0 | 2.92 | 1.56 |
| UNITED NATIONAL LIFE INS CO OF AM | IL | B | 3q 2017 | 27.2 | 14.8 | 13.3 | 5.7 | 1.04 | 0.77 |
| UNITED OF OMAHA LIFE INS CO | NE | • B | 3q 2017 | 22,326.3 | 4,430.6 | 1,644.7 | 1,460.5 | 1.85 | 1.05 |
| UNITED OHIO INS CO | OH | B- | 3q 2017 | 338.5 | 155.2 | 0.0 | 172.9 | 7.35 | 5.21 |
| ▲ UNITED SECURITY ASR CO OF PA | PA | E+ | 3q 2017 | 22.2 | 33.0 | 32.7 | 10.6 | 2.97 | 1.93 |
| UNITED SECURITY HEALTH & CASUALTY | IL | D | 3q 2017 | 5.5 | 0.5 | 0.4 | 4.1 | 2.66 | 2.20 |
| UNITED STATES LIFE INS CO IN NYC | NY | B | 3q 2017 | 28,940.0 | 1,952.6 | 167.2 | 1,939.9 | 2.47 | 1.21 |
| UNITED SURETY & INDEMNITY CO | PR | B | 3q 2017 | 106.6 | 38.4 | 0.8 | 63.9 | 2.28 | 1.48 |
| UNITED WORLD LIFE INS CO | NE | • B+ | 3q 2017 | 123.8 | 342.5 | 341.2 | 50.8 | 5.16 | 2.18 |
| ▼ UNITEDHEALTHCARE BENEFITS OF TEXAS | TX | • B- | 3q 2017 | 807.3 | 2,727.3 | 2,727.3 | 150.0 | 1.55 | 1.29 |
| UNITEDHEALTHCARE BENEFITS PLAN OF CA | CA | • C | 3q 2017 | 3.5 | 6.7 | 6.7 | 3.4 | 5.84 | 3.62 |
| UNITEDHEALTHCARE COMMUNITY PLAN INC | MI | • B | 3q 2017 | 301.2 | 1,242.1 | 1,242.1 | 132.8 | 2.58 | 2.15 |
| UNITEDHEALTHCARE COMMUNITY PLAN TX | TX | • B+ | 3q 2017 | 614.6 | 2,369.4 | 2,369.4 | 240.2 | 1.87 | 1.56 |
| UNITEDHEALTHCARE COMMUNITYPLAN OHIO | OH | • B | 3q 2017 | 500.0 | 2,059.4 | 2,059.4 | 245.4 | 2.37 | 1.98 |
| UNITEDHEALTHCARE INS CO RIVER VALLEY | IL | • B | 3q 2017 | 281.3 | 896.7 | 896.7 | 115.1 | 2.43 | 2.02 |
| UNITEDHEALTHCARE LIFE INS CO | WI | • C | 3q 2017 | 222.9 | 963.3 | 962.8 | 136.0 | 1.97 | 1.56 |
| UNITEDHEALTHCARE OF NEW MEXICO INC | NM | • E | 3q 2017 | 289.8 | 865.4 | 865.4 | 154.5 | 22.57 | 18.81 |
| UNITEDHEALTHCARE OF OKLAHOMA INC | OK | • B | 3q 2017 | 149.2 | 401.5 | 401.5 | 56.0 | 2.48 | 2.06 |
| UNITEDHEALTHCARE OF OREGON | OR | • B | 3q 2017 | 449.3 | 975.1 | 975.1 | 147.7 | 3.05 | 2.54 |
| UNITEDHEALTHCARE OF PENNSYLVANIA INC | PA | • B | 3q 2017 | 418.4 | 1,347.1 | 1,347.1 | 181.3 | 8.02 | 6.68 |
| UNITEDHEALTHCARE OF WASHINGTON INC | WA | • C | 3q 2017 | 367.6 | 1,027.2 | 1,027.2 | 158.1 | 3.00 | 2.50 |
| UNITEDHEALTHCARE PLAN RIVER VALLEY | IL | • B | 3q 2017 | 1,108.3 | 3,591.4 | 3,591.4 | 446.0 | 2.67 | 2.22 |



Arrows denote recent upgrades ▲ or downgrades ▼

• Bullets denote a more detailed analysis is available in Section II.

| INSURANCE COMPANY NAME | DOM. STATE | RATING | DATA DATE | TOTAL ASSETS ($MIL) | TOTAL PREMIUMS ($MIL) | HEALTH PREMIUMS ($MIL) | CAPITAL & SURPLUS ($MIL) | RISK ADJUSTED CAPITAL RATIO 1 | RISK ADJUSTED CAPITAL RATIO 2 |
|---|---|---|---|---|---|---|---|---|---|
| UNITY HEALTH PLANS INS CORP | WI | • C | 3q 2017 | 173.3 | 863.5 | 863.5 | 67.0 | 1.54 | 1.28 |
| UNIV OF MD HEALTH ADVANTAGE INC | MD | • E- | 3q 2017 | 24.7 | 41.6 | 41.6 | 2.2 | 0.20 | 0.17 |
| UNIVERSAL CARE | CA | • E- | 3q 2017 | 64.0 | 142.0 | 142.0 | -3.1 | 0.00 | 0.00 |
| UNIVERSAL FIDELITY LIFE INS CO | OK | D | 3q 2017 | 13.0 | 8.9 | 8.4 | 4.0 | 1.34 | 0.95 |
| UNIVERSAL GUARANTY LIFE INS CO | OH | C+ | 3q 2017 | 337.4 | 9.2 | 0.0 | 48.1 | 1.57 | 0.90 |
| UNIVERSAL LIFE INS CO | PR | B+ | 3q 2017 | 1,387.9 | 356.3 | 4.9 | 106.6 | 3.21 | 1.69 |
| UNIVERSITY HEALTH ALLIANCE | HI | • C+ | 3q 2017 | 110.8 | 272.7 | 272.7 | 63.2 | 1.85 | 1.54 |
| UNIVERSITY HEALTH CARE INC | KY | • B | 3q 2017 | 418.5 | 1,747.8 | 1,747.8 | 211.2 | 1.48 | 1.23 |
| UNIVERSITY OF ARIZONA HEALTH PLANS | AZ | U | | -- | -- | -- | -- | -- | -- |
| UNIVERSITY OF UTAH HEALTH INS PLANS | UT | • D+ | 3q 2017 | 27.3 | 19.1 | 19.1 | 14.0 | 2.94 | 2.45 |
| UNUM LIFE INS CO OF AMERICA | ME | • C+ | 3q 2017 | 21,366.1 | 4,601.7 | 3,219.5 | 1,702.3 | 2.30 | 1.22 |
| UPMC FOR YOU INC | PA | • B+ | 3q 2017 | 726.3 | 2,383.2 | 2,383.2 | 392.5 | 2.78 | 2.31 |
| UPMC HEALTH BENEFITS INC | PA | • D | 3q 2017 | 226.9 | 105.2 | 28.4 | 99.6 | 0.91 | 0.57 |
| UPMC HEALTH COVERAGE INC | PA | • B | 3q 2017 | 20.5 | 27.7 | 27.7 | 14.3 | 6.33 | 5.28 |
| UPMC HEALTH NETWORK INC | PA | • C | 3q 2017 | 44.5 | 82.2 | 82.2 | 20.4 | 2.68 | 2.23 |
| UPMC HEALTH OPTIONS INC | PA | • C+ | 3q 2017 | 485.2 | 1,548.2 | 1,548.2 | 210.4 | 2.09 | 1.75 |
| ▲ UPMC HEALTH PLAN INC | PA | • A- | 3q 2017 | 640.7 | 1,490.4 | 1,490.4 | 237.0 | 2.20 | 1.83 |
| ▲ UPPER PENINSULA HEALTH PLAN INC | MI | • A | 3q 2017 | 97.3 | 283.8 | 283.8 | 50.5 | 2.06 | 1.71 |
| US ALLIANCE LIFE & SECURITY CO | KS | D- | 3q 2017 | 23.1 | 4.6 | 0.1 | 4.3 | 1.28 | 0.79 |
| US FIRE INS CO | DE | • C | 3q 2017 | 4,021.4 | 891.9 | 265.2 | 1,243.0 | 1.27 | 0.97 |
| US SPECIALTY INS CO | TX | B- | 3q 2017 | 1,864.8 | 613.5 | 8.4 | 575.4 | 2.54 | 1.63 |
| USA INS CO | MS | C- | 3q 2017 | 3.7 | 0.4 | 0.3 | 2.8 | 2.53 | 2.28 |
| USAA LIFE INS CO | TX | A | 3q 2017 | 24,728.9 | 2,335.2 | 289.8 | 2,465.5 | 3.92 | 2.09 |
| USABLE LIFE | AR | • B+ | 3q 2017 | 510.9 | 248.3 | 123.7 | 263.9 | 2.62 | 1.95 |
| USABLE MUTUAL INS CO | AR | • A+ | 3q 2017 | 1,648.3 | 2,487.0 | 2,487.0 | 878.3 | 5.34 | 4.45 |
| USIC LIFE INS CO | PR | B | 3q 2017 | 10.1 | 5.2 | 4.0 | 8.1 | 1.59 | 1.16 |
| UTIC INS CO | AL | B | 3q 2017 | 92.7 | 18.1 | 18.1 | 22.8 | 2.44 | 1.59 |
| UTMB HEALTH PLANS INC | TX | • B- | 3q 2017 | 5.5 | 0.7 | 0.7 | 5.4 | 57.14 | 47.62 |
| VALUE BEHAVIORAL HEALTH OF PA | PA | • E | 3q 2017 | 29.8 | 83.8 | 83.8 | 16.8 | 1.95 | 1.63 |
| VALUEOPTIONS OF NEW JERSEY INC | NJ | • E | 4q 2016 | 16.1 | 203.6 | 203.6 | 5.4 | 0.00 | 0.00 |
| VALUEOPTIONS OF TEXAS INC | TX | • D | 2q 2017 | 14.0 | 146.3 | 146.3 | 5.7 | 0.95 | 0.79 |
| VANTAGE HEALTH PLAN INC | LA | • C- | 3q 2017 | 98.2 | 368.5 | 368.5 | 21.0 | 0.57 | 0.47 |
| VANTIS LIFE INS CO | CT | C+ | 3q 2017 | 368.1 | 67.4 | 0.0 | 47.6 | 2.93 | 1.75 |
| VENTURA COUNTY HEALTH CARE PLAN | CA | • E- | 3q 2017 | 18.4 | 63.5 | 63.5 | 1.4 | 0.20 | 0.12 |
| VERMONT HEALTH PLAN LLC | VT | • C+ | 3q 2017 | 37.8 | 30.6 | 30.6 | 33.3 | 8.88 | 7.40 |
| VERSANT LIFE INS CO | MS | B- | 3q 2017 | 6.3 | 1.2 | 0.2 | 4.8 | 2.79 | 2.51 |
| VIRGINIA FARM BUREAU MUTUAL INS CO | VA | B- | 3q 2017 | 412.5 | 141.4 | 0.0 | 203.7 | 2.22 | 1.82 |
| VIRGINIA PREMIER HEALTH PLAN INC | VA | • B+ | 3q 2017 | 317.9 | 1,070.4 | 1,070.4 | 184.3 | 1.82 | 1.51 |
| VISTA HEALTH PLAN INC | PA | • B- | 3q 2017 | 813.1 | 4,574.3 | 4,574.3 | 281.6 | 2.16 | 1.80 |
| VIVA HEALTH INC | AL | • B+ | 3q 2017 | 276.6 | 625.2 | 625.2 | 102.6 | 2.37 | 1.98 |
| VOLUNTARY EMPLOYEES BENEFIT | HI | U | | -- | -- | -- | -- | -- | -- |
| VOLUNTEER STATE HEALTH PLAN INC | TN | • A+ | 3q 2017 | 818.7 | 2,440.8 | 2,440.8 | 458.7 | 3.65 | 3.04 |
| VOYA INS & ANNUITY CO | IA | B- | 3q 2017 | 59,991.4 | 2,012.2 | 0.1 | 1,856.9 | 1.71 | 0.84 |
| VOYA RETIREMENT INS & ANNUITY CO | CT | B+ | 3q 2017 | 104,964.0 | 12,613.0 | 0.1 | 1,829.0 | 2.09 | 1.02 |
| WASHINGTON NATIONAL INS CO | IN | • D+ | 3q 2017 | 5,420.1 | 675.8 | 617.4 | 398.1 | 1.98 | 1.06 |
| WEA INS CORP | WI | • C | 3q 2017 | 665.7 | 500.1 | 500.1 | 155.5 | 1.72 | 1.18 |
| WELLCARE HEALTH INS OF ARIZONA INC | AZ | • C | 3q 2017 | 240.9 | 731.0 | 731.0 | 61.6 | 1.73 | 1.44 |
| WELLCARE HEALTH INS OF KENTUCKY INC | KY | • C | 3q 2017 | 835.8 | 2,753.4 | 2,753.4 | 302.0 | 2.08 | 1.74 |
| WELLCARE HEALTH PLANS OF KENTUCKY | KY | • C- | 1q 2017 | 5.2 | 2.5 | 2.5 | 4.1 | 3.11 | 2.59 |
| WELLCARE HEALTH PLANS OF NEW JERSEY | NJ | • C | 3q 2017 | 161.2 | 454.6 | 454.6 | 74.0 | 3.38 | 2.82 |
| WELLCARE OF CONNECTICUT INC | CT | • C+ | 3q 2017 | 48.2 | 81.2 | 81.2 | 22.5 | 4.25 | 3.54 |
| WELLCARE OF FLORIDA INC | FL | • E | 3q 2017 | 921.8 | 3,679.1 | 3,679.1 | 178.6 | 1.06 | 0.88 |

| INSURANCE COMPANY NAME | DOM. STATE | RATING | DATA DATE | TOTAL ASSETS ($MIL) | TOTAL PREMIUMS ($MIL) | HEALTH PREMIUMS ($MIL) | CAPITAL & SURPLUS ($MIL) | RISK ADJUSTED CAPITAL RATIO 1 | RISK ADJUSTED CAPITAL RATIO 2 |
|---|---|---|---|---|---|---|---|---|---|
| WELLCARE OF GEORGIA INC | GA | • C | 3q 2017 | 543.9 | 2,041.1 | 2,041.1 | 224.7 | 2.22 | 1.85 |
| WELLCARE OF NEVADA INC | NV | U | | -- | -- | -- | -- | -- | -- |
| WELLCARE OF OHIO INC | OH | U | | -- | -- | -- | -- | -- | -- |
| WELLCARE OF OKLAHOMA INC | OK | U | | -- | -- | -- | -- | -- | -- |
| WELLCARE OF SOUTH CAROLINA INC | SC | • C | 3q 2017 | 119.0 | 277.6 | 277.6 | 63.1 | 4.24 | 3.53 |
| WELLCARE OF TEXAS INC | TX | • C | 3q 2017 | 183.8 | 384.3 | 384.3 | 65.2 | 3.10 | 2.59 |
| WELLCARE PRESCRIPTION INS INC | FL | • E | 3q 2017 | 1,654.9 | 755.6 | 755.6 | 220.1 | 11.37 | 9.47 |
| WELLMARK HEALTH PLAN OF IOWA | IA | • B | 3q 2017 | 272.5 | 316.0 | 316.0 | 184.7 | 8.66 | 7.21 |
| WELLMARK INC | IA | • B- | 3q 2017 | 2,412.3 | 2,656.3 | 2,656.3 | 1,548.0 | 6.23 | 5.20 |
| WELLMARK OF SOUTH DAKOTA INC | SD | • B+ | 3q 2017 | 465.7 | 695.8 | 695.8 | 284.3 | 7.33 | 6.11 |
| WESCO INS CO | DE | B- | 3q 2017 | 1,949.3 | 2,341.5 | 28.7 | 440.8 | 1.19 | 0.74 |
| ▲ WEST COAST LIFE INS CO | NE | B- | 3q 2017 | 5,250.1 | 569.4 | 0.0 | 364.0 | 2.30 | 1.12 |
| WEST VIRGINIA FAMILY HEALTH PLAN INC | WV | • C- | 3q 2017 | 66.9 | 299.6 | 299.6 | 20.8 | 0.60 | 0.50 |
| WESTERN & SOUTHERN LIFE INS CO | OH | B | 3q 2017 | 10,626.1 | 257.7 | 26.1 | 5,103.2 | 1.97 | 1.64 |
| WESTERN AMERICAN LIFE INS CO | TX | D | 3q 2017 | 27.5 | 2.4 | 0.0 | 2.2 | 0.51 | 0.46 |
| WESTERN GROCERS EMPLOYEE BENEFITS | OR | • E | 3q 2017 | 7.3 | 16.4 | 16.4 | 3.6 | -0.92 | -0.77 |
| WESTERN HEALTH ADVANTAGE | CA | • E | 3q 2017 | 63.8 | 664.4 | 664.4 | 9.7 | 0.20 | 0.12 |
| WESTERN UNITED LIFE ASR CO | WA | B- | 3q 2017 | 1,194.8 | 164.3 | 0.2 | 76.7 | 1.67 | 0.80 |
| WESTPORT INS CORP | MO | B | 3q 2017 | 4,720.7 | 719.9 | 67.5 | 1,521.2 | 1.75 | 1.21 |
| WICHITA NATIONAL LIFE INS CO | OK | C- | 3q 2017 | 16.4 | 4.7 | 0.9 | 7.9 | 2.52 | 2.27 |
| WILCAC LIFE INS CO | IL | C | 3q 2017 | 2,342.2 | 42.6 | 0.1 | 149.4 | 3.88 | 1.95 |
| WILCO LIFE INS CO | IN | C | 3q 2017 | 3,005.1 | 172.9 | 24.7 | 167.1 | 1.55 | 0.80 |
| WILLIAM PENN LIFE INS CO OF NEW YORK | NY | C- | 3q 2017 | 1,185.0 | 220.8 | 0.0 | 143.3 | 2.95 | 1.37 |
| WILTON REASSURANCE LIFE CO OF NY | NY | B- | 3q 2017 | 897.1 | 55.4 | 0.1 | 102.2 | 2.87 | 1.44 |
| WINDSOR LIFE INS CO | TX | B- | 3q 2017 | 3.1 | 0.2 | 0.2 | 2.9 | 2.75 | 2.48 |
| WISCONSIN PHYSICIANS SERVICE INS | WI | • C | 3q 2017 | 284.9 | 435.4 | 435.4 | 121.4 | 2.01 | 1.67 |
| WMI MUTUAL INS CO | UT | • C | 3q 2017 | 14.6 | 18.0 | 18.0 | 9.8 | 2.82 | 2.35 |
| WPS HEALTH PLAN INC | WI | • C- | 3q 2017 | 35.2 | 185.8 | 185.8 | 18.5 | 1.16 | 0.97 |
| XL REINS AMERICA INC | NY | C | 3q 2017 | 6,423.3 | 22.3 | 1.6 | 2,055.8 | 2.31 | 1.85 |
| ZALE INDEMNITY CO | TX | C+ | 3q 2017 | 48.3 | 21.6 | 0.5 | 18.7 | 1.43 | 1.25 |
| ZALE LIFE INS CO | AZ | B- | 3q 2017 | 12.4 | 1.7 | 0.7 | 10.2 | 4.01 | 3.61 |
| ZOOM HEALTH PLAN INC | OR | F | 4q 2016 | 8.7 | 4.7 | 4.7 | 2.9 | 0.83 | 0.69 |
| ZURICH AMERICAN INS CO | NY | B- | 3q 2017 | 32,998.1 | 5,766.9 | 288.1 | 7,565.4 | 2.26 | 1.56 |
| ZURICH AMERICAN LIFE INS CO | IL | C | 3q 2017 | 14,265.7 | 450.8 | 5.9 | 118.4 | 1.66 | 0.91 |
| ZURICH AMERICAN LIFE INS CO OF NY | NY | B- | 3q 2017 | 71.3 | 22.7 | 0.3 | 21.8 | 2.88 | 2.59 |

# Section II

# Analysis of Largest Companies

A summary analysis of all rated

**U.S. Health Plans and Blue Cross Blue Shield Plans**

plus other **U.S. Insurers**
with capital in excess of $25 million and health insurance premiums equaling at least 25% of total premiums.

Companies are listed in alphabetical order.

# Section II Contents

This section contains rating factors, historical data, and general information on all rated health insurers and Blue Cross/Blue Shield plans plus other insurers with capital in excess of $25 million and health insurance premiums equaling at least 25% of total premiums.

A number of the contents listed below will only apply to health insurers filing the NAIC Health insurance financial statement.

1. **Safety Rating** The current Weiss rating appears to the right of the company name. Our ratings are designed to distinguish levels of insolvency risk and are measured on a scale from A (Excellent) to F (Failed). Highly rated companies are, in our opinion, less likely to experience financial difficulties than lower rated firms. See *About Weiss Safety Ratings* for more information.

2. **Major Rating Factors** A synopsis of the key indexes and sub-factors that have most influenced the rating of a particular insurer. Items are presented in the approximate order of their importance to the rating. There may be additional factors which have influenced the rating but do not appear due to space limitations or confidentiality agreements with insurers.

3. **Other Rating Factors** A summary of those Weiss Ratings indexes that were not included as Major Rating Factors, but nevertheless may have had some impact on the final grade.

4. **Principal Business** The major types of policies written by an insurer along with the percentages for each line in relation to the entire book of business, including direct premium, reinsurance assumed and deposit funds. Lines of business for health insurers include comprehensive medical, medical only, medicare supplemental, administrative service contracts, point of service, dental, vision, stop-loss, long-term care, disability, Federal Employee Health Benefits (FEHB), medicare, and medicaid.

5. **Member Physicians** The number of physicians who participated in the insurer's network of providers during the current and prior year.

6. **MLR (Medical Loss Ratio)** The percentage of total premium income paid out as benefits to members.

7. **Administrative Expense Ratio** The percentage of total premium income paid out for administrative expenses.

8. **Enrollment** The total number of members (policyholders) as of the current quarter, current year end and prior year end. The letter Q followed by a number represents the quarter (first, second, or third) from which the enrollment numbers were last available.

**9. Medical Expenses Per Member Per Month** The average dollar amount the insurer spends on a per member per month basis. Calculated as total medical expenses divided by the reported member months.

**10. Principal Investments** The major investments in an insurer's portfolio. These include investment grade bonds, noninvestment grade bonds, collateralized mortgage obligations (CMOs) and other structured securities, which consist primarily of mortgage-backed bonds, real estate, mortgages in good standing, nonperforming mortgages, common and preferred stocks, contract loans and other investments.

**11. Provider Compensation** The total annual amount the health insurer pays its providers (e.g., physicians, hospitals, etc.) and manner in which they are paid, including:

- fee-for-service (FFS) – amount paid for the services provided where the payment base is not fixed by contract
- contractual fees – amount paid for services whereby the amount is fixed by contract, e.g., hospital per diems, DRGs, etc.
- salary – amount paid providers who are direct employees of the HMO
- capitation – amount paid to providers on a per member basis as defined by contract
- other – amount paid under various contracts including bonus arrangements, stop-loss arrangements, etc.

**12. Total Member Encounters** The number of contacts members of the health insurer who are not confined to a health care facility have with the providers during the current year.

**13. Investments in Affiliates** The percentage of bonds, common and preferred stocks, and other financial instruments an insurer has invested with affiliated companies. This is not a subcategory of "Principal Investments."

**14. Group Affiliation** The name of the group of companies to which a particular insurer belongs.

**15. Licensed in** List of the states in which an insurer is licensed to conduct business.

**16. Address** The address of an insurer's corporate headquarters. This location may differ from the company's state of domicile.

**17. Phone** The telephone number of an insurer's corporate headquarters.

**18. Domicile State** The state that has primary regulatory responsibility for this company. You do not have to live in the domicile state to do business with this firm, provided it is registered to do business in your state.

**19. Commenced Business** The month and year the insurer started its operations

**20. NAIC Code** The identification number assigned to an insurer by the National Association of Insurance Commissioners (NAIC).

**21. Historical Data** Five years of background data for Weiss Safety Rating, risk-adjusted capital ratios (moderate and severe loss scenarios), total assets, capital (including capital stock and retained earnings), net premium, and net income. See the next page for more details on how to read the historical data table.

**22. Customized Graph (or Table)** A graph or table depicting one of the company's major strengths or weaknesses.

# How to Read the Historical Data Table

**Data Date:** The quarterly or annual date of the financial statements that provide the source of the data.

**RACR#1:** Ratio of the capital resources an insurer currently has to the resources that would be needed to deal with a modest loss scenario.

**Total Assets:** Total admitted assets in millions of dollars, including investments and other business assets.

**Net Premiums:** The total volume of premium dollars, in millions, retained by an insurer. This figure is equal to direct premiums written plus deposit funds, and reinsurance assumed, less reinsurance ceded.

| Data Date | Rating | RACR #1 | RACR #2 | Total Assets ($mil) | Capital ($mil) | Net Premium ($mil) | Net Income ($mil) |
|---|---|---|---|---|---|---|---|
| 09-17 | B+ | 3.89 | 2.56 | 58.6 | 48.5 | 8.2 | 2.2 |
| 09-16 | B+ | 3.96 | 2.63 | 56.4 | 46.6 | 8.1 | 1.0 |
| 2016 | B+ | 4.01 | 2.67 | 56.0 | 46.8 | 10.8 | 1.3 |
| 2015 | B+ | 3.91 | 2.59 | 54.0 | 45.3 | 10.6 | 2.2 |
| 2014 | B+ | 3.64 | 2.40 | 53.5 | 44.0 | 9.9 | 2.9 |
| 2013 | B+ | 3.51 | 2.32 | 51.4 | 41.5 | 9.6 | 1.6 |
| 2012 | B+ | 3.78 | 2.54 | 47.5 | 38.9 | 9.6 | 0.9 |

**Safety Rating:** Our opinion of the financial strength of an insurer based on data from that time period.

**RACR #2:** Ratio of the capital resources an insurer currently has to the resources that would be needed to deal with a severe loss scenario.

**Capital:** The equity or net worth of an insurer in millions of dollars.

**Net Income:** Profit gained on operations and investments, after expenses, taxes, and capital gains

## Row Descriptions:

**Row 1** contains the most recent quarterly data as filed with state regulators and is presented on a year-to-date basis. For example, the figure for third quarter premiums includes premiums received through the third quarter. **Row 2** consists of data from the same quarter of the prior year. Compare current quarterly results to those of a year ago.

**Row 3** contains data from the most recent annual statutory filing. **Rows 4-7** includes data from year-end statements going back four years from the most recent annual filing. Compare current year-end results to those of the previous four years. With the exception of Total Assets and Capital, quarterly data are not comparable with annual data.

# Customized Graphs

In the lower right-hand corner of each company section, a customized graph or text block highlights a key factor affecting that company's financial strength. One of twenty five types of information is found, identified by one of the following headings:

**# of Months of Claims and Expenses in Capital** illustrates the number of months' worth of medical and administrative expenses the company could cover by drawing solely on its current capital position.

**Adverse Trends in Operations** lists changes in key balance sheet and income statement items which may be leading indicators of deteriorating business performance.

**Allocation of Premium Income** shows what portion of the company's premium income is being spent on medical benefits and administrative expenses. Any income left after the payment of these two types of expense, is used to pay taxes and extraordinary expenditures; the remainder is profit.

**Capital History** plots the company's reported capital and surplus in millions of dollars over the last five years. Volatile changes in capital levels may indicate unstable operations.

**Detail of Risk-Adjusted Capital Ratio** provides a percentage breakdown of target capital components based on lines of business and investments in a moderate or severe loss scenario. Target capital is our opinion of the level of capital the company should have, based on the risk it assumes. For example, if the percentage of target capital for individual life is 33%, this means that 33% of the company's target capital relates to individual life. C2 refers to the pricing risk element of the risk-adjusted capital formula. C3 refers to disintermediation (interest rate) risk.

**Enrollment Trend** charts an insurer's year-end membership levels over the last five years.

**Exposure to Withdrawals Without Penalty** answers the question: For each dollar of capital and surplus, how much does the company have in annuity and deposit funds that can be withdrawn by policyholders with minimal or no penalty? The figures do not include the effects of reinsurance or funds subject to withdrawals from cash value life insurance policies.

**Group Ratings** shows the group name, a composite Weiss Safety Rating for the group, and a list of the largest members with their ratings. The composite Weiss Safety Rating is made up of the weighted average, by assets, of the individual ratings of each company in the group (including life/health companies, property/casualty companies, or HMOs) plus a factor for the financial strength of the holding company, where applicable.

**High Risk Assets as a % of Capital** answers the question: For each dollar of capital and surplus, how much does the company have in junk bonds, nonperforming mortgages and repossessed real estate? Accumulations in the Asset Valuation Reserve or AVR, which provide some protection against investment losses, have not been included in the figure for capital. These figures are based on year-end data.

**Income Trends** shows underwriting and net income results over the last five years.

**Investment Income Compared to Needs of Reserves** answers the question: Is the company earning enough investment income to meet the expectations of actuaries when they priced their policies and set reserve levels? According to state insurance regulators, it would be "unusual" if an insurer were to have less than $1.25 in actual investment income for each dollar of investment income that it projected in its actuarial forecasts. This provides an excess margin of at least 25 cents on the dollar to cover any unexpected decline in income or increase in claims. This graph shows whether or not the company is maintaining the appropriate 25% margin and is based on year-end data.

**Junk Bonds as a % of Capital** answers the question: For each dollar of capital and surplus, how much does the company have in junk bonds? In addition, it shows a breakdown of the junk bond portfolio by bond rating – BB, B, CCC or in default. Accumulations in the Asset Valuation Reserve or AVR, which provide some protection against investment losses, have not been included in the figure for capital. These figures are based on year-end data.

**Largest Net Exposure Per Risk** shows the ratio of the largest net aggregate amount insured in any one risk (excluding workers' compensation) as a percent of capital.

**Liquidity Index** evaluates a company's ability to raise the cash necessary to pay claims. Various cash flow scenarios are modeled to determine how the company might fare in the event of an unexpected spike in claims costs.

**Net Income History** plots operating gains and losses over the most recent five-year period.

**Nonperforming Mortgages (plus repossessed real estate) as a % of Capital** answers the question: For each dollar of capital and surplus, how much does the company have in nonperforming mortgages and repossessed real estate? Nonperforming mortgages include those overdue more than 90 days and mortgages currently in process of foreclosure. Accumulations in the Asset Valuation Reserve or AVR, which provide some protection against investment losses, have not been included in the figure for capital. These figures are based on year-end data.

**Policy Leverage** answers the question: To what degree is this insurer capable of handling an unexpected spike in claims? Low leverage indicates low exposure; high leverage is high exposure.

**Target leverage** represents the maximum exposure we feel would be appropriate for a top-rated company.

**Premium Growth History** depicts the change in the insurer's net premiums written. Such changes may be the result of issuing more policies or changes in reinsurance arrangements. In either case, growth rates above 20% per year are considered excessive. "Standard" growth is under 20%; "shrinkage" refers to net declines.

**Rating Indexes** illustrate the score and range – strong, good, fair, or weak – on each of Weiss indexes.

**Reserve Deficiency** shows whether the company has set aside sufficient funds to pay claims. A positive number indicates insufficient reserving and a negative number adequate reserving.

**Reserves to Capital** analyzes the relationship between loss and loss expense reserves to capital. Operating results and capital levels for companies with a high ratio are more susceptible to fluctuations than those with lower ratios.

**Risk-Adjusted Capital Ratio #1** answers the question: In each of the past five years, does the insurer have sufficient capital to cover potential losses in its investments and business operations in a *moderate* loss scenario?

**Risk-Adjusted Capital Ratio #2** answers the question: In each of the past five years, does the insurer have sufficient capital to cover potential losses in its investments and business operations in a *severe* loss scenario?

**Risk-Adjusted Capital Ratios** answers these questions for both a moderate loss scenario (RACR #1 shown by the dark bar), and a severe loss scenario (RACR #2, light bar).

## 4 EVER LIFE INSURANCE COMPANY B Good

**Major Rating Factors:** Good overall results on stability tests (6.2 on a scale of 0 to 10) despite negative cash flow from operations for 2016. Other stability subfactors include good operational trends and excellent risk diversification. Good quality investment portfolio (6.2) despite mixed results such as: no exposure to mortgages and substantial holdings of BBB bonds but minimal holdings in junk bonds. Good liquidity (6.6).
**Other Rating Factors:** Fair profitability (4.9). Strong capitalization (10.0) based on excellent risk adjusted capital (severe loss scenario).
**Principal Business:** Group health insurance (74%), reinsurance (22%), and group life insurance (3%).
**Principal Investments:** NonCMO investment grade bonds (49%), CMOs and structured securities (23%), common & preferred stock (10%), cash (7%), and noninv. grade bonds (5%).
**Investments in Affiliates:** None
**Group Affiliation:** BCS Financial Corp
**Licensed in:** All states, the District of Columbia and Puerto Rico
**Commenced Business:** November 1949
**Address:** 2 Mid America Plaza Suite 200, Oakbrook Terrace, IL 60181
**Phone:** (630) 472-7700 **Domicile State:** IL **NAIC Code:** 80985

| Data Date | Rating | RACR #1 | RACR #2 | Total Assets ($mil) | Capital ($mil) | Net Premium ($mil) | Net Income ($mil) |
|---|---|---|---|---|---|---|---|
| 9-17 | B | 5.46 | 3.55 | 217.2 | 86.6 | 59.0 | 3.5 |
| 9-16 | A | 5.50 | 3.63 | 207.9 | 85.8 | 69.9 | 2.8 |
| 2016 | B | 5.21 | 3.36 | 207.5 | 82.6 | 72.9 | 0.6 |
| 2015 | A | 5.63 | 3.67 | 200.0 | 93.1 | 86.9 | 5.5 |
| 2014 | A | 3.89 | 2.72 | 198.5 | 92.3 | 151.8 | 7.3 |
| 2013 | A | 3.92 | 2.79 | 186.9 | 89.9 | 148.4 | 6.4 |
| 2012 | A- | 3.43 | 2.51 | 187.2 | 84.4 | 170.1 | 6.2 |

**Adverse Trends in Operations**

Decrease in premium volume from 2015 to 2016 (16%)
Decrease in capital during 2016 (11%)
Decrease in premium volume from 2014 to 2015 (43%)
Decrease in premium volume from 2012 to 2013 (13%)

## ABSOLUTE TOTAL CARE INC C- Fair

**Major Rating Factors:** Weak profitability index (0.9 on a scale of 0 to 10). Good liquidity (6.7) with sufficient resources (cash flows and marketable investments) to handle a spike in claims. Strong capitalization (8.2) based on excellent current risk-adjusted capital (severe loss scenario).
**Other Rating Factors:** High quality investment portfolio (9.4).
**Principal Business:** Medicaid (96%), Medicare (4%)
**Mem Phys: 16:** 7,900 **15:** 8,261 **16 MLR** 87.3% **/ 16 Admin Exp** N/A
**Enroll(000): Q3 17:** 122 **16:** 125 **15:** 104 **Med Exp PMPM:** $309
**Principal Investments:** Long-term bonds (68%), cash and equiv (31%), affiliate common stock (1%)
**Provider Compensation ($000):** Contr fee ($385,081), salary ($29,796), capitation ($8,590), bonus arrang ($1,602)
**Total Member Encounters:** Phys (733,569), non-phys (515,976)
**Group Affiliation:** Centene Corporation
**Licensed in:** SC
**Address:** 1441 Main St Ste 900, Columbia, SC 29201
**Phone:** (314) 725-4477 **Dom State:** SC **Commenced Bus:** April 2007

| Data Date | Rating | RACR #1 | RACR #2 | Total Assets ($mil) | Capital ($mil) | Net Premium ($mil) | Net Income ($mil) |
|---|---|---|---|---|---|---|---|
| 9-17 | C- | 2.32 | 1.93 | 122.2 | 62.7 | 397.5 | 2.7 |
| 9-16 | C- | 1.96 | 1.63 | 99.1 | 46.8 | 352.0 | -5.4 |
| 2016 | C- | 2.14 | 1.79 | 113.4 | 57.9 | 492.5 | -1.7 |
| 2015 | C- | 2.09 | 1.74 | 107.9 | 50.1 | 435.7 | -1.4 |
| 2014 | C- | 2.07 | 1.72 | 92.1 | 45.4 | 396.3 | -8.4 |
| 2013 | C- | 1.99 | 1.66 | 83.8 | 41.0 | 329.4 | -20.2 |
| 2012 | C- | 1.73 | 1.44 | 74.4 | 35.5 | 319.7 | -16.9 |

**Rating Indexes**

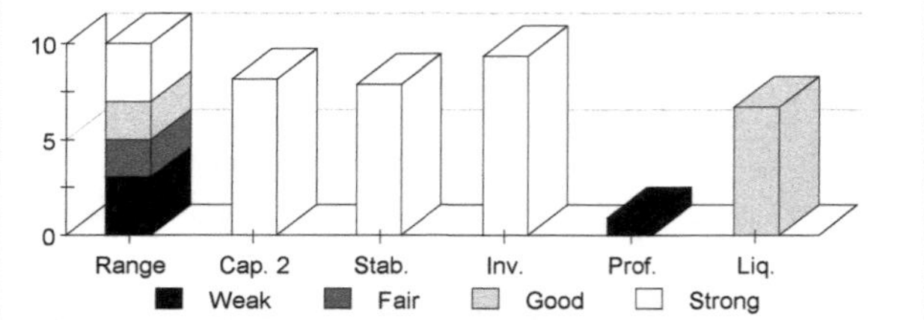


## ADVANCE INSURANCE COMPANY OF KANSAS * B+ Good

**Major Rating Factors:** Good overall results on stability tests (6.8 on a scale of 0 to 10). Stability strengths include excellent operational trends and excellent risk diversification. Fair quality investment portfolio (4.7). Strong capitalization (9.3) based on excellent risk adjusted capital (severe loss scenario). Moreover, capital levels have been consistently high over the last five years.
**Other Rating Factors:** Excellent profitability (8.4) with operating gains in each of the last five years. Excellent liquidity (7.4).
**Principal Business:** Group life insurance (55%), group health insurance (33%), and individual life insurance (12%).
**Principal Investments:** NonCMO investment grade bonds (46%), common & preferred stock (29%), and CMOs and structured securities (23%).
**Investments in Affiliates:** 2%
**Group Affiliation:** Blue Cross Blue Shield Kansas
**Licensed in:** KS
**Commenced Business:** July 2004
**Address:** 1133 SW Topeka Blvd, Topeka, KS 66629-0001
**Phone:** (785) 273-9804 **Domicile State:** KS **NAIC Code:** 12143

| Data Date | Rating | RACR #1 | RACR #2 | Total Assets ($mil) | Capital ($mil) | Net Premium ($mil) | Net Income ($mil) |
|---|---|---|---|---|---|---|---|
| 9-17 | B+ | 3.89 | 2.56 | 58.6 | 48.5 | 8.2 | 2.2 |
| 9-16 | B+ | 3.96 | 2.63 | 56.4 | 46.6 | 8.1 | 1.0 |
| 2016 | B+ | 4.01 | 2.67 | 56.0 | 46.8 | 10.8 | 1.3 |
| 2015 | B+ | 3.91 | 2.59 | 54.0 | 45.3 | 10.6 | 2.2 |
| 2014 | B+ | 3.64 | 2.40 | 53.5 | 44.0 | 9.9 | 2.9 |
| 2013 | B+ | 3.51 | 2.32 | 51.4 | 41.5 | 9.6 | 1.6 |
| 2012 | B+ | 3.78 | 2.54 | 47.5 | 38.9 | 9.6 | 0.9 |

**Rating Indexes**

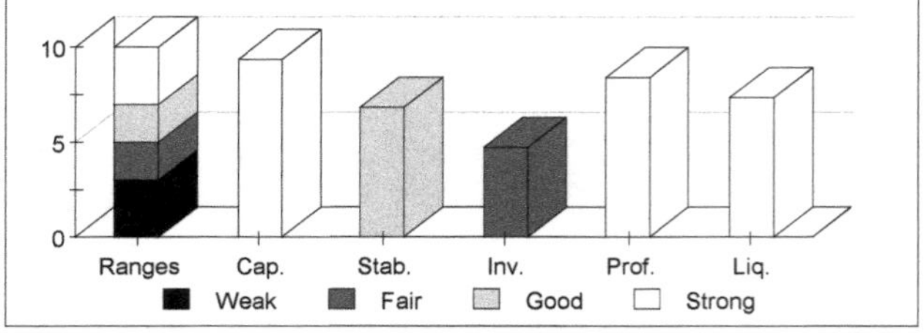

## ADVENTIST HEALTH PLAN INC — D — Weak

**Major Rating Factors:** Weak profitability index (0.8 on a scale of 0 to 10). Fair overall results on stability tests (3.0). Good capitalization index (5.6) based on fair current risk-adjusted capital (moderate loss scenario).
**Other Rating Factors:** Excellent liquidity (7.0) with ample operational cash flow and liquid investments.
**Principal Business:** Managed care (100%)
**Mem Phys: 16:** N/A **15:** N/A **16 MLR** 91.2% **/ 16 Admin Exp** N/A
**Enroll(000): Q3 17:** 17 **16:** 16 **15:** 0 **Med Exp PMPM:** $124
**Principal Investments ($000):** Cash and equiv ($1,882)
**Provider Compensation ($000):** None
**Total Member Encounters:** N/A
**Group Affiliation:** None
**Licensed in:** CA
**Address:** 2100 Douglas Blvd, Roseville, CA 95661
**Phone:** (916) 789-4252 **Dom State:** CA **Commenced Bus:** N/A

| Data Date | Rating | RACR #1 | RACR #2 | Total Assets ($mil) | Capital ($mil) | Net Premium ($mil) | Net Income ($mil) |
|---|---|---|---|---|---|---|---|
| 9-17 | D | 0.85 | 0.54 | 4.4 | 2.5 | 20.7 | 0.7 |
| 9-16 | U | 720.80 | 720.80 | 3.2 | 1.8 | 19.7 | 0.7 |
| 2016 | D | 0.61 | 0.39 | 3.3 | 1.8 | 26.2 | 0.7 |
| 2015 | E- | N/A | N/A | 1.5 | -1.9 | N/A | -1.7 |
| 2014 | N/A | N/A | N/A | 1.1 | -0.2 | N/A | -1.8 |
| 2013 | N/A | N/A | N/A | N/A | N/A | N/A | N/A |
| 2012 | N/A | N/A | N/A | N/A | N/A | N/A | N/A |

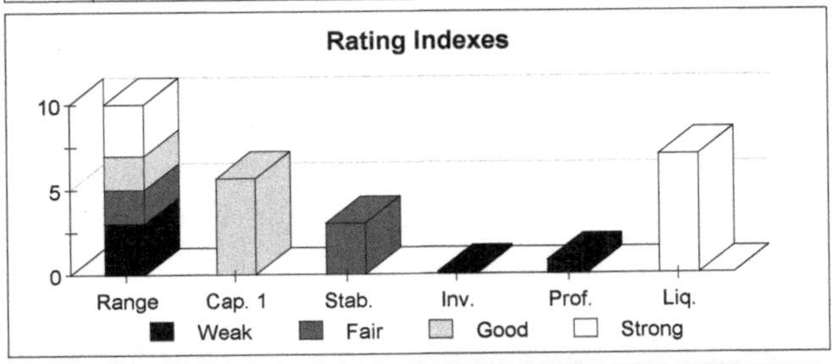


## ADVICARE CORP — C+ — Fair

**Major Rating Factors:** Fair profitability index (4.2 on a scale of 0 to 10). Strong capitalization (9.5) based on excellent current risk-adjusted capital (severe loss scenario). High quality investment portfolio (9.9).
**Other Rating Factors:** Excellent liquidity (8.0) with ample operational cash flow and liquid investments.
**Principal Business:** Medicaid (72%), Medicare (28%)
**Mem Phys: 16:** N/A **15:** N/A **16 MLR** 84.9% **/ 16 Admin Exp** N/A
**Enroll(000): Q1 17:** N/A **16:** N/A **15:** 33 **Med Exp PMPM:** N/A
**Principal Investments:** Cash and equiv (99%), long-term bonds (1%)
**Provider Compensation ($000):** FFS ($65,897), capitation ($231)
**Total Member Encounters:** N/A
**Group Affiliation:** Spartanburg Regional Health Services
**Licensed in:** SC
**Address:** 531 S Main St Ste RL-1, Greenville, SC 29601
**Phone:** (888) 781-4371 **Dom State:** SC **Commenced Bus:** January 2014

| Data Date | Rating | RACR #1 | RACR #2 | Total Assets ($mil) | Capital ($mil) | Net Premium ($mil) | Net Income ($mil) |
|---|---|---|---|---|---|---|---|
| 3-17 | C+ | 3.32 | 2.77 | 38.0 | 35.5 | 0.8 | 0.3 |
| 3-16 | D | 0.38 | 0.31 | 38.6 | 9.8 | 35.1 | -0.6 |
| 2016 | C+ | 3.15 | 2.62 | 37.1 | 33.8 | 77.9 | 17.3 |
| 2015 | D | 0.59 | 0.49 | 39.8 | 14.0 | 133.0 | -10.3 |
| 2014 | C- | 0.78 | 0.65 | 26.8 | 13.0 | 104.2 | 1.5 |
| 2013 | N/A | N/A | N/A | N/A | N/A | N/A | N/A |
| 2012 | N/A | N/A | N/A | N/A | N/A | N/A | N/A |

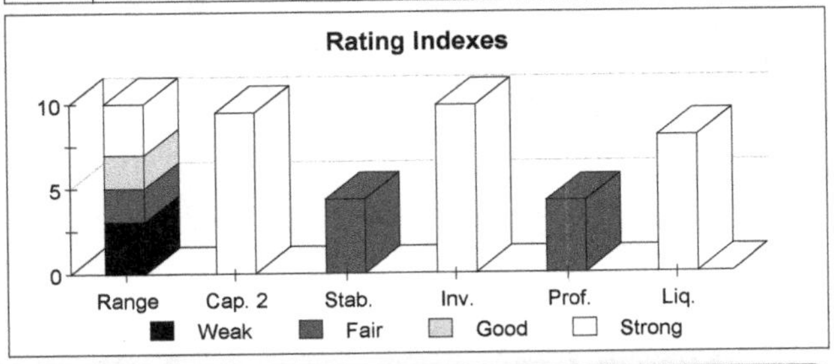


## AETNA BETTER HEALTH (AN OHIO CORP) — B — Good

**Major Rating Factors:** Good liquidity (6.3 on a scale of 0 to 10) with sufficient resources (cash flows and marketable investments) to handle a spike in claims. Fair profitability index (4.2). Strong capitalization (10.0) based on excellent current risk-adjusted capital (severe loss scenario).
**Other Rating Factors:** High quality investment portfolio (9.0).
**Principal Business:** Medicaid (68%), Medicare (32%)
**Mem Phys: 16:** 16,736 **15:** 15,666 **16 MLR** 80.0% **/ 16 Admin Exp** N/A
**Enroll(000): Q3 17:** 23 **16:** 22 **15:** 20 **Med Exp PMPM:** $2,756
**Principal Investments:** Long-term bonds (95%), cash and equiv (5%)
**Provider Compensation ($000):** Contr fee ($601,251), FFS ($81,999), capitation ($26,085)
**Total Member Encounters:** Phys (817,141), non-phys (2,667,533)
**Group Affiliation:** Aetna Inc
**Licensed in:** OH
**Address:** 7400 W CAMPUS Rd, NEW ALBANY, OH 43054
**Phone:** (800) 872-3862 **Dom State:** OH **Commenced Bus:** March 2012

| Data Date | Rating | RACR #1 | RACR #2 | Total Assets ($mil) | Capital ($mil) | Net Premium ($mil) | Net Income ($mil) |
|---|---|---|---|---|---|---|---|
| 9-17 | B | 4.14 | 3.45 | 391.2 | 172.2 | 698.8 | 48.3 |
| 9-16 | C+ | 3.83 | 3.19 | 334.5 | 154.7 | 633.0 | 25.4 |
| 2016 | C+ | 4.01 | 3.34 | 319.8 | 166.2 | 858.2 | 40.4 |
| 2015 | C+ | 2.86 | 2.38 | 310.5 | 107.4 | 783.0 | -10.1 |
| 2014 | U | 1.69 | 1.41 | 159.1 | 44.7 | 335.3 | -19.6 |
| 2013 | N/A | N/A | N/A | 3.0 | 3.0 | N/A | N/A |
| 2012 | N/A | N/A | N/A | 3.0 | 3.0 | N/A | N/A |

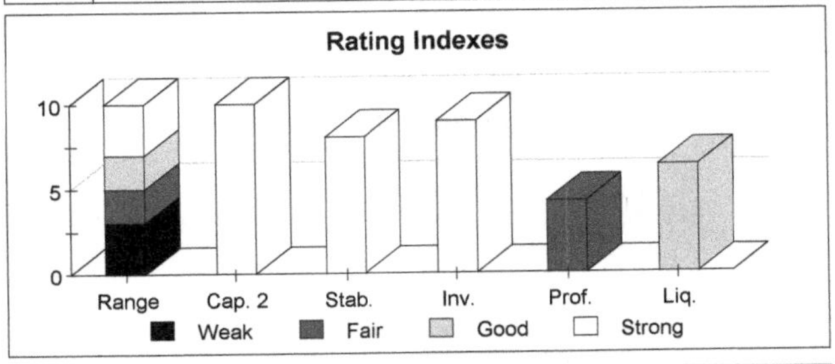

## AETNA BETTER HEALTH INC B- Good

**Major Rating Factors:** Fair profitability index (3.9 on a scale of 0 to 10). Good quality investment portfolio (6.5). Good liquidity (6.6) with sufficient resources (cash flows and marketable investments) to handle a spike in claims.
**Other Rating Factors:** Strong capitalization (7.9) based on excellent current risk-adjusted capital (severe loss scenario).
**Principal Business:** Medicaid (94%), Medicare (6%)
**Mem Phys: 16:** 23,359 **15:** 14,595 **16 MLR** 94.3% **/ 16 Admin Exp** N/A
**Enroll(000): Q3 17:** 238 **16:** 221 **15:** 181 **Med Exp PMPM:** $596
**Principal Investments:** Long-term bonds (106%)
**Provider Compensation ($000):** Contr fee ($1,302,253), FFS ($90,352), capitation ($38,175), bonus arrang ($593)
**Total Member Encounters:** Phys (2,059,361), non-phys (1,548,912)
**Group Affiliation:** Aetna Inc
**Licensed in:** IL
**Address:** 333 W WACKER Dr Ste 2100, CHICAGO, IL 60606
**Phone:** (800) 872-3862 **Dom State:** IL **Commenced Bus:** May 2011

| Data Date | Rating | RACR #1 | RACR #2 | Total Assets ($mil) | Capital ($mil) | Net Premium ($mil) | Net Income ($mil) |
|---|---|---|---|---|---|---|---|
| 9-17 | B- | 2.04 | 1.70 | 984.5 | 196.3 | 1,334.4 | 10.8 |
| 9-16 | B- | 1.98 | 1.65 | 468.0 | 163.2 | 1,103.0 | -16.5 |
| 2016 | B- | 1.97 | 1.64 | 591.8 | 189.5 | 1,539.8 | -14.8 |
| 2015 | B | 2.00 | 1.67 | 483.0 | 165.0 | 1,361.9 | -11.2 |
| 2014 | B | 2.42 | 2.02 | 252.6 | 87.3 | 645.5 | 10.3 |
| 2013 | B | 2.35 | 1.96 | 146.4 | 35.5 | 308.2 | 6.5 |
| 2012 | A- | 3.79 | 3.16 | 91.6 | 42.8 | 230.2 | 13.9 |

Rating Indexes

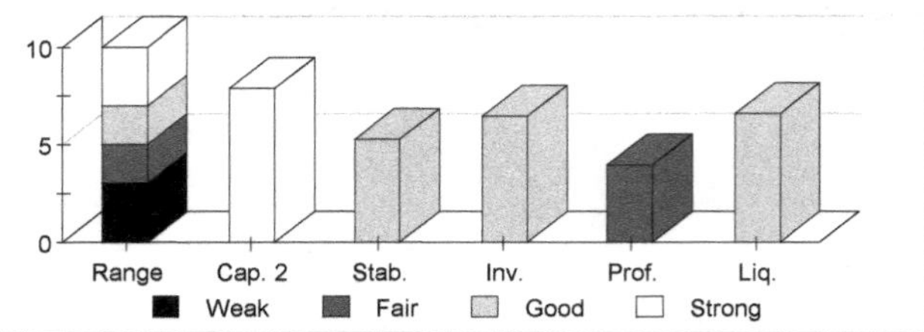


## AETNA BETTER HEALTH INC (A LA CORP) C+ Fair

**Major Rating Factors:** Good liquidity (6.0 on a scale of 0 to 10) with sufficient resources (cash flows and marketable investments) to handle a spike in claims. Weak profitability index (0.9). Strong capitalization (10.0) based on excellent current risk-adjusted capital (severe loss scenario).
**Other Rating Factors:** High quality investment portfolio (9.9).
**Principal Business:** Medicaid (100%)
**Mem Phys: 16:** 12,090 **15:** 9,842 **16 MLR** 87.8% **/ 16 Admin Exp** N/A
**Enroll(000): Q3 17:** 114 **16:** 106 **15:** 38 **Med Exp PMPM:** $382
**Principal Investments:** Long-term bonds (80%), cash and equiv (20%)
**Provider Compensation ($000):** Contr fee ($264,467), FFS ($38,672), capitation ($5,397)
**Total Member Encounters:** Phys (133,125), non-phys (85,795)
**Group Affiliation:** Aetna Inc
**Licensed in:** LA
**Address:** 2400 VETERANS MEMORIAL Blvd, KENNER, LA 70062
**Phone:** (504) 667-4461 **Dom State:** LA **Commenced Bus:** January 2015

| Data Date | Rating | RACR #1 | RACR #2 | Total Assets ($mil) | Capital ($mil) | Net Premium ($mil) | Net Income ($mil) |
|---|---|---|---|---|---|---|---|
| 9-17 | C+ | 3.92 | 3.27 | 213.6 | 90.8 | 440.5 | 27.5 |
| 9-16 | B- | 4.08 | 3.40 | 229.9 | 59.9 | 274.8 | -13.4 |
| 2016 | C+ | 2.94 | 2.45 | 213.9 | 65.1 | 421.9 | -7.9 |
| 2015 | C+ | 1.67 | 1.39 | 89.4 | 24.5 | 180.7 | -11.9 |
| 2014 | N/A | N/A | N/A | 3.0 | 3.0 | N/A | N/A |
| 2013 | N/A | N/A | N/A | N/A | N/A | N/A | N/A |
| 2012 | N/A | N/A | N/A | N/A | N/A | N/A | N/A |

Rating Indexes

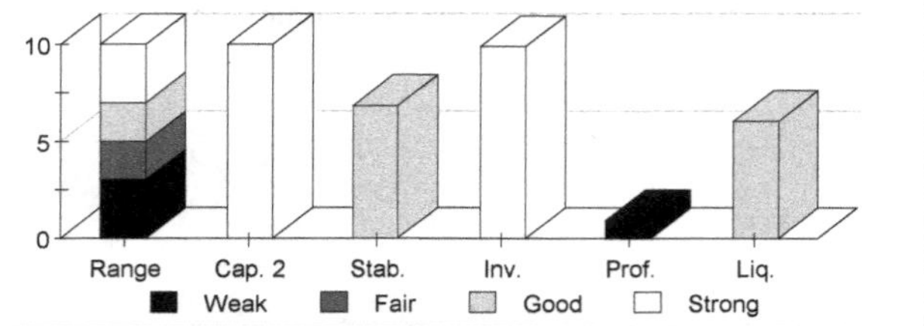


## AETNA BETTER HEALTH INC (A NJ CORP) * B+ Good

**Major Rating Factors:** Excellent profitability (8.2 on a scale of 0 to 10). Strong capitalization (10.0) based on excellent current risk-adjusted capital (severe loss scenario). High quality investment portfolio (9.8).
**Other Rating Factors:** Excellent liquidity (7.2) with ample operational cash flow and liquid investments.
**Principal Business:** Medicaid (100%)
**Mem Phys: 16:** 9,592 **15:** 8,361 **16 MLR** 68.1% **/ 16 Admin Exp** N/A
**Enroll(000): Q3 17:** 43 **16:** 33 **15:** 19 **Med Exp PMPM:** $264
**Principal Investments:** Long-term bonds (59%), cash and equiv (41%)
**Provider Compensation ($000):** FFS ($58,445), contr fee ($34,783), capitation ($3,891), bonus arrang ($269)
**Total Member Encounters:** Phys (129,583), non-phys (167,995)
**Group Affiliation:** Aetna Inc
**Licensed in:** NJ
**Address:** 3 INDEPENDENCE WAY Ste 400, PRINCETON, NJ 08540
**Phone:** (855) 232-3596 **Dom State:** NJ **Commenced Bus:** January 2015

| Data Date | Rating | RACR #1 | RACR #2 | Total Assets ($mil) | Capital ($mil) | Net Premium ($mil) | Net Income ($mil) |
|---|---|---|---|---|---|---|---|
| 9-17 | B+ | 9.00 | 7.50 | 136.9 | 47.9 | 164.5 | 13.6 |
| 9-16 | B- | 4.66 | 3.88 | 104.0 | 29.8 | 102.0 | 10.5 |
| 2016 | B | 7.41 | 6.18 | 119.6 | 35.3 | 138.0 | 16.1 |
| 2015 | C+ | 1.92 | 1.60 | 50.0 | 12.3 | 68.4 | -2.6 |
| 2014 | N/A | N/A | N/A | 5.0 | 5.0 | N/A | N/A |
| 2013 | N/A | N/A | N/A | N/A | N/A | N/A | N/A |
| 2012 | N/A | N/A | N/A | N/A | N/A | N/A | N/A |

Rating Indexes

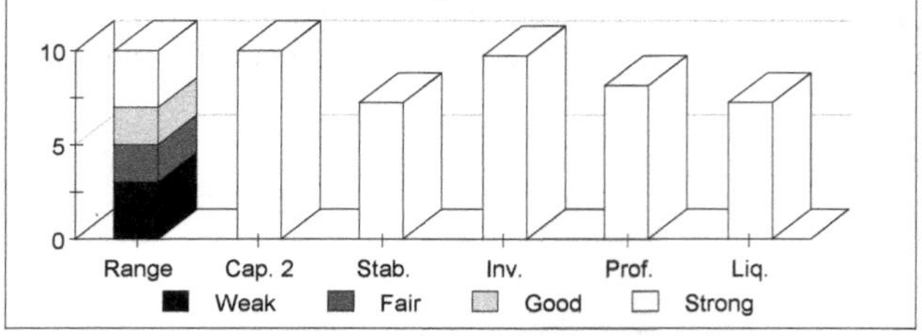

## AETNA BETTER HEALTH INC (A PA CORP) D- Weak

**Major Rating Factors:** Good overall profitability index (6.2 on a scale of 0 to 10). Good quality investment portfolio (6.6). Good liquidity (6.4) with sufficient resources (cash flows and marketable investments) to handle a spike in claims.
**Other Rating Factors:** Strong capitalization (9.5) based on excellent current risk-adjusted capital (severe loss scenario).
**Principal Business:** Medicaid (100%)
**Mem Phys: 16:** 30,530 **15:** 25,048 **16 MLR** 74.7% **/ 16 Admin Exp** N/A
**Enroll(000): Q3 17:** 205 **16:** 208 **15:** 190 **Med Exp PMPM:** $266
**Principal Investments:** Long-term bonds (78%), cash and equiv (21%), nonaffiliate common stock (1%)
**Provider Compensation ($000):** Contr fee ($599,969), FFS ($78,392), capitation ($33,055)
**Total Member Encounters:** Phys (982,366), non-phys (1,030,192)
**Group Affiliation:** Aetna Inc
**Licensed in:** PA
**Address:** 1425 UNION MEETING Rd, BLUE BELL, PA 19422
**Phone:** (800) 872-3862 **Dom State:** PA **Commenced Bus:** April 2010

| Data Date | Rating | RACR #1 | RACR #2 | Total Assets ($mil) | Capital ($mil) | Net Premium ($mil) | Net Income ($mil) |
|---|---|---|---|---|---|---|---|
| 9-17 | D- | 3.38 | 2.81 | 480.4 | 125.2 | 693.2 | 42.5 |
| 9-16 | D- | 2.76 | 2.30 | 522.8 | 119.5 | 634.9 | 32.3 |
| 2016 | D- | 3.76 | 3.13 | 574.8 | 141.3 | 867.8 | 58.2 |
| 2015 | D- | 2.57 | 2.14 | 419.0 | 111.4 | 818.5 | 32.7 |
| 2014 | D- | 4.38 | 3.65 | 304.8 | 108.6 | 467.1 | 11.1 |
| 2013 | D- | 2.06 | 1.72 | 133.6 | 31.6 | 305.9 | -7.0 |
| 2012 | D- | 2.33 | 1.94 | 115.9 | 39.3 | 289.5 | -13.1 |

Rating Indexes

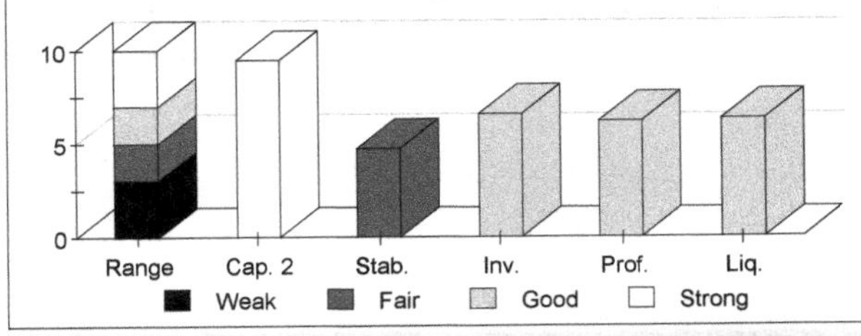


## AETNA BETTER HEALTH OF MICHIGAN INC B Good

**Major Rating Factors:** Fair profitability index (3.4 on a scale of 0 to 10). Strong capitalization (7.7) based on excellent current risk-adjusted capital (severe loss scenario). High quality investment portfolio (9.1).
**Other Rating Factors:** Excellent liquidity (7.0) with sufficient resources (cash flows and marketable investments) to handle a spike in claims.
**Principal Business:** Medicaid (74%), Medicare (26%)
**Mem Phys: 16:** 6,975 **15:** 5,953 **16 MLR** 84.7% **/ 16 Admin Exp** N/A
**Enroll(000): Q3 17:** 52 **16:** 52 **15:** 48 **Med Exp PMPM:** $473
**Principal Investments:** Cash and equiv (99%), long-term bonds (1%)
**Provider Compensation ($000):** Contr fee ($194,319), capitation ($65,441), FFS ($31,949)
**Total Member Encounters:** Phys (280,185), non-phys (251,996)
**Group Affiliation:** Aetna Inc
**Licensed in:** MI
**Address:** 1333 GRATIOT STE 400, DETROIT, MI 48207
**Phone:** (313) 465-1519 **Dom State:** MI **Commenced Bus:** October 2004

| Data Date | Rating | RACR #1 | RACR #2 | Total Assets ($mil) | Capital ($mil) | Net Premium ($mil) | Net Income ($mil) |
|---|---|---|---|---|---|---|---|
| 9-17 | B | 1.89 | 1.58 | 120.1 | 28.2 | 269.3 | -3.5 |
| 9-16 | B | 2.93 | 2.44 | 131.8 | 35.5 | 249.3 | -4.0 |
| 2016 | B | 2.22 | 1.85 | 120.5 | 34.2 | 340.2 | -3.5 |
| 2015 | B+ | 3.04 | 2.53 | 110.4 | 36.9 | 282.1 | 5.6 |
| 2014 | B | 2.98 | 2.49 | 49.1 | 23.6 | 187.5 | 6.2 |
| 2013 | B | 2.84 | 2.36 | 41.9 | 21.8 | 163.7 | 4.4 |
| 2012 | B | 3.02 | 2.52 | 46.7 | 24.3 | 173.2 | 7.1 |

Rating Indexes

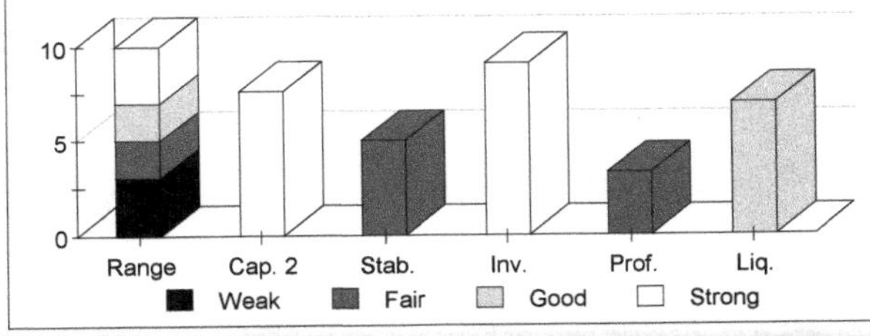


## AETNA BETTER HEALTH OF MISSOURI LLC B- Good

**Major Rating Factors:** Fair quality investment portfolio (3.7 on a scale of 0 to 10). Fair overall results on stability tests (4.6) based on inconsistent enrollment growth in the past five years due to declines in 2013 and 2014. Rating is significantly influenced by the good financial results of Aetna Inc. Excellent profitability (7.6).
**Other Rating Factors:** Strong capitalization index (9.4) based on excellent current risk-adjusted capital (severe loss scenario). Excellent liquidity (7.0) with sufficient resources (cash flows and marketable investments) to handle a spike in claims.
**Principal Business:** Medicaid (97%), comp med (3%)
**Mem Phys: 16:** 22,557 **15:** 17,534 **16 MLR** 85.6% **/ 16 Admin Exp** N/A
**Enroll(000): Q2 17:** N/A **16:** 279 **15:** 264 **Med Exp PMPM:** $205
**Principal Investments:** Long-term bonds (76%), cash and equiv (21%), nonaffiliate common stock (2%)
**Provider Compensation ($000):** Contr fee ($470,035), capitation ($192,213), FFS ($13,043)
**Total Member Encounters:** Phys (895,697), non-phys (877,772)
**Group Affiliation:** Aetna Inc
**Licensed in:** KS, MO
**Address:** 10 S BROADWAY SUITE 1200, ST LOUIS, MO 63102-1713
**Phone:** (314) 241-5300 **Dom State:** MO **Commenced Bus:** July 1995

| Data Date | Rating | RACR #1 | RACR #2 | Total Assets ($mil) | Capital ($mil) | Net Premium ($mil) | Net Income ($mil) |
|---|---|---|---|---|---|---|---|
| 6-17 | B- | 3.30 | 2.75 | 198.5 | 111.1 | 257.3 | -0.2 |
| 6-16 | B | 4.19 | 3.49 | 281.9 | 131.8 | 385.5 | 5.1 |
| 2016 | B | 4.66 | 3.88 | 280.3 | 164.4 | 780.7 | 32.7 |
| 2015 | B | 4.29 | 3.58 | 252.9 | 135.4 | 707.0 | 20.1 |
| 2014 | A- | 3.97 | 3.31 | 191.5 | 109.6 | 645.4 | 24.3 |
| 2013 | A- | 3.65 | 3.05 | 164.1 | 103.1 | 669.4 | 32.9 |
| 2012 | B+ | 3.33 | 2.77 | 152.1 | 95.2 | 658.5 | 19.7 |

Rating Indexes

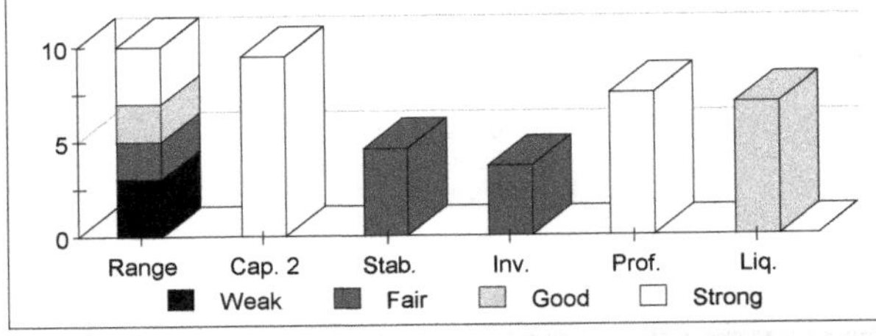

## AETNA BETTER HEALTH OF TEXAS INC * B+ Good

**Major Rating Factors:** Good liquidity (6.8 on a scale of 0 to 10) with sufficient resources (cash flows and marketable investments) to handle a spike in claims. Excellent profitability (9.4). Strong capitalization (9.7) based on excellent current risk-adjusted capital (severe loss scenario).
**Other Rating Factors:** High quality investment portfolio (8.7).
**Principal Business:** Medicaid (94%), comp med (6%)
**Mem Phys: 16:** 25,287 **15:** 24,390 **16 MLR** 80.8% **/ 16 Admin Exp** N/A
**Enroll(000): Q3 17:** 90 **16:** 89 **15:** 84 **Med Exp PMPM:** $201
**Principal Investments:** Long-term bonds (86%), cash and equiv (14%)
**Provider Compensation ($000):** Contr fee ($164,968), FFS ($20,832), bonus arrang ($261), capitation ($255)
**Total Member Encounters:** Phys (533,571), non-phys (355,554)
**Group Affiliation:** Aetna Inc
**Licensed in:** TX
**Address:** 2777 N STEMMONS FREEWAY #1450, DALLAS, TX 75207-2265
**Phone:** (800) 872-3862 **Dom State:** TX **Commenced Bus:** August 2015

| Data Date | Rating | RACR #1 | RACR #2 | Total Assets ($mil) | Capital ($mil) | Net Premium ($mil) | Net Income ($mil) |
|---|---|---|---|---|---|---|---|
| 9-17 | B+ | 3.54 | 2.95 | 120.2 | 48.6 | 215.9 | 13.8 |
| 9-16 | U | 8.44 | 7.03 | 88.8 | 46.1 | 178.2 | 12.3 |
| 2016 | C+ | 3.55 | 2.96 | 102.1 | 48.8 | 251.1 | 15.4 |
| 2015 | U | 5.62 | 4.68 | 92.7 | 30.7 | 70.3 | 4.6 |
| 2014 | N/A | N/A | N/A | N/A | N/A | N/A | N/A |
| 2013 | N/A | N/A | N/A | N/A | N/A | N/A | N/A |
| 2012 | N/A | N/A | N/A | N/A | N/A | N/A | N/A |

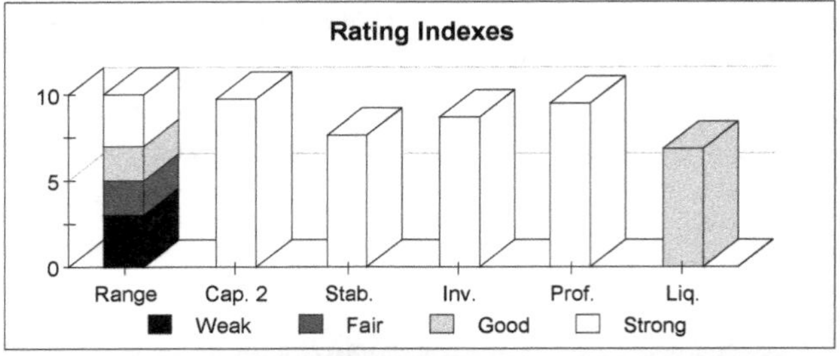


## AETNA BETTER HLTH OF KY INS CO * B+ Good

**Major Rating Factors:** Good quality investment portfolio (6.2 on a scale of 0 to 10). Good liquidity (6.5) with sufficient resources (cash flows and marketable investments) to handle a spike in claims. Excellent profitability (10.0).
**Other Rating Factors:** Strong capitalization (10.0) based on excellent current risk-adjusted capital (severe loss scenario).
**Principal Business:** Medicaid (96%), comp med (4%)
**Mem Phys: 16:** N/A **15:** N/A **16 MLR** 74.8% **/ 16 Admin Exp** N/A
**Enroll(000): Q3 17:** 251 **16:** 273 **15:** N/A **Med Exp PMPM:** $275
**Principal Investments:** Long-term bonds (99%), cash and equiv (1%)
**Provider Compensation ($000):** Contr fee ($606,168), FFS ($28,254), capitation ($11,339)
**Total Member Encounters:** Phys (1,379,013), non-phys (866,055)
**Group Affiliation:** Aetna Inc
**Licensed in:** KY
**Address:** 306 WEST MAIN St Ste 512, FRANKFORT, KY 40601
**Phone:** (800) 627-4702 **Dom State:** KY **Commenced Bus:** November 2015

| Data Date | Rating | RACR #1 | RACR #2 | Total Assets ($mil) | Capital ($mil) | Net Premium ($mil) | Net Income ($mil) |
|---|---|---|---|---|---|---|---|
| 9-17 | B+ | 3.72 | 3.10 | 489.7 | 241.3 | 832.5 | 29.1 |
| 9-16 | N/A | N/A | N/A | 596.7 | 190.8 | 817.9 | 94.7 |
| 2016 | C+ | 3.29 | 2.74 | 563.5 | 213.4 | 1,111.9 | 122.2 |
| 2015 | N/A | N/A | N/A | 3.3 | 3.3 | N/A | N/A |
| 2014 | N/A | N/A | N/A | N/A | N/A | N/A | N/A |
| 2013 | N/A | N/A | N/A | N/A | N/A | N/A | N/A |
| 2012 | N/A | N/A | N/A | N/A | N/A | N/A | N/A |

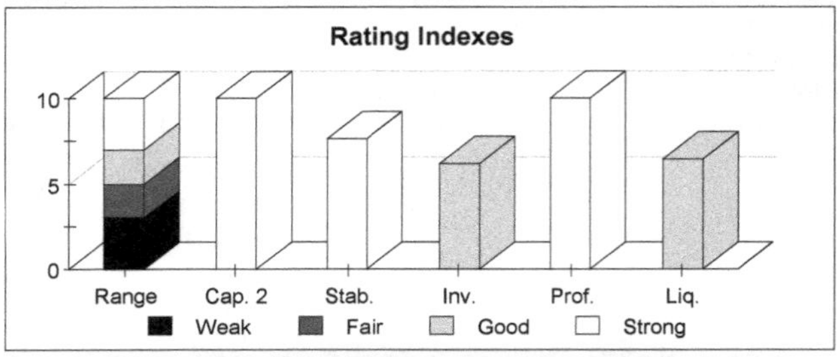


## AETNA HEALTH & LIFE INSURANCE COMPANY * B+ Good

**Major Rating Factors:** Good overall results on stability tests (6.5 on a scale of 0 to 10). Stability strengths include excellent operational trends and excellent risk diversification. Good quality investment portfolio (5.7) despite mixed results such as: substantial holdings of BBB bonds but junk bond exposure equal to 57% of capital. Good overall profitability (6.0) although investment income, in comparison to reserve requirements, is below regulatory standards.
**Other Rating Factors:** Strong capitalization (7.3) based on excellent risk adjusted capital (severe loss scenario). Excellent liquidity (7.1).
**Principal Business:** Reinsurance (77%) and individual health insurance (22%).
**Principal Investments:** NonCMO investment grade bonds (61%), CMOs and structured securities (13%), mortgages in good standing (10%), and noninv. grade bonds (6%).
**Investments in Affiliates:** 4%
**Group Affiliation:** Aetna Inc
**Licensed in:** All states except PR
**Commenced Business:** October 1971
**Address:** 151 FARMINGTON AVENUE, HARTFORD, CT 6156
**Phone:** (860) 273-0123 **Domicile State:** CT **NAIC Code:** 78700

| Data Date | Rating | RACR #1 | RACR #2 | Total Assets ($mil) | Capital ($mil) | Net Premium ($mil) | Net Income ($mil) |
|---|---|---|---|---|---|---|---|
| 9-17 | B+ | 1.88 | 1.17 | 2,403.1 | 262.1 | 671.5 | 12.2 |
| 9-16 | B+ | 2.11 | 1.30 | 2,362.3 | 271.7 | 593.0 | 6.0 |
| 2016 | B+ | 2.14 | 1.33 | 2,388.6 | 282.5 | 804.5 | 9.5 |
| 2015 | B+ | 2.59 | 1.58 | 2,290.6 | 299.9 | 655.8 | 76.8 |
| 2014 | B+ | 3.11 | 1.86 | 2,254.6 | 319.7 | 568.8 | 85.2 |
| 2013 | B+ | 3.04 | 1.80 | 2,148.2 | 280.6 | 501.0 | 71.2 |
| 2012 | B+ | 3.11 | 1.77 | 1,988.1 | 256.3 | 420.1 | 53.4 |

**Adverse Trends in Operations**

Decrease in capital during 2016 (6%)
Decrease in capital during 2015 (6%)

## AETNA HEALTH INC (A CT CORP) C Fair

**Major Rating Factors:** Fair profitability index (4.4 on a scale of 0 to 10). Good quality investment portfolio (6.4). Good overall results on stability tests (5.0). Rating is significantly influenced by the good financial results of Aetna Inc.
**Other Rating Factors:** Good liquidity (6.8) with sufficient resources (cash flows and marketable investments) to handle a spike in claims. Strong capitalization index (10.0) based on excellent current risk-adjusted capital (severe loss scenario).
**Principal Business:** Medicare (98%), comp med (2%)
**Mem Phys: 16:** 25,161 **15:** 24,004 **16 MLR** 80.3% **/ 16 Admin Exp** N/A
**Enroll(000): Q3 17:** 26 **16:** 26 **15:** 24 **Med Exp PMPM:** $643
**Principal Investments:** Long-term bonds (99%), cash and equiv (1%)
**Provider Compensation ($000):** Contr fee ($186,471), FFS ($7,299), bonus arrang ($1,707), capitation ($919)
**Total Member Encounters:** Phys (721,253), non-phys (431,045)
**Group Affiliation:** Aetna Inc
**Licensed in:** CT
**Address:** 151 FARMINGTON AVENUE, HARTFORD, CT 06156
**Phone:** (800) 872-3862 **Dom State:** CT **Commenced Bus:** June 1987

| Data Date | Rating | RACR #1 | RACR #2 | Total Assets ($mil) | Capital ($mil) | Net Premium ($mil) | Net Income ($mil) |
|---|---|---|---|---|---|---|---|
| 9-17 | C | 6.19 | 5.16 | 149.2 | 83.4 | 188.4 | 10.2 |
| 9-16 | C | 5.69 | 4.74 | 140.6 | 77.7 | 184.0 | 6.6 |
| 2016 | C | 6.11 | 5.09 | 122.2 | 82.2 | 245.6 | 13.0 |
| 2015 | C | 5.02 | 4.18 | 103.2 | 68.2 | 225.4 | 1.5 |
| 2014 | C | 3.68 | 3.07 | 102.8 | 67.2 | 298.1 | -8.6 |
| 2013 | B | 2.31 | 1.93 | 98.8 | 50.2 | 350.2 | -12.7 |
| 2012 | B | 1.22 | 1.02 | 75.4 | 23.5 | 314.3 | -5.5 |

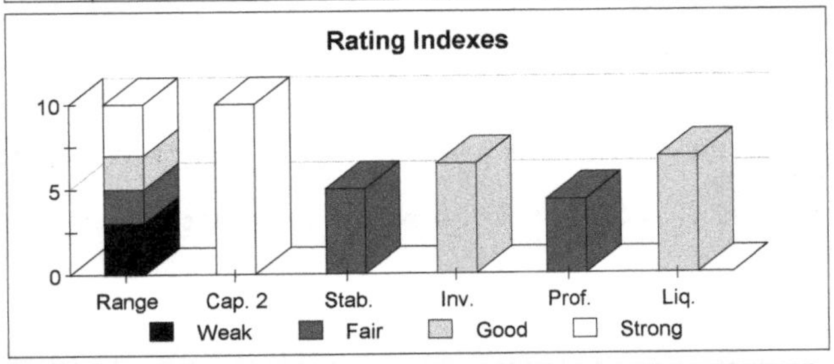


## AETNA HEALTH INC (A FLORIDA CORP) * B+ Good

**Major Rating Factors:** Good overall results on stability tests (6.3 on a scale of 0 to 10) based on healthy premium and capital growth during 2016 but a decline in the number of member physicians during 2017. Rating is significantly influenced by the good financial results of Aetna Inc. Good liquidity (6.5) with sufficient resources (cash flows and marketable investments) to handle a spike in claims. Excellent profitability (9.3).
**Other Rating Factors:** Strong capitalization index (8.8) based on excellent current risk-adjusted capital (severe loss scenario). High quality investment portfolio (8.5).
**Principal Business:** Comp med (52%), Medicare (48%)
**Mem Phys: 16:** 47,677 **15:** 56,057 **16 MLR** 82.3% **/ 16 Admin Exp** N/A
**Enroll(000): Q3 17:** 241 **16:** 286 **15:** 281 **Med Exp PMPM:** $475
**Principal Investments:** Long-term bonds (97%), cash and equiv (2%), nonaffiliate common stock (1%)
**Provider Compensation ($000):** Contr fee ($1,371,236), capitation ($149,952), FFS ($72,518), bonus arrang ($38,816)
**Total Member Encounters:** Phys (3,019,528), non-phys (2,748,957)
**Group Affiliation:** Aetna Inc
**Licensed in:** FL, IA
**Address:** 4630 WOODLANDS CORPORATE BOULE, TAMPA, FL 33614-2415
**Phone:** (813) 775-0000 **Dom State:** FL **Commenced Bus:** July 1985

| Data Date | Rating | RACR #1 | RACR #2 | Total Assets ($mil) | Capital ($mil) | Net Premium ($mil) | Net Income ($mil) |
|---|---|---|---|---|---|---|---|
| 9-17 | B+ | 2.76 | 2.30 | 590.4 | 269.1 | 1,401.8 | 37.7 |
| 9-16 | B | 2.57 | 2.14 | 586.2 | 211.6 | 1,494.4 | 55.6 |
| 2016 | B+ | 2.58 | 2.15 | 541.2 | 249.8 | 1,982.9 | 69.6 |
| 2015 | B | 2.21 | 1.84 | 512.6 | 180.0 | 1,631.5 | 41.3 |
| 2014 | A- | 2.43 | 2.02 | 266.5 | 130.4 | 1,101.5 | 53.9 |
| 2013 | A- | 1.84 | 1.53 | 273.7 | 116.4 | 1,220.0 | 77.7 |
| 2012 | A- | 1.42 | 1.18 | 310.4 | 103.2 | 1,374.2 | 59.8 |

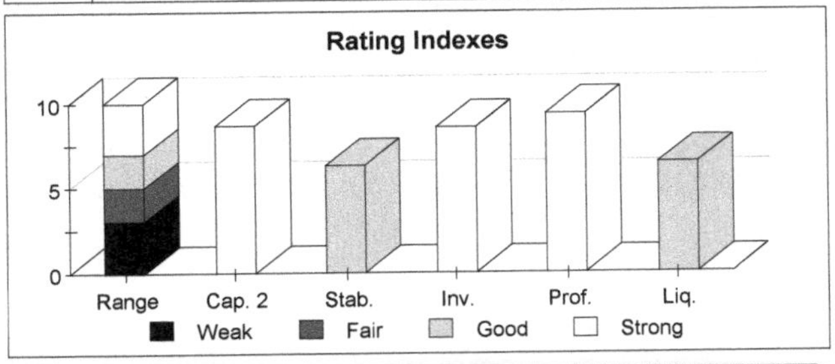


## AETNA HEALTH INC (A GEORGIA CORP) B Good

**Major Rating Factors:** Good liquidity (6.0 on a scale of 0 to 10) with sufficient resources (cash flows and marketable investments) to handle a spike in claims. Fair profitability index (4.5). Fair overall results on stability tests (4.5) based on a significant 22% decrease in enrollment during the period. Rating is significantly influenced by the good financial results of Aetna Inc.
**Other Rating Factors:** Strong capitalization index (9.3) based on excellent current risk-adjusted capital (severe loss scenario). High quality investment portfolio (9.7).
**Principal Business:** Comp med (89%), Medicare (7%), FEHB (4%)
**Mem Phys: 16:** 25,910 **15:** 23,102 **16 MLR** 82.6% **/ 16 Admin Exp** N/A
**Enroll(000): Q3 17:** 69 **16:** 149 **15:** 191 **Med Exp PMPM:** $253
**Principal Investments:** Long-term bonds (100%)
**Provider Compensation ($000):** FFS ($452,176), contr fee ($27,603), capitation ($11,676), bonus arrang ($400)
**Total Member Encounters:** Phys (1,094,131), non-phys (477,675)
**Group Affiliation:** Aetna Inc
**Licensed in:** GA
**Address:** 1100 ABERNATHY ROAD SUITE 375, ATLANTA, GA 30328
**Phone:** (800) 872-3862 **Dom State:** GA **Commenced Bus:** February 1986

| Data Date | Rating | RACR #1 | RACR #2 | Total Assets ($mil) | Capital ($mil) | Net Premium ($mil) | Net Income ($mil) |
|---|---|---|---|---|---|---|---|
| 9-17 | B | 3.23 | 2.69 | 280.3 | 114.9 | 242.8 | 0.6 |
| 9-16 | B | 3.40 | 2.84 | 286.8 | 132.3 | 468.2 | 17.6 |
| 2016 | B | 3.66 | 3.05 | 284.8 | 131.4 | 605.1 | 18.9 |
| 2015 | B | 3.01 | 2.51 | 298.3 | 116.0 | 642.9 | -4.6 |
| 2014 | B | 3.67 | 3.06 | 241.4 | 129.6 | 753.5 | 11.5 |
| 2013 | B | 2.79 | 2.33 | 232.8 | 120.4 | 877.3 | 14.3 |
| 2012 | B | 2.14 | 1.78 | 218.1 | 117.5 | 864.4 | 17.7 |

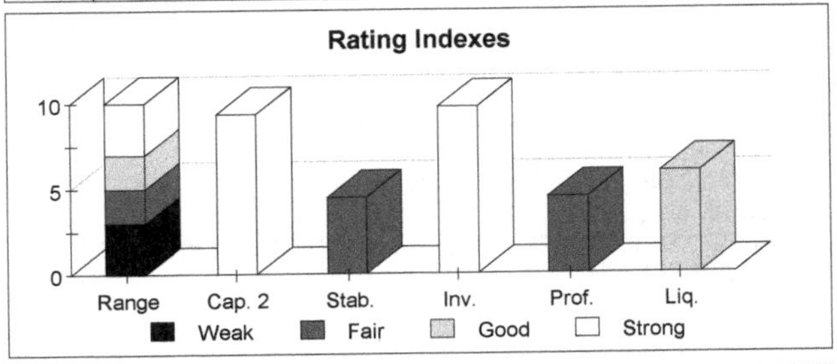

## AETNA HEALTH INC (A MAINE CORP) B- Good

**Major Rating Factors:** Fair overall results on stability tests (4.9 on a scale of 0 to 10). Rating is significantly influenced by the good financial results of Aetna Inc. Good overall profitability index (5.1). Good liquidity (6.8) with sufficient resources (cash flows and marketable investments) to handle a spike in claims.
**Other Rating Factors:** Strong capitalization index (10.0) based on excellent current risk-adjusted capital (severe loss scenario). High quality investment portfolio (9.9).
**Principal Business:** Medicare (74%), comp med (26%)
**Mem Phys: 16:** 11,115 **15:** 10,598 **16 MLR** 84.2% **/ 16 Admin Exp** N/A
**Enroll(000): Q3 17:** 11 **16:** 11 **15:** 12 **Med Exp PMPM:** $476
**Principal Investments:** Long-term bonds (85%), cash and equiv (15%)
**Provider Compensation ($000):** Contr fee ($60,027), FFS ($2,289), bonus arrang ($816), capitation ($239)
**Total Member Encounters:** Phys (229,880), non-phys (160,800)
**Group Affiliation:** Aetna Inc
**Licensed in:** ME
**Address:** 175 RUNNING HILL ROAD SUITE 30, SOUTH PORTLAND, ME 04106-3220
**Phone:** (800) 872-3862 **Dom State:** ME **Commenced Bus:** April 1996

| Data Date | Rating | RACR #1 | RACR #2 | Total Assets ($mil) | Capital ($mil) | Net Premium ($mil) | Net Income ($mil) |
|---|---|---|---|---|---|---|---|
| 9-17 | B- | 3.93 | 3.27 | 36.1 | 19.7 | 59.1 | 3.9 |
| 9-16 | B- | 2.72 | 2.27 | 33.6 | 14.7 | 55.6 | 1.3 |
| 2016 | B- | 3.13 | 2.61 | 27.6 | 15.5 | 75.3 | 2.5 |
| 2015 | B- | 2.36 | 1.97 | 26.2 | 12.7 | 80.1 | -1.2 |
| 2014 | B | 2.36 | 1.97 | 27.9 | 15.7 | 104.7 | 2.6 |
| 2013 | B- | 2.23 | 1.86 | 34.2 | 13.9 | 98.3 | -1.4 |
| 2012 | B- | 2.78 | 2.32 | 27.6 | 14.8 | 93.2 | 7.4 |

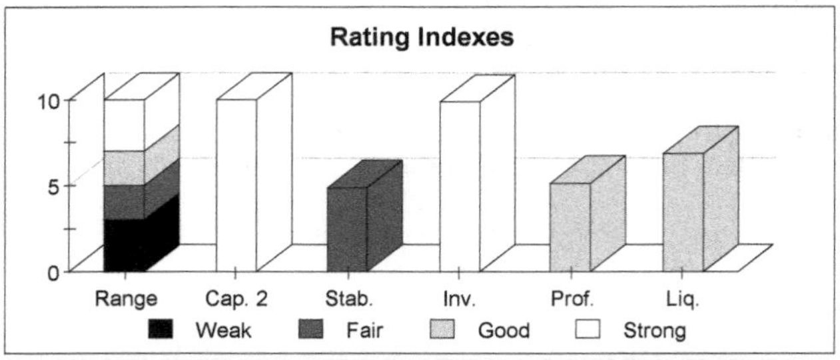


## AETNA HEALTH INC (A NEW JERSEY CORP) B Good

**Major Rating Factors:** Good overall profitability index (6.4 on a scale of 0 to 10). Good quality investment portfolio (4.9). Good liquidity (6.6) with sufficient resources (cash flows and marketable investments) to handle a spike in claims.
**Other Rating Factors:** Fair overall results on stability tests (4.5) based on a significant 52% decrease in enrollment during the period. Rating is significantly influenced by the good financial results of Aetna Inc. Strong capitalization index (10.0) based on excellent current risk-adjusted capital (severe loss scenario).
**Principal Business:** Medicare (56%), comp med (38%), FEHB (6%)
**Mem Phys: 16:** 37,114 **15:** 34,954 **16 MLR** 83.6% **/ 16 Admin Exp** N/A
**Enroll(000): Q3 17:** 64 **16:** 75 **15:** 155 **Med Exp PMPM:** $593
**Principal Investments:** Long-term bonds (100%)
**Provider Compensation ($000):** Contr fee ($707,972), FFS ($46,699), capitation ($26,196), bonus arrang ($3,581)
**Total Member Encounters:** Phys (2,223,967), non-phys (1,506,208)
**Group Affiliation:** Aetna Inc
**Licensed in:** NJ
**Address:** 9 ENTIN ROAD SUITE 203, PARSIPPANY, NJ 07054
**Phone:** (800) 872-3862 **Dom State:** NJ **Commenced Bus:** March 1983

| Data Date | Rating | RACR #1 | RACR #2 | Total Assets ($mil) | Capital ($mil) | Net Premium ($mil) | Net Income ($mil) |
|---|---|---|---|---|---|---|---|
| 9-17 | B | 3.87 | 3.23 | 315.9 | 188.0 | 490.4 | 11.6 |
| 9-16 | B | 3.13 | 2.61 | 334.7 | 183.2 | 703.8 | 8.2 |
| 2016 | B | 3.87 | 3.22 | 302.9 | 187.8 | 887.0 | 17.7 |
| 2015 | B | 2.94 | 2.45 | 340.4 | 171.6 | 1,123.5 | 13.4 |
| 2014 | B | 3.34 | 2.79 | 323.7 | 198.4 | 1,171.4 | 40.2 |
| 2013 | B | 2.11 | 1.76 | 341.3 | 149.2 | 1,355.1 | 21.7 |
| 2012 | B | 1.83 | 1.53 | 368.0 | 151.1 | 1,627.9 | 47.2 |

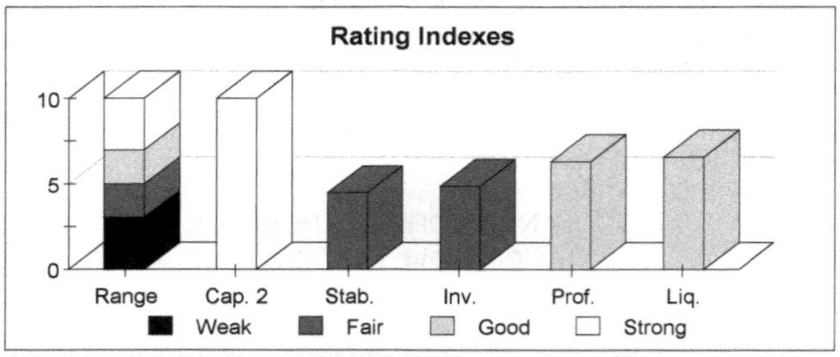


## AETNA HEALTH INC (A NEW YORK CORP) C+ Fair

**Major Rating Factors:** Fair overall results on stability tests (3.6 on a scale of 0 to 10) based on a steep decline in premium revenue in 2016, a significant 50% decrease in enrollment during the period. Rating is significantly influenced by the good financial results of Aetna Inc. Excellent profitability (7.3). Strong capitalization index (10.0) based on excellent current risk-adjusted capital (severe loss scenario).
**Other Rating Factors:** High quality investment portfolio (8.4). Excellent liquidity (7.0) with sufficient resources (cash flows and marketable investments) to handle a spike in claims.
**Principal Business:** Medicare (100%), comp med (2%)
**Mem Phys: 16:** 76,401 **15:** 74,588 **16 MLR** 77.9% **/ 16 Admin Exp** N/A
**Enroll(000): Q3 17:** 10 **16:** 15 **15:** 31 **Med Exp PMPM:** $704
**Principal Investments:** Long-term bonds (86%), affiliate common stock (10%), cash and equiv (2%), nonaffiliate common stock (2%)
**Provider Compensation ($000):** Contr fee ($138,934), FFS ($8,116), capitation ($2,466), bonus arrang ($577)
**Total Member Encounters:** Phys (492,740), non-phys (311,471)
**Group Affiliation:** Aetna Inc
**Licensed in:** NY
**Address:** 100 PARK AVENUE 12TH FLOOR, NEW YORK, NY 10178
**Phone:** (800) 872-3862 **Dom State:** NY **Commenced Bus:** May 1986

| Data Date | Rating | RACR #1 | RACR #2 | Total Assets ($mil) | Capital ($mil) | Net Premium ($mil) | Net Income ($mil) |
|---|---|---|---|---|---|---|---|
| 9-17 | C+ | 19.40 | 16.17 | 282.3 | 227.3 | 92.5 | 5.8 |
| 9-16 | C+ | 13.54 | 11.29 | 266.2 | 201.7 | 133.7 | 0.5 |
| 2016 | C+ | 18.31 | 15.26 | 264.7 | 214.4 | 172.3 | 13.2 |
| 2015 | C+ | 13.32 | 11.10 | 276.0 | 198.4 | 300.9 | 15.2 |
| 2014 | B | 4.53 | 3.78 | 285.2 | 176.5 | 489.9 | 25.4 |
| 2013 | B+ | 6.63 | 5.52 | 362.3 | 242.4 | 575.1 | 42.6 |
| 2012 | A- | 8.67 | 7.23 | 363.9 | 247.1 | 626.8 | 73.6 |

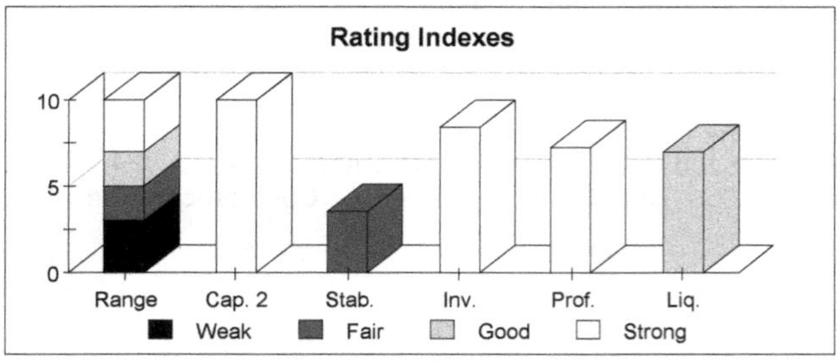

## AETNA HEALTH INC (A PA CORP) C+ Fair

**Major Rating Factors:** Good quality investment portfolio (6.6 on a scale of 0 to 10). Good liquidity (5.0) as cash resources may not be adequate to cover a spike in claims. Weak overall results on stability tests (2.6). Rating is significantly influenced by the good financial results of Aetna Inc.
**Other Rating Factors:** Excellent profitability (7.3). Strong capitalization index (9.6) based on excellent current risk-adjusted capital (severe loss scenario).
**Principal Business:** Comp med (47%), Medicare (35%), FEHB (18%)
**Mem Phys: 16:** 370,968 **15:** 407,130 **16 MLR** 94.6% **/ 16 Admin Exp** N/A
**Enroll(000): Q3 17:** 616 **16:** 763 **15:** 812 **Med Exp PMPM:** $373
**Principal Investments:** Long-term bonds (97%), affiliate common stock (1%), nonaffiliate common stock (1%), other (2%)
**Provider Compensation ($000):** Contr fee ($3,440,713), FFS ($188,631), capitation ($48,587), bonus arrang ($13,972)
**Total Member Encounters:** Phys (8,863,313), non-phys (6,191,173)
**Group Affiliation:** Aetna Inc
**Licensed in:** AZ, CO, DC, DE, IL, IN, KS, KY, MD, MA, MO, NE, NV, NC, OH, OK, PA, SC, TN, VA, WA, WV
**Address:** 1425 UNION MEETING ROAD, BLUE BELL, PA 19422
**Phone:** (800) 872-3862 **Dom State:** PA **Commenced Bus:** September 1981

| Data Date | Rating | RACR #1 | RACR #2 | Total Assets ($mil) | Capital ($mil) | Net Premium ($mil) | Net Income ($mil) |
|---|---|---|---|---|---|---|---|
| 9-17 | C+ | 3.41 | 2.84 | 1,372.7 | 596.0 | 2,693.5 | 76.3 |
| 9-16 | B | 5.27 | 4.39 | 1,503.4 | 540.4 | 3,012.7 | 73.1 |
| 2016 | C+ | 2.69 | 2.24 | 1,380.0 | 458.2 | 3,951.7 | 83.4 |
| 2015 | B | 4.17 | 3.47 | 1,479.3 | 672.3 | 4,192.9 | 113.8 |
| 2014 | B | 3.64 | 3.04 | 1,322.6 | 662.2 | 4,568.7 | 117.0 |
| 2013 | B | 2.54 | 2.12 | 1,202.3 | 495.1 | 4,332.3 | 101.0 |
| 2012 | A- | 2.15 | 1.79 | 1,144.5 | 554.2 | 4,792.1 | 159.3 |

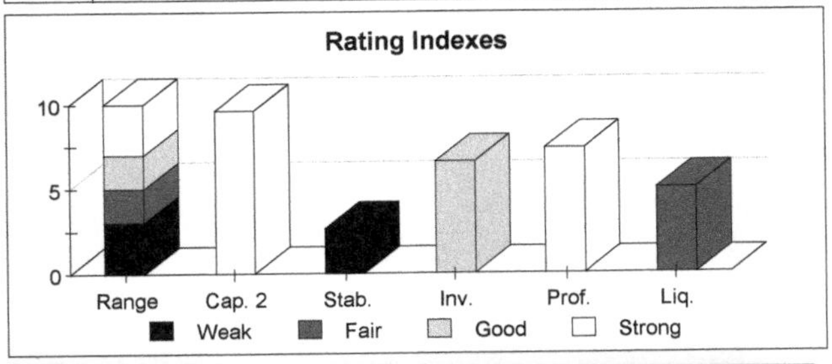


## AETNA HEALTH INC (A TEXAS CORP) C+ Fair

**Major Rating Factors:** Good liquidity (5.9 on a scale of 0 to 10) with sufficient resources (cash flows and marketable investments) to handle a spike in claims. Weak profitability index (2.2). Weak overall results on stability tests (2.4). Rating is significantly influenced by the good financial results of Aetna Inc.
**Other Rating Factors:** Strong capitalization index (9.2) based on excellent current risk-adjusted capital (severe loss scenario). High quality investment portfolio (9.9).
**Principal Business:** Medicare (62%), comp med (38%)
**Mem Phys: 16:** 56,451 **15:** 54,248 **16 MLR** 90.6% **/ 16 Admin Exp** N/A
**Enroll(000): Q3 17:** 53 **16:** 58 **15:** 52 **Med Exp PMPM:** $564
**Principal Investments:** Long-term bonds (95%), cash and equiv (3%), nonaffiliate common stock (2%)
**Provider Compensation ($000):** Contr fee ($324,821), FFS ($47,661), capitation ($2,938), bonus arrang ($2,426)
**Total Member Encounters:** Phys (778,027), non-phys (620,557)
**Group Affiliation:** Aetna Inc
**Licensed in:** TX
**Address:** 2777 N STEMMONS FREEWAY SUITE, DALLAS, TX 75207-2265
**Phone:** (800) 872-3862 **Dom State:** TX **Commenced Bus:** November 1987

| Data Date | Rating | RACR #1 | RACR #2 | Total Assets ($mil) | Capital ($mil) | Net Premium ($mil) | Net Income ($mil) |
|---|---|---|---|---|---|---|---|
| 9-17 | C+ | 3.13 | 2.60 | 159.1 | 77.1 | 304.8 | -9.5 |
| 9-16 | C+ | 3.60 | 3.00 | 192.1 | 99.4 | 326.3 | -8.0 |
| 2016 | C+ | 3.83 | 3.19 | 161.0 | 96.7 | 430.1 | -7.6 |
| 2015 | B | 4.13 | 3.44 | 166.9 | 116.0 | 514.8 | 13.9 |
| 2014 | B | 3.13 | 2.61 | 236.5 | 124.0 | 690.2 | 23.6 |
| 2013 | B | 2.28 | 1.90 | 199.2 | 100.6 | 704.9 | 6.5 |
| 2012 | B+ | 2.69 | 2.24 | 206.5 | 122.4 | 711.6 | 9.6 |

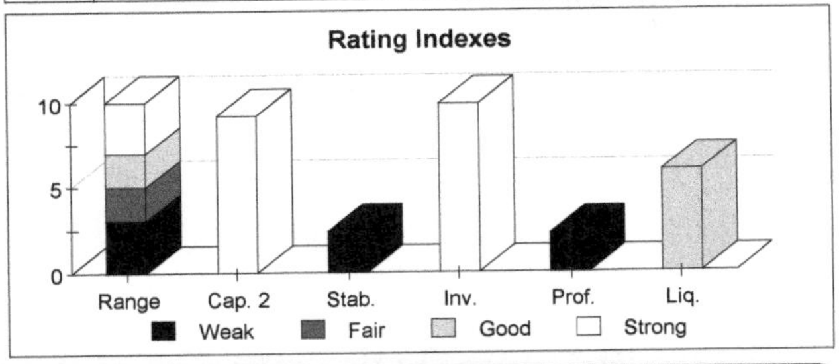


## AETNA HEALTH INC (LA) B- Good

**Major Rating Factors:** Fair profitability index (4.9 on a scale of 0 to 10). Fair overall results on stability tests (4.3). Rating is significantly influenced by the good financial results of Aetna Inc. Good liquidity (6.8) with sufficient resources (cash flows and marketable investments) to handle a spike in claims.
**Other Rating Factors:** Strong capitalization index (10.0) based on excellent current risk-adjusted capital (severe loss scenario). High quality investment portfolio (9.3).
**Principal Business:** Comp med (88%), Medicare (11%)
**Mem Phys: 16:** N/A **15:** 225,803 **16 MLR** 77.8% **/ 16 Admin Exp** N/A
**Enroll(000): Q3 17:** 16 **16:** 28 **15:** 29 **Med Exp PMPM:** $340
**Principal Investments:** Long-term bonds (91%), cash and equiv (9%)
**Provider Compensation ($000):** Contr fee ($66,076), capitation ($18,508), FFS ($5,478)
**Total Member Encounters:** Phys (146,473), non-phys (46,024)
**Group Affiliation:** Aetna Inc
**Licensed in:** LA
**Address:** 3838 N CAUSEWAY BLVD SUITE 335, METAIRIE, LA 70002
**Phone:** (504) 834-0840 **Dom State:** LA **Commenced Bus:** July 1985

| Data Date | Rating | RACR #1 | RACR #2 | Total Assets ($mil) | Capital ($mil) | Net Premium ($mil) | Net Income ($mil) |
|---|---|---|---|---|---|---|---|
| 9-17 | B- | 5.24 | 4.36 | 45.1 | 28.8 | 76.5 | 5.1 |
| 9-16 | B- | 2.71 | 2.26 | 41.8 | 21.7 | 84.8 | 4.4 |
| 2016 | B- | 4.51 | 3.76 | 43.7 | 24.4 | 111.1 | 6.1 |
| 2015 | B- | 2.29 | 1.91 | 45.9 | 17.6 | 139.7 | -5.5 |
| 2014 | B | 2.06 | 1.72 | 55.0 | 21.0 | 190.4 | 2.0 |
| 2013 | B | 2.75 | 2.30 | 47.0 | 24.0 | 171.1 | 5.2 |
| 2012 | B | 3.36 | 2.80 | 47.1 | 26.6 | 156.2 | 8.0 |

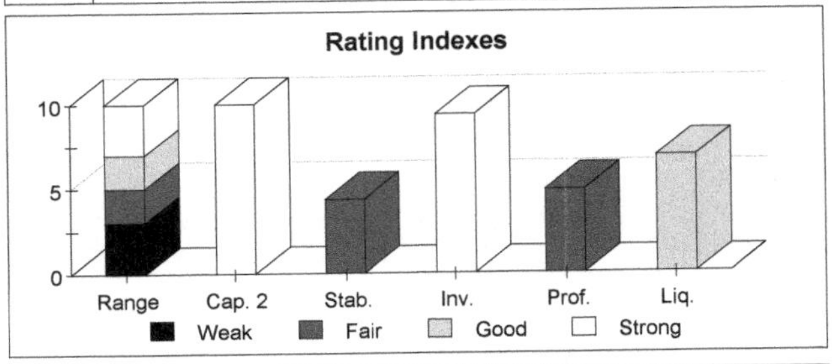

## AETNA HEALTH INS CO B- Good

**Major Rating Factors:** Good quality investment portfolio (6.7 on a scale of 0 to 10). Strong capitalization (10.0) based on excellent current risk-adjusted capital (severe loss scenario). Excellent liquidity (7.0) with ample operational cash flow and liquid investments.
**Other Rating Factors:** Weak profitability index (1.1).
**Principal Business:** Comp med (99%)
**Mem Phys: 16:** N/A **15:** N/A **16 MLR** 82.2% **/ 16 Admin Exp** N/A
**Enroll(000): Q3 17:** 149 **16:** 177 **15:** 201 **Med Exp PMPM:** $13
**Principal Investments:** Long-term bonds (84%), cash and equiv (16%)
**Provider Compensation ($000):** FFS ($31,278)
**Total Member Encounters:** N/A
**Group Affiliation:** Aetna Inc
**Licensed in:** All states except CA, CT, MS, NY, PR
**Address:** 1425 UNION MEETING Rd, BLUE BELL, PA 19422
**Phone:** (800) 872-3862 **Dom State:** PA **Commenced Bus:** December 1956

| Data Date | Rating | RACR #1 | RACR #2 | Total Assets ($mil) | Capital ($mil) | Net Premium ($mil) | Net Income ($mil) |
|---|---|---|---|---|---|---|---|
| 9-17 | B- | 10.00 | 8.33 | 40.4 | 34.9 | 12.3 | -1.6 |
| 9-16 | B- | 6.30 | 5.25 | 52.1 | 31.7 | 23.1 | -2.0 |
| 2016 | B- | 9.96 | 8.30 | 43.1 | 34.8 | 34.8 | 0.6 |
| 2015 | C+ | 6.42 | 5.35 | 59.0 | 32.3 | 33.8 | -6.8 |
| 2014 | B | 7.50 | 6.25 | 59.1 | 38.9 | 52.4 | -1.5 |
| 2013 | B | 6.23 | 5.20 | 61.6 | 40.3 | 86.9 | 5.6 |
| 2012 | B | 4.98 | 4.15 | 52.4 | 34.8 | 67.7 | -8.6 |

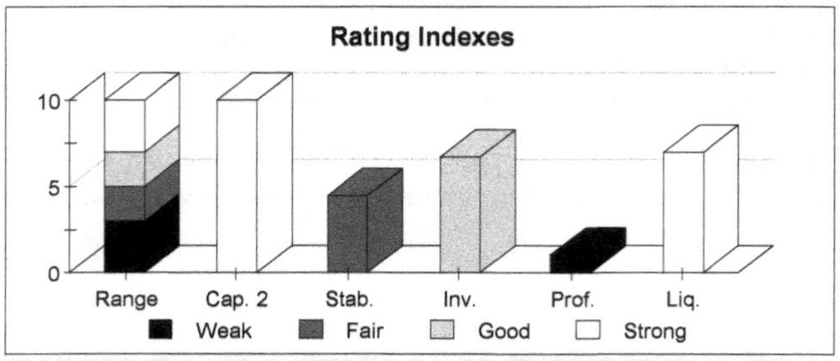


## AETNA HEALTH INS CO OF NY C+ Fair

**Major Rating Factors:** Weak profitability index (1.5 on a scale of 0 to 10). Strong capitalization (10.0) based on excellent current risk-adjusted capital (severe loss scenario). High quality investment portfolio (9.9).
**Other Rating Factors:** Excellent liquidity (10.0) with ample operational cash flow and liquid investments.
**Principal Business:** Comp med (100%)
**Mem Phys: 16:** N/A **15:** N/A **16 MLR** 53.8% **/ 16 Admin Exp** N/A
**Enroll(000): Q2 17:** N/A **16:** 0 **15:** 2 **Med Exp PMPM:** $52
**Principal Investments:** Long-term bonds (77%), cash and equiv (23%)
**Provider Compensation ($000):** FFS ($156)
**Total Member Encounters:** N/A
**Group Affiliation:** Aetna Inc
**Licensed in:** NY
**Address:** 101 PARK Ave 15TH Fl, NEW YORK, NY 10178
**Phone:** (800) 872-3862 **Dom State:** NY **Commenced Bus:** August 1986

| Data Date | Rating | RACR #1 | RACR #2 | Total Assets ($mil) | Capital ($mil) | Net Premium ($mil) | Net Income ($mil) |
|---|---|---|---|---|---|---|---|
| 6-17 | C+ | 7.74 | 6.45 | 10.3 | 10.3 | 0.0 | 0.1 |
| 6-16 | C+ | 7.58 | 6.31 | 10.4 | 10.1 | 0.0 | -0.1 |
| 2016 | C+ | 7.68 | 6.40 | 10.5 | 10.2 | 0.2 | 0.0 |
| 2015 | C+ | 7.59 | 6.33 | 10.5 | 10.2 | 0.5 | -0.1 |
| 2014 | B- | 7.58 | 6.32 | 10.7 | 10.2 | 1.2 | 0.0 |
| 2013 | B | 7.71 | 6.42 | 11.5 | 10.2 | 2.2 | -0.5 |
| 2012 | B | 8.04 | 6.70 | 12.0 | 10.6 | 3.6 | 0.5 |

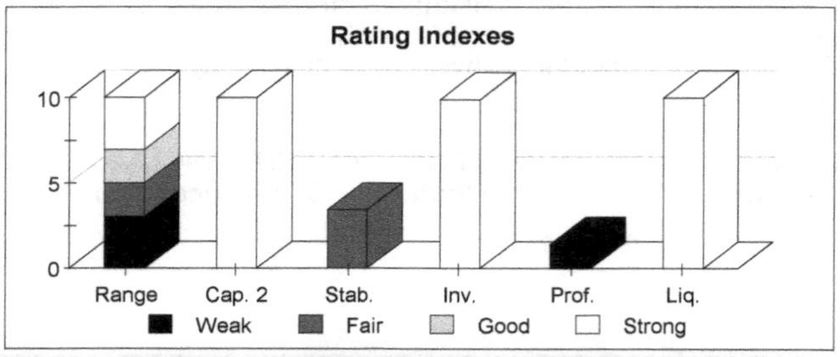


## AETNA HEALTH OF CALIFORNIA INC C+ Fair

**Major Rating Factors:** Good overall profitability index (5.5 on a scale of 0 to 10). Good capitalization index (6.6) based on fair current risk-adjusted capital (moderate loss scenario). Good liquidity (6.6) with sufficient resources (cash flows and marketable investments) to handle a spike in claims.
**Other Rating Factors:** Weak overall results on stability tests (2.8). Rating is significantly influenced by the good financial results of Aetna Inc.
**Principal Business:** Medicare (11%)
**Mem Phys: 16:** N/A **15:** N/A **16 MLR** 82.3% **/ 16 Admin Exp** N/A
**Enroll(000): Q3 17:** 279 **16:** 350 **15:** 368 **Med Exp PMPM:** $343
**Principal Investments ($000):** Cash and equiv ($53,436)
**Provider Compensation ($000):** None
**Total Member Encounters:** N/A
**Group Affiliation:** Aetna Inc
**Licensed in:** CA
**Address:** 2850 Shadelands Drive, Walnut Creek, CA 94598
**Phone:** (925) 948-4207 **Dom State:** CA **Commenced Bus:** October 1981

| Data Date | Rating | RACR #1 | RACR #2 | Total Assets ($mil) | Capital ($mil) | Net Premium ($mil) | Net Income ($mil) |
|---|---|---|---|---|---|---|---|
| 9-17 | C+ | 0.97 | 0.66 | 432.6 | 109.2 | 1,181.4 | 0.2 |
| 9-16 | C+ | 1.03 | 0.70 | 562.6 | 124.4 | 1,317.0 | 17.4 |
| 2016 | C+ | 1.16 | 0.79 | 483.7 | 135.8 | 1,775.7 | 35.0 |
| 2015 | C+ | 1.05 | 0.71 | 451.7 | 120.9 | 1,821.2 | 21.2 |
| 2014 | B | 1.12 | 0.74 | 448.5 | 128.6 | 1,958.3 | 36.1 |
| 2013 | B | 1.25 | 0.83 | 431.4 | 143.8 | 1,910.1 | 53.4 |
| 2012 | B | 1.53 | 1.02 | 422.8 | 177.7 | 1,893.8 | 80.3 |

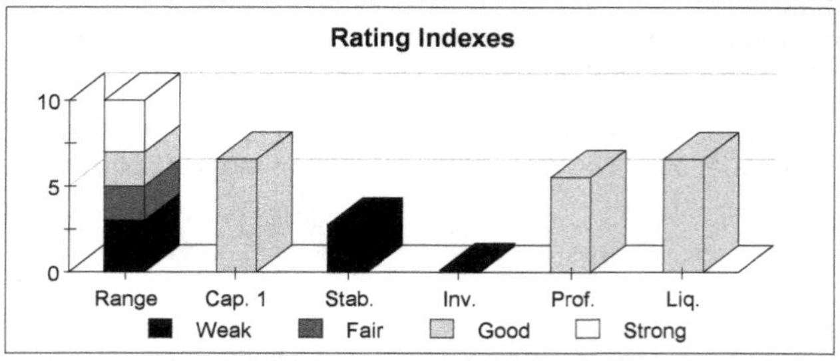

## AETNA HEALTH OF IOWA INC — C+ Fair

**Major Rating Factors:** Fair overall results on stability tests (3.3 on a scale of 0 to 10) based on a decline in the number of member physicians during 2017, a steep decline in premium revenue in 2016 and a significant 27% decrease in enrollment during the period. Rating is significantly influenced by the good financial results of Aetna Inc. Good liquidity (5.2) with sufficient resources (cash flows and marketable investments) to handle a spike in claims. Weak profitability index (2.7).
**Other Rating Factors:** Strong capitalization index (8.6) based on excellent current risk-adjusted capital (severe loss scenario). High quality investment portfolio (9.5).
**Principal Business:** Comp med (93%), Medicare (8%)
**Mem Phys: 16:** 26,786 **15:** 32,309 **16 MLR** 90.8% **/ 16 Admin Exp** N/A
**Enroll(000): Q3 17:** 40 **16:** 50 **15:** 69 **Med Exp PMPM:** $318
**Principal Investments:** Long-term bonds (98%), cash and equiv (2%)
**Provider Compensation ($000):** Contr fee ($202,674), FFS ($14,275), capitation ($10,622), bonus arrang ($433)
**Total Member Encounters:** Phys (292,080), non-phys (126,106)
**Group Affiliation:** Aetna Inc
**Licensed in:** IA
**Address:** 15950 WEST DODGE ROAD, OMAHA, NE 68118
**Phone:** (800) 471-0240 **Dom State:** IA **Commenced Bus:** January 1986

| Data Date | Rating | RACR #1 | RACR #2 | Total Assets ($mil) | Capital ($mil) | Net Premium ($mil) | Net Income ($mil) |
|---|---|---|---|---|---|---|---|
| 9-17 | C+ | 2.64 | 2.20 | 108.3 | 40.1 | 163.1 | 10.0 |
| 9-16 | B | 2.08 | 1.74 | 88.7 | 38.2 | 191.2 | -0.9 |
| 2016 | C+ | 1.92 | 1.60 | 87.5 | 29.4 | 240.4 | -7.3 |
| 2015 | B | 2.13 | 1.78 | 96.9 | 39.1 | 311.4 | -2.1 |
| 2014 | B | 2.16 | 1.80 | 70.9 | 25.6 | 198.5 | -3.6 |
| 2013 | B | 3.01 | 2.51 | 46.5 | 21.1 | 118.6 | 6.3 |
| 2012 | B | 3.88 | 3.24 | 43.1 | 24.3 | 110.6 | 9.4 |

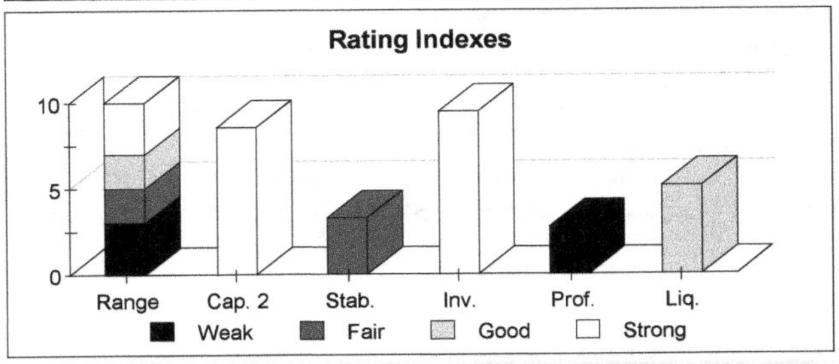


## AETNA HEALTH OF UTAH INC — C+ Fair

**Major Rating Factors:** Fair profitability index (3.4 on a scale of 0 to 10). Fair quality investment portfolio (4.8). Fair overall results on stability tests (3.3). Rating is significantly influenced by the good financial results of Aetna Inc.
**Other Rating Factors:** Good liquidity (6.3) with sufficient resources (cash flows and marketable investments) to handle a spike in claims. Strong capitalization index (9.7) based on excellent current risk-adjusted capital (severe loss scenario).
**Principal Business:** Comp med (43%), FEHB (38%), Medicare (19%)
**Mem Phys: 16:** 11,497 **15:** 10,088 **16 MLR** 88.5% **/ 16 Admin Exp** N/A
**Enroll(000): Q3 17:** 47 **16:** 57 **15:** 66 **Med Exp PMPM:** $333
**Principal Investments:** Long-term bonds (97%), cash and equiv (3%)
**Provider Compensation ($000):** Contr fee ($237,589), FFS ($16,925), capitation ($1,630)
**Total Member Encounters:** Phys (572,322), non-phys (343,772)
**Group Affiliation:** Aetna Inc
**Licensed in:** ID, NV, UT, WY
**Address:** 10150 S CENTENNIAL PARKWAY SUI, SANDY, UT 84070
**Phone:** (801) 933-3500 **Dom State:** UT **Commenced Bus:** March 1976

| Data Date | Rating | RACR #1 | RACR #2 | Total Assets ($mil) | Capital ($mil) | Net Premium ($mil) | Net Income ($mil) |
|---|---|---|---|---|---|---|---|
| 9-17 | C+ | 3.55 | 2.96 | 92.5 | 41.8 | 195.8 | 3.1 |
| 9-16 | B- | 3.04 | 2.54 | 121.7 | 50.3 | 227.1 | -5.9 |
| 2016 | B- | 4.51 | 3.76 | 113.8 | 54.4 | 293.5 | -2.7 |
| 2015 | B | 3.35 | 2.79 | 117.8 | 55.9 | 300.7 | 6.4 |
| 2014 | B | 1.93 | 1.61 | 124.2 | 50.6 | 477.8 | 5.0 |
| 2013 | B | 1.65 | 1.37 | 106.4 | 45.2 | 489.9 | 1.1 |
| 2012 | A- | 2.15 | 1.79 | 97.8 | 50.7 | 409.9 | 8.9 |

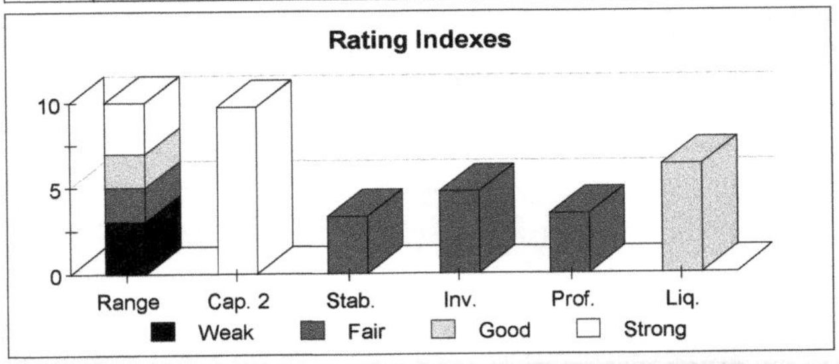


## AETNA HEALTHASSURANCE PA INC — D Weak

**Major Rating Factors:** Weak profitability index (0.9 on a scale of 0 to 10). Strong capitalization (7.7) based on excellent current risk-adjusted capital (severe loss scenario). High quality investment portfolio (9.9).
**Other Rating Factors:** Excellent liquidity (7.3) with ample operational cash flow and liquid investments.
**Principal Business:** Comp med (100%)
**Mem Phys: 16:** 53,569 **15:** N/A **16 MLR** 75.9% **/ 16 Admin Exp** N/A
**Enroll(000): Q3 17:** 51 **16:** 31 **15:** N/A **Med Exp PMPM:** $470
**Principal Investments:** Cash and equiv (100%)
**Provider Compensation ($000):** Contr fee ($44,088)
**Total Member Encounters:** Phys (374), non-phys (368)
**Group Affiliation:** Aetna Inc
**Licensed in:** PA
**Address:** 980 JOLLY Rd, BLUE BELL, PA 19422
**Phone:** (800) 788-6445 **Dom State:** PA **Commenced Bus:** November 2015

| Data Date | Rating | RACR #1 | RACR #2 | Total Assets ($mil) | Capital ($mil) | Net Premium ($mil) | Net Income ($mil) |
|---|---|---|---|---|---|---|---|
| 9-17 | D | 1.89 | 1.57 | 60.5 | 9.9 | 212.7 | -14.1 |
| 9-16 | N/A | N/A | N/A | 20.4 | 7.5 | 32.3 | 2.5 |
| 2016 | C+ | 1.90 | 1.58 | 26.9 | 9.9 | 71.6 | 4.9 |
| 2015 | N/A | N/A | N/A | 5.0 | 5.0 | N/A | N/A |
| 2014 | N/A | N/A | N/A | N/A | N/A | N/A | N/A |
| 2013 | N/A | N/A | N/A | N/A | N/A | N/A | N/A |
| 2012 | N/A | N/A | N/A | N/A | N/A | N/A | N/A |

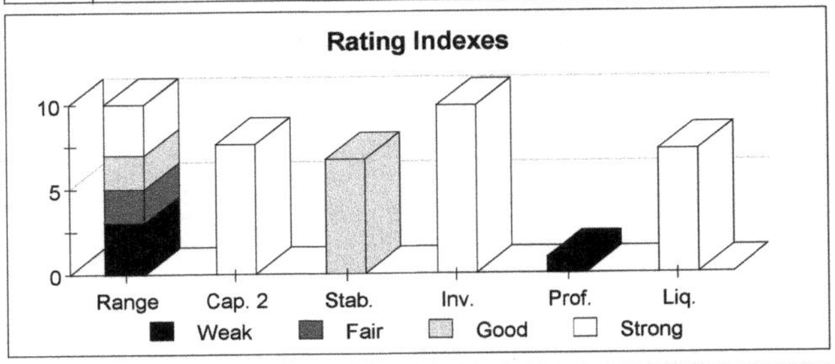

## AETNA LIFE INSURANCE COMPANY B Good

**Major Rating Factors:** Good overall capitalization (5.5 on a scale of 0 to 10) based on mixed results -- excessive policy leverage mitigated by excellent risk adjusted capital (severe loss scenario). Good quality investment portfolio (6.2) despite mixed results such as: minimal exposure to mortgages and large holdings of BBB rated bonds but small junk bond holdings. Good liquidity (6.3).
**Other Rating Factors:** Good overall results on stability tests (5.7) excellent operational trends, excellent risk adjusted capital for prior years and excellent risk diversification. Excellent profitability (7.5).
**Principal Business:** Group health insurance (60%), individual health insurance (36%), group life insurance (4%), and reinsurance (1%).
**Principal Investments:** NonCMO investment grade bonds (60%), CMOs and structured securities (13%), mortgages in good standing (10%), noninv. grade bonds (6%), and misc. investments (12%).
**Investments in Affiliates:** 4%
**Group Affiliation:** Aetna Inc
**Licensed in:** All states, the District of Columbia and Puerto Rico
**Commenced Business:** December 1850
**Address:** 151 FARMINGTON AVENUE, HARTFORD, CT 6156
**Phone:** (860) 273-0123 **Domicile State:** CT **NAIC Code:** 60054

| Data Date | Rating | RACR #1 | RACR #2 | Total Assets ($mil) | Capital ($mil) | Net Premium ($mil) | Net Income ($mil) |
|---|---|---|---|---|---|---|---|
| 9-17 | B | 1.53 | 1.14 | 22,767.9 | 3,979.7 | 14,388.4 | 1,565.0 |
| 9-16 | B | 1.51 | 1.11 | 23,083.6 | 3,678.3 | 13,875.4 | 1,107.4 |
| 2016 | B | 1.34 | 1.00 | 22,376.2 | 3,479.2 | 18,556.4 | 1,251.7 |
| 2015 | B | 1.57 | 1.15 | 21,214.1 | 3,770.8 | 17,155.4 | 1,211.9 |
| 2014 | B+ | 1.72 | 1.25 | 22,795.4 | 3,871.9 | 15,544.4 | 1,321.7 |
| 2013 | B+ | 1.76 | 1.25 | 21,793.1 | 3,199.9 | 12,354.0 | 911.1 |
| 2012 | B+ | 1.89 | 1.33 | 21,175.5 | 3,332.3 | 12,689.8 | 1,020.0 |

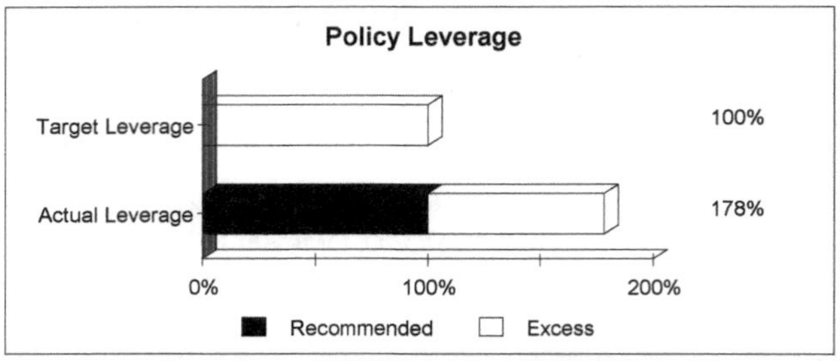


## AIDS HEALTHCARE FOUNDATION MCO OF FL E- Very Weak

**Major Rating Factors:** Weak profitability index (0.9 on a scale of 0 to 10). Poor capitalization (0.1) based on weak current risk-adjusted capital (moderate loss scenario). Good liquidity (6.9) with sufficient resources (cash flows and marketable investments) to handle a spike in claims.
**Other Rating Factors:** High quality investment portfolio (9.8).
**Principal Business:** Medicare (61%), Medicaid (39%)
**Mem Phys: 16:** N/A **15:** N/A **16 MLR** 99.0% **/ 16 Admin Exp** N/A
**Enroll(000): Q3 17:** 4 **16:** 3 **15:** 3 **Med Exp PMPM:** $3,101
**Principal Investments:** Cash and equiv (94%), real estate (6%)
**Provider Compensation ($000):** FFS ($114,468)
**Total Member Encounters:** Phys (16,029), non-phys (11,112)
**Group Affiliation:** AIDS Healthcare Foundation
**Licensed in:** FL
**Address:** 110 SE 6th St Ste 1960, Ft. Lauderdale, FL 33301
**Phone:** (323) 860-5200 **Dom State:** FL **Commenced Bus:** June 2007

| Data Date | Rating | RACR #1 | RACR #2 | Total Assets ($mil) | Capital ($mil) | Net Premium ($mil) | Net Income ($mil) |
|---|---|---|---|---|---|---|---|
| 9-17 | E- | 0.31 | 0.26 | 56.5 | 5.2 | 97.6 | -3.8 |
| 9-16 | E | 0.16 | 0.13 | 23.0 | 2.6 | 86.8 | -5.4 |
| 2016 | E+ | 0.41 | 0.34 | 37.9 | 7.1 | 121.8 | -13.9 |
| 2015 | E | 0.17 | 0.14 | 18.9 | 2.8 | 111.2 | -11.3 |
| 2014 | D- | 0.49 | 0.41 | 20.1 | 6.2 | 87.9 | -5.6 |
| 2013 | N/A | N/A | N/A | 9.5 | 2.3 | 51.8 | -1.9 |
| 2012 | N/A | N/A | N/A | 9.9 | 4.2 | 37.8 | 0.9 |

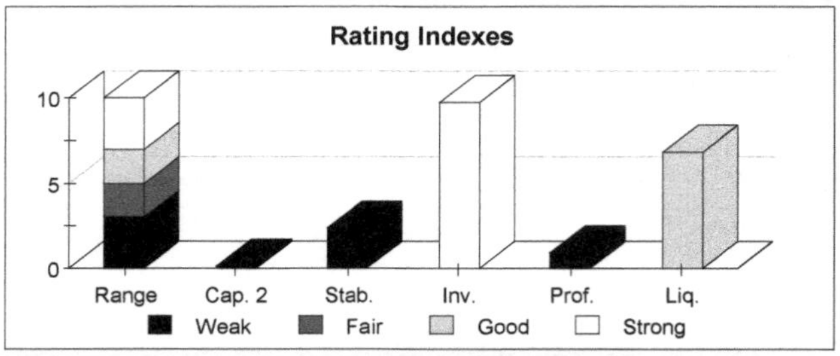


## ALIGNMENT HEALTH PLAN E Very Weak

**Major Rating Factors:** Weak profitability index (1.1 on a scale of 0 to 10). Poor capitalization index (0.0) based on weak current risk-adjusted capital (severe loss scenario). Weak liquidity (0.0) as a spike in claims may stretch capacity.
**Other Rating Factors:** Fair overall results on stability tests (4.1) based on fair risk diversification due to the company's size.
**Principal Business:** Medicare (100%)
**Mem Phys: 16:** N/A **15:** N/A **16 MLR** 89.6% **/ 16 Admin Exp** N/A
**Enroll(000): Q3 17:** 34 **16:** 21 **15:** 20 **Med Exp PMPM:** $861
**Principal Investments ($000):** Cash and equiv ($10,292)
**Provider Compensation ($000):** None
**Total Member Encounters:** N/A
**Group Affiliation:** Alignment Healthcare USA LLC
**Licensed in:** CA
**Address:** 1100 W Town & Country Rd #1600, Orange, CA 92868
**Phone:** (657) 218-7731 **Dom State:** CA **Commenced Bus:** May 2004

| Data Date | Rating | RACR #1 | RACR #2 | Total Assets ($mil) | Capital ($mil) | Net Premium ($mil) | Net Income ($mil) |
|---|---|---|---|---|---|---|---|
| 9-17 | E | 0.15 | 0.09 | 100.4 | 14.4 | 268.1 | -39.6 |
| 9-16 | E | 0.22 | 0.14 | 63.1 | 11.1 | 168.3 | -18.6 |
| 2016 | E | N/A | N/A | 46.4 | 10.0 | 227.8 | -24.6 |
| 2015 | E | 0.24 | 0.15 | 52.2 | 11.6 | 205.6 | -32.2 |
| 2014 | E | 0.21 | 0.13 | 36.6 | 9.6 | 133.8 | -18.0 |
| 2013 | E | N/A | N/A | 28.6 | 1.7 | 161.2 | -3.8 |
| 2012 | D- | 0.12 | 0.07 | 29.3 | 6.0 | 145.7 | 1.9 |

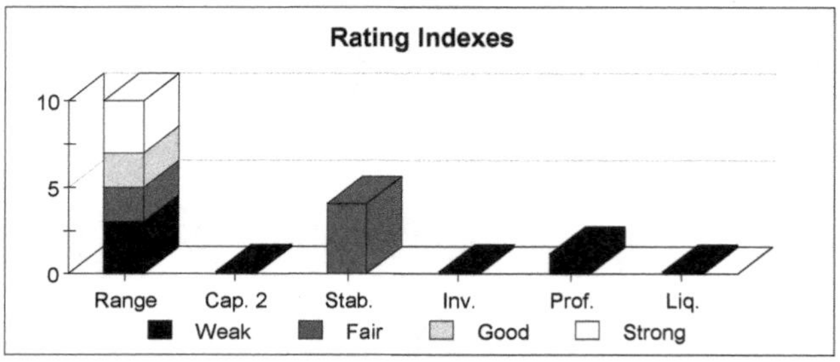

## ALL SAVERS INSURANCE COMPANY — C — Fair

**Major Rating Factors:** Good liquidity (6.3 on a scale of 0 to 10) with sufficient resources to handle a spike in claims. Weak profitability (2.0). Excellent expense controls. Weak overall results on stability tests (2.5) including weak results on operational trends, negative cash flow from operations for 2016.
**Other Rating Factors:** Strong capitalization (10.0) based on excellent risk adjusted capital (severe loss scenario). High quality investment portfolio (8.1).
**Principal Business:** Individual health insurance (73%) and group health insurance (27%).
**Principal Investments:** NonCMO investment grade bonds (72%), CMOs and structured securities (25%), and cash (1%).
**Investments in Affiliates:** None
**Group Affiliation:** UnitedHealth Group Inc
**Licensed in:** All states except CA, MA, MN, NJ, NY, PR
**Commenced Business:** February 1986
**Address:** 7440 WOODLAND DRIVE, INDIANAPOLIS, IN 46278-1719
**Phone:** (317) 290-8100 **Domicile State:** IN **NAIC Code:** 82406

| Data Date | Rating | RACR #1 | RACR #2 | Total Assets ($mil) | Capital ($mil) | Net Premium ($mil) | Net Income ($mil) |
|---|---|---|---|---|---|---|---|
| 9-17 | C | 11.79 | 8.41 | 1,368.8 | 1,240.2 | 382.0 | 183.9 |
| 9-16 | C | 5.92 | 4.62 | 1,607.2 | 1,049.6 | 1,235.7 | -110.9 |
| 2016 | C | 5.31 | 3.99 | 1,551.5 | 1,054.2 | 1,603.1 | -102.2 |
| 2015 | C | 5.60 | 4.41 | 1,067.5 | 600.8 | 891.4 | -339.5 |
| 2014 | B- | 1.51 | 1.25 | 61.6 | 31.1 | 111.9 | 5.0 |
| 2013 | B- | 1.19 | 0.99 | 29.6 | 16.4 | 76.3 | 1.5 |
| 2012 | B- | 1.31 | 1.09 | 18.9 | 11.1 | 46.8 | 2.0 |

**Adverse Trends in Operations**

Change in asset mix during 2016 (17%)
Change in premium mix from 2014 to 2015 (15%)

## ALLCARE HEALTH PLAN INC — E — Very Weak

**Major Rating Factors:** Weak profitability index (2.1 on a scale of 0 to 10). Good capitalization (6.2) based on good current risk-adjusted capital (severe loss scenario). High quality investment portfolio (7.6).
**Other Rating Factors:** Excellent liquidity (7.0) with sufficient resources (cash flows and marketable investments) to handle a spike in claims.
**Principal Business:** Medicare (65%), comp med (35%)
**Mem Phys: 16:** 1,488 **15:** 1,113 **16 MLR** 93.7% **/ 16 Admin Exp** N/A
**Enroll(000): Q3 17:** 4 **16:** 4 **15:** 4 **Med Exp PMPM:** $668
**Principal Investments:** Cash and equiv (75%), long-term bonds (25%)
**Provider Compensation ($000):** Contr fee ($28,183), FFS ($2,616)
**Total Member Encounters:** Phys (57,193), non-phys (17,787)
**Group Affiliation:** Mid Rogue AllCare Hlth Assurance Inc
**Licensed in:** OR
**Address:** 740 SE 7th St, Grants Pass, OR 97526-1635
**Phone:** (541) 471-4106 **Dom State:** OR **Commenced Bus:** January 2005

| Data Date | Rating | RACR #1 | RACR #2 | Total Assets ($mil) | Capital ($mil) | Net Premium ($mil) | Net Income ($mil) |
|---|---|---|---|---|---|---|---|
| 9-17 | E | 1.11 | 0.93 | 14.7 | 7.6 | 26.7 | 1.3 |
| 9-16 | E | 1.01 | 0.84 | 12.3 | 6.4 | 24.9 | -0.7 |
| 2016 | E | 0.87 | 0.73 | 11.3 | 6.4 | 33.5 | -0.8 |
| 2015 | E | 1.18 | 0.98 | 10.9 | 7.1 | 31.4 | 0.0 |
| 2014 | E | 0.67 | 0.56 | 11.8 | 6.5 | 41.2 | -2.6 |
| 2013 | E | 0.85 | 0.71 | 13.1 | 7.4 | 43.5 | -1.7 |
| 2012 | D- | 1.21 | 1.01 | 14.6 | 8.4 | 41.3 | 0.1 |

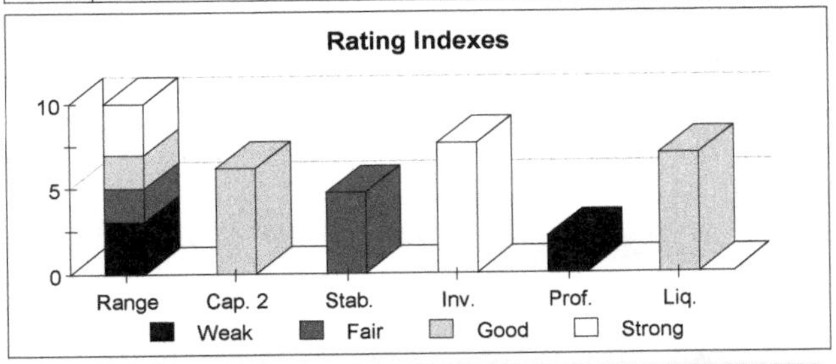


## ALLEGIAN INS CO — C — Fair

**Major Rating Factors:** Weak profitability index (2.0 on a scale of 0 to 10). Good liquidity (6.9) with sufficient resources (cash flows and marketable investments) to handle a spike in claims. Strong capitalization (7.9) based on excellent current risk-adjusted capital (severe loss scenario).
**Other Rating Factors:** High quality investment portfolio (9.9).
**Principal Business:** Comp med (78%), Medicare (22%)
**Mem Phys: 16:** 5,397 **15:** 5,397 **16 MLR** 94.5% **/ 16 Admin Exp** N/A
**Enroll(000): Q2 17:** 0 **16:** 19 **15:** 14 **Med Exp PMPM:** $314
**Principal Investments:** Cash and equiv (100%)
**Provider Compensation ($000):** Contr fee ($67,115), capitation ($7,944), FFS ($3,494)
**Total Member Encounters:** Phys (80,587), non-phys (76,067)
**Group Affiliation:** Tenet Healthcare Corp
**Licensed in:** TX
**Address:** 4801 NW Loop #410 Ste 380, San Antonio, TX 78229
**Phone:** (602) 200-6925 **Dom State:** TX **Commenced Bus:** March 2006

| Data Date | Rating | RACR #1 | RACR #2 | Total Assets ($mil) | Capital ($mil) | Net Premium ($mil) | Net Income ($mil) |
|---|---|---|---|---|---|---|---|
| 6-17 | C | 2.04 | 1.70 | 45.1 | 21.3 | 25.0 | 1.4 |
| 6-16 | D+ | 3.13 | 2.61 | 38.3 | 18.9 | 43.5 | -1.4 |
| 2016 | D+ | 1.63 | 1.36 | 34.4 | 16.1 | 89.3 | -3.9 |
| 2015 | D+ | 3.40 | 2.83 | 29.7 | 20.4 | 55.5 | 2.0 |
| 2014 | D+ | 2.72 | 2.27 | 26.1 | 18.3 | 57.0 | 1.4 |
| 2013 | C | 2.48 | 2.07 | 17.5 | 6.4 | 42.2 | -2.5 |
| 2012 | C | 3.51 | 2.92 | 21.7 | 15.4 | 35.6 | 2.6 |

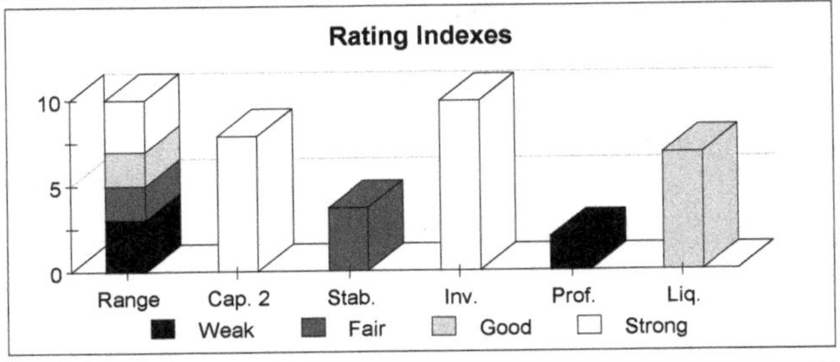

## ALLEGIANCE L&H INS CO — C — Fair

**Major Rating Factors:** Fair profitability index (4.6 on a scale of 0 to 10). Strong capitalization (10.0) based on excellent current risk-adjusted capital (severe loss scenario). High quality investment portfolio (9.2).
**Other Rating Factors:** Excellent liquidity (7.5) with ample operational cash flow and liquid investments.
**Principal Business:** Comp med (96%), dental (3%)
**Mem Phys: 16:** N/A **15:** N/A **16 MLR** 70.6% **/ 16 Admin Exp** N/A
**Enroll(000): Q3 17:** 3 **16:** 2 **15:** 4 **Med Exp PMPM:** $322
**Principal Investments:** Long-term bonds (65%), cash and equiv (35%)
**Provider Compensation ($000):** FFS ($11,595)
**Total Member Encounters:** Phys (12,873), non-phys (34,365)
**Group Affiliation:** Cigna Corporation
**Licensed in:** MT
**Address:** 2806 S GARFIELD St, MISSOULA, MT 59801
**Phone:** (406) 721-2222 **Dom State:** MT **Commenced Bus:** November 2006

| Data Date | Rating | RACR #1 | RACR #2 | Total Assets ($mil) | Capital ($mil) | Net Premium ($mil) | Net Income ($mil) |
|---|---|---|---|---|---|---|---|
| 9-17 | C | 11.31 | 9.42 | 14.4 | 12.2 | 9.7 | 0.8 |
| 9-16 | C | 4.70 | 3.92 | 14.0 | 11.0 | 10.5 | 1.5 |
| 2016 | C | 10.64 | 8.87 | 13.7 | 11.4 | 13.6 | 1.9 |
| 2015 | C | 4.13 | 3.44 | 12.5 | 9.5 | 22.9 | 1.3 |
| 2014 | C | 2.64 | 2.20 | 15.2 | 8.7 | 36.8 | 0.2 |
| 2013 | C | 1.51 | 1.26 | 19.3 | 7.4 | 53.0 | -3.0 |
| 2012 | C | 1.53 | 1.28 | 23.1 | 10.4 | 79.4 | -2.2 |

Rating Indexes

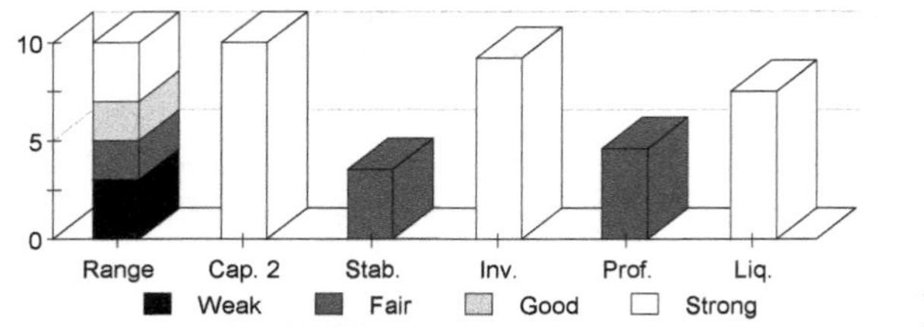


## ALLIANCE HEALTH & LIFE INS CO — C — Fair

**Major Rating Factors:** Fair capitalization (4.5 on a scale of 0 to 10) based on fair current risk-adjusted capital (moderate loss scenario). Weak profitability index (0.9). High quality investment portfolio (9.9).
**Other Rating Factors:** Excellent liquidity (6.9) with sufficient resources (cash flows and marketable investments) to handle a spike in claims.
**Principal Business:** Comp med (80%), Medicare (11%), other (9%)
**Mem Phys: 16:** 11,821 **15:** 11,486 **16 MLR** 79.4% **/ 16 Admin Exp** N/A
**Enroll(000): Q3 17:** 61 **16:** 73 **15:** 54 **Med Exp PMPM:** $368
**Principal Investments:** Cash and equiv (83%), long-term bonds (14%), other (3%)
**Provider Compensation ($000):** Contr fee ($274,985), FFS ($22,899), other ($20)
**Total Member Encounters:** Phys (266,827), non-phys (37,847)
**Group Affiliation:** Henry Ford Health System
**Licensed in:** MI
**Address:** 2850 West Grand Blvd, Detroit, MI 48202
**Phone:** (313) 872-8100 **Dom State:** MI **Commenced Bus:** September 1996

| Data Date | Rating | RACR #1 | RACR #2 | Total Assets ($mil) | Capital ($mil) | Net Premium ($mil) | Net Income ($mil) |
|---|---|---|---|---|---|---|---|
| 9-17 | C | 0.85 | 0.71 | 109.7 | 24.8 | 263.5 | -11.5 |
| 9-16 | C | 2.22 | 1.85 | 126.2 | 45.5 | 304.2 | -9.0 |
| 2016 | C | 1.19 | 0.99 | 111.2 | 36.2 | 399.0 | -17.0 |
| 2015 | C+ | 1.26 | 1.05 | 86.0 | 24.4 | 293.2 | -2.1 |
| 2014 | B | 1.60 | 1.33 | 70.1 | 26.0 | 235.6 | -2.0 |
| 2013 | A- | 1.81 | 1.50 | 64.2 | 27.9 | 209.3 | 0.6 |
| 2012 | B+ | 2.08 | 1.73 | 62.8 | 29.2 | 181.2 | 1.6 |

Rating Indexes

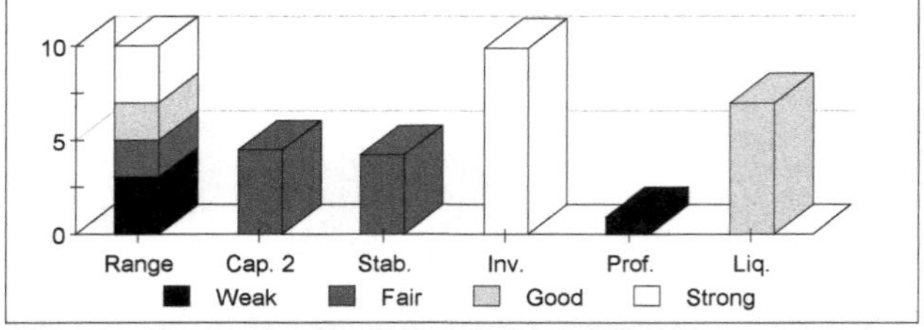


## ALLIANT HEALTH PLANS INC — D- — Weak

**Major Rating Factors:** Weak profitability index (2.2 on a scale of 0 to 10). Fair overall results on stability tests (4.2) based on a significant 21% decrease in enrollment during the period. Strong capitalization index (7.1) based on excellent current risk-adjusted capital (severe loss scenario).
**Other Rating Factors:** High quality investment portfolio (9.9). Excellent liquidity (6.9) with sufficient resources (cash flows and marketable investments) to handle a spike in claims.
**Principal Business:** Comp med (100%)
**Mem Phys: 16:** 16,085 **15:** N/A **16 MLR** 88.5% **/ 16 Admin Exp** N/A
**Enroll(000): Q3 17:** 35 **16:** 19 **15:** 24 **Med Exp PMPM:** $403
**Principal Investments:** Cash and equiv (97%), real estate (3%), nonaffiliate common stock (1%)
**Provider Compensation ($000):** Contr fee ($104,263)
**Total Member Encounters:** Phys (43,575), non-phys (8,235)
**Group Affiliation:** Health One Alliance LLC
**Licensed in:** GA
**Address:** 1503 N Tibbs Road, Dalton, GA 30720
**Phone:** (706) 629-8848 **Dom State:** GA **Commenced Bus:** December 1998

| Data Date | Rating | RACR #1 | RACR #2 | Total Assets ($mil) | Capital ($mil) | Net Premium ($mil) | Net Income ($mil) |
|---|---|---|---|---|---|---|---|
| 9-17 | D- | 1.42 | 1.19 | 58.8 | 17.3 | 190.8 | 5.6 |
| 9-16 | D- | 0.94 | 0.78 | 28.3 | 11.5 | 86.4 | -5.0 |
| 2016 | D- | 1.08 | 0.90 | 33.4 | 12.8 | 114.3 | -6.2 |
| 2015 | C | 1.19 | 0.99 | 36.0 | 15.2 | 129.8 | -1.7 |
| 2014 | C | 1.25 | 1.04 | 35.1 | 16.9 | 118.8 | -0.4 |
| 2013 | C+ | 1.52 | 1.27 | 29.1 | 16.5 | 94.1 | -4.3 |
| 2012 | B | 2.19 | 1.82 | 31.0 | 19.3 | 79.5 | 0.5 |

Rating Indexes

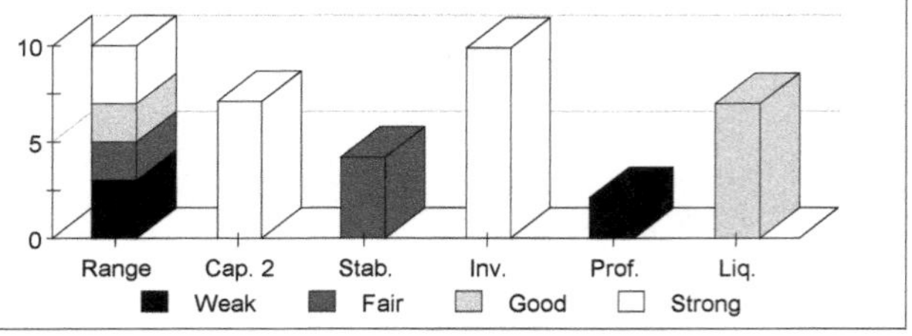

## ALOHACARE C+ Fair

**Major Rating Factors:** Good overall results on stability tests (5.2 on a scale of 0 to 10). Weak profitability index (2.5). Strong capitalization index (8.1) based on excellent current risk-adjusted capital (severe loss scenario).
**Other Rating Factors:** High quality investment portfolio (9.4). Excellent liquidity (7.2) with ample operational cash flow and liquid investments.
**Principal Business:** Medicaid (96%), Medicare (4%)
**Mem Phys: 16:** 6,636 **15:** 6,144 **16 MLR** 87.7% **/ 16 Admin Exp** N/A
**Enroll(000): Q3 17:** 70 **16:** 72 **15:** 68 **Med Exp PMPM:** $332
**Principal Investments:** Cash and equiv (67%), long-term bonds (27%), other (7%)
**Provider Compensation ($000):** Contr fee ($187,642), FFS ($68,117), capitation ($5,130)
**Total Member Encounters:** Phys (393,861), non-phys (220,124)
**Group Affiliation:** AlohaCare
**Licensed in:** HI
**Address:** 1357 Kapiolani Blvd Suite 1250, Honolulu, HI 96814
**Phone:** (808) 973-1650 **Dom State:** HI **Commenced Bus:** August 1994

| Data Date | Rating | RACR #1 | RACR #2 | Total Assets ($mil) | Capital ($mil) | Net Premium ($mil) | Net Income ($mil) |
|---|---|---|---|---|---|---|---|
| 9-17 | C+ | 2.26 | 1.88 | 149.8 | 66.9 | 277.4 | -0.3 |
| 9-16 | C+ | N/A | N/A | 123.5 | 48.7 | 233.8 | -2.9 |
| 2016 | C+ | 2.27 | 1.89 | 141.4 | 67.2 | 317.3 | 15.6 |
| 2015 | C+ | N/A | N/A | 113.8 | 51.6 | 271.0 | -19.2 |
| 2014 | B | 3.00 | 2.50 | 114.8 | 70.8 | 237.6 | -5.3 |
| 2013 | N/A | N/A | N/A | 139.2 | 76.3 | 225.3 | -9.4 |
| 2012 | A+ | 3.92 | 3.27 | 134.2 | 85.6 | 232.7 | 8.7 |

Rating Indexes

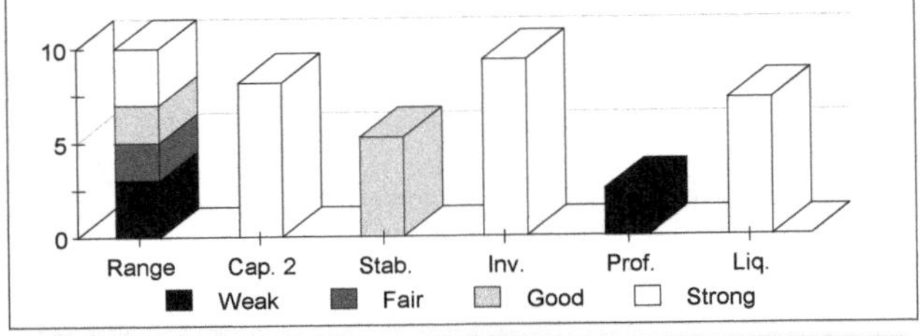


## ALPHACARE OF NEW YORK INC C- Fair

**Major Rating Factors:** Weak profitability index (0.6 on a scale of 0 to 10). Strong capitalization (7.7) based on excellent current risk-adjusted capital (severe loss scenario). High quality investment portfolio (9.9).
**Other Rating Factors:** Excellent liquidity (7.1) with ample operational cash flow and liquid investments.
**Principal Business:** Medicaid (91%), Medicare (7%), other (2%)
**Mem Phys: 16:** 10,159 **15:** 8,152 **16 MLR** 80.3% **/ 16 Admin Exp** N/A
**Enroll(000): Q3 17:** 4 **16:** 4 **15:** 3 **Med Exp PMPM:** $2,380
**Principal Investments:** Cash and equiv (89%), long-term bonds (11%)
**Provider Compensation ($000):** Contr fee ($96,440), capitation ($14,028)
**Total Member Encounters:** Phys (7,039), non-phys (5,584)
**Group Affiliation:** Magellan Health Inc
**Licensed in:** NY
**Address:** 335 Adams St 26th Fl, Brooklyn, NY 11201-9816
**Phone:** (212) 466-6000 **Dom State:** NY **Commenced Bus:** July 2013

| Data Date | Rating | RACR #1 | RACR #2 | Total Assets ($mil) | Capital ($mil) | Net Premium ($mil) | Net Income ($mil) |
|---|---|---|---|---|---|---|---|
| 9-17 | C- | 1.88 | 1.57 | 36.8 | 18.7 | 132.6 | -0.3 |
| 9-16 | C- | 2.02 | 1.68 | 44.8 | 15.0 | 99.8 | -7.7 |
| 2016 | C- | 1.85 | 1.54 | 47.0 | 18.6 | 138.5 | -4.0 |
| 2015 | C- | 2.01 | 1.67 | 48.2 | 15.0 | 102.2 | -10.9 |
| 2014 | D+ | 4.93 | 4.11 | 41.8 | 23.7 | 39.9 | -16.3 |
| 2013 | N/A | N/A | N/A | 14.2 | 10.0 | 3.3 | N/A |
| 2012 | N/A | N/A | N/A | N/A | N/A | N/A | N/A |

Rating Indexes

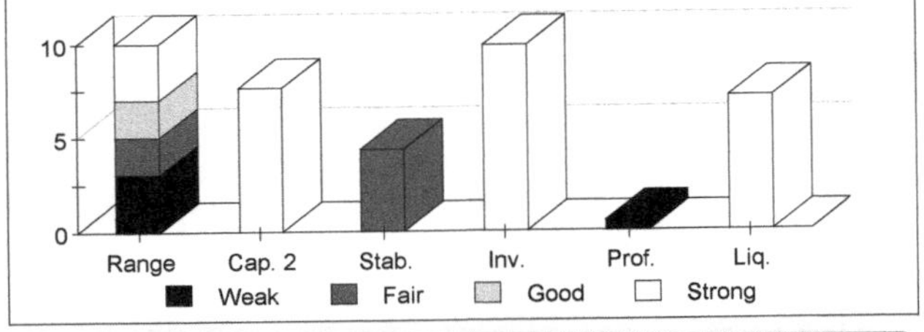


## AMALGAMATED LIFE INSURANCE COMPANY * A- Excellent

**Major Rating Factors:** Good liquidity (6.3 on a scale of 0 to 10) with sufficient resources to handle a spike in claims. Strong capitalization (10.0) based on excellent risk adjusted capital (severe loss scenario). Furthermore, this high level of risk adjusted capital has been consistently maintained over the last five years. High quality investment portfolio (8.2).
**Other Rating Factors:** Excellent profitability (7.8). Excellent overall results on stability tests (7.0) excellent operational trends and excellent risk diversification.
**Principal Business:** Reinsurance (41%), group life insurance (33%), group health insurance (24%), and individual health insurance (2%).
**Principal Investments:** NonCMO investment grade bonds (75%) and CMOs and structured securities (28%).
**Investments in Affiliates:** None
**Group Affiliation:** National Retirement Fund
**Licensed in:** All states except PR
**Commenced Business:** February 1944
**Address:** 333 WESTCHESTER AVENUE, WHITE PLAINS, NY 10604
**Phone:** (914) 367-5000 **Domicile State:** NY **NAIC Code:** 60216

| Data Date | Rating | RACR #1 | RACR #2 | Total Assets ($mil) | Capital ($mil) | Net Premium ($mil) | Net Income ($mil) |
|---|---|---|---|---|---|---|---|
| 9-17 | A- | 5.10 | 3.93 | 124.9 | 61.4 | 62.8 | 5.1 |
| 9-16 | A- | 4.26 | 3.37 | 124.1 | 56.1 | 59.1 | 2.0 |
| 2016 | A- | 4.85 | 3.74 | 122.9 | 57.8 | 80.7 | 3.5 |
| 2015 | A- | 4.12 | 3.27 | 119.9 | 55.6 | 75.6 | 3.0 |
| 2014 | A- | 3.82 | 3.03 | 111.8 | 51.0 | 72.4 | 3.5 |
| 2013 | A- | 3.45 | 2.72 | 99.9 | 47.2 | 64.3 | 3.5 |
| 2012 | A- | 3.31 | 2.64 | 88.6 | 42.2 | 56.3 | 3.7 |

Rating Indexes

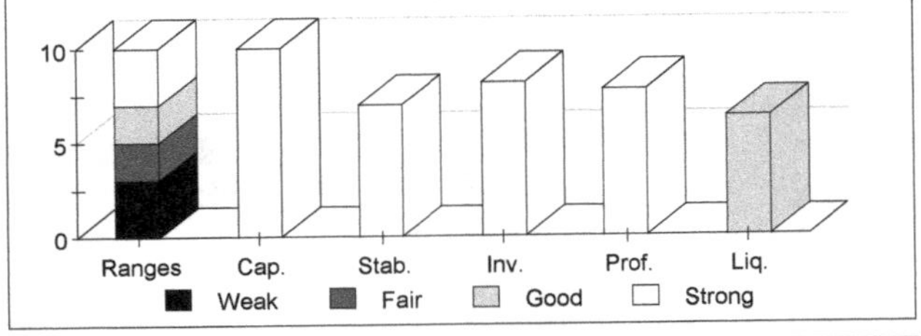



* Denotes a Weiss Ratings Recommended Company

## AMBETTER OF MAGNOLIA INC C+ Fair

**Major Rating Factors:** Good liquidity (6.8 on a scale of 0 to 10) with sufficient resources (cash flows and marketable investments) to handle a spike in claims. Excellent profitability (9.4). Strong capitalization (10.0) based on excellent current risk-adjusted capital (severe loss scenario).
**Other Rating Factors:** High quality investment portfolio (9.4).
**Principal Business:** Comp med (100%)
**Mem Phys: 16:** 7,695 **15:** 13,958 **16 MLR** 81.7% **/ 16 Admin Exp** N/A
**Enroll(000): Q3 17:** 52 **16:** 28 **15:** 15 **Med Exp PMPM:** $263
**Principal Investments:** Cash and equiv (57%), long-term bonds (43%)
**Provider Compensation ($000):** Contr fee ($88,151), capitation ($4,095), salary ($750)
**Total Member Encounters:** Phys (71,415), non-phys (78,844)
**Group Affiliation:** Centene Corporation
**Licensed in:** MS
**Address:** 111 East Capitol St Ste 500, Jackson, MS 39201
**Phone:** (314) 725-4477 **Dom State:** MS **Commenced Bus:** May 2015

| Data Date | Rating | RACR #1 | RACR #2 | Total Assets ($mil) | Capital ($mil) | Net Premium ($mil) | Net Income ($mil) |
|---|---|---|---|---|---|---|---|
| 9-17 | C+ | 3.80 | 3.17 | 77.0 | 26.1 | 225.0 | 17.8 |
| 9-16 | U | 14.48 | 12.07 | 49.3 | 7.1 | 100.5 | 3.3 |
| 2016 | C- | 1.35 | 1.12 | 49.7 | 8.4 | 126.1 | 0.1 |
| 2015 | U | 8.82 | 7.35 | 40.3 | 4.3 | 35.7 | 0.9 |
| 2014 | N/A | N/A | N/A | N/A | N/A | N/A | N/A |
| 2013 | N/A | N/A | N/A | N/A | N/A | N/A | N/A |
| 2012 | N/A | N/A | N/A | N/A | N/A | N/A | N/A |

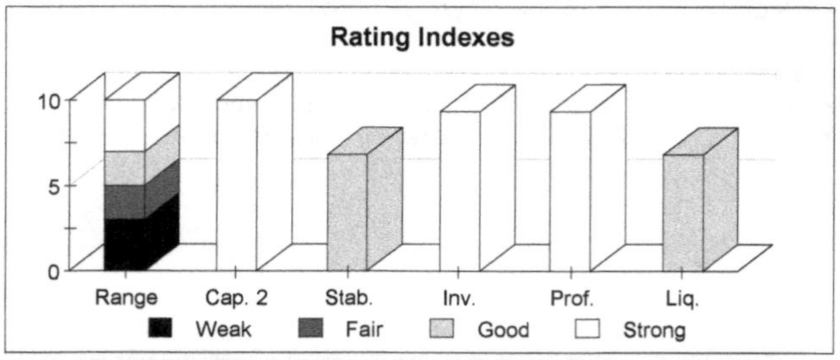


## AMBETTER OF PEACH STATE INC C+ Fair

**Major Rating Factors:** Excellent profitability (9.4 on a scale of 0 to 10). Strong capitalization (10.0) based on excellent current risk-adjusted capital (severe loss scenario). High quality investment portfolio (9.9).
**Other Rating Factors:** Excellent liquidity (7.7) with ample operational cash flow and liquid investments.
**Principal Business:** Comp med (100%)
**Mem Phys: 16:** 6,064 **15:** N/A **16 MLR** 66.9% **/ 16 Admin Exp** N/A
**Enroll(000): Q3 17:** 123 **16:** 64 **15:** N/A **Med Exp PMPM:** $145
**Principal Investments:** Cash and equiv (65%), long-term bonds (35%)
**Provider Compensation ($000):** Contr fee ($68,116), bonus arrang ($29,937), capitation ($6,381), salary ($988)
**Total Member Encounters:** Phys (329,880), non-phys (251,713)
**Group Affiliation:** Centene Corporation
**Licensed in:** GA
**Address:** 1100 Circle 75 Pkwy Ste 1100, Atlanta, GA 30339
**Phone:** (314) 725-4477 **Dom State:** GA **Commenced Bus:** April 2015

| Data Date | Rating | RACR #1 | RACR #2 | Total Assets ($mil) | Capital ($mil) | Net Premium ($mil) | Net Income ($mil) |
|---|---|---|---|---|---|---|---|
| 9-17 | C+ | 5.84 | 4.87 | 199.9 | 36.0 | 369.6 | 20.2 |
| 9-16 | N/A | N/A | N/A | 139.5 | 12.5 | 147.0 | 8.1 |
| 2016 | C- | 2.91 | 2.42 | 165.8 | 17.9 | 197.2 | 13.6 |
| 2015 | N/A | N/A | N/A | 6.3 | 3.0 | N/A | -0.2 |
| 2014 | N/A | N/A | N/A | N/A | N/A | N/A | N/A |
| 2013 | N/A | N/A | N/A | N/A | N/A | N/A | N/A |
| 2012 | N/A | N/A | N/A | N/A | N/A | N/A | N/A |

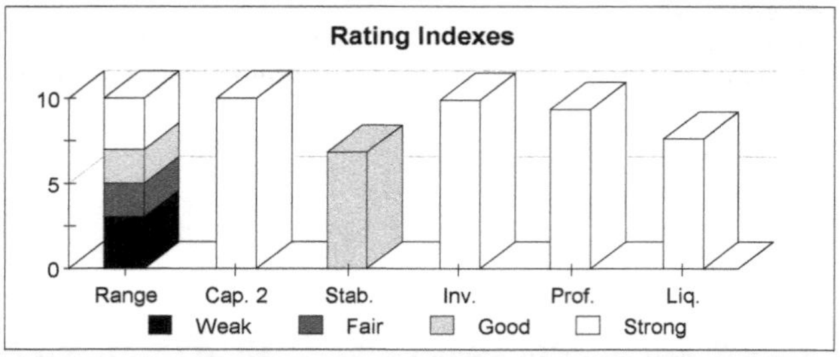


## AMERICAN BANKERS LIFE ASSURANCE COMPANY OF FLORID/ C+ Fair

**Major Rating Factors:** Fair overall results on stability tests (4.4 on a scale of 0 to 10) including negative cash flow from operations for 2016. Good quality investment portfolio (6.5) despite mixed results such as: minimal exposure to mortgages and substantial holdings of BBB bonds but minimal holdings in junk bonds. Good liquidity (6.9).
**Other Rating Factors:** Strong capitalization (10.0) based on excellent risk adjusted capital (severe loss scenario). Excellent profitability (7.3).
**Principal Business:** Credit life insurance (45%), credit health insurance (32%), reinsurance (14%), group health insurance (4%), and individual life insurance (3%).
**Principal Investments:** NonCMO investment grade bonds (58%), real estate (14%), CMOs and structured securities (11%), cash (7%), and misc. investments (10%).
**Investments in Affiliates:** None
**Group Affiliation:** Assurant Inc
**Licensed in:** All states except NY
**Commenced Business:** April 1952
**Address:** 11222 QUAIL ROOST DRIVE, MIAMI, FL 33157-6596
**Phone:** (305) 253-2244 **Domicile State:** FL **NAIC Code:** 60275

| Data Date | Rating | RACR #1 | RACR #2 | Total Assets ($mil) | Capital ($mil) | Net Premium ($mil) | Net Income ($mil) |
|---|---|---|---|---|---|---|---|
| 9-17 | C+ | 6.56 | 3.47 | 368.2 | 66.9 | 56.5 | 14.4 |
| 9-16 | C+ | 6.64 | 3.29 | 381.6 | 50.6 | 27.1 | 14.1 |
| 2016 | C+ | 7.11 | 3.50 | 378.7 | 54.7 | 35.7 | 21.5 |
| 2015 | C+ | 7.24 | 3.58 | 406.2 | 56.7 | 30.6 | 21.2 |
| 2014 | B | 5.37 | 2.87 | 489.6 | 55.9 | 67.9 | 18.6 |
| 2013 | B | 4.07 | 2.32 | 521.6 | 50.4 | 114.9 | 11.0 |
| 2012 | B | 3.76 | 2.25 | 553.8 | 67.3 | 127.7 | 13.4 |

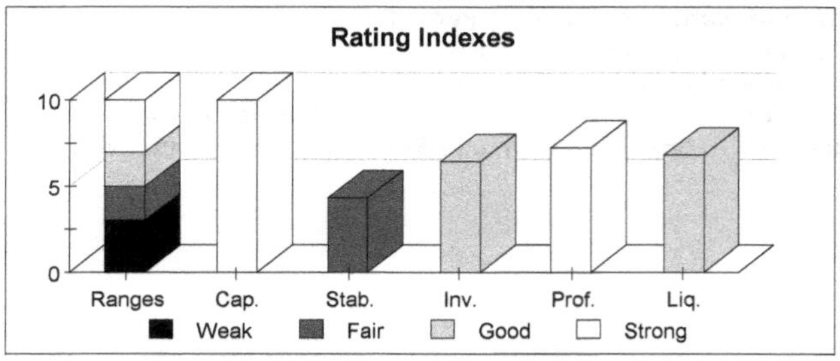

## AMERICAN CONTINENTAL INSURANCE COMPANY B- Good

**Major Rating Factors:** Good overall capitalization (5.7 on a scale of 0 to 10) based on mixed results -- excessive policy leverage mitigated by excellent risk adjusted capital (severe loss scenario). Capital levels have been relatively consistent over the last five years. Good liquidity (5.0) with sufficient resources to handle a spike in claims. Fair overall results on stability tests (4.9) including negative cash flow from operations for 2016.
**Other Rating Factors:** Weak profitability (1.9) with operating losses during the first nine months of 2017. High quality investment portfolio (7.7).
**Principal Business:** Individual health insurance (89%) and individual life insurance (11%).
**Principal Investments:** NonCMO investment grade bonds (73%) and CMOs and structured securities (34%).
**Investments in Affiliates:** None
**Group Affiliation:** Aetna Inc
**Licensed in:** AL, AZ, AR, CO, FL, GA, IL, IN, IA, KS, KY, LA, MI, MN, MS, MO, MT, NE, NV, NM, NC, ND, OH, OK, PA, SC, SD, TN, TX, UT, VA, WV, WI, WY
**Commenced Business:** September 2005
**Address:** 800 CRESENT CENTRE DR STE 200, FRANKLIN, TN 37067
**Phone:** (800) 264-4000 **Domicile State:** TN **NAIC Code:** 12321

| Data Date | Rating | RACR #1 | RACR #2 | Total Assets ($mil) | Capital ($mil) | Net Premium ($mil) | Net Income ($mil) |
|---|---|---|---|---|---|---|---|
| 9-17 | B- | 1.62 | 1.22 | 253.8 | 100.7 | 381.2 | -15.2 |
| 9-16 | B- | 1.35 | 1.03 | 208.6 | 77.2 | 353.9 | -15.9 |
| 2016 | B- | 1.60 | 1.21 | 229.0 | 94.0 | 472.9 | -17.7 |
| 2015 | B- | 1.49 | 1.14 | 203.1 | 79.7 | 430.1 | -15.3 |
| 2014 | B | 1.82 | 1.40 | 177.2 | 86.4 | 378.7 | -12.7 |
| 2013 | B | 1.32 | 1.03 | 127.2 | 51.3 | 300.6 | -13.5 |
| 2012 | B | 2.02 | 1.56 | 98.2 | 57.5 | 178.7 | -6.0 |

Policy Leverage

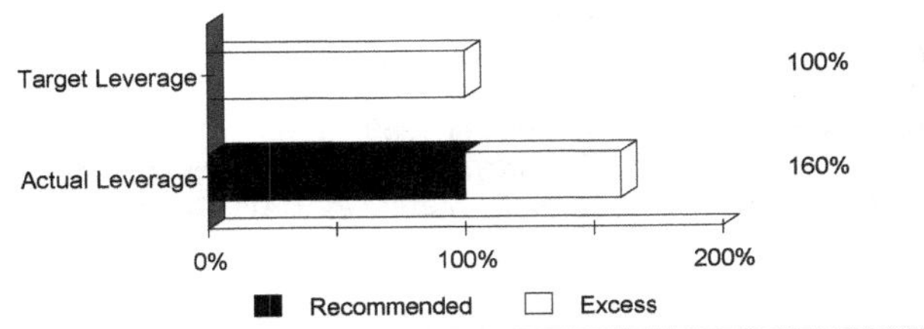


## AMERICAN FAMILY LIFE ASSUR COMPANY OF NEW YORK * A- Excellent

**Major Rating Factors:** Excellent overall results on stability tests (7.1 on a scale of 0 to 10). Strengths that enhance stability include excellent operational trends and excellent risk diversification. Strong capitalization (10.0) based on excellent risk adjusted capital (severe loss scenario). Furthermore, this high level of risk adjusted capital has been consistently maintained over the last five years. High quality investment portfolio (8.0).
**Other Rating Factors:** Excellent profitability (9.1). Excellent liquidity (7.8).
**Principal Business:** Individual health insurance (95%), individual life insurance (4%), and group health insurance (2%).
**Principal Investments:** NonCMO investment grade bonds (95%), noninv. grade bonds (3%), CMOs and structured securities (1%), and cash (1%).
**Investments in Affiliates:** None
**Group Affiliation:** AFLAC Inc
**Licensed in:** CT, MA, NJ, NY, ND, VT
**Commenced Business:** December 1964
**Address:** 22 Corporate Woods Blvd Ste 2, Albany, NY 12211
**Phone:** (518) 438-0764 **Domicile State:** NY **NAIC Code:** 60526

| Data Date | Rating | RACR #1 | RACR #2 | Total Assets ($mil) | Capital ($mil) | Net Premium ($mil) | Net Income ($mil) |
|---|---|---|---|---|---|---|---|
| 9-17 | A- | 5.56 | 3.70 | 945.4 | 298.3 | 244.7 | 43.9 |
| 9-16 | A- | 5.67 | 3.80 | 889.2 | 293.8 | 236.5 | 39.8 |
| 2016 | A- | 5.91 | 3.97 | 870.1 | 304.3 | 315.9 | 51.6 |
| 2015 | A- | 6.11 | 4.20 | 817.9 | 298.5 | 304.2 | 47.4 |
| 2014 | A- | 5.39 | 3.76 | 735.9 | 250.1 | 293.5 | 26.8 |
| 2013 | A- | 4.96 | 3.49 | 645.3 | 221.8 | 285.5 | 45.4 |
| 2012 | A- | 4.18 | 2.99 | 555.9 | 176.2 | 271.1 | 40.0 |

**Adverse Trends in Operations**

Increase in policy surrenders from 2014 to 2015 (30%)
Increase in policy surrenders from 2013 to 2014 (49%)
Increase in policy surrenders from 2012 to 2013 (34%)

## AMERICAN FAMILY LIFE ASSURANCE COMPANY OF COLUMBU B+ Good

**Major Rating Factors:** Good overall profitability (6.3 on a scale of 0 to 10) although investment income, in comparison to reserve requirements, is below regulatory standards. Good overall results on stability tests (6.7). Stability strengths include excellent operational trends and excellent risk diversification. Strong capitalization (7.6) based on excellent risk adjusted capital (severe loss scenario).
**Other Rating Factors:** High quality investment portfolio (7.1). Excellent liquidity (7.0).
**Principal Business:** Individual health insurance (72%), individual life insurance (23%), individual annuities (4%), and reinsurance (1%).
**Principal Investments:** NonCMO investment grade bonds (85%), common & preferred stock (4%), noninv. grade bonds (4%), CMOs and structured securities (4%), and cash (1%).
**Investments in Affiliates:** 4%
**Group Affiliation:** AFLAC Inc
**Licensed in:** All states except NY
**Commenced Business:** April 1956
**Address:** 10306 Regency Parkway Drive, Omaha, NE 68114-3743
**Phone:** (706) 323-3431 **Domicile State:** NE **NAIC Code:** 60380

| Data Date | Rating | RACR #1 | RACR #2 | Total Assets ($mil) | Capital ($mil) | Net Premium ($mil) | Net Income ($mil) |
|---|---|---|---|---|---|---|---|
| 9-17 | B+ | 1.81 | 1.41 | 113,507 | 11,350.2 | 13,671.6 | 2,012.9 |
| 9-16 | B+ | 2.45 | 1.71 | 119,307 | 11,297.9 | 14,326.9 | 2,200.2 |
| 2016 | B+ | 1.81 | 1.43 | 108,871 | 11,221.1 | 18,902.8 | 2,754.5 |
| 2015 | B+ | 2.75 | 2.00 | 101,566 | 11,297.9 | 17,495.2 | 2,273.6 |
| 2014 | B+ | 3.53 | 2.38 | 100,966 | 10,839.1 | 19,362.9 | 2,392.6 |
| 2013 | B+ | 3.23 | 2.09 | 107,913 | 9,630.1 | 20,550.2 | 2,360.6 |
| 2012 | B+ | 2.77 | 1.74 | 115,347 | 8,891.8 | 23,102.5 | 2,337.3 |

Investment Income Compared to Needs of Reserves

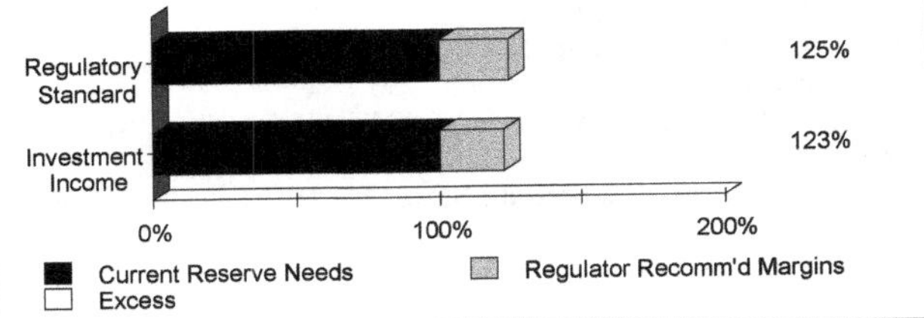

## AMERICAN FIDELITY ASSURANCE COMPANY * B+ Good

**Major Rating Factors:** Good quality investment portfolio (6.0 on a scale of 0 to 10) despite mixed results such as: large holdings of BBB rated bonds but moderate junk bond exposure. Good liquidity (6.2) with sufficient resources to cover a large increase in policy surrenders. Good overall results on stability tests (6.8) excellent operational trends, good risk adjusted capital for prior years and excellent risk diversification.

**Other Rating Factors:** Strong capitalization (7.2) based on excellent risk adjusted capital (severe loss scenario). Excellent profitability (8.6).

**Principal Business:** Group health insurance (41%), individual health insurance (26%), individual annuities (14%), individual life insurance (13%), and reinsurance (4%).

**Principal Investments:** NonCMO investment grade bonds (64%), CMOs and structured securities (18%), mortgages in good standing (10%), noninv. grade bonds (3%), and misc. investments (5%).

**Investments in Affiliates:** None

**Group Affiliation:** Cameron Associates Inc

**Licensed in:** All states except NY

**Commenced Business:** December 1960

**Address:** 9000 Cameron Parkway, Oklahoma City, OK 73114-3701

**Phone:** (405) 523-2000 **Domicile State:** OK **NAIC Code:** 60410

| Data Date | Rating | RACR #1 | RACR #2 | Total Assets ($mil) | Capital ($mil) | Net Premium ($mil) | Net Income ($mil) |
|---|---|---|---|---|---|---|---|
| 9-17 | B+ | 1.93 | 1.10 | 5,772.7 | 434.5 | 705.9 | 56.7 |
| 9-16 | B+ | 1.98 | 1.11 | 5,365.8 | 414.3 | 667.2 | 54.3 |
| 2016 | B+ | 1.88 | 1.07 | 5,446.8 | 414.6 | 906.6 | 76.4 |
| 2015 | B+ | 1.97 | 1.13 | 5,181.1 | 408.5 | 957.9 | 75.4 |
| 2014 | B+ | 1.93 | 1.11 | 4,959.0 | 380.4 | 822.5 | 69.3 |
| 2013 | B+ | 1.82 | 1.05 | 4,709.9 | 342.7 | 780.9 | 71.7 |
| 2012 | B+ | 1.60 | 0.95 | 4,358.1 | 308.9 | 765.7 | 58.5 |

**Adverse Trends in Operations**

Decrease in premium volume from 2015 to 2016 (5%)

## AMERICAN HEALTH & LIFE INSURANCE COMPANY * A- Excellent

**Major Rating Factors:** Good overall results on stability tests (5.5 on a scale of 0 to 10). Strengths that enhance stability include excellent risk diversification. Good quality investment portfolio (6.3) despite mixed results such as: large holdings of BBB rated bonds but moderate junk bond exposure. Strong capitalization (8.7) based on excellent risk adjusted capital (severe loss scenario).

**Other Rating Factors:** Excellent profitability (7.5). Excellent liquidity (8.0).

**Principal Business:** Credit life insurance (31%), credit health insurance (28%), reinsurance (26%), group health insurance (8%), and other lines (8%).

**Principal Investments:** NonCMO investment grade bonds (70%), CMOs and structured securities (21%), noninv. grade bonds (4%), common & preferred stock (1%), and cash (1%).

**Investments in Affiliates:** None

**Group Affiliation:** Citigroup Inc

**Licensed in:** All states except NY, PR

**Commenced Business:** June 1954

**Address:** 3001 Meacham Blvd Ste 100, Fort Worth, TX 76137

**Phone:** (800) 316-5607 **Domicile State:** TX **NAIC Code:** 60518

| Data Date | Rating | RACR #1 | RACR #2 | Total Assets ($mil) | Capital ($mil) | Net Premium ($mil) | Net Income ($mil) |
|---|---|---|---|---|---|---|---|
| 9-17 | A- | 3.54 | 2.13 | 840.1 | 142.1 | 152.5 | 34.9 |
| 9-16 | A- | 4.42 | 2.60 | 909.7 | 190.3 | 125.8 | 48.7 |
| 2016 | A- | 5.40 | 3.11 | 924.2 | 215.1 | 154.3 | 71.2 |
| 2015 | A- | 4.03 | 2.40 | 923.9 | 183.5 | 199.8 | 55.5 |
| 2014 | B | 2.88 | 1.96 | 912.8 | 188.6 | 209.9 | 70.0 |
| 2013 | B- | 3.08 | 2.11 | 941.1 | 208.6 | 221.8 | 84.1 |
| 2012 | B- | 3.52 | 2.39 | 972.0 | 234.7 | 213.5 | 110.0 |

**Rating Indexes**

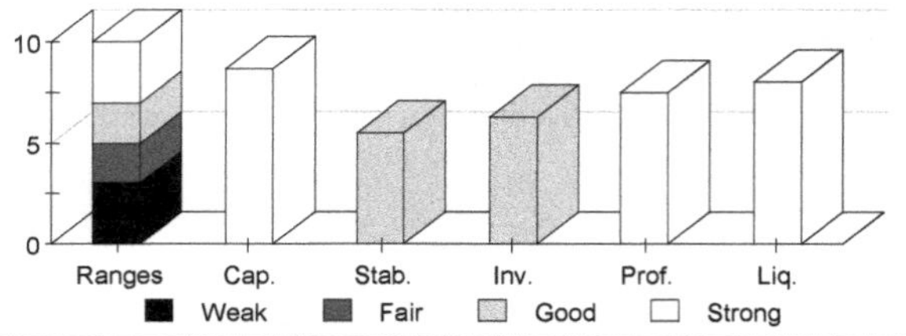


## AMERICAN HERITAGE LIFE INSURANCE COMPANY B Good

**Major Rating Factors:** Good overall results on stability tests (5.8 on a scale of 0 to 10). Stability strengths include excellent operational trends and excellent risk diversification. Good capitalization (5.8) based on good risk adjusted capital (severe loss scenario). Good quality investment portfolio (5.8).

**Other Rating Factors:** Good overall profitability (5.9) although investment income, in comparison to reserve requirements, is below regulatory standards. Good liquidity (6.5).

**Principal Business:** Group health insurance (60%), individual health insurance (23%), individual life insurance (9%), group life insurance (7%), and reinsurance (1%).

**Principal Investments:** NonCMO investment grade bonds (51%), policy loans (18%), common & preferred stock (13%), mortgages in good standing (9%), and misc. investments (9%).

**Investments in Affiliates:** 9%

**Group Affiliation:** Allstate Group

**Licensed in:** All states except NY

**Commenced Business:** December 1956

**Address:** 1776 AMERICAN HERITAGE LIFE DR, JACKSONVILLE, FL 32224-6688

**Phone:** (904) 992-1776 **Domicile State:** FL **NAIC Code:** 60534

| Data Date | Rating | RACR #1 | RACR #2 | Total Assets ($mil) | Capital ($mil) | Net Premium ($mil) | Net Income ($mil) |
|---|---|---|---|---|---|---|---|
| 9-17 | B | 1.10 | 0.85 | 1,915.6 | 323.1 | 681.6 | 42.3 |
| 9-16 | B | 1.15 | 0.93 | 1,850.2 | 324.5 | 649.6 | 46.8 |
| 2016 | B | 1.22 | 0.97 | 1,885.6 | 344.3 | 861.4 | 63.1 |
| 2015 | B | 1.19 | 0.96 | 1,830.9 | 329.7 | 785.9 | 56.3 |
| 2014 | B | 1.27 | 1.02 | 1,799.7 | 353.3 | 744.8 | 123.3 |
| 2013 | B | 1.18 | 0.97 | 1,770.2 | 337.7 | 707.7 | 57.0 |
| 2012 | B | 1.26 | 1.05 | 1,710.7 | 335.8 | 649.7 | 74.7 |

**Adverse Trends in Operations**

Decrease in capital during 2015 (7%)

## AMERICAN LIFE INSURANCE COMPANY C Fair

**Major Rating Factors:** Fair quality investment portfolio (3.1 on a scale of 0 to 10). Fair overall results on stability tests (3.4). Good profitability (5.0).
**Other Rating Factors:** Strong current capitalization (7.4) based on excellent risk adjusted capital (severe loss scenario) reflecting improvement over results in 2013. Excellent liquidity (7.7) with ample cash flow from premiums and investment income.
**Principal Business:** Individual life insurance (40%), group health insurance (26%), reinsurance (23%), individual health insurance (5%), and other lines (7%).
**Principal Investments:** Common & preferred stock (56%), nonCMO investment grade bonds (19%), noninv. grade bonds (14%), cash (8%), and misc. investments (4%).
**Investments in Affiliates:** 57%
**Group Affiliation:** MetLife Inc
**Licensed in:** DE
**Commenced Business:** August 1921
**Address:** 1209 Orange Street, Wilmington, DE 19801
**Phone:** (302) 594-2000 **Domicile State:** DE **NAIC Code:** 60690

| Data Date | Rating | RACR #1 | RACR #2 | Total Assets ($mil) | Capital ($mil) | Net Premium ($mil) | Net Income ($mil) |
|---|---|---|---|---|---|---|---|
| 9-17 | C | 1.30 | 1.24 | 12,555.4 | 6,472.0 | 1,041.2 | 1,165.1 |
| 9-16 | C | 1.11 | 1.07 | 11,959.5 | 6,244.1 | 1,003.9 | 487.4 |
| 2016 | C | 1.03 | 0.99 | 10,377.8 | 5,235.3 | 1,373.6 | 341.5 |
| 2015 | C | 1.02 | 0.99 | 11,097.5 | 6,115.1 | 1,204.5 | 334.6 |
| 2014 | C | 0.93 | 0.89 | 8,215.9 | 3,358.5 | 1,409.1 | -36.1 |
| 2013 | C | 0.92 | 0.88 | 7,296.4 | 2,711.2 | 1,140.4 | 630.5 |
| 2012 | C | 1.01 | 0.93 | 8,224.8 | 3,043.6 | 8,991.4 | 317.1 |

Rating Indexes

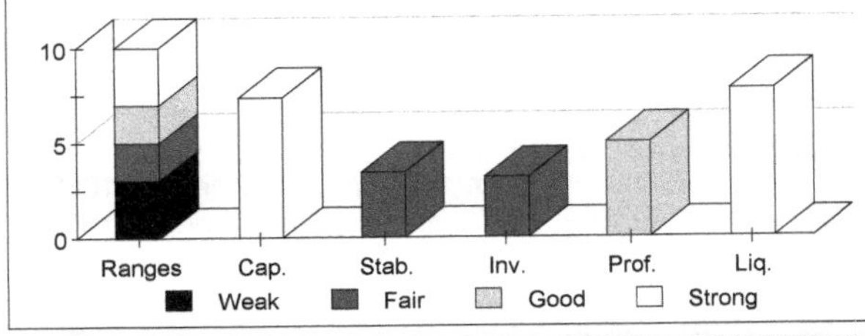


## AMERICAN MODERN LIFE INSURANCE COMPANY B Good

**Major Rating Factors:** Fair overall results on stability tests (4.3 on a scale of 0 to 10) including negative cash flow from operations for 2016. Strong capitalization (9.0) based on excellent risk adjusted capital (severe loss scenario). Moreover, capital levels have been consistently high over the last five years. High quality investment portfolio (8.0).
**Other Rating Factors:** Excellent profitability (8.1). Excellent liquidity (7.4).
**Principal Business:** Credit life insurance (56%), credit health insurance (43%), and reinsurance (1%).
**Principal Investments:** NonCMO investment grade bonds (61%), common & preferred stock (29%), CMOs and structured securities (9%), and cash (1%).
**Investments in Affiliates:** 29%
**Group Affiliation:** Securian Financial Group
**Licensed in:** All states except NH, NJ, PR
**Commenced Business:** January 1957
**Address:** 1300 EAST NINTH STREET, CLEVELAND, OH 44114
**Phone:** (800) 543-2644 **Domicile State:** OH **NAIC Code:** 65811

| Data Date | Rating | RACR #1 | RACR #2 | Total Assets ($mil) | Capital ($mil) | Net Premium ($mil) | Net Income ($mil) |
|---|---|---|---|---|---|---|---|
| 9-17 | B | 2.45 | 2.33 | 40.2 | 31.7 | 0.1 | 1.2 |
| 9-16 | B | 2.26 | 2.12 | 45.4 | 29.8 | 2.6 | 0.7 |
| 2016 | B | 2.31 | 2.19 | 44.7 | 30.5 | 3.1 | 1.2 |
| 2015 | B | 2.20 | 2.08 | 46.9 | 29.0 | 4.2 | 0.9 |
| 2014 | B | 2.09 | 1.96 | 47.8 | 27.9 | 5.1 | 2.1 |
| 2013 | B | 1.89 | 1.76 | 52.1 | 26.4 | 4.7 | 3.9 |
| 2012 | B | 1.55 | 1.43 | 58.8 | 23.1 | 8.1 | 1.9 |

Rating Indexes

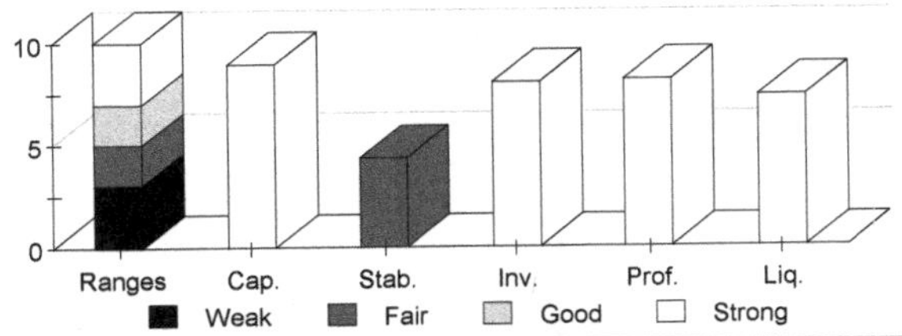


## AMERICAN NATIONAL LIFE INSURANCE COMPANY OF TEXAS B- Good

**Major Rating Factors:** Good liquidity (6.5 on a scale of 0 to 10) with sufficient resources to handle a spike in claims. Good overall results on stability tests (5.1) despite negative cash flow from operations for 2016. Strengths include good financial support from affiliation with American National Group Inc, good operational trends and excellent risk diversification. Weak profitability (2.1) with operating losses during the first nine months of 2017.
**Other Rating Factors:** Strong capitalization (10.0) based on excellent risk adjusted capital (severe loss scenario). High quality investment portfolio (7.1).
**Principal Business:** Group health insurance (51%), reinsurance (39%), individual life insurance (5%), individual health insurance (4%), and individual annuities (1%).
**Principal Investments:** NonCMO investment grade bonds (95%), policy loans (4%), and noninv. grade bonds (1%).
**Investments in Affiliates:** None
**Group Affiliation:** American National Group Inc
**Licensed in:** All states except ME, NJ, NY, VT, PR
**Commenced Business:** December 1954
**Address:** ONE MOODY PLAZA, GALVESTON, TX 77550
**Phone:** (409) 763-4661 **Domicile State:** TX **NAIC Code:** 71773

| Data Date | Rating | RACR #1 | RACR #2 | Total Assets ($mil) | Capital ($mil) | Net Premium ($mil) | Net Income ($mil) |
|---|---|---|---|---|---|---|---|
| 9-17 | B- | 3.77 | 3.19 | 121.7 | 33.5 | 20.9 | -0.9 |
| 9-16 | B- | 3.76 | 3.13 | 122.0 | 33.5 | 20.4 | -1.7 |
| 2016 | B- | 3.95 | 3.48 | 122.5 | 35.2 | 26.8 | -0.8 |
| 2015 | B- | 4.01 | 3.16 | 127.5 | 35.9 | 35.5 | -5.3 |
| 2014 | B- | 4.06 | 3.10 | 136.3 | 36.8 | 38.4 | 0.6 |
| 2013 | B- | 4.55 | 3.17 | 135.1 | 41.4 | 45.1 | 2.1 |
| 2012 | B- | 4.01 | 2.80 | 133.5 | 39.2 | 52.8 | -2.0 |

| American National Group Inc<br>Composite Group Rating: B<br>Largest Group Members | Assets ($mil) | Rating |
|---|---|---|
| AMERICAN NATIONAL INS CO | 18721 | B |
| FARM FAMILY LIFE INS CO | 1343 | B |
| AMERICAN NATIONAL PROPERTY CAS CO | 1320 | B |
| FARM FAMILY CASUALTY INS CO | 1164 | B+ |
| STANDARD LIFE ACCIDENT INS CO | 519 | A- |

## AMERICAN PROGRESSIVE L&H INSURANCE COMPANY OF NY C Fair

**Major Rating Factors:** Fair profitability (3.2 on a scale of 0 to 10) with operating losses during the first nine months of 2017. Good current capitalization (5.9) based on mixed results -- excessive policy leverage mitigated by good risk adjusted capital (severe loss scenario), although results have slipped from the excellent range during the last year. Weak overall results on stability tests (2.5) including potential financial drain due to affiliation with WellCare Health Plans Inc and negative cash flow from operations for 2016.
**Other Rating Factors:** Weak liquidity (0.5). High quality investment portfolio (7.4).
**Principal Business:** Individual health insurance (98%) and individual life insurance (2%).
**Principal Investments:** NonCMO investment grade bonds (86%), CMOs and structured securities (18%), and common & preferred stock (2%).
**Investments in Affiliates:** None
**Group Affiliation:** WellCare Health Plans Inc
**Licensed in:** AL, AR, CO, CT, DC, DE, GA, HI, IL, IN, LA, ME, MD, MA, MN, MO, NH, NJ, NY, NC, OH, OK, OR, PA, RI, SC, TX, VT, VA, WV
**Commenced Business:** March 1946
**Address:** 44 South Broadway Suite 1200, White Plains, NY 10601-4411
**Phone:** (813) 290-6200 **Domicile State:** NY **NAIC Code:** 80624

| Data Date | Rating | RACR #1 | RACR #2 | Total Assets ($mil) | Capital ($mil) | Net Premium ($mil) | Net Income ($mil) |
|---|---|---|---|---|---|---|---|
| 9-17 | C | 1.09 | 0.89 | 269.8 | 104.2 | 400.4 | -5.3 |
| 9-16 | C | 1.33 | 1.06 | 255.7 | 108.5 | 340.9 | 9.3 |
| 2016 | C | 1.25 | 1.02 | 215.0 | 109.3 | 463.9 | 10.0 |
| 2015 | C | 1.29 | 1.03 | 211.5 | 101.3 | 420.8 | -13.0 |
| 2014 | B | 1.49 | 1.18 | 227.7 | 116.4 | 412.9 | 2.7 |
| 2013 | B | 1.39 | 1.10 | 235.7 | 122.3 | 469.8 | 13.5 |
| 2012 | B | 1.84 | 1.46 | 263.8 | 145.4 | 419.3 | 14.8 |

| Universal American Corp<br>Composite Group Rating: D+<br>Largest Group Members | Assets ($mil) | Rating |
|---|---|---|
| WELLCARE PRESCRIPTION INS INC | 853 | E |
| WELLCARE OF FLORIDA INC | 689 | E |
| WELLCARE HEALTH INS OF KENTUCKY INC | 683 | C |
| WELLCARE OF GEORGIA INC | 494 | C |
| HARMONY HEALTH PLAN INC | 384 | C |

## AMERICAN PUBLIC LIFE INSURANCE COMPANY B Good

**Major Rating Factors:** Good overall results on stability tests (5.7 on a scale of 0 to 10). Stability strengths include excellent operational trends and excellent risk diversification. Strong capitalization (7.7) based on excellent risk adjusted capital (severe loss scenario). Moreover, capital levels have been consistently high over the last five years. High quality investment portfolio (7.9).
**Other Rating Factors:** Excellent profitability (8.3). Excellent liquidity (7.0).
**Principal Business:** Group health insurance (78%), individual health insurance (18%), reinsurance (3%), and individual life insurance (1%).
**Principal Investments:** NonCMO investment grade bonds (58%), CMOs and structured securities (25%), mortgages in good standing (11%), cash (3%), and misc. investments (3%).
**Investments in Affiliates:** None
**Group Affiliation:** Cameron Associates Inc
**Licensed in:** All states except NY, PR
**Commenced Business:** March 1946
**Address:** 9000 Cameron Parkway, Oklahoma City, OK 73114
**Phone:** (601) 936-6600 **Domicile State:** OK **NAIC Code:** 60801

| Data Date | Rating | RACR #1 | RACR #2 | Total Assets ($mil) | Capital ($mil) | Net Premium ($mil) | Net Income ($mil) |
|---|---|---|---|---|---|---|---|
| 9-17 | B | 1.95 | 1.47 | 98.4 | 29.9 | 67.5 | 3.0 |
| 9-16 | B | 2.03 | 1.51 | 94.1 | 27.4 | 54.2 | 3.8 |
| 2016 | B | 1.96 | 1.47 | 90.3 | 26.4 | 74.4 | 5.9 |
| 2015 | B | 1.95 | 1.44 | 86.7 | 23.6 | 61.4 | 5.0 |
| 2014 | B | 1.92 | 1.41 | 83.2 | 21.6 | 52.8 | 4.4 |
| 2013 | B | 2.02 | 1.46 | 80.3 | 21.7 | 46.9 | 3.7 |
| 2012 | B | 1.77 | 1.27 | 75.1 | 18.7 | 42.5 | 1.7 |

**Adverse Trends in Operations**

Increase in policy surrenders from 2014 to 2015 (36%)
Increase in policy surrenders from 2012 to 2013 (75%)

## AMERICAN REPUBLIC INSURANCE COMPANY * A- Excellent

**Major Rating Factors:** Good quality investment portfolio (6.9 on a scale of 0 to 10) despite mixed results such as: minimal exposure to mortgages and large holdings of BBB rated bonds but minimal holdings in junk bonds. Strong capitalization (10.0) based on excellent risk adjusted capital (severe loss scenario). Furthermore, this high level of risk adjusted capital has been consistently maintained over the last five years. Excellent profitability (9.3).
**Other Rating Factors:** Excellent liquidity (7.0). Excellent overall results on stability tests (7.0) excellent operational trends and excellent risk diversification.
**Principal Business:** Reinsurance (63%), individual health insurance (21%), group health insurance (12%), individual life insurance (3%), and credit health insurance (1%).
**Principal Investments:** NonCMO investment grade bonds (60%), CMOs and structured securities (17%), mortgages in good standing (8%), common & preferred stock (5%), and misc. investments (10%).
**Investments in Affiliates:** 4%
**Group Affiliation:** American Enterprise Mutual Holding
**Licensed in:** All states except NY, PR
**Commenced Business:** May 1929
**Address:** 601 Sixth Avenue, Des Moines, IA 50309
**Phone:** (800) 247-2190 **Domicile State:** IA **NAIC Code:** 60836

| Data Date | Rating | RACR #1 | RACR #2 | Total Assets ($mil) | Capital ($mil) | Net Premium ($mil) | Net Income ($mil) |
|---|---|---|---|---|---|---|---|
| 9-17 | A- | 4.74 | 3.38 | 933.1 | 502.9 | 329.1 | 15.5 |
| 9-16 | A- | 4.99 | 3.51 | 921.6 | 499.8 | 291.7 | 20.1 |
| 2016 | A- | 5.06 | 3.60 | 937.6 | 511.1 | 392.1 | 33.1 |
| 2015 | A- | 5.21 | 3.70 | 820.0 | 477.9 | 328.1 | 21.6 |
| 2014 | A- | 5.26 | 3.89 | 802.5 | 468.1 | 297.9 | 34.1 |
| 2013 | A- | 4.85 | 3.67 | 801.4 | 437.5 | 325.1 | 40.5 |
| 2012 | A- | 6.09 | 4.36 | 522.7 | 286.4 | 224.0 | 44.2 |

**Rating Indexes**

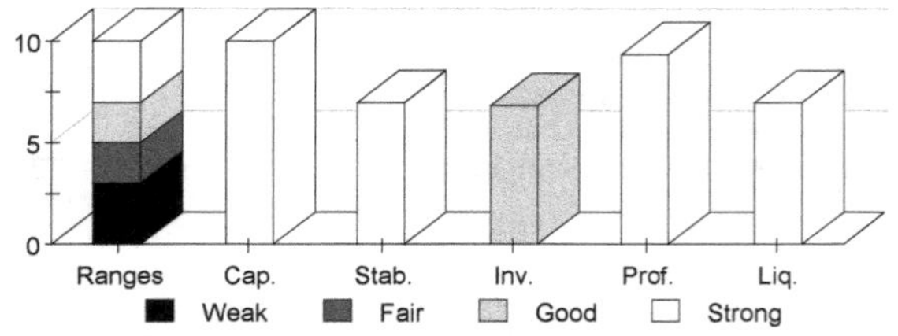

## AMERICAN RETIREMENT LIFE INSURANCE COMPANY C+ Fair

**Major Rating Factors:** Fair overall results on stability tests (3.3 on a scale of 0 to 10) including negative cash flow from operations for 2016, excessive premium growth and fair risk adjusted capital in prior years. Good current capitalization (5.1) based on mixed results -- excessive policy leverage mitigated by good risk adjusted capital (severe loss scenario) reflecting some improvement over results in 2016. Weak profitability (1.4) with operating losses during the first nine months of 2017.
**Other Rating Factors:** Weak liquidity (0.6). High quality investment portfolio (7.9).
**Principal Business:** Individual health insurance (100%).
**Principal Investments:** NonCMO investment grade bonds (113%).
**Investments in Affiliates:** None
**Group Affiliation:** CIGNA Corp
**Licensed in:** AL, AZ, AR, CA, CO, DE, FL, GA, IL, IN, IA, KS, KY, LA, MD, MN, MS, MO, MT, NE, NV, NH, NM, NC, ND, OH, OK, OR, PA, RI, SC, SD, TN, TX, UT, VA, WV, WI, WY
**Commenced Business:** November 1978
**Address:** 1300 East Ninth Street, Cleveland, OH 44114
**Phone:** (512) 451-2224 **Domicile State:** OH **NAIC Code:** 88366

| Data Date | Rating | RACR #1 | RACR #2 | Total Assets ($mil) | Capital ($mil) | Net Premium ($mil) | Net Income ($mil) |
|---|---|---|---|---|---|---|---|
| 9-17 | C+ | 0.99 | 0.80 | 104.3 | 55.1 | 254.3 | -28.4 |
| 9-16 | C+ | 0.99 | 0.76 | 76.5 | 41.6 | 187.4 | -20.5 |
| 2016 | C+ | 0.91 | 0.71 | 76.9 | 40.7 | 255.5 | -26.4 |
| 2015 | C+ | 1.36 | 1.05 | 77.4 | 47.3 | 192.2 | -22.1 |
| 2014 | B- | 1.11 | 0.86 | 55.7 | 31.0 | 120.4 | -17.7 |
| 2013 | B- | 1.61 | 1.25 | 18.0 | 8.4 | 16.7 | -4.3 |
| 2012 | B- | 3.32 | 2.99 | 5.7 | 5.4 | -0.7 | 0.1 |

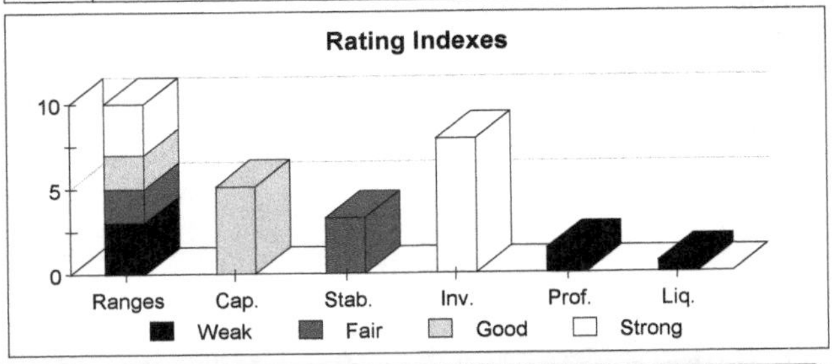


## AMERICAN SPECIALTY HEALTH INS CO B- Good

**Major Rating Factors:** Fair profitability index (4.3 on a scale of 0 to 10). Strong capitalization (10.0) based on excellent current risk-adjusted capital (severe loss scenario). High quality investment portfolio (9.9).
**Other Rating Factors:** Excellent liquidity (10.0) with ample operational cash flow and liquid investments.
**Principal Business:** Other (100%)
**Mem Phys: 16:** 26,577 **15:** 26,561 **16 MLR** 45.4% **/ 16 Admin Exp** N/A
**Enroll(000): Q3 17:** 153 **16:** 188 **15:** 234 **Med Exp PMPM:** $0
**Principal Investments:** Cash and equiv (100%)
**Provider Compensation ($000):** None
**Total Member Encounters:** Non-phys (32,046)
**Group Affiliation:** American Specialty Health Inc
**Licensed in:** All states except AK, CT, ME, NJ, NY, NC, RI, PR
**Address:** 70 West Madison Ste 3800, Chicago, IL 60602
**Phone:** (858) 754-2000 **Dom State:** IN **Commenced Bus:** August 1974

| Data Date | Rating | RACR #1 | RACR #2 | Total Assets ($mil) | Capital ($mil) | Net Premium ($mil) | Net Income ($mil) |
|---|---|---|---|---|---|---|---|
| 9-17 | B- | 34.13 | 28.44 | 9.1 | 8.3 | 1.0 | 0.0 |
| 9-16 | B- | 28.73 | 23.94 | 9.2 | 8.6 | 1.8 | 0.4 |
| 2016 | B- | 34.50 | 28.75 | 9.5 | 8.4 | 1.8 | 0.2 |
| 2015 | B | 27.13 | 22.61 | 8.5 | 8.1 | 3.0 | 0.7 |
| 2014 | C- | 19.15 | 15.96 | 8.1 | 7.5 | 3.0 | 0.4 |
| 2013 | E- | 8.98 | 7.49 | 8.1 | 7.3 | 5.2 | -0.3 |
| 2012 | N/A | N/A | N/A | 9.2 | 7.6 | 4.9 | -0.7 |

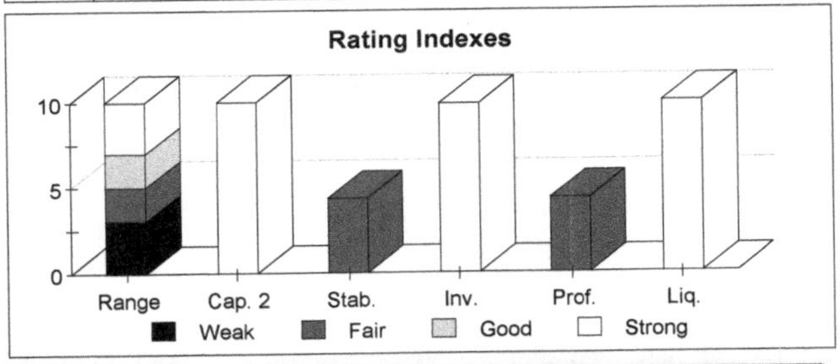


## AMERICAN SPECIALTY HEALTH ODS OF NJ C Fair

**Major Rating Factors:** Weak profitability index (1.7 on a scale of 0 to 10). Good capitalization (6.9) based on excellent current risk-adjusted capital (severe loss scenario). High quality investment portfolio (9.9).
**Other Rating Factors:** Excellent liquidity (7.4) with ample operational cash flow and liquid investments.
**Principal Business:** Other (100%)
**Mem Phys: 16:** 904 **15:** 1,799 **16 MLR** 77.8% **/ 16 Admin Exp** N/A
**Enroll(000): 16:** 845 **15:** 409 **Med Exp PMPM:** $0
**Principal Investments:** Cash and equiv (100%)
**Provider Compensation ($000):** FFS ($7,819)
**Total Member Encounters:** Non-phys (174,165)
**Group Affiliation:** American Specialty Health Incorporat
**Licensed in:** NJ
**Address:** 830 Bear Tavern Rd, West Trenton, NJ 08625
**Phone:** (858) 754-2000 **Dom State:** NJ **Commenced Bus:** April 2004

| Data Date | Rating | RACR #1 | RACR #2 | Total Assets ($mil) | Capital ($mil) | Net Premium ($mil) | Net Income ($mil) |
|---|---|---|---|---|---|---|---|
| 2016 | C | 1.26 | 1.05 | 2.7 | 2.1 | 10.1 | 0.1 |
| 2015 | U | 1.32 | 1.10 | 0.9 | 0.6 | 3.0 | 0.1 |
| 2014 | U | 1.19 | 0.99 | 0.7 | 0.5 | 2.9 | 0.1 |
| 2013 | U | 0.92 | 0.77 | 0.8 | 0.4 | 2.7 | -0.2 |
| 2012 | U | 3.69 | 3.07 | 0.6 | 0.3 | 0.2 | -0.2 |

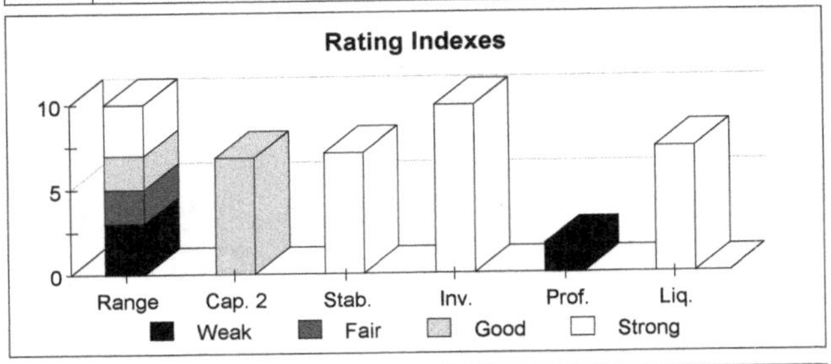

## AMERICAS 1ST CHOICE HEALTH PLANS INC — E+ — Very Weak

**Major Rating Factors:** Weak profitability index (2.0 on a scale of 0 to 10). Fair capitalization (4.7) based on fair current risk-adjusted capital (moderate loss scenario). Fair liquidity (4.1) as cash resources may not be adequate to cover a spike in claims.
**Other Rating Factors:** High quality investment portfolio (9.9).
**Principal Business:** Medicare (100%)
**Mem Phys: 16:** N/A **15:** 6,961 **16 MLR** 110.4% **/ 16 Admin Exp** N/A
**Enroll(000): 16:** 3 **15:** 4 **Med Exp PMPM:** $902
**Principal Investments:** Cash and equiv (74%), long-term bonds (26%)
**Provider Compensation ($000):** FFS ($33,113), capitation ($336)
**Total Member Encounters:** Phys (6,136), non-phys (6,692)
**Group Affiliation:** Americas 1st Choice Group
**Licensed in:** AZ, GA, SC
**Address:** 250 Berryhill Rd Ste 311, Columbia, SC 29210
**Phone:** (866) 321-3947 **Dom State:** SC **Commenced Bus:** March 2007

| Data Date | Rating | RACR #1 | RACR #2 | Total Assets ($mil) | Capital ($mil) | Net Premium ($mil) | Net Income ($mil) |
|---|---|---|---|---|---|---|---|
| 2016 | E+ | 0.89 | 0.74 | 11.8 | 5.6 | 30.6 | -3.5 |
| 2015 | E | 1.57 | 1.31 | 15.7 | 9.8 | 39.8 | -0.2 |
| 2014 | E | 1.35 | 1.12 | 16.4 | 10.3 | 52.9 | 0.7 |
| 2013 | E | 0.87 | 0.72 | 19.7 | 9.7 | 80.9 | 4.4 |
| 2012 | E | 0.37 | 0.31 | 19.2 | 5.1 | 99.6 | 3.3 |

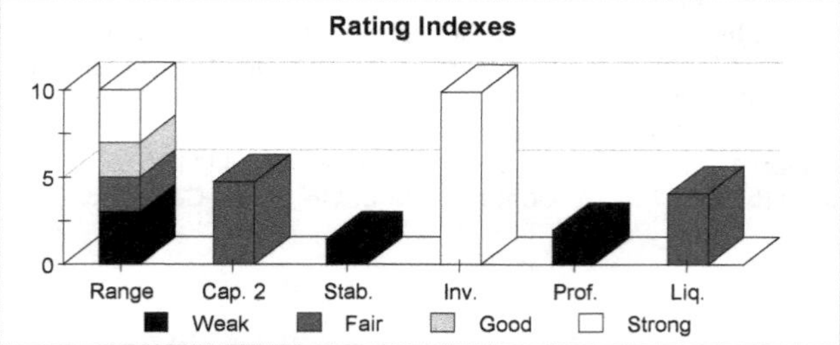


## AMERICAS 1ST CHOICE SOUTH CAROLINA — E- — Very Weak

**Major Rating Factors:** Weak profitability index (0.9 on a scale of 0 to 10). Strong capitalization (9.1) based on excellent current risk-adjusted capital (severe loss scenario). High quality investment portfolio (8.9).
**Other Rating Factors:** Excellent liquidity (7.3) with ample operational cash flow and liquid investments.
**Principal Business:** Medicare (100%)
**Mem Phys: 16:** 522 **15:** 397 **16 MLR** 74.7% **/ 16 Admin Exp** N/A
**Enroll(000): Q3 17:** 1 **16:** 0 **15:** 0 **Med Exp PMPM:** $538
**Principal Investments:** Long-term bonds (70%), cash and equiv (30%)
**Provider Compensation ($000):** FFS ($1,384), capitation ($17)
**Total Member Encounters:** Phys (129), non-phys (156)
**Group Affiliation:** Americas 1st Choice Group
**Licensed in:** SC
**Address:** 250 Berryhill Rd Ste 311, Columbia, South Caro, SC 29210
**Phone:** (888) 563-3289 **Dom State:** SC **Commenced Bus:** January 2015

| Data Date | Rating | RACR #1 | RACR #2 | Total Assets ($mil) | Capital ($mil) | Net Premium ($mil) | Net Income ($mil) |
|---|---|---|---|---|---|---|---|
| 9-17 | E- | 3.01 | 2.51 | 3.9 | 1.3 | 5.8 | -1.4 |
| 9-16 | D- | 3.63 | 3.03 | 2.5 | 1.7 | 1.4 | 0.0 |
| 2016 | D | 4.32 | 3.60 | 2.3 | 1.8 | 1.9 | 0.1 |
| 2015 | D- | 3.77 | 3.14 | 2.2 | 1.7 | 1.2 | 0.1 |
| 2014 | N/A | N/A | N/A | 1.9 | 1.6 | N/A | N/A |
| 2013 | N/A | N/A | N/A | N/A | N/A | N/A | N/A |
| 2012 | N/A | N/A | N/A | N/A | N/A | N/A | N/A |

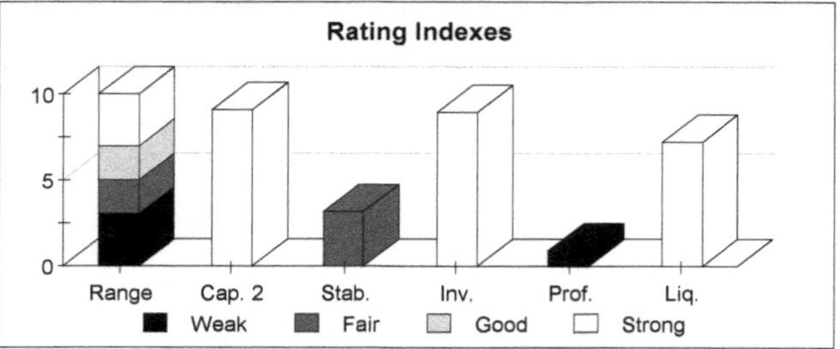


## AMERICASHEALTH PLAN INC — E+ — Very Weak

**Major Rating Factors:** Weak profitability index (0.9 on a scale of 0 to 10). Weak overall results on stability tests (0.5). Strong capitalization index (10.0) based on excellent current risk-adjusted capital (severe loss scenario).
**Other Rating Factors:** Excellent liquidity (7.3) with ample operational cash flow and liquid investments.
**Principal Business:** Managed care (100%)
**Mem Phys: 16:** N/A **15:** N/A **16 MLR** 82.8% **/ 16 Admin Exp** N/A
**Enroll(000): Q3 17:** 1 **16:** 0 **15:** N/A **Med Exp PMPM:** N/A
**Principal Investments ($000):** Cash and equiv ($1,835)
**Provider Compensation ($000):** None
**Total Member Encounters:** N/A
**Group Affiliation:** None
**Licensed in:** CA
**Address:** 200 South Wells Road Suite 200, Ventura, CA 93004
**Phone:** (615) 714-0232 **Dom State:** CA **Commenced Bus:** April 2013

| Data Date | Rating | RACR #1 | RACR #2 | Total Assets ($mil) | Capital ($mil) | Net Premium ($mil) | Net Income ($mil) |
|---|---|---|---|---|---|---|---|
| 9-17 | E+ | 5.55 | 3.66 | 3.5 | 0.6 | 3.8 | -0.6 |
| 9-16 | U | 773.20 | 463.90 | 2.0 | 1.7 | 0.4 | 0.0 |
| 2016 | C- | 14.90 | 9.82 | 2.3 | 1.7 | 0.9 | -0.1 |
| 2015 | N/A | N/A | N/A | 1.4 | 1.4 | N/A | N/A |
| 2014 | U | N/A | N/A | 1.5 | 1.5 | N/A | N/A |
| 2013 | N/A | N/A | N/A | 1.3 | 1.3 | N/A | N/A |
| 2012 | N/A | N/A | N/A | N/A | N/A | N/A | N/A |

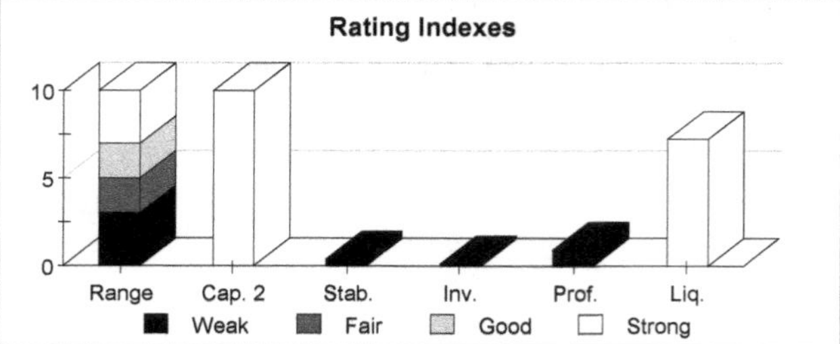

## AMERICHOICE OF NEW JERSEY INC B Good

**Major Rating Factors:** Good liquidity (6.8 on a scale of 0 to 10) with sufficient resources (cash flows and marketable investments) to handle a spike in claims. Excellent profitability (8.1). Strong capitalization index (8.2) based on excellent current risk-adjusted capital (severe loss scenario).
**Other Rating Factors:** High quality investment portfolio (9.4). Excellent overall results on stability tests (8.1). Rating is significantly influenced by the fair financial results of UnitedHealth Group Incorporated.
**Principal Business:** Medicaid (99%), comp med (1%)
**Mem Phys: 16:** 14,476 **15:** 12,914 **16 MLR** 82.5% **/ 16 Admin Exp** N/A
**Enroll(000): Q3 17:** 486 **16:** 492 **15:** 483 **Med Exp PMPM:** $357
**Principal Investments:** Long-term bonds (77%), cash and equiv (23%)
**Provider Compensation ($000):** Contr fee ($1,826,608), FFS ($195,459), capitation ($51,413), bonus arrang ($777)
**Total Member Encounters:** Phys (3,996,640), non-phys (2,976,701)
**Group Affiliation:** UnitedHealth Group Incorporated
**Licensed in:** NJ
**Address:** 333 THORNALL STREET 9TH FLOOR, EDISON, NJ 08837
**Phone:** (848) 200-3561 **Dom State:** NJ **Commenced Bus:** February 1996

| Data Date | Rating | RACR #1 | RACR #2 | Total Assets ($mil) | Capital ($mil) | Net Premium ($mil) | Net Income ($mil) |
|---|---|---|---|---|---|---|---|
| 9-17 | B | 2.31 | 1.92 | 592.3 | 309.8 | 1,928.9 | 35.9 |
| 9-16 | B | 2.21 | 1.84 | 593.5 | 277.8 | 1,896.9 | 58.2 |
| 2016 | B | 2.05 | 1.71 | 547.6 | 272.9 | 2,549.2 | 87.7 |
| 2015 | B | 2.07 | 1.72 | 523.6 | 258.7 | 2,388.2 | 99.1 |
| 2014 | B | 2.45 | 2.04 | 532.7 | 247.6 | 1,989.5 | 97.1 |
| 2013 | B | 2.19 | 1.83 | 460.6 | 204.1 | 1,726.7 | 62.3 |
| 2012 | B | 1.43 | 1.19 | 440.4 | 137.8 | 1,714.3 | -15.7 |

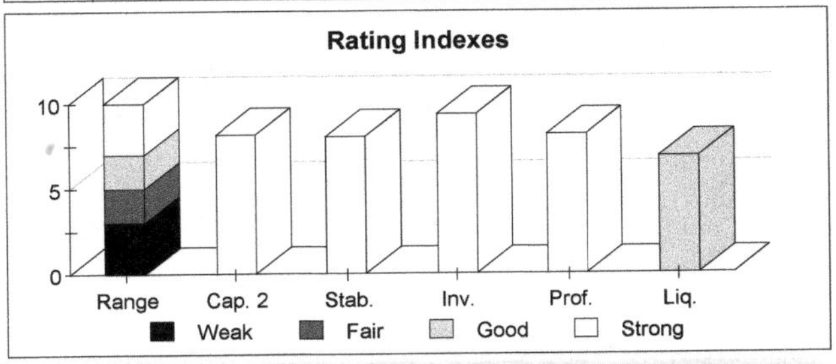


## AMERIGROUP COMMUNITY CARE NM B- Good

**Major Rating Factors:** Fair profitability index (3.6 on a scale of 0 to 10). Strong capitalization (10.0) based on excellent current risk-adjusted capital (severe loss scenario). High quality investment portfolio (9.4).
**Other Rating Factors:** Excellent liquidity (8.1) with ample operational cash flow and liquid investments.
**Principal Business:** Medicare (100%)
**Mem Phys: 16:** 5,850 **15:** 6,599 **16 MLR** 89.1% **/ 16 Admin Exp** N/A
**Enroll(000): Q2 17:** 2 **16:** 2 **15:** 2 **Med Exp PMPM:** $716
**Principal Investments:** Long-term bonds (89%), cash and equiv (10%), other (1%)
**Provider Compensation ($000):** Contr fee ($9,740), FFS ($4,854), capitation ($686), bonus arrang ($216)
**Total Member Encounters:** Phys (20,002), non-phys (21,985)
**Group Affiliation:** Anthem Inc
**Licensed in:** NM
**Address:** 6565 AMERICAS PARKWAY NE #200, ALBUQUERQUE, NM 87110
**Phone:** (757) 490-6900 **Dom State:** NM **Commenced Bus:** January 2008

| Data Date | Rating | RACR #1 | RACR #2 | Total Assets ($mil) | Capital ($mil) | Net Premium ($mil) | Net Income ($mil) |
|---|---|---|---|---|---|---|---|
| 6-17 | B- | 33.54 | 27.95 | 70.5 | 64.0 | 10.0 | 0.4 |
| 6-16 | B- | 34.43 | 28.69 | 70.0 | 62.4 | 9.7 | -0.4 |
| 2016 | B- | 33.33 | 27.77 | 99.8 | 63.5 | 18.8 | 0.6 |
| 2015 | B- | 34.71 | 28.93 | 68.2 | 62.9 | 20.2 | 2.4 |
| 2014 | B- | 16.89 | 14.07 | 71.1 | 60.2 | 37.8 | -2.5 |
| 2013 | B- | 2.71 | 2.26 | 123.2 | 69.3 | 492.9 | 6.5 |
| 2012 | C+ | 2.37 | 1.98 | 108.7 | 62.3 | 494.1 | 7.4 |

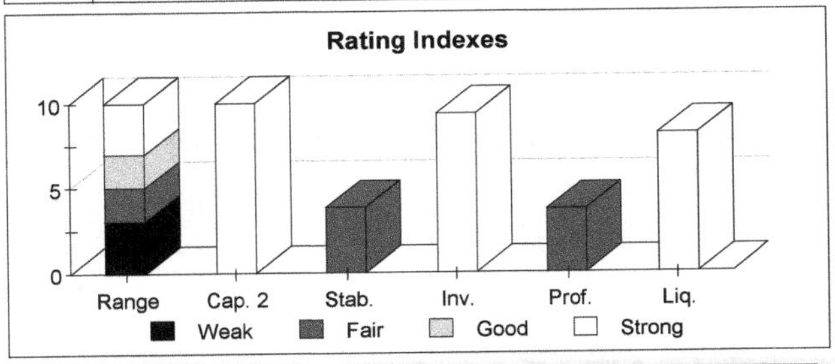


## AMERIGROUP INS CO B Good

**Major Rating Factors:** Good liquidity (6.7 on a scale of 0 to 10) with sufficient resources (cash flows and marketable investments) to handle a spike in claims. Fair profitability index (4.3). Strong capitalization (10.0) based on excellent current risk-adjusted capital (severe loss scenario).
**Other Rating Factors:** High quality investment portfolio (9.3).
**Principal Business:** Medicaid (100%)
**Mem Phys: 16:** 26,646 **15:** 24,016 **16 MLR** 87.7% **/ 16 Admin Exp** N/A
**Enroll(000): Q3 17:** 156 **16:** 159 **15:** 126 **Med Exp PMPM:** $348
**Principal Investments:** Long-term bonds (68%), cash and equiv (32%)
**Provider Compensation ($000):** Contr fee ($445,067), FFS ($39,426), capitation ($29,886), bonus arrang ($88)
**Total Member Encounters:** Phys (580,319), non-phys (1,011,263)
**Group Affiliation:** Anthem Inc
**Licensed in:** TX
**Address:** 3800 BUFFALO SPEEDWAY Ste 400, HOUSTON, TX 77098
**Phone:** (757) 490-6900 **Dom State:** TX **Commenced Bus:** March 2012

| Data Date | Rating | RACR #1 | RACR #2 | Total Assets ($mil) | Capital ($mil) | Net Premium ($mil) | Net Income ($mil) |
|---|---|---|---|---|---|---|---|
| 9-17 | B | 3.85 | 3.20 | 260.0 | 135.5 | 725.7 | 19.4 |
| 9-16 | B- | 3.71 | 3.09 | 176.0 | 99.3 | 407.6 | 5.3 |
| 2016 | B- | 2.86 | 2.39 | 209.3 | 99.2 | 624.2 | 6.0 |
| 2015 | B- | 3.52 | 2.93 | 167.5 | 93.6 | 491.8 | -0.1 |
| 2014 | B- | 4.51 | 3.76 | 141.7 | 96.9 | 383.1 | 1.5 |
| 2013 | B- | 4.46 | 3.72 | 136.8 | 96.3 | 394.1 | 16.3 |
| 2012 | B- | 3.11 | 2.59 | 119.7 | 79.6 | 325.9 | -21.4 |

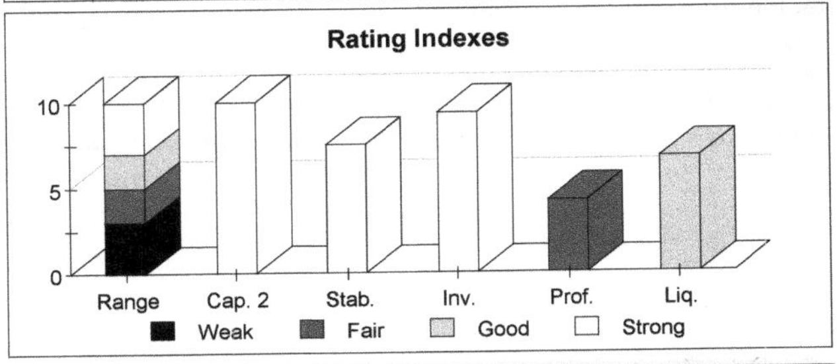

## AMERIGROUP IOWA INC — C — Fair

**Major Rating Factors:** Weak profitability index (0.8 on a scale of 0 to 10). Weak liquidity (0.8) as a spike in claims may stretch capacity. Strong capitalization (7.0) based on excellent current risk-adjusted capital (severe loss scenario).
**Other Rating Factors:** High quality investment portfolio (9.9).
**Principal Business:** Medicaid (98%), comp med (2%)
**Mem Phys: 16:** 30,924 **15:** N/A **16 MLR** 116.0% **/ 16 Admin Exp** N/A
**Enroll(000): Q3 17:** 194 **16:** 194 **15:** N/A **Med Exp PMPM:** $527
**Principal Investments:** Cash and equiv (100%)
**Provider Compensation ($000):** Contr fee ($445,290), FFS ($319,619), capitation ($4,726), bonus arrang ($625)
**Total Member Encounters:** Phys (1,107,621), non-phys (1,468,218)
**Group Affiliation:** Anthem Inc
**Licensed in:** IA
**Address:** 5550 WILD ROSE LANE Ste 400, DES MOINES, IA 50266
**Phone:** (757) 490-6900 **Dom State:** IA **Commenced Bus:** N/A

| Data Date | Rating | RACR #1 | RACR #2 | Total Assets ($mil) | Capital ($mil) | Net Premium ($mil) | Net Income ($mil) |
|---|---|---|---|---|---|---|---|
| 9-17 | C | 1.33 | 1.11 | 323.7 | 101.9 | 932.0 | -89.7 |
| 9-16 | N/A | N/A | N/A | 297.2 | 63.2 | 523.1 | -147.2 |
| 2016 | B- | 1.74 | 1.45 | 316.6 | 132.4 | 788.0 | -133.3 |
| 2015 | N/A | N/A | N/A | 74.0 | 19.1 | N/A | -50.5 |
| 2014 | N/A | N/A | N/A | N/A | N/A | N/A | N/A |
| 2013 | N/A | N/A | N/A | N/A | N/A | N/A | N/A |
| 2012 | N/A | N/A | N/A | N/A | N/A | N/A | N/A |

Rating Indexes

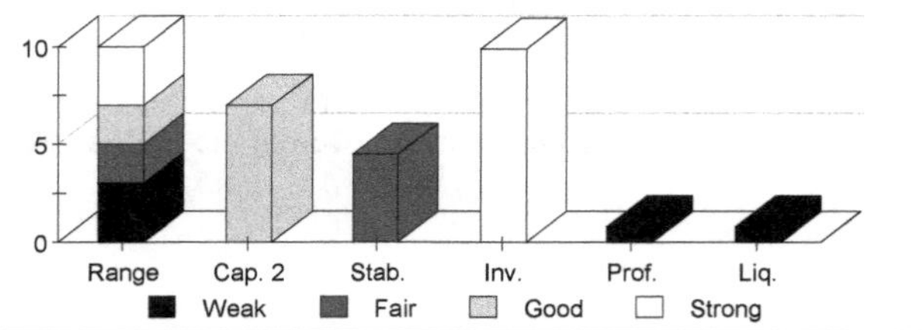


## AMERIGROUP KANSAS INC — B- — Good

**Major Rating Factors:** Strong capitalization (9.2 on a scale of 0 to 10) based on excellent current risk-adjusted capital (severe loss scenario). High quality investment portfolio (9.9). Excellent liquidity (7.1) with ample operational cash flow and liquid investments.
**Other Rating Factors:** Weak profitability index (0.9).
**Principal Business:** Medicaid (97%), comp med (3%)
**Mem Phys: 16:** 18,245 **15:** 17,234 **16 MLR** 86.3% **/ 16 Admin Exp** N/A
**Enroll(000): Q3 17:** 122 **16:** 131 **15:** 130 **Med Exp PMPM:** $539
**Principal Investments:** Cash and equiv (65%), long-term bonds (35%)
**Provider Compensation ($000):** Contr fee ($864,301), capitation ($4,380), FFS ($3,908), bonus arrang ($85)
**Total Member Encounters:** Phys (859,467), non-phys (2,428,753)
**Group Affiliation:** Anthem Inc
**Licensed in:** KS
**Address:** 9225 INDIAN CREEK PKWY STE 400, OVERLAND PARK, KS 66210
**Phone:** (913) 749-5955 **Dom State:** KS **Commenced Bus:** January 2013

| Data Date | Rating | RACR #1 | RACR #2 | Total Assets ($mil) | Capital ($mil) | Net Premium ($mil) | Net Income ($mil) |
|---|---|---|---|---|---|---|---|
| 9-17 | B- | 3.10 | 2.58 | 294.4 | 168.4 | 733.9 | -16.7 |
| 9-16 | C+ | 3.33 | 2.78 | 289.6 | 178.5 | 751.6 | 3.4 |
| 2016 | B- | 3.35 | 2.79 | 303.3 | 183.3 | 997.7 | 8.9 |
| 2015 | B- | 3.24 | 2.70 | 289.4 | 173.2 | 1,004.9 | 87.2 |
| 2014 | B- | 1.69 | 1.41 | 253.8 | 87.1 | 900.9 | -68.5 |
| 2013 | B- | 1.53 | 1.28 | 181.9 | 83.7 | 720.6 | -34.2 |
| 2012 | N/A | N/A | N/A | 7.7 | 2.4 | N/A | -3.5 |

Rating Indexes

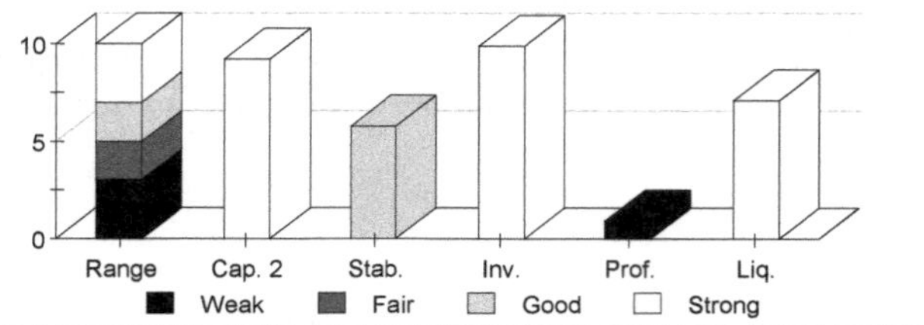


## AMERIGROUP MARYLAND INC — B — Good

**Major Rating Factors:** Good liquidity (6.9 on a scale of 0 to 10) with sufficient resources (cash flows and marketable investments) to handle a spike in claims. Fair quality investment portfolio (3.5). Excellent profitability (8.9).
**Other Rating Factors:** Strong capitalization (8.2) based on excellent current risk-adjusted capital (severe loss scenario).
**Principal Business:** Medicaid (95%), comp med (5%)
**Mem Phys: 16:** 17,469 **15:** 16,754 **16 MLR** 81.9% **/ 16 Admin Exp** N/A
**Enroll(000): Q3 17:** 279 **16:** 278 **15:** 253 **Med Exp PMPM:** $280
**Principal Investments:** Long-term bonds (90%), cash and equiv (8%), other (2%)
**Provider Compensation ($000):** Contr fee ($785,617), FFS ($95,015), capitation ($5,617), bonus arrang ($1,312)
**Total Member Encounters:** Phys (1,471,730), non-phys (912,184)
**Group Affiliation:** Anthem Inc
**Licensed in:** MD
**Address:** 7550 TEAGUE Rd Ste 500, HANOVER, MD 21076
**Phone:** (757) 490-6900 **Dom State:** MD **Commenced Bus:** June 1999

| Data Date | Rating | RACR #1 | RACR #2 | Total Assets ($mil) | Capital ($mil) | Net Premium ($mil) | Net Income ($mil) |
|---|---|---|---|---|---|---|---|
| 9-17 | B | 2.32 | 1.94 | 351.8 | 140.3 | 834.0 | 50.4 |
| 9-16 | B | 2.29 | 1.91 | 349.4 | 121.1 | 812.5 | 25.9 |
| 2016 | B | 2.14 | 1.78 | 346.3 | 128.7 | 1,088.1 | 54.3 |
| 2015 | B | 1.88 | 1.57 | 276.2 | 98.2 | 946.1 | 3.9 |
| 2014 | B | 2.09 | 1.74 | 307.2 | 114.2 | 1,069.6 | 51.3 |
| 2013 | B | 2.30 | 1.91 | 180.1 | 88.8 | 764.2 | 31.4 |
| 2012 | A- | 3.30 | 2.75 | 191.9 | 114.1 | 684.2 | 34.2 |

Rating Indexes

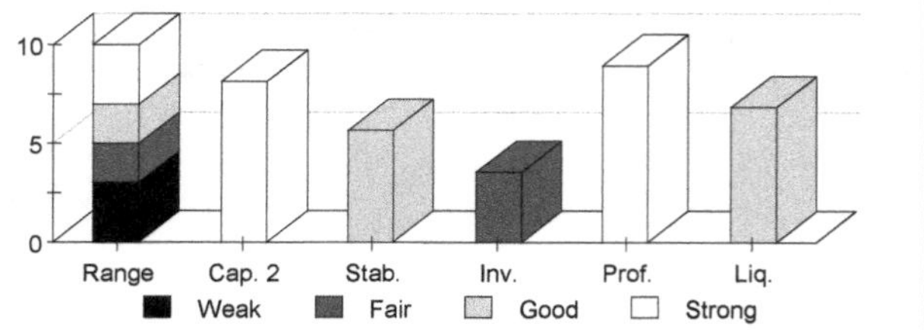

## AMERIGROUP NEVADA INC — B — Good

**Major Rating Factors:** Excellent profitability (8.7 on a scale of 0 to 10). Strong capitalization (7.9) based on excellent current risk-adjusted capital (severe loss scenario). High quality investment portfolio (9.9).
**Other Rating Factors:** Excellent liquidity (6.9) with sufficient resources (cash flows and marketable investments) to handle a spike in claims.
**Principal Business:** Medicaid (98%), comp med (2%)
**Mem Phys: 16:** 6,652 **15:** 5,484 **16 MLR** 85.5% **/ 16 Admin Exp** N/A
**Enroll(000): Q3 17:** 194 **16:** 195 **15:** 183 **Med Exp PMPM:** $240
**Principal Investments:** Cash and equiv (68%), long-term bonds (32%)
**Provider Compensation ($000):** Contr fee ($492,794), capitation ($33,570), FFS ($4,946), bonus arrang ($578)
**Total Member Encounters:** Phys (1,248,048), non-phys (551,731)
**Group Affiliation:** Anthem Inc
**Licensed in:** NV
**Address:** 9133 W RUSSELL RD, LAS VEGAS, NV 89148
**Phone:** (757) 490-6900 **Dom State:** NV **Commenced Bus:** February 2009

| Data Date | Rating | RACR #1 | RACR #2 | Total Assets ($mil) | Capital ($mil) | Net Premium ($mil) | Net Income ($mil) |
|---|---|---|---|---|---|---|---|
| 9-17 | B | 2.09 | 1.74 | 129.0 | 71.3 | 485.5 | 6.0 |
| 9-16 | B | 2.18 | 1.82 | 114.9 | 61.1 | 470.7 | 0.6 |
| 2016 | B | 1.91 | 1.59 | 122.1 | 64.7 | 635.1 | 4.9 |
| 2015 | B | 2.19 | 1.82 | 114.8 | 61.3 | 560.0 | 9.5 |
| 2014 | B | 2.23 | 1.86 | 92.1 | 41.9 | 400.8 | 14.1 |
| 2013 | B- | 3.12 | 2.60 | 45.1 | 28.0 | 188.1 | 7.0 |
| 2012 | B | 3.95 | 3.29 | 48.9 | 35.8 | 185.4 | 7.0 |

Rating Indexes

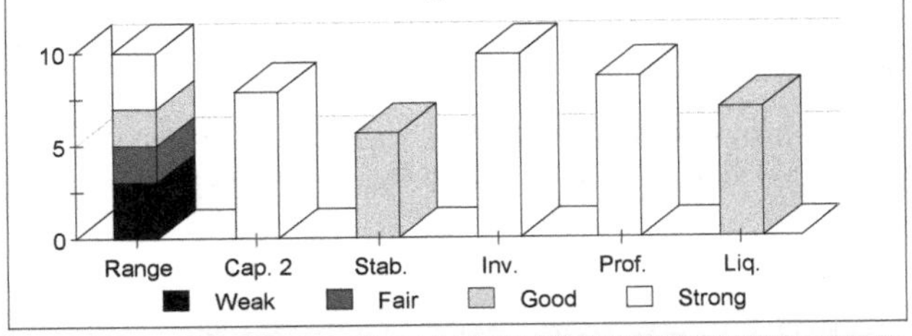


## AMERIGROUP NEW JERSEY INC * — B+ — Good

**Major Rating Factors:** Good overall results on stability tests (5.8 on a scale of 0 to 10). Rating is significantly influenced by the good financial results of Anthem Inc. Good liquidity (6.7) with sufficient resources (cash flows and marketable investments) to handle a spike in claims. Excellent profitability (8.8).
**Other Rating Factors:** Strong capitalization index (8.1) based on excellent current risk-adjusted capital (severe loss scenario). High quality investment portfolio (9.0).
**Principal Business:** Medicaid (86%), Medicare (12%), comp med (2%)
**Mem Phys: 16:** 14,145 **15:** 11,758 **16 MLR** 81.0% **/ 16 Admin Exp** N/A
**Enroll(000): Q3 17:** 199 **16:** 209 **15:** 209 **Med Exp PMPM:** $420
**Principal Investments:** Long-term bonds (100%)
**Provider Compensation ($000):** Contr fee ($985,295), capitation ($36,635), FFS ($22,474), bonus arrang ($5,906)
**Total Member Encounters:** Phys (1,349,143), non-phys (2,569,970)
**Group Affiliation:** Anthem Inc
**Licensed in:** NJ
**Address:** 101 WOOD AVENUE SOUTH 8TH FLOO, ISELIN, NJ 08830
**Phone:** (757) 490-6900 **Dom State:** NJ **Commenced Bus:** February 1996

| Data Date | Rating | RACR #1 | RACR #2 | Total Assets ($mil) | Capital ($mil) | Net Premium ($mil) | Net Income ($mil) |
|---|---|---|---|---|---|---|---|
| 9-17 | B+ | 2.21 | 1.84 | 329.0 | 146.6 | 1,030.5 | 27.3 |
| 9-16 | B | 3.12 | 2.60 | 372.5 | 191.9 | 970.2 | 37.1 |
| 2016 | A- | 2.52 | 2.10 | 318.0 | 168.8 | 1,304.3 | 65.2 |
| 2015 | B | 2.54 | 2.12 | 386.5 | 154.3 | 1,208.2 | 59.1 |
| 2014 | A- | 3.82 | 3.18 | 290.8 | 174.5 | 965.4 | 77.7 |
| 2013 | A- | 3.26 | 2.72 | 178.3 | 110.3 | 645.5 | 25.0 |
| 2012 | A- | 2.46 | 2.05 | 153.9 | 85.0 | 631.2 | 11.6 |

Rating Indexes

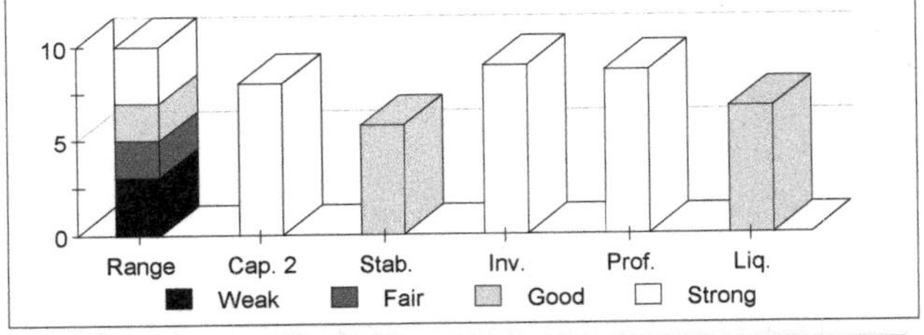


## AMERIGROUP TENNESSEE INC — B- — Good

**Major Rating Factors:** Fair quality investment portfolio (3.7 on a scale of 0 to 10). Good liquidity (6.1) with sufficient resources (cash flows and marketable investments) to handle a spike in claims. Excellent profitability (8.9).
**Other Rating Factors:** Strong capitalization (7.7) based on excellent current risk-adjusted capital (severe loss scenario).
**Principal Business:** Medicaid (94%), Medicare (6%)
**Mem Phys: 16:** 24,146 **15:** 20,449 **16 MLR** 84.2% **/ 16 Admin Exp** N/A
**Enroll(000): Q3 17:** 407 **16:** 450 **15:** 427 **Med Exp PMPM:** $291
**Principal Investments:** Long-term bonds (80%), cash and equiv (14%), other (6%)
**Provider Compensation ($000):** Contr fee ($1,522,992), capitation ($55,035), FFS ($17,843), bonus arrang ($2,084)
**Total Member Encounters:** Phys (2,725,626), non-phys (3,346,631)
**Group Affiliation:** Anthem Inc
**Licensed in:** TN
**Address:** 22 CENTURY Blvd Ste 220, NASHVILLE, TN 37214
**Phone:** (757) 490-6900 **Dom State:** TN **Commenced Bus:** April 2007

| Data Date | Rating | RACR #1 | RACR #2 | Total Assets ($mil) | Capital ($mil) | Net Premium ($mil) | Net Income ($mil) |
|---|---|---|---|---|---|---|---|
| 9-17 | B- | 1.92 | 1.60 | 524.5 | 195.4 | 1,296.4 | 16.8 |
| 9-16 | B- | 1.96 | 1.63 | 552.4 | 164.6 | 1,440.4 | -1.1 |
| 2016 | B- | 1.76 | 1.47 | 531.9 | 178.2 | 1,905.9 | 13.4 |
| 2015 | B | 2.02 | 1.68 | 591.6 | 169.6 | 1,688.4 | 22.7 |
| 2014 | B | 3.21 | 2.68 | 429.0 | 156.6 | 1,006.3 | 26.1 |
| 2013 | B | 2.42 | 2.01 | 236.7 | 108.1 | 917.0 | 23.8 |
| 2012 | B | 2.35 | 1.96 | 212.2 | 106.1 | 904.9 | 25.8 |

Rating Indexes

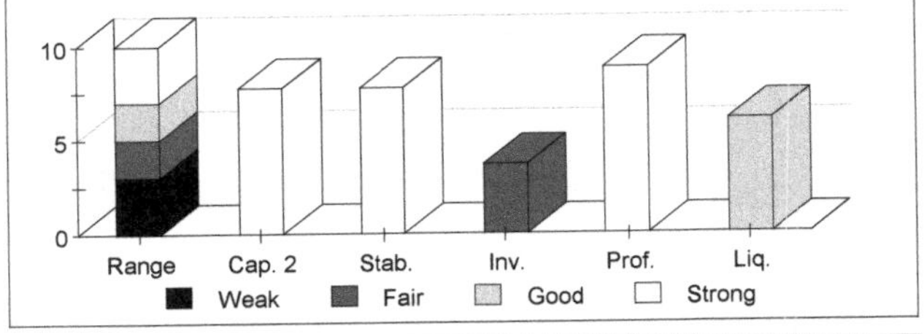



* Denotes a Weiss Ratings Recommended Company

## AMERIGROUP TEXAS INC * A- Excellent

**Major Rating Factors:** Excellent profitability (8.6 on a scale of 0 to 10). Strong capitalization index (8.3) based on excellent current risk-adjusted capital (severe loss scenario). High quality investment portfolio (9.1).
**Other Rating Factors:** Excellent overall results on stability tests (7.0). Rating is significantly influenced by the good financial results of Anthem Inc. Good liquidity (6.7) with sufficient resources (cash flows and marketable investments) to handle a spike in claims.
**Principal Business:** Medicaid (79%), Medicare (19%), comp med (3%)
**Mem Phys: 16:** 70,270 **15:** 62,584 **16 MLR** 83.0% **/ 16 Admin Exp** N/A
**Enroll(000): Q3 17:** 689 **16:** 701 **15:** 688 **Med Exp PMPM:** $383
**Principal Investments:** Long-term bonds (78%), cash and equiv (18%), other (3%)
**Provider Compensation ($000):** Contr fee ($2,908,650), FFS ($254,777), capitation ($72,823), bonus arrang ($9,604)
**Total Member Encounters:** Phys (4,206,314), non-phys (5,273,282)
**Group Affiliation:** Anthem Inc
**Licensed in:** TX
**Address:** 3800 BUFFALO SPEEDWAY SUITE 40, HOUSTON, TX 77098
**Phone:** (757) 490-6900 **Dom State:** TX **Commenced Bus:** October 1996

| Data Date | Rating | RACR #1 | RACR #2 | Total Assets ($mil) | Capital ($mil) | Net Premium ($mil) | Net Income ($mil) |
|---|---|---|---|---|---|---|---|
| 9-17 | A- | 2.42 | 2.01 | 1,042.5 | 477.2 | 2,865.7 | 69.9 |
| 9-16 | B+ | 2.10 | 1.75 | 1,017.8 | 403.2 | 2,921.7 | 50.3 |
| 2016 | A- | 2.06 | 1.72 | 912.7 | 400.5 | 3,861.6 | 87.0 |
| 2015 | B | 1.86 | 1.55 | 874.5 | 352.8 | 3,610.8 | 54.3 |
| 2014 | B | 2.15 | 1.79 | 629.8 | 312.0 | 2,747.5 | 37.7 |
| 2013 | A- | 2.45 | 2.04 | 666.8 | 348.3 | 2,627.5 | 69.3 |
| 2012 | A- | 2.08 | 1.73 | 500.7 | 275.3 | 2,373.1 | 23.5 |

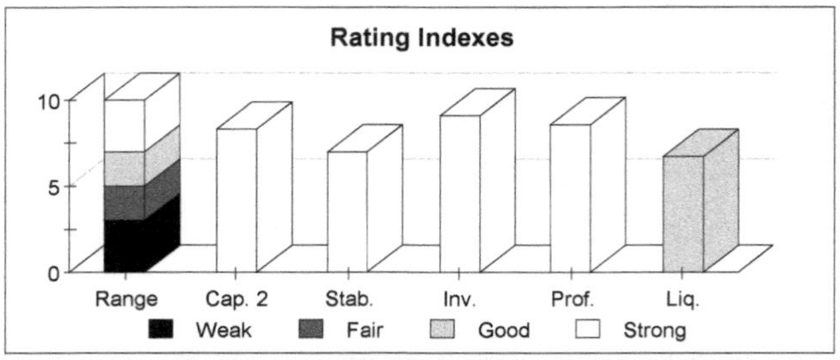


## AMERIGROUP WASHINGTON INC * A- Excellent

**Major Rating Factors:** Strong capitalization (10.0 on a scale of 0 to 10) based on excellent current risk-adjusted capital (severe loss scenario). High quality investment portfolio (8.0). Good overall profitability index (6.5).
**Other Rating Factors:** Good liquidity (6.8) with sufficient resources (cash flows and marketable investments) to handle a spike in claims.
**Principal Business:** Medicaid (97%), Medicare (2%)
**Mem Phys: 16:** 22,924 **15:** 20,063 **16 MLR** 81.9% **/ 16 Admin Exp** N/A
**Enroll(000): Q3 17:** 146 **16:** 151 **15:** 143 **Med Exp PMPM:** $266
**Principal Investments:** Long-term bonds (98%), cash and equiv (2%)
**Provider Compensation ($000):** Contr fee ($455,671), capitation ($8,953), FFS ($8,711), bonus arrang ($165)
**Total Member Encounters:** Phys (779,729), non-phys (564,066)
**Group Affiliation:** Anthem Inc
**Licensed in:** WA
**Address:** 705 FIFTH Ave S Ste 110, SEATTLE, WA 98104
**Phone:** (757) 490-6900 **Dom State:** WA **Commenced Bus:** July 2012

| Data Date | Rating | RACR #1 | RACR #2 | Total Assets ($mil) | Capital ($mil) | Net Premium ($mil) | Net Income ($mil) |
|---|---|---|---|---|---|---|---|
| 9-17 | A- | 4.73 | 3.94 | 267.7 | 146.2 | 459.5 | 25.2 |
| 9-16 | B | 4.51 | 3.76 | 260.4 | 126.3 | 427.5 | 16.5 |
| 2016 | A- | 4.36 | 3.63 | 259.0 | 134.1 | 570.7 | 24.8 |
| 2015 | B | 4.33 | 3.60 | 240.5 | 120.9 | 509.6 | 18.7 |
| 2014 | B- | 5.11 | 4.26 | 413.2 | 103.4 | 389.9 | -4.6 |
| 2013 | B- | 5.38 | 4.48 | 105.1 | 35.7 | 133.9 | 2.5 |
| 2012 | B- | 6.65 | 5.54 | 65.8 | 30.2 | 45.5 | -4.9 |

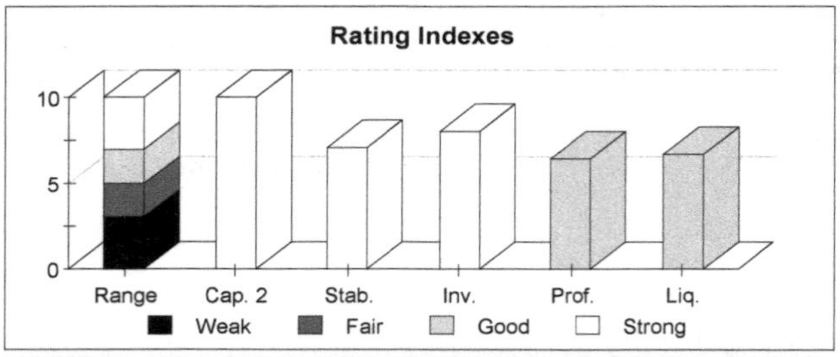


## AMERIHEALTH CARITAS IOWA INC C- Fair

**Major Rating Factors:** Fair liquidity (4.8 on a scale of 0 to 10) as cash resources may not be adequate to cover a spike in claims. Weak profitability index (0.9). Strong capitalization (7.0) based on excellent current risk-adjusted capital (severe loss scenario).
**Other Rating Factors:** High quality investment portfolio (9.9).
**Principal Business:** Medicaid (100%)
**Mem Phys: 16:** 42,298 **15:** N/A **16 MLR** 110.4% **/ 16 Admin Exp** N/A
**Enroll(000): Q3 17:** 219 **16:** 223 **15:** N/A **Med Exp PMPM:** $789
**Principal Investments:** Cash and equiv (100%)
**Provider Compensation ($000):** Contr fee ($1,305,055), capitation ($17,752)
**Total Member Encounters:** Phys (725,539), non-phys (170,923)
**Group Affiliation:** Independence Health Group Inc
**Licensed in:** IA
**Address:** 601 Locust St Ste 900, Des Moines, IA 50309
**Phone:** (215) 937-8000 **Dom State:** IA **Commenced Bus:** August 2015

| Data Date | Rating | RACR #1 | RACR #2 | Total Assets ($mil) | Capital ($mil) | Net Premium ($mil) | Net Income ($mil) |
|---|---|---|---|---|---|---|---|
| 9-17 | C- | 1.35 | 1.13 | 417.9 | 159.9 | 1,418.4 | -148.0 |
| 9-16 | N/A | N/A | N/A | 178.9 | 17.5 | 842.5 | -132.4 |
| 2016 | C- | 1.18 | 0.99 | 453.6 | 140.1 | 1,398.0 | -293.1 |
| 2015 | N/A | N/A | N/A | 41.2 | 8.2 | N/A | -33.0 |
| 2014 | N/A | N/A | N/A | N/A | N/A | N/A | N/A |
| 2013 | N/A | N/A | N/A | N/A | N/A | N/A | N/A |
| 2012 | N/A | N/A | N/A | N/A | N/A | N/A | N/A |

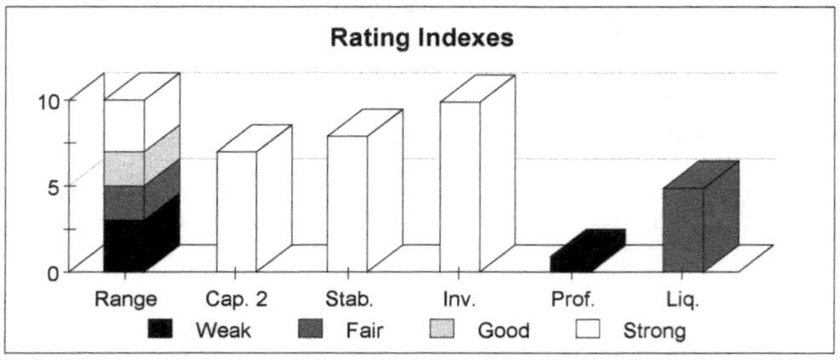

## AMERIHEALTH CARITAS OF LOUISIANA INC C Fair

**Major Rating Factors:** Low quality investment portfolio (1.0 on a scale of 0 to 10). Good overall profitability index (6.3). Strong capitalization (7.9) based on excellent current risk-adjusted capital (severe loss scenario).
**Other Rating Factors:** Excellent liquidity (7.0) with ample operational cash flow and liquid investments.
**Principal Business:** Medicaid (100%)
**Mem Phys: 16:** 29,212 **15:** 26,232 **16 MLR** 84.3% **/ 16 Admin Exp** N/A
**Enroll(000): Q3 17:** 214 **16:** 223 **15:** 176 **Med Exp PMPM:** $337
**Principal Investments:** Cash and equiv (99%), long-term bonds (1%)
**Provider Compensation ($000):** Contr fee ($526,710), capitation ($159,845), bonus arrang ($1,798)
**Total Member Encounters:** Phys (1,093,120), non-phys (783,083)
**Group Affiliation:** Independence Health Group Inc
**Licensed in:** LA
**Address:** 10000 Perkins Rowe G Ste 400, Baton Rouge, LA 70810
**Phone:** (215) 937-8000 **Dom State:** LA **Commenced Bus:** July 2011

| Data Date | Rating | RACR #1 | RACR #2 | Total Assets ($mil) | Capital ($mil) | Net Premium ($mil) | Net Income ($mil) |
|---|---|---|---|---|---|---|---|
| 9-17 | C | 2.10 | 1.75 | 257.9 | 92.7 | 755.6 | 25.3 |
| 9-16 | C | 2.14 | 1.78 | 251.3 | 65.8 | 637.1 | 4.9 |
| 2016 | C | 1.56 | 1.30 | 276.8 | 67.9 | 908.3 | 6.2 |
| 2015 | C | 1.96 | 1.63 | 155.6 | 59.8 | 622.8 | 9.7 |
| 2014 | C | 1.67 | 1.40 | 183.0 | 48.7 | 537.3 | -1.4 |
| 2013 | C | 1.56 | 1.30 | 105.7 | 40.3 | 490.6 | 12.4 |
| 2012 | C | 1.45 | 1.21 | 85.7 | 23.4 | 272.4 | -15.3 |

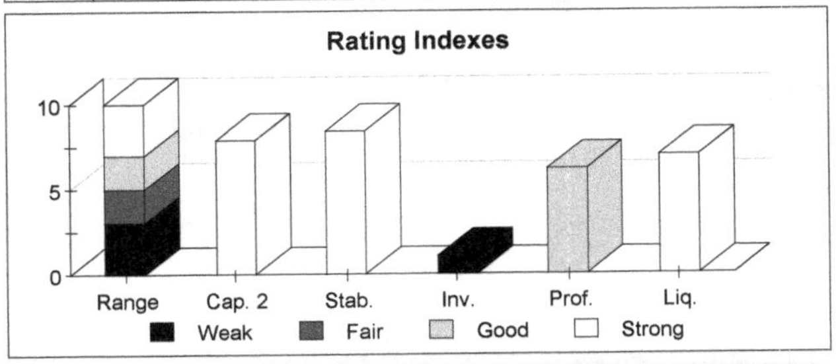


## AMERIHEALTH DISTRICT OF COLUMBIA INC B- Good

**Major Rating Factors:** Good overall profitability index (6.5 on a scale of 0 to 10). Strong capitalization (8.3) based on excellent current risk-adjusted capital (severe loss scenario). High quality investment portfolio (9.9).
**Other Rating Factors:** Excellent liquidity (7.2) with ample operational cash flow and liquid investments.
**Principal Business:** Medicaid (95%), comp med (5%)
**Mem Phys: 16:** 4,042 **15:** 4,000 **16 MLR** 78.4% **/ 16 Admin Exp** N/A
**Enroll(000): Q3 17:** 110 **16:** 104 **15:** 106 **Med Exp PMPM:** $307
**Principal Investments:** Cash and equiv (100%)
**Provider Compensation ($000):** Contr fee ($379,438), capitation ($10,869)
**Total Member Encounters:** Phys (706,634), non-phys (150,755)
**Group Affiliation:** Independence Health Group Inc
**Licensed in:** DC
**Address:** 1120 Vermont Ave Ste 200, Washington, DC 20005
**Phone:** (215) 937-8000 **Dom State:** DC **Commenced Bus:** March 2013

| Data Date | Rating | RACR #1 | RACR #2 | Total Assets ($mil) | Capital ($mil) | Net Premium ($mil) | Net Income ($mil) |
|---|---|---|---|---|---|---|---|
| 9-17 | B- | 2.40 | 2.00 | 132.2 | 57.5 | 375.9 | 18.1 |
| 9-16 | C+ | 2.63 | 2.19 | 144.0 | 65.4 | 370.0 | 12.8 |
| 2016 | B- | 2.95 | 2.46 | 155.1 | 72.2 | 493.9 | 19.2 |
| 2015 | B | 2.28 | 1.90 | 142.9 | 56.2 | 477.3 | 9.5 |
| 2014 | B | 2.25 | 1.87 | 115.5 | 45.1 | 447.0 | 16.4 |
| 2013 | C | 1.48 | 1.24 | 83.8 | 24.8 | 255.5 | -6.0 |
| 2012 | N/A | N/A | N/A | N/A | N/A | N/A | N/A |

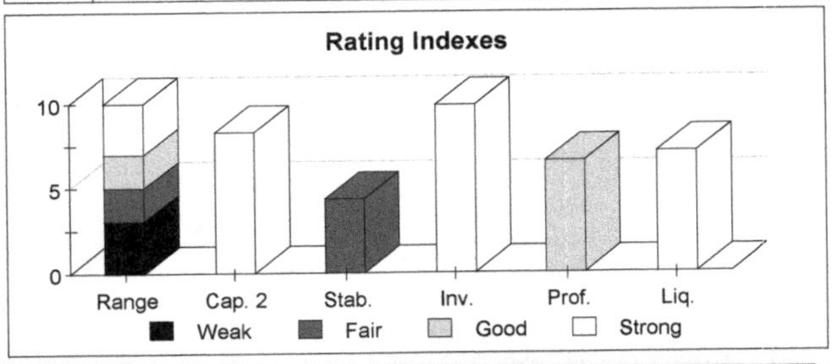


## AMERIHEALTH HMO INC C Fair

**Major Rating Factors:** Fair profitability index (4.7 on a scale of 0 to 10). Fair overall results on stability tests (3.6) based on an inordinate decline in premium revenue in 2016. Rating is significantly influenced by the fair financial results of Independence Health Group Inc. Weak liquidity (2.7) as a spike in claims may stretch capacity.
**Other Rating Factors:** Strong capitalization index (10.0) based on excellent current risk-adjusted capital (severe loss scenario). High quality investment portfolio (9.9).
**Principal Business:** Comp med (100%)
**Mem Phys: 16:** 52,014 **15:** 46,206 **16 MLR** 2572.1% **/ 16 Admin Exp** N/A
**Enroll(000): Q3 17:** 34 **16:** 59 **15:** 65 **Med Exp PMPM:** $508
**Principal Investments:** Long-term bonds (94%), cash and equiv (6%)
**Provider Compensation ($000):** Contr fee ($350,417), FFS ($30,404), capitation ($5,204), bonus arrang ($37)
**Total Member Encounters:** Phys (1,173,643), non-phys (188,836)
**Group Affiliation:** Independence Health Group Inc
**Licensed in:** DE, NJ, PA
**Address:** 1901 Market Street, Philadelphia, PA 19103-1480
**Phone:** (215) 241-2400 **Dom State:** PA **Commenced Bus:** April 1978

| Data Date | Rating | RACR #1 | RACR #2 | Total Assets ($mil) | Capital ($mil) | Net Premium ($mil) | Net Income ($mil) |
|---|---|---|---|---|---|---|---|
| 9-17 | C | 8.86 | 7.39 | 106.0 | 18.1 | 9.4 | 0.2 |
| 9-16 | C | 6.20 | 5.16 | 173.5 | 13.7 | 11.5 | 0.6 |
| 2016 | C | 9.04 | 7.53 | 162.0 | 18.6 | 14.9 | 1.9 |
| 2015 | C | 7.89 | 6.58 | 259.5 | 19.3 | 17.2 | 0.9 |
| 2014 | C | 3.25 | 2.71 | 293.8 | 51.4 | 335.9 | -0.8 |
| 2013 | B | 4.71 | 3.93 | 1,326.7 | 1,258.9 | 391.7 | 5.7 |
| 2012 | B | 4.19 | 3.49 | 1,151.2 | 1,094.7 | 337.4 | 215.2 |

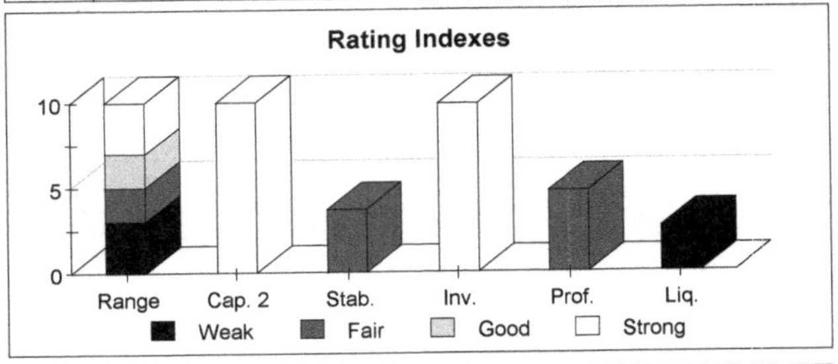

## AMERIHEALTH INSURANCE CO OF NJ C- Fair

**Major Rating Factors:** Weak profitability index (0.9 on a scale of 0 to 10). Good liquidity (6.7) with sufficient resources (cash flows and marketable investments) to handle a spike in claims. Strong capitalization (7.3) based on excellent current risk-adjusted capital (severe loss scenario).
**Other Rating Factors:** High quality investment portfolio (9.7).
**Principal Business:** Comp med (84%), Medicare (15%)
**Mem Phys: 16:** 49,217 **15:** 50,390 **16 MLR** 63.0% **/ 16 Admin Exp** N/A
**Enroll(000): 16:** 129 **15:** 125 **Med Exp PMPM:** $534
**Principal Investments:** Long-term bonds (98%), cash and equiv (2%)
**Provider Compensation ($000):** Contr fee ($607,655), FFS ($237,385), capitation ($3,728), bonus arrang ($1,128)
**Total Member Encounters:** Phys (3,491,174), non-phys (379,890)
**Group Affiliation:** Independence Health Group Inc
**Licensed in:** NJ
**Address:** 8000 Midlantic Dr Ste 333, Mount Laurel, NJ 08054-1560
**Phone:** (609) 662-2400 **Dom State:** NJ **Commenced Bus:** June 1995

| Data Date | Rating | RACR #1 | RACR #2 | Total Assets ($mil) | Capital ($mil) | Net Premium ($mil) | Net Income ($mil) |
|---|---|---|---|---|---|---|---|
| 2016 | C- | 1.59 | 1.32 | 421.3 | 126.6 | 1,356.1 | -63.5 |
| 2015 | C- | 2.41 | 2.01 | 492.6 | 173.8 | 1,241.3 | -46.9 |
| 2014 | C- | 2.39 | 1.99 | 431.9 | 143.6 | 1,057.6 | 15.1 |
| 2013 | C- | 3.44 | 2.87 | 169.1 | 83.7 | 415.8 | 2.7 |
| 2012 | C- | 4.02 | 3.35 | 143.0 | 79.9 | 332.6 | -2.5 |

Rating Indexes

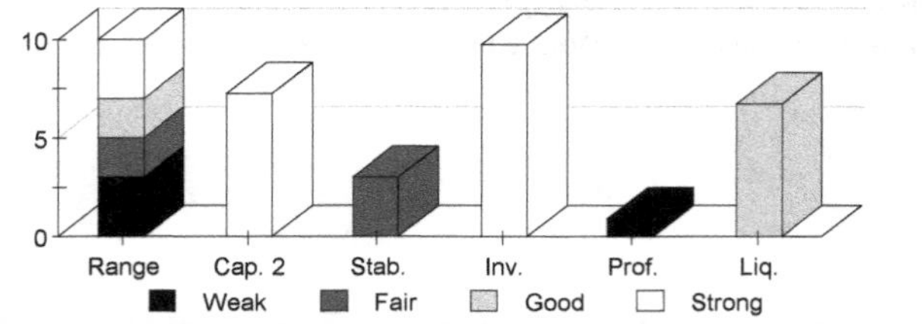


## AMERIHEALTH MICHIGAN INC C- Fair

**Major Rating Factors:** Weak profitability index (0.9 on a scale of 0 to 10). Good liquidity (6.8) with sufficient resources (cash flows and marketable investments) to handle a spike in claims. Strong capitalization (8.0) based on excellent current risk-adjusted capital (severe loss scenario).
**Other Rating Factors:** High quality investment portfolio (9.9).
**Principal Business:** Medicare (100%)
**Mem Phys: 16:** 4,274 **15:** 4,501 **16 MLR** 95.0% **/ 16 Admin Exp** N/A
**Enroll(000): Q3 17:** 3 **16:** 3 **15:** 3 **Med Exp PMPM:** $1,867
**Principal Investments:** Cash and equiv (96%), long-term bonds (4%)
**Provider Compensation ($000):** Contr fee ($72,696), capitation ($585)
**Total Member Encounters:** Phys (9,261), non-phys (12,593)
**Group Affiliation:** Independence Health Group Inc
**Licensed in:** MI
**Address:** 100 Galleria Officentre #210A, Southfield, MI 48034
**Phone:** (215) 937-8000 **Dom State:** MI **Commenced Bus:** April 2013

| Data Date | Rating | RACR #1 | RACR #2 | Total Assets ($mil) | Capital ($mil) | Net Premium ($mil) | Net Income ($mil) |
|---|---|---|---|---|---|---|---|
| 9-17 | C- | 2.12 | 1.77 | 31.9 | 12.4 | 64.7 | -4.5 |
| 9-16 | U | 1.85 | 1.55 | 28.4 | 8.3 | 57.9 | -8.4 |
| 2016 | C- | 2.03 | 1.69 | 28.4 | 11.9 | 78.1 | -10.7 |
| 2015 | U | 1.96 | 1.63 | 27.5 | 8.7 | 40.1 | -13.5 |
| 2014 | N/A | N/A | N/A | 2.1 | 2.0 | N/A | -2.6 |
| 2013 | N/A | N/A | N/A | 1.6 | 1.6 | N/A | N/A |
| 2012 | N/A | N/A | N/A | N/A | N/A | N/A | N/A |

Rating Indexes

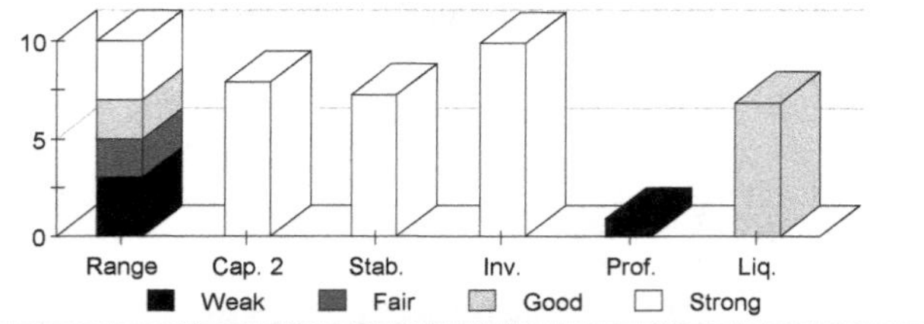


## AMERIHEALTH NEBRASKA INC E- Very Weak

**Major Rating Factors:** Weak profitability index (0.8 on a scale of 0 to 10). Weak liquidity (0.1) as a spike in claims may stretch capacity. Good capitalization (6.9) based on excellent current risk-adjusted capital (severe loss scenario).
**Other Rating Factors:** High quality investment portfolio (9.9).
**Principal Business:** Medicaid (100%)
**Mem Phys: 16:** 12,221 **15:** 8,479 **16 MLR** 95.0% **/ 16 Admin Exp** N/A
**Enroll(000): Q2 17:** N/A **16:** 26 **15:** 25 **Med Exp PMPM:** $262
**Principal Investments:** Cash and equiv (100%)
**Provider Compensation ($000):** Contr fee ($76,003), bonus arrang ($210)
**Total Member Encounters:** Phys (182,934), non-phys (85,263)
**Group Affiliation:** Independence Health Group Inc
**Licensed in:** NE
**Address:** 2120 S 72nd St, Omaha, NE 68124
**Phone:** (215) 937-8000 **Dom State:** NE **Commenced Bus:** February 2012

| Data Date | Rating | RACR #1 | RACR #2 | Total Assets ($mil) | Capital ($mil) | Net Premium ($mil) | Net Income ($mil) |
|---|---|---|---|---|---|---|---|
| 6-17 | E- | 1.25 | 1.04 | 14.2 | 9.0 | 0.6 | 1.3 |
| 6-16 | E | 2.05 | 1.71 | 27.1 | 10.8 | 42.9 | -1.4 |
| 2016 | E- | 0.51 | 0.43 | 23.9 | 4.2 | 85.6 | -7.9 |
| 2015 | E | 2.29 | 1.91 | 26.3 | 12.1 | 76.3 | -3.5 |
| 2014 | E | 2.59 | 2.16 | 21.3 | 11.1 | 65.7 | -0.1 |
| 2013 | C | 2.18 | 1.82 | 16.2 | 7.2 | 57.0 | 0.7 |
| 2012 | C | 2.39 | 1.99 | 21.9 | 7.2 | 25.0 | -3.7 |

Rating Indexes

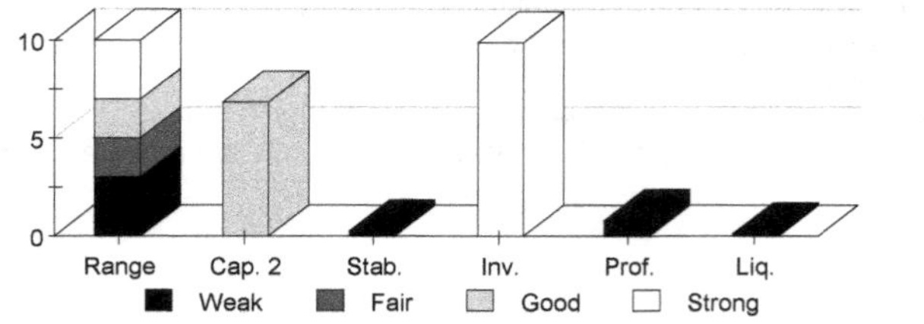

## AMERITAS LIFE INSURANCE CORP OF NEW YORK B- Good

**Major Rating Factors:** Good quality investment portfolio (6.1 on a scale of 0 to 10) despite large holdings of BBB rated bonds in addition to moderate junk bond exposure. Exposure to mortgages is significant, but the mortgage default rate has been low. Fair liquidity (4.8) due, in part, to cash value policies that are subject to withdrawals with minimal or no penalty. Fair overall results on stability tests (4.9).
**Other Rating Factors:** Weak profitability (2.2) with investment income below regulatory standards in relation to interest assumptions of reserves. Strong capitalization (7.3) based on excellent risk adjusted capital (severe loss scenario).
**Principal Business:** Individual life insurance (43%), group health insurance (21%), group retirement contracts (17%), reinsurance (11%), and other lines (7%).
**Principal Investments:** NonCMO investment grade bonds (65%), CMOs and structured securities (15%), mortgages in good standing (14%), noninv. grade bonds (3%), and policy loans (2%).
**Investments in Affiliates:** None
**Group Affiliation:** Ameritas Mutual Holding Co
**Licensed in:** NY
**Commenced Business:** May 1994
**Address:** 1350 Broadway Suite 2201, New York, NY 10018-7722
**Phone:** (845) 357-3816 **Domicile State:** NY **NAIC Code:** 60033

| Data Date | Rating | RACR #1 | RACR #2 | Total Assets ($mil) | Capital ($mil) | Net Premium ($mil) | Net Income ($mil) |
|---|---|---|---|---|---|---|---|
| 9-17 | B- | 2.20 | 1.18 | 1,249.8 | 100.8 | 113.6 | 1.0 |
| 9-16 | B- | N/A | N/A | 1,208.7 | 78.7 | 101.2 | -0.4 |
| 2016 | B- | 2.18 | 1.18 | 1,204.4 | 97.2 | 131.7 | 20.1 |
| 2015 | B- | 1.60 | 0.87 | 1,149.7 | 65.8 | 100.8 | -17.1 |
| 2014 | B- | 2.15 | 1.18 | 1,128.8 | 86.9 | 95.3 | -3.9 |
| 2013 | B- | 2.12 | 1.17 | 1,112.3 | 81.8 | 285.0 | -45.8 |
| 2012 | B- | 3.72 | 3.07 | 122.3 | 33.5 | 71.4 | -4.2 |

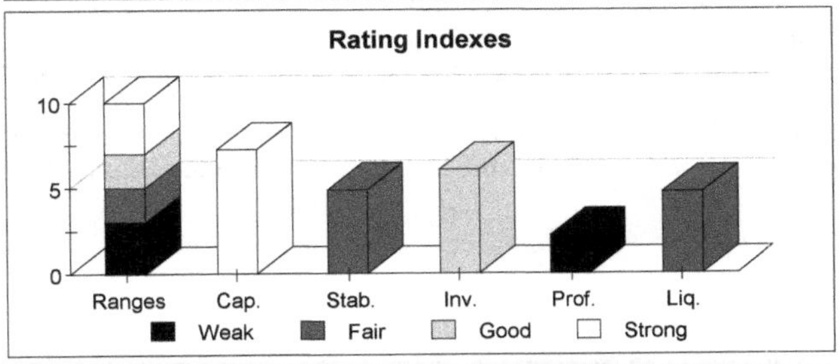


## AMERITAS LIFE INSURANCE CORPORATION B Good

**Major Rating Factors:** Good liquidity (6.1 on a scale of 0 to 10) with sufficient resources to cover a large increase in policy surrenders. Fair quality investment portfolio (4.9) with significant exposure to mortgages . Mortgage default rate has been low. Fair profitability (4.9).
**Other Rating Factors:** Fair overall results on stability tests (4.4). Strong capitalization (7.6) based on excellent risk adjusted capital (severe loss scenario).
**Principal Business:** Reinsurance (48%), group retirement contracts (14%), group health insurance (14%), individual life insurance (12%), and other lines (11%).
**Principal Investments:** NonCMO investment grade bonds (57%), mortgages in good standing (14%), CMOs and structured securities (13%), policy loans (5%), and misc. investments (12%).
**Investments in Affiliates:** 2%
**Group Affiliation:** Ameritas Mutual Holding Co
**Licensed in:** All states except NY, PR
**Commenced Business:** May 1887
**Address:** 5900 O Street, Lincoln, NE 68510-2234
**Phone:** (402) 467-1122 **Domicile State:** NE **NAIC Code:** 61301

| Data Date | Rating | RACR #1 | RACR #2 | Total Assets ($mil) | Capital ($mil) | Net Premium ($mil) | Net Income ($mil) |
|---|---|---|---|---|---|---|---|
| 9-17 | B | 2.39 | 1.42 | 19,676.1 | 1,575.8 | 2,016.3 | 92.6 |
| 9-16 | B | 2.17 | 1.31 | 18,589.5 | 1,458.8 | 3,811.9 | -30.4 |
| 2016 | B | 2.22 | 1.34 | 18,696.6 | 1,484.1 | 4,421.9 | -4.8 |
| 2015 | B | 2.40 | 1.45 | 18,148.8 | 1,511.5 | 3,359.6 | -9.5 |
| 2014 | B | 2.67 | 1.67 | 16,822.0 | 1,623.5 | 2,119.7 | 129.8 |
| 2013 | B | 1.30 | 1.13 | 9,187.8 | 1,501.8 | 1,622.4 | 64.9 |
| 2012 | B | 1.31 | 1.13 | 7,997.9 | 1,298.4 | 1,494.5 | 0.0 |

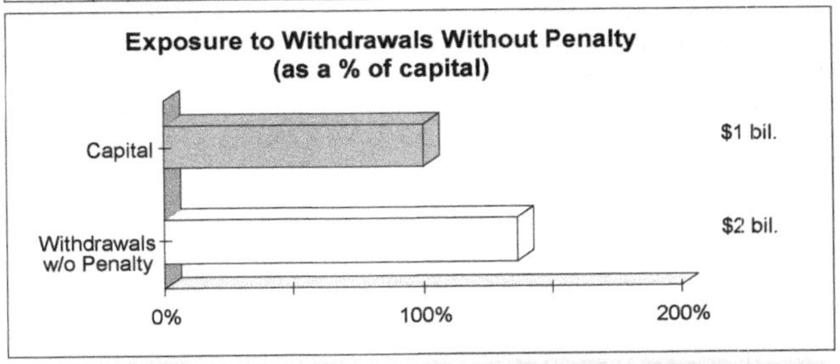


## AMEX ASSURANCE CO B Good

**Major Rating Factors:** Fair profitability index (4.2 on a scale of 0 to 10). Good expense controls. Return on equity has been fair, averaging 35.8% over the past five years. Fair overall results on stability tests (4.5) including weak results on operational trends. The largest net exposure for one risk is acceptable at 3.0% of capital.
**Other Rating Factors:** Strong long-term capitalization index (10.0) based on excellent current risk adjusted capital (severe and moderate loss scenarios), despite some fluctuation in capital levels. Ample reserve history (8.6) that helps to protect the company against sharp claims increases. Excellent liquidity (7.0) with ample operational cash flow and liquid investments.
**Principal Business:** Inland marine (62%) and group accident & health (38%).
**Principal Investments:** Investment grade bonds (96%) and misc. investments (4%).
**Investments in Affiliates:** None
**Group Affiliation:** American Express Company
**Licensed in:** All states, the District of Columbia and Puerto Rico
**Commenced Business:** February 1973
**Address:** 2 Pierce Place Suite 900, Itasca, IL 60143
**Phone:** (623) 492-3038 **Domicile State:** IL **NAIC Code:** 27928

| Data Date | Rating | RACR #1 | RACR #2 | Loss Ratio % | Total Assets ($mil) | Capital ($mil) | Net Premium ($mil) | Net Income ($mil) |
|---|---|---|---|---|---|---|---|---|
| 9-17 | B | 11.32 | 6.57 | N/A | 239.1 | 198.7 | 133.4 | 42.1 |
| 9-16 | B | 12.14 | 6.80 | N/A | 249.6 | 206.3 | 144.5 | 50.4 |
| 2016 | B | 10.58 | 6.07 | 39.0 | 227.8 | 181.4 | 177.4 | 59.7 |
| 2015 | B | 9.75 | 5.62 | 36.6 | 256.3 | 184.3 | 188.2 | 62.5 |
| 2014 | B | 10.09 | 5.82 | 38.7 | 280.2 | 188.8 | 183.4 | 70.7 |
| 2013 | B | 9.10 | 5.40 | 49.3 | 296.5 | 196.9 | 177.5 | 78.9 |
| 2012 | B | 7.41 | 4.31 | 42.8 | 269.2 | 196.7 | 244.3 | 78.9 |

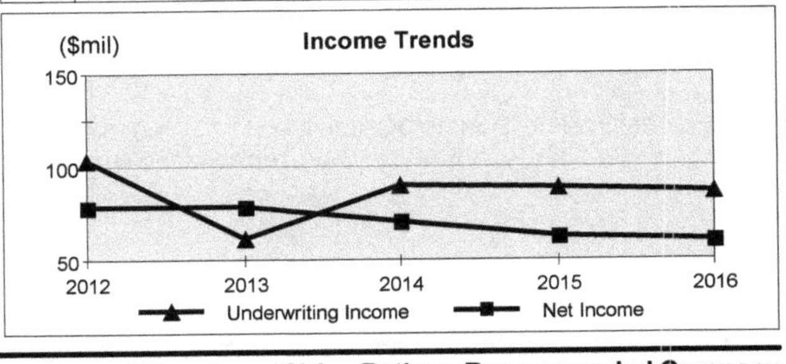

## AMFIRST INS CO * B+ Good

**Major Rating Factors:** Good quality investment portfolio (6.5 on a scale of 0 to 10). Excellent profitability (7.3). Strong capitalization (9.8) based on excellent current risk-adjusted capital (severe loss scenario).
**Other Rating Factors:** Excellent liquidity (7.6) with ample operational cash flow and liquid investments.
**Principal Business:** Dental (46%), other (54%)
**Mem Phys: 16:** N/A **15:** N/A **16 MLR** 20.7% **/ 16 Admin Exp** N/A
**Enroll(000): Q3 17:** 62 **16:** 33 **15:** 29 **Med Exp PMPM:** $29
**Principal Investments:** Affiliate common stock (46%), long-term bonds (19%), cash and equiv (17%), pref stock (9%), real estate (5%), nonaffiliate common stock (1%), other (4%)
**Provider Compensation ($000):** FFS ($10,520)
**Total Member Encounters:** Phys (33,513), non-phys (96,032)
**Group Affiliation:** Wheaton Management LLC
**Licensed in:** AL, AZ, AR, FL, GA, LA, MD, MI, MS, NC, OH, OK, PA, SC, TN, TX, VA, WV
**Address:** 201 Robert S Kerr Ave Ste 600, Oklahoma City, OK 73102
**Phone:** (601) 956-2028 **Dom State:** OK **Commenced Bus:** January 1999

| Data Date | Rating | RACR #1 | RACR #2 | Total Assets ($mil) | Capital ($mil) | Net Premium ($mil) | Net Income ($mil) |
|---|---|---|---|---|---|---|---|
| 9-17 | B+ | 3.61 | 3.00 | 57.6 | 50.0 | 46.4 | 1.8 |
| 9-16 | B | 3.17 | 2.64 | 52.6 | 45.6 | 39.9 | 1.8 |
| 2016 | B | 3.24 | 2.70 | 52.5 | 45.3 | 53.3 | 2.8 |
| 2015 | B | 2.84 | 2.37 | 47.4 | 41.3 | 52.4 | 5.8 |
| 2014 | B | 2.54 | 2.11 | 41.5 | 35.0 | 35.6 | 4.3 |
| 2013 | B | 2.92 | 2.43 | 32.4 | 23.3 | 11.6 | 2.7 |
| 2012 | B | 2.78 | 2.32 | 23.3 | 16.9 | 29.8 | 2.4 |

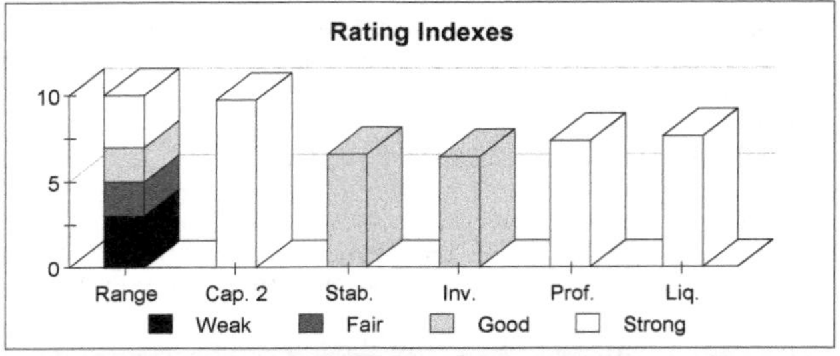


## AMGP GEORGIA MANAGED CARE CO INC * A- Excellent

**Major Rating Factors:** Excellent profitability (8.9 on a scale of 0 to 10). Strong capitalization (8.5) based on excellent current risk-adjusted capital (severe loss scenario). High quality investment portfolio (7.6).
**Other Rating Factors:** Good liquidity (6.8) with sufficient resources (cash flows and marketable investments) to handle a spike in claims.
**Principal Business:** Medicaid (95%), comp med (5%)
**Mem Phys: 16:** 29,935 **15:** 25,609 **16 MLR** 80.9% **/ 16 Admin Exp** N/A
**Enroll(000): Q3 17:** 347 **16:** 384 **15:** 381 **Med Exp PMPM:** $216
**Principal Investments:** Long-term bonds (92%), cash and equiv (4%), other (4%)
**Provider Compensation ($000):** Contr fee ($972,301), capitation ($15,320), FFS ($8,873), bonus arrang ($7,366)
**Total Member Encounters:** Phys (2,448,010), non-phys (1,465,170)
**Group Affiliation:** Anthem Inc
**Licensed in:** GA
**Address:** 4170 ASHFORD DUNWOODY RD, ATLANTA, GA 30319
**Phone:** (678) 587-4840 **Dom State:** GA **Commenced Bus:** June 2006

| Data Date | Rating | RACR #1 | RACR #2 | Total Assets ($mil) | Capital ($mil) | Net Premium ($mil) | Net Income ($mil) |
|---|---|---|---|---|---|---|---|
| 9-17 | A- | 2.56 | 2.14 | 295.6 | 160.6 | 880.8 | 12.4 |
| 9-16 | B+ | 2.54 | 2.12 | 301.8 | 150.0 | 911.3 | 1.1 |
| 2016 | A- | 2.37 | 1.97 | 296.4 | 147.4 | 1,228.3 | 16.0 |
| 2015 | A- | 2.55 | 2.13 | 291.7 | 150.7 | 1,202.7 | 26.1 |
| 2014 | A- | 2.70 | 2.25 | 270.7 | 136.3 | 1,054.7 | 36.7 |
| 2013 | B | 2.85 | 2.37 | 223.5 | 109.2 | 795.0 | 25.7 |
| 2012 | A- | 3.35 | 2.80 | 183.1 | 123.3 | 734.4 | 13.9 |

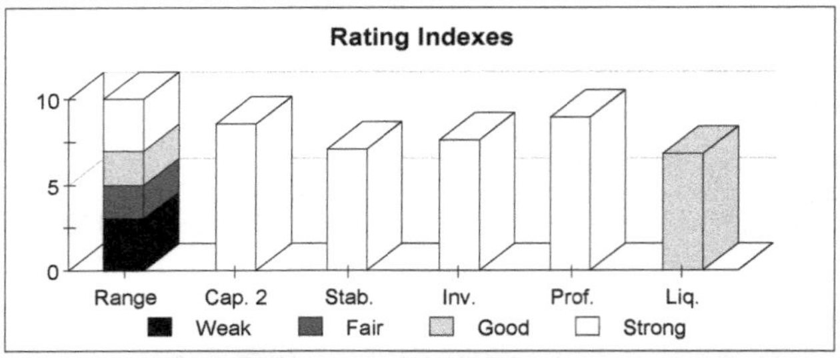


## ANTHEM BLUE CROSS LIFE & HEALTH INS B- Good

**Major Rating Factors:** Fair quality investment portfolio (3.7 on a scale of 0 to 10). Excellent profitability (8.4). Strong capitalization (10.0) based on excellent current risk-adjusted capital (severe loss scenario).
**Other Rating Factors:** Excellent liquidity (7.2) with ample operational cash flow and liquid investments.
**Principal Business:** Comp med (69%), dental (10%), Medicare (4%), vision (2%), other (14%)
**Mem Phys: 16:** 62,560 **15:** 61,811 **16 MLR** 75.7% **/ 16 Admin Exp** N/A
**Enroll(000): Q3 17:** 2,230 **16:** 2,261 **15:** 2,482 **Med Exp PMPM:** $62
**Principal Investments:** Long-term bonds (81%), cash and equiv (4%), pref stock (1%), other (13%)
**Provider Compensation ($000):** Contr fee ($1,078,191), FFS ($683,215), bonus arrang ($7,859), other ($87,482)
**Total Member Encounters:** Phys (2,014,783), non-phys (1,666,725)
**Group Affiliation:** Anthem Inc
**Licensed in:** CA
**Address:** 21555 OXNARD St, WOODLAND HILLS, CA 91367
**Phone:** (818) 234-2345 **Dom State:** CA **Commenced Bus:** August 1991

| Data Date | Rating | RACR #1 | RACR #2 | Total Assets ($mil) | Capital ($mil) | Net Premium ($mil) | Net Income ($mil) |
|---|---|---|---|---|---|---|---|
| 9-17 | B- | 7.66 | 6.38 | 2,337.2 | 1,371.3 | 1,450.5 | 94.8 |
| 9-16 | B- | 6.33 | 5.27 | 2,210.1 | 1,420.6 | 1,707.0 | 227.2 |
| 2016 | B- | 7.49 | 6.25 | 2,682.8 | 1,340.8 | 2,289.5 | 281.4 |
| 2015 | B | 5.69 | 4.75 | 2,521.6 | 1,274.7 | 3,631.5 | 243.6 |
| 2014 | B | 5.64 | 4.70 | 2,572.2 | 1,352.5 | 4,079.9 | 309.4 |
| 2013 | B | 3.81 | 3.17 | 2,838.2 | 1,216.8 | 5,393.8 | 168.9 |
| 2012 | B | 4.37 | 3.64 | 2,739.1 | 1,361.0 | 5,231.2 | 342.4 |

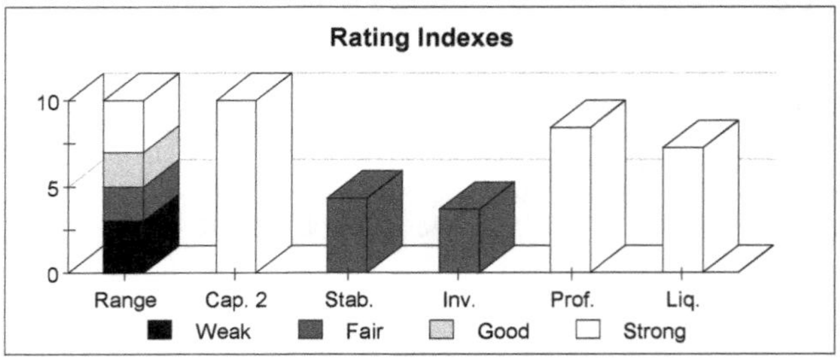

## ANTHEM HEALTH PLANS INC — B- Good

**Major Rating Factors:** Fair quality investment portfolio (3.8 on a scale of 0 to 10). Good liquidity (6.2) with sufficient resources (cash flows and marketable investments) to handle a spike in claims. Excellent profitability (7.7).
**Other Rating Factors:** Strong capitalization (9.0) based on excellent current risk-adjusted capital (severe loss scenario).
**Principal Business:** Comp med (58%), FEHB (16%), Medicare (12%), med supp (7%), dental (2%), other (4%)
**Mem Phys: 16:** 26,012 **15:** 24,458 **16 MLR** 87.9% **/ 16 Admin Exp** N/A
**Enroll(000): Q3 17:** 673 **16:** 617 **15:** 622 **Med Exp PMPM:** $198
**Principal Investments:** Long-term bonds (77%), other (32%)
**Provider Compensation ($000):** Contr fee ($1,216,074), FFS ($167,400), bonus arrang ($7,566), capitation ($2,399), other ($60,506)
**Total Member Encounters:** Phys (2,670,611), non-phys (1,321,008)
**Group Affiliation:** Anthem Inc
**Licensed in:** CT
**Address:** 108 LEIGUS Rd, WALLINGFORD, CT 06492-2518
**Phone:** (203) 677-4000 **Dom State:** CT **Commenced Bus:** August 1997

| Data Date | Rating | RACR #1 | RACR #2 | Total Assets ($mil) | Capital ($mil) | Net Premium ($mil) | Net Income ($mil) |
|---|---|---|---|---|---|---|---|
| 9-17 | B- | 2.91 | 2.43 | 718.5 | 281.0 | 1,480.1 | 44.7 |
| 9-16 | B- | 3.82 | 3.18 | 745.8 | 312.1 | 1,248.4 | 24.8 |
| 2016 | B- | 2.44 | 2.03 | 800.4 | 232.2 | 1,663.8 | 22.5 |
| 2015 | B- | 3.49 | 2.91 | 697.2 | 284.1 | 1,570.9 | 91.9 |
| 2014 | B | 3.39 | 2.82 | 719.5 | 311.7 | 1,801.1 | 108.4 |
| 2013 | B | 3.38 | 2.81 | 683.4 | 320.3 | 1,811.0 | 117.8 |
| 2012 | B+ | 3.30 | 2.75 | 720.7 | 328.9 | 1,891.0 | 133.3 |

Rating Indexes

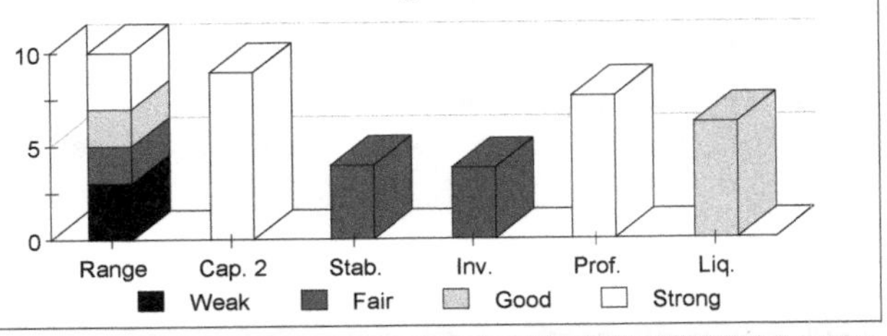


## ANTHEM HEALTH PLANS OF KENTUCKY INC * — B+ Good

**Major Rating Factors:** Good overall results on stability tests (6.2 on a scale of 0 to 10). Rating is significantly influenced by the good financial results of Anthem Inc. Good liquidity (6.3) with sufficient resources (cash flows and marketable investments) to handle a spike in claims. Excellent profitability (8.9).
**Other Rating Factors:** Strong capitalization index (9.6) based on excellent current risk-adjusted capital (severe loss scenario). High quality investment portfolio (8.6).
**Principal Business:** Comp med (67%), FEHB (19%), med supp (8%), Medicare (5%)
**Mem Phys: 16:** 30,762 **15:** 28,866 **16 MLR** 83.4% **/ 16 Admin Exp** N/A
**Enroll(000): Q3 17:** 830 **16:** 838 **15:** 855 **Med Exp PMPM:** $188
**Principal Investments:** Long-term bonds (95%), real estate (3%), other (3%)
**Provider Compensation ($000):** Contr fee ($1,073,611), FFS ($814,381), bonus arrang ($5,860), capitation ($1,027), other ($71)
**Total Member Encounters:** Phys (3,724,140), non-phys (2,992,794)
**Group Affiliation:** Anthem Inc
**Licensed in:** KY
**Address:** 13550 TRITON PARK BLVD, LOUISVILLE, KY 40223
**Phone:** (800) 331-1476 **Dom State:** KY **Commenced Bus:** July 1993

| Data Date | Rating | RACR #1 | RACR #2 | Total Assets ($mil) | Capital ($mil) | Net Premium ($mil) | Net Income ($mil) |
|---|---|---|---|---|---|---|---|
| 9-17 | B+ | 3.40 | 2.83 | 1,046.0 | 401.6 | 1,776.2 | 122.6 |
| 9-16 | B | 2.87 | 2.39 | 879.4 | 300.7 | 1,714.2 | 100.0 |
| 2016 | B+ | 2.69 | 2.24 | 1,069.4 | 313.6 | 2,285.7 | 112.0 |
| 2015 | B | 2.85 | 2.38 | 866.8 | 299.3 | 2,161.2 | 101.8 |
| 2014 | B | 3.05 | 2.54 | 897.5 | 331.4 | 2,311.1 | 123.4 |
| 2013 | A- | 3.45 | 2.87 | 871.1 | 371.9 | 2,205.0 | 142.2 |
| 2012 | A- | 3.28 | 2.73 | 849.2 | 344.0 | 2,138.0 | 175.5 |

Rating Indexes

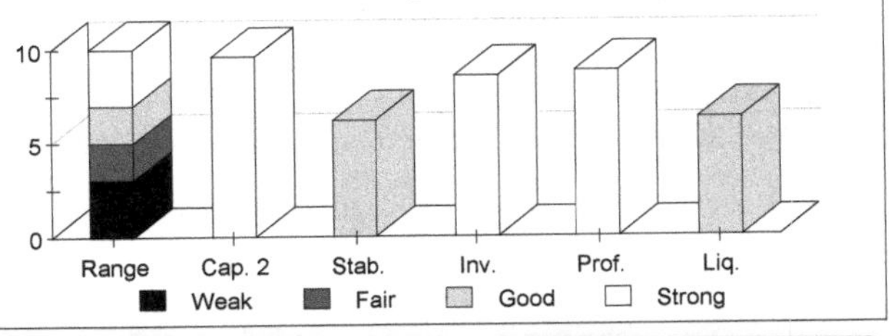


## ANTHEM HEALTH PLANS OF MAINE INC * — B+ Good

**Major Rating Factors:** Good quality investment portfolio (6.4 on a scale of 0 to 10). Good liquidity (6.8) with sufficient resources (cash flows and marketable investments) to handle a spike in claims. Excellent profitability (8.2).
**Other Rating Factors:** Strong capitalization (10.0) based on excellent current risk-adjusted capital (severe loss scenario).
**Principal Business:** Comp med (73%), FEHB (18%), med supp (4%), Medicare (2%)
**Mem Phys: 16:** 6,587 **15:** 5,805 **16 MLR** 87.9% **/ 16 Admin Exp** N/A
**Enroll(000): Q3 17:** 390 **16:** 380 **15:** 318 **Med Exp PMPM:** $221
**Principal Investments:** Long-term bonds (98%), other (5%)
**Provider Compensation ($000):** Contr fee ($757,508), FFS ($159,420), bonus arrang ($3,379), other ($4,697)
**Total Member Encounters:** Phys (1,345,890), non-phys (613,845)
**Group Affiliation:** Anthem Inc
**Licensed in:** ME
**Address:** 2 GANNETT Dr, SOUTH PORTLAND, ME 04106-6911
**Phone:** (866) 583-6182 **Dom State:** ME **Commenced Bus:** June 2000

| Data Date | Rating | RACR #1 | RACR #2 | Total Assets ($mil) | Capital ($mil) | Net Premium ($mil) | Net Income ($mil) |
|---|---|---|---|---|---|---|---|
| 9-17 | B+ | 3.75 | 3.13 | 489.5 | 182.6 | 860.7 | 35.6 |
| 9-16 | B- | 3.60 | 3.00 | 401.0 | 163.1 | 796.3 | 9.6 |
| 2016 | B | 3.12 | 2.60 | 408.4 | 150.4 | 1,062.9 | 19.1 |
| 2015 | B- | 3.40 | 2.84 | 397.9 | 154.0 | 1,034.5 | 22.2 |
| 2014 | B- | 3.91 | 3.26 | 386.3 | 141.2 | 1,017.4 | 19.2 |
| 2013 | B- | 4.55 | 3.79 | 417.6 | 163.1 | 1,030.8 | 48.4 |
| 2012 | B- | 3.22 | 2.69 | 414.9 | 142.8 | 1,019.2 | 39.9 |

Rating Indexes

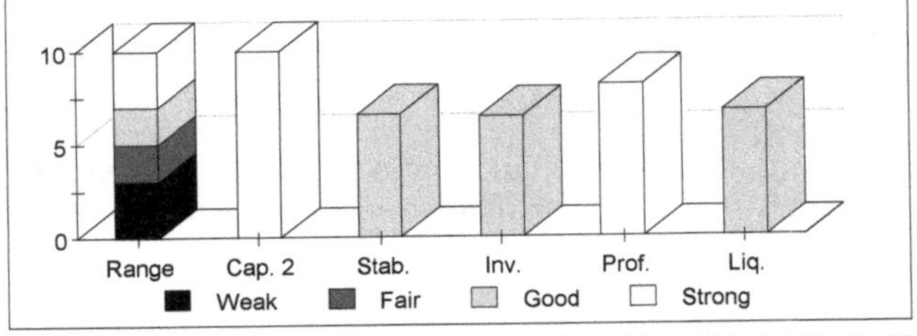




* Denotes a Weiss Ratings Recommended Company

## ANTHEM HEALTH PLANS OF NEW HAMPSHIRE — B — Good

**Major Rating Factors:** Fair quality investment portfolio (4.5 on a scale of 0 to 10). Excellent profitability (7.6). Strong capitalization (10.0) based on excellent current risk-adjusted capital (severe loss scenario).
**Other Rating Factors:** Excellent liquidity (6.9) with sufficient resources (cash flows and marketable investments) to handle a spike in claims.
**Principal Business:** FEHB (53%), comp med (25%), med supp (15%), Medicare (4%), dental (1%)
**Mem Phys: 16:** 17,774 **15:** 15,617 **16 MLR** 87.4% **/ 16 Admin Exp** N/A
**Enroll(000): Q3 17:** 133 **16:** 136 **15:** 129 **Med Exp PMPM:** $262
**Principal Investments:** Long-term bonds (53%), affiliate common stock (45%), other (2%)
**Provider Compensation ($000):** Contr fee ($333,339), FFS ($78,720), bonus arrang ($1,881), capitation ($87), other ($4,026)
**Total Member Encounters:** Phys (952,760), non-phys (586,503)
**Group Affiliation:** Anthem Inc
**Licensed in:** NH
**Address:** 1155 ELM St, MANCHESTER, NH 03101
**Phone:** (603) 541-2000 **Dom State:** NH **Commenced Bus:** October 1999

| Data Date | Rating | RACR #1 | RACR #2 | Total Assets ($mil) | Capital ($mil) | Net Premium ($mil) | Net Income ($mil) |
|---|---|---|---|---|---|---|---|
| 9-17 | B | 3.76 | 3.13 | 347.4 | 182.1 | 382.5 | 16.2 |
| 9-16 | B+ | 4.13 | 3.44 | 393.5 | 183.4 | 362.1 | 5.0 |
| 2016 | B | 2.96 | 2.46 | 316.0 | 142.7 | 488.2 | 35.2 |
| 2015 | B+ | 3.68 | 3.06 | 339.9 | 162.9 | 466.9 | 41.7 |
| 2014 | B+ | 3.15 | 2.62 | 327.7 | 157.9 | 493.8 | 31.8 |
| 2013 | B+ | 3.05 | 2.54 | 297.5 | 154.5 | 521.3 | 37.7 |
| 2012 | B+ | 3.31 | 2.75 | 297.9 | 166.5 | 507.1 | 44.0 |

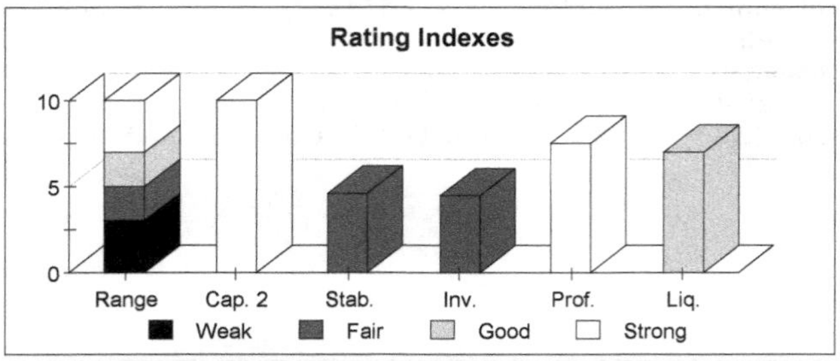


## ANTHEM HEALTH PLANS OF VIRGINIA — B- — Good

**Major Rating Factors:** Fair quality investment portfolio (4.5 on a scale of 0 to 10). Good liquidity (6.9) with sufficient resources (cash flows and marketable investments) to handle a spike in claims. Excellent profitability (8.2).
**Other Rating Factors:** Strong capitalization (9.5) based on excellent current risk-adjusted capital (severe loss scenario).
**Principal Business:** FEHB (47%), comp med (39%), med supp (7%), dental (2%), other (4%)
**Mem Phys: 16:** 33,315 **15:** 32,496 **16 MLR** 82.4% **/ 16 Admin Exp** N/A
**Enroll(000): Q3 17:** 1,514 **16:** 1,553 **15:** 1,894 **Med Exp PMPM:** $169
**Principal Investments:** Long-term bonds (50%), nonaffiliate common stock (26%), real estate (2%), affiliate common stock (1%), other (21%)
**Provider Compensation ($000):** Contr fee ($2,953,295), FFS ($92,062), bonus arrang ($8,020), other ($98,671)
**Total Member Encounters:** Phys (6,847,651), non-phys (2,867,093)
**Group Affiliation:** Anthem Inc
**Licensed in:** VA
**Address:** 2015 STAPLES MILL Rd, RICHMOND, VA 23230
**Phone:** (804) 354-7000 **Dom State:** VA **Commenced Bus:** October 1935

| Data Date | Rating | RACR #1 | RACR #2 | Total Assets ($mil) | Capital ($mil) | Net Premium ($mil) | Net Income ($mil) |
|---|---|---|---|---|---|---|---|
| 9-17 | B- | 3.34 | 2.78 | 2,166.2 | 619.8 | 2,746.1 | 166.2 |
| 9-16 | B- | 3.04 | 2.53 | 2,189.6 | 583.1 | 2,853.3 | 177.1 |
| 2016 | B- | 3.52 | 2.93 | 1,941.2 | 655.3 | 3,825.9 | 230.2 |
| 2015 | B- | 3.09 | 2.58 | 1,991.9 | 594.2 | 3,740.6 | 216.1 |
| 2014 | B | 3.15 | 2.62 | 1,962.5 | 623.1 | 3,947.9 | 242.5 |
| 2013 | B | 3.51 | 2.92 | 1,970.0 | 643.2 | 4,011.2 | 269.5 |
| 2012 | B | 3.76 | 3.13 | 1,986.9 | 724.0 | 4,156.9 | 345.1 |

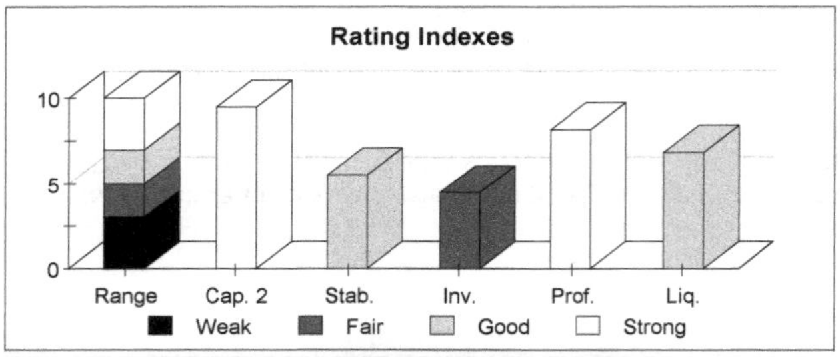


## ANTHEM INS COMPANIES INC — B- — Good

**Major Rating Factors:** Fair quality investment portfolio (3.7 on a scale of 0 to 10). Good liquidity (6.8) with sufficient resources (cash flows and marketable investments) to handle a spike in claims. Excellent profitability (9.2).
**Other Rating Factors:** Strong capitalization (9.0) based on excellent current risk-adjusted capital (severe loss scenario).
**Principal Business:** Comp med (28%), Medicaid (26%), Medicare (23%), FEHB (11%), med supp (2%), other (9%)
**Mem Phys: 16:** 41,239 **15:** 35,302 **16 MLR** 82.1% **/ 16 Admin Exp** N/A
**Enroll(000): Q3 17:** 2,653 **16:** 2,508 **15:** 2,693 **Med Exp PMPM:** $166
**Principal Investments:** Long-term bonds (76%), affiliate common stock (6%), other (21%)
**Provider Compensation ($000):** Contr fee ($2,721,074), FFS ($2,082,924), capitation ($52,710), bonus arrang ($10,486), other ($169,281)
**Total Member Encounters:** Phys (7,836,045), non-phys (6,617,435)
**Group Affiliation:** Anthem Inc
**Licensed in:** AL, AZ, AR, CO, CT, GA, ID, IL, IN, IA, KS, KY, LA, ME, MS, MO, MT, NE, NV, NH, NM, NC, ND, OH, OK, OR, SC, SD, TN, TX, UT, VA, WA, WI, WY
**Address:** 120 MONUMENT CIRCLE, INDIANAPOLIS, IN 46204-4903
**Phone:** (317) 488-6000 **Dom State:** IN **Commenced Bus:** November 1944

| Data Date | Rating | RACR #1 | RACR #2 | Total Assets ($mil) | Capital ($mil) | Net Premium ($mil) | Net Income ($mil) |
|---|---|---|---|---|---|---|---|
| 9-17 | B- | 2.94 | 2.45 | 3,613.9 | 1,187.4 | 5,172.4 | 280.4 |
| 9-16 | B- | 2.52 | 2.10 | 3,030.4 | 872.0 | 4,572.7 | 336.4 |
| 2016 | B- | 2.42 | 2.02 | 2,947.5 | 968.6 | 6,126.1 | 431.0 |
| 2015 | B- | 2.36 | 1.97 | 2,853.0 | 816.5 | 5,320.0 | 405.5 |
| 2014 | B- | 2.90 | 2.42 | 3,231.7 | 832.9 | 4,869.8 | 389.1 |
| 2013 | B | 3.51 | 2.93 | 2,781.5 | 1,004.8 | 5,008.5 | 374.4 |
| 2012 | B | 3.00 | 2.50 | 2,638.3 | 898.1 | 5,128.4 | 327.5 |

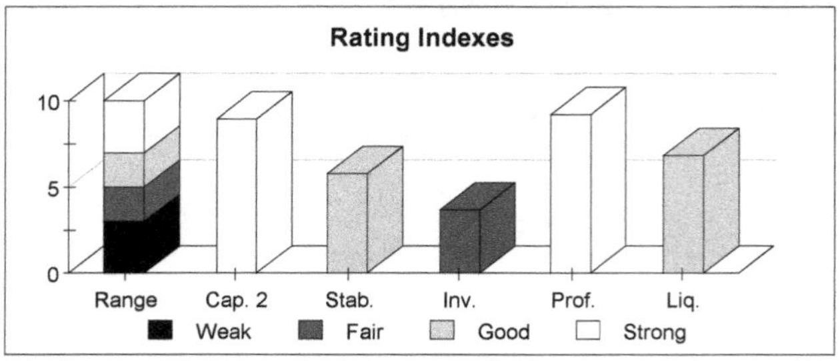

## ANTHEM KENTUCKY MANAGED CARE PLAN * A- Excellent

**Major Rating Factors:** Excellent profitability (10.0 on a scale of 0 to 10). Strong capitalization (10.0) based on excellent current risk-adjusted capital (severe loss scenario). High quality investment portfolio (9.8).
**Other Rating Factors:** Excellent liquidity (7.2) with ample operational cash flow and liquid investments.
**Principal Business:** Medicaid (99%)
**Mem Phys: 16:** 30,762 **15:** 28,866 **16 MLR** 84.2% **/ 16 Admin Exp** N/A
**Enroll(000): Q3 17:** 126 **16:** 115 **15:** 95 **Med Exp PMPM:** $388
**Principal Investments:** Cash and equiv (76%), long-term bonds (24%)
**Provider Compensation ($000):** Contr fee ($416,246), FFS ($68,995), capitation ($936), bonus arrang ($162)
**Total Member Encounters:** Phys (897,799), non-phys (493,816)
**Group Affiliation:** Anthem Inc
**Licensed in:** KY
**Address:** 13550 TRITON PARK BLVD, LOUISVILLE, KY 40223
**Phone:** (800) 331-1476 **Dom State:** KY **Commenced Bus:** October 2014

| Data Date | Rating | RACR #1 | RACR #2 | Total Assets ($mil) | Capital ($mil) | Net Premium ($mil) | Net Income ($mil) |
|---|---|---|---|---|---|---|---|
| 9-17 | A- | 4.22 | 3.52 | 237.7 | 143.3 | 486.4 | 21.2 |
| 9-16 | B+ | 4.88 | 4.07 | 222.2 | 120.6 | 444.8 | 17.1 |
| 2016 | A- | 3.62 | 3.02 | 216.1 | 122.0 | 588.9 | 18.7 |
| 2015 | B+ | 4.23 | 3.53 | 190.8 | 104.3 | 490.4 | 61.9 |
| 2014 | U | 4.39 | 3.66 | 70.7 | 26.9 | 87.5 | 8.9 |
| 2013 | N/A | N/A | N/A | N/A | N/A | N/A | N/A |
| 2012 | N/A | N/A | N/A | N/A | N/A | N/A | N/A |

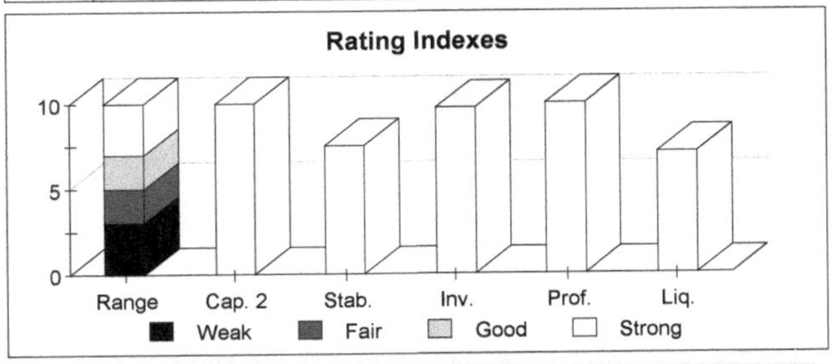


## ANTHEM LIFE INSURANCE COMPANY * A- Excellent

**Major Rating Factors:** Good liquidity (6.1 on a scale of 0 to 10) with sufficient resources to handle a spike in claims. Excellent overall results on stability tests (7.1). Strengths that enhance stability include excellent operational trends and excellent risk diversification. Strong capitalization (7.8) based on excellent risk adjusted capital (severe loss scenario). Furthermore, this high level of risk adjusted capital has been consistently maintained over the last five years.
**Other Rating Factors:** High quality investment portfolio (7.5). Excellent profitability (7.4).
**Principal Business:** Reinsurance (42%), group life insurance (32%), group health insurance (25%), and individual life insurance (1%).
**Principal Investments:** NonCMO investment grade bonds (64%), CMOs and structured securities (19%), noninv. grade bonds (1%), common & preferred stock (1%), and cash (1%).
**Investments in Affiliates:** None
**Group Affiliation:** Anthem Inc
**Licensed in:** All states except NY, RI, VT, PR
**Commenced Business:** June 1956
**Address:** 120 MONUMENT CIRCLE, INDIANAPOLIS, IN 46204
**Phone:** (614) 433-8800 **Domicile State:** IN **NAIC Code:** 61069

| Data Date | Rating | RACR #1 | RACR #2 | Total Assets ($mil) | Capital ($mil) | Net Premium ($mil) | Net Income ($mil) |
|---|---|---|---|---|---|---|---|
| 9-17 | A- | 2.26 | 1.55 | 738.1 | 118.5 | 305.8 | 5.0 |
| 9-16 | A- | 2.06 | 1.44 | 610.8 | 100.7 | 276.9 | 22.2 |
| 2016 | A- | 1.85 | 1.28 | 623.3 | 108.9 | 362.3 | 28.3 |
| 2015 | A- | 1.64 | 1.16 | 633.7 | 95.9 | 368.9 | 18.2 |
| 2014 | A- | 1.92 | 1.34 | 582.4 | 109.1 | 357.8 | 34.4 |
| 2013 | A- | 2.17 | 1.51 | 575.3 | 120.4 | 345.1 | 47.1 |
| 2012 | A- | 1.60 | 1.12 | 565.4 | 87.4 | 336.1 | 13.8 |

**Adverse Trends in Operations**

Decrease in premium volume from 2015 to 2016 (2%)
Decrease in asset base during 2016 (2%)
Decrease in capital during 2015 (12%)
Decrease in capital during 2014 (9%)

## ARCADIAN HEALTH PLAN INC B- Good

**Major Rating Factors:** Good liquidity (6.3 on a scale of 0 to 10) with sufficient resources (cash flows and marketable investments) to handle a spike in claims. Strong capitalization (10.0) based on excellent current risk-adjusted capital (severe loss scenario). High quality investment portfolio (9.9).
**Other Rating Factors:** Weak profitability index (0.9).
**Principal Business:** Medicare (100%)
**Mem Phys: 16:** 43,417 **15:** 180,729 **16 MLR** 95.5% **/ 16 Admin Exp** N/A
**Enroll(000): Q3 17:** 79 **16:** 82 **15:** 8 **Med Exp PMPM:** $801
**Principal Investments:** Long-term bonds (85%), cash and equiv (15%)
**Provider Compensation ($000):** Capitation ($480,507), contr fee ($231,608), FFS ($3,555)
**Total Member Encounters:** Phys (1,192,176), non-phys (551,413)
**Group Affiliation:** Humana Inc
**Licensed in:** AZ, AR, CA, IN, KY, ME, MO, NE, NH, SC, TX, VA, WA, WV
**Address:** 300 DESCHUTES WAY SW Ste 304, TUMWATER, WA 98501
**Phone:** (502) 580-1000 **Dom State:** WA **Commenced Bus:** January 2005

| Data Date | Rating | RACR #1 | RACR #2 | Total Assets ($mil) | Capital ($mil) | Net Premium ($mil) | Net Income ($mil) |
|---|---|---|---|---|---|---|---|
| 9-17 | B- | 6.42 | 5.35 | 417.7 | 227.0 | 614.0 | 6.9 |
| 9-16 | C+ | 30.32 | 25.27 | 349.5 | 156.8 | 610.3 | -50.7 |
| 2016 | B- | 4.86 | 4.05 | 275.8 | 171.0 | 812.9 | -41.2 |
| 2015 | C+ | 7.23 | 6.02 | 77.7 | 35.0 | 71.1 | -32.7 |
| 2014 | C | 12.03 | 10.03 | 69.1 | 57.9 | 70.1 | 7.5 |
| 2013 | B | 4.87 | 4.06 | 103.6 | 70.3 | 227.5 | -4.9 |
| 2012 | B | 1.78 | 1.48 | 143.3 | 72.1 | 399.8 | 0.3 |

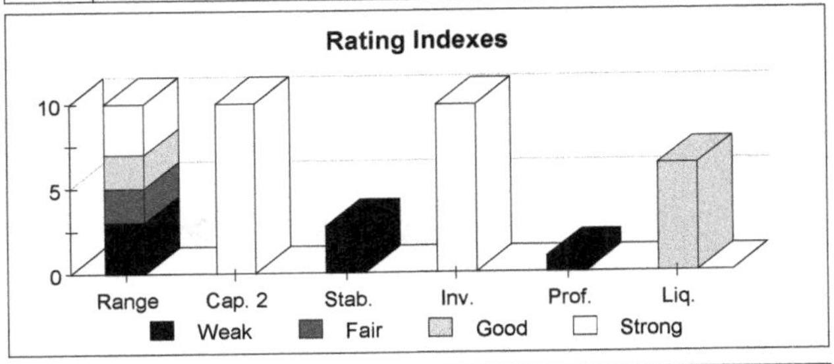

## ARKANSAS SUPERIOR SELECT INC — E — Very Weak

**Major Rating Factors:** Weak profitability index (0.2 on a scale of 0 to 10). Weak liquidity (2.0) as a spike in claims may stretch capacity. Strong capitalization (7.9) based on excellent current risk-adjusted capital (severe loss scenario).
**Other Rating Factors:** High quality investment portfolio (9.9).
**Principal Business:** Medicare (100%)
**Mem Phys: 16:** 6,670 **15:** 3,255 **16 MLR** 100.3% **/ 16 Admin Exp** N/A
**Enroll(000): Q3 17:** 1 **16:** 0 **15:** 0 **Med Exp PMPM:** $1,463
**Principal Investments:** Cash and equiv (99%), other (1%)
**Provider Compensation ($000):** Contr fee ($4,288)
**Total Member Encounters:** Phys (4,474), non-phys (6,230)
**Group Affiliation:** Select Founders LLC
**Licensed in:** AR
**Address:** 1401 West Capital Ste 430, Little Rock, AR 72201
**Phone:** (501) 372-1922 **Dom State:** AR **Commenced Bus:** May 2013

| Data Date | Rating | RACR #1 | RACR #2 | Total Assets ($mil) | Capital ($mil) | Net Premium ($mil) | Net Income ($mil) |
|---|---|---|---|---|---|---|---|
| 9-17 | E | 2.08 | 1.73 | 6.9 | 2.3 | 7.8 | -1.7 |
| 9-16 | E | 0.97 | 0.81 | 4.3 | 1.4 | 3.1 | -1.5 |
| 2016 | E | 1.25 | 1.04 | 4.6 | 1.3 | 5.1 | -3.5 |
| 2015 | E | 0.69 | 0.57 | 3.6 | 1.0 | 1.7 | -4.1 |
| 2014 | N/A | N/A | N/A | 2.4 | 2.4 | N/A | -1.2 |
| 2013 | N/A | N/A | N/A | 0.4 | 0.4 | N/A | -0.7 |
| 2012 | N/A | N/A | N/A | N/A | N/A | N/A | N/A |

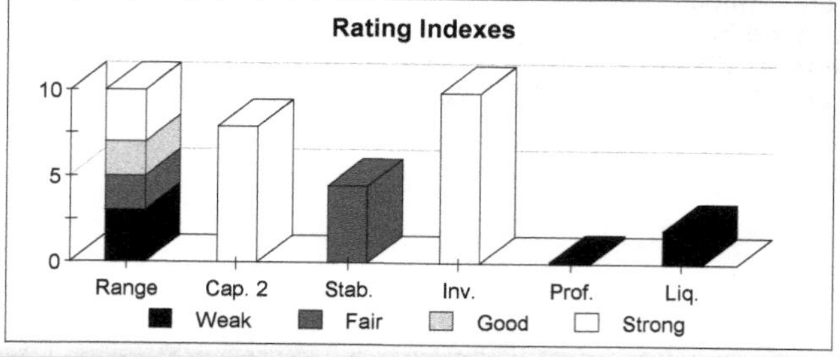


## ASPIRE HEALTH PLAN — E- — Very Weak

**Major Rating Factors:** Weak profitability index (0.0 on a scale of 0 to 10). Poor capitalization index (0.0) based on weak current risk-adjusted capital (severe loss scenario). overall results on stability tests (-0.3) based on a steep decline in capital during 2016, an excessive 80% enrollment growth during the period.
**Other Rating Factors:** Excellent liquidity (7.3) with ample operational cash flow and liquid investments.
**Principal Business:** Medicare (100%)
**Mem Phys: 16:** N/A **15:** N/A **16 MLR** 101.0% **/ 16 Admin Exp** N/A
**Enroll(000): Q3 17:** 2 **16:** 2 **15:** 1 **Med Exp PMPM:** $766
**Principal Investments ($000):** Cash and equiv ($1,377)
**Provider Compensation ($000):** None
**Total Member Encounters:** N/A
**Group Affiliation:** None
**Licensed in:** CA
**Address:** 23625 Holman Highway, Monterey, CA 93940
**Phone:** (831) 625-4965 **Dom State:** CA **Commenced Bus:** April 2013

| Data Date | Rating | RACR #1 | RACR #2 | Total Assets ($mil) | Capital ($mil) | Net Premium ($mil) | Net Income ($mil) |
|---|---|---|---|---|---|---|---|
| 9-17 | E- | N/A | N/A | 7.2 | -20.0 | 17.3 | -4.7 |
| 9-16 | E- | N/A | N/A | 4.1 | -2.8 | 10.2 | -5.2 |
| 2016 | E- | N/A | N/A | 8.5 | -15.2 | 13.7 | 1.6 |
| 2015 | E- | N/A | N/A | 3.8 | -1.6 | 7.8 | -6.0 |
| 2014 | E- | N/A | N/A | 2.6 | -2.7 | 4.1 | -4.3 |
| 2013 | N/A | N/A | N/A | 3.2 | -1.7 | N/A | -6.8 |
| 2012 | N/A | N/A | N/A | N/A | N/A | N/A | N/A |

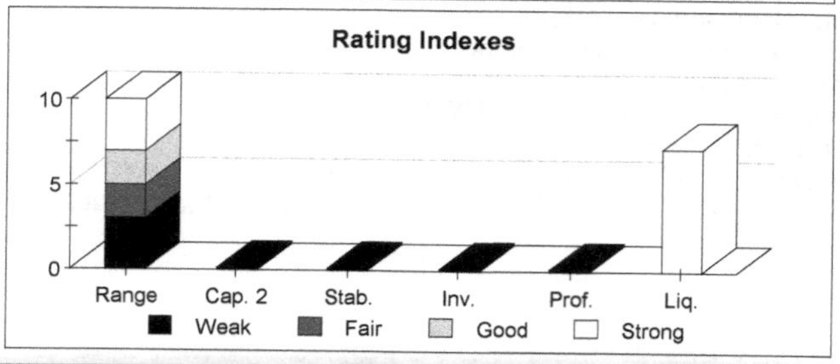


## ASSURITY LIFE INSURANCE COMPANY * — B+ — Good

**Major Rating Factors:** Good quality investment portfolio (5.5 on a scale of 0 to 10) despite significant exposure to mortgages . Mortgage default rate has been low. large holdings of BBB rated bonds in addition to small junk bond holdings. Good overall profitability (6.1). Good liquidity (5.6).
**Other Rating Factors:** Good overall results on stability tests (6.6) excellent operational trends and excellent risk diversification. Strong capitalization (7.8) based on excellent risk adjusted capital (severe loss scenario).
**Principal Business:** Individual life insurance (49%), individual health insurance (27%), group health insurance (13%), group life insurance (4%), and other lines (7%).
**Principal Investments:** NonCMO investment grade bonds (58%), mortgages in good standing (15%), CMOs and structured securities (11%), policy loans (5%), and misc. investments (10%).
**Investments in Affiliates:** 1%
**Group Affiliation:** Assurity Security Group Inc
**Licensed in:** All states except NY, PR
**Commenced Business:** March 1964
**Address:** 2000 Q STREET, LINCOLN, NE 68503
**Phone:** (402) 476-6500 **Domicile State:** NE **NAIC Code:** 71439

| Data Date | Rating | RACR #1 | RACR #2 | Total Assets ($mil) | Capital ($mil) | Net Premium ($mil) | Net Income ($mil) |
|---|---|---|---|---|---|---|---|
| 9-17 | B+ | 2.76 | 1.54 | 2,726.8 | 332.2 | 142.1 | 9.5 |
| 9-16 | B+ | 2.63 | 1.46 | 2,595.8 | 316.4 | 146.0 | 8.0 |
| 2016 | B+ | 2.70 | 1.51 | 2,605.0 | 324.9 | 193.3 | 12.0 |
| 2015 | B+ | 2.71 | 1.51 | 2,472.0 | 318.1 | 189.5 | 20.8 |
| 2014 | B+ | 3.03 | 1.61 | 2,463.6 | 300.5 | 189.7 | 19.2 |
| 2013 | B+ | 3.17 | 1.69 | 2,449.3 | 306.4 | 191.2 | 14.6 |
| 2012 | B+ | 3.00 | 1.57 | 2,419.2 | 262.7 | 225.0 | 21.9 |

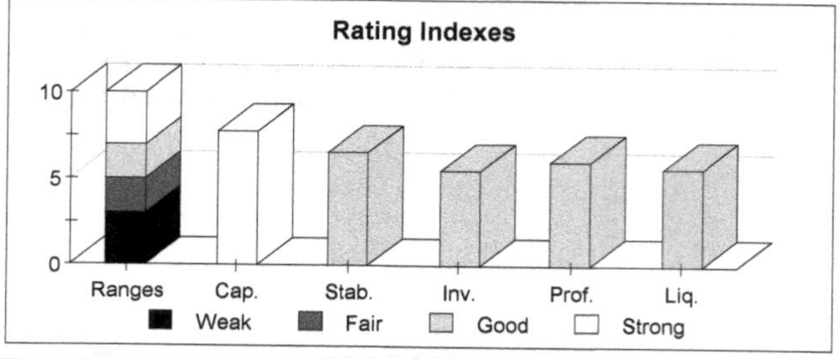

## ASURIS NORTHWEST HEALTH B- Good

**Major Rating Factors:** Fair profitability index (3.5 on a scale of 0 to 10). Good liquidity (6.7) with sufficient resources (cash flows and marketable investments) to handle a spike in claims. Strong capitalization (10.0) based on excellent current risk-adjusted capital (severe loss scenario).
**Other Rating Factors:** High quality investment portfolio (9.9).
**Principal Business:** Comp med (75%), Medicare (10%), med supp (9%), other (6%)
**Mem Phys: 16:** 6,581 **15:** 6,797 **16 MLR** 83.1% **/ 16 Admin Exp** N/A
**Enroll(000): Q3 17:** 45 **16:** 39 **15:** 36 **Med Exp PMPM:** $261
**Principal Investments:** Long-term bonds (94%), cash and equiv (6%)
**Provider Compensation ($000):** Contr fee ($64,976), FFS ($51,921), capitation ($16), bonus arrang ($6)
**Total Member Encounters:** Phys (325,096), non-phys (426,778)
**Group Affiliation:** Cambia Health Solutions Inc
**Licensed in:** OR, WA
**Address:** 1800 NINTH Ave, SEATTLE, WA 98101
**Phone:** (206) 464-3600 **Dom State:** WA **Commenced Bus:** July 1933

| Data Date | Rating | RACR #1 | RACR #2 | Total Assets ($mil) | Capital ($mil) | Net Premium ($mil) | Net Income ($mil) |
|---|---|---|---|---|---|---|---|
| 9-17 | B- | 7.12 | 5.93 | 106.0 | 67.6 | 137.5 | 2.2 |
| 9-16 | B- | 7.03 | 5.86 | 94.8 | 65.3 | 104.6 | 1.5 |
| 2016 | B- | 6.94 | 5.79 | 92.1 | 65.8 | 141.6 | 0.8 |
| 2015 | C+ | 6.94 | 5.78 | 91.7 | 64.5 | 145.4 | 5.1 |
| 2014 | B- | 5.47 | 4.56 | 90.5 | 60.2 | 167.0 | -2.6 |
| 2013 | B | 3.98 | 3.32 | 100.0 | 63.3 | 241.2 | -3.4 |
| 2012 | B | 4.50 | 3.75 | 100.9 | 66.2 | 240.8 | 11.9 |

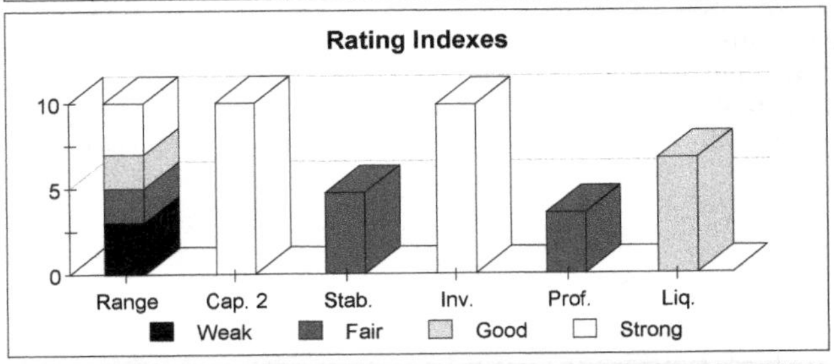


## ATRIO HEALTH PLANS INC C- Fair

**Major Rating Factors:** Weak profitability index (1.4 on a scale of 0 to 10). Good quality investment portfolio (6.5). Good liquidity (6.9) with sufficient resources (cash flows and marketable investments) to handle a spike in claims.
**Other Rating Factors:** Strong capitalization (6.9) based on excellent current risk-adjusted capital (severe loss scenario).
**Principal Business:** Medicare (97%), comp med (3%)
**Mem Phys: 16:** 6,090 **15:** 2,578 **16 MLR** 86.7% **/ 16 Admin Exp** N/A
**Enroll(000): Q3 17:** 28 **16:** 21 **15:** 16 **Med Exp PMPM:** $733
**Principal Investments:** Long-term bonds (56%), cash and equiv (38%), other (7%)
**Provider Compensation ($000):** Capitation ($166,909), FFS ($12,479)
**Total Member Encounters:** Phys (606,721), non-phys (252,030)
**Group Affiliation:** ATRIO Health Plans Inc
**Licensed in:** OR
**Address:** 2270 NW Aviation Dr Ste 3, Roseburg, OR 97470
**Phone:** (541) 672-8620 **Dom State:** OR **Commenced Bus:** January 2005

| Data Date | Rating | RACR #1 | RACR #2 | Total Assets ($mil) | Capital ($mil) | Net Premium ($mil) | Net Income ($mil) |
|---|---|---|---|---|---|---|---|
| 9-17 | C- | 1.28 | 1.07 | 82.9 | 19.6 | 200.5 | -5.5 |
| 9-16 | C- | 2.41 | 2.01 | 72.1 | 30.3 | 156.8 | -0.3 |
| 2016 | C- | 1.68 | 1.40 | 50.8 | 25.6 | 203.3 | -3.5 |
| 2015 | C- | 2.23 | 1.85 | 46.5 | 28.1 | 176.1 | 1.3 |
| 2014 | C- | 1.31 | 1.09 | 40.3 | 23.4 | 159.8 | 2.5 |
| 2013 | C- | 1.96 | 1.63 | 38.6 | 21.1 | 148.1 | 2.0 |
| 2012 | C- | 1.91 | 1.59 | 31.0 | 18.3 | 135.5 | 2.7 |

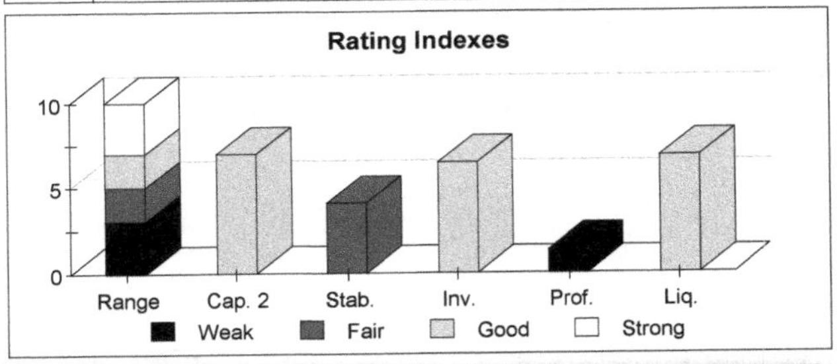


## AULTCARE HEALTH INSURING CORP B Good

**Major Rating Factors:** Good liquidity (6.9 on a scale of 0 to 10) with sufficient resources (cash flows and marketable investments) to handle a spike in claims. Fair profitability index (4.3). Strong capitalization (8.0) based on excellent current risk-adjusted capital (severe loss scenario).
**Other Rating Factors:** High quality investment portfolio (6.9).
**Principal Business:** Medicare (100%)
**Mem Phys: 16:** 1,813 **15:** 1,656 **16 MLR** 87.3% **/ 16 Admin Exp** N/A
**Enroll(000): Q3 17:** 21 **16:** 21 **15:** 20 **Med Exp PMPM:** $850
**Principal Investments:** Affiliate common stock (48%), long-term bonds (30%), cash and equiv (11%), nonaffiliate common stock (8%), other (2%)
**Provider Compensation ($000):** Contr fee ($129,339), capitation ($66,575), FFS ($18,533)
**Total Member Encounters:** Phys (86,863), non-phys (639,757)
**Group Affiliation:** Aultman Health Foundation
**Licensed in:** OH
**Address:** 2600 Sixth St SW, Canton, OH 44710
**Phone:** (330) 363-4057 **Dom State:** OH **Commenced Bus:** July 2013

| Data Date | Rating | RACR #1 | RACR #2 | Total Assets ($mil) | Capital ($mil) | Net Premium ($mil) | Net Income ($mil) |
|---|---|---|---|---|---|---|---|
| 9-17 | B | 2.18 | 1.81 | 126.9 | 87.0 | 183.4 | 3.5 |
| 9-16 | C | 1.71 | 1.43 | 116.3 | 72.6 | 182.2 | 4.6 |
| 2016 | B- | 1.92 | 1.60 | 97.3 | 76.9 | 245.0 | 5.1 |
| 2015 | C- | 1.52 | 1.26 | 82.6 | 64.6 | 226.7 | -3.9 |
| 2014 | N/A | N/A | N/A | 66.3 | 66.3 | N/A | N/A |
| 2013 | N/A | N/A | N/A | N/A | N/A | N/A | N/A |
| 2012 | N/A | N/A | N/A | N/A | N/A | N/A | N/A |

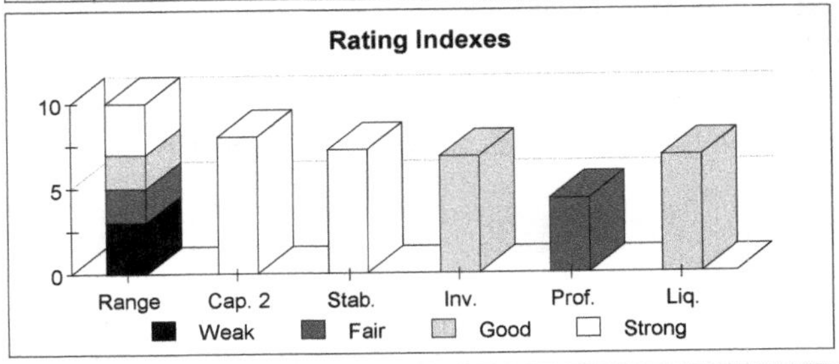

## AULTCARE INS CO C+ Fair

**Major Rating Factors:** Good overall profitability index (6.0 on a scale of 0 to 10). Good liquidity (6.8) with sufficient resources (cash flows and marketable investments) to handle a spike in claims. Strong capitalization (8.2) based on excellent current risk-adjusted capital (severe loss scenario).
**Other Rating Factors:** High quality investment portfolio (8.9).
**Principal Business:** Comp med (87%), FEHB (5%), dental (1%), other (6%)
**Mem Phys: 16:** 1,813 **15:** 1,656 **16 MLR** 85.4% **/ 16 Admin Exp** N/A
**Enroll(000): Q3 17:** 81 **16:** 81 **15:** 86 **Med Exp PMPM:** $221
**Principal Investments:** Long-term bonds (35%), cash and equiv (28%), nonaffiliate common stock (10%), other (26%)
**Provider Compensation ($000):** Contr fee ($139,257), capitation ($35,660), FFS ($33,088)
**Total Member Encounters:** Phys (202,585), non-phys (493,988)
**Group Affiliation:** Aultman Health Foundation
**Licensed in:** OH
**Address:** 2600 Sixth St SW, Canton, OH 44710
**Phone:** (330) 363-4057 **Dom State:** OH **Commenced Bus:** November 1989

| Data Date | Rating | RACR #1 | RACR #2 | Total Assets ($mil) | Capital ($mil) | Net Premium ($mil) | Net Income ($mil) |
|---|---|---|---|---|---|---|---|
| 9-17 | C+ | 2.29 | 1.91 | 100.7 | 48.7 | 193.4 | 5.5 |
| 9-16 | C- | 1.93 | 1.61 | 89.8 | 38.9 | 189.3 | 1.2 |
| 2016 | C | 2.01 | 1.68 | 86.1 | 42.7 | 259.3 | 5.5 |
| 2015 | C- | 1.79 | 1.49 | 84.0 | 36.0 | 250.2 | 7.7 |
| 2014 | C- | 1.59 | 1.33 | 116.1 | 62.4 | 465.7 | 5.4 |
| 2013 | C- | 1.57 | 1.31 | 115.2 | 61.7 | 454.1 | 4.7 |
| 2012 | U | 1.33 | 1.11 | 112.8 | 58.4 | 468.5 | -0.3 |

Rating Indexes

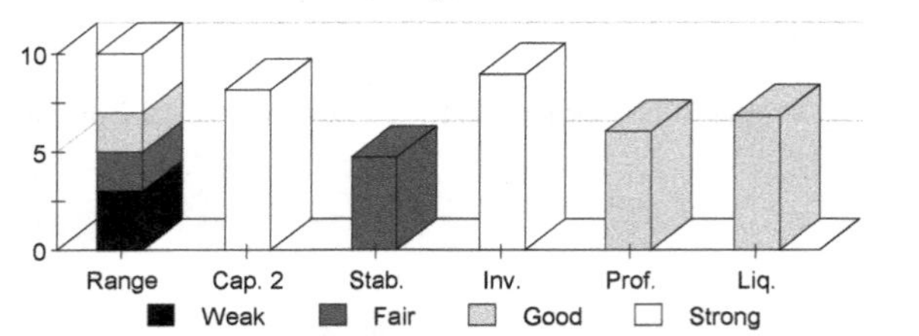


## AVALON INS CO C Fair

**Major Rating Factors:** Weak profitability index (0.7 on a scale of 0 to 10). Good liquidity (6.0) with sufficient resources (cash flows and marketable investments) to handle a spike in claims. Strong capitalization (7.2) based on excellent current risk-adjusted capital (severe loss scenario).
**Other Rating Factors:** High quality investment portfolio (9.9).
**Principal Business:** Med supp (3%), other (96%)
**Mem Phys: 16:** 781 **15:** 758 **16 MLR** 95.3% **/ 16 Admin Exp** N/A
**Enroll(000): Q3 17:** 303 **16:** 309 **15:** 301 **Med Exp PMPM:** $16
**Principal Investments:** Long-term bonds (52%), cash and equiv (45%), nonaffiliate common stock (3%)
**Provider Compensation ($000):** Contr fee ($8,402), other ($52,387)
**Total Member Encounters:** Phys (23,553), non-phys (262,698)
**Group Affiliation:** Capital Blue Cross
**Licensed in:** DC, DE, MD, PA, VA, WV
**Address:** 2500 Elmerton Ave, Harrisburg, PA 17177-9799
**Phone:** (717) 541-7000 **Dom State:** PA **Commenced Bus:** January 2006

| Data Date | Rating | RACR #1 | RACR #2 | Total Assets ($mil) | Capital ($mil) | Net Premium ($mil) | Net Income ($mil) |
|---|---|---|---|---|---|---|---|
| 9-17 | C | 1.52 | 1.27 | 33.2 | 11.4 | 47.2 | -4.3 |
| 9-16 | C | 2.32 | 1.93 | 39.3 | 15.1 | 49.9 | -3.7 |
| 2016 | C | 2.05 | 1.70 | 38.3 | 15.5 | 63.8 | -9.3 |
| 2015 | C | 2.81 | 2.35 | 41.4 | 18.4 | 62.4 | -4.7 |
| 2014 | C | 2.04 | 1.70 | 33.9 | 13.8 | 56.0 | -6.1 |
| 2013 | C | 4.32 | 3.60 | 33.5 | 19.8 | 46.0 | 3.0 |
| 2012 | C | 3.65 | 3.04 | 31.8 | 17.5 | 41.5 | 1.1 |

Rating Indexes

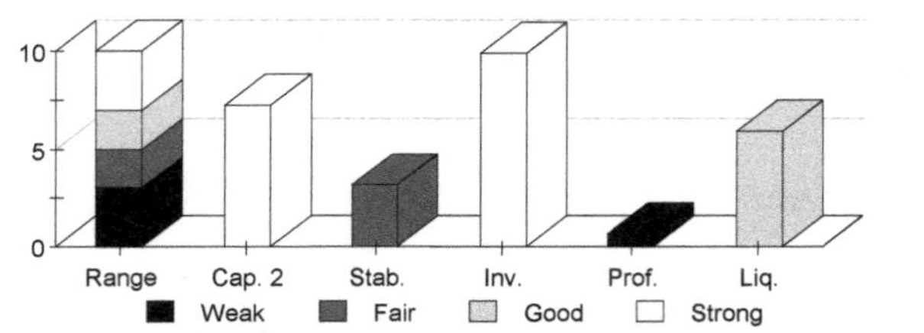


## AVERA HEALTH PLANS INC C Fair

**Major Rating Factors:** Fair profitability index (3.1 on a scale of 0 to 10). Good overall results on stability tests (5.8). Good liquidity (6.0) with sufficient resources (cash flows and marketable investments) to handle a spike in claims.
**Other Rating Factors:** Strong capitalization index (7.1) based on excellent current risk-adjusted capital (severe loss scenario). High quality investment portfolio (9.2).
**Principal Business:** Comp med (91%), med supp (9%)
**Mem Phys: 16:** 5,530 **15:** 5,480 **16 MLR** 95.3% **/ 16 Admin Exp** N/A
**Enroll(000): Q2 17:** 54 **16:** 49 **15:** 37 **Med Exp PMPM:** $303
**Principal Investments:** Long-term bonds (49%), cash and equiv (32%), nonaffiliate common stock (19%)
**Provider Compensation ($000):** FFS ($103,866), contr fee ($73,223)
**Total Member Encounters:** Phys (86,252), non-phys (44,799)
**Group Affiliation:** Avera Health
**Licensed in:** IA, NE, SD
**Address:** 3816 S Elmwood Ave Suite 100, Sioux Falls, SD 57105
**Phone:** (605) 322-4500 **Dom State:** SD **Commenced Bus:** October 1999

| Data Date | Rating | RACR #1 | RACR #2 | Total Assets ($mil) | Capital ($mil) | Net Premium ($mil) | Net Income ($mil) |
|---|---|---|---|---|---|---|---|
| 6-17 | C | 1.47 | 1.22 | 74.5 | 34.8 | 127.7 | 12.5 |
| 6-16 | C- | 1.62 | 1.35 | 59.5 | 29.6 | 98.2 | 7.2 |
| 2016 | C- | 0.91 | 0.76 | 56.6 | 22.2 | 191.6 | 0.6 |
| 2015 | C- | 1.19 | 0.99 | 47.7 | 22.1 | 123.5 | -17.9 |
| 2014 | C- | N/A | N/A | 32.5 | 11.5 | 118.0 | 0.6 |
| 2013 | C | 0.75 | 0.62 | 24.2 | 9.4 | 84.3 | -2.5 |
| 2012 | C+ | 1.03 | 0.86 | 25.2 | 11.7 | 75.9 | 0.9 |

Rating Indexes

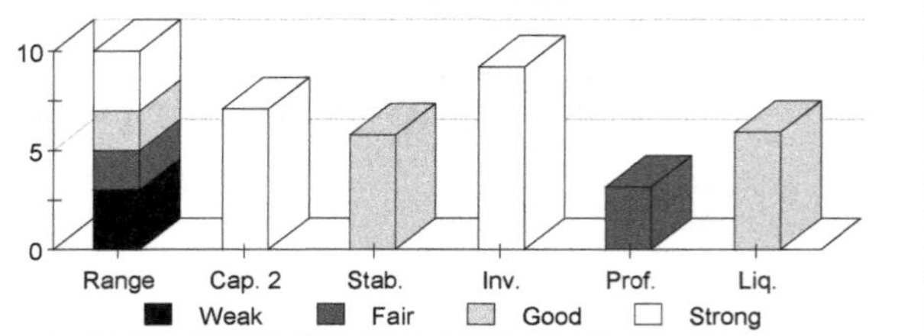

## AVMED INC — C — Fair

**Major Rating Factors:** Fair overall results on stability tests (4.0 on a scale of 0 to 10). Weak profitability index (1.4). Good capitalization index (6.7) based on good current risk-adjusted capital (severe loss scenario).
**Other Rating Factors:** Good liquidity (5.1) with sufficient resources (cash flows and marketable investments) to handle a spike in claims. High quality investment portfolio (7.5).
**Principal Business:** Comp med (55%), Medicare (42%), FEHB (3%)
**Mem Phys: 16:** 40,677 **15:** 37,487 **16 MLR** 88.4% **/ 16 Admin Exp** N/A
**Enroll(000): Q3 17:** 171 **16:** 150 **15:** 128 **Med Exp PMPM:** $489
**Principal Investments:** Long-term bonds (68%), nonaffiliate common stock (17%), cash and equiv (8%), real estate (7%)
**Provider Compensation ($000):** Contr fee ($552,853), FFS ($234,222), capitation ($58,195), bonus arrang ($1,864)
**Total Member Encounters:** N/A
**Group Affiliation:** SantaFe HealthCare Inc
**Licensed in:** FL
**Address:** 9400 South Dadeland Boulevard, Miami, FL 33156
**Phone:** (352) 372-8400 **Dom State:** FL **Commenced Bus:** October 1977

| Data Date | Rating | RACR #1 | RACR #2 | Total Assets ($mil) | Capital ($mil) | Net Premium ($mil) | Net Income ($mil) |
|---|---|---|---|---|---|---|---|
| 9-17 | C | 1.19 | 0.99 | 359.1 | 95.4 | 816.4 | 10.0 |
| 9-16 | B- | 1.43 | 1.19 | 315.2 | 94.3 | 728.3 | -4.3 |
| 2016 | C | 0.99 | 0.83 | 281.1 | 81.7 | 967.8 | -15.5 |
| 2015 | B- | 1.54 | 1.28 | 283.7 | 99.9 | 819.8 | -6.0 |
| 2014 | B | 1.94 | 1.61 | 253.6 | 115.2 | 723.8 | -48.5 |
| 2013 | B+ | 2.70 | 2.25 | 289.6 | 162.0 | 782.1 | 20.4 |
| 2012 | B+ | 2.03 | 1.69 | 292.4 | 146.2 | 908.8 | 25.4 |

Rating Indexes

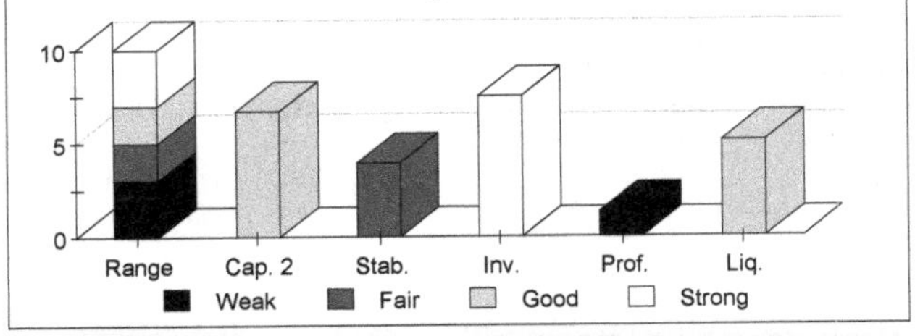


## BANKERS FIDELITY LIFE INSURANCE COMPANY — B — Good

**Major Rating Factors:** Good overall results on stability tests (5.6 on a scale of 0 to 10). Strengths include good financial strength of affiliated Atlantic American Corp, excellent operational trends and good risk diversification. Good capitalization (5.6) based on good risk adjusted capital (severe loss scenario). Good liquidity (5.3).
**Other Rating Factors:** Fair quality investment portfolio (4.7). Fair profitability (4.8) with operating losses during the first nine months of 2017.
**Principal Business:** Individual health insurance (83%), individual life insurance (9%), reinsurance (7%), and group health insurance (1%).
**Principal Investments:** NonCMO investment grade bonds (68%), common & preferred stock (11%), noninv. grade bonds (11%), CMOs and structured securities (5%), and misc. investments (6%).
**Investments in Affiliates:** 7%
**Group Affiliation:** Atlantic American Corp
**Licensed in:** All states except CA, CT, NY, VT, PR
**Commenced Business:** November 1955
**Address:** 4370 Peachtree Road NE, Atlanta, GA 30319
**Phone:** (800) 241-1439 **Domicile State:** GA **NAIC Code:** 61239

| Data Date | Rating | RACR #1 | RACR #2 | Total Assets ($mil) | Capital ($mil) | Net Premium ($mil) | Net Income ($mil) |
|---|---|---|---|---|---|---|---|
| 9-17 | B | 1.07 | 0.82 | 140.6 | 29.7 | 83.1 | -1.9 |
| 9-16 | B | 1.17 | 0.87 | 142.2 | 33.0 | 77.2 | 0.3 |
| 2016 | B | 1.24 | 0.94 | 144.3 | 33.4 | 99.6 | 1.2 |
| 2015 | B | 1.28 | 0.96 | 143.9 | 35.3 | 96.1 | 4.0 |
| 2014 | B | 1.21 | 0.92 | 139.1 | 34.0 | 100.2 | 2.7 |
| 2013 | B | 1.58 | 1.14 | 138.8 | 34.5 | 99.6 | 3.0 |
| 2012 | B | 2.03 | 1.48 | 128.7 | 33.1 | 89.6 | 2.3 |

| Atlantic American Corp<br>Composite Group Rating: B-<br>Largest Group Members | Assets ($mil) | Rating |
|---|---|---|
| BANKERS FIDELITY LIFE INS CO | 144 | B |
| AMERICAN SOUTHERN INS CO | 111 | C+ |
| AMERICAN SAFETY INS CO | 17 | C |
| BANKERS FIDELITY ASR CO | 10 | B- |

## BANKERS LIFE & CASUALTY COMPANY — D+ — Weak

**Major Rating Factors:** Weak overall results on stability tests (2.7 on a scale of 0 to 10). Fair quality investment portfolio (4.8) with large holdings of BBB rated bonds in addition to junk bond exposure equal to 59% of capital. Good liquidity (5.7) with sufficient resources to cover a large increase in policy surrenders.
**Other Rating Factors:** Strong capitalization (7.3) based on excellent risk adjusted capital (severe loss scenario). Excellent profitability (9.1).
**Principal Business:** Individual annuities (37%), individual health insurance (32%), individual life insurance (18%), reinsurance (13%), and group health insurance (1%).
**Principal Investments:** NonCMO investment grade bonds (56%), CMOs and structured securities (26%), mortgages in good standing (7%), noninv. grade bonds (5%), and misc. investments (6%).
**Investments in Affiliates:** 1%
**Group Affiliation:** CNO Financial Group Inc
**Licensed in:** All states except NY, PR
**Commenced Business:** January 1879
**Address:** 111 EAST WACKER DRIVE STE 2100, CHICAGO, IL 60601-4508
**Phone:** (312) 396-6000 **Domicile State:** IL **NAIC Code:** 61263

| Data Date | Rating | RACR #1 | RACR #2 | Total Assets ($mil) | Capital ($mil) | Net Premium ($mil) | Net Income ($mil) |
|---|---|---|---|---|---|---|---|
| 9-17 | D+ | 2.32 | 1.20 | 18,092.1 | 1,326.1 | 1,931.0 | 174.0 |
| 9-16 | D+ | 2.15 | 1.12 | 17,406.3 | 1,289.7 | 1,876.1 | 128.0 |
| 2016 | D+ | 2.32 | 1.20 | 17,602.0 | 1,300.3 | 2,535.9 | 171.2 |
| 2015 | D+ | 2.23 | 1.16 | 16,905.4 | 1,238.6 | 2,385.0 | 188.7 |
| 2014 | D+ | 2.12 | 1.10 | 16,590.7 | 1,193.1 | 2,387.1 | 211.6 |
| 2013 | D+ | 2.04 | 1.06 | 15,839.5 | 1,057.0 | 2,323.5 | 161.9 |
| 2012 | D+ | 1.83 | 0.96 | 14,941.3 | 914.6 | 2,282.5 | 231.3 |

Rating Indexes

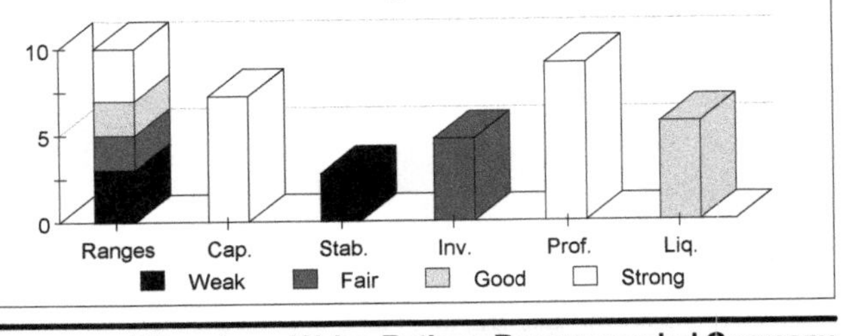

## BANKERS RESERVE LIFE INS CO OF WI C- Fair

**Major Rating Factors:** Weak profitability index (0.9 on a scale of 0 to 10). Good liquidity (6.8) with sufficient resources (cash flows and marketable investments) to handle a spike in claims. Strong capitalization (7.6) based on excellent current risk-adjusted capital (severe loss scenario).
**Other Rating Factors:** High quality investment portfolio (9.8).
**Principal Business:** Medicaid (89%), comp med (11%)
**Mem Phys: 16:** 53,273 **15:** N/A **16 MLR** 85.0% **/ 16 Admin Exp** N/A
**Enroll(000): Q3 17:** 516 **16:** 509 **15:** 517 **Med Exp PMPM:** $278
**Principal Investments:** Long-term bonds (64%), cash and equiv (32%), affiliate common stock (3%), other (2%)
**Provider Compensation ($000):** Contr fee ($1,554,424), bonus arrang ($112,419), salary ($68,987), capitation ($14,357)
**Total Member Encounters:** Phys (2,680,803), non-phys (5,397,419)
**Group Affiliation:** Centene Corporation
**Licensed in:** All states except AK, CA, CT, HI, MA, MN, NY, VT, PR
**Address:** 7700 Forsyth Blvd, St. Louis, MO 63105
**Phone:** (314) 505-6143 **Dom State:** WI **Commenced Bus:** July 1964

| Data Date | Rating | RACR #1 | RACR #2 | Total Assets ($mil) | Capital ($mil) | Net Premium ($mil) | Net Income ($mil) |
|---|---|---|---|---|---|---|---|
| 9-17 | C- | 1.87 | 1.55 | 368.2 | 192.3 | 1,410.2 | -23.6 |
| 9-16 | C- | 2.03 | 1.69 | 406.4 | 227.5 | 1,452.4 | -18.0 |
| 2016 | C- | 2.14 | 1.78 | 410.4 | 223.7 | 1,958.6 | -20.7 |
| 2015 | C- | 2.17 | 1.81 | 425.9 | 244.4 | 2,102.0 | -21.7 |
| 2014 | C- | 2.18 | 1.82 | 468.8 | 268.0 | 2,363.6 | 11.2 |
| 2013 | C- | 1.80 | 1.50 | 434.6 | 238.1 | 2,322.6 | -4.6 |
| 2012 | C- | 1.84 | 1.53 | 409.4 | 198.6 | 1,719.3 | -126.4 |

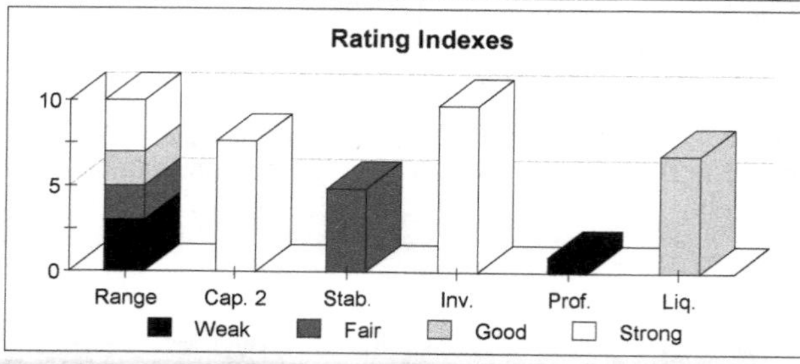


## BAPTIST HEALTH PLAN INC D Weak

**Major Rating Factors:** Weak profitability index (0.8 on a scale of 0 to 10). Poor capitalization index (1.8) based on weak current risk-adjusted capital (moderate loss scenario). Weak overall results on stability tests (1.8) based on an excessive 31% enrollment growth during the period, a steep decline in capital during 2016.
**Other Rating Factors:** Weak liquidity (1.4) as a spike in claims may stretch capacity. Good quality investment portfolio (5.2).
**Principal Business:** Comp med (95%), Medicare (5%)
**Mem Phys: 16:** 45,508 **15:** 36,927 **16 MLR** 100.7% **/ 16 Admin Exp** N/A
**Enroll(000): Q3 17:** 26 **16:** 39 **15:** 29 **Med Exp PMPM:** $342
**Principal Investments:** Long-term bonds (53%), nonaffiliate common stock (43%), cash and equiv (4%)
**Provider Compensation ($000):** Contr fee ($141,296), FFS ($2,026), capitation ($1,228)
**Total Member Encounters:** Phys (401,389), non-phys (110,745)
**Group Affiliation:** Baptist Healthcare System Inc
**Licensed in:** IL, IN, KY, OH, TN, WV
**Address:** 651 Perimeter Drive STE 300, Lexington, KY 40517
**Phone:** (859) 269-4475 **Dom State:** KY **Commenced Bus:** April 1993

| Data Date | Rating | RACR #1 | RACR #2 | Total Assets ($mil) | Capital ($mil) | Net Premium ($mil) | Net Income ($mil) |
|---|---|---|---|---|---|---|---|
| 9-17 | D | 0.48 | 0.40 | 50.1 | 17.8 | 106.4 | -4.5 |
| 9-16 | C- | 1.42 | 1.18 | 67.4 | 23.0 | 115.7 | -5.9 |
| 2016 | D+ | 0.63 | 0.53 | 76.1 | 20.9 | 153.8 | -24.8 |
| 2015 | C | 2.71 | 2.26 | 68.0 | 34.9 | 129.8 | -18.5 |
| 2014 | B | 4.08 | 3.40 | 100.6 | 71.7 | 145.8 | -6.3 |
| 2013 | A- | 4.46 | 3.72 | 99.5 | 75.6 | 144.8 | 2.7 |
| 2012 | A- | 3.56 | 2.97 | 93.7 | 67.9 | 169.6 | 12.9 |

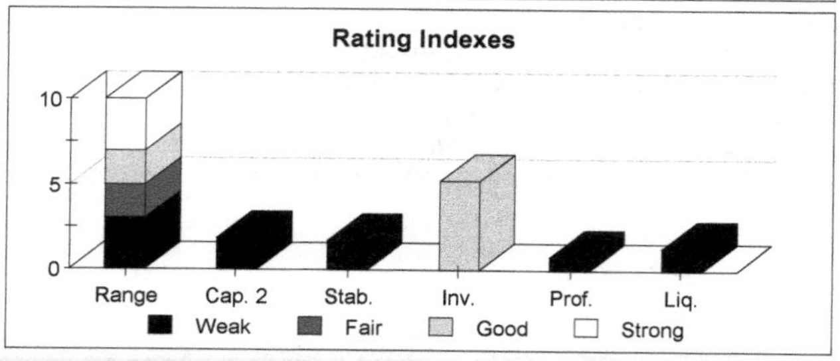


## BAY AREA ACCOUNTABLE CARE D+ Weak

**Major Rating Factors:** Weak profitability index (0.9 on a scale of 0 to 10). Weak overall results on stability tests (2.2). Strong capitalization index (7.1) based on excellent current risk-adjusted capital (severe loss scenario).
**Other Rating Factors:** Excellent liquidity (7.0) with sufficient resources (cash flows and marketable investments) to handle a spike in claims.
**Principal Business:** Managed care (100%)
**Mem Phys: 16:** N/A **15:** N/A **16 MLR** 89.5% **/ 16 Admin Exp** N/A
**Enroll(000): Q3 17:** 14 **16:** 14 **15:** N/A **Med Exp PMPM:** $662
**Principal Investments ($000):** Cash and equiv ($16,554)
**Provider Compensation ($000):** None
**Total Member Encounters:** N/A
**Group Affiliation:** None
**Licensed in:** CA
**Address:** 6475 Christie Avenue Suite 360, Emeryville, CA 94608
**Phone:** (415) 299-7840 **Dom State:** CA **Commenced Bus:** N/A

| Data Date | Rating | RACR #1 | RACR #2 | Total Assets ($mil) | Capital ($mil) | Net Premium ($mil) | Net Income ($mil) |
|---|---|---|---|---|---|---|---|
| 9-17 | D+ | 1.92 | 1.21 | 19.9 | 8.1 | 66.1 | -1.7 |
| 9-16 | N/A | N/A | N/A | N/A | N/A | N/A | N/A |
| 2016 | D+ | 2.43 | 1.53 | 18.1 | 9.7 | 31.5 | -1.9 |
| 2015 | N/A | N/A | N/A | N/A | N/A | N/A | N/A |
| 2014 | N/A | N/A | N/A | N/A | N/A | N/A | N/A |
| 2013 | N/A | N/A | N/A | N/A | N/A | N/A | N/A |
| 2012 | N/A | N/A | N/A | N/A | N/A | N/A | N/A |

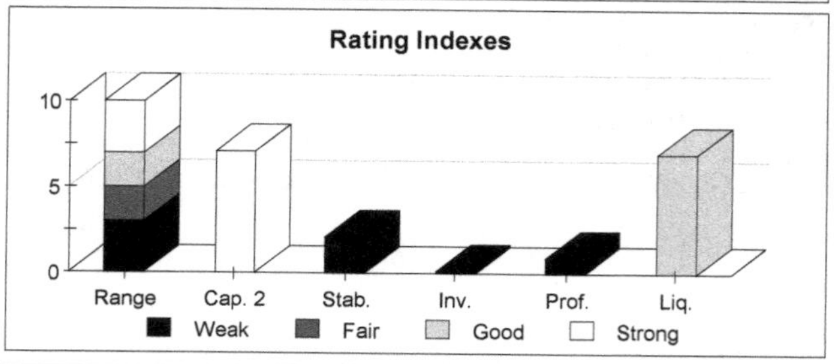

## BCS INS CO B Good

**Major Rating Factors:** History of adequate reserve strength (6.9 on a scale of 0 to 10) as reserves have been consistently at an acceptable level. Good overall profitability index (5.7). Fair expense controls. Return on equity has been fair, averaging 6.4% over the past five years.
**Other Rating Factors:** Good liquidity (6.4) with sufficient resources (cash flows and marketable investments) to handle a spike in claims. Fair overall results on stability tests (4.3) including weak results on operational trends and negative cash flow from operations for 2016. Strong long-term capitalization index (10.0) based on excellent current risk adjusted capital (severe and moderate loss scenarios), despite some fluctuation in capital levels.
**Principal Business:** Group accident & health (57%), inland marine (21%), other liability (14%), and commercial multiple peril (8%).
**Principal Investments:** Investment grade bonds (82%), misc. investments (17%), and non investment grade bonds (1%).
**Investments in Affiliates:** 1%
**Group Affiliation:** BCS Financial Corp
**Licensed in:** All states, the District of Columbia and Puerto Rico
**Commenced Business:** November 1952
**Address:** 6740 North High Street, Worthington, OH 43085
**Phone:** (630) 472-7700 **Domicile State:** OH **NAIC Code:** 38245

| Data Date | Rating | RACR #1 | RACR #2 | Loss Ratio % | Total Assets ($mil) | Capital ($mil) | Net Premium ($mil) | Net Income ($mil) |
|---|---|---|---|---|---|---|---|---|
| 9-17 | B | 9.90 | 5.63 | N/A | 273.3 | 160.3 | 75.3 | 10.3 |
| 9-16 | B | 9.41 | 5.35 | N/A | 272.8 | 163.7 | 75.5 | 9.4 |
| 2016 | B | 8.93 | 5.13 | 64.9 | 269.4 | 155.2 | 101.8 | 11.4 |
| 2015 | B | 8.58 | 4.87 | 60.5 | 272.2 | 161.3 | 95.3 | 13.3 |
| 2014 | B | 6.63 | 3.81 | 69.0 | 279.6 | 157.2 | 129.6 | 8.0 |
| 2013 | B | 7.43 | 4.22 | 70.2 | 267.9 | 152.9 | 131.9 | 6.4 |
| 2012 | B | 10.06 | 5.70 | 63.4 | 254.5 | 151.9 | 111.6 | 8.2 |

**Reserve Deficiency (as % of capital)**

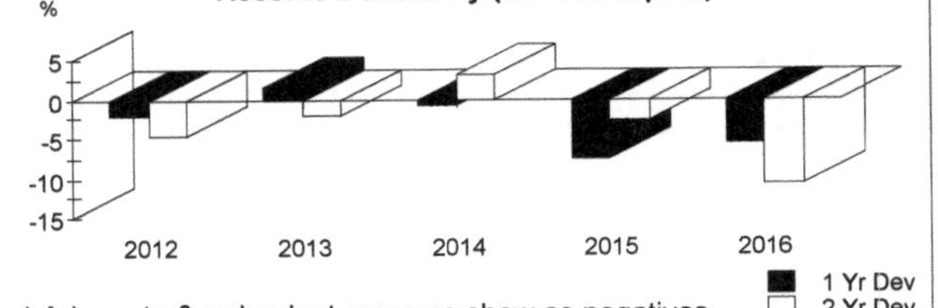


* Adequate & redundant reserves show as negatives

## BEHEALTHY FLORIDA INC D+ Weak

**Major Rating Factors:** Weak profitability index (0.2 on a scale of 0 to 10). Strong capitalization (10.0) based on excellent current risk-adjusted capital (severe loss scenario). High quality investment portfolio (9.9).
**Other Rating Factors:** Excellent liquidity (8.2) with ample operational cash flow and liquid investments.
**Principal Business:** Medicare (100%)
**Mem Phys: 16:** N/A **15:** 567 **16 MLR** 89.4% **/ 16 Admin Exp** N/A
**Enroll(000): Q3 17:** 9 **16:** 3 **15:** 1 **Med Exp PMPM:** $668
**Principal Investments:** Cash and equiv (100%)
**Provider Compensation ($000):** Capitation ($20,665), FFS ($875)
**Total Member Encounters:** Phys (12,406), non-phys (4,465)
**Group Affiliation:** GuideWell Mutual Holding Corporation
**Licensed in:** FL
**Address:** 4800 Deerwood Campus Parkway, Jacksonville, FL 32246
**Phone:** (904) 791-6111 **Dom State:** FL **Commenced Bus:** May 2013

| Data Date | Rating | RACR #1 | RACR #2 | Total Assets ($mil) | Capital ($mil) | Net Premium ($mil) | Net Income ($mil) |
|---|---|---|---|---|---|---|---|
| 9-17 | D+ | 6.25 | 5.21 | 37.8 | 9.8 | 69.6 | -1.2 |
| 9-16 | D | 3.98 | 3.32 | 10.5 | 4.0 | 17.2 | -1.3 |
| 2016 | D | 6.97 | 5.81 | 16.6 | 11.0 | 23.3 | -1.5 |
| 2015 | C- | 5.23 | 4.36 | 8.8 | 5.3 | 7.0 | -3.7 |
| 2014 | D | 0.88 | 0.74 | 3.6 | 2.2 | 5.1 | -3.0 |
| 2013 | N/A | N/A | N/A | 3.4 | 3.1 | N/A | -2.2 |
| 2012 | N/A | N/A | N/A | 5.7 | 5.7 | N/A | N/A |

**Rating Indexes**

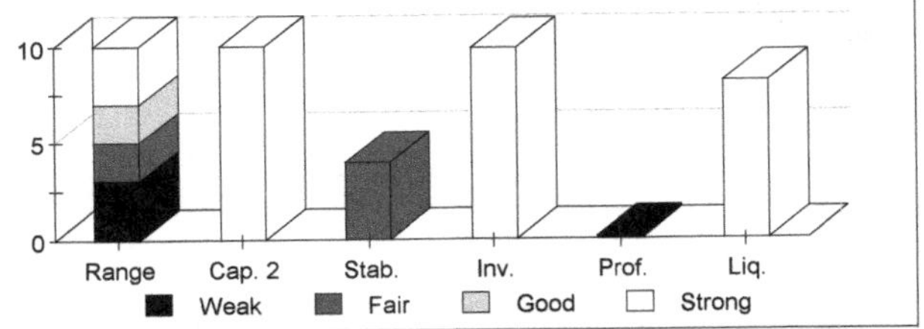


## BERKLEY LIFE & HEALTH INSURANCE COMPANY * A Excellent

**Major Rating Factors:** Excellent overall results on stability tests (7.8 on a scale of 0 to 10). Strengths that enhance stability include excellent operational trends and excellent risk diversification. Strong capitalization (10.0) based on excellent risk adjusted capital (severe loss scenario). Furthermore, this high level of risk adjusted capital has been consistently maintained over the last five years. High quality investment portfolio (7.8).
**Other Rating Factors:** Excellent profitability (8.8). Excellent liquidity (7.1).
**Principal Business:** Group health insurance (99%) and reinsurance (1%).
**Principal Investments:** NonCMO investment grade bonds (59%), CMOs and structured securities (38%), and cash (2%).
**Investments in Affiliates:** None
**Group Affiliation:** W R Berkley Corp
**Licensed in:** All states except PR
**Commenced Business:** July 1963
**Address:** 11201 DOUGLAS AVE, URBANDALE, IA 50322
**Phone:** (609) 584-6990 **Domicile State:** IA **NAIC Code:** 64890

| Data Date | Rating | RACR #1 | RACR #2 | Total Assets ($mil) | Capital ($mil) | Net Premium ($mil) | Net Income ($mil) |
|---|---|---|---|---|---|---|---|
| 9-17 | A | 4.66 | 3.48 | 286.6 | 148.9 | 181.2 | 5.5 |
| 9-16 | B | 4.77 | 3.68 | 258.7 | 139.5 | 181.3 | 11.2 |
| 2016 | B | 4.60 | 3.45 | 267.7 | 143.7 | 237.9 | 14.1 |
| 2015 | B- | 5.35 | 4.11 | 223.9 | 129.2 | 187.3 | 23.1 |
| 2014 | B- | 5.56 | 4.23 | 197.6 | 106.0 | 145.5 | 11.7 |
| 2013 | B- | 6.16 | 4.73 | 166.3 | 94.2 | 117.1 | 11.3 |
| 2012 | B | 5.25 | 4.11 | 148.7 | 83.3 | 123.9 | 7.7 |

**Adverse Trends in Operations**

Decrease in premium volume from 2012 to 2013 (5%)

## BERKSHIRE LIFE INSURANCE COMPANY OF AMERICA B Good

**Major Rating Factors:** Good overall profitability (5.4 on a scale of 0 to 10). Good overall results on stability tests (6.1). Strengths include potential support from affiliation with Guardian Group, excellent operational trends and excellent risk diversification. Fair quality investment portfolio (3.9) with large holdings of BBB rated bonds in addition to junk bond exposure equal to 93% of capital.
**Other Rating Factors:** Strong capitalization (7.5) based on excellent risk adjusted capital (severe loss scenario). Excellent liquidity (7.7).
**Principal Business:** Individual health insurance (73%), reinsurance (26%), and individual life insurance (1%).
**Principal Investments:** NonCMO investment grade bonds (92%), noninv. grade bonds (6%), CMOs and structured securities (1%), and real estate (1%).
**Investments in Affiliates:** None
**Group Affiliation:** Guardian Group
**Licensed in:** All states except PR
**Commenced Business:** July 2001
**Address:** 700 SOUTH STREET, PITTSFIELD, MA 1201
**Phone:** (413) 499-4321 **Domicile State:** MA **NAIC Code:** 71714

| Data Date | Rating | RACR #1 | RACR #2 | Total Assets ($mil) | Capital ($mil) | Net Premium ($mil) | Net Income ($mil) |
|---|---|---|---|---|---|---|---|
| 9-17 | B | 2.88 | 1.34 | 3,685.6 | 209.8 | 95.0 | 16.3 |
| 9-16 | B | 3.04 | 1.41 | 3,489.0 | 221.7 | 92.4 | 18.8 |
| 2016 | B | 2.97 | 1.36 | 3,526.7 | 201.6 | 123.3 | 17.8 |
| 2015 | B | 3.34 | 1.58 | 3,381.4 | 207.9 | 118.2 | 14.2 |
| 2014 | A- | 4.53 | 2.24 | 3,377.3 | 269.5 | 114.0 | 16.9 |
| 2013 | A | 8.68 | 4.24 | 3,461.4 | 583.0 | 115.9 | 60.0 |
| 2012 | A | 5.30 | 3.03 | 3,209.2 | 543.4 | 493.9 | 43.9 |

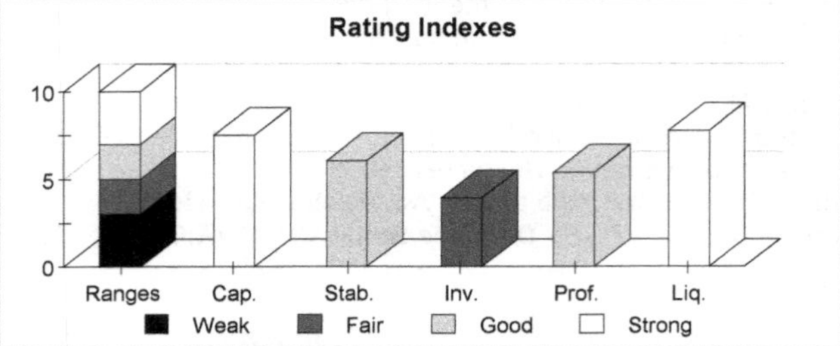


## BLUE ADVANTAGE PLUS OF KANSAS CITY C Fair

**Major Rating Factors:** Fair capitalization (2.9 on a scale of 0 to 10) based on good current risk-adjusted capital (moderate loss scenario). Fair liquidity (3.0) as a spike in claims may stretch capacity. Weak profitability index (0.0).
**Other Rating Factors:** High quality investment portfolio (9.9).
**Principal Business:** Medicare (100%)
**Mem Phys: 16:** 2,628 **15:** 1,681 **16 MLR** 99.7% **/ 16 Admin Exp** N/A
**Enroll(000): Q3 17:** 9 **16:** 4 **15:** N/A **Med Exp PMPM:** $732
**Principal Investments:** Long-term bonds (92%), cash and equiv (8%)
**Provider Compensation ($000):** Contr fee ($17,737), FFS ($6,428), capitation ($261)
**Total Member Encounters:** Phys (24,820), non-phys (5,108)
**Group Affiliation:** Blue Cross & Blue Shield of KS City
**Licensed in:** KS, MO
**Address:** 2301 Main St, Kansas City, MO 64108-2428
**Phone:** (816) 395-2222 **Dom State:** MO **Commenced Bus:** July 2005

| Data Date | Rating | RACR #1 | RACR #2 | Total Assets ($mil) | Capital ($mil) | Net Premium ($mil) | Net Income ($mil) |
|---|---|---|---|---|---|---|---|
| 9-17 | C | 1.68 | 1.40 | 40.0 | 14.8 | 58.5 | -5.5 |
| 9-16 | N/A | N/A | N/A | 23.5 | 9.4 | 22.4 | -5.9 |
| 2016 | C | 1.00 | 0.83 | 16.8 | 9.3 | 29.3 | -5.9 |
| 2015 | N/A | N/A | N/A | 21.2 | 15.3 | N/A | -8.7 |
| 2014 | N/A | N/A | N/A | 26.2 | 24.0 | N/A | -1.0 |
| 2013 | N/A | N/A | N/A | 25.1 | 25.0 | N/A | 0.2 |
| 2012 | N/A | N/A | N/A | 25.8 | 24.5 | 45.4 | 2.0 |

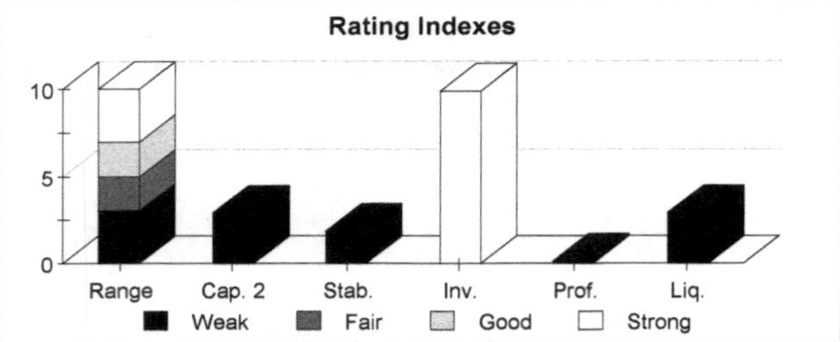


## BLUE CARE NETWORK OF MICHIGAN * B+ Good

**Major Rating Factors:** Good overall profitability index (6.9 on a scale of 0 to 10). Strong capitalization index (10.0) based on excellent current risk-adjusted capital (severe loss scenario). High quality investment portfolio (9.7).
**Other Rating Factors:** Excellent overall results on stability tests (8.2). Fair financial strength from affiliates. Excellent liquidity (7.0) with ample operational cash flow and liquid investments.
**Principal Business:** Comp med (72%), Medicare (24%), FEHB (3%)
**Mem Phys: 16:** 51,896 **15:** 47,800 **16 MLR** 84.3% **/ 16 Admin Exp** N/A
**Enroll(000): Q3 17:** 683 **16:** 670 **15:** 670 **Med Exp PMPM:** $354
**Principal Investments:** Long-term bonds (54%), cash and equiv (36%), nonaffiliate common stock (10%), affiliate common stock (1%)
**Provider Compensation ($000):** Bonus arrang ($1,782,219), contr fee ($843,880), capitation ($206,035), FFS ($54,067)
**Total Member Encounters:** Phys (4,061,690), non-phys (1,585,900)
**Group Affiliation:** Blue Cross Blue Shield of Michigan
**Licensed in:** MI
**Address:** 20500 Civic Center Drive, Southfield, MI 48076
**Phone:** (248) 799-6400 **Dom State:** MI **Commenced Bus:** May 1981

| Data Date | Rating | RACR #1 | RACR #2 | Total Assets ($mil) | Capital ($mil) | Net Premium ($mil) | Net Income ($mil) |
|---|---|---|---|---|---|---|---|
| 9-17 | B+ | 6.95 | 5.79 | 2,177.8 | 1,290.0 | 2,689.2 | 146.0 |
| 9-16 | B+ | 6.21 | 5.18 | 1,904.6 | 1,112.0 | 2,580.2 | 86.4 |
| 2016 | B+ | 6.05 | 5.04 | 1,864.2 | 1,123.0 | 3,399.3 | 93.8 |
| 2015 | B+ | 5.74 | 4.78 | 1,847.8 | 1,026.5 | 3,252.5 | 18.0 |
| 2014 | B+ | 5.74 | 4.78 | 1,799.3 | 1,013.5 | 2,992.1 | 17.3 |
| 2013 | B+ | 6.62 | 5.52 | 1,593.6 | 999.8 | 2,613.3 | 118.6 |
| 2012 | A- | 6.02 | 5.02 | 1,567.9 | 892.5 | 2,632.8 | 167.2 |

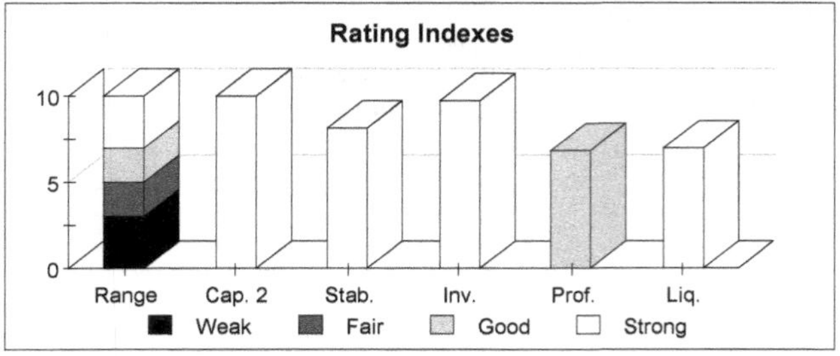

## BLUE CARE OF MICHIGAN INC C Fair

**Major Rating Factors:** Fair overall results on stability tests (4.0 on a scale of 0 to 10) based on a steep decline in premium revenue in 2016, a significant 23% decrease in enrollment during the period. Rating is significantly influenced by the fair financial results of Blue Cross Blue Shield of Michigan. Weak profitability index (1.4). Strong capitalization index (10.0) based on excellent current risk-adjusted capital (severe loss scenario).
**Other Rating Factors:** High quality investment portfolio (9.9). Excellent liquidity (9.7) with ample operational cash flow and liquid investments.
**Principal Business:** Comp med (100%)
**Mem Phys: 16:** N/A **15:** N/A **16 MLR** 96.4% **/ 16 Admin Exp** N/A
**Enroll(000): Q3 17:** 0 **16:** 0 **15:** 0 **Med Exp PMPM:** $419
**Principal Investments:** Cash and equiv (61%), long-term bonds (39%)
**Provider Compensation ($000):** Capitation ($721)
**Total Member Encounters:** N/A
**Group Affiliation:** Blue Cross Blue Shield of Michigan
**Licensed in:** MI
**Address:** 20500 Civic Center Drive, Southfield, MI 48076
**Phone:** (248) 799-6400 **Dom State:** MI **Commenced Bus:** July 1984

| Data Date | Rating | RACR #1 | RACR #2 | Total Assets ($mil) | Capital ($mil) | Net Premium ($mil) | Net Income ($mil) |
|---|---|---|---|---|---|---|---|
| 9-17 | C | 22.75 | 18.96 | 6.2 | 6.1 | 0.5 | -0.1 |
| 9-16 | C | 22.59 | 18.82 | 6.3 | 6.3 | 0.6 | -0.2 |
| 2016 | C | 23.10 | 19.25 | 6.3 | 6.2 | 0.7 | -0.2 |
| 2015 | C | 23.13 | 19.28 | 6.5 | 6.4 | 1.0 | -0.2 |
| 2014 | C+ | 9.38 | 7.81 | 6.6 | 6.5 | 1.6 | -0.2 |
| 2013 | C+ | 9.90 | 8.25 | 6.6 | 6.6 | 2.4 | -0.1 |
| 2012 | N/A | N/A | N/A | 6.7 | 6.6 | 3.0 | -0.1 |

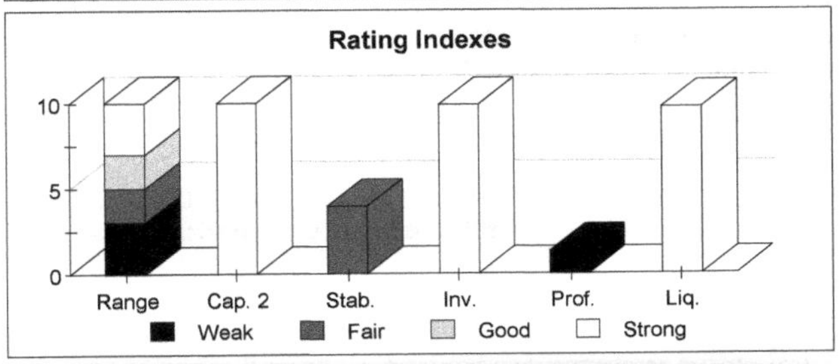


## BLUE CROSS & BLUE SHIELD MA HMO BLUE * A- Excellent

**Major Rating Factors:** Strong capitalization (10.0 on a scale of 0 to 10) based on excellent current risk-adjusted capital (severe loss scenario). High quality investment portfolio (7.2). Good overall profitability index (5.8).
**Other Rating Factors:** Good liquidity (6.6) with sufficient resources (cash flows and marketable investments) to handle a spike in claims.
**Principal Business:** Comp med (90%), Medicare (10%)
**Mem Phys: 16:** 24,444 **15:** 23,609 **16 MLR** 88.6% **/ 16 Admin Exp** N/A
**Enroll(000): Q3 17:** 796 **16:** 769 **15:** 758 **Med Exp PMPM:** $446
**Principal Investments:** Long-term bonds (46%), nonaffiliate common stock (11%), real estate (5%), cash and equiv (2%), other (36%)
**Provider Compensation ($000):** Bonus arrang ($2,289,496), contr fee ($1,357,092), FFS ($270,260), capitation ($133,214)
**Total Member Encounters:** Phys (2,978,734), non-phys (2,456,509)
**Group Affiliation:** Blue Cross and Blue Shield of MA Inc
**Licensed in:** MA
**Address:** 101 Huntington Ave, Boston, MA 02199
**Phone:** (617) 246-5000 **Dom State:** MA **Commenced Bus:** January 2005

| Data Date | Rating | RACR #1 | RACR #2 | Total Assets ($mil) | Capital ($mil) | Net Premium ($mil) | Net Income ($mil) |
|---|---|---|---|---|---|---|---|
| 9-17 | A- | 4.41 | 3.67 | 2,283.0 | 1,376.9 | 3,590.7 | 113.5 |
| 9-16 | B | 4.08 | 3.40 | 2,022.6 | 1,137.0 | 3,424.4 | 35.6 |
| 2016 | B+ | 3.89 | 3.24 | 2,098.2 | 1,207.7 | 4,596.5 | 74.2 |
| 2015 | B | 3.91 | 3.26 | 1,908.1 | 1,089.6 | 4,358.1 | 2.4 |
| 2014 | B | 3.99 | 3.33 | 1,928.6 | 1,124.2 | 4,130.2 | 3.2 |
| 2013 | B | 4.18 | 3.48 | 1,855.0 | 1,151.8 | 3,952.9 | 40.6 |
| 2012 | B | 4.09 | 3.41 | 1,780.7 | 1,077.1 | 3,895.2 | 117.8 |

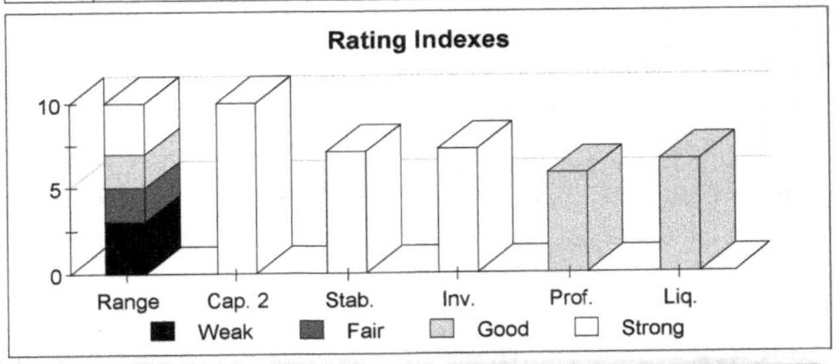


## BLUE CROSS & BLUE SHIELD OF FLORIDA B- Good

**Major Rating Factors:** Good overall profitability index (6.3 on a scale of 0 to 10). Good quality investment portfolio (5.3). Strong capitalization (10.0) based on excellent current risk-adjusted capital (severe loss scenario).
**Other Rating Factors:** Excellent liquidity (6.9) with sufficient resources (cash flows and marketable investments) to handle a spike in claims.
**Principal Business:** Comp med (63%), FEHB (25%), Medicare (6%), med supp (5%), other (2%)
**Mem Phys: 16:** 28,564 **15:** 28,564 **16 MLR** 79.0% **/ 16 Admin Exp** N/A
**Enroll(000): Q3 17:** 1,915 **16:** 1,808 **15:** 1,766 **Med Exp PMPM:** $329
**Principal Investments:** Long-term bonds (72%), nonaffiliate common stock (9%), cash and equiv (8%), real estate (5%), other (7%)
**Provider Compensation ($000):** Contr fee ($6,262,605), FFS ($1,016,614), capitation ($42,813), bonus arrang ($18,294)
**Total Member Encounters:** Phys (14,526,136), non-phys (9,520,220)
**Group Affiliation:** GuideWell Mutual Holding Corporation
**Licensed in:** FL, PA
**Address:** 4800 Deerwood Campus Parkway, Jacksonville, FL 32246
**Phone:** (904) 791-6111 **Dom State:** FL **Commenced Bus:** January 1980

| Data Date | Rating | RACR #1 | RACR #2 | Total Assets ($mil) | Capital ($mil) | Net Premium ($mil) | Net Income ($mil) |
|---|---|---|---|---|---|---|---|
| 9-17 | B- | 4.27 | 3.56 | 5,938.0 | 1,767.5 | 7,529.8 | 361.2 |
| 9-16 | B- | 5.13 | 4.27 | 5,756.1 | 2,019.1 | 7,040.6 | 338.2 |
| 2016 | B- | 5.46 | 4.55 | 5,974.6 | 2,271.7 | 9,387.5 | 552.8 |
| 2015 | C | 4.69 | 3.91 | 5,612.2 | 1,842.1 | 8,789.8 | 327.5 |
| 2014 | C | 3.89 | 3.24 | 4,969.1 | 1,439.0 | 8,102.4 | 64.9 |
| 2013 | B+ | 7.09 | 5.91 | 6,225.0 | 3,086.8 | 6,842.0 | 204.5 |
| 2012 | B+ | 7.08 | 5.90 | 5,583.0 | 2,789.9 | 6,564.7 | 159.1 |

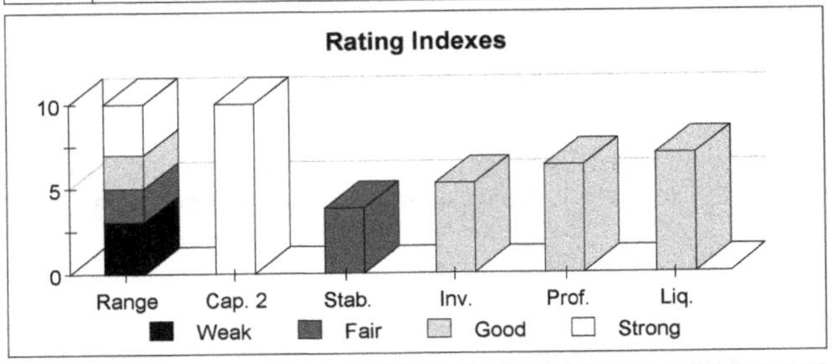

## BLUE CROSS BLUE SHIELD HEALTHCARE GA * A- Excellent

**Major Rating Factors:** Excellent profitability (9.0 on a scale of 0 to 10). Strong capitalization index (9.5) based on excellent current risk-adjusted capital (severe loss scenario). High quality investment portfolio (9.9).
**Other Rating Factors:** Excellent overall results on stability tests (8.0) based on healthy premium and capital growth during 2016. Rating is significantly influenced by the good financial results of Anthem Inc. Excellent liquidity (6.9) with sufficient resources (cash flows and marketable investments) to handle a spike in claims.
**Principal Business:** Comp med (97%), other (3%)
**Mem Phys: 16:** 19,766 **15:** 18,728 **16 MLR** 81.7% **/ 16 Admin Exp** N/A
**Enroll(000): Q3 17:** 718 **16:** 561 **15:** 515 **Med Exp PMPM:** $259
**Principal Investments:** Long-term bonds (66%), cash and equiv (33%), other (1%)
**Provider Compensation ($000):** Contr fee ($1,673,783), capitation ($7,119), bonus arrang ($3,035), other ($36,185)
**Total Member Encounters:** Phys (2,492,166), non-phys (969,534)
**Group Affiliation:** Anthem Inc
**Licensed in:** GA
**Address:** 3350 PEACHTREE ROAD NE, ATLANTA, GA 30326
**Phone:** (404) 842-8000 **Dom State:** GA **Commenced Bus:** September 1986

| Data Date | Rating | RACR #1 | RACR #2 | Total Assets ($mil) | Capital ($mil) | Net Premium ($mil) | Net Income ($mil) |
|---|---|---|---|---|---|---|---|
| 9-17 | A- | 3.35 | 2.79 | 1,109.3 | 419.4 | 2,512.0 | 150.7 |
| 9-16 | B+ | 2.95 | 2.46 | 719.5 | 310.0 | 1,594.4 | 77.3 |
| 2016 | A- | 2.51 | 2.10 | 764.0 | 310.7 | 2,134.3 | 71.7 |
| 2015 | A- | 2.47 | 2.06 | 612.2 | 257.6 | 1,782.8 | 50.9 |
| 2014 | A- | 2.79 | 2.32 | 717.8 | 261.5 | 1,593.9 | 46.8 |
| 2013 | A- | 3.19 | 2.66 | 486.2 | 251.6 | 1,445.8 | 70.5 |
| 2012 | A- | 3.01 | 2.51 | 449.0 | 238.8 | 1,465.7 | 57.2 |

Rating Indexes

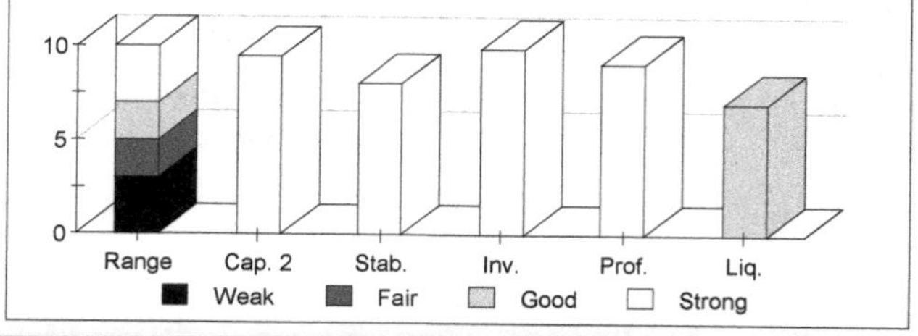


## BLUE CROSS BLUE SHIELD OF ALABAMA B Good

**Major Rating Factors:** Fair profitability index (4.5 on a scale of 0 to 10). Strong capitalization (10.0) based on excellent current risk-adjusted capital (severe loss scenario). High quality investment portfolio (8.8).
**Other Rating Factors:** Excellent liquidity (7.0) with ample operational cash flow and liquid investments.
**Principal Business:** Comp med (66%), FEHB (16%), Medicare (10%), med supp (5%), dental (3%)
**Mem Phys: 16:** 44,522 **15:** 42,455 **16 MLR** 89.2% **/ 16 Admin Exp** N/A
**Enroll(000): Q3 17:** 1,646 **16:** 1,611 **15:** 1,669 **Med Exp PMPM:** $234
**Principal Investments:** Long-term bonds (48%), cash and equiv (22%), nonaffiliate common stock (19%), real estate (5%), affiliate common stock (3%), other (3%)
**Provider Compensation ($000):** Contr fee ($4,515,571), capitation ($12,905), bonus arrang ($3,133), FFS ($2,373)
**Total Member Encounters:** Phys (21,970,878), non-phys (7,321,736)
**Group Affiliation:** Blue Cross and Blue Shield of AL
**Licensed in:** AL
**Address:** 450 Riverchase Parkway East, Birmingham, AL 35244
**Phone:** (205) 220-2100 **Dom State:** AL **Commenced Bus:** January 1936

| Data Date | Rating | RACR #1 | RACR #2 | Total Assets ($mil) | Capital ($mil) | Net Premium ($mil) | Net Income ($mil) |
|---|---|---|---|---|---|---|---|
| 9-17 | B | 6.07 | 5.06 | 3,656.3 | 1,640.0 | 4,351.3 | 289.1 |
| 9-16 | B- | 4.75 | 3.95 | 2,920.0 | 1,192.2 | 3,848.6 | 68.4 |
| 2016 | B- | 4.68 | 3.90 | 3,031.4 | 1,257.9 | 5,155.8 | 83.9 |
| 2015 | B | 4.55 | 3.79 | 2,840.7 | 1,142.2 | 4,864.7 | -138.3 |
| 2014 | B | 5.20 | 4.33 | 2,865.3 | 1,077.4 | 4,577.2 | 52.8 |
| 2013 | A- | 6.95 | 5.79 | 2,839.5 | 1,243.9 | 4,114.1 | 69.1 |
| 2012 | A- | 6.41 | 5.34 | 2,630.4 | 1,118.9 | 4,077.6 | 114.6 |

Rating Indexes

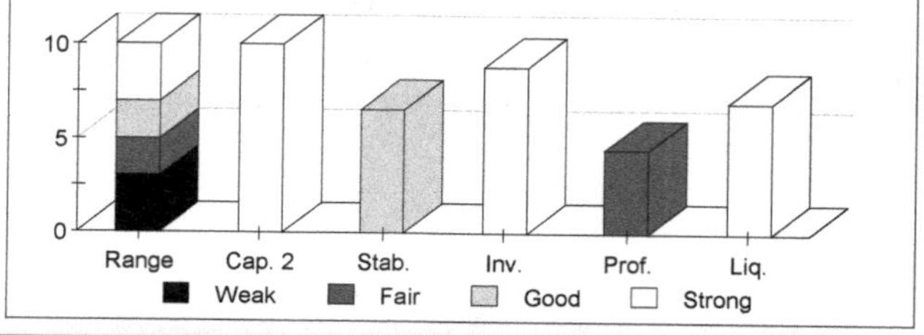


## BLUE CROSS BLUE SHIELD OF ARIZONA * A+ Excellent

**Major Rating Factors:** Strong capitalization (10.0 on a scale of 0 to 10) based on excellent current risk-adjusted capital (severe loss scenario). Good overall profitability index (6.3). Good quality investment portfolio (5.7).
**Other Rating Factors:** Good liquidity (6.9) with sufficient resources (cash flows and marketable investments) to handle a spike in claims.
**Principal Business:** Comp med (63%), FEHB (28%), med supp (5%), other (3%)
**Mem Phys: 16:** 24,995 **15:** 23,866 **16 MLR** 85.2% **/ 16 Admin Exp** N/A
**Enroll(000): Q3 17:** 1,523 **16:** 1,512 **15:** 1,467 **Med Exp PMPM:** $95
**Principal Investments:** Long-term bonds (45%), nonaffiliate common stock (26%), real estate (5%), affiliate common stock (4%), cash and equiv (1%), pref stock (1%), other (18%)
**Provider Compensation ($000):** Contr fee ($1,262,928), FFS ($392,490), capitation ($14,684), bonus arrang ($1,938)
**Total Member Encounters:** Phys (2,803,434), non-phys (1,578,210)
**Group Affiliation:** Blue Cross Blue Shield of AZ Inc
**Licensed in:** AZ
**Address:** 2444 W LAS PALMARITAS Dr, PHOENIX, AZ 85021
**Phone:** (602) 864-4100 **Dom State:** AZ **Commenced Bus:** February 1939

| Data Date | Rating | RACR #1 | RACR #2 | Total Assets ($mil) | Capital ($mil) | Net Premium ($mil) | Net Income ($mil) |
|---|---|---|---|---|---|---|---|
| 9-17 | A+ | 7.07 | 5.89 | 2,020.4 | 1,274.4 | 1,573.3 | 154.8 |
| 9-16 | A+ | 6.29 | 5.24 | 1,740.1 | 1,066.8 | 1,532.6 | 39.1 |
| 2016 | A+ | 6.02 | 5.02 | 1,782.4 | 1,084.4 | 2,048.1 | 61.0 |
| 2015 | A+ | 5.92 | 4.94 | 1,627.1 | 1,004.2 | 1,975.8 | 2.6 |
| 2014 | A+ | 6.42 | 5.35 | 1,657.1 | 1,030.1 | 1,716.5 | 4.4 |
| 2013 | A+ | 7.08 | 5.90 | 1,578.9 | 1,036.3 | 1,531.9 | 85.0 |
| 2012 | A+ | 6.78 | 5.65 | 1,456.7 | 908.5 | 1,448.4 | 67.7 |

Rating Indexes

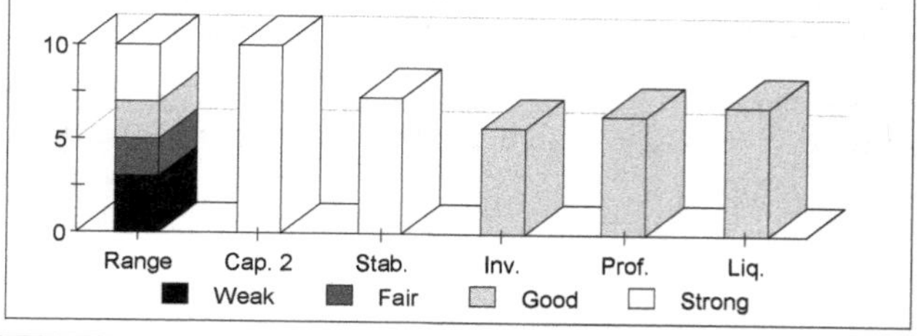

## BLUE CROSS BLUE SHIELD OF GEORGIA — B- — Good

**Major Rating Factors:** Excellent profitability (8.1 on a scale of 0 to 10). Strong capitalization (10.0) based on excellent current risk-adjusted capital (severe loss scenario). Excellent liquidity (7.0) with sufficient resources (cash flows and marketable investments) to handle a spike in claims.
**Other Rating Factors:** Low quality investment portfolio (2.8).
**Principal Business:** FEHB (66%), comp med (16%), med supp (9%), dental (5%), Medicare (1%), other (2%)
**Mem Phys: 16:** 21,710 **15:** 20,753 **16 MLR** 88.0% **/ 16 Admin Exp** N/A
**Enroll(000): Q3 17:** 1,288 **16:** 828 **15:** 781 **Med Exp PMPM:** $166
**Principal Investments:** Nonaffiliate common stock (47%), long-term bonds (46%), affiliate common stock (4%), other (9%)
**Provider Compensation ($000):** Contr fee ($1,403,159), FFS ($204,723), bonus arrang ($1,987), other ($27,324)
**Total Member Encounters:** Phys (3,541,255), non-phys (2,011,532)
**Group Affiliation:** Anthem Inc
**Licensed in:** GA
**Address:** 3350 PEACHTREE Rd NE, ATLANTA, GA 30326
**Phone:** (404) 842-8000 **Dom State:** GA **Commenced Bus:** November 1937

| Data Date | Rating | RACR #1 | RACR #2 | Total Assets ($mil) | Capital ($mil) | Net Premium ($mil) | Net Income ($mil) |
|---|---|---|---|---|---|---|---|
| 9-17 | B- | 5.15 | 4.29 | 1,240.9 | 441.1 | 1,369.7 | 21.7 |
| 9-16 | C+ | 4.86 | 4.05 | 1,307.8 | 411.4 | 1,369.3 | 59.1 |
| 2016 | B- | 5.15 | 4.29 | 1,367.6 | 440.9 | 1,847.1 | 86.2 |
| 2015 | B | 5.00 | 4.17 | 1,265.1 | 424.6 | 1,952.0 | 79.1 |
| 2014 | B | 2.85 | 2.38 | 1,364.7 | 430.3 | 3,038.0 | 73.6 |
| 2013 | B | 2.79 | 2.32 | 928.7 | 273.0 | 2,007.5 | 73.1 |
| 2012 | B | 2.83 | 2.36 | 985.9 | 306.0 | 2,197.1 | 79.5 |

**Rating Indexes**

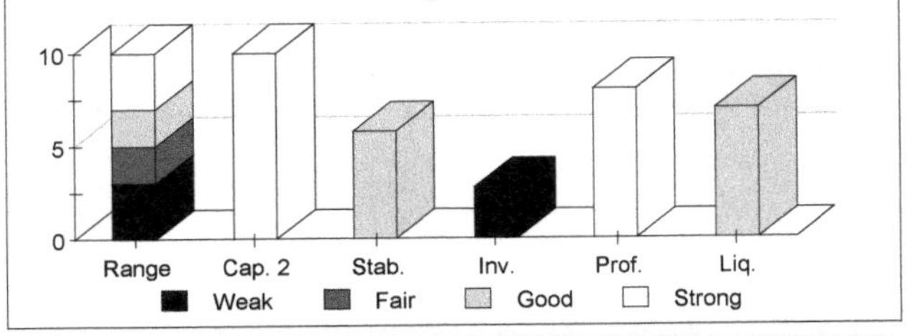


## BLUE CROSS BLUE SHIELD OF KANSAS INCORPORATED — B — Good

**Major Rating Factors:** Good liquidity (5.5 on a scale of 0 to 10) with sufficient resources to handle a spike in claims. Good overall results on stability tests (5.4). Stability strengths include excellent operational trends and excellent risk diversification. Fair quality investment portfolio (4.2).
**Other Rating Factors:** Fair profitability (4.0). Strong capitalization (7.8) based on excellent risk adjusted capital (severe loss scenario).
**Principal Business:** Group health insurance (73%) and individual health insurance (27%).
**Principal Investments:** NonCMO investment grade bonds (39%), common & preferred stock (34%), CMOs and structured securities (18%), noninv. grade bonds (2%), and misc. investments (4%).
**Investments in Affiliates:** 9%
**Group Affiliation:** Blue Cross Blue Shield Kansas
**Licensed in:** KS
**Commenced Business:** July 1942
**Address:** 1133 SW Topeka Boulevard, Topeka, KS 66629-0001
**Phone:** (785) 291-7000 **Domicile State:** KS **NAIC Code:** 70729

| Data Date | Rating | RACR #1 | RACR #2 | Total Assets ($mil) | Capital ($mil) | Net Premium ($mil) | Net Income ($mil) |
|---|---|---|---|---|---|---|---|
| 9-17 | B | 2.00 | 1.54 | 1,571.6 | 821.1 | 1,329.1 | 75.1 |
| 9-16 | B | 2.00 | 1.48 | 1,475.9 | 773.0 | 1,421.7 | 30.9 |
| 2016 | B | 1.74 | 1.35 | 1,452.3 | 728.9 | 1,899.8 | 59.1 |
| 2015 | B | 1.84 | 1.39 | 1,404.1 | 686.7 | 1,854.4 | -30.8 |
| 2014 | B | 2.05 | 1.50 | 1,555.1 | 753.6 | 1,797.7 | -11.5 |
| 2013 | B | 2.26 | 1.62 | 1,541.9 | 800.8 | 1,689.2 | 78.6 |
| 2012 | B | 2.23 | 1.62 | 1,433.2 | 762.3 | 1,680.3 | 55.9 |

**Adverse Trends in Operations**

Decrease in asset base during 2015 (9%)
Decrease in capital during 2015 (9%)
Decrease in capital during 2014 (6%)

## BLUE CROSS BLUE SHIELD OF KC — C+ — Fair

**Major Rating Factors:** Fair profitability index (3.9 on a scale of 0 to 10). Good quality investment portfolio (5.3). Good liquidity (6.8) with sufficient resources (cash flows and marketable investments) to handle a spike in claims.
**Other Rating Factors:** Strong capitalization (10.0) based on excellent current risk-adjusted capital (severe loss scenario).
**Principal Business:** Comp med (77%), FEHB (18%), med supp (4%), dental (1%)
**Mem Phys: 16:** 6,356 **15:** 6,288 **16 MLR** 82.5% **/ 16 Admin Exp** N/A
**Enroll(000): Q3 17:** 523 **16:** 532 **15:** 371 **Med Exp PMPM:** $221
**Principal Investments:** Long-term bonds (44%), nonaffiliate common stock (30%), affiliate common stock (8%), cash and equiv (5%), real estate (3%), other (11%)
**Provider Compensation ($000):** Contr fee ($1,211,198), FFS ($207,419), capitation ($4,485)
**Total Member Encounters:** Phys (2,014,050), non-phys (456,007)
**Group Affiliation:** Blue Cross & Blue Shield of KS City
**Licensed in:** KS, MO
**Address:** 2301 Main St, Kansas City, MO 64108-2428
**Phone:** (816) 395-2222 **Dom State:** MO **Commenced Bus:** May 1982

| Data Date | Rating | RACR #1 | RACR #2 | Total Assets ($mil) | Capital ($mil) | Net Premium ($mil) | Net Income ($mil) |
|---|---|---|---|---|---|---|---|
| 9-17 | C+ | 5.30 | 4.42 | 1,343.9 | 723.3 | 1,361.1 | 78.7 |
| 9-16 | C | 3.93 | 3.27 | 1,124.2 | 548.2 | 1,282.4 | 15.8 |
| 2016 | C | 4.22 | 3.52 | 1,157.0 | 604.7 | 1,718.1 | 23.1 |
| 2015 | C | 4.05 | 3.38 | 1,108.9 | 562.2 | 1,484.8 | -5.8 |
| 2014 | C+ | 3.73 | 3.11 | 1,008.1 | 502.0 | 1,347.9 | -82.5 |
| 2013 | B | 4.89 | 4.08 | 988.8 | 610.2 | 1,255.4 | -19.4 |
| 2012 | A+ | 5.77 | 4.81 | 1,039.5 | 651.9 | 1,226.1 | 26.8 |

**Rating Indexes**

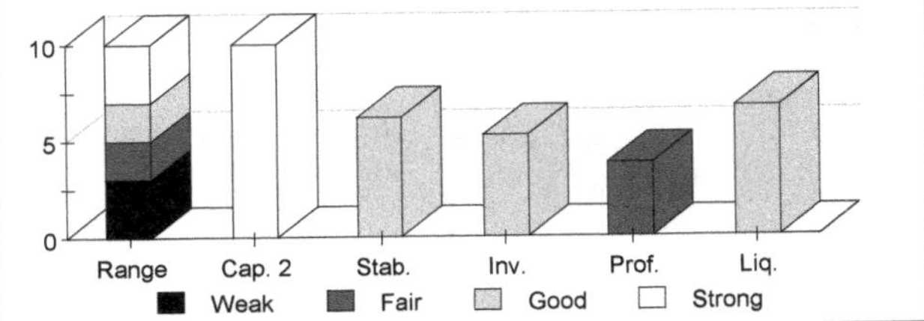

## BLUE CROSS BLUE SHIELD OF MA — B- — Good

**Major Rating Factors:** Fair profitability index (3.6 on a scale of 0 to 10). Good liquidity (6.3) with sufficient resources (cash flows and marketable investments) to handle a spike in claims. Strong capitalization (9.4) based on excellent current risk-adjusted capital (severe loss scenario).
**Other Rating Factors:** High quality investment portfolio (7.3).
**Principal Business:** Comp med (36%), FEHB (29%), med supp (19%), dental (6%), other (10%)
**Mem Phys: 16:** 24,444 **15:** 23,609 **16 MLR** 94.9% **/ 16 Admin Exp** N/A
**Enroll(000): Q3 17:** 1,344 **16:** 1,279 **15:** 1,247 **Med Exp PMPM:** $158
**Principal Investments:** Long-term bonds (47%), nonaffiliate common stock (10%), real estate (6%), cash and equiv (2%), other (34%)
**Provider Compensation ($000):** Contr fee ($1,721,628), FFS ($698,419)
**Total Member Encounters:** Phys (3,383,770), non-phys (2,460,336)
**Group Affiliation:** Blue Cross and Blue Shield of MA Inc
**Licensed in:** MA
**Address:** 101 Huntington Ave, Boston, MA 02199
**Phone:** (617) 246-5000 **Dom State:** MA **Commenced Bus:** October 1937

| Data Date | Rating | RACR #1 | RACR #2 | Total Assets ($mil) | Capital ($mil) | Net Premium ($mil) | Net Income ($mil) |
|---|---|---|---|---|---|---|---|
| 9-17 | B- | 3.25 | 2.71 | 2,238.0 | 781.3 | 2,002.5 | -16.8 |
| 9-16 | B- | 3.25 | 2.71 | 2,170.8 | 641.9 | 1,898.4 | -21.0 |
| 2016 | B | 3.00 | 2.50 | 2,237.4 | 728.2 | 2,522.4 | 3.9 |
| 2015 | B | 3.14 | 2.61 | 2,005.4 | 618.7 | 2,439.3 | 12.6 |
| 2014 | B | 3.17 | 2.64 | 1,994.1 | 671.2 | 2,370.5 | 4.7 |
| 2013 | B | 3.74 | 3.11 | 2,096.6 | 820.1 | 2,331.1 | 28.5 |
| 2012 | B+ | 3.67 | 3.05 | 2,018.4 | 740.8 | 2,401.6 | 46.1 |

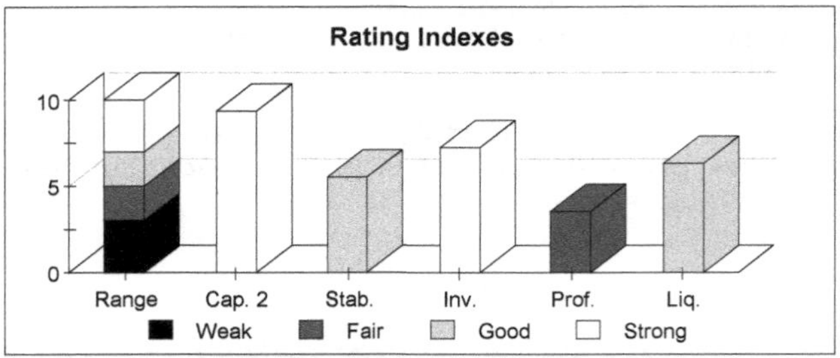


## BLUE CROSS BLUE SHIELD OF MICHIGAN — C — Fair

**Major Rating Factors:** Weak profitability index (2.9 on a scale of 0 to 10). Good quality investment portfolio (6.8). Good liquidity (6.7) with sufficient resources (cash flows and marketable investments) to handle a spike in claims.
**Other Rating Factors:** Strong capitalization (10.0) based on excellent current risk-adjusted capital (severe loss scenario).
**Principal Business:** Comp med (56%), Medicare (28%), FEHB (6%), med supp (4%), dental (1%), other (5%)
**Mem Phys: 16:** 55,888 **15:** 53,285 **16 MLR** 86.5% **/ 16 Admin Exp** N/A
**Enroll(000): Q3 17:** 1,275 **16:** 1,330 **15:** 1,358 **Med Exp PMPM:** $420
**Principal Investments:** Long-term bonds (40%), affiliate common stock (35%), nonaffiliate common stock (6%), cash and equiv (4%), real estate (2%), other (13%)
**Provider Compensation ($000):** Contr fee ($6,738,394), bonus arrang ($47,644)
**Total Member Encounters:** N/A
**Group Affiliation:** Blue Cross Blue Shield of Michigan
**Licensed in:** MI
**Address:** 600 Lafayette East, Detroit, MI 48226
**Phone:** (313) 225-9000 **Dom State:** MI **Commenced Bus:** January 1975

| Data Date | Rating | RACR #1 | RACR #2 | Total Assets ($mil) | Capital ($mil) | Net Premium ($mil) | Net Income ($mil) |
|---|---|---|---|---|---|---|---|
| 9-17 | C | 3.74 | 3.12 | 8,404.4 | 4,057.7 | 6,099.4 | 357.2 |
| 9-16 | C | 3.75 | 3.13 | 7,882.3 | 3,555.4 | 5,899.2 | -62.0 |
| 2016 | C | 3.17 | 2.64 | 7,543.7 | 3,432.5 | 7,899.3 | -226.1 |
| 2015 | C+ | 3.36 | 2.80 | 7,488.3 | 3,171.7 | 7,502.7 | -344.3 |
| 2014 | B | 3.97 | 3.31 | 7,646.2 | 3,340.1 | 7,445.8 | 295.0 |
| 2013 | B | 4.21 | 3.51 | 7,715.2 | 3,288.7 | 6,688.4 | -85.9 |
| 2012 | B+ | 4.18 | 3.49 | 7,469.4 | 3,060.6 | 6,412.7 | -2.5 |

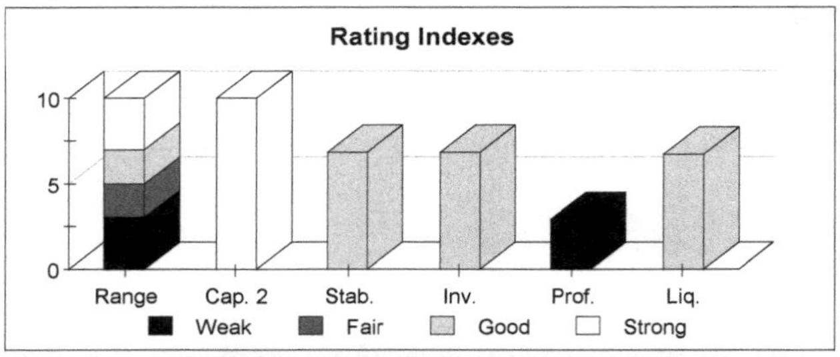


## BLUE CROSS BLUE SHIELD OF MINNESOTA — C — Fair

**Major Rating Factors:** Weak profitability index (2.0 on a scale of 0 to 10). Good quality investment portfolio (6.6). Good liquidity (6.8) with sufficient resources (cash flows and marketable investments) to handle a spike in claims.
**Other Rating Factors:** Strong capitalization (9.0) based on excellent current risk-adjusted capital (severe loss scenario).
**Principal Business:** Comp med (48%), Medicare (24%), FEHB (13%), med supp (6%), other (8%)
**Mem Phys: 16:** 48,000 **15:** 45,590 **16 MLR** 87.7% **/ 16 Admin Exp** N/A
**Enroll(000): Q3 17:** 673 **16:** 730 **15:** 764 **Med Exp PMPM:** $396
**Principal Investments:** Long-term bonds (38%), affiliate common stock (29%), nonaffiliate common stock (21%), cash and equiv (12%)
**Provider Compensation ($000):** Contr fee ($1,638,315), bonus arrang ($1,445,417), FFS ($308,475), other ($82,352)
**Total Member Encounters:** Phys (4,931,516), non-phys (1,973,896)
**Group Affiliation:** Aware Integrated Inc
**Licensed in:** MN
**Address:** 3535 Blue Cross Rd, Eagan, MN 55122
**Phone:** (651) 662-8000 **Dom State:** MN **Commenced Bus:** June 1972

| Data Date | Rating | RACR #1 | RACR #2 | Total Assets ($mil) | Capital ($mil) | Net Premium ($mil) | Net Income ($mil) |
|---|---|---|---|---|---|---|---|
| 9-17 | C | 2.93 | 2.44 | 2,540.3 | 1,128.5 | 2,710.8 | 50.2 |
| 9-16 | C+ | 3.57 | 2.98 | 2,679.4 | 1,066.0 | 2,930.3 | -13.3 |
| 2016 | C | 2.58 | 2.15 | 2,544.3 | 990.5 | 3,938.7 | -103.5 |
| 2015 | C+ | 3.69 | 3.07 | 2,751.4 | 1,100.7 | 3,762.9 | -178.4 |
| 2014 | B | 3.37 | 2.81 | 1,942.1 | 726.5 | 3,277.2 | -9.0 |
| 2013 | A | 3.92 | 3.27 | 1,996.8 | 808.0 | 3,082.6 | 25.7 |
| 2012 | A+ | 4.12 | 3.43 | 2,114.8 | 827.5 | 3,069.5 | 50.4 |

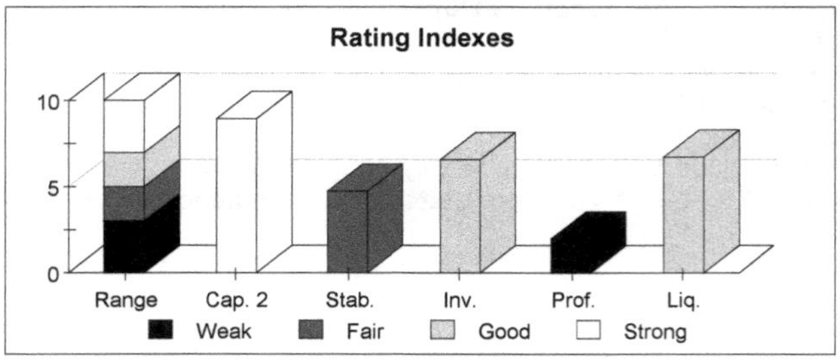

## BLUE CROSS BLUE SHIELD OF MS, MUTUAL B Good

**Major Rating Factors:** Good overall profitability index (5.3 on a scale of 0 to 10). Good liquidity (6.8) with sufficient resources (cash flows and marketable investments) to handle a spike in claims. Strong capitalization (10.0) based on excellent current risk-adjusted capital (severe loss scenario).
**Other Rating Factors:** High quality investment portfolio (7.6).
**Principal Business:** Comp med (72%), FEHB (25%), med supp (3%)
**Mem Phys: 16:** 12,144 **15:** 10,003 **16 MLR** 87.7% **/ 16 Admin Exp** N/A
**Enroll(000): Q2 17:** 634 **16:** 631 **15:** 631 **Med Exp PMPM:** $154
**Principal Investments:** Long-term bonds (71%), cash and equiv (10%), affiliate common stock (8%), nonaffiliate common stock (6%), real estate (5%)
**Provider Compensation ($000):** Contr fee ($1,145,140), FFS ($24,444)
**Total Member Encounters:** Phys (2,064,549), non-phys (1,546,053)
**Group Affiliation:** Blue Cross & Blue Shield of Mississi
**Licensed in:** MS
**Address:** 3545 Lakeland Dr, Flowood, MS 39232
**Phone:** (601) 932-3704 **Dom State:** MS **Commenced Bus:** January 1948

| Data Date | Rating | RACR #1 | RACR #2 | Total Assets ($mil) | Capital ($mil) | Net Premium ($mil) | Net Income ($mil) |
|---|---|---|---|---|---|---|---|
| 6-17 | B | 7.92 | 6.60 | 946.4 | 634.1 | 666.9 | 37.4 |
| 6-16 | B | 7.59 | 6.33 | 913.8 | 580.1 | 640.9 | -8.6 |
| 2016 | B | 7.35 | 6.12 | 899.1 | 597.3 | 1,334.1 | 23.6 |
| 2015 | B+ | 7.65 | 6.38 | 877.5 | 583.6 | 1,287.2 | 13.6 |
| 2014 | B+ | 7.85 | 6.54 | 845.2 | 564.8 | 1,213.2 | 18.3 |
| 2013 | B+ | 7.52 | 6.26 | 811.9 | 555.5 | 1,190.4 | 4.1 |
| 2012 | A- | 7.80 | 6.50 | 788.2 | 566.0 | 1,143.2 | -1.7 |

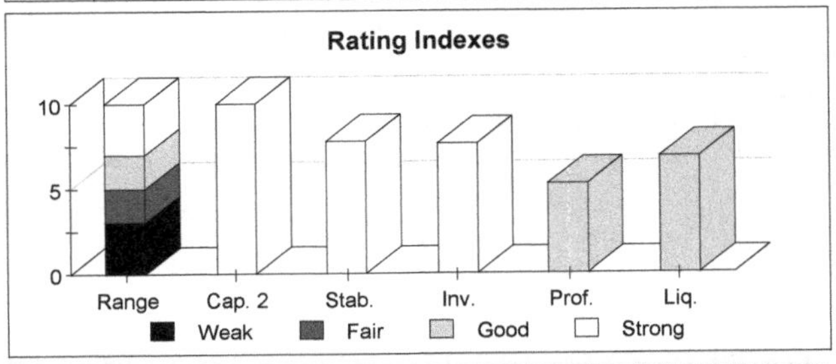


## BLUE CROSS BLUE SHIELD OF NC B Good

**Major Rating Factors:** Good quality investment portfolio (6.8 on a scale of 0 to 10). Good liquidity (6.5) with sufficient resources (cash flows and marketable investments) to handle a spike in claims. Fair profitability index (4.6).
**Other Rating Factors:** Strong capitalization (10.0) based on excellent current risk-adjusted capital (severe loss scenario).
**Principal Business:** Comp med (62%), FEHB (15%), Medicare (14%), med supp (5%), dental (1%), other (2%)
**Mem Phys: 16:** 56,067 **15:** 52,827 **16 MLR** 82.5% **/ 16 Admin Exp** N/A
**Enroll(000): Q3 17:** 1,667 **16:** 1,541 **15:** 1,773 **Med Exp PMPM:** $307
**Principal Investments:** Long-term bonds (63%), nonaffiliate common stock (16%), affiliate common stock (6%), pref stock (2%), other (14%)
**Provider Compensation ($000):** Contr fee ($4,133,012), FFS ($1,760,244), capitation ($48,988)
**Total Member Encounters:** Phys (8,983,672)
**Group Affiliation:** Blue Cross and Blue Shield of NC
**Licensed in:** NC
**Address:** 4705 University Dr Bldg 700, Durham, NC 27707-3460
**Phone:** (919) 489-7431 **Dom State:** NC **Commenced Bus:** January 1968

| Data Date | Rating | RACR #1 | RACR #2 | Total Assets ($mil) | Capital ($mil) | Net Premium ($mil) | Net Income ($mil) |
|---|---|---|---|---|---|---|---|
| 9-17 | B | 6.53 | 5.44 | 5,341.5 | 2,988.8 | 6,629.7 | 764.8 |
| 9-16 | B- | 4.47 | 3.72 | 4,200.9 | 2,217.7 | 5,420.9 | 288.5 |
| 2016 | B- | 4.85 | 4.04 | 4,110.2 | 2,210.5 | 7,189.0 | 272.0 |
| 2015 | B- | 4.16 | 3.47 | 4,102.7 | 2,067.1 | 7,457.1 | -5.7 |
| 2014 | B+ | 4.52 | 3.77 | 4,206.1 | 2,298.3 | 7,351.8 | -137.6 |
| 2013 | A | 5.94 | 4.95 | 3,786.8 | 2,388.5 | 5,816.1 | 180.1 |
| 2012 | A+ | 6.03 | 5.02 | 3,498.6 | 2,081.0 | 5,252.3 | 89.1 |

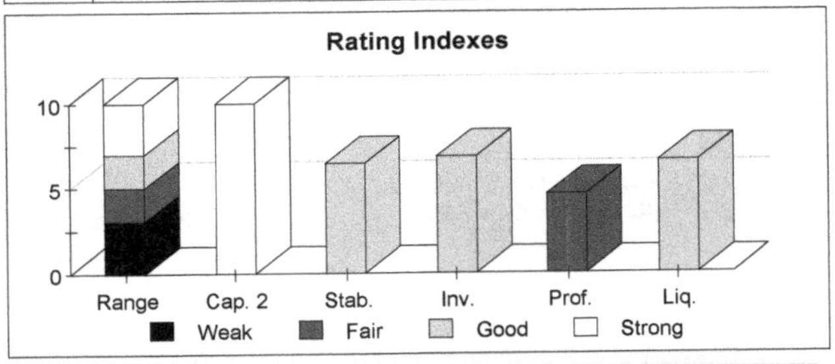


## BLUE CROSS BLUE SHIELD OF NEBRASKA C Fair

**Major Rating Factors:** Weak profitability index (2.6 on a scale of 0 to 10). Good liquidity (6.6) with sufficient resources (cash flows and marketable investments) to handle a spike in claims. Strong capitalization (10.0) based on excellent current risk-adjusted capital (severe loss scenario).
**Other Rating Factors:** High quality investment portfolio (7.4).
**Principal Business:** Comp med (72%), FEHB (14%), med supp (10%), other (4%)
**Mem Phys: 16:** 19,096 **15:** 18,099 **16 MLR** 90.5% **/ 16 Admin Exp** N/A
**Enroll(000): Q3 17:** 364 **16:** 402 **15:** 397 **Med Exp PMPM:** $329
**Principal Investments:** Long-term bonds (61%), nonaffiliate common stock (18%), cash and equiv (5%), affiliate common stock (4%), real estate (2%), other (9%)
**Provider Compensation ($000):** Contr fee ($1,574,039), other ($40,879)
**Total Member Encounters:** Phys (2,182,620), non-phys (81,321)
**Group Affiliation:** Blue Cross and Blue Shield of NB
**Licensed in:** NE
**Address:** 1919 Aksarben Dr, Omaha, NE 68180
**Phone:** (402) 982-7000 **Dom State:** NE **Commenced Bus:** January 1939

| Data Date | Rating | RACR #1 | RACR #2 | Total Assets ($mil) | Capital ($mil) | Net Premium ($mil) | Net Income ($mil) |
|---|---|---|---|---|---|---|---|
| 9-17 | C | 4.17 | 3.47 | 934.5 | 407.4 | 1,237.9 | 52.1 |
| 9-16 | C+ | 4.54 | 3.79 | 858.4 | 373.1 | 1,308.9 | 5.8 |
| 2016 | C | 3.57 | 2.98 | 875.3 | 355.7 | 1,744.1 | -21.6 |
| 2015 | B- | 4.80 | 4.00 | 880.3 | 391.9 | 1,648.2 | -31.5 |
| 2014 | A- | 5.91 | 4.92 | 896.8 | 429.9 | 1,636.0 | 5.4 |
| 2013 | A- | 5.83 | 4.86 | 871.3 | 439.0 | 1,578.1 | 24.5 |
| 2012 | A- | 5.47 | 4.56 | 831.6 | 390.3 | 1,510.6 | 8.3 |

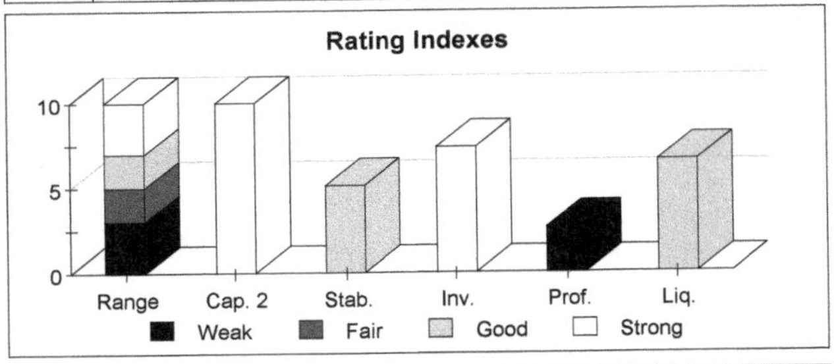

## BLUE CROSS BLUE SHIELD OF RI — C — Fair

**Major Rating Factors:** Weak profitability index (1.6 on a scale of 0 to 10). Good liquidity (6.2) with sufficient resources (cash flows and marketable investments) to handle a spike in claims. Strong capitalization (8.2) based on excellent current risk-adjusted capital (severe loss scenario).
**Other Rating Factors:** High quality investment portfolio (8.2).
**Principal Business:** Comp med (53%), Medicare (34%), FEHB (7%), med supp (3%), dental (2%), other (1%)
**Mem Phys: 16:** 5,282 **15:** 4,755 **16 MLR** 86.5% **/ 16 Admin Exp** N/A
**Enroll(000): Q3 17:** 403 **16:** 340 **15:** 334 **Med Exp PMPM:** $362
**Principal Investments:** Long-term bonds (68%), nonaffiliate common stock (20%), real estate (8%), other (4%)
**Provider Compensation ($000):** Contr fee ($1,439,882)
**Total Member Encounters:** Phys (1,908,885), non-phys (1,329,157)
**Group Affiliation:** Blue Cross & Blue Shield of RI
**Licensed in:** RI
**Address:** 500 EXCHANGE St, PROVIDENCE, RI 02903
**Phone:** (401) 459-1000 **Dom State:** RI **Commenced Bus:** September 1939

| Data Date | Rating | RACR #1 | RACR #2 | Total Assets ($mil) | Capital ($mil) | Net Premium ($mil) | Net Income ($mil) |
|---|---|---|---|---|---|---|---|
| 9-17 | C | 2.31 | 1.92 | 673.7 | 303.2 | 1,294.6 | 40.2 |
| 9-16 | C | 1.98 | 1.65 | 632.0 | 244.5 | 1,293.2 | -45.8 |
| 2016 | C | 2.01 | 1.68 | 618.4 | 266.5 | 1,714.1 | -34.5 |
| 2015 | C | 2.40 | 2.00 | 623.7 | 293.7 | 1,661.3 | -125.9 |
| 2014 | C | 2.02 | 1.68 | 614.6 | 264.0 | 1,640.5 | 0.1 |
| 2013 | C | 2.21 | 1.84 | 601.5 | 287.6 | 1,537.7 | 21.7 |
| 2012 | C | 2.05 | 1.71 | 583.7 | 260.2 | 1,558.1 | -41.5 |

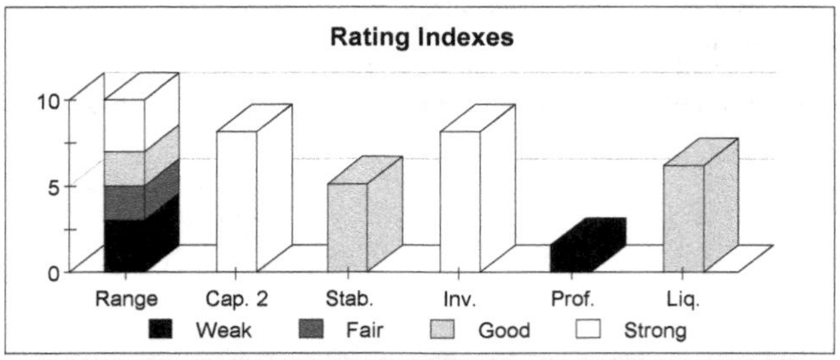


## BLUE CROSS BLUE SHIELD OF SC INC * — A- — Excellent

**Major Rating Factors:** Excellent profitability (7.7 on a scale of 0 to 10). Strong capitalization (10.0) based on excellent current risk-adjusted capital (severe loss scenario). Excellent liquidity (7.0) with ample operational cash flow and liquid investments.
**Other Rating Factors:** Fair quality investment portfolio (3.8).
**Principal Business:** Comp med (68%), FEHB (20%), med supp (5%), dental (3%), other (2%)
**Mem Phys: 16:** 20,117 **15:** 19,361 **16 MLR** 80.9% **/ 16 Admin Exp** N/A
**Enroll(000): Q3 17:** 1,423 **16:** 1,358 **15:** 1,310 **Med Exp PMPM:** $131
**Principal Investments:** Affiliate common stock (22%), long-term bonds (22%), nonaffiliate common stock (13%), cash and equiv (8%), real estate (5%), other (30%)
**Provider Compensation ($000):** Contr fee ($1,870,849), FFS ($241,452), capitation ($1,191), bonus arrang ($910), other ($1,177)
**Total Member Encounters:** Phys (4,253,347), non-phys (1,645,780)
**Group Affiliation:** Blue Cross and Blue Shield of SC
**Licensed in:** SC
**Address:** 2501 Faraway Dr, Columbia, SC 29219
**Phone:** (803) 788-3860 **Dom State:** SC **Commenced Bus:** April 1947

| Data Date | Rating | RACR #1 | RACR #2 | Total Assets ($mil) | Capital ($mil) | Net Premium ($mil) | Net Income ($mil) |
|---|---|---|---|---|---|---|---|
| 9-17 | A- | 5.93 | 4.95 | 4,019.7 | 2,580.5 | 2,530.0 | 78.0 |
| 9-16 | A- | 6.11 | 5.09 | 3,456.3 | 2,341.1 | 1,983.1 | 55.0 |
| 2016 | A- | 5.56 | 4.63 | 3,522.2 | 2,413.8 | 2,639.2 | 59.1 |
| 2015 | A- | 5.88 | 4.90 | 3,254.2 | 2,252.7 | 2,325.5 | 76.7 |
| 2014 | A- | 4.61 | 3.84 | 3,195.9 | 2,166.3 | 2,369.0 | 38.1 |
| 2013 | A- | 5.01 | 4.17 | 2,983.1 | 2,153.3 | 2,178.1 | 82.2 |
| 2012 | A- | 4.81 | 4.01 | 2,744.8 | 1,961.6 | 2,185.1 | 77.0 |

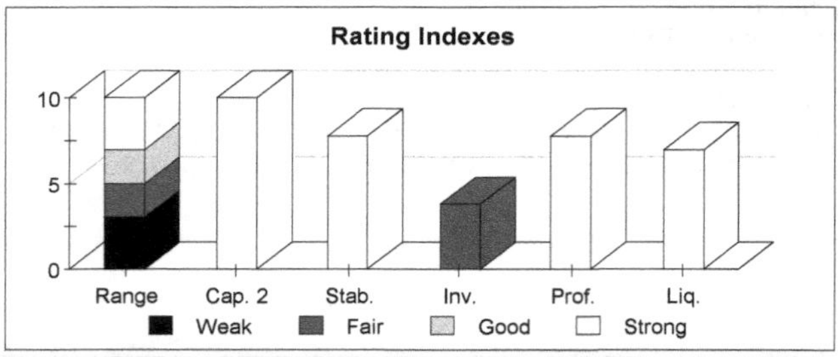


## BLUE CROSS BLUE SHIELD OF VERMONT — B — Good

**Major Rating Factors:** Good quality investment portfolio (5.9 on a scale of 0 to 10). Good liquidity (6.6) with sufficient resources (cash flows and marketable investments) to handle a spike in claims. Fair profitability index (3.5).
**Other Rating Factors:** Strong capitalization (8.8) based on excellent current risk-adjusted capital (severe loss scenario).
**Principal Business:** Comp med (83%), FEHB (15%), med supp (2%)
**Mem Phys: 16:** 7,751 **15:** 7,374 **16 MLR** 94.7% **/ 16 Admin Exp** N/A
**Enroll(000): Q3 17:** 212 **16:** 211 **15:** 209 **Med Exp PMPM:** $206
**Principal Investments:** Long-term bonds (48%), affiliate common stock (32%), nonaffiliate common stock (9%), cash and equiv (8%), real estate (4%)
**Provider Compensation ($000):** FFS ($231,462), contr fee ($201,771), capitation ($2,708), other ($79,453)
**Total Member Encounters:** Phys (305,781), non-phys (373,781)
**Group Affiliation:** Blue Cross and Blue Shield of VT
**Licensed in:** VT
**Address:** 445 Industrial Lane, Berlin, VT 05602
**Phone:** (802) 223-6131 **Dom State:** VT **Commenced Bus:** December 1980

| Data Date | Rating | RACR #1 | RACR #2 | Total Assets ($mil) | Capital ($mil) | Net Premium ($mil) | Net Income ($mil) |
|---|---|---|---|---|---|---|---|
| 9-17 | B | 2.77 | 2.31 | 278.5 | 148.6 | 435.5 | 18.7 |
| 9-16 | B+ | 2.80 | 2.34 | 266.8 | 147.9 | 412.4 | -0.2 |
| 2016 | B | 2.52 | 2.10 | 285.4 | 135.3 | 547.3 | -9.7 |
| 2015 | B+ | 2.81 | 2.34 | 266.6 | 148.4 | 539.9 | 12.2 |
| 2014 | B+ | 2.81 | 2.34 | 256.1 | 138.4 | 470.6 | 9.9 |
| 2013 | B+ | 2.42 | 2.02 | 214.1 | 132.4 | 420.8 | 3.8 |
| 2012 | A- | 2.47 | 2.06 | 208.2 | 126.0 | 382.5 | -4.7 |

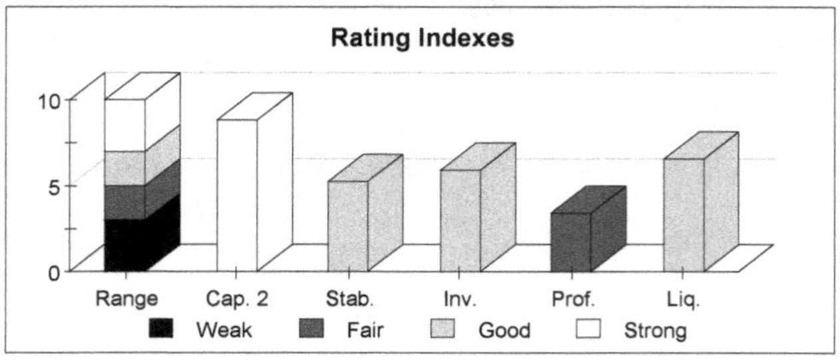

## BLUE CROSS BLUE SHIELD OF WISCONSIN B- Good

**Major Rating Factors:** Excellent profitability (9.2 on a scale of 0 to 10). Strong capitalization (9.1) based on excellent current risk-adjusted capital (severe loss scenario). Excellent liquidity (7.0) with sufficient resources (cash flows and marketable investments) to handle a spike in claims.
**Other Rating Factors:** Low quality investment portfolio (2.4).
**Principal Business:** FEHB (64%), comp med (18%), med supp (10%), dental (3%), other (5%)
**Mem Phys: 16:** 40,006 **15:** 38,397 **16 MLR** 84.6% **/ 16 Admin Exp** N/A
**Enroll(000): Q3 17:** 356 **16:** 378 **15:** 392 **Med Exp PMPM:** $150
**Principal Investments:** Long-term bonds (55%), affiliate common stock (53%), real estate (2%), other (2%)
**Provider Compensation ($000):** Contr fee ($465,734), FFS ($149,941), bonus arrang ($749), other ($24,364)
**Total Member Encounters:** Phys (864,193), non-phys (653,979)
**Group Affiliation:** Anthem Inc
**Licensed in:** WI
**Address:** N17 W24340 RIVERWOOD Dr, WAUKESHA, WI 53188
**Phone:** (262) 523-4020 **Dom State:** WI **Commenced Bus:** October 1939

| Data Date | Rating | RACR #1 | RACR #2 | Total Assets ($mil) | Capital ($mil) | Net Premium ($mil) | Net Income ($mil) |
|---|---|---|---|---|---|---|---|
| 9-17 | B- | 3.00 | 2.50 | 563.8 | 260.3 | 572.6 | 78.0 |
| 9-16 | C+ | 2.95 | 2.45 | 547.8 | 238.6 | 564.4 | 63.2 |
| 2016 | B- | 3.01 | 2.50 | 544.6 | 260.5 | 758.6 | 81.2 |
| 2015 | B- | 2.56 | 2.13 | 463.8 | 206.4 | 735.1 | 78.6 |
| 2014 | B- | 3.06 | 2.55 | 454.2 | 232.1 | 699.4 | 84.3 |
| 2013 | B- | 3.40 | 2.83 | 474.6 | 235.2 | 672.8 | 69.6 |
| 2012 | B- | 3.40 | 2.83 | 418.3 | 189.9 | 570.8 | 86.9 |

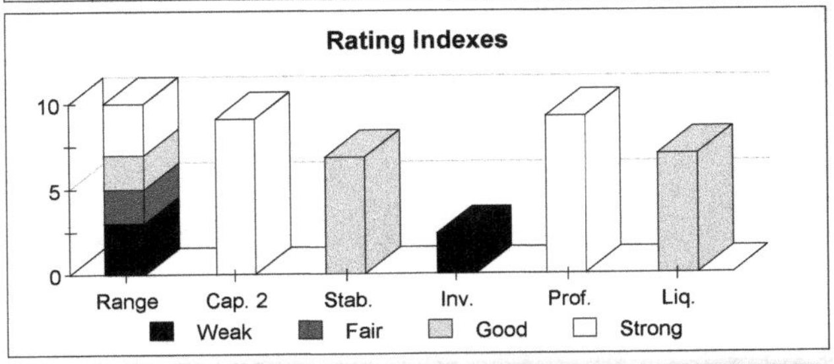


## BLUE CROSS BLUE SHIELD OF WYOMING B- Good

**Major Rating Factors:** Fair profitability index (4.9 on a scale of 0 to 10). Fair quality investment portfolio (3.4). Good liquidity (6.8) with sufficient resources (cash flows and marketable investments) to handle a spike in claims.
**Other Rating Factors:** Strong capitalization (10.0) based on excellent current risk-adjusted capital (severe loss scenario).
**Principal Business:** Comp med (72%), FEHB (22%), med supp (4%)
**Mem Phys: 16:** 3,574 **15:** 3,829 **16 MLR** 93.8% **/ 16 Admin Exp** N/A
**Enroll(000): Q3 17:** 89 **16:** 89 **15:** 77 **Med Exp PMPM:** $403
**Principal Investments:** Nonaffiliate common stock (49%), long-term bonds (43%), cash and equiv (2%), real estate (1%), other (5%)
**Provider Compensation ($000):** FFS ($394,646), contr fee ($31,858), bonus arrang ($78)
**Total Member Encounters:** Phys (802,996), non-phys (904,901)
**Group Affiliation:** Blue Cross Blue Shield of Wyoming
**Licensed in:** WY
**Address:** 4000 HOUSE Ave, CHEYENNE, WY 82001
**Phone:** (307) 634-1393 **Dom State:** WY **Commenced Bus:** August 1976

| Data Date | Rating | RACR #1 | RACR #2 | Total Assets ($mil) | Capital ($mil) | Net Premium ($mil) | Net Income ($mil) |
|---|---|---|---|---|---|---|---|
| 9-17 | B- | 5.65 | 4.71 | 518.7 | 314.6 | 364.7 | 26.7 |
| 9-16 | B | 6.46 | 5.39 | 475.1 | 288.8 | 347.6 | 5.9 |
| 2016 | B | 4.91 | 4.09 | 481.1 | 276.4 | 467.8 | -15.1 |
| 2015 | B | 6.13 | 5.11 | 437.3 | 275.1 | 369.1 | 20.1 |
| 2014 | B | 5.97 | 4.97 | 405.0 | 251.3 | 286.3 | 12.7 |
| 2013 | B+ | 6.08 | 5.06 | 384.6 | 242.3 | 270.5 | 11.8 |
| 2012 | B+ | 6.19 | 5.16 | 335.0 | 199.9 | 275.7 | 29.6 |

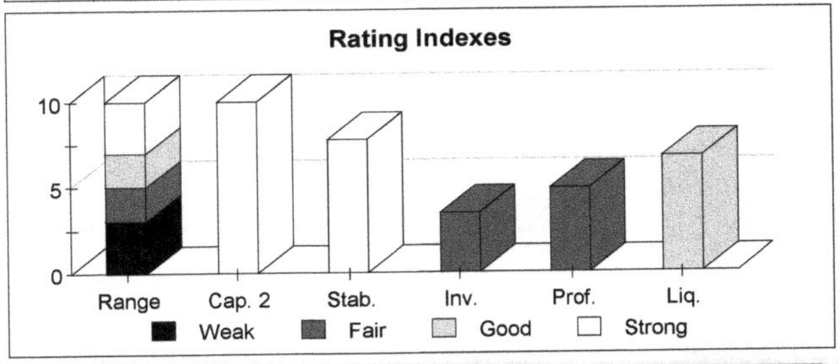


## BLUE CROSS COMPLETE OF MICHIGAN E Very Weak

**Major Rating Factors:** Weak profitability index (2.5 on a scale of 0 to 10). Strong capitalization (7.5) based on excellent current risk-adjusted capital (severe loss scenario). High quality investment portfolio (9.9).
**Other Rating Factors:** Excellent liquidity (7.1) with ample operational cash flow and liquid investments.
**Principal Business:** Medicaid (100%)
**Mem Phys: 16:** 24,709 **15:** 23,855 **16 MLR** 83.5% **/ 16 Admin Exp** N/A
**Enroll(000): Q3 17:** 200 **16:** 174 **15:** 89 **Med Exp PMPM:** $333
**Principal Investments:** Cash and equiv (100%)
**Provider Compensation ($000):** Contr fee ($411,116), capitation ($157,384), bonus arrang ($2,829)
**Total Member Encounters:** Phys (1,145,287), non-phys (195,318)
**Group Affiliation:** Blue Cross Complete of Michigan LLC
**Licensed in:** MI
**Address:** 100 Galleria Officentre #210, Southfield, MI 48034
**Phone:** (215) 937-8000 **Dom State:** MI **Commenced Bus:** January 2003

| Data Date | Rating | RACR #1 | RACR #2 | Total Assets ($mil) | Capital ($mil) | Net Premium ($mil) | Net Income ($mil) |
|---|---|---|---|---|---|---|---|
| 9-17 | E | 1.72 | 1.43 | 189.8 | 56.9 | 646.2 | 9.1 |
| 9-16 | E | 2.26 | 1.89 | 146.0 | 44.1 | 515.6 | 7.3 |
| 2016 | E | 1.46 | 1.22 | 154.9 | 47.9 | 709.4 | 10.8 |
| 2015 | E | 1.95 | 1.63 | 115.5 | 37.9 | 418.5 | -1.2 |
| 2014 | E | 1.33 | 1.11 | 89.2 | 30.7 | 259.3 | -13.7 |
| 2013 | E | 2.16 | 1.80 | 38.2 | 12.8 | 123.2 | -9.0 |
| 2012 | B | 1.77 | 1.47 | 13.1 | 4.8 | 65.9 | 0.2 |

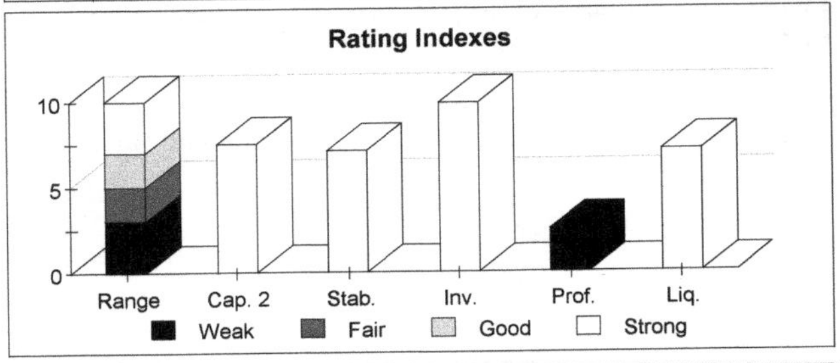

## BLUE CROSS OF CALIFORNIA * A+ Excellent

**Major Rating Factors:** Excellent profitability (9.1 on a scale of 0 to 10). Strong capitalization index (8.2) based on excellent current risk-adjusted capital (severe loss scenario). Excellent overall results on stability tests (8.4).
**Other Rating Factors:** Excellent liquidity (7.3) with ample operational cash flow and liquid investments.
**Principal Business:** Medicaid (30%), Medicare (2%)
**Mem Phys: 16:** N/A **15:** N/A **16 MLR** 81.4% **/ 16 Admin Exp** N/A
**Enroll(000): Q3 17:** 3,941 **16:** 4,067 **15:** 3,895 **Med Exp PMPM:** $304
**Principal Investments ($000):** Cash and equiv ($4,353,509)
**Provider Compensation ($000):** None
**Total Member Encounters:** N/A
**Group Affiliation:** Anthem Inc
**Licensed in:** CA
**Address:** 1 Wellpoint Way, Thousand Oaks, CA 91362
**Phone:** (916) 403-0526 **Dom State:** CA **Commenced Bus:** July 1982

| Data Date | Rating | RACR #1 | RACR #2 | Total Assets ($mil) | Capital ($mil) | Net Premium ($mil) | Net Income ($mil) |
|---|---|---|---|---|---|---|---|
| 9-17 | A+ | 3.06 | 1.94 | 7,951.3 | 2,554.1 | 12,586.6 | 552.5 |
| 9-16 | A+ | 2.91 | 1.83 | 6,905.9 | 2,124.3 | 12,317.3 | 563.8 |
| 2016 | A+ | 2.62 | 1.65 | 7,350.6 | 2,109.1 | 16,650.0 | 710.4 |
| 2015 | A+ | 2.49 | 1.57 | 6,611.5 | 1,801.2 | 14,977.4 | 502.0 |
| 2014 | A+ | 2.41 | 1.53 | 5,862.9 | 1,643.8 | 13,373.6 | 426.0 |
| 2013 | A+ | 2.37 | 1.49 | 4,372.2 | 1,349.4 | 10,762.3 | 453.2 |
| 2012 | A+ | 2.26 | 1.40 | 3,717.9 | 1,210.3 | 11,231.5 | 407.4 |

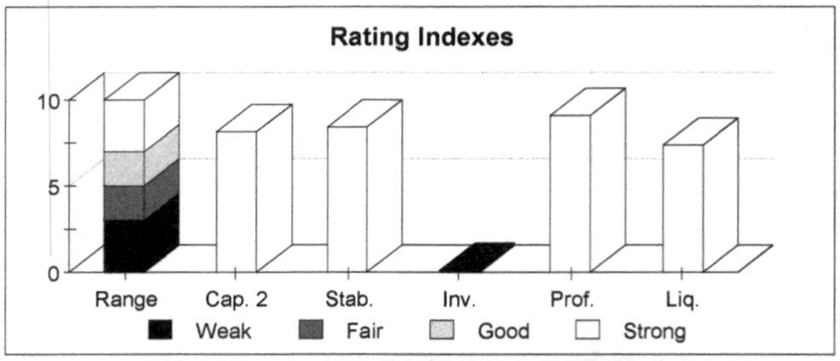


## BLUE CROSS OF IDAHO CARE PLUS INC C Fair

**Major Rating Factors:** Weak profitability index (1.9 on a scale of 0 to 10). Good liquidity (6.8) with sufficient resources (cash flows and marketable investments) to handle a spike in claims. Strong capitalization (8.2) based on excellent current risk-adjusted capital (severe loss scenario).
**Other Rating Factors:** High quality investment portfolio (9.8).
**Principal Business:** Medicare (100%)
**Mem Phys: 16:** 7,217 **15:** 6,464 **16 MLR** 84.0% **/ 16 Admin Exp** N/A
**Enroll(000): Q3 17:** 25 **16:** 27 **15:** 34 **Med Exp PMPM:** $829
**Principal Investments:** Long-term bonds (66%), cash and equiv (29%), other (5%)
**Provider Compensation ($000):** Contr fee ($164,081), bonus arrang ($102,695), capitation ($934)
**Total Member Encounters:** Phys (291,913), non-phys (418,028)
**Group Affiliation:** Blue Cross of Idaho Hth Service Inc
**Licensed in:** ID
**Address:** 3000 E Pine Ave, Meridian, ID 83642
**Phone:** (208) 345-4550 **Dom State:** ID **Commenced Bus:** February 2013

| Data Date | Rating | RACR #1 | RACR #2 | Total Assets ($mil) | Capital ($mil) | Net Premium ($mil) | Net Income ($mil) |
|---|---|---|---|---|---|---|---|
| 9-17 | C | 2.35 | 1.96 | 171.8 | 78.6 | 231.6 | 17.8 |
| 9-16 | C+ | 1.46 | 1.22 | 144.7 | 59.9 | 245.0 | 12.5 |
| 2016 | C | 1.42 | 1.18 | 123.3 | 59.6 | 320.4 | 13.3 |
| 2015 | C+ | 1.00 | 0.83 | 97.8 | 48.1 | 325.4 | -5.7 |
| 2014 | U | 0.19 | 0.16 | 35.8 | 3.5 | 75.1 | -14.2 |
| 2013 | N/A | N/A | N/A | 2.2 | 2.2 | N/A | -0.3 |
| 2012 | N/A | N/A | N/A | N/A | N/A | N/A | N/A |

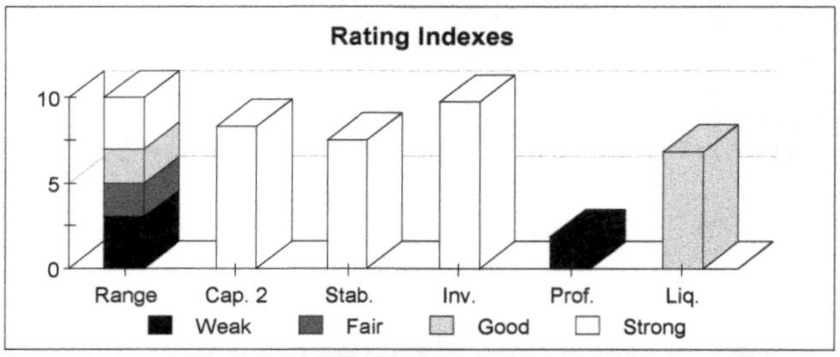


## BLUE CROSS OF IDAHO HEALTH SERVICE B Good

**Major Rating Factors:** Good overall profitability index (5.5 on a scale of 0 to 10). Good quality investment portfolio (5.0). Good liquidity (6.5) with sufficient resources (cash flows and marketable investments) to handle a spike in claims.
**Other Rating Factors:** Strong capitalization (10.0) based on excellent current risk-adjusted capital (severe loss scenario).
**Principal Business:** Comp med (78%), FEHB (11%), dental (8%), med supp (2%), other (2%)
**Mem Phys: 16:** 13,548 **15:** 12,404 **16 MLR** 88.3% **/ 16 Admin Exp** N/A
**Enroll(000): Q3 17:** 245 **16:** 565 **15:** 592 **Med Exp PMPM:** $153
**Principal Investments:** Long-term bonds (63%), nonaffiliate common stock (28%), cash and equiv (4%), real estate (3%), other (1%)
**Provider Compensation ($000):** Contr fee ($1,040,259), capitation ($3,387)
**Total Member Encounters:** Phys (1,536,381), non-phys (1,604,368)
**Group Affiliation:** Blue Cross of ID Health Service Inc
**Licensed in:** ID
**Address:** 3000 E Pine Ave, Meridian, ID 83642
**Phone:** (208) 345-4550 **Dom State:** ID **Commenced Bus:** January 1978

| Data Date | Rating | RACR #1 | RACR #2 | Total Assets ($mil) | Capital ($mil) | Net Premium ($mil) | Net Income ($mil) |
|---|---|---|---|---|---|---|---|
| 9-17 | B | 6.80 | 5.67 | 841.5 | 581.4 | 809.5 | 76.2 |
| 9-16 | B | 5.17 | 4.30 | 764.3 | 476.4 | 886.7 | 16.1 |
| 2016 | B | 5.47 | 4.56 | 770.1 | 486.6 | 1,173.6 | 11.0 |
| 2015 | B | 4.92 | 4.10 | 758.1 | 458.5 | 1,202.5 | -3.1 |
| 2014 | B+ | 4.89 | 4.08 | 821.5 | 524.8 | 1,367.2 | 5.9 |
| 2013 | A | 5.68 | 4.73 | 794.3 | 541.0 | 1,244.2 | 39.3 |
| 2012 | A+ | 5.09 | 4.24 | 718.7 | 485.7 | 1,260.4 | 46.7 |

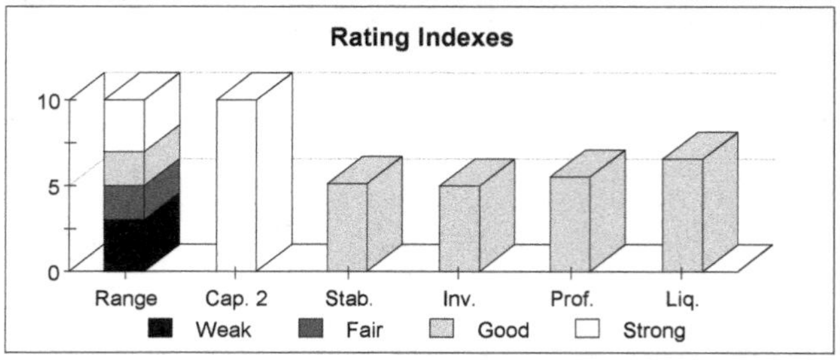

## BLUE SHIELD OF CALIFORNIA * A+ Excellent

**Major Rating Factors:** Strong capitalization index (8.7 on a scale of 0 to 10) based on excellent current risk-adjusted capital (severe loss scenario). Excellent overall results on stability tests (7.8). Good overall profitability index (6.2).
**Other Rating Factors:** Good liquidity (6.4) with sufficient resources (cash flows and marketable investments) to handle a spike in claims.
**Principal Business:** Medicare (8%)
**Mem Phys: 16:** N/A **15:** N/A **16 MLR** 89.1% **/ 16 Admin Exp** N/A
**Enroll(000): Q3 17:** 3,246 **16:** 3,416 **15:** 3,473 **Med Exp PMPM:** $397
**Principal Investments ($000):** Cash and equiv ($1,056,800)
**Provider Compensation ($000):** None
**Total Member Encounters:** N/A
**Group Affiliation:** Blue Shield of California
**Licensed in:** CA
**Address:** 50 Beale Street 22nd Floor, San Francisco, CA 94105
**Phone:** (415) 229-5195 **Dom State:** CA **Commenced Bus:** February 1939

| Data Date | Rating | RACR #1 | RACR #2 | Total Assets ($mil) | Capital ($mil) | Net Premium ($mil) | Net Income ($mil) |
|---|---|---|---|---|---|---|---|
| 9-17 | A+ | 3.34 | 2.25 | 8,119.3 | 4,669.3 | 10,716.2 | 293.3 |
| 9-16 | A+ | 3.42 | 2.27 | 7,828.0 | 4,238.4 | 10,811.4 | -13.5 |
| 2016 | A+ | 3.02 | 2.02 | 7,509.1 | 4,296.6 | 14,290.2 | 67.0 |
| 2015 | A+ | 3.42 | 2.26 | 7,358.4 | 4,170.4 | 12,531.2 | 86.9 |
| 2014 | A+ | 4.66 | 3.16 | 6,919.5 | 4,179.5 | 11,300.6 | 161.8 |
| 2013 | A | 5.41 | 3.72 | 6,028.0 | 4,143.3 | 8,316.4 | 170.6 |
| 2012 | A | 4.89 | 3.38 | 5,654.4 | 3,857.6 | 8,182.1 | 204.2 |

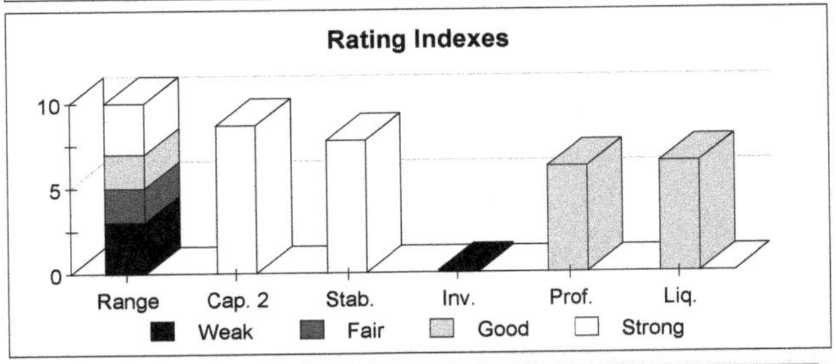


## BLUE SHIELD OF CALIFORNIA LIFE & HEALTH INS COMPANY B Good

**Major Rating Factors:** Fair profitability (3.0 on a scale of 0 to 10) with operating losses during the first nine months of 2017. Fair overall results on stability tests (4.9) including weak results on operational trends, negative cash flow from operations for 2016. Strong current capitalization (9.1) based on excellent risk adjusted capital (severe loss scenario) reflecting improvement over results in 2012.
**Other Rating Factors:** High quality investment portfolio (8.1). Excellent liquidity (7.1).
**Principal Business:** Individual health insurance (96%), group life insurance (3%), and individual life insurance (1%).
**Principal Investments:** CMOs and structured securities (47%), nonCMO investment grade bonds (46%), cash (3%), and noninv. grade bonds (1%).
**Investments in Affiliates:** None
**Group Affiliation:** Blue Shield of California
**Licensed in:** CA
**Commenced Business:** July 1954
**Address:** 50 Beale Street, San Francisco, CA 94105-0000
**Phone:** (800) 642-5599 **Domicile State:** CA **NAIC Code:** 61557

| Data Date | Rating | RACR #1 | RACR #2 | Total Assets ($mil) | Capital ($mil) | Net Premium ($mil) | Net Income ($mil) |
|---|---|---|---|---|---|---|---|
| 9-17 | B | 3.14 | 2.43 | 338.4 | 164.0 | 191.6 | -16.2 |
| 9-16 | B | 4.46 | 3.44 | 474.4 | 328.2 | 234.6 | 24.9 |
| 2016 | B | 5.28 | 4.03 | 462.9 | 320.1 | 309.6 | 22.4 |
| 2015 | B | 2.98 | 2.37 | 665.2 | 481.1 | 1,249.2 | 39.5 |
| 2014 | A- | 1.93 | 1.53 | 743.7 | 444.3 | 1,794.5 | 78.5 |
| 2013 | A- | 1.22 | 0.97 | 890.7 | 367.1 | 2,381.3 | 12.3 |
| 2012 | A- | 1.20 | 0.95 | 802.7 | 297.3 | 1,937.3 | -19.1 |

**Adverse Trends in Operations**

Decrease in premium volume from 2015 to 2016 (75%)
Decrease in asset base during 2016 (30%)
Decrease in capital during 2016 (33%)
Decrease in premium volume from 2014 to 2015 (30%)
Decrease in asset base during 2015 (11%)

## BLUECHOICE HEALTHPLAN OF SC INC B Good

**Major Rating Factors:** Good liquidity (5.1 on a scale of 0 to 10) with sufficient resources (cash flows and marketable investments) to handle a spike in claims. Fair profitability index (3.5). Fair overall results on stability tests (4.6).
**Other Rating Factors:** Strong capitalization index (10.0) based on excellent current risk-adjusted capital (severe loss scenario). High quality investment portfolio (9.6).
**Principal Business:** Comp med (85%), Medicaid (14%)
**Mem Phys: 16:** 23,685 **15:** 22,344 **16 MLR** 110.4% **/ 16 Admin Exp** N/A
**Enroll(000): Q3 17:** 182 **16:** 256 **15:** 204 **Med Exp PMPM:** $342
**Principal Investments:** Long-term bonds (65%), cash and equiv (20%), nonaffiliate common stock (8%), affiliate common stock (7%)
**Provider Compensation ($000):** Contr fee ($1,032,802), FFS ($10,426), capitation ($4,278), bonus arrang ($3,131)
**Total Member Encounters:** Phys (1,791,432), non-phys (562,821)
**Group Affiliation:** Blue Cross and Blue Shield of SC
**Licensed in:** SC
**Address:** I-20 at Alpine Road, Columbia, SC 29219
**Phone:** (803) 786-8466 **Dom State:** SC **Commenced Bus:** October 1984

| Data Date | Rating | RACR #1 | RACR #2 | Total Assets ($mil) | Capital ($mil) | Net Premium ($mil) | Net Income ($mil) |
|---|---|---|---|---|---|---|---|
| 9-17 | B | 3.85 | 3.21 | 352.1 | 227.9 | 421.8 | 26.5 |
| 9-16 | A | 5.90 | 4.92 | 382.7 | 223.3 | 735.5 | 0.9 |
| 2016 | B | 3.36 | 2.80 | 346.9 | 197.9 | 969.9 | -23.4 |
| 2015 | A | 5.95 | 4.96 | 347.4 | 225.4 | 664.4 | 14.4 |
| 2014 | A- | 7.25 | 6.04 | 306.2 | 215.1 | 490.4 | 11.3 |
| 2013 | A | 6.76 | 5.64 | 284.7 | 209.5 | 494.7 | 14.9 |
| 2012 | A | 7.41 | 6.18 | 257.9 | 192.1 | 403.5 | 21.3 |

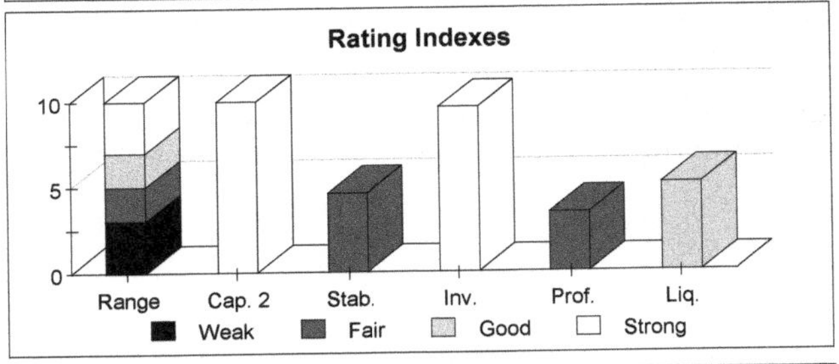

## BLUECROSS BLUESHIELD KANSAS SOLUTION C+ Fair

**Major Rating Factors:** Fair liquidity (3.8 on a scale of 0 to 10) as cash resources may not be adequate to cover a spike in claims. Weak profitability index (0.2). Strong capitalization (8.3) based on excellent current risk-adjusted capital (severe loss scenario).
**Other Rating Factors:** High quality investment portfolio (7.8).
**Principal Business:** Comp med (100%)
**Mem Phys: 16:** 13,669 **15:** 10,676 **16 MLR** 120.0% **/ 16 Admin Exp** N/A
**Enroll(000): Q3 17:** 68 **16:** 49 **15:** 20 **Med Exp PMPM:** $314
**Principal Investments:** Long-term bonds (79%), cash and equiv (12%), nonaffiliate common stock (9%)
**Provider Compensation ($000):** Contr fee ($175,771)
**Total Member Encounters:** Phys (111,289), non-phys (115,167)
**Group Affiliation:** Blue Cross & Blue Shield of KS City
**Licensed in:** KS
**Address:** 1133 SW Topeka Blvd, Topeka, KS 66629-0001
**Phone:** (785) 291-7000 **Dom State:** KS **Commenced Bus:** April 2014

| Data Date | Rating | RACR #1 | RACR #2 | Total Assets ($mil) | Capital ($mil) | Net Premium ($mil) | Net Income ($mil) |
|---|---|---|---|---|---|---|---|
| 9-17 | C+ | 2.39 | 1.99 | 142.3 | 40.3 | 258.2 | -1.2 |
| 9-16 | C+ | 12.46 | 10.38 | 146.4 | 79.6 | 118.0 | -3.1 |
| 2016 | C+ | 4.16 | 3.47 | 138.2 | 67.7 | 157.8 | 4.5 |
| 2015 | C | 2.53 | 2.11 | 98.4 | 17.0 | 43.1 | -61.3 |
| 2014 | N/A | N/A | N/A | 10.9 | 10.2 | N/A | -0.1 |
| 2013 | N/A | N/A | N/A | N/A | N/A | N/A | N/A |
| 2012 | N/A | N/A | N/A | N/A | N/A | N/A | N/A |

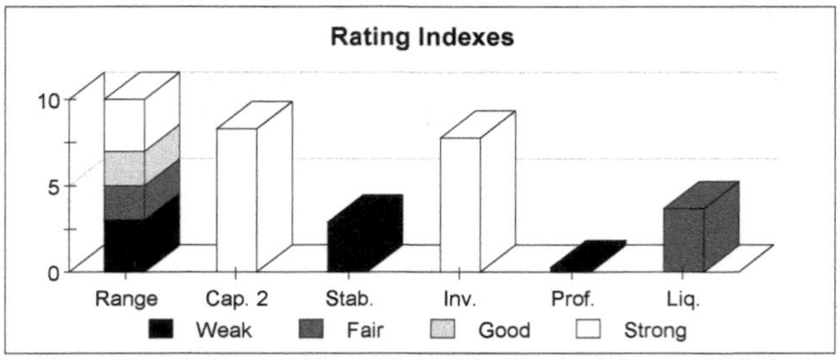


## BLUECROSS BLUESHIELD OF TENNESSEE B Good

**Major Rating Factors:** Good quality investment portfolio (5.5 on a scale of 0 to 10). Good liquidity (6.8) with sufficient resources (cash flows and marketable investments) to handle a spike in claims. Fair profitability index (4.6).
**Other Rating Factors:** Strong capitalization (10.0) based on excellent current risk-adjusted capital (severe loss scenario).
**Principal Business:** Comp med (60%), Medicare (19%), FEHB (14%), med supp (3%), dental (3%)
**Mem Phys: 16:** 30,088 **15:** 29,850 **16 MLR** 86.6% **/ 16 Admin Exp** N/A
**Enroll(000): Q3 17:** 1,597 **16:** 1,746 **15:** 1,780 **Med Exp PMPM:** $192
**Principal Investments:** Long-term bonds (65%), affiliate common stock (25%), cash and equiv (6%), real estate (4%), pref stock (3%), other (6%)
**Provider Compensation ($000):** Contr fee ($3,289,879), FFS ($826,106), capitation ($15,965), bonus arrang ($2,281)
**Total Member Encounters:** Phys (9,878,862), non-phys (1,673,058)
**Group Affiliation:** BlueCross BlueShield of Tennessee
**Licensed in:** TN
**Address:** 1 Cameron Hill Circle, Chattanooga, TN 37402-0001
**Phone:** (423) 535-5600 **Dom State:** TN **Commenced Bus:** October 1945

| Data Date | Rating | RACR #1 | RACR #2 | Total Assets ($mil) | Capital ($mil) | Net Premium ($mil) | Net Income ($mil) |
|---|---|---|---|---|---|---|---|
| 9-17 | B | 7.61 | 6.35 | 3,018.0 | 2,090.7 | 3,448.9 | 283.5 |
| 9-16 | B | 6.39 | 5.33 | 2,691.1 | 1,733.6 | 3,547.4 | 36.4 |
| 2016 | B | 6.32 | 5.27 | 2,556.7 | 1,733.5 | 4,739.9 | 2.4 |
| 2015 | B+ | 6.19 | 5.16 | 2,465.5 | 1,678.6 | 4,525.2 | -101.9 |
| 2014 | A | 6.86 | 5.72 | 2,442.4 | 1,733.5 | 4,222.3 | 63.4 |
| 2013 | A | 7.32 | 6.10 | 2,226.9 | 1,651.4 | 3,658.7 | 188.9 |
| 2012 | A | 7.21 | 6.00 | 2,090.4 | 1,514.9 | 3,368.4 | 142.3 |

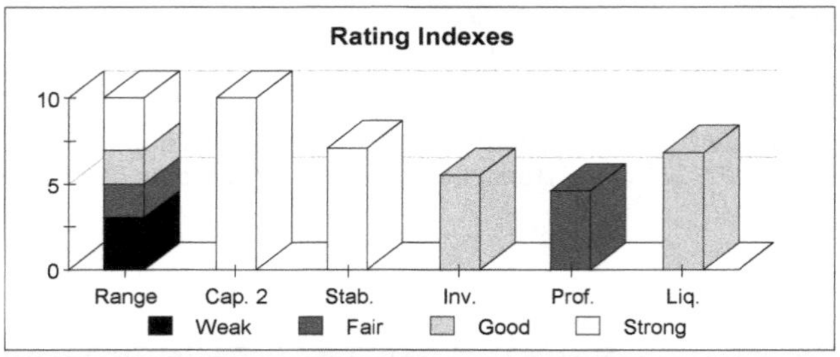


## BOSTON MEDICAL CENTER HEALTH PLAN B- Good

**Major Rating Factors:** Fair profitability index (3.1 on a scale of 0 to 10). Good quality investment portfolio (6.8). Good liquidity (6.8) with sufficient resources (cash flows and marketable investments) to handle a spike in claims.
**Other Rating Factors:** Strong capitalization (7.7) based on excellent current risk-adjusted capital (severe loss scenario).
**Principal Business:** Medicaid (92%), comp med (8%)
**Mem Phys: 16:** 26,901 **15:** 26,327 **16 MLR** 91.4% **/ 16 Admin Exp** N/A
**Enroll(000): Q3 17:** 316 **16:** 290 **15:** 308 **Med Exp PMPM:** $403
**Principal Investments:** Long-term bonds (46%), cash and equiv (36%), nonaffiliate common stock (18%)
**Provider Compensation ($000):** Contr fee ($1,313,677), capitation ($122,174), bonus arrang ($1,740)
**Total Member Encounters:** Phys (2,578,226), non-phys (5,545,545)
**Group Affiliation:** BMC Health System Inc
**Licensed in:** MA, NH
**Address:** Two Copley Place Ste 600, Boston, MA 02116
**Phone:** (617) 748-6000 **Dom State:** MA **Commenced Bus:** July 1997

| Data Date | Rating | RACR #1 | RACR #2 | Total Assets ($mil) | Capital ($mil) | Net Premium ($mil) | Net Income ($mil) |
|---|---|---|---|---|---|---|---|
| 9-17 | B- | 1.91 | 1.59 | 457.9 | 236.1 | 1,238.2 | 1.2 |
| 9-16 | B- | 1.80 | 1.50 | 456.1 | 218.0 | 1,176.7 | -23.9 |
| 2016 | B- | 1.91 | 1.59 | 471.3 | 236.2 | 1,574.5 | -4.5 |
| 2015 | B- | 2.12 | 1.77 | 459.4 | 253.6 | 1,564.1 | 47.8 |
| 2014 | C+ | 1.40 | 1.17 | 392.0 | 204.2 | 1,791.5 | -19.4 |
| 2013 | B- | 1.86 | 1.55 | 341.3 | 215.4 | 1,406.5 | -0.8 |
| 2012 | B- | 2.43 | 2.03 | 360.6 | 236.4 | 1,219.5 | -7.5 |

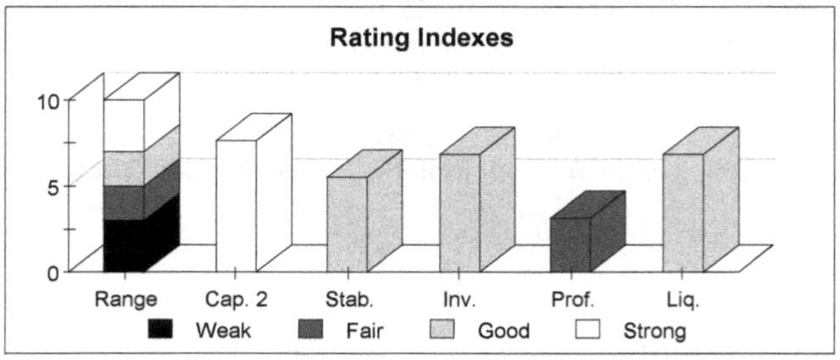

## BOSTON MUTUAL LIFE INSURANCE COMPANY * B+ Good

**Major Rating Factors:** Good quality investment portfolio (6.5 on a scale of 0 to 10) despite significant exposure to mortgages . Mortgage default rate has been low. substantial holdings of BBB bonds in addition to small junk bond holdings. Good overall profitability (6.0). Good liquidity (5.3).
**Other Rating Factors:** Good overall results on stability tests (6.4) excellent operational trends and excellent risk diversification. Strong capitalization (7.8) based on excellent risk adjusted capital (severe loss scenario).
**Principal Business:** Individual life insurance (58%), group health insurance (20%), group life insurance (17%), and individual health insurance (5%).
**Principal Investments:** NonCMO investment grade bonds (61%), mortgages in good standing (15%), policy loans (13%), common & preferred stock (5%), and misc. investments (7%).
**Investments in Affiliates:** 4%
**Group Affiliation:** Boston Mutual Group
**Licensed in:** All states, the District of Columbia and Puerto Rico
**Commenced Business:** February 1892
**Address:** 120 Royall Street, Canton, MA 02021-1098
**Phone:** (781) 828-7000 **Domicile State:** MA **NAIC Code:** 61476

| Data Date | Rating | RACR #1 | RACR #2 | Total Assets ($mil) | Capital ($mil) | Net Premium ($mil) | Net Income ($mil) |
|---|---|---|---|---|---|---|---|
| 9-17 | B+ | 2.31 | 1.51 | 1,424.8 | 209.6 | 147.6 | 12.6 |
| 9-16 | B+ | 2.04 | 1.33 | 1,349.6 | 170.2 | 141.0 | 7.2 |
| 2016 | B+ | 2.06 | 1.35 | 1,359.7 | 178.0 | 188.1 | 11.4 |
| 2015 | B+ | 1.98 | 1.31 | 1,297.1 | 159.1 | 185.7 | 12.8 |
| 2014 | B+ | 1.95 | 1.29 | 1,245.2 | 145.3 | 185.3 | 9.9 |
| 2013 | B+ | 2.07 | 1.36 | 1,188.8 | 142.5 | 182.6 | 16.0 |
| 2012 | B+ | 1.97 | 1.27 | 1,138.4 | 126.0 | 180.4 | 12.8 |

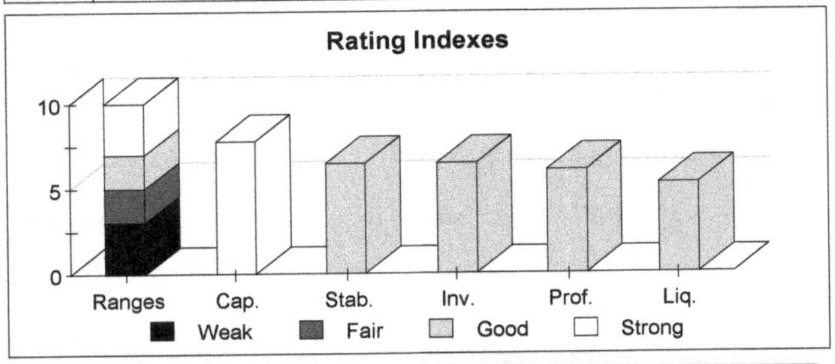


## BRAVO HEALTH MID-ATLANTIC INC C+ Fair

**Major Rating Factors:** Fair profitability index (4.0 on a scale of 0 to 10). Good quality investment portfolio (6.1). Good overall results on stability tests (5.2) despite a decline in enrollment during 2016. Rating is significantly influenced by the good financial results of Cigna Corporation.
**Other Rating Factors:** Weak liquidity (2.4) as a spike in claims may stretch capacity. Strong capitalization index (8.0) based on excellent current risk-adjusted capital (severe loss scenario).
**Principal Business:** Medicare (100%)
**Mem Phys: 16:** 13,462 **15:** 10,390 **16 MLR** 89.5% **/ 16 Admin Exp** N/A
**Enroll(000): Q3 17:** 15 **16:** 18 **15:** 21 **Med Exp PMPM:** $1,049
**Principal Investments:** Long-term bonds (97%), cash and equiv (3%)
**Provider Compensation ($000):** Contr fee ($194,254), capitation ($38,777), salary ($2,480), bonus arrang ($1,031), other ($8,443)
**Total Member Encounters:** Phys (348,282), non-phys (290,755)
**Group Affiliation:** Cigna Corporation
**Licensed in:** DC, DE, MD
**Address:** 3601 ODONNELL STREET, BALTIMORE, MD 21224-5238
**Phone:** (800) 235-9188 **Dom State:** MD **Commenced Bus:** January 2001

| Data Date | Rating | RACR #1 | RACR #2 | Total Assets ($mil) | Capital ($mil) | Net Premium ($mil) | Net Income ($mil) |
|---|---|---|---|---|---|---|---|
| 9-17 | C+ | 2.18 | 1.82 | 90.2 | 35.5 | 169.2 | -2.5 |
| 9-16 | B- | 2.40 | 2.00 | 100.4 | 36.5 | 216.0 | -0.1 |
| 2016 | C+ | 2.19 | 1.82 | 80.6 | 35.6 | 279.3 | -1.4 |
| 2015 | B- | 2.50 | 2.08 | 94.2 | 38.1 | 288.2 | 3.4 |
| 2014 | B- | 2.23 | 1.86 | 84.0 | 35.4 | 306.6 | 10.2 |
| 2013 | C | 1.28 | 1.07 | 72.9 | 25.0 | 329.2 | -4.1 |
| 2012 | C | 1.41 | 1.18 | 80.2 | 28.8 | 348.7 | 3.8 |

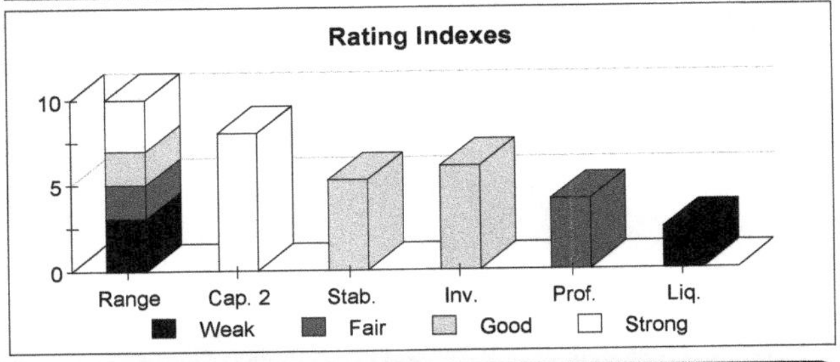


## BRAVO HEALTH PENNSYLVANIA INC B Good

**Major Rating Factors:** Good liquidity (6.6 on a scale of 0 to 10) with sufficient resources (cash flows and marketable investments) to handle a spike in claims. Fair profitability index (4.0). Strong capitalization (10.0) based on excellent current risk-adjusted capital (severe loss scenario).
**Other Rating Factors:** High quality investment portfolio (8.2).
**Principal Business:** Medicare (100%)
**Mem Phys: 16:** 25,175 **15:** 16,941 **16 MLR** 87.3% **/ 16 Admin Exp** N/A
**Enroll(000): Q3 17:** 41 **16:** 46 **15:** 54 **Med Exp PMPM:** $1,046
**Principal Investments:** Long-term bonds (79%), cash and equiv (21%)
**Provider Compensation ($000):** Contr fee ($478,283), capitation ($94,571), bonus arrang ($4,543), salary ($2,664), other ($44,943)
**Total Member Encounters:** Phys (903,960), non-phys (780,601)
**Group Affiliation:** Cigna Corporation
**Licensed in:** NJ, PA
**Address:** 1500 SPRING GARDEN St Ste 800, PHILADELPHIA, PA 19130-4071
**Phone:** (800) 235-9188 **Dom State:** PA **Commenced Bus:** December 2002

| Data Date | Rating | RACR #1 | RACR #2 | Total Assets ($mil) | Capital ($mil) | Net Premium ($mil) | Net Income ($mil) |
|---|---|---|---|---|---|---|---|
| 9-17 | B | 3.92 | 3.26 | 304.4 | 154.7 | 453.4 | 9.5 |
| 9-16 | B- | 3.23 | 2.69 | 292.6 | 147.4 | 559.3 | -1.0 |
| 2016 | B | 3.63 | 3.03 | 246.7 | 143.4 | 721.7 | -4.8 |
| 2015 | B | 3.27 | 2.72 | 244.3 | 149.1 | 776.2 | 20.8 |
| 2014 | B | 2.82 | 2.35 | 236.3 | 131.2 | 904.4 | 14.8 |
| 2013 | B | 1.77 | 1.48 | 263.3 | 101.6 | 1,070.2 | -19.3 |
| 2012 | A- | 2.48 | 2.07 | 257.6 | 136.0 | 1,069.5 | 18.8 |

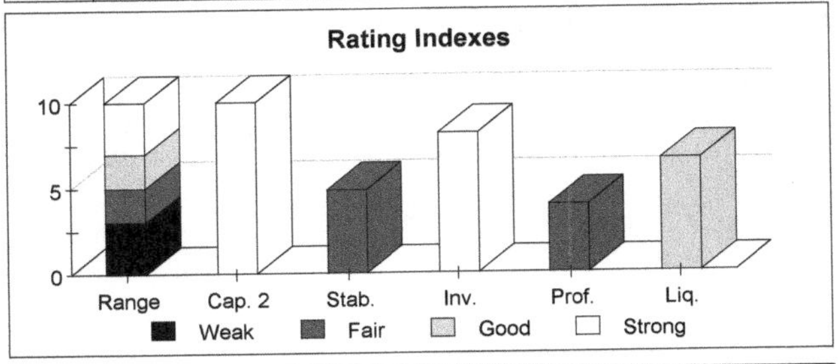

## BRIDGESPAN HEALTH CO E Very Weak

**Major Rating Factors:** Weak profitability index (0.1 on a scale of 0 to 10). Fair overall results on stability tests (4.1) based on a significant 26% decrease in enrollment during the period. Rating is significantly influenced by the good financial results of Cambia Health Solutions Inc. Strong capitalization index (10.0) based on excellent current risk-adjusted capital (severe loss scenario).
**Other Rating Factors:** High quality investment portfolio (9.8). Excellent liquidity (7.3) with ample operational cash flow and liquid investments.
**Principal Business:** Comp med (99%), med supp (1%)
**Mem Phys: 16:** N/A **15:** N/A **16 MLR** 80.8% **/ 16 Admin Exp** N/A
**Enroll(000): Q3 17:** 35 **16:** 15 **15:** 20 **Med Exp PMPM:** $282
**Principal Investments:** Long-term bonds (67%), cash and equiv (33%)
**Provider Compensation ($000):** Contr fee ($38,055), FFS ($19,637), bonus arrang ($25), capitation ($5)
**Total Member Encounters:** Phys (131,872), non-phys (180,367)
**Group Affiliation:** Cambia Health Solutions Inc
**Licensed in:** ID, OR, UT, WA
**Address:** 2890 EAST COTTONWOOD PARKWAY, SALT LAKE CITY, UT 84121-7035
**Phone:** (801) 333-2000 **Dom State:** UT **Commenced Bus:** September 1982

| Data Date | Rating | RACR #1 | RACR #2 | Total Assets ($mil) | Capital ($mil) | Net Premium ($mil) | Net Income ($mil) |
|---|---|---|---|---|---|---|---|
| 9-17 | E | 6.30 | 5.25 | 74.8 | 26.4 | 133.6 | -1.0 |
| 9-16 | E | 4.00 | 3.34 | 46.2 | 25.7 | 45.4 | 6.2 |
| 2016 | E | 5.71 | 4.76 | 50.1 | 23.9 | 61.3 | 3.5 |
| 2015 | E | 3.06 | 2.55 | 45.1 | 19.6 | 67.9 | -18.7 |
| 2014 | E | 0.91 | 0.76 | 17.0 | 3.0 | 22.1 | -7.4 |
| 2013 | B | 58.91 | 49.09 | 14.3 | 10.9 | 0.9 | -1.8 |
| 2012 | A- | 86.85 | 72.37 | 15.5 | 13.1 | 1.2 | 4.1 |

Rating Indexes

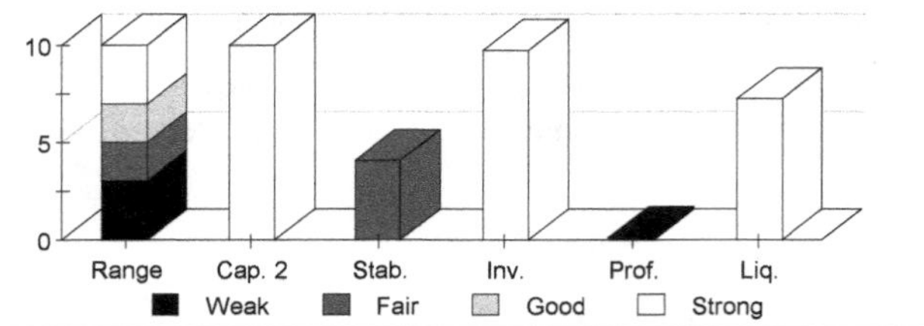


## BROWN & TOLAND HEALTH SERVICES E- Very Weak

**Major Rating Factors:** Weak profitability index (1.1 on a scale of 0 to 10). Poor capitalization index (0.0) based on weak current risk-adjusted capital (severe loss scenario). Weak overall results on stability tests (2.3).
**Other Rating Factors:** Excellent liquidity (7.0) with ample operational cash flow and liquid investments.
**Principal Business:** Managed care (100%)
**Mem Phys: 16:** N/A **15:** N/A **16 MLR** 103.4% **/ 16 Admin Exp** N/A
**Enroll(000): Q3 17:** 10 **16:** 9 **15:** 10 **Med Exp PMPM:** $748
**Principal Investments ($000):** Cash and equiv ($14,549)
**Provider Compensation ($000):** None
**Total Member Encounters:** N/A
**Group Affiliation:** None
**Licensed in:** CA
**Address:** 1221 Broadway Street Suite 700, Oakland, CA 94612
**Phone:** (415) 322-9897 **Dom State:** CA **Commenced Bus:** April 2013

| Data Date | Rating | RACR #1 | RACR #2 | Total Assets ($mil) | Capital ($mil) | Net Premium ($mil) | Net Income ($mil) |
|---|---|---|---|---|---|---|---|
| 9-17 | E- | 0.07 | 0.04 | 24.8 | 0.6 | 71.3 | 3.8 |
| 9-16 | E- | N/A | N/A | 18.1 | -1.1 | 63.1 | 2.1 |
| 2016 | E- | N/A | N/A | 24.1 | -3.1 | 82.2 | 0.1 |
| 2015 | E- | N/A | N/A | 20.1 | -3.3 | 85.3 | -2.8 |
| 2014 | E- | N/A | N/A | 15.2 | -0.5 | 19.4 | -0.7 |
| 2013 | E | 1.01 | 0.63 | 1.9 | 0.2 | 1.4 | -0.1 |
| 2012 | N/A | N/A | N/A | N/A | N/A | N/A | N/A |

Rating Indexes

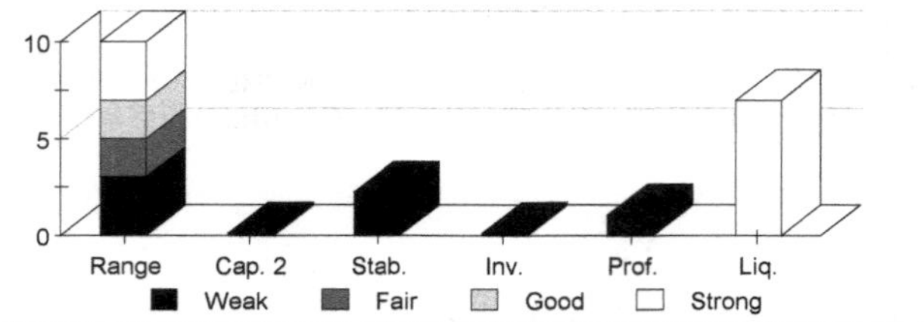


## BUCKEYE COMMUNITY HEALTH PLAN INC C+ Fair

**Major Rating Factors:** Good liquidity (6.5 on a scale of 0 to 10) with sufficient resources (cash flows and marketable investments) to handle a spike in claims. Excellent profitability (8.5). Strong capitalization (8.5) based on excellent current risk-adjusted capital (severe loss scenario).
**Other Rating Factors:** High quality investment portfolio (9.6).
**Principal Business:** Medicaid (88%), Medicare (11%), comp med (1%)
**Mem Phys: 16:** 48,014 **15:** 36,239 **16 MLR** 82.8% **/ 16 Admin Exp** N/A
**Enroll(000): Q3 17:** 350 **16:** 327 **15:** 311 **Med Exp PMPM:** $433
**Principal Investments:** Long-term bonds (80%), cash and equiv (16%), affiliate common stock (2%), other (2%)
**Provider Compensation ($000):** Contr fee ($1,203,284), bonus arrang ($313,682), capitation ($157,432), salary ($37,158), other ($20,828)
**Total Member Encounters:** Phys (2,498,597), non-phys (4,224,288)
**Group Affiliation:** Centene Corporation
**Licensed in:** OH
**Address:** 4349 Easton Way Ste 200, Columbus, OH 43219
**Phone:** (314) 725-4477 **Dom State:** OH **Commenced Bus:** January 2004

| Data Date | Rating | RACR #1 | RACR #2 | Total Assets ($mil) | Capital ($mil) | Net Premium ($mil) | Net Income ($mil) |
|---|---|---|---|---|---|---|---|
| 9-17 | C+ | 2.60 | 2.16 | 494.4 | 245.9 | 1,647.7 | 31.4 |
| 9-16 | C+ | 2.23 | 1.85 | 446.0 | 203.9 | 1,536.4 | 16.5 |
| 2016 | C+ | 2.26 | 1.88 | 429.4 | 211.0 | 2,048.4 | 22.8 |
| 2015 | C+ | 1.96 | 1.63 | 454.5 | 178.3 | 1,981.9 | 25.9 |
| 2014 | C+ | 2.01 | 1.68 | 368.2 | 123.1 | 1,325.9 | -0.9 |
| 2013 | C+ | 2.80 | 2.34 | 199.3 | 105.7 | 795.0 | 13.1 |
| 2012 | B- | 2.54 | 2.11 | 161.1 | 90.7 | 728.3 | 13.0 |

Rating Indexes

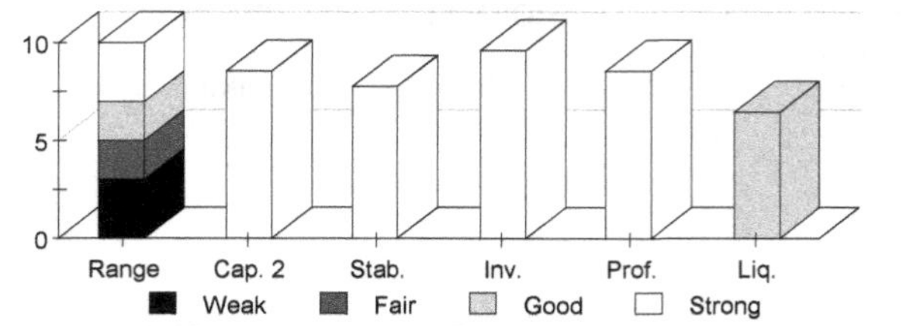

## BUPA INS CO — B — Good

**Major Rating Factors:** Fair profitability index (4.2 on a scale of 0 to 10). Strong capitalization (9.6) based on excellent current risk-adjusted capital (severe loss scenario). High quality investment portfolio (9.5).
**Other Rating Factors:** Excellent liquidity (8.5) with ample operational cash flow and liquid investments.
**Principal Business:** Comp med (100%)
**Mem Phys: 16:** 11,630 **15:** 8,760 **16 MLR** 26.7% **/ 16 Admin Exp** N/A
**Enroll(000): Q3 17:** 30 **16:** 31 **15:** 100 **Med Exp PMPM:** $205
**Principal Investments:** Cash and equiv (59%), long-term bonds (30%), affiliate common stock (5%), other (5%)
**Provider Compensation ($000):** FFS ($91,426)
**Total Member Encounters:** Phys (22,651), non-phys (10,275)
**Group Affiliation:** British United Provident Association
**Licensed in:** FL, PR
**Address:** 18001 Old Cutler Rd Ste 300, Palmetto Bay, FL 33157
**Phone:** (305) 275-1400 **Dom State:** FL **Commenced Bus:** July 1973

| Data Date | Rating | RACR #1 | RACR #2 | Total Assets ($mil) | Capital ($mil) | Net Premium ($mil) | Net Income ($mil) |
|---|---|---|---|---|---|---|---|
| 9-17 | B | 3.40 | 2.83 | 303.2 | 143.3 | 220.8 | -0.1 |
| 9-16 | B | 3.58 | 2.98 | 350.8 | 169.3 | 245.8 | 7.4 |
| 2016 | B | 3.63 | 3.02 | 320.0 | 153.0 | 315.4 | 12.7 |
| 2015 | C | 3.60 | 3.00 | 379.4 | 170.4 | 367.7 | 45.9 |
| 2014 | D+ | 2.70 | 2.25 | 401.2 | 124.7 | 413.2 | 17.9 |
| 2013 | D+ | 1.40 | 1.16 | 356.9 | 68.5 | 439.9 | -29.8 |
| 2012 | D+ | 1.70 | 1.42 | 187.4 | 59.7 | 215.7 | -9.2 |

Rating Indexes

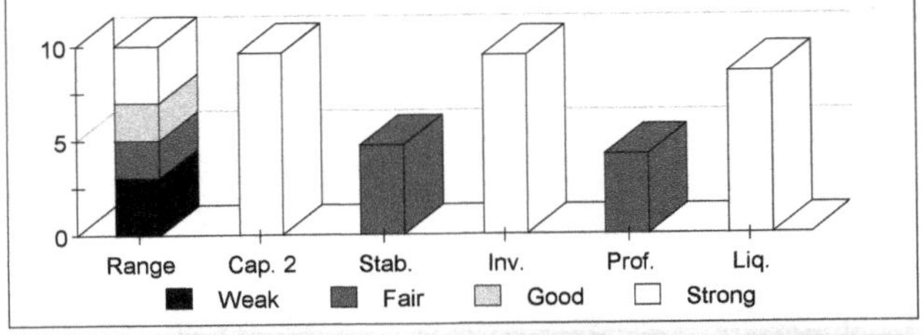


## CALIFORNIA HEALTH & WELLNESS PLAN — C — Fair

**Major Rating Factors:** Weak overall results on stability tests (2.1 on a scale of 0 to 10). Good overall profitability index (6.0). Good capitalization index (6.1) based on fair current risk-adjusted capital (moderate loss scenario).
**Other Rating Factors:** Excellent liquidity (7.2) with ample operational cash flow and liquid investments.
**Principal Business:** Medicaid (100%)
**Mem Phys: 16:** N/A **15:** N/A **16 MLR** 82.7% **/ 16 Admin Exp** N/A
**Enroll(000): Q3 17:** 191 **16:** 188 **15:** 185 **Med Exp PMPM:** $222
**Principal Investments ($000):** Cash and equiv ($88,411)
**Provider Compensation ($000):** None
**Total Member Encounters:** N/A
**Group Affiliation:** None
**Licensed in:** CA
**Address:** 1740 Creekside Oaks Drive, Sacramento, CA 95833
**Phone:** (818) 676-8486 **Dom State:** CA **Commenced Bus:** October 2013

| Data Date | Rating | RACR #1 | RACR #2 | Total Assets ($mil) | Capital ($mil) | Net Premium ($mil) | Net Income ($mil) |
|---|---|---|---|---|---|---|---|
| 9-17 | C | 0.91 | 0.64 | 373.5 | 68.3 | 467.3 | 2.7 |
| 9-16 | C | 0.95 | 0.67 | 290.0 | 71.5 | 448.9 | 12.2 |
| 2016 | C+ | 1.11 | 0.78 | 320.4 | 84.4 | 610.6 | 27.2 |
| 2015 | C | 0.85 | 0.59 | 274.8 | 57.5 | 581.5 | 15.0 |
| 2014 | C- | 1.80 | 1.16 | 172.6 | 42.6 | 330.3 | 22.2 |
| 2013 | D+ | 3.83 | 2.42 | 32.5 | 12.8 | 27.3 | -3.2 |
| 2012 | N/A | N/A | N/A | N/A | N/A | N/A | N/A |

Rating Indexes

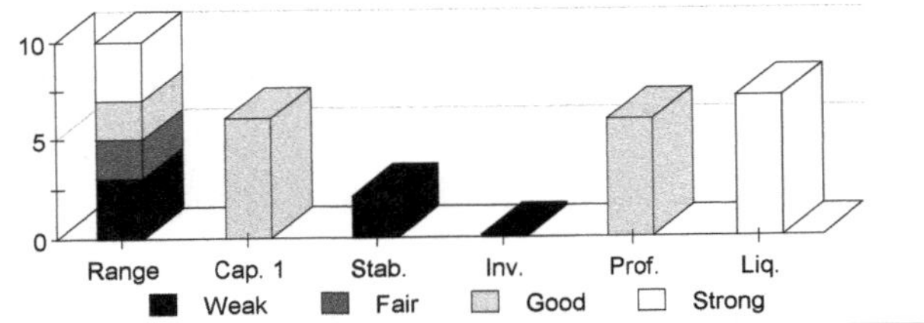


## CAPITAL ADVANTAGE ASR CO — C- — Fair

**Major Rating Factors:** Weak profitability index (1.5 on a scale of 0 to 10). Good liquidity (6.4) with sufficient resources (cash flows and marketable investments) to handle a spike in claims. Strong capitalization (9.3) based on excellent current risk-adjusted capital (severe loss scenario).
**Other Rating Factors:** High quality investment portfolio (8.6).
**Principal Business:** Comp med (82%), dental (2%), other (15%)
**Mem Phys: 16:** 25,831 **15:** 23,683 **16 MLR** 90.4% **/ 16 Admin Exp** N/A
**Enroll(000): Q3 17:** 245 **16:** 219 **15:** 187 **Med Exp PMPM:** $425
**Principal Investments:** Long-term bonds (81%), cash and equiv (19%)
**Provider Compensation ($000):** Contr fee ($1,053,239)
**Total Member Encounters:** Phys (2,113,237), non-phys (2,981,688)
**Group Affiliation:** Capital Blue Cross
**Licensed in:** PA
**Address:** 2500 Elmerton Ave, Harrisburg, PA 17177-9799
**Phone:** (717) 541-7000 **Dom State:** PA **Commenced Bus:** January 2013

| Data Date | Rating | RACR #1 | RACR #2 | Total Assets ($mil) | Capital ($mil) | Net Premium ($mil) | Net Income ($mil) |
|---|---|---|---|---|---|---|---|
| 9-17 | C- | 3.20 | 2.67 | 605.0 | 264.0 | 1,151.5 | 31.5 |
| 9-16 | C- | 1.32 | 1.10 | 441.1 | 146.4 | 902.9 | -36.6 |
| 2016 | C- | 2.82 | 2.35 | 529.1 | 231.6 | 1,218.0 | -44.7 |
| 2015 | C- | 1.94 | 1.62 | 423.6 | 185.8 | 965.1 | -28.4 |
| 2014 | C- | 1.92 | 1.60 | 412.2 | 191.0 | 1,023.4 | -38.3 |
| 2013 | C- | 2.18 | 1.81 | 336.0 | 181.0 | 735.1 | -13.8 |
| 2012 | N/A | N/A | N/A | 100.7 | 99.8 | N/A | -0.1 |

Rating Indexes

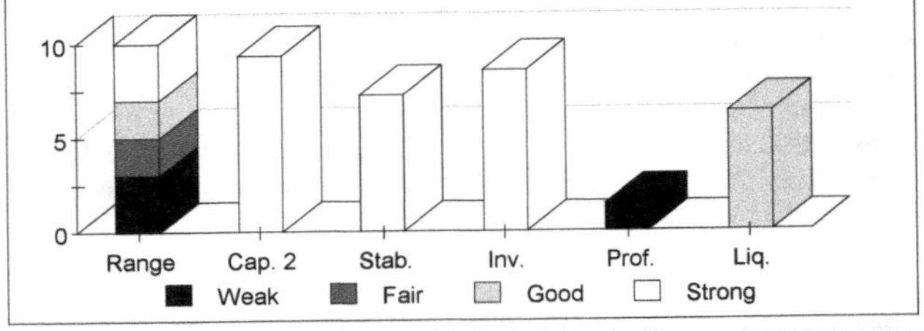

## CAPITAL ADVANTAGE INS CO — C — Fair

**Major Rating Factors:** Low quality investment portfolio (2.8 on a scale of 0 to 10). Good overall profitability index (5.4). Strong capitalization (9.0) based on excellent current risk-adjusted capital (severe loss scenario).
**Other Rating Factors:** Excellent liquidity (7.3) with ample operational cash flow and liquid investments.
**Principal Business:** Medicare (71%), med supp (14%), comp med (4%), other (10%)
**Mem Phys: 16:** 25,831 **15:** 23,683 **16 MLR** 85.5% **/ 16 Admin Exp** N/A
**Enroll(000): Q3 17:** 59 **16:** 58 **15:** 49 **Med Exp PMPM:** $291
**Principal Investments:** Affiliate common stock (92%), long-term bonds (16%), cash and equiv (1%)
**Provider Compensation ($000):** Contr fee ($165,120), other ($7,208)
**Total Member Encounters:** Phys (1,124,217), non-phys (142,653)
**Group Affiliation:** Capital Blue Cross
**Licensed in:** PA
**Address:** 2500 Elmerton Ave, Harrisburg, PA 17177-9799
**Phone:** (717) 541-7000 **Dom State:** PA **Commenced Bus:** May 1982

| Data Date | Rating | RACR #1 | RACR #2 | Total Assets ($mil) | Capital ($mil) | Net Premium ($mil) | Net Income ($mil) |
|---|---|---|---|---|---|---|---|
| 9-17 | C | 2.98 | 2.48 | 604.4 | 381.5 | 177.3 | -3.1 |
| 9-16 | C- | 1.70 | 1.42 | 375.9 | 223.3 | 164.9 | 2.2 |
| 2016 | C | 2.73 | 2.27 | 464.2 | 349.0 | 219.2 | 4.2 |
| 2015 | C | 2.40 | 2.00 | 418.0 | 292.7 | 203.0 | 31.8 |
| 2014 | C | 2.73 | 2.28 | 442.9 | 319.2 | 258.4 | 22.7 |
| 2013 | C | 2.35 | 1.96 | 503.8 | 340.5 | 573.1 | 1.1 |
| 2012 | C+ | 2.61 | 2.17 | 610.2 | 366.2 | 1,409.9 | -0.6 |

Rating Indexes

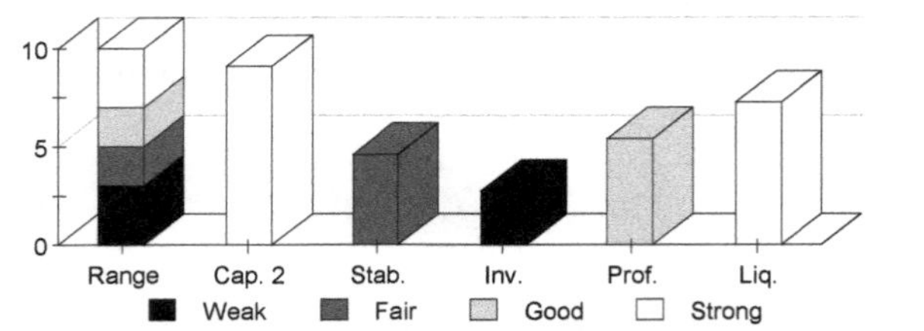


## CAPITAL BLUE CROSS — B- — Good

**Major Rating Factors:** Fair profitability index (4.3 on a scale of 0 to 10). Strong capitalization (10.0) based on excellent current risk-adjusted capital (severe loss scenario). Excellent liquidity (7.7) with ample operational cash flow and liquid investments.
**Other Rating Factors:** Low quality investment portfolio (2.6).
**Principal Business:** FEHB (90%), med supp (8%), other (2%)
**Mem Phys: 16:** 781 **15:** 758 **16 MLR** 89.5% **/ 16 Admin Exp** N/A
**Enroll(000): Q3 17:** 92 **16:** 94 **15:** 96 **Med Exp PMPM:** $234
**Principal Investments:** Affiliate common stock (40%), long-term bonds (24%), nonaffiliate common stock (21%), cash and equiv (5%), real estate (3%), other (6%)
**Provider Compensation ($000):** Contr fee ($267,353)
**Total Member Encounters:** Non-phys (438,680)
**Group Affiliation:** Capital Blue Cross
**Licensed in:** PA
**Address:** 2500 Elmerton Ave, Harrisburg, PA 17177-9799
**Phone:** (717) 541-7000 **Dom State:** PA **Commenced Bus:** March 1938

| Data Date | Rating | RACR #1 | RACR #2 | Total Assets ($mil) | Capital ($mil) | Net Premium ($mil) | Net Income ($mil) |
|---|---|---|---|---|---|---|---|
| 9-17 | B- | 4.33 | 3.60 | 1,138.4 | 737.6 | 217.5 | 18.5 |
| 9-16 | B- | 4.14 | 3.45 | 1,071.9 | 715.2 | 223.2 | 10.9 |
| 2016 | B- | 4.13 | 3.44 | 1,058.6 | 703.4 | 297.5 | 9.4 |
| 2015 | B- | 4.43 | 3.69 | 1,081.6 | 764.7 | 279.7 | 11.3 |
| 2014 | B- | 4.76 | 3.96 | 1,123.6 | 824.7 | 270.8 | 16.0 |
| 2013 | B- | 4.26 | 3.55 | 1,119.1 | 857.7 | 289.4 | 10.2 |
| 2012 | B- | 4.28 | 3.57 | 1,061.1 | 824.8 | 270.0 | 3.6 |

Rating Indexes

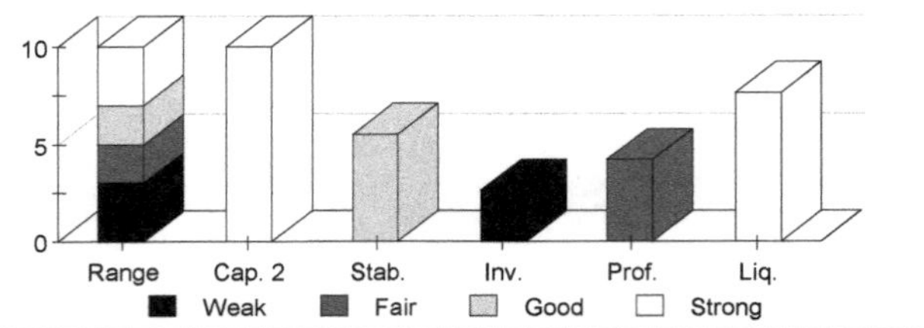


## CAPITAL DISTRICT PHYSICIANS HEALTH P — B — Good

**Major Rating Factors:** Good overall results on stability tests (5.3 on a scale of 0 to 10) despite a decline in enrollment during 2016. Good liquidity (6.9) with sufficient resources (cash flows and marketable investments) to handle a spike in claims. Excellent profitability (7.7).
**Other Rating Factors:** Strong capitalization index (8.9) based on excellent current risk-adjusted capital (severe loss scenario). High quality investment portfolio (7.8).
**Principal Business:** Comp med (34%), Medicaid (32%), Medicare (30%), other (4%)
**Mem Phys: 16:** 18,816 **15:** 18,372 **16 MLR** 88.8% **/ 16 Admin Exp** N/A
**Enroll(000): Q3 17:** 207 **16:** 212 **15:** 236 **Med Exp PMPM:** $487
**Principal Investments:** Long-term bonds (50%), cash and equiv (16%), affiliate common stock (5%), other (29%)
**Provider Compensation ($000):** Contr fee ($746,126), FFS ($405,993), bonus arrang ($69,395), capitation ($24,864), other ($30,346)
**Total Member Encounters:** Phys (1,938,444), non-phys (731,269)
**Group Affiliation:** Capital District Physicians Health
**Licensed in:** CA, NY
**Address:** 500 Patroon Creek Boulevard, Albany, NY 12206-1057
**Phone:** (518) 641-3000 **Dom State:** NY **Commenced Bus:** July 1984

| Data Date | Rating | RACR #1 | RACR #2 | Total Assets ($mil) | Capital ($mil) | Net Premium ($mil) | Net Income ($mil) |
|---|---|---|---|---|---|---|---|
| 9-17 | B | 2.85 | 2.38 | 576.7 | 350.8 | 1,088.0 | 29.0 |
| 9-16 | B- | 2.25 | 1.87 | 491.4 | 284.7 | 1,075.3 | 13.2 |
| 2016 | B | 2.47 | 2.05 | 506.9 | 308.4 | 1,444.6 | 33.8 |
| 2015 | B- | 2.33 | 1.94 | 478.7 | 292.9 | 1,512.3 | 85.7 |
| 2014 | B- | 2.06 | 1.72 | 440.7 | 248.9 | 1,426.9 | 23.7 |
| 2013 | B+ | 2.61 | 2.18 | 489.4 | 300.5 | 1,302.2 | 23.0 |
| 2012 | A+ | 2.97 | 2.48 | 529.4 | 325.0 | 1,237.9 | 41.7 |

Rating Indexes

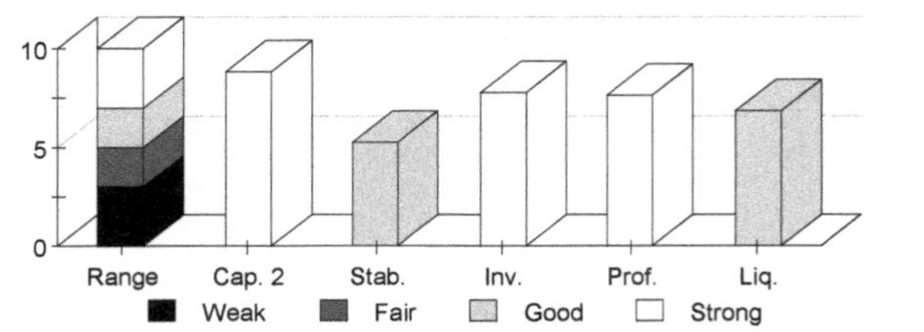

## CAPITAL HEALTH PLAN INC B Good

**Major Rating Factors:** Good liquidity (6.6 on a scale of 0 to 10) with sufficient resources (cash flows and marketable investments) to handle a spike in claims. Fair profitability index (4.8). Strong capitalization index (10.0) based on excellent current risk-adjusted capital (severe loss scenario).
**Other Rating Factors:** High quality investment portfolio (8.4). Excellent overall results on stability tests (7.6).
**Principal Business:** Comp med (71%), Medicare (26%), FEHB (2%)
**Mem Phys: 16:** 587 **15:** 572 **16 MLR** 94.9% **/ 16 Admin Exp** N/A
**Enroll(000): Q3 17:** 135 **16:** 134 **15:** 132 **Med Exp PMPM:** $457
**Principal Investments:** Long-term bonds (73%), nonaffiliate common stock (19%), real estate (5%), cash and equiv (2%), other (1%)
**Provider Compensation ($000):** Contr fee ($407,626), FFS ($240,734), salary ($39,332), capitation ($31,308)
**Total Member Encounters:** Phys (1,058,540), non-phys (540,224)
**Group Affiliation:** GuideWell Mutual Holding Corporation
**Licensed in:** FL
**Address:** 2140 Centerville Place, Tallahassee, FL 32308
**Phone:** (850) 383-3333 **Dom State:** FL **Commenced Bus:** June 1982

| Data Date | Rating | RACR #1 | RACR #2 | Total Assets ($mil) | Capital ($mil) | Net Premium ($mil) | Net Income ($mil) |
|---|---|---|---|---|---|---|---|
| 9-17 | B | 7.70 | 6.42 | 534.9 | 390.6 | 608.9 | 10.0 |
| 9-16 | B | 7.78 | 6.49 | 489.5 | 365.4 | 578.3 | -0.9 |
| 2016 | B | 7.32 | 6.10 | 489.9 | 371.0 | 766.3 | 4.6 |
| 2015 | B | 7.76 | 6.46 | 467.8 | 364.1 | 716.9 | 8.8 |
| 2014 | A- | N/A | N/A | 461.3 | 368.8 | 679.2 | 3.6 |
| 2013 | A | 8.67 | 7.23 | 450.7 | 365.9 | 640.2 | 13.8 |
| 2012 | A | 8.73 | 7.28 | 428.4 | 342.2 | 617.2 | 23.0 |

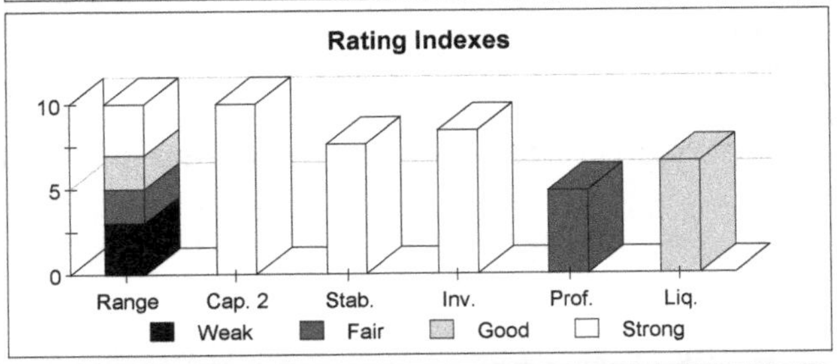


## CARE 1ST HEALTH PLAN INC * A+ Excellent

**Major Rating Factors:** Excellent profitability (9.2 on a scale of 0 to 10). Strong capitalization (9.1) based on excellent current risk-adjusted capital (severe loss scenario). High quality investment portfolio (9.6).
**Other Rating Factors:** Excellent liquidity (7.0) with sufficient resources (cash flows and marketable investments) to handle a spike in claims.
**Principal Business:** Medicaid (62%), Medicare (37%)
**Mem Phys: 16:** N/A **15:** N/A **16 MLR** 84.0% **/ 16 Admin Exp** N/A
**Enroll(000): Q3 17:** 496 **16:** 479 **15:** 437 **Med Exp PMPM:** $325
**Principal Investments:** Long-term bonds (50%), cash and equiv (48%), real estate (3%)
**Provider Compensation ($000):** Contr fee ($1,255,875), capitation ($625,749)
**Total Member Encounters:** Phys (809,729), non-phys (5,380,548)
**Group Affiliation:** Blue Shield of California
**Licensed in:** CA, TX
**Address:** 601 POTRERO GRANDE DR, MONTEREY PARK, CA 91755
**Phone:** (Phone number **Dom State:** CA **Commenced Bus:** January 2014

| Data Date | Rating | RACR #1 | RACR #2 | Total Assets ($mil) | Capital ($mil) | Net Premium ($mil) | Net Income ($mil) |
|---|---|---|---|---|---|---|---|
| 9-17 | A+ | 3.06 | 2.55 | 1,094.9 | 430.7 | 2,209.7 | 75.6 |
| 9-16 | B | 1.23 | 1.02 | 1,056.0 | 272.1 | 1,598.6 | 61.6 |
| 2016 | B+ | 2.63 | 2.19 | 894.2 | 381.8 | 2,143.2 | 234.5 |
| 2015 | C | 0.68 | 0.57 | 742.6 | 190.3 | 1,870.4 | 16.9 |
| 2014 | U | 0.97 | 0.81 | 435.2 | 90.6 | 1,345.8 | 48.5 |
| 2013 | N/A | N/A | N/A | N/A | N/A | N/A | N/A |
| 2012 | N/A | N/A | N/A | N/A | N/A | N/A | N/A |

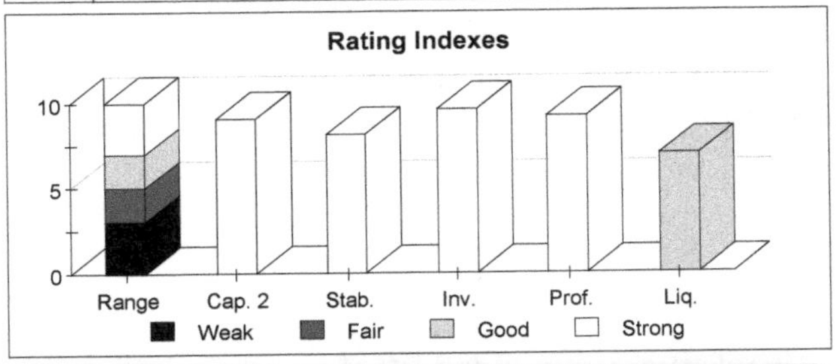


## CARE IMPROVEMENT PLUS OF TEXAS INS C Fair

**Major Rating Factors:** Weak liquidity (1.5 on a scale of 0 to 10) as a spike in claims may stretch capacity. Excellent profitability (8.7). Strong capitalization (9.1) based on excellent current risk-adjusted capital (severe loss scenario).
**Other Rating Factors:** High quality investment portfolio (9.3).
**Principal Business:** Medicare (100%)
**Mem Phys: 16:** 47,187 **15:** 130,023 **16 MLR** 80.3% **/ 16 Admin Exp** N/A
**Enroll(000): Q3 17:** 105 **16:** 86 **15:** 99 **Med Exp PMPM:** $951
**Principal Investments:** Long-term bonds (98%), cash and equiv (1%), other (1%)
**Provider Compensation ($000):** Contr fee ($453,262), FFS ($400,816), capitation ($5,164), bonus arrang ($2,791)
**Total Member Encounters:** Phys (1,973,032), non-phys (1,125,783)
**Group Affiliation:** UnitedHealth Group Incorporated
**Licensed in:** AL, IL, IN, IA, NE, NM, NY, NC, PA, TX
**Address:** 4350 LOCKHILL-SELMA Rd 3RD FL, SAN ANTONIO, TX 78249
**Phone:** (952) 936-1300 **Dom State:** TX **Commenced Bus:** April 2006

| Data Date | Rating | RACR #1 | RACR #2 | Total Assets ($mil) | Capital ($mil) | Net Premium ($mil) | Net Income ($mil) |
|---|---|---|---|---|---|---|---|
| 9-17 | C | 3.00 | 2.50 | 632.1 | 172.7 | 1,026.8 | 56.7 |
| 9-16 | B | 2.63 | 2.19 | 475.1 | 171.2 | 867.3 | 57.0 |
| 2016 | C | 2.10 | 1.75 | 378.9 | 120.9 | 1,155.1 | 49.6 |
| 2015 | B | 2.17 | 1.81 | 377.0 | 140.5 | 1,297.7 | 34.6 |
| 2014 | B | 2.84 | 2.36 | 287.3 | 165.1 | 1,164.9 | 42.4 |
| 2013 | B | 2.79 | 2.33 | 230.3 | 133.3 | 990.3 | 42.8 |
| 2012 | B | 3.34 | 2.78 | 184.1 | 100.9 | 643.4 | 62.1 |

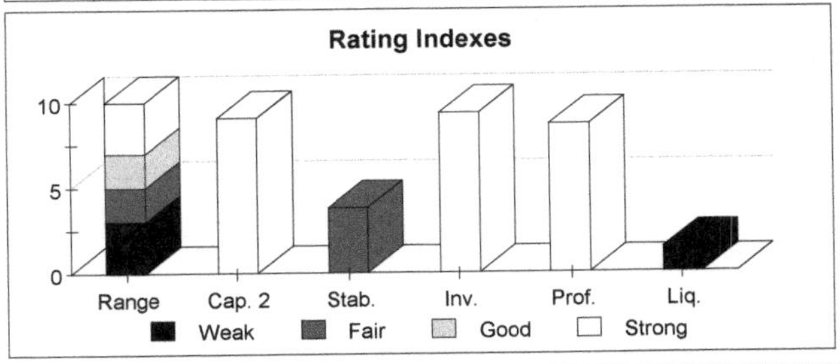

## CARE IMPROVEMENT PLUS SOUTH CENTRAL C Fair

**Major Rating Factors:** Good liquidity (6.4 on a scale of 0 to 10) with sufficient resources (cash flows and marketable investments) to handle a spike in claims. Excellent profitability (9.0). Strong capitalization (7.8) based on excellent current risk-adjusted capital (severe loss scenario).
**Other Rating Factors:** High quality investment portfolio (9.7).
**Principal Business:** Medicare (100%)
**Mem Phys: 16:** 220,453 **15:** 301,083 **16 MLR** 76.5% **/ 16 Admin Exp** N/A
**Enroll(000): Q3 17:** 96 **16:** 274 **15:** 260 **Med Exp PMPM:** $884
**Principal Investments:** Long-term bonds (58%), cash and equiv (42%)
**Provider Compensation ($000):** Contr fee ($1,438,717), FFS ($1,206,801), capitation ($17,594), bonus arrang ($4,927)
**Total Member Encounters:** Phys (6,007,164), non-phys (3,199,463)
**Group Affiliation:** UnitedHealth Group Incorporated
**Licensed in:** AL, AR, CO, FL, GA, IL, IN, IA, KS, KY, ME, MA, MO, NH, NJ, NM, NY, NC, OH, OK, PA, SC, TX, VA, WA
**Address:** 1401 CAPITOL Ave 3RD FIL #375, LITTLE ROCK, AR 77205
**Phone:** (952) 936-1300 **Dom State:** AR **Commenced Bus:** January 2007

| Data Date | Rating | RACR #1 | RACR #2 | Total Assets ($mil) | Capital ($mil) | Net Premium ($mil) | Net Income ($mil) |
|---|---|---|---|---|---|---|---|
| 9-17 | C | 1.97 | 1.64 | 761.0 | 384.0 | 915.4 | 63.9 |
| 9-16 | C | 2.59 | 2.16 | 1,345.5 | 433.1 | 2,782.7 | 177.3 |
| 2016 | C | 2.17 | 1.81 | 1,029.5 | 423.1 | 3,705.3 | 241.4 |
| 2015 | C | 1.91 | 1.59 | 900.9 | 315.2 | 3,290.3 | 35.3 |
| 2014 | C | 2.30 | 1.92 | 646.9 | 348.6 | 2,985.4 | 78.0 |
| 2013 | C | 2.84 | 2.37 | 565.9 | 340.5 | 2,464.4 | 81.5 |
| 2012 | C | 4.22 | 3.52 | 502.4 | 324.6 | 1,649.2 | 162.3 |

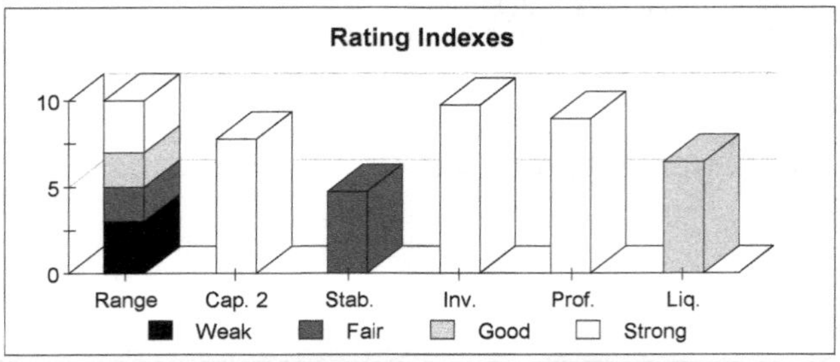


## CARE IMPROVEMENT PLUS WI INS C Fair

**Major Rating Factors:** Weak profitability index (1.8 on a scale of 0 to 10). Strong capitalization (10.0) based on excellent current risk-adjusted capital (severe loss scenario). High quality investment portfolio (9.9).
**Other Rating Factors:** Excellent liquidity (7.0) with ample operational cash flow and liquid investments.
**Principal Business:** Medicare (100%)
**Mem Phys: 16:** 21,376 **15:** 20,373 **16 MLR** 85.4% **/ 16 Admin Exp** N/A
**Enroll(000): Q3 17:** 12 **16:** 8 **15:** 8 **Med Exp PMPM:** $738
**Principal Investments:** Cash and equiv (100%)
**Provider Compensation ($000):** Contr fee ($42,911), FFS ($18,765), capitation ($330), bonus arrang ($56)
**Total Member Encounters:** Phys (149,701), non-phys (68,050)
**Group Affiliation:** UnitedHealth Group Incorporated
**Licensed in:** WI
**Address:** 10701 W RESEARCH DR, Wauwatosa, WI 53266-0649
**Phone:** (952) 979-6172 **Dom State:** WI **Commenced Bus:** January 2012

| Data Date | Rating | RACR #1 | RACR #2 | Total Assets ($mil) | Capital ($mil) | Net Premium ($mil) | Net Income ($mil) |
|---|---|---|---|---|---|---|---|
| 9-17 | C | 3.63 | 3.02 | 56.9 | 20.3 | 92.2 | 0.9 |
| 9-16 | C | 4.80 | 4.00 | 42.2 | 20.4 | 57.8 | -0.3 |
| 2016 | C | 3.53 | 2.94 | 35.7 | 19.8 | 79.1 | -0.9 |
| 2015 | C | 4.82 | 4.02 | 34.2 | 20.5 | 67.9 | 5.0 |
| 2014 | C | 3.36 | 2.80 | 22.2 | 11.6 | 45.1 | -3.1 |
| 2013 | C | 14.70 | 12.25 | 16.7 | 7.7 | 24.6 | -4.8 |
| 2012 | C | 11.53 | 9.61 | 11.9 | 8.8 | 2.0 | -2.6 |

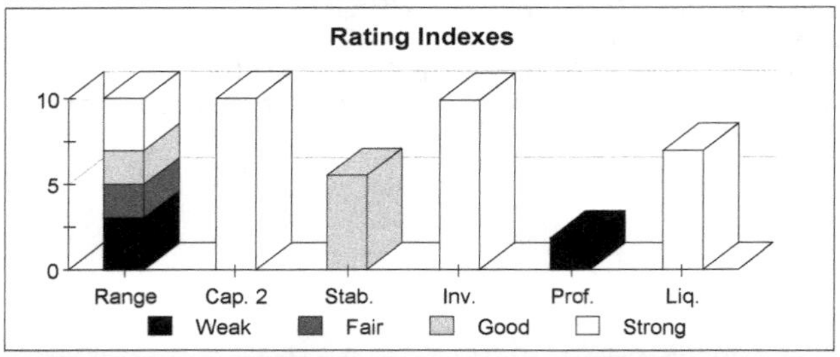


## CARE N CARE INS CO C Fair

**Major Rating Factors:** Fair profitability index (3.4 on a scale of 0 to 10). Good liquidity (6.9) with sufficient resources (cash flows and marketable investments) to handle a spike in claims. Strong capitalization (6.9) based on excellent current risk-adjusted capital (severe loss scenario).
**Other Rating Factors:** High quality investment portfolio (9.7).
**Principal Business:** Medicare (96%)
**Mem Phys: 16:** 2,493 **15:** 2,300 **16 MLR** 89.4% **/ 16 Admin Exp** N/A
**Enroll(000): Q3 17:** 11 **16:** 11 **15:** 10 **Med Exp PMPM:** $771
**Principal Investments:** Cash and equiv (92%), affiliate common stock (8%)
**Provider Compensation ($000):** Contr fee ($81,759), capitation ($16,885)
**Total Member Encounters:** Phys (13,753)
**Group Affiliation:** North Texas Specialty Physicians
**Licensed in:** TX
**Address:** 1701 River Run Rd Ste 402, Fort Worth, TX 76107
**Phone:** (817) 810-5213 **Dom State:** TX **Commenced Bus:** May 2008

| Data Date | Rating | RACR #1 | RACR #2 | Total Assets ($mil) | Capital ($mil) | Net Premium ($mil) | Net Income ($mil) |
|---|---|---|---|---|---|---|---|
| 9-17 | C | 1.29 | 1.08 | 49.0 | 16.0 | 75.1 | 5.3 |
| 9-16 | C | 0.96 | 0.80 | 35.1 | 12.2 | 81.5 | -4.1 |
| 2016 | C | 1.16 | 0.97 | 30.0 | 14.4 | 113.8 | -3.4 |
| 2015 | C | 1.31 | 1.09 | 30.3 | 16.6 | 101.6 | -0.4 |
| 2014 | D | 1.64 | 1.36 | 25.0 | 17.9 | 90.4 | 0.9 |
| 2013 | D | 1.61 | 1.34 | 18.8 | 14.7 | 74.2 | 0.5 |
| 2012 | D- | 1.92 | 1.60 | 16.1 | 11.6 | 50.2 | 0.5 |

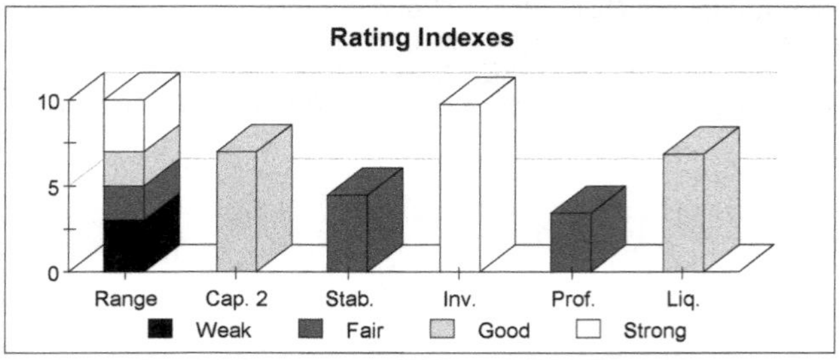

## CARE N CARE INS CO OF NORTH CAROLINA D+ Weak

**Major Rating Factors:** Weak profitability index (0.9 on a scale of 0 to 10). Good capitalization (5.8) based on good current risk-adjusted capital (severe loss scenario). High quality investment portfolio (9.6).
**Other Rating Factors:** Excellent liquidity (7.0) with sufficient resources (cash flows and marketable investments) to handle a spike in claims.
**Principal Business:** Medicare (100%)
**Mem Phys: 16:** N/A **15:** N/A **16 MLR** 96.7% **/ 16 Admin Exp** N/A
**Enroll(000): Q3 17:** 12 **16:** 7 **15:** N/A **Med Exp PMPM:** $732
**Principal Investments:** Cash and equiv (75%), long-term bonds (25%)
**Provider Compensation ($000):** Contr fee ($39,912), capitation ($8,903)
**Total Member Encounters:** Phys (13,659)
**Group Affiliation:** Wesley Long Community Health Service
**Licensed in:** NC
**Address:** 7800 Airport Center Dr Ste 401, Greensboro, NC 27409
**Phone:** (817) 810-5213 **Dom State:** NC **Commenced Bus:** January 2015

| Data Date | Rating | RACR #1 | RACR #2 | Total Assets ($mil) | Capital ($mil) | Net Premium ($mil) | Net Income ($mil) |
|---|---|---|---|---|---|---|---|
| 9-17 | D+ | 1.05 | 0.87 | 49.5 | 9.3 | 75.6 | -10.5 |
| 9-16 | N/A | N/A | N/A | 16.7 | 4.5 | 41.6 | -1.3 |
| 2016 | D+ | 0.89 | 0.74 | 21.0 | 8.1 | 56.8 | -3.6 |
| 2015 | N/A | N/A | N/A | 4.6 | 4.1 | N/A | -1.4 |
| 2014 | N/A | N/A | N/A | N/A | N/A | N/A | N/A |
| 2013 | N/A | N/A | N/A | N/A | N/A | N/A | N/A |
| 2012 | N/A | N/A | N/A | N/A | N/A | N/A | N/A |

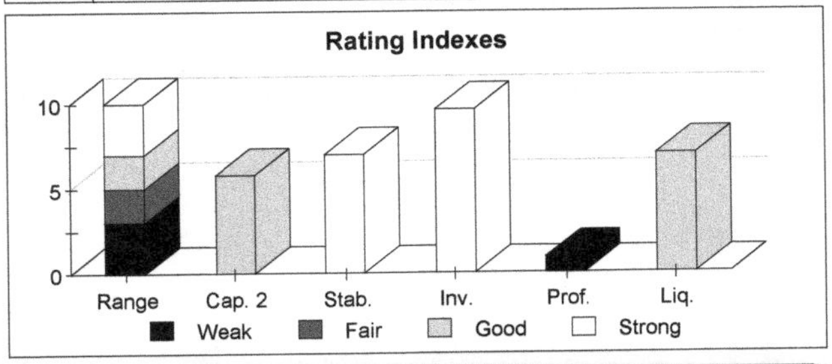


## CARE WISCONSIN HEALTH PLAN INC B Good

**Major Rating Factors:** Good overall profitability index (6.3 on a scale of 0 to 10). Strong capitalization (8.5) based on excellent current risk-adjusted capital (severe loss scenario). High quality investment portfolio (9.6).
**Other Rating Factors:** Excellent liquidity (7.1) with ample operational cash flow and liquid investments.
**Principal Business:** Medicaid (67%), Medicare (33%)
**Mem Phys: 16:** 12,254 **15:** 9,724 **16 MLR** 81.8% **/ 16 Admin Exp** N/A
**Enroll(000): Q3 17:** 3 **16:** 3 **15:** 3 **Med Exp PMPM:** $2,587
**Principal Investments:** Cash and equiv (59%), long-term bonds (36%), nonaffiliate common stock (5%)
**Provider Compensation ($000):** Contr fee ($81,804), FFS ($18,389), other ($1,237)
**Total Member Encounters:** Phys (123,085), non-phys (3,370,928)
**Group Affiliation:** Care Wisconsin First Inc
**Licensed in:** WI
**Address:** 1617 Sherman Ave, Madison, WI 53704
**Phone:** (608) 240-0020 **Dom State:** WI **Commenced Bus:** January 2005

| Data Date | Rating | RACR #1 | RACR #2 | Total Assets ($mil) | Capital ($mil) | Net Premium ($mil) | Net Income ($mil) |
|---|---|---|---|---|---|---|---|
| 9-17 | B | 2.55 | 2.13 | 56.8 | 34.1 | 96.5 | 6.2 |
| 9-16 | B | 2.00 | 1.67 | 42.9 | 26.6 | 94.1 | 5.0 |
| 2016 | B | 2.11 | 1.75 | 43.2 | 28.4 | 124.7 | 6.3 |
| 2015 | C | 1.63 | 1.36 | 34.5 | 21.8 | 118.8 | 11.0 |
| 2014 | C | 0.81 | 0.68 | 28.6 | 10.8 | 102.1 | -9.4 |
| 2013 | B | 1.90 | 1.59 | 30.1 | 20.5 | 92.7 | 4.5 |
| 2012 | C | 1.63 | 1.36 | 24.6 | 15.4 | 87.4 | 6.6 |

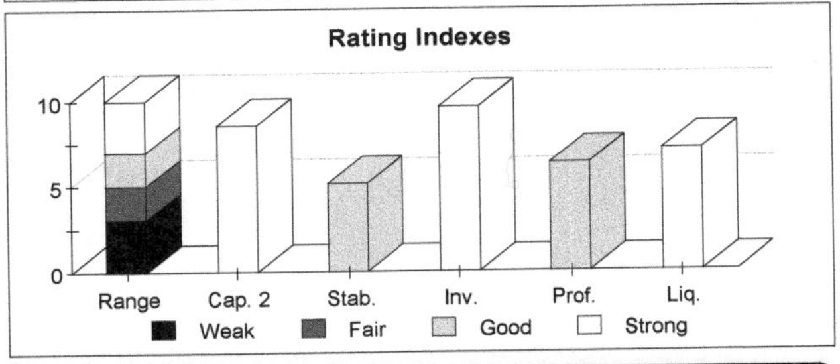


## CARECENTRIX OF NEW JERSEY INC D- Weak

**Major Rating Factors:** Low quality investment portfolio (0.0 on a scale of 0 to 10). Fair profitability index (3.3). Fair capitalization (3.2) based on weak current risk-adjusted capital (moderate loss scenario).
**Other Rating Factors:** Excellent liquidity (9.0) with ample operational cash flow and liquid investments.
**Principal Business:** Other (100%)
**Mem Phys: 16:** 7,000 **15:** 7,000 **16 MLR** 91.6% **/ 16 Admin Exp** N/A
**Enroll(000): 16:** 838 **15:** 871 **Med Exp PMPM:** $1
**Principal Investments:** Cash and equiv (100%)
**Provider Compensation ($000):** FFS ($16,501)
**Total Member Encounters:** N/A
**Group Affiliation:** NDES Holdings LLC
**Licensed in:** NJ
**Address:** 160 Greentree Dr Suite 101, Dover, DE 19904
**Phone:** (631) 501-7017 **Dom State:** NJ **Commenced Bus:** January 2012

| Data Date | Rating | RACR #1 | RACR #2 | Total Assets ($mil) | Capital ($mil) | Net Premium ($mil) | Net Income ($mil) |
|---|---|---|---|---|---|---|---|
| 2016 | D- | 0.66 | 0.55 | 30.9 | 3.4 | 18.0 | -0.4 |
| 2015 | U | 0.43 | 0.36 | 9.9 | 0.8 | 7.1 | -0.2 |
| 2014 | N/A | N/A | N/A | 2.8 | 0.9 | 0.6 | 0.1 |
| 2013 | N/A | N/A | N/A | 2.2 | 0.8 | 0.7 | 0.1 |
| 2012 | N/A | N/A | N/A | 1.5 | 0.7 | 1.4 | 0.6 |

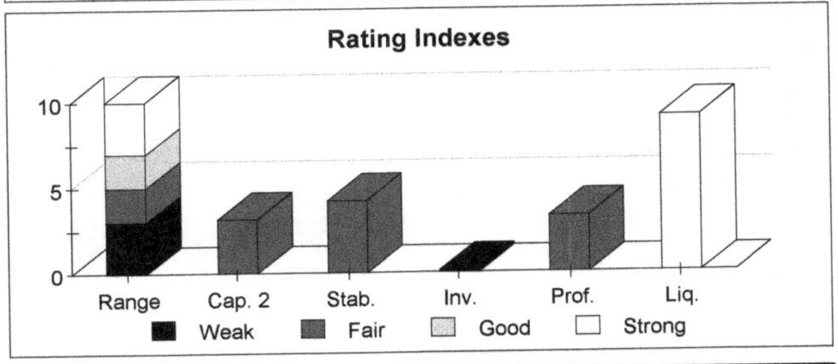

## CARECONNECT INS CO — E- Very Weak

**Major Rating Factors:** Weak profitability index (0.1 on a scale of 0 to 10). Poor capitalization (2.3) based on weak current risk-adjusted capital (moderate loss scenario). Weak liquidity (1.2) as a spike in claims may stretch capacity.
**Other Rating Factors:** High quality investment portfolio (9.9).
**Principal Business:** Comp med (100%)
**Mem Phys: 16:** 23,703 **15:** 19,842 **16 MLR** 122.2% **/ 16 Admin Exp** N/A
**Enroll(000): Q3 17:** 117 **16:** 112 **15:** 69 **Med Exp PMPM:** $384
**Principal Investments:** Cash and equiv (51%), long-term bonds (49%)
**Provider Compensation ($000):** Contr fee ($361,910), capitation ($1,241), bonus arrang ($527)
**Total Member Encounters:** Phys (428,818), non-phys (299,441)
**Group Affiliation:** Northwell Health Inc
**Licensed in:** NY
**Address:** 2200 Nern Blvd Ste 104, East Hills, NY 11548
**Phone:** (516) 405-7500 **Dom State:** NY **Commenced Bus:** October 2013

| Data Date | Rating | RACR #1 | RACR #2 | Total Assets ($mil) | Capital ($mil) | Net Premium ($mil) | Net Income ($mil) |
|---|---|---|---|---|---|---|---|
| 9-17 | E- | 0.53 | 0.44 | 256.0 | 29.2 | 414.3 | -82.5 |
| 9-16 | E- | 0.43 | 0.36 | 187.1 | 6.3 | 264.5 | -93.8 |
| 2016 | E- | 0.61 | 0.51 | 278.9 | 33.0 | 361.1 | -156.2 |
| 2015 | E | 1.50 | 1.25 | 80.3 | 20.5 | 124.6 | -29.8 |
| 2014 | E- | N/A | N/A | 28.5 | -1.8 | 44.4 | -26.8 |
| 2013 | N/A | N/A | N/A | 28.6 | 25.7 | N/A | -12.3 |
| 2012 | N/A | N/A | N/A | N/A | N/A | N/A | N/A |

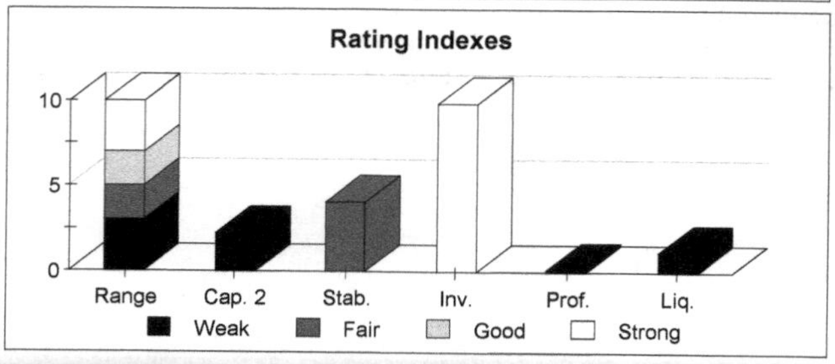


## CARECORE NJ LLC — D- Weak

**Major Rating Factors:** Excellent profitability (8.0 on a scale of 0 to 10). Strong capitalization (7.5) based on excellent current risk-adjusted capital (severe loss scenario). High quality investment portfolio (8.2).
**Other Rating Factors:** Excellent liquidity (6.9) with sufficient resources (cash flows and marketable investments) to handle a spike in claims.
**Principal Business:** Other (100%)
**Mem Phys: 16:** 1,073 **15:** 76 **16 MLR** 86.5% **/ 16 Admin Exp** N/A
**Enroll(000): 16:** 1,299 **15:** 1,155 **Med Exp PMPM:** $7
**Principal Investments:** Cash and equiv (100%)
**Provider Compensation ($000):** Contr fee ($10,612), other ($117,733)
**Total Member Encounters:** N/A
**Group Affiliation:** CareCore National Group LLC
**Licensed in:** NJ
**Address:** 400 Buckwalter Place Blvd, Bluffton, SC 29910
**Phone:** (800) 918-8924 **Dom State:** NJ **Commenced Bus:** March 2005

| Data Date | Rating | RACR #1 | RACR #2 | Total Assets ($mil) | Capital ($mil) | Net Premium ($mil) | Net Income ($mil) |
|---|---|---|---|---|---|---|---|
| 2016 | D- | 1.77 | 1.48 | 21.3 | 6.3 | 148.4 | 3.7 |
| 2015 | U | 9.43 | 7.86 | 21.0 | 12.5 | 140.6 | 18.3 |
| 2014 | N/A | N/A | N/A | 16.7 | 11.7 | 155.8 | 31.3 |
| 2013 | N/A | N/A | N/A | 22.0 | 20.1 | 186.5 | 34.3 |
| 2012 | N/A | N/A | N/A | 47.7 | 46.6 | 185.0 | 35.2 |

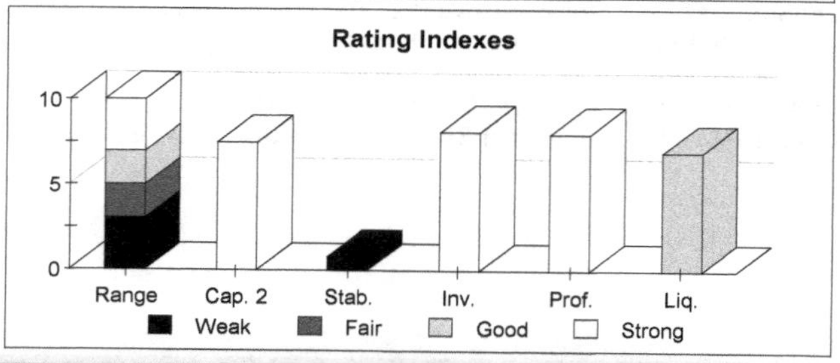


## CAREFIRST BLUECHOICE INC * — A- Excellent

**Major Rating Factors:** Strong capitalization index (10.0 on a scale of 0 to 10) based on excellent current risk-adjusted capital (severe loss scenario). High quality investment portfolio (7.8). Good overall results on stability tests (6.5).
**Other Rating Factors:** Good liquidity (6.8) with sufficient resources (cash flows and marketable investments) to handle a spike in claims. Weak profitability index (2.3).
**Principal Business:** Comp med (87%), FEHB (12%)
**Mem Phys: 16:** 43,663 **15:** 41,749 **16 MLR** 80.1% **/ 16 Admin Exp** N/A
**Enroll(000): Q3 17:** 658 **16:** 669 **15:** 691 **Med Exp PMPM:** $304
**Principal Investments:** Long-term bonds (80%), nonaffiliate common stock (19%), cash and equiv (1%)
**Provider Compensation ($000):** Contr fee ($2,470,977), FFS ($10,703), capitation ($3,294)
**Total Member Encounters:** Phys (4,045,026), non-phys (2,748,526)
**Group Affiliation:** CareFirst Inc
**Licensed in:** DC, MD, VA
**Address:** 840 FIRST STREET NE, WASHINGTON, DC 20065
**Phone:** (410) 581-3000 **Dom State:** DC **Commenced Bus:** March 1985

| Data Date | Rating | RACR #1 | RACR #2 | Total Assets ($mil) | Capital ($mil) | Net Premium ($mil) | Net Income ($mil) |
|---|---|---|---|---|---|---|---|
| 9-17 | A- | 4.70 | 3.91 | 1,137.7 | 694.0 | 2,426.5 | -7.2 |
| 9-16 | A | 5.13 | 4.27 | 1,130.8 | 716.2 | 2,335.1 | -20.4 |
| 2016 | A- | 4.72 | 3.93 | 1,145.5 | 697.5 | 3,102.9 | -46.1 |
| 2015 | A | 5.30 | 4.42 | 1,177.0 | 741.1 | 2,986.5 | -9.9 |
| 2014 | A+ | 5.81 | 4.85 | 1,152.3 | 757.1 | 2,700.8 | 22.1 |
| 2013 | A+ | 6.23 | 5.19 | 1,043.2 | 733.4 | 2,401.3 | 69.2 |
| 2012 | A+ | 6.01 | 5.01 | 992.4 | 671.2 | 2,163.6 | 25.9 |

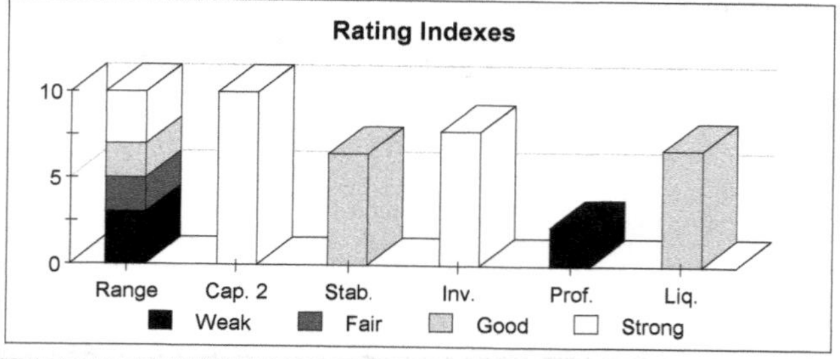

## CAREFIRST OF MARYLAND INC — C+ — Fair

**Major Rating Factors:** Good quality investment portfolio (5.1 on a scale of 0 to 10). Weak profitability index (2.4). Strong capitalization (10.0) based on excellent current risk-adjusted capital (severe loss scenario).
**Other Rating Factors:** Excellent liquidity (6.9) with sufficient resources (cash flows and marketable investments) to handle a spike in claims.
**Principal Business:** FEHB (65%), comp med (22%), med supp (7%), dental (3%), other (2%)
**Mem Phys: 16:** 48,475 **15:** 46,712 **16 MLR** 83.5% **/ 16 Admin Exp** N/A
**Enroll(000): Q3 17:** 561 **16:** 573 **15:** 614 **Med Exp PMPM:** $235
**Principal Investments:** Long-term bonds (29%), nonaffiliate common stock (7%), cash and equiv (3%), other (60%)
**Provider Compensation ($000):** Contr fee ($1,582,682), FFS ($27,835), capitation ($3,962)
**Total Member Encounters:** Phys (5,824,604), non-phys (5,338,187)
**Group Affiliation:** CareFirst Inc
**Licensed in:** DC, MD
**Address:** 1501 S CLINTON St, BALTIMORE, MD 21224
**Phone:** (410) 581-3000 **Dom State:** MD **Commenced Bus:** January 1985

| Data Date | Rating | RACR #1 | RACR #2 | Total Assets ($mil) | Capital ($mil) | Net Premium ($mil) | Net Income ($mil) |
|---|---|---|---|---|---|---|---|
| 9-17 | C+ | 3.69 | 3.07 | 1,419.7 | 563.1 | 1,408.2 | -12.9 |
| 9-16 | C+ | 3.89 | 3.24 | 1,361.0 | 554.7 | 1,461.2 | -19.9 |
| 2016 | C+ | 3.65 | 3.04 | 1,412.3 | 556.2 | 1,946.6 | -21.1 |
| 2015 | C+ | 3.88 | 3.24 | 1,406.7 | 553.5 | 1,914.6 | -9.8 |
| 2014 | B- | 3.78 | 3.15 | 1,369.0 | 537.6 | 1,950.4 | -15.8 |
| 2013 | B | 4.21 | 3.51 | 1,387.1 | 556.5 | 1,867.3 | 22.2 |
| 2012 | B | 3.95 | 3.29 | 1,336.2 | 528.4 | 1,872.1 | 8.1 |

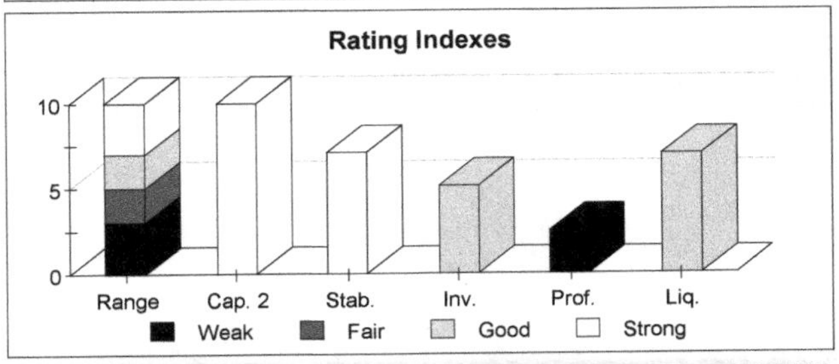


## CAREMORE HEALTH PLAN * — B+ — Good

**Major Rating Factors:** Excellent profitability (7.6 on a scale of 0 to 10). Strong capitalization index (8.3) based on excellent current risk-adjusted capital (severe loss scenario). Excellent overall results on stability tests (7.4). Rating is significantly influenced by the good financial results of Anthem Inc.
**Other Rating Factors:** Excellent liquidity (7.4) with ample operational cash flow and liquid investments.
**Principal Business:** Medicare (100%)
**Mem Phys: 16:** N/A **15:** N/A **16 MLR** 76.9% **/ 16 Admin Exp** N/A
**Enroll(000): Q3 17:** 58 **16:** 57 **15:** 56 **Med Exp PMPM:** $1,082
**Principal Investments ($000):** Cash and equiv ($217,311)
**Provider Compensation ($000):** None
**Total Member Encounters:** N/A
**Group Affiliation:** Anthem Inc
**Licensed in:** CA
**Address:** 12900 Park Plaza Dr Suite 150, Cerritos, CA 90703
**Phone:** (562) 677-2455 **Dom State:** CA **Commenced Bus:** November 2002

| Data Date | Rating | RACR #1 | RACR #2 | Total Assets ($mil) | Capital ($mil) | Net Premium ($mil) | Net Income ($mil) |
|---|---|---|---|---|---|---|---|
| 9-17 | B+ | 3.17 | 1.99 | 317.1 | 94.8 | 735.8 | 46.8 |
| 9-16 | U | 3.11 | 1.95 | 351.4 | 96.1 | 721.5 | 43.7 |
| 2016 | B- | 3.05 | 1.91 | 299.6 | 91.3 | 949.8 | 58.1 |
| 2015 | B+ | 2.78 | 1.75 | 263.4 | 84.4 | 928.2 | 34.6 |
| 2014 | B | 2.82 | 1.78 | 292.6 | 80.5 | 835.7 | 27.1 |
| 2013 | A- | 2.85 | 1.79 | 248.5 | 90.1 | 836.7 | 35.7 |
| 2012 | A- | 2.04 | 1.37 | 215.1 | 91.2 | 810.4 | 61.2 |

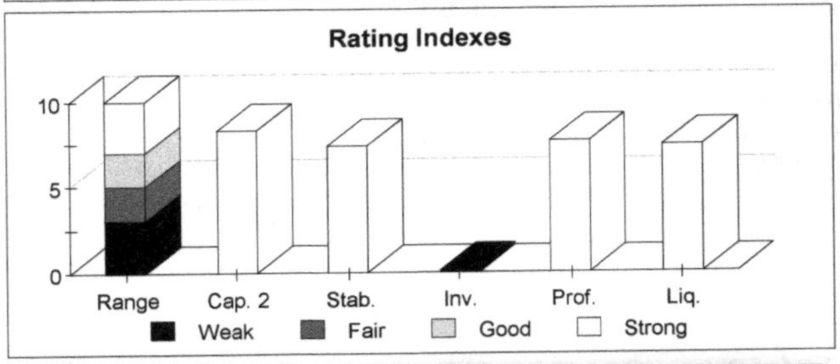


## CAREMORE HEALTH PLAN OF ARIZONA INC — B- — Good

**Major Rating Factors:** Good liquidity (6.2 on a scale of 0 to 10) with sufficient resources (cash flows and marketable investments) to handle a spike in claims. Strong capitalization (10.0) based on excellent current risk-adjusted capital (severe loss scenario). High quality investment portfolio (8.2).
**Other Rating Factors:** Weak profitability index (1.4).
**Principal Business:** Medicare (100%)
**Mem Phys: 16:** 2,945 **15:** 5,077 **16 MLR** 80.2% **/ 16 Admin Exp** N/A
**Enroll(000): Q3 17:** 13 **16:** 12 **15:** 16 **Med Exp PMPM:** $752
**Principal Investments:** Long-term bonds (98%), other (3%)
**Provider Compensation ($000):** Contr fee ($84,594), salary ($19,470), capitation ($9,186), bonus arrang ($2,847)
**Total Member Encounters:** Phys (46,571), non-phys (13,786)
**Group Affiliation:** Anthem Inc
**Licensed in:** AZ
**Address:** 322 WEST ROOSEVELT, PHOENIX, AZ 85003
**Phone:** (562) 622-2900 **Dom State:** AZ **Commenced Bus:** January 2010

| Data Date | Rating | RACR #1 | RACR #2 | Total Assets ($mil) | Capital ($mil) | Net Premium ($mil) | Net Income ($mil) |
|---|---|---|---|---|---|---|---|
| 9-17 | B- | 4.88 | 4.06 | 65.8 | 29.6 | 110.8 | -2.4 |
| 9-16 | B- | 3.03 | 2.53 | 71.1 | 27.9 | 102.6 | 0.0 |
| 2016 | B- | 5.07 | 4.23 | 63.6 | 30.9 | 134.8 | 3.1 |
| 2015 | B- | 3.05 | 2.54 | 66.5 | 28.1 | 199.8 | -7.6 |
| 2014 | B- | 3.96 | 3.30 | 67.2 | 34.6 | 187.6 | 2.0 |
| 2013 | B- | 3.22 | 2.69 | 74.6 | 31.4 | 204.0 | -6.6 |
| 2012 | B- | 3.48 | 2.90 | 64.3 | 32.2 | 164.7 | -7.4 |

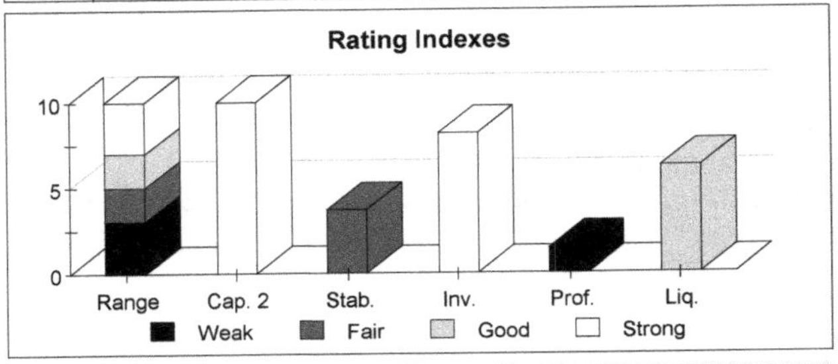

## CAREMORE HEALTH PLAN OF NEVADA — D — Weak

**Major Rating Factors:** Weak profitability index (0.9 on a scale of 0 to 10). Good quality investment portfolio (6.4). Good liquidity (6.9) with sufficient resources (cash flows and marketable investments) to handle a spike in claims.
**Other Rating Factors:** Strong capitalization (9.5) based on excellent current risk-adjusted capital (severe loss scenario).
**Principal Business:** Medicare (100%)
**Mem Phys: 16:** 1,865 **15:** 1,905 **16 MLR** 84.3% **/ 16 Admin Exp** N/A
**Enroll(000): Q3 17:** 8 **16:** 7 **15:** 6 **Med Exp PMPM:** $905
**Principal Investments:** Long-term bonds (53%), cash and equiv (47%)
**Provider Compensation ($000):** Contr fee ($58,029), salary ($9,003), capitation ($8,357), bonus arrang ($859)
**Total Member Encounters:** Phys (33,401), non-phys (7,920)
**Group Affiliation:** Anthem Inc
**Licensed in:** NV
**Address:** 12900 PK PLZ DR #150 M/S-7105, CERRITOS, CA 90703
**Phone:** (562) 622-2900 **Dom State:** NV **Commenced Bus:** January 2010

| Data Date | Rating | RACR #1 | RACR #2 | Total Assets ($mil) | Capital ($mil) | Net Premium ($mil) | Net Income ($mil) |
|---|---|---|---|---|---|---|---|
| 9-17 | D | 3.34 | 2.78 | 40.9 | 15.5 | 73.1 | -3.0 |
| 9-16 | D | 4.13 | 3.44 | 43.6 | 19.2 | 67.5 | 2.0 |
| 2016 | D | 3.75 | 3.13 | 33.7 | 17.6 | 89.4 | 0.8 |
| 2015 | D | 3.64 | 3.04 | 36.3 | 16.8 | 83.7 | -7.0 |
| 2014 | D | 3.94 | 3.29 | 32.7 | 17.9 | 72.0 | 1.0 |
| 2013 | D | 2.58 | 2.15 | 32.5 | 11.1 | 68.2 | -11.5 |
| 2012 | B- | 3.49 | 2.91 | 24.7 | 13.2 | 54.5 | -2.6 |

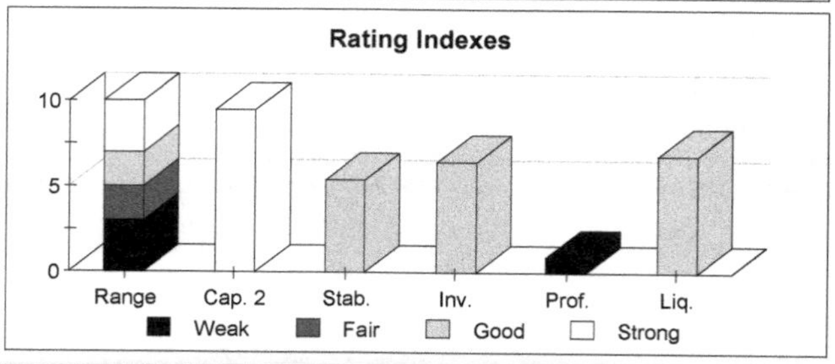


## CAREPLUS HEALTH PLANS INC — B- — Good

**Major Rating Factors:** Fair overall results on stability tests (3.6 on a scale of 0 to 10) based on a steep decline in capital during 2016. Rating is significantly influenced by the good financial results of Humana Inc. Good liquidity (6.7) with sufficient resources (cash flows and marketable investments) to handle a spike in claims. Excellent profitability (8.1).
**Other Rating Factors:** Strong capitalization index (8.9) based on excellent current risk-adjusted capital (severe loss scenario). High quality investment portfolio (9.7).
**Principal Business:** Medicare (100%)
**Mem Phys: 16:** 37,683 **15:** 36,418 **16 MLR** 81.1% **/ 16 Admin Exp** N/A
**Enroll(000): Q3 17:** 107 **16:** 110 **15:** 116 **Med Exp PMPM:** $1,055
**Principal Investments:** Long-term bonds (86%), cash and equiv (14%)
**Provider Compensation ($000):** Contr fee ($640,088), salary ($397,910), capitation ($357,924)
**Total Member Encounters:** Phys (2,297,353), non-phys (553,232)
**Group Affiliation:** Humana Inc
**Licensed in:** FL
**Address:** 11430 NW 20TH STREET SUITE 300, MIAMI, FL 33172
**Phone:** (305) 441-9400 **Dom State:** FL **Commenced Bus:** November 1986

| Data Date | Rating | RACR #1 | RACR #2 | Total Assets ($mil) | Capital ($mil) | Net Premium ($mil) | Net Income ($mil) |
|---|---|---|---|---|---|---|---|
| 9-17 | B- | 2.89 | 2.41 | 597.0 | 132.0 | 1,270.4 | 72.8 |
| 9-16 | C+ | 2.74 | 2.28 | 531.2 | 127.6 | 1,311.5 | 71.1 |
| 2016 | B- | 3.25 | 2.71 | 405.6 | 154.7 | 1,721.4 | 96.8 |
| 2015 | B | 3.86 | 3.21 | 450.5 | 199.7 | 1,754.0 | 142.9 |
| 2014 | B- | 3.25 | 2.71 | 336.1 | 111.4 | 1,379.2 | 56.9 |
| 2013 | C+ | 3.78 | 3.15 | 315.9 | 109.5 | 1,204.3 | 66.5 |
| 2012 | B | 3.00 | 2.50 | 370.7 | 153.5 | 1,186.4 | 108.0 |

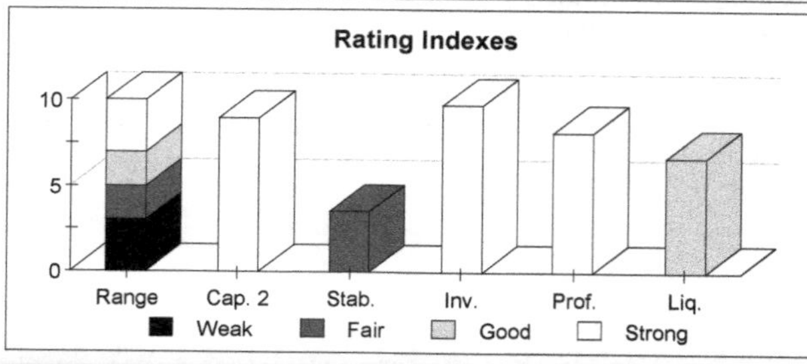


## CARESOURCE — B- — Good

**Major Rating Factors:** Fair profitability index (3.1 on a scale of 0 to 10). Fair overall results on stability tests (3.8) based on a steep decline in capital during 2016, a decline in the number of member physicians during 2017. Good liquidity (6.8) with sufficient resources (cash flows and marketable investments) to handle a spike in claims.
**Other Rating Factors:** Strong capitalization index (7.4) based on excellent current risk-adjusted capital (severe loss scenario). High quality investment portfolio (7.8).
**Principal Business:** Medicaid (93%), Medicare (4%), comp med (3%)
**Mem Phys: 16:** 45,274 **15:** 81,621 **16 MLR** 88.9% **/ 16 Admin Exp** N/A
**Enroll(000): Q3 17:** 1,379 **16:** 1,378 **15:** 1,307 **Med Exp PMPM:** $382
**Principal Investments:** Long-term bonds (48%), cash and equiv (40%), nonaffiliate common stock (11%)
**Provider Compensation ($000):** Contr fee ($5,836,440), capitation ($487,867)
**Total Member Encounters:** Phys (9,450,483), non-phys (8,715,897)
**Group Affiliation:** CareSource Management Group Company
**Licensed in:** OH
**Address:** 230 North Main Street, Dayton, OH 45402
**Phone:** (937) 531-3300 **Dom State:** OH **Commenced Bus:** October 1988

| Data Date | Rating | RACR #1 | RACR #2 | Total Assets ($mil) | Capital ($mil) | Net Premium ($mil) | Net Income ($mil) |
|---|---|---|---|---|---|---|---|
| 9-17 | B- | 1.68 | 1.40 | 1,692.5 | 725.8 | 5,869.1 | -39.9 |
| 9-16 | A- | 1.97 | 1.64 | 1,681.8 | 819.3 | 5,230.9 | -112.0 |
| 2016 | B | 1.71 | 1.42 | 1,608.7 | 740.9 | 7,030.7 | -186.2 |
| 2015 | A- | 2.32 | 1.93 | 1,762.0 | 929.2 | 6,723.9 | 191.0 |
| 2014 | A- | 2.19 | 1.82 | 1,720.9 | 743.5 | 5,607.9 | 160.7 |
| 2013 | A | 2.43 | 2.03 | 1,129.1 | 604.9 | 4,161.9 | 134.9 |
| 2012 | A- | 2.30 | 1.92 | 935.9 | 534.5 | 3,703.5 | 119.8 |

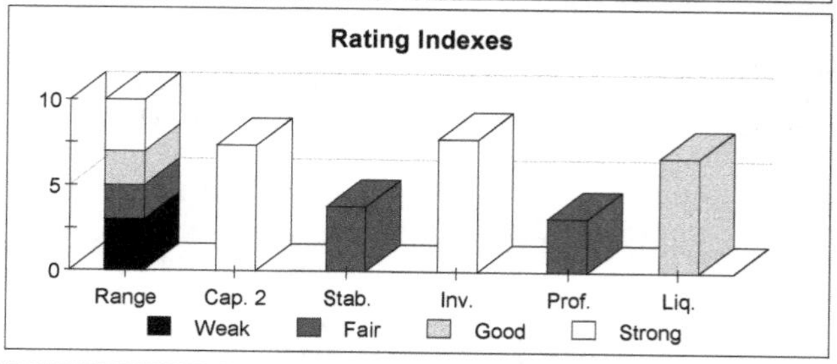

## CARESOURCE INDIANA INC — D+ — Weak

**Major Rating Factors:** Weak profitability index (0.9 on a scale of 0 to 10). Strong capitalization (10.0) based on excellent current risk-adjusted capital (severe loss scenario). High quality investment portfolio (9.9).
**Other Rating Factors:** Excellent liquidity (7.2) with ample operational cash flow and liquid investments.
**Principal Business:** Comp med (91%), Medicare (9%)
**Mem Phys: 16:** 12,014 **15:** 7,221 **16 MLR** 99.8% **/ 16 Admin Exp** N/A
**Enroll(000): Q3 17:** 109 **16:** 26 **15:** 17 **Med Exp PMPM:** $291
**Principal Investments:** Cash and equiv (100%)
**Provider Compensation ($000):** Contr fee ($90,855), capitation ($349)
**Total Member Encounters:** Phys (123,070), non-phys (77,403)
**Group Affiliation:** CareSource Management Group Company
**Licensed in:** IN
**Address:** 135 N Pennsylvania St Ste 1300, Indianapolis, IN 46204
**Phone:** (937) 531-3300 **Dom State:** IN **Commenced Bus:** January 2005

| Data Date | Rating | RACR #1 | RACR #2 | Total Assets ($mil) | Capital ($mil) | Net Premium ($mil) | Net Income ($mil) |
|---|---|---|---|---|---|---|---|
| 9-17 | D+ | 5.39 | 4.49 | 163.5 | 40.7 | 223.5 | 7.4 |
| 9-16 | C | 5.59 | 4.66 | 62.1 | 24.5 | 72.8 | -11.5 |
| 2016 | D+ | 2.15 | 1.79 | 64.6 | 15.9 | 92.4 | -21.6 |
| 2015 | B | 2.05 | 1.71 | 49.8 | 8.6 | 55.6 | -3.0 |
| 2014 | N/A | N/A | N/A | 3.0 | 2.2 | N/A | -0.3 |
| 2013 | N/A | N/A | N/A | 1.6 | 1.6 | N/A | N/A |
| 2012 | N/A | N/A | N/A | 1.9 | 1.9 | N/A | N/A |

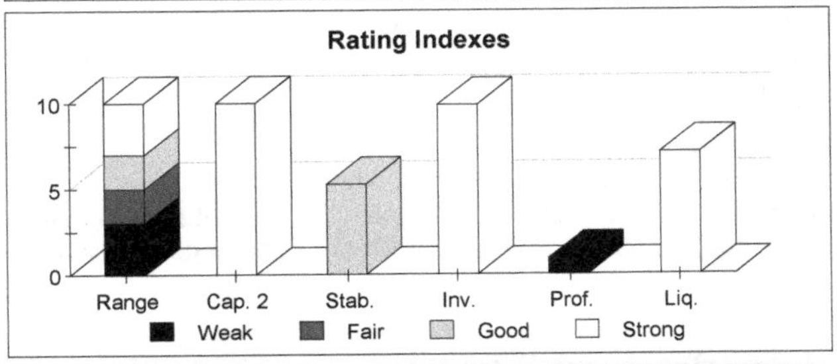


## CARESOURCE KENTUCKY CO — C — Fair

**Major Rating Factors:** Weak profitability index (0.9 on a scale of 0 to 10). Strong capitalization (10.0) based on excellent current risk-adjusted capital (severe loss scenario). High quality investment portfolio (9.9).
**Other Rating Factors:** Excellent liquidity (7.4) with ample operational cash flow and liquid investments.
**Principal Business:** Comp med (93%), Medicare (7%)
**Mem Phys: 16:** 7,428 **15:** 3,803 **16 MLR** 113.8% **/ 16 Admin Exp** N/A
**Enroll(000): Q3 17:** 28 **16:** 12 **15:** 5 **Med Exp PMPM:** $247
**Principal Investments:** Cash and equiv (100%)
**Provider Compensation ($000):** Contr fee ($32,786), capitation ($108)
**Total Member Encounters:** Phys (61,470), non-phys (39,447)
**Group Affiliation:** CareSource Management Group Company
**Licensed in:** KY
**Address:** 230 N Main St, Dayton, OH 45402
**Phone:** (937) 531-3300 **Dom State:** KY **Commenced Bus:** April 2014

| Data Date | Rating | RACR #1 | RACR #2 | Total Assets ($mil) | Capital ($mil) | Net Premium ($mil) | Net Income ($mil) |
|---|---|---|---|---|---|---|---|
| 9-17 | C | 3.64 | 3.03 | 48.3 | 14.2 | 74.3 | -2.2 |
| 9-16 | C | 5.60 | 4.67 | 22.3 | 6.8 | 23.7 | -6.3 |
| 2016 | C | 2.26 | 1.88 | 30.2 | 8.9 | 31.3 | -8.8 |
| 2015 | B | 5.02 | 4.18 | 12.4 | 5.8 | 10.0 | -3.6 |
| 2014 | N/A | N/A | N/A | 3.8 | 3.7 | N/A | -0.3 |
| 2013 | N/A | N/A | N/A | N/A | N/A | N/A | N/A |
| 2012 | N/A | N/A | N/A | N/A | N/A | N/A | N/A |

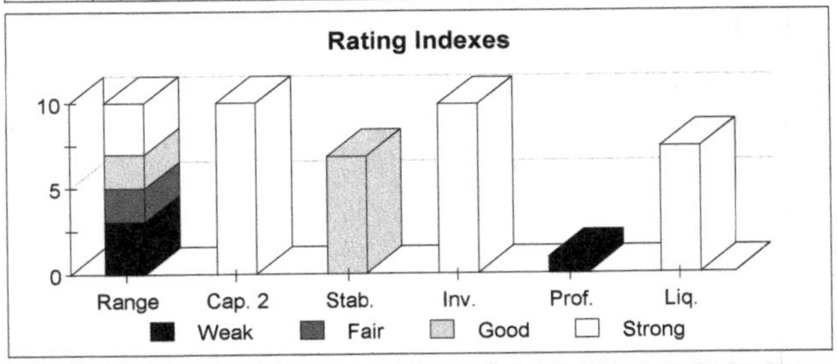


## CARESOURCE WEST VIRGINIA CO — C — Fair

**Major Rating Factors:** Weak profitability index (0.9 on a scale of 0 to 10). Strong capitalization (10.0) based on excellent current risk-adjusted capital (severe loss scenario). High quality investment portfolio (9.9).
**Other Rating Factors:** Excellent liquidity (8.3) with ample operational cash flow and liquid investments.
**Principal Business:** Comp med (100%)
**Mem Phys: 16:** 2,450 **15:** N/A **16 MLR** 101.9% **/ 16 Admin Exp** N/A
**Enroll(000): Q3 17:** 5 **16:** 1 **15:** N/A **Med Exp PMPM:** $350
**Principal Investments:** Cash and equiv (100%)
**Provider Compensation ($000):** Contr fee ($4,212), capitation ($11)
**Total Member Encounters:** Phys (5,424), non-phys (3,137)
**Group Affiliation:** CareSource Management Group Company
**Licensed in:** WV
**Address:** 230 N Main St, Dayton, OH 45402
**Phone:** (937) 531-3300 **Dom State:** WV **Commenced Bus:** April 2015

| Data Date | Rating | RACR #1 | RACR #2 | Total Assets ($mil) | Capital ($mil) | Net Premium ($mil) | Net Income ($mil) |
|---|---|---|---|---|---|---|---|
| 9-17 | C | 4.32 | 3.60 | 22.6 | 5.2 | 23.8 | -3.3 |
| 9-16 | N/A | N/A | N/A | 6.6 | 4.1 | 4.7 | N/A |
| 2016 | C+ | 2.95 | 2.46 | 7.4 | 3.6 | 5.2 | -0.5 |
| 2015 | N/A | N/A | N/A | 4.8 | 4.2 | N/A | -0.3 |
| 2014 | N/A | N/A | N/A | N/A | N/A | N/A | N/A |
| 2013 | N/A | N/A | N/A | N/A | N/A | N/A | N/A |
| 2012 | N/A | N/A | N/A | N/A | N/A | N/A | N/A |

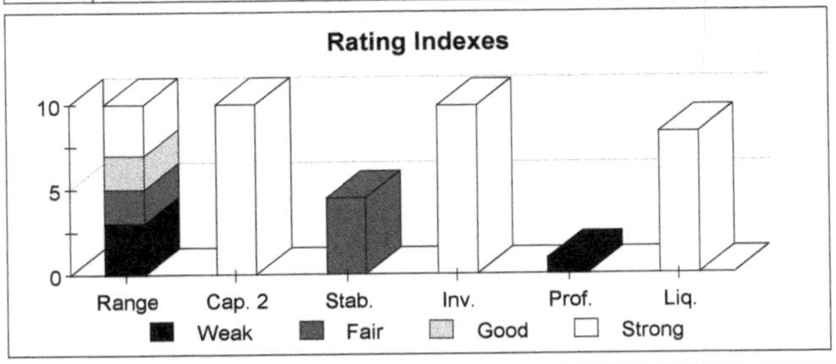

## CARITEN HEALTH PLAN INC B Good

**Major Rating Factors:** Good overall profitability index (6.7 on a scale of 0 to 10). Good overall results on stability tests (5.7) based on steady enrollment growth, averaging 7% over the past five years but a decline in the number of member physicians during 2017. Rating is significantly influenced by the good financial results of Humana Inc. Strong capitalization index (9.7) based on excellent current risk-adjusted capital (severe loss scenario).
**Other Rating Factors:** High quality investment portfolio (9.9). Excellent liquidity (6.9) with sufficient resources (cash flows and marketable investments) to handle a spike in claims.
**Principal Business:** Medicare (100%)
**Mem Phys: 16:** 22,212 **15:** 55,157 **16 MLR** 81.6% **/ 16 Admin Exp** N/A
**Enroll(000): Q3 17:** 117 **16:** 119 **15:** 115 **Med Exp PMPM:** $740
**Principal Investments:** Long-term bonds (58%), cash and equiv (42%)
**Provider Compensation ($000):** Contr fee ($707,592), capitation ($325,501), FFS ($5,653)
**Total Member Encounters:** Phys (2,539,446), non-phys (1,198,054)
**Group Affiliation:** Humana Inc
**Licensed in:** AL, TN
**Address:** 2160 LAKESIDE CENTRE WAY, KNOXVILLE, TN 37922
**Phone:** (865) 470-3993 **Dom State:** TN **Commenced Bus:** December 1995

| Data Date | Rating | RACR #1 | RACR #2 | Total Assets ($mil) | Capital ($mil) | Net Premium ($mil) | Net Income ($mil) |
|---|---|---|---|---|---|---|---|
| 9-17 | B | 3.52 | 2.93 | 527.1 | 203.5 | 1,028.8 | 70.0 |
| 9-16 | B- | 2.73 | 2.28 | 403.1 | 152.7 | 967.4 | 24.9 |
| 2016 | B | 3.03 | 2.53 | 300.4 | 174.0 | 1,283.3 | 44.7 |
| 2015 | B- | 2.59 | 2.16 | 243.2 | 144.6 | 1,173.7 | 12.7 |
| 2014 | B- | 3.07 | 2.56 | 258.4 | 162.2 | 1,094.1 | 12.2 |
| 2013 | B | 3.82 | 3.18 | 286.0 | 178.8 | 1,044.6 | 64.9 |
| 2012 | B- | 2.34 | 1.95 | 238.7 | 115.2 | 857.5 | -18.3 |

Rating Indexes

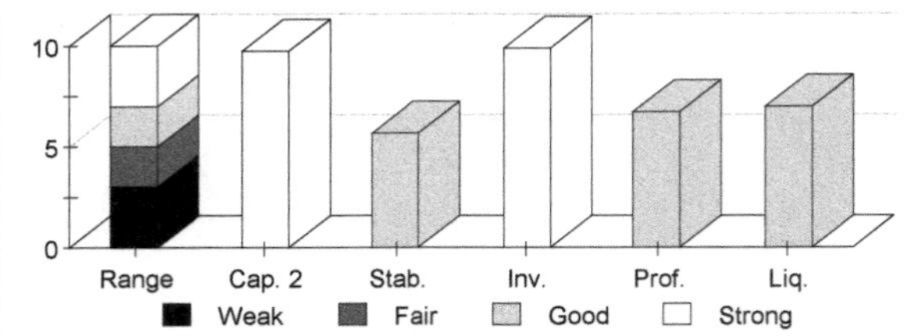


## CATHOLIC SPECIAL NEEDS PLAN LLC C Fair

**Major Rating Factors:** Fair capitalization (3.8 on a scale of 0 to 10) based on fair current risk-adjusted capital (moderate loss scenario). Weak profitability index (2.7). High quality investment portfolio (9.9).
**Other Rating Factors:** Excellent liquidity (7.1) with ample operational cash flow and liquid investments.
**Principal Business:** Medicare (100%)
**Mem Phys: 16:** N/A **15:** N/A **16 MLR** 82.9% **/ 16 Admin Exp** N/A
**Enroll(000): Q3 17:** 2 **16:** 2 **15:** 2 **Med Exp PMPM:** $2,059
**Principal Investments:** Cash and equiv (100%)
**Provider Compensation ($000):** Contr fee ($27,866), capitation ($11,252), bonus arrang ($483)
**Total Member Encounters:** N/A
**Group Affiliation:** Providence Health Services Inc
**Licensed in:** NY
**Address:** 205 Lexington Ave, New York, NY 10016
**Phone:** (646) 633-4702 **Dom State:** NY **Commenced Bus:** January 2008

| Data Date | Rating | RACR #1 | RACR #2 | Total Assets ($mil) | Capital ($mil) | Net Premium ($mil) | Net Income ($mil) |
|---|---|---|---|---|---|---|---|
| 9-17 | C | 0.75 | 0.62 | 18.1 | 5.9 | 33.8 | -0.6 |
| 9-16 | C | 0.76 | 0.63 | 19.5 | 6.0 | 36.3 | 0.2 |
| 2016 | C | 0.83 | 0.69 | 15.1 | 6.3 | 48.3 | 0.4 |
| 2015 | D+ | 0.71 | 0.59 | 14.9 | 5.8 | 46.1 | 0.8 |
| 2014 | D | 0.52 | 0.43 | 12.0 | 4.9 | 42.0 | 1.0 |
| 2013 | D | 0.46 | 0.39 | 10.6 | 4.1 | 39.1 | -0.9 |
| 2012 | B | 1.07 | 0.89 | 13.2 | 7.1 | 37.1 | 0.2 |

Rating Indexes

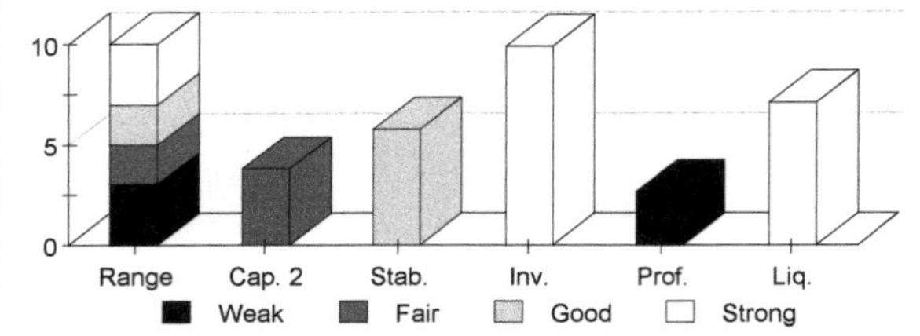


## CDPHP UNIVERSAL BENEFITS INC E+ Very Weak

**Major Rating Factors:** Weak profitability index (1.9 on a scale of 0 to 10). Good liquidity (6.5) with sufficient resources (cash flows and marketable investments) to handle a spike in claims. Strong capitalization (8.5) based on excellent current risk-adjusted capital (severe loss scenario).
**Other Rating Factors:** High quality investment portfolio (9.4).
**Principal Business:** Comp med (84%), FEHB (8%), Medicare (7%), med supp (1%)
**Mem Phys: 16:** 18,814 **15:** 18,372 **16 MLR** 89.2% **/ 16 Admin Exp** N/A
**Enroll(000): Q3 17:** 99 **16:** 118 **15:** 154 **Med Exp PMPM:** $398
**Principal Investments:** Long-term bonds (96%), cash and equiv (4%)
**Provider Compensation ($000):** Contr fee ($588,773), bonus arrang ($16,683), capitation ($3,614), other ($23,878)
**Total Member Encounters:** Phys (974,131), non-phys (363,713)
**Group Affiliation:** Capital District Physician Hlth Plan
**Licensed in:** NY
**Address:** 500 Patroon Creek Blvd, Albany, NY 12206-1057
**Phone:** (518) 641-3000 **Dom State:** NY **Commenced Bus:** January 1998

| Data Date | Rating | RACR #1 | RACR #2 | Total Assets ($mil) | Capital ($mil) | Net Premium ($mil) | Net Income ($mil) |
|---|---|---|---|---|---|---|---|
| 9-17 | E+ | 2.53 | 2.11 | 188.0 | 126.2 | 442.5 | 11.6 |
| 9-16 | E | 1.00 | 0.83 | 162.6 | 59.5 | 535.9 | -22.2 |
| 2016 | E+ | 2.23 | 1.86 | 175.3 | 113.7 | 703.4 | -17.5 |
| 2015 | E | 1.37 | 1.15 | 176.2 | 82.0 | 795.0 | -45.6 |
| 2014 | E | 1.35 | 1.12 | 154.0 | 77.5 | 759.3 | -62.0 |
| 2013 | E | 1.52 | 1.26 | 160.6 | 79.3 | 687.6 | -67.0 |
| 2012 | D | 0.22 | 0.18 | 84.5 | 15.4 | 537.7 | -26.1 |

Rating Indexes

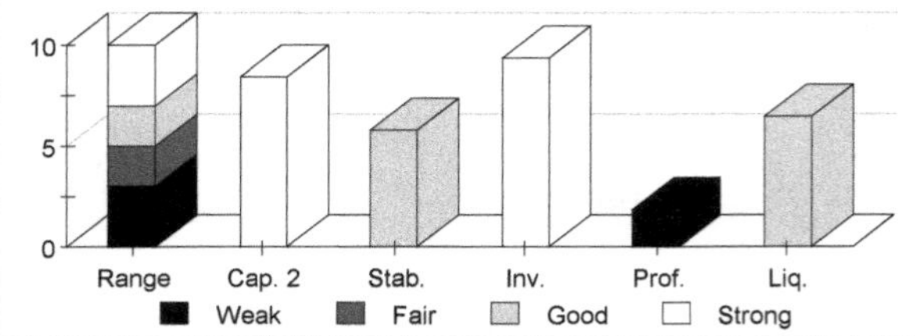

## CELTIC INS CO C+ Fair

**Major Rating Factors:** Excellent profitability (8.3 on a scale of 0 to 10). Strong capitalization (10.0) based on excellent current risk-adjusted capital (severe loss scenario). High quality investment portfolio (9.4).
**Other Rating Factors:** Excellent liquidity (7.2) with ample operational cash flow and liquid investments.
**Principal Business:** Comp med (100%)
**Mem Phys: 16:** 11,056 **15:** 840 **16 MLR** 80.2% **/ 16 Admin Exp** N/A
**Enroll(000): Q3 17:** 568 **16:** 251 **15:** 55 **Med Exp PMPM:** $189
**Principal Investments:** Cash and equiv (51%), long-term bonds (43%), affiliate common stock (6%)
**Provider Compensation ($000):** Contr fee ($438,104), bonus arrang ($80,051), capitation ($18,295), salary ($5,493)
**Total Member Encounters:** Phys (1,273,895), non-phys (1,145,347)
**Group Affiliation:** Centene Corporation
**Licensed in:** All states except PR
**Address:** 77 W Wacker Dr Ste 1200, Chicago, IL 60601
**Phone:** (800) 714-4658 **Dom State:** IL **Commenced Bus:** January 1950

| Data Date | Rating | RACR #1 | RACR #2 | Total Assets ($mil) | Capital ($mil) | Net Premium ($mil) | Net Income ($mil) |
|---|---|---|---|---|---|---|---|
| 9-17 | C+ | 4.01 | 3.34 | 1,115.4 | 179.4 | 1,560.8 | 87.1 |
| 9-16 | C | 13.91 | 11.59 | 498.8 | 68.7 | 601.5 | 18.8 |
| 2016 | C+ | 1.28 | 1.07 | 593.0 | 53.3 | 781.9 | 2.0 |
| 2015 | C- | 8.41 | 7.01 | 139.9 | 38.2 | 170.7 | 8.3 |
| 2014 | N/A | N/A | N/A | 136.6 | 29.4 | 129.8 | N/A |
| 2013 | N/A | N/A | N/A | 83.5 | 43.8 | 125.1 | N/A |
| 2012 | N/A | N/A | N/A | 100.0 | 43.7 | 154.7 | N/A |

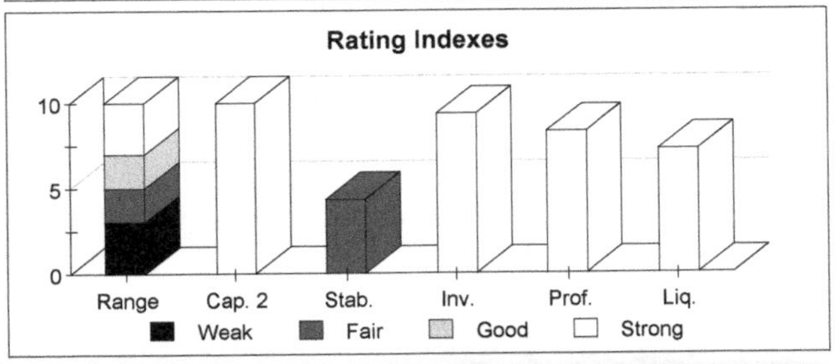


## CELTICARE HEALTH PLAN OF MA INC C Fair

**Major Rating Factors:** Good overall profitability index (6.4 on a scale of 0 to 10). Strong capitalization (9.6) based on excellent current risk-adjusted capital (severe loss scenario). High quality investment portfolio (8.4).
**Other Rating Factors:** Excellent liquidity (6.9) with sufficient resources (cash flows and marketable investments) to handle a spike in claims.
**Principal Business:** Medicaid (98%), comp med (2%)
**Mem Phys: 16:** 12,019 **15:** 9,060 **16 MLR** 81.9% **/ 16 Admin Exp** N/A
**Enroll(000): Q3 17:** 40 **16:** 40 **15:** 51 **Med Exp PMPM:** $293
**Principal Investments:** Long-term bonds (81%), cash and equiv (12%), other (7%)
**Provider Compensation ($000):** Contr fee ($123,824), bonus arrang ($14,918), salary ($4,739), capitation ($2,282)
**Total Member Encounters:** Phys (153,060), non-phys (152,347)
**Group Affiliation:** Centene Corporation
**Licensed in:** MA
**Address:** 200 West St Ste 250, Waltham, MA 02451
**Phone:** (314) 725-4706 **Dom State:** MA **Commenced Bus:** May 2009

| Data Date | Rating | RACR #1 | RACR #2 | Total Assets ($mil) | Capital ($mil) | Net Premium ($mil) | Net Income ($mil) |
|---|---|---|---|---|---|---|---|
| 9-17 | C | 3.46 | 2.88 | 67.8 | 33.6 | 134.3 | 1.8 |
| 9-16 | C | 5.05 | 4.20 | 74.6 | 45.6 | 133.9 | 4.9 |
| 2016 | C+ | 4.70 | 3.92 | 80.7 | 46.4 | 174.2 | 5.6 |
| 2015 | C+ | 6.11 | 5.09 | 99.6 | 55.7 | 220.1 | 26.6 |
| 2014 | C+ | 3.67 | 3.05 | 62.9 | 29.4 | 179.5 | 14.6 |
| 2013 | C | 3.00 | 2.50 | 18.2 | 11.6 | 54.4 | -1.5 |
| 2012 | B- | 1.69 | 1.41 | 32.2 | 13.2 | 119.8 | 0.1 |

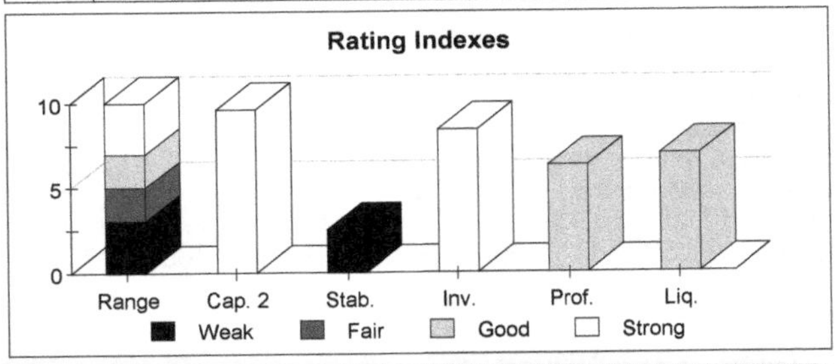


## CENPATICO OF ARIZONA INC C+ Fair

**Major Rating Factors:** Good liquidity (6.9 on a scale of 0 to 10) with sufficient resources (cash flows and marketable investments) to handle a spike in claims. Weak profitability index (2.5). Strong capitalization (7.8) based on excellent current risk-adjusted capital (severe loss scenario).
**Other Rating Factors:** High quality investment portfolio (9.9).
**Principal Business:** Medicaid (100%)
**Mem Phys: 16:** 6,843 **15:** 4,401 **16 MLR** 93.1% **/ 16 Admin Exp** N/A
**Enroll(000): Q3 17:** 443 **16:** 442 **15:** 434 **Med Exp PMPM:** $116
**Principal Investments:** Cash and equiv (51%), long-term bonds (49%)
**Provider Compensation ($000):** Capitation ($324,137), contr fee ($266,884), salary ($11,212), bonus arrang ($703), FFS ($262)
**Total Member Encounters:** Phys (693,793), non-phys (3,891,308)
**Group Affiliation:** Centene Corporation
**Licensed in:** AZ
**Address:** 1501 W Fountainhead Pkwy #360, Tempe, AZ 85282
**Phone:** (314) 725-4477 **Dom State:** AZ **Commenced Bus:** December 2013

| Data Date | Rating | RACR #1 | RACR #2 | Total Assets ($mil) | Capital ($mil) | Net Premium ($mil) | Net Income ($mil) |
|---|---|---|---|---|---|---|---|
| 9-17 | C+ | 1.97 | 1.64 | 128.2 | 60.3 | 513.4 | -6.0 |
| 9-16 | U | 7.97 | 6.64 | 105.6 | 61.9 | 484.4 | 2.3 |
| 2016 | C- | 2.14 | 1.78 | 111.6 | 65.4 | 655.7 | 2.3 |
| 2015 | U | 7.54 | 6.29 | 96.6 | 58.5 | 160.0 | 1.9 |
| 2014 | N/A | N/A | N/A | 1.5 | 1.5 | N/A | N/A |
| 2013 | N/A | N/A | N/A | 1.5 | 1.5 | N/A | N/A |
| 2012 | N/A | N/A | N/A | N/A | N/A | N/A | N/A |

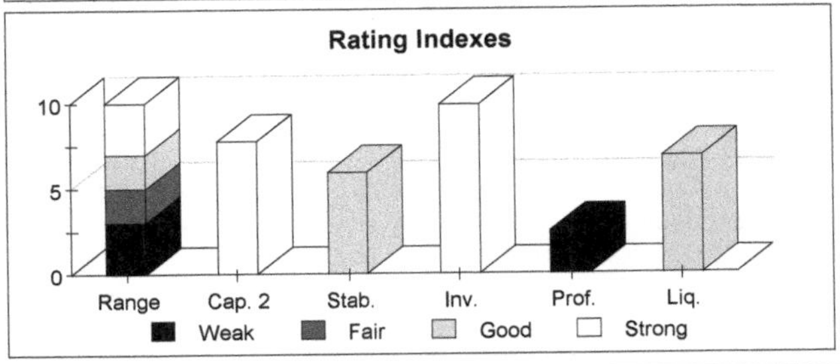

## CENTRAL HEALTH PLAN OF CALIFORNIA E+ Very Weak

**Major Rating Factors:** Poor capitalization index (0.0 on a scale of 0 to 10) based on weak current risk-adjusted capital (severe loss scenario). Weak liquidity (0.0) as a spike in claims may stretch capacity. Good overall results on stability tests (6.0) despite fair risk diversification due to the company's size.
**Other Rating Factors:** Excellent profitability (7.2).
**Principal Business:** Medicare (100%)
**Mem Phys: 16:** N/A **15:** N/A **16 MLR** 86.7% **/ 16 Admin Exp** N/A
**Enroll(000): Q3 17:** 36 **16:** 34 **15:** 30 **Med Exp PMPM:** $773
**Principal Investments ($000):** Cash and equiv ($34,921)
**Provider Compensation ($000):** None
**Total Member Encounters:** N/A
**Group Affiliation:** AHMC Central Health LLC
**Licensed in:** CA
**Address:** 1540 Bridgegate Drive, Diamond Bar, CA 91765
**Phone:** (626) 388-2390 **Dom State:** CA **Commenced Bus:** October 2004

| Data Date | Rating | RACR #1 | RACR #2 | Total Assets ($mil) | Capital ($mil) | Net Premium ($mil) | Net Income ($mil) |
|---|---|---|---|---|---|---|---|
| 9-17 | E+ | 0.39 | 0.24 | 101.1 | 16.7 | 273.4 | 4.2 |
| 9-16 | E+ | 0.30 | 0.19 | 72.2 | 13.9 | 255.8 | 1.9 |
| 2016 | E+ | 0.33 | 0.20 | 56.6 | 15.0 | 351.5 | 2.9 |
| 2015 | E+ | 0.29 | 0.18 | 43.8 | 13.6 | 298.5 | 3.5 |
| 2014 | E+ | 0.13 | 0.08 | 24.0 | 8.6 | 183.2 | -0.2 |
| 2013 | E+ | 0.18 | 0.11 | 25.0 | 8.8 | 128.6 | 1.2 |
| 2012 | E+ | 0.14 | 0.09 | 27.5 | 7.6 | 127.2 | 4.4 |

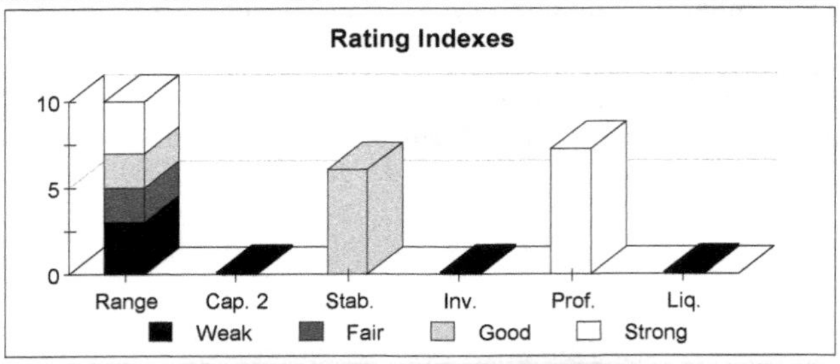


## CENTRAL STATES HEALTH & LIFE COMPANY OF OMAHA * A- Excellent

**Major Rating Factors:** Good quality investment portfolio (5.8 on a scale of 0 to 10) despite mixed results such as: minimal exposure to mortgages and substantial holdings of BBB bonds but minimal holdings in junk bonds. Good overall results on stability tests (5.5) despite negative cash flow from operations for 2016. Strengths that enhance stability include good operational trends and excellent risk diversification. Strong capitalization (10.0) based on excellent risk adjusted capital (severe loss scenario).
**Other Rating Factors:** Excellent profitability (8.1). Excellent liquidity (7.5).
**Principal Business:** Credit life insurance (54%), credit health insurance (31%), individual health insurance (11%), group health insurance (2%), and individual life insurance (2%).
**Principal Investments:** NonCMO investment grade bonds (43%), CMOs and structured securities (26%), common & preferred stock (12%), mortgages in good standing (5%), and misc. investments (15%).
**Investments in Affiliates:** 6%
**Group Affiliation:** Central States Group
**Licensed in:** All states except NY, PR
**Commenced Business:** June 1932
**Address:** 1212 North 96th Street, Omaha, NE 68114
**Phone:** (402) 397-1111 **Domicile State:** NE **NAIC Code:** 61751

| Data Date | Rating | RACR #1 | RACR #2 | Total Assets ($mil) | Capital ($mil) | Net Premium ($mil) | Net Income ($mil) |
|---|---|---|---|---|---|---|---|
| 9-17 | A- | 4.51 | 3.21 | 411.0 | 146.7 | 30.1 | 10.6 |
| 9-16 | A- | 4.14 | 2.94 | 419.8 | 130.7 | 40.3 | 7.1 |
| 2016 | A- | 4.28 | 3.06 | 420.0 | 134.3 | 51.3 | 10.5 |
| 2015 | A- | 3.99 | 2.88 | 419.9 | 122.9 | 66.1 | 6.4 |
| 2014 | A- | 3.79 | 2.71 | 414.7 | 119.6 | 72.7 | 5.5 |
| 2013 | A- | 3.98 | 2.85 | 395.5 | 119.6 | 77.1 | 0.2 |
| 2012 | A- | 4.26 | 3.06 | 372.0 | 111.0 | 72.2 | 3.8 |

**Adverse Trends in Operations**

Decrease in premium volume from 2015 to 2016 (22%)
Decrease in premium volume from 2014 to 2015 (9%)
Decrease in premium volume from 2013 to 2014 (6%)

## CENTRAL STATES INDEMNITY CO OF OMAHA C+ Fair

**Major Rating Factors:** Fair overall results on stability tests (4.5 on a scale of 0 to 10) including potential drain of affiliation with Berkshire-Hathaway and weak results on operational trends. Good overall profitability index (6.8). Weak expense controls. Return on equity has been fair, averaging 5.9% over the past five years.
**Other Rating Factors:** Strong long-term capitalization index (9.1) based on excellent current risk adjusted capital (severe and moderate loss scenarios), despite some fluctuation in capital levels. Ample reserve history (7.4) that can protect against increases in claims costs. Excellent liquidity (8.1) with ample operational cash flow and liquid investments.
**Principal Business:** Other accident & health (59%), inland marine (26%), aggregate write-ins for other lines of business (9%), credit accident & health (4%), and aircraft (2%).
**Principal Investments:** Misc. investments (72%), investment grade bonds (27%), and cash (1%).
**Investments in Affiliates:** 3%
**Group Affiliation:** Berkshire-Hathaway
**Licensed in:** All states, the District of Columbia and Puerto Rico
**Commenced Business:** June 1977
**Address:** 1212 North 96th Street, Omaha, NE 68114
**Phone:** (402) 997-8000 **Domicile State:** NE **NAIC Code:** 34274

| Data Date | Rating | RACR #1 | RACR #2 | Loss Ratio % | Total Assets ($mil) | Capital ($mil) | Net Premium ($mil) | Net Income ($mil) |
|---|---|---|---|---|---|---|---|---|
| 9-17 | C+ | 3.87 | 2.43 | N/A | 498.9 | 411.0 | 47.3 | 67.2 |
| 9-16 | C+ | 4.29 | 2.74 | N/A | 399.5 | 343.9 | 44.1 | 4.3 |
| 2016 | C+ | 3.82 | 2.42 | 60.2 | 447.9 | 378.0 | 59.6 | 8.0 |
| 2015 | C+ | 4.00 | 2.50 | 55.4 | 417.3 | 354.9 | 55.0 | 9.5 |
| 2014 | C+ | 4.12 | 2.63 | 44.6 | 435.0 | 363.7 | 50.2 | 11.4 |
| 2013 | B+ | 4.34 | 2.79 | 36.2 | 412.3 | 346.0 | 43.0 | 17.7 |
| 2012 | B+ | 4.34 | 2.69 | 18.3 | 335.1 | 285.5 | 32.2 | 13.1 |

**Berkshire-Hathaway**
**Composite Group Rating: B**

| Largest Group Members | Assets ($mil) | Rating |
|---|---|---|
| NATIONAL INDEMNITY CO | 178623 | B |
| GOVERNMENT EMPLOYEES INS CO | 27198 | B |
| COLUMBIA INS CO | 20707 | U |
| BERKSHIRE HATHAWAY LIFE INS CO OF NE | 17970 | C+ |
| GENERAL REINS CORP | 14780 | C+ |

## CENTRAL UNITED LIFE INSURANCE COMPANY C Fair

**Major Rating Factors:** Fair capitalization (3.6 on a scale of 0 to 10) based on fair risk adjusted capital (severe loss scenario). Fair overall results on stability tests (3.6) including fair risk adjusted capital in prior years. Good quality investment portfolio (5.2) despite significant exposure to mortgages . Mortgage default rate has been low. substantial holdings of BBB bonds in addition to minimal holdings in junk bonds.

**Other Rating Factors:** Good liquidity (6.1). Excellent profitability (7.6) despite modest operating losses during 2016.

**Principal Business:** Individual health insurance (65%), reinsurance (23%), group health insurance (9%), and individual life insurance (3%).

**Principal Investments:** Common & preferred stock (37%), nonCMO investment grade bonds (35%), mortgages in good standing (12%), real estate (7%), and misc. investments (4%).

**Investments in Affiliates:** 37%

**Group Affiliation:** Manhattan Life Group Inc

**Licensed in:** All states except CT, FL, NJ, NY, RI, PR

**Commenced Business:** September 1963

**Address:** 425 W Capitol Ave Ste 1800, Little Rock, AR 72201

**Phone:** (713) 529-0045 **Domicile State:** AR **NAIC Code:** 61883

| Data Date | Rating | RACR #1 | RACR #2 | Total Assets ($mil) | Capital ($mil) | Net Premium ($mil) | Net Income ($mil) |
|---|---|---|---|---|---|---|---|
| 9-17 | C | 0.64 | 0.58 | 390.7 | 102.0 | 84.0 | 5.5 |
| 9-16 | C | 0.62 | 0.56 | 380.8 | 92.1 | 75.1 | -4.0 |
| 2016 | C | 0.61 | 0.55 | 385.0 | 95.6 | 99.9 | -1.6 |
| 2015 | C | 0.64 | 0.59 | 327.0 | 92.9 | 100.0 | 2.6 |
| 2014 | C | 0.58 | 0.53 | 305.1 | 76.8 | 92.7 | 3.9 |
| 2013 | C | 0.59 | 0.54 | 307.2 | 76.6 | 88.8 | 3.8 |
| 2012 | C | 0.77 | 0.67 | 302.0 | 59.7 | 92.0 | 8.8 |

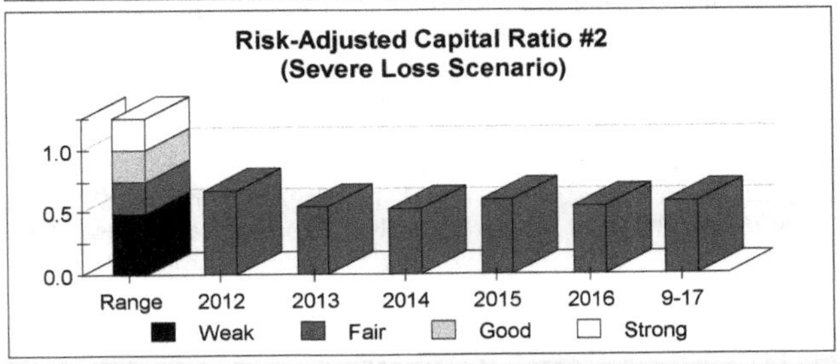


## CENTRE LIFE INSURANCE COMPANY B- Good

**Major Rating Factors:** Good quality investment portfolio (6.7 on a scale of 0 to 10) with no exposure to mortgages and minimal holdings in junk bonds. Fair overall results on stability tests (4.5) including fair financial strength of affiliated Zurich Financial Services Group and negative cash flow from operations for 2016. Weak profitability (2.7) with operating losses during the first nine months of 2017.

**Other Rating Factors:** Strong capitalization (9.2) based on excellent risk adjusted capital (severe loss scenario). Excellent liquidity (9.4).

**Principal Business:** Reinsurance (60%) and individual health insurance (40%).

**Principal Investments:** NonCMO investment grade bonds (82%) and CMOs and structured securities (17%).

**Investments in Affiliates:** None

**Group Affiliation:** Zurich Financial Services Group

**Licensed in:** All states except PR

**Commenced Business:** October 1927

**Address:** 1350 MAIN STREET SUITE 1600, SPRINGFIELD, MA 01103-1641

**Phone:** (212) 859-2640 **Domicile State:** MA **NAIC Code:** 80896

| Data Date | Rating | RACR #1 | RACR #2 | Total Assets ($mil) | Capital ($mil) | Net Premium ($mil) | Net Income ($mil) |
|---|---|---|---|---|---|---|---|
| 9-17 | B- | 4.01 | 2.49 | 1,834.2 | 93.3 | 1.0 | -0.8 |
| 9-16 | B- | 3.98 | 2.60 | 1,831.5 | 95.0 | 1.0 | 0.7 |
| 2016 | B- | 4.03 | 2.48 | 1,809.8 | 93.8 | 1.4 | -0.5 |
| 2015 | B- | 3.94 | 2.57 | 1,884.1 | 94.5 | 1.9 | -3.7 |
| 2014 | B- | 4.03 | 2.54 | 1,926.1 | 98.0 | 0.0 | -2.7 |
| 2013 | B- | 4.13 | 2.67 | 1,927.7 | 101.2 | 0.0 | 1.9 |
| 2012 | C+ | 4.15 | 2.72 | 1,815.1 | 98.8 | 0.0 | 0.3 |

| Zurich Financial Services Group<br>Composite Group Rating: C+<br>Largest Group Members | Assets ($mil) | Rating |
|---|---|---|
| ZURICH AMERICAN INS CO | 31003 | B- |
| ZURICH AMERICAN LIFE INS CO | 12330 | C |
| FARMERS NEW WORLD LIFE INS CO | 7155 | B- |
| CENTRE LIFE INS CO | 1810 | B- |
| RURAL COMMUNITY INS CO | 1754 | C+ |

## CENTURION LIFE INSURANCE COMPANY D+ Weak

**Major Rating Factors:** Weak profitability (2.0 on a scale of 0 to 10) with investment income below regulatory standards in relation to interest assumptions of reserves. Weak overall results on stability tests (2.8) including negative cash flow from operations for 2016. Good quality investment portfolio (6.9).

**Other Rating Factors:** Strong capitalization (9.4) based on excellent risk adjusted capital (severe loss scenario). Excellent liquidity (7.5).

**Principal Business:** Reinsurance (100%).

**Principal Investments:** NonCMO investment grade bonds (68%), CMOs and structured securities (26%), noninv. grade bonds (4%), and cash (2%).

**Investments in Affiliates:** None

**Group Affiliation:** Wells Fargo Group

**Licensed in:** All states except ME, NY, VT, PR

**Commenced Business:** July 1956

**Address:** 800 WALNUT STREET, DES MOINES, IA 50309

**Phone:** (515) 557-7321 **Domicile State:** IA **NAIC Code:** 62383

| Data Date | Rating | RACR #1 | RACR #2 | Total Assets ($mil) | Capital ($mil) | Net Premium ($mil) | Net Income ($mil) |
|---|---|---|---|---|---|---|---|
| 9-17 | D+ | 4.40 | 2.57 | 1,267.7 | 368.1 | 160.7 | 50.7 |
| 9-16 | D | 3.60 | 2.15 | 1,284.0 | 312.4 | 126.5 | 16.5 |
| 2016 | D | 3.82 | 2.23 | 1,288.2 | 317.7 | 172.8 | 22.5 |
| 2015 | D | 3.59 | 2.17 | 1,262.6 | 293.9 | 179.0 | 52.0 |
| 2014 | D | 2.64 | 1.59 | 1,259.3 | 251.2 | 314.0 | -165.5 |
| 2013 | D | 4.92 | 2.88 | 1,209.0 | 397.3 | 204.6 | -227.0 |
| 2012 | C+ | 20.93 | 10.33 | 1,475.0 | 599.9 | 13.7 | 39.4 |

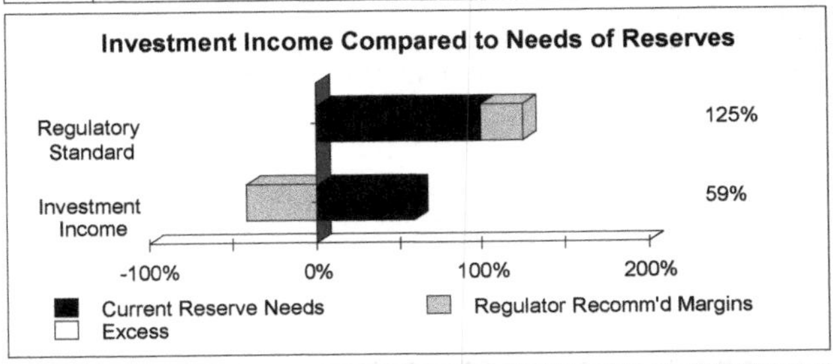

## CHA HMO INC — C+ Fair

**Major Rating Factors:** Fair overall results on stability tests (4.2 on a scale of 0 to 10) based on a decline in the number of member physicians during 2017, an excessive 44% enrollment growth during the period. Rating is significantly influenced by the good financial results of Humana Inc. Good liquidity (6.4) with sufficient resources (cash flows and marketable investments) to handle a spike in claims. Weak profitability index (1.1).
**Other Rating Factors:** Strong capitalization index (10.0) based on excellent current risk-adjusted capital (severe loss scenario). High quality investment portfolio (9.4).
**Principal Business:** Medicare (100%)
**Mem Phys: 16:** 23,057 **15:** 29,348 **16 MLR** 87.5% **/ 16 Admin Exp** N/A
**Enroll(000): Q3 17:** 18 **16:** 17 **15:** 11 **Med Exp PMPM:** $587
**Principal Investments:** Long-term bonds (93%), cash and equiv (7%)
**Provider Compensation ($000):** Capitation ($57,853), contr fee ($50,327), FFS ($1,092)
**Total Member Encounters:** Phys (269,789), non-phys (136,584)
**Group Affiliation:** Humana Inc
**Licensed in:** HI, IN, IA, KY, NE, SD
**Address:** 500 WEST MAIN STREET, LOUISVILLE, KY 40202
**Phone:** (502) 580-1000 **Dom State:** KY **Commenced Bus:** July 1995

| Data Date | Rating | RACR #1 | RACR #2 | Total Assets ($mil) | Capital ($mil) | Net Premium ($mil) | Net Income ($mil) |
|---|---|---|---|---|---|---|---|
| 9-17 | C+ | 3.83 | 3.19 | 59.2 | 23.5 | 121.1 | 0.4 |
| 9-16 | C+ | 5.44 | 4.54 | 49.9 | 21.4 | 95.6 | -2.4 |
| 2016 | C+ | 3.79 | 3.16 | 33.0 | 23.3 | 128.3 | 0.0 |
| 2015 | C+ | 6.07 | 5.06 | 32.6 | 24.0 | 77.6 | -4.5 |
| 2014 | C | 10.04 | 8.37 | 32.7 | 27.2 | 33.3 | -1.6 |
| 2013 | C | 9.65 | 8.04 | 33.3 | 29.2 | 25.8 | -2.6 |
| 2012 | N/A | N/A | N/A | 31.6 | 31.5 | N/A | 0.9 |

**Rating Indexes**

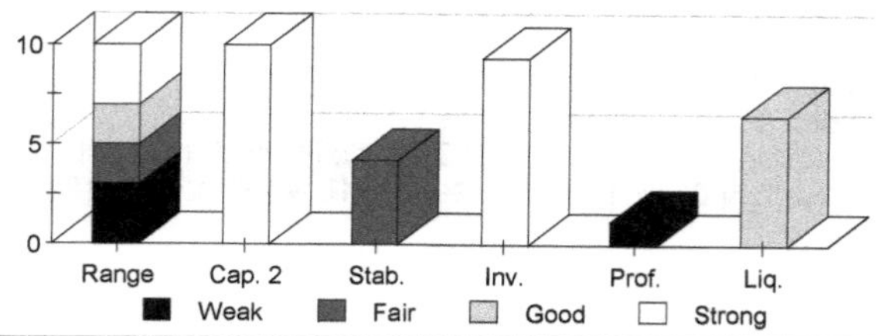


## CHESAPEAKE LIFE INSURANCE COMPANY — B Good

**Major Rating Factors:** Good overall profitability (6.0 on a scale of 0 to 10). Good overall results on stability tests (5.4) despite fair risk adjusted capital in prior years. Other stability subfactors include good operational trends and good risk diversification. Strong current capitalization (8.2) based on excellent risk adjusted capital (severe loss scenario) reflecting significant improvement over results in 2013.
**Other Rating Factors:** High quality investment portfolio (9.0). Excellent liquidity (8.3).
**Principal Business:** Individual health insurance (80%), individual life insurance (19%), and reinsurance (1%).
**Principal Investments:** NonCMO investment grade bonds (97%), cash (2%), and CMOs and structured securities (1%).
**Investments in Affiliates:** None
**Group Affiliation:** Blackstone Investor Group
**Licensed in:** All states except NJ, NY, VT, PR
**Commenced Business:** October 1956
**Address:** 1833 SOUTH MORGAN ROAD, OKLAHOMA CITY, OK 73128
**Phone:** (817) 255-3100 **Domicile State:** OK **NAIC Code:** 61832

| Data Date | Rating | RACR #1 | RACR #2 | Total Assets ($mil) | Capital ($mil) | Net Premium ($mil) | Net Income ($mil) |
|---|---|---|---|---|---|---|---|
| 9-17 | B | 2.28 | 1.81 | 157.9 | 91.0 | 150.0 | 12.9 |
| 9-16 | C+ | 1.89 | 1.51 | 128.0 | 70.4 | 137.9 | 9.3 |
| 2016 | C+ | 1.85 | 1.47 | 133.3 | 69.7 | 184.3 | 11.6 |
| 2015 | C+ | 1.38 | 1.11 | 99.8 | 46.8 | 159.6 | -0.9 |
| 2014 | C+ | 1.40 | 1.11 | 75.1 | 43.1 | 119.4 | 0.4 |
| 2013 | C+ | 0.85 | 0.67 | 42.5 | 20.9 | 82.6 | -3.2 |
| 2012 | C+ | 1.60 | 1.22 | 36.2 | 23.3 | 47.1 | -2.1 |

**Adverse Trends in Operations**

Increase in policy surrenders from 2015 to 2016 (122%)
Change in asset mix during 2016 (5%)
Increase in policy surrenders from 2014 to 2015 (922%)
Change in asset mix during 2014 (4.7%)
Decrease in capital during 2013 (11%)

## CHILDRENS COMMUNITY HEALTH PLAN INC — B Good

**Major Rating Factors:** Good overall profitability index (5.8 on a scale of 0 to 10). Strong capitalization (7.6) based on excellent current risk-adjusted capital (severe loss scenario). High quality investment portfolio (9.8).
**Other Rating Factors:** Excellent liquidity (7.0) with ample operational cash flow and liquid investments.
**Principal Business:** Medicaid (100%)
**Mem Phys: 16:** 13,173 **15:** 12,650 **16 MLR** 88.2% **/ 16 Admin Exp** N/A
**Enroll(000): Q3 17:** 131 **16:** 130 **15:** 133 **Med Exp PMPM:** $131
**Principal Investments:** Cash and equiv (69%), long-term bonds (31%)
**Provider Compensation ($000):** Contr fee ($195,311), capitation ($14,836)
**Total Member Encounters:** Phys (386,700), non-phys (93,993)
**Group Affiliation:** Childrens Hospital and Health System
**Licensed in:** WI
**Address:** 9000 W Wisconsin Ave, Milwaukee, WI 53226
**Phone:** (800) 482-8010 **Dom State:** WI **Commenced Bus:** January 2010

| Data Date | Rating | RACR #1 | RACR #2 | Total Assets ($mil) | Capital ($mil) | Net Premium ($mil) | Net Income ($mil) |
|---|---|---|---|---|---|---|---|
| 9-17 | B | 1.80 | 1.50 | 79.4 | 40.9 | 190.9 | -3.4 |
| 9-16 | B | 1.95 | 1.62 | 75.6 | 44.5 | 176.9 | 4.1 |
| 2016 | B | 1.95 | 1.63 | 85.3 | 44.1 | 235.8 | 4.2 |
| 2015 | B | 1.72 | 1.43 | 81.3 | 39.7 | 237.6 | 10.7 |
| 2014 | C- | 1.31 | 1.09 | 70.3 | 29.8 | 314.2 | 9.7 |
| 2013 | C- | 0.93 | 0.77 | 67.0 | 20.0 | 274.9 | -2.0 |
| 2012 | C- | 0.99 | 0.83 | 27.8 | 9.0 | 103.6 | -3.3 |

**Rating Indexes**

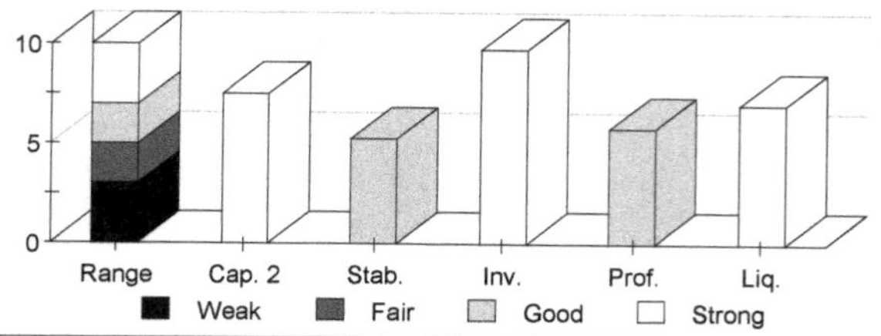

## CHILDRENS MEDICAL CENTER HEALTH PLAN E- Very Weak

**Major Rating Factors:** Weak profitability index (0.9 on a scale of 0 to 10). Good liquidity (5.5) with sufficient resources (cash flows and marketable investments) to handle a spike in claims. Strong capitalization (8.4) based on excellent current risk-adjusted capital (severe loss scenario).
**Other Rating Factors:** High quality investment portfolio (9.9).
**Principal Business:** Medicaid (100%)
**Mem Phys: 16:** 7,861 **15:** N/A **16 MLR** 94.5% **/ 16 Admin Exp** N/A
**Enroll(000): Q3 17:** 10 **16:** 9 **15:** N/A **Med Exp PMPM:** $1,900
**Principal Investments:** Cash and equiv (100%)
**Provider Compensation ($000):** FFS ($16,322), contr fee ($32), capitation ($24)
**Total Member Encounters:** Phys (19,368), non-phys (8,107)
**Group Affiliation:** Childrens Health System of Texas
**Licensed in:** TX
**Address:** 1320 GREENWAY DR Ste 1000, IRVING, TX 75038
**Phone:** (214) 456-7000 **Dom State:** TX **Commenced Bus:** April 2013

| Data Date | Rating | RACR #1 | RACR #2 | Total Assets ($mil) | Capital ($mil) | Net Premium ($mil) | Net Income ($mil) |
|---|---|---|---|---|---|---|---|
| 9-17 | E- | 2.48 | 2.07 | 54.8 | 21.5 | 175.8 | -34.3 |
| 9-16 | N/A | N/A | N/A | 6.8 | 4.6 | N/A | -7.9 |
| 2016 | D+ | 1.16 | 0.97 | 31.7 | 10.3 | 38.2 | -13.4 |
| 2015 | N/A | N/A | N/A | 4.5 | 3.7 | N/A | -4.6 |
| 2014 | N/A | N/A | N/A | 4.8 | 3.3 | N/A | -4.1 |
| 2013 | N/A | N/A | N/A | N/A | N/A | N/A | N/A |
| 2012 | N/A | N/A | N/A | N/A | N/A | N/A | N/A |

**Rating Indexes**

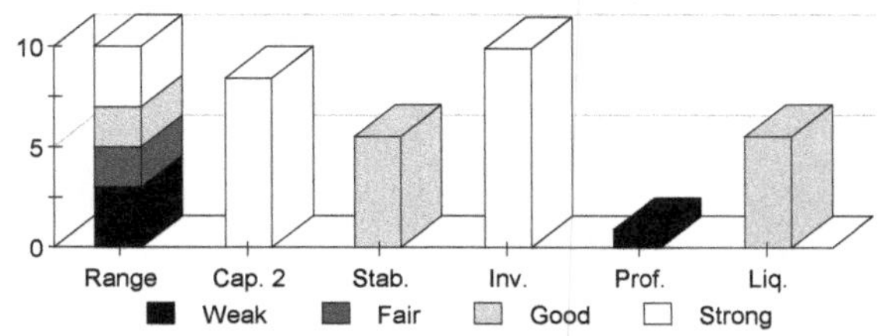


## CHOICE PHYSICIANS NETWORK E+ Very Weak

**Major Rating Factors:** Poor capitalization index (0.0 on a scale of 0 to 10) based on weak current risk-adjusted capital (severe loss scenario). Weak liquidity (1.0) as a spike in claims may stretch capacity. Fair profitability index (4.9).
**Other Rating Factors:** Fair overall results on stability tests (4.2) based on an excessive 55% enrollment growth during the period but healthy premium and capital growth during 2016.
**Principal Business:** Managed care (100%)
**Mem Phys: 16:** N/A **15:** N/A **16 MLR** 104.4% **/ 16 Admin Exp** N/A
**Enroll(000): Q3 17:** 14 **16:** 15 **15:** 10 **Med Exp PMPM:** N/A
**Principal Investments ($000):** Cash and equiv ($9,691)
**Provider Compensation ($000):** None
**Total Member Encounters:** N/A
**Group Affiliation:** None
**Licensed in:** CA
**Address:** 18564 Hwy 18 Ste 105, Apple Valley, CA 92307
**Phone:** (626) 229-9828 **Dom State:** CA **Commenced Bus:** September 2009

| Data Date | Rating | RACR #1 | RACR #2 | Total Assets ($mil) | Capital ($mil) | Net Premium ($mil) | Net Income ($mil) |
|---|---|---|---|---|---|---|---|
| 9-17 | E+ | 0.37 | 0.22 | 20.8 | 4.6 | 97.2 | 0.2 |
| 9-16 | E+ | 0.53 | 0.32 | 18.4 | 4.6 | 79.0 | -0.1 |
| 2016 | E+ | 0.34 | 0.21 | 17.3 | 4.3 | 105.6 | -0.5 |
| 2015 | D- | 0.38 | 0.23 | 12.0 | 3.4 | 78.5 | 0.0 |
| 2014 | D | 0.59 | 0.36 | 10.8 | 4.1 | 63.8 | 1.0 |
| 2013 | D+ | 0.59 | 0.36 | 8.4 | 3.1 | 50.0 | 2.4 |
| 2012 | D- | 0.58 | 0.35 | 6.4 | 2.6 | 43.4 | 0.2 |

**Rating Indexes**

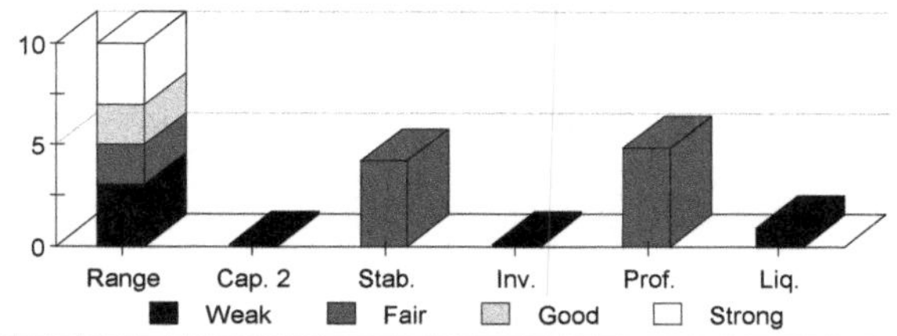


## CHRISTIAN FIDELITY LIFE INSURANCE COMPANY B Good

**Major Rating Factors:** Good overall results on stability tests (6.2 on a scale of 0 to 10). Stability strengths include excellent operational trends and good risk diversification. Good liquidity (6.9) with sufficient resources to handle a spike in claims. Strong capitalization (9.4) based on excellent risk adjusted capital (severe loss scenario).
**Other Rating Factors:** High quality investment portfolio (7.8). Excellent profitability (7.9).
**Principal Business:** Individual health insurance (88%), group health insurance (8%), and individual life insurance (4%).
**Principal Investments:** NonCMO investment grade bonds (89%), mortgages in good standing (4%), CMOs and structured securities (4%), policy loans (1%), and misc. investments (2%).
**Investments in Affiliates:** None
**Group Affiliation:** Amerco Corp
**Licensed in:** AL, AZ, AR, CO, FL, GA, ID, IL, IN, KS, KY, LA, MS, MO, MT, NE, NV, NM, ND, OH, OK, OR, SC, SD, TN, TX, UT, VA, WA, WV, WY
**Commenced Business:** December 1935
**Address:** 1999 Bryan Street Suite 900, Dallas, TX 75201
**Phone:** (602) 263-6666 **Domicile State:** TX **NAIC Code:** 61859

| Data Date | Rating | RACR #1 | RACR #2 | Total Assets ($mil) | Capital ($mil) | Net Premium ($mil) | Net Income ($mil) |
|---|---|---|---|---|---|---|---|
| 9-17 | B | 3.53 | 2.58 | 67.6 | 34.0 | 23.3 | 6.0 |
| 9-16 | B | 3.36 | 2.46 | 70.8 | 34.8 | 26.2 | 5.8 |
| 2016 | B | 2.75 | 2.03 | 63.9 | 28.0 | 34.5 | 8.1 |
| 2015 | B | 2.63 | 1.93 | 68.8 | 28.9 | 38.7 | 9.2 |
| 2014 | B- | 2.36 | 1.75 | 71.2 | 28.6 | 43.6 | 9.2 |
| 2013 | B- | 2.20 | 1.63 | 75.4 | 28.8 | 48.9 | 9.6 |
| 2012 | B- | 2.00 | 1.49 | 77.9 | 28.0 | 54.3 | 8.7 |

**Adverse Trends in Operations**

Decrease in premium volume from 2015 to 2016 (11%)
Decrease in premium volume from 2013 to 2014 (11%)
Increase in policy surrenders from 2013 to 2014 (138%)
Increase in policy surrenders from 2012 to 2013 (178%)
Decrease in premium volume from 2012 to 2013 (10%)

## CHRISTUS HEALTH PLAN C- Fair

**Major Rating Factors:** Weak profitability index (0.9 on a scale of 0 to 10). Good capitalization (6.4) based on good current risk-adjusted capital (severe loss scenario). High quality investment portfolio (9.9).
**Other Rating Factors:** Excellent liquidity (7.0) with sufficient resources (cash flows and marketable investments) to handle a spike in claims.
**Principal Business:** Comp med (69%), Medicaid (28%), Medicare (3%)
**Mem Phys: 16:** N/A **15:** 13,330 **16 MLR** 96.4% **/ 16 Admin Exp** N/A
**Enroll(000): Q3 17:** 35 **16:** 20 **15:** 8 **Med Exp PMPM:** $253
**Principal Investments:** Cash and equiv (100%)
**Provider Compensation ($000):** FFS ($50,613)
**Total Member Encounters:** N/A
**Group Affiliation:** CHRISTUS Health
**Licensed in:** NM, TX
**Address:** 919 Hidden Ridge Dr, Irving, TX 75038
**Phone:** (469) 282-2000 **Dom State:** TX **Commenced Bus:** March 2012

| Data Date | Rating | RACR #1 | RACR #2 | Total Assets ($mil) | Capital ($mil) | Net Premium ($mil) | Net Income ($mil) |
|---|---|---|---|---|---|---|---|
| 9-17 | C- | 1.14 | 0.95 | 48.9 | 12.5 | 95.7 | -2.5 |
| 9-16 | C- | 1.38 | 1.15 | 23.6 | 7.3 | 59.9 | 0.0 |
| 2016 | C- | 0.84 | 0.70 | 35.5 | 9.4 | 64.7 | -11.4 |
| 2015 | C- | 1.44 | 1.20 | 10.7 | 7.6 | 21.2 | -5.2 |
| 2014 | C+ | 3.15 | 2.62 | 15.8 | 12.8 | 20.5 | -2.8 |
| 2013 | B- | 3.91 | 3.26 | 18.4 | 15.4 | 29.7 | 1.7 |
| 2012 | C- | 4.12 | 3.43 | 21.9 | 13.1 | 17.9 | 0.6 |

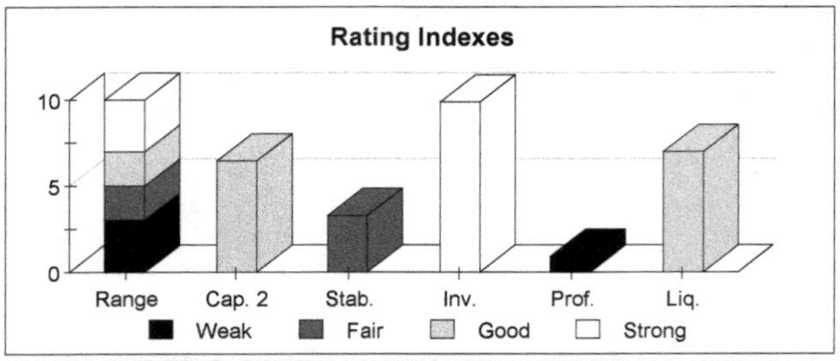


## CIGNA HEALTH & LIFE INSURANCE COMPANY B Good

**Major Rating Factors:** Good overall results on stability tests (5.6 on a scale of 0 to 10). Stability strengths include excellent operational trends and excellent risk diversification. Fair quality investment portfolio (3.7) with large holdings of BBB rated bonds in addition to moderate junk bond exposure. Fair liquidity (4.9).
**Other Rating Factors:** Strong capitalization (7.6) based on excellent risk adjusted capital (severe loss scenario). Excellent profitability (9.9).
**Principal Business:** Group health insurance (84%), individual health insurance (15%), and reinsurance (1%).
**Principal Investments:** NonCMO investment grade bonds (44%), noninv. grade bonds (20%), common & preferred stock (9%), mortgages in good standing (8%), and misc. investments (19%).
**Investments in Affiliates:** 17%
**Group Affiliation:** CIGNA Corp
**Licensed in:** All states, the District of Columbia and Puerto Rico
**Commenced Business:** February 1964
**Address:** 900 COTTAGE GROVE ROAD, BLOOMFIELD, CT 6002
**Phone:** (860) 226-6000 **Domicile State:** CT **NAIC Code:** 67369

| Data Date | Rating | RACR #1 | RACR #2 | Total Assets ($mil) | Capital ($mil) | Net Premium ($mil) | Net Income ($mil) |
|---|---|---|---|---|---|---|---|
| 9-17 | B | 1.82 | 1.40 | 8,705.3 | 3,606.0 | 10,344.4 | 1,336.5 |
| 9-16 | B | 1.80 | 1.42 | 7,124.9 | 3,240.3 | 8,680.1 | 1,054.0 |
| 2016 | B | 1.86 | 1.43 | 7,410.9 | 3,390.1 | 11,625.2 | 1,396.6 |
| 2015 | B | 1.66 | 1.31 | 6,559.9 | 3,008.9 | 11,457.7 | 1,187.2 |
| 2014 | B | 1.89 | 1.48 | 6,204.5 | 2,799.7 | 9,789.3 | 1,047.0 |
| 2013 | B | 1.68 | 1.37 | 4,139.3 | 1,713.2 | 6,456.2 | 489.1 |
| 2012 | B | 1.92 | 1.66 | 1,681.4 | 1,017.9 | 1,883.9 | 300.7 |

**Adverse Trends in Operations**

Increase in policy surrenders from 2015 to 2016 (27%)
Change in asset mix during 2014 (5.3%)
Change in asset mix during 2013 (5.1%)

## CIGNA HEALTHCARE OF ARIZONA INC E- Very Weak

**Major Rating Factors:** Weak profitability index (0.9 on a scale of 0 to 10). Fair overall results on stability tests (4.6) based on inconsistent enrollment growth in the past five years due to declines in 2014 and 2016, a decline in the number of member physicians during 2017. Rating is significantly influenced by the good financial results of Cigna Corporation. Good liquidity (6.2) with sufficient resources (cash flows and marketable investments) to handle a spike in claims.
**Other Rating Factors:** Strong capitalization index (7.6) based on excellent current risk-adjusted capital (severe loss scenario). High quality investment portfolio (9.9).
**Principal Business:** Medicare (95%), comp med (11%)
**Mem Phys: 16:** 15,916 **15:** 25,678 **16 MLR** 99.0% **/ 16 Admin Exp** N/A
**Enroll(000): Q3 17:** 48 **16:** 57 **15:** 60 **Med Exp PMPM:** $723
**Principal Investments:** Cash and equiv (66%), long-term bonds (21%), real estate (13%)
**Provider Compensation ($000):** Contr fee ($260,986), FFS ($144,649), capitation ($69,689), salary ($58,374), other ($22,166)
**Total Member Encounters:** Phys (471,465), non-phys (113,083)
**Group Affiliation:** Cigna Corporation
**Licensed in:** AZ
**Address:** 25500 NNORTERRA DR, PHOENIX, AZ 85085-8200
**Phone:** (860) 226-5076 **Dom State:** AZ **Commenced Bus:** March 1979

| Data Date | Rating | RACR #1 | RACR #2 | Total Assets ($mil) | Capital ($mil) | Net Premium ($mil) | Net Income ($mil) |
|---|---|---|---|---|---|---|---|
| 9-17 | E- | 1.80 | 1.50 | 161.2 | 58.0 | 337.7 | -11.4 |
| 9-16 | E- | 0.49 | 0.41 | 123.2 | 8.3 | 436.5 | -26.3 |
| 2016 | E- | 2.05 | 1.71 | 130.3 | 66.6 | 566.0 | -36.2 |
| 2015 | C | 1.46 | 1.21 | 94.6 | 39.0 | 536.7 | -19.7 |
| 2014 | C | 1.74 | 1.45 | 84.2 | 38.4 | 457.0 | -16.9 |
| 2013 | C+ | 1.82 | 1.51 | 107.1 | 48.4 | 507.6 | 1.1 |
| 2012 | C | 2.34 | 1.95 | 120.7 | 58.3 | 488.6 | 8.9 |

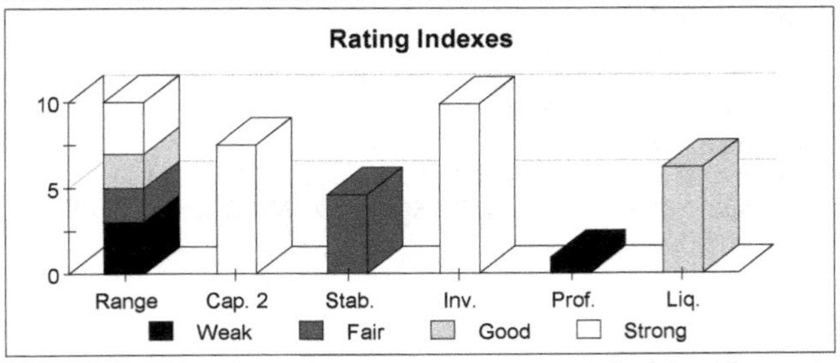

## CIGNA HEALTHCARE OF CALIFORNIA INC | C | Fair

**Major Rating Factors:** Weak profitability index (0.9 on a scale of 0 to 10). Good overall results on stability tests (5.1). Rating is significantly influenced by the good financial results of CIGNA Corp. Good liquidity (6.9) with sufficient resources (cash flows and marketable investments) to handle a spike in claims.
**Other Rating Factors:** Strong capitalization index (7.0) based on good current risk-adjusted capital (moderate loss scenario).
**Principal Business:** Managed care (100%)
**Mem Phys: 16:** N/A **15:** N/A **16 MLR** 91.9% **/ 16 Admin Exp** N/A
**Enroll(000): Q3 17:** 176 **16:** 174 **15:** 182 **Med Exp PMPM:** $1,629
**Principal Investments ($000):** Cash and equiv ($92,097)
**Provider Compensation ($000):** None
**Total Member Encounters:** N/A
**Group Affiliation:** CIGNA Corp
**Licensed in:** CA
**Address:** 400 N Brand Blvd Suite #400, Glendale, CA 91203
**Phone:** (818) 500-6276 **Dom State:** CA **Commenced Bus:** November 1978

| Data Date | Rating | RACR #1 | RACR #2 | Total Assets ($mil) | Capital ($mil) | Net Premium ($mil) | Net Income ($mil) |
|---|---|---|---|---|---|---|---|
| 9-17 | C | 1.16 | 0.71 | 146.6 | 36.1 | 741.5 | -11.3 |
| 9-16 | C | 1.24 | 0.76 | 163.1 | 39.4 | 692.4 | -10.8 |
| 2016 | C | 1.25 | 0.77 | 148.9 | 40.0 | 915.6 | -16.5 |
| 2015 | C | 1.18 | 0.72 | 134.5 | 37.0 | 950.8 | -18.6 |
| 2014 | B | 1.48 | 0.91 | 158.5 | 51.3 | 959.4 | 0.9 |
| 2013 | B | 1.43 | 0.87 | 156.0 | 49.9 | 944.4 | 5.9 |
| 2012 | C+ | 1.67 | 1.02 | 160.3 | 54.9 | 950.7 | 6.1 |

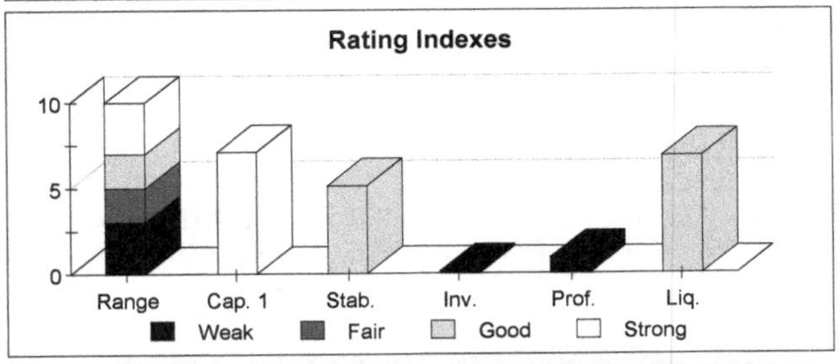


## CIGNA HEALTHCARE OF COLORADO INC | C | Fair

**Major Rating Factors:** Weak profitability index (1.6 on a scale of 0 to 10). Weak overall results on stability tests (2.2) based on a significant 38% decrease in enrollment during the period. Rating is significantly influenced by the good financial results of Cigna Corporation. Weak liquidity (2.1) as a spike in claims may stretch capacity.
**Other Rating Factors:** Strong capitalization index (10.0) based on excellent current risk-adjusted capital (severe loss scenario). High quality investment portfolio (9.3).
**Principal Business:** Comp med (100%)
**Mem Phys: 16:** 13,307 **15:** 14,316 **16 MLR** 133.9% **/ 16 Admin Exp** N/A
**Enroll(000): Q3 17:** 1 **16:** 1 **15:** 1 **Med Exp PMPM:** $602
**Principal Investments:** Long-term bonds (100%)
**Provider Compensation ($000):** Contr fee ($4,015), FFS ($1,081), capitation ($148)
**Total Member Encounters:** Phys (3,601), non-phys (1,233)
**Group Affiliation:** Cigna Corporation
**Licensed in:** CO
**Address:** 3900 EAST MEXICO AVENUE SUITE, DENVER, CO 80210
**Phone:** (860) 226-6000 **Dom State:** CO **Commenced Bus:** May 1986

| Data Date | Rating | RACR #1 | RACR #2 | Total Assets ($mil) | Capital ($mil) | Net Premium ($mil) | Net Income ($mil) |
|---|---|---|---|---|---|---|---|
| 9-17 | C | 6.68 | 5.57 | 5.8 | 3.8 | 3.8 | 1.6 |
| 9-16 | C | 4.13 | 3.44 | 3.6 | 2.5 | 3.6 | 0.2 |
| 2016 | C | 3.99 | 3.32 | 4.3 | 2.0 | 4.8 | -1.2 |
| 2015 | C | 3.88 | 3.24 | 4.1 | 2.3 | 7.1 | -0.9 |
| 2014 | C | 6.00 | 5.00 | 4.8 | 3.2 | 7.6 | 0.2 |
| 2013 | C | 7.07 | 5.90 | 5.5 | 4.4 | 9.8 | 1.1 |
| 2012 | C | 5.82 | 4.85 | 7.0 | 5.3 | 11.4 | 0.0 |

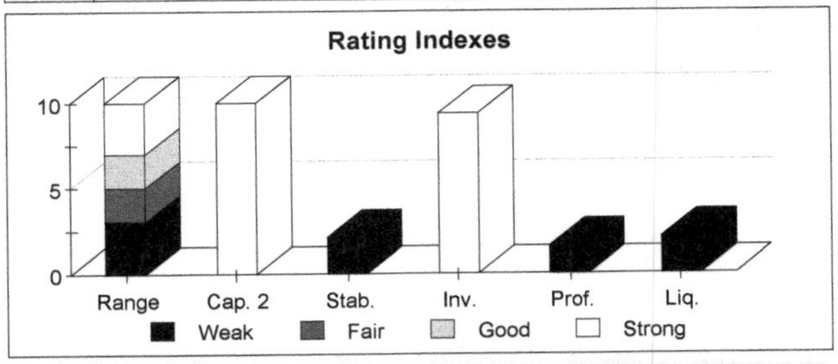


## CIGNA HEALTHCARE OF FLORIDA INC | C | Fair

**Major Rating Factors:** Fair overall results on stability tests (4.3 on a scale of 0 to 10) based on a significant 16% decrease in enrollment during the period. Rating is significantly influenced by the good financial results of Cigna Corporation. Weak profitability index (1.8). Strong capitalization index (10.0) based on excellent current risk-adjusted capital (severe loss scenario).
**Other Rating Factors:** High quality investment portfolio (9.9). Excellent liquidity (8.6) with ample operational cash flow and liquid investments.
**Principal Business:** Comp med (100%)
**Mem Phys: 16:** 89,623 **15:** 97,746 **16 MLR** 93.9% **/ 16 Admin Exp** N/A
**Enroll(000): Q3 17:** 0 **16:** 0 **15:** 0 **Med Exp PMPM:** $387
**Principal Investments:** Long-term bonds (58%), cash and equiv (42%)
**Provider Compensation ($000):** Contr fee ($692), FFS ($185), capitation ($58)
**Total Member Encounters:** Phys (950), non-phys (289)
**Group Affiliation:** Cigna Corporation
**Licensed in:** FL
**Address:** 2701 NORTH ROCKY POINT DRIVE S, TAMPA, FL 33607
**Phone:** (860) 226-4014 **Dom State:** FL **Commenced Bus:** February 1981

| Data Date | Rating | RACR #1 | RACR #2 | Total Assets ($mil) | Capital ($mil) | Net Premium ($mil) | Net Income ($mil) |
|---|---|---|---|---|---|---|---|
| 9-17 | C | 6.94 | 5.78 | 4.2 | 3.8 | 1.1 | 0.1 |
| 9-16 | C | 6.73 | 5.61 | 4.2 | 3.6 | 0.7 | -0.3 |
| 2016 | C | 6.97 | 5.81 | 4.2 | 3.8 | 1.0 | -0.1 |
| 2015 | C | 7.23 | 6.03 | 4.3 | 3.9 | 1.3 | -0.1 |
| 2014 | C | 7.85 | 6.54 | 4.4 | 4.0 | 1.3 | -0.2 |
| 2013 | C | 9.04 | 7.53 | 4.6 | 4.1 | 1.2 | 0.2 |
| 2012 | C | 9.58 | 7.98 | 5.1 | 3.9 | 5.6 | -0.2 |

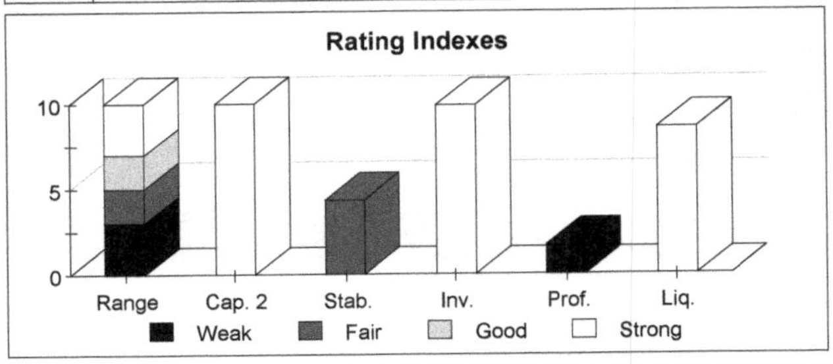

## CIGNA HEALTHCARE OF GEORGIA INC — E — Very Weak

**Major Rating Factors:** Weak profitability index (0.9 on a scale of 0 to 10). Fair overall results on stability tests (3.8) in spite of healthy premium and capital growth during 2016 but a decline in the number of member physicians during 2017 and an excessive 71% enrollment growth during the period. Rating is significantly influenced by the good financial results of Cigna Corporation. Good liquidity (6.3) with sufficient resources (cash flows and marketable investments) to handle a spike in claims.
**Other Rating Factors:** Strong capitalization index (7.5) based on excellent current risk-adjusted capital (severe loss scenario). High quality investment portfolio (9.9).
**Principal Business:** Medicare (99%)
**Mem Phys: 16:** 19,277 **15:** 41,656 **16 MLR** 96.3% **/ 16 Admin Exp** N/A
**Enroll(000): Q3 17:** 26 **16:** 38 **15:** 22 **Med Exp PMPM:** $771
**Principal Investments:** Cash and equiv (51%), long-term bonds (49%)
**Provider Compensation ($000):** FFS ($323,474), capitation ($19,770)
**Total Member Encounters:** Phys (867,285), non-phys (227,524)
**Group Affiliation:** Cigna Corporation
**Licensed in:** GA
**Address:** TWO SECURITIES CENTRE 3500 PIE, ATLANTA, GA 30305
**Phone:** (404) 443-8800 **Dom State:** GA **Commenced Bus:** December 1985

| Data Date | Rating | RACR #1 | RACR #2 | Total Assets ($mil) | Capital ($mil) | Net Premium ($mil) | Net Income ($mil) |
|---|---|---|---|---|---|---|---|
| 9-17 | E | 1.72 | 1.43 | 119.2 | 50.7 | 203.2 | -4.1 |
| 9-16 | E | 1.06 | 0.88 | 102.7 | 14.7 | 290.0 | -21.7 |
| 2016 | E | 1.85 | 1.54 | 111.7 | 54.5 | 383.6 | -17.8 |
| 2015 | E | 1.50 | 1.25 | 78.8 | 20.8 | 173.7 | -24.5 |
| 2014 | E | 2.70 | 2.25 | 13.2 | 3.8 | 12.5 | -7.4 |
| 2013 | C | 11.43 | 9.52 | 6.7 | 6.1 | 3.9 | 0.3 |
| 2012 | C | 10.98 | 9.15 | 6.8 | 5.9 | 6.1 | 0.5 |

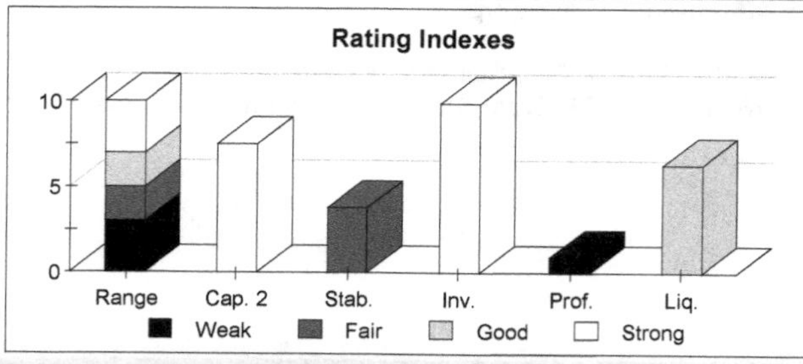


## CIGNA HEALTHCARE OF ILLINOIS INC — C- — Fair

**Major Rating Factors:** Fair overall results on stability tests (3.6 on a scale of 0 to 10) based on a significant 58% decrease in enrollment during the period. Rating is significantly influenced by the good financial results of Cigna Corporation. Weak profitability index (0.9). Strong capitalization index (10.0) based on excellent current risk-adjusted capital (severe loss scenario).
**Other Rating Factors:** High quality investment portfolio (9.9). Excellent liquidity (10.0) with ample operational cash flow and liquid investments.
**Principal Business:** Comp med (100%)
**Mem Phys: 16:** 48,762 **15:** 50,983 **16 MLR** 63.3% **/ 16 Admin Exp** N/A
**Enroll(000): Q3 17:** 22 **16:** 0 **15:** 0 **Med Exp PMPM:** $270
**Principal Investments:** Cash and equiv (77%), long-term bonds (23%)
**Provider Compensation ($000):** Contr fee ($194), FFS ($76), capitation ($33)
**Total Member Encounters:** Phys (379), non-phys (98)
**Group Affiliation:** Cigna Corporation
**Licensed in:** IL, IN
**Address:** 525 WEST MONROE SUITE 1650, CHICAGO, IL 60661
**Phone:** (860) 226-6000 **Dom State:** IL **Commenced Bus:** July 1986

| Data Date | Rating | RACR #1 | RACR #2 | Total Assets ($mil) | Capital ($mil) | Net Premium ($mil) | Net Income ($mil) |
|---|---|---|---|---|---|---|---|
| 9-17 | C- | 18.09 | 15.07 | 70.0 | 10.9 | 37.5 | -6.2 |
| 9-16 | C | 7.36 | 6.13 | 4.3 | 4.1 | 0.4 | 0.0 |
| 2016 | C | 8.71 | 7.26 | 12.1 | 5.3 | 0.5 | -4.1 |
| 2015 | C | 7.36 | 6.13 | 4.3 | 4.1 | 0.9 | 0.2 |
| 2014 | C | 7.07 | 5.89 | 4.1 | 3.9 | 1.1 | -0.1 |
| 2013 | C | 4.39 | 3.66 | 2.6 | 2.4 | 1.0 | 0.0 |
| 2012 | C- | 4.60 | 3.83 | 2.6 | 2.4 | 1.2 | 0.2 |

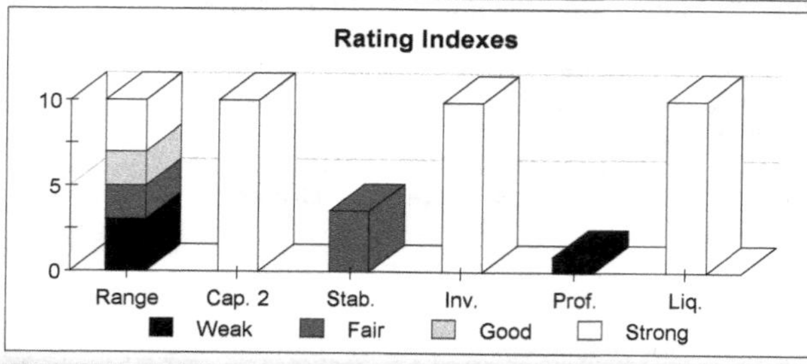


## CIGNA HEALTHCARE OF INDIANA INC — C+ — Fair

**Major Rating Factors:** Fair overall results on stability tests (3.6 on a scale of 0 to 10) based on a decline in the number of member physicians during 2017. Rating is significantly influenced by the good financial results of Cigna Corporation. Good liquidity (6.9) with sufficient resources (cash flows and marketable investments) to handle a spike in claims. Weak profitability index (2.3).
**Other Rating Factors:** Strong capitalization index (8.5) based on excellent current risk-adjusted capital (severe loss scenario). High quality investment portfolio (9.9).
**Principal Business:** Comp med (100%)
**Mem Phys: 16:** 9,385 **15:** 10,492 **16 MLR** 129.1% **/ 16 Admin Exp** N/A
**Enroll(000): Q3 17:** 0 **16:** 0 **15:** 0 **Med Exp PMPM:** $1,007
**Principal Investments:** Cash and equiv (54%), long-term bonds (46%)
**Provider Compensation ($000):** Contr fee ($1,186), FFS ($92), capitation ($44)
**Total Member Encounters:** Phys (551), non-phys (116)
**Group Affiliation:** Cigna Corporation
**Licensed in:** IN
**Address:** ONE PENN MARK PLAZA 11595 N ME, CARMEL, IN 46032
**Phone:** (215) 761-1000 **Dom State:** IN **Commenced Bus:** September 1986

| Data Date | Rating | RACR #1 | RACR #2 | Total Assets ($mil) | Capital ($mil) | Net Premium ($mil) | Net Income ($mil) |
|---|---|---|---|---|---|---|---|
| 9-17 | C+ | 2.58 | 2.15 | 1.8 | 1.4 | 0.9 | 0.3 |
| 9-16 | C+ | 2.17 | 1.81 | 1.7 | 1.2 | 0.8 | -0.3 |
| 2016 | C+ | 2.13 | 1.78 | 1.4 | 1.2 | 1.1 | -0.3 |
| 2015 | B- | 2.72 | 2.27 | 1.6 | 1.5 | 1.0 | 0.1 |
| 2014 | B- | 2.66 | 2.22 | 1.7 | 1.4 | 1.0 | -0.1 |
| 2013 | C+ | 2.74 | 2.28 | 1.5 | 1.5 | 0.8 | 0.0 |
| 2012 | C | 3.08 | 2.56 | 2.0 | 1.5 | 0.9 | 0.2 |

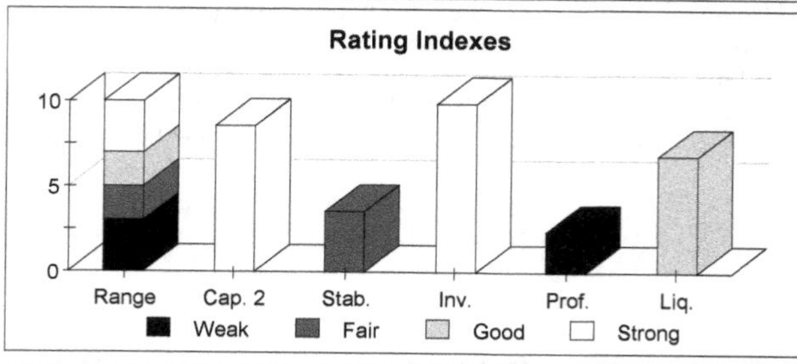

## CIGNA HEALTHCARE OF NEW JERSEY INC — E — Very Weak

**Major Rating Factors:** Weak profitability index (0.7 on a scale of 0 to 10). Weak overall results on stability tests (2.3). Rating is significantly influenced by the good financial results of Cigna Corporation. Strong capitalization index (10.0) based on excellent current risk-adjusted capital (severe loss scenario).
**Other Rating Factors:** High quality investment portfolio (9.9). Excellent liquidity (8.6) with ample operational cash flow and liquid investments.
**Principal Business:** Comp med (100%)
**Mem Phys: 16:** 111,346 **15:** 111,346 **16 MLR** 99.3% **/ 16 Admin Exp** N/A
**Enroll(000): Q3 17:** 0 **16:** 0 **15:** 0 **Med Exp PMPM:** $2,278
**Principal Investments:** Cash and equiv (50%), long-term bonds (50%)
**Provider Compensation ($000):** Contr fee ($3,239), FFS ($278), capitation ($48)
**Total Member Encounters:** Phys (2,271), non-phys (18,184)
**Group Affiliation:** Cigna Corporation
**Licensed in:** NJ
**Address:** 499 WASHINGTON BOULEVARD 5TH F, JERSEY CITY, NJ 07310-1608
**Phone:** (860) 226-6000 **Dom State:** NJ **Commenced Bus:** February 1988

| Data Date | Rating | RACR #1 | RACR #2 | Total Assets ($mil) | Capital ($mil) | Net Premium ($mil) | Net Income ($mil) |
|---|---|---|---|---|---|---|---|
| 9-17 | E | 9.14 | 7.61 | 9.0 | 5.1 | 3.2 | -2.2 |
| 9-16 | E | 9.03 | 7.53 | 8.5 | 5.0 | 1.6 | -0.4 |
| 2016 | E | 12.91 | 10.76 | 10.3 | 7.2 | 3.9 | 1.4 |
| 2015 | C | 5.19 | 4.33 | 5.2 | 2.9 | 1.6 | -2.7 |
| 2014 | C | 8.10 | 6.75 | 5.3 | 4.6 | 1.3 | -0.5 |
| 2013 | C | 7.28 | 6.07 | 4.7 | 4.0 | 3.2 | 0.4 |
| 2012 | C | 6.66 | 5.55 | 4.8 | 3.6 | 1.7 | -0.1 |

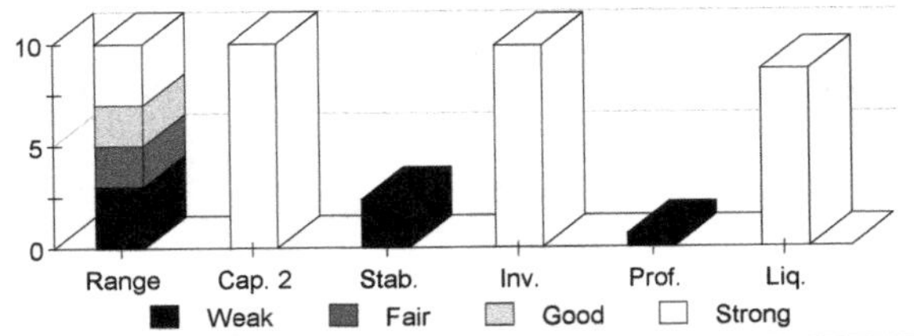


## CIGNA HEALTHCARE OF NORTH CAROLINA — C — Fair

**Major Rating Factors:** Fair overall results on stability tests (4.0 on a scale of 0 to 10) in spite of healthy premium and capital growth during 2016. Rating is significantly influenced by the good financial results of Cigna Corporation. Weak profitability index (2.7). Good liquidity (6.8) with sufficient resources (cash flows and marketable investments) to handle a spike in claims.
**Other Rating Factors:** Strong capitalization index (9.2) based on excellent current risk-adjusted capital (severe loss scenario). High quality investment portfolio (9.9).
**Principal Business:** Medicare (95%), comp med (5%)
**Mem Phys: 16:** 53,699 **15:** 41,656 **16 MLR** 87.9% **/ 16 Admin Exp** N/A
**Enroll(000): Q3 17:** 26 **16:** 9 **15:** 10 **Med Exp PMPM:** $702
**Principal Investments:** Long-term bonds (54%), cash and equiv (46%)
**Provider Compensation ($000):** FFS ($74,957), capitation ($1,338)
**Total Member Encounters:** Phys (171,974), non-phys (51,578)
**Group Affiliation:** Cigna Corporation
**Licensed in:** NC
**Address:** 701 CORPORATE CENTER DRIVE, RALEIGH, NC 27607
**Phone:** (860) 226-6000 **Dom State:** NC **Commenced Bus:** April 1986

| Data Date | Rating | RACR #1 | RACR #2 | Total Assets ($mil) | Capital ($mil) | Net Premium ($mil) | Net Income ($mil) |
|---|---|---|---|---|---|---|---|
| 9-17 | C | 3.14 | 2.61 | 93.0 | 22.8 | 112.8 | 8.7 |
| 9-16 | C | 1.66 | 1.38 | 27.9 | 9.9 | 67.7 | -2.8 |
| 2016 | C | 1.86 | 1.55 | 27.2 | 13.5 | 88.9 | -4.2 |
| 2015 | C | 1.31 | 1.09 | 18.2 | 7.7 | 74.9 | 0.6 |
| 2014 | C | 2.99 | 2.49 | 14.0 | 5.7 | 23.0 | -4.5 |
| 2013 | C | 7.45 | 6.20 | 11.3 | 9.7 | 15.3 | 1.1 |
| 2012 | C | 3.77 | 3.15 | 11.4 | 8.7 | 28.6 | 1.5 |

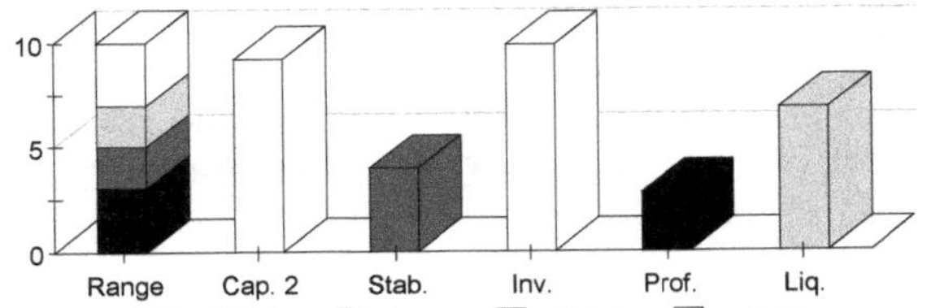


## CIGNA HEALTHCARE OF SOUTH CAROLINA — D- — Weak

**Major Rating Factors:** Weak profitability index (1.1 on a scale of 0 to 10). Good overall results on stability tests (6.5) based on healthy premium and capital growth during 2016. Rating is significantly influenced by the good financial results of Cigna Corporation. Strong capitalization index (8.2) based on excellent current risk-adjusted capital (severe loss scenario).
**Other Rating Factors:** High quality investment portfolio (9.9). Excellent liquidity (6.9) with sufficient resources (cash flows and marketable investments) to handle a spike in claims.
**Principal Business:** Medicare (100%)
**Mem Phys: 16:** 13,565 **15:** 14,659 **16 MLR** 86.2% **/ 16 Admin Exp** N/A
**Enroll(000): Q3 17:** 6 **16:** 10 **15:** 9 **Med Exp PMPM:** $684
**Principal Investments:** Cash and equiv (67%), long-term bonds (33%)
**Provider Compensation ($000):** FFS ($77,567), capitation ($1,079)
**Total Member Encounters:** Phys (180,572), non-phys (52,650)
**Group Affiliation:** Cigna Corporation
**Licensed in:** SC
**Address:** 4000 FABER PLACE DRIVE SUITE #, NORTH CHARLESTON, SC 29405
**Phone:** (860) 226-6000 **Dom State:** SC **Commenced Bus:** January 1987

| Data Date | Rating | RACR #1 | RACR #2 | Total Assets ($mil) | Capital ($mil) | Net Premium ($mil) | Net Income ($mil) |
|---|---|---|---|---|---|---|---|
| 9-17 | D- | 2.35 | 1.96 | 32.5 | 17.6 | 47.2 | 1.9 |
| 9-16 | D- | 1.41 | 1.18 | 28.7 | 8.8 | 70.9 | -4.2 |
| 2016 | D- | 2.09 | 1.74 | 29.6 | 15.7 | 95.4 | -2.4 |
| 2015 | D+ | 1.07 | 0.89 | 16.2 | 6.6 | 80.2 | -1.2 |
| 2014 | D+ | 1.26 | 1.05 | 13.1 | 6.1 | 55.3 | -2.2 |
| 2013 | C | 4.41 | 3.68 | 2.7 | 2.2 | 1.5 | 0.5 |
| 2012 | C | 3.98 | 3.32 | 2.3 | 1.7 | 1.5 | 0.1 |

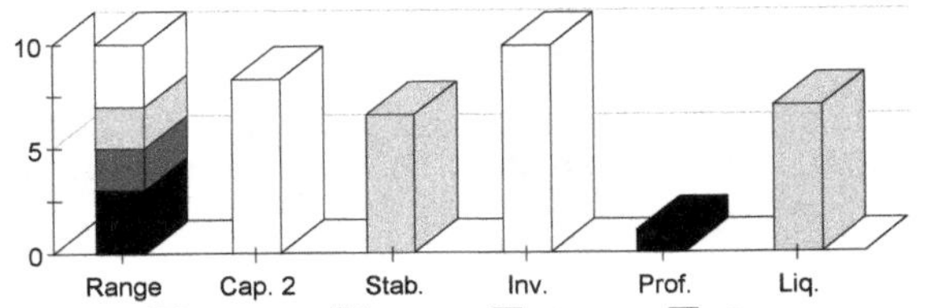

## CIGNA HEALTHCARE OF ST LOUIS D+ Weak

**Major Rating Factors:** Weak profitability index (0.9 on a scale of 0 to 10). Fair overall results on stability tests (4.0) based on an excessive 181% enrollment growth during the period. Rating is significantly influenced by the good financial results of Cigna Corporation. Strong capitalization index (8.5) based on excellent current risk-adjusted capital (severe loss scenario).
**Other Rating Factors:** High quality investment portfolio (9.9). Excellent liquidity (7.1) with ample operational cash flow and liquid investments.
**Principal Business:** Medicare (74%), comp med (26%)
**Mem Phys: 16:** N/A **15:** 50,284 **16 MLR** 95.5% **/ 16 Admin Exp** N/A
**Enroll(000): Q3 17:** 2 **16:** 3 **15:** 1 **Med Exp PMPM:** $624
**Principal Investments:** Cash and equiv (72%), long-term bonds (28%)
**Provider Compensation ($000):** FFS ($17,967), capitation ($520)
**Total Member Encounters:** Phys (40,879), non-phys (11,571)
**Group Affiliation:** Cigna Corporation
**Licensed in:** IL, KS, MO
**Address:** 231 S BEMISTON, CLAYTON, MO 63105
**Phone:** (860) 226-6000 **Dom State:** MO **Commenced Bus:** February 1986

| Data Date | Rating | RACR #1 | RACR #2 | Total Assets ($mil) | Capital ($mil) | Net Premium ($mil) | Net Income ($mil) |
|---|---|---|---|---|---|---|---|
| 9-17 | D+ | 2.54 | 2.12 | 14.0 | 6.9 | 13.3 | -0.3 |
| 9-16 | D+ | 13.80 | 11.50 | 16.2 | 7.8 | 16.9 | -0.9 |
| 2016 | D+ | 2.68 | 2.23 | 14.4 | 7.3 | 22.2 | -1.4 |
| 2015 | D+ | 15.69 | 13.07 | 13.3 | 8.9 | 6.3 | 0.0 |
| 2014 | D+ | 2.58 | 2.15 | 6.4 | 2.1 | 5.2 | -1.7 |
| 2013 | C | 4.28 | 3.57 | 5.1 | 2.3 | 5.5 | 0.2 |
| 2012 | C | 6.95 | 5.79 | 6.3 | 3.8 | 5.1 | -0.2 |

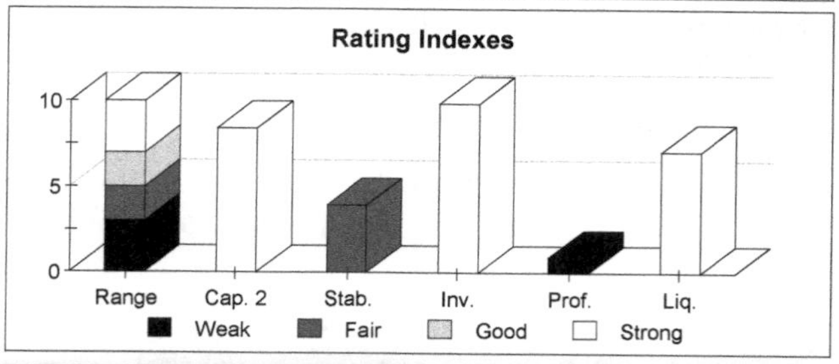


## CIGNA HEALTHCARE OF TENNESSEE INC C Fair

**Major Rating Factors:** Weak profitability index (0.7 on a scale of 0 to 10). Weak overall results on stability tests (2.2). Rating is significantly influenced by the good financial results of Cigna Corporation. Good liquidity (6.6) with sufficient resources (cash flows and marketable investments) to handle a spike in claims.
**Other Rating Factors:** Strong capitalization index (8.7) based on excellent current risk-adjusted capital (severe loss scenario). High quality investment portfolio (9.9).
**Principal Business:** Comp med (100%)
**Mem Phys: 16:** 61,331 **15:** 64,429 **16 MLR** 78.2% **/ 16 Admin Exp** N/A
**Enroll(000): Q3 17:** 5 **16:** 4 **15:** 3 **Med Exp PMPM:** $313
**Principal Investments:** Long-term bonds (72%), cash and equiv (28%)
**Provider Compensation ($000):** Contr fee ($8,144), FFS ($3,426), capitation ($1,172)
**Total Member Encounters:** Phys (12,185), non-phys (2,589)
**Group Affiliation:** Cigna Corporation
**Licensed in:** MS, TN
**Address:** 1000 CORPORATE CENTRE DRIVE, FRANKLIN, TN 37067
**Phone:** (860) 226-5634 **Dom State:** TN **Commenced Bus:** November 1985

| Data Date | Rating | RACR #1 | RACR #2 | Total Assets ($mil) | Capital ($mil) | Net Premium ($mil) | Net Income ($mil) |
|---|---|---|---|---|---|---|---|
| 9-17 | C | 2.73 | 2.28 | 7.1 | 3.2 | 16.3 | -0.7 |
| 9-16 | C | 3.62 | 3.02 | 7.9 | 4.8 | 11.7 | -0.4 |
| 2016 | C | 3.22 | 2.69 | 7.0 | 4.0 | 16.5 | -1.2 |
| 2015 | C | 3.52 | 2.94 | 7.8 | 4.6 | 19.0 | 0.2 |
| 2014 | C | 4.30 | 3.59 | 8.7 | 5.2 | 17.7 | -1.4 |
| 2013 | C | 3.74 | 3.12 | 12.8 | 8.2 | 35.4 | 2.3 |
| 2012 | C | 2.31 | 1.92 | 12.7 | 6.6 | 48.1 | -1.2 |

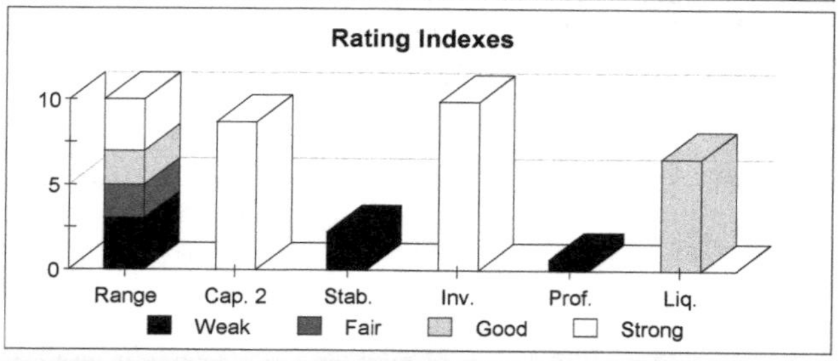


## CIGNA HEALTHCARE OF TEXAS INC C- Fair

**Major Rating Factors:** Weak profitability index (1.9 on a scale of 0 to 10). Good overall results on stability tests (6.2) despite a decline in the number of member physicians during 2017. Rating is significantly influenced by the good financial results of Cigna Corporation. Good liquidity (6.7) with sufficient resources (cash flows and marketable investments) to handle a spike in claims.
**Other Rating Factors:** Strong capitalization index (9.0) based on excellent current risk-adjusted capital (severe loss scenario). High quality investment portfolio (9.9).
**Principal Business:** Comp med (100%)
**Mem Phys: 16:** 83,880 **15:** 137,046 **16 MLR** 90.5% **/ 16 Admin Exp** N/A
**Enroll(000): Q3 17:** 10 **16:** 14 **15:** 12 **Med Exp PMPM:** $570
**Principal Investments:** Long-term bonds (52%), cash and equiv (48%)
**Provider Compensation ($000):** Contr fee ($64,617), FFS ($23,080), capitation ($9,192)
**Total Member Encounters:** Phys (31,805), non-phys (7,216)
**Group Affiliation:** Cigna Corporation
**Licensed in:** TX
**Address:** 6600 EAST CAMPUS CIRCLE DRIVE, IRVING, TX 75063
**Phone:** (860) 226-5634 **Dom State:** TX **Commenced Bus:** January 1996

| Data Date | Rating | RACR #1 | RACR #2 | Total Assets ($mil) | Capital ($mil) | Net Premium ($mil) | Net Income ($mil) |
|---|---|---|---|---|---|---|---|
| 9-17 | C- | 2.96 | 2.46 | 32.3 | 19.7 | 62.1 | 2.2 |
| 9-16 | C- | 2.10 | 1.75 | 28.0 | 9.3 | 84.5 | -6.1 |
| 2016 | C- | 2.39 | 1.99 | 37.6 | 15.6 | 110.8 | -7.5 |
| 2015 | B | 3.26 | 2.72 | 27.0 | 15.4 | 83.1 | -0.6 |
| 2014 | B- | 3.15 | 2.62 | 25.2 | 15.6 | 90.2 | 0.9 |
| 2013 | B- | 2.58 | 2.15 | 31.9 | 14.5 | 100.8 | 2.0 |
| 2012 | C | 2.62 | 2.18 | 21.9 | 12.8 | 95.2 | 1.1 |

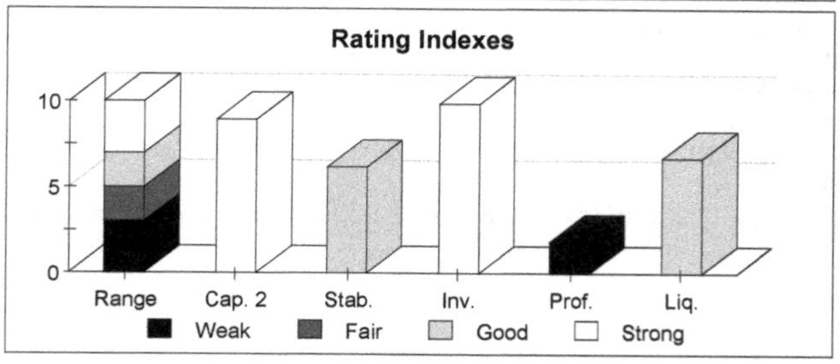

## CIGNA LIFE INSURANCE COMPANY OF NEW YORK * A- Excellent

**Major Rating Factors:** Good quality investment portfolio (6.4 on a scale of 0 to 10) despite mixed results such as: large holdings of BBB rated bonds but moderate junk bond exposure. Good overall profitability (6.2). Excellent overall results on stability tests (7.0) excellent operational trends and excellent risk diversification.
**Other Rating Factors:** Strong capitalization (7.9) based on excellent risk adjusted capital (severe loss scenario). Excellent liquidity (7.2).
**Principal Business:** Group health insurance (67%) and group life insurance (32%).
**Principal Investments:** NonCMO investment grade bonds (88%), noninv. grade bonds (9%), and CMOs and structured securities (4%).
**Investments in Affiliates:** None
**Group Affiliation:** CIGNA Corp
**Licensed in:** AL, DC, MO, NY, PA, TN
**Commenced Business:** December 1965
**Address:** 140 EAST 45TH STREET, NEW YORK, NY 10017
**Phone:** (215) 761-1000 **Domicile State:** NY **NAIC Code:** 64548

| Data Date | Rating | RACR #1 | RACR #2 | Total Assets ($mil) | Capital ($mil) | Net Premium ($mil) | Net Income ($mil) |
|---|---|---|---|---|---|---|---|
| 9-17 | A- | 2.47 | 1.61 | 403.0 | 95.7 | 134.4 | 10.1 |
| 9-16 | A- | 2.73 | 1.80 | 387.4 | 100.0 | 124.0 | 3.9 |
| 2016 | A- | 2.41 | 1.58 | 383.4 | 92.0 | 164.4 | 5.1 |
| 2015 | A- | 2.69 | 1.78 | 364.4 | 97.4 | 150.3 | 18.9 |
| 2014 | A- | 3.25 | 2.08 | 368.1 | 102.8 | 128.0 | 24.7 |
| 2013 | B+ | 3.21 | 2.03 | 375.9 | 93.5 | 119.9 | 16.9 |
| 2012 | B+ | 3.54 | 2.38 | 376.0 | 93.8 | 115.6 | 15.8 |

**Adverse Trends in Operations**

Decrease in capital during 2016 (5%)
Decrease in capital during 2015 (5%)
Decrease in asset base during 2015 (1%)
Decrease in asset base during 2014 (2%)

## CLEARRIVER HEALTH D Weak

**Major Rating Factors:** Weak profitability index (0.4 on a scale of 0 to 10). Good liquidity (6.3) with sufficient resources (cash flows and marketable investments) to handle a spike in claims. Strong capitalization (10.0) based on excellent current risk-adjusted capital (severe loss scenario).
**Other Rating Factors:** High quality investment portfolio (9.9).
**Principal Business:** Medicare (100%)
**Mem Phys: 16:** 2,209 **15:** 2,040 **16 MLR** 117.4% **/ 16 Admin Exp** N/A
**Enroll(000): Q2 17:** N/A **16:** 1 **15:** 0 **Med Exp PMPM:** $762
**Principal Investments:** Long-term bonds (98%), cash and equiv (2%)
**Provider Compensation ($000):** Contr fee ($4,598), capitation ($73), other ($249)
**Total Member Encounters:** Phys (9,583), non-phys (2,462)
**Group Affiliation:** Catholic Health Initiatives
**Licensed in:** TN
**Address:** PO Box 5788, Chattanooga, TN 37406
**Phone:** (866) 789-7747 **Dom State:** TN **Commenced Bus:** January 2015

| Data Date | Rating | RACR #1 | RACR #2 | Total Assets ($mil) | Capital ($mil) | Net Premium ($mil) | Net Income ($mil) |
|---|---|---|---|---|---|---|---|
| 6-17 | D | 6.59 | 5.49 | 6.1 | 5.2 | 0.0 | 0.2 |
| 6-16 | D | 11.62 | 9.68 | 7.4 | 5.4 | 2.1 | -0.3 |
| 2016 | D | 6.39 | 5.33 | 6.2 | 5.0 | 4.3 | -0.7 |
| 2015 | D | 12.50 | 10.42 | 7.2 | 5.6 | 2.0 | -1.3 |
| 2014 | N/A | N/A | N/A | 6.9 | 6.9 | N/A | N/A |
| 2013 | N/A | N/A | N/A | N/A | N/A | N/A | N/A |
| 2012 | N/A | N/A | N/A | N/A | N/A | N/A | N/A |

**Rating Indexes**

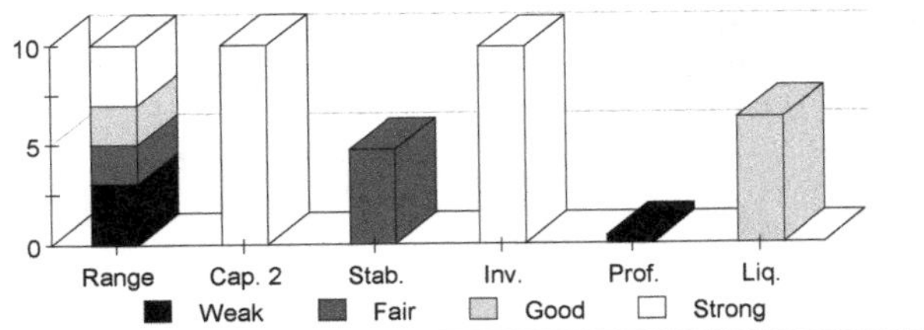


## CLOVER INSURANCE COMPANY C+ Fair

**Major Rating Factors:** Weak profitability index (0.8 on a scale of 0 to 10). Weak liquidity (2.5) as a spike in claims may stretch capacity. Strong capitalization (10.0) based on excellent current risk-adjusted capital (severe loss scenario).
**Other Rating Factors:** High quality investment portfolio (9.9).
**Principal Business:** Medicare (100%)
**Mem Phys: 16:** 10,080 **15:** N/A **16 MLR** 415.8% **/ 16 Admin Exp** N/A
**Enroll(000): Q3 17:** 27 **16:** 21 **15:** 7 **Med Exp PMPM:** $881
**Principal Investments:** Cash and equiv (97%), long-term bonds (3%)
**Provider Compensation ($000):** Contr fee ($153,946)
**Total Member Encounters:** N/A
**Group Affiliation:** Clover Health Investments Corp
**Licensed in:** All states except MI, NH, NY, NC, VT, PR
**Address:** Harborside Plaza Ten 3 2nd St, Jersey City, NJ 07311
**Phone:** (201) 432-2133 **Dom State:** NJ **Commenced Bus:** February 1948

| Data Date | Rating | RACR #1 | RACR #2 | Total Assets ($mil) | Capital ($mil) | Net Premium ($mil) | Net Income ($mil) |
|---|---|---|---|---|---|---|---|
| 9-17 | C+ | 4.39 | 3.66 | 110.3 | 53.9 | 201.0 | -31.6 |
| 9-16 | N/A | N/A | N/A | 96.8 | 18.0 | 35.3 | -1.8 |
| 2016 | B- | 6.41 | 5.34 | 189.0 | 67.9 | 46.0 | -34.6 |
| 2015 | N/A | N/A | N/A | 35.5 | 10.2 | 52.5 | N/A |
| 2014 | N/A | N/A | N/A | 13.1 | 5.1 | 24.8 | N/A |
| 2013 | N/A | N/A | N/A | 5.3 | 3.5 | 3.3 | N/A |
| 2012 | N/A | N/A | N/A | N/A | N/A | N/A | N/A |

**Rating Indexes**

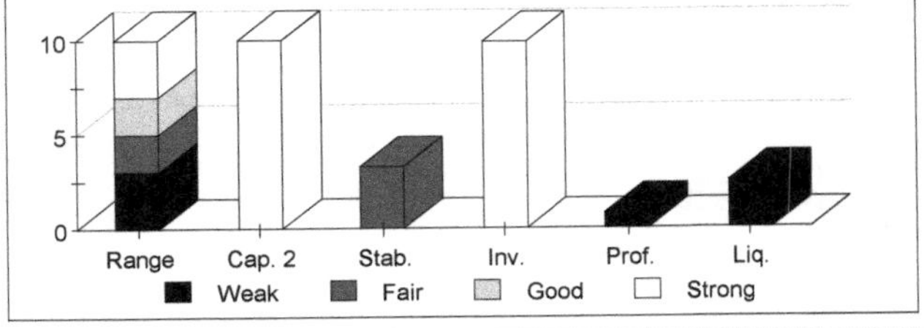

## CMNTY CARE HLTH PLAN INC (WI) — C — Fair

**Major Rating Factors:** Fair profitability index (3.1 on a scale of 0 to 10). Strong capitalization (7.0) based on excellent current risk-adjusted capital (severe loss scenario). High quality investment portfolio (9.9).

**Other Rating Factors:** Excellent liquidity (7.0) with sufficient resources (cash flows and marketable investments) to handle a spike in claims.

**Principal Business:** Medicaid (62%), Medicare (38%)

**Mem Phys: 16:** 13,843 **15:** 12,953 **16 MLR** 88.7% **/ 16 Admin Exp** N/A

**Enroll(000): Q3 17:** 2 **16:** 2 **15:** 2 **Med Exp PMPM:** $2,911

**Principal Investments:** Cash and equiv (52%), long-term bonds (48%)

**Provider Compensation ($000):** Contr fee ($57,189), salary ($20,185)

**Total Member Encounters:** Phys (27,141), non-phys (46,187)

**Group Affiliation:** Community Care Inc

**Licensed in:** WI

**Address:** 205 Bishops Way, Brookfield, WI 53005

**Phone:** (414) 385-6600 **Dom State:** WI **Commenced Bus:** July 2005

| Data Date | Rating | RACR #1 | RACR #2 | Total Assets ($mil) | Capital ($mil) | Net Premium ($mil) | Net Income ($mil) |
|---|---|---|---|---|---|---|---|
| 9-17 | C | 1.35 | 1.12 | 24.0 | 12.8 | 69.2 | 0.7 |
| 9-16 | C- | 1.21 | 1.01 | 21.7 | 11.9 | 72.5 | 2.7 |
| 2016 | C | 1.31 | 1.09 | 20.3 | 12.5 | 94.6 | 3.2 |
| 2015 | C- | 0.87 | 0.73 | 16.8 | 8.8 | 96.2 | -1.1 |
| 2014 | C- | 1.06 | 0.89 | 17.5 | 10.1 | 92.2 | -5.6 |
| 2013 | B | 1.80 | 1.50 | 24.4 | 16.1 | 94.8 | 0.6 |
| 2012 | B | 1.84 | 1.54 | 23.7 | 15.7 | 89.0 | 0.0 |

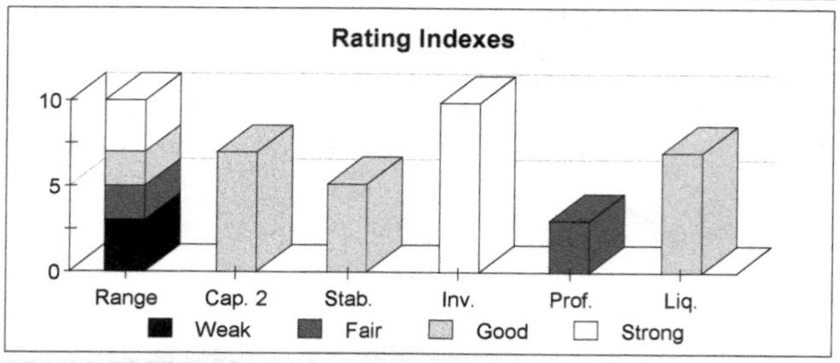


## CMNTY CARE HLTH PLAN OF LA INC — B — Good

**Major Rating Factors:** Fair profitability index (3.4 on a scale of 0 to 10). Strong capitalization (8.3) based on excellent current risk-adjusted capital (severe loss scenario). High quality investment portfolio (9.5).

**Other Rating Factors:** Excellent liquidity (6.9) with sufficient resources (cash flows and marketable investments) to handle a spike in claims.

**Principal Business:** Medicaid (95%), comp med (5%)

**Mem Phys: 16:** 16,695 **15:** 14,681 **16 MLR** 84.7% **/ 16 Admin Exp** N/A

**Enroll(000): Q3 17:** 241 **16:** 233 **15:** 172 **Med Exp PMPM:** $307

**Principal Investments:** Cash and equiv (61%), long-term bonds (38%)

**Provider Compensation ($000):** Contr fee ($578,060), capitation ($11,188), FFS ($9,233), bonus arrang ($403)

**Total Member Encounters:** Phys (1,068,333), non-phys (1,405,529)

**Group Affiliation:** Anthem Inc

**Licensed in:** LA

**Address:** 3850 N CAUSEWAY BLVD Ste 600, METAIRIE, LA 70002

**Phone:** (757) 490-6900 **Dom State:** LA **Commenced Bus:** February 2012

| Data Date | Rating | RACR #1 | RACR #2 | Total Assets ($mil) | Capital ($mil) | Net Premium ($mil) | Net Income ($mil) |
|---|---|---|---|---|---|---|---|
| 9-17 | B | 2.41 | 2.01 | 293.1 | 105.6 | 709.5 | 12.9 |
| 9-16 | B- | 1.99 | 1.65 | 222.7 | 57.0 | 531.0 | -17.5 |
| 2016 | B- | 1.61 | 1.34 | 282.8 | 68.9 | 785.3 | -3.3 |
| 2015 | B- | 1.86 | 1.55 | 137.9 | 53.2 | 506.3 | -3.9 |
| 2014 | B- | 2.15 | 1.79 | 102.7 | 47.5 | 396.0 | -1.6 |
| 2013 | B- | 1.92 | 1.60 | 94.8 | 47.4 | 411.0 | 9.9 |
| 2012 | B- | 1.97 | 1.64 | 69.0 | 37.5 | 247.1 | -20.4 |

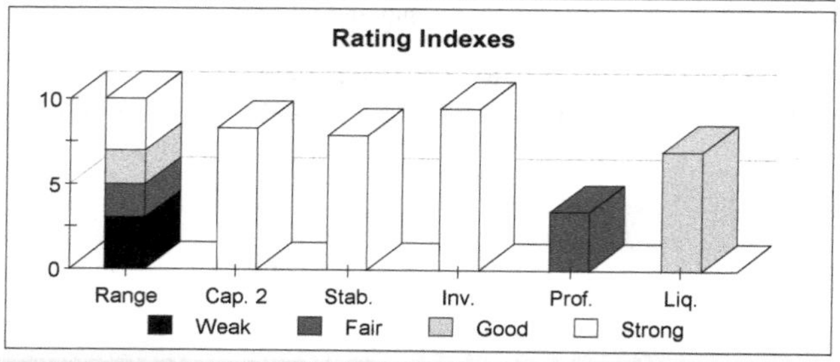


## COLONIAL LIFE & ACCIDENT INSURANCE COMPANY — C+ — Fair

**Major Rating Factors:** Fair overall results on stability tests (4.8 on a scale of 0 to 10) including fair financial strength of affiliated Unum Group. Good quality investment portfolio (5.9) despite large holdings of BBB rated bonds in addition to moderate junk bond exposure. Exposure to mortgages is significant, but the mortgage default rate has been low. Good liquidity (6.8).

**Other Rating Factors:** Strong capitalization (7.9) based on excellent risk adjusted capital (severe loss scenario). Excellent profitability (7.8).

**Principal Business:** Individual health insurance (68%), individual life insurance (21%), group health insurance (10%), and group life insurance (1%).

**Principal Investments:** NonCMO investment grade bonds (73%), mortgages in good standing (13%), noninv. grade bonds (6%), CMOs and structured securities (3%), and misc. investments (6%).

**Investments in Affiliates:** None

**Group Affiliation:** Unum Group

**Licensed in:** All states except NY

**Commenced Business:** September 1939

**Address:** 1200 COLONIAL LIFE BOULEVARD, COLUMBIA, SC 29210

**Phone:** (803) 798-7000 **Domicile State:** SC **NAIC Code:** 62049

| Data Date | Rating | RACR #1 | RACR #2 | Total Assets ($mil) | Capital ($mil) | Net Premium ($mil) | Net Income ($mil) |
|---|---|---|---|---|---|---|---|
| 9-17 | C+ | 2.54 | 1.59 | 3,274.2 | 580.7 | 1,129.7 | 116.8 |
| 9-16 | C+ | 2.57 | 1.59 | 3,129.2 | 569.5 | 1,059.0 | 101.8 |
| 2016 | C+ | 2.53 | 1.57 | 3,143.9 | 562.1 | 1,414.5 | 151.5 |
| 2015 | C+ | 2.65 | 1.64 | 3,018.8 | 566.0 | 1,333.8 | 157.8 |
| 2014 | C+ | 2.44 | 1.53 | 2,922.0 | 567.1 | 1,277.5 | 160.9 |
| 2013 | C+ | 2.71 | 1.66 | 2,752.7 | 538.2 | 1,238.8 | 134.4 |
| 2012 | C+ | 2.75 | 1.68 | 2,651.4 | 534.9 | 1,208.2 | 139.7 |

| Unum Group<br>Composite Group Rating: C+<br>Largest Group Members | Assets ($mil) | Rating |
|---|---|---|
| UNUM LIFE INS CO OF AMERICA | 21078 | C+ |
| PROVIDENT LIFE ACCIDENT INS CO | 8273 | C+ |
| PAUL REVERE LIFE INS CO | 3790 | C+ |
| FIRST UNUM LIFE INS CO | 3261 | C+ |
| COLONIAL LIFE ACCIDENT INS CO | 3144 | C+ |

## COLONIAL PENN LIFE INSURANCE COMPANY — D+ Weak

**Major Rating Factors:** Weak overall results on stability tests (2.7 on a scale of 0 to 10) including weak financial strength of affiliated CNO Financial Group Inc. Weak profitability (1.9) with operating losses during the first nine months of 2017. Weak liquidity (1.4) as a spike in claims or a run on policy withdrawals may stretch capacity.
**Other Rating Factors:** Fair quality investment portfolio (4.2). Good capitalization (5.4) based on good risk adjusted capital (moderate loss scenario).
**Principal Business:** Individual health insurance (62%), individual life insurance (22%), and group life insurance (16%).
**Principal Investments:** NonCMO investment grade bonds (66%), CMOs and structured securities (20%), noninv. grade bonds (5%), policy loans (3%), and misc. investments (6%).
**Investments in Affiliates:** None
**Group Affiliation:** CNO Financial Group Inc
**Licensed in:** All states except NY
**Commenced Business:** September 1959
**Address:** 399 MARKET STREET, PHILADELPHIA, PA 19181
**Phone:** (215) 928-8000 **Domicile State:** PA **NAIC Code:** 62065

| Data Date | Rating | RACR #1 | RACR #2 | Total Assets ($mil) | Capital ($mil) | Net Premium ($mil) | Net Income ($mil) |
|---|---|---|---|---|---|---|---|
| 9-17 | D+ | 1.27 | 0.73 | 860.4 | 97.4 | 285.7 | -12.7 |
| 9-16 | D+ | 1.37 | 0.79 | 854.7 | 104.9 | 275.5 | 4.2 |
| 2016 | D+ | 1.27 | 0.72 | 854.7 | 95.8 | 352.5 | -1.9 |
| 2015 | D+ | 1.13 | 0.66 | 816.0 | 79.3 | 330.3 | -18.8 |
| 2014 | D+ | 1.16 | 0.67 | 742.8 | 73.3 | 303.7 | -17.1 |
| 2013 | D+ | 1.05 | 0.60 | 740.3 | 62.0 | 277.8 | -19.1 |
| 2012 | D+ | 1.20 | 0.68 | 736.6 | 70.6 | 253.5 | -3.9 |

**CNO Financial Group Inc**
**Composite Group Rating: D+**

| Largest Group Members | Assets ($mil) | Rating |
|---|---|---|
| BANKERS LIFE CAS CO | 17602 | D+ |
| WASHINGTON NATIONAL INS CO | 5398 | D+ |
| COLONIAL PENN LIFE INS CO | 855 | D+ |
| BANKERS CONSECO LIFE INS CO | 450 | D |

## COLORADO ACCESS — E Very Weak

**Major Rating Factors:** Poor capitalization index (0.6 on a scale of 0 to 10) based on weak current risk-adjusted capital (moderate loss scenario). Fair profitability index (4.7). Fair overall results on stability tests (4.0) based on a decline in the number of member physicians during 2017.
**Other Rating Factors:** High quality investment portfolio (9.9). Excellent liquidity (7.2) with ample operational cash flow and liquid investments.
**Principal Business:** Medicaid (74%), other (25%)
**Mem Phys: 16:** 53,500 **15:** 59,506 **16 MLR** 91.1% **/ 16 Admin Exp** N/A
**Enroll(000): Q3 17:** 406 **16:** 403 **15:** 392 **Med Exp PMPM:** $46
**Principal Investments:** Cash and equiv (100%)
**Provider Compensation ($000):** Capitation ($116,702), contr fee ($100,911)
**Total Member Encounters:** Phys (994,498), non-phys (20,595)
**Group Affiliation:** Colorado Access
**Licensed in:** CO
**Address:** 11100 E BETHANY DR, AURORA, CO 80014-2630
**Phone:** (720) 744-5100 **Dom State:** CO **Commenced Bus:** January 1995

| Data Date | Rating | RACR #1 | RACR #2 | Total Assets ($mil) | Capital ($mil) | Net Premium ($mil) | Net Income ($mil) |
|---|---|---|---|---|---|---|---|
| 9-17 | E | 0.36 | 0.30 | 72.2 | 23.6 | 208.3 | 13.6 |
| 9-16 | N/A | N/A | N/A | 64.7 | 15.5 | 178.7 | 7.7 |
| 2016 | E | 0.23 | 0.19 | 67.7 | 15.7 | 244.1 | 7.9 |
| 2015 | N/A | N/A | N/A | 49.2 | 6.8 | 258.7 | -13.4 |
| 2014 | N/A | N/A | N/A | 55.6 | 19.3 | 222.5 | 3.8 |
| 2013 | N/A | N/A | N/A | 103.7 | 22.4 | 171.8 | -2.0 |
| 2012 | N/A | N/A | N/A | 75.5 | 27.3 | 174.0 | 9.7 |

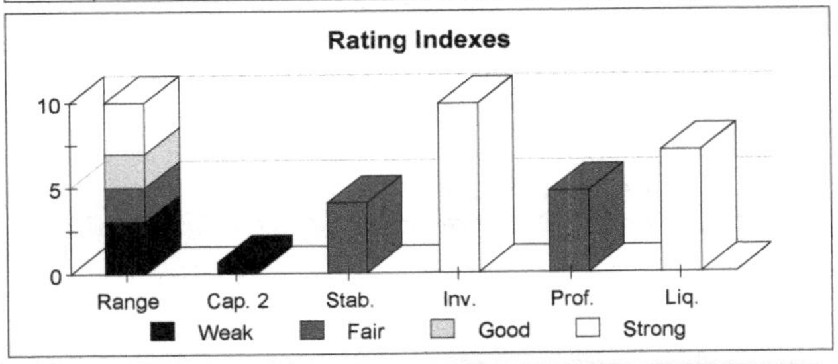


## COLUMBIA UNITED PROVIDERS INC — C Fair

**Major Rating Factors:** Weak profitability index (1.6 on a scale of 0 to 10). Strong capitalization (7.0) based on excellent current risk-adjusted capital (severe loss scenario). High quality investment portfolio (8.5).
**Other Rating Factors:** Excellent liquidity (7.1) with ample operational cash flow and liquid investments.
**Principal Business:** Medicaid (98%), comp med (1%)
**Mem Phys: 15:** 1,598 **14:** 1,693 **15 MLR** 93.0% **/ 15 Admin Exp** N/A
**Enroll(000): Q3 16:** N/A **15:** 57 **14:** 54 **Med Exp PMPM:** $208
**Principal Investments:** Cash and equiv (78%), long-term bonds (22%), nonaffiliate common stock (1%)
**Provider Compensation ($000):** FFS ($88,421), contr fee ($30,245), capitation ($12,800)
**Total Member Encounters:** N/A
**Group Affiliation:** Southwest Washington Health Systems
**Licensed in:** WA
**Address:** 1115 SE 164th Ave, Vancouver, WA 98683
**Phone:** (360) 729-1000 **Dom State:** WA **Commenced Bus:** January 1994

| Data Date | Rating | RACR #1 | RACR #2 | Total Assets ($mil) | Capital ($mil) | Net Premium ($mil) | Net Income ($mil) |
|---|---|---|---|---|---|---|---|
| 9-16 | C | 1.33 | 1.11 | 42.8 | 23.1 | 0.5 | -3.1 |
| 9-15 | C- | 0.81 | 0.68 | 47.2 | 13.0 | 108.9 | -5.8 |
| 2015 | C | 1.43 | 1.19 | 76.2 | 24.9 | 144.2 | 3.9 |
| 2014 | C | 1.03 | 0.86 | 32.8 | 19.0 | 128.9 | -7.6 |
| 2013 | B | 2.13 | 1.78 | 35.4 | 23.8 | 95.5 | -1.0 |
| 2012 | B | 2.19 | 1.83 | 36.1 | 24.6 | 108.7 | 2.3 |
| 2011 | N/A | N/A | N/A | 34.2 | 22.8 | 136.8 | N/A |

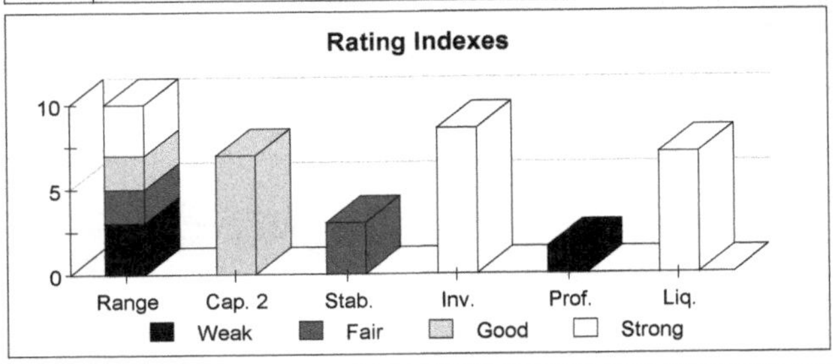

## COMBINED INSURANCE COMPANY OF AMERICA C+ Fair

**Major Rating Factors:** Fair overall results on stability tests (4.5 on a scale of 0 to 10) including fair risk adjusted capital in prior years. Good current capitalization (6.2) based on good risk adjusted capital (severe loss scenario) reflecting some improvement over results in 2015. Good quality investment portfolio (5.7).
**Other Rating Factors:** Weak profitability (2.8) with investment income below regulatory standards in relation to interest assumptions of reserves. Excellent liquidity (7.1).
**Principal Business:** Individual health insurance (63%), group health insurance (25%), individual life insurance (7%), group life insurance (3%), and reinsurance (2%).
**Principal Investments:** NonCMO investment grade bonds (61%), CMOs and structured securities (19%), noninv. grade bonds (10%), cash (5%), and misc. investments (6%).
**Investments in Affiliates:** 3%
**Group Affiliation:** Chubb Limited
**Licensed in:** All states except NY
**Commenced Business:** January 1922
**Address:** 111 E Wacker Drive, Chicago, IL 60601
**Phone:** (800) 225-4500 **Domicile State:** IL **NAIC Code:** 62146

| Data Date | Rating | RACR #1 | RACR #2 | Total Assets ($mil) | Capital ($mil) | Net Premium ($mil) | Net Income ($mil) |
|---|---|---|---|---|---|---|---|
| 9-17 | C+ | 1.30 | 0.90 | 1,507.0 | 159.5 | 358.2 | 23.1 |
| 9-16 | C+ | 1.07 | 0.72 | 1,387.6 | 114.5 | 334.0 | 21.5 |
| 2016 | C+ | 1.15 | 0.80 | 1,432.1 | 131.5 | 447.5 | 30.7 |
| 2015 | C | 0.80 | 0.54 | 1,316.7 | 79.9 | 439.9 | -14.1 |
| 2014 | C+ | 1.10 | 0.78 | 1,378.3 | 134.4 | 434.5 | 60.1 |
| 2013 | C+ | 1.99 | 1.54 | 1,588.9 | 324.6 | 428.1 | 71.8 |
| 2012 | C+ | 2.06 | 1.61 | 1,543.6 | 320.7 | 151.5 | 195.8 |

**Rating Indexes**

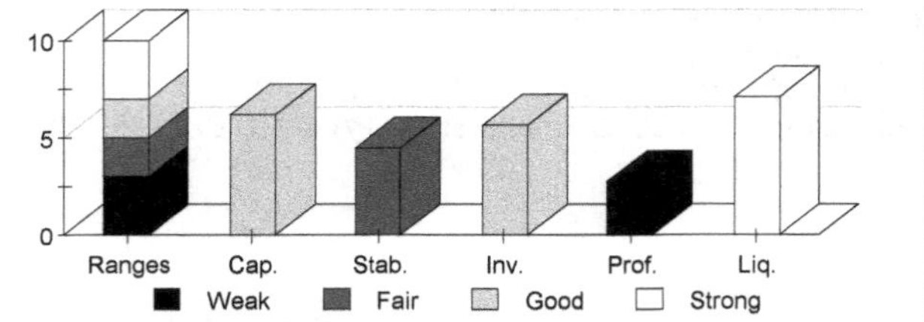


## COMBINED LIFE INSURANCE COMPANY OF NEW YORK C+ Fair

**Major Rating Factors:** Fair profitability (3.0 on a scale of 0 to 10) with investment income below regulatory standards in relation to interest assumptions of reserves. Fair overall results on stability tests (4.5) including weak risk adjusted capital in prior years. Good overall capitalization (5.6) based on mixed results -- excessive policy leverage mitigated by good risk adjusted capital (severe loss scenario).
**Other Rating Factors:** High quality investment portfolio (7.1). Excellent liquidity (7.4).
**Principal Business:** Individual health insurance (67%), reinsurance (12%), individual life insurance (11%), group health insurance (9%), and group life insurance (1%).
**Principal Investments:** NonCMO investment grade bonds (56%), CMOs and structured securities (42%), and policy loans (2%).
**Investments in Affiliates:** None
**Group Affiliation:** Chubb Limited
**Licensed in:** IL, NY
**Commenced Business:** June 1971
**Address:** 13 Cornell Road, Latham, NY 12110
**Phone:** (800) 951-6206 **Domicile State:** NY **NAIC Code:** 78697

| Data Date | Rating | RACR #1 | RACR #2 | Total Assets ($mil) | Capital ($mil) | Net Premium ($mil) | Net Income ($mil) |
|---|---|---|---|---|---|---|---|
| 9-17 | C+ | 1.16 | 0.82 | 442.6 | 42.8 | 122.7 | 7.3 |
| 9-16 | C+ | 0.94 | 0.67 | 411.2 | 33.1 | 116.4 | 6.5 |
| 2016 | C+ | 0.95 | 0.67 | 420.3 | 33.4 | 155.2 | 7.6 |
| 2015 | C | 0.63 | 0.45 | 397.3 | 21.9 | 156.2 | -9.7 |
| 2014 | B | 1.32 | 0.92 | 391.9 | 39.9 | 127.5 | 6.1 |
| 2013 | B | 1.85 | 1.29 | 402.9 | 56.4 | 126.0 | 3.7 |
| 2012 | B | 2.23 | 1.55 | 398.9 | 67.7 | 126.0 | 7.2 |

**Investment Income Compared to Needs of Reserves**

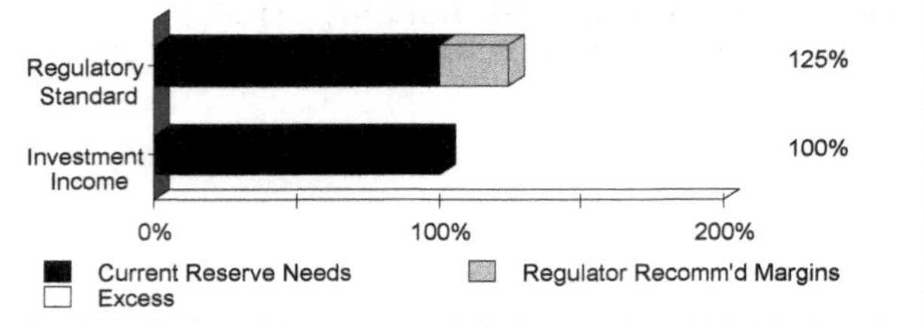


## COMMON GROUND HEALTHCARE COOPERATIVE D Weak

**Major Rating Factors:** Weak profitability index (0.7 on a scale of 0 to 10). Fair capitalization (2.9) based on good current risk-adjusted capital (moderate loss scenario). Good liquidity (5.3) with sufficient resources (cash flows and marketable investments) to handle a spike in claims.
**Other Rating Factors:** High quality investment portfolio (9.9).
**Principal Business:** Comp med (100%)
**Mem Phys: 16:** 25,616 **15:** 25,626 **16 MLR** 137.1% **/ 16 Admin Exp** N/A
**Enroll(000): Q3 17:** 29 **16:** 17 **15:** 33 **Med Exp PMPM:** $542
**Principal Investments:** Cash and equiv (100%)
**Provider Compensation ($000):** FFS ($87,003), contr fee ($47,055)
**Total Member Encounters:** N/A
**Group Affiliation:** Common Ground Healthcare Cooperative
**Licensed in:** WI
**Address:** 120 BISHOPS WAY Ste 150, BROOKFIELD, WI 53005-6271
**Phone:** (262) 754-9690 **Dom State:** WI **Commenced Bus:** March 2013

| Data Date | Rating | RACR #1 | RACR #2 | Total Assets ($mil) | Capital ($mil) | Net Premium ($mil) | Net Income ($mil) |
|---|---|---|---|---|---|---|---|
| 9-17 | D | 1.22 | 1.02 | 60.2 | 27.1 | 132.2 | 4.5 |
| 9-16 | D | 1.17 | 0.97 | 67.4 | 29.3 | 72.7 | -25.7 |
| 2016 | D | 1.13 | 0.95 | 59.2 | 24.6 | 88.8 | -36.0 |
| 2015 | D | 1.05 | 0.87 | 74.1 | 24.6 | 136.3 | -28.2 |
| 2014 | D | 0.89 | 0.74 | 105.6 | 36.9 | 123.5 | -36.5 |
| 2013 | N/A | N/A | N/A | 23.6 | 14.2 | N/A | -4.3 |
| 2012 | N/A | N/A | N/A | 2.6 | -1.6 | N/A | N/A |

**Rating Indexes**

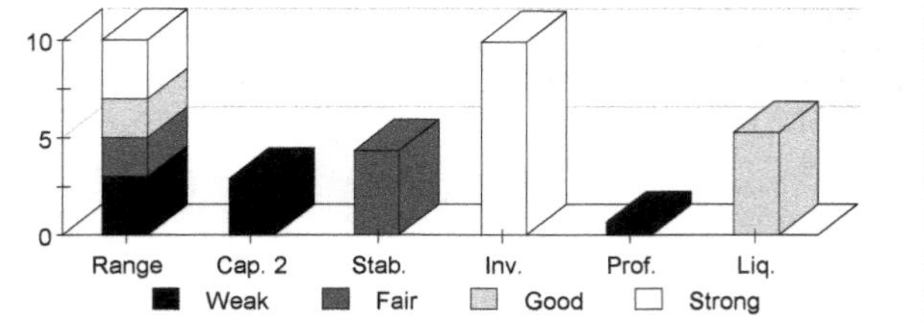

## COMMUNITY CARE ALLIANCE OF ILLINOIS C- Fair

**Major Rating Factors:** Fair profitability index (4.4 on a scale of 0 to 10). Fair capitalization (3.0) based on weak current risk-adjusted capital (moderate loss scenario). Good liquidity (6.9) with sufficient resources (cash flows and marketable investments) to handle a spike in claims.
**Other Rating Factors:** High quality investment portfolio (9.9).
**Principal Business:** Medicare (100%)
**Mem Phys: 16:** 10,302 **15:** 9,135 **16 MLR** 81.7% **/ 16 Admin Exp** N/A
**Enroll(000): Q3 17:** 6 **16:** 5 **15:** 2 **Med Exp PMPM:** $708
**Principal Investments:** Cash and equiv (97%), long-term bonds (3%)
**Provider Compensation ($000):** Contr fee ($28,495), capitation ($4,642), bonus arrang ($434)
**Total Member Encounters:** Phys (85,556), non-phys (4,160)
**Group Affiliation:** Family Health Network Inc
**Licensed in:** IL
**Address:** 322 S Green St Ste 400, Chicago, IL 60607
**Phone:** (312) 605-9847 **Dom State:** IL **Commenced Bus:** January 2014

| Data Date | Rating | RACR #1 | RACR #2 | Total Assets ($mil) | Capital ($mil) | Net Premium ($mil) | Net Income ($mil) |
|---|---|---|---|---|---|---|---|
| 9-17 | C- | 0.64 | 0.53 | 20.3 | 4.7 | 46.4 | 0.1 |
| 9-16 | D+ | 0.71 | 0.59 | 15.0 | 4.4 | 30.3 | 1.1 |
| 2016 | D+ | 0.66 | 0.55 | 14.0 | 4.8 | 42.7 | 1.2 |
| 2015 | D | 0.29 | 0.24 | 8.6 | 2.7 | 19.6 | 0.1 |
| 2014 | D+ | 1.38 | 1.15 | 5.2 | 2.6 | 7.2 | -0.4 |
| 2013 | N/A | N/A | N/A | 1.9 | 1.5 | N/A | -0.5 |
| 2012 | N/A | N/A | N/A | N/A | N/A | N/A | N/A |

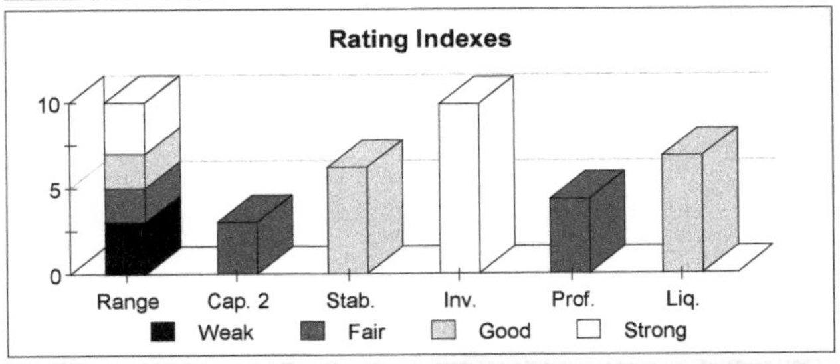


## COMMUNITY CARE BEHAVIORAL HEALTH B Good

**Major Rating Factors:** Excellent profitability (7.9 on a scale of 0 to 10). Strong capitalization (10.0) based on excellent current risk-adjusted capital (severe loss scenario). High quality investment portfolio (8.5).
**Other Rating Factors:** Excellent liquidity (7.1) with ample operational cash flow and liquid investments.
**Principal Business:** Medicaid (99%)
**Mem Phys: 16:** 3,573 **15:** 3,380 **16 MLR** 87.2% **/ 16 Admin Exp** N/A
**Enroll(000): Q3 17:** 765 **16:** 1,281 **15:** 1,195 **Med Exp PMPM:** $50
**Principal Investments:** Cash and equiv (52%), long-term bonds (35%), nonaffiliate common stock (10%), other (3%)
**Provider Compensation ($000):** Contr fee ($757,248), capitation ($14,295)
**Total Member Encounters:** Phys (25,674,255)
**Group Affiliation:** Univ of Pittsburgh Medical Center
**Licensed in:** PA
**Address:** 339 Sixth Ave Ste 1300, Pittsburgh, PA 15222
**Phone:** (412) 454-2120 **Dom State:** PA **Commenced Bus:** August 1997

| Data Date | Rating | RACR #1 | RACR #2 | Total Assets ($mil) | Capital ($mil) | Net Premium ($mil) | Net Income ($mil) |
|---|---|---|---|---|---|---|---|
| 9-17 | B | 4.02 | 3.35 | 326.3 | 199.6 | 688.8 | 15.1 |
| 9-16 | C+ | 3.42 | 2.85 | 299.6 | 169.4 | 662.8 | 13.9 |
| 2016 | C+ | 3.75 | 3.13 | 308.2 | 185.5 | 884.6 | 26.4 |
| 2015 | C | 3.10 | 2.59 | 244.5 | 156.9 | 811.3 | 4.5 |
| 2014 | C | 3.42 | 2.85 | 253.3 | 172.3 | 786.2 | 19.6 |
| 2013 | C | 3.20 | 2.66 | 234.9 | 155.4 | 735.7 | 15.6 |
| 2012 | C | 2.79 | 2.32 | 213.5 | 140.2 | 737.1 | 16.5 |

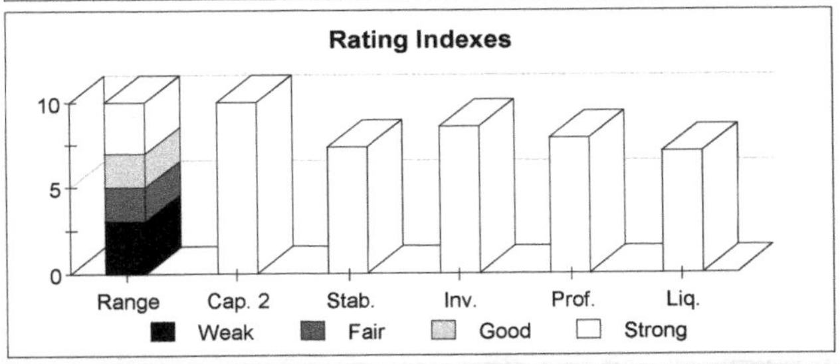


## COMMUNITY CARE HEALTH PLAN C- Fair

**Major Rating Factors:** Fair overall results on stability tests (4.1 on a scale of 0 to 10) based on poor risk diversification due to the company's size. Excellent profitability (7.2). Strong capitalization index (7.8) based on excellent current risk-adjusted capital (severe loss scenario).
**Other Rating Factors:** Excellent liquidity (7.4) with ample operational cash flow and liquid investments.
**Principal Business:** Managed care (100%)
**Mem Phys: 16:** N/A **15:** N/A **16 MLR** 81.4% **/ 16 Admin Exp** N/A
**Enroll(000): Q3 17:** 8 **16:** 5 **15:** 5 **Med Exp PMPM:** $290
**Principal Investments ($000):** Cash and equiv ($6,347)
**Provider Compensation ($000):** None
**Total Member Encounters:** N/A
**Group Affiliation:** Fresno Community Hosp & Med Center
**Licensed in:** CA
**Address:** 7370 N Palm Ave Ste 103, Fresno, CA 93711
**Phone:** (818) 458-2867 **Dom State:** CA **Commenced Bus:** March 2013

| Data Date | Rating | RACR #1 | RACR #2 | Total Assets ($mil) | Capital ($mil) | Net Premium ($mil) | Net Income ($mil) |
|---|---|---|---|---|---|---|---|
| 9-17 | C- | 2.66 | 1.69 | 9.3 | 6.7 | 22.5 | 1.8 |
| 9-16 | C- | 1.93 | 1.23 | 6.8 | 4.7 | 15.5 | 0.1 |
| 2016 | C- | 1.79 | 1.14 | 6.9 | 4.7 | 20.8 | 0.1 |
| 2015 | C- | 1.91 | 1.21 | 7.5 | 4.6 | 19.2 | 0.3 |
| 2014 | C- | 2.70 | 1.72 | 6.5 | 3.9 | 12.1 | 0.2 |
| 2013 | N/A | N/A | N/A | 5.3 | 3.5 | N/A | -0.2 |
| 2012 | N/A | N/A | N/A | N/A | N/A | N/A | N/A |

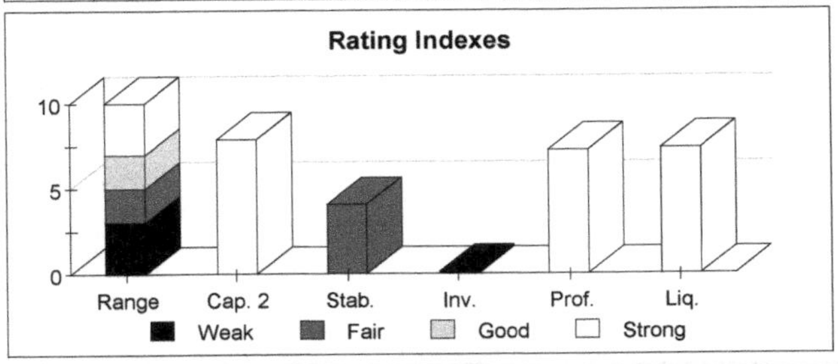

## COMMUNITY FIRST HEALTH PLANS INC * A Excellent

**Major Rating Factors:** Excellent profitability (8.9 on a scale of 0 to 10). Strong capitalization index (9.1) based on excellent current risk-adjusted capital (severe loss scenario). High quality investment portfolio (8.8).
**Other Rating Factors:** Excellent overall results on stability tests (8.1) based on healthy premium and capital growth during 2016. Excellent liquidity (7.0) with ample operational cash flow and liquid investments.
**Principal Business:** Medicaid (84%), comp med (16%)
**Mem Phys: 16:** 6,148 **15:** 4,697 **16 MLR** 86.1% **/ 16 Admin Exp** N/A
**Enroll(000): Q3 17:** 140 **16:** 144 **15:** 136 **Med Exp PMPM:** $218
**Principal Investments:** Cash and equiv (52%), long-term bonds (48%)
**Provider Compensation ($000):** Contr fee ($305,891), capitation ($34,615)
**Total Member Encounters:** Phys (565,036), non-phys (931,759)
**Group Affiliation:** Bexar County Hospital District
**Licensed in:** TX
**Address:** 12238 Silicon Drive Ste 100, San Antonio, TX 78249
**Phone:** (210) 227-2347 **Dom State:** TX **Commenced Bus:** October 1995

| Data Date | Rating | RACR #1 | RACR #2 | Total Assets ($mil) | Capital ($mil) | Net Premium ($mil) | Net Income ($mil) |
|---|---|---|---|---|---|---|---|
| 9-17 | A | 3.06 | 2.55 | 151.9 | 99.9 | 386.8 | 9.5 |
| 9-16 | A- | 2.90 | 2.42 | 124.9 | 83.0 | 296.7 | 8.6 |
| 2016 | A | 2.78 | 2.32 | 155.1 | 92.3 | 424.2 | 19.0 |
| 2015 | A- | 2.53 | 2.11 | 117.8 | 74.5 | 356.3 | 14.6 |
| 2014 | A- | 2.22 | 1.85 | 104.9 | 58.9 | 310.6 | 13.7 |
| 2013 | B+ | 1.75 | 1.46 | 78.1 | 45.5 | 264.7 | 4.6 |
| 2012 | B | 1.51 | 1.26 | 67.9 | 39.1 | 259.5 | 0.3 |

Rating Indexes

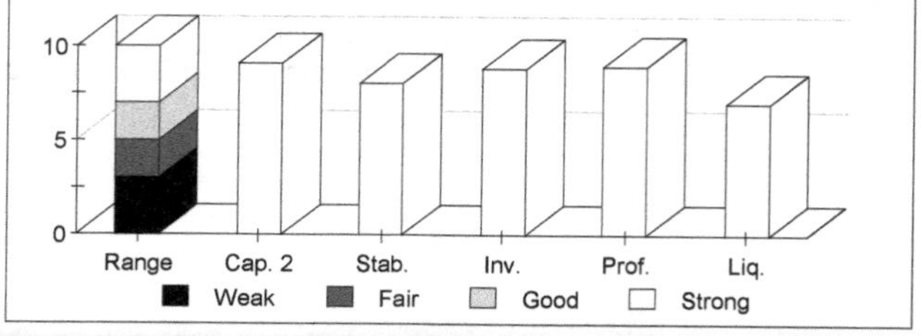


## COMMUNITY HEALTH CHOICE INC D Weak

**Major Rating Factors:** Weak profitability index (1.8 on a scale of 0 to 10). Poor capitalization index (0.0) based on weak current risk-adjusted capital (severe loss scenario). Weak overall results on stability tests (2.9).
**Other Rating Factors:** High quality investment portfolio (9.9). Excellent liquidity (7.1) with ample operational cash flow and liquid investments.
**Principal Business:** Medicaid (73%), comp med (27%)
**Mem Phys: 16:** 10,911 **15:** 10,895 **16 MLR** 91.5% **/ 16 Admin Exp** N/A
**Enroll(000): Q3 17:** 133 **16:** 359 **15:** 295 **Med Exp PMPM:** $237
**Principal Investments:** Cash and equiv (100%)
**Provider Compensation ($000):** Contr fee ($962,145), capitation ($36,075), bonus arrang ($4,930)
**Total Member Encounters:** Phys (3,110,422), non-phys (564,599)
**Group Affiliation:** Harris Health System
**Licensed in:** TX
**Address:** 2636 South Loop West Ste 700, Houston, TX 77054
**Phone:** (713) 295-2200 **Dom State:** TX **Commenced Bus:** July 1997

| Data Date | Rating | RACR #1 | RACR #2 | Total Assets ($mil) | Capital ($mil) | Net Premium ($mil) | Net Income ($mil) |
|---|---|---|---|---|---|---|---|
| 9-17 | D | 0.08 | 0.07 | 160.6 | 8.8 | 676.0 | 3.9 |
| 9-16 | B | 1.44 | 1.20 | 265.0 | 102.4 | 842.7 | 0.9 |
| 2016 | C+ | 0.84 | 0.70 | 305.6 | 83.7 | 1,121.5 | -18.3 |
| 2015 | B | 1.47 | 1.23 | 239.9 | 101.6 | 850.6 | 5.4 |
| 2014 | B- | 1.67 | 1.39 | 192.1 | 100.4 | 720.2 | 16.3 |
| 2013 | B- | 1.47 | 1.22 | 166.6 | 87.3 | 666.4 | -6.3 |
| 2012 | B | 1.62 | 1.35 | 172.8 | 91.2 | 636.2 | -15.5 |

Rating Indexes

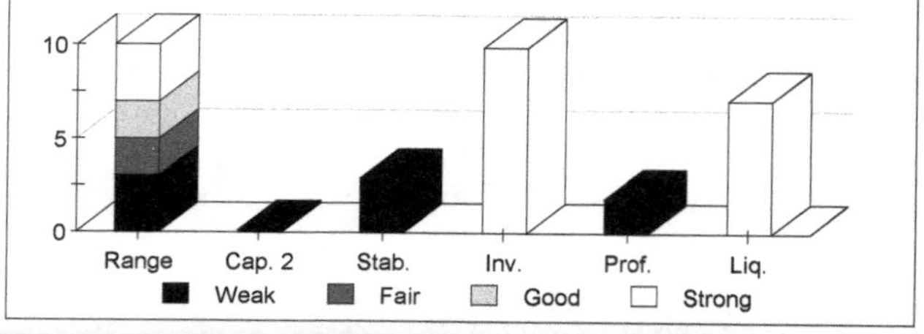


## COMMUNITY HEALTH GROUP B Good

**Major Rating Factors:** Good overall results on stability tests (5.5 on a scale of 0 to 10). Excellent profitability (7.6). Strong capitalization index (10.0) based on excellent current risk-adjusted capital (severe loss scenario).
**Other Rating Factors:** Excellent liquidity (8.6) with ample operational cash flow and liquid investments.
**Principal Business:** Medicaid (100%)
**Mem Phys: 16:** N/A **15:** N/A **16 MLR** 80.6% **/ 16 Admin Exp** N/A
**Enroll(000): Q3 17:** 292 **16:** 291 **15:** 271 **Med Exp PMPM:** $282
**Principal Investments ($000):** Cash and equiv ($732,492)
**Provider Compensation ($000):** None
**Total Member Encounters:** N/A
**Group Affiliation:** None
**Licensed in:** CA
**Address:** 2420 Fenton Street Suite 100, Chula Vista, CA 91914
**Phone:** (619) 498-6516 **Dom State:** CA **Commenced Bus:** N/A

| Data Date | Rating | RACR #1 | RACR #2 | Total Assets ($mil) | Capital ($mil) | Net Premium ($mil) | Net Income ($mil) |
|---|---|---|---|---|---|---|---|
| 9-17 | B | 8.21 | 4.97 | 928.8 | 527.7 | 898.6 | 143.2 |
| 9-16 | B- | 6.39 | 3.86 | 664.3 | 378.6 | 932.5 | 191.3 |
| 2016 | B | 5.72 | 3.46 | 776.0 | 384.5 | 1,184.5 | 197.3 |
| 2015 | B- | 3.02 | 1.83 | 529.4 | 187.3 | 1,038.5 | 113.7 |
| 2014 | C+ | 1.28 | 0.80 | 231.4 | 73.6 | 683.6 | 35.2 |
| 2013 | C | 1.02 | 0.64 | 94.5 | 38.3 | 340.7 | -11.9 |
| 2012 | B | 1.53 | 0.96 | 98.1 | 50.2 | 312.1 | -2.6 |

Rating Indexes

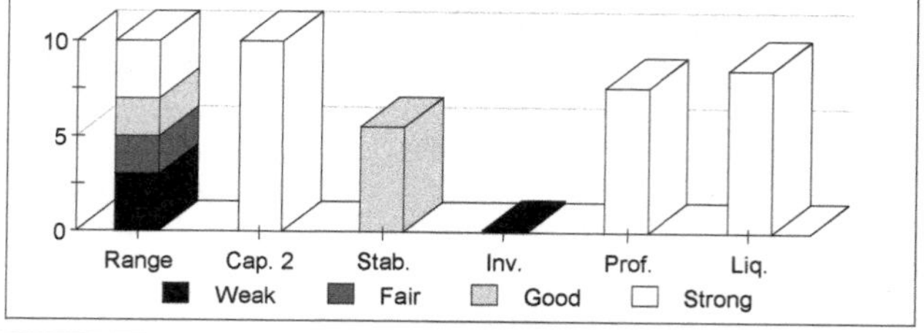

## COMMUNITY HEALTH PLAN OF WASHINGTON B Good

**Major Rating Factors:** Good liquidity (6.8 on a scale of 0 to 10) with sufficient resources (cash flows and marketable investments) to handle a spike in claims. Fair profitability index (4.2). Strong capitalization (8.0) based on excellent current risk-adjusted capital (severe loss scenario).
**Other Rating Factors:** High quality investment portfolio (9.4).
**Principal Business:** Medicaid (91%), Medicare (8%), comp med (1%)
**Mem Phys: 16:** 25,035 **15:** 23,346 **16 MLR** 88.8% **/ 16 Admin Exp** N/A
**Enroll(000): Q3 17:** 297 **16:** 311 **15:** 311 **Med Exp PMPM:** $256
**Principal Investments:** Long-term bonds (51%), cash and equiv (34%), nonaffiliate common stock (14%)
**Provider Compensation ($000):** FFS ($739,748), capitation ($192,314)
**Total Member Encounters:** Phys (1,215,784), non-phys (599,043)
**Group Affiliation:** Community Hlth Network of Washington
**Licensed in:** WA
**Address:** 1111 Third Ave Ste 400, Seattle, WA 98101
**Phone:** (206) 521-8833 **Dom State:** WA **Commenced Bus:** July 1996

| Data Date | Rating | RACR #1 | RACR #2 | Total Assets ($mil) | Capital ($mil) | Net Premium ($mil) | Net Income ($mil) |
|---|---|---|---|---|---|---|---|
| 9-17 | B | 2.13 | 1.78 | 453.9 | 180.1 | 822.4 | 11.4 |
| 9-16 | B | 2.46 | 2.05 | 511.7 | 161.9 | 792.4 | 20.8 |
| 2016 | B | 1.93 | 1.61 | 445.2 | 162.0 | 1,070.9 | 17.4 |
| 2015 | B- | 2.14 | 1.78 | 502.0 | 139.0 | 1,070.2 | 39.6 |
| 2014 | B | 1.62 | 1.35 | 562.1 | 98.6 | 999.1 | -25.2 |
| 2013 | A- | 2.04 | 1.70 | 376.9 | 137.8 | 872.7 | 18.4 |
| 2012 | B+ | 1.89 | 1.57 | 314.0 | 126.1 | 876.2 | 8.8 |

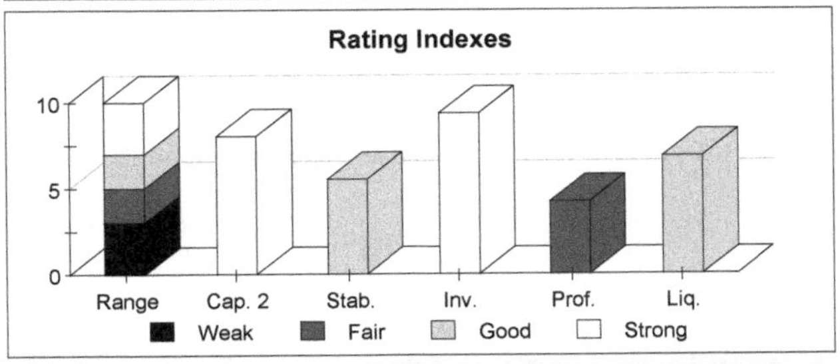


## COMMUNITY INS CO (OH) * B+ Good

**Major Rating Factors:** Good liquidity (6.2 on a scale of 0 to 10) with sufficient resources (cash flows and marketable investments) to handle a spike in claims. Excellent profitability (9.0). Strong capitalization (8.9) based on excellent current risk-adjusted capital (severe loss scenario).
**Other Rating Factors:** Fair quality investment portfolio (3.7).
**Principal Business:** Comp med (48%), Medicare (25%), FEHB (20%), med supp (2%), other (4%)
**Mem Phys: 16:** 71,966 **15:** 68,003 **16 MLR** 83.6% **/ 16 Admin Exp** N/A
**Enroll(000): Q3 17:** 2,026 **16:** 1,841 **15:** 1,854 **Med Exp PMPM:** $202
**Principal Investments:** Long-term bonds (84%), nonaffiliate common stock (21%), real estate (1%), other (12%)
**Provider Compensation ($000):** Contr fee ($2,543,360), FFS ($1,672,806), bonus arrang ($39,178), capitation ($12,649), other ($152,598)
**Total Member Encounters:** Phys (6,629,261), non-phys (5,579,180)
**Group Affiliation:** Anthem Inc
**Licensed in:** IN, OH
**Address:** 4361 IRWIN SIMPSON Rd, MASON, OH 45040-9498
**Phone:** (513) 872-8100 **Dom State:** OH **Commenced Bus:** October 1995

| Data Date | Rating | RACR #1 | RACR #2 | Total Assets ($mil) | Capital ($mil) | Net Premium ($mil) | Net Income ($mil) |
|---|---|---|---|---|---|---|---|
| 9-17 | B+ | 2.85 | 2.38 | 2,274.1 | 877.6 | 4,287.8 | 302.9 |
| 9-16 | B+ | 2.92 | 2.43 | 2,365.0 | 865.3 | 3,966.9 | 276.8 |
| 2016 | B+ | 2.64 | 2.20 | 2,138.7 | 807.8 | 5,297.0 | 319.1 |
| 2015 | B+ | 2.56 | 2.13 | 2,091.4 | 754.1 | 5,255.4 | 266.3 |
| 2014 | B+ | 2.74 | 2.28 | 2,014.3 | 812.2 | 5,309.2 | 276.9 |
| 2013 | B+ | 2.72 | 2.27 | 1,887.4 | 778.4 | 5,102.2 | 392.5 |
| 2012 | B+ | 2.55 | 2.13 | 1,988.7 | 754.8 | 5,229.5 | 380.1 |

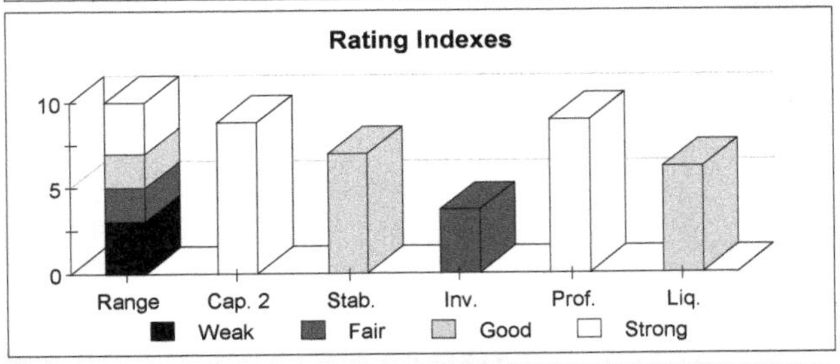


## COMMUNITYCARE GOVERNMENT PROGRAMS D+ Weak

**Major Rating Factors:** Weak profitability index (0.9 on a scale of 0 to 10). Good capitalization (5.0) based on good current risk-adjusted capital (severe loss scenario). High quality investment portfolio (9.9).
**Other Rating Factors:** Excellent liquidity (7.5) with ample operational cash flow and liquid investments.
**Principal Business:** Medicare (100%)
**Mem Phys: 16:** 3,431 **15:** N/A **16 MLR** 86.0% **/ 16 Admin Exp** N/A
**Enroll(000): Q3 17:** 2 **16:** 1 **15:** N/A **Med Exp PMPM:** $479
**Principal Investments:** Cash and equiv (84%), long-term bonds (16%)
**Provider Compensation ($000):** Contr fee ($3,546), capitation ($2,521), FFS ($9)
**Total Member Encounters:** Phys (7,674), non-phys (9,440)
**Group Affiliation:** CommunityCare Government Programs
**Licensed in:** OK
**Address:** 218 W 6th St, Tulsa, OK 74119
**Phone:** (918) 594-5295 **Dom State:** OK **Commenced Bus:** January 2015

| Data Date | Rating | RACR #1 | RACR #2 | Total Assets ($mil) | Capital ($mil) | Net Premium ($mil) | Net Income ($mil) |
|---|---|---|---|---|---|---|---|
| 9-17 | D+ | 0.94 | 0.78 | 6.0 | 3.0 | 10.0 | 0.4 |
| 9-16 | N/A | N/A | N/A | 5.0 | 3.8 | 4.0 | -0.6 |
| 2016 | D+ | 1.16 | 0.96 | 4.3 | 3.6 | 5.6 | -0.7 |
| 2015 | N/A | N/A | N/A | 1.8 | 1.7 | N/A | -1.3 |
| 2014 | N/A | N/A | N/A | N/A | N/A | N/A | N/A |
| 2013 | N/A | N/A | N/A | N/A | N/A | N/A | N/A |
| 2012 | N/A | N/A | N/A | N/A | N/A | N/A | N/A |

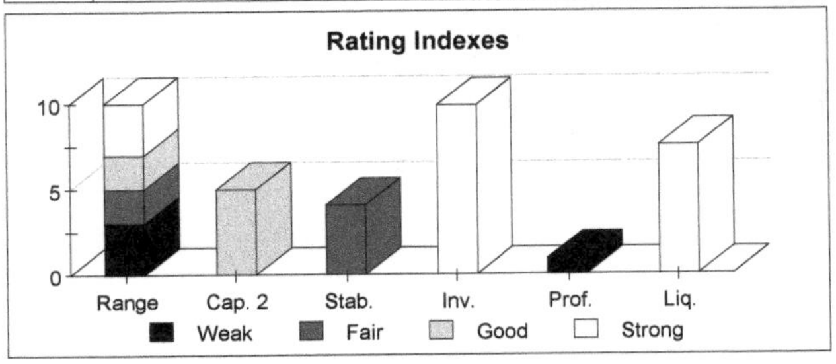

## COMMUNITYCARE HMO INC * B+ Good

**Major Rating Factors:** Good overall profitability index (6.6 on a scale of 0 to 10). Good overall results on stability tests (5.9). Strong capitalization index (9.4) based on excellent current risk-adjusted capital (severe loss scenario).
**Other Rating Factors:** High quality investment portfolio (9.9). Excellent liquidity (7.0) with ample operational cash flow and liquid investments.
**Principal Business:** Comp med (51%), Medicare (49%)
**Mem Phys: 16:** 9,042 **15:** 8,875 **16 MLR** 87.7% **/ 16 Admin Exp** N/A
**Enroll(000): Q3 17:** 98 **16:** 95 **15:** 95 **Med Exp PMPM:** $455
**Principal Investments:** Cash and equiv (61%), long-term bonds (37%), other (1%)
**Provider Compensation ($000):** Capitation ($267,385), contr fee ($234,869), FFS ($5,472)
**Total Member Encounters:** Phys (640,364), non-phys (699,845)
**Group Affiliation:** CommunityCare Mngd Healthcare Plan
**Licensed in:** OK
**Address:** 218 W 6th St, Tulsa, OK 74119
**Phone:** (918) 594-5200 **Dom State:** OK **Commenced Bus:** June 1994

| Data Date | Rating | RACR #1 | RACR #2 | Total Assets ($mil) | Capital ($mil) | Net Premium ($mil) | Net Income ($mil) |
|---|---|---|---|---|---|---|---|
| 9-17 | B+ | 3.30 | 2.75 | 231.6 | 118.0 | 469.8 | 7.2 |
| 9-16 | B | 3.18 | 2.65 | 201.2 | 119.8 | 448.6 | 0.1 |
| 2016 | B+ | 3.33 | 2.78 | 181.4 | 119.1 | 592.3 | 1.6 |
| 2015 | A- | 3.06 | 2.55 | 164.7 | 115.1 | 585.3 | -0.1 |
| 2014 | A | 2.97 | 2.48 | 193.7 | 121.0 | 676.3 | 8.3 |
| 2013 | A | 2.84 | 2.36 | 185.7 | 112.5 | 661.6 | 9.8 |
| 2012 | A | 2.78 | 2.32 | 153.9 | 102.9 | 606.6 | 8.9 |

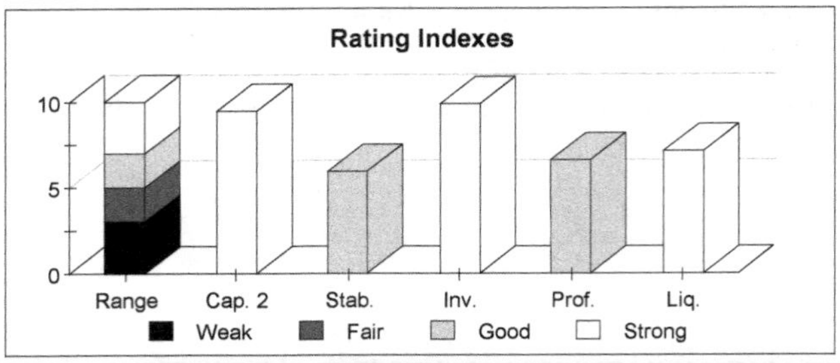


## COMMUNITYCARE L&H INS CO B- Good

**Major Rating Factors:** Strong capitalization (7.5 on a scale of 0 to 10) based on excellent current risk-adjusted capital (severe loss scenario). High quality investment portfolio (9.9). Excellent liquidity (7.0) with ample operational cash flow and liquid investments.
**Other Rating Factors:** Weak profitability index (1.3).
**Principal Business:** Comp med (98%), med supp (2%)
**Mem Phys: 16:** 10,382 **15:** 10,201 **16 MLR** 84.6% **/ 16 Admin Exp** N/A
**Enroll(000): Q3 17:** 11 **16:** 11 **15:** 13 **Med Exp PMPM:** $330
**Principal Investments:** Cash and equiv (82%), long-term bonds (18%)
**Provider Compensation ($000):** Contr fee ($43,944), FFS ($1,969)
**Total Member Encounters:** Phys (68,073), non-phys (49,079)
**Group Affiliation:** CommunityCare Managed Hlthcare Plan
**Licensed in:** OK
**Address:** 218 W 6th St, Tulsa, OK 74119
**Phone:** (918) 594-5200 **Dom State:** OK **Commenced Bus:** June 2000

| Data Date | Rating | RACR #1 | RACR #2 | Total Assets ($mil) | Capital ($mil) | Net Premium ($mil) | Net Income ($mil) |
|---|---|---|---|---|---|---|---|
| 9-17 | B- | 1.79 | 1.49 | 17.9 | 8.8 | 39.4 | 0.4 |
| 9-16 | B- | 1.53 | 1.28 | 18.1 | 9.0 | 42.0 | -1.0 |
| 2016 | B- | 1.77 | 1.48 | 20.2 | 8.7 | 54.0 | -1.3 |
| 2015 | B- | 1.68 | 1.40 | 20.0 | 10.1 | 66.0 | -2.0 |
| 2014 | B- | 1.86 | 1.55 | 22.5 | 12.0 | 75.5 | -1.0 |
| 2013 | B- | 2.02 | 1.69 | 23.0 | 12.8 | 73.9 | 0.9 |
| 2012 | B- | 1.90 | 1.58 | 22.6 | 11.8 | 69.7 | -0.6 |

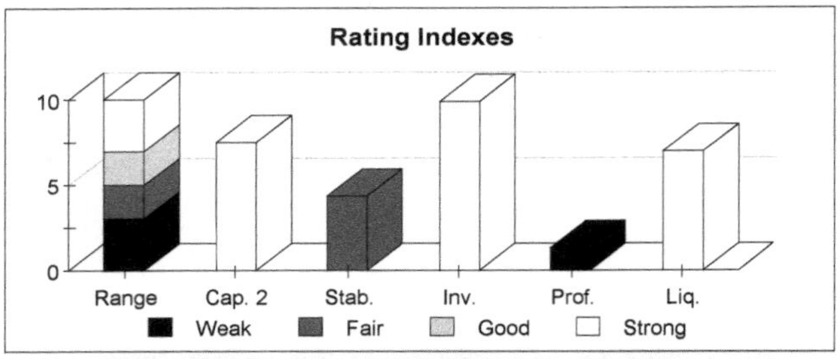


## COMPANION LIFE INSURANCE COMPANY * B+ Good

**Major Rating Factors:** Good liquidity (6.9 on a scale of 0 to 10) with sufficient resources to handle a spike in claims. Good overall results on stability tests (6.6). Strengths include good financial support from affiliation with Blue Cross Blue Shield of S Carolina, excellent operational trends and excellent risk diversification. Fair quality investment portfolio (4.4).
**Other Rating Factors:** Strong capitalization (8.6) based on excellent risk adjusted capital (severe loss scenario). Excellent profitability (8.6).
**Principal Business:** Group health insurance (87%), reinsurance (8%), group life insurance (4%), and individual health insurance (1%).
**Principal Investments:** NonCMO investment grade bonds (44%), common & preferred stock (37%), CMOs and structured securities (16%), and cash (2%).
**Investments in Affiliates:** 11%
**Group Affiliation:** Blue Cross Blue Shield of S Carolina
**Licensed in:** All states except CA, HI, NJ, NY, PR
**Commenced Business:** July 1970
**Address:** 2501 Faraway Drive, Columbia, SC 29219
**Phone:** (800) 753-0404 **Domicile State:** SC **NAIC Code:** 77828

| Data Date | Rating | RACR #1 | RACR #2 | Total Assets ($mil) | Capital ($mil) | Net Premium ($mil) | Net Income ($mil) |
|---|---|---|---|---|---|---|---|
| 9-17 | B+ | 2.68 | 2.07 | 359.8 | 206.2 | 185.7 | 13.9 |
| 9-16 | A- | 3.20 | 2.42 | 335.7 | 181.5 | 178.1 | 11.3 |
| 2016 | B+ | 2.55 | 1.99 | 338.7 | 186.2 | 237.4 | 16.4 |
| 2015 | A- | 3.15 | 2.44 | 300.4 | 160.4 | 221.6 | 13.7 |
| 2014 | A- | 2.95 | 2.30 | 284.9 | 149.0 | 220.5 | 15.6 |
| 2013 | A- | 2.92 | 2.31 | 251.7 | 138.0 | 202.8 | 14.5 |
| 2012 | A- | 2.75 | 2.19 | 203.8 | 120.7 | 181.8 | 12.5 |

**Blue Cross Blue Shield of S Carolina**
**Composite Group Rating: B+**

| Largest Group Members | Assets ($mil) | Rating |
|---|---|---|
| BLUE CROSS BLUE SHIELD OF SC INC | 3522 | A- |
| BLUECHOICE HEALTHPLAN OF SC INC | 347 | B |
| COMPANION LIFE INS CO | 339 | B+ |
| NIAGARA LIFE HEALTH INS CO | 18 | B |

## COMPCARE HEALTH SERVICES INS CORP * — A- Excellent

**Major Rating Factors:** Excellent profitability (8.7 on a scale of 0 to 10). Strong capitalization index (9.7) based on excellent current risk-adjusted capital (severe loss scenario). High quality investment portfolio (8.3).
**Other Rating Factors:** Excellent overall results on stability tests (7.2). Rating is significantly influenced by the good financial results of Anthem Inc. Good liquidity (6.7) with sufficient resources (cash flows and marketable investments) to handle a spike in claims.
**Principal Business:** Comp med (71%), Medicaid (24%), Medicare (3%), dental (1%)
**Mem Phys: 16:** 14,501 **15:** 14,121 **16 MLR** 81.5% **/ 16 Admin Exp** N/A
**Enroll(000): Q3 17:** 219 **16:** 215 **15:** 209 **Med Exp PMPM:** $240
**Principal Investments:** Long-term bonds (90%), cash and equiv (5%), other (4%)
**Provider Compensation ($000):** Contr fee ($445,971), FFS ($172,704), capitation ($5,553), bonus arrang ($2,957)
**Total Member Encounters:** Phys (1,208,505), non-phys (655,868)
**Group Affiliation:** Anthem Inc
**Licensed in:** WI
**Address:** N17 W24340 RIVERWOOD DRIVE, WAUKESHA, WI 53188
**Phone:** (262) 523-4020 **Dom State:** WI **Commenced Bus:** February 1976

| Data Date | Rating | RACR #1 | RACR #2 | Total Assets ($mil) | Capital ($mil) | Net Premium ($mil) | Net Income ($mil) |
|---|---|---|---|---|---|---|---|
| 9-17 | A- | 3.49 | 2.91 | 314.8 | 152.5 | 600.8 | 39.3 |
| 9-16 | B+ | 3.22 | 2.69 | 265.8 | 131.1 | 580.4 | 44.7 |
| 2016 | A- | 3.11 | 2.60 | 265.3 | 135.4 | 769.1 | 45.8 |
| 2015 | A- | 2.50 | 2.09 | 233.6 | 100.7 | 681.2 | 6.8 |
| 2014 | A- | 2.85 | 2.38 | 228.6 | 107.6 | 660.8 | 29.1 |
| 2013 | A- | 3.15 | 2.63 | 190.2 | 103.9 | 599.3 | 40.6 |
| 2012 | B+ | 3.28 | 2.73 | 163.7 | 86.0 | 471.3 | 32.9 |

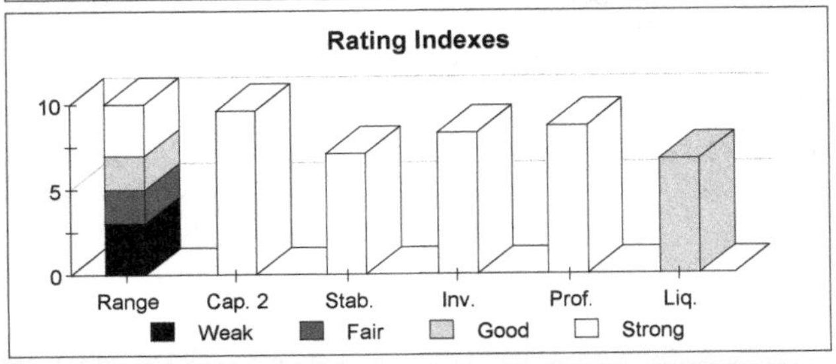


## COMPREHENSIVE MOBILE INS CO — B Good

**Major Rating Factors:** Good overall profitability index (5.5 on a scale of 0 to 10). Strong capitalization (10.0) based on excellent current risk-adjusted capital (severe loss scenario). High quality investment portfolio (9.8).
**Other Rating Factors:** Excellent liquidity (7.6) with ample operational cash flow and liquid investments.
**Principal Business:** Other (100%)
**Mem Phys: 16:** 45 **15:** 12 **16 MLR** 42.0% **/ 16 Admin Exp** N/A
**Enroll(000): Q3 17:** 2 **16:** 1 **15:** 1 **Med Exp PMPM:** $85
**Principal Investments:** Cash and equiv (49%), long-term bonds (30%), nonaffiliate common stock (21%)
**Provider Compensation ($000):** FFS ($1,226)
**Total Member Encounters:** Non-phys (2,996)
**Group Affiliation:** Comprehensive Mobile Insurance Group
**Licensed in:** AZ
**Address:** 19820 N 7TH St Ste 290, PHOENIX, AZ 85024
**Phone:** (877) 929-0030 **Dom State:** AZ **Commenced Bus:** November 2013

| Data Date | Rating | RACR #1 | RACR #2 | Total Assets ($mil) | Capital ($mil) | Net Premium ($mil) | Net Income ($mil) |
|---|---|---|---|---|---|---|---|
| 9-17 | B | 5.34 | 4.45 | 2.4 | 2.0 | 2.9 | 0.1 |
| 9-16 | B- | 8.75 | 7.29 | 1.4 | 1.0 | 2.1 | 0.2 |
| 2016 | B | 2.71 | 2.26 | 1.4 | 1.0 | 2.9 | 0.2 |
| 2015 | C- | 7.29 | 6.08 | 1.2 | 0.9 | 1.1 | 0.2 |
| 2014 | U | 5.59 | 4.66 | 0.7 | 0.7 | 0.1 | -0.1 |
| 2013 | N/A | N/A | N/A | 0.7 | 0.7 | N/A | N/A |
| 2012 | N/A | N/A | N/A | N/A | N/A | N/A | N/A |

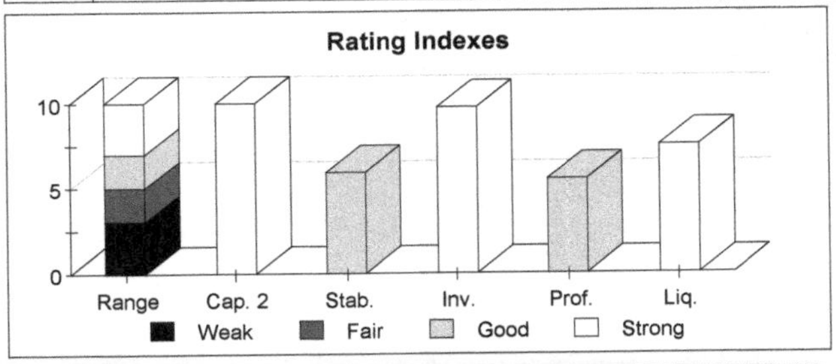


## CONNECTICARE BENEFITS INC — D+ Weak

**Major Rating Factors:** Fair profitability index (2.9 on a scale of 0 to 10). Good liquidity (6.8) with sufficient resources (cash flows and marketable investments) to handle a spike in claims. Strong capitalization (7.6) based on excellent current risk-adjusted capital (severe loss scenario).
**Other Rating Factors:** High quality investment portfolio (9.9).
**Principal Business:** Comp med (100%)
**Mem Phys: 16:** 23,850 **15:** 22,449 **16 MLR** 94.9% **/ 16 Admin Exp** N/A
**Enroll(000): Q3 17:** 63 **16:** 49 **15:** 35 **Med Exp PMPM:** $423
**Principal Investments:** Cash and equiv (82%), long-term bonds (18%)
**Provider Compensation ($000):** Contr fee ($194,947), FFS ($47,344), capitation ($6,932)
**Total Member Encounters:** Phys (218,298), non-phys (187,564)
**Group Affiliation:** EmblemHealth Inc
**Licensed in:** CT
**Address:** 175 Scott Swamp Rd, Farmington, CT 06032-3124
**Phone:** (860) 674-5700 **Dom State:** CT **Commenced Bus:** January 2013

| Data Date | Rating | RACR #1 | RACR #2 | Total Assets ($mil) | Capital ($mil) | Net Premium ($mil) | Net Income ($mil) |
|---|---|---|---|---|---|---|---|
| 9-17 | D+ | 1.85 | 1.55 | 107.9 | 28.9 | 298.6 | 1.7 |
| 9-16 | D+ | 3.05 | 2.54 | 76.2 | 23.6 | 207.1 | -12.9 |
| 2016 | D+ | 1.78 | 1.49 | 84.1 | 27.2 | 272.1 | -17.5 |
| 2015 | C | 4.80 | 4.00 | 81.5 | 42.4 | 198.8 | 13.6 |
| 2014 | C- | 3.34 | 2.79 | 59.5 | 29.7 | 140.1 | 12.3 |
| 2013 | N/A | N/A | N/A | 1.4 | 1.0 | N/A | N/A |
| 2012 | N/A | N/A | N/A | N/A | N/A | N/A | N/A |

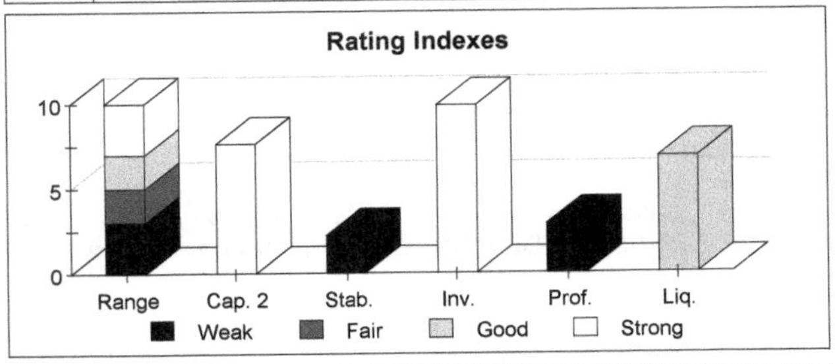

## CONNECTICARE INC — C — Fair

**Major Rating Factors:** Fair overall results on stability tests (4.5 on a scale of 0 to 10). Poor financial strength from affiliates. Good overall profitability index (5.8). Good liquidity (6.8) with sufficient resources (cash flows and marketable investments) to handle a spike in claims.
**Other Rating Factors:** Strong capitalization index (7.9) based on excellent current risk-adjusted capital (severe loss scenario). High quality investment portfolio (9.9).
**Principal Business:** Medicare (74%), comp med (26%)
**Mem Phys: 16:** 23,850 **15:** 22,449 **16 MLR** 84.0% **/ 16 Admin Exp** N/A
**Enroll(000): Q3 17:** 80 **16:** 88 **15:** 98 **Med Exp PMPM:** $628
**Principal Investments:** Long-term bonds (90%), cash and equiv (10%)
**Provider Compensation ($000):** Contr fee ($574,063), FFS ($78,818), capitation ($11,599)
**Total Member Encounters:** Phys (741,364), non-phys (600,910)
**Group Affiliation:** EmblemHealth Inc
**Licensed in:** CT
**Address:** 175 Scott Swamp Road, Farmington, CT 06032-3124
**Phone:** (860) 674-5700 **Dom State:** CT **Commenced Bus:** July 1999

| Data Date | Rating | RACR #1 | RACR #2 | Total Assets ($mil) | Capital ($mil) | Net Premium ($mil) | Net Income ($mil) |
|---|---|---|---|---|---|---|---|
| 9-17 | C | 2.08 | 1.73 | 236.1 | 90.4 | 536.3 | -0.7 |
| 9-16 | C | 1.67 | 1.39 | 220.8 | 73.3 | 597.5 | 2.6 |
| 2016 | C | 2.19 | 1.82 | 209.2 | 94.5 | 793.8 | 7.1 |
| 2015 | C+ | 2.51 | 2.09 | 214.0 | 108.9 | 835.4 | 5.1 |
| 2014 | B | 2.78 | 2.32 | 254.1 | 115.6 | 778.5 | -0.9 |
| 2013 | B+ | 3.08 | 2.57 | 246.6 | 138.7 | 834.3 | 16.8 |
| 2012 | B+ | 2.92 | 2.43 | 278.7 | 153.3 | 971.9 | 31.4 |

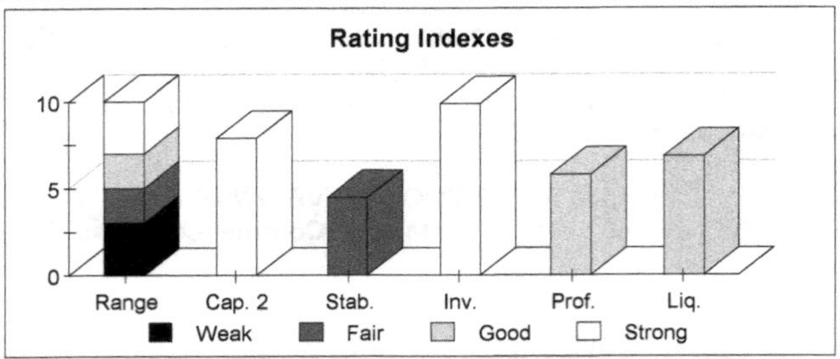


## CONNECTICARE INS CO — C — Fair

**Major Rating Factors:** Fair liquidity (4.5 on a scale of 0 to 10) as cash resources may not be adequate to cover a spike in claims. Weak profitability index (0.9). Strong capitalization (7.0) based on excellent current risk-adjusted capital (severe loss scenario).
**Other Rating Factors:** High quality investment portfolio (9.1).
**Principal Business:** Comp med (100%)
**Mem Phys: 16:** 23,850 **15:** 22,449 **16 MLR** 96.0% **/ 16 Admin Exp** N/A
**Enroll(000): Q3 17:** 111 **16:** 155 **15:** 153 **Med Exp PMPM:** $391
**Principal Investments:** Long-term bonds (74%), affiliate common stock (14%), cash and equiv (12%)
**Provider Compensation ($000):** Contr fee ($581,207), FFS ($122,440), capitation ($16,641)
**Total Member Encounters:** Phys (627,416), non-phys (541,391)
**Group Affiliation:** EmblemHealth Inc
**Licensed in:** CT
**Address:** 175 Scott Swamp Rd, Farmington, CT 06032-3124
**Phone:** (860) 674-5700 **Dom State:** CT **Commenced Bus:** October 2002

| Data Date | Rating | RACR #1 | RACR #2 | Total Assets ($mil) | Capital ($mil) | Net Premium ($mil) | Net Income ($mil) |
|---|---|---|---|---|---|---|---|
| 9-17 | C | 1.33 | 1.11 | 198.0 | 90.9 | 524.6 | 4.3 |
| 9-16 | C | 1.60 | 1.34 | 252.5 | 82.4 | 573.8 | -50.1 |
| 2016 | C | 1.28 | 1.06 | 249.3 | 86.3 | 765.3 | -49.8 |
| 2015 | C | 1.19 | 0.99 | 210.8 | 66.5 | 714.4 | -19.7 |
| 2014 | C | 1.79 | 1.49 | 158.4 | 68.4 | 544.9 | 2.7 |
| 2013 | C | 1.80 | 1.50 | 90.5 | 37.9 | 404.9 | 14.1 |
| 2012 | D+ | 1.92 | 1.60 | 61.7 | 23.7 | 224.5 | 4.1 |

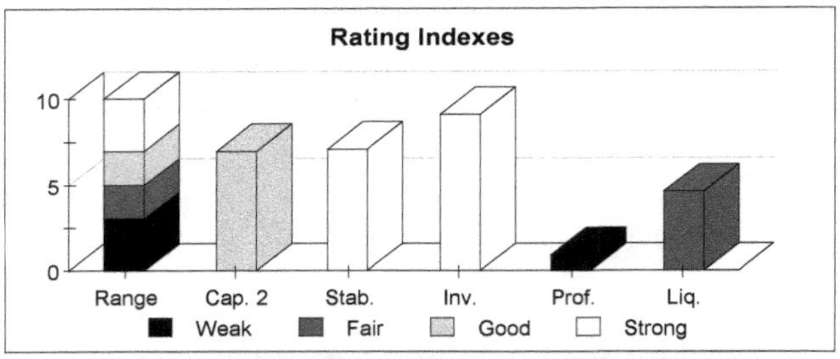


## CONNECTICARE OF MASSACHUSETTS INC — E- — Very Weak

**Major Rating Factors:** Weak profitability index (0.8 on a scale of 0 to 10). Weak overall results on stability tests (2.3) based on a significant 42% decrease in enrollment during the period, a steep decline in capital during 2016. Rating is significantly influenced by the poor financial results of EmblemHealth Inc. Good liquidity (6.3) with sufficient resources (cash flows and marketable investments) to handle a spike in claims.
**Other Rating Factors:** Strong capitalization index (6.9) based on excellent current risk-adjusted capital (severe loss scenario). High quality investment portfolio (9.9).
**Principal Business:** Comp med (100%)
**Mem Phys: 16:** 23,850 **15:** 22,449 **16 MLR** 104.5% **/ 16 Admin Exp** N/A
**Enroll(000): Q3 17:** 1 **16:** 1 **15:** 1 **Med Exp PMPM:** $465
**Principal Investments:** Long-term bonds (86%), cash and equiv (14%)
**Provider Compensation ($000):** Contr fee ($4,211), FFS ($901), capitation ($110)
**Total Member Encounters:** Phys (4,292), non-phys (3,047)
**Group Affiliation:** EmblemHealth Inc
**Licensed in:** MA
**Address:** c/o Leboeuf Lamb Greene & McRa, Boston, MA 02110-3173
**Phone:** (860) 674-5700 **Dom State:** MA **Commenced Bus:** July 2000

| Data Date | Rating | RACR #1 | RACR #2 | Total Assets ($mil) | Capital ($mil) | Net Premium ($mil) | Net Income ($mil) |
|---|---|---|---|---|---|---|---|
| 9-17 | E- | 1.31 | 1.09 | 2.6 | 1.6 | 3.3 | 0.2 |
| 9-16 | E- | 1.65 | 1.38 | 3.1 | 2.0 | 4.1 | -0.1 |
| 2016 | E- | 1.20 | 1.00 | 2.6 | 1.5 | 4.8 | -0.7 |
| 2015 | E- | 1.74 | 1.45 | 3.7 | 2.1 | 8.3 | -0.9 |
| 2014 | C | 2.55 | 2.13 | 6.7 | 3.1 | 10.1 | -0.4 |
| 2013 | C+ | 2.77 | 2.31 | 4.6 | 3.5 | 14.8 | 0.4 |
| 2012 | C+ | 4.45 | 3.71 | 7.1 | 5.6 | 17.2 | 2.5 |

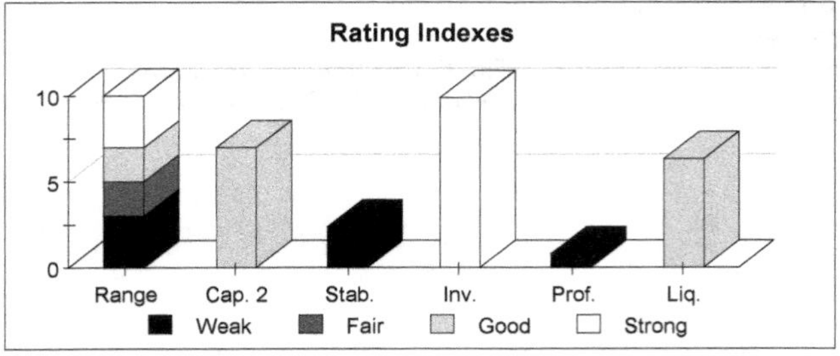

## CONNECTICUT GENERAL LIFE INSURANCE COMPANY B- Good

**Major Rating Factors:** Fair quality investment portfolio (4.4 on a scale of 0 to 10). Fair overall results on stability tests (4.9). Strong capitalization (7.3) based on excellent risk adjusted capital (severe loss scenario). Moreover, capital levels have been consistently high over the last five years.
**Other Rating Factors:** Excellent profitability (8.4). Excellent liquidity (7.3).
**Principal Business:** Individual life insurance (34%), group life insurance (29%), individual health insurance (24%), group health insurance (7%), and reinsurance (5%).
**Principal Investments:** Common & preferred stock (37%), nonCMO investment grade bonds (35%), policy loans (15%), mortgages in good standing (3%), and misc. investments (11%).
**Investments in Affiliates:** 39%
**Group Affiliation:** CIGNA Corp
**Licensed in:** All states, the District of Columbia and Puerto Rico
**Commenced Business:** October 1865
**Address:** 900 COTTAGE GROVE ROAD, BLOOMFIELD, CT 6002
**Phone:** (860) 226-6000 **Domicile State:** CT **NAIC Code:** 62308

| Data Date | Rating | RACR #1 | RACR #2 | Total Assets ($mil) | Capital ($mil) | Net Premium ($mil) | Net Income ($mil) |
|---|---|---|---|---|---|---|---|
| 9-17 | B- | 1.33 | 1.21 | 18,077.3 | 4,307.1 | 277.7 | 1,005.2 |
| 9-16 | B- | 1.36 | 1.21 | 17,661.0 | 3,902.6 | 303.6 | 908.6 |
| 2016 | B- | 1.32 | 1.20 | 17,646.3 | 4,074.4 | 402.2 | 1,180.4 |
| 2015 | B- | 1.33 | 1.19 | 17,374.4 | 3,631.0 | 490.7 | 916.2 |
| 2014 | B- | 1.34 | 1.19 | 17,768.9 | 3,473.3 | 1,107.4 | 212.6 |
| 2013 | B- | 1.63 | 1.33 | 18,573.6 | 3,246.4 | 3,380.1 | 601.8 |
| 2012 | B- | 1.78 | 1.35 | 20,921.6 | 3,040.9 | 7,272.6 | 588.9 |

Rating Indexes

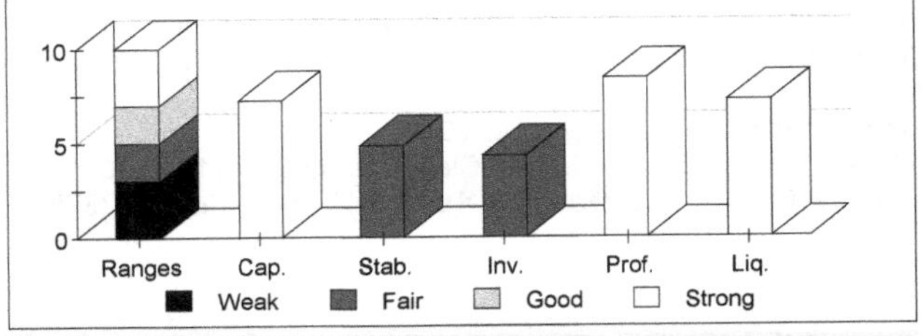


## CONSTELLATION HEALTH LLC E- Very Weak

**Major Rating Factors:** Weak profitability index (0.3 on a scale of 0 to 10). Poor capitalization index (0.0) based on weak current risk-adjusted capital (severe loss scenario). Weak liquidity (0.1) as a spike in claims may stretch capacity.
**Other Rating Factors:** High quality investment portfolio (9.9).
**Principal Business:** Medicare (100%)
**Mem Phys: 16:** 4,240 **15:** 3,774 **16 MLR** 89.5% **/ 16 Admin Exp** N/A
**Enroll(000): Q3 17:** 21 **16:** 20 **15:** 9 **Med Exp PMPM:** $733
**Principal Investments:** Cash and equiv (100%)
**Provider Compensation ($000):** Contr fee ($119,727), capitation ($12,345)
**Total Member Encounters:** Phys (299,023), non-phys (173,734)
**Group Affiliation:** Constellation Health LLC
**Licensed in:** PR
**Address:** 1064 Ponce de Leon Ave Ste 500, San Juan, PR 00907
**Phone:** (787) 304-4041 **Dom State:** PR **Commenced Bus:** January 2014

| Data Date | Rating | RACR #1 | RACR #2 | Total Assets ($mil) | Capital ($mil) | Net Premium ($mil) | Net Income ($mil) |
|---|---|---|---|---|---|---|---|
| 9-17 | E- | N/A | N/A | 41.1 | -10.3 | 154.4 | 0.5 |
| 9-16 | N/A | N/A | N/A | 23.8 | -12.9 | 115.4 | -0.2 |
| 2016 | E- | N/A | N/A | 25.4 | -10.4 | 169.8 | -1.2 |
| 2015 | N/A | N/A | N/A | 4.7 | -9.4 | 74.1 | -14.9 |
| 2014 | N/A | N/A | N/A | 0.3 | -8.6 | 18.4 | N/A |
| 2013 | N/A | N/A | N/A | 2.7 | 1.1 | N/A | N/A |
| 2012 | N/A | N/A | N/A | N/A | N/A | N/A | N/A |

Rating Indexes

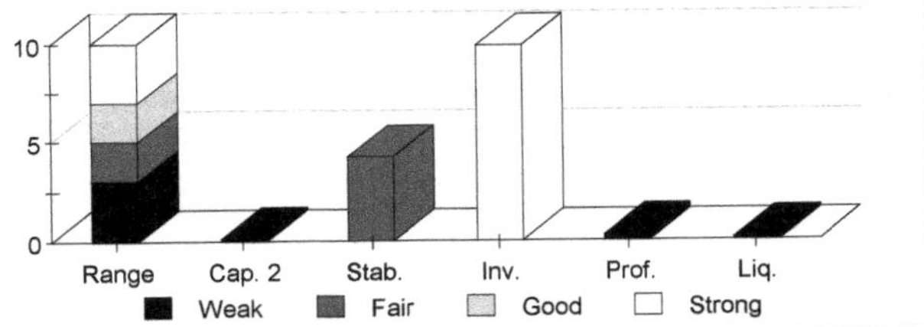


## CONSTITUTION LIFE INSURANCE COMPANY D Weak

**Major Rating Factors:** Weak overall results on stability tests (1.5 on a scale of 0 to 10) including potential financial drain due to affiliation with Nassau Reinsurance Group Holdings LP and negative cash flow from operations for 2016. Weak profitability (2.6) with investment income below regulatory standards in relation to interest assumptions of reserves. Good quality investment portfolio (6.7).
**Other Rating Factors:** Strong capitalization (7.9) based on excellent risk adjusted capital (severe loss scenario). Excellent liquidity (7.1).
**Principal Business:** Individual health insurance (51%), reinsurance (31%), group health insurance (9%), and individual life insurance (9%).
**Principal Investments:** NonCMO investment grade bonds (76%), CMOs and structured securities (21%), and noninv. grade bonds (2%).
**Investments in Affiliates:** 1%
**Group Affiliation:** Nassau Reinsurance Group Holdings LP
**Licensed in:** All states except NJ, NY, PR
**Commenced Business:** June 1929
**Address:** 4888 Loop Central Dr Ste 700, Houston, TX 77081
**Phone:** (407) 547-3800 **Domicile State:** TX **NAIC Code:** 62359

| Data Date | Rating | RACR #1 | RACR #2 | Total Assets ($mil) | Capital ($mil) | Net Premium ($mil) | Net Income ($mil) |
|---|---|---|---|---|---|---|---|
| 9-17 | D | 2.74 | 1.59 | 438.3 | 45.7 | 38.6 | 2.5 |
| 9-16 | D+ | 1.31 | 0.90 | 446.4 | 36.6 | 119.2 | -34.5 |
| 2016 | D | 2.71 | 1.71 | 444.1 | 55.6 | 90.0 | -11.8 |
| 2015 | C+ | 2.75 | 1.84 | 394.8 | 66.6 | 123.3 | 34.9 |
| 2014 | C+ | 1.88 | 1.23 | 316.5 | 37.0 | 94.4 | 11.1 |
| 2013 | C+ | 1.56 | 1.05 | 317.3 | 33.5 | 109.5 | 9.2 |
| 2012 | B- | 1.52 | 1.16 | 57.4 | 28.4 | 69.2 | 4.5 |

| Universal American Corp<br>Composite Group Rating: E+<br>Largest Group Members | Assets ($mil) | Rating |
|---|---|---|
| PHOENIX LIFE INS CO | 12451 | E |
| PHL VARIABLE INS CO | 6387 | D- |
| CONSTITUTION LIFE INS CO | 444 | D |
| PYRAMID LIFE INS CO | 77 | D- |
| PHOENIX LIFE ANNUITY CO | 32 | E+ |

## CONSUMERS LIFE INSURANCE COMPANY B Good

**Major Rating Factors:** Good overall profitability (5.3 on a scale of 0 to 10). Excellent expense controls. Good overall results on stability tests (6.2) despite excessive premium growth and fair risk adjusted capital in prior years. Strengths include excellent financial support from affiliation with Medical Mutual of Ohio, good operational trends and good risk diversification. Strong capitalization (8.1) based on excellent risk adjusted capital (severe loss scenario).
**Other Rating Factors:** High quality investment portfolio (9.4). Excellent liquidity (7.2).
**Principal Business:** Group life insurance (68%), group health insurance (19%), individual health insurance (12%), and individual life insurance (1%).
**Principal Investments:** NonCMO investment grade bonds (66%) and cash (34%).
**Investments in Affiliates:** None
**Group Affiliation:** Medical Mutual of Ohio
**Licensed in:** AZ, AR, CO, DC, DE, GA, IL, IN, IA, KS, KY, LA, MD, MI, MN, MS, MO, MT, NE, NV, NJ, NM, ND, OH, OK, OR, PA, SC, SD, TX, UT, VA, WV, WI, WY
**Commenced Business:** October 1955
**Address:** 2060 East Ninth Street, Cleveland, OH 44115-1355
**Phone:** (216) 687-7000 **Domicile State:** OH **NAIC Code:** 62375

| Data Date | Rating | RACR #1 | RACR #2 | Total Assets ($mil) | Capital ($mil) | Net Premium ($mil) | Net Income ($mil) |
|---|---|---|---|---|---|---|---|
| 9-17 | B | 2.20 | 1.70 | 47.3 | 27.4 | 36.2 | 3.1 |
| 9-16 | B | 2.21 | 1.70 | 41.8 | 22.9 | 23.1 | 0.8 |
| 2016 | B | 1.90 | 1.46 | 41.8 | 23.3 | 31.4 | 0.6 |
| 2015 | C+ | 1.91 | 1.46 | 37.6 | 21.6 | 29.0 | 1.3 |
| 2014 | C | 1.89 | 1.45 | 36.4 | 19.7 | 25.9 | -1.4 |
| 2013 | C | 1.17 | 0.92 | 39.7 | 19.7 | 60.9 | 1.2 |
| 2012 | C | 0.80 | 0.63 | 38.8 | 12.9 | 63.0 | -4.9 |

**Medical Mutual of Ohio**
**Composite Group Rating: A**

| Largest Group Members | Assets ($mil) | Rating |
|---|---|---|
| MEDICAL MUTUAL OF OHIO | 1992 | A |
| MEDICAL HEALTH INS CORP OF OHIO | 156 | B+ |
| CONSUMERS LIFE INS CO | 42 | B |

## CONTINENTAL AMERICAN INSURANCE COMPANY B Good

**Major Rating Factors:** Good overall profitability (5.4 on a scale of 0 to 10) despite operating losses during the first nine months of 2017. Good overall results on stability tests (5.7). Strengths include good financial support from affiliation with AFLAC Inc, good operational trends and excellent risk diversification. Strong capitalization (7.6) based on excellent risk adjusted capital (severe loss scenario).
**Other Rating Factors:** High quality investment portfolio (7.9). Excellent liquidity (7.3).
**Principal Business:** Group health insurance (63%), reinsurance (35%), and group life insurance (2%).
**Principal Investments:** NonCMO investment grade bonds (97%), noninv. grade bonds (2%), and policy loans (1%).
**Investments in Affiliates:** None
**Group Affiliation:** AFLAC Inc
**Licensed in:** All states except NY, PR
**Commenced Business:** January 1969
**Address:** 1600 Williams Street, Omaha, NE 68114-3743
**Phone:** (888) 730-2244 **Domicile State:** SC **NAIC Code:** 71730

| Data Date | Rating | RACR #1 | RACR #2 | Total Assets ($mil) | Capital ($mil) | Net Premium ($mil) | Net Income ($mil) |
|---|---|---|---|---|---|---|---|
| 9-17 | B | 1.94 | 1.40 | 671.3 | 173.3 | 401.2 | -14.4 |
| 9-16 | B | 2.00 | 1.46 | 598.9 | 171.2 | 404.7 | 39.3 |
| 2016 | B | 1.98 | 1.44 | 607.0 | 174.4 | 536.1 | 46.8 |
| 2015 | B | 1.84 | 1.37 | 512.3 | 138.0 | 436.8 | 26.2 |
| 2014 | B | 2.49 | 1.78 | 397.0 | 109.7 | 240.6 | -17.3 |
| 2013 | B | 3.47 | 2.49 | 382.4 | 138.0 | 233.4 | 18.8 |
| 2012 | B | 4.36 | 3.13 | 344.0 | 137.4 | 183.7 | -21.2 |

**AFLAC Inc**
**Composite Group Rating: B+**

| Largest Group Members | Assets ($mil) | Rating |
|---|---|---|
| AMERICAN FAMILY LIFE ASR CO OF COLUM | 108871 | B+ |
| AMERICAN FAMILY LIFE ASR CO OF NY | 870 | A- |
| CONTINENTAL AMERICAN INS CO | 607 | B |

## CONTINENTAL GENERAL INSURANCE COMPANY C+ Fair

**Major Rating Factors:** Fair current capitalization (4.9 on a scale of 0 to 10) based on fair risk adjusted capital (moderate loss scenario), although results have slipped from the good range during the last year. Fair quality investment portfolio (3.5) with large holdings of BBB rated bonds in addition to junk bond exposure equal to 97% of capital. Fair overall results on stability tests (4.7) including fair risk adjusted capital in prior years.
**Other Rating Factors:** Good overall profitability (6.0). Excellent liquidity (7.3).
**Principal Business:** Individual health insurance (82%), group health insurance (8%), individual life insurance (6%), reinsurance (2%), and group retirement contracts (1%).
**Principal Investments:** NonCMO investment grade bonds (65%), CMOs and structured securities (21%), common & preferred stock (6%), noninv. grade bonds (5%), and misc. investments (2%).
**Investments in Affiliates:** 3%
**Group Affiliation:** HC2 Holdings Inc
**Licensed in:** All states except FL, NY, PR
**Commenced Business:** July 1961
**Address:** 11001 Lakeline Blvd Ste 120, Austin, TX 78717
**Phone:** (866) 830-0607 **Domicile State:** OH **NAIC Code:** 71404

| Data Date | Rating | RACR #1 | RACR #2 | Total Assets ($mil) | Capital ($mil) | Net Premium ($mil) | Net Income ($mil) |
|---|---|---|---|---|---|---|---|
| 9-17 | C+ | 0.99 | 0.65 | 1,372.6 | 73.5 | 62.4 | 0.3 |
| 9-16 | C+ | 1.37 | 0.92 | 251.9 | 19.5 | 10.0 | -4.4 |
| 2016 | C+ | 1.10 | 0.72 | 1,344.1 | 76.9 | 82.2 | -15.3 |
| 2015 | C+ | 1.28 | 0.89 | 249.3 | 18.5 | 13.3 | 32.6 |
| 2014 | C | 2.35 | 1.38 | 242.4 | 21.5 | 14.3 | 1.9 |
| 2013 | C | 2.50 | 1.49 | 238.4 | 22.8 | 15.3 | 4.7 |
| 2012 | C | 1.99 | 1.19 | 231.9 | 20.5 | 27.6 | -0.1 |

**Risk-Adjusted Capital Ratio #1**
**(Moderate Loss Scenario)**

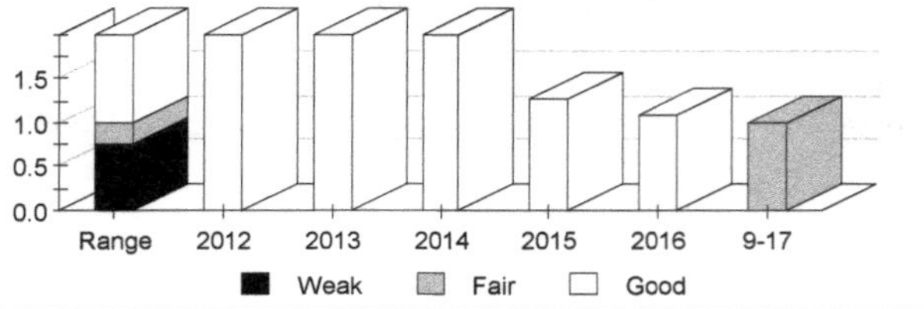

## CONTINENTAL LIFE INSURANCE COMPANY OF BRENTWOOD C+ Fair

**Major Rating Factors:** Fair overall results on stability tests (4.7 on a scale of 0 to 10) including negative cash flow from operations for 2016. Good quality investment portfolio (5.4) despite mixed results such as: no exposure to mortgages and large holdings of BBB rated bonds but minimal holdings in junk bonds. Good liquidity (6.2) with sufficient resources to handle a spike in claims.
**Other Rating Factors:** Weak profitability (2.5) with operating losses during the first nine months of 2017. Strong capitalization (7.1) based on excellent risk adjusted capital (severe loss scenario).
**Principal Business:** Individual health insurance (98%), group health insurance (1%), and individual life insurance (1%).
**Principal Investments:** NonCMO investment grade bonds (42%), common & preferred stock (33%), CMOs and structured securities (25%), and noninv. grade bonds (1%).
**Investments in Affiliates:** 33%
**Group Affiliation:** Aetna Inc
**Licensed in:** All states except AK, CT, DC, HI, ME, MA, NY, WA, PR
**Commenced Business:** December 1983
**Address:** 800 CRESCENT CENTRE DR STE 200, FRANKLIN, TN 37067
**Phone:** (800) 264-4000 **Domicile State:** TN **NAIC Code:** 68500

| Data Date | Rating | RACR #1 | RACR #2 | Total Assets ($mil) | Capital ($mil) | Net Premium ($mil) | Net Income ($mil) |
|---|---|---|---|---|---|---|---|
| 9-17 | C+ | 1.21 | 1.07 | 336.0 | 190.1 | 349.7 | -12.3 |
| 9-16 | B | 1.13 | 1.00 | 279.9 | 151.8 | 317.5 | -8.7 |
| 2016 | B | 1.16 | 1.03 | 307.1 | 173.8 | 427.2 | -7.8 |
| 2015 | B | 1.11 | 0.99 | 274.0 | 144.3 | 380.6 | -1.2 |
| 2014 | B | 1.19 | 1.08 | 277.8 | 156.4 | 330.6 | 3.0 |
| 2013 | B | 1.12 | 1.01 | 205.6 | 97.0 | 256.6 | 3.2 |
| 2012 | B | 0.97 | 0.89 | 175.6 | 80.2 | 166.4 | 9.7 |

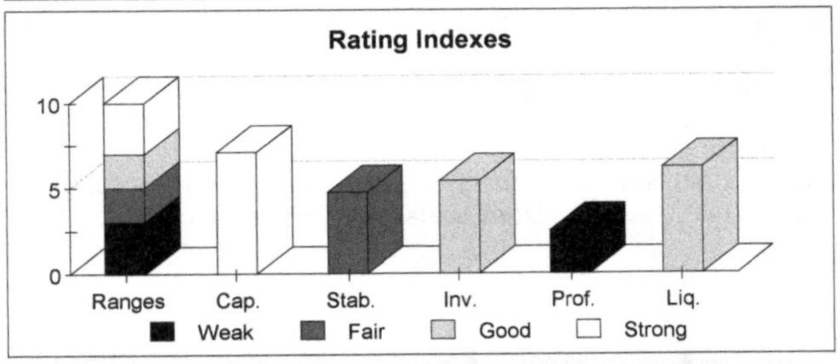


## CONTRA COSTA COUNTY MED SVCS C Fair

**Major Rating Factors:** Excellent profitability (8.2 on a scale of 0 to 10). Strong capitalization index (7.1) based on good current risk-adjusted capital (moderate loss scenario). Excellent overall results on stability tests (6.9).
**Other Rating Factors:** Excellent liquidity (7.6) with ample operational cash flow and liquid investments.
**Principal Business:** Medicaid (90%)
**Mem Phys: 16:** N/A **15:** N/A **16 MLR** 102.4% **/ 16 Admin Exp** N/A
**Enroll(000): Q3 17:** 193 **16:** 192 **15:** 172 **Med Exp PMPM:** $318
**Principal Investments ($000):** Cash and equiv ($197,734)
**Provider Compensation ($000):** None
**Total Member Encounters:** N/A
**Group Affiliation:** None
**Licensed in:** CA
**Address:** 595 Center Avenue Suite 100, Martinez, CA 94553
**Phone:** (925) 313-6004 **Dom State:** CA **Commenced Bus:** November 1973

| Data Date | Rating | RACR #1 | RACR #2 | Total Assets ($mil) | Capital ($mil) | Net Premium ($mil) | Net Income ($mil) |
|---|---|---|---|---|---|---|---|
| 9-17 | C | 1.19 | 0.75 | 379.8 | 53.9 | 553.0 | 5.1 |
| 9-16 | C | 1.13 | 0.72 | 288.4 | 44.5 | 517.5 | 11.2 |
| 2016 | C | 0.98 | 0.62 | 281.7 | 45.3 | 692.0 | 12.1 |
| 2015 | C | 1.16 | 0.74 | 206.2 | 45.5 | 622.6 | 24.6 |
| 2014 | D | 0.69 | 0.44 | 133.3 | 20.9 | 418.4 | 7.0 |
| 2013 | D | 0.53 | 0.35 | 139.4 | 13.9 | 356.1 | 1.8 |
| 2012 | D | 0.58 | 0.37 | 97.1 | 12.1 | 255.9 | 4.0 |

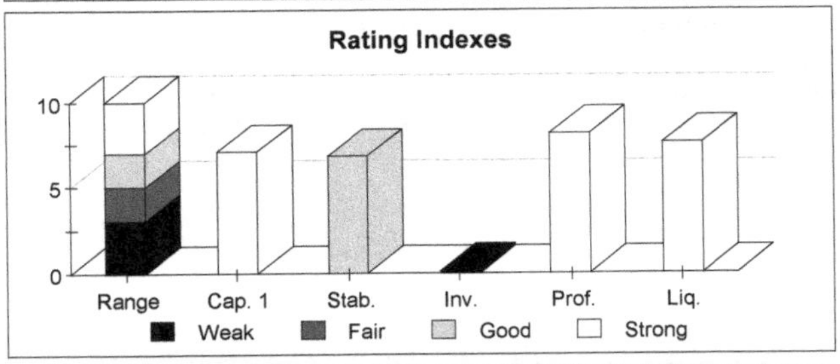


## COOK CHILDRENS HEALTH PLAN E+ Very Weak

**Major Rating Factors:** Fair overall results on stability tests (4.9 on a scale of 0 to 10). Good overall profitability index (6.5). Strong capitalization index (7.9) based on excellent current risk-adjusted capital (severe loss scenario).
**Other Rating Factors:** High quality investment portfolio (9.9). Excellent liquidity (7.1) with ample operational cash flow and liquid investments.
**Principal Business:** Medicaid (88%), comp med (12%)
**Mem Phys: 16:** 4,996 **15:** 3,242 **16 MLR** 82.1% **/ 16 Admin Exp** N/A
**Enroll(000): Q3 17:** 138 **16:** 134 **15:** 121 **Med Exp PMPM:** $190
**Principal Investments:** Cash and equiv (59%), long-term bonds (41%)
**Provider Compensation ($000):** Contr fee ($271,852), bonus arrang ($983)
**Total Member Encounters:** Phys (2,325,884), non-phys (342,968)
**Group Affiliation:** W I Cook Foundation
**Licensed in:** TX
**Address:** 801 Seventh Avenue, Fort Worth, TX 76104
**Phone:** (817) 334-2247 **Dom State:** TX **Commenced Bus:** April 1999

| Data Date | Rating | RACR #1 | RACR #2 | Total Assets ($mil) | Capital ($mil) | Net Premium ($mil) | Net Income ($mil) |
|---|---|---|---|---|---|---|---|
| 9-17 | E+ | 2.10 | 1.75 | 121.5 | 63.5 | 372.2 | -11.6 |
| 9-16 | E+ | 2.71 | 2.26 | 113.0 | 73.8 | 240.8 | 12.6 |
| 2016 | E+ | 2.71 | 2.25 | 129.7 | 79.2 | 345.7 | 18.5 |
| 2015 | E+ | 2.35 | 1.96 | 118.7 | 63.9 | 297.1 | 11.3 |
| 2014 | E+ | 1.97 | 1.65 | 96.3 | 54.4 | 295.7 | 18.3 |
| 2013 | E+ | 1.16 | 0.97 | 68.6 | 36.1 | 265.2 | 4.1 |
| 2012 | E+ | 1.27 | 1.05 | 57.3 | 31.2 | 237.4 | 8.4 |

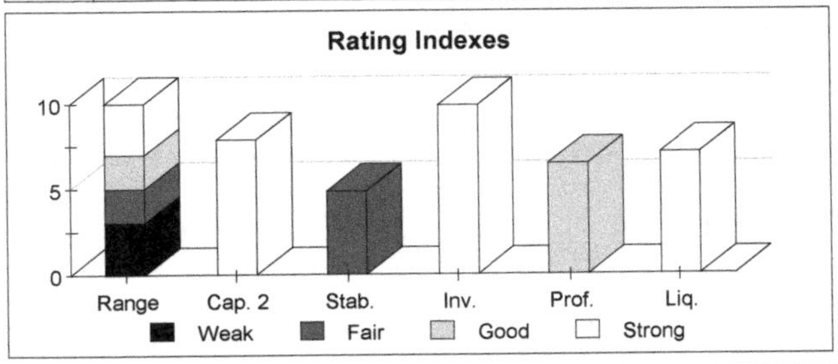

## COORDINATED CARE CORP — C+ Fair

**Major Rating Factors:** Good overall profitability index (6.5 on a scale of 0 to 10). Strong capitalization index (9.0) based on excellent current risk-adjusted capital (severe loss scenario). High quality investment portfolio (9.9).
**Other Rating Factors:** Excellent overall results on stability tests (7.3) based on healthy premium and capital growth during 2016. Rating is significantly influenced by the fair financial results of Centene Corporation. Excellent liquidity (7.0) with ample operational cash flow and liquid investments.
**Principal Business:** Medicaid (93%), comp med (7%)
**Mem Phys: 16:** 20,897 **15:** 13,620 **16 MLR** 85.5% **/ 16 Admin Exp** N/A
**Enroll(000): Q3 17:** 312 **16:** 301 **15:** 299 **Med Exp PMPM:** $258
**Principal Investments:** Cash and equiv (56%), long-term bonds (38%), affiliate common stock (3%), other (4%)
**Provider Compensation ($000):** Contr fee ($859,669), bonus arrang ($51,773), salary ($20,460), capitation ($13,399)
**Total Member Encounters:** Phys (1,629,391), non-phys (1,374,629)
**Group Affiliation:** Centene Corporation
**Licensed in:** IN, WA
**Address:** 1099 N Meridian Street Suite 4, Indianapolis, IN 46204-1041
**Phone:** (314) 725-4477 **Dom State:** IN **Commenced Bus:** August 1996

| Data Date | Rating | RACR #1 | RACR #2 | Total Assets ($mil) | Capital ($mil) | Net Premium ($mil) | Net Income ($mil) |
|---|---|---|---|---|---|---|---|
| 9-17 | C+ | 2.96 | 2.47 | 392.7 | 147.2 | 1,084.2 | 6.9 |
| 9-16 | C+ | 2.93 | 2.44 | 322.8 | 110.4 | 808.5 | 8.7 |
| 2016 | C+ | 2.30 | 1.92 | 330.6 | 111.8 | 1,091.2 | 6.7 |
| 2015 | C+ | 2.28 | 1.90 | 306.6 | 83.7 | 811.8 | 15.3 |
| 2014 | C+ | 1.73 | 1.44 | 462.9 | 67.1 | 931.0 | -3.1 |
| 2013 | C+ | 2.03 | 1.70 | 188.3 | 57.1 | 570.0 | 4.9 |
| 2012 | B- | 2.54 | 2.12 | 154.1 | 51.0 | 387.5 | 1.2 |

Rating Indexes

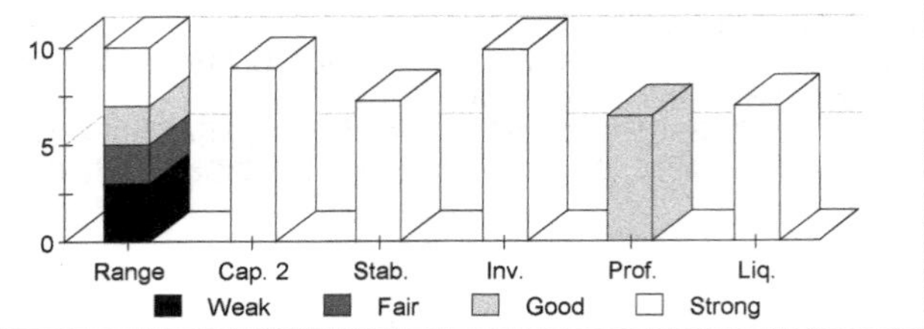


## COORDINATED CARE OF WASHINGTON INC — D+ Weak

**Major Rating Factors:** Weak profitability index (0.9 on a scale of 0 to 10). Good liquidity (6.7) with sufficient resources (cash flows and marketable investments) to handle a spike in claims. Strong capitalization (8.6) based on excellent current risk-adjusted capital (severe loss scenario).
**Other Rating Factors:** High quality investment portfolio (9.4).
**Principal Business:** Medicaid (99%)
**Mem Phys: 16:** 24,560 **15:** 19,259 **16 MLR** 90.6% **/ 16 Admin Exp** N/A
**Enroll(000): Q3 17:** 201 **16:** 207 **15:** 182 **Med Exp PMPM:** $257
**Principal Investments:** Long-term bonds (68%), cash and equiv (32%)
**Provider Compensation ($000):** Contr fee ($535,909), capitation ($38,824), bonus arrang ($17,160), salary ($10,259)
**Total Member Encounters:** Phys (776,134), non-phys (1,038,482)
**Group Affiliation:** Centene Corporation
**Licensed in:** WA
**Address:** 1145 BRdway Ste 300, Tacoma, WA 98402
**Phone:** (314) 725-4477 **Dom State:** WA **Commenced Bus:** January 2015

| Data Date | Rating | RACR #1 | RACR #2 | Total Assets ($mil) | Capital ($mil) | Net Premium ($mil) | Net Income ($mil) |
|---|---|---|---|---|---|---|---|
| 9-17 | D+ | 2.63 | 2.19 | 245.1 | 89.7 | 525.6 | 1.0 |
| 9-16 | D+ | 2.60 | 2.16 | 227.7 | 76.4 | 501.0 | -11.5 |
| 2016 | D+ | 1.90 | 1.59 | 247.2 | 60.6 | 680.3 | -38.4 |
| 2015 | D+ | 2.88 | 2.40 | 231.0 | 84.6 | 558.5 | -8.6 |
| 2014 | N/A | N/A | N/A | 167.6 | 86.6 | N/A | -30.3 |
| 2013 | N/A | N/A | N/A | 3.0 | 3.0 | N/A | N/A |
| 2012 | N/A | N/A | N/A | N/A | N/A | N/A | N/A |

Rating Indexes

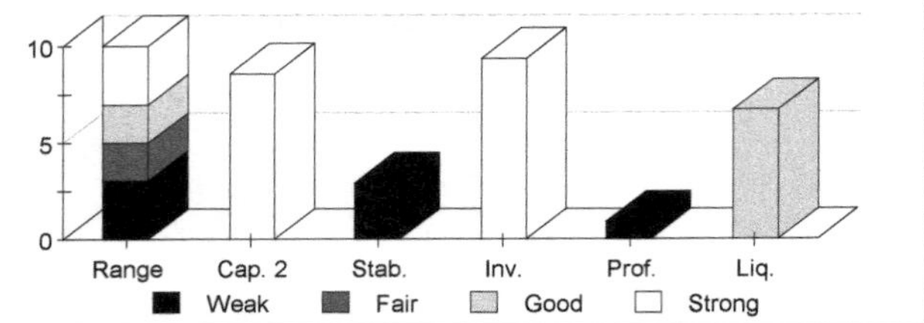


## COVENTRY HEALTH & LIFE INS CO — B Good

**Major Rating Factors:** Good quality investment portfolio (6.0 on a scale of 0 to 10). Good liquidity (6.8) with sufficient resources (cash flows and marketable investments) to handle a spike in claims. Excellent profitability (8.3).
**Other Rating Factors:** Strong capitalization (10.0) based on excellent current risk-adjusted capital (severe loss scenario).
**Principal Business:** Medicare (53%), comp med (42%), Medicaid (4%)
**Mem Phys: 16:** N/A **15:** N/A **16 MLR** 82.5% **/ 16 Admin Exp** N/A
**Enroll(000): Q3 17:** 184 **16:** 325 **15:** 759 **Med Exp PMPM:** $424
**Principal Investments:** Long-term bonds (79%), affiliate common stock (17%), cash and equiv (4%)
**Provider Compensation ($000):** Contr fee ($1,910,942), FFS ($198,626), capitation ($151,708), bonus arrang ($64,772)
**Total Member Encounters:** Phys (2,792,458), non-phys (737,700)
**Group Affiliation:** Aetna Inc
**Licensed in:** All states except NY, PR
**Address:** 550 MARYVILLE CENTRE Dr #300, ST. LOUIS, MO 63141
**Phone:** (800) 843-7421 **Dom State:** MO **Commenced Bus:** May 1968

| Data Date | Rating | RACR #1 | RACR #2 | Total Assets ($mil) | Capital ($mil) | Net Premium ($mil) | Net Income ($mil) |
|---|---|---|---|---|---|---|---|
| 9-17 | B | 7.15 | 5.96 | 1,487.5 | 1,083.8 | 1,257.3 | 97.8 |
| 9-16 | B | 5.35 | 4.46 | 1,602.1 | 1,064.2 | 1,937.5 | 28.7 |
| 2016 | B | 7.51 | 6.26 | 1,512.5 | 1,145.3 | 2,484.5 | 77.6 |
| 2015 | B | 4.82 | 4.01 | 1,699.7 | 949.3 | 4,066.1 | 260.2 |
| 2014 | B | 2.89 | 2.41 | 1,616.3 | 704.2 | 4,565.5 | 159.1 |
| 2013 | B+ | 3.08 | 2.57 | 1,162.5 | 585.9 | 3,441.1 | 117.9 |
| 2012 | B+ | 2.50 | 2.09 | 936.0 | 478.1 | 3,303.6 | 39.8 |

Rating Indexes

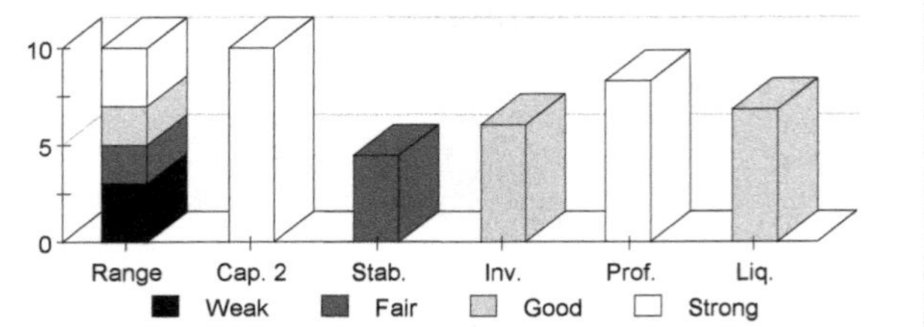

## COVENTRY HEALTH CARE OF FLORIDA INC — C+ Fair

**Major Rating Factors:** Fair profitability index (3.4 on a scale of 0 to 10). Good overall results on stability tests (5.0) based on a decline in the number of member physicians during 2017, inconsistent enrollment growth in the past five years due to declines in 2013, 2015 and 2016. Rating is significantly influenced by the good financial results of Aetna Inc. Good liquidity (5.8) with sufficient resources (cash flows and marketable investments) to handle a spike in claims.
**Other Rating Factors:** Strong capitalization index (9.1) based on excellent current risk-adjusted capital (severe loss scenario). High quality investment portfolio (9.0).
**Principal Business:** Comp med (69%), Medicaid (31%)
**Mem Phys: 16:** 44,208 **15:** 225,803 **16 MLR** 81.7% **/ 16 Admin Exp** N/A
**Enroll(000): Q3 17:** 109 **16:** 325 **15:** 335 **Med Exp PMPM:** $261
**Principal Investments:** Long-term bonds (94%), cash and equiv (3%), nonaffiliate common stock (2%)
**Provider Compensation ($000):** Contr fee ($803,237), capitation ($162,453), FFS ($150,605)
**Total Member Encounters:** Phys (1,720,950), non-phys (104,061)
**Group Affiliation:** Aetna Inc
**Licensed in:** FL
**Address:** 1340 CONCORD TERRACE, SUNRISE, FL 33323
**Phone:** (954) 858-3000 **Dom State:** FL **Commenced Bus:** January 1985

| Data Date | Rating | RACR #1 | RACR #2 | Total Assets ($mil) | Capital ($mil) | Net Premium ($mil) | Net Income ($mil) |
|---|---|---|---|---|---|---|---|
| 9-17 | C+ | 3.03 | 2.53 | 351.7 | 194.1 | 388.5 | 18.0 |
| 9-16 | C+ | 3.26 | 2.71 | 542.8 | 210.6 | 1,049.2 | 37.2 |
| 2016 | C+ | 3.05 | 2.54 | 547.7 | 195.6 | 1,368.1 | 42.9 |
| 2015 | C+ | 2.10 | 1.75 | 515.7 | 128.7 | 1,280.5 | 6.9 |
| 2014 | B | 1.04 | 0.87 | 476.5 | 54.8 | 1,110.3 | -44.6 |
| 2013 | B | 3.48 | 2.90 | 178.6 | 103.4 | 523.1 | 14.5 |
| 2012 | B | 2.61 | 2.18 | 167.4 | 92.4 | 692.6 | 32.3 |

Rating Indexes

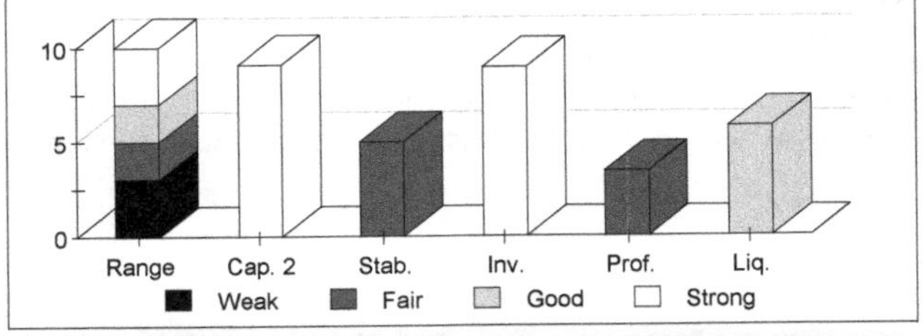


## COVENTRY HEALTH CARE OF ILLINOIS INC — C Fair

**Major Rating Factors:** Fair profitability index (4.7 on a scale of 0 to 10). Strong capitalization (9.5) based on excellent current risk-adjusted capital (severe loss scenario). High quality investment portfolio (9.1).
**Other Rating Factors:** Excellent liquidity (7.0) with ample operational cash flow and liquid investments.
**Principal Business:** Medicare (51%), comp med (49%)
**Mem Phys: 16:** 37,312 **15:** N/A **16 MLR** 74.5% **/ 16 Admin Exp** N/A
**Enroll(000): Q3 17:** 22 **16:** 51 **15:** 46 **Med Exp PMPM:** $550
**Principal Investments:** Long-term bonds (55%), cash and equiv (42%), other (3%)
**Provider Compensation ($000):** Contr fee ($240,787), bonus arrang ($31,817), capitation ($30,863), FFS ($29,433)
**Total Member Encounters:** Phys (385,433), non-phys (112,827)
**Group Affiliation:** Aetna Inc
**Licensed in:** IL
**Address:** 2110 FOX Dr, CHAMPAIGN, IL 61820
**Phone:** (217) 366-1226 **Dom State:** IL **Commenced Bus:** December 1988

| Data Date | Rating | RACR #1 | RACR #2 | Total Assets ($mil) | Capital ($mil) | Net Premium ($mil) | Net Income ($mil) |
|---|---|---|---|---|---|---|---|
| 9-17 | C | 3.39 | 2.82 | 174.7 | 90.0 | 245.4 | 10.3 |
| 9-16 | C | 2.61 | 2.17 | 159.4 | 43.0 | 339.5 | -19.2 |
| 2016 | C | 3.32 | 2.77 | 177.9 | 88.2 | 481.2 | 1.1 |
| 2015 | B- | 2.84 | 2.37 | 131.4 | 47.6 | 351.9 | 7.8 |
| 2014 | B | 2.20 | 1.83 | 117.6 | 34.3 | 320.1 | -2.4 |
| 2013 | B+ | 3.54 | 2.95 | 88.3 | 44.0 | 263.5 | 7.7 |
| 2012 | B+ | 3.33 | 2.77 | 99.2 | 43.8 | 272.1 | 9.2 |

Rating Indexes

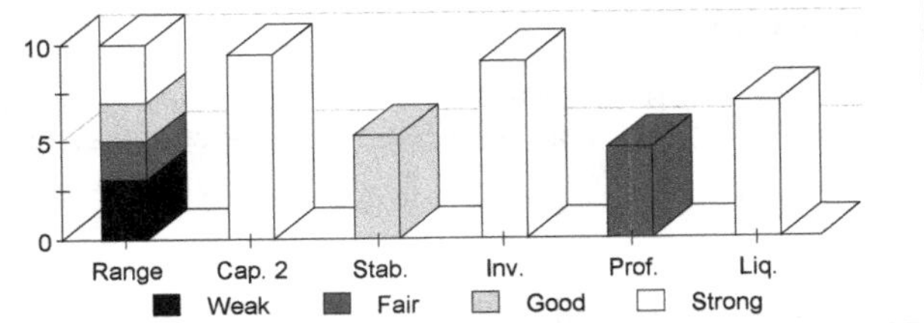


## COVENTRY HEALTH CARE OF KANSAS INC — C+ Fair

**Major Rating Factors:** Fair quality investment portfolio (3.7 on a scale of 0 to 10). Good overall profitability index (6.3). Weak overall results on stability tests (2.0) based on a significant 88% decrease in enrollment during the period, a steep decline in capital during 2016. Rating is significantly influenced by the good financial results of Aetna Inc.
**Other Rating Factors:** Strong capitalization index (9.1) based on excellent current risk-adjusted capital (severe loss scenario). Excellent liquidity (8.4) with ample operational cash flow and liquid investments.
**Principal Business:** Medicare (81%), comp med (18%)
**Mem Phys: 16:** 19,016 **15:** 18,357 **16 MLR** 28.7% **/ 16 Admin Exp** N/A
**Enroll(000): Q3 17:** 3 **16:** 7 **15:** 60 **Med Exp PMPM:** $397
**Principal Investments:** Long-term bonds (69%), cash and equiv (28%), nonaffiliate common stock (2%)
**Provider Compensation ($000):** Contr fee ($117,036), FFS ($17,755), capitation ($6,555), bonus arrang ($2,565)
**Total Member Encounters:** Phys (154,224), non-phys (41,892)
**Group Affiliation:** Aetna Inc
**Licensed in:** AR, KS, MO, OK
**Address:** 8535 E 21ST STREET N, WICHITA, KS 67206
**Phone:** (913) 202-5400 **Dom State:** KS **Commenced Bus:** October 1981

| Data Date | Rating | RACR #1 | RACR #2 | Total Assets ($mil) | Capital ($mil) | Net Premium ($mil) | Net Income ($mil) |
|---|---|---|---|---|---|---|---|
| 9-17 | C+ | 3.06 | 2.55 | 68.0 | 48.5 | 8.7 | 2.6 |
| 9-16 | C+ | 3.47 | 2.89 | 147.0 | 94.5 | 301.7 | 19.7 |
| 2016 | C+ | 4.28 | 3.57 | 116.0 | 73.8 | 367.9 | 25.7 |
| 2015 | C+ | 3.43 | 2.86 | 211.3 | 93.1 | 573.7 | 28.2 |
| 2014 | B | 3.50 | 2.92 | 230.2 | 109.4 | 615.0 | 24.5 |
| 2013 | B | 3.26 | 2.72 | 204.4 | 115.5 | 699.7 | 33.9 |
| 2012 | B | 2.03 | 1.69 | 248.1 | 113.7 | 1,040.2 | -29.7 |

Rating Indexes

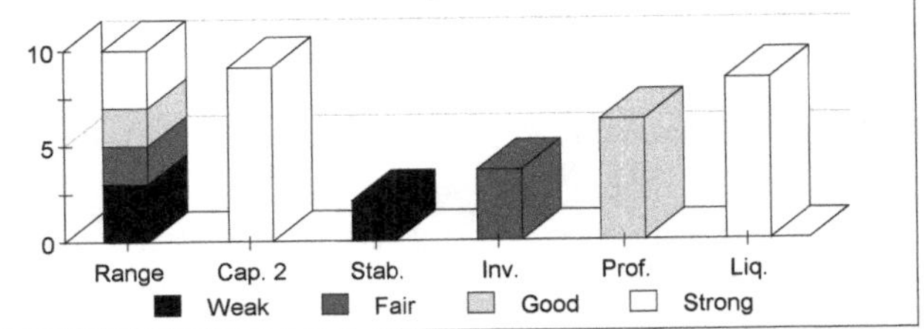

## COVENTRY HEALTH CARE OF MISSOURI INC C+ Fair

**Major Rating Factors:** Fair quality investment portfolio (4.1 on a scale of 0 to 10). Good overall results on stability tests (6.2). Rating is significantly influenced by the good financial results of Aetna Inc. Weak liquidity (2.6) as a spike in claims may stretch capacity.
**Other Rating Factors:** Excellent profitability (9.0). Strong capitalization index (10.0) based on excellent current risk-adjusted capital (severe loss scenario).
**Principal Business:** Medicare (98%), comp med (2%)
**Mem Phys: 16:** 14,658 **15:** N/A **16 MLR** 124.4% **/ 16 Admin Exp** N/A
**Enroll(000): Q3 17:** 87 **16:** 92 **15:** 78 **Med Exp PMPM:** $718
**Principal Investments:** Long-term bonds (87%), cash and equiv (12%), other (1%)
**Provider Compensation ($000):** Contr fee ($427,881), capitation ($215,133), bonus arrang ($66,487), FFS ($15,166)
**Total Member Encounters:** Phys (895,837), non-phys (203,069)
**Group Affiliation:** Aetna Inc
**Licensed in:** AR, IL, KS, MO, OK
**Address:** 550 MARYVILLE CENTRE DRIVE, ST LOUIS, MO 63141-5818
**Phone:** (314) 506-1700 **Dom State:** MO **Commenced Bus:** November 1985

| Data Date | Rating | RACR #1 | RACR #2 | Total Assets ($mil) | Capital ($mil) | Net Premium ($mil) | Net Income ($mil) |
|---|---|---|---|---|---|---|---|
| 9-17 | C+ | 5.75 | 4.80 | 401.3 | 155.5 | 670.4 | 46.4 |
| 9-16 | C+ | 5.58 | 4.65 | 371.1 | 145.2 | 434.1 | 22.4 |
| 2016 | C+ | 5.72 | 4.76 | 323.0 | 154.4 | 588.3 | 37.1 |
| 2015 | C+ | 4.55 | 3.79 | 236.3 | 116.9 | 563.5 | 32.4 |
| 2014 | B | 3.47 | 2.89 | 229.4 | 88.2 | 512.6 | 9.3 |
| 2013 | B | 3.92 | 3.27 | 201.4 | 79.6 | 456.8 | 18.1 |
| 2012 | B- | 4.81 | 4.01 | 207.7 | 97.6 | 458.9 | 34.6 |

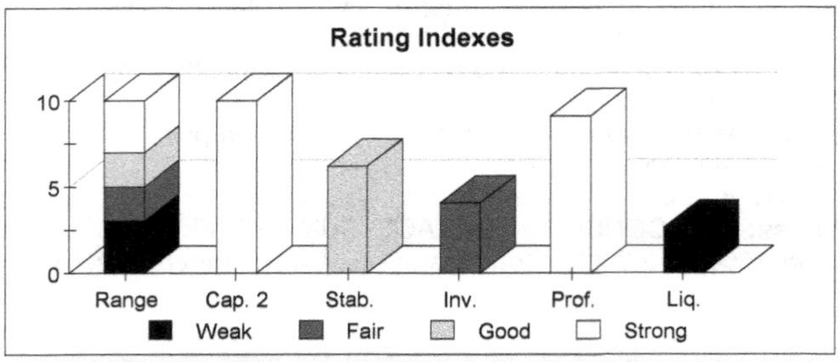


## COVENTRY HEALTH CARE OF NEBRASKA INC B Good

**Major Rating Factors:** Good quality investment portfolio (6.8 on a scale of 0 to 10). Good overall results on stability tests (6.7) despite a decline in enrollment during 2016. Rating is significantly influenced by the good financial results of Aetna Inc. Good liquidity (5.1) with sufficient resources (cash flows and marketable investments) to handle a spike in claims.
**Other Rating Factors:** Fair profitability index (4.6). Strong capitalization index (9.2) based on excellent current risk-adjusted capital (severe loss scenario).
**Principal Business:** Medicaid (52%), comp med (43%), Medicare (6%)
**Mem Phys: 16:** N/A **15:** 21,888 **16 MLR** 91.0% **/ 16 Admin Exp** N/A
**Enroll(000): Q3 17:** 5 **16:** 153 **15:** 178 **Med Exp PMPM:** $264
**Principal Investments:** Long-term bonds (91%), cash and equiv (8%)
**Provider Compensation ($000):** Contr fee ($460,975), capitation ($50,393), FFS ($23,293)
**Total Member Encounters:** Phys (798,711), non-phys (659,712)
**Group Affiliation:** Aetna Inc
**Licensed in:** IA, NE
**Address:** 15950 WEST DODGE ROAD SUITE 40, OMAHA, NE 68131-3406
**Phone:** (800) 471-0240 **Dom State:** NE **Commenced Bus:** October 1987

| Data Date | Rating | RACR #1 | RACR #2 | Total Assets ($mil) | Capital ($mil) | Net Premium ($mil) | Net Income ($mil) |
|---|---|---|---|---|---|---|---|
| 9-17 | B | 3.08 | 2.57 | 162.7 | 90.9 | 27.4 | 8.7 |
| 9-16 | B | 1.99 | 1.66 | 195.6 | 64.1 | 441.6 | -9.7 |
| 2016 | B | 2.80 | 2.34 | 200.5 | 81.7 | 567.0 | -8.3 |
| 2015 | B+ | 2.34 | 1.95 | 217.1 | 77.1 | 603.4 | -4.2 |
| 2014 | B+ | 2.78 | 2.32 | 148.6 | 60.4 | 422.1 | 11.1 |
| 2013 | B+ | 2.72 | 2.27 | 127.9 | 49.6 | 375.4 | 14.0 |
| 2012 | B- | 2.50 | 2.09 | 112.8 | 42.1 | 316.5 | 8.6 |

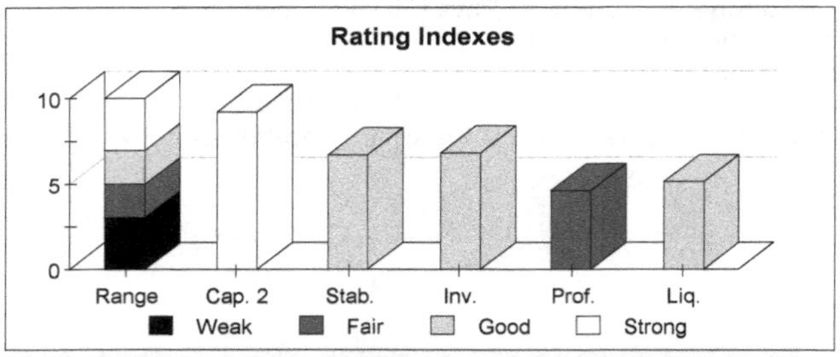


## COVENTRY HEALTH CARE OF VIRGINIA INC C+ Fair

**Major Rating Factors:** Fair profitability index (4.4 on a scale of 0 to 10). Good liquidity (5.5) with sufficient resources (cash flows and marketable investments) to handle a spike in claims. Weak overall results on stability tests (2.4) based on a steep decline in premium revenue in 2016, inconsistent enrollment growth in the past five years due to declines in 2015 and 2016 and a decline in the number of member physicians during 2017. Rating is significantly influenced by the good financial results of Aetna Inc.
**Other Rating Factors:** Strong capitalization index (8.3) based on excellent current risk-adjusted capital (severe loss scenario). High quality investment portfolio (9.2).
**Principal Business:** Medicaid (52%), comp med (48%)
**Mem Phys: 16:** 20,775 **15:** 225,803 **16 MLR** 89.0% **/ 16 Admin Exp** N/A
**Enroll(000): Q3 17:** 50 **16:** 79 **15:** 91 **Med Exp PMPM:** $300
**Principal Investments:** Long-term bonds (97%), real estate (3%), cash and equiv (1%)
**Provider Compensation ($000):** FFS ($256,981), capitation ($38,247), contr fee ($12,898)
**Total Member Encounters:** Phys (520,066), non-phys (232,020)
**Group Affiliation:** Aetna Inc
**Licensed in:** VA
**Address:** 9881 MAYLAND DRIVE, RICHMOND, VA 23233
**Phone:** (804) 747-3700 **Dom State:** VA **Commenced Bus:** April 1991

| Data Date | Rating | RACR #1 | RACR #2 | Total Assets ($mil) | Capital ($mil) | Net Premium ($mil) | Net Income ($mil) |
|---|---|---|---|---|---|---|---|
| 9-17 | C+ | 2.36 | 1.97 | 104.3 | 51.2 | 165.1 | 11.8 |
| 9-16 | B | 2.40 | 2.00 | 122.6 | 57.7 | 270.1 | -2.4 |
| 2016 | C+ | 1.88 | 1.57 | 109.5 | 40.1 | 348.4 | -4.3 |
| 2015 | B+ | 2.52 | 2.10 | 126.0 | 60.7 | 463.0 | 14.9 |
| 2014 | B | 2.38 | 1.98 | 125.7 | 59.4 | 414.2 | 2.6 |
| 2013 | B | 2.10 | 1.75 | 74.5 | 35.9 | 315.4 | 13.9 |
| 2012 | B- | 2.80 | 2.33 | 76.0 | 38.5 | 258.7 | 17.0 |

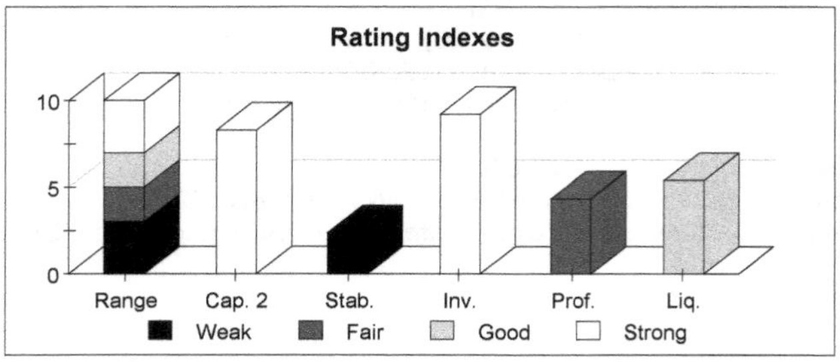

## COVENTRY HEALTH CARE OF WEST VA INC * B+ Good

**Major Rating Factors:** Good quality investment portfolio (6.7 on a scale of 0 to 10). Good overall results on stability tests (5.4). Rating is significantly influenced by the good financial results of Aetna Inc. Good liquidity (6.8) with sufficient resources (cash flows and marketable investments) to handle a spike in claims.
**Other Rating Factors:** Excellent profitability (9.2). Strong capitalization index (8.0) based on excellent current risk-adjusted capital (severe loss scenario).
**Principal Business:** Medicaid (90%), Medicare (10%)
**Mem Phys: 16:** 5,212 **15:** 5,211 **16 MLR** 86.5% **/ 16 Admin Exp** N/A
**Enroll(000): Q3 17:** 134 **16:** 126 **15:** 125 **Med Exp PMPM:** $308
**Principal Investments:** Long-term bonds (80%), cash and equiv (11%), nonaffiliate common stock (1%), other (8%)
**Provider Compensation ($000):** Contr fee ($388,542), FFS ($55,049), bonus arrang ($5,883), capitation ($1,003)
**Total Member Encounters:** Phys (725,693), non-phys (125,133)
**Group Affiliation:** Aetna Inc
**Licensed in:** WV
**Address:** 500 VIRGINIA STREET EAST SUITE, CHARLESTON, WV 25301
**Phone:** (804) 747-3700 **Dom State:** WV **Commenced Bus:** January 1995

| Data Date | Rating | RACR #1 | RACR #2 | Total Assets ($mil) | Capital ($mil) | Net Premium ($mil) | Net Income ($mil) |
|---|---|---|---|---|---|---|---|
| 9-17 | B+ | 2.18 | 1.82 | 152.7 | 64.8 | 436.1 | 8.6 |
| 9-16 | B+ | 3.08 | 2.57 | 143.9 | 54.9 | 400.6 | 5.3 |
| 2016 | B+ | 2.41 | 2.01 | 171.0 | 72.5 | 546.4 | 22.6 |
| 2015 | B+ | 3.56 | 2.97 | 120.5 | 64.5 | 342.8 | 18.6 |
| 2014 | A | 3.91 | 3.25 | 96.8 | 57.4 | 297.9 | 31.0 |
| 2013 | A- | 3.57 | 2.97 | 78.3 | 44.4 | 235.1 | 17.3 |
| 2012 | B+ | 3.46 | 2.88 | 69.0 | 37.0 | 189.0 | 8.5 |

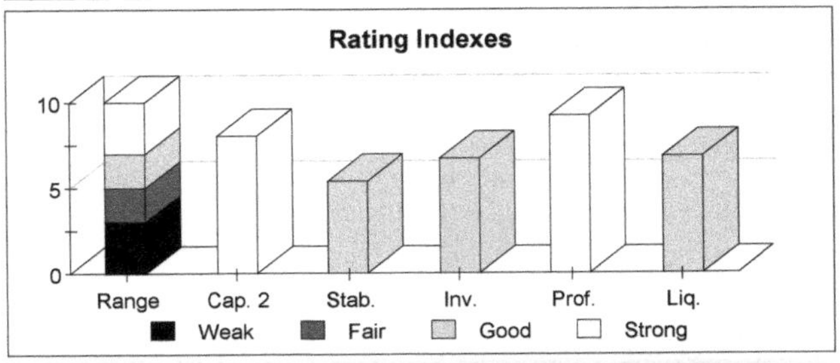


## COX HEALTH SYSTEMS INS CO D+ Weak

**Major Rating Factors:** Weak profitability index (0.8 on a scale of 0 to 10). Poor capitalization (1.9) based on weak current risk-adjusted capital (moderate loss scenario). Good liquidity (6.2) with sufficient resources (cash flows and marketable investments) to handle a spike in claims.
**Other Rating Factors:** High quality investment portfolio (9.9).
**Principal Business:** Comp med (100%)
**Mem Phys: 16:** 2,954 **15:** 2,677 **16 MLR** 92.9% **/ 16 Admin Exp** N/A
**Enroll(000): Q3 17:** 35 **16:** 35 **15:** 33 **Med Exp PMPM:** $288
**Principal Investments:** Cash and equiv (54%), long-term bonds (46%)
**Provider Compensation ($000):** Contr fee ($118,017), FFS ($3,288)
**Total Member Encounters:** Phys (171,136), non-phys (31,315)
**Group Affiliation:** Cox Health
**Licensed in:** MO
**Address:** 3200 S National Bldg B, Springfield, MO 65801-5750
**Phone:** (417) 269-6762 **Dom State:** MO **Commenced Bus:** January 1995

| Data Date | Rating | RACR #1 | RACR #2 | Total Assets ($mil) | Capital ($mil) | Net Premium ($mil) | Net Income ($mil) |
|---|---|---|---|---|---|---|---|
| 9-17 | D+ | 0.50 | 0.41 | 37.1 | 10.0 | 105.8 | -4.6 |
| 9-16 | C | 1.07 | 0.89 | 39.4 | 16.4 | 98.5 | -1.0 |
| 2016 | C | 1.03 | 0.86 | 41.5 | 17.2 | 131.8 | -3.7 |
| 2015 | C+ | 1.15 | 0.96 | 38.3 | 17.5 | 120.5 | -0.1 |
| 2014 | B- | 1.07 | 0.89 | 35.7 | 14.5 | 112.0 | 0.2 |
| 2013 | B- | 1.06 | 0.88 | 36.7 | 14.6 | 109.8 | 1.6 |
| 2012 | N/A | N/A | N/A | 29.9 | 10.5 | 101.8 | -4.8 |

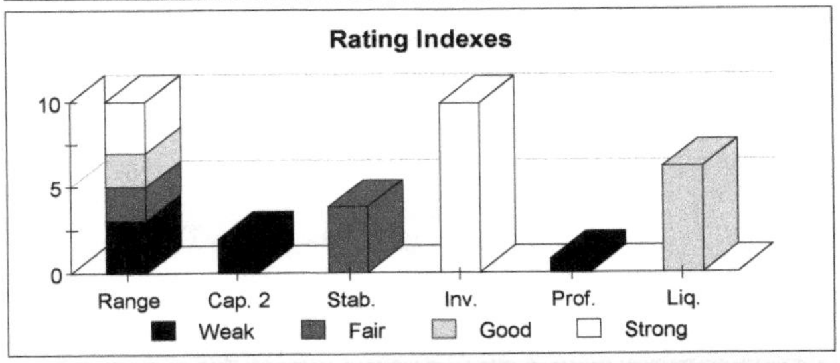


## CRESTPOINT HEALTH INS CO D Weak

**Major Rating Factors:** Weak profitability index (0.9 on a scale of 0 to 10). Good liquidity (6.7) with sufficient resources (cash flows and marketable investments) to handle a spike in claims. Strong capitalization (7.9) based on excellent current risk-adjusted capital (severe loss scenario).
**Other Rating Factors:** High quality investment portfolio (9.9).
**Principal Business:** Medicare (100%)
**Mem Phys: 16:** N/A **15:** 5,024 **16 MLR** 104.5% **/ 16 Admin Exp** N/A
**Enroll(000): Q1 17:** N/A **16:** N/A **15:** 5 **Med Exp PMPM:** N/A
**Principal Investments:** Long-term bonds (59%), cash and equiv (41%)
**Provider Compensation ($000):** Contr fee ($25,444)
**Total Member Encounters:** Phys (7,136), non-phys (8,963)
**Group Affiliation:** Mountain States Health Alliance
**Licensed in:** (No states)
**Address:** 509 Med Tech Parkway Ste 100, Johnson City, TN 37604
**Phone:** (423) 952-2111 **Dom State:** TN **Commenced Bus:** March 1930

| Data Date | Rating | RACR #1 | RACR #2 | Total Assets ($mil) | Capital ($mil) | Net Premium ($mil) | Net Income ($mil) |
|---|---|---|---|---|---|---|---|
| 3-17 | D | 2.08 | 1.74 | 12.0 | 8.6 | N/A | 0.0 |
| 3-16 | D | 1.15 | 0.96 | 18.2 | 7.9 | 13.4 | -2.3 |
| 2016 | D | 2.14 | 1.79 | 12.3 | 8.8 | 21.8 | -2.2 |
| 2015 | D | 1.03 | 0.86 | 17.0 | 7.1 | 41.4 | -8.5 |
| 2014 | D | 1.40 | 1.16 | 13.7 | 5.7 | 20.9 | -4.6 |
| 2013 | D | 3.09 | 2.57 | 8.0 | 3.4 | 2.2 | -8.6 |
| 2012 | N/A | N/A | N/A | 2.5 | 2.1 | N/A | N/A |

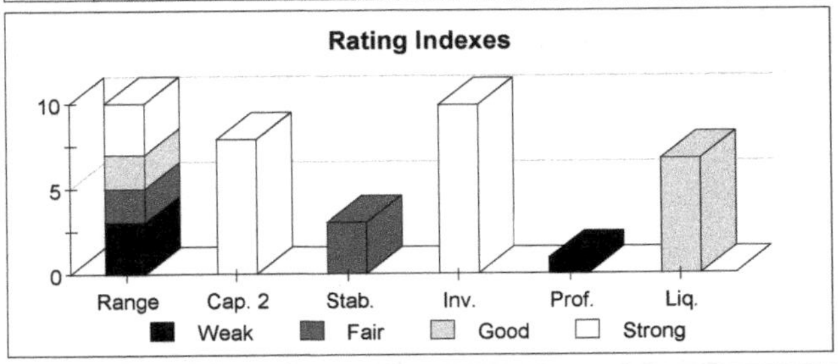

## CRYSTAL RUN HEALTH INS CO INC E- Very Weak

**Major Rating Factors:** Weak profitability index (0.0 on a scale of 0 to 10). Fair capitalization (3.7) based on weak current risk-adjusted capital (moderate loss scenario). Good liquidity (6.1) with sufficient resources (cash flows and marketable investments) to handle a spike in claims.
**Other Rating Factors:** High quality investment portfolio (9.9).
**Principal Business:** Comp med (100%)
**Mem Phys: 16:** N/A **15:** N/A **16 MLR** 97.2% **/ 16 Admin Exp** N/A
**Enroll(000): Q3 17:** 3 **16:** 4 **15:** 2 **Med Exp PMPM:** $327
**Principal Investments:** Cash and equiv (100%)
**Provider Compensation ($000):** Contr fee ($7,385)
**Total Member Encounters:** Phys (9,612), non-phys (1,821)
**Group Affiliation:** Crystal Run Healthcare LLP
**Licensed in:** (No states)
**Address:** 109 Rykowski Lane, Middletown, NY 10940
**Phone:** (845) 703-6422 **Dom State:** NY **Commenced Bus:** January 2015

| Data Date | Rating | RACR #1 | RACR #2 | Total Assets ($mil) | Capital ($mil) | Net Premium ($mil) | Net Income ($mil) |
|---|---|---|---|---|---|---|---|
| 9-17 | E- | 0.73 | 0.61 | 8.3 | 2.4 | 9.7 | -3.4 |
| 9-16 | E | 1.33 | 1.11 | 5.9 | 2.3 | 7.1 | -1.7 |
| 2016 | E- | 0.13 | 0.11 | 6.7 | 0.3 | 9.4 | -3.9 |
| 2015 | E | 2.17 | 1.81 | 6.9 | 2.4 | 2.1 | -3.5 |
| 2014 | N/A | N/A | N/A | N/A | N/A | N/A | N/A |
| 2013 | N/A | N/A | N/A | N/A | N/A | N/A | N/A |
| 2012 | N/A | N/A | N/A | N/A | N/A | N/A | N/A |

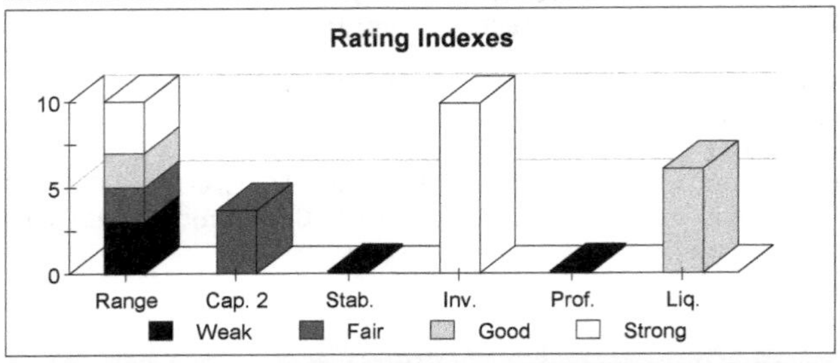


## CRYSTAL RUN HEALTH PLAN LLC D- Weak

**Major Rating Factors:** Weak profitability index (0.0 on a scale of 0 to 10). Strong capitalization (7.4) based on excellent current risk-adjusted capital (severe loss scenario). High quality investment portfolio (9.9).
**Other Rating Factors:** Excellent liquidity (7.0) with ample operational cash flow and liquid investments.
**Principal Business:** Comp med (87%), Medicaid (13%)
**Mem Phys: 16:** N/A **15:** N/A **16 MLR** 96.0% **/ 16 Admin Exp** N/A
**Enroll(000): Q3 17:** 4 **16:** 3 **15:** 0 **Med Exp PMPM:** $384
**Principal Investments:** Cash and equiv (100%)
**Provider Compensation ($000):** Contr fee ($7,893)
**Total Member Encounters:** Phys (15,059), non-phys (3,686)
**Group Affiliation:** Crystal Run Healthcare LLP
**Licensed in:** (No states)
**Address:** 109 Rykowski Lane, Middletown, NY 10941
**Phone:** (845) 703-6422 **Dom State:** NY **Commenced Bus:** September 2015

| Data Date | Rating | RACR #1 | RACR #2 | Total Assets ($mil) | Capital ($mil) | Net Premium ($mil) | Net Income ($mil) |
|---|---|---|---|---|---|---|---|
| 9-17 | D- | 1.67 | 1.39 | 10.0 | 4.6 | 11.8 | 0.9 |
| 9-16 | N/A | N/A | N/A | 10.6 | 4.0 | 8.9 | -3.8 |
| 2016 | D- | 1.21 | 1.01 | 12.0 | 3.5 | 13.2 | -4.2 |
| 2015 | N/A | N/A | N/A | 9.0 | 7.9 | 0.1 | N/A |
| 2014 | N/A | N/A | N/A | N/A | N/A | N/A | N/A |
| 2013 | N/A | N/A | N/A | N/A | N/A | N/A | N/A |
| 2012 | N/A | N/A | N/A | N/A | N/A | N/A | N/A |

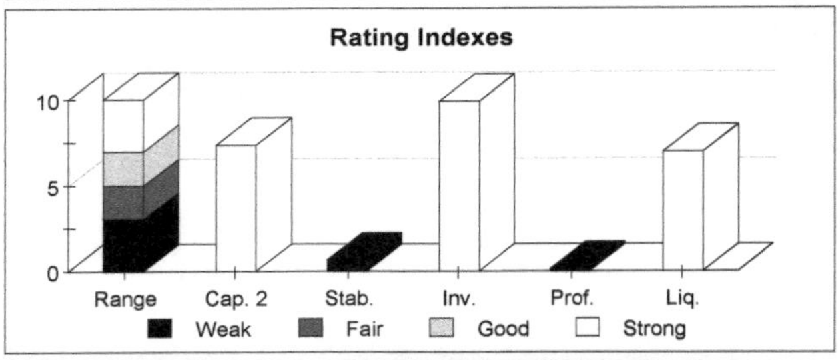


## DAVITA HEALTH PLAN OF CA INC D+ Weak

**Major Rating Factors:** Fair capitalization index (3.9 on a scale of 0 to 10) based on weak current risk-adjusted capital (moderate loss scenario). Good overall results on stability tests (6.8). Excellent profitability (9.0).
**Other Rating Factors:** Excellent liquidity (6.9) with sufficient resources (cash flows and marketable investments) to handle a spike in claims.
**Principal Business:** Managed care (97%)
**Mem Phys: 16:** N/A **15:** N/A **16 MLR** 93.8% **/ 16 Admin Exp** N/A
**Enroll(000): Q3 17:** 486 **16:** 495 **15:** 519 **Med Exp PMPM:** $226
**Principal Investments ($000):** Cash and equiv ($54,258)
**Provider Compensation ($000):** None
**Total Member Encounters:** N/A
**Group Affiliation:** HealthCare Partners Holdings LLC
**Licensed in:** CA
**Address:** 2220 E Gonzales Road Suite 210, Oxnard, CA 93036
**Phone:** (805) 981-5006 **Dom State:** CA **Commenced Bus:** January 2014

| Data Date | Rating | RACR #1 | RACR #2 | Total Assets ($mil) | Capital ($mil) | Net Premium ($mil) | Net Income ($mil) |
|---|---|---|---|---|---|---|---|
| 9-17 | D+ | 0.64 | 0.39 | 174.9 | 54.4 | 1,446.0 | 1.1 |
| 9-16 | C | 0.92 | 0.55 | 93.8 | 73.3 | 1,095.5 | 29.6 |
| 2016 | D+ | 0.63 | 0.38 | 98.4 | 53.4 | 1,462.1 | 39.7 |
| 2015 | D | 0.51 | 0.31 | 79.0 | 43.6 | 1,458.0 | 40.8 |
| 2014 | U | 0.35 | 0.21 | 56.8 | 27.5 | 1,284.0 | 40.2 |
| 2013 | N/A | N/A | N/A | N/A | N/A | N/A | N/A |
| 2012 | N/A | N/A | N/A | N/A | N/A | N/A | N/A |

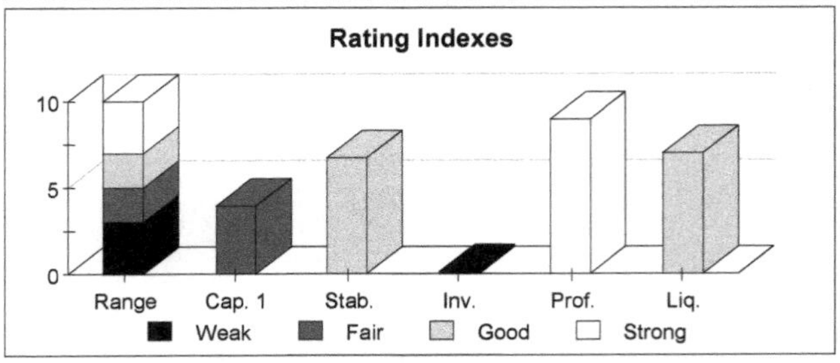

## DEAN HEALTH PLAN INC * B+ Good

**Major Rating Factors:** Good overall profitability index (6.4 on a scale of 0 to 10). Strong capitalization index (7.9) based on excellent current risk-adjusted capital (severe loss scenario). High quality investment portfolio (8.2).
**Other Rating Factors:** Excellent overall results on stability tests (7.3). Excellent liquidity (6.9) with sufficient resources (cash flows and marketable investments) to handle a spike in claims
**Principal Business:** Comp med (78%), Medicare (10%), Medicaid (6%), med supp (3%), FEHB (2%)
**Mem Phys: 16:** 3,933 **15:** 3,500 **16 MLR** 86.8% **/ 16 Admin Exp** N/A
**Enroll(000): Q3 17:** 268 **16:** 276 **15:** 272 **Med Exp PMPM:** $324
**Principal Investments:** Cash and equiv (44%), long-term bonds (29%), nonaffiliate common stock (16%), real estate (11%)
**Provider Compensation ($000):** Capitation ($1,005,256), contr fee ($47,781), FFS ($28,441)
**Total Member Encounters:** Phys (953,065), non-phys (875,129)
**Group Affiliation:** SSM Health Care Corporation
**Licensed in:** WI
**Address:** 1277 Deming Way, Madison, WI 53717
**Phone:** (608) 836-1400 **Dom State:** WI **Commenced Bus:** January 1984

| Data Date | Rating | RACR #1 | RACR #2 | Total Assets ($mil) | Capital ($mil) | Net Premium ($mil) | Net Income ($mil) |
|---|---|---|---|---|---|---|---|
| 9-17 | B+ | 2.11 | 1.76 | 225.0 | 128.2 | 938.5 | 5.5 |
| 9-16 | B | 1.74 | 1.45 | 207.0 | 103.0 | 944.0 | 4.4 |
| 2016 | B+ | 1.85 | 1.54 | 212.7 | 113.1 | 1,250.9 | 15.9 |
| 2015 | B | 1.60 | 1.33 | 209.0 | 95.9 | 1,220.6 | 5.3 |
| 2014 | B | 1.64 | 1.36 | 178.3 | 93.3 | 1,160.6 | 0.2 |
| 2013 | B | 1.55 | 1.29 | 159.6 | 86.6 | 1,076.7 | 32.0 |
| 2012 | A- | 1.74 | 1.45 | 151.8 | 89.0 | 1,042.3 | -1.3 |

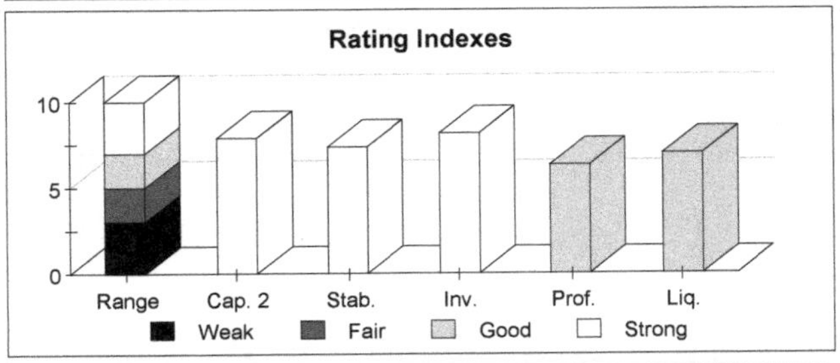


## DEARBORN NATIONAL LIFE INSURANCE COMPANY * B+ Good

**Major Rating Factors:** Good overall results on stability tests (6.5 on a scale of 0 to 10) despite negative cash flow from operations for 2016. Other stability subfactors include good operational trends and excellent risk diversification. Good quality investment portfolio (6.4) despite mixed results such as: large holdings of BBB rated bonds but moderate junk bond exposure. Good overall profitability (6.3).
**Other Rating Factors:** Good liquidity (6.4). Strong capitalization (8.7) based on excellent risk adjusted capital (severe loss scenario).
**Principal Business:** Group life insurance (63%), group health insurance (34%), individual life insurance (2%), and individual annuities (1%).
**Principal Investments:** NonCMO investment grade bonds (65%), CMOs and structured securities (20%), noninv. grade bonds (9%), mortgages in good standing (4%), and common & preferred stock (1%).
**Investments in Affiliates:** 1%
**Group Affiliation:** HCSC Group
**Licensed in:** All states except NY
**Commenced Business:** April 1969
**Address:** 300 East Randolph Street, Chicago, IL 60601-5099
**Phone:** (800) 633-3696 **Domicile State:** IL **NAIC Code:** 71129

| Data Date | Rating | RACR #1 | RACR #2 | Total Assets ($mil) | Capital ($mil) | Net Premium ($mil) | Net Income ($mil) |
|---|---|---|---|---|---|---|---|
| 9-17 | B+ | 3.42 | 2.15 | 1,849.7 | 510.9 | 328.1 | 14.8 |
| 9-16 | B+ | 3.73 | 2.32 | 1,940.0 | 537.0 | 304.1 | 12.9 |
| 2016 | B+ | 3.36 | 2.11 | 1,872.5 | 497.0 | 408.0 | 19.7 |
| 2015 | B+ | 3.63 | 2.25 | 1,990.5 | 522.1 | 382.5 | 59.1 |
| 2014 | A- | 2.86 | 1.91 | 2,145.5 | 514.7 | 379.9 | 54.8 |
| 2013 | A- | 2.27 | 1.52 | 2,324.1 | 439.7 | 495.5 | 42.3 |
| 2012 | A- | 1.85 | 1.21 | 2,621.0 | 402.8 | 563.1 | -6.1 |

**Adverse Trends in Operations**

Decrease in asset base during 2016 (6%)
Decrease in asset base during 2015 (7%)
Decrease in premium volume from 2013 to 2014 (23%)
Decrease in premium volume from 2012 to 2013 (12%)
Decrease in asset base during 2013 (11%)

## DELAWARE AMERICAN LIFE INSURANCE COMPANY * B+ Good

**Major Rating Factors:** Good overall results on stability tests (5.3 on a scale of 0 to 10). Stability strengths include good operational trends and excellent risk diversification. Strong overall capitalization (10.0) based on excellent risk adjusted capital (severe loss scenario). However, capital levels have fluctuated somewhat during past years. High quality investment portfolio (7.6).
**Other Rating Factors:** Excellent profitability (7.3). Excellent liquidity (7.1).
**Principal Business:** Group health insurance (72%), reinsurance (15%), group life insurance (11%), and individual life insurance (1%).
**Principal Investments:** NonCMO investment grade bonds (63%), CMOs and structured securities (26%), cash (4%), and noninv. grade bonds (2%).
**Investments in Affiliates:** 4%
**Group Affiliation:** MetLife Inc
**Licensed in:** All states except PR
**Commenced Business:** August 1966
**Address:** 1209 Orange Street, Wilmington, DE 19801
**Phone:** (302) 594-2000 **Domicile State:** DE **NAIC Code:** 62634

| Data Date | Rating | RACR #1 | RACR #2 | Total Assets ($mil) | Capital ($mil) | Net Premium ($mil) | Net Income ($mil) |
|---|---|---|---|---|---|---|---|
| 9-17 | B+ | 4.69 | 3.47 | 137.9 | 76.3 | 72.8 | 6.1 |
| 9-16 | A- | 3.63 | 2.66 | 163.7 | 70.3 | 94.3 | 8.0 |
| 2016 | B+ | 4.56 | 3.33 | 132.8 | 72.5 | 89.9 | 15.2 |
| 2015 | A- | 3.53 | 2.60 | 136.6 | 63.5 | 108.7 | 1.8 |
| 2014 | A- | 3.88 | 2.81 | 136.7 | 69.3 | 102.1 | 10.0 |
| 2013 | B | 4.89 | 3.54 | 137.1 | 74.3 | 91.1 | 17.1 |
| 2012 | B | 3.60 | 2.62 | 128.7 | 54.6 | 76.1 | 7.7 |

**Adverse Trends in Operations**

Change in premium mix from 2015 to 2016 (6.7%)
Decrease in premium volume from 2015 to 2016 (17%)
Decrease in asset base during 2016 (3%)
Decrease in capital during 2015 (8%)
Decrease in capital during 2014 (7%)

## DENVER HEALTH MEDICAL PLAN INC — B — Good

**Major Rating Factors:** Good overall results on stability tests (6.5 on a scale of 0 to 10). Good liquidity (6.4) with sufficient resources (cash flows and marketable investments) to handle a spike in claims. Fair profitability index (3.7).
**Other Rating Factors:** Strong capitalization index (8.1) based on excellent current risk-adjusted capital (severe loss scenario). High quality investment portfolio (9.2).
**Principal Business:** Comp med (62%), Medicare (38%)
**Mem Phys: 16:** 15,841 **15:** 14,471 **16 MLR** 87.0% **/ 16 Admin Exp** N/A
**Enroll(000): Q3 17:** 29 **16:** 26 **15:** 20 **Med Exp PMPM:** $422
**Principal Investments:** Long-term bonds (99%), cash and equiv (1%)
**Provider Compensation ($000):** FFS ($50,533), contr fee ($45,737), capitation ($22,037)
**Total Member Encounters:** Phys (164,386), non-phys (51,636)
**Group Affiliation:** Denver Health and Hospital Authority
**Licensed in:** CO
**Address:** 777 Bannock Street MC 6000, Denver, CO 80204
**Phone:** (303) 602-2100 **Dom State:** CO **Commenced Bus:** January 1997

| Data Date | Rating | RACR #1 | RACR #2 | Total Assets ($mil) | Capital ($mil) | Net Premium ($mil) | Net Income ($mil) |
|---|---|---|---|---|---|---|---|
| 9-17 | B | 2.23 | 1.86 | 60.0 | 31.3 | 114.0 | -0.6 |
| 9-16 | B | 3.02 | 2.52 | 61.9 | 37.2 | 101.0 | 6.4 |
| 2016 | B | 2.29 | 1.91 | 52.1 | 32.0 | 137.6 | 6.1 |
| 2015 | B | 2.50 | 2.08 | 48.5 | 31.0 | 119.3 | 1.2 |
| 2014 | B | 2.48 | 2.06 | 45.9 | 29.9 | 114.1 | -5.0 |
| 2013 | B | 3.39 | 2.82 | 45.9 | 34.9 | 108.9 | 7.2 |
| 2012 | B | 3.74 | 3.12 | 47.8 | 34.8 | 101.5 | 12.8 |

Rating Indexes

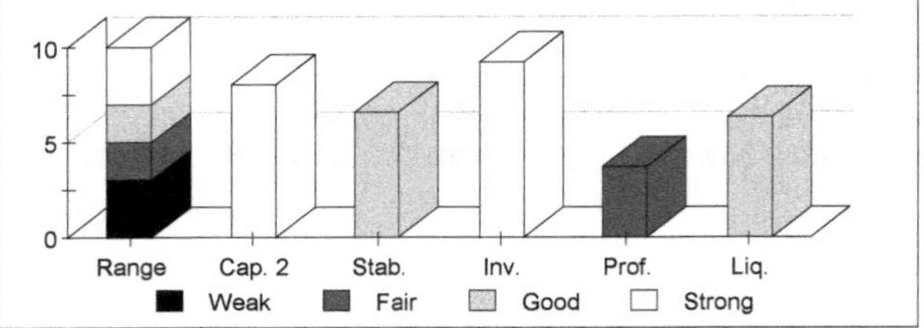


## DRISCOLL CHILDRENS HEALTH PLAN — C+ — Fair

**Major Rating Factors:** Fair profitability index (3.8 on a scale of 0 to 10). Good overall results on stability tests (5.3) despite a decline in the number of member physicians during 2017. Strong capitalization index (7.4) based on excellent current risk-adjusted capital (severe loss scenario).
**Other Rating Factors:** High quality investment portfolio (9.9). Excellent liquidity (7.0) with sufficient resources (cash flows and marketable investments) to handle a spike in claims.
**Principal Business:** Medicaid (97%), other (3%)
**Mem Phys: 16:** 2,973 **15:** 3,542 **16 MLR** 86.9% **/ 16 Admin Exp** N/A
**Enroll(000): Q3 17:** 167 **16:** 165 **15:** 144 **Med Exp PMPM:** $244
**Principal Investments:** Cash and equiv (77%), nonaffiliate common stock (23%)
**Provider Compensation ($000):** Contr fee ($295,458), FFS ($109,693), bonus arrang ($20,810), capitation ($12,287)
**Total Member Encounters:** Phys (1,390,222), non-phys (98,310)
**Group Affiliation:** Driscoll Childrens Hospital Inc
**Licensed in:** TX
**Address:** Corpus Christi, Corpus Christi, TX 78401
**Phone:** (361) 694-6432 **Dom State:** TX **Commenced Bus:** April 1997

| Data Date | Rating | RACR #1 | RACR #2 | Total Assets ($mil) | Capital ($mil) | Net Premium ($mil) | Net Income ($mil) |
|---|---|---|---|---|---|---|---|
| 9-17 | C+ | 1.66 | 1.39 | 142.2 | 81.5 | 500.3 | 31.8 |
| 9-16 | C- | 0.92 | 0.77 | 90.0 | 44.7 | 365.2 | 1.0 |
| 2016 | C- | 0.99 | 0.82 | 116.9 | 51.5 | 522.6 | 6.4 |
| 2015 | C- | 0.61 | 0.51 | 81.2 | 30.2 | 435.6 | -15.6 |
| 2014 | D | 0.54 | 0.45 | 74.4 | 23.3 | 384.7 | -9.3 |
| 2013 | D | 0.96 | 0.80 | 63.1 | 30.3 | 315.6 | 1.4 |
| 2012 | D | 1.17 | 0.98 | 63.0 | 30.2 | 290.0 | 22.0 |

Rating Indexes

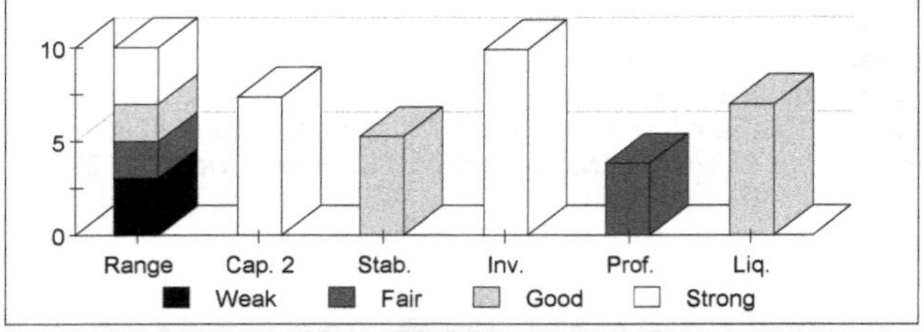


## EASY CHOICE HEALTH PLAN — C- — Fair

**Major Rating Factors:** Fair overall results on stability tests (4.5 on a scale of 0 to 10). Weak profitability index (1.9). Good capitalization index (6.9) based on good current risk-adjusted capital (moderate loss scenario).
**Other Rating Factors:** Excellent liquidity (7.2) with ample operational cash flow and liquid investments.
**Principal Business:** Medicare (100%)
**Mem Phys: 16:** N/A **15:** N/A **16 MLR** 86.9% **/ 16 Admin Exp** N/A
**Enroll(000): Q3 17:** 26 **16:** 31 **15:** 32 **Med Exp PMPM:** $874
**Principal Investments ($000):** Cash and equiv ($84,361)
**Provider Compensation ($000):** None
**Total Member Encounters:** N/A
**Group Affiliation:** None
**Licensed in:** CA
**Address:** 4550 California Ave Suite 100, Bakersfield, CA 93309
**Phone:** (310) 228-3745 **Dom State:** CA **Commenced Bus:** September 2006

| Data Date | Rating | RACR #1 | RACR #2 | Total Assets ($mil) | Capital ($mil) | Net Premium ($mil) | Net Income ($mil) |
|---|---|---|---|---|---|---|---|
| 9-17 | C- | 1.06 | 0.66 | 155.8 | 31.4 | 260.0 | 11.4 |
| 9-16 | E+ | 0.54 | 0.34 | 130.1 | 20.5 | 291.3 | 1.2 |
| 2016 | D | 0.68 | 0.42 | 100.4 | 20.1 | 382.1 | 0.8 |
| 2015 | E | 0.50 | 0.31 | 62.2 | 19.3 | 380.0 | -13.0 |
| 2014 | E | 0.41 | 0.25 | 90.7 | 26.3 | 629.8 | -32.9 |
| 2013 | D- | 0.41 | 0.25 | 89.4 | 23.2 | 567.3 | -4.4 |
| 2012 | E+ | 0.47 | 0.29 | 56.4 | 16.1 | 352.9 | -4.3 |

Rating Indexes

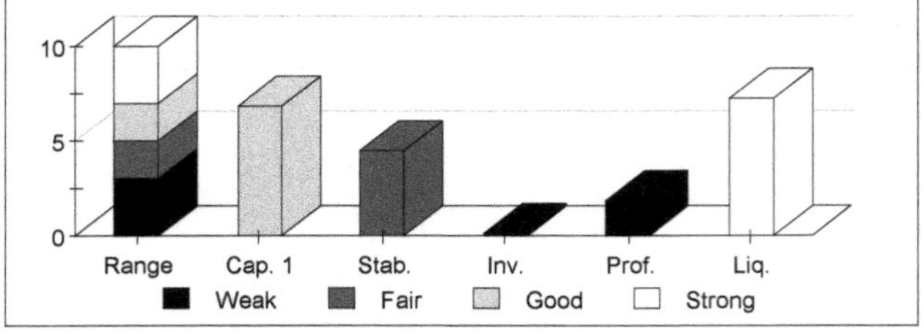

## EDUCATORS HEALTH PLANS LIFE ACCIDENT B Good

**Major Rating Factors:** Good overall profitability index (5.9 on a scale of 0 to 10). Strong capitalization (8.9) based on excellent current risk-adjusted capital (severe loss scenario). High quality investment portfolio (9.9).
**Other Rating Factors:** Excellent liquidity (7.3) with ample operational cash flow and liquid investments.
**Principal Business:** Dental (44%), comp med (13%), vision (3%), other (40%)
**Mem Phys: 16:** 17,252 **15:** 15,221 **16 MLR** 89.5% **/ 16 Admin Exp** N/A
**Enroll(000): Q3 17:** 138 **16:** 117 **15:** 87 **Med Exp PMPM:** $28
**Principal Investments:** Cash and equiv (53%), long-term bonds (47%)
**Provider Compensation ($000):** Contr fee ($27,655), FFS ($4,275)
**Total Member Encounters:** Phys (208,745), non-phys (195,960)
**Group Affiliation:** Educators Mutual Insurance Assoc
**Licensed in:** AZ, FL, NV, OH, PA, TX, UT
**Address:** 852 East Arrowhead Lane, Murray, UT 84107
**Phone:** (801) 262-7476 **Dom State:** UT **Commenced Bus:** February 2006

| Data Date | Rating | RACR #1 | RACR #2 | Total Assets ($mil) | Capital ($mil) | Net Premium ($mil) | Net Income ($mil) |
|---|---|---|---|---|---|---|---|
| 9-17 | B | 2.84 | 2.37 | 40.8 | 20.4 | 41.4 | 2.5 |
| 9-16 | B | 4.01 | 3.34 | 33.9 | 17.8 | 28.2 | 2.7 |
| 2016 | B | 2.48 | 2.07 | 36.0 | 17.9 | 39.3 | 2.5 |
| 2015 | B- | 3.29 | 2.74 | 26.7 | 14.9 | 28.2 | 2.8 |
| 2014 | C+ | 2.90 | 2.42 | 21.7 | 12.2 | 25.9 | -2.0 |
| 2013 | N/A | N/A | N/A | 12.6 | 7.0 | 21.1 | N/A |
| 2012 | N/A | N/A | N/A | 10.3 | 6.3 | 19.5 | N/A |

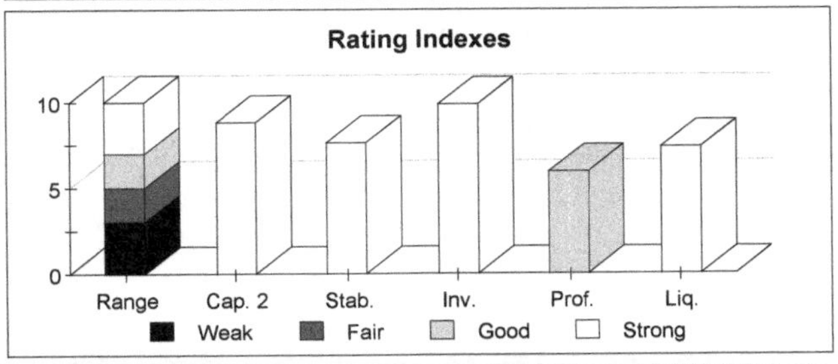


## EL PASO HEALTH * A- Excellent

**Major Rating Factors:** Excellent profitability (8.7 on a scale of 0 to 10). Strong capitalization index (8.1) based on excellent current risk-adjusted capital (severe loss scenario). High quality investment portfolio (9.5).
**Other Rating Factors:** Excellent overall results on stability tests (7.7). Excellent liquidity (7.2) with ample operational cash flow and liquid investments
**Principal Business:** Medicaid (92%), comp med (7%)
**Mem Phys: 16:** 2,162 **15:** 2,242 **16 MLR** 86.8% **/ 16 Admin Exp** N/A
**Enroll(000): Q3 17:** 76 **16:** 77 **15:** 76 **Med Exp PMPM:** $190
**Principal Investments:** Cash and equiv (85%), real estate (15%)
**Provider Compensation ($000):** Contr fee ($140,994), capitation ($26,190), FFS ($6,786), other ($1,883)
**Total Member Encounters:** Phys (557,933), non-phys (143,065)
**Group Affiliation:** El Paso County Hospital District
**Licensed in:** TX
**Address:** 1145 Westmoreland, El Paso, TX 79925
**Phone:** (915) 298-7198 **Dom State:** TX **Commenced Bus:** October 2000

| Data Date | Rating | RACR #1 | RACR #2 | Total Assets ($mil) | Capital ($mil) | Net Premium ($mil) | Net Income ($mil) |
|---|---|---|---|---|---|---|---|
| 9-17 | A- | 2.23 | 1.86 | 64.2 | 43.1 | 142.3 | 6.7 |
| 9-16 | B | 2.01 | 1.67 | 57.3 | 39.1 | 149.9 | 6.0 |
| 2016 | A- | 2.20 | 1.83 | 60.3 | 42.5 | 201.0 | 8.6 |
| 2015 | B | 1.69 | 1.41 | 51.2 | 33.5 | 192.0 | 2.6 |
| 2014 | B | 2.08 | 1.74 | 47.8 | 30.8 | 150.6 | 5.2 |
| 2013 | B | 2.07 | 1.72 | 38.2 | 28.0 | 126.9 | 3.7 |
| 2012 | B | 1.86 | 1.55 | 37.4 | 24.2 | 126.7 | 6.8 |

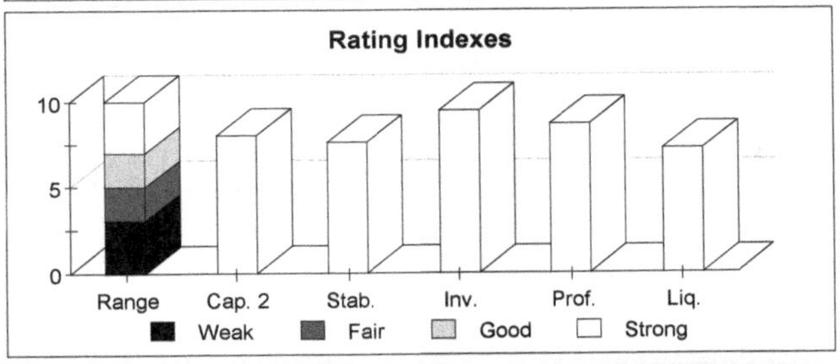


## ELDERPLAN INC C Fair

**Major Rating Factors:** Fair profitability index (3.3 on a scale of 0 to 10). Good capitalization index (5.6) based on good current risk-adjusted capital (severe loss scenario). Good overall results on stability tests (5.2).
**Other Rating Factors:** Good liquidity (6.8) with sufficient resources (cash flows and marketable investments) to handle a spike in claims. High quality investment portfolio (9.0).
**Principal Business:** Medicaid (80%), Medicare (20%)
**Mem Phys: 16:** 25,773 **15:** 23,533 **16 MLR** 83.7% **/ 16 Admin Exp** N/A
**Enroll(000): Q3 17:** 23 **16:** 24 **15:** 27 **Med Exp PMPM:** $2,515
**Principal Investments:** Long-term bonds (41%), cash and equiv (32%), nonaffiliate common stock (7%), other (20%)
**Provider Compensation ($000):** FFS ($621,250), contr fee ($61,742), capitation ($15,538)
**Total Member Encounters:** Phys (275,296), non-phys (246,100)
**Group Affiliation:** Elderplan Inc
**Licensed in:** NY
**Address:** 6323 Seventh Ave, Brooklyn, NY 11220
**Phone:** (718) 921-7990 **Dom State:** NY **Commenced Bus:** March 1985

| Data Date | Rating | RACR #1 | RACR #2 | Total Assets ($mil) | Capital ($mil) | Net Premium ($mil) | Net Income ($mil) |
|---|---|---|---|---|---|---|---|
| 9-17 | C | 1.02 | 0.85 | 236.3 | 78.2 | 728.5 | 18.2 |
| 9-16 | D+ | 0.81 | 0.67 | 193.7 | 61.3 | 626.9 | 9.0 |
| 2016 | C- | 0.73 | 0.60 | 189.7 | 56.6 | 843.5 | 5.6 |
| 2015 | D+ | 0.58 | 0.48 | 170.4 | 43.8 | 811.9 | -30.7 |
| 2014 | C | 1.27 | 1.06 | 198.6 | 86.6 | 778.1 | 4.4 |
| 2013 | D+ | 1.90 | 1.58 | 200.2 | 103.0 | 645.9 | 28.9 |
| 2012 | D | 1.52 | 1.27 | 151.0 | 72.5 | 514.7 | 12.0 |

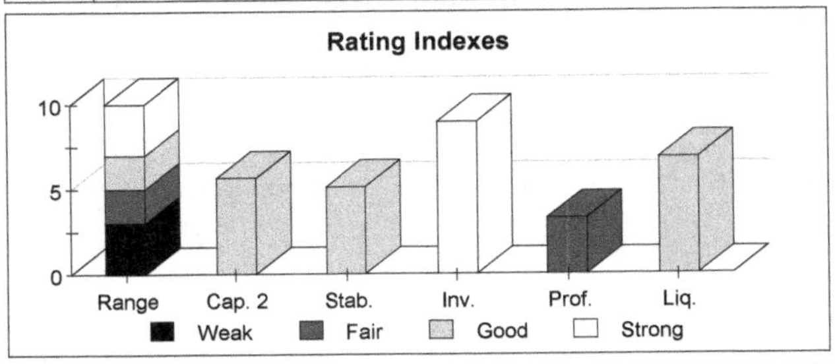

## EMI HEALTH * — A — Excellent

**Major Rating Factors:** Excellent profitability (8.4 on a scale of 0 to 10). Strong capitalization (10.0) based on excellent current risk-adjusted capital (severe loss scenario). High quality investment portfolio (7.5).
**Other Rating Factors:** Excellent liquidity (8.4) with ample operational cash flow and liquid investments.
**Principal Business:** Dental (16%), med supp (11%), comp med (5%), vision (2%), other (65%)
**Mem Phys: 16:** 17,252 **15:** 15,221 **16 MLR** 82.6% **/ 16 Admin Exp** N/A
**Enroll(000): Q3 17:** 61 **16:** 70 **15:** 72 **Med Exp PMPM:** $32
**Principal Investments:** Long-term bonds (53%), cash and equiv (21%), affiliate common stock (18%), real estate (6%), nonaffiliate common stock (2%)
**Provider Compensation ($000):** Contr fee ($19,747), FFS ($5,989)
**Total Member Encounters:** Phys (479,233), non-phys (300,639)
**Group Affiliation:** Educators Mutual Insurance Assoc
**Licensed in:** ID, UT
**Address:** 852 East Arrowhead Lane, Murray, UT 84107
**Phone:** (801) 262-7476 **Dom State:** UT **Commenced Bus:** June 1935

| Data Date | Rating | RACR #1 | RACR #2 | Total Assets ($mil) | Capital ($mil) | Net Premium ($mil) | Net Income ($mil) |
|---|---|---|---|---|---|---|---|
| 9-17 | A | 5.05 | 4.21 | 107.5 | 81.2 | 22.1 | 0.8 |
| 9-16 | B+ | 5.42 | 4.52 | 99.0 | 72.5 | 22.9 | 4.0 |
| 2016 | A | 4.81 | 4.01 | 104.1 | 78.1 | 32.1 | 9.3 |
| 2015 | A- | 4.74 | 3.95 | 91.7 | 65.0 | 31.8 | 3.7 |
| 2014 | B+ | 4.75 | 3.96 | 86.7 | 58.4 | 32.3 | 7.8 |
| 2013 | C- | 4.21 | 3.51 | 75.9 | 52.8 | 35.1 | 4.1 |
| 2012 | N/A | N/A | N/A | 72.1 | 46.4 | 35.4 | N/A |

**Rating Indexes**

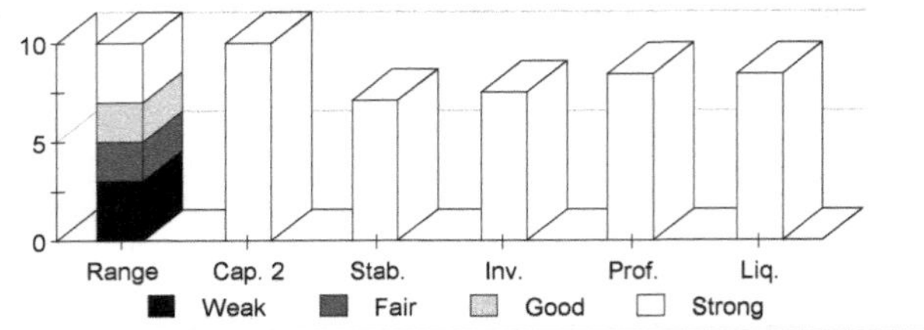


## EMPIRE HEALTHCHOICE ASSURANCE INC — B- — Good

**Major Rating Factors:** Fair quality investment portfolio (3.7 on a scale of 0 to 10). Good overall profitability index (6.8). Good liquidity (6.8) with sufficient resources (cash flows and marketable investments) to handle a spike in claims.
**Other Rating Factors:** Strong capitalization (10.0) based on excellent current risk-adjusted capital (severe loss scenario).
**Principal Business:** Comp med (51%), FEHB (37%), Medicare (4%), med supp (4%), dental (2%), other (3%)
**Mem Phys: 16:** 82,540 **15:** 78,609 **16 MLR** 84.9% **/ 16 Admin Exp** N/A
**Enroll(000): Q3 17:** 768 **16:** 775 **15:** 863 **Med Exp PMPM:** $193
**Principal Investments:** Long-term bonds (64%), affiliate common stock (15%), pref stock (1%), other (23%)
**Provider Compensation ($000):** Contr fee ($1,581,750), FFS ($329,409), bonus arrang ($8,333), capitation ($3,196), other ($36,942)
**Total Member Encounters:** Phys (2,750,220), non-phys (1,706,009)
**Group Affiliation:** Anthem Inc
**Licensed in:** NY
**Address:** 1 LIBERTY PLAZA 165 BROADWAY, NEW YORK, NY 10006
**Phone:** (212) 476-1000 **Dom State:** NY **Commenced Bus:** June 1974

| Data Date | Rating | RACR #1 | RACR #2 | Total Assets ($mil) | Capital ($mil) | Net Premium ($mil) | Net Income ($mil) |
|---|---|---|---|---|---|---|---|
| 9-17 | B- | 4.86 | 4.05 | 2,273.8 | 941.5 | 1,557.8 | 101.0 |
| 9-16 | C+ | 3.79 | 3.16 | 2,186.7 | 829.1 | 1,667.1 | 140.3 |
| 2016 | B- | 4.54 | 3.78 | 2,501.0 | 877.4 | 2,228.7 | 193.0 |
| 2015 | B- | 4.23 | 3.52 | 2,378.9 | 928.5 | 2,598.2 | 145.1 |
| 2014 | B- | 5.55 | 4.62 | 2,709.0 | 1,130.7 | 2,493.0 | 326.0 |
| 2013 | B | 5.14 | 4.28 | 3,533.3 | 1,711.9 | 4,591.4 | 263.0 |
| 2012 | B+ | 4.58 | 3.82 | 3,655.5 | 1,712.2 | 5,130.5 | 291.0 |

**Rating Indexes**

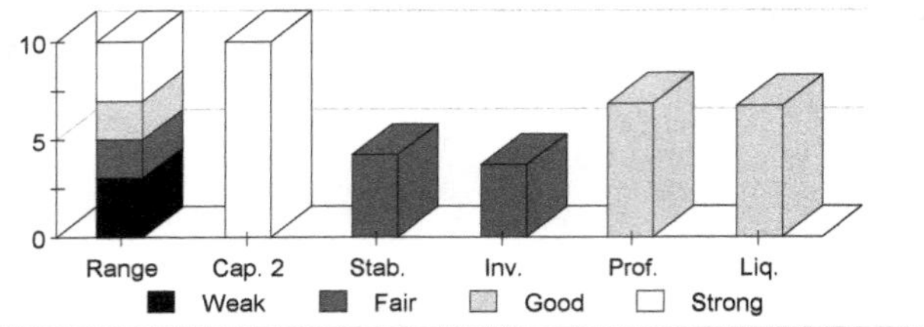


## EMPIRE HEALTHCHOICE HMO INC — C+ — Fair

**Major Rating Factors:** Fair overall results on stability tests (4.2 on a scale of 0 to 10). Rating is significantly influenced by the good financial results of Anthem Inc. Good liquidity (6.0) with sufficient resources (cash flows and marketable investments) to handle a spike in claims. Weak profitability index (1.2).
**Other Rating Factors:** Strong capitalization index (8.6) based on excellent current risk-adjusted capital (severe loss scenario). High quality investment portfolio (7.7).
**Principal Business:** Medicare (55%), comp med (45%)
**Mem Phys: 16:** 81,448 **15:** 77,365 **16 MLR** 90.5% **/ 16 Admin Exp** N/A
**Enroll(000): Q3 17:** 137 **16:** 142 **15:** 164 **Med Exp PMPM:** $686
**Principal Investments:** Long-term bonds (95%), other (5%)
**Provider Compensation ($000):** Contr fee ($929,328), FFS ($303,334), capitation ($36,884), bonus arrang ($14,758), other ($260)
**Total Member Encounters:** Phys (1,859,292), non-phys (909,730)
**Group Affiliation:** Anthem Inc
**Licensed in:** NY
**Address:** 1 LIBERTY PLAZA 165 BROADWAY, NEW YORK, NY 10006
**Phone:** (212) 476-1000 **Dom State:** NY **Commenced Bus:** March 1996

| Data Date | Rating | RACR #1 | RACR #2 | Total Assets ($mil) | Capital ($mil) | Net Premium ($mil) | Net Income ($mil) |
|---|---|---|---|---|---|---|---|
| 9-17 | C+ | 2.64 | 2.20 | 589.2 | 196.6 | 969.9 | -31.1 |
| 9-16 | C+ | 3.36 | 2.80 | 668.6 | 228.5 | 1,066.1 | -9.0 |
| 2016 | C+ | 2.96 | 2.47 | 616.1 | 223.9 | 1,381.4 | -8.0 |
| 2015 | B | 3.53 | 2.94 | 615.5 | 241.8 | 1,248.0 | -36.6 |
| 2014 | B | 3.83 | 3.19 | 692.9 | 295.0 | 1,390.9 | -20.0 |
| 2013 | B+ | 5.53 | 4.61 | 750.6 | 477.3 | 1,539.6 | 22.3 |
| 2012 | A- | 5.79 | 4.83 | 850.1 | 548.8 | 1,699.5 | 83.8 |

**Rating Indexes**

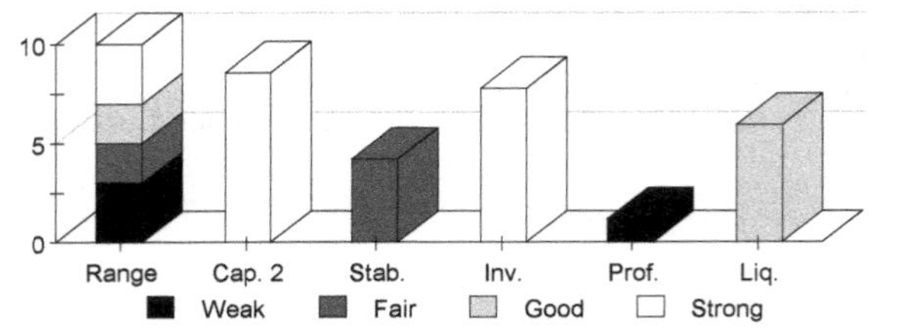

## ENTERPRISE LIFE INSURANCE COMPANY B- Good

**Major Rating Factors:** Good overall results on stability tests (5.1 on a scale of 0 to 10) despite fair financial strength of affiliated Credit Suisse Group and excessive premium growth. Other stability subfactors include excellent operational trends, good risk adjusted capital for prior years and good risk diversification. Good quality investment portfolio (5.7) with no exposure to mortgages and minimal holdings in junk bonds. Strong capitalization (7.0) based on excellent risk adjusted capital (severe loss scenario).
**Other Rating Factors:** Excellent profitability (8.9) despite modest operating losses during 2012. Excellent liquidity (7.2).
**Principal Business:** Reinsurance (98%), group health insurance (1%), and individual health insurance (1%).
**Principal Investments:** Common & preferred stock (58%), nonCMO investment grade bonds (20%), cash (19%), CMOs and structured securities (2%), and noninv. grade bonds (1%).
**Investments in Affiliates:** 58%
**Group Affiliation:** Credit Suisse Group
**Licensed in:** AZ, AR, IL, KS, LA, MS, NE, NM, OK, OR, TX, WI
**Commenced Business:** September 1978
**Address:** 300 Burnett Street Suite 200, Fort Worth, TX 76102-2734
**Phone:** (817) 878-3300 **Domicile State:** TX **NAIC Code:** 89087

| Data Date | Rating | RACR #1 | RACR #2 | Total Assets ($mil) | Capital ($mil) | Net Premium ($mil) | Net Income ($mil) |
|---|---|---|---|---|---|---|---|
| 9-17 | B- | 1.16 | 1.03 | 50.0 | 32.2 | 73.7 | 4.9 |
| 9-16 | B- | 1.01 | 0.90 | 32.4 | 22.8 | 44.6 | 0.0 |
| 2016 | B- | 0.84 | 0.75 | 34.9 | 23.5 | 62.7 | 0.1 |
| 2015 | C | 0.88 | 0.79 | 28.2 | 19.9 | 38.9 | 0.0 |
| 2014 | C | 0.95 | 0.90 | 19.8 | 14.9 | 21.1 | 1.3 |
| 2013 | C | 1.10 | 1.05 | 17.0 | 13.9 | 10.7 | 0.6 |
| 2012 | C | 1.32 | 1.32 | 13.4 | 12.9 | -0.3 | 0.0 |

**Credit Suisse Group**
**Composite Group Rating: C+**

| Largest Group Members | Assets ($mil) | Rating |
|---|---|---|
| FREEDOM LIFE INS CO OF AMERICA | 100 | C+ |
| ENTERPRISE LIFE INS CO | 35 | B- |
| NATIONAL FOUNDATION LIFE INS CO | 34 | B |

## EPIC HEALTH PLAN D- Weak

**Major Rating Factors:** Poor capitalization index (0.0 on a scale of 0 to 10) based on weak current risk-adjusted capital (severe loss scenario). Weak liquidity (0.0) as a spike in claims may stretch capacity. Good overall results on stability tests (5.5).
**Other Rating Factors:** Excellent profitability (8.8).
**Principal Business:** Managed care (100%)
**Mem Phys: 16:** N/A **15:** N/A **16 MLR** 97.5% **/ 16 Admin Exp** N/A
**Enroll(000): Q3 17:** 63 **16:** 58 **15:** 58 **Med Exp PMPM:** $482
**Principal Investments ($000):** Cash and equiv ($24,716)
**Provider Compensation ($000):** None
**Total Member Encounters:** N/A
**Group Affiliation:** None
**Licensed in:** CA
**Address:** 10803 Hope St Ste B, Cypress, CA 90630
**Phone:** (813) 206-7668 **Dom State:** CA **Commenced Bus:** October 2010

| Data Date | Rating | RACR #1 | RACR #2 | Total Assets ($mil) | Capital ($mil) | Net Premium ($mil) | Net Income ($mil) |
|---|---|---|---|---|---|---|---|
| 9-17 | D- | 0.03 | 0.02 | 34.1 | 13.9 | 288.1 | 3.2 |
| 9-16 | D- | 0.13 | 0.08 | 29.5 | 10.5 | 258.4 | 1.9 |
| 2016 | D- | N/A | N/A | 28.9 | 10.7 | 343.1 | 2.2 |
| 2015 | D- | 0.06 | 0.04 | 29.3 | 8.5 | 348.2 | 2.4 |
| 2014 | D- | 0.10 | 0.06 | 23.8 | 5.6 | 301.9 | N/A |
| 2013 | D+ | 0.55 | 0.33 | 11.6 | 4.1 | 65.4 | 0.7 |
| 2012 | C- | 1.20 | 0.73 | 6.3 | 2.9 | 21.0 | N/A |

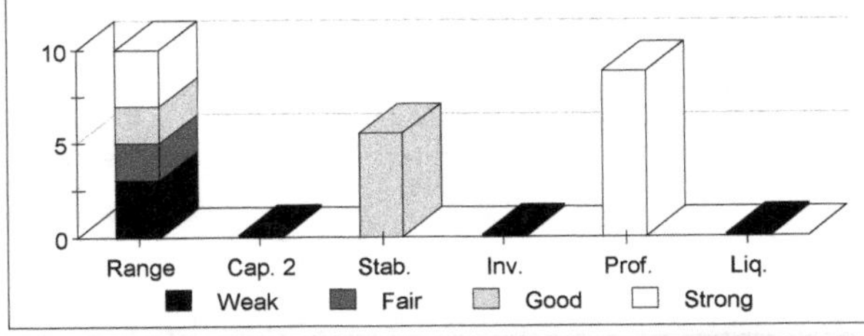


## EQUITABLE LIFE & CASUALTY INSURANCE COMPANY B- Good

**Major Rating Factors:** Good quality investment portfolio (5.4 on a scale of 0 to 10) despite mixed results such as: minimal exposure to mortgages and large holdings of BBB rated bonds but minimal holdings in junk bonds. Good overall results on stability tests (5.3). Stability strengths include excellent operational trends and good risk diversification. Fair profitability (4.2) with operating losses during the first nine months of 2017.
**Other Rating Factors:** Strong capitalization (7.3) based on excellent risk adjusted capital (severe loss scenario). Excellent liquidity (7.1).
**Principal Business:** Individual health insurance (93%), individual life insurance (6%), and reinsurance (1%).
**Principal Investments:** NonCMO investment grade bonds (75%), CMOs and structured securities (20%), and mortgages in good standing (5%).
**Investments in Affiliates:** None
**Group Affiliation:** SILAC LLC
**Licensed in:** All states except CA, MN, NJ, NY, PR
**Commenced Business:** June 1935
**Address:** 3 TRIAD CENTER, SALT LAKE CITY, UT 84180-1200
**Phone:** (801) 579-3400 **Domicile State:** UT **NAIC Code:** 62952

| Data Date | Rating | RACR #1 | RACR #2 | Total Assets ($mil) | Capital ($mil) | Net Premium ($mil) | Net Income ($mil) |
|---|---|---|---|---|---|---|---|
| 9-17 | B- | 1.91 | 1.20 | 328.0 | 49.8 | 45.0 | -8.7 |
| 9-16 | B | 3.21 | 2.10 | 316.1 | 48.9 | 48.2 | 0.9 |
| 2016 | B | 2.86 | 1.90 | 313.6 | 44.8 | 64.7 | -2.1 |
| 2015 | B | 2.94 | 1.96 | 306.4 | 46.2 | 69.7 | 9.5 |
| 2014 | B | 2.72 | 1.84 | 295.9 | 41.8 | 70.4 | 10.3 |
| 2013 | D+ | 2.15 | 1.51 | 275.8 | 39.1 | 91.1 | -0.3 |
| 2012 | C- | 1.51 | 1.08 | 243.0 | 30.3 | 111.1 | 1.8 |

**Adverse Trends in Operations**

Decrease in capital during 2016 (3%)
Decrease in premium volume from 2015 to 2016 (7%)
Decrease in premium volume from 2013 to 2014 (23%)
Decrease in premium volume from 2012 to 2013 (18%)
Increase in policy surrenders from 2012 to 2013 (75%)

## ESSENCE HEALTHCARE INC * B+ Good

**Major Rating Factors:** Good liquidity (6.8 on a scale of 0 to 10) with sufficient resources (cash flows and marketable investments) to handle a spike in claims. Excellent profitability (8.4). Strong capitalization (7.4) based on excellent current risk-adjusted capital (severe loss scenario).
**Other Rating Factors:** High quality investment portfolio (9.3).
**Principal Business:** Medicare (100%)
**Mem Phys: 16:** N/A **15:** 5,240 **16 MLR** 83.0% **/ 16 Admin Exp** N/A
**Enroll(000): Q3 17:** 64 **16:** 62 **15:** 53 **Med Exp PMPM:** $756
**Principal Investments:** Long-term bonds (73%), cash and equiv (23%), nonaffiliate common stock (4%)
**Provider Compensation ($000):** Contr fee ($414,142), capitation ($97,342)
**Total Member Encounters:** Phys (486,515), non-phys (105,930)
**Group Affiliation:** Essence Group Holdings Corp
**Licensed in:** IL, MO, TX, WA
**Address:** 13900 Riverport Dr, St. Louis, MO 63043
**Phone:** (314) 209-2780 **Dom State:** MO **Commenced Bus:** July 2004

| Data Date | Rating | RACR #1 | RACR #2 | Total Assets ($mil) | Capital ($mil) | Net Premium ($mil) | Net Income ($mil) |
|---|---|---|---|---|---|---|---|
| 9-17 | B+ | 1.65 | 1.38 | 288.5 | 86.8 | 527.4 | 14.2 |
| 9-16 | B+ | 1.61 | 1.35 | 246.5 | 75.4 | 492.0 | 12.6 |
| 2016 | B+ | 1.53 | 1.27 | 193.0 | 81.4 | 657.2 | 22.9 |
| 2015 | B+ | 1.36 | 1.13 | 132.6 | 65.3 | 552.5 | 11.4 |
| 2014 | B | 1.33 | 1.11 | 106.6 | 51.3 | 435.8 | 10.7 |
| 2013 | B | 1.23 | 1.02 | 111.3 | 44.3 | 411.8 | 20.3 |
| 2012 | B | 1.40 | 1.17 | 135.2 | 51.1 | 432.7 | 20.8 |

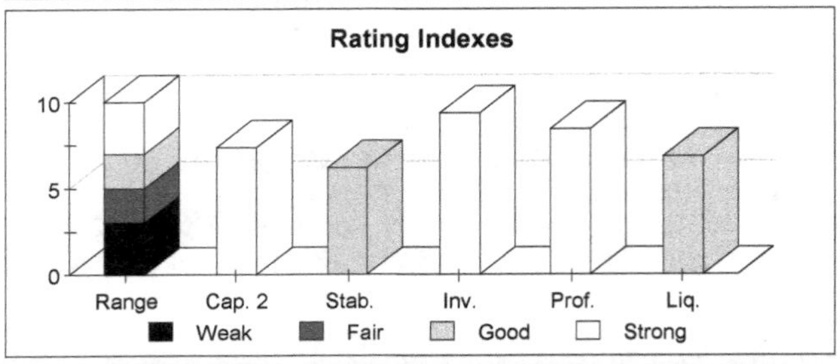


## EXCELLUS HEALTH PLAN INC * B+ Good

**Major Rating Factors:** Good overall profitability index (6.1 on a scale of 0 to 10). Good liquidity (6.8) with sufficient resources (cash flows and marketable investments) to handle a spike in claims. Strong capitalization (10.0) based on excellent current risk-adjusted capital (severe loss scenario).
**Other Rating Factors:** High quality investment portfolio (7.0).
**Principal Business:** Comp med (58%), Medicare (19%), Medicaid (17%), FEHB (3%), dental (1%), other (1%)
**Mem Phys: 16:** 27,749 **15:** 27,224 **16 MLR** 85.9% **/ 16 Admin Exp** N/A
**Enroll(000): Q3 17:** 1,106 **16:** 1,135 **15:** 1,238 **Med Exp PMPM:** $357
**Principal Investments:** Long-term bonds (65%), nonaffiliate common stock (20%), affiliate common stock (7%), cash and equiv (2%), real estate (2%), other (5%)
**Provider Compensation ($000):** Contr fee ($5,070,812), capitation ($43,526), bonus arrang ($9,493)
**Total Member Encounters:** Phys (9,913,545), non-phys (2,655,932)
**Group Affiliation:** Lifetime Healthcare Inc
**Licensed in:** NY
**Address:** 165 Court St, Rochester, NY 14647
**Phone:** (585) 454-1700 **Dom State:** NY **Commenced Bus:** January 1936

| Data Date | Rating | RACR #1 | RACR #2 | Total Assets ($mil) | Capital ($mil) | Net Premium ($mil) | Net Income ($mil) |
|---|---|---|---|---|---|---|---|
| 9-17 | B+ | 3.84 | 3.20 | 3,365.4 | 1,424.5 | 4,213.7 | 167.3 |
| 9-16 | B+ | 3.20 | 2.67 | 3,084.1 | 1,139.3 | 4,572.3 | 65.0 |
| 2016 | B+ | 3.29 | 2.74 | 3,086.3 | 1,210.7 | 5,983.7 | 99.5 |
| 2015 | A- | 2.99 | 2.50 | 3,026.5 | 1,059.4 | 5,923.2 | 57.9 |
| 2014 | A- | 3.23 | 2.69 | 3,046.4 | 1,157.6 | 5,944.0 | 24.2 |
| 2013 | A+ | 3.48 | 2.90 | 3,044.0 | 1,352.6 | 6,290.4 | 52.6 |
| 2012 | A+ | 3.71 | 3.09 | 2,818.6 | 1,282.5 | 6,000.8 | 105.7 |

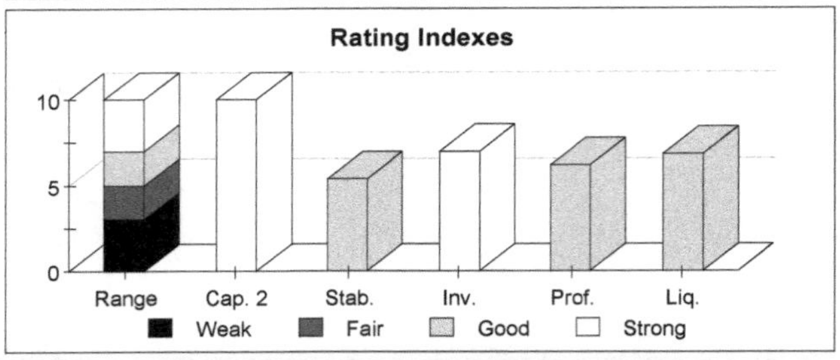


## FALLON COMMUNITY HEALTH PLAN B- Good

**Major Rating Factors:** Good overall results on stability tests (6.1 on a scale of 0 to 10). Good liquidity (5.5) with sufficient resources (cash flows and marketable investments) to handle a spike in claims. Strong capitalization index (7.5) based on excellent current risk-adjusted capital (severe loss scenario).
**Other Rating Factors:** High quality investment portfolio (7.0). Weak profitability index (2.5).
**Principal Business:** Comp med (71%), Medicaid (15%), Medicare (14%)
**Mem Phys: 16:** 52,817 **15:** 43,927 **16 MLR** 90.7% **/ 16 Admin Exp** N/A
**Enroll(000): Q3 17:** 140 **16:** 139 **15:** 140 **Med Exp PMPM:** $650
**Principal Investments:** Long-term bonds (57%), nonaffiliate common stock (29%), affiliate common stock (7%), cash and equiv (6%), other (1%)
**Provider Compensation ($000):** Contr fee ($872,082), capitation ($148,145), salary ($17,268), bonus arrang ($4,894)
**Total Member Encounters:** Phys (527,076), non-phys (358,823)
**Group Affiliation:** Fallon Community Health Plan Inc
**Licensed in:** MA
**Address:** 10 Chestnut Street, Worcester, MA 01608-2810
**Phone:** (508) 799-2100 **Dom State:** MA **Commenced Bus:** February 1977

| Data Date | Rating | RACR #1 | RACR #2 | Total Assets ($mil) | Capital ($mil) | Net Premium ($mil) | Net Income ($mil) |
|---|---|---|---|---|---|---|---|
| 9-17 | B- | 1.72 | 1.44 | 394.2 | 158.0 | 928.4 | 8.5 |
| 9-16 | B | 1.84 | 1.53 | 363.8 | 152.5 | 855.6 | -13.7 |
| 2016 | B- | 1.59 | 1.33 | 347.2 | 145.8 | 1,149.0 | -21.3 |
| 2015 | B | 1.82 | 1.52 | 368.4 | 151.3 | 1,095.9 | 8.8 |
| 2014 | B | 1.96 | 1.64 | 390.9 | 168.4 | 1,103.7 | 26.7 |
| 2013 | B- | 1.78 | 1.49 | 396.4 | 167.0 | 1,195.4 | 28.9 |
| 2012 | B- | 1.73 | 1.44 | 367.7 | 154.5 | 1,107.5 | 23.7 |

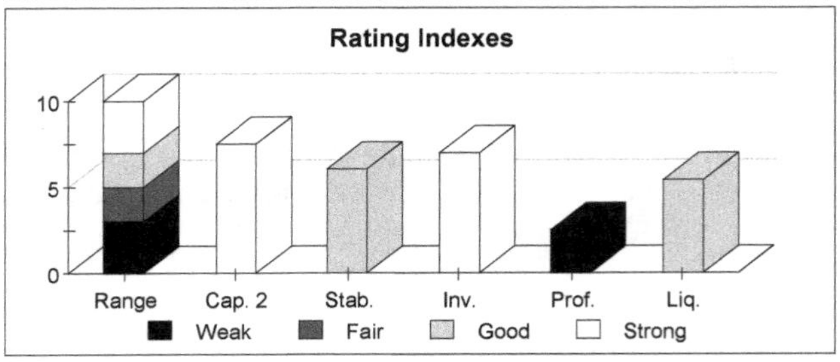

## FALLON HEALTH & LIFE ASR CO — E — Very Weak

**Major Rating Factors:** Weak profitability index (0.4 on a scale of 0 to 10). Good capitalization (6.9) based on excellent current risk-adjusted capital (severe loss scenario). High quality investment portfolio (9.9).
**Other Rating Factors:** Excellent liquidity (7.5) with ample operational cash flow and liquid investments.
**Principal Business:** Comp med (75%), med supp (25%)
**Mem Phys: 16:** 52,817 **15:** 43,927 **16 MLR** 94.8% **/ 16 Admin Exp** N/A
**Enroll(000): Q3 17:** 6 **16:** 6 **15:** 7 **Med Exp PMPM:** $396
**Principal Investments:** Cash and equiv (100%), affiliate common stock (25%)
**Provider Compensation ($000):** Contr fee ($31,353), capitation ($55), bonus arrang ($32)
**Total Member Encounters:** Phys (28,333), non-phys (7,472)
**Group Affiliation:** Fallon Community Health Plan Inc
**Licensed in:** MA
**Address:** 10 Chestnut St, Worcester, MA 01608-2810
**Phone:** (508) 799-2100 **Dom State:** MA **Commenced Bus:** January 1993

| Data Date | Rating | RACR #1 | RACR #2 | Total Assets ($mil) | Capital ($mil) | Net Premium ($mil) | Net Income ($mil) |
|---|---|---|---|---|---|---|---|
| 9-17 | E | 1.27 | 1.06 | 22.5 | 5.1 | 21.6 | -3.5 |
| 9-16 | E | 1.10 | 0.92 | 26.4 | 6.5 | 23.2 | 0.0 |
| 2016 | E | 2.02 | 1.68 | 25.9 | 8.4 | 30.1 | 1.8 |
| 2015 | E | 0.97 | 0.81 | 31.6 | 5.7 | 37.3 | -11.0 |
| 2014 | E | 1.10 | 0.92 | 31.4 | 6.4 | 40.2 | -12.1 |
| 2013 | E | 1.08 | 0.90 | 30.8 | 5.6 | 35.2 | -9.3 |
| 2012 | C | 1.31 | 1.09 | 25.8 | 6.4 | 28.2 | -8.9 |

**Rating Indexes**

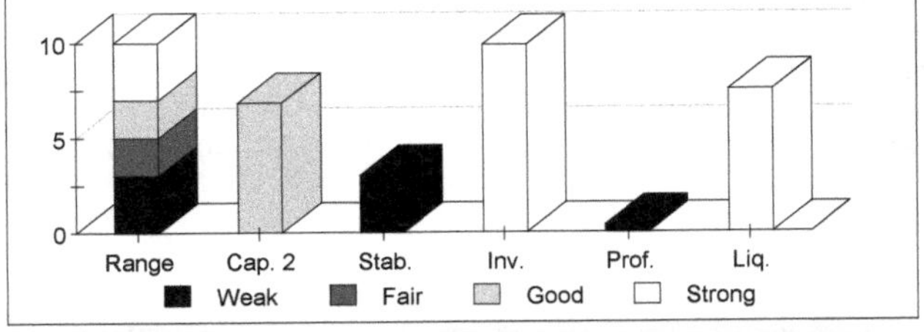


## FAMILY HEALTH NETWORK INC — C — Fair

**Major Rating Factors:** Fair capitalization (4.6 on a scale of 0 to 10) based on fair current risk-adjusted capital (moderate loss scenario). Excellent profitability (7.8). High quality investment portfolio (9.3).
**Other Rating Factors:** Excellent liquidity (7.0) with sufficient resources (cash flows and marketable investments) to handle a spike in claims.
**Principal Business:** Medicaid (100%)
**Mem Phys: 16:** 13,123 **15:** 3,848 **16 MLR** 92.7% **/ 16 Admin Exp** N/A
**Enroll(000): Q3 17:** 210 **16:** 239 **15:** 228 **Med Exp PMPM:** $164
**Principal Investments:** Cash and equiv (55%), affiliate common stock (26%), long-term bonds (19%)
**Provider Compensation ($000):** Contr fee ($408,146), capitation ($50,206), bonus arrang ($1,469)
**Total Member Encounters:** Phys (1,302,134), non-phys (180,225)
**Group Affiliation:** Family Health Network Inc
**Licensed in:** IL
**Address:** 322 S Green St Ste 400, Chicago, IL 60607
**Phone:** (312) 491-1956 **Dom State:** IL **Commenced Bus:** April 1995

| Data Date | Rating | RACR #1 | RACR #2 | Total Assets ($mil) | Capital ($mil) | Net Premium ($mil) | Net Income ($mil) |
|---|---|---|---|---|---|---|---|
| 9-17 | C | 0.87 | 0.73 | 278.6 | 62.4 | 357.1 | 1.8 |
| 9-16 | U | 0.80 | 0.67 | 162.1 | 59.1 | 369.8 | 2.3 |
| 2016 | C- | 0.84 | 0.70 | 197.8 | 60.9 | 504.1 | 2.3 |
| 2015 | U | 0.43 | 0.36 | 171.7 | 27.6 | 466.1 | 1.8 |
| 2014 | N/A | N/A | N/A | N/A | N/A | N/A | N/A |
| 2013 | N/A | N/A | N/A | N/A | N/A | N/A | N/A |
| 2012 | N/A | N/A | N/A | N/A | N/A | N/A | N/A |

**Rating Indexes**

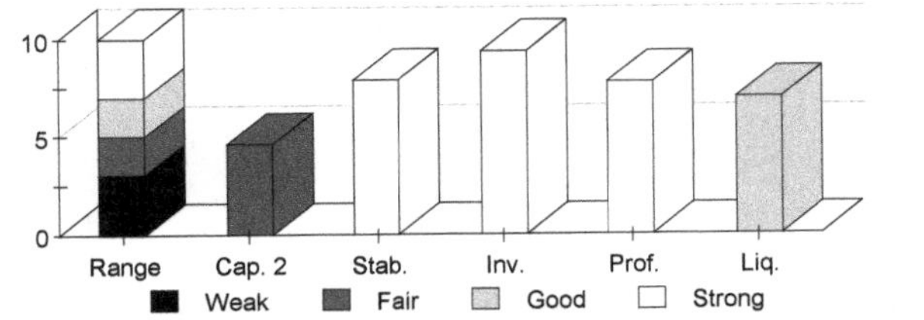


## FAMILY HERITAGE LIFE INSURANCE COMPANY OF AMERICA * — B+ — Good

**Major Rating Factors:** Good overall results on stability tests (6.5 on a scale of 0 to 10). Stability strengths include excellent operational trends and excellent risk diversification. Good quality investment portfolio (6.4) despite mixed results such as: no exposure to mortgages and large holdings of BBB rated bonds but minimal holdings in junk bonds. Good profitability (5.0) although investment income, in comparison to reserve requirements, is below regulatory standards.
**Other Rating Factors:** Strong capitalization (7.2) based on excellent risk adjusted capital (severe loss scenario). Excellent liquidity (7.9).
**Principal Business:** Individual health insurance (56%), reinsurance (41%), group health insurance (2%), and individual life insurance (1%).
**Principal Investments:** NonCMO investment grade bonds (96%), CMOs and structured securities (1%), and noninv. grade bonds (1%).
**Investments in Affiliates:** None
**Group Affiliation:** Torchmark Corp
**Licensed in:** All states except NY
**Commenced Business:** November 1989
**Address:** 6001 East Royalton Rd Ste 200, Cleveland, OH 44147-3529
**Phone:** (440) 922-5200 **Domicile State:** OH **NAIC Code:** 77968

| Data Date | Rating | RACR #1 | RACR #2 | Total Assets ($mil) | Capital ($mil) | Net Premium ($mil) | Net Income ($mil) |
|---|---|---|---|---|---|---|---|
| 9-17 | B+ | 1.82 | 1.15 | 1,249.5 | 103.8 | 214.4 | 13.6 |
| 9-16 | A- | 2.17 | 1.40 | 1,081.2 | 109.7 | 201.8 | 15.3 |
| 2016 | B+ | 1.96 | 1.25 | 1,108.8 | 104.2 | 264.6 | 23.8 |
| 2015 | A- | 1.92 | 1.27 | 921.0 | 78.3 | 254.1 | 19.1 |
| 2014 | A- | 1.87 | 1.27 | 775.2 | 67.4 | 237.0 | 18.1 |
| 2013 | A- | 2.09 | 1.48 | 641.5 | 66.9 | 192.7 | 17.0 |
| 2012 | B+ | 2.15 | 1.57 | 571.1 | 62.1 | 177.0 | 16.5 |

**Adverse Trends in Operations**

Increase in policy surrenders from 2014 to 2015 (118%)
Increase in policy surrenders from 2012 to 2013 (77%)

## FAMILY LIFE INSURANCE COMPANY C Fair

**Major Rating Factors:** Fair profitability (3.0 on a scale of 0 to 10) with investment income below regulatory standards in relation to interest assumptions of reserves. Fair overall results on stability tests (4.2). Good liquidity (6.5) with sufficient resources to handle a spike in claims as well as a significant increase in policy surrenders.
**Other Rating Factors:** Strong capitalization (9.8) based on excellent risk adjusted capital (severe loss scenario). High quality investment portfolio (8.3).
**Principal Business:** Individual health insurance (65%) and individual life insurance (35%).
**Principal Investments:** NonCMO investment grade bonds (72%), policy loans (10%), CMOs and structured securities (3%), mortgages in good standing (2%), and common & preferred stock (1%).
**Investments in Affiliates:** None
**Group Affiliation:** Manhattan Life Group Inc
**Licensed in:** All states except NY, PR
**Commenced Business:** June 1949
**Address:** 10777 Northwest Freeway, Houston, TX 77092
**Phone:** (713) 529-0045 **Domicile State:** TX **NAIC Code:** 63053

| Data Date | Rating | RACR #1 | RACR #2 | Total Assets ($mil) | Capital ($mil) | Net Premium ($mil) | Net Income ($mil) |
|---|---|---|---|---|---|---|---|
| 9-17 | C | 3.43 | 2.86 | 153.4 | 32.2 | 19.2 | 2.1 |
| 9-16 | C | 3.48 | 2.79 | 155.9 | 32.9 | 19.8 | 1.3 |
| 2016 | C | 3.61 | 3.03 | 155.8 | 34.0 | 26.0 | 1.0 |
| 2015 | C | 3.79 | 3.13 | 158.7 | 35.8 | 26.5 | 2.7 |
| 2014 | C | 3.87 | 3.33 | 146.5 | 36.2 | 25.2 | 1.7 |
| 2013 | C | 3.41 | 2.69 | 147.6 | 31.9 | 26.0 | 3.5 |
| 2012 | C | 3.39 | 2.63 | 147.4 | 31.7 | 27.9 | 5.8 |

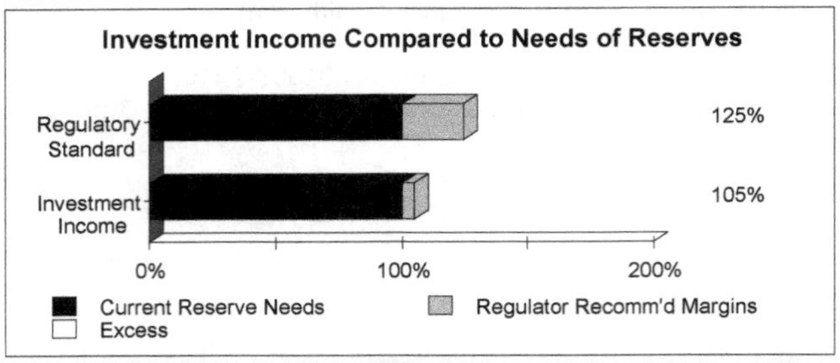


## FAMILYCARE HEALTH PLANS INC E- Very Weak

**Major Rating Factors:** Weak profitability index (0.7 on a scale of 0 to 10). Weak liquidity (1.1) as a spike in claims may stretch capacity. Strong capitalization (7.5) based on excellent current risk-adjusted capital (severe loss scenario).
**Other Rating Factors:** High quality investment portfolio (9.9).
**Principal Business:** Medicare (100%)
**Mem Phys: 16:** 3,184 **15:** 2,946 **16 MLR** 110.5% **/ 16 Admin Exp** N/A
**Enroll(000): Q3 17:** 4 **16:** 5 **15:** 4 **Med Exp PMPM:** $961
**Principal Investments:** Long-term bonds (64%), cash and equiv (36%)
**Provider Compensation ($000):** Contr fee ($45,325), FFS ($6,514), bonus arrang ($343), capitation ($208)
**Total Member Encounters:** Phys (75,334), non-phys (49,067)
**Group Affiliation:** FamilyCare Inc
**Licensed in:** OR
**Address:** 825 NE Multnomah Ste 1400, Portland, OR 97232
**Phone:** (503) 222-3205 **Dom State:** OR **Commenced Bus:** June 1997

| Data Date | Rating | RACR #1 | RACR #2 | Total Assets ($mil) | Capital ($mil) | Net Premium ($mil) | Net Income ($mil) |
|---|---|---|---|---|---|---|---|
| 9-17 | E- | 1.77 | 1.47 | 29.2 | 14.9 | 30.6 | -5.6 |
| 9-16 | E- | 1.54 | 1.28 | 25.1 | 10.3 | 35.0 | -12.5 |
| 2016 | E- | 1.14 | 0.95 | 19.4 | 9.7 | 47.3 | -13.4 |
| 2015 | D | 1.26 | 1.05 | 17.9 | 8.6 | 39.3 | -9.9 |
| 2014 | C- | 3.50 | 2.92 | 26.2 | 19.5 | 32.1 | -5.0 |
| 2013 | C- | 0.99 | 0.82 | 10.7 | 4.7 | 31.1 | -0.2 |
| 2012 | C- | 0.85 | 0.71 | 10.3 | 3.9 | 28.6 | -0.4 |

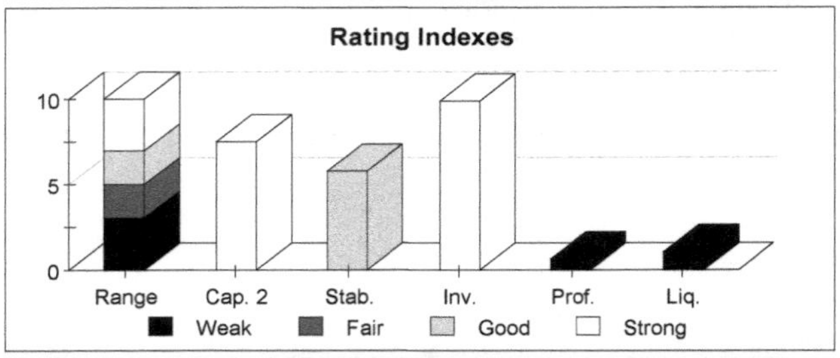


## FEDERATED MUTUAL INS CO B Good

**Major Rating Factors:** Good overall results on stability tests (5.1 on a scale of 0 to 10) despite potential drain of affiliation with Federated Mutual Ins Group and weak results on operational trends. Good liquidity (6.9) with sufficient resources (cash flows and marketable investments) to handle a spike in claims.
**Other Rating Factors:** Strong long-term capitalization index (9.8) based on excellent current risk adjusted capital (severe and moderate loss scenarios). Moreover, capital levels have been consistent in recent years. Ample reserve history (9.0) that helps to protect the company against sharp claims increases. Excellent profitability (8.6) with operating gains in each of the last five years.
**Principal Business:** Group accident & health (33%), workers compensation (17%), other liability (14%), auto liability (12%), commercial multiple peril (5%), auto physical damage (5%), and other lines (13%).
**Principal Investments:** Investment grade bonds (67%), misc. investments (32%), non investment grade bonds (1%), and real estate (1%).
**Investments in Affiliates:** 15%
**Group Affiliation:** Federated Mutual Ins Group
**Licensed in:** All states except HI, PR
**Commenced Business:** August 1904
**Address:** 121 EAST PARK SQUARE, Owatonna, MN 55060
**Phone:** (507) 455-5200 **Domicile State:** MN **NAIC Code:** 13935

| Data Date | Rating | RACR #1 | RACR #2 | Loss Ratio % | Total Assets ($mil) | Capital ($mil) | Net Premium ($mil) | Net Income ($mil) |
|---|---|---|---|---|---|---|---|---|
| 9-17 | B | 3.52 | 2.80 | N/A | 5,784.4 | 3,296.2 | 1,125.1 | 127.7 |
| 9-16 | B | 3.88 | 3.11 | N/A | 5,361.4 | 3,070.2 | 1,053.7 | 131.4 |
| 2016 | B | 3.61 | 2.97 | 68.8 | 5,456.8 | 3,091.1 | 1,460.6 | 185.4 |
| 2015 | B | 3.82 | 3.13 | 66.9 | 5,076.2 | 2,862.4 | 1,301.0 | 189.1 |
| 2014 | B | 3.79 | 3.11 | 63.2 | 4,783.7 | 2,657.1 | 1,183.9 | 187.6 |
| 2013 | A- | 3.67 | 3.00 | 69.6 | 4,523.5 | 2,518.3 | 1,083.5 | 127.9 |
| 2012 | A- | 3.86 | 3.19 | 74.6 | 4,233.8 | 2,365.4 | 942.3 | 106.1 |

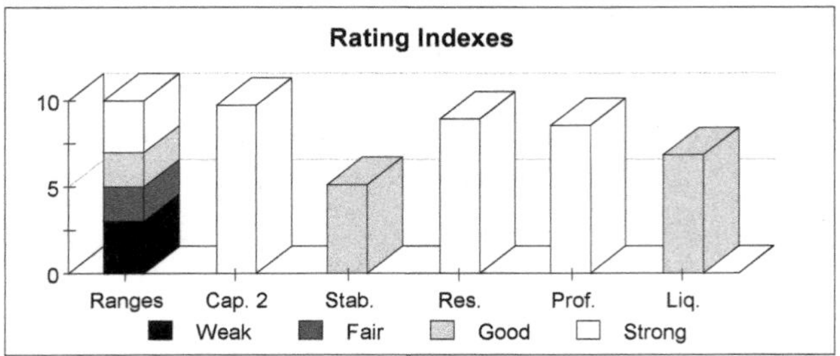

## FIDELITY SECURITY LIFE INSURANCE COMPANY B Good

**Major Rating Factors:** Good quality investment portfolio (6.7 on a scale of 0 to 10) despite mixed results such as: minimal exposure to mortgages and large holdings of BBB rated bonds but small junk bond holdings. Good liquidity (6.5) with sufficient resources to cover a large increase in policy surrenders. Fair overall results on stability tests (4.5).
**Other Rating Factors:** Strong capitalization (8.8) based on excellent risk adjusted capital (severe loss scenario). Excellent profitability (7.2).
**Principal Business:** Group health insurance (90%), reinsurance (5%), individual health insurance (2%), group life insurance (1%), and other lines (2%).
**Principal Investments:** NonCMO investment grade bonds (45%), CMOs and structured securities (44%), noninv. grade bonds (3%), common & preferred stock (3%), and misc. investments (4%).
**Investments in Affiliates:** 2%
**Group Affiliation:** Fidelity Security Group
**Licensed in:** All states except PR
**Commenced Business:** July 1969
**Address:** 3130 Broadway, Kansas City, MO 64111-2452
**Phone:** (816) 750-1060 **Domicile State:** MO **NAIC Code:** 71870

| Data Date | Rating | RACR #1 | RACR #2 | Total Assets ($mil) | Capital ($mil) | Net Premium ($mil) | Net Income ($mil) |
|---|---|---|---|---|---|---|---|
| 9-17 | B | 3.66 | 2.18 | 930.2 | 201.8 | 87.4 | 18.0 |
| 9-16 | B | 3.01 | 1.99 | 864.7 | 179.6 | 91.9 | 10.6 |
| 2016 | B | 3.46 | 2.07 | 875.1 | 186.8 | 121.6 | 17.5 |
| 2015 | B | 2.02 | 1.44 | 864.2 | 169.0 | 420.4 | 18.1 |
| 2014 | B- | 2.65 | 1.73 | 831.7 | 151.9 | 204.6 | 18.4 |
| 2013 | B- | 2.99 | 1.83 | 819.5 | 135.3 | 109.2 | 13.9 |
| 2012 | B | 2.79 | 1.67 | 789.7 | 123.2 | 202.7 | 2.3 |

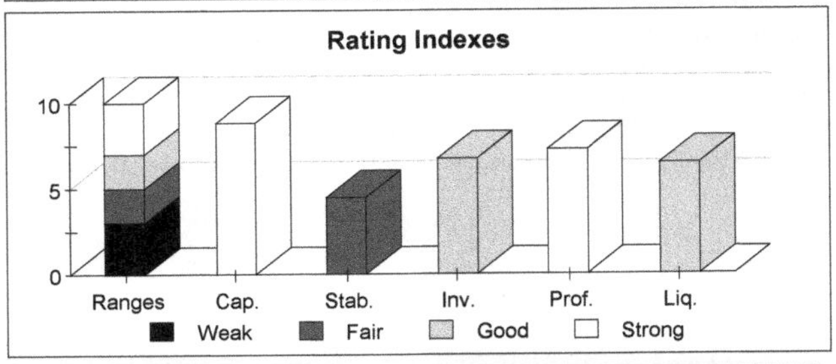


## FIRST CARE INC C+ Fair

**Major Rating Factors:** Weak profitability index (1.9 on a scale of 0 to 10). Strong capitalization (10.0) based on excellent current risk-adjusted capital (severe loss scenario). High quality investment portfolio (9.9).
**Other Rating Factors:** Excellent liquidity (10.0) with ample operational cash flow and liquid investments.
**Principal Business:** Med supp (100%)
**Mem Phys: 16:** 43,488 **15:** N/A **16 MLR** 69.1% **/ 16 Admin Exp** N/A
**Enroll(000): Q3 17:** 5 **16:** 1 **15:** N/A **Med Exp PMPM:** $102
**Principal Investments:** Cash and equiv (75%), long-term bonds (25%)
**Provider Compensation ($000):** Contr fee ($150), FFS ($10)
**Total Member Encounters:** Phys (2,617), non-phys (937)
**Group Affiliation:** CareFirst Inc
**Licensed in:** DC, DE, MD, VA
**Address:** 1501 S CLINTON St, BALTIMORE, MD 21224
**Phone:** (410) 581-3000 **Dom State:** MD **Commenced Bus:** February 1996

| Data Date | Rating | RACR #1 | RACR #2 | Total Assets ($mil) | Capital ($mil) | Net Premium ($mil) | Net Income ($mil) |
|---|---|---|---|---|---|---|---|
| 9-17 | C+ | 111.68 | 93.07 | 7.4 | 6.5 | 5.0 | -1.2 |
| 9-16 | N/A | N/A | N/A | 13.6 | 6.0 | N/A | 0.1 |
| 2016 | C | 106.20 | 88.46 | 14.0 | 6.2 | 0.6 | 0.0 |
| 2015 | N/A | N/A | N/A | 13.2 | 5.9 | N/A | 0.1 |
| 2014 | U | N/A | N/A | 11.1 | 5.2 | N/A | 0.8 |
| 2013 | U | 19.02 | 15.85 | 16.7 | 4.7 | N/A | 0.0 |
| 2012 | U | 14.65 | 12.21 | 18.2 | 3.7 | N/A | 0.1 |

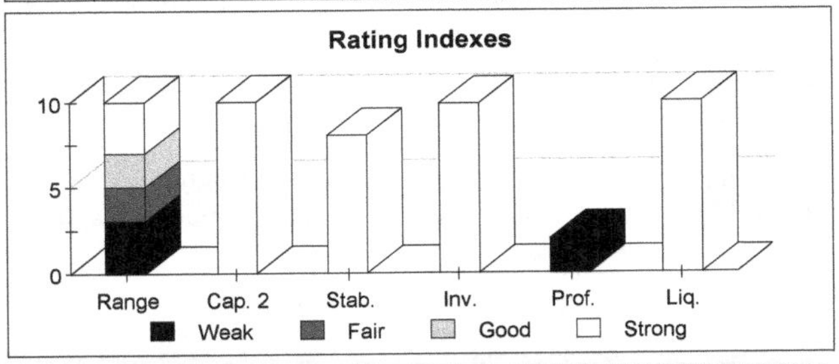


## FIRST COMMUNITY HEALTH PLAN INC B Good

**Major Rating Factors:** Excellent profitability (7.7 on a scale of 0 to 10). Strong capitalization (10.0) based on excellent current risk-adjusted capital (severe loss scenario). High quality investment portfolio (9.6).
**Other Rating Factors:** Excellent liquidity (7.6) with ample operational cash flow and liquid investments.
**Principal Business:** Med supp (100%)
**Mem Phys: 16:** N/A **15:** N/A **16 MLR** 73.6% **/ 16 Admin Exp** N/A
**Enroll(000): Q3 17:** 4 **16:** 4 **15:** 4 **Med Exp PMPM:** $120
**Principal Investments:** Cash and equiv (55%), long-term bonds (45%)
**Provider Compensation ($000):** Contr fee ($5,663)
**Total Member Encounters:** Phys (52,937), non-phys (221,528)
**Group Affiliation:** FirstCommunity Health Plan Inc
**Licensed in:** AL
**Address:** 699 Gallatin St SW Ste A2, Huntsville, AL 35801-4912
**Phone:** (256) 532-2780 **Dom State:** AL **Commenced Bus:** January 1996

| Data Date | Rating | RACR #1 | RACR #2 | Total Assets ($mil) | Capital ($mil) | Net Premium ($mil) | Net Income ($mil) |
|---|---|---|---|---|---|---|---|
| 9-17 | B | 9.09 | 7.57 | 7.8 | 6.3 | 6.0 | 0.1 |
| 9-16 | B | 9.37 | 7.81 | 7.4 | 6.0 | 5.8 | -0.1 |
| 2016 | B | 8.93 | 7.44 | 7.6 | 6.2 | 7.7 | 0.2 |
| 2015 | B | 9.58 | 7.99 | 7.4 | 6.0 | 7.5 | 0.5 |
| 2014 | B | 8.91 | 7.42 | 6.9 | 5.6 | 7.1 | 0.3 |
| 2013 | B | 8.35 | 6.96 | 6.5 | 5.3 | 6.8 | 0.8 |
| 2012 | B- | 6.92 | 5.76 | 6.3 | 5.0 | 6.3 | 0.3 |

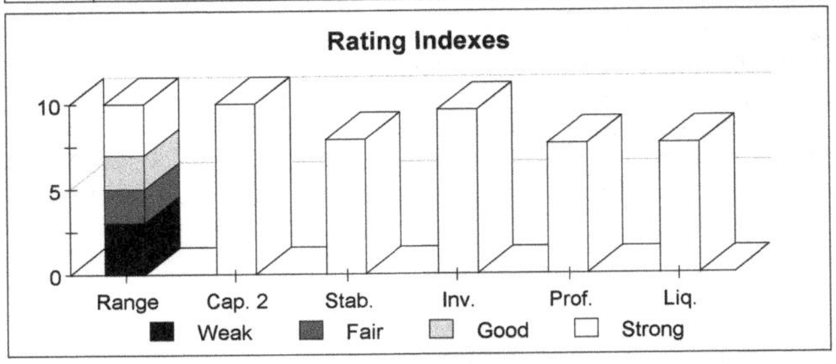

## FIRST HEALTH LIFE & HEALTH INSURANCE COMPANY B- Good

**Major Rating Factors:** Good current capitalization (6.9 on a scale of 0 to 10) based on excellent risk adjusted capital (severe loss scenario) reflecting improvement over results in 2013. Fair liquidity (4.7) as cash from operations and sale of marketable assets may not be adequate to cover a spike in claims. Fair overall results on stability tests (3.5) including weak results on operational trends.
**Other Rating Factors:** Weak profitability (1.9) with operating losses during the first nine months of 2017. High quality investment portfolio (8.7).
**Principal Business:** Individual health insurance (98%) and group health insurance (2%).
**Principal Investments:** Cash (66%), nonCMO investment grade bonds (23%), CMOs and structured securities (10%), and noninv. grade bonds (2%).
**Investments in Affiliates:** None
**Group Affiliation:** Aetna Inc
**Licensed in:** All states except PR
**Commenced Business:** June 1979
**Address:** DOWNERS GROVE, IL 60515
**Phone:** (630) 737-7900 **Domicile State:** TX **NAIC Code:** 90328

| Data Date | Rating | RACR #1 | RACR #2 | Total Assets ($mil) | Capital ($mil) | Net Premium ($mil) | Net Income ($mil) |
|---|---|---|---|---|---|---|---|
| 9-17 | B- | 1.49 | 1.22 | 515.7 | 207.8 | 587.1 | -3.6 |
| 9-16 | B- | 1.31 | 1.09 | 606.2 | 182.1 | 610.6 | -30.9 |
| 2016 | B- | 1.50 | 1.24 | 454.9 | 211.1 | 798.3 | -1.7 |
| 2015 | B- | 2.24 | 1.85 | 581.8 | 289.2 | 700.0 | 16.1 |
| 2014 | B | 1.15 | 0.96 | 475.0 | 226.0 | 925.3 | -6.6 |
| 2013 | B | 1.02 | 0.85 | 505.6 | 233.3 | 1,420.5 | -175.3 |
| 2012 | C+ | 1.46 | 1.22 | 600.2 | 412.2 | 1,494.9 | 48.3 |

**Risk-Adjusted Capital Ratio #2 (Severe Loss Scenario)**

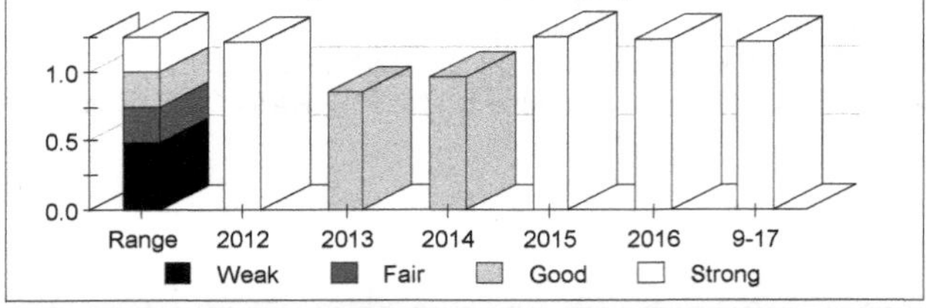


## FIRST MEDICAL HEALTH PLAN INC E Very Weak

**Major Rating Factors:** Poor capitalization index (1.2 on a scale of 0 to 10) based on weak current risk-adjusted capital (moderate loss scenario). Fair profitability index (3.6). Good overall results on stability tests (5.4) despite inconsistent enrollment growth in the past five years due to declines in 2013, 2014 and 2016.
**Other Rating Factors:** Good liquidity (6.8) with sufficient resources (cash flows and marketable investments) to handle a spike in claims. High quality investment portfolio (7.3).
**Principal Business:** Medicaid (56%), comp med (44%)
**Mem Phys: 16:** N/A **15:** N/A **16 MLR** 90.2% **/ 16 Admin Exp** N/A
**Enroll(000): Q3 17:** 560 **16:** 562 **15:** 567 **Med Exp PMPM:** $139
**Principal Investments:** Cash and equiv (83%), nonaffiliate common stock (17%)
**Provider Compensation ($000):** Capitation ($558,811), contr fee ($402,564)
**Total Member Encounters:** Phys (3,060,929), non-phys (4,139)
**Group Affiliation:** First Medical Health Plan Inc
**Licensed in:** PR
**Address:** 530 Marginal Buchanan, Guaynabo, PR 00966
**Phone:** (787) 474-3999 **Dom State:** PR **Commenced Bus:** March 1977

| Data Date | Rating | RACR #1 | RACR #2 | Total Assets ($mil) | Capital ($mil) | Net Premium ($mil) | Net Income ($mil) |
|---|---|---|---|---|---|---|---|
| 9-17 | E | 0.42 | 0.35 | 195.6 | 43.1 | 810.4 | 10.0 |
| 9-16 | E- | 0.18 | 0.15 | 180.3 | 26.7 | 776.8 | 4.4 |
| 2016 | E- | 0.28 | 0.23 | 183.5 | 32.8 | 1,048.9 | 10.6 |
| 2015 | E- | 0.12 | 0.10 | 191.9 | 21.5 | 882.7 | -12.5 |
| 2014 | E+ | 0.41 | 0.34 | 123.6 | 35.3 | 586.2 | 2.7 |
| 2013 | E | 0.34 | 0.28 | 122.7 | 33.0 | 643.4 | 7.2 |
| 2012 | E | 0.18 | 0.15 | 129.6 | 23.7 | 614.7 | 6.5 |

**Rating Indexes**

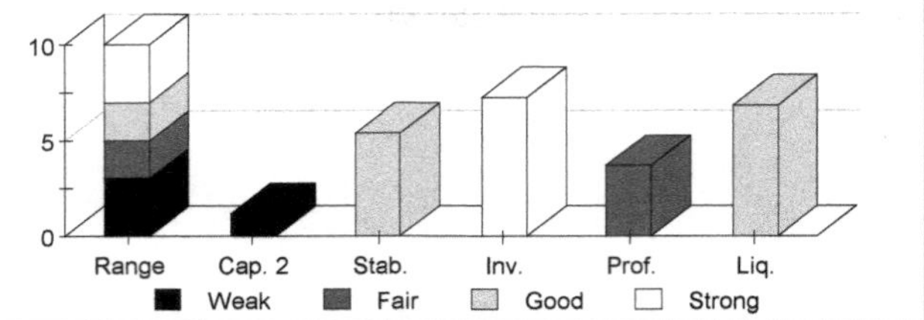


## FIRST RELIANCE STANDARD LIFE INSURANCE COMPANY * A Excellent

**Major Rating Factors:** Good overall results on stability tests (6.0 on a scale of 0 to 10). Strengths that enhance stability include excellent operational trends and excellent risk diversification. Good quality investment portfolio (6.7) despite mixed results such as: no exposure to mortgages and substantial holdings of BBB bonds but small junk bond holdings. Good overall profitability (6.9) despite operating losses during the first nine months of 2017.
**Other Rating Factors:** Strong capitalization (10.0) based on excellent risk adjusted capital (severe loss scenario). Excellent liquidity (7.0).
**Principal Business:** Group health insurance (59%) and group life insurance (40%).
**Principal Investments:** NonCMO investment grade bonds (72%), CMOs and structured securities (21%), and noninv. grade bonds (6%).
**Investments in Affiliates:** None
**Group Affiliation:** Tokio Marine Holdings Inc
**Licensed in:** DC, DE, NY
**Commenced Business:** October 1984
**Address:** 590 Madison Avenue 29th Floor, New York, NY 10022
**Phone:** (215) 787-4000 **Domicile State:** NY **NAIC Code:** 71005

| Data Date | Rating | RACR #1 | RACR #2 | Total Assets ($mil) | Capital ($mil) | Net Premium ($mil) | Net Income ($mil) |
|---|---|---|---|---|---|---|---|
| 9-17 | A | 5.84 | 3.71 | 197.5 | 66.7 | 45.5 | -0.9 |
| 9-16 | A | 6.51 | 4.36 | 194.2 | 73.9 | 47.7 | 8.3 |
| 2016 | A | 6.14 | 4.05 | 188.9 | 68.3 | 63.0 | 9.5 |
| 2015 | A | 5.72 | 3.61 | 184.0 | 65.5 | 57.9 | 6.5 |
| 2014 | A | 5.62 | 3.53 | 184.1 | 66.4 | 57.0 | 7.8 |
| 2013 | A | 5.71 | 3.72 | 182.7 | 64.2 | 56.8 | 5.9 |
| 2012 | A | 6.69 | 4.70 | 176.2 | 63.6 | 53.5 | 6.7 |

**Adverse Trends in Operations**

Increase in policy surrenders from 2015 to 2016 (27%)
Decrease in capital during 2015 (1%)

## FIRST UNITED AMERICAN LIFE INSURANCE COMPANY * B+ Good

**Major Rating Factors:** Good overall results on stability tests (6.7 on a scale of 0 to 10). Stability strengths include excellent operational trends and excellent risk diversification. Good quality investment portfolio (5.0) despite mixed results such as: large holdings of BBB rated bonds but moderate junk bond exposure. Good liquidity (5.1).
**Other Rating Factors:** Strong capitalization (7.5) based on excellent risk adjusted capital (severe loss scenario). Excellent profitability (8.2).
**Principal Business:** Individual health insurance (51%), individual life insurance (34%), reinsurance (6%), individual annuities (6%), and group health insurance (2%).
**Principal Investments:** NonCMO investment grade bonds (80%), noninv. grade bonds (8%), CMOs and structured securities (5%), policy loans (4%), and cash (1%).
**Investments in Affiliates:** None
**Group Affiliation:** Torchmark Corp
**Licensed in:** NY
**Commenced Business:** December 1984
**Address:** 1020 SEVENTH NORTH ST STE 130, LIVERPOOL, NY 13212
**Phone:** (315) 451-2544 **Domicile State:** NY **NAIC Code:** 74101

| Data Date | Rating | RACR #1 | RACR #2 | Total Assets ($mil) | Capital ($mil) | Net Premium ($mil) | Net Income ($mil) |
|---|---|---|---|---|---|---|---|
| 9-17 | B+ | 2.17 | 1.36 | 237.8 | 36.3 | 52.9 | 3.4 |
| 9-16 | B+ | 2.34 | 1.47 | 226.9 | 38.6 | 58.6 | 5.7 |
| 2016 | B+ | 2.25 | 1.41 | 229.1 | 39.0 | 76.7 | 6.2 |
| 2015 | B+ | 2.26 | 1.43 | 209.7 | 35.6 | 72.9 | 3.0 |
| 2014 | B+ | 2.40 | 1.54 | 194.7 | 35.9 | 72.7 | 4.9 |
| 2013 | B+ | 2.18 | 1.42 | 178.0 | 34.2 | 78.7 | 3.1 |
| 2012 | B+ | 2.31 | 1.49 | 165.4 | 34.3 | 88.7 | 9.9 |

**Adverse Trends in Operations**

Decrease in premium volume from 2013 to 2014 (8%)
Decrease in premium volume from 2012 to 2013 (11%)

## FIRST UNUM LIFE INSURANCE COMPANY C+ Fair

**Major Rating Factors:** Fair overall results on stability tests (4.8 on a scale of 0 to 10) including fair financial strength of affiliated Unum Group. Fair quality investment portfolio (4.2) with large holdings of BBB rated bonds in addition to significant exposure to junk bonds. Good overall profitability (6.9). Excellent expense controls.
**Other Rating Factors:** Strong capitalization (7.6) based on excellent risk adjusted capital (severe loss scenario). Excellent liquidity (7.1).
**Principal Business:** Group health insurance (55%), individual health insurance (24%), group life insurance (18%), individual life insurance (2%), and reinsurance (1%).
**Principal Investments:** NonCMO investment grade bonds (77%), noninv. grade bonds (11%), mortgages in good standing (6%), and CMOs and structured securities (6%).
**Investments in Affiliates:** None
**Group Affiliation:** Unum Group
**Licensed in:** NY
**Commenced Business:** January 1960
**Address:** 666 THIRD AVENUE SUITE 301, NEW YORK, NY 10017
**Phone:** (212) 328-8830 **Domicile State:** NY **NAIC Code:** 64297

| Data Date | Rating | RACR #1 | RACR #2 | Total Assets ($mil) | Capital ($mil) | Net Premium ($mil) | Net Income ($mil) |
|---|---|---|---|---|---|---|---|
| 9-17 | C+ | 2.76 | 1.39 | 3,352.5 | 306.9 | 296.5 | 25.6 |
| 9-16 | C+ | 2.39 | 1.19 | 3,212.0 | 254.0 | 281.3 | 54.9 |
| 2016 | C+ | 2.63 | 1.32 | 3,260.8 | 282.4 | 375.7 | 82.4 |
| 2015 | C+ | 2.54 | 1.27 | 3,130.4 | 263.5 | 363.2 | 26.5 |
| 2014 | C+ | 2.63 | 1.33 | 2,976.2 | 272.1 | 360.0 | -5.4 |
| 2013 | C+ | 2.75 | 1.42 | 2,704.1 | 266.3 | 348.7 | 20.4 |
| 2012 | C+ | 2.65 | 1.41 | 2,682.6 | 251.8 | 360.2 | 11.3 |

| Unum Group<br>Composite Group Rating: C+<br>Largest Group Members | Assets ($mil) | Rating |
|---|---|---|
| UNUM LIFE INS CO OF AMERICA | 21078 | C+ |
| PROVIDENT LIFE ACCIDENT INS CO | 8273 | C+ |
| PAUL REVERE LIFE INS CO | 3790 | C+ |
| FIRST UNUM LIFE INS CO | 3261 | C+ |
| COLONIAL LIFE ACCIDENT INS CO | 3144 | C+ |

## FIRSTCAROLINACARE INS CO D Weak

**Major Rating Factors:** Weak profitability index (0.8 on a scale of 0 to 10). Weak liquidity (0.0) as a spike in claims may stretch capacity. Fair capitalization (3.8) based on fair current risk-adjusted capital (moderate loss scenario).
**Other Rating Factors:** High quality investment portfolio (8.9).
**Principal Business:** Comp med (54%), Medicare (46%)
**Mem Phys: 16:** 3,000 **15:** 2,900 **16 MLR** 101.6% **/ 16 Admin Exp** N/A
**Enroll(000): Q3 17:** 18 **16:** 20 **15:** 17 **Med Exp PMPM:** $537
**Principal Investments:** Long-term bonds (54%), cash and equiv (32%), nonaffiliate common stock (14%)
**Provider Compensation ($000):** Contr fee ($108,671), FFS ($5,611)
**Total Member Encounters:** Phys (286,573), non-phys (34,754)
**Group Affiliation:** FirstHealth of the Carolinas Inc
**Licensed in:** NC, SC
**Address:** 42 MEMORIAL Dr, PINEHURST, NC 28374
**Phone:** (910) 715-8100 **Dom State:** NC **Commenced Bus:** April 2007

| Data Date | Rating | RACR #1 | RACR #2 | Total Assets ($mil) | Capital ($mil) | Net Premium ($mil) | Net Income ($mil) |
|---|---|---|---|---|---|---|---|
| 9-17 | D | 0.76 | 0.63 | 35.1 | 12.1 | 100.4 | -6.1 |
| 9-16 | D+ | 0.53 | 0.44 | 24.5 | 6.6 | 86.8 | -7.2 |
| 2016 | D | 0.47 | 0.39 | 25.9 | 7.9 | 117.7 | -17.6 |
| 2015 | B- | 1.11 | 0.92 | 30.1 | 13.7 | 98.0 | -12.7 |
| 2014 | B | 1.01 | 0.85 | 23.2 | 9.7 | 74.2 | -10.1 |
| 2013 | B | 1.74 | 1.45 | 24.0 | 14.4 | 65.2 | -4.0 |
| 2012 | B+ | 2.15 | 1.79 | 21.1 | 13.6 | 49.4 | -0.1 |

**Rating Indexes**

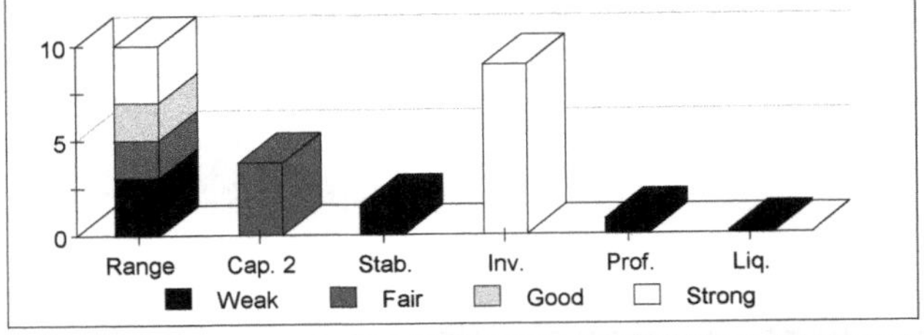

## FLORIDA COMBINED LIFE INSURANCE COMPANY INCORPORA C Fair

**Major Rating Factors:** Fair quality investment portfolio (4.8 on a scale of 0 to 10). Fair profitability (4.3). Fair overall results on stability tests (4.4) including negative cash flow from operations for 2016.
**Other Rating Factors:** Strong capitalization (8.0) based on excellent risk adjusted capital (severe loss scenario). Moreover, capital levels have been consistently high over the last five years. Excellent liquidity (7.2).
**Principal Business:** Group health insurance (44%), individual health insurance (36%), group life insurance (18%), individual life insurance (2%), and reinsurance (1%).
**Principal Investments:** NonCMO investment grade bonds (18%), cash (4%), and CMOs and structured securities (3%).
**Investments in Affiliates:** 75%
**Group Affiliation:** Blue Cross Blue Shield of Florida
**Licensed in:** AL, FL, GA, NC, SC
**Commenced Business:** May 1988
**Address:** 4800 Deerwood Campus Parkway, Jacksonville, FL 32246
**Phone:** (800) 333-3256 **Domicile State:** FL **NAIC Code:** 76031

| Data Date | Rating | RACR #1 | RACR #2 | Total Assets ($mil) | Capital ($mil) | Net Premium ($mil) | Net Income ($mil) |
|---|---|---|---|---|---|---|---|
| 9-17 | C | 5.24 | 3.24 | 52.4 | 31.0 | 0.0 | 0.6 |
| 9-16 | C | 4.90 | 3.24 | 50.3 | 29.0 | 0.0 | 0.1 |
| 2016 | C | 4.94 | 3.29 | 50.7 | 28.9 | 0.0 | 0.1 |
| 2015 | C | 4.60 | 3.45 | 50.2 | 27.1 | 0.0 | 0.3 |
| 2014 | B | 4.59 | 3.64 | 46.9 | 25.8 | 0.0 | 0.1 |
| 2013 | B+ | 4.40 | 3.96 | 42.8 | 23.4 | 0.0 | 0.2 |
| 2012 | B+ | 4.87 | 4.24 | 35.3 | 22.4 | 0.0 | 0.1 |

Rating Indexes

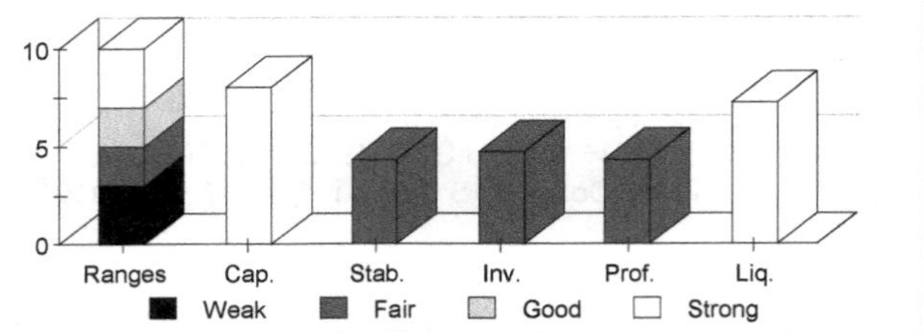


## FLORIDA HEALTH CARE PLAN INC * B+ Good

**Major Rating Factors:** Good liquidity (6.8 on a scale of 0 to 10) with sufficient resources (cash flows and marketable investments) to handle a spike in claims. Excellent profitability (7.8). Strong capitalization (10.0) based on excellent current risk-adjusted capital (severe loss scenario).
**Other Rating Factors:** High quality investment portfolio (9.8).
**Principal Business:** Comp med (60%), Medicare (40%)
**Mem Phys: 16:** 932 **15:** 808 **16 MLR** 83.7% **/ 16 Admin Exp** N/A
**Enroll(000): Q3 17:** 78 **16:** 68 **15:** 50 **Med Exp PMPM:** $445
**Principal Investments:** Long-term bonds (57%), cash and equiv (35%), real estate (7%)
**Provider Compensation ($000):** Contr fee ($200,396), salary ($42,381), FFS ($26,609), capitation ($22,398), other ($46,410)
**Total Member Encounters:** Phys (247,458), non-phys (77,475)
**Group Affiliation:** GuideWell Mutual Holding Corporation
**Licensed in:** FL
**Address:** 1340 Ridgewood Ave, Holly Hill, FL 32117
**Phone:** (386) 676-7100 **Dom State:** FL **Commenced Bus:** January 2009

| Data Date | Rating | RACR #1 | RACR #2 | Total Assets ($mil) | Capital ($mil) | Net Premium ($mil) | Net Income ($mil) |
|---|---|---|---|---|---|---|---|
| 9-17 | B+ | 5.68 | 4.74 | 204.7 | 90.4 | 377.1 | 16.8 |
| 9-16 | C | N/A | N/A | 162.0 | 79.5 | 320.7 | 5.6 |
| 2016 | B- | 5.50 | 4.58 | 166.4 | 87.4 | 428.0 | 12.0 |
| 2015 | C | N/A | N/A | 115.8 | 75.5 | 358.1 | 7.5 |
| 2014 | B- | 4.20 | 3.50 | 117.3 | 74.6 | 342.7 | 5.0 |
| 2013 | A | 5.14 | 4.28 | 114.1 | 81.7 | 310.8 | 12.3 |
| 2012 | A | 4.45 | 3.71 | 101.3 | 69.4 | 306.0 | 13.8 |

Rating Indexes

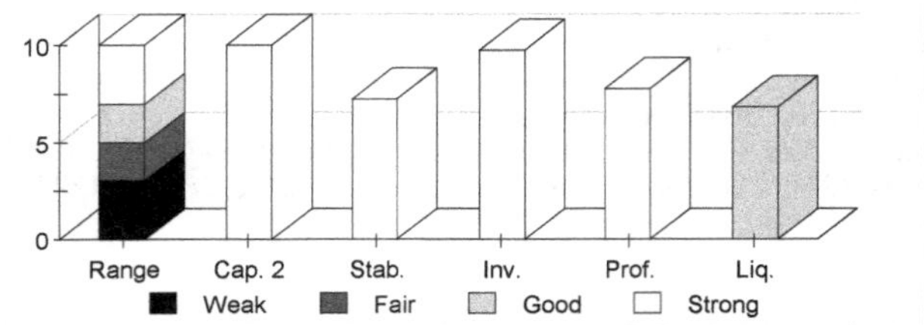


## FLORIDA MHS INC D Weak

**Major Rating Factors:** Fair profitability index (4.4 on a scale of 0 to 10). Strong capitalization (8.4) based on excellent current risk-adjusted capital (severe loss scenario). High quality investment portfolio (9.9).
**Other Rating Factors:** Excellent liquidity (7.3) with ample operational cash flow and liquid investments.
**Principal Business:** Medicaid (100%)
**Mem Phys: 16:** 31,736 **15:** 28,695 **16 MLR** 78.6% **/ 16 Admin Exp** N/A
**Enroll(000): Q3 17:** 68 **16:** 59 **15:** 42 **Med Exp PMPM:** $636
**Principal Investments:** Cash and equiv (93%), long-term bonds (7%)
**Provider Compensation ($000):** FFS ($412,307), capitation ($30,556)
**Total Member Encounters:** Phys (481,012), non-phys (868,914)
**Group Affiliation:** Magellan Health Inc
**Licensed in:** FL
**Address:** 6950 Columbia Gateway Dr, Columbia, MD 21046
**Phone:** (314) 387-5044 **Dom State:** FL **Commenced Bus:** July 2012

| Data Date | Rating | RACR #1 | RACR #2 | Total Assets ($mil) | Capital ($mil) | Net Premium ($mil) | Net Income ($mil) |
|---|---|---|---|---|---|---|---|
| 9-17 | D | 2.51 | 2.09 | 237.3 | 107.6 | 457.4 | 30.8 |
| 9-16 | D | 1.19 | 0.99 | 141.9 | 52.8 | 403.6 | 13.8 |
| 2016 | D | 1.81 | 1.51 | 177.5 | 76.1 | 549.1 | 38.5 |
| 2015 | D | 0.90 | 0.75 | 122.9 | 39.2 | 440.9 | -21.5 |
| 2014 | U | 1.33 | 1.11 | 124.5 | 29.3 | 190.1 | -14.8 |
| 2013 | N/A | N/A | N/A | 16.9 | 16.5 | 0.6 | -1.9 |
| 2012 | N/A | N/A | N/A | 4.8 | 4.8 | N/A | N/A |

Rating Indexes

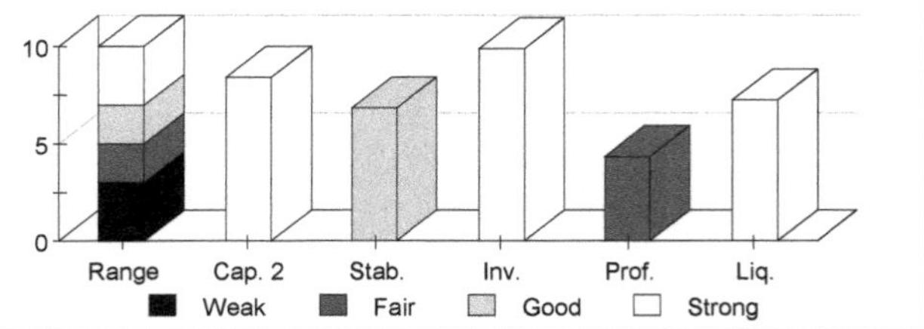

## FLORIDA TRUE HEALTH INC — E — Very Weak

**Major Rating Factors:** Weak profitability index (0.7 on a scale of 0 to 10). Strong capitalization (7.2) based on excellent current risk-adjusted capital (severe loss scenario). High quality investment portfolio (8.8).
**Other Rating Factors:** Excellent liquidity (7.0) with sufficient resources (cash flows and marketable investments) to handle a spike in claims.
**Principal Business:** Medicaid (100%)
**Mem Phys: 16:** 39,248 **15:** 28,017 **16 MLR** 88.9% **/ 16 Admin Exp** N/A
**Enroll(000): Q3 17:** 328 **16:** 327 **15:** 315 **Med Exp PMPM:** $260
**Principal Investments:** Cash and equiv (99%), long-term bonds (1%)
**Provider Compensation ($000):** Contr fee ($829,566), capitation ($177,965)
**Total Member Encounters:** Phys (7,247,211), non-phys (885,326)
**Group Affiliation:** Florida True Health Inc
**Licensed in:** FL
**Address:** 11631 Kew Gardens Ave Ste 200, Palm Beach Gardens, FL 33410
**Phone:** (215) 937-8000 **Dom State:** FL **Commenced Bus:** July 2012

| Data Date | Rating | RACR #1 | RACR #2 | Total Assets ($mil) | Capital ($mil) | Net Premium ($mil) | Net Income ($mil) |
|---|---|---|---|---|---|---|---|
| 9-17 | E | 1.53 | 1.28 | 222.2 | 86.6 | 921.8 | -12.1 |
| 9-16 | E | 1.35 | 1.13 | 223.3 | 80.9 | 800.5 | 5.8 |
| 2016 | E | 1.68 | 1.40 | 219.2 | 95.2 | 1,104.9 | 18.3 |
| 2015 | E | 1.31 | 1.09 | 247.0 | 78.4 | 942.3 | -152.5 |
| 2014 | E | N/A | N/A | 139.5 | -1.7 | 648.0 | -14.7 |
| 2013 | E | 2.01 | 1.67 | 67.6 | 10.3 | 263.6 | -13.8 |
| 2012 | N/A | N/A | N/A | 19.2 | 10.3 | N/A | -9.5 |

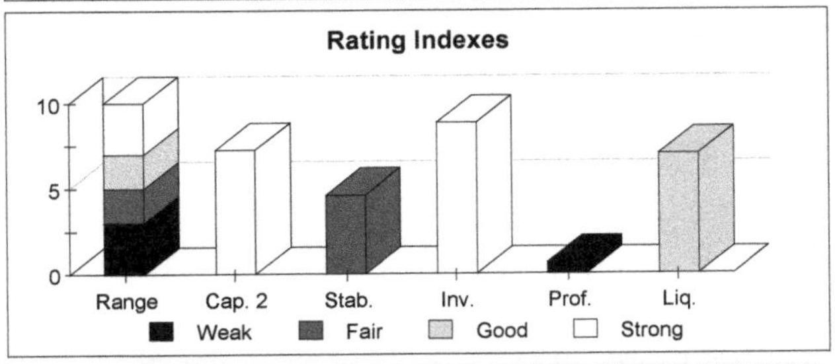


## FREEDOM HEALTH INC — D- — Weak

**Major Rating Factors:** Poor capitalization (1.6 on a scale of 0 to 10) based on weak current risk-adjusted capital (moderate loss scenario). Excellent profitability (8.2). High quality investment portfolio (9.7).
**Other Rating Factors:** Excellent liquidity (6.9) with sufficient resources (cash flows and marketable investments) to handle a spike in claims.
**Principal Business:** Medicare (100%)
**Mem Phys: 16:** 28,465 **15:** 32,388 **16 MLR** 84.1% **/ 16 Admin Exp** N/A
**Enroll(000): Q3 17:** 74 **16:** 70 **15:** 64 **Med Exp PMPM:** $875
**Principal Investments:** Cash and equiv (86%), long-term bonds (10%), nonaffiliate common stock (3%)
**Provider Compensation ($000):** FFS ($374,047), contr fee ($160,064), bonus arrang ($116,272), capitation ($70,408)
**Total Member Encounters:** Phys (49,639), non-phys (50,129)
**Group Affiliation:** Americas 1st Choice Group
**Licensed in:** FL
**Address:** 5600 Mariner St Ste 227, Tampa, FL 33609
**Phone:** (813) 506-6000 **Dom State:** FL **Commenced Bus:** September 2005

| Data Date | Rating | RACR #1 | RACR #2 | Total Assets ($mil) | Capital ($mil) | Net Premium ($mil) | Net Income ($mil) |
|---|---|---|---|---|---|---|---|
| 9-17 | D- | 0.45 | 0.38 | 282.0 | 41.7 | 724.2 | 17.6 |
| 9-16 | E | 0.39 | 0.32 | 240.3 | 33.4 | 681.4 | -1.4 |
| 2016 | E | 0.32 | 0.27 | 165.5 | 32.2 | 871.2 | 3.4 |
| 2015 | E | 0.40 | 0.33 | 135.0 | 33.7 | 770.8 | 10.4 |
| 2014 | E+ | 0.32 | 0.26 | 103.7 | 25.0 | 663.7 | 0.5 |
| 2013 | N/A | N/A | N/A | 95.7 | 23.6 | 651.0 | 2.7 |
| 2012 | N/A | N/A | N/A | 82.7 | 20.2 | 587.4 | 5.8 |

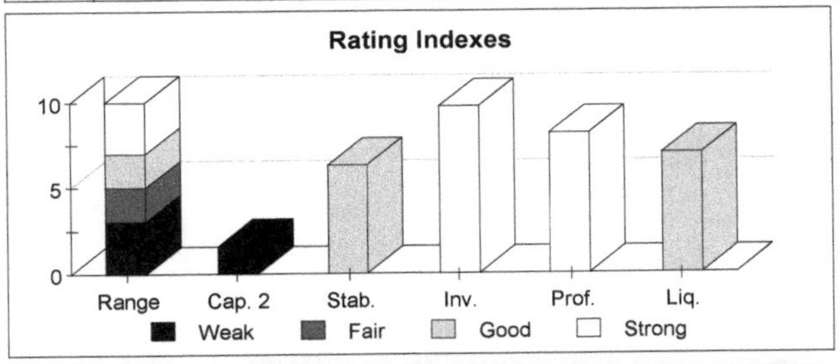


## FREEDOM LIFE INSURANCE COMPANY OF AMERICA — C+ — Fair

**Major Rating Factors:** Fair overall results on stability tests (4.6 on a scale of 0 to 10) including excessive premium growth and fair risk adjusted capital in prior years. Good current capitalization (5.3) based on good risk adjusted capital (severe loss scenario) reflecting some improvement over results in 2013. High quality investment portfolio (7.3).
**Other Rating Factors:** Excellent profitability (8.3). Excellent liquidity (7.2).
**Principal Business:** Group health insurance (68%), individual health insurance (22%), and individual life insurance (11%).
**Principal Investments:** NonCMO investment grade bonds (54%), common & preferred stock (29%), cash (10%), CMOs and structured securities (6%), and noninv. grade bonds (1%).
**Investments in Affiliates:** 29%
**Group Affiliation:** Credit Suisse Group
**Licensed in:** AL, AZ, AR, CO, DE, FL, GA, IL, IN, IA, KS, KY, LA, MD, MI, MN, MS, MO, NE, NV, NM, NC, OH, OK, OR, PA, SC, SD, TN, TX, UT, VA, WA, WV, WY
**Commenced Business:** June 1956
**Address:** 300 Burnett Street Suite 200, Fort Worth, TX 76102-2734
**Phone:** (817) 878-3300 **Domicile State:** TX **NAIC Code:** 62324

| Data Date | Rating | RACR #1 | RACR #2 | Total Assets ($mil) | Capital ($mil) | Net Premium ($mil) | Net Income ($mil) |
|---|---|---|---|---|---|---|---|
| 9-17 | C+ | 0.95 | 0.79 | 132.9 | 71.1 | 202.6 | 10.4 |
| 9-16 | C+ | 0.81 | 0.69 | 90.9 | 46.8 | 141.5 | 7.7 |
| 2016 | C+ | 0.83 | 0.71 | 100.2 | 51.1 | 196.9 | 12.0 |
| 2015 | C+ | 0.75 | 0.65 | 77.3 | 37.0 | 140.1 | 14.9 |
| 2014 | C | 0.69 | 0.60 | 59.9 | 25.7 | 109.7 | 10.1 |
| 2013 | C | 0.67 | 0.59 | 56.2 | 22.6 | 98.1 | 12.3 |
| 2012 | C | 0.73 | 0.65 | 41.5 | 19.6 | 68.8 | 5.9 |

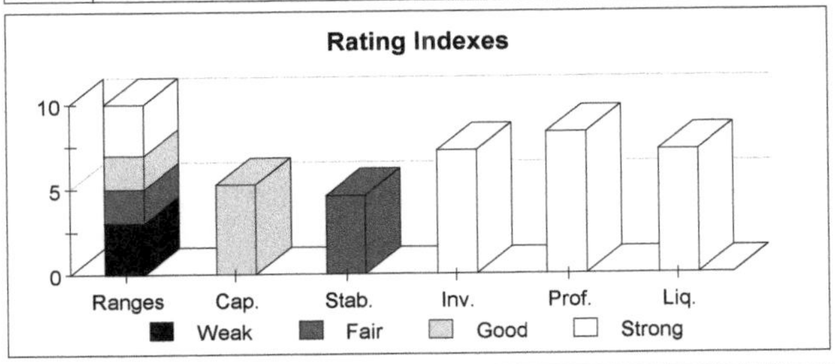

## FRESENIUS HEALTH PLANS INS CO D Weak

**Major Rating Factors:** Weak profitability index (0.5 on a scale of 0 to 10). Strong capitalization (9.5) based on excellent current risk-adjusted capital (severe loss scenario). High quality investment portfolio (9.9).
**Other Rating Factors:** Excellent liquidity (8.1) with ample operational cash flow and liquid investments.
**Principal Business:** Medicare (100%)
**Mem Phys: 16:** 3,631 **15:** N/A **16 MLR** 88.2% **/ 16 Admin Exp** N/A
**Enroll(000): Q3 17:** 0 **16:** 0 **15:** N/A **Med Exp PMPM:** $6,751
**Principal Investments:** Cash and equiv (82%), long-term bonds (18%)
**Provider Compensation ($000):** Contr fee ($10,283), FFS ($4,225)
**Total Member Encounters:** Phys (6,731), non-phys (265)
**Group Affiliation:** Fresenius Medical Care Holdings Inc
**Licensed in:** All states except NY, PR
**Address:** 1320 CITY CENTER Dr Ste 250, CARMEL, IN 46032
**Phone:** (512) 359-7366 **Dom State:** IN **Commenced Bus:** March 1975

| Data Date | Rating | RACR #1 | RACR #2 | Total Assets ($mil) | Capital ($mil) | Net Premium ($mil) | Net Income ($mil) |
|---|---|---|---|---|---|---|---|
| 9-17 | D | 3.35 | 2.79 | 38.2 | 15.1 | 18.8 | -0.7 |
| 9-16 | N/A | N/A | N/A | 31.0 | 16.7 | 15.0 | -1.6 |
| 2016 | D | 3.49 | 2.91 | 30.9 | 15.8 | 20.9 | -2.4 |
| 2015 | N/A | N/A | N/A | 21.1 | 18.4 | N/A | -0.8 |
| 2014 | N/A | N/A | N/A | 13.3 | 12.9 | N/A | 1.5 |
| 2013 | N/A | N/A | N/A | 13.8 | 13.4 | N/A | -0.7 |
| 2012 | N/A | N/A | N/A | 83.0 | 81.8 | N/A | 2.8 |

Rating Indexes

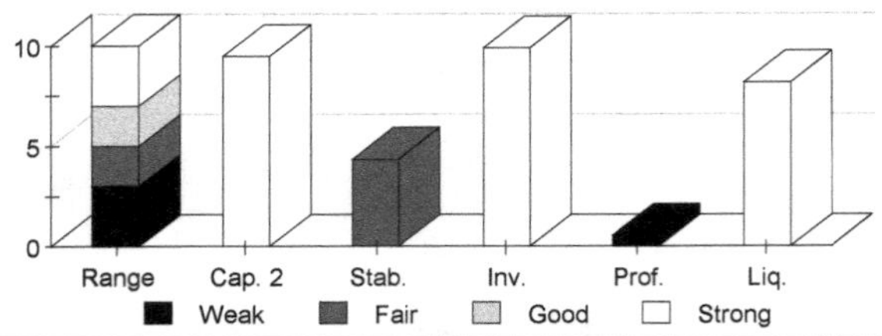


## FRESENIUS HEALTH PLANS OF NC INC D+ Weak

**Major Rating Factors:** Weak profitability index (0.9 on a scale of 0 to 10). Good capitalization (6.2) based on good current risk-adjusted capital (severe loss scenario). High quality investment portfolio (9.9).
**Other Rating Factors:** Excellent liquidity (7.9) with ample operational cash flow and liquid investments.
**Principal Business:** Medicaid (100%)
**Mem Phys: 16:** 2,607 **15:** N/A **16 MLR** 95.3% **/ 16 Admin Exp** N/A
**Enroll(000): Q3 17:** 0 **16:** 0 **15:** N/A **Med Exp PMPM:** $6,077
**Principal Investments:** Cash and equiv (100%)
**Provider Compensation ($000):** Contr fee ($4,234), FFS ($1,212)
**Total Member Encounters:** Phys (2,310), non-phys (225)
**Group Affiliation:** Fresenius Medical Care Holdings Inc
**Licensed in:** NC
**Address:** 3711 S MOPAC EXPY Bldg 2 #300, AUSTIN, TX 78746
**Phone:** (512) 359-7296 **Dom State:** NC **Commenced Bus:** July 2005

| Data Date | Rating | RACR #1 | RACR #2 | Total Assets ($mil) | Capital ($mil) | Net Premium ($mil) | Net Income ($mil) |
|---|---|---|---|---|---|---|---|
| 9-17 | D+ | 1.11 | 0.92 | 14.3 | 2.9 | 7.3 | -1.3 |
| 9-16 | N/A | N/A | N/A | 9.3 | 3.4 | 5.0 | -1.1 |
| 2016 | D+ | 1.03 | 0.86 | 9.0 | 2.7 | 7.0 | -1.8 |
| 2015 | N/A | N/A | N/A | 6.7 | 5.0 | -0.1 | -1.6 |
| 2014 | D+ | N/A | N/A | 1.3 | 1.3 | N/A | N/A |
| 2013 | D+ | 3.92 | 3.26 | 2.3 | 2.0 | 2.6 | -0.8 |
| 2012 | C | 4.51 | 3.76 | 4.5 | 3.9 | 5.8 | -0.2 |

Rating Indexes

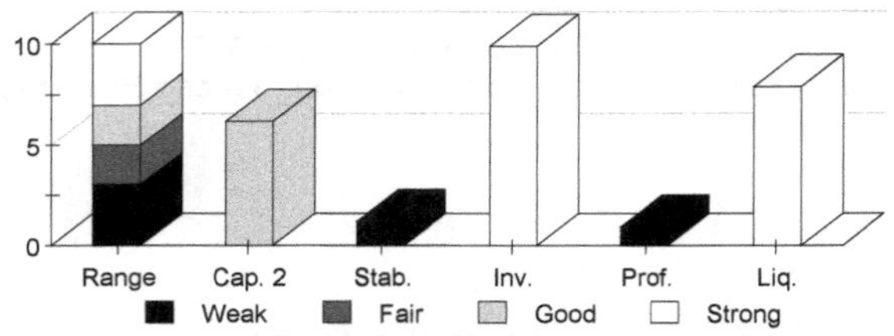


## FRESNO-KINGS-MADERA REGIONAL HEALTH D+ Weak

**Major Rating Factors:** Good capitalization index (5.4 on a scale of 0 to 10) based on fair current risk-adjusted capital (moderate loss scenario). Excellent profitability (9.0). Excellent overall results on stability tests (7.1).
**Other Rating Factors:** Excellent liquidity (6.9) with sufficient resources (cash flows and marketable investments) to handle a spike in claims.
**Principal Business:** Medicaid (100%)
**Mem Phys: 16:** N/A **15:** N/A **16 MLR** 91.4% **/ 16 Admin Exp** N/A
**Enroll(000): Q3 17:** 361 **16:** 352 **15:** 316 **Med Exp PMPM:** $246
**Principal Investments ($000):** Cash and equiv ($31,700)
**Provider Compensation ($000):** None
**Total Member Encounters:** N/A
**Group Affiliation:** None
**Licensed in:** CA
**Address:** 1615 Orange Tree Lane, Redlands, CA 92374
**Phone:** (909) 786-0702 **Dom State:** CA **Commenced Bus:** March 2011

| Data Date | Rating | RACR #1 | RACR #2 | Total Assets ($mil) | Capital ($mil) | Net Premium ($mil) | Net Income ($mil) |
|---|---|---|---|---|---|---|---|
| 9-17 | D+ | 0.82 | 0.50 | 346.0 | 52.8 | 792.7 | 7.8 |
| 9-16 | E+ | 0.57 | 0.34 | 154.9 | 35.3 | 794.9 | 8.4 |
| 2016 | E+ | 0.58 | 0.35 | 151.4 | 38.4 | 1,092.6 | 11.5 |
| 2015 | E+ | 0.43 | 0.26 | 124.8 | 26.8 | 1,010.4 | 13.3 |
| 2014 | E | 0.36 | 0.22 | 86.1 | 13.5 | 573.2 | 3.6 |
| 2013 | E | 0.33 | 0.20 | 70.4 | 9.9 | 454.5 | 4.6 |
| 2012 | E | 0.20 | 0.12 | 48.0 | 5.3 | 361.0 | 4.9 |

Rating Indexes

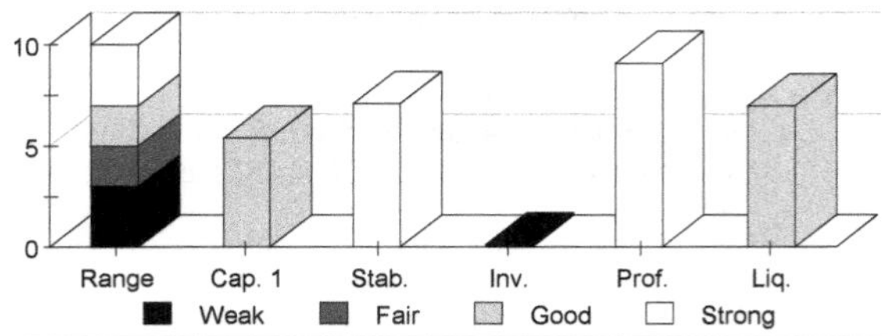

## FRIDAY HEALTH PLANS OF CO INC E- Very Weak

**Major Rating Factors:** Weak profitability index (0.9 on a scale of 0 to 10). Poor capitalization index (0.0) based on weak current risk-adjusted capital (severe loss scenario). Weak overall results on stability tests (0.2) based on an excessive 58% enrollment growth during the period.
**Other Rating Factors:** Weak liquidity (0.7) as a spike in claims may stretch capacity. High quality investment portfolio (9.9).
**Principal Business:** Comp med (93%), Medicaid (4%), Medicare (3%)
**Mem Phys: 16:** 7,898 **15:** 7,892 **16 MLR** 93.8% **/ 16 Admin Exp** N/A
**Enroll(000): Q3 17:** 18 **16:** 20 **15:** 13 **Med Exp PMPM:** $351
**Principal Investments:** Cash and equiv (100%)
**Provider Compensation ($000):** Contr fee ($76,815), FFS ($861)
**Total Member Encounters:** N/A
**Group Affiliation:** Friday Health Plans Inc
**Licensed in:** CO
**Address:** 700 Main Street Suite 100, Alamosa, CO 81101
**Phone:** (719) 589-3696 **Dom State:** CO **Commenced Bus:** May 1975

| Data Date | Rating | RACR #1 | RACR #2 | Total Assets ($mil) | Capital ($mil) | Net Premium ($mil) | Net Income ($mil) |
|---|---|---|---|---|---|---|---|
| 9-17 | E- | 0.12 | 0.10 | 22.3 | 3.3 | 71.1 | 0.6 |
| 9-16 | C | 0.60 | 0.50 | 23.9 | 4.5 | 69.0 | -0.9 |
| 2016 | E- | 0.07 | 0.06 | 24.3 | 1.6 | 92.5 | -4.8 |
| 2015 | C | 0.68 | 0.57 | 22.2 | 5.1 | 49.5 | -1.9 |
| 2014 | C+ | 1.13 | 0.94 | 19.7 | 7.7 | 49.1 | 2.4 |
| 2013 | C+ | 0.93 | 0.77 | 9.3 | 4.4 | 24.6 | -1.4 |
| 2012 | B | 2.03 | 1.69 | 11.2 | 6.5 | 20.8 | 1.1 |

Rating Indexes

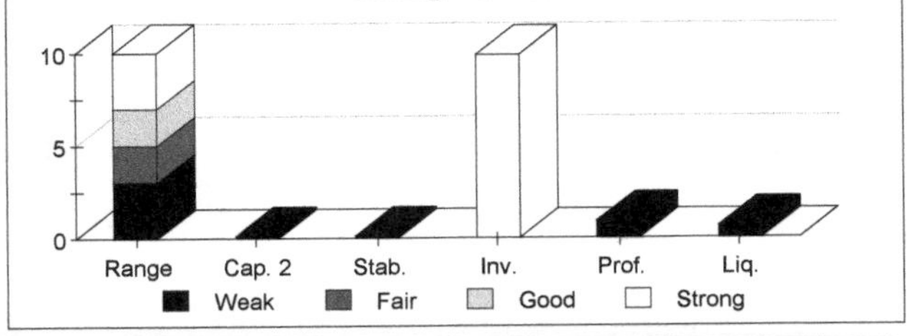


## GATEWAY HEALTH PLAN INC B- Good

**Major Rating Factors:** Good overall profitability index (5.2 on a scale of 0 to 10). Good overall results on stability tests (6.5). Fair financial strength from affiliates. Strong capitalization index (8.8) based on excellent current risk-adjusted capital (severe loss scenario).
**Other Rating Factors:** High quality investment portfolio (9.9). Excellent liquidity (7.0) with sufficient resources (cash flows and marketable investments) to handle a spike in claims.
**Principal Business:** Medicaid (70%), Medicare (30%)
**Mem Phys: 16:** 22,084 **15:** 22,221 **16 MLR** 84.2% **/ 16 Admin Exp** N/A
**Enroll(000): Q3 17:** 353 **16:** 360 **15:** 361 **Med Exp PMPM:** $460
**Principal Investments:** Cash and equiv (58%), long-term bonds (25%), nonaffiliate common stock (17%)
**Provider Compensation ($000):** Contr fee ($1,912,770), capitation ($99,066)
**Total Member Encounters:** Phys (2,020,672), non-phys (852,484)
**Group Affiliation:** Gateway Health Plan LP
**Licensed in:** PA
**Address:** 4 Gateway Center 444 Liberty, Pittsburgh, PA 15222-1222
**Phone:** (412) 255-4640 **Dom State:** PA **Commenced Bus:** August 1986

| Data Date | Rating | RACR #1 | RACR #2 | Total Assets ($mil) | Capital ($mil) | Net Premium ($mil) | Net Income ($mil) |
|---|---|---|---|---|---|---|---|
| 9-17 | B- | 2.79 | 2.32 | 829.4 | 359.7 | 1,740.6 | 51.8 |
| 9-16 | B- | 2.31 | 1.93 | 810.3 | 286.3 | 1,802.0 | 47.4 |
| 2016 | B- | 2.34 | 1.95 | 754.7 | 299.6 | 2,380.6 | 57.9 |
| 2015 | B- | 1.91 | 1.59 | 581.7 | 236.2 | 2,168.8 | 10.9 |
| 2014 | B | 1.94 | 1.62 | 448.4 | 207.4 | 1,910.6 | -22.5 |
| 2013 | B | 2.52 | 2.10 | 470.7 | 236.7 | 1,809.5 | 20.2 |
| 2012 | B | 2.42 | 2.02 | 440.0 | 197.6 | 1,616.6 | 28.9 |

Rating Indexes

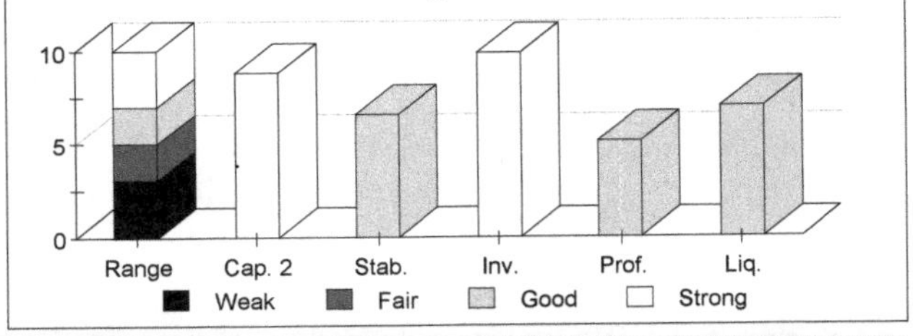


## GATEWAY HEALTH PLAN OF OHIO INC C Fair

**Major Rating Factors:** Weak profitability index (1.9 on a scale of 0 to 10). Strong capitalization (8.8) based on excellent current risk-adjusted capital (severe loss scenario). High quality investment portfolio (9.9).
**Other Rating Factors:** Excellent liquidity (7.1) with ample operational cash flow and liquid investments.
**Principal Business:** Medicare (100%)
**Mem Phys: 16:** 26,682 **15:** 13,004 **16 MLR** 84.6% **/ 16 Admin Exp** N/A
**Enroll(000): Q3 17:** 10 **16:** 8 **15:** 7 **Med Exp PMPM:** $747
**Principal Investments:** Cash and equiv (95%), long-term bonds (5%)
**Provider Compensation ($000):** Contr fee ($65,831), capitation ($1,935)
**Total Member Encounters:** Phys (67,510), non-phys (37,001)
**Group Affiliation:** Gateway Health Plan LP
**Licensed in:** KY, NC, OH
**Address:** 444 Liberty Ave Ste 2100, Pittsburgh, PA 15222-1222
**Phone:** (412) 255-4640 **Dom State:** OH **Commenced Bus:** September 2005

| Data Date | Rating | RACR #1 | RACR #2 | Total Assets ($mil) | Capital ($mil) | Net Premium ($mil) | Net Income ($mil) |
|---|---|---|---|---|---|---|---|
| 9-17 | C | 2.81 | 2.35 | 46.3 | 13.3 | 78.1 | -2.1 |
| 9-16 | C | 2.07 | 1.73 | 35.6 | 9.5 | 58.4 | 0.5 |
| 2016 | C | 2.69 | 2.24 | 29.6 | 12.7 | 78.5 | 0.8 |
| 2015 | C | 1.78 | 1.48 | 26.0 | 8.2 | 59.9 | -1.0 |
| 2014 | U | 3.73 | 3.11 | 9.0 | 4.2 | 7.5 | -6.6 |
| 2013 | N/A | N/A | N/A | 8.3 | 2.5 | N/A | -7.1 |
| 2012 | N/A | N/A | N/A | 2.4 | 2.4 | N/A | N/A |

Rating Indexes

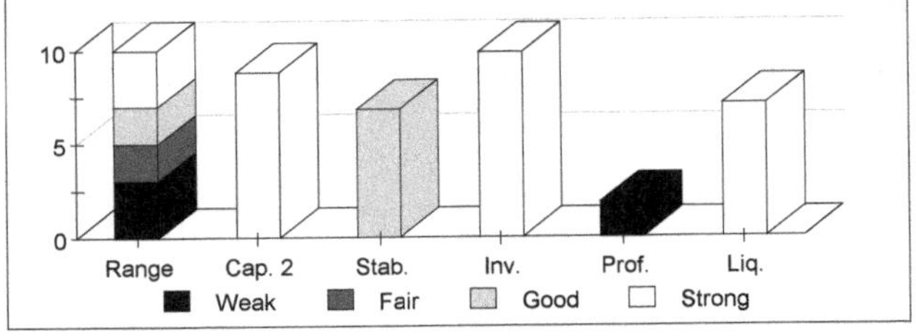

## GEISINGER HEALTH PLAN * B+ Good

**Major Rating Factors:** Excellent profitability (7.7 on a scale of 0 to 10). Strong capitalization index (7.8) based on excellent current risk-adjusted capital (severe loss scenario). High quality investment portfolio (7.9).
**Other Rating Factors:** Excellent overall results on stability tests (7.6). Excellent liquidity (6.9) with sufficient resources (cash flows and marketable investments) to handle a spike in claims
**Principal Business:** Medicaid (40%), Medicare (39%), comp med (21%)
**Mem Phys: 16:** 41,281 **15:** 36,042 **16 MLR** 86.4% **/ 16 Admin Exp** N/A
**Enroll(000): Q3 17:** 358 **16:** 340 **15:** 329 **Med Exp PMPM:** $453
**Principal Investments:** Cash and equiv (38%), long-term bonds (37%), nonaffiliate common stock (23%), real estate (2%)
**Provider Compensation ($000):** Contr fee ($1,534,313), FFS ($193,022), capitation ($72,875), bonus arrang ($36,841)
**Total Member Encounters:** Phys (2,535,352), non-phys (506,094)
**Group Affiliation:** Geisinger Health System Foundation
**Licensed in:** NJ, PA
**Address:** 100 North Academy Avenue, Danville, PA 17822
**Phone:** (570) 271-8777 **Dom State:** PA **Commenced Bus:** March 1985

| Data Date | Rating | RACR #1 | RACR #2 | Total Assets ($mil) | Capital ($mil) | Net Premium ($mil) | Net Income ($mil) |
|---|---|---|---|---|---|---|---|
| 9-17 | B+ | 1.97 | 1.64 | 688.5 | 313.5 | 1,772.0 | 101.6 |
| 9-16 | B | 1.63 | 1.36 | 602.7 | 239.8 | 1,593.3 | 54.9 |
| 2016 | B | 1.33 | 1.11 | 545.3 | 216.5 | 2,132.4 | 50.3 |
| 2015 | B | 1.32 | 1.10 | 465.4 | 195.5 | 1,884.8 | 16.3 |
| 2014 | B | 1.32 | 1.10 | 388.9 | 170.4 | 1,612.8 | 8.1 |
| 2013 | B | 1.46 | 1.21 | 338.1 | 166.9 | 1,466.3 | 44.0 |
| 2012 | B | 1.75 | 1.46 | 239.3 | 125.6 | 935.6 | 46.5 |

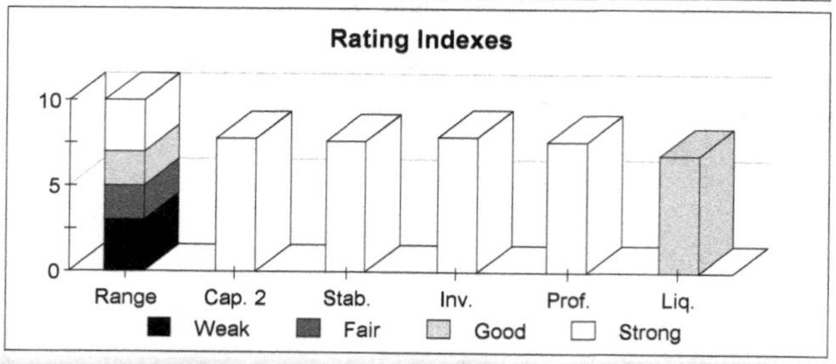


## GEISINGER INDEMNITY INS CO C+ Fair

**Major Rating Factors:** Good capitalization (5.6 on a scale of 0 to 10) based on good current risk-adjusted capital (severe loss scenario). Good liquidity (5.1) with sufficient resources (cash flows and marketable investments) to handle a spike in claims. Weak profitability index (0.9).
**Other Rating Factors:** High quality investment portfolio (9.4).
**Principal Business:** Medicare (97%), med supp (3%)
**Mem Phys: 16:** 49,259 **15:** 44,534 **16 MLR** 97.1% **/ 16 Admin Exp** N/A
**Enroll(000): Q3 17:** 28 **16:** 22 **15:** 22 **Med Exp PMPM:** $535
**Principal Investments:** Long-term bonds (67%), cash and equiv (33%)
**Provider Compensation ($000):** Contr fee ($127,672), FFS ($9,667), capitation ($2,092), bonus arrang ($715)
**Total Member Encounters:** Phys (217,419), non-phys (50,145)
**Group Affiliation:** Geisinger Health System Foundation
**Licensed in:** PA, WV
**Address:** 100 N Academy Ave MC 32-51, Danville, PA 17822
**Phone:** (570) 271-8777 **Dom State:** PA **Commenced Bus:** February 1996

| Data Date | Rating | RACR #1 | RACR #2 | Total Assets ($mil) | Capital ($mil) | Net Premium ($mil) | Net Income ($mil) |
|---|---|---|---|---|---|---|---|
| 9-17 | C+ | 1.02 | 0.85 | 79.8 | 17.5 | 149.3 | -3.3 |
| 9-16 | C | 0.73 | 0.61 | 57.3 | 10.5 | 103.0 | -4.7 |
| 2016 | C | 1.13 | 0.94 | 58.3 | 19.6 | 138.8 | -8.1 |
| 2015 | C | 1.07 | 0.89 | 44.8 | 14.6 | 128.3 | 7.7 |
| 2014 | C | 1.13 | 0.94 | 63.0 | 20.4 | 199.6 | 0.6 |
| 2013 | C | 1.43 | 1.19 | 51.0 | 18.1 | 158.1 | -7.8 |
| 2012 | C | 1.64 | 1.37 | 40.7 | 17.8 | 122.0 | -8.7 |

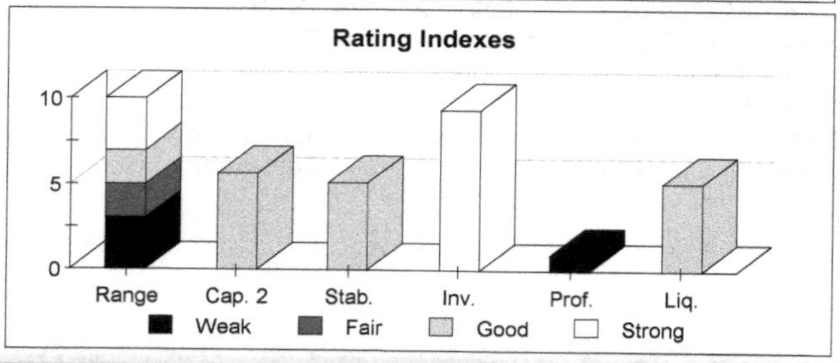


## GEISINGER QUALITY OPTIONS INC C+ Fair

**Major Rating Factors:** Good liquidity (5.8 on a scale of 0 to 10) with sufficient resources (cash flows and marketable investments) to handle a spike in claims. Weak profitability index (1.8). Strong capitalization (7.2) based on excellent current risk-adjusted capital (severe loss scenario).
**Other Rating Factors:** High quality investment portfolio (9.5).
**Principal Business:** Comp med (96%), Medicare (4%)
**Mem Phys: 16:** 40,640 **15:** 25,737 **16 MLR** 93.0% **/ 16 Admin Exp** N/A
**Enroll(000): Q3 17:** 51 **16:** 54 **15:** 44 **Med Exp PMPM:** $407
**Principal Investments:** Long-term bonds (80%), cash and equiv (20%)
**Provider Compensation ($000):** Contr fee ($141,955), FFS ($81,126), capitation ($8,820), bonus arrang ($2,536)
**Total Member Encounters:** Phys (262,027), non-phys (36,174)
**Group Affiliation:** Geisinger Health System Foundation
**Licensed in:** NJ, PA
**Address:** 100 N Academy Ave MC 32-51, Danville, PA 17822
**Phone:** (570) 271-8777 **Dom State:** PA **Commenced Bus:** March 2007

| Data Date | Rating | RACR #1 | RACR #2 | Total Assets ($mil) | Capital ($mil) | Net Premium ($mil) | Net Income ($mil) |
|---|---|---|---|---|---|---|---|
| 9-17 | C+ | 1.54 | 1.29 | 73.7 | 36.6 | 213.6 | 4.5 |
| 9-16 | C | 1.31 | 1.09 | 77.6 | 25.8 | 194.4 | -4.3 |
| 2016 | C | 1.30 | 1.08 | 83.7 | 31.9 | 265.0 | -6.2 |
| 2015 | C | 1.53 | 1.28 | 68.6 | 30.5 | 231.1 | 0.4 |
| 2014 | C | 1.53 | 1.27 | 87.8 | 38.6 | 287.8 | -6.2 |
| 2013 | C | 1.65 | 1.38 | 99.1 | 45.9 | 341.5 | 2.4 |
| 2012 | C | 1.52 | 1.27 | 92.4 | 43.5 | 354.8 | 1.7 |

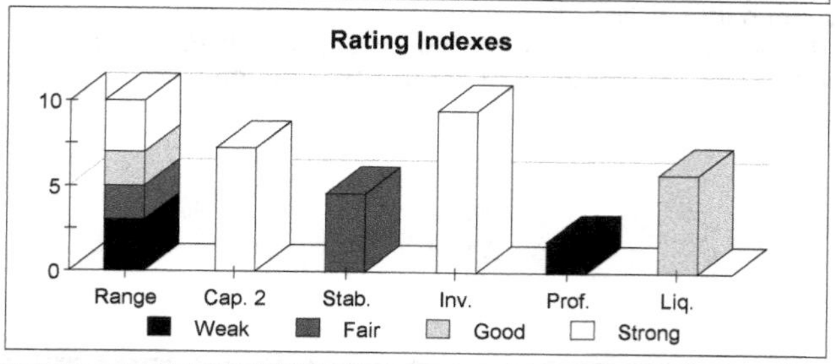

## GENWORTH LIFE INSURANCE COMPANY C+ Fair

**Major Rating Factors:** Fair profitability (3.3 on a scale of 0 to 10) with operating losses during the first nine months of 2017. Fair overall results on stability tests (3.8). Good quality investment portfolio (6.2) despite mixed results such as: large holdings of BBB rated bonds but moderate junk bond exposure.
**Other Rating Factors:** Strong capitalization (7.0) based on excellent risk adjusted capital (severe loss scenario). Excellent liquidity (7.2).
**Principal Business:** Individual health insurance (74%), individual life insurance (11%), group health insurance (9%), reinsurance (3%), and individual annuities (2%).
**Principal Investments:** NonCMO investment grade bonds (62%), CMOs and structured securities (13%), mortgages in good standing (10%), common & preferred stock (5%), and misc. investments (8%).
**Investments in Affiliates:** 5%
**Group Affiliation:** Genworth Financial
**Licensed in:** All states except NY
**Commenced Business:** October 1956
**Address:** 2711 CENTERVILLE ROAD STE 400, WILMINGTON, DE 19808
**Phone:** (800) 255-7836 **Domicile State:** DE **NAIC Code:** 70025

| Data Date | Rating | RACR #1 | RACR #2 | Total Assets ($mil) | Capital ($mil) | Net Premium ($mil) | Net Income ($mil) |
|---|---|---|---|---|---|---|---|
| 9-17 | C+ | 1.36 | 1.00 | 40,425.9 | 3,257.4 | -7,422.9 | -74.6 |
| 9-16 | C+ | 0.89 | 0.67 | 40,061.0 | 2,386.7 | 945.0 | -166.7 |
| 2016 | C+ | 1.17 | 0.87 | 40,172.5 | 3,099.6 | 2,084.8 | -39.1 |
| 2015 | B- | 1.02 | 0.78 | 38,504.3 | 2,740.7 | 1,587.2 | 35.2 |
| 2014 | B- | 1.02 | 0.81 | 38,163.2 | 3,224.4 | 1,713.3 | -179.7 |
| 2013 | C+ | 1.06 | 0.85 | 36,445.4 | 3,487.2 | 2,569.0 | 329.8 |
| 2012 | C+ | 1.01 | 0.80 | 36,783.8 | 3,410.5 | 1,659.0 | 201.0 |

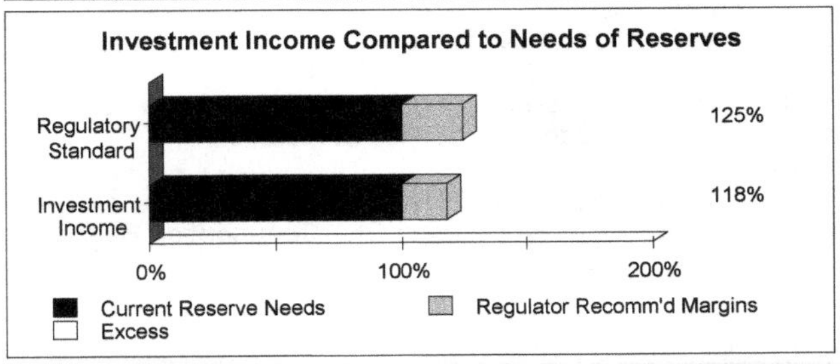


## GENWORTH LIFE INSURANCE COMPANY OF NEW YORK C Fair

**Major Rating Factors:** Fair overall results on stability tests (3.7 on a scale of 0 to 10) including negative cash flow from operations for 2016. Good quality investment portfolio (5.0) despite mixed results such as: large holdings of BBB rated bonds but junk bond exposure equal to 51% of capital. Good liquidity (6.4) with sufficient resources to handle a spike in claims as well as a significant increase in policy surrenders.
**Other Rating Factors:** Weak profitability (2.8) with investment income below regulatory standards in relation to interest assumptions of reserves. Strong capitalization (7.2) based on excellent risk adjusted capital (severe loss scenario).
**Principal Business:** Individual health insurance (59%), individual life insurance (18%), reinsurance (16%), individual annuities (4%), and group health insurance (3%).
**Principal Investments:** NonCMO investment grade bonds (59%), CMOs and structured securities (23%), mortgages in good standing (9%), noninv. grade bonds (3%), and common & preferred stock (1%).
**Investments in Affiliates:** None
**Group Affiliation:** Genworth Financial
**Licensed in:** CT, DC, DE, FL, IL, NJ, NY, RI, VA
**Commenced Business:** October 1988
**Address:** 600 THIRD AVENUE SUITE 2400, NEW YORK, NY 10016
**Phone:** (800) 357-1066 **Domicile State:** NY **NAIC Code:** 72990

| Data Date | Rating | RACR #1 | RACR #2 | Total Assets ($mil) | Capital ($mil) | Net Premium ($mil) | Net Income ($mil) |
|---|---|---|---|---|---|---|---|
| 9-17 | C | 2.17 | 1.10 | 8,167.4 | 473.5 | 190.7 | 9.3 |
| 9-16 | C+ | 2.39 | 1.20 | 8,493.6 | 532.1 | 207.8 | 35.0 |
| 2016 | C | 2.20 | 1.12 | 8,495.5 | 481.2 | 276.9 | -20.0 |
| 2015 | C+ | 2.22 | 1.12 | 8,372.2 | 494.8 | 356.1 | -39.8 |
| 2014 | B- | 2.14 | 1.08 | 8,474.6 | 481.1 | 521.7 | -93.3 |
| 2013 | B | 2.29 | 1.15 | 8,139.0 | 527.3 | 610.9 | 13.1 |
| 2012 | B | 2.36 | 1.18 | 7,815.8 | 540.1 | 542.6 | 19.1 |

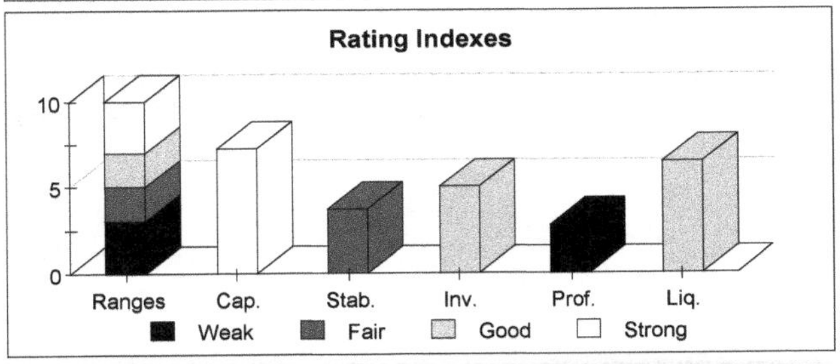


## GERBER LIFE INSURANCE COMPANY * B+ Good

**Major Rating Factors:** Good quality investment portfolio (5.9 on a scale of 0 to 10) despite mixed results such as: large holdings of BBB rated bonds but moderate junk bond exposure. Good overall profitability (5.3) despite operating losses during the first nine months of 2017. Good liquidity (5.4) with sufficient resources to handle a spike in claims as well as a significant increase in policy surrenders.
**Other Rating Factors:** Good overall results on stability tests (6.5) excellent operational trends and excellent risk diversification. Strong capitalization (7.1) based on excellent risk adjusted capital (severe loss scenario).
**Principal Business:** Individual life insurance (44%), group health insurance (36%), individual health insurance (12%), and reinsurance (9%).
**Principal Investments:** NonCMO investment grade bonds (66%), CMOs and structured securities (22%), policy loans (5%), common & preferred stock (3%), and noninv. grade bonds (3%).
**Investments in Affiliates:** None
**Group Affiliation:** Nestle SA
**Licensed in:** All states, the District of Columbia and Puerto Rico
**Commenced Business:** September 1968
**Address:** 1311 Mamaroneck Avenue, White Plains, NY 10605
**Phone:** (914) 272-4000 **Domicile State:** NY **NAIC Code:** 70939

| Data Date | Rating | RACR #1 | RACR #2 | Total Assets ($mil) | Capital ($mil) | Net Premium ($mil) | Net Income ($mil) |
|---|---|---|---|---|---|---|---|
| 9-17 | B+ | 1.74 | 1.04 | 3,650.7 | 311.4 | 554.5 | -10.2 |
| 9-16 | B+ | 1.88 | 1.12 | 3,324.6 | 303.5 | 530.9 | 7.4 |
| 2016 | B+ | 1.78 | 1.06 | 3,397.6 | 307.0 | 690.0 | 15.3 |
| 2015 | B+ | 1.90 | 1.14 | 3,088.3 | 295.8 | 604.2 | 18.5 |
| 2014 | A- | 1.97 | 1.20 | 2,812.2 | 285.3 | 565.3 | 24.2 |
| 2013 | A- | 2.00 | 1.21 | 2,548.1 | 263.5 | 506.8 | 22.7 |
| 2012 | A- | 1.96 | 1.17 | 2,306.7 | 237.9 | 464.1 | 20.2 |

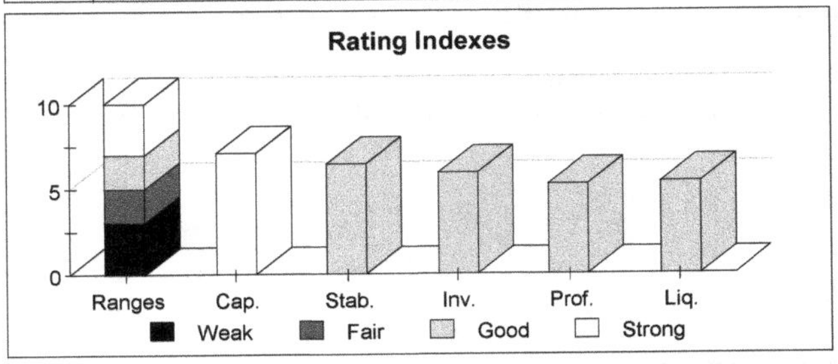

## GHS HEALTH MAINTENANCE ORGANIZATION B- Good

**Major Rating Factors:** Strong capitalization index (8.4 on a scale of 0 to 10) based on excellent current risk-adjusted capital (severe loss scenario). High quality investment portfolio (9.7). Weak profitability index (0.5).
**Other Rating Factors:** Weak overall results on stability tests (2.8) based on inconsistent enrollment growth in the past five years due to declines in 2013 and 2014. Rating is significantly influenced by the good financial results of Health Care Service Corporation. Weak liquidity (2.4) as a spike in claims may stretch capacity.
**Principal Business:** Medicare (100%)
**Mem Phys: 16:** 10,865 **15:** 9,426 **16 MLR** 161.7% **/ 16 Admin Exp** N/A
**Enroll(000): Q3 17:** 10 **16:** 9 **15:** 8 **Med Exp PMPM:** $559
**Principal Investments:** Affiliate common stock (45%), long-term bonds (36%), cash and equiv (18%)
**Provider Compensation ($000):** Contr fee ($43,432), FFS ($17,404), bonus arrang ($519), capitation ($155), other ($184)
**Total Member Encounters:** Phys (60,549), non-phys (20,509)
**Group Affiliation:** Health Care Service Corporation
**Licensed in:** OK
**Address:** 1400 South Boston, Tulsa, OK 74119
**Phone:** (312) 653-6000 **Dom State:** OK **Commenced Bus:** August 1984

| Data Date | Rating | RACR #1 | RACR #2 | Total Assets ($mil) | Capital ($mil) | Net Premium ($mil) | Net Income ($mil) |
|---|---|---|---|---|---|---|---|
| 9-17 | B- | 2.47 | 2.05 | 62.3 | 19.7 | 46.2 | -5.8 |
| 9-16 | C+ | 4.39 | 3.66 | 48.4 | 31.9 | 29.4 | -1.9 |
| 2016 | C+ | 3.57 | 2.97 | 43.5 | 28.5 | 38.7 | -3.8 |
| 2015 | B- | 4.10 | 3.42 | 42.2 | 29.8 | 27.6 | -15.5 |
| 2014 | B | 11.36 | 9.47 | 42.1 | 38.2 | 4.2 | -1.1 |
| 2013 | U | 17.71 | 14.76 | 42.2 | 32.4 | N/A | 0.2 |
| 2012 | U | 116.20 | 96.81 | 25.9 | 25.5 | N/A | 0.0 |

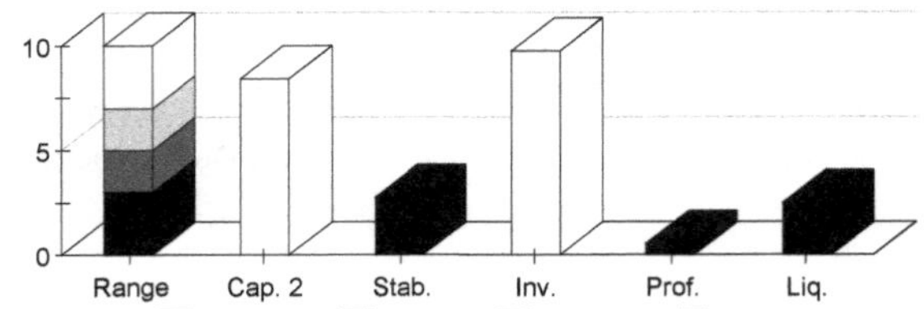


## GHS INS CO E- Very Weak

**Major Rating Factors:** Weak profitability index (0.0 on a scale of 0 to 10). Strong capitalization (8.7) based on excellent current risk-adjusted capital (severe loss scenario). High quality investment portfolio (9.9).
**Other Rating Factors:** Excellent liquidity (7.0) with sufficient resources (cash flows and marketable investments) to handle a spike in claims.
**Principal Business:** Medicare (97%)
**Mem Phys: 16:** 11,759 **15:** 3,806 **16 MLR** 95.0% **/ 16 Admin Exp** N/A
**Enroll(000): Q3 17:** 7 **16:** 4 **15:** 1 **Med Exp PMPM:** $681
**Principal Investments:** Long-term bonds (58%), cash and equiv (42%)
**Provider Compensation ($000):** Contr fee ($12,076), capitation ($7,940), FFS ($3,770), bonus arrang ($2), other ($540)
**Total Member Encounters:** Phys (8,773), non-phys (4,593)
**Group Affiliation:** Health Care Service Corporation
**Licensed in:** AR, CO, IL, IN, KS, NM, OK, TX
**Address:** 3817 Nwest Expressway Ste 300, Oklahoma City, OK 73112
**Phone:** (312) 653-6000 **Dom State:** OK **Commenced Bus:** July 1988

| Data Date | Rating | RACR #1 | RACR #2 | Total Assets ($mil) | Capital ($mil) | Net Premium ($mil) | Net Income ($mil) |
|---|---|---|---|---|---|---|---|
| 9-17 | E- | 2.73 | 2.28 | 35.5 | 4.2 | 32.2 | -3.5 |
| 9-16 | E | 6.44 | 5.37 | 26.3 | 7.4 | 19.5 | 3.8 |
| 2016 | E | 4.46 | 3.71 | 30.9 | 8.5 | 27.4 | 1.7 |
| 2015 | E | 4.59 | 3.83 | 24.6 | 4.4 | 6.8 | -13.6 |
| 2014 | N/A | N/A | N/A | 18.5 | 8.1 | 0.6 | N/A |
| 2013 | N/A | N/A | N/A | 23.9 | 9.9 | 3.9 | N/A |
| 2012 | N/A | N/A | N/A | 35.9 | 13.6 | 17.9 | N/A |

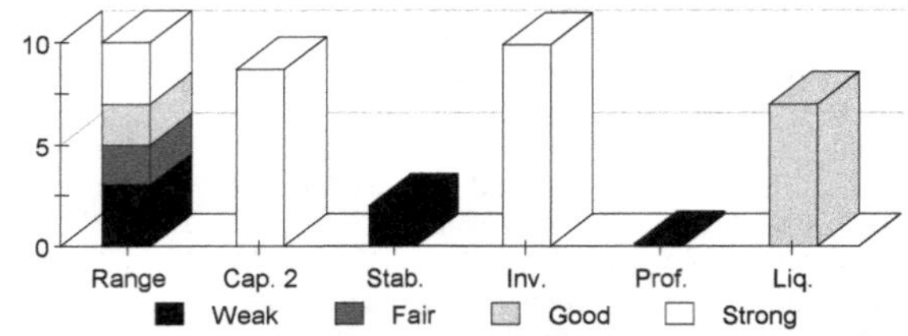


## GHS MANAGED HEALTH CARE PLANS INC E Very Weak

**Major Rating Factors:** Weak profitability index (0.9 on a scale of 0 to 10). Good liquidity (6.1) with sufficient resources (cash flows and marketable investments) to handle a spike in claims. Strong capitalization (8.7) based on excellent current risk-adjusted capital (severe loss scenario).
**Other Rating Factors:** High quality investment portfolio (9.9).
**Principal Business:** Medicare (100%)
**Mem Phys: 16:** 3,591 **15:** 1,753 **16 MLR** 115.2% **/ 16 Admin Exp** N/A
**Enroll(000): Q2 17:** N/A **16:** 5 **15:** 4 **Med Exp PMPM:** $736
**Principal Investments:** Long-term bonds (70%), cash and equiv (30%)
**Provider Compensation ($000):** Contr fee ($33,536), FFS ($4,484), bonus arrang ($984), other ($93)
**Total Member Encounters:** Phys (28,199), non-phys (17,825)
**Group Affiliation:** Health Care Service Corporation a Mu
**Licensed in:** OK
**Address:** 1400 S Boston Ave, Tulsa, OK 74119
**Phone:** (312) 653-6000 **Dom State:** OK **Commenced Bus:** February 2011

| Data Date | Rating | RACR #1 | RACR #2 | Total Assets ($mil) | Capital ($mil) | Net Premium ($mil) | Net Income ($mil) |
|---|---|---|---|---|---|---|---|
| 6-17 | E | 2.75 | 2.29 | 27.7 | 11.2 | 15.4 | -2.2 |
| 6-16 | E- | 3.89 | 3.24 | 40.2 | 16.1 | 18.7 | 4.7 |
| 2016 | E- | 3.26 | 2.71 | 37.1 | 13.3 | 35.3 | 1.9 |
| 2015 | E- | 2.74 | 2.29 | 40.7 | 11.4 | 37.3 | -22.4 |
| 2014 | B- | 2.55 | 2.12 | 20.2 | 8.8 | 25.2 | -1.6 |
| 2013 | D | 1.22 | 1.02 | 8.6 | 2.6 | 12.9 | -7.9 |
| 2012 | C+ | 2.54 | 2.12 | 3.5 | 2.2 | 3.2 | -1.6 |

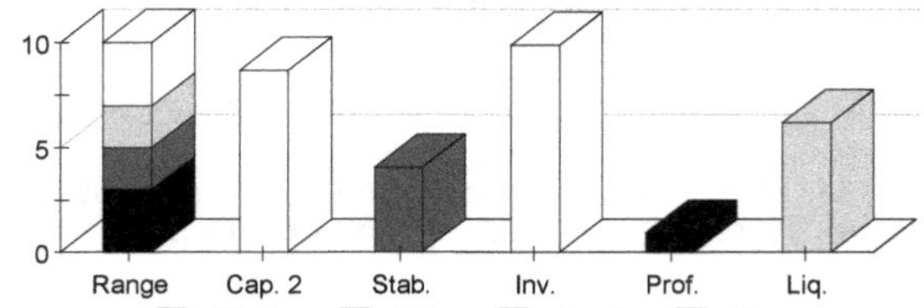

## GLOBALHEALTH INC — D Weak

**Major Rating Factors:** Weak profitability index (1.0 on a scale of 0 to 10). Good capitalization (6.1) based on good current risk-adjusted capital (severe loss scenario). Good quality investment portfolio (6.6).
**Other Rating Factors:** Good liquidity (6.9) with sufficient resources (cash flows and marketable investments) to handle a spike in claims.
**Principal Business:** Comp med (65%), Medicare (32%), FEHB (3%)
**Mem Phys: 16:** 3,747 **15:** 3,168 **16 MLR** 85.7% **/ 16 Admin Exp** N/A
**Enroll(000): Q3 17:** 43 **16:** 42 **15:** 45 **Med Exp PMPM:** $428
**Principal Investments:** Cash and equiv (36%), long-term bonds (5%), other (59%)
**Provider Compensation ($000):** Capitation ($155,616), contr fee ($54,732), FFS ($7,246)
**Total Member Encounters:** Phys (103,051)
**Group Affiliation:** Kinderhook Capital Fund III LP
**Licensed in:** OK
**Address:** 701 NE 10TH St Ste 300, OKLAHOMA CITY, OK 73104
**Phone:** (405) 280-5656 **Dom State:** OK **Commenced Bus:** July 2009

| Data Date | Rating | RACR #1 | RACR #2 | Total Assets ($mil) | Capital ($mil) | Net Premium ($mil) | Net Income ($mil) |
|---|---|---|---|---|---|---|---|
| 9-17 | D | 1.09 | 0.91 | 49.3 | 19.3 | 212.4 | -0.8 |
| 9-16 | D | 1.42 | 1.19 | 41.3 | 16.7 | 190.7 | -2.1 |
| 2016 | D | 1.04 | 0.87 | 35.3 | 18.5 | 256.4 | -1.4 |
| 2015 | D | 1.02 | 0.85 | 36.7 | 20.4 | 245.4 | -5.9 |
| 2014 | C+ | 1.00 | 0.83 | 36.1 | 17.8 | 246.4 | -1.4 |
| 2013 | B | 1.16 | 0.97 | 30.8 | 21.4 | 219.3 | 0.8 |
| 2012 | C- | 0.97 | 0.81 | 27.3 | 17.1 | 182.9 | 0.9 |

Rating Indexes

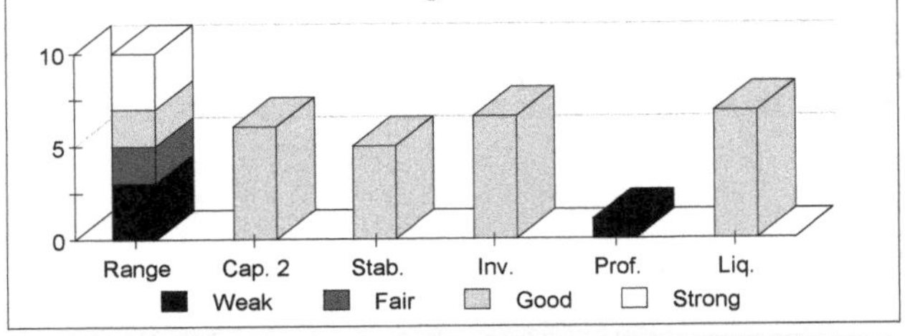


## GOLDEN RULE INSURANCE COMPANY — B Good

**Major Rating Factors:** Good overall results on stability tests (5.1 on a scale of 0 to 10) despite fair financial strength of affiliated UnitedHealth Group Inc. Other stability subfactors include good operational trends, good risk adjusted capital for prior years and excellent risk diversification. Good overall profitability (6.4). Excellent expense controls. Good liquidity (6.1).
**Other Rating Factors:** Fair overall capitalization (4.7) based on mixed results -- excessive policy leverage mitigated by excellent risk adjusted capital (severe loss scenario). High quality investment portfolio (8.1).
**Principal Business:** Group health insurance (84%), individual health insurance (13%), and individual life insurance (2%).
**Principal Investments:** NonCMO investment grade bonds (80%), CMOs and structured securities (15%), cash (1%), and real estate (1%).
**Investments in Affiliates:** None
**Group Affiliation:** UnitedHealth Group Inc
**Licensed in:** All states except NY, PR
**Commenced Business:** June 1961
**Address:** 7440 WOODLAND DRIVE, INDIANAPOLIS, IN 46278
**Phone:** (317) 290-8100 **Domicile State:** IN **NAIC Code:** 62286

| Data Date | Rating | RACR #1 | RACR #2 | Total Assets ($mil) | Capital ($mil) | Net Premium ($mil) | Net Income ($mil) |
|---|---|---|---|---|---|---|---|
| 9-17 | B | 1.28 | 1.01 | 508.5 | 222.7 | 1,010.9 | 105.6 |
| 9-16 | B | 1.35 | 1.06 | 628.8 | 243.8 | 1,013.4 | 86.2 |
| 2016 | B | 0.99 | 0.78 | 529.5 | 170.1 | 1,354.2 | 65.2 |
| 2015 | B | 1.37 | 1.07 | 635.6 | 268.0 | 1,501.3 | 106.8 |
| 2014 | B | 1.30 | 1.03 | 718.2 | 313.2 | 1,850.6 | 76.7 |
| 2013 | B | 1.12 | 0.89 | 759.8 | 293.5 | 2,020.6 | 129.4 |
| 2012 | B | 1.19 | 0.94 | 782.5 | 292.3 | 1,879.5 | 127.6 |

| UnitedHealth Group Inc<br>Composite Group Rating: C+<br>Largest Group Members | Assets ($mil) | Rating |
|---|---|---|
| UNITED HEALTHCARE INS CO | 17923 | C |
| SIERRA HEALTH AND LIFE INS CO INC | 2397 | B |
| OXFORD HEALTH INS INC | 2211 | B |
| ALL SAVERS INS CO | 1552 | C |
| UNITED HEALTHCARE OF WISCONSIN INC | 1224 | B |

## GOLDEN SECURITY INS CO — B Good

**Major Rating Factors:** Excellent profitability (10.0 on a scale of 0 to 10). Strong capitalization (8.6) based on excellent current risk-adjusted capital (severe loss scenario). High quality investment portfolio (9.0).
**Other Rating Factors:** Excellent liquidity (7.3) with ample operational cash flow and liquid investments.
**Principal Business:** Other (100%)
**Mem Phys: 16:** N/A **15:** N/A **16 MLR** 69.5% **/ 16 Admin Exp** N/A
**Enroll(000): Q3 17:** 267 **16:** 248 **15:** 249 **Med Exp PMPM:** $13
**Principal Investments:** Long-term bonds (56%), cash and equiv (39%), nonaffiliate common stock (5%)
**Provider Compensation ($000):** Other ($36,323)
**Total Member Encounters:** N/A
**Group Affiliation:** BlueCross BlueShield of Tennessee
**Licensed in:** AR, MS, TN
**Address:** 1 Cameron Hill Circle, Chattanooga, TN 37402-0001
**Phone:** (423) 535-5600 **Dom State:** TN **Commenced Bus:** January 1984

| Data Date | Rating | RACR #1 | RACR #2 | Total Assets ($mil) | Capital ($mil) | Net Premium ($mil) | Net Income ($mil) |
|---|---|---|---|---|---|---|---|
| 9-17 | B | 2.62 | 2.19 | 44.2 | 31.3 | 44.6 | 2.6 |
| 9-16 | B | 2.51 | 2.09 | 43.0 | 26.5 | 42.1 | 3.1 |
| 2016 | B | 2.38 | 1.98 | 43.0 | 28.3 | 56.6 | 5.2 |
| 2015 | B | 2.18 | 1.82 | 34.2 | 22.9 | 51.3 | 5.6 |
| 2014 | B | 1.57 | 1.31 | 20.8 | 10.5 | 35.7 | 4.2 |
| 2013 | B | 1.75 | 1.46 | 18.6 | 7.9 | 24.0 | 2.7 |
| 2012 | N/A | N/A | N/A | 15.3 | 5.2 | 16.4 | 1.8 |

Rating Indexes

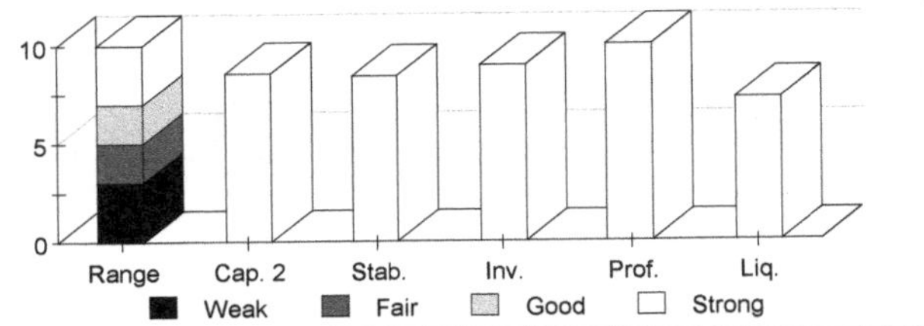

## GOLDEN STATE MEDICARE HEALTH PLAN — E+ Very Weak

**Major Rating Factors:** Weak profitability index (2.0 on a scale of 0 to 10). Poor capitalization index (0.0) based on weak current risk-adjusted capital (severe loss scenario). Weak overall results on stability tests (0.5) based on an excessive 275% enrollment growth during the period, a steep decline in capital during 2016.
**Other Rating Factors:** Excellent liquidity (6.9) with sufficient resources (cash flows and marketable investments) to handle a spike in claims.
**Principal Business:** Medicare (100%)
**Mem Phys: 16:** N/A **15:** N/A **16 MLR** 90.3% **/ 16 Admin Exp** N/A
**Enroll(000): Q3 17:** 8 **16:** 7 **15:** 2 **Med Exp PMPM:** $1,452
**Principal Investments ($000):** Cash and equiv ($5,646)
**Provider Compensation ($000):** None
**Total Member Encounters:** N/A
**Group Affiliation:** None
**Licensed in:** CA
**Address:** 3030 Old Ranch Pkwy Suite 155, Seal Beach, CA 90740
**Phone:** (608) 347-4897 **Dom State:** CA **Commenced Bus:** May 2009

| Data Date | Rating | RACR #1 | RACR #2 | Total Assets ($mil) | Capital ($mil) | Net Premium ($mil) | Net Income ($mil) |
|---|---|---|---|---|---|---|---|
| 9-17 | E+ | 0.19 | 0.12 | 6.5 | 1.3 | 51.4 | 0.7 |
| 9-16 | N/A | N/A | N/A | N/A | N/A | N/A | N/A |
| 2016 | D- | 0.50 | 0.31 | 8.3 | 3.4 | 66.0 | -0.4 |
| 2015 | D+ | 1.55 | 0.96 | 7.6 | 6.4 | 33.4 | -1.0 |
| 2014 | C- | 2.41 | 1.51 | 5.8 | 5.5 | 18.1 | -2.1 |
| 2013 | C- | 4.99 | 3.19 | 5.8 | 5.3 | 8.7 | -0.8 |
| 2012 | C- | 1.12 | 0.70 | 1.5 | 1.3 | 10.7 | 0.7 |

**Rating Indexes**

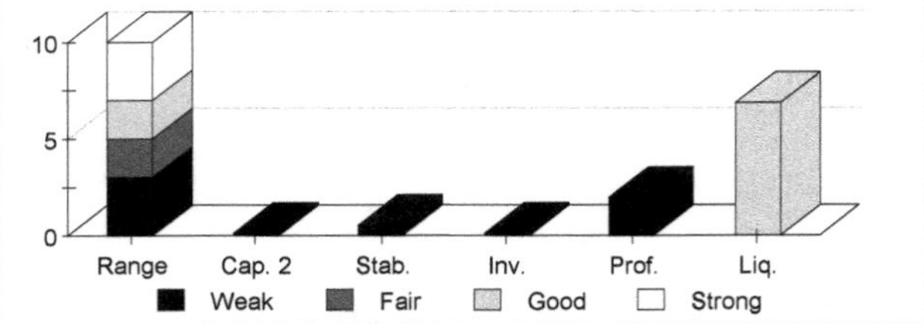


## GOOD HEALTH HMO INC — C Fair

**Major Rating Factors:** Weak profitability index (1.4 on a scale of 0 to 10). Good overall results on stability tests (5.1). Good liquidity (6.7) with sufficient resources (cash flows and marketable investments) to handle a spike in claims.
**Other Rating Factors:** Strong capitalization index (10.0) based on excellent current risk-adjusted capital (severe loss scenario). High quality investment portfolio (9.9).
**Principal Business:** Comp med (100%)
**Mem Phys: 16:** 5,431 **15:** 5,404 **16 MLR** 88.2% **/ 16 Admin Exp** N/A
**Enroll(000): Q3 17:** 51 **16:** 59 **15:** 29 **Med Exp PMPM:** $255
**Principal Investments:** Long-term bonds (88%), cash and equiv (12%)
**Provider Compensation ($000):** Contr fee ($147,513), FFS ($14,589), capitation ($1,494)
**Total Member Encounters:** Phys (266,755), non-phys (141,674)
**Group Affiliation:** Blue Cross & Blue Shield of KS City
**Licensed in:** KS, MO
**Address:** 2301 Main Street, Kansas City, MO 64108-2428
**Phone:** (816) 395-2222 **Dom State:** MO **Commenced Bus:** January 1989

| Data Date | Rating | RACR #1 | RACR #2 | Total Assets ($mil) | Capital ($mil) | Net Premium ($mil) | Net Income ($mil) |
|---|---|---|---|---|---|---|---|
| 9-17 | C | 4.24 | 3.53 | 78.4 | 56.1 | 143.2 | -1.6 |
| 9-16 | C | 5.51 | 4.60 | 79.5 | 53.0 | 138.4 | -4.4 |
| 2016 | C | 4.13 | 3.44 | 86.7 | 57.7 | 189.5 | -3.8 |
| 2015 | C | 5.86 | 4.88 | 73.9 | 56.0 | 138.0 | 0.5 |
| 2014 | C | 4.39 | 3.66 | 67.5 | 51.8 | 155.5 | -6.8 |
| 2013 | B | 3.76 | 3.14 | 89.1 | 63.4 | 252.0 | -6.5 |
| 2012 | N/A | N/A | N/A | 118.8 | 74.5 | 389.4 | -5.1 |

**Rating Indexes**

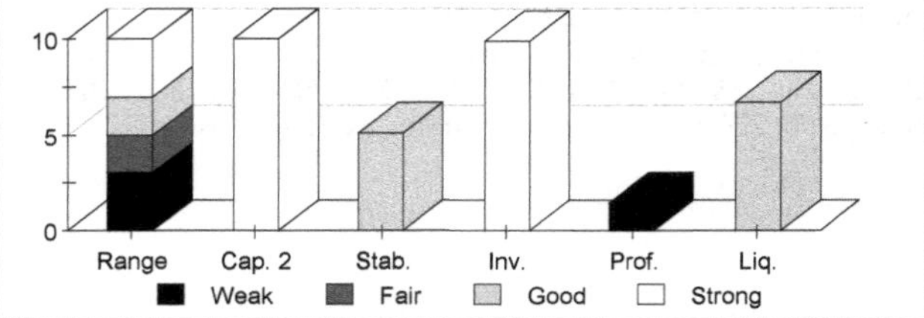


## GOVERNMENT PERSONNEL MUTUAL LIFE INSURANCE CO * — B+ Good

**Major Rating Factors:** Good quality investment portfolio (6.6 on a scale of 0 to 10) despite significant exposure to mortgages . Mortgage default rate has been low. large holdings of BBB rated bonds in addition to small junk bond holdings. Good overall profitability (6.9). Good liquidity (5.5).
**Other Rating Factors:** Good overall results on stability tests (6.4) excellent operational trends and excellent risk diversification. Strong capitalization (7.9) based on excellent risk adjusted capital (severe loss scenario).
**Principal Business:** Individual life insurance (58%), individual health insurance (40%), individual annuities (1%), and reinsurance (1%).
**Principal Investments:** NonCMO investment grade bonds (67%), mortgages in good standing (15%), policy loans (9%), common & preferred stock (3%), and misc. investments (7%).
**Investments in Affiliates:** 2%
**Group Affiliation:** GPM Life Group
**Licensed in:** All states except NJ, NY, PR
**Commenced Business:** October 1934
**Address:** 2211 NE Loop 410, San Antonio, TX 78217
**Phone:** (800) 938-9765 **Domicile State:** TX **NAIC Code:** 63967

| Data Date | Rating | RACR #1 | RACR #2 | Total Assets ($mil) | Capital ($mil) | Net Premium ($mil) | Net Income ($mil) |
|---|---|---|---|---|---|---|---|
| 9-17 | B+ | 2.50 | 1.62 | 832.3 | 122.3 | 33.9 | 3.0 |
| 9-16 | B+ | 2.82 | 1.75 | 835.8 | 118.1 | 34.5 | 2.8 |
| 2016 | B+ | 2.51 | 1.62 | 835.1 | 120.9 | 44.9 | 4.0 |
| 2015 | B+ | 2.81 | 1.76 | 836.1 | 116.2 | 46.3 | 2.6 |
| 2014 | B+ | 2.72 | 1.73 | 837.5 | 112.4 | 46.2 | 3.3 |
| 2013 | B+ | 2.69 | 1.72 | 830.9 | 109.2 | 46.9 | 4.1 |
| 2012 | B+ | 2.64 | 1.69 | 833.7 | 104.8 | 51.1 | 4.9 |

**Rating Indexes**

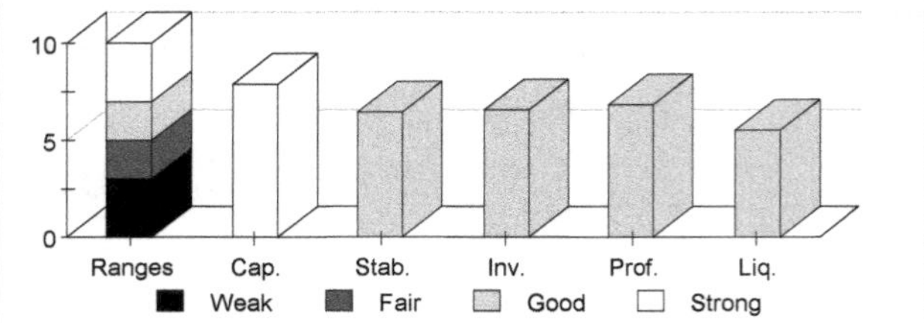

## GRAND VALLEY HEALTH PLAN INC — E- Very Weak

**Major Rating Factors:** Weak profitability index (0.8 on a scale of 0 to 10). Poor capitalization index (0.0) based on weak current risk-adjusted capital (severe loss scenario). Weak overall results on stability tests (2.3) based on a significant 48% decrease in enrollment during the period.
**Other Rating Factors:** High quality investment portfolio (9.5). Excellent liquidity (6.9) with sufficient resources (cash flows and marketable investments) to handle a spike in claims.
**Principal Business:** Comp med (70%), FEHB (30%)
**Mem Phys: 16:** 6,299 **15:** 5,575 **16 MLR** 91.9% **/ 16 Admin Exp** N/A
**Enroll(000): Q2 17:** 0 **16:** 3 **15:** 5 **Med Exp PMPM:** $373
**Principal Investments:** Cash and equiv (100%)
**Provider Compensation ($000):** Contr fee ($9,150), salary ($7,747), FFS ($236), capitation ($134)
**Total Member Encounters:** Phys (5,570), non-phys (1,296)
**Group Affiliation:** Grand Valley Health Corporation
**Licensed in:** MI
**Address:** 2680 Leonard NE Suite 2, Grand Rapids, MI 49525
**Phone:** (616) 949-2410 **Dom State:** MI **Commenced Bus:** February 1982

| Data Date | Rating | RACR #1 | RACR #2 | Total Assets ($mil) | Capital ($mil) | Net Premium ($mil) | Net Income ($mil) |
|---|---|---|---|---|---|---|---|
| 6-17 | E- | 0.06 | 0.05 | 1.2 | 0.4 | 1.3 | -0.9 |
| 6-16 | N/A | N/A | N/A | N/A | N/A | N/A | N/A |
| 2016 | D | 0.35 | 0.29 | 3.4 | 1.4 | 17.0 | -0.1 |
| 2015 | D | 0.30 | 0.25 | 5.9 | 1.3 | 22.0 | -0.8 |
| 2014 | D+ | 0.60 | 0.50 | 5.0 | 1.8 | 22.2 | -0.3 |
| 2013 | D+ | 0.81 | 0.68 | 5.0 | 2.0 | 22.0 | -0.4 |
| 2012 | D | 0.81 | 0.67 | 5.8 | 2.6 | 25.9 | 0.3 |

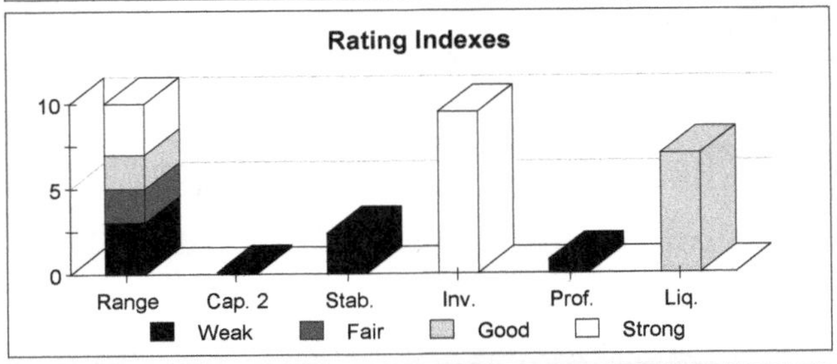


## GRANITE STATE HEALTH PLAN INC — D+ Weak

**Major Rating Factors:** Weak profitability index (0.9 on a scale of 0 to 10). Strong capitalization (10.0) based on excellent current risk-adjusted capital (severe loss scenario). High quality investment portfolio (9.9).
**Other Rating Factors:** Excellent liquidity (7.0) with ample operational cash flow and liquid investments.
**Principal Business:** Medicaid (100%)
**Mem Phys: 16:** 10,755 **15:** 6,144 **16 MLR** 93.2% **/ 16 Admin Exp** N/A
**Enroll(000): Q3 17:** 60 **16:** 61 **15:** 72 **Med Exp PMPM:** $358
**Principal Investments:** Cash and equiv (100%)
**Provider Compensation ($000):** Contr fee ($200,881), bonus arrang ($54,011), capitation ($6,761), salary ($6,624)
**Total Member Encounters:** Phys (277,218), non-phys (409,697)
**Group Affiliation:** Centene Corporation
**Licensed in:** NH
**Address:** 2 Executive Park Dr, Bedford, NH 03110
**Phone:** (314) 725-4477 **Dom State:** NH **Commenced Bus:** December 2013

| Data Date | Rating | RACR #1 | RACR #2 | Total Assets ($mil) | Capital ($mil) | Net Premium ($mil) | Net Income ($mil) |
|---|---|---|---|---|---|---|---|
| 9-17 | D+ | 6.53 | 5.44 | 92.3 | 22.8 | 206.6 | -13.7 |
| 9-16 | D+ | 3.82 | 3.18 | 106.7 | 22.0 | 208.2 | -11.1 |
| 2016 | D+ | 6.52 | 5.43 | 82.4 | 22.7 | 280.8 | -15.7 |
| 2015 | D+ | 4.31 | 3.59 | 91.1 | 25.1 | 325.8 | -16.7 |
| 2014 | D+ | 2.03 | 1.69 | 59.5 | 21.3 | 204.2 | -7.0 |
| 2013 | N/A | N/A | N/A | 13.0 | 6.1 | 10.3 | N/A |
| 2012 | N/A | N/A | N/A | 7.0 | 7.0 | N/A | N/A |

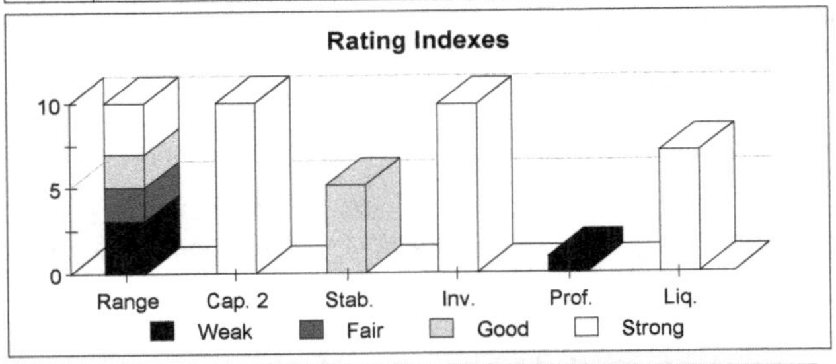


## GREAT MIDWEST INS CO — B Good

**Major Rating Factors:** Fair reserve development (4.2 on a scale of 0 to 10) as reserves have generally been sufficient to cover claims. In 2016, the one year reserve development was 18% deficient. Fair profitability index (3.5) with operating losses during 2012 and the first nine months of 2017. Average return on equity over the last five years has been poor at -1.5%.
**Other Rating Factors:** Fair overall results on stability tests (4.2) including weak results on operational trends and negative cash flow from operations for 2016. The largest net exposure for one risk is conservative at 1.1% of capital. Strong long-term capitalization index (7.9) based on excellent current risk adjusted capital (severe and moderate loss scenarios), despite some fluctuation in capital levels. Excellent liquidity (7.4) with ample operational cash flow and liquid investments.
**Principal Business:** Group accident & health (47%), other liability (19%), auto liability (10%), workers compensation (9%), commercial multiple peril (7%), auto physical damage (3%), and inland marine (3%).
**Principal Investments:** Investment grade bonds (91%), cash (5%), misc. investments (3%), and non investment grade bonds (1%).
**Investments in Affiliates:** 0%
**Group Affiliation:** Houston International Ins Group Ltd
**Licensed in:** All states except PR
**Commenced Business:** November 1985
**Address:** 800 Gessner Suite 600, Houston, TX 77024
**Phone:** (713) 935-0226 **Domicile State:** TX **NAIC Code:** 18694

| Data Date | Rating | RACR #1 | RACR #2 | Loss Ratio % | Total Assets ($mil) | Capital ($mil) | Net Premium ($mil) | Net Income ($mil) |
|---|---|---|---|---|---|---|---|---|
| 9-17 | B | 2.67 | 1.74 | N/A | 206.6 | 103.4 | 53.8 | -2.0 |
| 9-16 | B | 3.20 | 1.93 | N/A | 204.1 | 106.4 | 73.0 | -0.8 |
| 2016 | B | 2.29 | 1.51 | 94.5 | 215.8 | 104.8 | 86.2 | -20.2 |
| 2015 | B | 2.42 | 1.50 | 63.8 | 211.1 | 107.6 | 93.5 | 6.1 |
| 2014 | B- | 3.37 | 2.10 | 59.1 | 191.8 | 103.0 | 71.2 | 5.8 |
| 2013 | B- | 2.46 | 1.62 | 64.3 | 128.3 | 56.1 | 63.0 | 1.5 |
| 2012 | B- | 4.09 | 2.56 | 63.8 | 86.9 | 53.1 | 25.6 | -0.9 |

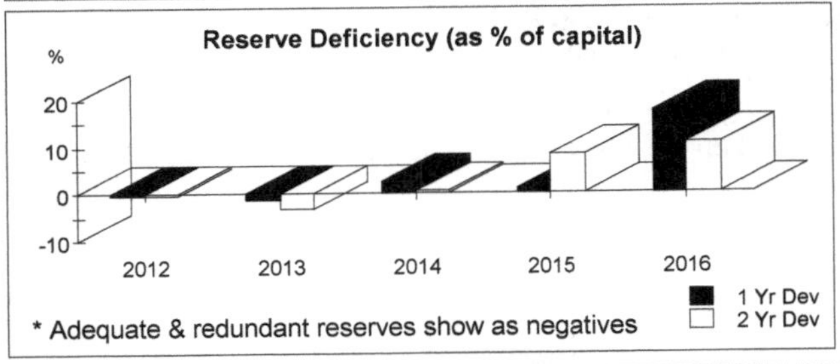

## GROUP HEALTH COOP OF EAU CLAIRE E+ Very Weak

**Major Rating Factors:** Fair profitability index (3.7 on a scale of 0 to 10). Fair overall results on stability tests (3.7) based on inconsistent enrollment growth in the past five years due to declines in 2013 and 2014. Good capitalization index (6.6) based on good current risk-adjusted capital (severe loss scenario).
**Other Rating Factors:** Good liquidity (5.4) with sufficient resources (cash flows and marketable investments) to handle a spike in claims. High quality investment portfolio (9.4).
**Principal Business:** Medicaid (74%), comp med (26%)
**Mem Phys: 16:** 11,630 **15:** 11,984 **16 MLR** 90.3% **/ 16 Admin Exp** N/A
**Enroll(000): Q3 17:** 49 **16:** 48 **15:** 46 **Med Exp PMPM:** $272
**Principal Investments:** Long-term bonds (87%), cash and equiv (13%)
**Provider Compensation ($000):** Contr fee ($114,644), FFS ($42,434), capitation ($888)
**Total Member Encounters:** Phys (285,532), non-phys (208,756)
**Group Affiliation:** Group Health Coop of Eau Claire
**Licensed in:** WI
**Address:** 2503 N Hillcrest Parkway, Altoona, WI 54720
**Phone:** (715) 552-4300 **Dom State:** WI **Commenced Bus:** November 1976

| Data Date | Rating | RACR #1 | RACR #2 | Total Assets ($mil) | Capital ($mil) | Net Premium ($mil) | Net Income ($mil) |
|---|---|---|---|---|---|---|---|
| 9-17 | E+ | 1.17 | 0.97 | 51.1 | 22.3 | 133.1 | -5.8 |
| 9-16 | E+ | 1.67 | 1.39 | 55.6 | 28.7 | 130.0 | -2.4 |
| 2016 | E+ | 1.46 | 1.22 | 56.5 | 28.0 | 174.1 | -2.9 |
| 2015 | E+ | 1.81 | 1.51 | 58.2 | 31.0 | 163.7 | 6.5 |
| 2014 | E+ | 1.73 | 1.44 | 49.0 | 24.3 | 138.7 | 12.5 |
| 2013 | E+ | 0.91 | 0.76 | 42.2 | 18.2 | 170.9 | 4.4 |
| 2012 | E+ | 0.54 | 0.45 | 40.6 | 13.9 | 198.3 | 2.2 |

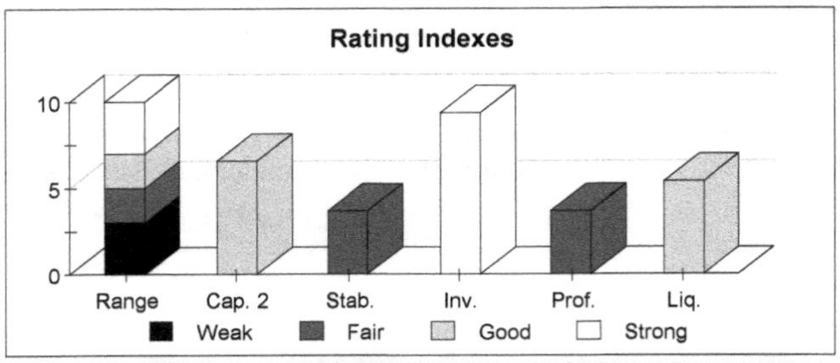


## GROUP HEALTH COOP OF S CENTRAL WI D Weak

**Major Rating Factors:** Weak profitability index (1.7 on a scale of 0 to 10). Low quality investment portfolio (2.8). Good overall results on stability tests (5.0) based on inconsistent enrollment growth in the past five years due to declines in 2015 and 2016.
**Other Rating Factors:** Good liquidity (6.5) with sufficient resources (cash flows and marketable investments) to handle a spike in claims. Strong capitalization index (7.3) based on excellent current risk-adjusted capital (severe loss scenario).
**Principal Business:** Comp med (88%), FEHB (8%), Medicaid (3%)
**Mem Phys: 16:** 3,588 **15:** 1,809 **16 MLR** 91.1% **/ 16 Admin Exp** N/A
**Enroll(000): Q3 17:** 74 **16:** 76 **15:** 78 **Med Exp PMPM:** $368
**Principal Investments:** Cash and equiv (28%), nonaffiliate common stock (28%), long-term bonds (22%), real estate (21%), other (1%)
**Provider Compensation ($000):** FFS ($138,776), capitation ($94,045), salary ($59,491), contr fee ($43,935)
**Total Member Encounters:** Phys (380,156), non-phys (157,929)
**Group Affiliation:** Group Health Coop of S Central WI
**Licensed in:** WI
**Address:** 1265 JOHN Q HAMMONS DRIVE, MADISON, WI 53717
**Phone:** (608) 251-4156 **Dom State:** WI **Commenced Bus:** March 1976

| Data Date | Rating | RACR #1 | RACR #2 | Total Assets ($mil) | Capital ($mil) | Net Premium ($mil) | Net Income ($mil) |
|---|---|---|---|---|---|---|---|
| 9-17 | D | 1.57 | 1.31 | 91.8 | 48.3 | 270.5 | 6.5 |
| 9-16 | D | 1.06 | 0.88 | 84.2 | 35.9 | 272.9 | -2.6 |
| 2016 | D | 1.25 | 1.04 | 86.0 | 39.6 | 364.9 | 0.9 |
| 2015 | D | 1.17 | 0.97 | 84.3 | 39.2 | 383.6 | 0.2 |
| 2014 | D | 1.02 | 0.85 | 87.6 | 38.1 | 372.8 | -18.7 |
| 2013 | D+ | 1.92 | 1.60 | 101.5 | 58.1 | 316.9 | -13.5 |
| 2012 | C | 1.71 | 1.43 | 116.4 | 76.5 | 296.7 | -5.5 |

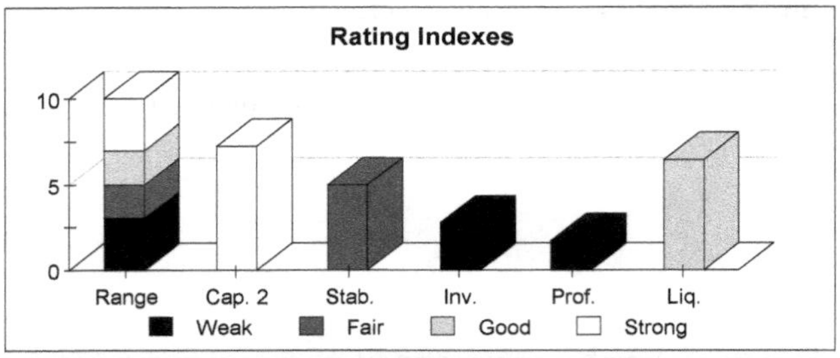


## GROUP HEALTH INCORPORATED E Very Weak

**Major Rating Factors:** Fair profitability index (3.3 on a scale of 0 to 10). Strong capitalization (9.2) based on excellent current risk-adjusted capital (severe loss scenario). High quality investment portfolio (9.9).
**Other Rating Factors:** Excellent liquidity (7.9) with ample operational cash flow and liquid investments.
**Principal Business:** Comp med (32%), FEHB (27%), dental (12%), Medicare (11%), other (16%)
**Mem Phys: 16:** 82,523 **15:** 85,161 **16 MLR** 81.9% **/ 16 Admin Exp** N/A
**Enroll(000): Q3 17:** 1,718 **16:** 1,489 **15:** 1,463 **Med Exp PMPM:** $41
**Principal Investments:** Cash and equiv (81%), long-term bonds (19%)
**Provider Compensation ($000):** FFS ($384,390), contr fee ($270,466), capitation ($345), other ($70,497)
**Total Member Encounters:** N/A
**Group Affiliation:** EmblemHealth Inc
**Licensed in:** NY
**Address:** 55 Water St, New York, NY 10041
**Phone:** (646) 447-5000 **Dom State:** NY **Commenced Bus:** December 1940

| Data Date | Rating | RACR #1 | RACR #2 | Total Assets ($mil) | Capital ($mil) | Net Premium ($mil) | Net Income ($mil) |
|---|---|---|---|---|---|---|---|
| 9-17 | E | 3.10 | 2.58 | 652.7 | 229.6 | 583.8 | 16.6 |
| 9-16 | E | 2.27 | 1.89 | 608.7 | 176.8 | 683.5 | -42.6 |
| 2016 | E | 3.65 | 3.04 | 672.2 | 260.8 | 908.8 | 260.3 |
| 2015 | E | 2.86 | 2.39 | 602.4 | 213.8 | 912.7 | 30.2 |
| 2014 | E | 0.89 | 0.74 | 722.8 | 127.5 | 1,894.7 | -128.6 |
| 2013 | D | 1.06 | 0.89 | 991.9 | 276.3 | 3,614.6 | -66.2 |
| 2012 | D | 0.37 | 0.30 | 967.1 | 120.2 | 3,571.3 | -51.9 |

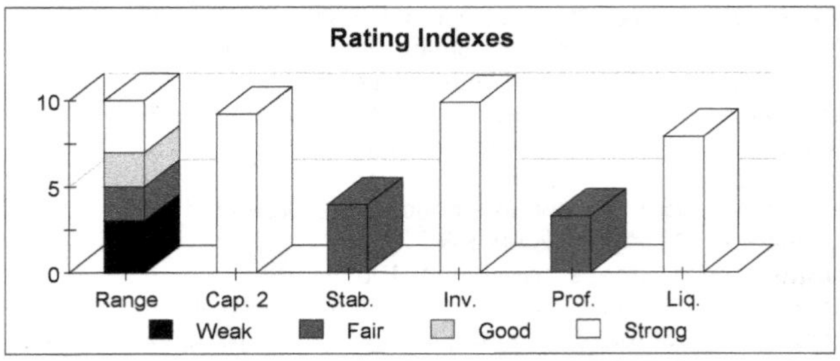

## GROUP HEALTH PLAN INC * A- Excellent

**Major Rating Factors:** Strong capitalization index (8.8 on a scale of 0 to 10) based on excellent current risk-adjusted capital (severe loss scenario). High quality investment portfolio (7.8). Excellent liquidity (7.1) with ample operational cash flow and liquid investments.
**Other Rating Factors:** Fair profitability index (3.8). Fair overall results on stability tests (3.9). Potential support from affiliation with HealthPartners Inc.
**Principal Business:** Comp med (58%), Medicare (34%), FEHB (4%), dental (4%)
**Mem Phys: 16:** 64,919 **15:** 57,617 **16 MLR** 96.3% **/ 16 Admin Exp** N/A
**Enroll(000): Q3 17:** 89 **16:** 80 **15:** 69 **Med Exp PMPM:** $1,289
**Principal Investments:** Long-term bonds (35%), nonaffiliate common stock (27%), cash and equiv (19%), real estate (19%), other (1%)
**Provider Compensation ($000):** Bonus arrang ($324,086), contr fee ($95,810)
**Total Member Encounters:** Phys (1,300,593), non-phys (134,232)
**Group Affiliation:** HealthPartners Inc
**Licensed in:** MN
**Address:** 8170 33RD AVENUE SOUTH POBOX 1, MINNEAPOLIS, MN 55440-1309
**Phone:** (952) 883-6000 **Dom State:** MN **Commenced Bus:** August 1957

| Data Date | Rating | RACR #1 | RACR #2 | Total Assets ($mil) | Capital ($mil) | Net Premium ($mil) | Net Income ($mil) |
|---|---|---|---|---|---|---|---|
| 9-17 | A- | 2.80 | 2.33 | 902.1 | 165.3 | 1,036.3 | 0.7 |
| 9-16 | A+ | 4.17 | 3.48 | 786.5 | 183.7 | 937.5 | -1.4 |
| 2016 | A- | 2.84 | 2.37 | 822.2 | 168.2 | 1,262.9 | -13.9 |
| 2015 | A+ | 4.68 | 3.90 | 882.2 | 206.8 | 1,130.3 | 12.1 |
| 2014 | A+ | 4.75 | 3.96 | 844.0 | 188.4 | 1,088.6 | 41.7 |
| 2013 | A- | 4.37 | 3.65 | 764.3 | 158.8 | 1,040.2 | 43.0 |
| 2012 | C- | 3.10 | 2.58 | 606.1 | 98.8 | 968.4 | 20.3 |

Rating Indexes

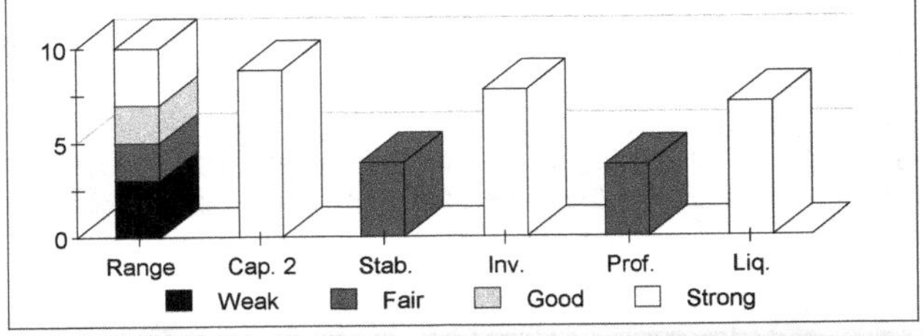


## GROUP HOSP & MEDICAL SERVICES INC B- Good

**Major Rating Factors:** Fair profitability index (4.2 on a scale of 0 to 10). Good quality investment portfolio (5.2). Good liquidity (6.8) with sufficient resources (cash flows and marketable investments) to handle a spike in claims.
**Other Rating Factors:** Strong capitalization (10.0) based on excellent current risk-adjusted capital (severe loss scenario).
**Principal Business:** FEHB (60%), comp med (37%), dental (2%)
**Mem Phys: 16:** 48,475 **15:** 46,712 **16 MLR** 88.5% **/ 16 Admin Exp** N/A
**Enroll(000): Q3 17:** 681 **16:** 722 **15:** 786 **Med Exp PMPM:** $350
**Principal Investments:** Long-term bonds (42%), nonaffiliate common stock (11%), cash and equiv (1%), other (46%)
**Provider Compensation ($000):** Contr fee ($3,000,248), FFS ($82,506), capitation ($6,499)
**Total Member Encounters:** Phys (8,915,925), non-phys (5,547,549)
**Group Affiliation:** CareFirst Inc
**Licensed in:** DC, MD, VA
**Address:** 840 FIRST St NE, WASHINGTON, DC 20065
**Phone:** (410) 581-3000 **Dom State:** DC **Commenced Bus:** March 1934

| Data Date | Rating | RACR #1 | RACR #2 | Total Assets ($mil) | Capital ($mil) | Net Premium ($mil) | Net Income ($mil) |
|---|---|---|---|---|---|---|---|
| 9-17 | B- | 5.16 | 4.30 | 2,297.6 | 1,016.8 | 2,522.9 | 40.5 |
| 9-16 | B- | 4.99 | 4.16 | 2,367.9 | 947.0 | 2,628.5 | -30.0 |
| 2016 | B- | 4.89 | 4.07 | 2,284.1 | 963.2 | 3,502.0 | -9.5 |
| 2015 | B- | 5.06 | 4.22 | 2,292.7 | 960.2 | 3,465.3 | 35.0 |
| 2014 | B- | 5.02 | 4.18 | 2,209.6 | 934.4 | 3,347.3 | -15.7 |
| 2013 | B | 5.36 | 4.47 | 2,216.0 | 934.8 | 3,161.9 | 9.0 |
| 2012 | A- | 5.34 | 4.45 | 2,251.3 | 941.1 | 3,165.9 | -7.5 |

Rating Indexes

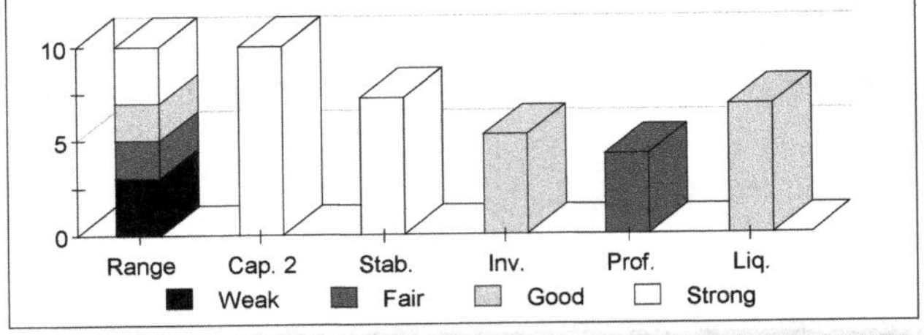


## GUARANTEE TRUST LIFE INSURANCE COMPANY B Good

**Major Rating Factors:** Good quality investment portfolio (6.5 on a scale of 0 to 10) despite mixed results such as: minimal exposure to mortgages and substantial holdings of BBB bonds but small junk bond holdings. Good overall results on stability tests (6.2). Stability strengths include excellent operational trends, good risk adjusted capital for prior years and excellent risk diversification. Strong capitalization (7.3) based on excellent risk adjusted capital (severe loss scenario).
**Other Rating Factors:** Excellent profitability (8.2). Excellent liquidity (7.3).
**Principal Business:** Individual health insurance (75%), group health insurance (16%), individual life insurance (7%), and reinsurance (1%).
**Principal Investments:** NonCMO investment grade bonds (54%), CMOs and structured securities (31%), mortgages in good standing (8%), noninv. grade bonds (3%), and misc. investments (4%).
**Investments in Affiliates:** 2%
**Group Affiliation:** Guarantee Trust
**Licensed in:** All states except NY
**Commenced Business:** June 1936
**Address:** 1275 Milwaukee Avenue, Glenview, IL 60025
**Phone:** (847) 699-0600 **Domicile State:** IL **NAIC Code:** 64211

| Data Date | Rating | RACR #1 | RACR #2 | Total Assets ($mil) | Capital ($mil) | Net Premium ($mil) | Net Income ($mil) |
|---|---|---|---|---|---|---|---|
| 9-17 | B | 1.83 | 1.20 | 592.0 | 79.6 | 166.8 | 7.3 |
| 9-16 | B | 1.74 | 1.16 | 545.4 | 72.8 | 170.5 | 4.1 |
| 2016 | B | 1.85 | 1.23 | 550.7 | 77.0 | 219.2 | 9.1 |
| 2015 | B | 1.75 | 1.18 | 495.8 | 70.0 | 221.4 | 8.7 |
| 2014 | B | 1.67 | 1.15 | 433.3 | 62.3 | 210.7 | 9.7 |
| 2013 | B | 1.49 | 1.03 | 366.1 | 54.3 | 196.4 | 7.1 |
| 2012 | B | 1.36 | 0.97 | 325.0 | 44.2 | 182.9 | 3.3 |

**Adverse Trends in Operations**

Increase in policy surrenders from 2015 to 2016 (46%)
Increase in policy surrenders from 2012 to 2013 (127%)

## GUARDIAN LIFE INSURANCE COMPANY OF AMERICA * A Excellent

**Major Rating Factors:** Good quality investment portfolio (6.7 on a scale of 0 to 10) despite mixed results such as: large holdings of BBB rated bonds but moderate junk bond exposure. Good liquidity (5.8) with sufficient resources to handle a spike in claims as well as a significant increase in policy surrenders. Strong capitalization (8.3) based on excellent risk adjusted capital (severe loss scenario).
**Other Rating Factors:** Excellent profitability (7.6). Excellent overall results on stability tests (7.5) excellent operational trends and excellent risk diversification.
**Principal Business:** Individual life insurance (49%), group health insurance (36%), group life insurance (7%), reinsurance (6%), and individual health insurance (2%).
**Principal Investments:** NonCMO investment grade bonds (64%), CMOs and structured securities (8%), policy loans (7%), mortgages in good standing (7%), and misc. investments (13%).
**Investments in Affiliates:** 4%
**Group Affiliation:** Guardian Group
**Licensed in:** All states except PR
**Commenced Business:** July 1860
**Address:** 7 HANOVER SQUARE, NEW YORK, NY 10004-4025
**Phone:** (212) 598-8000 **Domicile State:** NY **NAIC Code:** 64246

| Data Date | Rating | RACR #1 | RACR #2 | Total Assets ($mil) | Capital ($mil) | Net Premium ($mil) | Net Income ($mil) |
|---|---|---|---|---|---|---|---|
| 9-17 | A | 2.87 | 1.84 | 55,226.5 | 6,864.6 | 6,027.9 | 269.8 |
| 9-16 | A | 2.49 | 1.60 | 51,194.9 | 6,259.5 | 5,731.1 | 303.4 |
| 2016 | A | 2.77 | 1.79 | 51,883.7 | 6,172.5 | 7,772.7 | 367.7 |
| 2015 | A | 2.55 | 1.66 | 48,120.9 | 6,089.7 | 7,337.7 | 433.1 |
| 2014 | A | 2.76 | 1.80 | 45,297.4 | 5,691.6 | 7,000.0 | 711.8 |
| 2013 | A | 2.64 | 1.73 | 42,066.0 | 5,011.9 | 6,705.6 | 285.5 |
| 2012 | A | 2.59 | 1.70 | 37,530.7 | 4,752.0 | 6,011.2 | 253.3 |

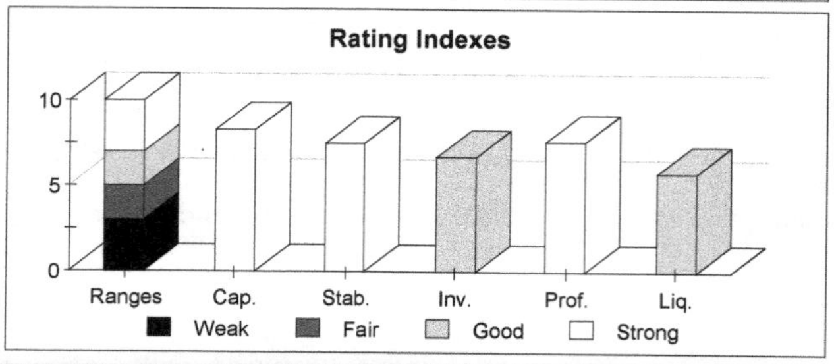


## GUNDERSEN HEALTH PLAN INC C- Fair

**Major Rating Factors:** Weak profitability index (1.1 on a scale of 0 to 10). Good overall results on stability tests (5.3). Strong capitalization index (7.0) based on excellent current risk-adjusted capital (severe loss scenario).
**Other Rating Factors:** High quality investment portfolio (9.9). Excellent liquidity (6.9) with sufficient resources (cash flows and marketable investments) to handle a spike in claims.
**Principal Business:** Medicare (45%), comp med (45%), Medicaid (10%)
**Mem Phys: 16:** 2,301 **15:** 2,160 **16 MLR** 91.8% **/ 16 Admin Exp** N/A
**Enroll(000): Q3 17:** 48 **16:** 57 **15:** 58 **Med Exp PMPM:** $403
**Principal Investments:** Cash and equiv (64%), long-term bonds (31%), affiliate common stock (6%)
**Provider Compensation ($000):** Capitation ($239,709), contr fee ($37,817)
**Total Member Encounters:** Phys (243,559), non-phys (163,582)
**Group Affiliation:** University Health Care Inc
**Licensed in:** IA, WI
**Address:** 1836 South Avenue, La Crosse, WI 54601
**Phone:** (608) 881-8279 **Dom State:** WI **Commenced Bus:** September 1995

| Data Date | Rating | RACR #1 | RACR #2 | Total Assets ($mil) | Capital ($mil) | Net Premium ($mil) | Net Income ($mil) |
|---|---|---|---|---|---|---|---|
| 9-17 | C- | 1.38 | 1.15 | 53.9 | 23.3 | 206.1 | 0.3 |
| 9-16 | C | 1.51 | 1.26 | 57.8 | 28.0 | 228.0 | 0.3 |
| 2016 | C- | 1.20 | 1.00 | 47.3 | 20.8 | 301.4 | -5.7 |
| 2015 | C+ | 0.65 | 0.54 | 38.8 | 16.1 | 297.4 | -5.0 |
| 2014 | B | 1.12 | 0.93 | 39.7 | 22.1 | 295.5 | 2.3 |
| 2013 | B | 1.23 | 1.03 | 35.2 | 19.8 | 283.9 | 1.5 |
| 2012 | B | 1.02 | 0.85 | 28.0 | 18.5 | 280.4 | 1.7 |

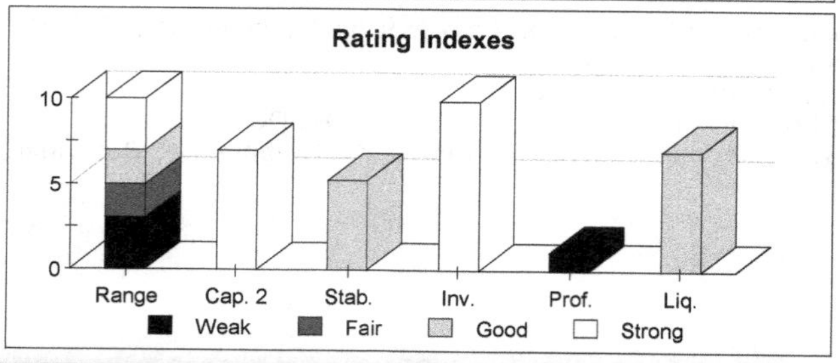


## GUNDERSEN HLTH PLAN MN INC C Fair

**Major Rating Factors:** Weak profitability index (1.8 on a scale of 0 to 10). Good capitalization (6.8) based on excellent current risk-adjusted capital (severe loss scenario). High quality investment portfolio (9.9).
**Other Rating Factors:** Excellent liquidity (7.5) with ample operational cash flow and liquid investments.
**Principal Business:** Medicare (75%), comp med (25%)
**Mem Phys: 16:** 682 **15:** 845 **16 MLR** 90.0% **/ 16 Admin Exp** N/A
**Enroll(000): Q3 17:** 1 **16:** 1 **15:** 1 **Med Exp PMPM:** $472
**Principal Investments:** Cash and equiv (100%)
**Provider Compensation ($000):** Capitation ($5,681), contr fee ($267)
**Total Member Encounters:** Phys (5,198), non-phys (3,175)
**Group Affiliation:** University Health Care Inc
**Licensed in:** MN
**Address:** 1900 S Ave, La Crosse, WI 54601
**Phone:** (800) 370-9718 **Dom State:** MN **Commenced Bus:** February 2012

| Data Date | Rating | RACR #1 | RACR #2 | Total Assets ($mil) | Capital ($mil) | Net Premium ($mil) | Net Income ($mil) |
|---|---|---|---|---|---|---|---|
| 9-17 | C | 1.23 | 1.02 | 3.0 | 2.1 | 5.8 | 0.0 |
| 9-16 | C | 1.21 | 1.01 | 2.6 | 2.0 | 4.8 | 0.1 |
| 2016 | C | 1.20 | 1.00 | 2.4 | 2.1 | 6.4 | 0.2 |
| 2015 | C | 1.00 | 0.83 | 2.5 | 1.9 | 5.3 | -0.7 |
| 2014 | B- | 0.78 | 0.65 | 1.7 | 1.5 | 4.1 | 0.1 |
| 2013 | B- | 0.76 | 0.63 | 1.6 | 1.5 | 2.2 | 0.0 |
| 2012 | U | 0.74 | 0.62 | 1.6 | 1.5 | 0.0 | 0.0 |

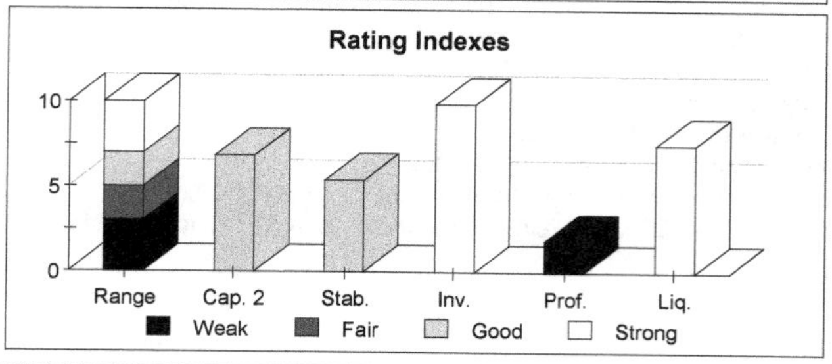

## HAP MIDWEST HEALTH PLAN INC C Fair

**Major Rating Factors:** Weak overall results on stability tests (0.6 on a scale of 0 to 10) based on a steep decline in capital during 2016, a significant 91% decrease in enrollment during the period. Potentially strong support from affiliation with Henry Ford Health System. Excellent overall profitability index (7.0). Strong capitalization index (8.8) based on excellent current risk-adjusted capital (severe loss scenario).
**Other Rating Factors:** High quality investment portfolio (9.9). Excellent liquidity (7.2) with ample operational cash flow and liquid investments.
**Principal Business:** Medicare (70%), Medicaid (30%)
**Mem Phys: 16:** 2,443 **15:** 1,808 **16 MLR** 84.9% **/ 16 Admin Exp** N/A
**Enroll(000): Q3 17:** 8 **16:** 8 **15:** 94 **Med Exp PMPM:** $1,075
**Principal Investments:** Cash and equiv (99%), long-term bonds (1%)
**Provider Compensation ($000):** Contr fee ($109,875), FFS ($19,502), capitation ($16,605), bonus arrang ($218), other ($6,267)
**Total Member Encounters:** Phys (142,200), non-phys (119,487)
**Group Affiliation:** Henry Ford Health System
**Licensed in:** MI
**Address:** 2850 West Grand Blvd, Detroit, MI 48202
**Phone:** (888) 654-2200 **Dom State:** MI **Commenced Bus:** January 1994

| Data Date | Rating | RACR #1 | RACR #2 | Total Assets ($mil) | Capital ($mil) | Net Premium ($mil) | Net Income ($mil) |
|---|---|---|---|---|---|---|---|
| 9-17 | C | 2.79 | 2.32 | 62.4 | 24.8 | 86.5 | -0.5 |
| 9-16 | B- | 1.65 | 1.38 | 94.6 | 48.8 | 91.0 | 22.8 |
| 2016 | C | 2.73 | 2.28 | 85.4 | 24.3 | 122.4 | 23.0 |
| 2015 | B | 1.91 | 1.59 | 180.6 | 57.4 | 501.9 | 27.5 |
| 2014 | B- | 1.70 | 1.42 | 101.4 | 39.8 | 381.7 | 19.1 |
| 2013 | B- | 1.62 | 1.35 | 82.1 | 31.4 | 294.6 | 9.4 |
| 2012 | B- | 1.49 | 1.24 | 66.7 | 26.8 | 274.5 | 7.1 |

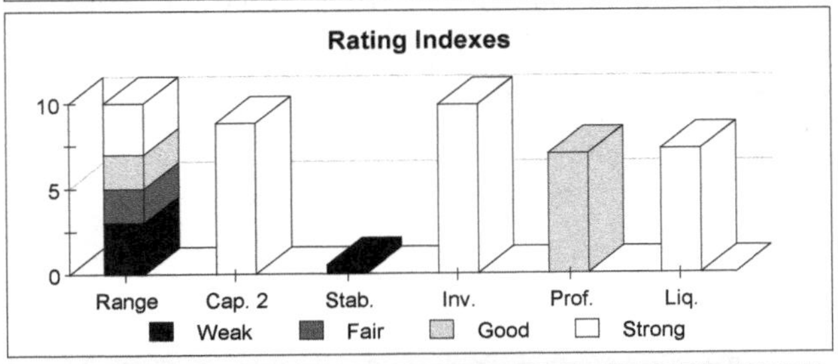


## HARBOR HEALTH PLAN INC E Very Weak

**Major Rating Factors:** Fair overall results on stability tests (3.8 on a scale of 0 to 10) based on a steep decline in capital during 2016, an excessive 53% enrollment growth during the period. Good overall profitability index (6.1). Strong capitalization index (7.1) based on excellent current risk-adjusted capital (severe loss scenario).
**Other Rating Factors:** High quality investment portfolio (9.9). Excellent liquidity (7.6) with ample operational cash flow and liquid investments.
**Principal Business:** Medicaid (78%), comp med (11%), Medicare (11%)
**Mem Phys: 16:** 2,937 **15:** 2,937 **16 MLR** 76.8% **/ 16 Admin Exp** N/A
**Enroll(000): Q3 17:** 9 **16:** 10 **15:** 7 **Med Exp PMPM:** $296
**Principal Investments:** Cash and equiv (100%)
**Provider Compensation ($000):** Contr fee ($16,957), capitation ($15,086), FFS ($5,774)
**Total Member Encounters:** Phys (51,991), non-phys (133,501)
**Group Affiliation:** Trusted Health Plans Inc
**Licensed in:** MI
**Address:** 3663 Woodward Suite 120, Detroit, MI 48201
**Phone:** (800) 543-0161 **Dom State:** MI **Commenced Bus:** December 2000

| Data Date | Rating | RACR #1 | RACR #2 | Total Assets ($mil) | Capital ($mil) | Net Premium ($mil) | Net Income ($mil) |
|---|---|---|---|---|---|---|---|
| 9-17 | E | 1.42 | 1.19 | 17.1 | 7.0 | 35.7 | 0.0 |
| 9-16 | E | 4.75 | 3.96 | 27.9 | 13.7 | 39.0 | 2.0 |
| 2016 | E | 1.70 | 1.42 | 31.0 | 7.9 | 51.8 | 2.5 |
| 2015 | E- | 3.56 | 2.97 | 17.8 | 10.0 | 36.6 | 4.3 |
| 2014 | E- | 2.22 | 1.85 | 14.5 | 7.0 | 21.9 | 0.4 |
| 2013 | E- | 3.55 | 2.96 | 6.5 | 4.8 | 8.9 | -0.3 |
| 2012 | C+ | 1.75 | 1.46 | 3.4 | 1.7 | 8.0 | -0.1 |

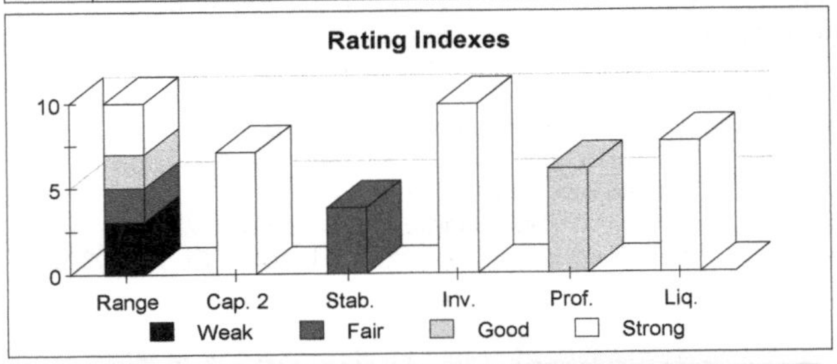


## HARKEN HEALTH INS CO C Fair

**Major Rating Factors:** Weak profitability index (0.6 on a scale of 0 to 10). Weak liquidity (0.0) as a spike in claims may stretch capacity. Strong capitalization (8.6) based on excellent current risk-adjusted capital (severe loss scenario).
**Other Rating Factors:** High quality investment portfolio (9.9).
**Principal Business:** Comp med (100%)
**Mem Phys: 16:** 64,031 **15:** N/A **16 MLR** 173.5% **/ 16 Admin Exp** N/A
**Enroll(000): Q3 17:** 3 **16:** 35 **15:** N/A **Med Exp PMPM:** $656
**Principal Investments:** Cash and equiv (98%), long-term bonds (2%)
**Provider Compensation ($000):** Contr fee ($178,836), capitation ($18,049), FFS ($6,285), bonus arrang ($34)
**Total Member Encounters:** Phys (156,881), non-phys (123,971)
**Group Affiliation:** UnitedHealth Group Incorporated
**Licensed in:** FL, GA, IL, IN, IA, MI, NE, OH, TX, WI
**Address:** 2700 MIDWEST Dr, ONALASKA, WI 54650-8764
**Phone:** (608) 783-7130 **Dom State:** WI **Commenced Bus:** March 1973

| Data Date | Rating | RACR #1 | RACR #2 | Total Assets ($mil) | Capital ($mil) | Net Premium ($mil) | Net Income ($mil) |
|---|---|---|---|---|---|---|---|
| 9-17 | C | 2.67 | 2.22 | 62.9 | 54.1 | 13.6 | 12.9 |
| 9-16 | N/A | N/A | N/A | 138.9 | 25.9 | 110.7 | -78.3 |
| 2016 | C | 2.01 | 1.68 | 112.5 | 40.7 | 147.2 | -63.7 |
| 2015 | N/A | N/A | N/A | 58.1 | 10.3 | N/A | N/A |
| 2014 | N/A | N/A | N/A | 7.6 | 6.7 | N/A | N/A |
| 2013 | N/A | N/A | N/A | 7.2 | 6.2 | N/A | N/A |
| 2012 | N/A | N/A | N/A | 22.2 | 20.8 | N/A | N/A |

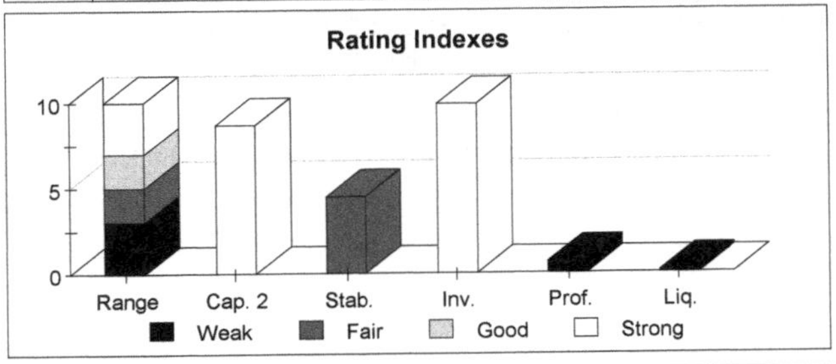

## HARMONY HEALTH PLAN INC C Fair

**Major Rating Factors:** Fair overall results on stability tests (4.2 on a scale of 0 to 10). Fair financial strength from affiliates. Excellent profitability (7.8). Strong capitalization index (9.3) based on excellent current risk-adjusted capital (severe loss scenario).
**Other Rating Factors:** High quality investment portfolio (9.9). Excellent liquidity (7.1) with ample operational cash flow and liquid investments.
**Principal Business:** Medicare (63%), Medicaid (35%), other (3%)
**Mem Phys: 16:** 68,800 **15:** 58,800 **16 MLR** 81.7% **/ 16 Admin Exp** N/A
**Enroll(000): Q3 17:** 217 **16:** 264 **15:** 249 **Med Exp PMPM:** $279
**Principal Investments:** Cash and equiv (95%), long-term bonds (5%)
**Provider Compensation ($000):** Contr fee ($730,950), capitation ($127,047)
**Total Member Encounters:** Phys (1,121,668), non-phys (487,707)
**Group Affiliation:** WellCare Health Plans Inc
**Licensed in:** AL, AR, IL, IN, MS, MO, MT, OK, SC, TN, VA
**Address:** 29 North Wacker Drive Suite 30, Chicago, IL 60606
**Phone:** (813) 290-6200 **Dom State:** IL **Commenced Bus:** July 1996

| Data Date | Rating | RACR #1 | RACR #2 | Total Assets ($mil) | Capital ($mil) | Net Premium ($mil) | Net Income ($mil) |
|---|---|---|---|---|---|---|---|
| 9-17 | C | 3.20 | 2.67 | 514.9 | 158.6 | 918.5 | 4.1 |
| 9-16 | C | 3.08 | 2.57 | 463.9 | 144.0 | 800.3 | 7.5 |
| 2016 | C | 3.07 | 2.56 | 384.3 | 151.7 | 1,069.7 | 16.6 |
| 2015 | C | 3.78 | 3.15 | 334.1 | 180.9 | 968.2 | 30.4 |
| 2014 | B- | 3.54 | 2.95 | 340.9 | 192.2 | 877.3 | 9.3 |
| 2013 | B | 3.13 | 2.61 | 97.3 | 43.2 | 368.1 | 6.6 |
| 2012 | B+ | 4.09 | 3.41 | 98.9 | 49.5 | 323.1 | 14.0 |

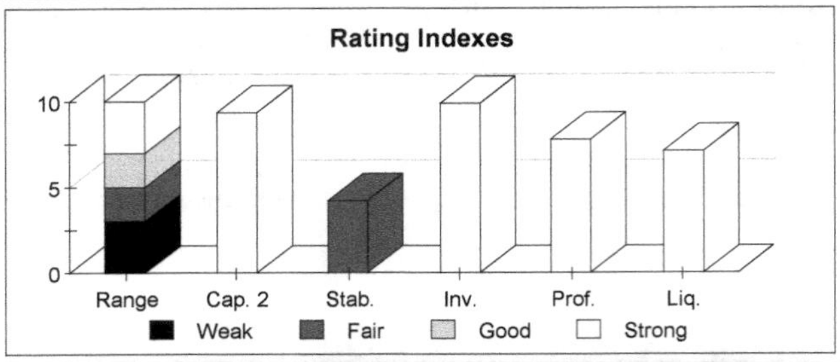


## HARTFORD LIFE & ACCIDENT INSURANCE COMPANY B- Good

**Major Rating Factors:** Good overall results on stability tests (5.3 on a scale of 0 to 10) despite fair financial strength of affiliated Hartford Financial Services Inc and negative cash flow from operations for 2016. Other stability subfactors include good operational trends and excellent risk diversification. Good quality investment portfolio (6.6) despite significant exposure to mortgages . Mortgage default rate has been low. large holdings of BBB rated bonds in addition to small junk bond holdings. Good overall profitability (5.2).
**Other Rating Factors:** Good liquidity (6.9). Strong capitalization (9.3) based on excellent risk adjusted capital (severe loss scenario).
**Principal Business:** Group health insurance (54%), group life insurance (40%), reinsurance (5%), and individual life insurance (1%).
**Principal Investments:** NonCMO investment grade bonds (67%), CMOs and structured securities (15%), mortgages in good standing (11%), noninv. grade bonds (3%), and common & preferred stock (1%).
**Investments in Affiliates:** None
**Group Affiliation:** Hartford Financial Services Inc
**Licensed in:** All states, the District of Columbia and Puerto Rico
**Commenced Business:** February 1967
**Address:** One Hartford Plaza, Hartford, CT 06155-0001
**Phone:** (860) 547-5000 **Domicile State:** CT **NAIC Code:** 70815

| Data Date | Rating | RACR #1 | RACR #2 | Total Assets ($mil) | Capital ($mil) | Net Premium ($mil) | Net Income ($mil) |
|---|---|---|---|---|---|---|---|
| 9-17 | B- | 4.00 | 2.53 | 9,168.5 | 1,624.3 | 1,790.6 | 185.3 |
| 9-16 | C+ | 3.96 | 2.45 | 8,783.0 | 1,615.9 | 1,636.6 | 160.5 |
| 2016 | B- | 4.15 | 2.61 | 8,785.9 | 1,623.8 | 2,241.9 | 208.3 |
| 2015 | C | 3.96 | 2.47 | 8,992.2 | 1,651.4 | 2,296.5 | 168.1 |
| 2014 | C | 3.43 | 2.15 | 9,086.9 | 1,592.3 | 2,486.3 | -331.3 |
| 2013 | B- | 1.05 | 1.00 | 13,890.8 | 5,595.2 | 1,974.0 | -174.0 |
| 2012 | B- | 1.07 | 1.01 | 14,404.8 | 5,767.3 | 2,878.5 | -397.8 |

**Hartford Financial Services Inc**
**Composite Group Rating: C+**

| Largest Group Members | Assets ($mil) | Rating |
|---|---|---|
| HARTFORD LIFE INS CO | 111450 | C+ |
| HARTFORD LIFE ANNUITY INS CO | 36793 | B- |
| HARTFORD FIRE INS CO | 25541 | B |
| HARTFORD ACCIDENT INDEMNITY CO | 11605 | B |
| HARTFORD LIFE ACCIDENT INS CO | 8786 | B- |

## HARVARD PILGRIM HC OF NEW ENGLAND C Fair

**Major Rating Factors:** Fair profitability index (3.9 on a scale of 0 to 10). Fair overall results on stability tests (4.6). Good liquidity (6.1) with sufficient resources (cash flows and marketable investments) to handle a spike in claims.
**Other Rating Factors:** Strong capitalization index (8.7) based on excellent current risk-adjusted capital (severe loss scenario). High quality investment portfolio (9.2).
**Principal Business:** Comp med (96%), Medicare (4%)
**Mem Phys: 16:** 79,113 **15:** 73,621 **16 MLR** 86.0% **/ 16 Admin Exp** N/A
**Enroll(000): Q3 17:** 95 **16:** 94 **15:** 73 **Med Exp PMPM:** $386
**Principal Investments:** Long-term bonds (95%), cash and equiv (5%)
**Provider Compensation ($000):** Capitation ($262,223), contr fee ($94,145), bonus arrang ($61,507), FFS ($7,925)
**Total Member Encounters:** Phys (341,226), non-phys (282,277)
**Group Affiliation:** Harvard Pilgrim Health Care Inc
**Licensed in:** MA, NH
**Address:** 93 WORCESTER STREET, WELLESLEY, MA 02481-9181
**Phone:** (781) 263-6000 **Dom State:** MA **Commenced Bus:** October 1980

| Data Date | Rating | RACR #1 | RACR #2 | Total Assets ($mil) | Capital ($mil) | Net Premium ($mil) | Net Income ($mil) |
|---|---|---|---|---|---|---|---|
| 9-17 | C | 2.74 | 2.29 | 142.9 | 63.0 | 421.6 | 6.0 |
| 9-16 | C | 2.68 | 2.23 | 140.9 | 63.8 | 359.4 | -3.8 |
| 2016 | C | 2.59 | 2.15 | 151.3 | 60.1 | 482.2 | -7.7 |
| 2015 | B | 2.94 | 2.45 | 127.9 | 68.0 | 374.6 | 18.4 |
| 2014 | B+ | 3.43 | 2.86 | 103.1 | 59.1 | 284.1 | 6.9 |
| 2013 | B | 4.12 | 3.43 | 84.8 | 59.4 | 230.8 | 13.3 |
| 2012 | B | 3.97 | 3.31 | 72.9 | 50.1 | 195.0 | 7.3 |

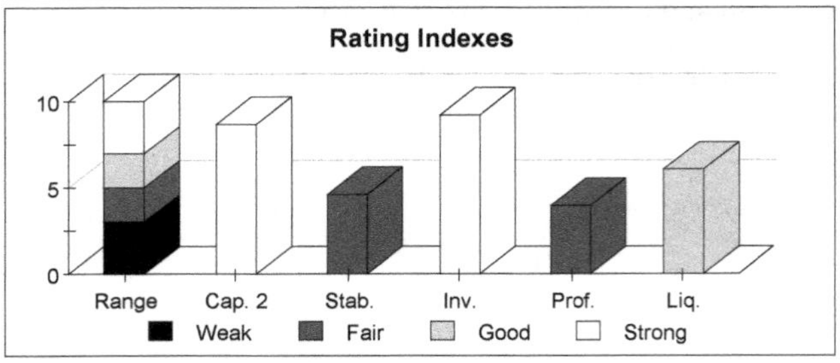

## HARVARD PILGRIM HEALTH CARE INC C+ Fair

**Major Rating Factors:** Fair quality investment portfolio (4.4 on a scale of 0 to 10). Good overall results on stability tests (5.3) despite a decline in enrollment during 2016. Good liquidity (6.8) with sufficient resources (cash flows and marketable investments) to handle a spike in claims.
**Other Rating Factors:** Weak profitability index (2.1). Strong capitalization index (8.4) based on excellent current risk-adjusted capital (severe loss scenario).
**Principal Business:** Comp med (99%), Medicare (1%)
**Mem Phys: 16:** 79,113 **15:** 73,621 **16 MLR** 88.9% **/ 16 Admin Exp** N/A
**Enroll(000): Q3 17:** 252 **16:** 287 **15:** 304 **Med Exp PMPM:** $436
**Principal Investments:** Long-term bonds (36%), affiliate common stock (23%), nonaffiliate common stock (18%), cash and equiv (8%), real estate (3%), other (11%)
**Provider Compensation ($000):** Bonus arrang ($672,552), contr fee ($518,177), capitation ($334,565), FFS ($40,583), other ($13,064)
**Total Member Encounters:** Phys (1,286,210), non-phys (1,022,208)
**Group Affiliation:** Harvard Pilgrim Health Care Inc
**Licensed in:** ME, MA
**Address:** 93 WORCESTER STREET, WELLESLEY, MA 02481-9181
**Phone:** (781) 263-6000 **Dom State:** MA **Commenced Bus:** February 1969

| Data Date | Rating | RACR #1 | RACR #2 | Total Assets ($mil) | Capital ($mil) | Net Premium ($mil) | Net Income ($mil) |
|---|---|---|---|---|---|---|---|
| 9-17 | C+ | 2.44 | 2.03 | 923.5 | 478.7 | 1,243.1 | -15.1 |
| 9-16 | C+ | 2.10 | 1.75 | 851.2 | 405.7 | 1,365.3 | 1.6 |
| 2016 | C+ | 2.30 | 1.92 | 916.8 | 456.8 | 1,782.3 | 18.5 |
| 2015 | B- | 2.41 | 2.01 | 930.6 | 458.1 | 1,684.1 | -35.2 |
| 2014 | B+ | 3.36 | 2.80 | 921.6 | 548.7 | 1,645.1 | 14.3 |
| 2013 | B+ | 3.08 | 2.56 | 853.5 | 496.6 | 1,786.0 | 11.5 |
| 2012 | A | 3.03 | 2.52 | 882.6 | 481.1 | 1,923.0 | 16.4 |

Rating Indexes

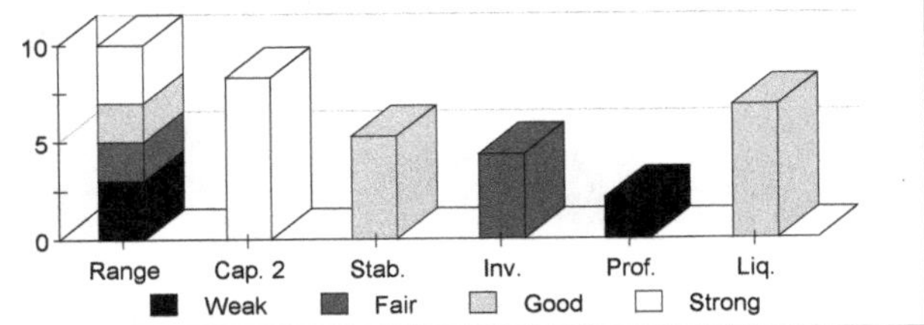


## HARVARD PILGRIM HEALTH CARE OF CT D+ Weak

**Major Rating Factors:** Weak profitability index (0.5 on a scale of 0 to 10). Good liquidity (6.9) with sufficient resources (cash flows and marketable investments) to handle a spike in claims. Strong capitalization (10.0) based on excellent current risk-adjusted capital (severe loss scenario).
**Other Rating Factors:** High quality investment portfolio (9.1).
**Principal Business:** Comp med (100%)
**Mem Phys: 16:** 79,113 **15:** 73,621 **16 MLR** 88.6% **/ 16 Admin Exp** N/A
**Enroll(000): Q3 17:** 0 **16:** 1 **15:** 1 **Med Exp PMPM:** $403
**Principal Investments:** Long-term bonds (96%), cash and equiv (4%)
**Provider Compensation ($000):** Contr fee ($3,343), capitation ($141), FFS ($61), other ($43)
**Total Member Encounters:** Phys (2,493), non-phys (1,497)
**Group Affiliation:** Harvard Pilgrim Health Care Inc
**Licensed in:** CT
**Address:** CITYPLACE II 185 ASYLUM St, HARTFORD, CT 06103
**Phone:** (781) 263-6000 **Dom State:** CT **Commenced Bus:** July 2014

| Data Date | Rating | RACR #1 | RACR #2 | Total Assets ($mil) | Capital ($mil) | Net Premium ($mil) | Net Income ($mil) |
|---|---|---|---|---|---|---|---|
| 9-17 | D+ | 9.33 | 7.77 | 14.9 | 14.5 | 2.1 | -0.4 |
| 9-16 | C- | 8.06 | 6.72 | 15.6 | 13.1 | 2.0 | -2.2 |
| 2016 | C- | 9.45 | 7.87 | 15.4 | 14.8 | 4.0 | -0.5 |
| 2015 | C | 9.72 | 8.10 | 16.6 | 15.4 | 1.4 | -1.6 |
| 2014 | U | 7.89 | 6.58 | 14.1 | 14.0 | 0.0 | -2.0 |
| 2013 | N/A | N/A | N/A | N/A | N/A | N/A | N/A |
| 2012 | N/A | N/A | N/A | N/A | N/A | N/A | N/A |

Rating Indexes

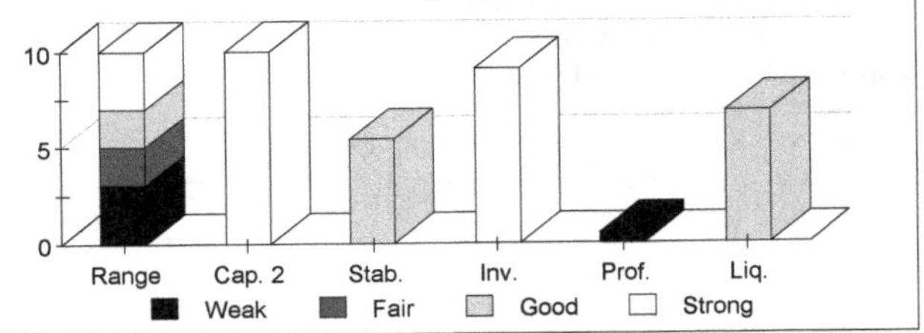


## HARVESTPLAINS HEALTH OF IOWA C- Fair

**Major Rating Factors:** Fair profitability index (3.2 on a scale of 0 to 10). Good liquidity (6.9) with sufficient resources (cash flows and marketable investments) to handle a spike in claims. Strong capitalization (10.0) based on excellent current risk-adjusted capital (severe loss scenario).
**Other Rating Factors:** High quality investment portfolio (9.9).
**Principal Business:** Medicare (100%)
**Mem Phys: 16:** 1,449 **15:** N/A **16 MLR** 85.8% **/ 16 Admin Exp** N/A
**Enroll(000): Q2 17:** N/A **16:** 0 **15:** N/A **Med Exp PMPM:** $502
**Principal Investments:** Long-term bonds (89%), cash and equiv (11%)
**Provider Compensation ($000):** Contr fee ($2,003), capitation ($51), other ($225)
**Total Member Encounters:** Phys (3,851), non-phys (2,461)
**Group Affiliation:** Catholic Health Initiatives
**Licensed in:** IA
**Address:** PO Box 8250, Des Moines, IA 50301
**Phone:** (866) 789-7747 **Dom State:** IA **Commenced Bus:** April 2015

| Data Date | Rating | RACR #1 | RACR #2 | Total Assets ($mil) | Capital ($mil) | Net Premium ($mil) | Net Income ($mil) |
|---|---|---|---|---|---|---|---|
| 6-17 | C- | 6.40 | 5.33 | 3.2 | 3.0 | 0.0 | 0.0 |
| 6-16 | N/A | N/A | N/A | 3.4 | 2.7 | 1.3 | -0.3 |
| 2016 | C- | 6.32 | 5.27 | 3.4 | 3.0 | 2.7 | 0.0 |
| 2015 | N/A | N/A | N/A | 3.0 | 3.0 | N/A | N/A |
| 2014 | N/A | N/A | N/A | N/A | N/A | N/A | N/A |
| 2013 | N/A | N/A | N/A | N/A | N/A | N/A | N/A |
| 2012 | N/A | N/A | N/A | N/A | N/A | N/A | N/A |

Rating Indexes

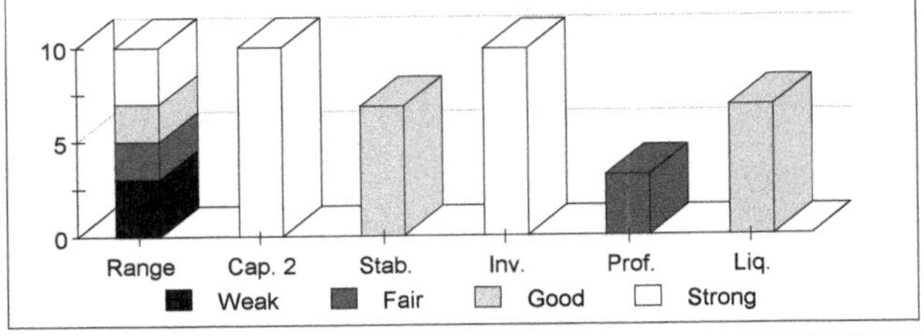

## HAWAII MANAGEMENT ALLIANCE ASSOC C- Fair

**Major Rating Factors:** Fair profitability index (3.7 on a scale of 0 to 10). Weak liquidity (2.1) as a spike in claims may stretch capacity. Good capitalization (5.2) based on good current risk-adjusted capital (severe loss scenario).
**Other Rating Factors:** High quality investment portfolio (8.7).
**Principal Business:** Comp med (82%), dental (2%), other (16%)
**Mem Phys: 16:** 8,484 **15:** N/A **16 MLR** 113.0% **/ 16 Admin Exp** N/A
**Enroll(000): Q3 17:** 44 **16:** 41 **15:** 42 **Med Exp PMPM:** $301
**Principal Investments:** Long-term bonds (54%), cash and equiv (41%), nonaffiliate common stock (5%)
**Provider Compensation ($000):** Contr fee ($143,020), FFS ($4,423)
**Total Member Encounters:** N/A
**Group Affiliation:** Hawaii Management Alliance Assoc
**Licensed in:** HI
**Address:** 733 Bishop St Ste 1560, Honolulu, HI 96813
**Phone:** (808) 791-7550 **Dom State:** HI **Commenced Bus:** October 1990

| Data Date | Rating | RACR #1 | RACR #2 | Total Assets ($mil) | Capital ($mil) | Net Premium ($mil) | Net Income ($mil) |
|---|---|---|---|---|---|---|---|
| 9-17 | C- | 0.96 | 0.80 | 43.3 | 16.8 | 112.1 | 1.6 |
| 9-16 | C- | 0.88 | 0.73 | 37.2 | 14.7 | 98.5 | 0.7 |
| 2016 | C- | 0.84 | 0.70 | 34.8 | 15.0 | 131.2 | 1.0 |
| 2015 | C- | 0.79 | 0.66 | 38.2 | 13.7 | 126.1 | 0.2 |
| 2014 | C- | 0.79 | 0.66 | 33.0 | 11.6 | 90.8 | -4.4 |
| 2013 | C | 1.21 | 1.01 | 34.9 | 12.9 | 79.0 | 0.5 |
| 2012 | C | 1.45 | 1.21 | 29.1 | 11.4 | 58.8 | 0.0 |

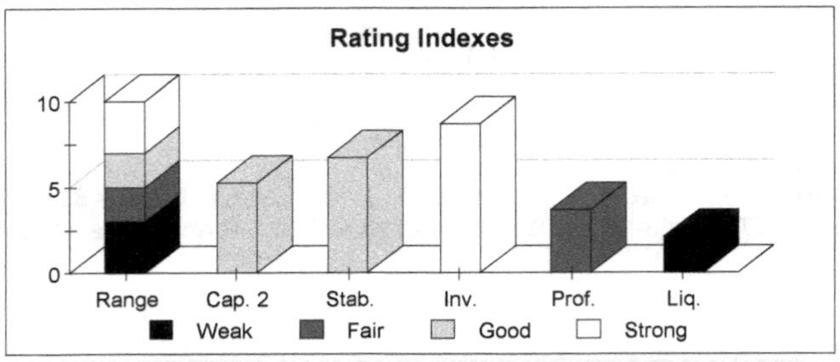


## HAWAII MEDICAL SERVICE ASSOCIATION B- Good

**Major Rating Factors:** Fair profitability index (4.0 on a scale of 0 to 10). Good liquidity (6.8) with sufficient resources (cash flows and marketable investments) to handle a spike in claims. Strong capitalization (8.0) based on excellent current risk-adjusted capital (severe loss scenario).
**Other Rating Factors:** High quality investment portfolio (8.7).
**Principal Business:** Comp med (56%), Medicaid (20%), Medicare (13%), FEHB (11%)
**Mem Phys: 16:** 7,705 **15:** 7,490 **16 MLR** 89.5% **/ 16 Admin Exp** N/A
**Enroll(000): Q3 17:** 723 **16:** 725 **15:** 718 **Med Exp PMPM:** $325
**Principal Investments:** Cash and equiv (27%), nonaffiliate common stock (27%), long-term bonds (25%), real estate (14%), affiliate common stock (3%), other (4%)
**Provider Compensation ($000):** Contr fee ($2,212,514), bonus arrang ($377,180), salary ($77,194), capitation ($71,007)
**Total Member Encounters:** Phys (5,169,832)
**Group Affiliation:** Hawaii Medical Service Association
**Licensed in:** HI
**Address:** 818 Keeaumoku St, Honolulu, HI 96814
**Phone:** (808) 948-5145 **Dom State:** HI **Commenced Bus:** June 1938

| Data Date | Rating | RACR #1 | RACR #2 | Total Assets ($mil) | Capital ($mil) | Net Premium ($mil) | Net Income ($mil) |
|---|---|---|---|---|---|---|---|
| 9-17 | B- | 2.15 | 1.79 | 1,155.2 | 462.1 | 2,504.0 | 45.8 |
| 9-16 | C | 1.68 | 1.40 | 967.2 | 372.6 | 2,364.5 | -0.2 |
| 2016 | C+ | 1.92 | 1.60 | 1,004.0 | 417.6 | 3,158.0 | 28.5 |
| 2015 | C | 1.70 | 1.42 | 972.6 | 371.9 | 2,978.7 | 7.6 |
| 2014 | C | 1.81 | 1.50 | 932.8 | 393.4 | 2,873.0 | 4.2 |
| 2013 | C | 1.87 | 1.56 | 945.2 | 391.5 | 2,640.0 | -44.4 |
| 2012 | C | 2.32 | 1.93 | 864.4 | 452.2 | 2,481.8 | 36.0 |

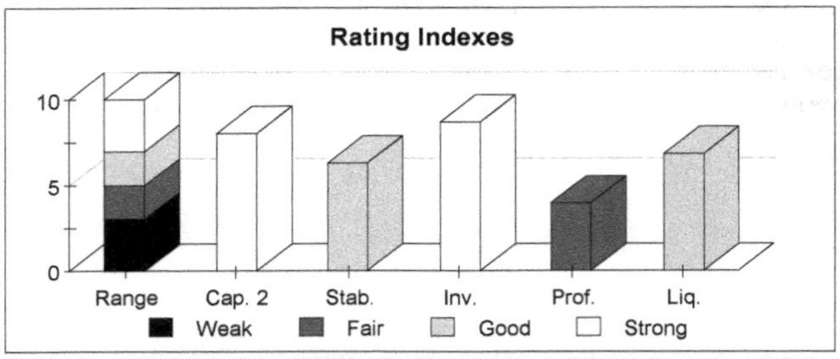


## HCC LIFE INSURANCE COMPANY B Good

**Major Rating Factors:** Good overall results on stability tests (6.0 on a scale of 0 to 10). Stability strengths include excellent operational trends and excellent risk diversification. Good liquidity (6.9) with sufficient resources to handle a spike in claims. Strong capitalization (10.0) based on excellent risk adjusted capital (severe loss scenario).
**Other Rating Factors:** High quality investment portfolio (8.3). Excellent profitability (9.2).
**Principal Business:** Group health insurance (91%) and individual health insurance (9%).
**Principal Investments:** NonCMO investment grade bonds (55%) and CMOs and structured securities (44%).
**Investments in Affiliates:** None
**Group Affiliation:** HCC Ins Holdings Inc
**Licensed in:** All states except PR
**Commenced Business:** March 1981
**Address:** 150 West Market Street Ste 800, Indianapolis, IN 46204
**Phone:** (770) 973-9851 **Domicile State:** IN **NAIC Code:** 92711

| Data Date | Rating | RACR #1 | RACR #2 | Total Assets ($mil) | Capital ($mil) | Net Premium ($mil) | Net Income ($mil) |
|---|---|---|---|---|---|---|---|
| 9-17 | B | 5.38 | 4.15 | 1,058.7 | 689.6 | 767.1 | 89.1 |
| 9-16 | B | 5.01 | 3.81 | 1,011.9 | 629.2 | 738.0 | 79.0 |
| 2016 | B | 4.81 | 3.71 | 981.6 | 601.8 | 987.7 | 104.8 |
| 2015 | B | 4.44 | 3.40 | 921.5 | 552.7 | 973.3 | 112.1 |
| 2014 | B | 4.61 | 3.60 | 923.5 | 554.3 | 956.4 | 116.1 |
| 2013 | B | 3.61 | 2.96 | 750.2 | 436.9 | 854.6 | 142.1 |
| 2012 | B | 2.72 | 2.34 | 731.2 | 413.7 | 821.0 | 100.2 |

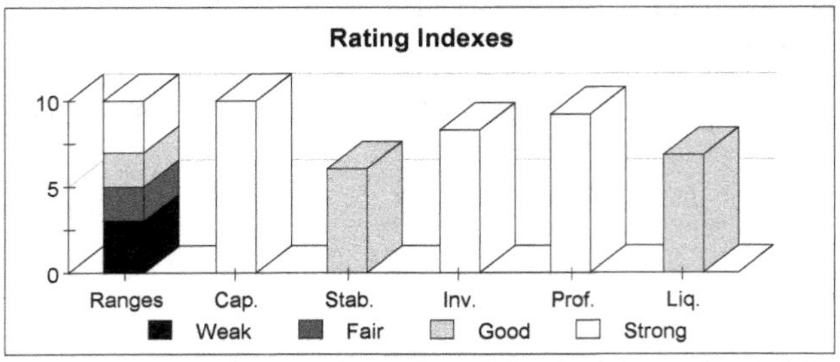

## HCSC INS SERVICES CO — D- — Weak

**Major Rating Factors:** Weak profitability index (0.9 on a scale of 0 to 10). Good liquidity (6.4) with sufficient resources (cash flows and marketable investments) to handle a spike in claims. Strong capitalization (8.4) based on excellent current risk-adjusted capital (severe loss scenario).
**Other Rating Factors:** High quality investment portfolio (9.9).
**Principal Business:** Medicaid (65%), Medicare (8%), other (27%)
**Mem Phys: 16:** 44,337 **15:** 33,769 **16 MLR** 85.0% **/ 16 Admin Exp** N/A
**Enroll(000): Q3 17:** 523 **16:** 516 **15:** 515 **Med Exp PMPM:** $192
**Principal Investments:** Long-term bonds (60%), cash and equiv (40%)
**Provider Compensation ($000):** FFS ($484,415), contr fee ($363,698), capitation ($11,603), bonus arrang ($60), other ($319,159)
**Total Member Encounters:** Phys (703,490), non-phys (1,143,321)
**Group Affiliation:** Health Care Service Corporation
**Licensed in:** All states except CT, HI, ME, NH, NJ, NY, VT, PR
**Address:** 300 East Randolph St, Chicago, IL 60601-5099
**Phone:** (312) 653-6000 **Dom State:** IL **Commenced Bus:** February 1958

| Data Date | Rating | RACR #1 | RACR #2 | Total Assets ($mil) | Capital ($mil) | Net Premium ($mil) | Net Income ($mil) |
|---|---|---|---|---|---|---|---|
| 9-17 | D- | 2.51 | 2.09 | 788.7 | 218.0 | 1,061.3 | -69.3 |
| 9-16 | D | 2.53 | 2.11 | 596.6 | 203.2 | 1,037.1 | -15.4 |
| 2016 | D | 2.19 | 1.83 | 581.5 | 189.8 | 1,391.7 | -37.3 |
| 2015 | D | 2.79 | 2.33 | 560.2 | 225.0 | 1,306.9 | -122.1 |
| 2014 | B | 3.81 | 3.18 | 464.9 | 249.7 | 1,020.7 | -45.0 |
| 2013 | B+ | 7.86 | 6.55 | 300.3 | 205.9 | 442.8 | -43.3 |
| 2012 | A- | 5.92 | 4.93 | 188.5 | 143.5 | 425.1 | 8.9 |

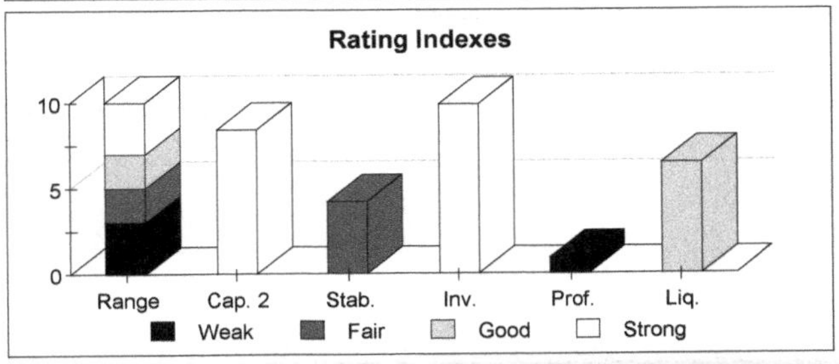


## HEALTH ALLIANCE CONNECT INC — C — Fair

**Major Rating Factors:** Weak profitability index (1.7 on a scale of 0 to 10). Good capitalization (5.4) based on good current risk-adjusted capital (severe loss scenario). High quality investment portfolio (9.8).
**Other Rating Factors:** Excellent liquidity (6.9) with sufficient resources (cash flows and marketable investments) to handle a spike in claims.
**Principal Business:** Medicaid (70%), Medicare (30%)
**Mem Phys: 16:** 35,596 **15:** N/A **16 MLR** 94.5% **/ 16 Admin Exp** N/A
**Enroll(000): Q3 17:** 20 **16:** 108 **15:** 141 **Med Exp PMPM:** $358
**Principal Investments:** Cash and equiv (79%), long-term bonds (21%)
**Provider Compensation ($000):** Contr fee ($479,388), capitation ($128,404), FFS ($19,095)
**Total Member Encounters:** Phys (544,692), non-phys (1,983,933)
**Group Affiliation:** Carle Foundation
**Licensed in:** IL, IN, OH
**Address:** 301 S Vine St, Urbana, IL 61801
**Phone:** (800) 851-3379 **Dom State:** IL **Commenced Bus:** August 2014

| Data Date | Rating | RACR #1 | RACR #2 | Total Assets ($mil) | Capital ($mil) | Net Premium ($mil) | Net Income ($mil) |
|---|---|---|---|---|---|---|---|
| 9-17 | C | 0.99 | 0.82 | 130.2 | 69.4 | 154.2 | 4.6 |
| 9-16 | C | N/A | N/A | 171.3 | 70.6 | 496.3 | 3.2 |
| 2016 | C | 0.96 | 0.80 | 166.1 | 72.3 | 647.4 | 4.9 |
| 2015 | N/A | N/A | N/A | 183.0 | 58.9 | 547.3 | N/A |
| 2014 | U | 1.97 | 1.64 | 39.8 | 11.4 | 31.5 | -6.5 |
| 2013 | N/A | N/A | N/A | N/A | N/A | N/A | N/A |
| 2012 | N/A | N/A | N/A | N/A | N/A | N/A | N/A |

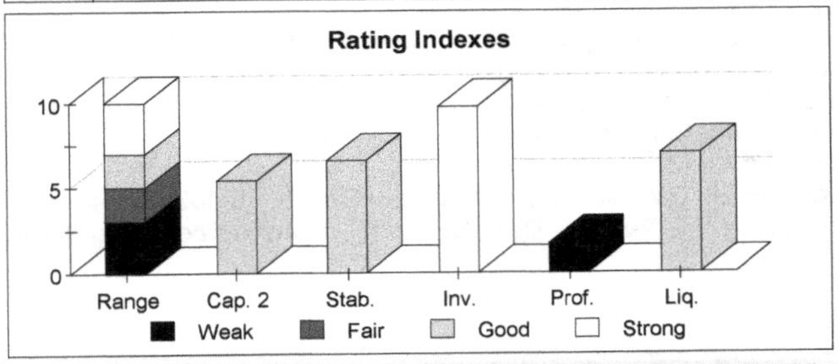


## HEALTH ALLIANCE MEDICAL PLANS — B- — Good

**Major Rating Factors:** Fair profitability index (3.7 on a scale of 0 to 10). Good quality investment portfolio (5.5). Strong capitalization (8.8) based on excellent current risk-adjusted capital (severe loss scenario).
**Other Rating Factors:** Excellent liquidity (7.0) with sufficient resources (cash flows and marketable investments) to handle a spike in claims.
**Principal Business:** Comp med (93%), Medicare (2%), Medicaid (2%), FEHB (2%)
**Mem Phys: 16:** 43,943 **15:** N/A **16 MLR** 88.1% **/ 16 Admin Exp** N/A
**Enroll(000): Q3 17:** 171 **16:** 172 **15:** 169 **Med Exp PMPM:** $479
**Principal Investments:** Long-term bonds (42%), nonaffiliate common stock (37%), cash and equiv (12%), affiliate common stock (3%), other (6%)
**Provider Compensation ($000):** Contr fee ($632,399), capitation ($332,137), FFS ($13,094)
**Total Member Encounters:** Phys (514,963), non-phys (1,617,099)
**Group Affiliation:** Carle Foundation
**Licensed in:** IL, MO
**Address:** 301 S Vine, Urbana, IL 61801
**Phone:** (800) 851-3379 **Dom State:** IL **Commenced Bus:** December 1989

| Data Date | Rating | RACR #1 | RACR #2 | Total Assets ($mil) | Capital ($mil) | Net Premium ($mil) | Net Income ($mil) |
|---|---|---|---|---|---|---|---|
| 9-17 | B- | 2.75 | 2.30 | 645.7 | 213.8 | 926.3 | 19.7 |
| 9-16 | B- | N/A | N/A | 598.3 | 185.7 | 845.5 | -3.9 |
| 2016 | B- | 2.52 | 2.10 | 505.1 | 195.7 | 1,133.1 | 2.2 |
| 2015 | N/A | N/A | N/A | 526.3 | 184.5 | 1,156.4 | N/A |
| 2014 | B+ | 2.13 | 1.78 | 517.1 | 179.1 | 1,234.7 | -14.0 |
| 2013 | A | 2.75 | 2.29 | 509.3 | 200.8 | 1,119.0 | 11.4 |
| 2012 | B+ | 2.36 | 1.97 | 477.1 | 165.3 | 1,069.8 | 11.8 |

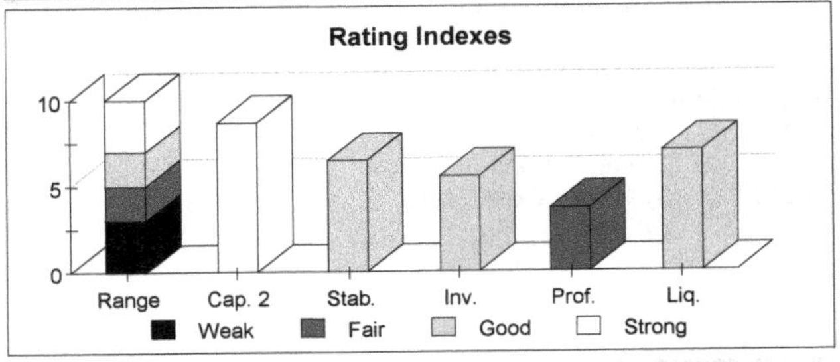

## HEALTH ALLIANCE NORTHWEST HEALTH PL — B- — Good

**Major Rating Factors:** Fair profitability index (3.8 on a scale of 0 to 10). Strong capitalization (9.6) based on excellent current risk-adjusted capital (severe loss scenario). High quality investment portfolio (9.8).
**Other Rating Factors:** Excellent liquidity (7.1) with ample operational cash flow and liquid investments.
**Principal Business:** Medicare (100%)
**Mem Phys: 16:** 8,484 **15:** 5,296 **16 MLR** 85.3% **/ 16 Admin Exp** N/A
**Enroll(000): Q3 17:** 7 **16:** 5 **15:** 4 **Med Exp PMPM:** $597
**Principal Investments:** Cash and equiv (81%), long-term bonds (19%)
**Provider Compensation ($000):** Capitation ($34,111), contr fee ($742), FFS ($229)
**Total Member Encounters:** Phys (14,829), non-phys (116,472)
**Group Affiliation:** Carle Foundation
**Licensed in:** WA
**Address:** 316 Fifth St, Wenatchee, WA 98801
**Phone:** (800) 851-3379 **Dom State:** WA **Commenced Bus:** January 2014

| Data Date | Rating | RACR #1 | RACR #2 | Total Assets ($mil) | Capital ($mil) | Net Premium ($mil) | Net Income ($mil) |
|---|---|---|---|---|---|---|---|
| 9-17 | B- | 3.43 | 2.86 | 23.8 | 9.6 | 42.7 | 0.6 |
| 9-16 | C+ | 3.58 | 2.99 | 18.9 | 8.6 | 33.3 | 0.4 |
| 2016 | C+ | 3.39 | 2.82 | 16.0 | 9.5 | 44.5 | 0.5 |
| 2015 | C | 3.79 | 3.16 | 16.5 | 9.1 | 30.1 | -0.2 |
| 2014 | B- | 2.49 | 2.07 | 9.3 | 4.5 | 23.8 | -0.3 |
| 2013 | N/A | N/A | N/A | 5.1 | 4.9 | N/A | -0.2 |
| 2012 | N/A | N/A | N/A | N/A | N/A | N/A | N/A |

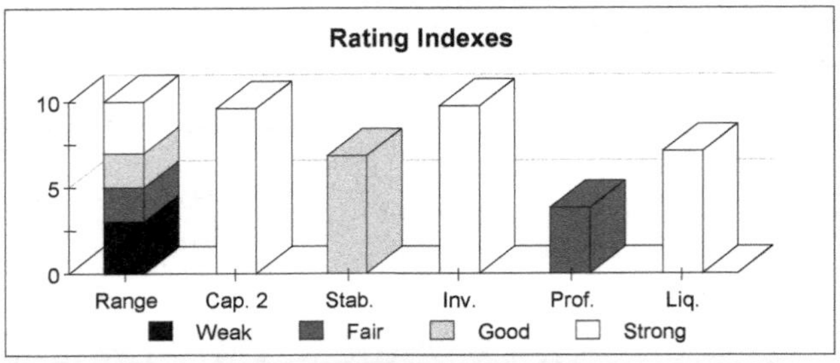


## HEALTH ALLIANCE PLAN OF MICHIGAN — C+ — Fair

**Major Rating Factors:** Good capitalization index (6.9 on a scale of 0 to 10) based on excellent current risk-adjusted capital (severe loss scenario). Good overall results on stability tests (6.1) despite a decline in enrollment during 2016. Weak profitability index (2.4).
**Other Rating Factors:** High quality investment portfolio (9.9). Excellent liquidity (6.9) with sufficient resources (cash flows and marketable investments) to handle a spike in claims.
**Principal Business:** Comp med (57%), Medicare (36%), FEHB (7%)
**Mem Phys: 16:** 24,009 **15:** 10,476 **16 MLR** 90.2% **/ 16 Admin Exp** N/A
**Enroll(000): Q3 17:** 262 **16:** 288 **15:** 317 **Med Exp PMPM:** $494
**Principal Investments:** Cash and equiv (51%), affiliate common stock (20%), long-term bonds (14%), nonaffiliate common stock (11%), real estate (1%), other (3%)
**Provider Compensation ($000):** Contr fee ($1,334,791), capitation ($325,307), FFS ($62,575), bonus arrang ($14,029)
**Total Member Encounters:** Phys (1,300,104), non-phys (610,644)
**Group Affiliation:** Henry Ford Health System
**Licensed in:** MI
**Address:** 2850 West Grand Boulevard, Detroit, MI 48202
**Phone:** (313) 872-8100 **Dom State:** MI **Commenced Bus:** February 1979

| Data Date | Rating | RACR #1 | RACR #2 | Total Assets ($mil) | Capital ($mil) | Net Premium ($mil) | Net Income ($mil) |
|---|---|---|---|---|---|---|---|
| 9-17 | C+ | 1.25 | 1.04 | 587.2 | 214.7 | 1,383.6 | 7.6 |
| 9-16 | C+ | 1.34 | 1.12 | 593.4 | 216.2 | 1,455.5 | 40.8 |
| 2016 | C+ | 1.20 | 1.00 | 515.5 | 204.4 | 1,924.3 | 38.4 |
| 2015 | C+ | 1.31 | 1.09 | 530.9 | 206.5 | 2,069.8 | -33.1 |
| 2014 | B | 1.33 | 1.11 | 469.0 | 208.3 | 1,749.5 | -5.0 |
| 2013 | B | 1.45 | 1.21 | 456.7 | 210.2 | 1,869.0 | 17.9 |
| 2012 | B+ | 1.57 | 1.31 | 500.0 | 231.5 | 1,895.1 | 21.8 |

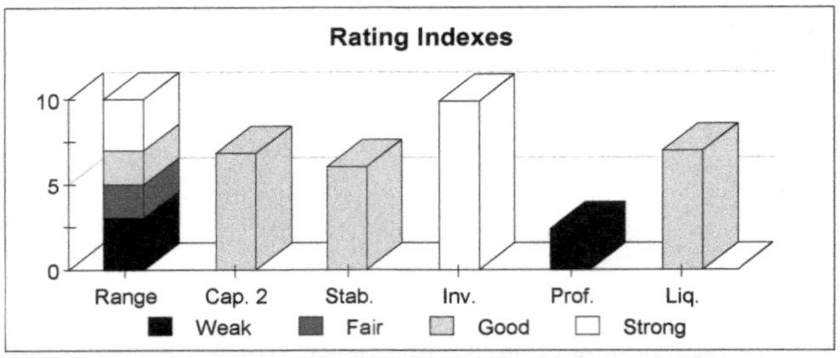


## HEALTH ALLIANCE-MIDWEST INC — E — Very Weak

**Major Rating Factors:** Weak profitability index (1.2 on a scale of 0 to 10). Good overall results on stability tests (5.0) despite a decline in enrollment during 2016. Rating is significantly influenced by the good financial results of Carle Foundation. Good liquidity (6.4) with sufficient resources (cash flows and marketable investments) to handle a spike in claims.
**Other Rating Factors:** Strong capitalization index (8.3) based on excellent current risk-adjusted capital (severe loss scenario). High quality investment portfolio (9.0).
**Principal Business:** Medicare (57%), comp med (42%)
**Mem Phys: 16:** 49,105 **15:** 43,290 **16 MLR** 92.2% **/ 16 Admin Exp** N/A
**Enroll(000): Q3 17:** 2 **16:** 3 **15:** 3 **Med Exp PMPM:** $501
**Principal Investments:** Long-term bonds (75%), cash and equiv (25%)
**Provider Compensation ($000):** Contr fee ($13,828), capitation ($3,074), FFS ($413)
**Total Member Encounters:** Phys (11,680), non-phys (35,910)
**Group Affiliation:** Carle Foundation
**Licensed in:** IL, IA, NE
**Address:** 301 S Vine, Urbana, IL 61801
**Phone:** (800) 851-3379 **Dom State:** IL **Commenced Bus:** May 1997

| Data Date | Rating | RACR #1 | RACR #2 | Total Assets ($mil) | Capital ($mil) | Net Premium ($mil) | Net Income ($mil) |
|---|---|---|---|---|---|---|---|
| 9-17 | E | 2.36 | 1.97 | 21.0 | 7.6 | 0.0 | 0.8 |
| 9-16 | E | 1.11 | 0.92 | 8.8 | 3.1 | 14.1 | -0.8 |
| 2016 | E | 2.01 | 1.67 | 10.2 | 6.8 | 18.8 | -1.1 |
| 2015 | E | 1.42 | 1.18 | 8.2 | 4.0 | 17.1 | -1.1 |
| 2014 | E | 2.69 | 2.24 | 8.7 | 5.1 | 13.5 | -3.0 |
| 2013 | D | 1.78 | 1.49 | 8.6 | 3.1 | 11.8 | -1.5 |
| 2012 | D+ | 2.52 | 2.10 | 7.9 | 4.6 | 12.2 | -1.1 |

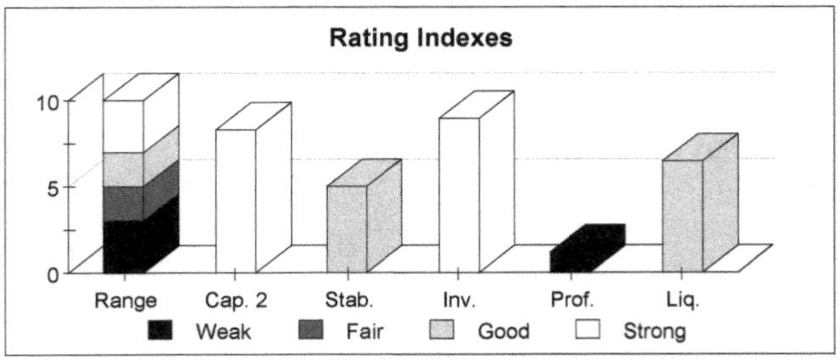

## HEALTH CARE SVC CORP A MUT LEG RES — B — Good

**Major Rating Factors:** Good profitability index (4.9 on a scale of 0 to 10). Good liquidity (6.7) with sufficient resources (cash flows and marketable investments) to handle a spike in claims. Strong capitalization (10.0) based on excellent current risk-adjusted capital (severe loss scenario).
**Other Rating Factors:** High quality investment portfolio (7.1).
**Principal Business:** Comp med (68%), FEHB (16%), med supp (5%), Medicaid (4%), Medicare (4%), other (2%)
**Mem Phys: 16:** 200,847 **15:** 190,385 **16 MLR** 88.3% **/ 16 Admin Exp** N/A
**Enroll(000): Q3 17:** 8,476 **16:** 8,817 **15:** 9,706 **Med Exp PMPM:** $246
**Principal Investments:** Long-term bonds (76%), nonaffiliate common stock (11%), real estate (9%), affiliate common stock (8%), other (1%)
**Provider Compensation ($000):** FFS ($15,906,271), contr fee ($9,004,775), capitation ($1,038,477), bonus arrang ($220,558), other ($526,380)
**Total Member Encounters:** Phys (48,941,623), non-phys (18,749,519)
**Group Affiliation:** Health Care Service Corporation
**Licensed in:** AK, AZ, AR, CO, CT, DC, DE, FL, GA, ID, IL, IN, KY, ME, MD, MA, MI, MN, MO, MT, NE, NJ, NM, OH, OK, OR, PA, SC, TX, UT, VA, WV, WI
**Address:** 300 East Randolph St, Chicago, IL 60601-5099
**Phone:** (312) 653-6000 **Dom State:** IL **Commenced Bus:** January 1937

| Data Date | Rating | RACR #1 | RACR #2 | Total Assets ($mil) | Capital ($mil) | Net Premium ($mil) | Net Income ($mil) |
|---|---|---|---|---|---|---|---|
| 9-17 | B | 5.73 | 4.77 | 21,258.2 | 11,588.1 | 24,467.5 | 1,645.3 |
| 9-16 | B | 4.45 | 3.71 | 18,769.5 | 9,402.2 | 22,791.6 | -255.9 |
| 2016 | B | 4.74 | 3.95 | 18,036.1 | 9,535.9 | 30,335.8 | 106.3 |
| 2015 | B | 4.47 | 3.72 | 17,661.1 | 9,445.0 | 31,185.3 | -65.9 |
| 2014 | A+ | 5.55 | 4.63 | 17,829.4 | 9,942.2 | 27,705.5 | -281.9 |
| 2013 | A+ | 7.13 | 5.94 | 16,713.6 | 10,271.6 | 22,686.7 | 684.3 |
| 2012 | A+ | 7.22 | 6.02 | 15,517.6 | 9,553.7 | 20,653.4 | 1,007.1 |

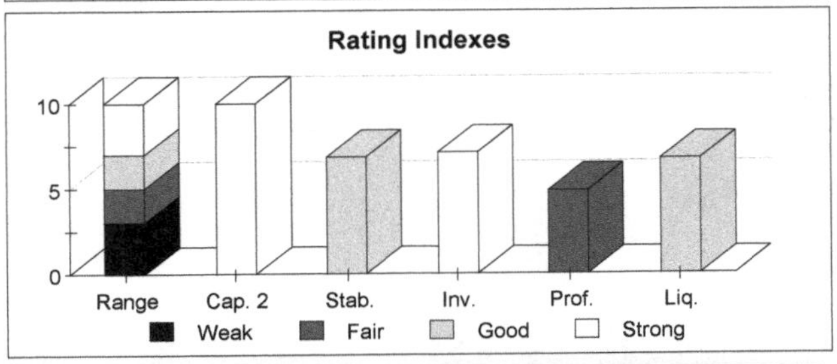


## HEALTH CHOICE INS CO — E- — Very Weak

**Major Rating Factors:** Weak profitability index (0.1 on a scale of 0 to 10). Poor capitalization (1.9) based on weak current risk-adjusted capital (moderate loss scenario). Weak liquidity (0.0) as a spike in claims may stretch capacity.
**Other Rating Factors:** High quality investment portfolio (9.9).
**Principal Business:** Comp med (100%)
**Mem Phys: 16:** 4,290 **15:** 3,323 **16 MLR** 168.9% **/ 16 Admin Exp** N/A
**Enroll(000): Q1 17:** N/A **16:** 8 **15:** 4 **Med Exp PMPM:** $365
**Principal Investments:** Cash and equiv (100%)
**Provider Compensation ($000):** FFS ($18,598), contr fee ($14,196), capitation ($206)
**Total Member Encounters:** Phys (31,250), non-phys (38,559)
**Group Affiliation:** TPG IASIS IV LLC
**Licensed in:** AZ
**Address:** 410 N 44th St Ste 900, Phoenix, AZ 85008
**Phone:** (480) 968-6866 **Dom State:** AZ **Commenced Bus:** April 2013

| Data Date | Rating | RACR #1 | RACR #2 | Total Assets ($mil) | Capital ($mil) | Net Premium ($mil) | Net Income ($mil) |
|---|---|---|---|---|---|---|---|
| 3-17 | E- | 0.49 | 0.41 | 22.8 | 4.4 | 0.0 | 0.1 |
| 3-16 | C- | 4.58 | 3.82 | 21.7 | 10.8 | 10.0 | 1.3 |
| 2016 | E- | 0.45 | 0.37 | 28.0 | 4.1 | 26.9 | -16.3 |
| 2015 | C- | 3.43 | 2.86 | 13.5 | 8.2 | 10.1 | -0.8 |
| 2014 | D+ | 2.02 | 1.68 | 4.2 | 1.8 | 2.8 | -0.2 |
| 2013 | N/A | N/A | N/A | 2.1 | 2.0 | N/A | N/A |
| 2012 | N/A | N/A | N/A | N/A | N/A | N/A | N/A |

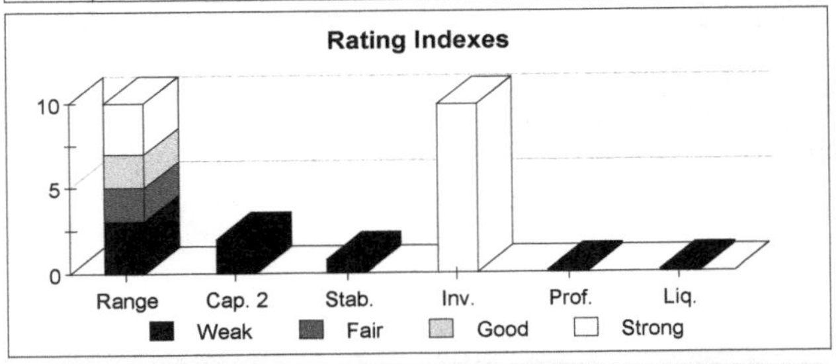


## HEALTH CHOICE UTAH INC — E- — Very Weak

**Major Rating Factors:** Fair profitability index (4.5 on a scale of 0 to 10). Strong capitalization (7.3) based on excellent current risk-adjusted capital (severe loss scenario). High quality investment portfolio (9.9).
**Other Rating Factors:** Excellent liquidity (6.9) with sufficient resources (cash flows and marketable investments) to handle a spike in claims.
**Principal Business:** Medicaid (100%)
**Mem Phys: 16:** 2,475 **15:** 2,217 **16 MLR** 101.0% **/ 16 Admin Exp** N/A
**Enroll(000): Q3 17:** 18 **16:** 18 **15:** 17 **Med Exp PMPM:** $264
**Principal Investments:** Cash and equiv (100%)
**Provider Compensation ($000):** Contr fee ($43,336), FFS ($4,748)
**Total Member Encounters:** Phys (83,009), non-phys (79,694)
**Group Affiliation:** TPG IASIS IV LLC
**Licensed in:** UT
**Address:** 406 W S Jordan Parkway Ste 500, South Jordan, UT 84095
**Phone:** (801) 984-3388 **Dom State:** UT **Commenced Bus:** April 2012

| Data Date | Rating | RACR #1 | RACR #2 | Total Assets ($mil) | Capital ($mil) | Net Premium ($mil) | Net Income ($mil) |
|---|---|---|---|---|---|---|---|
| 9-17 | E- | 1.59 | 1.33 | 21.7 | 13.9 | 40.2 | 3.5 |
| 9-16 | E- | 0.94 | 0.78 | 19.5 | 6.4 | 41.1 | -2.5 |
| 2016 | E- | 1.13 | 0.94 | 34.2 | 10.2 | 55.6 | -1.2 |
| 2015 | E- | 1.30 | 1.08 | 20.5 | 8.4 | 32.9 | 0.8 |
| 2014 | D+ | 0.49 | 0.41 | 7.3 | 1.8 | 13.5 | -0.6 |
| 2013 | D+ | 2.04 | 1.70 | 5.5 | 1.5 | 6.2 | 0.6 |
| 2012 | D | 0.47 | 0.39 | 2.5 | 1.5 | 0.7 | 0.0 |

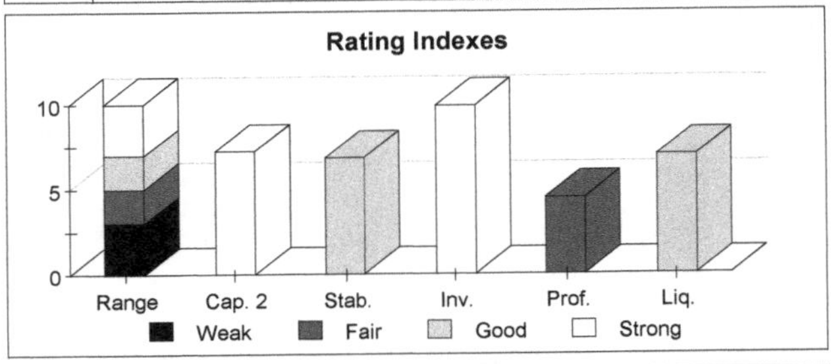

## HEALTH FIRST COMMERCIAL PLANS INC B- Good

**Major Rating Factors:** Excellent profitability (7.8 on a scale of 0 to 10). Strong capitalization (10.0) based on excellent current risk-adjusted capital (severe loss scenario). High quality investment portfolio (9.9).
**Other Rating Factors:** Excellent liquidity (7.0) with ample operational cash flow and liquid investments.
**Principal Business:** Comp med (100%)
**Mem Phys: 16:** 1,678 **15:** N/A **16 MLR** 80.7% **/ 16 Admin Exp** N/A
**Enroll(000): Q3 17:** 39 **16:** 14 **15:** N/A **Med Exp PMPM:** $348
**Principal Investments:** Long-term bonds (54%), cash and equiv (46%)
**Provider Compensation ($000):** Contr fee ($35,158), FFS ($22,495), capitation ($716)
**Total Member Encounters:** Phys (88,777), non-phys (30,370)
**Group Affiliation:** Health First Inc
**Licensed in:** FL
**Address:** 6450 US HIGHWAY 1, ROCKLEDGE, FL 32955
**Phone:** (321) 434-5600 **Dom State:** FL **Commenced Bus:** January 2016

| Data Date | Rating | RACR #1 | RACR #2 | Total Assets ($mil) | Capital ($mil) | Net Premium ($mil) | Net Income ($mil) |
|---|---|---|---|---|---|---|---|
| 9-17 | B- | 5.72 | 4.76 | 74.3 | 40.5 | 161.0 | 9.9 |
| 9-16 | N/A | N/A | N/A | 28.9 | 18.3 | 54.5 | -0.3 |
| 2016 | C- | 2.74 | 2.28 | 31.9 | 19.1 | 72.6 | 1.3 |
| 2015 | N/A | N/A | N/A | 1.8 | 1.8 | N/A | N/A |
| 2014 | N/A | N/A | N/A | N/A | N/A | N/A | N/A |
| 2013 | N/A | N/A | N/A | N/A | N/A | N/A | N/A |
| 2012 | N/A | N/A | N/A | N/A | N/A | N/A | N/A |

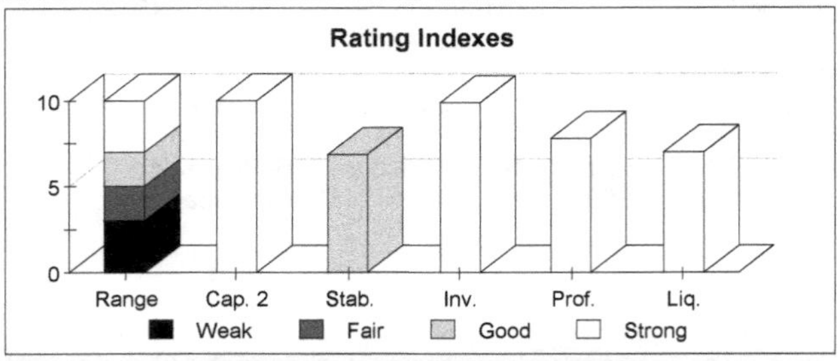


## HEALTH FIRST HEALTH PLANS INC B Good

**Major Rating Factors:** Excellent profitability (7.6 on a scale of 0 to 10). Strong capitalization (7.8) based on excellent current risk-adjusted capital (severe loss scenario). High quality investment portfolio (9.9).
**Other Rating Factors:** Excellent liquidity (7.1) with ample operational cash flow and liquid investments.
**Principal Business:** Medicare (79%), comp med (21%)
**Mem Phys: 16:** 4,926 **15:** N/A **16 MLR** 81.7% **/ 16 Admin Exp** N/A
**Enroll(000): Q3 17:** 37 **16:** 53 **15:** N/A **Med Exp PMPM:** $569
**Principal Investments:** Cash and equiv (67%), long-term bonds (23%), nonaffiliate common stock (10%)
**Provider Compensation ($000):** Contr fee ($282,970), FFS ($61,822), capitation ($7,571)
**Total Member Encounters:** Phys (776,706), non-phys (357,226)
**Group Affiliation:** Health First Inc
**Licensed in:** FL
**Address:** 6450 US HIGHWAY 1, ROCKLEDGE, FL 32955
**Phone:** (321) 434-5600 **Dom State:** FL **Commenced Bus:** January 2016

| Data Date | Rating | RACR #1 | RACR #2 | Total Assets ($mil) | Capital ($mil) | Net Premium ($mil) | Net Income ($mil) |
|---|---|---|---|---|---|---|---|
| 9-17 | B | 2.01 | 1.68 | 157.3 | 69.2 | 284.3 | 12.8 |
| 9-16 | N/A | N/A | N/A | 140.1 | 62.4 | 334.3 | 18.9 |
| 2016 | C- | 2.01 | 1.68 | 130.8 | 70.6 | 443.3 | 22.5 |
| 2015 | N/A | N/A | N/A | 1.8 | 1.8 | N/A | N/A |
| 2014 | N/A | N/A | N/A | N/A | N/A | N/A | N/A |
| 2013 | N/A | N/A | N/A | N/A | N/A | N/A | N/A |
| 2012 | N/A | N/A | N/A | N/A | N/A | N/A | N/A |

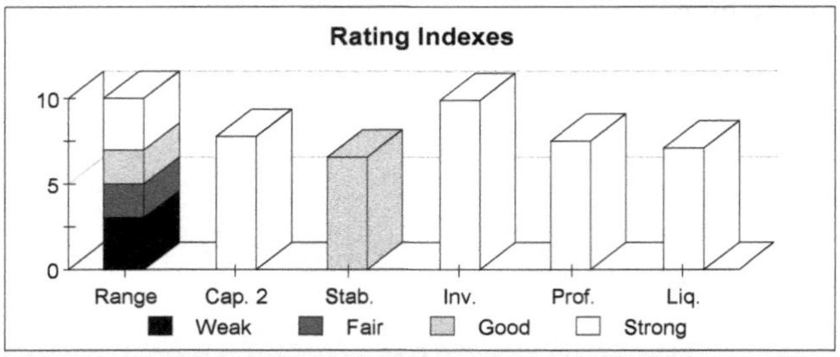


## HEALTH FIRST INS INC D Weak

**Major Rating Factors:** Weak profitability index (0.8 on a scale of 0 to 10). Strong capitalization (10.0) based on excellent current risk-adjusted capital (severe loss scenario). High quality investment portfolio (9.9).
**Other Rating Factors:** Excellent liquidity (6.9) with sufficient resources (cash flows and marketable investments) to handle a spike in claims.
**Principal Business:** Comp med (98%), med supp (2%)
**Mem Phys: 16:** 1,552 **15:** 1,635 **16 MLR** 76.1% **/ 16 Admin Exp** N/A
**Enroll(000): Q3 17:** 1 **16:** 1 **15:** 2 **Med Exp PMPM:** $317
**Principal Investments:** Cash and equiv (100%)
**Provider Compensation ($000):** FFS ($2,945), contr fee ($1,931), capitation ($50)
**Total Member Encounters:** Phys (6,264), non-phys (3,179)
**Group Affiliation:** Health First Inc
**Licensed in:** FL
**Address:** 6450 US HIGHWAY 1, ROCKLEDGE, FL 32955
**Phone:** (321) 434-5600 **Dom State:** FL **Commenced Bus:** January 2012

| Data Date | Rating | RACR #1 | RACR #2 | Total Assets ($mil) | Capital ($mil) | Net Premium ($mil) | Net Income ($mil) |
|---|---|---|---|---|---|---|---|
| 9-17 | D | 4.13 | 3.44 | 5.6 | 4.6 | 2.5 | 0.0 |
| 9-16 | E | 1.95 | 1.63 | 6.2 | 4.3 | 3.9 | 0.0 |
| 2016 | E | 4.06 | 3.38 | 6.0 | 4.7 | 5.3 | 0.3 |
| 2015 | E- | 1.58 | 1.32 | 6.4 | 3.6 | 10.4 | -2.0 |
| 2014 | D+ | 0.86 | 0.71 | 10.2 | 2.8 | 22.1 | -1.9 |
| 2013 | D+ | 5.41 | 4.51 | 5.4 | 4.3 | 1.0 | -1.2 |
| 2012 | U | 22.72 | 18.94 | 2.6 | 2.5 | 0.0 | -0.5 |

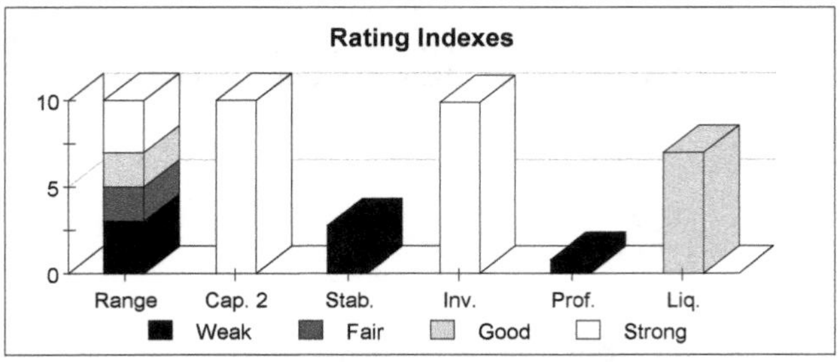

## HEALTH INS CO OF AM INC — D — Weak

**Major Rating Factors:** Weak profitability index (0.1 on a scale of 0 to 10). Strong capitalization (10.0) based on excellent current risk-adjusted capital (severe loss scenario). High quality investment portfolio (9.9).
**Other Rating Factors:** Excellent liquidity (7.8) with ample operational cash flow and liquid investments.
**Principal Business:** Dental (53%), other (47%)
**Mem Phys: 16:** N/A **15:** N/A **16 MLR** 36.8% **/ 16 Admin Exp** N/A
**Enroll(000): Q3 17:** 16 **16:** 17 **15:** 17 **Med Exp PMPM:** $1
**Principal Investments:** Cash and equiv (81%), long-term bonds (19%)
**Provider Compensation ($000):** None
**Total Member Encounters:** N/A
**Group Affiliation:** Ausman Management Company LLC
**Licensed in:** NY
**Address:** 2363 JAMES St, SYRACUSE, NY 13206
**Phone:** (315) 413-4941 **Dom State:** NY **Commenced Bus:** November 2010

| Data Date | Rating | RACR #1 | RACR #2 | Total Assets ($mil) | Capital ($mil) | Net Premium ($mil) | Net Income ($mil) |
|---|---|---|---|---|---|---|---|
| 9-17 | D | 7.67 | 6.39 | 1.5 | 0.5 | 0.3 | -0.3 |
| 9-16 | N/A | N/A | N/A | 1.7 | 0.5 | 0.4 | -0.2 |
| 2016 | D | 8.64 | 7.20 | 1.6 | 0.7 | 0.6 | 0.0 |
| 2015 | N/A | N/A | N/A | 1.8 | 0.7 | 0.7 | -0.3 |
| 2014 | N/A | N/A | N/A | 1.9 | 0.7 | 0.8 | -0.6 |
| 2013 | N/A | N/A | N/A | 1.8 | 0.8 | 0.9 | -0.3 |
| 2012 | N/A | N/A | N/A | 1.7 | 0.8 | 0.8 | -0.2 |

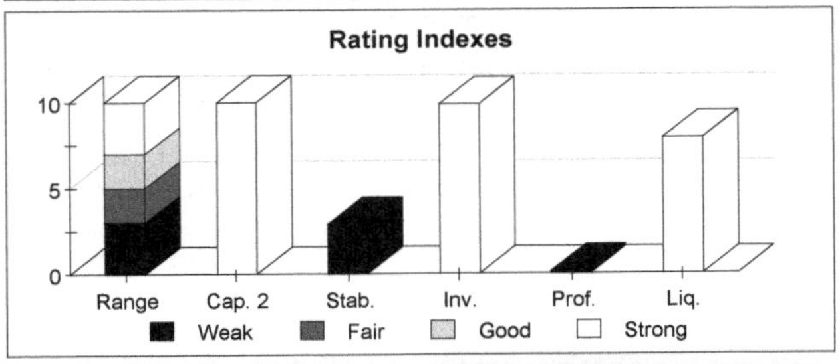


## HEALTH INSURANCE PLAN OF GREATER NY — C- — Fair

**Major Rating Factors:** Fair quality investment portfolio (3.7 on a scale of 0 to 10). Weak profitability index (0.9). Good capitalization (6.4) based on good current risk-adjusted capital (severe loss scenario).
**Other Rating Factors:** Good liquidity (5.9) with sufficient resources (cash flows and marketable investments) to handle a spike in claims.
**Principal Business:** Comp med (41%), Medicare (33%), Medicaid (24%), FEHB (2%)
**Mem Phys: 16:** 93,899 **15:** 75,119 **16 MLR** 92.8% **/ 16 Admin Exp** N/A
**Enroll(000): Q3 17:** 604 **16:** 627 **15:** 690 **Med Exp PMPM:** $575
**Principal Investments:** Affiliate common stock (46%), long-term bonds (34%), real estate (17%), cash and equiv (13%)
**Provider Compensation ($000):** Capitation ($1,609,495), contr fee ($1,601,308), FFS ($1,178,904), bonus arrang ($59,324)
**Total Member Encounters:** Phys (8,429,768), non-phys (3,721,823)
**Group Affiliation:** EmblemHealth Inc
**Licensed in:** NY
**Address:** 55 Water St, New York, NY 10041-8190
**Phone:** (646) 447-5000 **Dom State:** NY **Commenced Bus:** March 1947

| Data Date | Rating | RACR #1 | RACR #2 | Total Assets ($mil) | Capital ($mil) | Net Premium ($mil) | Net Income ($mil) |
|---|---|---|---|---|---|---|---|
| 9-17 | C- | 1.14 | 0.95 | 1,413.4 | 470.7 | 3,585.5 | -86.0 |
| 9-16 | C- | 1.40 | 1.17 | 1,498.6 | 565.1 | 3,682.0 | -35.6 |
| 2016 | C- | 1.15 | 0.96 | 1,424.4 | 469.9 | 4,855.3 | -239.2 |
| 2015 | C- | 1.70 | 1.42 | 1,644.4 | 684.1 | 5,065.0 | -143.2 |
| 2014 | B- | 2.45 | 2.04 | 1,894.6 | 897.6 | 5,088.7 | -365.3 |
| 2013 | B+ | 4.14 | 3.45 | 2,111.3 | 1,435.5 | 4,981.2 | 179.0 |
| 2012 | B+ | 4.32 | 3.60 | 2,310.2 | 1,498.9 | 5,026.5 | 173.7 |

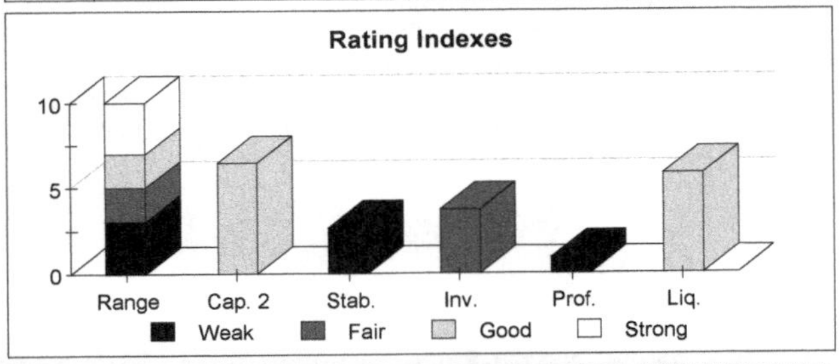


## HEALTH NET COMMUNITY SOLUTIONS INC — B — Good

**Major Rating Factors:** Excellent profitability (8.9 on a scale of 0 to 10). Strong capitalization index (7.4) based on excellent current risk-adjusted capital (severe loss scenario). Excellent overall results on stability tests (7.6) based on healthy premium and capital growth during 2016.
**Other Rating Factors:** Excellent liquidity (7.2) with ample operational cash flow and liquid investments.
**Principal Business:** Medicaid (84%), Medicare (2%)
**Mem Phys: 16:** N/A **15:** N/A **16 MLR** 82.3% **/ 16 Admin Exp** N/A
**Enroll(000): Q3 17:** 1,888 **16:** 1,873 **15:** 811 **Med Exp PMPM:** $273
**Principal Investments ($000):** Cash and equiv ($1,468,556)
**Provider Compensation ($000):** None
**Total Member Encounters:** N/A
**Group Affiliation:** Health Net Inc
**Licensed in:** CA
**Address:** 11971 Foundation Place, Rancho Cordova, CA 95670
**Phone:** (818) 676-8394 **Dom State:** CA **Commenced Bus:** June 2005

| Data Date | Rating | RACR #1 | RACR #2 | Total Assets ($mil) | Capital ($mil) | Net Premium ($mil) | Net Income ($mil) |
|---|---|---|---|---|---|---|---|
| 9-17 | B | 2.02 | 1.37 | 3,147.0 | 944.7 | 5,612.9 | 347.6 |
| 9-16 | B- | 1.81 | 1.12 | 2,533.0 | 486.9 | 5,325.2 | 269.8 |
| 2016 | B | 1.62 | 1.09 | 3,043.0 | 737.2 | 7,482.8 | 541.9 |
| 2015 | B | 2.03 | 1.26 | 2,321.8 | 549.1 | 6,467.1 | 533.2 |
| 2014 | B- | 1.75 | 1.08 | 1,593.8 | 369.1 | 4,427.6 | 195.7 |
| 2013 | C | 2.32 | 1.44 | 577.6 | 233.0 | 2,158.4 | 75.3 |
| 2012 | N/A | N/A | N/A | 358.2 | 158.5 | 1,722.8 | 4.5 |

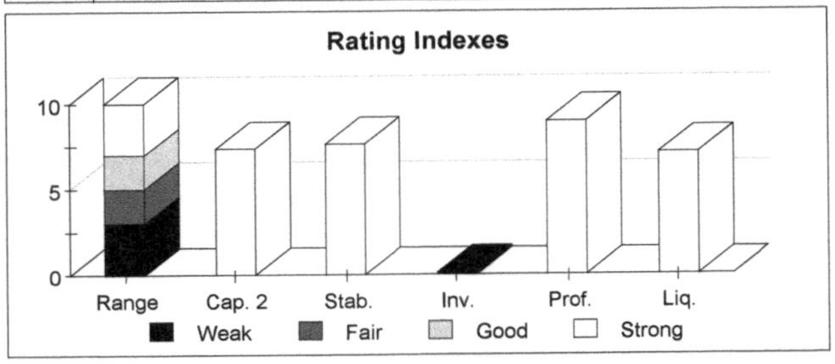

## HEALTH NET HEALTH PLAN OF OREGON INC — E- Very Weak

**Major Rating Factors:** Weak profitability index (1.3 on a scale of 0 to 10). Good overall results on stability tests (5.5). Rating is significantly influenced by the fair financial results of Centene Corporation. Good liquidity (6.1) with sufficient resources (cash flows and marketable investments) to handle a spike in claims.
**Other Rating Factors:** Strong capitalization index (8.5) based on excellent current risk-adjusted capital (severe loss scenario). High quality investment portfolio (9.9).
**Principal Business:** Medicare (54%), comp med (45%)
**Mem Phys: 16:** 53,403 **15:** 39,512 **16 MLR** 95.2% **/ 16 Admin Exp** N/A
**Enroll(000): Q3 17:** 82 **16:** 94 **15:** 80 **Med Exp PMPM:** $441
**Principal Investments:** Long-term bonds (85%), cash and equiv (15%)
**Provider Compensation ($000):** FFS ($471,227), capitation ($10,401)
**Total Member Encounters:** Phys (509,180), non-phys (445,814)
**Group Affiliation:** Centene Corporation
**Licensed in:** OR, WA
**Address:** 13221 SW 68th Parkway Suite 20, Tigard, OR 97223-8328
**Phone:** (314) 724-4477 **Dom State:** OR **Commenced Bus:** September 1989

| Data Date | Rating | RACR #1 | RACR #2 | Total Assets ($mil) | Capital ($mil) | Net Premium ($mil) | Net Income ($mil) |
|---|---|---|---|---|---|---|---|
| 9-17 | E- | 2.58 | 2.15 | 210.2 | 101.5 | 400.4 | 5.7 |
| 9-16 | E- | 2.65 | 2.20 | 194.4 | 85.6 | 374.9 | -27.6 |
| 2016 | E- | 2.53 | 2.11 | 181.6 | 99.7 | 506.2 | -31.8 |
| 2015 | E+ | 1.68 | 1.40 | 152.1 | 68.1 | 418.8 | -25.4 |
| 2014 | E | 1.92 | 1.60 | 131.6 | 55.7 | 327.9 | -43.8 |
| 2013 | B- | 2.11 | 1.76 | 94.6 | 53.3 | 294.1 | 4.6 |
| 2012 | B | 2.21 | 1.85 | 121.4 | 66.7 | 368.8 | 10.6 |

Rating Indexes

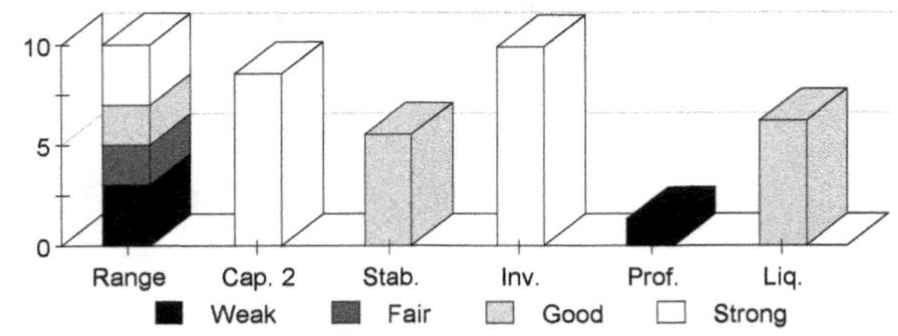


## HEALTH NET LIFE INSURANCE COMPANY — C Fair

**Major Rating Factors:** Fair overall results on stability tests (3.9 on a scale of 0 to 10) including fair financial strength of affiliated Centene Corporation. Weak profitability (2.9). Excellent expense controls. Weak liquidity (2.0) as a spike in claims may stretch capacity.
**Other Rating Factors:** Strong capitalization (10.0) based on excellent risk adjusted capital (severe loss scenario). High quality investment portfolio (9.0).
**Principal Business:** Group health insurance (64%) and individual health insurance (36%).
**Principal Investments:** NonCMO investment grade bonds (61%), cash (23%), and CMOs and structured securities (8%).
**Investments in Affiliates:** None
**Group Affiliation:** Centene Corporation
**Licensed in:** All states except MI, NY, PR
**Commenced Business:** January 1987
**Address:** 21281 Burbank Boulevard B3, Woodland Hills, CA 91367
**Phone:** (314) 725-4477 **Domicile State:** CA **NAIC Code:** 66141

| Data Date | Rating | RACR #1 | RACR #2 | Total Assets ($mil) | Capital ($mil) | Net Premium ($mil) | Net Income ($mil) |
|---|---|---|---|---|---|---|---|
| 9-17 | C | 3.78 | 3.10 | 748.6 | 423.9 | 594.2 | 6.3 |
| 9-16 | C | 2.46 | 2.00 | 760.9 | 338.4 | 585.3 | -190.7 |
| 2016 | C | 3.59 | 2.94 | 727.2 | 410.0 | 809.8 | -171.8 |
| 2015 | C | 1.84 | 1.52 | 618.5 | 331.3 | 1,181.3 | -93.2 |
| 2014 | C | 2.26 | 1.84 | 624.0 | 363.9 | 1,040.9 | -9.3 |
| 2013 | B | 1.88 | 1.52 | 485.1 | 257.2 | 916.1 | 22.9 |
| 2012 | C+ | 2.25 | 1.82 | 632.0 | 365.6 | 1,079.4 | 107.7 |

**Centene Corporation**
**Composite Group Rating: C-**

| Largest Group Members | Assets ($mil) | Rating |
|---|---|---|
| HEALTH NET LIFE INS CO | 727 | C |
| SUNSHINE HEALTH | 676 | E |
| SUPERIOR HEALTHPLAN INC | 664 | C+ |
| CELTIC INS CO | 593 | C+ |
| HEALTH NET OF ARIZONA INC | 455 | C |

## HEALTH NET OF ARIZONA INC — C Fair

**Major Rating Factors:** Fair overall results on stability tests (4.0 on a scale of 0 to 10) based on a significant 42% decrease in enrollment during the period, a steep decline in premium revenue in 2016. Weak profitability index (1.0). Weak liquidity (1.4) as a spike in claims may stretch capacity.
**Other Rating Factors:** Strong capitalization index (9.6) based on excellent current risk-adjusted capital (severe loss scenario). High quality investment portfolio (9.9).
**Principal Business:** Medicare (73%), comp med (16%), FEHB (11%)
**Mem Phys: 16:** 18,635 **15:** 17,396 **16 MLR** 116.2% **/ 16 Admin Exp** N/A
**Enroll(000): Q3 17:** 129 **16:** 57 **15:** 98 **Med Exp PMPM:** $555
**Principal Investments:** Long-term bonds (52%), cash and equiv (48%)
**Provider Compensation ($000):** Contr fee ($306,870), capitation ($128,202)
**Total Member Encounters:** Phys (534,187), non-phys (48,265)
**Group Affiliation:** Centene Corporation
**Licensed in:** AZ
**Address:** 1230 West Washington St Suite, Tempe, AZ 85281-1245
**Phone:** (314) 725-4477 **Dom State:** AZ **Commenced Bus:** November 1981

| Data Date | Rating | RACR #1 | RACR #2 | Total Assets ($mil) | Capital ($mil) | Net Premium ($mil) | Net Income ($mil) |
|---|---|---|---|---|---|---|---|
| 9-17 | C | 3.47 | 2.89 | 415.0 | 171.9 | 749.4 | 19.4 |
| 9-16 | C | 2.92 | 2.43 | 510.0 | 111.1 | 257.4 | -65.8 |
| 2016 | C | 2.63 | 2.19 | 455.4 | 130.5 | 360.9 | -54.8 |
| 2015 | C | 1.39 | 1.16 | 451.0 | 65.8 | 684.2 | -55.2 |
| 2014 | D+ | 2.25 | 1.87 | 538.4 | 120.5 | 838.1 | -79.0 |
| 2013 | C | 1.84 | 1.54 | 350.3 | 85.3 | 721.0 | -4.7 |
| 2012 | C+ | 1.34 | 1.11 | 218.1 | 77.5 | 724.9 | -10.2 |

Rating Indexes

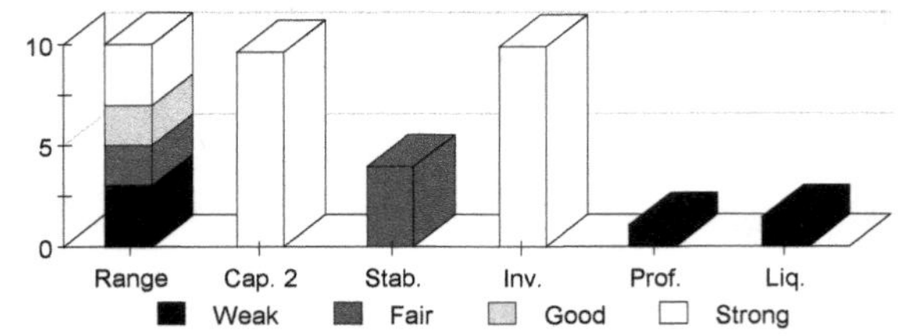

## HEALTH NET OF CALIFORNIA INC — C — Fair

**Major Rating Factors:** Weak profitability index (0.9 on a scale of 0 to 10). Good overall results on stability tests (5.7). Potentially strong support from affiliation with Health Net Inc. Good liquidity (6.2) with sufficient resources (cash flows and marketable investments) to handle a spike in claims.
**Other Rating Factors:** Strong capitalization index (7.1) based on excellent current risk-adjusted capital (severe loss scenario).
**Principal Business:** Medicare (32%)
**Mem Phys: 16:** N/A **15:** N/A **16 MLR** 94.3% **/ 16 Admin Exp** N/A
**Enroll(000): Q3 17:** 1,035 **16:** 1,102 **15:** 1,260 **Med Exp PMPM:** $456
**Principal Investments ($000):** Cash and equiv ($510,814)
**Provider Compensation ($000):** None
**Total Member Encounters:** N/A
**Group Affiliation:** Health Net Inc
**Licensed in:** CA
**Address:** 21281 Burbank Blvd, Woodland Hills, CA 91367
**Phone:** (818) 676-8394 **Dom State:** CA **Commenced Bus:** March 1979

| Data Date | Rating | RACR #1 | RACR #2 | Total Assets ($mil) | Capital ($mil) | Net Premium ($mil) | Net Income ($mil) |
|---|---|---|---|---|---|---|---|
| 9-17 | C | 1.80 | 1.20 | 2,341.4 | 987.9 | 4,754.1 | -24.6 |
| 9-16 | C- | 2.01 | 1.25 | 2,338.2 | 868.6 | 5,080.9 | -430.2 |
| 2016 | C | 1.88 | 1.25 | 2,280.5 | 1,001.6 | 6,751.6 | -459.2 |
| 2015 | C+ | 2.42 | 1.51 | 2,592.5 | 1,045.0 | 7,591.8 | -189.6 |
| 2014 | B- | 2.35 | 1.46 | 2,312.8 | 977.9 | 7,418.6 | 6.6 |
| 2013 | C+ | 2.42 | 1.50 | 1,948.3 | 922.2 | 7,078.8 | 65.4 |
| 2012 | B- | 2.54 | 1.57 | 2,196.0 | 1,068.9 | 7,836.5 | 113.9 |

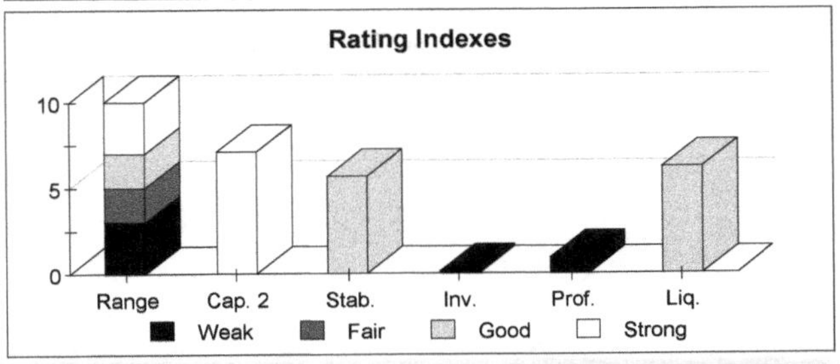


## HEALTH NEW ENGLAND INC — C- — Fair

**Major Rating Factors:** Fair profitability index (3.7 on a scale of 0 to 10). Fair capitalization index (3.6) based on weak current risk-adjusted capital (moderate loss scenario). Good overall results on stability tests (6.0).
**Other Rating Factors:** Good liquidity (6.8) with sufficient resources (cash flows and marketable investments) to handle a spike in claims. High quality investment portfolio (8.9).
**Principal Business:** Comp med (47%), Medicaid (43%), Medicare (10%)
**Mem Phys: 16:** 10,620 **15:** 9,289 **16 MLR** 90.0% **/ 16 Admin Exp** N/A
**Enroll(000): Q3 17:** 158 **16:** 164 **15:** 179 **Med Exp PMPM:** $422
**Principal Investments:** Long-term bonds (63%), cash and equiv (22%), nonaffiliate common stock (7%), affiliate common stock (5%), other (3%)
**Provider Compensation ($000):** Contr fee ($547,326), FFS ($155,967), bonus arrang ($148,354), capitation ($8,538)
**Total Member Encounters:** Phys (1,589,212), non-phys (167,323)
**Group Affiliation:** Baystate Health Inc
**Licensed in:** MA
**Address:** One Monarch Place Suite 1500, Springfield, MA 01144
**Phone:** (413) 787-4000 **Dom State:** MA **Commenced Bus:** January 1986

| Data Date | Rating | RACR #1 | RACR #2 | Total Assets ($mil) | Capital ($mil) | Net Premium ($mil) | Net Income ($mil) |
|---|---|---|---|---|---|---|---|
| 9-17 | C- | 0.72 | 0.60 | 204.3 | 69.6 | 678.3 | 8.8 |
| 9-16 | D- | 0.43 | 0.36 | 166.0 | 46.9 | 699.2 | 10.1 |
| 2016 | D | 0.53 | 0.44 | 179.0 | 54.1 | 930.1 | 18.1 |
| 2015 | D | 0.36 | 0.30 | 165.5 | 40.1 | 898.5 | -20.5 |
| 2014 | B- | 0.84 | 0.70 | 151.0 | 48.0 | 585.0 | -6.7 |
| 2013 | B- | 1.02 | 0.85 | 137.0 | 52.6 | 546.6 | 2.3 |
| 2012 | A- | 1.17 | 0.98 | 127.6 | 50.3 | 494.2 | 2.2 |

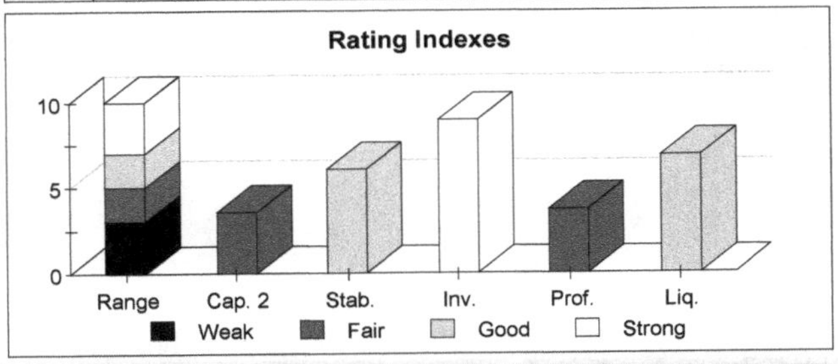


## HEALTH OPTIONS INC * — B+ — Good

**Major Rating Factors:** Good liquidity (6.9 on a scale of 0 to 10) with sufficient resources (cash flows and marketable investments) to handle a spike in claims. Excellent profitability (9.2). Strong capitalization index (10.0) based on excellent current risk-adjusted capital (severe loss scenario).
**Other Rating Factors:** High quality investment portfolio (9.9). Excellent overall results on stability tests (7.4) based on healthy premium and capital growth during 2016. Good financial strength from affiliates.
**Principal Business:** Comp med (79%), Medicare (21%)
**Mem Phys: 16:** N/A **15:** N/A **16 MLR** 77.7% **/ 16 Admin Exp** N/A
**Enroll(000): Q3 17:** 722 **16:** 508 **15:** 371 **Med Exp PMPM:** $322
**Principal Investments:** Long-term bonds (68%), cash and equiv (26%), other (6%)
**Provider Compensation ($000):** Contr fee ($1,834,866), FFS ($61,202), capitation ($49,978), bonus arrang ($5,229)
**Total Member Encounters:** Phys (3,661,079), non-phys (2,320,144)
**Group Affiliation:** GuideWell Mutual Holding Corporation
**Licensed in:** FL
**Address:** 4800 Deerwood Campus Parkway, Jacksonville, FL 32246
**Phone:** (904) 791-6111 **Dom State:** FL **Commenced Bus:** October 1984

| Data Date | Rating | RACR #1 | RACR #2 | Total Assets ($mil) | Capital ($mil) | Net Premium ($mil) | Net Income ($mil) |
|---|---|---|---|---|---|---|---|
| 9-17 | B+ | 4.33 | 3.61 | 1,453.7 | 568.9 | 2,846.7 | 152.5 |
| 9-16 | U | 3.55 | 2.96 | 857.3 | 386.4 | 1,949.9 | 66.4 |
| 2016 | C | 3.15 | 2.63 | 879.8 | 412.0 | 2,585.6 | 101.0 |
| 2015 | U | 3.01 | 2.50 | 689.5 | 326.9 | 2,014.2 | 24.6 |
| 2014 | N/A | N/A | N/A | 560.2 | 241.0 | 1,592.5 | 19.6 |
| 2013 | N/A | N/A | N/A | 387.6 | 216.0 | 1,012.1 | 35.5 |
| 2012 | N/A | N/A | N/A | 268.4 | 181.1 | 671.5 | 16.1 |

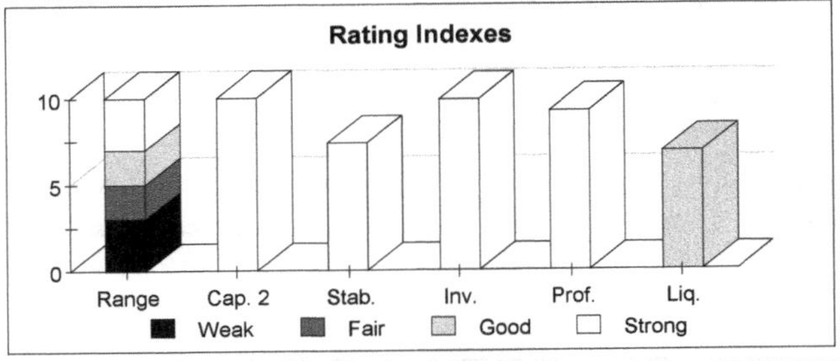

## HEALTH PARTNERS PLANS INC — B- Good

**Major Rating Factors:** Fair profitability index (4.7 on a scale of 0 to 10). Good capitalization index (5.2) based on good current risk-adjusted capital (severe loss scenario). Good overall results on stability tests (6.8).
**Other Rating Factors:** High quality investment portfolio (9.9). Excellent liquidity (7.1) with ample operational cash flow and liquid investments.
**Principal Business:** Medicaid (84%), Medicare (15%)
**Mem Phys: 16:** 8,339 **15:** 6,681 **16 MLR** 80.1% **/ 16 Admin Exp** N/A
**Enroll(000): Q3 17:** 280 **16:** 273 **15:** 253 **Med Exp PMPM:** $485
**Principal Investments:** Cash and equiv (83%), long-term bonds (17%)
**Provider Compensation ($000):** Contr fee ($1,350,419), capitation ($64,605)
**Total Member Encounters:** Phys (2,161,244), non-phys (421,772)
**Group Affiliation:** Health Partners Plans Inc
**Licensed in:** PA
**Address:** 901 MARKET STREET SUITE 500, PHILADELPHIA, PA 19107
**Phone:** (215) 849-9606 **Dom State:** PA **Commenced Bus:** October 1988

| Data Date | Rating | RACR #1 | RACR #2 | Total Assets ($mil) | Capital ($mil) | Net Premium ($mil) | Net Income ($mil) |
|---|---|---|---|---|---|---|---|
| 9-17 | B- | 0.96 | 0.80 | 681.2 | 134.5 | 1,456.0 | 6.6 |
| 9-16 | B- | 1.05 | 0.88 | 609.9 | 120.1 | 1,420.7 | 19.7 |
| 2016 | B- | 0.90 | 0.75 | 620.7 | 126.8 | 1,917.0 | 27.3 |
| 2015 | B- | 0.83 | 0.69 | 469.9 | 96.9 | 1,502.9 | N/A |
| 2014 | B | N/A | N/A | 294.8 | 79.2 | 909.7 | -8.5 |
| 2013 | B | 1.30 | 1.08 | 296.5 | 89.9 | 1,000.3 | -0.2 |
| 2012 | B | 1.25 | 1.04 | 273.6 | 86.7 | 1,034.9 | -1.6 |

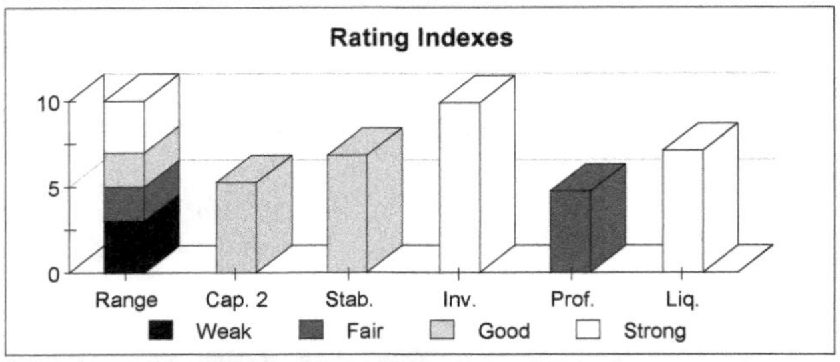


## HEALTH PLAN OF CAREOREGON INC — C Fair

**Major Rating Factors:** Fair liquidity (4.5 on a scale of 0 to 10) as cash resources may not be adequate to cover a spike in claims. Weak profitability index (0.8). Good capitalization (5.8) based on good current risk-adjusted capital (severe loss scenario).
**Other Rating Factors:** High quality investment portfolio (9.9).
**Principal Business:** Medicare (100%)
**Mem Phys: 16:** 1,952 **15:** 1,889 **16 MLR** 94.7% **/ 16 Admin Exp** N/A
**Enroll(000): Q3 17:** 13 **16:** 13 **15:** 12 **Med Exp PMPM:** $998
**Principal Investments:** Long-term bonds (95%), cash and equiv (5%)
**Provider Compensation ($000):** Contr fee ($121,427), FFS ($36,237)
**Total Member Encounters:** Phys (87,890), non-phys (56,005)
**Group Affiliation:** CareOregon Inc
**Licensed in:** OR
**Address:** 315 SW FIFTH AVE Ste 900, PORTLAND, OR 97204-1753
**Phone:** (503) 416-4100 **Dom State:** OR **Commenced Bus:** March 2005

| Data Date | Rating | RACR #1 | RACR #2 | Total Assets ($mil) | Capital ($mil) | Net Premium ($mil) | Net Income ($mil) |
|---|---|---|---|---|---|---|---|
| 9-17 | C | 1.06 | 0.88 | 73.8 | 20.3 | 132.9 | -10.2 |
| 9-16 | C | 1.82 | 1.52 | 72.2 | 32.9 | 120.3 | -6.3 |
| 2016 | C | 1.59 | 1.32 | 60.5 | 30.4 | 163.3 | -8.6 |
| 2015 | C | 2.27 | 1.89 | 69.9 | 40.5 | 145.3 | -16.2 |
| 2014 | B | 2.24 | 1.86 | 57.8 | 34.5 | 130.9 | -5.0 |
| 2013 | B | 3.13 | 2.61 | 66.9 | 40.1 | 115.5 | 0.5 |
| 2012 | B | 3.35 | 2.79 | 57.9 | 38.7 | 105.6 | 3.9 |

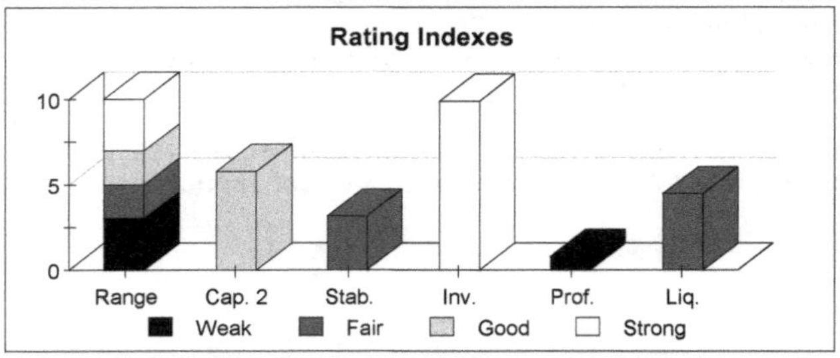


## HEALTH PLAN OF NEVADA INC — B Good

**Major Rating Factors:** Good overall results on stability tests (6.8 on a scale of 0 to 10). Rating is significantly influenced by the fair financial results of UnitedHealth Group Incorporated. Good liquidity (6.7) with sufficient resources (cash flows and marketable investments) to handle a spike in claims. Excellent profitability (9.1).
**Other Rating Factors:** Strong capitalization index (8.6) based on excellent current risk-adjusted capital (severe loss scenario). High quality investment portfolio (9.9).
**Principal Business:** Comp med (38%), Medicaid (35%), Medicare (26%)
**Mem Phys: 16:** 9,840 **15:** 10,160 **16 MLR** 84.2% **/ 16 Admin Exp** N/A
**Enroll(000): Q3 17:** 604 **16:** 595 **15:** 566 **Med Exp PMPM:** $309
**Principal Investments:** Long-term bonds (78%), cash and equiv (17%), real estate (4%), pref stock (1%)
**Provider Compensation ($000):** Contr fee ($1,078,919), capitation ($908,815), FFS ($163,563), bonus arrang ($182)
**Total Member Encounters:** Phys (3,534,561), non-phys (1,665,603)
**Group Affiliation:** UnitedHealth Group Incorporated
**Licensed in:** NV
**Address:** 2720 NORTH TENAYA WAY, LAS VEGAS, NV 89128
**Phone:** (702) 242-7732 **Dom State:** NV **Commenced Bus:** August 1982

| Data Date | Rating | RACR #1 | RACR #2 | Total Assets ($mil) | Capital ($mil) | Net Premium ($mil) | Net Income ($mil) |
|---|---|---|---|---|---|---|---|
| 9-17 | B | 2.64 | 2.20 | 690.0 | 299.0 | 2,081.2 | 126.7 |
| 9-16 | B | 2.50 | 2.08 | 578.6 | 233.4 | 1,919.8 | 48.4 |
| 2016 | B | 1.94 | 1.62 | 524.4 | 216.4 | 2,569.9 | 78.0 |
| 2015 | B | 2.43 | 2.02 | 505.6 | 226.5 | 2,345.0 | 99.5 |
| 2014 | B | 2.82 | 2.35 | 454.5 | 213.4 | 1,931.3 | 89.2 |
| 2013 | B | 3.63 | 3.02 | 381.5 | 224.3 | 1,564.2 | 97.6 |
| 2012 | B | 3.56 | 2.97 | 342.4 | 201.7 | 1,493.7 | 115.1 |

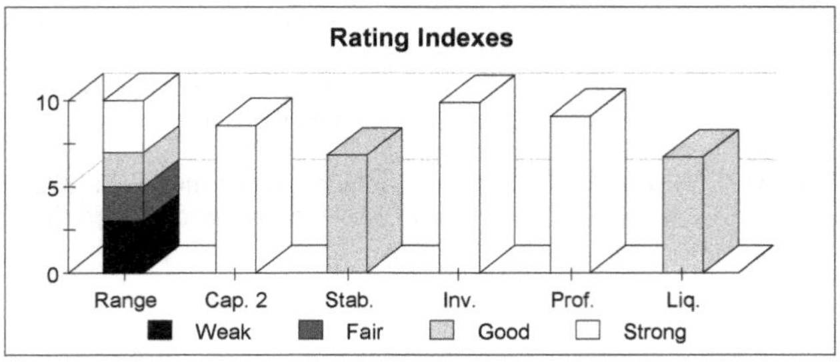

## HEALTH PLAN OF WV INC — C — Fair

**Major Rating Factors:** Fair quality investment portfolio (4.2 on a scale of 0 to 10). Fair overall results on stability tests (4.6) based on a decline in the number of member physicians during 2017. Weak profitability index (1.3).
**Other Rating Factors:** Good liquidity (6.5) with sufficient resources (cash flows and marketable investments) to handle a spike in claims. Strong capitalization index (8.2) based on excellent current risk-adjusted capital (severe loss scenario).
**Principal Business:** Medicaid (52%), Medicare (26%), comp med (22%)
**Mem Phys: 16:** 17,602 **15:** 19,680 **16 MLR** 96.7% **/ 16 Admin Exp** N/A
**Enroll(000): Q3 17:** 123 **16:** 115 **15:** 110 **Med Exp PMPM:** $400
**Principal Investments:** Long-term bonds (53%), nonaffiliate common stock (27%), affiliate common stock (15%), real estate (3%), cash and equiv (2%)
**Provider Compensation ($000):** Contr fee ($532,925)
**Total Member Encounters:** Phys (1,397,432), non-phys (437,030)
**Group Affiliation:** Health Plan of the Upper Ohio Valley
**Licensed in:** OH, WV
**Address:** 52160 National Road E, St Clairsville, OH 43950-9306
**Phone:** (740) 695-3585 **Dom State:** WV **Commenced Bus:** November 1979

| Data Date | Rating | RACR #1 | RACR #2 | Total Assets ($mil) | Capital ($mil) | Net Premium ($mil) | Net Income ($mil) |
|---|---|---|---|---|---|---|---|
| 9-17 | C | 2.35 | 1.96 | 260.8 | 148.3 | 474.4 | -7.8 |
| 9-16 | C | 3.20 | 2.67 | 273.4 | 151.8 | 422.5 | -23.7 |
| 2016 | C | 2.37 | 1.98 | 265.2 | 149.7 | 567.1 | -18.0 |
| 2015 | B | 3.81 | 3.17 | 274.0 | 171.0 | 407.8 | -8.4 |
| 2014 | B+ | 3.60 | 3.00 | 259.9 | 194.8 | 381.5 | 10.9 |
| 2013 | B+ | 3.58 | 2.98 | 245.9 | 191.4 | 363.5 | 16.2 |
| 2012 | B+ | 3.76 | 3.14 | 243.1 | 190.0 | 376.9 | 9.0 |

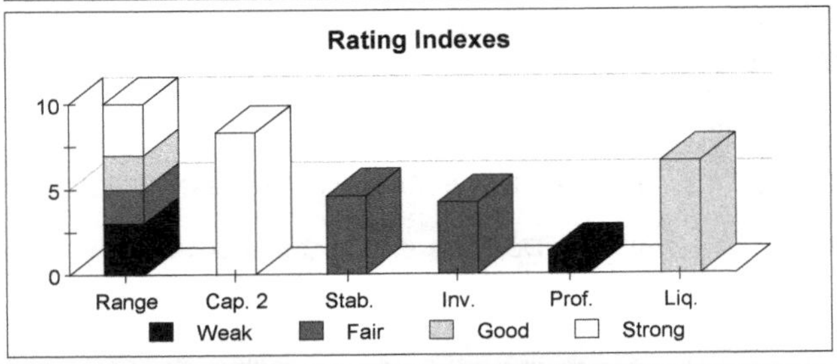


## HEALTH REPUBLIC INS CO — E — Very Weak

**Major Rating Factors:** Weak profitability index (0.0 on a scale of 0 to 10). Poor capitalization (0.0) based on weak current risk-adjusted capital (severe loss scenario). Weak liquidity (0.0) as a spike in claims may stretch capacity.
**Other Rating Factors:** High quality investment portfolio (9.9).
**Principal Business:** Comp med (100%)
**Mem Phys: 15:** N/A **14:** 23,611 **15 MLR** 150.0% **/ 15 Admin Exp** N/A
**Enroll(000): Q3 16:** N/A **15:** 12 **14:** 9 **Med Exp PMPM:** $451
**Principal Investments:** Cash and equiv (98%), long-term bonds (2%)
**Provider Compensation ($000):** Contr fee ($65,021), capitation ($781)
**Total Member Encounters:** N/A
**Group Affiliation:** None
**Licensed in:** OR
**Address:** 2373 NW 185th Ave #701, Hillsboro, OR 97124
**Phone:** (888) 990-6635 **Dom State:** OR **Commenced Bus:** February 2012

| Data Date | Rating | RACR #1 | RACR #2 | Total Assets ($mil) | Capital ($mil) | Net Premium ($mil) | Net Income ($mil) |
|---|---|---|---|---|---|---|---|
| 9-16 | E | 0.29 | 0.24 | 8.8 | 4.1 | -0.5 | -0.6 |
| 9-15 | D+ | 0.64 | 0.54 | 32.6 | 8.2 | 48.3 | -10.9 |
| 2015 | E | 0.30 | 0.25 | 21.5 | 4.2 | 46.2 | -29.3 |
| 2014 | D+ | 0.93 | 0.78 | 38.1 | 11.4 | 25.4 | -12.9 |
| 2013 | N/A | N/A | N/A | 16.1 | 6.3 | N/A | -7.4 |
| 2012 | N/A | N/A | N/A | 3.0 | -1.0 | N/A | N/A |
| 2011 | N/A | N/A | N/A | N/A | N/A | N/A | N/A |

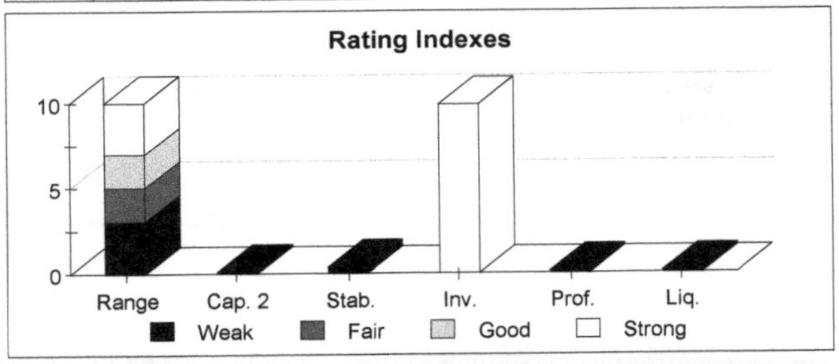


## HEALTH TRADITION HEALTH PLAN — B — Good

**Major Rating Factors:** Good overall profitability index (5.3 on a scale of 0 to 10). Good capitalization index (6.8) based on excellent current risk-adjusted capital (severe loss scenario). Good overall results on stability tests (5.8) despite inconsistent enrollment growth in the past five years due to declines in 2013 and 2015.
**Other Rating Factors:** High quality investment portfolio (9.9). Excellent liquidity (7.0) with ample operational cash flow and liquid investments.
**Principal Business:** Comp med (86%), Medicaid (11%), med supp (3%)
**Mem Phys: 16:** 1,615 **15:** 1,578 **16 MLR** 90.3% **/ 16 Admin Exp** N/A
**Enroll(000): Q3 17:** 36 **16:** 38 **15:** 34 **Med Exp PMPM:** $279
**Principal Investments:** Cash and equiv (88%), long-term bonds (12%)
**Provider Compensation ($000):** Capitation ($82,261), FFS ($24,526), other ($12,377)
**Total Member Encounters:** Phys (228,339), non-phys (154,539)
**Group Affiliation:** Mayo Clinic
**Licensed in:** WI
**Address:** 1808 East Main Street, Onalaska, WI 54650
**Phone:** (507) 538-5212 **Dom State:** WI **Commenced Bus:** April 1986

| Data Date | Rating | RACR #1 | RACR #2 | Total Assets ($mil) | Capital ($mil) | Net Premium ($mil) | Net Income ($mil) |
|---|---|---|---|---|---|---|---|
| 9-17 | B | 1.21 | 1.01 | 47.7 | 12.2 | 113.0 | 0.4 |
| 9-16 | B | 1.25 | 1.04 | 34.9 | 11.9 | 104.9 | -0.3 |
| 2016 | B | 1.20 | 1.00 | 40.6 | 12.1 | 142.2 | 0.0 |
| 2015 | B | 1.27 | 1.06 | 30.1 | 12.1 | 142.3 | -0.3 |
| 2014 | B | 1.09 | 0.90 | 35.8 | 12.8 | 168.3 | 0.4 |
| 2013 | B | 1.07 | 0.89 | 30.2 | 12.5 | 151.3 | 0.3 |
| 2012 | B | 1.04 | 0.87 | 27.7 | 12.2 | 144.5 | 0.5 |

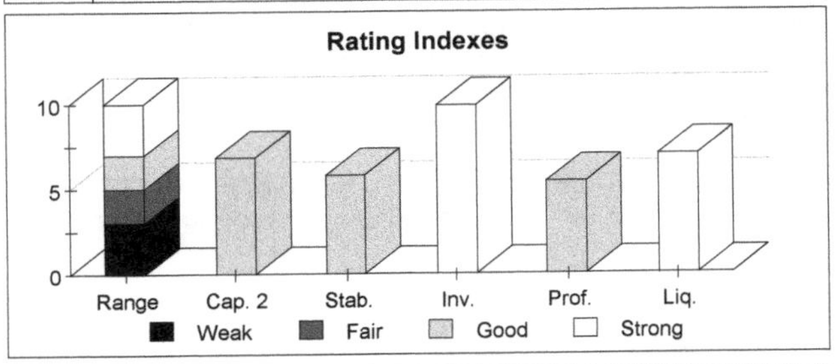

## HEALTHASSURANCE PENNSYLVANIA INC B- Good

**Major Rating Factors:** Fair quality investment portfolio (4.1 on a scale of 0 to 10). Fair overall results on stability tests (4.4) based on a significant 39% decrease in enrollment during the period. Rating is significantly influenced by the good financial results of Aetna Inc. Good liquidity (6.7) with sufficient resources (cash flows and marketable investments) to handle a spike in claims.
**Other Rating Factors:** Excellent profitability (7.2). Strong capitalization index (9.5) based on excellent current risk-adjusted capital (severe loss scenario).
**Principal Business:** Medicare (74%), comp med (26%)
**Mem Phys: 16:** 53,569 **15:** 53,528 **16 MLR** 80.2% **/ 16 Admin Exp** N/A
**Enroll(000): Q3 17:** 76 **16:** 97 **15:** 159 **Med Exp PMPM:** $558
**Principal Investments:** Long-term bonds (101%), nonaffiliate common stock (1%)
**Provider Compensation ($000):** Contr fee ($777,941), FFS ($42,152), capitation ($13,336)
**Total Member Encounters:** Phys (1,085,352), non-phys (244,520)
**Group Affiliation:** Aetna Inc
**Licensed in:** PA
**Address:** 3721 TECPORT DRIVE PO BOX 6710, HARRISBURG, PA 17106-7103
**Phone:** (800) 788-6445 **Dom State:** PA **Commenced Bus:** June 2001

| Data Date | Rating | RACR #1 | RACR #2 | Total Assets ($mil) | Capital ($mil) | Net Premium ($mil) | Net Income ($mil) |
|---|---|---|---|---|---|---|---|
| 9-17 | B- | 3.37 | 2.81 | 417.8 | 170.2 | 595.5 | 29.3 |
| 9-16 | B- | 2.67 | 2.23 | 381.6 | 170.6 | 798.7 | 28.2 |
| 2016 | B- | 3.56 | 2.97 | 323.3 | 180.7 | 1,015.7 | 43.3 |
| 2015 | B- | 2.56 | 2.13 | 335.6 | 162.4 | 1,243.3 | 25.6 |
| 2014 | B | 2.77 | 2.31 | 318.7 | 159.8 | 1,124.5 | 19.6 |
| 2013 | B | 3.02 | 2.52 | 283.5 | 170.5 | 1,065.1 | 30.0 |
| 2012 | B+ | 3.42 | 2.85 | 315.6 | 192.2 | 1,051.0 | 39.4 |

Rating Indexes

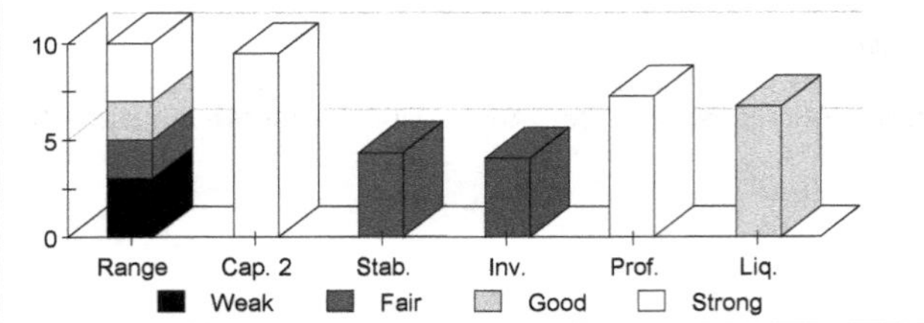


## HEALTHFIRST HEALTH PLAN INC C+ Fair

**Major Rating Factors:** Good liquidity (6.3 on a scale of 0 to 10) with sufficient resources (cash flows and marketable investments) to handle a spike in claims. Weak profitability index (2.3). Strong capitalization index (7.2) based on excellent current risk-adjusted capital (severe loss scenario).
**Other Rating Factors:** High quality investment portfolio (9.9). Excellent overall results on stability tests (7.6) based on steady enrollment growth, averaging 7% over the past five years.
**Principal Business:** Medicare (100%)
**Mem Phys: 16:** 32,873 **15:** 31,334 **16 MLR** 86.4% **/ 16 Admin Exp** N/A
**Enroll(000): Q3 17:** 147 **16:** 139 **15:** 130 **Med Exp PMPM:** $1,179
**Principal Investments:** Long-term bonds (53%), cash and equiv (44%), affiliate common stock (2%)
**Provider Compensation ($000):** Contr fee ($1,713,094), FFS ($76,120), capitation ($22,907)
**Total Member Encounters:** Phys (4,025,975), non-phys (3,896,368)
**Group Affiliation:** HealthFirst Inc
**Licensed in:** NY
**Address:** 100 Church St, New York, NY 10007
**Phone:** (212) 801-6000 **Dom State:** NY **Commenced Bus:** October 1990

| Data Date | Rating | RACR #1 | RACR #2 | Total Assets ($mil) | Capital ($mil) | Net Premium ($mil) | Net Income ($mil) |
|---|---|---|---|---|---|---|---|
| 9-17 | C+ | 1.53 | 1.27 | 993.2 | 286.7 | 1,703.0 | -8.9 |
| 9-16 | B- | 1.38 | 1.15 | 864.3 | 230.5 | 1,636.9 | -4.0 |
| 2016 | B- | 1.38 | 1.15 | 782.8 | 262.5 | 2,238.2 | 6.5 |
| 2015 | B- | 1.45 | 1.21 | 614.3 | 241.5 | 2,022.5 | 5.8 |
| 2014 | B- | 1.43 | 1.19 | 548.7 | 206.9 | 1,775.9 | -32.3 |
| 2013 | B+ | 1.59 | 1.32 | 476.3 | 195.1 | 1,613.4 | -10.2 |
| 2012 | B+ | 1.89 | 1.58 | 502.9 | 207.4 | 1,472.4 | 16.7 |

Rating Indexes

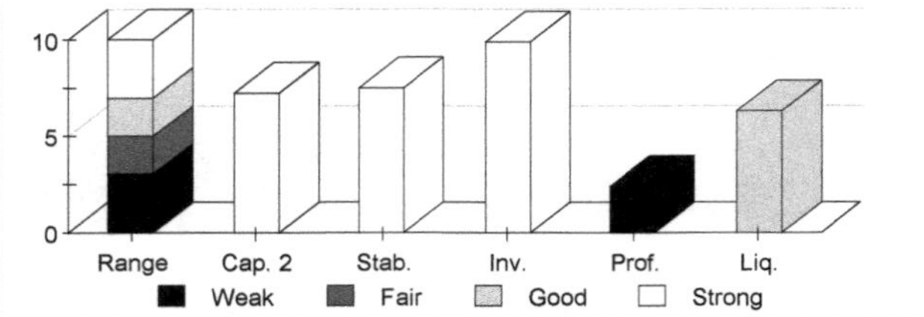


## HEALTHKEEPERS INC * B+ Good

**Major Rating Factors:** Good liquidity (6.8 on a scale of 0 to 10) with sufficient resources (cash flows and marketable investments) to handle a spike in claims. Excellent profitability (8.8). Strong capitalization index (9.7) based on excellent current risk-adjusted capital (severe loss scenario).
**Other Rating Factors:** Excellent overall results on stability tests (7.4). Rating is significantly influenced by the good financial results of Anthem Inc. Fair quality investment portfolio (4.2).
**Principal Business:** Comp med (53%), Medicaid (36%), Medicare (11%)
**Mem Phys: 16:** 26,959 **15:** 26,000 **16 MLR** 85.4% **/ 16 Admin Exp** N/A
**Enroll(000): Q3 17:** 665 **16:** 632 **15:** 629 **Med Exp PMPM:** $344
**Principal Investments:** Long-term bonds (40%), nonaffiliate common stock (23%), cash and equiv (1%), other (36%)
**Provider Compensation ($000):** Contr fee ($2,542,743), FFS ($79,264), capitation ($52,679), bonus arrang ($7,863)
**Total Member Encounters:** Phys (4,462,688), non-phys (2,527,764)
**Group Affiliation:** Anthem Inc
**Licensed in:** VA
**Address:** 2015 STAPLES MILL ROAD, RICHMOND, VA 23230
**Phone:** (804) 354-7000 **Dom State:** VA **Commenced Bus:** September 1986

| Data Date | Rating | RACR #1 | RACR #2 | Total Assets ($mil) | Capital ($mil) | Net Premium ($mil) | Net Income ($mil) |
|---|---|---|---|---|---|---|---|
| 9-17 | B+ | 3.51 | 2.93 | 1,218.8 | 643.9 | 2,555.2 | 186.9 |
| 9-16 | B+ | 2.96 | 2.47 | 1,042.8 | 470.1 | 2,364.5 | 118.7 |
| 2016 | B+ | 2.46 | 2.05 | 1,132.9 | 442.7 | 3,120.5 | 123.8 |
| 2015 | A- | 2.17 | 1.81 | 896.5 | 340.7 | 2,806.1 | 46.2 |
| 2014 | A- | 2.50 | 2.09 | 716.9 | 281.5 | 2,081.4 | 65.3 |
| 2013 | A- | 2.65 | 2.21 | 490.8 | 249.2 | 1,658.7 | 70.3 |
| 2012 | A+ | 2.78 | 2.32 | 515.3 | 278.8 | 1,762.2 | 104.4 |

Rating Indexes

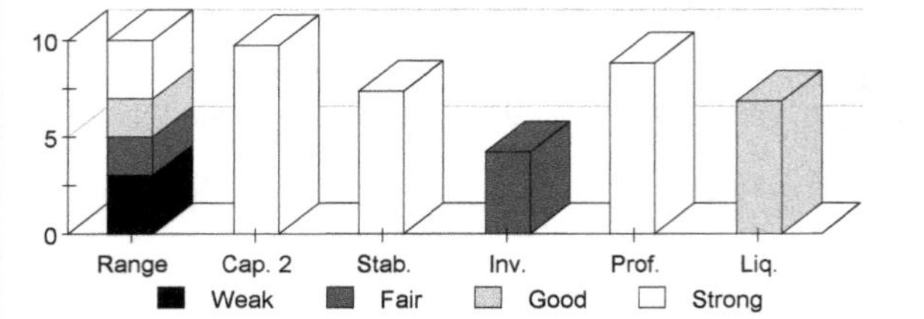

## HEALTHNOW NY INC C+ Fair

**Major Rating Factors:** Fair profitability index (3.5 on a scale of 0 to 10). Good liquidity (6.8) with sufficient resources (cash flows and marketable investments) to handle a spike in claims. Strong capitalization (10.0) based on excellent current risk-adjusted capital (severe loss scenario).
**Other Rating Factors:** High quality investment portfolio (9.4).
**Principal Business:** Comp med (64%), Medicare (25%), Medicaid (6%), FEHB (3%)
**Mem Phys: 16:** 30,076 **15:** 29,255 **16 MLR** 88.6% **/ 16 Admin Exp** N/A
**Enroll(000): Q3 17:** 405 **16:** 392 **15:** 399 **Med Exp PMPM:** $439
**Principal Investments:** Long-term bonds (76%), nonaffiliate common stock (19%), cash and equiv (1%), pref stock (1%), affiliate common stock (1%), other (2%)
**Provider Compensation ($000):** Contr fee ($2,019,982), capitation ($20,419)
**Total Member Encounters:** Phys (3,127,993), non-phys (1,381,510)
**Group Affiliation:** HealthNow Systems Inc
**Licensed in:** NY
**Address:** 257 West Genesee St, Buffalo, NY 14202
**Phone:** (716) 887-6900 **Dom State:** NY **Commenced Bus:** March 1940

| Data Date | Rating | RACR #1 | RACR #2 | Total Assets ($mil) | Capital ($mil) | Net Premium ($mil) | Net Income ($mil) |
|---|---|---|---|---|---|---|---|
| 9-17 | C+ | 3.87 | 3.23 | 1,140.1 | 609.2 | 1,878.1 | 64.0 |
| 9-16 | C+ | 3.68 | 3.07 | 1,069.1 | 564.2 | 1,729.8 | 23.8 |
| 2016 | C+ | 3.37 | 2.81 | 1,062.3 | 541.5 | 2,311.2 | 4.2 |
| 2015 | C+ | 3.53 | 2.94 | 1,037.8 | 544.4 | 2,242.3 | 63.8 |
| 2014 | B- | 2.64 | 2.20 | 1,041.3 | 486.5 | 2,443.8 | -53.2 |
| 2013 | A | 3.27 | 2.72 | 1,009.5 | 591.7 | 2,463.2 | 31.7 |
| 2012 | A | 3.20 | 2.66 | 1,010.3 | 556.8 | 2,455.4 | 31.5 |

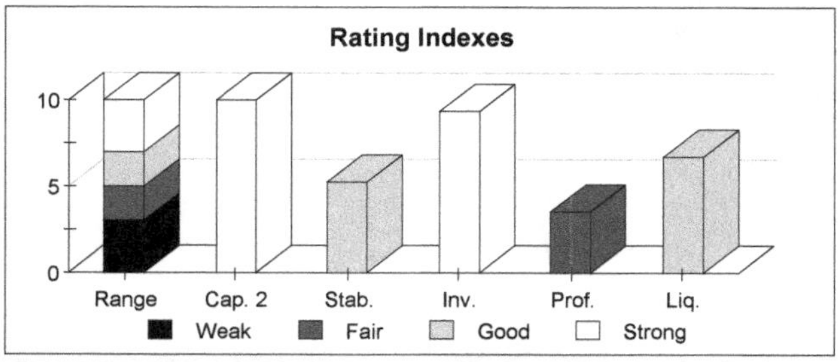


## HEALTHPARTNERS * A+ Excellent

**Major Rating Factors:** Strong capitalization index (9.7 on a scale of 0 to 10) based on excellent current risk-adjusted capital (severe loss scenario). High quality investment portfolio (9.5). Excellent liquidity (7.2) with ample operational cash flow and liquid investments.
**Other Rating Factors:** Good overall profitability index (6.7). Good overall results on stability tests (6.7).
**Principal Business:** Comp med (50%), Medicaid (46%), dental (4%)
**Mem Phys: 16:** 64,919 **15:** 57,617 **16 MLR** 90.7% **/ 16 Admin Exp** N/A
**Enroll(000): Q3 17:** 320 **16:** 239 **15:** 249 **Med Exp PMPM:** $428
**Principal Investments:** Long-term bonds (51%), cash and equiv (25%), nonaffiliate common stock (16%), other (8%)
**Provider Compensation ($000):** Bonus arrang ($847,517), contr fee ($354,224)
**Total Member Encounters:** Phys (2,014,674), non-phys (264,367)
**Group Affiliation:** HealthPartners Inc
**Licensed in:** MN
**Address:** 8170 33RD AVENUE SOUTH, MINNEAPOLIS, MN 55440-1309
**Phone:** (952) 883-6000 **Dom State:** MN **Commenced Bus:** March 1984

| Data Date | Rating | RACR #1 | RACR #2 | Total Assets ($mil) | Capital ($mil) | Net Premium ($mil) | Net Income ($mil) |
|---|---|---|---|---|---|---|---|
| 9-17 | A+ | 3.55 | 2.96 | 1,213.6 | 953.4 | 1,248.4 | 3.2 |
| 9-16 | A+ | 3.82 | 3.18 | 1,135.5 | 919.8 | 1,019.2 | 17.7 |
| 2016 | A+ | 3.40 | 2.83 | 1,179.5 | 911.4 | 1,371.7 | 22.2 |
| 2015 | A+ | 3.89 | 3.24 | 1,247.4 | 938.1 | 1,425.0 | 76.8 |
| 2014 | A | 3.60 | 3.00 | 1,236.0 | 908.6 | 1,350.2 | 16.8 |
| 2013 | B+ | 3.71 | 3.09 | 1,055.6 | 846.4 | 1,279.2 | 65.6 |
| 2012 | C- | 3.30 | 2.75 | 866.7 | 709.1 | 1,379.2 | 106.4 |

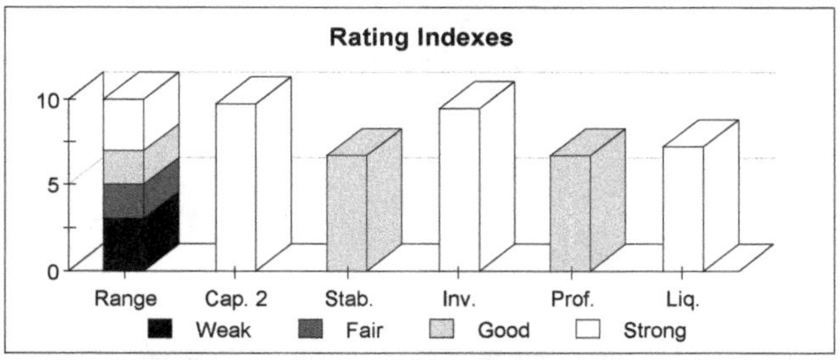


## HEALTHPARTNERS INS CO B Good

**Major Rating Factors:** Good liquidity (6.8 on a scale of 0 to 10) with sufficient resources (cash flows and marketable investments) to handle a spike in claims. Fair profitability index (3.4). Strong capitalization (8.8) based on excellent current risk-adjusted capital (severe loss scenario).
**Other Rating Factors:** High quality investment portfolio (9.9).
**Principal Business:** Comp med (91%), other (8%)
**Mem Phys: 16:** 64,822 **15:** 57,617 **16 MLR** 89.4% **/ 16 Admin Exp** N/A
**Enroll(000): Q3 17:** 607 **16:** 680 **15:** 672 **Med Exp PMPM:** $114
**Principal Investments:** Long-term bonds (48%), cash and equiv (40%), nonaffiliate common stock (12%)
**Provider Compensation ($000):** Bonus arrang ($561,529), contr fee ($360,371)
**Total Member Encounters:** Phys (1,325,639), non-phys (155,332)
**Group Affiliation:** HealthPartners Inc
**Licensed in:** IA, MN, NE, ND, WI
**Address:** 8170 33RD Ave S, MINNEAPOLIS, MN 55440-1309
**Phone:** (952) 883-6000 **Dom State:** MN **Commenced Bus:** January 1991

| Data Date | Rating | RACR #1 | RACR #2 | Total Assets ($mil) | Capital ($mil) | Net Premium ($mil) | Net Income ($mil) |
|---|---|---|---|---|---|---|---|
| 9-17 | B | 2.80 | 2.33 | 386.9 | 193.5 | 784.8 | 29.7 |
| 9-16 | B | 2.41 | 2.01 | 375.1 | 152.7 | 785.8 | 2.2 |
| 2016 | B | 2.33 | 1.94 | 372.7 | 159.1 | 1,053.8 | -11.8 |
| 2015 | B+ | 2.35 | 1.96 | 331.1 | 148.8 | 1,014.0 | -10.5 |
| 2014 | A- | 2.89 | 2.41 | 319.0 | 160.5 | 943.2 | 10.1 |
| 2013 | A- | 2.75 | 2.29 | 279.0 | 148.9 | 892.7 | 1.3 |
| 2012 | A- | 2.76 | 2.30 | 272.3 | 148.9 | 880.7 | 14.0 |

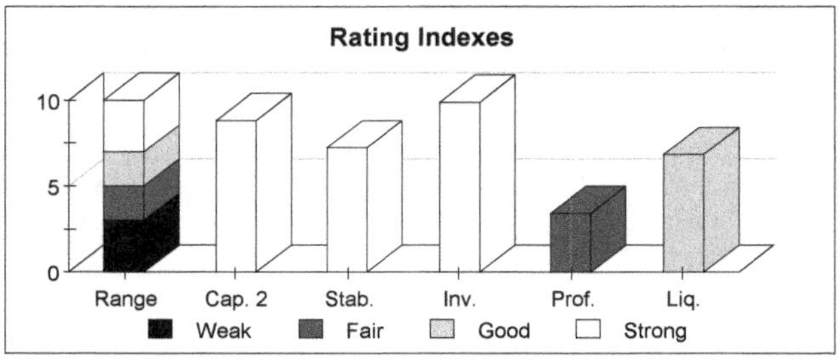

## HEALTHPLEX OF NJ INC — D+ Weak

**Major Rating Factors:** Weak profitability index (1.1 on a scale of 0 to 10). Good capitalization (6.1) based on good current risk-adjusted capital (severe loss scenario). High quality investment portfolio (9.9).
**Other Rating Factors:** Excellent liquidity (7.0) with ample operational cash flow and liquid investments.
**Principal Business:** Dental (100%)
**Mem Phys: 16:** N/A **15:** N/A **16 MLR** 95.9% **/ 16 Admin Exp** N/A
**Enroll(000): 16:** 209 **15:** 272 **Med Exp PMPM:** $10
**Principal Investments:** Cash and equiv (100%)
**Provider Compensation ($000):** FFS ($26,877), capitation ($2,660)
**Total Member Encounters:** Non-phys (236,649)
**Group Affiliation:** Healthplex Inc
**Licensed in:** NJ
**Address:** 333 Earle Ovington Blvd #300, Uniondale, NY 11553
**Phone:** (516) 542-2200 **Dom State:** NJ **Commenced Bus:** May 2007

| Data Date | Rating | RACR #1 | RACR #2 | Total Assets ($mil) | Capital ($mil) | Net Premium ($mil) | Net Income ($mil) |
|---|---|---|---|---|---|---|---|
| 2016 | D+ | 1.09 | 0.91 | 6.0 | 4.2 | 29.7 | -0.3 |
| 2015 | N/A | N/A | N/A | 6.1 | 2.9 | 37.9 | N/A |
| 2014 | N/A | N/A | N/A | 7.0 | 2.5 | 30.5 | N/A |
| 2013 | N/A | N/A | N/A | 2.6 | 1.6 | 16.3 | N/A |
| 2012 | N/A | N/A | N/A | 2.5 | 1.2 | 14.3 | N/A |

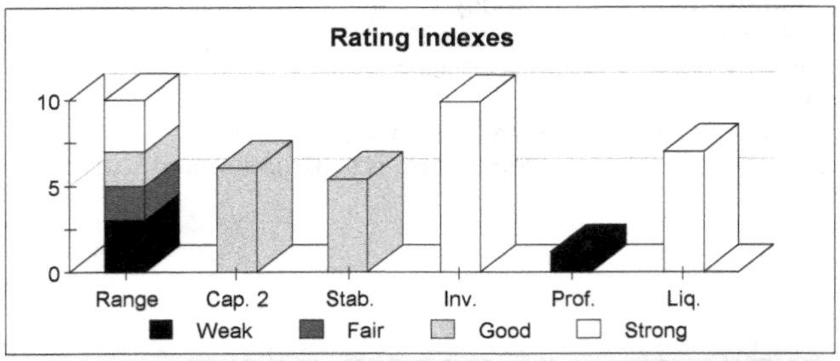


## HEALTHSPRING L&H INS CO — C+ Fair

**Major Rating Factors:** Good quality investment portfolio (6.8 on a scale of 0 to 10). Good liquidity (6.3) with sufficient resources (cash flows and marketable investments) to handle a spike in claims. Weak profitability index (1.9).
**Other Rating Factors:** Strong capitalization (7.8) based on excellent current risk-adjusted capital (severe loss scenario).
**Principal Business:** Medicare (63%), Medicaid (37%)
**Mem Phys: 16:** 22,721 **15:** 20,733 **16 MLR** 85.7% **/ 16 Admin Exp** N/A
**Enroll(000): Q3 17:** 146 **16:** 162 **15:** 167 **Med Exp PMPM:** $999
**Principal Investments:** Long-term bonds (79%), cash and equiv (21%)
**Provider Compensation ($000):** FFS ($1,492,318), capitation ($531,900)
**Total Member Encounters:** Phys (6,423,723), non-phys (1,784,347)
**Group Affiliation:** Cigna Corporation
**Licensed in:** All states except PR
**Address:** 2900 N LOOP WEST Ste 1300, HOUSTON, TX 77092
**Phone:** (615) 291-7000 **Dom State:** TX **Commenced Bus:** February 2007

| Data Date | Rating | RACR #1 | RACR #2 | Total Assets ($mil) | Capital ($mil) | Net Premium ($mil) | Net Income ($mil) |
|---|---|---|---|---|---|---|---|
| 9-17 | C+ | 1.96 | 1.63 | 643.1 | 252.6 | 1,562.2 | -35.3 |
| 9-16 | B | 2.89 | 2.41 | 765.9 | 341.2 | 1,793.0 | 20.9 |
| 2016 | B | 2.16 | 1.80 | 602.8 | 280.2 | 2,367.0 | -50.8 |
| 2015 | B | 2.78 | 2.32 | 614.0 | 327.4 | 2,213.5 | 46.1 |
| 2014 | B- | 3.04 | 2.54 | 586.1 | 328.7 | 2,205.4 | -7.9 |
| 2013 | B | 4.22 | 3.52 | 671.9 | 384.7 | 2,124.3 | 57.4 |
| 2012 | B | 5.04 | 4.20 | 796.2 | 439.3 | 2,167.8 | 118.0 |

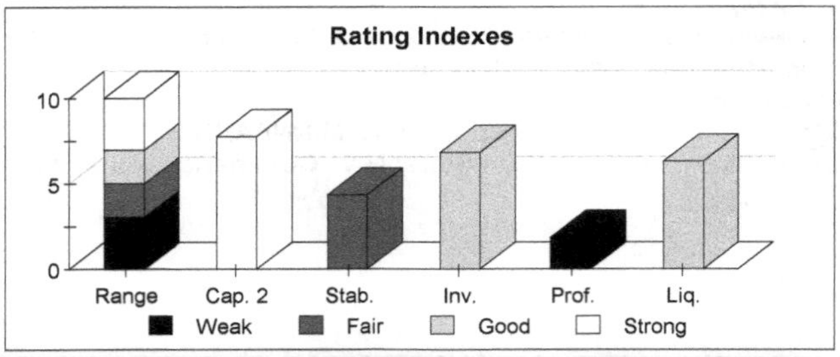


## HEALTHSPRING OF ALABAMA INC — B Good

**Major Rating Factors:** Good overall results on stability tests (5.4 on a scale of 0 to 10). Rating is significantly influenced by the good financial results of Cigna Corporation. Good liquidity (6.7) with sufficient resources (cash flows and marketable investments) to handle a spike in claims. Fair profitability index (4.5).
**Other Rating Factors:** Strong capitalization index (8.2) based on excellent current risk-adjusted capital (severe loss scenario). High quality investment portfolio (8.4).
**Principal Business:** Medicare (100%)
**Mem Phys: 16:** 4,889 **15:** 4,816 **16 MLR** 83.2% **/ 16 Admin Exp** N/A
**Enroll(000): Q3 17:** 47 **16:** 53 **15:** 56 **Med Exp PMPM:** $856
**Principal Investments:** Long-term bonds (79%), cash and equiv (21%)
**Provider Compensation ($000):** Contr fee ($294,165), capitation ($176,543), FFS ($92,098)
**Total Member Encounters:** Phys (434,792), non-phys (498,930)
**Group Affiliation:** Cigna Corporation
**Licensed in:** AL
**Address:** 2 CHASE CORPORATE DRIVE, BIRMINGHAM, AL 35244
**Phone:** (205) 423-1000 **Dom State:** AL **Commenced Bus:** May 1986

| Data Date | Rating | RACR #1 | RACR #2 | Total Assets ($mil) | Capital ($mil) | Net Premium ($mil) | Net Income ($mil) |
|---|---|---|---|---|---|---|---|
| 9-17 | B | 2.32 | 1.93 | 213.1 | 77.6 | 463.8 | 16.1 |
| 9-16 | B- | 2.35 | 1.96 | 204.8 | 75.8 | 534.7 | 19.2 |
| 2016 | B- | 1.83 | 1.53 | 154.5 | 60.3 | 694.8 | 3.3 |
| 2015 | B- | 1.80 | 1.50 | 138.2 | 57.3 | 637.7 | -8.9 |
| 2014 | B | 2.57 | 2.14 | 124.7 | 73.6 | 528.2 | 7.3 |
| 2013 | B | 3.28 | 2.73 | 139.8 | 81.0 | 502.9 | 14.9 |
| 2012 | B | 4.12 | 3.43 | 141.5 | 92.3 | 473.7 | 26.2 |

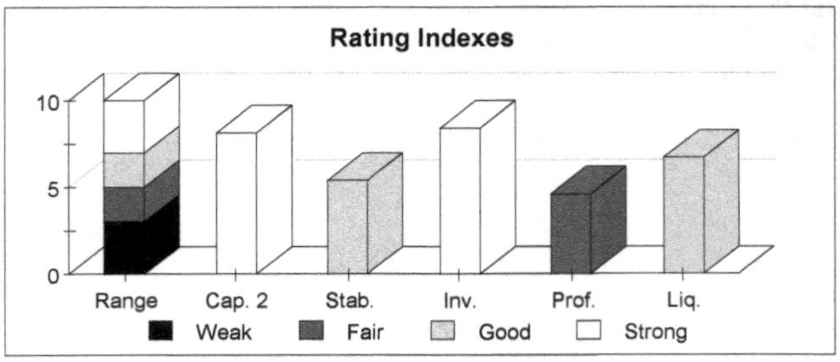

## HEALTHSPRING OF FLORIDA INC * B+ Good

**Major Rating Factors:** Good liquidity (6.7 on a scale of 0 to 10) with sufficient resources (cash flows and marketable investments) to handle a spike in claims. Excellent profitability (8.9). Strong capitalization (8.5) based on excellent current risk-adjusted capital (severe loss scenario).
**Other Rating Factors:** High quality investment portfolio (6.9).
**Principal Business:** Medicare (100%)
**Mem Phys: 16:** 2,081 **15:** 1,958 **16 MLR** 81.9% **/ 16 Admin Exp** N/A
**Enroll(000): Q3 17:** 46 **16:** 48 **15:** 51 **Med Exp PMPM:** $1,184
**Principal Investments:** Long-term bonds (99%), cash and equiv (1%)
**Provider Compensation ($000):** Capitation ($386,962), contr fee ($240,396), FFS ($105,844)
**Total Member Encounters:** Phys (947,236), non-phys (653,184)
**Group Affiliation:** Cigna Corporation
**Licensed in:** FL
**Address:** 8600 NW 41ST St Ste 201, DORAL, FL 33166
**Phone:** (305) 229-7461 **Dom State:** FL **Commenced Bus:** August 2002

| Data Date | Rating | RACR #1 | RACR #2 | Total Assets ($mil) | Capital ($mil) | Net Premium ($mil) | Net Income ($mil) |
|---|---|---|---|---|---|---|---|
| 9-17 | B+ | 2.52 | 2.10 | 233.5 | 93.1 | 578.9 | 2.9 |
| 9-16 | B | 2.05 | 1.71 | 223.1 | 79.3 | 662.6 | 17.0 |
| 2016 | B+ | 2.42 | 2.02 | 157.0 | 89.5 | 866.7 | 26.9 |
| 2015 | B | 1.62 | 1.35 | 144.1 | 62.3 | 886.0 | 9.2 |
| 2014 | B | 1.56 | 1.30 | 123.7 | 54.7 | 784.0 | 6.4 |
| 2013 | B | 1.55 | 1.29 | 98.7 | 48.5 | 752.5 | 14.8 |
| 2012 | B- | 1.11 | 0.92 | 78.3 | 33.5 | 711.2 | 6.9 |

Rating Indexes

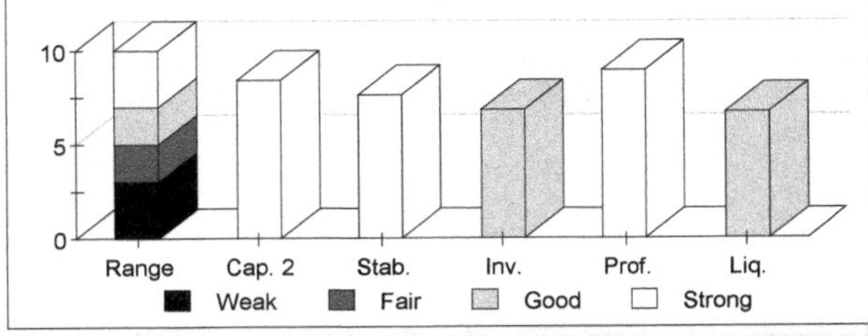


## HEALTHSPRING OF TENNESSEE INC * B+ Good

**Major Rating Factors:** Good overall results on stability tests (6.0 on a scale of 0 to 10). Rating is significantly influenced by the good financial results of Cigna Corporation. Good liquidity (6.2) with sufficient resources (cash flows and marketable investments) to handle a spike in claims. Excellent profitability (8.0).
**Other Rating Factors:** Strong capitalization index (7.9) based on excellent current risk-adjusted capital (severe loss scenario). High quality investment portfolio (7.3).
**Principal Business:** Medicare (91%), Medicaid (9%)
**Mem Phys: 16:** 29,730 **15:** 20,264 **16 MLR** 82.1% **/ 16 Admin Exp** N/A
**Enroll(000): Q3 17:** 105 **16:** 126 **15:** 130 **Med Exp PMPM:** $853
**Principal Investments:** Long-term bonds (83%), cash and equiv (17%)
**Provider Compensation ($000):** FFS ($1,038,022), capitation ($325,080)
**Total Member Encounters:** Phys (2,455,079), non-phys (687,702)
**Group Affiliation:** Cigna Corporation
**Licensed in:** AR, IL, MS, TN
**Address:** 530 GREAT CIRCLE ROAD, NASHVILLE, TN 37228-1513
**Phone:** (615) 291-7000 **Dom State:** TN **Commenced Bus:** July 1995

| Data Date | Rating | RACR #1 | RACR #2 | Total Assets ($mil) | Capital ($mil) | Net Premium ($mil) | Net Income ($mil) |
|---|---|---|---|---|---|---|---|
| 9-17 | B+ | 2.06 | 1.72 | 460.4 | 198.8 | 1,065.6 | 19.6 |
| 9-16 | B | 1.86 | 1.55 | 470.0 | 176.5 | 1,282.5 | 12.5 |
| 2016 | B+ | 1.83 | 1.52 | 364.2 | 176.2 | 1,667.7 | 14.2 |
| 2015 | B | 1.67 | 1.40 | 345.4 | 159.3 | 1,589.6 | 21.2 |
| 2014 | B | 1.40 | 1.16 | 286.1 | 117.6 | 1,366.2 | 3.4 |
| 2013 | C+ | 1.64 | 1.37 | 260.0 | 116.0 | 1,170.1 | 9.5 |
| 2012 | B | 2.76 | 2.30 | 270.2 | 157.4 | 1,052.2 | 51.0 |

Rating Indexes

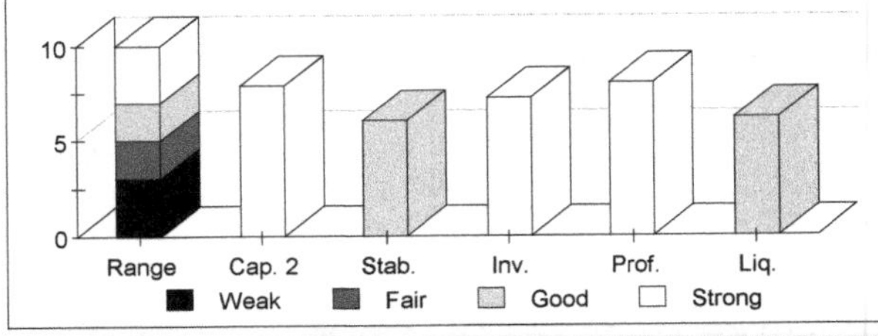


## HEALTHSUN HEALTH PLANS INC C- Fair

**Major Rating Factors:** Fair capitalization (3.7 on a scale of 0 to 10) based on weak current risk-adjusted capital (moderate loss scenario). Excellent profitability (8.7). High quality investment portfolio (9.9).
**Other Rating Factors:** Excellent liquidity (7.1) with ample operational cash flow and liquid investments.
**Principal Business:** Medicare (100%)
**Mem Phys: 15:** 4,034 **14:** 3,551 **15 MLR** 88.7% **/ 15 Admin Exp** N/A
**Enroll(000): Q3 16:** 36 **15:** 31 **14:** 28 **Med Exp PMPM:** $1,775
**Principal Investments:** Cash and equiv (100%)
**Provider Compensation ($000):** Capitation ($313,117), FFS ($207,594), contr fee ($99,430)
**Total Member Encounters:** Phys (573,365), non-phys (249,434)
**Group Affiliation:** None
**Licensed in:** FL
**Address:** 3250 MARY ST #400, COCONUT GROVE, FL 33133
**Phone:** (305) 448-8100 **Dom State:** FL **Commenced Bus:** August 2005

| Data Date | Rating | RACR #1 | RACR #2 | Total Assets ($mil) | Capital ($mil) | Net Premium ($mil) | Net Income ($mil) |
|---|---|---|---|---|---|---|---|
| 9-16 | C- | 0.73 | 0.61 | 156.7 | 35.9 | 587.4 | 13.5 |
| 9-15 | C- | 0.70 | 0.58 | 109.7 | 25.3 | 509.7 | 19.4 |
| 2015 | C- | 0.62 | 0.51 | 130.1 | 30.8 | 695.7 | 23.5 |
| 2014 | C | 0.64 | 0.53 | 74.0 | 23.3 | 503.8 | 20.7 |
| 2013 | C- | 0.48 | 0.40 | 55.7 | 13.2 | 414.0 | 11.3 |
| 2012 | C+ | 0.73 | 0.61 | 56.3 | 13.3 | 309.5 | 12.1 |
| 2011 | N/A | N/A | N/A | 23.9 | 4.6 | 129.3 | N/A |

Rating Indexes

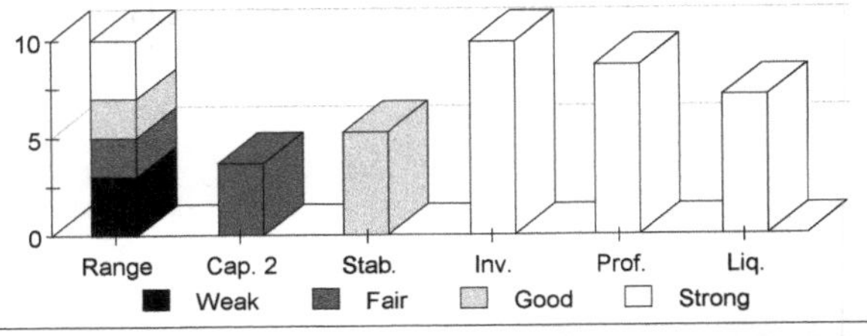

## HEALTHY ALLIANCE LIFE INS CO * A- Excellent

**Major Rating Factors:** Excellent profitability (9.1 on a scale of 0 to 10). Strong capitalization (10.0) based on excellent current risk-adjusted capital (severe loss scenario). High quality investment portfolio (7.6).
**Other Rating Factors:** Good liquidity (6.9) with sufficient resources (cash flows and marketable investments) to handle a spike in claims.
**Principal Business:** Comp med (71%), FEHB (21%), med supp (4%), dental (1%), other (2%)
**Mem Phys: 16:** 20,127 **15:** 19,135 **16 MLR** 79.5% **/ 16 Admin Exp** N/A
**Enroll(000): Q3 17:** 817 **16:** 692 **15:** 681 **Med Exp PMPM:** $183
**Principal Investments:** Long-term bonds (77%), other (23%)
**Provider Compensation ($000):** Contr fee ($857,671), FFS ($641,354), bonus arrang ($4,591), capitation ($127), other ($28,289)
**Total Member Encounters:** Phys (2,360,898), non-phys (1,755,234)
**Group Affiliation:** Anthem Inc
**Licensed in:** KS, MO
**Address:** 1831 CHESTNUT St, ST. LOUIS, MO 63103-2275
**Phone:** (314) 923-4444 **Dom State:** MO **Commenced Bus:** June 1971

| Data Date | Rating | RACR #1 | RACR #2 | Total Assets ($mil) | Capital ($mil) | Net Premium ($mil) | Net Income ($mil) |
|---|---|---|---|---|---|---|---|
| 9-17 | A- | 4.58 | 3.81 | 1,295.0 | 467.9 | 1,930.8 | 172.1 |
| 9-16 | B+ | 4.46 | 3.72 | 875.0 | 399.4 | 1,450.5 | 128.7 |
| 2016 | A- | 4.13 | 3.44 | 890.1 | 420.4 | 1,942.0 | 142.8 |
| 2015 | A- | 4.25 | 3.54 | 829.4 | 379.6 | 1,811.5 | 106.3 |
| 2014 | A- | 4.50 | 3.75 | 870.8 | 397.8 | 1,872.9 | 109.8 |
| 2013 | A- | 3.89 | 3.24 | 862.2 | 380.8 | 1,883.4 | 133.4 |
| 2012 | A- | 3.70 | 3.08 | 774.4 | 342.7 | 1,845.0 | 107.9 |

Rating Indexes

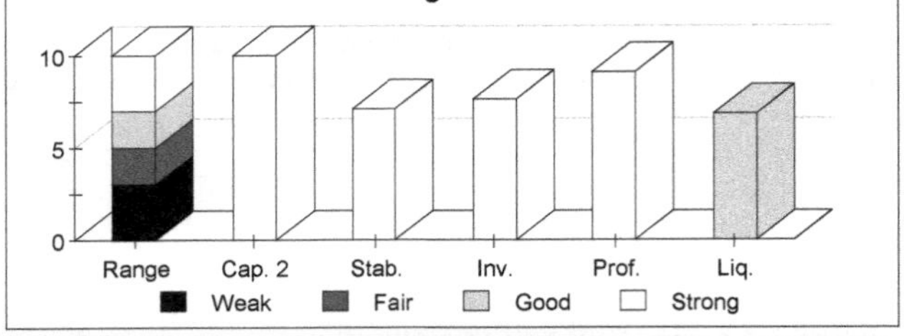


## HEARTLANDPLAINS HEALTH E- Very Weak

**Major Rating Factors:** Weak profitability index (0.2 on a scale of 0 to 10). Fair liquidity (4.0) as cash resources may not be adequate to cover a spike in claims. Strong capitalization (7.6) based on excellent current risk-adjusted capital (severe loss scenario).
**Other Rating Factors:** High quality investment portfolio (9.9).
**Principal Business:** Medicare (100%)
**Mem Phys: 16:** 3,881 **15:** 3,651 **16 MLR** 111.2% **/ 16 Admin Exp** N/A
**Enroll(000): Q3 17:** 1 **16:** 1 **15:** 1 **Med Exp PMPM:** $654
**Principal Investments:** Long-term bonds (98%), cash and equiv (2%)
**Provider Compensation ($000):** Contr fee ($6,317), capitation ($121), other ($487)
**Total Member Encounters:** Phys (11,696), non-phys (4,017)
**Group Affiliation:** Catholic Health Initiatives
**Licensed in:** NE
**Address:** PO Box 31457, Omaha, NE 68131
**Phone:** (866) 789-7747 **Dom State:** NE **Commenced Bus:** January 2015

| Data Date | Rating | RACR #1 | RACR #2 | Total Assets ($mil) | Capital ($mil) | Net Premium ($mil) | Net Income ($mil) |
|---|---|---|---|---|---|---|---|
| 9-17 | E- | 1.88 | 1.56 | 5.0 | 2.0 | 4.2 | -0.2 |
| 9-16 | N/A | N/A | N/A | 5.4 | 2.4 | 4.7 | -1.3 |
| 2016 | E- | 1.59 | 1.33 | 4.6 | 1.7 | 6.3 | -2.0 |
| 2015 | N/A | N/A | N/A | 4.4 | 2.2 | 3.5 | -1.9 |
| 2014 | N/A | N/A | N/A | 3.3 | 3.3 | N/A | N/A |
| 2013 | N/A | N/A | N/A | N/A | N/A | N/A | N/A |
| 2012 | N/A | N/A | N/A | N/A | N/A | N/A | N/A |

Rating Indexes

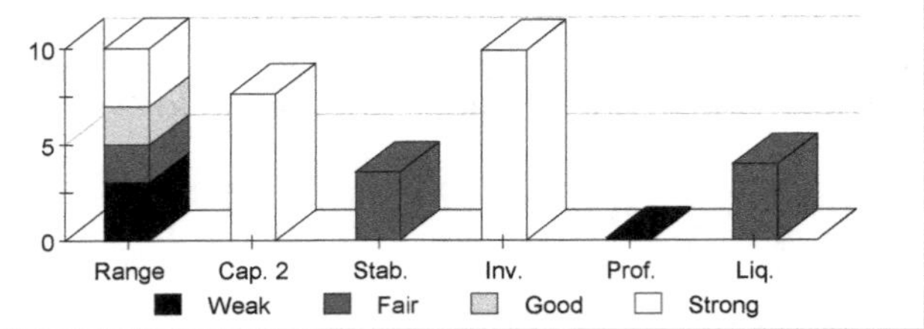


## HENNEPIN HEALTH C Fair

**Major Rating Factors:** Fair profitability index (4.3 on a scale of 0 to 10). Good overall results on stability tests (5.3) despite a decline in the number of member physicians during 2017. Strong capitalization index (8.8) based on excellent current risk-adjusted capital (severe loss scenario).
**Other Rating Factors:** High quality investment portfolio (8.4). Excellent liquidity (7.4) with ample operational cash flow and liquid investments.
**Principal Business:** Medicaid (99%), other (1%)
**Mem Phys: 16:** 2,065 **15:** 4,428 **16 MLR** 87.1% **/ 16 Admin Exp** N/A
**Enroll(000): Q3 17:** 30 **16:** 12 **15:** 13 **Med Exp PMPM:** $820
**Principal Investments:** Cash and equiv (98%), real estate (2%)
**Provider Compensation ($000):** Contr fee ($63,105), bonus arrang ($46,324)
**Total Member Encounters:** Phys (79,897), non-phys (53,576)
**Group Affiliation:** Hennepin Health
**Licensed in:** MN
**Address:** 400 South 4th Street Suite 201, Minneapolis, MN 55415
**Phone:** (612) 596-1036 **Dom State:** MN **Commenced Bus:** June 1984

| Data Date | Rating | RACR #1 | RACR #2 | Total Assets ($mil) | Capital ($mil) | Net Premium ($mil) | Net Income ($mil) |
|---|---|---|---|---|---|---|---|
| 9-17 | C | 2.79 | 2.32 | 88.9 | 37.0 | 169.7 | 2.9 |
| 9-16 | C- | 2.54 | 2.12 | 63.6 | 33.7 | 95.6 | 0.6 |
| 2016 | C- | 2.60 | 2.17 | 72.1 | 34.6 | 127.0 | 0.6 |
| 2015 | C- | 2.57 | 2.14 | 93.0 | 34.1 | 143.6 | -3.4 |
| 2014 | C- | N/A | N/A | 86.7 | 28.5 | 158.2 | -0.3 |
| 2013 | C- | 1.95 | 1.63 | 64.6 | 28.3 | 154.5 | 4.0 |
| 2012 | C- | 1.98 | 1.65 | 57.1 | 24.7 | 132.4 | 5.5 |

Rating Indexes

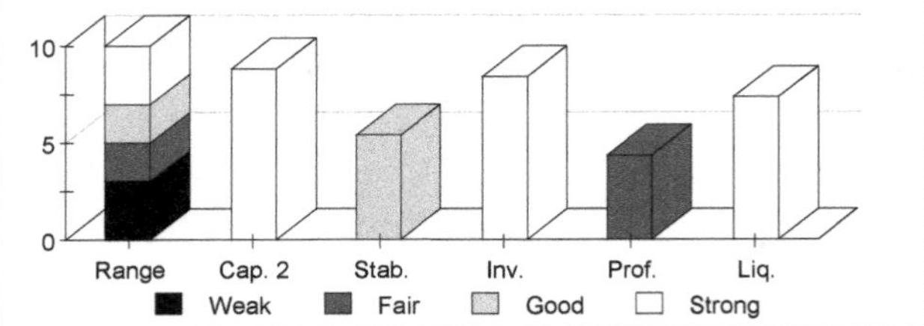

## HERITAGE PROVIDER NETWORK INC — D — Weak

**Major Rating Factors:** Fair capitalization index (3.6 on a scale of 0 to 10) based on weak current risk-adjusted capital (moderate loss scenario). Good overall profitability index (5.9). Good overall results on stability tests (5.1).
**Other Rating Factors:** Excellent liquidity (6.9) with sufficient resources (cash flows and marketable investments) to handle a spike in claims.
**Principal Business:** Managed care (99%)
**Mem Phys: 16:** N/A **15:** N/A **16 MLR** 93.3% **/ 16 Admin Exp** N/A
**Enroll(000): Q3 17:** 658 **16:** 595 **15:** 534 **Med Exp PMPM:** $336
**Principal Investments ($000):** Cash and equiv ($473,456)
**Provider Compensation ($000):** None
**Total Member Encounters:** N/A
**Group Affiliation:** Heritage California Medical Groups
**Licensed in:** CA
**Address:** 1 Park Plaza Suite 450, Irvine, CA 92614
**Phone:** (502) 580-1575 **Dom State:** CA **Commenced Bus:** May 1996

| Data Date | Rating | RACR #1 | RACR #2 | Total Assets ($mil) | Capital ($mil) | Net Premium ($mil) | Net Income ($mil) |
|---|---|---|---|---|---|---|---|
| 9-17 | D | 0.60 | 0.37 | 544.2 | 120.1 | 1,997.2 | 2.0 |
| 9-16 | D | 0.70 | 0.43 | 691.7 | 132.7 | 1,810.2 | 2.3 |
| 2016 | D | 0.66 | 0.41 | 575.3 | 127.8 | 2,432.2 | 2.3 |
| 2015 | D | 0.69 | 0.42 | 661.8 | 131.5 | 2,380.8 | 14.5 |
| 2014 | D | 0.72 | 0.44 | 496.1 | 123.4 | 2,098.1 | 17.7 |
| 2013 | D | 0.64 | 0.39 | 333.8 | 105.9 | 1,857.4 | 2.4 |
| 2012 | D- | 0.57 | 0.35 | 363.0 | 97.6 | 1,751.0 | 2.8 |

Rating Indexes

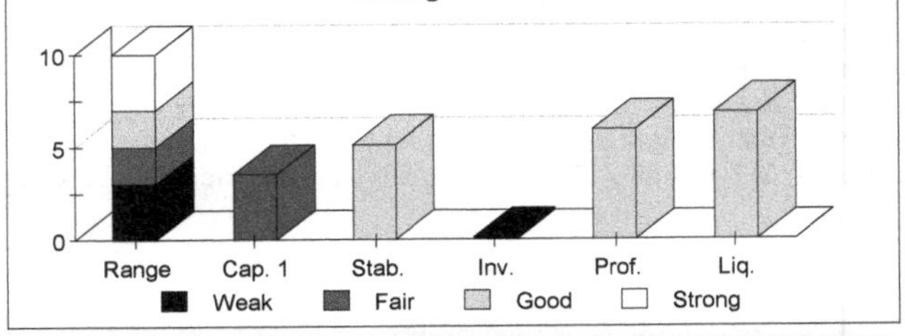


## HIGHMARK BCBSD INC — B- — Good

**Major Rating Factors:** Fair profitability index (3.6 on a scale of 0 to 10). Good quality investment portfolio (6.1). Good liquidity (6.8) with sufficient resources (cash flows and marketable investments) to handle a spike in claims.
**Other Rating Factors:** Strong capitalization (10.0) based on excellent current risk-adjusted capital (severe loss scenario).
**Principal Business:** Comp med (79%), FEHB (19%), med supp (2%)
**Mem Phys: 16:** 8,854 **15:** 6,763 **16 MLR** 89.2% **/ 16 Admin Exp** N/A
**Enroll(000): Q3 17:** 104 **16:** 121 **15:** 126 **Med Exp PMPM:** $423
**Principal Investments:** Long-term bonds (58%), nonaffiliate common stock (27%), cash and equiv (12%), other (4%)
**Provider Compensation ($000):** Contr fee ($596,491), FFS ($15,293), bonus arrang ($1,974), capitation ($1,193)
**Total Member Encounters:** Phys (785,322), non-phys (508,073)
**Group Affiliation:** Highmark Health
**Licensed in:** DE
**Address:** 800 Delaware Ave, Wilmington, DE 19801
**Phone:** (302) 421-3000 **Dom State:** DE **Commenced Bus:** September 1935

| Data Date | Rating | RACR #1 | RACR #2 | Total Assets ($mil) | Capital ($mil) | Net Premium ($mil) | Net Income ($mil) |
|---|---|---|---|---|---|---|---|
| 9-17 | B- | 5.07 | 4.22 | 407.7 | 210.1 | 476.5 | 50.2 |
| 9-16 | B- | 3.67 | 3.06 | 361.2 | 141.9 | 531.7 | 14.0 |
| 2016 | B- | 3.61 | 3.01 | 363.0 | 149.6 | 705.8 | 19.1 |
| 2015 | B- | 3.13 | 2.61 | 336.9 | 120.8 | 638.8 | -26.5 |
| 2014 | B | 4.14 | 3.45 | 335.7 | 138.4 | 583.2 | -4.2 |
| 2013 | B | 5.45 | 4.54 | 334.2 | 157.7 | 512.1 | -8.4 |
| 2012 | A | 6.08 | 5.07 | 312.5 | 168.7 | 532.2 | -11.1 |

Rating Indexes

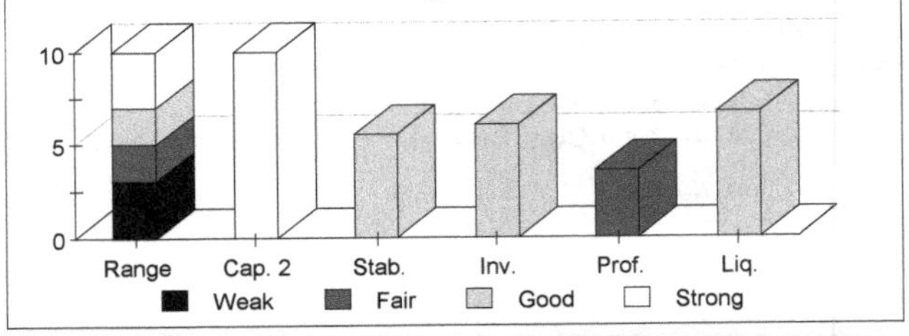


## HIGHMARK CASUALTY INS CO — C — Fair

**Major Rating Factors:** Fair overall results on stability tests (4.2 on a scale of 0 to 10) including fair financial strength of affiliated Highmark Inc, weak results on operational trends and negative cash flow from operations for 2016. The largest net exposure for one risk is conservative at 1.1% of capital. Vulnerable liquidity (0.9) as a spike in claims may stretch capacity.
**Other Rating Factors:** History of adequate reserve strength (6.9) as reserves have been consistently at an acceptable level. Strong long-term capitalization index (9.0) based on excellent current risk adjusted capital (severe and moderate loss scenarios). Moreover, capital levels have been consistent in recent years. Excellent profitability (8.1) with operating gains in each of the last five years.
**Principal Business:** Group accident & health (84%) and workers compensation (16%).
**Principal Investments:** Investment grade bonds (72%), misc. investments (15%), non investment grade bonds (12%), and cash (1%).
**Investments in Affiliates:** None
**Group Affiliation:** Highmark Inc
**Licensed in:** AL, FL, GA, ID, IL, IN, KS, KY, MD, MI, MS, MO, NV, NJ, NM, NC, OR, PA, SC, TX, UT, VA, WA, WV
**Commenced Business:** February 1978
**Address:** Fifth Ave Place 120 Fifth Ave, Pittsburgh, PA 15222-3099
**Phone:** (800) 328-5433 **Domicile State:** PA **NAIC Code:** 35599

| Data Date | Rating | RACR #1 | RACR #2 | Loss Ratio % | Total Assets ($mil) | Capital ($mil) | Net Premium ($mil) | Net Income ($mil) |
|---|---|---|---|---|---|---|---|---|
| 9-17 | C | 4.91 | 3.22 | N/A | 282.1 | 185.5 | 141.0 | 6.1 |
| 9-16 | C | 3.63 | 2.79 | N/A | 282.3 | 168.1 | 193.9 | -4.9 |
| 2016 | C | 4.28 | 2.84 | 74.5 | 274.7 | 179.2 | 218.0 | 1.9 |
| 2015 | C | 2.56 | 1.77 | 76.6 | 457.2 | 173.1 | 282.9 | 7.2 |
| 2014 | C | 2.11 | 1.47 | 80.1 | 439.0 | 166.3 | 298.4 | 5.0 |
| 2013 | C | 1.23 | 0.84 | 75.7 | 398.5 | 160.9 | 290.7 | 12.6 |
| 2012 | C | 1.37 | 0.93 | 72.1 | 344.9 | 148.5 | 253.0 | 20.0 |

Rating Indexes

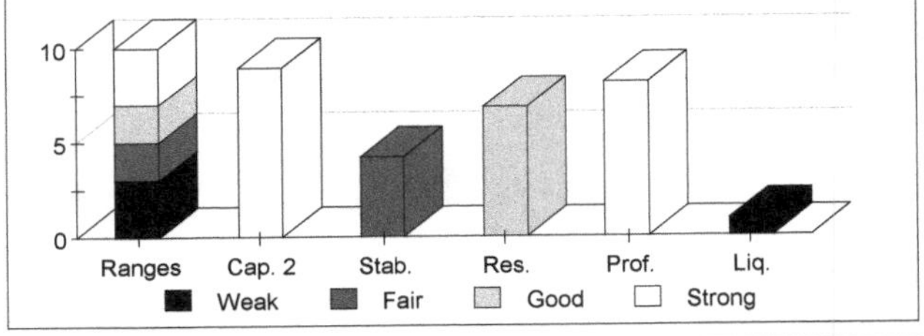

## HIGHMARK INC — C — Fair

**Major Rating Factors:** Fair profitability index (3.5 on a scale of 0 to 10). Fair quality investment portfolio (4.1). Strong capitalization (10.0) based on excellent current risk-adjusted capital (severe loss scenario).
**Other Rating Factors:** Excellent liquidity (8.3) with ample operational cash flow and liquid investments.
**Principal Business:** Medicare (44%), comp med (40%), FEHB (10%), med supp (3%), other (2%)
**Mem Phys: 16:** 81,781 **15:** 78,120 **16 MLR** 34.8% **/ 16 Admin Exp** N/A
**Enroll(000): Q3 17:** 827 **16:** 888 **15:** 1,112 **Med Exp PMPM:** $281
**Principal Investments:** Affiliate common stock (40%), long-term bonds (21%), nonaffiliate common stock (12%), cash and equiv (6%), real estate (1%), other (19%)
**Provider Compensation ($000):** Contr fee ($2,780,000), FFS ($323,266), bonus arrang ($22,695), capitation ($397)
**Total Member Encounters:** Phys (5,459,540), non-phys (3,533,787)
**Group Affiliation:** Highmark Health
**Licensed in:** PA
**Address:** 1800 Center St, Camp Hill, PA 17011
**Phone:** (412) 544-7000 **Dom State:** PA **Commenced Bus:** December 1996

| Data Date | Rating | RACR #1 | RACR #2 | Total Assets ($mil) | Capital ($mil) | Net Premium ($mil) | Net Income ($mil) |
|---|---|---|---|---|---|---|---|
| 9-17 | C | 3.61 | 3.01 | 7,778.7 | 4,327.3 | 6,008.2 | 503.9 |
| 9-16 | C | 3.08 | 2.56 | 7,539.0 | 3,732.6 | 6,582.8 | -126.3 |
| 2016 | C | 3.24 | 2.70 | 7,526.6 | 3,886.3 | 8,742.8 | -73.9 |
| 2015 | C | 3.18 | 2.65 | 7,565.3 | 3,860.6 | 8,745.5 | -405.2 |
| 2014 | B- | 3.44 | 2.86 | 7,729.6 | 4,252.0 | 9,259.3 | -81.1 |
| 2013 | B- | 3.75 | 3.13 | 7,624.1 | 4,386.3 | 6,204.9 | 340.7 |
| 2012 | B | 3.56 | 2.97 | 7,286.3 | 4,138.1 | 2,063.0 | 163.2 |

Rating Indexes

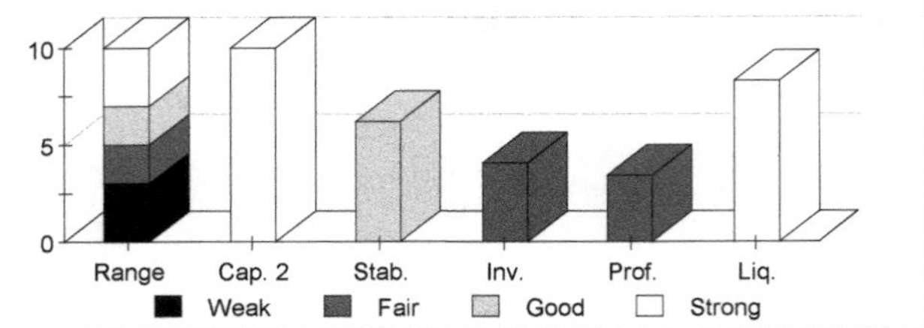


## HIGHMARK WEST VIRGINIA INC — B — Good

**Major Rating Factors:** Good profitability index (4.9 on a scale of 0 to 10). Good quality investment portfolio (6.5). Strong capitalization (10.0) based on excellent current risk-adjusted capital (severe loss scenario).
**Other Rating Factors:** Excellent liquidity (6.9) with sufficient resources (cash flows and marketable investments) to handle a spike in claims.
**Principal Business:** Comp med (64%), FEHB (28%), Medicare (4%), med supp (2%), other (2%)
**Mem Phys: 16:** 15,700 **15:** 13,278 **16 MLR** 86.3% **/ 16 Admin Exp** N/A
**Enroll(000): Q3 17:** 178 **16:** 197 **15:** 205 **Med Exp PMPM:** $426
**Principal Investments:** Long-term bonds (68%), cash and equiv (14%), nonaffiliate common stock (5%), real estate (4%), other (8%)
**Provider Compensation ($000):** Contr fee ($640,610), FFS ($373,423), bonus arrang ($3,985), capitation ($953)
**Total Member Encounters:** Phys (1,219,931), non-phys (852,333)
**Group Affiliation:** Highmark Health
**Licensed in:** WV
**Address:** 614 Market St, Parkersburg, WV 26101
**Phone:** (304) 424-7700 **Dom State:** WV **Commenced Bus:** January 1983

| Data Date | Rating | RACR #1 | RACR #2 | Total Assets ($mil) | Capital ($mil) | Net Premium ($mil) | Net Income ($mil) |
|---|---|---|---|---|---|---|---|
| 9-17 | B | 5.65 | 4.71 | 730.0 | 383.3 | 883.3 | 66.9 |
| 9-16 | B | 4.68 | 3.90 | 677.0 | 304.7 | 895.7 | 17.5 |
| 2016 | B | 4.62 | 3.85 | 675.7 | 312.7 | 1,192.5 | -4.2 |
| 2015 | B | 4.59 | 3.82 | 617.5 | 290.2 | 1,121.8 | -12.6 |
| 2014 | B+ | 5.82 | 4.85 | 598.1 | 308.1 | 991.6 | 9.5 |
| 2013 | B+ | 6.16 | 5.13 | 574.6 | 308.1 | 894.3 | 1.4 |
| 2012 | A- | 7.42 | 6.18 | 545.0 | 322.6 | 824.0 | 32.2 |

Rating Indexes

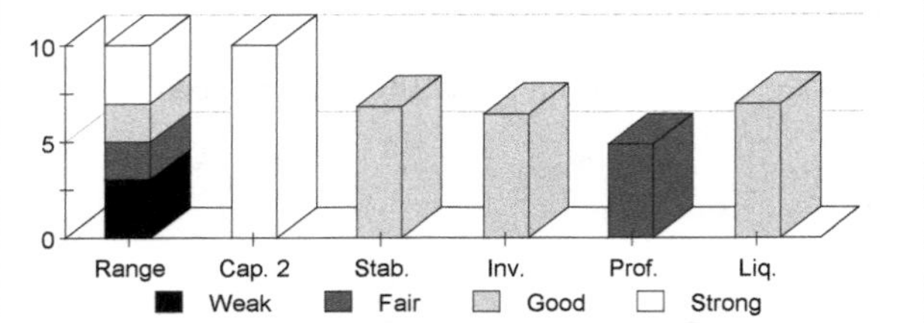


## HIP INS CO OF NEW YORK — D- — Weak

**Major Rating Factors:** Weak profitability index (1.7 on a scale of 0 to 10). Strong capitalization (10.0) based on excellent current risk-adjusted capital (severe loss scenario). High quality investment portfolio (8.5).
**Other Rating Factors:** Excellent liquidity (7.1) with ample operational cash flow and liquid investments.
**Principal Business:** Comp med (100%)
**Mem Phys: 16:** 50,592 **15:** 47,579 **16 MLR** 76.9% **/ 16 Admin Exp** N/A
**Enroll(000): Q3 17:** 7 **16:** 7 **15:** 10 **Med Exp PMPM:** $64
**Principal Investments:** Long-term bonds (96%), cash and equiv (4%)
**Provider Compensation ($000):** FFS ($4,362), contr fee ($2,374), capitation ($569), bonus arrang ($382)
**Total Member Encounters:** Phys (51,112), non-phys (22,729)
**Group Affiliation:** EmblemHealth Inc
**Licensed in:** NY
**Address:** 55 Water St, New York, NY 10041-8190
**Phone:** (646) 447-5000 **Dom State:** NY **Commenced Bus:** September 1994

| Data Date | Rating | RACR #1 | RACR #2 | Total Assets ($mil) | Capital ($mil) | Net Premium ($mil) | Net Income ($mil) |
|---|---|---|---|---|---|---|---|
| 9-17 | D- | 36.66 | 30.55 | 55.2 | 40.3 | 6.9 | 0.1 |
| 9-16 | D- | 30.41 | 25.34 | 51.8 | 45.1 | 10.3 | 2.6 |
| 2016 | D- | 38.10 | 31.75 | 53.7 | 41.6 | 8.3 | 1.2 |
| 2015 | D- | 28.95 | 24.12 | 51.6 | 42.5 | 20.1 | 4.4 |
| 2014 | D- | 9.63 | 8.02 | 68.5 | 39.5 | 60.1 | -5.1 |
| 2013 | D- | 4.47 | 3.72 | 67.3 | 43.3 | 146.8 | 4.3 |
| 2012 | E+ | 3.23 | 2.69 | 75.1 | 40.0 | 169.6 | -13.6 |

Rating Indexes

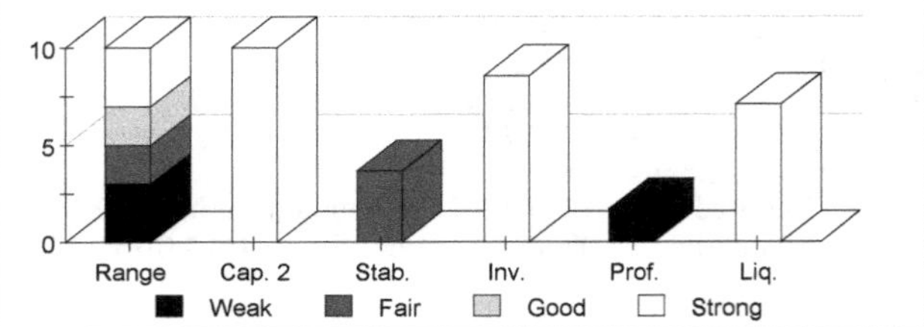

## HM LIFE INSURANCE COMPANY B- Good

**Major Rating Factors:** Good overall results on stability tests (5.3 on a scale of 0 to 10) despite fair financial strength of affiliated Highmark Inc. Other stability subfactors include excellent operational trends and excellent risk diversification. Fair quality investment portfolio (4.9). Strong capitalization (9.1) based on excellent risk adjusted capital (severe loss scenario).
**Other Rating Factors:** Excellent profitability (8.4) despite operating losses during the first nine months of 2017. Excellent liquidity (7.0).
**Principal Business:** Group health insurance (88%) and reinsurance (12%).
**Principal Investments:** NonCMO investment grade bonds (55%), CMOs and structured securities (13%), noninv. grade bonds (11%), common & preferred stock (10%), and cash (5%).
**Investments in Affiliates:** None
**Group Affiliation:** Highmark Inc
**Licensed in:** All states except NY, PR
**Commenced Business:** May 1981
**Address:** Fifth AvePlace 120 Fifth Ave, Pittsburgh, PA 15222-3099
**Phone:** (800) 328-5433 **Domicile State:** PA **NAIC Code:** 93440

| Data Date | Rating | RACR #1 | RACR #2 | Total Assets ($mil) | Capital ($mil) | Net Premium ($mil) | Net Income ($mil) |
|---|---|---|---|---|---|---|---|
| 9-17 | B- | 3.33 | 2.39 | 687.4 | 377.1 | 554.9 | -2.8 |
| 9-16 | B- | 3.33 | 2.40 | 658.3 | 355.4 | 514.1 | 5.0 |
| 2016 | B- | 3.39 | 2.43 | 643.3 | 360.7 | 673.4 | 17.8 |
| 2015 | B | 3.73 | 2.73 | 620.8 | 348.6 | 640.3 | 37.3 |
| 2014 | B | 3.28 | 2.49 | 574.5 | 309.2 | 647.9 | 24.1 |
| 2013 | B | 3.07 | 2.35 | 557.9 | 284.6 | 634.0 | 35.5 |
| 2012 | B | 2.87 | 2.20 | 491.3 | 250.0 | 588.8 | 25.4 |

**Highmark Inc**
**Composite Group Rating: C**

| Largest Group Members | Assets ($mil) | Rating |
|---|---|---|
| HIGHMARK INC | 7527 | C |
| GATEWAY HEALTH PLAN INC | 755 | B- |
| HIGHMARK WEST VIRGINIA INC | 676 | B |
| HM LIFE INS CO | 643 | B- |
| HIGHMARK BCBSD INC | 363 | B- |

## HM LIFE INSURANCE COMPANY OF NEW YORK B Good

**Major Rating Factors:** Good overall results on stability tests (5.3 on a scale of 0 to 10) despite fair financial strength of affiliated Highmark Inc. Other stability subfactors include excellent operational trends and excellent risk diversification. Good overall profitability (6.8). Strong capitalization (9.7) based on excellent risk adjusted capital (severe loss scenario).
**Other Rating Factors:** High quality investment portfolio (8.8). Excellent liquidity (7.2).
**Principal Business:** Group health insurance (96%) and reinsurance (4%).
**Principal Investments:** NonCMO investment grade bonds (74%), CMOs and structured securities (20%), and cash (4%).
**Investments in Affiliates:** None
**Group Affiliation:** Highmark Inc
**Licensed in:** DC, NY, RI
**Commenced Business:** March 1997
**Address:** 420 Fifth Avenue 3rd Floor, New York, NY 10018
**Phone:** (800) 328-5433 **Domicile State:** NY **NAIC Code:** 60213

| Data Date | Rating | RACR #1 | RACR #2 | Total Assets ($mil) | Capital ($mil) | Net Premium ($mil) | Net Income ($mil) |
|---|---|---|---|---|---|---|---|
| 9-17 | B | 3.53 | 2.81 | 69.1 | 45.2 | 56.6 | 5.2 |
| 9-16 | B | 3.23 | 2.55 | 72.9 | 40.7 | 54.7 | 1.8 |
| 2016 | B | 3.23 | 2.57 | 67.0 | 40.2 | 72.4 | 1.7 |
| 2015 | B | 3.33 | 2.64 | 65.7 | 38.9 | 66.2 | -1.1 |
| 2014 | B+ | 3.12 | 2.47 | 71.4 | 39.2 | 75.4 | 8.0 |
| 2013 | B+ | 2.28 | 1.81 | 76.1 | 31.9 | 85.4 | -0.4 |
| 2012 | B+ | 2.00 | 1.59 | 66.5 | 31.8 | 88.4 | 9.0 |

**Highmark Inc**
**Composite Group Rating: C**

| Largest Group Members | Assets ($mil) | Rating |
|---|---|---|
| HIGHMARK INC | 7527 | C |
| GATEWAY HEALTH PLAN INC | 755 | B- |
| HIGHMARK WEST VIRGINIA INC | 676 | B |
| HM LIFE INS CO | 643 | B- |
| HIGHMARK BCBSD INC | 363 | B- |

## HMO COLORADO B- Good

**Major Rating Factors:** Fair overall results on stability tests (4.1 on a scale of 0 to 10) in spite of healthy premium and capital growth during 2016 but a decline in the number of member physicians during 2017. Rating is significantly influenced by the good financial results of Anthem Inc. Good overall profitability index (5.7). Strong capitalization index (10.0) based on excellent current risk-adjusted capital (severe loss scenario).
**Other Rating Factors:** High quality investment portfolio (9.6). Excellent liquidity (7.1) with ample operational cash flow and liquid investments.
**Principal Business:** Comp med (98%), Medicare (1%)
**Mem Phys: 16:** 20,457 **15:** 28,112 **16 MLR** 89.9% **/ 16 Admin Exp** N/A
**Enroll(000): Q3 17:** 115 **16:** 65 **15:** 56 **Med Exp PMPM:** $315
**Principal Investments:** Cash and equiv (65%), long-term bonds (34%), affiliate common stock (1%), other (1%)
**Provider Compensation ($000):** Contr fee ($250,229), bonus arrang ($2,741), capitation ($1,104), other ($220)
**Total Member Encounters:** Phys (287,972), non-phys (125,231)
**Group Affiliation:** Anthem Inc
**Licensed in:** CO, NV
**Address:** 700 BROADWAY, DENVER, CO 80273
**Phone:** (303) 831-2131 **Dom State:** CO **Commenced Bus:** January 1980

| Data Date | Rating | RACR #1 | RACR #2 | Total Assets ($mil) | Capital ($mil) | Net Premium ($mil) | Net Income ($mil) |
|---|---|---|---|---|---|---|---|
| 9-17 | B- | 4.58 | 3.82 | 216.9 | 83.0 | 502.7 | 32.4 |
| 9-16 | C+ | 2.34 | 1.95 | 123.6 | 34.3 | 215.5 | -2.9 |
| 2016 | B- | 2.85 | 2.38 | 153.5 | 51.4 | 285.2 | 2.3 |
| 2015 | C+ | 2.53 | 2.11 | 102.1 | 37.0 | 240.4 | -4.1 |
| 2014 | B- | 3.25 | 2.71 | 92.9 | 42.2 | 209.2 | 3.9 |
| 2013 | B- | 4.90 | 4.08 | 65.7 | 47.2 | 145.1 | 8.5 |
| 2012 | B- | 6.01 | 5.01 | 75.0 | 55.0 | 155.5 | 15.6 |

Rating Indexes

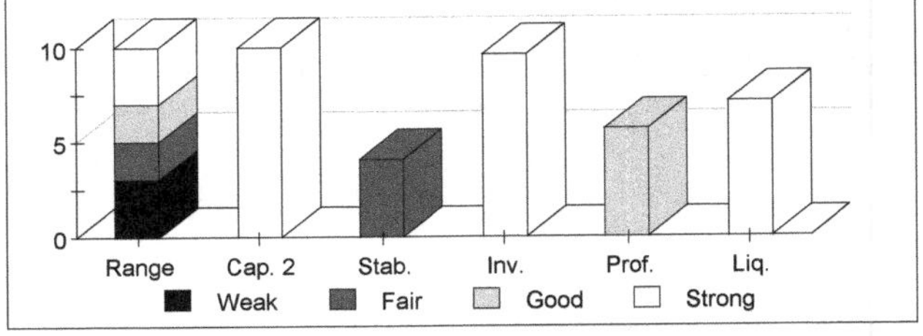

## HMO LOUISIANA INC * A+ Excellent

**Major Rating Factors:** Strong capitalization index (10.0 on a scale of 0 to 10) based on excellent current risk-adjusted capital (severe loss scenario). High quality investment portfolio (8.3). Excellent overall results on stability tests (7.2).
**Other Rating Factors:** Excellent liquidity (7.1) with ample operational cash flow and liquid investments. Fair profitability index (4.2).
**Principal Business:** Comp med (98%), Medicare (2%)
**Mem Phys: 16:** 25,954 **15:** 19,614 **16 MLR** 86.6% **/ 16 Admin Exp** N/A
**Enroll(000): Q3 17:** 163 **16:** 143 **15:** 125 **Med Exp PMPM:** $349
**Principal Investments:** Long-term bonds (54%), cash and equiv (21%), nonaffiliate common stock (20%), other (5%)
**Provider Compensation ($000):** Contr fee ($609,480)
**Total Member Encounters:** Phys (1,498,346), non-phys (806,726)
**Group Affiliation:** LA Health Service and Indemnity Co
**Licensed in:** LA
**Address:** 5525 Reitz Avenue, Baton Rouge, LA 70809
**Phone:** (225) 295-3307 **Dom State:** LA **Commenced Bus:** July 1986

| Data Date | Rating | RACR #1 | RACR #2 | Total Assets ($mil) | Capital ($mil) | Net Premium ($mil) | Net Income ($mil) |
|---|---|---|---|---|---|---|---|
| 9-17 | A+ | 8.41 | 7.01 | 669.8 | 388.5 | 708.2 | 34.5 |
| 9-16 | A+ | 9.01 | 7.50 | 591.0 | 346.2 | 536.7 | 10.4 |
| 2016 | A+ | 7.53 | 6.27 | 570.5 | 347.5 | 719.2 | 10.3 |
| 2015 | A+ | 8.70 | 7.25 | 513.2 | 334.4 | 584.5 | -28.8 |
| 2014 | A+ | 10.84 | 9.04 | 502.3 | 362.4 | 508.9 | 15.3 |
| 2013 | A+ | 11.94 | 9.95 | 434.9 | 347.9 | 472.4 | 47.9 |
| 2012 | A+ | 9.67 | 8.06 | 395.7 | 296.2 | 499.6 | 32.9 |

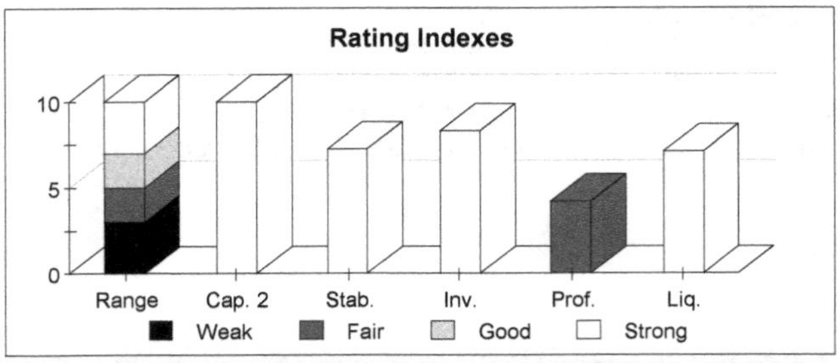


## HMO MINNESOTA C Fair

**Major Rating Factors:** Fair overall results on stability tests (3.3 on a scale of 0 to 10) based on an excessive 184% enrollment growth during the period. Weak profitability index (2.6). Good quality investment portfolio (6.6).
**Other Rating Factors:** Good liquidity (5.9) with sufficient resources (cash flows and marketable investments) to handle a spike in claims. Strong capitalization index (10.0) based on excellent current risk-adjusted capital (severe loss scenario).
**Principal Business:** Medicaid (97%), comp med (3%)
**Mem Phys: 16:** 11,727 **15:** 11,286 **16 MLR** 99.3% **/ 16 Admin Exp** N/A
**Enroll(000): Q3 17:** 413 **16:** 333 **15:** 117 **Med Exp PMPM:** $465
**Principal Investments:** Long-term bonds (62%), nonaffiliate common stock (21%), cash and equiv (16%)
**Provider Compensation ($000):** Contr fee ($953,169), bonus arrang ($594,169), FFS ($125,553)
**Total Member Encounters:** Phys (1,923,365), non-phys (2,124,174)
**Group Affiliation:** Aware Integrated Inc
**Licensed in:** MN
**Address:** 3535 Blue Cross Road, Eagan, MN 55122
**Phone:** (651) 662-8000 **Dom State:** MN **Commenced Bus:** November 1974

| Data Date | Rating | RACR #1 | RACR #2 | Total Assets ($mil) | Capital ($mil) | Net Premium ($mil) | Net Income ($mil) |
|---|---|---|---|---|---|---|---|
| 9-17 | C | 3.71 | 3.09 | 851.4 | 458.9 | 1,812.1 | 20.5 |
| 9-16 | C | 8.51 | 7.09 | 797.0 | 510.1 | 1,350.5 | -76.9 |
| 2016 | C | 3.46 | 2.88 | 858.3 | 426.8 | 1,816.2 | -156.7 |
| 2015 | B- | 9.49 | 7.91 | 825.1 | 570.2 | 895.0 | 52.0 |
| 2014 | B | 10.04 | 8.37 | 725.4 | 530.6 | 820.4 | 85.7 |
| 2013 | A- | 6.84 | 5.70 | 629.8 | 448.9 | 1,016.7 | 73.2 |
| 2012 | A- | 5.56 | 4.63 | 572.8 | 359.6 | 956.9 | -4.4 |

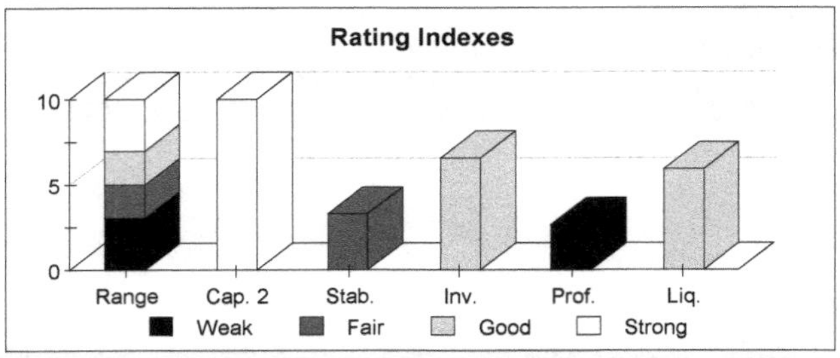


## HMO MISSOURI INC B Good

**Major Rating Factors:** Fair overall results on stability tests (4.9 on a scale of 0 to 10). Rating is significantly influenced by the good financial results of Anthem Inc. Excellent profitability (8.4). Strong capitalization index (10.0) based on excellent current risk-adjusted capital (severe loss scenario).
**Other Rating Factors:** High quality investment portfolio (9.3). Excellent liquidity (7.1) with ample operational cash flow and liquid investments.
**Principal Business:** Comp med (39%), FEHB (35%), Medicare (26%)
**Mem Phys: 16:** 17,226 **15:** 16,291 **16 MLR** 79.1% **/ 16 Admin Exp** N/A
**Enroll(000): Q3 17:** 28 **16:** 25 **15:** 23 **Med Exp PMPM:** $393
**Principal Investments:** Long-term bonds (68%), cash and equiv (32%)
**Provider Compensation ($000):** Contr fee ($74,122), FFS ($40,852), bonus arrang ($1,230), capitation ($494)
**Total Member Encounters:** Phys (161,934), non-phys (140,679)
**Group Affiliation:** Anthem Inc
**Licensed in:** IL, MO
**Address:** 1831 CHESTNUT STREET, ST LOUIS, MO 63103-2275
**Phone:** (314) 923-4444 **Dom State:** MO **Commenced Bus:** December 1987

| Data Date | Rating | RACR #1 | RACR #2 | Total Assets ($mil) | Capital ($mil) | Net Premium ($mil) | Net Income ($mil) |
|---|---|---|---|---|---|---|---|
| 9-17 | B | 7.58 | 6.31 | 96.5 | 50.9 | 134.4 | 6.0 |
| 9-16 | B- | 7.99 | 6.66 | 78.0 | 43.3 | 110.0 | 5.9 |
| 2016 | B | 6.74 | 5.61 | 75.1 | 45.2 | 149.5 | 8.8 |
| 2015 | B- | 7.08 | 5.90 | 68.9 | 38.3 | 134.8 | 9.9 |
| 2014 | B- | 5.72 | 4.77 | 61.2 | 29.7 | 135.6 | 10.4 |
| 2013 | B- | 5.31 | 4.42 | 71.2 | 39.3 | 169.1 | 9.1 |
| 2012 | B- | 8.52 | 7.10 | 115.9 | 65.5 | 184.3 | 13.6 |

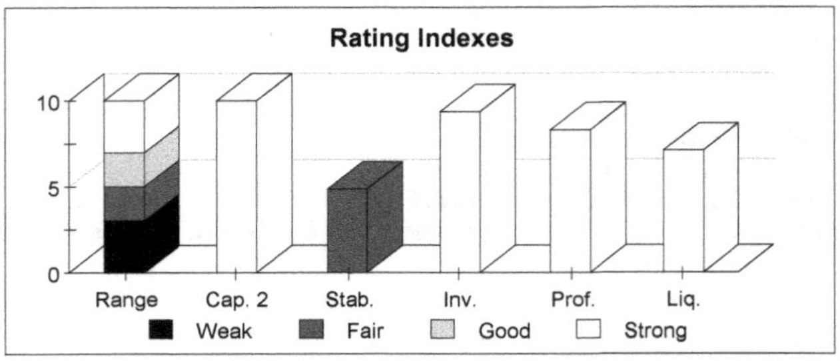

## HMO PARTNERS INC * A+ Excellent

**Major Rating Factors:** Strong capitalization index (10.0 on a scale of 0 to 10) based on excellent current risk-adjusted capital (severe loss scenario). High quality investment portfolio (9.0). Good overall profitability index (5.9).
**Other Rating Factors:** Good overall results on stability tests (5.3) despite inconsistent enrollment growth in the past five years due to declines in 2014 and 2015. Potential support from affiliation with HMO Partners Inc. Fair liquidity (3.6) as cash resources may not be adequate to cover a spike in claims.
**Principal Business:** Comp med (97%), Medicare (3%)
**Mem Phys: 16:** 16,096 **15:** 15,261 **16 MLR** 129.0% **/ 16 Admin Exp** N/A
**Enroll(000): Q3 17:** 72 **16:** 72 **15:** 69 **Med Exp PMPM:** $285
**Principal Investments:** Long-term bonds (44%), cash and equiv (37%), nonaffiliate common stock (18%)
**Provider Compensation ($000):** Bonus arrang ($255,354), FFS ($2,527)
**Total Member Encounters:** Phys (68,724), non-phys (81,743)
**Group Affiliation:** HMO Partners Inc
**Licensed in:** AR
**Address:** 320 West Capitol, Little Rock, AR 72203-8069
**Phone:** (501) 221-1800 **Dom State:** AR **Commenced Bus:** January 1994

| Data Date | Rating | RACR #1 | RACR #2 | Total Assets ($mil) | Capital ($mil) | Net Premium ($mil) | Net Income ($mil) |
|---|---|---|---|---|---|---|---|
| 9-17 | A+ | 5.59 | 4.66 | 135.4 | 66.5 | 154.4 | 4.9 |
| 9-16 | A+ | 5.67 | 4.73 | 108.6 | 60.1 | 142.6 | 1.1 |
| 2016 | A+ | 4.93 | 4.11 | 114.1 | 58.3 | 191.1 | 0.7 |
| 2015 | A+ | 5.38 | 4.48 | 113.7 | 56.7 | 177.3 | 4.8 |
| 2014 | A+ | 10.48 | 8.73 | 186.7 | 119.4 | 171.5 | 3.1 |
| 2013 | A+ | 11.17 | 9.31 | 157.2 | 116.9 | 153.8 | 7.5 |
| 2012 | A+ | 11.32 | 9.43 | 148.0 | 109.3 | 143.2 | 8.4 |

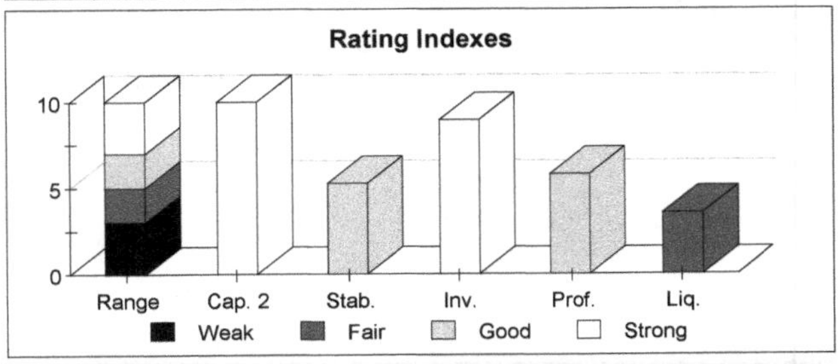


## HN1 THERAPY NETWORK NEW JERSEY LLC C- Fair

**Major Rating Factors:** Fair capitalization (4.5 on a scale of 0 to 10) based on fair current risk-adjusted capital (moderate loss scenario). Good overall profitability index (6.8). High quality investment portfolio (9.9).
**Other Rating Factors:** Excellent liquidity (9.0) with ample operational cash flow and liquid investments.
**Principal Business:** Medicaid (96%), Medicare (4%)
**Mem Phys: 16:** 251 **15:** 244 **16 MLR** 35.2% **/ 16 Admin Exp** N/A
**Enroll(000): 16:** 209 **15:** 209 **Med Exp PMPM:** $0
**Principal Investments:** Cash and equiv (100%)
**Provider Compensation ($000):** FFS ($1,276), bonus arrang ($49)
**Total Member Encounters:** N/A
**Group Affiliation:** HN1 Therapy Network LLC
**Licensed in:** (No states)
**Address:** 801 E Hallandale Beach Blv 200, Hallandale, FL 33009
**Phone:** (305) 614-0109 **Dom State:** NJ **Commenced Bus:** June 2011

| Data Date | Rating | RACR #1 | RACR #2 | Total Assets ($mil) | Capital ($mil) | Net Premium ($mil) | Net Income ($mil) |
|---|---|---|---|---|---|---|---|
| 2016 | C- | 0.86 | 0.71 | 2.8 | 2.3 | 3.0 | 0.9 |
| 2015 | N/A | N/A | N/A | 3.7 | 3.0 | 3.7 | 1.6 |
| 2014 | N/A | N/A | N/A | 4.8 | 2.0 | 5.8 | 1.8 |
| 2013 | N/A | N/A | N/A | 0.3 | 0.2 | 0.2 | -0.1 |
| 2012 | N/A | N/A | N/A | 0.1 | 0.1 | N/A | N/A |

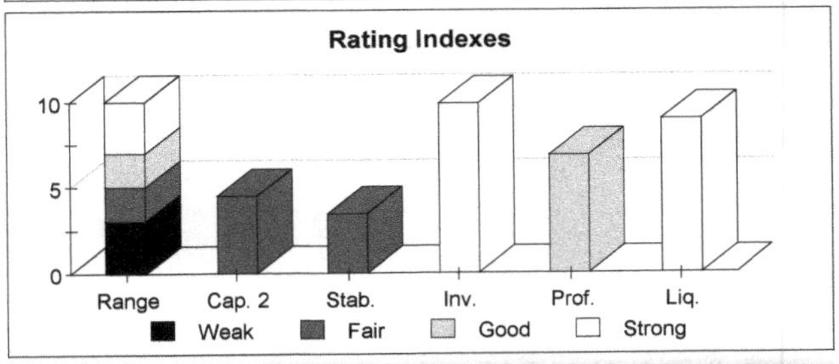


## HNE INS CO C Fair

**Major Rating Factors:** Weak profitability index (2.7 on a scale of 0 to 10). Strong capitalization (10.0) based on excellent current risk-adjusted capital (severe loss scenario). High quality investment portfolio (9.9).
**Other Rating Factors:** Excellent liquidity (10.0) with ample operational cash flow and liquid investments.
**Principal Business:** Med supp (100%)
**Mem Phys: 16:** 5,488 **15:** 4,680 **16 MLR** 81.5% **/ 16 Admin Exp** N/A
**Enroll(000): Q3 17:** 0 **16:** 0 **15:** 0 **Med Exp PMPM:** $124
**Principal Investments:** Cash and equiv (100%)
**Provider Compensation ($000):** Contr fee ($428)
**Total Member Encounters:** Phys (2,902), non-phys (225)
**Group Affiliation:** Baystate Health Inc
**Licensed in:** MA
**Address:** 1 Monarch Place Ste 1500, Springfield, MA 01144
**Phone:** (413) 787-4000 **Dom State:** MA **Commenced Bus:** January 2013

| Data Date | Rating | RACR #1 | RACR #2 | Total Assets ($mil) | Capital ($mil) | Net Premium ($mil) | Net Income ($mil) |
|---|---|---|---|---|---|---|---|
| 9-17 | C | 71.70 | 59.75 | 5.1 | 5.0 | 0.5 | 0.1 |
| 9-16 | D | 67.27 | 56.06 | 5.0 | 4.9 | 0.4 | 0.0 |
| 2016 | D+ | 68.24 | 56.87 | 5.0 | 4.9 | 0.5 | 0.1 |
| 2015 | D+ | 65.74 | 54.79 | 5.0 | 4.9 | 0.4 | 0.0 |
| 2014 | C | 65.52 | 54.60 | 5.0 | 4.9 | 0.2 | -0.1 |
| 2013 | U | 58.31 | 48.59 | 4.8 | 4.7 | 0.1 | 0.0 |
| 2012 | N/A | N/A | N/A | 5.0 | 5.0 | N/A | N/A |

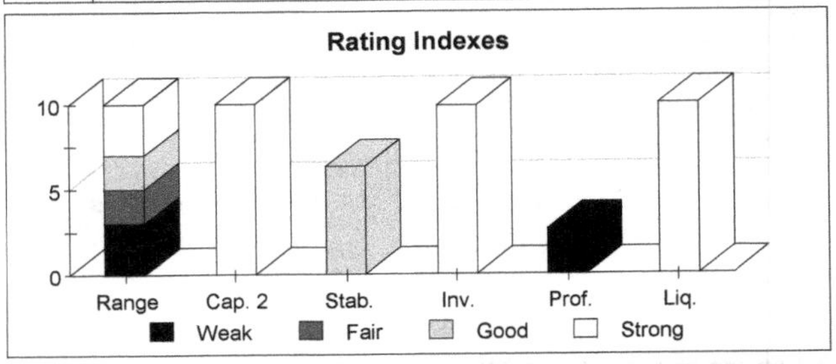

## HNE OF CONNECTICUT INC — D — Weak

**Major Rating Factors:** Weak profitability index (0.2 on a scale of 0 to 10). Strong capitalization (7.7) based on excellent current risk-adjusted capital (severe loss scenario). High quality investment portfolio (9.9).
**Other Rating Factors:** Excellent liquidity (9.2) with ample operational cash flow and liquid investments.
**Principal Business:** Medicare (100%)
**Mem Phys: 16:** 5,471 **15:** 4,654 **16 MLR** 89.6% **/ 16 Admin Exp** N/A
**Enroll(000): Q3 17:** 0 **16:** 0 **15:** 0 **Med Exp PMPM:** $416
**Principal Investments:** Cash and equiv (90%), long-term bonds (10%)
**Provider Compensation ($000):** Contr fee ($1,095)
**Total Member Encounters:** Phys (1,376), non-phys (114)
**Group Affiliation:** Baystate Health Inc
**Licensed in:** CT
**Address:** One Monarch Place, Springfield, MA 01104
**Phone:** (800) 310-2835 **Dom State:** CT **Commenced Bus:** January 2015

| Data Date | Rating | RACR #1 | RACR #2 | Total Assets ($mil) | Capital ($mil) | Net Premium ($mil) | Net Income ($mil) |
|---|---|---|---|---|---|---|---|
| 9-17 | D | 1.90 | 1.58 | 4.5 | 3.8 | 0.6 | -0.8 |
| 9-16 | D | 1.82 | 1.52 | 5.0 | 4.3 | 0.8 | -0.3 |
| 2016 | D | 2.19 | 1.82 | 5.0 | 4.5 | 1.1 | -0.1 |
| 2015 | D | 1.95 | 1.63 | 5.3 | 4.7 | 0.7 | -0.6 |
| 2014 | N/A | N/A | N/A | 5.4 | 5.3 | N/A | -0.2 |
| 2013 | N/A | N/A | N/A | N/A | N/A | N/A | N/A |
| 2012 | N/A | N/A | N/A | N/A | N/A | N/A | N/A |

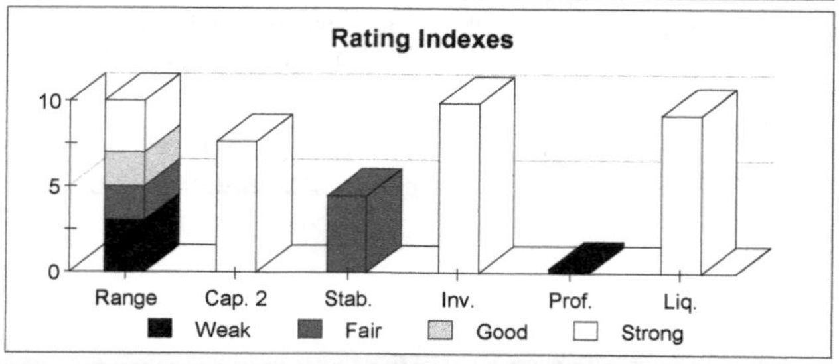


## HOME STATE HEALTH PLAN INC — C- — Fair

**Major Rating Factors:** Weak profitability index (1.9 on a scale of 0 to 10). Good liquidity (6.8) with sufficient resources (cash flows and marketable investments) to handle a spike in claims. Strong capitalization (8.1) based on excellent current risk-adjusted capital (severe loss scenario).
**Other Rating Factors:** High quality investment portfolio (9.9).
**Principal Business:** Medicaid (100%)
**Mem Phys: 16:** 16,486 **15:** 14,677 **16 MLR** 97.0% **/ 16 Admin Exp** N/A
**Enroll(000): Q3 17:** 273 **16:** 105 **15:** 94 **Med Exp PMPM:** $273
**Principal Investments:** Cash and equiv (51%), long-term bonds (44%), affiliate common stock (5%)
**Provider Compensation ($000):** Contr fee ($302,511), capitation ($10,324), bonus arrang ($6,993), salary ($4,961)
**Total Member Encounters:** Phys (408,489), non-phys (513,374)
**Group Affiliation:** Centene Corporation
**Licensed in:** MO
**Address:** 16090 Swingley Ridge Rd #450, Chesterfield, MO 63017
**Phone:** (314) 725-4477 **Dom State:** MO **Commenced Bus:** July 2012

| Data Date | Rating | RACR #1 | RACR #2 | Total Assets ($mil) | Capital ($mil) | Net Premium ($mil) | Net Income ($mil) |
|---|---|---|---|---|---|---|---|
| 9-17 | C- | 2.26 | 1.88 | 186.7 | 44.5 | 498.2 | -26.2 |
| 9-16 | C- | 2.45 | 2.04 | 98.4 | 36.0 | 258.3 | -20.3 |
| 2016 | C- | 2.21 | 1.84 | 102.3 | 43.4 | 344.4 | -12.9 |
| 2015 | C- | 2.35 | 1.96 | 86.4 | 34.3 | 266.6 | -15.6 |
| 2014 | C- | 2.58 | 2.15 | 60.2 | 22.6 | 179.2 | -19.8 |
| 2013 | C- | 2.44 | 2.03 | 47.4 | 17.2 | 185.2 | -2.8 |
| 2012 | C- | 2.77 | 2.31 | 52.8 | 20.3 | 77.8 | -15.6 |

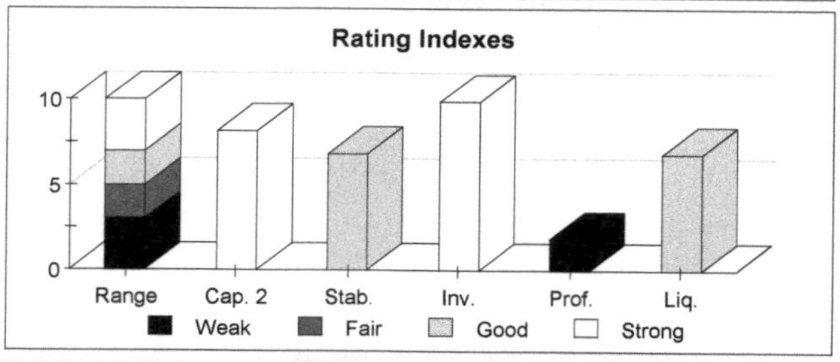


## HOMETOWN HEALTH PLAN INC — C- — Fair

**Major Rating Factors:** Fair overall results on stability tests (3.7 on a scale of 0 to 10) based on a steep decline in capital during 2016, inconsistent enrollment growth in the past five years due to declines in 2015 and 2016. Weak profitability index (2.3). Good liquidity (6.9) with sufficient resources (cash flows and marketable investments) to handle a spike in claims.
**Other Rating Factors:** Strong capitalization index (7.0) based on excellent current risk-adjusted capital (severe loss scenario). High quality investment portfolio (9.9).
**Principal Business:** Medicare (62%), comp med (38%)
**Mem Phys: 16:** 2,466 **15:** 2,196 **16 MLR** 91.5% **/ 16 Admin Exp** N/A
**Enroll(000): Q3 17:** 34 **16:** 33 **15:** 34 **Med Exp PMPM:** $614
**Principal Investments:** Cash and equiv (57%), long-term bonds (36%), real estate (7%)
**Provider Compensation ($000):** FFS ($238,391), capitation ($3,765)
**Total Member Encounters:** Phys (401,350), non-phys (257,009)
**Group Affiliation:** Renown Health
**Licensed in:** NV
**Address:** 830 Harvard Way, Reno, NV 89502
**Phone:** (775) 982-3100 **Dom State:** NV **Commenced Bus:** February 1988

| Data Date | Rating | RACR #1 | RACR #2 | Total Assets ($mil) | Capital ($mil) | Net Premium ($mil) | Net Income ($mil) |
|---|---|---|---|---|---|---|---|
| 9-17 | C- | 1.37 | 1.14 | 121.1 | 41.2 | 208.7 | 11.1 |
| 9-16 | C- | 1.16 | 0.97 | 101.9 | 35.1 | 202.2 | -3.0 |
| 2016 | C- | 1.01 | 0.84 | 86.1 | 30.6 | 266.5 | -7.5 |
| 2015 | C- | 1.29 | 1.07 | 79.0 | 38.9 | 271.5 | 2.7 |
| 2014 | C | 0.75 | 0.62 | 69.0 | 22.2 | 254.2 | -15.2 |
| 2013 | C | 1.39 | 1.16 | 87.4 | 34.8 | 237.4 | 4.8 |
| 2012 | C | 1.11 | 0.93 | 84.9 | 32.5 | 245.2 | 8.2 |

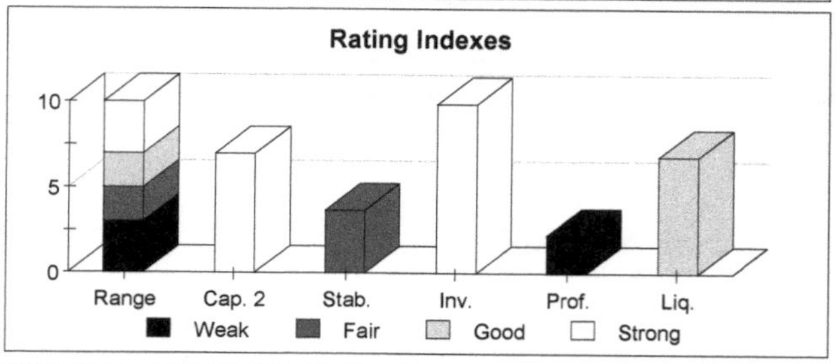

## HOMETOWN HEALTH PROVIDERS INS CO — B- — Good

**Major Rating Factors:** Fair profitability index (4.4 on a scale of 0 to 10). Strong capitalization (8.7) based on excellent current risk-adjusted capital (severe loss scenario). High quality investment portfolio (9.5).
**Other Rating Factors:** Excellent liquidity (7.0) with sufficient resources (cash flows and marketable investments) to handle a spike in claims.
**Principal Business:** Comp med (98%), Medicare (2%)
**Mem Phys: 16:** 2,484 **15:** 2,219 **16 MLR** 81.1% **/ 16 Admin Exp** N/A
**Enroll(000): Q3 17:** 39 **16:** 32 **15:** 29 **Med Exp PMPM:** $211
**Principal Investments:** Long-term bonds (52%), cash and equiv (37%), real estate (10%)
**Provider Compensation ($000):** FFS ($78,509)
**Total Member Encounters:** Phys (122,040), non-phys (80,825)
**Group Affiliation:** Renown Health
**Licensed in:** NV
**Address:** 830 Harvard Way, Reno, NV 89502
**Phone:** (775) 982-3100 **Dom State:** NV **Commenced Bus:** March 1982

| Data Date | Rating | RACR #1 | RACR #2 | Total Assets ($mil) | Capital ($mil) | Net Premium ($mil) | Net Income ($mil) |
|---|---|---|---|---|---|---|---|
| 9-17 | B- | 2.71 | 2.26 | 57.0 | 29.8 | 96.8 | -0.6 |
| 9-16 | C+ | 3.41 | 2.84 | 49.3 | 30.6 | 71.4 | -0.2 |
| 2016 | B- | 2.75 | 2.29 | 50.3 | 30.9 | 97.4 | 0.2 |
| 2015 | B- | 3.48 | 2.90 | 45.6 | 30.9 | 72.4 | 0.8 |
| 2014 | B | 4.14 | 3.45 | 44.5 | 30.7 | 58.1 | 2.2 |
| 2013 | B | 4.18 | 3.48 | 46.1 | 29.1 | 53.6 | 0.3 |
| 2012 | N/A | N/A | N/A | 40.8 | 29.3 | 59.6 | 1.6 |

Rating Indexes

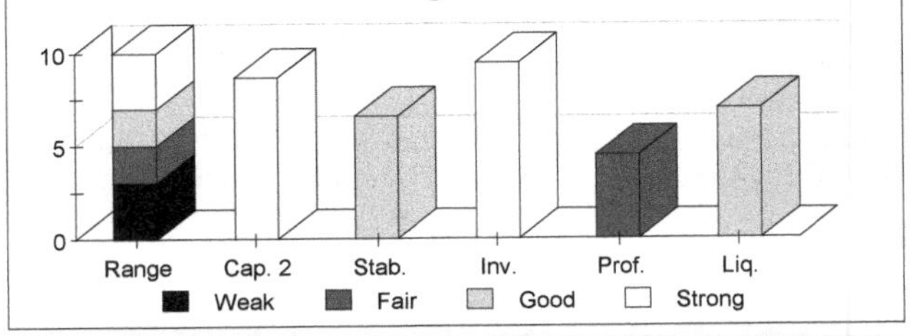


## HOOSIER MOTOR MUTUAL INS CO — B — Good

**Major Rating Factors:** Good quality investment portfolio (6.7 on a scale of 0 to 10). Fair profitability index (4.3). Strong capitalization (10.0) based on excellent current risk-adjusted capital (severe loss scenario).
**Other Rating Factors:** Excellent liquidity (10.0) with ample operational cash flow and liquid investments.
**Principal Business:** Other (100%)
**Mem Phys: 16:** N/A **15:** N/A **16 MLR** 0.7% **/ 16 Admin Exp** N/A
**Enroll(000): Q3 17:** 438 **16:** 436 **15:** 429 **Med Exp PMPM:** N/A
**Principal Investments:** Long-term bonds (48%), nonaffiliate common stock (32%), real estate (13%), cash and equiv (5%), other (2%)
**Provider Compensation ($000):** Other ($6)
**Total Member Encounters:** Phys (4)
**Group Affiliation:** Hoosier Motor Mutual Insurance Co
**Licensed in:** IN
**Address:** 3750 Guion Rd, Indianapolis, IN 46222
**Phone:** (317) 923-1500 **Dom State:** IN **Commenced Bus:** December 1972

| Data Date | Rating | RACR #1 | RACR #2 | Total Assets ($mil) | Capital ($mil) | Net Premium ($mil) | Net Income ($mil) |
|---|---|---|---|---|---|---|---|
| 9-17 | B | 11.15 | 9.29 | 12.0 | 11.5 | 0.5 | 0.8 |
| 9-16 | C+ | 11.24 | 9.37 | 11.9 | 11.4 | 0.5 | 0.5 |
| 2016 | C+ | 10.33 | 8.61 | 11.4 | 10.7 | 0.6 | -0.3 |
| 2015 | C- | 10.58 | 8.81 | 11.2 | 10.8 | 0.6 | -0.2 |
| 2014 | C+ | 5.98 | 3.15 | 11.7 | 11.2 | 0.6 | 0.1 |
| 2013 | C+ | 5.82 | 3.07 | 11.9 | 11.3 | 0.6 | -0.4 |
| 2012 | C+ | 6.81 | 3.54 | 12.0 | 11.4 | 0.6 | 0.1 |

Rating Indexes

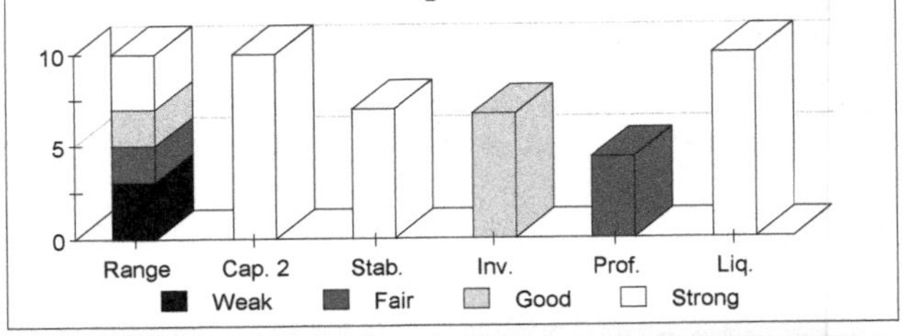


## HOPKINS HEALTH ADV INC — E — Very Weak

**Major Rating Factors:** Weak profitability index (0.1 on a scale of 0 to 10). Poor capitalization (0.0) based on weak current risk-adjusted capital (severe loss scenario). Good liquidity (6.8) with sufficient resources (cash flows and marketable investments) to handle a spike in claims.
**Other Rating Factors:** High quality investment portfolio (9.9).
**Principal Business:** Medicare (100%)
**Mem Phys: 16:** N/A **15:** N/A **16 MLR** 95.2% **/ 16 Admin Exp** N/A
**Enroll(000): Q3 17:** 8 **16:** 5 **15:** N/A **Med Exp PMPM:** $759
**Principal Investments:** Cash and equiv (100%)
**Provider Compensation ($000):** Contr fee ($32,093), capitation ($426)
**Total Member Encounters:** Phys (115,762), non-phys (41,572)
**Group Affiliation:** Johns Hopkins HealthCare LLC
**Licensed in:** MD
**Address:** 6704 Curtis Court, Glen Burnie, MD 21060
**Phone:** (410) 424-4948 **Dom State:** MD **Commenced Bus:** November 2014

| Data Date | Rating | RACR #1 | RACR #2 | Total Assets ($mil) | Capital ($mil) | Net Premium ($mil) | Net Income ($mil) |
|---|---|---|---|---|---|---|---|
| 9-17 | E | 0.25 | 0.21 | 27.1 | 2.4 | 63.0 | -10.2 |
| 9-16 | N/A | N/A | N/A | 17.9 | 4.4 | 31.3 | -9.9 |
| 2016 | D+ | 0.69 | 0.57 | 22.4 | 6.1 | 42.4 | -19.7 |
| 2015 | N/A | N/A | N/A | 1.9 | 1.9 | N/A | N/A |
| 2014 | N/A | N/A | N/A | N/A | N/A | N/A | N/A |
| 2013 | N/A | N/A | N/A | N/A | N/A | N/A | N/A |
| 2012 | N/A | N/A | N/A | N/A | N/A | N/A | N/A |

Rating Indexes

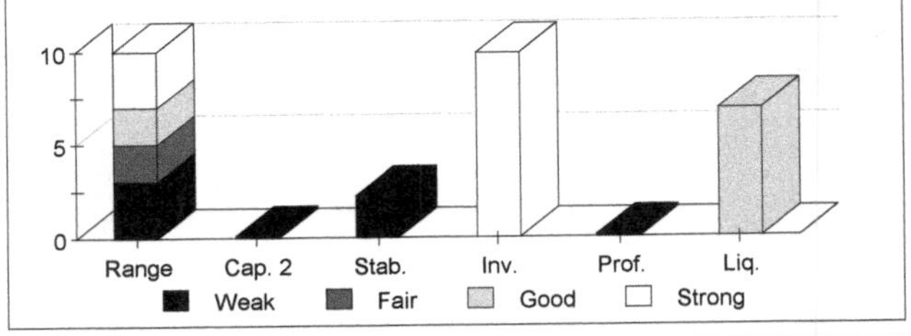

## HORIZON HEALTHCARE OF NEW JERSEY INC * A- Excellent

**Major Rating Factors:** Strong capitalization index (9.7 on a scale of 0 to 10) based on excellent current risk-adjusted capital (severe loss scenario). High quality investment portfolio (9.9). Good overall profitability index (6.8).
**Other Rating Factors:** Good overall results on stability tests (6.7) despite a decline in the number of member physicians during 2017. Good liquidity (6.7) with sufficient resources (cash flows and marketable investments) to handle a spike in claims.
**Principal Business:** Medicaid (99%)
**Mem Phys: 16:** 33,598 **15:** 38,917 **16 MLR** 86.8% **/ 16 Admin Exp** N/A
**Enroll(000): Q3 17:** 884 **16:** 897 **15:** 850 **Med Exp PMPM:** $399
**Principal Investments:** Long-term bonds (79%), nonaffiliate common stock (16%), cash and equiv (5%)
**Provider Compensation ($000):** Contr fee ($3,639,684), FFS ($335,792), capitation ($214,103)
**Total Member Encounters:** Phys (8,304,248), non-phys (3,992,493)
**Group Affiliation:** Horizon Healthcare Services Inc
**Licensed in:** NJ
**Address:** 3 Penn Plz E Ste PP-15D, Newark, NJ 07105-2248
**Phone:** (973) 466-5954 **Dom State:** NJ **Commenced Bus:** June 1986

| Data Date | Rating | RACR #1 | RACR #2 | Total Assets ($mil) | Capital ($mil) | Net Premium ($mil) | Net Income ($mil) |
|---|---|---|---|---|---|---|---|
| 9-17 | A- | 3.55 | 2.96 | 1,358.6 | 988.6 | 380.3 | 32.5 |
| 9-16 | A- | 3.51 | 2.93 | 1,619.2 | 923.3 | 3,608.0 | 84.0 |
| 2016 | A- | 3.58 | 2.99 | 1,601.5 | 998.0 | 4,868.0 | 151.2 |
| 2015 | A- | 3.24 | 2.70 | 1,439.4 | 850.1 | 4,561.5 | 72.0 |
| 2014 | A- | 2.63 | 2.19 | 1,339.5 | 585.9 | 3,916.6 | 21.4 |
| 2013 | A | 2.44 | 2.04 | 1,318.4 | 577.6 | 4,115.5 | 36.1 |
| 2012 | A | 2.39 | 1.99 | 1,235.9 | 542.6 | 4,099.9 | 50.4 |

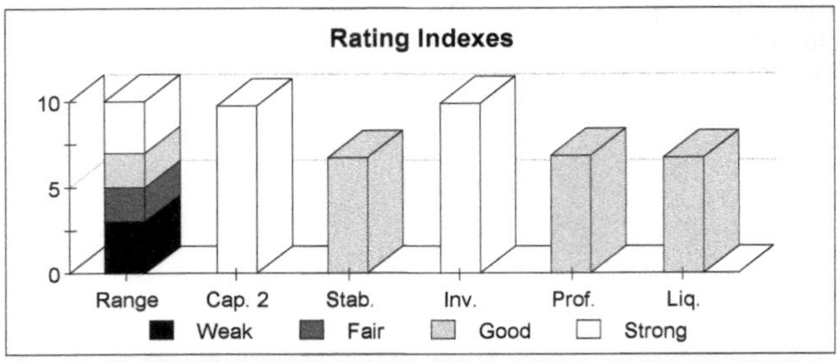


## HORIZON HEALTHCARE SERVICES INC B Good

**Major Rating Factors:** Good liquidity (6.6 on a scale of 0 to 10) with sufficient resources (cash flows and marketable investments) to handle a spike in claims. Fair profitability index (4.2). Fair quality investment portfolio (3.8).
**Other Rating Factors:** Strong capitalization (9.8) based on excellent current risk-adjusted capital (severe loss scenario).
**Principal Business:** Comp med (77%), FEHB (12%), Medicare (4%), med supp (4%), dental (2%)
**Mem Phys: 16:** 83,594 **15:** 91,005 **16 MLR** 78.6% **/ 16 Admin Exp** N/A
**Enroll(000): 16:** 1,284 **15:** 1,358 **Med Exp PMPM:** $334
**Principal Investments:** Long-term bonds (59%), affiliate common stock (38%), nonaffiliate common stock (6%), other (6%)
**Provider Compensation ($000):** Contr fee ($4,870,509), capitation ($260,394), FFS ($81,754)
**Total Member Encounters:** Phys (11,346,535), non-phys (10,390,379)
**Group Affiliation:** Horizon Healthcare Services Inc
**Licensed in:** NJ
**Address:** 3 Penn Plaza East, PP-15D, Newark, NJ 07105-2248
**Phone:** (973) 466-5607 **Dom State:** NJ **Commenced Bus:** December 1932

| Data Date | Rating | RACR #1 | RACR #2 | Total Assets ($mil) | Capital ($mil) | Net Premium ($mil) | Net Income ($mil) |
|---|---|---|---|---|---|---|---|
| 2016 | B | 3.59 | 3.00 | 4,257.6 | 2,385.9 | 6,692.7 | -83.0 |
| 2015 | B+ | 3.79 | 3.16 | 4,089.2 | 2,305.9 | 6,123.6 | 20.6 |
| 2014 | B+ | 4.03 | 3.36 | 3,795.8 | 2,230.2 | 5,812.8 | 59.7 |
| 2013 | B+ | 4.11 | 3.42 | 3,679.0 | 2,212.0 | 5,243.6 | 519.9 |
| 2012 | B | 3.87 | 3.23 | 3,624.1 | 2,106.9 | 4,940.8 | 152.6 |

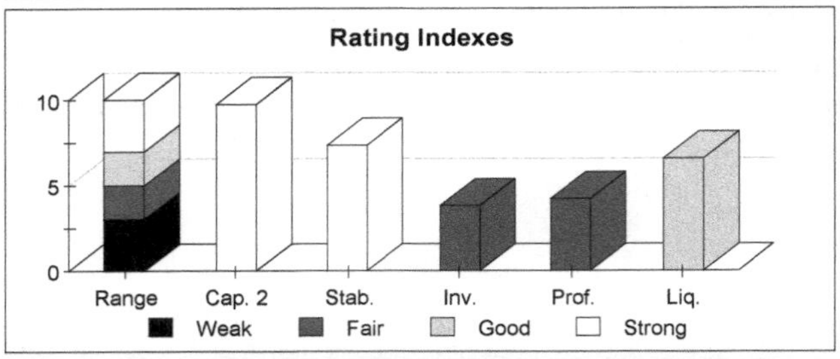


## HORIZON INS CO B- Good

**Major Rating Factors:** Excellent profitability (8.2 on a scale of 0 to 10). Strong capitalization (10.0) based on excellent current risk-adjusted capital (severe loss scenario). High quality investment portfolio (8.6).
**Other Rating Factors:** Weak liquidity (2.0) as a spike in claims may stretch capacity.
**Principal Business:** Medicare (46%), med supp (43%), vision (4%), other (6%)
**Mem Phys: 16:** 40,292 **15:** 38,617 **16 MLR** 835.6% **/ 16 Admin Exp** N/A
**Enroll(000): 16:** 196 **15:** 174 **Med Exp PMPM:** $231
**Principal Investments:** Long-term bonds (98%), cash and equiv (2%)
**Provider Compensation ($000):** Contr fee ($487,665), FFS ($31,786), capitation ($17,604)
**Total Member Encounters:** Phys (3,320,847), non-phys (1,509,199)
**Group Affiliation:** Horizon Healthcare Services Inc
**Licensed in:** NJ
**Address:** 3 Penn Plaza East PP-15D, Newark, NJ 07105-2248
**Phone:** (973) 466-5607 **Dom State:** NJ **Commenced Bus:** December 2012

| Data Date | Rating | RACR #1 | RACR #2 | Total Assets ($mil) | Capital ($mil) | Net Premium ($mil) | Net Income ($mil) |
|---|---|---|---|---|---|---|---|
| 2016 | B- | 8.75 | 7.29 | 123.8 | 27.3 | 64.1 | 3.2 |
| 2015 | B | 3.79 | 3.16 | 141.4 | 25.5 | 220.3 | 9.1 |
| 2014 | B+ | 1.68 | 1.40 | 71.5 | 16.3 | 258.7 | 7.4 |
| 2013 | B | 1.40 | 1.16 | 68.0 | 9.9 | 122.6 | 1.5 |
| 2012 | N/A | N/A | N/A | N/A | N/A | N/A | N/A |

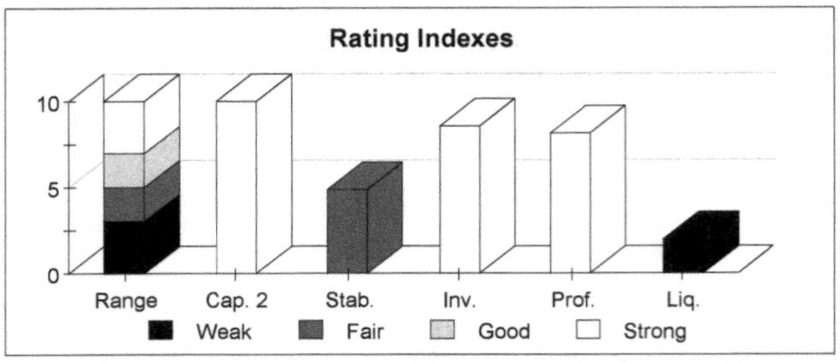

## HPHC INS CO — D- Weak

**Major Rating Factors:** Weak profitability index (0.9 on a scale of 0 to 10). Fair liquidity (4.6) as cash resources may not be adequate to cover a spike in claims. Strong capitalization (7.3) based on excellent current risk-adjusted capital (severe loss scenario).
**Other Rating Factors:** High quality investment portfolio (8.9).
**Principal Business:** Comp med (71%), med supp (27%), other (2%)
**Mem Phys: 16:** 79,113 **15:** 73,621 **16 MLR** 91.5% **/ 16 Admin Exp** N/A
**Enroll(000): Q3 17:** 187 **16:** 202 **15:** 194 **Med Exp PMPM:** $291
**Principal Investments:** Long-term bonds (95%), cash and equiv (5%), other (1%)
**Provider Compensation ($000):** Contr fee ($576,152), capitation ($74,790), FFS ($15,070), bonus arrang ($49), other ($38,772)
**Total Member Encounters:** Phys (1,086,561), non-phys (958,643)
**Group Affiliation:** Harvard Pilgrim Health Care Inc
**Licensed in:** CT, ME, MA, NH
**Address:** 93 WORCESTER St, WELLESLEY, MA 02481-9181
**Phone:** (781) 263-6000 **Dom State:** MA **Commenced Bus:** January 1992

| Data Date | Rating | RACR #1 | RACR #2 | Total Assets ($mil) | Capital ($mil) | Net Premium ($mil) | Net Income ($mil) |
|---|---|---|---|---|---|---|---|
| 9-17 | D- | 1.61 | 1.34 | 283.2 | 79.1 | 614.1 | 11.7 |
| 9-16 | D- | 0.82 | 0.68 | 240.1 | 33.9 | 580.9 | -42.8 |
| 2016 | D- | 1.43 | 1.19 | 268.9 | 70.6 | 774.5 | -57.8 |
| 2015 | C | 1.23 | 1.02 | 226.3 | 51.8 | 665.4 | -37.3 |
| 2014 | B- | 1.48 | 1.24 | 194.7 | 51.1 | 610.1 | -12.1 |
| 2013 | B | 1.02 | 0.85 | 158.0 | 42.0 | 616.1 | -3.8 |
| 2012 | B | 1.24 | 1.03 | 150.3 | 40.7 | 542.5 | -2.0 |

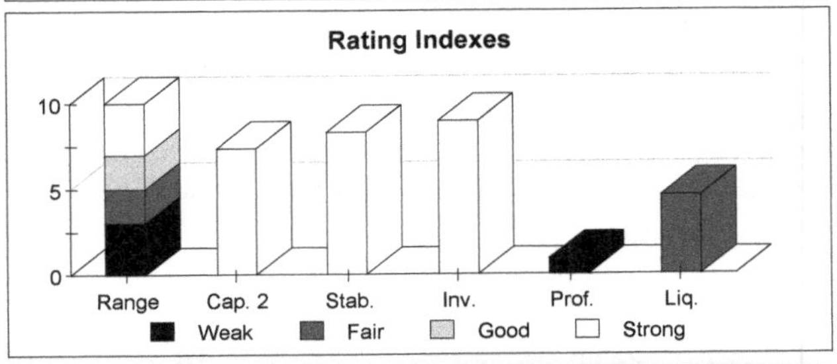


## HSA HEALTH INS CO — D Weak

**Major Rating Factors:** Weak profitability index (0.3 on a scale of 0 to 10). Fair liquidity (4.2) as cash resources may not be adequate to cover a spike in claims. Good capitalization (6.9) based on excellent current risk-adjusted capital (severe loss scenario).
**Other Rating Factors:** High quality investment portfolio (9.9).
**Principal Business:** Comp med (97%), other (3%)
**Mem Phys: 16:** 14,410 **15:** 4,300 **16 MLR** 97.5% **/ 16 Admin Exp** N/A
**Enroll(000): Q3 17:** 10 **16:** 5 **15:** N/A **Med Exp PMPM:** $116
**Principal Investments:** Long-term bonds (54%), cash and equiv (46%)
**Provider Compensation ($000):** Contr fee ($3,141)
**Total Member Encounters:** Phys (1,435), non-phys (3,579)
**Group Affiliation:** HSA Health Insurance Company
**Licensed in:** UT
**Address:** 10437 S Jordan Gateway, South Jordan, UT 84095
**Phone:** (844) 234-4472 **Dom State:** UT **Commenced Bus:** May 2015

| Data Date | Rating | RACR #1 | RACR #2 | Total Assets ($mil) | Capital ($mil) | Net Premium ($mil) | Net Income ($mil) |
|---|---|---|---|---|---|---|---|
| 9-17 | D | 1.27 | 1.06 | 6.1 | 2.1 | 9.0 | 1.2 |
| 9-16 | N/A | N/A | N/A | 3.0 | 1.5 | 3.8 | -0.7 |
| 2016 | D | 0.78 | 0.65 | 5.0 | 1.3 | 4.8 | -3.2 |
| 2015 | N/A | N/A | N/A | 2.4 | 2.2 | N/A | -0.9 |
| 2014 | N/A | N/A | N/A | N/A | N/A | N/A | N/A |
| 2013 | N/A | N/A | N/A | N/A | N/A | N/A | N/A |
| 2012 | N/A | N/A | N/A | N/A | N/A | N/A | N/A |

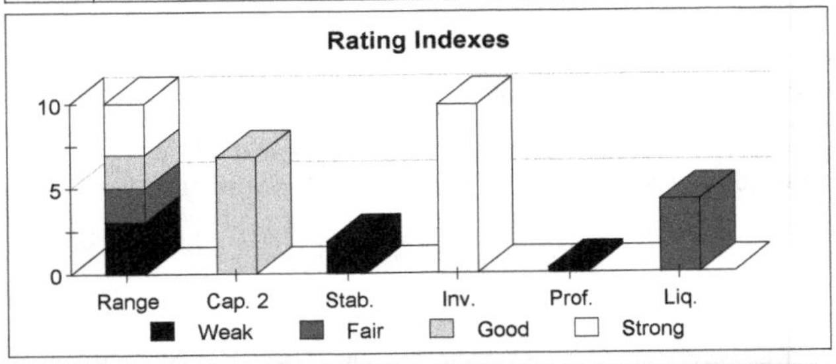


## HUMANA BENEFIT PLAN OF ILLINOIS * — A- Excellent

**Major Rating Factors:** Excellent profitability (8.8 on a scale of 0 to 10). Strong capitalization (10.0) based on excellent current risk-adjusted capital (severe loss scenario). High quality investment portfolio (9.9).
**Other Rating Factors:** Good liquidity (6.8) with sufficient resources (cash flows and marketable investments) to handle a spike in claims.
**Principal Business:** Medicare (100%)
**Mem Phys: 16:** 280,648 **15:** 119,803 **16 MLR** 82.9% **/ 16 Admin Exp** N/A
**Enroll(000): Q3 17:** 88 **16:** 88 **15:** 69 **Med Exp PMPM:** $773
**Principal Investments:** Long-term bonds (85%), cash and equiv (15%)
**Provider Compensation ($000):** Contr fee ($716,282), capitation ($45,146), FFS ($17,008), salary ($15,299)
**Total Member Encounters:** Phys (1,765,939), non-phys (1,080,694)
**Group Affiliation:** Humana Inc
**Licensed in:** All states except CA, FL, NY, UT, PR
**Address:** 7915 N HALE AVE STE D, PEORIA, IL 61615
**Phone:** (502) 580-1000 **Dom State:** IL **Commenced Bus:** February 1995

| Data Date | Rating | RACR #1 | RACR #2 | Total Assets ($mil) | Capital ($mil) | Net Premium ($mil) | Net Income ($mil) |
|---|---|---|---|---|---|---|---|
| 9-17 | A- | 3.79 | 3.16 | 394.7 | 196.5 | 767.4 | 36.1 |
| 9-16 | B | 3.77 | 3.14 | 319.0 | 149.7 | 727.8 | 19.0 |
| 2016 | A- | 3.13 | 2.61 | 248.6 | 161.8 | 969.5 | 32.1 |
| 2015 | B | 3.29 | 2.74 | 197.6 | 130.4 | 700.1 | -0.9 |
| 2014 | B- | 4.36 | 3.63 | 88.5 | 61.9 | 280.2 | 19.5 |
| 2013 | B | 4.99 | 4.16 | 66.4 | 45.9 | 172.3 | 4.7 |
| 2012 | C+ | 4.40 | 3.66 | 64.3 | 44.6 | 164.5 | 3.8 |

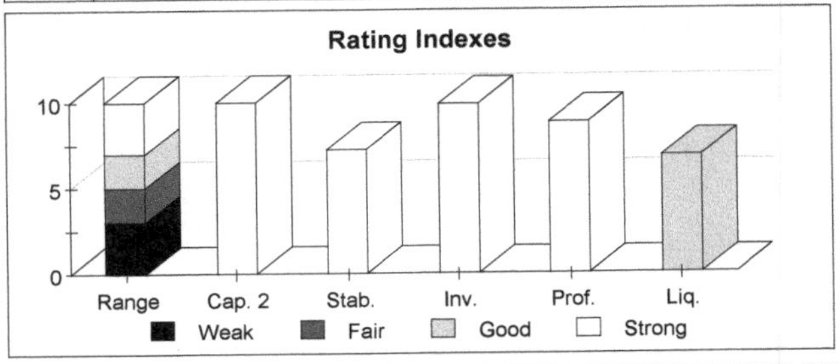

## HUMANA EMPLOYERS HEALTH PLAN OF GA — C — Fair

**Major Rating Factors:** Weak profitability index (0.9 on a scale of 0 to 10). Weak liquidity (2.5) as a spike in claims may stretch capacity. Good overall results on stability tests (5.1) despite a decline in enrollment during 2016. Potentially strong support from affiliation with Humana Inc.
**Other Rating Factors:** Strong capitalization index (10.0) based on excellent current risk-adjusted capital (severe loss scenario). High quality investment portfolio (9.3).
**Principal Business:** Comp med (75%), Medicare (24%), FEHB (1%)
**Mem Phys: 16:** 52,329 **15:** 49,922 **16 MLR** 105.4% **/ 16 Admin Exp** N/A
**Enroll(000): Q3 17:** 256 **16:** 405 **15:** 496 **Med Exp PMPM:** $385
**Principal Investments:** Long-term bonds (100%)
**Provider Compensation ($000):** Contr fee ($1,417,441), FFS ($439,550), capitation ($142,426), salary ($50,422)
**Total Member Encounters:** Phys (3,418,990), non-phys (1,485,141)
**Group Affiliation:** Humana Inc
**Licensed in:** GA
**Address:** 1200 ASHWOOD PKWY STE 250, ATLANTA, GA 30338
**Phone:** (770) 393-9226 **Dom State:** GA **Commenced Bus:** February 1997

| Data Date | Rating | RACR #1 | RACR #2 | Total Assets ($mil) | Capital ($mil) | Net Premium ($mil) | Net Income ($mil) |
|---|---|---|---|---|---|---|---|
| 9-17 | C | 4.03 | 3.36 | 755.0 | 531.0 | 900.3 | 28.6 |
| 9-16 | C | 3.36 | 2.80 | 900.5 | 461.4 | 1,655.4 | 53.0 |
| 2016 | C | 4.23 | 3.52 | 862.2 | 557.2 | 1,903.8 | -118.4 |
| 2015 | C- | 2.17 | 1.81 | 985.9 | 300.8 | 2,273.5 | -205.7 |
| 2014 | D | 2.20 | 1.83 | 408.3 | 196.9 | 1,623.8 | -6.5 |
| 2013 | D | 2.21 | 1.84 | 194.7 | 73.9 | 628.6 | -31.9 |
| 2012 | D | 1.72 | 1.43 | 105.4 | 34.0 | 393.2 | -7.5 |

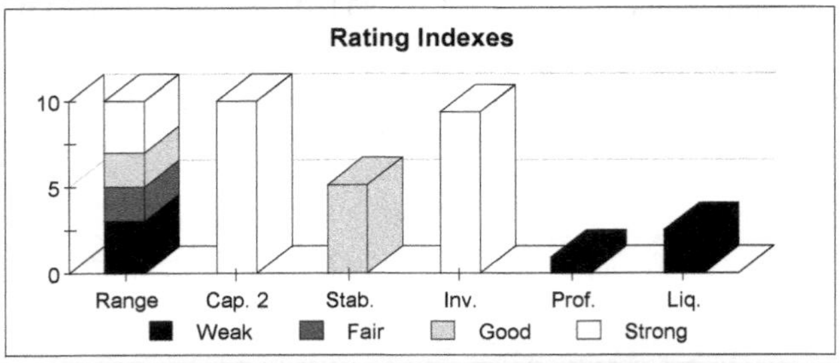


## HUMANA HEALTH BENEFIT PLAN LA — B — Good

**Major Rating Factors:** Good overall results on stability tests (5.7 on a scale of 0 to 10). Rating is significantly influenced by the good financial results of Humana Inc. Good liquidity (6.7) with sufficient resources (cash flows and marketable investments) to handle a spike in claims. Excellent profitability (8.6).
**Other Rating Factors:** Strong capitalization index (9.1) based on excellent current risk-adjusted capital (severe loss scenario). High quality investment portfolio (9.2).
**Principal Business:** Medicare (78%), comp med (22%)
**Mem Phys: 16:** 36,183 **15:** 35,503 **16 MLR** 81.5% **/ 16 Admin Exp** N/A
**Enroll(000): Q3 17:** 322 **16:** 319 **15:** 277 **Med Exp PMPM:** $439
**Principal Investments:** Long-term bonds (88%), cash and equiv (12%)
**Provider Compensation ($000):** Contr fee ($1,088,522), capitation ($422,408), FFS ($134,836), salary ($15,302)
**Total Member Encounters:** Phys (3,812,559), non-phys (2,008,989)
**Group Affiliation:** Humana Inc
**Licensed in:** LA
**Address:** ONE GALLERIA BLVD SUITE 1200, METAIRIE, LA 70001-7542
**Phone:** (504) 219-6600 **Dom State:** LA **Commenced Bus:** November 1994

| Data Date | Rating | RACR #1 | RACR #2 | Total Assets ($mil) | Capital ($mil) | Net Premium ($mil) | Net Income ($mil) |
|---|---|---|---|---|---|---|---|
| 9-17 | B | 3.07 | 2.55 | 744.0 | 285.6 | 1,571.4 | 69.1 |
| 9-16 | B- | 2.59 | 2.16 | 633.6 | 226.2 | 1,539.3 | 44.4 |
| 2016 | B | 2.65 | 2.21 | 495.5 | 244.2 | 2,031.7 | 60.2 |
| 2015 | B- | 2.09 | 1.75 | 396.4 | 179.7 | 1,837.4 | 36.6 |
| 2014 | B- | 2.95 | 2.46 | 406.4 | 223.3 | 1,646.3 | 56.2 |
| 2013 | B | 3.74 | 3.11 | 388.0 | 236.6 | 1,464.8 | 88.3 |
| 2012 | B | 3.44 | 2.86 | 357.8 | 204.7 | 1,371.7 | 79.7 |

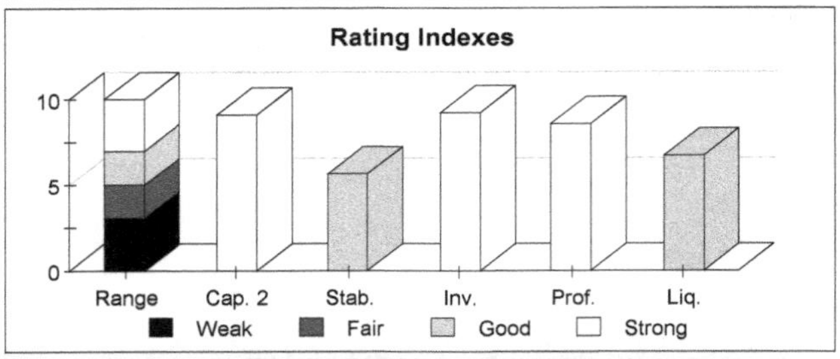


## HUMANA HEALTH CO OF NEW YORK INC — D- — Weak

**Major Rating Factors:** Weak profitability index (0.9 on a scale of 0 to 10). Strong capitalization (8.4) based on excellent current risk-adjusted capital (severe loss scenario). High quality investment portfolio (9.9).
**Other Rating Factors:** Excellent liquidity (7.0) with ample operational cash flow and liquid investments.
**Principal Business:** Medicare (100%)
**Mem Phys: 16:** 29,318 **15:** 25,198 **16 MLR** 90.7% **/ 16 Admin Exp** N/A
**Enroll(000): Q3 17:** 14 **16:** 12 **15:** 5 **Med Exp PMPM:** $728
**Principal Investments:** Cash and equiv (100%)
**Provider Compensation ($000):** Contr fee ($69,053), capitation ($19,625), FFS ($3,036)
**Total Member Encounters:** Phys (208,166), non-phys (92,469)
**Group Affiliation:** Humana Inc
**Licensed in:** NY
**Address:** 845 THIRD Ave 7TH Fl, NEW YORK, NY 10022
**Phone:** (800) 201-3687 **Dom State:** NY **Commenced Bus:** January 2009

| Data Date | Rating | RACR #1 | RACR #2 | Total Assets ($mil) | Capital ($mil) | Net Premium ($mil) | Net Income ($mil) |
|---|---|---|---|---|---|---|---|
| 9-17 | D- | 2.49 | 2.07 | 53.1 | 17.1 | 96.0 | -4.3 |
| 9-16 | D- | 5.06 | 4.21 | 40.7 | 18.0 | 79.6 | -4.7 |
| 2016 | D- | 3.10 | 2.58 | 40.1 | 21.3 | 108.1 | -12.1 |
| 2015 | D- | 6.33 | 5.27 | 27.9 | 22.5 | 42.6 | -1.0 |
| 2014 | E | 17.18 | 14.32 | 28.3 | 24.1 | 13.2 | -2.5 |
| 2013 | E | 19.34 | 16.12 | 27.5 | 26.8 | 4.5 | 1.4 |
| 2012 | E | 2.92 | 2.43 | 8.3 | 5.0 | 6.7 | -3.2 |

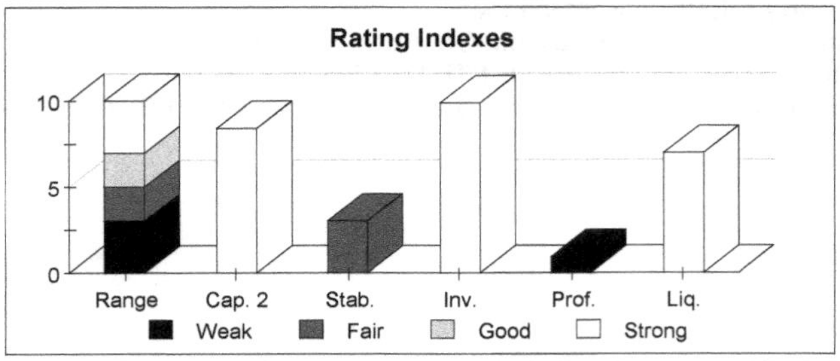

## HUMANA HEALTH INS CO OF FL INC — B- Good

**Major Rating Factors:** Good overall profitability index (6.8 on a scale of 0 to 10). Good liquidity (6.7) with sufficient resources (cash flows and marketable investments) to handle a spike in claims. Strong capitalization (10.0) based on excellent current risk-adjusted capital (severe loss scenario).
**Other Rating Factors:** High quality investment portfolio (9.2).
**Principal Business:** Medicare (65%), comp med (25%), med supp (6%), other (4%)
**Mem Phys: 16:** 112,839 **15:** 114,369 **16 MLR** 82.7% **/ 16 Admin Exp** N/A
**Enroll(000): Q3 17:** 174 **16:** 113 **15:** 88 **Med Exp PMPM:** $121
**Principal Investments:** Long-term bonds (97%), cash and equiv (3%)
**Provider Compensation ($000):** Contr fee ($154,985), FFS ($22,503)
**Total Member Encounters:** Phys (531,369), non-phys (217,566)
**Group Affiliation:** Humana Inc
**Licensed in:** AL, FL, KY
**Address:** 3501 SW 160TH Ave, MIRAMAR, FL 33027
**Phone:** (305) 626-5616 **Dom State:** FL **Commenced Bus:** May 1984

| Data Date | Rating | RACR #1 | RACR #2 | Total Assets ($mil) | Capital ($mil) | Net Premium ($mil) | Net Income ($mil) |
|---|---|---|---|---|---|---|---|
| 9-17 | B- | 4.48 | 3.73 | 293.5 | 58.8 | 725.8 | 4.1 |
| 9-16 | B- | 3.37 | 2.81 | 119.7 | 54.4 | 158.2 | 4.3 |
| 2016 | B- | 4.03 | 3.36 | 107.3 | 52.6 | 206.8 | 8.0 |
| 2015 | C+ | 4.43 | 3.69 | 133.5 | 72.5 | 265.6 | 12.8 |
| 2014 | C+ | 3.56 | 2.97 | 134.6 | 59.1 | 287.2 | 6.0 |
| 2013 | C | 3.28 | 2.73 | 125.8 | 56.4 | 323.7 | 10.2 |
| 2012 | B | 5.50 | 4.59 | 167.9 | 95.1 | 326.9 | 25.9 |

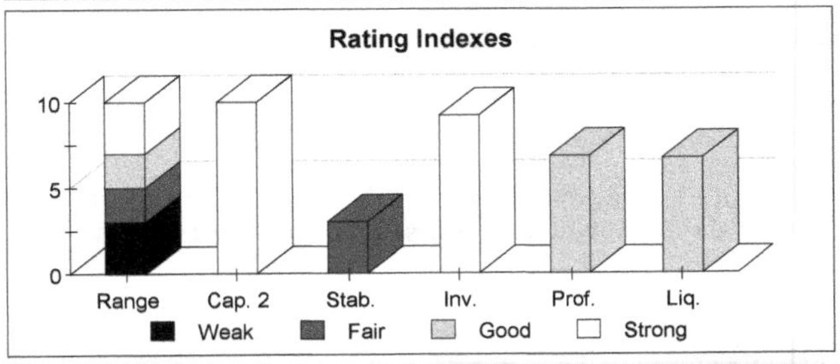


## HUMANA HEALTH PLAN INC — B- Good

**Major Rating Factors:** Fair profitability index (3.8 on a scale of 0 to 10). Good liquidity (5.5) with sufficient resources (cash flows and marketable investments) to handle a spike in claims. Strong capitalization index (9.3) based on excellent current risk-adjusted capital (severe loss scenario).
**Other Rating Factors:** High quality investment portfolio (9.6). Excellent overall results on stability tests (7.7) based on healthy premium and capital growth during 2016.
**Principal Business:** Medicare (82%), comp med (12%), Medicaid (4%), FEHB (2%)
**Mem Phys: 16:** 581,173 **15:** 574,650 **16 MLR** 95.7% **/ 16 Admin Exp** N/A
**Enroll(000): Q3 17:** 931 **16:** 968 **15:** 861 **Med Exp PMPM:** $612
**Principal Investments:** Long-term bonds (85%), cash and equiv (11%), mortgs (2%), affiliate common stock (2%)
**Provider Compensation ($000):** Contr fee ($3,887,182), capitation ($2,076,695), salary ($635,253), FFS ($294,951)
**Total Member Encounters:** Phys (15,534,780), non-phys (8,448,064)
**Group Affiliation:** Humana Inc
**Licensed in:** AL, AZ, AR, CO, ID, IL, IN, KS, KY, MO, NE, NV, NM, OH, SC, TN, TX, VA, WA, WV
**Address:** 321 WEST MAIN STREET - 12TH FL, LOUISVILLE, KY 40202
**Phone:** (502) 580-1000 **Dom State:** KY **Commenced Bus:** September 1983

| Data Date | Rating | RACR #1 | RACR #2 | Total Assets ($mil) | Capital ($mil) | Net Premium ($mil) | Net Income ($mil) |
|---|---|---|---|---|---|---|---|
| 9-17 | B- | 3.17 | 2.64 | 2,619.9 | 1,039.6 | 5,465.0 | 145.4 |
| 9-16 | C+ | 2.26 | 1.88 | 2,185.2 | 632.1 | 5,481.6 | -15.5 |
| 2016 | B- | 2.65 | 2.21 | 1,678.6 | 866.7 | 7,278.9 | 37.0 |
| 2015 | C+ | 2.15 | 1.79 | 1,385.6 | 601.3 | 5,790.9 | -102.9 |
| 2014 | C | 2.55 | 2.13 | 1,275.1 | 585.6 | 4,947.1 | -49.1 |
| 2013 | C | 2.29 | 1.91 | 811.6 | 379.2 | 3,694.2 | -38.5 |
| 2012 | B- | 2.19 | 1.82 | 645.2 | 307.9 | 2,992.3 | -28.9 |

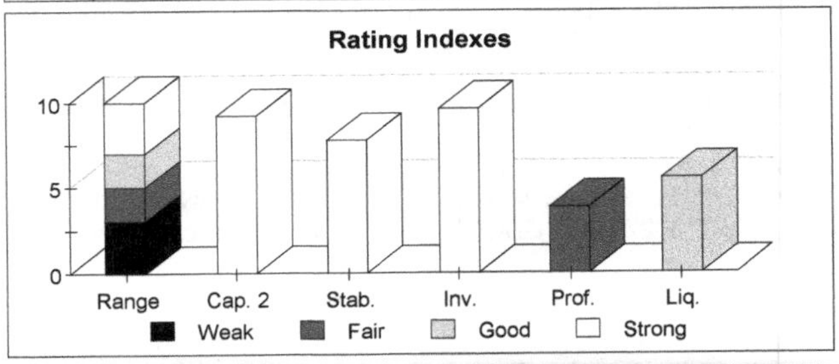


## HUMANA HEALTH PLAN OF OHIO INC — B- Good

**Major Rating Factors:** Good liquidity (6.3 on a scale of 0 to 10) with sufficient resources (cash flows and marketable investments) to handle a spike in claims. Strong capitalization index (9.2) based on excellent current risk-adjusted capital (severe loss scenario). High quality investment portfolio (9.9).
**Other Rating Factors:** Excellent overall results on stability tests (7.1) based on healthy premium and capital growth during 2016 but a decline in the number of member physicians during 2017. Rating is significantly influenced by the good financial results of Humana Inc. Weak profitability index (2.6).
**Principal Business:** Medicare (70%), comp med (29%)
**Mem Phys: 16:** 92,220 **15:** 112,141 **16 MLR** 86.7% **/ 16 Admin Exp** N/A
**Enroll(000): Q3 17:** 51 **16:** 105 **15:** 97 **Med Exp PMPM:** $508
**Principal Investments:** Long-term bonds (87%), cash and equiv (13%)
**Provider Compensation ($000):** Contr fee ($430,631), capitation ($138,713), FFS ($57,083)
**Total Member Encounters:** Phys (1,283,328), non-phys (723,653)
**Group Affiliation:** Humana Inc
**Licensed in:** IN, KY, OH
**Address:** 640 EDEN PARK DRIVE, CINCINNATI, OH 45202-6056
**Phone:** (513) 784-5320 **Dom State:** OH **Commenced Bus:** March 1979

| Data Date | Rating | RACR #1 | RACR #2 | Total Assets ($mil) | Capital ($mil) | Net Premium ($mil) | Net Income ($mil) |
|---|---|---|---|---|---|---|---|
| 9-17 | B- | 3.10 | 2.58 | 153.8 | 118.7 | 174.8 | 13.6 |
| 9-16 | B- | 2.57 | 2.14 | 235.4 | 85.7 | 552.8 | -2.8 |
| 2016 | B- | 2.68 | 2.23 | 180.5 | 102.5 | 728.8 | 8.4 |
| 2015 | C+ | 2.32 | 1.93 | 176.8 | 77.3 | 591.0 | -27.3 |
| 2014 | C | 2.22 | 1.85 | 140.9 | 63.5 | 497.0 | -25.5 |
| 2013 | C | 2.41 | 2.01 | 90.7 | 48.6 | 367.0 | 5.6 |
| 2012 | C | 2.49 | 2.08 | 77.4 | 41.2 | 284.7 | 5.4 |

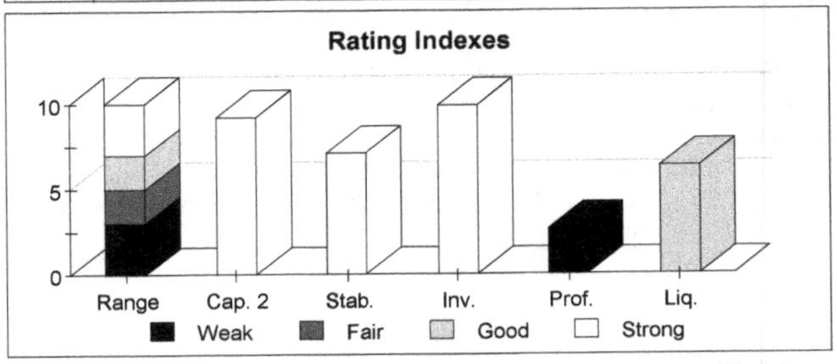

## HUMANA HEALTH PLAN OF TEXAS INC — C — Fair

**Major Rating Factors:** Weak profitability index (0.8 on a scale of 0 to 10). Weak overall results on stability tests (2.8) based on a significant 43% decrease in enrollment during the period. Rating is significantly influenced by the good financial results of Humana Inc. Good liquidity (5.4) with sufficient resources (cash flows and marketable investments) to handle a spike in claims.
**Other Rating Factors:** Strong capitalization index (8.8) based on excellent current risk-adjusted capital (severe loss scenario). High quality investment portfolio (9.8).
**Principal Business:** Comp med (91%), FEHB (9%)
**Mem Phys: 16:** 128,357 **15:** 121,076 **16 MLR** 94.8% **/ 16 Admin Exp** N/A
**Enroll(000): Q3 17:** 178 **16:** 214 **15:** 372 **Med Exp PMPM:** $285
**Principal Investments:** Long-term bonds (98%), cash and equiv (2%), real estate (1%)
**Provider Compensation ($000):** Contr fee ($644,629), FFS ($232,624), capitation ($2,544)
**Total Member Encounters:** Phys (1,386,606), non-phys (520,321)
**Group Affiliation:** Humana Inc
**Licensed in:** TX
**Address:** 1221 S MO PAC EXPY SUITE 200, AUSTIN, TX 78746-7625
**Phone:** (502) 580-1000 **Dom State:** TX **Commenced Bus:** July 1984

| Data Date | Rating | RACR #1 | RACR #2 | Total Assets ($mil) | Capital ($mil) | Net Premium ($mil) | Net Income ($mil) |
|---|---|---|---|---|---|---|---|
| 9-17 | C | 2.82 | 2.35 | 253.1 | 139.1 | 588.7 | 34.1 |
| 9-16 | C | 2.24 | 1.86 | 398.5 | 218.7 | 672.7 | -19.2 |
| 2016 | C | 4.65 | 3.87 | 404.6 | 233.9 | 805.9 | -69.0 |
| 2015 | C | 2.28 | 1.90 | 584.5 | 199.6 | 2,044.9 | -86.4 |
| 2014 | B- | 2.91 | 2.43 | 473.8 | 237.4 | 1,838.5 | 6.7 |
| 2013 | B | 3.20 | 2.66 | 335.2 | 174.7 | 1,362.4 | 9.6 |
| 2012 | B | 1.87 | 1.55 | 243.9 | 102.6 | 1,171.2 | 6.4 |

**Rating Indexes**

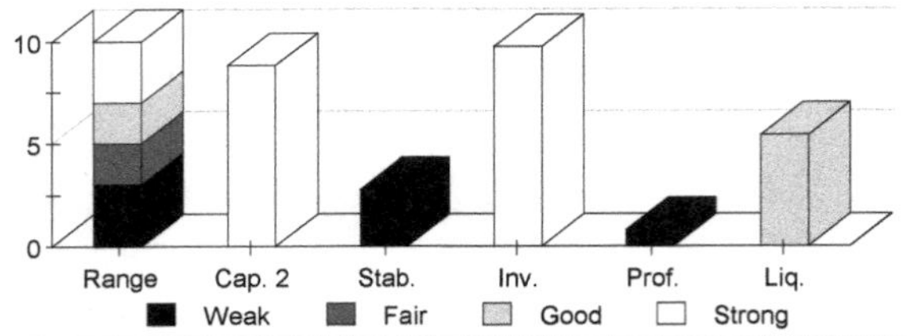


## HUMANA HEALTH PLANS OF PUERTO RICO — C+ — Fair

**Major Rating Factors:** Good liquidity (5.3 on a scale of 0 to 10) with sufficient resources (cash flows and marketable investments) to handle a spike in claims. Weak profitability index (0.7). Weak overall results on stability tests (1.5) based on a significant 20% decrease in enrollment during the period, a steep decline in capital during 2016. Rating is significantly influenced by the good financial results of Humana Inc.
**Other Rating Factors:** Strong capitalization index (8.4) based on excellent current risk-adjusted capital (severe loss scenario). High quality investment portfolio (9.9).
**Principal Business:** Medicare (90%), FEHB (6%), comp med (4%)
**Mem Phys: 16:** 13,474 **15:** 7,253 **16 MLR** 93.9% **/ 16 Admin Exp** N/A
**Enroll(000): Q3 17:** 48 **16:** 47 **15:** 58 **Med Exp PMPM:** $509
**Principal Investments:** Long-term bonds (61%), cash and equiv (39%)
**Provider Compensation ($000):** Capitation ($153,310), contr fee ($137,555), FFS ($15,283)
**Total Member Encounters:** Phys (946,931), non-phys (473,858)
**Group Affiliation:** Humana Inc
**Licensed in:** PR
**Address:** 383 FD ROOSEVELT AVENUE, SAN JUAN, PR 00918-2131
**Phone:** (787) 282-7900 **Dom State:** PR **Commenced Bus:** May 1986

| Data Date | Rating | RACR #1 | RACR #2 | Total Assets ($mil) | Capital ($mil) | Net Premium ($mil) | Net Income ($mil) |
|---|---|---|---|---|---|---|---|
| 9-17 | C+ | 2.51 | 2.09 | 145.5 | 32.1 | 231.8 | -11.3 |
| 9-16 | C+ | 3.88 | 3.23 | 138.2 | 56.2 | 248.2 | -16.6 |
| 2016 | C+ | 3.21 | 2.67 | 114.7 | 42.8 | 312.2 | -32.2 |
| 2015 | C+ | 4.97 | 4.14 | 140.8 | 75.6 | 417.7 | 7.7 |
| 2014 | C | 4.49 | 3.74 | 150.1 | 69.5 | 391.5 | -18.2 |
| 2013 | B | 1.75 | 1.46 | 189.5 | 87.0 | 907.2 | -15.0 |
| 2012 | B | 1.82 | 1.52 | 260.8 | 102.5 | 1,025.2 | 19.3 |

**Rating Indexes**

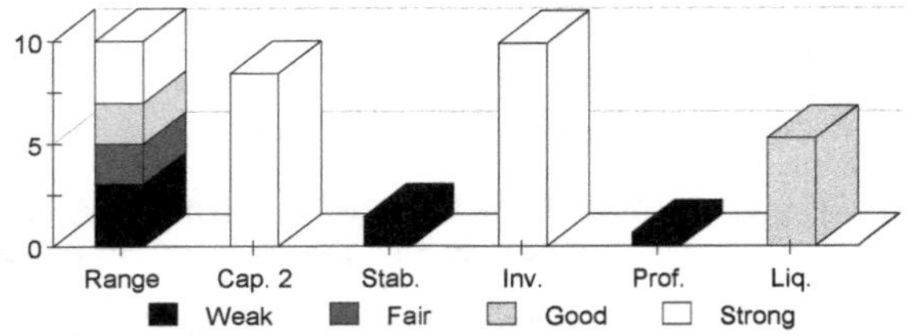


## HUMANA INS CO (WI) * — A- — Excellent

**Major Rating Factors:** Excellent profitability (8.0 on a scale of 0 to 10). Strong capitalization (8.8) based on excellent current risk-adjusted capital (severe loss scenario). High quality investment portfolio (9.7).
**Other Rating Factors:** Excellent liquidity (6.9) with sufficient resources (cash flows and marketable investments) to handle a spike in claims.
**Principal Business:** Medicare (69%), comp med (11%), med supp (2%), other (17%)
**Mem Phys: 16:** 1,458,699 **15:** 1,358,209 **16 MLR** 82.9% **/ 16 Admin Exp** N/A
**Enroll(000): Q3 17:** 10,334 **16:** 9,692 **15:** 9,319 **Med Exp PMPM:** $165
**Principal Investments:** Long-term bonds (47%), cash and equiv (31%), affiliate common stock (22%)
**Provider Compensation ($000):** Contr fee ($16,704,066), capitation ($1,311,910), FFS ($1,210,441)
**Total Member Encounters:** Phys (37,026,045), non-phys (21,362,075)
**Group Affiliation:** Humana Inc
**Licensed in:** All states except NY, PR
**Address:** 1100 EMPLOYERS Blvd, DEPERE, WI 54115
**Phone:** (920) 336-1100 **Dom State:** WI **Commenced Bus:** December 1968

| Data Date | Rating | RACR #1 | RACR #2 | Total Assets ($mil) | Capital ($mil) | Net Premium ($mil) | Net Income ($mil) |
|---|---|---|---|---|---|---|---|
| 9-17 | A- | 2.76 | 2.30 | 10,120.6 | 4,043.5 | 17,310.7 | 786.6 |
| 9-16 | B+ | 2.58 | 2.15 | 8,522.8 | 3,816.3 | 17,372.5 | 288.3 |
| 2016 | A- | 2.88 | 2.40 | 6,870.6 | 4,224.7 | 22,960.9 | 506.1 |
| 2015 | B+ | 2.47 | 2.06 | 6,583.3 | 3,642.1 | 23,141.9 | 421.8 |
| 2014 | C- | 2.47 | 2.06 | 6,237.0 | 3,307.5 | 22,315.2 | 505.3 |
| 2013 | N/A | N/A | N/A | 5,620.4 | 3,075.2 | 19,802.9 | N/A |
| 2012 | N/A | N/A | N/A | 5,197.5 | 2,665.5 | 18,473.9 | N/A |

**Rating Indexes**

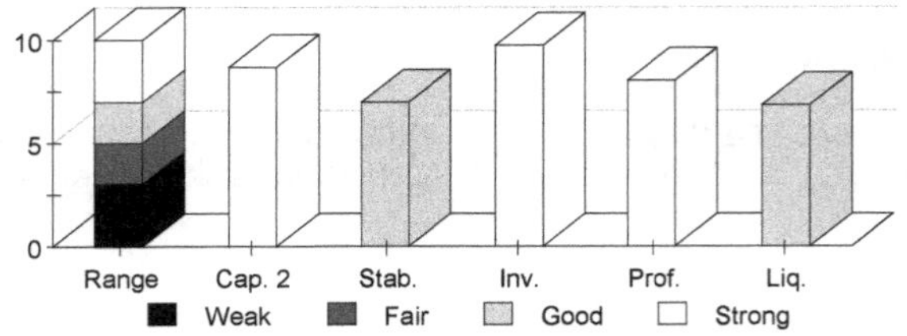

## HUMANA INS CO OF NY B- Good

**Major Rating Factors:** Strong capitalization (10.0 on a scale of 0 to 10) based on excellent current risk-adjusted capital (severe loss scenario). High quality investment portfolio (9.9). Excellent liquidity (7.0) with ample operational cash flow and liquid investments.
**Other Rating Factors:** Weak profitability index (2.1).
**Principal Business:** Medicare (42%), med supp (5%), other (52%)
**Mem Phys: 16:** 42,960 **15:** 25,198 **16 MLR** 86.0% **/ 16 Admin Exp** N/A
**Enroll(000): Q3 17:** 179 **16:** 172 **15:** 156 **Med Exp PMPM:** $121
**Principal Investments:** Cash and equiv (87%), long-term bonds (12%)
**Provider Compensation ($000):** Contr fee ($243,924), FFS ($4,914), capitation ($4,086)
**Total Member Encounters:** Phys (431,268), non-phys (207,264)
**Group Affiliation:** Humana Inc
**Licensed in:** NY
**Address:** 845 THIRD Ave 7TH Fl, NEW YORK, NY 10022
**Phone:** (800) 201-3687 **Dom State:** NY **Commenced Bus:** August 2006

| Data Date | Rating | RACR #1 | RACR #2 | Total Assets ($mil) | Capital ($mil) | Net Premium ($mil) | Net Income ($mil) |
|---|---|---|---|---|---|---|---|
| 9-17 | B- | 4.53 | 3.78 | 198.9 | 68.8 | 211.5 | 0.0 |
| 9-16 | B- | 4.91 | 4.09 | 157.8 | 63.2 | 222.3 | -8.2 |
| 2016 | B- | 4.49 | 3.74 | 105.5 | 68.1 | 291.8 | -3.4 |
| 2015 | C+ | 4.40 | 3.66 | 106.4 | 56.6 | 253.4 | -4.9 |
| 2014 | B- | 5.20 | 4.34 | 98.5 | 59.4 | 230.7 | -2.0 |
| 2013 | B | 6.73 | 5.61 | 82.8 | 64.0 | 185.5 | -1.8 |
| 2012 | B | 9.18 | 7.65 | 78.3 | 64.2 | 146.7 | 3.1 |

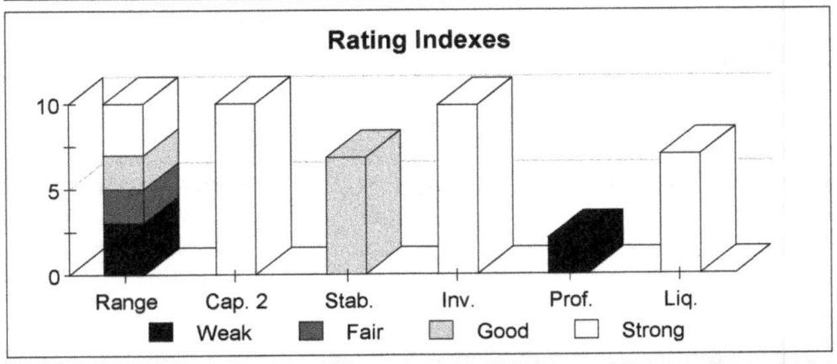


## HUMANA INSURANCE COMPANY OF KENTUCKY C Fair

**Major Rating Factors:** Fair overall results on stability tests (3.2 on a scale of 0 to 10) including excessive premium growth. Strong capitalization (10.0) based on excellent risk adjusted capital (severe loss scenario). Moreover, capital levels have been consistently high over the last five years. High quality investment portfolio (8.0).
**Other Rating Factors:** Excellent profitability (7.2) despite modest operating losses during 2015. Excellent liquidity (7.8).
**Principal Business:** Reinsurance (43%), individual health insurance (34%), group life insurance (21%), and group health insurance (2%).
**Principal Investments:** NonCMO investment grade bonds (58%) and CMOs and structured securities (41%).
**Investments in Affiliates:** None
**Group Affiliation:** Humana Inc
**Licensed in:** KY
**Commenced Business:** January 2001
**Address:** 500 WEST MAIN STREET, LOUISVILLE, KY 40202
**Phone:** (502) 580-1000 **Domicile State:** KY **NAIC Code:** 60219

| Data Date | Rating | RACR #1 | RACR #2 | Total Assets ($mil) | Capital ($mil) | Net Premium ($mil) | Net Income ($mil) |
|---|---|---|---|---|---|---|---|
| 9-17 | C | 6.51 | 4.69 | 214.6 | 169.2 | 94.2 | 19.3 |
| 9-16 | C | 4.68 | 3.40 | 206.6 | 158.4 | 58.8 | 36.3 |
| 2016 | C | 6.43 | 4.69 | 204.5 | 149.9 | 90.9 | 37.4 |
| 2015 | C | 2.61 | 1.95 | 432.9 | 122.2 | 269.9 | -2.8 |
| 2014 | B- | 2.71 | 2.11 | 418.0 | 107.6 | 157.8 | -5.8 |
| 2013 | B- | 2.03 | 1.57 | 108.6 | 61.1 | 111.5 | 15.7 |
| 2012 | B- | 1.73 | 1.35 | 42.3 | 24.8 | 40.8 | 6.4 |

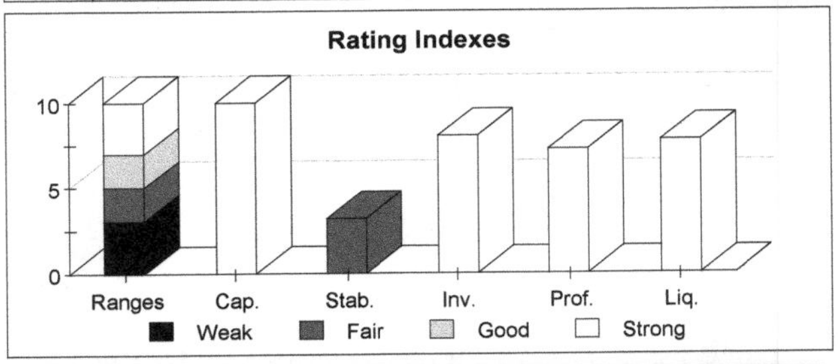


## HUMANA INSURANCE COMPANY OF PUERTO RICO INCORPOR/ B- Good

**Major Rating Factors:** Good liquidity (6.4 on a scale of 0 to 10) with sufficient resources to handle a spike in claims. Good overall results on stability tests (5.0). Strengths include good financial support from affiliation with Humana Inc, good operational trends and good risk diversification. Weak profitability (2.8). Excellent expense controls.
**Other Rating Factors:** Strong capitalization (8.2) based on excellent risk adjusted capital (severe loss scenario). High quality investment portfolio (8.4).
**Principal Business:** Group health insurance (89%) and individual health insurance (10%).
**Principal Investments:** NonCMO investment grade bonds (45%), CMOs and structured securities (37%), cash (14%), and noninv. grade bonds (1%).
**Investments in Affiliates:** None
**Group Affiliation:** Humana Inc
**Licensed in:** PR
**Commenced Business:** September 1971
**Address:** 383 FD ROOSEVELT AVENUE, SAN JUAN, PR 00918-2131
**Phone:** (787) 282-7900 **Domicile State:** PR **NAIC Code:** 84603

| Data Date | Rating | RACR #1 | RACR #2 | Total Assets ($mil) | Capital ($mil) | Net Premium ($mil) | Net Income ($mil) |
|---|---|---|---|---|---|---|---|
| 9-17 | B- | 2.28 | 1.82 | 73.9 | 50.9 | 97.7 | 5.0 |
| 9-16 | C+ | 2.49 | 1.95 | 70.7 | 49.2 | 83.8 | -1.6 |
| 2016 | C+ | 2.29 | 1.84 | 67.3 | 46.2 | 110.8 | -4.4 |
| 2015 | B- | 2.85 | 2.28 | 69.3 | 51.2 | 96.9 | 1.5 |
| 2014 | B- | 2.80 | 2.22 | 70.2 | 49.8 | 93.3 | -6.6 |
| 2013 | B- | 3.20 | 2.52 | 73.3 | 57.0 | 93.2 | 4.7 |
| 2012 | C+ | 2.86 | 2.27 | 70.2 | 52.1 | 98.6 | 4.6 |

| Humana Inc<br>Composite Group Rating: B<br>Largest Group Members | Assets ($mil) | Rating |
|---|---|---|
| HUMANA INS CO (WI) | 6871 | A- |
| KANAWHA INS CO | 2343 | B- |
| HUMANA MEDICAL PLAN INC | 1939 | B |
| HUMANA HEALTH PLAN INC | 1679 | B- |
| HUMANA EMPLOYERS HEALTH PLAN OF GA | 862 | C |

## HUMANA MEDICAL PLAN INC — B — Good

**Major Rating Factors:** Good overall results on stability tests (5.4 on a scale of 0 to 10) despite a decline in the number of member physicians during 2017. Good liquidity (5.5) with sufficient resources (cash flows and marketable investments) to handle a spike in claims. Excellent profitability (9.1)
**Other Rating Factors:** Strong capitalization index (8.6) based on excellent current risk-adjusted capital (severe loss scenario). High quality investment portfolio (9.5).
**Principal Business:** Medicare (64%), comp med (18%), Medicaid (17%)
**Mem Phys: 16:** 171,427 **15:** 238,812 **16 MLR** 84.2% **/ 16 Admin Exp** N/A
**Enroll(000): Q3 17:** 944 **16:** 1,160 **15:** 1,204 **Med Exp PMPM:** $543
**Principal Investments:** Long-term bonds (95%), cash and equiv (4%)
**Provider Compensation ($000):** Capitation ($3,126,139), contr fee ($2,759,092), salary ($1,145,929), FFS ($676,911)
**Total Member Encounters:** Phys (16,497,670), non-phys (8,163,987)
**Group Affiliation:** Humana Inc
**Licensed in:** FL, KY, MS, NC, OR, VA
**Address:** 3501 SW 160TH AVENUE, MIRAMAR, FL 33027
**Phone:** (305) 626-5616 **Dom State:** FL **Commenced Bus:** June 1987

| Data Date | Rating | RACR #1 | RACR #2 | Total Assets ($mil) | Capital ($mil) | Net Premium ($mil) | Net Income ($mil) |
|---|---|---|---|---|---|---|---|
| 9-17 | B | 2.64 | 2.20 | 2,681.0 | 882.7 | 6,613.1 | 214.9 |
| 9-16 | B | 2.42 | 2.02 | 2,669.6 | 754.5 | 6,787.8 | 99.2 |
| 2016 | B | 2.32 | 1.93 | 1,939.0 | 768.5 | 9,065.9 | 153.3 |
| 2015 | B | 2.21 | 1.84 | 2,013.8 | 683.1 | 8,867.8 | 328.3 |
| 2014 | B- | 2.60 | 2.17 | 1,742.2 | 591.5 | 6,965.8 | 332.9 |
| 2013 | B | 3.77 | 3.14 | 1,595.0 | 530.7 | 5,391.4 | 348.6 |
| 2012 | B | 4.80 | 4.00 | 1,618.6 | 631.5 | 5,242.2 | 461.2 |

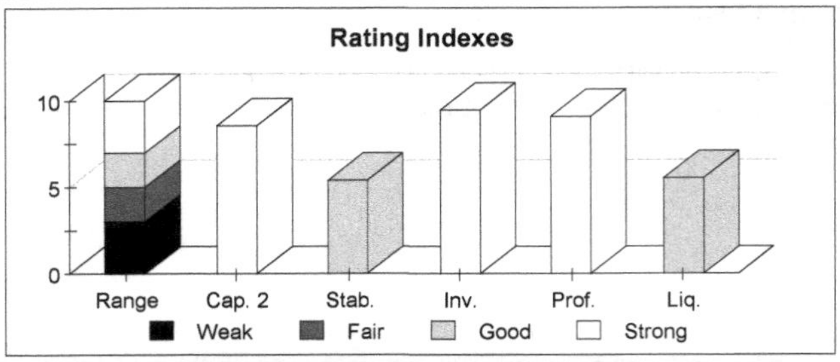


## HUMANA MEDICAL PLAN OF MICHIGAN INC — C+ — Fair

**Major Rating Factors:** Good liquidity (6.9 on a scale of 0 to 10) with sufficient resources (cash flows and marketable investments) to handle a spike in claims. Weak profitability index (0.9). Strong capitalization (10.0) based on excellent current risk-adjusted capital (severe loss scenario).
**Other Rating Factors:** High quality investment portfolio (9.9).
**Principal Business:** Comp med (59%), Medicare (41%)
**Mem Phys: 16:** 68,574 **15:** 36,424 **16 MLR** 87.3% **/ 16 Admin Exp** N/A
**Enroll(000): Q3 17:** 11 **16:** 30 **15:** 17 **Med Exp PMPM:** $249
**Principal Investments:** Cash and equiv (57%), long-term bonds (43%)
**Provider Compensation ($000):** Contr fee ($76,452), FFS ($15,824), capitation ($6,311)
**Total Member Encounters:** Phys (247,463), non-phys (107,487)
**Group Affiliation:** Humana Inc
**Licensed in:** MI
**Address:** 250 MONROE NW STE 400, GRAND RAPIDS, MI 49503
**Phone:** (502) 580-1000 **Dom State:** MI **Commenced Bus:** February 2012

| Data Date | Rating | RACR #1 | RACR #2 | Total Assets ($mil) | Capital ($mil) | Net Premium ($mil) | Net Income ($mil) |
|---|---|---|---|---|---|---|---|
| 9-17 | C+ | 4.11 | 3.43 | 50.2 | 30.1 | 58.6 | -1.3 |
| 9-16 | C+ | 4.79 | 3.99 | 74.5 | 24.6 | 91.7 | -4.4 |
| 2016 | C+ | 4.26 | 3.55 | 70.0 | 31.1 | 115.1 | -8.0 |
| 2015 | C+ | 4.10 | 3.41 | 56.6 | 21.0 | 80.1 | 1.3 |
| 2014 | C | 8.15 | 6.80 | 69.4 | 31.0 | 50.5 | -4.3 |
| 2013 | C | 3.49 | 2.91 | 5.6 | 5.2 | 1.8 | 0.2 |
| 2012 | N/A | N/A | N/A | 5.0 | 5.0 | N/A | N/A |

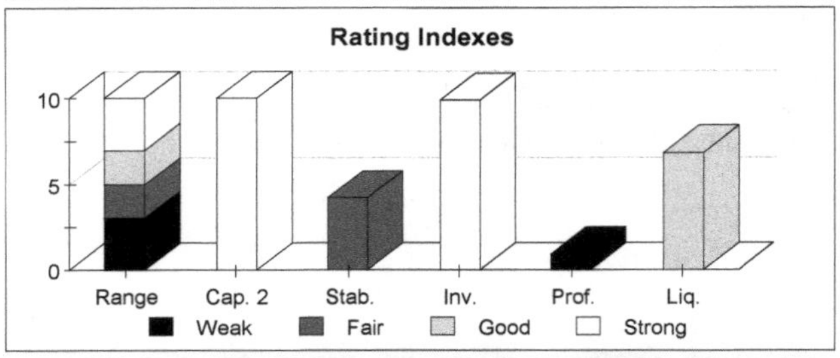


## HUMANA MEDICAL PLAN OF PENNSYLVANIA — B — Good

**Major Rating Factors:** Fair profitability index (4.1 on a scale of 0 to 10). Strong capitalization (10.0) based on excellent current risk-adjusted capital (severe loss scenario). High quality investment portfolio (9.9).
**Other Rating Factors:** Excellent liquidity (7.4) with ample operational cash flow and liquid investments.
**Principal Business:** Medicare (100%)
**Mem Phys: 16:** 25,143 **15:** 23,271 **16 MLR** 86.5% **/ 16 Admin Exp** N/A
**Enroll(000): Q3 17:** 10 **16:** 7 **15:** 4 **Med Exp PMPM:** $678
**Principal Investments:** Cash and equiv (100%)
**Provider Compensation ($000):** Contr fee ($37,439), capitation ($7,889), FFS ($78)
**Total Member Encounters:** Phys (94,978), non-phys (51,487)
**Group Affiliation:** Humana Inc
**Licensed in:** PA
**Address:** 5000 RITTER Rd Ste 101, MECHANICSBURG, PA 17055
**Phone:** (502) 580-1000 **Dom State:** PA **Commenced Bus:** October 2013

| Data Date | Rating | RACR #1 | RACR #2 | Total Assets ($mil) | Capital ($mil) | Net Premium ($mil) | Net Income ($mil) |
|---|---|---|---|---|---|---|---|
| 9-17 | B | 5.65 | 4.71 | 46.0 | 21.7 | 71.1 | 0.6 |
| 9-16 | B | 8.71 | 7.26 | 33.4 | 22.7 | 41.5 | 0.3 |
| 2016 | B | 5.59 | 4.66 | 28.6 | 21.5 | 56.1 | -1.1 |
| 2015 | B | 8.66 | 7.22 | 26.2 | 22.6 | 35.2 | 0.1 |
| 2014 | C- | 4.92 | 4.10 | 8.2 | 7.4 | 8.3 | 0.5 |
| 2013 | N/A | N/A | N/A | 4.0 | 3.9 | N/A | N/A |
| 2012 | N/A | N/A | N/A | N/A | N/A | N/A | N/A |

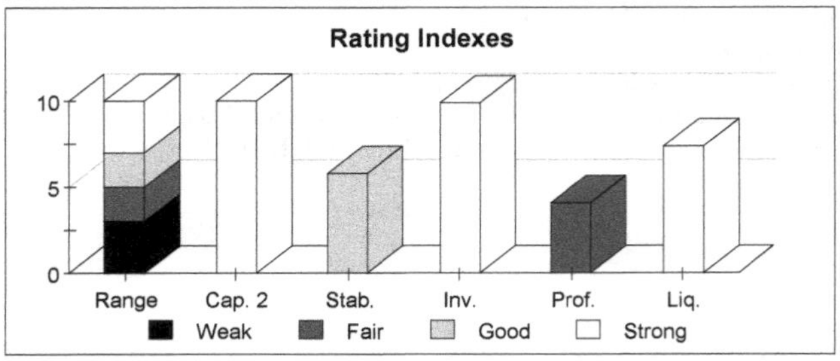

## HUMANA MEDICAL PLAN OF UTAH INC C+ Fair

**Major Rating Factors:** Good liquidity (5.5 on a scale of 0 to 10) with sufficient resources (cash flows and marketable investments) to handle a spike in claims. Weak profitability index (0.6). Strong capitalization (10.0) based on excellent current risk-adjusted capital (severe loss scenario).
**Other Rating Factors:** High quality investment portfolio (9.9).
**Principal Business:** Medicare (99%)
**Mem Phys: 16:** 13,002 **15:** 7,788 **16 MLR** 115.5% **/ 16 Admin Exp** N/A
**Enroll(000): Q3 17:** 6 **16:** 12 **15:** 19 **Med Exp PMPM:** $339
**Principal Investments:** Long-term bonds (90%), cash and equiv (10%)
**Provider Compensation ($000):** Contr fee ($27,777), capitation ($20,578), FFS ($6,497)
**Total Member Encounters:** Phys (116,535), non-phys (64,632)
**Group Affiliation:** Humana Inc
**Licensed in:** UT
**Address:** 9815 S MONROE St Ste 300, SANDY, UT 84070
**Phone:** (801) 256-6200 **Dom State:** UT **Commenced Bus:** March 2007

| Data Date | Rating | RACR #1 | RACR #2 | Total Assets ($mil) | Capital ($mil) | Net Premium ($mil) | Net Income ($mil) |
|---|---|---|---|---|---|---|---|
| 9-17 | C+ | 4.53 | 3.77 | 30.9 | 17.6 | 30.4 | 0.2 |
| 9-16 | C | 3.98 | 3.32 | 37.7 | 17.0 | 41.8 | -6.0 |
| 2016 | C+ | 4.44 | 3.70 | 31.8 | 17.2 | 46.0 | -10.9 |
| 2015 | C- | 4.47 | 3.73 | 43.4 | 19.2 | 68.6 | -8.3 |
| 2014 | D | 7.59 | 6.32 | 40.2 | 27.5 | 75.5 | 0.5 |
| 2013 | D | 9.42 | 7.85 | 32.0 | 25.9 | 37.3 | 4.4 |
| 2012 | D | 3.08 | 2.57 | 39.3 | 21.7 | 93.1 | -13.5 |

**Rating Indexes**

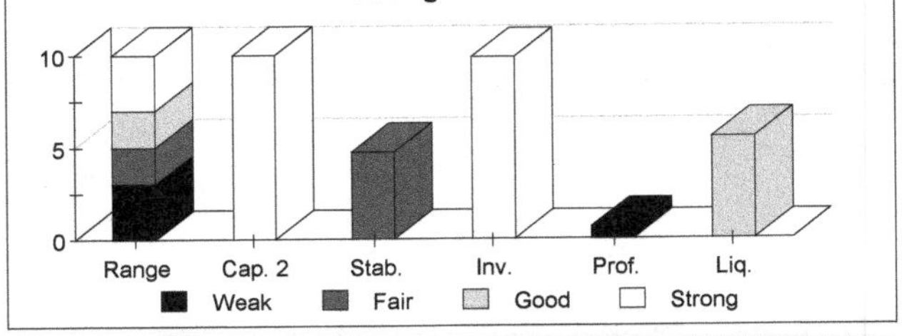


## HUMANA REGIONAL HEALTH PLAN INC B- Good

**Major Rating Factors:** Strong capitalization (10.0 on a scale of 0 to 10) based on excellent current risk-adjusted capital (severe loss scenario). High quality investment portfolio (9.9). Excellent liquidity (7.1) with ample operational cash flow and liquid investments.
**Other Rating Factors:** Weak profitability index (1.9).
**Principal Business:** Medicare (100%)
**Mem Phys: 16:** 72,284 **15:** 62,376 **16 MLR** 86.5% **/ 16 Admin Exp** N/A
**Enroll(000): Q3 17:** 3 **16:** 3 **15:** 2 **Med Exp PMPM:** $777
**Principal Investments:** Cash and equiv (54%), long-term bonds (46%)
**Provider Compensation ($000):** Contr fee ($18,686), capitation ($6,626), FFS ($104)
**Total Member Encounters:** Phys (54,338), non-phys (32,546)
**Group Affiliation:** Humana Inc
**Licensed in:** AR, OK, TX
**Address:** 300 ST STE 900, LITTLE ROCK, AR 72201
**Phone:** (502) 580-1000 **Dom State:** AR **Commenced Bus:** March 2005

| Data Date | Rating | RACR #1 | RACR #2 | Total Assets ($mil) | Capital ($mil) | Net Premium ($mil) | Net Income ($mil) |
|---|---|---|---|---|---|---|---|
| 9-17 | B- | 6.21 | 5.18 | 22.1 | 14.1 | 25.9 | 1.3 |
| 9-16 | B- | 6.92 | 5.77 | 19.5 | 13.5 | 22.7 | 0.9 |
| 2016 | B- | 5.69 | 4.74 | 16.4 | 12.8 | 30.6 | 0.3 |
| 2015 | C+ | 6.48 | 5.40 | 14.9 | 12.6 | 22.0 | -1.1 |
| 2014 | C+ | 10.51 | 8.76 | 16.0 | 15.1 | 5.7 | 1.4 |
| 2013 | N/A | N/A | N/A | 16.1 | 15.2 | -0.1 | 1.6 |
| 2012 | C+ | 2.35 | 1.96 | 26.6 | 14.0 | 90.8 | -2.0 |

**Rating Indexes**

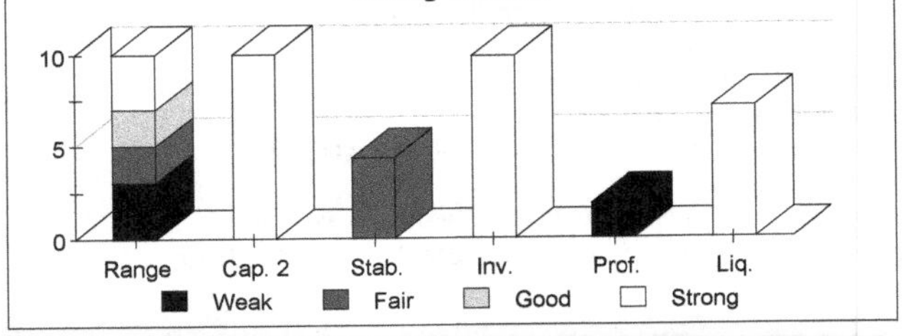


## HUMANA WISCONSIN HEALTH ORGANIZATION B- Good

**Major Rating Factors:** Fair profitability index (3.4 on a scale of 0 to 10). Good overall results on stability tests (6.3) despite a decline in enrollment during 2016. Rating is significantly influenced by the good financial results of Humana Inc. Good liquidity (6.5) with sufficient resources (cash flows and marketable investments) to handle a spike in claims.
**Other Rating Factors:** Strong capitalization index (10.0) based on excellent current risk-adjusted capital (severe loss scenario). High quality investment portfolio (9.9).
**Principal Business:** Medicare (79%), comp med (21%)
**Mem Phys: 16:** 72,284 **15:** 45,900 **16 MLR** 85.8% **/ 16 Admin Exp** N/A
**Enroll(000): Q3 17:** 134 **16:** 76 **15:** 84 **Med Exp PMPM:** $580
**Principal Investments:** Long-term bonds (79%), cash and equiv (21%)
**Provider Compensation ($000):** Contr fee ($434,680), FFS ($34,247), salary ($29,045), capitation ($16,774)
**Total Member Encounters:** Phys (1,084,548), non-phys (569,414)
**Group Affiliation:** Humana Inc
**Licensed in:** DE, KY, MT, NJ, OH, RI, VA, WI
**Address:** N19W24133 RIVERWOOD DR SUITE 3, WAUKESHA, WI 53188-1145
**Phone:** (262) 408-4300 **Dom State:** WI **Commenced Bus:** September 1985

| Data Date | Rating | RACR #1 | RACR #2 | Total Assets ($mil) | Capital ($mil) | Net Premium ($mil) | Net Income ($mil) |
|---|---|---|---|---|---|---|---|
| 9-17 | B- | 4.18 | 3.48 | 440.4 | 144.6 | 980.9 | 31.6 |
| 9-16 | B- | 2.39 | 1.99 | 227.4 | 86.0 | 460.2 | -1.1 |
| 2016 | B- | 3.27 | 2.73 | 200.3 | 113.2 | 614.4 | 2.7 |
| 2015 | C+ | 2.43 | 2.02 | 179.4 | 87.4 | 592.9 | -17.6 |
| 2014 | B- | 2.14 | 1.78 | 69.9 | 35.7 | 287.6 | -0.9 |
| 2013 | B | 2.63 | 2.19 | 76.2 | 39.2 | 241.8 | 2.3 |
| 2012 | B | 2.38 | 1.98 | 73.3 | 37.4 | 286.3 | 0.6 |

**Rating Indexes**

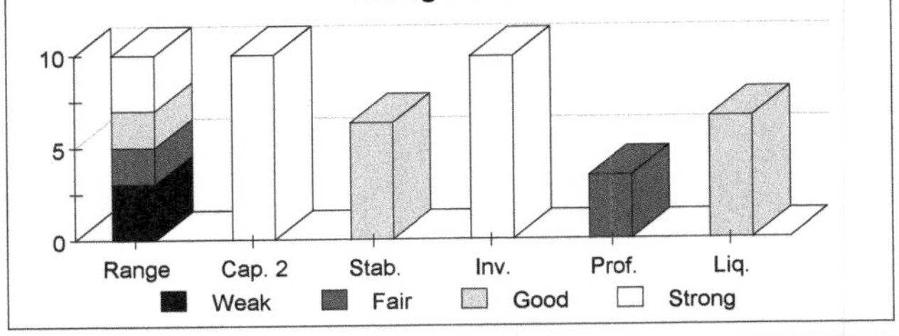

## ILLINICARE HEALTH PLAN INC C- Fair

**Major Rating Factors:** Weak profitability index (0.9 on a scale of 0 to 10). Good liquidity (6.8) with sufficient resources (cash flows and marketable investments) to handle a spike in claims. Strong capitalization (7.6) based on excellent current risk-adjusted capital (severe loss scenario).
**Other Rating Factors:** High quality investment portfolio (9.9).
**Principal Business:** Medicaid (94%), Medicare (6%)
**Mem Phys: 16:** 15,088 **15:** 15,884 **16 MLR** 99.7% **/ 16 Admin Exp** N/A
**Enroll(000): Q3 17:** 223 **16:** 217 **15:** 209 **Med Exp PMPM:** $476
**Principal Investments:** Cash and equiv (296%)
**Provider Compensation ($000):** Contr fee ($1,078,801), salary ($46,835), capitation ($24,291), other ($19,707)
**Total Member Encounters:** Phys (1,300,331), non-phys (1,273,876)
**Group Affiliation:** Centene Corporation
**Licensed in:** IL
**Address:** 999 Oakmont Plaza Dr, Westmont, IL 60559
**Phone:** (314) 725-4477 **Dom State:** IL **Commenced Bus:** May 2011

| Data Date | Rating | RACR #1 | RACR #2 | Total Assets ($mil) | Capital ($mil) | Net Premium ($mil) | Net Income ($mil) |
|---|---|---|---|---|---|---|---|
| 9-17 | C- | 1.86 | 1.55 | 697.8 | 124.9 | 1,027.1 | 3.7 |
| 9-16 | C- | 1.44 | 1.20 | 272.3 | 79.4 | 879.9 | -65.8 |
| 2016 | C- | 1.85 | 1.54 | 360.9 | 123.9 | 1,201.2 | -73.7 |
| 2015 | C- | 1.69 | 1.41 | 295.8 | 95.0 | 1,078.8 | -33.4 |
| 2014 | C+ | 2.83 | 2.36 | 199.9 | 67.8 | 528.0 | 10.9 |
| 2013 | C+ | 1.93 | 1.61 | 114.7 | 28.6 | 309.4 | 1.8 |
| 2012 | B- | 1.22 | 1.01 | 46.8 | 19.0 | 227.1 | 5.9 |

Rating Indexes

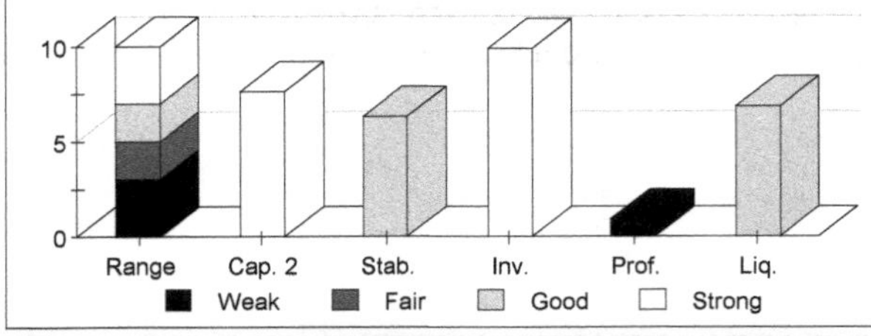


## ILLINOIS MUTUAL LIFE INSURANCE COMPANY B Good

**Major Rating Factors:** Good quality investment portfolio (6.6 on a scale of 0 to 10) despite mixed results such as: minimal exposure to mortgages and large holdings of BBB rated bonds but small junk bond holdings. Good liquidity (6.5) with sufficient resources to handle a spike in claims as well as a significant increase in policy surrenders. Good overall results on stability tests (6.2) excellent operational trends and excellent risk diversification.
**Other Rating Factors:** Fair profitability (4.3) with investment income below regulatory standards in relation to interest assumptions of reserves. Strong capitalization (8.7) based on excellent risk adjusted capital (severe loss scenario).
**Principal Business:** Individual health insurance (49%), individual life insurance (48%), group health insurance (2%), and individual annuities (1%).
**Principal Investments:** NonCMO investment grade bonds (64%), CMOs and structured securities (24%), noninv. grade bonds (4%), common & preferred stock (4%), and misc. investments (4%).
**Investments in Affiliates:** None
**Group Affiliation:** None
**Licensed in:** All states except AK, DC, HI, NY, PR
**Commenced Business:** July 1912
**Address:** 300 SW Adams Street, Peoria, IL 61634
**Phone:** (309) 674-8255 **Domicile State:** IL **NAIC Code:** 64580

| Data Date | Rating | RACR #1 | RACR #2 | Total Assets ($mil) | Capital ($mil) | Net Premium ($mil) | Net Income ($mil) |
|---|---|---|---|---|---|---|---|
| 9-17 | B | 3.77 | 2.13 | 1,444.5 | 232.7 | 80.2 | 9.3 |
| 9-16 | A- | 3.57 | 2.00 | 1,435.2 | 220.7 | 77.6 | 8.4 |
| 2016 | B | 3.70 | 2.08 | 1,434.3 | 226.0 | 102.8 | 9.4 |
| 2015 | A- | 3.53 | 1.99 | 1,388.9 | 211.7 | 100.3 | 14.8 |
| 2014 | A- | 3.27 | 1.84 | 1,367.7 | 196.3 | 100.5 | 28.2 |
| 2013 | A- | 3.57 | 2.05 | 1,329.4 | 173.7 | 104.2 | 26.7 |
| 2012 | B | 3.07 | 1.76 | 1,289.1 | 144.2 | 102.0 | 27.0 |

**Adverse Trends in Operations**

Decrease in premium volume from 2013 to 2014 (4%)

## IMPERIAL HEALTH PLAN OF CALIFORNIA C- Fair

**Major Rating Factors:** Fair overall results on stability tests (3.5 on a scale of 0 to 10). Excellent profitability (8.5). Strong capitalization index (8.0) based on excellent current risk-adjusted capital (severe loss scenario).
**Other Rating Factors:** Excellent liquidity (7.2) with ample operational cash flow and liquid investments.
**Principal Business:** Managed care (100%)
**Mem Phys: 16:** N/A **15:** N/A **16 MLR** 74.8% **/ 16 Admin Exp** N/A
**Enroll(000): Q3 17:** 3 **16:** 14 **15:** N/A **Med Exp PMPM:** $274
**Principal Investments ($000):** Cash and equiv ($2,661)
**Provider Compensation ($000):** None
**Total Member Encounters:** N/A
**Group Affiliation:** None
**Licensed in:** CA
**Address:** 10801 6th Street Suite 120, Rancho Cucamonga, CA 91730
**Phone:** (951) 335-3987 **Dom State:** CA **Commenced Bus:** N/A

| Data Date | Rating | RACR #1 | RACR #2 | Total Assets ($mil) | Capital ($mil) | Net Premium ($mil) | Net Income ($mil) |
|---|---|---|---|---|---|---|---|
| 9-17 | C- | 2.71 | 1.79 | 2.7 | 1.5 | 12.0 | 0.2 |
| 9-16 | N/A | N/A | N/A | N/A | N/A | N/A | N/A |
| 2016 | C- | 2.38 | 1.57 | 3.0 | 1.3 | 5.1 | 0.1 |
| 2015 | N/A | N/A | N/A | N/A | N/A | N/A | N/A |
| 2014 | N/A | N/A | N/A | N/A | N/A | N/A | N/A |
| 2013 | N/A | N/A | N/A | N/A | N/A | N/A | N/A |
| 2012 | N/A | N/A | N/A | N/A | N/A | N/A | N/A |

Rating Indexes

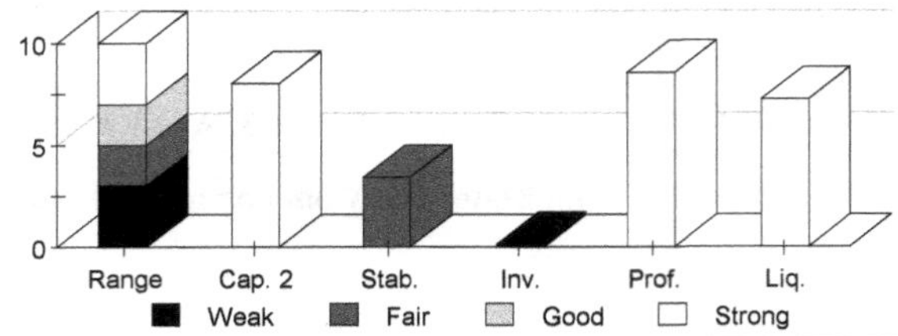

## INDEPENDENCE AMERICAN INS CO B- Good

**Major Rating Factors:** Fair overall results on stability tests (3.9 on a scale of 0 to 10) including potential drain of affiliation with Geneve Holdings Inc, weak results on operational trends, negative cash flow from operations for 2016 and excessive premium growth. The largest net exposure for one risk is acceptable at 2.1% of capital. History of adequate reserve strength (5.8) as reserves have been consistently at an acceptable level.

**Other Rating Factors:** Strong long-term capitalization index (8.4) based on excellent current risk adjusted capital (severe and moderate loss scenarios). Moreover, capital levels have been consistent in recent years. Excellent profitability (8.8) with operating gains in each of the last five years. Vulnerable liquidity (2.8) as a spike in claims may stretch capacity.

**Principal Business:** Group accident & health (40%), aggregate write-ins for other lines of business (28%), inland marine (26%), other liability (3%), and other accident & health (3%).

**Principal Investments:** Investment grade bonds (84%), misc. investments (13%), and cash (3%).

**Investments in Affiliates:** None

**Group Affiliation:** Geneve Holdings Inc

**Licensed in:** All states except PR

**Commenced Business:** March 1973

**Address:** 1209 Orange Street, Wilmington, DE 19801

**Phone:** (212) 355-4141 **Domicile State:** DE **NAIC Code:** 26581

| Data Date | Rating | RACR #1 | RACR #2 | Loss Ratio % | Total Assets ($mil) | Capital ($mil) | Net Premium ($mil) | Net Income ($mil) |
|---|---|---|---|---|---|---|---|---|
| 9-17 | B- | 4.42 | 2.56 | N/A | 112.7 | 70.8 | 83.5 | 5.7 |
| 9-16 | C+ | 3.13 | 1.86 | N/A | 120.0 | 66.0 | 65.9 | 2.3 |
| 2016 | B- | 4.41 | 2.55 | 62.5 | 114.4 | 66.8 | 91.2 | 4.0 |
| 2015 | C+ | 2.35 | 1.39 | 66.8 | 115.9 | 63.4 | 149.8 | 3.0 |
| 2014 | C | 2.34 | 1.39 | 66.7 | 102.9 | 60.2 | 133.6 | 3.1 |
| 2013 | C | 2.39 | 1.41 | 68.7 | 102.1 | 57.9 | 128.8 | 3.2 |
| 2012 | C | 3.72 | 2.14 | 67.9 | 84.7 | 54.4 | 85.8 | 3.3 |

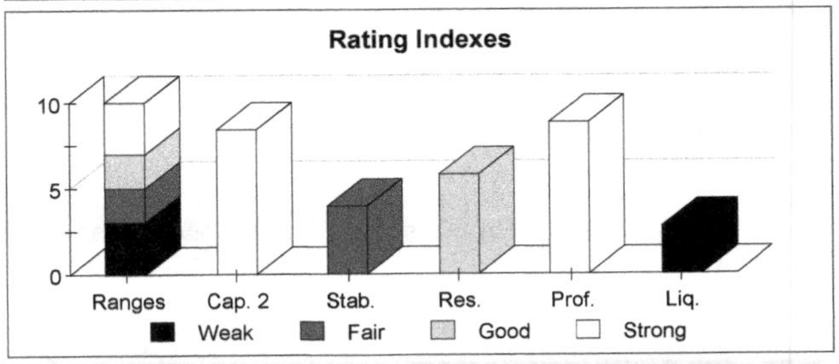


## INDEPENDENCE BLUE CROSS C- Fair

**Major Rating Factors:** Weak profitability index (1.0 on a scale of 0 to 10). Strong capitalization (10.0) based on excellent current risk-adjusted capital (severe loss scenario). High quality investment portfolio (8.3).

**Other Rating Factors:** Excellent liquidity (7.3) with ample operational cash flow and liquid investments.

**Principal Business:** FEHB (78%), med supp (14%), comp med (6%)

**Mem Phys: 16:** 794 **15:** 794 **16 MLR** 90.3% **/ 16 Admin Exp** N/A

**Enroll(000): Q3 17:** 121 **16:** 124 **15:** 127 **Med Exp PMPM:** $236

**Principal Investments:** Long-term bonds (57%), cash and equiv (18%), nonaffiliate common stock (11%), other (14%)

**Provider Compensation ($000):** Contr fee ($321,839), FFS ($33,363), bonus arrang ($3,471), other ($5,335)

**Total Member Encounters:** Non-phys (767,789)

**Group Affiliation:** Independence Health Group Inc

**Licensed in:** PA

**Address:** 1901 Market St, Philadelphia, PA 19103-1480

**Phone:** (215) 241-2400 **Dom State:** PA **Commenced Bus:** November 1938

| Data Date | Rating | RACR #1 | RACR #2 | Total Assets ($mil) | Capital ($mil) | Net Premium ($mil) | Net Income ($mil) |
|---|---|---|---|---|---|---|---|
| 9-17 | C- | 6.96 | 5.80 | 259.0 | 71.5 | 273.3 | -1.0 |
| 9-16 | C- | 5.55 | 4.63 | 267.8 | 57.6 | 295.7 | -2.7 |
| 2016 | C- | 6.74 | 5.62 | 285.0 | 68.7 | 391.8 | 7.0 |
| 2015 | C- | 5.44 | 4.53 | 303.9 | 56.0 | 358.8 | -24.4 |
| 2014 | C | 6.57 | 5.48 | 423.1 | 81.4 | 373.2 | 18.8 |
| 2013 | C | 4.02 | 3.35 | 2,866.2 | 2,250.1 | 363.5 | -74.4 |
| 2012 | C | 3.86 | 3.21 | 2,693.0 | 2,014.9 | 402.7 | 126.2 |

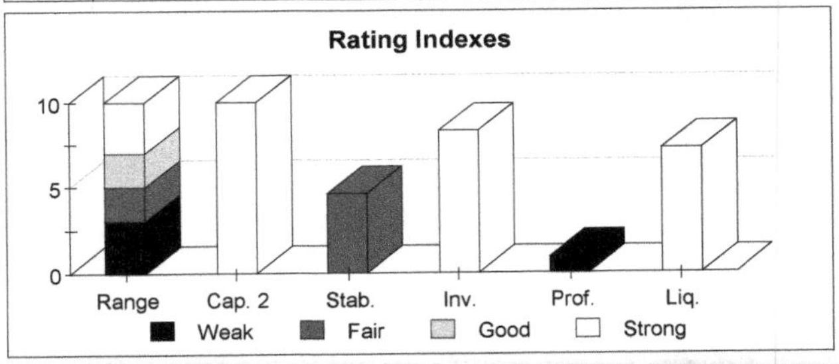


## INDEPENDENT CARE HEALTH PLAN * A- Excellent

**Major Rating Factors:** Excellent profitability (7.7 on a scale of 0 to 10). Strong capitalization (8.9) based on excellent current risk-adjusted capital (severe loss scenario). High quality investment portfolio (9.9).

**Other Rating Factors:** Good liquidity (6.0) with sufficient resources (cash flows and marketable investments) to handle a spike in claims.

**Principal Business:** Medicaid (51%), Medicare (49%)

**Mem Phys: 16:** 4,955 **15:** 4,616 **16 MLR** 84.1% **/ 16 Admin Exp** N/A

**Enroll(000): Q3 17:** 29 **16:** 27 **15:** 26 **Med Exp PMPM:** $565

**Principal Investments:** Long-term bonds (63%), cash and equiv (37%)

**Provider Compensation ($000):** Contr fee ($174,305), capitation ($2,130)

**Total Member Encounters:** Phys (308,600), non-phys (228,731)

**Group Affiliation:** Independent Care Health Plan

**Licensed in:** IL, WI

**Address:** 1555 N RiverCenter Dr Ste 206, Milwaukee, WI 53212

**Phone:** (414) 223-4847 **Dom State:** WI **Commenced Bus:** June 2003

| Data Date | Rating | RACR #1 | RACR #2 | Total Assets ($mil) | Capital ($mil) | Net Premium ($mil) | Net Income ($mil) |
|---|---|---|---|---|---|---|---|
| 9-17 | A- | 2.90 | 2.42 | 89.0 | 30.2 | 168.9 | 3.0 |
| 9-16 | B+ | 2.89 | 2.40 | 78.9 | 27.1 | 161.0 | -0.5 |
| 2016 | A- | 2.68 | 2.23 | 71.2 | 27.4 | 215.1 | -0.5 |
| 2015 | B+ | 2.92 | 2.43 | 68.2 | 27.5 | 210.9 | 5.3 |
| 2014 | B | 2.87 | 2.39 | 55.4 | 22.2 | 175.5 | 1.8 |
| 2013 | B | 2.66 | 2.22 | 56.1 | 20.8 | 174.3 | 0.6 |
| 2012 | B | 2.87 | 2.39 | 54.5 | 20.3 | 162.8 | 1.6 |

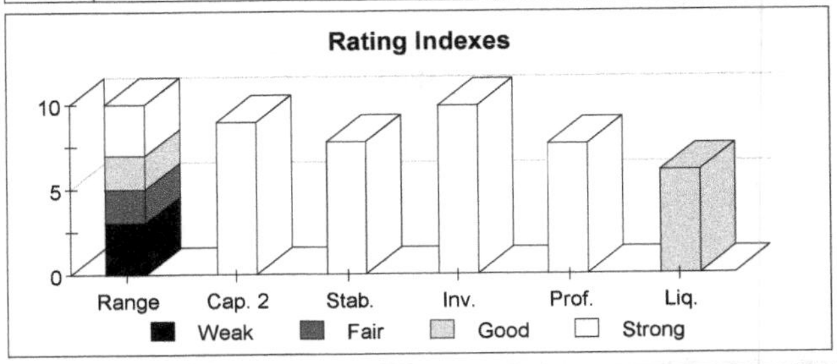

## INDEPENDENT HEALTH ASSOC INC — B- — Good

**Major Rating Factors:** Good overall results on stability tests (5.3 on a scale of 0 to 10). Strong capitalization index (9.6) based on excellent current risk-adjusted capital (severe loss scenario). High quality investment portfolio (8.5).
**Other Rating Factors:** Excellent liquidity (6.9) with sufficient resources (cash flows and marketable investments) to handle a spike in claims. Weak profitability index (1.6).
**Principal Business:** Medicare (63%), Medicaid (24%), comp med (13%)
**Mem Phys: 16:** 4,071 **15:** 3,969 **16 MLR** 90.6% **/ 16 Admin Exp** N/A
**Enroll(000): Q3 17:** 171 **16:** 194 **15:** 204 **Med Exp PMPM:** $592
**Principal Investments:** Long-term bonds (59%), nonaffiliate common stock (8%), cash and equiv (6%), real estate (5%), affiliate common stock (2%), other (19%)
**Provider Compensation ($000):** Capitation ($1,046,694), FFS ($326,006), other ($15,505)
**Total Member Encounters:** Phys (396,163), non-phys (450,126)
**Group Affiliation:** Independent Health Association Inc
**Licensed in:** NY
**Address:** 511 Farber Lakes Drive, Buffalo, NY 14221
**Phone:** (716) 631-3001 **Dom State:** NY **Commenced Bus:** January 1980

| Data Date | Rating | RACR #1 | RACR #2 | Total Assets ($mil) | Capital ($mil) | Net Premium ($mil) | Net Income ($mil) |
|---|---|---|---|---|---|---|---|
| 9-17 | B- | 3.44 | 2.86 | 689.3 | 376.9 | 1,018.3 | -12.2 |
| 9-16 | B- | 3.11 | 2.59 | 650.2 | 351.8 | 1,125.6 | 7.7 |
| 2016 | B- | 3.23 | 2.69 | 710.1 | 367.1 | 1,511.3 | 26.1 |
| 2015 | B- | 2.99 | 2.49 | 764.7 | 337.3 | 1,507.7 | -43.9 |
| 2014 | B- | 4.05 | 3.38 | 668.6 | 384.2 | 1,339.4 | -72.8 |
| 2013 | B+ | 5.03 | 4.19 | 658.7 | 461.6 | 1,356.1 | 26.7 |
| 2012 | B+ | 4.63 | 3.86 | 606.3 | 411.8 | 1,354.9 | -49.4 |

**Rating Indexes**

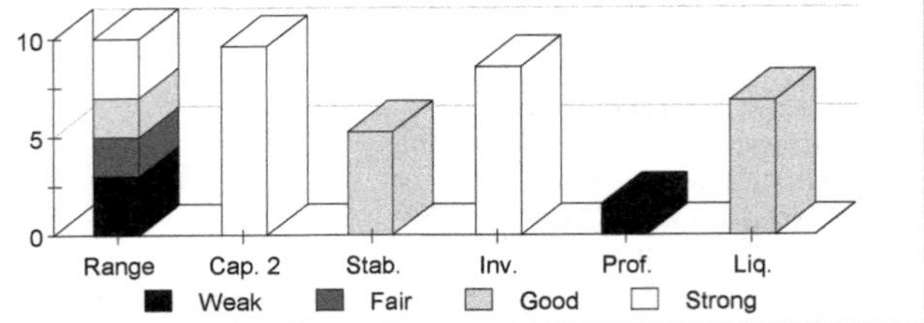


## INDEPENDENT HEALTH BENEFITS CORP — C — Fair

**Major Rating Factors:** Weak profitability index (1.7 on a scale of 0 to 10). Strong capitalization (7.7) based on excellent current risk-adjusted capital (severe loss scenario). High quality investment portfolio (9.2).
**Other Rating Factors:** Excellent liquidity (7.1) with ample operational cash flow and liquid investments.
**Principal Business:** Comp med (77%), FEHB (14%), Medicare (9%)
**Mem Phys: 16:** 4,051 **15:** 3,954 **16 MLR** 88.5% **/ 16 Admin Exp** N/A
**Enroll(000): Q3 17:** 114 **16:** 115 **15:** 108 **Med Exp PMPM:** $392
**Principal Investments:** Long-term bonds (90%), cash and equiv (10%)
**Provider Compensation ($000):** FFS ($502,531), capitation ($2,032), other ($19,369)
**Total Member Encounters:** Phys (1,851,525), non-phys (4,227,225)
**Group Affiliation:** Independent Health Association Inc
**Licensed in:** NY
**Address:** 511 Farber Lakes Dr, Buffalo, NY 14221
**Phone:** (716) 631-3001 **Dom State:** NY **Commenced Bus:** December 1995

| Data Date | Rating | RACR #1 | RACR #2 | Total Assets ($mil) | Capital ($mil) | Net Premium ($mil) | Net Income ($mil) |
|---|---|---|---|---|---|---|---|
| 9-17 | C | 1.91 | 1.59 | 227.8 | 90.3 | 463.1 | -4.1 |
| 9-16 | C | 2.10 | 1.75 | 216.1 | 90.0 | 441.3 | -20.6 |
| 2016 | C | 1.75 | 1.46 | 238.3 | 96.0 | 606.8 | -13.1 |
| 2015 | B- | 2.48 | 2.07 | 270.2 | 107.0 | 584.3 | -0.1 |
| 2014 | B- | 2.63 | 2.19 | 167.8 | 107.1 | 504.8 | 12.6 |
| 2013 | C+ | 2.60 | 2.16 | 174.5 | 98.9 | 485.9 | -7.0 |
| 2012 | B | 2.39 | 1.99 | 164.4 | 100.2 | 508.2 | -0.7 |

**Rating Indexes**

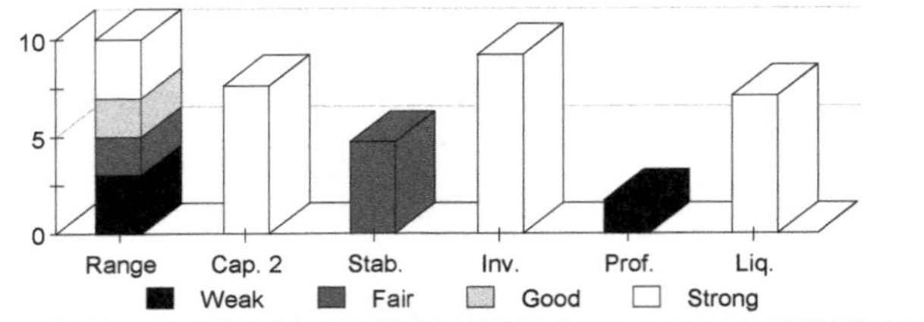


## INDIANA UNIVERSITY HEALTH PLANS INC — E- — Very Weak

**Major Rating Factors:** Weak profitability index (0.9 on a scale of 0 to 10). Strong capitalization (7.8) based on excellent current risk-adjusted capital (severe loss scenario). High quality investment portfolio (9.9).
**Other Rating Factors:** Excellent liquidity (7.3) with ample operational cash flow and liquid investments.
**Principal Business:** Comp med (100%)
**Mem Phys: 16:** 12,210 **15:** 5,601 **16 MLR** 83.5% **/ 16 Admin Exp** N/A
**Enroll(000): Q3 17:** 14 **16:** 28 **15:** 13 **Med Exp PMPM:** $184
**Principal Investments:** Cash and equiv (100%)
**Provider Compensation ($000):** Capitation ($62,758)
**Total Member Encounters:** N/A
**Group Affiliation:** Indiana University Health Inc
**Licensed in:** IN
**Address:** 950 N Meridian St Ste 200, Indianapolis, IN 46204
**Phone:** (317) 963-9780 **Dom State:** IN **Commenced Bus:** May 2008

| Data Date | Rating | RACR #1 | RACR #2 | Total Assets ($mil) | Capital ($mil) | Net Premium ($mil) | Net Income ($mil) |
|---|---|---|---|---|---|---|---|
| 9-17 | E- | 1.99 | 1.66 | 21.6 | 8.5 | 46.4 | -6.4 |
| 9-16 | E- | 0.60 | 0.50 | 57.8 | 4.3 | 59.2 | -13.1 |
| 2016 | E- | 1.88 | 1.57 | 42.8 | 8.0 | 75.1 | -19.7 |
| 2015 | D | 1.92 | 1.60 | 22.2 | 14.2 | 141.9 | -3.7 |
| 2014 | D- | 1.22 | 1.02 | 13.2 | 10.0 | 134.8 | -2.0 |
| 2013 | D- | 1.21 | 1.01 | 9.0 | 7.3 | 98.3 | 0.6 |
| 2012 | D- | 1.04 | 0.86 | 10.1 | 7.4 | 118.3 | -1.1 |

**Rating Indexes**

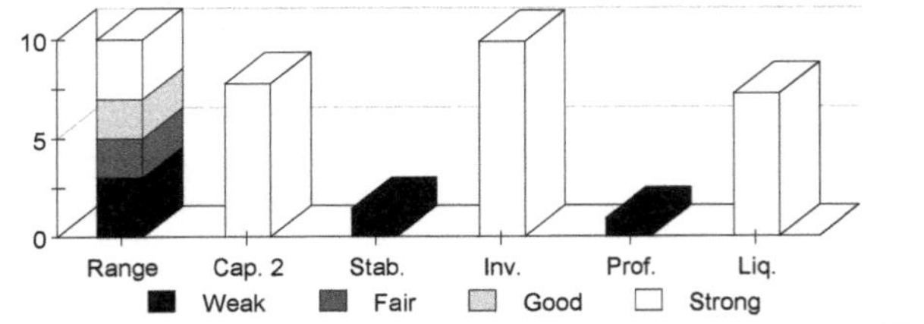

## INDIANA UNIVERSITY HEALTH PLANS NFP C+ Fair

**Major Rating Factors:** Weak profitability index (2.5 on a scale of 0 to 10). Strong capitalization (7.2) based on excellent current risk-adjusted capital (severe loss scenario). High quality investment portfolio (9.9).
**Other Rating Factors:** Excellent liquidity (7.0) with ample operational cash flow and liquid investments.
**Principal Business:** Medicare (100%)
**Mem Phys: 16:** 12,733 **15:** N/A **16 MLR** 89.1% **/ 16 Admin Exp** N/A
**Enroll(000): Q3 17:** 15 **16:** 16 **15:** N/A **Med Exp PMPM:** $816
**Principal Investments:** Cash and equiv (100%)
**Provider Compensation ($000):** Capitation ($160,503)
**Total Member Encounters:** N/A
**Group Affiliation:** Indiana University Health Inc
**Licensed in:** IN
**Address:** 950 N Meridian St Ste 200, Indianapolis, IN 46204
**Phone:** (317) 963-9780 **Dom State:** IN **Commenced Bus:** September 2013

| Data Date | Rating | RACR #1 | RACR #2 | Total Assets ($mil) | Capital ($mil) | Net Premium ($mil) | Net Income ($mil) |
|---|---|---|---|---|---|---|---|
| 9-17 | C+ | 1.54 | 1.28 | 46.6 | 15.6 | 120.8 | -1.3 |
| 9-16 | N/A | N/A | N/A | 26.9 | 11.3 | 142.7 | 2.0 |
| 2016 | C | 1.46 | 1.21 | 19.3 | 14.8 | 180.0 | 0.6 |
| 2015 | N/A | N/A | N/A | 1.5 | 1.5 | N/A | N/A |
| 2014 | N/A | N/A | N/A | 1.5 | 1.5 | N/A | N/A |
| 2013 | N/A | N/A | N/A | N/A | N/A | N/A | N/A |
| 2012 | N/A | N/A | N/A | N/A | N/A | N/A | N/A |

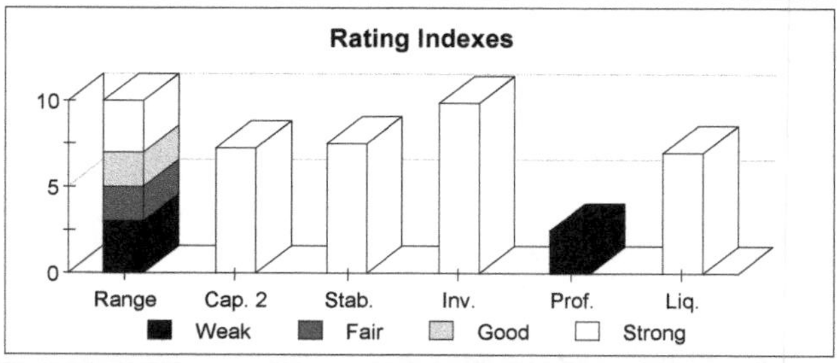


## INLAND EMPIRE HEALTH PLAN * A Excellent

**Major Rating Factors:** Excellent profitability (9.5 on a scale of 0 to 10). Strong capitalization index (9.0) based on excellent current risk-adjusted capital (severe loss scenario). Excellent overall results on stability tests (7.7).
**Other Rating Factors:** Excellent liquidity (7.1) with ample operational cash flow and liquid investments.
**Principal Business:** Medicaid (92%), Medicare (8%)
**Mem Phys: 16:** N/A **15:** N/A **16 MLR** 87.5% **/ 16 Admin Exp** N/A
**Enroll(000): Q3 17:** 1,429 **16:** 1,168 **15:** 1,090 **Med Exp PMPM:** $276
**Principal Investments ($000):** Cash and equiv ($871,209)
**Provider Compensation ($000):** None
**Total Member Encounters:** N/A
**Group Affiliation:** None
**Licensed in:** CA
**Address:** 300 S Park Avenue, Pomona, CA 91769
**Phone:** (909) 623-6333 **Dom State:** CA **Commenced Bus:** September 1996

| Data Date | Rating | RACR #1 | RACR #2 | Total Assets ($mil) | Capital ($mil) | Net Premium ($mil) | Net Income ($mil) |
|---|---|---|---|---|---|---|---|
| 9-17 | A | 3.77 | 2.43 | 1,779.5 | 831.9 | 3,828.4 | 52.6 |
| 9-16 | A | N/A | N/A | 1,505.2 | 660.6 | 3,194.3 | 188.6 |
| 2016 | A | 3.02 | 1.95 | 1,782.2 | 688.7 | 4,298.5 | 216.7 |
| 2015 | B+ | 2.31 | 1.46 | 1,402.3 | 472.0 | 3,887.3 | 317.3 |
| 2014 | B | 1.31 | 0.83 | 476.0 | 160.3 | 1,847.9 | 41.9 |
| 2013 | B | 1.39 | 0.87 | 280.5 | 118.5 | 1,240.9 | 10.8 |
| 2012 | B | 1.78 | 1.09 | 237.7 | 107.7 | 990.3 | 37.1 |

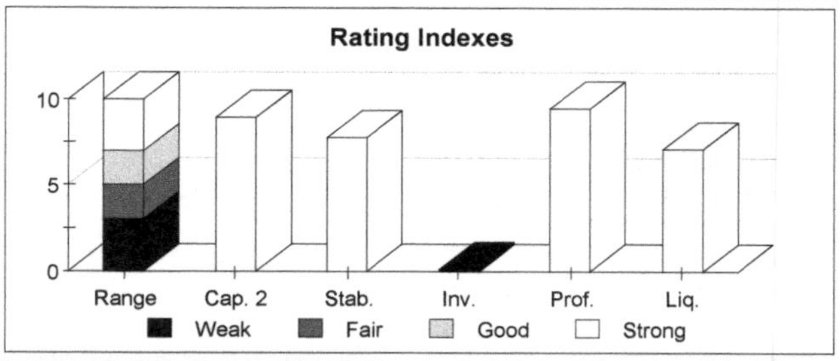


## INNOVATION HEALTH INS CO C- Fair

**Major Rating Factors:** Weak profitability index (0.7 on a scale of 0 to 10). Good liquidity (5.8) with sufficient resources (cash flows and marketable investments) to handle a spike in claims. Strong capitalization (7.5) based on excellent current risk-adjusted capital (severe loss scenario).
**Other Rating Factors:** High quality investment portfolio (8.5).
**Principal Business:** Comp med (100%)
**Mem Phys: 16:** 69,530 **15:** 65,263 **16 MLR** 89.7% **/ 16 Admin Exp** N/A
**Enroll(000): Q3 17:** 80 **16:** 70 **15:** 52 **Med Exp PMPM:** $247
**Principal Investments:** Long-term bonds (70%), affiliate common stock (18%), cash and equiv (12%)
**Provider Compensation ($000):** FFS ($202,141)
**Total Member Encounters:** Phys (14,220), non-phys (13,401)
**Group Affiliation:** Innovation Health Holdings LLC
**Licensed in:** DC, MD, VA
**Address:** 3190 FAIRVIEW PARK Dr Ste 570, FALLS CHURCH, VA 22042
**Phone:** (703) 914-2925 **Dom State:** VA **Commenced Bus:** April 2013

| Data Date | Rating | RACR #1 | RACR #2 | Total Assets ($mil) | Capital ($mil) | Net Premium ($mil) | Net Income ($mil) |
|---|---|---|---|---|---|---|---|
| 9-17 | C- | 1.76 | 1.47 | 206.6 | 38.9 | 242.8 | -33.7 |
| 9-16 | B- | 3.24 | 2.70 | 156.9 | 58.0 | 187.1 | -5.1 |
| 2016 | C+ | 1.97 | 1.64 | 157.4 | 44.2 | 244.0 | -26.0 |
| 2015 | C+ | 3.52 | 2.93 | 120.4 | 63.2 | 204.6 | 3.1 |
| 2014 | B | 3.42 | 2.85 | 76.2 | 41.1 | 129.5 | -1.0 |
| 2013 | B | 3.99 | 3.33 | 15.8 | 12.6 | 4.3 | -6.2 |
| 2012 | N/A | N/A | N/A | N/A | -0.2 | N/A | N/A |

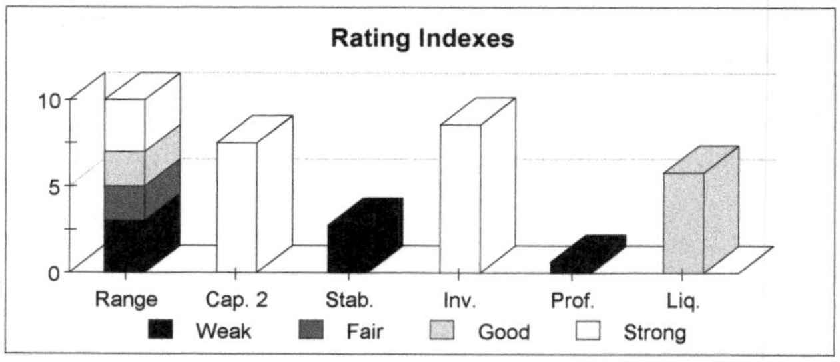

## INNOVATION HEALTH PLAN INC — C- — Fair

**Major Rating Factors:** Weak profitability index (0.9 on a scale of 0 to 10). Good liquidity (6.8) with sufficient resources (cash flows and marketable investments) to handle a spike in claims. Strong capitalization (9.4) based on excellent current risk-adjusted capital (severe loss scenario).
**Other Rating Factors:** High quality investment portfolio (9.3).
**Principal Business:** Comp med (100%)
**Mem Phys: 16:** 72,651 **15:** 65,263 **16 MLR** 87.5% **/ 16 Admin Exp** N/A
**Enroll(000): Q3 17:** 24 **16:** 28 **15:** 23 **Med Exp PMPM:** $273
**Principal Investments:** Long-term bonds (57%), cash and equiv (43%)
**Provider Compensation ($000):** Contr fee ($48,627), FFS ($30,103), capitation ($172)
**Total Member Encounters:** Phys (5,184), non-phys (5,014)
**Group Affiliation:** Innovation Health Holdings LLC
**Licensed in:** DC, MD, VA
**Address:** 3190 FAIRVIEW PARK Dr Ste 570, FALLS CHURCH, VA 22042
**Phone:** (703) 914-2925 **Dom State:** VA **Commenced Bus:** April 2013

| Data Date | Rating | RACR #1 | RACR #2 | Total Assets ($mil) | Capital ($mil) | Net Premium ($mil) | Net Income ($mil) |
|---|---|---|---|---|---|---|---|
| 9-17 | C- | 3.29 | 2.74 | 42.7 | 22.3 | 79.2 | 0.2 |
| 9-16 | C- | 3.40 | 2.83 | 62.9 | 15.3 | 71.2 | -2.8 |
| 2016 | C- | 2.74 | 2.28 | 44.1 | 18.4 | 95.7 | -4.9 |
| 2015 | C+ | 3.85 | 3.21 | 30.7 | 17.6 | 79.6 | 3.4 |
| 2014 | B | 3.60 | 3.00 | 20.8 | 12.1 | 51.3 | 1.1 |
| 2013 | B | 3.70 | 3.08 | 9.9 | 5.8 | 8.8 | -2.3 |
| 2012 | N/A | N/A | N/A | N/A | -0.2 | N/A | N/A |

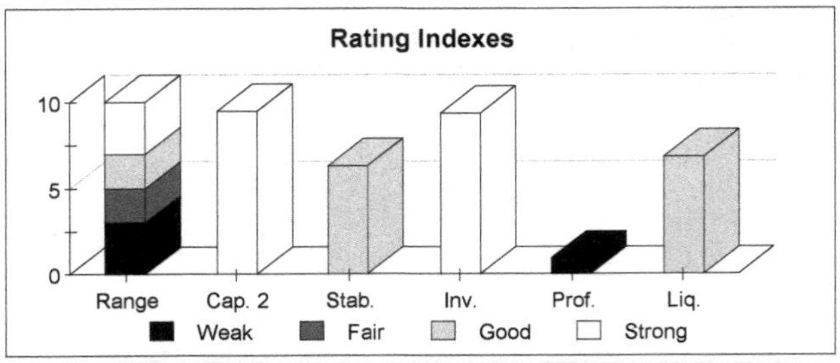


## INS CO OF NORTH AMERICA — C — Fair

**Major Rating Factors:** Fair overall results on stability tests (3.6 on a scale of 0 to 10) including fair financial strength of affiliated Chubb Limited and weak results on operational trends. The largest net exposure for one risk is high at 3.2% of capital. History of adequate reserve strength (6.4) as reserves have been consistently at an acceptable level.
**Other Rating Factors:** Strong long-term capitalization index (7.6) based on excellent current risk adjusted capital (severe and moderate loss scenarios), despite some fluctuation in capital levels. Excellent profitability (7.7) with operating gains in each of the last five years. Excellent liquidity (7.1) with ample operational cash flow and liquid investments.
**Principal Business:** Other accident & health (24%), other liability (20%), fire (18%), international (14%), group accident & health (10%), ocean marine (5%), and other lines (9%).
**Principal Investments:** Investment grade bonds (77%), cash (24%), and real estate (3%).
**Investments in Affiliates:** None
**Group Affiliation:** Chubb Limited
**Licensed in:** All states, the District of Columbia and Puerto Rico
**Commenced Business:** January 1792
**Address:** 436 WALNUT STREET, Philadelphia, PA 19106
**Phone:** (215) 640-1000 **Domicile State:** PA **NAIC Code:** 22713

| Data Date | Rating | RACR #1 | RACR #2 | Loss Ratio % | Total Assets ($mil) | Capital ($mil) | Net Premium ($mil) | Net Income ($mil) |
|---|---|---|---|---|---|---|---|---|
| 9-17 | C | 2.10 | 1.40 | N/A | 1,007.3 | 252.6 | 205.2 | 1.9 |
| 9-16 | C | 1.97 | 1.32 | N/A | 936.3 | 244.9 | 194.2 | 10.8 |
| 2016 | C | 2.29 | 1.53 | 76.5 | 944.2 | 250.2 | 249.8 | 16.5 |
| 2015 | C | 2.08 | 1.40 | 72.8 | 883.8 | 233.6 | 237.9 | 8.6 |
| 2014 | C | 2.29 | 1.53 | 77.6 | 869.9 | 225.2 | 223.9 | 12.7 |
| 2013 | C | 1.88 | 1.26 | 72.2 | 787.1 | 182.8 | 217.7 | 15.3 |
| 2012 | C | 2.22 | 1.46 | 89.9 | 831.8 | 195.6 | 224.1 | 3.2 |

| Chubb Limited<br>Composite Group Rating: B-<br>Largest Group Members | Assets ($mil) | Rating |
|---|---|---|
| FEDERAL INS CO | 27371 | B- |
| ACE AMERICAN INS CO | 13036 | B- |
| ACE PC INS CO | 8192 | B- |
| PACIFIC INDEMNITY CO | 6555 | B- |
| PACIFIC EMPLOYERS INS CO | 3774 | B- |

## INS CO OF SCOTT & WHITE — E- — Very Weak

**Major Rating Factors:** Weak profitability index (0.7 on a scale of 0 to 10). Fair capitalization (4.2) based on fair current risk-adjusted capital (moderate loss scenario). High quality investment portfolio (9.9).
**Other Rating Factors:** Excellent liquidity (7.2) with ample operational cash flow and liquid investments.
**Principal Business:** Medicare (50%), comp med (50%)
**Mem Phys: 15:** 9,028 **14:** 6,134 **15 MLR** 83.5% **/ 15 Admin Exp** N/A
**Enroll(000): Q3 16:** 61 **15:** 10 **14:** 7 **Med Exp PMPM:** $300
**Principal Investments:** Cash and equiv (91%), long-term bonds (5%), nonaffiliate common stock (4%)
**Provider Compensation ($000):** Contr fee ($28,351), FFS ($3,822), bonus arrang ($854), capitation ($260)
**Total Member Encounters:** Phys (215,891), non-phys (43,818)
**Group Affiliation:** Scott & White Group
**Licensed in:** TX
**Address:** 1206 WEST CAMPUS Dr, TEMPLE, TX 76502
**Phone:** (254) 298-3000 **Dom State:** TX **Commenced Bus:** May 2003

| Data Date | Rating | RACR #1 | RACR #2 | Total Assets ($mil) | Capital ($mil) | Net Premium ($mil) | Net Income ($mil) |
|---|---|---|---|---|---|---|---|
| 9-16 | E- | 0.82 | 0.68 | 67.9 | 4.3 | 213.2 | -77.7 |
| 9-15 | E | 1.33 | 1.10 | 12.6 | 5.0 | 29.6 | -3.0 |
| 2015 | E | 1.36 | 1.13 | 17.5 | 6.8 | 40.5 | -5.3 |
| 2014 | C- | 1.37 | 1.15 | 9.8 | 3.6 | 24.7 | -3.5 |
| 2013 | C+ | 1.98 | 1.65 | 8.3 | 3.8 | 14.2 | -0.5 |
| 2012 | N/A | N/A | N/A | 6.6 | 4.2 | 8.3 | N/A |
| 2011 | N/A | N/A | N/A | 3.0 | 2.9 | 1.0 | N/A |

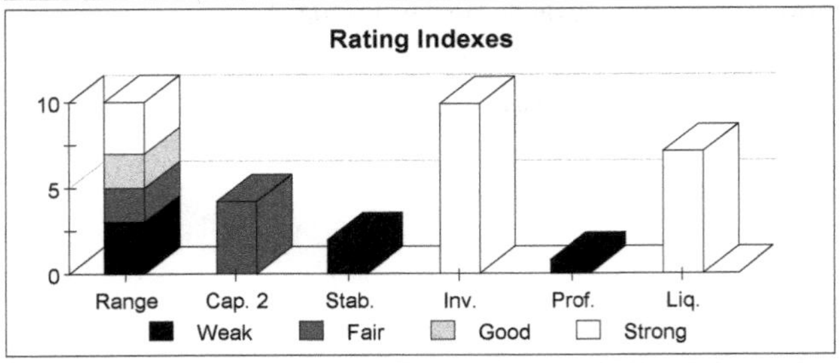

## INTERVALLEY HEALTH PLAN — D — Weak

**Major Rating Factors:** Weak profitability index (2.8 on a scale of 0 to 10). Fair overall results on stability tests (4.3) in spite of steady enrollment growth, averaging 6% over the past five years. Good capitalization index (5.6) based on fair current risk-adjusted capital (moderate loss scenario).
**Other Rating Factors:** Excellent liquidity (7.1) with ample operational cash flow and liquid investments.
**Principal Business:** Medicare (100%)
**Mem Phys: 16:** N/A **15:** N/A **16 MLR** 91.2% **/ 16 Admin Exp** N/A
**Enroll(000): Q3 17:** 25 **16:** 23 **15:** 22 **Med Exp PMPM:** $986
**Principal Investments ($000):** Cash and equiv ($14,224)
**Provider Compensation ($000):** None
**Total Member Encounters:** N/A
**Group Affiliation:** None
**Licensed in:** CA
**Address:** 1800 Harrison Street 20th Fl, Oakland, CA 94612
**Phone:** (510) 393-6574 **Dom State:** CA **Commenced Bus:** July 1979

| Data Date | Rating | RACR #1 | RACR #2 | Total Assets ($mil) | Capital ($mil) | Net Premium ($mil) | Net Income ($mil) |
|---|---|---|---|---|---|---|---|
| 9-17 | D | 0.85 | 0.54 | 64.0 | 22.4 | 219.1 | -2.8 |
| 9-16 | D | 1.08 | 0.69 | 29.5 | 24.9 | 207.1 | 1.8 |
| 2016 | D | 1.00 | 0.63 | 41.6 | 26.0 | 289.7 | 2.8 |
| 2015 | D | 1.01 | 0.64 | 38.6 | 23.2 | 262.5 | 2.4 |
| 2014 | D | 0.95 | 0.60 | 26.1 | 20.8 | 238.4 | -2.1 |
| 2013 | D | 1.15 | 0.73 | 30.4 | 23.0 | 225.2 | 1.7 |
| 2012 | D | 1.16 | 0.74 | 48.6 | 21.3 | 201.8 | 2.5 |

Rating Indexes

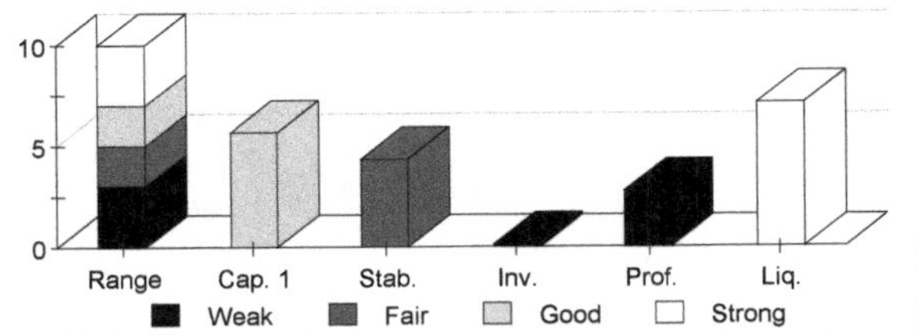


## INVOVA HEALH PLAN LLC — C — Fair

**Major Rating Factors:** Weak profitability index (2.0 on a scale of 0 to 10). Strong capitalization (8.4) based on excellent current risk-adjusted capital (severe loss scenario). High quality investment portfolio (9.9).
**Other Rating Factors:** Excellent liquidity (6.9) with sufficient resources (cash flows and marketable investments) to handle a spike in claims.
**Principal Business:** Medicaid (100%)
**Mem Phys: 16:** 15,151 **15:** 15,619 **16 MLR** 90.4% **/ 16 Admin Exp** N/A
**Enroll(000): Q3 17:** 63 **16:** 61 **15:** 58 **Med Exp PMPM:** $249
**Principal Investments:** Cash and equiv (74%), long-term bonds (26%)
**Provider Compensation ($000):** Capitation ($4,689), other ($170,249)
**Total Member Encounters:** Phys (442,097), non-phys (175,104)
**Group Affiliation:** Inova Health System Foundation
**Licensed in:** VA
**Address:** 8110 Gatehouse Rd Ste 400W, Falls Church, VA 22042
**Phone:** (703) 289-2455 **Dom State:** VA **Commenced Bus:** September 2005

| Data Date | Rating | RACR #1 | RACR #2 | Total Assets ($mil) | Capital ($mil) | Net Premium ($mil) | Net Income ($mil) |
|---|---|---|---|---|---|---|---|
| 9-17 | C | 2.50 | 2.09 | 61.3 | 23.9 | 157.4 | -1.2 |
| 9-16 | C+ | 2.56 | 2.13 | 58.7 | 22.9 | 146.7 | -4.1 |
| 2016 | C+ | 2.56 | 2.13 | 56.3 | 24.5 | 196.3 | -2.2 |
| 2015 | B | 2.95 | 2.46 | 51.5 | 26.5 | 188.6 | 1.9 |
| 2014 | B | 2.85 | 2.38 | 50.7 | 25.5 | 176.7 | -4.1 |
| 2013 | B+ | 3.75 | 3.12 | 54.4 | 32.1 | 178.2 | 0.4 |
| 2012 | B | 1.43 | 1.19 | 39.9 | 24.0 | 147.4 | 5.4 |

Rating Indexes

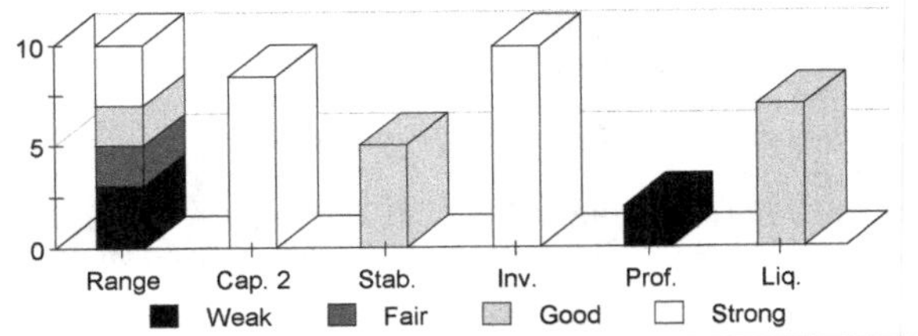


## JOHN HANCOCK LIFE & HEALTH INSURANCE COMPANY — B — Good

**Major Rating Factors:** Good quality investment portfolio (5.2 on a scale of 0 to 10) with minimal exposure to mortgages and minimal holdings in junk bonds. Fair overall results on stability tests (4.0) including negative cash flow from operations for 2016. Strong capitalization (8.0) based on excellent risk adjusted capital (severe loss scenario).
**Other Rating Factors:** Excellent profitability (7.3). Excellent liquidity (8.7).
**Principal Business:** Group health insurance (71%), individual health insurance (24%), and reinsurance (4%).
**Principal Investments:** NonCMO investment grade bonds (54%), mortgages in good standing (7%), CMOs and structured securities (5%), real estate (4%), and misc. investments (20%).
**Investments in Affiliates:** 1%
**Group Affiliation:** Manulife Financial Group
**Licensed in:** All states, the District of Columbia and Puerto Rico
**Commenced Business:** October 1981
**Address:** 197 Clarendon Street, Boston, MA 02116-5010
**Phone:** (617) 572-6000 **Domicile State:** MA **NAIC Code:** 93610

| Data Date | Rating | RACR #1 | RACR #2 | Total Assets ($mil) | Capital ($mil) | Net Premium ($mil) | Net Income ($mil) |
|---|---|---|---|---|---|---|---|
| 9-17 | B | 2.90 | 1.65 | 12,953.4 | 805.5 | 513.9 | 90.2 |
| 9-16 | B | 3.08 | 1.68 | 12,346.3 | 722.9 | 430.3 | -10.4 |
| 2016 | B | 3.12 | 1.71 | 11,875.2 | 723.6 | 351.9 | 101.6 |
| 2015 | B | 3.22 | 1.76 | 11,150.5 | 704.6 | 575.4 | 40.3 |
| 2014 | B | 3.85 | 2.14 | 10,700.1 | 745.8 | 576.0 | 2.8 |
| 2013 | B | 3.05 | 1.81 | 9,737.6 | 682.7 | 565.5 | 82.4 |
| 2012 | B | 3.50 | 1.94 | 10,039.5 | 664.9 | 562.3 | 12.0 |

Rating Indexes

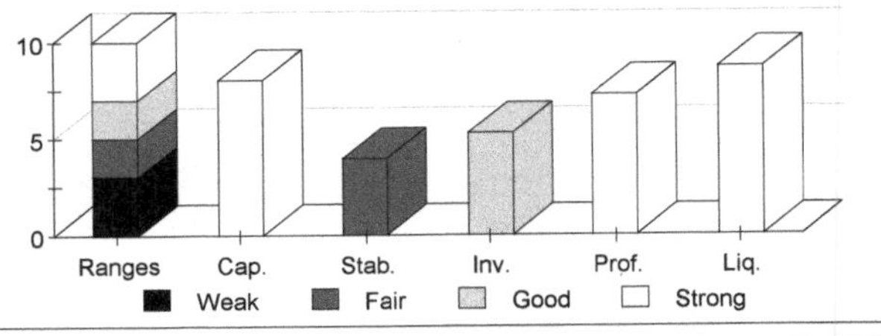

## K S PLAN ADMINISTRATORS LLC * B+ Good

**Major Rating Factors:** Good quality investment portfolio (6.8 on a scale of 0 to 10). Excellent profitability (9.0). Strong capitalization (7.8) based on excellent current risk-adjusted capital (severe loss scenario).
**Other Rating Factors:** Excellent liquidity (7.0) with ample operational cash flow and liquid investments.
**Principal Business:** Medicare (100%)
**Mem Phys: 16:** 732 **15:** 756 **16 MLR** 90.0% **/ 16 Admin Exp** N/A
**Enroll(000): Q3 17:** 31 **16:** 31 **15:** 30 **Med Exp PMPM:** $823
**Principal Investments:** Cash and equiv (57%), nonaffiliate common stock (43%)
**Provider Compensation ($000):** FFS ($157,586), capitation ($137,058), bonus arrang ($3,645)
**Total Member Encounters:** Phys (496,879), non-phys (14,872)
**Group Affiliation:** Kelsey-Seybold Medical Group PLLC
**Licensed in:** TX
**Address:** 2727 West Holcombe Blvd, Houston, TX 77025
**Phone:** (713) 442-1700 **Dom State:** TX **Commenced Bus:** December 2006

| Data Date | Rating | RACR #1 | RACR #2 | Total Assets ($mil) | Capital ($mil) | Net Premium ($mil) | Net Income ($mil) |
|---|---|---|---|---|---|---|---|
| 9-17 | B+ | 1.96 | 1.64 | 116.8 | 60.0 | 260.4 | 3.1 |
| 9-16 | B+ | 1.88 | 1.56 | 106.6 | 53.3 | 250.9 | 2.2 |
| 2016 | B+ | 1.87 | 1.56 | 83.5 | 57.2 | 334.8 | 5.9 |
| 2015 | B+ | 1.77 | 1.47 | 77.2 | 50.3 | 320.2 | 11.5 |
| 2014 | B+ | 1.42 | 1.18 | 65.8 | 39.5 | 295.0 | 2.8 |
| 2013 | C | 1.58 | 1.31 | 60.6 | 36.3 | 268.1 | 11.5 |
| 2012 | C- | 1.10 | 0.91 | 50.8 | 24.8 | 259.1 | 9.1 |

**Rating Indexes**

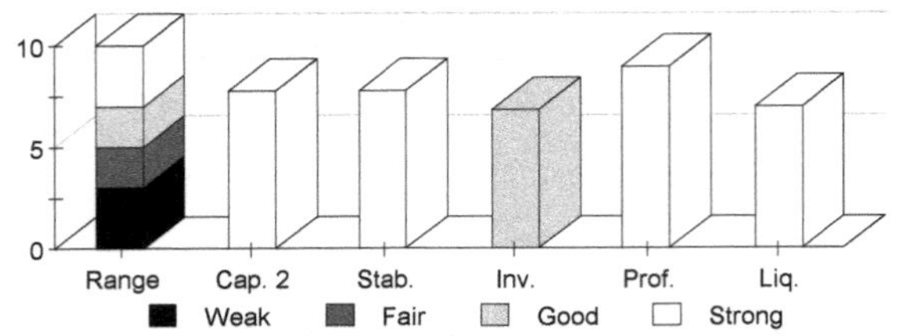


## KAISER FNDTN HLTH PLAN OF WA * B+ Good

**Major Rating Factors:** Good overall profitability index (6.4 on a scale of 0 to 10). Good quality investment portfolio (5.1). Good overall results on stability tests (6.1). Rating is significantly influenced by the strong financial results of Kaiser Foundation Health Plan Inc.
**Other Rating Factors:** Good liquidity (6.9) with sufficient resources (cash flows and marketable investments) to handle a spike in claims. Strong capitalization index (10.0) based on excellent current risk-adjusted capital (severe loss scenario).
**Principal Business:** Comp med (49%), Medicare (42%), FEHB (10%)
**Mem Phys: 16:** 17,576 **15:** 18,496 **16 MLR** 90.5% **/ 16 Admin Exp** N/A
**Enroll(000): Q3 17:** 389 **16:** 363 **15:** 355 **Med Exp PMPM:** $508
**Principal Investments:** Long-term bonds (42%), real estate (22%), nonaffiliate common stock (16%), affiliate common stock (9%), cash and equiv (4%), other (7%)
**Provider Compensation ($000):** Contr fee ($1,000,586), capitation ($362,779), FFS ($330,710), bonus arrang ($4,582), other ($514,344)
**Total Member Encounters:** Phys (1,492,914), non-phys (201,209)
**Group Affiliation:** Kaiser Foundation Health Plan Inc
**Licensed in:** WA
**Address:** 320 Westlake Ave N Suite 100, Seattle, WA 98109-5233
**Phone:** (206) 448-5600 **Dom State:** WA **Commenced Bus:** December 1945

| Data Date | Rating | RACR #1 | RACR #2 | Total Assets ($mil) | Capital ($mil) | Net Premium ($mil) | Net Income ($mil) |
|---|---|---|---|---|---|---|---|
| 9-17 | B+ | 4.48 | 3.73 | 1,673.0 | 925.1 | 1,971.9 | 0.5 |
| 9-16 | A- | 5.54 | 4.61 | 1,818.6 | 956.7 | 1,833.8 | 63.5 |
| 2016 | A- | 4.69 | 3.91 | 1,718.3 | 970.5 | 2,447.0 | 81.1 |
| 2015 | A- | 5.10 | 4.25 | 1,692.2 | 879.3 | 2,334.4 | 118.4 |
| 2014 | A- | 4.46 | 3.72 | 1,645.5 | 792.1 | 2,338.0 | 112.5 |
| 2013 | A- | 4.57 | 3.81 | 1,531.0 | 803.5 | 2,245.8 | 107.8 |
| 2012 | A- | 2.03 | 1.69 | 1,255.4 | 431.3 | 2,122.0 | 4.4 |

**Rating Indexes**

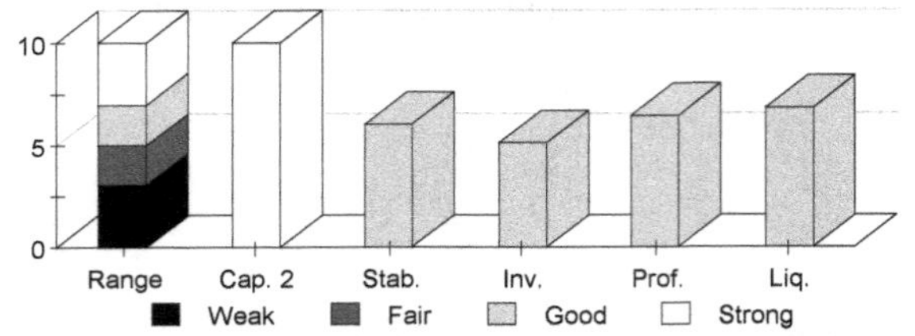


## KAISER FNDTN HLTH PLAN WA OPTN B Good

**Major Rating Factors:** Good liquidity (6.2 on a scale of 0 to 10) with sufficient resources (cash flows and marketable investments) to handle a spike in claims. Fair profitability index (3.8). Strong capitalization (9.0) based on excellent current risk-adjusted capital (severe loss scenario).
**Other Rating Factors:** High quality investment portfolio (9.1).
**Principal Business:** Comp med (92%), FEHB (8%)
**Mem Phys: 16:** 48,680 **15:** 56,255 **16 MLR** 87.4% **/ 16 Admin Exp** N/A
**Enroll(000): Q3 17:** 184 **16:** 186 **15:** 159 **Med Exp PMPM:** $375
**Principal Investments:** Long-term bonds (90%), cash and equiv (10%)
**Provider Compensation ($000):** FFS ($783,329), capitation ($5,203)
**Total Member Encounters:** Phys (568,330), non-phys (36,061)
**Group Affiliation:** Kaiser Foundation Health Plan Inc
**Licensed in:** ID, WA
**Address:** 320 Westlake Ave N Ste 100, Seattle, WA 98109-5233
**Phone:** (206) 448-5600 **Dom State:** WA **Commenced Bus:** October 1990

| Data Date | Rating | RACR #1 | RACR #2 | Total Assets ($mil) | Capital ($mil) | Net Premium ($mil) | Net Income ($mil) |
|---|---|---|---|---|---|---|---|
| 9-17 | B | 2.93 | 2.44 | 298.9 | 148.9 | 726.7 | 18.9 |
| 9-16 | B | 3.64 | 3.04 | 289.6 | 138.8 | 681.1 | -2.7 |
| 2016 | B | 2.59 | 2.16 | 289.3 | 131.0 | 903.9 | -7.7 |
| 2015 | B | 3.73 | 3.11 | 292.3 | 142.3 | 842.1 | 1.4 |
| 2014 | B- | 3.66 | 3.05 | 299.0 | 143.0 | 859.6 | 10.4 |
| 2013 | B- | 2.65 | 2.21 | 219.4 | 111.5 | 893.6 | 2.0 |
| 2012 | C+ | 1.54 | 1.29 | 219.2 | 109.9 | 1,010.9 | -8.2 |

**Rating Indexes**

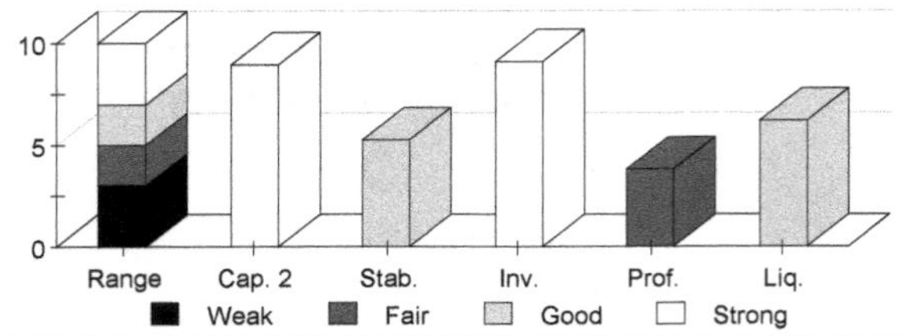

## KAISER FOUNDATION HEALTH PLAN INC * | A | Excellent

**Major Rating Factors:** Strong capitalization index (9.5 on a scale of 0 to 10) based on excellent current risk-adjusted capital (severe loss scenario). Excellent overall results on stability tests (7.5) based on steady enrollment growth, averaging 4% over the past five years. Excellent liquidity (7.1) with ample operational cash flow and liquid investments.
**Other Rating Factors:** Good overall profitability index (6.4).
**Principal Business:** Medicare (25%), Medicaid (4%)
**Mem Phys: 16:** N/A **15:** N/A **16 MLR** 96.3% **/ 16 Admin Exp** N/A
**Enroll(000): Q3 17:** 8,634 **16:** 8,363 **15:** 8,065 **Med Exp PMPM:** $588
**Principal Investments ($000):** Cash and equiv ($9,111,290)
**Provider Compensation ($000):** None
**Total Member Encounters:** N/A
**Group Affiliation:** Kaiser Foundation
**Licensed in:** CA
**Address:** 9700 Stockdale Highway, Bakersfield, CA 93311
**Phone:** (661) 664-5016 **Dom State:** CA **Commenced Bus:** N/A

| Data Date | Rating | RACR #1 | RACR #2 | Total Assets ($mil) | Capital ($mil) | Net Premium ($mil) | Net Income ($mil) |
|---|---|---|---|---|---|---|---|
| 9-17 | A | 3.87 | 2.80 | 72,940.0 | 32,223.2 | 51,265.0 | 3,832.8 |
| 9-16 | A | 4.03 | 2.88 | 65,227.7 | 28,182.8 | 45,474.1 | 2,334.7 |
| 2016 | A | 3.86 | 2.76 | 64,612.7 | 27,089.8 | 60,874.0 | 3,119.6 |
| 2015 | A- | 3.58 | 2.57 | 62,625.8 | 24,897.0 | 57,241.2 | 1,867.9 |
| 2014 | B+ | 3.08 | 2.21 | 61,914.6 | 20,827.2 | 53,137.7 | 3,073.3 |
| 2013 | A | 3.71 | 2.64 | 56,878.4 | 23,048.8 | 49,772.6 | 2,684.8 |
| 2012 | A- | 2.56 | 1.81 | 52,812.8 | 14,283.6 | 47,488.3 | 2,595.6 |

**Rating Indexes**

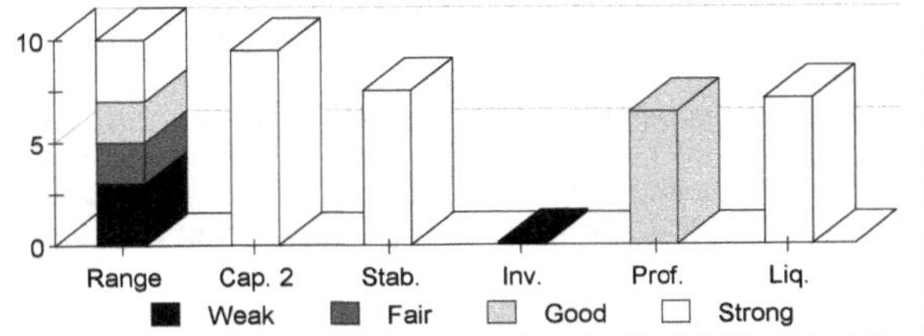


## KAISER FOUNDATION HP INC HI | C | Fair

**Major Rating Factors:** Weak profitability index (0.9 on a scale of 0 to 10). Good overall results on stability tests (5.4). Rating is significantly influenced by the strong financial results of Kaiser Foundation Health Plan Inc. Strong capitalization index (8.2) based on excellent current risk-adjusted capital (severe loss scenario).
**Other Rating Factors:** High quality investment portfolio (9.9). Excellent liquidity (7.1) with ample operational cash flow and liquid investments.
**Principal Business:** Comp med (60%), Medicare (27%), Medicaid (7%), FEHB (5%)
**Mem Phys: 16:** 461 **15:** 445 **16 MLR** 95.2% **/ 16 Admin Exp** N/A
**Enroll(000): Q3 17:** 251 **16:** 250 **15:** 246 **Med Exp PMPM:** $437
**Principal Investments:** Real estate (58%), cash and equiv (42%)
**Provider Compensation ($000):** Salary ($734,856), contr fee ($137,890), FFS ($10,378), other ($422,539)
**Total Member Encounters:** Phys (768,064), non-phys (444,054)
**Group Affiliation:** Kaiser Foundation Health Plan Inc
**Licensed in:** HI
**Address:** 711 Kapiolani Boulevard, Honolulu, HI 96813
**Phone:** (808) 432-5955 **Dom State:** HI **Commenced Bus:** February 1958

| Data Date | Rating | RACR #1 | RACR #2 | Total Assets ($mil) | Capital ($mil) | Net Premium ($mil) | Net Income ($mil) |
|---|---|---|---|---|---|---|---|
| 9-17 | C | 2.28 | 1.90 | 439.3 | 89.5 | 1,102.0 | 2.4 |
| 9-16 | C | 2.67 | 2.23 | 461.4 | 99.4 | 1,027.0 | -10.1 |
| 2016 | C | 2.19 | 1.83 | 421.6 | 86.2 | 1,369.0 | -22.8 |
| 2015 | B- | 2.02 | 1.69 | 424.5 | 75.2 | 1,270.6 | -17.4 |
| 2014 | B | 2.26 | 1.88 | 380.8 | 81.7 | 1,203.5 | -2.1 |
| 2013 | B | 3.89 | 3.24 | 356.3 | 130.7 | 1,159.0 | -1.0 |
| 2012 | B | 3.41 | 2.84 | 334.5 | 107.0 | 1,126.1 | 1.7 |

**Rating Indexes**

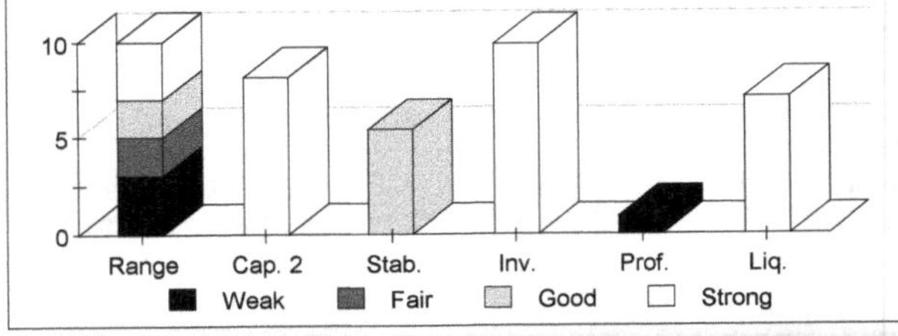


## KAISER FOUNDATION HP MID-ATL STATES | B | Good

**Major Rating Factors:** Good quality investment portfolio (6.7 on a scale of 0 to 10). Good overall results on stability tests (6.0) based on steady enrollment growth, averaging 9% over the past five years. Rating is significantly influenced by the strong financial results of Kaiser Foundation Health Plan Inc. Good liquidity (6.8) with sufficient resources (cash flows and marketable investments) to handle a spike in claims.
**Other Rating Factors:** Fair profitability index (3.9). Fair capitalization index (2.9) based on good current risk-adjusted capital (moderate loss scenario).
**Principal Business:** Comp med (54%), FEHB (23%), Medicare (15%), Medicaid (7%)
**Mem Phys: 16:** 20,507 **15:** 19,970 **16 MLR** 89.5% **/ 16 Admin Exp** N/A
**Enroll(000): Q3 17:** 699 **16:** 660 **15:** 610 **Med Exp PMPM:** $374
**Principal Investments:** Real estate (68%), long-term bonds (28%), cash and equiv (4%)
**Provider Compensation ($000):** Salary ($811,060), contr fee ($437,390), FFS ($276,371), capitation ($9,714), other ($1,339,545)
**Total Member Encounters:** Phys (1,956,625), non-phys (928,139)
**Group Affiliation:** Kaiser Foundation Health Plan Inc
**Licensed in:** DC, MD, VA
**Address:** 2101 East Jefferson Street, Rockville, MD 20852
**Phone:** (301) 816-2424 **Dom State:** MD **Commenced Bus:** October 1972

| Data Date | Rating | RACR #1 | RACR #2 | Total Assets ($mil) | Capital ($mil) | Net Premium ($mil) | Net Income ($mil) |
|---|---|---|---|---|---|---|---|
| 9-17 | B | 1.06 | 0.88 | 1,213.6 | 219.0 | 2,672.9 | 31.2 |
| 9-16 | B | 1.23 | 1.02 | 1,149.1 | 235.5 | 2,445.4 | 29.6 |
| 2016 | B | 0.97 | 0.80 | 1,172.5 | 198.7 | 3,264.8 | 16.8 |
| 2015 | B | 1.10 | 0.91 | 1,148.5 | 209.2 | 2,981.7 | -5.1 |
| 2014 | B | 0.80 | 0.66 | 1,196.4 | 147.2 | 2,621.1 | -12.3 |
| 2013 | B | 1.32 | 1.10 | 1,120.9 | 176.0 | 2,409.1 | -19.4 |
| 2012 | B | 1.41 | 1.18 | 1,121.8 | 182.3 | 2,302.0 | -21.3 |

**Rating Indexes**

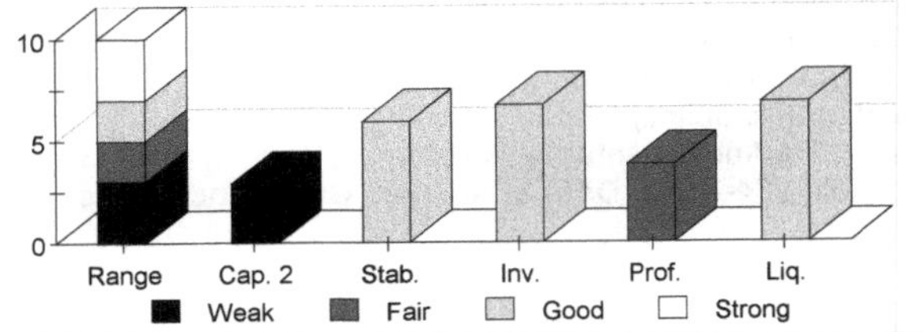

## KAISER FOUNDATION HP NORTHWEST B Good

**Major Rating Factors:** Good overall results on stability tests (5.4 on a scale of 0 to 10). Rating is significantly influenced by the strong financial results of Kaiser Foundation Health Plan Inc. Good liquidity (6.8) with sufficient resources (cash flows and marketable investments) to handle a spike in claims. Fair profitability index (3.0).
**Other Rating Factors:** Strong capitalization index (10.0) based on excellent current risk-adjusted capital (severe loss scenario). High quality investment portfolio (9.3).
**Principal Business:** Comp med (59%), Medicare (28%), FEHB (4%), dental (4%), other (5%)
**Mem Phys: 16:** 1,349 **15:** 1,310 **16 MLR** 92.3% **/ 16 Admin Exp** N/A
**Enroll(000): Q3 17:** 520 **16:** 498 **15:** 476 **Med Exp PMPM:** $558
**Principal Investments:** Long-term bonds (80%), real estate (18%), cash and equiv (2%)
**Provider Compensation ($000):** Salary ($1,398,731), contr fee ($425,530), FFS ($124,645), capitation ($5,541), other ($1,326,297)
**Total Member Encounters:** Phys (2,037,061), non-phys (813,367)
**Group Affiliation:** Kaiser Foundation Health Plan Inc
**Licensed in:** OR, WA
**Address:** 500 NE Multnomah Street Suite, Portland, OR 97232-2099
**Phone:** (503) 813-2800 **Dom State:** OR **Commenced Bus:** May 1942

| Data Date | Rating | RACR #1 | RACR #2 | Total Assets ($mil) | Capital ($mil) | Net Premium ($mil) | Net Income ($mil) |
|---|---|---|---|---|---|---|---|
| 9-17 | B | 5.18 | 4.32 | 1,440.8 | 567.4 | 2,816.7 | 62.2 |
| 9-16 | B | 4.71 | 3.92 | 1,454.6 | 495.2 | 2,650.1 | 51.4 |
| 2016 | B | 4.39 | 3.66 | 1,399.4 | 479.9 | 3,558.6 | 40.4 |
| 2015 | B- | 3.99 | 3.32 | 1,477.6 | 419.3 | 3,357.5 | -13.5 |
| 2014 | B | 2.03 | 1.69 | 1,300.8 | 203.2 | 3,137.6 | -15.6 |
| 2013 | B | 5.36 | 4.46 | 1,216.5 | 480.1 | 3,008.0 | -14.9 |
| 2012 | A- | 5.89 | 4.91 | 1,152.7 | 471.7 | 2,862.6 | 22.0 |

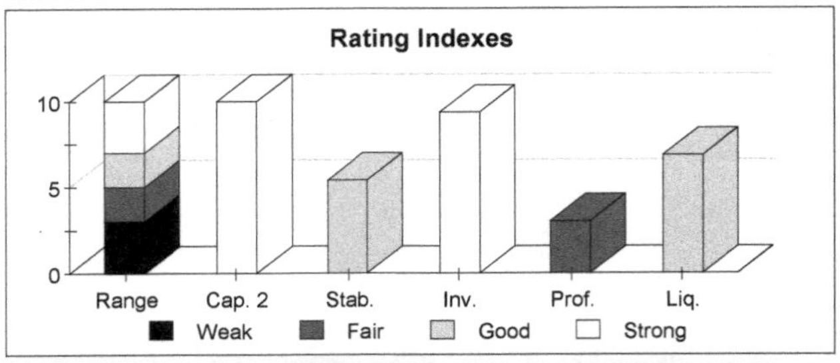


## KAISER FOUNDATION HP OF CO B Good

**Major Rating Factors:** Good overall results on stability tests (5.3 on a scale of 0 to 10). Rating is significantly influenced by the strong financial results of Kaiser Foundation Health Plan Inc. Good liquidity (6.8) with sufficient resources (cash flows and marketable investments) to handle a spike in claims. Fair profitability index (2.9).
**Other Rating Factors:** Strong capitalization index (8.2) based on excellent current risk-adjusted capital (severe loss scenario). High quality investment portfolio (7.8).
**Principal Business:** Comp med (61%), Medicare (32%), FEHB (5%), other (2%)
**Mem Phys: 16:** 1,126 **15:** 1,080 **16 MLR** 93.1% **/ 16 Admin Exp** N/A
**Enroll(000): Q3 17:** 599 **16:** 588 **15:** 541 **Med Exp PMPM:** $460
**Principal Investments:** Long-term bonds (61%), real estate (24%), nonaffiliate common stock (14%), cash and equiv (1%)
**Provider Compensation ($000):** Contr fee ($1,221,334), salary ($554,766), FFS ($103,708), capitation ($9,269), other ($1,376,388)
**Total Member Encounters:** Phys (3,237,311), non-phys (1,392,333)
**Group Affiliation:** Kaiser Foundation Health Plan Inc
**Licensed in:** CO
**Address:** 10350 E DAKOTA AVENUE, DENVER, CO 80231-1314
**Phone:** (800) 632-9700 **Dom State:** CO **Commenced Bus:** July 1969

| Data Date | Rating | RACR #1 | RACR #2 | Total Assets ($mil) | Capital ($mil) | Net Premium ($mil) | Net Income ($mil) |
|---|---|---|---|---|---|---|---|
| 9-17 | B | 2.28 | 1.90 | 1,262.9 | 338.5 | 2,764.3 | 4.4 |
| 9-16 | B | 3.33 | 2.78 | 1,452.9 | 465.2 | 2,651.4 | 23.5 |
| 2016 | B | 2.53 | 2.10 | 1,383.0 | 375.5 | 3,507.4 | 1.1 |
| 2015 | B- | 2.82 | 2.35 | 1,392.5 | 393.6 | 3,285.8 | -17.0 |
| 2014 | B | 1.83 | 1.52 | 1,305.1 | 222.0 | 3,190.3 | 78.7 |
| 2013 | B+ | 3.04 | 2.53 | 1,182.0 | 419.8 | 2,958.0 | 83.9 |
| 2012 | B+ | 3.58 | 2.99 | 1,128.7 | 451.5 | 2,830.7 | 64.0 |

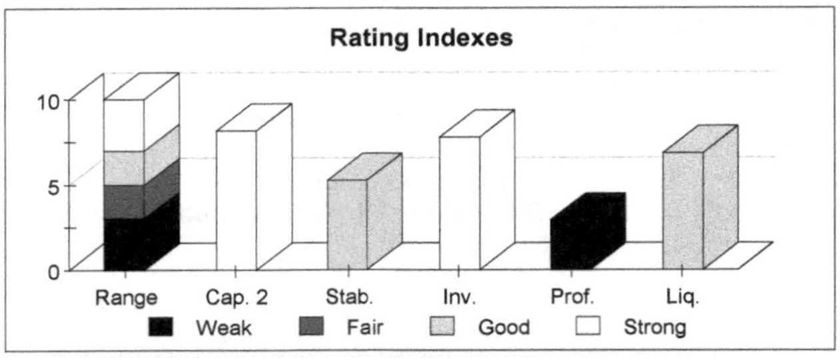


## KAISER FOUNDATION HP OF GA C- Fair

**Major Rating Factors:** Fair capitalization index (2.9 on a scale of 0 to 10) based on good current risk-adjusted capital (moderate loss scenario). Weak profitability index (1.9). Good liquidity (6.5) with sufficient resources (cash flows and marketable investments) to handle a spike in claims.
**Other Rating Factors:** High quality investment portfolio (7.5). Excellent overall results on stability tests (8.1) based on steady enrollment growth, averaging 5% over the past five years. Rating is significantly influenced by the strong financial results of Kaiser Foundation Health Plan Inc.
**Principal Business:** Comp med (69%), Medicare (19%), FEHB (11%)
**Mem Phys: 16:** 633 **15:** 587 **16 MLR** 94.7% **/ 16 Admin Exp** N/A
**Enroll(000): Q3 17:** 296 **16:** 274 **15:** 257 **Med Exp PMPM:** $414
**Principal Investments:** Long-term bonds (54%), real estate (43%), cash and equiv (3%)
**Provider Compensation ($000):** Contr fee ($485,784), FFS ($90,896), capitation ($404), other ($801,152)
**Total Member Encounters:** Phys (277,821), non-phys (70,359)
**Group Affiliation:** Kaiser Foundation Health Plan Inc
**Licensed in:** (No states)
**Address:** 9 Piedmont Center 3495 Piedmon, Atlanta, GA 30305-1736
**Phone:** (404) 364-7000 **Dom State:** GA **Commenced Bus:** October 1985

| Data Date | Rating | RACR #1 | RACR #2 | Total Assets ($mil) | Capital ($mil) | Net Premium ($mil) | Net Income ($mil) |
|---|---|---|---|---|---|---|---|
| 9-17 | C- | 1.42 | 1.18 | 491.3 | 164.8 | 1,253.5 | 38.5 |
| 9-16 | D+ | 1.21 | 1.01 | 496.9 | 128.8 | 1,090.5 | 11.2 |
| 2016 | C- | 1.08 | 0.90 | 494.4 | 125.7 | 1,458.6 | -9.1 |
| 2015 | D | 1.12 | 0.93 | 487.8 | 118.5 | 1,319.7 | -30.1 |
| 2014 | D | 1.04 | 0.86 | 511.1 | 106.2 | 1,200.1 | -170.2 |
| 2013 | D | 1.02 | 0.85 | 479.8 | 88.4 | 1,099.4 | -80.6 |
| 2012 | C- | 1.04 | 0.87 | 455.7 | 89.7 | 1,084.5 | -71.6 |

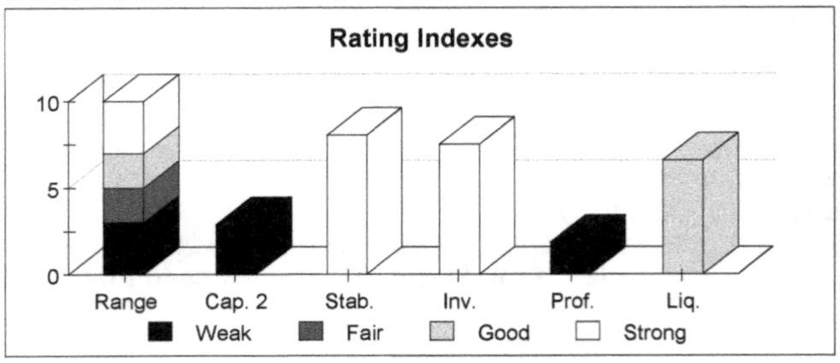

## KAISER PERMANENTE INS CO — B — Good

**Major Rating Factors:** Excellent profitability (8.6 on a scale of 0 to 10). Strong capitalization (10.0) based on excellent current risk-adjusted capital (severe loss scenario). High quality investment portfolio (9.7).
**Other Rating Factors:** Excellent liquidity (7.0) with ample operational cash flow and liquid investments.
**Principal Business:** Comp med (68%), dental (30%), other (2%)
**Mem Phys: 16:** 819,688 **15:** 778,702 **16 MLR** 73.3% **/ 16 Admin Exp** N/A
**Enroll(000): Q3 17:** 228 **16:** 239 **15:** 238 **Med Exp PMPM:** $31
**Principal Investments:** Long-term bonds (89%), cash and equiv (11%), other (1%)
**Provider Compensation ($000):** Contr fee ($61,056), bonus arrang ($16,445), FFS ($16,006), other ($755)
**Total Member Encounters:** Phys (42,572), non-phys (153,466)
**Group Affiliation:** Kaiser Foundation Health Plan Inc
**Licensed in:** CA, CO, DC, GA, HI, KS, MD, MO, OH, OR, SC, VA, WA
**Address:** 300 Lakeside Dr 13th Fl, Oakland, CA 94612
**Phone:** (877) 847-7572 **Dom State:** CA **Commenced Bus:** January 1995

| Data Date | Rating | RACR #1 | RACR #2 | Total Assets ($mil) | Capital ($mil) | Net Premium ($mil) | Net Income ($mil) |
|---|---|---|---|---|---|---|---|
| 9-17 | B | 14.17 | 11.81 | 195.9 | 117.0 | 85.5 | 4.6 |
| 9-16 | B | 13.35 | 11.12 | 183.1 | 109.6 | 93.3 | 6.4 |
| 2016 | B | 13.54 | 11.28 | 179.2 | 111.7 | 123.1 | 8.4 |
| 2015 | B | 12.65 | 10.54 | 174.3 | 103.7 | 126.2 | 7.2 |
| 2014 | B+ | 10.19 | 8.50 | 169.6 | 94.8 | 141.2 | 8.2 |
| 2013 | A | 5.99 | 4.99 | 180.0 | 88.5 | 245.8 | 5.1 |
| 2012 | A | 5.03 | 4.19 | 160.8 | 83.1 | 291.9 | 10.3 |

**Rating Indexes**

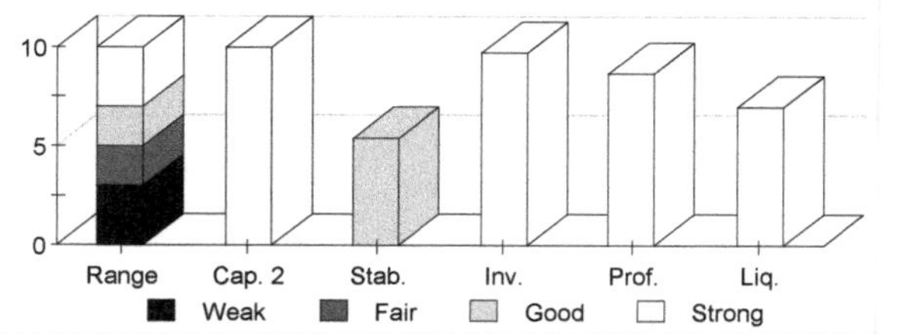


## KANAWHA INSURANCE COMPANY — B- — Good

**Major Rating Factors:** Good quality investment portfolio (5.6 on a scale of 0 to 10) despite mixed results such as: minimal exposure to mortgages and large holdings of BBB rated bonds but small junk bond holdings. Fair overall results on stability tests (3.6) including weak results on operational trends. Weak profitability (1.0) with operating losses during the first nine months of 2017.
**Other Rating Factors:** Strong capitalization (7.6) based on excellent risk adjusted capital (severe loss scenario). Excellent liquidity (7.5).
**Principal Business:** Individual health insurance (44%), group health insurance (38%), individual life insurance (12%), group life insurance (4%), and reinsurance (2%).
**Principal Investments:** NonCMO investment grade bonds (91%), CMOs and structured securities (6%), noninv. grade bonds (2%), policy loans (1%), and cash (1%).
**Investments in Affiliates:** None
**Group Affiliation:** Humana Inc
**Licensed in:** All states except AK, ME, NY, PR
**Commenced Business:** December 1958
**Address:** 210 SOUTH WHITE STREET, LANCASTER, SC 29720
**Phone:** (803) 283-5300 **Domicile State:** SC **NAIC Code:** 65110

| Data Date | Rating | RACR #1 | RACR #2 | Total Assets ($mil) | Capital ($mil) | Net Premium ($mil) | Net Income ($mil) |
|---|---|---|---|---|---|---|---|
| 9-17 | B- | 2.59 | 1.38 | 2,383.6 | 148.2 | 116.5 | -5.7 |
| 9-16 | C+ | 1.70 | 0.96 | 1,801.0 | 102.7 | 158.1 | -31.6 |
| 2016 | C+ | 2.65 | 1.46 | 2,343.0 | 147.0 | 193.8 | -523.2 |
| 2015 | C | 4.41 | 2.12 | 1,518.9 | 133.2 | 38.5 | 0.7 |
| 2014 | C | 3.63 | 1.94 | 1,458.8 | 122.1 | 169.5 | -38.5 |
| 2013 | C | 2.68 | 1.67 | 1,623.0 | 155.1 | 228.1 | -174.9 |
| 2012 | C | 4.02 | 2.54 | 1,456.8 | 255.5 | 252.2 | -112.4 |

**Adverse Trends in Operations**

Increase in policy surrenders from 2015 to 2016 (1273%)
Decrease in premium volume from 2014 to 2015 (77%)
Decrease in premium volume from 2013 to 2014 (26%)
Decrease in asset base during 2014 (10%)
Decrease in capital during 2013 (39%)

## KERN HEALTH SYSTEMS — B- — Good

**Major Rating Factors:** Excellent profitability (7.6 on a scale of 0 to 10). Strong capitalization index (10.0) based on excellent current risk-adjusted capital (severe loss scenario). Excellent overall results on stability tests (7.2) based on healthy premium and capital growth during 2016.
**Other Rating Factors:** Excellent liquidity (7.7) with ample operational cash flow and liquid investments.
**Principal Business:** Medicaid (100%)
**Mem Phys: 16:** N/A **15:** N/A **16 MLR** 83.5% **/ 16 Admin Exp** N/A
**Enroll(000): Q3 17:** 241 **16:** 234 **15:** 217 **Med Exp PMPM:** $205
**Principal Investments ($000):** Cash and equiv ($291,870)
**Provider Compensation ($000):** None
**Total Member Encounters:** N/A
**Group Affiliation:** None
**Licensed in:** CA
**Address:** 1055 West 7th Street, Los Angeles, CA 90017
**Phone:** (213) 694-1250 **Dom State:** CA **Commenced Bus:** June 1996

| Data Date | Rating | RACR #1 | RACR #2 | Total Assets ($mil) | Capital ($mil) | Net Premium ($mil) | Net Income ($mil) |
|---|---|---|---|---|---|---|---|
| 9-17 | B- | 5.34 | 3.25 | 425.6 | 194.4 | 541.0 | 22.1 |
| 9-16 | C+ | 4.68 | 2.85 | 345.6 | 154.8 | 493.3 | 43.8 |
| 2016 | B- | 4.85 | 2.96 | 349.3 | 172.3 | 671.5 | 61.3 |
| 2015 | C+ | 3.41 | 2.08 | 267.4 | 111.0 | 559.6 | 33.8 |
| 2014 | C | 3.02 | 1.85 | 205.9 | 81.7 | 407.1 | 3.8 |
| 2013 | C | 3.70 | 2.26 | 134.6 | 72.6 | 232.1 | 5.5 |
| 2012 | C | 3.39 | 2.12 | 105.1 | 67.1 | 198.4 | -31.3 |

**Rating Indexes**

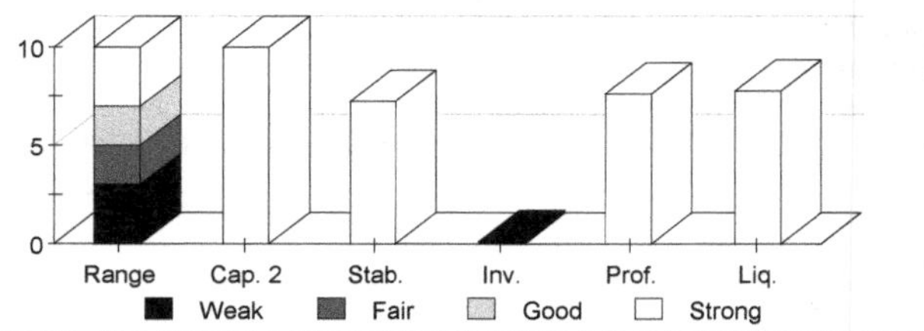

## KEYSTONE HEALTH PLAN CENTRAL INC C+ Fair

**Major Rating Factors:** Fair overall results on stability tests (3.9 on a scale of 0 to 10) based on an excessive 94% enrollment growth during the period. Good liquidity (6.1) with sufficient resources (cash flows and marketable investments) to handle a spike in claims. Weak profitability index (1.5).
**Other Rating Factors:** Strong capitalization index (8.7) based on excellent current risk-adjusted capital (severe loss scenario). High quality investment portfolio (7.9).
**Principal Business:** Medicare (46%), comp med (45%), other (8%)
**Mem Phys: 16:** 4,000 **15:** 3,954 **16 MLR** 92.1% **/ 16 Admin Exp** N/A
**Enroll(000): Q3 17:** 36 **16:** 63 **15:** 33 **Med Exp PMPM:** $366
**Principal Investments:** Long-term bonds (82%), cash and equiv (18%)
**Provider Compensation ($000):** Contr fee ($252,252), capitation ($15,934)
**Total Member Encounters:** Phys (721,413), non-phys (428,098)
**Group Affiliation:** Capital Blue Cross
**Licensed in:** PA
**Address:** 2500 Elmerton Avenue, Harrisburg, PA 17177-9799
**Phone:** (717) 541-7000 **Dom State:** PA **Commenced Bus:** November 1988

| Data Date | Rating | RACR #1 | RACR #2 | Total Assets ($mil) | Capital ($mil) | Net Premium ($mil) | Net Income ($mil) |
|---|---|---|---|---|---|---|---|
| 9-17 | C+ | 2.74 | 2.28 | 87.1 | 53.8 | 173.8 | 6.6 |
| 9-16 | C+ | 3.67 | 3.06 | 133.1 | 50.7 | 250.4 | -4.5 |
| 2016 | C+ | 2.32 | 1.93 | 146.1 | 45.1 | 307.9 | -14.0 |
| 2015 | C+ | 4.03 | 3.35 | 119.0 | 55.8 | 239.0 | -11.3 |
| 2014 | B | 6.50 | 5.42 | 125.7 | 84.9 | 228.2 | 5.9 |
| 2013 | B | 6.03 | 5.02 | 126.8 | 88.1 | 258.1 | 10.1 |
| 2012 | B | 5.79 | 4.83 | 129.3 | 92.5 | 283.3 | 13.2 |

Rating Indexes

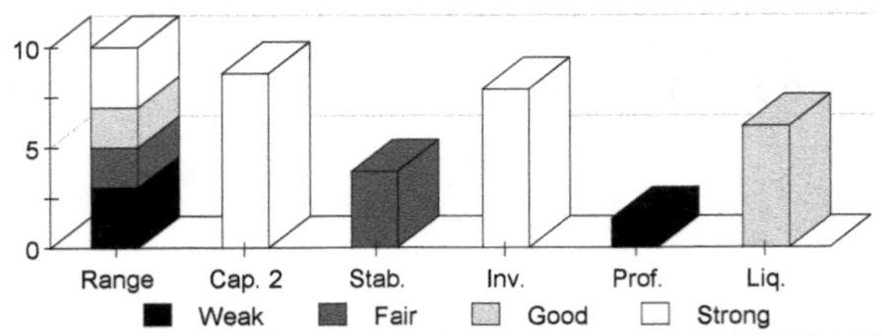


## KEYSTONE HEALTH PLAN EAST INC C+ Fair

**Major Rating Factors:** Fair overall results on stability tests (4.3 on a scale of 0 to 10) based on inconsistent enrollment growth in the past five years due to declines in 2013 and 2015. Good overall profitability index (6.8). Good quality investment portfolio (5.1).
**Other Rating Factors:** Good liquidity (6.3) with sufficient resources (cash flows and marketable investments) to handle a spike in claims. Strong capitalization index (9.6) based on excellent current risk-adjusted capital (severe loss scenario).
**Principal Business:** Comp med (62%), Medicare (38%)
**Mem Phys: 16:** 34,779 **15:** 32,624 **16 MLR** 81.9% **/ 16 Admin Exp** N/A
**Enroll(000): Q3 17:** 455 **16:** 447 **15:** 438 **Med Exp PMPM:** $451
**Principal Investments:** Long-term bonds (73%), nonaffiliate common stock (10%), pref stock (4%), cash and equiv (3%), other (9%)
**Provider Compensation ($000):** Contr fee ($1,688,607), capitation ($817,303), FFS ($49,858), bonus arrang ($40,434)
**Total Member Encounters:** Phys (5,594,288), non-phys (1,644,720)
**Group Affiliation:** Independence Health Group Inc
**Licensed in:** PA
**Address:** 1901 Market Street, Philadelphia, PA 19103-1480
**Phone:** (215) 241-2400 **Dom State:** PA **Commenced Bus:** January 1987

| Data Date | Rating | RACR #1 | RACR #2 | Total Assets ($mil) | Capital ($mil) | Net Premium ($mil) | Net Income ($mil) |
|---|---|---|---|---|---|---|---|
| 9-17 | C+ | 3.43 | 2.85 | 1,299.3 | 528.8 | 2,351.3 | 86.0 |
| 9-16 | C | 2.45 | 2.04 | 1,204.2 | 339.2 | 2,346.2 | -7.9 |
| 2016 | C+ | 2.64 | 2.20 | 1,221.4 | 397.5 | 3,072.9 | 44.3 |
| 2015 | C | 3.26 | 2.71 | 1,179.9 | 465.8 | 2,959.7 | 32.9 |
| 2014 | B- | 4.13 | 3.44 | 1,267.7 | 636.3 | 2,938.4 | 87.3 |
| 2013 | B+ | 5.78 | 4.82 | 1,325.1 | 916.5 | 2,685.7 | 145.5 |
| 2012 | B+ | 4.82 | 4.02 | 1,257.4 | 763.2 | 2,844.6 | 168.9 |

Rating Indexes

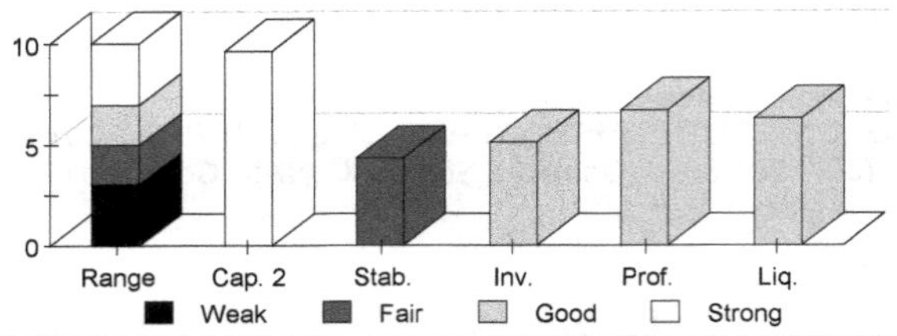


## LA HEALTH SERVICE & INDEMNITY CO B Good

**Major Rating Factors:** Good quality investment portfolio (5.8 on a scale of 0 to 10). Fair profitability index (4.2). Strong capitalization (10.0) based on excellent current risk-adjusted capital (severe loss scenario).
**Other Rating Factors:** Excellent liquidity (6.9) with sufficient resources (cash flows and marketable investments) to handle a spike in claims.
**Principal Business:** Comp med (78%), FEHB (16%), med supp (4%)
**Mem Phys: 16:** 31,837 **15:** 29,503 **16 MLR** 87.2% **/ 16 Admin Exp** N/A
**Enroll(000): Q3 17:** 679 **16:** 632 **15:** 650 **Med Exp PMPM:** $254
**Principal Investments:** Long-term bonds (37%), affiliate common stock (27%), nonaffiliate common stock (14%), cash and equiv (12%), real estate (4%), other (5%)
**Provider Compensation ($000):** FFS ($1,268,841), contr fee ($912,488), other ($13,924)
**Total Member Encounters:** Phys (6,298,041), non-phys (2,939,624)
**Group Affiliation:** LA Health Service and Indemnity Co
**Licensed in:** LA
**Address:** 5525 Reitz Ave, Baton Rouge, LA 70809
**Phone:** (225) 295-3307 **Dom State:** LA **Commenced Bus:** January 1975

| Data Date | Rating | RACR #1 | RACR #2 | Total Assets ($mil) | Capital ($mil) | Net Premium ($mil) | Net Income ($mil) |
|---|---|---|---|---|---|---|---|
| 9-17 | B | 6.31 | 5.26 | 1,988.3 | 1,267.7 | 1,784.6 | 108.4 |
| 9-16 | B | 5.66 | 4.72 | 1,761.9 | 1,121.1 | 1,902.8 | 16.9 |
| 2016 | B | 5.54 | 4.62 | 1,789.8 | 1,113.1 | 2,526.0 | -4.8 |
| 2015 | B | 5.46 | 4.55 | 1,671.2 | 1,080.1 | 2,555.3 | -50.6 |
| 2014 | A- | 6.44 | 5.37 | 1,736.9 | 1,145.3 | 2,408.8 | 36.3 |
| 2013 | A+ | 6.98 | 5.82 | 1,644.0 | 1,102.4 | 2,181.0 | 68.7 |
| 2012 | A+ | 6.50 | 5.42 | 1,505.4 | 992.5 | 2,094.6 | 58.1 |

Rating Indexes

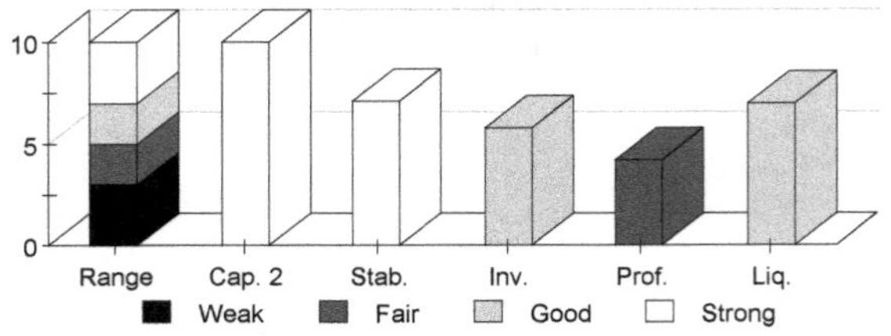

## LEGAL SERVICE PLANS OF VIRGINIA INC — B — Good

**Major Rating Factors:** Excellent profitability (8.8 on a scale of 0 to 10). Strong capitalization (7.6) based on excellent current risk-adjusted capital (severe loss scenario). High quality investment portfolio (9.5).
**Other Rating Factors:** Excellent liquidity (7.2) with ample operational cash flow and liquid investments.
**Principal Business:** Other (100%)
**Mem Phys: 16:** N/A **15:** N/A **16 MLR** 32.2% **/ 16 Admin Exp** N/A
**Enroll(000): Q3 17:** 38 **16:** 37 **15:** 36 **Med Exp PMPM:** $78
**Principal Investments:** Long-term bonds (72%), cash and equiv (28%)
**Provider Compensation ($000):** Capitation ($2,932)
**Total Member Encounters:** N/A
**Group Affiliation:** Ultramar Capital Ltd
**Licensed in:** VA
**Address:** One Pre-Paid Way, Ada, OK 74820
**Phone:** (580) 436-1234 **Dom State:** VA **Commenced Bus:** February 1997

| Data Date | Rating | RACR #1 | RACR #2 | Total Assets ($mil) | Capital ($mil) | Net Premium ($mil) | Net Income ($mil) |
|---|---|---|---|---|---|---|---|
| 9-17 | B | 1.84 | 1.53 | 2.4 | 1.2 | 7.0 | 0.9 |
| 9-16 | B | 2.14 | 1.78 | 2.4 | 1.4 | 6.8 | 0.8 |
| 2016 | B | 2.05 | 1.71 | 2.4 | 1.3 | 9.1 | 1.1 |
| 2015 | B | 1.72 | 1.43 | 2.4 | 1.1 | 8.7 | 0.8 |
| 2014 | N/A | N/A | N/A | 2.4 | 1.0 | 8.4 | 1.0 |
| 2013 | N/A | N/A | N/A | 2.3 | 1.2 | 8.6 | 1.2 |
| 2012 | N/A | N/A | N/A | 2.2 | 1.0 | 8.4 | 1.0 |

**Rating Indexes**

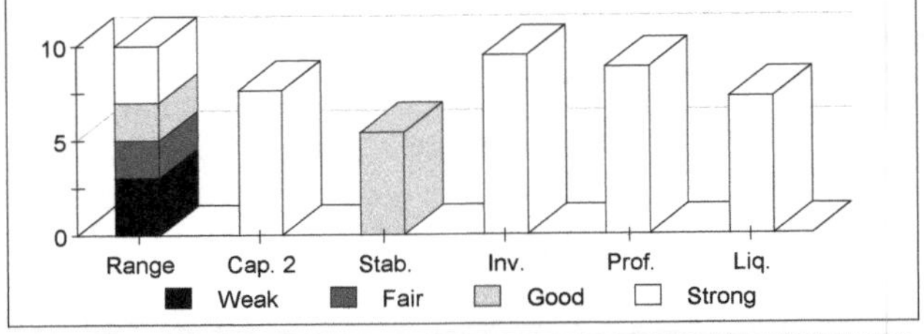


## LIBERTY LIFE ASSURANCE COMPANY OF BOSTON — B — Good

**Major Rating Factors:** Good overall results on stability tests (6.2 on a scale of 0 to 10). Stability strengths include excellent operational trends and excellent risk diversification. Good quality investment portfolio (6.1) despite mixed results such as: large holdings of BBB rated bonds but moderate junk bond exposure. Good overall profitability (5.8) although investment income, in comparison to reserve requirements, is below regulatory standards.
**Other Rating Factors:** Good liquidity (6.5). Strong capitalization (7.1) based on excellent risk adjusted capital (severe loss scenario).
**Principal Business:** Group health insurance (34%), individual annuities (25%), individual life insurance (24%), and group life insurance (17%).
**Principal Investments:** NonCMO investment grade bonds (79%), CMOs and structured securities (8%), mortgages in good standing (6%), noninv. grade bonds (2%), and policy loans (1%).
**Investments in Affiliates:** None
**Group Affiliation:** Liberty Mutual Group
**Licensed in:** All states except PR
**Commenced Business:** January 1964
**Address:** 175 Berkeley Street, Boston, MA 2116
**Phone:** (617) 357-9500 **Domicile State:** NH **NAIC Code:** 65315

| Data Date | Rating | RACR #1 | RACR #2 | Total Assets ($mil) | Capital ($mil) | Net Premium ($mil) | Net Income ($mil) |
|---|---|---|---|---|---|---|---|
| 9-17 | B | 1.88 | 1.09 | 18,681.2 | 1,174.7 | 2,272.4 | 21.4 |
| 9-16 | B | 1.70 | 0.98 | 16,978.4 | 957.7 | 2,053.8 | 5.0 |
| 2016 | B | 1.90 | 1.11 | 17,479.3 | 1,161.0 | 2,714.5 | 5.3 |
| 2015 | B | 1.77 | 1.04 | 16,054.1 | 966.4 | 2,501.1 | 69.9 |
| 2014 | B | 1.88 | 1.09 | 14,628.8 | 902.4 | 2,410.6 | 37.0 |
| 2013 | B | 1.83 | 1.07 | 13,115.1 | 716.9 | 2,095.9 | 39.2 |
| 2012 | B | 1.63 | 1.03 | 12,403.2 | 688.6 | 1,807.1 | 31.3 |

**Adverse Trends in Operations**

Increase in policy surrenders from 2012 to 2013 (38%)

## LIBERTY UNION LIFE ASR CO — C — Fair

**Major Rating Factors:** Fair profitability index (4.4 on a scale of 0 to 10). Weak liquidity (2.0) as a spike in claims may stretch capacity. Strong capitalization (9.8) based on excellent current risk-adjusted capital (severe loss scenario).
**Other Rating Factors:** High quality investment portfolio (9.4).
**Principal Business:** Comp med (73%), dental (8%), other (17%)
**Mem Phys: 16:** N/A **15:** N/A **16 MLR** 66.2% **/ 16 Admin Exp** N/A
**Enroll(000): Q3 17:** 9 **16:** 10 **15:** 13 **Med Exp PMPM:** $109
**Principal Investments:** Long-term bonds (91%), nonaffiliate common stock (4%), cash and equiv (4%), other (1%)
**Provider Compensation ($000):** Contr fee ($13,386), FFS ($428)
**Total Member Encounters:** Phys (41,429), non-phys (44,037)
**Group Affiliation:** Liberty Union Life Assurance Company
**Licensed in:** MI, WV
**Address:** 560 Kirts Blvd Ste 125, Troy, MI 48084-4133
**Phone:** (248) 583-7123 **Dom State:** MI **Commenced Bus:** June 1964

| Data Date | Rating | RACR #1 | RACR #2 | Total Assets ($mil) | Capital ($mil) | Net Premium ($mil) | Net Income ($mil) |
|---|---|---|---|---|---|---|---|
| 9-17 | C | 3.60 | 3.00 | 15.9 | 3.9 | 14.1 | 0.1 |
| 9-16 | C- | 3.33 | 2.78 | 14.1 | 4.2 | 17.1 | 0.2 |
| 2016 | C- | 3.76 | 3.13 | 14.0 | 4.2 | 22.2 | 0.2 |
| 2015 | C- | 3.24 | 2.70 | 14.5 | 4.0 | 24.8 | 0.0 |
| 2014 | C- | 2.15 | 1.79 | 14.1 | 4.7 | 21.5 | 0.6 |
| 2013 | C- | 2.12 | 1.76 | 11.6 | 4.7 | 21.7 | 0.5 |
| 2012 | C- | 2.73 | 2.28 | 11.2 | 4.5 | 21.2 | 0.9 |

**Rating Indexes**

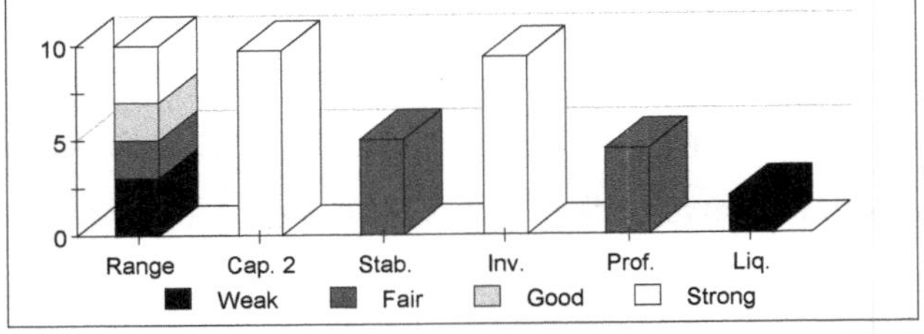

## LIFE INSURANCE COMPANY OF ALABAMA B Good

**Major Rating Factors:** Good liquidity (6.6 on a scale of 0 to 10) with sufficient resources to handle a spike in claims. Good overall results on stability tests (5.7). Stability strengths include excellent operational trends and good risk diversification. Fair quality investment portfolio (3.7) with large holdings of BBB rated bonds in addition to moderate junk bond exposure.
**Other Rating Factors:** Strong capitalization (8.8) based on excellent risk adjusted capital (severe loss scenario). Excellent profitability (8.9).
**Principal Business:** Individual health insurance (74%), individual life insurance (18%), and group health insurance (8%).
**Principal Investments:** NonCMO investment grade bonds (75%), noninv. grade bonds (15%), common & preferred stock (4%), policy loans (3%), and misc. investments (3%).
**Investments in Affiliates:** None
**Group Affiliation:** None
**Licensed in:** AL, AR, FL, GA, KY, LA, MS, NC, OK, SC, TN
**Commenced Business:** August 1952
**Address:** 302 Broad Street, Gadsden, AL 35901
**Phone:** (256) 543-2022 **Domicile State:** AL **NAIC Code:** 65412

| Data Date | Rating | RACR #1 | RACR #2 | Total Assets ($mil) | Capital ($mil) | Net Premium ($mil) | Net Income ($mil) |
|---|---|---|---|---|---|---|---|
| 9-17 | B | 3.56 | 2.22 | 126.5 | 41.9 | 27.6 | 1.4 |
| 9-16 | A- | 3.41 | 2.06 | 119.6 | 40.4 | 27.2 | 2.1 |
| 2016 | B | 3.39 | 2.03 | 120.8 | 40.6 | 36.0 | 2.2 |
| 2015 | A- | 3.37 | 2.10 | 116.6 | 38.7 | 36.3 | 2.8 |
| 2014 | A- | 3.33 | 2.22 | 113.5 | 37.3 | 37.4 | 7.0 |
| 2013 | A- | 2.88 | 1.95 | 108.0 | 33.0 | 37.2 | 2.7 |
| 2012 | A- | 2.52 | 1.74 | 102.6 | 29.4 | 38.0 | 3.0 |

**Adverse Trends in Operations**

Decrease in premium volume from 2014 to 2015 (3%)
Decrease in premium volume from 2012 to 2013 (2%)

## LIFE INSURANCE COMPANY OF BOSTON & NEW YORK * A- Excellent

**Major Rating Factors:** Good overall profitability (6.4 on a scale of 0 to 10). Good liquidity (6.6) with sufficient resources to handle a spike in claims as well as a significant increase in policy surrenders. Excellent overall results on stability tests (7.0). Strengths that enhance stability include excellent operational trends and good risk diversification.
**Other Rating Factors:** Strong capitalization (9.3) based on excellent risk adjusted capital (severe loss scenario). High quality investment portfolio (7.4).
**Principal Business:** Individual life insurance (58%), group health insurance (22%), and individual health insurance (20%).
**Principal Investments:** NonCMO investment grade bonds (67%), policy loans (21%), CMOs and structured securities (6%), common & preferred stock (2%), and misc. investments (4%).
**Investments in Affiliates:** None
**Group Affiliation:** Boston Mutual Group
**Licensed in:** NY
**Commenced Business:** March 1990
**Address:** 4300 Camp Road PO Box 331, Athol Springs, NY 14010
**Phone:** (212) 684-2000 **Domicile State:** NY **NAIC Code:** 78140

| Data Date | Rating | RACR #1 | RACR #2 | Total Assets ($mil) | Capital ($mil) | Net Premium ($mil) | Net Income ($mil) |
|---|---|---|---|---|---|---|---|
| 9-17 | A- | 3.33 | 2.50 | 148.4 | 30.3 | 16.1 | 1.5 |
| 9-16 | A- | 3.16 | 2.43 | 138.4 | 28.8 | 15.6 | 1.4 |
| 2016 | A- | 3.15 | 2.49 | 141.4 | 28.9 | 22.0 | 1.5 |
| 2015 | A- | 2.91 | 2.40 | 130.4 | 26.6 | 21.5 | 3.3 |
| 2014 | A- | 2.64 | 2.07 | 124.1 | 23.9 | 24.8 | 1.8 |
| 2013 | A- | 2.42 | 2.00 | 117.3 | 21.8 | 23.9 | -1.4 |
| 2012 | A- | 2.06 | 1.85 | 103.0 | 18.3 | 18.8 | 1.4 |

**Adverse Trends in Operations**

Decrease in premium volume from 2014 to 2015 (13%)
Increase in policy surrenders from 2013 to 2014 (41%)

## LIFE INSURANCE COMPANY OF NORTH AMERICA B Good

**Major Rating Factors:** Good overall results on stability tests (5.8 on a scale of 0 to 10). Stability strengths include excellent operational trends and excellent risk diversification. Good quality investment portfolio (5.4) despite large holdings of BBB rated bonds in addition to moderate junk bond exposure. Exposure to mortgages is significant, but the mortgage default rate has been low. Good liquidity (6.6).
**Other Rating Factors:** Strong capitalization (7.9) based on excellent risk adjusted capital (severe loss scenario). Excellent profitability (8.0).
**Principal Business:** Group health insurance (56%), group life insurance (41%), and reinsurance (3%).
**Principal Investments:** NonCMO investment grade bonds (69%), mortgages in good standing (12%), noninv. grade bonds (9%), CMOs and structured securities (2%), and misc. investments (8%).
**Investments in Affiliates:** 8%
**Group Affiliation:** CIGNA Corp
**Licensed in:** All states, the District of Columbia and Puerto Rico
**Commenced Business:** September 1957
**Address:** 2 LIBERTY PLC 1601 CHESTNUT ST, PHILADELPHIA, PA 19192-2362
**Phone:** (215) 761-1000 **Domicile State:** PA **NAIC Code:** 65498

| Data Date | Rating | RACR #1 | RACR #2 | Total Assets ($mil) | Capital ($mil) | Net Premium ($mil) | Net Income ($mil) |
|---|---|---|---|---|---|---|---|
| 9-17 | B | 2.52 | 1.62 | 8,856.7 | 1,728.4 | 2,793.7 | 234.6 |
| 9-16 | B | 2.16 | 1.39 | 8,457.8 | 1,407.4 | 2,812.5 | 22.1 |
| 2016 | B | 2.20 | 1.41 | 8,604.4 | 1,477.8 | 3,751.3 | 111.9 |
| 2015 | B | 2.34 | 1.51 | 8,141.6 | 1,495.3 | 3,674.5 | 236.6 |
| 2014 | B | 2.42 | 1.54 | 7,562.6 | 1,346.0 | 3,192.3 | 287.8 |
| 2013 | B | 2.20 | 1.39 | 6,711.9 | 1,103.5 | 3,232.7 | 173.3 |
| 2012 | B | 2.10 | 1.34 | 6,089.4 | 884.4 | 2,705.9 | 198.7 |

**Adverse Trends in Operations**

Decrease in capital during 2016 (1%)
Increase in policy surrenders from 2015 to 2016 (392%)
Change in premium mix from 2014 to 2015 (6%)
Increase in policy surrenders from 2014 to 2015 (994%)
Change in premium mix from 2013 to 2014 (5.7%)

## LIFEMAP ASSURANCE COMPANY B- Good

**Major Rating Factors:** Good quality investment portfolio (5.3 on a scale of 0 to 10) with no exposure to mortgages and minimal holdings in junk bonds. Good liquidity (6.6) with sufficient resources to handle a spike in claims. Good overall results on stability tests (5.2). Strengths include good financial support from affiliation with Regence Group, excellent operational trends and excellent risk diversification.

**Other Rating Factors:** Weak profitability (2.6). Strong capitalization (7.4) based on excellent risk adjusted capital (severe loss scenario).

**Principal Business:** Group health insurance (66%), group life insurance (27%), and individual health insurance (7%).

**Principal Investments:** NonCMO investment grade bonds (40%), CMOs and structured securities (31%), common & preferred stock (21%), and cash (8%).

**Investments in Affiliates:** 2%

**Group Affiliation:** Regence Group

**Licensed in:** AK, AZ, CA, ID, MT, OR, RI, UT, WA, WY

**Commenced Business:** July 1966

**Address:** 100 SW MARKET STREET, PORTLAND, OR 97201

**Phone:** (503) 225-6069 **Domicile State:** OR **NAIC Code:** 97985

| Data Date | Rating | RACR #1 | RACR #2 | Total Assets ($mil) | Capital ($mil) | Net Premium ($mil) | Net Income ($mil) |
|---|---|---|---|---|---|---|---|
| 9-17 | B- | 1.72 | 1.26 | 97.5 | 45.7 | 63.6 | 0.3 |
| 9-16 | B- | 1.46 | 1.08 | 83.4 | 37.4 | 60.4 | -0.9 |
| 2016 | B- | 1.50 | 1.11 | 84.0 | 38.4 | 81.0 | -0.3 |
| 2015 | B- | 1.55 | 1.14 | 83.1 | 39.4 | 76.4 | -1.4 |
| 2014 | B | 1.80 | 1.32 | 85.1 | 43.1 | 68.9 | -0.1 |
| 2013 | B | 1.96 | 1.41 | 89.6 | 45.3 | 64.1 | -0.5 |
| 2012 | B+ | 2.17 | 1.56 | 86.1 | 44.9 | 55.0 | -1.8 |

| Regence Group<br>Composite Group Rating: B<br>Largest Group Members | Assets ($mil) | Rating |
|---|---|---|
| REGENCE BLUESHIELD | 1652 | B |
| REGENCE BL CROSS BL SHIELD OREGON | 1093 | B+ |
| REGENCE BLUE CROSS BLUE SHIELD OF UT | 564 | B- |
| REGENCE BLUESHIELD OF IDAHO INC | 265 | C+ |
| ASURIS NORTHWEST HEALTH | 92 | B- |

## LIFESECURE INSURANCE COMPANY D Weak

**Major Rating Factors:** Weak profitability (1.8 on a scale of 0 to 10) with operating losses during the first nine months of 2017. Weak overall results on stability tests (2.3). Strong current capitalization (7.3) based on excellent risk adjusted capital (severe loss scenario) reflecting improvement over results in 2015.

**Other Rating Factors:** High quality investment portfolio (7.2). Excellent liquidity (8.7).

**Principal Business:** Individual health insurance (58%), reinsurance (32%), individual life insurance (8%), and individual annuities (2%).

**Principal Investments:** NonCMO investment grade bonds (83%) and CMOs and structured securities (17%).

**Investments in Affiliates:** None

**Group Affiliation:** Blue Cross Blue Shield of Michigan

**Licensed in:** All states except ME, MA, NH, NY, PR

**Commenced Business:** July 1954

**Address:** 10559 CItation Drive Suite 300, Brighton, MI 48116

**Phone:** (810) 220-7700 **Domicile State:** MI **NAIC Code:** 77720

| Data Date | Rating | RACR #1 | RACR #2 | Total Assets ($mil) | Capital ($mil) | Net Premium ($mil) | Net Income ($mil) |
|---|---|---|---|---|---|---|---|
| 9-17 | D | 1.82 | 1.20 | 353.9 | 31.1 | 54.1 | -3.0 |
| 9-16 | D | 1.71 | 1.11 | 300.1 | 26.6 | 45.3 | -6.7 |
| 2016 | D | 2.05 | 1.33 | 309.2 | 32.5 | 61.9 | -0.5 |
| 2015 | D | 1.32 | 0.85 | 262.3 | 18.0 | 50.4 | -10.3 |
| 2014 | D- | 1.76 | 1.16 | 226.9 | 20.4 | 42.5 | -13.0 |
| 2013 | D- | 2.10 | 1.34 | 189.7 | 20.2 | 33.4 | -3.9 |
| 2012 | E+ | 2.50 | 1.79 | 174.9 | 23.8 | 28.2 | -6.2 |

Investment Income Compared to Needs of Reserves

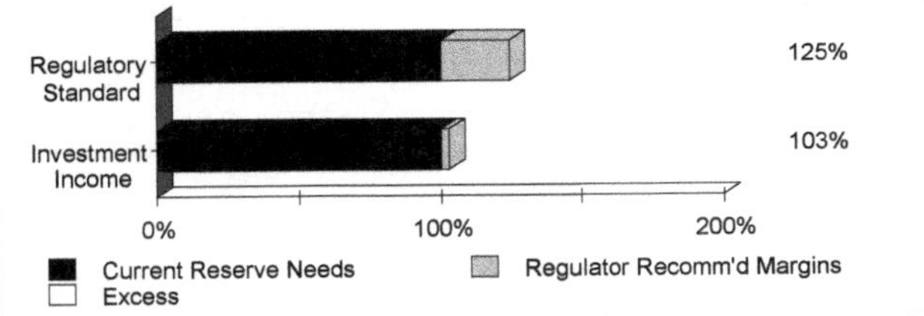


## LIFEWISE ASSURANCE COMPANY * A Excellent

**Major Rating Factors:** Good liquidity (6.9 on a scale of 0 to 10) with sufficient resources to handle a spike in claims. Excellent overall results on stability tests (7.1). Strengths that enhance stability include excellent operational trends and excellent risk diversification. Strong capitalization (10.0) based on excellent risk adjusted capital (severe loss scenario). Furthermore, this high level of risk adjusted capital has been consistently maintained over the last five years.

**Other Rating Factors:** High quality investment portfolio (8.0). Excellent profitability (9.3).

**Principal Business:** Group health insurance (100%).

**Principal Investments:** NonCMO investment grade bonds (52%), CMOs and structured securities (45%), noninv. grade bonds (2%), and cash (1%).

**Investments in Affiliates:** None

**Group Affiliation:** PREMERA

**Licensed in:** AK, CA, ID, MD, OR, WA

**Commenced Business:** November 1981

**Address:** 7001 220th Street SW, Mountlake Terrace, WA 98043

**Phone:** (425) 918-4575 **Domicile State:** WA **NAIC Code:** 94188

| Data Date | Rating | RACR #1 | RACR #2 | Total Assets ($mil) | Capital ($mil) | Net Premium ($mil) | Net Income ($mil) |
|---|---|---|---|---|---|---|---|
| 9-17 | A | 7.11 | 5.27 | 166.6 | 123.1 | 96.7 | 15.2 |
| 9-16 | A | 6.61 | 4.95 | 141.8 | 103.9 | 89.8 | 7.4 |
| 2016 | A | 6.77 | 5.05 | 142.7 | 108.1 | 118.3 | 11.6 |
| 2015 | A | 6.80 | 5.11 | 133.5 | 96.5 | 105.7 | 6.7 |
| 2014 | A | 7.38 | 5.56 | 127.0 | 89.9 | 90.9 | 9.3 |
| 2013 | A | 6.19 | 4.70 | 119.4 | 81.1 | 85.4 | 9.5 |
| 2012 | A | 5.90 | 4.42 | 118.4 | 71.6 | 84.3 | 12.8 |

Rating Indexes

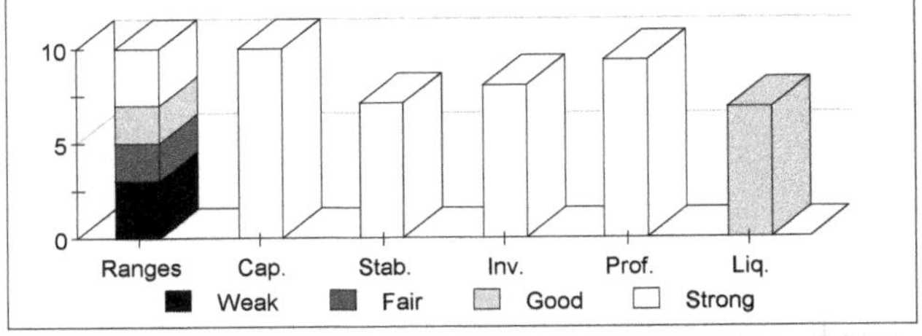

## LIFEWISE HEALTH PLAN OF OREGON — C — Fair

**Major Rating Factors:** Weak profitability index (0.8 on a scale of 0 to 10). Weak liquidity (1.1) as a spike in claims may stretch capacity. Strong capitalization (7.6) based on excellent current risk-adjusted capital (severe loss scenario).
**Other Rating Factors:** High quality investment portfolio (9.1).
**Principal Business:** Comp med (97%), med supp (2%), dental (1%)
**Mem Phys: 16:** 12,884 **15:** 12,570 **16 MLR** 97.9% **/ 16 Admin Exp** N/A
**Enroll(000): Q3 17:** 0 **16:** 28 **15:** 66 **Med Exp PMPM:** $303
**Principal Investments:** Long-term bonds (87%), cash and equiv (13%)
**Provider Compensation ($000):** Contr fee ($132,110), FFS ($13,337)
**Total Member Encounters:** Phys (225,267), non-phys (84,643)
**Group Affiliation:** PREMERA
**Licensed in:** ID, OR
**Address:** 2020 SW 4th St Ste 1000, Portland, OR 97201
**Phone:** (425) 918-4000 **Dom State:** OR **Commenced Bus:** January 1987

| Data Date | Rating | RACR #1 | RACR #2 | Total Assets ($mil) | Capital ($mil) | Net Premium ($mil) | Net Income ($mil) |
|---|---|---|---|---|---|---|---|
| 9-17 | C | 1.81 | 1.51 | 18.0 | 14.0 | 5.7 | -1.3 |
| 9-16 | C | 1.05 | 0.87 | 61.7 | 13.8 | 108.2 | -7.8 |
| 2016 | C | 1.95 | 1.63 | 51.3 | 15.3 | 135.9 | -6.7 |
| 2015 | C | 1.54 | 1.28 | 107.3 | 21.4 | 198.3 | -35.7 |
| 2014 | B | 4.12 | 3.44 | 93.7 | 40.8 | 150.3 | -24.3 |
| 2013 | B | 7.47 | 6.22 | 97.9 | 65.6 | 151.3 | 1.0 |
| 2012 | B | 6.87 | 5.72 | 99.7 | 64.7 | 160.1 | -0.2 |

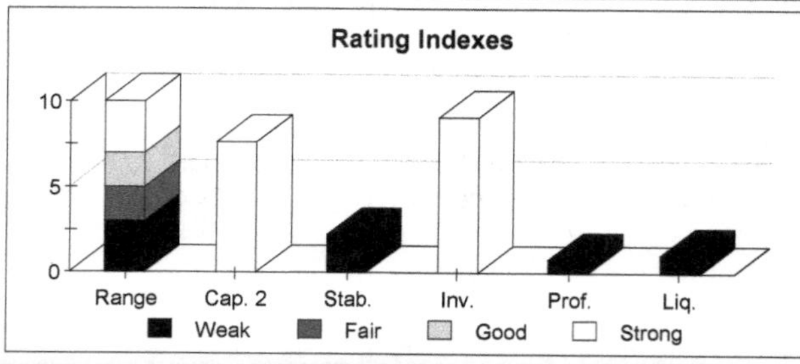


## LIFEWISE HEALTH PLAN OF WASHINGTON — B — Good

**Major Rating Factors:** Good liquidity (6.5 on a scale of 0 to 10) with sufficient resources (cash flows and marketable investments) to handle a spike in claims. Fair profitability index (4.5). Strong capitalization (10.0) based on excellent current risk-adjusted capital (severe loss scenario).
**Other Rating Factors:** High quality investment portfolio (9.1).
**Principal Business:** Comp med (98%), dental (2%)
**Mem Phys: 16:** 46,497 **15:** 39,105 **16 MLR** 91.5% **/ 16 Admin Exp** N/A
**Enroll(000): Q3 17:** 41 **16:** 45 **15:** 71 **Med Exp PMPM:** $260
**Principal Investments:** Long-term bonds (87%), cash and equiv (13%)
**Provider Compensation ($000):** Contr fee ($161,322), FFS ($7,602)
**Total Member Encounters:** Phys (367,511), non-phys (142,475)
**Group Affiliation:** PREMERA
**Licensed in:** WA
**Address:** 7001 220th St SW, Mountlake Terrace, WA 98043-2124
**Phone:** (425) 918-4000 **Dom State:** WA **Commenced Bus:** April 2001

| Data Date | Rating | RACR #1 | RACR #2 | Total Assets ($mil) | Capital ($mil) | Net Premium ($mil) | Net Income ($mil) |
|---|---|---|---|---|---|---|---|
| 9-17 | B | 7.40 | 6.17 | 123.5 | 77.5 | 145.8 | 6.4 |
| 9-16 | B | 5.68 | 4.73 | 124.4 | 70.0 | 136.2 | -4.3 |
| 2016 | B | 6.84 | 5.70 | 121.1 | 71.2 | 176.0 | -3.1 |
| 2015 | B+ | 6.08 | 5.07 | 147.6 | 75.4 | 243.2 | 4.9 |
| 2014 | B+ | 5.08 | 4.23 | 171.0 | 70.8 | 285.4 | 7.1 |
| 2013 | B+ | 3.66 | 3.05 | 117.8 | 61.8 | 345.0 | 15.7 |
| 2012 | B+ | 2.54 | 2.12 | 110.5 | 46.2 | 326.0 | -1.4 |

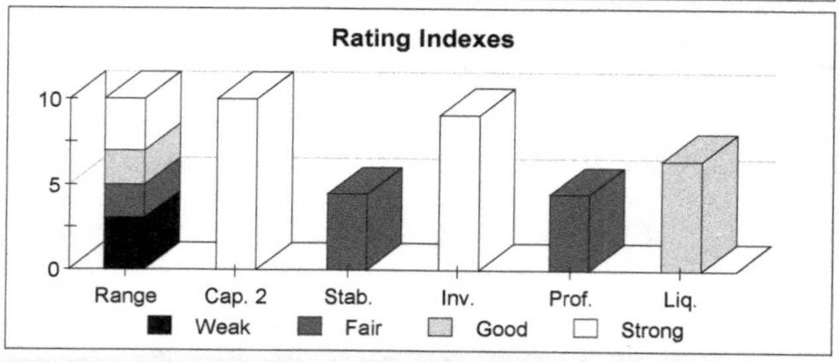


## LOCAL INITIATIVE HEALTH AUTH LA — C — Fair

**Major Rating Factors:** Weak liquidity (0.0 on a scale of 0 to 10) as a spike in claims may stretch capacity. Excellent profitability (8.1). Strong capitalization index (7.0) based on good current risk-adjusted capital (moderate loss scenario).
**Other Rating Factors:** Excellent overall results on stability tests (7.7).
**Principal Business:** Medicaid (95%), Medicare (2%)
**Mem Phys: 16:** N/A **15:** N/A **16 MLR** 95.8% **/ 16 Admin Exp** N/A
**Enroll(000): Q3 17:** 2,130 **16:** 1,983 **15:** 1,842 **Med Exp PMPM:** $312
**Principal Investments ($000):** Cash and equiv ($2,703,504)
**Provider Compensation ($000):** None
**Total Member Encounters:** N/A
**Group Affiliation:** None
**Licensed in:** CA
**Address:** 750 Medical Center Court Ste 2, Chula Vista, CA 91911
**Phone:** (619) 421-1659 **Dom State:** CA **Commenced Bus:** April 1997

| Data Date | Rating | RACR #1 | RACR #2 | Total Assets ($mil) | Capital ($mil) | Net Premium ($mil) | Net Income ($mil) |
|---|---|---|---|---|---|---|---|
| 9-17 | C | 1.16 | 0.70 | 5,958.0 | 677.0 | 6,802.3 | 131.9 |
| 9-16 | C | 1.46 | 0.88 | 3,903.9 | 563.2 | 5,789.9 | 70.2 |
| 2016 | C | 0.69 | 0.42 | 4,136.1 | 523.8 | 7,755.3 | 30.9 |
| 2015 | C | 1.20 | 0.73 | 2,857.7 | 492.9 | 6,366.0 | 272.9 |
| 2014 | C | 0.64 | 0.39 | 1,354.7 | 220.1 | 4,137.2 | 44.1 |
| 2013 | C | 0.91 | 0.55 | 1,233.9 | 175.9 | 2,687.4 | 36.7 |
| 2012 | C | 1.13 | 0.68 | 509.3 | 139.3 | 1,933.6 | -11.5 |

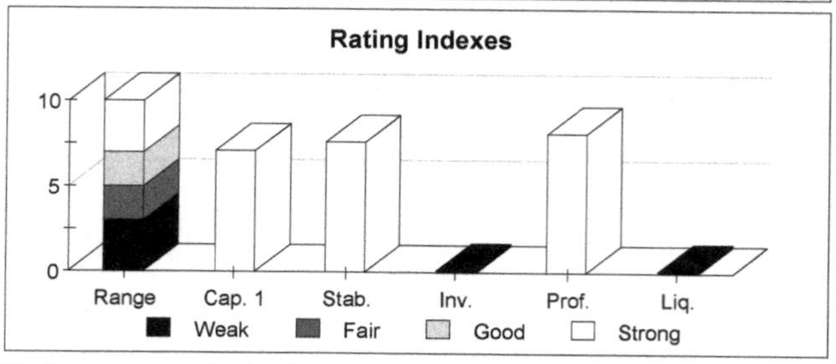

## LONDON LIFE REINSURANCE COMPANY C+ Fair

**Major Rating Factors:** Fair overall results on stability tests (3.7 on a scale of 0 to 10). Good overall profitability (6.8). Excellent expense controls. Strong capitalization (10.0) based on excellent risk adjusted capital (severe loss scenario).
**Other Rating Factors:** High quality investment portfolio (7.7). Excellent liquidity (8.0) with ample cash flow from premiums and investment income.
**Principal Business:** Reinsurance (100%).
**Principal Investments:** NonCMO investment grade bonds (77%), CMOs and structured securities (8%), cash (8%), common & preferred stock (1%), and noninv. grade bonds (1%).
**Investments in Affiliates:** None
**Group Affiliation:** Great West Life Asr
**Licensed in:** All states, the District of Columbia and Puerto Rico
**Commenced Business:** December 1969
**Address:** 1787 Sentry Pkwy W Bldg 16, Blue Bell, PA 19422-2240
**Phone:** (215) 542-7200 **Domicile State:** PA **NAIC Code:** 76694

| Data Date | Rating | RACR #1 | RACR #2 | Total Assets ($mil) | Capital ($mil) | Net Premium ($mil) | Net Income ($mil) |
|---|---|---|---|---|---|---|---|
| 9-17 | C+ | 5.82 | 3.59 | 201.2 | 58.5 | 0.9 | 0.5 |
| 9-16 | C+ | 5.51 | 3.00 | 285.2 | 58.2 | 1.2 | 1.6 |
| 2016 | C+ | 5.58 | 3.21 | 289.3 | 58.5 | 1.5 | 2.3 |
| 2015 | C+ | 5.43 | 2.91 | 301.3 | 57.4 | 1.9 | 2.1 |
| 2014 | C+ | 5.29 | 2.81 | 316.2 | 56.6 | 2.2 | 4.2 |
| 2013 | C+ | 4.74 | 2.39 | 344.1 | 52.9 | -8.1 | 2.3 |
| 2012 | C+ | 4.67 | 2.38 | 424.6 | 67.2 | 29.9 | 1.6 |

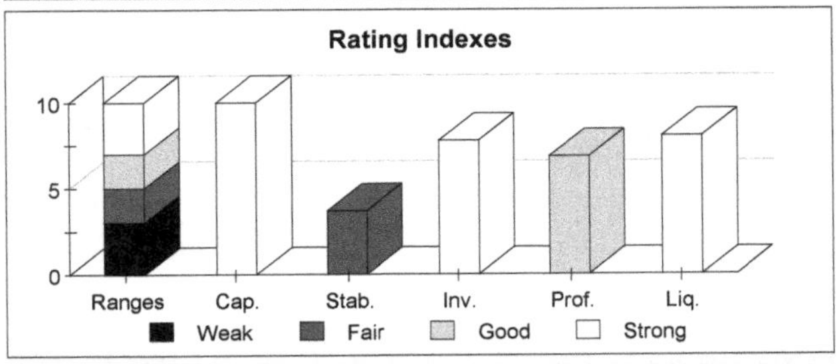


## LOUISIANA HEALTHCARE CONNECTIONS INC E Very Weak

**Major Rating Factors:** Weak profitability index (0.9 on a scale of 0 to 10). Strong capitalization (7.1) based on excellent current risk-adjusted capital (severe loss scenario). High quality investment portfolio (9.9).
**Other Rating Factors:** Excellent liquidity (7.0) with sufficient resources (cash flows and marketable investments) to handle a spike in claims.
**Principal Business:** Medicaid (100%)
**Mem Phys: 16:** 19,442 **15:** 14,150 **16 MLR** 86.4% **/ 16 Admin Exp** N/A
**Enroll(000): Q3 17:** 486 **16:** 473 **15:** 382 **Med Exp PMPM:** $295
**Principal Investments:** Cash and equiv (83%), long-term bonds (17%)
**Provider Compensation ($000):** Contr fee ($1,113,921), salary ($281,208), capitation ($30,769), bonus arrang ($10,868)
**Total Member Encounters:** Phys (1,977,087), non-phys (3,510,074)
**Group Affiliation:** Centene Corporation
**Licensed in:** LA
**Address:** 7700 Forsyth Blvd, Saint Louis, MO 63105
**Phone:** (314) 725-4477 **Dom State:** LA **Commenced Bus:** July 2011

| Data Date | Rating | RACR #1 | RACR #2 | Total Assets ($mil) | Capital ($mil) | Net Premium ($mil) | Net Income ($mil) |
|---|---|---|---|---|---|---|---|
| 9-17 | E | 1.45 | 1.21 | 440.3 | 99.8 | 1,575.7 | -16.7 |
| 9-16 | E | 1.52 | 1.27 | 360.1 | 86.3 | 1,232.1 | -28.0 |
| 2016 | E | 1.40 | 1.17 | 451.1 | 96.5 | 1,740.3 | -22.9 |
| 2015 | E | 1.56 | 1.30 | 247.5 | 88.4 | 1,188.1 | -17.1 |
| 2014 | C- | 2.74 | 2.28 | 117.7 | 64.6 | 451.1 | -5.0 |
| 2013 | C- | 1.92 | 1.60 | 88.4 | 47.6 | 456.7 | 4.1 |
| 2012 | C- | 1.68 | 1.40 | 89.3 | 35.2 | 271.1 | -16.4 |

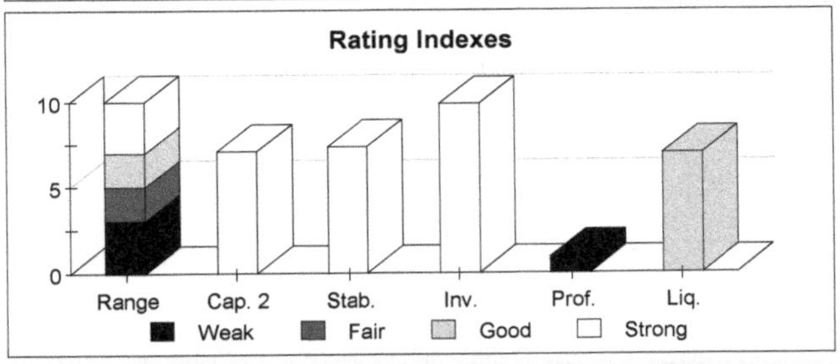


## LOYAL AMERICAN LIFE INSURANCE COMPANY B- Good

**Major Rating Factors:** Good capitalization (6.9 on a scale of 0 to 10) based on good risk adjusted capital (severe loss scenario). Capital levels have been relatively consistent over the last five years. Good quality investment portfolio (6.1) despite mixed results such as: no exposure to mortgages and large holdings of BBB rated bonds but minimal holdings in junk bonds. Good overall profitability (5.4) although investment income, in comparison to reserve requirements, is below regulatory standards.
**Other Rating Factors:** Good liquidity (6.7). Fair overall results on stability tests (4.9).
**Principal Business:** Individual health insurance (59%), reinsurance (37%), group health insurance (2%), and individual life insurance (2%).
**Principal Investments:** NonCMO investment grade bonds (83%), common & preferred stock (17%), noninv. grade bonds (1%), and CMOs and structured securities (1%).
**Investments in Affiliates:** 17%
**Group Affiliation:** CIGNA Corp
**Licensed in:** All states except NY, PR
**Commenced Business:** July 1955
**Address:** 1300 East Ninth Street, Cleveland, OH 44114
**Phone:** (512) 451-2224 **Domicile State:** OH **NAIC Code:** 65722

| Data Date | Rating | RACR #1 | RACR #2 | Total Assets ($mil) | Capital ($mil) | Net Premium ($mil) | Net Income ($mil) |
|---|---|---|---|---|---|---|---|
| 9-17 | B- | 1.20 | 0.99 | 304.3 | 104.9 | 232.2 | 5.6 |
| 9-16 | C+ | 0.97 | 0.83 | 264.0 | 83.0 | 210.8 | 11.5 |
| 2016 | C+ | 1.08 | 0.91 | 272.9 | 86.3 | 281.7 | 15.6 |
| 2015 | C+ | 1.00 | 0.86 | 266.7 | 85.6 | 278.5 | 16.5 |
| 2014 | C | 1.11 | 0.93 | 249.3 | 73.5 | 243.7 | 20.2 |
| 2013 | C | 1.53 | 1.18 | 244.0 | 71.5 | 260.0 | 14.3 |
| 2012 | C | 1.71 | 1.32 | 282.3 | 78.2 | -80.2 | -22.2 |

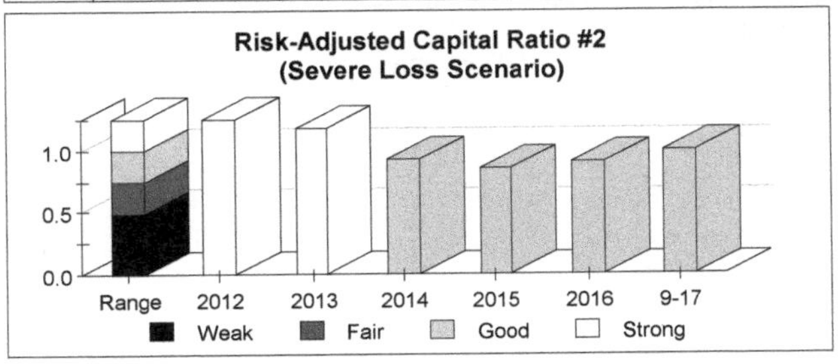

## MADISON NATIONAL LIFE INSURANCE COMPANY INCORPORAT C+ Fair

**Major Rating Factors:** Fair quality investment portfolio (4.7 on a scale of 0 to 10). Fair overall results on stability tests (4.6). Good liquidity (6.5) with sufficient resources to handle a spike in claims.
**Other Rating Factors:** Strong current capitalization (7.7) based on excellent risk adjusted capital (severe loss scenario) reflecting improvement over results in 2012. Excellent profitability (8.2).
**Principal Business:** Group health insurance (55%), group life insurance (18%), reinsurance (9%), individual life insurance (9%), and individual annuities (8%).
**Principal Investments:** NonCMO investment grade bonds (50%), common & preferred stock (41%), cash (1%), and CMOs and structured securities (1%).
**Investments in Affiliates:** 40%
**Group Affiliation:** Geneve Holdings Inc
**Licensed in:** All states except NY, PR
**Commenced Business:** March 1962
**Address:** 1241 John Q Hammons Drive, Madison, WI 53717-1929
**Phone:** (608) 830-2000 **Domicile State:** WI **NAIC Code:** 65781

| Data Date | Rating | RACR #1 | RACR #2 | Total Assets ($mil) | Capital ($mil) | Net Premium ($mil) | Net Income ($mil) |
|---|---|---|---|---|---|---|---|
| 9-17 | C+ | 1.53 | 1.46 | 335.6 | 185.8 | 64.9 | 8.2 |
| 9-16 | C+ | 2.46 | 1.91 | 337.5 | 187.4 | 65.1 | 9.7 |
| 2016 | C+ | 1.48 | 1.41 | 329.7 | 179.0 | 86.9 | -1.6 |
| 2015 | B- | 1.95 | 1.71 | 256.9 | 116.7 | 126.4 | 20.3 |
| 2014 | C+ | 1.26 | 1.06 | 496.7 | 81.5 | 147.5 | 9.9 |
| 2013 | C+ | 1.20 | 1.00 | 488.6 | 78.0 | 168.8 | 11.7 |
| 2012 | B | 1.12 | 0.89 | 689.7 | 72.3 | 136.4 | 11.9 |

Rating Indexes

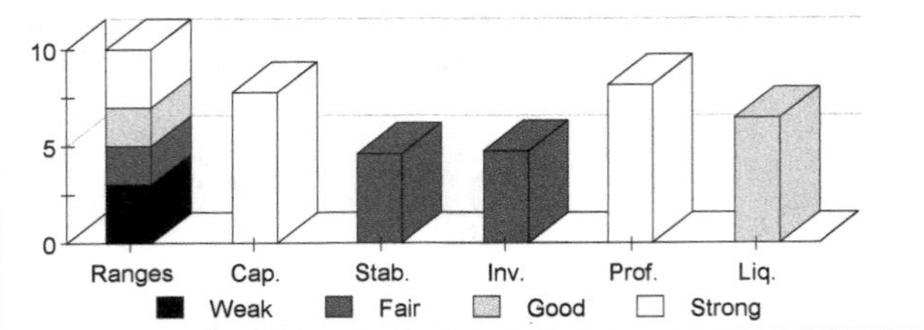


## MAGELLAN BEHAVIORAL HEALTH OF NE B- Good

**Major Rating Factors:** Excellent profitability (7.0 on a scale of 0 to 10). Strong capitalization (10.0) based on excellent current risk-adjusted capital (severe loss scenario). High quality investment portfolio (9.9).
**Other Rating Factors:** Excellent liquidity (7.6) with ample operational cash flow and liquid investments.
**Principal Business:** Medicaid (100%)
**Mem Phys: 16:** 1,736 **15:** 1,673 **16 MLR** 81.8% **/ 16 Admin Exp** N/A
**Enroll(000): Q1 17:** N/A **16:** 235 **15:** 246 **Med Exp PMPM:** $33
**Principal Investments:** Cash and equiv (100%)
**Provider Compensation ($000):** FFS ($92,991)
**Total Member Encounters:** Phys (262,869), non-phys (1,462,389)
**Group Affiliation:** Magellan Health Inc
**Licensed in:** NE
**Address:** 1221 N St Ste 325, Lincoln, NE 68508
**Phone:** (402) 437-4214 **Dom State:** NE **Commenced Bus:** July 2012

| Data Date | Rating | RACR #1 | RACR #2 | Total Assets ($mil) | Capital ($mil) | Net Premium ($mil) | Net Income ($mil) |
|---|---|---|---|---|---|---|---|
| 3-17 | B- | 7.97 | 6.64 | 39.4 | 14.9 | 1.8 | 0.2 |
| 3-16 | B- | 5.57 | 4.64 | 43.9 | 9.9 | 27.4 | -0.8 |
| 2016 | B- | 7.80 | 6.50 | 48.7 | 14.7 | 115.4 | 6.0 |
| 2015 | B- | 6.93 | 5.78 | 43.0 | 12.6 | 106.0 | 3.7 |
| 2014 | C- | 4.24 | 3.54 | 22.3 | 8.9 | 105.0 | 0.0 |
| 2013 | D+ | 1.98 | 1.65 | 17.1 | 4.4 | 33.2 | -0.6 |
| 2012 | N/A | N/A | N/A | 0.1 | 0.1 | N/A | N/A |

Rating Indexes

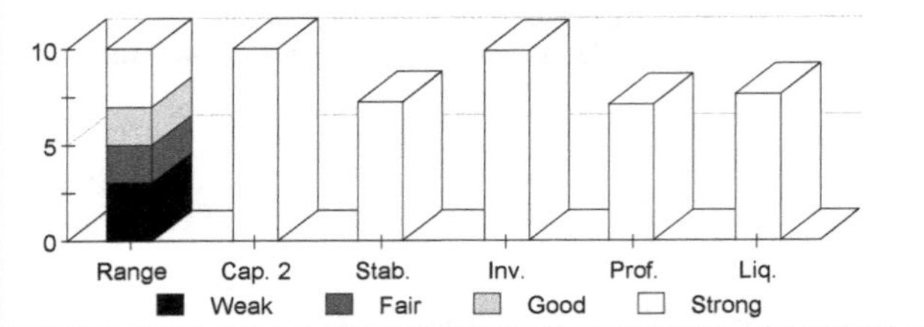


## MAGELLAN BEHAVIORAL HEALTH OF NJ LLC D+ Weak

**Major Rating Factors:** Weak profitability index (2.5 on a scale of 0 to 10). Strong capitalization (10.0) based on excellent current risk-adjusted capital (severe loss scenario). High quality investment portfolio (8.4).
**Other Rating Factors:** Excellent liquidity (10.0) with ample operational cash flow and liquid investments.
**Principal Business:** Other (100%)
**Mem Phys: 16:** 4,904 **15:** N/A **16 MLR** 73.9% **/ 16 Admin Exp** N/A
**Enroll(000): 16:** 1 **15:** N/A **Med Exp PMPM:** $19
**Principal Investments:** Cash and equiv (100%)
**Provider Compensation ($000):** FFS ($180), contr fee ($96)
**Total Member Encounters:** N/A
**Group Affiliation:** Magellan Health Inc
**Licensed in:** NJ
**Address:** 199 Pomeroy Rd, Parsippany, NJ 07054
**Phone:** (314) 387-4688 **Dom State:** MD **Commenced Bus:** January 2006

| Data Date | Rating | RACR #1 | RACR #2 | Total Assets ($mil) | Capital ($mil) | Net Premium ($mil) | Net Income ($mil) |
|---|---|---|---|---|---|---|---|
| 2016 | D+ | 88.03 | 73.36 | 2.5 | 2.3 | 0.1 | 0.0 |
| 2015 | N/A | N/A | N/A | 7.2 | 6.8 | 4.2 | -0.5 |
| 2014 | N/A | N/A | N/A | 21.8 | 10.6 | 109.5 | 5.6 |
| 2013 | N/A | N/A | N/A | 30.5 | 10.0 | 194.9 | -5.6 |
| 2012 | N/A | N/A | N/A | 15.5 | 8.8 | 167.4 | 2.3 |

Rating Indexes

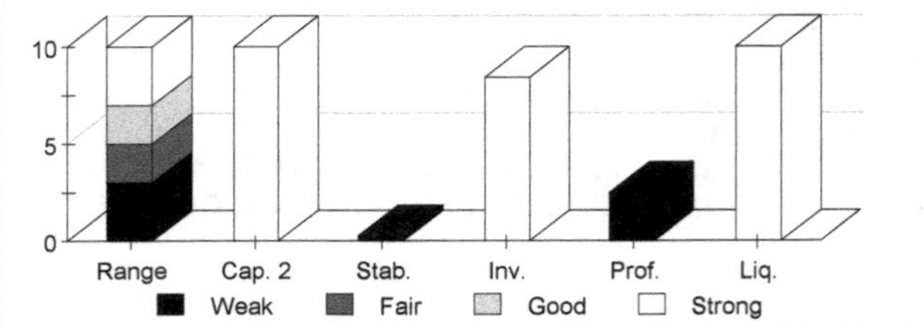

## MAGELLAN BEHAVIORAL HEALTH OF PA INC — C+ Fair

**Major Rating Factors:** Excellent profitability (7.9 on a scale of 0 to 10). Strong capitalization (7.1) based on excellent current risk-adjusted capital (severe loss scenario). High quality investment portfolio (9.9).
**Other Rating Factors:** Excellent liquidity (7.1) with ample operational cash flow and liquid investments.
**Principal Business:** Medicaid (100%)
**Mem Phys: 16:** 496 **15:** 491 **16 MLR** 87.8% **/ 16 Admin Exp** N/A
**Enroll(000): Q3 17:** 436 **16:** 396 **15:** 375 **Med Exp PMPM:** $86
**Principal Investments:** Cash and equiv (100%)
**Provider Compensation ($000):** Contr fee ($398,020)
**Total Member Encounters:** Phys (466,891), non-phys (1,025,525)
**Group Affiliation:** Magellan Health Inc
**Licensed in:** PA
**Address:** 105 Terry Dr Ste 103, Newtown, PA 18940
**Phone:** (215) 504-3907 **Dom State:** PA **Commenced Bus:** February 1997

| Data Date | Rating | RACR #1 | RACR #2 | Total Assets ($mil) | Capital ($mil) | Net Premium ($mil) | Net Income ($mil) |
|---|---|---|---|---|---|---|---|
| 9-17 | C+ | 1.41 | 1.18 | 109.6 | 51.7 | 356.5 | 3.1 |
| 9-16 | C | 1.48 | 1.24 | 100.3 | 46.8 | 342.1 | 2.0 |
| 2016 | C+ | 1.37 | 1.14 | 107.9 | 50.6 | 460.3 | 5.7 |
| 2015 | B- | 1.41 | 1.18 | 92.7 | 44.9 | 395.2 | 5.4 |
| 2014 | C+ | 1.52 | 1.26 | 98.1 | 46.5 | 369.3 | 5.2 |
| 2013 | E+ | 19.86 | 16.55 | 89.7 | 45.3 | 358.5 | 4.8 |
| 2012 | N/A | N/A | N/A | 84.0 | 44.9 | 355.1 | 4.6 |

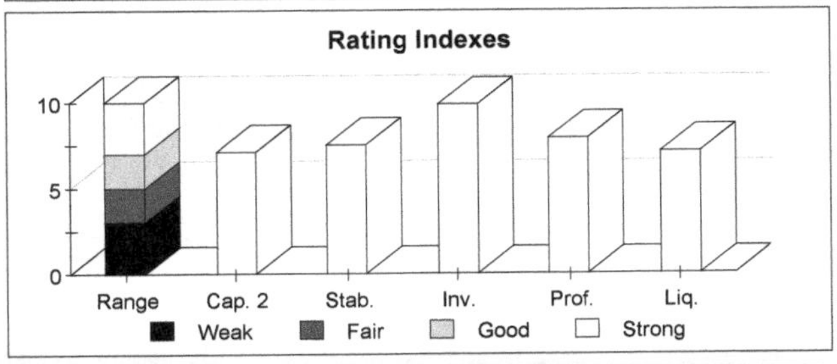


## MAGELLAN LIFE INS CO — B- Good

**Major Rating Factors:** Excellent profitability (7.6 on a scale of 0 to 10). Strong capitalization (7.6) based on excellent current risk-adjusted capital (severe loss scenario). High quality investment portfolio (9.9).
**Other Rating Factors:** Excellent liquidity (8.9) with ample operational cash flow and liquid investments.
**Principal Business:** Other (100%)
**Mem Phys: 16:** N/A **15:** N/A **16 MLR** 16.3% **/ 16 Admin Exp** N/A
**Enroll(000): Q3 17:** 213 **16:** 211 **15:** 185 **Med Exp PMPM:** $3
**Principal Investments:** Cash and equiv (90%), long-term bonds (10%)
**Provider Compensation ($000):** Other ($10,123)
**Total Member Encounters:** N/A
**Group Affiliation:** Magellan Health Inc
**Licensed in:** AZ, CA, DE, GA, HI, IN, KS, MS, MT, NE, NM, ND, SC, SD, TN, TX, UT, WV, WY
**Address:** 1209 Orange St, Wilmington, DE 19801
**Phone:** (314) 387-5602 **Dom State:** DE **Commenced Bus:** August 1982

| Data Date | Rating | RACR #1 | RACR #2 | Total Assets ($mil) | Capital ($mil) | Net Premium ($mil) | Net Income ($mil) |
|---|---|---|---|---|---|---|---|
| 9-17 | B- | 1.81 | 1.51 | 22.6 | 12.8 | 46.6 | 1.1 |
| 9-16 | U | 3.22 | 2.68 | 11.9 | 9.6 | 44.9 | 4.9 |
| 2016 | C- | 1.62 | 1.35 | 16.2 | 11.5 | 61.3 | 7.1 |
| 2015 | U | 3.05 | 2.54 | 13.1 | 9.1 | 25.6 | 3.5 |
| 2014 | N/A | N/A | N/A | 6.2 | 3.9 | 14.2 | 0.2 |
| 2013 | N/A | N/A | N/A | 6.3 | 3.7 | 18.4 | -0.2 |
| 2012 | N/A | N/A | N/A | 7.3 | 3.9 | 16.3 | 0.2 |

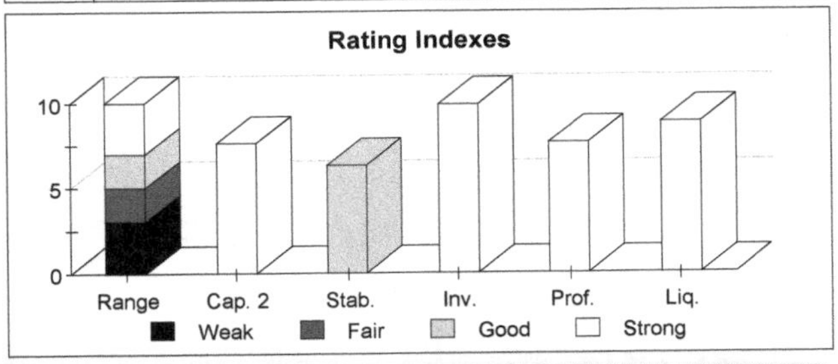


## MAGNA INS CO — C- Fair

**Major Rating Factors:** Weak profitability index (1.1 on a scale of 0 to 10). Strong capitalization (10.0) based on excellent current risk-adjusted capital (severe loss scenario). High quality investment portfolio (9.3).
**Other Rating Factors:** Excellent liquidity (9.5) with ample operational cash flow and liquid investments.
**Principal Business:** Other (100%)
**Mem Phys: 16:** N/A **15:** N/A **16 MLR** -8.0% **/ 16 Admin Exp** N/A
**Enroll(000): Q2 17:** N/A **16:** N/A **15:** N/A **Med Exp PMPM:** N/A
**Principal Investments:** Long-term bonds (67%), cash and equiv (33%)
**Provider Compensation ($000):** None
**Total Member Encounters:** N/A
**Group Affiliation:** PRAM LLC
**Licensed in:** AL, AR, FL, IL, IN, KY, LA, MS, MO, SC, TN, TX
**Address:** 190 CAPITOL St Ste 800, JACKSON, MS 39201-2155
**Phone:** (985) 206-5113 **Dom State:** MS **Commenced Bus:** November 1962

| Data Date | Rating | RACR #1 | RACR #2 | Total Assets ($mil) | Capital ($mil) | Net Premium ($mil) | Net Income ($mil) |
|---|---|---|---|---|---|---|---|
| 6-17 | C- | 13.58 | 11.31 | 2.6 | 2.2 | 1.4 | -0.1 |
| 6-16 | N/A | N/A | N/A | 2.8 | 2.5 | N/A | N/A |
| 2016 | C- | 14.53 | 12.10 | 2.7 | 2.4 | 0.4 | 0.0 |
| 2015 | N/A | N/A | N/A | 3.0 | 2.6 | 2.8 | N/A |
| 2014 | N/A | N/A | N/A | 2.6 | 2.4 | 0.9 | N/A |
| 2013 | N/A | N/A | N/A | 2.6 | 2.4 | 0.6 | N/A |
| 2012 | N/A | N/A | N/A | 2.9 | 2.4 | N/A | N/A |

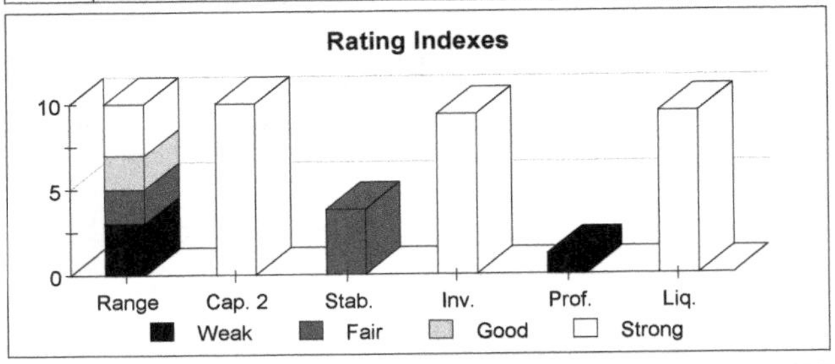

## MAGNOLIA HEALTH PLAN INC — D — Weak

**Major Rating Factors:** Weak profitability index (0.9 on a scale of 0 to 10). Good capitalization (6.9) based on excellent current risk-adjusted capital (severe loss scenario). Good liquidity (6.3) with sufficient resources (cash flows and marketable investments) to handle a spike in claims.
**Other Rating Factors:** High quality investment portfolio (9.4).
**Principal Business:** Medicaid (100%)
**Mem Phys: 16:** 10,851 **15:** 8,868 **16 MLR** 89.8% **/ 16 Admin Exp** N/A
**Enroll(000): Q3 17:** 266 **16:** 263 **15:** 268 **Med Exp PMPM:** $348
**Principal Investments:** Cash and equiv (60%), long-term bonds (40%)
**Provider Compensation ($000):** Contr fee ($1,069,177), capitation ($35,407), salary ($14,179)
**Total Member Encounters:** Phys (1,317,922), non-phys (1,588,618)
**Group Affiliation:** Centene Corporation
**Licensed in:** MS
**Address:** 111 East Capitol St Ste 500, Jackson, MS 39201
**Phone:** (314) 725-4477 **Dom State:** MS **Commenced Bus:** January 2011

| Data Date | Rating | RACR #1 | RACR #2 | Total Assets ($mil) | Capital ($mil) | Net Premium ($mil) | Net Income ($mil) |
|---|---|---|---|---|---|---|---|
| 9-17 | D | 1.24 | 1.03 | 200.2 | 86.8 | 942.3 | -13.5 |
| 9-16 | D | 1.69 | 1.41 | 164.0 | 76.5 | 915.6 | -31.7 |
| 2016 | D | 1.21 | 1.01 | 197.6 | 85.1 | 1,248.5 | -43.3 |
| 2015 | D | 1.26 | 1.05 | 167.0 | 56.2 | 879.6 | -28.8 |
| 2014 | D | N/A | N/A | 149.0 | 61.1 | 547.3 | -14.9 |
| 2013 | C- | 1.75 | 1.46 | 57.1 | 36.3 | 406.6 | -10.1 |
| 2012 | C | 2.26 | 1.89 | 40.3 | 19.3 | 195.6 | 10.1 |

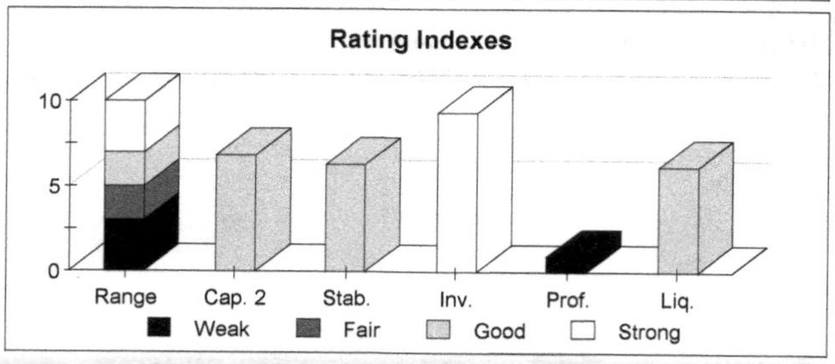


## MAINE COMMUNITY HEALTH OPTIONS — D — Weak

**Major Rating Factors:** Weak profitability index (0.8 on a scale of 0 to 10). Poor capitalization (2.2) based on weak current risk-adjusted capital (moderate loss scenario). Weak liquidity (0.0) as a spike in claims may stretch capacity.
**Other Rating Factors:** High quality investment portfolio (8.9).
**Principal Business:** Comp med (100%)
**Mem Phys: 16:** 23,898 **15:** 15,795 **16 MLR** 105.7% **/ 16 Admin Exp** N/A
**Enroll(000): Q3 17:** 39 **16:** 68 **15:** 75 **Med Exp PMPM:** $431
**Principal Investments:** Long-term bonds (70%), cash and equiv (30%)
**Provider Compensation ($000):** FFS ($412,378), bonus arrang ($457)
**Total Member Encounters:** Phys (340,051), non-phys (174,920)
**Group Affiliation:** Maine Community Health Options
**Licensed in:** ME, NH
**Address:** 150 MILL St THIRD Fl, LEWISTON, ME 04240
**Phone:** (207) 402-3330 **Dom State:** ME **Commenced Bus:** January 2014

| Data Date | Rating | RACR #1 | RACR #2 | Total Assets ($mil) | Capital ($mil) | Net Premium ($mil) | Net Income ($mil) |
|---|---|---|---|---|---|---|---|
| 9-17 | D | 0.52 | 0.43 | 86.4 | 46.8 | 205.5 | 6.5 |
| 9-16 | C- | N/A | N/A | 120.3 | 48.2 | 299.6 | -3.3 |
| 2016 | D | 0.43 | 0.36 | 102.0 | 38.6 | 377.8 | -14.0 |
| 2015 | C- | N/A | N/A | 167.6 | 49.8 | 287.0 | -74.0 |
| 2014 | D+ | 0.58 | 0.49 | 77.4 | 27.4 | 167.4 | 5.9 |
| 2013 | N/A | N/A | N/A | 18.2 | 5.9 | 0.5 | N/A |
| 2012 | N/A | N/A | N/A | N/A | N/A | N/A | N/A |

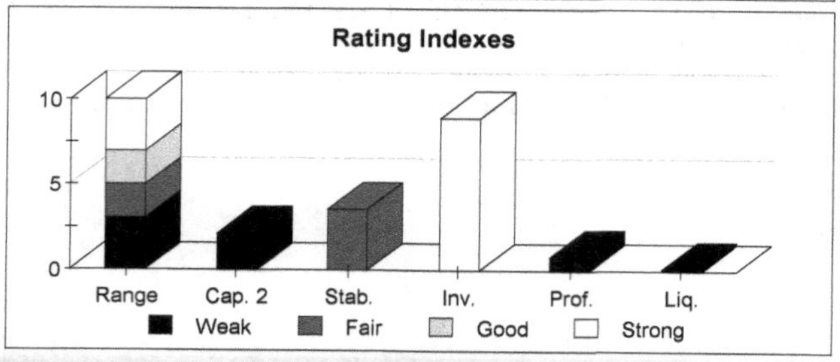


## MAMSI L&H INS CO — C+ — Fair

**Major Rating Factors:** Excellent profitability (8.1 on a scale of 0 to 10). Strong capitalization (10.0) based on excellent current risk-adjusted capital (severe loss scenario). High quality investment portfolio (9.9).
**Other Rating Factors:** Excellent liquidity (7.3) with ample operational cash flow and liquid investments.
**Principal Business:** Comp med (100%)
**Mem Phys: 16:** 48,611 **15:** 45,388 **16 MLR** 69.5% **/ 16 Admin Exp** N/A
**Enroll(000): Q3 17:** 19 **16:** 15 **15:** 12 **Med Exp PMPM:** $272
**Principal Investments:** Cash and equiv (94%), long-term bonds (6%)
**Provider Compensation ($000):** Contr fee ($41,811), bonus arrang ($19), capitation ($10), FFS ($2)
**Total Member Encounters:** Phys (104,131), non-phys (4,756)
**Group Affiliation:** UnitedHealth Group Incorporated
**Licensed in:** DC, DE, LA, MD, MO, ND, TX, VA, WV
**Address:** 800 KING FARM BLVD, ROCKVILLE, MD 20850
**Phone:** (301) 762-8205 **Dom State:** MD **Commenced Bus:** November 1955

| Data Date | Rating | RACR #1 | RACR #2 | Total Assets ($mil) | Capital ($mil) | Net Premium ($mil) | Net Income ($mil) |
|---|---|---|---|---|---|---|---|
| 9-17 | C+ | 4.19 | 3.49 | 25.9 | 13.4 | 56.9 | 4.6 |
| 9-16 | C+ | 7.27 | 6.06 | 24.8 | 16.2 | 46.5 | 4.6 |
| 2016 | C+ | 2.90 | 2.42 | 21.9 | 8.8 | 61.6 | 4.2 |
| 2015 | C+ | 5.42 | 4.52 | 21.1 | 11.7 | 52.6 | 4.9 |
| 2014 | B | 4.31 | 3.60 | 25.7 | 17.2 | 66.4 | 2.3 |
| 2013 | B- | 4.00 | 3.34 | 24.4 | 15.7 | 73.3 | 6.6 |
| 2012 | C+ | 3.39 | 2.83 | 15.7 | 9.2 | 54.4 | 4.7 |

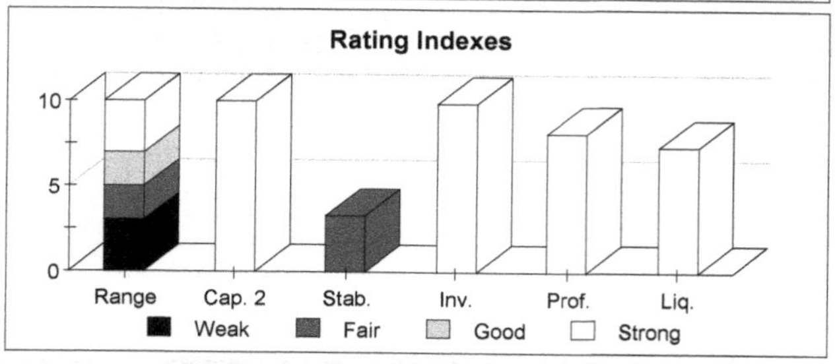

## MANHATTAN LIFE INSURANCE COMPANY B Good

**Major Rating Factors:** Good overall results on stability tests (5.4 on a scale of 0 to 10) despite fair financial strength of affiliated Manhattan Life Group Inc. Other stability subfactors include good operational trends and good risk diversification. Good capitalization (6.4) based on good risk adjusted capital (severe loss scenario). Capital levels have been relatively consistent over the last five years. Good quality investment portfolio (6.1).
**Other Rating Factors:** Good liquidity (6.4). Fair profitability (4.0) with investment income below regulatory standards in relation to interest assumptions of reserves.
**Principal Business:** Individual annuities (49%), individual health insurance (43%), individual life insurance (6%), group health insurance (2%), and reinsurance (1%).
**Principal Investments:** NonCMO investment grade bonds (65%), CMOs and structured securities (9%), common & preferred stock (7%), mortgages in good standing (5%), and misc. investments (10%).
**Investments in Affiliates:** 6%
**Group Affiliation:** Manhattan Life Group Inc
**Licensed in:** All states, the District of Columbia and Puerto Rico
**Commenced Business:** August 1850
**Address:** 225 Community Drive Suite 11, Great Neck, NY 11021
**Phone:** (713) 529-0045 **Domicile State:** NY **NAIC Code:** 65870

| Data Date | Rating | RACR #1 | RACR #2 | Total Assets ($mil) | Capital ($mil) | Net Premium ($mil) | Net Income ($mil) |
|---|---|---|---|---|---|---|---|
| 9-17 | B | 1.28 | 0.93 | 577.7 | 53.0 | 73.1 | 7.4 |
| 9-16 | B | 1.23 | 0.94 | 509.4 | 49.9 | 87.4 | 13.7 |
| 2016 | B | 1.26 | 0.94 | 543.1 | 51.1 | 125.6 | 13.9 |
| 2015 | B | 1.18 | 0.91 | 484.6 | 47.1 | 152.1 | 11.2 |
| 2014 | B | 1.17 | 0.96 | 362.4 | 41.0 | 71.1 | 2.8 |
| 2013 | B | 1.23 | 1.03 | 310.4 | 36.9 | 12.1 | 3.7 |
| 2012 | C+ | 1.32 | 1.15 | 320.8 | 39.4 | 12.4 | 2.4 |

| Manhattan Life Group Inc<br>Composite Group Rating: C+<br>Largest Group Members | Assets ($mil) | Rating |
|---|---|---|
| WESTERN UNITED LIFE ASR CO | 1158 | B- |
| MANHATTAN LIFE INS CO | 543 | B |
| MANHATTANLIFE ASSR CO OF AM | 385 | C |
| FAMILY LIFE INS CO | 156 | C |

## MARTINS POINT GENERATIONS ADVANTAGE C- Fair

**Major Rating Factors:** Weak profitability index (1.3 on a scale of 0 to 10). Good liquidity (6.2) with sufficient resources (cash flows and marketable investments) to handle a spike in claims. Strong capitalization (7.2) based on excellent current risk-adjusted capital (severe loss scenario).
**Other Rating Factors:** High quality investment portfolio (9.2).
**Principal Business:** Medicare (100%)
**Mem Phys: 16:** 12,947 **15:** N/A **16 MLR** 93.5% **/ 16 Admin Exp** N/A
**Enroll(000): Q3 17:** 42 **16:** 40 **15:** 36 **Med Exp PMPM:** $668
**Principal Investments:** Long-term bonds (55%), cash and equiv (23%), nonaffiliate common stock (22%)
**Provider Compensation ($000):** Bonus arrang ($207,651), contr fee ($95,795), capitation ($1,294)
**Total Member Encounters:** Phys (497,407), non-phys (239,118)
**Group Affiliation:** Penobscot Bay Medical Associates
**Licensed in:** ME, NH
**Address:** 331 Veranda St, Portland, ME 04103
**Phone:** (207) 774-5801 **Dom State:** ME **Commenced Bus:** January 2016

| Data Date | Rating | RACR #1 | RACR #2 | Total Assets ($mil) | Capital ($mil) | Net Premium ($mil) | Net Income ($mil) |
|---|---|---|---|---|---|---|---|
| 9-17 | C- | 1.47 | 1.23 | 129.6 | 49.4 | 289.3 | 4.5 |
| 9-16 | N/A | N/A | N/A | 105.7 | 35.3 | 242.5 | -13.8 |
| 2016 | D+ | 1.28 | 1.07 | 88.4 | 43.3 | 329.3 | -13.2 |
| 2015 | N/A | N/A | N/A | 73.6 | 36.9 | 275.1 | N/A |
| 2014 | N/A | N/A | N/A | 62.8 | 34.5 | 231.6 | N/A |
| 2013 | N/A | N/A | N/A | 40.6 | 17.7 | 171.0 | N/A |
| 2012 | N/A | N/A | N/A | 31.6 | 13.9 | 132.1 | N/A |

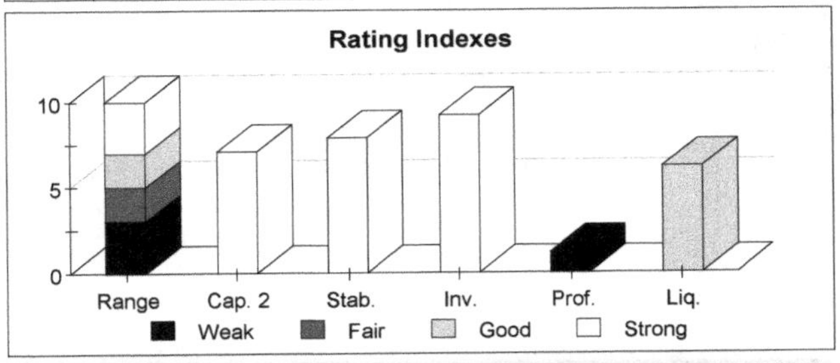


## MATTHEW THORNTON HEALTH PLAN B Good

**Major Rating Factors:** Good liquidity (6.8 on a scale of 0 to 10) with sufficient resources (cash flows and marketable investments) to handle a spike in claims. Fair overall results on stability tests (4.3). Rating is significantly influenced by the good financial results of Anthem Inc. Excellent profitability (9.0).
**Other Rating Factors:** Strong capitalization index (10.0) based on excellent current risk-adjusted capital (severe loss scenario). High quality investment portfolio (8.2).
**Principal Business:** Comp med (98%), Medicare (2%)
**Mem Phys: 16:** 17,752 **15:** 15,624 **16 MLR** 82.6% **/ 16 Admin Exp** N/A
**Enroll(000): Q3 17:** 94 **16:** 94 **15:** 96 **Med Exp PMPM:** $357
**Principal Investments:** Long-term bonds (96%), other (6%)
**Provider Compensation ($000):** Contr fee ($339,969), FFS ($77,195), bonus arrang ($3,365), capitation ($107), other ($249)
**Total Member Encounters:** Phys (597,399), non-phys (181,624)
**Group Affiliation:** Anthem Inc
**Licensed in:** NH
**Address:** 1155 ELM STREET, MANCHESTER, NH 03101
**Phone:** (603) 541-2000 **Dom State:** NH **Commenced Bus:** November 1971

| Data Date | Rating | RACR #1 | RACR #2 | Total Assets ($mil) | Capital ($mil) | Net Premium ($mil) | Net Income ($mil) |
|---|---|---|---|---|---|---|---|
| 9-17 | B | 4.08 | 3.40 | 232.5 | 117.3 | 398.7 | 20.9 |
| 9-16 | B+ | 4.69 | 3.91 | 238.6 | 126.4 | 381.4 | 17.2 |
| 2016 | B | 3.32 | 2.77 | 202.4 | 94.1 | 508.0 | 13.3 |
| 2015 | A- | 4.17 | 3.47 | 218.8 | 111.3 | 514.6 | 33.9 |
| 2014 | A- | 3.44 | 2.87 | 230.3 | 106.9 | 585.8 | 36.7 |
| 2013 | A- | 3.03 | 2.52 | 187.5 | 92.2 | 492.1 | 25.3 |
| 2012 | B | 2.84 | 2.37 | 155.2 | 89.3 | 511.6 | 28.0 |

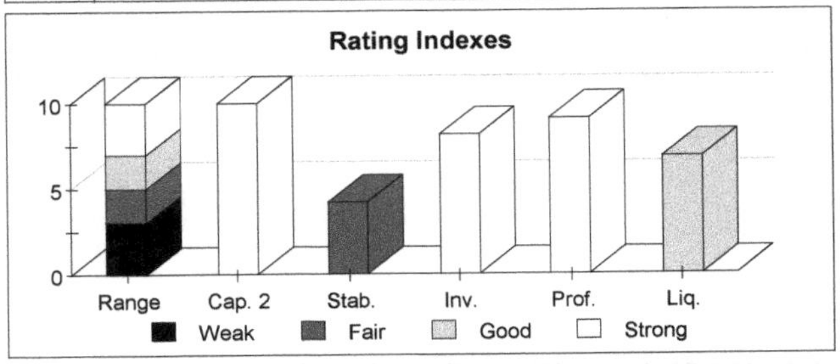

## MCLAREN HEALTH PLAN COMMUNITY B- Good

**Major Rating Factors:** Fair profitability index (3.0 on a scale of 0 to 10). Strong capitalization (8.2) based on excellent current risk-adjusted capital (severe loss scenario). High quality investment portfolio (9.9).
**Other Rating Factors:** Excellent liquidity (7.2) with ample operational cash flow and liquid investments.
**Principal Business:** Comp med (100%)
**Mem Phys: 16:** 26,656 **15:** 23,760 **16 MLR** 92.0% **/ 16 Admin Exp** N/A
**Enroll(000): Q3 17:** 28 **16:** 27 **15:** N/A **Med Exp PMPM:** $335
**Principal Investments:** Cash and equiv (95%), long-term bonds (4%), other (1%)
**Provider Compensation ($000):** Contr fee ($39,486), FFS ($1,567), capitation ($495)
**Total Member Encounters:** Phys (97,643), non-phys (16,704)
**Group Affiliation:** McLaren Health Care Corporation
**Licensed in:** MI
**Address:** G3245 Beecher Rd, Flint, MI 48532
**Phone:** (888) 327-0671 **Dom State:** MI **Commenced Bus:** February 2012

| Data Date | Rating | RACR #1 | RACR #2 | Total Assets ($mil) | Capital ($mil) | Net Premium ($mil) | Net Income ($mil) |
|---|---|---|---|---|---|---|---|
| 9-17 | B- | 2.31 | 1.92 | 35.2 | 18.0 | 88.1 | 1.2 |
| 9-16 | N/A | N/A | N/A | 23.5 | 15.4 | 31.1 | -2.4 |
| 2016 | C+ | 1.75 | 1.46 | 32.3 | 13.9 | 61.0 | -1.0 |
| 2015 | N/A | N/A | N/A | 3.1 | 3.0 | N/A | N/A |
| 2014 | N/A | N/A | N/A | 3.0 | 3.0 | N/A | N/A |
| 2013 | N/A | N/A | N/A | 3.0 | 3.0 | N/A | N/A |
| 2012 | N/A | N/A | N/A | 3.0 | 3.0 | N/A | N/A |

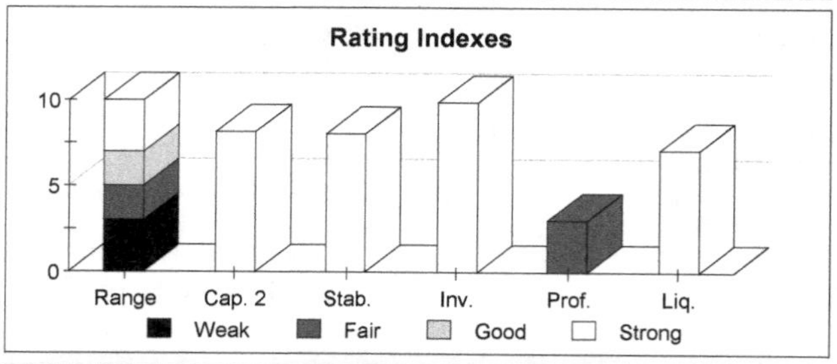


## MCLAREN HEALTH PLAN INC * A- Excellent

**Major Rating Factors:** Excellent profitability (8.9 on a scale of 0 to 10). Strong capitalization index (7.2) based on excellent current risk-adjusted capital (severe loss scenario). High quality investment portfolio (9.0).
**Other Rating Factors:** Excellent overall results on stability tests (8.3). Excellent liquidity (6.9) with sufficient resources (cash flows and marketable investments) to handle a spike in claims
**Principal Business:** Medicaid (94%), comp med (5%)
**Mem Phys: 16:** 26,656 **15:** 23,760 **16 MLR** 88.5% **/ 16 Admin Exp** N/A
**Enroll(000): Q3 17:** 195 **16:** 186 **15:** 204 **Med Exp PMPM:** $347
**Principal Investments:** Cash and equiv (79%), nonaffiliate common stock (11%), affiliate common stock (8%), real estate (1%)
**Provider Compensation ($000):** Contr fee ($606,639), capitation ($214,900), FFS ($24,044)
**Total Member Encounters:** Phys (1,538,569), non-phys (319,375)
**Group Affiliation:** McLaren Health Care Corporation
**Licensed in:** MI
**Address:** G-3245 Beecher Rd, FLINT, MI 48532
**Phone:** (810) 733-9723 **Dom State:** MI **Commenced Bus:** August 1996

| Data Date | Rating | RACR #1 | RACR #2 | Total Assets ($mil) | Capital ($mil) | Net Premium ($mil) | Net Income ($mil) |
|---|---|---|---|---|---|---|---|
| 9-17 | A- | 1.50 | 1.25 | 239.2 | 102.8 | 655.5 | 14.7 |
| 9-16 | B | 1.15 | 0.96 | 209.6 | 79.3 | 709.3 | 13.3 |
| 2016 | B | 1.20 | 1.00 | 207.5 | 83.0 | 929.6 | 20.5 |
| 2015 | B | 1.01 | 0.84 | 231.5 | 70.8 | 902.6 | 23.4 |
| 2014 | B- | 0.87 | 0.72 | 170.2 | 51.9 | 722.6 | 12.2 |
| 2013 | C | 0.92 | 0.77 | 130.3 | 44.2 | 532.6 | -0.2 |
| 2012 | C | 1.32 | 1.10 | 116.7 | 42.4 | 453.2 | 14.8 |

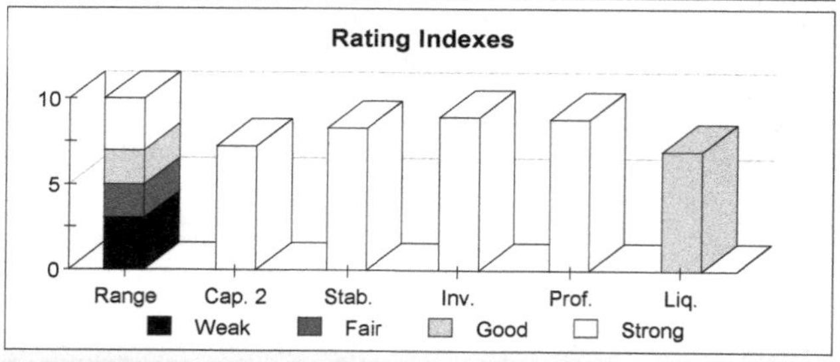


## MCS ADVANTAGE INC E+ Very Weak

**Major Rating Factors:** Fair capitalization (3.7 on a scale of 0 to 10) based on weak current risk-adjusted capital (moderate loss scenario). Good overall profitability index (5.7). Good liquidity (6.9) with sufficient resources (cash flows and marketable investments) to handle a spike in claims.
**Other Rating Factors:** High quality investment portfolio (9.9).
**Principal Business:** Medicare (100%)
**Mem Phys: 16:** 9,869 **15:** 11,485 **16 MLR** 86.8% **/ 16 Admin Exp** N/A
**Enroll(000): Q3 17:** 194 **16:** 215 **15:** 180 **Med Exp PMPM:** $618
**Principal Investments:** Cash and equiv (58%), long-term bonds (42%)
**Provider Compensation ($000):** Contr fee ($1,172,587), capitation ($379,640)
**Total Member Encounters:** Phys (3,022,852), non-phys (135,921)
**Group Affiliation:** Medical Card System Inc
**Licensed in:** PR
**Address:** Ste 203 255 Ponce de LeÃ³n Ave, San Juan, PR 00917
**Phone:** (787) 758-2500 **Dom State:** PR **Commenced Bus:** February 2007

| Data Date | Rating | RACR #1 | RACR #2 | Total Assets ($mil) | Capital ($mil) | Net Premium ($mil) | Net Income ($mil) |
|---|---|---|---|---|---|---|---|
| 9-17 | E+ | 0.73 | 0.61 | 469.1 | 83.6 | 1,259.3 | 20.3 |
| 9-16 | E- | 0.38 | 0.32 | 392.7 | 41.9 | 1,300.9 | 4.0 |
| 2016 | E | 0.64 | 0.53 | 251.7 | 74.0 | 1,756.1 | 19.5 |
| 2015 | E | 0.47 | 0.40 | 287.3 | 55.7 | 1,535.4 | 6.3 |
| 2014 | E+ | 0.45 | 0.38 | 217.7 | 51.6 | 1,462.8 | -21.1 |
| 2013 | C- | 0.75 | 0.63 | 189.0 | 63.1 | 1,173.8 | 3.7 |
| 2012 | C- | 0.84 | 0.70 | 200.1 | 62.8 | 1,146.4 | 27.3 |

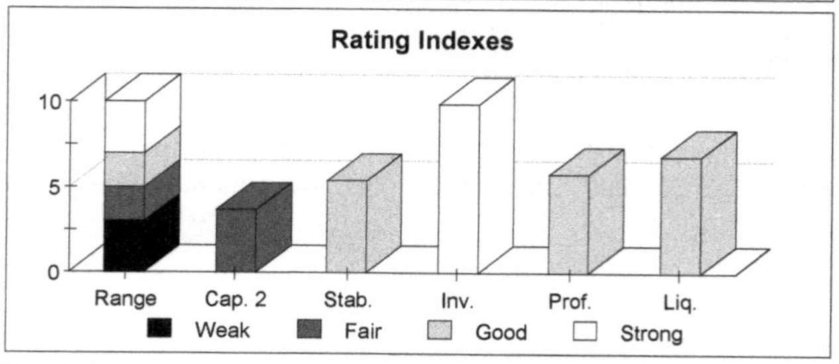

## MCS LIFE INSURANCE COMPANY D- Weak

**Major Rating Factors:** Weak overall results on stability tests (1.0 on a scale of 0 to 10) including potential financial drain due to affiliation with Medical Card System Inc and weak risk adjusted capital in prior years. Poor overall capitalization (2.9) based on excessive policy leverage and weak risk adjusted capital (moderate loss scenario). Weak liquidity (2.0).
**Other Rating Factors:** Fair profitability (3.1). High quality investment portfolio (8.7).
**Principal Business:** Group health insurance (91%), individual health insurance (9%), and group life insurance (1%).
**Principal Investments:** Cash (80%), nonCMO investment grade bonds (17%), common & preferred stock (1%), CMOs and structured securities (1%), and noninv. grade bonds (1%).
**Investments in Affiliates:** None
**Group Affiliation:** Medical Card System Inc
**Licensed in:** PR
**Commenced Business:** January 1996
**Address:** Ste 900 255 Ponce de Leon Ave, San Juan, PR 917
**Phone:** (787) 758-2500 **Domicile State:** PR **NAIC Code:** 60030

| Data Date | Rating | RACR #1 | RACR #2 | Total Assets ($mil) | Capital ($mil) | Net Premium ($mil) | Net Income ($mil) |
|---|---|---|---|---|---|---|---|
| 9-17 | D- | 0.56 | 0.49 | 83.9 | 30.3 | 233.3 | 9.1 |
| 9-16 | E | 0.23 | 0.20 | 63.7 | 13.1 | 228.3 | 0.7 |
| 2016 | E | 0.38 | 0.34 | 68.7 | 20.6 | 308.4 | 9.2 |
| 2015 | E | 0.18 | 0.16 | 71.7 | 10.4 | 306.4 | -10.7 |
| 2014 | E+ | 0.42 | 0.37 | 60.9 | 20.2 | 277.5 | -1.7 |
| 2013 | D- | 0.44 | 0.36 | 67.3 | 22.2 | 252.4 | 1.2 |
| 2012 | D- | 0.44 | 0.37 | 55.4 | 17.3 | 215.5 | 1.8 |

| Medical Card System Inc<br>Composite Group Rating: E+<br>Largest Group Members | Assets ($mil) | Rating |
|---|---|---|
| MCS ADVANTAGE INC | 252 | E |
| MCS LIFE INS CO | 69 | D- |

## MD INDIVIDUAL PRACTICE ASSOC INC B- Good

**Major Rating Factors:** Fair overall results on stability tests (4.5 on a scale of 0 to 10) based on a significant 19% decrease in enrollment during the period. Rating is significantly influenced by the fair financial results of UnitedHealth Group Incorporated. Excellent profitability (8.3). Strong capitalization index (10.0) based on excellent current risk-adjusted capital (severe loss scenario).
**Other Rating Factors:** High quality investment portfolio (9.9). Excellent liquidity (7.1) with ample operational cash flow and liquid investments.
**Principal Business:** FEHB (100%)
**Mem Phys: 16:** 40,566 **15:** 38,327 **16 MLR** 82.7% **/ 16 Admin Exp** N/A
**Enroll(000): Q3 17:** 42 **16:** 48 **15:** 60 **Med Exp PMPM:** $432
**Principal Investments:** Cash and equiv (98%), long-term bonds (2%)
**Provider Compensation ($000):** Contr fee ($251,463), capitation ($6,854), bonus arrang ($225), FFS ($3)
**Total Member Encounters:** Phys (446,071), non-phys (38,232)
**Group Affiliation:** UnitedHealth Group Incorporated
**Licensed in:** DC, MD, VA
**Address:** 800 KING FARM BLVD, ROCKVILLE, MD 20850
**Phone:** (240) 683-5250 **Dom State:** MD **Commenced Bus:** December 1980

| Data Date | Rating | RACR #1 | RACR #2 | Total Assets ($mil) | Capital ($mil) | Net Premium ($mil) | Net Income ($mil) |
|---|---|---|---|---|---|---|---|
| 9-17 | B- | 11.24 | 9.36 | 79.8 | 46.1 | 214.7 | 20.6 |
| 9-16 | C | 6.44 | 5.37 | 79.8 | 37.0 | 229.9 | 12.4 |
| 2016 | B- | 8.30 | 6.92 | 72.3 | 33.1 | 307.8 | 17.1 |
| 2015 | C | 5.68 | 4.74 | 76.3 | 32.2 | 350.0 | 16.5 |
| 2014 | B- | 10.88 | 9.07 | 107.9 | 66.3 | 401.5 | 35.6 |
| 2013 | B- | 8.17 | 6.81 | 93.4 | 50.7 | 417.3 | 34.8 |
| 2012 | C+ | 5.24 | 4.37 | 76.4 | 31.2 | 485.7 | 42.4 |

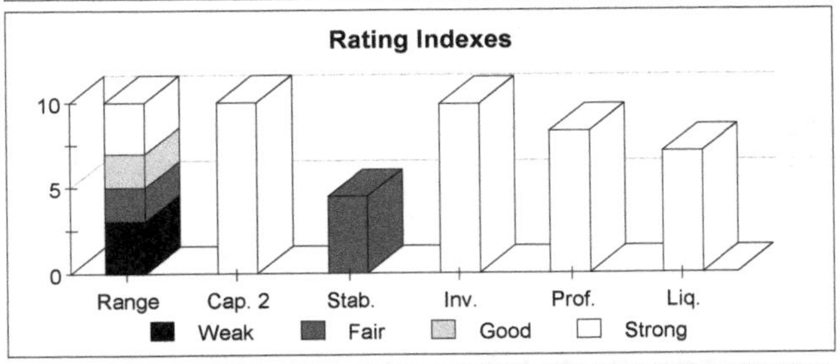


## MDWISE INC B Good

**Major Rating Factors:** Excellent profitability (7.2 on a scale of 0 to 10). Strong capitalization index (7.0) based on excellent current risk-adjusted capital (severe loss scenario). High quality investment portfolio (9.9).
**Other Rating Factors:** Excellent overall results on stability tests (6.9). Excellent liquidity (7.1) with ample operational cash flow and liquid investments
**Principal Business:** Medicaid (100%)
**Mem Phys: 16:** 24,245 **15:** 20,210 **16 MLR** 95.2% **/ 16 Admin Exp** N/A
**Enroll(000): Q3 17:** 345 **16:** 423 **15:** 379 **Med Exp PMPM:** $278
**Principal Investments:** Cash and equiv (67%), long-term bonds (32%), nonaffiliate common stock (1%)
**Provider Compensation ($000):** Capitation ($1,364,767)
**Total Member Encounters:** Phys (1,915,205)
**Group Affiliation:** MDwise Inc
**Licensed in:** IN
**Address:** 1200 Madison Avenue Suite 400, Indianapolis, IN 46225
**Phone:** (317) 822-7300 **Dom State:** IN **Commenced Bus:** May 1989

| Data Date | Rating | RACR #1 | RACR #2 | Total Assets ($mil) | Capital ($mil) | Net Premium ($mil) | Net Income ($mil) |
|---|---|---|---|---|---|---|---|
| 9-17 | B | 1.35 | 1.13 | 207.9 | 96.4 | 1,093.5 | 7.1 |
| 9-16 | B | 1.78 | 1.49 | 219.5 | 88.3 | 1,070.6 | 23.0 |
| 2016 | B | 1.32 | 1.10 | 199.6 | 93.8 | 1,433.7 | 28.8 |
| 2015 | B | 1.47 | 1.23 | 144.2 | 69.4 | 1,033.2 | 20.3 |
| 2014 | B- | 1.28 | 1.07 | 76.6 | 39.0 | 583.8 | 3.2 |
| 2013 | C+ | 1.25 | 1.04 | 47.9 | 31.0 | 449.9 | -2.7 |
| 2012 | B- | 1.56 | 1.30 | 45.6 | 37.4 | 445.4 | 2.5 |

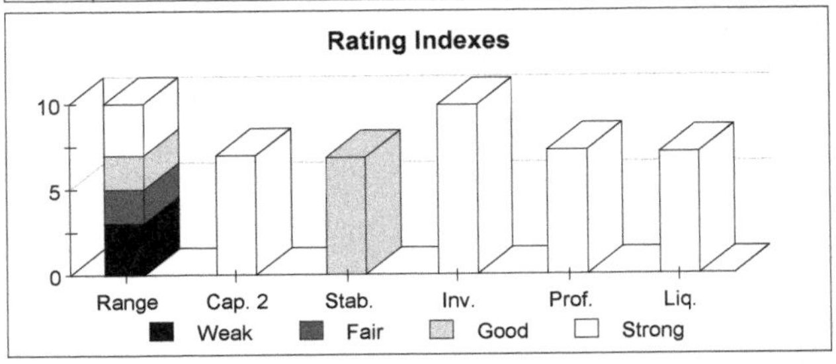

## MDWISE MARKETPLACE INC — C — Fair

**Major Rating Factors:** Weak profitability index (0.9 on a scale of 0 to 10). Strong capitalization (7.1) based on excellent current risk-adjusted capital (severe loss scenario). High quality investment portfolio (9.9).
**Other Rating Factors:** Excellent liquidity (7.5) with ample operational cash flow and liquid investments.
**Principal Business:** Comp med (100%)
**Mem Phys: 16:** 18,056 **15:** 13,422 **16 MLR** 86.2% **/ 16 Admin Exp** N/A
**Enroll(000): Q3 17:** 28 **16:** 38 **15:** 15 **Med Exp PMPM:** $324
**Principal Investments:** Cash and equiv (100%)
**Provider Compensation ($000):** Capitation ($117,786)
**Total Member Encounters:** Phys (158,236)
**Group Affiliation:** Indiana University Health Inc
**Licensed in:** IN
**Address:** 1200 Madison Ave Ste 400, Indianapolis, IN 46225
**Phone:** (317) 822-7300 **Dom State:** IN **Commenced Bus:** August 2014

| Data Date | Rating | RACR #1 | RACR #2 | Total Assets ($mil) | Capital ($mil) | Net Premium ($mil) | Net Income ($mil) |
|---|---|---|---|---|---|---|---|
| 9-17 | C | 1.46 | 1.22 | 51.4 | 9.8 | 113.0 | 0.4 |
| 9-16 | C | 1.74 | 1.45 | 45.6 | 8.9 | 103.8 | -0.9 |
| 2016 | C | 1.40 | 1.17 | 47.4 | 9.4 | 136.8 | -3.4 |
| 2015 | C | 1.32 | 1.10 | 61.7 | 6.8 | 104.5 | -1.9 |
| 2014 | U | 1.72 | 1.43 | 19.8 | 3.7 | 22.9 | -1.2 |
| 2013 | N/A | N/A | N/A | N/A | N/A | N/A | N/A |
| 2012 | N/A | N/A | N/A | N/A | N/A | N/A | N/A |

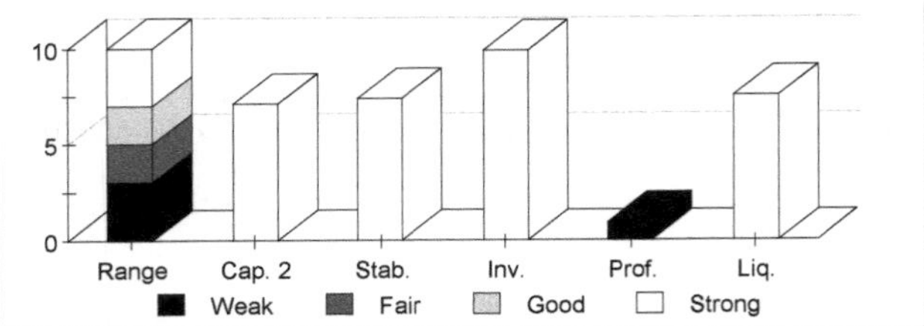


## MEDAMERICA INSURANCE COMPANY — C — Fair

**Major Rating Factors:** Fair current capitalization (4.9 on a scale of 0 to 10) based on fair risk adjusted capital (moderate loss scenario), although results have slipped from the good range during the last year. Fair overall results on stability tests (4.1) including fair risk adjusted capital in prior years. Low quality investment portfolio (0.8).
**Other Rating Factors:** Weak profitability (1.7) with operating losses during the first nine months of 2017. Excellent liquidity (8.7).
**Principal Business:** Individual health insurance (65%), reinsurance (27%), and group health insurance (8%).
**Principal Investments:** NonCMO investment grade bonds (84%), CMOs and structured securities (5%), noninv. grade bonds (5%), and cash (1%).
**Investments in Affiliates:** None
**Group Affiliation:** Lifetime Healthcare Inc
**Licensed in:** All states except FL, NY, PR
**Commenced Business:** August 1966
**Address:** 651 Holiday Drive Foster Plaza, Pittsburgh, PA 15220-2740
**Phone:** (585) 238-4659 **Domicile State:** PA **NAIC Code:** 69515

| Data Date | Rating | RACR #1 | RACR #2 | Total Assets ($mil) | Capital ($mil) | Net Premium ($mil) | Net Income ($mil) |
|---|---|---|---|---|---|---|---|
| 9-17 | C | 0.99 | 0.54 | 939.5 | 28.0 | 47.0 | -2.0 |
| 9-16 | C | 1.21 | 0.65 | 921.2 | 33.3 | 48.6 | 0.7 |
| 2016 | B- | 1.14 | 0.62 | 939.2 | 31.7 | 64.6 | -1.2 |
| 2015 | B | 1.23 | 0.67 | 890.9 | 34.4 | 63.2 | -45.8 |
| 2014 | B | 1.66 | 0.91 | 859.4 | 43.2 | 60.9 | -1.9 |
| 2013 | B | 1.85 | 1.00 | 866.2 | 43.6 | 54.6 | 1.7 |
| 2012 | B | 1.44 | 0.78 | 733.7 | 28.7 | 49.0 | -7.7 |

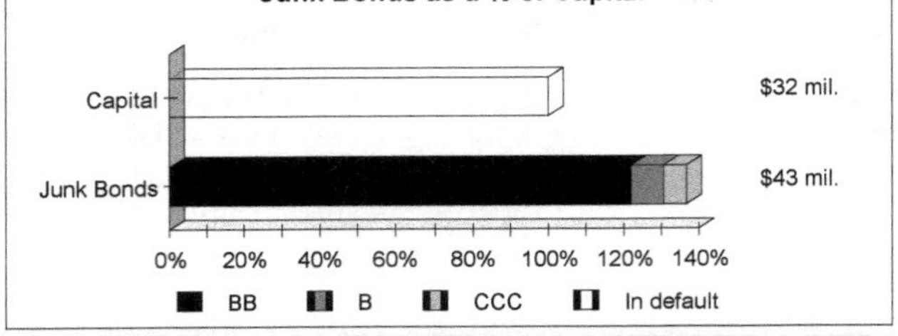


## MEDCO CONTAINMENT INS CO OF NY — B — Good

**Major Rating Factors:** Fair profitability index (3.2 on a scale of 0 to 10). Strong capitalization (10.0) based on excellent current risk-adjusted capital (severe loss scenario). High quality investment portfolio (9.9).
**Other Rating Factors:** Excellent liquidity (7.9) with ample operational cash flow and liquid investments.
**Principal Business:** Other (100%)
**Mem Phys: 16:** N/A **15:** N/A **16 MLR** 73.8% **/ 16 Admin Exp** N/A
**Enroll(000): Q3 17:** 97 **16:** 95 **15:** 84 **Med Exp PMPM:** $81
**Principal Investments:** Cash and equiv (100%)
**Provider Compensation ($000):** FFS ($105,209)
**Total Member Encounters:** N/A
**Group Affiliation:** Express Scripts Holding Company
**Licensed in:** NY
**Address:** 433 River St Ste 800, Troy, NY 12180
**Phone:** (800) 322-5455 **Dom State:** NY **Commenced Bus:** July 1989

| Data Date | Rating | RACR #1 | RACR #2 | Total Assets ($mil) | Capital ($mil) | Net Premium ($mil) | Net Income ($mil) |
|---|---|---|---|---|---|---|---|
| 9-17 | B | 5.03 | 4.19 | 124.1 | 50.2 | 102.1 | -5.5 |
| 9-16 | B | 9.91 | 8.26 | 122.8 | 48.4 | 92.9 | -2.0 |
| 2016 | B | 5.71 | 4.76 | 67.4 | 55.8 | 123.8 | 5.2 |
| 2015 | B- | 9.27 | 7.72 | 59.4 | 47.6 | 102.3 | -0.5 |
| 2014 | B+ | 11.11 | 9.26 | 59.1 | 50.4 | 100.0 | -3.3 |
| 2013 | A- | 17.98 | 14.98 | 62.0 | 53.8 | 77.2 | 6.2 |
| 2012 | B+ | 14.63 | 12.19 | 54.9 | 48.3 | 83.3 | 5.5 |

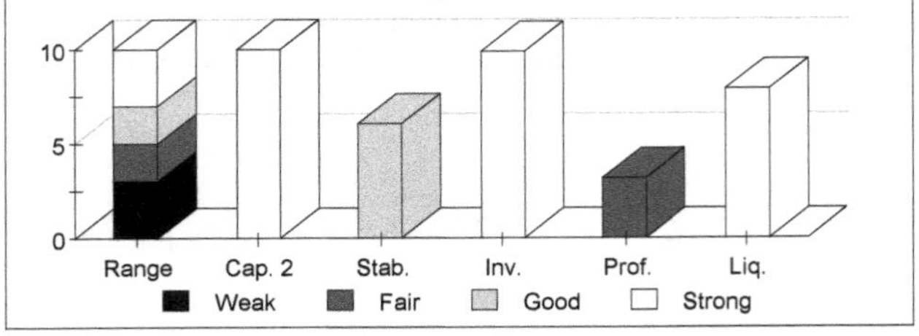

## MEDCO CONTAINMENT LIFE INS CO * A- Excellent

**Major Rating Factors:** Excellent profitability (8.9 on a scale of 0 to 10). Strong capitalization (10.0) based on excellent current risk-adjusted capital (severe loss scenario). High quality investment portfolio (9.9).
**Other Rating Factors:** Excellent liquidity (9.3) with ample operational cash flow and liquid investments.
**Principal Business:** Other (100%)
**Mem Phys: 16:** N/A **15:** N/A **16 MLR** 77.9% **/ 16 Admin Exp** N/A
**Enroll(000): Q3 17:** 595 **16:** 524 **15:** 515 **Med Exp PMPM:** $84
**Principal Investments:** Cash and equiv (99%), long-term bonds (1%)
**Provider Compensation ($000):** FFS ($574,504)
**Total Member Encounters:** N/A
**Group Affiliation:** Express Scripts Holding Company
**Licensed in:** All states except NY
**Address:** 4415 Lewis Rd Ste #1, Harrisburg, PA 17111
**Phone:** (800) 332-5455 **Dom State:** PA **Commenced Bus:** July 1955

| Data Date | Rating | RACR #1 | RACR #2 | Total Assets ($mil) | Capital ($mil) | Net Premium ($mil) | Net Income ($mil) |
|---|---|---|---|---|---|---|---|
| 9-17 | A- | 5.63 | 4.69 | 1,113.2 | 406.5 | 623.9 | 4.4 |
| 9-16 | B | 9.59 | 7.99 | 1,114.4 | 422.2 | 515.1 | 41.6 |
| 2016 | A- | 6.54 | 5.45 | 1,689.0 | 462.5 | 672.2 | 80.5 |
| 2015 | B | 6.25 | 5.21 | 1,391.5 | 403.5 | 657.7 | 28.5 |
| 2014 | B+ | 8.29 | 6.91 | 1,180.8 | 309.6 | 584.0 | 23.6 |
| 2013 | B+ | 9.38 | 7.82 | 807.0 | 284.4 | 513.3 | 70.9 |
| 2012 | B+ | 7.00 | 5.83 | 396.9 | 226.3 | 598.0 | 42.6 |

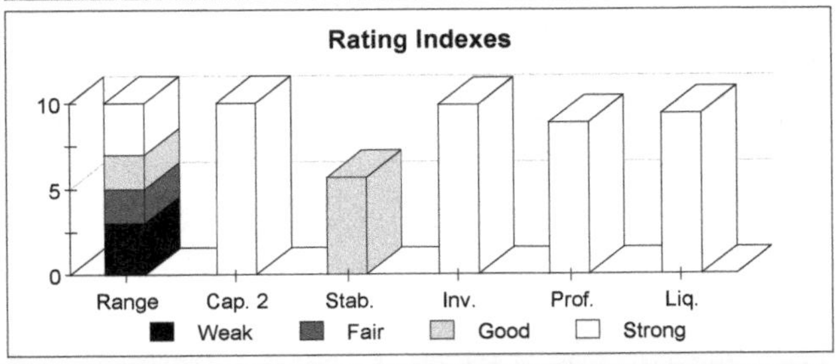


## MEDICA HEALTH PLANS C Fair

**Major Rating Factors:** Weak profitability index (1.3 on a scale of 0 to 10). Weak overall results on stability tests (2.1) based on an excessive 71% enrollment growth during the period. Good liquidity (6.8) with sufficient resources (cash flows and marketable investments) to handle a spike in claims.
**Other Rating Factors:** Strong capitalization index (7.9) based on excellent current risk-adjusted capital (severe loss scenario). High quality investment portfolio (8.1).
**Principal Business:** Medicaid (94%), comp med (6%)
**Mem Phys: 16:** 101,764 **15:** 97,294 **16 MLR** 96.0% **/ 16 Admin Exp** N/A
**Enroll(000): Q3 17:** 33 **16:** 346 **15:** 203 **Med Exp PMPM:** $532
**Principal Investments:** Long-term bonds (37%), cash and equiv (33%), real estate (15%), nonaffiliate common stock (12%), other (4%)
**Provider Compensation ($000):** Contr fee ($1,470,931), bonus arrang ($685,743), capitation ($2,804), other ($42,566)
**Total Member Encounters:** Phys (5,008,996), non-phys (2,605,289)
**Group Affiliation:** Medica Holding Company
**Licensed in:** IA, MN, ND, SD
**Address:** 401 CARLSON PARKWAY, MINNETONKA, MN 55305
**Phone:** (952) 992-2900 **Dom State:** MN **Commenced Bus:** December 1974

| Data Date | Rating | RACR #1 | RACR #2 | Total Assets ($mil) | Capital ($mil) | Net Premium ($mil) | Net Income ($mil) |
|---|---|---|---|---|---|---|---|
| 9-17 | C | 2.12 | 1.76 | 535.5 | 353.9 | 1,064.4 | 57.0 |
| 9-16 | B- | 3.44 | 2.87 | 714.9 | 410.2 | 1,747.0 | -92.9 |
| 2016 | C | 1.80 | 1.50 | 803.3 | 317.4 | 2,327.5 | -189.9 |
| 2015 | B+ | 4.37 | 3.64 | 896.8 | 504.0 | 1,777.0 | 45.4 |
| 2014 | B+ | 4.10 | 3.41 | 856.9 | 460.1 | 1,719.6 | 46.9 |
| 2013 | A- | 3.20 | 2.66 | 686.5 | 404.5 | 1,778.6 | -4.3 |
| 2012 | A | 4.09 | 3.41 | 681.8 | 442.1 | 1,594.5 | 44.5 |

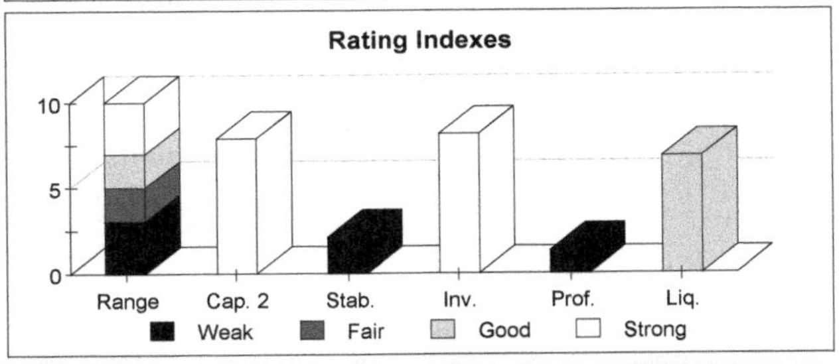


## MEDICA HEALTH PLANS OF WI C Fair

**Major Rating Factors:** Weak profitability index (0.9 on a scale of 0 to 10). Weak overall results on stability tests (2.7) based on an excessive 273% enrollment growth during the period. Potentially strong support from affiliation with Medica Holding Company. Good liquidity (6.1) with sufficient resources (cash flows and marketable investments) to handle a spike in claims.
**Other Rating Factors:** Strong capitalization index (8.3) based on excellent current risk-adjusted capital (severe loss scenario). High quality investment portfolio (9.9).
**Principal Business:** Comp med (100%)
**Mem Phys: 16:** 101,764 **15:** 97,294 **16 MLR** 107.1% **/ 16 Admin Exp** N/A
**Enroll(000): Q3 17:** 36 **16:** 49 **15:** 13 **Med Exp PMPM:** $395
**Principal Investments:** Long-term bonds (54%), cash and equiv (46%)
**Provider Compensation ($000):** Contr fee ($137,478), bonus arrang ($79,069)
**Total Member Encounters:** Phys (372,100), non-phys (39,061)
**Group Affiliation:** Medica Holding Company
**Licensed in:** MN, WI
**Address:** 401 CARLSON PARKWAY, MINNETONKA, MN 55305
**Phone:** (952) 992-2900 **Dom State:** WI **Commenced Bus:** January 1998

| Data Date | Rating | RACR #1 | RACR #2 | Total Assets ($mil) | Capital ($mil) | Net Premium ($mil) | Net Income ($mil) |
|---|---|---|---|---|---|---|---|
| 9-17 | C | 2.37 | 1.98 | 116.1 | 58.3 | 208.9 | 0.3 |
| 9-16 | B | 2.26 | 1.88 | 84.1 | 25.8 | 165.6 | -14.1 |
| 2016 | C | 0.75 | 0.63 | 98.2 | 27.6 | 221.6 | -32.3 |
| 2015 | B | 4.32 | 3.60 | 67.8 | 40.1 | 66.5 | -12.4 |
| 2014 | B- | 11.22 | 9.35 | 57.8 | 47.6 | 30.6 | 4.8 |
| 2013 | N/A | N/A | N/A | 50.0 | 47.9 | N/A | N/A |
| 2012 | N/A | N/A | N/A | 3.0 | 3.0 | N/A | N/A |

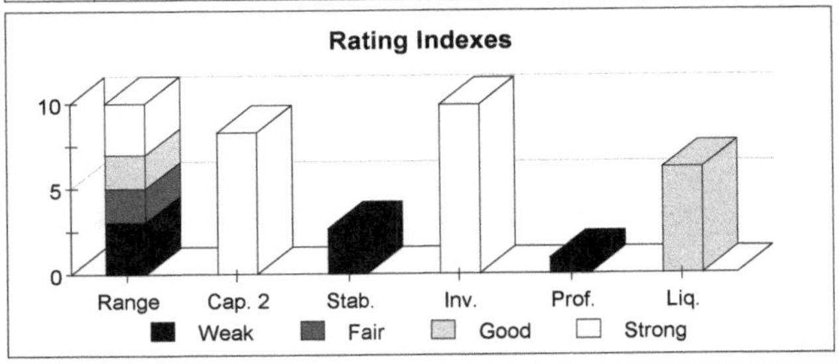

## MEDICA HEALTHCARE PLANS INC — E — Very Weak

**Major Rating Factors:** Fair profitability index (4.5 on a scale of 0 to 10). Good liquidity (6.9) with sufficient resources (cash flows and marketable investments) to handle a spike in claims. Strong capitalization (8.6) based on excellent current risk-adjusted capital (severe loss scenario).
**Other Rating Factors:** High quality investment portfolio (9.3).
**Principal Business:** Medicare (100%)
**Mem Phys: 16:** 31,620 **15:** 27,983 **16 MLR** 82.8% **/ 16 Admin Exp** N/A
**Enroll(000): Q3 17:** 42 **16:** 39 **15:** 36 **Med Exp PMPM:** $972
**Principal Investments:** Long-term bonds (72%), cash and equiv (28%)
**Provider Compensation ($000):** Contr fee ($308,171), capitation ($84,646), FFS ($23,591), bonus arrang ($6,506)
**Total Member Encounters:** Phys (592,099), non-phys (396,289)
**Group Affiliation:** UnitedHealth Group Incorporated
**Licensed in:** FL
**Address:** 9100 S DADELAND Blvd Ste 1250, MIAMI, FL 33156
**Phone:** (305) 670-8440 **Dom State:** FL **Commenced Bus:** June 2005

| Data Date | Rating | RACR #1 | RACR #2 | Total Assets ($mil) | Capital ($mil) | Net Premium ($mil) | Net Income ($mil) |
|---|---|---|---|---|---|---|---|
| 9-17 | E | 2.60 | 2.17 | 222.9 | 69.2 | 409.2 | 8.1 |
| 9-16 | E | 2.48 | 2.07 | 188.3 | 73.9 | 398.8 | 20.8 |
| 2016 | E | 2.32 | 1.93 | 139.6 | 61.4 | 533.9 | 24.9 |
| 2015 | E- | 1.82 | 1.52 | 132.9 | 54.1 | 523.1 | 11.6 |
| 2014 | E- | 0.61 | 0.51 | 118.8 | 20.4 | 486.6 | -7.4 |
| 2013 | E- | 0.66 | 0.55 | 100.3 | 20.0 | 513.4 | -21.6 |
| 2012 | E- | 0.47 | 0.39 | 84.9 | 21.3 | 554.3 | -8.4 |

Rating Indexes

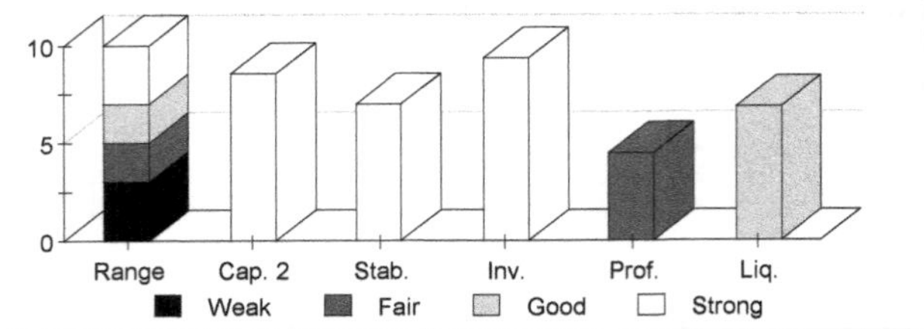


## MEDICA INS CO — B — Good

**Major Rating Factors:** Good liquidity (5.5 on a scale of 0 to 10) with sufficient resources (cash flows and marketable investments) to handle a spike in claims. Fair profitability index (4.3). Strong capitalization (9.1) based on excellent current risk-adjusted capital (severe loss scenario).
**Other Rating Factors:** High quality investment portfolio (8.0).
**Principal Business:** Medicare (49%), comp med (47%), other (4%)
**Mem Phys: 16:** 101,764 **15:** 97,294 **16 MLR** 90.6% **/ 16 Admin Exp** N/A
**Enroll(000): Q3 17:** 420 **16:** 379 **15:** 367 **Med Exp PMPM:** $392
**Principal Investments:** Long-term bonds (81%), nonaffiliate common stock (12%), pref stock (5%), cash and equiv (1%)
**Provider Compensation ($000):** Contr fee ($934,562), bonus arrang ($763,888), other ($68,247)
**Total Member Encounters:** Phys (5,253,697), non-phys (1,783,951)
**Group Affiliation:** Medica Holding Company
**Licensed in:** IA, KS, MN, NE, ND, SD, WI
**Address:** 401 CARLSON PARKWAY, MINNETONKA, MN 55305
**Phone:** (952) 992-2900 **Dom State:** MN **Commenced Bus:** June 1984

| Data Date | Rating | RACR #1 | RACR #2 | Total Assets ($mil) | Capital ($mil) | Net Premium ($mil) | Net Income ($mil) |
|---|---|---|---|---|---|---|---|
| 9-17 | B | 3.01 | 2.51 | 809.4 | 349.8 | 1,633.6 | 65.9 |
| 9-16 | A- | 3.11 | 2.60 | 700.5 | 322.6 | 1,467.4 | 8.2 |
| 2016 | B | 2.29 | 1.91 | 595.0 | 277.2 | 1,967.7 | -28.7 |
| 2015 | A- | 3.17 | 2.64 | 623.1 | 313.7 | 1,790.2 | -2.3 |
| 2014 | B | 3.48 | 2.90 | 545.0 | 309.7 | 1,664.5 | 74.8 |
| 2013 | B | 2.79 | 2.32 | 544.3 | 267.5 | 1,463.9 | 32.9 |
| 2012 | A- | 2.76 | 2.30 | 582.8 | 255.3 | 1,381.0 | -2.6 |

Rating Indexes

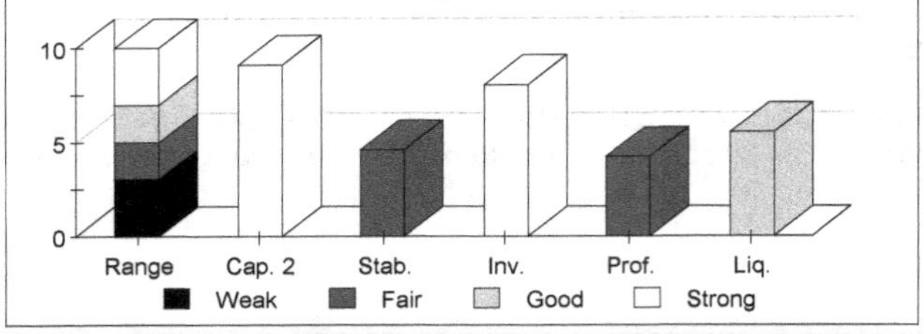


## MEDICAL ASSOC CLINIC HEALTH PLAN — C+ — Fair

**Major Rating Factors:** Fair profitability index (3.2 on a scale of 0 to 10). Good overall results on stability tests (5.1) despite inconsistent enrollment growth in the past five years due to declines in 2013 and 2016. Strong capitalization index (7.0) based on excellent current risk-adjusted capital (severe loss scenario).
**Other Rating Factors:** High quality investment portfolio (8.5). Excellent liquidity (6.9) with sufficient resources (cash flows and marketable investments) to handle a spike in claims.
**Principal Business:** Comp med (80%), Medicare (20%)
**Mem Phys: 16:** 369 **15:** 366 **16 MLR** 88.3% **/ 16 Admin Exp** N/A
**Enroll(000): Q3 17:** 7 **16:** 7 **15:** 8 **Med Exp PMPM:** $251
**Principal Investments:** Long-term bonds (58%), cash and equiv (35%), nonaffiliate common stock (8%)
**Provider Compensation ($000):** Capitation ($22,534)
**Total Member Encounters:** Phys (108,855)
**Group Affiliation:** Medical Associates Clinic PC
**Licensed in:** WI
**Address:** 1605 Associates Drive Suite 10, Dubuque, IA 52002-2270
**Phone:** (563) 556-8070 **Dom State:** WI **Commenced Bus:** January 1985

| Data Date | Rating | RACR #1 | RACR #2 | Total Assets ($mil) | Capital ($mil) | Net Premium ($mil) | Net Income ($mil) |
|---|---|---|---|---|---|---|---|
| 9-17 | C+ | 1.39 | 1.16 | 3.8 | 3.1 | 19.3 | 0.3 |
| 9-16 | C+ | 1.16 | 0.97 | 4.3 | 2.7 | 19.3 | 0.1 |
| 2016 | C+ | 1.22 | 1.01 | 3.2 | 2.7 | 25.5 | 0.1 |
| 2015 | C+ | 1.08 | 0.90 | 4.0 | 2.6 | 25.7 | -0.7 |
| 2014 | B- | 1.71 | 1.43 | 4.3 | 3.4 | 22.3 | 0.3 |
| 2013 | B- | 1.17 | 0.97 | 3.9 | 3.0 | 21.7 | 0.1 |
| 2012 | B- | 1.17 | 0.97 | 3.4 | 3.0 | 30.0 | 0.2 |

Rating Indexes

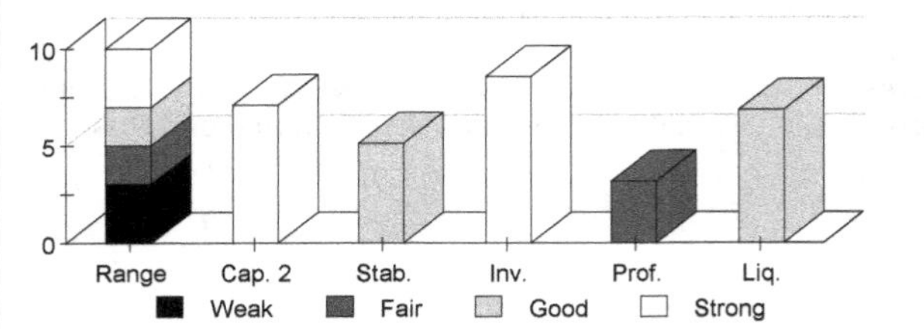

## MEDICAL ASSOCIATES HEALTH PLAN INC B- Good

**Major Rating Factors:** Fair profitability index (4.0 on a scale of 0 to 10). Good overall results on stability tests (5.2). Good liquidity (6.8) with sufficient resources (cash flows and marketable investments) to handle a spike in claims.
**Other Rating Factors:** Strong capitalization index (8.7) based on excellent current risk-adjusted capital (severe loss scenario). High quality investment portfolio (7.4).
**Principal Business:** Comp med (78%), Medicare (22%)
**Mem Phys: 16:** 369 **15:** 366 **16 MLR** 85.5% **/ 16 Admin Exp** N/A
**Enroll(000): Q3 17:** 24 **16:** 24 **15:** 23 **Med Exp PMPM:** $248
**Principal Investments:** Long-term bonds (69%), nonaffiliate common stock (17%), cash and equiv (14%)
**Provider Compensation ($000):** Contr fee ($47,773), capitation ($23,553)
**Total Member Encounters:** Phys (346,939)
**Group Affiliation:** Medical Associates Clinic PC
**Licensed in:** IL, IA
**Address:** 1605 Associates Drive Ste 101, Dubuque, IA 52002-2270
**Phone:** (563) 556-8070 **Dom State:** IA **Commenced Bus:** August 1987

| Data Date | Rating | RACR #1 | RACR #2 | Total Assets ($mil) | Capital ($mil) | Net Premium ($mil) | Net Income ($mil) |
|---|---|---|---|---|---|---|---|
| 9-17 | B- | 2.71 | 2.26 | 38.5 | 20.5 | 64.2 | 0.4 |
| 9-16 | B- | 2.34 | 1.95 | 37.5 | 20.1 | 61.4 | 1.3 |
| 2016 | B- | 2.62 | 2.18 | 32.4 | 19.8 | 82.5 | 1.4 |
| 2015 | B- | 2.12 | 1.77 | 32.2 | 18.1 | 80.3 | -1.1 |
| 2014 | B | 2.03 | 1.69 | 32.8 | 19.3 | 86.3 | -1.2 |
| 2013 | B | 1.96 | 1.63 | 30.8 | 20.9 | 85.4 | 3.6 |
| 2012 | B | 1.81 | 1.51 | 32.0 | 19.0 | 109.7 | 1.7 |

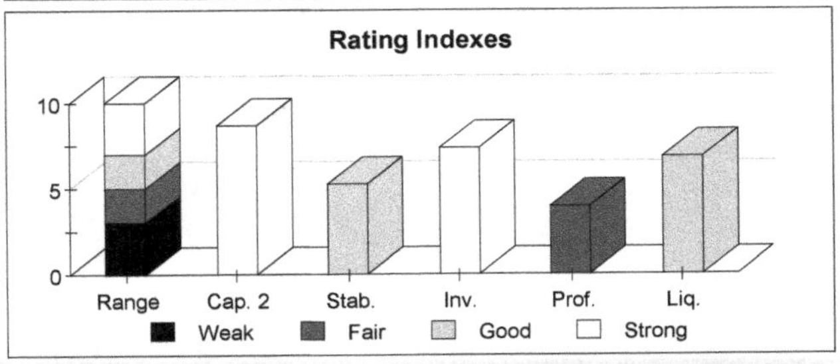


## MEDICAL HEALTH INS CORP OF OHIO * B+ Good

**Major Rating Factors:** Good liquidity (6.6 on a scale of 0 to 10) with sufficient resources (cash flows and marketable investments) to handle a spike in claims. Strong capitalization index (9.3) based on excellent current risk-adjusted capital (severe loss scenario). High quality investment portfolio (9.9).
**Other Rating Factors:** Fair overall results on stability tests (3.7) based on an excessive 60% enrollment growth during the period. Potentially strong support from affiliation with Medical Mutual of Ohio. Weak profitability index (0.7).
**Principal Business:** Comp med (85%), med supp (15%)
**Mem Phys: 16:** 48,453 **15:** 48,205 **16 MLR** 96.8% **/ 16 Admin Exp** N/A
**Enroll(000): Q3 17:** 86 **16:** 77 **15:** 48 **Med Exp PMPM:** $371
**Principal Investments:** Long-term bonds (50%), cash and equiv (50%)
**Provider Compensation ($000):** Contr fee ($296,023), FFS ($2,127), bonus arrang ($220), capitation ($2)
**Total Member Encounters:** Phys (706,260), non-phys (477,418)
**Group Affiliation:** Medical Mutual of Ohio
**Licensed in:** OH
**Address:** 2060 East Ninth Street, Cleveland, OH 44115-1355
**Phone:** (216) 687-7000 **Dom State:** OH **Commenced Bus:** January 1985

| Data Date | Rating | RACR #1 | RACR #2 | Total Assets ($mil) | Capital ($mil) | Net Premium ($mil) | Net Income ($mil) |
|---|---|---|---|---|---|---|---|
| 9-17 | B+ | 3.20 | 2.67 | 138.6 | 60.7 | 229.7 | -9.1 |
| 9-16 | B+ | 5.11 | 4.25 | 147.9 | 77.0 | 235.6 | -9.1 |
| 2016 | B+ | 3.48 | 2.90 | 155.6 | 66.5 | 328.2 | -18.1 |
| 2015 | B+ | 3.99 | 3.33 | 123.3 | 59.6 | 252.8 | -8.4 |
| 2014 | B+ | 6.10 | 5.08 | 118.6 | 69.5 | 159.8 | -20.3 |
| 2013 | B+ | 64.64 | 53.86 | 92.4 | 88.6 | 12.3 | 2.0 |
| 2012 | B+ | 52.34 | 43.62 | 90.3 | 86.7 | 24.0 | 3.8 |

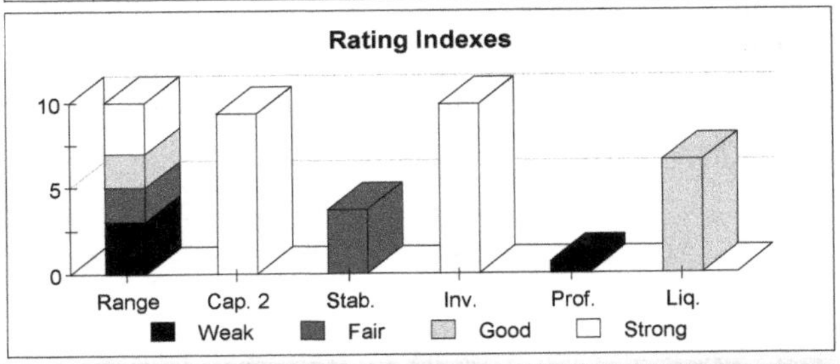


## MEDICAL MUTUAL OF OHIO * A Excellent

**Major Rating Factors:** Excellent profitability (7.5 on a scale of 0 to 10). Strong capitalization (10.0) based on excellent current risk-adjusted capital (severe loss scenario). High quality investment portfolio (7.4).
**Other Rating Factors:** Good liquidity (6.9) with sufficient resources (cash flows and marketable investments) to handle a spike in claims.
**Principal Business:** Comp med (85%), Medicare (6%), med supp (1%), FEHB (1%), other (5%)
**Mem Phys: 16:** 54,964 **15:** 54,439 **16 MLR** 83.6% **/ 16 Admin Exp** N/A
**Enroll(000): Q3 17:** 983 **16:** 1,027 **15:** 997 **Med Exp PMPM:** $160
**Principal Investments:** Long-term bonds (57%), nonaffiliate common stock (13%), cash and equiv (9%), affiliate common stock (5%), other (15%)
**Provider Compensation ($000):** Contr fee ($1,804,021), FFS ($14,312), capitation ($3,998), bonus arrang ($3,722), other ($89,680)
**Total Member Encounters:** Phys (3,420,845), non-phys (2,329,465)
**Group Affiliation:** Medical Mutual of Ohio
**Licensed in:** GA, IN, MI, NC, OH, PA, SC, WV, WI
**Address:** 2060 East Ninth St, Cleveland, OH 44115-1355
**Phone:** (216) 687-7000 **Dom State:** OH **Commenced Bus:** January 1934

| Data Date | Rating | RACR #1 | RACR #2 | Total Assets ($mil) | Capital ($mil) | Net Premium ($mil) | Net Income ($mil) |
|---|---|---|---|---|---|---|---|
| 9-17 | A | 7.06 | 5.89 | 2,136.4 | 1,525.3 | 1,838.2 | 112.1 |
| 9-16 | A- | 7.62 | 6.35 | 2,020.4 | 1,435.7 | 1,760.2 | 96.0 |
| 2016 | A | 6.47 | 5.39 | 1,991.5 | 1,395.8 | 2,368.3 | 57.9 |
| 2015 | A- | 7.18 | 5.99 | 1,853.2 | 1,352.8 | 2,146.9 | 126.7 |
| 2014 | A- | 6.64 | 5.53 | 1,766.9 | 1,279.9 | 2,238.2 | 97.3 |
| 2013 | A- | 5.85 | 4.87 | 1,684.6 | 1,221.8 | 2,473.5 | 97.7 |
| 2012 | A | 5.28 | 4.40 | 1,634.4 | 1,133.6 | 2,371.9 | 43.4 |

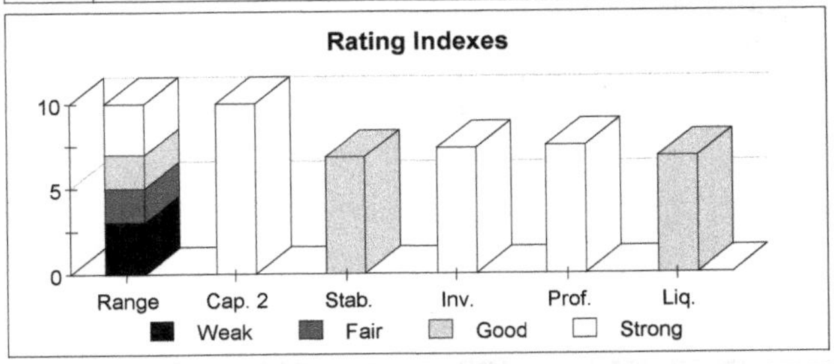

## MEDICO INSURANCE COMPANY B Good

**Major Rating Factors:** Fair profitability (4.5 on a scale of 0 to 10). Fair overall results on stability tests (4.7). Strong overall capitalization (10.0) based on excellent risk adjusted capital (severe loss scenario). However, capital levels have fluctuated somewhat during past years.
**Other Rating Factors:** High quality investment portfolio (7.7). Excellent liquidity (7.4) with ample cash flow from premiums and investment income.
**Principal Business:** Individual health insurance (78%), group health insurance (21%), individual life insurance (1%), and reinsurance (1%).
**Principal Investments:** NonCMO investment grade bonds (71%), CMOs and structured securities (21%), and cash (8%).
**Investments in Affiliates:** None
**Group Affiliation:** American Enterprise Mutual Holding
**Licensed in:** All states except CT, NJ, NY, PR
**Commenced Business:** April 1930
**Address:** 1010 North 102nd St Ste 201, Omaha, IA 50309
**Phone:** (800) 228-6080 **Domicile State:** NE **NAIC Code:** 31119

| Data Date | Rating | RACR #1 | RACR #2 | Total Assets ($mil) | Capital ($mil) | Net Premium ($mil) | Net Income ($mil) |
|---|---|---|---|---|---|---|---|
| 9-17 | B | 4.13 | 3.72 | 82.1 | 34.6 | 0.4 | 1.0 |
| 9-16 | B | 4.52 | 4.07 | 80.8 | 35.2 | 0.5 | 1.5 |
| 2016 | B | 4.63 | 4.16 | 87.3 | 38.8 | 0.6 | 1.8 |
| 2015 | B | 4.12 | 3.71 | 74.3 | 31.9 | 0.7 | 2.1 |
| 2014 | B | 4.14 | 3.73 | 69.1 | 30.9 | 0.9 | -0.2 |
| 2013 | B | 4.06 | 3.66 | 65.7 | 29.7 | 0.9 | 0.8 |
| 2012 | B | 4.07 | 2.82 | 55.1 | 31.5 | 25.4 | -12.4 |

Rating Indexes

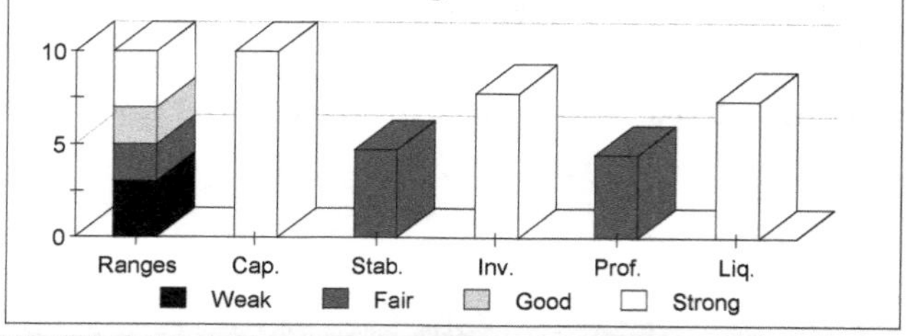


## MEDISUN INC B- Good

**Major Rating Factors:** Good overall profitability index (5.4 on a scale of 0 to 10). Good capitalization index (6.1) based on good current risk-adjusted capital (severe loss scenario). Good overall results on stability tests (6.8).
**Other Rating Factors:** Good liquidity (6.0) with sufficient resources (cash flows and marketable investments) to handle a spike in claims. High quality investment portfolio (9.4).
**Principal Business:** Medicare (100%)
**Mem Phys: 16:** 9,376 **15:** 6,388 **16 MLR** 89.2% **/ 16 Admin Exp** N/A
**Enroll(000): Q3 17:** 66 **16:** 62 **15:** 48 **Med Exp PMPM:** $714
**Principal Investments:** Cash and equiv (78%), long-term bonds (22%)
**Provider Compensation ($000):** Contr fee ($384,434), capitation ($142,781)
**Total Member Encounters:** Phys (1,353,873), non-phys (353,485)
**Group Affiliation:** Veritage LLC
**Licensed in:** AZ
**Address:** 2901 N Central Ave Suite 160, Phoenix, AZ 85012
**Phone:** (480) 684-7744 **Dom State:** AZ **Commenced Bus:** May 1985

| Data Date | Rating | RACR #1 | RACR #2 | Total Assets ($mil) | Capital ($mil) | Net Premium ($mil) | Net Income ($mil) |
|---|---|---|---|---|---|---|---|
| 9-17 | B- | 1.09 | 0.91 | 168.8 | 55.2 | 497.3 | 11.3 |
| 9-16 | B- | 1.02 | 0.85 | 120.2 | 42.2 | 439.4 | 3.6 |
| 2016 | C+ | 0.76 | 0.63 | 72.4 | 39.8 | 590.9 | 4.3 |
| 2015 | B- | 0.83 | 0.69 | 69.3 | 35.0 | 467.6 | -3.7 |
| 2014 | B | 0.97 | 0.81 | 38.9 | 24.0 | 229.2 | -0.5 |
| 2013 | B | 0.95 | 0.79 | 37.2 | 24.7 | 238.1 | 4.9 |
| 2012 | B | 0.91 | 0.76 | 33.0 | 18.8 | 239.0 | 2.8 |

Rating Indexes

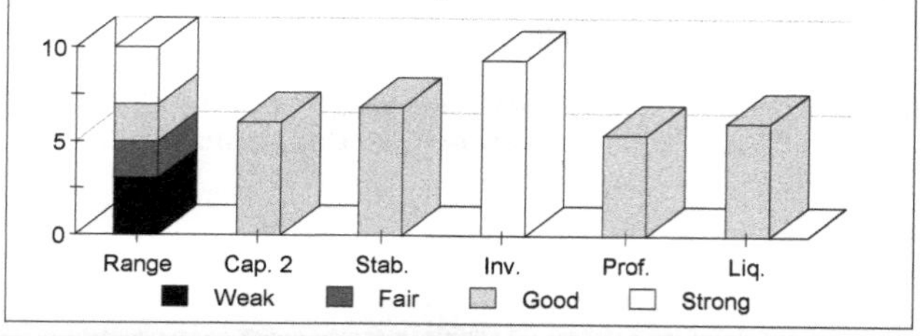


## MEDSTAR FAMILY CHOICE INC C Fair

**Major Rating Factors:** Weak profitability index (1.7 on a scale of 0 to 10). Good capitalization (6.0) based on good current risk-adjusted capital (severe loss scenario). High quality investment portfolio (9.9).
**Other Rating Factors:** Excellent liquidity (7.1) with ample operational cash flow and liquid investments.
**Principal Business:** Medicaid (85%), Medicare (15%)
**Mem Phys: 16:** N/A **15:** N/A **16 MLR** 91.3% **/ 16 Admin Exp** N/A
**Enroll(000): Q3 17:** 160 **16:** 147 **15:** 122 **Med Exp PMPM:** $415
**Principal Investments:** Cash and equiv (100%)
**Provider Compensation ($000):** FFS ($427,892), contr fee ($237,514), capitation ($7,707)
**Total Member Encounters:** N/A
**Group Affiliation:** MedStar Health Inc
**Licensed in:** DC, MD
**Address:** 5233 King Ave Ste 400, Baltimore, MD 21237
**Phone:** (410) 933-2215 **Dom State:** MD **Commenced Bus:** July 1997

| Data Date | Rating | RACR #1 | RACR #2 | Total Assets ($mil) | Capital ($mil) | Net Premium ($mil) | Net Income ($mil) |
|---|---|---|---|---|---|---|---|
| 9-17 | C | 1.08 | 0.90 | 263.1 | 78.9 | 643.0 | -5.3 |
| 9-16 | C- | N/A | N/A | 237.8 | 65.6 | 547.8 | -20.0 |
| 2016 | C- | 1.17 | 0.97 | 244.5 | 84.5 | 749.3 | -16.2 |
| 2015 | N/A | N/A | N/A | 219.7 | 84.2 | 599.6 | N/A |
| 2014 | C- | 0.51 | 0.42 | 131.1 | 27.1 | 478.2 | 4.6 |
| 2013 | C- | 0.79 | 0.66 | 63.7 | 21.5 | 224.8 | -1.4 |
| 2012 | C- | 1.43 | 1.20 | 40.8 | 23.8 | 115.4 | 0.1 |

Rating Indexes

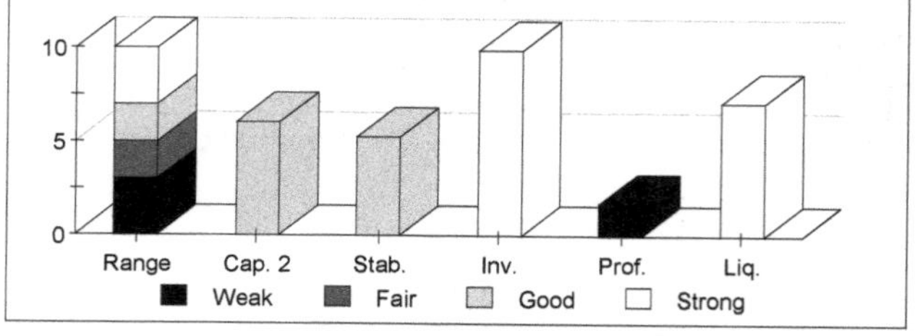

## MEMBERS HEALTH INS CO — C — Fair

**Major Rating Factors:** Weak profitability index (0.9 on a scale of 0 to 10). Strong capitalization (10.0) based on excellent current risk-adjusted capital (severe loss scenario). High quality investment portfolio (9.2).
**Other Rating Factors:** Excellent liquidity (8.3) with ample operational cash flow and liquid investments.
**Principal Business:** Med supp (100%)
**Mem Phys: 16:** N/A **15:** N/A **16 MLR** 69.5% **/ 16 Admin Exp** N/A
**Enroll(000): Q3 17:** 4 **16:** 1 **15:** 1 **Med Exp PMPM:** $107
**Principal Investments:** Long-term bonds (72%), cash and equiv (14%), nonaffiliate common stock (14%)
**Provider Compensation ($000):** FFS ($1,714)
**Total Member Encounters:** Phys (21,260), non-phys (6,273)
**Group Affiliation:** TN Rural Health Improvement Assoc
**Licensed in:** AL, AZ, AR, CO, GA, ID, IL, IN, KY, MD, MN, MS, MO, MT, NE, NM, ND, OK, OR, PA, SC, SD, TN, TX, UT, WA, WV
**Address:** 24 West Camelback Ave Ste A546, Phoenix, AZ 85013
**Phone:** (931) 560-0041 **Dom State:** AZ **Commenced Bus:** May 1982

| Data Date | Rating | RACR #1 | RACR #2 | Total Assets ($mil) | Capital ($mil) | Net Premium ($mil) | Net Income ($mil) |
|---|---|---|---|---|---|---|---|
| 9-17 | C | 16.99 | 14.16 | 34.2 | 30.7 | 4.3 | -1.9 |
| 9-16 | C | 18.38 | 15.32 | 33.2 | 31.6 | 1.8 | -0.4 |
| 2016 | C | 17.30 | 14.42 | 32.8 | 30.9 | 2.5 | -1.1 |
| 2015 | C | 18.55 | 15.46 | 33.4 | 31.9 | 2.0 | -0.1 |
| 2014 | C | 17.19 | 14.32 | 33.1 | 31.9 | 1.5 | 0.8 |
| 2013 | C | 17.27 | 14.39 | 32.7 | 31.1 | 0.7 | -0.9 |
| 2012 | N/A | N/A | N/A | 32.0 | 31.8 | N/A | 0.4 |

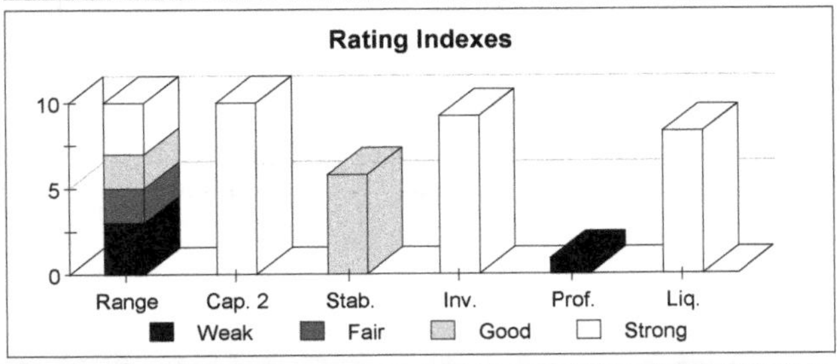


## MEMORIAL HERMANN HEALTH INS CO — C- — Fair

**Major Rating Factors:** Weak profitability index (0.9 on a scale of 0 to 10). Good liquidity (5.7) with sufficient resources (cash flows and marketable investments) to handle a spike in claims. Strong capitalization (7.3) based on excellent current risk-adjusted capital (severe loss scenario).
**Other Rating Factors:** High quality investment portfolio (9.9).
**Principal Business:** Comp med (85%), Medicare (15%)
**Mem Phys: 16:** 18,347 **15:** 17,196 **16 MLR** 112.8% **/ 16 Admin Exp** N/A
**Enroll(000): Q3 17:** 12 **16:** 21 **15:** 13 **Med Exp PMPM:** $401
**Principal Investments:** Cash and equiv (100%)
**Provider Compensation ($000):** FFS ($97,561)
**Total Member Encounters:** Phys (111,801), non-phys (109,654)
**Group Affiliation:** Memorial Hermann Health System
**Licensed in:** TX
**Address:** 929 Gessner Ste 1500, Houston, TX 77024
**Phone:** (713) 338-6480 **Dom State:** TX **Commenced Bus:** January 2001

| Data Date | Rating | RACR #1 | RACR #2 | Total Assets ($mil) | Capital ($mil) | Net Premium ($mil) | Net Income ($mil) |
|---|---|---|---|---|---|---|---|
| 9-17 | C- | 1.56 | 1.30 | 47.1 | 22.5 | 52.9 | -1.6 |
| 9-16 | C- | 1.71 | 1.43 | 35.8 | 14.8 | 71.6 | -9.4 |
| 2016 | C- | 1.74 | 1.45 | 53.3 | 25.0 | 92.8 | -15.0 |
| 2015 | C- | 1.87 | 1.55 | 31.0 | 16.2 | 50.2 | -9.7 |
| 2014 | C- | 2.36 | 1.96 | 27.9 | 18.1 | 42.6 | -4.9 |
| 2013 | C- | 1.68 | 1.40 | 18.7 | 8.7 | 20.9 | -3.4 |
| 2012 | C- | 2.48 | 2.06 | 9.4 | 3.9 | 5.2 | -0.7 |

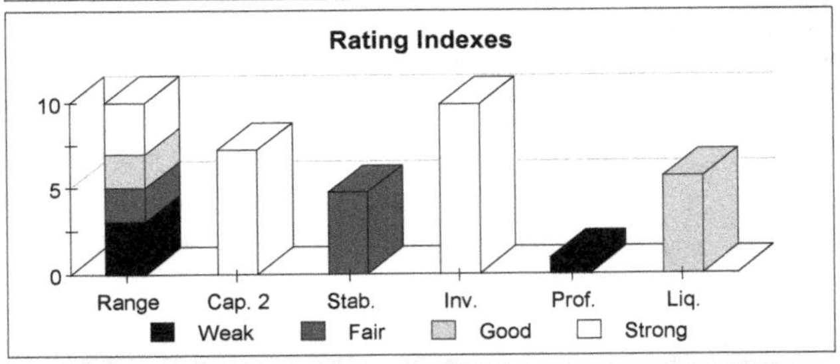


## MEMORIAL HERMANN HEALTH PLAN INC — D+ — Weak

**Major Rating Factors:** Weak profitability index (0.9 on a scale of 0 to 10). Weak liquidity (1.2) as a spike in claims may stretch capacity. Good capitalization (5.9) based on good current risk-adjusted capital (severe loss scenario).
**Other Rating Factors:** High quality investment portfolio (9.9).
**Principal Business:** Medicare (71%), comp med (29%)
**Mem Phys: 16:** 15,589 **15:** 12,495 **16 MLR** 95.6% **/ 16 Admin Exp** N/A
**Enroll(000): Q3 17:** 20 **16:** 11 **15:** 4 **Med Exp PMPM:** $437
**Principal Investments:** Cash and equiv (100%)
**Provider Compensation ($000):** FFS ($48,819)
**Total Member Encounters:** Phys (72,450), non-phys (68,088)
**Group Affiliation:** Memorial Hermann Health System
**Licensed in:** TX
**Address:** 929 Gessner Ste 1500, Houston, TX 77024
**Phone:** (713) 338-6480 **Dom State:** TX **Commenced Bus:** April 2014

| Data Date | Rating | RACR #1 | RACR #2 | Total Assets ($mil) | Capital ($mil) | Net Premium ($mil) | Net Income ($mil) |
|---|---|---|---|---|---|---|---|
| 9-17 | D+ | 1.06 | 0.89 | 35.5 | 10.2 | 78.5 | 0.1 |
| 9-16 | D+ | 1.44 | 1.20 | 22.5 | 7.3 | 43.8 | -6.3 |
| 2016 | D+ | 1.10 | 0.92 | 26.7 | 10.5 | 55.7 | -10.9 |
| 2015 | D+ | 1.50 | 1.25 | 11.9 | 7.5 | 18.0 | -8.3 |
| 2014 | N/A | N/A | N/A | 7.3 | 6.5 | N/A | -4.8 |
| 2013 | N/A | N/A | N/A | N/A | N/A | N/A | N/A |
| 2012 | N/A | N/A | N/A | N/A | N/A | N/A | N/A |

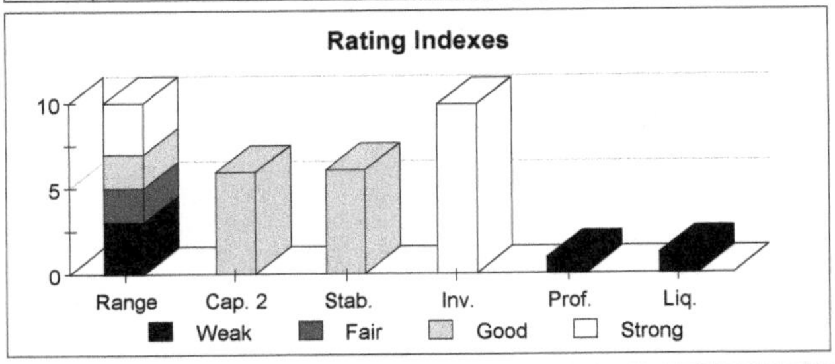

## MERCYCARE HMO C Fair

**Major Rating Factors:** Fair profitability index (3.5 on a scale of 0 to 10). Fair quality investment portfolio (3.7). Good liquidity (5.5) with sufficient resources (cash flows and marketable investments) to handle a spike in claims.
**Other Rating Factors:** Strong capitalization (7.6) based on excellent current risk-adjusted capital (severe loss scenario).
**Principal Business:** Comp med (65%), Medicaid (31%), med supp (3%), FEHB (2%)
**Mem Phys: 16:** 436 **15:** 277 **16 MLR** 91.8% **/ 16 Admin Exp** N/A
**Enroll(000): Q3 17:** 30 **16:** 27 **15:** 28 **Med Exp PMPM:** $232
**Principal Investments:** Nonaffiliate common stock (59%), long-term bonds (32%), cash and equiv (9%)
**Provider Compensation ($000):** Contr fee ($61,484), capitation ($10,790), FFS ($2,068)
**Total Member Encounters:** Phys (220,641), non-phys (28,328)
**Group Affiliation:** Mercy Health Corporation
**Licensed in:** IL, WI
**Address:** 580 N Washington, Janesville, WI 53545
**Phone:** (608) 752-3431 **Dom State:** WI **Commenced Bus:** September 2004

| Data Date | Rating | RACR #1 | RACR #2 | Total Assets ($mil) | Capital ($mil) | Net Premium ($mil) | Net Income ($mil) |
|---|---|---|---|---|---|---|---|
| 9-17 | C | 1.81 | 1.50 | 38.1 | 18.3 | 73.6 | 1.3 |
| 9-16 | C | 1.43 | 1.19 | 28.6 | 13.8 | 61.7 | 0.2 |
| 2016 | C | 1.54 | 1.29 | 31.0 | 15.8 | 82.0 | 1.5 |
| 2015 | C | 1.47 | 1.23 | 27.3 | 14.2 | 79.5 | 0.0 |
| 2014 | C | 1.34 | 1.12 | 28.9 | 15.1 | 98.6 | -1.9 |
| 2013 | C | 1.59 | 1.32 | 30.6 | 17.7 | 109.0 | 0.2 |
| 2012 | C | 1.24 | 1.03 | 26.2 | 14.2 | 114.3 | 0.4 |

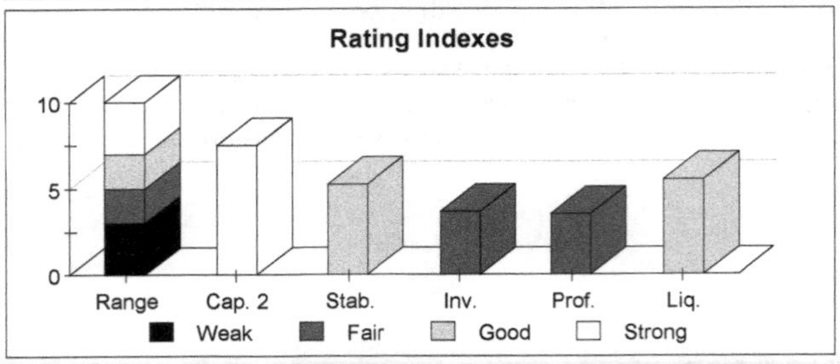


## MERCYCARE INS CO D+ Weak

**Major Rating Factors:** Weak profitability index (1.4 on a scale of 0 to 10). Low quality investment portfolio (2.3). Good liquidity (6.3) with sufficient resources (cash flows and marketable investments) to handle a spike in claims.
**Other Rating Factors:** Strong capitalization (7.2) based on excellent current risk-adjusted capital (severe loss scenario).
**Principal Business:** Comp med (100%)
**Mem Phys: 16:** 436 **15:** N/A **16 MLR** 288.2% **/ 16 Admin Exp** N/A
**Enroll(000): Q3 17:** 1 **16:** 2 **15:** 2 **Med Exp PMPM:** $86
**Principal Investments:** Affiliate common stock (92%), long-term bonds (12%)
**Provider Compensation ($000):** FFS ($1,546)
**Total Member Encounters:** Phys (378), non-phys (55)
**Group Affiliation:** Mercy Health Corporation
**Licensed in:** IL, WI
**Address:** 580 N Washington, Janesville, WI 53545
**Phone:** (800) 895-2421 **Dom State:** WI **Commenced Bus:** January 1994

| Data Date | Rating | RACR #1 | RACR #2 | Total Assets ($mil) | Capital ($mil) | Net Premium ($mil) | Net Income ($mil) |
|---|---|---|---|---|---|---|---|
| 9-17 | D+ | 1.50 | 1.25 | 20.5 | 17.6 | 0.5 | -0.2 |
| 9-16 | C- | 1.22 | 1.01 | 16.7 | 14.0 | 0.5 | -0.9 |
| 2016 | D+ | 1.29 | 1.08 | 17.4 | 15.4 | 0.6 | -1.4 |
| 2015 | C- | 1.33 | 1.11 | 16.1 | 15.2 | 2.2 | -1.0 |
| 2014 | C- | N/A | N/A | 17.2 | 16.9 | 1.2 | -0.1 |
| 2013 | C- | 1.57 | 1.31 | 19.8 | 19.6 | 0.7 | 0.0 |
| 2012 | C- | 1.26 | 1.05 | 16.4 | 16.0 | 0.7 | 0.0 |

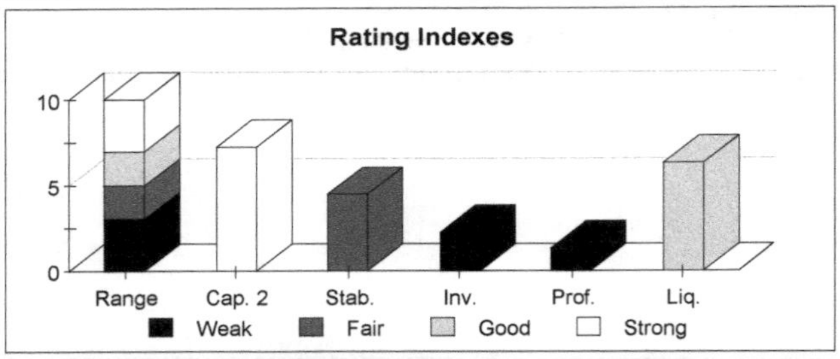


## MERIDIAN HEALTH PLAN OF ILLINOIS INC C+ Fair

**Major Rating Factors:** Fair capitalization (4.2 on a scale of 0 to 10) based on fair current risk-adjusted capital (moderate loss scenario). Good liquidity (6.8) with sufficient resources (cash flows and marketable investments) to handle a spike in claims. Weak profitability index (1.0).
**Other Rating Factors:** High quality investment portfolio (9.9).
**Principal Business:** Medicaid (86%), Medicare (14%)
**Mem Phys: 16:** 28,179 **15:** 39,208 **16 MLR** 94.6% **/ 16 Admin Exp** N/A
**Enroll(000): Q3 17:** 391 **16:** 374 **15:** 244 **Med Exp PMPM:** $266
**Principal Investments:** Cash and equiv (100%)
**Provider Compensation ($000):** Contr fee ($735,073), FFS ($229,890), bonus arrang ($6,113)
**Total Member Encounters:** Phys (2,316,837), non-phys (1,387,998)
**Group Affiliation:** Caidan Enterprises Inc
**Licensed in:** IL
**Address:** 333 S Wabash Ste 2900, Chicago, IL 60604
**Phone:** (313) 324-3700 **Dom State:** IL **Commenced Bus:** December 2008

| Data Date | Rating | RACR #1 | RACR #2 | Total Assets ($mil) | Capital ($mil) | Net Premium ($mil) | Net Income ($mil) |
|---|---|---|---|---|---|---|---|
| 9-17 | C+ | 0.82 | 0.68 | 747.8 | 85.6 | 1,067.9 | -13.0 |
| 9-16 | B | 0.98 | 0.82 | 295.7 | 77.5 | 974.2 | -9.9 |
| 2016 | B- | 0.93 | 0.78 | 405.5 | 96.5 | 1,125.7 | -30.4 |
| 2015 | B | 1.11 | 0.92 | 282.6 | 87.3 | 1,017.2 | 7.2 |
| 2014 | B | 1.02 | 0.85 | 130.5 | 31.6 | 320.5 | -0.2 |
| 2013 | B- | 0.94 | 0.78 | 24.2 | 4.9 | 40.9 | 0.4 |
| 2012 | B- | 1.52 | 1.26 | 6.7 | 2.3 | 11.4 | 0.1 |

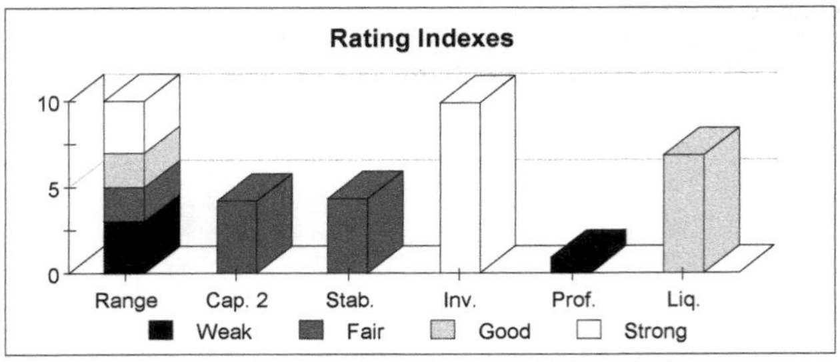

## MERIDIAN HEALTH PLAN OF IOWA INC — E+ Very Weak

**Major Rating Factors:** Weak profitability index (1.9 on a scale of 0 to 10). Strong capitalization (10.0) based on excellent current risk-adjusted capital (severe loss scenario). High quality investment portfolio (9.9).
**Other Rating Factors:** Excellent liquidity (10.0) with ample operational cash flow and liquid investments.
**Principal Business:** Medicaid (102%)
**Mem Phys: 16:** N/A **15:** 13,007 **16 MLR** ****.*% **/ 16 Admin Exp** N/A
**Enroll(000): Q1 17:** N/A **16:** N/A **15:** 61 **Med Exp PMPM:** N/A
**Principal Investments:** Cash and equiv (100%)
**Provider Compensation ($000):** Contr fee ($13,446), FFS ($2,021)
**Total Member Encounters:** N/A
**Group Affiliation:** Caidan Enterprises Inc
**Licensed in:** IA
**Address:** 1 Campus Martius Ste 700, Detroit, MI 48226
**Phone:** (313) 324-3700 **Dom State:** IA **Commenced Bus:** March 2012

| Data Date | Rating | RACR #1 | RACR #2 | Total Assets ($mil) | Capital ($mil) | Net Premium ($mil) | Net Income ($mil) |
|---|---|---|---|---|---|---|---|
| 3-17 | E+ | 4.63 | 3.86 | 8.9 | 7.2 | N/A | 0.0 |
| 3-16 | E | N/A | N/A | 19.8 | 10.1 | 0.3 | -1.7 |
| 2016 | E+ | 4.66 | 3.88 | 9.1 | 7.2 | 0.3 | 2.4 |
| 2015 | E | 0.85 | 0.71 | 33.2 | 11.8 | 151.7 | -3.6 |
| 2014 | E | 0.84 | 0.70 | 41.0 | 13.4 | 145.0 | -6.8 |
| 2013 | E | 1.31 | 1.09 | 20.1 | 10.3 | 57.0 | -4.6 |
| 2012 | B- | 1.11 | 0.92 | 3.8 | 1.4 | 8.5 | 0.2 |

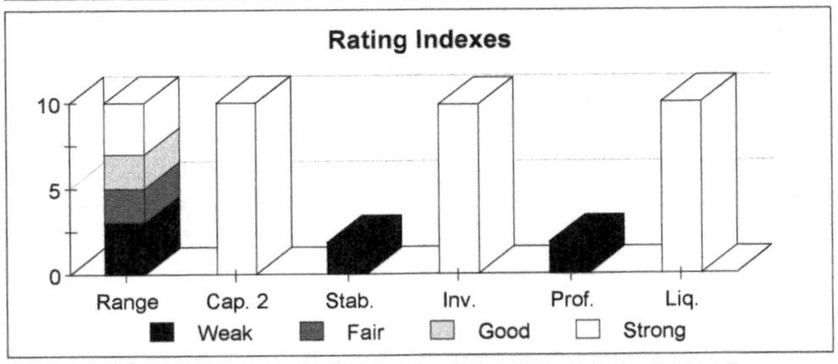


## MERIDIAN HEALTH PLAN OF MICHIGAN INC — B Good

**Major Rating Factors:** Good capitalization index (6.2 on a scale of 0 to 10) based on good current risk-adjusted capital (severe loss scenario). Good overall results on stability tests (6.8) despite a decline in the number of member physicians during 2017. Good liquidity (6.9) with sufficient resources (cash flows and marketable investments) to handle a spike in claims.
**Other Rating Factors:** Fair profitability index (4.0). High quality investment portfolio (9.8).
**Principal Business:** Medicaid (94%), Medicare (5%)
**Mem Phys: 16:** 33,865 **15:** 56,280 **16 MLR** 84.0% **/ 16 Admin Exp** N/A
**Enroll(000): Q3 17:** 514 **16:** 505 **15:** 455 **Med Exp PMPM:** $346
**Principal Investments:** Cash and equiv (73%), long-term bonds (24%), nonaffiliate common stock (3%)
**Provider Compensation ($000):** Contr fee ($1,360,767), capitation ($505,472), FFS ($137,630), bonus arrang ($12,024)
**Total Member Encounters:** Phys (6,241,740), non-phys (5,215,974)
**Group Affiliation:** Caidan Enterprises Inc
**Licensed in:** DC, DE, IL, IN, KY, ME, MI, OH
**Address:** 1 Campus Martius Suite 700, Detroit, MI 48226
**Phone:** (313) 324-3700 **Dom State:** MI **Commenced Bus:** December 1995

| Data Date | Rating | RACR #1 | RACR #2 | Total Assets ($mil) | Capital ($mil) | Net Premium ($mil) | Net Income ($mil) |
|---|---|---|---|---|---|---|---|
| 9-17 | B | 1.10 | 0.92 | 515.8 | 177.0 | 1,755.7 | -10.0 |
| 9-16 | B+ | 1.15 | 0.96 | 491.0 | 162.0 | 1,810.8 | 0.8 |
| 2016 | B+ | 1.16 | 0.97 | 537.4 | 185.3 | 2,420.8 | 3.9 |
| 2015 | B+ | 1.09 | 0.91 | 477.6 | 153.4 | 2,113.2 | 6.8 |
| 2014 | B+ | 1.09 | 0.91 | 324.5 | 107.4 | 1,443.3 | 3.4 |
| 2013 | B | 1.16 | 0.97 | 210.5 | 88.6 | 1,058.6 | 5.7 |
| 2012 | B | 1.14 | 0.95 | 191.6 | 82.0 | 957.4 | 5.2 |

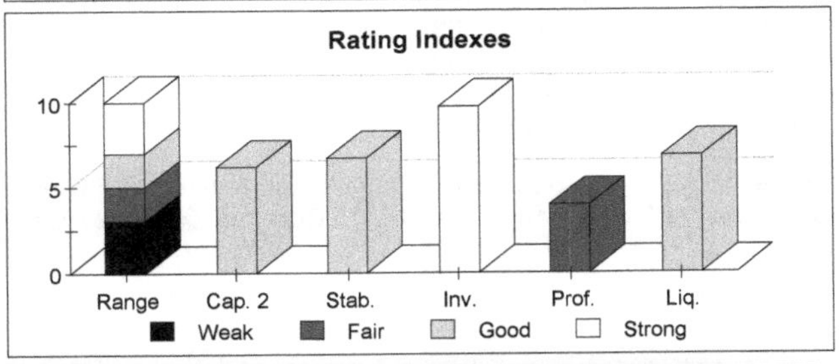


## MERIT HEALTH INS CO — C Fair

**Major Rating Factors:** Excellent profitability (7.5 on a scale of 0 to 10). Strong capitalization (10.0) based on excellent current risk-adjusted capital (severe loss scenario). High quality investment portfolio (9.1).
**Other Rating Factors:** Excellent liquidity (8.8) with ample operational cash flow and liquid investments.
**Principal Business:** Medicaid (5%), other (95%)
**Mem Phys: 16:** N/A **15:** 3,863 **16 MLR** 79.2% **/ 16 Admin Exp** N/A
**Enroll(000): Q3 17:** 107 **16:** 63 **15:** 4 **Med Exp PMPM:** $76
**Principal Investments:** Affiliate common stock (52%), cash and equiv (36%), long-term bonds (12%)
**Provider Compensation ($000):** Contr fee ($4,910), other ($50,861)
**Total Member Encounters:** N/A
**Group Affiliation:** Magellan Health Inc
**Licensed in:** AL, AK, AZ, AR, CO, DC, DE, GA, HI, ID, IL, IN, IA, KY, LA, ME, MD, MA, MI, MN, MS, MO, MT, NE, NH, NM, NC, ND, OK, OR, PA, SC, SD, TN, TX, UT, VT, VA, WV, WI
**Address:** 5215 Old Orchard Rd Ste 600, Skokie, IL 60077
**Phone:** (224) 935-9809 **Dom State:** IL **Commenced Bus:** January 1993

| Data Date | Rating | RACR #1 | RACR #2 | Total Assets ($mil) | Capital ($mil) | Net Premium ($mil) | Net Income ($mil) |
|---|---|---|---|---|---|---|---|
| 9-17 | C | 4.82 | 4.01 | 182.1 | 50.4 | 85.9 | -1.8 |
| 9-16 | C+ | 4.02 | 3.35 | 138.1 | 56.1 | 45.5 | 6.7 |
| 2016 | C+ | 5.46 | 4.55 | 147.0 | 58.3 | 59.8 | 8.8 |
| 2015 | B- | 3.57 | 2.98 | 65.0 | 47.9 | 118.5 | 10.4 |
| 2014 | C+ | 5.84 | 4.87 | 67.2 | 27.0 | 128.8 | 7.5 |
| 2013 | D+ | 6.45 | 5.38 | 78.4 | 37.8 | 128.6 | 12.6 |
| 2012 | N/A | N/A | N/A | 76.4 | 34.9 | 106.7 | 11.7 |

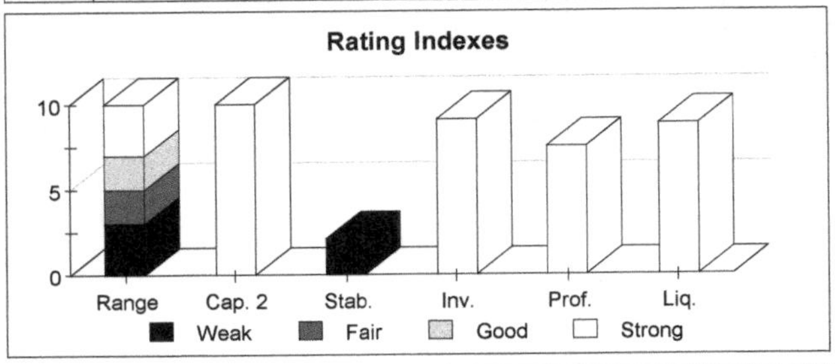

## MERIT LIFE INSURANCE COMPANY B Good

**Major Rating Factors:** Good quality investment portfolio (6.7 on a scale of 0 to 10) despite mixed results such as: minimal exposure to mortgages and large holdings of BBB rated bonds but minimal holdings in junk bonds. Good overall results on stability tests (5.6). Stability strengths include good operational trends and excellent risk diversification. Fair profitability (4.7).
**Other Rating Factors:** Strong capitalization (10.0) based on excellent risk adjusted capital (severe loss scenario). Excellent liquidity (8.5).
**Principal Business:** Credit health insurance (38%), credit life insurance (36%), individual life insurance (16%), and individual health insurance (10%).
**Principal Investments:** NonCMO investment grade bonds (72%), CMOs and structured securities (20%), mortgages in good standing (5%), noninv. grade bonds (2%), and common & preferred stock (1%).
**Investments in Affiliates:** None
**Group Affiliation:** Fortress Investment Group LLC
**Licensed in:** All states except AK, MA, NY, VT, PR
**Commenced Business:** October 1957
**Address:** 601 NW 2ND ST, EVANSVILLE, IN 47708-1013
**Phone:** (800) 325-2147 **Domicile State:** IN **NAIC Code:** 65951

| Data Date | Rating | RACR #1 | RACR #2 | Total Assets ($mil) | Capital ($mil) | Net Premium ($mil) | Net Income ($mil) |
|---|---|---|---|---|---|---|---|
| 9-17 | B | 6.19 | 3.63 | 560.7 | 155.6 | 61.3 | 22.7 |
| 9-16 | B | 4.62 | 2.80 | 577.6 | 133.2 | 94.3 | 12.4 |
| 2016 | B | 4.82 | 2.90 | 559.3 | 133.4 | 127.4 | 19.8 |
| 2015 | B | 4.11 | 2.56 | 588.8 | 122.8 | 150.1 | -0.9 |
| 2014 | B+ | 5.53 | 3.47 | 588.2 | 171.4 | 157.1 | -2.4 |
| 2013 | B+ | 6.34 | 4.09 | 532.0 | 184.5 | 128.1 | 3.3 |
| 2012 | B+ | 10.53 | 5.92 | 549.0 | 245.4 | 85.9 | 10.1 |

**Adverse Trends in Operations**

Decrease in premium volume from 2015 to 2016 (15%)
Decrease in premium volume from 2014 to 2015 (4%)
Decrease in capital during 2015 (28%)
Decrease in capital during 2013 (25%)
Decrease in asset base during 2013 (3%)

## MHS HEALTH WISCONSIN C+ Fair

**Major Rating Factors:** Good overall results on stability tests (5.4 on a scale of 0 to 10). Rating is significantly influenced by the fair financial results of Centene Corporation. Good liquidity (6.9) with sufficient resources (cash flows and marketable investments) to handle a spike in claims. Excellent profitability (9.3).
**Other Rating Factors:** Strong capitalization index (10.0) based on excellent current risk-adjusted capital (severe loss scenario). High quality investment portfolio (8.7).
**Principal Business:** Medicaid (88%), Medicare (6%), comp med (6%)
**Mem Phys: 16:** 26,072 **15:** 24,646 **16 MLR** 82.1% **/ 16 Admin Exp** N/A
**Enroll(000): Q3 17:** 36 **16:** 38 **15:** 40 **Med Exp PMPM:** $316
**Principal Investments:** Long-term bonds (77%), cash and equiv (19%), affiliate common stock (2%), other (3%)
**Provider Compensation ($000):** Contr fee ($144,382), salary ($6,092), capitation ($2,533), bonus arrang ($402)
**Total Member Encounters:** Phys (224,606), non-phys (233,613)
**Group Affiliation:** Centene Corporation
**Licensed in:** WI
**Address:** 10700 W Research Drive Suite 3, Milwaukee, WI 53226
**Phone:** (314) 505-6143 **Dom State:** WI **Commenced Bus:** December 1990

| Data Date | Rating | RACR #1 | RACR #2 | Total Assets ($mil) | Capital ($mil) | Net Premium ($mil) | Net Income ($mil) |
|---|---|---|---|---|---|---|---|
| 9-17 | C+ | 4.65 | 3.88 | 71.0 | 48.5 | 123.2 | 6.5 |
| 9-16 | C | 5.12 | 4.27 | 77.8 | 52.3 | 140.9 | 6.9 |
| 2016 | C+ | 4.92 | 4.10 | 72.3 | 51.5 | 183.6 | 9.5 |
| 2015 | C+ | 4.59 | 3.83 | 75.7 | 46.6 | 196.8 | 15.8 |
| 2014 | C+ | 3.51 | 2.93 | 69.0 | 30.9 | 174.6 | 6.7 |
| 2013 | C+ | 3.09 | 2.57 | 56.9 | 26.5 | 203.7 | 8.2 |
| 2012 | C | 2.01 | 1.67 | 53.1 | 18.2 | 201.9 | 7.1 |

**Rating Indexes**

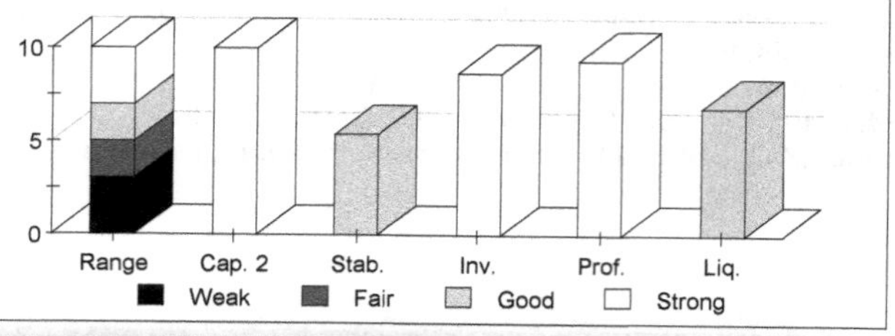


## MICHIGAN COMPLETE HEALTH INC C- Fair

**Major Rating Factors:** Weak profitability index (0.9 on a scale of 0 to 10). Strong capitalization (8.6) based on excellent current risk-adjusted capital (severe loss scenario). High quality investment portfolio (9.9).
**Other Rating Factors:** Excellent liquidity (7.1) with ample operational cash flow and liquid investments.
**Principal Business:** Medicare (76%), Medicaid (24%)
**Mem Phys: 16:** 5,900 **15:** 5,496 **16 MLR** 89.1% **/ 16 Admin Exp** N/A
**Enroll(000): Q3 17:** 2 **16:** 4 **15:** 8 **Med Exp PMPM:** $766
**Principal Investments:** Cash and equiv (64%), long-term bonds (36%)
**Provider Compensation ($000):** Capitation ($38,551), contr fee ($5,417), salary ($506)
**Total Member Encounters:** Phys (52,827), non-phys (100,261)
**Group Affiliation:** Centene Corporation
**Licensed in:** MI
**Address:** 800 Tower Rd Ste 200, Troy, MI 48098
**Phone:** (314) 725-4477 **Dom State:** MI **Commenced Bus:** July 2005

| Data Date | Rating | RACR #1 | RACR #2 | Total Assets ($mil) | Capital ($mil) | Net Premium ($mil) | Net Income ($mil) |
|---|---|---|---|---|---|---|---|
| 9-17 | C- | 2.65 | 2.20 | 16.6 | 7.4 | 40.0 | 1.3 |
| 9-16 | C- | 2.29 | 1.91 | 12.8 | 6.7 | 35.4 | -0.5 |
| 2016 | C- | 2.34 | 1.95 | 10.6 | 6.5 | 46.9 | -0.6 |
| 2015 | C | 1.77 | 1.47 | 11.3 | 5.0 | 60.5 | -3.4 |
| 2014 | C | 1.32 | 1.10 | 8.8 | 4.9 | 30.7 | N/A |
| 2013 | C | 1.53 | 1.27 | 6.8 | 4.5 | 20.5 | -0.1 |
| 2012 | C | 1.59 | 1.33 | 7.5 | 4.4 | 20.4 | 0.3 |

**Rating Indexes**

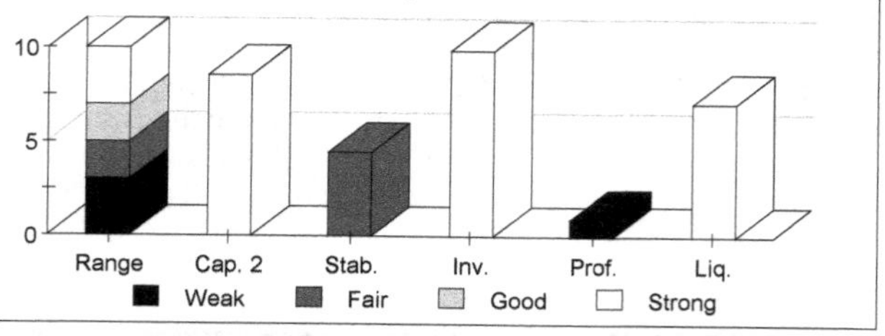

## MII LIFE INC — B- Good

**Major Rating Factors:** Fair quality investment portfolio (4.7 on a scale of 0 to 10). Good overall profitability index (5.3). Strong capitalization (9.5) based on excellent current risk-adjusted capital (severe loss scenario).
**Other Rating Factors:** Excellent liquidity (8.1) with ample operational cash flow and liquid investments.
**Principal Business:** Other (4%)
**Mem Phys: 16:** N/A **15:** N/A **16 MLR** 117.4% **/ 16 Admin Exp** N/A
**Enroll(000): Q3 17:** 34 **16:** 25 **15:** 22 **Med Exp PMPM:** $70
**Principal Investments:** Long-term bonds (83%), nonaffiliate common stock (9%), cash and equiv (8%)
**Provider Compensation ($000):** Other ($18,039)
**Total Member Encounters:** N/A
**Group Affiliation:** Aware Integrated Inc
**Licensed in:** IA, MI, MN, MT, NE, ND, SD, WI, WY
**Address:** 3535 BLUE CROSS Rd, EAGAN, MN 55122
**Phone:** (651) 662-8000 **Dom State:** MN **Commenced Bus:** September 1959

| Data Date | Rating | RACR #1 | RACR #2 | Total Assets ($mil) | Capital ($mil) | Net Premium ($mil) | Net Income ($mil) |
|---|---|---|---|---|---|---|---|
| 9-17 | B- | 3.36 | 2.80 | 952.4 | 46.1 | 3.3 | 2.8 |
| 9-16 | B- | 3.93 | 3.28 | 756.7 | 41.0 | 0.5 | 9.4 |
| 2016 | B- | 2.91 | 2.43 | 813.0 | 39.9 | 17.2 | 9.5 |
| 2015 | B | 2.66 | 2.21 | 596.6 | 27.7 | 16.2 | 3.2 |
| 2014 | B | 2.68 | 2.24 | 511.4 | 27.4 | 15.6 | 1.9 |
| 2013 | B | 1.29 | 1.08 | 438.0 | 15.7 | 15.1 | 3.5 |
| 2012 | N/A | N/A | N/A | 405.2 | 14.4 | 11.9 | 2.8 |

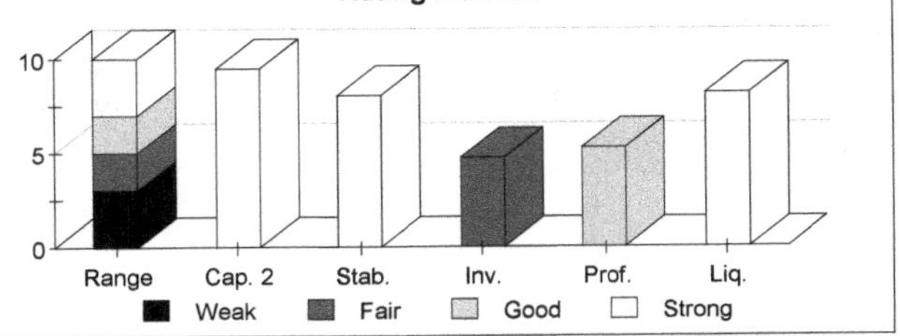


## MISSOURI CARE INC — E Very Weak

**Major Rating Factors:** Good overall profitability index (5.2 on a scale of 0 to 10). Strong capitalization (10.0) based on excellent current risk-adjusted capital (severe loss scenario). High quality investment portfolio (9.9).
**Other Rating Factors:** Excellent liquidity (7.0) with ample operational cash flow and liquid investments.
**Principal Business:** Medicaid (98%), comp med (2%)
**Mem Phys: 16:** 28,500 **15:** 23,100 **16 MLR** 84.9% **/ 16 Admin Exp** N/A
**Enroll(000): Q3 17:** 291 **16:** 121 **15:** 114 **Med Exp PMPM:** $210
**Principal Investments:** Cash and equiv (98%), long-term bonds (2%)
**Provider Compensation ($000):** Contr fee ($222,409), capitation ($69,469)
**Total Member Encounters:** Phys (385,540), non-phys (172,956)
**Group Affiliation:** WellCare Health Plans Inc
**Licensed in:** MO
**Address:** 2404 Forum Blvd, Columbia, MO 65203
**Phone:** (813) 206-6200 **Dom State:** MO **Commenced Bus:** July 2006

| Data Date | Rating | RACR #1 | RACR #2 | Total Assets ($mil) | Capital ($mil) | Net Premium ($mil) | Net Income ($mil) |
|---|---|---|---|---|---|---|---|
| 9-17 | E | 4.33 | 3.61 | 191.1 | 71.9 | 461.6 | 10.0 |
| 9-16 | E | 2.38 | 1.98 | 79.0 | 35.1 | 257.6 | -3.5 |
| 2016 | E | 2.73 | 2.27 | 87.6 | 42.6 | 349.5 | 3.5 |
| 2015 | E | 2.35 | 1.96 | 74.1 | 34.5 | 308.9 | -0.7 |
| 2014 | E | 3.47 | 2.90 | 79.9 | 47.1 | 275.2 | 4.0 |
| 2013 | E | 2.28 | 1.90 | 86.1 | 42.7 | 305.2 | 11.4 |
| 2012 | C | 0.92 | 0.76 | 57.1 | 17.6 | 228.4 | -2.7 |

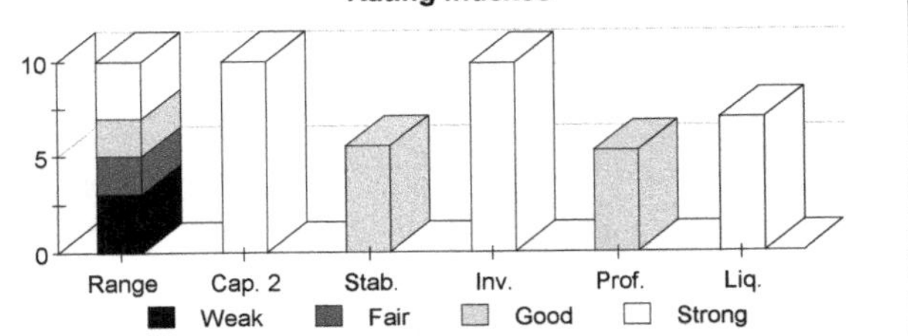


## MISSOURI MEDICARE SELECT LLC — C- Fair

**Major Rating Factors:** Weak profitability index (2.3 on a scale of 0 to 10). Poor capitalization (2.8) based on weak current risk-adjusted capital (moderate loss scenario). High quality investment portfolio (9.9).
**Other Rating Factors:** Excellent liquidity (7.1) with ample operational cash flow and liquid investments.
**Principal Business:** Medicare (100%)
**Mem Phys: 16:** N/A **15:** N/A **16 MLR** 87.2% **/ 16 Admin Exp** N/A
**Enroll(000): Q3 17:** 0 **16:** 0 **15:** N/A **Med Exp PMPM:** $2,300
**Principal Investments:** Cash and equiv (56%), long-term bonds (44%)
**Provider Compensation ($000):** FFS ($5,302)
**Total Member Encounters:** N/A
**Group Affiliation:** MO Select LLC
**Licensed in:** MO
**Address:** 10954 Kennerly Rd, St. Louis, MO 63128
**Phone:** (615) 308-7191 **Dom State:** MO **Commenced Bus:** April 2015

| Data Date | Rating | RACR #1 | RACR #2 | Total Assets ($mil) | Capital ($mil) | Net Premium ($mil) | Net Income ($mil) |
|---|---|---|---|---|---|---|---|
| 9-17 | C- | 0.60 | 0.50 | 2.1 | 0.8 | 3.5 | -0.1 |
| 9-16 | N/A | N/A | N/A | 2.2 | 1.2 | 4.7 | 0.2 |
| 2016 | C- | 1.11 | 0.93 | 1.5 | 1.2 | 6.1 | 0.2 |
| 2015 | N/A | N/A | N/A | 1.2 | 1.2 | N/A | -0.2 |
| 2014 | N/A | N/A | N/A | N/A | N/A | N/A | N/A |
| 2013 | N/A | N/A | N/A | N/A | N/A | N/A | N/A |
| 2012 | N/A | N/A | N/A | N/A | N/A | N/A | N/A |

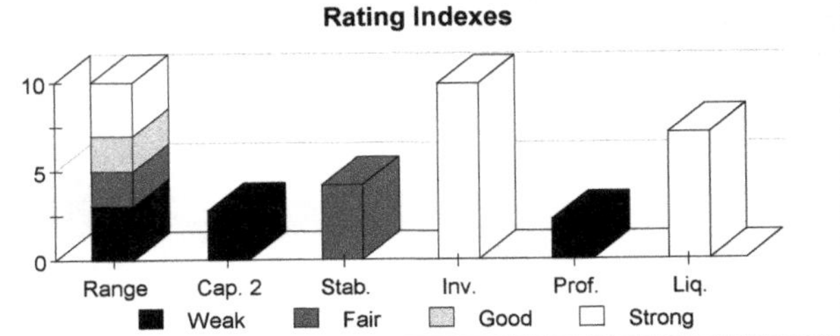

## MMM HEALTHCARE LLC — E- Very Weak

**Major Rating Factors:** Good overall profitability index (6.3 on a scale of 0 to 10). Good capitalization (6.8) based on excellent current risk-adjusted capital (severe loss scenario). Good liquidity (6.8) with sufficient resources (cash flows and marketable investments) to handle a spike in claims.
**Other Rating Factors:** High quality investment portfolio (9.8).
**Principal Business:** Medicare (100%)
**Mem Phys: 16:** N/A **15:** N/A **16 MLR** 82.5% **/ 16 Admin Exp** N/A
**Enroll(000): Q3 17:** 207 **16:** 192 **15:** 179 **Med Exp PMPM:** $607
**Principal Investments:** Long-term bonds (57%), cash and equiv (26%), other (17%)
**Provider Compensation ($000):** FFS ($707,266), capitation ($268,431), bonus arrang ($42,571), other ($405,876)
**Total Member Encounters:** N/A
**Group Affiliation:** InnovaCare Inc
**Licensed in:** PR
**Address:** 350 CHARDON AVE STE 500, SAN JUAN, PR 00918
**Phone:** (787) 622-3000 **Dom State:** PR **Commenced Bus:** January 2001

| Data Date | Rating | RACR #1 | RACR #2 | Total Assets ($mil) | Capital ($mil) | Net Premium ($mil) | Net Income ($mil) |
|---|---|---|---|---|---|---|---|
| 9-17 | E- | 1.20 | 1.00 | 490.8 | 137.3 | 1,371.9 | 34.0 |
| 9-16 | E- | 1.18 | 0.98 | 508.9 | 143.4 | 1,171.0 | 32.2 |
| 2016 | E- | 1.01 | 0.85 | 310.7 | 117.0 | 1,593.6 | 37.3 |
| 2015 | E- | 0.99 | 0.82 | 272.5 | 120.8 | 1,531.9 | 11.2 |
| 2014 | C | 0.71 | 0.60 | 272.3 | 104.1 | 1,463.7 | -28.9 |
| 2013 | C+ | 0.87 | 0.72 | 314.2 | 123.7 | 1,733.0 | 46.8 |
| 2012 | C | 0.63 | 0.53 | 306.5 | 89.8 | 1,698.3 | 77.4 |

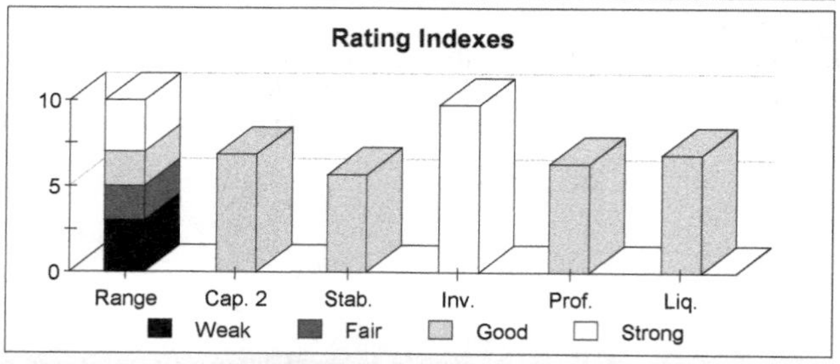


## MMM MULTI HEALTH LLC — D Weak

**Major Rating Factors:** Weak profitability index (1.5 on a scale of 0 to 10). Good liquidity (6.8) with sufficient resources (cash flows and marketable investments) to handle a spike in claims. Strong capitalization (8.7) based on excellent current risk-adjusted capital (severe loss scenario).
**Other Rating Factors:** High quality investment portfolio (9.9).
**Principal Business:** Medicaid (100%)
**Mem Phys: 16:** N/A **15:** N/A **16 MLR** 90.1% **/ 16 Admin Exp** N/A
**Enroll(000): Q3 17:** 260 **16:** 126 **15:** 130 **Med Exp PMPM:** $148
**Principal Investments:** Cash and equiv (56%), long-term bonds (44%)
**Provider Compensation ($000):** FFS ($99,424), capitation ($44,040), bonus arrang ($5,153), other ($70,478)
**Total Member Encounters:** N/A
**Group Affiliation:** InnovaCare Inc
**Licensed in:** PR
**Address:** 350 CHARDON AVE STE 350, SAN JUAN, PR 00918
**Phone:** (787) 622-3000 **Dom State:** PR **Commenced Bus:** February 2005

| Data Date | Rating | RACR #1 | RACR #2 | Total Assets ($mil) | Capital ($mil) | Net Premium ($mil) | Net Income ($mil) |
|---|---|---|---|---|---|---|---|
| 9-17 | D | 2.74 | 2.28 | 151.2 | 53.0 | 401.5 | 0.0 |
| 9-16 | N/A | N/A | N/A | 61.8 | 18.0 | 182.9 | 4.3 |
| 2016 | D | 1.10 | 0.92 | 63.5 | 18.8 | 249.6 | -1.3 |
| 2015 | N/A | N/A | N/A | 67.5 | 15.6 | 193.4 | -2.3 |
| 2014 | N/A | N/A | N/A | 0.6 | N/A | N/A | N/A |
| 2013 | N/A | N/A | N/A | 0.6 | N/A | N/A | N/A |
| 2012 | N/A | N/A | N/A | 0.6 | N/A | N/A | N/A |

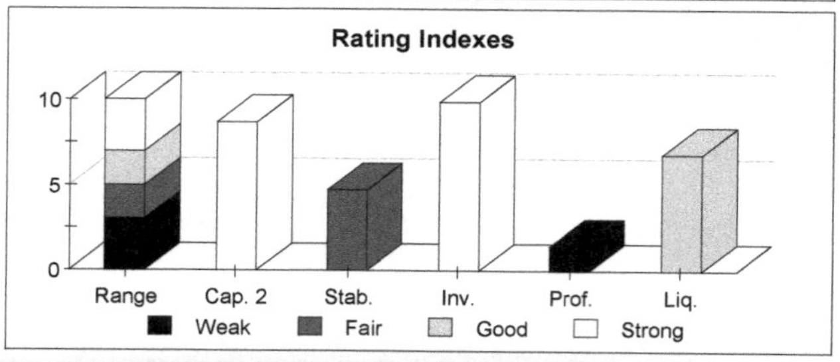


## MODA HEALTH PLAN INC — E Very Weak

**Major Rating Factors:** Weak profitability index (1.7 on a scale of 0 to 10). Weak liquidity (0.2) as a spike in claims may stretch capacity. Fair capitalization (3.1) based on weak current risk-adjusted capital (moderate loss scenario).
**Other Rating Factors:** Fair quality investment portfolio (4.0).
**Principal Business:** Comp med (84%), Medicare (16%)
**Mem Phys: 16:** 30,006 **15:** 30,682 **16 MLR** 99.1% **/ 16 Admin Exp** N/A
**Enroll(000): Q3 17:** 75 **16:** 130 **15:** 216 **Med Exp PMPM:** $521
**Principal Investments:** Affiliate common stock (61%), long-term bonds (23%), nonaffiliate common stock (9%), other (10%)
**Provider Compensation ($000):** Contr fee ($793,483), FFS ($67,407)
**Total Member Encounters:** Phys (70,859), non-phys (57,545)
**Group Affiliation:** Oregon Dental Service
**Licensed in:** AK, CA, ID, OR, TX, WA
**Address:** 601 SW SECOND AVE, PORTLAND, OR 97204
**Phone:** (503) 228-6554 **Dom State:** OR **Commenced Bus:** December 1988

| Data Date | Rating | RACR #1 | RACR #2 | Total Assets ($mil) | Capital ($mil) | Net Premium ($mil) | Net Income ($mil) |
|---|---|---|---|---|---|---|---|
| 9-17 | E | 0.65 | 0.54 | 291.8 | 94.1 | 422.4 | 31.0 |
| 9-16 | E- | 0.37 | 0.31 | 595.1 | 59.5 | 666.1 | -33.5 |
| 2016 | E | 0.45 | 0.38 | 366.4 | 77.6 | 903.9 | -12.9 |
| 2015 | E- | 0.42 | 0.35 | 558.7 | 67.0 | 777.1 | -49.5 |
| 2014 | C | 1.41 | 1.17 | 353.7 | 121.1 | 749.5 | -5.2 |
| 2013 | B- | 2.17 | 1.81 | 208.8 | 74.9 | 293.0 | 7.5 |
| 2012 | B- | 2.45 | 2.04 | 284.1 | 75.9 | 249.4 | 5.3 |

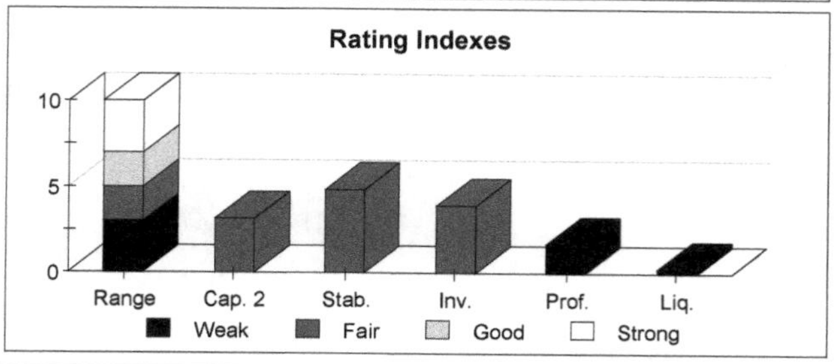

## MOLINA HEALTHCARE OF CALIFORNIA C- Fair

**Major Rating Factors:** Weak overall results on stability tests (2.2 on a scale of 0 to 10). Good overall profitability index (6.2). Strong capitalization index (7.1) based on good current risk-adjusted capital (moderate loss scenario).
**Other Rating Factors:** Excellent liquidity (7.2) with ample operational cash flow and liquid investments.
**Principal Business:** Medicaid (74%), Medicare (9%)
**Mem Phys: 16:** N/A **15:** N/A **16 MLR** 82.6% **/ 16 Admin Exp** N/A
**Enroll(000): Q3 17:** 757 **16:** 684 **15:** 618 **Med Exp PMPM:** $250
**Principal Investments ($000):** Cash and equiv ($738,546)
**Provider Compensation ($000):** None
**Total Member Encounters:** N/A
**Group Affiliation:** Molina Healthcare Inc
**Licensed in:** CA
**Address:** 200 Oceangate Ste 100, Long Beach, CA 90802
**Phone:** (800) 562-5442 **Dom State:** CA **Commenced Bus:** April 1989

| Data Date | Rating | RACR #1 | RACR #2 | Total Assets ($mil) | Capital ($mil) | Net Premium ($mil) | Net Income ($mil) |
|---|---|---|---|---|---|---|---|
| 9-17 | C- | 1.18 | 0.73 | 1,139.4 | 152.4 | 2,107.7 | 43.5 |
| 9-16 | C- | 1.32 | 0.81 | 990.4 | 166.2 | 1,775.1 | 39.0 |
| 2016 | C- | 1.63 | 1.01 | 973.4 | 208.6 | 2,470.4 | 82.3 |
| 2015 | C- | 1.40 | 0.86 | 683.8 | 175.7 | 2,272.2 | 65.2 |
| 2014 | C- | 1.18 | 0.77 | 566.4 | 124.7 | 1,566.2 | 67.9 |
| 2013 | C- | 0.81 | 0.52 | 246.8 | 56.9 | 770.4 | -1.3 |
| 2012 | C- | 0.76 | 0.47 | 119.0 | 47.5 | 671.3 | -4.0 |

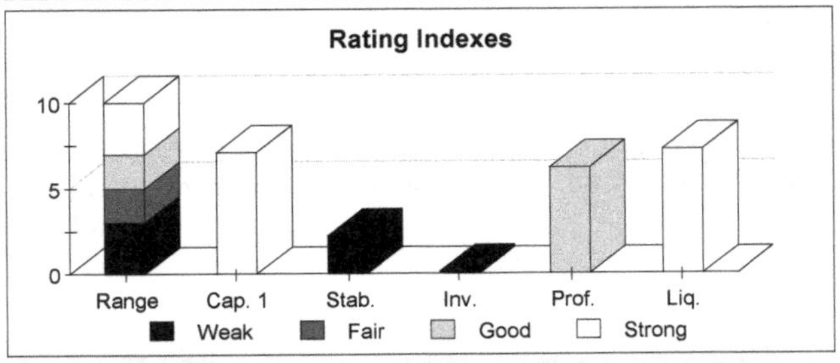


## MOLINA HEALTHCARE OF FLORIDA INC E Very Weak

**Major Rating Factors:** Weak profitability index (1.2 on a scale of 0 to 10). Strong capitalization (7.6) based on excellent current risk-adjusted capital (severe loss scenario). High quality investment portfolio (9.9).
**Other Rating Factors:** Excellent liquidity (7.0) with ample operational cash flow and liquid investments.
**Principal Business:** Medicaid (57%), comp med (30%), Medicare (1%), other (12%)
**Mem Phys: 16:** 33,502 **15:** 24,639 **16 MLR** 89.5% **/ 16 Admin Exp** N/A
**Enroll(000): Q3 17:** 641 **16:** 553 **15:** 440 **Med Exp PMPM:** $263
**Principal Investments:** Cash and equiv (78%), long-term bonds (22%)
**Provider Compensation ($000):** Contr fee ($1,378,911), capitation ($171,149), FFS ($166,433)
**Total Member Encounters:** Phys (2,975,562), non-phys (3,661,614)
**Group Affiliation:** Molina Healthcare Inc
**Licensed in:** FL
**Address:** 8300 NW 33rd St Ste 400, Doral, FL 33122
**Phone:** (866) 422-2541 **Dom State:** FL **Commenced Bus:** March 2008

| Data Date | Rating | RACR #1 | RACR #2 | Total Assets ($mil) | Capital ($mil) | Net Premium ($mil) | Net Income ($mil) |
|---|---|---|---|---|---|---|---|
| 9-17 | E | 1.82 | 1.51 | 1,058.3 | 198.4 | 1,962.3 | -132.2 |
| 9-16 | E | 2.33 | 1.94 | 640.9 | 164.0 | 1,473.3 | -27.0 |
| 2016 | E | 1.83 | 1.53 | 802.9 | 200.0 | 1,961.9 | -62.0 |
| 2015 | E | 1.94 | 1.62 | 632.8 | 137.0 | 1,217.3 | -38.7 |
| 2014 | E | 0.20 | 0.17 | 113.8 | 8.1 | 454.3 | -20.2 |
| 2013 | D | 0.79 | 0.66 | 53.1 | 17.3 | 264.9 | -5.6 |
| 2012 | D | 1.15 | 0.95 | 42.7 | 19.1 | 228.6 | 0.0 |

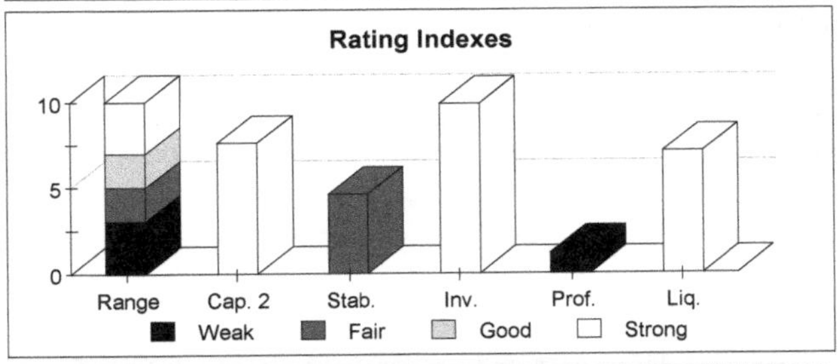


## MOLINA HEALTHCARE OF ILLINOIS INC E Very Weak

**Major Rating Factors:** Weak profitability index (0.9 on a scale of 0 to 10). Weak liquidity (1.0) as a spike in claims may stretch capacity. Strong capitalization (7.7) based on excellent current risk-adjusted capital (severe loss scenario).
**Other Rating Factors:** High quality investment portfolio (9.7).
**Principal Business:** Medicaid (92%), Medicare (8%)
**Mem Phys: 16:** 11,559 **15:** 4,588 **16 MLR** 90.6% **/ 16 Admin Exp** N/A
**Enroll(000): Q3 17:** 163 **16:** 195 **15:** 98 **Med Exp PMPM:** $310
**Principal Investments:** Cash and equiv (114%)
**Provider Compensation ($000):** Contr fee ($377,390), capitation ($221,989), FFS ($100,742)
**Total Member Encounters:** Phys (1,029,107), non-phys (1,270,692)
**Group Affiliation:** Molina Healthcare Inc
**Licensed in:** IL
**Address:** 1520 Kensington Rd # 212, Oakbrook, IL 60523
**Phone:** (888) 858-2156 **Dom State:** IL **Commenced Bus:** June 2011

| Data Date | Rating | RACR #1 | RACR #2 | Total Assets ($mil) | Capital ($mil) | Net Premium ($mil) | Net Income ($mil) |
|---|---|---|---|---|---|---|---|
| 9-17 | E | 1.92 | 1.60 | 258.3 | 70.8 | 569.3 | -45.4 |
| 9-16 | E | N/A | N/A | 145.8 | 58.9 | 570.9 | -0.1 |
| 2016 | E | 1.40 | 1.16 | 146.1 | 51.3 | 796.9 | -20.6 |
| 2015 | E | N/A | N/A | 125.0 | 46.4 | 467.4 | -5.9 |
| 2014 | E | 1.81 | 1.51 | 80.6 | 18.5 | 170.7 | -3.8 |
| 2013 | C+ | 2.01 | 1.67 | 13.8 | 5.0 | 8.3 | -5.8 |
| 2012 | N/A | N/A | N/A | 2.3 | 2.2 | N/A | N/A |

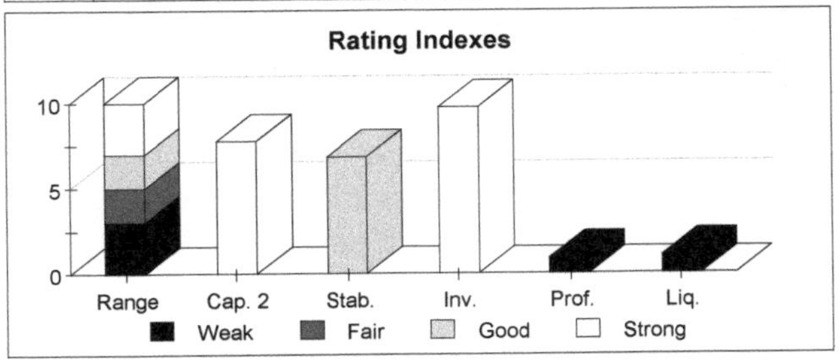

## MOLINA HEALTHCARE OF MICHIGAN INC — B- Good

**Major Rating Factors:** Excellent profitability (9.1 on a scale of 0 to 10). Strong capitalization index (8.2) based on excellent current risk-adjusted capital (severe loss scenario). High quality investment portfolio (9.6).
**Other Rating Factors:** Excellent overall results on stability tests (8.0) based on healthy premium and capital growth during 2016. Fair financial strength from affiliates. Excellent liquidity (6.9) with sufficient resources (cash flows and marketable investments) to handle a spike in claims.
**Principal Business:** Medicaid (86%), Medicare (14%)
**Mem Phys: 16:** 30,281 **15:** 27,646 **16 MLR** 82.1% **/ 16 Admin Exp** N/A
**Enroll(000): Q3 17:** 399 **16:** 391 **15:** 328 **Med Exp PMPM:** $366
**Principal Investments:** Cash and equiv (77%), long-term bonds (23%)
**Provider Compensation ($000):** Contr fee ($1,124,822), capitation ($470,335), FFS ($82,068)
**Total Member Encounters:** Phys (2,577,733), non-phys (3,569,694)
**Group Affiliation:** Molina Healthcare Inc
**Licensed in:** MI
**Address:** 880 W Long Lake Rd Suite 600, Troy, MI 48098-4504
**Phone:** (248) 925-1700 **Dom State:** MI **Commenced Bus:** January 1998

| Data Date | Rating | RACR #1 | RACR #2 | Total Assets ($mil) | Capital ($mil) | Net Premium ($mil) | Net Income ($mil) |
|---|---|---|---|---|---|---|---|
| 9-17 | B- | 2.34 | 1.95 | 569.7 | 200.8 | 1,525.3 | 15.2 |
| 9-16 | B- | 2.65 | 2.21 | 493.2 | 153.4 | 1,594.9 | 15.7 |
| 2016 | B- | 2.01 | 1.68 | 476.9 | 172.3 | 2,104.8 | 30.9 |
| 2015 | B- | 2.40 | 2.00 | 376.0 | 138.7 | 1,467.9 | 53.8 |
| 2014 | B | 2.71 | 2.26 | 254.5 | 125.1 | 1,059.7 | 26.7 |
| 2013 | B | 1.98 | 1.65 | 193.7 | 102.7 | 883.4 | 18.6 |
| 2012 | B | 1.57 | 1.31 | 174.4 | 80.5 | 841.2 | 9.4 |

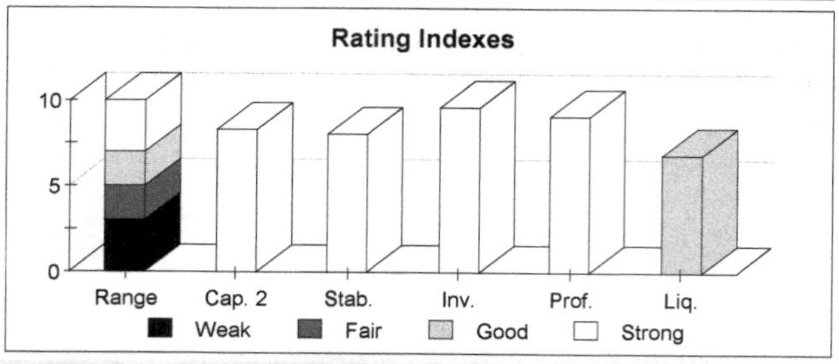


## MOLINA HEALTHCARE OF NEW MEXICO — C Fair

**Major Rating Factors:** Weak profitability index (0.9 on a scale of 0 to 10). Good overall results on stability tests (5.1). Potential support from affiliation with Molina Healthcare Inc. Strong capitalization index (7.2) based on excellent current risk-adjusted capital (severe loss scenario).
**Other Rating Factors:** High quality investment portfolio (9.9). Excellent liquidity (7.1) with ample operational cash flow and liquid investments.
**Principal Business:** Medicaid (93%), comp med (4%), Medicare (2%)
**Mem Phys: 16:** 15,552 **15:** 13,717 **16 MLR** 82.9% **/ 16 Admin Exp** N/A
**Enroll(000): Q3 17:** 256 **16:** 254 **15:** 231 **Med Exp PMPM:** $379
**Principal Investments:** Cash and equiv (76%), long-term bonds (23%)
**Provider Compensation ($000):** Contr fee ($1,061,572), FFS ($62,379), capitation ($34,841)
**Total Member Encounters:** Phys (930,066), non-phys (3,581,635)
**Group Affiliation:** Molina Healthcare Inc
**Licensed in:** NM
**Address:** 400 Tijeras Ave NW Suite 200, Albuquerque, NM 87102-3234
**Phone:** (505) 348-0410 **Dom State:** NM **Commenced Bus:** December 1993

| Data Date | Rating | RACR #1 | RACR #2 | Total Assets ($mil) | Capital ($mil) | Net Premium ($mil) | Net Income ($mil) |
|---|---|---|---|---|---|---|---|
| 9-17 | C | 1.54 | 1.28 | 383.1 | 111.4 | 1,050.1 | -25.8 |
| 9-16 | C | 1.65 | 1.37 | 435.6 | 112.4 | 1,089.4 | 2.6 |
| 2016 | C | 1.68 | 1.40 | 468.3 | 122.7 | 1,386.6 | -28.5 |
| 2015 | C | 1.61 | 1.34 | 409.1 | 109.7 | 1,318.0 | -1.6 |
| 2014 | C+ | 1.33 | 1.10 | 304.3 | 86.1 | 1,121.2 | -24.9 |
| 2013 | B | 1.53 | 1.27 | 95.3 | 40.9 | 499.7 | 1.0 |
| 2012 | B | 2.50 | 2.09 | 74.1 | 47.5 | 337.5 | 6.0 |

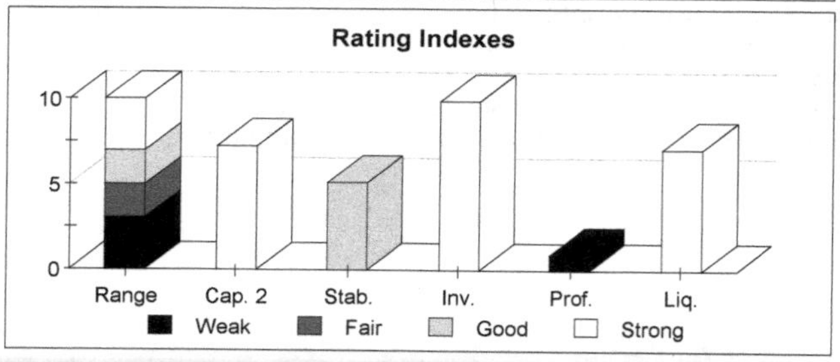


## MOLINA HEALTHCARE OF OHIO INC — B- Good

**Major Rating Factors:** Excellent profitability (9.4 on a scale of 0 to 10). Strong capitalization (8.4) based on excellent current risk-adjusted capital (severe loss scenario). High quality investment portfolio (9.9).
**Other Rating Factors:** Excellent liquidity (7.0) with sufficient resources (cash flows and marketable investments) to handle a spike in claims.
**Principal Business:** Medicaid (88%), Medicare (10%), comp med (2%)
**Mem Phys: 16:** 39,637 **15:** 37,528 **16 MLR** 78.0% **/ 16 Admin Exp** N/A
**Enroll(000): Q3 17:** 343 **16:** 332 **15:** 327 **Med Exp PMPM:** $424
**Principal Investments:** Cash and equiv (72%), long-term bonds (28%)
**Provider Compensation ($000):** Contr fee ($1,365,822), capitation ($269,395), FFS ($90,744)
**Total Member Encounters:** Phys (1,675,698), non-phys (4,760,003)
**Group Affiliation:** Molina Healthcare Inc
**Licensed in:** OH
**Address:** 3000 Corporate Exchange Dr, Columbus, OH 43231
**Phone:** (888) 562-5442 **Dom State:** OH **Commenced Bus:** October 2005

| Data Date | Rating | RACR #1 | RACR #2 | Total Assets ($mil) | Capital ($mil) | Net Premium ($mil) | Net Income ($mil) |
|---|---|---|---|---|---|---|---|
| 9-17 | B- | 2.50 | 2.08 | 548.1 | 257.2 | 1,805.5 | 18.2 |
| 9-16 | B- | 2.21 | 1.84 | 509.9 | 221.5 | 1,662.0 | 33.6 |
| 2016 | B- | 2.29 | 1.91 | 507.2 | 234.9 | 2,198.5 | 45.9 |
| 2015 | B- | 1.92 | 1.60 | 440.4 | 190.7 | 2,270.8 | 110.0 |
| 2014 | B | 2.25 | 1.87 | 464.1 | 182.7 | 1,781.8 | 55.9 |
| 2013 | B | 1.90 | 1.58 | 267.3 | 128.9 | 1,248.2 | 34.0 |
| 2012 | B- | 1.35 | 1.12 | 199.9 | 96.4 | 1,216.3 | 18.8 |

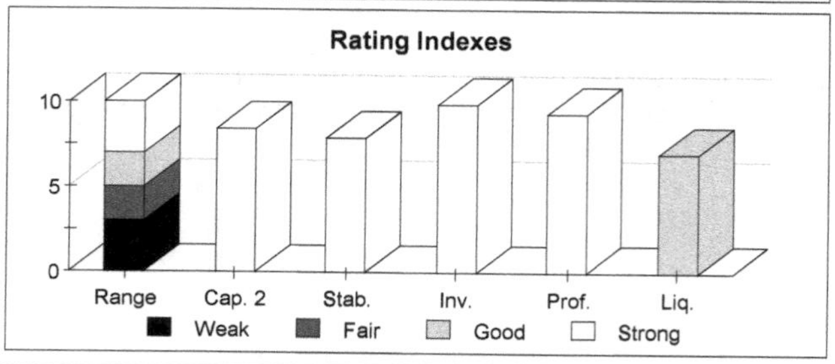

## MOLINA HEALTHCARE OF PUERTO RICO INC C- Fair

**Major Rating Factors:** Weak profitability index (1.2 on a scale of 0 to 10). Strong capitalization (7.8) based on excellent current risk-adjusted capital (severe loss scenario). High quality investment portfolio (9.9).
**Other Rating Factors:** Excellent liquidity (7.0) with sufficient resources (cash flows and marketable investments) to handle a spike in claims.
**Principal Business:** Medicaid (100%)
**Mem Phys: 16:** 3,235 **15:** N/A **16 MLR** 90.8% **/ 16 Admin Exp** N/A
**Enroll(000): Q3 17:** 306 **16:** 330 **15:** 348 **Med Exp PMPM:** $168
**Principal Investments:** Cash and equiv (100%)
**Provider Compensation ($000):** Contr fee ($501,912), capitation ($123,565), FFS ($50,289)
**Total Member Encounters:** Phys (2,013,214), non-phys (1,684,185)
**Group Affiliation:** Molina Healthcare Inc
**Licensed in:** PR
**Address:** 654 Plaza 654 Munoz Rivera Ave, San Juan, PR 00918-4123
**Phone:** (787) 200-3300 **Dom State:** PR **Commenced Bus:** September 2014

| Data Date | Rating | RACR #1 | RACR #2 | Total Assets ($mil) | Capital ($mil) | Net Premium ($mil) | Net Income ($mil) |
|---|---|---|---|---|---|---|---|
| 9-17 | C- | 1.97 | 1.64 | 166.7 | 74.2 | 553.1 | 3.4 |
| 9-16 | U | 1.78 | 1.48 | 156.3 | 67.3 | 554.8 | -3.2 |
| 2016 | C- | 1.79 | 1.49 | 158.8 | 66.4 | 746.3 | -9.9 |
| 2015 | U | 1.56 | 1.30 | 130.6 | 49.1 | 556.6 | -5.3 |
| 2014 | N/A | N/A | N/A | 5.1 | 5.0 | N/A | N/A |
| 2013 | N/A | N/A | N/A | N/A | N/A | N/A | N/A |
| 2012 | N/A | N/A | N/A | N/A | N/A | N/A | N/A |

Rating Indexes

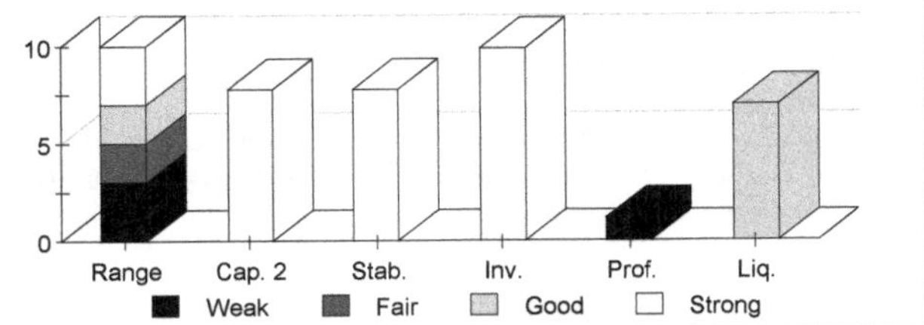


## MOLINA HEALTHCARE OF SOUTH CAROLINA C Fair

**Major Rating Factors:** Good overall profitability index (5.2 on a scale of 0 to 10). Strong capitalization (8.4) based on excellent current risk-adjusted capital (severe loss scenario). High quality investment portfolio (9.7).
**Other Rating Factors:** Excellent liquidity (6.9) with sufficient resources (cash flows and marketable investments) to handle a spike in claims.
**Principal Business:** Medicaid (96%), Medicare (4%)
**Mem Phys: 16:** 14,620 **15:** 11,717 **16 MLR** 80.7% **/ 16 Admin Exp** N/A
**Enroll(000): Q3 17:** 113 **16:** 109 **15:** 100 **Med Exp PMPM:** $260
**Principal Investments:** Cash and equiv (55%), long-term bonds (43%), other (2%)
**Provider Compensation ($000):** Contr fee ($261,445), FFS ($35,146), capitation ($29,307)
**Total Member Encounters:** Phys (567,812), non-phys (549,003)
**Group Affiliation:** Molina Healthcare Inc
**Licensed in:** SC
**Address:** 4105 Faber Place Dr Ste 120, North Charleston, SC 29405
**Phone:** (843) 740-1780 **Dom State:** SC **Commenced Bus:** October 2013

| Data Date | Rating | RACR #1 | RACR #2 | Total Assets ($mil) | Capital ($mil) | Net Premium ($mil) | Net Income ($mil) |
|---|---|---|---|---|---|---|---|
| 9-17 | C | 2.50 | 2.09 | 117.0 | 48.9 | 342.5 | -5.7 |
| 9-16 | B- | 5.53 | 4.61 | 150.8 | 97.2 | 301.7 | 7.1 |
| 2016 | C | 2.51 | 2.09 | 102.3 | 49.0 | 411.8 | 13.4 |
| 2015 | B- | 4.79 | 3.99 | 125.5 | 83.0 | 369.3 | 17.3 |
| 2014 | C | 2.06 | 1.72 | 120.4 | 59.2 | 398.2 | 14.9 |
| 2013 | N/A | N/A | N/A | 66.3 | 10.3 | N/A | N/A |
| 2012 | N/A | N/A | N/A | N/A | N/A | N/A | N/A |

Rating Indexes

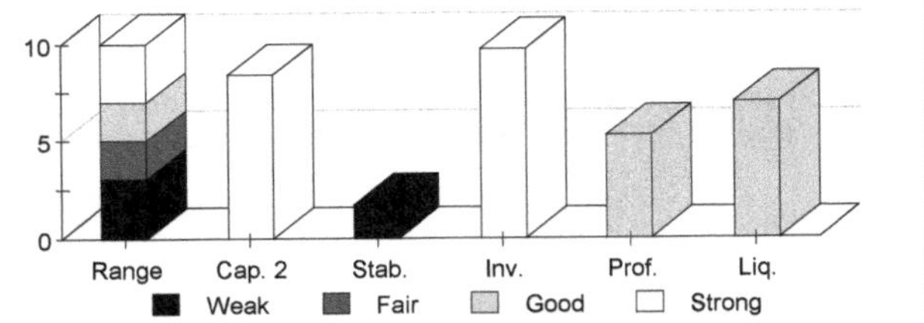


## MOLINA HEALTHCARE OF TEXAS INC B- Good

**Major Rating Factors:** Good overall profitability index (6.4 on a scale of 0 to 10). Strong capitalization (7.9) based on excellent current risk-adjusted capital (severe loss scenario). High quality investment portfolio (9.9).
**Other Rating Factors:** Excellent liquidity (7.1) with ample operational cash flow and liquid investments.
**Principal Business:** Medicaid (77%), comp med (14%), Medicare (10%)
**Mem Phys: 16:** 68,804 **15:** 66,456 **16 MLR** 79.3% **/ 16 Admin Exp** N/A
**Enroll(000): Q3 17:** 420 **16:** 310 **15:** 225 **Med Exp PMPM:** $531
**Principal Investments:** Cash and equiv (79%), long-term bonds (21%)
**Provider Compensation ($000):** Contr fee ($1,852,109), FFS ($146,497), capitation ($83,639)
**Total Member Encounters:** Phys (1,849,488), non-phys (4,543,216)
**Group Affiliation:** Molina Healthcare Inc
**Licensed in:** TX
**Address:** 5605 N MacArthur Blvd Ste 400, Irving, TX 75038
**Phone:** (877) 665-4622 **Dom State:** TX **Commenced Bus:** June 2005

| Data Date | Rating | RACR #1 | RACR #2 | Total Assets ($mil) | Capital ($mil) | Net Premium ($mil) | Net Income ($mil) |
|---|---|---|---|---|---|---|---|
| 9-17 | B- | 2.07 | 1.72 | 891.1 | 281.5 | 2,147.7 | 40.3 |
| 9-16 | B- | 1.86 | 1.55 | 714.4 | 219.5 | 1,991.3 | 56.9 |
| 2016 | B- | 1.75 | 1.46 | 696.6 | 237.5 | 2,606.1 | 82.4 |
| 2015 | C | 1.26 | 1.05 | 477.2 | 148.7 | 2,056.4 | -12.3 |
| 2014 | C | 1.70 | 1.41 | 301.0 | 141.7 | 1,359.4 | -7.3 |
| 2013 | C | 1.28 | 1.07 | 227.3 | 110.0 | 1,312.4 | 16.7 |
| 2012 | C | 0.97 | 0.81 | 232.4 | 88.3 | 1,257.3 | -21.5 |

Rating Indexes

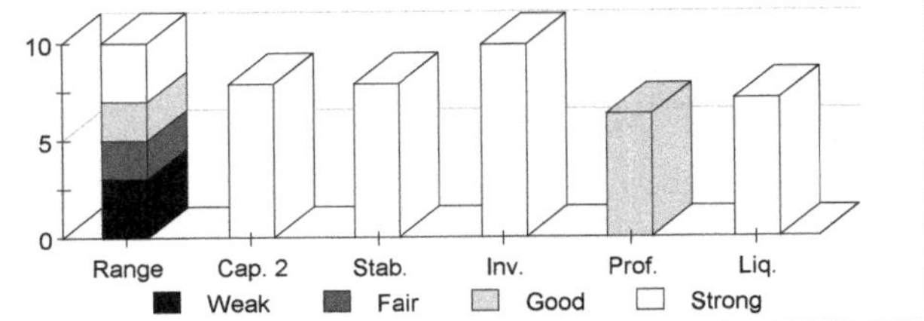

## MOLINA HEALTHCARE OF UTAH INC C- Fair

**Major Rating Factors:** Weak profitability index (0.9 on a scale of 0 to 10). Good overall results on stability tests (6.7). Rating is significantly influenced by the fair financial results of Molina Healthcare Inc. Good liquidity (6.9) with sufficient resources (cash flows and marketable investments) to handle a spike in claims.
**Other Rating Factors:** Strong capitalization index (8.2) based on excellent current risk-adjusted capital (severe loss scenario). High quality investment portfolio (9.1).
**Principal Business:** Medicaid (50%), comp med (25%), Medicare (25%)
**Mem Phys: 16:** 10,809 **15:** 8,982 **16 MLR** 91.3% **/ 16 Admin Exp** N/A
**Enroll(000): Q3 17:** 160 **16:** 146 **15:** 102 **Med Exp PMPM:** $233
**Principal Investments:** Cash and equiv (64%), long-term bonds (36%)
**Provider Compensation ($000):** Contr fee ($368,148), FFS ($18,724), capitation ($4,292)
**Total Member Encounters:** Phys (750,127), non-phys (676,282)
**Group Affiliation:** Molina Healthcare Inc
**Licensed in:** UT
**Address:** 7050 Union Park Center Ste 200, Midvale, UT 84047
**Phone:** (801) 858-0400 **Dom State:** UT **Commenced Bus:** May 1996

| Data Date | Rating | RACR #1 | RACR #2 | Total Assets ($mil) | Capital ($mil) | Net Premium ($mil) | Net Income ($mil) |
|---|---|---|---|---|---|---|---|
| 9-17 | C- | 2.33 | 1.95 | 238.2 | 64.9 | 402.3 | -8.5 |
| 9-16 | C+ | 2.00 | 1.67 | 153.9 | 38.9 | 339.1 | -10.7 |
| 2016 | C | 1.84 | 1.53 | 191.3 | 50.7 | 453.9 | -19.1 |
| 2015 | B- | 2.58 | 2.15 | 122.7 | 50.8 | 343.7 | 0.6 |
| 2014 | B | 2.53 | 2.10 | 107.4 | 51.2 | 320.4 | -4.3 |
| 2013 | B | 2.50 | 2.09 | 107.5 | 57.6 | 347.3 | 10.8 |
| 2012 | B | 2.48 | 2.07 | 82.6 | 50.8 | 310.8 | 18.0 |

**Rating Indexes**

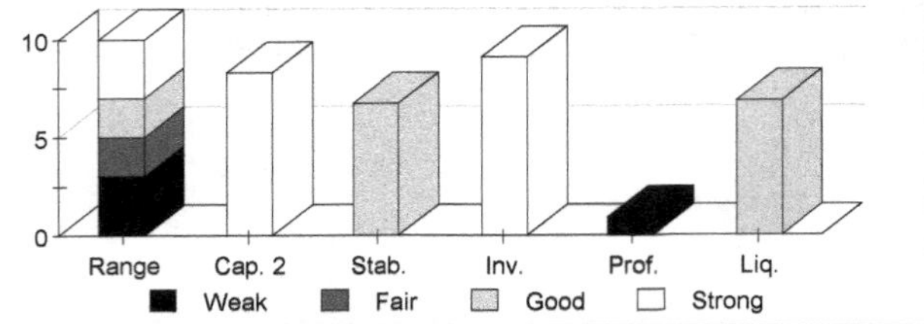


## MOLINA HEALTHCARE OF WASHINGTON INC B Good

**Major Rating Factors:** Good overall profitability index (5.2 on a scale of 0 to 10). Strong capitalization index (8.1) based on excellent current risk-adjusted capital (severe loss scenario). High quality investment portfolio (9.4).
**Other Rating Factors:** Excellent overall results on stability tests (8.1) based on healthy premium and capital growth during 2016. Fair financial strength from affiliates. Excellent liquidity (7.0) with ample operational cash flow and liquid investments.
**Principal Business:** Medicaid (90%), Medicare (5%), comp med (5%)
**Mem Phys: 16:** 34,132 **15:** 29,496 **16 MLR** 86.1% **/ 16 Admin Exp** N/A
**Enroll(000): Q3 17:** 770 **16:** 736 **15:** 582 **Med Exp PMPM:** $235
**Principal Investments:** Cash and equiv (70%), long-term bonds (30%)
**Provider Compensation ($000):** Contr fee ($1,226,796), FFS ($629,411), capitation ($113,797)
**Total Member Encounters:** Phys (3,240,331), non-phys (3,909,820)
**Group Affiliation:** Molina Healthcare Inc
**Licensed in:** WA
**Address:** 21540 - 30th Drive SE Suite, Bothell, WA 98021
**Phone:** (425) 424-1100 **Dom State:** WA **Commenced Bus:** December 1986

| Data Date | Rating | RACR #1 | RACR #2 | Total Assets ($mil) | Capital ($mil) | Net Premium ($mil) | Net Income ($mil) |
|---|---|---|---|---|---|---|---|
| 9-17 | B | 2.19 | 1.83 | 852.4 | 293.0 | 1,996.7 | 41.7 |
| 9-16 | B | 1.99 | 1.66 | 723.5 | 195.8 | 1,710.8 | 10.5 |
| 2016 | B | 1.78 | 1.48 | 685.6 | 235.9 | 2,307.8 | 8.2 |
| 2015 | B | 1.99 | 1.66 | 589.8 | 190.8 | 1,671.7 | -3.4 |
| 2014 | B | 1.69 | 1.41 | 669.2 | 145.8 | 1,357.0 | -24.6 |
| 2013 | A- | 1.50 | 1.25 | 331.7 | 120.0 | 1,201.2 | 5.0 |
| 2012 | A- | 1.67 | 1.39 | 294.0 | 113.8 | 1,050.1 | 19.3 |

**Rating Indexes**

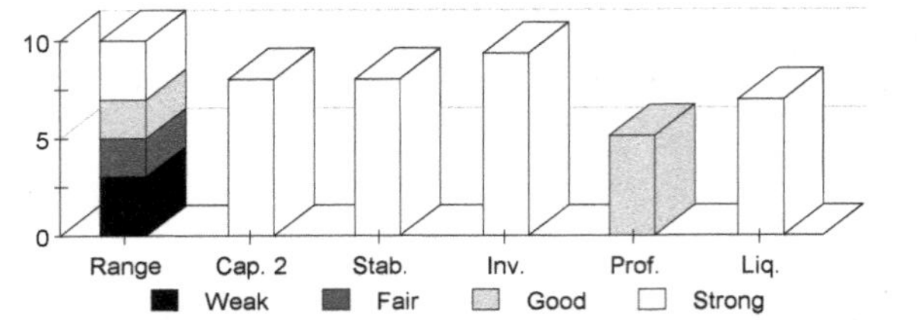


## MOLINA HEALTHCARE OF WISCONSIN INC E+ Very Weak

**Major Rating Factors:** Weak profitability index (0.9 on a scale of 0 to 10). Good liquidity (6.1) with sufficient resources (cash flows and marketable investments) to handle a spike in claims. Strong capitalization (8.2) based on excellent current risk-adjusted capital (severe loss scenario).
**Other Rating Factors:** High quality investment portfolio (9.9).
**Principal Business:** Comp med (64%), Medicaid (34%), Medicare (2%)
**Mem Phys: 16:** 16,774 **15:** 13,194 **16 MLR** 97.1% **/ 16 Admin Exp** N/A
**Enroll(000): Q3 17:** 124 **16:** 126 **15:** 98 **Med Exp PMPM:** $250
**Principal Investments:** Cash and equiv (99%), long-term bonds (1%)
**Provider Compensation ($000):** Contr fee ($349,305), FFS ($21,507), capitation ($1,379)
**Total Member Encounters:** Phys (646,046), non-phys (680,501)
**Group Affiliation:** Molina Healthcare Inc
**Licensed in:** WI
**Address:** 11200 W Parkland Ave, Milwaukee, WI 53224-3127
**Phone:** (414) 847-1777 **Dom State:** WI **Commenced Bus:** May 2004

| Data Date | Rating | RACR #1 | RACR #2 | Total Assets ($mil) | Capital ($mil) | Net Premium ($mil) | Net Income ($mil) |
|---|---|---|---|---|---|---|---|
| 9-17 | E+ | 2.34 | 1.95 | 169.6 | 60.1 | 375.7 | -20.4 |
| 9-16 | E+ | 1.55 | 1.29 | 104.9 | 22.5 | 305.8 | -14.4 |
| 2016 | E+ | 1.86 | 1.55 | 141.0 | 47.2 | 403.1 | -34.2 |
| 2015 | D | 2.04 | 1.70 | 69.7 | 29.9 | 266.0 | 4.2 |
| 2014 | D | 2.22 | 1.85 | 53.3 | 22.4 | 161.0 | -0.9 |
| 2013 | D | 1.60 | 1.33 | 47.4 | 22.7 | 195.1 | 6.1 |
| 2012 | D | 1.66 | 1.38 | 32.1 | 14.6 | 96.5 | -5.9 |

**Rating Indexes**

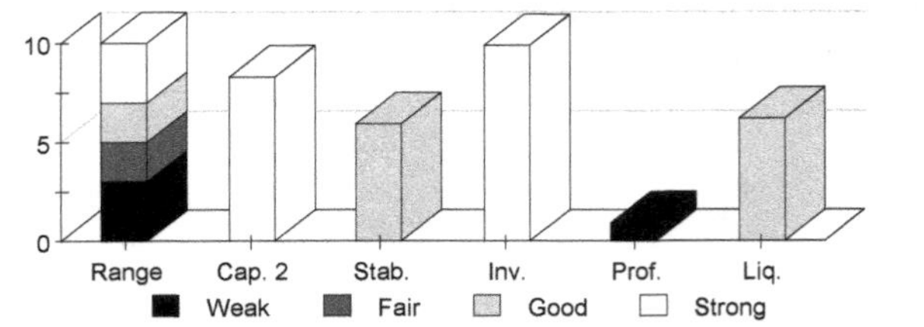

## MONARCH HEALTH PLAN E- Very Weak

**Major Rating Factors:** Poor capitalization index (0.0 on a scale of 0 to 10) based on weak current risk-adjusted capital (severe loss scenario). Weak liquidity (0.0) as a spike in claims may stretch capacity. Fair overall results on stability tests (4.1).
**Other Rating Factors:** Good overall profitability index (6.1).
**Principal Business:** Managed care (100%)
**Mem Phys: 16:** N/A **15:** N/A **16 MLR** 96.3% **/ 16 Admin Exp** N/A
**Enroll(000): Q3 17:** 156 **16:** 52 **15:** 55 **Med Exp PMPM:** $545
**Principal Investments ($000):** Cash and equiv ($69,172)
**Provider Compensation ($000):** None
**Total Member Encounters:** N/A
**Group Affiliation:** None
**Licensed in:** CA
**Address:** 11 Technology Drive, Irvine, CA 92618
**Phone:** (949) 923-3350 **Dom State:** CA **Commenced Bus:** January 2008

| Data Date | Rating | RACR #1 | RACR #2 | Total Assets ($mil) | Capital ($mil) | Net Premium ($mil) | Net Income ($mil) |
|---|---|---|---|---|---|---|---|
| 9-17 | E- | 0.29 | 0.17 | 113.5 | 38.2 | 500.6 | 20.3 |
| 9-16 | E- | 0.11 | 0.06 | 70.6 | 19.0 | 274.5 | 6.5 |
| 2016 | E- | N/A | N/A | 72.9 | 17.7 | 359.8 | 5.5 |
| 2015 | E- | N/A | N/A | 75.0 | 12.5 | 359.9 | 10.8 |
| 2014 | E- | N/A | N/A | 35.2 | 1.7 | 181.9 | 0.5 |
| 2013 | E- | N/A | N/A | 24.1 | 1.2 | 133.1 | -1.4 |
| 2012 | E- | N/A | N/A | 23.7 | 2.6 | 117.7 | 0.8 |

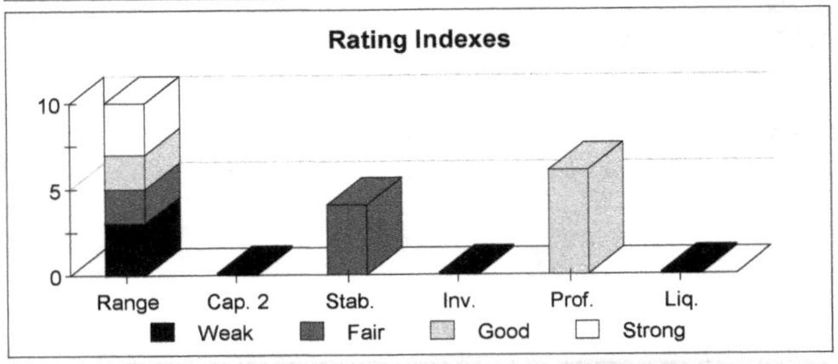


## MONTANA HEALTH COOPERATIVE D Weak

**Major Rating Factors:** Weak profitability index (0.9 on a scale of 0 to 10). Weak liquidity (1.3) as a spike in claims may stretch capacity. Fair capitalization (2.9) based on good current risk-adjusted capital (moderate loss scenario).
**Other Rating Factors:** High quality investment portfolio (8.5).
**Principal Business:** Comp med (100%)
**Mem Phys: 16:** N/A **15:** 9,506 **16 MLR** 104.0% **/ 16 Admin Exp** N/A
**Enroll(000): Q3 17:** 31 **16:** 28 **15:** 41 **Med Exp PMPM:** $343
**Principal Investments:** Cash and equiv (55%), nonaffiliate common stock (24%), long-term bonds (20%)
**Provider Compensation ($000):** FFS ($69,062), contr fee ($68,846)
**Total Member Encounters:** N/A
**Group Affiliation:** Montana Health Cooperative
**Licensed in:** ID, MT
**Address:** 1005 PARTRIDGE PLACE, HELENA, MT 59601
**Phone:** (406) 447-9510 **Dom State:** MT **Commenced Bus:** January 2013

| Data Date | Rating | RACR #1 | RACR #2 | Total Assets ($mil) | Capital ($mil) | Net Premium ($mil) | Net Income ($mil) |
|---|---|---|---|---|---|---|---|
| 9-17 | D | 1.19 | 0.99 | 79.9 | 42.0 | 119.8 | 18.6 |
| 9-16 | D- | 0.54 | 0.45 | 50.7 | 23.0 | 90.9 | -13.5 |
| 2016 | D | 0.62 | 0.51 | 51.8 | 24.0 | 123.0 | -19.7 |
| 2015 | D+ | 0.77 | 0.64 | 67.2 | 33.0 | 135.3 | -40.7 |
| 2014 | D+ | 1.27 | 1.06 | 54.4 | 25.9 | 50.8 | -3.5 |
| 2013 | N/A | N/A | N/A | 9.7 | 8.8 | N/A | -3.8 |
| 2012 | N/A | N/A | N/A | N/A | N/A | N/A | N/A |

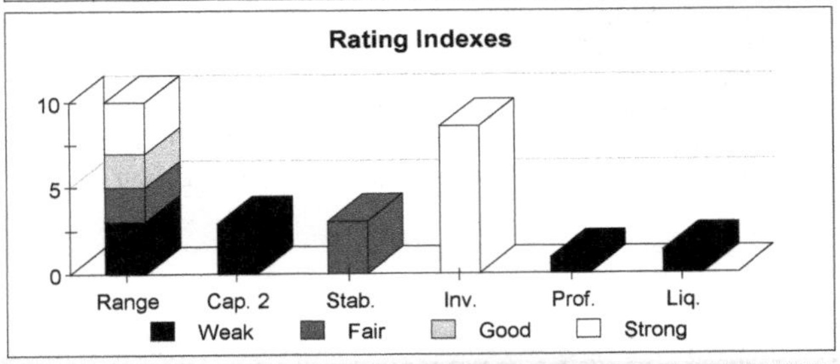


## MOUNT CARMEL HEALTH INS CO D Weak

**Major Rating Factors:** Weak profitability index (0.9 on a scale of 0 to 10). Good liquidity (6.9) with sufficient resources (cash flows and marketable investments) to handle a spike in claims. Strong capitalization (7.4) based on excellent current risk-adjusted capital (severe loss scenario).
**Other Rating Factors:** High quality investment portfolio (9.9).
**Principal Business:** Medicare (100%)
**Mem Phys: 16:** 5,652 **15:** 5,264 **16 MLR** 95.4% **/ 16 Admin Exp** N/A
**Enroll(000): Q3 17:** 1 **16:** 2 **15:** 1 **Med Exp PMPM:** $796
**Principal Investments:** Cash and equiv (64%), long-term bonds (36%)
**Provider Compensation ($000):** Contr fee ($17,986), FFS ($4,579), capitation ($82)
**Total Member Encounters:** Phys (31,565), non-phys (10,522)
**Group Affiliation:** Trinity Health Corporation
**Licensed in:** OH
**Address:** 6150 East BRd St EE320, Columbus, OH 43213
**Phone:** (614) 546-3211 **Dom State:** OH **Commenced Bus:** January 2009

| Data Date | Rating | RACR #1 | RACR #2 | Total Assets ($mil) | Capital ($mil) | Net Premium ($mil) | Net Income ($mil) |
|---|---|---|---|---|---|---|---|
| 9-17 | D | 1.67 | 1.39 | 8.7 | 6.3 | 6.0 | 0.0 |
| 9-16 | D | 2.64 | 2.20 | 11.8 | 6.0 | 19.7 | -0.2 |
| 2016 | D | 1.40 | 1.17 | 9.0 | 5.4 | 24.8 | -1.3 |
| 2015 | D | 1.67 | 1.39 | 6.6 | 3.6 | 14.2 | -1.1 |
| 2014 | D | 2.75 | 2.29 | 7.3 | 5.9 | 12.5 | -1.0 |
| 2013 | D | 4.04 | 3.37 | 7.9 | 6.9 | 9.3 | 0.1 |
| 2012 | D | 4.00 | 3.33 | 7.5 | 6.8 | 7.3 | 1.0 |

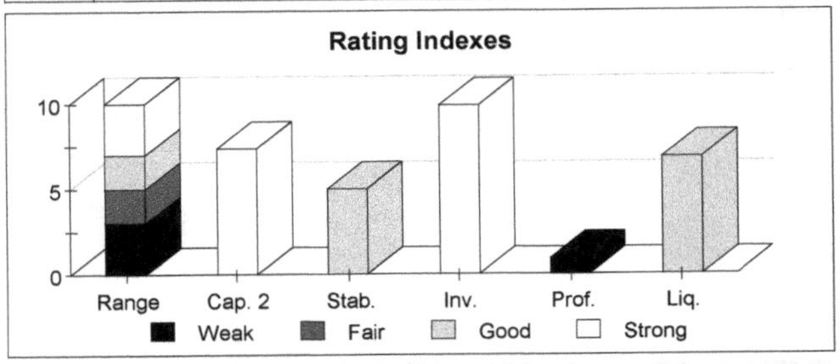

## MOUNT CARMEL HEALTH PLAN INC — C — Fair

**Major Rating Factors:** Fair profitability index (3.1 on a scale of 0 to 10). Good overall results on stability tests (5.3). Strong capitalization index (9.6) based on excellent current risk-adjusted capital (severe loss scenario).
**Other Rating Factors:** High quality investment portfolio (9.4). Excellent liquidity (6.9) with sufficient resources (cash flows and marketable investments) to handle a spike in claims.
**Principal Business:** Medicare (100%)
**Mem Phys: 16:** 5,652 **15:** 5,264 **16 MLR** 93.1% **/ 16 Admin Exp** N/A
**Enroll(000): Q3 17:** 55 **16:** 54 **15:** 49 **Med Exp PMPM:** $810
**Principal Investments:** Long-term bonds (45%), cash and equiv (34%), nonaffiliate common stock (21%)
**Provider Compensation ($000):** Contr fee ($465,712), FFS ($48,872), capitation ($2,122)
**Total Member Encounters:** Phys (529,411), non-phys (114,996)
**Group Affiliation:** Trinity Health Corporation
**Licensed in:** OH
**Address:** 6150 East Broad Street EE320, Columbus, OH 43213
**Phone:** (614) 546-3211 **Dom State:** OH **Commenced Bus:** April 1997

| Data Date | Rating | RACR #1 | RACR #2 | Total Assets ($mil) | Capital ($mil) | Net Premium ($mil) | Net Income ($mil) |
|---|---|---|---|---|---|---|---|
| 9-17 | C | 3.45 | 2.87 | 356.2 | 184.0 | 458.8 | 29.8 |
| 9-16 | C | 3.16 | 2.63 | 320.1 | 147.4 | 426.8 | -6.2 |
| 2016 | C | 2.75 | 2.29 | 277.9 | 148.8 | 566.2 | -9.6 |
| 2015 | C | 3.33 | 2.78 | 275.3 | 155.1 | 509.8 | -1.2 |
| 2014 | B- | 4.19 | 3.50 | 251.3 | 210.6 | 473.1 | 6.8 |
| 2013 | A | 6.99 | 5.83 | 327.1 | 291.4 | 424.8 | 43.4 |
| 2012 | A | 7.81 | 6.51 | 294.6 | 264.7 | 359.3 | 49.6 |

Rating Indexes

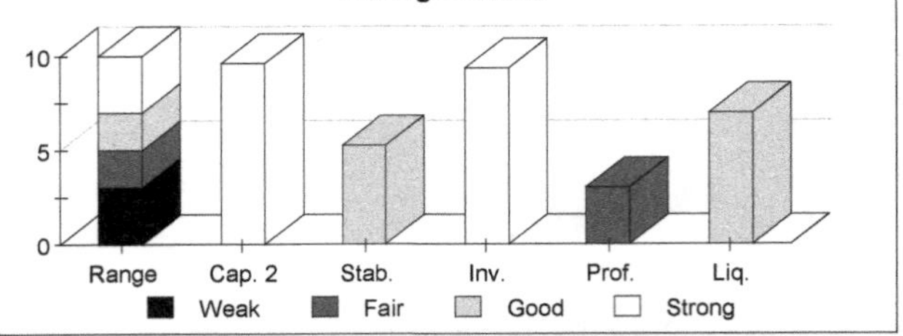


## MUTUAL OF OMAHA INSURANCE COMPANY * — B+ — Good

**Major Rating Factors:** Good overall results on stability tests (6.5 on a scale of 0 to 10). Stability strengths include excellent operational trends and excellent risk diversification. Good capitalization (6.9) based on good risk adjusted capital (severe loss scenario). Moreover, capital levels have been consistent over the last five years. Good quality investment portfolio (6.1).
**Other Rating Factors:** Excellent profitability (8.2) despite operating losses during the first nine months of 2017. Excellent liquidity (7.0).
**Principal Business:** Reinsurance (53%), individual health insurance (40%), and group health insurance (7%).
**Principal Investments:** NonCMO investment grade bonds (42%), common & preferred stock (37%), CMOs and structured securities (12%), mortgages in good standing (3%), and misc. investments (6%).
**Investments in Affiliates:** 39%
**Group Affiliation:** Mutual Of Omaha Group
**Licensed in:** All states, the District of Columbia and Puerto Rico
**Commenced Business:** January 1910
**Address:** MUTUAL OF OMAHA PLAZA, OMAHA, NE 68175
**Phone:** (402) 342-7600 **Domicile State:** NE **NAIC Code:** 71412

| Data Date | Rating | RACR #1 | RACR #2 | Total Assets ($mil) | Capital ($mil) | Net Premium ($mil) | Net Income ($mil) |
|---|---|---|---|---|---|---|---|
| 9-17 | B+ | 1.07 | 0.99 | 7,661.2 | 3,083.3 | 2,256.0 | -19.9 |
| 9-16 | B+ | 1.01 | 0.94 | 7,223.1 | 2,851.3 | 2,008.7 | 98.2 |
| 2016 | B+ | 1.07 | 0.99 | 7,278.9 | 3,048.3 | 2,726.5 | 103.4 |
| 2015 | B+ | 1.02 | 0.95 | 6,945.1 | 2,862.8 | 2,411.8 | 11.2 |
| 2014 | B+ | 1.02 | 0.96 | 6,426.8 | 2,795.7 | 2,186.3 | 30.4 |
| 2013 | B+ | 1.11 | 1.04 | 5,795.4 | 2,674.5 | 2,071.2 | 105.8 |
| 2012 | B+ | 1.09 | 1.02 | 5,549.8 | 2,406.0 | 1,946.8 | 56.8 |

Rating Indexes

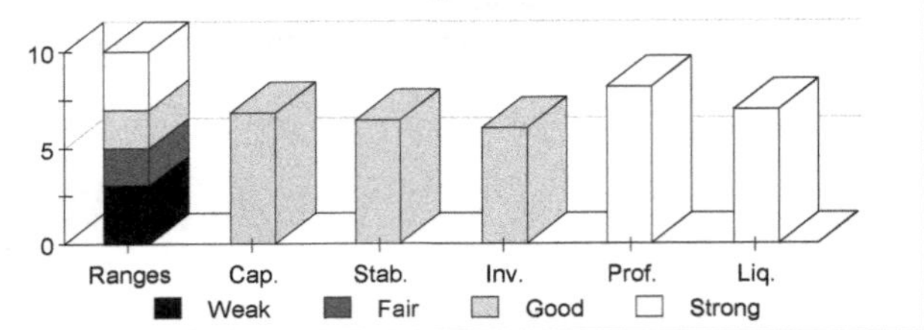


## MVP HEALTH INS CO — E+ — Very Weak

**Major Rating Factors:** Weak profitability index (2.1 on a scale of 0 to 10). Strong capitalization (10.0) based on excellent current risk-adjusted capital (severe loss scenario). High quality investment portfolio (9.9).
**Other Rating Factors:** Excellent liquidity (7.0) with ample operational cash flow and liquid investments.
**Principal Business:** Comp med (100%)
**Mem Phys: 16:** 47,314 **15:** 44,869 **16 MLR** 82.4% **/ 16 Admin Exp** N/A
**Enroll(000): Q3 17:** 4 **16:** 5 **15:** 51 **Med Exp PMPM:** $375
**Principal Investments:** Long-term bonds (61%), cash and equiv (39%)
**Provider Compensation ($000):** Contr fee ($72,245), salary ($2,757), capitation ($932), bonus arrang ($616), FFS ($302)
**Total Member Encounters:** Phys (160,022), non-phys (69,891)
**Group Affiliation:** MVP Health Care Inc
**Licensed in:** NY, VT
**Address:** 625 State St, Schenectady, NY 12305
**Phone:** (518) 370-4793 **Dom State:** NY **Commenced Bus:** July 2001

| Data Date | Rating | RACR #1 | RACR #2 | Total Assets ($mil) | Capital ($mil) | Net Premium ($mil) | Net Income ($mil) |
|---|---|---|---|---|---|---|---|
| 9-17 | E+ | 4.96 | 4.14 | 29.1 | 25.1 | 15.8 | -0.4 |
| 9-16 | E+ | 1.55 | 1.29 | 35.7 | 22.0 | 60.1 | 6.1 |
| 2016 | E+ | 4.98 | 4.15 | 31.9 | 25.0 | 69.4 | 10.5 |
| 2015 | E | 2.54 | 2.12 | 112.0 | 64.1 | 251.3 | -9.8 |
| 2014 | E | 2.30 | 1.92 | 117.8 | 77.4 | 351.5 | 5.2 |
| 2013 | E | 1.45 | 1.21 | 155.5 | 72.6 | 527.1 | -29.6 |
| 2012 | E | 1.67 | 1.39 | 182.0 | 102.9 | 695.6 | -22.7 |

Rating Indexes

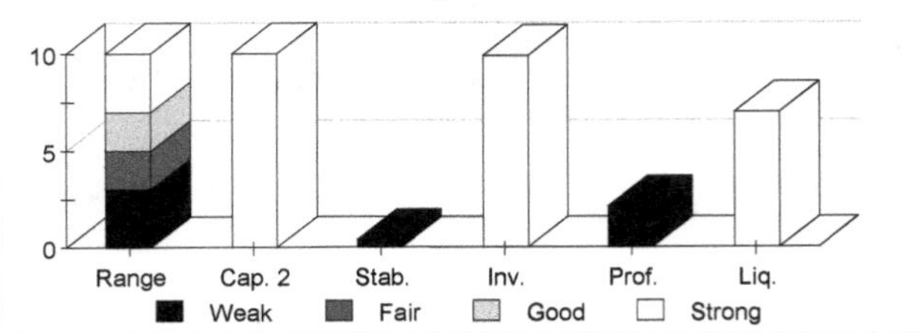

## MVP HEALTH PLAN INC B- Good

**Major Rating Factors:** Fair profitability index (3.9 on a scale of 0 to 10). Good overall results on stability tests (6.3). Strong capitalization index (8.2) based on excellent current risk-adjusted capital (severe loss scenario).
**Other Rating Factors:** High quality investment portfolio (9.1). Excellent liquidity (7.0) with sufficient resources (cash flows and marketable investments) to handle a spike in claims.
**Principal Business:** Medicaid (42%), Medicare (31%), comp med (21%), FEHB (5%)
**Mem Phys: 16:** 46,206 **15:** 44,352 **16 MLR** 91.2% **/ 16 Admin Exp** N/A
**Enroll(000): Q3 17:** 361 **16:** 365 **15:** 212 **Med Exp PMPM:** $517
**Principal Investments:** Long-term bonds (33%), cash and equiv (32%), nonaffiliate common stock (11%), other (24%)
**Provider Compensation ($000):** Contr fee ($1,925,078), capitation ($80,305), bonus arrang ($70,413), FFS ($23,971), other ($48,872)
**Total Member Encounters:** Phys (5,665,549), non-phys (2,092,114)
**Group Affiliation:** MVP Health Care Inc
**Licensed in:** NY, VT
**Address:** 625 State Street, Schenectady, NY 12305
**Phone:** (518) 370-4793 **Dom State:** NY **Commenced Bus:** July 1983

| Data Date | Rating | RACR #1 | RACR #2 | Total Assets ($mil) | Capital ($mil) | Net Premium ($mil) | Net Income ($mil) |
|---|---|---|---|---|---|---|---|
| 9-17 | B- | 2.30 | 1.92 | 741.8 | 407.1 | 1,878.7 | 23.6 |
| 9-16 | B- | 3.60 | 3.00 | 718.0 | 387.7 | 1,854.7 | -6.2 |
| 2016 | B- | 2.30 | 1.92 | 750.0 | 403.9 | 2,501.8 | 9.7 |
| 2015 | B- | 3.63 | 3.02 | 570.7 | 389.9 | 1,560.1 | 5.8 |
| 2014 | B- | 3.42 | 2.85 | 485.7 | 328.0 | 1,656.7 | -23.7 |
| 2013 | B | 3.97 | 3.31 | 538.2 | 380.9 | 1,678.6 | 27.5 |
| 2012 | B | 3.02 | 2.51 | 535.7 | 345.1 | 1,959.8 | 61.4 |

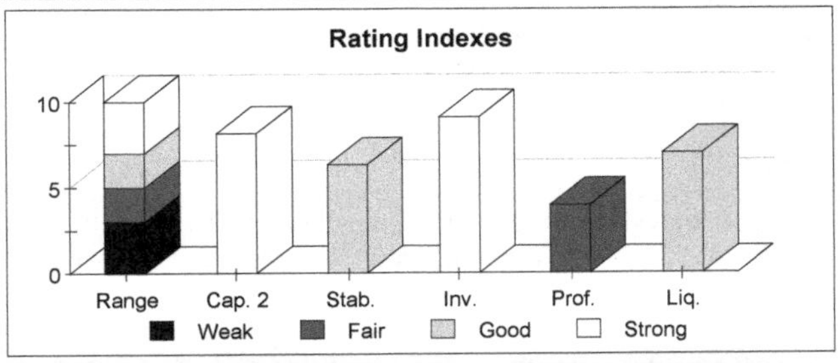


## MVP HEALTH SERVICES CORP C Fair

**Major Rating Factors:** Fair capitalization (2.9 on a scale of 0 to 10) based on weak current risk-adjusted capital (moderate loss scenario). Weak profitability index (1.3). Good liquidity (6.8) with sufficient resources (cash flows and marketable investments) to handle a spike in claims.
**Other Rating Factors:** High quality investment portfolio (9.9).
**Principal Business:** Comp med (100%)
**Mem Phys: 16:** 35,084 **15:** 33,071 **16 MLR** 85.9% **/ 16 Admin Exp** N/A
**Enroll(000): Q3 17:** 142 **16:** 109 **15:** 51 **Med Exp PMPM:** $354
**Principal Investments:** Long-term bonds (77%), cash and equiv (23%)
**Provider Compensation ($000):** Contr fee ($284,395), FFS ($81,525), capitation ($7,964), bonus arrang ($2,347), other ($22,460)
**Total Member Encounters:** Phys (1,005,890), non-phys (315,470)
**Group Affiliation:** MVP Health Care Inc
**Licensed in:** NY
**Address:** 625 State St, Schenectady, NY 12305
**Phone:** (518) 370-4793 **Dom State:** NY **Commenced Bus:** June 1993

| Data Date | Rating | RACR #1 | RACR #2 | Total Assets ($mil) | Capital ($mil) | Net Premium ($mil) | Net Income ($mil) |
|---|---|---|---|---|---|---|---|
| 9-17 | C | 0.70 | 0.58 | 134.5 | 52.8 | 497.4 | -16.7 |
| 9-16 | C | 2.23 | 1.86 | 145.4 | 68.4 | 357.3 | 5.4 |
| 2016 | C | 0.92 | 0.77 | 135.1 | 69.6 | 491.4 | 6.4 |
| 2015 | C- | 0.93 | 0.78 | 64.6 | 28.0 | 187.6 | 0.3 |
| 2014 | N/A | N/A | N/A | 65.2 | 27.4 | 101.3 | -25.1 |
| 2013 | N/A | N/A | N/A | 13.4 | 12.4 | 2.0 | N/A |
| 2012 | N/A | N/A | N/A | 13.3 | 12.8 | 2.4 | N/A |

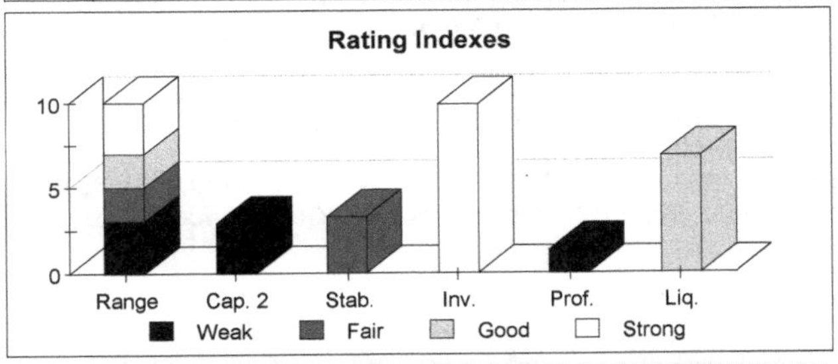


## NATIONAL GUARDIAN LIFE INSURANCE COMPANY B- Good

**Major Rating Factors:** Good quality investment portfolio (5.7 on a scale of 0 to 10) despite mixed results such as: large holdings of BBB rated bonds but moderate junk bond exposure. Good overall profitability (5.6) although investment income, in comparison to reserve requirements, is below regulatory standards. Good liquidity (6.0).
**Other Rating Factors:** Good overall results on stability tests (5.3) good operational trends, good risk adjusted capital for prior years and excellent risk diversification. Strong capitalization (7.1) based on excellent risk adjusted capital (severe loss scenario).
**Principal Business:** Group health insurance (38%), group life insurance (32%), individual life insurance (19%), reinsurance (8%), and other lines (4%).
**Principal Investments:** NonCMO investment grade bonds (78%), CMOs and structured securities (5%), noninv. grade bonds (3%), common & preferred stock (3%), and misc. investments (7%).
**Investments in Affiliates:** 2%
**Group Affiliation:** NGL Ins Group
**Licensed in:** All states except NY, PR
**Commenced Business:** October 1910
**Address:** 2 East Gilman Street, Madison, WI 53703-1494
**Phone:** (608) 257-5611 **Domicile State:** WI **NAIC Code:** 66583

| Data Date | Rating | RACR #1 | RACR #2 | Total Assets ($mil) | Capital ($mil) | Net Premium ($mil) | Net Income ($mil) |
|---|---|---|---|---|---|---|---|
| 9-17 | B- | 1.67 | 1.04 | 3,859.7 | 336.0 | 467.3 | 18.9 |
| 9-16 | B- | 1.58 | 0.98 | 3,615.5 | 295.5 | 449.3 | 11.8 |
| 2016 | B- | 1.52 | 0.95 | 3,657.9 | 293.3 | 553.0 | 18.1 |
| 2015 | B- | 1.45 | 0.91 | 3,422.2 | 271.1 | 790.0 | -4.5 |
| 2014 | B | 1.47 | 0.96 | 2,948.3 | 250.1 | 476.1 | 24.4 |
| 2013 | B | 1.51 | 0.99 | 2,730.8 | 241.3 | 416.1 | 28.8 |
| 2012 | B | 1.43 | 0.93 | 2,532.8 | 196.4 | 395.8 | 18.9 |

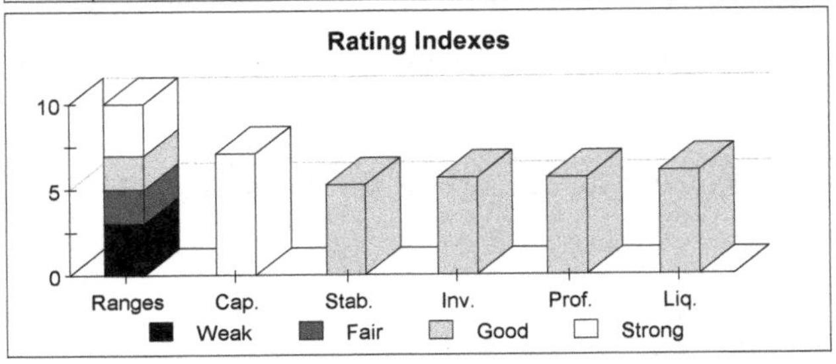

## NATIONAL TEACHERS ASSOCIATES LIFE INSURANCE COMPAN B Good

**Major Rating Factors:** Good quality investment portfolio (6.8 on a scale of 0 to 10) despite mixed results such as: minimal exposure to mortgages and substantial holdings of BBB bonds but small junk bond holdings. Good overall results on stability tests (6.0). Stability strengths include excellent operational trends and excellent risk diversification. Fair profitability (3.7) with investment income below regulatory standards in relation to interest assumptions of reserves.
**Other Rating Factors:** Strong capitalization (8.5) based on excellent risk adjusted capital (severe loss scenario). Excellent liquidity (8.2).
**Principal Business:** Individual health insurance (98%) and individual life insurance (2%).
**Principal Investments:** NonCMO investment grade bonds (52%), CMOs and structured securities (34%), noninv. grade bonds (5%), common & preferred stock (4%), and misc. investments (5%).
**Investments in Affiliates:** 1%
**Group Affiliation:** Ellard Family Holdings Inc
**Licensed in:** All states except NY, PR
**Commenced Business:** July 1938
**Address:** 4949 Keller Springs Rd, Addison, TX 75001
**Phone:** (972) 532-2100 **Domicile State:** TX **NAIC Code:** 87963

| Data Date | Rating | RACR #1 | RACR #2 | Total Assets ($mil) | Capital ($mil) | Net Premium ($mil) | Net Income ($mil) |
|---|---|---|---|---|---|---|---|
| 9-17 | B | 3.03 | 2.03 | 535.3 | 110.4 | 98.1 | 13.4 |
| 9-16 | B | N/A | N/A | 501.0 | 99.7 | 96.6 | 7.5 |
| 2016 | B | 2.86 | 1.94 | 510.5 | 102.4 | 129.2 | 11.2 |
| 2015 | B | N/A | N/A | 464.1 | 92.1 | 123.6 | 11.1 |
| 2014 | B | 2.47 | 1.73 | 422.9 | 80.9 | 117.5 | 7.8 |
| 2013 | B | 2.55 | 1.84 | 381.8 | 73.1 | 108.1 | 7.0 |
| 2012 | B+ | 3.40 | 2.34 | 347.2 | 67.1 | 99.0 | 9.2 |

**Adverse Trends in Operations**

Increase in policy surrenders from 2012 to 2013 (29%)

## NEIGHBORHOOD HEALTH PARTNERSHIP INC B Good

**Major Rating Factors:** Good overall results on stability tests (5.6 on a scale of 0 to 10). Rating is significantly influenced by the fair financial results of UnitedHealth Group Incorporated. Good liquidity (6.7) with sufficient resources (cash flows and marketable investments) to handle a spike in claims. Excellent profitability (8.9).
**Other Rating Factors:** Strong capitalization index (8.4) based on excellent current risk-adjusted capital (severe loss scenario). High quality investment portfolio (9.9).
**Principal Business:** Comp med (100%)
**Mem Phys: 16:** 17,372 **15:** 13,030 **16 MLR** 74.8% **/ 16 Admin Exp** N/A
**Enroll(000): Q3 17:** 130 **16:** 122 **15:** 116 **Med Exp PMPM:** $299
**Principal Investments:** Long-term bonds (70%), cash and equiv (30%)
**Provider Compensation ($000):** Contr fee ($385,904), FFS ($23,592), capitation ($11,981)
**Total Member Encounters:** Phys (649,882), non-phys (16,339)
**Group Affiliation:** UnitedHealth Group Incorporated
**Licensed in:** FL
**Address:** 7600 CORPORATE CENTER DRIVE, MIAMI, FL 33126-1216
**Phone:** (800) 825-8792 **Dom State:** FL **Commenced Bus:** November 2000

| Data Date | Rating | RACR #1 | RACR #2 | Total Assets ($mil) | Capital ($mil) | Net Premium ($mil) | Net Income ($mil) |
|---|---|---|---|---|---|---|---|
| 9-17 | B | 2.46 | 2.05 | 162.6 | 70.6 | 462.3 | 37.0 |
| 9-16 | B- | 1.89 | 1.58 | 132.8 | 51.6 | 433.3 | 25.1 |
| 2016 | B | 2.11 | 1.76 | 149.0 | 60.2 | 578.0 | 41.4 |
| 2015 | B | 1.48 | 1.24 | 121.7 | 39.9 | 528.5 | 26.1 |
| 2014 | B- | 1.18 | 0.99 | 93.4 | 28.4 | 485.6 | 21.9 |
| 2013 | B- | 1.63 | 1.36 | 94.4 | 35.0 | 477.4 | 30.6 |
| 2012 | B | 2.27 | 1.89 | 106.1 | 43.3 | 448.2 | 42.1 |

**Rating Indexes**

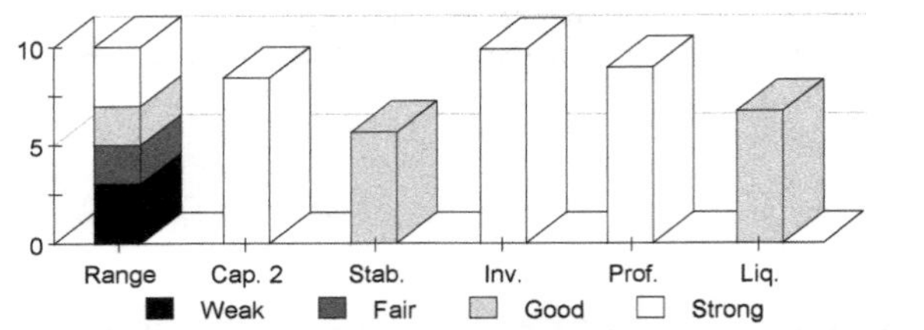


## NEIGHBORHOOD HEALTH PLAN D Weak

**Major Rating Factors:** Weak profitability index (0.9 on a scale of 0 to 10). Low quality investment portfolio (1.6). Weak liquidity (1.3) as a spike in claims may stretch capacity.
**Other Rating Factors:** Good overall results on stability tests (6.1). Strong capitalization index (7.2) based on excellent current risk-adjusted capital (severe loss scenario).
**Principal Business:** Medicaid (71%), comp med (29%)
**Mem Phys: 16:** 32,693 **15:** 29,947 **16 MLR** 98.6% **/ 16 Admin Exp** N/A
**Enroll(000): Q3 17:** 368 **16:** 438 **15:** 422 **Med Exp PMPM:** $471
**Principal Investments:** Nonaffiliate common stock (85%), cash and equiv (8%), long-term bonds (7%)
**Provider Compensation ($000):** Contr fee ($1,731,164), capitation ($625,953), FFS ($21,928), other ($86,301)
**Total Member Encounters:** Phys (3,352,151), non-phys (3,512,704)
**Group Affiliation:** Partners HealthCare System Inc
**Licensed in:** MA
**Address:** 253 Summer St, Boston, MA 02210-1120
**Phone:** (800) 433-5556 **Dom State:** MA **Commenced Bus:** January 1988

| Data Date | Rating | RACR #1 | RACR #2 | Total Assets ($mil) | Capital ($mil) | Net Premium ($mil) | Net Income ($mil) |
|---|---|---|---|---|---|---|---|
| 9-17 | D | 1.54 | 1.28 | 556.1 | 296.1 | 1,844.9 | 62.8 |
| 9-16 | D | 1.05 | 0.87 | 533.0 | 180.0 | 1,917.0 | -113.2 |
| 2016 | D | 0.99 | 0.83 | 531.0 | 192.4 | 2,560.0 | -130.9 |
| 2015 | D | 1.09 | 0.91 | 450.2 | 186.9 | 2,163.0 | -25.5 |
| 2014 | D | 0.89 | 0.74 | 420.4 | 128.7 | 1,717.8 | -101.3 |
| 2013 | C+ | 1.54 | 1.28 | 340.4 | 97.2 | 1,363.0 | 19.4 |
| 2012 | C+ | 1.41 | 1.18 | 321.9 | 154.0 | 1,268.8 | 10.7 |

**Rating Indexes**

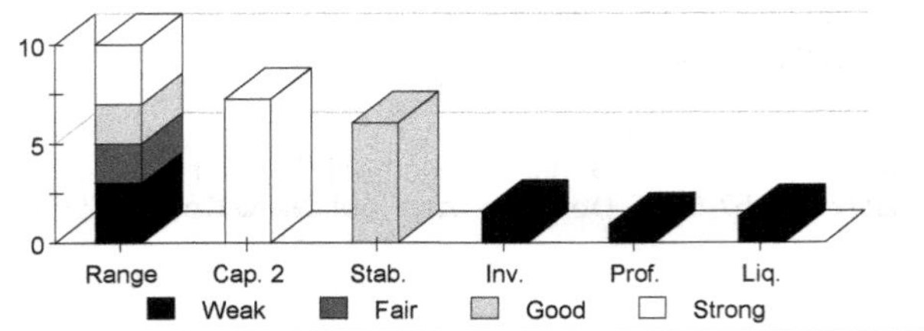

## NEIGHBORHOOD HEALTH PLAN OF RI INC B Good

**Major Rating Factors:** Good overall profitability index (6.3 on a scale of 0 to 10). Good capitalization index (6.1) based on good current risk-adjusted capital (severe loss scenario). Good overall results on stability tests (6.6).
**Other Rating Factors:** High quality investment portfolio (9.9). Excellent liquidity (7.0) with sufficient resources (cash flows and marketable investments) to handle a spike in claims.
**Principal Business:** Medicaid (95%), comp med (5%)
**Mem Phys: 16:** 5,951 **15:** 5,480 **16 MLR** 87.8% **/ 16 Admin Exp** N/A
**Enroll(000): Q3 17:** 200 **16:** 193 **15:** 178 **Med Exp PMPM:** $441
**Principal Investments:** Cash and equiv (67%), long-term bonds (32%), other (1%)
**Provider Compensation ($000):** Contr fee ($930,560), capitation ($13,723), bonus arrang ($4,392)
**Total Member Encounters:** Phys (5,348,370), non-phys (790,512)
**Group Affiliation:** Neighborhood Health Plan of RI
**Licensed in:** RI
**Address:** 910 Douglas Pike, Smithfield, RI 02917
**Phone:** (401) 459-6000 **Dom State:** RI **Commenced Bus:** December 1994

| Data Date | Rating | RACR #1 | RACR #2 | Total Assets ($mil) | Capital ($mil) | Net Premium ($mil) | Net Income ($mil) |
|---|---|---|---|---|---|---|---|
| 9-17 | B | 1.09 | 0.91 | 422.9 | 102.9 | 1,015.4 | 1.2 |
| 9-16 | B | 1.23 | 1.02 | 328.2 | 101.5 | 813.3 | 16.6 |
| 2016 | B | 1.09 | 0.91 | 348.8 | 102.7 | 1,121.9 | 19.7 |
| 2015 | B- | 1.00 | 0.83 | 369.5 | 85.6 | 1,011.4 | 28.6 |
| 2014 | C | 0.68 | 0.57 | 252.0 | 58.1 | 894.4 | 21.1 |
| 2013 | B- | 0.83 | 0.69 | 134.5 | 35.7 | 428.2 | -3.8 |
| 2012 | B- | 0.99 | 0.83 | 149.5 | 42.1 | 427.6 | -0.7 |

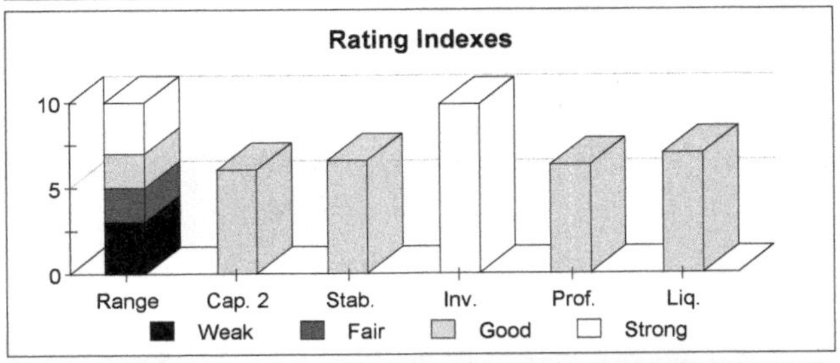


## NETWORK HEALTH INS CORP C Fair

**Major Rating Factors:** Weak profitability index (2.0 on a scale of 0 to 10). Good liquidity (6.1) with sufficient resources (cash flows and marketable investments) to handle a spike in claims. Strong capitalization (7.3) based on excellent current risk-adjusted capital (severe loss scenario).
**Other Rating Factors:** High quality investment portfolio (9.9).
**Principal Business:** Medicare (98%)
**Mem Phys: 16:** 12,556 **15:** 10,522 **16 MLR** 91.7% **/ 16 Admin Exp** N/A
**Enroll(000): Q3 17:** 68 **16:** 87 **15:** 78 **Med Exp PMPM:** $564
**Principal Investments:** Long-term bonds (64%), cash and equiv (36%)
**Provider Compensation ($000):** Contr fee ($434,395), FFS ($58,787), bonus arrang ($1,133)
**Total Member Encounters:** Phys (404,811), non-phys (131,555)
**Group Affiliation:** Network Health Inc
**Licensed in:** WI
**Address:** 1570 Midway Place, Menasha, WI 54952
**Phone:** (920) 720-1452 **Dom State:** WI **Commenced Bus:** April 2013

| Data Date | Rating | RACR #1 | RACR #2 | Total Assets ($mil) | Capital ($mil) | Net Premium ($mil) | Net Income ($mil) |
|---|---|---|---|---|---|---|---|
| 9-17 | C | 1.62 | 1.35 | 231.6 | 79.9 | 429.1 | -0.3 |
| 9-16 | C | 1.70 | 1.42 | 234.9 | 84.5 | 420.0 | 0.8 |
| 2016 | C | 1.65 | 1.37 | 185.0 | 81.5 | 550.6 | -3.3 |
| 2015 | C | 1.65 | 1.37 | 176.0 | 81.7 | 556.5 | -5.7 |
| 2014 | C- | 1.44 | 1.20 | 155.2 | 64.7 | 499.1 | -33.2 |
| 2013 | C- | 1.59 | 1.33 | 122.1 | 64.4 | 474.2 | 4.2 |
| 2012 | N/A | N/A | N/A | 110.8 | 55.5 | 446.3 | N/A |

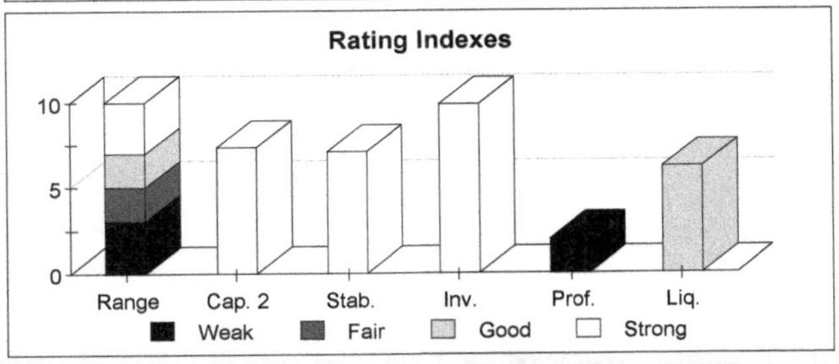


## NETWORK HEALTH PLAN B- Good

**Major Rating Factors:** Fair overall results on stability tests (4.8 on a scale of 0 to 10). Good liquidity (6.7) with sufficient resources (cash flows and marketable investments) to handle a spike in claims. Excellent profitability (7.1).
**Other Rating Factors:** Strong capitalization index (7.7) based on excellent current risk-adjusted capital (severe loss scenario). High quality investment portfolio (9.9).
**Principal Business:** Comp med (80%), Medicaid (20%)
**Mem Phys: 16:** 12,550 **15:** 12,352 **16 MLR** 87.8% **/ 16 Admin Exp** N/A
**Enroll(000): Q3 17:** 75 **16:** 92 **15:** 101 **Med Exp PMPM:** $287
**Principal Investments:** Long-term bonds (59%), cash and equiv (38%), real estate (3%)
**Provider Compensation ($000):** Contr fee ($241,794), capitation ($66,128), FFS ($13,370)
**Total Member Encounters:** Phys (341,106), non-phys (257,065)
**Group Affiliation:** Network Health Inc
**Licensed in:** WI
**Address:** 1570 Midway Place, Menasha, WI 54952
**Phone:** (920) 720-1200 **Dom State:** WI **Commenced Bus:** April 1983

| Data Date | Rating | RACR #1 | RACR #2 | Total Assets ($mil) | Capital ($mil) | Net Premium ($mil) | Net Income ($mil) |
|---|---|---|---|---|---|---|---|
| 9-17 | B- | 1.89 | 1.57 | 90.1 | 51.8 | 214.9 | 7.1 |
| 9-16 | C | 1.64 | 1.37 | 104.5 | 46.4 | 279.6 | 1.2 |
| 2016 | B- | 1.52 | 1.27 | 102.6 | 41.4 | 370.9 | 0.6 |
| 2015 | B- | 1.60 | 1.34 | 103.2 | 45.3 | 403.4 | 6.0 |
| 2014 | C- | 1.33 | 1.11 | 83.8 | 39.3 | 402.6 | 2.5 |
| 2013 | D+ | 1.30 | 1.09 | 94.3 | 40.6 | 418.0 | 13.1 |
| 2012 | B | 1.24 | 1.03 | 144.9 | 91.2 | 435.4 | 5.1 |

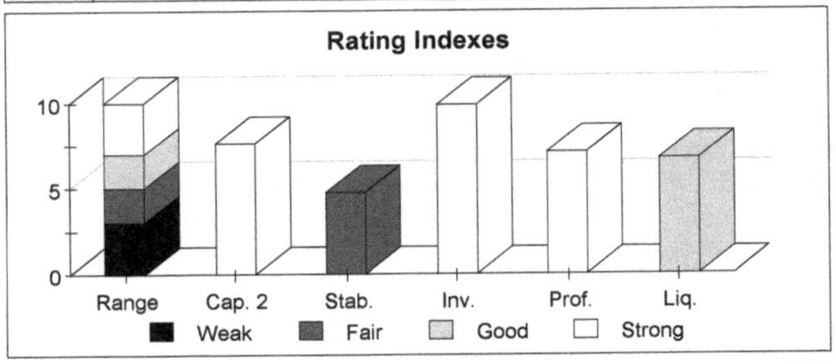

## NEW ERA LIFE INSURANCE COMPANY C Fair

**Major Rating Factors:** Fair overall results on stability tests (4.1 on a scale of 0 to 10) including fair risk adjusted capital in prior years. Good current capitalization (5.0) based on good risk adjusted capital (severe loss scenario) reflecting some improvement over results in 2012. Good quality investment portfolio (5.3).
**Other Rating Factors:** Good liquidity (6.8). Excellent profitability (8.9).
**Principal Business:** Individual health insurance (51%), individual annuities (47%), and individual life insurance (1%).
**Principal Investments:** NonCMO investment grade bonds (47%), mortgages in good standing (19%), common & preferred stock (10%), CMOs and structured securities (8%), and misc. investments (15%).
**Investments in Affiliates:** 10%
**Group Affiliation:** New Era Life Group
**Licensed in:** AL, AZ, AR, CA, CO, DE, FL, GA, IN, KS, KY, LA, MI, MS, MO, MT, NE, NM, NC, ND, OH, OK, PA, SC, SD, TN, TX, UT, WA, WV
**Commenced Business:** June 1924
**Address:** 11720 Katy Freeway Suite 1700, Houston, TX 77079
**Phone:** (281) 368-7200 **Domicile State:** TX **NAIC Code:** 78743

| Data Date | Rating | RACR #1 | RACR #2 | Total Assets ($mil) | Capital ($mil) | Net Premium ($mil) | Net Income ($mil) |
|---|---|---|---|---|---|---|---|
| 9-17 | C | 0.99 | 0.75 | 533.5 | 79.9 | 138.8 | 3.0 |
| 9-16 | C | 0.93 | 0.71 | 488.0 | 73.2 | 143.4 | 2.7 |
| 2016 | C | 0.94 | 0.72 | 504.2 | 75.1 | 190.3 | 4.5 |
| 2015 | C | 0.95 | 0.73 | 463.5 | 70.7 | 111.2 | 5.1 |
| 2014 | C | 0.95 | 0.73 | 402.5 | 66.2 | 99.3 | 4.3 |
| 2013 | C | 0.90 | 0.69 | 371.3 | 58.0 | 77.3 | 4.6 |
| 2012 | C | 0.86 | 0.65 | 352.2 | 52.0 | 68.3 | 2.1 |

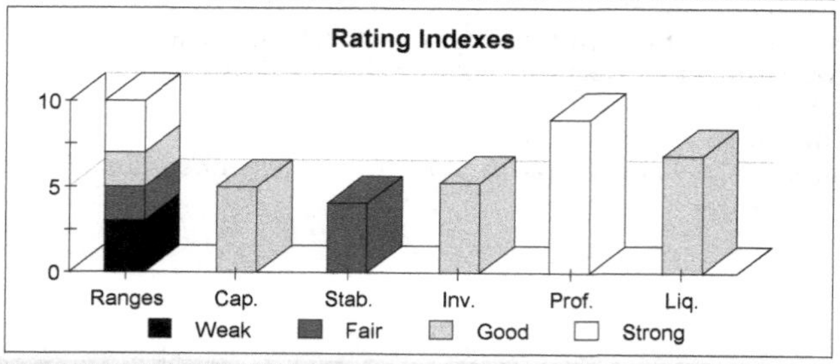


## NEW MEXICO HEALTH CONNECTIONS E- Very Weak

**Major Rating Factors:** Weak profitability index (0.6 on a scale of 0 to 10). Poor capitalization (0.0) based on weak current risk-adjusted capital (severe loss scenario). Weak liquidity (0.0) as a spike in claims may stretch capacity.
**Other Rating Factors:** High quality investment portfolio (9.8).
**Principal Business:** Comp med (100%)
**Mem Phys: 16:** 8,841 **15:** 8,110 **16 MLR** 89.1% **/ 16 Admin Exp** N/A
**Enroll(000): Q3 17:** 40 **16:** 43 **15:** 34 **Med Exp PMPM:** $262
**Principal Investments:** Long-term bonds (88%), cash and equiv (12%)
**Provider Compensation ($000):** Contr fee ($132,176), FFS ($5,729)
**Total Member Encounters:** Phys (286,751), non-phys (40,675)
**Group Affiliation:** New Mexico Health Connections
**Licensed in:** NM
**Address:** 2440 LOUISIANA BLVD NE Ste 601, ALBUQUERQUE, NM 87110
**Phone:** (505) 633-8023 **Dom State:** NM **Commenced Bus:** September 2011

| Data Date | Rating | RACR #1 | RACR #2 | Total Assets ($mil) | Capital ($mil) | Net Premium ($mil) | Net Income ($mil) |
|---|---|---|---|---|---|---|---|
| 9-17 | E- | 0.16 | 0.13 | 43.3 | 3.5 | 106.1 | -10.4 |
| 9-16 | D- | 0.81 | 0.67 | 43.7 | 18.1 | 106.7 | -12.6 |
| 2016 | E- | 0.43 | 0.36 | 36.8 | 12.1 | 153.0 | -17.9 |
| 2015 | D | 1.39 | 1.16 | 61.0 | 31.4 | 96.2 | -23.0 |
| 2014 | D | 1.89 | 1.57 | 58.1 | 23.2 | 29.9 | -4.3 |
| 2013 | N/A | N/A | N/A | 47.9 | 27.8 | N/A | -14.5 |
| 2012 | N/A | N/A | N/A | N/A | N/A | N/A | N/A |

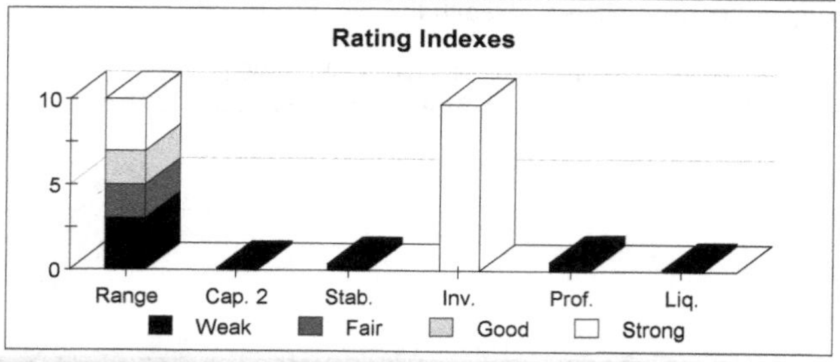


## NEW WEST HEALTH SERVICES E- Very Weak

**Major Rating Factors:** Weak profitability index (0.8 on a scale of 0 to 10). Poor capitalization index (0.0) based on weak current risk-adjusted capital (severe loss scenario). Weak overall results on stability tests (0.7) based on a steep decline in capital during 2016, a significant 23% decrease in enrollment during the period.
**Other Rating Factors:** Weak liquidity (0.0) as a spike in claims may stretch capacity. High quality investment portfolio (9.9).
**Principal Business:** Medicare (99%), med supp (1%)
**Mem Phys: 16:** 5,395 **15:** 5,420 **16 MLR** 97.3% **/ 16 Admin Exp** N/A
**Enroll(000): Q1 17:** 0 **16:** 15 **15:** 19 **Med Exp PMPM:** $650
**Principal Investments:** Cash and equiv (100%)
**Provider Compensation ($000):** Contr fee ($114,876), FFS ($11,499), capitation ($187)
**Total Member Encounters:** Phys (171,980), non-phys (273,644)
**Group Affiliation:** Billings Clinic
**Licensed in:** MT
**Address:** 130 Neill Avenue, Helena, MT 59601
**Phone:** (406) 457-2200 **Dom State:** MT **Commenced Bus:** March 1998

| Data Date | Rating | RACR #1 | RACR #2 | Total Assets ($mil) | Capital ($mil) | Net Premium ($mil) | Net Income ($mil) |
|---|---|---|---|---|---|---|---|
| 3-17 | E- | 0.13 | 0.11 | 8.7 | 4.9 | 0.0 | 0.3 |
| 3-16 | E+ | 0.23 | 0.19 | 29.3 | 10.1 | 30.9 | -4.9 |
| 2016 | E- | 0.13 | 0.11 | 20.0 | 5.1 | 121.2 | -17.9 |
| 2015 | E+ | 0.24 | 0.20 | 34.6 | 10.6 | 157.1 | -19.7 |
| 2014 | E+ | 0.24 | 0.20 | 43.0 | 11.9 | 189.5 | -21.7 |
| 2013 | E+ | 0.26 | 0.21 | 27.6 | 9.9 | 155.2 | -15.7 |
| 2012 | D- | 0.40 | 0.33 | 23.6 | 9.9 | 92.6 | -14.3 |

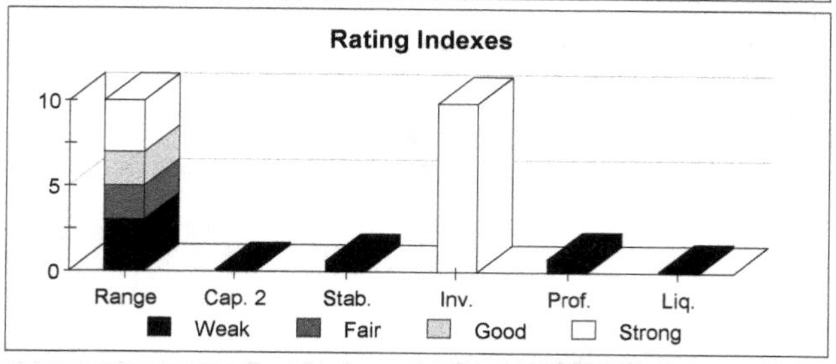

## NIPPON LIFE INSURANCE COMPANY OF AMERICA * A- Excellent

**Major Rating Factors:** Good overall profitability (6.8 on a scale of 0 to 10). Good liquidity (6.6) with sufficient resources to handle a spike in claims. Strong capitalization (10.0) based on excellent risk adjusted capital (severe loss scenario). Furthermore, this high level of risk adjusted capital has been consistently maintained over the last five years.
**Other Rating Factors:** High quality investment portfolio (8.3). Excellent overall results on stability tests (7.0) excellent operational trends and excellent risk diversification.
**Principal Business:** Group health insurance (100%).
**Principal Investments:** NonCMO investment grade bonds (75%), CMOs and structured securities (11%), cash (3%), and common & preferred stock (2%).
**Investments in Affiliates:** None
**Group Affiliation:** Nippon Life Ins Co Japan
**Licensed in:** All states except ME, NH, WY, PR
**Commenced Business:** July 1973
**Address:** 7115 Vista Drive, West Des Moines, IA 50266
**Phone:** (212) 682-3000 **Domicile State:** IA **NAIC Code:** 81264

| Data Date | Rating | RACR #1 | RACR #2 | Total Assets ($mil) | Capital ($mil) | Net Premium ($mil) | Net Income ($mil) |
|---|---|---|---|---|---|---|---|
| 9-17 | A- | 3.78 | 2.99 | 219.6 | 141.7 | 231.0 | 2.0 |
| 9-16 | A- | 4.00 | 3.17 | 211.3 | 139.6 | 212.6 | 0.6 |
| 2016 | A- | 3.73 | 2.96 | 212.3 | 139.6 | 285.7 | 0.5 |
| 2015 | A- | 3.92 | 3.11 | 212.6 | 140.8 | 277.0 | 4.6 |
| 2014 | A- | 3.39 | 2.71 | 216.4 | 141.1 | 315.7 | 8.2 |
| 2013 | A- | 2.96 | 2.35 | 225.1 | 136.7 | 351.2 | 6.7 |
| 2012 | A- | 3.44 | 2.71 | 213.7 | 134.6 | 295.4 | 8.4 |

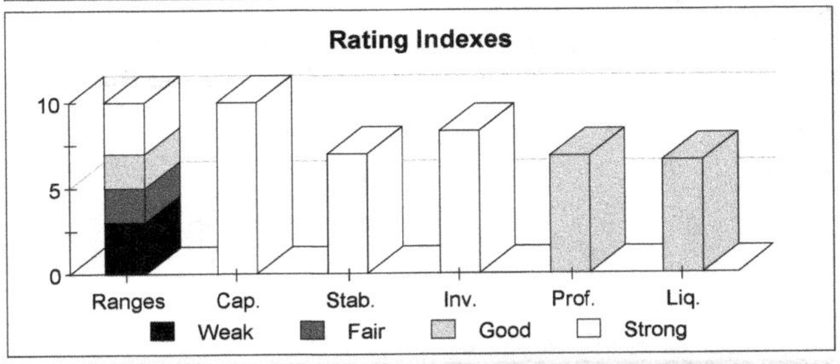


## NORIDIAN MUTUAL INS CO B Good

**Major Rating Factors:** Good overall profitability index (5.3 on a scale of 0 to 10). Strong capitalization (10.0) based on excellent current risk-adjusted capital (severe loss scenario). High quality investment portfolio (7.1).
**Other Rating Factors:** Excellent liquidity (6.9) with sufficient resources (cash flows and marketable investments) to handle a spike in claims.
**Principal Business:** Comp med (67%), FEHB (11%), med supp (8%), dental (2%), other (12%)
**Mem Phys: 16:** 6,548 **15:** 6,288 **16 MLR** 85.2% **/ 16 Admin Exp** N/A
**Enroll(000): Q3 17:** 317 **16:** 308 **15:** 341 **Med Exp PMPM:** $242
**Principal Investments:** Long-term bonds (64%), nonaffiliate common stock (10%), cash and equiv (8%), affiliate common stock (8%), real estate (4%), pref stock (3%), other (4%)
**Provider Compensation ($000):** FFS ($465,204), contr fee ($457,820)
**Total Member Encounters:** Phys (2,382,817), non-phys (2,401,636)
**Group Affiliation:** Noridian Mutual Insurance Company
**Licensed in:** ND
**Address:** 4510 13th Ave S, Fargo, ND 58121
**Phone:** (701) 282-1100 **Dom State:** ND **Commenced Bus:** April 1940

| Data Date | Rating | RACR #1 | RACR #2 | Total Assets ($mil) | Capital ($mil) | Net Premium ($mil) | Net Income ($mil) |
|---|---|---|---|---|---|---|---|
| 9-17 | B | 4.47 | 3.73 | 719.6 | 477.3 | 820.3 | 64.9 |
| 9-16 | B | 3.40 | 2.83 | 620.5 | 404.2 | 808.4 | 81.4 |
| 2016 | B | 3.66 | 3.05 | 640.5 | 399.2 | 1,080.4 | 70.3 |
| 2015 | B | 2.49 | 2.07 | 521.5 | 302.9 | 1,243.3 | 63.8 |
| 2014 | C+ | 1.68 | 1.40 | 513.5 | 231.1 | 1,328.2 | 26.8 |
| 2013 | C+ | 1.58 | 1.31 | 458.2 | 199.1 | 1,195.6 | -80.8 |
| 2012 | B+ | 2.29 | 1.91 | 506.8 | 272.0 | 1,106.3 | 22.1 |

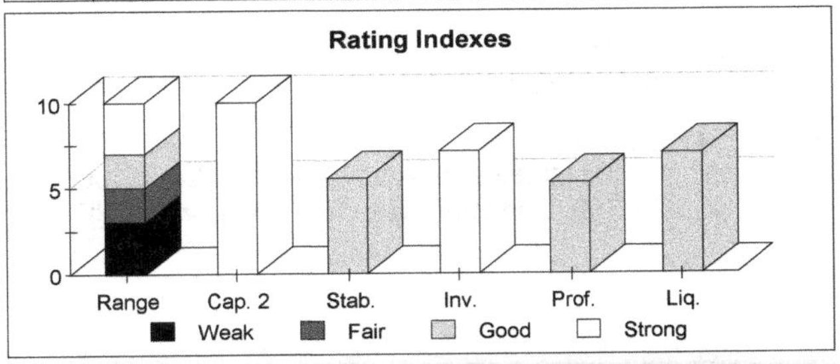


## NORTHWESTERN LONG TERM CARE INSURANCE COMPANY B Good

**Major Rating Factors:** Good liquidity (6.1 on a scale of 0 to 10) with sufficient resources to handle a spike in claims. Fair profitability (4.0). Fair overall results on stability tests (4.9) including negative cash flow from operations for 2016.
**Other Rating Factors:** Strong capitalization (10.0) based on excellent risk adjusted capital (severe loss scenario). High quality investment portfolio (9.6).
**Principal Business:** Individual health insurance (100%).
**Principal Investments:** NonCMO investment grade bonds (94%) and cash (6%).
**Investments in Affiliates:** None
**Group Affiliation:** Northwestern Mutual Group
**Licensed in:** All states except PR
**Commenced Business:** October 1953
**Address:** 720 EAST WISCONSIN AVENUE, MILWAUKEE, WI 53202
**Phone:** (414) 661-2510 **Domicile State:** WI **NAIC Code:** 69000

| Data Date | Rating | RACR #1 | RACR #2 | Total Assets ($mil) | Capital ($mil) | Net Premium ($mil) | Net Income ($mil) |
|---|---|---|---|---|---|---|---|
| 9-17 | B | 7.89 | 3.17 | 196.0 | 104.8 | -0.1 | 6.7 |
| 9-16 | B | 6.44 | 2.59 | 167.4 | 81.8 | 0.1 | 2.1 |
| 2016 | B | 6.46 | 2.60 | 172.7 | 82.2 | 0.2 | 2.6 |
| 2015 | B | 6.57 | 2.65 | 166.0 | 79.5 | 0.3 | 2.5 |
| 2014 | B | 8.08 | 7.27 | 161.4 | 77.2 | -1,548.3 | 403.6 |
| 2013 | B | 1.76 | 0.99 | 2,220.1 | 213.8 | 457.3 | -84.2 |
| 2012 | B | 2.45 | 1.40 | 1,861.6 | 274.7 | 387.1 | -192.9 |

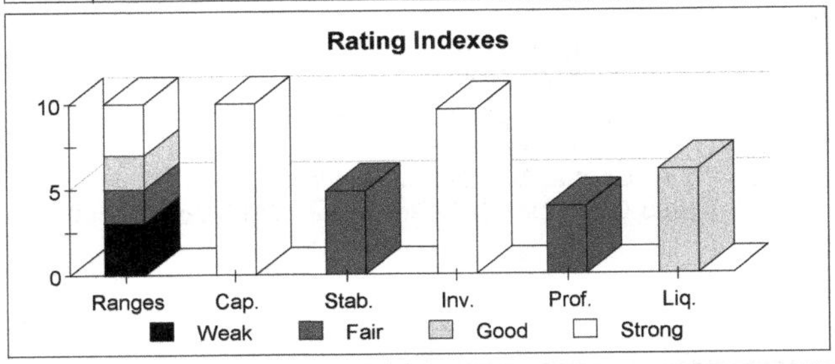

## OKLAHOMA SUPERIOR SELECT INC — E Very Weak

**Major Rating Factors:** Weak profitability index (0.5 on a scale of 0 to 10). Good capitalization (6.2) based on good current risk-adjusted capital (severe loss scenario). Good liquidity (6.6) with sufficient resources (cash flows and marketable investments) to handle a spike in claims.
**Other Rating Factors:** High quality investment portfolio (9.9).
**Principal Business:** Medicare (100%)
**Mem Phys: 16:** 1,088 **15:** 196 **16 MLR** 70.7% **/ 16 Admin Exp** N/A
**Enroll(000): Q3 17:** 0 **16:** 0 **15:** 0 **Med Exp PMPM:** $1,378
**Principal Investments:** Cash and equiv (78%), long-term bonds (22%)
**Provider Compensation ($000):** Contr fee ($2,419)
**Total Member Encounters:** Phys (2,086), non-phys (2,662)
**Group Affiliation:** Healthcare Investors LLC
**Licensed in:** OK
**Address:** 909 S Meridian Ave Ste 425, Oklahoma City, OK 73108
**Phone:** (405) 602-5488 **Dom State:** OK **Commenced Bus:** December 2004

| Data Date | Rating | RACR #1 | RACR #2 | Total Assets ($mil) | Capital ($mil) | Net Premium ($mil) | Net Income ($mil) |
|---|---|---|---|---|---|---|---|
| 9-17 | E | 1.10 | 0.92 | 3.5 | 1.5 | 3.4 | -0.6 |
| 9-16 | E- | 1.56 | 1.30 | 3.6 | 1.8 | 2.9 | -0.6 |
| 2016 | E | 1.40 | 1.16 | 3.7 | 1.6 | 4.0 | -1.9 |
| 2015 | E- | 0.50 | 0.42 | 2.3 | 0.6 | 2.9 | -3.1 |
| 2014 | B- | 3.13 | 2.61 | 2.3 | 2.1 | 3.1 | 0.3 |
| 2013 | C | 2.55 | 2.12 | 2.4 | 1.8 | 3.2 | 0.0 |
| 2012 | C | 2.95 | 2.46 | 2.2 | 1.8 | 3.3 | 0.1 |

**Rating Indexes**

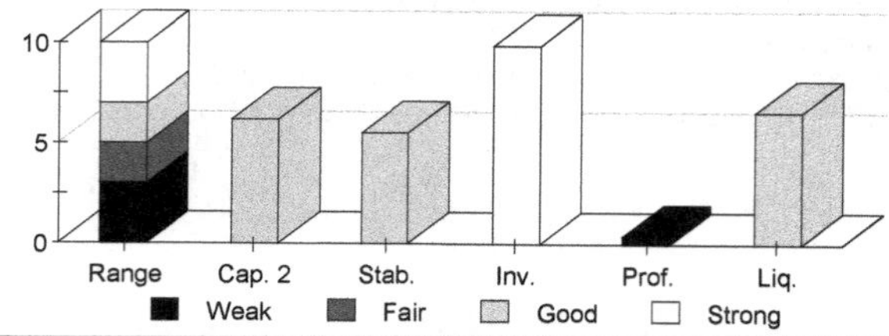


## OLD REPUBLIC LIFE INSURANCE COMPANY — B- Good

**Major Rating Factors:** Good quality investment portfolio (5.7 on a scale of 0 to 10) despite mixed results such as: no exposure to mortgages and substantial holdings of BBB bonds but small junk bond holdings. Good overall results on stability tests (5.2). Strengths include good financial support from affiliation with Old Republic Group, good operational trends and excellent risk diversification. Weak profitability (2.8) with operating losses during the first nine months of 2017.
**Other Rating Factors:** Strong capitalization (8.8) based on excellent risk adjusted capital (severe loss scenario). Excellent liquidity (7.7).
**Principal Business:** Group health insurance (55%), individual life insurance (31%), and reinsurance (13%).
**Principal Investments:** NonCMO investment grade bonds (80%), common & preferred stock (13%), noninv. grade bonds (3%), cash (2%), and policy loans (1%).
**Investments in Affiliates:** None
**Group Affiliation:** Old Republic Group
**Licensed in:** All states except NY
**Commenced Business:** April 1923
**Address:** 307 NORTH MICHIGAN AVENUE, CHICAGO, IL 60601
**Phone:** (312) 346-8100 **Domicile State:** IL **NAIC Code:** 67261

| Data Date | Rating | RACR #1 | RACR #2 | Total Assets ($mil) | Capital ($mil) | Net Premium ($mil) | Net Income ($mil) |
|---|---|---|---|---|---|---|---|
| 9-17 | B- | 3.52 | 2.19 | 120.8 | 33.1 | 13.9 | -0.2 |
| 9-16 | B- | 3.07 | 1.90 | 123.9 | 29.9 | 13.1 | 0.5 |
| 2016 | B- | 3.43 | 2.12 | 125.0 | 31.4 | 19.4 | 2.3 |
| 2015 | B- | 2.84 | 1.77 | 126.9 | 27.0 | 18.1 | -0.3 |
| 2014 | B- | 3.22 | 2.02 | 125.1 | 30.6 | 20.1 | 0.8 |
| 2013 | B- | 4.30 | 2.81 | 131.7 | 36.4 | 21.2 | 2.2 |
| 2012 | B | 4.68 | 3.13 | 138.4 | 40.6 | 21.0 | 1.6 |

**Old Republic Group**
**Composite Group Rating: B**

| Largest Group Members | Assets ($mil) | Rating |
|---|---|---|
| OLD REPUB INS CO | 2814 | B |
| OLD REPUBLIC GENERAL INS CORP | 2021 | B |
| GREAT WEST CASUALTY CO | 2016 | B |
| OLD REPUBLIC SECURITY ASR CO | 1057 | B |
| PENNSYLVANIA MANUFACTURERS ASN INS | 930 | C |

## OLD UNITED LIFE INSURANCE COMPANY — B Good

**Major Rating Factors:** Good overall results on stability tests (5.1 on a scale of 0 to 10) despite negative cash flow from operations for 2016. Other stability subfactors include good operational trends and excellent risk diversification. Good quality investment portfolio (6.1) despite mixed results such as: no exposure to mortgages and large holdings of BBB rated bonds but minimal holdings in junk bonds. Good overall profitability (6.5).
**Other Rating Factors:** Strong capitalization (10.0) based on excellent risk adjusted capital (severe loss scenario). Excellent liquidity (10.0).
**Principal Business:** Credit health insurance (50%) and credit life insurance (50%).
**Principal Investments:** NonCMO investment grade bonds (74%), common & preferred stock (13%), CMOs and structured securities (11%), and noninv. grade bonds (3%).
**Investments in Affiliates:** None
**Group Affiliation:** Berkshire Hathaway Inc
**Licensed in:** All states except ME, NH, NY, PR
**Commenced Business:** January 1964
**Address:** 3800 N Central Ave Ste 460, Phoenix, AZ 85012
**Phone:** (913) 895-0200 **Domicile State:** AZ **NAIC Code:** 76007

| Data Date | Rating | RACR #1 | RACR #2 | Total Assets ($mil) | Capital ($mil) | Net Premium ($mil) | Net Income ($mil) |
|---|---|---|---|---|---|---|---|
| 9-17 | B | 6.41 | 4.32 | 83.3 | 46.6 | 4.6 | 2.4 |
| 9-16 | B | 5.73 | 5.15 | 81.9 | 43.4 | 6.1 | 1.2 |
| 2016 | B | 5.88 | 4.49 | 81.6 | 43.9 | 7.9 | 1.8 |
| 2015 | B | 5.56 | 5.01 | 82.5 | 42.0 | 6.2 | 4.2 |
| 2014 | B | 6.13 | 3.70 | 91.4 | 46.3 | 8.2 | 2.4 |
| 2013 | B | 6.08 | 3.55 | 87.4 | 44.9 | 8.5 | 0.4 |
| 2012 | B | 5.95 | 3.86 | 82.3 | 43.9 | 9.8 | 1.0 |

**Adverse Trends in Operations**

Change in asset mix during 2016 (6%)
Increase in policy surrenders from 2015 to 2016 (152%)
Decrease in premium volume from 2014 to 2015 (24%)
Change in asset mix during 2015 (5%)
Decrease in premium volume from 2012 to 2013 (13%)

## OMAHA INS CO B- Good

**Major Rating Factors:** Good liquidity (5.8 on a scale of 0 to 10) with sufficient resources to handle a spike in claims. Fair overall results on stability tests (3.7) including negative cash flow from operations for 2016 and excessive premium growth. Weak profitability (1.9) with operating losses during the first nine months of 2017. Return on equity has been low, averaging -12.5%.
**Other Rating Factors:** Strong capitalization (7.2) based on excellent risk adjusted capital (severe loss scenario). High quality investment portfolio (7.8).
**Principal Business:** Individual health insurance (100%).
**Principal Investments:** NonCMO investment grade bonds (60%) and CMOs and structured securities (39%).
**Investments in Affiliates:** None
**Group Affiliation:** Mutual Of Omaha Group
**Licensed in:** AK, AZ, AR, CT, DC, DE, GA, HI, IN, IA, KS, KY, ME, MD, MA, MI, MN, MS, MO, MT, NE, NJ, NM, ND, OH, OK, OR, PA, SC, SD, TN, TX, UT, VA, WA, WV, WY
**Commenced Business:** November 2006
**Address:** MUTUAL OF OMAHA PLAZA, OMAHA, NE 68175
**Phone:** (402) 342-7600 **Domicile State:** NE **NAIC Code:** 13100

| Data Date | Rating | RACR #1 | RACR #2 | Total Assets ($mil) | Capital ($mil) | Net Premium ($mil) | Net Income ($mil) |
|---|---|---|---|---|---|---|---|
| 9-17 | B- | 2.10 | 1.11 | 95.3 | 48.4 | 41.5 | -3.3 |
| 9-16 | C+ | 2.65 | 1.42 | 85.8 | 51.5 | 32.2 | -3.8 |
| 2016 | C+ | 2.48 | 1.31 | 99.2 | 49.2 | 44.4 | -5.4 |
| 2015 | C+ | 3.70 | 1.97 | 88.2 | 54.1 | 29.3 | -5.4 |
| 2014 | B- | 2.47 | 1.33 | 43.8 | 21.1 | 14.3 | -3.9 |
| 2013 | B- | 4.16 | 2.72 | 22.9 | 15.9 | 5.1 | -2.0 |
| 2012 | B- | 4.64 | 4.18 | 19.9 | 16.3 | 0.6 | -2.2 |

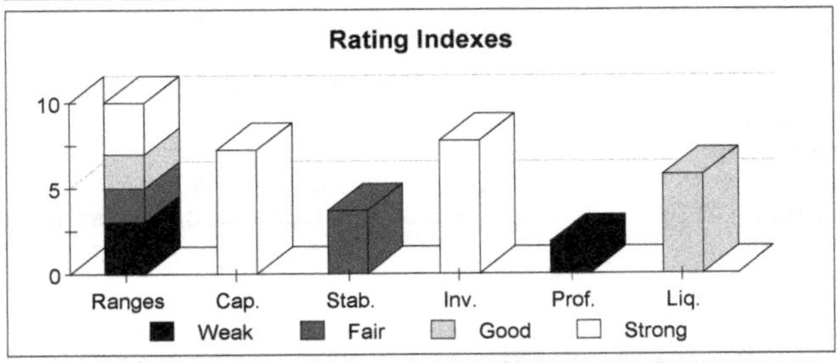


## ON LOK SENIOR HEALTH SERVICES B Good

**Major Rating Factors:** Good overall results on stability tests (6.6 on a scale of 0 to 10) based on steady enrollment growth, averaging 6% over the past five years. Excellent profitability (7.5). Strong capitalization index (10.0) based on excellent current risk-adjusted capital (severe loss scenario).
**Other Rating Factors:** Excellent liquidity (7.5) with ample operational cash flow and liquid investments.
**Principal Business:** Medicaid (68%), Medicare (31%)
**Mem Phys: 16:** N/A **15:** N/A **16 MLR** 83.6% **/ 16 Admin Exp** N/A
**Enroll(000): Q3 17:** 1 **16:** 1 **15:** 1 **Med Exp PMPM:** $6,466
**Principal Investments ($000):** Cash and equiv ($7,597)
**Provider Compensation ($000):** None
**Total Member Encounters:** N/A
**Group Affiliation:** None
**Licensed in:** CA
**Address:** 1333 Bush Street, San Francisco, CA 94109
**Phone:** (415) 292-8722 **Dom State:** CA **Commenced Bus:** September 1971

| Data Date | Rating | RACR #1 | RACR #2 | Total Assets ($mil) | Capital ($mil) | Net Premium ($mil) | Net Income ($mil) |
|---|---|---|---|---|---|---|---|
| 9-17 | B | 4.84 | 3.51 | 176.3 | 133.4 | 111.3 | 18.7 |
| 9-16 | B | 3.79 | 2.75 | 132.0 | 96.8 | 94.7 | 1.8 |
| 2016 | B | 3.94 | 2.85 | 141.6 | 106.0 | 133.2 | 11.0 |
| 2015 | B | 3.79 | 2.75 | 133.7 | 98.0 | 115.6 | 8.5 |
| 2014 | B+ | 3.90 | 2.84 | 129.0 | 99.5 | 105.9 | 10.1 |
| 2013 | B | 3.55 | 2.59 | 118.8 | 89.4 | 97.0 | 5.7 |
| 2012 | B | 3.70 | 2.69 | 115.4 | 83.7 | 95.7 | 1.6 |

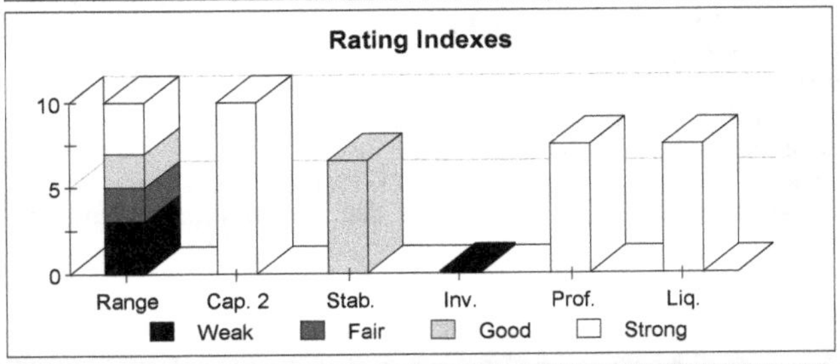


## OPTIMA HEALTH INS CO C Fair

**Major Rating Factors:** Weak profitability index (0.6 on a scale of 0 to 10). Good liquidity (6.8) with sufficient resources (cash flows and marketable investments) to handle a spike in claims. Strong capitalization (8.9) based on excellent current risk-adjusted capital (severe loss scenario).
**Other Rating Factors:** High quality investment portfolio (9.9).
**Principal Business:** Comp med (100%)
**Mem Phys: 16:** 8,386 **15:** 8,832 **16 MLR** 87.1% **/ 16 Admin Exp** N/A
**Enroll(000): Q3 17:** 8 **16:** 9 **15:** 11 **Med Exp PMPM:** $397
**Principal Investments:** Long-term bonds (74%), cash and equiv (19%), nonaffiliate common stock (7%)
**Provider Compensation ($000):** Contr fee ($45,403), capitation ($208)
**Total Member Encounters:** Phys (1,650), non-phys (16,011)
**Group Affiliation:** Sentara Healthcare
**Licensed in:** VA
**Address:** 4417 Corporation Lane, Virginia Beach, VA 23462
**Phone:** (757) 552-7401 **Dom State:** VA **Commenced Bus:** October 1992

| Data Date | Rating | RACR #1 | RACR #2 | Total Assets ($mil) | Capital ($mil) | Net Premium ($mil) | Net Income ($mil) |
|---|---|---|---|---|---|---|---|
| 9-17 | C | 2.88 | 2.40 | 33.6 | 14.5 | 36.2 | -1.5 |
| 9-16 | C | 2.64 | 2.20 | 28.0 | 16.6 | 39.4 | -1.1 |
| 2016 | C | 3.15 | 2.62 | 28.8 | 16.1 | 51.6 | -1.5 |
| 2015 | C | 2.75 | 2.29 | 28.7 | 17.4 | 71.0 | -1.5 |
| 2014 | C | 1.39 | 1.16 | 31.4 | 15.0 | 110.5 | -14.5 |
| 2013 | B | 1.74 | 1.45 | 36.0 | 18.2 | 113.6 | -6.0 |
| 2012 | B- | 2.81 | 2.34 | 41.3 | 25.3 | 93.2 | -4.5 |

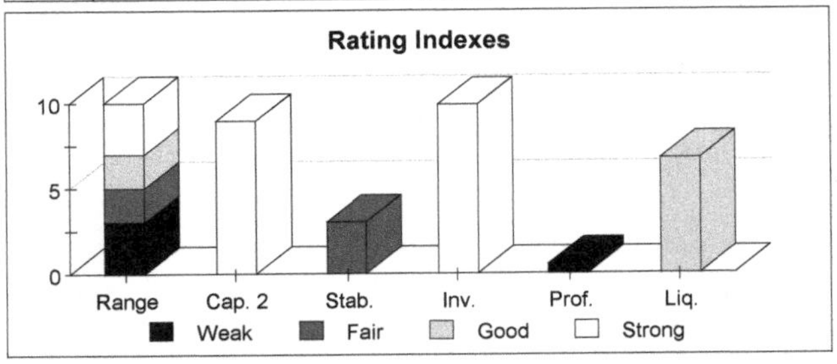

## OPTIMA HEALTH PLAN * A- Excellent

**Major Rating Factors:** Excellent profitability (7.6 on a scale of 0 to 10). Strong capitalization index (8.0) based on excellent current risk-adjusted capital (severe loss scenario). High quality investment portfolio (9.9).
**Other Rating Factors:** Excellent overall results on stability tests (7.3). Good liquidity (6.8) with sufficient resources (cash flows and marketable investments) to handle a spike in claims.
**Principal Business:** Medicaid (53%), comp med (44%), Medicare (2%), FEHB (1%)
**Mem Phys: 16:** 15,931 **15:** 15,836 **16 MLR** 92.0% **/ 16 Admin Exp** N/A
**Enroll(000): Q3 17:** 294 **16:** 295 **15:** 293 **Med Exp PMPM:** $371
**Principal Investments:** Long-term bonds (60%), cash and equiv (29%), nonaffiliate common stock (10%)
**Provider Compensation ($000):** Contr fee ($1,268,002), capitation ($25,452), bonus arrang ($8)
**Total Member Encounters:** Phys (1,616,828), non-phys (5,385,679)
**Group Affiliation:** Sentara Healthcare
**Licensed in:** VA
**Address:** 4417 Corporation Lane, Virginia Beach, VA 23462
**Phone:** (757) 552-7401 **Dom State:** VA **Commenced Bus:** December 1984

| Data Date | Rating | RACR #1 | RACR #2 | Total Assets ($mil) | Capital ($mil) | Net Premium ($mil) | Net Income ($mil) |
|---|---|---|---|---|---|---|---|
| 9-17 | A- | 2.19 | 1.82 | 445.1 | 251.4 | 1,075.9 | 34.5 |
| 9-16 | B+ | 2.02 | 1.69 | 358.0 | 218.9 | 1,061.0 | 5.8 |
| 2016 | B+ | 1.92 | 1.60 | 372.9 | 222.6 | 1,423.6 | 9.6 |
| 2015 | B+ | 1.96 | 1.63 | 352.3 | 212.4 | 1,357.3 | 15.5 |
| 2014 | B+ | 1.96 | 1.64 | 329.6 | 197.7 | 1,382.1 | 51.5 |
| 2013 | A- | 2.07 | 1.72 | 349.5 | 196.6 | 1,302.4 | 48.9 |
| 2012 | A- | 1.85 | 1.54 | 316.0 | 170.2 | 1,238.4 | 29.6 |

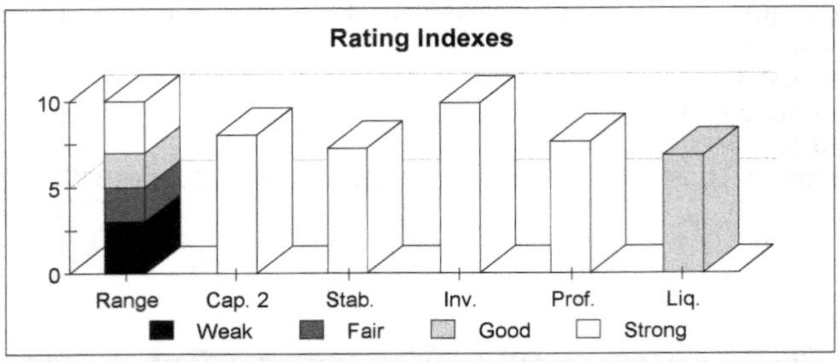


## OPTIMUM CHOICE INC C+ Fair

**Major Rating Factors:** Fair overall results on stability tests (4.5 on a scale of 0 to 10). Rating is significantly influenced by the fair financial results of UnitedHealth Group Incorporated. Excellent profitability (8.0). Strong capitalization index (10.0) based on excellent current risk-adjusted capital (severe loss scenario).
**Other Rating Factors:** High quality investment portfolio (9.9). Excellent liquidity (6.9) with sufficient resources (cash flows and marketable investments) to handle a spike in claims.
**Principal Business:** Comp med (100%)
**Mem Phys: 16:** 48,611 **15:** 45,388 **16 MLR** 69.4% **/ 16 Admin Exp** N/A
**Enroll(000): Q3 17:** 49 **16:** 42 **15:** 43 **Med Exp PMPM:** $267
**Principal Investments:** Long-term bonds (83%), cash and equiv (17%)
**Provider Compensation ($000):** Contr fee ($124,030), capitation ($7,375), bonus arrang ($90), FFS ($15)
**Total Member Encounters:** Phys (214,771), non-phys (12,445)
**Group Affiliation:** UnitedHealth Group Incorporated
**Licensed in:** DC, DE, MD, VA, WV
**Address:** 800 KING FARM BLVD, ROCKVILLE, MD 20850
**Phone:** (240) 632-8109 **Dom State:** MD **Commenced Bus:** September 1988

| Data Date | Rating | RACR #1 | RACR #2 | Total Assets ($mil) | Capital ($mil) | Net Premium ($mil) | Net Income ($mil) |
|---|---|---|---|---|---|---|---|
| 9-17 | C+ | 4.76 | 3.97 | 62.9 | 21.7 | 160.2 | 10.1 |
| 9-16 | C | 5.19 | 4.32 | 59.6 | 25.3 | 137.1 | 12.6 |
| 2016 | C+ | 4.40 | 3.67 | 58.2 | 19.9 | 182.8 | 15.4 |
| 2015 | C | 4.71 | 3.93 | 60.6 | 22.8 | 197.2 | 15.9 |
| 2014 | B- | 7.39 | 6.16 | 83.7 | 54.1 | 219.9 | 25.6 |
| 2013 | C+ | 4.41 | 3.67 | 70.1 | 41.0 | 233.5 | 24.5 |
| 2012 | C+ | 2.81 | 2.35 | 56.3 | 26.5 | 242.9 | 22.1 |

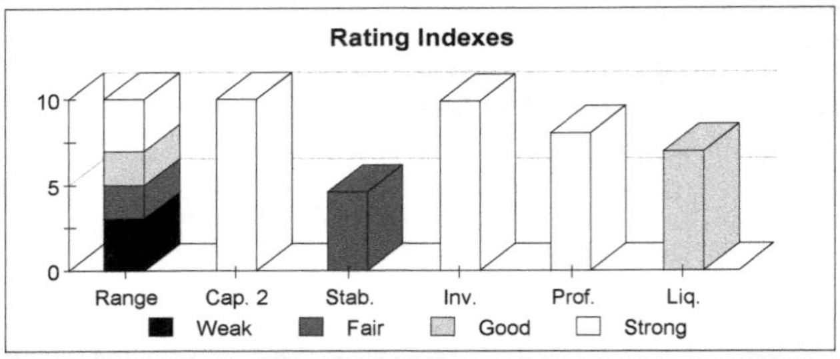


## OPTIMUM HEALTHCARE INC E Very Weak

**Major Rating Factors:** Fair capitalization (4.7 on a scale of 0 to 10) based on fair current risk-adjusted capital (moderate loss scenario). Excellent profitability (9.1). High quality investment portfolio (9.9).
**Other Rating Factors:** Excellent liquidity (7.0) with sufficient resources (cash flows and marketable investments) to handle a spike in claims.
**Principal Business:** Medicare (100%)
**Mem Phys: 16:** 16,381 **15:** 14,502 **16 MLR** 83.2% **/ 16 Admin Exp** N/A
**Enroll(000): Q3 17:** 53 **16:** 46 **15:** 40 **Med Exp PMPM:** $823
**Principal Investments:** Cash and equiv (89%), long-term bonds (11%)
**Provider Compensation ($000):** Contr fee ($213,327), bonus arrang ($87,623), salary ($69,009), capitation ($45,564)
**Total Member Encounters:** Phys (20,960), non-phys (22,951)
**Group Affiliation:** Americas 1st Choice Group
**Licensed in:** FL
**Address:** 5600 Mariner St Ste 227, Tampa, FL 33609
**Phone:** (813) 506-6000 **Dom State:** FL **Commenced Bus:** August 2004

| Data Date | Rating | RACR #1 | RACR #2 | Total Assets ($mil) | Capital ($mil) | Net Premium ($mil) | Net Income ($mil) |
|---|---|---|---|---|---|---|---|
| 9-17 | E | 0.88 | 0.74 | 189.9 | 35.0 | 469.4 | 10.3 |
| 9-16 | E- | 0.81 | 0.67 | 152.9 | 31.6 | 406.6 | 6.0 |
| 2016 | E- | 0.75 | 0.62 | 112.5 | 30.5 | 529.9 | 6.7 |
| 2015 | E- | 0.67 | 0.56 | 73.7 | 25.9 | 415.7 | 2.6 |
| 2014 | D+ | 0.57 | 0.48 | 77.7 | 23.2 | 440.7 | 5.5 |
| 2013 | N/A | N/A | N/A | 60.3 | 17.2 | 379.1 | 2.6 |
| 2012 | N/A | N/A | N/A | 43.8 | 14.6 | 244.4 | 5.7 |

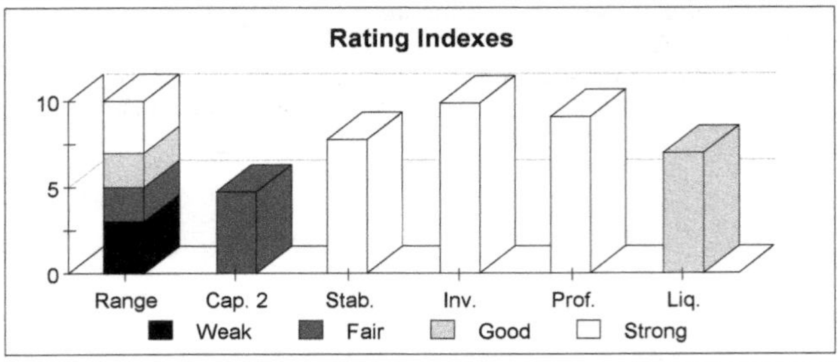

## ORANGE PREVENTION & TREATMENT INTEGR * A- Excellent

**Major Rating Factors:** Excellent profitability (9.0 on a scale of 0 to 10). Strong capitalization index (8.0) based on excellent current risk-adjusted capital (severe loss scenario). Excellent overall results on stability tests (7.3).
**Other Rating Factors:** Good liquidity (6.8) with sufficient resources (cash flows and marketable investments) to handle a spike in claims.
**Principal Business:** Medicaid (95%), Medicare (5%)
**Mem Phys: 16:** N/A **15:** N/A **16 MLR** 96.0% **/ 16 Admin Exp** N/A
**Enroll(000): Q3 17:** 796 **16:** 807 **15:** 753 **Med Exp PMPM:** $323
**Principal Investments ($000):** Cash and equiv ($1,273,438)
**Provider Compensation ($000):** None
**Total Member Encounters:** N/A
**Group Affiliation:** None
**Licensed in:** CA
**Address:** 505 City Parkway West, Orange, CA 92868
**Phone:** (714) 796-6122 **Dom State:** CA **Commenced Bus:** June 2000

| Data Date | Rating | RACR #1 | RACR #2 | Total Assets ($mil) | Capital ($mil) | Net Premium ($mil) | Net Income ($mil) |
|---|---|---|---|---|---|---|---|
| 9-17 | A- | 2.77 | 1.82 | 2,819.9 | 724.8 | 2,728.4 | 60.2 |
| 9-16 | A- | 2.84 | 1.87 | 2,172.8 | 650.2 | 2,272.7 | 23.1 |
| 2016 | A- | 2.54 | 1.66 | 2,304.9 | 659.6 | 3,163.8 | 32.5 |
| 2015 | A- | 2.75 | 1.81 | 1,866.5 | 627.0 | 3,236.6 | 231.1 |
| 2014 | A- | 2.77 | 1.77 | 1,007.5 | 400.3 | 2,002.0 | 188.4 |
| 2013 | B | 1.58 | 1.01 | 690.4 | 211.9 | 1,743.2 | 55.1 |
| 2012 | B- | 1.17 | 0.75 | 464.9 | 156.9 | 1,493.1 | 3.5 |

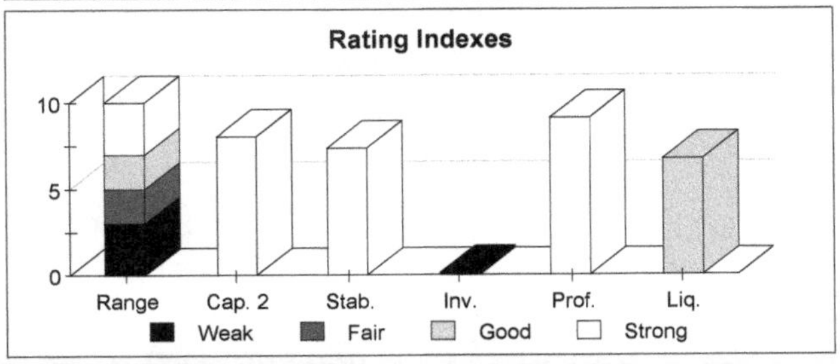


## ORTHONET OF THE MID-ATLANTIC C Fair

**Major Rating Factors:** Excellent profitability (8.1 on a scale of 0 to 10). Strong capitalization (10.0) based on excellent current risk-adjusted capital (severe loss scenario). High quality investment portfolio (9.9).
**Other Rating Factors:** Excellent liquidity (8.9) with ample operational cash flow and liquid investments.
**Principal Business:** Other (100%)
**Mem Phys: 16:** 343 **15:** 631 **16 MLR** 48.5% **/ 16 Admin Exp** N/A
**Enroll(000): 16:** 55 **15:** 121 **Med Exp PMPM:** $2
**Principal Investments:** Cash and equiv (100%)
**Provider Compensation ($000):** Contr fee ($1,424)
**Total Member Encounters:** Non-phys (41,707)
**Group Affiliation:** UnitedHealth Group Incorporated
**Licensed in:** NJ
**Address:** 1311 Mamaroneck Ave, White Plains, NY 10605
**Phone:** (914) 681-8800 **Dom State:** NJ **Commenced Bus:** January 2003

| Data Date | Rating | RACR #1 | RACR #2 | Total Assets ($mil) | Capital ($mil) | Net Premium ($mil) | Net Income ($mil) |
|---|---|---|---|---|---|---|---|
| 2016 | C | 45.60 | 38.00 | 16.5 | 11.4 | 4.2 | 1.1 |
| 2015 | U | 22.29 | 18.58 | 18.3 | 9.9 | 5.5 | 0.9 |
| 2014 | N/A | N/A | N/A | 7.7 | 6.3 | 5.9 | 1.4 |
| 2013 | N/A | N/A | N/A | 13.8 | 12.0 | 6.2 | 1.7 |
| 2012 | N/A | N/A | N/A | 15.4 | 10.4 | 8.5 | 2.0 |

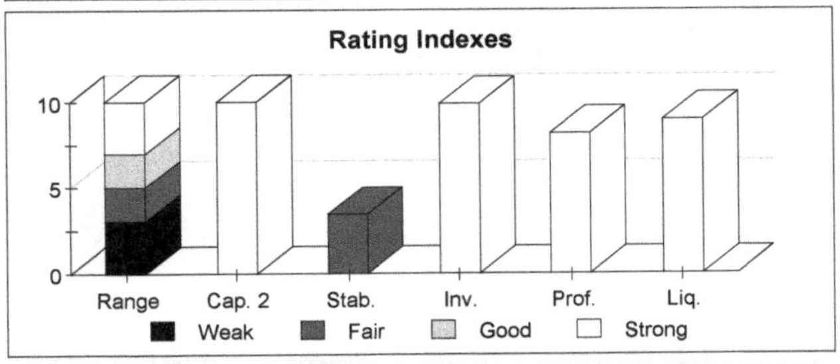


## OSCAR HEALTH PLAN OF CALIFORNIA E- Very Weak

**Major Rating Factors:** Weak profitability index (0.0 on a scale of 0 to 10). Poor capitalization index (0.0) based on weak current risk-adjusted capital (severe loss scenario). Weak overall results on stability tests (0.4).
**Other Rating Factors:** Weak liquidity (0.1) as a spike in claims may stretch capacity.
**Principal Business:** Managed care (100%)
**Mem Phys: 16:** N/A **15:** N/A **16 MLR** 116.9% **/ 16 Admin Exp** N/A
**Enroll(000): Q3 17:** 10 **16:** 4 **15:** N/A **Med Exp PMPM:** $97
**Principal Investments ($000):** Cash and equiv ($15,060)
**Provider Compensation ($000):** None
**Total Member Encounters:** N/A
**Group Affiliation:** None
**Licensed in:** CA
**Address:** 3535 Hayden Avenue Suite 230, Culver City, CA 90232
**Phone:** (424) 261-4363 **Dom State:** CA **Commenced Bus:** N/A

| Data Date | Rating | RACR #1 | RACR #2 | Total Assets ($mil) | Capital ($mil) | Net Premium ($mil) | Net Income ($mil) |
|---|---|---|---|---|---|---|---|
| 9-17 | E- | N/A | N/A | 15.7 | -41.4 | 25.4 | -14.4 |
| 9-16 | N/A | N/A | N/A | N/A | N/A | N/A | N/A |
| 2016 | E- | N/A | N/A | 16.4 | -27.0 | 9.1 | -20.8 |
| 2015 | N/A | N/A | N/A | N/A | N/A | N/A | N/A |
| 2014 | N/A | N/A | N/A | N/A | N/A | N/A | N/A |
| 2013 | N/A | N/A | N/A | N/A | N/A | N/A | N/A |
| 2012 | N/A | N/A | N/A | N/A | N/A | N/A | N/A |

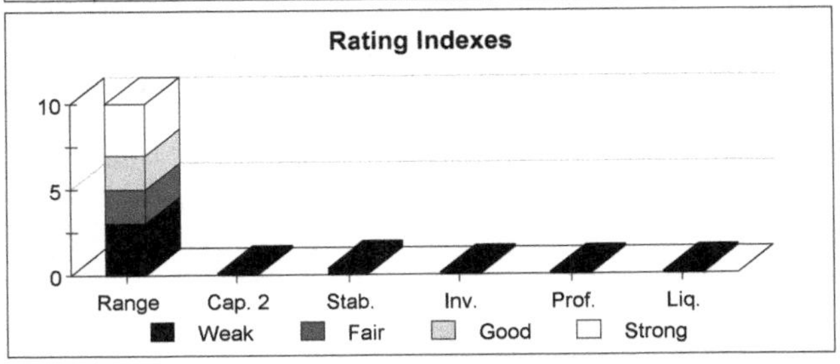

## OSCAR INS CO OF TEXAS D- Weak

**Major Rating Factors:** Weak profitability index (0.1 on a scale of 0 to 10). Fair capitalization (4.4) based on fair current risk-adjusted capital (moderate loss scenario). Good liquidity (5.5) with sufficient resources (cash flows and marketable investments) to handle a spike in claims.
**Other Rating Factors:** High quality investment portfolio (9.9).
**Principal Business:** Comp med (100%)
**Mem Phys: 16:** 1,243 **15:** N/A **16 MLR** 123.9% **/ 16 Admin Exp** N/A
**Enroll(000): Q3 17:** 30 **16:** 29 **15:** N/A **Med Exp PMPM:** $290
**Principal Investments:** Cash and equiv (100%)
**Provider Compensation ($000):** FFS ($82,812), capitation ($9)
**Total Member Encounters:** Phys (121,867), non-phys (49,017)
**Group Affiliation:** Mulberry Health Inc
**Licensed in:** TX
**Address:** 3102 Oak Lawn Ste 602, Dallas, TX 75206
**Phone:** (646) 403-3677 **Dom State:** TX **Commenced Bus:** N/A

| Data Date | Rating | RACR #1 | RACR #2 | Total Assets ($mil) | Capital ($mil) | Net Premium ($mil) | Net Income ($mil) |
|---|---|---|---|---|---|---|---|
| 9-17 | D- | 0.84 | 0.70 | 51.3 | 15.1 | 72.6 | -26.1 |
| 9-16 | N/A | N/A | N/A | 79.1 | 18.7 | 68.7 | -31.5 |
| 2016 | D | 1.80 | 1.50 | 88.1 | 29.5 | 88.6 | -45.2 |
| 2015 | N/A | N/A | N/A | 17.9 | 11.6 | N/A | -9.1 |
| 2014 | N/A | N/A | N/A | N/A | N/A | N/A | N/A |
| 2013 | N/A | N/A | N/A | N/A | N/A | N/A | N/A |
| 2012 | N/A | N/A | N/A | N/A | N/A | N/A | N/A |

Rating Indexes

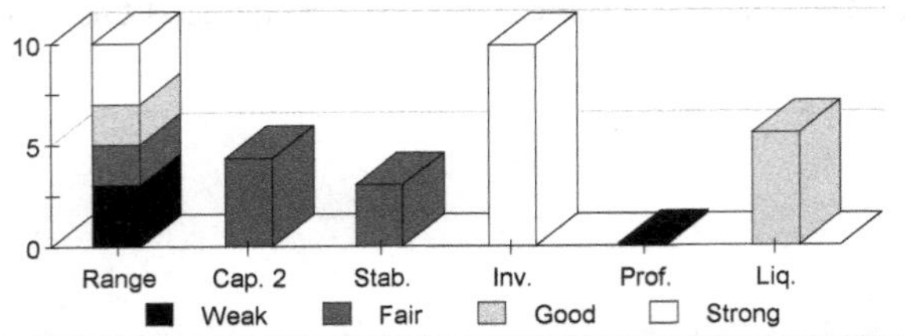


## OSCAR INS CORP E- Very Weak

**Major Rating Factors:** Weak profitability index (0.0 on a scale of 0 to 10). Weak liquidity (0.0) as a spike in claims may stretch capacity. Fair capitalization (4.3) based on fair current risk-adjusted capital (moderate loss scenario).
**Other Rating Factors:** High quality investment portfolio (9.9).
**Principal Business:** Comp med (100%)
**Mem Phys: 16:** 9,611 **15:** 34,576 **16 MLR** 133.2% **/ 16 Admin Exp** N/A
**Enroll(000): Q3 17:** 42 **16:** 54 **15:** 53 **Med Exp PMPM:** $452
**Principal Investments:** Cash and equiv (100%)
**Provider Compensation ($000):** FFS ($296,995), capitation ($514)
**Total Member Encounters:** Phys (295,913), non-phys (174,748)
**Group Affiliation:** Mulberry Health Inc
**Licensed in:** NY
**Address:** 295 Lafayette St, New York, NY 10012
**Phone:** (646) 403-3677 **Dom State:** NY **Commenced Bus:** January 2014

| Data Date | Rating | RACR #1 | RACR #2 | Total Assets ($mil) | Capital ($mil) | Net Premium ($mil) | Net Income ($mil) |
|---|---|---|---|---|---|---|---|
| 9-17 | E- | 0.83 | 0.69 | 109.6 | 25.7 | 114.8 | -55.2 |
| 9-16 | E- | 1.63 | 1.35 | 123.2 | 32.2 | 192.5 | -78.9 |
| 2016 | E- | 1.42 | 1.18 | 148.8 | 45.2 | 246.3 | -123.7 |
| 2015 | D | 1.10 | 0.92 | 118.6 | 21.3 | 117.4 | -92.4 |
| 2014 | D | 2.32 | 1.93 | 60.0 | 27.3 | 56.9 | -27.6 |
| 2013 | N/A | N/A | N/A | 47.8 | 46.6 | N/A | -8.2 |
| 2012 | N/A | N/A | N/A | N/A | N/A | N/A | N/A |

Rating Indexes

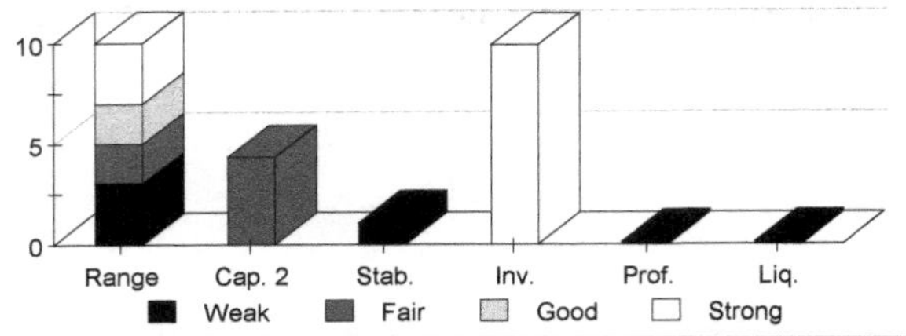


## OSCAR INS CORP OF NEW JERSEY D Weak

**Major Rating Factors:** Weak profitability index (0.9 on a scale of 0 to 10). Good capitalization (6.1) based on good current risk-adjusted capital (severe loss scenario). High quality investment portfolio (9.9).
**Other Rating Factors:** Excellent liquidity (7.3) with ample operational cash flow and liquid investments.
**Principal Business:** Comp med (100%)
**Mem Phys: 16:** 4,703 **15:** 30,273 **16 MLR** 95.2% **/ 16 Admin Exp** N/A
**Enroll(000): 16:** 21 **15:** 3 **Med Exp PMPM:** $283
**Principal Investments:** Cash and equiv (100%)
**Provider Compensation ($000):** FFS ($61,655), capitation ($14)
**Total Member Encounters:** Phys (105,574), non-phys (8,513)
**Group Affiliation:** Mulberry Health Inc
**Licensed in:** NJ
**Address:** 295 Lafayette St, New York, NY 10012-2701
**Phone:** (646) 403-3677 **Dom State:** NJ **Commenced Bus:** January 2015

| Data Date | Rating | RACR #1 | RACR #2 | Total Assets ($mil) | Capital ($mil) | Net Premium ($mil) | Net Income ($mil) |
|---|---|---|---|---|---|---|---|
| 2016 | D | 1.09 | 0.91 | 70.4 | 10.2 | 82.1 | -15.0 |
| 2015 | N/A | N/A | N/A | 14.9 | 4.6 | 9.0 | -12.8 |
| 2014 | N/A | N/A | N/A | 4.4 | 3.6 | N/A | -3.4 |
| 2013 | N/A | N/A | N/A | N/A | N/A | N/A | N/A |
| 2012 | N/A | N/A | N/A | N/A | N/A | N/A | N/A |

Rating Indexes

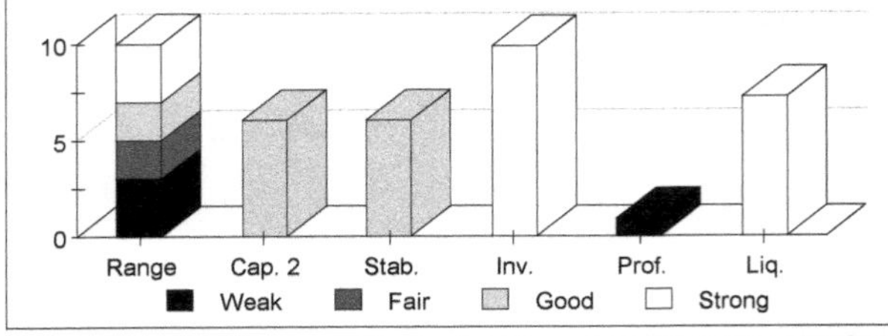

## OXFORD HEALTH INS INC B Good

**Major Rating Factors:** Good liquidity (6.9 on a scale of 0 to 10) with sufficient resources (cash flows and marketable investments) to handle a spike in claims. Excellent profitability (9.0). Strong capitalization (10.0) based on excellent current risk-adjusted capital (severe loss scenario).
**Other Rating Factors:** High quality investment portfolio (9.5).
**Principal Business:** Comp med (100%)
**Mem Phys: 16:** 103,448 **15:** 159,000 **16 MLR** 78.1% **/ 16 Admin Exp** N/A
**Enroll(000): Q3 17:** 960 **16:** 909 **15:** 862 **Med Exp PMPM:** $472
**Principal Investments:** Long-term bonds (82%), cash and equiv (16%), other (2%)
**Provider Compensation ($000):** Contr fee ($3,866,270), FFS ($801,066), capitation ($327,023), bonus arrang ($23,788)
**Total Member Encounters:** Phys (4,198,109), non-phys (3,534,455)
**Group Affiliation:** UnitedHealth Group Incorporated
**Licensed in:** CT, NJ, NY, PA
**Address:** ONE PENN PLAZA Fl 8, NEW YORK, NY 10119
**Phone:** (203) 447-4500 **Dom State:** NY **Commenced Bus:** July 1987

| Data Date | Rating | RACR #1 | RACR #2 | Total Assets ($mil) | Capital ($mil) | Net Premium ($mil) | Net Income ($mil) |
|---|---|---|---|---|---|---|---|
| 9-17 | B | 4.82 | 4.02 | 2,629.9 | 1,502.5 | 5,353.2 | 314.3 |
| 9-16 | B | 4.69 | 3.91 | 2,292.2 | 1,358.3 | 4,887.6 | 259.7 |
| 2016 | B | 3.86 | 3.21 | 2,210.8 | 1,192.6 | 6,431.1 | 363.6 |
| 2015 | B | 4.35 | 3.62 | 2,195.0 | 1,257.2 | 5,819.0 | 418.5 |
| 2014 | B | 3.52 | 2.93 | 1,946.6 | 917.3 | 4,922.3 | 237.0 |
| 2013 | C+ | 5.65 | 4.70 | 2,078.4 | 855.2 | 2,862.9 | 141.4 |
| 2012 | C+ | 4.83 | 4.03 | 2,004.7 | 721.8 | 2,832.7 | 160.7 |

Rating Indexes

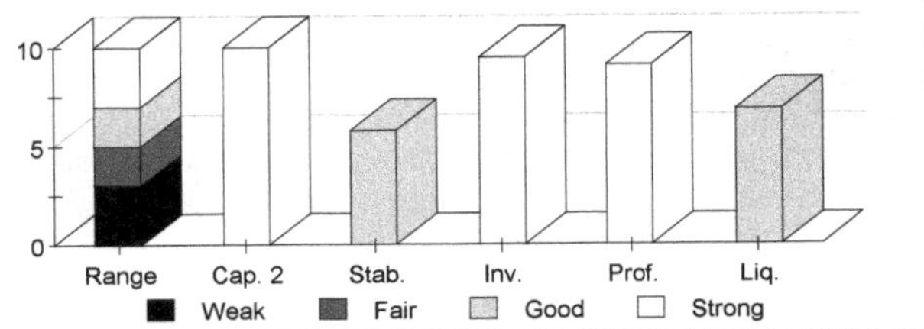


## OXFORD HEALTH PLANS (CT) INC B- Good

**Major Rating Factors:** Fair overall results on stability tests (4.7 on a scale of 0 to 10) based on a decline in the number of member physicians during 2017. Rating is significantly influenced by the fair financial results of UnitedHealth Group Incorporated. Excellent profitability (8.5). Strong capitalization index (10.0) based on excellent current risk-adjusted capital (severe loss scenario).
**Other Rating Factors:** High quality investment portfolio (9.9). Excellent liquidity (6.9) with sufficient resources (cash flows and marketable investments) to handle a spike in claims.
**Principal Business:** Medicare (95%), comp med (5%)
**Mem Phys: 16:** 49,202 **15:** 109,881 **16 MLR** 81.4% **/ 16 Admin Exp** N/A
**Enroll(000): Q3 17:** 139 **16:** 48 **15:** 41 **Med Exp PMPM:** $692
**Principal Investments:** Long-term bonds (67%), cash and equiv (33%)
**Provider Compensation ($000):** Contr fee ($332,671), FFS ($28,619), capitation ($4,494), bonus arrang ($3,042)
**Total Member Encounters:** Phys (868,581), non-phys (359,761)
**Group Affiliation:** UnitedHealth Group Incorporated
**Licensed in:** CT, NJ
**Address:** 4 RESEARCH DRIVE, SHELTON, CT 06484
**Phone:** (203) 447-4500 **Dom State:** CT **Commenced Bus:** October 1993

| Data Date | Rating | RACR #1 | RACR #2 | Total Assets ($mil) | Capital ($mil) | Net Premium ($mil) | Net Income ($mil) |
|---|---|---|---|---|---|---|---|
| 9-17 | B- | 5.07 | 4.22 | 595.4 | 128.2 | 1,078.1 | 52.9 |
| 9-16 | C | 4.39 | 3.66 | 255.9 | 91.0 | 358.6 | 7.6 |
| 2016 | B- | 3.61 | 3.01 | 220.1 | 88.7 | 476.1 | 8.2 |
| 2015 | C | 3.73 | 3.11 | 178.6 | 79.7 | 456.1 | 32.2 |
| 2014 | B- | 3.96 | 3.30 | 240.3 | 102.6 | 499.5 | 19.6 |
| 2013 | B | 3.28 | 2.73 | 245.1 | 120.5 | 653.1 | 7.0 |
| 2012 | B- | 2.79 | 2.33 | 237.5 | 108.3 | 652.4 | 27.5 |

Rating Indexes

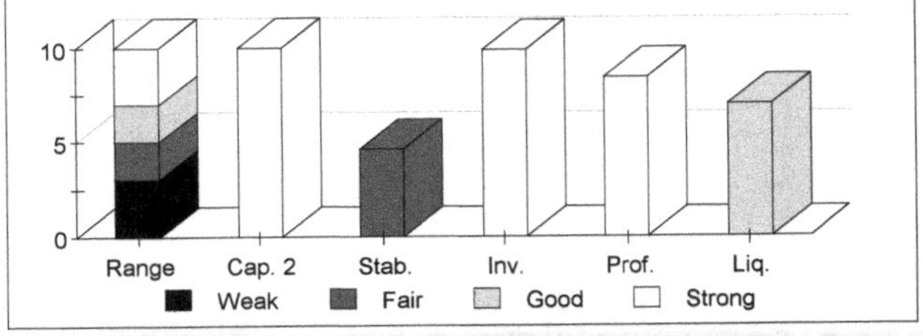


## OXFORD HEALTH PLANS (NJ) INC B Good

**Major Rating Factors:** Good overall results on stability tests (5.0 on a scale of 0 to 10). Rating is significantly influenced by the fair financial results of UnitedHealth Group Incorporated. Good liquidity (6.6) with sufficient resources (cash flows and marketable investments) to handle a spike in claims. Excellent profitability (8.4).
**Other Rating Factors:** Strong capitalization index (8.3) based on excellent current risk-adjusted capital (severe loss scenario). High quality investment portfolio (9.9).
**Principal Business:** Medicare (91%), comp med (9%)
**Mem Phys: 16:** 109,705 **15:** 109,881 **16 MLR** 79.5% **/ 16 Admin Exp** N/A
**Enroll(000): Q3 17:** 31 **16:** 107 **15:** 109 **Med Exp PMPM:** $658
**Principal Investments:** Long-term bonds (83%), cash and equiv (10%), other (7%)
**Provider Compensation ($000):** Contr fee ($618,601), FFS ($189,790), capitation ($15,200), bonus arrang ($6,640)
**Total Member Encounters:** Phys (1,859,049), non-phys (640,248)
**Group Affiliation:** UnitedHealth Group Incorporated
**Licensed in:** DE, MO, NJ, OR, PA, RI
**Address:** 170 WOOD AVENUE FLOOR 3, ISELIN, NJ 08830
**Phone:** (203) 447-4500 **Dom State:** NJ **Commenced Bus:** September 1985

| Data Date | Rating | RACR #1 | RACR #2 | Total Assets ($mil) | Capital ($mil) | Net Premium ($mil) | Net Income ($mil) |
|---|---|---|---|---|---|---|---|
| 9-17 | B | 2.41 | 2.01 | 311.7 | 129.0 | 285.3 | 20.8 |
| 9-16 | B | 2.48 | 2.07 | 408.4 | 128.2 | 791.9 | 33.9 |
| 2016 | B | 2.21 | 1.84 | 302.8 | 117.2 | 1,057.0 | 48.9 |
| 2015 | B | 2.35 | 1.96 | 289.5 | 121.0 | 970.1 | 14.6 |
| 2014 | B | 2.34 | 1.95 | 284.6 | 126.6 | 1,018.8 | 22.5 |
| 2013 | B+ | 2.33 | 1.94 | 337.3 | 140.8 | 1,143.7 | 34.0 |
| 2012 | B+ | 2.05 | 1.71 | 317.3 | 124.1 | 1,118.0 | 62.8 |

Rating Indexes

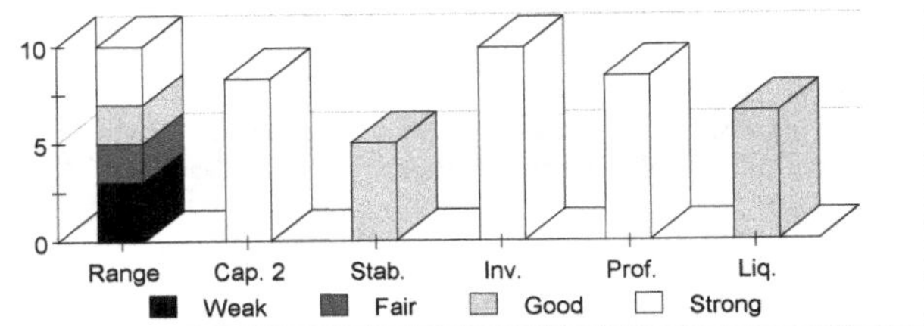

## OXFORD HEALTH PLANS (NY) INC * B+ Good

**Major Rating Factors:** Good overall profitability index (6.6 on a scale of 0 to 10). Good liquidity (6.6) with sufficient resources (cash flows and marketable investments) to handle a spike in claims. Strong capitalization index (9.2) based on excellent current risk-adjusted capital (severe loss scenario).
**Other Rating Factors:** High quality investment portfolio (9.1). Weak overall results on stability tests (1.8) based on a steep decline in capital during 2016. Rating is significantly influenced by the fair financial results of UnitedHealth Group Incorporated.
**Principal Business:** Comp med (53%), Medicare (47%)
**Mem Phys: 16:** 149,765 **15:** 150,981 **16 MLR** 85.4% **/ 16 Admin Exp** N/A
**Enroll(000): Q3 17:** 106 **16:** 181 **15:** 204 **Med Exp PMPM:** $627
**Principal Investments:** Long-term bonds (94%), cash and equiv (6%)
**Provider Compensation ($000):** Contr fee ($1,062,677), FFS ($333,911), capitation ($27,657), bonus arrang ($14,759)
**Total Member Encounters:** Phys (2,237,767), non-phys (828,367)
**Group Affiliation:** UnitedHealth Group Incorporated
**Licensed in:** NY
**Address:** ONE PENN PLAZA FLOOR 8, NEW YORK, NY 10119
**Phone:** (203) 447-4500 **Dom State:** NY **Commenced Bus:** June 1986

| Data Date | Rating | RACR #1 | RACR #2 | Total Assets ($mil) | Capital ($mil) | Net Premium ($mil) | Net Income ($mil) |
|---|---|---|---|---|---|---|---|
| 9-17 | B+ | 3.12 | 2.60 | 646.3 | 293.7 | 897.1 | 14.1 |
| 9-16 | A | 5.67 | 4.72 | 1,002.1 | 507.8 | 1,310.6 | 31.6 |
| 2016 | B+ | 3.01 | 2.51 | 614.8 | 282.4 | 1,707.7 | 22.4 |
| 2015 | A | 5.32 | 4.43 | 821.9 | 474.7 | 1,793.4 | 110.0 |
| 2014 | A | 3.60 | 3.00 | 750.1 | 406.6 | 2,028.4 | 4.9 |
| 2013 | A+ | 4.58 | 3.82 | 1,820.5 | 1,386.7 | 2,524.6 | 77.7 |
| 2012 | A+ | 3.95 | 3.29 | 1,626.5 | 1,175.8 | 2,524.0 | 108.3 |

Rating Indexes

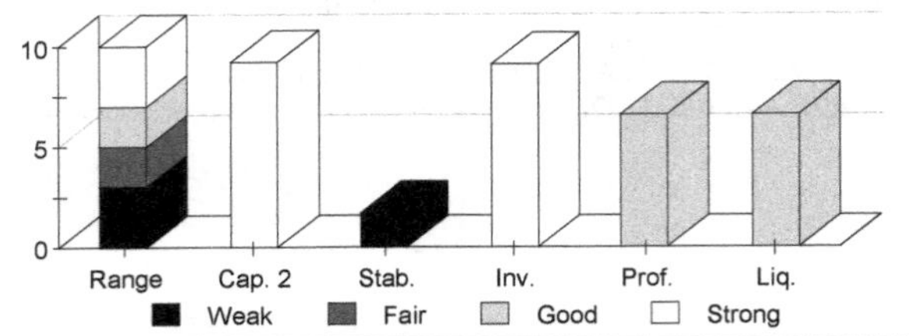


## PACIFIC CENTURY LIFE INSURANCE CORPORATION B Good

**Major Rating Factors:** Good overall profitability (6.6 on a scale of 0 to 10). Fair overall results on stability tests (4.7). Strong overall capitalization (10.0) based on excellent risk adjusted capital (severe loss scenario). However, capital levels have fluctuated somewhat during past years.
**Other Rating Factors:** High quality investment portfolio (7.4). Excellent liquidity (10.0).
**Principal Business:** Reinsurance (98%) and credit health insurance (2%).
**Principal Investments:** Mortgages in good standing (86%), cash (13%), and nonCMO investment grade bonds (2%).
**Investments in Affiliates:** None
**Group Affiliation:** Bank of Hawaii Corp
**Licensed in:** AZ, HI
**Commenced Business:** February 1982
**Address:** 2910 North 44th Street 2nd Fl, Phoenix, AZ 85018-7269
**Phone:** (602) 200-6900 **Domicile State:** AZ **NAIC Code:** 93815

| Data Date | Rating | RACR #1 | RACR #2 | Total Assets ($mil) | Capital ($mil) | Net Premium ($mil) | Net Income ($mil) |
|---|---|---|---|---|---|---|---|
| 9-17 | B | 31.95 | 25.36 | 362.5 | 360.5 | 0.1 | 5.1 |
| 9-16 | B | 31.47 | 23.67 | 356.2 | 353.3 | 0.2 | 5.3 |
| 2016 | B | 31.49 | 22.90 | 357.6 | 355.2 | 0.2 | 7.3 |
| 2015 | B | 31.00 | 21.87 | 351.3 | 347.9 | 0.4 | 7.7 |
| 2014 | B | 30.50 | 21.00 | 344.3 | 340.2 | 0.8 | 7.5 |
| 2013 | B | 30.00 | 22.50 | 336.8 | 332.8 | 1.1 | 7.4 |
| 2012 | B- | 30.00 | 25.79 | 336.7 | 332.8 | 1.1 | 7.3 |

Rating Indexes

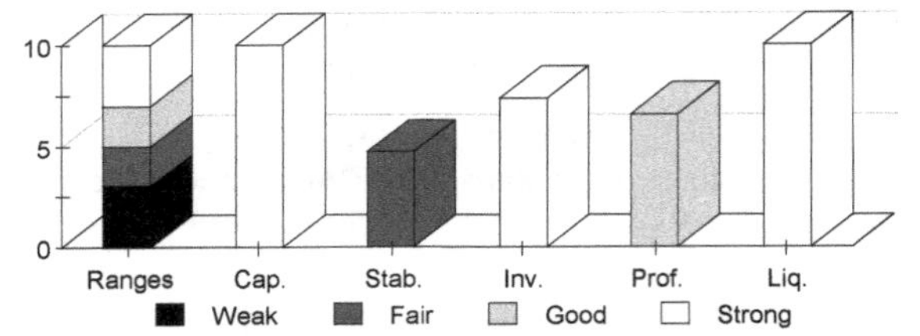


## PACIFIC GUARDIAN LIFE INSURANCE COMPANY LIMITED * A- Excellent

**Major Rating Factors:** Good quality investment portfolio (6.6 on a scale of 0 to 10) despite large exposure to mortgages . Mortgage default rate has been low. substantial holdings of BBB bonds in addition to no exposure to junk bonds. Good overall profitability (6.0). Good liquidity (6.2).
**Other Rating Factors:** Excellent overall results on stability tests (7.0) excellent operational trends and excellent risk diversification. Strong capitalization (9.0) based on excellent risk adjusted capital (severe loss scenario).
**Principal Business:** Group health insurance (51%), individual life insurance (37%), and group life insurance (11%).
**Principal Investments:** NonCMO investment grade bonds (37%), mortgages in good standing (36%), CMOs and structured securities (19%), policy loans (6%), and cash (2%).
**Investments in Affiliates:** None
**Group Affiliation:** Meiji Yasuda Life Ins Co
**Licensed in:** AK, AZ, CA, CO, HI, ID, IA, LA, MO, MT, NE, NV, NM, OK, OR, SD, TX, UT, WA, WY
**Commenced Business:** June 1962
**Address:** 1440 Kapiolani Blvd Ste 1600, Honolulu, HI 96814-3698
**Phone:** (808) 955-2236 **Domicile State:** HI **NAIC Code:** 64343

| Data Date | Rating | RACR #1 | RACR #2 | Total Assets ($mil) | Capital ($mil) | Net Premium ($mil) | Net Income ($mil) |
|---|---|---|---|---|---|---|---|
| 9-17 | A- | 4.03 | 2.33 | 552.3 | 103.7 | 57.4 | 3.1 |
| 9-16 | A- | 4.22 | 2.43 | 538.7 | 106.0 | 57.2 | 4.2 |
| 2016 | A- | 4.30 | 2.51 | 543.1 | 107.1 | 74.3 | 5.2 |
| 2015 | A- | 4.52 | 2.62 | 528.4 | 108.5 | 70.2 | 6.7 |
| 2014 | A- | 4.72 | 2.73 | 515.6 | 108.8 | 68.4 | 8.1 |
| 2013 | A- | 5.09 | 2.93 | 504.7 | 108.0 | 69.8 | 6.9 |
| 2012 | A- | 4.98 | 2.91 | 486.8 | 99.8 | 70.5 | 6.2 |

Rating Indexes

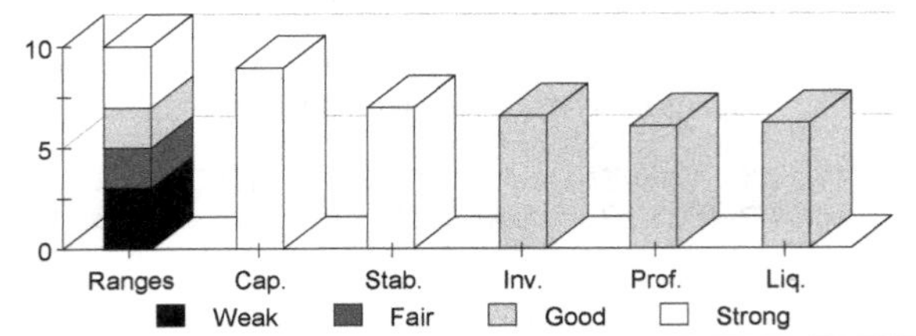

## PACIFICARE LIFE & HEALTH INSURANCE COMPANY C+ Fair

**Major Rating Factors:** Fair overall results on stability tests (4.3 on a scale of 0 to 10) including fair financial strength of affiliated UnitedHealth Group Inc. Good overall profitability (5.8). Excellent expense controls. Strong overall capitalization (10.0) based on excellent risk adjusted capital (severe loss scenario). Nevertheless, capital levels have fluctuated during prior years.
**Other Rating Factors:** High quality investment portfolio (8.2). Excellent liquidity (10.0).
**Principal Business:** Individual health insurance (74%) and group health insurance (26%).
**Principal Investments:** NonCMO investment grade bonds (79%) and CMOs and structured securities (22%).
**Investments in Affiliates:** None
**Group Affiliation:** UnitedHealth Group Inc
**Licensed in:** All states except NY, PR
**Commenced Business:** September 1967
**Address:** 7440 WOODLAND DRIVE, INDIANAPOLIS, IN 46278
**Phone:** (608) 783-8610 **Domicile State:** IN **NAIC Code:** 70785

| Data Date | Rating | RACR #1 | RACR #2 | Total Assets ($mil) | Capital ($mil) | Net Premium ($mil) | Net Income ($mil) |
|---|---|---|---|---|---|---|---|
| 9-17 | C+ | 18.46 | 16.62 | 187.0 | 180.4 | 10.4 | 2.3 |
| 9-16 | C+ | 18.24 | 16.42 | 187.7 | 180.8 | 10.8 | 3.2 |
| 2016 | C+ | 18.52 | 16.67 | 189.2 | 180.8 | 14.3 | 3.2 |
| 2015 | C+ | 19.90 | 17.91 | 205.7 | 197.4 | 15.8 | 4.1 |
| 2014 | C+ | 19.49 | 17.54 | 204.8 | 193.3 | 36.3 | 7.9 |
| 2013 | C+ | 29.46 | 19.62 | 616.2 | 592.6 | 104.7 | 13.2 |
| 2012 | C+ | 23.08 | 15.56 | 622.2 | 582.0 | 139.3 | 18.7 |

| UnitedHealth Group Inc<br>Composite Group Rating: C+<br>Largest Group Members | Assets ($mil) | Rating |
|---|---|---|
| UNITED HEALTHCARE INS CO | 17923 | C |
| SIERRA HEALTH AND LIFE INS CO INC | 2397 | B |
| OXFORD HEALTH INS INC | 2211 | B |
| ALL SAVERS INS CO | 1552 | C |
| UNITED HEALTHCARE OF WISCONSIN INC | 1224 | B |

## PACIFICARE OF COLORADO INC B Good

**Major Rating Factors:** Good overall results on stability tests (5.3 on a scale of 0 to 10) based on healthy premium and capital growth during 2016. Rating is significantly influenced by the fair financial results of UnitedHealth Group Incorporated. Good liquidity (6.7) with sufficient resources (cash flows and marketable investments) to handle a spike in claims. Excellent profitability (9.1).
**Other Rating Factors:** Strong capitalization index (8.3) based on excellent current risk-adjusted capital (severe loss scenario). High quality investment portfolio (9.5).
**Principal Business:** Medicare (100%)
**Mem Phys: 16:** 33,686 **15:** 11,171 **16 MLR** 82.6% **/ 16 Admin Exp** N/A
**Enroll(000): Q3 17:** 273 **16:** 249 **15:** 100 **Med Exp PMPM:** $697
**Principal Investments:** Long-term bonds (99%), cash and equiv (1%)
**Provider Compensation ($000):** Contr fee ($972,324), capitation ($933,281), bonus arrang ($25,184), FFS ($23,506)
**Total Member Encounters:** Phys (981,076), non-phys (122,713)
**Group Affiliation:** UnitedHealth Group Incorporated
**Licensed in:** AZ, CO, NV
**Address:** 6465 GREENWOOD PLAZA BLVD SUIT, CENTENNIAL, CO 80111
**Phone:** (952) 936-1300 **Dom State:** CO **Commenced Bus:** November 1987

| Data Date | Rating | RACR #1 | RACR #2 | Total Assets ($mil) | Capital ($mil) | Net Premium ($mil) | Net Income ($mil) |
|---|---|---|---|---|---|---|---|
| 9-17 | B | 2.37 | 1.97 | 813.9 | 246.7 | 2,132.4 | 65.8 |
| 9-16 | B | 4.24 | 3.53 | 582.5 | 168.5 | 1,843.7 | 59.6 |
| 2016 | B | 1.75 | 1.46 | 412.6 | 182.6 | 2,469.4 | 73.4 |
| 2015 | B | 2.78 | 2.32 | 209.8 | 109.3 | 973.1 | 43.1 |
| 2014 | B | 3.21 | 2.68 | 211.4 | 128.6 | 929.4 | 45.0 |
| 2013 | B | 3.65 | 3.04 | 211.3 | 134.2 | 849.8 | 50.9 |
| 2012 | B- | 2.39 | 1.99 | 164.0 | 83.7 | 813.0 | 62.5 |

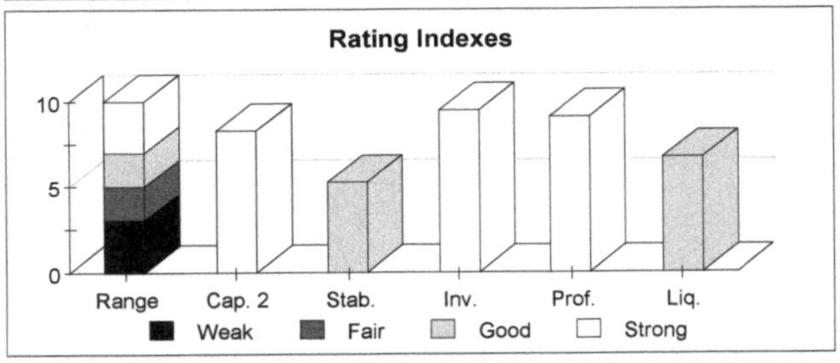


## PACIFICARE OF NEVADA INC E Very Weak

**Major Rating Factors:** Weak profitability index (1.2 on a scale of 0 to 10). Weak overall results on stability tests (1.2). Rating is significantly influenced by the fair financial results of UnitedHealth Group Inc. Strong capitalization index (7.7) based on excellent current risk-adjusted capital (severe loss scenario).
**Other Rating Factors:** High quality investment portfolio (9.9). Excellent liquidity (7.0) with ample operational cash flow and liquid investments.
**Principal Business:** Medicare (100%)
**Mem Phys: 15:** 5,239 **14:** 4,280 **15 MLR** 87.1% **/ 15 Admin Exp** N/A
**Enroll(000): Q3 16:** N/A **15:** 14 **14:** 12 **Med Exp PMPM:** $682
**Principal Investments:** Cash and equiv (85%), long-term bonds (15%)
**Provider Compensation ($000):** Capitation ($103,775), FFS ($6,304), contr fee ($2,770), bonus arrang ($3)
**Total Member Encounters:** N/A
**Group Affiliation:** UnitedHealth Group Inc
**Licensed in:** NV
**Address:** 2720 N TENAYA WAY, LAS VEGAS, NV 89128
**Phone:** (952) 936-1300 **Dom State:** NV **Commenced Bus:** September 1997

| Data Date | Rating | RACR #1 | RACR #2 | Total Assets ($mil) | Capital ($mil) | Net Premium ($mil) | Net Income ($mil) |
|---|---|---|---|---|---|---|---|
| 9-16 | E | 1.95 | 1.62 | 16.1 | 7.6 | -1.1 | -1.3 |
| 9-15 | E | 5.45 | 4.54 | 28.1 | 23.8 | 96.4 | 6.4 |
| 2015 | E | 4.00 | 3.33 | 29.8 | 16.6 | 128.6 | 6.1 |
| 2014 | E | 4.34 | 3.62 | 30.9 | 18.7 | 113.1 | -1.1 |
| 2013 | E | 1.86 | 1.55 | 26.0 | 8.3 | 86.6 | -11.3 |
| 2012 | C | 4.84 | 4.03 | 10.5 | 5.9 | 28.5 | -0.2 |
| 2011 | N/A | N/A | N/A | 17.4 | 15.9 | 20.0 | N/A |

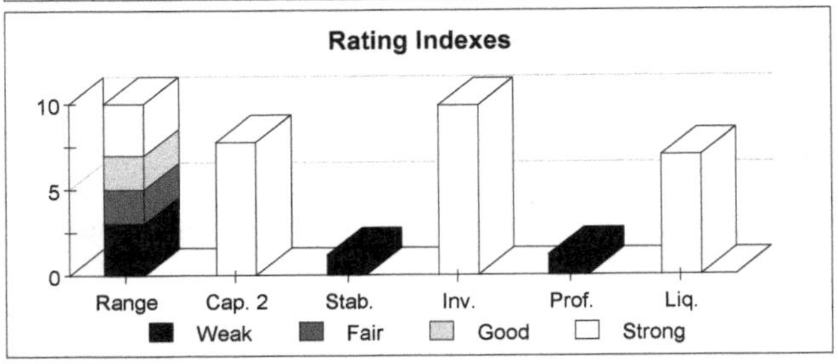

## PACIFICSOURCE COMMUNITY HEALTH PLANS B- Good

**Major Rating Factors:** Fair profitability index (3.9 on a scale of 0 to 10). Good quality investment portfolio (6.4). Good liquidity (6.8) with sufficient resources (cash flows and marketable investments) to handle a spike in claims.
**Other Rating Factors:** Strong capitalization (8.2) based on excellent current risk-adjusted capital (severe loss scenario).
**Principal Business:** Medicare (100%)
**Mem Phys: 16:** 16,900 **15:** 16,900 **16 MLR** 89.5% **/ 16 Admin Exp** N/A
**Enroll(000): Q3 17:** 35 **16:** 38 **15:** 34 **Med Exp PMPM:** $682
**Principal Investments:** Affiliate common stock (49%), cash and equiv (34%), long-term bonds (17%)
**Provider Compensation ($000):** Bonus arrang ($176,389), contr fee ($117,374), FFS ($12,759), capitation ($959)
**Total Member Encounters:** Phys (296,638), non-phys (80,383)
**Group Affiliation:** PacificSource
**Licensed in:** ID, MT, OR
**Address:** 2965 NE Conners Ave, Bend, OR 97701
**Phone:** (541) 385-5315 **Dom State:** OR **Commenced Bus:** March 2007

| Data Date | Rating | RACR #1 | RACR #2 | Total Assets ($mil) | Capital ($mil) | Net Premium ($mil) | Net Income ($mil) |
|---|---|---|---|---|---|---|---|
| 9-17 | B- | 2.31 | 1.92 | 171.4 | 78.3 | 270.5 | 25.6 |
| 9-16 | C | 1.95 | 1.62 | 146.1 | 62.2 | 260.7 | 0.6 |
| 2016 | C | 1.92 | 1.60 | 123.1 | 66.4 | 345.1 | 5.5 |
| 2015 | C | 1.86 | 1.55 | 101.6 | 59.3 | 301.1 | 4.2 |
| 2014 | C | 1.48 | 1.24 | 100.8 | 51.0 | 328.2 | -5.6 |
| 2013 | C | 1.33 | 1.11 | 78.8 | 41.5 | 300.4 | -6.6 |
| 2012 | C | 2.15 | 1.79 | 70.4 | 44.0 | 165.5 | -4.1 |

Rating Indexes

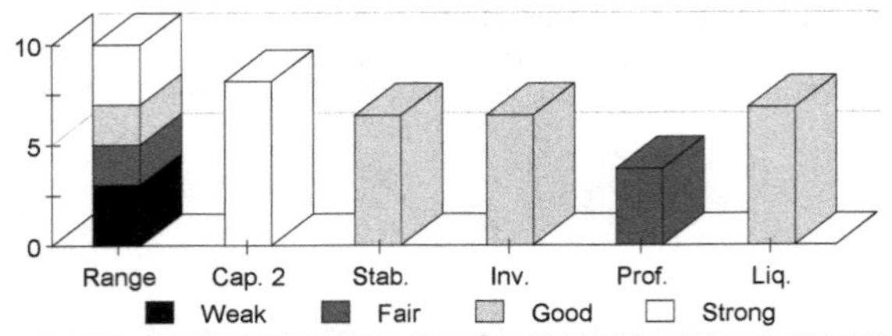


## PACIFICSOURCE HEALTH PLANS C Fair

**Major Rating Factors:** Weak profitability index (2.5 on a scale of 0 to 10). Good quality investment portfolio (5.3). Good liquidity (6.1) with sufficient resources (cash flows and marketable investments) to handle a spike in claims.
**Other Rating Factors:** Strong capitalization (8.2) based on excellent current risk-adjusted capital (severe loss scenario).
**Principal Business:** Comp med (95%), dental (4%), other (1%)
**Mem Phys: 16:** 47,359 **15:** 47,359 **16 MLR** 90.9% **/ 16 Admin Exp** N/A
**Enroll(000): Q3 17:** 213 **16:** 162 **15:** 168 **Med Exp PMPM:** $257
**Principal Investments:** Affiliate common stock (38%), long-term bonds (34%), cash and equiv (15%), nonaffiliate common stock (12%)
**Provider Compensation ($000):** Contr fee ($306,747), FFS ($177,189), bonus arrang ($19,926), capitation ($474)
**Total Member Encounters:** Phys (394,064), non-phys (342,407)
**Group Affiliation:** PacificSource
**Licensed in:** ID, MT, OR, WA
**Address:** 110 INTERNATIONAL WAY, SPRINGFIELD, OR 97477
**Phone:** (541) 686-1242 **Dom State:** OR **Commenced Bus:** July 1939

| Data Date | Rating | RACR #1 | RACR #2 | Total Assets ($mil) | Capital ($mil) | Net Premium ($mil) | Net Income ($mil) |
|---|---|---|---|---|---|---|---|
| 9-17 | C | 2.28 | 1.90 | 304.0 | 192.0 | 513.8 | 22.1 |
| 9-16 | C | 1.63 | 1.36 | 221.0 | 136.8 | 409.0 | -10.5 |
| 2016 | C | 1.84 | 1.54 | 238.1 | 157.4 | 547.9 | -21.1 |
| 2015 | C | 1.72 | 1.43 | 228.9 | 144.4 | 564.8 | -10.2 |
| 2014 | C+ | 1.62 | 1.35 | 235.1 | 148.2 | 610.6 | -16.9 |
| 2013 | B- | 1.57 | 1.31 | 230.1 | 151.3 | 724.1 | 14.7 |
| 2012 | B- | 1.23 | 1.02 | 209.2 | 109.8 | 722.2 | -25.9 |

Rating Indexes

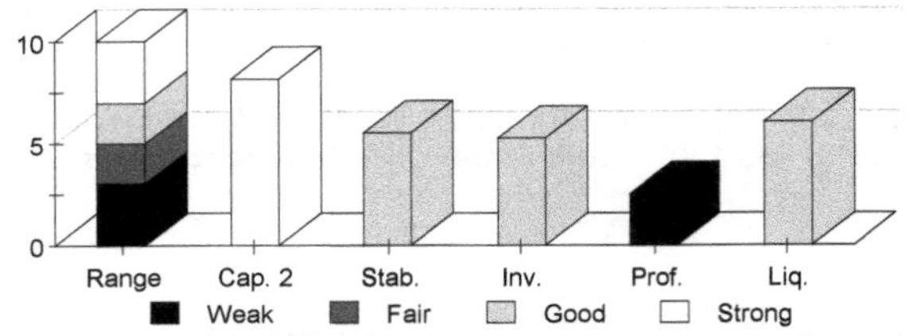


## PAN-AMERICAN LIFE INSURANCE COMPANY B Good

**Major Rating Factors:** Good overall results on stability tests (6.0 on a scale of 0 to 10). Stability strengths include excellent operational trends and excellent risk diversification. Good quality investment portfolio (5.4) despite mixed results such as: large holdings of BBB rated bonds but moderate junk bond exposure. Good overall profitability (6.5).
**Other Rating Factors:** Good liquidity (6.5). Strong capitalization (8.1) based on excellent risk adjusted capital (severe loss scenario).
**Principal Business:** Group health insurance (71%), reinsurance (11%), individual life insurance (9%), individual health insurance (6%), and group life insurance (3%).
**Principal Investments:** NonCMO investment grade bonds (59%), CMOs and structured securities (16%), noninv. grade bonds (8%), common & preferred stock (5%), and misc. investments (11%).
**Investments in Affiliates:** 2%
**Group Affiliation:** Pan-American Life
**Licensed in:** All states except ME, NY, VT
**Commenced Business:** March 1912
**Address:** PAN-AMERICAN LIFE CENTER, NEW ORLEANS, LA 70130-6060
**Phone:** (504) 566-1300 **Domicile State:** LA **NAIC Code:** 67539

| Data Date | Rating | RACR #1 | RACR #2 | Total Assets ($mil) | Capital ($mil) | Net Premium ($mil) | Net Income ($mil) |
|---|---|---|---|---|---|---|---|
| 9-17 | B | 2.73 | 1.74 | 1,249.1 | 261.0 | 160.9 | 19.2 |
| 9-16 | B | 2.61 | 1.67 | 1,276.6 | 253.2 | 172.5 | 15.6 |
| 2016 | B | 2.53 | 1.60 | 1,260.9 | 244.6 | 226.5 | 21.3 |
| 2015 | B | 2.52 | 1.62 | 1,293.7 | 244.9 | 237.9 | 22.0 |
| 2014 | B | 2.20 | 1.40 | 1,345.4 | 237.5 | 238.9 | 23.8 |
| 2013 | B | 2.29 | 1.43 | 1,425.5 | 244.6 | 270.3 | 27.3 |
| 2012 | B | 2.12 | 1.31 | 1,444.4 | 226.6 | 255.0 | 15.3 |

**Adverse Trends in Operations**

Decrease in asset base during 2016 (3%)
Decrease in asset base during 2015 (4%)
Decrease in premium volume from 2013 to 2014 (12%)
Decrease in capital during 2014 (3%)
Decrease in asset base during 2013 (1%)

## PARAMOUNT ADVANTAGE * A- Excellent

**Major Rating Factors:** Strong capitalization (8.1 on a scale of 0 to 10) based on excellent current risk-adjusted capital (severe loss scenario). High quality investment portfolio (9.5). Good overall profitability index (5.4).
**Other Rating Factors:** Good liquidity (6.7) with sufficient resources (cash flows and marketable investments) to handle a spike in claims.
**Principal Business:** Medicaid (100%)
**Mem Phys: 16:** 22,784 **15:** 21,761 **16 MLR** 86.9% **/ 16 Admin Exp** N/A
**Enroll(000): Q3 17:** 243 **16:** 233 **15:** 228 **Med Exp PMPM:** $311
**Principal Investments:** Long-term bonds (58%), cash and equiv (28%), nonaffiliate common stock (14%)
**Provider Compensation ($000):** Contr fee ($557,126), FFS ($242,936), capitation ($69,322)
**Total Member Encounters:** Phys (314,589), non-phys (34,017)
**Group Affiliation:** ProMedica Health System Inc
**Licensed in:** OH
**Address:** 1901 Indian Wood Circle, Maumee, OH 43537
**Phone:** (419) 887-2500 **Dom State:** OH **Commenced Bus:** December 2005

| Data Date | Rating | RACR #1 | RACR #2 | Total Assets ($mil) | Capital ($mil) | Net Premium ($mil) | Net Income ($mil) |
|---|---|---|---|---|---|---|---|
| 9-17 | A- | 2.25 | 1.88 | 305.9 | 168.1 | 846.2 | 27.5 |
| 9-16 | A- | 2.34 | 1.95 | 276.1 | 160.0 | 748.9 | 12.0 |
| 2016 | A- | 1.81 | 1.51 | 290.4 | 135.3 | 1,000.4 | -12.8 |
| 2015 | A- | 2.13 | 1.78 | 269.5 | 146.2 | 1,004.2 | 47.2 |
| 2014 | A- | 1.84 | 1.53 | 256.0 | 100.9 | 727.1 | 10.5 |
| 2013 | B+ | 2.08 | 1.73 | 130.2 | 63.7 | 390.0 | 5.5 |
| 2012 | B+ | 2.37 | 1.97 | 95.1 | 58.0 | 294.8 | 9.6 |

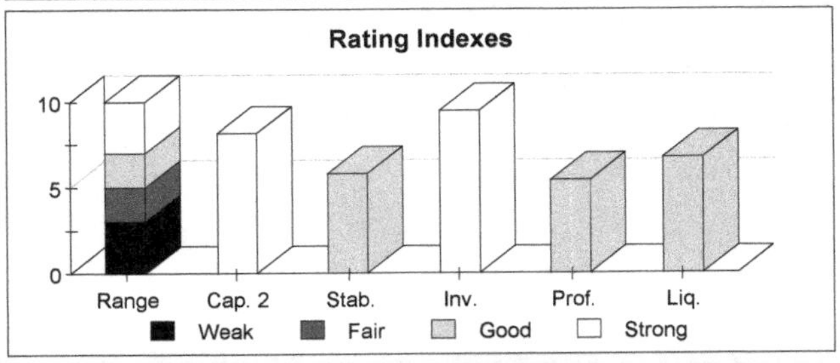


## PARAMOUNT CARE INC C+ Fair

**Major Rating Factors:** Fair profitability index (3.8 on a scale of 0 to 10). Good overall results on stability tests (5.0). Strong capitalization index (10.0) based on excellent current risk-adjusted capital (severe loss scenario).
**Other Rating Factors:** High quality investment portfolio (9.9). Excellent liquidity (7.0) with ample operational cash flow and liquid investments.
**Principal Business:** Medicare (100%)
**Mem Phys: 16:** 2,403 **15:** 2,290 **16 MLR** 87.1% **/ 16 Admin Exp** N/A
**Enroll(000): Q3 17:** 14 **16:** 14 **15:** 13 **Med Exp PMPM:** $884
**Principal Investments:** Long-term bonds (77%), cash and equiv (23%)
**Provider Compensation ($000):** Contr fee ($126,505), FFS ($24,043)
**Total Member Encounters:** Phys (33,371), non-phys (2,514)
**Group Affiliation:** ProMedica Health System Inc
**Licensed in:** OH
**Address:** 1901 Indian Wood Circle, Maumee, OH 43537
**Phone:** (419) 887-2500 **Dom State:** OH **Commenced Bus:** January 1988

| Data Date | Rating | RACR #1 | RACR #2 | Total Assets ($mil) | Capital ($mil) | Net Premium ($mil) | Net Income ($mil) |
|---|---|---|---|---|---|---|---|
| 9-17 | C+ | 5.34 | 4.45 | 139.4 | 79.5 | 128.8 | 4.9 |
| 9-16 | C | 4.55 | 3.79 | 119.2 | 71.1 | 133.3 | 6.7 |
| 2016 | C | 4.79 | 3.99 | 102.3 | 72.2 | 173.5 | 10.4 |
| 2015 | C | 4.10 | 3.42 | 91.6 | 64.5 | 150.8 | -6.5 |
| 2014 | C | 3.80 | 3.17 | 105.1 | 55.8 | 143.0 | 0.9 |
| 2013 | C | 3.13 | 2.61 | 98.8 | 64.4 | 212.8 | 7.2 |
| 2012 | C- | 2.06 | 1.72 | 111.6 | 58.2 | 270.3 | -8.6 |

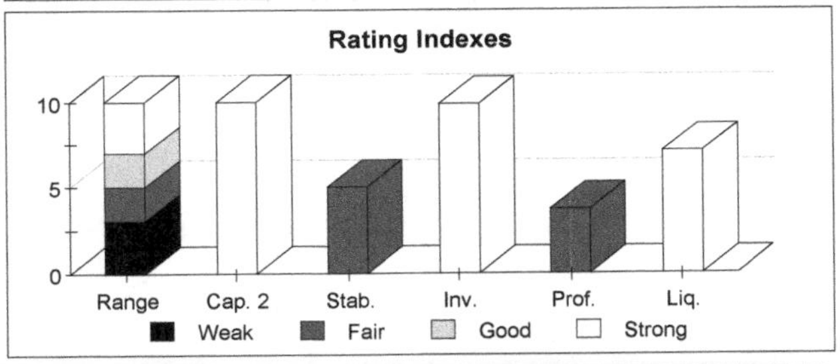


## PARAMOUNT CARE OF MI INC B Good

**Major Rating Factors:** Good overall profitability index (5.4 on a scale of 0 to 10). Good overall results on stability tests (5.1). Rating is significantly influenced by the good financial results of ProMedica Health System Inc. Strong capitalization index (10.0) based on excellent current risk-adjusted capital (severe loss scenario).
**Other Rating Factors:** High quality investment portfolio (9.9). Excellent liquidity (7.8) with ample operational cash flow and liquid investments.
**Principal Business:** Medicare (100%)
**Mem Phys: 16:** 1,700 **15:** 1,567 **16 MLR** 74.7% **/ 16 Admin Exp** N/A
**Enroll(000): Q3 17:** 2 **16:** 2 **15:** 2 **Med Exp PMPM:** $717
**Principal Investments:** Cash and equiv (65%), long-term bonds (35%)
**Provider Compensation ($000):** Contr fee ($13,645), FFS ($2,697)
**Total Member Encounters:** Phys (3,683), non-phys (306)
**Group Affiliation:** ProMedica Health System Inc
**Licensed in:** MI
**Address:** 106 Park Place, Dundee, MI 48131
**Phone:** (734) 529-7800 **Dom State:** MI **Commenced Bus:** June 1996

| Data Date | Rating | RACR #1 | RACR #2 | Total Assets ($mil) | Capital ($mil) | Net Premium ($mil) | Net Income ($mil) |
|---|---|---|---|---|---|---|---|
| 9-17 | B | 4.88 | 4.07 | 15.8 | 12.3 | 16.5 | 0.6 |
| 9-16 | B | 4.03 | 3.36 | 14.4 | 10.8 | 16.4 | 2.1 |
| 2016 | B | 4.46 | 3.72 | 14.5 | 11.4 | 21.9 | 2.8 |
| 2015 | B- | 3.17 | 2.64 | 11.1 | 8.5 | 18.7 | 1.2 |
| 2014 | B- | 2.82 | 2.35 | 10.5 | 7.2 | 16.8 | -0.3 |
| 2013 | C+ | 2.06 | 1.72 | 10.8 | 7.5 | 23.1 | 0.0 |
| 2012 | C+ | 1.78 | 1.48 | 13.3 | 8.0 | 30.4 | -1.9 |

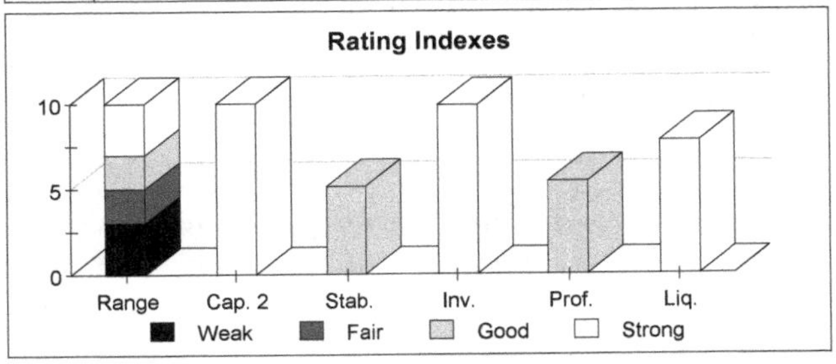

## PARAMOUNT INS CO (OH) * A- Excellent

**Major Rating Factors:** Excellent profitability (7.4 on a scale of 0 to 10). Strong capitalization (8.5) based on excellent current risk-adjusted capital (severe loss scenario). High quality investment portfolio (9.5).
**Other Rating Factors:** Excellent liquidity (7.1) with ample operational cash flow and liquid investments.
**Principal Business:** Comp med (98%), med supp (2%)
**Mem Phys: 16:** 2,403 **15:** 2,290 **16 MLR** 82.9% **/ 16 Admin Exp** N/A
**Enroll(000): Q3 17:** 36 **16:** 40 **15:** 36 **Med Exp PMPM:** $278
**Principal Investments:** Long-term bonds (45%), cash and equiv (38%), nonaffiliate common stock (17%)
**Provider Compensation ($000):** FFS ($77,907), contr fee ($51,481)
**Total Member Encounters:** Phys (34,839), non-phys (3,298)
**Group Affiliation:** ProMedica Health System Inc
**Licensed in:** MI, OH
**Address:** 1901 Indian Wood Circle, Maumee, OH 43537
**Phone:** (419) 887-2500 **Dom State:** OH **Commenced Bus:** September 2002

| Data Date | Rating | RACR #1 | RACR #2 | Total Assets ($mil) | Capital ($mil) | Net Premium ($mil) | Net Income ($mil) |
|---|---|---|---|---|---|---|---|
| 9-17 | A- | 2.57 | 2.15 | 88.2 | 37.3 | 122.8 | 5.2 |
| 9-16 | B+ | 2.33 | 1.95 | 81.3 | 30.1 | 120.0 | 4.6 |
| 2016 | B+ | 2.10 | 1.75 | 87.5 | 30.7 | 158.0 | 5.3 |
| 2015 | B | 1.94 | 1.62 | 68.8 | 25.1 | 146.9 | 4.6 |
| 2014 | B | 1.52 | 1.27 | 44.6 | 20.6 | 151.6 | 6.3 |
| 2013 | C+ | 1.87 | 1.56 | 35.0 | 14.6 | 79.2 | 1.9 |
| 2012 | C | 3.32 | 2.77 | 18.6 | 12.8 | 26.9 | -0.9 |

Rating Indexes

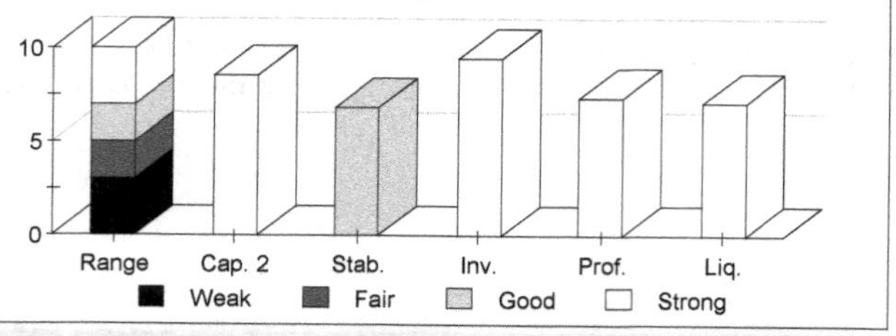


## PARKLAND COMMUNITY HEALTH PLAN INC B- Good

**Major Rating Factors:** Fair profitability index (3.3 on a scale of 0 to 10). Good overall results on stability tests (4.9). Good liquidity (6.3) with sufficient resources (cash flows and marketable investments) to handle a spike in claims.
**Other Rating Factors:** Strong capitalization index (7.9) based on excellent current risk-adjusted capital (severe loss scenario). High quality investment portfolio (9.9).
**Principal Business:** Medicaid (90%), comp med (10%)
**Mem Phys: 16:** 6,543 **15:** 6,012 **16 MLR** 87.5% **/ 16 Admin Exp** N/A
**Enroll(000): Q3 17:** 195 **16:** 198 **15:** 208 **Med Exp PMPM:** $190
**Principal Investments:** Long-term bonds (78%), cash and equiv (22%)
**Provider Compensation ($000):** Contr fee ($454,655), capitation ($2,760)
**Total Member Encounters:** Phys (1,467,148), non-phys (520,736)
**Group Affiliation:** Parkland Community Health Plan Inc
**Licensed in:** TX
**Address:** 2777 N Stemmons Freeway Suite, Dallas, TX 75207
**Phone:** (214) 266-2100 **Dom State:** TX **Commenced Bus:** January 1998

| Data Date | Rating | RACR #1 | RACR #2 | Total Assets ($mil) | Capital ($mil) | Net Premium ($mil) | Net Income ($mil) |
|---|---|---|---|---|---|---|---|
| 9-17 | B- | 2.10 | 1.75 | 152.0 | 88.8 | 402.6 | 9.2 |
| 9-16 | B- | 2.37 | 1.97 | 142.2 | 97.0 | 386.0 | 1.2 |
| 2016 | B- | 2.45 | 2.04 | 144.4 | 101.4 | 520.7 | 3.2 |
| 2015 | B | 2.85 | 2.38 | 168.8 | 98.3 | 525.7 | -13.5 |
| 2014 | B+ | 3.36 | 2.80 | 175.0 | 130.3 | 500.6 | 23.6 |
| 2013 | B | 2.63 | 2.19 | 157.6 | 106.7 | 518.6 | 27.3 |
| 2012 | B | 1.88 | 1.57 | 130.3 | 79.4 | 514.1 | 24.2 |

Rating Indexes

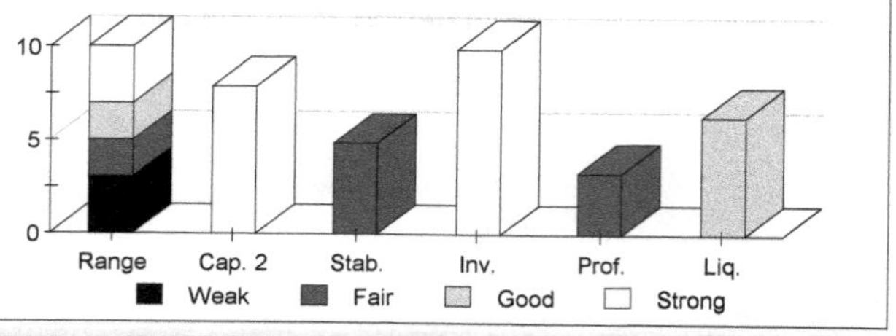


## PARTNERRE AMERICA INS CO C+ Fair

**Major Rating Factors:** Fair overall results on stability tests (4.4 on a scale of 0 to 10) including potential drain of affiliation with Giovanni Agnelli e C Sapaz, weak results on operational trends and negative cash flow from operations for 2016. Fair profitability index (3.5) with operating losses during the first nine months of 2017. Return on equity has been fair, averaging 6.7% over the past five years.
**Other Rating Factors:** History of adequate reserve strength (5.9) as reserves have been consistently at an acceptable level. Strong long-term capitalization index (10.0) based on excellent current risk adjusted capital (severe and moderate loss scenarios), despite some fluctuation in capital levels. Excellent liquidity (7.9) with ample operational cash flow and liquid investments.
**Principal Business:** Other liability (52%), other accident & health (46%), aircraft (1%), and allied lines (1%).
**Principal Investments:** Investment grade bonds (95%) and cash (6%).
**Investments in Affiliates:** None
**Group Affiliation:** Giovanni Agnelli e C Sapaz
**Licensed in:** All states, the District of Columbia and Puerto Rico
**Commenced Business:** August 1919
**Address:** 1209 ORANGE STREET, Wilmington, DE 19801
**Phone:** (203) 485-4200 **Domicile State:** DE **NAIC Code:** 11835

| Data Date | Rating | RACR #1 | RACR #2 | Loss Ratio % | Total Assets ($mil) | Capital ($mil) | Net Premium ($mil) | Net Income ($mil) |
|---|---|---|---|---|---|---|---|---|
| 9-17 | C+ | 8.77 | 5.34 | N/A | 374.8 | 114.4 | 27.0 | -1.5 |
| 9-16 | C+ | 11.45 | 6.89 | N/A | 384.9 | 130.2 | 22.9 | 2.1 |
| 2016 | C+ | 10.77 | 6.63 | 85.8 | 370.9 | 116.0 | 32.1 | 0.8 |
| 2015 | C+ | 11.97 | 7.29 | 90.3 | 375.8 | 128.4 | 32.2 | 5.6 |
| 2014 | C | 14.47 | 10.40 | 75.4 | 298.4 | 133.6 | 25.7 | 8.2 |
| 2013 | C | 23.52 | 21.17 | 64.9 | 169.4 | 128.5 | -0.2 | 0.8 |
| 2012 | C | 13.77 | 9.39 | N/A | 185.7 | 121.8 | 2.1 | 34.1 |

**Giovanni Agnelli e C Sapaz**
**Composite Group Rating: C+**

| Largest Group Members | Assets ($mil) | Rating |
|---|---|---|
| PARTNER REINSURANCE CO OF THE US | 4823 | C+ |
| PARTNERRE AMERICA INS CO | 371 | C+ |
| PARTNERRE INS CO OF NY | 126 | C |
| PARTNERRE LIFE RE CO OF AM | 46 | C |

## PARTNERSHIP HEALTHPLAN OF CALIFORNIA * A- Excellent

**Major Rating Factors:** Excellent profitability (7.9 on a scale of 0 to 10). Strong capitalization index (10.0) based on excellent current risk-adjusted capital (severe loss scenario). Excellent liquidity (7.9) with ample operational cash flow and liquid investments.
**Other Rating Factors:** Good overall results on stability tests (5.6) despite a decline in enrollment during 2016.
**Principal Business:** Medicaid (100%)
**Mem Phys: 16:** N/A **15:** N/A **16 MLR** 85.0% **/ 16 Admin Exp** N/A
**Enroll(000): Q3 17:** 571 **16:** 572 **15:** 677 **Med Exp PMPM:** $309
**Principal Investments ($000):** Cash and equiv ($1,233,816)
**Provider Compensation ($000):** None
**Total Member Encounters:** N/A
**Group Affiliation:** None
**Licensed in:** CA
**Address:** 4665 Business Center Drive, Fairfield, CA 94534
**Phone:** (707) 863-4218 **Dom State:** CA **Commenced Bus:** November 2005

| Data Date | Rating | RACR #1 | RACR #2 | Total Assets ($mil) | Capital ($mil) | Net Premium ($mil) | Net Income ($mil) |
|---|---|---|---|---|---|---|---|
| 9-17 | A- | 9.06 | 5.54 | 1,697.8 | 814.8 | 1,871.2 | -42.2 |
| 9-16 | A- | 10.93 | 6.68 | 1,495.7 | 819.7 | 1,811.0 | 138.2 |
| 2016 | A | 9.68 | 5.92 | 1,717.6 | 848.1 | 2,436.1 | 166.7 |
| 2015 | A- | 8.79 | 5.36 | 1,483.2 | 681.5 | 2,251.2 | 267.4 |
| 2014 | A- | 6.72 | 4.10 | 727.2 | 414.1 | 1,614.5 | 178.0 |
| 2013 | A- | 6.00 | 3.68 | 378.0 | 236.0 | 928.9 | 62.0 |
| 2012 | B+ | 4.23 | 2.58 | 351.9 | 174.1 | 906.2 | 51.4 |

Rating Indexes

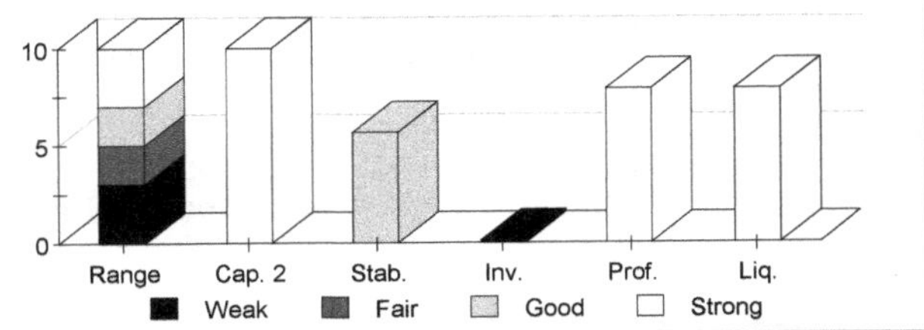


## PAUL REVERE LIFE INSURANCE COMPANY C+ Fair

**Major Rating Factors:** Fair overall results on stability tests (4.8 on a scale of 0 to 10) including fair financial strength of affiliated Unum Group and negative cash flow from operations for 2016. Fair quality investment portfolio (3.5) with large holdings of BBB rated bonds in addition to significant exposure to junk bonds. Good capitalization (6.2) based on good risk adjusted capital (severe loss scenario).
**Other Rating Factors:** Good overall profitability (6.2). Excellent liquidity (7.4).
**Principal Business:** Individual health insurance (67%), reinsurance (25%), group health insurance (4%), individual life insurance (3%), and group life insurance (1%).
**Principal Investments:** NonCMO investment grade bonds (81%), noninv. grade bonds (8%), common & preferred stock (4%), CMOs and structured securities (4%), and mortgages in good standing (3%).
**Investments in Affiliates:** 2%
**Group Affiliation:** Unum Group
**Licensed in:** All states except PR
**Commenced Business:** July 1930
**Address:** 1 MERCANTILE STREET, WORCESTER, MA 1608
**Phone:** (423) 294-1011 **Domicile State:** MA **NAIC Code:** 67598

| Data Date | Rating | RACR #1 | RACR #2 | Total Assets ($mil) | Capital ($mil) | Net Premium ($mil) | Net Income ($mil) |
|---|---|---|---|---|---|---|---|
| 9-17 | C+ | 1.49 | 0.90 | 3,653.7 | 213.5 | 71.2 | 31.2 |
| 9-16 | C+ | 1.60 | 0.94 | 3,820.7 | 235.7 | 72.6 | 47.9 |
| 2016 | C+ | 1.71 | 1.01 | 3,790.4 | 251.4 | 95.2 | 65.6 |
| 2015 | C+ | 1.72 | 1.02 | 3,977.0 | 257.7 | 96.8 | 63.1 |
| 2014 | C+ | 1.85 | 1.09 | 4,145.1 | 278.0 | 91.0 | 76.5 |
| 2013 | C+ | 1.78 | 1.13 | 4,301.8 | 336.1 | 90.4 | 66.5 |
| 2012 | C+ | 1.99 | 1.23 | 4,458.2 | 368.3 | 91.9 | 81.7 |

**Unum Group**
**Composite Group Rating: C+**

| Largest Group Members | Assets ($mil) | Rating |
|---|---|---|
| UNUM LIFE INS CO OF AMERICA | 21078 | C+ |
| PROVIDENT LIFE ACCIDENT INS CO | 8273 | C+ |
| PAUL REVERE LIFE INS CO | 3790 | C+ |
| FIRST UNUM LIFE INS CO | 3261 | C+ |
| COLONIAL LIFE ACCIDENT INS CO | 3144 | C+ |

## PEACH STATE HEALTH PLAN INC C+ Fair

**Major Rating Factors:** Good overall profitability index (6.5 on a scale of 0 to 10). Strong capitalization (9.2) based on excellent current risk-adjusted capital (severe loss scenario). High quality investment portfolio (9.1).
**Other Rating Factors:** Excellent liquidity (6.9) with sufficient resources (cash flows and marketable investments) to handle a spike in claims.
**Principal Business:** Medicaid (99%)
**Mem Phys: 16:** 29,728 **15:** 22,231 **16 MLR** 79.4% **/ 16 Admin Exp** N/A
**Enroll(000): Q3 17:** 353 **16:** 424 **15:** 409 **Med Exp PMPM:** $195
**Principal Investments:** Long-term bonds (63%), cash and equiv (32%), affiliate common stock (5%)
**Provider Compensation ($000):** Contr fee ($929,238), capitation ($22,806), salary ($14,159), bonus arrang ($4,568)
**Total Member Encounters:** Phys (357,117), non-phys (301,576)
**Group Affiliation:** Centene Corporation
**Licensed in:** GA
**Address:** 1100 Circle 75 Parkway #1100, Atlanta, GA 30339
**Phone:** (314) 725-4477 **Dom State:** GA **Commenced Bus:** June 2006

| Data Date | Rating | RACR #1 | RACR #2 | Total Assets ($mil) | Capital ($mil) | Net Premium ($mil) | Net Income ($mil) |
|---|---|---|---|---|---|---|---|
| 9-17 | C+ | 3.14 | 2.62 | 310.0 | 184.7 | 858.4 | 17.0 |
| 9-16 | C+ | 3.37 | 2.80 | 281.2 | 179.0 | 895.5 | 49.3 |
| 2016 | C+ | 3.17 | 2.64 | 286.7 | 186.4 | 1,207.0 | 69.1 |
| 2015 | C+ | 2.77 | 2.31 | 314.6 | 145.6 | 1,101.6 | 39.1 |
| 2014 | C+ | 2.10 | 1.75 | 244.4 | 107.2 | 1,041.9 | 12.4 |
| 2013 | C | 2.23 | 1.86 | 170.5 | 89.5 | 799.0 | -3.9 |
| 2012 | C | 2.07 | 1.72 | 155.2 | 85.0 | 764.1 | -18.0 |

Rating Indexes

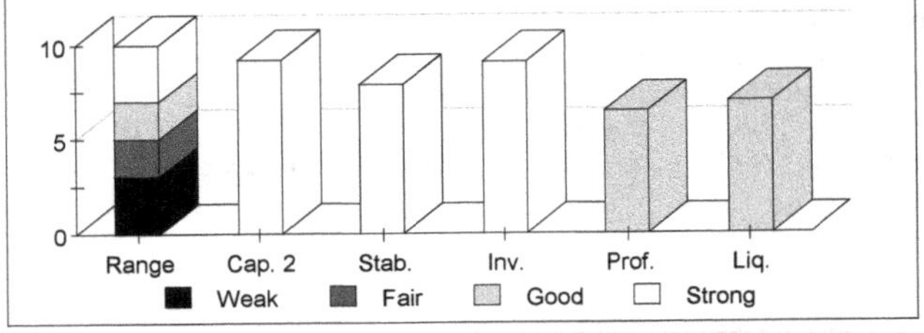

## PEKIN LIFE INSURANCE COMPANY — B Good

**Major Rating Factors:** Good quality investment portfolio (6.6 on a scale of 0 to 10) despite mixed results such as: minimal exposure to mortgages and substantial holdings of BBB bonds but minimal holdings in junk bonds. Good overall profitability (5.2). Good liquidity (5.7).
**Other Rating Factors:** Good overall results on stability tests (6.2) excellent operational trends and excellent risk diversification. Strong capitalization (7.4) based on excellent risk adjusted capital (severe loss scenario).
**Principal Business:** Individual life insurance (34%), group life insurance (19%), group health insurance (17%), individual health insurance (13%), and other lines (17%).
**Principal Investments:** NonCMO investment grade bonds (64%), CMOs and structured securities (28%), mortgages in good standing (2%), policy loans (1%), and misc. investments (2%).
**Investments in Affiliates:** None
**Group Affiliation:** Farmers Automobile Ins Assn
**Licensed in:** AL, AZ, AR, GA, IL, IN, IA, KS, KY, LA, MI, MN, MS, MO, NE, OH, PA, TN, TX, VA, WI
**Commenced Business:** September 1965
**Address:** 2505 COURT STREET, PEKIN, IL 61558-0001
**Phone:** (309) 346-1161 **Domicile State:** IL **NAIC Code:** 67628

| Data Date | Rating | RACR #1 | RACR #2 | Total Assets ($mil) | Capital ($mil) | Net Premium ($mil) | Net Income ($mil) |
|---|---|---|---|---|---|---|---|
| 9-17 | B | 2.09 | 1.24 | 1,465.6 | 129.3 | 152.1 | 5.2 |
| 9-16 | B | 1.90 | 1.13 | 1,454.0 | 119.7 | 168.1 | -2.2 |
| 2016 | B | 2.03 | 1.21 | 1,459.6 | 124.6 | 222.5 | -1.0 |
| 2015 | B | 1.98 | 1.19 | 1,393.6 | 120.2 | 215.7 | -1.3 |
| 2014 | B | 2.11 | 1.28 | 1,324.1 | 120.3 | 206.2 | 5.9 |
| 2013 | B | 2.24 | 1.37 | 1,301.6 | 122.7 | 227.0 | 2.4 |
| 2012 | B | 2.24 | 1.39 | 1,209.2 | 119.2 | 221.1 | 7.6 |

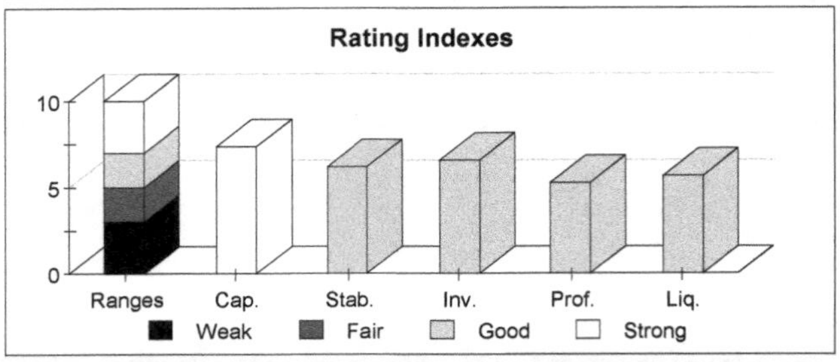


## PEOPLES HEALTH INC — D Weak

**Major Rating Factors:** Low quality investment portfolio (0.1 on a scale of 0 to 10). Fair capitalization (3.8) based on fair current risk-adjusted capital (moderate loss scenario). Excellent profitability (7.3).
**Other Rating Factors:** Excellent liquidity (7.0) with sufficient resources (cash flows and marketable investments) to handle a spike in claims.
**Principal Business:** Medicare (100%)
**Mem Phys: 16:** 4,755 **15:** 4,158 **16 MLR** 85.0% **/ 16 Admin Exp** N/A
**Enroll(000): Q3 17:** 60 **16:** 55 **15:** 54 **Med Exp PMPM:** $955
**Principal Investments:** Cash and equiv (100%)
**Provider Compensation ($000):** Capitation ($626,094)
**Total Member Encounters:** Phys (1,015,932), non-phys (594,593)
**Group Affiliation:** PH Holdings LLC
**Licensed in:** LA
**Address:** 3838 N Causeway Blvd Ste 2200, Metairie, LA 70002
**Phone:** (504) 849-4500 **Dom State:** LA **Commenced Bus:** March 2009

| Data Date | Rating | RACR #1 | RACR #2 | Total Assets ($mil) | Capital ($mil) | Net Premium ($mil) | Net Income ($mil) |
|---|---|---|---|---|---|---|---|
| 9-17 | D | 0.75 | 0.63 | 151.6 | 35.9 | 579.4 | 1.0 |
| 9-16 | D | 0.73 | 0.61 | 125.7 | 34.6 | 556.7 | 1.0 |
| 2016 | D | 0.73 | 0.61 | 65.6 | 34.9 | 736.6 | 1.3 |
| 2015 | D | 0.71 | 0.59 | 55.3 | 33.6 | 710.4 | 1.3 |
| 2014 | D | 0.72 | 0.60 | 52.4 | 32.3 | 696.2 | 1.2 |
| 2013 | D+ | 0.69 | 0.58 | 50.9 | 31.1 | 699.7 | 1.2 |
| 2012 | D+ | 0.69 | 0.58 | 55.3 | 29.9 | 678.0 | 1.1 |

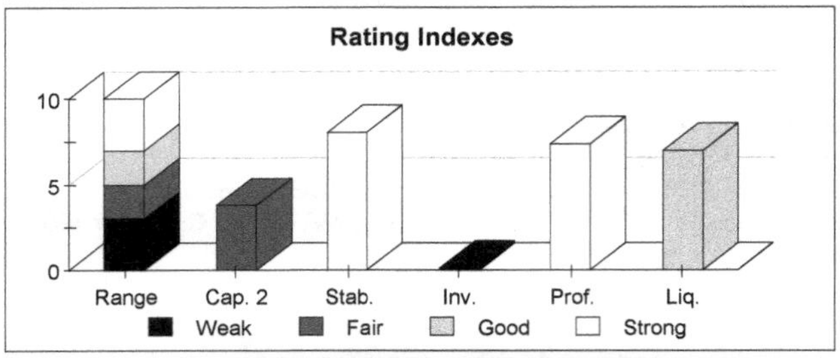


## PHILADELPHIA AMERICAN LIFE INSURANCE COMPANY — B Good

**Major Rating Factors:** Good overall results on stability tests (5.5 on a scale of 0 to 10) despite fair financial strength of affiliated New Era Life Group. Other stability subfactors include excellent operational trends, good risk adjusted capital for prior years and good risk diversification. Good liquidity (6.2) with sufficient resources to handle a spike in claims as well as a significant increase in policy surrenders. Fair quality investment portfolio (4.7).
**Other Rating Factors:** Strong capitalization (7.0) based on excellent risk adjusted capital (severe loss scenario). Excellent profitability (9.2).
**Principal Business:** Individual health insurance (81%), individual annuities (14%), individual life insurance (3%), and group health insurance (2%).
**Principal Investments:** NonCMO investment grade bonds (72%), CMOs and structured securities (13%), noninv. grade bonds (10%), and mortgages in good standing (5%).
**Investments in Affiliates:** None
**Group Affiliation:** New Era Life Group
**Licensed in:** All states except NY, RI, PR
**Commenced Business:** March 1978
**Address:** 11720 Katy Freeway Suite 1700, Houston, TX 77079
**Phone:** (281) 368-7200 **Domicile State:** TX **NAIC Code:** 67784

| Data Date | Rating | RACR #1 | RACR #2 | Total Assets ($mil) | Capital ($mil) | Net Premium ($mil) | Net Income ($mil) |
|---|---|---|---|---|---|---|---|
| 9-17 | B | 1.59 | 1.02 | 290.6 | 35.5 | 115.5 | 3.1 |
| 9-16 | B | 1.55 | 0.99 | 257.3 | 34.0 | 108.1 | 0.7 |
| 2016 | B | 1.62 | 1.03 | 263.3 | 34.2 | 141.1 | 1.4 |
| 2015 | B | 1.46 | 0.95 | 235.2 | 33.9 | 160.1 | 1.1 |
| 2014 | B- | 1.50 | 0.96 | 220.2 | 33.2 | 144.1 | 5.9 |
| 2013 | B- | 1.38 | 0.88 | 205.7 | 29.0 | 120.4 | 3.1 |
| 2012 | B- | 1.68 | 0.99 | 197.6 | 26.1 | 69.5 | 4.3 |

**New Era Life Group**
**Composite Group Rating: C+**

| Largest Group Members | Assets ($mil) | Rating |
|---|---|---|
| NEW ERA LIFE INS CO | 504 | C |
| PHILADELPHIA AMERICAN LIFE INS CO | 263 | B |
| NEW ERA LIFE INS CO OF THE MIDWEST | 117 | C |
| LIFE OF AMERICA INS CO | 12 | C |

## PHOENIX HEALTH PLANS INC — E — Very Weak

**Major Rating Factors:** Weak profitability index (0.9 on a scale of 0 to 10). Strong capitalization (7.3) based on excellent current risk-adjusted capital (severe loss scenario). High quality investment portfolio (9.9).
**Other Rating Factors:** Excellent liquidity (7.1) with ample operational cash flow and liquid investments.
**Principal Business:** Medicare (72%), comp med (28%)
**Mem Phys: 16:** 3,518 **15:** 3,518 **16 MLR** 107.2% **/ 16 Admin Exp** N/A
**Enroll(000): Q3 17:** 0 **16:** 41 **15:** 13 **Med Exp PMPM:** $340
**Principal Investments:** Affiliate common stock (435%), cash and equiv (98%), long-term bonds (2%)
**Provider Compensation ($000):** Contr fee ($153,184), FFS ($21,537)
**Total Member Encounters:** Phys (237,374), non-phys (187,437)
**Group Affiliation:** Tenet Healthcare Corp
**Licensed in:** AZ
**Address:** 7878 N 16th St Ste 105, Phoenix, AZ 85020
**Phone:** (602) 824-3700 **Dom State:** AZ **Commenced Bus:** July 2005

| Data Date | Rating | RACR #1 | RACR #2 | Total Assets ($mil) | Capital ($mil) | Net Premium ($mil) | Net Income ($mil) |
|---|---|---|---|---|---|---|---|
| 9-17 | E | 1.61 | 1.34 | 43.1 | 34.6 | -3.6 | -8.7 |
| 9-16 | E | 0.85 | 0.71 | 87.6 | 10.8 | 141.6 | -9.6 |
| 2016 | E | 1.19 | 0.99 | 101.8 | 26.0 | 167.9 | -21.9 |
| 2015 | E | 1.69 | 1.41 | 50.9 | 21.7 | 113.2 | 5.4 |
| 2014 | E | 1.24 | 1.04 | 38.7 | 17.9 | 86.5 | -16.1 |
| 2013 | C- | 1.26 | 1.05 | 36.9 | 13.1 | 68.7 | -6.5 |
| 2012 | B | 3.18 | 2.65 | 38.5 | 19.7 | 41.0 | 0.0 |

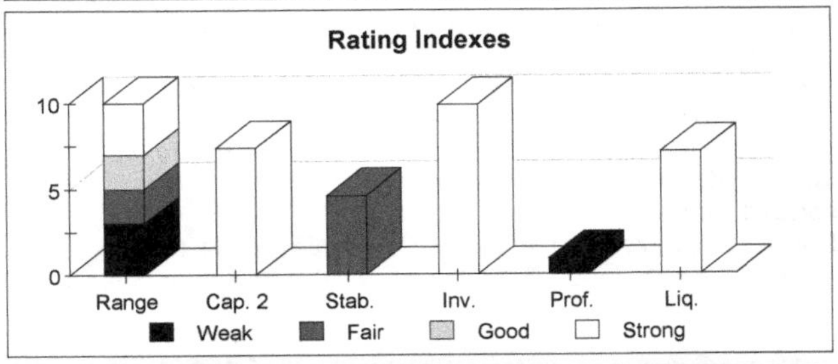


## PHP INS CO — B — Good

**Major Rating Factors:** Fair profitability index (4.4 on a scale of 0 to 10). Strong capitalization (9.3) based on excellent current risk-adjusted capital (severe loss scenario). High quality investment portfolio (9.9).
**Other Rating Factors:** Excellent liquidity (7.6) with ample operational cash flow and liquid investments.
**Principal Business:** Comp med (100%)
**Mem Phys: 16:** 3,407 **15:** N/A **16 MLR** 74.1% **/ 16 Admin Exp** N/A
**Enroll(000): Q3 17:** 6 **16:** 5 **15:** 9 **Med Exp PMPM:** $314
**Principal Investments:** Cash and equiv (98%), long-term bonds (2%)
**Provider Compensation ($000):** Contr fee ($26,596), FFS ($1,843)
**Total Member Encounters:** Phys (79,462), non-phys (39,751)
**Group Affiliation:** Sparrow Health System
**Licensed in:** MI
**Address:** 1400 EAST MICHIGAN Ave, LANSING, MI 48912
**Phone:** (517) 364-8400 **Dom State:** MI **Commenced Bus:** December 2006

| Data Date | Rating | RACR #1 | RACR #2 | Total Assets ($mil) | Capital ($mil) | Net Premium ($mil) | Net Income ($mil) |
|---|---|---|---|---|---|---|---|
| 9-17 | B | 3.21 | 2.68 | 16.5 | 12.8 | 22.9 | 1.4 |
| 9-16 | C+ | 2.08 | 1.74 | 16.4 | 10.9 | 27.8 | 2.4 |
| 2016 | C+ | 3.08 | 2.57 | 16.2 | 11.6 | 35.7 | 2.9 |
| 2015 | C | 1.59 | 1.33 | 14.0 | 8.4 | 42.9 | -2.4 |
| 2014 | C | 1.55 | 1.29 | 16.3 | 8.6 | 46.0 | -0.2 |
| 2013 | C+ | 1.55 | 1.29 | 14.9 | 8.4 | 41.2 | -1.0 |
| 2012 | B | 2.46 | 2.05 | 13.7 | 9.2 | 27.9 | 0.6 |

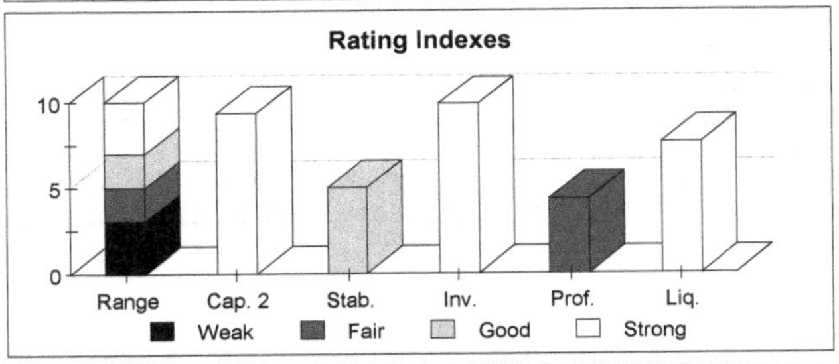


## PHYSICIANS HEALTH CHOICE OF TEXAS — C — Fair

**Major Rating Factors:** Weak profitability index (2.0 on a scale of 0 to 10). Good capitalization (6.0) based on good current risk-adjusted capital (severe loss scenario). Good liquidity (6.7) with sufficient resources (cash flows and marketable investments) to handle a spike in claims.
**Other Rating Factors:** High quality investment portfolio (9.6).
**Principal Business:** Medicare (100%)
**Mem Phys: 16:** 343 **15:** 390 **16 MLR** 89.8% **/ 16 Admin Exp** N/A
**Enroll(000): Q3 17:** 65 **16:** 32 **15:** 28 **Med Exp PMPM:** $1,031
**Principal Investments:** Long-term bonds (78%), cash and equiv (22%)
**Provider Compensation ($000):** Capitation ($330,826), contr fee ($46,034), FFS ($1,225), bonus arrang ($439)
**Total Member Encounters:** Phys (456,508), non-phys (393,807)
**Group Affiliation:** UnitedHealth Group Incorporated
**Licensed in:** TX
**Address:** 1311 W PRESIDENT GEORGE BUSH, RICHARDSON, TX 75080
**Phone:** (952) 936-1300 **Dom State:** TX **Commenced Bus:** August 2002

| Data Date | Rating | RACR #1 | RACR #2 | Total Assets ($mil) | Capital ($mil) | Net Premium ($mil) | Net Income ($mil) |
|---|---|---|---|---|---|---|---|
| 9-17 | C | 1.08 | 0.90 | 212.8 | 14.7 | 563.9 | -0.9 |
| 9-16 | C+ | 3.21 | 2.67 | 119.6 | 35.7 | 310.4 | -3.4 |
| 2016 | C+ | 2.32 | 1.93 | 64.0 | 33.5 | 417.5 | -5.5 |
| 2015 | C+ | 3.46 | 2.88 | 67.7 | 38.6 | 372.6 | 4.4 |
| 2014 | B- | 4.17 | 3.48 | 80.2 | 54.0 | 338.9 | -2.2 |
| 2013 | B- | 3.00 | 2.50 | 73.5 | 56.4 | 404.1 | 9.6 |
| 2012 | N/A | N/A | N/A | 123.5 | 38.8 | 410.8 | 6.9 |

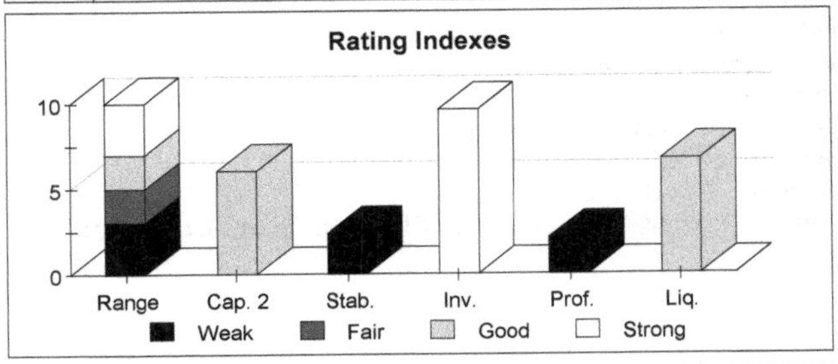

## PHYSICIANS HEALTH PLAN OF NO IN — B Good

**Major Rating Factors:** Good overall profitability index (5.7 on a scale of 0 to 10). Good overall results on stability tests (5.3) despite a decline in enrollment during 2016, a decline in the number of member physicians during 2017. Good liquidity (6.7) with sufficient resources (cash flows and marketable investments) to handle a spike in claims.
**Other Rating Factors:** Strong capitalization index (8.9) based on excellent current risk-adjusted capital (severe loss scenario). High quality investment portfolio (8.6).
**Principal Business:** Comp med (100%)
**Mem Phys: 16:** 4,096 **15:** 5,415 **16 MLR** 85.2% **/ 16 Admin Exp** N/A
**Enroll(000): Q3 17:** 31 **16:** 37 **15:** 41 **Med Exp PMPM:** $342
**Principal Investments:** Long-term bonds (53%), nonaffiliate common stock (21%), cash and equiv (17%), affiliate common stock (3%), real estate (3%), other (4%)
**Provider Compensation ($000):** FFS ($128,988), contr fee ($19,065), bonus arrang ($7,061), capitation ($1,209)
**Total Member Encounters:** Phys (179,759), non-phys (145,967)
**Group Affiliation:** Physicians Hlth Plan of Northern IN
**Licensed in:** IN
**Address:** 8101 West Jefferson Blvd, Fort Wayne, IN 46804
**Phone:** (260) 432-6690 **Dom State:** IN **Commenced Bus:** December 1983

| Data Date | Rating | RACR #1 | RACR #2 | Total Assets ($mil) | Capital ($mil) | Net Premium ($mil) | Net Income ($mil) |
|---|---|---|---|---|---|---|---|
| 9-17 | B | 2.90 | 2.42 | 86.3 | 59.9 | 117.9 | 8.9 |
| 9-16 | B | 2.43 | 2.03 | 85.4 | 53.1 | 134.1 | 5.1 |
| 2016 | B | 2.32 | 1.94 | 82.3 | 49.1 | 180.1 | -0.2 |
| 2015 | B | 1.97 | 1.64 | 84.6 | 43.9 | 192.5 | 2.7 |
| 2014 | B | 1.80 | 1.50 | 87.6 | 44.8 | 212.8 | 1.8 |
| 2013 | B | 2.22 | 1.85 | 74.6 | 44.9 | 167.1 | 0.4 |
| 2012 | B- | 2.34 | 1.95 | 70.0 | 42.4 | 151.8 | 2.9 |

Rating Indexes

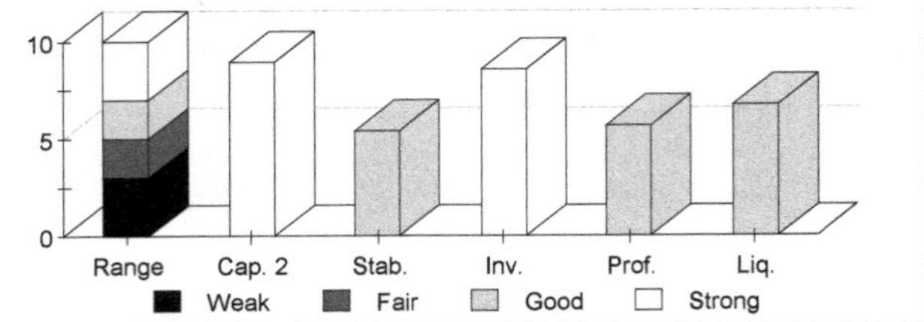


## PHYSICIANS HP OF MID-MICHIGAN — B Good

**Major Rating Factors:** Good quality investment portfolio (5.0 on a scale of 0 to 10). Good liquidity (6.9) with sufficient resources (cash flows and marketable investments) to handle a spike in claims. Fair profitability index (3.8).
**Other Rating Factors:** Fair overall results on stability tests (4.3) based on inconsistent enrollment growth in the past five years due to declines in 2013 and 2014. Strong capitalization index (7.4) based on excellent current risk-adjusted capital (severe loss scenario).
**Principal Business:** Comp med (100%)
**Mem Phys: 16:** 4,077 **15:** N/A **16 MLR** 89.5% **/ 16 Admin Exp** N/A
**Enroll(000): Q3 17:** 37 **16:** 36 **15:** 34 **Med Exp PMPM:** $365
**Principal Investments:** Nonaffiliate common stock (42%), cash and equiv (28%), affiliate common stock (14%), real estate (2%), other (14%)
**Provider Compensation ($000):** Contr fee ($90,953), FFS ($70,217), bonus arrang ($593)
**Total Member Encounters:** Phys (244,632), non-phys (120,979)
**Group Affiliation:** Sparrow Health System
**Licensed in:** MI
**Address:** 1400 EAST MICHIGAN AVENUE, LANSING, MI 48912
**Phone:** (517) 364-8400 **Dom State:** MI **Commenced Bus:** October 1981

| Data Date | Rating | RACR #1 | RACR #2 | Total Assets ($mil) | Capital ($mil) | Net Premium ($mil) | Net Income ($mil) |
|---|---|---|---|---|---|---|---|
| 9-17 | B | 1.70 | 1.41 | 81.5 | 49.7 | 139.1 | 7.1 |
| 9-16 | B | 2.33 | 1.94 | 92.0 | 64.2 | 133.7 | -1.6 |
| 2016 | B | 2.22 | 1.85 | 91.1 | 62.1 | 177.4 | -1.2 |
| 2015 | B | 2.07 | 1.72 | 80.3 | 58.2 | 162.9 | 0.5 |
| 2014 | B | 1.96 | 1.63 | 86.3 | 59.8 | 157.9 | 2.9 |
| 2013 | B | 1.91 | 1.60 | 83.2 | 58.2 | 195.3 | 3.0 |
| 2012 | B | 1.74 | 1.45 | 79.9 | 52.7 | 214.6 | 0.0 |

Rating Indexes

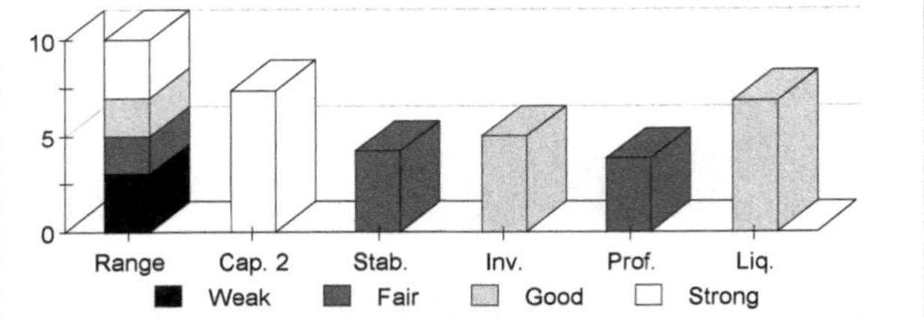


## PHYSICIANS MUTUAL INSURANCE COMPANY * — A+ Excellent

**Major Rating Factors:** Good quality investment portfolio (6.2 on a scale of 0 to 10) despite mixed results such as: no exposure to mortgages and large holdings of BBB rated bonds but small junk bond holdings. Strong capitalization (9.4) based on excellent risk adjusted capital (severe loss scenario). Furthermore, this high level of risk adjusted capital has been consistently maintained over the last five years. Excellent profitability (8.1).
**Other Rating Factors:** Excellent liquidity (7.4). Excellent overall results on stability tests (7.9) excellent operational trends and excellent risk diversification.
**Principal Business:** Individual health insurance (65%), reinsurance (26%), and group health insurance (9%).
**Principal Investments:** NonCMO investment grade bonds (62%), common & preferred stock (16%), CMOs and structured securities (16%), and noninv. grade bonds (5%).
**Investments in Affiliates:** 7%
**Group Affiliation:** Physicians Mutual Group
**Licensed in:** All states except PR
**Commenced Business:** February 1902
**Address:** 2600 Dodge Street, Omaha, NE 68131-2671
**Phone:** (402) 633-1000 **Domicile State:** NE **NAIC Code:** 80578

| Data Date | Rating | RACR #1 | RACR #2 | Total Assets ($mil) | Capital ($mil) | Net Premium ($mil) | Net Income ($mil) |
|---|---|---|---|---|---|---|---|
| 9-17 | A+ | 3.48 | 2.62 | 2,289.0 | 957.4 | 325.5 | 31.0 |
| 9-16 | A+ | 3.51 | 2.63 | 2,185.2 | 911.0 | 352.4 | 21.5 |
| 2016 | A+ | 3.41 | 2.58 | 2,208.6 | 919.2 | 454.5 | 29.1 |
| 2015 | A+ | 3.51 | 2.65 | 2,106.2 | 885.5 | 454.2 | 39.6 |
| 2014 | A+ | 3.67 | 2.78 | 2,026.2 | 845.5 | 424.5 | 42.8 |
| 2013 | A+ | 4.23 | 3.22 | 1,920.5 | 931.1 | 453.9 | 33.6 |
| 2012 | A+ | 4.02 | 3.04 | 1,829.7 | 866.1 | 447.6 | 30.2 |

Rating Indexes

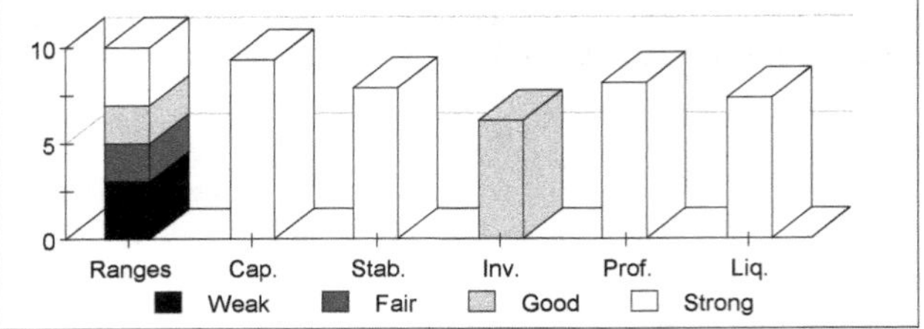

## PHYSICIANS PLUS INS CORP — D+ Weak

**Major Rating Factors:** Weak profitability index (0.9 on a scale of 0 to 10). Fair overall results on stability tests (4.8). Good liquidity (6.4) with sufficient resources (cash flows and marketable investments) to handle a spike in claims.
**Other Rating Factors:** Strong capitalization index (10.0) based on excellent current risk-adjusted capital (severe loss scenario). High quality investment portfolio (7.8).
**Principal Business:** Comp med (87%), Medicaid (8%), FEHB (4%), med supp (1%)
**Mem Phys: 16:** 5,189 **15:** 4,815 **16 MLR** 89.7% **/ 16 Admin Exp** N/A
**Enroll(000): Q3 17:** 61 **16:** 62 **15:** 65 **Med Exp PMPM:** $290
**Principal Investments:** Long-term bonds (64%), nonaffiliate common stock (19%), cash and equiv (17%)
**Provider Compensation ($000):** Contr fee ($146,316), capitation ($36,297), FFS ($27,124)
**Total Member Encounters:** Phys (302,611), non-phys (284,883)
**Group Affiliation:** Iowa Health System Inc
**Licensed in:** IL, WI
**Address:** 2650 Novation Parkway, Madison, WI 53713
**Phone:** (608) 282-8900 **Dom State:** WI **Commenced Bus:** October 1986

| Data Date | Rating | RACR #1 | RACR #2 | Total Assets ($mil) | Capital ($mil) | Net Premium ($mil) | Net Income ($mil) |
|---|---|---|---|---|---|---|---|
| 9-17 | D+ | 4.05 | 3.37 | 128.7 | 87.4 | 180.4 | -1.8 |
| 9-16 | D+ | 1.14 | 0.95 | 76.6 | 38.3 | 183.8 | 7.5 |
| 2016 | D+ | 0.84 | 0.70 | 75.4 | 33.4 | 244.1 | 1.9 |
| 2015 | D+ | 0.75 | 0.62 | 64.6 | 29.9 | 252.0 | -9.2 |
| 2014 | D+ | 1.18 | 0.98 | 74.5 | 39.2 | 232.3 | 2.8 |
| 2013 | D | 0.55 | 0.46 | 89.9 | 33.5 | 352.4 | -16.5 |
| 2012 | D | 0.52 | 0.43 | 80.5 | 25.9 | 438.3 | -30.3 |

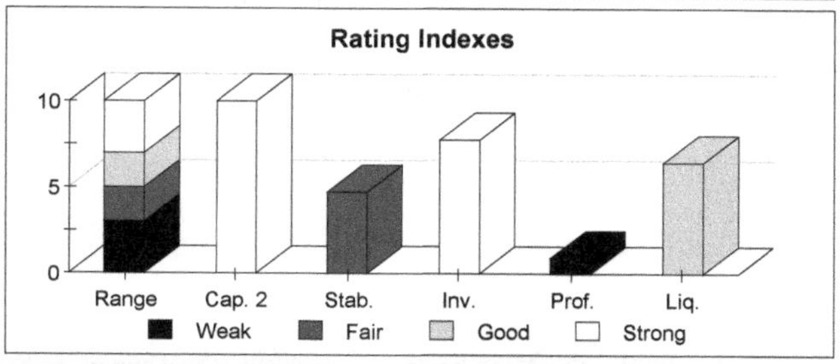


## PIEDMONT COMMUNITY HEALTHCARE — D+ Weak

**Major Rating Factors:** Weak profitability index (0.9 on a scale of 0 to 10). Weak liquidity (0.1) as a spike in claims may stretch capacity. Fair capitalization index (4.9) based on good current risk-adjusted capital (severe loss scenario).
**Other Rating Factors:** High quality investment portfolio (9.9). Excellent overall results on stability tests (8.3).
**Principal Business:** Medicare (55%), comp med (45%)
**Mem Phys: 16:** 981 **15:** 873 **16 MLR** 93.2% **/ 16 Admin Exp** N/A
**Enroll(000): Q3 17:** 13 **16:** 14 **15:** 15 **Med Exp PMPM:** $517
**Principal Investments:** Cash and equiv (100%)
**Provider Compensation ($000):** Contr fee ($81,973), FFS ($4,176)
**Total Member Encounters:** Phys (138,017), non-phys (99,651)
**Group Affiliation:** Centra Health Inc
**Licensed in:** VA
**Address:** 2316 Atherholt Road, Lynchburg, VA 24501
**Phone:** (434) 947-4463 **Dom State:** VA **Commenced Bus:** January 1999

| Data Date | Rating | RACR #1 | RACR #2 | Total Assets ($mil) | Capital ($mil) | Net Premium ($mil) | Net Income ($mil) |
|---|---|---|---|---|---|---|---|
| 9-17 | D+ | 0.92 | 0.76 | 27.8 | 12.0 | 68.9 | -3.5 |
| 9-16 | C | 0.67 | 0.56 | 22.9 | 8.0 | 70.1 | -2.9 |
| 2016 | D+ | 0.88 | 0.73 | 24.2 | 11.5 | 94.3 | -2.5 |
| 2015 | B- | 0.96 | 0.80 | 26.7 | 10.7 | 84.7 | -0.8 |
| 2014 | B- | 0.89 | 0.74 | 18.7 | 7.8 | 64.7 | 0.4 |
| 2013 | B | 0.93 | 0.77 | 16.6 | 7.5 | 57.8 | 0.2 |
| 2012 | B | 0.94 | 0.79 | 15.4 | 6.4 | 47.9 | 0.1 |

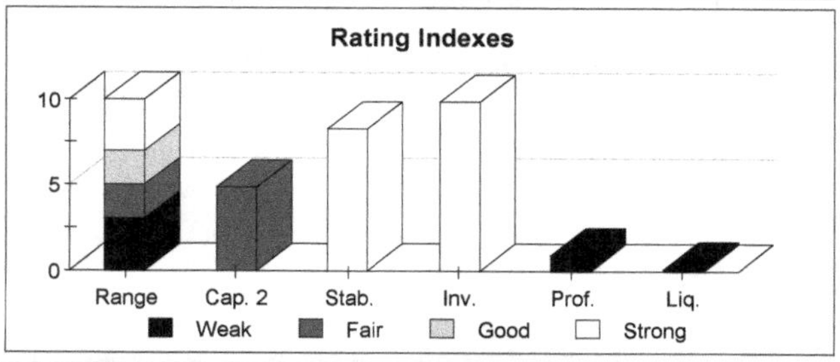


## PIEDMONT COMMUNITY HEALTHCARE HMO — C- Fair

**Major Rating Factors:** Weak profitability index (0.8 on a scale of 0 to 10). Good capitalization (6.9) based on excellent current risk-adjusted capital (severe loss scenario). Good liquidity (6.7) with sufficient resources (cash flows and marketable investments) to handle a spike in claims.
**Other Rating Factors:** High quality investment portfolio (9.9).
**Principal Business:** Comp med (100%)
**Mem Phys: 16:** 935 **15:** 688 **16 MLR** 111.7% **/ 16 Admin Exp** N/A
**Enroll(000): Q3 17:** 4 **16:** 2 **15:** N/A **Med Exp PMPM:** $434
**Principal Investments:** Cash and equiv (100%)
**Provider Compensation ($000):** Contr fee ($10,612), FFS ($367)
**Total Member Encounters:** Phys (15,035), non-phys (9,046)
**Group Affiliation:** Centra Health Inc
**Licensed in:** VA
**Address:** 2316 Atherholt Rd, Lynchburg, VA 24501
**Phone:** (434) 947-4463 **Dom State:** VA **Commenced Bus:** October 2015

| Data Date | Rating | RACR #1 | RACR #2 | Total Assets ($mil) | Capital ($mil) | Net Premium ($mil) | Net Income ($mil) |
|---|---|---|---|---|---|---|---|
| 9-17 | C- | 1.28 | 1.06 | 5.0 | 3.1 | 14.4 | 0.4 |
| 9-16 | N/A | N/A | N/A | 4.7 | 3.3 | 7.8 | -1.2 |
| 2016 | D | 1.29 | 1.08 | 4.6 | 3.2 | 10.7 | -1.6 |
| 2015 | N/A | N/A | N/A | 4.6 | 4.5 | N/A | N/A |
| 2014 | N/A | N/A | N/A | N/A | N/A | N/A | N/A |
| 2013 | N/A | N/A | N/A | N/A | N/A | N/A | N/A |
| 2012 | N/A | N/A | N/A | N/A | N/A | N/A | N/A |

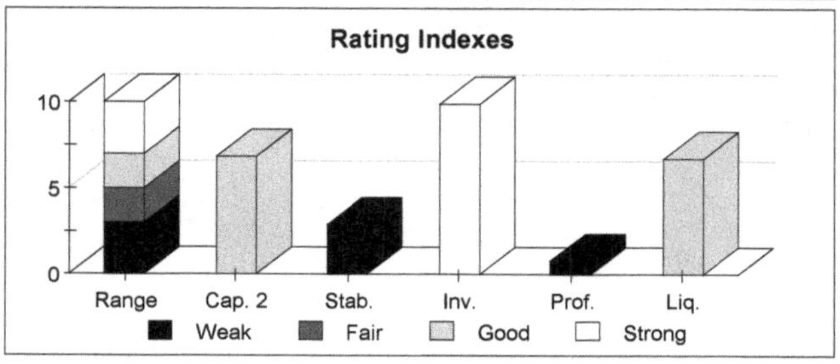

## PIEDMONT WELLSTAR HEALTHPLANS INC — E — Very Weak

**Major Rating Factors:** Weak profitability index (0.0 on a scale of 0 to 10). Strong capitalization (10.0) based on excellent current risk-adjusted capital (severe loss scenario). High quality investment portfolio (9.9).
**Other Rating Factors:** Excellent liquidity (8.0) with ample operational cash flow and liquid investments.
**Principal Business:** Comp med (93%), Medicare (7%)
**Mem Phys: 16:** 5,150 **15:** 5,150 **16 MLR** 33.5% **/ 16 Admin Exp** N/A
**Enroll(000): Q1 17:** N/A **16:** N/A **15:** 15 **Med Exp PMPM:** N/A
**Principal Investments:** Cash and equiv (99%), long-term bonds (1%)
**Provider Compensation ($000):** Capitation ($11,537)
**Total Member Encounters:** Phys (102), non-phys (72)
**Group Affiliation:** Piedmont WellStar HealthPlans Inc
**Licensed in:** GA
**Address:** 1800 Howell Mill Rd Ste 850, Atlanta, GA 30318
**Phone:** (678) 505-2895 **Dom State:** GA **Commenced Bus:** January 2014

| Data Date | Rating | RACR #1 | RACR #2 | Total Assets ($mil) | Capital ($mil) | Net Premium ($mil) | Net Income ($mil) |
|---|---|---|---|---|---|---|---|
| 3-17 | E | 6.32 | 5.26 | 17.6 | 8.2 | 0.0 | -0.1 |
| 3-16 | E | 0.90 | 0.75 | 25.1 | 5.9 | 1.0 | -1.6 |
| 2016 | E | 6.37 | 5.31 | 17.5 | 8.2 | 1.6 | 0.8 |
| 2015 | E | 1.04 | 0.87 | 39.2 | 6.9 | 115.6 | -24.4 |
| 2014 | D | 1.63 | 1.36 | 38.9 | 17.1 | 69.8 | -11.4 |
| 2013 | N/A | N/A | N/A | 27.2 | 21.9 | N/A | -19.6 |
| 2012 | N/A | N/A | N/A | N/A | N/A | N/A | N/A |

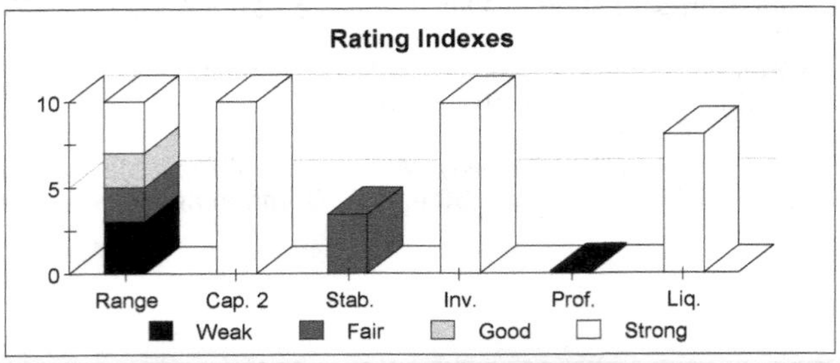


## PIONEER EDUCATORS HEALTH TRUST — E — Very Weak

**Major Rating Factors:** Weak profitability index (0.8 on a scale of 0 to 10). Poor capitalization (0.0) based on weak current risk-adjusted capital (severe loss scenario). Good liquidity (6.9) with sufficient resources (cash flows and marketable investments) to handle a spike in claims.
**Other Rating Factors:** High quality investment portfolio (9.9).
**Principal Business:** Comp med (91%), dental (9%)
**Mem Phys: 16:** N/A **15:** N/A **16 MLR** 101.1% **/ 16 Admin Exp** N/A
**Enroll(000): Q3 17:** 4 **16:** 5 **15:** 7 **Med Exp PMPM:** $263
**Principal Investments:** Cash and equiv (78%), long-term bonds (22%)
**Provider Compensation ($000):** FFS ($17,241)
**Total Member Encounters:** Phys (55,181), non-phys (82,031)
**Group Affiliation:** Pioneer Educators Health Trust
**Licensed in:** OR
**Address:** 700 NE MULTNOMAH ST Ste 1300, PORTLAND, OR 97232
**Phone:** (503) 224-8390 **Dom State:** OR **Commenced Bus:** April 2003

| Data Date | Rating | RACR #1 | RACR #2 | Total Assets ($mil) | Capital ($mil) | Net Premium ($mil) | Net Income ($mil) |
|---|---|---|---|---|---|---|---|
| 9-17 | E | 0.28 | 0.23 | 3.8 | 1.2 | 11.1 | -0.3 |
| 9-16 | N/A | N/A | N/A | 4.2 | 1.8 | 13.5 | -0.1 |
| 2016 | E | 0.34 | 0.28 | 4.5 | 1.5 | 17.4 | -0.4 |
| 2015 | N/A | N/A | N/A | 3.3 | 1.9 | 21.0 | -1.8 |
| 2014 | N/A | N/A | N/A | 4.3 | 2.6 | 16.7 | -4.8 |
| 2013 | N/A | N/A | N/A | 8.6 | 7.4 | 19.2 | 2.3 |
| 2012 | N/A | N/A | N/A | 7.4 | 6.0 | 19.6 | 2.2 |

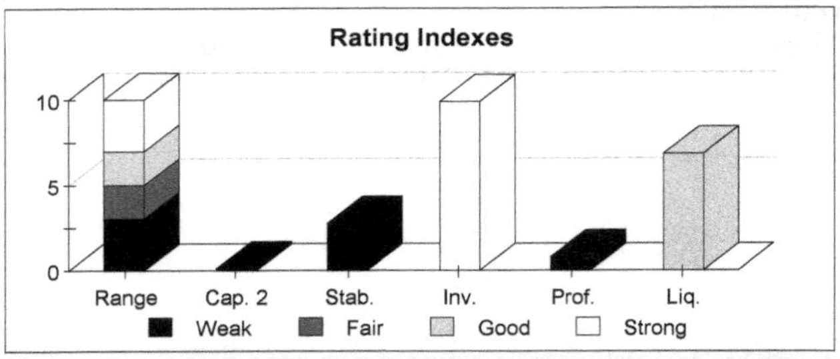


## PL MEDICO SERV DE SALUD BELLA VISTA — C- — Fair

**Major Rating Factors:** Fair profitability index (3.7 on a scale of 0 to 10). Fair capitalization index (3.4) based on weak current risk-adjusted capital (moderate loss scenario). Fair quality investment portfolio (3.6).
**Other Rating Factors:** Fair overall results on stability tests (3.7) based on a steep decline in capital during 2016. Excellent liquidity (7.0) with sufficient resources (cash flows and marketable investments) to handle a spike in claims.
**Principal Business:** Comp med (97%)
**Mem Phys: 16:** 1,000 **15:** 1,000 **16 MLR** 89.1% **/ 16 Admin Exp** N/A
**Enroll(000): Q3 17:** 18 **16:** 18 **15:** 17 **Med Exp PMPM:** $75
**Principal Investments:** Cash and equiv (97%), long-term bonds (3%)
**Provider Compensation ($000):** None
**Total Member Encounters:** N/A
**Group Affiliation:** Medico Servicios de Salud Bella Vist
**Licensed in:** (No states)
**Address:** 770 Avenida Hostos, Mayaguez, PR 00683-1538
**Phone:** (787) 833-8070 **Dom State:** PR **Commenced Bus:** February 1986

| Data Date | Rating | RACR #1 | RACR #2 | Total Assets ($mil) | Capital ($mil) | Net Premium ($mil) | Net Income ($mil) |
|---|---|---|---|---|---|---|---|
| 9-17 | C- | 0.69 | 0.57 | 2.8 | 1.1 | 4.6 | 0.3 |
| 9-16 | U | 0.72 | 0.60 | 2.8 | 1.0 | 4.4 | 0.0 |
| 2016 | D | 0.50 | 0.42 | 2.6 | 0.8 | 6.1 | -0.2 |
| 2015 | U | 0.73 | 0.61 | 2.7 | 1.0 | 5.6 | 0.2 |
| 2014 | N/A | N/A | N/A | 2.5 | 0.7 | 5.3 | 0.1 |
| 2013 | N/A | N/A | N/A | 2.6 | 0.9 | 5.4 | 0.3 |
| 2012 | N/A | N/A | N/A | 2.1 | 0.6 | 5.8 | N/A |

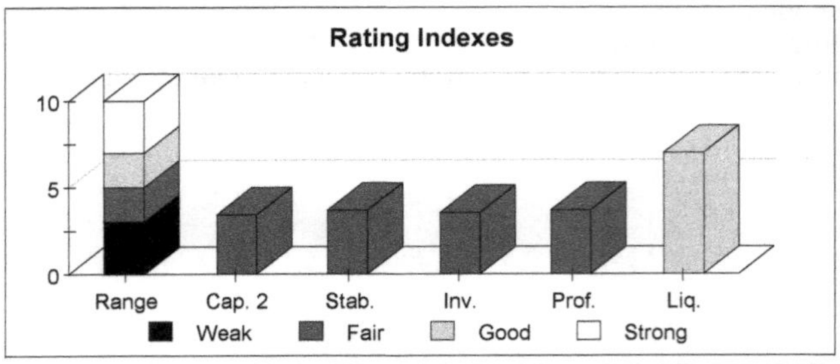

## PLAN DE SALUD MENONITA — C- — Fair

**Major Rating Factors:** Fair overall results on stability tests (3.8 on a scale of 0 to 10). Weak profitability index (2.4). Good capitalization index (6.9) based on excellent current risk-adjusted capital (severe loss scenario).
**Other Rating Factors:** Good liquidity (6.9) with sufficient resources (cash flows and marketable investments) to handle a spike in claims. High quality investment portfolio (9.5).
**Principal Business:** Comp med (91%)
**Mem Phys: 16:** 2,147 **15:** N/A **16 MLR** 74.6% **/ 16 Admin Exp** N/A
**Enroll(000): Q3 17:** 17 **16:** 16 **15:** 14 **Med Exp PMPM:** $62
**Principal Investments:** Long-term bonds (62%), cash and equiv (38%)
**Provider Compensation ($000):** Contr fee ($11,531)
**Total Member Encounters:** N/A
**Group Affiliation:** Mennonite General Hospital Inc
**Licensed in:** PR
**Address:** P O BOX 44, AIBONITO, PR 00705-0000
**Phone:** (787) 735-4520 **Dom State:** PR **Commenced Bus:** November 1979

| Data Date | Rating | RACR #1 | RACR #2 | Total Assets ($mil) | Capital ($mil) | Net Premium ($mil) | Net Income ($mil) |
|---|---|---|---|---|---|---|---|
| 9-17 | C- | 1.27 | 1.06 | 6.5 | 3.5 | 12.8 | -0.2 |
| 9-16 | N/A | N/A | N/A | 5.6 | 2.8 | 11.5 | 0.1 |
| 2016 | U | 0.77 | 0.64 | 4.3 | 2.2 | 15.4 | 0.0 |
| 2015 | N/A | N/A | N/A | 5.0 | 2.7 | 13.6 | 0.1 |
| 2014 | N/A | N/A | N/A | 4.0 | 2.6 | 11.7 | N/A |
| 2013 | N/A | N/A | N/A | 2.3 | 0.6 | 9.7 | N/A |
| 2012 | N/A | N/A | N/A | 1.9 | 0.6 | 18.8 | N/A |

Rating Indexes

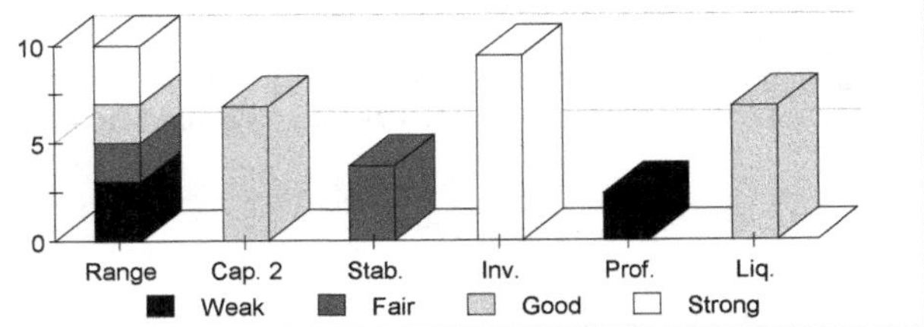


## PMC MEDICARE CHOICE LLC — D — Weak

**Major Rating Factors:** Fair profitability index (3.8 on a scale of 0 to 10). Fair capitalization (4.8) based on good current risk-adjusted capital (severe loss scenario). Good liquidity (6.9) with sufficient resources (cash flows and marketable investments) to handle a spike in claims.
**Other Rating Factors:** High quality investment portfolio (9.9).
**Principal Business:** Medicaid (67%), Medicare (33%)
**Mem Phys: 16:** N/A **15:** N/A **16 MLR** 87.6% **/ 16 Admin Exp** N/A
**Enroll(000): Q1 17:** N/A **16:** 147 **15:** 181 **Med Exp PMPM:** $202
**Principal Investments:** Cash and equiv (62%), long-term bonds (38%)
**Provider Compensation ($000):** FFS ($222,821), capitation ($62,310), bonus arrang ($11,192), other ($120,470)
**Total Member Encounters:** N/A
**Group Affiliation:** InnovaCare Inc
**Licensed in:** PR
**Address:** 350 ChardÃ³n Ave, San Juan, PR 00917
**Phone:** (787) 622-3000 **Dom State:** PR **Commenced Bus:** August 2004

| Data Date | Rating | RACR #1 | RACR #2 | Total Assets ($mil) | Capital ($mil) | Net Premium ($mil) | Net Income ($mil) |
|---|---|---|---|---|---|---|---|
| 3-17 | D | 0.90 | 0.75 | 44.4 | 35.3 | N/A | -0.2 |
| 3-16 | D- | 0.93 | 0.78 | 154.0 | 40.6 | 136.9 | 3.5 |
| 2016 | D | 0.87 | 0.73 | 92.3 | 34.6 | 456.4 | 2.7 |
| 2015 | D- | 0.97 | 0.81 | 140.0 | 42.2 | 522.8 | -1.8 |
| 2014 | B- | 0.98 | 0.82 | 80.8 | 31.6 | 345.9 | -5.4 |
| 2013 | B- | 0.99 | 0.82 | 83.1 | 33.7 | 402.7 | 6.2 |
| 2012 | C | 0.83 | 0.69 | 87.5 | 29.6 | 415.5 | 16.9 |

Rating Indexes

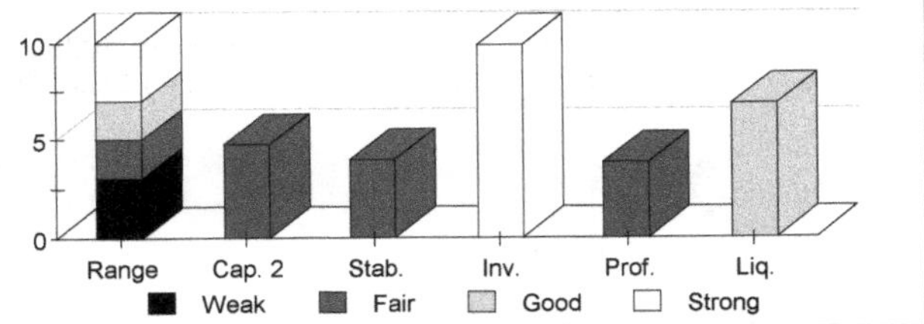


## PREFERRED CARE PARTNERS INC — E — Very Weak

**Major Rating Factors:** Good overall profitability index (5.4 on a scale of 0 to 10). Good liquidity (6.4) with sufficient resources (cash flows and marketable investments) to handle a spike in claims. Strong capitalization (7.2) based on excellent current risk-adjusted capital (severe loss scenario).
**Other Rating Factors:** High quality investment portfolio (9.1).
**Principal Business:** Medicare (100%)
**Mem Phys: 16:** 11,725 **15:** 9,698 **16 MLR** 86.0% **/ 16 Admin Exp** N/A
**Enroll(000): Q3 17:** 161 **16:** 131 **15:** 60 **Med Exp PMPM:** $856
**Principal Investments:** Long-term bonds (60%), cash and equiv (27%), other (13%)
**Provider Compensation ($000):** Contr fee ($670,013), capitation ($399,947), FFS ($67,058), bonus arrang ($18,951)
**Total Member Encounters:** Phys (842,371), non-phys (328,510)
**Group Affiliation:** UnitedHealth Group Incorporated
**Licensed in:** FL
**Address:** 9100 S DADELAND Blvd Ste 1250, MIAMI, FL 33156
**Phone:** (305) 670-8438 **Dom State:** FL **Commenced Bus:** August 2002

| Data Date | Rating | RACR #1 | RACR #2 | Total Assets ($mil) | Capital ($mil) | Net Premium ($mil) | Net Income ($mil) |
|---|---|---|---|---|---|---|---|
| 9-17 | E | 1.49 | 1.24 | 600.4 | 92.7 | 1,301.7 | 13.8 |
| 9-16 | E | 1.76 | 1.47 | 424.0 | 55.0 | 1,103.2 | 11.0 |
| 2016 | E | 1.34 | 1.11 | 325.0 | 82.7 | 1,484.4 | 13.8 |
| 2015 | E- | 1.76 | 1.47 | 169.4 | 54.9 | 732.4 | 24.2 |
| 2014 | E- | 3.51 | 2.92 | 196.9 | 109.6 | 585.1 | 19.9 |
| 2013 | E- | 0.68 | 0.57 | 110.5 | 23.9 | 566.5 | 14.1 |
| 2012 | E- | N/A | N/A | 110.2 | -8.9 | 671.1 | N/A |

Rating Indexes

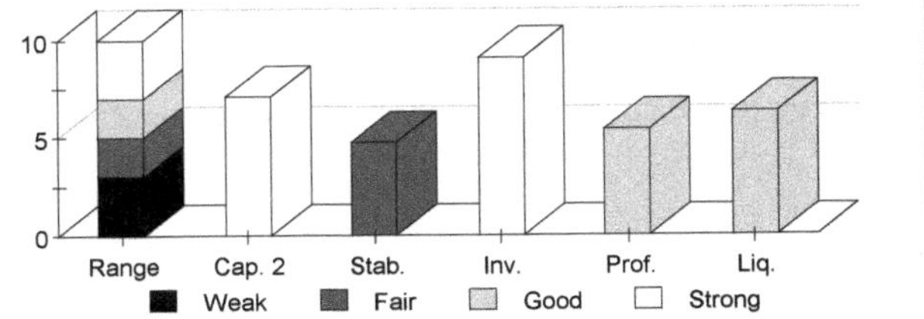

## PREFERREDONE COMMUNITY HEALTH PLAN — D — Weak

**Major Rating Factors:** Weak profitability index (0.7 on a scale of 0 to 10). Weak overall results on stability tests (1.8) based on a significant 73% decrease in enrollment during the period. Good liquidity (6.7) with sufficient resources (cash flows and marketable investments) to handle a spike in claims.
**Other Rating Factors:** Strong capitalization index (7.7) based on excellent current risk-adjusted capital (severe loss scenario). High quality investment portfolio (9.5).
**Principal Business:** Comp med (100%)
**Mem Phys: 16:** 39,815 **15:** 41,017 **16 MLR** 89.3% **/ 16 Admin Exp** N/A
**Enroll(000): Q3 17:** 1 **16:** 1 **15:** 4 **Med Exp PMPM:** $329
**Principal Investments:** Long-term bonds (77%), cash and equiv (23%)
**Provider Compensation ($000):** Contr fee ($7,737), FFS ($2,816), bonus arrang ($449)
**Total Member Encounters:** N/A
**Group Affiliation:** Fairview Health Services
**Licensed in:** MN
**Address:** 6105 Golden Hills Drive, Golden Valley, MN 55416-1023
**Phone:** (763) 847-4477 **Dom State:** MN **Commenced Bus:** January 1996

| Data Date | Rating | RACR #1 | RACR #2 | Total Assets ($mil) | Capital ($mil) | Net Premium ($mil) | Net Income ($mil) |
|---|---|---|---|---|---|---|---|
| 9-17 | D | 1.90 | 1.58 | 3.8 | 2.8 | 2.8 | -0.7 |
| 9-16 | D | 0.59 | 0.49 | 5.4 | 2.6 | 9.0 | -0.8 |
| 2016 | D | 2.26 | 1.88 | 5.7 | 3.5 | 10.3 | 0.1 |
| 2015 | D | 0.75 | 0.63 | 7.6 | 3.4 | 26.1 | -0.9 |
| 2014 | D | 0.68 | 0.57 | 11.8 | 4.8 | 57.4 | -2.8 |
| 2013 | D | 1.01 | 0.84 | 14.1 | 7.7 | 59.6 | -2.7 |
| 2012 | D+ | 1.28 | 1.07 | 18.4 | 10.2 | 62.9 | -0.8 |

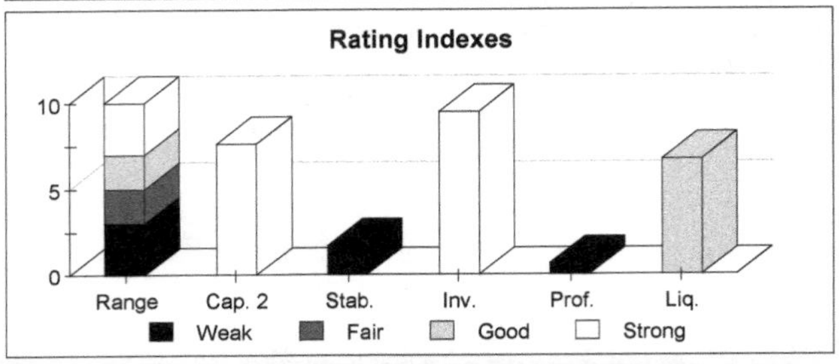


## PREFERREDONE INS CO — D+ — Weak

**Major Rating Factors:** Weak profitability index (0.9 on a scale of 0 to 10). Good liquidity (6.2) with sufficient resources (cash flows and marketable investments) to handle a spike in claims. Strong capitalization (7.6) based on excellent current risk-adjusted capital (severe loss scenario).
**Other Rating Factors:** High quality investment portfolio (9.4).
**Principal Business:** Comp med (84%), other (16%)
**Mem Phys: 16:** 39,815 **15:** 41,017 **16 MLR** 95.4% **/ 16 Admin Exp** N/A
**Enroll(000): Q3 17:** 143 **16:** 126 **15:** 140 **Med Exp PMPM:** $114
**Principal Investments:** Long-term bonds (69%), nonaffiliate common stock (18%), cash and equiv (13%)
**Provider Compensation ($000):** Contr fee ($110,318), FFS ($26,329), bonus arrang ($8,222), other ($24,417)
**Total Member Encounters:** N/A
**Group Affiliation:** Fairview Health Services
**Licensed in:** IA, MN, NE, ND, SD, WI
**Address:** 6105 Golden Hills Dr, Golden Valley, MN 55416-1023
**Phone:** (763) 847-4477 **Dom State:** MN **Commenced Bus:** October 2003

| Data Date | Rating | RACR #1 | RACR #2 | Total Assets ($mil) | Capital ($mil) | Net Premium ($mil) | Net Income ($mil) |
|---|---|---|---|---|---|---|---|
| 9-17 | D+ | 1.85 | 1.55 | 101.7 | 50.6 | 186.8 | 5.3 |
| 9-16 | D+ | 1.30 | 1.09 | 71.4 | 37.0 | 142.7 | 1.6 |
| 2016 | D+ | 1.40 | 1.17 | 78.3 | 38.9 | 178.2 | -5.8 |
| 2015 | D+ | 0.76 | 0.63 | 62.9 | 30.8 | 153.3 | -43.6 |
| 2014 | C+ | 0.68 | 0.57 | 146.8 | 47.9 | 430.2 | -20.9 |
| 2013 | B+ | 1.33 | 1.11 | 58.1 | 29.8 | 165.7 | -1.6 |
| 2012 | B+ | 1.66 | 1.38 | 51.5 | 30.5 | 144.8 | 3.1 |

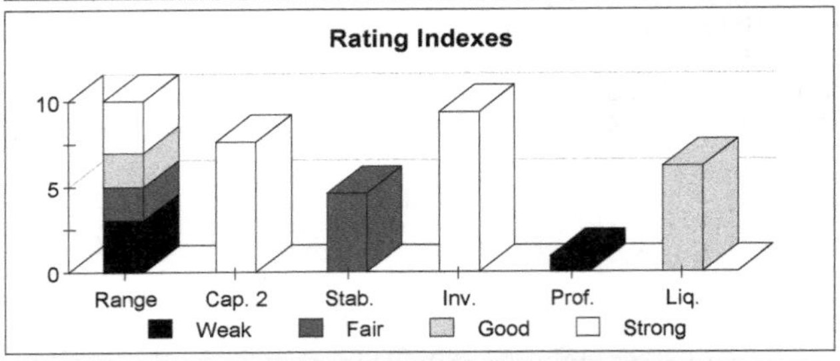


## PREMERA BLUE CROSS * — B+ — Good

**Major Rating Factors:** Good overall profitability index (6.1 on a scale of 0 to 10). Good liquidity (6.6) with sufficient resources (cash flows and marketable investments) to handle a spike in claims. Strong capitalization (10.0) based on excellent current risk-adjusted capital (severe loss scenario).
**Other Rating Factors:** Fair quality investment portfolio (4.5).
**Principal Business:** Comp med (72%), FEHB (18%), Medicare (5%), med supp (3%)
**Mem Phys: 16:** 50,626 **15:** 42,331 **16 MLR** 88.3% **/ 16 Admin Exp** N/A
**Enroll(000): Q3 17:** 660 **16:** 772 **15:** 796 **Med Exp PMPM:** $351
**Principal Investments:** Long-term bonds (43%), nonaffiliate common stock (26%), affiliate common stock (11%), real estate (2%), pref stock (1%), other (18%)
**Provider Compensation ($000):** Contr fee ($3,117,533), FFS ($180,016)
**Total Member Encounters:** Phys (5,333,415), non-phys (2,299,730)
**Group Affiliation:** PREMERA
**Licensed in:** AK, WA
**Address:** 7001 220th St SW, Mountlake Terrace, WA 98043
**Phone:** (425) 918-4000 **Dom State:** WA **Commenced Bus:** May 1945

| Data Date | Rating | RACR #1 | RACR #2 | Total Assets ($mil) | Capital ($mil) | Net Premium ($mil) | Net Income ($mil) |
|---|---|---|---|---|---|---|---|
| 9-17 | B+ | 5.78 | 4.82 | 2,574.6 | 1,653.9 | 2,566.0 | 116.6 |
| 9-16 | B+ | 5.40 | 4.50 | 2,399.4 | 1,424.3 | 2,810.6 | 13.8 |
| 2016 | B+ | 5.17 | 4.31 | 2,428.9 | 1,476.2 | 3,780.1 | 45.2 |
| 2015 | B+ | 5.27 | 4.39 | 2,276.0 | 1,388.4 | 3,489.4 | 12.9 |
| 2014 | A- | 5.80 | 4.83 | 2,211.0 | 1,415.3 | 3,072.7 | 65.9 |
| 2013 | A- | 6.45 | 5.38 | 2,009.4 | 1,359.9 | 2,556.1 | 86.3 |
| 2012 | A- | 6.02 | 5.02 | 1,781.7 | 1,160.4 | 2,574.5 | 93.1 |

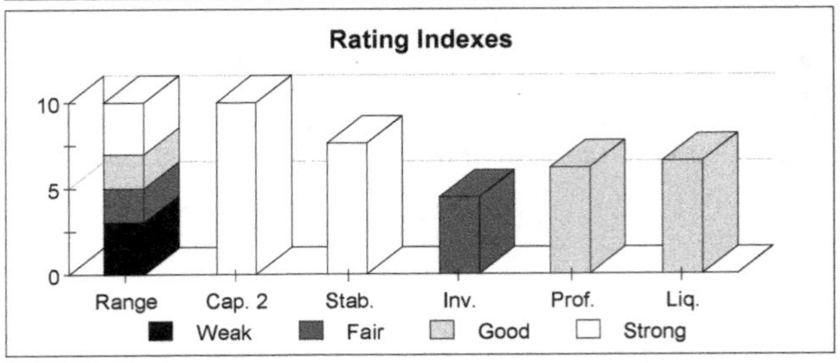

## PREMIER HEALTH INSURING CORP — E — Very Weak

**Major Rating Factors:** Weak profitability index (0.3 on a scale of 0 to 10). Weak liquidity (0.5) as a spike in claims may stretch capacity. Good capitalization (6.6) based on good current risk-adjusted capital (severe loss scenario).
**Other Rating Factors:** High quality investment portfolio (9.4).
**Principal Business:** Medicare (100%)
**Mem Phys: 16:** N/A **15:** 4,168 **16 MLR** 103.3% **/ 16 Admin Exp** N/A
**Enroll(000): Q3 17:** 10 **16:** 9 **15:** 8 **Med Exp PMPM:** $711
**Principal Investments:** Long-term bonds (43%), cash and equiv (31%), affiliate common stock (27%)
**Provider Compensation ($000):** Contr fee ($65,662), FFS ($3,712), other ($6,832)
**Total Member Encounters:** Phys (47,577), non-phys (8,746)
**Group Affiliation:** Premier Health Partners
**Licensed in:** OH
**Address:** 110 N MAIN ST STE 1200, DAYTON, OH 45402
**Phone:** (937) 499-9588 **Dom State:** OH **Commenced Bus:** April 2014

| Data Date | Rating | RACR #1 | RACR #2 | Total Assets ($mil) | Capital ($mil) | Net Premium ($mil) | Net Income ($mil) |
|---|---|---|---|---|---|---|---|
| 9-17 | E | 1.17 | 0.98 | 38.4 | 12.6 | 67.3 | -13.6 |
| 9-16 | E | 1.05 | 0.88 | 33.6 | 11.8 | 59.3 | -13.4 |
| 2016 | E | 1.41 | 1.18 | 30.0 | 15.2 | 77.0 | -21.3 |
| 2015 | E | 1.25 | 1.04 | 25.3 | 14.8 | 59.5 | -14.4 |
| 2014 | N/A | N/A | N/A | 32.8 | 32.5 | N/A | -3.2 |
| 2013 | N/A | N/A | N/A | N/A | N/A | N/A | N/A |
| 2012 | N/A | N/A | N/A | N/A | N/A | N/A | N/A |

Rating Indexes

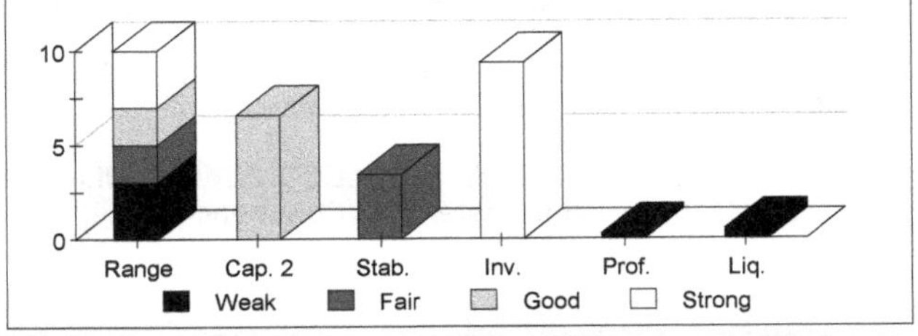


## PREMIER HEALTH PLAN INC — D- — Weak

**Major Rating Factors:** Weak profitability index (0.0 on a scale of 0 to 10). Weak liquidity (2.2) as a spike in claims may stretch capacity. Strong capitalization (7.1) based on excellent current risk-adjusted capital (severe loss scenario).
**Other Rating Factors:** High quality investment portfolio (9.9).
**Principal Business:** Comp med (100%)
**Mem Phys: 16:** 5,938 **15:** 4,306 **16 MLR** 133.4% **/ 16 Admin Exp** N/A
**Enroll(000): Q3 17:** 5 **16:** 6 **15:** 3 **Med Exp PMPM:** $377
**Principal Investments:** Cash and equiv (93%), long-term bonds (7%)
**Provider Compensation ($000):** Contr fee ($17,815), FFS ($810), other ($2,969)
**Total Member Encounters:** Phys (14,330), non-phys (3,154)
**Group Affiliation:** Premier Health Partners
**Licensed in:** OH
**Address:** 110 N MAIN ST STE 1200, Dayton, OH 45402
**Phone:** (937) 499-9588 **Dom State:** OH **Commenced Bus:** March 2014

| Data Date | Rating | RACR #1 | RACR #2 | Total Assets ($mil) | Capital ($mil) | Net Premium ($mil) | Net Income ($mil) |
|---|---|---|---|---|---|---|---|
| 9-17 | D- | 1.46 | 1.22 | 14.8 | 6.7 | 22.1 | -1.8 |
| 9-16 | E+ | 2.08 | 1.73 | 14.2 | 5.2 | 16.3 | -6.2 |
| 2016 | D- | 1.44 | 1.20 | 16.9 | 6.5 | 20.7 | -9.9 |
| 2015 | E+ | 2.29 | 1.91 | 11.7 | 5.8 | 8.2 | -3.2 |
| 2014 | N/A | N/A | N/A | 22.7 | 22.5 | N/A | -7.9 |
| 2013 | N/A | N/A | N/A | N/A | N/A | N/A | N/A |
| 2012 | N/A | N/A | N/A | N/A | N/A | N/A | N/A |

Rating Indexes

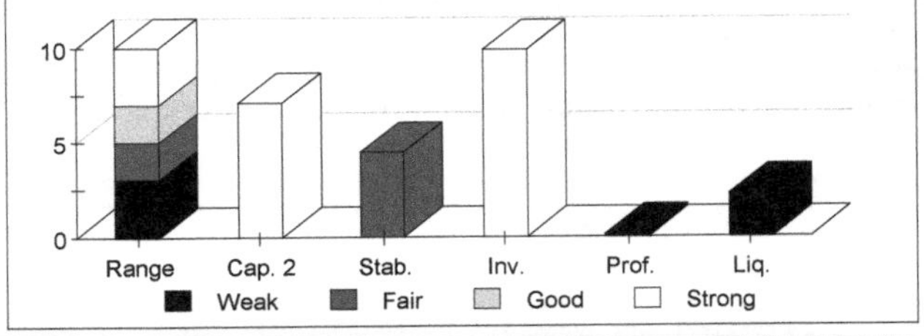


## PREMIER HEALTH PLAN SERVICES INC — D — Weak

**Major Rating Factors:** Weak overall results on stability tests (0.7 on a scale of 0 to 10) based on a steep decline in capital during 2016. Fair profitability index (3.8). Fair capitalization index (3.6) based on weak current risk-adjusted capital (moderate loss scenario).
**Other Rating Factors:** Excellent liquidity (7.1) with ample operational cash flow and liquid investments.
**Principal Business:** Managed care (100%)
**Mem Phys: 16:** N/A **15:** N/A **16 MLR** 85.6% **/ 16 Admin Exp** N/A
**Enroll(000): Q3 17:** 37 **16:** 39 **15:** 42 **Med Exp PMPM:** $182
**Principal Investments ($000):** Cash and equiv ($27,485)
**Provider Compensation ($000):** None
**Total Member Encounters:** N/A
**Group Affiliation:** Lakewood IPA
**Licensed in:** CA
**Address:** 10833 Valley View St Suite 300, Cypress, CA 90630
**Phone:** (310) 277-9003 **Dom State:** CA **Commenced Bus:** June 2009

| Data Date | Rating | RACR #1 | RACR #2 | Total Assets ($mil) | Capital ($mil) | Net Premium ($mil) | Net Income ($mil) |
|---|---|---|---|---|---|---|---|
| 9-17 | D | 0.60 | 0.38 | 21.8 | 5.2 | 66.5 | -0.8 |
| 9-16 | U | -454.00 | -15.00 | 34.2 | 15.5 | 79.6 | 6.3 |
| 2016 | C- | 0.79 | 0.49 | 29.2 | 6.6 | 99.6 | 0.5 |
| 2015 | U | -262.00 | -8.66 | 27.0 | 9.2 | 0.0 | 1.8 |
| 2014 | C | 1.29 | 0.82 | 24.5 | 8.2 | 77.4 | 3.0 |
| 2013 | C- | 2.81 | 1.85 | 4.6 | 2.1 | 17.9 | 0.0 |
| 2012 | C- | 9.88 | 9.49 | 5.1 | 2.1 | 17.3 | 0.6 |

Rating Indexes

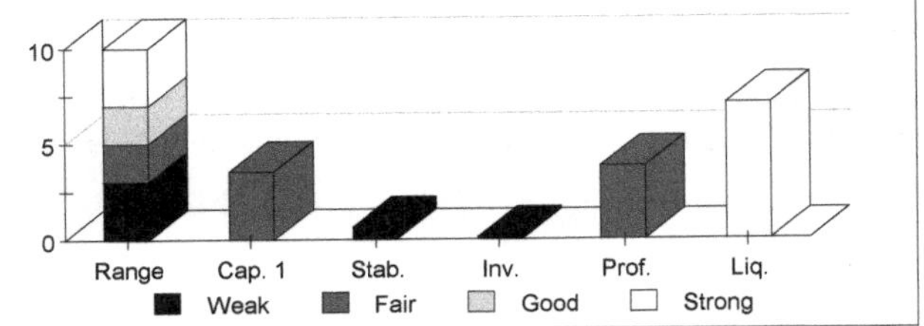

## PRESBYTERIAN HEALTH PLAN INC — B — Good

**Major Rating Factors:** Good overall results on stability tests (5.4 on a scale of 0 to 10) based on steady enrollment growth, averaging 6% over the past five years. Excellent profitability (8.2). Strong capitalization index (7.8) based on excellent current risk-adjusted capital (severe loss scenario).
**Other Rating Factors:** High quality investment portfolio (8.8). Excellent liquidity (7.0) with sufficient resources (cash flows and marketable investments) to handle a spike in claims.
**Principal Business:** Medicaid (67%), Medicare (16%), comp med (13%), FEHB (4%)
**Mem Phys: 16:** 7,472 **15:** N/A **16 MLR** 84.7% **/ 16 Admin Exp** N/A
**Enroll(000): Q3 17:** 318 **16:** 331 **15:** 309 **Med Exp PMPM:** $393
**Principal Investments:** Long-term bonds (48%), cash and equiv (35%), nonaffiliate common stock (17%), other (1%)
**Provider Compensation ($000):** Contr fee ($1,055,617), capitation ($429,517), FFS ($81,191)
**Total Member Encounters:** Phys (2,952,443), non-phys (1,562,671)
**Group Affiliation:** Presbyterian Healthcare Services
**Licensed in:** AZ, NM
**Address:** 9521 SAN MATEO BLVD NE, ALBUQUERQUE, NM 87113
**Phone:** (505) 923-6522 **Dom State:** NM **Commenced Bus:** July 1987

| Data Date | Rating | RACR #1 | RACR #2 | Total Assets ($mil) | Capital ($mil) | Net Premium ($mil) | Net Income ($mil) |
|---|---|---|---|---|---|---|---|
| 9-17 | B | 1.96 | 1.63 | 539.5 | 239.3 | 1,383.8 | 40.8 |
| 9-16 | B | 2.25 | 1.87 | 696.9 | 240.2 | 1,381.5 | 39.8 |
| 2016 | B | 1.95 | 1.62 | 664.9 | 238.2 | 1,838.9 | 31.8 |
| 2015 | B | 1.96 | 1.63 | 606.0 | 209.9 | 1,658.6 | 29.8 |
| 2014 | A- | 2.78 | 2.31 | 506.8 | 246.1 | 1,447.8 | 71.0 |
| 2013 | B+ | 2.45 | 2.05 | 305.7 | 169.1 | 1,092.5 | 16.6 |
| 2012 | A- | 2.25 | 1.87 | 319.2 | 153.4 | 1,069.4 | 37.6 |

**Rating Indexes**

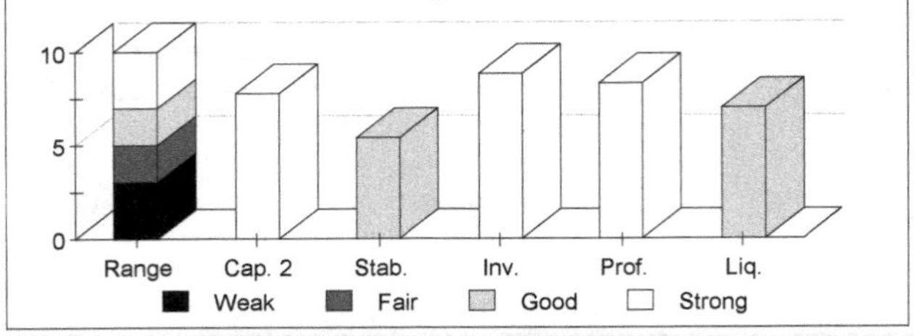


## PRESBYTERIAN INS CO — B- — Good

**Major Rating Factors:** Good liquidity (5.4 on a scale of 0 to 10) with sufficient resources (cash flows and marketable investments) to handle a spike in claims. Strong capitalization (7.2) based on excellent current risk-adjusted capital (severe loss scenario). High quality investment portfolio (8.8).
**Other Rating Factors:** Weak profitability index (1.0).
**Principal Business:** Comp med (47%), Medicare (46%), other (7%)
**Mem Phys: 16:** 6,085 **15:** 6,862 **16 MLR** 92.4% **/ 16 Admin Exp** N/A
**Enroll(000): Q3 17:** 21 **16:** 33 **15:** 24 **Med Exp PMPM:** $428
**Principal Investments:** Long-term bonds (61%), nonaffiliate common stock (30%), cash and equiv (7%), other (1%)
**Provider Compensation ($000):** Contr fee ($126,393), FFS ($33,802), capitation ($2,265)
**Total Member Encounters:** Phys (240,671), non-phys (104,757)
**Group Affiliation:** Presbyterian Healthcare Services
**Licensed in:** NM
**Address:** 9521 SAN MATEO BLVD NE, ALBUQUERQUE, NM 87113
**Phone:** (505) 923-6522 **Dom State:** NM **Commenced Bus:** July 2002

| Data Date | Rating | RACR #1 | RACR #2 | Total Assets ($mil) | Capital ($mil) | Net Premium ($mil) | Net Income ($mil) |
|---|---|---|---|---|---|---|---|
| 9-17 | B- | 1.54 | 1.29 | 54.8 | 29.0 | 96.9 | -5.9 |
| 9-16 | B- | 1.81 | 1.51 | 55.4 | 25.7 | 133.0 | -6.1 |
| 2016 | B- | 1.22 | 1.02 | 46.5 | 22.8 | 177.6 | -9.1 |
| 2015 | B | 2.19 | 1.82 | 53.3 | 31.6 | 168.0 | 1.8 |
| 2014 | B+ | 2.22 | 1.85 | 61.9 | 35.9 | 202.1 | 6.8 |
| 2013 | B | 2.07 | 1.72 | 49.7 | 28.4 | 151.6 | 5.4 |
| 2012 | B | 1.40 | 1.17 | 54.4 | 22.0 | 181.8 | 4.1 |

**Rating Indexes**

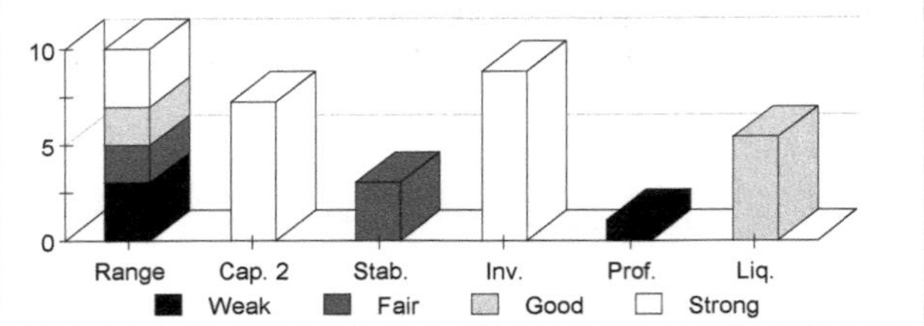


## PRIMECARE MEDICAL NETWORK INC — B — Good

**Major Rating Factors:** Good overall results on stability tests (5.4 on a scale of 0 to 10) despite inconsistent enrollment growth in the past five years due to declines in 2013 and 2016. Rating is significantly influenced by the fair financial results of UnitedHealth Group Inc. Excellent profitability (7.2). Strong capitalization index (7.3) based on excellent current risk-adjusted capital (severe loss scenario).
**Other Rating Factors:** Excellent liquidity (7.2) with ample operational cash flow and liquid investments.
**Principal Business:** Managed care (100%)
**Mem Phys: 16:** N/A **15:** N/A **16 MLR** 86.7% **/ 16 Admin Exp** N/A
**Enroll(000): Q3 17:** 195 **16:** 202 **15:** 507 **Med Exp PMPM:** $299
**Principal Investments ($000):** Cash and equiv ($198,055)
**Provider Compensation ($000):** None
**Total Member Encounters:** N/A
**Group Affiliation:** UnitedHealth Group Inc
**Licensed in:** CA
**Address:** 3990 Concours Street 5th Floor, Ontario, CA 91764
**Phone:** (909) 605-8000 **Dom State:** CA **Commenced Bus:** October 1998

| Data Date | Rating | RACR #1 | RACR #2 | Total Assets ($mil) | Capital ($mil) | Net Premium ($mil) | Net Income ($mil) |
|---|---|---|---|---|---|---|---|
| 9-17 | B | 2.10 | 1.30 | 238.0 | 66.6 | 659.5 | 23.4 |
| 9-16 | C+ | 2.14 | 1.33 | 218.1 | 62.3 | 640.4 | 17.3 |
| 2016 | B | 1.98 | 1.23 | 214.0 | 62.5 | 846.4 | 18.3 |
| 2015 | B- | 1.53 | 0.95 | 192.9 | 44.4 | 809.8 | 26.4 |
| 2014 | B | 2.56 | 1.59 | 178.6 | 62.7 | 674.7 | 19.5 |
| 2013 | C | 1.15 | 0.72 | 154.5 | 42.7 | 620.8 | 21.7 |
| 2012 | C | 0.62 | 0.38 | 127.3 | 21.6 | 559.2 | 25.5 |

**Rating Indexes**

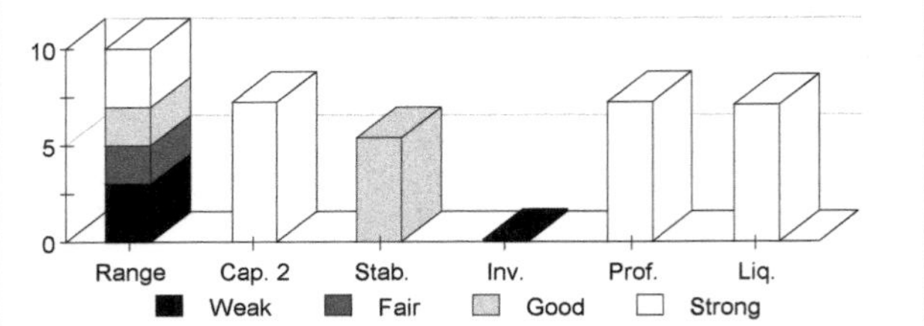

## PRIORITY HEALTH * — A — Excellent

**Major Rating Factors:** Excellent profitability (8.4 on a scale of 0 to 10). Strong capitalization index (9.2) based on excellent current risk-adjusted capital (severe loss scenario). High quality investment portfolio (9.9).
**Other Rating Factors:** Excellent overall results on stability tests (7.9). Excellent liquidity (6.9) with sufficient resources (cash flows and marketable investments) to handle a spike in claims
**Principal Business:** Comp med (59%), Medicare (40%)
**Mem Phys: 16:** 17,931 **15:** 17,501 **16 MLR** 88.2% **/ 16 Admin Exp** N/A
**Enroll(000): Q3 17:** 529 **16:** 494 **15:** 412 **Med Exp PMPM:** $408
**Principal Investments:** Long-term bonds (40%), cash and equiv (37%), nonaffiliate common stock (12%), affiliate common stock (12%)
**Provider Compensation ($000):** Contr fee ($1,427,865), bonus arrang ($768,014), FFS ($62,404), capitation ($2,881)
**Total Member Encounters:** Phys (5,521,696), non-phys (712,531)
**Group Affiliation:** Spectrum Health System
**Licensed in:** MI
**Address:** 1231 East Beltline NE, Grand Rapids, MI 49525-4501
**Phone:** (616) 942-0954 **Dom State:** MI **Commenced Bus:** October 1986

| Data Date | Rating | RACR #1 | RACR #2 | Total Assets ($mil) | Capital ($mil) | Net Premium ($mil) | Net Income ($mil) |
|---|---|---|---|---|---|---|---|
| 9-17 | A | 3.13 | 2.61 | 1,290.9 | 685.4 | 2,251.1 | 104.9 |
| 9-16 | A- | 3.05 | 2.54 | 1,081.5 | 577.7 | 1,979.9 | 43.4 |
| 2016 | A- | 2.49 | 2.07 | 1,000.4 | 574.5 | 2,663.2 | 51.1 |
| 2015 | A- | 2.71 | 2.26 | 910.2 | 529.8 | 2,187.7 | 91.1 |
| 2014 | B+ | 2.63 | 2.19 | 746.6 | 470.6 | 1,984.6 | 91.4 |
| 2013 | B | 2.22 | 1.85 | 624.0 | 394.9 | 1,878.2 | 58.6 |
| 2012 | B | 1.60 | 1.34 | 542.5 | 307.2 | 1,936.8 | 60.7 |

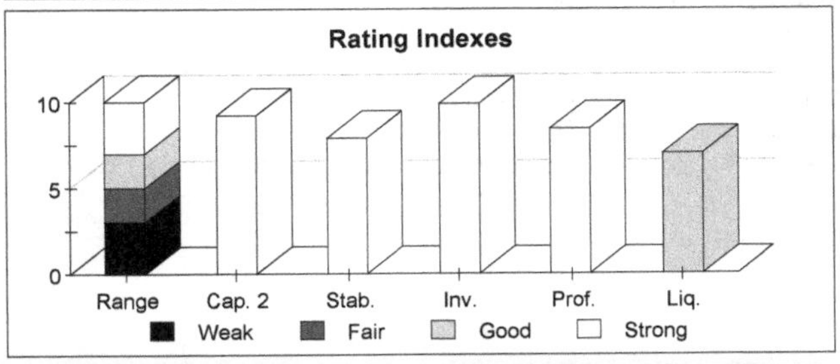


## PRIORITY HEALTH CHOICE INC * — B+ — Good

**Major Rating Factors:** Excellent profitability (7.1 on a scale of 0 to 10). Strong capitalization (8.3) based on excellent current risk-adjusted capital (severe loss scenario). High quality investment portfolio (9.9).
**Other Rating Factors:** Excellent liquidity (6.9) with sufficient resources (cash flows and marketable investments) to handle a spike in claims.
**Principal Business:** Medicaid (100%)
**Mem Phys: 16:** 6,899 **15:** 6,516 **16 MLR** 86.6% **/ 16 Admin Exp** N/A
**Enroll(000): Q3 17:** 124 **16:** 119 **15:** 116 **Med Exp PMPM:** $311
**Principal Investments:** Cash and equiv (66%), nonaffiliate common stock (33%), long-term bonds (1%)
**Provider Compensation ($000):** Capitation ($176,991), contr fee ($157,359), bonus arrang ($71,937), FFS ($11,571)
**Total Member Encounters:** Phys (1,378,150), non-phys (156,290)
**Group Affiliation:** Spectrum Health System
**Licensed in:** MI
**Address:** 1231 East Beltline NE, Grand Rapids, MI 49525-4501
**Phone:** (616) 942-0954 **Dom State:** MI **Commenced Bus:** October 2002

| Data Date | Rating | RACR #1 | RACR #2 | Total Assets ($mil) | Capital ($mil) | Net Premium ($mil) | Net Income ($mil) |
|---|---|---|---|---|---|---|---|
| 9-17 | B+ | 2.41 | 2.01 | 143.4 | 58.2 | 384.2 | 1.5 |
| 9-16 | B+ | 2.24 | 1.87 | 133.9 | 54.2 | 362.4 | 8.1 |
| 2016 | B+ | 2.18 | 1.82 | 132.3 | 55.3 | 484.5 | 10.5 |
| 2015 | B+ | 1.82 | 1.51 | 122.8 | 44.9 | 452.0 | 15.2 |
| 2014 | B+ | 1.47 | 1.23 | 85.4 | 29.8 | 341.1 | 0.2 |
| 2013 | B+ | 1.97 | 1.64 | 62.0 | 29.5 | 231.5 | -0.1 |
| 2012 | B | 2.44 | 2.04 | 52.0 | 29.7 | 192.6 | 4.0 |

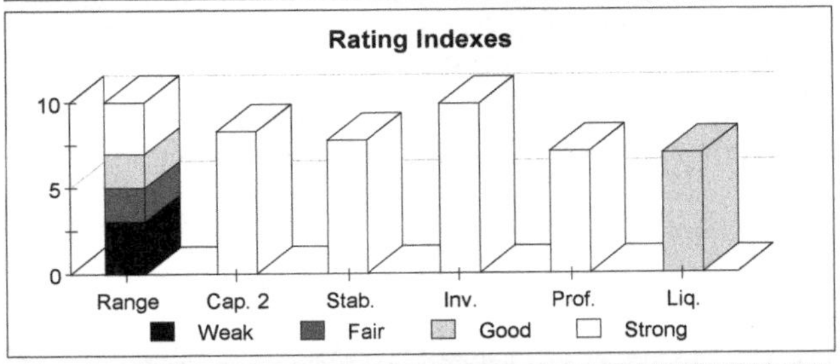


## PRIORITY HEALTH INS CO — B — Good

**Major Rating Factors:** Excellent profitability (7.5 on a scale of 0 to 10). Strong capitalization (8.6) based on excellent current risk-adjusted capital (severe loss scenario). High quality investment portfolio (8.7).
**Other Rating Factors:** Excellent liquidity (7.0) with ample operational cash flow and liquid investments.
**Principal Business:** Comp med (90%), dental (2%), other (9%)
**Mem Phys: 16:** 18,117 **15:** 17,729 **16 MLR** 81.2% **/ 16 Admin Exp** N/A
**Enroll(000): Q3 17:** 55 **16:** 64 **15:** 60 **Med Exp PMPM:** $285
**Principal Investments:** Nonaffiliate common stock (60%), cash and equiv (39%), other (1%)
**Provider Compensation ($000):** Contr fee ($115,414), FFS ($44,755), bonus arrang ($42,191)
**Total Member Encounters:** Phys (433,786), non-phys (25,969)
**Group Affiliation:** Spectrum Health System
**Licensed in:** MI
**Address:** 1231 East Beltline NE, Grand Rapids, MI 49525-4501
**Phone:** (616) 942-0954 **Dom State:** MI **Commenced Bus:** September 2004

| Data Date | Rating | RACR #1 | RACR #2 | Total Assets ($mil) | Capital ($mil) | Net Premium ($mil) | Net Income ($mil) |
|---|---|---|---|---|---|---|---|
| 9-17 | B | 2.63 | 2.19 | 122.8 | 51.8 | 179.4 | 3.3 |
| 9-16 | B- | 2.86 | 2.38 | 116.2 | 49.1 | 189.8 | 3.0 |
| 2016 | B- | 2.31 | 1.93 | 110.9 | 47.7 | 259.2 | 5.8 |
| 2015 | B- | 2.54 | 2.11 | 107.0 | 44.6 | 218.7 | 9.3 |
| 2014 | C+ | 3.55 | 2.96 | 120.3 | 59.5 | 216.9 | 5.5 |
| 2013 | C | 2.88 | 2.40 | 88.3 | 45.5 | 197.3 | 14.5 |
| 2012 | C | 1.65 | 1.38 | 74.8 | 30.9 | 224.4 | 1.1 |

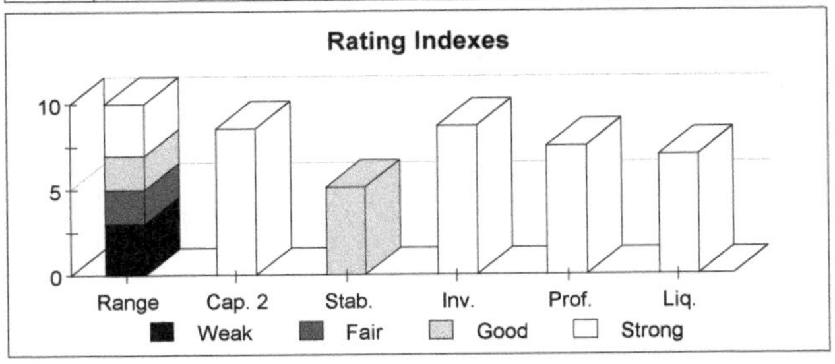

## PROFESSIONAL INSURANCE COMPANY D Weak

**Major Rating Factors:** Weak overall results on stability tests (1.6 on a scale of 0 to 10) including potential financial drain due to affiliation with Sun Life Assurance Group. Good quality investment portfolio (6.7) despite mixed results such as: no exposure to mortgages and large holdings of BBB rated bonds but minimal holdings in junk bonds. Good liquidity (6.9).
**Other Rating Factors:** Strong capitalization (10.0) based on excellent risk adjusted capital (severe loss scenario). Excellent profitability (8.1).
**Principal Business:** Individual health insurance (94%) and individual life insurance (6%).
**Principal Investments:** NonCMO investment grade bonds (78%), CMOs and structured securities (16%), policy loans (3%), and noninv. grade bonds (1%).
**Investments in Affiliates:** None
**Group Affiliation:** Sun Life Assurance Group
**Licensed in:** All states except AK, DE, ME, NH, NJ, NY, RI, VT, PR
**Commenced Business:** September 1937
**Address:** 350 North St Paul Street, Dallas, TX 75201
**Phone:** (781) 237-6030 **Domicile State:** TX **NAIC Code:** 68047

| Data Date | Rating | RACR #1 | RACR #2 | Total Assets ($mil) | Capital ($mil) | Net Premium ($mil) | Net Income ($mil) |
|---|---|---|---|---|---|---|---|
| 9-17 | D | 5.21 | 4.69 | 111.4 | 46.7 | 16.1 | 3.7 |
| 9-16 | D- | 4.62 | 3.73 | 110.8 | 41.2 | 18.4 | 2.6 |
| 2016 | D- | 4.68 | 4.11 | 110.0 | 42.0 | 24.5 | 4.5 |
| 2015 | C | 4.32 | 3.34 | 109.2 | 38.6 | 27.7 | 2.7 |
| 2014 | C | 4.02 | 2.88 | 108.9 | 35.9 | 31.6 | 1.8 |
| 2013 | C- | 3.16 | 2.21 | 105.1 | 29.5 | 37.1 | 3.4 |
| 2012 | D | 2.61 | 1.84 | 108.6 | 28.6 | 44.6 | 1.1 |

**Sun Life Assurance Group**
**Composite Group Rating: E+**

| Largest Group Members | Assets ($mil) | Rating |
|---|---|---|
| SUN LIFE ASR CO OF CANADA | 19563 | E+ |
| INDEPENDENCE LIFE ANNUITY CO | 3028 | D |
| SUN LIFE HEALTH INS CO | 485 | D |
| PROFESSIONAL INS CO | 110 | D |

## PROMINENCE HEALTHFIRST E Very Weak

**Major Rating Factors:** Weak profitability index (0.9 on a scale of 0 to 10). Fair liquidity (3.8) as cash resources may not be adequate to cover a spike in claims. Good quality investment portfolio (5.9).
**Other Rating Factors:** Good overall results on stability tests (6.0) based on healthy premium and capital growth during 2016. Strong capitalization index (8.0) based on excellent current risk-adjusted capital (severe loss scenario).
**Principal Business:** Comp med (80%), Medicare (20%)
**Mem Phys: 16:** 5,394 **15:** 5,444 **16 MLR** 94.9% **/ 16 Admin Exp** N/A
**Enroll(000): Q3 17:** 32 **16:** 41 **15:** 24 **Med Exp PMPM:** $360
**Principal Investments:** Cash and equiv (45%), affiliate common stock (38%), nonaffiliate common stock (15%), real estate (2%)
**Provider Compensation ($000):** Contr fee ($138,459), capitation ($4,941)
**Total Member Encounters:** Phys (167,899), non-phys (48,476)
**Group Affiliation:** Universal Health Services Inc
**Licensed in:** NV
**Address:** 1510 Meadow Wood Lane, Reno, NV 89502
**Phone:** (775) 770-9300 **Dom State:** NV **Commenced Bus:** June 1993

| Data Date | Rating | RACR #1 | RACR #2 | Total Assets ($mil) | Capital ($mil) | Net Premium ($mil) | Net Income ($mil) |
|---|---|---|---|---|---|---|---|
| 9-17 | E | 2.12 | 1.77 | 93.3 | 48.5 | 137.9 | -11.1 |
| 9-16 | E | 0.66 | 0.55 | 60.6 | 13.1 | 128.4 | -12.6 |
| 2016 | E | 1.41 | 1.17 | 91.9 | 34.3 | 169.5 | -29.7 |
| 2015 | E | 1.22 | 1.01 | 55.5 | 25.8 | 89.2 | -15.8 |
| 2014 | E | 1.15 | 0.96 | 52.7 | 26.1 | 105.4 | -10.0 |
| 2013 | D+ | 1.00 | 0.83 | 43.5 | 19.4 | 84.4 | -3.7 |
| 2012 | D+ | 0.82 | 0.69 | 31.2 | 15.3 | 84.7 | 0.0 |

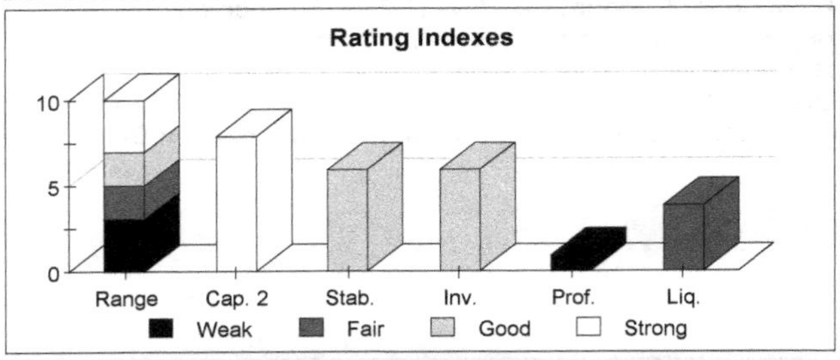


## PROMINENCE HEALTHFIRST OF TEXAS INC D+ Weak

**Major Rating Factors:** Weak profitability index (0.9 on a scale of 0 to 10). Good liquidity (6.9) with sufficient resources (cash flows and marketable investments) to handle a spike in claims. Strong capitalization (8.7) based on excellent current risk-adjusted capital (severe loss scenario).
**Other Rating Factors:** High quality investment portfolio (9.9).
**Principal Business:** Comp med (53%), Medicare (47%)
**Mem Phys: 16:** 1,654 **15:** 744 **16 MLR** 104.5% **/ 16 Admin Exp** N/A
**Enroll(000): Q3 17:** 7 **16:** 5 **15:** 0 **Med Exp PMPM:** $449
**Principal Investments:** Cash and equiv (97%), long-term bonds (3%)
**Provider Compensation ($000):** Contr fee ($19,796), capitation ($284)
**Total Member Encounters:** Phys (24,249), non-phys (6,324)
**Group Affiliation:** Universal Health Services Inc
**Licensed in:** TX
**Address:** 367 S Gulph Rd, King of Prussia, PA 19406
**Phone:** (775) 770-9320 **Dom State:** TX **Commenced Bus:** February 2014

| Data Date | Rating | RACR #1 | RACR #2 | Total Assets ($mil) | Capital ($mil) | Net Premium ($mil) | Net Income ($mil) |
|---|---|---|---|---|---|---|---|
| 9-17 | D+ | 2.73 | 2.28 | 23.1 | 10.7 | 32.0 | -3.0 |
| 9-16 | D | 4.54 | 3.79 | 11.3 | 3.8 | 17.6 | -4.1 |
| 2016 | D+ | 1.66 | 1.38 | 14.7 | 6.9 | 23.1 | -6.4 |
| 2015 | D | 9.14 | 7.61 | 8.9 | 7.4 | 3.6 | -2.6 |
| 2014 | N/A | N/A | N/A | 5.4 | 5.4 | N/A | -0.1 |
| 2013 | N/A | N/A | N/A | N/A | N/A | N/A | N/A |
| 2012 | N/A | N/A | N/A | N/A | N/A | N/A | N/A |

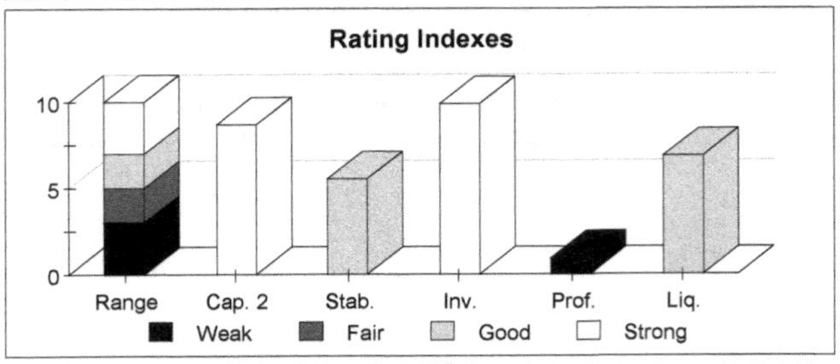

## PROMINENCE PREFERRED HEALTH INS CO — E — Very Weak

**Major Rating Factors:** Weak profitability index (1.9 on a scale of 0 to 10). Strong capitalization (10.0) based on excellent current risk-adjusted capital (severe loss scenario). High quality investment portfolio (9.9).
**Other Rating Factors:** Excellent liquidity (7.5) with ample operational cash flow and liquid investments.
**Principal Business:** Comp med (97%), dental (3%)
**Mem Phys: 16:** 10,591 **15:** 10,922 **16 MLR** 101.8% **/ 16 Admin Exp** N/A
**Enroll(000): Q3 17:** 2 **16:** 5 **15:** 12 **Med Exp PMPM:** $426
**Principal Investments:** Cash and equiv (95%), real estate (5%)
**Provider Compensation ($000):** Contr fee ($49,439), capitation ($650)
**Total Member Encounters:** Phys (64,263), non-phys (15,802)
**Group Affiliation:** Universal Health Services Inc
**Licensed in:** NV
**Address:** 1510 Meadow Wood Lane, Reno, NV 89502
**Phone:** (775) 770-9320 **Dom State:** NV **Commenced Bus:** April 2000

| Data Date | Rating | RACR #1 | RACR #2 | Total Assets ($mil) | Capital ($mil) | Net Premium ($mil) | Net Income ($mil) |
|---|---|---|---|---|---|---|---|
| 9-17 | E | 5.94 | 4.95 | 37.3 | 33.2 | 10.7 | 1.3 |
| 9-16 | E | 2.94 | 2.45 | 38.0 | 25.1 | 35.8 | -7.5 |
| 2016 | E | 4.88 | 4.06 | 37.0 | 28.7 | 44.4 | -4.7 |
| 2015 | E | 2.80 | 2.33 | 40.0 | 24.3 | 63.1 | -11.4 |
| 2014 | E | 2.05 | 1.71 | 36.2 | 19.7 | 74.2 | -11.1 |
| 2013 | D | 1.22 | 1.02 | 26.6 | 10.2 | 69.2 | -7.8 |
| 2012 | D | 0.72 | 0.60 | 17.0 | 6.7 | 80.9 | -3.4 |

Rating Indexes

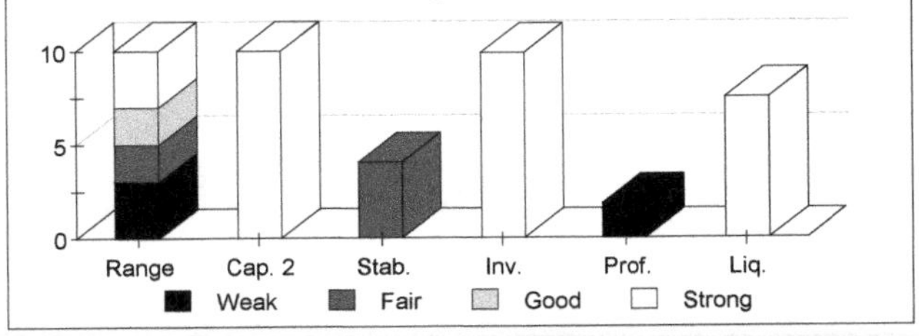


## PROSPECT HEALTH PLAN — E+ — Very Weak

**Major Rating Factors:** Fair capitalization index (3.4 on a scale of 0 to 10) based on weak current risk-adjusted capital (moderate loss scenario). Fair overall results on stability tests (3.9) based on poor risk diversification due to the company's size, an excessive 88% enrollment growth during the period. Excellent profitability (7.8)
**Other Rating Factors:** Excellent liquidity (7.0) with sufficient resources (cash flows and marketable investments) to handle a spike in claims.
**Principal Business:** Managed care (103%)
**Mem Phys: 16:** N/A **15:** N/A **16 MLR** 96.9% **/ 16 Admin Exp** N/A
**Enroll(000): Q3 17:** 51 **16:** 8 **15:** 4 **Med Exp PMPM:** $671
**Principal Investments ($000):** Cash and equiv ($7,985)
**Provider Compensation ($000):** None
**Total Member Encounters:** N/A
**Group Affiliation:** PHP Holdings Inc
**Licensed in:** CA
**Address:** 10780 Santa Monica Blvd #400, Los Angeles, CA 90025
**Phone:** (310) 228-3745 **Dom State:** CA **Commenced Bus:** November 2014

| Data Date | Rating | RACR #1 | RACR #2 | Total Assets ($mil) | Capital ($mil) | Net Premium ($mil) | Net Income ($mil) |
|---|---|---|---|---|---|---|---|
| 9-17 | E+ | 0.57 | 0.36 | 10.5 | 4.5 | 116.5 | 1.2 |
| 9-16 | U | 2.47 | 1.50 | 8.3 | 2.4 | 40.5 | 0.1 |
| 2016 | E | 0.31 | 0.20 | 21.4 | 2.6 | 58.1 | 0.3 |
| 2015 | U | 2.34 | 1.42 | 6.0 | 2.3 | 7.1 | 0.0 |
| 2014 | N/A | N/A | N/A | N/A | N/A | N/A | N/A |
| 2013 | N/A | N/A | N/A | N/A | N/A | N/A | N/A |
| 2012 | N/A | N/A | N/A | N/A | N/A | N/A | N/A |

Rating Indexes

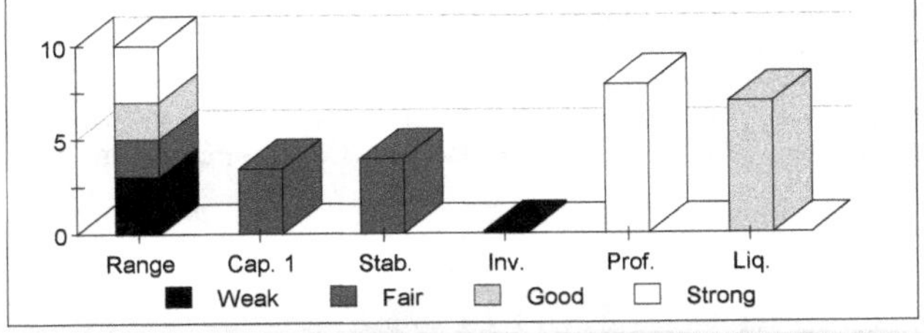


## PROVIDENCE HEALTH ASR — B — Good

**Major Rating Factors:** Good overall profitability index (6.2 on a scale of 0 to 10). Strong capitalization (10.0) based on excellent current risk-adjusted capital (severe loss scenario). High quality investment portfolio (9.9).
**Other Rating Factors:** Excellent liquidity (7.0) with ample operational cash flow and liquid investments.
**Principal Business:** Medicare (81%), Medicaid (19%)
**Mem Phys: 16:** 21,235 **15:** N/A **16 MLR** 91.3% **/ 16 Admin Exp** N/A
**Enroll(000): Q3 17:** 88 **16:** 85 **15:** 36 **Med Exp PMPM:** $594
**Principal Investments:** Long-term bonds (74%), cash and equiv (23%), nonaffiliate common stock (1%), other (2%)
**Provider Compensation ($000):** Bonus arrang ($256,978), contr fee ($204,110), FFS ($143,973), capitation ($17,035), other ($2,388)
**Total Member Encounters:** Phys (659,236), non-phys (779,873)
**Group Affiliation:** Providence Health & Services
**Licensed in:** OR, WA
**Address:** 4400 NE Halsey Bldg 2 Ste 690, Portland, OR 97213-1545
**Phone:** (503) 574-7500 **Dom State:** OR **Commenced Bus:** January 2004

| Data Date | Rating | RACR #1 | RACR #2 | Total Assets ($mil) | Capital ($mil) | Net Premium ($mil) | Net Income ($mil) |
|---|---|---|---|---|---|---|---|
| 9-17 | B | 5.01 | 4.17 | 489.9 | 250.8 | 539.0 | 38.4 |
| 9-16 | B | 24.13 | 20.11 | 409.3 | 246.9 | 500.4 | 14.2 |
| 2016 | B+ | 5.18 | 4.32 | 376.5 | 262.4 | 670.1 | 24.5 |
| 2015 | B- | 1.91 | 1.59 | 40.2 | 21.3 | 130.6 | 4.5 |
| 2014 | N/A | N/A | N/A | 29.0 | 17.1 | 117.6 | 7.6 |
| 2013 | N/A | N/A | N/A | 14.0 | 10.1 | 56.7 | -2.3 |
| 2012 | N/A | N/A | N/A | 20.2 | 10.4 | 62.6 | N/A |

Rating Indexes

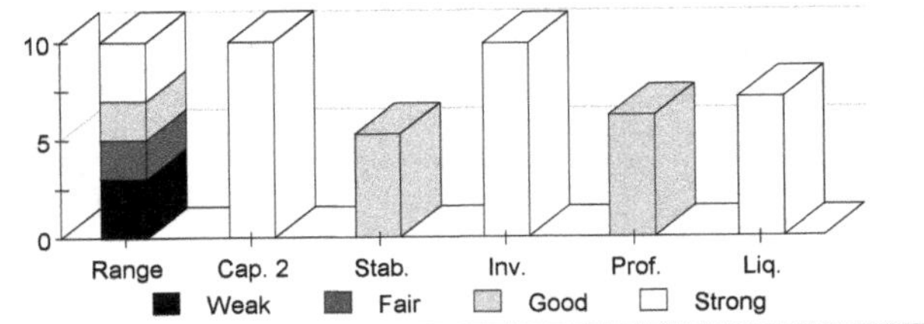

## PROVIDENCE HEALTH NETWORK E- Very Weak

**Major Rating Factors:** Weak profitability index (0.9 on a scale of 0 to 10). Poor capitalization index (0.0) based on weak current risk-adjusted capital (severe loss scenario). Weak overall results on stability tests (0.0).
**Other Rating Factors:** Weak liquidity (0.1) as a spike in claims may stretch capacity.
**Principal Business:** Managed care (98%)
**Mem Phys: 16:** N/A **15:** N/A **16 MLR** 112.7% **/ 16 Admin Exp** N/A
**Enroll(000): Q3 17:** 23 **16:** 15 **15:** 4 **Med Exp PMPM:** $599
**Principal Investments ($000):** Cash and equiv ($11,156)
**Provider Compensation ($000):** None
**Total Member Encounters:** N/A
**Group Affiliation:** None
**Licensed in:** CA
**Address:** 20555 Earl Street, Torrance, CA 90503
**Phone:** (805) 705-4451 **Dom State:** CA **Commenced Bus:** November 2013

| Data Date | Rating | RACR #1 | RACR #2 | Total Assets ($mil) | Capital ($mil) | Net Premium ($mil) | Net Income ($mil) |
|---|---|---|---|---|---|---|---|
| 9-17 | E- | 0.32 | 0.19 | 21.5 | 4.0 | 79.8 | -5.3 |
| 9-16 | E- | 0.01 | N/A | 19.0 | 0.1 | 68.2 | -3.5 |
| 2016 | E- | N/A | N/A | 11.7 | -10.1 | 89.7 | -13.7 |
| 2015 | E+ | 0.30 | 0.18 | 7.1 | 1.6 | 38.6 | -2.1 |
| 2014 | U | 0.40 | 0.24 | 5.4 | 1.7 | 33.8 | -0.6 |
| 2013 | N/A | N/A | N/A | 2.3 | 2.3 | N/A | N/A |
| 2012 | N/A | N/A | N/A | N/A | N/A | N/A | N/A |

Rating Indexes

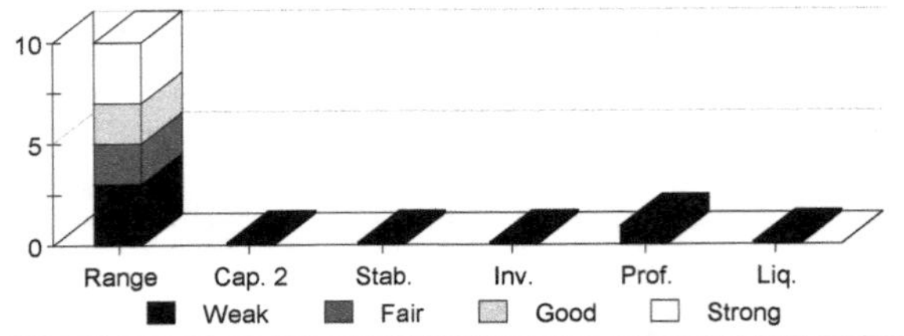


## PROVIDENCE HEALTH PLAN * A+ Excellent

**Major Rating Factors:** Strong capitalization index (10.0 on a scale of 0 to 10) based on excellent current risk-adjusted capital (severe loss scenario). High quality investment portfolio (7.2). Good overall results on stability tests (6.5).
**Other Rating Factors:** Good liquidity (6.4) with sufficient resources (cash flows and marketable investments) to handle a spike in claims. Weak profitability index (2.4).
**Principal Business:** Comp med (100%)
**Mem Phys: 16:** 31,942 **15:** 30,107 **16 MLR** 99.4% **/ 16 Admin Exp** N/A
**Enroll(000): Q3 17:** 269 **16:** 272 **15:** 218 **Med Exp PMPM:** $351
**Principal Investments:** Long-term bonds (44%), affiliate common stock (37%), cash and equiv (9%), real estate (8%), nonaffiliate common stock (1%), other (1%)
**Provider Compensation ($000):** Contr fee ($707,065), FFS ($264,457), capitation ($51,839), bonus arrang ($13,688), other ($1,559)
**Total Member Encounters:** Phys (884,454), non-phys (1,293,307)
**Group Affiliation:** Providence Health & Services
**Licensed in:** OR, WA
**Address:** 4400 NE Halsey Bldg # 2 Ste #, Portland, OR 97213-1545
**Phone:** (503) 574-7500 **Dom State:** OR **Commenced Bus:** January 1985

| Data Date | Rating | RACR #1 | RACR #2 | Total Assets ($mil) | Capital ($mil) | Net Premium ($mil) | Net Income ($mil) |
|---|---|---|---|---|---|---|---|
| 9-17 | A+ | 4.01 | 3.34 | 910.5 | 507.1 | 974.9 | 3.9 |
| 9-16 | A+ | 4.80 | 4.00 | 769.1 | 471.6 | 827.0 | 2.5 |
| 2016 | A+ | 3.65 | 3.05 | 750.7 | 466.2 | 1,107.6 | -28.1 |
| 2015 | A+ | 4.31 | 3.59 | 799.3 | 464.6 | 1,193.2 | -63.0 |
| 2014 | A+ | 5.73 | 4.77 | 762.1 | 530.4 | 1,102.1 | 22.3 |
| 2013 | A+ | 5.85 | 4.88 | 692.9 | 506.8 | 1,076.2 | 47.2 |
| 2012 | A+ | 4.43 | 3.69 | 654.4 | 470.3 | 1,057.6 | 49.8 |

Rating Indexes

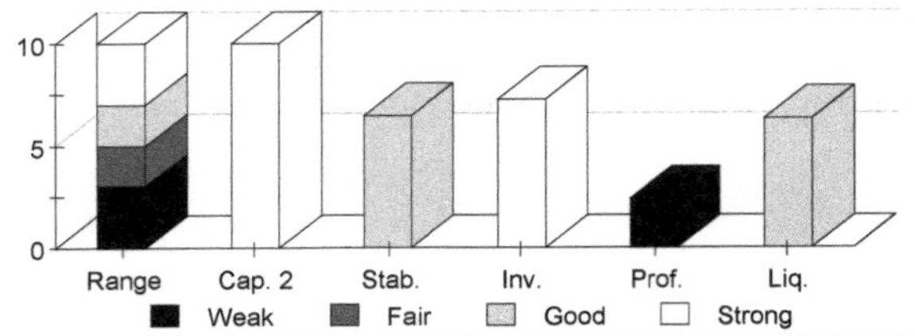


## PROVIDENT LIFE & ACCIDENT INSURANCE COMPANY C+ Fair

**Major Rating Factors:** Fair quality investment portfolio (4.8 on a scale of 0 to 10) with large holdings of BBB rated bonds in addition to junk bond exposure equal to 78% of capital. Fair overall results on stability tests (4.5). Strong overall capitalization (7.6) based on excellent risk adjusted capital (severe loss scenario). However, capital levels have fluctuated somewhat during past years.
**Other Rating Factors:** Excellent profitability (7.1). Excellent liquidity (7.4).
**Principal Business:** Individual health insurance (69%), individual life insurance (30%), and reinsurance (1%).
**Principal Investments:** NonCMO investment grade bonds (74%), noninv. grade bonds (8%), mortgages in good standing (6%), CMOs and structured securities (6%), and misc. investments (6%).
**Investments in Affiliates:** None
**Group Affiliation:** Unum Group
**Licensed in:** All states except NY
**Commenced Business:** May 1887
**Address:** 1 FOUNTAIN SQUARE, CHATTANOOGA, TN 37402-1330
**Phone:** (423) 294-1011 **Domicile State:** TN **NAIC Code:** 68195

| Data Date | Rating | RACR #1 | RACR #2 | Total Assets ($mil) | Capital ($mil) | Net Premium ($mil) | Net Income ($mil) |
|---|---|---|---|---|---|---|---|
| 9-17 | C+ | 2.81 | 1.41 | 8,207.4 | 738.0 | 600.2 | 128.5 |
| 9-16 | C+ | 2.75 | 1.39 | 8,283.2 | 737.1 | 669.9 | 143.5 |
| 2016 | C+ | 2.76 | 1.38 | 8,272.6 | 728.2 | 840.8 | 191.7 |
| 2015 | C+ | 2.74 | 1.38 | 8,325.3 | 727.5 | 869.4 | 178.9 |
| 2014 | C+ | 2.72 | 1.37 | 8,297.3 | 720.0 | 889.8 | 187.1 |
| 2013 | C+ | 2.55 | 1.28 | 8,347.6 | 699.7 | 898.5 | 166.4 |
| 2012 | C+ | 2.30 | 1.16 | 8,452.0 | 642.8 | 960.1 | 168.9 |

Rating Indexes

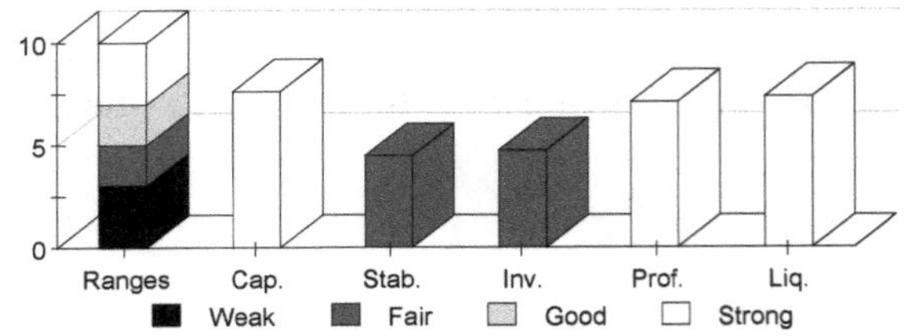

## PROVIDENT LIFE & CASUALTY INSURANCE COMPANY — B- — Good

**Major Rating Factors:** Good overall results on stability tests (5.3 on a scale of 0 to 10) despite fair financial strength of affiliated Unum Group. Other stability subfactors include excellent operational trends and excellent risk diversification. Fair quality investment portfolio (4.6) with large holdings of BBB rated bonds in addition to moderate junk bond exposure. Strong capitalization (9.6) based on excellent risk adjusted capital (severe loss scenario).
**Other Rating Factors:** Excellent profitability (7.2). Excellent liquidity (7.1).
**Principal Business:** Individual health insurance (93%), reinsurance (4%), and individual life insurance (2%).
**Principal Investments:** NonCMO investment grade bonds (80%), noninv. grade bonds (9%), CMOs and structured securities (6%), and mortgages in good standing (3%).
**Investments in Affiliates:** None
**Group Affiliation:** Unum Group
**Licensed in:** AK, AR, CO, CT, DC, DE, GA, HI, ID, IL, IA, KY, LA, MA, MS, MO, NE, NH, NJ, NM, NY, NC, ND, OH, OK, PA, RI, SC, SD, TN, VA, WA
**Commenced Business:** January 1952
**Address:** 1 FOUNTAIN SQUARE, CHATTANOOGA, TN 37402-1330
**Phone:** (423) 294-1011 **Domicile State:** TN **NAIC Code:** 68209

| Data Date | Rating | RACR #1 | RACR #2 | Total Assets ($mil) | Capital ($mil) | Net Premium ($mil) | Net Income ($mil) |
|---|---|---|---|---|---|---|---|
| 9-17 | B- | 4.96 | 2.72 | 760.2 | 165.3 | 69.9 | 23.0 |
| 9-16 | B- | 4.65 | 2.49 | 772.1 | 156.2 | 68.2 | 9.1 |
| 2016 | B- | 4.43 | 2.38 | 753.2 | 141.7 | 90.3 | 13.7 |
| 2015 | B- | 4.65 | 2.50 | 755.8 | 147.2 | 87.0 | 21.3 |
| 2014 | B- | 4.38 | 2.32 | 767.2 | 139.4 | 84.5 | 6.8 |
| 2013 | B- | 4.65 | 2.46 | 764.1 | 150.9 | 86.2 | 18.3 |
| 2012 | B- | 4.43 | 2.33 | 777.6 | 145.9 | 87.8 | 17.8 |

**Unum Group**
**Composite Group Rating: C+**

| Largest Group Members | Assets ($mil) | Rating |
|---|---|---|
| UNUM LIFE INS CO OF AMERICA | 21078 | C+ |
| PROVIDENT LIFE ACCIDENT INS CO | 8273 | C+ |
| PAUL REVERE LIFE INS CO | 3790 | C+ |
| FIRST UNUM LIFE INS CO | 3261 | C+ |
| COLONIAL LIFE ACCIDENT INS CO | 3144 | C+ |

## PROVIDER PARTNERS HEALTH PLAN INC — E- — Very Weak

**Major Rating Factors:** Weak profitability index (0.0 on a scale of 0 to 10). Poor capitalization (0.0) based on weak current risk-adjusted capital (severe loss scenario). Weak liquidity (1.3) as a spike in claims may stretch capacity.
**Other Rating Factors:** High quality investment portfolio (8.7).
**Principal Business:** Medicare (100%)
**Mem Phys: 16:** 1,492 **15:** N/A **16 MLR** 88.3% **/ 16 Admin Exp** N/A
**Enroll(000): Q3 17:** 0 **16:** 0 **15:** N/A **Med Exp PMPM:** $1,762
**Principal Investments:** Cash and equiv (100%)
**Provider Compensation ($000):** Contr fee ($148), capitation ($117)
**Total Member Encounters:** N/A
**Group Affiliation:** Provider Partners Health Group
**Licensed in:** MD
**Address:** 1922 GREENSPRING DR STE 6, TIMONIUM, MD 21093
**Phone:** (410) 308-2300 **Dom State:** MD **Commenced Bus:** February 2015

| Data Date | Rating | RACR #1 | RACR #2 | Total Assets ($mil) | Capital ($mil) | Net Premium ($mil) | Net Income ($mil) |
|---|---|---|---|---|---|---|---|
| 9-17 | E- | 0.29 | 0.24 | 3.3 | 0.8 | 4.9 | -1.1 |
| 9-16 | N/A | N/A | N/A | 1.9 | 1.6 | 0.2 | -0.7 |
| 2016 | E- | 0.31 | 0.26 | 1.8 | 0.8 | 0.7 | -1.8 |
| 2015 | N/A | N/A | N/A | 1.8 | 1.5 | N/A | -0.9 |
| 2014 | N/A | N/A | N/A | N/A | N/A | N/A | N/A |
| 2013 | N/A | N/A | N/A | N/A | N/A | N/A | N/A |
| 2012 | N/A | N/A | N/A | N/A | N/A | N/A | N/A |

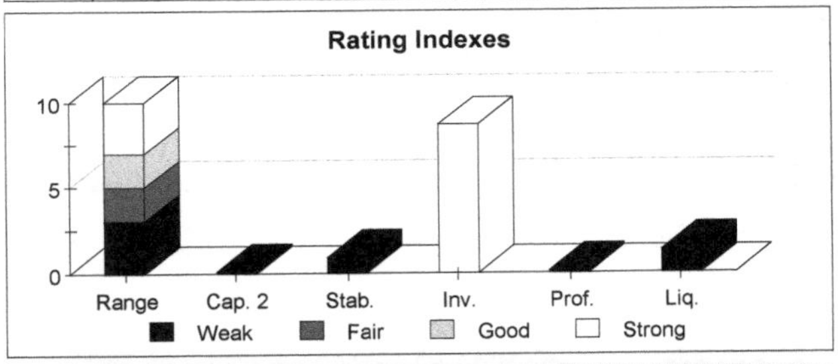


## PUPIL BENEFITS PLAN INC — C- — Fair

**Major Rating Factors:** Good quality investment portfolio (6.1 on a scale of 0 to 10). Excellent profitability (8.0). Strong capitalization (10.0) based on excellent current risk-adjusted capital (severe loss scenario).
**Other Rating Factors:** Excellent liquidity (7.7) with ample operational cash flow and liquid investments.
**Principal Business:** Other (100%)
**Mem Phys: 16:** N/A **15:** N/A **16 MLR** 55.4% **/ 16 Admin Exp** N/A
**Enroll(000): Q3 17:** 657 **16:** 684 **15:** 794 **Med Exp PMPM:** $0
**Principal Investments:** Cash and equiv (62%), long-term bonds (29%), nonaffiliate common stock (8%), real estate (2%)
**Provider Compensation ($000):** FFS ($6,220)
**Total Member Encounters:** N/A
**Group Affiliation:** Pupil Benefits Plan Inc
**Licensed in:** NY
**Address:** 101 DUTCH MEADOWS LANE, GLENVILLE, NY 12302
**Phone:** (518) 377-5144 **Dom State:** NE **Commenced Bus:** July 1941

| Data Date | Rating | RACR #1 | RACR #2 | Total Assets ($mil) | Capital ($mil) | Net Premium ($mil) | Net Income ($mil) |
|---|---|---|---|---|---|---|---|
| 9-17 | C- | 4.52 | 3.77 | 16.6 | 6.1 | 6.7 | 1.2 |
| 9-16 | C- | 2.85 | 2.38 | 16.6 | 4.6 | 7.4 | 1.5 |
| 2016 | C- | 3.48 | 2.90 | 14.3 | 4.7 | 9.6 | 1.6 |
| 2015 | C- | 1.88 | 1.56 | 14.3 | 3.1 | 9.8 | 1.2 |
| 2014 | C- | 0.98 | 0.82 | 12.4 | 1.9 | 9.0 | -0.1 |
| 2013 | C- | 1.25 | 1.04 | 11.5 | 1.9 | 8.3 | 0.0 |
| 2012 | C- | 1.34 | 1.11 | 10.6 | 1.7 | 7.3 | 0.1 |

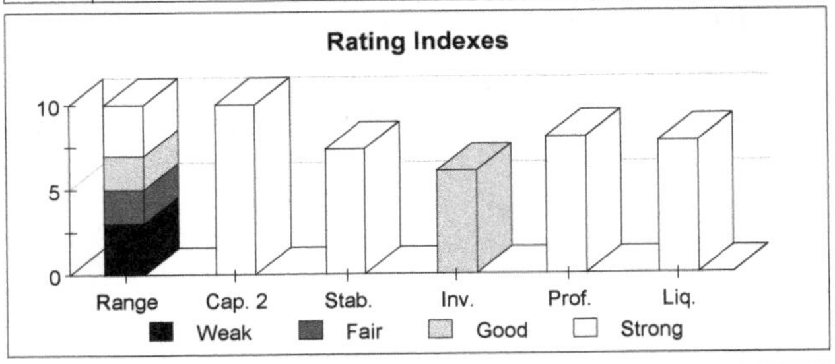

## QCA HEALTH PLAN INC — C- — Fair

**Major Rating Factors:** Fair overall results on stability tests (3.9 on a scale of 0 to 10) based on inconsistent enrollment growth in the past five years due to declines in 2013 and 2015. Fair liquidity (4.2) as cash resources may not be adequate to cover a spike in claims. Weak profitability index (1.5).
**Other Rating Factors:** Strong capitalization index (7.6) based on excellent current risk-adjusted capital (severe loss scenario). High quality investment portfolio (9.9).
**Principal Business:** Comp med (99%), FEHB (1%)
**Mem Phys: 16:** 18,028 **15:** 16,399 **16 MLR** 97.1% **/ 16 Admin Exp** N/A
**Enroll(000): Q3 17:** 46 **16:** 57 **15:** 46 **Med Exp PMPM:** $322
**Principal Investments:** Long-term bonds (68%), cash and equiv (29%), other (3%)
**Provider Compensation ($000):** Contr fee ($174,179), FFS ($33,626)
**Total Member Encounters:** Phys (496,490), non-phys (289,483)
**Group Affiliation:** Catholic Health Initiatives
**Licensed in:** AR
**Address:** 12615 Chenal Parkway Suite 300, Little Rock, AR 72211
**Phone:** (501) 228-7111 **Dom State:** AR **Commenced Bus:** July 1996

| Data Date | Rating | RACR #1 | RACR #2 | Total Assets ($mil) | Capital ($mil) | Net Premium ($mil) | Net Income ($mil) |
|---|---|---|---|---|---|---|---|
| 9-17 | C- | 1.85 | 1.54 | 72.5 | 40.4 | 147.6 | 8.2 |
| 9-16 | D+ | 1.60 | 1.33 | 68.0 | 29.0 | 162.4 | -8.3 |
| 2016 | D+ | 1.46 | 1.22 | 75.2 | 31.9 | 214.8 | -18.3 |
| 2015 | C- | 2.21 | 1.84 | 81.3 | 39.6 | 205.8 | 9.3 |
| 2014 | C- | 1.05 | 0.87 | 64.0 | 20.3 | 159.8 | -5.2 |
| 2013 | C- | 0.78 | 0.65 | 31.0 | 12.8 | 141.3 | -3.6 |
| 2012 | C- | 0.80 | 0.66 | 39.1 | 12.9 | 147.2 | -6.2 |

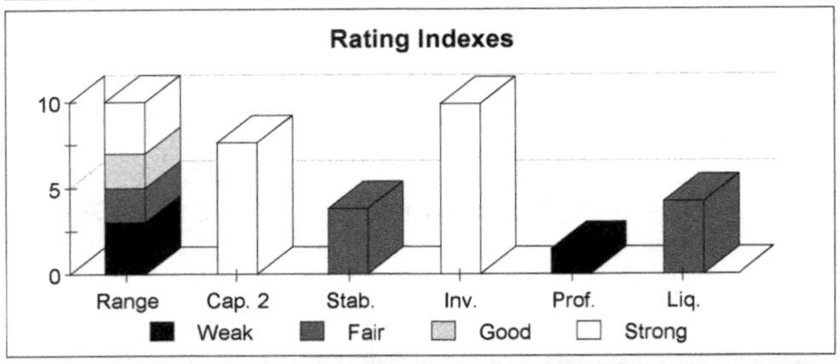


## QCC INS CO — C — Fair

**Major Rating Factors:** Weak profitability index (2.3 on a scale of 0 to 10). Good quality investment portfolio (5.5). Good liquidity (6.5) with sufficient resources (cash flows and marketable investments) to handle a spike in claims.
**Other Rating Factors:** Strong capitalization (9.6) based on excellent current risk-adjusted capital (severe loss scenario).
**Principal Business:** Comp med (90%), Medicare (6%), dental (2%), other (3%)
**Mem Phys: 16:** 59,300 **15:** 55,924 **16 MLR** 80.0% **/ 16 Admin Exp** N/A
**Enroll(000): Q3 17:** 314 **16:** 354 **15:** 363 **Med Exp PMPM:** $414
**Principal Investments:** Long-term bonds (58%), nonaffiliate common stock (36%), cash and equiv (3%), other (3%)
**Provider Compensation ($000):** Contr fee ($1,742,834), FFS ($47,063), capitation ($23,064), bonus arrang ($8,340)
**Total Member Encounters:** Phys (7,079,372), non-phys (1,267,783)
**Group Affiliation:** Independence Health Group Inc
**Licensed in:** AZ, CO, DC, DE, FL, GA, IN, KS, KY, LA, MD, MA, MS, MT, NE, NV, NM, ND, OH, OK, PA, SC, SD, TN, TX, UT, VT, WA, WV
**Address:** 1901 Market St, Philadelphia, PA 19103-1480
**Phone:** (215) 241-2400 **Dom State:** PA **Commenced Bus:** December 1981

| Data Date | Rating | RACR #1 | RACR #2 | Total Assets ($mil) | Capital ($mil) | Net Premium ($mil) | Net Income ($mil) |
|---|---|---|---|---|---|---|---|
| 9-17 | C | 3.44 | 2.87 | 1,160.7 | 473.9 | 1,658.3 | 43.1 |
| 9-16 | C | 2.81 | 2.35 | 1,151.9 | 361.4 | 1,704.0 | -37.0 |
| 2016 | C | 2.96 | 2.46 | 1,157.6 | 401.0 | 2,248.6 | -10.6 |
| 2015 | C | 3.13 | 2.61 | 1,161.6 | 408.5 | 2,246.3 | -57.6 |
| 2014 | C+ | 3.68 | 3.07 | 1,100.8 | 496.0 | 2,309.2 | 5.5 |
| 2013 | B | 4.93 | 4.11 | 1,211.6 | 730.7 | 2,002.2 | 36.1 |
| 2012 | B | 5.23 | 4.36 | 1,335.2 | 711.5 | 2,146.4 | 58.3 |

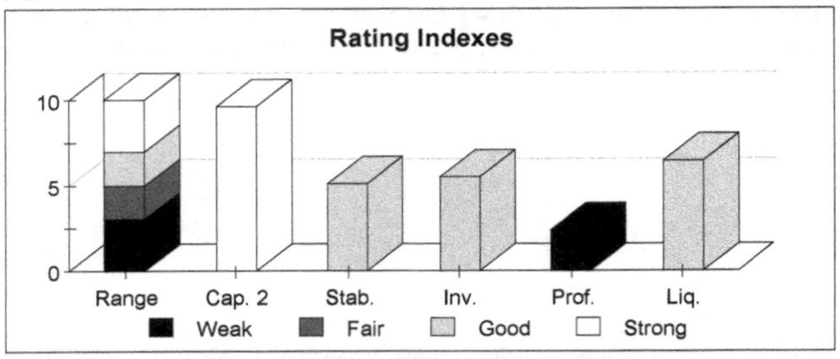


## QUALCHOICE ADVANTAGE INC — C- — Fair

**Major Rating Factors:** Fair profitability index (3.4 on a scale of 0 to 10). Good liquidity (6.7) with sufficient resources (cash flows and marketable investments) to handle a spike in claims. Strong capitalization (7.8) based on excellent current risk-adjusted capital (severe loss scenario).
**Other Rating Factors:** High quality investment portfolio (9.9).
**Principal Business:** Medicare (100%)
**Mem Phys: 16:** 1,860 **15:** N/A **16 MLR** 86.8% **/ 16 Admin Exp** N/A
**Enroll(000): Q3 17:** 2 **16:** 2 **15:** N/A **Med Exp PMPM:** $475
**Principal Investments:** Long-term bonds (74%), cash and equiv (26%)
**Provider Compensation ($000):** Contr fee ($8,712), capitation ($199), other ($1,530)
**Total Member Encounters:** Phys (18,460), non-phys (5,489)
**Group Affiliation:** Catholic Health Initiatives
**Licensed in:** AR
**Address:** 12615 Chenal Parkway Ste 300, Little Rock, AR 72211
**Phone:** (866) 789-7747 **Dom State:** AR **Commenced Bus:** April 2015

| Data Date | Rating | RACR #1 | RACR #2 | Total Assets ($mil) | Capital ($mil) | Net Premium ($mil) | Net Income ($mil) |
|---|---|---|---|---|---|---|---|
| 9-17 | C- | 1.96 | 1.63 | 6.7 | 3.7 | 8.6 | 0.4 |
| 9-16 | N/A | N/A | N/A | 6.2 | 3.8 | 9.1 | 0.3 |
| 2016 | C- | 1.74 | 1.45 | 5.1 | 3.3 | 12.0 | -0.2 |
| 2015 | N/A | N/A | N/A | 3.5 | 3.5 | N/A | N/A |
| 2014 | N/A | N/A | N/A | N/A | N/A | N/A | N/A |
| 2013 | N/A | N/A | N/A | N/A | N/A | N/A | N/A |
| 2012 | N/A | N/A | N/A | N/A | N/A | N/A | N/A |

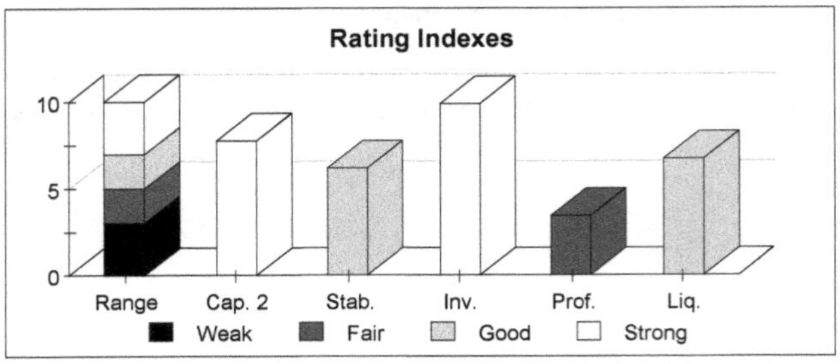

## QUALCHOICE L&H INS CO — D — Weak

**Major Rating Factors:** Weak profitability index (0.9 on a scale of 0 to 10). Good liquidity (5.4) with sufficient resources (cash flows and marketable investments) to handle a spike in claims. Strong capitalization (7.6) based on excellent current risk-adjusted capital (severe loss scenario).
**Other Rating Factors:** High quality investment portfolio (9.9).
**Principal Business:** Comp med (97%), med supp (3%)
**Mem Phys: 16:** 18,028 **15:** 16,399 **16 MLR** 102.8% **/ 16 Admin Exp** N/A
**Enroll(000): Q3 17:** 28 **16:** 38 **15:** 23 **Med Exp PMPM:** $345
**Principal Investments:** Long-term bonds (51%), cash and equiv (49%)
**Provider Compensation ($000):** Contr fee ($106,656), FFS ($20,585)
**Total Member Encounters:** Phys (321,709), non-phys (151,220)
**Group Affiliation:** Catholic Health Initiatives
**Licensed in:** AR, NE
**Address:** 12615 Chenal Parkway Ste 300, Little Rock, AR 72211
**Phone:** (501) 219-5109 **Dom State:** AR **Commenced Bus:** April 1965

| Data Date | Rating | RACR #1 | RACR #2 | Total Assets ($mil) | Capital ($mil) | Net Premium ($mil) | Net Income ($mil) |
|---|---|---|---|---|---|---|---|
| 9-17 | D | 1.83 | 1.53 | 50.0 | 28.1 | 87.6 | -2.1 |
| 9-16 | D- | 1.21 | 1.01 | 34.4 | 11.2 | 92.4 | -16.0 |
| 2016 | D- | 1.97 | 1.64 | 51.1 | 29.9 | 129.2 | -15.5 |
| 2015 | C | 2.57 | 2.15 | 44.7 | 21.3 | 61.9 | -5.1 |
| 2014 | C | 1.82 | 1.52 | 7.5 | 6.3 | 6.1 | -0.9 |
| 2013 | C | 0.90 | 0.75 | 2.4 | 1.7 | 6.1 | 0.0 |
| 2012 | C- | 1.00 | 0.84 | 2.5 | 1.7 | 5.9 | -0.1 |

Rating Indexes

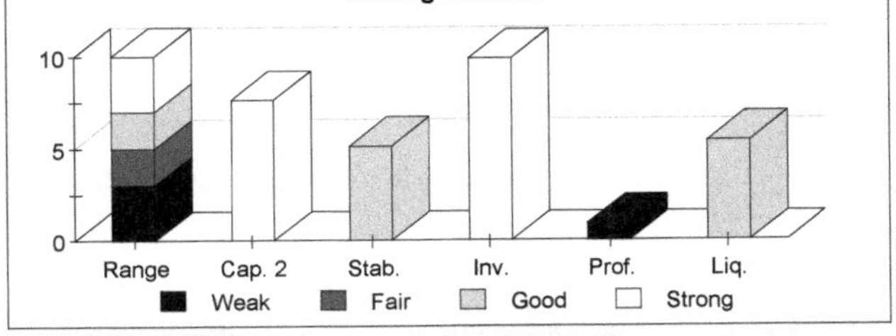


## QUALITY HEALTH PLANS OF NEW YORK INC — E+ — Very Weak

**Major Rating Factors:** Weak profitability index (0.0 on a scale of 0 to 10). Poor capitalization (0.0) based on weak current risk-adjusted capital (severe loss scenario). Weak liquidity (0.0) as a spike in claims may stretch capacity.
**Other Rating Factors:** High quality investment portfolio (9.9).
**Principal Business:** Medicare (100%)
**Mem Phys: 15:** 4,667 **14:** 2,962 **15 MLR** 97.6% **/ 15 Admin Exp** N/A
**Enroll(000): Q3 16:** 2 **15:** 1 **14:** 0 **Med Exp PMPM:** $777
**Principal Investments:** Cash and equiv (100%)
**Provider Compensation ($000):** FFS ($3,353), capitation ($256), other ($903)
**Total Member Encounters:** Phys (14,251), non-phys (1,479)
**Group Affiliation:** QHP Group Inc
**Licensed in:** NY
**Address:** 2805 Veterans Memorial Hwy #17, Ronkonkoma, NY 11779
**Phone:** (813) 463-0099 **Dom State:** NY **Commenced Bus:** January 2010

| Data Date | Rating | RACR #1 | RACR #2 | Total Assets ($mil) | Capital ($mil) | Net Premium ($mil) | Net Income ($mil) |
|---|---|---|---|---|---|---|---|
| 9-16 | E+ | 0.18 | 0.15 | 5.4 | 0.7 | 16.1 | 1.6 |
| 9-15 | D- | 0.46 | 0.38 | 2.1 | 0.6 | 4.9 | 0.2 |
| 2015 | E+ | 0.18 | 0.15 | 5.3 | 0.7 | 6.7 | -2.8 |
| 2014 | D- | 0.62 | 0.51 | 2.1 | 0.8 | 2.4 | -0.7 |
| 2013 | E | 0.41 | 0.34 | 2.5 | 0.2 | 1.2 | -2.9 |
| 2012 | E- | 2.42 | 2.02 | 2.4 | 1.5 | 0.2 | -2.6 |
| 2011 | N/A | N/A | N/A | 1.7 | 1.5 | 0.1 | N/A |

Rating Indexes

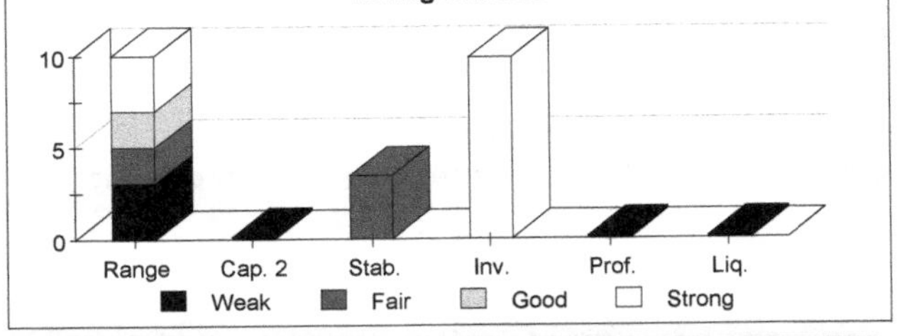


## REGENCE BL CROSS BL SHIELD OREGON * — B+ — Good

**Major Rating Factors:** Good overall profitability index (6.1 on a scale of 0 to 10). Good quality investment portfolio (6.3). Good liquidity (6.8) with sufficient resources (cash flows and marketable investments) to handle a spike in claims.
**Other Rating Factors:** Strong capitalization (10.0) based on excellent current risk-adjusted capital (severe loss scenario).
**Principal Business:** Comp med (41%), Medicare (32%), FEHB (21%), med supp (1%), other (3%)
**Mem Phys: 16:** 25,686 **15:** 21,875 **16 MLR** 83.4% **/ 16 Admin Exp** N/A
**Enroll(000): Q3 17:** 517 **16:** 483 **15:** 486 **Med Exp PMPM:** $259
**Principal Investments:** Long-term bonds (69%), nonaffiliate common stock (29%), real estate (1%), affiliate common stock (1%)
**Provider Compensation ($000):** Contr fee ($1,048,580), FFS ($421,291), bonus arrang ($1,351), capitation ($91), other ($14,376)
**Total Member Encounters:** Phys (4,641,081), non-phys (5,272,582)
**Group Affiliation:** Cambia Health Solutions Inc
**Licensed in:** OR, WA
**Address:** 100 SW MARKET St, PORTLAND, OR 97201
**Phone:** (503) 225-5221 **Dom State:** OR **Commenced Bus:** June 1942

| Data Date | Rating | RACR #1 | RACR #2 | Total Assets ($mil) | Capital ($mil) | Net Premium ($mil) | Net Income ($mil) |
|---|---|---|---|---|---|---|---|
| 9-17 | B+ | 7.24 | 6.04 | 1,253.4 | 730.8 | 1,431.6 | 65.0 |
| 9-16 | B+ | 6.19 | 5.16 | 1,142.2 | 661.1 | 1,339.5 | 22.9 |
| 2016 | B+ | 6.57 | 5.48 | 1,092.9 | 661.0 | 1,780.8 | 30.2 |
| 2015 | B+ | 5.99 | 4.99 | 1,045.8 | 639.2 | 1,877.6 | 25.8 |
| 2014 | B+ | 5.91 | 4.93 | 1,039.7 | 635.3 | 1,871.4 | 35.9 |
| 2013 | B+ | 5.87 | 4.89 | 1,008.2 | 627.3 | 1,891.2 | 18.0 |
| 2012 | B+ | 5.92 | 4.94 | 938.4 | 565.0 | 1,852.5 | 43.2 |

Rating Indexes

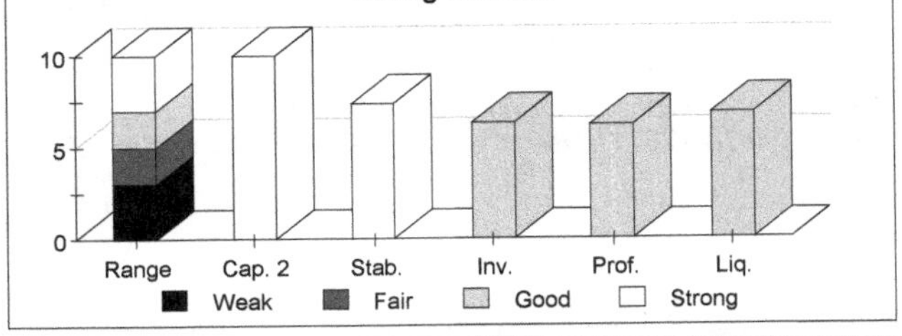

## REGENCE BLUE CROSS BLUE SHIELD OF UT — B- — Good

**Major Rating Factors:** Good overall profitability index (5.5 on a scale of 0 to 10). Good quality investment portfolio (5.5). Good liquidity (6.8) with sufficient resources (cash flows and marketable investments) to handle a spike in claims.
**Other Rating Factors:** Strong capitalization (10.0) based on excellent current risk-adjusted capital (severe loss scenario).
**Principal Business:** Comp med (42%), FEHB (40%), Medicare (12%), med supp (4%), other (2%)
**Mem Phys: 16:** 12,838 **15:** 12,800 **16 MLR** 86.8% **/ 16 Admin Exp** N/A
**Enroll(000): Q3 17:** 216 **16:** 217 **15:** 236 **Med Exp PMPM:** $333
**Principal Investments:** Long-term bonds (77%), nonaffiliate common stock (17%), affiliate common stock (5%), real estate (1%), cash and equiv (1%)
**Provider Compensation ($000):** Contr fee ($586,232), FFS ($302,512), bonus arrang ($794), capitation ($176), other ($5,945)
**Total Member Encounters:** Phys (2,839,838), non-phys (2,890,426)
**Group Affiliation:** Cambia Health Solutions Inc
**Licensed in:** UT
**Address:** 2890 EAST COTTONWOOD PARKWAY, SALT LAKE CITY, UT 84121-7035
**Phone:** (801) 333-2000 **Dom State:** UT **Commenced Bus:** January 1945

| Data Date | Rating | RACR #1 | RACR #2 | Total Assets ($mil) | Capital ($mil) | Net Premium ($mil) | Net Income ($mil) |
|---|---|---|---|---|---|---|---|
| 9-17 | B- | 6.63 | 5.52 | 622.8 | 323.9 | 771.9 | 48.3 |
| 9-16 | C+ | 4.79 | 3.99 | 586.7 | 252.3 | 772.2 | -9.3 |
| 2016 | B- | 5.59 | 4.66 | 564.0 | 271.2 | 1,020.1 | 8.6 |
| 2015 | B- | 4.97 | 4.14 | 529.7 | 261.8 | 1,084.9 | 3.1 |
| 2014 | B | 5.11 | 4.26 | 524.1 | 269.8 | 1,120.7 | -3.3 |
| 2013 | B | 5.44 | 4.53 | 534.8 | 287.5 | 1,086.4 | 8.6 |
| 2012 | B | 5.98 | 4.99 | 511.8 | 279.9 | 1,000.0 | 112.7 |

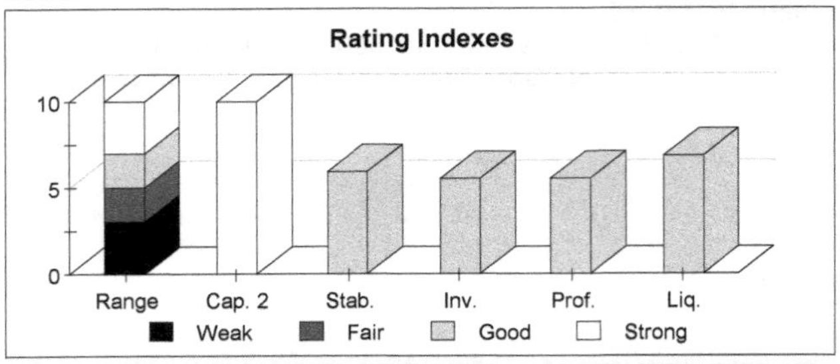


## REGENCE BLUESHIELD — B — Good

**Major Rating Factors:** Good overall profitability index (5.4 on a scale of 0 to 10). Good quality investment portfolio (5.6). Good liquidity (6.8) with sufficient resources (cash flows and marketable investments) to handle a spike in claims.
**Other Rating Factors:** Strong capitalization (10.0) based on excellent current risk-adjusted capital (severe loss scenario).
**Principal Business:** Comp med (65%), FEHB (15%), Medicare (14%), med supp (5%)
**Mem Phys: 16:** 36,728 **15:** 36,558 **16 MLR** 80.3% **/ 16 Admin Exp** N/A
**Enroll(000): Q3 17:** 427 **16:** 390 **15:** 403 **Med Exp PMPM:** $295
**Principal Investments:** Long-term bonds (60%), nonaffiliate common stock (24%), affiliate common stock (10%), pref stock (3%), cash and equiv (2%), real estate (1%)
**Provider Compensation ($000):** Contr fee ($946,980), FFS ($410,423), bonus arrang ($1,364), capitation ($153)
**Total Member Encounters:** Phys (4,710,684), non-phys (5,639,705)
**Group Affiliation:** Cambia Health Solutions Inc
**Licensed in:** WA
**Address:** 1800 NINTH Ave, SEATTLE, WA 98101
**Phone:** (206) 464-3600 **Dom State:** WA **Commenced Bus:** April 1933

| Data Date | Rating | RACR #1 | RACR #2 | Total Assets ($mil) | Capital ($mil) | Net Premium ($mil) | Net Income ($mil) |
|---|---|---|---|---|---|---|---|
| 9-17 | B | 9.01 | 7.51 | 1,806.9 | 1,181.5 | 1,484.4 | 75.9 |
| 9-16 | B | 8.33 | 6.95 | 1,713.9 | 1,136.4 | 1,246.9 | 43.3 |
| 2016 | B | 8.78 | 7.31 | 1,652.3 | 1,150.7 | 1,673.9 | 53.7 |
| 2015 | B | 8.18 | 6.81 | 1,611.9 | 1,114.6 | 1,784.1 | 11.8 |
| 2014 | B | 8.12 | 6.77 | 1,640.5 | 1,145.6 | 1,826.3 | 17.1 |
| 2013 | B+ | 7.22 | 6.02 | 1,692.1 | 1,178.5 | 2,190.6 | 48.3 |
| 2012 | B+ | 7.15 | 5.96 | 1,583.5 | 1,079.7 | 2,157.8 | 30.0 |

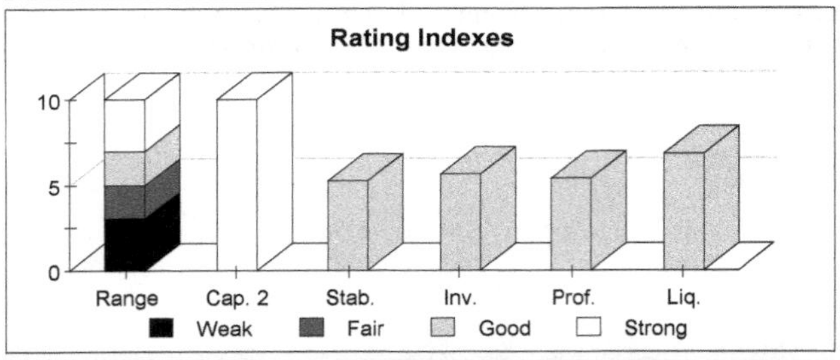


## REGENCE BLUESHIELD OF IDAHO INC — B — Good

**Major Rating Factors:** Good quality investment portfolio (6.0 on a scale of 0 to 10). Good liquidity (6.7) with sufficient resources (cash flows and marketable investments) to handle a spike in claims. Fair profitability index (4.7).
**Other Rating Factors:** Strong capitalization (10.0) based on excellent current risk-adjusted capital (severe loss scenario).
**Principal Business:** Comp med (74%), Medicare (15%), FEHB (4%), med supp (3%), other (3%)
**Mem Phys: 16:** 9,285 **15:** 8,863 **16 MLR** 79.0% **/ 16 Admin Exp** N/A
**Enroll(000): Q3 17:** 110 **16:** 107 **15:** 107 **Med Exp PMPM:** $261
**Principal Investments:** Long-term bonds (72%), nonaffiliate common stock (17%), real estate (6%), cash and equiv (4%), affiliate common stock (1%)
**Provider Compensation ($000):** Contr fee ($204,743), FFS ($122,084), capitation ($545), bonus arrang ($429), other ($6,585)
**Total Member Encounters:** Phys (1,009,547), non-phys (1,262,929)
**Group Affiliation:** Cambia Health Solutions Inc
**Licensed in:** ID, WA
**Address:** 1602 21ST Ave, LEWISTON, ID 83501-4061
**Phone:** (208) 746-2671 **Dom State:** ID **Commenced Bus:** April 1946

| Data Date | Rating | RACR #1 | RACR #2 | Total Assets ($mil) | Capital ($mil) | Net Premium ($mil) | Net Income ($mil) |
|---|---|---|---|---|---|---|---|
| 9-17 | B | 7.17 | 5.98 | 302.1 | 173.5 | 346.4 | 21.6 |
| 9-16 | C+ | 5.22 | 4.35 | 256.8 | 143.7 | 313.1 | 8.8 |
| 2016 | C+ | 6.30 | 5.25 | 265.4 | 152.1 | 418.7 | 15.6 |
| 2015 | B- | 4.92 | 4.10 | 237.7 | 135.3 | 433.4 | -10.2 |
| 2014 | B | 5.73 | 4.77 | 248.1 | 149.9 | 441.2 | -5.6 |
| 2013 | B | 6.33 | 5.28 | 273.8 | 158.5 | 479.6 | 14.0 |
| 2012 | B | 6.23 | 5.19 | 258.9 | 146.1 | 460.6 | 15.1 |

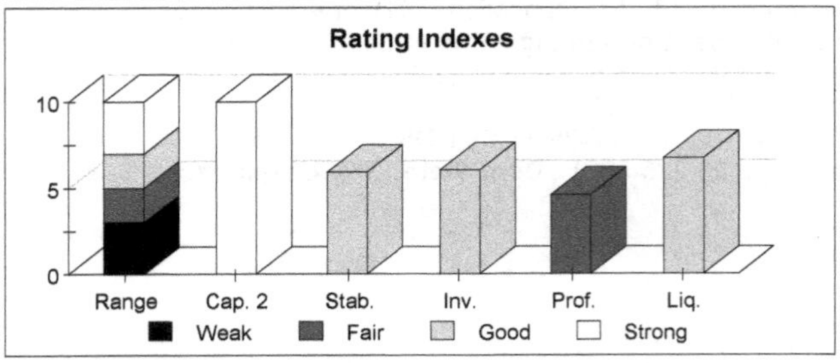

## RELIANCE STANDARD LIFE INSURANCE COMPANY — B — Good

**Major Rating Factors:** Good overall results on stability tests (5.9 on a scale of 0 to 10) despite excessive premium growth. Other stability subfactors include excellent operational trends and excellent risk diversification. Good current capitalization (6.9) based on good risk adjusted capital (severe loss scenario), although results have slipped from the excellent range during the last year. Good liquidity (6.9).
**Other Rating Factors:** Fair quality investment portfolio (4.2). Excellent profitability (8.5).
**Principal Business:** Group health insurance (38%), individual annuities (33%), group life insurance (20%), group retirement contracts (5%), and reinsurance (3%).
**Principal Investments:** CMOs and structured securities (37%), nonCMO investment grade bonds (30%), mortgages in good standing (20%), noninv. grade bonds (6%), and common & preferred stock (3%).
**Investments in Affiliates:** 2%
**Group Affiliation:** Tokio Marine Holdings Inc
**Licensed in:** All states, the District of Columbia and Puerto Rico
**Commenced Business:** April 1907
**Address:** 1100 East Woodfield Road, Schaumburg, IL 60173
**Phone:** (215) 787-4000 **Domicile State:** IL **NAIC Code:** 68381

| Data Date | Rating | RACR #1 | RACR #2 | Total Assets ($mil) | Capital ($mil) | Net Premium ($mil) | Net Income ($mil) |
|---|---|---|---|---|---|---|---|
| 9-17 | B | 1.84 | 0.99 | 11,909.1 | 1,089.1 | 1,678.6 | 118.0 |
| 9-16 | B | 1.75 | 0.94 | 10,435.2 | 1,010.3 | 1,308.2 | 109.2 |
| 2016 | B | 1.91 | 1.06 | 10,889.4 | 1,066.1 | 1,801.1 | 166.0 |
| 2015 | B | 1.64 | 0.89 | 9,580.8 | 923.9 | 1,536.0 | 124.5 |
| 2014 | B | 1.70 | 0.92 | 7,583.8 | 713.3 | 1,787.2 | 166.9 |
| 2013 | B | 1.78 | 1.06 | 5,980.4 | 598.4 | 1,642.5 | 134.6 |
| 2012 | B | 1.74 | 1.02 | 5,186.9 | 561.5 | 1,386.6 | 88.4 |

**Adverse Trends in Operations**

Increase in policy surrenders from 2015 to 2016 (47%)
Decrease in premium volume from 2014 to 2015 (14%)
Increase in policy surrenders from 2012 to 2013 (50%)

## RELIASTAR LIFE INSURANCE COMPANY — C+ — Fair

**Major Rating Factors:** Fair overall results on stability tests (4.7 on a scale of 0 to 10). Good quality investment portfolio (6.2) despite large holdings of BBB rated bonds in addition to moderate junk bond exposure. Exposure to mortgages is significant, but the mortgage default rate has been low. Good liquidity (5.0) with sufficient resources to handle a spike in claims as well as a significant increase in policy surrenders.
**Other Rating Factors:** Weak profitability (2.5). Strong capitalization (7.3) based on excellent risk adjusted capital (severe loss scenario).
**Principal Business:** Individual life insurance (36%), group health insurance (33%), group life insurance (16%), individual annuities (10%), and other lines (6%).
**Principal Investments:** NonCMO investment grade bonds (62%), mortgages in good standing (13%), CMOs and structured securities (10%), noninv. grade bonds (4%), and misc. investments (9%).
**Investments in Affiliates:** 3%
**Group Affiliation:** Voya Financial Inc
**Licensed in:** All states, the District of Columbia and Puerto Rico
**Commenced Business:** September 1885
**Address:** 20 WASHINGTON AVENUE SOUTH, MINNEAPOLIS, MN 55401
**Phone:** (770) 980-5100 **Domicile State:** MN **NAIC Code:** 67105

| Data Date | Rating | RACR #1 | RACR #2 | Total Assets ($mil) | Capital ($mil) | Net Premium ($mil) | Net Income ($mil) |
|---|---|---|---|---|---|---|---|
| 9-17 | C+ | 1.96 | 1.18 | 20,125.4 | 1,547.1 | 533.6 | 182.3 |
| 9-16 | C+ | 1.93 | 1.16 | 19,844.2 | 1,536.7 | 593.0 | 6.4 |
| 2016 | C+ | 2.09 | 1.26 | 19,828.5 | 1,662.0 | 777.1 | -506.6 |
| 2015 | C+ | 2.03 | 1.23 | 19,805.1 | 1,609.2 | 740.9 | 74.2 |
| 2014 | C+ | 2.40 | 1.42 | 21,468.7 | 1,944.7 | -149.0 | 103.9 |
| 2013 | C | 2.29 | 1.38 | 21,621.2 | 1,942.5 | 840.3 | 215.9 |
| 2012 | C- | 2.57 | 1.54 | 21,526.1 | 2,284.6 | 858.8 | -155.3 |

**Rating Indexes**

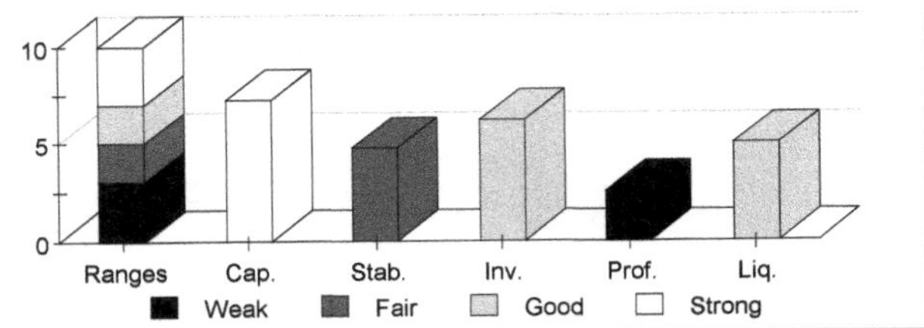


## RESERVE NATIONAL INSURANCE COMPANY — B- — Good

**Major Rating Factors:** Good liquidity (5.8 on a scale of 0 to 10) with sufficient resources to handle a spike in claims. Fair overall results on stability tests (4.9). Weak profitability (2.0) with operating losses during the first nine months of 2017.
**Other Rating Factors:** Strong capitalization (7.1) based on excellent risk adjusted capital (severe loss scenario). High quality investment portfolio (7.7).
**Principal Business:** Individual health insurance (79%), individual life insurance (15%), reinsurance (4%), and group health insurance (2%).
**Principal Investments:** NonCMO investment grade bonds (88%), cash (6%), CMOs and structured securities (2%), and noninv. grade bonds (1%).
**Investments in Affiliates:** None
**Group Affiliation:** Kemper Corporation
**Licensed in:** All states except NY, PR
**Commenced Business:** September 1956
**Address:** 601 EAST BRITTON ROAD, OKLAHOMA CITY, OK 73114
**Phone:** (405) 848-7931 **Domicile State:** OK **NAIC Code:** 68462

| Data Date | Rating | RACR #1 | RACR #2 | Total Assets ($mil) | Capital ($mil) | Net Premium ($mil) | Net Income ($mil) |
|---|---|---|---|---|---|---|---|
| 9-17 | B- | 1.41 | 1.06 | 118.6 | 31.6 | 112.6 | -6.6 |
| 9-16 | A- | 1.96 | 1.49 | 123.7 | 40.8 | 106.7 | -1.7 |
| 2016 | B+ | 1.77 | 1.34 | 126.9 | 40.2 | 143.6 | -2.0 |
| 2015 | A | 2.18 | 1.66 | 122.8 | 45.1 | 132.7 | -0.5 |
| 2014 | A | 2.44 | 1.88 | 118.2 | 51.0 | 131.8 | 1.7 |
| 2013 | A | 2.27 | 1.76 | 111.2 | 52.4 | 143.6 | 4.9 |
| 2012 | A | 2.66 | 2.04 | 116.0 | 58.4 | 135.2 | 8.8 |

**Rating Indexes**

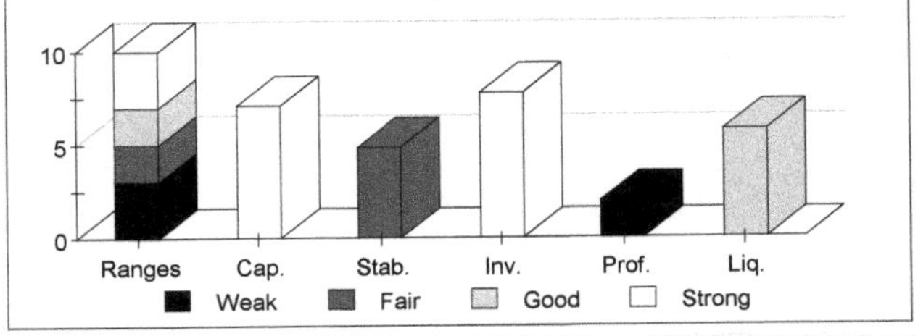

## RGA REINSURANCE COMPANY B- Good

**Major Rating Factors:** Good capitalization (5.8 on a scale of 0 to 10) based on good risk adjusted capital (moderate loss scenario). Good quality investment portfolio (5.2) despite large holdings of BBB rated bonds in addition to junk bond exposure equal to 87% of capital. Exposure to mortgages is significant, but the mortgage default rate has been low. Good overall profitability (6.7). Excellent expense controls.
**Other Rating Factors:** Good liquidity (5.7). Good overall results on stability tests (5.3) good operational trends and excellent risk diversification.
**Principal Business:** Reinsurance (100%).
**Principal Investments:** NonCMO investment grade bonds (47%), mortgages in good standing (18%), CMOs and structured securities (14%), policy loans (7%), and misc. investments (13%).
**Investments in Affiliates:** 3%
**Group Affiliation:** Reinsurance Group of America Inc
**Licensed in:** All states, the District of Columbia and Puerto Rico
**Commenced Business:** October 1982
**Address:** 16600 Swingley Ridge Road, Chesterfield, MO 63017-1706
**Phone:** (636) 736-7000 **Domicile State:** MO **NAIC Code:** 93572

| Data Date | Rating | RACR #1 | RACR #2 | Total Assets ($mil) | Capital ($mil) | Net Premium ($mil) | Net Income ($mil) |
|---|---|---|---|---|---|---|---|
| 9-17 | B- | 1.50 | 0.83 | 29,084.7 | 1,535.8 | 4,297.7 | 53.1 |
| 9-16 | B- | 1.45 | 0.82 | 25,381.4 | 1,523.3 | 1,879.0 | 91.1 |
| 2016 | B- | 1.61 | 0.87 | 25,432.8 | 1,521.6 | 2,636.1 | 148.6 |
| 2015 | B- | 1.42 | 0.81 | 24,593.0 | 1,503.4 | 3,364.2 | -23.6 |
| 2014 | B | 1.69 | 0.88 | 24,178.4 | 1,528.3 | 3,494.2 | 17.1 |
| 2013 | B | 1.70 | 0.90 | 23,259.8 | 1,550.1 | 2,305.6 | 115.8 |
| 2012 | B | 1.75 | 0.95 | 22,835.1 | 1,644.6 | 5,213.8 | 3.5 |

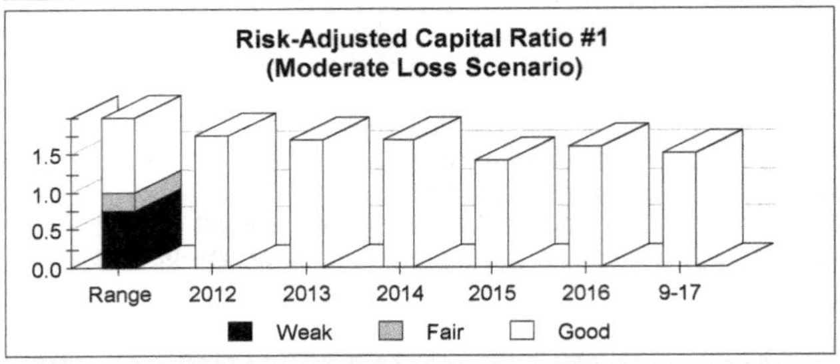


## RIVERLINK HEALTH E+ Very Weak

**Major Rating Factors:** Weak profitability index (0.7 on a scale of 0 to 10). Fair liquidity (4.8) as cash resources may not be adequate to cover a spike in claims. Strong capitalization (7.8) based on excellent current risk-adjusted capital (severe loss scenario).
**Other Rating Factors:** High quality investment portfolio (9.9).
**Principal Business:** Medicare (100%)
**Mem Phys: 16:** 5,773 **15:** 4,417 **16 MLR** 115.1% **/ 16 Admin Exp** N/A
**Enroll(000): Q3 17:** 1 **16:** 1 **15:** 1 **Med Exp PMPM:** $690
**Principal Investments:** Long-term bonds (101%)
**Provider Compensation ($000):** Contr fee ($9,568), capitation ($310), other ($479)
**Total Member Encounters:** Phys (18,208), non-phys (6,768)
**Group Affiliation:** Catholic Health Initiatives
**Licensed in:** OH
**Address:** PO Box 8849, Cincinnati, OH 45208
**Phone:** (866) 789-7747 **Dom State:** OH **Commenced Bus:** January 2015

| Data Date | Rating | RACR #1 | RACR #2 | Total Assets ($mil) | Capital ($mil) | Net Premium ($mil) | Net Income ($mil) |
|---|---|---|---|---|---|---|---|
| 9-17 | E+ | 1.97 | 1.64 | 6.2 | 2.9 | 6.7 | -0.4 |
| 9-16 | D+ | 4.27 | 3.56 | 6.2 | 3.4 | 6.9 | -1.1 |
| 2016 | E+ | 1.30 | 1.08 | 5.4 | 1.8 | 9.3 | -2.6 |
| 2015 | D+ | 4.37 | 3.64 | 5.0 | 3.5 | 4.1 | -1.2 |
| 2014 | N/A | N/A | N/A | 3.4 | 3.4 | N/A | N/A |
| 2013 | N/A | N/A | N/A | N/A | N/A | N/A | N/A |
| 2012 | N/A | N/A | N/A | N/A | N/A | N/A | N/A |

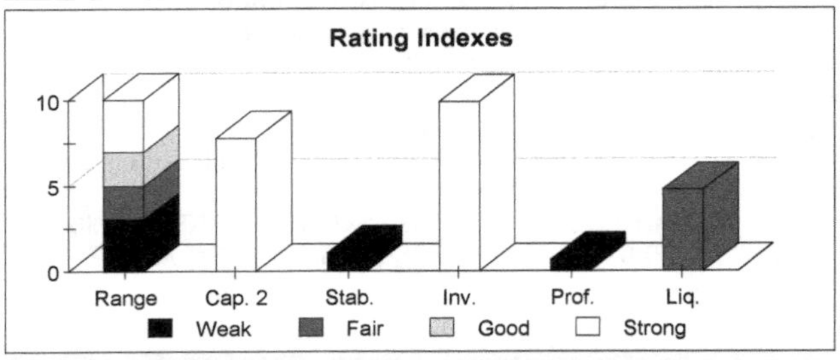


## RIVERLINK HEALTH OF KENTUCKY INC D- Weak

**Major Rating Factors:** Weak profitability index (0.8 on a scale of 0 to 10). Good liquidity (6.3) with sufficient resources (cash flows and marketable investments) to handle a spike in claims. Strong capitalization (8.6) based on excellent current risk-adjusted capital (severe loss scenario).
**Other Rating Factors:** High quality investment portfolio (9.9).
**Principal Business:** Medicare (100%)
**Mem Phys: 16:** 5,773 **15:** 4,417 **16 MLR** 109.2% **/ 16 Admin Exp** N/A
**Enroll(000): Q3 17:** 1 **16:** 1 **15:** 0 **Med Exp PMPM:** $686
**Principal Investments:** Long-term bonds (90%), cash and equiv (10%)
**Provider Compensation ($000):** Contr fee ($8,720), capitation ($153), other ($314)
**Total Member Encounters:** Phys (15,483), non-phys (6,960)
**Group Affiliation:** Catholic Health Initiatives
**Licensed in:** KY
**Address:** PO Box 1109, Lexington, KY 40588
**Phone:** (866) 789-7747 **Dom State:** KY **Commenced Bus:** April 2014

| Data Date | Rating | RACR #1 | RACR #2 | Total Assets ($mil) | Capital ($mil) | Net Premium ($mil) | Net Income ($mil) |
|---|---|---|---|---|---|---|---|
| 9-17 | D- | 2.62 | 2.18 | 6.8 | 3.7 | 6.3 | -0.8 |
| 9-16 | D- | 4.80 | 4.00 | 6.2 | 2.7 | 6.4 | -2.5 |
| 2016 | D- | 3.18 | 2.65 | 6.5 | 4.5 | 8.5 | -1.8 |
| 2015 | C- | 9.29 | 7.74 | 6.0 | 5.2 | 3.1 | -0.4 |
| 2014 | N/A | N/A | N/A | 5.5 | 5.5 | N/A | N/A |
| 2013 | N/A | N/A | N/A | N/A | N/A | N/A | N/A |
| 2012 | N/A | N/A | N/A | N/A | N/A | N/A | N/A |

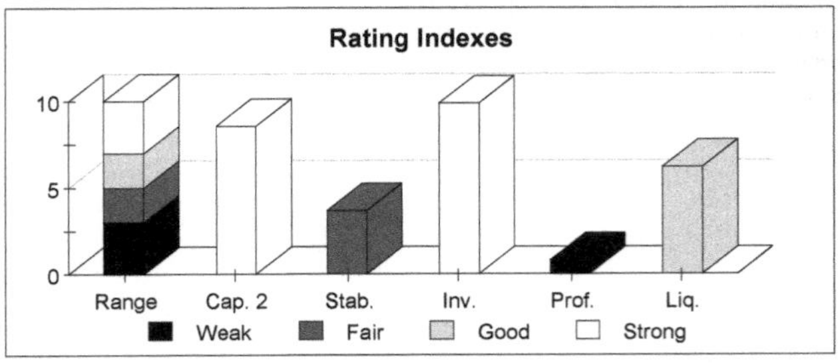

## ROCKY MOUNTAIN HEALTH MAINT ORG — C — Fair

**Major Rating Factors:** Fair overall results on stability tests (4.8 on a scale of 0 to 10). Rating is significantly influenced by the fair financial results of UnitedHealth Group Incorporated. Fair liquidity (3.3) as cash resources may not be adequate to cover a spike in claims. Weak profitability index (0.9).
**Other Rating Factors:** Strong capitalization index (7.5) based on excellent current risk-adjusted capital (severe loss scenario). High quality investment portfolio (9.2).
**Principal Business:** Comp med (48%), Medicaid (41%), Medicare (10%)
**Mem Phys: 16:** 20,360 **15:** 18,018 **16 MLR** 87.5% **/ 16 Admin Exp** N/A
**Enroll(000): Q3 17:** 229 **16:** 234 **15:** 231 **Med Exp PMPM:** $140
**Principal Investments:** Cash and equiv (48%), long-term bonds (28%), real estate (7%), affiliate common stock (5%), other (13%)
**Provider Compensation ($000):** Bonus arrang ($227,979), contr fee ($152,356), FFS ($14,609), capitation ($8,064)
**Total Member Encounters:** Phys (1,214,500)
**Group Affiliation:** UnitedHealth Group Incorporated
**Licensed in:** CO
**Address:** 2775 Crossroads Blvd, Grand Junction, CO 81506
**Phone:** (970) 244-7760 **Dom State:** CO **Commenced Bus:** June 1974

| Data Date | Rating | RACR #1 | RACR #2 | Total Assets ($mil) | Capital ($mil) | Net Premium ($mil) | Net Income ($mil) |
|---|---|---|---|---|---|---|---|
| 9-17 | C | 1.76 | 1.47 | 137.6 | 47.6 | 289.6 | 4.2 |
| 9-16 | C | 0.84 | 0.70 | 158.0 | 44.1 | 339.9 | 3.8 |
| 2016 | C | 1.09 | 0.91 | 152.3 | 46.9 | 449.2 | -6.8 |
| 2015 | C | 0.75 | 0.62 | 186.5 | 39.6 | 481.0 | -21.8 |
| 2014 | B | 1.62 | 1.35 | 164.1 | 63.2 | 332.4 | -13.6 |
| 2013 | A- | 5.79 | 4.83 | 142.6 | 91.0 | 160.4 | 4.1 |
| 2012 | A+ | 6.88 | 5.73 | 168.1 | 106.5 | 171.8 | 14.2 |

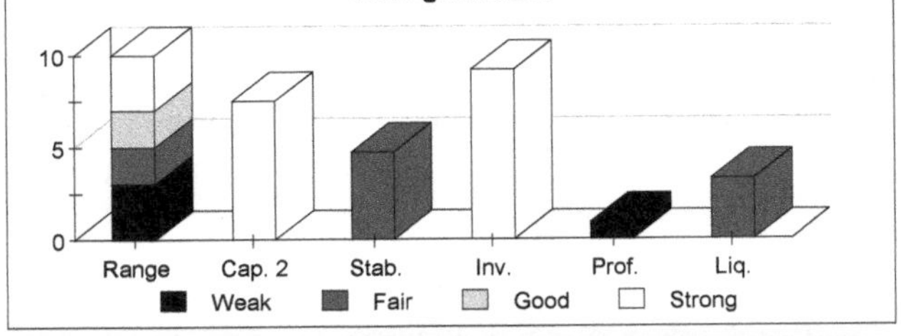


## ROCKY MOUNTAIN HEALTHCARE OPTIONS — D — Weak

**Major Rating Factors:** Weak profitability index (0.9 on a scale of 0 to 10). Fair capitalization (2.9) based on fair current risk-adjusted capital (moderate loss scenario). Good liquidity (6.4) with sufficient resources (cash flows and marketable investments) to handle a spike in claims.
**Other Rating Factors:** High quality investment portfolio (7.9).
**Principal Business:** Comp med (99%), other (1%)
**Mem Phys: 16:** 20,354 **15:** 18,016 **16 MLR** 89.5% **/ 16 Admin Exp** N/A
**Enroll(000): Q3 17:** 7 **16:** 10 **15:** 14 **Med Exp PMPM:** $469
**Principal Investments:** Long-term bonds (63%), affiliate common stock (7%), cash and equiv (4%), other (26%)
**Provider Compensation ($000):** Contr fee ($52,541), bonus arrang ($9,264), FFS ($7,423), capitation ($448), other ($1,191)
**Total Member Encounters:** Phys (85,101)
**Group Affiliation:** UnitedHealth Group Incorporated
**Licensed in:** CO
**Address:** 2775 CROSSRdS BLVD, GRAND JUNCTION, CO 81506
**Phone:** (970) 244-7760 **Dom State:** CO **Commenced Bus:** May 1993

| Data Date | Rating | RACR #1 | RACR #2 | Total Assets ($mil) | Capital ($mil) | Net Premium ($mil) | Net Income ($mil) |
|---|---|---|---|---|---|---|---|
| 9-17 | D | 0.98 | 0.81 | 21.2 | 10.8 | 36.6 | -4.4 |
| 9-16 | E | 0.51 | 0.42 | 22.7 | 10.4 | 56.3 | -0.7 |
| 2016 | E+ | 0.72 | 0.60 | 27.6 | 12.7 | 73.7 | -4.6 |
| 2015 | E | 0.53 | 0.44 | 28.4 | 10.9 | 85.3 | -4.2 |
| 2014 | E | 0.39 | 0.33 | 34.8 | 10.7 | 106.1 | -5.3 |
| 2013 | E | 0.50 | 0.41 | 40.8 | 13.6 | 170.4 | -4.2 |
| 2012 | E | 0.59 | 0.49 | 44.7 | 13.8 | 168.5 | -14.2 |

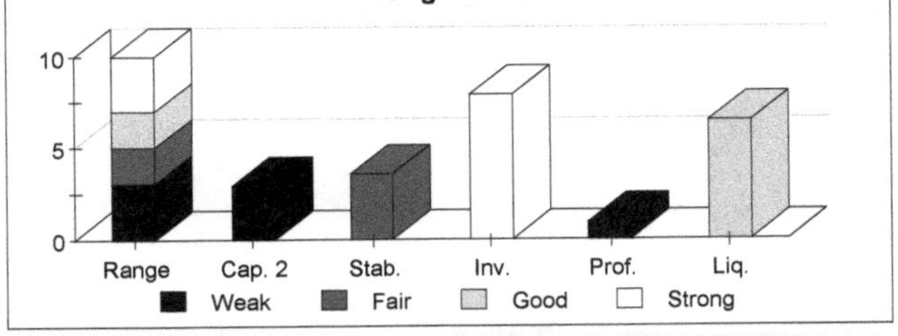


## ROCKY MOUNTAIN HOSPITAL & MEDICAL — B — Good

**Major Rating Factors:** Good liquidity (6.6 on a scale of 0 to 10) with sufficient resources (cash flows and marketable investments) to handle a spike in claims. Fair quality investment portfolio (3.7). Excellent profitability (8.2).
**Other Rating Factors:** Strong capitalization (9.2) based on excellent current risk-adjusted capital (severe loss scenario).
**Principal Business:** Comp med (59%), FEHB (34%), med supp (4%), dental (2%), other (2%)
**Mem Phys: 16:** 20,555 **15:** 25,603 **16 MLR** 86.9% **/ 16 Admin Exp** N/A
**Enroll(000): Q3 17:** 644 **16:** 710 **15:** 624 **Med Exp PMPM:** $237
**Principal Investments:** Long-term bonds (81%), affiliate common stock (31%), other (2%)
**Provider Compensation ($000):** Contr fee ($1,896,582), FFS ($59,225), bonus arrang ($8,684), capitation ($234), other ($30,273)
**Total Member Encounters:** Phys (2,768,590), non-phys (1,521,766)
**Group Affiliation:** Anthem Inc
**Licensed in:** CO, NV
**Address:** 700 Broadway, DENVER, CO 80273
**Phone:** (303) 831-2131 **Dom State:** CO **Commenced Bus:** October 1938

| Data Date | Rating | RACR #1 | RACR #2 | Total Assets ($mil) | Capital ($mil) | Net Premium ($mil) | Net Income ($mil) |
|---|---|---|---|---|---|---|---|
| 9-17 | B | 3.10 | 2.59 | 1,040.9 | 468.2 | 1,447.4 | 55.2 |
| 9-16 | B | 4.42 | 3.68 | 1,061.0 | 462.3 | 1,751.4 | 81.0 |
| 2016 | B | 2.50 | 2.09 | 1,007.6 | 374.9 | 2,337.6 | 87.7 |
| 2015 | B | 3.71 | 3.09 | 907.0 | 387.1 | 1,907.8 | 89.7 |
| 2014 | B+ | 3.53 | 2.94 | 861.7 | 440.9 | 1,960.5 | 108.4 |
| 2013 | B+ | 3.46 | 2.89 | 815.5 | 405.7 | 1,921.6 | 110.9 |
| 2012 | A- | 3.01 | 2.51 | 826.9 | 370.2 | 1,992.2 | 95.9 |

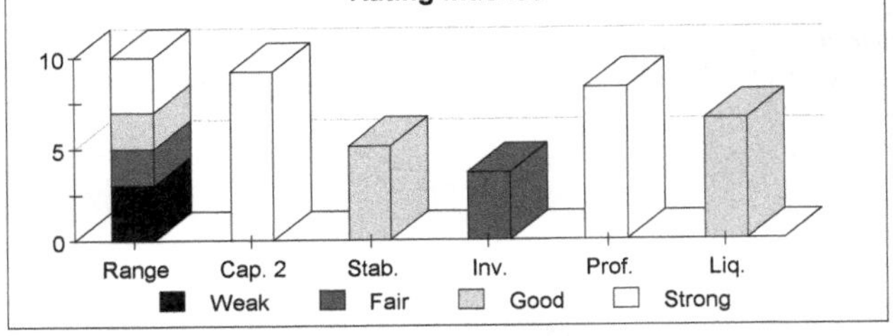

## ROYAL STATE NATIONAL INSURANCE COMPANY LIMITED — C — Fair

**Major Rating Factors:** Fair profitability (4.0 on a scale of 0 to 10). Fair overall results on stability tests (4.2). Good quality investment portfolio (6.1) despite mixed results such as: no exposure to mortgages and large holdings of BBB rated bonds but no exposure to junk bonds.
**Other Rating Factors:** Strong capitalization (10.0) based on excellent risk adjusted capital (severe loss scenario). Excellent liquidity (7.1).
**Principal Business:** Group health insurance (53%), group life insurance (35%), individual life insurance (10%), and reinsurance (1%).
**Principal Investments:** NonCMO investment grade bonds (67%), common & preferred stock (17%), CMOs and structured securities (14%), cash (2%), and policy loans (1%).
**Investments in Affiliates:** 3%
**Group Affiliation:** Royal State Group
**Licensed in:** HI
**Commenced Business:** August 1961
**Address:** 819 SOUTH BERETANIA STREET, HONOLULU, HI 96813
**Phone:** (808) 539-1600 **Domicile State:** HI **NAIC Code:** 68551

| Data Date | Rating | RACR #1 | RACR #2 | Total Assets ($mil) | Capital ($mil) | Net Premium ($mil) | Net Income ($mil) |
|---|---|---|---|---|---|---|---|
| 9-17 | C | 4.95 | 3.30 | 46.1 | 29.5 | 3.8 | 0.1 |
| 9-16 | C | 4.98 | 3.33 | 46.2 | 29.1 | 4.0 | 0.3 |
| 2016 | C | 5.11 | 3.41 | 46.5 | 29.6 | 5.3 | 0.8 |
| 2015 | C | 4.91 | 3.29 | 45.3 | 28.6 | 7.0 | -0.4 |
| 2014 | B- | 3.27 | 2.29 | 47.1 | 29.3 | 10.8 | 0.7 |
| 2013 | B- | 3.29 | 2.33 | 45.6 | 28.9 | 10.6 | 0.4 |
| 2012 | B- | 3.29 | 2.38 | 44.6 | 28.9 | 10.5 | -0.1 |

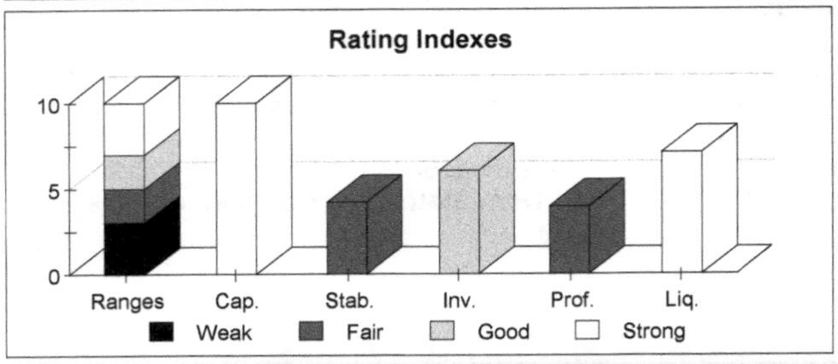


## RYDER HEALTH PLAN INC — C — Fair

**Major Rating Factors:** Weak profitability index (2.6 on a scale of 0 to 10). Good overall results on stability tests (4.9). Strong capitalization index (7.2) based on excellent current risk-adjusted capital (severe loss scenario).
**Other Rating Factors:** High quality investment portfolio (9.8). Excellent liquidity (7.5) with ample operational cash flow and liquid investments.
**Principal Business:** Comp med (99%)
**Mem Phys: 16:** N/A **15:** N/A **16 MLR** 83.0% **/ 16 Admin Exp** N/A
**Enroll(000): Q3 17:** 3 **16:** 3 **15:** 3 **Med Exp PMPM:** $52
**Principal Investments:** Cash and equiv (80%), long-term bonds (20%)
**Provider Compensation ($000):** Capitation ($1,734), other ($351)
**Total Member Encounters:** N/A
**Group Affiliation:** Ryder Health Plan Inc
**Licensed in:** PR
**Address:** 353 FONT MARTELO AVE SUITE 1, HUMACAO, PR 00791
**Phone:** (787) 852-0846 **Dom State:** PR **Commenced Bus:** October 1984

| Data Date | Rating | RACR #1 | RACR #2 | Total Assets ($mil) | Capital ($mil) | Net Premium ($mil) | Net Income ($mil) |
|---|---|---|---|---|---|---|---|
| 9-17 | C | 1.54 | 1.28 | 1.6 | 0.6 | 1.9 | 0.1 |
| 9-16 | C- | 1.56 | 1.30 | 1.4 | 0.6 | 2.0 | 0.1 |
| 2016 | C- | 1.24 | 1.03 | 1.5 | 0.5 | 2.6 | 0.0 |
| 2015 | C- | 1.28 | 1.07 | 1.3 | 0.5 | 1.9 | -0.2 |
| 2014 | C- | 1.61 | 1.34 | 1.5 | 0.7 | 2.5 | 0.0 |
| 2013 | D | 0.60 | 0.50 | 1.5 | 0.7 | 2.6 | 0.0 |
| 2012 | D | 0.23 | 0.19 | 1.5 | 0.7 | 2.8 | 0.0 |

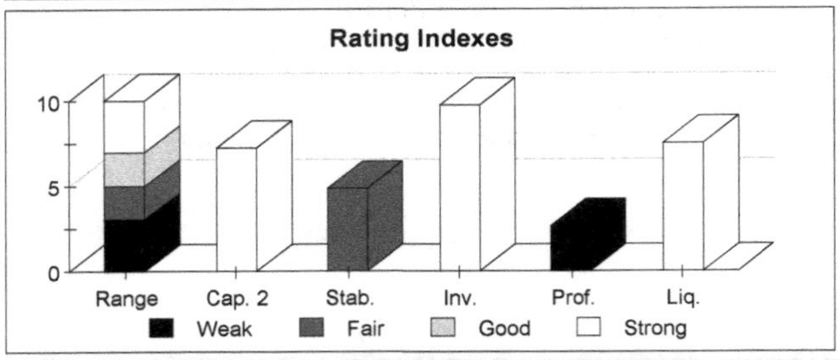


## SAMARITAN HEALTH PLANS INC — B — Good

**Major Rating Factors:** Good overall profitability index (6.1 on a scale of 0 to 10). Good capitalization (6.9) based on excellent current risk-adjusted capital (severe loss scenario). Good liquidity (6.8) with sufficient resources (cash flows and marketable investments) to handle a spike in claims.
**Other Rating Factors:** High quality investment portfolio (9.9).
**Principal Business:** Medicare (83%), comp med (17%)
**Mem Phys: 16:** 6,212 **15:** 4,830 **16 MLR** 82.5% **/ 16 Admin Exp** N/A
**Enroll(000): Q3 17:** 10 **16:** 9 **15:** 6 **Med Exp PMPM:** $639
**Principal Investments:** Long-term bonds (50%), cash and equiv (44%), nonaffiliate common stock (6%)
**Provider Compensation ($000):** Contr fee ($60,645)
**Total Member Encounters:** Phys (101,718), non-phys (64,869)
**Group Affiliation:** Samaritan Health Services Inc
**Licensed in:** OR
**Address:** 3600 NW Samaritan Dr, Corvallis, OR 97330
**Phone:** (541) 768-5328 **Dom State:** OR **Commenced Bus:** January 2005

| Data Date | Rating | RACR #1 | RACR #2 | Total Assets ($mil) | Capital ($mil) | Net Premium ($mil) | Net Income ($mil) |
|---|---|---|---|---|---|---|---|
| 9-17 | B | 1.28 | 1.06 | 35.8 | 12.4 | 71.6 | 2.8 |
| 9-16 | C | 0.89 | 0.74 | 24.5 | 8.4 | 55.3 | 1.4 |
| 2016 | C+ | 0.94 | 0.79 | 20.7 | 9.5 | 73.4 | 2.8 |
| 2015 | C | 0.85 | 0.71 | 17.4 | 8.1 | 61.1 | -0.9 |
| 2014 | B | 1.08 | 0.90 | 19.1 | 9.1 | 57.8 | 0.8 |
| 2013 | B- | 0.97 | 0.81 | 16.6 | 8.0 | 55.4 | -0.5 |
| 2012 | C+ | 0.95 | 0.79 | 15.7 | 7.7 | 55.6 | 1.3 |

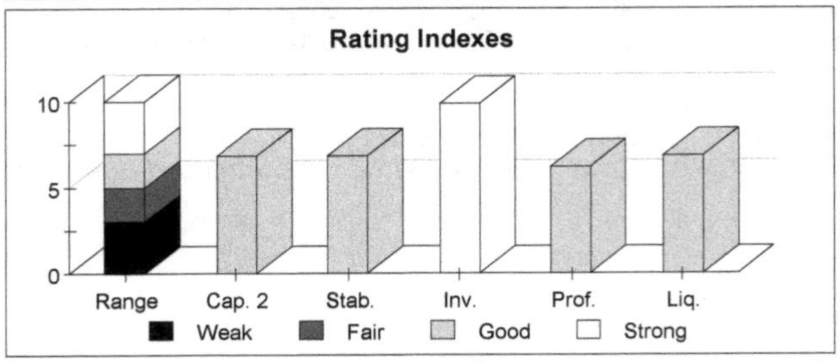

## SAN FRANCISCO HEALTH AUTHORITY — B — Good

**Major Rating Factors:** Excellent profitability (8.1 on a scale of 0 to 10). Strong capitalization index (8.3) based on excellent current risk-adjusted capital (severe loss scenario). Excellent overall results on stability tests (7.2).
**Other Rating Factors:** Excellent liquidity (8.6) with ample operational cash flow and liquid investments.
**Principal Business:** Medicaid (92%)
**Mem Phys: 16:** N/A **15:** N/A **16 MLR** 89.1% **/ 16 Admin Exp** N/A
**Enroll(000): Q3 17:** 149 **16:** 145 **15:** 136 **Med Exp PMPM:** $294
**Principal Investments ($000):** Cash and equiv ($166,288)
**Provider Compensation ($000):** None
**Total Member Encounters:** N/A
**Group Affiliation:** None
**Licensed in:** (No states)
**Address:** 50 Beale Street 12th Floor, San Francisco, CA 94105
**Phone:** (415) 615-4217 **Dom State:** CA **Commenced Bus:** March 1996

| Data Date | Rating | RACR #1 | RACR #2 | Total Assets ($mil) | Capital ($mil) | Net Premium ($mil) | Net Income ($mil) |
|---|---|---|---|---|---|---|---|
| 9-17 | B | 3.17 | 1.98 | 742.2 | 123.5 | 478.0 | 9.9 |
| 9-16 | B | 2.96 | 1.87 | 427.6 | 106.6 | 422.8 | 23.8 |
| 2016 | B | 2.91 | 1.83 | 484.8 | 112.6 | 572.8 | 29.9 |
| 2015 | B | 2.20 | 1.39 | 346.1 | 82.7 | 545.1 | 37.8 |
| 2014 | B | 1.75 | 1.13 | 217.4 | 47.4 | 311.9 | 11.2 |
| 2013 | C+ | 1.49 | 0.97 | 159.5 | 36.2 | 250.1 | 10.5 |
| 2012 | C | 1.21 | 0.79 | 121.7 | 25.7 | 201.1 | -4.5 |

Rating Indexes

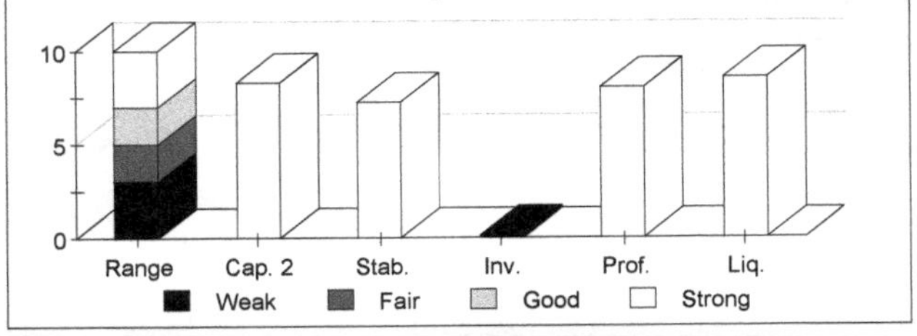


## SAN JOAQUIN CNTY HEALTH — C+ — Fair

**Major Rating Factors:** Fair overall results on stability tests (4.7 on a scale of 0 to 10) in spite of healthy premium and capital growth during 2016. Good overall profitability index (6.6). Strong capitalization index (9.5) based on excellent current risk-adjusted capital (severe loss scenario).
**Other Rating Factors:** Excellent liquidity (7.9) with ample operational cash flow and liquid investments.
**Principal Business:** Medicaid (100%)
**Mem Phys: 16:** N/A **15:** N/A **16 MLR** 93.6% **/ 16 Admin Exp** N/A
**Enroll(000): Q3 17:** 350 **16:** 338 **15:** 312 **Med Exp PMPM:** $221
**Principal Investments ($000):** Cash and equiv ($414,666)
**Provider Compensation ($000):** None
**Total Member Encounters:** N/A
**Group Affiliation:** None
**Licensed in:** CA
**Address:** 7751 S Manthey Rd, French Camp, CA 95231-9802
**Phone:** (888) 936-7526 **Dom State:** CA **Commenced Bus:** N/A

| Data Date | Rating | RACR #1 | RACR #2 | Total Assets ($mil) | Capital ($mil) | Net Premium ($mil) | Net Income ($mil) |
|---|---|---|---|---|---|---|---|
| 9-17 | C+ | 4.62 | 2.81 | 847.4 | 282.9 | 788.1 | 77.8 |
| 9-16 | C+ | 2.38 | 1.45 | 516.1 | 122.5 | 678.3 | 8.3 |
| 2016 | C+ | 1.89 | 1.15 | 561.1 | 140.8 | 920.6 | 26.7 |
| 2015 | C+ | 2.18 | 1.33 | 455.2 | 114.2 | 729.1 | 79.9 |
| 2014 | C+ | 1.22 | 0.75 | 169.0 | 39.4 | 446.4 | -14.0 |
| 2013 | B | 2.23 | 1.38 | 115.1 | 53.4 | 301.5 | 3.0 |
| 2012 | B | 2.92 | 1.81 | 81.3 | 50.4 | 204.0 | 0.8 |

Rating Indexes

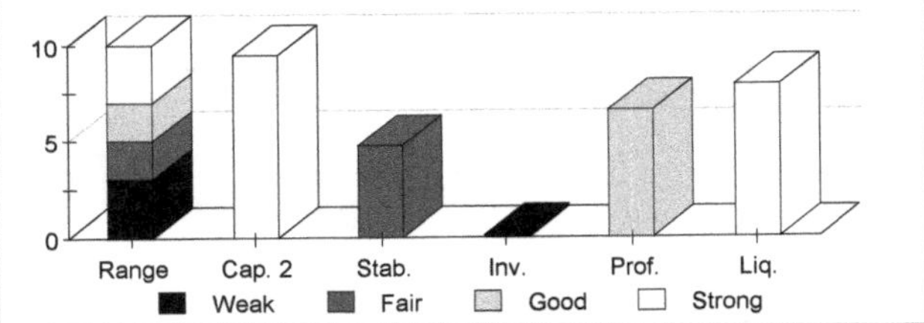


## SAN MATEO HEALTH COMMISSION * — B+ — Good

**Major Rating Factors:** Good overall results on stability tests (5.1 on a scale of 0 to 10). Excellent overall profitability index (6.9). Strong capitalization index (10.0) based on excellent current risk-adjusted capital (severe loss scenario).
**Other Rating Factors:** Excellent liquidity (7.6) with ample operational cash flow and liquid investments.
**Principal Business:** Medicaid (77%), Medicare (23%)
**Mem Phys: 16:** N/A **15:** N/A **16 MLR** 92.6% **/ 16 Admin Exp** N/A
**Enroll(000): Q3 17:** 134 **16:** 136 **15:** 138 **Med Exp PMPM:** $446
**Principal Investments ($000):** Cash and equiv ($602,497)
**Provider Compensation ($000):** None
**Total Member Encounters:** N/A
**Group Affiliation:** None
**Licensed in:** CA
**Address:** 7751 S Manthey Road, French Camp, CA 95231
**Phone:** (209) 461-2211 **Dom State:** CA **Commenced Bus:** December 1987

| Data Date | Rating | RACR #1 | RACR #2 | Total Assets ($mil) | Capital ($mil) | Net Premium ($mil) | Net Income ($mil) |
|---|---|---|---|---|---|---|---|
| 9-17 | B+ | 5.66 | 3.48 | 657.3 | 301.9 | 640.8 | 4.4 |
| 9-16 | A- | 7.11 | 4.36 | 550.4 | 343.4 | 608.6 | 25.6 |
| 2016 | B+ | 5.55 | 3.41 | 800.6 | 297.4 | 792.3 | -20.3 |
| 2015 | A- | 6.65 | 4.08 | 641.5 | 317.8 | 911.0 | 103.4 |
| 2014 | A- | 5.38 | 3.31 | 408.4 | 214.3 | 728.9 | 69.2 |
| 2013 | B+ | 5.12 | 3.13 | 256.2 | 145.2 | 503.9 | 57.4 |
| 2012 | B | 2.78 | 1.70 | 209.9 | 87.8 | 478.7 | 11.9 |

Rating Indexes

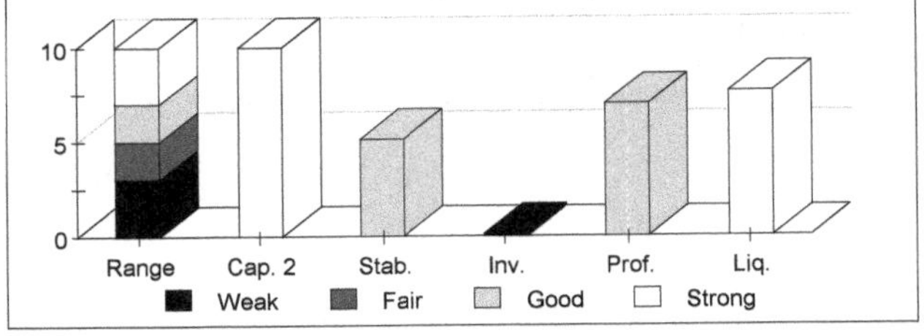

## SANFORD HEALTH PLAN C Fair

**Major Rating Factors:** Weak profitability index (0.9 on a scale of 0 to 10). Good overall results on stability tests (6.5) based on healthy premium and capital growth during 2016. Good liquidity (6.3) with sufficient resources (cash flows and marketable investments) to handle a spike in claims.
**Other Rating Factors:** Strong capitalization index (7.1) based on excellent current risk-adjusted capital (severe loss scenario). High quality investment portfolio (9.7).
**Principal Business:** Comp med (64%), Medicaid (35%)
**Mem Phys: 16:** 47,998 **15:** 40,490 **16 MLR** 99.7% **/ 16 Admin Exp** N/A
**Enroll(000): Q3 17:** 129 **16:** 136 **15:** 130 **Med Exp PMPM:** $498
**Principal Investments:** Long-term bonds (51%), cash and equiv (34%), nonaffiliate common stock (14%), pref stock (1%), other (1%)
**Provider Compensation ($000):** Contr fee ($828,265)
**Total Member Encounters:** Phys (550,787), non-phys (535,502)
**Group Affiliation:** Sanford
**Licensed in:** IA, ND, SD
**Address:** 300 Cherapa Place Suite 201, Sioux Falls, SD 57103
**Phone:** (605) 328-6868 **Dom State:** SD **Commenced Bus:** January 1998

| Data Date | Rating | RACR #1 | RACR #2 | Total Assets ($mil) | Capital ($mil) | Net Premium ($mil) | Net Income ($mil) |
|---|---|---|---|---|---|---|---|
| 9-17 | C | 1.43 | 1.20 | 263.9 | 125.2 | 625.5 | 18.9 |
| 9-16 | C | 0.51 | 0.42 | 192.2 | 39.1 | 620.4 | -14.7 |
| 2016 | C | 0.96 | 0.80 | 230.5 | 86.4 | 823.7 | -8.9 |
| 2015 | C | 0.74 | 0.62 | 223.0 | 55.1 | 613.2 | -73.2 |
| 2014 | C+ | 0.70 | 0.58 | 78.1 | 24.1 | 295.6 | -1.6 |
| 2013 | B | 1.56 | 1.30 | 51.3 | 26.0 | 143.3 | 1.8 |
| 2012 | B | 1.69 | 1.41 | 47.8 | 26.8 | 138.2 | 2.8 |

Rating Indexes

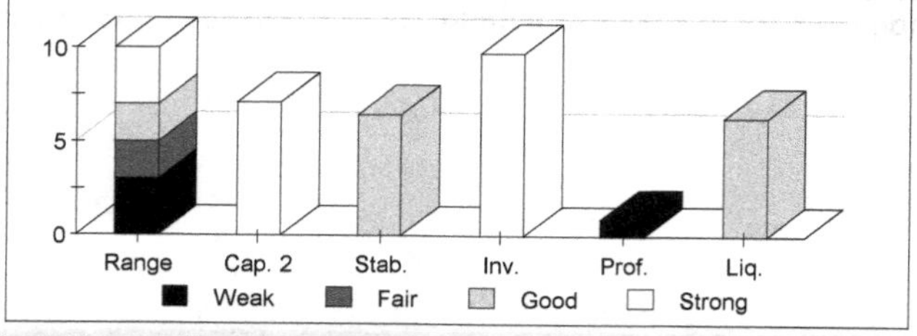


## SANFORD HEALTH PLAN OF MINNESOTA E+ Very Weak

**Major Rating Factors:** Weak profitability index (0.9 on a scale of 0 to 10). Fair overall results on stability tests (4.6). Rating is significantly influenced by the fair financial results of Sanford. Strong capitalization index (7.9) based on excellent current risk-adjusted capital (severe loss scenario).
**Other Rating Factors:** High quality investment portfolio (9.9). Excellent liquidity (7.4) with ample operational cash flow and liquid investments.
**Principal Business:** Comp med (87%), med supp (13%)
**Mem Phys: 16:** 47,988 **15:** 40,490 **16 MLR** 125.5% **/ 16 Admin Exp** N/A
**Enroll(000): Q3 17:** 0 **16:** 1 **15:** 1 **Med Exp PMPM:** $477
**Principal Investments:** Cash and equiv (100%)
**Provider Compensation ($000):** Contr fee ($2,439)
**Total Member Encounters:** Phys (1,750), non-phys (1,965)
**Group Affiliation:** Sanford
**Licensed in:** MN
**Address:** 300 Cherapa Place Suite 201, Sioux Falls, SD 57109-1110
**Phone:** (605) 328-6868 **Dom State:** MN **Commenced Bus:** January 1998

| Data Date | Rating | RACR #1 | RACR #2 | Total Assets ($mil) | Capital ($mil) | Net Premium ($mil) | Net Income ($mil) |
|---|---|---|---|---|---|---|---|
| 9-17 | E+ | 2.05 | 1.71 | 2.0 | 1.6 | 1.3 | 0.1 |
| 9-16 | E | 1.58 | 1.32 | 2.3 | 1.4 | 1.8 | -0.3 |
| 2016 | E+ | 1.88 | 1.57 | 2.2 | 1.5 | 2.4 | -0.2 |
| 2015 | E | 2.00 | 1.67 | 2.5 | 1.7 | 2.6 | -0.4 |
| 2014 | E | 1.34 | 1.12 | 1.8 | 1.2 | 2.2 | 0.0 |
| 2013 | E | 1.35 | 1.13 | 2.0 | 1.3 | 3.0 | -0.4 |
| 2012 | E | 0.42 | 0.35 | 1.8 | 0.7 | 3.1 | -1.2 |

Rating Indexes

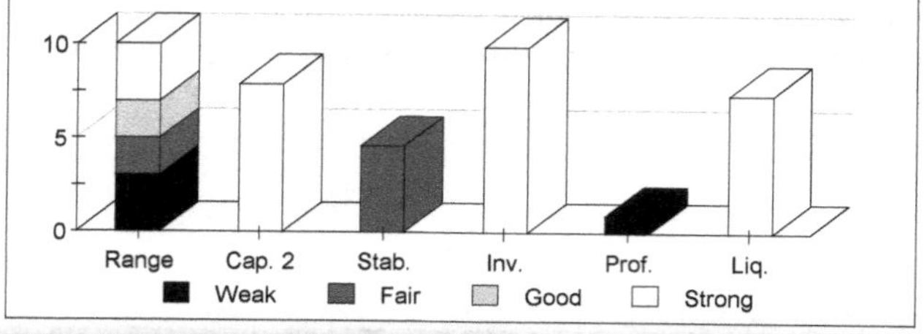


## SANFORD HEART OF AMERICA HEALTH PLAN D+ Weak

**Major Rating Factors:** Weak profitability index (1.1 on a scale of 0 to 10). Good overall results on stability tests (5.0) despite a decline in enrollment during 2016. Rating is significantly influenced by the fair financial results of Sanford. Strong capitalization index (8.8) based on excellent current risk-adjusted capital (severe loss scenario).
**Other Rating Factors:** High quality investment portfolio (9.9). Excellent liquidity (7.1) with ample operational cash flow and liquid investments.
**Principal Business:** Comp med (58%), other (42%)
**Mem Phys: 16:** 18,286 **15:** 14,811 **16 MLR** 84.4% **/ 16 Admin Exp** N/A
**Enroll(000): Q3 17:** 1 **16:** 1 **15:** 1 **Med Exp PMPM:** $339
**Principal Investments:** Long-term bonds (69%), cash and equiv (31%)
**Provider Compensation ($000):** FFS ($2,936)
**Total Member Encounters:** Phys (2,289), non-phys (2,456)
**Group Affiliation:** Sanford
**Licensed in:** ND
**Address:** 1749 38th Street South, Fargo, ND 58104
**Phone:** (605) 328-6868 **Dom State:** ND **Commenced Bus:** August 1982

| Data Date | Rating | RACR #1 | RACR #2 | Total Assets ($mil) | Capital ($mil) | Net Premium ($mil) | Net Income ($mil) |
|---|---|---|---|---|---|---|---|
| 9-17 | D+ | 2.76 | 2.30 | 3.5 | 2.6 | 2.5 | 0.4 |
| 9-16 | D+ | 1.73 | 1.44 | 3.2 | 2.1 | 2.7 | 0.2 |
| 2016 | D+ | 2.22 | 1.85 | 3.1 | 2.2 | 3.4 | 0.2 |
| 2015 | D+ | 1.67 | 1.39 | 3.1 | 1.9 | 3.5 | -0.6 |
| 2014 | E | 0.34 | 0.29 | 1.5 | 0.5 | 3.7 | -0.7 |
| 2013 | D+ | 0.87 | 0.72 | 2.0 | 1.2 | 3.8 | -0.4 |
| 2012 | C- | 0.96 | 0.80 | 1.5 | 0.9 | 4.1 | -0.3 |

Rating Indexes

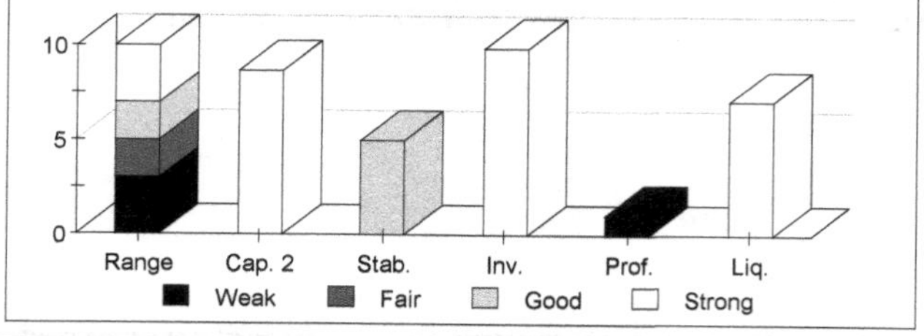

## SANTA BARBARA SAN LUIS OBISPO REGION — B — Good

**Major Rating Factors:** Good liquidity (6.6 on a scale of 0 to 10) with sufficient resources (cash flows and marketable investments) to handle a spike in claims. Excellent profitability (9.9). Strong capitalization index (9.5) based on excellent current risk-adjusted capital (severe loss scenario).
**Other Rating Factors:** Excellent overall results on stability tests (7.4).
**Principal Business:** Medicaid (100%)
**Mem Phys: 16:** N/A **15:** N/A **16 MLR** 83.9% **/ 16 Admin Exp** N/A
**Enroll(000): Q3 17:** 178 **16:** 178 **15:** 164 **Med Exp PMPM:** $267
**Principal Investments ($000):** Cash and equiv ($202,771)
**Provider Compensation ($000):** None
**Total Member Encounters:** N/A
**Group Affiliation:** None
**Licensed in:** CA
**Address:** 801 Gateway Blvd Suite 100, So. San Francisco, CA 94080
**Phone:** (650) 616-2151 **Dom State:** CA **Commenced Bus:** September 1983

| Data Date | Rating | RACR #1 | RACR #2 | Total Assets ($mil) | Capital ($mil) | Net Premium ($mil) | Net Income ($mil) |
|---|---|---|---|---|---|---|---|
| 9-17 | B | 4.64 | 2.79 | 518.2 | 211.5 | 534.0 | 29.2 |
| 9-16 | C- | 3.25 | 1.96 | 308.1 | 141.9 | 504.0 | 52.5 |
| 2016 | C | 2.97 | 1.79 | 359.9 | 150.6 | 658.3 | 61.2 |
| 2015 | D- | 1.58 | 0.96 | 250.1 | 89.4 | 597.5 | 58.9 |
| 2014 | E+ | 0.14 | 0.09 | 135.4 | 37.8 | 383.7 | 2.8 |
| 2013 | E+ | 0.08 | 0.05 | 121.5 | 35.0 | 343.9 | 13.4 |
| 2012 | E+ | N/A | N/A | 81.5 | 21.6 | 328.7 | 0.7 |

Rating Indexes

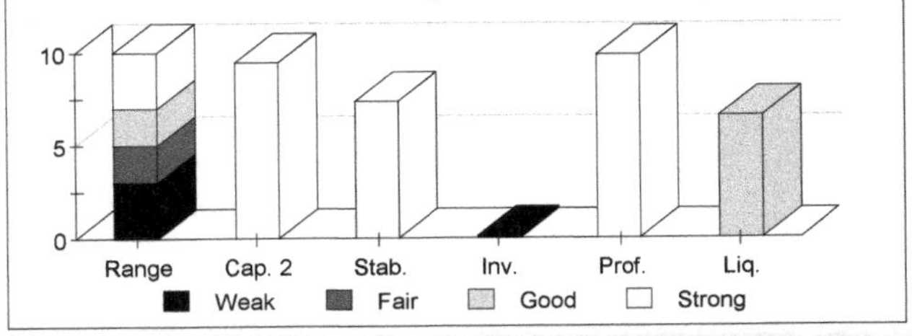


## SANTA CLARA COUNTY — D — Weak

**Major Rating Factors:** Fair capitalization index (4.4 on a scale of 0 to 10) based on weak current risk-adjusted capital (moderate loss scenario). Fair overall results on stability tests (4.3). Good overall profitability index (6.9).
**Other Rating Factors:** Excellent liquidity (7.0) with sufficient resources (cash flows and marketable investments) to handle a spike in claims.
**Principal Business:** Managed care (100%)
**Mem Phys: 16:** N/A **15:** N/A **16 MLR** 92.7% **/ 16 Admin Exp** N/A
**Enroll(000): Q3 17:** 164 **16:** 165 **15:** 151 **Med Exp PMPM:** $245
**Principal Investments ($000):** Cash and equiv ($107,123)
**Provider Compensation ($000):** None
**Total Member Encounters:** N/A
**Group Affiliation:** None
**Licensed in:** CA
**Address:** 2480 North 1st St Suite 200, San Jose, CA 95131
**Phone:** (408) 885-5606 **Dom State:** CA **Commenced Bus:** September 1985

| Data Date | Rating | RACR #1 | RACR #2 | Total Assets ($mil) | Capital ($mil) | Net Premium ($mil) | Net Income ($mil) |
|---|---|---|---|---|---|---|---|
| 9-17 | D | 0.70 | 0.43 | 152.5 | 28.2 | 389.5 | 2.1 |
| 9-16 | D | 0.61 | 0.38 | 162.8 | 23.9 | 385.0 | 8.4 |
| 2016 | D | 0.62 | 0.38 | 130.8 | 25.3 | 514.9 | 9.8 |
| 2015 | C | 0.78 | 0.48 | 96.0 | 29.4 | 487.9 | 8.4 |
| 2014 | C | 0.99 | 0.61 | 56.8 | 21.1 | 281.6 | 5.7 |
| 2013 | C | 1.05 | 0.64 | 29.6 | 15.3 | 212.1 | 7.3 |
| 2012 | C | 1.72 | 1.05 | 35.0 | 21.5 | 182.7 | 7.1 |

Rating Indexes

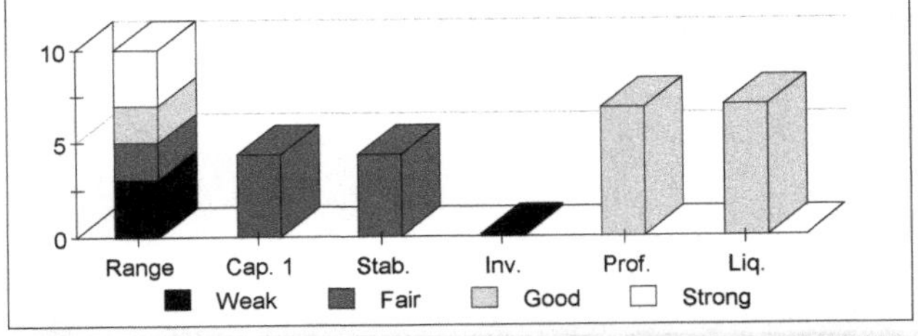


## SANTA CLARA COUNTY HEALTH AUTHORITY — C — Fair

**Major Rating Factors:** Excellent profitability (10.0 on a scale of 0 to 10). Strong capitalization index (7.8) based on excellent current risk-adjusted capital (severe loss scenario). Excellent overall results on stability tests (7.2) based on healthy premium and capital growth during 2016.
**Other Rating Factors:** Excellent liquidity (8.2) with ample operational cash flow and liquid investments.
**Principal Business:** Medicaid (91%), Medicare (9%)
**Mem Phys: 16:** N/A **15:** N/A **16 MLR** 87.7% **/ 16 Admin Exp** N/A
**Enroll(000): Q3 17:** 271 **16:** 273 **15:** 247 **Med Exp PMPM:** $346
**Principal Investments ($000):** Cash and equiv ($145,777)
**Provider Compensation ($000):** None
**Total Member Encounters:** N/A
**Group Affiliation:** None
**Licensed in:** CA
**Address:** 4050 Calle Real, Santa Barbara, CA 93110
**Phone:** (805) 685-9525 **Dom State:** CA **Commenced Bus:** February 1997

| Data Date | Rating | RACR #1 | RACR #2 | Total Assets ($mil) | Capital ($mil) | Net Premium ($mil) | Net Income ($mil) |
|---|---|---|---|---|---|---|---|
| 9-17 | C | 2.73 | 1.65 | 993.8 | 166.3 | 1,196.4 | 55.1 |
| 9-16 | C | 1.69 | 1.02 | 437.9 | 83.6 | 882.4 | 11.0 |
| 2016 | C | 1.67 | 1.01 | 576.5 | 100.3 | 1,259.2 | 27.7 |
| 2015 | C | 1.43 | 0.86 | 295.9 | 72.6 | 959.7 | 37.4 |
| 2014 | C | 1.39 | 0.85 | 114.5 | 40.9 | 452.2 | 8.3 |
| 2013 | C- | 1.39 | 0.85 | 95.4 | 32.6 | 384.2 | 8.3 |
| 2012 | D+ | 1.12 | 0.71 | 60.0 | 24.2 | 246.4 | 0.1 |

Rating Indexes

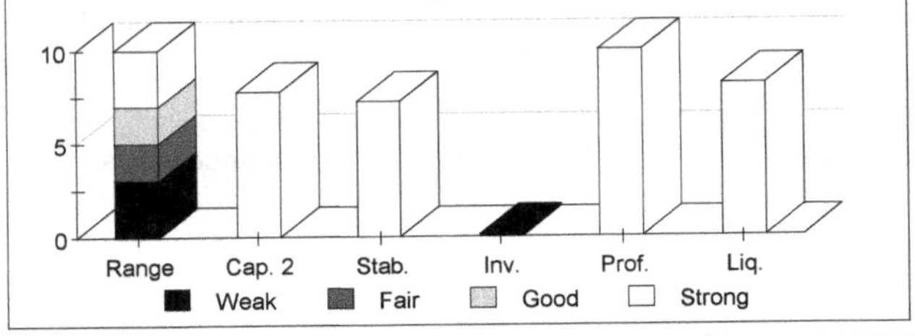

## SANTA CRUZ-MONTEREY-MERCED MGD MED B- Good

**Major Rating Factors:** Excellent profitability (9.5 on a scale of 0 to 10). Strong capitalization index (10.0) based on excellent current risk-adjusted capital (severe loss scenario). Excellent overall results on stability tests (7.7).
**Other Rating Factors:** Excellent liquidity (8.7) with ample operational cash flow and liquid investments.
**Principal Business:** Medicaid (100%)
**Mem Phys: 16:** N/A **15:** N/A **16 MLR** 87.3% **/ 16 Admin Exp** N/A
**Enroll(000): Q3 17:** 355 **16:** 352 **15:** 340 **Med Exp PMPM:** $226
**Principal Investments ($000):** Cash and equiv ($872,706)
**Provider Compensation ($000):** None
**Total Member Encounters:** N/A
**Group Affiliation:** None
**Licensed in:** CA
**Address:** 210 East Hacienda Avenue, Campbell, CA 95008
**Phone:** (408) 874-1701 **Dom State:** CA **Commenced Bus:** N/A

| Data Date | Rating | RACR #1 | RACR #2 | Total Assets ($mil) | Capital ($mil) | Net Premium ($mil) | Net Income ($mil) |
|---|---|---|---|---|---|---|---|
| 9-17 | B- | 12.87 | 7.88 | 1,450.9 | 642.3 | 854.5 | 49.9 |
| 9-16 | B- | 13.91 | 8.50 | 1,237.4 | 576.5 | 803.6 | 57.2 |
| 2016 | B- | 11.77 | 7.21 | 1,393.4 | 592.4 | 1,075.9 | 73.1 |
| 2015 | B- | 12.48 | 7.62 | 1,097.2 | 519.2 | 985.4 | 118.4 |
| 2014 | B- | 11.20 | 6.92 | 714.0 | 400.9 | 789.8 | 87.7 |
| 2013 | B- | 10.15 | 6.25 | 418.3 | 313.2 | 684.4 | 127.6 |
| 2012 | B- | 5.73 | 3.51 | 325.9 | 185.6 | 588.3 | 26.0 |

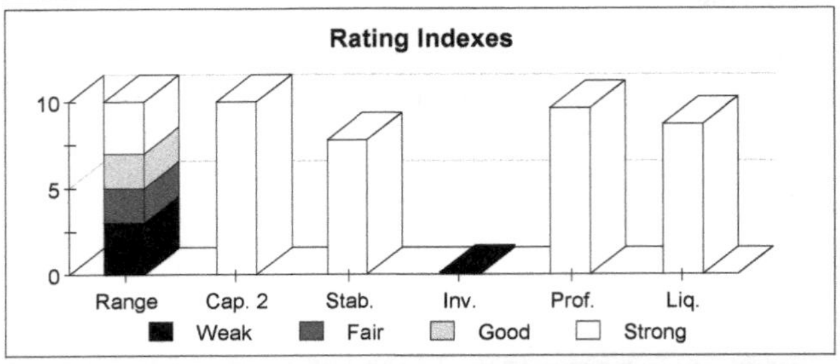


## SCAN HEALTH PLAN C Fair

**Major Rating Factors:** Weak profitability index (2.9 on a scale of 0 to 10). Good overall results on stability tests (5.2). Strong capitalization index (8.3) based on excellent current risk-adjusted capital (severe loss scenario).
**Other Rating Factors:** Excellent liquidity (7.4) with ample operational cash flow and liquid investments.
**Principal Business:** Medicare (97%), Medicaid (3%)
**Mem Phys: 16:** N/A **15:** N/A **16 MLR** 88.5% **/ 16 Admin Exp** N/A
**Enroll(000): Q3 17:** 187 **16:** 171 **15:** 162 **Med Exp PMPM:** $978
**Principal Investments ($000):** Cash and equiv ($467,112)
**Provider Compensation ($000):** None
**Total Member Encounters:** N/A
**Group Affiliation:** SCAN Group
**Licensed in:** CA
**Address:** 300 Santana Row Suite 300, San Jose, CA 95128
**Phone:** (650) 404-3798 **Dom State:** CA **Commenced Bus:** March 1985

| Data Date | Rating | RACR #1 | RACR #2 | Total Assets ($mil) | Capital ($mil) | Net Premium ($mil) | Net Income ($mil) |
|---|---|---|---|---|---|---|---|
| 9-17 | C | 3.23 | 2.01 | 829.1 | 359.9 | 1,922.8 | 16.6 |
| 9-16 | U | 3.62 | 2.26 | 813.8 | 404.6 | 1,711.1 | 52.4 |
| 2016 | C- | 2.96 | 1.84 | 571.9 | 332.1 | 2,251.5 | 41.2 |
| 2015 | C | 3.10 | 1.93 | 569.8 | 352.2 | 2,165.1 | 24.8 |
| 2014 | C | 3.83 | 2.38 | 575.5 | 402.4 | 2,013.4 | -59.1 |
| 2013 | C | 5.00 | 3.10 | 647.6 | 461.5 | 1,862.2 | 38.0 |
| 2012 | C | 6.11 | 3.78 | 721.7 | 498.5 | 1,682.1 | 59.8 |

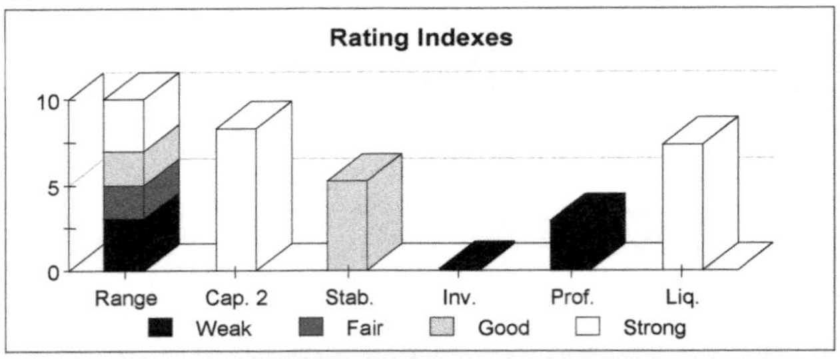


## SCOTT & WHITE HEALTH PLAN C- Fair

**Major Rating Factors:** Fair capitalization index (3.4 on a scale of 0 to 10) based on weak current risk-adjusted capital (moderate loss scenario). Weak profitability index (0.9). Good quality investment portfolio (5.9).
**Other Rating Factors:** Good liquidity (5.3) with sufficient resources (cash flows and marketable investments) to handle a spike in claims. Excellent overall results on stability tests (7.6) despite a decline in enrollment during 2016.
**Principal Business:** Comp med (59%), Medicare (22%), Medicaid (18%)
**Mem Phys: 16:** 12,551 **15:** 9,916 **16 MLR** 95.5% **/ 16 Admin Exp** N/A
**Enroll(000): Q3 17:** 157 **16:** 165 **15:** 182 **Med Exp PMPM:** $317
**Principal Investments:** Cash and equiv (26%), long-term bonds (17%), real estate (9%), nonaffiliate common stock (8%), affiliate common stock (6%), other (34%)
**Provider Compensation ($000):** Contr fee ($536,114), capitation ($61,886), FFS ($42,184), bonus arrang ($45)
**Total Member Encounters:** Phys (627,290), non-phys (206,798)
**Group Affiliation:** Baylor Scott & White Holdings
**Licensed in:** TX
**Address:** 1206 WEST CAMPUS DRIVE, TEMPLE, TX 76502
**Phone:** (254) 298-3000 **Dom State:** TX **Commenced Bus:** January 1982

| Data Date | Rating | RACR #1 | RACR #2 | Total Assets ($mil) | Capital ($mil) | Net Premium ($mil) | Net Income ($mil) |
|---|---|---|---|---|---|---|---|
| 9-17 | C- | 0.70 | 0.58 | 287.2 | 100.8 | 523.0 | 2.2 |
| 9-16 | C- | 0.72 | 0.60 | 193.8 | 51.4 | 514.3 | -30.6 |
| 2016 | C- | 0.66 | 0.55 | 270.8 | 97.1 | 670.1 | -59.1 |
| 2015 | B | 1.28 | 1.07 | 218.5 | 83.3 | 688.9 | -12.2 |
| 2014 | B | 1.79 | 1.49 | 174.3 | 84.8 | 662.4 | 24.2 |
| 2013 | B | 1.53 | 1.28 | 149.9 | 63.1 | 589.6 | 2.9 |
| 2012 | B- | 1.37 | 1.14 | 140.6 | 57.4 | 579.4 | 6.1 |

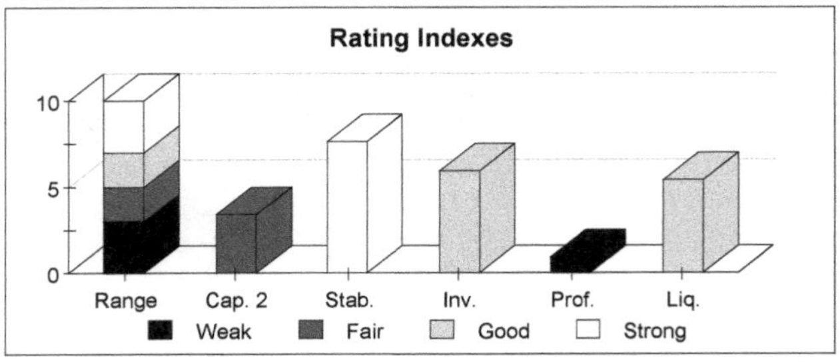

## SCRIPPS HEALTH PLAN SERVICES INC — C- — Fair

**Major Rating Factors:** Good capitalization index (5.8 on a scale of 0 to 10) based on fair current risk-adjusted capital (moderate loss scenario). Good overall results on stability tests (6.3) despite fair risk diversification due to the company's size. Excellent profitability (7.7).
**Other Rating Factors:** Excellent liquidity (7.0) with sufficient resources (cash flows and marketable investments) to handle a spike in claims.
**Principal Business:** Managed care (100%)
**Mem Phys: 16:** N/A **15:** N/A **16 MLR** 100.0% **/ 16 Admin Exp** N/A
**Enroll(000): Q3 17:** 116 **16:** 104 **15:** 44 **Med Exp PMPM:** $424
**Principal Investments ($000):** Cash and equiv ($87,626)
**Provider Compensation ($000):** None
**Total Member Encounters:** N/A
**Group Affiliation:** Scripps Health
**Licensed in:** CA
**Address:** 3800 Kilroy Airport Way #100, Long Beach, CA 90801-5616
**Phone:** (562) 989-8320 **Dom State:** CA **Commenced Bus:** October 1997

| Data Date | Rating | RACR #1 | RACR #2 | Total Assets ($mil) | Capital ($mil) | Net Premium ($mil) | Net Income ($mil) |
|---|---|---|---|---|---|---|---|
| 9-17 | C- | 0.88 | 0.54 | 125.3 | 33.3 | 453.0 | 1.9 |
| 9-16 | D+ | 0.82 | 0.49 | 90.1 | 28.5 | 377.4 | 1.5 |
| 2016 | D+ | 0.77 | 0.46 | 90.7 | 29.1 | 515.3 | 2.1 |
| 2015 | D+ | 0.64 | 0.39 | 85.1 | 22.3 | 475.0 | 0.2 |
| 2014 | D | 0.73 | 0.44 | 78.8 | 18.7 | 338.1 | 0.2 |
| 2013 | E+ | 0.46 | 0.28 | 56.8 | 9.3 | 249.8 | 0.2 |
| 2012 | E | 0.42 | 0.26 | 36.3 | 8.1 | 229.3 | 0.3 |

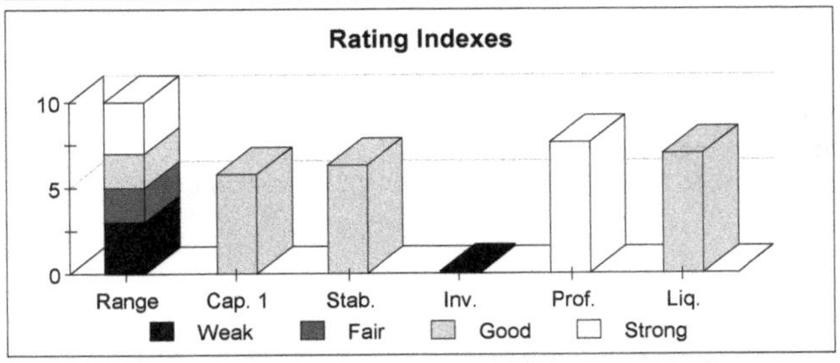


## SD STATE MEDICAL HOLDING CO — D — Weak

**Major Rating Factors:** Weak profitability index (0.6 on a scale of 0 to 10). Weak overall results on stability tests (1.9) based on a decline in the number of member physicians during 2017, a significant 50% decrease in enrollment during the period. Weak liquidity (2.0) as a spike in claims may stretch capacity.
**Other Rating Factors:** Fair capitalization index (2.9) based on weak current risk-adjusted capital (moderate loss scenario). Fair quality investment portfolio (4.4).
**Principal Business:** Comp med (100%)
**Mem Phys: 16:** 2,022 **15:** 2,418 **16 MLR** 133.6% **/ 16 Admin Exp** N/A
**Enroll(000): Q3 17:** 10 **16:** 18 **15:** 36 **Med Exp PMPM:** $391
**Principal Investments:** Cash and equiv (62%), affiliate common stock (27%), long-term bonds (12%)
**Provider Compensation ($000):** Contr fee ($92,286), FFS ($22,765), bonus arrang ($2,526)
**Total Member Encounters:** Phys (180,752), non-phys (20,624)
**Group Affiliation:** Avera Health
**Licensed in:** SD
**Address:** 2600 W 49th St, Sioux Falls, SD 57105
**Phone:** (605) 334-4000 **Dom State:** SD **Commenced Bus:** April 1985

| Data Date | Rating | RACR #1 | RACR #2 | Total Assets ($mil) | Capital ($mil) | Net Premium ($mil) | Net Income ($mil) |
|---|---|---|---|---|---|---|---|
| 9-17 | D | 0.63 | 0.52 | 23.4 | 12.7 | 44.5 | 5.4 |
| 9-16 | D | N/A | N/A | 32.4 | 12.0 | 53.3 | -1.3 |
| 2016 | D | 0.46 | 0.39 | 26.8 | 9.3 | 79.2 | -4.5 |
| 2015 | D | N/A | N/A | 50.3 | 11.5 | 107.9 | -19.7 |
| 2014 | B | 1.47 | 1.23 | 40.2 | 20.5 | 111.8 | 0.4 |
| 2013 | B | 1.66 | 1.38 | 42.4 | 23.3 | 113.9 | 3.2 |
| 2012 | B | 1.73 | 1.44 | 41.5 | 23.7 | 110.3 | 4.4 |

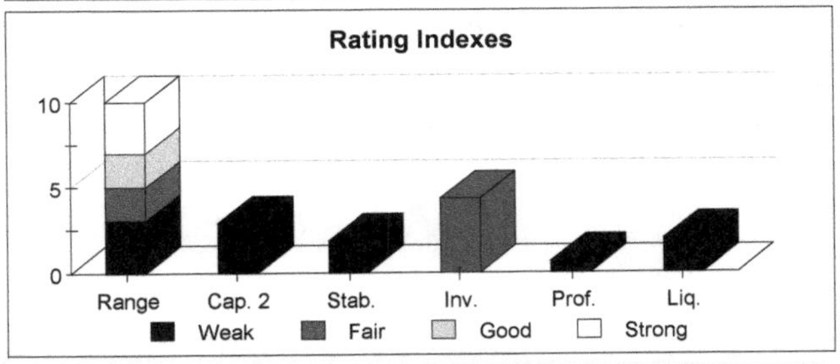


## SEASIDE HEALTH PLAN — D- — Weak

**Major Rating Factors:** Weak profitability index (0.8 on a scale of 0 to 10). Poor capitalization index (0.0) based on weak current risk-adjusted capital (severe loss scenario). Weak liquidity (0.0) as a spike in claims may stretch capacity.
**Other Rating Factors:** Fair overall results on stability tests (3.3) in spite of healthy premium and capital growth during 2016 but an excessive 51% enrollment growth during the period.
**Principal Business:** Managed care (100%)
**Mem Phys: 16:** N/A **15:** N/A **16 MLR** 108.3% **/ 16 Admin Exp** N/A
**Enroll(000): Q3 17:** 40 **16:** 40 **15:** 27 **Med Exp PMPM:** $78
**Principal Investments ($000):** Cash and equiv ($8,852)
**Provider Compensation ($000):** None
**Total Member Encounters:** N/A
**Group Affiliation:** None
**Licensed in:** CA
**Address:** 10790 Rancho Bernardo Road, San Diego, CA 92127
**Phone:** (858) 927-5360 **Dom State:** CA **Commenced Bus:** May 2013

| Data Date | Rating | RACR #1 | RACR #2 | Total Assets ($mil) | Capital ($mil) | Net Premium ($mil) | Net Income ($mil) |
|---|---|---|---|---|---|---|---|
| 9-17 | D- | 0.34 | 0.22 | 14.5 | 8.0 | 30.6 | -4.9 |
| 9-16 | D | 0.96 | 0.66 | 14.1 | 7.3 | 22.6 | -8.7 |
| 2016 | D | 0.59 | 0.38 | 15.1 | 9.1 | 31.4 | -9.8 |
| 2015 | D | 0.55 | 0.38 | 11.2 | 5.9 | 21.5 | -9.7 |
| 2014 | U | 2.22 | 1.53 | 11.0 | 7.6 | 10.1 | -5.1 |
| 2013 | N/A | N/A | N/A | 0.4 | 0.1 | N/A | -0.2 |
| 2012 | N/A | N/A | N/A | N/A | N/A | N/A | N/A |

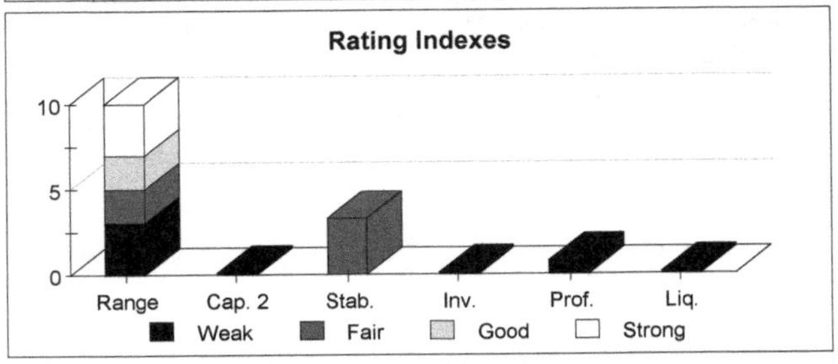

## SECURITY HEALTH PLAN OF WI INC * A- Excellent

**Major Rating Factors:** Strong capitalization index (7.9 on a scale of 0 to 10) based on excellent current risk-adjusted capital (severe loss scenario). Good overall results on stability tests (5.7). Good liquidity (6.7) with sufficient resources (cash flows and marketable investments) to handle a spike in claims.
**Other Rating Factors:** Fair profitability index (4.3). Fair quality investment portfolio (4.2).
**Principal Business:** Comp med (49%), Medicare (40%), Medicaid (10%)
**Mem Phys: 16:** 4,860 **15:** 4,342 **16 MLR** 91.3% **/ 16 Admin Exp** N/A
**Enroll(000): Q3 17:** 204 **16:** 201 **15:** 201 **Med Exp PMPM:** $445
**Principal Investments:** Nonaffiliate common stock (30%), cash and equiv (19%), long-term bonds (17%), real estate (2%), other (32%)
**Provider Compensation ($000):** Contr fee ($566,018), FFS ($261,801), capitation ($248,015)
**Total Member Encounters:** N/A
**Group Affiliation:** Marshfield Clinic Health System Inc
**Licensed in:** WI
**Address:** 1515 St Joseph Ave, Marshfield, WI 54449
**Phone:** (715) 221-9555 **Dom State:** WI **Commenced Bus:** September 1986

| Data Date | Rating | RACR #1 | RACR #2 | Total Assets ($mil) | Capital ($mil) | Net Premium ($mil) | Net Income ($mil) |
|---|---|---|---|---|---|---|---|
| 9-17 | A- | 2.07 | 1.73 | 427.3 | 207.9 | 918.2 | 35.4 |
| 9-16 | A- | 2.28 | 1.90 | 411.7 | 222.5 | 883.2 | 21.1 |
| 2016 | A- | 2.25 | 1.88 | 384.0 | 225.1 | 1,178.1 | 11.4 |
| 2015 | A- | 2.06 | 1.72 | 350.6 | 202.4 | 1,158.3 | 18.6 |
| 2014 | A- | 1.95 | 1.62 | 320.2 | 187.9 | 1,098.0 | 28.3 |
| 2013 | A- | 1.72 | 1.43 | 280.1 | 152.5 | 1,001.8 | -19.3 |
| 2012 | A+ | 2.13 | 1.78 | 308.6 | 176.3 | 978.0 | 8.5 |

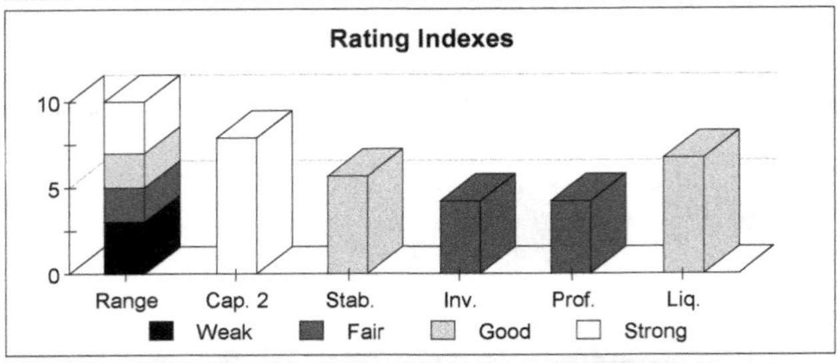


## SECURITYCARE OF TENNESSEE INC B Good

**Major Rating Factors:** Strong capitalization (9.0 on a scale of 0 to 10) based on excellent current risk-adjusted capital (severe loss scenario). High quality investment portfolio (9.9). Weak profitability index (0.9).
**Other Rating Factors:** Weak liquidity (0.9) as a spike in claims may stretch capacity.
**Principal Business:** Medicare (100%)
**Mem Phys: 16:** 14,285 **15:** 11,760 **16 MLR** 90.2% **/ 16 Admin Exp** N/A
**Enroll(000): Q3 17:** 3 **16:** 3 **15:** 2 **Med Exp PMPM:** $593
**Principal Investments:** Cash and equiv (88%), long-term bonds (12%)
**Provider Compensation ($000):** Contr fee ($19,923), capitation ($4), bonus arrang ($3)
**Total Member Encounters:** Phys (70,755), non-phys (6,153)
**Group Affiliation:** BlueCross BlueShield of Tennessee
**Licensed in:** TN
**Address:** 1 Cameron Hill Circle, Chattanooga, TN 37402-0001
**Phone:** (423) 535-5600 **Dom State:** TN **Commenced Bus:** December 2012

| Data Date | Rating | RACR #1 | RACR #2 | Total Assets ($mil) | Capital ($mil) | Net Premium ($mil) | Net Income ($mil) |
|---|---|---|---|---|---|---|---|
| 9-17 | B | 2.98 | 2.49 | 11.5 | 6.8 | 21.1 | 0.2 |
| 9-16 | B | 2.69 | 2.24 | 9.6 | 5.0 | 16.1 | -0.7 |
| 2016 | B | 3.01 | 2.51 | 9.3 | 6.8 | 21.7 | -0.6 |
| 2015 | B | 1.93 | 1.61 | 6.1 | 3.7 | 15.4 | -1.3 |
| 2014 | B | 2.00 | 1.67 | 2.8 | 2.6 | 1.8 | -0.4 |
| 2013 | N/A | N/A | N/A | 3.0 | 3.0 | N/A | N/A |
| 2012 | N/A | N/A | N/A | 3.0 | 3.0 | N/A | N/A |

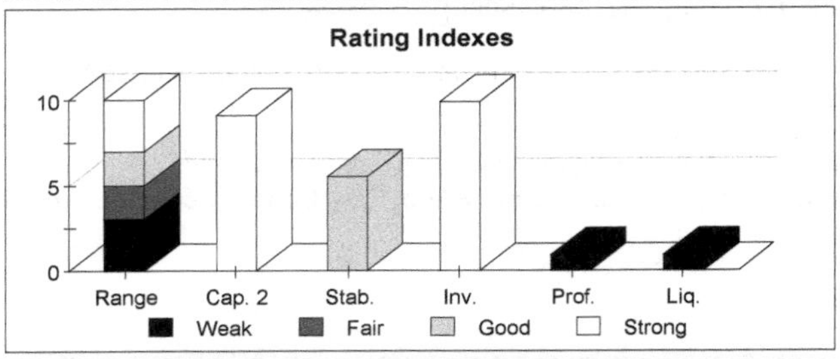


## SELECT HEALTH OF SOUTH CAROLINA INC B- Good

**Major Rating Factors:** Excellent profitability (9.3 on a scale of 0 to 10). Strong capitalization index (8.3) based on excellent current risk-adjusted capital (severe loss scenario). High quality investment portfolio (9.3).
**Other Rating Factors:** Excellent overall results on stability tests (8.4). Fair financial strength from affiliates. Excellent liquidity (6.9) with sufficient resources (cash flows and marketable investments) to handle a spike in claims.
**Principal Business:** Medicaid (96%), Medicare (4%)
**Mem Phys: 16:** 22,355 **15:** 16,881 **16 MLR** 84.3% **/ 16 Admin Exp** N/A
**Enroll(000): Q3 17:** 364 **16:** 361 **15:** 332 **Med Exp PMPM:** $268
**Principal Investments:** Cash and equiv (54%), long-term bonds (33%), nonaffiliate common stock (13%)
**Provider Compensation ($000):** Contr fee ($1,013,806), capitation ($70,824)
**Total Member Encounters:** Phys (2,590,738), non-phys (733,172)
**Group Affiliation:** Independence Health Group Inc
**Licensed in:** KY, MS, RI, SC
**Address:** 4390 Belle Oaks Drive Suite 40, North Charleston, SC 29405
**Phone:** (843) 569-1759 **Dom State:** SC **Commenced Bus:** December 1996

| Data Date | Rating | RACR #1 | RACR #2 | Total Assets ($mil) | Capital ($mil) | Net Premium ($mil) | Net Income ($mil) |
|---|---|---|---|---|---|---|---|
| 9-17 | B- | 2.38 | 1.98 | 340.4 | 170.4 | 1,019.5 | 24.9 |
| 9-16 | B- | 2.35 | 1.96 | 315.9 | 149.0 | 974.9 | 26.9 |
| 2016 | B- | 2.37 | 1.97 | 354.0 | 169.7 | 1,337.3 | 46.8 |
| 2015 | B- | 2.12 | 1.77 | 271.5 | 133.3 | 1,175.8 | 32.2 |
| 2014 | B | 1.89 | 1.58 | 277.7 | 119.3 | 1,135.5 | 36.1 |
| 2013 | B | 1.61 | 1.34 | 198.2 | 82.5 | 848.7 | 9.7 |
| 2012 | B | 2.01 | 1.68 | 166.2 | 78.5 | 678.4 | 14.7 |

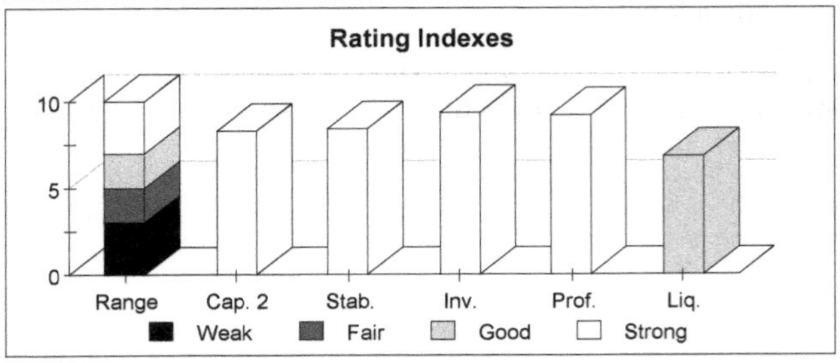

## SELECTCARE HEALTH PLANS INC — C+ — Fair

**Major Rating Factors:** Good overall profitability index (5.2 on a scale of 0 to 10). Good liquidity (6.9) with sufficient resources (cash flows and marketable investments) to handle a spike in claims. Strong capitalization (10.0) based on excellent current risk-adjusted capital (severe loss scenario).
**Other Rating Factors:** High quality investment portfolio (9.7).
**Principal Business:** Medicare (100%)
**Mem Phys: 16:** 128 **15:** 186 **16 MLR** 82.5% **/ 16 Admin Exp** N/A
**Enroll(000): Q3 17:** 2 **16:** 3 **15:** 4 **Med Exp PMPM:** $764
**Principal Investments:** Long-term bonds (97%), cash and equiv (3%)
**Provider Compensation ($000):** Contr fee ($27,415), capitation ($1,016)
**Total Member Encounters:** Phys (41,447), non-phys (11,157)
**Group Affiliation:** WellCare Health Plans Inc
**Licensed in:** TX
**Address:** 4888 Loop Central Dr Ste 700, Houston, TX 77081-2181
**Phone:** (713) 965-9444 **Dom State:** TX **Commenced Bus:** July 2005

| Data Date | Rating | RACR #1 | RACR #2 | Total Assets ($mil) | Capital ($mil) | Net Premium ($mil) | Net Income ($mil) |
|---|---|---|---|---|---|---|---|
| 9-17 | C+ | 3.96 | 3.30 | 22.7 | 15.6 | 18.5 | 0.7 |
| 9-16 | C+ | 3.18 | 2.65 | 22.0 | 13.9 | 25.7 | -0.2 |
| 2016 | C+ | 3.90 | 3.25 | 18.9 | 14.7 | 33.7 | 0.7 |
| 2015 | C+ | 3.30 | 2.75 | 19.0 | 14.0 | 42.7 | 0.7 |
| 2014 | C | 2.70 | 2.25 | 20.4 | 13.5 | 51.4 | -0.4 |
| 2013 | C | 2.73 | 2.28 | 20.3 | 14.7 | 56.0 | 1.6 |
| 2012 | C | 4.03 | 3.36 | 23.5 | 17.6 | 54.2 | 4.9 |

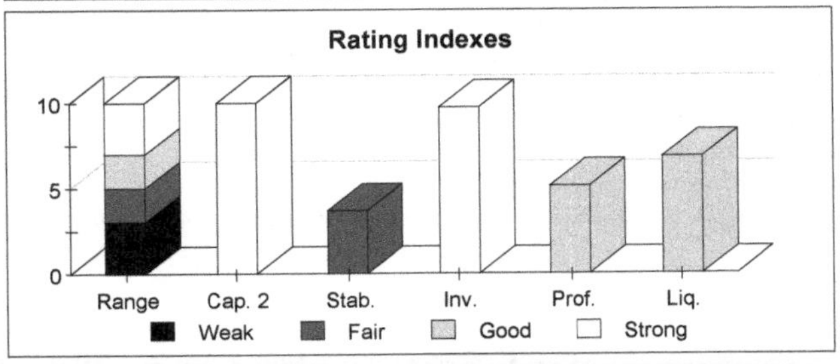


## SELECTCARE OF TEXAS INC — B — Good

**Major Rating Factors:** Good overall results on stability tests (6.1 on a scale of 0 to 10) based on steady enrollment growth, averaging 10% over the past five years. Good liquidity (6.9) with sufficient resources (cash flows and marketable investments) to handle a spike in claims. Excellent profitability (7.7).
**Other Rating Factors:** Strong capitalization index (7.1) based on excellent current risk-adjusted capital (severe loss scenario). High quality investment portfolio (8.7).
**Principal Business:** Medicare (100%)
**Mem Phys: 16:** 6,073 **15:** 5,378 **16 MLR** 83.9% **/ 16 Admin Exp** N/A
**Enroll(000): Q3 17:** 68 **16:** 66 **15:** 63 **Med Exp PMPM:** $890
**Principal Investments:** Long-term bonds (93%), cash and equiv (5%), pref stock (2%)
**Provider Compensation ($000):** Contr fee ($359,787), capitation ($341,123)
**Total Member Encounters:** Phys (837,529), non-phys (77,927)
**Group Affiliation:** WellCare Health Plans Inc
**Licensed in:** TX
**Address:** 4888 Loop Central Dr Ste 700, Houston, TX 77081-2181
**Phone:** (713) 965-9444 **Dom State:** TX **Commenced Bus:** May 2001

| Data Date | Rating | RACR #1 | RACR #2 | Total Assets ($mil) | Capital ($mil) | Net Premium ($mil) | Net Income ($mil) |
|---|---|---|---|---|---|---|---|
| 9-17 | B | 1.41 | 1.17 | 278.3 | 73.2 | 633.9 | 3.9 |
| 9-16 | B | 1.21 | 1.01 | 218.6 | 55.5 | 628.2 | 3.0 |
| 2016 | B | 1.27 | 1.06 | 160.6 | 62.6 | 833.8 | 10.3 |
| 2015 | B | 1.37 | 1.14 | 146.4 | 61.5 | 799.0 | 9.6 |
| 2014 | C | 1.60 | 1.34 | 138.8 | 62.9 | 728.5 | 9.0 |
| 2013 | C | 1.81 | 1.51 | 133.1 | 64.2 | 652.0 | 11.7 |
| 2012 | B | 3.35 | 2.79 | 180.5 | 103.7 | 614.3 | 15.6 |

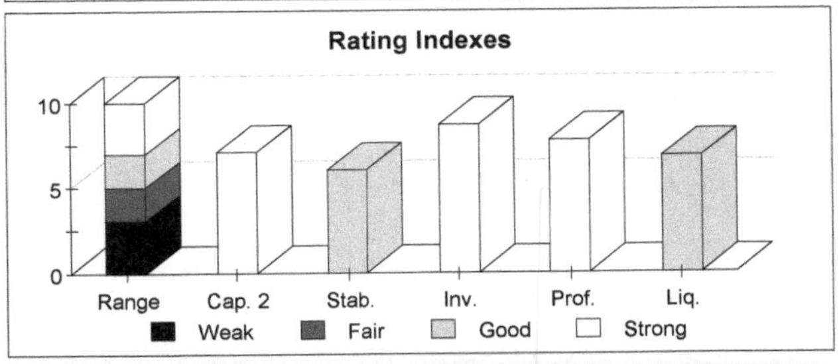


## SELECTHEALTH BENEFIT ASR CO INC — C — Fair

**Major Rating Factors:** Excellent profitability (8.9 on a scale of 0 to 10). Strong capitalization (10.0) based on excellent current risk-adjusted capital (severe loss scenario). High quality investment portfolio (9.9).
**Other Rating Factors:** Excellent liquidity (8.4) with ample operational cash flow and liquid investments.
**Principal Business:** Other (100%)
**Mem Phys: 16:** N/A **15:** N/A **16 MLR** 12.1% **/ 16 Admin Exp** N/A
**Enroll(000): Q3 17:** 0 **16:** 1 **15:** 3 **Med Exp PMPM:** $305
**Principal Investments:** Long-term bonds (52%), cash and equiv (48%)
**Provider Compensation ($000):** FFS ($5,572)
**Total Member Encounters:** Phys (319), non-phys (260)
**Group Affiliation:** Intermountain Health Care Inc
**Licensed in:** ID, UT
**Address:** 5381Green St, Murray, UT 84123
**Phone:** (801) 442-5000 **Dom State:** UT **Commenced Bus:** July 1992

| Data Date | Rating | RACR #1 | RACR #2 | Total Assets ($mil) | Capital ($mil) | Net Premium ($mil) | Net Income ($mil) |
|---|---|---|---|---|---|---|---|
| 9-17 | C | 3.69 | 3.08 | 28.6 | 17.0 | 27.3 | 1.2 |
| 9-16 | C | 3.04 | 2.54 | 25.9 | 16.5 | 25.1 | 1.9 |
| 2016 | C | 3.35 | 2.79 | 25.1 | 16.0 | 34.4 | 1.2 |
| 2015 | B- | 2.80 | 2.33 | 23.1 | 15.0 | 30.7 | 2.2 |
| 2014 | B | 5.02 | 4.18 | 21.1 | 14.0 | 14.1 | 0.8 |
| 2013 | B | 6.74 | 5.61 | 18.0 | 13.1 | 7.3 | 2.6 |
| 2012 | B | 5.45 | 4.54 | 15.8 | 10.4 | 7.4 | 1.0 |

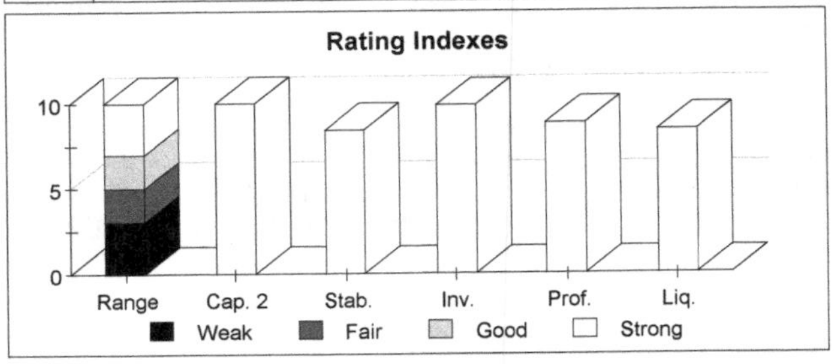

## SELECTHEALTH INC — C — Fair

**Major Rating Factors:** Weak profitability index (0.9 on a scale of 0 to 10). Good overall results on stability tests (5.3). Good liquidity (5.9) with sufficient resources (cash flows and marketable investments) to handle a spike in claims.
**Other Rating Factors:** Strong capitalization index (7.9) based on excellent current risk-adjusted capital (severe loss scenario). High quality investment portfolio (7.1).
**Principal Business:** Comp med (75%), Medicaid (12%), Medicare (11%), FEHB (1%)
**Mem Phys: 16:** 9,618 **15:** 9,979 **16 MLR** 97.6% **/ 16 Admin Exp** N/A
**Enroll(000): Q3 17:** 653 **16:** 685 **15:** 639 **Med Exp PMPM:** $304
**Principal Investments:** Long-term bonds (41%), nonaffiliate common stock (34%), cash and equiv (17%), other (7%)
**Provider Compensation ($000):** Contr fee ($1,390,808), bonus arrang ($713,926), FFS ($401,565), capitation ($6,445)
**Total Member Encounters:** Phys (3,417,465), non-phys (1,637,066)
**Group Affiliation:** Intermountain Health Care Inc
**Licensed in:** ID, UT
**Address:** 5381 Green Street, Murray, UT 84123
**Phone:** (801) 442-5000 **Dom State:** UT **Commenced Bus:** February 1984

| Data Date | Rating | RACR #1 | RACR #2 | Total Assets ($mil) | Capital ($mil) | Net Premium ($mil) | Net Income ($mil) |
|---|---|---|---|---|---|---|---|
| 9-17 | C | 2.05 | 1.71 | 1,078.3 | 446.0 | 1,966.2 | 58.2 |
| 9-16 | C | 1.46 | 1.21 | 881.1 | 270.8 | 1,944.2 | -47.8 |
| 2016 | C | 1.49 | 1.24 | 1,085.9 | 332.0 | 2,611.6 | -136.6 |
| 2015 | C | 1.61 | 1.35 | 912.5 | 298.8 | 2,029.2 | -374.0 |
| 2014 | A | 2.94 | 2.45 | 848.5 | 444.8 | 1,891.4 | 26.9 |
| 2013 | A | 3.78 | 3.15 | 767.6 | 464.8 | 1,461.4 | 50.8 |
| 2012 | A | 3.88 | 3.23 | 573.3 | 376.0 | 1,160.2 | 33.4 |

**Rating Indexes**

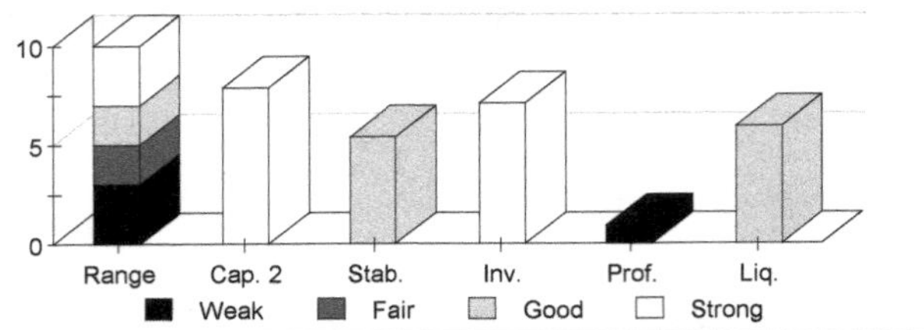


## SENDERO HEALTH PLANS INC — E- — Very Weak

**Major Rating Factors:** Weak profitability index (1.9 on a scale of 0 to 10). Fair capitalization (2.9) based on fair current risk-adjusted capital (moderate loss scenario). High quality investment portfolio (9.9).
**Other Rating Factors:** Excellent liquidity (7.6) with ample operational cash flow and liquid investments.
**Principal Business:** Comp med (52%), Medicaid (43%), other (5%)
**Mem Phys: 16:** N/A **15:** N/A **16 MLR** 80.3% **/ 16 Admin Exp** N/A
**Enroll(000): Q3 17:** 51 **16:** 34 **15:** 20 **Med Exp PMPM:** $162
**Principal Investments:** Cash and equiv (100%)
**Provider Compensation ($000):** FFS ($47,683), capitation ($15,484)
**Total Member Encounters:** Phys (166,665), non-phys (43,409)
**Group Affiliation:** Travis County Healthcare District
**Licensed in:** TX
**Address:** 2028 E Ben White Blvd Ste 400, Austin, TX 78741
**Phone:** (512) 978-8147 **Dom State:** TX **Commenced Bus:** March 2012

| Data Date | Rating | RACR #1 | RACR #2 | Total Assets ($mil) | Capital ($mil) | Net Premium ($mil) | Net Income ($mil) |
|---|---|---|---|---|---|---|---|
| 9-17 | E- | 0.79 | 0.66 | 58.7 | 12.4 | 124.3 | 3.6 |
| 9-16 | E- | 0.47 | 0.39 | 47.7 | 6.3 | 55.5 | -4.2 |
| 2016 | E- | 0.74 | 0.62 | 56.9 | 11.5 | 85.1 | 4.5 |
| 2015 | E- | 0.79 | 0.66 | 31.8 | 11.0 | 58.6 | -4.8 |
| 2014 | D+ | 0.89 | 0.74 | 30.4 | 8.7 | 49.0 | -17.7 |
| 2013 | N/A | N/A | N/A | 16.3 | 5.8 | 38.2 | -1.5 |
| 2012 | N/A | N/A | N/A | 16.7 | 5.2 | 19.2 | -9.2 |

**Rating Indexes**

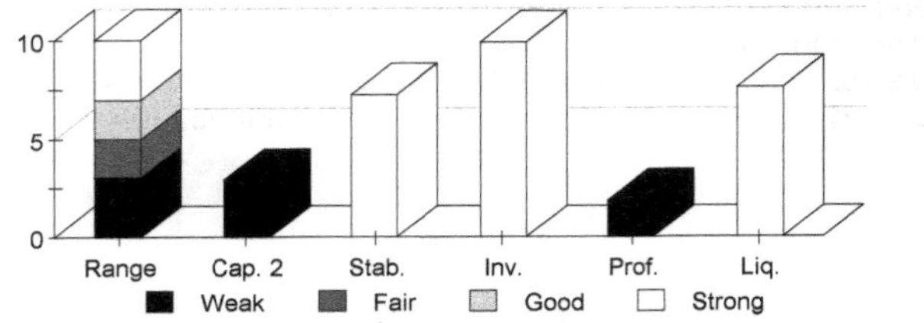


## SENIOR HEALTH INSURANCE COMPANY OF PENNSYLVANIA — E- — Very Weak

**Major Rating Factors:** Low quality investment portfolio (0.0 on a scale of 0 to 10) containing large holdings of BBB rated bonds in addition to significant exposure to junk bonds. Weak profitability (1.0) with operating losses during 2016. Weak overall results on stability tests (0.1) including weak risk adjusted capital in prior years, negative cash flow from operations for 2016.
**Other Rating Factors:** Strong overall capitalization (7.4) based on mixed results -- excessive policy leverage mitigated by excellent risk adjusted capital (severe loss scenario). Excellent liquidity (7.2).
**Principal Business:** Individual health insurance (88%), reinsurance (11%), and group health insurance (1%).
**Principal Investments:** NonCMO investment grade bonds (66%), CMOs and structured securities (11%), noninv. grade bonds (8%), common & preferred stock (5%), and mortgages in good standing (2%).
**Investments in Affiliates:** None
**Group Affiliation:** Senior Health Care Oversight Trust
**Licensed in:** All states except CT, NY, RI, VT, PR
**Commenced Business:** February 1965
**Address:** 27 North Front Street, Harrisburg, PA 17101-1606
**Phone:** (317) 566-7500 **Domicile State:** PA **NAIC Code:** 76325

| Data Date | Rating | RACR #1 | RACR #2 | Total Assets ($mil) | Capital ($mil) | Net Premium ($mil) | Net Income ($mil) |
|---|---|---|---|---|---|---|---|
| 2016 | E- | 1.42 | 1.27 | 2,736.1 | 28.3 | -1,153.0 | -39.4 |
| 2015 | D | 0.59 | 0.29 | 2,879.8 | 55.8 | 136.7 | -9.0 |
| 2014 | D+ | 0.87 | 0.42 | 2,907.0 | 80.0 | 155.2 | -56.1 |
| 2013 | D+ | 1.25 | 0.62 | 2,985.9 | 98.2 | 173.7 | -3.4 |
| 2012 | D+ | 1.22 | 0.60 | 3,080.7 | 105.5 | 194.0 | -4.0 |

**Junk Bonds as a % of Capital**

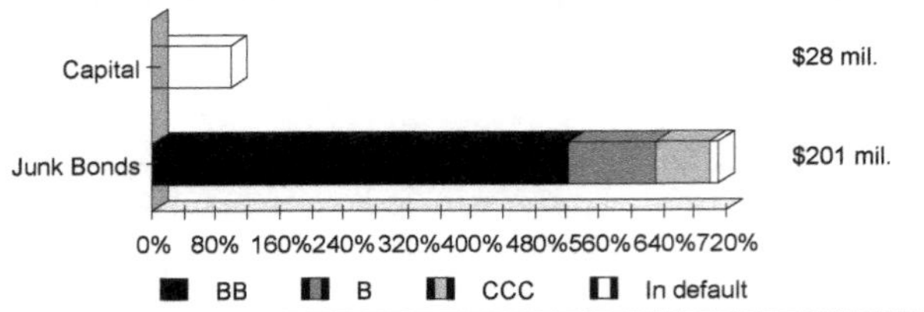

## SENIOR WHOLE HEALTH OF NEW YORK INC E Very Weak

**Major Rating Factors:** Weak profitability index (0.9 on a scale of 0 to 10). Good capitalization (6.3) based on good current risk-adjusted capital (severe loss scenario). High quality investment portfolio (9.9).
**Other Rating Factors:** Excellent liquidity (7.2) with ample operational cash flow and liquid investments.
**Principal Business:** Medicaid (93%), Medicare (4%), other (3%)
**Mem Phys: 16:** 18,831 **15:** 10,064 **16 MLR** 87.1% **/ 16 Admin Exp** N/A
**Enroll(000): Q3 17:** 9 **16:** 7 **15:** 4 **Med Exp PMPM:** $3,265
**Principal Investments:** Cash and equiv (100%)
**Provider Compensation ($000):** None
**Total Member Encounters:** Non-phys (424,627)
**Group Affiliation:** TA XI LP
**Licensed in:** NY
**Address:** 111 Broadway Ste 1505, NEW YORK, NY 10006
**Phone:** (617) 494-5353 **Dom State:** NY **Commenced Bus:** January 2007

| Data Date | Rating | RACR #1 | RACR #2 | Total Assets ($mil) | Capital ($mil) | Net Premium ($mil) | Net Income ($mil) |
|---|---|---|---|---|---|---|---|
| 9-17 | E | 1.13 | 0.94 | 90.2 | 32.5 | 291.8 | 5.1 |
| 9-16 | E | 1.65 | 1.38 | 68.0 | 26.3 | 172.0 | 9.4 |
| 2016 | E | 0.93 | 0.78 | 78.0 | 26.8 | 245.7 | 9.5 |
| 2015 | E | 1.10 | 0.92 | 53.6 | 17.5 | 133.1 | 10.6 |
| 2014 | E | 0.63 | 0.53 | 23.1 | 5.6 | 53.2 | -2.1 |
| 2013 | D- | 1.23 | 1.02 | 11.3 | 5.2 | 17.8 | -0.7 |
| 2012 | E | 0.01 | 0.01 | 8.7 | 0.1 | 27.6 | -8.7 |

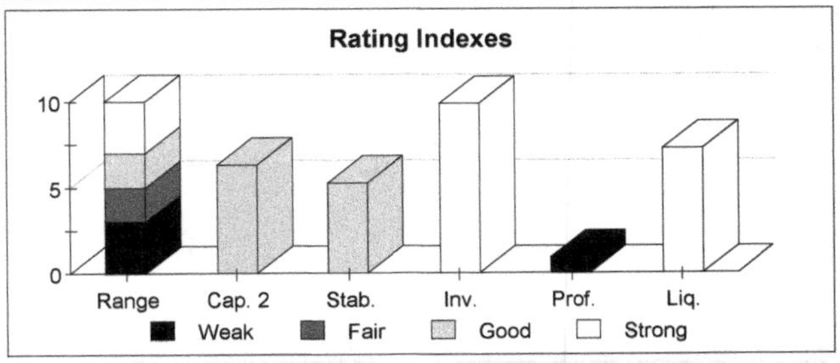


## SETON HEALTH PLAN INC B- Good

**Major Rating Factors:** Good overall profitability index (5.5 on a scale of 0 to 10). Good quality investment portfolio (5.4). Good overall results on stability tests (5.3).
**Other Rating Factors:** Strong capitalization index (8.5) based on excellent current risk-adjusted capital (severe loss scenario). Excellent liquidity (7.0) with ample operational cash flow and liquid investments.
**Principal Business:** Medicaid (76%), comp med (24%)
**Mem Phys: 16:** 3,996 **15:** 3,662 **16 MLR** 89.3% **/ 16 Admin Exp** N/A
**Enroll(000): Q3 17:** 25 **16:** 26 **15:** 26 **Med Exp PMPM:** $164
**Principal Investments:** Nonaffiliate common stock (49%), cash and equiv (45%), long-term bonds (6%)
**Provider Compensation ($000):** Contr fee ($35,544), FFS ($4,698), capitation ($646), other ($9,451)
**Total Member Encounters:** Phys (240,794), non-phys (43,615)
**Group Affiliation:** Ascension Health
**Licensed in:** TX
**Address:** 1345 Philomena Strret, Austin, TX 78723
**Phone:** (512) 324-3350 **Dom State:** TX **Commenced Bus:** July 1995

| Data Date | Rating | RACR #1 | RACR #2 | Total Assets ($mil) | Capital ($mil) | Net Premium ($mil) | Net Income ($mil) |
|---|---|---|---|---|---|---|---|
| 9-17 | B- | 2.52 | 2.10 | 53.3 | 23.7 | 22.3 | 5.8 |
| 9-16 | C | 1.81 | 1.51 | 23.9 | 15.8 | 44.9 | 0.8 |
| 2016 | C+ | 1.84 | 1.53 | 28.0 | 17.4 | 58.3 | 1.9 |
| 2015 | C | 1.73 | 1.45 | 32.6 | 15.1 | 53.5 | 1.5 |
| 2014 | B- | 1.97 | 1.64 | 35.7 | 23.5 | 50.0 | -0.3 |
| 2013 | C | 2.24 | 1.86 | 32.7 | 23.6 | 54.0 | 7.4 |
| 2012 | B | 2.61 | 2.17 | 25.7 | 16.0 | 40.2 | -2.1 |

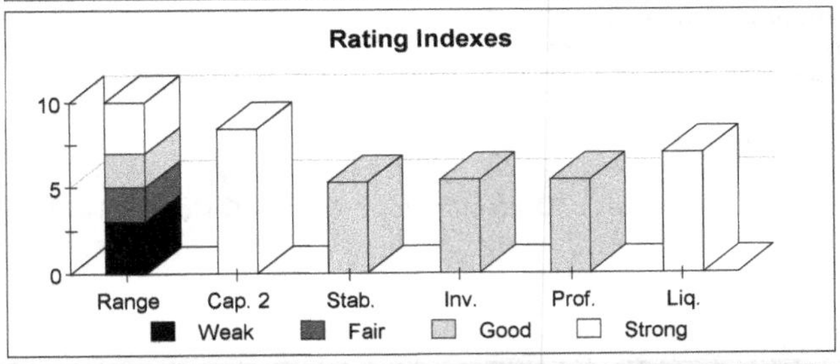


## SHA LLC E Very Weak

**Major Rating Factors:** Weak profitability index (0.9 on a scale of 0 to 10). Weak liquidity (2.2) as a spike in claims may stretch capacity. Good capitalization index (5.0) based on good current risk-adjusted capital (severe loss scenario).
**Other Rating Factors:** Good quality investment portfolio (6.6). Good overall results on stability tests (5.2).
**Principal Business:** Medicaid (53%), comp med (41%), Medicare (6%)
**Mem Phys: 16:** 21,293 **15:** 20,931 **16 MLR** 91.7% **/ 16 Admin Exp** N/A
**Enroll(000): Q3 17:** 171 **16:** 184 **15:** 158 **Med Exp PMPM:** $271
**Principal Investments:** Long-term bonds (42%), nonaffiliate common stock (29%), cash and equiv (16%), affiliate common stock (10%), real estate (3%)
**Provider Compensation ($000):** Contr fee ($542,188), FFS ($12,034), capitation ($1,479)
**Total Member Encounters:** Phys (864,634), non-phys (718,375)
**Group Affiliation:** Providence St Joseph Health
**Licensed in:** TX
**Address:** 12940 N Hwy 183, Austin, TX 78750-3203
**Phone:** (512) 257-6001 **Dom State:** TX **Commenced Bus:** August 1994

| Data Date | Rating | RACR #1 | RACR #2 | Total Assets ($mil) | Capital ($mil) | Net Premium ($mil) | Net Income ($mil) |
|---|---|---|---|---|---|---|---|
| 9-17 | E | 0.92 | 0.77 | 101.4 | 56.4 | 425.7 | -16.3 |
| 9-16 | E | 1.34 | 1.11 | 130.0 | 65.0 | 437.9 | -16.7 |
| 2016 | E | 1.11 | 0.92 | 131.5 | 66.4 | 614.6 | -18.2 |
| 2015 | E | 1.51 | 1.26 | 136.3 | 72.2 | 510.0 | -1.2 |
| 2014 | E | 1.09 | 0.90 | 121.1 | 56.4 | 490.6 | -31.9 |
| 2013 | E | 1.09 | 0.90 | 115.3 | 55.4 | 478.0 | -9.1 |
| 2012 | C+ | 1.12 | 0.94 | 116.5 | 49.1 | 414.1 | 2.9 |

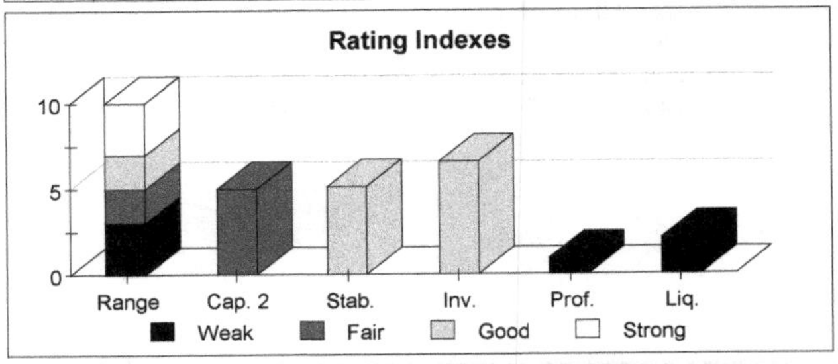

## SHARP HEALTH PLAN — B Good

**Major Rating Factors:** Good capitalization index (6.9 on a scale of 0 to 10) based on excellent current risk-adjusted capital (severe loss scenario). Excellent profitability (8.4). Excellent overall results on stability tests (7.1).
**Other Rating Factors:** Excellent liquidity (7.0) with ample operational cash flow and liquid investments.
**Principal Business:** Managed care (99%)
**Mem Phys: 16:** N/A **15:** N/A **16 MLR** 87.9% **/ 16 Admin Exp** N/A
**Enroll(000): Q3 17:** 137 **16:** 130 **15:** 107 **Med Exp PMPM:** $360
**Principal Investments ($000):** Cash and equiv ($42,021)
**Provider Compensation ($000):** None
**Total Member Encounters:** N/A
**Group Affiliation:** San Diego Hospital Assoc
**Licensed in:** CA
**Address:** 2801 Atlantic Avenue, Long Beach, CA 90806
**Phone:** (714) 377-3215 **Dom State:** CA **Commenced Bus:** November 1992

| Data Date | Rating | RACR #1 | RACR #2 | Total Assets ($mil) | Capital ($mil) | Net Premium ($mil) | Net Income ($mil) |
|---|---|---|---|---|---|---|---|
| 9-17 | B | 1.63 | 1.06 | 136.6 | 82.7 | 522.5 | 12.4 |
| 9-16 | B | 1.56 | 1.01 | 130.3 | 69.4 | 456.4 | 5.2 |
| 2016 | B | 1.38 | 0.89 | 115.3 | 70.4 | 612.1 | 6.7 |
| 2015 | B | 1.43 | 0.93 | 103.4 | 64.1 | 498.5 | 7.9 |
| 2014 | B | 1.55 | 1.01 | 86.7 | 56.4 | 382.6 | 9.4 |
| 2013 | B | 1.41 | 0.92 | 65.8 | 47.2 | 320.4 | 7.1 |
| 2012 | B- | 1.32 | 0.86 | 60.1 | 40.0 | 277.3 | 5.8 |

Rating Indexes

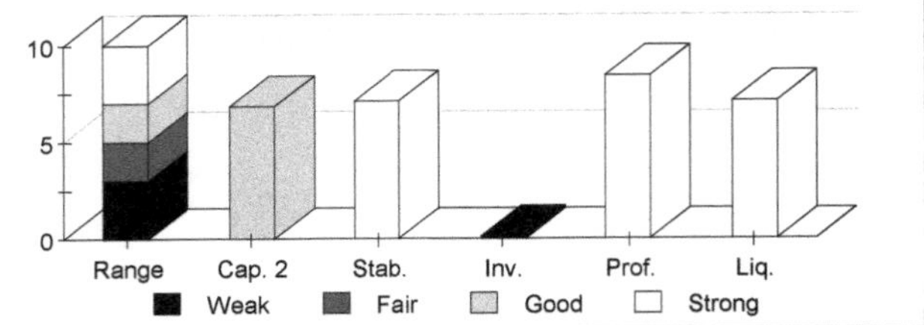


## SHELTERPOINT LIFE INSURANCE COMPANY * — A Excellent

**Major Rating Factors:** Good overall results on stability tests (6.8 on a scale of 0 to 10). Strengths that enhance stability include excellent operational trends and good risk diversification. Strong capitalization (8.7) based on excellent risk adjusted capital (severe loss scenario). Furthermore, this high level of risk adjusted capital has been consistently maintained over the last five years. High quality investment portfolio (7.5).
**Other Rating Factors:** Excellent profitability (7.9). Excellent liquidity (7.0).
**Principal Business:** Group health insurance (98%) and group life insurance (2%).
**Principal Investments:** NonCMO investment grade bonds (68%), CMOs and structured securities (16%), common & preferred stock (10%), noninv. grade bonds (3%), and cash (2%).
**Investments in Affiliates:** 10%
**Group Affiliation:** ShelterPoint Group Inc
**Licensed in:** CA, CO, CT, DC, DE, FL, IL, MD, MA, MI, MN, NJ, NY, NC, PA, RI, SC, TN
**Commenced Business:** November 1972
**Address:** 600 NORTHERN BLVD, GREAT NECK, NY 11530
**Phone:** (516) 829-8100 **Domicile State:** NY **NAIC Code:** 81434

| Data Date | Rating | RACR #1 | RACR #2 | Total Assets ($mil) | Capital ($mil) | Net Premium ($mil) | Net Income ($mil) |
|---|---|---|---|---|---|---|---|
| 9-17 | A | 2.51 | 2.11 | 110.1 | 62.2 | 75.7 | 3.8 |
| 9-16 | A | 2.44 | 2.06 | 103.0 | 57.5 | 71.0 | 3.7 |
| 2016 | A | 2.47 | 2.09 | 106.5 | 58.8 | 91.8 | 5.5 |
| 2015 | A | 2.38 | 2.01 | 107.5 | 54.9 | 88.6 | 5.6 |
| 2014 | A | 2.40 | 2.03 | 104.4 | 54.9 | 86.7 | 10.0 |
| 2013 | A | 3.82 | 2.91 | 100.4 | 48.2 | 82.4 | 5.7 |
| 2012 | A- | 4.13 | 3.18 | 93.5 | 47.3 | 71.9 | 4.5 |

Rating Indexes

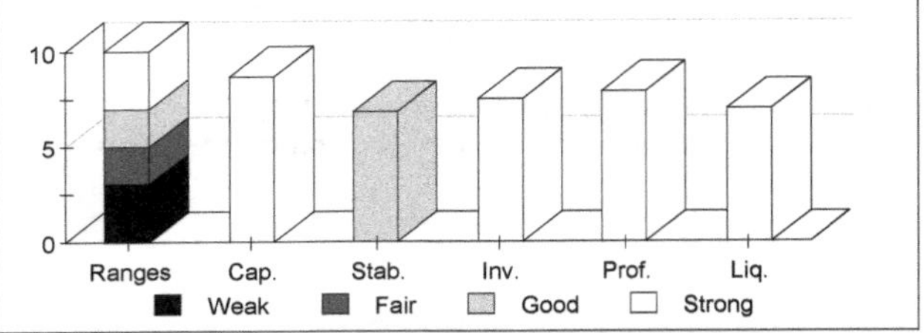


## SIERRA HEALTH AND LIFE INS CO INC — B Good

**Major Rating Factors:** Good liquidity (6.9 on a scale of 0 to 10) with sufficient resources (cash flows and marketable investments) to handle a spike in claims. Excellent profitability (9.3). Strong capitalization (9.2) based on excellent current risk-adjusted capital (severe loss scenario).
**Other Rating Factors:** High quality investment portfolio (9.8).
**Principal Business:** Medicare (95%), comp med (4%)
**Mem Phys: 16:** 1,025,812 **15:** 946,185 **16 MLR** 80.4% **/ 16 Admin Exp** N/A
**Enroll(000): Q3 17:** 1,235 **16:** 877 **15:** 749 **Med Exp PMPM:** $689
**Principal Investments:** Long-term bonds (91%), cash and equiv (9%)
**Provider Compensation ($000):** Contr fee ($4,385,452), FFS ($2,488,282), capitation ($44,358), bonus arrang ($35,201)
**Total Member Encounters:** Phys (10,355,998), non-phys (3,440,271)
**Group Affiliation:** UnitedHealth Group Incorporated
**Licensed in:** All states except PR
**Address:** 2720 N TENAYA WAY, LAS VEGAS, NV 89128
**Phone:** (702) 242-7732 **Dom State:** NV **Commenced Bus:** August 1906

| Data Date | Rating | RACR #1 | RACR #2 | Total Assets ($mil) | Capital ($mil) | Net Premium ($mil) | Net Income ($mil) |
|---|---|---|---|---|---|---|---|
| 9-17 | B | 3.11 | 2.59 | 4,140.2 | 1,490.2 | 10,119.9 | 451.0 |
| 9-16 | B | 2.81 | 2.34 | 2,851.2 | 1,081.5 | 6,656.5 | 338.2 |
| 2016 | B | 2.46 | 2.05 | 2,396.9 | 1,177.4 | 8,918.3 | 438.3 |
| 2015 | B | 2.03 | 1.69 | 1,676.6 | 779.0 | 6,732.9 | 96.0 |
| 2014 | B | 3.71 | 3.09 | 170.1 | 75.6 | 426.9 | 15.8 |
| 2013 | C | 5.65 | 4.71 | 127.0 | 70.8 | 257.1 | 11.6 |
| 2012 | N/A | N/A | N/A | 133.6 | 65.5 | 317.3 | N/A |

Rating Indexes

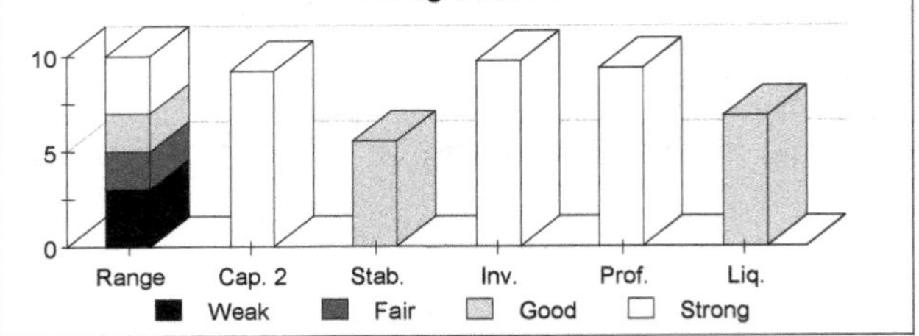

## SIGNATURE ADVANTAGE LLC D+ Weak

**Major Rating Factors:** Weak profitability index (0.9 on a scale of 0 to 10). Good capitalization (6.2) based on good current risk-adjusted capital (severe loss scenario). High quality investment portfolio (9.9).
**Other Rating Factors:** Excellent liquidity (7.3) with ample operational cash flow and liquid investments.
**Principal Business:** Medicare (100%)
**Mem Phys: 16:** N/A **15:** N/A **16 MLR** 81.8% **/ 16 Admin Exp** N/A
**Enroll(000): Q3 17:** 0 **16:** 0 **15:** N/A **Med Exp PMPM:** $2,086
**Principal Investments:** Cash and equiv (83%), long-term bonds (17%)
**Provider Compensation ($000):** Contr fee ($3,361)
**Total Member Encounters:** N/A
**Group Affiliation:** Las Palmas I-SNP LLC
**Licensed in:** KY
**Address:** 12201 Bluegrass Parkway, Louisville, KY 40299
**Phone:** (615) 308-7191 **Dom State:** KY **Commenced Bus:** March 2015

| Data Date | Rating | RACR #1 | RACR #2 | Total Assets ($mil) | Capital ($mil) | Net Premium ($mil) | Net Income ($mil) |
|---|---|---|---|---|---|---|---|
| 9-17 | D+ | 1.10 | 0.92 | 2.5 | 1.3 | 3.4 | -0.1 |
| 9-16 | N/A | N/A | N/A | 2.3 | 1.3 | 3.5 | -0.2 |
| 2016 | D+ | 1.36 | 1.13 | 2.2 | 1.5 | 4.1 | 0.1 |
| 2015 | N/A | N/A | N/A | 1.5 | 1.5 | N/A | -1.0 |
| 2014 | N/A | N/A | N/A | N/A | N/A | N/A | N/A |
| 2013 | N/A | N/A | N/A | N/A | N/A | N/A | N/A |
| 2012 | N/A | N/A | N/A | N/A | N/A | N/A | N/A |

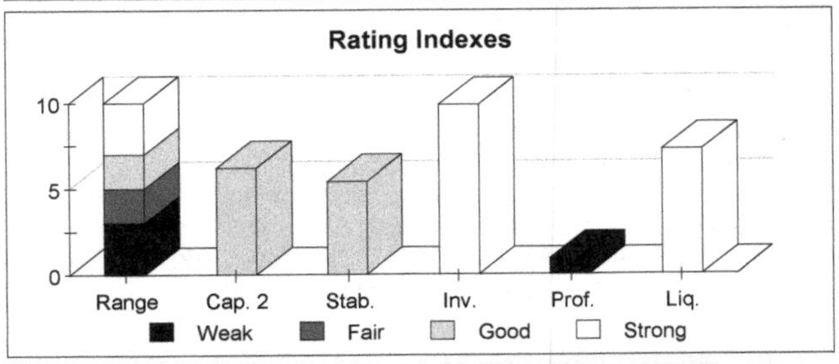


## SILVERSCRIPT INS CO D Weak

**Major Rating Factors:** Excellent profitability (9.1 on a scale of 0 to 10). Strong capitalization (10.0) based on excellent current risk-adjusted capital (severe loss scenario). High quality investment portfolio (9.9).
**Other Rating Factors:** Excellent liquidity (8.5) with ample operational cash flow and liquid investments.
**Principal Business:** Other (100%)
**Mem Phys: 16:** 68,000 **15:** 69,615 **16 MLR** 88.1% **/ 16 Admin Exp** N/A
**Enroll(000): Q3 17:** 4,500 **16:** 4,286 **15:** 3,486 **Med Exp PMPM:** $43
**Principal Investments:** Cash and equiv (100%)
**Provider Compensation ($000):** Other ($2,613,540)
**Total Member Encounters:** N/A
**Group Affiliation:** CVS Health Corp
**Licensed in:** All states, the District of Columbia and Puerto Rico
**Address:** 445 GREAT CIRCLE RD, NASHVILLE, TN 37228
**Phone:** (615) 743-6600 **Dom State:** TN **Commenced Bus:** January 2006

| Data Date | Rating | RACR #1 | RACR #2 | Total Assets ($mil) | Capital ($mil) | Net Premium ($mil) | Net Income ($mil) |
|---|---|---|---|---|---|---|---|
| 9-17 | D | 6.77 | 5.64 | 4,421.7 | 793.6 | 2,210.4 | 20.0 |
| 9-16 | D | 6.13 | 5.11 | 4,638.1 | 514.7 | 2,003.6 | 86.9 |
| 2016 | D | 6.84 | 5.70 | 2,823.6 | 799.2 | 2,483.6 | 206.1 |
| 2015 | D | 7.54 | 6.29 | 2,385.7 | 613.7 | 2,337.3 | 38.0 |
| 2014 | D | 3.99 | 3.32 | 2,764.2 | 448.1 | 2,516.2 | 124.6 |
| 2013 | D | 2.71 | 2.25 | 2,479.4 | 331.9 | 2,965.6 | 100.1 |
| 2012 | B- | 4.26 | 3.55 | 775.9 | 286.0 | 1,389.7 | 111.4 |

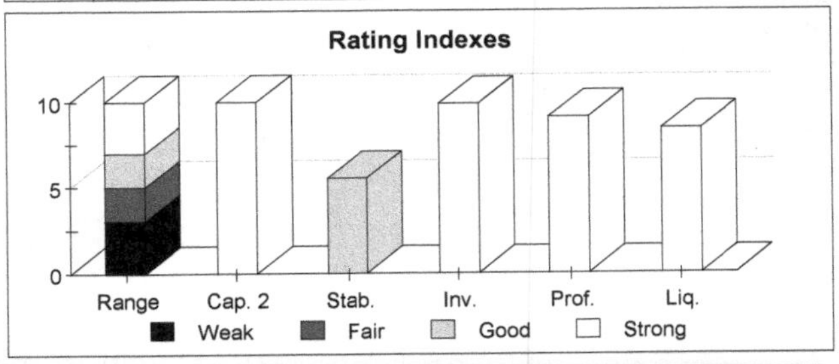


## SIMPLY HEALTHCARE PLANS INC * A- Excellent

**Major Rating Factors:** Excellent profitability (9.3 on a scale of 0 to 10). Strong capitalization (8.2) based on excellent current risk-adjusted capital (severe loss scenario). High quality investment portfolio (9.8).
**Other Rating Factors:** Excellent liquidity (7.0) with ample operational cash flow and liquid investments.
**Principal Business:** Medicaid (55%), Medicare (45%)
**Mem Phys: 16:** 20,907 **15:** 19,102 **16 MLR** 81.7% **/ 16 Admin Exp** N/A
**Enroll(000): Q3 17:** 134 **16:** 133 **15:** 116 **Med Exp PMPM:** $645
**Principal Investments:** Cash and equiv (75%), long-term bonds (25%)
**Provider Compensation ($000):** Contr fee ($754,154), capitation ($134,853), bonus arrang ($76,471)
**Total Member Encounters:** Phys (1,565,764), non-phys (124,208)
**Group Affiliation:** Anthem Inc
**Licensed in:** FL
**Address:** 9250 W FLAGLER St Ste 600, MIAMI, FL 33174
**Phone:** (757) 490-6900 **Dom State:** FL **Commenced Bus:** January 2010

| Data Date | Rating | RACR #1 | RACR #2 | Total Assets ($mil) | Capital ($mil) | Net Premium ($mil) | Net Income ($mil) |
|---|---|---|---|---|---|---|---|
| 9-17 | A- | 2.31 | 1.92 | 434.0 | 149.2 | 1,026.7 | 32.1 |
| 9-16 | B- | 1.34 | 1.12 | 323.1 | 91.9 | 898.6 | 32.2 |
| 2016 | B | 1.73 | 1.44 | 294.0 | 113.4 | 1,213.9 | 55.6 |
| 2015 | B- | 0.60 | 0.50 | 183.3 | 46.1 | 986.2 | 21.8 |
| 2014 | N/A | N/A | N/A | 199.8 | 27.3 | 834.6 | 11.9 |
| 2013 | N/A | N/A | N/A | 77.6 | 13.3 | 423.4 | 8.1 |
| 2012 | N/A | N/A | N/A | 43.5 | 11.0 | 150.0 | 2.1 |

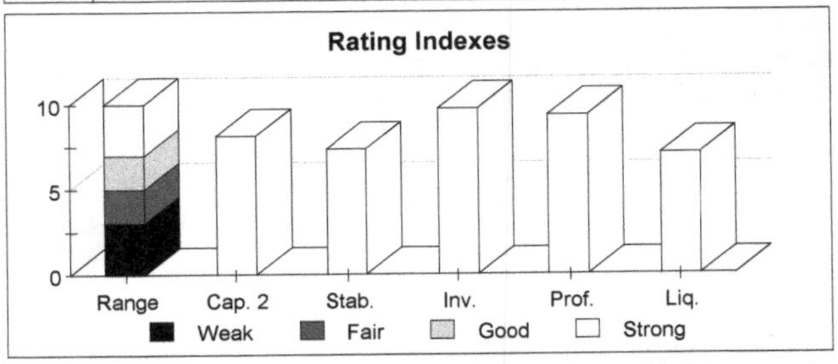


 * Denotes a Weiss Ratings Recommended Company

## SIRIUS AMERICA INS CO — B- Good

**Major Rating Factors:** Fair long-term capitalization (3.9 on a scale of 0 to 10) based on good current risk adjusted capital (moderate loss scenario) reflecting some improvement over results in 2016. Fair overall results on stability tests (3.5) including weak results on operational trends, negative cash flow from operations for 2016 and fair risk adjusted capital in prior years. The largest net exposure for one risk is high at 4.3% of capital.
**Other Rating Factors:** History of adequate reserve strength (6.6) as reserves have been consistently at an acceptable level. Good overall profitability index (5.2) despite modest operating losses during the first nine months of 2017. Return on equity has been fair, averaging 9.3% over the past five years. Excellent liquidity (7.4) with ample operational cash flow and liquid investments.
**Principal Business:** Group accident & health (99%) and commercial multiple peril (1%).
**Principal Investments:** Investment grade bonds (90%), misc. investments (9%), and cash (1%).
**Investments in Affiliates:** None
**Group Affiliation:** China Minsheng Investment Co Ltd
**Licensed in:** All states, the District of Columbia and Puerto Rico
**Commenced Business:** January 1980
**Address:** 140 BROADWAY - 32ND FLOOR, New York, NY 10005-1108
**Phone:** (212) 312-2500 **Domicile State:** NY **NAIC Code:** 38776

| Data Date | Rating | RACR #1 | RACR #2 | Loss Ratio % | Total Assets ($mil) | Capital ($mil) | Net Premium ($mil) | Net Income ($mil) |
|---|---|---|---|---|---|---|---|---|
| 9-17 | B- | 1.11 | 0.79 | N/A | 1,364.8 | 544.0 | 69.3 | -2.4 |
| 9-16 | C+ | 1.46 | 0.89 | N/A | 1,392.5 | 526.5 | 224.9 | 54.8 |
| 2016 | B- | 0.96 | 0.69 | 73.8 | 1,395.1 | 544.3 | 217.3 | 82.7 |
| 2015 | C+ | 1.42 | 0.87 | 53.7 | 1,387.6 | 517.6 | 283.9 | 74.7 |
| 2014 | C+ | 1.58 | 0.94 | 45.1 | 1,550.5 | 620.6 | 267.2 | 56.1 |
| 2013 | C+ | 2.14 | 1.21 | 48.9 | 1,559.4 | 548.4 | 252.8 | 55.9 |
| 2012 | C | 1.64 | 1.03 | 76.8 | 1,669.7 | 528.3 | 271.2 | 26.2 |

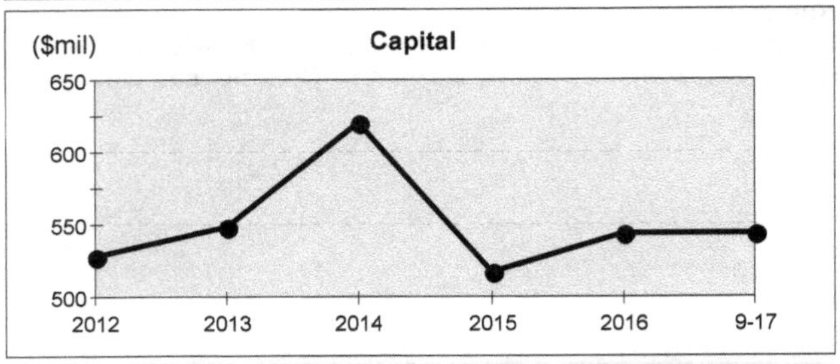


## SISTEMAS MEDICOS NACIONALES SA DE CV — C+ Fair

**Major Rating Factors:** Good overall results on stability tests (6.8 on a scale of 0 to 10) based on steady enrollment growth, averaging 9% over the past five years. Excellent profitability (10.0). Strong capitalization index (9.4) based on excellent current risk-adjusted capital (severe loss scenario).
**Other Rating Factors:** Excellent liquidity (7.6) with ample operational cash flow and liquid investments.
**Principal Business:** Managed care (94%), indemnity (6%)
**Mem Phys: 16:** N/A **15:** N/A **16 MLR** 57.2% **/ 16 Admin Exp** N/A
**Enroll(000): Q3 17:** 46 **16:** 45 **15:** 41 **Med Exp PMPM:** $86
**Principal Investments ($000):** Cash and equiv ($17,154)
**Provider Compensation ($000):** None
**Total Member Encounters:** N/A
**Group Affiliation:** None
**Licensed in:** CA
**Address:** 8520 Tech Way Suite 200, San Diego, CA 92123-1450
**Phone:** (858) 499-8240 **Dom State:** CA **Commenced Bus:** January 2000

| Data Date | Rating | RACR #1 | RACR #2 | Total Assets ($mil) | Capital ($mil) | Net Premium ($mil) | Net Income ($mil) |
|---|---|---|---|---|---|---|---|
| 9-17 | C+ | 4.10 | 2.71 | 52.2 | 32.7 | 66.0 | 10.5 |
| 9-16 | C+ | 3.90 | 2.59 | 40.1 | 25.6 | 58.9 | 9.5 |
| 2016 | C+ | 3.05 | 2.02 | 37.8 | 22.7 | 78.6 | 7.1 |
| 2015 | C+ | 2.69 | 1.79 | 28.6 | 17.6 | 69.1 | 6.8 |
| 2014 | C+ | 1.62 | 1.08 | 19.1 | 10.8 | 64.7 | 3.7 |
| 2013 | C+ | 1.76 | 1.17 | 15.1 | 9.2 | 52.8 | 4.7 |
| 2012 | C+ | 1.94 | 1.29 | 14.1 | 9.0 | 44.5 | 3.2 |

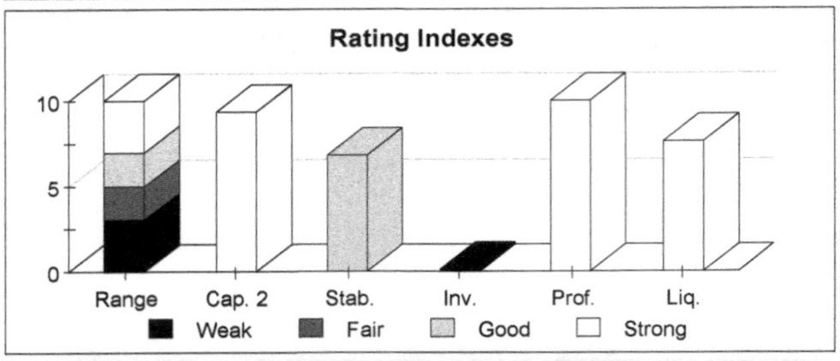


## SOUNDPATH HEALTH — E- Very Weak

**Major Rating Factors:** Weak profitability index (0.8 on a scale of 0 to 10). Poor capitalization (1.4) based on weak current risk-adjusted capital (moderate loss scenario). Good liquidity (5.3) with sufficient resources (cash flows and marketable investments) to handle a spike in claims.
**Other Rating Factors:** High quality investment portfolio (9.9).
**Principal Business:** Medicare (100%)
**Mem Phys: 16:** 11,853 **15:** 10,291 **16 MLR** 93.9% **/ 16 Admin Exp** N/A
**Enroll(000): Q3 17:** 23 **16:** 27 **15:** 21 **Med Exp PMPM:** $578
**Principal Investments:** Long-term bonds (90%), cash and equiv (10%)
**Provider Compensation ($000):** Contr fee ($138,143), capitation ($49,945)
**Total Member Encounters:** Phys (274,486), non-phys (162,466)
**Group Affiliation:** Catholic Health Initiatives
**Licensed in:** WA
**Address:** 33820 Weyerhaeuser Way S, Federal Way, WA 98001
**Phone:** (866) 789-7747 **Dom State:** WA **Commenced Bus:** January 2008

| Data Date | Rating | RACR #1 | RACR #2 | Total Assets ($mil) | Capital ($mil) | Net Premium ($mil) | Net Income ($mil) |
|---|---|---|---|---|---|---|---|
| 9-17 | E- | 0.44 | 0.37 | 64.4 | 14.5 | 132.3 | -20.3 |
| 9-16 | E | 1.65 | 1.37 | 76.4 | 32.3 | 148.7 | -4.7 |
| 2016 | E | 1.55 | 1.29 | 55.6 | 34.8 | 198.1 | -0.9 |
| 2015 | E | 0.38 | 0.32 | 50.6 | 10.6 | 155.2 | -17.3 |
| 2014 | C | 0.80 | 0.67 | 32.8 | 15.6 | 137.9 | -3.3 |
| 2013 | C | 1.61 | 1.34 | 31.4 | 18.9 | 150.0 | 2.4 |
| 2012 | D- | 0.36 | 0.30 | 19.7 | 2.4 | 128.0 | -0.4 |

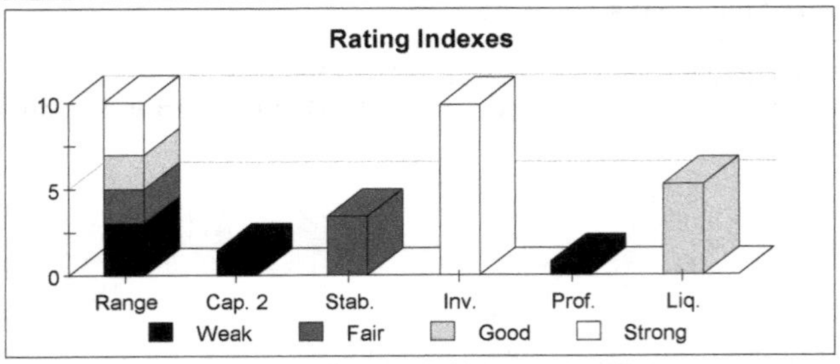

## SOUTHEASTERN INDIANA HEALTH ORG INC — C — Fair

**Major Rating Factors:** Fair profitability index (3.7 on a scale of 0 to 10). Weak overall results on stability tests (2.7) based on a steep decline in capital during 2016, a significant 19% decrease in enrollment during the period and a decline in the number of member physicians during 2017. Strong capitalization index (7.5) based on excellent current risk-adjusted capital (severe loss scenario).
**Other Rating Factors:** High quality investment portfolio (9.9). Excellent liquidity (7.1) with ample operational cash flow and liquid investments.
**Principal Business:** Comp med (99%)
**Mem Phys: 16:** 10,212 **15:** 29,150 **16 MLR** 89.3% / **16 Admin Exp** N/A
**Enroll(000): Q3 17:** 5 **16:** 6 **15:** 7 **Med Exp PMPM:** $396
**Principal Investments:** Cash and equiv (100%)
**Provider Compensation ($000):** Contr fee ($22,477), bonus arrang ($6,670), capitation ($508), FFS ($48), other ($1,005)
**Total Member Encounters:** Phys (31,691), non-phys (13,295)
**Group Affiliation:** SIHO Holding Inc
**Licensed in:** IN
**Address:** 417 WASHINGTON STREET, COLUMBUS, IN 47201
**Phone:** (812) 378-7000 **Dom State:** IN **Commenced Bus:** December 1986

| Data Date | Rating | RACR #1 | RACR #2 | Total Assets ($mil) | Capital ($mil) | Net Premium ($mil) | Net Income ($mil) |
|---|---|---|---|---|---|---|---|
| 9-17 | C | 1.72 | 1.43 | 15.1 | 8.7 | 22.3 | 0.2 |
| 9-16 | C+ | 1.54 | 1.29 | 16.0 | 8.0 | 25.8 | 0.2 |
| 2016 | C | 1.21 | 1.01 | 12.6 | 6.3 | 34.1 | 0.6 |
| 2015 | B | 1.75 | 1.46 | 16.4 | 9.1 | 36.4 | -1.6 |
| 2014 | B | 1.74 | 1.45 | 18.8 | 10.3 | 47.4 | 0.7 |
| 2013 | B | 1.56 | 1.30 | 16.5 | 9.4 | 50.4 | 1.9 |
| 2012 | B | 1.29 | 1.07 | 15.3 | 7.9 | 47.4 | 2.0 |

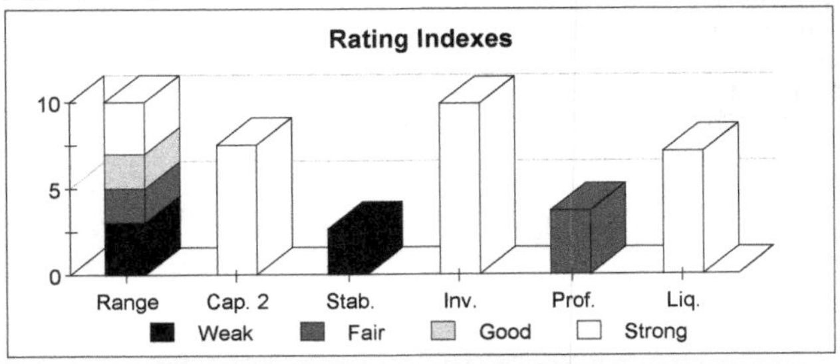


## SOUTHLAND NATIONAL INSURANCE CORPORATION — C- — Fair

**Major Rating Factors:** Fair quality investment portfolio (4.2 on a scale of 0 to 10). Fair profitability (4.2) with operating losses during the first three months of 2017. Weak overall results on stability tests (2.3) including weak results on operational trends.
**Other Rating Factors:** Good capitalization (5.9) based on good risk adjusted capital (severe loss scenario). Excellent liquidity (9.1).
**Principal Business:** Reinsurance (93%), group health insurance (5%), individual life insurance (1%), and group life insurance (1%).
**Principal Investments:** CMOs and structured securities (43%), nonCMO investment grade bonds (20%), cash (19%), common & preferred stock (13%), and misc. investments (5%).
**Investments in Affiliates:** 16%
**Group Affiliation:** SNA Capital LLC
**Licensed in:** AL, AZ, AR, CO, GA, IN, KY, LA, MS, NM, NC, OH, OK, SC, TN, TX, VA
**Commenced Business:** January 1969
**Address:** 2222 Sedwick Rd, Durham, NC 27713
**Phone:** (205) 343-1250 **Domicile State:** NC **NAIC Code:** 79057

| Data Date | Rating | RACR #1 | RACR #2 | Total Assets ($mil) | Capital ($mil) | Net Premium ($mil) | Net Income ($mil) |
|---|---|---|---|---|---|---|---|
| 3-17 | C- | 1.42 | 0.86 | 381.0 | 35.4 | 0.5 | -0.6 |
| 3-16 | C- | 2.12 | 0.94 | 305.0 | 32.7 | 1.4 | -1.3 |
| 2016 | C- | 1.50 | 0.96 | 385.4 | 36.6 | 94.4 | -1.7 |
| 2015 | C- | 2.18 | 0.93 | 307.4 | 34.0 | -152.4 | 16.4 |
| 2014 | D | 1.83 | 0.89 | 318.1 | 22.9 | 145.2 | -7.2 |
| 2013 | C | 0.96 | 0.82 | 167.1 | 9.5 | 6.5 | 0.2 |
| 2012 | C | 0.98 | 0.72 | 176.6 | 9.7 | 7.8 | 0.2 |

**Adverse Trends in Operations**

Increase in policy surrenders from 2015 to 2016 (83%)
Decrease in premium volume from 2014 to 2015 (205%)
Change in asset mix during 2014 (5.3%)
Decrease in asset base during 2013 (5%)
Decrease in premium volume from 2012 to 2013 (16%)

## SOUTHWEST L&H INS CO — C- — Fair

**Major Rating Factors:** Weak profitability index (0.9 on a scale of 0 to 10). Good liquidity (6.0) with sufficient resources (cash flows and marketable investments) to handle a spike in claims. Strong capitalization (10.0) based on excellent current risk-adjusted capital (severe loss scenario).
**Other Rating Factors:** High quality investment portfolio (7.1).
**Principal Business:** Comp med (99%), other (1%)
**Mem Phys: 16:** 18,615 **15:** 19,220 **16 MLR** 107.6% / **16 Admin Exp** N/A
**Enroll(000): Q3 17:** 1 **16:** 2 **15:** 4 **Med Exp PMPM:** $390
**Principal Investments:** Long-term bonds (60%), nonaffiliate common stock (38%), cash and equiv (2%)
**Provider Compensation ($000):** Contr fee ($12,600), FFS ($228), capitation ($138)
**Total Member Encounters:** Phys (11,949), non-phys (7,199)
**Group Affiliation:** Providence St Joseph Health
**Licensed in:** LA, NM, TX
**Address:** 12940 N Hwy 183, Austin, TX 78750-3203
**Phone:** (512) 257-6001 **Dom State:** TX **Commenced Bus:** March 1962

| Data Date | Rating | RACR #1 | RACR #2 | Total Assets ($mil) | Capital ($mil) | Net Premium ($mil) | Net Income ($mil) |
|---|---|---|---|---|---|---|---|
| 9-17 | C- | 4.48 | 3.73 | 11.7 | 10.2 | 6.0 | -1.1 |
| 9-16 | C- | 1.95 | 1.63 | 11.9 | 5.9 | 8.5 | -1.7 |
| 2016 | C- | 3.33 | 2.77 | 11.0 | 7.5 | 11.1 | -2.9 |
| 2015 | C | 1.91 | 1.59 | 10.4 | 5.7 | 14.6 | -5.1 |
| 2014 | C | 2.29 | 1.91 | 11.3 | 7.8 | 20.4 | -2.7 |
| 2013 | C | 2.26 | 1.88 | 10.8 | 7.6 | 21.7 | -0.2 |
| 2012 | C | 1.72 | 1.43 | 11.9 | 7.8 | 26.5 | -1.4 |

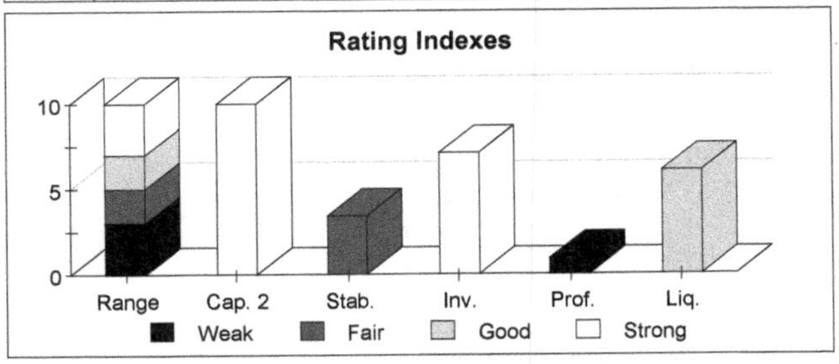

## STABLEVIEW HEALTH INC D+ Weak

**Major Rating Factors:** Weak profitability index (1.1 on a scale of 0 to 10). Good liquidity (6.8) with sufficient resources (cash flows and marketable investments) to handle a spike in claims. Strong capitalization (10.0) based on excellent current risk-adjusted capital (severe loss scenario).
**Other Rating Factors:** High quality investment portfolio (9.9).
**Principal Business:** Medicare (100%)
**Mem Phys: 16:** 1,444 **15:** 1,260 **16 MLR** 101.4% **/ 16 Admin Exp** N/A
**Enroll(000): Q1 17:** N/A **16:** 0 **15:** 0 **Med Exp PMPM:** $688
**Principal Investments:** Long-term bonds (90%), cash and equiv (10%)
**Provider Compensation ($000):** Contr fee ($1,389), capitation ($25), other ($116)
**Total Member Encounters:** Phys (2,591), non-phys (1,048)
**Group Affiliation:** Catholic Health Initiatives
**Licensed in:** KY
**Address:** PO Box 1109, Lexington, KY 40588
**Phone:** (866) 789-7747 **Dom State:** KY **Commenced Bus:** January 2015

| Data Date | Rating | RACR #1 | RACR #2 | Total Assets ($mil) | Capital ($mil) | Net Premium ($mil) | Net Income ($mil) |
|---|---|---|---|---|---|---|---|
| 3-17 | D+ | 12.15 | 10.13 | 5.2 | 5.2 | 0.0 | 0.1 |
| 3-16 | N/A | N/A | N/A | 6.0 | 5.0 | 0.4 | N/A |
| 2016 | D+ | 11.97 | 9.97 | 5.4 | 5.1 | 1.6 | 0.1 |
| 2015 | N/A | N/A | N/A | 5.9 | 5.0 | 0.6 | -0.5 |
| 2014 | N/A | N/A | N/A | 5.5 | 5.5 | N/A | N/A |
| 2013 | N/A | N/A | N/A | N/A | N/A | N/A | N/A |
| 2012 | N/A | N/A | N/A | N/A | N/A | N/A | N/A |

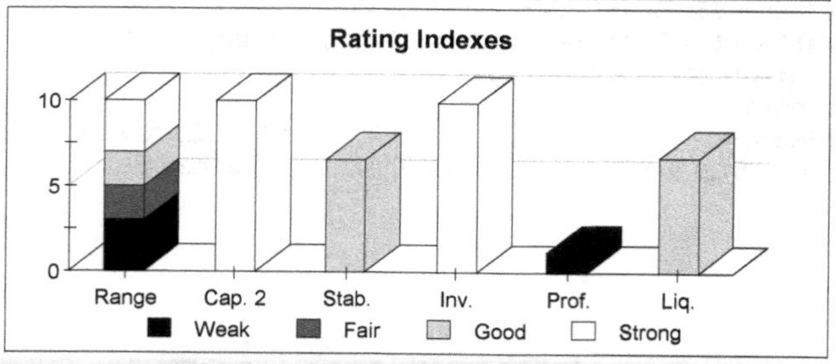


## STANDARD INSURANCE COMPANY * B+ Good

**Major Rating Factors:** Good quality investment portfolio (5.1 on a scale of 0 to 10) despite substantial holdings of BBB bonds in addition to junk bond exposure equal to 50% of capital. Exposure to mortgages is large, but the mortgage default rate has been low. Good overall profitability (6.1). Good overall results on stability tests (6.5) excellent operational trends and excellent risk diversification.
**Other Rating Factors:** Strong capitalization (7.1) based on excellent risk adjusted capital (severe loss scenario). Excellent liquidity (7.0).
**Principal Business:** Group retirement contracts (44%), group health insurance (24%), group life insurance (16%), individual annuities (8%), and other lines (7%).
**Principal Investments:** NonCMO investment grade bonds (48%), mortgages in good standing (41%), noninv. grade bonds (4%), and CMOs and structured securities (4%).
**Investments in Affiliates:** None
**Group Affiliation:** Meiji Yasuda Life Ins Company
**Licensed in:** All states except NY
**Commenced Business:** April 1906
**Address:** 1100 SOUTHWEST SIXTH AVENUE, PORTLAND, OR 97204-1093
**Phone:** (503) 321-7000 **Domicile State:** OR **NAIC Code:** 69019

| Data Date | Rating | RACR #1 | RACR #2 | Total Assets ($mil) | Capital ($mil) | Net Premium ($mil) | Net Income ($mil) |
|---|---|---|---|---|---|---|---|
| 9-17 | B+ | 2.10 | 1.09 | 23,414.5 | 1,091.1 | 3,073.6 | 116.2 |
| 9-16 | B+ | 2.10 | 1.09 | 21,609.6 | 1,079.6 | 2,807.3 | 108.3 |
| 2016 | B+ | 2.04 | 1.06 | 21,792.1 | 1,040.4 | 4,075.8 | 144.8 |
| 2015 | B+ | 2.21 | 1.16 | 20,781.6 | 1,085.0 | 3,528.4 | 160.1 |
| 2014 | B+ | 2.38 | 1.26 | 20,361.1 | 1,151.8 | 4,019.8 | 209.4 |
| 2013 | B+ | 2.37 | 1.32 | 19,118.7 | 1,287.3 | 3,489.3 | 195.8 |
| 2012 | B+ | 2.36 | 1.33 | 17,250.3 | 1,190.3 | 3,506.4 | 125.4 |

**Adverse Trends in Operations**

Increase in policy surrenders from 2015 to 2016 (26%)
Decrease in capital during 2016 (4%)
Decrease in premium volume from 2014 to 2015 (12%)
Decrease in capital during 2014 (11%)
Increase in policy surrenders from 2013 to 2014 (66%)

## STANDARD LIFE & ACCIDENT INSURANCE COMPANY * A- Excellent

**Major Rating Factors:** Good overall results on stability tests (6.9 on a scale of 0 to 10). Strengths that enhance stability include excellent operational trends and excellent risk diversification. Good liquidity (6.9) with sufficient resources to handle a spike in claims as well as a significant increase in policy surrenders. Fair quality investment portfolio (4.9).
**Other Rating Factors:** Strong capitalization (10.0) based on excellent risk adjusted capital (severe loss scenario). Excellent profitability (8.5).
**Principal Business:** Individual health insurance (40%), reinsurance (32%), group health insurance (21%), and individual life insurance (7%).
**Principal Investments:** NonCMO investment grade bonds (74%), common & preferred stock (17%), mortgages in good standing (6%), noninv. grade bonds (2%), and policy loans (1%).
**Investments in Affiliates:** None
**Group Affiliation:** American National Group Inc
**Licensed in:** All states except ME, NH, NJ, NY, PR
**Commenced Business:** June 1976
**Address:** ONE MOODY PLAZA, GALVESTON, TX 77550
**Phone:** (409) 763-4661 **Domicile State:** TX **NAIC Code:** 86355

| Data Date | Rating | RACR #1 | RACR #2 | Total Assets ($mil) | Capital ($mil) | Net Premium ($mil) | Net Income ($mil) |
|---|---|---|---|---|---|---|---|
| 9-17 | A- | 6.18 | 3.79 | 516.7 | 287.7 | 73.0 | 8.2 |
| 9-16 | A- | 6.01 | 3.67 | 514.8 | 282.6 | 71.2 | 9.9 |
| 2016 | A- | 6.21 | 3.82 | 518.8 | 287.1 | 95.1 | 13.6 |
| 2015 | A- | 5.93 | 3.68 | 514.5 | 278.1 | 105.2 | 8.6 |
| 2014 | A- | 5.09 | 3.17 | 530.2 | 259.1 | 120.7 | 20.6 |
| 2013 | A- | 5.22 | 3.20 | 527.6 | 252.2 | 108.7 | 18.0 |
| 2012 | A- | 5.88 | 3.59 | 527.8 | 255.8 | 106.2 | 22.4 |

**Adverse Trends in Operations**

Decrease in premium volume from 2015 to 2016 (10%)
Decrease in asset base during 2015 (3%)
Decrease in premium volume from 2014 to 2015 (13%)
Decrease in capital during 2013 (1%)

## STANDARD LIFE INSURANCE COMPANY OF NEW YORK * A- Excellent

**Major Rating Factors:** Excellent overall results on stability tests (7.2 on a scale of 0 to 10). Strengths that enhance stability include excellent operational trends and excellent risk diversification. Strong capitalization (10.0) based on excellent risk adjusted capital (severe loss scenario). Furthermore, this high level of risk adjusted capital has been consistently maintained over the last five years. High quality investment portfolio (7.4).
**Other Rating Factors:** Excellent profitability (7.9). Excellent liquidity (7.3).
**Principal Business:** Group health insurance (56%), group life insurance (40%), and individual health insurance (3%).
**Principal Investments:** Mortgages in good standing (49%), nonCMO investment grade bonds (48%), and cash (3%).
**Investments in Affiliates:** None
**Group Affiliation:** Meiji Yasuda Life Ins Company
**Licensed in:** NY
**Commenced Business:** January 2001
**Address:** 360 HAMILTON AVENUE SUITE 210, WHITE PLAINS, NY 10601-1871
**Phone:** (914) 989-4400 **Domicile State:** NY **NAIC Code:** 89009

| Data Date | Rating | RACR #1 | RACR #2 | Total Assets ($mil) | Capital ($mil) | Net Premium ($mil) | Net Income ($mil) |
|---|---|---|---|---|---|---|---|
| 9-17 | A- | 4.68 | 3.05 | 292.4 | 96.3 | 68.2 | 10.8 |
| 9-16 | A- | 4.23 | 2.75 | 282.7 | 84.4 | 67.1 | 2.1 |
| 2016 | A- | 4.25 | 2.80 | 286.6 | 85.9 | 89.1 | 3.6 |
| 2015 | A- | 4.14 | 2.73 | 282.7 | 80.9 | 89.4 | 6.3 |
| 2014 | A- | 3.57 | 2.37 | 275.3 | 76.6 | 95.2 | 4.0 |
| 2013 | A- | 3.28 | 2.19 | 265.6 | 71.6 | 98.0 | 2.7 |
| 2012 | A- | 3.07 | 2.10 | 251.1 | 69.3 | 100.1 | 6.1 |

**Adverse Trends in Operations**

Increase in policy surrenders from 2015 to 2016 (415%)
Decrease in premium volume from 2014 to 2015 (6%)
Decrease in premium volume from 2013 to 2014 (3%)
Decrease in premium volume from 2012 to 2013 (2%)
Increase in policy surrenders from 2012 to 2013 (771%)

## STANDARD SECURITY LIFE INSURANCE CO OF NEW YORK B Good

**Major Rating Factors:** Good overall profitability (5.4 on a scale of 0 to 10). Good liquidity (6.5) with sufficient resources to handle a spike in claims. Fair overall results on stability tests (4.6) including negative cash flow from operations for 2016.
**Other Rating Factors:** Strong capitalization (10.0) based on excellent risk adjusted capital (severe loss scenario). High quality investment portfolio (8.3).
**Principal Business:** Group health insurance (93%), individual health insurance (4%), and reinsurance (2%).
**Principal Investments:** NonCMO investment grade bonds (78%), common & preferred stock (14%), cash (3%), and CMOs and structured securities (1%).
**Investments in Affiliates:** 9%
**Group Affiliation:** Geneve Holdings Inc
**Licensed in:** All states, the District of Columbia and Puerto Rico
**Commenced Business:** December 1958
**Address:** 485 Madison Avenue 14th Floor, New York, NY 10022-5872
**Phone:** (212) 355-4141 **Domicile State:** NY **NAIC Code:** 69078

| Data Date | Rating | RACR #1 | RACR #2 | Total Assets ($mil) | Capital ($mil) | Net Premium ($mil) | Net Income ($mil) |
|---|---|---|---|---|---|---|---|
| 9-17 | B | 6.62 | 5.11 | 133.1 | 66.5 | 62.3 | 2.8 |
| 9-16 | A- | 5.84 | 4.70 | 238.5 | 127.0 | 64.9 | 10.2 |
| 2016 | B+ | 6.84 | 5.28 | 154.9 | 70.6 | 84.7 | -10.5 |
| 2015 | A- | 3.95 | 3.20 | 269.9 | 125.1 | 211.0 | 13.2 |
| 2014 | B | 3.55 | 2.81 | 252.4 | 116.5 | 207.3 | 12.1 |
| 2013 | B | 3.29 | 2.67 | 249.5 | 114.0 | 214.4 | 9.2 |
| 2012 | B | 4.05 | 3.25 | 239.5 | 116.3 | 148.4 | 15.8 |

**Rating Indexes**

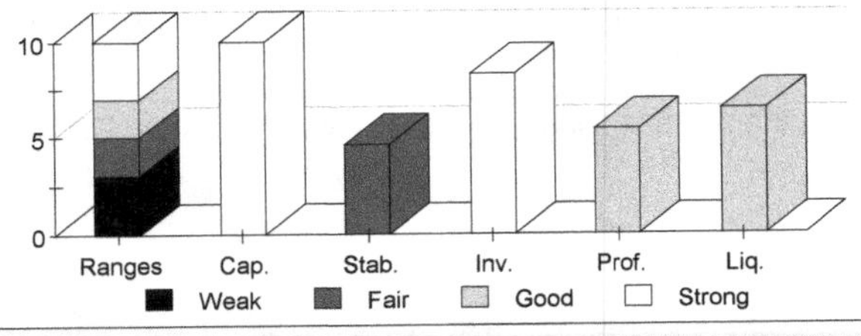


## STANFORD HEALTH CARE ADVANTAGE E- Very Weak

**Major Rating Factors:** Weak profitability index (0.9 on a scale of 0 to 10). Weak overall results on stability tests (0.3) based on an excessive 1188% enrollment growth during the period. Weak liquidity (0.0) as a spike in claims may stretch capacity.
**Other Rating Factors:** Good capitalization index (6.1) based on good current risk-adjusted capital (severe loss scenario).
**Principal Business:** Medicare (100%)
**Mem Phys: 16:** N/A **15:** N/A **16 MLR** 113.4% **/ 16 Admin Exp** N/A
**Enroll(000): Q3 17:** 2 **16:** 1 **15:** 0 **Med Exp PMPM:** $1,176
**Principal Investments ($000):** Cash and equiv ($4,544)
**Provider Compensation ($000):** None
**Total Member Encounters:** N/A
**Group Affiliation:** None
**Licensed in:** CA
**Address:** 4365 Executive Drive Suite 500, San Diego, CA 92121
**Phone:** (858) 658-8662 **Dom State:** CA **Commenced Bus:** August 2013

| Data Date | Rating | RACR #1 | RACR #2 | Total Assets ($mil) | Capital ($mil) | Net Premium ($mil) | Net Income ($mil) |
|---|---|---|---|---|---|---|---|
| 9-17 | E- | 1.33 | 0.91 | 6.5 | 2.2 | 12.1 | -8.0 |
| 9-16 | N/A | N/A | N/A | N/A | N/A | N/A | N/A |
| 2016 | D | 1.82 | 1.25 | 5.1 | 3.0 | 6.7 | -5.7 |
| 2015 | U | 5.31 | 4.78 | 3.2 | 2.6 | 0.5 | -4.2 |
| 2014 | N/A | N/A | N/A | 1.3 | 1.3 | N/A | N/A |
| 2013 | N/A | N/A | N/A | N/A | N/A | N/A | N/A |
| 2012 | N/A | N/A | N/A | N/A | N/A | N/A | N/A |

**Rating Indexes**

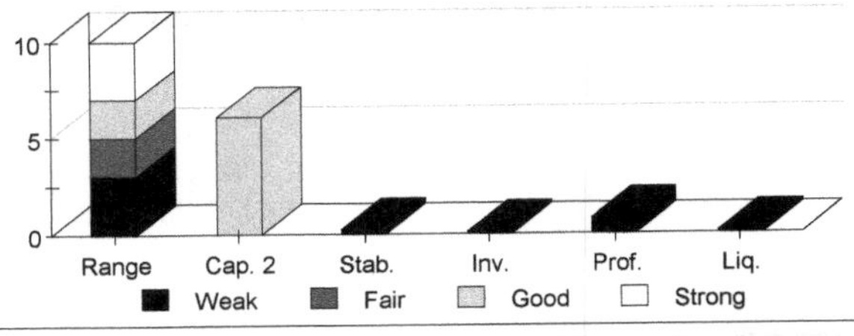

## STARMOUNT LIFE INSURANCE COMPANY B Good

**Major Rating Factors:** Good overall results on stability tests (5.4 on a scale of 0 to 10) despite fair financial strength of affiliated Unum Group. Other stability subfactors include excellent operational trends and excellent risk diversification. Good overall capitalization (5.9) based on mixed results -- excessive policy leverage mitigated by good risk adjusted capital (severe loss scenario). Moreover, capital levels have been consistent over the last five years. Good overall profitability (6.6) despite operating losses during the first nine months of 2017.

**Other Rating Factors:** Good liquidity (5.8). High quality investment portfolio (7.6).

**Principal Business:** Group health insurance (49%), reinsurance (32%), individual health insurance (14%), and individual life insurance (6%).

**Principal Investments:** NonCMO investment grade bonds (62%), cash (31%), real estate (4%), noninv. grade bonds (3%), and policy loans (1%).

**Investments in Affiliates:** None

**Group Affiliation:** Unum Group

**Licensed in:** All states except NY, PR

**Commenced Business:** August 1983

**Address:** 8485 Goodwood Blvd, Baton Rouge, LA 70806

**Phone:** (225) 926-2888 **Domicile State:** LA **NAIC Code:** 68985

| Data Date | Rating | RACR #1 | RACR #2 | Total Assets ($mil) | Capital ($mil) | Net Premium ($mil) | Net Income ($mil) |
|---|---|---|---|---|---|---|---|
| 9-17 | B | 1.11 | 0.86 | 76.4 | 34.8 | 133.0 | -2.6 |
| 9-16 | B | N/A | N/A | 64.8 | 26.6 | 100.6 | -0.7 |
| 2016 | B | 1.20 | 0.94 | 76.2 | 32.3 | 144.3 | -0.4 |
| 2015 | B | N/A | N/A | 65.9 | 28.3 | 121.0 | 4.0 |
| 2014 | B | 1.35 | 1.02 | 59.1 | 25.0 | 95.2 | 3.8 |
| 2013 | B | 1.46 | 1.08 | 51.1 | 22.3 | 79.7 | 4.2 |
| 2012 | B | 1.52 | 1.12 | 45.3 | 19.5 | 66.1 | 2.2 |

**H J Capital LLC**
**Composite Group Rating: C+**

| Largest Group Members | Assets ($mil) | Rating |
|---|---|---|
| UNUM LIFE INS CO OF AMERICA | 21078 | C+ |
| PROVIDENT LIFE ACCIDENT INS CO | 8273 | C+ |
| PAUL REVERE LIFE INS CO | 3790 | C+ |
| FIRST UNUM LIFE INS CO | 3261 | C+ |
| COLONIAL LIFE ACCIDENT INS CO | 3144 | C+ |

## STATE MUTUAL INSURANCE COMPANY C- Fair

**Major Rating Factors:** Fair quality investment portfolio (3.7 on a scale of 0 to 10) with large holdings of BBB rated bonds in addition to moderate junk bond exposure. Fair overall results on stability tests (3.2) including negative cash flow from operations for 2016, fair risk adjusted capital in prior years. Weak profitability (2.6) with operating losses during the first nine months of 2017.

**Other Rating Factors:** Good capitalization (5.4) based on good risk adjusted capital (severe loss scenario). Good liquidity (6.2).

**Principal Business:** Individual health insurance (46%), individual life insurance (36%), and reinsurance (18%).

**Principal Investments:** NonCMO investment grade bonds (44%), CMOs and structured securities (16%), common & preferred stock (9%), mortgages in good standing (6%), and misc. investments (24%).

**Investments in Affiliates:** 9%

**Group Affiliation:** None

**Licensed in:** All states except AK, CA, CT, ME, MA, MI, NH, NJ, NY, PR

**Commenced Business:** October 1890

**Address:** 210 E Second Avenue Suite 301, Rome, GA 30161

**Phone:** (706) 291-1054 **Domicile State:** GA **NAIC Code:** 69132

| Data Date | Rating | RACR #1 | RACR #2 | Total Assets ($mil) | Capital ($mil) | Net Premium ($mil) | Net Income ($mil) |
|---|---|---|---|---|---|---|---|
| 9-17 | C- | 1.21 | 0.80 | 274.1 | 29.9 | -30.9 | -2.2 |
| 9-16 | C- | 1.82 | 1.01 | 278.7 | 29.3 | 16.6 | -2.7 |
| 2016 | C- | 1.05 | 0.73 | 279.4 | 26.1 | 22.8 | -9.0 |
| 2015 | D+ | 2.31 | 1.27 | 286.7 | 33.7 | 18.7 | 1.0 |
| 2014 | C | 1.64 | 1.02 | 292.5 | 33.9 | 0.4 | 0.2 |
| 2013 | C | 1.73 | 1.04 | 296.8 | 30.0 | 21.5 | 0.8 |
| 2012 | C | 1.93 | 1.11 | 298.0 | 29.4 | 16.3 | 1.4 |

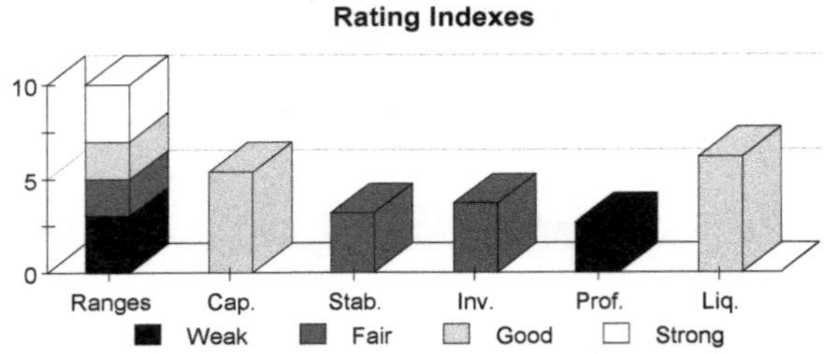


## SUMMA INS CO C- Fair

**Major Rating Factors:** Weak profitability index (0.9 on a scale of 0 to 10). Good liquidity (6.6) with sufficient resources (cash flows and marketable investments) to handle a spike in claims. Strong capitalization (7.3) based on excellent current risk-adjusted capital (severe loss scenario).

**Other Rating Factors:** High quality investment portfolio (9.9).

**Principal Business:** Comp med (99%)

**Mem Phys: 16:** 14,500 **15:** 7,000 **16 MLR** 85.4% **/ 16 Admin Exp** N/A

**Enroll(000): Q3 17:** 32 **16:** 36 **15:** 43 **Med Exp PMPM:** $358

**Principal Investments:** Long-term bonds (86%), cash and equiv (14%)

**Provider Compensation ($000):** Contr fee ($167,671), capitation ($441)

**Total Member Encounters:** Phys (57,215), non-phys (89,249)

**Group Affiliation:** Summa Health System Community

**Licensed in:** OH

**Address:** 10 N Main St, Akron, OH 44308

**Phone:** (330) 996-8410 **Dom State:** OH **Commenced Bus:** February 1996

| Data Date | Rating | RACR #1 | RACR #2 | Total Assets ($mil) | Capital ($mil) | Net Premium ($mil) | Net Income ($mil) |
|---|---|---|---|---|---|---|---|
| 9-17 | C- | 1.63 | 1.36 | 53.7 | 27.2 | 129.2 | -1.1 |
| 9-16 | C- | 1.31 | 1.09 | 55.0 | 25.6 | 141.9 | 1.2 |
| 2016 | C- | 1.73 | 1.44 | 54.9 | 28.4 | 190.6 | 4.0 |
| 2015 | C- | 1.25 | 1.04 | 59.7 | 24.4 | 214.9 | -7.6 |
| 2014 | D | 1.41 | 1.17 | 71.5 | 31.5 | 234.6 | -13.5 |
| 2013 | D+ | 0.69 | 0.57 | 61.7 | 29.8 | 219.6 | -10.6 |
| 2012 | C | 1.99 | 1.66 | 95.3 | 58.0 | 205.2 | -1.6 |

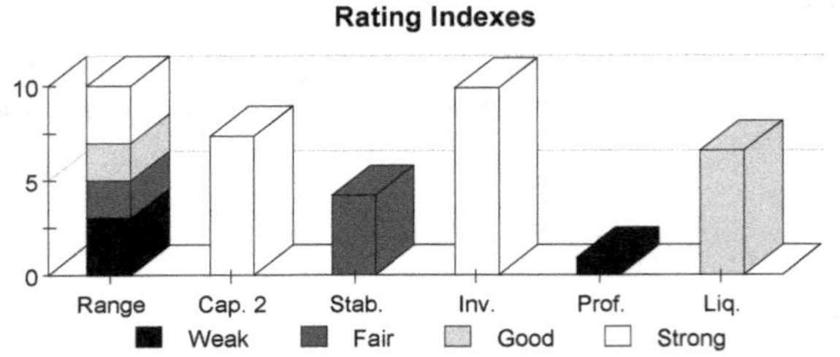

## SUMMACARE INC — C+ — Fair

**Major Rating Factors:** Fair overall results on stability tests (4.8 on a scale of 0 to 10) based on inconsistent enrollment growth in the past five years due to declines in 2015 and 2016. Good liquidity (6.8) with sufficient resources (cash flows and marketable investments) to handle a spike in claims. Weak profitability index (2.4).

**Other Rating Factors:** Strong capitalization index (7.3) based on excellent current risk-adjusted capital (severe loss scenario). High quality investment portfolio (9.9).

**Principal Business:** Medicare (100%)

**Mem Phys: 16:** 14,500 **15:** 7,000 **16 MLR** 86.0% **/ 16 Admin Exp** N/A

**Enroll(000): Q3 17:** 24 **16:** 24 **15:** 26 **Med Exp PMPM:** $753

**Principal Investments:** Long-term bonds (42%), affiliate common stock (34%), cash and equiv (24%)

**Provider Compensation ($000):** Contr fee ($218,709), capitation ($1,811), bonus arrang ($58)

**Total Member Encounters:** Phys (107,265), non-phys (159,700)

**Group Affiliation:** Summa Health System Community

**Licensed in:** OH

**Address:** 10 North Main Street, Akron, OH 44308

**Phone:** (330) 996-8410 **Dom State:** OH **Commenced Bus:** March 1993

| Data Date | Rating | RACR #1 | RACR #2 | Total Assets ($mil) | Capital ($mil) | Net Premium ($mil) | Net Income ($mil) |
|---|---|---|---|---|---|---|---|
| 9-17 | C+ | 1.63 | 1.36 | 113.4 | 49.5 | 179.4 | -4.5 |
| 9-16 | B- | 1.50 | 1.25 | 106.8 | 51.6 | 186.7 | -1.1 |
| 2016 | B- | 1.85 | 1.54 | 91.4 | 55.5 | 252.6 | -0.5 |
| 2015 | B- | 1.49 | 1.24 | 90.6 | 51.6 | 271.4 | -5.2 |
| 2014 | C | 1.09 | 0.91 | 85.2 | 42.8 | 315.7 | 2.0 |
| 2013 | C | 1.30 | 1.09 | 105.3 | 30.6 | 277.6 | 9.1 |
| 2012 | B | 2.43 | 2.02 | 88.3 | 52.2 | 283.3 | 3.9 |

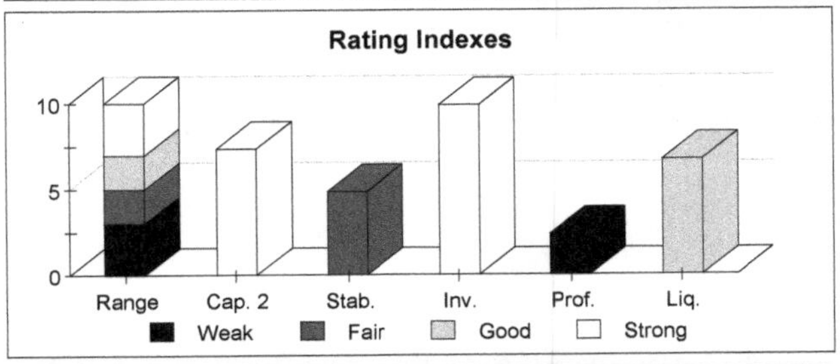


## SUN LIFE & HEALTH INSURANCE COMPANY — D — Weak

**Major Rating Factors:** Weak overall results on stability tests (1.6 on a scale of 0 to 10) including potential financial drain due to affiliation with Sun Life Assurance Group and negative cash flow from operations for 2016. Weak profitability (2.0). Good liquidity (6.8) with sufficient resources to handle a spike in claims.

**Other Rating Factors:** Strong capitalization (10.0) based on excellent risk adjusted capital (severe loss scenario). High quality investment portfolio (7.2).

**Principal Business:** Group health insurance (50%), reinsurance (26%), and group life insurance (23%).

**Principal Investments:** NonCMO investment grade bonds (49%), CMOs and structured securities (30%), mortgages in good standing (14%), noninv. grade bonds (2%), and misc. investments (3%).

**Investments in Affiliates:** None

**Group Affiliation:** Sun Life Assurance Group

**Licensed in:** All states, the District of Columbia and Puerto Rico

**Commenced Business:** January 1975

**Address:** 201 Townsend Street Ste 900, Lansing, MI 48933

**Phone:** (781) 237-6030 **Domicile State:** MI **NAIC Code:** 80926

| Data Date | Rating | RACR #1 | RACR #2 | Total Assets ($mil) | Capital ($mil) | Net Premium ($mil) | Net Income ($mil) |
|---|---|---|---|---|---|---|---|
| 9-17 | D | 5.37 | 3.36 | 504.8 | 205.6 | 83.1 | 8.7 |
| 9-16 | D- | 4.39 | 2.91 | 509.9 | 202.2 | 223.1 | -43.3 |
| 2016 | D- | 4.36 | 2.91 | 485.3 | 198.5 | 248.1 | -44.8 |
| 2015 | C | 6.46 | 4.17 | 447.7 | 241.5 | 173.5 | 17.2 |
| 2014 | C- | 4.77 | 3.13 | 371.8 | 175.5 | 168.0 | -1.4 |
| 2013 | C- | 5.38 | 3.67 | 353.7 | 182.0 | 166.8 | -35.8 |
| 2012 | C- | 6.10 | 2.98 | 64.6 | 48.1 | 0.0 | 1.8 |

**Sun Life Assurance Group**
**Composite Group Rating: E+**

| Largest Group Members | Assets ($mil) | Rating |
|---|---|---|
| SUN LIFE ASR CO OF CANADA | 19563 | E+ |
| INDEPENDENCE LIFE ANNUITY CO | 3028 | D |
| SUN LIFE HEALTH INS CO | 485 | D |
| PROFESSIONAL INS CO | 110 | D |

## SUN LIFE ASSURANCE COMPANY OF CANADA — D- — Weak

**Major Rating Factors:** Poor current capitalization (2.1 on a scale of 0 to 10) based on weak risk adjusted capital (moderate loss scenario), although results have slipped from the good range over the last two years. Low quality investment portfolio (1.9) containing large holdings of BBB rated bonds in addition to moderate junk bond exposure. Exposure to mortgages is significant, but the mortgage default rate has been low. Weak profitability (1.9).

**Other Rating Factors:** Weak overall results on stability tests (0.9) including weak risk adjusted capital in prior years, negative cash flow from operations for 2016. Good liquidity (5.2).

**Principal Business:** Reinsurance (48%), group health insurance (32%), individual life insurance (10%), and group life insurance (10%).

**Principal Investments:** NonCMO investment grade bonds (55%), mortgages in good standing (17%), CMOs and structured securities (10%), real estate (6%), and misc. investments (11%).

**Investments in Affiliates:** 1%

**Group Affiliation:** Sun Life Assurance Group

**Licensed in:** All states except NY

**Commenced Business:** May 1871

**Address:** 150 King Street West, Toronto, Ontario, MA 2481

**Phone:** (781) 237-6030 **Domicile State:** MI **NAIC Code:** 80802

| Data Date | Rating | RACR #1 | RACR #2 | Total Assets ($mil) | Capital ($mil) | Net Premium ($mil) | Net Income ($mil) |
|---|---|---|---|---|---|---|---|
| 9-17 | D- | 0.64 | 0.38 | 20,032.5 | 1,142.6 | 1,769.5 | 127.9 |
| 9-16 | E | 0.63 | 0.37 | 20,677.4 | 1,106.3 | 3,218.1 | -949.9 |
| 2016 | E | 0.53 | 0.32 | 19,562.8 | 1,019.0 | 3,803.2 | -535.1 |
| 2015 | D | 1.27 | 0.74 | 18,222.4 | 1,925.8 | 2,207.2 | 86.4 |
| 2014 | D | 0.75 | 0.43 | 17,090.5 | 940.3 | 2,349.1 | -64.3 |
| 2013 | D | 0.53 | 0.30 | 15,368.9 | 766.7 | -919.7 | 234.8 |
| 2012 | C- | 0.79 | 0.45 | 17,403.4 | 1,037.6 | 2,283.3 | 119.1 |

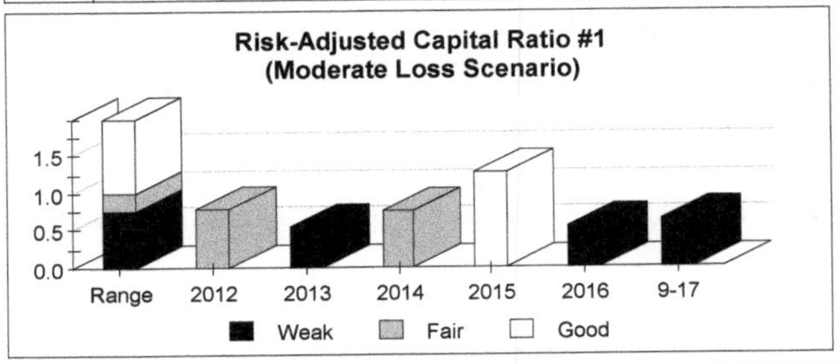

## SUNFLOWER STATE HEALTH PLAN INC C- Fair

**Major Rating Factors:** Weak profitability index (0.9 on a scale of 0 to 10). Strong capitalization (8.2) based on excellent current risk-adjusted capital (severe loss scenario). High quality investment portfolio (9.5).
**Other Rating Factors:** Excellent liquidity (7.0) with sufficient resources (cash flows and marketable investments) to handle a spike in claims.
**Principal Business:** Medicaid (97%), comp med (3%)
**Mem Phys: 16:** 7,453 **15:** 7,146 **16 MLR** 87.3% **/ 16 Admin Exp** N/A
**Enroll(000): Q3 17:** 127 **16:** 140 **15:** 141 **Med Exp PMPM:** $556
**Principal Investments:** Cash and equiv (51%), long-term bonds (49%)
**Provider Compensation ($000):** Contr fee ($941,438), salary ($18,908), capitation ($5,565), bonus arrang ($1,339)
**Total Member Encounters:** Phys (677,420), non-phys (2,212,828)
**Group Affiliation:** Centene Corporation
**Licensed in:** KS
**Address:** 8325 Lenexa Dr, Lenexa, KS 66214
**Phone:** (314) 725-4477 **Dom State:** KS **Commenced Bus:** January 2013

| Data Date | Rating | RACR #1 | RACR #2 | Total Assets ($mil) | Capital ($mil) | Net Premium ($mil) | Net Income ($mil) |
|---|---|---|---|---|---|---|---|
| 9-17 | C- | 2.33 | 1.94 | 238.0 | 131.5 | 827.5 | 7.3 |
| 9-16 | C- | 2.29 | 1.91 | 253.9 | 140.3 | 830.9 | 5.5 |
| 2016 | C- | 2.36 | 1.96 | 254.0 | 133.3 | 1,106.7 | 9.7 |
| 2015 | C- | 2.21 | 1.84 | 265.6 | 134.8 | 1,115.0 | 20.8 |
| 2014 | D+ | 1.98 | 1.65 | 273.0 | 112.8 | 1,039.9 | -39.3 |
| 2013 | D+ | 1.45 | 1.21 | 215.1 | 81.5 | 801.7 | -91.0 |
| 2012 | N/A | N/A | N/A | 3.2 | 3.0 | N/A | N/A |

Rating Indexes

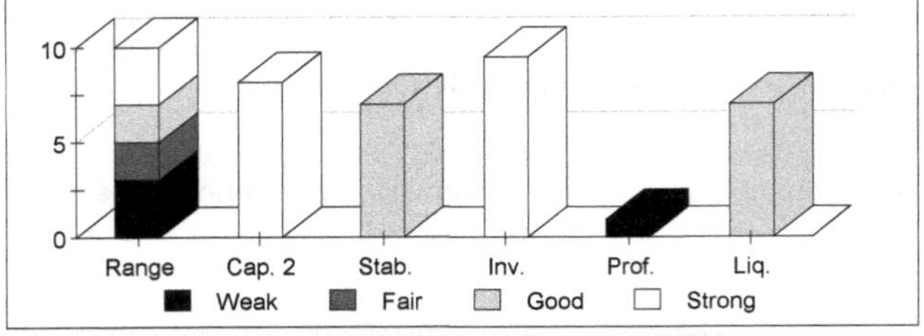


## SUNSHINE HEALTH E Very Weak

**Major Rating Factors:** Weak profitability index (0.9 on a scale of 0 to 10). Good liquidity (6.4) with sufficient resources (cash flows and marketable investments) to handle a spike in claims. Strong capitalization (7.6) based on excellent current risk-adjusted capital (severe loss scenario).
**Other Rating Factors:** High quality investment portfolio (9.9).
**Principal Business:** Comp med (50%), Medicaid (50%)
**Mem Phys: 16:** 29,106 **15:** 27,198 **16 MLR** 92.6% **/ 16 Admin Exp** N/A
**Enroll(000): Q3 17:** 571 **16:** 569 **15:** 529 **Med Exp PMPM:** $504
**Principal Investments:** Long-term bonds (80%), cash and equiv (20%)
**Provider Compensation ($000):** Contr fee ($2,496,738), capitation ($388,179), bonus arrang ($387,257), salary ($76,902)
**Total Member Encounters:** Phys (3,018,894), non-phys (5,588,842)
**Group Affiliation:** Centene Corporation
**Licensed in:** FL
**Address:** 1301 International Parkway, Sunrise, FL 33323
**Phone:** (314) 725-4477 **Dom State:** FL **Commenced Bus:** February 2009

| Data Date | Rating | RACR #1 | RACR #2 | Total Assets ($mil) | Capital ($mil) | Net Premium ($mil) | Net Income ($mil) |
|---|---|---|---|---|---|---|---|
| 9-17 | E | 1.84 | 1.53 | 724.8 | 363.5 | 2,815.9 | -3.8 |
| 9-16 | E | 1.93 | 1.61 | 654.5 | 339.7 | 2,684.1 | 2.3 |
| 2016 | E | 1.81 | 1.51 | 676.5 | 357.9 | 3,627.5 | 23.0 |
| 2015 | E | 1.88 | 1.57 | 692.8 | 330.9 | 3,125.4 | 27.1 |
| 2014 | E | 0.84 | 0.70 | 541.5 | 116.2 | 2,268.5 | -119.3 |
| 2013 | E | 1.31 | 1.10 | 195.9 | 55.8 | 771.3 | 5.9 |
| 2012 | E | 1.25 | 1.04 | 86.9 | 40.8 | 559.1 | 0.4 |

Rating Indexes

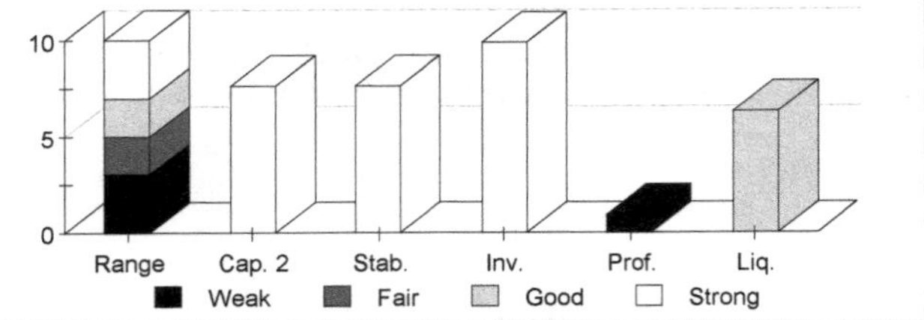


## SUPERIOR HEALTHPLAN INC C+ Fair

**Major Rating Factors:** Good overall profitability index (6.2 on a scale of 0 to 10). Good liquidity (6.8) with sufficient resources (cash flows and marketable investments) to handle a spike in claims. Strong capitalization index (7.6) based on excellent current risk-adjusted capital (severe loss scenario).
**Other Rating Factors:** High quality investment portfolio (9.9). Excellent overall results on stability tests (8.2) based on healthy premium and capital growth during 2016. Fair financial strength from affiliates.
**Principal Business:** Medicaid (84%), comp med (11%), Medicare (4%)
**Mem Phys: 16:** 53,273 **15:** 46,068 **16 MLR** 87.6% **/ 16 Admin Exp** N/A
**Enroll(000): Q3 17:** 535 **16:** 518 **15:** 498 **Med Exp PMPM:** $519
**Principal Investments:** Long-term bonds (54%), cash and equiv (42%), affiliate common stock (2%), other (2%)
**Provider Compensation ($000):** Contr fee ($2,653,595), bonus arrang ($229,388), salary ($142,508), capitation ($38,917)
**Total Member Encounters:** Phys (3,178,804), non-phys (6,662,582)
**Group Affiliation:** Centene Corporation
**Licensed in:** TX
**Address:** 2100 South IH 35 Suite 202, Austin, TX 78704
**Phone:** (314) 725-4477 **Dom State:** TX **Commenced Bus:** February 1997

| Data Date | Rating | RACR #1 | RACR #2 | Total Assets ($mil) | Capital ($mil) | Net Premium ($mil) | Net Income ($mil) |
|---|---|---|---|---|---|---|---|
| 9-17 | C+ | 1.88 | 1.56 | 708.3 | 355.8 | 2,925.4 | 46.0 |
| 9-16 | C+ | 1.79 | 1.49 | 635.6 | 279.0 | 2,586.0 | 22.7 |
| 2016 | C+ | 1.64 | 1.37 | 664.3 | 308.4 | 3,522.0 | 52.2 |
| 2015 | C+ | 1.68 | 1.40 | 620.4 | 260.9 | 2,882.1 | 13.6 |
| 2014 | C+ | 2.12 | 1.77 | 384.7 | 208.8 | 1,856.8 | 32.1 |
| 2013 | C | 1.95 | 1.63 | 349.1 | 188.0 | 1,703.5 | 16.8 |
| 2012 | C | 1.72 | 1.43 | 332.2 | 162.9 | 1,559.3 | -40.6 |

Rating Indexes

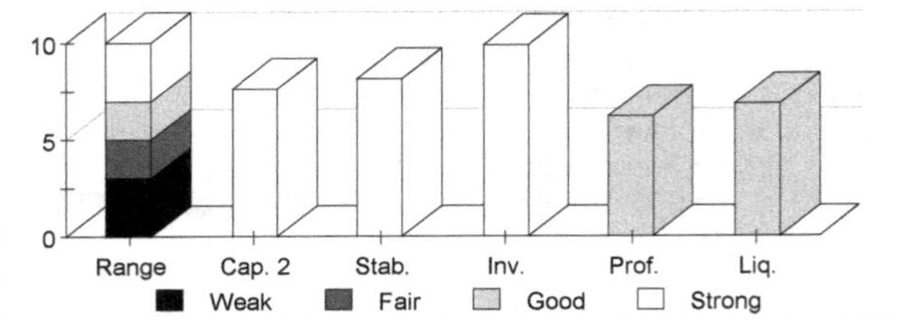

## SUTTER HEALTH PLAN — D- — Weak

**Major Rating Factors:** Weak profitability index (0.1 on a scale of 0 to 10). Fair overall results on stability tests (3.3) in spite of healthy premium and capital growth during 2016 but an excessive 83% enrollment growth during the period. Strong capitalization index (7.2) based on good current risk-adjusted capital (moderate loss scenario)
**Other Rating Factors:** Excellent liquidity (7.1) with ample operational cash flow and liquid investments.
**Principal Business:** Managed care (100%)
**Mem Phys: 16:** N/A **15:** N/A **16 MLR** 95.2% **/ 16 Admin Exp** N/A
**Enroll(000): Q3 17:** 65 **16:** 48 **15:** 26 **Med Exp PMPM:** $362
**Principal Investments ($000):** Cash and equiv ($51,173)
**Provider Compensation ($000):** None
**Total Member Encounters:** N/A
**Group Affiliation:** None
**Licensed in:** CA
**Address:** 2088 OtayLakesRd #102, Chula Vista, CA 91915
**Phone:** (619) 407-4082 **Dom State:** CA **Commenced Bus:** April 2013

| Data Date | Rating | RACR #1 | RACR #2 | Total Assets ($mil) | Capital ($mil) | Net Premium ($mil) | Net Income ($mil) |
|---|---|---|---|---|---|---|---|
| 9-17 | D- | 1.23 | 0.78 | 91.1 | 22.2 | 233.8 | -19.9 |
| 9-16 | E | N/A | N/A | 48.9 | -0.2 | 133.2 | -29.8 |
| 2016 | E+ | 0.72 | 0.46 | 76.2 | 13.1 | 188.2 | -40.6 |
| 2015 | E | 1.11 | 0.74 | 41.4 | 10.2 | 77.1 | -27.5 |
| 2014 | U | 5.04 | 3.53 | 41.2 | 23.7 | 30.9 | -19.0 |
| 2013 | U | 257.80 | 171.80 | 43.1 | 28.7 | N/A | -46.4 |
| 2012 | N/A | N/A | N/A | N/A | N/A | N/A | N/A |

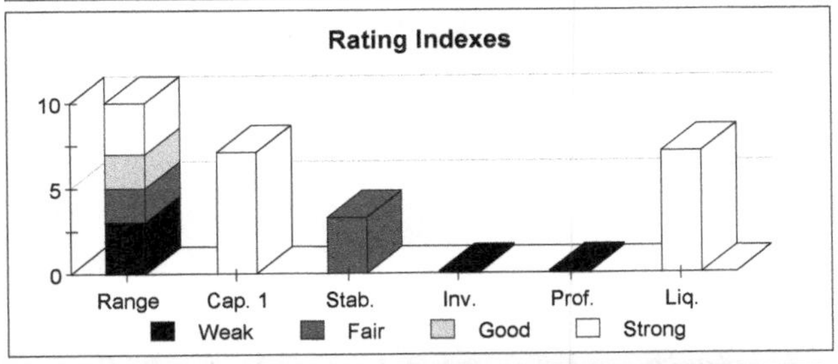


## SWISS RE LIFE & HEALTH AMERICA INCORPORATED — C — Fair

**Major Rating Factors:** Fair overall results on stability tests (3.8 on a scale of 0 to 10). Good quality investment portfolio (6.4) despite mixed results such as: large holdings of BBB rated bonds but moderate junk bond exposure. Good liquidity (6.1) with sufficient resources to handle a spike in claims as well as a significant increase in policy surrenders.
**Other Rating Factors:** Weak profitability (2.8). Strong capitalization (7.1) based on excellent risk adjusted capital (severe loss scenario).
**Principal Business:** Reinsurance (100%).
**Principal Investments:** NonCMO investment grade bonds (71%), CMOs and structured securities (14%), mortgages in good standing (6%), noninv. grade bonds (3%), and common & preferred stock (1%).
**Investments in Affiliates:** 7%
**Group Affiliation:** Swiss Reinsurance Group
**Licensed in:** All states, the District of Columbia and Puerto Rico
**Commenced Business:** September 1967
**Address:** 237 EAST HIGH STREET, JEFFERSON CITY, MO 65101
**Phone:** (914) 828-8000 **Domicile State:** MO **NAIC Code:** 82627

| Data Date | Rating | RACR #1 | RACR #2 | Total Assets ($mil) | Capital ($mil) | Net Premium ($mil) | Net Income ($mil) |
|---|---|---|---|---|---|---|---|
| 9-17 | C | 1.74 | 1.09 | 14,355.3 | 1,457.4 | 1,827.3 | 189.9 |
| 9-16 | C | 1.61 | 0.94 | 13,998.7 | 1,275.8 | 1,756.8 | 62.2 |
| 2016 | C | 1.57 | 0.99 | 14,226.8 | 1,380.9 | 2,289.7 | -5.8 |
| 2015 | C | 1.83 | 1.08 | 12,264.0 | 1,318.3 | 2,983.5 | 85.8 |
| 2014 | C | 1.69 | 1.12 | 11,247.5 | 1,461.0 | 2,107.9 | -924.1 |
| 2013 | C | 1.86 | 1.31 | 9,994.7 | 1,644.0 | 1,644.4 | 95.4 |
| 2012 | D+ | 1.35 | 0.97 | 9,138.9 | 1,185.3 | 1,557.8 | 95.4 |

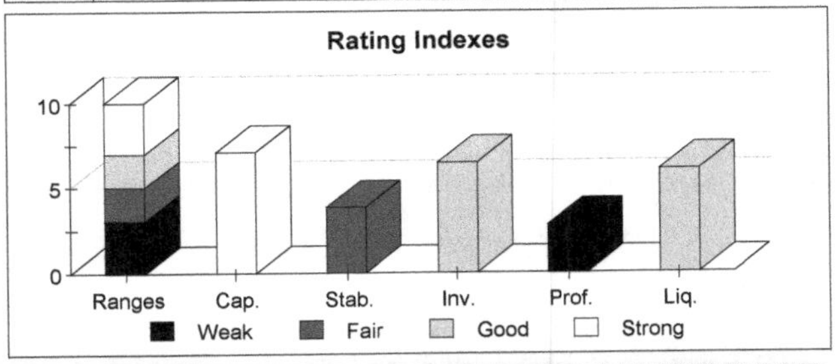


## SYMPHONIX HEALTH INS INC — E+ — Very Weak

**Major Rating Factors:** Weak profitability index (0.9 on a scale of 0 to 10). Strong capitalization (8.7) based on excellent current risk-adjusted capital (severe loss scenario). High quality investment portfolio (9.9).
**Other Rating Factors:** Excellent liquidity (7.4) with ample operational cash flow and liquid investments.
**Principal Business:** Other (100%)
**Mem Phys: 16:** 65,495 **15:** 75,843 **16 MLR** 78.7% **/ 16 Admin Exp** N/A
**Enroll(000): Q3 17:** 791 **16:** 422 **15:** 199 **Med Exp PMPM:** $62
**Principal Investments:** Long-term bonds (68%), cash and equiv (32%)
**Provider Compensation ($000):** FFS ($404,145)
**Total Member Encounters:** N/A
**Group Affiliation:** UnitedHealth Group Incorporated
**Licensed in:** All states except NY, PR
**Address:** 1900 EAST GOLF RD, SCHAUMBURG, IL 60173
**Phone:** (847) 585-4058 **Dom State:** IL **Commenced Bus:** September 1974

| Data Date | Rating | RACR #1 | RACR #2 | Total Assets ($mil) | Capital ($mil) | Net Premium ($mil) | Net Income ($mil) |
|---|---|---|---|---|---|---|---|
| 9-17 | E+ | 2.73 | 2.27 | 293.4 | 32.6 | 353.1 | -36.1 |
| 9-16 | C | 2.20 | 1.83 | 514.2 | 23.3 | 268.4 | -5.7 |
| 2016 | C | 4.96 | 4.13 | 531.6 | 59.1 | 357.9 | -38.8 |
| 2015 | D- | 1.23 | 1.03 | 228.3 | 22.6 | 173.0 | -1.8 |
| 2014 | N/A | N/A | N/A | 64.9 | 7.6 | 80.1 | N/A |
| 2013 | N/A | N/A | N/A | 9.8 | 7.6 | N/A | N/A |
| 2012 | N/A | N/A | N/A | 41.4 | 40.7 | N/A | N/A |

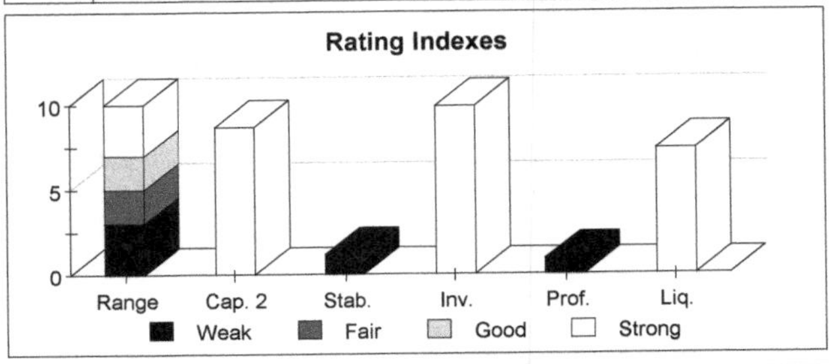

## TAKECARE INS CO D+ Weak

**Major Rating Factors:** Poor capitalization (2.8 on a scale of 0 to 10) based on weak current risk-adjusted capital (moderate loss scenario). Weak liquidity (0.1) as a spike in claims may stretch capacity. Fair profitability index (4.5).
**Other Rating Factors:** Fair quality investment portfolio (3.8).
**Principal Business:** Comp med (66%), FEHB (34%)
**Mem Phys: 16:** 404 **15:** 398 **16 MLR** 94.8% **/ 16 Admin Exp** N/A
**Enroll(000): Q3 17:** 27 **16:** 33 **15:** 35 **Med Exp PMPM:** $241
**Principal Investments:** Cash and equiv (20%), real estate (10%), other (70%)
**Provider Compensation ($000):** Contr fee ($55,518), capitation ($41,385)
**Total Member Encounters:** N/A
**Group Affiliation:** TakeCare Health Systems LLP
**Licensed in:** (No states)
**Address:** STE 308 415 CHN SAN ANTONIO, TAMUNING, GU 96913
**Phone:** (671) 646-6956 **Dom State:** GU **Commenced Bus:** January 2001

| Data Date | Rating | RACR #1 | RACR #2 | Total Assets ($mil) | Capital ($mil) | Net Premium ($mil) | Net Income ($mil) |
|---|---|---|---|---|---|---|---|
| 9-17 | D+ | 0.58 | 0.48 | 32.5 | 8.3 | 73.3 | 0.5 |
| 9-16 | C+ | 1.02 | 0.85 | 37.7 | 14.6 | 76.2 | 0.6 |
| 2016 | C | 1.06 | 0.89 | 32.3 | 14.0 | 101.0 | -0.7 |
| 2015 | C+ | 1.25 | 1.04 | 38.5 | 18.0 | 106.3 | 5.0 |
| 2014 | U | 1.07 | 0.89 | 34.1 | 14.8 | 100.7 | 4.7 |
| 2013 | N/A | N/A | N/A | 30.7 | 12.3 | 99.2 | 2.2 |
| 2012 | N/A | N/A | N/A | 26.8 | 11.8 | 95.9 | 7.4 |

Rating Indexes

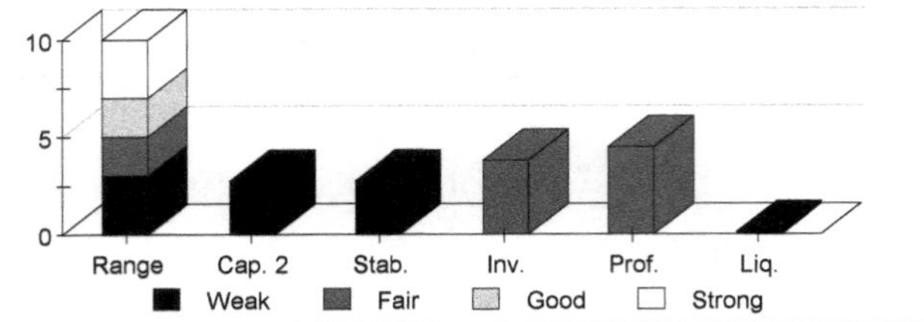


## TEXAS CHILDRENS HEALTH PLAN INC D+ Weak

**Major Rating Factors:** Weak profitability index (0.9 on a scale of 0 to 10). Fair capitalization index (4.1) based on fair current risk-adjusted capital (moderate loss scenario). Fair overall results on stability tests (3.2).
**Other Rating Factors:** Good liquidity (6.4) with sufficient resources (cash flows and marketable investments) to handle a spike in claims. High quality investment portfolio (9.9).
**Principal Business:** Medicaid (87%), comp med (13%)
**Mem Phys: 16:** 15,381 **15:** 12,661 **16 MLR** 90.1% **/ 16 Admin Exp** N/A
**Enroll(000): Q3 17:** 431 **16:** 431 **15:** 392 **Med Exp PMPM:** $196
**Principal Investments:** Long-term bonds (48%), cash and equiv (39%), affiliate common stock (13%)
**Provider Compensation ($000):** FFS ($477,250), contr fee ($399,135), capitation ($45,130), bonus arrang ($7,070)
**Total Member Encounters:** Phys (1,872,546), non-phys (1,164,878)
**Group Affiliation:** Texas Childrens
**Licensed in:** TX
**Address:** 6330 West Loop South, Bellaire, TX 77401
**Phone:** (832) 828-1020 **Dom State:** TX **Commenced Bus:** February 1996

| Data Date | Rating | RACR #1 | RACR #2 | Total Assets ($mil) | Capital ($mil) | Net Premium ($mil) | Net Income ($mil) |
|---|---|---|---|---|---|---|---|
| 9-17 | D+ | 0.79 | 0.66 | 221.9 | 80.3 | 1,144.1 | -45.3 |
| 9-16 | B- | 1.22 | 1.01 | 184.0 | 102.0 | 729.4 | -11.6 |
| 2016 | B- | 1.08 | 0.90 | 226.3 | 104.9 | 1,067.6 | -17.7 |
| 2015 | B | 1.49 | 1.24 | 210.4 | 125.1 | 958.4 | 15.7 |
| 2014 | B- | 1.01 | 0.84 | 167.7 | 86.4 | 918.4 | 2.2 |
| 2013 | B- | 1.23 | 1.02 | 150.4 | 90.1 | 792.8 | 2.8 |
| 2012 | B | 1.67 | 1.39 | 175.4 | 108.2 | 734.6 | 18.7 |

Rating Indexes

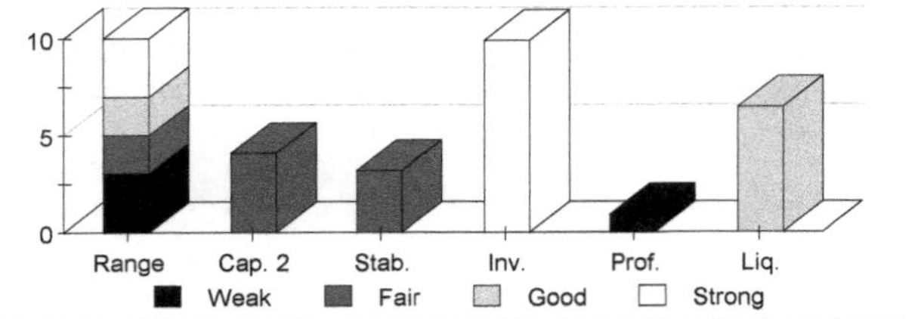


## THP INS CO D Weak

**Major Rating Factors:** Weak profitability index (1.9 on a scale of 0 to 10). Strong capitalization (9.6) based on excellent current risk-adjusted capital (severe loss scenario). High quality investment portfolio (9.9).
**Other Rating Factors:** Excellent liquidity (7.2) with ample operational cash flow and liquid investments.
**Principal Business:** Comp med (60%), med supp (19%), Medicare (16%), other (5%)
**Mem Phys: 16:** 17,602 **15:** 19,308 **16 MLR** 91.4% **/ 16 Admin Exp** N/A
**Enroll(000): Q3 17:** 19 **16:** 17 **15:** 12 **Med Exp PMPM:** $343
**Principal Investments:** Cash and equiv (61%), nonaffiliate common stock (37%), long-term bonds (2%)
**Provider Compensation ($000):** Contr fee ($61,897)
**Total Member Encounters:** Phys (213,212), non-phys (51,218)
**Group Affiliation:** Health Plan of the Upper Ohio Valley
**Licensed in:** OH, PA, WV
**Address:** 52160 National Rd East E, St. Clairsville, OH 43950-9306
**Phone:** (740) 695-3585 **Dom State:** WV **Commenced Bus:** March 1999

| Data Date | Rating | RACR #1 | RACR #2 | Total Assets ($mil) | Capital ($mil) | Net Premium ($mil) | Net Income ($mil) |
|---|---|---|---|---|---|---|---|
| 9-17 | D | 3.40 | 2.83 | 48.8 | 27.2 | 69.1 | 2.1 |
| 9-16 | D | 3.83 | 3.19 | 43.4 | 26.0 | 50.6 | 1.5 |
| 2016 | D | 3.00 | 2.50 | 43.0 | 24.1 | 71.7 | 2.3 |
| 2015 | D | 3.58 | 2.99 | 38.8 | 24.7 | 52.8 | -1.8 |
| 2014 | D | 2.45 | 2.04 | 34.8 | 18.9 | 52.0 | -13.1 |
| 2013 | D | 1.78 | 1.48 | 30.3 | 14.9 | 53.1 | -12.3 |
| 2012 | D | 3.28 | 2.73 | 28.2 | 19.0 | 46.5 | -7.4 |

Rating Indexes

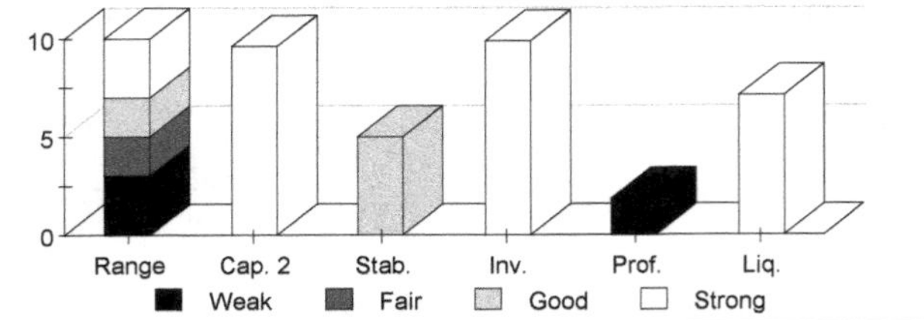

## TIMBER PRODUCTS MANUFACTURERS TRUST D- Weak

**Major Rating Factors:** Weak profitability index (1.5 on a scale of 0 to 10). Weak liquidity (1.1) as a spike in claims may stretch capacity. Fair capitalization (3.2) based on weak current risk-adjusted capital (moderate loss scenario).
**Other Rating Factors:** High quality investment portfolio (9.6).
**Principal Business:** Comp med (97%), dental (3%)
**Mem Phys: 16:** N/A **15:** N/A **16 MLR** 102.2% **/ 16 Admin Exp** N/A
**Enroll(000): Q3 17:** 15 **16:** 22 **15:** 22 **Med Exp PMPM:** $220
**Principal Investments:** Long-term bonds (48%), cash and equiv (46%), nonaffiliate common stock (4%), other (3%)
**Provider Compensation ($000):** Contr fee ($60,276)
**Total Member Encounters:** Phys (84,526), non-phys (12,998)
**Group Affiliation:** Timber Products Manufacturers Trust
**Licensed in:** ID, MT, OR, WA, WY
**Address:** 951 EAST THIRD Ave, SPOKANE, WA 99202
**Phone:** (509) 535-4646 **Dom State:** WA **Commenced Bus:** August 1960

| Data Date | Rating | RACR #1 | RACR #2 | Total Assets ($mil) | Capital ($mil) | Net Premium ($mil) | Net Income ($mil) |
|---|---|---|---|---|---|---|---|
| 9-17 | D- | 0.66 | 0.55 | 10.7 | 6.1 | 37.1 | 3.2 |
| 9-16 | E+ | 0.37 | 0.31 | 9.5 | 2.6 | 43.7 | -3.1 |
| 2016 | E+ | 0.32 | 0.26 | 10.0 | 2.9 | 57.7 | -4.3 |
| 2015 | C | 0.71 | 0.59 | 14.2 | 5.4 | 54.6 | -2.5 |
| 2014 | C+ | 1.30 | 1.08 | 14.3 | 8.1 | 43.7 | 1.1 |
| 2013 | C+ | 1.22 | 1.01 | 12.4 | 7.1 | 35.3 | 0.7 |
| 2012 | C | 1.27 | 1.06 | 11.2 | 6.4 | 29.8 | 1.4 |

Rating Indexes

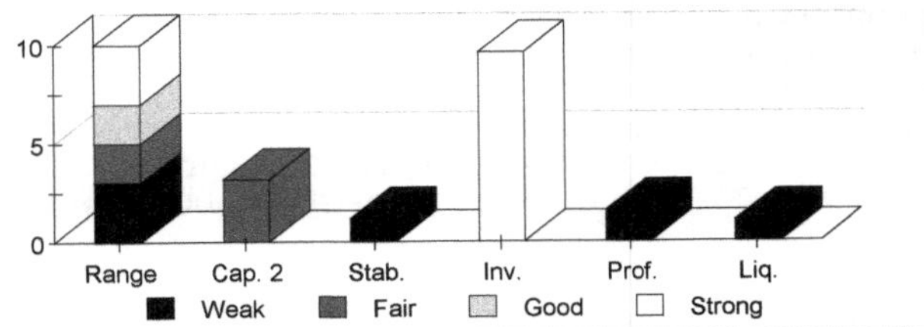


## TIME INSURANCE COMPANY C+ Fair

**Major Rating Factors:** Fair overall results on stability tests (3.0 on a scale of 0 to 10) including weak results on operational trends. Good liquidity (6.9) with sufficient resources to handle a spike in claims. Weak profitability (1.8).
**Other Rating Factors:** Strong capitalization (10.0) based on excellent risk adjusted capital (severe loss scenario). High quality investment portfolio (7.3).
**Principal Business:** Group health insurance (48%), individual health insurance (38%), and individual life insurance (13%).
**Principal Investments:** NonCMO investment grade bonds (85%), CMOs and structured securities (7%), real estate (7%), common & preferred stock (1%), and noninv. grade bonds (1%).
**Investments in Affiliates:** None
**Group Affiliation:** Assurant Inc
**Licensed in:** All states except NY, PR
**Commenced Business:** March 1910
**Address:** 501 WEST MICHIGAN STREET, MILWAUKEE, WI 53203
**Phone:** (414) 271-3011 **Domicile State:** WI **NAIC Code:** 69477

| Data Date | Rating | RACR #1 | RACR #2 | Total Assets ($mil) | Capital ($mil) | Net Premium ($mil) | Net Income ($mil) |
|---|---|---|---|---|---|---|---|
| 9-17 | C+ | 5.57 | 4.84 | 108.9 | 50.1 | 5.3 | 35.1 |
| 9-16 | C+ | 1.98 | 1.55 | 336.2 | 169.4 | 7.1 | 13.2 |
| 2016 | C+ | 9.64 | 7.15 | 219.8 | 91.0 | 18.2 | 37.5 |
| 2015 | C+ | 1.44 | 1.16 | 1,157.9 | 471.7 | 2,031.9 | -389.3 |
| 2014 | C+ | 1.46 | 1.15 | 991.0 | 389.7 | 1,755.5 | -64.6 |
| 2013 | B- | 1.14 | 0.88 | 691.5 | 212.0 | 1,269.5 | 5.6 |
| 2012 | B- | 1.20 | 0.92 | 645.4 | 205.8 | 1,164.5 | 48.7 |

**Adverse Trends in Operations**

Increase in policy surrenders from 2015 to 2016 (738%)
Decrease in asset base during 2016 (81%)
Decrease in premium volume from 2015 to 2016 (99%)
Decrease in capital during 2016 (81%)
Increase in policy surrenders from 2012 to 2013 (116%)

## TODAYS OPTIONS OF TEXAS INC C Fair

**Major Rating Factors:** Excellent profitability (9.3 on a scale of 0 to 10). Strong capitalization (10.0) based on excellent current risk-adjusted capital (severe loss scenario). High quality investment portfolio (9.9).
**Other Rating Factors:** Excellent liquidity (9.1) with ample operational cash flow and liquid investments.
**Principal Business:** Medicare (100%)
**Mem Phys: 16:** 1,943 **15:** N/A **16 MLR** 60.3% **/ 16 Admin Exp** N/A
**Enroll(000): Q3 17:** 1 **16:** 0 **15:** N/A **Med Exp PMPM:** $742
**Principal Investments:** Cash and equiv (98%), long-term bonds (2%)
**Provider Compensation ($000):** Contr fee ($1,651), capitation ($40)
**Total Member Encounters:** Phys (2,963), non-phys (299)
**Group Affiliation:** WellCare Health Plans Inc
**Licensed in:** TX
**Address:** 4888 Loop Central Dr Ste 300, Houston, TX 77081-2181
**Phone:** (713) 965-9444 **Dom State:** TX **Commenced Bus:** April 2014

| Data Date | Rating | RACR #1 | RACR #2 | Total Assets ($mil) | Capital ($mil) | Net Premium ($mil) | Net Income ($mil) |
|---|---|---|---|---|---|---|---|
| 9-17 | C | 7.90 | 6.58 | 10.2 | 6.9 | 6.5 | 1.0 |
| 9-16 | N/A | N/A | N/A | 6.4 | 5.0 | 2.3 | -0.2 |
| 2016 | C | 6.97 | 5.81 | 6.8 | 5.8 | 3.5 | 0.6 |
| 2015 | N/A | N/A | N/A | 5.0 | 5.0 | N/A | N/A |
| 2014 | N/A | N/A | N/A | 1.6 | 1.5 | N/A | N/A |
| 2013 | N/A | N/A | N/A | N/A | N/A | N/A | N/A |
| 2012 | N/A | N/A | N/A | N/A | N/A | N/A | N/A |

Rating Indexes

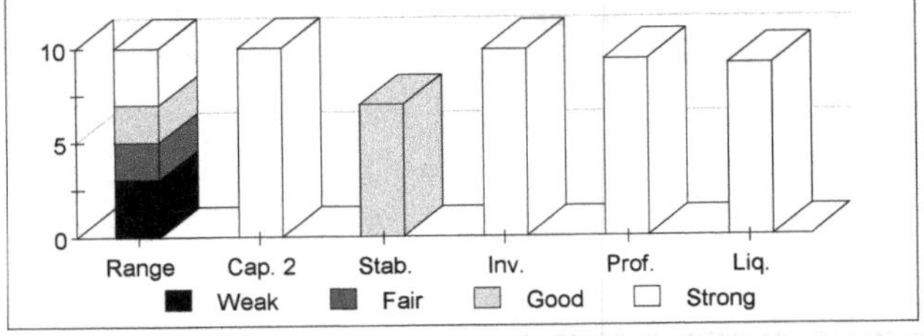

## TOKIO MARINE PACIFIC INS LTD — C — Fair

**Major Rating Factors:** Fair overall results on stability tests (3.4 on a scale of 0 to 10) including negative cash flow from operations for 2016. Vulnerable liquidity (1.0) as a spike in claims may stretch capacity.
**Other Rating Factors:** Good overall profitability index (6.4). Good expense controls. Return on equity has been good over the last five years, averaging 11.6%. Strong long-term capitalization index (8.9) based on excellent current risk adjusted capital (severe and moderate loss scenarios), despite some fluctuation in capital levels. Ample reserve history (7.9) that can protect against increases in claims costs.
**Principal Business:** Group accident & health (90%), auto physical damage (3%), auto liability (2%), commercial multiple peril (1%), workers compensation (1%), homeowners multiple peril (1%), and other lines (2%).
**Principal Investments:** Investment grade bonds (75%), cash (24%), and misc. investments (1%).
**Investments in Affiliates:** None
**Group Affiliation:** Tokio Marine Holdings Inc
**Licensed in:** (No states)
**Commenced Business:** February 2002
**Address:** 250 ROUTE 4 STE 202, Hagatna, GU 96910
**Phone:** (671) 475-8671 **Domicile State:** GU **NAIC Code:** 11216

| Data Date | Rating | RACR #1 | RACR #2 | Loss Ratio % | Total Assets ($mil) | Capital ($mil) | Net Premium ($mil) | Net Income ($mil) |
|---|---|---|---|---|---|---|---|---|
| 9-17 | C | 4.66 | 2.50 | N/A | 116.6 | 78.4 | 113.8 | 3.2 |
| 9-16 | C | 4.65 | 2.50 | N/A | 119.1 | 77.7 | 104.7 | 10.4 |
| 2016 | C | 3.82 | 2.05 | 82.5 | 105.0 | 62.8 | 143.9 | 7.5 |
| 2015 | C | 4.01 | 2.18 | 81.1 | 109.3 | 67.0 | 135.2 | 5.3 |
| 2014 | C | 3.31 | 1.87 | 81.5 | 98.5 | 61.0 | 121.8 | 4.3 |
| 2013 | B- | 3.79 | 2.11 | 80.4 | 105.9 | 60.5 | 122.5 | 5.2 |
| 2012 | B | 4.52 | 2.46 | 75.8 | 105.7 | 61.7 | 125.2 | 16.7 |

**Tokio Marine Holdings Inc**
**Composite Group Rating: B**

| Largest Group Members | Assets ($mil) | Rating |
|---|---|---|
| RELIANCE STANDARD LIFE INS CO | 10889 | B |
| PHILADELPHIA INDEMNITY INS CO | 8081 | B- |
| SAFETY NATIONAL CASUALTY CORP | 6450 | C |
| HOUSTON CASUALTY CO | 3330 | B- |
| US SPECIALTY INS CO | 1792 | B- |

## TOTAL HEALTH CARE INC — C+ — Fair

**Major Rating Factors:** Fair overall results on stability tests (4.8 on a scale of 0 to 10). Good liquidity (6.9) with sufficient resources (cash flows and marketable investments) to handle a spike in claims. Weak profitability index (2.2).
**Other Rating Factors:** Strong capitalization index (7.3) based on excellent current risk-adjusted capital (severe loss scenario). High quality investment portfolio (8.0).
**Principal Business:** Medicaid (100%)
**Mem Phys: 16:** 5,545 **15:** 6,011 **16 MLR** 84.9% **/ 16 Admin Exp** N/A
**Enroll(000): Q3 17:** 53 **16:** 54 **15:** 62 **Med Exp PMPM:** $359
**Principal Investments:** Cash and equiv (61%), affiliate common stock (38%), long-term bonds (1%)
**Provider Compensation ($000):** Contr fee ($133,829), capitation ($110,420), FFS ($235)
**Total Member Encounters:** Phys (390,425), non-phys (183,073)
**Group Affiliation:** Total Health Care Inc
**Licensed in:** MI
**Address:** 3011 W GRAND BLVD SUITE 1600, DETROIT, MI 48202
**Phone:** (313) 871-2000 **Dom State:** MI **Commenced Bus:** May 1976

| Data Date | Rating | RACR #1 | RACR #2 | Total Assets ($mil) | Capital ($mil) | Net Premium ($mil) | Net Income ($mil) |
|---|---|---|---|---|---|---|---|
| 9-17 | C+ | 1.60 | 1.33 | 81.5 | 48.9 | 191.4 | -7.4 |
| 9-16 | B- | 1.40 | 1.17 | 81.6 | 49.9 | 214.2 | 2.8 |
| 2016 | B- | 1.48 | 1.23 | 83.2 | 46.5 | 284.1 | -1.8 |
| 2015 | B- | 1.14 | 0.95 | 84.2 | 41.7 | 322.4 | 5.9 |
| 2014 | C | 0.82 | 0.69 | 60.5 | 29.9 | 272.3 | 5.0 |
| 2013 | D+ | 0.72 | 0.60 | 44.6 | 23.2 | 224.0 | -6.4 |
| 2012 | D+ | 1.16 | 0.96 | 50.5 | 29.6 | 200.3 | 0.1 |

Rating Indexes

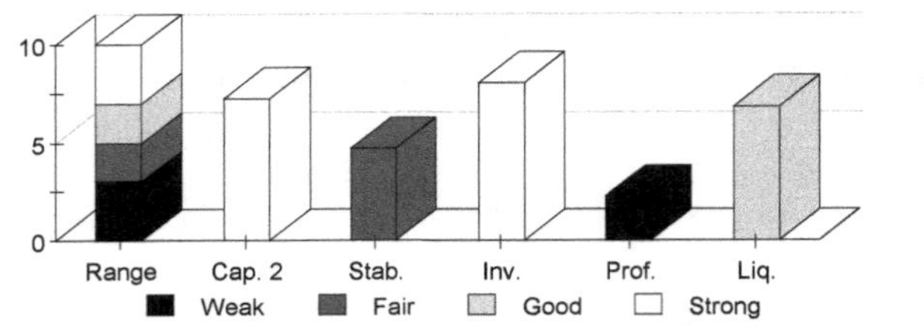


## TOTAL HEALTH CARE USA INC * — B+ — Good

**Major Rating Factors:** Excellent profitability (8.8 on a scale of 0 to 10). Strong capitalization (9.6) based on excellent current risk-adjusted capital (severe loss scenario). High quality investment portfolio (9.9).
**Other Rating Factors:** Excellent liquidity (7.4) with ample operational cash flow and liquid investments.
**Principal Business:** Comp med (100%)
**Mem Phys: 16:** 5,253 **15:** 6,204 **16 MLR** 77.8% **/ 16 Admin Exp** N/A
**Enroll(000): Q3 17:** 35 **16:** 33 **15:** 41 **Med Exp PMPM:** $269
**Principal Investments:** Cash and equiv (98%), long-term bonds (2%)
**Provider Compensation ($000):** Contr fee ($104,890), capitation ($3,475), FFS ($324)
**Total Member Encounters:** Phys (206,948), non-phys (74,814)
**Group Affiliation:** Total Health Care Inc
**Licensed in:** MI
**Address:** 3011 W GRAND BLVD Ste 1600, DETROIT, MI 48202
**Phone:** (313) 871-2000 **Dom State:** MI **Commenced Bus:** February 1994

| Data Date | Rating | RACR #1 | RACR #2 | Total Assets ($mil) | Capital ($mil) | Net Premium ($mil) | Net Income ($mil) |
|---|---|---|---|---|---|---|---|
| 9-17 | B+ | 3.47 | 2.89 | 68.3 | 39.9 | 112.9 | 9.9 |
| 9-16 | B | 2.27 | 1.90 | 54.2 | 28.8 | 105.9 | 5.7 |
| 2016 | B+ | 2.54 | 2.12 | 55.4 | 29.9 | 139.3 | 6.7 |
| 2015 | B | 1.80 | 1.50 | 53.5 | 23.4 | 154.9 | 5.5 |
| 2014 | C+ | 1.20 | 1.00 | 45.0 | 17.6 | 160.5 | 2.3 |
| 2013 | C+ | 1.38 | 1.15 | 30.1 | 15.5 | 114.8 | 0.1 |
| 2012 | B- | 1.64 | 1.36 | 26.8 | 15.5 | 96.9 | 0.2 |

Rating Indexes

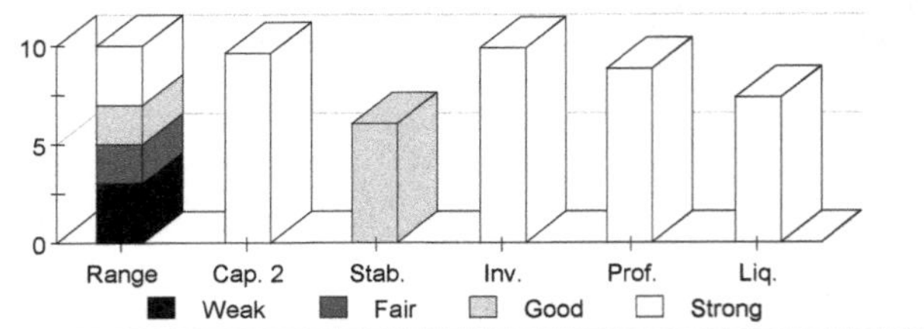

## TOUCHSTONE HEALTH HMO INC E+ Very Weak

**Major Rating Factors:** Weak profitability index (0.9 on a scale of 0 to 10). Poor capitalization (1.2) based on weak current risk-adjusted capital (moderate loss scenario). High quality investment portfolio (9.9).
**Other Rating Factors:** Excellent liquidity (8.4) with ample operational cash flow and liquid investments.
**Principal Business:** Medicare (100%)
**Mem Phys: 16:** N/A **15:** N/A **16 MLR** -553.8% **/ 16 Admin Exp** N/A
**Enroll(000): Q1 17:** N/A **16:** N/A **15:** 10 **Med Exp PMPM:** N/A
**Principal Investments:** Cash and equiv (83%), long-term bonds (17%)
**Provider Compensation ($000):** None
**Total Member Encounters:** N/A
**Group Affiliation:** Touchstone Health Partnership Inc
**Licensed in:** NY
**Address:** 1 N LEXINGTON Ave 12TH Fl, WHITE PLAINS, NY 10601
**Phone:** (914) 288-1000 **Dom State:** NY **Commenced Bus:** September 2007

| Data Date | Rating | RACR #1 | RACR #2 | Total Assets ($mil) | Capital ($mil) | Net Premium ($mil) | Net Income ($mil) |
|---|---|---|---|---|---|---|---|
| 3-17 | E+ | 0.42 | 0.35 | 12.5 | 2.6 | 0.0 | -0.4 |
| 3-16 | E | N/A | N/A | 13.3 | 2.3 | N/A | -0.1 |
| 2016 | E+ | 0.41 | 0.35 | 10.3 | 2.5 | 0.3 | 0.1 |
| 2015 | E | 0.09 | 0.08 | 24.5 | 2.4 | 129.9 | -6.0 |
| 2014 | E | 0.36 | 0.30 | 18.5 | 9.6 | 157.9 | 0.4 |
| 2013 | N/A | N/A | N/A | 12.9 | -0.5 | 152.9 | -1.3 |
| 2012 | E | N/A | N/A | 14.8 | 0.9 | 157.1 | -1.5 |

Rating Indexes

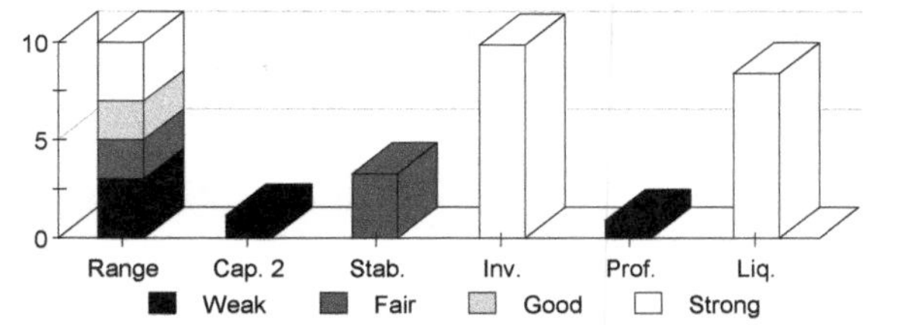


## TRANS OCEANIC LIFE INSURANCE COMPANY * A- Excellent

**Major Rating Factors:** Good quality investment portfolio (5.1 on a scale of 0 to 10) with no exposure to mortgages and minimal holdings in junk bonds. Good overall results on stability tests (6.4). Strengths that enhance stability include excellent operational trends and good risk diversification. Strong capitalization (7.8) based on excellent risk adjusted capital (severe loss scenario).
**Other Rating Factors:** Excellent profitability (8.4). Excellent liquidity (8.2).
**Principal Business:** Individual health insurance (92%) and individual life insurance (7%).
**Principal Investments:** NonCMO investment grade bonds (52%), CMOs and structured securities (11%), real estate (10%), common & preferred stock (9%), and misc. investments (12%).
**Investments in Affiliates:** None
**Group Affiliation:** Trans-Oceanic Group Inc
**Licensed in:** FL, PR
**Commenced Business:** December 1959
**Address:** # 121 ONEILL, SAN JUAN, PR 00918-2404
**Phone:** (787) 620-2680 **Domicile State:** PR **NAIC Code:** 69523

| Data Date | Rating | RACR #1 | RACR #2 | Total Assets ($mil) | Capital ($mil) | Net Premium ($mil) | Net Income ($mil) |
|---|---|---|---|---|---|---|---|
| 9-17 | A- | 2.45 | 1.55 | 71.4 | 32.7 | 22.7 | 0.9 |
| 9-16 | A- | 2.61 | 1.63 | 69.2 | 34.7 | 23.1 | 1.1 |
| 2016 | A- | 2.54 | 1.61 | 70.6 | 32.8 | 30.7 | 1.2 |
| 2015 | A | 3.12 | 1.95 | 67.4 | 35.2 | 30.4 | 4.7 |
| 2014 | A | 3.09 | 2.06 | 65.1 | 33.7 | 29.8 | 4.6 |
| 2013 | B+ | 2.67 | 1.83 | 58.9 | 29.5 | 29.8 | 6.0 |
| 2012 | B+ | 2.11 | 1.46 | 49.6 | 22.5 | 28.5 | 3.7 |

**Adverse Trends in Operations**

Increase in policy surrenders from 2015 to 2016 (8879%)
Decrease in capital during 2016 (9%)
Change in asset mix during 2016 (4%)
Increase in policy surrenders from 2012 to 2013 (257%)

## TRH HEALTH INS CO C Fair

**Major Rating Factors:** Weak profitability index (1.7 on a scale of 0 to 10). Good liquidity (5.8) with sufficient resources (cash flows and marketable investments) to handle a spike in claims. Strong capitalization (8.1) based on excellent current risk-adjusted capital (severe loss scenario).
**Other Rating Factors:** High quality investment portfolio (9.6).
**Principal Business:** Comp med (55%), med supp (45%)
**Mem Phys: 16:** 744,874 **15:** 610,745 **16 MLR** 89.2% **/ 16 Admin Exp** N/A
**Enroll(000): Q3 17:** 134 **16:** 116 **15:** 116 **Med Exp PMPM:** $188
**Principal Investments:** Long-term bonds (77%), cash and equiv (18%), nonaffiliate common stock (4%)
**Provider Compensation ($000):** FFS ($261,472)
**Total Member Encounters:** Phys (2,463,437), non-phys (371,281)
**Group Affiliation:** TN Rural Health Improvement Assoc
**Licensed in:** TN
**Address:** 147 Bear Creek Pike, Columbia, TN 38401-2266
**Phone:** (931) 560-0041 **Dom State:** TN **Commenced Bus:** February 1999

| Data Date | Rating | RACR #1 | RACR #2 | Total Assets ($mil) | Capital ($mil) | Net Premium ($mil) | Net Income ($mil) |
|---|---|---|---|---|---|---|---|
| 9-17 | C | 2.21 | 1.85 | 127.7 | 66.0 | 308.6 | -9.7 |
| 9-16 | B- | 3.03 | 2.53 | 120.2 | 78.5 | 222.4 | -0.1 |
| 2016 | C+ | 2.41 | 2.01 | 127.5 | 71.1 | 296.7 | -12.3 |
| 2015 | B- | 3.06 | 2.55 | 120.7 | 79.3 | 287.6 | 9.8 |
| 2014 | C+ | 2.98 | 2.49 | 82.9 | 53.3 | 159.7 | -0.7 |
| 2013 | B- | 2.86 | 2.39 | 87.3 | 55.1 | 175.9 | -6.3 |
| 2012 | B- | 2.89 | 2.41 | 82.6 | 58.6 | 182.2 | 13.5 |

Rating Indexes

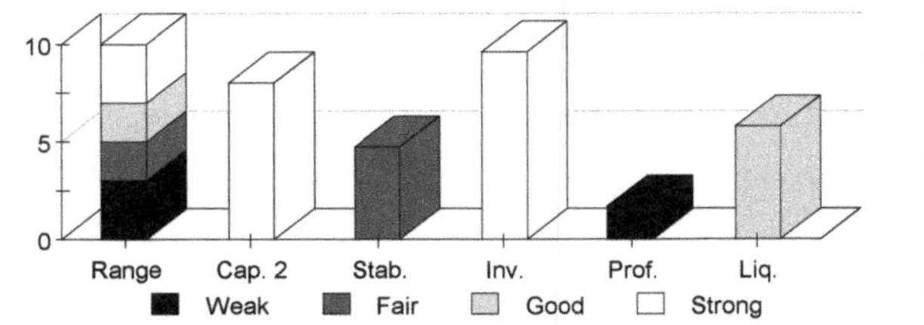

## TRILLIUM COMMUNITY HEALTH PLAN INC C+ Fair

**Major Rating Factors:** Good liquidity (6.3 on a scale of 0 to 10) with sufficient resources (cash flows and marketable investments) to handle a spike in claims. Excellent profitability (8.7). Strong capitalization (8.5) based on excellent current risk-adjusted capital (severe loss scenario).
**Other Rating Factors:** High quality investment portfolio (9.2).
**Principal Business:** Medicaid (91%), Medicare (9%)
**Mem Phys: 16:** 3,569 **15:** 3,301 **16 MLR** 90.8% **/ 16 Admin Exp** N/A
**Enroll(000): Q3 17:** 92 **16:** 93 **15:** 101 **Med Exp PMPM:** $397
**Principal Investments:** Long-term bonds (64%), cash and equiv (36%)
**Provider Compensation ($000):** Contr fee ($375,000), capitation ($51,937), salary ($24,520), bonus arrang ($9,639)
**Total Member Encounters:** Phys (517,074), non-phys (590,518)
**Group Affiliation:** Centene Corporation
**Licensed in:** OR
**Address:** 1800 Millrace Dr, Eugene, OR 97403
**Phone:** (877) 600-5472 **Dom State:** OR **Commenced Bus:** February 2006

| Data Date | Rating | RACR #1 | RACR #2 | Total Assets ($mil) | Capital ($mil) | Net Premium ($mil) | Net Income ($mil) |
|---|---|---|---|---|---|---|---|
| 9-17 | C+ | 2.59 | 2.16 | 175.8 | 67.2 | 370.5 | 3.9 |
| 9-16 | C | 2.35 | 1.96 | 179.8 | 62.3 | 394.5 | 2.2 |
| 2016 | C+ | 2.49 | 2.08 | 174.7 | 64.5 | 519.7 | 5.0 |
| 2015 | C+ | 1.61 | 1.34 | 154.8 | 41.3 | 522.9 | 14.1 |
| 2014 | B | 1.20 | 1.00 | 118.8 | 43.5 | 407.5 | 22.2 |
| 2013 | C | 0.78 | 0.65 | 62.5 | 20.9 | 244.5 | 3.9 |
| 2012 | E+ | 0.37 | 0.31 | 40.4 | 6.0 | 134.0 | 1.2 |

Rating Indexes

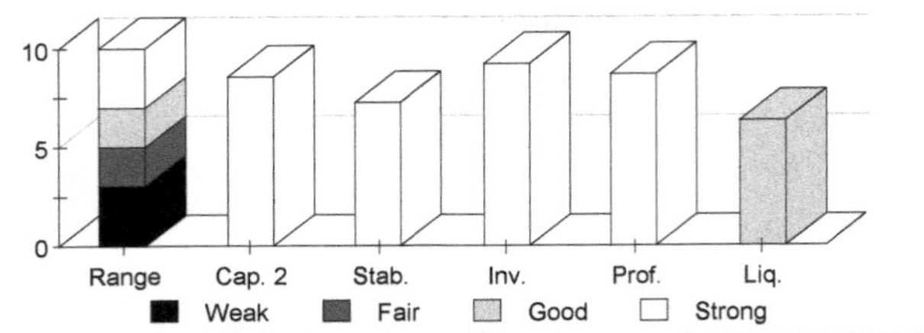


## TRILOGY HEALTH INS INC C Fair

**Major Rating Factors:** Fair profitability index (3.0 on a scale of 0 to 10). Fair capitalization (4.8) based on good current risk-adjusted capital (severe loss scenario). High quality investment portfolio (9.9).
**Other Rating Factors:** Excellent liquidity (7.0) with ample operational cash flow and liquid investments.
**Principal Business:** Medicaid (100%)
**Mem Phys: 16:** 11,863 **15:** 10,787 **16 MLR** 85.9% **/ 16 Admin Exp** N/A
**Enroll(000): Q3 17:** 9 **16:** 9 **15:** 7 **Med Exp PMPM:** $182
**Principal Investments:** Cash and equiv (96%), long-term bonds (4%)
**Provider Compensation ($000):** Contr fee ($16,749), capitation ($330)
**Total Member Encounters:** Phys (56,384), non-phys (11,993)
**Group Affiliation:** Trilogy Health Holdings LLC
**Licensed in:** WI
**Address:** 18000 West Sarah Lane Ste 310, Brookfield, WI 53045-5842
**Phone:** (262) 432-9145 **Dom State:** WI **Commenced Bus:** January 2007

| Data Date | Rating | RACR #1 | RACR #2 | Total Assets ($mil) | Capital ($mil) | Net Premium ($mil) | Net Income ($mil) |
|---|---|---|---|---|---|---|---|
| 9-17 | C | 0.90 | 0.75 | 6.1 | 3.2 | 16.5 | -0.5 |
| 9-16 | C | 1.49 | 1.24 | 7.2 | 4.0 | 15.2 | 0.1 |
| 2016 | C | 1.05 | 0.87 | 7.3 | 3.8 | 20.4 | 0.1 |
| 2015 | C | 1.61 | 1.34 | 7.3 | 4.7 | 17.7 | 3.1 |
| 2014 | E+ | 0.68 | 0.57 | 3.1 | 1.2 | 5.1 | -1.7 |
| 2013 | N/A | N/A | N/A | 2.0 | 1.5 | N/A | 1.3 |
| 2012 | E | 0.02 | 0.02 | 5.4 | 0.3 | 25.8 | 0.1 |

Rating Indexes

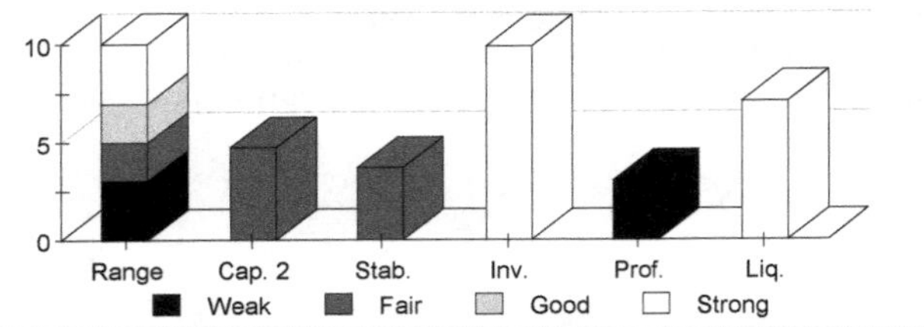


## TRIPLE S VIDA INCORPORATED B- Good

**Major Rating Factors:** Good overall results on stability tests (5.2 on a scale of 0 to 10) despite fair risk adjusted capital in prior years. Other stability subfactors include excellent operational trends and good risk diversification. Good current capitalization (5.2) based on good risk adjusted capital (moderate loss scenario) reflecting some improvement over results in 2013. Good overall profitability (6.6).
**Other Rating Factors:** Fair quality investment portfolio (4.5). Fair liquidity (4.1).
**Principal Business:** Individual life insurance (53%), individual health insurance (31%), group health insurance (5%), group life insurance (4%), and other lines (7%).
**Principal Investments:** NonCMO investment grade bonds (83%), common & preferred stock (14%), policy loans (2%), and noninv. grade bonds (2%).
**Investments in Affiliates:** 1%
**Group Affiliation:** Triple-S Management Corp
**Licensed in:** PR
**Commenced Business:** September 1964
**Address:** 1052 Munoz Rivera, San Juan, PR 927
**Phone:** (787) 777-8432 **Domicile State:** PR **NAIC Code:** 73814

| Data Date | Rating | RACR #1 | RACR #2 | Total Assets ($mil) | Capital ($mil) | Net Premium ($mil) | Net Income ($mil) |
|---|---|---|---|---|---|---|---|
| 9-17 | B- | 1.14 | 0.75 | 637.5 | 59.6 | 129.0 | 3.9 |
| 9-16 | B- | N/A | N/A | 593.1 | 55.2 | 126.0 | 5.2 |
| 2016 | B- | 1.16 | 0.75 | 601.8 | 62.0 | 170.9 | 9.5 |
| 2015 | B- | N/A | N/A | 572.2 | 59.1 | 161.0 | 5.3 |
| 2014 | B- | 1.19 | 0.81 | 550.3 | 64.8 | 158.3 | 12.3 |
| 2013 | B- | 1.00 | 0.69 | 512.7 | 61.1 | 147.3 | 6.0 |
| 2012 | B- | 1.16 | 0.75 | 480.8 | 57.4 | 172.6 | 4.5 |

**Adverse Trends in Operations**

Decrease in premium volume from 2012 to 2013 (15%)

## TRIPLE-S ADVANTAGE INC — C — Fair

**Major Rating Factors:** Fair liquidity (3.0 on a scale of 0 to 10) as a spike in claims may stretch capacity. Weak profitability index (0.9). Poor capitalization (1.3) based on weak current risk-adjusted capital (moderate loss scenario).
**Other Rating Factors:** High quality investment portfolio (8.9).
**Principal Business:** Medicare (100%)
**Mem Phys: 16:** N/A **15:** N/A **16 MLR** 90.3% **/ 16 Admin Exp** N/A
**Enroll(000): Q3 17:** 123 **16:** 110 **15:** 124 **Med Exp PMPM:** $663
**Principal Investments:** Long-term bonds (81%), nonaffiliate common stock (11%), cash and equiv (8%)
**Provider Compensation ($000):** FFS ($844,989), capitation ($89,663)
**Total Member Encounters:** Phys (2,426,896), non-phys (443,787)
**Group Affiliation:** Triple-S Management Corporation
**Licensed in:** PR
**Address:** FD ROOSEVELT AVE 1441, SAN JUAN, PR 00920
**Phone:** (787) 620-1919 **Dom State:** PR **Commenced Bus:** May 2001

| Data Date | Rating | RACR #1 | RACR #2 | Total Assets ($mil) | Capital ($mil) | Net Premium ($mil) | Net Income ($mil) |
|---|---|---|---|---|---|---|---|
| 9-17 | C | 0.43 | 0.36 | 379.8 | 67.9 | 788.5 | -10.0 |
| 9-16 | N/A | N/A | N/A | 311.0 | 24.7 | 789.4 | -32.9 |
| 2016 | C | 0.44 | 0.36 | 265.8 | 67.1 | 1,024.0 | -40.2 |
| 2015 | N/A | N/A | N/A | 280.7 | 87.0 | 1,097.3 | N/A |
| 2014 | B | 1.08 | 0.90 | 227.7 | 45.4 | 539.8 | 10.4 |
| 2013 | C | 0.86 | 0.72 | 152.2 | 52.8 | 519.9 | 19.7 |
| 2012 | D- | 0.37 | 0.31 | 121.3 | 30.7 | 539.3 | -11.8 |

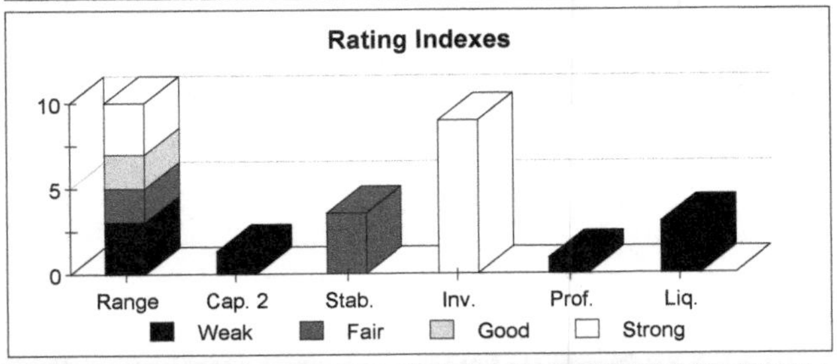


## TRIPLE-S SALUD INC — B- — Good

**Major Rating Factors:** Good overall profitability index (5.9 on a scale of 0 to 10). Good liquidity (6.6) with sufficient resources (cash flows and marketable investments) to handle a spike in claims. Strong capitalization (8.0) based on excellent current risk-adjusted capital (severe loss scenario).
**Other Rating Factors:** High quality investment portfolio (8.6).
**Principal Business:** Medicaid (48%), comp med (40%), FEHB (11%), med supp (1%)
**Mem Phys: 16:** N/A **15:** N/A **16 MLR** 87.6% **/ 16 Admin Exp** N/A
**Enroll(000): Q3 17:** 888 **16:** 923 **15:** 986 **Med Exp PMPM:** $125
**Principal Investments:** Long-term bonds (58%), nonaffiliate common stock (25%), cash and equiv (12%), affiliate common stock (3%), other (2%)
**Provider Compensation ($000):** Contr fee ($1,323,959), capitation ($93,593)
**Total Member Encounters:** Phys (4,412,780), non-phys (142,404)
**Group Affiliation:** Triple-S Management Corporation
**Licensed in:** PR
**Address:** FD Roosevelt Ave 1441, San Juan, PR 00920
**Phone:** (787) 749-4949 **Dom State:** PR **Commenced Bus:** March 1960

| Data Date | Rating | RACR #1 | RACR #2 | Total Assets ($mil) | Capital ($mil) | Net Premium ($mil) | Net Income ($mil) |
|---|---|---|---|---|---|---|---|
| 9-17 | B- | 2.13 | 1.77 | 619.9 | 261.8 | 1,169.7 | 51.9 |
| 9-16 | N/A | N/A | N/A | 712.3 | 345.5 | 1,222.7 | 17.7 |
| 2016 | B | 3.10 | 2.58 | 701.1 | 371.2 | 1,626.3 | 38.4 |
| 2015 | N/A | N/A | N/A | 734.6 | 404.8 | 1,453.6 | N/A |
| 2014 | B+ | 3.31 | 2.76 | 653.6 | 395.1 | 1,355.7 | 39.9 |
| 2013 | A- | 2.94 | 2.45 | 714.2 | 381.8 | 1,455.1 | 17.8 |
| 2012 | A- | 2.47 | 2.06 | 702.5 | 334.3 | 1,497.2 | 43.0 |

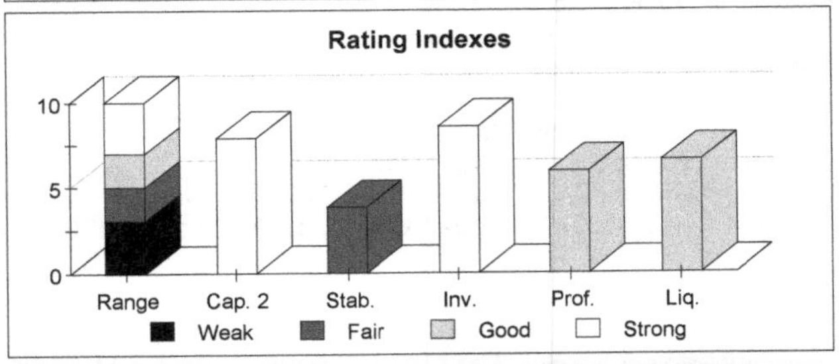


## TRITON INS CO — C+ — Fair

**Major Rating Factors:** Fair overall results on stability tests (4.2 on a scale of 0 to 10) including weak results on operational trends. Weak profitability index (2.9). Fair expense controls. Return on equity has been fair, averaging 23.9% over the past five years.
**Other Rating Factors:** Strong long-term capitalization index (10.0) based on excellent current risk adjusted capital (severe and moderate loss scenarios), despite some fluctuation in capital levels. Ample reserve history (7.5) that can protect against increases in claims costs. Excellent liquidity (7.2) with ample operational cash flow and liquid investments.
**Principal Business:** Aggregate write-ins for other lines of business (58%), credit accident & health (33%), and inland marine (8%).
**Principal Investments:** Investment grade bonds (83%), misc. investments (11%), cash (3%), and non investment grade bonds (3%).
**Investments in Affiliates:** None
**Group Affiliation:** Citigroup Inc
**Licensed in:** All states except PR
**Commenced Business:** July 1982
**Address:** 3001 Meacham Boulevard Ste 100, Fort Worth, TX 76137
**Phone:** (800) 316-5607 **Domicile State:** TX **NAIC Code:** 41211

| Data Date | Rating | RACR #1 | RACR #2 | Loss Ratio % | Total Assets ($mil) | Capital ($mil) | Net Premium ($mil) | Net Income ($mil) |
|---|---|---|---|---|---|---|---|---|
| 9-17 | C+ | 5.77 | 3.94 | N/A | 440.5 | 168.1 | 76.2 | 24.4 |
| 9-16 | B- | 7.15 | 4.12 | N/A | 425.3 | 141.7 | 83.4 | 12.5 |
| 2016 | C+ | 4.76 | 3.33 | 41.3 | 426.1 | 139.5 | 101.5 | 13.9 |
| 2015 | B- | 8.82 | 5.08 | 39.7 | 482.4 | 180.8 | 117.8 | 34.0 |
| 2014 | C+ | 9.84 | 5.43 | 31.2 | 492.8 | 190.4 | 115.1 | 55.0 |
| 2013 | C+ | 10.15 | 5.58 | 32.3 | 527.8 | 205.9 | 138.6 | 64.0 |
| 2012 | C+ | 10.46 | 5.85 | 30.9 | 554.4 | 219.4 | 147.3 | 74.9 |

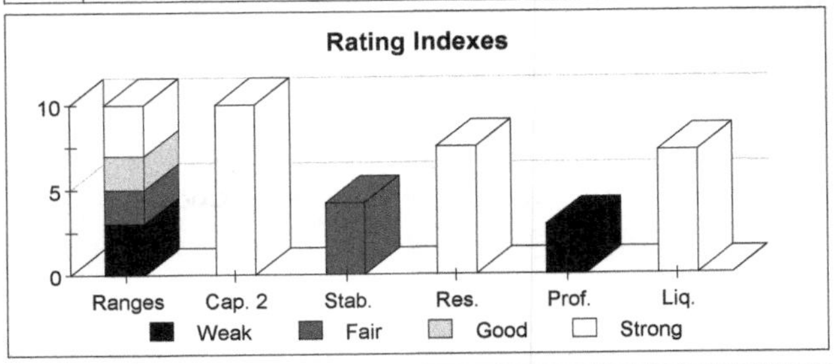

## TRUSTED HEALTH PLAN INC — C+ Fair

**Major Rating Factors:** Fair liquidity (4.1 on a scale of 0 to 10) as cash resources may not be adequate to cover a spike in claims. Good capitalization (5.6) based on good current risk-adjusted capital (severe loss scenario). Excellent profitability (7.6).
**Other Rating Factors:** High quality investment portfolio (9.0).
**Principal Business:** Medicaid (92%), comp med (8%)
**Mem Phys: 16:** 6,365 **15:** 2,581 **16 MLR** 78.9% **/ 16 Admin Exp** N/A
**Enroll(000): Q3 17:** 37 **16:** 34 **15:** 31 **Med Exp PMPM:** $300
**Principal Investments:** Long-term bonds (67%), cash and equiv (33%)
**Provider Compensation ($000):** Contr fee ($108,884), capitation ($3,869)
**Total Member Encounters:** Phys (233,282), non-phys (51,417)
**Group Affiliation:** Trusted Health Plans Inc
**Licensed in:** DC
**Address:** 1100 New Jersey Ave SE Ste 840, Washington, DC 20003
**Phone:** (202) 821-1100 **Dom State:** DC **Commenced Bus:** March 2012

| Data Date | Rating | RACR #1 | RACR #2 | Total Assets ($mil) | Capital ($mil) | Net Premium ($mil) | Net Income ($mil) |
|---|---|---|---|---|---|---|---|
| 9-17 | C+ | 1.02 | 0.85 | 56.5 | 17.3 | 116.1 | 2.3 |
| 9-16 | C | 0.97 | 0.81 | 45.7 | 16.3 | 108.9 | 4.1 |
| 2016 | C | 0.83 | 0.70 | 45.0 | 14.8 | 147.4 | 4.2 |
| 2015 | D+ | 0.66 | 0.55 | 39.8 | 12.3 | 131.6 | 4.3 |
| 2014 | D | 0.34 | 0.28 | 26.0 | 8.7 | 119.1 | 3.0 |
| 2013 | D- | 0.43 | 0.36 | 12.7 | 3.5 | 50.5 | -0.2 |
| 2012 | N/A | N/A | N/A | 1.5 | 1.5 | N/A | -0.2 |

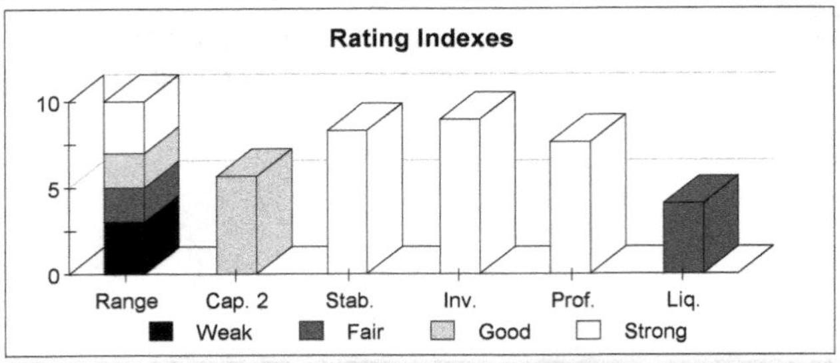


## TRUSTMARK INSURANCE COMPANY * — B+ Good

**Major Rating Factors:** Good overall profitability (6.1 on a scale of 0 to 10). Good overall results on stability tests (6.8). Stability strengths include excellent operational trends and excellent risk diversification. Fair quality investment portfolio (4.9) with substantial holdings of BBB bonds in addition to moderate junk bond exposure.
**Other Rating Factors:** Strong capitalization (7.9) based on excellent risk adjusted capital (severe loss scenario). Excellent liquidity (7.2).
**Principal Business:** Group life insurance (42%), group health insurance (25%), individual health insurance (22%), individual life insurance (10%), and reinsurance (1%).
**Principal Investments:** NonCMO investment grade bonds (43%), CMOs and structured securities (28%), common & preferred stock (10%), noninv. grade bonds (7%), and misc. investments (11%).
**Investments in Affiliates:** None
**Group Affiliation:** Trustmark Group Inc
**Licensed in:** All states, the District of Columbia and Puerto Rico
**Commenced Business:** January 1913
**Address:** 400 FIELD DRIVE, LAKE FOREST, IL 60045-2581
**Phone:** (847) 615-1500 **Domicile State:** IL **NAIC Code:** 61425

| Data Date | Rating | RACR #1 | RACR #2 | Total Assets ($mil) | Capital ($mil) | Net Premium ($mil) | Net Income ($mil) |
|---|---|---|---|---|---|---|---|
| 9-17 | B+ | 2.83 | 1.60 | 1,532.5 | 317.5 | 253.3 | 19.8 |
| 9-16 | B+ | 2.89 | 1.64 | 1,455.4 | 297.2 | 237.8 | 18.3 |
| 2016 | B+ | 3.12 | 1.77 | 1,460.2 | 294.8 | 322.0 | 21.0 |
| 2015 | B+ | 3.15 | 1.77 | 1,406.8 | 286.7 | 293.6 | 16.3 |
| 2014 | B+ | 3.02 | 1.75 | 1,393.5 | 287.7 | 312.2 | 18.9 |
| 2013 | B+ | 3.24 | 1.89 | 1,369.8 | 297.8 | 294.0 | 30.0 |
| 2012 | B+ | 3.00 | 1.78 | 1,320.0 | 266.5 | 307.6 | 22.3 |

**Adverse Trends in Operations**

Decrease in premium volume from 2014 to 2015 (6%)
Decrease in capital during 2014 (3%)
Decrease in premium volume from 2012 to 2013 (4%)

## TRUSTMARK LIFE INSURANCE COMPANY * — B+ Good

**Major Rating Factors:** Good quality investment portfolio (5.5 on a scale of 0 to 10) despite mixed results such as: no exposure to mortgages and substantial holdings of BBB bonds but small junk bond holdings. Good liquidity (6.9) with sufficient resources to handle a spike in claims. Good overall results on stability tests (6.1) good operational trends and excellent risk diversification.
**Other Rating Factors:** Strong capitalization (10.0) based on excellent risk adjusted capital (severe loss scenario). Excellent profitability (7.6).
**Principal Business:** Group health insurance (98%) and group life insurance (2%).
**Principal Investments:** NonCMO investment grade bonds (74%), noninv. grade bonds (10%), CMOs and structured securities (9%), and common & preferred stock (6%).
**Investments in Affiliates:** None
**Group Affiliation:** Trustmark Group Inc
**Licensed in:** All states except PR
**Commenced Business:** February 1925
**Address:** 400 FIELD DRIVE, LAKE FOREST, IL 60045-2581
**Phone:** (847) 615-1500 **Domicile State:** IL **NAIC Code:** 62863

| Data Date | Rating | RACR #1 | RACR #2 | Total Assets ($mil) | Capital ($mil) | Net Premium ($mil) | Net Income ($mil) |
|---|---|---|---|---|---|---|---|
| 9-17 | B+ | 7.86 | 5.00 | 320.1 | 178.0 | 85.6 | 13.5 |
| 9-16 | B+ | 6.69 | 4.39 | 328.1 | 174.2 | 108.6 | 12.2 |
| 2016 | B+ | 6.63 | 4.33 | 308.6 | 162.7 | 137.4 | 16.7 |
| 2015 | B+ | 5.62 | 3.77 | 321.3 | 159.8 | 163.7 | 8.4 |
| 2014 | B+ | 4.41 | 3.01 | 353.2 | 162.6 | 206.9 | 14.0 |
| 2013 | B+ | 3.61 | 2.53 | 365.5 | 160.6 | 264.5 | 13.9 |
| 2012 | B+ | 3.28 | 2.34 | 367.8 | 165.8 | 320.1 | 15.1 |

**Adverse Trends in Operations**

Decrease in asset base during 2016 (4%)
Decrease in premium volume from 2015 to 2016 (16%)
Decrease in premium volume from 2014 to 2015 (21%)
Decrease in premium volume from 2013 to 2014 (22%)
Decrease in premium volume from 2012 to 2013 (17%)

## TUFTS ASSOCIATED HEALTH MAINT ORG — B — Good

**Major Rating Factors:** Good overall results on stability tests (6.8 on a scale of 0 to 10). Good liquidity (6.4) with sufficient resources (cash flows and marketable investments) to handle a spike in claims. Fair quality investment portfolio (3.1).
**Other Rating Factors:** Excellent profitability (7.1). Strong capitalization index (9.7) based on excellent current risk-adjusted capital (severe loss scenario).
**Principal Business:** Medicare (54%), comp med (42%), Medicaid (2%), other (2%)
**Mem Phys: 16:** 49,118 **15:** 46,200 **16 MLR** 88.3% **/ 16 Admin Exp** N/A
**Enroll(000): Q3 17:** 297 **16:** 305 **15:** 306 **Med Exp PMPM:** $624
**Principal Investments:** Affiliate common stock (35%), nonaffiliate common stock (26%), long-term bonds (21%), real estate (9%), cash and equiv (1%), other (8%)
**Provider Compensation ($000):** Capitation ($1,036,968), contr fee ($688,012), FFS ($280,236), bonus arrang ($229,852)
**Total Member Encounters:** Phys (2,095,966), non-phys (532,449)
**Group Affiliation:** Tufts Associated Health Maintenance
**Licensed in:** MA, RI
**Address:** 705 Mount Auburn Street, Watertown, MA 02472-1508
**Phone:** (617) 972-9400 **Dom State:** MA **Commenced Bus:** October 1981

| Data Date | Rating | RACR #1 | RACR #2 | Total Assets ($mil) | Capital ($mil) | Net Premium ($mil) | Net Income ($mil) |
|---|---|---|---|---|---|---|---|
| 9-17 | B | 3.49 | 2.91 | 1,517.3 | 937.0 | 1,902.4 | 98.5 |
| 9-16 | B | 2.95 | 2.46 | 1,247.6 | 717.3 | 1,910.4 | 27.1 |
| 2016 | B | 2.95 | 2.45 | 1,245.3 | 786.5 | 2,553.4 | -3.2 |
| 2015 | B | 3.12 | 2.60 | 1,126.6 | 745.4 | 2,519.1 | 54.6 |
| 2014 | B | 3.44 | 2.86 | 1,112.2 | 765.0 | 2,641.8 | 65.8 |
| 2013 | B | 3.14 | 2.62 | 1,030.3 | 715.4 | 2,509.4 | 62.4 |
| 2012 | B | 3.11 | 2.59 | 1,062.2 | 661.6 | 2,528.0 | 65.0 |

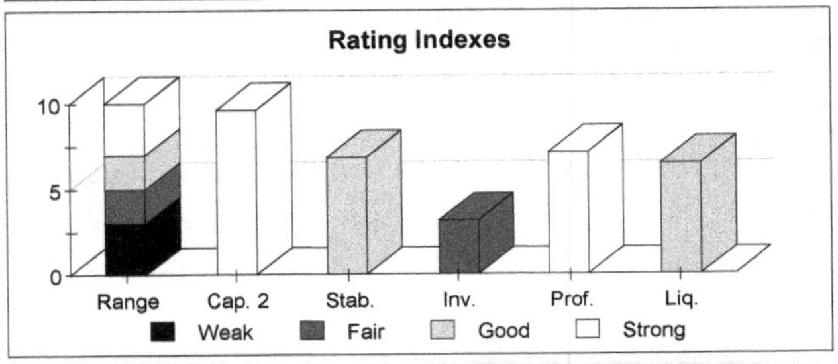


## TUFTS HEALTH FREEDOM INS CO — C — Fair

**Major Rating Factors:** Weak profitability index (0.2 on a scale of 0 to 10). Strong capitalization (10.0) based on excellent current risk-adjusted capital (severe loss scenario). High quality investment portfolio (9.9).
**Other Rating Factors:** Excellent liquidity (9.1) with ample operational cash flow and liquid investments.
**Principal Business:** Comp med (100%)
**Mem Phys: 16:** 49,118 **15:** N/A **16 MLR** 81.6% **/ 16 Admin Exp** N/A
**Enroll(000): Q3 17:** 9 **16:** 3 **15:** N/A **Med Exp PMPM:** $395
**Principal Investments:** Cash and equiv (100%)
**Provider Compensation ($000):** Contr fee ($2,338), FFS ($499)
**Total Member Encounters:** Phys (2,217), non-phys (740)
**Group Affiliation:** Tufts Assoc Hlth Maintenance Org Inc
**Licensed in:** NH
**Address:** 705 Mount Auburn St, Watertown, MA 02472
**Phone:** (617) 972-9400 **Dom State:** NH **Commenced Bus:** April 2015

| Data Date | Rating | RACR #1 | RACR #2 | Total Assets ($mil) | Capital ($mil) | Net Premium ($mil) | Net Income ($mil) |
|---|---|---|---|---|---|---|---|
| 9-17 | C | 8.15 | 6.79 | 26.2 | 12.6 | 29.4 | -0.6 |
| 9-16 | N/A | N/A | N/A | 18.9 | 13.9 | 1.9 | -1.6 |
| 2016 | C | 8.60 | 7.17 | 20.3 | 13.3 | 5.3 | -2.2 |
| 2015 | N/A | N/A | N/A | 15.7 | 12.5 | N/A | -6.5 |
| 2014 | N/A | N/A | N/A | N/A | N/A | N/A | N/A |
| 2013 | N/A | N/A | N/A | N/A | N/A | N/A | N/A |
| 2012 | N/A | N/A | N/A | N/A | N/A | N/A | N/A |

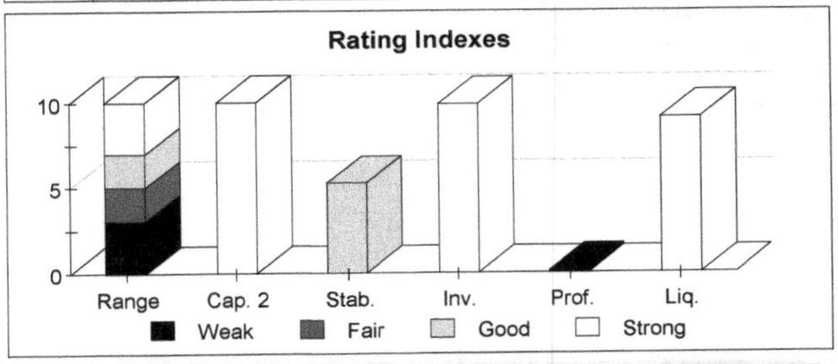


## TUFTS HEALTH PUBLIC PLANS INC — C+ — Fair

**Major Rating Factors:** Fair profitability index (3.4 on a scale of 0 to 10). Fair quality investment portfolio (3.2). Good liquidity (6.2) with sufficient resources (cash flows and marketable investments) to handle a spike in claims.
**Other Rating Factors:** Strong capitalization (8.2) based on excellent current risk-adjusted capital (severe loss scenario).
**Principal Business:** Medicaid (83%), comp med (17%)
**Mem Phys: 16:** 25,786 **15:** 26,123 **16 MLR** 91.2% **/ 16 Admin Exp** N/A
**Enroll(000): Q3 17:** 355 **16:** 330 **15:** 279 **Med Exp PMPM:** $370
**Principal Investments:** Nonaffiliate common stock (63%), cash and equiv (20%), long-term bonds (14%), other (3%)
**Provider Compensation ($000):** Contr fee ($1,163,476), bonus arrang ($160,280), FFS ($44,730)
**Total Member Encounters:** Phys (4,005,378), non-phys (1,198,291)
**Group Affiliation:** Tufts Assoc Hlth Maintenance Org Inc
**Licensed in:** MA, RI
**Address:** 705 Mount Auburn St, Watertown, MA 02472
**Phone:** (617) 972-9400 **Dom State:** MA **Commenced Bus:** November 2011

| Data Date | Rating | RACR #1 | RACR #2 | Total Assets ($mil) | Capital ($mil) | Net Premium ($mil) | Net Income ($mil) |
|---|---|---|---|---|---|---|---|
| 9-17 | C+ | 2.35 | 1.96 | 559.0 | 231.9 | 1,340.8 | 2.5 |
| 9-16 | C+ | 2.23 | 1.86 | 512.0 | 190.4 | 1,124.6 | -22.1 |
| 2016 | C+ | 1.98 | 1.65 | 529.7 | 193.5 | 1,528.3 | -9.6 |
| 2015 | C+ | 2.39 | 1.99 | 490.6 | 202.2 | 1,326.7 | 34.0 |
| 2014 | C+ | 2.37 | 1.98 | 358.6 | 179.9 | 1,245.8 | 33.1 |
| 2013 | C+ | 1.86 | 1.55 | 268.0 | 136.8 | 1,072.8 | -66.1 |
| 2012 | C+ | 1.78 | 1.48 | 217.6 | 113.7 | 999.1 | -5.1 |

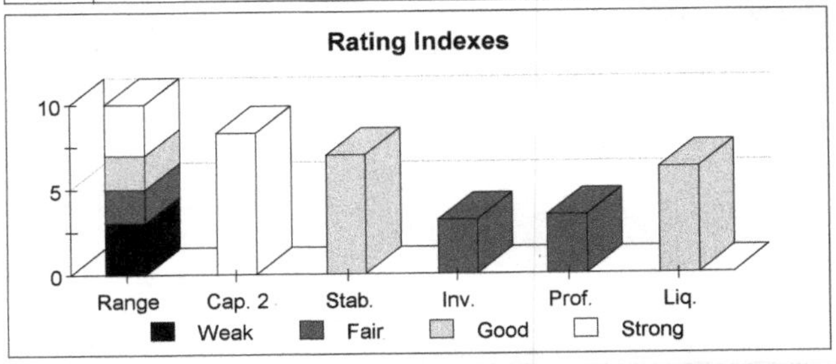

## TUFTS INS CO C- Fair

**Major Rating Factors:** Weak profitability index (0.9 on a scale of 0 to 10). Good liquidity (6.8) with sufficient resources (cash flows and marketable investments) to handle a spike in claims. Strong capitalization (9.2) based on excellent current risk-adjusted capital (severe loss scenario).
**Other Rating Factors:** High quality investment portfolio (9.9).
**Principal Business:** Comp med (75%), med supp (13%), other (13%)
**Mem Phys: 16:** 49,118 **15:** 46,200 **16 MLR** 91.1% **/ 16 Admin Exp** N/A
**Enroll(000): Q3 17:** 64 **16:** 82 **15:** 69 **Med Exp PMPM:** $288
**Principal Investments:** Cash and equiv (47%), long-term bonds (33%), nonaffiliate common stock (20%)
**Provider Compensation ($000):** Contr fee ($166,726), FFS ($32,642), other ($32,944)
**Total Member Encounters:** Phys (315,481), non-phys (108,386)
**Group Affiliation:** Tufts Assoc Hlth Maintenance Org Inc
**Licensed in:** AZ, CA, CT, DC, FL, GA, IL, IN, ME, MD, MA, MI, NH, NY, NC, OH, PA, RI, TX, VT, VA
**Address:** 705 Mount Auburn St, Watertown, MA 02472-1508
**Phone:** (617) 972-9400 **Dom State:** MA **Commenced Bus:** August 1996

| Data Date | Rating | RACR #1 | RACR #2 | Total Assets ($mil) | Capital ($mil) | Net Premium ($mil) | Net Income ($mil) |
|---|---|---|---|---|---|---|---|
| 9-17 | C- | 3.10 | 2.59 | 100.1 | 52.4 | 208.9 | -9.9 |
| 9-16 | C- | 3.16 | 2.63 | 97.5 | 51.8 | 189.7 | -16.0 |
| 2016 | C- | 3.01 | 2.51 | 101.6 | 50.7 | 258.4 | -21.9 |
| 2015 | D+ | 3.32 | 2.77 | 97.8 | 53.4 | 263.1 | -5.9 |
| 2014 | D+ | 3.16 | 2.63 | 97.5 | 50.5 | 248.2 | -17.8 |
| 2013 | D+ | 3.03 | 2.53 | 87.6 | 48.6 | 233.9 | 1.2 |
| 2012 | D+ | 3.10 | 2.58 | 92.1 | 48.4 | 207.0 | 2.0 |

Rating Indexes

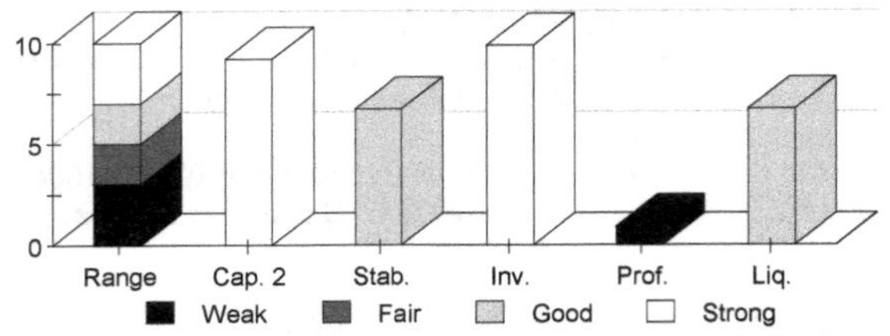


## U S HEALTH & LIFE INS CO B Good

**Major Rating Factors:** Good overall profitability index (5.6 on a scale of 0 to 10). Strong capitalization (9.0) based on excellent current risk-adjusted capital (severe loss scenario). High quality investment portfolio (9.9).
**Other Rating Factors:** Excellent liquidity (7.7) with ample operational cash flow and liquid investments.
**Principal Business:** Comp med (83%), dental (1%), other (14%)
**Mem Phys: 16:** N/A **15:** N/A **16 MLR** 60.1% **/ 16 Admin Exp** N/A
**Enroll(000): Q3 17:** 11 **16:** 9 **15:** 12 **Med Exp PMPM:** $185
**Principal Investments:** Cash and equiv (61%), long-term bonds (33%), real estate (6%)
**Provider Compensation ($000):** Contr fee ($21,840)
**Total Member Encounters:** Phys (41,470), non-phys (17,779)
**Group Affiliation:** Ascension Health Alliance
**Licensed in:** AK, AZ, DC, DE, ID, IL, IN, LA, MI, NE, NM, ND, OH, OR, SC, SD, TN, TX, UT, VA, WI
**Address:** 8220 Irving Rd, Sterling Heights, MI 48312
**Phone:** (586) 693-4400 **Dom State:** MI **Commenced Bus:** January 1984

| Data Date | Rating | RACR #1 | RACR #2 | Total Assets ($mil) | Capital ($mil) | Net Premium ($mil) | Net Income ($mil) |
|---|---|---|---|---|---|---|---|
| 9-17 | B | 2.98 | 2.49 | 25.7 | 14.2 | 23.5 | 0.3 |
| 9-16 | B | 3.03 | 2.52 | 31.6 | 13.5 | 24.7 | 2.1 |
| 2016 | B | 2.94 | 2.45 | 31.2 | 14.0 | 33.7 | 2.6 |
| 2015 | B | 2.60 | 2.16 | 29.5 | 11.3 | 38.4 | 3.0 |
| 2014 | C- | 1.49 | 1.25 | 26.8 | 8.3 | 56.9 | -1.0 |
| 2013 | C- | 1.48 | 1.23 | 26.2 | 8.0 | 67.8 | -1.4 |
| 2012 | N/A | N/A | N/A | 26.3 | 8.8 | 52.1 | -0.2 |

Rating Indexes

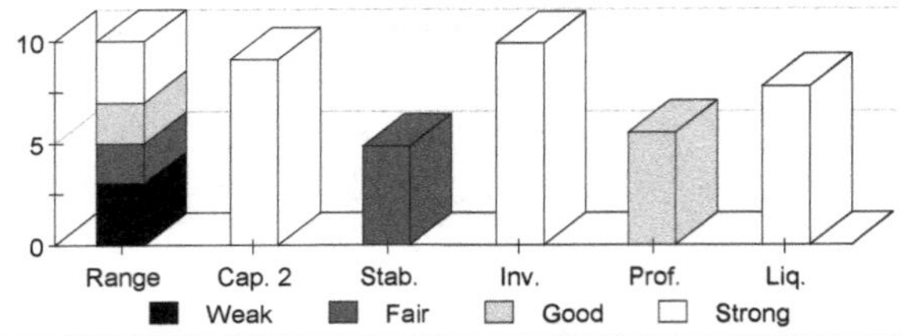


## UCARE HEALTH INC E Very Weak

**Major Rating Factors:** Weak profitability index (1.7 on a scale of 0 to 10). Fair capitalization (2.9) based on good current risk-adjusted capital (moderate loss scenario). High quality investment portfolio (9.9).
**Other Rating Factors:** Excellent liquidity (10.0) with ample operational cash flow and liquid investments.
**Principal Business:** Comp med (116%)
**Mem Phys: 16:** N/A **15:** 49,356 **16 MLR** -186.8% **/ 16 Admin Exp** N/A
**Enroll(000): Q2 17:** N/A **16:** N/A **15:** 8 **Med Exp PMPM:** N/A
**Principal Investments:** Cash and equiv (100%)
**Provider Compensation ($000):** Contr fee ($5,946), FFS ($1,566)
**Total Member Encounters:** Phys (2,276), non-phys (1,493)
**Group Affiliation:** UCare Minnesota
**Licensed in:** MN, WI
**Address:** 500 Stinson Blvd NE, Minneapolis, MN 55413-2615
**Phone:** (612) 676-6500 **Dom State:** WI **Commenced Bus:** January 2008

| Data Date | Rating | RACR #1 | RACR #2 | Total Assets ($mil) | Capital ($mil) | Net Premium ($mil) | Net Income ($mil) |
|---|---|---|---|---|---|---|---|
| 6-17 | E | 7.86 | 6.55 | 19.5 | 18.4 | 5.6 | 3.8 |
| 6-16 | E | N/A | N/A | 16.4 | 10.5 | 0.7 | 0.6 |
| 2016 | E | 6.24 | 5.20 | 15.7 | 14.5 | 1.6 | 4.7 |
| 2015 | E | 0.77 | 0.64 | 22.9 | 9.7 | 55.8 | -9.1 |
| 2014 | E | 0.30 | 0.25 | 23.5 | 3.6 | 73.9 | -10.7 |
| 2013 | D | 0.80 | 0.67 | 19.9 | 9.5 | 59.0 | -5.3 |
| 2012 | D | 1.36 | 1.13 | 26.7 | 14.7 | 66.4 | -0.5 |

Rating Indexes

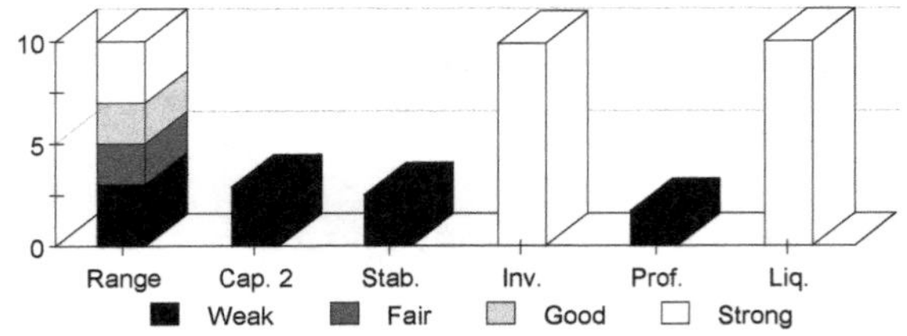

## UCARE MINNESOTA B Good

**Major Rating Factors:** Good liquidity (6.8 on a scale of 0 to 10) with sufficient resources (cash flows and marketable investments) to handle a spike in claims. Fair profitability index (4.7). Fair overall results on stability tests (4.0) based on a significant 69% decrease in enrollment during the period, a decline in the number of member physicians during 2017.
**Other Rating Factors:** Strong capitalization index (10.0) based on excellent current risk-adjusted capital (severe loss scenario). High quality investment portfolio (9.3).
**Principal Business:** Medicaid (49%), Medicare (49%), comp med (2%)
**Mem Phys: 16:** 38,194 **15:** 53,074 **16 MLR** 93.5% **/ 16 Admin Exp** N/A
**Enroll(000): Q3 17:** 371 **16:** 152 **15:** 492 **Med Exp PMPM:** $868
**Principal Investments:** Long-term bonds (62%), cash and equiv (24%), nonaffiliate common stock (12%), real estate (3%)
**Provider Compensation ($000):** Contr fee ($1,670,439), FFS ($88,727), capitation ($4,202)
**Total Member Encounters:** Phys (789,194), non-phys (475,062)
**Group Affiliation:** UCare Minnesota
**Licensed in:** MN
**Address:** 500 Stinson Boulevard NE, Minneapolis, MN 55413
**Phone:** (612) 676-6500 **Dom State:** MN **Commenced Bus:** April 1988

| Data Date | Rating | RACR #1 | RACR #2 | Total Assets ($mil) | Capital ($mil) | Net Premium ($mil) | Net Income ($mil) |
|---|---|---|---|---|---|---|---|
| 9-17 | B | 4.70 | 3.92 | 1,170.5 | 575.1 | 1,920.8 | 36.1 |
| 9-16 | A | 2.28 | 1.90 | 960.8 | 571.5 | 1,266.4 | 20.4 |
| 2016 | B+ | 4.14 | 3.45 | 938.5 | 516.2 | 1,686.7 | -25.0 |
| 2015 | A | 2.16 | 1.80 | 1,233.9 | 546.4 | 3,513.9 | 27.7 |
| 2014 | A- | 2.49 | 2.07 | 1,314.9 | 536.4 | 3,053.3 | 107.8 |
| 2013 | A- | 2.45 | 2.04 | 856.4 | 443.2 | 2,413.2 | 47.2 |
| 2012 | A- | 2.30 | 1.91 | 781.3 | 387.7 | 2,229.5 | 70.7 |

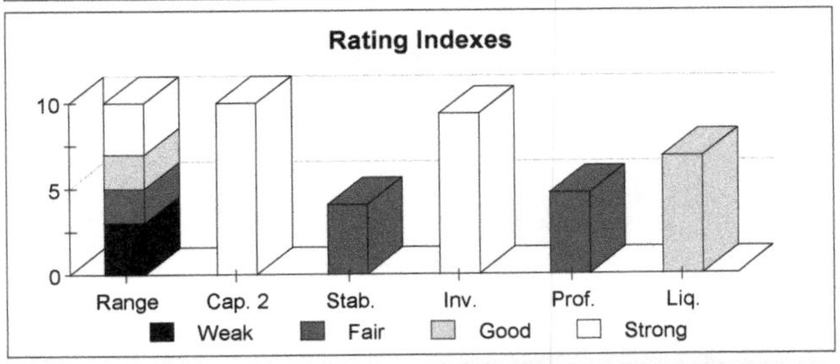


## UHC OF CALIFORNIA INC C Fair

**Major Rating Factors:** Fair capitalization index (4.5 on a scale of 0 to 10) based on weak current risk-adjusted capital (moderate loss scenario). Fair overall results on stability tests (3.3). Rating is significantly influenced by the fair financial results of UnitedHealth Group Inc. Good overall profitability index (6.0).
**Other Rating Factors:** Excellent liquidity (7.0) with sufficient resources (cash flows and marketable investments) to handle a spike in claims.
**Principal Business:** Medicare (61%)
**Mem Phys: 16:** N/A **15:** N/A **16 MLR** 86.3% **/ 16 Admin Exp** N/A
**Enroll(000): Q3 17:** 872 **16:** 836 **15:** 790 **Med Exp PMPM:** $583
**Principal Investments ($000):** Cash and equiv ($291,966)
**Provider Compensation ($000):** None
**Total Member Encounters:** N/A
**Group Affiliation:** UnitedHealth Group Inc
**Licensed in:** CA
**Address:** 1221 Broadway 3rd Floor, Oakland, CA 94612
**Phone:** (510) 470-0590 **Dom State:** CA **Commenced Bus:** March 1975

| Data Date | Rating | RACR #1 | RACR #2 | Total Assets ($mil) | Capital ($mil) | Net Premium ($mil) | Net Income ($mil) |
|---|---|---|---|---|---|---|---|
| 9-17 | C | 0.71 | 0.44 | 1,242.4 | 224.6 | 4,967.6 | 77.0 |
| 9-16 | C+ | 1.14 | 0.71 | 1,172.9 | 303.9 | 5,018.6 | 113.2 |
| 2016 | C+ | 0.98 | 0.61 | 837.4 | 293.1 | 6,668.2 | 114.0 |
| 2015 | C+ | 1.18 | 0.73 | 778.4 | 314.4 | 6,267.3 | 143.7 |
| 2014 | C+ | 1.45 | 0.90 | 824.7 | 354.2 | 6,195.4 | 209.1 |
| 2013 | B- | 1.57 | 0.97 | 903.9 | 386.7 | 6,487.2 | 277.2 |
| 2012 | C+ | 1.54 | 0.95 | 1,018.6 | 351.1 | 6,404.9 | 327.4 |

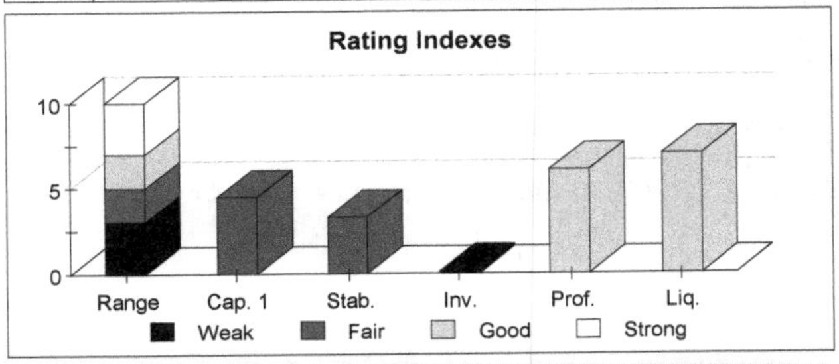


## ULTIMATE HEALTH PLANS INC E Very Weak

**Major Rating Factors:** Weak profitability index (0.7 on a scale of 0 to 10). Fair capitalization (3.8) based on weak current risk-adjusted capital (moderate loss scenario). High quality investment portfolio (9.9).
**Other Rating Factors:** Excellent liquidity (7.0) with ample operational cash flow and liquid investments.
**Principal Business:** Medicare (100%)
**Mem Phys: 16:** 800 **15:** 631 **16 MLR** 79.8% **/ 16 Admin Exp** N/A
**Enroll(000): Q3 17:** 6 **16:** 6 **15:** 4 **Med Exp PMPM:** $608
**Principal Investments:** Cash and equiv (97%), other (3%)
**Provider Compensation ($000):** FFS ($33,488), capitation ($3,455), bonus arrang ($2,196), contr fee ($1,504)
**Total Member Encounters:** Phys (160,123), non-phys (7,244)
**Group Affiliation:** Ultimate Healthcare Holdings LLC
**Licensed in:** FL
**Address:** 1244 Mariner Blvd, Spring Hill, FL 33609
**Phone:** (352) 835-7151 **Dom State:** FL **Commenced Bus:** October 2011

| Data Date | Rating | RACR #1 | RACR #2 | Total Assets ($mil) | Capital ($mil) | Net Premium ($mil) | Net Income ($mil) |
|---|---|---|---|---|---|---|---|
| 9-17 | E | 0.74 | 0.62 | 22.4 | 5.8 | 42.7 | -0.1 |
| 9-16 | E | 1.01 | 0.85 | 16.2 | 6.5 | 39.7 | 1.6 |
| 2016 | E | 0.83 | 0.69 | 12.8 | 6.5 | 52.0 | 0.4 |
| 2015 | E | 0.77 | 0.64 | 9.9 | 5.1 | 39.2 | -0.5 |
| 2014 | E | 0.75 | 0.62 | 8.8 | 4.8 | 26.7 | -1.9 |
| 2013 | E | 1.24 | 1.03 | 5.2 | 1.8 | 4.5 | -7.6 |
| 2012 | N/A | N/A | N/A | 4.8 | 4.7 | N/A | -1.8 |

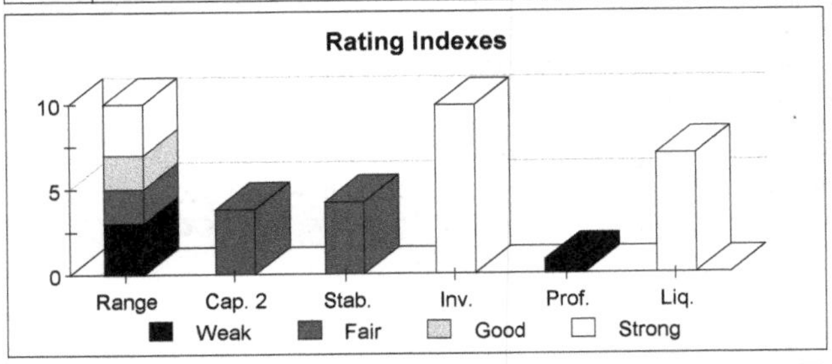

## UNICARE HEALTH PLAN OF WEST VIRGINIA * A- Excellent

**Major Rating Factors:** Excellent profitability (8.0 on a scale of 0 to 10). Strong capitalization (8.4) based on excellent current risk-adjusted capital (severe loss scenario). High quality investment portfolio (9.4).
**Other Rating Factors:** Good liquidity (6.9) with sufficient resources (cash flows and marketable investments) to handle a spike in claims.
**Principal Business:** Medicaid (100%)
**Mem Phys: 16:** 1,389 **15:** 1,440 **16 MLR** 87.5% **/ 16 Admin Exp** N/A
**Enroll(000): Q3 17:** 142 **16:** 131 **15:** 127 **Med Exp PMPM:** $269
**Principal Investments:** Long-term bonds (100%)
**Provider Compensation ($000):** Contr fee ($416,897), capitation ($4,890)
**Total Member Encounters:** Phys (863,959), non-phys (351,744)
**Group Affiliation:** Anthem Inc
**Licensed in:** WV
**Address:** 200 ASSOCIATION Dr Ste 200, CHARLESTON, WV 25311
**Phone:** (877) 864-2273 **Dom State:** WV **Commenced Bus:** November 2003

| Data Date | Rating | RACR #1 | RACR #2 | Total Assets ($mil) | Capital ($mil) | Net Premium ($mil) | Net Income ($mil) |
|---|---|---|---|---|---|---|---|
| 9-17 | A- | 2.45 | 2.04 | 110.0 | 69.6 | 394.4 | -2.4 |
| 9-16 | B | 2.62 | 2.19 | 106.6 | 48.0 | 349.0 | -12.6 |
| 2016 | B+ | 2.52 | 2.10 | 120.0 | 71.7 | 484.5 | 15.7 |
| 2015 | A- | 3.20 | 2.67 | 100.9 | 58.8 | 314.7 | 2.0 |
| 2014 | A- | 4.16 | 3.47 | 83.0 | 59.9 | 275.5 | 24.5 |
| 2013 | A- | 3.29 | 2.74 | 70.1 | 40.5 | 215.5 | 11.7 |
| 2012 | A- | 3.13 | 2.61 | 55.1 | 31.8 | 167.1 | 5.8 |

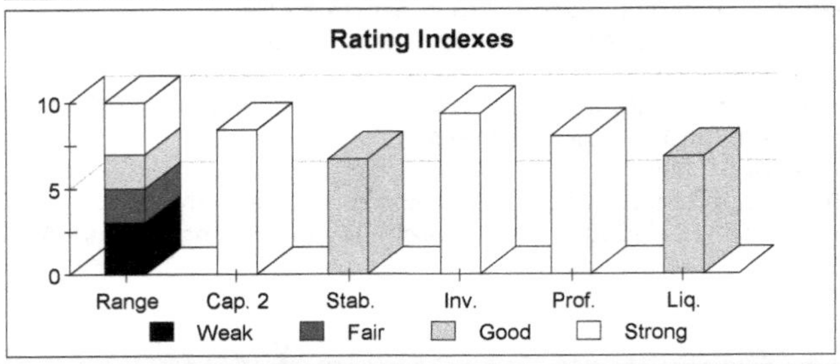


## UNICARE LIFE & HEALTH INSURANCE COMPANY B- Good

**Major Rating Factors:** Good overall profitability (6.6 on a scale of 0 to 10). Excellent expense controls. Good liquidity (5.8) with sufficient resources to handle a spike in claims. Good overall results on stability tests (5.3). Strengths include good financial support from affiliation with Anthem Inc, good operational trends and good risk diversification.
**Other Rating Factors:** Fair quality investment portfolio (4.4). Strong capitalization (7.6) based on excellent risk adjusted capital (severe loss scenario).
**Principal Business:** Reinsurance (44%), group life insurance (37%), group health insurance (13%), and individual health insurance (6%).
**Principal Investments:** NonCMO investment grade bonds (88%), noninv. grade bonds (12%), and CMOs and structured securities (1%).
**Investments in Affiliates:** None
**Group Affiliation:** Anthem Inc
**Licensed in:** All states, the District of Columbia and Puerto Rico
**Commenced Business:** December 1980
**Address:** 120 MONUMENT CIRCLE, INDIANAPOLIS, IN 46204
**Phone:** (877) 864-2273 **Domicile State:** IN **NAIC Code:** 80314

| Data Date | Rating | RACR #1 | RACR #2 | Total Assets ($mil) | Capital ($mil) | Net Premium ($mil) | Net Income ($mil) |
|---|---|---|---|---|---|---|---|
| 9-17 | B- | 1.82 | 1.37 | 305.5 | 70.8 | 234.5 | 15.6 |
| 9-16 | B- | 2.13 | 1.57 | 306.7 | 80.5 | 204.2 | 21.7 |
| 2016 | B- | 2.81 | 2.12 | 306.0 | 88.1 | 275.2 | 28.3 |
| 2015 | B- | 3.06 | 2.27 | 373.8 | 108.4 | 291.9 | 21.5 |
| 2014 | B- | 1.77 | 1.32 | 413.3 | 63.8 | 329.6 | 25.0 |
| 2013 | B | 3.13 | 2.32 | 469.1 | 126.3 | 321.7 | 43.7 |
| 2012 | B | 2.83 | 2.05 | 554.2 | 158.8 | 439.4 | 74.4 |

**Anthem Inc**
**Composite Group Rating: B**

| Largest Group Members | Assets ($mil) | Rating |
|---|---|---|
| BLUE CROSS OF CALIFORNIA | 7351 | A+ |
| ANTHEM INS COMPANIES INC | 2947 | B- |
| ANTHEM BLUE CROSS LIFE HEALTH INS | 2683 | B- |
| EMPIRE HEALTHCHOICE ASSURANCE INC | 2501 | B- |
| COMMUNITY INS CO | 2139 | B+ |

## UNIFIED LIFE INSURANCE COMPANY B Good

**Major Rating Factors:** Good overall profitability (5.8 on a scale of 0 to 10) despite operating losses during the first nine months of 2017. Return on equity has been fair, averaging 8.9%. Good liquidity (5.5) with sufficient resources to cover a large increase in policy surrenders. Good overall results on stability tests (6.3) good operational trends and good risk diversification.
**Other Rating Factors:** Fair quality investment portfolio (4.6). Strong capitalization (7.3) based on excellent risk adjusted capital (severe loss scenario).
**Principal Business:** Group health insurance (76%), individual health insurance (10%), reinsurance (9%), and individual life insurance (5%).
**Principal Investments:** NonCMO investment grade bonds (63%), CMOs and structured securities (24%), policy loans (5%), noninv. grade bonds (5%), and cash (3%).
**Investments in Affiliates:** None
**Group Affiliation:** William M Buchanan Group
**Licensed in:** All states except NY, PR
**Commenced Business:** May 2001
**Address:** CSC-Lawyers Inc Serv 211 E 7th, Austin, TX 78701-3218
**Phone:** (877) 492-4678 **Domicile State:** TX **NAIC Code:** 11121

| Data Date | Rating | RACR #1 | RACR #2 | Total Assets ($mil) | Capital ($mil) | Net Premium ($mil) | Net Income ($mil) |
|---|---|---|---|---|---|---|---|
| 9-17 | B | 1.94 | 1.17 | 213.5 | 25.3 | 36.0 | -0.6 |
| 9-16 | B | 1.91 | 1.18 | 219.8 | 26.2 | 46.5 | 2.8 |
| 2016 | B | 1.78 | 1.09 | 219.0 | 25.9 | 60.4 | 1.2 |
| 2015 | B | 1.86 | 1.14 | 184.1 | 21.8 | 46.7 | 0.0 |
| 2014 | B | 2.55 | 1.55 | 183.5 | 24.9 | 33.7 | 2.7 |
| 2013 | B | 2.29 | 1.30 | 179.6 | 22.8 | 30.4 | 3.2 |
| 2012 | B | 2.20 | 1.23 | 170.6 | 20.4 | 29.1 | 1.9 |

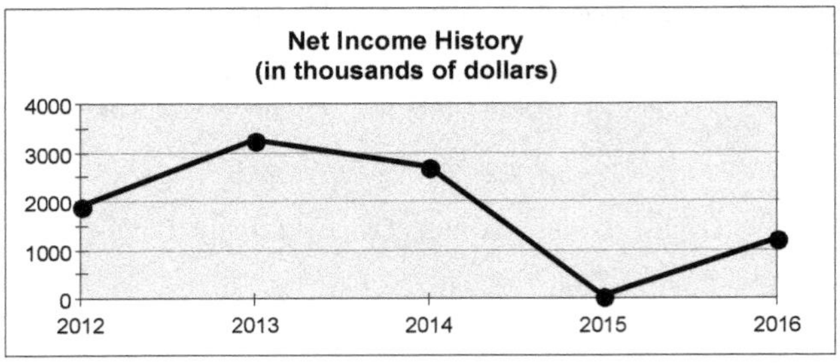

## UNIMERICA INSURANCE COMPANY B Good

**Major Rating Factors:** Good overall results on stability tests (5.5 on a scale of 0 to 10) despite fair financial strength of affiliated UnitedHealth Group Inc. Other stability subfactors include excellent operational trends, excellent risk adjusted capital for prior years and excellent risk diversification. Good overall capitalization (5.4) based on mixed results -- excessive policy leverage mitigated by excellent risk adjusted capital (severe loss scenario). Nevertheless, capital levels have fluctuated during prior years. Good overall profitability (6.9).

**Other Rating Factors:** Good liquidity (5.6). High quality investment portfolio (8.5).

**Principal Business:** Reinsurance (60%), group health insurance (38%), and group life insurance (2%).

**Principal Investments:** NonCMO investment grade bonds (86%) and CMOs and structured securities (14%).

**Investments in Affiliates:** None

**Group Affiliation:** UnitedHealth Group Inc

**Licensed in:** All states except NY, PR

**Commenced Business:** December 1980

**Address:** 10701 WEST RESEARCH DRIVE, MILWAUKEE, WI 53226-0649

**Phone:** (763) 732-8837 **Domicile State:** WI **NAIC Code:** 91529

| Data Date | Rating | RACR #1 | RACR #2 | Total Assets ($mil) | Capital ($mil) | Net Premium ($mil) | Net Income ($mil) |
|---|---|---|---|---|---|---|---|
| 9-17 | B | 1.67 | 1.35 | 473.4 | 169.9 | 652.3 | 14.0 |
| 9-16 | B | 1.61 | 1.29 | 538.2 | 152.8 | 656.4 | 19.4 |
| 2016 | B | 1.43 | 1.15 | 476.4 | 154.7 | 877.0 | 21.1 |
| 2015 | B | 1.99 | 1.59 | 435.9 | 167.7 | 669.4 | 65.7 |
| 2014 | B | 2.54 | 2.02 | 415.0 | 187.8 | 582.4 | 76.9 |
| 2013 | B | 2.82 | 2.24 | 410.1 | 181.1 | 489.2 | 43.3 |
| 2012 | B | 3.17 | 2.48 | 326.6 | 153.2 | 319.8 | 32.2 |

| UnitedHealth Group Inc<br>Composite Group Rating: C+<br>Largest Group Members | Assets ($mil) | Rating |
|---|---|---|
| UNITED HEALTHCARE INS CO | 17923 | C |
| SIERRA HEALTH AND LIFE INS CO INC | 2397 | B |
| OXFORD HEALTH INS INC | 2211 | B |
| ALL SAVERS INS CO | 1552 | C |
| UNITED HEALTHCARE OF WISCONSIN INC | 1224 | B |

## UNION FIDELITY LIFE INSURANCE COMPANY C Fair

**Major Rating Factors:** Fair quality investment portfolio (3.6 on a scale of 0 to 10) with large holdings of BBB rated bonds in addition to junk bond exposure equal to 94% of capital. Fair overall results on stability tests (3.7) including weak risk adjusted capital in prior years, negative cash flow from operations for 2016. Good capitalization (5.9) based on good risk adjusted capital (moderate loss scenario).

**Other Rating Factors:** Weak profitability (2.9) with operating losses during the first nine months of 2017. Excellent liquidity (8.7).

**Principal Business:** Reinsurance (89%), group health insurance (5%), group life insurance (3%), individual life insurance (2%), and individual health insurance (1%).

**Principal Investments:** NonCMO investment grade bonds (78%), CMOs and structured securities (12%), noninv. grade bonds (4%), and mortgages in good standing (4%).

**Investments in Affiliates:** 1%

**Group Affiliation:** General Electric Corp Group

**Licensed in:** All states except NY, PR

**Commenced Business:** February 1926

**Address:** 7101 College Blvd Ste 1400, Overland Park, KS 66210

**Phone:** (913) 982-3700 **Domicile State:** KS **NAIC Code:** 62596

| Data Date | Rating | RACR #1 | RACR #2 | Total Assets ($mil) | Capital ($mil) | Net Premium ($mil) | Net Income ($mil) |
|---|---|---|---|---|---|---|---|
| 9-17 | C | 1.58 | 0.79 | 19,526.8 | 748.4 | 192.4 | -24.0 |
| 9-16 | D+ | 0.83 | 0.43 | 19,428.3 | 402.3 | 197.1 | -171.7 |
| 2016 | D+ | 1.53 | 0.76 | 19,644.5 | 765.8 | 266.4 | -65.0 |
| 2015 | D+ | 0.89 | 0.46 | 19,365.0 | 428.3 | 276.3 | -60.9 |
| 2014 | D+ | 1.04 | 0.54 | 19,673.7 | 518.4 | 285.9 | -280.8 |
| 2013 | D+ | 1.07 | 0.55 | 19,510.6 | 569.3 | 305.7 | 6.3 |
| 2012 | D | 1.01 | 0.52 | 19,585.3 | 560.1 | 316.1 | -430.4 |

Rating Indexes

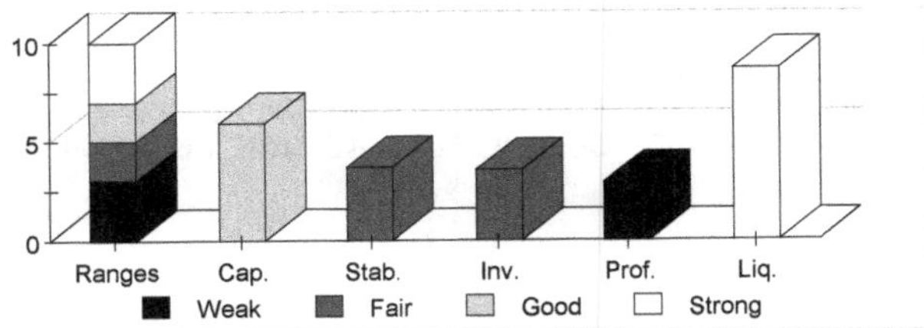


## UNION HEALTH SERVICE INC B Good

**Major Rating Factors:** Good overall profitability index (6.0 on a scale of 0 to 10). Good capitalization index (6.3) based on good current risk-adjusted capital (severe loss scenario). Good liquidity (6.9) with sufficient resources (cash flows and marketable investments) to handle a spike in claims.

**Other Rating Factors:** High quality investment portfolio (8.0). Excellent overall results on stability tests (7.4).

**Principal Business:** FEHB (8%), Medicare (4%), other (88%)

**Mem Phys: 16:** 300 **15:** 280 **16 MLR** 97.9% **/ 16 Admin Exp** N/A

**Enroll(000): Q3 17:** 46 **16:** 45 **15:** 44 **Med Exp PMPM:** $135

**Principal Investments:** Long-term bonds (40%), nonaffiliate common stock (29%), cash and equiv (26%), other (5%)

**Provider Compensation ($000):** FFS ($22,029), contr fee ($1,764), other ($48,673)

**Total Member Encounters:** Phys (132,637), non-phys (11,710)

**Group Affiliation:** Union Health Service Inc

**Licensed in:** IL

**Address:** 1634 W POLK STREET, CHICAGO, IL 60612

**Phone:** (312) 423-4200 **Dom State:** IL **Commenced Bus:** April 1955

| Data Date | Rating | RACR #1 | RACR #2 | Total Assets ($mil) | Capital ($mil) | Net Premium ($mil) | Net Income ($mil) |
|---|---|---|---|---|---|---|---|
| 9-17 | B | 1.13 | 0.94 | 26.7 | 16.8 | 56.8 | 1.5 |
| 9-16 | B | 1.11 | 0.92 | 25.2 | 16.1 | 56.0 | 2.3 |
| 2016 | B | 1.00 | 0.83 | 25.6 | 14.8 | 73.7 | 1.0 |
| 2015 | B | 1.02 | 0.85 | 23.7 | 14.9 | 70.0 | 0.5 |
| 2014 | B | 1.21 | 1.01 | 23.5 | 14.8 | 68.2 | 0.3 |
| 2013 | B | 1.26 | 1.05 | 26.0 | 14.4 | 63.9 | 1.4 |
| 2012 | B | 1.17 | 0.98 | 23.0 | 11.9 | 62.8 | 2.1 |

Rating Indexes

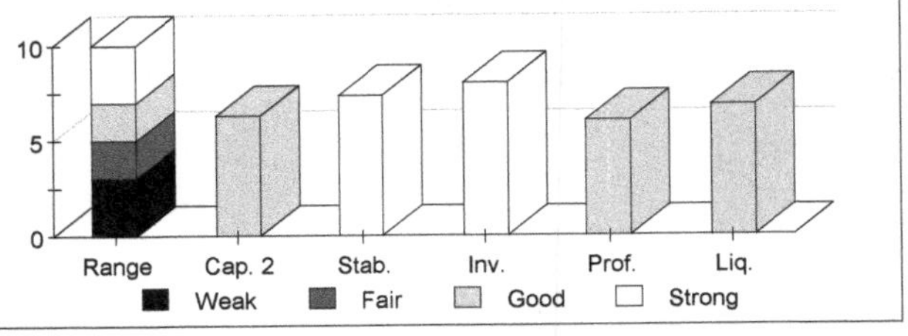

## UNION LABOR LIFE INSURANCE COMPANY B Good

**Major Rating Factors:** Good overall profitability (5.4 on a scale of 0 to 10). Good overall results on stability tests (5.7). Stability strengths include excellent operational trends and excellent risk diversification. Strong capitalization (7.5) based on excellent risk adjusted capital (severe loss scenario). Capital levels have been relatively consistent over the last five years.
**Other Rating Factors:** High quality investment portfolio (7.1). Excellent liquidity (7.5).
**Principal Business:** Group health insurance (56%), group life insurance (30%), reinsurance (10%), and group retirement contracts (4%).
**Principal Investments:** NonCMO investment grade bonds (57%), CMOs and structured securities (27%), mortgages in good standing (8%), and common & preferred stock (6%).
**Investments in Affiliates:** 4%
**Group Affiliation:** ULLICO Inc
**Licensed in:** All states except PR
**Commenced Business:** May 1927
**Address:** 8403 COLESVILLE ROAD, SILVER SPRING, MD 20910
**Phone:** (202) 682-0900 **Domicile State:** MD **NAIC Code:** 69744

| Data Date | Rating | RACR #1 | RACR #2 | Total Assets ($mil) | Capital ($mil) | Net Premium ($mil) | Net Income ($mil) |
|---|---|---|---|---|---|---|---|
| 9-17 | B | 2.01 | 1.30 | 3,544.9 | 93.9 | 104.0 | 6.4 |
| 9-16 | B- | 1.62 | 1.13 | 3,334.5 | 84.6 | 102.6 | 8.1 |
| 2016 | B- | 2.04 | 1.32 | 3,354.7 | 89.2 | 124.2 | 10.2 |
| 2015 | B- | 1.52 | 1.07 | 3,238.8 | 79.6 | 138.3 | 3.5 |
| 2014 | B- | 1.42 | 1.00 | 3,337.5 | 76.4 | 142.1 | 1.4 |
| 2013 | B- | 1.66 | 1.20 | 2,813.7 | 87.7 | 139.5 | -11.1 |
| 2012 | B- | 2.22 | 1.50 | 2,905.9 | 96.9 | 148.8 | 7.9 |

**Adverse Trends in Operations**

Decrease in premium volume from 2015 to 2016 (10%)
Decrease in asset base during 2015 (3%)
Decrease in capital during 2014 (13%)
Decrease in premium volume from 2012 to 2013 (6%)
Decrease in asset base during 2013 (3%)

## UNION SECURITY INSURANCE COMPANY B Good

**Major Rating Factors:** Good quality investment portfolio (5.4 on a scale of 0 to 10) despite mixed results such as: large holdings of BBB rated bonds but moderate junk bond exposure. Good overall profitability (6.1). Excellent expense controls. Fair overall results on stability tests (4.2).
**Other Rating Factors:** Fair overall capitalization (4.0) based on mixed results -- excessive policy leverage mitigated by excellent risk adjusted capital (severe loss scenario). Excellent liquidity (8.1).
**Principal Business:** Group health insurance (61%), group life insurance (18%), individual health insurance (8%), reinsurance (7%), and other lines (7%).
**Principal Investments:** NonCMO investment grade bonds (70%), mortgages in good standing (9%), common & preferred stock (7%), noninv. grade bonds (5%), and misc. investments (10%).
**Investments in Affiliates:** None
**Group Affiliation:** Assurant Inc
**Licensed in:** All states except NY, PR
**Commenced Business:** September 1910
**Address:** 2323 GRAND BOULEVARD, TOPEKA, KS 66614
**Phone:** (651) 361-4000 **Domicile State:** KS **NAIC Code:** 70408

| Data Date | Rating | RACR #1 | RACR #2 | Total Assets ($mil) | Capital ($mil) | Net Premium ($mil) | Net Income ($mil) |
|---|---|---|---|---|---|---|---|
| 9-17 | B | 2.61 | 1.37 | 2,690.2 | 129.1 | 3.3 | 81.9 |
| 9-16 | B | 3.70 | 2.21 | 2,946.2 | 289.6 | -1,469.4 | 445.0 |
| 2016 | B | 3.14 | 1.62 | 2,690.3 | 158.5 | -1,468.9 | 481.7 |
| 2015 | B | 1.91 | 1.26 | 4,711.8 | 428.4 | 1,028.4 | 71.5 |
| 2014 | B | 1.82 | 1.18 | 4,937.1 | 415.7 | 1,016.0 | 67.3 |
| 2013 | B | 1.88 | 1.21 | 5,085.8 | 434.7 | 986.2 | 85.4 |
| 2012 | B | 2.10 | 1.28 | 5,015.5 | 438.8 | 986.8 | 95.3 |

**Rating Indexes**

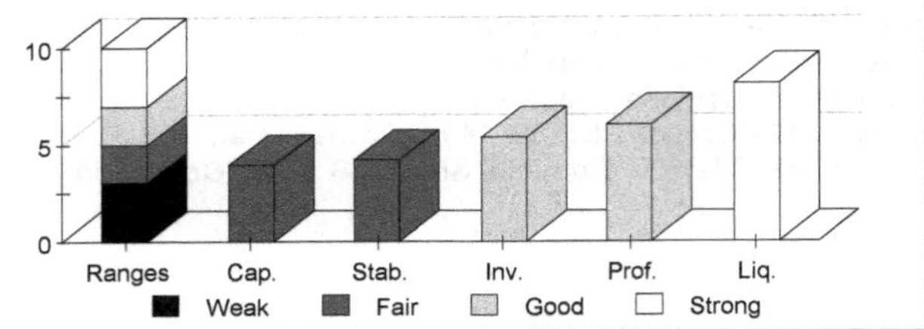


## UNION SECURITY LIFE INSURANCE COMPANY OF NEW YORK C+ Fair

**Major Rating Factors:** Fair overall capitalization (4.0 on a scale of 0 to 10) based on mixed results -- excessive policy leverage mitigated by excellent risk adjusted capital (severe loss scenario). However, capital levels have fluctuated somewhat during past years. Fair overall results on stability tests (3.0) including weak results on operational trends. High quality investment portfolio (8.6).
**Other Rating Factors:** Excellent profitability (7.9). Excellent liquidity (10.0).
**Principal Business:** Group health insurance (40%), individual health insurance (30%), reinsurance (13%), group life insurance (10%), and other lines (7%).
**Principal Investments:** NonCMO investment grade bonds (92%), CMOs and structured securities (6%), noninv. grade bonds (1%), and cash (1%).
**Investments in Affiliates:** None
**Group Affiliation:** Assurant Inc
**Licensed in:** NY
**Commenced Business:** April 1974
**Address:** 212 HIGHBRIDGE STREET SUITE D, FAYETTEVILLE, NY 13066
**Phone:** (315) 637-4232 **Domicile State:** NY **NAIC Code:** 81477

| Data Date | Rating | RACR #1 | RACR #2 | Total Assets ($mil) | Capital ($mil) | Net Premium ($mil) | Net Income ($mil) |
|---|---|---|---|---|---|---|---|
| 9-17 | C+ | 6.51 | 5.86 | 74.4 | 52.8 | 0.7 | 4.7 |
| 9-16 | B+ | 7.19 | 6.47 | 83.5 | 66.3 | -72.3 | 19.2 |
| 2016 | B- | 8.30 | 7.47 | 81.0 | 67.4 | -72.0 | 22.0 |
| 2015 | B+ | 4.34 | 3.91 | 128.3 | 39.5 | 21.6 | 3.3 |
| 2014 | B+ | 4.66 | 4.19 | 138.7 | 42.8 | 23.8 | 5.6 |
| 2013 | B+ | 4.44 | 4.00 | 147.7 | 40.9 | 27.4 | 5.4 |
| 2012 | B | 5.02 | 4.21 | 160.6 | 46.9 | 30.1 | 5.5 |

**Policy Leverage**

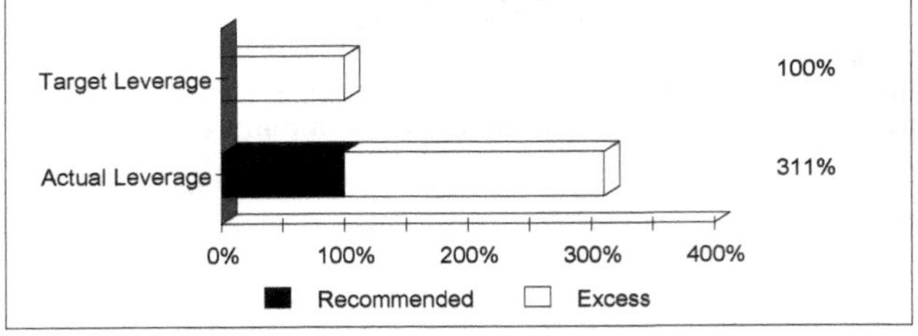

## UNITED AMERICAN INSURANCE COMPANY B- Good

**Major Rating Factors:** Good current capitalization (5.9 on a scale of 0 to 10) based on mixed results -- excessive policy leverage mitigated by excellent risk adjusted capital (severe loss scenario) reflecting improvement over results in 2016. Good quality investment portfolio (6.2) despite mixed results such as: large holdings of BBB rated bonds but moderate junk bond exposure. Good overall profitability (6.5).
**Other Rating Factors:** Good liquidity (6.6). Fair overall results on stability tests (4.6).
**Principal Business:** Individual health insurance (49%), group health insurance (30%), reinsurance (16%), individual annuities (3%), and individual life insurance (2%).
**Principal Investments:** NonCMO investment grade bonds (77%), common & preferred stock (4%), noninv. grade bonds (4%), CMOs and structured securities (3%), and misc. investments (3%).
**Investments in Affiliates:** 12%
**Group Affiliation:** Torchmark Corp
**Licensed in:** All states except NY, PR
**Commenced Business:** August 1981
**Address:** 10306 REGENCY PARKWAY DR, OMAHA, NE 68114
**Phone:** (972) 529-5085 **Domicile State:** NE **NAIC Code:** 92916

| Data Date | Rating | RACR #1 | RACR #2 | Total Assets ($mil) | Capital ($mil) | Net Premium ($mil) | Net Income ($mil) |
|---|---|---|---|---|---|---|---|
| 9-17 | B- | 1.65 | 1.23 | 1,006.6 | 206.2 | 359.5 | 65.8 |
| 9-16 | B- | 1.34 | 0.97 | 1,613.2 | 180.2 | 524.9 | 15.6 |
| 2016 | B- | 1.07 | 0.78 | 1,563.3 | 157.7 | 706.0 | 37.1 |
| 2015 | B- | 1.24 | 0.90 | 1,559.7 | 192.7 | 815.3 | 80.1 |
| 2014 | B- | 1.01 | 0.74 | 1,694.9 | 178.4 | 870.9 | 29.5 |
| 2013 | B | 1.27 | 0.91 | 1,683.4 | 211.6 | 745.1 | 58.1 |
| 2012 | B | 1.47 | 1.05 | 1,722.8 | 256.1 | 779.2 | 78.8 |

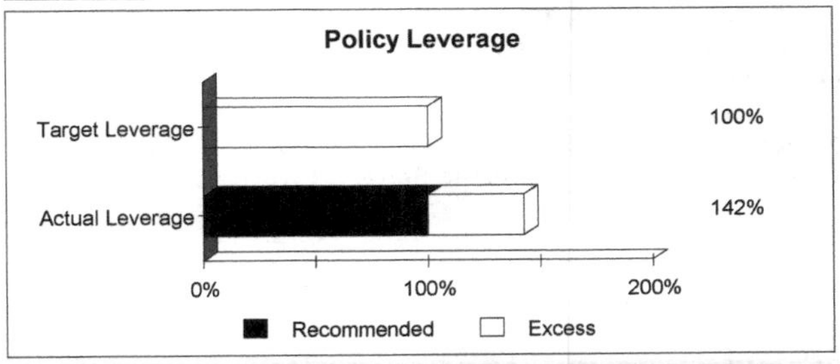


## UNITED HEALTHCARE INS CO OF IL B Good

**Major Rating Factors:** Good liquidity (6.6 on a scale of 0 to 10) with sufficient resources (cash flows and marketable investments) to handle a spike in claims. Excellent profitability (9.4). Strong capitalization (8.8) based on excellent current risk-adjusted capital (severe loss scenario).
**Other Rating Factors:** High quality investment portfolio (9.5).
**Principal Business:** Comp med (100%)
**Mem Phys: 16:** 63,392 **15:** 38,096 **16 MLR** 80.7% **/ 16 Admin Exp** N/A
**Enroll(000): Q3 17:** 229 **16:** 214 **15:** 192 **Med Exp PMPM:** $351
**Principal Investments:** Long-term bonds (80%), cash and equiv (17%), other (3%)
**Provider Compensation ($000):** Contr fee ($840,974), bonus arrang ($869), capitation ($438), FFS ($1)
**Total Member Encounters:** Phys (1,347,523), non-phys (387,109)
**Group Affiliation:** UnitedHealth Group Incorporated
**Licensed in:** IL
**Address:** 200 EAST RANDOLPH St Ste 5300, CHICAGO, IL 60601
**Phone:** (312) 424-4460 **Dom State:** IL **Commenced Bus:** December 1991

| Data Date | Rating | RACR #1 | RACR #2 | Total Assets ($mil) | Capital ($mil) | Net Premium ($mil) | Net Income ($mil) |
|---|---|---|---|---|---|---|---|
| 9-17 | B | 2.77 | 2.31 | 336.3 | 156.9 | 898.3 | 76.0 |
| 9-16 | B | 2.55 | 2.12 | 272.5 | 120.9 | 793.1 | 37.7 |
| 2016 | B | 1.95 | 1.63 | 302.3 | 109.9 | 1,065.1 | 44.0 |
| 2015 | B | 2.47 | 2.06 | 266.0 | 117.3 | 939.9 | 60.5 |
| 2014 | B | 2.09 | 1.74 | 246.7 | 106.3 | 932.7 | 24.7 |
| 2013 | B | 1.70 | 1.41 | 193.5 | 80.8 | 890.6 | 33.2 |
| 2012 | B | 2.56 | 2.13 | 159.5 | 79.0 | 626.0 | 40.0 |

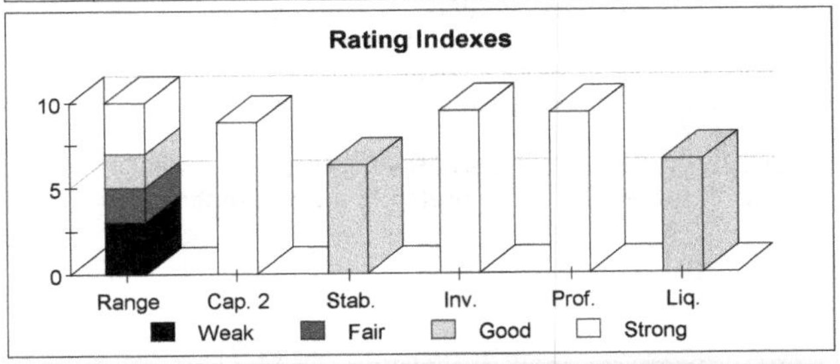


## UNITED HEALTHCARE INS CO OF NY B- Good

**Major Rating Factors:** Excellent profitability (7.6 on a scale of 0 to 10). Strong capitalization (10.0) based on excellent current risk-adjusted capital (severe loss scenario). High quality investment portfolio (9.5).
**Other Rating Factors:** Weak liquidity (2.1) as a spike in claims may stretch capacity.
**Principal Business:** Medicare (30%), med supp (29%), comp med (26%), dental (2%), other (13%)
**Mem Phys: 16:** 86,015 **15:** 103,624 **16 MLR** 157.0% **/ 16 Admin Exp** N/A
**Enroll(000): Q3 17:** 1,403 **16:** 1,393 **15:** 1,390 **Med Exp PMPM:** $157
**Principal Investments:** Long-term bonds (79%), cash and equiv (21%)
**Provider Compensation ($000):** Contr fee ($2,023,209), FFS ($470,386), capitation ($45,896), bonus arrang ($7,508), other ($15,676)
**Total Member Encounters:** Phys (9,772,364), non-phys (1,205,202)
**Group Affiliation:** UnitedHealth Group Incorporated
**Licensed in:** DC, NY
**Address:** 2950 EXPRESSWAY Dr S Ste 240, ISLANDIA, NY 11749-1412
**Phone:** (877) 832-7734 **Dom State:** NY **Commenced Bus:** December 1995

| Data Date | Rating | RACR #1 | RACR #2 | Total Assets ($mil) | Capital ($mil) | Net Premium ($mil) | Net Income ($mil) |
|---|---|---|---|---|---|---|---|
| 9-17 | B- | 21.78 | 18.15 | 1,497.9 | 498.2 | 1,359.5 | 38.4 |
| 9-16 | B- | 32.83 | 27.36 | 1,260.7 | 426.7 | 1,243.1 | 39.1 |
| 2016 | B- | 19.57 | 16.30 | 1,212.3 | 446.5 | 1,664.4 | 61.4 |
| 2015 | B- | 36.40 | 30.33 | 1,223.3 | 474.4 | 1,448.9 | 48.2 |
| 2014 | B- | 38.77 | 32.31 | 1,180.3 | 475.1 | 1,386.3 | 55.5 |
| 2013 | B- | 55.00 | 45.83 | 1,983.0 | 615.8 | 1,536.2 | 101.6 |
| 2012 | B- | 60.13 | 50.10 | 2,299.1 | 571.0 | 1,928.7 | 93.7 |

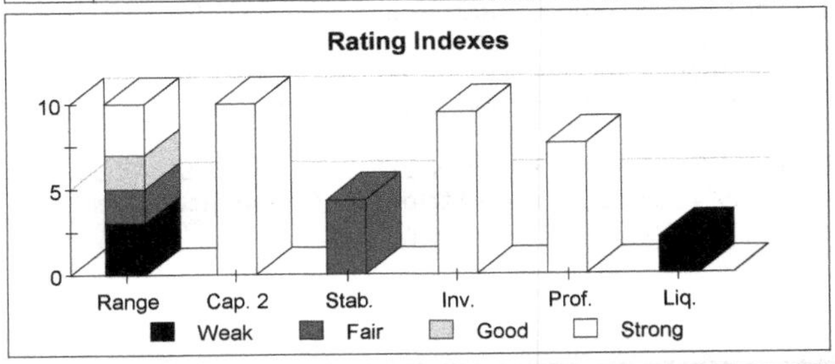

## UNITED HEALTHCARE INSURANCE COMPANY C Fair

**Major Rating Factors:** Fair current capitalization (4.3 on a scale of 0 to 10) based on mixed results -- excessive policy leverage mitigated by fair risk adjusted capital (severe loss scenario), although results have slipped from the good range over the last two years. Fair overall results on stability tests (3.9) including fair risk adjusted capital in prior years. Good quality investment portfolio (6.6).
**Other Rating Factors:** Weak liquidity (2.0). Excellent profitability (7.9).
**Principal Business:** Group health insurance (83%), individual health insurance (11%), and reinsurance (5%).
**Principal Investments:** NonCMO investment grade bonds (55%), common & preferred stock (20%), CMOs and structured securities (17%), noninv. grade bonds (5%), and misc. investments (2%).
**Investments in Affiliates:** 17%
**Group Affiliation:** UnitedHealth Group Inc
**Licensed in:** All states except NY
**Commenced Business:** April 1972
**Address:** 185 ASYLUM STREET, HARTFORD, CT 06103-3408
**Phone:** (877) 832-7734 **Domicile State:** CT **NAIC Code:** 79413

| Data Date | Rating | RACR #1 | RACR #2 | Total Assets ($mil) | Capital ($mil) | Net Premium ($mil) | Net Income ($mil) |
|---|---|---|---|---|---|---|---|
| 9-17 | C | 0.85 | 0.72 | 20,075.9 | 5,039.7 | 38,027.9 | 1,692.6 |
| 9-16 | C | 0.85 | 0.72 | 16,184.0 | 4,481.6 | 34,099.6 | 1,238.6 |
| 2016 | C | 0.79 | 0.67 | 17,922.6 | 5,250.4 | 44,379.2 | 1,924.6 |
| 2015 | C | 0.89 | 0.75 | 15,791.2 | 5,589.7 | 41,950.2 | 1,930.3 |
| 2014 | C | 0.82 | 0.69 | 15,113.4 | 5,595.8 | 43,936.4 | 2,658.1 |
| 2013 | C | 0.76 | 0.64 | 14,512.6 | 5,039.5 | 44,680.4 | 2,384.0 |
| 2012 | C | 0.76 | 0.64 | 14,118.3 | 4,711.9 | 42,602.9 | 2,531.0 |

**Policy Leverage**

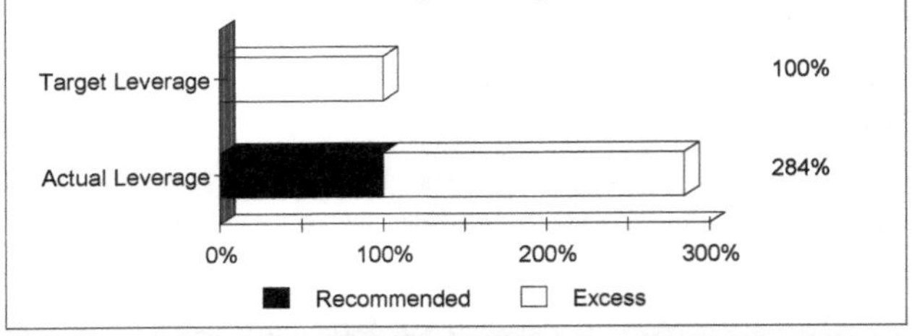


## UNITED HEALTHCARE OF ALABAMA INC B- Good

**Major Rating Factors:** Fair overall results on stability tests (3.6 on a scale of 0 to 10). Rating is significantly influenced by the fair financial results of UnitedHealth Group Incorporated. Good liquidity (6.8) with sufficient resources (cash flows and marketable investments) to handle a spike in claims. Excellent profitability (8.0).
**Other Rating Factors:** Strong capitalization index (7.5) based on excellent current risk-adjusted capital (severe loss scenario). High quality investment portfolio (9.9).
**Principal Business:** Medicare (74%), comp med (26%)
**Mem Phys: 16:** 41,619 **15:** 10,963 **16 MLR** 82.7% **/ 16 Admin Exp** N/A
**Enroll(000): Q3 17:** 3 **16:** 71 **15:** 56 **Med Exp PMPM:** $539
**Principal Investments:** Long-term bonds (71%), cash and equiv (29%)
**Provider Compensation ($000):** Contr fee ($371,748), FFS ($57,107), capitation ($11,748), bonus arrang ($5,454)
**Total Member Encounters:** Phys (1,307,518), non-phys (429,158)
**Group Affiliation:** UnitedHealth Group Incorporated
**Licensed in:** AL
**Address:** 33 INVERNESS CENTER PARKWAY, BIRMINGHAM, AL 35242
**Phone:** (205) 437-8500 **Dom State:** AL **Commenced Bus:** March 1986

| Data Date | Rating | RACR #1 | RACR #2 | Total Assets ($mil) | Capital ($mil) | Net Premium ($mil) | Net Income ($mil) |
|---|---|---|---|---|---|---|---|
| 9-17 | B- | 1.79 | 1.49 | 78.0 | 39.4 | -0.7 | 4.7 |
| 9-16 | B- | 3.52 | 2.94 | 206.1 | 48.9 | 424.9 | -1.8 |
| 2016 | B | 2.46 | 2.05 | 176.2 | 56.4 | 559.7 | 10.2 |
| 2015 | B | 3.66 | 3.05 | 142.7 | 51.2 | 455.7 | 20.6 |
| 2014 | B | 3.40 | 2.83 | 121.1 | 61.3 | 426.0 | 29.9 |
| 2013 | B | 3.07 | 2.56 | 132.7 | 62.4 | 406.2 | 26.7 |
| 2012 | B | 3.76 | 3.14 | 134.0 | 71.3 | 411.1 | 39.3 |

**Rating Indexes**

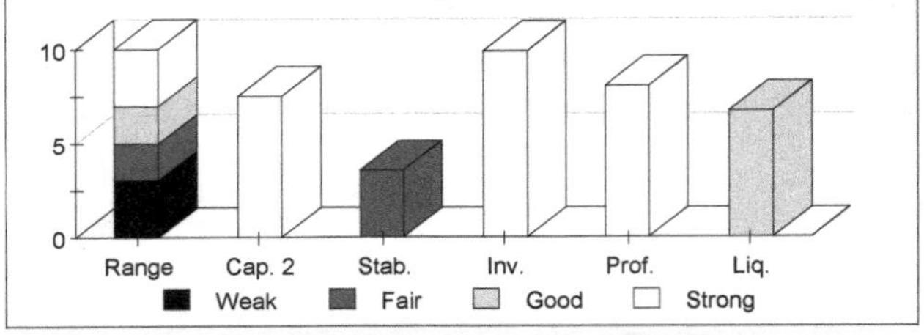


## UNITED HEALTHCARE OF ARIZONA INC C Fair

**Major Rating Factors:** Weak overall results on stability tests (1.2 on a scale of 0 to 10) based on a steep decline in capital during 2016, a significant 39% decrease in enrollment during the period. Rating is significantly influenced by the fair financial results of UnitedHealth Group Incorporated. Excellent profitability (7.6). Strong capitalization index (10.0) based on excellent current risk-adjusted capital (severe loss scenario).
**Other Rating Factors:** High quality investment portfolio (9.9). Excellent liquidity (7.1) with ample operational cash flow and liquid investments.
**Principal Business:** Comp med (99%)
**Mem Phys: 16:** 20,592 **15:** 19,033 **16 MLR** 86.8% **/ 16 Admin Exp** N/A
**Enroll(000): Q3 17:** 24 **16:** 19 **15:** 32 **Med Exp PMPM:** $443
**Principal Investments:** Cash and equiv (91%), long-term bonds (9%)
**Provider Compensation ($000):** Contr fee ($95,555), FFS ($9,636), capitation ($1,907), bonus arrang ($1,195)
**Total Member Encounters:** Phys (225,163), non-phys (11,716)
**Group Affiliation:** UnitedHealth Group Incorporated
**Licensed in:** AZ
**Address:** 1 EAST WASHINGTON STREET, PHOENIX, AZ 85004
**Phone:** (952) 936-1300 **Dom State:** AZ **Commenced Bus:** July 1985

| Data Date | Rating | RACR #1 | RACR #2 | Total Assets ($mil) | Capital ($mil) | Net Premium ($mil) | Net Income ($mil) |
|---|---|---|---|---|---|---|---|
| 9-17 | C | 5.32 | 4.43 | 49.2 | 21.8 | 95.4 | 5.6 |
| 9-16 | C | 2.63 | 2.19 | 48.3 | 29.4 | 83.6 | 2.5 |
| 2016 | C | 4.41 | 3.67 | 39.4 | 17.4 | 111.4 | 0.6 |
| 2015 | C | 2.85 | 2.38 | 64.9 | 32.3 | 256.3 | 14.0 |
| 2014 | B | 3.14 | 2.62 | 89.9 | 53.5 | 325.3 | 16.6 |
| 2013 | B- | 2.07 | 1.73 | 74.4 | 36.9 | 338.9 | 13.9 |
| 2012 | C | 1.35 | 1.13 | 71.4 | 23.8 | 320.5 | 12.3 |

**Rating Indexes**

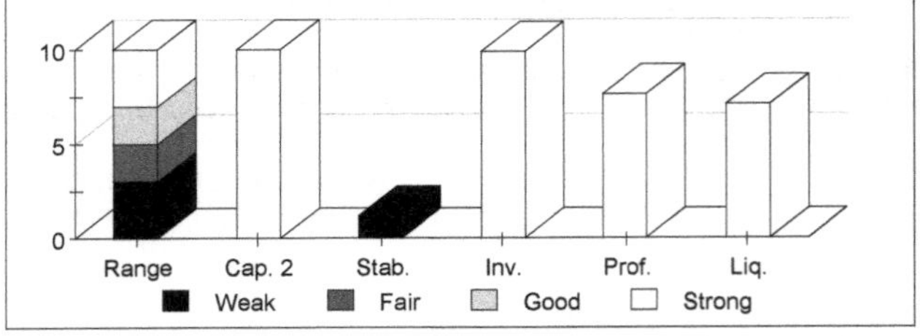

## UNITED HEALTHCARE OF ARKANSAS INC D- Weak

**Major Rating Factors:** Weak profitability index (1.5 on a scale of 0 to 10). Fair overall results on stability tests (4.6) based on an excessive 291% enrollment growth during the period. Rating is significantly influenced by the fair financial results of UnitedHealth Group Incorporated. Strong capitalization index (10.0) based on excellent current risk-adjusted capital (severe loss scenario).
**Other Rating Factors:** High quality investment portfolio (9.9). Excellent liquidity (7.7) with ample operational cash flow and liquid investments.
**Principal Business:** Comp med (100%)
**Mem Phys: 16:** 7,952 **15:** 7,715 **16 MLR** 112.4% **/ 16 Admin Exp** N/A
**Enroll(000): Q3 17:** 5 **16:** 12 **15:** 3 **Med Exp PMPM:** $365
**Principal Investments:** Cash and equiv (99%), long-term bonds (1%)
**Provider Compensation ($000):** Contr fee ($35,967), FFS ($3,094), capitation ($937), bonus arrang ($87)
**Total Member Encounters:** Phys (106,333), non-phys (6,536)
**Group Affiliation:** UnitedHealth Group Incorporated
**Licensed in:** AR
**Address:** 1401 CAPITOL AVE 3RD FLOOR STE, LITTLE ROCK, AR 72205
**Phone:** (501) 664-7700 **Dom State:** AR **Commenced Bus:** April 1992

| Data Date | Rating | RACR #1 | RACR #2 | Total Assets ($mil) | Capital ($mil) | Net Premium ($mil) | Net Income ($mil) |
|---|---|---|---|---|---|---|---|
| 9-17 | D- | 5.14 | 4.28 | 25.2 | 21.6 | 16.8 | 5.3 |
| 9-16 | D- | 3.58 | 2.98 | 23.5 | 3.4 | 26.2 | -11.3 |
| 2016 | D- | 2.49 | 2.08 | 43.1 | 10.1 | 41.1 | -9.7 |
| 2015 | B | 6.74 | 5.61 | 10.0 | 7.1 | 10.2 | 0.9 |
| 2014 | B | 9.23 | 7.69 | 10.0 | 7.8 | 8.2 | 0.6 |
| 2013 | B | 3.17 | 2.64 | 15.1 | 9.1 | 44.9 | 1.9 |
| 2012 | B | 3.28 | 2.73 | 15.6 | 8.9 | 43.7 | 3.3 |

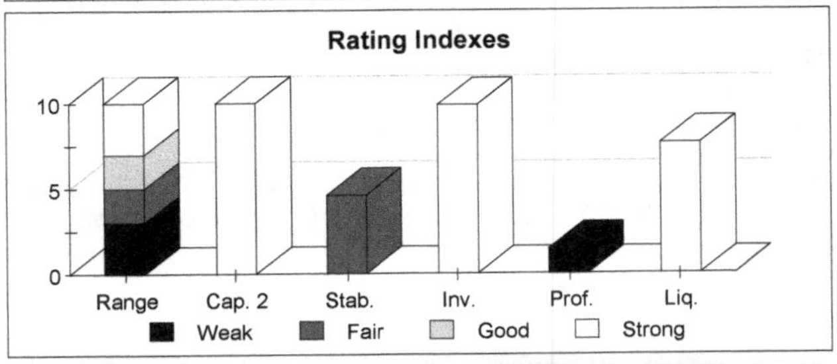


## UNITED HEALTHCARE OF COLORADO INC D- Weak

**Major Rating Factors:** Fair profitability index (4.3 on a scale of 0 to 10). Fair overall results on stability tests (4.7) based on an excessive 94% enrollment growth during the period. Rating is significantly influenced by the fair financial results of UnitedHealth Group Incorporated. Strong capitalization index (8.2) based on excellent current risk-adjusted capital (severe loss scenario).
**Other Rating Factors:** High quality investment portfolio (9.9). Excellent liquidity (7.1) with ample operational cash flow and liquid investments.
**Principal Business:** Comp med (100%)
**Mem Phys: 16:** 17,702 **15:** 15,564 **16 MLR** 86.5% **/ 16 Admin Exp** N/A
**Enroll(000): Q3 17:** 21 **16:** 22 **15:** 12 **Med Exp PMPM:** $309
**Principal Investments:** Cash and equiv (94%), long-term bonds (6%)
**Provider Compensation ($000):** Contr fee ($62,236), FFS ($4,602), capitation ($3,926), bonus arrang ($31)
**Total Member Encounters:** Phys (133,276), non-phys (5,196)
**Group Affiliation:** UnitedHealth Group Incorporated
**Licensed in:** CO
**Address:** 6465 SOUTH GREENWOOD PLAZA BLV, CENTENNIAL, CO 80111
**Phone:** (952) 936-1300 **Dom State:** CO **Commenced Bus:** March 1986

| Data Date | Rating | RACR #1 | RACR #2 | Total Assets ($mil) | Capital ($mil) | Net Premium ($mil) | Net Income ($mil) |
|---|---|---|---|---|---|---|---|
| 9-17 | D- | 2.32 | 1.93 | 32.6 | 13.3 | 52.8 | 3.4 |
| 9-16 | D- | 5.31 | 4.43 | 31.2 | 10.3 | 66.8 | -0.6 |
| 2016 | D- | 1.74 | 1.45 | 31.8 | 9.8 | 87.9 | 0.0 |
| 2015 | C | 3.12 | 2.60 | 18.4 | 5.9 | 36.4 | -0.9 |
| 2014 | B | 5.38 | 4.48 | 16.0 | 10.9 | 32.1 | 2.3 |
| 2013 | B- | 5.86 | 4.88 | 11.5 | 8.6 | 19.5 | 3.7 |
| 2012 | C | 3.87 | 3.22 | 9.4 | 4.8 | 12.1 | -1.7 |

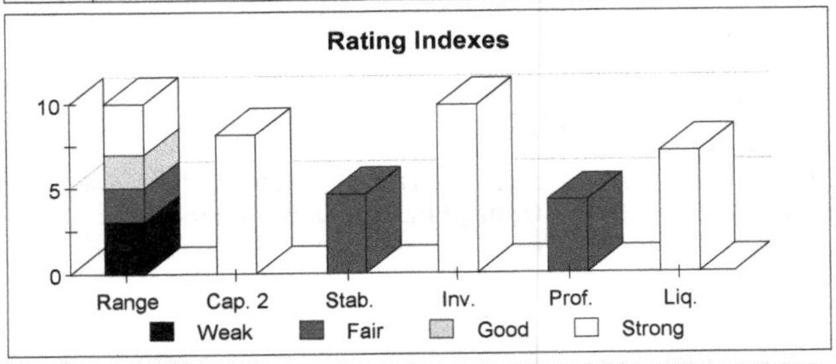


## UNITED HEALTHCARE OF FLORIDA INC D+ Weak

**Major Rating Factors:** Weak profitability index (1.8 on a scale of 0 to 10). Good overall results on stability tests (5.4). Rating is significantly influenced by the fair financial results of UnitedHealth Group Incorporated. Good liquidity (6.7) with sufficient resources (cash flows and marketable investments) to handle a spike in claims.
**Other Rating Factors:** Strong capitalization index (7.6) based on excellent current risk-adjusted capital (severe loss scenario). High quality investment portfolio (9.9).
**Principal Business:** Medicaid (65%), comp med (35%)
**Mem Phys: 16:** 46,634 **15:** 44,349 **16 MLR** 87.5% **/ 16 Admin Exp** N/A
**Enroll(000): Q3 17:** 398 **16:** 485 **15:** 557 **Med Exp PMPM:** $459
**Principal Investments:** Long-term bonds (65%), cash and equiv (28%), other (7%)
**Provider Compensation ($000):** Contr fee ($2,329,957), FFS ($175,920), capitation ($128,685), bonus arrang ($8,699)
**Total Member Encounters:** Phys (4,163,059), non-phys (2,015,476)
**Group Affiliation:** UnitedHealth Group Incorporated
**Licensed in:** FL
**Address:** 495 NORTH KELLER ROAD SUITE 20, MAITLAND, FL 32751
**Phone:** (407) 659-6900 **Dom State:** FL **Commenced Bus:** March 1973

| Data Date | Rating | RACR #1 | RACR #2 | Total Assets ($mil) | Capital ($mil) | Net Premium ($mil) | Net Income ($mil) |
|---|---|---|---|---|---|---|---|
| 9-17 | D+ | 1.87 | 1.56 | 632.5 | 300.2 | 1,843.5 | 60.5 |
| 9-16 | D+ | 1.62 | 1.35 | 744.6 | 302.1 | 2,246.1 | 30.7 |
| 2016 | D+ | 2.15 | 1.79 | 792.7 | 348.7 | 3,000.4 | 84.7 |
| 2015 | C | 1.48 | 1.23 | 808.6 | 274.5 | 3,248.8 | -12.9 |
| 2014 | C | 0.78 | 0.65 | 651.3 | 105.0 | 2,349.5 | -165.1 |
| 2013 | C | 0.82 | 0.68 | 351.2 | 71.4 | 1,668.7 | -40.0 |
| 2012 | C | 1.37 | 1.14 | 291.5 | 92.4 | 1,364.4 | 47.9 |

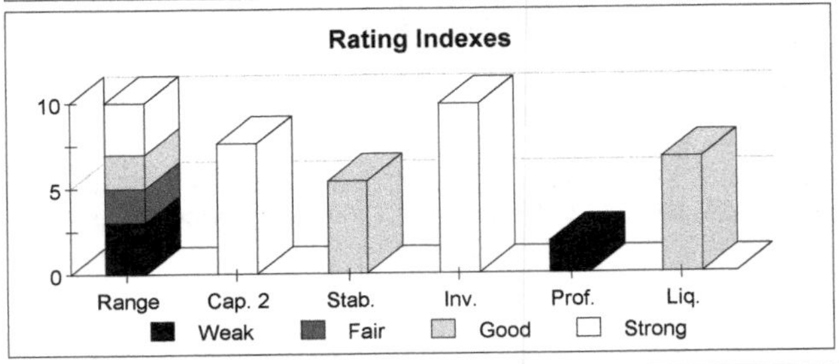

## UNITED HEALTHCARE OF GEORGIA INC B Good

**Major Rating Factors:** Good overall results on stability tests (6.1 on a scale of 0 to 10) based on healthy premium and capital growth during 2016. Rating is significantly influenced by the fair financial results of UnitedHealth Group Incorporated. Good liquidity (6.8) with sufficient resources (cash flows and marketable investments) to handle a spike in claims. Fair profitability index (4.6).
**Other Rating Factors:** Strong capitalization index (9.4) based on excellent current risk-adjusted capital (severe loss scenario). High quality investment portfolio (9.9).
**Principal Business:** Comp med (68%), Medicare (32%)
**Mem Phys: 16:** 24,768 **15:** 24,485 **16 MLR** 93.3% **/ 16 Admin Exp** N/A
**Enroll(000): Q3 17:** 50 **16:** 48 **15:** 29 **Med Exp PMPM:** $519
**Principal Investments:** Cash and equiv (50%), long-term bonds (50%)
**Provider Compensation ($000):** Contr fee ($223,913), FFS ($24,832), capitation ($3,776), bonus arrang ($786)
**Total Member Encounters:** Phys (514,239), non-phys (93,271)
**Group Affiliation:** UnitedHealth Group Incorporated
**Licensed in:** GA
**Address:** 3720 DAVINCI COURT SUITE 300, NORCROSS, GA 30092
**Phone:** (770) 300-3501 **Dom State:** GA **Commenced Bus:** April 1986

| Data Date | Rating | RACR #1 | RACR #2 | Total Assets ($mil) | Capital ($mil) | Net Premium ($mil) | Net Income ($mil) |
|---|---|---|---|---|---|---|---|
| 9-17 | B | 3.24 | 2.70 | 112.2 | 58.2 | 201.8 | 13.0 |
| 9-16 | C+ | 3.39 | 2.83 | 106.8 | 35.4 | 211.4 | 12.7 |
| 2016 | C+ | 2.54 | 2.12 | 105.0 | 45.2 | 287.3 | 21.9 |
| 2015 | C | 2.72 | 2.27 | 91.5 | 28.0 | 174.0 | -35.2 |
| 2014 | B- | 4.45 | 3.71 | 45.5 | 30.2 | 123.6 | 8.4 |
| 2013 | B- | 3.18 | 2.65 | 41.1 | 24.1 | 138.1 | 6.6 |
| 2012 | C | 2.04 | 1.70 | 35.0 | 16.0 | 146.8 | 6.6 |

Rating Indexes

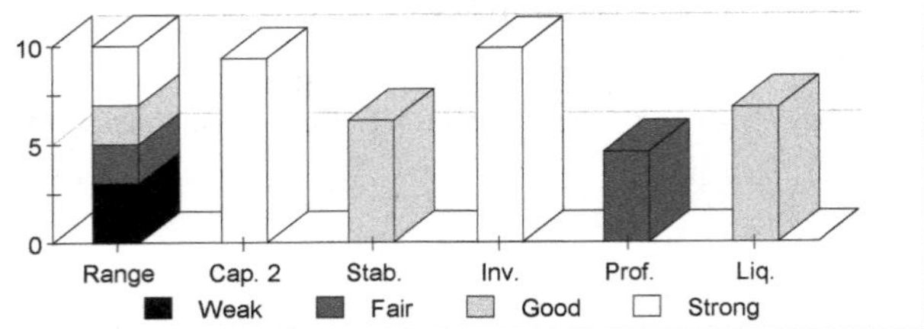


## UNITED HEALTHCARE OF ILLINOIS INC B- Good

**Major Rating Factors:** Fair overall results on stability tests (4.8 on a scale of 0 to 10) based on an excessive 40% enrollment growth during the period. Rating is significantly influenced by the fair financial results of UnitedHealth Group Incorporated. Excellent profitability (8.8). Strong capitalization index (10.0) based on excellent current risk-adjusted capital (severe loss scenario).
**Other Rating Factors:** High quality investment portfolio (9.9). Excellent liquidity (7.0) with sufficient resources (cash flows and marketable investments) to handle a spike in claims.
**Principal Business:** Comp med (100%)
**Mem Phys: 16:** 40,760 **15:** 38,096 **16 MLR** 73.5% **/ 16 Admin Exp** N/A
**Enroll(000): Q3 17:** 35 **16:** 31 **15:** 22 **Med Exp PMPM:** $314
**Principal Investments:** Long-term bonds (58%), cash and equiv (42%)
**Provider Compensation ($000):** Contr fee ($87,395), FFS ($5,873), capitation ($2,450), bonus arrang ($144)
**Total Member Encounters:** Phys (229,580), non-phys (9,349)
**Group Affiliation:** UnitedHealth Group Incorporated
**Licensed in:** IL, IN
**Address:** 200 EAST RANDOLPH STREET, CHICAGO, IL 60601
**Phone:** (312) 803-5900 **Dom State:** IL **Commenced Bus:** January 1984

| Data Date | Rating | RACR #1 | RACR #2 | Total Assets ($mil) | Capital ($mil) | Net Premium ($mil) | Net Income ($mil) |
|---|---|---|---|---|---|---|---|
| 9-17 | B- | 3.65 | 3.04 | 51.6 | 25.3 | 128.5 | 7.6 |
| 9-16 | C | 4.17 | 3.48 | 41.0 | 23.6 | 97.2 | 7.7 |
| 2016 | B- | 2.56 | 2.13 | 38.5 | 17.5 | 135.1 | 10.2 |
| 2015 | C | 2.89 | 2.41 | 32.1 | 16.0 | 108.0 | 7.2 |
| 2014 | C | 3.35 | 2.79 | 35.4 | 20.4 | 105.9 | 5.1 |
| 2013 | B- | 5.02 | 4.19 | 32.7 | 21.9 | 76.5 | 6.6 |
| 2012 | C | 5.65 | 4.71 | 19.8 | 15.3 | 44.4 | 4.5 |

Rating Indexes

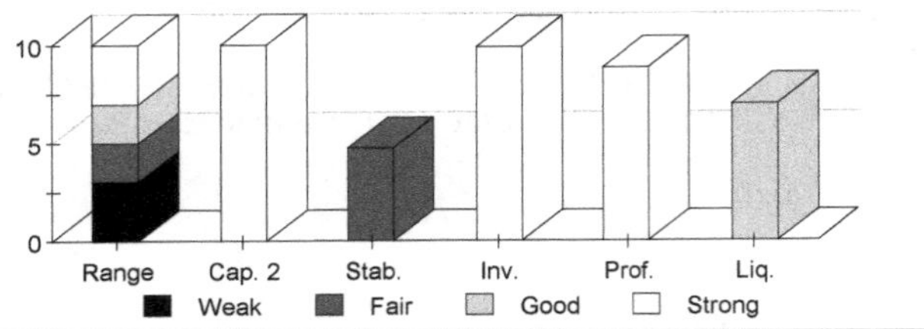


## UNITED HEALTHCARE OF KENTUCKY LTD C Fair

**Major Rating Factors:** Fair profitability index (3.3 on a scale of 0 to 10). Weak overall results on stability tests (2.6). Rating is significantly influenced by the fair financial results of UnitedHealth Group Incorporated. Good liquidity (6.4) with sufficient resources (cash flows and marketable investments) to handle a spike in claims.
**Other Rating Factors:** Strong capitalization index (8.0) based on excellent current risk-adjusted capital (severe loss scenario). High quality investment portfolio (9.9).
**Principal Business:** Comp med (100%)
**Mem Phys: 16:** 15,957 **15:** 15,044 **16 MLR** 88.6% **/ 16 Admin Exp** N/A
**Enroll(000): Q3 17:** 23 **16:** 24 **15:** 21 **Med Exp PMPM:** $350
**Principal Investments:** Long-term bonds (67%), cash and equiv (33%)
**Provider Compensation ($000):** Contr fee ($82,533), FFS ($5,677), capitation ($1,673)
**Total Member Encounters:** Phys (174,152), non-phys (7,912)
**Group Affiliation:** UnitedHealth Group Incorporated
**Licensed in:** IN, KY
**Address:** 230 LEXINGTON GREEN CIRCLE, LEXINGTON, KY 40503
**Phone:** (859) 825-6132 **Dom State:** KY **Commenced Bus:** May 1986

| Data Date | Rating | RACR #1 | RACR #2 | Total Assets ($mil) | Capital ($mil) | Net Premium ($mil) | Net Income ($mil) |
|---|---|---|---|---|---|---|---|
| 9-17 | C | 2.13 | 1.78 | 31.2 | 14.2 | 85.5 | 4.6 |
| 9-16 | B- | 2.45 | 2.04 | 32.9 | 12.4 | 79.3 | -0.9 |
| 2016 | C | 1.53 | 1.28 | 31.7 | 9.9 | 105.1 | -2.5 |
| 2015 | B | 2.85 | 2.38 | 29.8 | 14.7 | 90.1 | 3.4 |
| 2014 | B | 2.13 | 1.78 | 26.1 | 11.6 | 86.9 | -4.2 |
| 2013 | B | 2.36 | 1.97 | 24.1 | 12.8 | 95.8 | 4.9 |
| 2012 | B- | 1.69 | 1.41 | 18.7 | 8.1 | 86.9 | 4.1 |

Rating Indexes

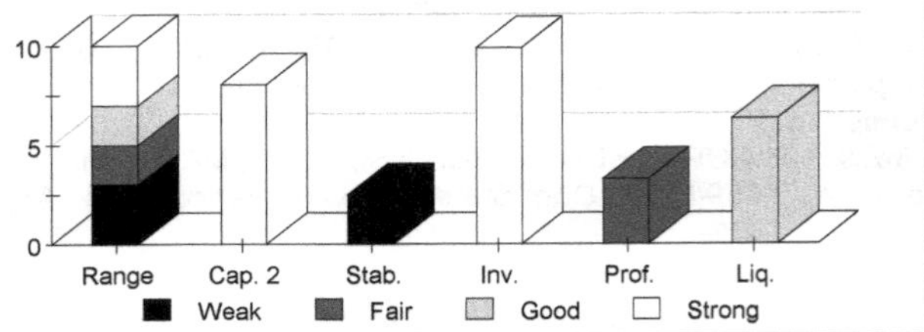

## UNITED HEALTHCARE OF LOUISIANA INC — D — Weak

**Major Rating Factors:** Good overall results on stability tests (5.9 on a scale of 0 to 10) based on healthy premium and capital growth during 2016 but a decline in the number of member physicians during 2017. Rating is significantly influenced by the fair financial results of UnitedHealth Group Incorporated. Good liquidity (6.9) with sufficient resources (cash flows and marketable investments) to handle a spike in claims. Excellent profitability (8.0).
**Other Rating Factors:** Strong capitalization index (8.1) based on excellent current risk-adjusted capital (severe loss scenario). High quality investment portfolio (9.9).
**Principal Business:** Medicaid (84%), comp med (16%)
**Mem Phys: 16:** 17,349 **15:** 27,647 **16 MLR** 90.6% **/ 16 Admin Exp** N/A
**Enroll(000): Q3 17:** 441 **16:** 456 **15:** 356 **Med Exp PMPM:** $301
**Principal Investments:** Cash and equiv (68%), long-term bonds (32%)
**Provider Compensation ($000):** Contr fee ($1,055,253), capitation ($229,679), FFS ($94,696), bonus arrang ($7,369)
**Total Member Encounters:** Phys (4,090,637), non-phys (2,006,075)
**Group Affiliation:** UnitedHealth Group Incorporated
**Licensed in:** LA
**Address:** 3838 N CAUSEWAY BLVD SUITE 260, METAIRIE, LA 70002
**Phone:** (504) 849-1603 **Dom State:** LA **Commenced Bus:** November 1986

| Data Date | Rating | RACR #1 | RACR #2 | Total Assets ($mil) | Capital ($mil) | Net Premium ($mil) | Net Income ($mil) |
|---|---|---|---|---|---|---|---|
| 9-17 | D | 2.21 | 1.84 | 557.7 | 180.5 | 1,446.6 | 60.0 |
| 9-16 | D | 1.94 | 1.62 | 474.3 | 113.6 | 1,121.3 | 27.7 |
| 2016 | D | 1.56 | 1.30 | 479.2 | 126.5 | 1,644.8 | 43.9 |
| 2015 | D | 1.45 | 1.21 | 275.9 | 84.5 | 1,069.8 | 29.5 |
| 2014 | D | 17.39 | 14.50 | 37.1 | 18.9 | 7.5 | -2.2 |
| 2013 | D | 10.28 | 8.57 | 15.4 | 12.4 | 5.1 | 3.0 |
| 2012 | D | 4.19 | 3.49 | 10.3 | 5.1 | 4.7 | -4.7 |

Rating Indexes

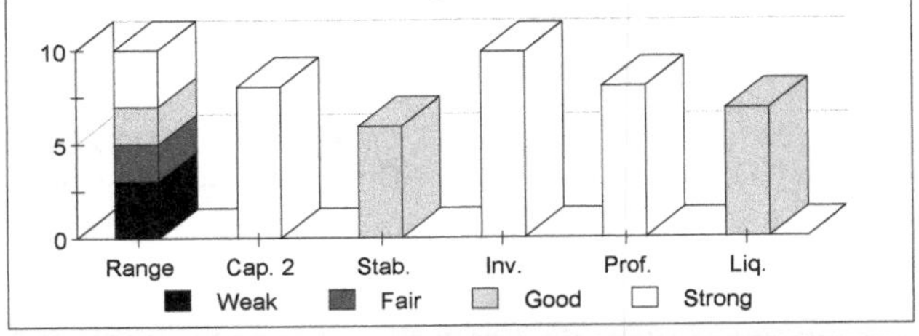


## UNITED HEALTHCARE OF MID-ATLANTIC — B — Good

**Major Rating Factors:** Good overall profitability index (5.1 on a scale of 0 to 10). Good overall results on stability tests (5.2). Rating is significantly influenced by the fair financial results of UnitedHealth Group Incorporated. Strong capitalization index (9.1) based on excellent current risk-adjusted capital (severe loss scenario).
**Other Rating Factors:** High quality investment portfolio (9.9). Excellent liquidity (7.0) with sufficient resources (cash flows and marketable investments) to handle a spike in claims.
**Principal Business:** Medicaid (86%), comp med (14%)
**Mem Phys: 16:** 43,435 **15:** 40,524 **16 MLR** 79.1% **/ 16 Admin Exp** N/A
**Enroll(000): Q3 17:** 182 **16:** 195 **15:** 177 **Med Exp PMPM:** $301
**Principal Investments:** Long-term bonds (67%), cash and equiv (33%)
**Provider Compensation ($000):** Contr fee ($656,897), FFS ($50,119), capitation ($3,204), bonus arrang ($12)
**Total Member Encounters:** Phys (1,542,093), non-phys (750,748)
**Group Affiliation:** UnitedHealth Group Incorporated
**Licensed in:** DC, MD, VA
**Address:** 800 KING FARM BOULEVARD, ROCKVILLE, MD 20850
**Phone:** (866) 297-9264 **Dom State:** MD **Commenced Bus:** December 1978

| Data Date | Rating | RACR #1 | RACR #2 | Total Assets ($mil) | Capital ($mil) | Net Premium ($mil) | Net Income ($mil) |
|---|---|---|---|---|---|---|---|
| 9-17 | B | 3.06 | 2.55 | 306.4 | 141.7 | 620.9 | 29.0 |
| 9-16 | C+ | 2.64 | 2.20 | 337.0 | 147.2 | 678.1 | 48.4 |
| 2016 | B | 3.02 | 2.51 | 321.2 | 139.8 | 896.7 | 62.4 |
| 2015 | C+ | 2.33 | 1.94 | 350.5 | 138.5 | 894.5 | -64.2 |
| 2014 | B | 2.20 | 1.84 | 368.0 | 141.0 | 1,159.7 | 12.6 |
| 2013 | B | 2.92 | 2.44 | 226.7 | 114.4 | 737.0 | -0.1 |
| 2012 | B | 3.40 | 2.83 | 210.8 | 124.6 | 701.6 | 22.5 |

Rating Indexes

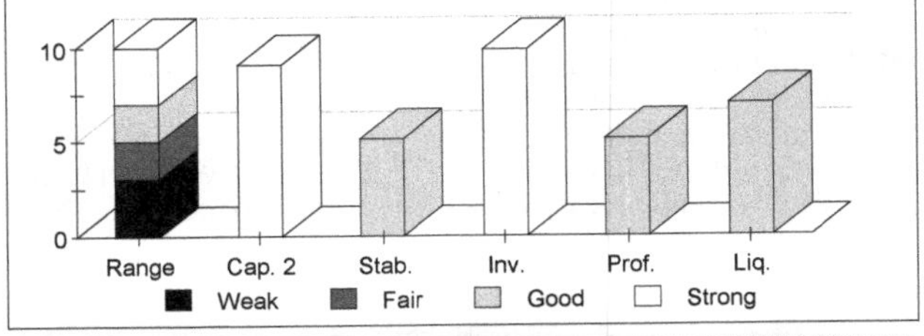


## UNITED HEALTHCARE OF MISSISSIPPI INC — C — Fair

**Major Rating Factors:** Weak profitability index (0.9 on a scale of 0 to 10). Good liquidity (6.5) with sufficient resources (cash flows and marketable investments) to handle a spike in claims. Strong capitalization index (7.7) based on excellent current risk-adjusted capital (severe loss scenario).
**Other Rating Factors:** High quality investment portfolio (9.9). Excellent overall results on stability tests (7.2) based on healthy premium and capital growth during 2016 but a decline in enrollment during 2016. Rating is significantly influenced by the fair financial results of UnitedHealth Group Incorporated.
**Principal Business:** Medicaid (84%), comp med (16%)
**Mem Phys: 16:** 9,928 **15:** 9,064 **16 MLR** 93.8% **/ 16 Admin Exp** N/A
**Enroll(000): Q3 17:** 266 **16:** 289 **15:** 310 **Med Exp PMPM:** $322
**Principal Investments:** Cash and equiv (53%), long-term bonds (47%)
**Provider Compensation ($000):** Contr fee ($1,046,908), FFS ($68,159), capitation ($23,437), bonus arrang ($76)
**Total Member Encounters:** Phys (2,719,263), non-phys (1,520,809)
**Group Affiliation:** UnitedHealth Group Incorporated
**Licensed in:** MS
**Address:** 795 WOODLANDS PARKWAY SUITE 30, RIDGELAND, MS 39157
**Phone:** (504) 849-1603 **Dom State:** MS **Commenced Bus:** January 1993

| Data Date | Rating | RACR #1 | RACR #2 | Total Assets ($mil) | Capital ($mil) | Net Premium ($mil) | Net Income ($mil) |
|---|---|---|---|---|---|---|---|
| 9-17 | C | 1.89 | 1.57 | 284.9 | 137.6 | 831.8 | -28.6 |
| 9-16 | B- | 1.70 | 1.41 | 233.4 | 87.8 | 912.4 | -2.4 |
| 2016 | B- | 1.33 | 1.11 | 223.4 | 96.8 | 1,233.0 | 8.9 |
| 2015 | B- | 1.32 | 1.10 | 220.6 | 66.8 | 897.1 | -14.6 |
| 2014 | C+ | 2.31 | 1.92 | 113.9 | 54.7 | 400.3 | 13.4 |
| 2013 | C | 1.67 | 1.40 | 106.8 | 45.0 | 360.6 | -11.8 |
| 2012 | C | 2.34 | 1.95 | 73.3 | 18.8 | 126.1 | 3.1 |

Rating Indexes

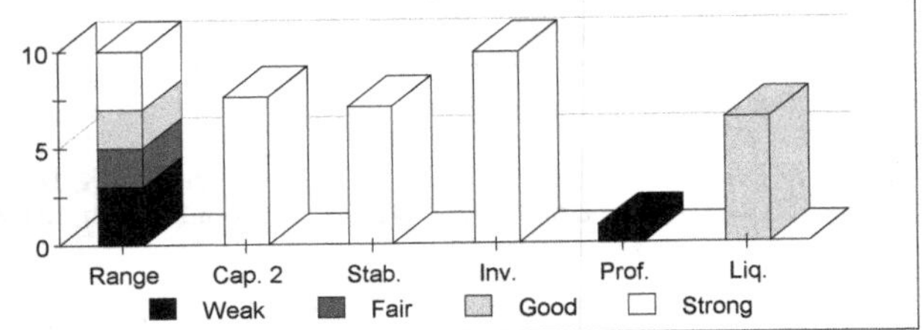

## UNITED HEALTHCARE OF NC INC B Good

**Major Rating Factors:** Good overall results on stability tests (5.3 on a scale of 0 to 10) despite inconsistent enrollment growth in the past five years due to declines in 2013 and 2014. Rating is significantly influenced by the fair financial results of UnitedHealth Group Incorporated. Excellent profitability (8.5). Strong capitalization index (9.4) based on excellent current risk-adjusted capital (severe loss scenario).
**Other Rating Factors:** High quality investment portfolio (9.9). Excellent liquidity (7.0) with ample operational cash flow and liquid investments.
**Principal Business:** Comp med (100%)
**Mem Phys: 16:** 28,732 **15:** 27,531 **16 MLR** 82.1% **/ 16 Admin Exp** N/A
**Enroll(000): Q3 17:** 86 **16:** 195 **15:** 163 **Med Exp PMPM:** $350
**Principal Investments:** Cash and equiv (61%), long-term bonds (39%)
**Provider Compensation ($000):** Contr fee ($723,475), FFS ($36,181), bonus arrang ($20,189), capitation ($12,572)
**Total Member Encounters:** Phys (1,817,593), non-phys (77,230)
**Group Affiliation:** UnitedHealth Group Incorporated
**Licensed in:** NC
**Address:** 3803 NORTH ELM STREET, GREENSBORO, NC 27455
**Phone:** (336) 282-0900 **Dom State:** NC **Commenced Bus:** May 1985

| Data Date | Rating | RACR #1 | RACR #2 | Total Assets ($mil) | Capital ($mil) | Net Premium ($mil) | Net Income ($mil) |
|---|---|---|---|---|---|---|---|
| 9-17 | B | 3.30 | 2.75 | 218.4 | 151.4 | 283.2 | 26.4 |
| 9-16 | B | 2.19 | 1.83 | 367.1 | 139.5 | 707.7 | 3.5 |
| 2016 | B | 3.24 | 2.70 | 403.7 | 148.4 | 931.0 | 26.4 |
| 2015 | B | 2.00 | 1.67 | 375.5 | 126.9 | 1,280.4 | 6.5 |
| 2014 | B | 2.53 | 2.11 | 263.6 | 130.8 | 1,013.8 | 39.6 |
| 2013 | B | 2.60 | 2.17 | 249.7 | 130.5 | 969.0 | 40.0 |
| 2012 | B- | 1.97 | 1.64 | 228.2 | 86.0 | 986.5 | 59.5 |

Rating Indexes

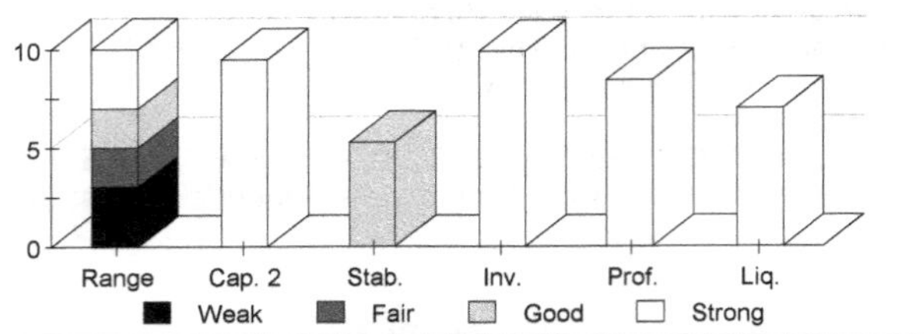


## UNITED HEALTHCARE OF NEW ENGLAND INC B- Good

**Major Rating Factors:** Fair overall results on stability tests (3.9 on a scale of 0 to 10). Rating is significantly influenced by the fair financial results of UnitedHealth Group Incorporated. Good overall profitability index (5.6). Good liquidity (6.6) with sufficient resources (cash flows and marketable investments) to handle a spike in claims.
**Other Rating Factors:** Strong capitalization index (9.0) based on excellent current risk-adjusted capital (severe loss scenario). High quality investment portfolio (9.5).
**Principal Business:** Medicaid (58%), Medicare (41%)
**Mem Phys: 16:** 116,101 **15:** 45,542 **16 MLR** 87.5% **/ 16 Admin Exp** N/A
**Enroll(000): Q3 17:** 143 **16:** 128 **15:** 114 **Med Exp PMPM:** $511
**Principal Investments:** Long-term bonds (90%), nonaffiliate common stock (6%), cash and equiv (4%)
**Provider Compensation ($000):** Contr fee ($621,250), capitation ($101,426), FFS ($59,340), bonus arrang ($4,642)
**Total Member Encounters:** Phys (1,520,188), non-phys (757,539)
**Group Affiliation:** UnitedHealth Group Incorporated
**Licensed in:** MA, NH, PA, RI, VT
**Address:** 475 KILVERT STREET SUITE 310, WARWICK, RI 02886-1392
**Phone:** (203) 447-4444 **Dom State:** RI **Commenced Bus:** December 1984

| Data Date | Rating | RACR #1 | RACR #2 | Total Assets ($mil) | Capital ($mil) | Net Premium ($mil) | Net Income ($mil) |
|---|---|---|---|---|---|---|---|
| 9-17 | B- | 2.99 | 2.49 | 390.3 | 129.1 | 733.4 | 23.4 |
| 9-16 | B | 3.53 | 2.95 | 347.7 | 147.5 | 638.9 | 15.9 |
| 2016 | B- | 2.76 | 2.30 | 313.5 | 119.0 | 866.6 | 12.7 |
| 2015 | B | 3.53 | 2.94 | 363.9 | 147.2 | 768.5 | 27.5 |
| 2014 | B | 4.37 | 3.64 | 314.9 | 160.7 | 691.5 | 36.7 |
| 2013 | B | 3.67 | 3.05 | 230.9 | 124.5 | 587.5 | -2.8 |
| 2012 | B | 4.38 | 3.65 | 245.7 | 140.1 | 568.8 | 16.7 |

Rating Indexes

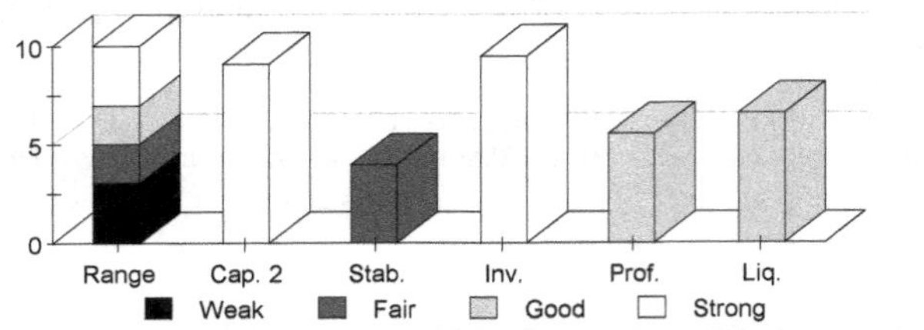


## UNITED HEALTHCARE OF NY INC * B+ Good

**Major Rating Factors:** Good liquidity (6.9 on a scale of 0 to 10) with sufficient resources (cash flows and marketable investments) to handle a spike in claims. Excellent profitability (9.9). Strong capitalization index (8.5) based on excellent current risk-adjusted capital (severe loss scenario).
**Other Rating Factors:** High quality investment portfolio (9.7). Excellent overall results on stability tests (8.0) based on healthy premium and capital growth during 2016. Rating is significantly influenced by the fair financial results of UnitedHealth Group Incorporated.
**Principal Business:** Medicaid (61%), Medicare (24%), comp med (4%), other (11%)
**Mem Phys: 16:** 90,361 **15:** 79,658 **16 MLR** 82.7% **/ 16 Admin Exp** N/A
**Enroll(000): Q3 17:** 710 **16:** 676 **15:** 574 **Med Exp PMPM:** $417
**Principal Investments:** Long-term bonds (66%), cash and equiv (34%)
**Provider Compensation ($000):** Contr fee ($2,796,479), FFS ($176,325), bonus arrang ($93,115), capitation ($33,201)
**Total Member Encounters:** Phys (6,204,362), non-phys (3,278,376)
**Group Affiliation:** UnitedHealth Group Incorporated
**Licensed in:** NY
**Address:** 77 WATER STREET 14TH / 15TH FL, NEW YORK, NY 10005
**Phone:** (203) 447-4439 **Dom State:** NY **Commenced Bus:** January 1987

| Data Date | Rating | RACR #1 | RACR #2 | Total Assets ($mil) | Capital ($mil) | Net Premium ($mil) | Net Income ($mil) |
|---|---|---|---|---|---|---|---|
| 9-17 | B+ | 2.57 | 2.15 | 1,277.0 | 574.0 | 3,267.7 | 112.6 |
| 9-16 | B+ | 3.05 | 2.54 | 1,112.6 | 503.5 | 2,752.0 | 43.5 |
| 2016 | B+ | 2.55 | 2.12 | 1,096.2 | 568.0 | 3,870.2 | 115.2 |
| 2015 | B+ | 2.77 | 2.31 | 846.1 | 455.9 | 3,025.2 | 106.0 |
| 2014 | B+ | 2.82 | 2.35 | 648.2 | 363.0 | 2,481.1 | 112.3 |
| 2013 | B+ | 3.65 | 3.04 | 606.2 | 345.2 | 1,879.0 | 79.9 |
| 2012 | B+ | 4.02 | 3.35 | 564.5 | 323.9 | 1,607.3 | 111.7 |

Rating Indexes

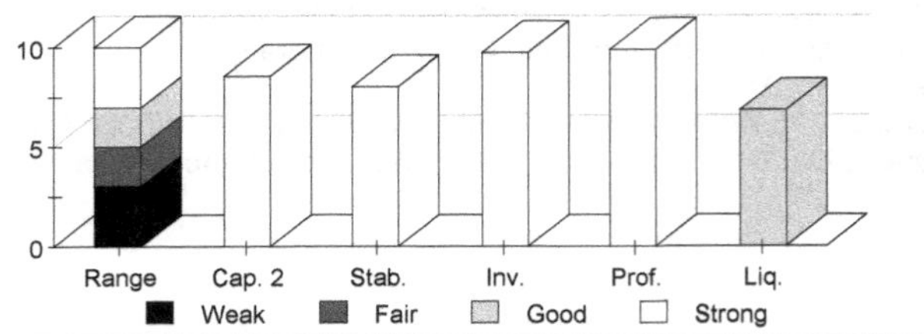

## UNITED HEALTHCARE OF OHIO INC — C — Fair

**Major Rating Factors:** Weak overall results on stability tests (2.3 on a scale of 0 to 10) based on a significant 72% decrease in enrollment during the period. Rating is significantly influenced by the fair financial results of UnitedHealth Group Incorporated. Good overall profitability index (5.9). Strong capitalization index (10.0) based on excellent current risk-adjusted capital (severe loss scenario).
**Other Rating Factors:** High quality investment portfolio (9.9). Excellent liquidity (7.7) with ample operational cash flow and liquid investments.
**Principal Business:** Comp med (100%)
**Mem Phys: 16:** 58,039 **15:** 54,078 **16 MLR** 94.7% **/ 16 Admin Exp** N/A
**Enroll(000): Q3 17:** 9 **16:** 17 **15:** 61 **Med Exp PMPM:** $399
**Principal Investments:** Cash and equiv (97%), long-term bonds (3%)
**Provider Compensation ($000):** Contr fee ($107,858), FFS ($8,759), bonus arrang ($7,025), capitation ($1,657)
**Total Member Encounters:** Phys (138,720), non-phys (9,029)
**Group Affiliation:** UnitedHealth Group Incorporated
**Licensed in:** KY, OH
**Address:** OH020-3010 9200 WORTHINGTON RO, WESTERVILLE, OH 43082-8823
**Phone:** (614) 410-7000 **Dom State:** OH **Commenced Bus:** August 1985

| Data Date | Rating | RACR #1 | RACR #2 | Total Assets ($mil) | Capital ($mil) | Net Premium ($mil) | Net Income ($mil) |
|---|---|---|---|---|---|---|---|
| 9-17 | C | 19.25 | 16.04 | 79.3 | 68.7 | 30.2 | 3.4 |
| 9-16 | C | 2.54 | 2.12 | 113.2 | 82.8 | 60.4 | 3.5 |
| 2016 | C | 18.09 | 15.07 | 88.6 | 64.1 | 81.6 | 5.4 |
| 2015 | C | 2.43 | 2.02 | 177.5 | 78.5 | 682.6 | 37.7 |
| 2014 | B | 2.82 | 2.35 | 257.9 | 134.9 | 879.6 | 21.6 |
| 2013 | B | 2.22 | 1.85 | 286.3 | 126.6 | 1,041.1 | 3.9 |
| 2012 | B | 2.64 | 2.20 | 256.4 | 122.7 | 926.1 | 34.3 |

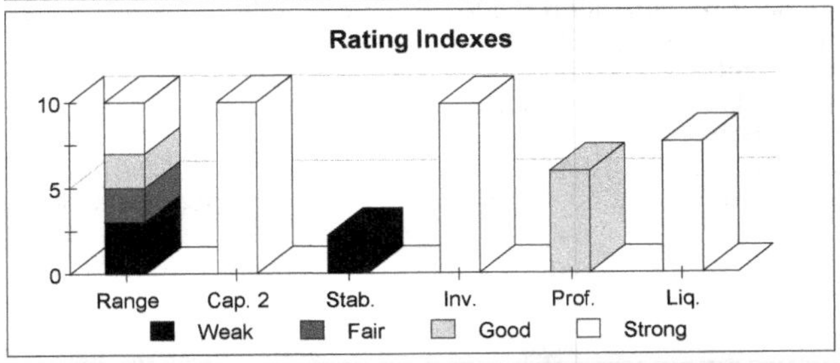


## UNITED HEALTHCARE OF THE MIDLANDS — B — Good

**Major Rating Factors:** Good liquidity (6.7 on a scale of 0 to 10) with sufficient resources (cash flows and marketable investments) to handle a spike in claims. Fair profitability index (4.9). Fair overall results on stability tests (4.9) based on an excessive 69% enrollment growth during the period. Rating is significantly influenced by the fair financial results of UnitedHealth Group Incorporated.
**Other Rating Factors:** Strong capitalization index (10.0) based on excellent current risk-adjusted capital (severe loss scenario). High quality investment portfolio (9.9).
**Principal Business:** Medicare (49%), Medicaid (33%), comp med (18%)
**Mem Phys: 16:** 39,583 **15:** 21,142 **16 MLR** 88.5% **/ 16 Admin Exp** N/A
**Enroll(000): Q3 17:** 273 **16:** 118 **15:** 70 **Med Exp PMPM:** $363
**Principal Investments:** Long-term bonds (51%), cash and equiv (49%)
**Provider Compensation ($000):** Contr fee ($417,745), FFS ($29,539), capitation ($14,481), bonus arrang ($4,427)
**Total Member Encounters:** Phys (1,270,284), non-phys (508,831)
**Group Affiliation:** UnitedHealth Group Incorporated
**Licensed in:** AL, AR, IL, IN, IA, KS, MO, NE
**Address:** 2717 NORTH 118TH STREET, OMAHA, NE 68164-9672
**Phone:** (402) 445-5600 **Dom State:** NE **Commenced Bus:** October 1984

| Data Date | Rating | RACR #1 | RACR #2 | Total Assets ($mil) | Capital ($mil) | Net Premium ($mil) | Net Income ($mil) |
|---|---|---|---|---|---|---|---|
| 9-17 | B | 4.59 | 3.83 | 790.1 | 152.9 | 1,889.1 | 87.2 |
| 9-16 | B | 1.81 | 1.51 | 161.6 | 27.0 | 429.4 | 3.4 |
| 2016 | B | 2.21 | 1.84 | 207.3 | 72.2 | 573.2 | -8.4 |
| 2015 | B+ | 1.75 | 1.46 | 90.9 | 26.0 | 286.4 | -11.6 |
| 2014 | B+ | 2.53 | 2.11 | 69.9 | 32.6 | 261.8 | 12.1 |
| 2013 | B+ | 2.92 | 2.43 | 65.8 | 30.0 | 207.0 | 9.8 |
| 2012 | B+ | 2.33 | 1.94 | 53.8 | 20.3 | 186.9 | 8.7 |

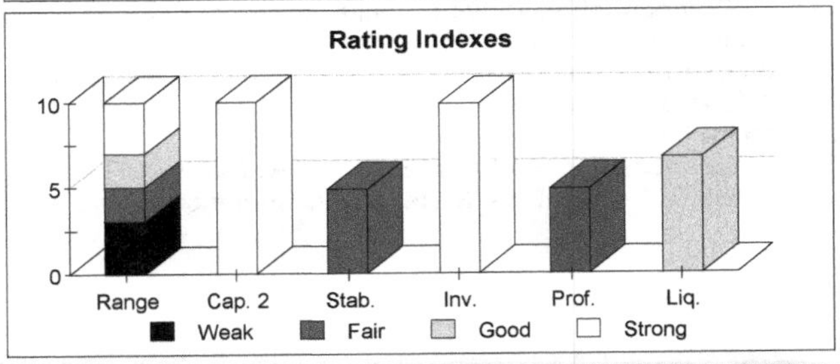


## UNITED HEALTHCARE OF THE MIDWEST INC — C+ — Fair

**Major Rating Factors:** Good overall results on stability tests (6.2 on a scale of 0 to 10) based on healthy premium and capital growth during 2016. Rating is significantly influenced by the fair financial results of UnitedHealth Group Incorporated. Weak liquidity (2.1) as a spike in claims may stretch capacity. Excellent profitability (8.7).
**Other Rating Factors:** Strong capitalization index (8.8) based on excellent current risk-adjusted capital (severe loss scenario). High quality investment portfolio (9.9).
**Principal Business:** Medicare (68%), Medicaid (29%), comp med (3%)
**Mem Phys: 16:** 79,536 **15:** 75,757 **16 MLR** 119.5% **/ 16 Admin Exp** N/A
**Enroll(000): Q3 17:** 292 **16:** 234 **15:** 196 **Med Exp PMPM:** $533
**Principal Investments:** Long-term bonds (67%), cash and equiv (33%)
**Provider Compensation ($000):** Contr fee ($1,236,113), capitation ($129,397), FFS ($93,437), bonus arrang ($41,023)
**Total Member Encounters:** Phys (2,759,769), non-phys (1,736,225)
**Group Affiliation:** UnitedHealth Group Incorporated
**Licensed in:** IL, KS, MO
**Address:** 13655 RIVERPORT DRIVE MO050-10, MARYLAND HEIGHTS, MO 63043
**Phone:** (314) 592-7000 **Dom State:** MO **Commenced Bus:** August 1985

| Data Date | Rating | RACR #1 | RACR #2 | Total Assets ($mil) | Capital ($mil) | Net Premium ($mil) | Net Income ($mil) |
|---|---|---|---|---|---|---|---|
| 9-17 | C+ | 2.80 | 2.33 | 417.1 | 178.1 | 368.6 | -2.8 |
| 9-16 | C+ | 3.31 | 2.76 | 570.7 | 180.8 | 957.2 | 37.1 |
| 2016 | C+ | 2.82 | 2.35 | 490.5 | 179.6 | 1,275.7 | 56.5 |
| 2015 | C+ | 2.67 | 2.22 | 408.7 | 144.1 | 1,025.2 | 14.0 |
| 2014 | C+ | 3.42 | 2.85 | 344.3 | 155.0 | 911.6 | 47.1 |
| 2013 | B- | 2.31 | 1.92 | 306.9 | 93.7 | 827.7 | 38.0 |
| 2012 | B | 3.77 | 3.14 | 198.3 | 88.8 | 536.6 | 38.9 |

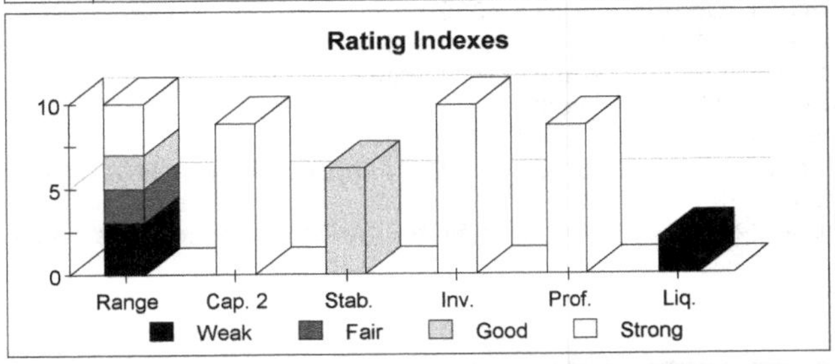

## UNITED HEALTHCARE OF TX INC — B- — Good

**Major Rating Factors:** Fair overall results on stability tests (4.5 on a scale of 0 to 10) in spite of healthy premium and capital growth during 2016 but an excessive 142% enrollment growth during the period. Rating is significantly influenced by the fair financial results of UnitedHealth Group Incorporated. Excellent profitability (7.5). Strong capitalization index (9.4) based on excellent current risk-adjusted capital (severe loss scenario).
**Other Rating Factors:** High quality investment portfolio (9.9). Excellent liquidity (7.3) with ample operational cash flow and liquid investments.
**Principal Business:** Comp med (100%)
**Mem Phys: 16:** 63,392 **15:** 58,993 **16 MLR** 75.5% **/ 16 Admin Exp** N/A
**Enroll(000): Q3 17:** 27 **16:** 23 **15:** 9 **Med Exp PMPM:** $254
**Principal Investments:** Cash and equiv (100%)
**Provider Compensation ($000):** Contr fee ($50,770), FFS ($5,569), capitation ($40), bonus arrang ($24)
**Total Member Encounters:** Phys (137,928), non-phys (3,853)
**Group Affiliation:** UnitedHealth Group Incorporated
**Licensed in:** TX
**Address:** 1311 W PRESIDENT GEORGE BUSH H, RICHARDSON, TX 75080
**Phone:** (952) 936-1300 **Dom State:** TX **Commenced Bus:** August 1985

| Data Date | Rating | RACR #1 | RACR #2 | Total Assets ($mil) | Capital ($mil) | Net Premium ($mil) | Net Income ($mil) |
|---|---|---|---|---|---|---|---|
| 9-17 | B- | 3.26 | 2.72 | 39.8 | 15.9 | 83.0 | 9.3 |
| 9-16 | C+ | 3.97 | 3.31 | 25.7 | 10.3 | 58.9 | 4.6 |
| 2016 | B- | 2.18 | 1.82 | 29.7 | 10.6 | 80.2 | 5.4 |
| 2015 | C | 2.17 | 1.81 | 14.4 | 5.5 | 27.9 | -1.1 |
| 2014 | C | 4.92 | 4.10 | 6.5 | 6.1 | 0.8 | 0.1 |
| 2013 | C | 5.09 | 4.24 | 6.1 | 6.0 | 0.8 | 0.2 |
| 2012 | C | 5.18 | 4.32 | 6.1 | 5.8 | 2.0 | 0.6 |

Rating Indexes

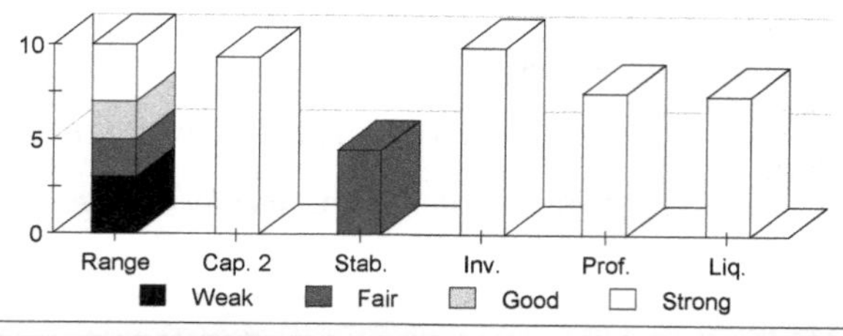


## UNITED HEALTHCARE OF UTAH — B — Good

**Major Rating Factors:** Good overall results on stability tests (5.5 on a scale of 0 to 10). Rating is significantly influenced by the fair financial results of UnitedHealth Group Incorporated. Fair profitability index (4.6). Strong capitalization index (8.8) based on excellent current risk-adjusted capital (severe loss scenario).
**Other Rating Factors:** High quality investment portfolio (9.9). Excellent liquidity (6.9) with sufficient resources (cash flows and marketable investments) to handle a spike in claims.
**Principal Business:** Medicare (97%), comp med (3%)
**Mem Phys: 16:** 9,242 **15:** 8,704 **16 MLR** 86.4% **/ 16 Admin Exp** N/A
**Enroll(000): Q3 17:** 70 **16:** 62 **15:** 54 **Med Exp PMPM:** $619
**Principal Investments:** Long-term bonds (75%), cash and equiv (25%)
**Provider Compensation ($000):** Capitation ($399,911), contr fee ($32,802), FFS ($4,364), bonus arrang ($77)
**Total Member Encounters:** Phys (942,972), non-phys (444,536)
**Group Affiliation:** UnitedHealth Group Incorporated
**Licensed in:** UT
**Address:** 2525 LAKE PARK BOULEVARD, SALT LAKE CITY, UT 84120
**Phone:** (952) 936-1300 **Dom State:** UT **Commenced Bus:** March 1984

| Data Date | Rating | RACR #1 | RACR #2 | Total Assets ($mil) | Capital ($mil) | Net Premium ($mil) | Net Income ($mil) |
|---|---|---|---|---|---|---|---|
| 9-17 | B | 2.77 | 2.31 | 195.6 | 56.8 | 496.6 | 3.1 |
| 9-16 | B- | 3.27 | 2.72 | 150.3 | 54.7 | 388.9 | 3.6 |
| 2016 | B | 2.68 | 2.24 | 121.8 | 55.0 | 514.7 | 3.5 |
| 2015 | B- | 3.55 | 2.96 | 110.1 | 59.9 | 443.6 | 31.4 |
| 2014 | C | 2.07 | 1.73 | 110.5 | 38.3 | 343.1 | -21.6 |
| 2013 | B- | 2.56 | 2.14 | 107.4 | 48.8 | 360.5 | 11.3 |
| 2012 | C+ | 2.08 | 1.74 | 96.4 | 35.7 | 294.0 | -2.3 |

Rating Indexes

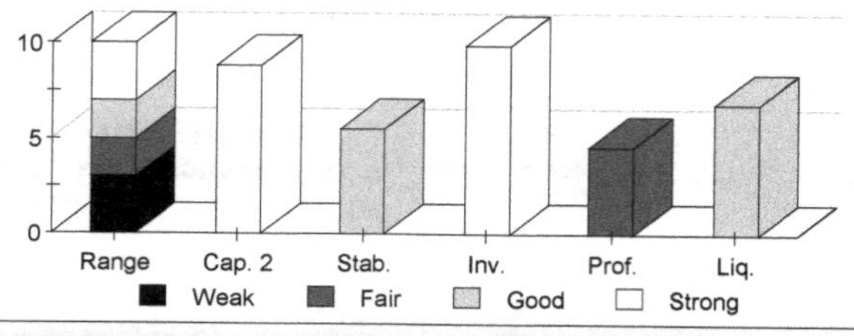


## UNITED HEALTHCARE OF WISCONSIN INC — B — Good

**Major Rating Factors:** Good liquidity (6.9 on a scale of 0 to 10) with sufficient resources (cash flows and marketable investments) to handle a spike in claims. Excellent profitability (10.0). Strong capitalization index (9.4) based on excellent current risk-adjusted capital (severe loss scenario).
**Other Rating Factors:** High quality investment portfolio (9.9). Excellent overall results on stability tests (7.4) based on healthy premium and capital growth during 2016. Rating is significantly influenced by the fair financial results of UnitedHealth Group Incorporated.
**Principal Business:** Medicare (88%), Medicaid (8%), comp med (4%)
**Mem Phys: 16:** 36,575 **15:** 29,138 **16 MLR** 78.4% **/ 16 Admin Exp** N/A
**Enroll(000): Q3 17:** 613 **16:** 536 **15:** 276 **Med Exp PMPM:** $557
**Principal Investments:** Long-term bonds (75%), cash and equiv (25%)
**Provider Compensation ($000):** Contr fee ($2,715,705), FFS ($215,763), capitation ($100,330), bonus arrang ($40,995)
**Total Member Encounters:** Phys (8,689,087), non-phys (3,749,641)
**Group Affiliation:** UnitedHealth Group Incorporated
**Licensed in:** AZ, IL, IA, KY, NC, OH, TN, VA, WI
**Address:** WI030-1000 10701 WEST RESEARCH, WAUWATOSA, WI 53226-0649
**Phone:** (414) 443-4000 **Dom State:** WI **Commenced Bus:** June 1986

| Data Date | Rating | RACR #1 | RACR #2 | Total Assets ($mil) | Capital ($mil) | Net Premium ($mil) | Net Income ($mil) |
|---|---|---|---|---|---|---|---|
| 9-17 | B | 3.26 | 2.72 | 2,191.8 | 656.2 | 4,093.7 | 248.8 |
| 9-16 | B | 4.57 | 3.81 | 1,445.3 | 331.3 | 3,350.2 | 141.0 |
| 2016 | B | 2.26 | 1.89 | 1,223.8 | 452.6 | 4,484.3 | 199.9 |
| 2015 | B | 3.76 | 3.13 | 489.4 | 270.3 | 1,502.6 | 53.6 |
| 2014 | B | 2.62 | 2.19 | 373.2 | 171.1 | 1,433.4 | 31.0 |
| 2013 | B | 2.52 | 2.10 | 346.3 | 157.0 | 1,328.8 | 20.4 |
| 2012 | B | 2.22 | 1.85 | 323.3 | 139.7 | 1,430.7 | 27.1 |

Rating Indexes

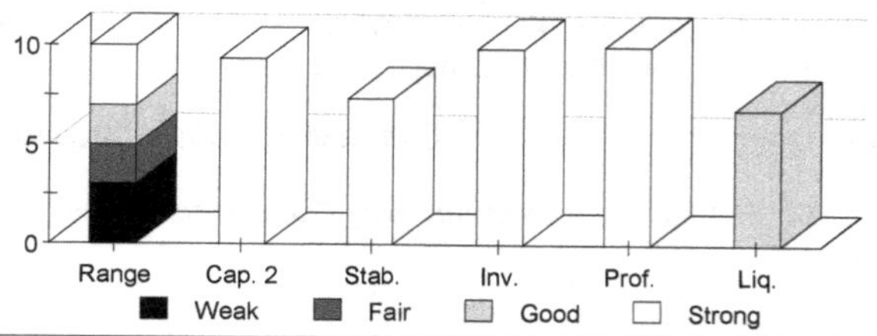

## UNITED OF OMAHA LIFE INSURANCE COMPANY — B — Good

**Major Rating Factors:** Good quality investment portfolio (5.1 on a scale of 0 to 10) despite large holdings of BBB rated bonds in addition to moderate junk bond exposure. Exposure to mortgages is significant, but the mortgage default rate has been low. Good liquidity (6.0) with sufficient resources to cover a large increase in policy surrenders. Good overall results on stability tests (6.0) good operational trends, good risk adjusted capital for prior years and excellent risk diversification.
**Other Rating Factors:** Strong capitalization (7.1) based on excellent risk adjusted capital (severe loss scenario). Excellent profitability (7.6) despite modest operating losses during 2012.
**Principal Business:** Individual life insurance (34%), individual health insurance (25%), group retirement contracts (14%), group health insurance (12%), and other lines (15%).
**Principal Investments:** NonCMO investment grade bonds (56%), CMOs and structured securities (23%), mortgages in good standing (12%), noninv. grade bonds (4%), and misc. investments (3%).
**Investments in Affiliates:** 1%
**Group Affiliation:** Mutual Of Omaha Group
**Licensed in:** All states except NY
**Commenced Business:** November 1926
**Address:** MUTUAL OF OMAHA PLAZA, OMAHA, NE 68175
**Phone:** (402) 342-7600 **Domicile State:** NE **NAIC Code:** 69868

| Data Date | Rating | RACR #1 | RACR #2 | Total Assets ($mil) | Capital ($mil) | Net Premium ($mil) | Net Income ($mil) |
|---|---|---|---|---|---|---|---|
| 9-17 | B | 1.85 | 1.05 | 22,326.3 | 1,460.5 | 2,913.5 | 55.3 |
| 9-16 | B | 1.73 | 0.99 | 20,497.8 | 1,338.1 | 2,901.3 | -7.4 |
| 2016 | B | 1.89 | 1.06 | 20,698.2 | 1,429.5 | 3,692.0 | 9.0 |
| 2015 | B | 1.90 | 1.11 | 19,622.5 | 1,441.7 | 3,572.3 | 153.6 |
| 2014 | B | 1.95 | 1.15 | 18,786.7 | 1,422.7 | 2,712.4 | 164.4 |
| 2013 | B | 1.71 | 1.00 | 18,122.5 | 1,226.9 | 3,428.2 | 69.9 |
| 2012 | B | 1.42 | 0.83 | 16,698.1 | 1,027.2 | 3,464.0 | -31.5 |

**Adverse Trends in Operations**

Change in premium mix from 2014 to 2015 (5%)
Increase in policy surrenders from 2013 to 2014 (30%)
Change in premium mix from 2013 to 2014 (5.1%)
Decrease in premium volume from 2013 to 2014 (21%)
Decrease in premium volume from 2012 to 2013 (1%)

## UNITED WORLD LIFE INSURANCE COMPANY * — B+ — Good

**Major Rating Factors:** Good overall results on stability tests (6.7 on a scale of 0 to 10). Stability strengths include excellent operational trends and excellent risk diversification. Good overall profitability (6.1). Good liquidity (6.9) with sufficient resources to handle a spike in claims.
**Other Rating Factors:** Strong capitalization (8.8) based on excellent risk adjusted capital (severe loss scenario). High quality investment portfolio (7.6).
**Principal Business:** Individual health insurance (100%).
**Principal Investments:** NonCMO investment grade bonds (67%), CMOs and structured securities (25%), cash (5%), noninv. grade bonds (2%), and policy loans (1%).
**Investments in Affiliates:** None
**Group Affiliation:** Mutual Of Omaha Group
**Licensed in:** All states except CT, NY, PR
**Commenced Business:** April 1970
**Address:** MUTUAL OF OMAHA PLAZA, OMAHA, NE 68175
**Phone:** (402) 342-7600 **Domicile State:** NE **NAIC Code:** 72850

| Data Date | Rating | RACR #1 | RACR #2 | Total Assets ($mil) | Capital ($mil) | Net Premium ($mil) | Net Income ($mil) |
|---|---|---|---|---|---|---|---|
| 9-17 | B+ | 5.16 | 2.18 | 123.8 | 50.8 | 0.9 | 0.5 |
| 9-16 | B+ | 4.84 | 2.05 | 121.3 | 49.9 | 0.9 | 2.0 |
| 2016 | B+ | 5.42 | 2.30 | 119.8 | 51.4 | 1.3 | 4.8 |
| 2015 | B+ | 4.92 | 2.09 | 123.7 | 48.9 | 1.4 | -0.5 |
| 2014 | B+ | 4.62 | 1.95 | 119.4 | 49.4 | 1.5 | 1.6 |
| 2013 | B+ | 4.19 | 1.76 | 114.9 | 48.6 | 1.6 | 1.2 |
| 2012 | B+ | 3.89 | 1.63 | 103.1 | 47.3 | 1.7 | 0.1 |

**Adverse Trends in Operations**

Decrease in premium volume from 2015 to 2016 (5%)
Decrease in asset base during 2016 (3%)
Increase in policy surrenders from 2014 to 2015 (38%)
Decrease in premium volume from 2012 to 2013 (7%)
Change in asset mix during 2013 (4.1%)

## UNITEDHEALTHCARE BENEFITS OF TEXAS — B- — Good

**Major Rating Factors:** Fair overall results on stability tests (3.2 on a scale of 0 to 10). Rating is significantly influenced by the fair financial results of UnitedHealth Group Incorporated. Excellent profitability (7.8). Strong capitalization index (7.2) based on excellent current risk-adjusted capital (severe loss scenario).
**Other Rating Factors:** High quality investment portfolio (9.9). Excellent liquidity (6.9) with sufficient resources (cash flows and marketable investments) to handle a spike in claims.
**Principal Business:** Medicare (100%)
**Mem Phys: 16:** 68,228 **15:** 63,548 **16 MLR** 86.9% **/ 16 Admin Exp** N/A
**Enroll(000): Q3 17:** 228 **16:** 214 **15:** 205 **Med Exp PMPM:** $933
**Principal Investments:** Long-term bonds (70%), cash and equiv (30%)
**Provider Compensation ($000):** Capitation ($1,800,133), contr fee ($582,375), bonus arrang ($21,660), FFS ($15,409)
**Total Member Encounters:** Phys (477,393), non-phys (49,859)
**Group Affiliation:** UnitedHealth Group Incorporated
**Licensed in:** TX
**Address:** 1311 W PRESIDENT GEORGE BUSH H, RICHARDSON, TX 75080
**Phone:** (952) 936-1300 **Dom State:** TX **Commenced Bus:** July 1986

| Data Date | Rating | RACR #1 | RACR #2 | Total Assets ($mil) | Capital ($mil) | Net Premium ($mil) | Net Income ($mil) |
|---|---|---|---|---|---|---|---|
| 9-17 | B- | 1.55 | 1.29 | 807.3 | 150.0 | 2,333.7 | 49.6 |
| 9-16 | B | 2.21 | 1.84 | 640.5 | 210.6 | 2,040.3 | 19.2 |
| 2016 | B | 2.28 | 1.90 | 403.3 | 226.9 | 2,727.3 | 35.8 |
| 2015 | B | 2.51 | 2.09 | 459.2 | 241.3 | 2,609.2 | 84.5 |
| 2014 | B+ | 3.06 | 2.55 | 530.8 | 309.5 | 2,482.3 | 144.1 |
| 2013 | B+ | 3.11 | 2.59 | 599.2 | 315.8 | 2,412.0 | 151.4 |
| 2012 | B+ | 2.80 | 2.34 | 585.8 | 242.3 | 2,274.1 | 189.2 |

**Rating Indexes**

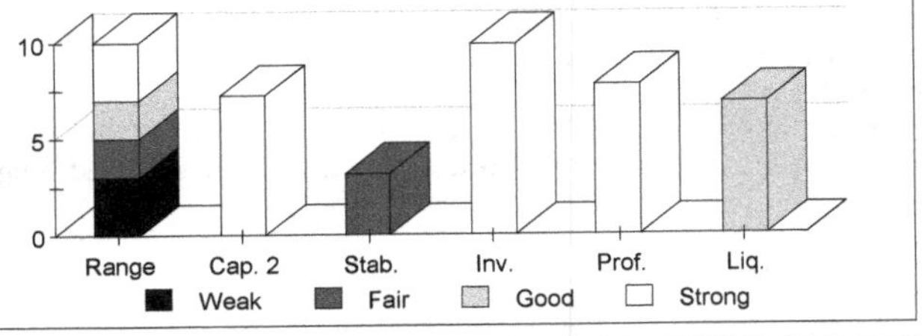

## UNITEDHEALTHCARE BENEFITS PLAN OF CA — C — Fair

**Major Rating Factors:** Weak profitability index (0.1 on a scale of 0 to 10). Weak overall results on stability tests (1.7). Rating is significantly influenced by the fair financial results of UnitedHealth Group Inc. Strong capitalization index (10.0) based on excellent current risk-adjusted capital (severe loss scenario).
**Other Rating Factors:** Excellent liquidity (7.0) with ample operational cash flow and liquid investments.
**Principal Business:** Managed care (100%)
**Mem Phys: 16:** N/A **15:** N/A **16 MLR** 135.3% **/ 16 Admin Exp** N/A
**Enroll(000): Q3 17:** N/A **16:** 1 **15:** N/A **Med Exp PMPM:** $718
**Principal Investments ($000):** Cash and equiv ($2,852)
**Provider Compensation ($000):** None
**Total Member Encounters:** N/A
**Group Affiliation:** UnitedHealth Group Inc
**Licensed in:** CA
**Address:** 2480 Natomas Park Dr Suite 150, Sacramento, CA 95833
**Phone:** (916) 286-6562 **Dom State:** CA **Commenced Bus:** August 2015

| Data Date | Rating | RACR #1 | RACR #2 | Total Assets ($mil) | Capital ($mil) | Net Premium ($mil) | Net Income ($mil) |
|---|---|---|---|---|---|---|---|
| 9-17 | C | 5.84 | 3.62 | 3.5 | 3.4 | -0.1 | 0.6 |
| 9-16 | U | N/A | N/A | 6.3 | 3.1 | 5.0 | -1.6 |
| 2016 | C | 4.82 | 2.99 | 5.1 | 2.8 | 6.7 | -1.9 |
| 2015 | N/A | N/A | N/A | 5.3 | 4.7 | N/A | -0.3 |
| 2014 | N/A | N/A | N/A | N/A | N/A | N/A | N/A |
| 2013 | N/A | N/A | N/A | N/A | N/A | N/A | N/A |
| 2012 | N/A | N/A | N/A | N/A | N/A | N/A | N/A |

**Rating Indexes**

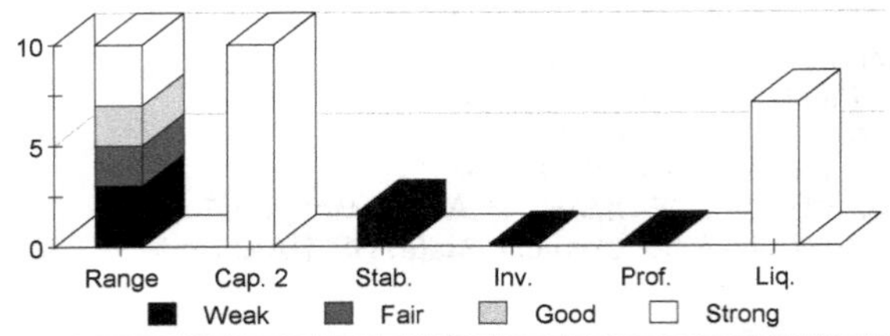


## UNITEDHEALTHCARE COMMUNITY PLAN INC — B — Good

**Major Rating Factors:** Good liquidity (6.9 on a scale of 0 to 10) with sufficient resources (cash flows and marketable investments) to handle a spike in claims. Excellent profitability (7.0). Strong capitalization index (8.5) based on excellent current risk-adjusted capital (severe loss scenario).
**Other Rating Factors:** High quality investment portfolio (9.9). Excellent overall results on stability tests (7.0). Rating is significantly influenced by the fair financial results of UnitedHealth Group Incorporated.
**Principal Business:** Medicaid (99%), comp med (1%)
**Mem Phys: 16:** 6,800 **15:** 6,469 **16 MLR** 80.1% **/ 16 Admin Exp** N/A
**Enroll(000): Q3 17:** 254 **16:** 259 **15:** 261 **Med Exp PMPM:** $318
**Principal Investments:** Cash and equiv (69%), long-term bonds (31%)
**Provider Compensation ($000):** Contr fee ($610,660), capitation ($311,909), FFS ($62,746), bonus arrang ($4,331)
**Total Member Encounters:** Phys (2,274,930), non-phys (1,244,352)
**Group Affiliation:** UnitedHealth Group Incorporated
**Licensed in:** MI
**Address:** 26957 NORTHWESTERN HIGHWAY SUI, SOUTHFIELD, MI 48033
**Phone:** (248) 559-5656 **Dom State:** MI **Commenced Bus:** October 1994

| Data Date | Rating | RACR #1 | RACR #2 | Total Assets ($mil) | Capital ($mil) | Net Premium ($mil) | Net Income ($mil) |
|---|---|---|---|---|---|---|---|
| 9-17 | B | 2.58 | 2.15 | 301.2 | 132.8 | 843.6 | 11.7 |
| 9-16 | B | 2.38 | 1.99 | 287.4 | 121.6 | 942.2 | 26.9 |
| 2016 | B | 2.38 | 1.98 | 289.8 | 122.2 | 1,242.1 | 26.8 |
| 2015 | B | 1.89 | 1.58 | 282.9 | 95.8 | 1,232.2 | 44.2 |
| 2014 | B | 2.10 | 1.75 | 250.8 | 104.6 | 1,090.8 | 30.4 |
| 2013 | B | 1.71 | 1.43 | 213.4 | 76.0 | 897.8 | -3.2 |
| 2012 | B | 1.82 | 1.52 | 175.6 | 70.7 | 875.4 | 4.2 |

**Rating Indexes**

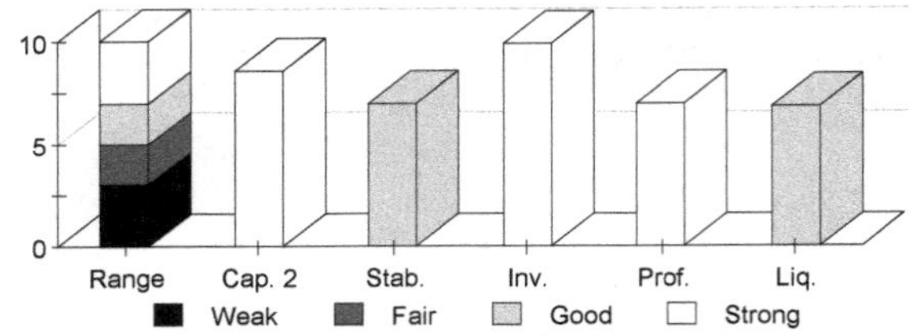


## UNITEDHEALTHCARE COMMUNITY PLAN TX * — B+ — Good

**Major Rating Factors:** Good liquidity (5.6 on a scale of 0 to 10) with sufficient resources (cash flows and marketable investments) to handle a spike in claims. Excellent profitability (8.5). Strong capitalization index (7.6) based on excellent current risk-adjusted capital (severe loss scenario).
**Other Rating Factors:** High quality investment portfolio (9.4). Excellent overall results on stability tests (7.2) based on steady enrollment growth, averaging 6% over the past five years. Rating is significantly influenced by the fair financial results of UnitedHealth Group Incorporated.
**Principal Business:** Medicaid (75%), Medicare (24%), comp med (1%)
**Mem Phys: 16:** 54,660 **15:** 48,834 **16 MLR** 88.4% **/ 16 Admin Exp** N/A
**Enroll(000): Q3 17:** 257 **16:** 255 **15:** 241 **Med Exp PMPM:** $701
**Principal Investments:** Long-term bonds (95%), cash and equiv (5%)
**Provider Compensation ($000):** Contr fee ($1,897,319), FFS ($154,455), capitation ($16,211), bonus arrang ($2,969)
**Total Member Encounters:** Phys (2,719,594), non-phys (2,805,107)
**Group Affiliation:** UnitedHealth Group Incorporated
**Licensed in:** TX
**Address:** 14141 S W FREEWAY, SUGAR LAND, TX 77478
**Phone:** (832) 500-6437 **Dom State:** TX **Commenced Bus:** August 2001

| Data Date | Rating | RACR #1 | RACR #2 | Total Assets ($mil) | Capital ($mil) | Net Premium ($mil) | Net Income ($mil) |
|---|---|---|---|---|---|---|---|
| 9-17 | B+ | 1.87 | 1.56 | 614.6 | 240.2 | 1,722.7 | 22.1 |
| 9-16 | B+ | 2.03 | 1.69 | 638.1 | 205.9 | 1,774.8 | 23.8 |
| 2016 | B+ | 1.72 | 1.43 | 549.9 | 220.1 | 2,369.4 | 33.8 |
| 2015 | B+ | 2.25 | 1.88 | 571.4 | 229.7 | 2,072.5 | 73.4 |
| 2014 | B+ | 2.40 | 2.00 | 411.3 | 187.5 | 1,546.0 | 43.5 |
| 2013 | B+ | 2.24 | 1.87 | 373.4 | 160.7 | 1,454.2 | 44.8 |
| 2012 | B+ | 1.85 | 1.54 | 287.4 | 115.8 | 1,185.7 | 8.8 |

**Rating Indexes**

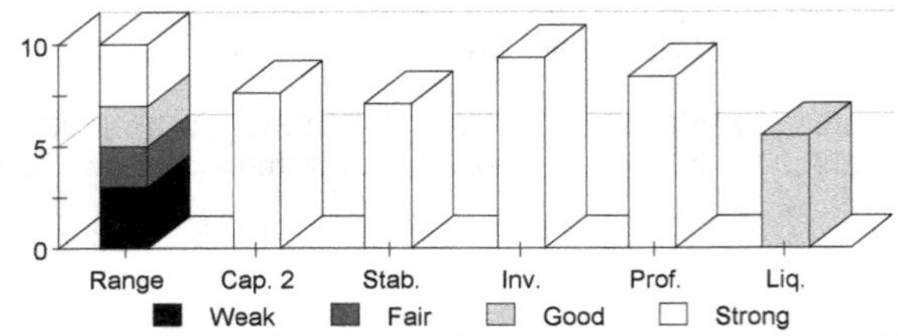

## UNITEDHEALTHCARE COMMUNITYPLAN OHIO B Good

**Major Rating Factors:** Good liquidity (6.7 on a scale of 0 to 10) with sufficient resources (cash flows and marketable investments) to handle a spike in claims. Excellent profitability (9.0). Strong capitalization (8.3) based on excellent current risk-adjusted capital (severe loss scenario).
**Other Rating Factors:** High quality investment portfolio (9.9).
**Principal Business:** Medicaid (100%)
**Mem Phys: 16:** 45,631 **15:** 42,450 **16 MLR** 82.5% **/ 16 Admin Exp** N/A
**Enroll(000): Q3 17:** 316 **16:** 294 **15:** 291 **Med Exp PMPM:** $479
**Principal Investments:** Long-term bonds (77%), cash and equiv (23%)
**Provider Compensation ($000):** Contr fee ($1,488,743), FFS ($116,187), capitation ($97,782), bonus arrang ($924)
**Total Member Encounters:** Phys (3,043,264), non-phys (2,261,368)
**Group Affiliation:** UnitedHealth Group Incorporated
**Licensed in:** OH
**Address:** 9200 WORTHINGTON Rd OH020-1000, WESTERVILLE, OH 43082
**Phone:** (952) 979-6171 **Dom State:** OH **Commenced Bus:** October 2005

| Data Date | Rating | RACR #1 | RACR #2 | Total Assets ($mil) | Capital ($mil) | Net Premium ($mil) | Net Income ($mil) |
|---|---|---|---|---|---|---|---|
| 9-17 | B | 2.37 | 1.98 | 500.0 | 245.4 | 1,652.8 | 50.9 |
| 9-16 | B | 2.02 | 1.68 | 425.0 | 200.7 | 1,534.4 | 3.7 |
| 2016 | B | 2.14 | 1.78 | 449.4 | 219.7 | 2,059.4 | 22.9 |
| 2015 | B | 2.27 | 1.89 | 430.3 | 226.9 | 2,145.2 | 120.5 |
| 2014 | B | 3.45 | 2.88 | 409.0 | 154.2 | 1,363.9 | 47.8 |
| 2013 | B | 4.11 | 3.43 | 242.6 | 130.9 | 667.4 | 22.2 |
| 2012 | B | 4.37 | 3.65 | 163.4 | 107.1 | 532.7 | 36.2 |

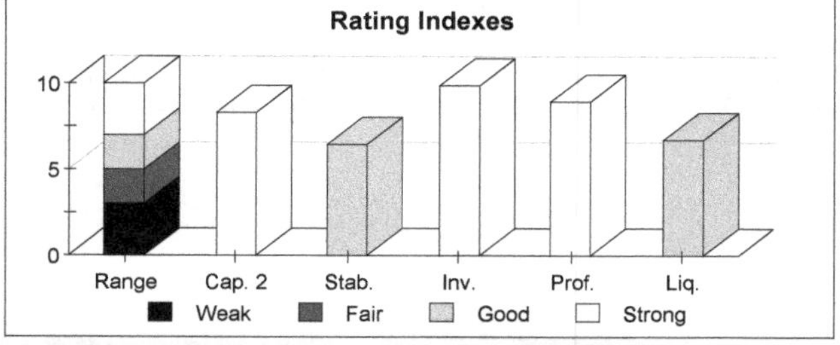


## UNITEDHEALTHCARE INS CO RIVER VALLEY B Good

**Major Rating Factors:** Good overall profitability index (5.3 on a scale of 0 to 10). Good liquidity (6.8) with sufficient resources (cash flows and marketable investments) to handle a spike in claims. Strong capitalization (8.3) based on excellent current risk-adjusted capital (severe loss scenario).
**Other Rating Factors:** High quality investment portfolio (9.9).
**Principal Business:** Comp med (100%)
**Mem Phys: 16:** 205,220 **15:** 177,949 **16 MLR** 81.2% **/ 16 Admin Exp** N/A
**Enroll(000): Q3 17:** 201 **16:** 209 **15:** 181 **Med Exp PMPM:** $303
**Principal Investments:** Long-term bonds (59%), cash and equiv (41%)
**Provider Compensation ($000):** Contr fee ($668,258), FFS ($42,056), capitation ($2,388), bonus arrang ($209)
**Total Member Encounters:** Phys (774,046), non-phys (142,894)
**Group Affiliation:** UnitedHealth Group Incorporated
**Licensed in:** AR, GA, IL, IA, LA, NC, OH, SC, TN, VA
**Address:** 1300 RIVER Dr Ste 200, MOLINE, IL 61265
**Phone:** (309) 736-4600 **Dom State:** IL **Commenced Bus:** December 2004

| Data Date | Rating | RACR #1 | RACR #2 | Total Assets ($mil) | Capital ($mil) | Net Premium ($mil) | Net Income ($mil) |
|---|---|---|---|---|---|---|---|
| 9-17 | B | 2.43 | 2.02 | 281.3 | 115.1 | 732.7 | 22.8 |
| 9-16 | B | 2.61 | 2.17 | 242.0 | 103.3 | 666.8 | 10.7 |
| 2016 | B | 1.97 | 1.64 | 261.9 | 92.1 | 896.7 | 0.8 |
| 2015 | B | 2.36 | 1.97 | 219.5 | 93.1 | 722.6 | -12.2 |
| 2014 | B | 1.96 | 1.63 | 154.7 | 60.7 | 594.7 | 10.7 |
| 2013 | B | 2.15 | 1.79 | 115.5 | 50.8 | 443.3 | 14.6 |
| 2012 | B- | 2.11 | 1.75 | 89.4 | 37.4 | 327.8 | 8.4 |

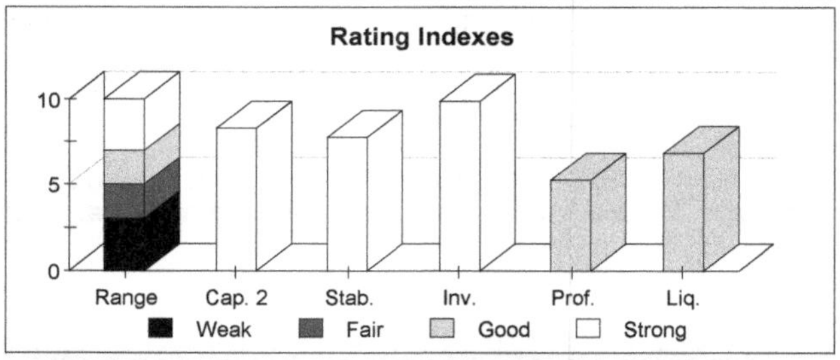


## UNITEDHEALTHCARE LIFE INSURANCE COMPANY C Fair

**Major Rating Factors:** Good overall capitalization (5.4 on a scale of 0 to 10) based on mixed results -- excessive policy leverage mitigated by excellent risk adjusted capital (severe loss scenario). However, capital levels have fluctuated somewhat during past years. Weak profitability (1.8). Excellent expense controls. Weak liquidity (0.5).
**Other Rating Factors:** Weak overall results on stability tests (2.5) including weak results on operational trends, negative cash flow from operations for 2016. High quality investment portfolio (8.5).
**Principal Business:** Individual health insurance (62%) and group health insurance (38%).
**Principal Investments:** NonCMO investment grade bonds (75%), CMOs and structured securities (24%), and cash (1%).
**Investments in Affiliates:** None
**Group Affiliation:** UnitedHealth Group Inc
**Licensed in:** All states except MA, NY, PR
**Commenced Business:** December 1982
**Address:** 3100 AMS BOULEVARD, GREEN BAY, WI 54313
**Phone:** (800) 232-5432 **Domicile State:** WI **NAIC Code:** 97179

| Data Date | Rating | RACR #1 | RACR #2 | Total Assets ($mil) | Capital ($mil) | Net Premium ($mil) | Net Income ($mil) |
|---|---|---|---|---|---|---|---|
| 9-17 | C | 1.97 | 1.56 | 222.9 | 136.0 | 328.9 | 30.8 |
| 9-16 | C | 1.35 | 1.07 | 484.7 | 150.3 | 727.0 | -25.5 |
| 2016 | C | 1.44 | 1.14 | 508.1 | 167.5 | 960.8 | -9.0 |
| 2015 | C | 1.61 | 1.28 | 488.4 | 137.1 | 700.9 | -143.0 |
| 2014 | B | 1.51 | 1.23 | 132.6 | 41.4 | 245.0 | -15.4 |
| 2013 | B | 2.11 | 1.69 | 57.0 | 29.3 | 84.8 | 7.3 |
| 2012 | B | 1.50 | 1.21 | 49.0 | 23.8 | 99.9 | 8.9 |

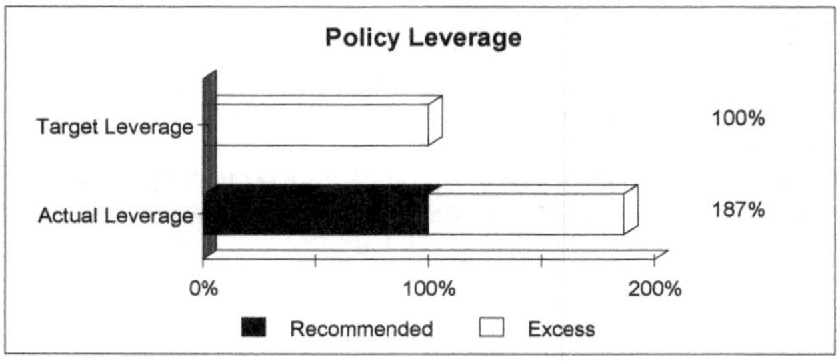

## UNITEDHEALTHCARE OF NEW MEXICO INC — E — Very Weak

**Major Rating Factors:** Excellent profitability (8.9 on a scale of 0 to 10). Strong capitalization (10.0) based on excellent current risk-adjusted capital (severe loss scenario). High quality investment portfolio (9.9).
**Other Rating Factors:** Excellent liquidity (7.1) with ample operational cash flow and liquid investments.
**Principal Business:** Medicaid (100%)
**Mem Phys: 16:** 5,985 **15:** 6,671 **16 MLR** 78.1% **/ 16 Admin Exp** N/A
**Enroll(000): Q3 17:** 87 **16:** 89 **15:** 87 **Med Exp PMPM:** $643
**Principal Investments:** Cash and equiv (57%), long-term bonds (43%)
**Provider Compensation ($000):** Contr fee ($643,497), FFS ($47,341), capitation ($20,637), bonus arrang ($117)
**Total Member Encounters:** Phys (975,332), non-phys (1,291,136)
**Group Affiliation:** UnitedHealth Group Incorporated
**Licensed in:** NM
**Address:** 8220 SAN PEDRO NE Ste 300, ALBUQUERQUE, NM 87113
**Phone:** (505) 449-4131 **Dom State:** NM **Commenced Bus:** October 2008

| Data Date | Rating | RACR #1 | RACR #2 | Total Assets ($mil) | Capital ($mil) | Net Premium ($mil) | Net Income ($mil) |
|---|---|---|---|---|---|---|---|
| 9-17 | E | 22.57 | 18.81 | 289.8 | 154.5 | 582.1 | 21.1 |
| 9-16 | E | 11.44 | 9.53 | 369.0 | 156.0 | 674.4 | 29.6 |
| 2016 | E | 20.02 | 16.69 | 355.2 | 136.0 | 865.4 | 34.4 |
| 2015 | E | 9.31 | 7.75 | 362.6 | 126.2 | 918.9 | 14.9 |
| 2014 | E | 9.24 | 7.70 | 312.4 | 130.2 | 812.4 | 34.2 |
| 2013 | E | 4.81 | 4.01 | 172.5 | 115.6 | 457.1 | 16.0 |
| 2012 | E | 5.14 | 4.29 | 157.0 | 107.9 | 416.5 | 21.9 |

Rating Indexes

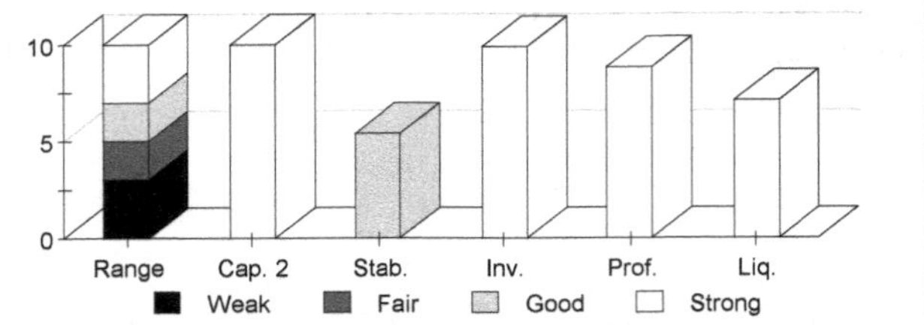


## UNITEDHEALTHCARE OF OKLAHOMA INC — B — Good

**Major Rating Factors:** Good overall results on stability tests (5.2 on a scale of 0 to 10). Rating is significantly influenced by the fair financial results of UnitedHealth Group Incorporated. Good liquidity (6.1) with sufficient resources (cash flows and marketable investments) to handle a spike in claims. Excellent profitability (8.4).
**Other Rating Factors:** Strong capitalization index (8.4) based on excellent current risk-adjusted capital (severe loss scenario). High quality investment portfolio (9.0).
**Principal Business:** Medicare (74%), comp med (26%)
**Mem Phys: 16:** 10,815 **15:** 10,060 **16 MLR** 85.6% **/ 16 Admin Exp** N/A
**Enroll(000): Q3 17:** 47 **16:** 46 **15:** 38 **Med Exp PMPM:** $636
**Principal Investments:** Long-term bonds (98%), cash and equiv (2%)
**Provider Compensation ($000):** Contr fee ($324,076), bonus arrang ($6,291), capitation ($4,397), FFS ($4,122)
**Total Member Encounters:** Phys (381,340), non-phys (45,078)
**Group Affiliation:** UnitedHealth Group Incorporated
**Licensed in:** OK
**Address:** 7666 E 61ST STREET SUITE 500, TULSA, OK 74133
**Phone:** (512) 347-2600 **Dom State:** OK **Commenced Bus:** September 1985

| Data Date | Rating | RACR #1 | RACR #2 | Total Assets ($mil) | Capital ($mil) | Net Premium ($mil) | Net Income ($mil) |
|---|---|---|---|---|---|---|---|
| 9-17 | B | 2.48 | 2.06 | 149.2 | 56.0 | 318.0 | 23.8 |
| 9-16 | B- | 2.27 | 1.89 | 132.0 | 42.4 | 303.4 | 5.3 |
| 2016 | B | 1.91 | 1.59 | 106.7 | 42.9 | 401.5 | 6.6 |
| 2015 | B- | 2.21 | 1.84 | 106.5 | 41.2 | 353.5 | 2.1 |
| 2014 | B | 2.72 | 2.27 | 94.4 | 53.5 | 371.5 | 16.5 |
| 2013 | B | 2.95 | 2.46 | 105.0 | 58.2 | 362.3 | 21.4 |
| 2012 | B | 2.26 | 1.88 | 97.3 | 48.8 | 418.7 | 25.8 |

Rating Indexes

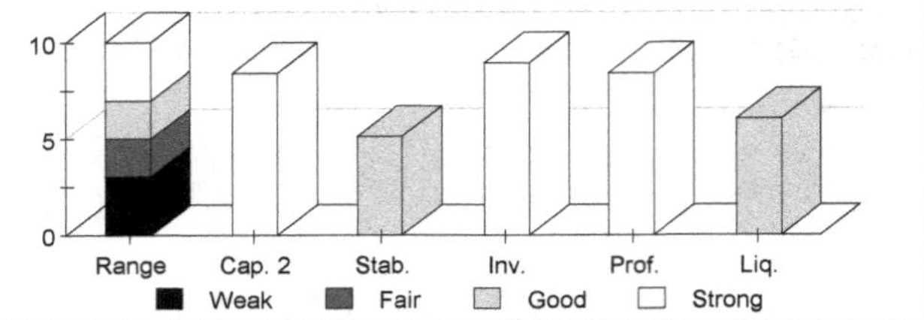


## UNITEDHEALTHCARE OF OREGON — B — Good

**Major Rating Factors:** Good liquidity (6.4 on a scale of 0 to 10) with sufficient resources (cash flows and marketable investments) to handle a spike in claims. Excellent profitability (9.6). Strong capitalization index (9.1) based on excellent current risk-adjusted capital (severe loss scenario).
**Other Rating Factors:** High quality investment portfolio (9.9). Excellent overall results on stability tests (7.1) based on healthy premium and capital growth during 2016. Rating is significantly influenced by the fair financial results of UnitedHealth Group Incorporated.
**Principal Business:** Medicare (100%)
**Mem Phys: 16:** 41,519 **15:** 37,054 **16 MLR** 84.2% **/ 16 Admin Exp** N/A
**Enroll(000): Q3 17:** 121 **16:** 97 **15:** 25 **Med Exp PMPM:** $724
**Principal Investments:** Long-term bonds (89%), cash and equiv (11%)
**Provider Compensation ($000):** Contr fee ($559,978), capitation ($166,041), FFS ($7,891), bonus arrang ($4,199)
**Total Member Encounters:** Phys (631,903), non-phys (87,639)
**Group Affiliation:** UnitedHealth Group Incorporated
**Licensed in:** OR, WA
**Address:** FIVE CENTERPOINTE DRIVE, LAKE OSWEGO, OR 97035
**Phone:** (952) 936-1300 **Dom State:** OR **Commenced Bus:** February 1987

| Data Date | Rating | RACR #1 | RACR #2 | Total Assets ($mil) | Capital ($mil) | Net Premium ($mil) | Net Income ($mil) |
|---|---|---|---|---|---|---|---|
| 9-17 | B | 3.05 | 2.54 | 449.3 | 147.7 | 922.6 | 21.4 |
| 9-16 | B- | 8.62 | 7.19 | 319.0 | 106.8 | 726.2 | 8.7 |
| 2016 | B | 2.22 | 1.85 | 260.1 | 107.4 | 975.1 | 4.1 |
| 2015 | B- | 7.21 | 6.01 | 126.9 | 89.1 | 256.0 | 8.4 |
| 2014 | B- | 3.51 | 2.93 | 64.2 | 38.6 | 229.1 | 12.6 |
| 2013 | B- | 3.32 | 2.77 | 56.4 | 32.9 | 202.0 | 12.4 |
| 2012 | C | 2.45 | 2.05 | 44.4 | 20.3 | 186.3 | 14.0 |

Rating Indexes

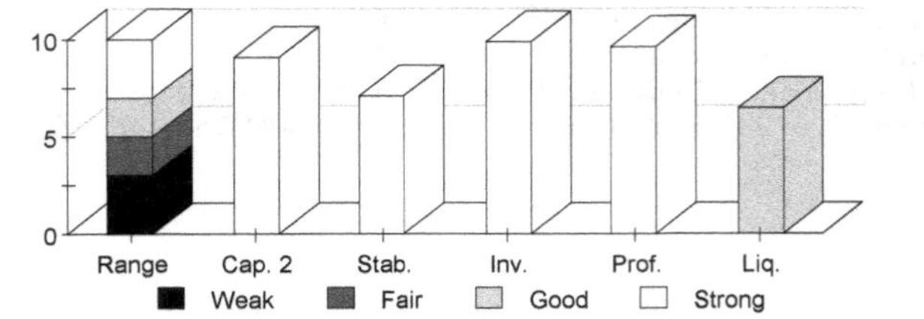

## UNITEDHEALTHCARE OF PENNSYLVANIA INC — B — Good

**Major Rating Factors:** Good overall results on stability tests (6.5 on a scale of 0 to 10) based on healthy premium and capital growth during 2016. Rating is significantly influenced by the fair financial results of UnitedHealth Group Incorporated. Excellent profitability (8.3). Strong capitalization index (10.0) based on excellent current risk-adjusted capital (severe loss scenario).
**Other Rating Factors:** High quality investment portfolio (9.9). Excellent liquidity (7.0) with ample operational cash flow and liquid investments.
**Principal Business:** Medicaid (90%), comp med (10%)
**Mem Phys: 16:** 45,974 **15:** 36,430 **16 MLR** 78.1% **/ 16 Admin Exp** N/A
**Enroll(000): Q3 17:** 262 **16:** 277 **15:** 275 **Med Exp PMPM:** $318
**Principal Investments:** Cash and equiv (50%), long-term bonds (50%)
**Provider Compensation ($000):** Contr fee ($868,379), FFS ($54,492), capitation ($31,482), bonus arrang ($1,092), other ($88,322)
**Total Member Encounters:** Phys (1,952,295), non-phys (988,812)
**Group Affiliation:** UnitedHealth Group Incorporated
**Licensed in:** PA
**Address:** 1001 BRINTON ROAD, PITTSBURGH, PA 15221
**Phone:** (412) 858-4000 **Dom State:** PA **Commenced Bus:** April 1996

| Data Date | Rating | RACR #1 | RACR #2 | Total Assets ($mil) | Capital ($mil) | Net Premium ($mil) | Net Income ($mil) |
|---|---|---|---|---|---|---|---|
| 9-17 | B | 8.02 | 6.68 | 418.4 | 181.3 | 923.3 | 39.4 |
| 9-16 | B | 2.64 | 2.20 | 453.5 | 150.7 | 996.3 | 6.7 |
| 2016 | B | 7.66 | 6.39 | 525.8 | 173.0 | 1,347.1 | 30.5 |
| 2015 | B | 2.51 | 2.09 | 428.2 | 143.0 | 1,123.0 | 8.8 |
| 2014 | B | 2.95 | 2.46 | 278.4 | 145.0 | 919.9 | 10.1 |
| 2013 | B | 2.58 | 2.15 | 279.8 | 148.4 | 1,101.8 | 12.3 |
| 2012 | B | 2.32 | 1.93 | 282.4 | 135.3 | 1,160.9 | 16.8 |

**Rating Indexes**

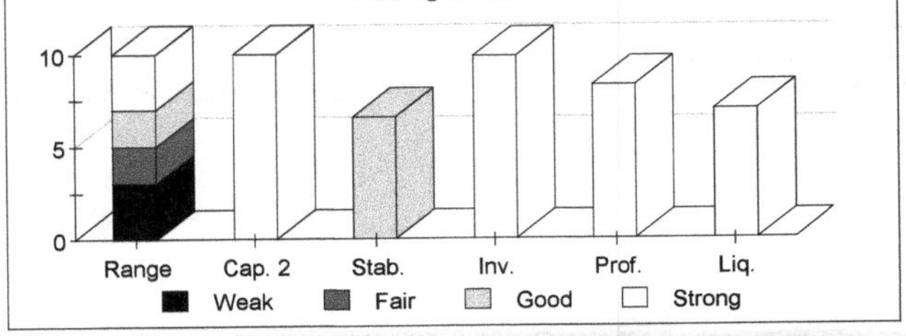


## UNITEDHEALTHCARE OF WASHINGTON INC — C — Fair

**Major Rating Factors:** Fair profitability index (4.2 on a scale of 0 to 10). Good liquidity (6.8) with sufficient resources (cash flows and marketable investments) to handle a spike in claims. Strong capitalization (9.1) based on excellent current risk-adjusted capital (severe loss scenario).
**Other Rating Factors:** High quality investment portfolio (9.2).
**Principal Business:** Medicaid (80%), comp med (20%)
**Mem Phys: 16:** 31,641 **15:** 31,497 **16 MLR** 84.7% **/ 16 Admin Exp** N/A
**Enroll(000): Q3 17:** 267 **16:** 271 **15:** 300 **Med Exp PMPM:** $283
**Principal Investments:** Long-term bonds (80%), cash and equiv (20%)
**Provider Compensation ($000):** Contr fee ($777,993), capitation ($82,493), FFS ($36,147), bonus arrang ($7,531)
**Total Member Encounters:** Phys (1,794,236), non-phys (800,788)
**Group Affiliation:** UnitedHealth Group Incorporated
**Licensed in:** WA
**Address:** 7525 SE 24TH Ste 200, MERCER ISLAND, WA 98040
**Phone:** (952) 936-1300 **Dom State:** WA **Commenced Bus:** December 1986

| Data Date | Rating | RACR #1 | RACR #2 | Total Assets ($mil) | Capital ($mil) | Net Premium ($mil) | Net Income ($mil) |
|---|---|---|---|---|---|---|---|
| 9-17 | C | 3.00 | 2.50 | 367.6 | 158.1 | 814.7 | 17.2 |
| 9-16 | B- | 2.68 | 2.24 | 411.8 | 188.9 | 771.2 | 12.3 |
| 2016 | C | 2.68 | 2.23 | 358.1 | 140.7 | 1,027.2 | 16.3 |
| 2015 | B | 3.14 | 2.62 | 480.4 | 222.4 | 1,428.2 | 15.0 |
| 2014 | B | 24.37 | 20.31 | 638.8 | 212.3 | 1,334.4 | 22.5 |
| 2013 | B | 2.73 | 2.28 | 276.1 | 117.5 | 783.7 | -15.9 |
| 2012 | B | 3.24 | 2.70 | 195.9 | 88.7 | 567.8 | 17.3 |

**Rating Indexes**

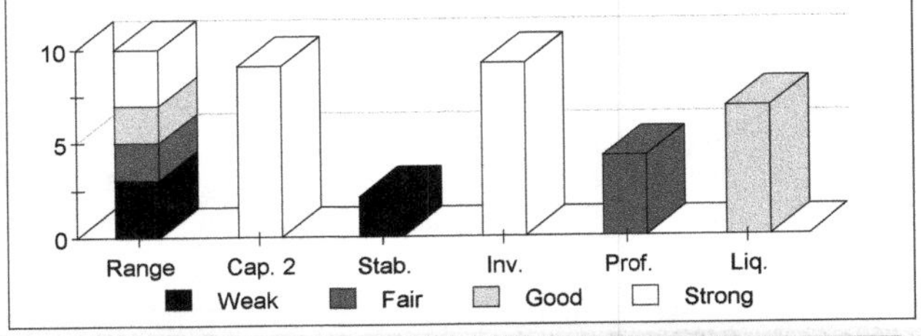


## UNITEDHEALTHCARE PLAN RIVER VALLEY — B — Good

**Major Rating Factors:** Good overall results on stability tests (5.1 on a scale of 0 to 10) despite inconsistent enrollment growth in the past five years due to declines in 2013 and 2015. Rating is significantly influenced by the fair financial results of UnitedHealth Group Incorporated. Good liquidity (6.8) with sufficient resources (cash flows and marketable investments) to handle a spike in claims. Excellent profitability (8.1).
**Other Rating Factors:** Strong capitalization index (8.6) based on excellent current risk-adjusted capital (severe loss scenario). High quality investment portfolio (9.9).
**Principal Business:** Medicaid (76%), Medicare (18%), comp med (6%)
**Mem Phys: 16:** 104,855 **15:** 96,584 **16 MLR** 81.1% **/ 16 Admin Exp** N/A
**Enroll(000): Q3 17:** 710 **16:** 749 **15:** 626 **Med Exp PMPM:** $337
**Principal Investments:** Long-term bonds (84%), cash and equiv (13%), other (3%)
**Provider Compensation ($000):** Contr fee ($2,659,348), FFS ($150,967), capitation ($41,660), bonus arrang ($11,722)
**Total Member Encounters:** Phys (6,715,270), non-phys (4,390,015)
**Group Affiliation:** UnitedHealth Group Incorporated
**Licensed in:** IL, IA, TN, VA
**Address:** 1300 RIVER DRIVE SUITE 200, MOLINE, IL 61265
**Phone:** (309) 736-4600 **Dom State:** IL **Commenced Bus:** December 1985

| Data Date | Rating | RACR #1 | RACR #2 | Total Assets ($mil) | Capital ($mil) | Net Premium ($mil) | Net Income ($mil) |
|---|---|---|---|---|---|---|---|
| 9-17 | B | 2.67 | 2.22 | 1,108.3 | 446.0 | 2,865.2 | 70.9 |
| 9-16 | B- | 2.63 | 2.19 | 980.1 | 396.7 | 2,596.5 | 45.7 |
| 2016 | B | 2.61 | 2.17 | 1,063.1 | 434.3 | 3,591.4 | 126.0 |
| 2015 | B- | 2.79 | 2.33 | 1,131.1 | 423.3 | 3,404.1 | 62.5 |
| 2014 | B+ | 2.98 | 2.48 | 1,342.9 | 600.3 | 4,245.8 | 237.0 |
| 2013 | B+ | 2.43 | 2.02 | 1,093.7 | 513.4 | 4,071.6 | 152.0 |
| 2012 | B+ | 2.15 | 1.79 | 1,017.4 | 441.2 | 4,011.4 | 170.0 |

**Rating Indexes**

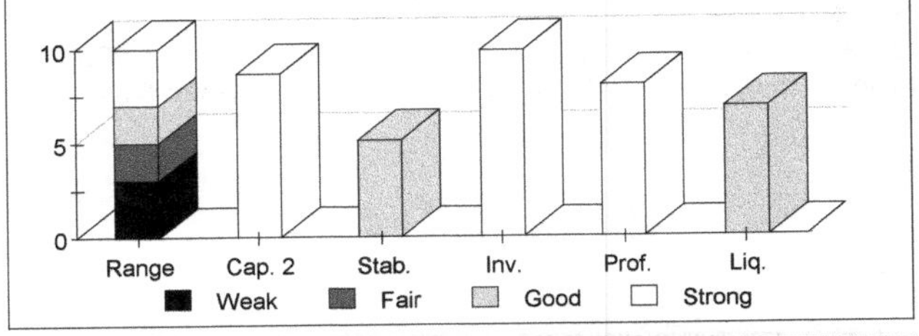

## UNITY HEALTH PLANS INS CORP — C — Fair

**Major Rating Factors:** Fair profitability index (3.1 on a scale of 0 to 10). Good liquidity (6.6) with sufficient resources (cash flows and marketable investments) to handle a spike in claims. Strong capitalization index (7.2) based on excellent current risk-adjusted capital (severe loss scenario).
**Other Rating Factors:** High quality investment portfolio (7.4). Excellent overall results on stability tests (7.4).
**Principal Business:** Comp med (96%), Medicaid (4%)
**Mem Phys: 16:** 5,011 **15:** 3,961 **16 MLR** 89.5% **/ 16 Admin Exp** N/A
**Enroll(000): Q3 17:** 200 **16:** 186 **15:** 176 **Med Exp PMPM:** $351
**Principal Investments:** Long-term bonds (59%), cash and equiv (30%), nonaffiliate common stock (11%), real estate (1%)
**Provider Compensation ($000):** Capitation ($783,816)
**Total Member Encounters:** Phys (805,379), non-phys (796,673)
**Group Affiliation:** University Health Care Inc
**Licensed in:** WI
**Address:** 840 Carolina Street, Sauk City, WI 53583
**Phone:** (608) 643-2491 **Dom State:** WI **Commenced Bus:** January 1984

| Data Date | Rating | RACR #1 | RACR #2 | Total Assets ($mil) | Capital ($mil) | Net Premium ($mil) | Net Income ($mil) |
|---|---|---|---|---|---|---|---|
| 9-17 | C | 1.54 | 1.28 | 173.3 | 67.0 | 710.4 | 4.6 |
| 9-16 | C | 1.57 | 1.31 | 160.2 | 64.9 | 639.7 | -4.5 |
| 2016 | C | 1.38 | 1.15 | 167.4 | 61.3 | 863.5 | -8.0 |
| 2015 | B- | 1.23 | 1.03 | 148.2 | 54.1 | 829.9 | -2.7 |
| 2014 | B- | 1.47 | 1.22 | 143.1 | 59.1 | 755.1 | 4.6 |
| 2013 | B | 1.61 | 1.34 | 154.9 | 55.8 | 637.0 | -0.7 |
| 2012 | B | 1.14 | 0.95 | 97.8 | 45.6 | 485.2 | -0.1 |

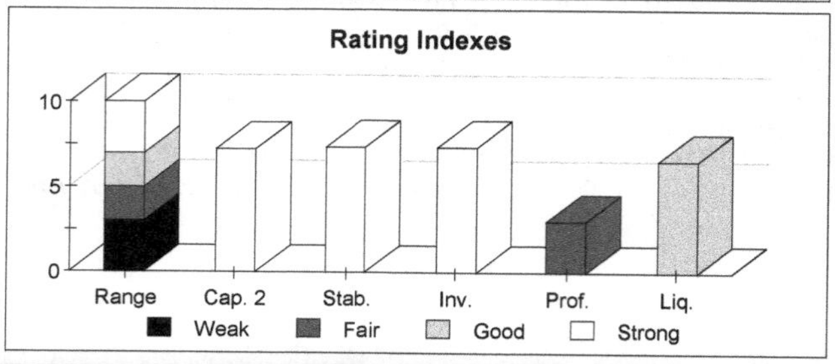


## UNIV OF MD HEALTH ADVANTAGE INC — E- — Very Weak

**Major Rating Factors:** Weak profitability index (0.0 on a scale of 0 to 10). Poor capitalization (0.0) based on weak current risk-adjusted capital (severe loss scenario). Weak liquidity (0.0) as a spike in claims may stretch capacity.
**Other Rating Factors:** High quality investment portfolio (8.9).
**Principal Business:** Medicare (100%)
**Mem Phys: 16:** 6,000 **15:** N/A **16 MLR** 107.4% **/ 16 Admin Exp** N/A
**Enroll(000): Q3 17:** 6 **16:** 4 **15:** N/A **Med Exp PMPM:** $1,209
**Principal Investments:** Cash and equiv (79%), long-term bonds (21%)
**Provider Compensation ($000):** Contr fee ($43,760), FFS ($3,266)
**Total Member Encounters:** Phys (4,995,043), non-phys (6,887,469)
**Group Affiliation:** Univ of Maryland Medical Systems
**Licensed in:** MD
**Address:** 1966 Greenspring Dr Ste 600, Timonium, MD 21093
**Phone:** (410) 878-7709 **Dom State:** MD **Commenced Bus:** January 2016

| Data Date | Rating | RACR #1 | RACR #2 | Total Assets ($mil) | Capital ($mil) | Net Premium ($mil) | Net Income ($mil) |
|---|---|---|---|---|---|---|---|
| 9-17 | E- | 0.20 | 0.17 | 24.7 | 2.2 | 65.6 | -14.4 |
| 9-16 | N/A | N/A | N/A | 12.9 | 2.9 | 28.4 | -8.8 |
| 2016 | D | 0.49 | 0.41 | 15.9 | 5.1 | 41.6 | -18.0 |
| 2015 | N/A | N/A | N/A | N/A | N/A | N/A | N/A |
| 2014 | N/A | N/A | N/A | N/A | N/A | N/A | N/A |
| 2013 | N/A | N/A | N/A | N/A | N/A | N/A | N/A |
| 2012 | N/A | N/A | N/A | N/A | N/A | N/A | N/A |

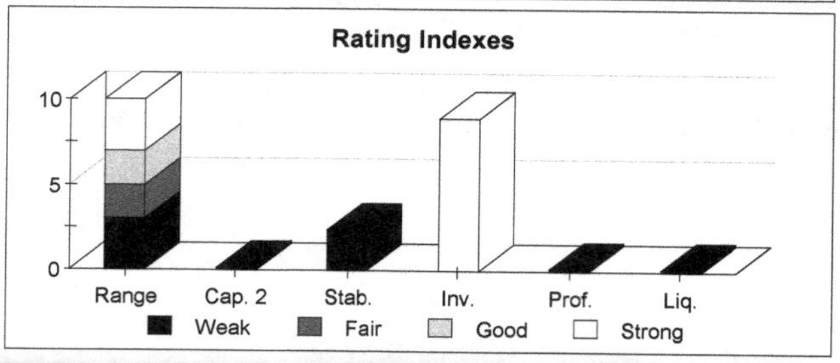


## UNIVERSAL CARE — E- — Very Weak

**Major Rating Factors:** Weak profitability index (0.8 on a scale of 0 to 10). Poor capitalization index (0.0) based on weak current risk-adjusted capital (severe loss scenario). Weak overall results on stability tests (2.5) in spite of healthy premium and capital growth during 2016 but an excessive 33% enrollment growth during the period.
**Other Rating Factors:** Excellent liquidity (7.0) with ample operational cash flow and liquid investments.
**Principal Business:** Medicare (94%), Medicaid (6%)
**Mem Phys: 16:** N/A **15:** N/A **16 MLR** 87.4% **/ 16 Admin Exp** N/A
**Enroll(000): Q3 17:** 18 **16:** 13 **15:** 10 **Med Exp PMPM:** $888
**Principal Investments ($000):** Cash and equiv ($17,896)
**Provider Compensation ($000):** None
**Total Member Encounters:** N/A
**Group Affiliation:** None
**Licensed in:** CA
**Address:** 5701 Katella Ave MS CA120-0368, Cypress, CA 90630
**Phone:** (916) 451-1592 **Dom State:** CA **Commenced Bus:** November 1985

| Data Date | Rating | RACR #1 | RACR #2 | Total Assets ($mil) | Capital ($mil) | Net Premium ($mil) | Net Income ($mil) |
|---|---|---|---|---|---|---|---|
| 9-17 | E- | N/A | N/A | 64.0 | -3.1 | 138.1 | -2.2 |
| 9-16 | E- | 0.13 | 0.08 | 45.6 | 1.4 | 100.2 | 2.5 |
| 2016 | E- | N/A | N/A | 52.9 | -4.6 | 142.0 | -1.6 |
| 2015 | E- | N/A | N/A | 30.4 | -13.7 | 95.3 | -3.2 |
| 2014 | E- | N/A | N/A | 23.6 | -4.5 | 65.5 | 0.4 |
| 2013 | E- | N/A | N/A | 22.1 | -4.9 | 50.1 | -3.3 |
| 2012 | E- | N/A | N/A | 13.5 | -1.6 | 40.5 | -2.4 |

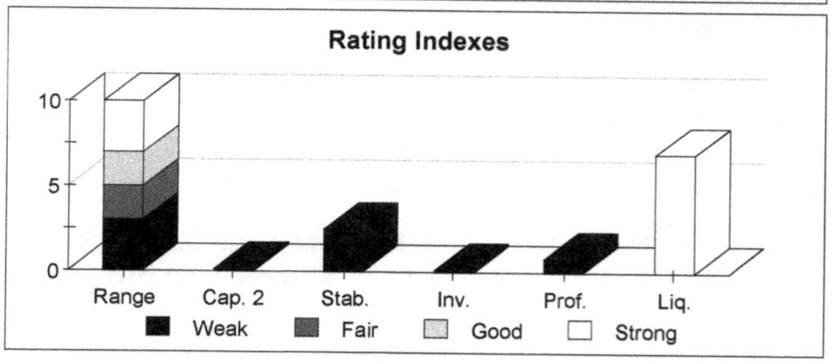

## UNIVERSITY HEALTH ALLIANCE C+ Fair

**Major Rating Factors:** Good overall profitability index (6.1 on a scale of 0 to 10). Good liquidity (6.4) with sufficient resources (cash flows and marketable investments) to handle a spike in claims. Low quality investment portfolio (2.5).
**Other Rating Factors:** Strong capitalization (7.6) based on excellent current risk-adjusted capital (severe loss scenario).
**Principal Business:** Comp med (78%), dental (2%), other (18%)
**Mem Phys: 16:** 5,955 **15:** 5,870 **16 MLR** 86.7% **/ 16 Admin Exp** N/A
**Enroll(000): Q3 17:** 55 **16:** 57 **15:** 53 **Med Exp PMPM:** $356
**Principal Investments:** Nonaffiliate common stock (72%), cash and equiv (16%), long-term bonds (12%)
**Provider Compensation ($000):** FFS ($172,983), contr fee ($54,874), capitation ($4,899), bonus arrang ($804)
**Total Member Encounters:** Phys (324,142), non-phys (153,052)
**Group Affiliation:** University Health Alliance
**Licensed in:** HI
**Address:** 700 BISHOP ST Ste 300, HONOLULU, HI 96813
**Phone:** (808) 532-4000 **Dom State:** HI **Commenced Bus:** March 1988

| Data Date | Rating | RACR #1 | RACR #2 | Total Assets ($mil) | Capital ($mil) | Net Premium ($mil) | Net Income ($mil) |
|---|---|---|---|---|---|---|---|
| 9-17 | C+ | 1.85 | 1.54 | 110.8 | 63.2 | 214.2 | 11.9 |
| 9-16 | C+ | 1.61 | 1.35 | 91.8 | 52.1 | 201.9 | 4.4 |
| 2016 | C+ | 1.40 | 1.17 | 96.0 | 49.5 | 272.7 | 3.6 |
| 2015 | C+ | 1.43 | 1.19 | 83.6 | 46.3 | 240.8 | -0.9 |
| 2014 | C+ | 1.65 | 1.38 | 81.0 | 48.6 | 227.9 | 2.3 |
| 2013 | C+ | 1.72 | 1.43 | 78.2 | 46.8 | 214.1 | 9.1 |
| 2012 | C+ | 1.57 | 1.30 | 66.7 | 36.8 | 185.5 | 7.8 |

Rating Indexes

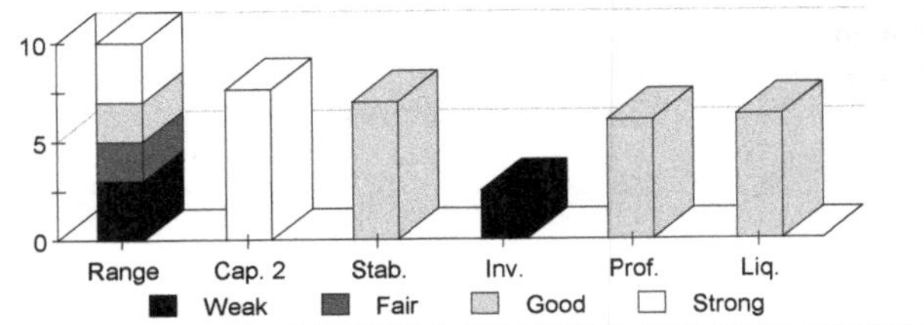


## UNIVERSITY HEALTH CARE INC B Good

**Major Rating Factors:** Good liquidity (5.9 on a scale of 0 to 10) with sufficient resources (cash flows and marketable investments) to handle a spike in claims. Fair profitability index (3.2). Fair overall results on stability tests (3.7) based on a steep decline in capital during 2016.
**Other Rating Factors:** Strong capitalization index (7.2) based on excellent current risk-adjusted capital (severe loss scenario). High quality investment portfolio (8.2).
**Principal Business:** Medicaid (99%), Medicare (1%)
**Mem Phys: 16:** 24,887 **15:** 22,086 **16 MLR** 95.5% **/ 16 Admin Exp** N/A
**Enroll(000): Q3 17:** 319 **16:** 298 **15:** 281 **Med Exp PMPM:** $467
**Principal Investments:** Cash and equiv (45%), long-term bonds (29%), nonaffiliate common stock (26%)
**Provider Compensation ($000):** Contr fee ($1,420,133), capitation ($189,313), FFS ($53,151)
**Total Member Encounters:** Phys (2,081,001), non-phys (2,163,288)
**Group Affiliation:** University of Louisville Physicians
**Licensed in:** KY
**Address:** 5100 Commerce Crossings Drive, Louisville, KY 40229
**Phone:** (502) 585-7900 **Dom State:** KY **Commenced Bus:** October 2000

| Data Date | Rating | RACR #1 | RACR #2 | Total Assets ($mil) | Capital ($mil) | Net Premium ($mil) | Net Income ($mil) |
|---|---|---|---|---|---|---|---|
| 9-17 | B | 1.48 | 1.23 | 418.5 | 211.2 | 1,419.1 | 6.8 |
| 9-16 | B+ | 1.72 | 1.44 | 431.2 | 222.9 | 1,320.1 | -39.2 |
| 2016 | B | 1.37 | 1.15 | 414.6 | 196.8 | 1,747.8 | -57.9 |
| 2015 | B+ | 1.94 | 1.62 | 444.2 | 249.9 | 1,653.1 | 39.1 |
| 2014 | B+ | 2.30 | 1.92 | 357.2 | 214.9 | 1,290.3 | 115.0 |
| 2013 | B+ | 1.80 | 1.50 | 177.6 | 100.7 | 685.4 | -3.5 |
| 2012 | B+ | 1.47 | 1.23 | 184.1 | 94.1 | 795.7 | -1.8 |

Rating Indexes

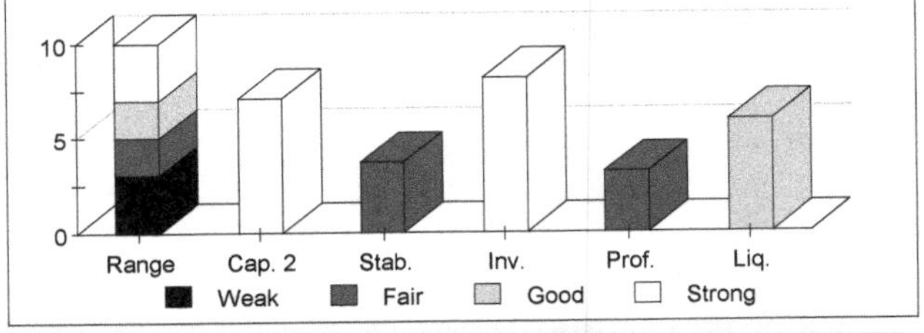


## UNIVERSITY OF UTAH HEALTH INS PLANS D+ Weak

**Major Rating Factors:** Weak profitability index (0.9 on a scale of 0 to 10). Fair quality investment portfolio (4.0). Good liquidity (6.9) with sufficient resources (cash flows and marketable investments) to handle a spike in claims.
**Other Rating Factors:** Strong capitalization (9.0) based on excellent current risk-adjusted capital (severe loss scenario).
**Principal Business:** Comp med (100%)
**Mem Phys: 16:** 6,794 **15:** N/A **16 MLR** 113.5% **/ 16 Admin Exp** N/A
**Enroll(000): Q3 17:** 9 **16:** 4 **15:** N/A **Med Exp PMPM:** $656
**Principal Investments:** Long-term bonds (46%), nonaffiliate common stock (40%), cash and equiv (8%), pref stock (7%)
**Provider Compensation ($000):** Contr fee ($19,463), FFS ($405)
**Total Member Encounters:** Phys (17,840), non-phys (18,131)
**Group Affiliation:** University of Utah
**Licensed in:** UT
**Address:** 6053 Fashion Square Dr Ste 110, Murray, UT 84107
**Phone:** (801) 587-6480 **Dom State:** UT **Commenced Bus:** January 2015

| Data Date | Rating | RACR #1 | RACR #2 | Total Assets ($mil) | Capital ($mil) | Net Premium ($mil) | Net Income ($mil) |
|---|---|---|---|---|---|---|---|
| 9-17 | D+ | 2.94 | 2.45 | 27.3 | 14.0 | 32.0 | -4.7 |
| 9-16 | N/A | N/A | N/A | 11.3 | 6.8 | 12.7 | -4.1 |
| 2016 | D+ | 2.22 | 1.85 | 17.1 | 10.6 | 19.1 | -4.2 |
| 2015 | N/A | N/A | N/A | 4.8 | 3.8 | N/A | -1.2 |
| 2014 | N/A | N/A | N/A | 2.0 | 2.0 | N/A | N/A |
| 2013 | N/A | N/A | N/A | N/A | N/A | N/A | N/A |
| 2012 | N/A | N/A | N/A | N/A | N/A | N/A | N/A |

Rating Indexes

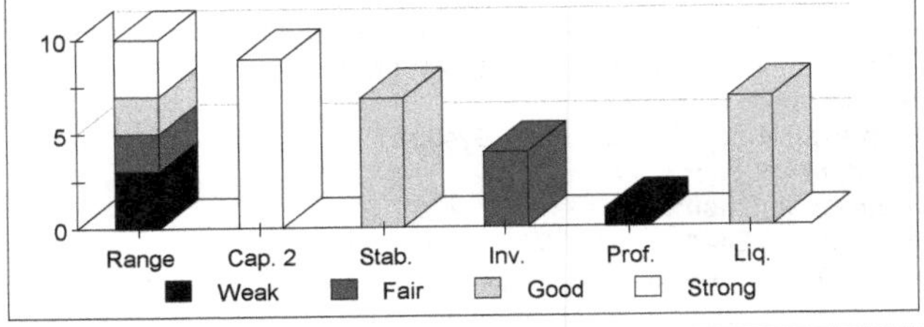

## UNUM LIFE INSURANCE COMPANY OF AMERICA C+ Fair

**Major Rating Factors:** Fair quality investment portfolio (3.8 on a scale of 0 to 10) with large holdings of BBB rated bonds in addition to significant exposure to junk bonds. Fair overall results on stability tests (4.8). Strong capitalization (7.3) based on excellent risk adjusted capital (severe loss scenario). Capital levels have been relatively consistent over the last five years.
**Other Rating Factors:** Excellent profitability (7.8). Excellent liquidity (7.1).
**Principal Business:** Group health insurance (62%), group life insurance (29%), individual health insurance (6%), and reinsurance (2%).
**Principal Investments:** NonCMO investment grade bonds (72%), noninv. grade bonds (12%), CMOs and structured securities (8%), and mortgages in good standing (5%).
**Investments in Affiliates:** None
**Group Affiliation:** Unum Group
**Licensed in:** All states except NY
**Commenced Business:** September 1966
**Address:** 2211 CONGRESS STREET, PORTLAND, ME 4122
**Phone:** (207) 575-2211 **Domicile State:** ME **NAIC Code:** 62235

| Data Date | Rating | RACR #1 | RACR #2 | Total Assets ($mil) | Capital ($mil) | Net Premium ($mil) | Net Income ($mil) |
|---|---|---|---|---|---|---|---|
| 9-17 | C+ | 2.30 | 1.22 | 21,366.1 | 1,702.3 | 2,615.1 | 271.2 |
| 9-16 | C+ | 2.21 | 1.17 | 20,869.0 | 1,582.5 | 2,507.0 | 245.1 |
| 2016 | C+ | 2.33 | 1.23 | 21,077.8 | 1,686.5 | 3,348.0 | 349.3 |
| 2015 | C+ | 2.28 | 1.22 | 20,552.3 | 1,567.3 | 3,168.1 | 203.5 |
| 2014 | C+ | 2.42 | 1.29 | 19,701.4 | 1,546.1 | 2,914.6 | 195.0 |
| 2013 | C+ | 2.49 | 1.34 | 19,078.5 | 1,557.9 | 2,794.2 | 176.2 |
| 2012 | C+ | 2.57 | 1.38 | 18,879.8 | 1,573.5 | 2,702.0 | 202.9 |

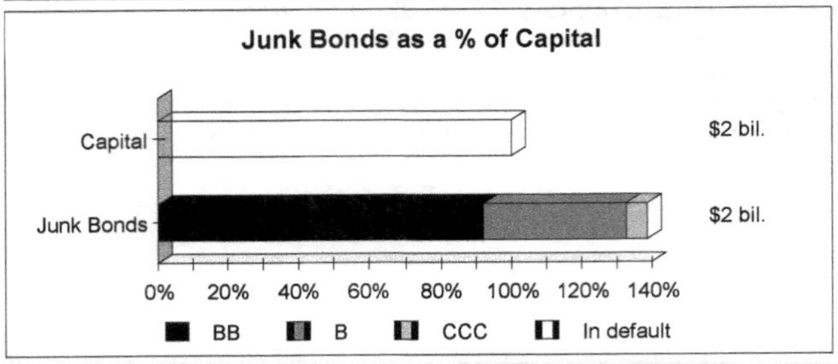


## UPMC FOR YOU INC * B+ Good

**Major Rating Factors:** Excellent profitability (8.6 on a scale of 0 to 10). Strong capitalization (8.8) based on excellent current risk-adjusted capital (severe loss scenario). High quality investment portfolio (9.9).
**Other Rating Factors:** Excellent liquidity (7.3) with ample operational cash flow and liquid investments.
**Principal Business:** Medicaid (87%), Medicare (13%)
**Mem Phys: 16:** 15,919 **15:** 13,895 **16 MLR** 87.1% **/ 16 Admin Exp** N/A
**Enroll(000): Q3 17:** 440 **16:** 426 **15:** 388 **Med Exp PMPM:** $418
**Principal Investments:** Cash and equiv (82%), long-term bonds (17%), other (1%)
**Provider Compensation ($000):** Contr fee ($2,106,880), capitation ($857)
**Total Member Encounters:** Phys (3,561,046), non-phys (2,913,854)
**Group Affiliation:** Univ of Pittsburgh Medical Center
**Licensed in:** PA
**Address:** 600 Grant St, Pittsburgh, PA 15219
**Phone:** (412) 434-1200 **Dom State:** PA **Commenced Bus:** July 2004

| Data Date | Rating | RACR #1 | RACR #2 | Total Assets ($mil) | Capital ($mil) | Net Premium ($mil) | Net Income ($mil) |
|---|---|---|---|---|---|---|---|
| 9-17 | B+ | 2.78 | 2.31 | 726.3 | 392.5 | 1,963.2 | 41.8 |
| 9-16 | B+ | 2.16 | 1.80 | 692.0 | 317.8 | 1,864.0 | 70.7 |
| 2016 | B+ | 2.49 | 2.07 | 750.6 | 351.4 | 2,383.2 | 105.6 |
| 2015 | B | 1.64 | 1.37 | 527.8 | 247.6 | 2,061.8 | 66.4 |
| 2014 | B+ | 2.12 | 1.76 | 428.1 | 228.2 | 1,687.5 | 59.0 |
| 2013 | B+ | 1.62 | 1.35 | 338.8 | 172.7 | 1,553.3 | 30.0 |
| 2012 | B+ | 2.40 | 2.00 | 303.3 | 174.8 | 1,052.5 | 32.4 |

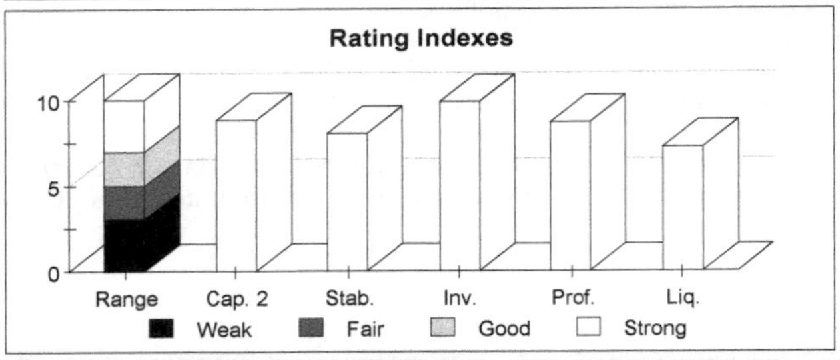


## UPMC HEALTH BENEFITS INC D Weak

**Major Rating Factors:** Poor long-term capitalization (1.7 on a scale of 0 to 10) based on fair current risk adjusted capital (moderate loss scenario) reflecting improvement over results in 2016. Weak overall results on stability tests (2.3) including weak risk adjusted capital in prior years and weak results on operational trends.
**Other Rating Factors:** Fair reserve development (4.9) as the level of reserves has at times been insufficient to cover claims. In 2016 and 2014 the two year reserve development was 17% and 42% deficient respectively. Fair profitability index (3.8) with operating losses during 2013 and the first nine months of 2017. Average return on equity over the last five years has been poor at -1.3%. Good liquidity (5.5) with sufficient resources (cash flows and marketable investments) to handle a spike in claims.
**Principal Business:** Workers compensation (73%) and other accident & health (27%).
**Principal Investments:** Investment grade bonds (42%), misc. investments (32%), cash (25%), and non investment grade bonds (1%).
**Investments in Affiliates:** None
**Group Affiliation:** UPMC Health System
**Licensed in:** OH, PA, WV
**Commenced Business:** February 2000
**Address:** 600 Grant Street, Pittsburgh, PA 15219
**Phone:** (412) 434-1200 **Domicile State:** PA **NAIC Code:** 11018

| Data Date | Rating | RACR #1 | RACR #2 | Loss Ratio % | Total Assets ($mil) | Capital ($mil) | Net Premium ($mil) | Net Income ($mil) |
|---|---|---|---|---|---|---|---|---|
| 9-17 | D | 0.91 | 0.57 | N/A | 226.9 | 99.6 | 82.0 | -1.1 |
| 9-16 | D+ | 0.83 | 0.52 | N/A | 166.4 | 66.8 | 70.1 | 1.4 |
| 2016 | D+ | 0.58 | 0.36 | 74.5 | 170.3 | 51.6 | 101.0 | -2.8 |
| 2015 | D+ | 0.96 | 0.59 | 76.9 | 148.7 | 64.1 | 91.2 | 0.8 |
| 2014 | C | 0.27 | 0.17 | 73.9 | 85.4 | 17.9 | 88.6 | 2.6 |
| 2013 | N/A | N/A | N/A | 87.3 | 70.6 | 14.7 | 85.6 | -3.0 |
| 2012 | N/A | N/A | N/A | 81.8 | 38.8 | 17.6 | 56.6 | 0.6 |

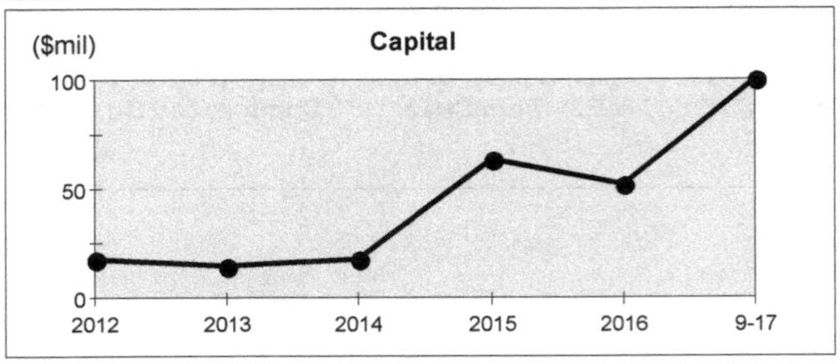

## UPMC HEALTH COVERAGE INC B Good

**Major Rating Factors:** Excellent profitability (9.2 on a scale of 0 to 10). Strong capitalization (10.0) based on excellent current risk-adjusted capital (severe loss scenario). High quality investment portfolio (9.6).
**Other Rating Factors:** Excellent liquidity (7.9) with ample operational cash flow and liquid investments.
**Principal Business:** Comp med (100%)
**Mem Phys: 16:** 20,379 **15:** 17,957 **16 MLR** 82.1% **/ 16 Admin Exp** N/A
**Enroll(000): Q3 17:** 7 **16:** 8 **15:** 7 **Med Exp PMPM:** $315
**Principal Investments:** Cash and equiv (99%), long-term bonds (1%)
**Provider Compensation ($000):** Contr fee ($23,152)
**Total Member Encounters:** Phys (41,280), non-phys (26,770)
**Group Affiliation:** Univ of Pittsburgh Medical Center
**Licensed in:** PA
**Address:** 600 Grant St, Pittsburgh, PA 15219
**Phone:** (412) 434-1200 **Dom State:** PA **Commenced Bus:** August 2014

| Data Date | Rating | RACR #1 | RACR #2 | Total Assets ($mil) | Capital ($mil) | Net Premium ($mil) | Net Income ($mil) |
|---|---|---|---|---|---|---|---|
| 9-17 | B | 6.33 | 5.28 | 20.5 | 14.3 | 24.8 | 2.7 |
| 9-16 | B | 8.81 | 7.34 | 14.6 | 11.6 | 19.9 | 1.8 |
| 2016 | B | 5.27 | 4.39 | 15.9 | 11.6 | 27.7 | 1.8 |
| 2015 | B | 6.57 | 5.48 | 14.7 | 9.8 | 27.5 | 7.7 |
| 2014 | U | 1.59 | 1.33 | 7.1 | 2.1 | 5.2 | -0.6 |
| 2013 | N/A | N/A | N/A | N/A | N/A | N/A | N/A |
| 2012 | N/A | N/A | N/A | N/A | N/A | N/A | N/A |

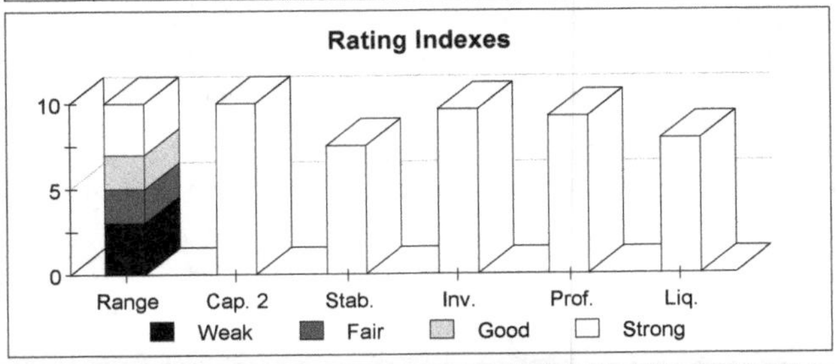


## UPMC HEALTH NETWORK INC C Fair

**Major Rating Factors:** Fair profitability index (3.2 on a scale of 0 to 10). Fair capitalization (2.9) based on good current risk-adjusted capital (moderate loss scenario). High quality investment portfolio (8.6).
**Other Rating Factors:** Excellent liquidity (7.6) with ample operational cash flow and liquid investments.
**Principal Business:** Medicare (100%)
**Mem Phys: 16:** 18,947 **15:** 15,447 **16 MLR** 88.3% **/ 16 Admin Exp** N/A
**Enroll(000): Q3 17:** 9 **16:** 9 **15:** 9 **Med Exp PMPM:** $688
**Principal Investments:** Cash and equiv (85%), other (15%)
**Provider Compensation ($000):** Contr fee ($73,075)
**Total Member Encounters:** Phys (121,174), non-phys (127,125)
**Group Affiliation:** Univ of Pittsburgh Medical Center
**Licensed in:** PA
**Address:** 600 Grant St, Pittsburgh, PA 15219
**Phone:** (412) 434-1200 **Dom State:** PA **Commenced Bus:** January 2005

| Data Date | Rating | RACR #1 | RACR #2 | Total Assets ($mil) | Capital ($mil) | Net Premium ($mil) | Net Income ($mil) |
|---|---|---|---|---|---|---|---|
| 9-17 | C | 2.68 | 2.23 | 44.5 | 20.4 | 64.7 | 2.8 |
| 9-16 | C | 2.17 | 1.81 | 38.6 | 18.0 | 62.7 | 2.2 |
| 2016 | C | 3.00 | 2.50 | 42.1 | 24.2 | 82.2 | 8.5 |
| 2015 | D+ | 2.68 | 2.23 | 40.9 | 25.6 | 92.2 | 2.6 |
| 2014 | D+ | 3.12 | 2.60 | 57.3 | 40.9 | 104.1 | -1.9 |
| 2013 | C+ | 0.76 | 0.64 | 281.4 | 142.1 | 1,208.2 | -48.1 |
| 2012 | B | 0.84 | 0.70 | 240.8 | 110.9 | 969.5 | -23.1 |

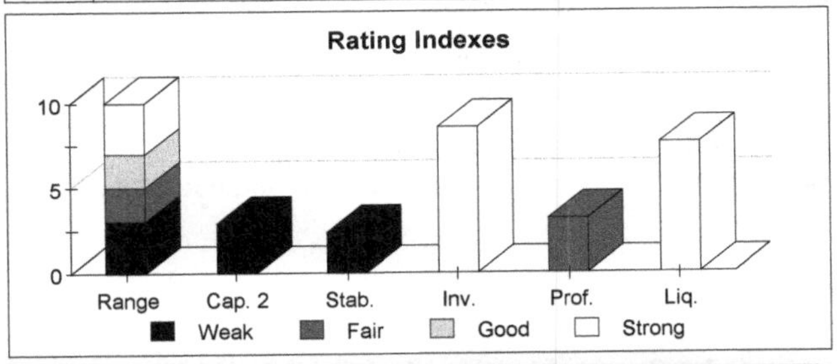


## UPMC HEALTH OPTIONS INC C+ Fair

**Major Rating Factors:** Good liquidity (6.9 on a scale of 0 to 10) with sufficient resources (cash flows and marketable investments) to handle a spike in claims. Weak profitability index (1.4). Strong capitalization (7.9) based on excellent current risk-adjusted capital (severe loss scenario).
**Other Rating Factors:** High quality investment portfolio (9.3).
**Principal Business:** Comp med (100%)
**Mem Phys: 16:** 16,366 **15:** 15,538 **16 MLR** 97.0% **/ 16 Admin Exp** N/A
**Enroll(000): Q3 17:** 416 **16:** 375 **15:** 316 **Med Exp PMPM:** $342
**Principal Investments:** Cash and equiv (56%), long-term bonds (33%), nonaffiliate common stock (11%), other (1%)
**Provider Compensation ($000):** Contr fee ($1,487,309)
**Total Member Encounters:** Phys (2,742,991), non-phys (1,681,600)
**Group Affiliation:** Univ of Pittsburgh Medical Center
**Licensed in:** PA
**Address:** 600 Grant St, Pittsburgh, PA 15219
**Phone:** (412) 434-1200 **Dom State:** PA **Commenced Bus:** January 2014

| Data Date | Rating | RACR #1 | RACR #2 | Total Assets ($mil) | Capital ($mil) | Net Premium ($mil) | Net Income ($mil) |
|---|---|---|---|---|---|---|---|
| 9-17 | C+ | 2.09 | 1.75 | 485.2 | 210.4 | 1,490.4 | 77.2 |
| 9-16 | C+ | 1.21 | 1.01 | 315.1 | 112.9 | 1,153.3 | -56.6 |
| 2016 | C+ | 1.88 | 1.57 | 359.4 | 189.1 | 1,548.2 | -49.6 |
| 2015 | C | 0.89 | 0.74 | 344.0 | 167.7 | 1,312.9 | -76.3 |
| 2014 | C | 0.77 | 0.64 | 257.2 | 132.2 | 1,046.5 | -37.8 |
| 2013 | N/A | N/A | N/A | 1.2 | 1.2 | N/A | N/A |
| 2012 | N/A | N/A | N/A | N/A | N/A | N/A | N/A |

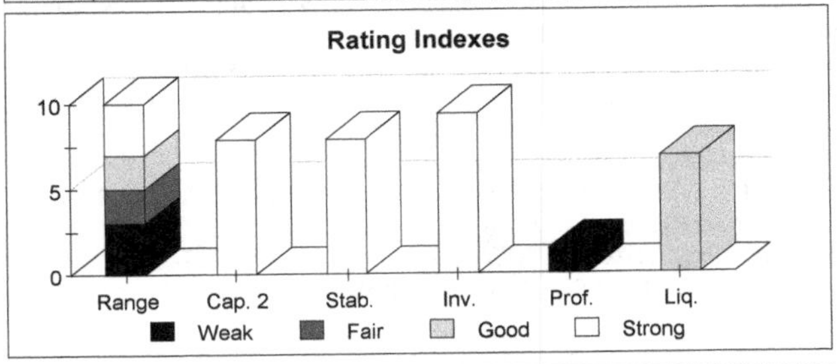

## UPMC HEALTH PLAN INC * A- Excellent

**Major Rating Factors:** Excellent profitability (8.0 on a scale of 0 to 10). Strong capitalization index (8.1) based on excellent current risk-adjusted capital (severe loss scenario). High quality investment portfolio (9.9).
**Other Rating Factors:** Excellent overall results on stability tests (8.0) based on steady enrollment growth, averaging 10% over the past five years. Good financial strength from affiliates. Excellent liquidity (7.0) with ample operational cash flow and liquid investments.
**Principal Business:** Medicare (90%), comp med (5%), FEHB (5%)
**Mem Phys: 16:** 20,379 **15:** 17,957 **16 MLR** 88.6% **/ 16 Admin Exp** N/A
**Enroll(000): Q3 17:** 181 **16:** 173 **15:** 160 **Med Exp PMPM:** $647
**Principal Investments:** Long-term bonds (85%), cash and equiv (9%), other (6%)
**Provider Compensation ($000):** Contr fee ($1,325,506), capitation ($41)
**Total Member Encounters:** Phys (2,139,301), non-phys (2,090,210)
**Group Affiliation:** Univ of Pittsburgh Medical Center
**Licensed in:** OH, PA, WV
**Address:** 600 Grant Street, Pittsburgh, PA 15219
**Phone:** (412) 434-1200 **Dom State:** PA **Commenced Bus:** March 1996

| Data Date | Rating | RACR #1 | RACR #2 | Total Assets ($mil) | Capital ($mil) | Net Premium ($mil) | Net Income ($mil) |
|---|---|---|---|---|---|---|---|
| 9-17 | A- | 2.20 | 1.83 | 640.7 | 237.0 | 1,220.7 | 27.3 |
| 9-16 | B | 1.56 | 1.30 | 554.3 | 200.6 | 1,128.0 | 32.6 |
| 2016 | B+ | 1.92 | 1.60 | 454.0 | 213.1 | 1,490.4 | 27.1 |
| 2015 | B | 1.21 | 1.00 | 341.2 | 167.9 | 1,371.4 | 3.3 |
| 2014 | B | 1.16 | 0.97 | 376.2 | 149.7 | 1,193.0 | 12.6 |
| 2013 | B | 1.50 | 1.25 | 343.6 | 151.6 | 1,036.2 | 41.7 |
| 2012 | C+ | 0.97 | 0.81 | 275.8 | 127.5 | 1,151.0 | 10.9 |

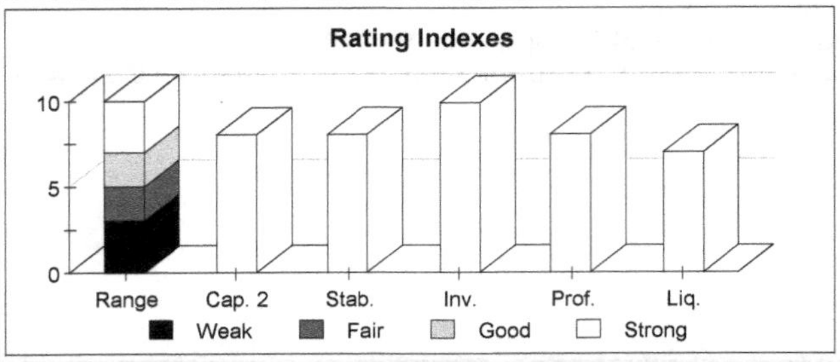


## UPPER PENINSULA HEALTH PLAN INC * A Excellent

**Major Rating Factors:** Excellent profitability (8.9 on a scale of 0 to 10). Strong capitalization index (7.9) based on excellent current risk-adjusted capital (severe loss scenario). High quality investment portfolio (9.5).
**Other Rating Factors:** Excellent overall results on stability tests (8.3). Excellent liquidity (7.0) with sufficient resources (cash flows and marketable investments) to handle a spike in claims
**Principal Business:** Medicaid (83%), Medicare (17%)
**Mem Phys: 16:** 1,370 **15:** 1,173 **16 MLR** 86.6% **/ 16 Admin Exp** N/A
**Enroll(000): Q3 17:** 49 **16:** 48 **15:** 47 **Med Exp PMPM:** $433
**Principal Investments:** Cash and equiv (64%), long-term bonds (18%), real estate (17%)
**Provider Compensation ($000):** Contr fee ($181,358), capitation ($46,786), FFS ($17,761)
**Total Member Encounters:** Phys (186,210), non-phys (141,876)
**Group Affiliation:** LifePoint Health Inc
**Licensed in:** MI
**Address:** 853 W Washington St, Marquette, MI 49855
**Phone:** (906) 225-7500 **Dom State:** MI **Commenced Bus:** August 1998

| Data Date | Rating | RACR #1 | RACR #2 | Total Assets ($mil) | Capital ($mil) | Net Premium ($mil) | Net Income ($mil) |
|---|---|---|---|---|---|---|---|
| 9-17 | A | 2.06 | 1.71 | 97.3 | 50.5 | 220.9 | 7.4 |
| 9-16 | B- | 1.48 | 1.23 | 83.5 | 32.1 | 208.7 | -3.3 |
| 2016 | B | 1.80 | 1.50 | 82.6 | 44.7 | 283.6 | 8.9 |
| 2015 | B- | 1.68 | 1.40 | 77.4 | 36.3 | 248.1 | 13.1 |
| 2014 | B- | 1.73 | 1.44 | 46.2 | 23.5 | 150.4 | 4.6 |
| 2013 | B- | 1.77 | 1.47 | 31.9 | 19.2 | 107.1 | 0.7 |
| 2012 | B- | 1.87 | 1.56 | 31.9 | 18.7 | 97.6 | 0.2 |

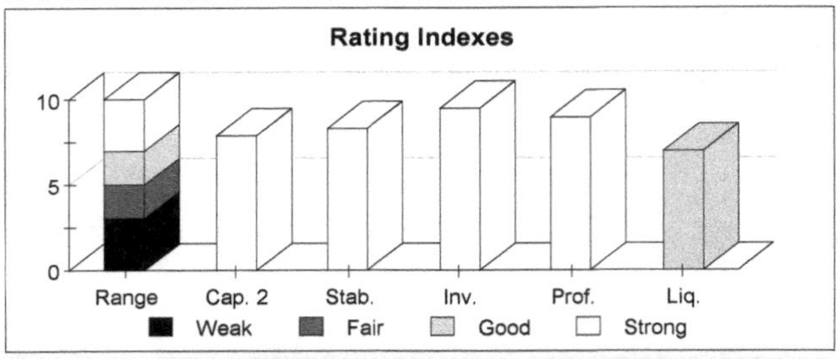


## US FIRE INS CO C Fair

**Major Rating Factors:** Fair overall results on stability tests (3.7 on a scale of 0 to 10) including potential drain of affiliation with Fairfax Financial and weak results on operational trends. Fair profitability index (3.9) with operating losses during 2012, 2013 and the first nine months of 2017. Return on equity has been low, averaging 0.5% over the past five years.
**Other Rating Factors:** Good long-term capitalization index (6.9) based on good current risk adjusted capital (moderate loss scenario), despite some fluctuation in capital levels. History of adequate reserve strength (5.8) as reserves have been consistently at an acceptable level. Good liquidity (6.9) with sufficient resources (cash flows and marketable investments) to handle a spike in claims.
**Principal Business:** Group accident & health (30%), inland marine (20%), other liability (11%), workers compensation (11%), auto liability (9%), commercial multiple peril (6%), and other lines (14%).
**Principal Investments:** Investment grade bonds (54%), misc. investments (37%), cash (3%), non investment grade bonds (3%), and real estate (3%).
**Investments in Affiliates:** 22%
**Group Affiliation:** Fairfax Financial
**Licensed in:** All states, the District of Columbia and Puerto Rico
**Commenced Business:** April 1824
**Address:** 1209 ORANGE STREET, Wilmington, DE 19801
**Phone:** (973) 490-6600 **Domicile State:** DE **NAIC Code:** 21113

| Data Date | Rating | RACR #1 | RACR #2 | Loss Ratio % | Total Assets ($mil) | Capital ($mil) | Net Premium ($mil) | Net Income ($mil) |
|---|---|---|---|---|---|---|---|---|
| 9-17 | C | 1.27 | 0.97 | N/A | 4,021.4 | 1,243.0 | 1,046.6 | -179.6 |
| 9-16 | C | 1.41 | 1.09 | N/A | 3,926.9 | 1,226.9 | 997.3 | 55.8 |
| 2016 | C | 1.35 | 1.04 | 63.7 | 3,949.6 | 1,218.9 | 1,370.7 | 32.3 |
| 2015 | C | 1.45 | 1.14 | 64.1 | 3,736.1 | 1,178.0 | 1,262.9 | 94.5 |
| 2014 | C | 1.62 | 1.14 | 67.5 | 3,248.6 | 898.6 | 1,025.1 | 195.7 |
| 2013 | C | 1.14 | 0.87 | 71.4 | 3,154.5 | 812.1 | 971.7 | -75.7 |
| 2012 | C | 1.42 | 1.07 | 81.2 | 2,924.1 | 881.7 | 810.0 | -50.1 |

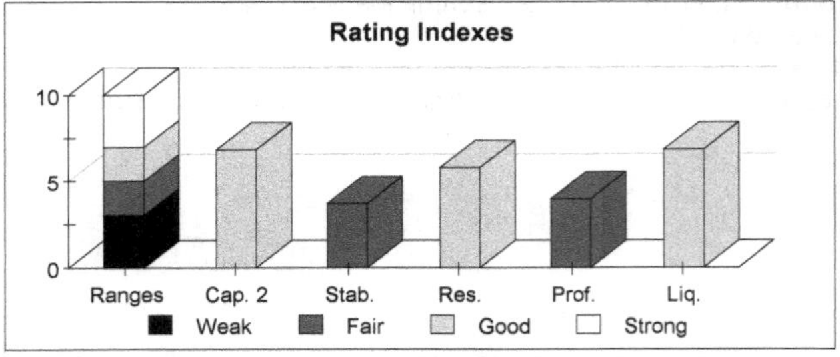

## USABLE LIFE * B+ Good

**Major Rating Factors:** Good quality investment portfolio (6.7 on a scale of 0 to 10) despite mixed results such as: minimal exposure to mortgages and large holdings of BBB rated bonds but minimal holdings in junk bonds. Good liquidity (6.5) with sufficient resources to handle a spike in claims. Good overall results on stability tests (6.7) excellent operational trends and excellent risk diversification.
**Other Rating Factors:** Strong capitalization (8.4) based on excellent risk adjusted capital (severe loss scenario). Excellent profitability (8.8).
**Principal Business:** Reinsurance (59%), group life insurance (20%), group health insurance (15%), individual health insurance (5%), and individual life insurance (1%).
**Principal Investments:** NonCMO investment grade bonds (75%), CMOs and structured securities (13%), common & preferred stock (7%), mortgages in good standing (2%), and misc. investments (4%).
**Investments in Affiliates:** None
**Group Affiliation:** Arkansas Bl Cross Bl Shield Group
**Licensed in:** All states except NY, PR
**Commenced Business:** December 1980
**Address:** 320 W Capitol Suite 700, Little Rock, AR 72201
**Phone:** (501) 375-7200 **Domicile State:** AR **NAIC Code:** 94358

| Data Date | Rating | RACR #1 | RACR #2 | Total Assets ($mil) | Capital ($mil) | Net Premium ($mil) | Net Income ($mil) |
|---|---|---|---|---|---|---|---|
| 9-17 | B+ | 2.62 | 1.95 | 510.9 | 263.9 | 436.0 | 19.9 |
| 9-16 | B+ | 2.22 | 1.64 | 485.9 | 233.5 | 444.0 | 18.0 |
| 2016 | B+ | 2.41 | 1.80 | 498.2 | 241.6 | 587.8 | 24.3 |
| 2015 | B+ | 2.07 | 1.52 | 467.9 | 215.3 | 580.2 | 27.3 |
| 2014 | B+ | 1.83 | 1.34 | 446.0 | 194.3 | 591.7 | 24.6 |
| 2013 | B+ | 1.60 | 1.17 | 408.3 | 166.3 | 570.0 | 11.5 |
| 2012 | B+ | 1.64 | 1.21 | 381.2 | 156.3 | 505.7 | 15.4 |

**Adverse Trends in Operations**

Decrease in premium volume from 2014 to 2015 (2%)

## USABLE MUTUAL INS CO * A+ Excellent

**Major Rating Factors:** Strong capitalization (10.0 on a scale of 0 to 10) based on excellent current risk-adjusted capital (severe loss scenario). High quality investment portfolio (9.2). Excellent liquidity (6.9) with sufficient resources (cash flows and marketable investments) to handle a spike in claims.
**Other Rating Factors:** Good overall profitability index (5.7).
**Principal Business:** Comp med (71%), FEHB (11%), med supp (10%), Medicare (7%), other (2%)
**Mem Phys: 16:** 16,527 **15:** 16,152 **16 MLR** 86.8% **/ 16 Admin Exp** N/A
**Enroll(000): Q3 17:** 673 **16:** 668 **15:** 647 **Med Exp PMPM:** $270
**Principal Investments:** Long-term bonds (48%), cash and equiv (19%), affiliate common stock (13%), nonaffiliate common stock (9%), real estate (4%), other (8%)
**Provider Compensation ($000):** Contr fee ($2,117,534), bonus arrang ($12,795)
**Total Member Encounters:** Phys (3,162,934), non-phys (4,478,839)
**Group Affiliation:** USAble Mutual Insurance Company
**Licensed in:** AR, TX
**Address:** 601 S Gaines, Little Rock, AR 72201
**Phone:** (501) 378-2000 **Dom State:** AR **Commenced Bus:** March 1949

| Data Date | Rating | RACR #1 | RACR #2 | Total Assets ($mil) | Capital ($mil) | Net Premium ($mil) | Net Income ($mil) |
|---|---|---|---|---|---|---|---|
| 9-17 | A+ | 5.34 | 4.45 | 1,648.3 | 878.3 | 1,878.9 | 26.3 |
| 9-16 | A+ | 5.41 | 4.51 | 1,603.0 | 801.8 | 1,844.1 | -19.7 |
| 2016 | A+ | 4.98 | 4.15 | 1,597.7 | 815.2 | 2,487.0 | 9.8 |
| 2015 | A+ | 5.52 | 4.60 | 1,579.9 | 817.8 | 2,239.7 | 4.3 |
| 2014 | A+ | 5.86 | 4.88 | 1,580.8 | 820.0 | 1,983.6 | 46.0 |
| 2013 | A+ | 6.72 | 5.60 | 1,454.5 | 767.2 | 1,393.0 | 37.7 |
| 2012 | A+ | 5.90 | 4.92 | 1,283.2 | 678.7 | 1,309.6 | 48.0 |

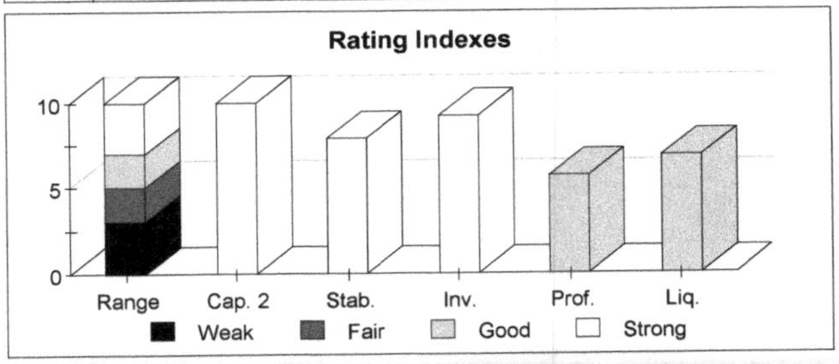


## UTMB HEALTH PLANS INC B- Good

**Major Rating Factors:** Fair overall results on stability tests (4.7 on a scale of 0 to 10). Excellent overall profitability index (7.0). Strong capitalization index (10.0) based on excellent current risk-adjusted capital (severe loss scenario).
**Other Rating Factors:** High quality investment portfolio (9.0). Excellent liquidity (10.0) with ample operational cash flow and liquid investments.
**Principal Business:** Med supp (100%)
**Mem Phys: 16:** 29 **15:** 27 **16 MLR** 38.0% **/ 16 Admin Exp** N/A
**Enroll(000): Q3 17:** 0 **16:** 0 **15:** 0 **Med Exp PMPM:** $83
**Principal Investments:** Cash and equiv (100%)
**Provider Compensation ($000):** Capitation ($190), FFS ($83)
**Total Member Encounters:** Phys (487), non-phys (555)
**Group Affiliation:** University of Texas Medical Branch
**Licensed in:** TX
**Address:** 301 University Blvd Rte 0985, Galveston, TX 77555-0985
**Phone:** (409) 766-4000 **Dom State:** TX **Commenced Bus:** April 1994

| Data Date | Rating | RACR #1 | RACR #2 | Total Assets ($mil) | Capital ($mil) | Net Premium ($mil) | Net Income ($mil) |
|---|---|---|---|---|---|---|---|
| 9-17 | B- | 57.14 | 47.62 | 5.5 | 5.4 | 1.0 | 0.7 |
| 9-16 | C+ | 49.51 | 41.26 | 5.7 | 5.1 | 0.5 | 0.2 |
| 2016 | B- | 49.96 | 41.63 | 5.7 | 5.1 | 0.7 | 0.3 |
| 2015 | B- | 51.16 | 42.63 | 6.3 | 5.6 | 0.7 | 0.3 |
| 2014 | B- | N/A | N/A | 7.2 | 6.6 | 1.8 | 1.3 |
| 2013 | B- | 38.84 | 32.37 | 8.2 | 6.2 | 0.8 | 0.2 |
| 2012 | C+ | 37.09 | 30.91 | 8.7 | 6.7 | 0.9 | 0.1 |

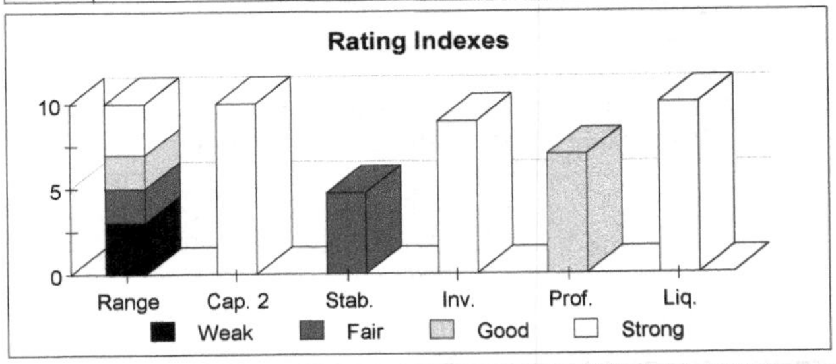

## VALUE BEHAVIORAL HEALTH OF PA — E — Very Weak

**Major Rating Factors:** Excellent profitability (8.1 on a scale of 0 to 10). Strong capitalization (7.8) based on excellent current risk-adjusted capital (severe loss scenario). High quality investment portfolio (9.9).
**Other Rating Factors:** Excellent liquidity (7.8) with ample operational cash flow and liquid investments.
**Principal Business:** Medicaid (98%), other (2%)
**Mem Phys: 16:** 994 **15:** 967 **16 MLR** 82.9% **/ 16 Admin Exp** N/A
**Enroll(000): Q3 17:** 9 **16:** 39 **15:** 87 **Med Exp PMPM:** $88
**Principal Investments:** Cash and equiv (100%)
**Provider Compensation ($000):** Contr fee ($73,360)
**Total Member Encounters:** Phys (19,096), non-phys (574,768)
**Group Affiliation:** DCP 2014 GP-GP LLC
**Licensed in:** PA
**Address:** 240 Corporate Blvd, Norfolk, VA 23502
**Phone:** (757) 459-5200 **Dom State:** PA **Commenced Bus:** January 1999

| Data Date | Rating | RACR #1 | RACR #2 | Total Assets ($mil) | Capital ($mil) | Net Premium ($mil) | Net Income ($mil) |
|---|---|---|---|---|---|---|---|
| 9-17 | E | 1.95 | 1.63 | 29.8 | 16.8 | 25.8 | 6.6 |
| 9-16 | E | 1.91 | 1.59 | 42.9 | 19.5 | 71.0 | 7.6 |
| 2016 | E | 2.26 | 1.89 | 42.2 | 19.7 | 83.8 | 7.5 |
| 2015 | E | 1.87 | 1.56 | 46.5 | 19.1 | 105.2 | 7.4 |
| 2014 | E | 1.57 | 1.31 | 34.8 | 16.2 | 101.4 | 3.7 |
| 2013 | E | 1.50 | 1.25 | 34.0 | 14.3 | 97.8 | 1.6 |
| 2012 | E | 2.73 | 2.27 | 48.5 | 27.9 | 101.0 | 4.8 |

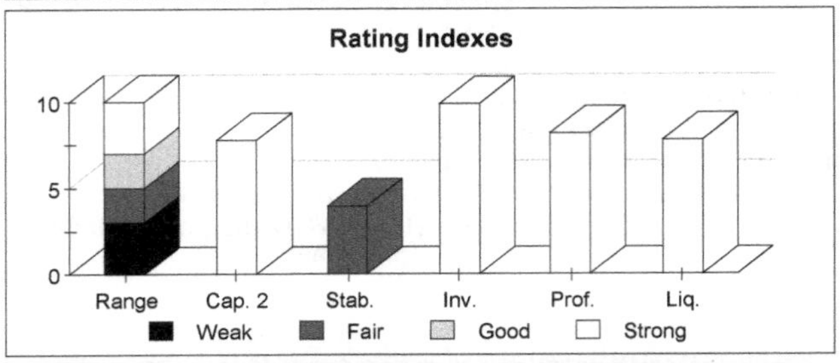


## VALUEOPTIONS OF NEW JERSEY INC — E — Very Weak

**Major Rating Factors:** Weak profitability index (1.8 on a scale of 0 to 10). Poor capitalization index (0.0) based on weak current risk-adjusted capital (severe loss scenario). Weak liquidity (0.0) as a spike in claims may stretch capacity.
**Other Rating Factors:** High quality investment portfolio (9.9).
**Principal Business:** Other (100%)
**Mem Phys: 16:** 19,159 **15:** 16,472 **16 MLR** 97.2% **/ 16 Admin Exp** N/A
**Enroll(000): 16:** 998 **15:** 628 **Med Exp PMPM:** $16
**Principal Investments:** Cash and equiv (100%)
**Provider Compensation ($000):** Contr fee ($197,143)
**Total Member Encounters:** Phys (138,028), non-phys (637,127)
**Group Affiliation:** DCP 2014 GP-GP LLC
**Licensed in:** NJ
**Address:** 103 Eisenhower Pkwy, Parkway, NJ 07068
**Phone:** (757) 459-5397 **Dom State:** NJ **Commenced Bus:** January 2014

| Data Date | Rating | RACR #1 | RACR #2 | Total Assets ($mil) | Capital ($mil) | Net Premium ($mil) | Net Income ($mil) |
|---|---|---|---|---|---|---|---|
| 2016 | E | N/A | N/A | 16.1 | 5.4 | 203.9 | -0.1 |
| 2015 | U | N/A | N/A | 12.0 | 3.0 | 111.3 | 0.1 |
| 2014 | N/A | N/A | N/A | 10.2 | 1.7 | 65.0 | -0.4 |
| 2013 | N/A | N/A | N/A | N/A | N/A | N/A | N/A |
| 2012 | N/A | N/A | N/A | N/A | N/A | N/A | N/A |

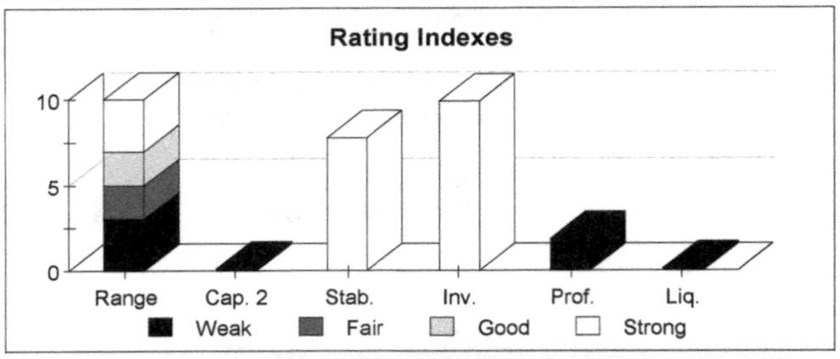


## VALUEOPTIONS OF TEXAS INC — D — Weak

**Major Rating Factors:** Good overall profitability index (6.2 on a scale of 0 to 10). Good capitalization index (5.1) based on good current risk-adjusted capital (severe loss scenario). Good overall results on stability tests (5.2) despite a decline in enrollment during 2016.
**Other Rating Factors:** High quality investment portfolio (9.9). Excellent liquidity (7.0) with sufficient resources (cash flows and marketable investments) to handle a spike in claims.
**Principal Business:** Medicaid (58%), other (42%)
**Mem Phys: 16:** 248 **15:** 219 **16 MLR** 85.7% **/ 16 Admin Exp** N/A
**Enroll(000): Q2 17:** N/A **16:** 493 **15:** 544 **Med Exp PMPM:** $20
**Principal Investments:** Cash and equiv (100%)
**Provider Compensation ($000):** Contr fee ($123,123)
**Total Member Encounters:** Phys (1,905), non-phys (563,452)
**Group Affiliation:** DCP 2014 GP-GP LLC
**Licensed in:** TX
**Address:** 1199 South Beltline Road Suite, Coppell, TX 75019
**Phone:** (757) 459-5397 **Dom State:** TX **Commenced Bus:** July 1999

| Data Date | Rating | RACR #1 | RACR #2 | Total Assets ($mil) | Capital ($mil) | Net Premium ($mil) | Net Income ($mil) |
|---|---|---|---|---|---|---|---|
| 6-17 | D | 0.95 | 0.79 | 14.0 | 5.7 | 0.3 | 0.3 |
| 6-16 | N/A | N/A | N/A | 27.8 | 4.9 | 74.8 | 0.1 |
| 2016 | E | 0.92 | 0.77 | 20.3 | 5.4 | 146.3 | 0.3 |
| 2015 | N/A | N/A | N/A | 20.1 | 5.6 | 164.7 | 1.7 |
| 2014 | N/A | N/A | N/A | 17.3 | 5.6 | 168.8 | N/A |
| 2013 | N/A | N/A | N/A | 15.5 | 4.7 | 161.9 | -0.1 |
| 2012 | N/A | N/A | N/A | 14.4 | 4.7 | 164.6 | N/A |

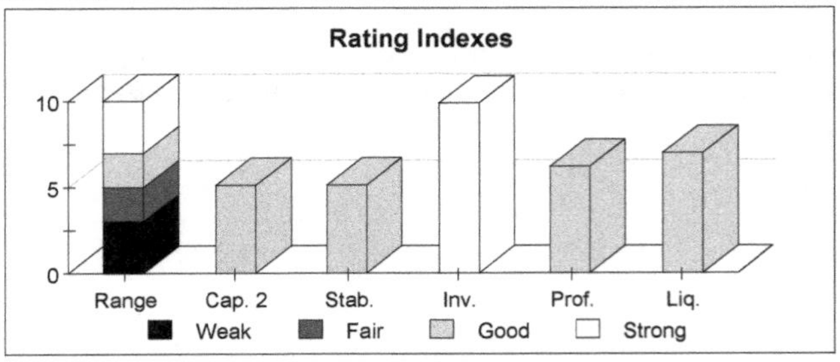

## VANTAGE HEALTH PLAN INC C- Fair

**Major Rating Factors:** Fair overall results on stability tests (4.4 on a scale of 0 to 10) based on an excessive 35% enrollment growth during the period. Poor capitalization index (2.6) based on weak current risk-adjusted capital (moderate loss scenario). Good overall profitability index (5.6).
**Other Rating Factors:** Good quality investment portfolio (5.7). Good liquidity (6.8) with sufficient resources (cash flows and marketable investments) to handle a spike in claims.
**Principal Business:** Medicare (51%), comp med (49%)
**Mem Phys: 16:** 10,916 **15:** 6,928 **16 MLR** 86.6% **/ 16 Admin Exp** N/A
**Enroll(000): Q3 17:** 48 **16:** 49 **15:** 36 **Med Exp PMPM:** $519
**Principal Investments:** Real estate (47%), cash and equiv (31%), other (21%)
**Provider Compensation ($000):** Contr fee ($265,808), FFS ($34,876), capitation ($484)
**Total Member Encounters:** Phys (641,822), non-phys (107,446)
**Group Affiliation:** Vantage Holdings Inc
**Licensed in:** LA
**Address:** 130 DeSiard Street Suite 300, Monroe, LA 71201
**Phone:** (318) 361-0900 **Dom State:** LA **Commenced Bus:** January 1995

| Data Date | Rating | RACR #1 | RACR #2 | Total Assets ($mil) | Capital ($mil) | Net Premium ($mil) | Net Income ($mil) |
|---|---|---|---|---|---|---|---|
| 9-17 | C- | 0.57 | 0.47 | 98.2 | 21.0 | 309.6 | 1.8 |
| 9-16 | D+ | 0.64 | 0.53 | 95.6 | 17.8 | 285.6 | 0.7 |
| 2016 | C- | 0.75 | 0.63 | 93.8 | 28.2 | 368.6 | 17.3 |
| 2015 | C | 0.85 | 0.70 | 64.1 | 24.0 | 270.0 | 1.2 |
| 2014 | B- | 0.91 | 0.76 | 53.4 | 21.2 | 227.7 | 5.5 |
| 2013 | B | 1.01 | 0.85 | 44.7 | 20.2 | 183.7 | 6.0 |
| 2012 | B | 1.18 | 0.99 | 43.8 | 21.5 | 177.5 | 9.9 |

Rating Indexes

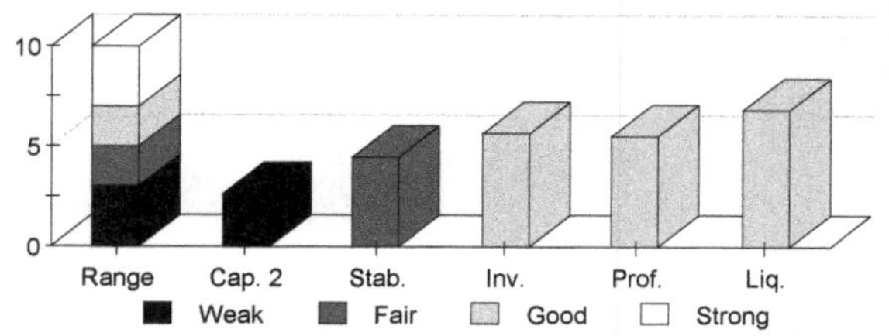


## VENTURA COUNTY HEALTH CARE PLAN E- Very Weak

**Major Rating Factors:** Weak profitability index (0.8 on a scale of 0 to 10). Poor capitalization index (0.0) based on weak current risk-adjusted capital (severe loss scenario). Weak overall results on stability tests (0.0).
**Other Rating Factors:** Weak liquidity (0.3) as a spike in claims may stretch capacity.
**Principal Business:** Managed care (100%)
**Mem Phys: 16:** N/A **15:** N/A **16 MLR** 95.3% **/ 16 Admin Exp** N/A
**Enroll(000): Q3 17:** 0 **16:** 16 **15:** 16 **Med Exp PMPM:** $317
**Principal Investments ($000):** Cash and equiv ($5,211)
**Provider Compensation ($000):** None
**Total Member Encounters:** N/A
**Group Affiliation:** None
**Licensed in:** CA
**Address:** 5455 Garden Grove Blvd Ste 500, Westminster, CA 92683
**Phone:** (562) 981-4004 **Dom State:** CA **Commenced Bus:** June 1996

| Data Date | Rating | RACR #1 | RACR #2 | Total Assets ($mil) | Capital ($mil) | Net Premium ($mil) | Net Income ($mil) |
|---|---|---|---|---|---|---|---|
| 9-17 | E- | 0.20 | 0.12 | 18.4 | 1.4 | 56.2 | 0.4 |
| 9-16 | D | 0.71 | 0.45 | 19.8 | 4.5 | 46.8 | -1.9 |
| 2016 | E- | 0.19 | 0.12 | 17.9 | 1.3 | 63.5 | -5.0 |
| 2015 | B- | 1.31 | 0.82 | 17.4 | 8.7 | 57.6 | -1.6 |
| 2014 | B | 1.87 | 1.18 | 23.5 | 10.4 | 53.9 | 0.1 |
| 2013 | B | 1.85 | 1.16 | 22.2 | 10.2 | 57.5 | 1.0 |
| 2012 | B | 1.79 | 1.12 | 22.1 | 9.2 | 53.7 | 1.7 |

Rating Indexes

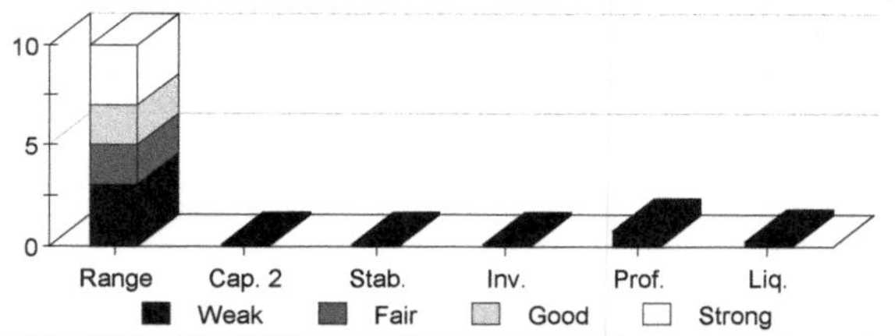


## VERMONT HEALTH PLAN LLC C+ Fair

**Major Rating Factors:** Fair overall results on stability tests (4.0 on a scale of 0 to 10) based on a steep decline in premium revenue in 2016, a significant 25% decrease in enrollment during the period. Weak profitability index (2.5). Strong capitalization index (10.0) based on excellent current risk-adjusted capital (severe loss scenario).
**Other Rating Factors:** High quality investment portfolio (9.7). Excellent liquidity (7.1) with ample operational cash flow and liquid investments.
**Principal Business:** Comp med (63%), med supp (35%), other (2%)
**Mem Phys: 16:** 7,751 **15:** 7,374 **16 MLR** 81.0% **/ 16 Admin Exp** N/A
**Enroll(000): Q3 17:** 10 **16:** 9 **15:** 13 **Med Exp PMPM:** $213
**Principal Investments:** Long-term bonds (86%), cash and equiv (14%)
**Provider Compensation ($000):** FFS ($19,354), contr fee ($6,982)
**Total Member Encounters:** Phys (14,373), non-phys (18,722)
**Group Affiliation:** Blue Cross and Blue Shield of VT
**Licensed in:** VT
**Address:** 445 Industrial Lane, Berlin, VT 05602
**Phone:** (802) 223-6131 **Dom State:** VT **Commenced Bus:** January 1997

| Data Date | Rating | RACR #1 | RACR #2 | Total Assets ($mil) | Capital ($mil) | Net Premium ($mil) | Net Income ($mil) |
|---|---|---|---|---|---|---|---|
| 9-17 | C+ | 8.88 | 7.40 | 37.8 | 33.3 | 21.1 | -1.1 |
| 9-16 | B | 5.81 | 4.84 | 40.5 | 35.0 | 23.2 | 1.8 |
| 2016 | B- | 9.12 | 7.60 | 40.1 | 34.4 | 30.6 | 1.1 |
| 2015 | B- | 5.53 | 4.61 | 43.1 | 33.2 | 50.9 | -0.7 |
| 2014 | B | 4.47 | 3.73 | 47.8 | 33.7 | 69.6 | 0.7 |
| 2013 | B | 2.00 | 1.67 | 63.9 | 33.2 | 173.0 | -2.8 |
| 2012 | B+ | 2.22 | 1.85 | 68.4 | 36.8 | 183.7 | 7.5 |

Rating Indexes

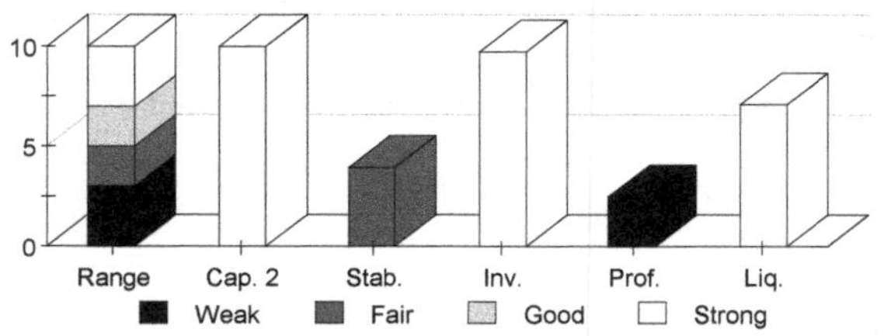

## VIRGINIA PREMIER HEALTH PLAN INC * B+ Good

**Major Rating Factors:** Good overall profitability index (6.8 on a scale of 0 to 10). Good overall results on stability tests (5.0). Strong capitalization index (7.6) based on excellent current risk-adjusted capital (severe loss scenario).
**Other Rating Factors:** High quality investment portfolio (8.0). Excellent liquidity (7.0) with sufficient resources (cash flows and marketable investments) to handle a spike in claims.
**Principal Business:** Medicaid (100%)
**Mem Phys: 16:** N/A **15:** N/A **16 MLR** 88.9% **/ 16 Admin Exp** N/A
**Enroll(000): Q3 17:** 206 **16:** 195 **15:** 194 **Med Exp PMPM:** $409
**Principal Investments:** Cash and equiv (30%), nonaffiliate common stock (25%), long-term bonds (24%), other (20%)
**Provider Compensation ($000):** Bonus arrang ($876,787), capitation ($65,071)
**Total Member Encounters:** N/A
**Group Affiliation:** VA Commonwealth University Health
**Licensed in:** VA
**Address:** 600 E Broad St Suite 400, Richmond, VA 23219
**Phone:** (804) 819-5151 **Dom State:** VA **Commenced Bus:** November 1995

| Data Date | Rating | RACR #1 | RACR #2 | Total Assets ($mil) | Capital ($mil) | Net Premium ($mil) | Net Income ($mil) |
|---|---|---|---|---|---|---|---|
| 9-17 | B+ | 1.82 | 1.51 | 317.9 | 184.3 | 860.8 | 8.4 |
| 9-16 | B | 1.76 | 1.47 | 320.6 | 189.5 | 807.2 | 22.2 |
| 2016 | B+ | 1.85 | 1.54 | 302.8 | 199.8 | 1,070.4 | 30.7 |
| 2015 | B+ | 1.51 | 1.26 | 281.9 | 168.3 | 1,024.6 | 16.3 |
| 2014 | A- | 1.79 | 1.49 | 282.3 | 157.7 | 825.1 | 7.6 |
| 2013 | A- | 1.56 | 1.30 | 183.6 | 99.8 | 714.9 | 26.8 |
| 2012 | B+ | 1.37 | 1.14 | 167.5 | 73.9 | 586.1 | 10.0 |

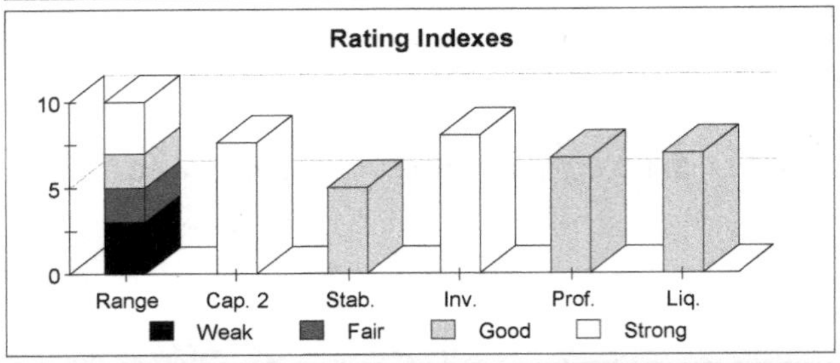


## VISTA HEALTH PLAN INC B- Good

**Major Rating Factors:** Good overall profitability index (6.9 on a scale of 0 to 10). Strong capitalization index (8.0) based on excellent current risk-adjusted capital (severe loss scenario). High quality investment portfolio (9.9).
**Other Rating Factors:** Excellent overall results on stability tests (8.4) based on healthy premium and capital growth during 2016. Fair financial strength from affiliates. Excellent liquidity (7.2) with ample operational cash flow and liquid investments.
**Principal Business:** Medicaid (98%), Medicare (2%)
**Mem Phys: 16:** 45,584 **15:** 40,517 **16 MLR** 90.2% **/ 16 Admin Exp** N/A
**Enroll(000): Q3 17:** 707 **16:** 690 **15:** 648 **Med Exp PMPM:** $510
**Principal Investments:** Cash and equiv (73%), long-term bonds (27%)
**Provider Compensation ($000):** Capitation ($4,126,083)
**Total Member Encounters:** Phys (4,786,267), non-phys (1,039,727)
**Group Affiliation:** Independence Health Group Inc
**Licensed in:** PA
**Address:** 1901 Market Street, Philadelphia, PA 19103-1480
**Phone:** (215) 241-2400 **Dom State:** PA **Commenced Bus:** November 1986

| Data Date | Rating | RACR #1 | RACR #2 | Total Assets ($mil) | Capital ($mil) | Net Premium ($mil) | Net Income ($mil) |
|---|---|---|---|---|---|---|---|
| 9-17 | B- | 2.16 | 1.80 | 813.1 | 281.6 | 3,293.8 | 2.9 |
| 9-16 | C+ | 2.02 | 1.68 | 702.8 | 262.5 | 3,308.3 | -13.7 |
| 2016 | B- | 2.14 | 1.78 | 1,158.0 | 278.5 | 4,574.3 | 3.2 |
| 2015 | B- | 1.75 | 1.46 | 453.3 | 227.9 | 3,750.6 | 3.0 |
| 2014 | B | 2.04 | 1.70 | 546.1 | 188.0 | 3,079.1 | 2.2 |
| 2013 | B | 1.98 | 1.65 | 447.4 | 160.5 | 2,750.9 | 2.9 |
| 2012 | N/A | N/A | N/A | 512.0 | 157.5 | 2,575.5 | 2.6 |

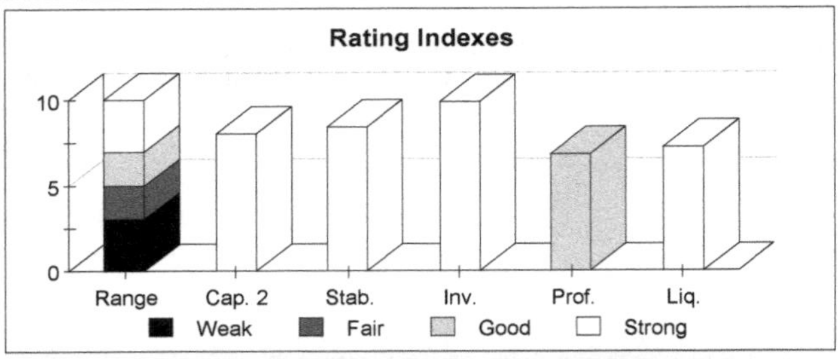


## VIVA HEALTH INC * B+ Good

**Major Rating Factors:** Good overall profitability index (5.8 on a scale of 0 to 10). Good overall results on stability tests (6.6). Strong capitalization index (8.3) based on excellent current risk-adjusted capital (severe loss scenario).
**Other Rating Factors:** High quality investment portfolio (7.3). Excellent liquidity (7.0) with ample operational cash flow and liquid investments.
**Principal Business:** Medicare (82%), comp med (18%)
**Mem Phys: 16:** 13,834 **15:** 12,385 **16 MLR** 85.8% **/ 16 Admin Exp** N/A
**Enroll(000): Q3 17:** 75 **16:** 74 **15:** 74 **Med Exp PMPM:** $612
**Principal Investments:** Cash and equiv (53%), nonaffiliate common stock (38%), long-term bonds (9%)
**Provider Compensation ($000):** Contr fee ($406,657), capitation ($140,201), FFS ($12,577)
**Total Member Encounters:** Phys (1,316,681), non-phys (1,439,173)
**Group Affiliation:** University of Alabama
**Licensed in:** AL
**Address:** 417 20TH STREET NORTH SUITE 11, BIRMINGHAM, AL 35203
**Phone:** (205) 939-1718 **Dom State:** AL **Commenced Bus:** February 1996

| Data Date | Rating | RACR #1 | RACR #2 | Total Assets ($mil) | Capital ($mil) | Net Premium ($mil) | Net Income ($mil) |
|---|---|---|---|---|---|---|---|
| 9-17 | B+ | 2.37 | 1.98 | 276.6 | 102.6 | 533.7 | 5.4 |
| 9-16 | B | 2.01 | 1.68 | 226.3 | 93.7 | 474.6 | 8.5 |
| 2016 | B+ | 2.23 | 1.86 | 181.0 | 97.2 | 625.2 | 10.6 |
| 2015 | B | 1.74 | 1.45 | 161.1 | 83.1 | 610.4 | -3.6 |
| 2014 | B+ | 2.11 | 1.76 | 153.8 | 94.2 | 603.3 | 6.4 |
| 2013 | B+ | 2.15 | 1.79 | 147.2 | 87.9 | 554.8 | 13.7 |
| 2012 | B+ | 1.85 | 1.54 | 132.5 | 78.2 | 559.8 | 11.0 |

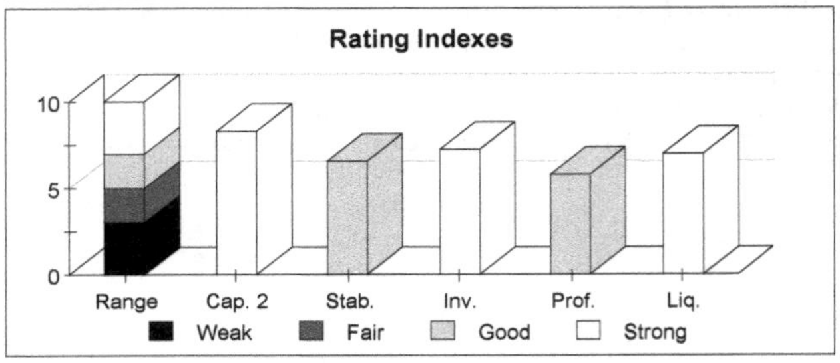

## VOLUNTEER STATE HEALTH PLAN INC * A+ Excellent

**Major Rating Factors:** Excellent profitability (9.8 on a scale of 0 to 10). Strong capitalization index (10.0) based on excellent current risk-adjusted capital (severe loss scenario). High quality investment portfolio (8.6).
**Other Rating Factors:** Excellent overall results on stability tests (8.1). Good financial strength from affiliates. Excellent liquidity (6.9) with sufficient resources (cash flows and marketable investments) to handle a spike in claims.
**Principal Business:** Medicaid (94%), Medicare (6%)
**Mem Phys: 16:** 27,705 **15:** 27,173 **16 MLR** 78.8% **/ 16 Admin Exp** N/A
**Enroll(000): Q3 17:** 531 **16:** 552 **15:** 529 **Med Exp PMPM:** $293
**Principal Investments:** Long-term bonds (62%), cash and equiv (27%), nonaffiliate common stock (9%), pref stock (2%)
**Provider Compensation ($000):** Contr fee ($1,874,038), capitation ($44,730), bonus arrang ($2,538)
**Total Member Encounters:** Phys (5,286,737), non-phys (459,717)
**Group Affiliation:** BlueCross BlueShield of Tennessee
**Licensed in:** (No states)
**Address:** 1 Cameron Hill Circle, Chattanooga, TN 37402-0001
**Phone:** (423) 535-5600 **Dom State:** TN **Commenced Bus:** November 1996

| Data Date | Rating | RACR #1 | RACR #2 | Total Assets ($mil) | Capital ($mil) | Net Premium ($mil) | Net Income ($mil) |
|---|---|---|---|---|---|---|---|
| 9-17 | A+ | 3.65 | 3.04 | 818.7 | 458.7 | 1,855.5 | 29.3 |
| 9-16 | A+ | 3.38 | 2.82 | 710.4 | 376.2 | 1,808.8 | 65.7 |
| 2016 | A+ | 3.36 | 2.80 | 737.6 | 420.8 | 2,440.8 | 109.6 |
| 2015 | A+ | 3.00 | 2.50 | 805.5 | 330.8 | 2,196.7 | 75.2 |
| 2014 | A+ | 3.58 | 2.99 | 729.4 | 330.1 | 1,815.8 | 60.3 |
| 2013 | B+ | 2.93 | 2.44 | 478.2 | 256.9 | 1,673.1 | 42.0 |
| 2012 | B | 2.48 | 2.06 | 450.4 | 217.7 | 1,690.8 | 42.8 |

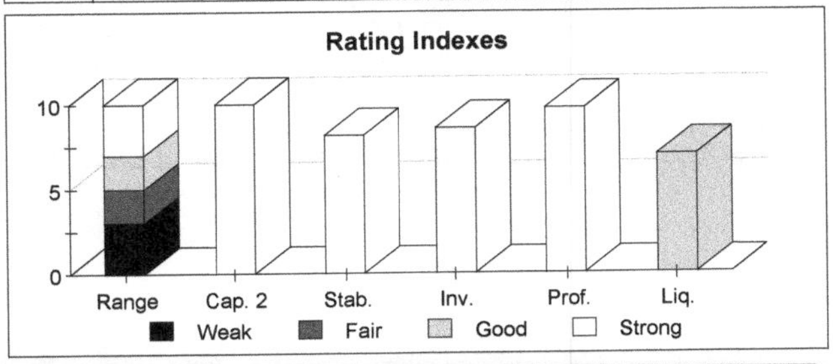


## WASHINGTON NATIONAL INSURANCE COMPANY D+ Weak

**Major Rating Factors:** Weak overall results on stability tests (2.7 on a scale of 0 to 10) including potential financial drain due to affiliation with CNO Financial Group Inc. Fair quality investment portfolio (4.6) with large holdings of BBB rated bonds in addition to junk bond exposure equal to 80% of capital. Good overall profitability (5.8). Excellent expense controls.
**Other Rating Factors:** Good liquidity (6.7). Strong capitalization (7.1) based on excellent risk adjusted capital (severe loss scenario).
**Principal Business:** Individual health insurance (60%), group health insurance (27%), individual life insurance (7%), reinsurance (4%), and individual annuities (1%).
**Principal Investments:** NonCMO investment grade bonds (56%), CMOs and structured securities (24%), noninv. grade bonds (6%), mortgages in good standing (6%), and misc. investments (8%).
**Investments in Affiliates:** 1%
**Group Affiliation:** CNO Financial Group Inc
**Licensed in:** All states except NY
**Commenced Business:** September 1923
**Address:** 11825 NORTH PENNSYLVANIA STREE, CARMEL, IN 46032
**Phone:** (317) 817-6100 **Domicile State:** IN **NAIC Code:** 70319

| Data Date | Rating | RACR #1 | RACR #2 | Total Assets ($mil) | Capital ($mil) | Net Premium ($mil) | Net Income ($mil) |
|---|---|---|---|---|---|---|---|
| 9-17 | D+ | 1.98 | 1.06 | 5,420.1 | 398.1 | 516.8 | 20.6 |
| 9-16 | D+ | 2.09 | 1.08 | 5,396.8 | 439.1 | 493.7 | -42.1 |
| 2016 | D+ | 2.09 | 1.09 | 5,397.6 | 431.1 | 663.1 | -53.0 |
| 2015 | D+ | 1.70 | 0.93 | 4,807.8 | 333.1 | 649.7 | 60.9 |
| 2014 | D+ | 1.67 | 0.90 | 4,775.3 | 327.0 | 610.0 | 50.8 |
| 2013 | D+ | 2.20 | 1.15 | 5,286.1 | 431.9 | 540.7 | 59.6 |
| 2012 | D+ | 2.28 | 1.23 | 5,247.6 | 469.4 | 522.4 | 58.6 |

**CNO Financial Group Inc**
**Composite Group Rating: D+**

| Largest Group Members | Assets ($mil) | Rating |
|---|---|---|
| BANKERS LIFE CAS CO | 17602 | D+ |
| WASHINGTON NATIONAL INS CO | 5398 | D+ |
| COLONIAL PENN LIFE INS CO | 855 | D+ |
| BANKERS CONSECO LIFE INS CO | 450 | D |

## WEA INSURANCE CORPORATION C Fair

**Major Rating Factors:** Fair quality investment portfolio (4.0 on a scale of 0 to 10). Fair overall results on stability tests (3.7) including negative cash flow from operations for 2016. Good liquidity (6.3) with sufficient resources to handle a spike in claims.
**Other Rating Factors:** Weak profitability (1.4) with operating losses during the first nine months of 2017. Strong capitalization (7.3) based on excellent risk adjusted capital (severe loss scenario).
**Principal Business:** Group health insurance (100%).
**Principal Investments:** NonCMO investment grade bonds (51%), CMOs and structured securities (24%), common & preferred stock (23%), and cash (1%).
**Investments in Affiliates:** None
**Group Affiliation:** Wisconsin Education Assn Ins Trust
**Licensed in:** WI
**Commenced Business:** July 1985
**Address:** 45 NOB HILL ROAD, MADISON, WI 53713-0000
**Phone:** (608) 276-4000 **Domicile State:** WI **NAIC Code:** 72273

| Data Date | Rating | RACR #1 | RACR #2 | Total Assets ($mil) | Capital ($mil) | Net Premium ($mil) | Net Income ($mil) |
|---|---|---|---|---|---|---|---|
| 9-17 | C | 1.72 | 1.18 | 665.7 | 155.5 | 350.8 | -3.7 |
| 9-16 | C | 1.63 | 1.13 | 641.4 | 149.6 | 372.4 | -0.5 |
| 2016 | C | 1.57 | 1.09 | 644.9 | 140.9 | 496.6 | 1.1 |
| 2015 | C | 1.70 | 1.20 | 644.2 | 160.7 | 550.6 | -34.2 |
| 2014 | C | 1.97 | 1.40 | 683.9 | 200.2 | 593.3 | -28.0 |
| 2013 | C | 2.28 | 1.61 | 720.9 | 243.0 | 594.6 | -15.1 |
| 2012 | B- | 2.19 | 1.59 | 686.8 | 232.1 | 635.9 | 19.1 |

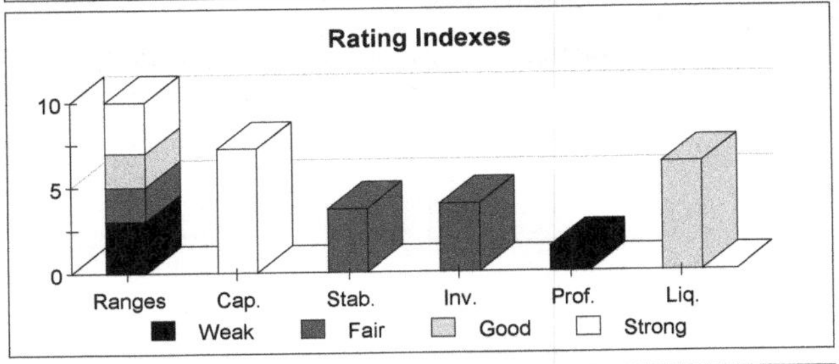

## WELLCARE HEALTH INS OF ARIZONA INC C Fair

**Major Rating Factors:** Good overall profitability index (5.9 on a scale of 0 to 10). Strong capitalization (7.5) based on excellent current risk-adjusted capital (severe loss scenario). High quality investment portfolio (9.9).
**Other Rating Factors:** Excellent liquidity (7.1) with ample operational cash flow and liquid investments.
**Principal Business:** Medicaid (71%), Medicare (29%)
**Mem Phys: 16:** 23,400 **15:** 20,100 **16 MLR** 82.3% **/ 16 Admin Exp** N/A
**Enroll(000): Q3 17:** 66 **16:** 69 **15:** 70 **Med Exp PMPM:** $746
**Principal Investments:** Cash and equiv (91%), long-term bonds (9%)
**Provider Compensation ($000):** Contr fee ($559,945), capitation ($39,307)
**Total Member Encounters:** Phys (380,105), non-phys (393,867)
**Group Affiliation:** WellCare Health Plans Inc
**Licensed in:** AL, AK, AZ, AR, CO, DC, DE, FL, GA, HI, ID, IL, IN, IA, KS, KY, LA, MD, MI, MN, MS, MO, MT, NE, NV, NM, NC, ND, OK, OR, SC, SD, TN, TX, UT, VA, WA, WY
**Address:** 3800 N Central Ave Ste 460, Phoenix, AZ 85012
**Phone:** (813) 290-6200 **Dom State:** AZ **Commenced Bus:** January 1973

| Data Date | Rating | RACR #1 | RACR #2 | Total Assets ($mil) | Capital ($mil) | Net Premium ($mil) | Net Income ($mil) |
|---|---|---|---|---|---|---|---|
| 9-17 | C | 1.73 | 1.44 | 240.9 | 61.6 | 531.5 | 3.2 |
| 9-16 | C | 2.46 | 2.05 | 256.6 | 93.7 | 543.2 | 5.9 |
| 2016 | C | 2.63 | 2.19 | 223.9 | 97.4 | 731.0 | 10.4 |
| 2015 | C | 2.28 | 1.90 | 217.6 | 86.1 | 739.3 | 1.0 |
| 2014 | B- | 2.26 | 1.89 | 192.8 | 82.0 | 701.8 | -2.4 |
| 2013 | B- | 2.83 | 2.36 | 167.8 | 74.4 | 519.4 | 13.0 |
| 2012 | C+ | 3.48 | 2.90 | 151.1 | 77.6 | 440.9 | 12.6 |

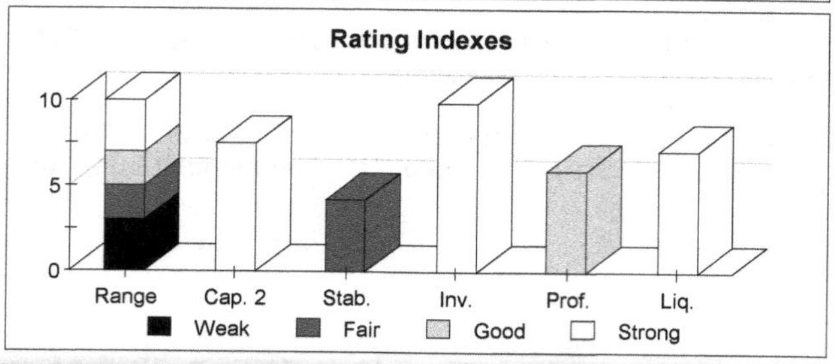


## WELLCARE HEALTH INS OF KENTUCKY INC C Fair

**Major Rating Factors:** Good overall profitability index (6.6 on a scale of 0 to 10). Strong capitalization (7.9) based on excellent current risk-adjusted capital (severe loss scenario). High quality investment portfolio (9.9).
**Other Rating Factors:** Excellent liquidity (7.0) with ample operational cash flow and liquid investments.
**Principal Business:** Medicaid (94%), Medicare (4%), other (2%)
**Mem Phys: 16:** 41,400 **15:** 35,600 **16 MLR** 86.2% **/ 16 Admin Exp** N/A
**Enroll(000): Q3 17:** 556 **16:** 529 **15:** 525 **Med Exp PMPM:** $373
**Principal Investments:** Cash and equiv (96%), long-term bonds (4%)
**Provider Compensation ($000):** Contr fee ($2,260,664), capitation ($124,226)
**Total Member Encounters:** Phys (2,921,445), non-phys (2,471,694)
**Group Affiliation:** WellCare Health Plans Inc
**Licensed in:** All states except FL, ME, MI, NH, NY, NC, TX, VT, PR
**Address:** 13551Triton Park Blvd Ste 1800, Louisville, KY 40223
**Phone:** (813) 290-6200 **Dom State:** KY **Commenced Bus:** August 1962

| Data Date | Rating | RACR #1 | RACR #2 | Total Assets ($mil) | Capital ($mil) | Net Premium ($mil) | Net Income ($mil) |
|---|---|---|---|---|---|---|---|
| 9-17 | C | 2.08 | 1.74 | 835.8 | 302.0 | 2,087.2 | 40.5 |
| 9-16 | C | 1.89 | 1.58 | 682.2 | 269.9 | 2,079.2 | 27.5 |
| 2016 | C | 1.97 | 1.64 | 682.9 | 283.2 | 2,753.4 | 42.2 |
| 2015 | C+ | 2.10 | 1.75 | 691.8 | 301.3 | 2,763.2 | 119.0 |
| 2014 | B- | 1.65 | 1.37 | 522.6 | 211.7 | 2,419.4 | 89.0 |
| 2013 | C | 1.53 | 1.27 | 291.4 | 123.5 | 1,403.7 | 38.9 |
| 2012 | C | 1.40 | 1.17 | 184.6 | 68.6 | 743.7 | -50.7 |

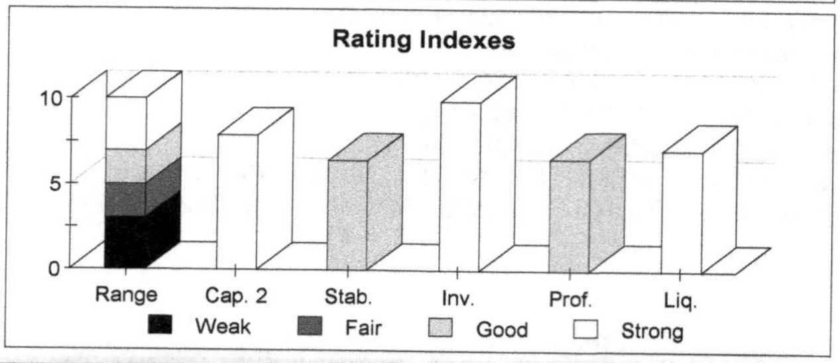


## WELLCARE HEALTH PLANS OF KENTUCKY C- Fair

**Major Rating Factors:** Weak profitability index (2.4 on a scale of 0 to 10). Strong capitalization (9.2) based on excellent current risk-adjusted capital (severe loss scenario). High quality investment portfolio (9.9).
**Other Rating Factors:** Excellent liquidity (8.9) with ample operational cash flow and liquid investments.
**Principal Business:** Comp med (100%)
**Mem Phys: 16:** 16,600 **15:** 13,100 **16 MLR** 112.0% **/ 16 Admin Exp** N/A
**Enroll(000): Q1 17:** N/A **16:** 1 **15:** 0 **Med Exp PMPM:** $286
**Principal Investments:** Cash and equiv (90%), long-term bonds (10%)
**Provider Compensation ($000):** Contr fee ($2,302), capitation ($75)
**Total Member Encounters:** Phys (3,250), non-phys (1,993)
**Group Affiliation:** WellCare Health Plans Inc
**Licensed in:** KY
**Address:** 13551 Triton Park Blvd #1800, Louisville, KY 40223
**Phone:** (813) 290-6200 **Dom State:** KY **Commenced Bus:** January 2015

| Data Date | Rating | RACR #1 | RACR #2 | Total Assets ($mil) | Capital ($mil) | Net Premium ($mil) | Net Income ($mil) |
|---|---|---|---|---|---|---|---|
| 3-17 | C- | 3.11 | 2.59 | 5.2 | 4.1 | 0.6 | 0.5 |
| 3-16 | C | 2.52 | 2.10 | 4.6 | 3.7 | 0.7 | -0.1 |
| 2016 | C- | 2.71 | 2.26 | 5.8 | 3.6 | 2.5 | -0.2 |
| 2015 | C- | 2.55 | 2.13 | 3.8 | 3.8 | 0.2 | 0.0 |
| 2014 | N/A | N/A | N/A | 3.5 | 3.5 | N/A | N/A |
| 2013 | N/A | N/A | N/A | N/A | N/A | N/A | N/A |
| 2012 | N/A | N/A | N/A | N/A | N/A | N/A | N/A |

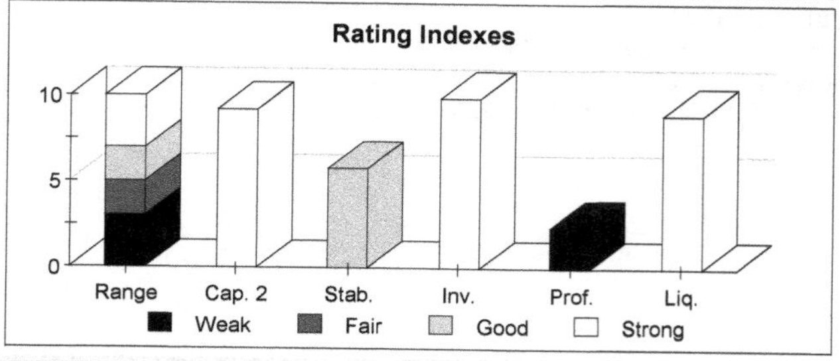

## WELLCARE HEALTH PLANS OF NEW JERSEY C Fair

**Major Rating Factors:** Weak profitability index (2.5 on a scale of 0 to 10). Strong capitalization (9.5) based on excellent current risk-adjusted capital (severe loss scenario). High quality investment portfolio (9.9).
**Other Rating Factors:** Excellent liquidity (7.0) with ample operational cash flow and liquid investments.
**Principal Business:** Medicaid (97%), Medicare (3%)
**Mem Phys: 16:** 23,600 **15:** 18,200 **16 MLR** 79.2% **/ 16 Admin Exp** N/A
**Enroll(000): Q3 17:** 68 **16:** 63 **15:** 57 **Med Exp PMPM:** $493
**Principal Investments:** Cash and equiv (66%), long-term bonds (34%)
**Provider Compensation ($000):** Contr fee ($363,279), capitation ($11,006)
**Total Member Encounters:** Phys (402,293), non-phys (481,623)
**Group Affiliation:** WellCare Health Plans Inc
**Licensed in:** NJ
**Address:** 550 BRd St Ste 1200, Newark, NJ 07102
**Phone:** (813) 290-6200 **Dom State:** NJ **Commenced Bus:** January 2008

| Data Date | Rating | RACR #1 | RACR #2 | Total Assets ($mil) | Capital ($mil) | Net Premium ($mil) | Net Income ($mil) |
|---|---|---|---|---|---|---|---|
| 9-17 | C | 3.38 | 2.82 | 161.2 | 74.0 | 435.3 | 0.1 |
| 9-16 | C- | 3.83 | 3.19 | 168.2 | 74.7 | 332.0 | 12.8 |
| 2016 | C- | 3.34 | 2.79 | 159.5 | 73.1 | 454.6 | 10.0 |
| 2015 | C- | 2.46 | 2.05 | 140.4 | 46.5 | 350.0 | 1.3 |
| 2014 | C- | 1.46 | 1.22 | 70.4 | 15.8 | 179.2 | -6.5 |
| 2013 | C | 5.72 | 4.77 | 9.8 | 6.8 | 12.0 | -1.6 |
| 2012 | B- | 3.63 | 3.02 | 9.9 | 5.9 | 19.4 | -1.3 |

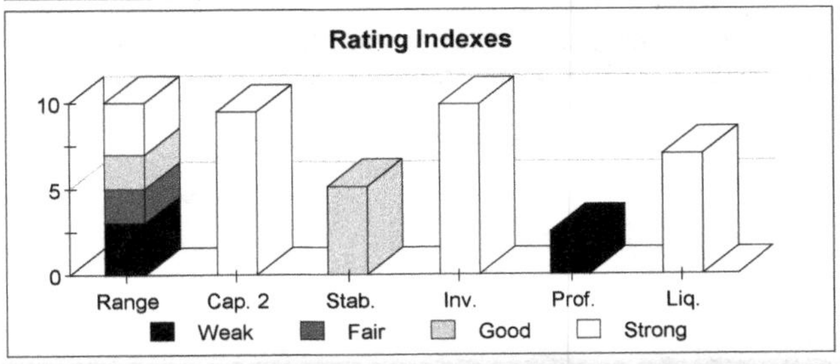


## WELLCARE OF CONNECTICUT INC C+ Fair

**Major Rating Factors:** Fair profitability index (3.4 on a scale of 0 to 10). Fair overall results on stability tests (4.6) based on a significant 42% decrease in enrollment during the period. Rating is significantly influenced by the fair financial results of WellCare Health Plans Inc. Strong capitalization index (10.0) based on excellent current risk-adjusted capital (severe loss scenario).
**Other Rating Factors:** High quality investment portfolio (9.9). Excellent liquidity (7.3) with ample operational cash flow and liquid investments.
**Principal Business:** Medicare (100%)
**Mem Phys: 16:** 20,600 **15:** 17,700 **16 MLR** 86.0% **/ 16 Admin Exp** N/A
**Enroll(000): Q3 17:** 7 **16:** 7 **15:** 12 **Med Exp PMPM:** $841,248
**Principal Investments:** Cash and equiv (97%), long-term bonds (3%)
**Provider Compensation ($000):** Contr fee ($71,394), capitation ($539)
**Total Member Encounters:** Phys (92,662), non-phys (53,018)
**Group Affiliation:** WellCare Health Plans Inc
**Licensed in:** CT
**Address:** 902 Chapel Street, New Haven, CT 06510
**Phone:** (813) 290-6200 **Dom State:** CT **Commenced Bus:** March 1995

| Data Date | Rating | RACR #1 | RACR #2 | Total Assets ($mil) | Capital ($mil) | Net Premium ($mil) | Net Income ($mil) |
|---|---|---|---|---|---|---|---|
| 9-17 | C+ | 4.25 | 3.54 | 48.2 | 22.5 | 65.1 | -1.7 |
| 9-16 | C+ | 2.76 | 2.30 | 48.2 | 24.6 | 62.3 | -3.4 |
| 2016 | C+ | 4.55 | 3.79 | 39.1 | 24.2 | 81.2 | -3.4 |
| 2015 | C+ | 3.07 | 2.56 | 45.0 | 27.5 | 146.5 | 6.1 |
| 2014 | C | 2.67 | 2.23 | 37.4 | 20.7 | 115.1 | 0.9 |
| 2013 | C | 3.47 | 2.89 | 28.8 | 20.1 | 83.2 | 3.5 |
| 2012 | B- | 3.17 | 2.65 | 23.3 | 13.3 | 51.1 | -1.7 |

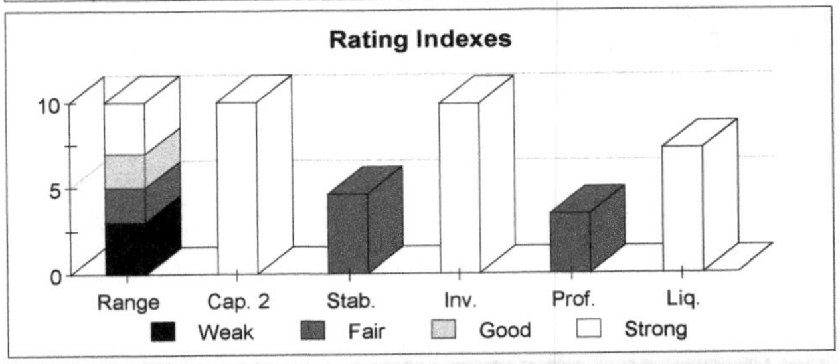


## WELLCARE OF FLORIDA INC E Very Weak

**Major Rating Factors:** Good overall profitability index (5.8 on a scale of 0 to 10). Good capitalization index (5.8) based on good current risk-adjusted capital (severe loss scenario). Good overall results on stability tests (5.8).
**Other Rating Factors:** High quality investment portfolio (9.9). Excellent liquidity (6.9) with sufficient resources (cash flows and marketable investments) to handle a spike in claims.
**Principal Business:** Medicaid (66%), Medicare (32%), comp med (2%)
**Mem Phys: 16:** 44,100 **15:** 38,400 **16 MLR** 82.9% **/ 16 Admin Exp** N/A
**Enroll(000): Q3 17:** 858 **16:** 874 **15:** 888 **Med Exp PMPM:** $305,042,357
**Principal Investments:** Cash and equiv (89%), long-term bonds (11%)
**Provider Compensation ($000):** Contr fee ($2,723,375), capitation ($249,017)
**Total Member Encounters:** Phys (5,185,672), non-phys (2,468,824)
**Group Affiliation:** WellCare Health Plans Inc
**Licensed in:** FL
**Address:** 8735 Henderson Road, Tampa, FL 33634
**Phone:** (813) 290-6200 **Dom State:** FL **Commenced Bus:** March 1986

| Data Date | Rating | RACR #1 | RACR #2 | Total Assets ($mil) | Capital ($mil) | Net Premium ($mil) | Net Income ($mil) |
|---|---|---|---|---|---|---|---|
| 9-17 | E | 1.06 | 0.88 | 921.8 | 178.6 | 2,895.4 | 126.1 |
| 9-16 | E | 1.15 | 0.96 | 797.6 | 191.1 | 2,747.6 | 66.6 |
| 2016 | E | 1.02 | 0.85 | 688.9 | 170.8 | 3,679.1 | 128.0 |
| 2015 | E- | 1.03 | 0.86 | 568.1 | 167.1 | 3,554.9 | 49.6 |
| 2014 | C- | 0.65 | 0.55 | 537.4 | 76.5 | 2,812.0 | -55.3 |
| 2013 | B+ | 1.56 | 1.30 | 402.1 | 150.7 | 2,021.8 | 42.8 |
| 2012 | B+ | 1.93 | 1.61 | 392.9 | 153.3 | 1,696.5 | 80.9 |

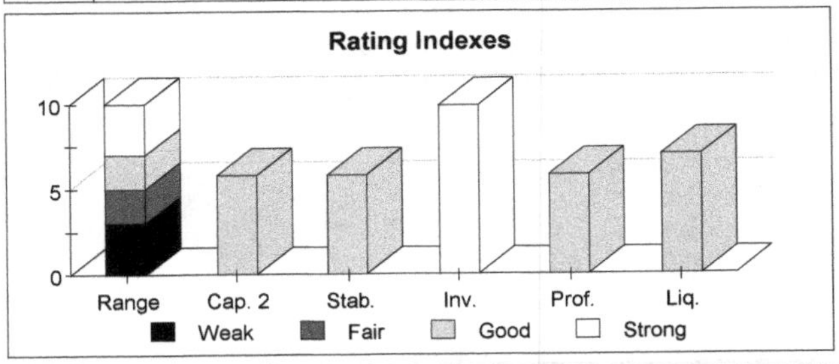

## WELLCARE OF GEORGIA INC C Fair

**Major Rating Factors:** Excellent profitability (8.6 on a scale of 0 to 10). Strong capitalization (8.1) based on excellent current risk-adjusted capital (severe loss scenario). High quality investment portfolio (9.9).
**Other Rating Factors:** Excellent liquidity (7.0) with ample operational cash flow and liquid investments.
**Principal Business:** Medicaid (73%), Medicare (21%), comp med (6%)
**Mem Phys: 16:** 43,200 **15:** 39,500 **16 MLR** 84.6% **/ 16 Admin Exp** N/A
**Enroll(000): Q3 17:** 543 **16:** 611 **15:** 621 **Med Exp PMPM:** $246,808,971
**Principal Investments:** Cash and equiv (100%)
**Provider Compensation ($000):** Contr fee ($1,564,029), capitation ($153,277)
**Total Member Encounters:** Phys (3,066,458), non-phys (1,496,721)
**Group Affiliation:** WellCare Health Plans Inc
**Licensed in:** GA
**Address:** 211 Perimeter Ctr Pkwy NW #800, Atlanta, GA 30346
**Phone:** (813) 290-6200 **Dom State:** GA **Commenced Bus:** July 2006

| Data Date | Rating | RACR #1 | RACR #2 | Total Assets ($mil) | Capital ($mil) | Net Premium ($mil) | Net Income ($mil) |
|---|---|---|---|---|---|---|---|
| 9-17 | C | 2.22 | 1.85 | 543.9 | 224.7 | 1,623.2 | 91.3 |
| 9-16 | C | 2.08 | 1.74 | 484.8 | 203.6 | 1,562.0 | 22.6 |
| 2016 | C | 1.96 | 1.63 | 493.6 | 195.2 | 2,041.1 | 16.7 |
| 2015 | C | 1.83 | 1.52 | 374.6 | 175.4 | 1,991.3 | 1.2 |
| 2014 | B- | 1.58 | 1.31 | 355.4 | 154.0 | 1,972.6 | 0.4 |
| 2013 | B | 1.55 | 1.29 | 336.8 | 145.4 | 1,805.8 | 10.9 |
| 2012 | B+ | 1.55 | 1.29 | 286.1 | 132.5 | 1,657.4 | 0.7 |

Rating Indexes

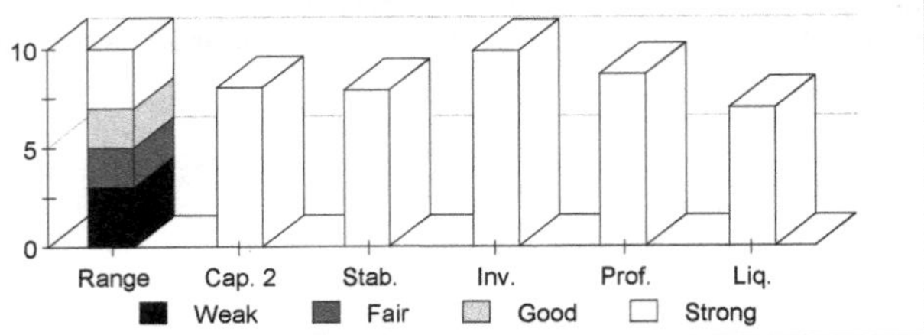


## WELLCARE OF SOUTH CAROLINA INC C Fair

**Major Rating Factors:** Excellent profitability (8.7 on a scale of 0 to 10). Strong capitalization (10.0) based on excellent current risk-adjusted capital (severe loss scenario). High quality investment portfolio (9.9).
**Other Rating Factors:** Excellent liquidity (7.2) with ample operational cash flow and liquid investments.
**Principal Business:** Medicaid (100%)
**Mem Phys: 16:** 24,100 **15:** 18,800 **16 MLR** 82.2% **/ 16 Admin Exp** N/A
**Enroll(000): Q3 17:** 83 **16:** 87 **15:** 60 **Med Exp PMPM:** $246,133
**Principal Investments:** Cash and equiv (100%)
**Provider Compensation ($000):** Contr fee ($206,572), capitation ($3,114)
**Total Member Encounters:** Phys (363,595), non-phys (103,215)
**Group Affiliation:** WellCare Health Plans Inc
**Licensed in:** SC
**Address:** 200 Center Point Circle #180, Columbia, SC 29210
**Phone:** (813) 206-6200 **Dom State:** SC **Commenced Bus:** November 2004

| Data Date | Rating | RACR #1 | RACR #2 | Total Assets ($mil) | Capital ($mil) | Net Premium ($mil) | Net Income ($mil) |
|---|---|---|---|---|---|---|---|
| 9-17 | C | 4.24 | 3.53 | 119.0 | 63.1 | 220.7 | 7.0 |
| 9-16 | C- | 4.22 | 3.51 | 104.2 | 47.7 | 200.4 | -0.2 |
| 2016 | C | 3.64 | 3.03 | 110.1 | 53.4 | 277.6 | 4.9 |
| 2015 | C | 3.85 | 3.21 | 78.7 | 43.2 | 222.7 | 12.5 |
| 2014 | B- | 3.78 | 3.15 | 75.5 | 43.7 | 217.3 | 10.4 |
| 2013 | B- | 3.54 | 2.95 | 59.2 | 35.4 | 162.9 | 7.7 |
| 2012 | C+ | 2.53 | 2.11 | 59.5 | 29.2 | 218.7 | 9.8 |

Rating Indexes

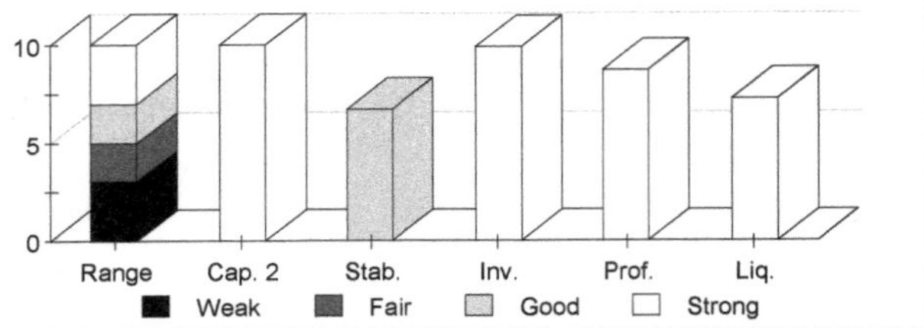


## WELLCARE OF TEXAS INC C Fair

**Major Rating Factors:** Fair profitability index (4.8 on a scale of 0 to 10). Strong capitalization (9.2) based on excellent current risk-adjusted capital (severe loss scenario). High quality investment portfolio (9.9).
**Other Rating Factors:** Excellent liquidity (7.1) with ample operational cash flow and liquid investments.
**Principal Business:** Medicare (100%)
**Mem Phys: 16:** 25,900 **15:** 22,800 **16 MLR** 83.2% **/ 16 Admin Exp** N/A
**Enroll(000): Q3 17:** 49 **16:** 49 **15:** 48 **Med Exp PMPM:** $567,051
**Principal Investments:** Cash and equiv (99%), long-term bonds (1%)
**Provider Compensation ($000):** Contr fee ($300,435), capitation ($10,366)
**Total Member Encounters:** Phys (541,052), non-phys (239,861)
**Group Affiliation:** WellCare Health Plans Inc
**Licensed in:** AZ, TX
**Address:** 11200 Richmond Ave Ste 450, Houston, TX 77082
**Phone:** (813) 290-6200 **Dom State:** TX **Commenced Bus:** January 2008

| Data Date | Rating | RACR #1 | RACR #2 | Total Assets ($mil) | Capital ($mil) | Net Premium ($mil) | Net Income ($mil) |
|---|---|---|---|---|---|---|---|
| 9-17 | C | 3.10 | 2.59 | 183.8 | 65.2 | 301.5 | 11.3 |
| 9-16 | C- | 2.60 | 2.17 | 158.7 | 51.0 | 288.6 | -1.8 |
| 2016 | C | 2.51 | 2.09 | 123.3 | 52.2 | 384.3 | 1.1 |
| 2015 | C | 2.57 | 2.14 | 100.1 | 50.3 | 366.8 | 2.1 |
| 2014 | C+ | 1.56 | 1.30 | 75.4 | 26.5 | 299.5 | -13.8 |
| 2013 | B | 1.63 | 1.35 | 66.1 | 24.2 | 271.9 | 7.0 |
| 2012 | B | 2.21 | 1.84 | 39.5 | 15.2 | 133.2 | 4.0 |

Rating Indexes

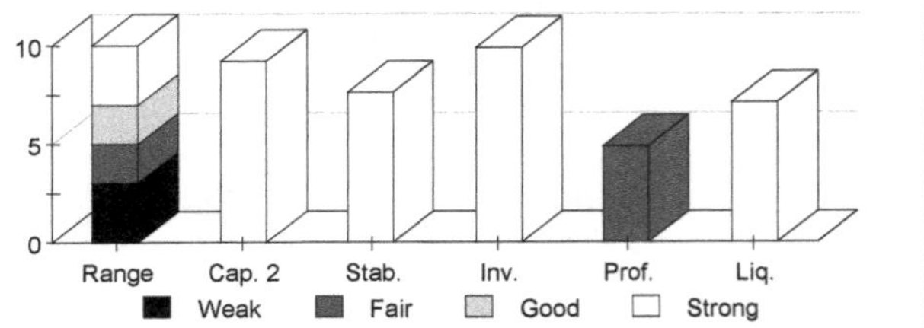

## WELLCARE PRESCRIPTION INS INC — E — Very Weak

**Major Rating Factors:** Good overall profitability index (6.5 on a scale of 0 to 10). Strong capitalization (10.0) based on excellent current risk-adjusted capital (severe loss scenario). High quality investment portfolio (9.9).
**Other Rating Factors:** Excellent liquidity (8.7) with ample operational cash flow and liquid investments.
**Principal Business:** Other (100%)
**Mem Phys: 16:** N/A **15:** N/A **16 MLR** 73.7% **/ 16 Admin Exp** N/A
**Enroll(000): Q3 17:** 1,039 **16:** 894 **15:** 930 **Med Exp PMPM:** $55,736,954
**Principal Investments:** Cash and equiv (97%), long-term bonds (3%)
**Provider Compensation ($000):** Contr fee ($447,038)
**Total Member Encounters:** N/A
**Group Affiliation:** WellCare Health Plans Inc
**Licensed in:** All states except AL, AR, CO, CT, MN, MT, RI, PR
**Address:** 8735 Henderson Rd, Tampa, FL 33634
**Phone:** (813) 290-6200 **Dom State:** FL **Commenced Bus:** October 2005

| Data Date | Rating | RACR #1 | RACR #2 | Total Assets ($mil) | Capital ($mil) | Net Premium ($mil) | Net Income ($mil) |
|---|---|---|---|---|---|---|---|
| 9-17 | E | 11.37 | 9.47 | 1,654.9 | 220.1 | 634.1 | 7.6 |
| 9-16 | E | 7.30 | 6.09 | 1,179.5 | 170.9 | 581.1 | 30.8 |
| 2016 | E | 10.83 | 9.02 | 852.9 | 209.5 | 755.6 | 68.4 |
| 2015 | E- | 6.07 | 5.06 | 721.2 | 141.3 | 814.8 | 23.6 |
| 2014 | D | 3.81 | 3.18 | 822.2 | 109.0 | 986.8 | -14.8 |
| 2013 | B | 5.57 | 4.64 | 205.6 | 118.6 | 715.8 | 17.1 |
| 2012 | B+ | 5.53 | 4.61 | 274.8 | 148.1 | 929.3 | 62.4 |

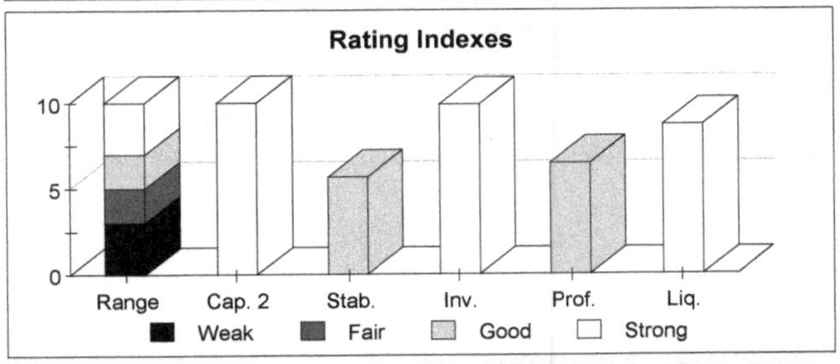


## WELLMARK HEALTH PLAN OF IOWA — B — Good

**Major Rating Factors:** Good quality investment portfolio (6.6 on a scale of 0 to 10). Good overall results on stability tests (5.5) despite a decline in enrollment during 2016. Good liquidity (6.7) with sufficient resources (cash flows and marketable investments) to handle a spike in claims.
**Other Rating Factors:** Fair profitability index (4.8). Strong capitalization index (10.0) based on excellent current risk-adjusted capital (severe loss scenario).
**Principal Business:** Comp med (100%)
**Mem Phys: 16:** 10,227 **15:** 9,054 **16 MLR** 79.2% **/ 16 Admin Exp** N/A
**Enroll(000): Q3 17:** 82 **16:** 74 **15:** 96 **Med Exp PMPM:** $288,752
**Principal Investments:** Long-term bonds (77%), nonaffiliate common stock (21%), cash and equiv (2%)
**Provider Compensation ($000):** Contr fee ($131,135), bonus arrang ($110,947), FFS ($11,873), capitation ($1,150)
**Total Member Encounters:** Phys (333,877), non-phys (204,955)
**Group Affiliation:** Wellmark Inc
**Licensed in:** IA
**Address:** 1331 Grand Avenue, Des Moines, IA 50309-2901
**Phone:** (515) 376-4500 **Dom State:** IA **Commenced Bus:** January 1997

| Data Date | Rating | RACR #1 | RACR #2 | Total Assets ($mil) | Capital ($mil) | Net Premium ($mil) | Net Income ($mil) |
|---|---|---|---|---|---|---|---|
| 9-17 | B | 8.66 | 7.21 | 272.5 | 184.7 | 289.0 | 25.8 |
| 9-16 | B | 6.00 | 5.00 | 216.6 | 146.2 | 235.1 | -0.8 |
| 2016 | B | 7.23 | 6.03 | 232.7 | 153.6 | 316.0 | 5.5 |
| 2015 | B+ | 6.08 | 5.07 | 227.6 | 148.2 | 358.7 | -9.4 |
| 2014 | B+ | 7.14 | 5.95 | 218.0 | 159.3 | 342.4 | 10.7 |
| 2013 | B+ | 6.81 | 5.67 | 207.9 | 147.6 | 338.0 | 25.5 |
| 2012 | B+ | 7.27 | 6.06 | 224.5 | 157.8 | 335.7 | 34.4 |

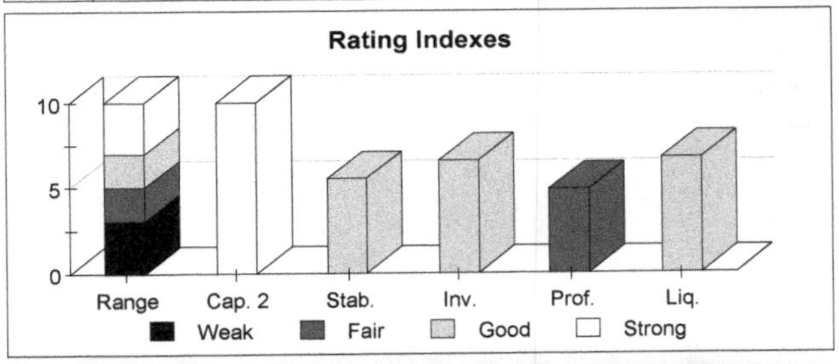


## WELLMARK INC — B- — Good

**Major Rating Factors:** Fair profitability index (4.7 on a scale of 0 to 10). Fair quality investment portfolio (4.4). Good liquidity (6.6) with sufficient resources (cash flows and marketable investments) to handle a spike in claims.
**Other Rating Factors:** Strong capitalization (10.0) based on excellent current risk-adjusted capital (severe loss scenario).
**Principal Business:** Comp med (67%), med supp (14%), FEHB (9%), other (9%)
**Mem Phys: 16:** 8,736 **15:** 6,463 **16 MLR** 87.1% **/ 16 Admin Exp** N/A
**Enroll(000): Q3 17:** 1,253 **16:** 1,274 **15:** 1,299 **Med Exp PMPM:** $154,377,847
**Principal Investments:** Long-term bonds (43%), affiliate common stock (23%), nonaffiliate common stock (17%), real estate (10%), cash and equiv (6%), other (1%)
**Provider Compensation ($000):** Contr fee ($1,528,677), bonus arrang ($428,993), FFS ($110,678), other ($153,009)
**Total Member Encounters:** Phys (3,693,727), non-phys (2,184,181)
**Group Affiliation:** Wellmark Inc
**Licensed in:** IA, SD
**Address:** 1331 Grand Ave, Des Moines, IA 50309-2901
**Phone:** (515) 376-4500 **Dom State:** IA **Commenced Bus:** October 1939

| Data Date | Rating | RACR #1 | RACR #2 | Total Assets ($mil) | Capital ($mil) | Net Premium ($mil) | Net Income ($mil) |
|---|---|---|---|---|---|---|---|
| 9-17 | B- | 6.23 | 5.20 | 2,412.3 | 1,548.0 | 1,984.0 | 72.1 |
| 9-16 | B | 5.41 | 4.51 | 2,088.9 | 1,326.0 | 1,986.2 | -9.7 |
| 2016 | B- | 5.36 | 4.47 | 2,129.5 | 1,330.3 | 2,656.3 | -26.5 |
| 2015 | B | 5.40 | 4.50 | 2,043.9 | 1,322.0 | 2,535.8 | -1.8 |
| 2014 | B | 5.86 | 4.88 | 2,018.0 | 1,359.7 | 2,409.4 | 15.4 |
| 2013 | B+ | 6.44 | 5.36 | 2,065.8 | 1,393.8 | 2,335.8 | 154.1 |
| 2012 | B | 5.61 | 4.68 | 1,873.8 | 1,231.2 | 2,316.8 | 85.2 |

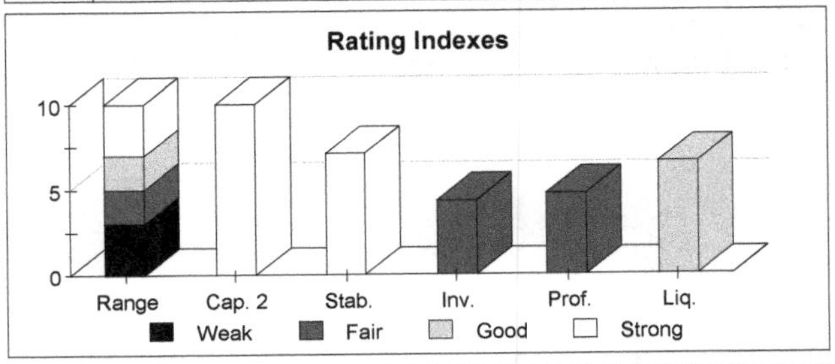

## WELLMARK OF SOUTH DAKOTA INC * B+ Good

**Major Rating Factors:** Good quality investment portfolio (6.6 on a scale of 0 to 10). Good liquidity (6.8) with sufficient resources (cash flows and marketable investments) to handle a spike in claims. Strong capitalization (10.0) based on excellent current risk-adjusted capital (severe loss scenario).
**Other Rating Factors:** Fair profitability index (4.8).
**Principal Business:** Comp med (69%), FEHB (22%), med supp (8%), other (2%)
**Mem Phys: 16:** 2,421 **15:** 2,010 **16 MLR** 88.5% **/ 16 Admin Exp** N/A
**Enroll(000): Q3 17:** 175 **16:** 177 **15:** 183 **Med Exp PMPM:** $308,332,299
**Principal Investments:** Long-term bonds (67%), nonaffiliate common stock (26%), cash and equiv (6%), real estate (1%)
**Provider Compensation ($000):** Contr fee ($564,848), FFS ($65,250)
**Total Member Encounters:** Phys (910,823), non-phys (375,477)
**Group Affiliation:** Wellmark Inc
**Licensed in:** SD
**Address:** 1601 West Madison St, Sioux Falls, SD 57104-5710
**Phone:** (605) 373-7200 **Dom State:** SD **Commenced Bus:** August 1996

| Data Date | Rating | RACR #1 | RACR #2 | Total Assets ($mil) | Capital ($mil) | Net Premium ($mil) | Net Income ($mil) |
|---|---|---|---|---|---|---|---|
| 9-17 | B+ | 7.33 | 6.11 | 465.7 | 284.3 | 555.5 | 37.2 |
| 9-16 | B+ | 6.13 | 5.11 | 394.5 | 237.2 | 515.5 | 2.7 |
| 2016 | B+ | 6.17 | 5.14 | 414.4 | 238.6 | 696.1 | 4.5 |
| 2015 | B+ | 6.02 | 5.01 | 407.3 | 232.7 | 694.8 | 27.7 |
| 2014 | B+ | 6.22 | 5.18 | 420.4 | 228.0 | 670.1 | -9.4 |
| 2013 | B+ | 6.93 | 5.77 | 402.5 | 235.8 | 639.9 | 29.9 |
| 2012 | B | 5.94 | 4.95 | 358.7 | 201.8 | 627.1 | 20.7 |

Rating Indexes

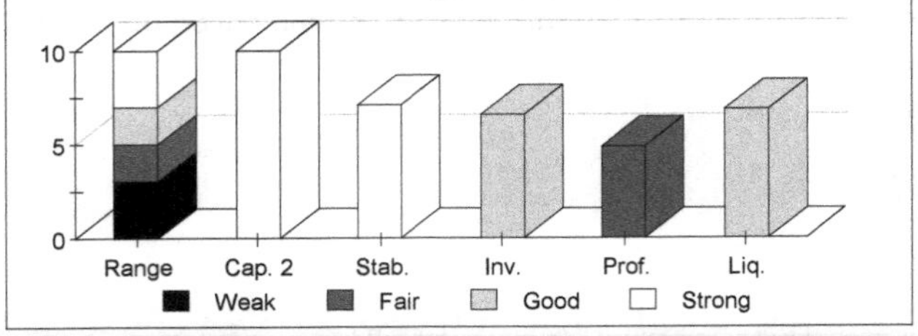


## WEST VIRGINIA FAMILY HEALTH PLAN INC C- Fair

**Major Rating Factors:** Poor capitalization (2.8 on a scale of 0 to 10) based on weak current risk-adjusted capital (moderate loss scenario). Good overall profitability index (5.0). Good liquidity (6.9) with sufficient resources (cash flows and marketable investments) to handle a spike in claims.
**Other Rating Factors:** High quality investment portfolio (9.9).
**Principal Business:** Medicaid (100%)
**Mem Phys: 16:** 8,226 **15:** 7,071 **16 MLR** 93.9% **/ 16 Admin Exp** N/A
**Enroll(000): Q3 17:** 69 **16:** 62 **15:** 53 **Med Exp PMPM:** $393,626
**Principal Investments:** Cash and equiv (100%)
**Provider Compensation ($000):** Contr fee ($275,739), capitation ($2,692), bonus arrang ($240)
**Total Member Encounters:** Phys (255,996), non-phys (120,028)
**Group Affiliation:** West Virginia Family Health Plan Inc
**Licensed in:** WV
**Address:** 614 Market St, Parkersburg, WV 26101
**Phone:** (304) 424-7700 **Dom State:** WV **Commenced Bus:** September 2014

| Data Date | Rating | RACR #1 | RACR #2 | Total Assets ($mil) | Capital ($mil) | Net Premium ($mil) | Net Income ($mil) |
|---|---|---|---|---|---|---|---|
| 9-17 | C- | 0.60 | 0.50 | 66.9 | 20.8 | 257.7 | 15.8 |
| 9-16 | C | 0.56 | 0.47 | 56.8 | 6.9 | 224.7 | 2.2 |
| 2016 | C- | 0.28 | 0.23 | 60.7 | 8.3 | 299.6 | 4.9 |
| 2015 | C | 1.36 | 1.14 | 51.0 | 4.9 | 102.6 | 0.8 |
| 2014 | U | 1.19 | 0.99 | 5.4 | 3.6 | 1.7 | -2.8 |
| 2013 | N/A | N/A | N/A | N/A | N/A | N/A | N/A |
| 2012 | N/A | N/A | N/A | N/A | N/A | N/A | N/A |

Rating Indexes

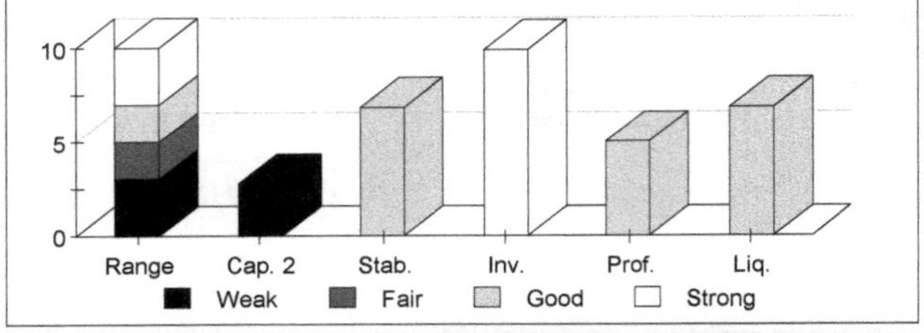


## WESTERN GROCERS EMPLOYEE BENEFITS E Very Weak

**Major Rating Factors:** Weak profitability index (1.5 on a scale of 0 to 10). Poor capitalization index (0.0) based on weak current risk-adjusted capital (severe loss scenario). Weak liquidity (2.4) as a spike in claims may stretch capacity.
**Other Rating Factors:** High quality investment portfolio (9.4).
**Principal Business:** Comp med (92%), dental (8%)
**Mem Phys: 16:** N/A **15:** N/A **16 MLR** 108.0% **/ 16 Admin Exp** N/A
**Enroll(000): Q3 17:** 6 **16:** 6 **15:** 6 **Med Exp PMPM:** $249,619
**Principal Investments:** Long-term bonds (75%), cash and equiv (25%)
**Provider Compensation ($000):** FFS ($17,132)
**Total Member Encounters:** Phys (36,973), non-phys (67,726)
**Group Affiliation:** Western Grocers Employee Benefits Tr
**Licensed in:** AK, OR, WA
**Address:** 12901 SE 97TH AVE #200, CLACKAMAS, OR 97015
**Phone:** (503) 968-2360 **Dom State:** OR **Commenced Bus:** October 1979

| Data Date | Rating | RACR #1 | RACR #2 | Total Assets ($mil) | Capital ($mil) | Net Premium ($mil) | Net Income ($mil) |
|---|---|---|---|---|---|---|---|
| 9-17 | E | -0.92 | -0.77 | 7.3 | 3.6 | 14.3 | 0.7 |
| 9-16 | N/A | N/A | N/A | 6.5 | 3.4 | 12.4 | -1.2 |
| 2016 | E | -0.77 | -0.64 | 6.0 | 2.9 | 16.4 | -1.7 |
| 2015 | N/A | N/A | N/A | 7.6 | 4.6 | 15.6 | -1.3 |
| 2014 | N/A | N/A | N/A | 8.3 | 5.9 | 15.8 | 1.1 |
| 2013 | N/A | N/A | N/A | 8.2 | 4.8 | 16.1 | 0.6 |
| 2012 | N/A | N/A | N/A | 7.8 | 4.2 | 16.3 | 1.4 |

Rating Indexes

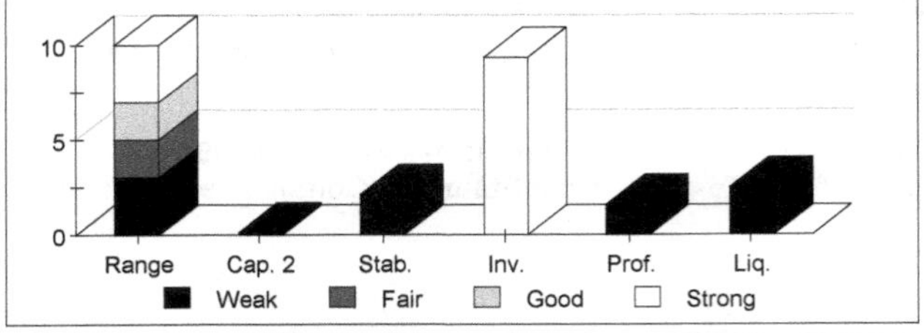

## WESTERN HEALTH ADVANTAGE E Very Weak

**Major Rating Factors:** Weak profitability index (2.5 on a scale of 0 to 10). Poor capitalization index (0.0) based on weak current risk-adjusted capital (severe loss scenario). Fair overall results on stability tests (4.6) in spite of steady enrollment growth, averaging 8% over the past five years.
**Other Rating Factors:** Excellent liquidity (6.9) with sufficient resources (cash flows and marketable investments) to handle a spike in claims.
**Principal Business:** Managed care (100%)
**Mem Phys: 16:** N/A **15:** N/A **16 MLR** 91.1% **/ 16 Admin Exp** N/A
**Enroll(000): Q3 17:** 0 **16:** 126 **15:** 117 **Med Exp PMPM:** $414
**Principal Investments ($000):** Cash and equiv ($57,081)
**Provider Compensation ($000):** None
**Total Member Encounters:** N/A
**Group Affiliation:** None
**Licensed in:** CA
**Address:** 2349 Gateway Oaks Suite 100, Sacramento, CA 95833
**Phone:** (916) 563-3183 **Dom State:** CA **Commenced Bus:** May 1997

| Data Date | Rating | RACR #1 | RACR #2 | Total Assets ($mil) | Capital ($mil) | Net Premium ($mil) | Net Income ($mil) |
|---|---|---|---|---|---|---|---|
| 9-17 | E | 0.20 | 0.12 | 63.8 | 9.7 | 569.3 | 3.4 |
| 9-16 | E | 0.20 | 0.12 | 76.9 | 9.2 | 492.5 | 2.0 |
| 2016 | E | 0.18 | 0.11 | 83.5 | 8.8 | 664.4 | 1.5 |
| 2015 | E | 0.15 | 0.09 | 93.9 | 7.3 | 594.9 | -13.2 |
| 2014 | D | 0.55 | 0.34 | 68.0 | 20.6 | 515.5 | 0.9 |
| 2013 | D | 0.58 | 0.36 | 49.9 | 19.4 | 444.6 | 0.9 |
| 2012 | D- | 0.59 | 0.36 | 51.0 | 18.5 | 396.9 | 1.5 |

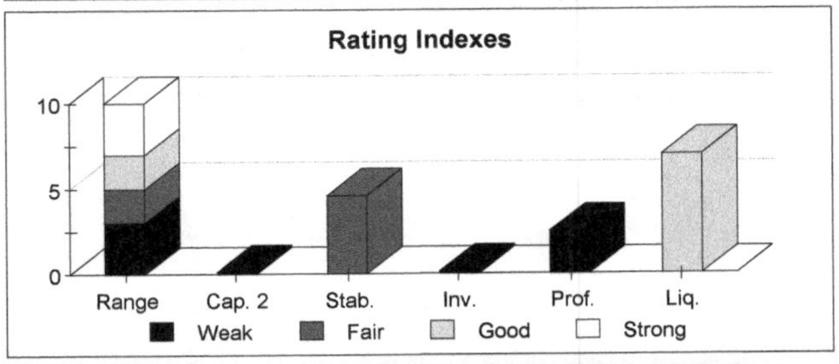


## WISCONSIN PHYSICIANS SERVICE INS C Fair

**Major Rating Factors:** Fair profitability index (2.9 on a scale of 0 to 10). Fair quality investment portfolio (4.8). Good liquidity (6.6) with sufficient resources (cash flows and marketable investments) to handle a spike in claims.
**Other Rating Factors:** Strong capitalization (7.8) based on excellent current risk-adjusted capital (severe loss scenario).
**Principal Business:** Comp med (59%), med supp (29%), dental (2%), other (10%)
**Mem Phys: 16:** N/A **15:** N/A **16 MLR** 80.4% **/ 16 Admin Exp** N/A
**Enroll(000): Q3 17:** 112 **16:** 123 **15:** 147 **Med Exp PMPM:** $350,147,713
**Principal Investments:** Long-term bonds (36%), affiliate common stock (25%), real estate (21%), nonaffiliate common stock (14%), cash and equiv (5%)
**Provider Compensation ($000):** Contr fee ($213,661), FFS ($131,008), other ($9,980)
**Total Member Encounters:** Phys (931,437), non-phys (316,339)
**Group Affiliation:** WI Physicians Service Ins Corp
**Licensed in:** IL, IN, MI, OH, WI
**Address:** 1717 WEST BRdWAY, MADISON, WI 53713-1895
**Phone:** (608) 977-5000 **Dom State:** WI **Commenced Bus:** April 1977

| Data Date | Rating | RACR #1 | RACR #2 | Total Assets ($mil) | Capital ($mil) | Net Premium ($mil) | Net Income ($mil) |
|---|---|---|---|---|---|---|---|
| 9-17 | C | 2.01 | 1.67 | 284.9 | 121.4 | 312.8 | 7.9 |
| 9-16 | C- | 1.26 | 1.05 | 247.5 | 87.0 | 325.5 | -1.2 |
| 2016 | C | 1.83 | 1.53 | 267.8 | 109.8 | 435.4 | 8.8 |
| 2015 | C- | 1.35 | 1.12 | 265.5 | 93.9 | 547.5 | -7.1 |
| 2014 | C | 1.91 | 1.59 | 315.6 | 145.4 | 560.9 | 3.6 |
| 2013 | C+ | 2.54 | 2.12 | 345.1 | 172.7 | 499.0 | 10.4 |
| 2012 | B- | 2.19 | 1.83 | 332.5 | 135.5 | 480.9 | -9.0 |

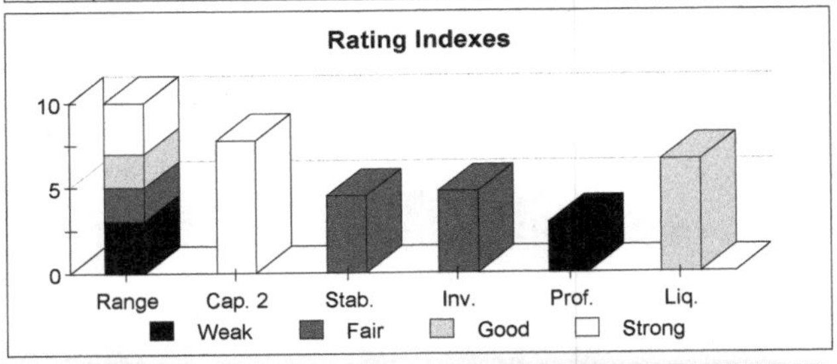


## WMI MUTUAL INS CO C Fair

**Major Rating Factors:** Fair profitability index (3.2 on a scale of 0 to 10). Good liquidity (5.9) with sufficient resources (cash flows and marketable investments) to handle a spike in claims. Strong capitalization (8.8) based on excellent current risk-adjusted capital (severe loss scenario).
**Other Rating Factors:** High quality investment portfolio (7.3).
**Principal Business:** Comp med (93%), dental (4%), med supp (3%)
**Mem Phys: 16:** N/A **15:** N/A **16 MLR** 104.1% **/ 16 Admin Exp** N/A
**Enroll(000): Q3 17:** 6 **16:** 6 **15:** 7 **Med Exp PMPM:** $250,398
**Principal Investments:** Long-term bonds (66%), nonaffiliate common stock (20%), cash and equiv (11%), affiliate common stock (3%)
**Provider Compensation ($000):** None
**Total Member Encounters:** N/A
**Group Affiliation:** WMI Mutual Insurance Company
**Licensed in:** AZ, ID, MT, NV, NM, UT, WA
**Address:** 4393 S RIVERBOAT RD #380, TAYLORSVILLE, UT 84123
**Phone:** (801) 263-8000 **Dom State:** UT **Commenced Bus:** December 1988

| Data Date | Rating | RACR #1 | RACR #2 | Total Assets ($mil) | Capital ($mil) | Net Premium ($mil) | Net Income ($mil) |
|---|---|---|---|---|---|---|---|
| 9-17 | C | 2.82 | 2.35 | 14.6 | 9.8 | 13.7 | 1.2 |
| 9-16 | N/A | N/A | N/A | 13.2 | 7.7 | 13.5 | -2.1 |
| 2016 | C | 2.40 | 2.00 | 13.8 | 8.4 | 18.0 | -1.1 |
| 2015 | N/A | N/A | N/A | 14.7 | 9.3 | 18.4 | N/A |
| 2014 | N/A | N/A | N/A | 13.5 | 709.8 | 19.8 | N/A |
| 2013 | N/A | N/A | N/A | 13.0 | 6.9 | 20.4 | N/A |
| 2012 | N/A | N/A | N/A | 13.0 | 6.7 | 20.0 | N/A |

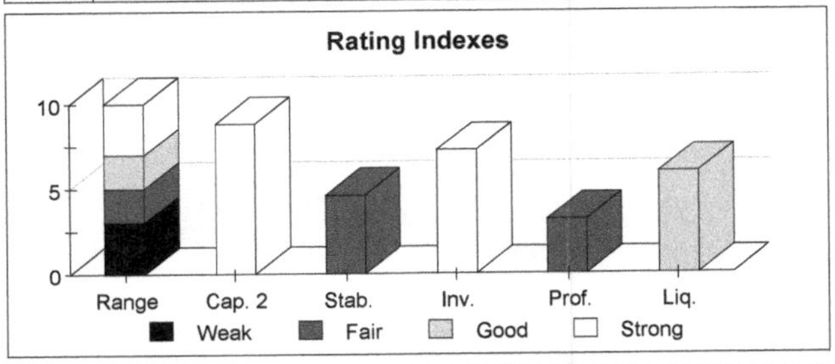

## WPS HEALTH PLAN INC C- Fair

**Major Rating Factors:** Weak profitability index (0.9 on a scale of 0 to 10). Weak liquidity (2.4) as a spike in claims may stretch capacity. Good capitalization (6.6) based on good current risk-adjusted capital (severe loss scenario).
**Other Rating Factors:** High quality investment portfolio (9.3).
**Principal Business:** Comp med (100%)
**Mem Phys: 16:** 8,602 **15:** 4,822 **16 MLR** 98.2% **/ 16 Admin Exp** N/A
**Enroll(000): Q3 17:** 22 **16:** 36 **15:** 29 **Med Exp PMPM:** $437,854
**Principal Investments:** Long-term bonds (83%), cash and equiv (17%)
**Provider Compensation ($000):** Contr fee ($137,199), FFS ($41,814)
**Total Member Encounters:** Phys (217,002), non-phys (80,129)
**Group Affiliation:** Wisconsin Physicians Service Ins
**Licensed in:** WI
**Address:** 421 LAWRENCE Dr STE 100, DEPERE, WI 54115
**Phone:** (920) 490-6900 **Dom State:** WI **Commenced Bus:** June 2005

| Data Date | Rating | RACR #1 | RACR #2 | Total Assets ($mil) | Capital ($mil) | Net Premium ($mil) | Net Income ($mil) |
|---|---|---|---|---|---|---|---|
| 9-17 | C- | 1.16 | 0.97 | 35.2 | 18.5 | 80.6 | -4.6 |
| 9-16 | C- | 1.28 | 1.07 | 51.9 | 19.1 | 137.6 | -4.6 |
| 2016 | C- | 1.40 | 1.17 | 50.4 | 23.1 | 185.8 | -6.0 |
| 2015 | C- | 1.36 | 1.13 | 50.2 | 20.2 | 150.2 | -22.4 |
| 2014 | C | 1.12 | 0.93 | 28.4 | 14.6 | 140.0 | -7.4 |
| 2013 | C | 1.07 | 0.89 | 23.1 | 7.9 | 78.8 | -3.7 |
| 2012 | C | 1.23 | 1.02 | 30.3 | 9.9 | 97.3 | -1.6 |

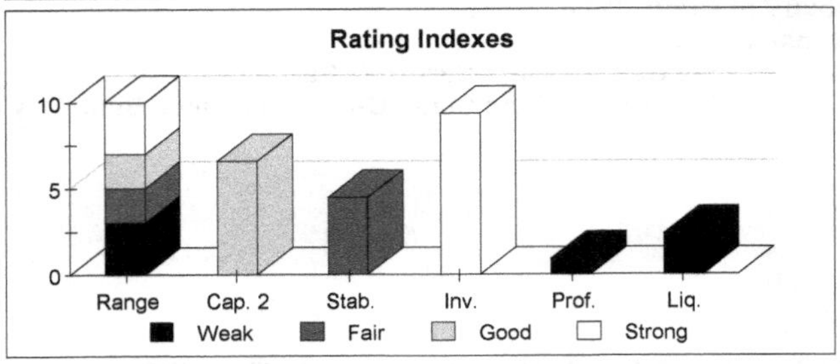

# Section III

# Weiss Recommended Companies

A compilation of those

**U.S. Health Insurers**

receiving a Weiss Safety Rating
of A+, A, A-, or B+.

Companies are listed in alphabetical order.

# Section III Contents

This section provides contact addresses and phone numbers for all recommended carriers analyzed by Weiss Ratings. It contains all insurers receiving a Safety Rating of A+, A, A-, or B+. If an insurer is not on this list, it should not automatically be assumed that the firm is weak. Indeed, there are many firms that have not achieved a B+ or better rating but are in relatively good condition with adequate resources to cover their risk during an average recession. Not being included in this list should not be construed as a recommendation to cancel policies.

1. **Safety Rating** — Our rating is measured on a scale from A to F and considers a wide range of factors. Highly-rated companies are, in our opinion, less likely to experience financial difficulties than lower-rated firms. See *About Weiss Safety Ratings* for more information.

2. **Insurance Company Name** — The legally-registered name, which can sometimes differ from the name that the company uses for advertising. An insurer's name can be very similar to the name of other companies, so make sure you note the exact name before contacting your agent.

3. **Address** — The address of the main office where you can contact the firm for additional financial data or for the location of local branches and/or registered agents.

4. **Telephone Number** — The number to call for additional financial data or for the phone numbers of local branches and/or registered agents.

**Weiss Safety Ratings are not deemed to be a recommendation concerning the purchase or sale of the securities of any insurance company that is publicly owned**

| RATING | INSURANCE COMPANY NAME | ADDRESS | CITY | STATE | ZIP | PHONE |
|---|---|---|---|---|---|---|
| B+ | ADVANCE INS CO OF KANSAS | 1133 SW TOPEKA BLVD | TOPEKA | KS | 66629 | (785) 273-9804 |
| B+ | AETNA BETTER HEALTH INC (A NJ CORP) | 3 INDEPENDENCE WAY STE 400 | PRINCETON | NJ | 08540 | (855) 232-3596 |
| B+ | AETNA BETTER HEALTH OF TEXAS INC | 2777 N STEMMONS FREEWAY #1450 | DALLAS | TX | 75207 | (800) 872-3862 |
| B+ | AETNA BETTER HLTH OF KY INS CO | 306 WEST MAIN ST STE 512 | FRANKFORT | KY | 40601 | (800) 627-4702 |
| B+ | AETNA HEALTH & LIFE INS CO | 151 FARMINGTON AVENUE | HARTFORD | CT | 6156 | (860) 273-0123 |
| B+ | AETNA HEALTH INC (A FLORIDA CORP) | 4630 WOODLANDS CORPORATE | TAMPA | FL | 33614 | (813) 775-0000 |
| A | ALLIANZ LIFE INS CO OF NY | 28 LIBERTY STREET 38TH FLOOR | NEW YORK | NY | 10005 | (763) 765-2913 |
| A- | AMALGAMATED LIFE INS CO | 333 WESTCHESTER AVENUE | WHITE PLAINS | NY | 10604 | (914) 367-5000 |
| B+ | AMERICAN FAMILY LIFE ASR CO OF COLUM | 10306 REGENCY PARKWAY DRIVE | OMAHA | NE | 68114 | (706) 323-3431 |
| A- | AMERICAN FAMILY LIFE ASR CO OF NY | 22 CORPORATE WOODS BLVD STE 2 | ALBANY | NY | 12211 | (518) 438-0764 |
| B+ | AMERICAN FAMILY MUTL INS CO SI | 6000 AMERICAN PARKWAY | MADISON | WI | 53783 | (608) 249-2111 |
| B+ | AMERICAN FIDELITY ASR CO | 9000 CAMERON PARKWAY | OKLAHOMA CITY | OK | 73114 | (405) 523-2000 |
| A- | AMERICAN HEALTH & LIFE INS CO | 3001 MEACHAM BLVD STE 100 | FORT WORTH | TX | 76137 | (800) 316-5607 |
| A- | AMERICAN REPUBLIC INS CO | 601 SIXTH AVENUE | DES MOINES | IA | 50309 | (800) 247-2190 |
| B+ | AMERICAN UNITED LIFE INS CO | ONE AMERICAN SQUARE | INDIANAPOLIS | IN | 46282 | (317) 285-1877 |
| B+ | AMERIGROUP NEW JERSEY INC | 101 WOOD AVENUE SOUTH 8TH | ISELIN | NJ | 08830 | (757) 490-6900 |
| A- | AMERIGROUP TEXAS INC | 3800 BUFFALO SPEEDWAY SUITE 40 | HOUSTON | TX | 77098 | (757) 490-6900 |
| A- | AMERIGROUP WASHINGTON INC | 705 FIFTH AVE S STE 110 | SEATTLE | WA | 98104 | (757) 490-6900 |
| B+ | AMFIRST INS CO | 201 ROBERT S KERR AVE STE 600 | OKLAHOMA CITY | OK | 73102 | (601) 956-2028 |
| A- | AMGP GEORGIA MANAGED CARE CO INC | 4170 ASHFORD DUNWOODY RD | ATLANTA | GA | 30319 | (678) 587-4840 |
| B+ | ANTHEM HEALTH PLANS OF KENTUCKY INC | 13550 TRITON PARK BLVD | LOUISVILLE | KY | 40223 | (800) 331-1476 |
| B+ | ANTHEM HEALTH PLANS OF MAINE INC | 2 GANNETT DR | SOUTH PORTLAND | ME | 04106 | (866) 583-6182 |
| A- | ANTHEM KENTUCKY MANAGED CARE PLAN | 13550 TRITON PARK BLVD | LOUISVILLE | KY | 40223 | (800) 331-1476 |
| A- | ANTHEM LIFE INS CO | 120 MONUMENT CIRCLE | INDIANAPOLIS | IN | 46204 | (614) 433-8800 |
| B+ | ASSURITY LIFE INS CO | 2000 Q STREET | LINCOLN | NE | 68503 | (402) 476-6500 |
| A- | AUTO-OWNERS LIFE INS CO | 6101 ANACAPRI BOULEVARD | LANSING | MI | 48917 | (517) 323-1200 |
| B+ | AXA EQUITABLE LIFE INS CO | 1290 AVENUE OF THE AMERICAS | NEW YORK | NY | 10104 | (212) 554-1234 |
| A | BERKLEY LIFE & HEALTH INS CO | 11201 DOUGLAS AVE | URBANDALE | IA | 50322 | (609) 584-6990 |
| B+ | BEST LIFE & HEALTH INS CO | AUSTIN | AUSTIN | TX | 78752 | (949) 253-4080 |
| B+ | BLUE CARE NETWORK OF MICHIGAN | 20500 CIVIC CENTER DRIVE | SOUTHFIELD | MI | 48076 | (248) 799-6400 |
| A- | BLUE CROSS & BLUE SHIELD MA HMO BLUE | 101 HUNTINGTON AVE | BOSTON | MA | 02199 | (617) 246-5000 |
| A- | BLUE CROSS BLUE SHIELD HEALTHCARE GA | 3350 PEACHTREE ROAD NE | ATLANTA | GA | 30326 | (404) 842-8000 |
| A+ | BLUE CROSS BLUE SHIELD OF ARIZONA | 2444 W LAS PALMARITAS DR | PHOENIX | AZ | 85021 | (602) 864-4100 |
| A- | BLUE CROSS BLUE SHIELD OF SC INC | 2501 FARAWAY DR | COLUMBIA | SC | 29219 | (803) 788-3860 |
| A+ | BLUE CROSS OF CALIFORNIA | 1 WELLPOINT WAY | THOUSAND OAKS | CA | 91362 | (916) 403-0526 |
| A+ | BLUE SHIELD OF CALIFORNIA | 50 BEALE STREET 22ND FLOOR | SAN FRANCISCO | CA | 94105 | (415) 229-5195 |
| B+ | BLUEBONNET LIFE INS CO | 3545 LAKELAND DR | FLOWOOD | MS | 39232 | (601) 664-4218 |
| B+ | BOSTON MUTUAL LIFE INS CO | 120 ROYALL STREET | CANTON | MA | 02021 | (781) 828-7000 |
| A+ | CARE 1ST HEALTH PLAN INC | 601 POTRERO GRANDE DR | MONTEREY PARK | CA | 91755 | (qq ) - |
| A- | CAREFIRST BLUECHOICE INC | 840 FIRST STREET NE | WASHINGTON | DC | 20065 | (410) 581-3000 |
| B+ | CAREMORE HEALTH PLAN | 12900 PARK PLAZA DR SUITE 150 | CERRITOS | CA | 90703 | (562) 677-2455 |
| A- | CENTRAL STATES H & L CO OF OMAHA | 1212 NORTH 96TH STREET | OMAHA | NE | 68114 | (402) 397-1111 |
| A- | CIGNA LIFE INS CO OF NEW YORK | 140 EAST 45TH STREET | NEW YORK | NY | 10017 | (215) 761-1000 |
| A | COMMUNITY FIRST HEALTH PLANS INC | 12238 SILICON DRIVE STE 100 | SAN ANTONIO | TX | 78249 | (210) 227-2347 |
| B+ | COMMUNITY INS CO (OH) | 4361 IRWIN SIMPSON RD | MASON | OH | 45040 | (513) 872-8100 |
| B+ | COMMUNITYCARE HMO INC | 218 W 6TH ST | TULSA | OK | 74119 | (918) 594-5200 |
| B+ | COMPANION LIFE INS CO | 2501 FARAWAY DRIVE | COLUMBIA | SC | 29219 | (803) 735-1251 |
| A- | COMPCARE HEALTH SERVICES INS CORP | N17 W24340 RIVERWOOD DRIVE | WAUKESHA | WI | 53188 | (262) 523-4020 |

| RATING | INSURANCE COMPANY NAME | ADDRESS | CITY | STATE | ZIP | PHONE |
|---|---|---|---|---|---|---|
| A- | COPIC INS CO | 7351 E LOWRY BLVD SUITE 400 | DENVER | CO | 80230 | (720) 858-6000 |
| A+ | COUNTRY LIFE INS CO | 1701 N TOWANDA AVENUE | BLOOMINGTON | IL | 61701 | (309) 821-3000 |
| B+ | COVENTRY HEALTH CARE OF WEST VA INC | 500 VIRGINIA STREET EAST SUITE | CHARLESTON | WV | 25301 | (804) 747-3700 |
| B+ | DEAN HEALTH PLAN INC | 1277 DEMING WAY | MADISON | WI | 53717 | (608) 836-1400 |
| B+ | DEARBORN NATIONAL LIFE INS CO | 300 EAST RANDOLPH STREET | CHICAGO | IL | 60601 | (800) 348-4512 |
| B+ | DEARBORN NATIONAL LIFE INS CO OF NY | 1250 PITTSFORD VICTOR ROAD | PITTSFORD | NY | 14534 | (800) 348-4512 |
| B+ | DELAWARE AMERICAN LIFE INS CO | 1209 ORANGE STREET | WILMINGTON | DE | 19801 | (302) 594-2000 |
| A- | EL PASO HEALTH | 1145 WESTMORELAND | EL PASO | TX | 79925 | (915) 298-7198 |
| A | EMI HEALTH | 852 EAST ARROWHEAD LANE | MURRAY | UT | 84107 | (801) 262-7476 |
| A- | ERIE FAMILY LIFE INS CO | 100 ERIE INSURANCE PLACE | ERIE | PA | 16530 | (814) 870-2000 |
| B+ | ESSENCE HEALTHCARE INC | 13900 RIVERPORT DR | ST. LOUIS | MO | 63043 | (314) 209-2780 |
| B+ | EXCELLUS HEALTH PLAN INC | 165 COURT ST | ROCHESTER | NY | 14647 | (585) 454-1700 |
| B+ | FAMILY HERITAGE LIFE INS CO OF AMER | 6001 EAST ROYALTON RD STE 200 | CLEVELAND | OH | 44147 | (440) 922-5200 |
| B+ | FARM BUREAU LIFE INS CO | 5400 UNIVERSITY AVENUE | WEST DES MOINES | IA | 50266 | (515) 225-5400 |
| A- | FARM BUREAU LIFE INS CO OF MISSOURI | 701 SOUTH COUNTRY CLUB DRIVE | JEFFERSON CITY | MO | 65109 | (573) 893-1400 |
| A | FEDERATED LIFE INS CO | 121 EAST PARK SQUARE | OWATONNA | MN | 55060 | (507) 455-5200 |
| A | FIRST RELIANCE STANDARD LIFE INS CO | 590 MADISON AVENUE 29TH FLOOR | NEW YORK | NY | 10022 | (212) 303-8400 |
| B+ | FIRST SYMETRA NATL LIFE INS CO OF NY | 420 LEXINGTON AVE SUITE 300 | NEW YORK | NY | 10170 | (425) 256-8000 |
| B+ | FLORIDA HEALTH CARE PLAN INC | 1340 RIDGEWOOD AVE | HOLLY HILL | FL | 32117 | (386) 676-7100 |
| A- | GARDEN STATE LIFE INS CO | ONE MOODY PLAZA | GALVESTON | TX | 77550 | (409) 763-4661 |
| B+ | GEISINGER HEALTH PLAN | 100 NORTH ACADEMY AVENUE | DANVILLE | PA | 17822 | (570) 271-8777 |
| B+ | GERBER LIFE INS CO | 1311 MAMARONECK AVENUE | WHITE PLAINS | NY | 10605 | (914) 272-4000 |
| B+ | GLOBE LIFE INSURANCE CO OF NY | 301 PLAINFIELD RD STE 150 | SYRACUSE | NY | 13212 | (315) 451-2544 |
| B+ | GOVERNMENT PERSONNEL MUTUAL L I C | 2211 NE LOOP 410 | SAN ANTONIO | TX | 78217 | (210) 357-2222 |
| A- | GROUP HEALTH PLAN INC | 8170 33RD AVENUE SOUTH POBOX 1 | MINNEAPOLIS | MN | 55440 | (952) 883-6000 |
| A | GUARDIAN LIFE INS CO OF AMERICA | 7 HANOVER SQUARE | NEW YORK | NY | 10004 | (212) 598-8000 |
| B+ | HEALTH OPTIONS INC | 4800 DEERWOOD CAMPUS | JACKSONVILLE | FL | 32246 | (904) 791-6111 |
| B+ | HEALTHKEEPERS INC | 2015 STAPLES MILL ROAD | RICHMOND | VA | 23230 | (804) 354-7000 |
| A+ | HEALTHPARTNERS | 8170 33RD AVENUE SOUTH | MINNEAPOLIS | MN | 55440 | (952) 883-6000 |
| B+ | HEALTHSPRING OF FLORIDA INC | 8600 NW 41ST ST STE 201 | DORAL | FL | 33166 | (305) 229-7461 |
| B+ | HEALTHSPRING OF TENNESSEE INC | 530 GREAT CIRCLE ROAD | NASHVILLE | TN | 37228 | (615) 291-7000 |
| A- | HEALTHY ALLIANCE LIFE INS CO | 1831 CHESTNUT ST | ST. LOUIS | MO | 63103 | (314) 923-4444 |
| A+ | HMO LOUISIANA INC | 5525 REITZ AVENUE | BATON ROUGE | LA | 70809 | (225) 295-3307 |
| A+ | HMO PARTNERS INC | 320 WEST CAPITOL | LITTLE ROCK | AR | 72203 | (501) 221-1800 |
| A- | HORIZON HEALTHCARE OF NEW JERSEY INC | 3 PENN PLZ E STE PP-15D | NEWARK | NJ | 07105 | (973) 466-5954 |
| A- | HUMANA BENEFIT PLAN OF ILLINOIS | 7915 N HALE AVE STE D | PEORIA | IL | 61615 | (502) 580-1000 |
| A- | HUMANA INS CO (WI) | 1100 EMPLOYERS BLVD | DEPERE | WI | 54115 | (920) 336-1100 |
| A- | INDEPENDENT CARE HEALTH PLAN | 1555 N RIVERCENTER DR STE 206 | MILWAUKEE | WI | 53212 | (414) 223-4847 |
| A | INLAND EMPIRE HEALTH PLAN | 300 S PARK AVENUE | POMONA | CA | 91769 | (909) 623-6333 |
| B+ | JACKSON NATIONAL LIFE INS CO | 1 CORPORATE WAY | LANSING | MI | 48951 | (517) 381-5500 |
| B+ | K S PLAN ADMINISTRATORS LLC | 2727 WEST HOLCOMBE BLVD | HOUSTON | TX | 77025 | (713) 442-1700 |
| B+ | KAISER FNDTN HLTH PLAN OF WA | 320 WESTLAKE AVE N SUITE 100 | SEATTLE | WA | 98109 | (206) 448-5600 |
| A | KAISER FOUNDATION HEALTH PLAN INC | 9700 STOCKDALE HIGHWAY | BAKERSFIELD | CA | 93311 | (661) 664-5016 |
| A- | LIFE INS CO OF BOSTON & NEW YORK | 4300 CAMP ROAD PO BOX 331 | ATHOL SPRINGS | NY | 14010 | (800) 645-2317 |
| A | LIFEWISE ASR CO | 7001 220TH STREET SW | MOUNTLAKE TERRACE | WA | 98043 | (425) 918-4575 |
| A- | MASSACHUSETTS MUTUAL LIFE INS CO | 1295 STATE STREET | SPRINGFIELD | MA | 1111 | (413) 788-8411 |
| A- | MCLAREN HEALTH PLAN INC | G-3245 BEECHER RD | FLINT | MI | 48532 | (810) 733-9723 |
| A- | MEDCO CONTAINMENT LIFE INS CO | 4415 LEWIS RD STE #1 | HARRISBURG | PA | 17111 | (800) 332-5455 |

| RATING | INSURANCE COMPANY NAME | ADDRESS | CITY | STATE | ZIP | PHONE |
|---|---|---|---|---|---|---|
| B+ | MEDICAL HEALTH INS CORP OF OHIO | 2060 EAST NINTH STREET | CLEVELAND | OH | 44115 | (216) 687-7000 |
| A | MEDICAL MUTUAL OF OHIO | 2060 EAST NINTH ST | CLEVELAND | OH | 44115 | (216) 687-7000 |
| A- | MEDICO CORP LIFE INS CO | 601 SIXTH AVE | DES MOINES | IA | 50309 | (800) 822-9993 |
| B+ | MIDLAND NATIONAL LIFE INS CO | 4350 WESTOWN PARKWAY | WEST DES MOINES | IA | 50266 | (515) 273-0874 |
| A | MIDWESTERN UNITED LIFE INS CO | 8761 BUFFETT PARKWAY | FISHERS | IN | 46038 | (770) 980-5100 |
| B+ | MINNESOTA LIFE INS CO | 400 ROBERT STREET NORTH | ST. PAUL | MN | 55101 | (651) 665-3500 |
| A- | MOTORISTS COMMERCIAL MUTUAL INS CO | 471 EAST BROAD STREET | COLUMBUS | OH | 43215 | (614) 225-8211 |
| A- | MUTUAL OF AMERICA LIFE INS CO | 320 PARK AVENUE | NEW YORK | NY | 10022 | (212) 224-1600 |
| B+ | MUTUAL OF OMAHA INS CO | MUTUAL OF OMAHA PLAZA | OMAHA | NE | 68175 | (402) 342-7600 |
| B+ | NATIONAL BENEFIT LIFE INS CO | ONE COURT SQUARE | LONG ISLAND CITY | NY | 11120 | (718) 361-3636 |
| B+ | NATIONAL CASUALTY CO | ONE W NATIONWIDE BLVD 1-04-701 | COLUMBUS | OH | 43215 | (480) 365-4000 |
| B+ | NATIONAL INCOME LIFE INS CO | 301 PLAINFIELD RD STE 150 | SYRACUSE | NY | 13212 | (315) 451-8180 |
| A | NATIONAL WESTERN LIFE INS CO | 1675 BROADWAY #1200 | DENVER | CO | 80202 | (512) 836-1010 |
| A- | NEW YORK LIFE INS CO | 51 MADISON AVENUE | NEW YORK | NY | 10010 | (212) 576-7000 |
| A- | NIPPON LIFE INS CO OF AMERICA | 7115 VISTA DRIVE | WEST DES MOINES | IA | 50266 | (212) 682-3000 |
| A- | NORTHWESTERN MUTUAL LIFE INS CO | 720 EAST WISCONSIN AVENUE | MILWAUKEE | WI | 53202 | (414) 271-1444 |
| B+ | OHIO NATIONAL LIFE ASR CORP | ONE FINANCIAL WAY | CINCINNATI | OH | 45242 | (513) 794-6100 |
| A- | OPTIMA HEALTH PLAN | 4417 CORPORATION LANE | VIRGINIA BEACH | VA | 23462 | (757) 552-7401 |
| A- | ORANGE PREVENTION & TREATMENT | 505 CITY PARKWAY WEST | ORANGE | CA | 92868 | (714) 796-6122 |
| B+ | OXFORD HEALTH PLANS (NY) INC | ONE PENN PLAZA FLOOR 8 | NEW YORK | NY | 10119 | (203) 447-4500 |
| A- | PACIFIC GUARDIAN LIFE INS CO LTD | 1440 KAPIOLANI BLVD STE 1600 | HONOLULU | HI | 96814 | (808) 955-2236 |
| A- | PARAMOUNT ADVANTAGE | 1901 INDIAN WOOD CIRCLE | MAUMEE | OH | 43537 | (419) 887-2500 |
| A- | PARAMOUNT INS CO (OH) | 1901 INDIAN WOOD CIRCLE | MAUMEE | OH | 43537 | (419) 887-2500 |
| A- | PARTNERSHIP HEALTHPLAN OF CALIFORNIA | 4665 BUSINESS CENTER DRIVE | FAIRFIELD | CA | 94534 | (707) 863-4218 |
| A- | PHYSICIANS LIFE INS CO | 2600 DODGE STREET | OMAHA | NE | 68131 | (402) 633-1000 |
| A+ | PHYSICIANS MUTUAL INS CO | 2600 DODGE STREET | OMAHA | NE | 68131 | (402) 633-1000 |
| B+ | PREMERA BLUE CROSS | 7001 220TH ST SW | MOUNTLAKE TERRACE | WA | 98043 | (425) 918-4000 |
| B+ | PRINCIPAL LIFE INS CO | 711 HIGH STREET | DES MOINES | IA | 50392 | (515) 247-5111 |
| A | PRIORITY HEALTH | 1231 EAST BELTLINE NE | GRAND RAPIDS | MI | 49525 | (616) 942-0954 |
| B+ | PRIORITY HEALTH CHOICE INC | 1231 EAST BELTLINE NE | GRAND RAPIDS | MI | 49525 | (616) 942-0954 |
| A- | PROTECTIVE INS CO | 111 CONGRESSIONAL BLVD STE 500 | CARMEL | IN | 46032 | (317) 636-9800 |
| A+ | PROVIDENCE HEALTH PLAN | 4400 NE HALSEY BLDG # 2 STE # | PORTLAND | OR | 97213 | (503) 574-7500 |
| B+ | REGENCE BL CROSS BL SHIELD OREGON | 100 SW MARKET ST | PORTLAND | OR | 97201 | (503) 225-5221 |
| B+ | SAN MATEO HEALTH COMMISSION | 7751 S MANTHEY ROAD | FRENCH CAMP | CA | 95231 | (209) 461-2211 |
| B+ | SB MUTL LIFE INS CO OF MA | ONE LINSCOTT ROAD | WOBURN | MA | 1801 | (781) 938-3500 |
| A- | SECURITY HEALTH PLAN OF WI INC | 1515 ST JOSEPH AVE | MARSHFIELD | WI | 54449 | (715) 221-9555 |
| A | SENTRY INS A MUTUAL CO | 1800 NORTH POINT DRIVE | STEVENS POINT | WI | 54481 | (715) 346-6000 |
| A | SENTRY LIFE INS CO | 1800 NORTH POINT DRIVE | STEVENS POINT | WI | 54481 | (715) 346-6000 |
| B+ | SENTRY SELECT INS CO | 1800 NORTH POINT DRIVE | STEVENS POINT | WI | 54481 | (715) 346-6000 |
| B+ | SHELTER LIFE INS CO | 1817 WEST BROADWAY | COLUMBIA | MO | 65218 | (573) 445-8441 |
| A | SHELTERPOINT LIFE INS CO | 1225 FRANKLIN AVE STE 475 | GARDEN CITY | NY | 11530 | (516) 829-8100 |
| A- | SIMPLY HEALTHCARE PLANS INC | 9250 W FLAGLER ST STE 600 | MIAMI | FL | 33174 | (757) 490-6900 |
| A | SOUTHERN FARM BUREAU LIFE INS CO | 1401 LIVINGSTON LANE | JACKSON | MS | 39213 | (601) 981-7422 |
| B+ | SOUTHERN PIONEER LIFE INS CO | 124 WEST CAPITOL AVE STE 1900 | LITTLE ROCK | AR | 72201 | (651) 665-3500 |
| B+ | STANDARD INS CO | 1100 SOUTHWEST SIXTH AVENUE | PORTLAND | OR | 97204 | (971) 321-7000 |
| A- | STANDARD LIFE & ACCIDENT INS CO | ONE MOODY PLAZA | GALVESTON | TX | 77550 | (409) 763-4661 |
| A- | STANDARD LIFE INS CO OF NY | 360 HAMILTON AVENUE SUITE 210 | WHITE PLAINS | NY | 10601 | (914) 989-4400 |
| B+ | STATE FARM FIRE & CAS CO | ONE STATE FARM PLAZA | BLOOMINGTON | IL | 61710 | (309) 766-2311 |

| RATING | INSURANCE COMPANY NAME | ADDRESS | CITY | STATE | ZIP | PHONE |
|---|---|---|---|---|---|---|
| B+ | STATE FARM MUTUAL AUTOMOBILE INS CO | ONE STATE FARM PLAZA | BLOOMINGTON | IL | 61710 | (309) 766-2311 |
| B+ | SYMETRA LIFE INS CO | 4125 WESTOWN PARKWAY SUITE | WEST DES MOINES | IA | 50266 | (425) 256-8000 |
| A+ | TEACHERS INS & ANNUITY ASN OF AM | 730 THIRD AVENUE | NEW YORK | NY | 10017 | (212) 490-9000 |
| B+ | TOTAL HEALTH CARE USA INC | 3011 W GRAND BLVD STE 1600 | DETROIT | MI | 48202 | (313) 871-2000 |
| A- | TRANS OCEANIC LIFE INS CO | #121 ONEILL | SAN JUAN | PR | 00918 | (787) 620-2680 |
| B+ | TRUSTMARK INS CO | 400 FIELD DRIVE | LAKE FOREST | IL | 60045 | (847) 615-1500 |
| B+ | TRUSTMARK LIFE INS CO | 400 FIELD DRIVE | LAKE FOREST | IL | 60045 | (847) 615-1500 |
| A- | UNICARE HEALTH PLAN OF WEST VIRGINIA | 200 ASSOCIATION DR STE 200 | CHARLESTON | WV | 25311 | (877) 864-2273 |
| A | UNITED FARM FAMILY LIFE INS CO | 225 SOUTH EAST STREET | INDIANAPOLIS | IN | 46202 | (317) 692-7200 |
| B+ | UNITED HEALTHCARE OF NY INC | 77 WATER STREET 14TH / 15TH FL | NEW YORK | NY | 10005 | (203) 447-4439 |
| B+ | UNITED WORLD LIFE INS CO | MUTUAL OF OMAHA PLAZA | OMAHA | NE | 68175 | (402) 342-7600 |
| B+ | UNITEDHEALTHCARE COMMUNITY PLAN TX | 14141 S W FREEWAY | SUGAR LAND | TX | 77478 | (832) 500-6437 |
| B+ | UNIVERSAL LIFE INS CO | CALLE BOLIVIA #33 6TO PISO | SAN JUAN | PR | 917 | (787) 706-7337 |
| B+ | UPMC FOR YOU INC | 600 GRANT ST | PITTSBURGH | PA | 15219 | (412) 434-1200 |
| A- | UPMC HEALTH PLAN INC | 600 GRANT STREET | PITTSBURGH | PA | 15219 | (412) 434-1200 |
| A | UPPER PENINSULA HEALTH PLAN INC | 853 W WASHINGTON ST | MARQUETTE | MI | 49855 | (906) 225-7500 |
| A | USAA LIFE INS CO | 9800 FREDERICKSBURG RD | SAN ANTONIO | TX | 78288 | (210) 498-1411 |
| B+ | USABLE LIFE | 320 W CAPITOL SUITE 700 | LITTLE ROCK | AR | 72201 | (501) 375-7200 |
| A+ | USABLE MUTUAL INS CO | 601 S GAINES | LITTLE ROCK | AR | 72201 | (501) 378-2000 |
| B+ | VIRGINIA PREMIER HEALTH PLAN INC | 600 E BROAD ST SUITE 400 | RICHMOND | VA | 23219 | (804) 819-5151 |
| B+ | VIVA HEALTH INC | 417 20TH STREET NORTH SUITE 11 | BIRMINGHAM | AL | 35203 | (205) 939-1718 |
| A+ | VOLUNTEER STATE HEALTH PLAN INC | 1 CAMERON HILL CIRCLE | CHATTANOOGA | TN | 37402 | (423) 535-5600 |
| B+ | VOYA RETIREMENT INS & ANNUITY CO | ONE ORANGE WAY | WINDSOR | CT | 06095 | (860) 580-4646 |
| B+ | WELLMARK OF SOUTH DAKOTA INC | 1601 WEST MADISON ST | SIOUX FALLS | SD | 57104 | (605) 373-7200 |

# Section IV

# Weiss Recommended Companies by State

A summary analysis of those

**U.S. Health Insurers**

receiving a Weiss Safety Rating
of A+, A, A-, or B+.

Companies are ranked by Safety Rating
in each state where they are licensed to do business.

# Section IV Contents

This section provides a list of the recommended carriers licensed to do business in each state. It contains all insurers receiving a Safety Rating of A+, A, A-, or B+. If an insurer is not on this list, it should not automatically be assumed that the firm is weak. Indeed, there are many firms that have not achieved a B+ or better rating but are in relatively good condition with adequate resources to cover their risk during an average recession. Not being included in this list should not be construed as a recommendation to cancel policies.

Companies are ranked within each state by their Safety Rating, and are listed alphabetically within each rating category. Companies with the same rating should be viewed as having the same relative strength regardless of their ranking in this table.

1. **Insurance Company Name** — The legally-registered name, which can sometimes differ from the name that the company uses for advertising. An insurer's name can be very similar to the name of other companies which may not be on our Recommended List, so make sure you note the exact name before contacting your agent.

2. **Domicile State** — The state which has primary regulatory responsibility for the company. It may differ from the location of the company's corporate headquarters. You do not have to be living in the domicile state to purchase insurance from this firm, provided it is licensed to do business in your state.

3. **Total Assets** — All assets admitted by state insurance regulators in millions of dollars as of the most recent year end. This includes investments and current business assets such as receivables from agents, reinsurers and subscribers.

Weiss Safety Ratings are not deemed to be a recommendation concerning the purchase or sale of the securities of any insurance company that is publicly owned.

## Alabama

| INSURANCE COMPANY NAME | DOM. STATE | TOTAL ASSETS ($MIL) |
|---|---|---|
| **Rating: A+** | | |
| COUNTRY LIFE INS CO | IL | 9,441.1 |
| PHYSICIANS MUTUAL INS CO | NE | 2,289.0 |
| TEACHERS INS & ANNUITY ASN OF AM | NY | 293,835.0 |
| **Rating: A** | | |
| BERKLEY LIFE & HEALTH INS CO | IA | 286.6 |
| FEDERATED LIFE INS CO | MN | 1,849.9 |
| GUARDIAN LIFE INS CO OF AMERICA | NY | 55,226.5 |
| MIDWESTERN UNITED LIFE INS CO | IN | 233.4 |
| NATIONAL WESTERN LIFE INS CO | CO | 11,058.8 |
| SENTRY INS A MUTUAL CO | WI | 8,232.3 |
| SENTRY LIFE INS CO | WI | 6,735.9 |
| SOUTHERN FARM BUREAU LIFE INS CO | MS | 14,163.7 |
| USAA LIFE INS CO | TX | 24,728.9 |
| **Rating: A-** | | |
| AMALGAMATED LIFE INS CO | NY | 124.9 |
| AMERICAN HEALTH & LIFE INS CO | TX | 840.1 |
| AMERICAN REPUBLIC INS CO | IA | 933.1 |
| ANTHEM LIFE INS CO | IN | 738.1 |
| AUTO-OWNERS LIFE INS CO | MI | 4,021.4 |
| CENTRAL STATES H & L CO OF OMAHA | NE | 411.0 |
| CIGNA LIFE INS CO OF NEW YORK | NY | 403.0 |
| GARDEN STATE LIFE INS CO | TX | 131.8 |
| HUMANA BENEFIT PLAN OF ILLINOIS | IL | 394.7 |
| HUMANA INS CO (WI) | WI | 10,120.6 |
| MASSACHUSETTS MUTUAL LIFE INS CO | MA | 235,570.0 |
| MEDCO CONTAINMENT LIFE INS CO | PA | 1,113.2 |
| MEDICO CORP LIFE INS CO | NE | 63.9 |
| MUTUAL OF AMERICA LIFE INS CO | NY | 20,499.3 |
| NEW YORK LIFE INS CO | NY | 176,417.0 |
| NIPPON LIFE INS CO OF AMERICA | IA | 219.6 |
| NORTHWESTERN MUTUAL LIFE INS CO | WI | 264,165.0 |
| PHYSICIANS LIFE INS CO | NE | 1,625.7 |
| PROTECTIVE INS CO | IN | 848.6 |
| STANDARD LIFE & ACCIDENT INS CO | TX | 516.7 |
| **Rating: B+** | | |
| AETNA HEALTH & LIFE INS CO | CT | 2,403.1 |
| AMERICAN FAMILY LIFE ASR CO OF COLUM | NE | 113,507.0 |
| AMERICAN FIDELITY ASR CO | OK | 5,772.7 |
| AMERICAN UNITED LIFE INS CO | IN | 27,567.2 |
| AMFIRST INS CO | OK | 57.6 |
| ASSURITY LIFE INS CO | NE | 2,726.8 |
| AXA EQUITABLE LIFE INS CO | NY | 187,479.0 |
| BEST LIFE & HEALTH INS CO | TX | 20.9 |
| BLUEBONNET LIFE INS CO | MS | 62.2 |
| BOSTON MUTUAL LIFE INS CO | MA | 1,424.8 |
| COMPANION LIFE INS CO | SC | 359.8 |
| DEARBORN NATIONAL LIFE INS CO | IL | 1,849.7 |
| DELAWARE AMERICAN LIFE INS CO | DE | 137.9 |
| FAMILY HERITAGE LIFE INS CO OF AMER | OH | 1,249.5 |
| GERBER LIFE INS CO | NY | 3,650.7 |
| GOVERNMENT PERSONNEL MUTUAL L I C | TX | 832.3 |
| JACKSON NATIONAL LIFE INS CO | MI | 222,617.0 |
| MIDLAND NATIONAL LIFE INS CO | IA | 55,140.0 |
| MINNESOTA LIFE INS CO | MN | 44,369.0 |
| MUTUAL OF OMAHA INS CO | NE | 7,661.2 |
| NATIONAL BENEFIT LIFE INS CO | NY | 537.3 |
| NATIONAL CASUALTY CO | OH | 406.6 |
| OHIO NATIONAL LIFE ASR CORP | OH | 4,048.6 |
| PRINCIPAL LIFE INS CO | IA | 185,959.0 |
| SB MUTL LIFE INS CO OF MA | MA | 3,015.1 |
| SENTRY SELECT INS CO | WI | 810.3 |
| SOUTHERN PIONEER LIFE INS CO | AR | 15.7 |
| STANDARD INS CO | OR | 23,414.5 |
| STATE FARM FIRE & CAS CO | IL | 39,417.8 |
| STATE FARM MUTUAL AUTOMOBILE INS CO | IL | 154,684.0 |
| SYMETRA LIFE INS CO | IA | 36,133.8 |
| TRUSTMARK INS CO | IL | 1,532.5 |
| TRUSTMARK LIFE INS CO | IL | 320.1 |
| UNITED WORLD LIFE INS CO | NE | 123.8 |
| USABLE LIFE | AR | 510.9 |
| VIVA HEALTH INC | AL | 276.6 |
| VOYA RETIREMENT INS & ANNUITY CO | CT | 104,964.0 |

## Alaska

| INSURANCE COMPANY NAME | DOM. STATE | TOTAL ASSETS ($MIL) |
|---|---|---|
| **Rating: A+** | | |
| COUNTRY LIFE INS CO | IL | 9,441.1 |
| PHYSICIANS MUTUAL INS CO | NE | 2,289.0 |
| TEACHERS INS & ANNUITY ASN OF AM | NY | 293,835.0 |
| **Rating: A** | | |
| BERKLEY LIFE & HEALTH INS CO | IA | 286.6 |
| GUARDIAN LIFE INS CO OF AMERICA | NY | 55,226.5 |
| LIFEWISE ASR CO | WA | 166.6 |
| MIDWESTERN UNITED LIFE INS CO | IN | 233.4 |
| NATIONAL WESTERN LIFE INS CO | CO | 11,058.8 |
| SENTRY INS A MUTUAL CO | WI | 8,232.3 |
| SENTRY LIFE INS CO | WI | 6,735.9 |
| USAA LIFE INS CO | TX | 24,728.9 |
| **Rating: A-** | | |
| AMALGAMATED LIFE INS CO | NY | 124.9 |
| AMERICAN HEALTH & LIFE INS CO | TX | 840.1 |
| AMERICAN REPUBLIC INS CO | IA | 933.1 |
| ANTHEM LIFE INS CO | IN | 738.1 |
| CENTRAL STATES H & L CO OF OMAHA | NE | 411.0 |
| GARDEN STATE LIFE INS CO | TX | 131.8 |
| HUMANA BENEFIT PLAN OF ILLINOIS | IL | 394.7 |
| HUMANA INS CO (WI) | WI | 10,120.6 |
| MASSACHUSETTS MUTUAL LIFE INS CO | MA | 235,570.0 |
| MEDCO CONTAINMENT LIFE INS CO | PA | 1,113.2 |
| MEDICO CORP LIFE INS CO | NE | 63.9 |
| MUTUAL OF AMERICA LIFE INS CO | NY | 20,499.3 |
| NEW YORK LIFE INS CO | NY | 176,417.0 |
| NIPPON LIFE INS CO OF AMERICA | IA | 219.6 |
| NORTHWESTERN MUTUAL LIFE INS CO | WI | 264,165.0 |
| PACIFIC GUARDIAN LIFE INS CO LTD | HI | 552.3 |
| PHYSICIANS LIFE INS CO | NE | 1,625.7 |
| PROTECTIVE INS CO | IN | 848.6 |
| STANDARD LIFE & ACCIDENT INS CO | TX | 516.7 |
| **Rating: B+** | | |
| AETNA HEALTH & LIFE INS CO | CT | 2,403.1 |
| AMERICAN FAMILY LIFE ASR CO OF COLUM | NE | 113,507.0 |
| AMERICAN FIDELITY ASR CO | OK | 5,772.7 |
| AMERICAN UNITED LIFE INS CO | IN | 27,567.2 |
| ASSURITY LIFE INS CO | NE | 2,726.8 |
| AXA EQUITABLE LIFE INS CO | NY | 187,479.0 |
| BOSTON MUTUAL LIFE INS CO | MA | 1,424.8 |
| COMPANION LIFE INS CO | SC | 359.8 |
| DEARBORN NATIONAL LIFE INS CO | IL | 1,849.7 |
| DELAWARE AMERICAN LIFE INS CO | DE | 137.9 |
| FAMILY HERITAGE LIFE INS CO OF AMER | OH | 1,249.5 |
| GERBER LIFE INS CO | NY | 3,650.7 |
| GOVERNMENT PERSONNEL MUTUAL L I C | TX | 832.3 |
| JACKSON NATIONAL LIFE INS CO | MI | 222,617.0 |
| MIDLAND NATIONAL LIFE INS CO | IA | 55,140.0 |
| MINNESOTA LIFE INS CO | MN | 44,369.0 |
| MUTUAL OF OMAHA INS CO | NE | 7,661.2 |
| NATIONAL BENEFIT LIFE INS CO | NY | 537.3 |
| NATIONAL CASUALTY CO | OH | 406.6 |
| OHIO NATIONAL LIFE ASR CORP | OH | 4,048.6 |
| PREMERA BLUE CROSS | WA | 2,574.6 |
| PRINCIPAL LIFE INS CO | IA | 185,959.0 |
| SB MUTL LIFE INS CO OF MA | MA | 3,015.1 |
| SENTRY SELECT INS CO | WI | 810.3 |
| STANDARD INS CO | OR | 23,414.5 |
| STATE FARM FIRE & CAS CO | IL | 39,417.8 |
| STATE FARM MUTUAL AUTOMOBILE INS CO | IL | 154,684.0 |
| SYMETRA LIFE INS CO | IA | 36,133.8 |
| TRUSTMARK INS CO | IL | 1,532.5 |
| TRUSTMARK LIFE INS CO | IL | 320.1 |
| UNITED WORLD LIFE INS CO | NE | 123.8 |
| USABLE LIFE | AR | 510.9 |
| VOYA RETIREMENT INS & ANNUITY CO | CT | 104,964.0 |

## Arizona

| INSURANCE COMPANY NAME | DOM. STATE | TOTAL ASSETS ($MIL) |
|---|---|---|
| **Rating: A+** | | |
| BLUE CROSS BLUE SHIELD OF ARIZONA | AZ | 2,020.4 |
| COUNTRY LIFE INS CO | IL | 9,441.1 |
| PHYSICIANS MUTUAL INS CO | NE | 2,289.0 |
| TEACHERS INS & ANNUITY ASN OF AM | NY | 293,835.0 |
| **Rating: A** | | |
| BERKLEY LIFE & HEALTH INS CO | IA | 286.6 |
| FEDERATED LIFE INS CO | MN | 1,849.9 |
| GUARDIAN LIFE INS CO OF AMERICA | NY | 55,226.5 |
| MIDWESTERN UNITED LIFE INS CO | IN | 233.4 |
| NATIONAL WESTERN LIFE INS CO | CO | 11,058.8 |
| SENTRY INS A MUTUAL CO | WI | 8,232.3 |
| SENTRY LIFE INS CO | WI | 6,735.9 |
| UNITED FARM FAMILY LIFE INS CO | IN | 2,312.3 |
| USAA LIFE INS CO | TX | 24,728.9 |
| **Rating: A-** | | |
| AMALGAMATED LIFE INS CO | NY | 124.9 |
| AMERICAN HEALTH & LIFE INS CO | TX | 840.1 |
| AMERICAN REPUBLIC INS CO | IA | 933.1 |
| ANTHEM LIFE INS CO | IN | 738.1 |
| AUTO-OWNERS LIFE INS CO | MI | 4,021.4 |
| CENTRAL STATES H & L CO OF OMAHA | NE | 411.0 |
| COPIC INS CO | CO | 765.4 |
| GARDEN STATE LIFE INS CO | TX | 131.8 |
| HUMANA BENEFIT PLAN OF ILLINOIS | IL | 394.7 |
| HUMANA INS CO (WI) | WI | 10,120.6 |
| MASSACHUSETTS MUTUAL LIFE INS CO | MA | 235,570.0 |
| MEDCO CONTAINMENT LIFE INS CO | PA | 1,113.2 |
| MEDICO CORP LIFE INS CO | NE | 63.9 |
| MOTORISTS COMMERCIAL MUTUAL INS CO | OH | 393.5 |
| MUTUAL OF AMERICA LIFE INS CO | NY | 20,499.3 |
| NEW YORK LIFE INS CO | NY | 176,417.0 |
| NIPPON LIFE INS CO OF AMERICA | IA | 219.6 |
| NORTHWESTERN MUTUAL LIFE INS CO | WI | 264,165.0 |
| PACIFIC GUARDIAN LIFE INS CO LTD | HI | 552.3 |
| PHYSICIANS LIFE INS CO | NE | 1,625.7 |
| PROTECTIVE INS CO | IN | 848.6 |
| STANDARD LIFE & ACCIDENT INS CO | TX | 516.7 |
| **Rating: B+** | | |
| AETNA HEALTH & LIFE INS CO | CT | 2,403.1 |
| AMERICAN FAMILY LIFE ASR CO OF COLUM | NE | 113,507.0 |
| AMERICAN FAMILY MUTL INS CO SI | WI | 17,048.2 |
| AMERICAN FIDELITY ASR CO | OK | 5,772.7 |
| AMERICAN UNITED LIFE INS CO | IN | 27,567.2 |
| AMFIRST INS CO | OK | 57.6 |
| ASSURITY LIFE INS CO | NE | 2,726.8 |
| AXA EQUITABLE LIFE INS CO | NY | 187,479.0 |
| BEST LIFE & HEALTH INS CO | TX | 20.9 |
| BOSTON MUTUAL LIFE INS CO | MA | 1,424.8 |
| COMPANION LIFE INS CO | SC | 359.8 |
| DEARBORN NATIONAL LIFE INS CO | IL | 1,849.7 |
| DELAWARE AMERICAN LIFE INS CO | DE | 137.9 |
| FAMILY HERITAGE LIFE INS CO OF AMER | OH | 1,249.5 |
| FARM BUREAU LIFE INS CO | IA | 8,948.8 |
| GERBER LIFE INS CO | NY | 3,650.7 |
| GOVERNMENT PERSONNEL MUTUAL L I C | TX | 832.3 |
| JACKSON NATIONAL LIFE INS CO | MI | 222,617.0 |
| MIDLAND NATIONAL LIFE INS CO | IA | 55,140.0 |
| MINNESOTA LIFE INS CO | MN | 44,369.0 |
| MUTUAL OF OMAHA INS CO | NE | 7,661.2 |
| NATIONAL BENEFIT LIFE INS CO | NY | 537.3 |
| NATIONAL CASUALTY CO | OH | 406.6 |
| OHIO NATIONAL LIFE ASR CORP | OH | 4,048.6 |
| PRINCIPAL LIFE INS CO | IA | 185,959.0 |
| SB MUTL LIFE INS CO OF MA | MA | 3,015.1 |
| SENTRY SELECT INS CO | WI | 810.3 |
| STANDARD INS CO | OR | 23,414.5 |
| STATE FARM FIRE & CAS CO | IL | 39,417.8 |
| STATE FARM MUTUAL AUTOMOBILE INS CO | IL | 154,684.0 |
| SYMETRA LIFE INS CO | IA | 36,133.8 |
| TRUSTMARK INS CO | IL | 1,532.5 |
| TRUSTMARK LIFE INS CO | IL | 320.1 |
| UNITED WORLD LIFE INS CO | NE | 123.8 |
| USABLE LIFE | AR | 510.9 |
| VOYA RETIREMENT INS & ANNUITY CO | CT | 104,964.0 |

## Arkansas

| INSURANCE COMPANY NAME | DOM. STATE | TOTAL ASSETS ($MIL) |
|---|---|---|
| **Rating: A+** | | |
| COUNTRY LIFE INS CO | IL | 9,441.1 |
| HMO PARTNERS INC | AR | 135.4 |
| PHYSICIANS MUTUAL INS CO | NE | 2,289.0 |
| TEACHERS INS & ANNUITY ASN OF AM | NY | 293,835.0 |
| USABLE MUTUAL INS CO | AR | 1,648.3 |
| **Rating: A** | | |
| BERKLEY LIFE & HEALTH INS CO | IA | 286.6 |
| FEDERATED LIFE INS CO | MN | 1,849.9 |
| GUARDIAN LIFE INS CO OF AMERICA | NY | 55,226.5 |
| MIDWESTERN UNITED LIFE INS CO | IN | 233.4 |
| NATIONAL WESTERN LIFE INS CO | CO | 11,058.8 |
| SENTRY INS A MUTUAL CO | WI | 8,232.3 |
| SENTRY LIFE INS CO | WI | 6,735.9 |
| SOUTHERN FARM BUREAU LIFE INS CO | MS | 14,163.7 |
| USAA LIFE INS CO | TX | 24,728.9 |
| **Rating: A-** | | |
| AMALGAMATED LIFE INS CO | NY | 124.9 |
| AMERICAN HEALTH & LIFE INS CO | TX | 840.1 |
| AMERICAN REPUBLIC INS CO | IA | 933.1 |
| ANTHEM LIFE INS CO | IN | 738.1 |
| AUTO-OWNERS LIFE INS CO | MI | 4,021.4 |
| CENTRAL STATES H & L CO OF OMAHA | NE | 411.0 |
| GARDEN STATE LIFE INS CO | TX | 131.8 |
| HUMANA BENEFIT PLAN OF ILLINOIS | IL | 394.7 |
| HUMANA INS CO (WI) | WI | 10,120.6 |
| MASSACHUSETTS MUTUAL LIFE INS CO | MA | 235,570.0 |
| MEDCO CONTAINMENT LIFE INS CO | PA | 1,113.2 |
| MEDICO CORP LIFE INS CO | NE | 63.9 |
| MUTUAL OF AMERICA LIFE INS CO | NY | 20,499.3 |
| NEW YORK LIFE INS CO | NY | 176,417.0 |
| NIPPON LIFE INS CO OF AMERICA | IA | 219.6 |
| NORTHWESTERN MUTUAL LIFE INS CO | WI | 264,165.0 |
| PHYSICIANS LIFE INS CO | NE | 1,625.7 |
| PROTECTIVE INS CO | IN | 848.6 |
| STANDARD LIFE & ACCIDENT INS CO | TX | 516.7 |
| **Rating: B+** | | |
| AETNA HEALTH & LIFE INS CO | CT | 2,403.1 |
| AMERICAN FAMILY LIFE ASR CO OF COLUM | NE | 113,507.0 |
| AMERICAN FIDELITY ASR CO | OK | 5,772.7 |
| AMERICAN UNITED LIFE INS CO | IN | 27,567.2 |
| AMFIRST INS CO | OK | 57.6 |
| ASSURITY LIFE INS CO | NE | 2,726.8 |
| AXA EQUITABLE LIFE INS CO | NY | 187,479.0 |
| BLUEBONNET LIFE INS CO | MS | 62.2 |
| BOSTON MUTUAL LIFE INS CO | MA | 1,424.8 |
| COMPANION LIFE INS CO | SC | 359.8 |
| DEARBORN NATIONAL LIFE INS CO | IL | 1,849.7 |
| DELAWARE AMERICAN LIFE INS CO | DE | 137.9 |
| FAMILY HERITAGE LIFE INS CO OF AMER | OH | 1,249.5 |
| GERBER LIFE INS CO | NY | 3,650.7 |
| GOVERNMENT PERSONNEL MUTUAL L I C | TX | 832.3 |
| HEALTHSPRING OF TENNESSEE INC | TN | 460.4 |
| JACKSON NATIONAL LIFE INS CO | MI | 222,617.0 |
| MIDLAND NATIONAL LIFE INS CO | IA | 55,140.0 |
| MINNESOTA LIFE INS CO | MN | 44,369.0 |
| MUTUAL OF OMAHA INS CO | NE | 7,661.2 |
| NATIONAL BENEFIT LIFE INS CO | NY | 537.3 |
| NATIONAL CASUALTY CO | OH | 406.6 |
| OHIO NATIONAL LIFE ASR CORP | OH | 4,048.6 |
| PRINCIPAL LIFE INS CO | IA | 185,959.0 |
| SB MUTL LIFE INS CO OF MA | MA | 3,015.1 |
| SENTRY SELECT INS CO | WI | 810.3 |
| SHELTER LIFE INS CO | MO | 1,238.3 |
| SOUTHERN PIONEER LIFE INS CO | AR | 15.7 |
| STANDARD INS CO | OR | 23,414.5 |
| STATE FARM FIRE & CAS CO | IL | 39,417.8 |
| STATE FARM MUTUAL AUTOMOBILE INS CO | IL | 154,684.0 |
| SYMETRA LIFE INS CO | IA | 36,133.8 |
| TRUSTMARK INS CO | IL | 1,532.5 |
| TRUSTMARK LIFE INS CO | IL | 320.1 |
| UNITED WORLD LIFE INS CO | NE | 123.8 |
| USABLE LIFE | AR | 510.9 |
| VOYA RETIREMENT INS & ANNUITY CO | CT | 104,964.0 |

## California

| INSURANCE COMPANY NAME | DOM. STATE | TOTAL ASSETS ($MIL) |
|---|---|---|
| **Rating: A+** | | |
| BLUE CROSS OF CALIFORNIA | CA | 7,951.3 |
| BLUE SHIELD OF CALIFORNIA | CA | 8,119.3 |
| CARE 1ST HEALTH PLAN INC | CA | 1,094.9 |
| PHYSICIANS MUTUAL INS CO | NE | 2,289.0 |
| TEACHERS INS & ANNUITY ASN OF AM | NY | 293,835.0 |
| **Rating: A** | | |
| BERKLEY LIFE & HEALTH INS CO | IA | 286.6 |
| FEDERATED LIFE INS CO | MN | 1,849.9 |
| GUARDIAN LIFE INS CO OF AMERICA | NY | 55,226.5 |
| INLAND EMPIRE HEALTH PLAN | CA | 1,779.5 |
| KAISER FOUNDATION HEALTH PLAN INC | CA | 72,940.0 |
| LIFEWISE ASR CO | WA | 166.6 |
| MIDWESTERN UNITED LIFE INS CO | IN | 233.4 |
| NATIONAL WESTERN LIFE INS CO | CO | 11,058.8 |
| SENTRY INS A MUTUAL CO | WI | 8,232.3 |
| SENTRY LIFE INS CO | WI | 6,735.9 |
| SHELTERPOINT LIFE INS CO | NY | 110.1 |
| UNITED FARM FAMILY LIFE INS CO | IN | 2,312.3 |
| USAA LIFE INS CO | TX | 24,728.9 |
| **Rating: A-** | | |
| AMALGAMATED LIFE INS CO | NY | 124.9 |
| AMERICAN HEALTH & LIFE INS CO | TX | 840.1 |
| AMERICAN REPUBLIC INS CO | IA | 933.1 |
| ANTHEM LIFE INS CO | IN | 738.1 |
| CENTRAL STATES H & L CO OF OMAHA | NE | 411.0 |
| GARDEN STATE LIFE INS CO | TX | 131.8 |
| HUMANA INS CO (WI) | WI | 10,120.6 |
| MASSACHUSETTS MUTUAL LIFE INS CO | MA | 235,570.0 |
| MEDCO CONTAINMENT LIFE INS CO | PA | 1,113.2 |
| MOTORISTS COMMERCIAL MUTUAL INS CO | OH | 393.5 |
| MUTUAL OF AMERICA LIFE INS CO | NY | 20,499.3 |
| NEW YORK LIFE INS CO | NY | 176,417.0 |
| NIPPON LIFE INS CO OF AMERICA | IA | 219.6 |
| NORTHWESTERN MUTUAL LIFE INS CO | WI | 264,165.0 |
| ORANGE PREVENTION & TREATMENT INTEGR | CA | 2,819.9 |
| PACIFIC GUARDIAN LIFE INS CO LTD | HI | 552.3 |
| PARTNERSHIP HEALTHPLAN OF CALIFORNIA | CA | 1,697.8 |
| PHYSICIANS LIFE INS CO | NE | 1,625.7 |
| PROTECTIVE INS CO | IN | 848.6 |
| STANDARD LIFE & ACCIDENT INS CO | TX | 516.7 |
| **Rating: B+** | | |
| AETNA HEALTH & LIFE INS CO | CT | 2,403.1 |
| AMERICAN FAMILY LIFE ASR CO OF COLUM | NE | 113,507.0 |
| AMERICAN FIDELITY ASR CO | OK | 5,772.7 |
| AMERICAN UNITED LIFE INS CO | IN | 27,567.2 |
| ASSURITY LIFE INS CO | NE | 2,726.8 |
| AXA EQUITABLE LIFE INS CO | NY | 187,479.0 |
| BEST LIFE & HEALTH INS CO | TX | 20.9 |
| BOSTON MUTUAL LIFE INS CO | MA | 1,424.8 |
| CAREMORE HEALTH PLAN | CA | 317.1 |
| DEARBORN NATIONAL LIFE INS CO | IL | 1,849.7 |
| DELAWARE AMERICAN LIFE INS CO | DE | 137.9 |
| FAMILY HERITAGE LIFE INS CO OF AMER | OH | 1,249.5 |
| GERBER LIFE INS CO | NY | 3,650.7 |
| GOVERNMENT PERSONNEL MUTUAL L I C | TX | 832.3 |
| JACKSON NATIONAL LIFE INS CO | MI | 222,617.0 |
| MIDLAND NATIONAL LIFE INS CO | IA | 55,140.0 |
| MINNESOTA LIFE INS CO | MN | 44,369.0 |
| MUTUAL OF OMAHA INS CO | NE | 7,661.2 |
| NATIONAL BENEFIT LIFE INS CO | NY | 537.3 |
| NATIONAL CASUALTY CO | OH | 406.6 |
| OHIO NATIONAL LIFE ASR CORP | OH | 4,048.6 |
| PRINCIPAL LIFE INS CO | IA | 185,959.0 |
| SAN MATEO HEALTH COMMISSION | CA | 657.3 |
| SB MUTL LIFE INS CO OF MA | MA | 3,015.1 |
| SENTRY SELECT INS CO | WI | 810.3 |
| STANDARD INS CO | OR | 23,414.5 |
| STATE FARM FIRE & CAS CO | IL | 39,417.8 |
| STATE FARM MUTUAL AUTOMOBILE INS CO | IL | 154,684.0 |
| SYMETRA LIFE INS CO | IA | 36,133.8 |
| TRUSTMARK INS CO | IL | 1,532.5 |
| TRUSTMARK LIFE INS CO | IL | 320.1 |
| UNITED WORLD LIFE INS CO | NE | 123.8 |
| USABLE LIFE | AR | 510.9 |
| VOYA RETIREMENT INS & ANNUITY CO | CT | 104,964.0 |

## Colorado

| INSURANCE COMPANY NAME | DOM. STATE | TOTAL ASSETS ($MIL) |
|---|---|---|
| **Rating: A+** | | |
| COUNTRY LIFE INS CO | IL | 9,441.1 |
| PHYSICIANS MUTUAL INS CO | NE | 2,289.0 |
| TEACHERS INS & ANNUITY ASN OF AM | NY | 293,835.0 |
| **Rating: A** | | |
| BERKLEY LIFE & HEALTH INS CO | IA | 286.6 |
| FEDERATED LIFE INS CO | MN | 1,849.9 |
| GUARDIAN LIFE INS CO OF AMERICA | NY | 55,226.5 |
| MIDWESTERN UNITED LIFE INS CO | IN | 233.4 |
| NATIONAL WESTERN LIFE INS CO | CO | 11,058.8 |
| SENTRY INS A MUTUAL CO | WI | 8,232.3 |
| SENTRY LIFE INS CO | WI | 6,735.9 |
| SHELTERPOINT LIFE INS CO | NY | 110.1 |
| SOUTHERN FARM BUREAU LIFE INS CO | MS | 14,163.7 |
| USAA LIFE INS CO | TX | 24,728.9 |
| **Rating: A-** | | |
| AMALGAMATED LIFE INS CO | NY | 124.9 |
| AMERICAN HEALTH & LIFE INS CO | TX | 840.1 |
| AMERICAN REPUBLIC INS CO | IA | 933.1 |
| ANTHEM LIFE INS CO | IN | 738.1 |
| AUTO-OWNERS LIFE INS CO | MI | 4,021.4 |
| CENTRAL STATES H & L CO OF OMAHA | NE | 411.0 |
| COPIC INS CO | CO | 765.4 |
| GARDEN STATE LIFE INS CO | TX | 131.8 |
| HUMANA BENEFIT PLAN OF ILLINOIS | IL | 394.7 |
| HUMANA INS CO (WI) | WI | 10,120.6 |
| MASSACHUSETTS MUTUAL LIFE INS CO | MA | 235,570.0 |
| MEDCO CONTAINMENT LIFE INS CO | PA | 1,113.2 |
| MEDICO CORP LIFE INS CO | NE | 63.9 |
| MOTORISTS COMMERCIAL MUTUAL INS CO | OH | 393.5 |
| MUTUAL OF AMERICA LIFE INS CO | NY | 20,499.3 |
| NEW YORK LIFE INS CO | NY | 176,417.0 |
| NIPPON LIFE INS CO OF AMERICA | IA | 219.6 |
| NORTHWESTERN MUTUAL LIFE INS CO | WI | 264,165.0 |
| PACIFIC GUARDIAN LIFE INS CO LTD | HI | 552.3 |
| PHYSICIANS LIFE INS CO | NE | 1,625.7 |
| PROTECTIVE INS CO | IN | 848.6 |
| STANDARD LIFE & ACCIDENT INS CO | TX | 516.7 |
| **Rating: B+** | | |
| AETNA HEALTH & LIFE INS CO | CT | 2,403.1 |
| AMERICAN FAMILY LIFE ASR CO OF COLUM | NE | 113,507.0 |
| AMERICAN FAMILY MUTL INS CO SI | WI | 17,048.2 |
| AMERICAN FIDELITY ASR CO | OK | 5,772.7 |
| AMERICAN UNITED LIFE INS CO | IN | 27,567.2 |
| ASSURITY LIFE INS CO | NE | 2,726.8 |
| AXA EQUITABLE LIFE INS CO | NY | 187,479.0 |
| BEST LIFE & HEALTH INS CO | TX | 20.9 |
| BOSTON MUTUAL LIFE INS CO | MA | 1,424.8 |
| COMPANION LIFE INS CO | SC | 359.8 |
| DEARBORN NATIONAL LIFE INS CO | IL | 1,849.7 |
| DELAWARE AMERICAN LIFE INS CO | DE | 137.9 |
| FAMILY HERITAGE LIFE INS CO OF AMER | OH | 1,249.5 |
| FARM BUREAU LIFE INS CO | IA | 8,948.8 |
| GERBER LIFE INS CO | NY | 3,650.7 |
| GOVERNMENT PERSONNEL MUTUAL L I C | TX | 832.3 |
| JACKSON NATIONAL LIFE INS CO | MI | 222,617.0 |
| MIDLAND NATIONAL LIFE INS CO | IA | 55,140.0 |
| MINNESOTA LIFE INS CO | MN | 44,369.0 |
| MUTUAL OF OMAHA INS CO | NE | 7,661.2 |
| NATIONAL BENEFIT LIFE INS CO | NY | 537.3 |
| NATIONAL CASUALTY CO | OH | 406.6 |
| OHIO NATIONAL LIFE ASR CORP | OH | 4,048.6 |
| PRINCIPAL LIFE INS CO | IA | 185,959.0 |
| SB MUTL LIFE INS CO OF MA | MA | 3,015.1 |
| SENTRY SELECT INS CO | WI | 810.3 |
| SHELTER LIFE INS CO | MO | 1,238.3 |
| STANDARD INS CO | OR | 23,414.5 |
| STATE FARM FIRE & CAS CO | IL | 39,417.8 |
| STATE FARM MUTUAL AUTOMOBILE INS CO | IL | 154,684.0 |
| SYMETRA LIFE INS CO | IA | 36,133.8 |
| TRUSTMARK INS CO | IL | 1,532.5 |
| TRUSTMARK LIFE INS CO | IL | 320.1 |
| UNITED WORLD LIFE INS CO | NE | 123.8 |
| USABLE LIFE | AR | 510.9 |
| VOYA RETIREMENT INS & ANNUITY CO | CT | 104,964.0 |

## Connecticut

| INSURANCE COMPANY NAME | DOM. STATE | TOTAL ASSETS ($MIL) |
|---|---|---|
| **Rating: A+** | | |
| COUNTRY LIFE INS CO | IL | 9,441.1 |
| PHYSICIANS MUTUAL INS CO | NE | 2,289.0 |
| TEACHERS INS & ANNUITY ASN OF AM | NY | 293,835.0 |
| **Rating: A** | | |
| ALLIANZ LIFE INS CO OF NY | NY | 3,347.7 |
| BERKLEY LIFE & HEALTH INS CO | IA | 286.6 |
| FEDERATED LIFE INS CO | MN | 1,849.9 |
| GUARDIAN LIFE INS CO OF AMERICA | NY | 55,226.5 |
| MIDWESTERN UNITED LIFE INS CO | IN | 233.4 |
| NATIONAL WESTERN LIFE INS CO | CO | 11,058.8 |
| SENTRY INS A MUTUAL CO | WI | 8,232.3 |
| SENTRY LIFE INS CO | WI | 6,735.9 |
| SHELTERPOINT LIFE INS CO | NY | 110.1 |
| USAA LIFE INS CO | TX | 24,728.9 |
| **Rating: A-** | | |
| AMALGAMATED LIFE INS CO | NY | 124.9 |
| AMERICAN FAMILY LIFE ASR CO OF NY | NY | 945.4 |
| AMERICAN HEALTH & LIFE INS CO | TX | 840.1 |
| AMERICAN REPUBLIC INS CO | IA | 933.1 |
| ANTHEM LIFE INS CO | IN | 738.1 |
| CENTRAL STATES H & L CO OF OMAHA | NE | 411.0 |
| GARDEN STATE LIFE INS CO | TX | 131.8 |
| HUMANA BENEFIT PLAN OF ILLINOIS | IL | 394.7 |
| HUMANA INS CO (WI) | WI | 10,120.6 |
| MASSACHUSETTS MUTUAL LIFE INS CO | MA | 235,570.0 |
| MEDCO CONTAINMENT LIFE INS CO | PA | 1,113.2 |
| MOTORISTS COMMERCIAL MUTUAL INS CO | OH | 393.5 |
| MUTUAL OF AMERICA LIFE INS CO | NY | 20,499.3 |
| NEW YORK LIFE INS CO | NY | 176,417.0 |
| NIPPON LIFE INS CO OF AMERICA | IA | 219.6 |
| NORTHWESTERN MUTUAL LIFE INS CO | WI | 264,165.0 |
| PHYSICIANS LIFE INS CO | NE | 1,625.7 |
| PROTECTIVE INS CO | IN | 848.6 |
| STANDARD LIFE & ACCIDENT INS CO | TX | 516.7 |
| **Rating: B+** | | |
| AETNA HEALTH & LIFE INS CO | CT | 2,403.1 |
| AMERICAN FAMILY LIFE ASR CO OF COLUM | NE | 113,507.0 |
| AMERICAN FIDELITY ASR CO | OK | 5,772.7 |
| AMERICAN UNITED LIFE INS CO | IN | 27,567.2 |
| ASSURITY LIFE INS CO | NE | 2,726.8 |
| AXA EQUITABLE LIFE INS CO | NY | 187,479.0 |
| BOSTON MUTUAL LIFE INS CO | MA | 1,424.8 |
| COMPANION LIFE INS CO | SC | 359.8 |
| DEARBORN NATIONAL LIFE INS CO | IL | 1,849.7 |
| DELAWARE AMERICAN LIFE INS CO | DE | 137.9 |
| FAMILY HERITAGE LIFE INS CO OF AMER | OH | 1,249.5 |
| GERBER LIFE INS CO | NY | 3,650.7 |
| GOVERNMENT PERSONNEL MUTUAL L I C | TX | 832.3 |
| JACKSON NATIONAL LIFE INS CO | MI | 222,617.0 |
| MIDLAND NATIONAL LIFE INS CO | IA | 55,140.0 |
| MINNESOTA LIFE INS CO | MN | 44,369.0 |
| MUTUAL OF OMAHA INS CO | NE | 7,661.2 |
| NATIONAL BENEFIT LIFE INS CO | NY | 537.3 |
| NATIONAL CASUALTY CO | OH | 406.6 |
| OHIO NATIONAL LIFE ASR CORP | OH | 4,048.6 |
| PRINCIPAL LIFE INS CO | IA | 185,959.0 |
| SB MUTL LIFE INS CO OF MA | MA | 3,015.1 |
| SENTRY SELECT INS CO | WI | 810.3 |
| STANDARD INS CO | OR | 23,414.5 |
| STATE FARM FIRE & CAS CO | IL | 39,417.8 |
| STATE FARM MUTUAL AUTOMOBILE INS CO | IL | 154,684.0 |
| SYMETRA LIFE INS CO | IA | 36,133.8 |
| TRUSTMARK INS CO | IL | 1,532.5 |
| TRUSTMARK LIFE INS CO | IL | 320.1 |
| USABLE LIFE | AR | 510.9 |
| VOYA RETIREMENT INS & ANNUITY CO | CT | 104,964.0 |

## Delaware

| INSURANCE COMPANY NAME | DOM. STATE | TOTAL ASSETS ($MIL) |
|---|---|---|
| **Rating: A+** | | |
| COUNTRY LIFE INS CO | IL | 9,441.1 |
| PHYSICIANS MUTUAL INS CO | NE | 2,289.0 |
| TEACHERS INS & ANNUITY ASN OF AM | NY | 293,835.0 |
| **Rating: A** | | |
| BERKLEY LIFE & HEALTH INS CO | IA | 286.6 |
| FEDERATED LIFE INS CO | MN | 1,849.9 |
| FIRST RELIANCE STANDARD LIFE INS CO | NY | 197.5 |
| GUARDIAN LIFE INS CO OF AMERICA | NY | 55,226.5 |
| MIDWESTERN UNITED LIFE INS CO | IN | 233.4 |
| NATIONAL WESTERN LIFE INS CO | CO | 11,058.8 |
| SENTRY INS A MUTUAL CO | WI | 8,232.3 |
| SENTRY LIFE INS CO | WI | 6,735.9 |
| SHELTERPOINT LIFE INS CO | NY | 110.1 |
| USAA LIFE INS CO | TX | 24,728.9 |
| **Rating: A-** | | |
| AMALGAMATED LIFE INS CO | NY | 124.9 |
| AMERICAN HEALTH & LIFE INS CO | TX | 840.1 |
| AMERICAN REPUBLIC INS CO | IA | 933.1 |
| ANTHEM LIFE INS CO | IN | 738.1 |
| CENTRAL STATES H & L CO OF OMAHA | NE | 411.0 |
| GARDEN STATE LIFE INS CO | TX | 131.8 |
| HUMANA BENEFIT PLAN OF ILLINOIS | IL | 394.7 |
| HUMANA INS CO (WI) | WI | 10,120.6 |
| MASSACHUSETTS MUTUAL LIFE INS CO | MA | 235,570.0 |
| MEDCO CONTAINMENT LIFE INS CO | PA | 1,113.2 |
| MEDICO CORP LIFE INS CO | NE | 63.9 |
| MOTORISTS COMMERCIAL MUTUAL INS CO | OH | 393.5 |
| MUTUAL OF AMERICA LIFE INS CO | NY | 20,499.3 |
| NEW YORK LIFE INS CO | NY | 176,417.0 |
| NIPPON LIFE INS CO OF AMERICA | IA | 219.6 |
| NORTHWESTERN MUTUAL LIFE INS CO | WI | 264,165.0 |
| PHYSICIANS LIFE INS CO | NE | 1,625.7 |
| PROTECTIVE INS CO | IN | 848.6 |
| STANDARD LIFE & ACCIDENT INS CO | TX | 516.7 |
| **Rating: B+** | | |
| AETNA HEALTH & LIFE INS CO | CT | 2,403.1 |
| AMERICAN FAMILY LIFE ASR CO OF COLUM | NE | 113,507.0 |
| AMERICAN FIDELITY ASR CO | OK | 5,772.7 |
| AMERICAN UNITED LIFE INS CO | IN | 27,567.2 |
| ASSURITY LIFE INS CO | NE | 2,726.8 |
| AXA EQUITABLE LIFE INS CO | NY | 187,479.0 |
| BOSTON MUTUAL LIFE INS CO | MA | 1,424.8 |
| COMPANION LIFE INS CO | SC | 359.8 |
| DEARBORN NATIONAL LIFE INS CO | IL | 1,849.7 |
| DELAWARE AMERICAN LIFE INS CO | DE | 137.9 |
| FAMILY HERITAGE LIFE INS CO OF AMER | OH | 1,249.5 |
| GERBER LIFE INS CO | NY | 3,650.7 |
| GOVERNMENT PERSONNEL MUTUAL L I C | TX | 832.3 |
| JACKSON NATIONAL LIFE INS CO | MI | 222,617.0 |
| MIDLAND NATIONAL LIFE INS CO | IA | 55,140.0 |
| MINNESOTA LIFE INS CO | MN | 44,369.0 |
| MUTUAL OF OMAHA INS CO | NE | 7,661.2 |
| NATIONAL BENEFIT LIFE INS CO | NY | 537.3 |
| NATIONAL CASUALTY CO | OH | 406.6 |
| OHIO NATIONAL LIFE ASR CORP | OH | 4,048.6 |
| PRINCIPAL LIFE INS CO | IA | 185,959.0 |
| SB MUTL LIFE INS CO OF MA | MA | 3,015.1 |
| SENTRY SELECT INS CO | WI | 810.3 |
| STANDARD INS CO | OR | 23,414.5 |
| STATE FARM FIRE & CAS CO | IL | 39,417.8 |
| STATE FARM MUTUAL AUTOMOBILE INS CO | IL | 154,684.0 |
| SYMETRA LIFE INS CO | IA | 36,133.8 |
| TRUSTMARK INS CO | IL | 1,532.5 |
| TRUSTMARK LIFE INS CO | IL | 320.1 |
| UNITED WORLD LIFE INS CO | NE | 123.8 |
| USABLE LIFE | AR | 510.9 |
| VOYA RETIREMENT INS & ANNUITY CO | CT | 104,964.0 |

## District of Columbia

| INSURANCE COMPANY NAME | DOM. STATE | TOTAL ASSETS ($MIL) |
|---|---|---|
| **Rating: A+** | | |
| PHYSICIANS MUTUAL INS CO | NE | 2,289.0 |
| TEACHERS INS & ANNUITY ASN OF AM | NY | 293,835.0 |
| **Rating: A** | | |
| ALLIANZ LIFE INS CO OF NY | NY | 3,347.7 |
| BERKLEY LIFE & HEALTH INS CO | IA | 286.6 |
| FIRST RELIANCE STANDARD LIFE INS CO | NY | 197.5 |
| GUARDIAN LIFE INS CO OF AMERICA | NY | 55,226.5 |
| MIDWESTERN UNITED LIFE INS CO | IN | 233.4 |
| NATIONAL WESTERN LIFE INS CO | CO | 11,058.8 |
| SENTRY INS A MUTUAL CO | WI | 8,232.3 |
| SENTRY LIFE INS CO | WI | 6,735.9 |
| SHELTERPOINT LIFE INS CO | NY | 110.1 |
| USAA LIFE INS CO | TX | 24,728.9 |
| **Rating: A-** | | |
| AMALGAMATED LIFE INS CO | NY | 124.9 |
| AMERICAN HEALTH & LIFE INS CO | TX | 840.1 |
| AMERICAN REPUBLIC INS CO | IA | 933.1 |
| ANTHEM LIFE INS CO | IN | 738.1 |
| CAREFIRST BLUECHOICE INC | DC | 1,137.7 |
| CENTRAL STATES H & L CO OF OMAHA | NE | 411.0 |
| CIGNA LIFE INS CO OF NEW YORK | NY | 403.0 |
| ERIE FAMILY LIFE INS CO | PA | 2,448.7 |
| GARDEN STATE LIFE INS CO | TX | 131.8 |
| HUMANA BENEFIT PLAN OF ILLINOIS | IL | 394.7 |
| HUMANA INS CO (WI) | WI | 10,120.6 |
| MASSACHUSETTS MUTUAL LIFE INS CO | MA | 235,570.0 |
| MEDCO CONTAINMENT LIFE INS CO | PA | 1,113.2 |
| MEDICO CORP LIFE INS CO | NE | 63.9 |
| MOTORISTS COMMERCIAL MUTUAL INS CO | OH | 393.5 |
| MUTUAL OF AMERICA LIFE INS CO | NY | 20,499.3 |
| NEW YORK LIFE INS CO | NY | 176,417.0 |
| NIPPON LIFE INS CO OF AMERICA | IA | 219.6 |
| NORTHWESTERN MUTUAL LIFE INS CO | WI | 264,165.0 |
| PHYSICIANS LIFE INS CO | NE | 1,625.7 |
| PROTECTIVE INS CO | IN | 848.6 |
| STANDARD LIFE & ACCIDENT INS CO | TX | 516.7 |
| **Rating: B+** | | |
| AETNA HEALTH & LIFE INS CO | CT | 2,403.1 |
| AMERICAN FAMILY LIFE ASR CO OF COLUM | NE | 113,507.0 |
| AMERICAN FIDELITY ASR CO | OK | 5,772.7 |
| AMERICAN UNITED LIFE INS CO | IN | 27,567.2 |
| ASSURITY LIFE INS CO | NE | 2,726.8 |
| AXA EQUITABLE LIFE INS CO | NY | 187,479.0 |
| BEST LIFE & HEALTH INS CO | TX | 20.9 |
| BOSTON MUTUAL LIFE INS CO | MA | 1,424.8 |
| COMPANION LIFE INS CO | SC | 359.8 |
| DEARBORN NATIONAL LIFE INS CO | IL | 1,849.7 |
| DELAWARE AMERICAN LIFE INS CO | DE | 137.9 |
| FAMILY HERITAGE LIFE INS CO OF AMER | OH | 1,249.5 |
| GERBER LIFE INS CO | NY | 3,650.7 |
| GOVERNMENT PERSONNEL MUTUAL L I C | TX | 832.3 |
| JACKSON NATIONAL LIFE INS CO | MI | 222,617.0 |
| MIDLAND NATIONAL LIFE INS CO | IA | 55,140.0 |
| MINNESOTA LIFE INS CO | MN | 44,369.0 |
| MUTUAL OF OMAHA INS CO | NE | 7,661.2 |
| NATIONAL BENEFIT LIFE INS CO | NY | 537.3 |
| NATIONAL CASUALTY CO | OH | 406.6 |
| OHIO NATIONAL LIFE ASR CORP | OH | 4,048.6 |
| PRINCIPAL LIFE INS CO | IA | 185,959.0 |
| SB MUTL LIFE INS CO OF MA | MA | 3,015.1 |
| SENTRY SELECT INS CO | WI | 810.3 |
| STANDARD INS CO | OR | 23,414.5 |
| STATE FARM FIRE & CAS CO | IL | 39,417.8 |
| STATE FARM MUTUAL AUTOMOBILE INS CO | IL | 154,684.0 |
| SYMETRA LIFE INS CO | IA | 36,133.8 |
| TRUSTMARK INS CO | IL | 1,532.5 |
| TRUSTMARK LIFE INS CO | IL | 320.1 |
| UNITED WORLD LIFE INS CO | NE | 123.8 |
| USABLE LIFE | AR | 510.9 |
| VOYA RETIREMENT INS & ANNUITY CO | CT | 104,964.0 |

## Florida

| INSURANCE COMPANY NAME | DOM. STATE | TOTAL ASSETS ($MIL) |
|---|---|---|
| **Rating: A+** | | |
| COUNTRY LIFE INS CO | IL | 9,441.1 |
| PHYSICIANS MUTUAL INS CO | NE | 2,289.0 |
| TEACHERS INS & ANNUITY ASN OF AM | NY | 293,835.0 |
| **Rating: A** | | |
| BERKLEY LIFE & HEALTH INS CO | IA | 286.6 |
| FEDERATED LIFE INS CO | MN | 1,849.9 |
| GUARDIAN LIFE INS CO OF AMERICA | NY | 55,226.5 |
| MIDWESTERN UNITED LIFE INS CO | IN | 233.4 |
| NATIONAL WESTERN LIFE INS CO | CO | 11,058.8 |
| SENTRY INS A MUTUAL CO | WI | 8,232.3 |
| SENTRY LIFE INS CO | WI | 6,735.9 |
| SHELTERPOINT LIFE INS CO | NY | 110.1 |
| SOUTHERN FARM BUREAU LIFE INS CO | MS | 14,163.7 |
| USAA LIFE INS CO | TX | 24,728.9 |
| **Rating: A-** | | |
| AMALGAMATED LIFE INS CO | NY | 124.9 |
| AMERICAN HEALTH & LIFE INS CO | TX | 840.1 |
| AMERICAN REPUBLIC INS CO | IA | 933.1 |
| ANTHEM LIFE INS CO | IN | 738.1 |
| AUTO-OWNERS LIFE INS CO | MI | 4,021.4 |
| CENTRAL STATES H & L CO OF OMAHA | NE | 411.0 |
| GARDEN STATE LIFE INS CO | TX | 131.8 |
| HUMANA INS CO (WI) | WI | 10,120.6 |
| MASSACHUSETTS MUTUAL LIFE INS CO | MA | 235,570.0 |
| MEDCO CONTAINMENT LIFE INS CO | PA | 1,113.2 |
| MEDICO CORP LIFE INS CO | NE | 63.9 |
| MUTUAL OF AMERICA LIFE INS CO | NY | 20,499.3 |
| NEW YORK LIFE INS CO | NY | 176,417.0 |
| NIPPON LIFE INS CO OF AMERICA | IA | 219.6 |
| NORTHWESTERN MUTUAL LIFE INS CO | WI | 264,165.0 |
| PHYSICIANS LIFE INS CO | NE | 1,625.7 |
| PROTECTIVE INS CO | IN | 848.6 |
| SIMPLY HEALTHCARE PLANS INC | FL | 434.0 |
| STANDARD LIFE & ACCIDENT INS CO | TX | 516.7 |
| TRANS OCEANIC LIFE INS CO | PR | 71.4 |
| **Rating: B+** | | |
| AETNA HEALTH & LIFE INS CO | CT | 2,403.1 |
| AETNA HEALTH INC (A FLORIDA CORP) | FL | 590.4 |
| AMERICAN FAMILY LIFE ASR CO OF COLUM | NE | 113,507.0 |
| AMERICAN FAMILY MUTL INS CO SI | WI | 17,048.2 |
| AMERICAN FIDELITY ASR CO | OK | 5,772.7 |
| AMERICAN UNITED LIFE INS CO | IN | 27,567.2 |
| AMFIRST INS CO | OK | 57.6 |
| ASSURITY LIFE INS CO | NE | 2,726.8 |
| AXA EQUITABLE LIFE INS CO | NY | 187,479.0 |
| BEST LIFE & HEALTH INS CO | TX | 20.9 |
| BOSTON MUTUAL LIFE INS CO | MA | 1,424.8 |
| COMPANION LIFE INS CO | SC | 359.8 |
| DEARBORN NATIONAL LIFE INS CO | IL | 1,849.7 |
| DELAWARE AMERICAN LIFE INS CO | DE | 137.9 |
| FAMILY HERITAGE LIFE INS CO OF AMER | OH | 1,249.5 |
| FLORIDA HEALTH CARE PLAN INC | FL | 204.7 |
| GERBER LIFE INS CO | NY | 3,650.7 |
| GOVERNMENT PERSONNEL MUTUAL L I C | TX | 832.3 |
| HEALTH OPTIONS INC | FL | 1,453.7 |
| HEALTHSPRING OF FLORIDA INC | FL | 233.5 |
| JACKSON NATIONAL LIFE INS CO | MI | 222,617.0 |
| MIDLAND NATIONAL LIFE INS CO | IA | 55,140.0 |
| MINNESOTA LIFE INS CO | MN | 44,369.0 |
| MUTUAL OF OMAHA INS CO | NE | 7,661.2 |
| NATIONAL BENEFIT LIFE INS CO | NY | 537.3 |
| NATIONAL CASUALTY CO | OH | 406.6 |
| OHIO NATIONAL LIFE ASR CORP | OH | 4,048.6 |
| PRINCIPAL LIFE INS CO | IA | 185,959.0 |
| SB MUTL LIFE INS CO OF MA | MA | 3,015.1 |
| SENTRY SELECT INS CO | WI | 810.3 |
| STANDARD INS CO | OR | 23,414.5 |
| STATE FARM FIRE & CAS CO | IL | 39,417.8 |
| STATE FARM MUTUAL AUTOMOBILE INS CO | IL | 154,684.0 |
| SYMETRA LIFE INS CO | IA | 36,133.8 |
| TRUSTMARK INS CO | IL | 1,532.5 |
| TRUSTMARK LIFE INS CO | IL | 320.1 |
| UNITED WORLD LIFE INS CO | NE | 123.8 |
| USABLE LIFE | AR | 510.9 |
| VOYA RETIREMENT INS & ANNUITY CO | CT | 104,964.0 |

## Georgia

| INSURANCE COMPANY NAME | DOM. STATE | TOTAL ASSETS ($MIL) |
|---|---|---|
| **Rating: A+** | | |
| COUNTRY LIFE INS CO | IL | 9,441.1 |
| PHYSICIANS MUTUAL INS CO | NE | 2,289.0 |
| TEACHERS INS & ANNUITY ASN OF AM | NY | 293,835.0 |
| **Rating: A** | | |
| BERKLEY LIFE & HEALTH INS CO | IA | 286.6 |
| FEDERATED LIFE INS CO | MN | 1,849.9 |
| GUARDIAN LIFE INS CO OF AMERICA | NY | 55,226.5 |
| MEDICAL MUTUAL OF OHIO | OH | 2,136.4 |
| MIDWESTERN UNITED LIFE INS CO | IN | 233.4 |
| NATIONAL WESTERN LIFE INS CO | CO | 11,058.8 |
| SENTRY INS A MUTUAL CO | WI | 8,232.3 |
| SENTRY LIFE INS CO | WI | 6,735.9 |
| SOUTHERN FARM BUREAU LIFE INS CO | MS | 14,163.7 |
| USAA LIFE INS CO | TX | 24,728.9 |
| **Rating: A-** | | |
| AMALGAMATED LIFE INS CO | NY | 124.9 |
| AMERICAN HEALTH & LIFE INS CO | TX | 840.1 |
| AMERICAN REPUBLIC INS CO | IA | 933.1 |
| AMGP GEORGIA MANAGED CARE CO INC | GA | 295.6 |
| ANTHEM LIFE INS CO | IN | 738.1 |
| AUTO-OWNERS LIFE INS CO | MI | 4,021.4 |
| BLUE CROSS BLUE SHIELD HEALTHCARE GA | GA | 1,109.3 |
| CENTRAL STATES H & L CO OF OMAHA | NE | 411.0 |
| COPIC INS CO | CO | 765.4 |
| GARDEN STATE LIFE INS CO | TX | 131.8 |
| HUMANA BENEFIT PLAN OF ILLINOIS | IL | 394.7 |
| HUMANA INS CO (WI) | WI | 10,120.6 |
| MASSACHUSETTS MUTUAL LIFE INS CO | MA | 235,570.0 |
| MEDCO CONTAINMENT LIFE INS CO | PA | 1,113.2 |
| MEDICO CORP LIFE INS CO | NE | 63.9 |
| MOTORISTS COMMERCIAL MUTUAL INS CO | OH | 393.5 |
| MUTUAL OF AMERICA LIFE INS CO | NY | 20,499.3 |
| NEW YORK LIFE INS CO | NY | 176,417.0 |
| NIPPON LIFE INS CO OF AMERICA | IA | 219.6 |
| NORTHWESTERN MUTUAL LIFE INS CO | WI | 264,165.0 |
| PHYSICIANS LIFE INS CO | NE | 1,625.7 |
| PROTECTIVE INS CO | IN | 848.6 |
| STANDARD LIFE & ACCIDENT INS CO | TX | 516.7 |
| **Rating: B+** | | |
| AETNA HEALTH & LIFE INS CO | CT | 2,403.1 |
| AMERICAN FAMILY LIFE ASR CO OF COLUM | NE | 113,507.0 |
| AMERICAN FAMILY MUTL INS CO SI | WI | 17,048.2 |
| AMERICAN FIDELITY ASR CO | OK | 5,772.7 |
| AMERICAN UNITED LIFE INS CO | IN | 27,567.2 |
| AMFIRST INS CO | OK | 57.6 |
| ASSURITY LIFE INS CO | NE | 2,726.8 |
| AXA EQUITABLE LIFE INS CO | NY | 187,479.0 |
| BEST LIFE & HEALTH INS CO | TX | 20.9 |
| BOSTON MUTUAL LIFE INS CO | MA | 1,424.8 |
| COMPANION LIFE INS CO | SC | 359.8 |
| DEARBORN NATIONAL LIFE INS CO | IL | 1,849.7 |
| DELAWARE AMERICAN LIFE INS CO | DE | 137.9 |
| FAMILY HERITAGE LIFE INS CO OF AMER | OH | 1,249.5 |
| GERBER LIFE INS CO | NY | 3,650.7 |
| GOVERNMENT PERSONNEL MUTUAL L I C | TX | 832.3 |
| JACKSON NATIONAL LIFE INS CO | MI | 222,617.0 |
| MIDLAND NATIONAL LIFE INS CO | IA | 55,140.0 |
| MINNESOTA LIFE INS CO | MN | 44,369.0 |
| MUTUAL OF OMAHA INS CO | NE | 7,661.2 |
| NATIONAL BENEFIT LIFE INS CO | NY | 537.3 |
| NATIONAL CASUALTY CO | OH | 406.6 |
| OHIO NATIONAL LIFE ASR CORP | OH | 4,048.6 |
| PRINCIPAL LIFE INS CO | IA | 185,959.0 |
| SB MUTL LIFE INS CO OF MA | MA | 3,015.1 |
| SENTRY SELECT INS CO | WI | 810.3 |
| SOUTHERN PIONEER LIFE INS CO | AR | 15.7 |
| STANDARD INS CO | OR | 23,414.5 |
| STATE FARM FIRE & CAS CO | IL | 39,417.8 |
| STATE FARM MUTUAL AUTOMOBILE INS CO | IL | 154,684.0 |
| SYMETRA LIFE INS CO | IA | 36,133.8 |
| TRUSTMARK INS CO | IL | 1,532.5 |
| TRUSTMARK LIFE INS CO | IL | 320.1 |
| UNITED WORLD LIFE INS CO | NE | 123.8 |
| USABLE LIFE | AR | 510.9 |
| VOYA RETIREMENT INS & ANNUITY CO | CT | 104,964.0 |

## Hawaii

| INSURANCE COMPANY NAME | DOM. STATE | TOTAL ASSETS ($MIL) |
|---|---|---|
| **Rating: A+** | | |
| PHYSICIANS MUTUAL INS CO | NE | 2,289.0 |
| TEACHERS INS & ANNUITY ASN OF AM | NY | 293,835.0 |
| **Rating: A** | | |
| BERKLEY LIFE & HEALTH INS CO | IA | 286.6 |
| GUARDIAN LIFE INS CO OF AMERICA | NY | 55,226.5 |
| MIDWESTERN UNITED LIFE INS CO | IN | 233.4 |
| NATIONAL WESTERN LIFE INS CO | CO | 11,058.8 |
| SENTRY INS A MUTUAL CO | WI | 8,232.3 |
| SENTRY LIFE INS CO | WI | 6,735.9 |
| USAA LIFE INS CO | TX | 24,728.9 |
| **Rating: A-** | | |
| AMALGAMATED LIFE INS CO | NY | 124.9 |
| AMERICAN HEALTH & LIFE INS CO | TX | 840.1 |
| AMERICAN REPUBLIC INS CO | IA | 933.1 |
| ANTHEM LIFE INS CO | IN | 738.1 |
| CENTRAL STATES H & L CO OF OMAHA | NE | 411.0 |
| GARDEN STATE LIFE INS CO | TX | 131.8 |
| HUMANA BENEFIT PLAN OF ILLINOIS | IL | 394.7 |
| HUMANA INS CO (WI) | WI | 10,120.6 |
| MASSACHUSETTS MUTUAL LIFE INS CO | MA | 235,570.0 |
| MEDCO CONTAINMENT LIFE INS CO | PA | 1,113.2 |
| MEDICO CORP LIFE INS CO | NE | 63.9 |
| MUTUAL OF AMERICA LIFE INS CO | NY | 20,499.3 |
| NEW YORK LIFE INS CO | NY | 176,417.0 |
| NIPPON LIFE INS CO OF AMERICA | IA | 219.6 |
| NORTHWESTERN MUTUAL LIFE INS CO | WI | 264,165.0 |
| PACIFIC GUARDIAN LIFE INS CO LTD | HI | 552.3 |
| PHYSICIANS LIFE INS CO | NE | 1,625.7 |
| PROTECTIVE INS CO | IN | 848.6 |
| STANDARD LIFE & ACCIDENT INS CO | TX | 516.7 |
| **Rating: B+** | | |
| AETNA HEALTH & LIFE INS CO | CT | 2,403.1 |
| AMERICAN FAMILY LIFE ASR CO OF COLUM | NE | 113,507.0 |
| AMERICAN FIDELITY ASR CO | OK | 5,772.7 |
| AMERICAN UNITED LIFE INS CO | IN | 27,567.2 |
| ASSURITY LIFE INS CO | NE | 2,726.8 |
| AXA EQUITABLE LIFE INS CO | NY | 187,479.0 |
| BEST LIFE & HEALTH INS CO | TX | 20.9 |
| BOSTON MUTUAL LIFE INS CO | MA | 1,424.8 |
| DEARBORN NATIONAL LIFE INS CO | IL | 1,849.7 |
| DELAWARE AMERICAN LIFE INS CO | DE | 137.9 |
| FAMILY HERITAGE LIFE INS CO OF AMER | OH | 1,249.5 |
| GERBER LIFE INS CO | NY | 3,650.7 |
| GOVERNMENT PERSONNEL MUTUAL L I C | TX | 832.3 |
| JACKSON NATIONAL LIFE INS CO | MI | 222,617.0 |
| MIDLAND NATIONAL LIFE INS CO | IA | 55,140.0 |
| MINNESOTA LIFE INS CO | MN | 44,369.0 |
| MUTUAL OF OMAHA INS CO | NE | 7,661.2 |
| NATIONAL BENEFIT LIFE INS CO | NY | 537.3 |
| NATIONAL CASUALTY CO | OH | 406.6 |
| OHIO NATIONAL LIFE ASR CORP | OH | 4,048.6 |
| PRINCIPAL LIFE INS CO | IA | 185,959.0 |
| SB MUTL LIFE INS CO OF MA | MA | 3,015.1 |
| SENTRY SELECT INS CO | WI | 810.3 |
| STANDARD INS CO | OR | 23,414.5 |
| STATE FARM FIRE & CAS CO | IL | 39,417.8 |
| STATE FARM MUTUAL AUTOMOBILE INS CO | IL | 154,684.0 |
| SYMETRA LIFE INS CO | IA | 36,133.8 |
| TRUSTMARK INS CO | IL | 1,532.5 |
| TRUSTMARK LIFE INS CO | IL | 320.1 |
| UNITED WORLD LIFE INS CO | NE | 123.8 |
| USABLE LIFE | AR | 510.9 |
| VOYA RETIREMENT INS & ANNUITY CO | CT | 104,964.0 |

## Idaho

### Rating: A+

| INSURANCE COMPANY NAME | DOM. STATE | TOTAL ASSETS ($MIL) |
|---|---|---|
| COUNTRY LIFE INS CO | IL | 9,441.1 |
| PHYSICIANS MUTUAL INS CO | NE | 2,289.0 |
| TEACHERS INS & ANNUITY ASN OF AM | NY | 293,835.0 |

### Rating: A

| INSURANCE COMPANY NAME | DOM. STATE | TOTAL ASSETS ($MIL) |
|---|---|---|
| BERKLEY LIFE & HEALTH INS CO | IA | 286.6 |
| EMI HEALTH | UT | 107.5 |
| FEDERATED LIFE INS CO | MN | 1,849.9 |
| GUARDIAN LIFE INS CO OF AMERICA | NY | 55,226.5 |
| LIFEWISE ASR CO | WA | 166.6 |
| MIDWESTERN UNITED LIFE INS CO | IN | 233.4 |
| NATIONAL WESTERN LIFE INS CO | CO | 11,058.8 |
| SENTRY INS A MUTUAL CO | WI | 8,232.3 |
| SENTRY LIFE INS CO | WI | 6,735.9 |
| USAA LIFE INS CO | TX | 24,728.9 |

### Rating: A-

| INSURANCE COMPANY NAME | DOM. STATE | TOTAL ASSETS ($MIL) |
|---|---|---|
| AMALGAMATED LIFE INS CO | NY | 124.9 |
| AMERICAN HEALTH & LIFE INS CO | TX | 840.1 |
| AMERICAN REPUBLIC INS CO | IA | 933.1 |
| ANTHEM LIFE INS CO | IN | 738.1 |
| AUTO-OWNERS LIFE INS CO | MI | 4,021.4 |
| CENTRAL STATES H & L CO OF OMAHA | NE | 411.0 |
| COPIC INS CO | CO | 765.4 |
| GARDEN STATE LIFE INS CO | TX | 131.8 |
| HUMANA BENEFIT PLAN OF ILLINOIS | IL | 394.7 |
| HUMANA INS CO (WI) | WI | 10,120.6 |
| MASSACHUSETTS MUTUAL LIFE INS CO | MA | 235,570.0 |
| MEDCO CONTAINMENT LIFE INS CO | PA | 1,113.2 |
| MEDICO CORP LIFE INS CO | NE | 63.9 |
| MOTORISTS COMMERCIAL MUTUAL INS CO | OH | 393.5 |
| MUTUAL OF AMERICA LIFE INS CO | NY | 20,499.3 |
| NEW YORK LIFE INS CO | NY | 176,417.0 |
| NIPPON LIFE INS CO OF AMERICA | IA | 219.6 |
| NORTHWESTERN MUTUAL LIFE INS CO | WI | 264,165.0 |
| PACIFIC GUARDIAN LIFE INS CO LTD | HI | 552.3 |
| PHYSICIANS LIFE INS CO | NE | 1,625.7 |
| PROTECTIVE INS CO | IN | 848.6 |
| STANDARD LIFE & ACCIDENT INS CO | TX | 516.7 |

### Rating: B+

| INSURANCE COMPANY NAME | DOM. STATE | TOTAL ASSETS ($MIL) |
|---|---|---|
| AETNA HEALTH & LIFE INS CO | CT | 2,403.1 |
| AMERICAN FAMILY LIFE ASR CO OF COLUM | NE | 113,507.0 |
| AMERICAN FAMILY MUTL INS CO SI | WI | 17,048.2 |
| AMERICAN FIDELITY ASR CO | OK | 5,772.7 |
| AMERICAN UNITED LIFE INS CO | IN | 27,567.2 |
| ASSURITY LIFE INS CO | NE | 2,726.8 |
| AXA EQUITABLE LIFE INS CO | NY | 187,479.0 |
| BEST LIFE & HEALTH INS CO | TX | 20.9 |
| BOSTON MUTUAL LIFE INS CO | MA | 1,424.8 |
| COMPANION LIFE INS CO | SC | 359.8 |
| DEARBORN NATIONAL LIFE INS CO | IL | 1,849.7 |
| DELAWARE AMERICAN LIFE INS CO | DE | 137.9 |
| FAMILY HERITAGE LIFE INS CO OF AMER | OH | 1,249.5 |
| FARM BUREAU LIFE INS CO | IA | 8,948.8 |
| GERBER LIFE INS CO | NY | 3,650.7 |
| GOVERNMENT PERSONNEL MUTUAL L I C | TX | 832.3 |
| JACKSON NATIONAL LIFE INS CO | MI | 222,617.0 |
| MIDLAND NATIONAL LIFE INS CO | IA | 55,140.0 |
| MINNESOTA LIFE INS CO | MN | 44,369.0 |
| MUTUAL OF OMAHA INS CO | NE | 7,661.2 |
| NATIONAL BENEFIT LIFE INS CO | NY | 537.3 |
| NATIONAL CASUALTY CO | OH | 406.6 |
| OHIO NATIONAL LIFE ASR CORP | OH | 4,048.6 |
| PRINCIPAL LIFE INS CO | IA | 185,959.0 |
| SB MUTL LIFE INS CO OF MA | MA | 3,015.1 |
| SENTRY SELECT INS CO | WI | 810.3 |
| STANDARD INS CO | OR | 23,414.5 |
| STATE FARM FIRE & CAS CO | IL | 39,417.8 |
| STATE FARM MUTUAL AUTOMOBILE INS CO | IL | 154,684.0 |
| SYMETRA LIFE INS CO | IA | 36,133.8 |
| TRUSTMARK INS CO | IL | 1,532.5 |
| TRUSTMARK LIFE INS CO | IL | 320.1 |
| UNITED WORLD LIFE INS CO | NE | 123.8 |
| USABLE LIFE | AR | 510.9 |
| VOYA RETIREMENT INS & ANNUITY CO | CT | 104,964.0 |

## Illinois

| INSURANCE COMPANY NAME | DOM. STATE | TOTAL ASSETS ($MIL) |
|---|---|---|
| **Rating: A+** | | |
| COUNTRY LIFE INS CO | IL | 9,441.1 |
| PHYSICIANS MUTUAL INS CO | NE | 2,289.0 |
| TEACHERS INS & ANNUITY ASN OF AM | NY | 293,835.0 |
| **Rating: A** | | |
| ALLIANZ LIFE INS CO OF NY | NY | 3,347.7 |
| BERKLEY LIFE & HEALTH INS CO | IA | 286.6 |
| FEDERATED LIFE INS CO | MN | 1,849.9 |
| GUARDIAN LIFE INS CO OF AMERICA | NY | 55,226.5 |
| MIDWESTERN UNITED LIFE INS CO | IN | 233.4 |
| NATIONAL WESTERN LIFE INS CO | CO | 11,058.8 |
| SENTRY INS A MUTUAL CO | WI | 8,232.3 |
| SENTRY LIFE INS CO | WI | 6,735.9 |
| SHELTERPOINT LIFE INS CO | NY | 110.1 |
| UNITED FARM FAMILY LIFE INS CO | IN | 2,312.3 |
| USAA LIFE INS CO | TX | 24,728.9 |
| **Rating: A-** | | |
| AMALGAMATED LIFE INS CO | NY | 124.9 |
| AMERICAN HEALTH & LIFE INS CO | TX | 840.1 |
| AMERICAN REPUBLIC INS CO | IA | 933.1 |
| ANTHEM LIFE INS CO | IN | 738.1 |
| AUTO-OWNERS LIFE INS CO | MI | 4,021.4 |
| CENTRAL STATES H & L CO OF OMAHA | NE | 411.0 |
| ERIE FAMILY LIFE INS CO | PA | 2,448.7 |
| GARDEN STATE LIFE INS CO | TX | 131.8 |
| HUMANA BENEFIT PLAN OF ILLINOIS | IL | 394.7 |
| HUMANA INS CO (WI) | WI | 10,120.6 |
| INDEPENDENT CARE HEALTH PLAN | WI | 89.0 |
| MASSACHUSETTS MUTUAL LIFE INS CO | MA | 235,570.0 |
| MEDCO CONTAINMENT LIFE INS CO | PA | 1,113.2 |
| MEDICO CORP LIFE INS CO | NE | 63.9 |
| MOTORISTS COMMERCIAL MUTUAL INS CO | OH | 393.5 |
| MUTUAL OF AMERICA LIFE INS CO | NY | 20,499.3 |
| NEW YORK LIFE INS CO | NY | 176,417.0 |
| NIPPON LIFE INS CO OF AMERICA | IA | 219.6 |
| NORTHWESTERN MUTUAL LIFE INS CO | WI | 264,165.0 |
| PHYSICIANS LIFE INS CO | NE | 1,625.7 |
| PROTECTIVE INS CO | IN | 848.6 |
| STANDARD LIFE & ACCIDENT INS CO | TX | 516.7 |
| **Rating: B+** | | |
| AETNA HEALTH & LIFE INS CO | CT | 2,403.1 |
| AMERICAN FAMILY LIFE ASR CO OF COLUM | NE | 113,507.0 |
| AMERICAN FAMILY MUTL INS CO SI | WI | 17,048.2 |
| AMERICAN FIDELITY ASR CO | OK | 5,772.7 |
| AMERICAN UNITED LIFE INS CO | IN | 27,567.2 |
| ASSURITY LIFE INS CO | NE | 2,726.8 |
| AXA EQUITABLE LIFE INS CO | NY | 187,479.0 |
| BEST LIFE & HEALTH INS CO | TX | 20.9 |
| BOSTON MUTUAL LIFE INS CO | MA | 1,424.8 |
| COMPANION LIFE INS CO | SC | 359.8 |
| DEARBORN NATIONAL LIFE INS CO | IL | 1,849.7 |
| DELAWARE AMERICAN LIFE INS CO | DE | 137.9 |
| ESSENCE HEALTHCARE INC | MO | 288.5 |
| FAMILY HERITAGE LIFE INS CO OF AMER | OH | 1,249.5 |
| GERBER LIFE INS CO | NY | 3,650.7 |
| GOVERNMENT PERSONNEL MUTUAL L I C | TX | 832.3 |
| HEALTHSPRING OF TENNESSEE INC | TN | 460.4 |
| JACKSON NATIONAL LIFE INS CO | MI | 222,617.0 |
| MIDLAND NATIONAL LIFE INS CO | IA | 55,140.0 |
| MINNESOTA LIFE INS CO | MN | 44,369.0 |
| MUTUAL OF OMAHA INS CO | NE | 7,661.2 |
| NATIONAL BENEFIT LIFE INS CO | NY | 537.3 |
| NATIONAL CASUALTY CO | OH | 406.6 |
| OHIO NATIONAL LIFE ASR CORP | OH | 4,048.6 |
| PRINCIPAL LIFE INS CO | IA | 185,959.0 |
| SB MUTL LIFE INS CO OF MA | MA | 3,015.1 |
| SENTRY SELECT INS CO | WI | 810.3 |
| SHELTER LIFE INS CO | MO | 1,238.3 |
| STANDARD INS CO | OR | 23,414.5 |
| STATE FARM FIRE & CAS CO | IL | 39,417.8 |
| STATE FARM MUTUAL AUTOMOBILE INS CO | IL | 154,684.0 |
| SYMETRA LIFE INS CO | IA | 36,133.8 |
| TRUSTMARK INS CO | IL | 1,532.5 |
| TRUSTMARK LIFE INS CO | IL | 320.1 |
| UNITED WORLD LIFE INS CO | NE | 123.8 |
| USABLE LIFE | AR | 510.9 |
| VOYA RETIREMENT INS & ANNUITY CO | CT | 104,964.0 |

## Indiana

| INSURANCE COMPANY NAME | DOM. STATE | TOTAL ASSETS ($MIL) |
|---|---|---|
| **Rating: A+** | | |
| COUNTRY LIFE INS CO | IL | 9,441.1 |
| PHYSICIANS MUTUAL INS CO | NE | 2,289.0 |
| TEACHERS INS & ANNUITY ASN OF AM | NY | 293,835.0 |
| **Rating: A** | | |
| BERKLEY LIFE & HEALTH INS CO | IA | 286.6 |
| FEDERATED LIFE INS CO | MN | 1,849.9 |
| GUARDIAN LIFE INS CO OF AMERICA | NY | 55,226.5 |
| MEDICAL MUTUAL OF OHIO | OH | 2,136.4 |
| MIDWESTERN UNITED LIFE INS CO | IN | 233.4 |
| NATIONAL WESTERN LIFE INS CO | CO | 11,058.8 |
| SENTRY INS A MUTUAL CO | WI | 8,232.3 |
| SENTRY LIFE INS CO | WI | 6,735.9 |
| UNITED FARM FAMILY LIFE INS CO | IN | 2,312.3 |
| USAA LIFE INS CO | TX | 24,728.9 |
| **Rating: A-** | | |
| AMALGAMATED LIFE INS CO | NY | 124.9 |
| AMERICAN HEALTH & LIFE INS CO | TX | 840.1 |
| AMERICAN REPUBLIC INS CO | IA | 933.1 |
| ANTHEM LIFE INS CO | IN | 738.1 |
| AUTO-OWNERS LIFE INS CO | MI | 4,021.4 |
| CENTRAL STATES H & L CO OF OMAHA | NE | 411.0 |
| ERIE FAMILY LIFE INS CO | PA | 2,448.7 |
| GARDEN STATE LIFE INS CO | TX | 131.8 |
| HUMANA BENEFIT PLAN OF ILLINOIS | IL | 394.7 |
| HUMANA INS CO (WI) | WI | 10,120.6 |
| MASSACHUSETTS MUTUAL LIFE INS CO | MA | 235,570.0 |
| MEDCO CONTAINMENT LIFE INS CO | PA | 1,113.2 |
| MEDICO CORP LIFE INS CO | NE | 63.9 |
| MOTORISTS COMMERCIAL MUTUAL INS CO | OH | 393.5 |
| MUTUAL OF AMERICA LIFE INS CO | NY | 20,499.3 |
| NEW YORK LIFE INS CO | NY | 176,417.0 |
| NIPPON LIFE INS CO OF AMERICA | IA | 219.6 |
| NORTHWESTERN MUTUAL LIFE INS CO | WI | 264,165.0 |
| PHYSICIANS LIFE INS CO | NE | 1,625.7 |
| PROTECTIVE INS CO | IN | 848.6 |
| STANDARD LIFE & ACCIDENT INS CO | TX | 516.7 |
| **Rating: B+** | | |
| AETNA HEALTH & LIFE INS CO | CT | 2,403.1 |
| AMERICAN FAMILY LIFE ASR CO OF COLUM | NE | 113,507.0 |
| AMERICAN FAMILY MUTL INS CO SI | WI | 17,048.2 |
| AMERICAN FIDELITY ASR CO | OK | 5,772.7 |
| AMERICAN UNITED LIFE INS CO | IN | 27,567.2 |
| ASSURITY LIFE INS CO | NE | 2,726.8 |
| AXA EQUITABLE LIFE INS CO | NY | 187,479.0 |
| BEST LIFE & HEALTH INS CO | TX | 20.9 |
| BOSTON MUTUAL LIFE INS CO | MA | 1,424.8 |
| COMMUNITY INS CO (OH) | OH | 2,274.1 |
| COMPANION LIFE INS CO | SC | 359.8 |
| DEARBORN NATIONAL LIFE INS CO | IL | 1,849.7 |
| DELAWARE AMERICAN LIFE INS CO | DE | 137.9 |
| FAMILY HERITAGE LIFE INS CO OF AMER | OH | 1,249.5 |
| GERBER LIFE INS CO | NY | 3,650.7 |
| GOVERNMENT PERSONNEL MUTUAL L I C | TX | 832.3 |
| JACKSON NATIONAL LIFE INS CO | MI | 222,617.0 |
| MIDLAND NATIONAL LIFE INS CO | IA | 55,140.0 |
| MINNESOTA LIFE INS CO | MN | 44,369.0 |
| MUTUAL OF OMAHA INS CO | NE | 7,661.2 |
| NATIONAL BENEFIT LIFE INS CO | NY | 537.3 |
| NATIONAL CASUALTY CO | OH | 406.6 |
| OHIO NATIONAL LIFE ASR CORP | OH | 4,048.6 |
| PRINCIPAL LIFE INS CO | IA | 185,959.0 |
| SB MUTL LIFE INS CO OF MA | MA | 3,015.1 |
| SENTRY SELECT INS CO | WI | 810.3 |
| SHELTER LIFE INS CO | MO | 1,238.3 |
| SOUTHERN PIONEER LIFE INS CO | AR | 15.7 |
| STANDARD INS CO | OR | 23,414.5 |
| STATE FARM FIRE & CAS CO | IL | 39,417.8 |
| STATE FARM MUTUAL AUTOMOBILE INS CO | IL | 154,684.0 |
| SYMETRA LIFE INS CO | IA | 36,133.8 |
| TRUSTMARK INS CO | IL | 1,532.5 |
| TRUSTMARK LIFE INS CO | IL | 320.1 |
| UNITED WORLD LIFE INS CO | NE | 123.8 |
| USABLE LIFE | AR | 510.9 |
| VOYA RETIREMENT INS & ANNUITY CO | CT | 104,964.0 |

## Iowa

| INSURANCE COMPANY NAME | DOM. STATE | TOTAL ASSETS ($MIL) |
|---|---|---|
| **Rating: A+** | | |
| COUNTRY LIFE INS CO | IL | 9,441.1 |
| PHYSICIANS MUTUAL INS CO | NE | 2,289.0 |
| TEACHERS INS & ANNUITY ASN OF AM | NY | 293,835.0 |
| **Rating: A** | | |
| BERKLEY LIFE & HEALTH INS CO | IA | 286.6 |
| FEDERATED LIFE INS CO | MN | 1,849.9 |
| GUARDIAN LIFE INS CO OF AMERICA | NY | 55,226.5 |
| MIDWESTERN UNITED LIFE INS CO | IN | 233.4 |
| NATIONAL WESTERN LIFE INS CO | CO | 11,058.8 |
| SENTRY INS A MUTUAL CO | WI | 8,232.3 |
| SENTRY LIFE INS CO | WI | 6,735.9 |
| USAA LIFE INS CO | TX | 24,728.9 |
| **Rating: A-** | | |
| AMALGAMATED LIFE INS CO | NY | 124.9 |
| AMERICAN HEALTH & LIFE INS CO | TX | 840.1 |
| AMERICAN REPUBLIC INS CO | IA | 933.1 |
| ANTHEM LIFE INS CO | IN | 738.1 |
| AUTO-OWNERS LIFE INS CO | MI | 4,021.4 |
| CENTRAL STATES H & L CO OF OMAHA | NE | 411.0 |
| COPIC INS CO | CO | 765.4 |
| GARDEN STATE LIFE INS CO | TX | 131.8 |
| HUMANA BENEFIT PLAN OF ILLINOIS | IL | 394.7 |
| HUMANA INS CO (WI) | WI | 10,120.6 |
| MASSACHUSETTS MUTUAL LIFE INS CO | MA | 235,570.0 |
| MEDCO CONTAINMENT LIFE INS CO | PA | 1,113.2 |
| MEDICO CORP LIFE INS CO | NE | 63.9 |
| MOTORISTS COMMERCIAL MUTUAL INS CO | OH | 393.5 |
| MUTUAL OF AMERICA LIFE INS CO | NY | 20,499.3 |
| NEW YORK LIFE INS CO | NY | 176,417.0 |
| NIPPON LIFE INS CO OF AMERICA | IA | 219.6 |
| NORTHWESTERN MUTUAL LIFE INS CO | WI | 264,165.0 |
| PACIFIC GUARDIAN LIFE INS CO LTD | HI | 552.3 |
| PHYSICIANS LIFE INS CO | NE | 1,625.7 |
| PROTECTIVE INS CO | IN | 848.6 |
| STANDARD LIFE & ACCIDENT INS CO | TX | 516.7 |
| **Rating: B+** | | |
| AETNA HEALTH & LIFE INS CO | CT | 2,403.1 |
| AETNA HEALTH INC (A FLORIDA CORP) | FL | 590.4 |
| AMERICAN FAMILY LIFE ASR CO OF COLUM | NE | 113,507.0 |
| AMERICAN FAMILY MUTL INS CO SI | WI | 17,048.2 |
| AMERICAN FIDELITY ASR CO | OK | 5,772.7 |
| AMERICAN UNITED LIFE INS CO | IN | 27,567.2 |
| ASSURITY LIFE INS CO | NE | 2,726.8 |
| AXA EQUITABLE LIFE INS CO | NY | 187,479.0 |
| BEST LIFE & HEALTH INS CO | TX | 20.9 |
| BOSTON MUTUAL LIFE INS CO | MA | 1,424.8 |
| COMPANION LIFE INS CO | SC | 359.8 |
| DEARBORN NATIONAL LIFE INS CO | IL | 1,849.7 |
| DELAWARE AMERICAN LIFE INS CO | DE | 137.9 |
| FAMILY HERITAGE LIFE INS CO OF AMER | OH | 1,249.5 |
| FARM BUREAU LIFE INS CO | IA | 8,948.8 |
| GERBER LIFE INS CO | NY | 3,650.7 |
| GOVERNMENT PERSONNEL MUTUAL L I C | TX | 832.3 |
| JACKSON NATIONAL LIFE INS CO | MI | 222,617.0 |
| MIDLAND NATIONAL LIFE INS CO | IA | 55,140.0 |
| MINNESOTA LIFE INS CO | MN | 44,369.0 |
| MUTUAL OF OMAHA INS CO | NE | 7,661.2 |
| NATIONAL BENEFIT LIFE INS CO | NY | 537.3 |
| NATIONAL CASUALTY CO | OH | 406.6 |
| OHIO NATIONAL LIFE ASR CORP | OH | 4,048.6 |
| PRINCIPAL LIFE INS CO | IA | 185,959.0 |
| SB MUTL LIFE INS CO OF MA | MA | 3,015.1 |
| SENTRY SELECT INS CO | WI | 810.3 |
| SHELTER LIFE INS CO | MO | 1,238.3 |
| STANDARD INS CO | OR | 23,414.5 |
| STATE FARM FIRE & CAS CO | IL | 39,417.8 |
| STATE FARM MUTUAL AUTOMOBILE INS CO | IL | 154,684.0 |
| SYMETRA LIFE INS CO | IA | 36,133.8 |
| TRUSTMARK INS CO | IL | 1,532.5 |
| TRUSTMARK LIFE INS CO | IL | 320.1 |
| UNITED WORLD LIFE INS CO | NE | 123.8 |
| USABLE LIFE | AR | 510.9 |
| VOYA RETIREMENT INS & ANNUITY CO | CT | 104,964.0 |

## Kansas

| INSURANCE COMPANY NAME | DOM. STATE | TOTAL ASSETS ($MIL) |
|---|---|---|
| **Rating: A+** | | |
| COUNTRY LIFE INS CO | IL | 9,441.1 |
| PHYSICIANS MUTUAL INS CO | NE | 2,289.0 |
| TEACHERS INS & ANNUITY ASN OF AM | NY | 293,835.0 |
| **Rating: A** | | |
| BERKLEY LIFE & HEALTH INS CO | IA | 286.6 |
| FEDERATED LIFE INS CO | MN | 1,849.9 |
| GUARDIAN LIFE INS CO OF AMERICA | NY | 55,226.5 |
| MIDWESTERN UNITED LIFE INS CO | IN | 233.4 |
| NATIONAL WESTERN LIFE INS CO | CO | 11,058.8 |
| SENTRY INS A MUTUAL CO | WI | 8,232.3 |
| SENTRY LIFE INS CO | WI | 6,735.9 |
| USAA LIFE INS CO | TX | 24,728.9 |
| **Rating: A-** | | |
| AMALGAMATED LIFE INS CO | NY | 124.9 |
| AMERICAN HEALTH & LIFE INS CO | TX | 840.1 |
| AMERICAN REPUBLIC INS CO | IA | 933.1 |
| ANTHEM LIFE INS CO | IN | 738.1 |
| AUTO-OWNERS LIFE INS CO | MI | 4,021.4 |
| CENTRAL STATES H & L CO OF OMAHA | NE | 411.0 |
| COPIC INS CO | CO | 765.4 |
| GARDEN STATE LIFE INS CO | TX | 131.8 |
| HEALTHY ALLIANCE LIFE INS CO | MO | 1,295.0 |
| HUMANA BENEFIT PLAN OF ILLINOIS | IL | 394.7 |
| HUMANA INS CO (WI) | WI | 10,120.6 |
| MASSACHUSETTS MUTUAL LIFE INS CO | MA | 235,570.0 |
| MEDCO CONTAINMENT LIFE INS CO | PA | 1,113.2 |
| MEDICO CORP LIFE INS CO | NE | 63.9 |
| MOTORISTS COMMERCIAL MUTUAL INS CO | OH | 393.5 |
| MUTUAL OF AMERICA LIFE INS CO | NY | 20,499.3 |
| NEW YORK LIFE INS CO | NY | 176,417.0 |
| NIPPON LIFE INS CO OF AMERICA | IA | 219.6 |
| NORTHWESTERN MUTUAL LIFE INS CO | WI | 264,165.0 |
| PHYSICIANS LIFE INS CO | NE | 1,625.7 |
| PROTECTIVE INS CO | IN | 848.6 |
| STANDARD LIFE & ACCIDENT INS CO | TX | 516.7 |
| **Rating: B+** | | |
| ADVANCE INS CO OF KANSAS | KS | 58.6 |
| AETNA HEALTH & LIFE INS CO | CT | 2,403.1 |
| AMERICAN FAMILY LIFE ASR CO OF COLUM | NE | 113,507.0 |
| AMERICAN FAMILY MUTL INS CO SI | WI | 17,048.2 |
| AMERICAN FIDELITY ASR CO | OK | 5,772.7 |
| AMERICAN UNITED LIFE INS CO | IN | 27,567.2 |
| ASSURITY LIFE INS CO | NE | 2,726.8 |
| AXA EQUITABLE LIFE INS CO | NY | 187,479.0 |
| BEST LIFE & HEALTH INS CO | TX | 20.9 |
| BOSTON MUTUAL LIFE INS CO | MA | 1,424.8 |
| COMPANION LIFE INS CO | SC | 359.8 |
| DEARBORN NATIONAL LIFE INS CO | IL | 1,849.7 |
| DELAWARE AMERICAN LIFE INS CO | DE | 137.9 |
| FAMILY HERITAGE LIFE INS CO OF AMER | OH | 1,249.5 |
| FARM BUREAU LIFE INS CO | IA | 8,948.8 |
| GERBER LIFE INS CO | NY | 3,650.7 |
| GOVERNMENT PERSONNEL MUTUAL L I C | TX | 832.3 |
| JACKSON NATIONAL LIFE INS CO | MI | 222,617.0 |
| MIDLAND NATIONAL LIFE INS CO | IA | 55,140.0 |
| MINNESOTA LIFE INS CO | MN | 44,369.0 |
| MUTUAL OF OMAHA INS CO | NE | 7,661.2 |
| NATIONAL BENEFIT LIFE INS CO | NY | 537.3 |
| NATIONAL CASUALTY CO | OH | 406.6 |
| OHIO NATIONAL LIFE ASR CORP | OH | 4,048.6 |
| PRINCIPAL LIFE INS CO | IA | 185,959.0 |
| SB MUTL LIFE INS CO OF MA | MA | 3,015.1 |
| SENTRY SELECT INS CO | WI | 810.3 |
| SHELTER LIFE INS CO | MO | 1,238.3 |
| SOUTHERN PIONEER LIFE INS CO | AR | 15.7 |
| STANDARD INS CO | OR | 23,414.5 |
| STATE FARM FIRE & CAS CO | IL | 39,417.8 |
| STATE FARM MUTUAL AUTOMOBILE INS CO | IL | 154,684.0 |
| SYMETRA LIFE INS CO | IA | 36,133.8 |
| TRUSTMARK INS CO | IL | 1,532.5 |
| TRUSTMARK LIFE INS CO | IL | 320.1 |
| UNITED WORLD LIFE INS CO | NE | 123.8 |
| USABLE LIFE | AR | 510.9 |
| VOYA RETIREMENT INS & ANNUITY CO | CT | 104,964.0 |

## Kentucky

| INSURANCE COMPANY NAME | DOM. STATE | TOTAL ASSETS ($MIL) |
|---|---|---|
| **Rating: A+** | | |
| COUNTRY LIFE INS CO | IL | 9,441.1 |
| PHYSICIANS MUTUAL INS CO | NE | 2,289.0 |
| TEACHERS INS & ANNUITY ASN OF AM | NY | 293,835.0 |
| **Rating: A** | | |
| BERKLEY LIFE & HEALTH INS CO | IA | 286.6 |
| FEDERATED LIFE INS CO | MN | 1,849.9 |
| GUARDIAN LIFE INS CO OF AMERICA | NY | 55,226.5 |
| MIDWESTERN UNITED LIFE INS CO | IN | 233.4 |
| NATIONAL WESTERN LIFE INS CO | CO | 11,058.8 |
| SENTRY INS A MUTUAL CO | WI | 8,232.3 |
| SENTRY LIFE INS CO | WI | 6,735.9 |
| SOUTHERN FARM BUREAU LIFE INS CO | MS | 14,163.7 |
| USAA LIFE INS CO | TX | 24,728.9 |
| **Rating: A-** | | |
| AMALGAMATED LIFE INS CO | NY | 124.9 |
| AMERICAN HEALTH & LIFE INS CO | TX | 840.1 |
| AMERICAN REPUBLIC INS CO | IA | 933.1 |
| ANTHEM KENTUCKY MANAGED CARE PLAN | KY | 237.7 |
| ANTHEM LIFE INS CO | IN | 738.1 |
| AUTO-OWNERS LIFE INS CO | MI | 4,021.4 |
| CENTRAL STATES H & L CO OF OMAHA | NE | 411.0 |
| ERIE FAMILY LIFE INS CO | PA | 2,448.7 |
| GARDEN STATE LIFE INS CO | TX | 131.8 |
| HUMANA BENEFIT PLAN OF ILLINOIS | IL | 394.7 |
| HUMANA INS CO (WI) | WI | 10,120.6 |
| MASSACHUSETTS MUTUAL LIFE INS CO | MA | 235,570.0 |
| MEDCO CONTAINMENT LIFE INS CO | PA | 1,113.2 |
| MEDICO CORP LIFE INS CO | NE | 63.9 |
| MOTORISTS COMMERCIAL MUTUAL INS CO | OH | 393.5 |
| MUTUAL OF AMERICA LIFE INS CO | NY | 20,499.3 |
| NEW YORK LIFE INS CO | NY | 176,417.0 |
| NIPPON LIFE INS CO OF AMERICA | IA | 219.6 |
| NORTHWESTERN MUTUAL LIFE INS CO | WI | 264,165.0 |
| PHYSICIANS LIFE INS CO | NE | 1,625.7 |
| PROTECTIVE INS CO | IN | 848.6 |
| STANDARD LIFE & ACCIDENT INS CO | TX | 516.7 |
| **Rating: B+** | | |
| AETNA BETTER HLTH OF KY INS CO | KY | 489.7 |
| AETNA HEALTH & LIFE INS CO | CT | 2,403.1 |
| AMERICAN FAMILY LIFE ASR CO OF COLUM | NE | 113,507.0 |
| AMERICAN FIDELITY ASR CO | OK | 5,772.7 |
| AMERICAN UNITED LIFE INS CO | IN | 27,567.2 |
| ANTHEM HEALTH PLANS OF KENTUCKY INC | KY | 1,046.0 |
| ASSURITY LIFE INS CO | NE | 2,726.8 |
| AXA EQUITABLE LIFE INS CO | NY | 187,479.0 |
| BEST LIFE & HEALTH INS CO | TX | 20.9 |
| BOSTON MUTUAL LIFE INS CO | MA | 1,424.8 |
| COMPANION LIFE INS CO | SC | 359.8 |
| DEARBORN NATIONAL LIFE INS CO | IL | 1,849.7 |
| DELAWARE AMERICAN LIFE INS CO | DE | 137.9 |
| FAMILY HERITAGE LIFE INS CO OF AMER | OH | 1,249.5 |
| GERBER LIFE INS CO | NY | 3,650.7 |
| GOVERNMENT PERSONNEL MUTUAL L I C | TX | 832.3 |
| JACKSON NATIONAL LIFE INS CO | MI | 222,617.0 |
| MIDLAND NATIONAL LIFE INS CO | IA | 55,140.0 |
| MINNESOTA LIFE INS CO | MN | 44,369.0 |
| MUTUAL OF OMAHA INS CO | NE | 7,661.2 |
| NATIONAL BENEFIT LIFE INS CO | NY | 537.3 |
| NATIONAL CASUALTY CO | OH | 406.6 |
| OHIO NATIONAL LIFE ASR CORP | OH | 4,048.6 |
| PRINCIPAL LIFE INS CO | IA | 185,959.0 |
| SB MUTL LIFE INS CO OF MA | MA | 3,015.1 |
| SENTRY SELECT INS CO | WI | 810.3 |
| SHELTER LIFE INS CO | MO | 1,238.3 |
| SOUTHERN PIONEER LIFE INS CO | AR | 15.7 |
| STANDARD INS CO | OR | 23,414.5 |
| STATE FARM FIRE & CAS CO | IL | 39,417.8 |
| STATE FARM MUTUAL AUTOMOBILE INS CO | IL | 154,684.0 |
| SYMETRA LIFE INS CO | IA | 36,133.8 |
| TRUSTMARK INS CO | IL | 1,532.5 |
| TRUSTMARK LIFE INS CO | IL | 320.1 |
| UNITED WORLD LIFE INS CO | NE | 123.8 |
| USABLE LIFE | AR | 510.9 |
| VOYA RETIREMENT INS & ANNUITY CO | CT | 104,964.0 |

## Louisiana

| INSURANCE COMPANY NAME | DOM. STATE | TOTAL ASSETS ($MIL) |
|---|---|---|
| **Rating: A+** | | |
| COUNTRY LIFE INS CO | IL | 9,441.1 |
| HMO LOUISIANA INC | LA | 669.8 |
| PHYSICIANS MUTUAL INS CO | NE | 2,289.0 |
| TEACHERS INS & ANNUITY ASN OF AM | NY | 293,835.0 |
| **Rating: A** | | |
| BERKLEY LIFE & HEALTH INS CO | IA | 286.6 |
| FEDERATED LIFE INS CO | MN | 1,849.9 |
| GUARDIAN LIFE INS CO OF AMERICA | NY | 55,226.5 |
| MIDWESTERN UNITED LIFE INS CO | IN | 233.4 |
| NATIONAL WESTERN LIFE INS CO | CO | 11,058.8 |
| SENTRY INS A MUTUAL CO | WI | 8,232.3 |
| SENTRY LIFE INS CO | WI | 6,735.9 |
| SOUTHERN FARM BUREAU LIFE INS CO | MS | 14,163.7 |
| USAA LIFE INS CO | TX | 24,728.9 |
| **Rating: A-** | | |
| AMALGAMATED LIFE INS CO | NY | 124.9 |
| AMERICAN HEALTH & LIFE INS CO | TX | 840.1 |
| AMERICAN REPUBLIC INS CO | IA | 933.1 |
| ANTHEM LIFE INS CO | IN | 738.1 |
| CENTRAL STATES H & L CO OF OMAHA | NE | 411.0 |
| GARDEN STATE LIFE INS CO | TX | 131.8 |
| HUMANA BENEFIT PLAN OF ILLINOIS | IL | 394.7 |
| HUMANA INS CO (WI) | WI | 10,120.6 |
| MASSACHUSETTS MUTUAL LIFE INS CO | MA | 235,570.0 |
| MEDCO CONTAINMENT LIFE INS CO | PA | 1,113.2 |
| MEDICO CORP LIFE INS CO | NE | 63.9 |
| MUTUAL OF AMERICA LIFE INS CO | NY | 20,499.3 |
| NEW YORK LIFE INS CO | NY | 176,417.0 |
| NIPPON LIFE INS CO OF AMERICA | IA | 219.6 |
| NORTHWESTERN MUTUAL LIFE INS CO | WI | 264,165.0 |
| PACIFIC GUARDIAN LIFE INS CO LTD | HI | 552.3 |
| PHYSICIANS LIFE INS CO | NE | 1,625.7 |
| PROTECTIVE INS CO | IN | 848.6 |
| STANDARD LIFE & ACCIDENT INS CO | TX | 516.7 |
| **Rating: B+** | | |
| AETNA HEALTH & LIFE INS CO | CT | 2,403.1 |
| AMERICAN FAMILY LIFE ASR CO OF COLUM | NE | 113,507.0 |
| AMERICAN FIDELITY ASR CO | OK | 5,772.7 |
| AMERICAN UNITED LIFE INS CO | IN | 27,567.2 |
| AMFIRST INS CO | OK | 57.6 |
| ASSURITY LIFE INS CO | NE | 2,726.8 |
| AXA EQUITABLE LIFE INS CO | NY | 187,479.0 |
| BEST LIFE & HEALTH INS CO | TX | 20.9 |
| BLUEBONNET LIFE INS CO | MS | 62.2 |
| BOSTON MUTUAL LIFE INS CO | MA | 1,424.8 |
| COMPANION LIFE INS CO | SC | 359.8 |
| DEARBORN NATIONAL LIFE INS CO | IL | 1,849.7 |
| DELAWARE AMERICAN LIFE INS CO | DE | 137.9 |
| FAMILY HERITAGE LIFE INS CO OF AMER | OH | 1,249.5 |
| GERBER LIFE INS CO | NY | 3,650.7 |
| GOVERNMENT PERSONNEL MUTUAL L I C | TX | 832.3 |
| JACKSON NATIONAL LIFE INS CO | MI | 222,617.0 |
| MIDLAND NATIONAL LIFE INS CO | IA | 55,140.0 |
| MINNESOTA LIFE INS CO | MN | 44,369.0 |
| MUTUAL OF OMAHA INS CO | NE | 7,661.2 |
| NATIONAL BENEFIT LIFE INS CO | NY | 537.3 |
| NATIONAL CASUALTY CO | OH | 406.6 |
| OHIO NATIONAL LIFE ASR CORP | OH | 4,048.6 |
| PRINCIPAL LIFE INS CO | IA | 185,959.0 |
| SB MUTL LIFE INS CO OF MA | MA | 3,015.1 |
| SENTRY SELECT INS CO | WI | 810.3 |
| SHELTER LIFE INS CO | MO | 1,238.3 |
| SOUTHERN PIONEER LIFE INS CO | AR | 15.7 |
| STANDARD INS CO | OR | 23,414.5 |
| STATE FARM FIRE & CAS CO | IL | 39,417.8 |
| STATE FARM MUTUAL AUTOMOBILE INS CO | IL | 154,684.0 |
| SYMETRA LIFE INS CO | IA | 36,133.8 |
| TRUSTMARK INS CO | IL | 1,532.5 |
| TRUSTMARK LIFE INS CO | IL | 320.1 |
| UNITED WORLD LIFE INS CO | NE | 123.8 |
| USABLE LIFE | AR | 510.9 |
| VOYA RETIREMENT INS & ANNUITY CO | CT | 104,964.0 |

## Maine

| INSURANCE COMPANY NAME | DOM. STATE | TOTAL ASSETS ($MIL) |
|---|---|---|
| **Rating: A+** | | |
| COUNTRY LIFE INS CO | IL | 9,441.1 |
| PHYSICIANS MUTUAL INS CO | NE | 2,289.0 |
| TEACHERS INS & ANNUITY ASN OF AM | NY | 293,835.0 |
| **Rating: A** | | |
| BERKLEY LIFE & HEALTH INS CO | IA | 286.6 |
| FEDERATED LIFE INS CO | MN | 1,849.9 |
| GUARDIAN LIFE INS CO OF AMERICA | NY | 55,226.5 |
| MIDWESTERN UNITED LIFE INS CO | IN | 233.4 |
| NATIONAL WESTERN LIFE INS CO | CO | 11,058.8 |
| SENTRY INS A MUTUAL CO | WI | 8,232.3 |
| SENTRY LIFE INS CO | WI | 6,735.9 |
| USAA LIFE INS CO | TX | 24,728.9 |
| **Rating: A-** | | |
| AMALGAMATED LIFE INS CO | NY | 124.9 |
| AMERICAN HEALTH & LIFE INS CO | TX | 840.1 |
| AMERICAN REPUBLIC INS CO | IA | 933.1 |
| ANTHEM LIFE INS CO | IN | 738.1 |
| AUTO-OWNERS LIFE INS CO | MI | 4,021.4 |
| CENTRAL STATES H & L CO OF OMAHA | NE | 411.0 |
| GARDEN STATE LIFE INS CO | TX | 131.8 |
| HUMANA BENEFIT PLAN OF ILLINOIS | IL | 394.7 |
| HUMANA INS CO (WI) | WI | 10,120.6 |
| MASSACHUSETTS MUTUAL LIFE INS CO | MA | 235,570.0 |
| MEDCO CONTAINMENT LIFE INS CO | PA | 1,113.2 |
| MEDICO CORP LIFE INS CO | NE | 63.9 |
| MOTORISTS COMMERCIAL MUTUAL INS CO | OH | 393.5 |
| MUTUAL OF AMERICA LIFE INS CO | NY | 20,499.3 |
| NEW YORK LIFE INS CO | NY | 176,417.0 |
| NORTHWESTERN MUTUAL LIFE INS CO | WI | 264,165.0 |
| PHYSICIANS LIFE INS CO | NE | 1,625.7 |
| PROTECTIVE INS CO | IN | 848.6 |
| **Rating: B+** | | |
| AETNA HEALTH & LIFE INS CO | CT | 2,403.1 |
| AMERICAN FAMILY LIFE ASR CO OF COLUM | NE | 113,507.0 |
| AMERICAN FIDELITY ASR CO | OK | 5,772.7 |
| AMERICAN UNITED LIFE INS CO | IN | 27,567.2 |
| ANTHEM HEALTH PLANS OF MAINE INC | ME | 489.5 |
| ASSURITY LIFE INS CO | NE | 2,726.8 |
| AXA EQUITABLE LIFE INS CO | NY | 187,479.0 |
| BOSTON MUTUAL LIFE INS CO | MA | 1,424.8 |
| COMPANION LIFE INS CO | SC | 359.8 |
| DEARBORN NATIONAL LIFE INS CO | IL | 1,849.7 |
| DELAWARE AMERICAN LIFE INS CO | DE | 137.9 |
| FAMILY HERITAGE LIFE INS CO OF AMER | OH | 1,249.5 |
| GERBER LIFE INS CO | NY | 3,650.7 |
| GOVERNMENT PERSONNEL MUTUAL L I C | TX | 832.3 |
| JACKSON NATIONAL LIFE INS CO | MI | 222,617.0 |
| MIDLAND NATIONAL LIFE INS CO | IA | 55,140.0 |
| MINNESOTA LIFE INS CO | MN | 44,369.0 |
| MUTUAL OF OMAHA INS CO | NE | 7,661.2 |
| NATIONAL BENEFIT LIFE INS CO | NY | 537.3 |
| NATIONAL CASUALTY CO | OH | 406.6 |
| OHIO NATIONAL LIFE ASR CORP | OH | 4,048.6 |
| PRINCIPAL LIFE INS CO | IA | 185,959.0 |
| SB MUTL LIFE INS CO OF MA | MA | 3,015.1 |
| SENTRY SELECT INS CO | WI | 810.3 |
| STANDARD INS CO | OR | 23,414.5 |
| STATE FARM FIRE & CAS CO | IL | 39,417.8 |
| STATE FARM MUTUAL AUTOMOBILE INS CO | IL | 154,684.0 |
| SYMETRA LIFE INS CO | IA | 36,133.8 |
| TRUSTMARK INS CO | IL | 1,532.5 |
| TRUSTMARK LIFE INS CO | IL | 320.1 |
| UNITED WORLD LIFE INS CO | NE | 123.8 |
| USABLE LIFE | AR | 510.9 |
| VOYA RETIREMENT INS & ANNUITY CO | CT | 104,964.0 |

## Maryland

| INSURANCE COMPANY NAME | DOM. STATE | TOTAL ASSETS ($MIL) |
|---|---|---|
| **Rating: A+** | | |
| COUNTRY LIFE INS CO | IL | 9,441.1 |
| PHYSICIANS MUTUAL INS CO | NE | 2,289.0 |
| TEACHERS INS & ANNUITY ASN OF AM | NY | 293,835.0 |
| **Rating: A** | | |
| BERKLEY LIFE & HEALTH INS CO | IA | 286.6 |
| FEDERATED LIFE INS CO | MN | 1,849.9 |
| GUARDIAN LIFE INS CO OF AMERICA | NY | 55,226.5 |
| LIFEWISE ASR CO | WA | 166.6 |
| MIDWESTERN UNITED LIFE INS CO | IN | 233.4 |
| NATIONAL WESTERN LIFE INS CO | CO | 11,058.8 |
| SENTRY INS A MUTUAL CO | WI | 8,232.3 |
| SENTRY LIFE INS CO | WI | 6,735.9 |
| SHELTERPOINT LIFE INS CO | NY | 110.1 |
| UNITED FARM FAMILY LIFE INS CO | IN | 2,312.3 |
| USAA LIFE INS CO | TX | 24,728.9 |
| **Rating: A-** | | |
| AMALGAMATED LIFE INS CO | NY | 124.9 |
| AMERICAN HEALTH & LIFE INS CO | TX | 840.1 |
| AMERICAN REPUBLIC INS CO | IA | 933.1 |
| ANTHEM LIFE INS CO | IN | 738.1 |
| CAREFIRST BLUECHOICE INC | DC | 1,137.7 |
| CENTRAL STATES H & L CO OF OMAHA | NE | 411.0 |
| ERIE FAMILY LIFE INS CO | PA | 2,448.7 |
| GARDEN STATE LIFE INS CO | TX | 131.8 |
| HUMANA BENEFIT PLAN OF ILLINOIS | IL | 394.7 |
| HUMANA INS CO (WI) | WI | 10,120.6 |
| MASSACHUSETTS MUTUAL LIFE INS CO | MA | 235,570.0 |
| MEDCO CONTAINMENT LIFE INS CO | PA | 1,113.2 |
| MEDICO CORP LIFE INS CO | NE | 63.9 |
| MOTORISTS COMMERCIAL MUTUAL INS CO | OH | 393.5 |
| MUTUAL OF AMERICA LIFE INS CO | NY | 20,499.3 |
| NEW YORK LIFE INS CO | NY | 176,417.0 |
| NIPPON LIFE INS CO OF AMERICA | IA | 219.6 |
| NORTHWESTERN MUTUAL LIFE INS CO | WI | 264,165.0 |
| PHYSICIANS LIFE INS CO | NE | 1,625.7 |
| PROTECTIVE INS CO | IN | 848.6 |
| STANDARD LIFE & ACCIDENT INS CO | TX | 516.7 |
| **Rating: B+** | | |
| AETNA HEALTH & LIFE INS CO | CT | 2,403.1 |
| AMERICAN FAMILY LIFE ASR CO OF COLUM | NE | 113,507.0 |
| AMERICAN FIDELITY ASR CO | OK | 5,772.7 |
| AMERICAN UNITED LIFE INS CO | IN | 27,567.2 |
| AMFIRST INS CO | OK | 57.6 |
| ASSURITY LIFE INS CO | NE | 2,726.8 |
| AXA EQUITABLE LIFE INS CO | NY | 187,479.0 |
| BEST LIFE & HEALTH INS CO | TX | 20.9 |
| BOSTON MUTUAL LIFE INS CO | MA | 1,424.8 |
| COMPANION LIFE INS CO | SC | 359.8 |
| DEARBORN NATIONAL LIFE INS CO | IL | 1,849.7 |
| DELAWARE AMERICAN LIFE INS CO | DE | 137.9 |
| FAMILY HERITAGE LIFE INS CO OF AMER | OH | 1,249.5 |
| GERBER LIFE INS CO | NY | 3,650.7 |
| GOVERNMENT PERSONNEL MUTUAL L I C | TX | 832.3 |
| JACKSON NATIONAL LIFE INS CO | MI | 222,617.0 |
| MIDLAND NATIONAL LIFE INS CO | IA | 55,140.0 |
| MINNESOTA LIFE INS CO | MN | 44,369.0 |
| MUTUAL OF OMAHA INS CO | NE | 7,661.2 |
| NATIONAL BENEFIT LIFE INS CO | NY | 537.3 |
| NATIONAL CASUALTY CO | OH | 406.6 |
| OHIO NATIONAL LIFE ASR CORP | OH | 4,048.6 |
| PRINCIPAL LIFE INS CO | IA | 185,959.0 |
| SB MUTL LIFE INS CO OF MA | MA | 3,015.1 |
| SENTRY SELECT INS CO | WI | 810.3 |
| STANDARD INS CO | OR | 23,414.5 |
| STATE FARM FIRE & CAS CO | IL | 39,417.8 |
| STATE FARM MUTUAL AUTOMOBILE INS CO | IL | 154,684.0 |
| SYMETRA LIFE INS CO | IA | 36,133.8 |
| TRUSTMARK INS CO | IL | 1,532.5 |
| TRUSTMARK LIFE INS CO | IL | 320.1 |
| UNITED WORLD LIFE INS CO | NE | 123.8 |
| USABLE LIFE | AR | 510.9 |
| VOYA RETIREMENT INS & ANNUITY CO | CT | 104,964.0 |

## Massachusetts

| INSURANCE COMPANY NAME | DOM. STATE | TOTAL ASSETS ($MIL) |
|---|---|---|
| **Rating: A+** | | |
| COUNTRY LIFE INS CO | IL | 9,441.1 |
| PHYSICIANS MUTUAL INS CO | NE | 2,289.0 |
| TEACHERS INS & ANNUITY ASN OF AM | NY | 293,835.0 |
| **Rating: A** | | |
| BERKLEY LIFE & HEALTH INS CO | IA | 286.6 |
| FEDERATED LIFE INS CO | MN | 1,849.9 |
| GUARDIAN LIFE INS CO OF AMERICA | NY | 55,226.5 |
| MIDWESTERN UNITED LIFE INS CO | IN | 233.4 |
| NATIONAL WESTERN LIFE INS CO | CO | 11,058.8 |
| SENTRY INS A MUTUAL CO | WI | 8,232.3 |
| SENTRY LIFE INS CO | WI | 6,735.9 |
| SHELTERPOINT LIFE INS CO | NY | 110.1 |
| UNITED FARM FAMILY LIFE INS CO | IN | 2,312.3 |
| USAA LIFE INS CO | TX | 24,728.9 |
| **Rating: A-** | | |
| AMALGAMATED LIFE INS CO | NY | 124.9 |
| AMERICAN FAMILY LIFE ASR CO OF NY | NY | 945.4 |
| AMERICAN HEALTH & LIFE INS CO | TX | 840.1 |
| AMERICAN REPUBLIC INS CO | IA | 933.1 |
| ANTHEM LIFE INS CO | IN | 738.1 |
| AUTO-OWNERS LIFE INS CO | MI | 4,021.4 |
| BLUE CROSS & BLUE SHIELD MA HMO BLUE | MA | 2,283.0 |
| CENTRAL STATES H & L CO OF OMAHA | NE | 411.0 |
| GARDEN STATE LIFE INS CO | TX | 131.8 |
| HUMANA BENEFIT PLAN OF ILLINOIS | IL | 394.7 |
| HUMANA INS CO (WI) | WI | 10,120.6 |
| MASSACHUSETTS MUTUAL LIFE INS CO | MA | 235,570.0 |
| MEDCO CONTAINMENT LIFE INS CO | PA | 1,113.2 |
| MOTORISTS COMMERCIAL MUTUAL INS CO | OH | 393.5 |
| MUTUAL OF AMERICA LIFE INS CO | NY | 20,499.3 |
| NEW YORK LIFE INS CO | NY | 176,417.0 |
| NIPPON LIFE INS CO OF AMERICA | IA | 219.6 |
| NORTHWESTERN MUTUAL LIFE INS CO | WI | 264,165.0 |
| PHYSICIANS LIFE INS CO | NE | 1,625.7 |
| PROTECTIVE INS CO | IN | 848.6 |
| STANDARD LIFE & ACCIDENT INS CO | TX | 516.7 |
| **Rating: B+** | | |
| AETNA HEALTH & LIFE INS CO | CT | 2,403.1 |
| AMERICAN FAMILY LIFE ASR CO OF COLUM | NE | 113,507.0 |
| AMERICAN FIDELITY ASR CO | OK | 5,772.7 |
| AMERICAN UNITED LIFE INS CO | IN | 27,567.2 |
| ASSURITY LIFE INS CO | NE | 2,726.8 |
| AXA EQUITABLE LIFE INS CO | NY | 187,479.0 |
| BOSTON MUTUAL LIFE INS CO | MA | 1,424.8 |
| COMPANION LIFE INS CO | SC | 359.8 |
| DEARBORN NATIONAL LIFE INS CO | IL | 1,849.7 |
| DELAWARE AMERICAN LIFE INS CO | DE | 137.9 |
| FAMILY HERITAGE LIFE INS CO OF AMER | OH | 1,249.5 |
| GERBER LIFE INS CO | NY | 3,650.7 |
| GOVERNMENT PERSONNEL MUTUAL L I C | TX | 832.3 |
| JACKSON NATIONAL LIFE INS CO | MI | 222,617.0 |
| MIDLAND NATIONAL LIFE INS CO | IA | 55,140.0 |
| MINNESOTA LIFE INS CO | MN | 44,369.0 |
| MUTUAL OF OMAHA INS CO | NE | 7,661.2 |
| NATIONAL BENEFIT LIFE INS CO | NY | 537.3 |
| NATIONAL CASUALTY CO | OH | 406.6 |
| OHIO NATIONAL LIFE ASR CORP | OH | 4,048.6 |
| PRINCIPAL LIFE INS CO | IA | 185,959.0 |
| SB MUTL LIFE INS CO OF MA | MA | 3,015.1 |
| SENTRY SELECT INS CO | WI | 810.3 |
| STANDARD INS CO | OR | 23,414.5 |
| STATE FARM FIRE & CAS CO | IL | 39,417.8 |
| STATE FARM MUTUAL AUTOMOBILE INS CO | IL | 154,684.0 |
| SYMETRA LIFE INS CO | IA | 36,133.8 |
| TRUSTMARK INS CO | IL | 1,532.5 |
| TRUSTMARK LIFE INS CO | IL | 320.1 |
| UNITED WORLD LIFE INS CO | NE | 123.8 |
| USABLE LIFE | AR | 510.9 |
| VOYA RETIREMENT INS & ANNUITY CO | CT | 104,964.0 |

## Michigan

| INSURANCE COMPANY NAME | DOM. STATE | TOTAL ASSETS ($MIL) |
|---|---|---|
| **Rating: A+** | | |
| COUNTRY LIFE INS CO | IL | 9,441.1 |
| PHYSICIANS MUTUAL INS CO | NE | 2,289.0 |
| TEACHERS INS & ANNUITY ASN OF AM | NY | 293,835.0 |
| **Rating: A** | | |
| BERKLEY LIFE & HEALTH INS CO | IA | 286.6 |
| FEDERATED LIFE INS CO | MN | 1,849.9 |
| GUARDIAN LIFE INS CO OF AMERICA | NY | 55,226.5 |
| MEDICAL MUTUAL OF OHIO | OH | 2,136.4 |
| MIDWESTERN UNITED LIFE INS CO | IN | 233.4 |
| NATIONAL WESTERN LIFE INS CO | CO | 11,058.8 |
| PRIORITY HEALTH | MI | 1,290.9 |
| SENTRY INS A MUTUAL CO | WI | 8,232.3 |
| SENTRY LIFE INS CO | WI | 6,735.9 |
| SHELTERPOINT LIFE INS CO | NY | 110.1 |
| UPPER PENINSULA HEALTH PLAN INC | MI | 97.3 |
| USAA LIFE INS CO | TX | 24,728.9 |
| **Rating: A-** | | |
| AMALGAMATED LIFE INS CO | NY | 124.9 |
| AMERICAN HEALTH & LIFE INS CO | TX | 840.1 |
| AMERICAN REPUBLIC INS CO | IA | 933.1 |
| ANTHEM LIFE INS CO | IN | 738.1 |
| AUTO-OWNERS LIFE INS CO | MI | 4,021.4 |
| CENTRAL STATES H & L CO OF OMAHA | NE | 411.0 |
| GARDEN STATE LIFE INS CO | TX | 131.8 |
| HUMANA BENEFIT PLAN OF ILLINOIS | IL | 394.7 |
| HUMANA INS CO (WI) | WI | 10,120.6 |
| MASSACHUSETTS MUTUAL LIFE INS CO | MA | 235,570.0 |
| MCLAREN HEALTH PLAN INC | MI | 239.2 |
| MEDCO CONTAINMENT LIFE INS CO | PA | 1,113.2 |
| MEDICO CORP LIFE INS CO | NE | 63.9 |
| MOTORISTS COMMERCIAL MUTUAL INS CO | OH | 393.5 |
| MUTUAL OF AMERICA LIFE INS CO | NY | 20,499.3 |
| NEW YORK LIFE INS CO | NY | 176,417.0 |
| NIPPON LIFE INS CO OF AMERICA | IA | 219.6 |
| NORTHWESTERN MUTUAL LIFE INS CO | WI | 264,165.0 |
| PARAMOUNT INS CO (OH) | OH | 88.2 |
| PHYSICIANS LIFE INS CO | NE | 1,625.7 |
| PROTECTIVE INS CO | IN | 848.6 |
| STANDARD LIFE & ACCIDENT INS CO | TX | 516.7 |
| **Rating: B+** | | |
| AETNA HEALTH & LIFE INS CO | CT | 2,403.1 |
| AMERICAN FAMILY LIFE ASR CO OF COLUM | NE | 113,507.0 |
| AMERICAN FIDELITY ASR CO | OK | 5,772.7 |
| AMERICAN UNITED LIFE INS CO | IN | 27,567.2 |
| AMFIRST INS CO | OK | 57.6 |
| ASSURITY LIFE INS CO | NE | 2,726.8 |
| AXA EQUITABLE LIFE INS CO | NY | 187,479.0 |
| BEST LIFE & HEALTH INS CO | TX | 20.9 |
| BLUE CARE NETWORK OF MICHIGAN | MI | 2,177.8 |
| BOSTON MUTUAL LIFE INS CO | MA | 1,424.8 |
| COMPANION LIFE INS CO | SC | 359.8 |
| DEARBORN NATIONAL LIFE INS CO | IL | 1,849.7 |
| DELAWARE AMERICAN LIFE INS CO | DE | 137.9 |
| FAMILY HERITAGE LIFE INS CO OF AMER | OH | 1,249.5 |
| GERBER LIFE INS CO | NY | 3,650.7 |
| GOVERNMENT PERSONNEL MUTUAL L I C | TX | 832.3 |
| JACKSON NATIONAL LIFE INS CO | MI | 222,617.0 |
| MIDLAND NATIONAL LIFE INS CO | IA | 55,140.0 |
| MINNESOTA LIFE INS CO | MN | 44,369.0 |
| MUTUAL OF OMAHA INS CO | NE | 7,661.2 |
| NATIONAL BENEFIT LIFE INS CO | NY | 537.3 |
| NATIONAL CASUALTY CO | OH | 406.6 |
| OHIO NATIONAL LIFE ASR CORP | OH | 4,048.6 |
| PRINCIPAL LIFE INS CO | IA | 185,959.0 |
| PRIORITY HEALTH CHOICE INC | MI | 143.4 |
| SB MUTL LIFE INS CO OF MA | MA | 3,015.1 |
| SENTRY SELECT INS CO | WI | 810.3 |
| STANDARD INS CO | OR | 23,414.5 |
| STATE FARM FIRE & CAS CO | IL | 39,417.8 |
| STATE FARM MUTUAL AUTOMOBILE INS CO | IL | 154,684.0 |
| SYMETRA LIFE INS CO | IA | 36,133.8 |
| TOTAL HEALTH CARE USA INC | MI | 68.3 |
| TRUSTMARK INS CO | IL | 1,532.5 |
| TRUSTMARK LIFE INS CO | IL | 320.1 |
| UNITED WORLD LIFE INS CO | NE | 123.8 |
| USABLE LIFE | AR | 510.9 |
| VOYA RETIREMENT INS & ANNUITY CO | CT | 104,964.0 |

## Minnesota

| INSURANCE COMPANY NAME | DOM. STATE | TOTAL ASSETS ($MIL) |
|---|---|---|
| **Rating: A+** | | |
| COUNTRY LIFE INS CO | IL | 9,441.1 |
| HEALTHPARTNERS | MN | 1,213.6 |
| PHYSICIANS MUTUAL INS CO | NE | 2,289.0 |
| TEACHERS INS & ANNUITY ASN OF AM | NY | 293,835.0 |
| **Rating: A** | | |
| ALLIANZ LIFE INS CO OF NY | NY | 3,347.7 |
| BERKLEY LIFE & HEALTH INS CO | IA | 286.6 |
| FEDERATED LIFE INS CO | MN | 1,849.9 |
| GUARDIAN LIFE INS CO OF AMERICA | NY | 55,226.5 |
| MIDWESTERN UNITED LIFE INS CO | IN | 233.4 |
| NATIONAL WESTERN LIFE INS CO | CO | 11,058.8 |
| SENTRY INS A MUTUAL CO | WI | 8,232.3 |
| SENTRY LIFE INS CO | WI | 6,735.9 |
| SHELTERPOINT LIFE INS CO | NY | 110.1 |
| USAA LIFE INS CO | TX | 24,728.9 |
| **Rating: A-** | | |
| AMALGAMATED LIFE INS CO | NY | 124.9 |
| AMERICAN HEALTH & LIFE INS CO | TX | 840.1 |
| AMERICAN REPUBLIC INS CO | IA | 933.1 |
| ANTHEM LIFE INS CO | IN | 738.1 |
| AUTO-OWNERS LIFE INS CO | MI | 4,021.4 |
| CENTRAL STATES H & L CO OF OMAHA | NE | 411.0 |
| COPIC INS CO | CO | 765.4 |
| ERIE FAMILY LIFE INS CO | PA | 2,448.7 |
| GARDEN STATE LIFE INS CO | TX | 131.8 |
| GROUP HEALTH PLAN INC | MN | 902.1 |
| HUMANA BENEFIT PLAN OF ILLINOIS | IL | 394.7 |
| HUMANA INS CO (WI) | WI | 10,120.6 |
| MASSACHUSETTS MUTUAL LIFE INS CO | MA | 235,570.0 |
| MEDCO CONTAINMENT LIFE INS CO | PA | 1,113.2 |
| MEDICO CORP LIFE INS CO | NE | 63.9 |
| MOTORISTS COMMERCIAL MUTUAL INS CO | OH | 393.5 |
| MUTUAL OF AMERICA LIFE INS CO | NY | 20,499.3 |
| NEW YORK LIFE INS CO | NY | 176,417.0 |
| NIPPON LIFE INS CO OF AMERICA | IA | 219.6 |
| NORTHWESTERN MUTUAL LIFE INS CO | WI | 264,165.0 |
| PHYSICIANS LIFE INS CO | NE | 1,625.7 |
| PROTECTIVE INS CO | IN | 848.6 |
| STANDARD LIFE & ACCIDENT INS CO | TX | 516.7 |
| **Rating: B+** | | |
| AETNA HEALTH & LIFE INS CO | CT | 2,403.1 |
| AMERICAN FAMILY LIFE ASR CO OF COLUM | NE | 113,507.0 |
| AMERICAN FAMILY MUTL INS CO SI | WI | 17,048.2 |
| AMERICAN FIDELITY ASR CO | OK | 5,772.7 |
| AMERICAN UNITED LIFE INS CO | IN | 27,567.2 |
| ASSURITY LIFE INS CO | NE | 2,726.8 |
| AXA EQUITABLE LIFE INS CO | NY | 187,479.0 |
| BOSTON MUTUAL LIFE INS CO | MA | 1,424.8 |
| COMPANION LIFE INS CO | SC | 359.8 |
| DEARBORN NATIONAL LIFE INS CO | IL | 1,849.7 |
| DELAWARE AMERICAN LIFE INS CO | DE | 137.9 |
| FAMILY HERITAGE LIFE INS CO OF AMER | OH | 1,249.5 |
| FARM BUREAU LIFE INS CO | IA | 8,948.8 |
| GERBER LIFE INS CO | NY | 3,650.7 |
| GOVERNMENT PERSONNEL MUTUAL L I C | TX | 832.3 |
| JACKSON NATIONAL LIFE INS CO | MI | 222,617.0 |
| MIDLAND NATIONAL LIFE INS CO | IA | 55,140.0 |
| MINNESOTA LIFE INS CO | MN | 44,369.0 |
| MUTUAL OF OMAHA INS CO | NE | 7,661.2 |
| NATIONAL BENEFIT LIFE INS CO | NY | 537.3 |
| NATIONAL CASUALTY CO | OH | 406.6 |
| OHIO NATIONAL LIFE ASR CORP | OH | 4,048.6 |
| PRINCIPAL LIFE INS CO | IA | 185,959.0 |
| SB MUTL LIFE INS CO OF MA | MA | 3,015.1 |
| SENTRY SELECT INS CO | WI | 810.3 |
| STANDARD INS CO | OR | 23,414.5 |
| STATE FARM FIRE & CAS CO | IL | 39,417.8 |
| STATE FARM MUTUAL AUTOMOBILE INS CO | IL | 154,684.0 |
| SYMETRA LIFE INS CO | IA | 36,133.8 |
| TRUSTMARK INS CO | IL | 1,532.5 |
| TRUSTMARK LIFE INS CO | IL | 320.1 |
| UNITED WORLD LIFE INS CO | NE | 123.8 |
| USABLE LIFE | AR | 510.9 |
| VOYA RETIREMENT INS & ANNUITY CO | CT | 104,964.0 |

## Mississippi

| INSURANCE COMPANY NAME | DOM. STATE | TOTAL ASSETS ($MIL) |
|---|---|---|
| **Rating: A+** | | |
| COUNTRY LIFE INS CO | IL | 9,441.1 |
| PHYSICIANS MUTUAL INS CO | NE | 2,289.0 |
| TEACHERS INS & ANNUITY ASN OF AM | NY | 293,835.0 |
| **Rating: A** | | |
| BERKLEY LIFE & HEALTH INS CO | IA | 286.6 |
| FEDERATED LIFE INS CO | MN | 1,849.9 |
| GUARDIAN LIFE INS CO OF AMERICA | NY | 55,226.5 |
| MIDWESTERN UNITED LIFE INS CO | IN | 233.4 |
| NATIONAL WESTERN LIFE INS CO | CO | 11,058.8 |
| SENTRY INS A MUTUAL CO | WI | 8,232.3 |
| SENTRY LIFE INS CO | WI | 6,735.9 |
| SOUTHERN FARM BUREAU LIFE INS CO | MS | 14,163.7 |
| USAA LIFE INS CO | TX | 24,728.9 |
| **Rating: A-** | | |
| AMALGAMATED LIFE INS CO | NY | 124.9 |
| AMERICAN HEALTH & LIFE INS CO | TX | 840.1 |
| AMERICAN REPUBLIC INS CO | IA | 933.1 |
| ANTHEM LIFE INS CO | IN | 738.1 |
| AUTO-OWNERS LIFE INS CO | MI | 4,021.4 |
| CENTRAL STATES H & L CO OF OMAHA | NE | 411.0 |
| GARDEN STATE LIFE INS CO | TX | 131.8 |
| HUMANA BENEFIT PLAN OF ILLINOIS | IL | 394.7 |
| HUMANA INS CO (WI) | WI | 10,120.6 |
| MASSACHUSETTS MUTUAL LIFE INS CO | MA | 235,570.0 |
| MEDCO CONTAINMENT LIFE INS CO | PA | 1,113.2 |
| MEDICO CORP LIFE INS CO | NE | 63.9 |
| MUTUAL OF AMERICA LIFE INS CO | NY | 20,499.3 |
| NEW YORK LIFE INS CO | NY | 176,417.0 |
| NIPPON LIFE INS CO OF AMERICA | IA | 219.6 |
| NORTHWESTERN MUTUAL LIFE INS CO | WI | 264,165.0 |
| PHYSICIANS LIFE INS CO | NE | 1,625.7 |
| PROTECTIVE INS CO | IN | 848.6 |
| STANDARD LIFE & ACCIDENT INS CO | TX | 516.7 |
| **Rating: B+** | | |
| AETNA HEALTH & LIFE INS CO | CT | 2,403.1 |
| AMERICAN FAMILY LIFE ASR CO OF COLUM | NE | 113,507.0 |
| AMERICAN FIDELITY ASR CO | OK | 5,772.7 |
| AMERICAN UNITED LIFE INS CO | IN | 27,567.2 |
| AMFIRST INS CO | OK | 57.6 |
| ASSURITY LIFE INS CO | NE | 2,726.8 |
| AXA EQUITABLE LIFE INS CO | NY | 187,479.0 |
| BEST LIFE & HEALTH INS CO | TX | 20.9 |
| BLUEBONNET LIFE INS CO | MS | 62.2 |
| BOSTON MUTUAL LIFE INS CO | MA | 1,424.8 |
| COMPANION LIFE INS CO | SC | 359.8 |
| DEARBORN NATIONAL LIFE INS CO | IL | 1,849.7 |
| DELAWARE AMERICAN LIFE INS CO | DE | 137.9 |
| FAMILY HERITAGE LIFE INS CO OF AMER | OH | 1,249.5 |
| GERBER LIFE INS CO | NY | 3,650.7 |
| GOVERNMENT PERSONNEL MUTUAL L I C | TX | 832.3 |
| HEALTHSPRING OF TENNESSEE INC | TN | 460.4 |
| JACKSON NATIONAL LIFE INS CO | MI | 222,617.0 |
| MIDLAND NATIONAL LIFE INS CO | IA | 55,140.0 |
| MINNESOTA LIFE INS CO | MN | 44,369.0 |
| MUTUAL OF OMAHA INS CO | NE | 7,661.2 |
| NATIONAL BENEFIT LIFE INS CO | NY | 537.3 |
| NATIONAL CASUALTY CO | OH | 406.6 |
| OHIO NATIONAL LIFE ASR CORP | OH | 4,048.6 |
| PRINCIPAL LIFE INS CO | IA | 185,959.0 |
| SB MUTL LIFE INS CO OF MA | MA | 3,015.1 |
| SENTRY SELECT INS CO | WI | 810.3 |
| SHELTER LIFE INS CO | MO | 1,238.3 |
| SOUTHERN PIONEER LIFE INS CO | AR | 15.7 |
| STANDARD INS CO | OR | 23,414.5 |
| STATE FARM FIRE & CAS CO | IL | 39,417.8 |
| STATE FARM MUTUAL AUTOMOBILE INS CO | IL | 154,684.0 |
| SYMETRA LIFE INS CO | IA | 36,133.8 |
| TRUSTMARK INS CO | IL | 1,532.5 |
| TRUSTMARK LIFE INS CO | IL | 320.1 |
| UNITED WORLD LIFE INS CO | NE | 123.8 |
| USABLE LIFE | AR | 510.9 |
| VOYA RETIREMENT INS & ANNUITY CO | CT | 104,964.0 |

## Missouri

| INSURANCE COMPANY NAME | DOM. STATE | TOTAL ASSETS ($MIL) |
|---|---|---|
| **Rating: A+** | | |
| COUNTRY LIFE INS CO | IL | 9,441.1 |
| PHYSICIANS MUTUAL INS CO | NE | 2,289.0 |
| TEACHERS INS & ANNUITY ASN OF AM | NY | 293,835.0 |
| **Rating: A** | | |
| ALLIANZ LIFE INS CO OF NY | NY | 3,347.7 |
| BERKLEY LIFE & HEALTH INS CO | IA | 286.6 |
| FEDERATED LIFE INS CO | MN | 1,849.9 |
| GUARDIAN LIFE INS CO OF AMERICA | NY | 55,226.5 |
| MIDWESTERN UNITED LIFE INS CO | IN | 233.4 |
| NATIONAL WESTERN LIFE INS CO | CO | 11,058.8 |
| SENTRY INS A MUTUAL CO | WI | 8,232.3 |
| SENTRY LIFE INS CO | WI | 6,735.9 |
| USAA LIFE INS CO | TX | 24,728.9 |
| **Rating: A-** | | |
| AMALGAMATED LIFE INS CO | NY | 124.9 |
| AMERICAN HEALTH & LIFE INS CO | TX | 840.1 |
| AMERICAN REPUBLIC INS CO | IA | 933.1 |
| ANTHEM LIFE INS CO | IN | 738.1 |
| AUTO-OWNERS LIFE INS CO | MI | 4,021.4 |
| CENTRAL STATES H & L CO OF OMAHA | NE | 411.0 |
| CIGNA LIFE INS CO OF NEW YORK | NY | 403.0 |
| COPIC INS CO | CO | 765.4 |
| FARM BUREAU LIFE INS CO OF MISSOURI | MO | 582.3 |
| GARDEN STATE LIFE INS CO | TX | 131.8 |
| HEALTHY ALLIANCE LIFE INS CO | MO | 1,295.0 |
| HUMANA BENEFIT PLAN OF ILLINOIS | IL | 394.7 |
| HUMANA INS CO (WI) | WI | 10,120.6 |
| MASSACHUSETTS MUTUAL LIFE INS CO | MA | 235,570.0 |
| MEDCO CONTAINMENT LIFE INS CO | PA | 1,113.2 |
| MEDICO CORP LIFE INS CO | NE | 63.9 |
| MOTORISTS COMMERCIAL MUTUAL INS CO | OH | 393.5 |
| MUTUAL OF AMERICA LIFE INS CO | NY | 20,499.3 |
| NEW YORK LIFE INS CO | NY | 176,417.0 |
| NIPPON LIFE INS CO OF AMERICA | IA | 219.6 |
| NORTHWESTERN MUTUAL LIFE INS CO | WI | 264,165.0 |
| PACIFIC GUARDIAN LIFE INS CO LTD | HI | 552.3 |
| PHYSICIANS LIFE INS CO | NE | 1,625.7 |
| PROTECTIVE INS CO | IN | 848.6 |
| STANDARD LIFE & ACCIDENT INS CO | TX | 516.7 |
| **Rating: B+** | | |
| AETNA HEALTH & LIFE INS CO | CT | 2,403.1 |
| AMERICAN FAMILY LIFE ASR CO OF COLUM | NE | 113,507.0 |
| AMERICAN FAMILY MUTL INS CO SI | WI | 17,048.2 |
| AMERICAN FIDELITY ASR CO | OK | 5,772.7 |
| AMERICAN UNITED LIFE INS CO | IN | 27,567.2 |
| ASSURITY LIFE INS CO | NE | 2,726.8 |
| AXA EQUITABLE LIFE INS CO | NY | 187,479.0 |
| BEST LIFE & HEALTH INS CO | TX | 20.9 |
| BOSTON MUTUAL LIFE INS CO | MA | 1,424.8 |
| COMPANION LIFE INS CO | SC | 359.8 |
| DEARBORN NATIONAL LIFE INS CO | IL | 1,849.7 |
| DELAWARE AMERICAN LIFE INS CO | DE | 137.9 |
| ESSENCE HEALTHCARE INC | MO | 288.5 |
| FAMILY HERITAGE LIFE INS CO OF AMER | OH | 1,249.5 |
| GERBER LIFE INS CO | NY | 3,650.7 |
| GOVERNMENT PERSONNEL MUTUAL L I C | TX | 832.3 |
| JACKSON NATIONAL LIFE INS CO | MI | 222,617.0 |
| MIDLAND NATIONAL LIFE INS CO | IA | 55,140.0 |
| MINNESOTA LIFE INS CO | MN | 44,369.0 |
| MUTUAL OF OMAHA INS CO | NE | 7,661.2 |
| NATIONAL BENEFIT LIFE INS CO | NY | 537.3 |
| NATIONAL CASUALTY CO | OH | 406.6 |
| OHIO NATIONAL LIFE ASR CORP | OH | 4,048.6 |
| PRINCIPAL LIFE INS CO | IA | 185,959.0 |
| SB MUTL LIFE INS CO OF MA | MA | 3,015.1 |
| SENTRY SELECT INS CO | WI | 810.3 |
| SHELTER LIFE INS CO | MO | 1,238.3 |
| SOUTHERN PIONEER LIFE INS CO | AR | 15.7 |
| STANDARD INS CO | OR | 23,414.5 |
| STATE FARM FIRE & CAS CO | IL | 39,417.8 |
| STATE FARM MUTUAL AUTOMOBILE INS CO | IL | 154,684.0 |
| SYMETRA LIFE INS CO | IA | 36,133.8 |
| TRUSTMARK INS CO | IL | 1,532.5 |
| TRUSTMARK LIFE INS CO | IL | 320.1 |
| UNITED WORLD LIFE INS CO | NE | 123.8 |
| USABLE LIFE | AR | 510.9 |
| VOYA RETIREMENT INS & ANNUITY CO | CT | 104,964.0 |

## Montana

| INSURANCE COMPANY NAME | DOM. STATE | TOTAL ASSETS ($MIL) |
|---|---|---|
| **Rating: A+** | | |
| COUNTRY LIFE INS CO | IL | 9,441.1 |
| PHYSICIANS MUTUAL INS CO | NE | 2,289.0 |
| TEACHERS INS & ANNUITY ASN OF AM | NY | 293,835.0 |
| **Rating: A** | | |
| BERKLEY LIFE & HEALTH INS CO | IA | 286.6 |
| FEDERATED LIFE INS CO | MN | 1,849.9 |
| GUARDIAN LIFE INS CO OF AMERICA | NY | 55,226.5 |
| MIDWESTERN UNITED LIFE INS CO | IN | 233.4 |
| NATIONAL WESTERN LIFE INS CO | CO | 11,058.8 |
| SENTRY INS A MUTUAL CO | WI | 8,232.3 |
| SENTRY LIFE INS CO | WI | 6,735.9 |
| USAA LIFE INS CO | TX | 24,728.9 |
| **Rating: A-** | | |
| AMALGAMATED LIFE INS CO | NY | 124.9 |
| AMERICAN HEALTH & LIFE INS CO | TX | 840.1 |
| AMERICAN REPUBLIC INS CO | IA | 933.1 |
| ANTHEM LIFE INS CO | IN | 738.1 |
| CENTRAL STATES H & L CO OF OMAHA | NE | 411.0 |
| COPIC INS CO | CO | 765.4 |
| GARDEN STATE LIFE INS CO | TX | 131.8 |
| HUMANA BENEFIT PLAN OF ILLINOIS | IL | 394.7 |
| HUMANA INS CO (WI) | WI | 10,120.6 |
| MASSACHUSETTS MUTUAL LIFE INS CO | MA | 235,570.0 |
| MEDCO CONTAINMENT LIFE INS CO | PA | 1,113.2 |
| MEDICO CORP LIFE INS CO | NE | 63.9 |
| MUTUAL OF AMERICA LIFE INS CO | NY | 20,499.3 |
| NEW YORK LIFE INS CO | NY | 176,417.0 |
| NIPPON LIFE INS CO OF AMERICA | IA | 219.6 |
| NORTHWESTERN MUTUAL LIFE INS CO | WI | 264,165.0 |
| PACIFIC GUARDIAN LIFE INS CO LTD | HI | 552.3 |
| PHYSICIANS LIFE INS CO | NE | 1,625.7 |
| PROTECTIVE INS CO | IN | 848.6 |
| STANDARD LIFE & ACCIDENT INS CO | TX | 516.7 |
| **Rating: B+** | | |
| AETNA HEALTH & LIFE INS CO | CT | 2,403.1 |
| AMERICAN FAMILY LIFE ASR CO OF COLUM | NE | 113,507.0 |
| AMERICAN FAMILY MUTL INS CO SI | WI | 17,048.2 |
| AMERICAN FIDELITY ASR CO | OK | 5,772.7 |
| AMERICAN UNITED LIFE INS CO | IN | 27,567.2 |
| ASSURITY LIFE INS CO | NE | 2,726.8 |
| AXA EQUITABLE LIFE INS CO | NY | 187,479.0 |
| BEST LIFE & HEALTH INS CO | TX | 20.9 |
| BOSTON MUTUAL LIFE INS CO | MA | 1,424.8 |
| COMPANION LIFE INS CO | SC | 359.8 |
| DEARBORN NATIONAL LIFE INS CO | IL | 1,849.7 |
| DELAWARE AMERICAN LIFE INS CO | DE | 137.9 |
| FAMILY HERITAGE LIFE INS CO OF AMER | OH | 1,249.5 |
| FARM BUREAU LIFE INS CO | IA | 8,948.8 |
| GERBER LIFE INS CO | NY | 3,650.7 |
| GOVERNMENT PERSONNEL MUTUAL L I C | TX | 832.3 |
| JACKSON NATIONAL LIFE INS CO | MI | 222,617.0 |
| MIDLAND NATIONAL LIFE INS CO | IA | 55,140.0 |
| MINNESOTA LIFE INS CO | MN | 44,369.0 |
| MUTUAL OF OMAHA INS CO | NE | 7,661.2 |
| NATIONAL BENEFIT LIFE INS CO | NY | 537.3 |
| NATIONAL CASUALTY CO | OH | 406.6 |
| OHIO NATIONAL LIFE ASR CORP | OH | 4,048.6 |
| PRINCIPAL LIFE INS CO | IA | 185,959.0 |
| SB MUTL LIFE INS CO OF MA | MA | 3,015.1 |
| SENTRY SELECT INS CO | WI | 810.3 |
| STANDARD INS CO | OR | 23,414.5 |
| STATE FARM FIRE & CAS CO | IL | 39,417.8 |
| STATE FARM MUTUAL AUTOMOBILE INS CO | IL | 154,684.0 |
| SYMETRA LIFE INS CO | IA | 36,133.8 |
| TRUSTMARK INS CO | IL | 1,532.5 |
| TRUSTMARK LIFE INS CO | IL | 320.1 |
| UNITED WORLD LIFE INS CO | NE | 123.8 |
| USABLE LIFE | AR | 510.9 |
| VOYA RETIREMENT INS & ANNUITY CO | CT | 104,964.0 |

## Nebraska

| INSURANCE COMPANY NAME | DOM. STATE | TOTAL ASSETS ($MIL) |
|---|---|---|
| **Rating: A+** | | |
| COUNTRY LIFE INS CO | IL | 9,441.1 |
| PHYSICIANS MUTUAL INS CO | NE | 2,289.0 |
| TEACHERS INS & ANNUITY ASN OF AM | NY | 293,835.0 |
| **Rating: A** | | |
| BERKLEY LIFE & HEALTH INS CO | IA | 286.6 |
| FEDERATED LIFE INS CO | MN | 1,849.9 |
| GUARDIAN LIFE INS CO OF AMERICA | NY | 55,226.5 |
| MIDWESTERN UNITED LIFE INS CO | IN | 233.4 |
| NATIONAL WESTERN LIFE INS CO | CO | 11,058.8 |
| SENTRY INS A MUTUAL CO | WI | 8,232.3 |
| SENTRY LIFE INS CO | WI | 6,735.9 |
| USAA LIFE INS CO | TX | 24,728.9 |
| **Rating: A-** | | |
| AMALGAMATED LIFE INS CO | NY | 124.9 |
| AMERICAN HEALTH & LIFE INS CO | TX | 840.1 |
| AMERICAN REPUBLIC INS CO | IA | 933.1 |
| ANTHEM LIFE INS CO | IN | 738.1 |
| AUTO-OWNERS LIFE INS CO | MI | 4,021.4 |
| CENTRAL STATES H & L CO OF OMAHA | NE | 411.0 |
| COPIC INS CO | CO | 765.4 |
| GARDEN STATE LIFE INS CO | TX | 131.8 |
| HUMANA BENEFIT PLAN OF ILLINOIS | IL | 394.7 |
| HUMANA INS CO (WI) | WI | 10,120.6 |
| MASSACHUSETTS MUTUAL LIFE INS CO | MA | 235,570.0 |
| MEDCO CONTAINMENT LIFE INS CO | PA | 1,113.2 |
| MEDICO CORP LIFE INS CO | NE | 63.9 |
| MOTORISTS COMMERCIAL MUTUAL INS CO | OH | 393.5 |
| MUTUAL OF AMERICA LIFE INS CO | NY | 20,499.3 |
| NEW YORK LIFE INS CO | NY | 176,417.0 |
| NIPPON LIFE INS CO OF AMERICA | IA | 219.6 |
| NORTHWESTERN MUTUAL LIFE INS CO | WI | 264,165.0 |
| PACIFIC GUARDIAN LIFE INS CO LTD | HI | 552.3 |
| PHYSICIANS LIFE INS CO | NE | 1,625.7 |
| PROTECTIVE INS CO | IN | 848.6 |
| STANDARD LIFE & ACCIDENT INS CO | TX | 516.7 |
| **Rating: B+** | | |
| AETNA HEALTH & LIFE INS CO | CT | 2,403.1 |
| AMERICAN FAMILY LIFE ASR CO OF COLUM | NE | 113,507.0 |
| AMERICAN FAMILY MUTL INS CO SI | WI | 17,048.2 |
| AMERICAN FIDELITY ASR CO | OK | 5,772.7 |
| AMERICAN UNITED LIFE INS CO | IN | 27,567.2 |
| ASSURITY LIFE INS CO | NE | 2,726.8 |
| AXA EQUITABLE LIFE INS CO | NY | 187,479.0 |
| BEST LIFE & HEALTH INS CO | TX | 20.9 |
| BOSTON MUTUAL LIFE INS CO | MA | 1,424.8 |
| COMPANION LIFE INS CO | SC | 359.8 |
| DEARBORN NATIONAL LIFE INS CO | IL | 1,849.7 |
| DELAWARE AMERICAN LIFE INS CO | DE | 137.9 |
| FAMILY HERITAGE LIFE INS CO OF AMER | OH | 1,249.5 |
| FARM BUREAU LIFE INS CO | IA | 8,948.8 |
| GERBER LIFE INS CO | NY | 3,650.7 |
| GOVERNMENT PERSONNEL MUTUAL L I C | TX | 832.3 |
| JACKSON NATIONAL LIFE INS CO | MI | 222,617.0 |
| MIDLAND NATIONAL LIFE INS CO | IA | 55,140.0 |
| MINNESOTA LIFE INS CO | MN | 44,369.0 |
| MUTUAL OF OMAHA INS CO | NE | 7,661.2 |
| NATIONAL BENEFIT LIFE INS CO | NY | 537.3 |
| NATIONAL CASUALTY CO | OH | 406.6 |
| OHIO NATIONAL LIFE ASR CORP | OH | 4,048.6 |
| PRINCIPAL LIFE INS CO | IA | 185,959.0 |
| SB MUTL LIFE INS CO OF MA | MA | 3,015.1 |
| SENTRY SELECT INS CO | WI | 810.3 |
| SHELTER LIFE INS CO | MO | 1,238.3 |
| STANDARD INS CO | OR | 23,414.5 |
| STATE FARM FIRE & CAS CO | IL | 39,417.8 |
| STATE FARM MUTUAL AUTOMOBILE INS CO | IL | 154,684.0 |
| SYMETRA LIFE INS CO | IA | 36,133.8 |
| TRUSTMARK INS CO | IL | 1,532.5 |
| TRUSTMARK LIFE INS CO | IL | 320.1 |
| UNITED WORLD LIFE INS CO | NE | 123.8 |
| USABLE LIFE | AR | 510.9 |
| VOYA RETIREMENT INS & ANNUITY CO | CT | 104,964.0 |

## Nevada

| INSURANCE COMPANY NAME | DOM. STATE | TOTAL ASSETS ($MIL) |
|---|---|---|
| **Rating: A+** | | |
| COUNTRY LIFE INS CO | IL | 9,441.1 |
| PHYSICIANS MUTUAL INS CO | NE | 2,289.0 |
| TEACHERS INS & ANNUITY ASN OF AM | NY | 293,835.0 |
| **Rating: A** | | |
| BERKLEY LIFE & HEALTH INS CO | IA | 286.6 |
| FEDERATED LIFE INS CO | MN | 1,849.9 |
| GUARDIAN LIFE INS CO OF AMERICA | NY | 55,226.5 |
| MIDWESTERN UNITED LIFE INS CO | IN | 233.4 |
| NATIONAL WESTERN LIFE INS CO | CO | 11,058.8 |
| SENTRY INS A MUTUAL CO | WI | 8,232.3 |
| SENTRY LIFE INS CO | WI | 6,735.9 |
| USAA LIFE INS CO | TX | 24,728.9 |
| **Rating: A-** | | |
| AMALGAMATED LIFE INS CO | NY | 124.9 |
| AMERICAN HEALTH & LIFE INS CO | TX | 840.1 |
| AMERICAN REPUBLIC INS CO | IA | 933.1 |
| ANTHEM LIFE INS CO | IN | 738.1 |
| AUTO-OWNERS LIFE INS CO | MI | 4,021.4 |
| CENTRAL STATES H & L CO OF OMAHA | NE | 411.0 |
| GARDEN STATE LIFE INS CO | TX | 131.8 |
| HUMANA BENEFIT PLAN OF ILLINOIS | IL | 394.7 |
| HUMANA INS CO (WI) | WI | 10,120.6 |
| MASSACHUSETTS MUTUAL LIFE INS CO | MA | 235,570.0 |
| MEDCO CONTAINMENT LIFE INS CO | PA | 1,113.2 |
| MEDICO CORP LIFE INS CO | NE | 63.9 |
| MOTORISTS COMMERCIAL MUTUAL INS CO | OH | 393.5 |
| MUTUAL OF AMERICA LIFE INS CO | NY | 20,499.3 |
| NEW YORK LIFE INS CO | NY | 176,417.0 |
| NIPPON LIFE INS CO OF AMERICA | IA | 219.6 |
| NORTHWESTERN MUTUAL LIFE INS CO | WI | 264,165.0 |
| PACIFIC GUARDIAN LIFE INS CO LTD | HI | 552.3 |
| PHYSICIANS LIFE INS CO | NE | 1,625.7 |
| PROTECTIVE INS CO | IN | 848.6 |
| STANDARD LIFE & ACCIDENT INS CO | TX | 516.7 |
| **Rating: B+** | | |
| AETNA HEALTH & LIFE INS CO | CT | 2,403.1 |
| AMERICAN FAMILY LIFE ASR CO OF COLUM | NE | 113,507.0 |
| AMERICAN FAMILY MUTL INS CO SI | WI | 17,048.2 |
| AMERICAN FIDELITY ASR CO | OK | 5,772.7 |
| AMERICAN UNITED LIFE INS CO | IN | 27,567.2 |
| ASSURITY LIFE INS CO | NE | 2,726.8 |
| AXA EQUITABLE LIFE INS CO | NY | 187,479.0 |
| BEST LIFE & HEALTH INS CO | TX | 20.9 |
| BOSTON MUTUAL LIFE INS CO | MA | 1,424.8 |
| COMPANION LIFE INS CO | SC | 359.8 |
| DEARBORN NATIONAL LIFE INS CO | IL | 1,849.7 |
| DELAWARE AMERICAN LIFE INS CO | DE | 137.9 |
| FAMILY HERITAGE LIFE INS CO OF AMER | OH | 1,249.5 |
| FARM BUREAU LIFE INS CO | IA | 8,948.8 |
| GERBER LIFE INS CO | NY | 3,650.7 |
| GOVERNMENT PERSONNEL MUTUAL L I C | TX | 832.3 |
| JACKSON NATIONAL LIFE INS CO | MI | 222,617.0 |
| MIDLAND NATIONAL LIFE INS CO | IA | 55,140.0 |
| MINNESOTA LIFE INS CO | MN | 44,369.0 |
| MUTUAL OF OMAHA INS CO | NE | 7,661.2 |
| NATIONAL BENEFIT LIFE INS CO | NY | 537.3 |
| NATIONAL CASUALTY CO | OH | 406.6 |
| OHIO NATIONAL LIFE ASR CORP | OH | 4,048.6 |
| PRINCIPAL LIFE INS CO | IA | 185,959.0 |
| SB MUTL LIFE INS CO OF MA | MA | 3,015.1 |
| SENTRY SELECT INS CO | WI | 810.3 |
| SHELTER LIFE INS CO | MO | 1,238.3 |
| STANDARD INS CO | OR | 23,414.5 |
| STATE FARM FIRE & CAS CO | IL | 39,417.8 |
| STATE FARM MUTUAL AUTOMOBILE INS CO | IL | 154,684.0 |
| SYMETRA LIFE INS CO | IA | 36,133.8 |
| TRUSTMARK INS CO | IL | 1,532.5 |
| TRUSTMARK LIFE INS CO | IL | 320.1 |
| UNITED WORLD LIFE INS CO | NE | 123.8 |
| USABLE LIFE | AR | 510.9 |
| VOYA RETIREMENT INS & ANNUITY CO | CT | 104,964.0 |

## New Hampshire

| INSURANCE COMPANY NAME | DOM. STATE | TOTAL ASSETS ($MIL) |
|---|---|---|
| **Rating: A+** | | |
| PHYSICIANS MUTUAL INS CO | NE | 2,289.0 |
| TEACHERS INS & ANNUITY ASN OF AM | NY | 293,835.0 |
| **Rating: A** | | |
| BERKLEY LIFE & HEALTH INS CO | IA | 286.6 |
| FEDERATED LIFE INS CO | MN | 1,849.9 |
| GUARDIAN LIFE INS CO OF AMERICA | NY | 55,226.5 |
| MIDWESTERN UNITED LIFE INS CO | IN | 233.4 |
| NATIONAL WESTERN LIFE INS CO | CO | 11,058.8 |
| SENTRY INS A MUTUAL CO | WI | 8,232.3 |
| SENTRY LIFE INS CO | WI | 6,735.9 |
| UNITED FARM FAMILY LIFE INS CO | IN | 2,312.3 |
| USAA LIFE INS CO | TX | 24,728.9 |
| **Rating: A-** | | |
| AMALGAMATED LIFE INS CO | NY | 124.9 |
| AMERICAN HEALTH & LIFE INS CO | TX | 840.1 |
| AMERICAN REPUBLIC INS CO | IA | 933.1 |
| ANTHEM LIFE INS CO | IN | 738.1 |
| AUTO-OWNERS LIFE INS CO | MI | 4,021.4 |
| CENTRAL STATES H & L CO OF OMAHA | NE | 411.0 |
| GARDEN STATE LIFE INS CO | TX | 131.8 |
| HUMANA BENEFIT PLAN OF ILLINOIS | IL | 394.7 |
| HUMANA INS CO (WI) | WI | 10,120.6 |
| MASSACHUSETTS MUTUAL LIFE INS CO | MA | 235,570.0 |
| MEDCO CONTAINMENT LIFE INS CO | PA | 1,113.2 |
| MOTORISTS COMMERCIAL MUTUAL INS CO | OH | 393.5 |
| MUTUAL OF AMERICA LIFE INS CO | NY | 20,499.3 |
| NEW YORK LIFE INS CO | NY | 176,417.0 |
| NORTHWESTERN MUTUAL LIFE INS CO | WI | 264,165.0 |
| PHYSICIANS LIFE INS CO | NE | 1,625.7 |
| PROTECTIVE INS CO | IN | 848.6 |
| **Rating: B+** | | |
| AETNA HEALTH & LIFE INS CO | CT | 2,403.1 |
| AMERICAN FAMILY LIFE ASR CO OF COLUM | NE | 113,507.0 |
| AMERICAN FIDELITY ASR CO | OK | 5,772.7 |
| AMERICAN UNITED LIFE INS CO | IN | 27,567.2 |
| ASSURITY LIFE INS CO | NE | 2,726.8 |
| AXA EQUITABLE LIFE INS CO | NY | 187,479.0 |
| BOSTON MUTUAL LIFE INS CO | MA | 1,424.8 |
| COMPANION LIFE INS CO | SC | 359.8 |
| DEARBORN NATIONAL LIFE INS CO | IL | 1,849.7 |
| DELAWARE AMERICAN LIFE INS CO | DE | 137.9 |
| FAMILY HERITAGE LIFE INS CO OF AMER | OH | 1,249.5 |
| GERBER LIFE INS CO | NY | 3,650.7 |
| GOVERNMENT PERSONNEL MUTUAL L I C | TX | 832.3 |
| JACKSON NATIONAL LIFE INS CO | MI | 222,617.0 |
| MIDLAND NATIONAL LIFE INS CO | IA | 55,140.0 |
| MINNESOTA LIFE INS CO | MN | 44,369.0 |
| MUTUAL OF OMAHA INS CO | NE | 7,661.2 |
| NATIONAL BENEFIT LIFE INS CO | NY | 537.3 |
| NATIONAL CASUALTY CO | OH | 406.6 |
| OHIO NATIONAL LIFE ASR CORP | OH | 4,048.6 |
| PRINCIPAL LIFE INS CO | IA | 185,959.0 |
| SB MUTL LIFE INS CO OF MA | MA | 3,015.1 |
| SENTRY SELECT INS CO | WI | 810.3 |
| STANDARD INS CO | OR | 23,414.5 |
| STATE FARM FIRE & CAS CO | IL | 39,417.8 |
| STATE FARM MUTUAL AUTOMOBILE INS CO | IL | 154,684.0 |
| SYMETRA LIFE INS CO | IA | 36,133.8 |
| TRUSTMARK INS CO | IL | 1,532.5 |
| TRUSTMARK LIFE INS CO | IL | 320.1 |
| UNITED WORLD LIFE INS CO | NE | 123.8 |
| USABLE LIFE | AR | 510.9 |
| VOYA RETIREMENT INS & ANNUITY CO | CT | 104,964.0 |

## New Jersey

| INSURANCE COMPANY NAME | DOM. STATE | TOTAL ASSETS ($MIL) |
|---|---|---|
| **Rating: A+** | | |
| PHYSICIANS MUTUAL INS CO | NE | 2,289.0 |
| TEACHERS INS & ANNUITY ASN OF AM | NY | 293,835.0 |
| **Rating: A** | | |
| BERKLEY LIFE & HEALTH INS CO | IA | 286.6 |
| FEDERATED LIFE INS CO | MN | 1,849.9 |
| GUARDIAN LIFE INS CO OF AMERICA | NY | 55,226.5 |
| MIDWESTERN UNITED LIFE INS CO | IN | 233.4 |
| NATIONAL WESTERN LIFE INS CO | CO | 11,058.8 |
| SENTRY INS A MUTUAL CO | WI | 8,232.3 |
| SENTRY LIFE INS CO | WI | 6,735.9 |
| SHELTERPOINT LIFE INS CO | NY | 110.1 |
| UNITED FARM FAMILY LIFE INS CO | IN | 2,312.3 |
| USAA LIFE INS CO | TX | 24,728.9 |
| **Rating: A-** | | |
| AMALGAMATED LIFE INS CO | NY | 124.9 |
| AMERICAN FAMILY LIFE ASR CO OF NY | NY | 945.4 |
| AMERICAN HEALTH & LIFE INS CO | TX | 840.1 |
| AMERICAN REPUBLIC INS CO | IA | 933.1 |
| ANTHEM LIFE INS CO | IN | 738.1 |
| CENTRAL STATES H & L CO OF OMAHA | NE | 411.0 |
| GARDEN STATE LIFE INS CO | TX | 131.8 |
| HORIZON HEALTHCARE OF NEW JERSEY INC | NJ | 1,358.6 |
| HUMANA BENEFIT PLAN OF ILLINOIS | IL | 394.7 |
| HUMANA INS CO (WI) | WI | 10,120.6 |
| MASSACHUSETTS MUTUAL LIFE INS CO | MA | 235,570.0 |
| MEDCO CONTAINMENT LIFE INS CO | PA | 1,113.2 |
| MOTORISTS COMMERCIAL MUTUAL INS CO | OH | 393.5 |
| MUTUAL OF AMERICA LIFE INS CO | NY | 20,499.3 |
| NEW YORK LIFE INS CO | NY | 176,417.0 |
| NIPPON LIFE INS CO OF AMERICA | IA | 219.6 |
| NORTHWESTERN MUTUAL LIFE INS CO | WI | 264,165.0 |
| PHYSICIANS LIFE INS CO | NE | 1,625.7 |
| PROTECTIVE INS CO | IN | 848.6 |
| **Rating: B+** | | |
| AETNA BETTER HEALTH INC (A NJ CORP) | NJ | 136.9 |
| AETNA HEALTH & LIFE INS CO | CT | 2,403.1 |
| AMERICAN FAMILY LIFE ASR CO OF COLUM | NE | 113,507.0 |
| AMERICAN FIDELITY ASR CO | OK | 5,772.7 |
| AMERICAN UNITED LIFE INS CO | IN | 27,567.2 |
| AMERIGROUP NEW JERSEY INC | NJ | 329.0 |
| ASSURITY LIFE INS CO | NE | 2,726.8 |
| AXA EQUITABLE LIFE INS CO | NY | 187,479.0 |
| BOSTON MUTUAL LIFE INS CO | MA | 1,424.8 |
| DEARBORN NATIONAL LIFE INS CO | IL | 1,849.7 |
| DELAWARE AMERICAN LIFE INS CO | DE | 137.9 |
| FAMILY HERITAGE LIFE INS CO OF AMER | OH | 1,249.5 |
| GEISINGER HEALTH PLAN | PA | 688.5 |
| GERBER LIFE INS CO | NY | 3,650.7 |
| JACKSON NATIONAL LIFE INS CO | MI | 222,617.0 |
| MIDLAND NATIONAL LIFE INS CO | IA | 55,140.0 |
| MINNESOTA LIFE INS CO | MN | 44,369.0 |
| MUTUAL OF OMAHA INS CO | NE | 7,661.2 |
| NATIONAL BENEFIT LIFE INS CO | NY | 537.3 |
| NATIONAL CASUALTY CO | OH | 406.6 |
| OHIO NATIONAL LIFE ASR CORP | OH | 4,048.6 |
| PRINCIPAL LIFE INS CO | IA | 185,959.0 |
| SB MUTL LIFE INS CO OF MA | MA | 3,015.1 |
| SENTRY SELECT INS CO | WI | 810.3 |
| STANDARD INS CO | OR | 23,414.5 |
| STATE FARM FIRE & CAS CO | IL | 39,417.8 |
| STATE FARM MUTUAL AUTOMOBILE INS CO | IL | 154,684.0 |
| SYMETRA LIFE INS CO | IA | 36,133.8 |
| TRUSTMARK INS CO | IL | 1,532.5 |
| TRUSTMARK LIFE INS CO | IL | 320.1 |
| UNITED WORLD LIFE INS CO | NE | 123.8 |
| USABLE LIFE | AR | 510.9 |
| VOYA RETIREMENT INS & ANNUITY CO | CT | 104,964.0 |

## New Mexico

| INSURANCE COMPANY NAME | DOM. STATE | TOTAL ASSETS ($MIL) |
|---|---|---|
| **Rating: A+** | | |
| COUNTRY LIFE INS CO | IL | 9,441.1 |
| PHYSICIANS MUTUAL INS CO | NE | 2,289.0 |
| TEACHERS INS & ANNUITY ASN OF AM | NY | 293,835.0 |
| **Rating: A** | | |
| BERKLEY LIFE & HEALTH INS CO | IA | 286.6 |
| FEDERATED LIFE INS CO | MN | 1,849.9 |
| GUARDIAN LIFE INS CO OF AMERICA | NY | 55,226.5 |
| MIDWESTERN UNITED LIFE INS CO | IN | 233.4 |
| NATIONAL WESTERN LIFE INS CO | CO | 11,058.8 |
| SENTRY INS A MUTUAL CO | WI | 8,232.3 |
| SENTRY LIFE INS CO | WI | 6,735.9 |
| USAA LIFE INS CO | TX | 24,728.9 |
| **Rating: A-** | | |
| AMALGAMATED LIFE INS CO | NY | 124.9 |
| AMERICAN HEALTH & LIFE INS CO | TX | 840.1 |
| AMERICAN REPUBLIC INS CO | IA | 933.1 |
| ANTHEM LIFE INS CO | IN | 738.1 |
| AUTO-OWNERS LIFE INS CO | MI | 4,021.4 |
| CENTRAL STATES H & L CO OF OMAHA | NE | 411.0 |
| GARDEN STATE LIFE INS CO | TX | 131.8 |
| HUMANA BENEFIT PLAN OF ILLINOIS | IL | 394.7 |
| HUMANA INS CO (WI) | WI | 10,120.6 |
| MASSACHUSETTS MUTUAL LIFE INS CO | MA | 235,570.0 |
| MEDCO CONTAINMENT LIFE INS CO | PA | 1,113.2 |
| MEDICO CORP LIFE INS CO | NE | 63.9 |
| MOTORISTS COMMERCIAL MUTUAL INS CO | OH | 393.5 |
| MUTUAL OF AMERICA LIFE INS CO | NY | 20,499.3 |
| NEW YORK LIFE INS CO | NY | 176,417.0 |
| NIPPON LIFE INS CO OF AMERICA | IA | 219.6 |
| NORTHWESTERN MUTUAL LIFE INS CO | WI | 264,165.0 |
| PACIFIC GUARDIAN LIFE INS CO LTD | HI | 552.3 |
| PHYSICIANS LIFE INS CO | NE | 1,625.7 |
| PROTECTIVE INS CO | IN | 848.6 |
| STANDARD LIFE & ACCIDENT INS CO | TX | 516.7 |
| **Rating: B+** | | |
| AETNA HEALTH & LIFE INS CO | CT | 2,403.1 |
| AMERICAN FAMILY LIFE ASR CO OF COLUM | NE | 113,507.0 |
| AMERICAN FAMILY MUTL INS CO SI | WI | 17,048.2 |
| AMERICAN FIDELITY ASR CO | OK | 5,772.7 |
| AMERICAN UNITED LIFE INS CO | IN | 27,567.2 |
| ASSURITY LIFE INS CO | NE | 2,726.8 |
| AXA EQUITABLE LIFE INS CO | NY | 187,479.0 |
| BEST LIFE & HEALTH INS CO | TX | 20.9 |
| BOSTON MUTUAL LIFE INS CO | MA | 1,424.8 |
| COMPANION LIFE INS CO | SC | 359.8 |
| DEARBORN NATIONAL LIFE INS CO | IL | 1,849.7 |
| DELAWARE AMERICAN LIFE INS CO | DE | 137.9 |
| FAMILY HERITAGE LIFE INS CO OF AMER | OH | 1,249.5 |
| FARM BUREAU LIFE INS CO | IA | 8,948.8 |
| GERBER LIFE INS CO | NY | 3,650.7 |
| GOVERNMENT PERSONNEL MUTUAL L I C | TX | 832.3 |
| JACKSON NATIONAL LIFE INS CO | MI | 222,617.0 |
| MIDLAND NATIONAL LIFE INS CO | IA | 55,140.0 |
| MINNESOTA LIFE INS CO | MN | 44,369.0 |
| MUTUAL OF OMAHA INS CO | NE | 7,661.2 |
| NATIONAL BENEFIT LIFE INS CO | NY | 537.3 |
| NATIONAL CASUALTY CO | OH | 406.6 |
| OHIO NATIONAL LIFE ASR CORP | OH | 4,048.6 |
| PRINCIPAL LIFE INS CO | IA | 185,959.0 |
| SB MUTL LIFE INS CO OF MA | MA | 3,015.1 |
| SENTRY SELECT INS CO | WI | 810.3 |
| SOUTHERN PIONEER LIFE INS CO | AR | 15.7 |
| STANDARD INS CO | OR | 23,414.5 |
| STATE FARM FIRE & CAS CO | IL | 39,417.8 |
| STATE FARM MUTUAL AUTOMOBILE INS CO | IL | 154,684.0 |
| SYMETRA LIFE INS CO | IA | 36,133.8 |
| TRUSTMARK INS CO | IL | 1,532.5 |
| TRUSTMARK LIFE INS CO | IL | 320.1 |
| UNITED WORLD LIFE INS CO | NE | 123.8 |
| USABLE LIFE | AR | 510.9 |
| VOYA RETIREMENT INS & ANNUITY CO | CT | 104,964.0 |

## New York

| INSURANCE COMPANY NAME | DOM. STATE | TOTAL ASSETS ($MIL) |
|---|---|---|
| **Rating: A+** | | |
| PHYSICIANS MUTUAL INS CO | NE | 2,289.0 |
| TEACHERS INS & ANNUITY ASN OF AM | NY | 293,835.0 |
| **Rating: A** | | |
| ALLIANZ LIFE INS CO OF NY | NY | 3,347.7 |
| BERKLEY LIFE & HEALTH INS CO | IA | 286.6 |
| FEDERATED LIFE INS CO | MN | 1,849.9 |
| FIRST RELIANCE STANDARD LIFE INS CO | NY | 197.5 |
| GUARDIAN LIFE INS CO OF AMERICA | NY | 55,226.5 |
| SENTRY INS A MUTUAL CO | WI | 8,232.3 |
| SHELTERPOINT LIFE INS CO | NY | 110.1 |
| **Rating: A-** | | |
| AMALGAMATED LIFE INS CO | NY | 124.9 |
| AMERICAN FAMILY LIFE ASR CO OF NY | NY | 945.4 |
| CIGNA LIFE INS CO OF NEW YORK | NY | 403.0 |
| GARDEN STATE LIFE INS CO | TX | 131.8 |
| LIFE INS CO OF BOSTON & NEW YORK | NY | 148.4 |
| MASSACHUSETTS MUTUAL LIFE INS CO | MA | 235,570.0 |
| MOTORISTS COMMERCIAL MUTUAL INS CO | OH | 393.5 |
| MUTUAL OF AMERICA LIFE INS CO | NY | 20,499.3 |
| NEW YORK LIFE INS CO | NY | 176,417.0 |
| NIPPON LIFE INS CO OF AMERICA | IA | 219.6 |
| NORTHWESTERN MUTUAL LIFE INS CO | WI | 264,165.0 |
| PROTECTIVE INS CO | IN | 848.6 |
| STANDARD LIFE INS CO OF NY | NY | 292.4 |
| **Rating: B+** | | |
| AETNA HEALTH & LIFE INS CO | CT | 2,403.1 |
| AMERICAN UNITED LIFE INS CO | IN | 27,567.2 |
| AXA EQUITABLE LIFE INS CO | NY | 187,479.0 |
| BOSTON MUTUAL LIFE INS CO | MA | 1,424.8 |
| DEARBORN NATIONAL LIFE INS CO OF NY | NY | 37.5 |
| DELAWARE AMERICAN LIFE INS CO | DE | 137.9 |
| EXCELLUS HEALTH PLAN INC | NY | 3,365.4 |
| FIRST SYMETRA NATL LIFE INS CO OF NY | NY | 1,776.8 |
| GERBER LIFE INS CO | NY | 3,650.7 |
| GLOBE LIFE INSURANCE CO OF NY | NY | 237.8 |
| MUTUAL OF OMAHA INS CO | NE | 7,661.2 |
| NATIONAL BENEFIT LIFE INS CO | NY | 537.3 |
| NATIONAL CASUALTY CO | OH | 406.6 |
| NATIONAL INCOME LIFE INS CO | NY | 223.3 |
| OXFORD HEALTH PLANS (NY) INC | NY | 646.3 |
| PRINCIPAL LIFE INS CO | IA | 185,959.0 |
| SENTRY SELECT INS CO | WI | 810.3 |
| STATE FARM FIRE & CAS CO | IL | 39,417.8 |
| STATE FARM MUTUAL AUTOMOBILE INS CO | IL | 154,684.0 |
| TRUSTMARK INS CO | IL | 1,532.5 |
| TRUSTMARK LIFE INS CO | IL | 320.1 |
| UNITED HEALTHCARE OF NY INC | NY | 1,277.0 |
| VOYA RETIREMENT INS & ANNUITY CO | CT | 104,964.0 |

## North Carolina

| INSURANCE COMPANY NAME | DOM. STATE | TOTAL ASSETS ($MIL) |
|---|---|---|
| **Rating: A+** | | |
| COUNTRY LIFE INS CO | IL | 9,441.1 |
| PHYSICIANS MUTUAL INS CO | NE | 2,289.0 |
| TEACHERS INS & ANNUITY ASN OF AM | NY | 293,835.0 |
| **Rating: A** | | |
| BERKLEY LIFE & HEALTH INS CO | IA | 286.6 |
| FEDERATED LIFE INS CO | MN | 1,849.9 |
| GUARDIAN LIFE INS CO OF AMERICA | NY | 55,226.5 |
| MEDICAL MUTUAL OF OHIO | OH | 2,136.4 |
| MIDWESTERN UNITED LIFE INS CO | IN | 233.4 |
| NATIONAL WESTERN LIFE INS CO | CO | 11,058.8 |
| SENTRY INS A MUTUAL CO | WI | 8,232.3 |
| SENTRY LIFE INS CO | WI | 6,735.9 |
| SHELTERPOINT LIFE INS CO | NY | 110.1 |
| SOUTHERN FARM BUREAU LIFE INS CO | MS | 14,163.7 |
| UNITED FARM FAMILY LIFE INS CO | IN | 2,312.3 |
| USAA LIFE INS CO | TX | 24,728.9 |
| **Rating: A-** | | |
| AMALGAMATED LIFE INS CO | NY | 124.9 |
| AMERICAN HEALTH & LIFE INS CO | TX | 840.1 |
| AMERICAN REPUBLIC INS CO | IA | 933.1 |
| ANTHEM LIFE INS CO | IN | 738.1 |
| AUTO-OWNERS LIFE INS CO | MI | 4,021.4 |
| CENTRAL STATES H & L CO OF OMAHA | NE | 411.0 |
| ERIE FAMILY LIFE INS CO | PA | 2,448.7 |
| GARDEN STATE LIFE INS CO | TX | 131.8 |
| HUMANA BENEFIT PLAN OF ILLINOIS | IL | 394.7 |
| HUMANA INS CO (WI) | WI | 10,120.6 |
| MASSACHUSETTS MUTUAL LIFE INS CO | MA | 235,570.0 |
| MEDCO CONTAINMENT LIFE INS CO | PA | 1,113.2 |
| MEDICO CORP LIFE INS CO | NE | 63.9 |
| MOTORISTS COMMERCIAL MUTUAL INS CO | OH | 393.5 |
| MUTUAL OF AMERICA LIFE INS CO | NY | 20,499.3 |
| NEW YORK LIFE INS CO | NY | 176,417.0 |
| NIPPON LIFE INS CO OF AMERICA | IA | 219.6 |
| NORTHWESTERN MUTUAL LIFE INS CO | WI | 264,165.0 |
| PHYSICIANS LIFE INS CO | NE | 1,625.7 |
| PROTECTIVE INS CO | IN | 848.6 |
| STANDARD LIFE & ACCIDENT INS CO | TX | 516.7 |
| **Rating: B+** | | |
| AETNA HEALTH & LIFE INS CO | CT | 2,403.1 |
| AMERICAN FAMILY LIFE ASR CO OF COLUM | NE | 113,507.0 |
| AMERICAN FAMILY MUTL INS CO SI | WI | 17,048.2 |
| AMERICAN FIDELITY ASR CO | OK | 5,772.7 |
| AMERICAN UNITED LIFE INS CO | IN | 27,567.2 |
| AMFIRST INS CO | OK | 57.6 |
| ASSURITY LIFE INS CO | NE | 2,726.8 |
| AXA EQUITABLE LIFE INS CO | NY | 187,479.0 |
| BEST LIFE & HEALTH INS CO | TX | 20.9 |
| BOSTON MUTUAL LIFE INS CO | MA | 1,424.8 |
| COMPANION LIFE INS CO | SC | 359.8 |
| DEARBORN NATIONAL LIFE INS CO | IL | 1,849.7 |
| DELAWARE AMERICAN LIFE INS CO | DE | 137.9 |
| FAMILY HERITAGE LIFE INS CO OF AMER | OH | 1,249.5 |
| GERBER LIFE INS CO | NY | 3,650.7 |
| GOVERNMENT PERSONNEL MUTUAL L I C | TX | 832.3 |
| JACKSON NATIONAL LIFE INS CO | MI | 222,617.0 |
| MIDLAND NATIONAL LIFE INS CO | IA | 55,140.0 |
| MINNESOTA LIFE INS CO | MN | 44,369.0 |
| MUTUAL OF OMAHA INS CO | NE | 7,661.2 |
| NATIONAL BENEFIT LIFE INS CO | NY | 537.3 |
| NATIONAL CASUALTY CO | OH | 406.6 |
| OHIO NATIONAL LIFE ASR CORP | OH | 4,048.6 |
| PRINCIPAL LIFE INS CO | IA | 185,959.0 |
| SB MUTL LIFE INS CO OF MA | MA | 3,015.1 |
| SENTRY SELECT INS CO | WI | 810.3 |
| STANDARD INS CO | OR | 23,414.5 |
| STATE FARM FIRE & CAS CO | IL | 39,417.8 |
| STATE FARM MUTUAL AUTOMOBILE INS CO | IL | 154,684.0 |
| SYMETRA LIFE INS CO | IA | 36,133.8 |
| TRUSTMARK INS CO | IL | 1,532.5 |
| TRUSTMARK LIFE INS CO | IL | 320.1 |
| UNITED WORLD LIFE INS CO | NE | 123.8 |
| USABLE LIFE | AR | 510.9 |
| VOYA RETIREMENT INS & ANNUITY CO | CT | 104,964.0 |

## North Dakota

| INSURANCE COMPANY NAME | DOM. STATE | TOTAL ASSETS ($MIL) |
|---|---|---|
| **Rating: A+** | | |
| COUNTRY LIFE INS CO | IL | 9,441.1 |
| PHYSICIANS MUTUAL INS CO | NE | 2,289.0 |
| TEACHERS INS & ANNUITY ASN OF AM | NY | 293,835.0 |
| **Rating: A** | | |
| ALLIANZ LIFE INS CO OF NY | NY | 3,347.7 |
| BERKLEY LIFE & HEALTH INS CO | IA | 286.6 |
| FEDERATED LIFE INS CO | MN | 1,849.9 |
| GUARDIAN LIFE INS CO OF AMERICA | NY | 55,226.5 |
| MIDWESTERN UNITED LIFE INS CO | IN | 233.4 |
| NATIONAL WESTERN LIFE INS CO | CO | 11,058.8 |
| SENTRY INS A MUTUAL CO | WI | 8,232.3 |
| SENTRY LIFE INS CO | WI | 6,735.9 |
| UNITED FARM FAMILY LIFE INS CO | IN | 2,312.3 |
| USAA LIFE INS CO | TX | 24,728.9 |
| **Rating: A-** | | |
| AMALGAMATED LIFE INS CO | NY | 124.9 |
| AMERICAN FAMILY LIFE ASR CO OF NY | NY | 945.4 |
| AMERICAN HEALTH & LIFE INS CO | TX | 840.1 |
| AMERICAN REPUBLIC INS CO | IA | 933.1 |
| ANTHEM LIFE INS CO | IN | 738.1 |
| AUTO-OWNERS LIFE INS CO | MI | 4,021.4 |
| CENTRAL STATES H & L CO OF OMAHA | NE | 411.0 |
| GARDEN STATE LIFE INS CO | TX | 131.8 |
| HUMANA BENEFIT PLAN OF ILLINOIS | IL | 394.7 |
| HUMANA INS CO (WI) | WI | 10,120.6 |
| MASSACHUSETTS MUTUAL LIFE INS CO | MA | 235,570.0 |
| MEDCO CONTAINMENT LIFE INS CO | PA | 1,113.2 |
| MEDICO CORP LIFE INS CO | NE | 63.9 |
| MOTORISTS COMMERCIAL MUTUAL INS CO | OH | 393.5 |
| MUTUAL OF AMERICA LIFE INS CO | NY | 20,499.3 |
| NEW YORK LIFE INS CO | NY | 176,417.0 |
| NIPPON LIFE INS CO OF AMERICA | IA | 219.6 |
| NORTHWESTERN MUTUAL LIFE INS CO | WI | 264,165.0 |
| PHYSICIANS LIFE INS CO | NE | 1,625.7 |
| PROTECTIVE INS CO | IN | 848.6 |
| STANDARD LIFE & ACCIDENT INS CO | TX | 516.7 |
| **Rating: B+** | | |
| AETNA HEALTH & LIFE INS CO | CT | 2,403.1 |
| AMERICAN FAMILY LIFE ASR CO OF COLUM | NE | 113,507.0 |
| AMERICAN FAMILY MUTL INS CO SI | WI | 17,048.2 |
| AMERICAN FIDELITY ASR CO | OK | 5,772.7 |
| AMERICAN UNITED LIFE INS CO | IN | 27,567.2 |
| ASSURITY LIFE INS CO | NE | 2,726.8 |
| AXA EQUITABLE LIFE INS CO | NY | 187,479.0 |
| BEST LIFE & HEALTH INS CO | TX | 20.9 |
| BOSTON MUTUAL LIFE INS CO | MA | 1,424.8 |
| COMPANION LIFE INS CO | SC | 359.8 |
| DEARBORN NATIONAL LIFE INS CO | IL | 1,849.7 |
| DELAWARE AMERICAN LIFE INS CO | DE | 137.9 |
| FAMILY HERITAGE LIFE INS CO OF AMER | OH | 1,249.5 |
| FARM BUREAU LIFE INS CO | IA | 8,948.8 |
| GERBER LIFE INS CO | NY | 3,650.7 |
| GOVERNMENT PERSONNEL MUTUAL L I C | TX | 832.3 |
| JACKSON NATIONAL LIFE INS CO | MI | 222,617.0 |
| MIDLAND NATIONAL LIFE INS CO | IA | 55,140.0 |
| MINNESOTA LIFE INS CO | MN | 44,369.0 |
| MUTUAL OF OMAHA INS CO | NE | 7,661.2 |
| NATIONAL BENEFIT LIFE INS CO | NY | 537.3 |
| NATIONAL CASUALTY CO | OH | 406.6 |
| OHIO NATIONAL LIFE ASR CORP | OH | 4,048.6 |
| PRINCIPAL LIFE INS CO | IA | 185,959.0 |
| SB MUTL LIFE INS CO OF MA | MA | 3,015.1 |
| SENTRY SELECT INS CO | WI | 810.3 |
| STANDARD INS CO | OR | 23,414.5 |
| STATE FARM FIRE & CAS CO | IL | 39,417.8 |
| STATE FARM MUTUAL AUTOMOBILE INS CO | IL | 154,684.0 |
| SYMETRA LIFE INS CO | IA | 36,133.8 |
| TRUSTMARK INS CO | IL | 1,532.5 |
| TRUSTMARK LIFE INS CO | IL | 320.1 |
| UNITED WORLD LIFE INS CO | NE | 123.8 |
| USABLE LIFE | AR | 510.9 |
| VOYA RETIREMENT INS & ANNUITY CO | CT | 104,964.0 |

## Ohio

| INSURANCE COMPANY NAME | DOM. STATE | TOTAL ASSETS ($MIL) |
|---|---|---|
| **Rating: A+** | | |
| COUNTRY LIFE INS CO | IL | 9,441.1 |
| PHYSICIANS MUTUAL INS CO | NE | 2,289.0 |
| TEACHERS INS & ANNUITY ASN OF AM | NY | 293,835.0 |
| **Rating: A** | | |
| BERKLEY LIFE & HEALTH INS CO | IA | 286.6 |
| FEDERATED LIFE INS CO | MN | 1,849.9 |
| GUARDIAN LIFE INS CO OF AMERICA | NY | 55,226.5 |
| MEDICAL MUTUAL OF OHIO | OH | 2,136.4 |
| MIDWESTERN UNITED LIFE INS CO | IN | 233.4 |
| NATIONAL WESTERN LIFE INS CO | CO | 11,058.8 |
| SENTRY INS A MUTUAL CO | WI | 8,232.3 |
| SENTRY LIFE INS CO | WI | 6,735.9 |
| UNITED FARM FAMILY LIFE INS CO | IN | 2,312.3 |
| USAA LIFE INS CO | TX | 24,728.9 |
| **Rating: A-** | | |
| AMALGAMATED LIFE INS CO | NY | 124.9 |
| AMERICAN HEALTH & LIFE INS CO | TX | 840.1 |
| AMERICAN REPUBLIC INS CO | IA | 933.1 |
| ANTHEM LIFE INS CO | IN | 738.1 |
| AUTO-OWNERS LIFE INS CO | MI | 4,021.4 |
| CENTRAL STATES H & L CO OF OMAHA | NE | 411.0 |
| ERIE FAMILY LIFE INS CO | PA | 2,448.7 |
| GARDEN STATE LIFE INS CO | TX | 131.8 |
| HUMANA BENEFIT PLAN OF ILLINOIS | IL | 394.7 |
| HUMANA INS CO (WI) | WI | 10,120.6 |
| MASSACHUSETTS MUTUAL LIFE INS CO | MA | 235,570.0 |
| MEDCO CONTAINMENT LIFE INS CO | PA | 1,113.2 |
| MEDICO CORP LIFE INS CO | NE | 63.9 |
| MOTORISTS COMMERCIAL MUTUAL INS CO | OH | 393.5 |
| MUTUAL OF AMERICA LIFE INS CO | NY | 20,499.3 |
| NEW YORK LIFE INS CO | NY | 176,417.0 |
| NIPPON LIFE INS CO OF AMERICA | IA | 219.6 |
| NORTHWESTERN MUTUAL LIFE INS CO | WI | 264,165.0 |
| PARAMOUNT ADVANTAGE | OH | 305.9 |
| PARAMOUNT INS CO (OH) | OH | 88.2 |
| PHYSICIANS LIFE INS CO | NE | 1,625.7 |
| PROTECTIVE INS CO | IN | 848.6 |
| STANDARD LIFE & ACCIDENT INS CO | TX | 516.7 |
| UPMC HEALTH PLAN INC | PA | 640.7 |
| **Rating: B+** | | |
| AETNA HEALTH & LIFE INS CO | CT | 2,403.1 |
| AMERICAN FAMILY LIFE ASR CO OF COLUM | NE | 113,507.0 |
| AMERICAN FAMILY MUTL INS CO SI | WI | 17,048.2 |
| AMERICAN FIDELITY ASR CO | OK | 5,772.7 |
| AMERICAN UNITED LIFE INS CO | IN | 27,567.2 |
| AMFIRST INS CO | OK | 57.6 |
| ASSURITY LIFE INS CO | NE | 2,726.8 |
| AXA EQUITABLE LIFE INS CO | NY | 187,479.0 |
| BEST LIFE & HEALTH INS CO | TX | 20.9 |
| BOSTON MUTUAL LIFE INS CO | MA | 1,424.8 |
| COMMUNITY INS CO (OH) | OH | 2,274.1 |
| COMPANION LIFE INS CO | SC | 359.8 |
| DEARBORN NATIONAL LIFE INS CO | IL | 1,849.7 |
| DELAWARE AMERICAN LIFE INS CO | DE | 137.9 |
| FAMILY HERITAGE LIFE INS CO OF AMER | OH | 1,249.5 |
| GERBER LIFE INS CO | NY | 3,650.7 |
| GOVERNMENT PERSONNEL MUTUAL L I C | TX | 832.3 |
| JACKSON NATIONAL LIFE INS CO | MI | 222,617.0 |
| MEDICAL HEALTH INS CORP OF OHIO | OH | 138.6 |
| MIDLAND NATIONAL LIFE INS CO | IA | 55,140.0 |
| MINNESOTA LIFE INS CO | MN | 44,369.0 |
| MUTUAL OF OMAHA INS CO | NE | 7,661.2 |
| NATIONAL BENEFIT LIFE INS CO | NY | 537.3 |
| NATIONAL CASUALTY CO | OH | 406.6 |
| OHIO NATIONAL LIFE ASR CORP | OH | 4,048.6 |
| PRINCIPAL LIFE INS CO | IA | 185,959.0 |
| SB MUTL LIFE INS CO OF MA | MA | 3,015.1 |
| SENTRY SELECT INS CO | WI | 810.3 |
| SHELTER LIFE INS CO | MO | 1,238.3 |
| STANDARD INS CO | OR | 23,414.5 |
| STATE FARM FIRE & CAS CO | IL | 39,417.8 |
| STATE FARM MUTUAL AUTOMOBILE INS CO | IL | 154,684.0 |
| SYMETRA LIFE INS CO | IA | 36,133.8 |
| TRUSTMARK INS CO | IL | 1,532.5 |
| TRUSTMARK LIFE INS CO | IL | 320.1 |
| UNITED WORLD LIFE INS CO | NE | 123.8 |
| USABLE LIFE | AR | 510.9 |
| VOYA RETIREMENT INS & ANNUITY CO | CT | 104,964.0 |

## Oklahoma

| INSURANCE COMPANY NAME | DOM. STATE | TOTAL ASSETS ($MIL) |
|---|---|---|
| **Rating: A+** | | |
| COUNTRY LIFE INS CO | IL | 9,441.1 |
| PHYSICIANS MUTUAL INS CO | NE | 2,289.0 |
| TEACHERS INS & ANNUITY ASN OF AM | NY | 293,835.0 |
| **Rating: A** | | |
| BERKLEY LIFE & HEALTH INS CO | IA | 286.6 |
| FEDERATED LIFE INS CO | MN | 1,849.9 |
| GUARDIAN LIFE INS CO OF AMERICA | NY | 55,226.5 |
| MIDWESTERN UNITED LIFE INS CO | IN | 233.4 |
| NATIONAL WESTERN LIFE INS CO | CO | 11,058.8 |
| SENTRY INS A MUTUAL CO | WI | 8,232.3 |
| SENTRY LIFE INS CO | WI | 6,735.9 |
| USAA LIFE INS CO | TX | 24,728.9 |
| **Rating: A-** | | |
| AMALGAMATED LIFE INS CO | NY | 124.9 |
| AMERICAN HEALTH & LIFE INS CO | TX | 840.1 |
| AMERICAN REPUBLIC INS CO | IA | 933.1 |
| ANTHEM LIFE INS CO | IN | 738.1 |
| CENTRAL STATES H & L CO OF OMAHA | NE | 411.0 |
| GARDEN STATE LIFE INS CO | TX | 131.8 |
| HUMANA BENEFIT PLAN OF ILLINOIS | IL | 394.7 |
| HUMANA INS CO (WI) | WI | 10,120.6 |
| MASSACHUSETTS MUTUAL LIFE INS CO | MA | 235,570.0 |
| MEDCO CONTAINMENT LIFE INS CO | PA | 1,113.2 |
| MEDICO CORP LIFE INS CO | NE | 63.9 |
| MOTORISTS COMMERCIAL MUTUAL INS CO | OH | 393.5 |
| MUTUAL OF AMERICA LIFE INS CO | NY | 20,499.3 |
| NEW YORK LIFE INS CO | NY | 176,417.0 |
| NIPPON LIFE INS CO OF AMERICA | IA | 219.6 |
| NORTHWESTERN MUTUAL LIFE INS CO | WI | 264,165.0 |
| PACIFIC GUARDIAN LIFE INS CO LTD | HI | 552.3 |
| PHYSICIANS LIFE INS CO | NE | 1,625.7 |
| PROTECTIVE INS CO | IN | 848.6 |
| STANDARD LIFE & ACCIDENT INS CO | TX | 516.7 |
| **Rating: B+** | | |
| AETNA HEALTH & LIFE INS CO | CT | 2,403.1 |
| AMERICAN FAMILY LIFE ASR CO OF COLUM | NE | 113,507.0 |
| AMERICAN FIDELITY ASR CO | OK | 5,772.7 |
| AMERICAN UNITED LIFE INS CO | IN | 27,567.2 |
| AMFIRST INS CO | OK | 57.6 |
| ASSURITY LIFE INS CO | NE | 2,726.8 |
| AXA EQUITABLE LIFE INS CO | NY | 187,479.0 |
| BEST LIFE & HEALTH INS CO | TX | 20.9 |
| BOSTON MUTUAL LIFE INS CO | MA | 1,424.8 |
| COMMUNITYCARE HMO INC | OK | 231.6 |
| COMPANION LIFE INS CO | SC | 359.8 |
| DEARBORN NATIONAL LIFE INS CO | IL | 1,849.7 |
| DELAWARE AMERICAN LIFE INS CO | DE | 137.9 |
| FAMILY HERITAGE LIFE INS CO OF AMER | OH | 1,249.5 |
| FARM BUREAU LIFE INS CO | IA | 8,948.8 |
| GERBER LIFE INS CO | NY | 3,650.7 |
| GOVERNMENT PERSONNEL MUTUAL L I C | TX | 832.3 |
| JACKSON NATIONAL LIFE INS CO | MI | 222,617.0 |
| MIDLAND NATIONAL LIFE INS CO | IA | 55,140.0 |
| MINNESOTA LIFE INS CO | MN | 44,369.0 |
| MUTUAL OF OMAHA INS CO | NE | 7,661.2 |
| NATIONAL BENEFIT LIFE INS CO | NY | 537.3 |
| NATIONAL CASUALTY CO | OH | 406.6 |
| OHIO NATIONAL LIFE ASR CORP | OH | 4,048.6 |
| PRINCIPAL LIFE INS CO | IA | 185,959.0 |
| SB MUTL LIFE INS CO OF MA | MA | 3,015.1 |
| SENTRY SELECT INS CO | WI | 810.3 |
| SHELTER LIFE INS CO | MO | 1,238.3 |
| SOUTHERN PIONEER LIFE INS CO | AR | 15.7 |
| STANDARD INS CO | OR | 23,414.5 |
| STATE FARM FIRE & CAS CO | IL | 39,417.8 |
| STATE FARM MUTUAL AUTOMOBILE INS CO | IL | 154,684.0 |
| SYMETRA LIFE INS CO | IA | 36,133.8 |
| TRUSTMARK INS CO | IL | 1,532.5 |
| TRUSTMARK LIFE INS CO | IL | 320.1 |
| UNITED WORLD LIFE INS CO | NE | 123.8 |
| USABLE LIFE | AR | 510.9 |
| VOYA RETIREMENT INS & ANNUITY CO | CT | 104,964.0 |

## Oregon

| INSURANCE COMPANY NAME | DOM. STATE | TOTAL ASSETS ($MIL) |
|---|---|---|
| **Rating: A+** | | |
| COUNTRY LIFE INS CO | IL | 9,441.1 |
| PHYSICIANS MUTUAL INS CO | NE | 2,289.0 |
| PROVIDENCE HEALTH PLAN | OR | 910.5 |
| TEACHERS INS & ANNUITY ASN OF AM | NY | 293,835.0 |
| **Rating: A** | | |
| BERKLEY LIFE & HEALTH INS CO | IA | 286.6 |
| FEDERATED LIFE INS CO | MN | 1,849.9 |
| GUARDIAN LIFE INS CO OF AMERICA | NY | 55,226.5 |
| LIFEWISE ASR CO | WA | 166.6 |
| MIDWESTERN UNITED LIFE INS CO | IN | 233.4 |
| NATIONAL WESTERN LIFE INS CO | CO | 11,058.8 |
| SENTRY INS A MUTUAL CO | WI | 8,232.3 |
| SENTRY LIFE INS CO | WI | 6,735.9 |
| USAA LIFE INS CO | TX | 24,728.9 |
| **Rating: A-** | | |
| AMALGAMATED LIFE INS CO | NY | 124.9 |
| AMERICAN HEALTH & LIFE INS CO | TX | 840.1 |
| AMERICAN REPUBLIC INS CO | IA | 933.1 |
| ANTHEM LIFE INS CO | IN | 738.1 |
| AUTO-OWNERS LIFE INS CO | MI | 4,021.4 |
| CENTRAL STATES H & L CO OF OMAHA | NE | 411.0 |
| GARDEN STATE LIFE INS CO | TX | 131.8 |
| HUMANA BENEFIT PLAN OF ILLINOIS | IL | 394.7 |
| HUMANA INS CO (WI) | WI | 10,120.6 |
| MASSACHUSETTS MUTUAL LIFE INS CO | MA | 235,570.0 |
| MEDCO CONTAINMENT LIFE INS CO | PA | 1,113.2 |
| MEDICO CORP LIFE INS CO | NE | 63.9 |
| MOTORISTS COMMERCIAL MUTUAL INS CO | OH | 393.5 |
| MUTUAL OF AMERICA LIFE INS CO | NY | 20,499.3 |
| NEW YORK LIFE INS CO | NY | 176,417.0 |
| NIPPON LIFE INS CO OF AMERICA | IA | 219.6 |
| NORTHWESTERN MUTUAL LIFE INS CO | WI | 264,165.0 |
| PACIFIC GUARDIAN LIFE INS CO LTD | HI | 552.3 |
| PHYSICIANS LIFE INS CO | NE | 1,625.7 |
| PROTECTIVE INS CO | IN | 848.6 |
| STANDARD LIFE & ACCIDENT INS CO | TX | 516.7 |
| **Rating: B+** | | |
| AETNA HEALTH & LIFE INS CO | CT | 2,403.1 |
| AMERICAN FAMILY LIFE ASR CO OF COLUM | NE | 113,507.0 |
| AMERICAN FAMILY MUTL INS CO SI | WI | 17,048.2 |
| AMERICAN FIDELITY ASR CO | OK | 5,772.7 |
| AMERICAN UNITED LIFE INS CO | IN | 27,567.2 |
| ASSURITY LIFE INS CO | NE | 2,726.8 |
| AXA EQUITABLE LIFE INS CO | NY | 187,479.0 |
| BEST LIFE & HEALTH INS CO | TX | 20.9 |
| BOSTON MUTUAL LIFE INS CO | MA | 1,424.8 |
| COMPANION LIFE INS CO | SC | 359.8 |
| DEARBORN NATIONAL LIFE INS CO | IL | 1,849.7 |
| DELAWARE AMERICAN LIFE INS CO | DE | 137.9 |
| FAMILY HERITAGE LIFE INS CO OF AMER | OH | 1,249.5 |
| FARM BUREAU LIFE INS CO | IA | 8,948.8 |
| GERBER LIFE INS CO | NY | 3,650.7 |
| GOVERNMENT PERSONNEL MUTUAL L I C | TX | 832.3 |
| JACKSON NATIONAL LIFE INS CO | MI | 222,617.0 |
| MIDLAND NATIONAL LIFE INS CO | IA | 55,140.0 |
| MINNESOTA LIFE INS CO | MN | 44,369.0 |
| MUTUAL OF OMAHA INS CO | NE | 7,661.2 |
| NATIONAL BENEFIT LIFE INS CO | NY | 537.3 |
| NATIONAL CASUALTY CO | OH | 406.6 |
| OHIO NATIONAL LIFE ASR CORP | OH | 4,048.6 |
| PRINCIPAL LIFE INS CO | IA | 185,959.0 |
| REGENCE BL CROSS BL SHIELD OREGON | OR | 1,253.4 |
| SB MUTL LIFE INS CO OF MA | MA | 3,015.1 |
| SENTRY SELECT INS CO | WI | 810.3 |
| STANDARD INS CO | OR | 23,414.5 |
| STATE FARM FIRE & CAS CO | IL | 39,417.8 |
| STATE FARM MUTUAL AUTOMOBILE INS CO | IL | 154,684.0 |
| SYMETRA LIFE INS CO | IA | 36,133.8 |
| TRUSTMARK INS CO | IL | 1,532.5 |
| TRUSTMARK LIFE INS CO | IL | 320.1 |
| UNITED WORLD LIFE INS CO | NE | 123.8 |
| USABLE LIFE | AR | 510.9 |
| VOYA RETIREMENT INS & ANNUITY CO | CT | 104,964.0 |

## Pennsylvania

| INSURANCE COMPANY NAME | DOM. STATE | TOTAL ASSETS ($MIL) |
|---|---|---|
| **Rating: A+** | | |
| COUNTRY LIFE INS CO | IL | 9,441.1 |
| PHYSICIANS MUTUAL INS CO | NE | 2,289.0 |
| TEACHERS INS & ANNUITY ASN OF AM | NY | 293,835.0 |
| **Rating: A** | | |
| BERKLEY LIFE & HEALTH INS CO | IA | 286.6 |
| FEDERATED LIFE INS CO | MN | 1,849.9 |
| GUARDIAN LIFE INS CO OF AMERICA | NY | 55,226.5 |
| MEDICAL MUTUAL OF OHIO | OH | 2,136.4 |
| MIDWESTERN UNITED LIFE INS CO | IN | 233.4 |
| NATIONAL WESTERN LIFE INS CO | CO | 11,058.8 |
| SENTRY INS A MUTUAL CO | WI | 8,232.3 |
| SENTRY LIFE INS CO | WI | 6,735.9 |
| SHELTERPOINT LIFE INS CO | NY | 110.1 |
| UNITED FARM FAMILY LIFE INS CO | IN | 2,312.3 |
| USAA LIFE INS CO | TX | 24,728.9 |
| **Rating: A-** | | |
| AMALGAMATED LIFE INS CO | NY | 124.9 |
| AMERICAN HEALTH & LIFE INS CO | TX | 840.1 |
| AMERICAN REPUBLIC INS CO | IA | 933.1 |
| ANTHEM LIFE INS CO | IN | 738.1 |
| AUTO-OWNERS LIFE INS CO | MI | 4,021.4 |
| CENTRAL STATES H & L CO OF OMAHA | NE | 411.0 |
| CIGNA LIFE INS CO OF NEW YORK | NY | 403.0 |
| ERIE FAMILY LIFE INS CO | PA | 2,448.7 |
| GARDEN STATE LIFE INS CO | TX | 131.8 |
| HUMANA BENEFIT PLAN OF ILLINOIS | IL | 394.7 |
| HUMANA INS CO (WI) | WI | 10,120.6 |
| MASSACHUSETTS MUTUAL LIFE INS CO | MA | 235,570.0 |
| MEDCO CONTAINMENT LIFE INS CO | PA | 1,113.2 |
| MEDICO CORP LIFE INS CO | NE | 63.9 |
| MOTORISTS COMMERCIAL MUTUAL INS CO | OH | 393.5 |
| MUTUAL OF AMERICA LIFE INS CO | NY | 20,499.3 |
| NEW YORK LIFE INS CO | NY | 176,417.0 |
| NIPPON LIFE INS CO OF AMERICA | IA | 219.6 |
| NORTHWESTERN MUTUAL LIFE INS CO | WI | 264,165.0 |
| PHYSICIANS LIFE INS CO | NE | 1,625.7 |
| PROTECTIVE INS CO | IN | 848.6 |
| STANDARD LIFE & ACCIDENT INS CO | TX | 516.7 |
| UPMC HEALTH PLAN INC | PA | 640.7 |
| **Rating: B+** | | |
| AETNA HEALTH & LIFE INS CO | CT | 2,403.1 |
| AMERICAN FAMILY LIFE ASR CO OF COLUM | NE | 113,507.0 |
| AMERICAN FIDELITY ASR CO | OK | 5,772.7 |
| AMERICAN UNITED LIFE INS CO | IN | 27,567.2 |
| AMFIRST INS CO | OK | 57.6 |
| ASSURITY LIFE INS CO | NE | 2,726.8 |
| AXA EQUITABLE LIFE INS CO | NY | 187,479.0 |
| BEST LIFE & HEALTH INS CO | TX | 20.9 |
| BOSTON MUTUAL LIFE INS CO | MA | 1,424.8 |
| COMPANION LIFE INS CO | SC | 359.8 |
| DEARBORN NATIONAL LIFE INS CO | IL | 1,849.7 |
| DELAWARE AMERICAN LIFE INS CO | DE | 137.9 |
| FAMILY HERITAGE LIFE INS CO OF AMER | OH | 1,249.5 |
| GEISINGER HEALTH PLAN | PA | 688.5 |
| GERBER LIFE INS CO | NY | 3,650.7 |
| GOVERNMENT PERSONNEL MUTUAL L I C | TX | 832.3 |
| JACKSON NATIONAL LIFE INS CO | MI | 222,617.0 |
| MIDLAND NATIONAL LIFE INS CO | IA | 55,140.0 |
| MINNESOTA LIFE INS CO | MN | 44,369.0 |
| MUTUAL OF OMAHA INS CO | NE | 7,661.2 |
| NATIONAL BENEFIT LIFE INS CO | NY | 537.3 |
| NATIONAL CASUALTY CO | OH | 406.6 |
| OHIO NATIONAL LIFE ASR CORP | OH | 4,048.6 |
| PRINCIPAL LIFE INS CO | IA | 185,959.0 |
| SB MUTL LIFE INS CO OF MA | MA | 3,015.1 |
| SENTRY SELECT INS CO | WI | 810.3 |
| STANDARD INS CO | OR | 23,414.5 |
| STATE FARM FIRE & CAS CO | IL | 39,417.8 |
| STATE FARM MUTUAL AUTOMOBILE INS CO | IL | 154,684.0 |
| SYMETRA LIFE INS CO | IA | 36,133.8 |
| TRUSTMARK INS CO | IL | 1,532.5 |
| TRUSTMARK LIFE INS CO | IL | 320.1 |
| UNITED WORLD LIFE INS CO | NE | 123.8 |
| UPMC FOR YOU INC | PA | 726.3 |
| USABLE LIFE | AR | 510.9 |
| VOYA RETIREMENT INS & ANNUITY CO | CT | 104,964.0 |

## Puerto Rico

| INSURANCE COMPANY NAME | DOM. STATE | TOTAL ASSETS ($MIL) |
|---|---|---|
| **Rating: A+** | | |
| TEACHERS INS & ANNUITY ASN OF AM | NY | 293,835.0 |
| **Rating: A** | | |
| NATIONAL WESTERN LIFE INS CO | CO | 11,058.8 |
| SENTRY INS A MUTUAL CO | WI | 8,232.3 |
| SOUTHERN FARM BUREAU LIFE INS CO | MS | 14,163.7 |
| **Rating: A-** | | |
| MASSACHUSETTS MUTUAL LIFE INS CO | MA | 235,570.0 |
| MEDCO CONTAINMENT LIFE INS CO | PA | 1,113.2 |
| NEW YORK LIFE INS CO | NY | 176,417.0 |
| PROTECTIVE INS CO | IN | 848.6 |
| TRANS OCEANIC LIFE INS CO | PR | 71.4 |
| **Rating: B+** | | |
| AMERICAN FAMILY LIFE ASR CO OF COLUM | NE | 113,507.0 |
| AMERICAN FIDELITY ASR CO | OK | 5,772.7 |
| AXA EQUITABLE LIFE INS CO | NY | 187,479.0 |
| BOSTON MUTUAL LIFE INS CO | MA | 1,424.8 |
| DEARBORN NATIONAL LIFE INS CO | IL | 1,849.7 |
| FAMILY HERITAGE LIFE INS CO OF AMER | OH | 1,249.5 |
| GERBER LIFE INS CO | NY | 3,650.7 |
| MIDLAND NATIONAL LIFE INS CO | IA | 55,140.0 |
| MINNESOTA LIFE INS CO | MN | 44,369.0 |
| MUTUAL OF OMAHA INS CO | NE | 7,661.2 |
| OHIO NATIONAL LIFE ASR CORP | OH | 4,048.6 |
| PRINCIPAL LIFE INS CO | IA | 185,959.0 |
| STANDARD INS CO | OR | 23,414.5 |
| SYMETRA LIFE INS CO | IA | 36,133.8 |
| TRUSTMARK INS CO | IL | 1,532.5 |
| UNIVERSAL LIFE INS CO | PR | 1,387.9 |
| VOYA RETIREMENT INS & ANNUITY CO | CT | 104,964.0 |

## Rhode Island

| INSURANCE COMPANY NAME | DOM. STATE | TOTAL ASSETS ($MIL) |
|---|---|---|
| **Rating: A+** | | |
| COUNTRY LIFE INS CO | IL | 9,441.1 |
| PHYSICIANS MUTUAL INS CO | NE | 2,289.0 |
| TEACHERS INS & ANNUITY ASN OF AM | NY | 293,835.0 |
| **Rating: A** | | |
| BERKLEY LIFE & HEALTH INS CO | IA | 286.6 |
| FEDERATED LIFE INS CO | MN | 1,849.9 |
| GUARDIAN LIFE INS CO OF AMERICA | NY | 55,226.5 |
| MIDWESTERN UNITED LIFE INS CO | IN | 233.4 |
| NATIONAL WESTERN LIFE INS CO | CO | 11,058.8 |
| SENTRY INS A MUTUAL CO | WI | 8,232.3 |
| SENTRY LIFE INS CO | WI | 6,735.9 |
| SHELTERPOINT LIFE INS CO | NY | 110.1 |
| USAA LIFE INS CO | TX | 24,728.9 |
| **Rating: A-** | | |
| AMALGAMATED LIFE INS CO | NY | 124.9 |
| AMERICAN HEALTH & LIFE INS CO | TX | 840.1 |
| AMERICAN REPUBLIC INS CO | IA | 933.1 |
| CENTRAL STATES H & L CO OF OMAHA | NE | 411.0 |
| GARDEN STATE LIFE INS CO | TX | 131.8 |
| HUMANA BENEFIT PLAN OF ILLINOIS | IL | 394.7 |
| HUMANA INS CO (WI) | WI | 10,120.6 |
| MASSACHUSETTS MUTUAL LIFE INS CO | MA | 235,570.0 |
| MEDCO CONTAINMENT LIFE INS CO | PA | 1,113.2 |
| MEDICO CORP LIFE INS CO | NE | 63.9 |
| MOTORISTS COMMERCIAL MUTUAL INS CO | OH | 393.5 |
| MUTUAL OF AMERICA LIFE INS CO | NY | 20,499.3 |
| NEW YORK LIFE INS CO | NY | 176,417.0 |
| NIPPON LIFE INS CO OF AMERICA | IA | 219.6 |
| NORTHWESTERN MUTUAL LIFE INS CO | WI | 264,165.0 |
| PHYSICIANS LIFE INS CO | NE | 1,625.7 |
| PROTECTIVE INS CO | IN | 848.6 |
| STANDARD LIFE & ACCIDENT INS CO | TX | 516.7 |
| **Rating: B+** | | |
| AETNA HEALTH & LIFE INS CO | CT | 2,403.1 |
| AMERICAN FAMILY LIFE ASR CO OF COLUM | NE | 113,507.0 |
| AMERICAN FIDELITY ASR CO | OK | 5,772.7 |
| AMERICAN UNITED LIFE INS CO | IN | 27,567.2 |
| ASSURITY LIFE INS CO | NE | 2,726.8 |
| AXA EQUITABLE LIFE INS CO | NY | 187,479.0 |
| BOSTON MUTUAL LIFE INS CO | MA | 1,424.8 |
| COMPANION LIFE INS CO | SC | 359.8 |
| DEARBORN NATIONAL LIFE INS CO | IL | 1,849.7 |
| DELAWARE AMERICAN LIFE INS CO | DE | 137.9 |
| FAMILY HERITAGE LIFE INS CO OF AMER | OH | 1,249.5 |
| GERBER LIFE INS CO | NY | 3,650.7 |
| GOVERNMENT PERSONNEL MUTUAL L I C | TX | 832.3 |
| JACKSON NATIONAL LIFE INS CO | MI | 222,617.0 |
| MIDLAND NATIONAL LIFE INS CO | IA | 55,140.0 |
| MINNESOTA LIFE INS CO | MN | 44,369.0 |
| MUTUAL OF OMAHA INS CO | NE | 7,661.2 |
| NATIONAL BENEFIT LIFE INS CO | NY | 537.3 |
| NATIONAL CASUALTY CO | OH | 406.6 |
| OHIO NATIONAL LIFE ASR CORP | OH | 4,048.6 |
| PRINCIPAL LIFE INS CO | IA | 185,959.0 |
| SB MUTL LIFE INS CO OF MA | MA | 3,015.1 |
| SENTRY SELECT INS CO | WI | 810.3 |
| STANDARD INS CO | OR | 23,414.5 |
| STATE FARM FIRE & CAS CO | IL | 39,417.8 |
| STATE FARM MUTUAL AUTOMOBILE INS CO | IL | 154,684.0 |
| SYMETRA LIFE INS CO | IA | 36,133.8 |
| TRUSTMARK INS CO | IL | 1,532.5 |
| TRUSTMARK LIFE INS CO | IL | 320.1 |
| UNITED WORLD LIFE INS CO | NE | 123.8 |
| USABLE LIFE | AR | 510.9 |
| VOYA RETIREMENT INS & ANNUITY CO | CT | 104,964.0 |

## South Carolina

| INSURANCE COMPANY NAME | DOM. STATE | TOTAL ASSETS ($MIL) |
|---|---|---|
| **Rating: A+** | | |
| COUNTRY LIFE INS CO | IL | 9,441.1 |
| PHYSICIANS MUTUAL INS CO | NE | 2,289.0 |
| TEACHERS INS & ANNUITY ASN OF AM | NY | 293,835.0 |
| **Rating: A** | | |
| BERKLEY LIFE & HEALTH INS CO | IA | 286.6 |
| FEDERATED LIFE INS CO | MN | 1,849.9 |
| GUARDIAN LIFE INS CO OF AMERICA | NY | 55,226.5 |
| MEDICAL MUTUAL OF OHIO | OH | 2,136.4 |
| MIDWESTERN UNITED LIFE INS CO | IN | 233.4 |
| NATIONAL WESTERN LIFE INS CO | CO | 11,058.8 |
| SENTRY INS A MUTUAL CO | WI | 8,232.3 |
| SENTRY LIFE INS CO | WI | 6,735.9 |
| SHELTERPOINT LIFE INS CO | NY | 110.1 |
| SOUTHERN FARM BUREAU LIFE INS CO | MS | 14,163.7 |
| USAA LIFE INS CO | TX | 24,728.9 |
| **Rating: A-** | | |
| AMALGAMATED LIFE INS CO | NY | 124.9 |
| AMERICAN HEALTH & LIFE INS CO | TX | 840.1 |
| AMERICAN REPUBLIC INS CO | IA | 933.1 |
| ANTHEM LIFE INS CO | IN | 738.1 |
| AUTO-OWNERS LIFE INS CO | MI | 4,021.4 |
| BLUE CROSS BLUE SHIELD OF SC INC | SC | 4,019.7 |
| CENTRAL STATES H & L CO OF OMAHA | NE | 411.0 |
| GARDEN STATE LIFE INS CO | TX | 131.8 |
| HUMANA BENEFIT PLAN OF ILLINOIS | IL | 394.7 |
| HUMANA INS CO (WI) | WI | 10,120.6 |
| MASSACHUSETTS MUTUAL LIFE INS CO | MA | 235,570.0 |
| MEDCO CONTAINMENT LIFE INS CO | PA | 1,113.2 |
| MEDICO CORP LIFE INS CO | NE | 63.9 |
| MOTORISTS COMMERCIAL MUTUAL INS CO | OH | 393.5 |
| MUTUAL OF AMERICA LIFE INS CO | NY | 20,499.3 |
| NEW YORK LIFE INS CO | NY | 176,417.0 |
| NIPPON LIFE INS CO OF AMERICA | IA | 219.6 |
| NORTHWESTERN MUTUAL LIFE INS CO | WI | 264,165.0 |
| PHYSICIANS LIFE INS CO | NE | 1,625.7 |
| PROTECTIVE INS CO | IN | 848.6 |
| STANDARD LIFE & ACCIDENT INS CO | TX | 516.7 |
| **Rating: B+** | | |
| AETNA HEALTH & LIFE INS CO | CT | 2,403.1 |
| AMERICAN FAMILY LIFE ASR CO OF COLUM | NE | 113,507.0 |
| AMERICAN FAMILY MUTL INS CO SI | WI | 17,048.2 |
| AMERICAN FIDELITY ASR CO | OK | 5,772.7 |
| AMERICAN UNITED LIFE INS CO | IN | 27,567.2 |
| AMFIRST INS CO | OK | 57.6 |
| ASSURITY LIFE INS CO | NE | 2,726.8 |
| AXA EQUITABLE LIFE INS CO | NY | 187,479.0 |
| BEST LIFE & HEALTH INS CO | TX | 20.9 |
| BOSTON MUTUAL LIFE INS CO | MA | 1,424.8 |
| COMPANION LIFE INS CO | SC | 359.8 |
| DEARBORN NATIONAL LIFE INS CO | IL | 1,849.7 |
| DELAWARE AMERICAN LIFE INS CO | DE | 137.9 |
| FAMILY HERITAGE LIFE INS CO OF AMER | OH | 1,249.5 |
| GERBER LIFE INS CO | NY | 3,650.7 |
| GOVERNMENT PERSONNEL MUTUAL L I C | TX | 832.3 |
| JACKSON NATIONAL LIFE INS CO | MI | 222,617.0 |
| MIDLAND NATIONAL LIFE INS CO | IA | 55,140.0 |
| MINNESOTA LIFE INS CO | MN | 44,369.0 |
| MUTUAL OF OMAHA INS CO | NE | 7,661.2 |
| NATIONAL BENEFIT LIFE INS CO | NY | 537.3 |
| NATIONAL CASUALTY CO | OH | 406.6 |
| OHIO NATIONAL LIFE ASR CORP | OH | 4,048.6 |
| PRINCIPAL LIFE INS CO | IA | 185,959.0 |
| SB MUTL LIFE INS CO OF MA | MA | 3,015.1 |
| SENTRY SELECT INS CO | WI | 810.3 |
| SOUTHERN PIONEER LIFE INS CO | AR | 15.7 |
| STANDARD INS CO | OR | 23,414.5 |
| STATE FARM FIRE & CAS CO | IL | 39,417.8 |
| STATE FARM MUTUAL AUTOMOBILE INS CO | IL | 154,684.0 |
| SYMETRA LIFE INS CO | IA | 36,133.8 |
| TRUSTMARK INS CO | IL | 1,532.5 |
| TRUSTMARK LIFE INS CO | IL | 320.1 |
| UNITED WORLD LIFE INS CO | NE | 123.8 |
| USABLE LIFE | AR | 510.9 |
| VOYA RETIREMENT INS & ANNUITY CO | CT | 104,964.0 |

## South Dakota

| INSURANCE COMPANY NAME | DOM. STATE | TOTAL ASSETS ($MIL) |
|---|---|---|
| **Rating: A+** | | |
| COUNTRY LIFE INS CO | IL | 9,441.1 |
| PHYSICIANS MUTUAL INS CO | NE | 2,289.0 |
| TEACHERS INS & ANNUITY ASN OF AM | NY | 293,835.0 |
| **Rating: A** | | |
| BERKLEY LIFE & HEALTH INS CO | IA | 286.6 |
| FEDERATED LIFE INS CO | MN | 1,849.9 |
| GUARDIAN LIFE INS CO OF AMERICA | NY | 55,226.5 |
| MIDWESTERN UNITED LIFE INS CO | IN | 233.4 |
| NATIONAL WESTERN LIFE INS CO | CO | 11,058.8 |
| SENTRY INS A MUTUAL CO | WI | 8,232.3 |
| SENTRY LIFE INS CO | WI | 6,735.9 |
| USAA LIFE INS CO | TX | 24,728.9 |
| **Rating: A-** | | |
| AMALGAMATED LIFE INS CO | NY | 124.9 |
| AMERICAN HEALTH & LIFE INS CO | TX | 840.1 |
| AMERICAN REPUBLIC INS CO | IA | 933.1 |
| ANTHEM LIFE INS CO | IN | 738.1 |
| AUTO-OWNERS LIFE INS CO | MI | 4,021.4 |
| CENTRAL STATES H & L CO OF OMAHA | NE | 411.0 |
| COPIC INS CO | CO | 765.4 |
| GARDEN STATE LIFE INS CO | TX | 131.8 |
| HUMANA BENEFIT PLAN OF ILLINOIS | IL | 394.7 |
| HUMANA INS CO (WI) | WI | 10,120.6 |
| MASSACHUSETTS MUTUAL LIFE INS CO | MA | 235,570.0 |
| MEDCO CONTAINMENT LIFE INS CO | PA | 1,113.2 |
| MEDICO CORP LIFE INS CO | NE | 63.9 |
| MOTORISTS COMMERCIAL MUTUAL INS CO | OH | 393.5 |
| MUTUAL OF AMERICA LIFE INS CO | NY | 20,499.3 |
| NEW YORK LIFE INS CO | NY | 176,417.0 |
| NIPPON LIFE INS CO OF AMERICA | IA | 219.6 |
| NORTHWESTERN MUTUAL LIFE INS CO | WI | 264,165.0 |
| PACIFIC GUARDIAN LIFE INS CO LTD | HI | 552.3 |
| PHYSICIANS LIFE INS CO | NE | 1,625.7 |
| PROTECTIVE INS CO | IN | 848.6 |
| STANDARD LIFE & ACCIDENT INS CO | TX | 516.7 |
| **Rating: B+** | | |
| AETNA HEALTH & LIFE INS CO | CT | 2,403.1 |
| AMERICAN FAMILY LIFE ASR CO OF COLUM | NE | 113,507.0 |
| AMERICAN FAMILY MUTL INS CO SI | WI | 17,048.2 |
| AMERICAN FIDELITY ASR CO | OK | 5,772.7 |
| AMERICAN UNITED LIFE INS CO | IN | 27,567.2 |
| ASSURITY LIFE INS CO | NE | 2,726.8 |
| AXA EQUITABLE LIFE INS CO | NY | 187,479.0 |
| BEST LIFE & HEALTH INS CO | TX | 20.9 |
| BOSTON MUTUAL LIFE INS CO | MA | 1,424.8 |
| COMPANION LIFE INS CO | SC | 359.8 |
| DEARBORN NATIONAL LIFE INS CO | IL | 1,849.7 |
| DELAWARE AMERICAN LIFE INS CO | DE | 137.9 |
| FAMILY HERITAGE LIFE INS CO OF AMER | OH | 1,249.5 |
| FARM BUREAU LIFE INS CO | IA | 8,948.8 |
| GERBER LIFE INS CO | NY | 3,650.7 |
| GOVERNMENT PERSONNEL MUTUAL L I C | TX | 832.3 |
| JACKSON NATIONAL LIFE INS CO | MI | 222,617.0 |
| MIDLAND NATIONAL LIFE INS CO | IA | 55,140.0 |
| MINNESOTA LIFE INS CO | MN | 44,369.0 |
| MUTUAL OF OMAHA INS CO | NE | 7,661.2 |
| NATIONAL BENEFIT LIFE INS CO | NY | 537.3 |
| NATIONAL CASUALTY CO | OH | 406.6 |
| OHIO NATIONAL LIFE ASR CORP | OH | 4,048.6 |
| PRINCIPAL LIFE INS CO | IA | 185,959.0 |
| SB MUTL LIFE INS CO OF MA | MA | 3,015.1 |
| SENTRY SELECT INS CO | WI | 810.3 |
| STANDARD INS CO | OR | 23,414.5 |
| STATE FARM FIRE & CAS CO | IL | 39,417.8 |
| STATE FARM MUTUAL AUTOMOBILE INS CO | IL | 154,684.0 |
| SYMETRA LIFE INS CO | IA | 36,133.8 |
| TRUSTMARK INS CO | IL | 1,532.5 |
| TRUSTMARK LIFE INS CO | IL | 320.1 |
| UNITED WORLD LIFE INS CO | NE | 123.8 |
| USABLE LIFE | AR | 510.9 |
| VOYA RETIREMENT INS & ANNUITY CO | CT | 104,964.0 |
| WELLMARK OF SOUTH DAKOTA INC | SD | 465.7 |

## Tennessee

| INSURANCE COMPANY NAME | DOM. STATE | TOTAL ASSETS ($MIL) |
|---|---|---|
| **Rating: A+** | | |
| COUNTRY LIFE INS CO | IL | 9,441.1 |
| PHYSICIANS MUTUAL INS CO | NE | 2,289.0 |
| TEACHERS INS & ANNUITY ASN OF AM | NY | 293,835.0 |
| **Rating: A** | | |
| BERKLEY LIFE & HEALTH INS CO | IA | 286.6 |
| FEDERATED LIFE INS CO | MN | 1,849.9 |
| GUARDIAN LIFE INS CO OF AMERICA | NY | 55,226.5 |
| MIDWESTERN UNITED LIFE INS CO | IN | 233.4 |
| NATIONAL WESTERN LIFE INS CO | CO | 11,058.8 |
| SENTRY INS A MUTUAL CO | WI | 8,232.3 |
| SENTRY LIFE INS CO | WI | 6,735.9 |
| SHELTERPOINT LIFE INS CO | NY | 110.1 |
| SOUTHERN FARM BUREAU LIFE INS CO | MS | 14,163.7 |
| USAA LIFE INS CO | TX | 24,728.9 |
| **Rating: A-** | | |
| AMALGAMATED LIFE INS CO | NY | 124.9 |
| AMERICAN HEALTH & LIFE INS CO | TX | 840.1 |
| AMERICAN REPUBLIC INS CO | IA | 933.1 |
| ANTHEM LIFE INS CO | IN | 738.1 |
| AUTO-OWNERS LIFE INS CO | MI | 4,021.4 |
| CENTRAL STATES H & L CO OF OMAHA | NE | 411.0 |
| CIGNA LIFE INS CO OF NEW YORK | NY | 403.0 |
| ERIE FAMILY LIFE INS CO | PA | 2,448.7 |
| GARDEN STATE LIFE INS CO | TX | 131.8 |
| HUMANA BENEFIT PLAN OF ILLINOIS | IL | 394.7 |
| HUMANA INS CO (WI) | WI | 10,120.6 |
| MASSACHUSETTS MUTUAL LIFE INS CO | MA | 235,570.0 |
| MEDCO CONTAINMENT LIFE INS CO | PA | 1,113.2 |
| MEDICO CORP LIFE INS CO | NE | 63.9 |
| MOTORISTS COMMERCIAL MUTUAL INS CO | OH | 393.5 |
| MUTUAL OF AMERICA LIFE INS CO | NY | 20,499.3 |
| NEW YORK LIFE INS CO | NY | 176,417.0 |
| NIPPON LIFE INS CO OF AMERICA | IA | 219.6 |
| NORTHWESTERN MUTUAL LIFE INS CO | WI | 264,165.0 |
| PHYSICIANS LIFE INS CO | NE | 1,625.7 |
| PROTECTIVE INS CO | IN | 848.6 |
| STANDARD LIFE & ACCIDENT INS CO | TX | 516.7 |
| **Rating: B+** | | |
| AETNA HEALTH & LIFE INS CO | CT | 2,403.1 |
| AMERICAN FAMILY LIFE ASR CO OF COLUM | NE | 113,507.0 |
| AMERICAN FAMILY MUTL INS CO SI | WI | 17,048.2 |
| AMERICAN FIDELITY ASR CO | OK | 5,772.7 |
| AMERICAN UNITED LIFE INS CO | IN | 27,567.2 |
| AMFIRST INS CO | OK | 57.6 |
| ASSURITY LIFE INS CO | NE | 2,726.8 |
| AXA EQUITABLE LIFE INS CO | NY | 187,479.0 |
| BEST LIFE & HEALTH INS CO | TX | 20.9 |
| BLUEBONNET LIFE INS CO | MS | 62.2 |
| BOSTON MUTUAL LIFE INS CO | MA | 1,424.8 |
| COMPANION LIFE INS CO | SC | 359.8 |
| DEARBORN NATIONAL LIFE INS CO | IL | 1,849.7 |
| DELAWARE AMERICAN LIFE INS CO | DE | 137.9 |
| FAMILY HERITAGE LIFE INS CO OF AMER | OH | 1,249.5 |
| GERBER LIFE INS CO | NY | 3,650.7 |

| INSURANCE COMPANY NAME | DOM. STATE | TOTAL ASSETS ($MIL) |
|---|---|---|
| GOVERNMENT PERSONNEL MUTUAL L I C | TX | 832.3 |
| HEALTHSPRING OF TENNESSEE INC | TN | 460.4 |
| JACKSON NATIONAL LIFE INS CO | MI | 222,617.0 |
| MIDLAND NATIONAL LIFE INS CO | IA | 55,140.0 |
| MINNESOTA LIFE INS CO | MN | 44,369.0 |
| MUTUAL OF OMAHA INS CO | NE | 7,661.2 |
| NATIONAL BENEFIT LIFE INS CO | NY | 537.3 |
| NATIONAL CASUALTY CO | OH | 406.6 |
| OHIO NATIONAL LIFE ASR CORP | OH | 4,048.6 |
| PRINCIPAL LIFE INS CO | IA | 185,959.0 |
| SB MUTL LIFE INS CO OF MA | MA | 3,015.1 |
| SENTRY SELECT INS CO | WI | 810.3 |
| SHELTER LIFE INS CO | MO | 1,238.3 |
| SOUTHERN PIONEER LIFE INS CO | AR | 15.7 |
| STANDARD INS CO | OR | 23,414.5 |
| STATE FARM FIRE & CAS CO | IL | 39,417.8 |
| STATE FARM MUTUAL AUTOMOBILE INS CO | IL | 154,684.0 |
| SYMETRA LIFE INS CO | IA | 36,133.8 |
| TRUSTMARK INS CO | IL | 1,532.5 |
| TRUSTMARK LIFE INS CO | IL | 320.1 |
| UNITED WORLD LIFE INS CO | NE | 123.8 |
| USABLE LIFE | AR | 510.9 |
| VOYA RETIREMENT INS & ANNUITY CO | CT | 104,964.0 |

## Texas

| INSURANCE COMPANY NAME | DOM. STATE | TOTAL ASSETS ($MIL) |
|---|---|---|
| **Rating: A+** | | |
| CARE 1ST HEALTH PLAN INC | CA | 1,094.9 |
| COUNTRY LIFE INS CO | IL | 9,441.1 |
| PHYSICIANS MUTUAL INS CO | NE | 2,289.0 |
| TEACHERS INS & ANNUITY ASN OF AM | NY | 293,835.0 |
| USABLE MUTUAL INS CO | AR | 1,648.3 |
| **Rating: A** | | |
| BERKLEY LIFE & HEALTH INS CO | IA | 286.6 |
| COMMUNITY FIRST HEALTH PLANS INC | TX | 151.9 |
| FEDERATED LIFE INS CO | MN | 1,849.9 |
| GUARDIAN LIFE INS CO OF AMERICA | NY | 55,226.5 |
| MIDWESTERN UNITED LIFE INS CO | IN | 233.4 |
| NATIONAL WESTERN LIFE INS CO | CO | 11,058.8 |
| SENTRY INS A MUTUAL CO | WI | 8,232.3 |
| SENTRY LIFE INS CO | WI | 6,735.9 |
| SOUTHERN FARM BUREAU LIFE INS CO | MS | 14,163.7 |
| USAA LIFE INS CO | TX | 24,728.9 |
| **Rating: A-** | | |
| AMALGAMATED LIFE INS CO | NY | 124.9 |
| AMERICAN HEALTH & LIFE INS CO | TX | 840.1 |
| AMERICAN REPUBLIC INS CO | IA | 933.1 |
| AMERIGROUP TEXAS INC | TX | 1,042.5 |
| ANTHEM LIFE INS CO | IN | 738.1 |
| CENTRAL STATES H & L CO OF OMAHA | NE | 411.0 |
| EL PASO HEALTH | TX | 64.2 |
| GARDEN STATE LIFE INS CO | TX | 131.8 |
| HUMANA BENEFIT PLAN OF ILLINOIS | IL | 394.7 |
| HUMANA INS CO (WI) | WI | 10,120.6 |
| MASSACHUSETTS MUTUAL LIFE INS CO | MA | 235,570.0 |
| MEDCO CONTAINMENT LIFE INS CO | PA | 1,113.2 |
| MEDICO CORP LIFE INS CO | NE | 63.9 |
| MOTORISTS COMMERCIAL MUTUAL INS CO | OH | 393.5 |
| MUTUAL OF AMERICA LIFE INS CO | NY | 20,499.3 |
| NEW YORK LIFE INS CO | NY | 176,417.0 |
| NIPPON LIFE INS CO OF AMERICA | IA | 219.6 |
| NORTHWESTERN MUTUAL LIFE INS CO | WI | 264,165.0 |
| PACIFIC GUARDIAN LIFE INS CO LTD | HI | 552.3 |
| PHYSICIANS LIFE INS CO | NE | 1,625.7 |
| PROTECTIVE INS CO | IN | 848.6 |
| STANDARD LIFE & ACCIDENT INS CO | TX | 516.7 |
| **Rating: B+** | | |
| AETNA BETTER HEALTH OF TEXAS INC | TX | 120.2 |
| AETNA HEALTH & LIFE INS CO | CT | 2,403.1 |
| AMERICAN FAMILY LIFE ASR CO OF COLUM | NE | 113,507.0 |
| AMERICAN FAMILY MUTL INS CO SI | WI | 17,048.2 |
| AMERICAN FIDELITY ASR CO | OK | 5,772.7 |
| AMERICAN UNITED LIFE INS CO | IN | 27,567.2 |
| AMFIRST INS CO | OK | 57.6 |
| ASSURITY LIFE INS CO | NE | 2,726.8 |
| AXA EQUITABLE LIFE INS CO | NY | 187,479.0 |
| BEST LIFE & HEALTH INS CO | TX | 20.9 |
| BOSTON MUTUAL LIFE INS CO | MA | 1,424.8 |
| COMPANION LIFE INS CO | SC | 359.8 |
| DEARBORN NATIONAL LIFE INS CO | IL | 1,849.7 |
| DELAWARE AMERICAN LIFE INS CO | DE | 137.9 |
| ESSENCE HEALTHCARE INC | MO | 288.5 |
| FAMILY HERITAGE LIFE INS CO OF AMER | OH | 1,249.5 |
| GERBER LIFE INS CO | NY | 3,650.7 |
| GOVERNMENT PERSONNEL MUTUAL L I C | TX | 832.3 |
| JACKSON NATIONAL LIFE INS CO | MI | 222,617.0 |
| K S PLAN ADMINISTRATORS LLC | TX | 116.8 |
| MIDLAND NATIONAL LIFE INS CO | IA | 55,140.0 |
| MINNESOTA LIFE INS CO | MN | 44,369.0 |
| MUTUAL OF OMAHA INS CO | NE | 7,661.2 |
| NATIONAL BENEFIT LIFE INS CO | NY | 537.3 |
| NATIONAL CASUALTY CO | OH | 406.6 |
| OHIO NATIONAL LIFE ASR CORP | OH | 4,048.6 |
| PRINCIPAL LIFE INS CO | IA | 185,959.0 |
| SB MUTL LIFE INS CO OF MA | MA | 3,015.1 |
| SENTRY SELECT INS CO | WI | 810.3 |
| SOUTHERN PIONEER LIFE INS CO | AR | 15.7 |
| STANDARD INS CO | OR | 23,414.5 |
| STATE FARM FIRE & CAS CO | IL | 39,417.8 |
| STATE FARM MUTUAL AUTOMOBILE INS CO | IL | 154,684.0 |
| SYMETRA LIFE INS CO | IA | 36,133.8 |
| TRUSTMARK INS CO | IL | 1,532.5 |
| TRUSTMARK LIFE INS CO | IL | 320.1 |
| UNITED WORLD LIFE INS CO | NE | 123.8 |
| UNITEDHEALTHCARE COMMUNITY PLAN TX | TX | 614.6 |
| USABLE LIFE | AR | 510.9 |
| VOYA RETIREMENT INS & ANNUITY CO | CT | 104,964.0 |

## Utah

| INSURANCE COMPANY NAME | DOM. STATE | TOTAL ASSETS ($MIL) |
|---|---|---|
| **Rating: A+** | | |
| COUNTRY LIFE INS CO | IL | 9,441.1 |
| PHYSICIANS MUTUAL INS CO | NE | 2,289.0 |
| TEACHERS INS & ANNUITY ASN OF AM | NY | 293,835.0 |
| **Rating: A** | | |
| BERKLEY LIFE & HEALTH INS CO | IA | 286.6 |
| EMI HEALTH | UT | 107.5 |
| FEDERATED LIFE INS CO | MN | 1,849.9 |
| GUARDIAN LIFE INS CO OF AMERICA | NY | 55,226.5 |
| MIDWESTERN UNITED LIFE INS CO | IN | 233.4 |
| NATIONAL WESTERN LIFE INS CO | CO | 11,058.8 |
| SENTRY INS A MUTUAL CO | WI | 8,232.3 |
| SENTRY LIFE INS CO | WI | 6,735.9 |
| USAA LIFE INS CO | TX | 24,728.9 |
| **Rating: A-** | | |
| AMALGAMATED LIFE INS CO | NY | 124.9 |
| AMERICAN HEALTH & LIFE INS CO | TX | 840.1 |
| AMERICAN REPUBLIC INS CO | IA | 933.1 |
| ANTHEM LIFE INS CO | IN | 738.1 |
| AUTO-OWNERS LIFE INS CO | MI | 4,021.4 |
| CENTRAL STATES H & L CO OF OMAHA | NE | 411.0 |
| COPIC INS CO | CO | 765.4 |
| GARDEN STATE LIFE INS CO | TX | 131.8 |
| HUMANA INS CO (WI) | WI | 10,120.6 |
| MASSACHUSETTS MUTUAL LIFE INS CO | MA | 235,570.0 |
| MEDCO CONTAINMENT LIFE INS CO | PA | 1,113.2 |
| MEDICO CORP LIFE INS CO | NE | 63.9 |
| MOTORISTS COMMERCIAL MUTUAL INS CO | OH | 393.5 |
| MUTUAL OF AMERICA LIFE INS CO | NY | 20,499.3 |
| NEW YORK LIFE INS CO | NY | 176,417.0 |
| NIPPON LIFE INS CO OF AMERICA | IA | 219.6 |
| NORTHWESTERN MUTUAL LIFE INS CO | WI | 264,165.0 |
| PACIFIC GUARDIAN LIFE INS CO LTD | HI | 552.3 |
| PHYSICIANS LIFE INS CO | NE | 1,625.7 |
| PROTECTIVE INS CO | IN | 848.6 |
| STANDARD LIFE & ACCIDENT INS CO | TX | 516.7 |
| **Rating: B+** | | |
| AETNA HEALTH & LIFE INS CO | CT | 2,403.1 |
| AMERICAN FAMILY LIFE ASR CO OF COLUM | NE | 113,507.0 |
| AMERICAN FAMILY MUTL INS CO SI | WI | 17,048.2 |
| AMERICAN FIDELITY ASR CO | OK | 5,772.7 |
| AMERICAN UNITED LIFE INS CO | IN | 27,567.2 |
| ASSURITY LIFE INS CO | NE | 2,726.8 |
| AXA EQUITABLE LIFE INS CO | NY | 187,479.0 |
| BEST LIFE & HEALTH INS CO | TX | 20.9 |
| BOSTON MUTUAL LIFE INS CO | MA | 1,424.8 |
| COMPANION LIFE INS CO | SC | 359.8 |
| DEARBORN NATIONAL LIFE INS CO | IL | 1,849.7 |
| DELAWARE AMERICAN LIFE INS CO | DE | 137.9 |
| FAMILY HERITAGE LIFE INS CO OF AMER | OH | 1,249.5 |
| FARM BUREAU LIFE INS CO | IA | 8,948.8 |
| GERBER LIFE INS CO | NY | 3,650.7 |
| GOVERNMENT PERSONNEL MUTUAL L I C | TX | 832.3 |
| JACKSON NATIONAL LIFE INS CO | MI | 222,617.0 |
| MIDLAND NATIONAL LIFE INS CO | IA | 55,140.0 |
| MINNESOTA LIFE INS CO | MN | 44,369.0 |
| MUTUAL OF OMAHA INS CO | NE | 7,661.2 |
| NATIONAL BENEFIT LIFE INS CO | NY | 537.3 |
| NATIONAL CASUALTY CO | OH | 406.6 |
| OHIO NATIONAL LIFE ASR CORP | OH | 4,048.6 |
| PRINCIPAL LIFE INS CO | IA | 185,959.0 |
| SB MUTL LIFE INS CO OF MA | MA | 3,015.1 |
| SENTRY SELECT INS CO | WI | 810.3 |
| STANDARD INS CO | OR | 23,414.5 |
| STATE FARM FIRE & CAS CO | IL | 39,417.8 |
| STATE FARM MUTUAL AUTOMOBILE INS CO | IL | 154,684.0 |
| SYMETRA LIFE INS CO | IA | 36,133.8 |
| TRUSTMARK INS CO | IL | 1,532.5 |
| TRUSTMARK LIFE INS CO | IL | 320.1 |
| UNITED WORLD LIFE INS CO | NE | 123.8 |
| USABLE LIFE | AR | 510.9 |
| VOYA RETIREMENT INS & ANNUITY CO | CT | 104,964.0 |

## Vermont

| INSURANCE COMPANY NAME | DOM. STATE | TOTAL ASSETS ($MIL) |
|---|---|---|
| **Rating: A+** | | |
| PHYSICIANS MUTUAL INS CO | NE | 2,289.0 |
| TEACHERS INS & ANNUITY ASN OF AM | NY | 293,835.0 |
| **Rating: A** | | |
| BERKLEY LIFE & HEALTH INS CO | IA | 286.6 |
| FEDERATED LIFE INS CO | MN | 1,849.9 |
| GUARDIAN LIFE INS CO OF AMERICA | NY | 55,226.5 |
| MIDWESTERN UNITED LIFE INS CO | IN | 233.4 |
| NATIONAL WESTERN LIFE INS CO | CO | 11,058.8 |
| SENTRY INS A MUTUAL CO | WI | 8,232.3 |
| SENTRY LIFE INS CO | WI | 6,735.9 |
| USAA LIFE INS CO | TX | 24,728.9 |
| **Rating: A-** | | |
| AMALGAMATED LIFE INS CO | NY | 124.9 |
| AMERICAN FAMILY LIFE ASR CO OF NY | NY | 945.4 |
| AMERICAN HEALTH & LIFE INS CO | TX | 840.1 |
| AMERICAN REPUBLIC INS CO | IA | 933.1 |
| AUTO-OWNERS LIFE INS CO | MI | 4,021.4 |
| CENTRAL STATES H & L CO OF OMAHA | NE | 411.0 |
| GARDEN STATE LIFE INS CO | TX | 131.8 |
| HUMANA BENEFIT PLAN OF ILLINOIS | IL | 394.7 |
| HUMANA INS CO (WI) | WI | 10,120.6 |
| MASSACHUSETTS MUTUAL LIFE INS CO | MA | 235,570.0 |
| MEDCO CONTAINMENT LIFE INS CO | PA | 1,113.2 |
| MEDICO CORP LIFE INS CO | NE | 63.9 |
| MOTORISTS COMMERCIAL MUTUAL INS CO | OH | 393.5 |
| MUTUAL OF AMERICA LIFE INS CO | NY | 20,499.3 |
| NEW YORK LIFE INS CO | NY | 176,417.0 |
| NIPPON LIFE INS CO OF AMERICA | IA | 219.6 |
| NORTHWESTERN MUTUAL LIFE INS CO | WI | 264,165.0 |
| PHYSICIANS LIFE INS CO | NE | 1,625.7 |
| PROTECTIVE INS CO | IN | 848.6 |
| STANDARD LIFE & ACCIDENT INS CO | TX | 516.7 |
| **Rating: B+** | | |
| AETNA HEALTH & LIFE INS CO | CT | 2,403.1 |
| AMERICAN FAMILY LIFE ASR CO OF COLUM | NE | 113,507.0 |
| AMERICAN FIDELITY ASR CO | OK | 5,772.7 |
| AMERICAN UNITED LIFE INS CO | IN | 27,567.2 |
| ASSURITY LIFE INS CO | NE | 2,726.8 |
| AXA EQUITABLE LIFE INS CO | NY | 187,479.0 |
| BOSTON MUTUAL LIFE INS CO | MA | 1,424.8 |
| COMPANION LIFE INS CO | SC | 359.8 |
| DEARBORN NATIONAL LIFE INS CO | IL | 1,849.7 |
| DELAWARE AMERICAN LIFE INS CO | DE | 137.9 |
| FAMILY HERITAGE LIFE INS CO OF AMER | OH | 1,249.5 |
| GERBER LIFE INS CO | NY | 3,650.7 |
| GOVERNMENT PERSONNEL MUTUAL L I C | TX | 832.3 |
| JACKSON NATIONAL LIFE INS CO | MI | 222,617.0 |
| MIDLAND NATIONAL LIFE INS CO | IA | 55,140.0 |
| MINNESOTA LIFE INS CO | MN | 44,369.0 |
| MUTUAL OF OMAHA INS CO | NE | 7,661.2 |
| NATIONAL BENEFIT LIFE INS CO | NY | 537.3 |
| NATIONAL CASUALTY CO | OH | 406.6 |
| OHIO NATIONAL LIFE ASR CORP | OH | 4,048.6 |
| PRINCIPAL LIFE INS CO | IA | 185,959.0 |
| SB MUTL LIFE INS CO OF MA | MA | 3,015.1 |
| SENTRY SELECT INS CO | WI | 810.3 |
| STANDARD INS CO | OR | 23,414.5 |
| STATE FARM FIRE & CAS CO | IL | 39,417.8 |
| STATE FARM MUTUAL AUTOMOBILE INS CO | IL | 154,684.0 |
| SYMETRA LIFE INS CO | IA | 36,133.8 |
| TRUSTMARK INS CO | IL | 1,532.5 |
| TRUSTMARK LIFE INS CO | IL | 320.1 |
| UNITED WORLD LIFE INS CO | NE | 123.8 |
| USABLE LIFE | AR | 510.9 |
| VOYA RETIREMENT INS & ANNUITY CO | CT | 104,964.0 |

## Virginia

| INSURANCE COMPANY NAME | DOM. STATE | TOTAL ASSETS ($MIL) |
|---|---|---|
| **Rating: A+** | | |
| COUNTRY LIFE INS CO | IL | 9,441.1 |
| PHYSICIANS MUTUAL INS CO | NE | 2,289.0 |
| TEACHERS INS & ANNUITY ASN OF AM | NY | 293,835.0 |
| **Rating: A** | | |
| BERKLEY LIFE & HEALTH INS CO | IA | 286.6 |
| FEDERATED LIFE INS CO | MN | 1,849.9 |
| GUARDIAN LIFE INS CO OF AMERICA | NY | 55,226.5 |
| MIDWESTERN UNITED LIFE INS CO | IN | 233.4 |
| NATIONAL WESTERN LIFE INS CO | CO | 11,058.8 |
| SENTRY INS A MUTUAL CO | WI | 8,232.3 |
| SENTRY LIFE INS CO | WI | 6,735.9 |
| SOUTHERN FARM BUREAU LIFE INS CO | MS | 14,163.7 |
| USAA LIFE INS CO | TX | 24,728.9 |
| **Rating: A-** | | |
| AMALGAMATED LIFE INS CO | NY | 124.9 |
| AMERICAN HEALTH & LIFE INS CO | TX | 840.1 |
| AMERICAN REPUBLIC INS CO | IA | 933.1 |
| ANTHEM LIFE INS CO | IN | 738.1 |
| AUTO-OWNERS LIFE INS CO | MI | 4,021.4 |
| CAREFIRST BLUECHOICE INC | DC | 1,137.7 |
| CENTRAL STATES H & L CO OF OMAHA | NE | 411.0 |
| ERIE FAMILY LIFE INS CO | PA | 2,448.7 |
| GARDEN STATE LIFE INS CO | TX | 131.8 |
| HUMANA BENEFIT PLAN OF ILLINOIS | IL | 394.7 |
| HUMANA INS CO (WI) | WI | 10,120.6 |
| MASSACHUSETTS MUTUAL LIFE INS CO | MA | 235,570.0 |
| MEDCO CONTAINMENT LIFE INS CO | PA | 1,113.2 |
| MEDICO CORP LIFE INS CO | NE | 63.9 |
| MOTORISTS COMMERCIAL MUTUAL INS CO | OH | 393.5 |
| MUTUAL OF AMERICA LIFE INS CO | NY | 20,499.3 |
| NEW YORK LIFE INS CO | NY | 176,417.0 |
| NIPPON LIFE INS CO OF AMERICA | IA | 219.6 |
| NORTHWESTERN MUTUAL LIFE INS CO | WI | 264,165.0 |
| OPTIMA HEALTH PLAN | VA | 445.1 |
| PHYSICIANS LIFE INS CO | NE | 1,625.7 |
| PROTECTIVE INS CO | IN | 848.6 |
| STANDARD LIFE & ACCIDENT INS CO | TX | 516.7 |
| **Rating: B+** | | |
| AETNA HEALTH & LIFE INS CO | CT | 2,403.1 |
| AMERICAN FAMILY LIFE ASR CO OF COLUM | NE | 113,507.0 |
| AMERICAN FAMILY MUTL INS CO SI | WI | 17,048.2 |
| AMERICAN FIDELITY ASR CO | OK | 5,772.7 |
| AMERICAN UNITED LIFE INS CO | IN | 27,567.2 |
| AMFIRST INS CO | OK | 57.6 |
| ASSURITY LIFE INS CO | NE | 2,726.8 |
| AXA EQUITABLE LIFE INS CO | NY | 187,479.0 |
| BEST LIFE & HEALTH INS CO | TX | 20.9 |
| BOSTON MUTUAL LIFE INS CO | MA | 1,424.8 |
| COMPANION LIFE INS CO | SC | 359.8 |
| DEARBORN NATIONAL LIFE INS CO | IL | 1,849.7 |
| DELAWARE AMERICAN LIFE INS CO | DE | 137.9 |
| FAMILY HERITAGE LIFE INS CO OF AMER | OH | 1,249.5 |
| GERBER LIFE INS CO | NY | 3,650.7 |
| GOVERNMENT PERSONNEL MUTUAL L I C | TX | 832.3 |
| HEALTHKEEPERS INC | VA | 1,218.8 |
| JACKSON NATIONAL LIFE INS CO | MI | 222,617.0 |
| MIDLAND NATIONAL LIFE INS CO | IA | 55,140.0 |
| MINNESOTA LIFE INS CO | MN | 44,369.0 |
| MUTUAL OF OMAHA INS CO | NE | 7,661.2 |
| NATIONAL BENEFIT LIFE INS CO | NY | 537.3 |
| NATIONAL CASUALTY CO | OH | 406.6 |
| OHIO NATIONAL LIFE ASR CORP | OH | 4,048.6 |
| PRINCIPAL LIFE INS CO | IA | 185,959.0 |
| SB MUTL LIFE INS CO OF MA | MA | 3,015.1 |
| SENTRY SELECT INS CO | WI | 810.3 |
| STANDARD INS CO | OR | 23,414.5 |
| STATE FARM FIRE & CAS CO | IL | 39,417.8 |
| STATE FARM MUTUAL AUTOMOBILE INS CO | IL | 154,684.0 |
| SYMETRA LIFE INS CO | IA | 36,133.8 |
| TRUSTMARK INS CO | IL | 1,532.5 |
| TRUSTMARK LIFE INS CO | IL | 320.1 |
| UNITED WORLD LIFE INS CO | NE | 123.8 |
| USABLE LIFE | AR | 510.9 |
| VIRGINIA PREMIER HEALTH PLAN INC | VA | 317.9 |
| VOYA RETIREMENT INS & ANNUITY CO | CT | 104,964.0 |

## Washington

| INSURANCE COMPANY NAME | DOM. STATE | TOTAL ASSETS ($MIL) |
|---|---|---|
| **Rating: A+** | | |
| COUNTRY LIFE INS CO | IL | 9,441.1 |
| PHYSICIANS MUTUAL INS CO | NE | 2,289.0 |
| PROVIDENCE HEALTH PLAN | OR | 910.5 |
| TEACHERS INS & ANNUITY ASN OF AM | NY | 293,835.0 |
| **Rating: A** | | |
| BERKLEY LIFE & HEALTH INS CO | IA | 286.6 |
| FEDERATED LIFE INS CO | MN | 1,849.9 |
| GUARDIAN LIFE INS CO OF AMERICA | NY | 55,226.5 |
| LIFEWISE ASR CO | WA | 166.6 |
| MIDWESTERN UNITED LIFE INS CO | IN | 233.4 |
| NATIONAL WESTERN LIFE INS CO | CO | 11,058.8 |
| SENTRY INS A MUTUAL CO | WI | 8,232.3 |
| SENTRY LIFE INS CO | WI | 6,735.9 |
| USAA LIFE INS CO | TX | 24,728.9 |
| **Rating: A-** | | |
| AMALGAMATED LIFE INS CO | NY | 124.9 |
| AMERICAN HEALTH & LIFE INS CO | TX | 840.1 |
| AMERICAN REPUBLIC INS CO | IA | 933.1 |
| AMERIGROUP WASHINGTON INC | WA | 267.7 |
| ANTHEM LIFE INS CO | IN | 738.1 |
| AUTO-OWNERS LIFE INS CO | MI | 4,021.4 |
| CENTRAL STATES H & L CO OF OMAHA | NE | 411.0 |
| GARDEN STATE LIFE INS CO | TX | 131.8 |
| HUMANA BENEFIT PLAN OF ILLINOIS | IL | 394.7 |
| HUMANA INS CO (WI) | WI | 10,120.6 |
| MASSACHUSETTS MUTUAL LIFE INS CO | MA | 235,570.0 |
| MEDCO CONTAINMENT LIFE INS CO | PA | 1,113.2 |
| MEDICO CORP LIFE INS CO | NE | 63.9 |
| MOTORISTS COMMERCIAL MUTUAL INS CO | OH | 393.5 |
| MUTUAL OF AMERICA LIFE INS CO | NY | 20,499.3 |
| NEW YORK LIFE INS CO | NY | 176,417.0 |
| NIPPON LIFE INS CO OF AMERICA | IA | 219.6 |
| NORTHWESTERN MUTUAL LIFE INS CO | WI | 264,165.0 |
| PACIFIC GUARDIAN LIFE INS CO LTD | HI | 552.3 |
| PHYSICIANS LIFE INS CO | NE | 1,625.7 |
| PROTECTIVE INS CO | IN | 848.6 |
| STANDARD LIFE & ACCIDENT INS CO | TX | 516.7 |
| **Rating: B+** | | |
| AETNA HEALTH & LIFE INS CO | CT | 2,403.1 |
| AMERICAN FAMILY LIFE ASR CO OF COLUM | NE | 113,507.0 |
| AMERICAN FAMILY MUTL INS CO SI | WI | 17,048.2 |
| AMERICAN FIDELITY ASR CO | OK | 5,772.7 |
| AMERICAN UNITED LIFE INS CO | IN | 27,567.2 |
| ASSURITY LIFE INS CO | NE | 2,726.8 |
| AXA EQUITABLE LIFE INS CO | NY | 187,479.0 |
| BEST LIFE & HEALTH INS CO | TX | 20.9 |
| BOSTON MUTUAL LIFE INS CO | MA | 1,424.8 |
| COMPANION LIFE INS CO | SC | 359.8 |
| DEARBORN NATIONAL LIFE INS CO | IL | 1,849.7 |
| DELAWARE AMERICAN LIFE INS CO | DE | 137.9 |
| ESSENCE HEALTHCARE INC | MO | 288.5 |
| FAMILY HERITAGE LIFE INS CO OF AMER | OH | 1,249.5 |
| FARM BUREAU LIFE INS CO | IA | 8,948.8 |
| GERBER LIFE INS CO | NY | 3,650.7 |
| GOVERNMENT PERSONNEL MUTUAL L I C | TX | 832.3 |
| JACKSON NATIONAL LIFE INS CO | MI | 222,617.0 |
| KAISER FNDTN HLTH PLAN OF WA | WA | 1,673.0 |
| MIDLAND NATIONAL LIFE INS CO | IA | 55,140.0 |
| MINNESOTA LIFE INS CO | MN | 44,369.0 |
| MUTUAL OF OMAHA INS CO | NE | 7,661.2 |
| NATIONAL BENEFIT LIFE INS CO | NY | 537.3 |
| NATIONAL CASUALTY CO | OH | 406.6 |
| OHIO NATIONAL LIFE ASR CORP | OH | 4,048.6 |
| PREMERA BLUE CROSS | WA | 2,574.6 |
| PRINCIPAL LIFE INS CO | IA | 185,959.0 |
| REGENCE BL CROSS BL SHIELD OREGON | OR | 1,253.4 |
| SB MUTL LIFE INS CO OF MA | MA | 3,015.1 |
| SENTRY SELECT INS CO | WI | 810.3 |
| STANDARD INS CO | OR | 23,414.5 |
| STATE FARM FIRE & CAS CO | IL | 39,417.8 |
| STATE FARM MUTUAL AUTOMOBILE INS CO | IL | 154,684.0 |
| SYMETRA LIFE INS CO | IA | 36,133.8 |
| TRUSTMARK INS CO | IL | 1,532.5 |
| TRUSTMARK LIFE INS CO | IL | 320.1 |
| UNITED WORLD LIFE INS CO | NE | 123.8 |
| USABLE LIFE | AR | 510.9 |
| VOYA RETIREMENT INS & ANNUITY CO | CT | 104,964.0 |

## West Virginia

| INSURANCE COMPANY NAME | DOM. STATE | TOTAL ASSETS ($MIL) |
|---|---|---|
| **Rating: A+** | | |
| COUNTRY LIFE INS CO | IL | 9,441.1 |
| PHYSICIANS MUTUAL INS CO | NE | 2,289.0 |
| TEACHERS INS & ANNUITY ASN OF AM | NY | 293,835.0 |
| **Rating: A** | | |
| BERKLEY LIFE & HEALTH INS CO | IA | 286.6 |
| FEDERATED LIFE INS CO | MN | 1,849.9 |
| GUARDIAN LIFE INS CO OF AMERICA | NY | 55,226.5 |
| MEDICAL MUTUAL OF OHIO | OH | 2,136.4 |
| MIDWESTERN UNITED LIFE INS CO | IN | 233.4 |
| NATIONAL WESTERN LIFE INS CO | CO | 11,058.8 |
| SENTRY INS A MUTUAL CO | WI | 8,232.3 |
| SENTRY LIFE INS CO | WI | 6,735.9 |
| USAA LIFE INS CO | TX | 24,728.9 |
| **Rating: A-** | | |
| AMALGAMATED LIFE INS CO | NY | 124.9 |
| AMERICAN HEALTH & LIFE INS CO | TX | 840.1 |
| AMERICAN REPUBLIC INS CO | IA | 933.1 |
| ANTHEM LIFE INS CO | IN | 738.1 |
| CENTRAL STATES H & L CO OF OMAHA | NE | 411.0 |
| ERIE FAMILY LIFE INS CO | PA | 2,448.7 |
| GARDEN STATE LIFE INS CO | TX | 131.8 |
| HUMANA BENEFIT PLAN OF ILLINOIS | IL | 394.7 |
| HUMANA INS CO (WI) | WI | 10,120.6 |
| MASSACHUSETTS MUTUAL LIFE INS CO | MA | 235,570.0 |
| MEDCO CONTAINMENT LIFE INS CO | PA | 1,113.2 |
| MEDICO CORP LIFE INS CO | NE | 63.9 |
| MOTORISTS COMMERCIAL MUTUAL INS CO | OH | 393.5 |
| MUTUAL OF AMERICA LIFE INS CO | NY | 20,499.3 |
| NEW YORK LIFE INS CO | NY | 176,417.0 |
| NIPPON LIFE INS CO OF AMERICA | IA | 219.6 |
| NORTHWESTERN MUTUAL LIFE INS CO | WI | 264,165.0 |
| PHYSICIANS LIFE INS CO | NE | 1,625.7 |
| PROTECTIVE INS CO | IN | 848.6 |
| STANDARD LIFE & ACCIDENT INS CO | TX | 516.7 |
| UNICARE HEALTH PLAN OF WEST VIRGINIA | WV | 110.0 |
| UPMC HEALTH PLAN INC | PA | 640.7 |
| **Rating: B+** | | |
| AETNA HEALTH & LIFE INS CO | CT | 2,403.1 |
| AMERICAN FAMILY LIFE ASR CO OF COLUM | NE | 113,507.0 |
| AMERICAN FIDELITY ASR CO | OK | 5,772.7 |
| AMERICAN UNITED LIFE INS CO | IN | 27,567.2 |
| AMFIRST INS CO | OK | 57.6 |
| ASSURITY LIFE INS CO | NE | 2,726.8 |
| AXA EQUITABLE LIFE INS CO | NY | 187,479.0 |
| BOSTON MUTUAL LIFE INS CO | MA | 1,424.8 |
| COMPANION LIFE INS CO | SC | 359.8 |
| COVENTRY HEALTH CARE OF WEST VA INC | WV | 152.7 |
| DEARBORN NATIONAL LIFE INS CO | IL | 1,849.7 |
| DELAWARE AMERICAN LIFE INS CO | DE | 137.9 |
| FAMILY HERITAGE LIFE INS CO OF AMER | OH | 1,249.5 |
| GERBER LIFE INS CO | NY | 3,650.7 |
| GOVERNMENT PERSONNEL MUTUAL L I C | TX | 832.3 |
| JACKSON NATIONAL LIFE INS CO | MI | 222,617.0 |
| MIDLAND NATIONAL LIFE INS CO | IA | 55,140.0 |
| MINNESOTA LIFE INS CO | MN | 44,369.0 |
| MUTUAL OF OMAHA INS CO | NE | 7,661.2 |
| NATIONAL BENEFIT LIFE INS CO | NY | 537.3 |
| NATIONAL CASUALTY CO | OH | 406.6 |
| OHIO NATIONAL LIFE ASR CORP | OH | 4,048.6 |
| PRINCIPAL LIFE INS CO | IA | 185,959.0 |
| SB MUTL LIFE INS CO OF MA | MA | 3,015.1 |
| SENTRY SELECT INS CO | WI | 810.3 |
| STANDARD INS CO | OR | 23,414.5 |
| STATE FARM FIRE & CAS CO | IL | 39,417.8 |
| STATE FARM MUTUAL AUTOMOBILE INS CO | IL | 154,684.0 |
| SYMETRA LIFE INS CO | IA | 36,133.8 |
| TRUSTMARK INS CO | IL | 1,532.5 |
| TRUSTMARK LIFE INS CO | IL | 320.1 |
| UNITED WORLD LIFE INS CO | NE | 123.8 |
| USABLE LIFE | AR | 510.9 |
| VOYA RETIREMENT INS & ANNUITY CO | CT | 104,964.0 |

## Wisconsin

| INSURANCE COMPANY NAME | DOM. STATE | TOTAL ASSETS ($MIL) |
|---|---|---|
| **Rating: A+** | | |
| COUNTRY LIFE INS CO | IL | 9,441.1 |
| PHYSICIANS MUTUAL INS CO | NE | 2,289.0 |
| TEACHERS INS & ANNUITY ASN OF AM | NY | 293,835.0 |
| **Rating: A** | | |
| BERKLEY LIFE & HEALTH INS CO | IA | 286.6 |
| FEDERATED LIFE INS CO | MN | 1,849.9 |
| GUARDIAN LIFE INS CO OF AMERICA | NY | 55,226.5 |
| MEDICAL MUTUAL OF OHIO | OH | 2,136.4 |
| MIDWESTERN UNITED LIFE INS CO | IN | 233.4 |
| NATIONAL WESTERN LIFE INS CO | CO | 11,058.8 |
| SENTRY INS A MUTUAL CO | WI | 8,232.3 |
| SENTRY LIFE INS CO | WI | 6,735.9 |
| USAA LIFE INS CO | TX | 24,728.9 |
| **Rating: A-** | | |
| AMALGAMATED LIFE INS CO | NY | 124.9 |
| AMERICAN HEALTH & LIFE INS CO | TX | 840.1 |
| AMERICAN REPUBLIC INS CO | IA | 933.1 |
| ANTHEM LIFE INS CO | IN | 738.1 |
| AUTO-OWNERS LIFE INS CO | MI | 4,021.4 |
| CENTRAL STATES H & L CO OF OMAHA | NE | 411.0 |
| COMPCARE HEALTH SERVICES INS CORP | WI | 314.8 |
| ERIE FAMILY LIFE INS CO | PA | 2,448.7 |
| GARDEN STATE LIFE INS CO | TX | 131.8 |
| HUMANA BENEFIT PLAN OF ILLINOIS | IL | 394.7 |
| HUMANA INS CO (WI) | WI | 10,120.6 |
| INDEPENDENT CARE HEALTH PLAN | WI | 89.0 |
| MASSACHUSETTS MUTUAL LIFE INS CO | MA | 235,570.0 |
| MEDCO CONTAINMENT LIFE INS CO | PA | 1,113.2 |
| MEDICO CORP LIFE INS CO | NE | 63.9 |
| MOTORISTS COMMERCIAL MUTUAL INS CO | OH | 393.5 |
| MUTUAL OF AMERICA LIFE INS CO | NY | 20,499.3 |
| NEW YORK LIFE INS CO | NY | 176,417.0 |
| NIPPON LIFE INS CO OF AMERICA | IA | 219.6 |
| NORTHWESTERN MUTUAL LIFE INS CO | WI | 264,165.0 |
| PHYSICIANS LIFE INS CO | NE | 1,625.7 |
| PROTECTIVE INS CO | IN | 848.6 |
| SECURITY HEALTH PLAN OF WI INC | WI | 427.3 |
| STANDARD LIFE & ACCIDENT INS CO | TX | 516.7 |
| **Rating: B+** | | |
| AETNA HEALTH & LIFE INS CO | CT | 2,403.1 |
| AMERICAN FAMILY LIFE ASR CO OF COLUM | NE | 113,507.0 |
| AMERICAN FAMILY MUTL INS CO SI | WI | 17,048.2 |
| AMERICAN FIDELITY ASR CO | OK | 5,772.7 |
| AMERICAN UNITED LIFE INS CO | IN | 27,567.2 |
| ASSURITY LIFE INS CO | NE | 2,726.8 |
| AXA EQUITABLE LIFE INS CO | NY | 187,479.0 |
| BOSTON MUTUAL LIFE INS CO | MA | 1,424.8 |
| COMPANION LIFE INS CO | SC | 359.8 |
| DEAN HEALTH PLAN INC | WI | 225.0 |
| DEARBORN NATIONAL LIFE INS CO | IL | 1,849.7 |
| DELAWARE AMERICAN LIFE INS CO | DE | 137.9 |
| FAMILY HERITAGE LIFE INS CO OF AMER | OH | 1,249.5 |
| FARM BUREAU LIFE INS CO | IA | 8,948.8 |
| GERBER LIFE INS CO | NY | 3,650.7 |
| GOVERNMENT PERSONNEL MUTUAL L I C | TX | 832.3 |
| JACKSON NATIONAL LIFE INS CO | MI | 222,617.0 |
| MIDLAND NATIONAL LIFE INS CO | IA | 55,140.0 |
| MINNESOTA LIFE INS CO | MN | 44,369.0 |
| MUTUAL OF OMAHA INS CO | NE | 7,661.2 |
| NATIONAL BENEFIT LIFE INS CO | NY | 537.3 |
| NATIONAL CASUALTY CO | OH | 406.6 |
| OHIO NATIONAL LIFE ASR CORP | OH | 4,048.6 |
| PRINCIPAL LIFE INS CO | IA | 185,959.0 |
| SB MUTL LIFE INS CO OF MA | MA | 3,015.1 |
| SENTRY SELECT INS CO | WI | 810.3 |
| STANDARD INS CO | OR | 23,414.5 |
| STATE FARM FIRE & CAS CO | IL | 39,417.8 |
| STATE FARM MUTUAL AUTOMOBILE INS CO | IL | 154,684.0 |
| SYMETRA LIFE INS CO | IA | 36,133.8 |
| TRUSTMARK INS CO | IL | 1,532.5 |
| TRUSTMARK LIFE INS CO | IL | 320.1 |
| UNITED WORLD LIFE INS CO | NE | 123.8 |
| USABLE LIFE | AR | 510.9 |
| VOYA RETIREMENT INS & ANNUITY CO | CT | 104,964.0 |

## Wyoming

| INSURANCE COMPANY NAME | DOM. STATE | TOTAL ASSETS ($MIL) |
|---|---|---|
| **Rating: A+** | | |
| COUNTRY LIFE INS CO | IL | 9,441.1 |
| PHYSICIANS MUTUAL INS CO | NE | 2,289.0 |
| TEACHERS INS & ANNUITY ASN OF AM | NY | 293,835.0 |
| **Rating: A** | | |
| BERKLEY LIFE & HEALTH INS CO | IA | 286.6 |
| FEDERATED LIFE INS CO | MN | 1,849.9 |
| GUARDIAN LIFE INS CO OF AMERICA | NY | 55,226.5 |
| MIDWESTERN UNITED LIFE INS CO | IN | 233.4 |
| NATIONAL WESTERN LIFE INS CO | CO | 11,058.8 |
| SENTRY INS A MUTUAL CO | WI | 8,232.3 |
| SENTRY LIFE INS CO | WI | 6,735.9 |
| USAA LIFE INS CO | TX | 24,728.9 |
| **Rating: A-** | | |
| AMALGAMATED LIFE INS CO | NY | 124.9 |
| AMERICAN HEALTH & LIFE INS CO | TX | 840.1 |
| AMERICAN REPUBLIC INS CO | IA | 933.1 |
| ANTHEM LIFE INS CO | IN | 738.1 |
| CENTRAL STATES H & L CO OF OMAHA | NE | 411.0 |
| COPIC INS CO | CO | 765.4 |
| GARDEN STATE LIFE INS CO | TX | 131.8 |
| HUMANA BENEFIT PLAN OF ILLINOIS | IL | 394.7 |
| HUMANA INS CO (WI) | WI | 10,120.6 |
| MASSACHUSETTS MUTUAL LIFE INS CO | MA | 235,570.0 |
| MEDCO CONTAINMENT LIFE INS CO | PA | 1,113.2 |
| MEDICO CORP LIFE INS CO | NE | 63.9 |
| MOTORISTS COMMERCIAL MUTUAL INS CO | OH | 393.5 |
| MUTUAL OF AMERICA LIFE INS CO | NY | 20,499.3 |
| NEW YORK LIFE INS CO | NY | 176,417.0 |
| NORTHWESTERN MUTUAL LIFE INS CO | WI | 264,165.0 |
| PACIFIC GUARDIAN LIFE INS CO LTD | HI | 552.3 |
| PHYSICIANS LIFE INS CO | NE | 1,625.7 |
| PROTECTIVE INS CO | IN | 848.6 |
| STANDARD LIFE & ACCIDENT INS CO | TX | 516.7 |
| **Rating: B+** | | |
| AETNA HEALTH & LIFE INS CO | CT | 2,403.1 |
| AMERICAN FAMILY LIFE ASR CO OF COLUM | NE | 113,507.0 |
| AMERICAN FAMILY MUTL INS CO SI | WI | 17,048.2 |
| AMERICAN FIDELITY ASR CO | OK | 5,772.7 |
| AMERICAN UNITED LIFE INS CO | IN | 27,567.2 |
| ASSURITY LIFE INS CO | NE | 2,726.8 |
| AXA EQUITABLE LIFE INS CO | NY | 187,479.0 |
| BEST LIFE & HEALTH INS CO | TX | 20.9 |
| BOSTON MUTUAL LIFE INS CO | MA | 1,424.8 |
| COMPANION LIFE INS CO | SC | 359.8 |
| DEARBORN NATIONAL LIFE INS CO | IL | 1,849.7 |
| DELAWARE AMERICAN LIFE INS CO | DE | 137.9 |
| FAMILY HERITAGE LIFE INS CO OF AMER | OH | 1,249.5 |
| FARM BUREAU LIFE INS CO | IA | 8,948.8 |
| GERBER LIFE INS CO | NY | 3,650.7 |
| GOVERNMENT PERSONNEL MUTUAL L I C | TX | 832.3 |
| JACKSON NATIONAL LIFE INS CO | MI | 222,617.0 |
| MIDLAND NATIONAL LIFE INS CO | IA | 55,140.0 |
| MINNESOTA LIFE INS CO | MN | 44,369.0 |
| MUTUAL OF OMAHA INS CO | NE | 7,661.2 |
| NATIONAL BENEFIT LIFE INS CO | NY | 537.3 |
| NATIONAL CASUALTY CO | OH | 406.6 |
| OHIO NATIONAL LIFE ASR CORP | OH | 4,048.6 |
| PRINCIPAL LIFE INS CO | IA | 185,959.0 |
| SB MUTL LIFE INS CO OF MA | MA | 3,015.1 |
| SENTRY SELECT INS CO | WI | 810.3 |
| STANDARD INS CO | OR | 23,414.5 |
| STATE FARM FIRE & CAS CO | IL | 39,417.8 |
| STATE FARM MUTUAL AUTOMOBILE INS CO | IL | 154,684.0 |
| SYMETRA LIFE INS CO | IA | 36,133.8 |
| TRUSTMARK INS CO | IL | 1,532.5 |
| TRUSTMARK LIFE INS CO | IL | 320.1 |
| UNITED WORLD LIFE INS CO | NE | 123.8 |
| USABLE LIFE | AR | 510.9 |
| VOYA RETIREMENT INS & ANNUITY CO | CT | 104,964.0 |

# Section V

# Long-Term Care Insurers

A list of rated companies providing

**Long-Term Care Insurance**

Companies are listed in alphabetical order.

# Section V Contents

This section provides contact addresses and phone numbers for all companies who sell long-term care insurance. The long-term care insurers in this section are listed in alphabetical order.

1. **Safety Rating** — Our rating is measured on a scale from A to F and considers a wide range of factors. Highly-rated companies are, in our opinion, less likely to experience financial difficulties than lower-rated firms. See *About Weiss Safety Ratings* for more information.

2. **Insurance Company Name** — The legally registered name, which can sometimes differ from the name that the company uses for advertising. An insurer's name can be very similar to the name of other companies, so make sure you note the exact name before contacting your agent.

3. **Address** — The address of the main office where you can contact the firm for additional financial data or for the location of local branches and/or registered agents.

4. **Telephone Number** — The number to call for additional financial data or for the phone numbers of local branches and/or registered agents.

To compare long-term care insurance policies and to walk through the maze of options, prices, and insurers, see the *Long-Term Care Insurance Planner*. It helps narrow down the choices available by addressing questions such as:

- What can you afford to pay for insurance?
- What type of care and living arrangement will suit your needs?
- When will you most likely need to utilize the insurance benefits?
- How much can you afford to pay from your own savings?
- Do you want a tax-qualified or non-qualified policy?
- What kind of insurance agent are you working with?

The planner offers an easy-to-use analysis tool to help identify the policy that best meets your needs. Based on information provided by insurance agents and literature from the provider, it addresses questions such as:

- How safe is the insurer?
- How are the coverage and facility options defined?
- What are the terms of coverage and reimbursement?
- How will the benefits be triggered?
- What other features are included in the policy?

| RATING | INSURANCE COMPANY NAME | ADDRESS | CITY | STATE | ZIP | PHONE |
|---|---|---|---|---|---|---|
| A- | AUTO-OWNERS LIFE INS CO | 6101 ANACAPRI BOULEVARD | LANSING | MI | 48917 | (517) 323-1200 |
| D | BANKERS CONSECO LIFE INS CO | 350 JERICHO TURNPIKE SUITE 304 | JERICHO | NY | 11753 | (317) 817-6100 |
| D+ | BANKERS LIFE & CAS CO | 111 EAST WACKER DRIVE STE 2100 | CHICAGO | IL | 60601 | (312) 396-6000 |
| B | BLUE CROSS BLUE SHIELD OF KANSAS INC | 1133 SW TOPEKA BOULEVARD | TOPEKA | KS | 66629 | (785) 291-7000 |
| A+ | COUNTRY LIFE INS CO | 1701 N TOWANDA AVENUE | BLOOMINGTON | IL | 61701 | (309) 821-3000 |
| B- | EQUITABLE LIFE & CASUALTY INS CO | 3 TRIAD CENTER | SALT LAKE CITY | UT | 84180 | (801) 579-3400 |
| B | FORETHOUGHT LIFE INS CO | 10 W MARKET ST STE 2300 | INDIANAPOLIS | IN | 46204 | (317) 223-2700 |
| C+ | GENWORTH LIFE INS CO | 251 LITTLE FALLS DR | WILMINGTON | DE | 19808 | (804) 662-2400 |
| C | GENWORTH LIFE INS CO OF NEW YORK | 600 THIRD AVENUE SUITE 2400 | NEW YORK | NY | 10016 | (212) 895-4137 |
| B | JOHN HANCOCK LIFE & HEALTH INS CO | 197 CLARENDON STREET | BOSTON | MA | 02116 | (617) 572-6000 |
| B | JOHN HANCOCK LIFE INS CO (USA) | 201 TOWNSEND STREET SUITE 900 | LANSING | MI | 48933 | (617) 572-6000 |
| D | LIFESECURE INS CO | 10559 CITATION DRIVE SUITE 300 | BRIGHTON | MI | 48116 | (810) 220-7700 |
| C+ | MADISON NATIONAL LIFE INS CO INC | 1241 JOHN Q HAMMONS DRIVE | MADISON | WI | 53717 | (608) 830-2000 |
| A- | MASSACHUSETTS MUTUAL LIFE INS CO | 1295 STATE STREET | SPRINGFIELD | MA | 1111 | (413) 788-8411 |
| C | MEDAMERICA INS CO | 651 HOLIDAY DRIVE FOSTER PLAZA | PITTSBURGH | PA | 15220 | (585) 238-4659 |
| D- | MEDAMERICA INS CO OF NEW YORK | 165 COURT STREET | ROCHESTER | NY | 14647 | (585) 238-4464 |
| B+ | MUTUAL OF OMAHA INS CO | MUTUAL OF OMAHA PLAZA | OMAHA | NE | 68175 | (402) 342-7600 |
| C | NATIONAL INS CO OF WI INC | 250 S EXECUTIVE DR | BROOKFIELD | WI | 53005 | (262) 785-9995 |
| A- | NEW YORK LIFE INS CO | 51 MADISON AVENUE | NEW YORK | NY | 10010 | (212) 576-7000 |
| B | NORTHWESTERN LONG TERM CARE INS CO | 720 EAST WISCONSIN AVENUE | MILWAUKEE | WI | 53202 | (414) 661-2510 |
| B- | RESERVE NATIONAL INS CO | 601 EAST BRITTON ROAD | OKLAHOMA CITY | OK | 73114 | (405) 848-7931 |
| B+ | STATE FARM MUTUAL AUTOMOBILE INS CO | ONE STATE FARM PLAZA | BLOOMINGTON | IL | 61710 | (309) 766-2311 |
| B | TRANSAMERICA FINANCIAL LIFE INS CO | 440 MAMARONECK AVENUE | HARRISON | NY | 10528 | (914) 627-3630 |
| B | TRANSAMERICA LIFE INS CO | 4333 EDGEWOOD RD NE | CEDAR RAPIDS | IA | 52499 | (319) 355-8511 |
| B | UNITED OF OMAHA LIFE INS CO | MUTUAL OF OMAHA PLAZA | OMAHA | NE | 68175 | (402) 342-7600 |
| E+ | UNITED SECURITY ASR CO OF PA | 673 EAST CHERRY LANE | SOUDERTON | PA | 18964 | (215) 723-3044 |

# Section VI

# Medicare Supplement Insurance

# Section VI Contents

# Part I:
# Answers to Your Questions About Medigap

The choices you make today about your health coverage – or the coverage of someone you care for – can have a major impact on both your health and your wealth. Since you are over 65, Medicare will provide you with a basic level of coverage, but there are many gaps in Medicare coverage that you will likely need to fill with a Medicare supplement insurance (Medigap) policy if you decide not to join a Medicare Advantage plan. The purpose of this report is to help you make coverage choices based on the most objective and broadest amount of information possible.

***First,*** you want to understand what the federal Medicare program does and does not cover. We provide you with a clear layout starting on the following page.

***Second,*** you will need to decide whether you want to fill the gaps in coverage by joining a Medicare Advantage plan or by combining Medicare supplement insurance with Medicare benefits. In Part 1 of this guide, we explain the differences between the two approaches.

***Third,*** if you decide to use Medigap, your next step is to find out which plan best suits your needs. To help you figure this out, review Part II of this guide.

***Fourth,*** check out the specific benefits for each plan along with the premium rates charged for those plans in Part III.

***Finally,*** once you've found a couple of alternatives you like the best, call the companies to find the authorized agent nearest you. Phone numbers for the companies' main offices are listed in Part IV. If you need additional information on health insurance and related topics, call the agencies listed under Reference Organizations.

# What Does Medicare Cover?

**Table 1**
**MEDICARE (PART A): HOSPITAL INSURANCE-COVERED SERVICES FOR 2018**

| Service | Benefit | Medicare Pays | You Pay |
|---|---|---|---|
| **HOSPITAL CARE (IN PATIENT CARE)** | | | |
| Semi-private rooms, meals, general nursing, and drugs as part of your inpatient treatment, and other hospital services and supplies. Limited to 190 days in a lifetime, inpatient psychiatric care in a freestanding psychiatric hospital. | First 60 days | All but $1,340 | $1,340 |
| | 61st to 90th day | All but $335 a day | $335 a day |
| | 91st to 150th day* | All but $670 a day | $670 a day |
| | Beyond 150 days | Nothing | All costs |
| **SKILLED NURSING FACILITY CARE** | | | |
| You must have been in a hospital for at least 3 days, enter a Medicare-approved facility generally within 30 days after hospital discharge, and meet other program requirements. ** | First 20 days | 100% of approved amount | Nothing |
| | Additional 80 days | All but $167.50 a day | Up to $167.50 a day |
| | Beyond 100 days | Nothing | All costs |
| **HOME HEALTH CARE** | | | |
| Part-time or intermittent skilled care, home health services, physical and occupational therapy, durable medical equipment and supplies and other services | For as long as you meet Medicare requirements for home health care benefits | 100% of approved amount; 80% of approved amount for durable medical equipment | Nothing for services; 20% of approved amount for durable medical equipment |
| **HOSPICE CARE** | | | |
| Includes drugs for symptom control and pain relief, medical and support services from a Medicare-approved hospice, and other services not otherwise covered by Medicare. Hospice care is usually given in your home. | For as long as doctor certifies need | All but limited costs for outpatient drugs and inpatient respite care | Limited cost sharing for outpatient drugs and inpatient respite care |
| **BLOOD** | | | |
| When furnished by a hospital or a skilled nursing facility during a covered stay | Unlimited during a benefit period if medically necessary | 80% of the Medicare-approved after the first 3 pints per calendar year | ***100% of the first 3 pints then 20% of the approved cost of additional pints. |

* 60 reserve days may be used only once.

** Neither Medicare nor Medicare supplement insurance will pay for most nursing home care.

*** To the extent the three pints of blood are paid for or replaced under one part of Medicare during the calendar year, they do not have to be paid for or replaced under the other part.

**Table 2**
**MEDICARE (PART B): PREVENTIVE SERVICES FOR 2018**

| Service | Benefit | Medicare Pays | You Pay |
|---|---|---|---|
| **"WELCOME TO MEDICARE" PHYSICAL EXAM (ONE-TIME)** | | | |
| | During the first 12 months that you have Part B, you can get a "Welcome to Medicare" preventive visit. | 100% if provider accepts assignment. | If health care provider performs additional test or services during the same visit, you may have to pay coinsurance, and Part B deductible may apply |
| **YEARLY "WELLNESS" VISIT** | | | |
| | This visit is covered once every 12 months. If you've had Part B for longer than 12 months, you can get a yearly "Wellness" visit. | 100% if provider accepts assignment. | If health care provider performs additional test or services during the same visit, you may have to pay coinsurance, and Part B deductible may apply |
| **ABDOMINAL AORTIC ANEURYSM SCREENING** | | | |
| | A one-time screening ultrasound for people at risk. You must get a referral for it as part of your one-time "Welcome to Medicare" preventive visit. | 100% if provider accepts assignment | Nothing for services |
| **ALCOHOL MISUSE SCREENING AND COUNSELING** | | | |
| | Once every 12 months for adults with Medicare (including pregnant women) who use alcohol, but don't meet the medical criteria for alcohol dependency. | 100% if provider accepts assignment | Nothing for services |
| **BONE MASS MEASUREMENT (BONE DENSITY)** | | | |
| | Once every 24 months (more often if medically necessary) for people who have certain medical conditions or meet certain criteria. | 100% if provider accepts assignment | Nothing for services |
| **BREAST CANCER SCREENING (MAMMOGRAMS)** | | | |
| | Once every 12 months for all women with Medicare who are 40 and older. Medicare covers one baseline mammogram for women between 35 - 39. | 100% if provider accepts assignment | Nothing for services |
| **CARDIOVASCULAR DISEASE (BEHAVIORAL THERAPY)** | | | |
| | One visit per year with a primary care doctor in a primary care setting (like a doctor's office) to help lower your risk | 100% if provider accepts assignment | Nothing for services |
| **CARDIOVASCULAR DISEASE SCREENINGS** | | | |
| | Once every 5 years to test your cholesterol, lipid, lipoprotein, and triglyceride levels. | 100% if provider accepts assignment | Nothing for services |

**Table 2**
**MEDICARE (PART B): PREVENTIVE SERVICES FOR 2018 (cont'd.)**

| Service | Benefit | Medicare Pays | You Pay |
|---|---|---|---|
| **CERVICAL AND VAGINAL CANCER SCREENING** | | | |
| | Once every 24 months. Every 12 months if you're at high risk for cervical or vaginal cancer or child-bearing age and had an abnormal Pap test in the past 36 months | 100% if the doctor or provider accepts assignment | Nothing for services |
| **COLORECTAL CANCER SCREENING** | | | |
| **Multi-target stool DNA test** | Once every 3 years if you meet all conditions: between ages 50-85, show no symptoms of colorectal disease, at average risk for developing colorectal cancer | 100% if the doctor or other qualified health care provider accepts assignment. | Nothing for services |
| **Screening facal occult blood test** | Once every 12 months if you're 50 or older | 100% if the doctor or other qualified health care provider accepts assignment. | Nothing for services |
| **Screening flexible sigmoidoscopy** | Once every 48 months if you're 50 or older, or 120 months after a previous screening colonoscopy for those not at high risk. | 100% if the doctor or other qualified health care provider accepts assignment. | Nothing for services |
| **Screening colonoscopy** | Once every 120 months (high risk every 24 months) or 48 months after a previous flexible sigmoidoscopy. There's no minimum age. | 100% if the doctor or other qualified health care provider accepts assignment. | If a polyp or other tissue is found and removed during the colonoscopy, you may have to pay 20% of the Medicare-approved amount for the doctor's services and a copayment in a hospital outpatient setting. |
| **Screening barium enema** | Once every 48 months if you're 50 or older (high risk every 24 months) when used instead of a sigmoidoscopy or colonoscopy. | 80% of the approved amount | You pay 20% for the doctor's services. In a hospital outpatient setting, you also pay the hospital a copayment. |
| **DERPRESSION SCREENING** | | | |
| | One screening per year. The screening must be done in a primary care setting (like a doctor's office) that can provide follow-up treatment and referrals. | 100% if provider accepts assignment | Nothing for services |

**Table 2**
**MEDICARE (PART B): PREVENTIVE SERVICES FOR 2018 (cont'd.)**

| Service | Benefit | Medicare Pays | You Pay |
|---|---|---|---|
| **DIABETES SCREENING** | | | |
| | Covers these screenings if your doctor determines you're at risk for diabetes. Up to 2 diabetes screenings each year. | 100% if your doctor or provider accepts assignment | Nothing for services |
| **DIABETES SELF-MANAGEMENT TRAINING** | | | |
| | Covers diabetes outpatient self-management training to teach you to cope with and manage your diabetes. | 80% of the approved amount | 20% of the Medicare approved amount, and the Part B deductible applies |
| **FLU SHOTS** | | | |
| | Covers one flu shot per flu season | 100% if the doctor or provider accepts assignment | Nothing for services |
| **GLAUCOMA TESTING** | | | |
| | Once every 12 months for those at high risk for glaucoma. | 80% of approved amount | 20% of the approved amount after the yearly Part B deductible. Copayment in a hospital outpatient setting |
| **HEPATITIS B SHOTS** | | | |
| | Covers these shots for people at medium or high risk for Hepatitis B | 100% if the doctor or provider accepts assignment | Nothing for services |
| **HEPATITIS C SCREENING TEST** | | | |
| | Covers one Hepatitis C screening test if you meet one of these conditions:<br>– Current or past history of illicit injection drug use<br>– Blood transfusion before 1992<br>– Born between 1945-1965 | 100% if the doctor or other qualified health care provider accepts assignment | Nothing for services |
| **HIV SCREENING** | | | |
| | Once per year for people at increased risk for HIV screenings for pregnant women up to 3 times during a pregnancy | 100% if the doctor or provider accepts assignment | Nothing for services |

**Table 2**
**MEDICARE (PART B): PREVENTIVE SERVICES FOR 2018 (cont'd.)**

| Service | Benefit | Medicare Pays | You Pay |
|---|---|---|---|
| **LUNG CANCER SCREENING** | | | |
| | Covers a lung cancer screening with Low Dose Computed Tomography (LDCT) once per year | 100% if the primary care doctor or other qualified primary care practitioner accepts assignment | Nothing for services |
| **MEDICAL NUTRITION THERAPY SERVICES** | | | |
| | Covers medical nutrition therapy and certain related services if you have diabetes or kidney disease, or you have had a kidney transplant in the last 36 months | 100% if the doctor or provider accepts assignment | Nothing for services |
| **OBESITY SCREENING AND COUNSELING** | | | |
| | If you have a body mass index (BMI) of 30 or more, Medicare covers face-to-face individual behavioral therapy sessions to help you lose weight. | 100% if the primary care doctor or other qualified primary care practitioner accepts assignment | Nothing for services |
| **PNEUMOCOCCAL SHOT** | | | |
| | Covers pneumococcal shots to help prevent pneumococcal infections (like certain types of pneumonia). Most people only need a shot once in their lifetime. | 100% if the doctor or provider accepts assignment | Nothing for services |
| **PROSTATE CANCER SCREENING** | | | |
| | Prostate Specific Antigen (PSA) and a digital rectal exam once every 12 months for men over 50 (beginning the day after your 50th birthday) | 100% for the PSA test | 20% of the Medicare-approved amount, and the Part B deductible applies for the digital rectal exam. In a hospital outpatient setting, you also pay the hospital a copayment. |

**Table 2**
**MEDICARE (PART B): PREVENTIVE SERVICES FOR 2018 (cont'd.)**

| Service | Benefit | Medicare Pays | You Pay |
|---|---|---|---|
| **SEXUALLY TRANSMITTED INFECTIONS SCREENING AND COUNSELING** | | | |
| | Covers screenings for Chlamydia, gonorrhea, syphilis, and Hepatitis B. Covered for people who are pregnant and for certain people who are at increased risk for an STI. Once every 12 months or at certain times during a pregnancy. Covers up to 2 individual, 20-30 minute, face-to-face, high-intensity behavioral counseling sessions each year for sexually active adults. | 100% if the primary care doctor or other qualified primary care practitioner accepts assignment | Nothing for services |
| **SMOKING AND TOBACCO-USE CESSATION** | | | |
| | Includes up to 8 face-to-face visits in a 12-month period | 100% if the doctor or other qualified health care provider accepts assignment | Nothing for services |

**Table 3**
**MEDICARE (PART B): MEDICAL INSURANCE-COVERED SERVICES FOR 2018**

| Service | Benefit | Medicare Pays | You Pay |
|---|---|---|---|
| **AMBULANCE SERVICES** | | | |
| | Covers ground ambulance transportation when you need to be transported to a hospital, critical access hospital, or skilled nursing facility for medically necessary services, and transportation in any other vehicle could endanger your health | 80% of approved amount (after deductible) | 20% of the Medicare-approved amount, and the Part B deductible applies |
| **AMBULATORY SURGICAL CENTERS** | | | |
| | Covers ground ambulance transportation when you need to be transported to a hospital, critical access hospital, or skilled nursing facility for medically necessary services. | 100% for certain preventive services | 20% of the Medicare approved amount to both the ambulatory surgical center and the doctor who treats you, and Part B deductible applies. |
| **BLOOD** | | | |
| | | 100% if the provider gets blood from a blood bank | A copayment for the blood processing and handling services for each unit of blood you get, and the Part B deductible applies. If the provider has to buy blood for you, you must either pay the provider costs for the first 3 units in a calendar year or have the blood donated by you or someone else. |

**Table 3**
**MEDICARE (PART B): MEDICAL INSURANCE-COVERED SERVICES FOR 2018**

| Service | Benefit | Medicare Pays | You Pay |
|---|---|---|---|
| **CARDIAC REHABILITATION** | | | |
| | Cover comprehensive programs that include exercise, education, and counseling for patients who meet certain conditions. Medicare also covers intensive cardiac rehabilitation programs that are typically more rigorous or more intense than regular cardiac rehabilitation programs. | 80% of the approved amount. | 20% of the Medicare-approved amount if you get the services in a doctor's office. In a hospital outpatient setting, you also pay the hospital a copayment. The Part B deductible applies. |
| **CHEMOTHERAPY** | | | |
| | Covers chemotherapy in a doctor's office, freestanding clinic, or hospital outpatient setting for people with cancer. | 80% of approved amount | A copayment for chemotherapy in a hospital outpatient setting. Chemotherapy given in a doctor's office or freestanding clinic you pay 20% of the Medicare-approved amount, and the Part B deductible applies. |
| **CHIROPRACTIC SERVICES (LIMITED COVERAGE)** | | | |
| | Covers manipulation of the spine if medically necessary to correct a subluxation (when one or more of the bones of your spine move out of position) | 80% of the approved amount | 20% of the Medicare-approved amount, and the Part B deductible applies. **Note:** You pay all costs for any other services or tests ordered by a chiropractor (including X-rays and massage therapy) |
| **CLINICAL RESEARCH STUDIES** | | | |
| | Covers some costs, like office visits and tests, in qualifying clinical research studies. | 80% of the approved amount | 20% of the Medicare-approved amount, and the Part B deductible may apply |

**Table 3**
**MEDICARE (PART B): MEDICAL INSURANCE-COVERED SERVICES FOR 2018**

| Service | Benefit | Medicare Pays | You Pay |
|---|---|---|---|
| **CONCIERGE CARE** | | | |
| | When a doctor or group of doctors charges you a membership fee before they'll see you or accept you into their practice. | Not Covered | 100% of the membership fees for concierge care (also called concierge medicine, retainer-based medicine, boutique medicine, platinum practice, or direct care) |
| **CONTINUOUS POSITIVE AIRWAY PRESSURE (CPAP) THERAPY** | | | |
| | A 3-month trial of CPAP therapy if you've been diagnosed with obstructive sleep apnea. | 80% of the approved amount | 20% of the Medicare-approved amount for rental of the machine and purchase of related supplies (like masks and tubing) and the Part B deductible applies. |
| **DEFIBRILLATOR (IMPLANTABLE AUTOMATIC)** | | | |
| | Covers these devices for some people diagnosed with heart failure. | 80% of the approved amount | 20% of the Medicare-approved amount, if the surgery takes place in a outpatient setting. The doctor's services. If you get the device as a hospital outpatient, you also pay the hospital a copayment. The Part B deductible applies. |

**Table 3**
**MEDICARE (PART B): MEDICAL INSURANCE-COVERED SERVICES FOR 2018**

| Service | Benefit | Medicare Pays | You Pay |
|---|---|---|---|
| **DIABETES SUPPLIES** | | | |
| | Covers blood sugar testing monitors, test strips, lancet devices and lancets, blood sugar control solutions, and therapeutic shoes (in some cases). Covers insulin if it's medically necessary to use with an external insulin pump. | 80% of the approved amount. | 20% of the Medicare approved amount, the Part B deductible applies |
| **DOCTOR AND OTHER HEALTH CARE PROVIDER SERVICES** | | | |
| | Covers medically necessary doctor services (including outpatient services and some doctor services you get when you're a hospital inpatient) and covered preventive services. | 80% of the approved amount. | 20% of the Medicare approved amount, the Part B deductible applies |
| **DURABLE MEDICAL EQUIPMENT (LIKE WALKERS)** | | | |
| | Covers items like oxygen equipment and supplies, wheelchairs, walkers, and hospital beds ordered by a doctor or other health care provider enrolled in Medicare for use in the home | 80% of the approved amount. | 20% of the Medicare approved amount, the Part B deductible applies |
| **EKG OR ECG (ELECTROCARDIOGRAM) SCREENING** | | | |
| | One time screening EKG/ECG if referred by your doctor or other health care provider as part of your one-time "Welcome to Medicare" preventive visit | 80% of the approved amount. | 20% of the Medicare approved amount, the Part B deductible applies. An EKG/ECG is also covered as a diagnostic test. |

**Table 3**
**MEDICARE (PART B): MEDICAL INSURANCE-COVERED SERVICES FOR 2018**

| Service | Benefit | Medicare Pays | You Pay |
|---|---|---|---|
| **EMERGENCY DEPARTMENT SERVICES** | | | |
| | When you have an injury, a sudden illness, or an illness that quickly gets much worse | 80% of the approved amount. | A specified copayment for the hospital emergency department visit, and you pay 20% of the Medicare-approved amount for the doctor's or other health care provider's services. The Part B deductible applies. Cost may be different if you're admitted. |
| **EYEGLASSES (LIMITED)** | | | |
| | One pair of eyeglasses with standard frames (or one set of contact lenses) after cataract surgery that implants an intraocular lens. | 80% of the approved amount. Medicare will only pay for contact lenses or eye glasses from a supplier enrolled in Medicare | 20% of Medicare-approved amount, and the Part B deductible applies. |
| **FEDERALLY-QUALIFIED HEALTH CENTER SERVICES** | | | |
| | Covers many outpatient primary care and preventive health services. | 80% of the approved amount. | No deductible, and generally, you're responsible for paying 20% of your charges or 20% of the Medicare-approved amount. |
| **FOOT EXAMS AND TREATMENT** | | | |
| | Covers foot exams and treatment if you have diabetes-related nerve damage and/or meet certain conditions | 80% of the approved amount. | 20% of the Medicare-approved amount, and the Part B deductible applies. In a hospital outpatient setting, you also pay the hospital copayment. |
| **HEARING AND BALANCE EXAMS** | | | |
| | Covers these exams if your doctor or other health care provider orders them to see if your need medical treatment. | 80% of the approved amount. | 20% of the Medicare-approved amount, and the Part B deductible applies. In a hospital outpatient setting, you also pay the hospital a copayment. |

**Table 3**
**MEDICARE (PART B): MEDICAL INSURANCE-COVERED SERVICES FOR 2018**

| Service | Benefit | Medicare Pays | You Pay |
|---|---|---|---|
| **HOME HEALTH SERVICES** | | | |
| | Covers medically necessary part-time or intermittent skilled nursing care, and/or physical therapy, speech-language pathology services, and/or services if you have a continuing need for occupation therapy. | 100% for health services. | Nothing for services |
| **KIDNEY DIALYSIS SERVICES AND SUPPLIES** | | | |
| | Covers 3 dialysis treatments per week if you have End-Stage Renal Disease (ESRD). This includes all ESRD-related drugs and biological, laboratory tests, home dialysis training, support services, equipment, and supplies | 80% of the approved amount. | 20% of approved Medicare-approved amount, and the Part B applies. |
| **KIDNEY DISEASE EDUCATION SERVICES** | | | |
| | Covers up to 6 sessions of kidney disease education services if you have Stage IV chronic kidney disease, and your doctor or other health care provider refers you for the service. | 80% of the approved amount. | 20% of approved Medicare-approved amount, and the Part B applies |
| **LABORATORY SERVICES** | | | |
| | Covers laboratory services including certain blood tests, urinalysis, certain tests on tissue specimens, and some screening tests. | Generally 100% of approved amount | Nothing for services |

**Table 3**
**MEDICARE (PART B): MEDICAL INSURANCE-COVERED SERVICES FOR 2018**

| Service | Benefit | Medicare Pays | You Pay |
|---|---|---|---|
| **MENTAL HEALTH CARE (OUTPATIENT)** | | | |
| | Covers mental health care services to help with conditions like depression or anxiety. Includes services generally provided in an outpatient setting (like a doctor's or other health care provider's office or hospital outpatient department). | 100% of lab tests. 80% of the approved amount. **Note:** Inpatient mental health care is covered under Part A | 20% of the Medicare-approved amount and the Part B deductible applies for:<br>• Visits to a doctor or other health care provider to diagnose your condition or monitor or change your prescriptions<br>• Outpatient treatment of your condition (like counseling or psychotherapy) |
| **OCCUPATIONAL THERAPY** | | | |
| | Covers evaluation and treatment to help you perform activities of daily living (like dressing or bathing) when your doctor or other health care provider certifies you need it. | 80% of the approved amount. | 20% of the Medicare-approved amount and the Part B deductible applies. |
| **OUTPATIENT HOSPITAL SERVICES** | | | |
| | Covers many diagnostic and treatment services in hospital outpatient departments. | 80% of the approved amount. | 20% of the Medicare-approved amount and the Part B deductible applies. |
| **OUTPATIENT MEDICAL AND SURGICAL SERVICES AND SUPPLIES** | | | |
| | Covers approved procedures like X-rays, casts, stitches, or outpatient surgeries. | 80% of the approved amount. | 20% of the Medicare-approved amount, and the Part B deductible applies. In a hospital outpatient setting, you also pay the hospital a copayment. |
| **PHYSICAL THERAPY** | | | |
| | Covers evaluation and treatment for injuries and diseases that change your ability to function when your doctor or other health care provider certifies your need for it. | 80% of the approved amount. | 20% of the Medicare-approved amount, and the Part B deductible applies. |

**Table 3**
**MEDICARE (PART B): MEDICAL INSURANCE-COVERED SERVICES FOR 2018**

| Service | Benefit | Medicare Pays | You Pay |
|---|---|---|---|
| **PRESCRIPTION DRUGS (LIMITED)** | | | |
| | Covers a limited number of drugs like injections you get in a doctor's office, certain oral anti-cancer drugs, drugs used with some types of durable medical equipment (like a nebulizer or external infusion pump), immunosuppressant drugs and under very limited circumstances. | 80% of the approved amount. | 20% of the Medicare-approved amount, and the Part B deductible applies. |
| **PROSTHETIC/ORTHOTIC ITEMS** | | | |
| | Covers arm, leg, back, and neck braces; artificial eyes; artificial limbs (and their replacement parts); some types of breast prostheses (after mastectomy); and prosthetic devices needed to replace an internal body part or function. | 80% of the approved amount. | 20% of the Medicare-approved amount, and the Part B deductible applies. |
| **PULMONARY REHABILITATION** | | | |
| | Covers a comprehensive pulmonary rehabilitation program if you have moderate to very severe chronic obstructive pulmonary disease (COPD) and have a referral from the doctor treating this chronic respiratory disease. | 80% of the approved amount. | 20% of the Medicare-approved amount, and the Part B deductible applies. In a hospital outpatient setting, you also pay the hospital a copayment. |
| **RURAL HEALTH CLINIC SERVICES** | | | |
| | Covers many outpatient primary care and preventive services in rural health clinics. | 80% of the approved amount. 100% for most preventive services. | 20% of the Medicare-approved amount, and the Part B deductible applies. |

**Table 3**
**MEDICARE (PART B): MEDICAL INSURANCE-COVERED SERVICES FOR 2018**

| Service | Benefit | Medicare Pays | You Pay |
|---|---|---|---|
| **SECOND SURGICAL OPINIONS** | | | |
| | Covers second surgical opinions for surgery that isn't an emergency. | 80% of the approved amount. | 20% of the Medicare-approved amount, and the Part B deductible applies. |
| **SPEECH-LANGUAGE PATHOLOGY SERVICES** | | | |
| | Covers evaluation and treatment to regain and strengthen speech and language skills, including cognitive and swallowing skills, when your doctor or other health care provider certifies you need it. | 80% of the approved amount. | 20% of the Medicare-approved amount, and the Part B deductible applies. |
| **SURGICAL DRESSING SERVICES** | | | |
| | Covers medically necessary treatment of a surgical or surgically treated wound. | 80% of the approved amount. | 20% of the Medicare-approved amount for the doctor's or other health care provider's services |
| **TELEHEALTH** | | | |
| | Covers limited medical or other health services, like office visits and consultations provided using an interactive, two-way telecommunications system (like real-time audio and video) by an eligible provider who isn't at your location. | 80% of the approved amount. | 20% of the Medicare-approved amount, and the Part B deductible applies. |
| **TESTS (OTHER THAN LAB TEST)** | | | |
| | Covers X-rays, MRIs, CT scans, ECG/EKGs, and some other diagnostic tests. | 80% of the approved amount. | 20% of the Medicare-approved amount, and the Part B deductible applies. You also pay the hospital a copayment that may be more than 20% of the Medicare-approved amount, but in most cases this amount can't be more than the Part A hospital stay deductible. |

**Table 3**
**MEDICARE (PART B): MEDICAL INSURANCE-COVERED SERVICES FOR 2018**

| Service | Benefit | Medicare Pays | You Pay |
|---|---|---|---|
| **TRANSPLANTS AND IMMUNOSUPPRESSIVE DRUGS** | | | |
| | Covers doctor services for heart, lung, kidney, pancreas, intestine, and liver transplants under certain conditions and only in a Medicare-certified facility. Covers bone marrow and cornea transplants under certain conditions. | 80% of the approved amount. | 20% of the Medicare-approved amount for the drugs, and the Part B deductible applies. |
| **TRAVEL (HEALTH CARE NEEDED WHEN TRAVELING OUTSIDE THE U.S.)** | | | |
| | Generally doesn't cover health care while you're traveling outside the U.S., there are some exceptions, including cases where Medicare may pay for services that you get while on board a ship within the territorial waters adjoining the land areas of the U.S. | 80% of the approved amount. | 20% of the Medicare-approved amount, and the Part B deductible applies. |
| **URGENTLY NEEDED CARE** | | | |
| | Covers urgently needed care to treat a sudden illness or injury that isn't a medical emergency. | 80% of the approved amount. | 20% of the Medicare-approved amount for the doctor's or other health care provider's services and the Part B deductible applies. In a hospital outpatient setting, you also pay the hospital a copayment |

In addition to the services listed, Medicare also helps cover the following: ambulance services, artificial eyes, artificial limbs (prosthetic devices and replacement parts), braces (arm, leg, back, and neck), chiropractic services (limited), eyeglasses (one pair of standard frames after cataract surgery with an intraocular lens), hearing and balance exams ordered by your doctor, kidney dialysis and prosthetic/orthodontic devices (including breast prosthesis after mastectomy).

In some cases and under certain conditions, Medicare may also cover these services: a second surgical opinion by a doctor, telemedicine services (in rural areas), and therapeutic shoes for people with diabetes, and transplants (heart, lung, kidney, pancreas, intestine, bone marrow, cornea, and liver).

**Table 4**
**MEDICARE (PART D): PRESCRIPTION DRUG COVERAGE FOR 2018**
**Coverage is provided by private companies that have been approved by Medicare**

| Service | Costs | Medicare Provider Pays | You Pay |
|---|---|---|---|
| Medicare approved drug plans will cover generic and brand-name drugs. Most plans will have a formulary, which is a list of drugs covered by the plan. This list must always meet Medicare's requirements, including:<br><br>- Inclusion of at least two drugs in every drug category.<br><br>- Access to retail pharmacies.<br><br>- For drugs not covered, a procedure must be in place to obtain, if medically necessary. | Premium | --- | On average, $39.32 per month for basic coverage, and $63.65 per month for enhanced coverage |
| | First $405 in costs | Nothing | Up to $405 (this is the deductible) |
| | Costs between $405 and $3,750 | $2,491 | $836 (35% for branded companies, 44% for generic) |
| | Next $1,250 drug costs | Nothing | Until out of pocket spending, including drug company discount total $5,000 |
| | All additional drug costs | All but co-pay | Co-pay $3.35 generic $8.35 all other drugs |

Your plan must, at a minimum, offer this standard level of service and cost coverage outlined here, however, some plans may offer more coverage. Premiums will vary depending on any additional coverage provided by the plan.

## What are the Gaps in Medicare Coverage?

Medicare has never covered all medical expenses and never will. The gap between what the doctors charge and the government pays is big and getting bigger. In fact, Medicare was never designed to cover chronic conditions or prolonged medical treatments. It was directed toward Americans age 65 or older who need minor or short-term care – little more. Be sure to understand where Medicare falls short. We can't list all the possible gaps, but here are the ones that affect almost everyone (see the tables on the previous pages for more details):

### Gap #1: Deductibles

Medicare has two parts: **Part A** *acts as hospital insurance* and **Part B** *acts as medical insurance.* You are responsible for deductibles under both parts. Under Part A, for instance, you would be responsible for the $1,340 deductible for the first 60 days of a hospital stay. Plus, this $1,340 deductible applies each time you re-enter the hospital after a greater than 60-day span between admissions.

Under Part B, Medicare will pick up 80% of approved medical expenses after you pay a $183 deductible.

### Gap #2: Co-Payments

You are responsible for a share of the daily costs if your hospital stay lasts more than 60 days. In 2018, you would be responsible for paying a $335 daily "coinsurance" fee if you stay in the hospital longer than 60 days but less than 90 days. Worse yet, Medicare Part A pays nothing after 90 days – unless you take advantage of the 60 "lifetime reserve days." The 60 reserve days can be used only once, and even then, you would still pay $670 daily for those 60 days.

### Gap #3: Shortfalls

A national fee schedule established what physicians on Medicare assignment can charge for their services; Medicare will generally pay 80% of that amount. However, not all physicians are on Medicare assignment. Those who are not on assignment may charge more than the approved amount, leaving you responsible for the shortfall.

### Gap #4: Nonpayment

The Original Medicare program does not directly provide any coverage whatsoever for certain services and expenses such as prescription drugs, hearing aids, treatment in foreign countries, and much more.

The bottom line: When all is said and done, the federal Medicare program will cover no more than half to three quarters of your medical expenses. That's why private Medicare supplement insurance, or Medigap, makes sense; its goal is to cover a portion of what Medicare doesn't. But in order for Medigap to make sense for you, you need to find the right policy, from the right company, for a reasonable price.

## What about Medicare Prescription Drug Coverage?

The Medicare Prescription Drug, Improvement and Modernization (MMA) Act was passed in 2003. This legislation created Medicare Part D: Prescription Drug Coverage effective January 2006. Coverage is only available by private companies that have been approved by Medicare, not through the Medicare program directly. You can obtain coverage by either directly purchasing Part D coverage through a plan sponsor or in combination with enrollment in a Medicare Advantage health plan offering drug coverage. These drug plans are standardized across providers but they are required to offer a minimum level of coverage. Plans may vary in co-pays, premiums, deductibles, and drug coverage and pharmacy networks. (See Table 4 for an outline of the required coverage.)

To assist you in the selection of a health benefit package complete with prescription drug coverage refer to our *Consumer Guide to Medicare Prescription Drug Coverage* that includes:

- Information on the Medicare prescription drug benefit.
- Help in making a choice about prescription drug coverage.
- What to consider once you enroll.
- An index of Medicare approved prescription drug plans.

# Medicare, Medicare Advantage, Part D Sponsors, Medigap – What Does It All Mean?

The various terms used regarding coverage of health benefits for seniors is downright confusing. Let us take a moment here to review some of the terminology. The health insurance program for seniors managed by the federal government consists of the Original Medicare, Medicare Advantage, and Part D Prescription Drug Sponsors. Tables 1 through 3 on the preceding pages outline your coverage and coverage gaps under the Original Medicare plan. With this plan you seek services from Medicare providers who then receive payment from the government for the costs they incur for your care.

The Medicare Advantage program allows you to join a private health insurance plan that has contracted with Medicare to provide Part A and B coverage. The Medicare Advantage plans in turn receive funds from the government for providing you with benefits. These plans typically provide coverage beyond what Medicare offers, making supplemental policy unnecessary.

Medicare Part D will allow you to get prescription drug benefits in two ways. One option is to enroll with a Prescription Drug Plan sponsor in combination with your Original Medicare benefits. You will receive benefits from and pay a premium to the plan sponsor who then receives funds from the government. The second option is to enroll with a Medicare Advantage plan that is offering prescription drug coverage. Here you will receive all your benefits from the plan and pay only one premium. Refer to Table 4 for an outline of the minimum coverage that a plan sponsor must offer.

Medicare Supplement insurance, or Medigap as it is commonly referred to, is available through private insurers for those enrollees of the Original Medicare plan to fill the coverage 'gaps' in the Part A and B coverage. Basically, Medigap insurance will reimburse you for the out-of-pocket costs you incur that are not covered under Medicare. This insurance is completely optional.

Of course, if you're lucky, and your employer or union is continuing to cover your health benefits when you retire you won't need any of these types of insurance. But you want to stay educated because you never know when your old employer may discontinue retirement benefits.

Now let's take a closer look at the difference between Medicare supplement insurance policies and Medicare Advantage plans.

## Medigap

To make comparing policies from one insurer to another easier Congress standardized and simplified Medigap plans so that there were just 10 to choose from – Plan 'A,' which is the bare bones, through Plan 'N,' the top of the line. This means that all Medigap insurers offer the same exact policy (though some companies may offer only a few of the plans). If you live in Wisconsin, Massachusetts, or Minnesota there are different types of Medigap plans that are sold in your state but are still standardized across insurers in each state.

Starting in 2006, two new plans, K and L, were introduced. These policies are structured to increase the portion of costs born by the policyholder while still providing the security of a cap on out-of-pocket expenses. These plans will be attractive to those individuals not able or willing to pay a higher premium for one of the other plans or expect to have minimal health expenses but still want the comfort of having costs capped. In June, 2010, plans E, H, I and J were discontinued and two new plans M and N were introduced. In Part II we provide you a table that outlines what each of the 10 plans cover.

You will have to pay a premium which can vary greatly, depending on the plan you choose and from which company you buy. Coverage is more expansive than through a Medicare Advantage plan but at a higher price. With a Medigap policy you have the freedom to choose your own doctors or specialists, and you will be covered regardless of which clinic or hospital you attend.

Medicare Select plans, a type of Medigap policy, are available in some areas which offer the same benefits but require you to use providers within the policy's network, similar to an HMO. These policies should be cheaper than non-Select plans since your choice of providers is restricted. Medigap plans do not cover long-term/custodial care at home or in a nursing home, hearing aids, vision care, private-duty nursing, dental care, or prescription medicine.

Even if you decide that you want a Medigap policy you may find that you will not be approved depending on your health, or you may not find an insurer in your area that sells these types of policies. However, once you do purchase a policy, Medigap policies are guaranteed renewable. This means that an insurance company cannot refuse to renew your policy unless you do not pay the premiums, or you made material misrepresentations on your application. You are typically able to obtain coverage each year once you are approved; however, the premium may change.

Prior to 2006, Medigap plans H, I, and J offered some prescription drug coverage. Effective in 2006 these plans were stripped of the prescription drug coverage benefit. If you purchased one of these plans prior to January 2006 and decided not to enroll in Medicare Part D, then you have been allowed to continue to renew the policy. If you decide to enroll in Part D, then you are allowed to switch to another Medigap plan (A, B, C, or F) without additional underwriting if one is offered by the insurer.

You are eligible to purchase a Medigap policy when you have enrolled in Medicare Parts A and B. In all states, there is an open enrollment period that lasts for six months and begins on the first day of the month in which you are both age 65 or older and enrolled in Part B. During this open enrollment period, the insurer cannot deny you coverage for any reason including pre-existing conditions. The insurer can, however, charge you a higher premium for the pre-existing condition or other health and lifestyle factors.

## Medicare Advantage Plans

Under Medicare Part C, Medicare Advantage plans were introduced to offer seniors choices in coverage, more benefits at minimal cost, and to reduce the burden on the Medicare program. Insurers will often offer benefits not covered by Medicare, such as dental and vision services, at a lower price than a Medigap policy.

Prior to 2006 most offered some type of prescription drug coverage, but it varied from plan to plan. With the Medicare Prescription drug bill that took effect in 2006, health insurers may still offer prescription drug coverage but the benefits must match or exceed the requirements outlined in Medicare Part D (Refer Table). The insurers will then receive funding from the government for providing the benefits. All coverage is included in one premium charge.

With a Medicare Advantage plan you will not have to file any forms for reimbursement. You may or may not have to pay a premium and/or a co-pay for doctor's visits. In most cases you are restricted to the doctors in the plan's network, and you will need a referral before you see a specialist. Several new types of Medicare Advantage plans (PPOs, Special Need plans, Private Fee-for-Service plans, Medicare Medical Savings Account Plans, and Cost plans) have been introduced recently that vary from the current HMO plans offered including, in some cases, expanded options for accessing providers. Make sure to understand how these plans work before signing on.

There may be limited insurers offering a Medicare Advantage plan in your area and your benefits can be discontinued after the contract period (usually one year). At that time you would have to either choose a new insurer/plan or join the Original Medicare Plan.

# Part II: Steps to Follow When Selecting a Medigap Policy

# Follow These Steps When Selecting a Medigap Policy

1. **Determine what benefits you need.** Consider the following:

- **Income.** If you are living on a **fixed income** and are able to afford only the most basic coverage, favor Plan A, the core plan. Among other things, you'll get an extra 30 days hospitalization per year beyond what Medicare pays. It also covers 100% of the Medicare Part B coinsurance for approved medical services, which is usually 20% of the approved amount.

  You may also want to consider plans, K or L, if they are available in your area. These policies help limit out-of-pocket costs for doctor's services and hospital care at a lower premium; however, you will have to pay more of Medicare's coinsurance and deductibles before the policy pays its share of the costs. These policies also do not cover 'excess' charges billed by your physician. Wisconsin, Massachusetts, and Minnesota also offer a core or basic plan to choose from.

- **Family History.** You or your family's medical history is such that you want to be prepared to pay for nursing care, consider Plan C. Your $167.50 per-day co-payment under Medicare would be covered up to 100 days for skilled nursing facility care.

- **Foreign Travel.** If you travel overseas extensively, you can get coverage for emergency care in a foreign country with Plan C through G, M and N. In Massachusetts and Minnesota foreign travel coverage can be found in the Supplement 1 and 2 Plans and to the Basic Medigap Coverage, respectively. In Wisconsin, a Foreign Travel rider can be added.
- **Plan F is the most popular one.** In 2016, 58.6% of enrollees chose this plan. The next popular, Plan G, had 18.2% of the enrollees.

The chart below shows basic information about the different benefits Medigap policies cover.

X = the plan covers 100% of this benefit

Blank = the policy doesn't cover that benefit
% = the plan covers the percentage of this benefit

| | Medigap Plans | | | | | | | | | |
|---|---|---|---|---|---|---|---|---|---|---|
| **Medigap Benefits** | **A** | **B** | **C** | **D** | **F*** | **G** | **K** | **L** | **M** | **N** |
| Part A coinsurance and hospital costs up to an additional 365 days after Medicare benefits are used up | X | X | X | X | X | X | X | X | X | X |
| Part B coinsurance or copayment | X | X | X | X | X | X | 50% | 75% | X | X*** |
| Blood (first 3 pints) | X | X | X | X | X | X | 50% | 75% | X | X |
| Part A hospice care coinsurance or copayment | X | X | X | X | X | X | 50% | 75% | X | X |
| Skilled nursing facility care coinsurance | | | X | X | X | X | 50% | 75% | X | X |
| Part A deductible | | X | X | X | X | X | 50% | 75% | 50% | X |
| Part B deductible | | | X | | X | | | | | |
| Part B excess charges | | | | | X | X | | | | |
| Foreign travel exchange (up to plan limits) | | | 80% | 80% | 80% | 80% | | | 80% | 80% |
| Out-of-pocket limit** | | | | | | | $5,240 | $2,620 | | |

*Plan F also offers a high-deductible plan. If you choose this option, this means you must pay for Medicare-covered cost up to the deductible amount of $2,240 in 2018 before your Medigap plan pays anything.

**After you meet your out-of-pocket yearly limit and your yearly Part B deductible, the Medigap plan pays 100% of covered services for the rest of the calendar year.

***Plan N pays 100% of the Part B coinsurance, except for a copayment of up to $20 for some office visits and up to a $50 copayment for emergency room visits that don't result in inpatient admission.

In Massachusetts, Minnesota, and Wisconsin medigap policies are standardized in a different way. They consist of a core plan/core plans and additional riders can be selected to provide additional coverage at a cost.

## 2. Find out which policies are available to you.

- Not all insurers offer all plans in all areas.

- Will you be denied coverage by some insurers due to your health? Find out which ones and eliminate them from your choices.

- Does the insurer deny coverage for pre-existing conditions? If you are past the 6-month window following enrollment in Medicare Part B, companies most often deny you coverage for a specific period of time. However, some companies do not do this so their annual premium may be higher. You need to consider whether or not the higher premium is worth the coverage.

- Are you a member of AARP? If so, you may be able to obtain a policy through its sponsored insurer. Other affinity organizations also offer coverage through a Medigap insurer. Be sure to check with any groups of which you are a member.

- Do you want a Medicare Select plan? If you buy a Medicare Select policy, you are buying one of the 10 standardized Medigap plans A through N. With a Medicare Select plan, however, you must use the network providers to get full insurance benefits (except in an emergency). For this reason, Medicare Select policies generally cost less. If you don't use a Medicare Select hospital for non-emergency services, you will have to pay what a traditional Medicare plan doesn't pay. Medicare will pay its share of the approved charges no matter what hospital you choose.

**3. Compare the premiums.** Not only will you want to check out the premium you would be charged for different plans, but it is important to understand that there are three ways that insurance companies set the prices for policies. In order to compare the premium charged by two insurers for the same plan you need to make sure you are comparing apples to apples. No matter which type of pricing your Medigap insurer uses, the price of your policy will likely go up each year because of inflation and rising health care costs.

- **Attained-Age Rating.** With this type of policy the premium will rise as you age. For example: if you buy at 65, you pay what the company charges 65-year-old customers. Then at 66, you will pay whatever the company is charging a 66-year-old. The Medigap policy will go up in cost due to age, in addition to the increased cost of medical care.
- **Issue-Age Rating.** With this policy, the insurance company will charge you based on the age you were when you first signed up; you will always pay the same premium that someone that age pays. Unlike attained-age policies, issue-age policies do not go up because you are another year older. For example: if you first buy at 65, you will always pay the premium the company charges 65-year-old customers—no matter what your age. If you first buy at 70, you will always pay the premium the company charges 70-year-old customers. This is not to say that your premium won't go up. It will increase as the insurer raises rates for that particular age.
- **No-Age Rating or Community Rating.** This is the least common way that policies are priced. No matter how old you are, the policy costs the same. With this structure, younger people pay more than what they would pay for other polices and older people may pay less. The premium is the same for all people who buy this plan regardless of age. For example: XYZ Company will charge a 65-year-old $140, a 75-year-old $140 and an 85-year-old $140.

**4. You may only be concerned with catastrophic illness.** If so, you may not need to buy a Medigap policy at all, especially if you are relatively healthy, live a healthy lifestyle, and currently only incur routine medical expenses that would cost less than the premiums for a Medigap policy. You could purchase a catastrophic or high-deductible health insurance policy that would kick in when your medical bills exceeded a predetermined level, such as $5,000.

The Medigap K and L plans may also be a good choice. They should cost less than other Medigap plans but will provide a cap on out-of-pocket expenses.

**5. What is the insurer's safety rating?** If you were to experience the double misfortune of becoming seriously ill and having your insurer fail, you may be responsible for much of your unpaid claims, and it would be difficult to find replacement coverage.
We recommend you choose a company with a B+ or higher Weiss Safety Rating if you can. You should also consider an insurer's level of customer service and timeliness in reimbursing claims. Ask friends about their experiences and contact your state's insurance department or counsel for aging to find out if they keep public complaint records. As an industry, Medigap insurers have a good reputation for paying claims.

## How to Switch Medigap Policies

If you are currently holding a Medigap policy and become uncomfortable with your company's financial stability, or if you find a cheaper policy at a stronger company, here are some steps to take before switching policies:

**Step 1:** Determine if your policy was issued prior to January 1, 1992. If it was, and if it was guaranteed renewable, you did not switch to one of the standard plans. This policy should be compared carefully to the newer standardized plans before switching. Remember: once you switch to one of the new standardized plans, you can never switch back to a non-standard plan.

Furthermore, you should know that if you already have a Medigap policy, it is against federal law for a company to sell you another one. When you buy another policy, you must sign a statement indicating that you are replacing your current policy and do not intend to keep both.

**Step 2:** Before switching policies, compare benefits and premiums. It is important to note that some of the older non-standard policies may provide superior coverage, and your increased age may make comparable coverage more expensive.

**Step 3:** Determine any impact on pre-existing conditions. Any portion of a pre-existing condition satisfied under the old policy will be credited to the new policy. Example: The old policy specified that it would not cover a pre-existing condition for the first six months. You switch policies after just two months. As a result, you only have four months to wait under the new policy to be covered for your pre-existing condition.
(Exception: If your new policy has a benefit that was not included in your old policy, a new six-month waiting period may be imposed on that particular benefit.)

**Step 4:** Use the "free-look" provision which allows you 30 days to review a Medigap policy once you've paid the first premium. If, during the first 30 days, you decide you don't want or need the policy you can return it to the company for a full refund.

**Step 5:** Do not cancel your old policy until your new policy is in force.

# Part III:
# Medigap Premium Rates

## Basic Medigap Coverage
## PLAN A

If you stay in the hospital for longer than 60 days, but less than 90 days, Plan A covers Medicare Part A coinsurance amount of $335 per day (in 2018) for each benefit period.

For each Medicare "hospital reserve day" you use, Plan A pays the $670 (in 2018) per day Medicare Part A coinsurance amount. "Hospital reserve days" are 60 nonrenewable hospital days that Medicare provides which can only be used once in a lifetime. After all Medicare hospital benefits are exhausted, Plan A will cover 100% of Medicare Part A eligible hospital expenses.

If the need arises, Plan A covers costs for the first three pints of blood or equivalent quantities of packed red blood cells received each year in connection with Medicare Parts A and B covered services. Once you have met this 3-pint blood deductible under Medicare Part A, it does not have to be met again under Part B.

After your $183 annual Medicare Part B deductible is met Plan A will cover the coinsurance amount for Medicare approved medical services, which is generally 20% of the approved amount.

Plan A now includes coverage of cost sharing for all Part A Medicare-eligible hospice care and respite care expenses.

If you feel that Plan A fits your needs, take a look at the two tables below to find out what price you should expect to be charged for this plan. The tables outline the typical annual premiums charged for Plan A depending on age and gender. These rates are based on our 2018 nationwide collection of insurance premiums.

## PLAN A

### *Female*

| Age | Average Premium | Lowest Premium | Highest Premium | Median Premium |
|---|---|---|---|---|
| 65 | $1,631 | $606 | $15,228 | $1,498 |
| 70 | $1,837 | $763 | $17,325 | $1,689 |
| 75 | $2,087 | $883 | $18,683 | $1,928 |
| 80 | $2,289 | $993 | $21,980 | $2,117 |
| 85 | $2,460 | $1,035 | $23,945 | $2,274 |
| 90 | $2,580 | $1,035 | $25,416 | $2,386 |
| 95 | $2,666 | $1,035 | $25,416 | $2,472 |

### *Male*

| Age | Average Premium | Lowest Premium | Highest Premium | Median Premium |
|---|---|---|---|---|
| 65 | $1,781 | $656 | $16,221 | $1,657 |
| 70 | $2,011 | $827 | $18,454 | $1,869 |
| 75 | $2,285 | $958 | $19,900 | $2,121 |
| 80 | $2,515 | $1,076 | $23,589 | $2,326 |
| 85 | $2,714 | $1,116 | $26,689 | $2,514 |
| 90 | $2,841 | $1,116 | $28,329 | $2,645 |
| 95 | $2,939 | $1,116 | $28,329 | $2,753 |

## Basic Medigap Coverage
## PLAN B

If you stay in the hospital for longer than 60 days, but less than 90 days, Plan B covers Medicare Part A coinsurance amount of $335 per day (in 2018) for each benefit period.

For each Medicare "hospital reserve day" you use, Plan B pays the $670 (in 2018) per day Medicare Part A coinsurance amount. "Hospital reserve days" are 60 nonrenewable hospital days that Medicare provides which can only be used once in a lifetime. After all Medicare hospital benefits are exhausted, Plan B will cover 100% of Medicare Part A eligible hospital expenses.

If the need arises, Plan B covers costs for the first three pints of blood or equivalent quantities of packed red blood cells received each year in connection with Medicare Parts A and B covered services. Once you have met this 3-pint blood deductible under Medicare Part A, it does not have to be met again under Part B.

After your $183 annual Medicare Part B deductible is met Plan B will cover the coinsurance amount for Medicare approved medical services, which is generally 20% of the approved amount.

Plan B now includes coverage of cost sharing for all Part A Medicare-eligible hospice care and respite care expenses.

***Additional Features***

Plan B includes the core Medigap coverage PLUS one extra benefit:

- It will pay for the $1,340 Medicare Part A in-patient hospital deductible (per benefit period in 2018).

If you feel that Plan B fits your needs, take a look at the two tables below to find out what price you should expect to be charged for this plan. The tables outline the typical annual premiums charged for Plan B depending on age and gender. These rates are based on our 2018 nationwide collection of insurance premiums.

## PLAN B

### *Female*

| Age | Average Premium | Lowest Premium | Highest Premium | Median Premium |
|---|---|---|---|---|
| 65 | $1,996 | $947 | $9,737 | $1,813 |
| 70 | $2,281 | $989 | $9,737 | $2,127 |
| 75 | $2,624 | $1,059 | $9,737 | $2,499 |
| 80 | $2,844 | $1,257 | $9,737 | $2,713 |
| 85 | $3,029 | $1,562 | $9,737 | $2,892 |
| 90 | $3,162 | $1,562 | $9,737 | $3,022 |
| 95 | $3,236 | $1,562 | $9,737 | $3,083 |

### *Male*

| Age | Average Premium | Lowest Premium | Highest Premium | Median Premium |
|---|---|---|---|---|
| 65 | $2,150 | $947 | $9,737 | $1,991 |
| 70 | $2,468 | $1,116 | $9,737 | $2,305 |
| 75 | $2,825 | $1,283 | $9,737 | $2,676 |
| 80 | $3,075 | $1,541 | $9,737 | $2,947 |
| 85 | $3,287 | $1,562 | $9,767 | $3,134 |
| 90 | $3,434 | $1,562 | $9,767 | $3,273 |
| 95 | $3,518 | $1,562 | $9,914 | $3,345 |

## Basic Medigap Coverage
## PLAN C

If you stay in the hospital for longer than 60 days, but less than 90 days, Plan C covers Medicare Part A coinsurance amount of $335 per day (in 2018) for each benefit period.

For each Medicare "hospital reserve day" you use, Plan C pays the $670 (in 2018) per day Medicare Part A coinsurance amount. "Hospital reserve days" are 60 nonrenewable hospital days that Medicare provides you which can only be used once in a lifetime. After all Medicare hospital benefits are exhausted, Plan C will cover 100% of Medicare Part A eligible hospital expenses.

If the need arises, Plan C covers costs for the first three pints of blood or equivalent quantities of packed red blood cells received each year in connection with Medicare Parts A and B covered services. Once you have met this 3-pint blood deductible under Medicare Part A, it does not have to be met again under Part B.

After your $183 annual Medicare Part B deductible is met, Plan C will cover the coinsurance amount of Medicare approved medical services, which is generally 20% of the approved amount

Plan C now includes coverage of cost sharing for all Part A Medicare-eligible hospice care and respite care expenses.

### *Additional Features*

Plan C includes the core Medigap coverage, plus four extra benefits.

- Your $1,340 Medicare Part A in-patient hospital deductible (per benefit period in 2018)
- Your coinsurance amount for skilled nursing facility care for the 21st through the 100th day of your stay (the amount is $167.50 per day in 2018).
- Your Medicare Part B deductible ($183 per calendar year in 2018).
- Any emergency care you may require when you are in a foreign country after a $250 deductible. This benefit pays 80% of the cost of your care for the first 60 days of each trip, up to $50,000 in your lifetime.

**Note:** The only difference between Plan C and Plan D is the Part B deductible. Compare the prices between the plans before making your choice.

If you feel that Plan C fits your needs, take a look at the two tables below to find out what price you should expect to be charged for this plan. The tables outline the typical annual premiums charged for Plan C depending on age and gender. These rates are based on our 2018 nationwide collection of insurance premiums.

## PLAN C

### *Female*

| Age | Average Premium | Lowest Premium | Highest Premium | Median Premium |
|---|---|---|---|---|
| 65 | $2,381 | $1,081 | $6,266 | $2,142 |
| 70 | $2,713 | $1,231 | $6,423 | $2,508 |
| 75 | $3,136 | $1,478 | $7,352 | $2,988 |
| 80 | $3,403 | $1,699 | $8,354 | $3,253 |
| 85 | $3,612 | $1,699 | $10,404 | $3,466 |
| 90 | $3,736 | $1,699 | $10,404 | $3,595 |
| 95 | $3,824 | $1,699 | $10,404 | $3,681 |

### *Male*

| Age | Average Premium | Lowest Premium | Highest Premium | Median Premium |
|---|---|---|---|---|
| 65 | $2,539 | $1,142 | $6,266 | $2,335 |
| 70 | $2,905 | $1,378 | $7,320 | $2,712 |
| 75 | $3,339 | $1,656 | $8,421 | $3,195 |
| 80 | $3,640 | $1,699 | $10,006 | $3,500 |
| 85 | $3,878 | $1,699 | $12,588 | $3,731 |
| 90 | $4,014 | $1,699 | $12,588 | $3,881 |
| 95 | $4,113 | $1,699 | $12,588 | $3,982 |

# Basic Medigap Coverage
# PLAN D

If you stay in the hospital for longer than 60 days, but less than 90 days, Plan D covers Medicare Part A coinsurance amount of $335 per day (in 2018) for each benefit period.

For each Medicare "hospital reserve day" you use, Plan D pays the $670 (in 2018) per day Medicare Part A coinsurance amount. "Hospital reserve days" are 60 nonrenewable hospital days that Medicare provides you which can only be used once in a lifetime. After all Medicare hospital benefits are exhausted, Plan D will cover 100% of Medicare Part A eligible hospital expenses.

If the need arises, Plan D covers costs for the first three pints of blood or equivalent quantities of packed red blood cells received each year in connection with Medicare Parts A and B covered services. Once you have met this 3-pint blood deductible under Medicare Part A, it does not have to be met again under Part B.

After your $183 annual Medicare Part B deductible is met, Plan D will cover the coinsurance amount of Medicare approved medical services, which is generally 20% of the approved amount

Plan D now includes coverage of cost sharing for all Part A Medicare-eligible hospice care and respite care expenses.

### *Additional Features*

Plan D includes the core Medigap coverage, plus three extra benefits.

- Your $1,340 Medicare Part A in-patient hospital deductible (per benefit period in 2018).
- Your coinsurance amount for skilled nursing facility care for the 21st through the 100th day of your stay (the amount is $167.50 per day in 2018).
- Any emergency care you may require when you are in a foreign country after a $250 deductible. This benefit pays 80% of the cost of your care for the first 60 days of each trip, up to $50,000 in your lifetime.

**Note:** The only difference between Plan D and Plan C is the Part B deductible. Compare the prices between the plans before making your choice.

If you feel that Plan D fits your needs, take a look at the two tables below to find out what price you should expect to be charged for this plan. The tables outline the typical annual premiums charged for Plan D depending on age and gender. These rates are based on our 2018 nationwide collection of insurance premiums.

## PLAN D

### *Female*

| Age | Average Premium | Lowest Premium | Highest Premium | Median Premium |
|---|---|---|---|---|
| 65 | $1,901 | $950 | $5,391 | $1,828 |
| 70 | $2,214 | $1,062 | $5,617 | $2,137 |
| 75 | $2,579 | $1,279 | $6,564 | $2,490 |
| 80 | $2,890 | $1,508 | $7,228 | $2,824 |
| 85 | $3,145 | $1,547 | $7,710 | $3,093 |
| 90 | $3,311 | $1,547 | $8,101 | $3,250 |
| 95 | $3,440 | $1,547 | $8,394 | $3,339 |

### *Male*

| Age | Average Premium | Lowest Premium | Highest Premium | Median Premium |
|---|---|---|---|---|
| 65 | $2,119 | $1,026 | $5,391 | $2,023 |
| 70 | $2,479 | $1,147 | $6,459 | $2,373 |
| 75 | $2,897 | $1,381 | $7,545 | $2,818 |
| 80 | $3,252 | $1,547 | $8,311 | $3,177 |
| 85 | $3,539 | $1,547 | $8,866 | $3,453 |
| 90 | $3,725 | $1,547 | $9,317 | $3,622 |
| 95 | $3,871 | $1,547 | $9,655 | $3,753 |

## Basic Medigap Coverage
## PLAN F

If you stay in the hospital for longer than 60 days, but less than 90 days, Plan F covers Medicare Part A coinsurance amount of $335 per day (in 2018) for each benefit period.

For each Medicare "hospital reserve day" you use, Plan F pays the $670 (in 2018) per day Medicare Part A coinsurance amount. "Hospital reserve days" are 60 nonrenewable hospital days that Medicare provides you which can only be used once in a lifetime. After all Medicare hospital benefits are exhausted, Plan F will cover 100% of Medicare Part A eligible hospital expenses.

If the need arises, Plan F covers costs for the first three pints of blood or equivalent quantities of packed red blood cells received each year in connection with Medicare Parts A and B covered services. Once you have met this 3-pint blood deductible under Medicare Part A, it does not have to be met again under Part B.

After your $183 annual Medicare Part B deductible is met, Plan F will cover the coinsurance amount of Medicare approved medical services, which is generally 20% of the approved amount. A high deductible option is available, requiring you to pay the first $2,240 of Medicare covered costs before your Medigap policy pays anything.

Plan F now includes coverage of cost sharing for all Part A Medicare-eligible hospice care and respite care expenses.

### *Additional Features*

Plan F includes all of the basic Medigap coverage plus five extra benefits.

- Your $1,340 Medicare Part A in-patient hospital deductible (per benefit period in 2018).
- Your coinsurance amount for skilled nursing facility care for the 21$^{st}$ through the 100$^{th}$ day of your stay (the amount is $167.50 per day in 2018).
- Any emergency care you may require when you are in a foreign country after a $250 deductible. This benefit pays 80% of the cost of your care for the first 60 days of each trip, up to $50,000 in your lifetime.
- Your deductible for Medicare Part B ($183 in 2018).
- 100% of any excess charges under Medicare Part B. This is the difference between the approved amount for Part B services and the actual charges (up to the charge limitations set by either Medicare or state law).

**Note:** The only difference between Plan F and Plan G is the Part B deductible. Compare the prices between the plans before making your choice.

If you feel that Plan F fits your needs, take a look at the two tables below to find out what price you should expect to be charged for this plan. The tables outline the typical annual premiums charged for Plan F depending on age and gender. These rates are based on our 2018 nationwide collection of insurance premiums.

## PLAN F

### *Female*

| Age | Average Premium | Lowest Premium | Highest Premium | Median Premium |
|---|---|---|---|---|
| 65 | $2,252 | $1,155 | $7,405 | $2,053 |
| 70 | $2,548 | $1,244 | $7,405 | $2,358 |
| 75 | $2,957 | $1,494 | $8,033 | $2,772 |
| 80 | $3,268 | $1,620 | $8,524 | $3,094 |
| 85 | $3,546 | $1,620 | $9,409 | $3,365 |
| 90 | $3,751 | $1,620 | $9,656 | $3,580 |
| 95 | $3,908 | $1,620 | $10,076 | $3,728 |

### *Male*

| Age | Average Premium | Lowest Premium | Highest Premium | Median Premium |
|---|---|---|---|---|
| 65 | $2,449 | $1,226 | $7,405 | $2,251 |
| 70 | $2,777 | $1,393 | $7,405 | $2,571 |
| 75 | $3,216 | $1,620 | $8,479 | $3,024 |
| 80 | $3,568 | $1,620 | $9,595 | $3,368 |
| 85 | $3,885 | $1,620 | $11,119 | $3,695 |
| 90 | $4,105 | $1,620 | $11,119 | $3,929 |
| 95 | $4,282 | $1,620 | $11,590 | $4,094 |

## Basic Medigap Coverage PLAN F with High Deductible

If you stay in the hospital for longer than 60 days, but less than 90 days, Plan F-High Deductible covers Medicare Part A coinsurance amount of $335 per day (in 2018) for each benefit period.

For each Medicare "hospital reserve day" you use, Plan F-High Deductible pays the $670 (in 2018) per day Medicare Part A coinsurance amount. "Hospital reserve days" are 60 nonrenewable hospital days that Medicare provides you which can only be used once in a lifetime. After all Medicare hospital benefits are exhausted, Plan F – High Deductible will cover 100% of Medicare Part A eligible hospital expenses.

If the need arises, Plan F-High Deductible covers costs for the first three pints of blood or equivalent quantities of packed red blood cells received each year in connection with Medicare Parts A and B covered services. Once you have met this 3-pint blood deductible under Medicare Part A, it does not have to be met again under Part B.

After your $183 annual Medicare Part B deductible is met, Plan F-High Deductible will cover the coinsurance amount of Medicare approved medical services, which is generally 20% of the approved amount.

Plan F High Deductible includes coverage of cost sharing for all Part A Medicare-eligible hospice care and respite care expenses.

### *Additional Features*

Plan F includes all of the basic Medigap coverage plus five extra benefits.

- Your $1,340 Medicare Part A in-patient hospital deductible (per benefit period in 2018).
- Your coinsurance amount for skilled nursing facility care for the 21st through the 100th day of your stay (the amount is $167.50 per day in 2018).
- Any emergency care you may require when you are in a foreign country after a $250 deductible. This benefit pays 80% of the cost of your care for the first 60 days of each trip, up to $50,000 in your lifetime.
- Your deductible for Medicare Part B ($183 in 2018).
- 100% of any excess charges under Medicare Part B. This is the difference between the approved amount for Part B services and the actual charges (up to the charge limitations set by either Medicare or state law).

### Important Notice:

You must meet a $2,240 deductible of unpaid Medicare eligible expenses before benefits are paid by this plan.

If you feel that Plan F with High Deductible fits your needs, take a look at the two tables below to find out what price you should expect to be charged for this plan. The tables outline the typical annual premiums charged for Plan F depending on age and gender. These rates are based on our 2018 nationwide collection of insurance premiums.

## PLAN F: with High Deductible

### *Female*

| Age | Average Premium | Lowest Premium | Highest Premium | Median Premium |
|---|---|---|---|---|
| 65 | $646 | $244 | $2,008 | $600 |
| 70 | $744 | $284 | $2,143 | $685 |
| 75 | $876 | $304 | $2,368 | $807 |
| 80 | $996 | $308 | $2,547 | $924 |
| 85 | $1,098 | $308 | $2,758 | $1,029 |
| 90 | $1,160 | $308 | $2,979 | $1,092 |
| 95 | $1,211 | $308 | $3,418 | $1,139 |

### *Male*

| Age | Average Premium | Lowest Premium | Highest Premium | Median Premium |
|---|---|---|---|---|
| 65 | $700 | $277 | $2,304 | $645 |
| 70 | $812 | $308 | $2,465 | $743 |
| 75 | $964 | $308 | $2,722 | $881 |
| 80 | $1,102 | $308 | $2,931 | $1,009 |
| 85 | $1,223 | $308 | $3,101 | $1,127 |
| 90 | $1,279 | $308 | $3,483 | $1,212 |
| 95 | $1,336 | $308 | $4,054 | $1,262 |

# Basic Medigap Coverage
# PLAN G

If you stay in the hospital for longer than 60 days, but less than 90 days, Plan G covers Medicare Part A coinsurance amount of $335 per day (in 2018) for each benefit period.

For each Medicare "hospital reserve day" you use, Plan G pays the $670 (in 2018) per day Medicare Part A coinsurance amount. "Hospital reserve days" are 60 nonrenewable hospital days that Medicare provides you which can only be used once in a lifetime. After all Medicare hospital benefits are exhausted, Plan G will cover 100% of Medicare Part A eligible hospital expenses.

If the need arises, Plan G covers costs for the first three pints of blood or equivalent quantities of packed red blood cells received each year in connection with Medicare Parts A and B covered services. Once you have met this 3-pint blood deductible under Medicare Part A, it does not have to be met again under Part B.

After your $183 annual Medicare Part B deductible is met, Plan G will cover the coinsurance amount of Medicare approved medical services, which is generally 20% of the approved amount.

Plan G now includes coverage of cost sharing for all Part A Medicare-eligible hospice care and respite care

### *Additional Features*

Plan G includes the core Medigap coverage plus four extra benefits.

- Your $1,340 Medicare Part A in-patient hospital deductible (per benefit period in 2018).
- Your coinsurance amount for skilled nursing care for the 21st through the 100th day of your stay (the amount is $167.50 per day in 2018).
- Any emergency care you may require when you are in a foreign country after a $250 deductible. This benefit pays 80% of the cost of your care for the first 60 days of each trip, up to $50,000 in your lifetime.
- 100% of any excess charges under Medicare Part B. Excess charges are the difference between the approved amount for Part B services and the actual charges (up to the charge limitations set by either Medicare or state law).

**Note:** The only difference between Plan G and Plan F is the Part B deductible.

Compare the prices between the plans before making your choice.

If you feel that Plan G fits your needs, take a look at the two tables below to find out what price you should expect to be charged for this plan. The tables outline the typical annual premiums charged for Plan G depending on age and gender. These rates are based on our 2018 nationwide collection of insurance premiums.

## PLAN G

### *Female*

| Age | Average Premium | Lowest Premium | Highest Premium | Median Premium |
|---|---|---|---|---|
| 65 | $1,795 | $858 | $6,540 | $1,620 |
| 70 | $2,028 | $972 | $6,540 | $1,853 |
| 75 | $2,393 | $1,157 | $6,540 | $2,205 |
| 80 | $2,669 | $1,267 | $6,994 | $2,476 |
| 85 | $2,934 | $1,344 | $7,458 | $2,745 |
| 90 | $3,162 | $1,382 | $7,835 | $2,980 |
| 95 | $3,320 | $1,382 | $8,534 | $3,161 |

### *Male*

| Age | Average Premium | Lowest Premium | Highest Premium | Median Premium |
|---|---|---|---|---|
| 65 | $1,971 | $986 | $6,540 | $1,784 |
| 70 | $2,231 | $1,089 | $6,540 | $2,033 |
| 75 | $2,632 | $1,327 | $7,301 | $2,421 |
| 80 | $2,932 | $1,382 | $8,042 | $2,723 |
| 85 | $3,229 | $1,382 | $8,576 | $3,044 |
| 90 | $3,484 | $1,382 | $9,013 | $3,328 |
| 95 | $3,664 | $1,382 | $9,482 | $3,524 |

## Basic Medigap Coverage
## PLAN K

If you stay in the hospital for longer than 60 days, but less than 90 days, Plan K covers Medicare Part A coinsurance amount of $335 per day (in 2018) for each benefit period.

For each Medicare "hospital reserve day" you use, Plan K pays the $670 (in 2018) per day Medicare Part A coinsurance amount. "Hospital reserve days" are 60 nonrenewable hospital days that Medicare provides you which can only be used once in a lifetime. After all Medicare hospital benefits are exhausted, Plan K will cover 100% of Medicare Part A eligible hospital expenses up to 365 days.

If the need arises, Plan K covers 50% of the costs for the first three pints of blood or equivalent quantities of packed red blood cells received each year in connection with Medicare Parts A and B covered services. Once you have met this 3-pint blood deductible under Medicare Part A, it does not have to be met again under Part B.

After your $183 annual Medicare Part B deductible is met, Plan K will cover 50% of the coinsurance amount of Medicare approved medical services, which is generally 20% of the approved amount.

### *Additional Features*

Plan K includes four additional benefits.

- 50% of your $1,340 Medicare Part A in-patient hospital deductible (per benefit period in 2018).
- 50% of your coinsurance amount for skilled nursing facility care for the 21st through the 100th day of your stay (the amount is $167.50 per day in 2018).
- 100% coinsurance for medicare-covered preventive medical care. Preventive care would include physical examinations, flu shots, serum cholesterol screening, hearing tests, diabetes screening, and thyroid function tests.
- 50% of hospice cost-sharing for all Part A Medicare covered expenses and respite care.

Note: There is a $5,240 out-of-pocket annual limit. Once you meet the annual limit, the plans pays 100% of the Medicare Part A and Part B co-payments and coinsurance for the rest of the calendar year. "Excess charges" are not covered and do not count toward the out-of-pocket limit.

If you feel that Plan K fits your needs, take a look at the two tables below to find out what price you should expect to be charged for this plan. The tables outline the typical annual premiums charged for Plan K depending on age and gender. These rates are based on our 2018 nationwide collection of insurance premiums.

## PLAN K

### *Female*

| Age | Average Premium | Lowest Premium | Highest Premium | Median Premium |
|---|---|---|---|---|
| 65 | $1,011 | $376 | $2,778 | $939 |
| 70 | $1,170 | $465 | $3,279 | $1,127 |
| 75 | $1,317 | $553 | $3,798 | $1,277 |
| 80 | $1,433 | $588 | $4,314 | $1,394 |
| 85 | $1,526 | $588 | $4,760 | $1,497 |
| 90 | $1,566 | $588 | $4,760 | $1,530 |
| 95 | $1,596 | $588 | $4,760 | $1,555 |

### *Male*

| Age | Average Premium | Lowest Premium | Highest Premium | Median Premium |
|---|---|---|---|---|
| 65 | $1,061 | $376 | $2,785 | $998 |
| 70 | $1,237 | $465 | $3,383 | $1,200 |
| 75 | $1,392 | $553 | $4,111 | $1,356 |
| 80 | $1,529 | $588 | $4,854 | $1,480 |
| 85 | $1,645 | $588 | $5,623 | $1,575 |
| 90 | $1,673 | $588 | $5,623 | $1,584 |
| 95 | $1,707 | $588 | $5,623 | $1,600 |

# Basic Medigap Coverage
# PLAN L

If you stay in the hospital for longer than 60 days, but less than 90 days, Plan L covers Medicare Part A coinsurance amount of $335 per day (in 2018) for each benefit period.

For each Medicare "hospital reserve day" you use, Plan L pays the $670 (in 2018) per day Medicare Part A coinsurance amount. "Hospital reserve days" are 60 nonrenewable hospital days that Medicare provides you which can only be used once in a lifetime. After all Medicare hospital benefits are exhausted, Plan L will cover 100% of Medicare Part A eligible hospital expenses up to 365 days.

If the need arises, Plan L covers 75% of the costs for the first three pints of blood or equivalent quantities of packed red blood cells received each year in connection with Medicare Parts A and B covered services. Once you have met this 3-pint blood deductible under Medicare Part A, it does not have to be met again under Part B.

After your $183 annual Medicare Part B deductible is met, Plan L will cover 75% of the coinsurance amount of Medicare approved medical services, which is generally 20% of the approved amount.

### *Additional Features*

Plan L includes four additional benefits.

- 75% of your $1,340 Medicare Part A in-patient hospital deductible (per benefit period in 2018).
- 75% of your coinsurance amount for skilled nursing facility care for the 21$^{st}$ through the 100$^{th}$ day of your stay (the amount is $167.50 per day in 2018).
- 100% coinsurance for medicare-covered preventive medical care. Preventive care would include physical examinations, flu shots, serum cholesterol screening, hearing tests, diabetes screening, and thyroid function tests.
- 75% of hospice cost-sharing for all Part A Medicare covered expenses and respite care.

**Note**: There is a $2,620 out-of-pocket annual limit. Once you meet the annual limit, the plans pays 100% of the Medicare Part A and Part B co-payments and coinsurance for the rest of the calendar year. "Excess charges" are not covered and do not count toward the out-of-pocket limit.

If you feel that Plan L fits your needs, take a look at the two tables below to find out what price you should expect to be charged for this plan. The tables outline the typical annual premiums charged for Plan L depending on age and gender. These rates are based on our 2018 nationwide collection of insurance premiums.

## PLAN L

### *Female*

| Age | Average Premium | Lowest Premium | Highest Premium | Median Premium |
|---|---|---|---|---|
| 65 | $1,628 | $674 | $4,177 | $1,527 |
| 70 | $1,870 | $832 | $4,193 | $1,810 |
| 75 | $2,095 | $990 | $4,857 | $2,086 |
| 80 | $2,255 | $1,053 | $5,518 | $2,236 |
| 85 | $2,377 | $1,053 | $6,090 | $2,314 |
| 90 | $2,448 | $1,053 | $6,090 | $2,313 |
| 95 | $2,492 | $1,053 | $6,453 | $2,313 |

### *Male*

| Age | Average Premium | Lowest Premium | Highest Premium | Median Premium |
|---|---|---|---|---|
| 65 | $1,713 | $674 | $4,177 | $1,670 |
| 70 | $1,980 | $832 | $4,326 | $1,971 |
| 75 | $2,207 | $990 | $5,258 | $2,212 |
| 80 | $2,395 | $1,053 | $6,210 | $2,343 |
| 85 | $2,546 | $1,053 | $7,195 | $2,433 |
| 90 | $2,602 | $1,053 | $7,195 | $2,394 |
| 95 | $2,650 | $1,053 | $7,195 | $2,394 |

# Basic Medigap Coverage

## PLAN M

If you stay in the hospital for longer than 60 days, but less than 90 days, Plan M covers the Medicare Part A coinsurance amount, $335 per day (in 2018) for each benefit period.

For each Medicare "hospital reserve day" you use, Plan M pays the Medicare Part A coinsurance amount, $670 (in 2018) per day. "Hospital reserve days" are 60 nonrenewable hospital days that Medicare provides you which can only be used once in a lifetime. After all Medicare hospital benefits are exhausted, Plan M will cover 100% of Medicare Part A eligible hospital expenses.

If the need arises, Plan M covers costs for the first three pints of blood or equivalent quantities of packed red blood cells received each year in connection with Medicare Parts A and B covered services. Once you have met this 3-pint blood deductible under Medicare Part A, it does not have to be met again under Part B.

After your $183 annual Medicare Part B deductible is met, Plan M will cover the coinsurance amount of Medicare approved medical services, which is generally 20% of the approved amount.

Coverage of cost sharing for all Part A Medicare eligible hospice care and respite care expense is included.

### *Additional Features*

Plan M includes the core Medigap coverage, plus three extra benefits.

- 50% of your Medicare Part A in-patient hospital deductible ($1,340 per benefit period in 2018).
- Your coinsurance amount for skilled nursing facility care for the 21st through the 100th day of your stay (the amount is $167.50 per day in 2018).
- Any emergency care you may require when you are in a foreign country after a $250 deductible. This benefit pays 80% of the cost of your care for the first 60 days of each trip, up to $50,000 in your lifetime.

If you feel that Plan M fits your needs, take a look at the two tables below to find out what price you should expect to be charged for this plan. The tables outline the typical annual premiums charged for Plan M depending on age and gender. These rates are based on our 2018 nationwide collection of insurance premiums.

## PLAN M

### *Female*

| Age | Average Premium | Lowest Premium | Highest Premium | Median Premium |
|---|---|---|---|---|
| 65 | $1,863 | $954 | $5,774 | $1,774 |
| 70 | $2,218 | $1,224 | $5,774 | $2,122 |
| 75 | $2,633 | $1,347 | $5,774 | $2,566 |
| 80 | $3,026 | $1,460 | $6,662 | $2,985 |
| 85 | $3,362 | $1,544 | $7,257 | $3,286 |
| 90 | $3,633 | $1,609 | $7,703 | $3,439 |
| 95 | $3,798 | $1,650 | $7,727 | $3,557 |

### *Male*

| Age | Average Premium | Lowest Premium | Highest Premium | Median Premium |
|---|---|---|---|---|
| 65 | $2,050 | $954 | $5,774 | $1,943 |
| 70 | $2,448 | $1,335 | $5,774 | $2,346 |
| 75 | $2,918 | $1,550 | $6,032 | $2,859 |
| 80 | $3,358 | $1,650 | $7,150 | $3,312 |
| 85 | $3,733 | $1,650 | $8,089 | $3,696 |
| 90 | $4,033 | $1,650 | $8,586 | $3,842 |
| 95 | $4,216 | $1,650 | $8,856 | $3,973 |

# Basic Medigap Coverage

# PLAN N

If you stay in the hospital for longer than 60 days, but less than 90 days, Plan N covers the Medicare Part A coinsurance amount, $335 per day (in 2018) for each benefit period.

For each Medicare "hospital reserve day" you use, Plan N pays the Medicare Part A coinsurance amount, $670 (in 2018) per day. "Hospital reserve days" are 60 nonrenewable hospital days that Medicare provides you which can only be used once in a lifetime. After all Medicare hospital benefits are exhausted, Plan N will cover 100% of Medicare Part A eligible hospital expenses.

If the need arises, Plan N covers costs for the first three pints of blood or equivalent quantities of packed red blood cells received each year in connection with Medicare Parts A and B covered services. Once you have met this 3-pint blood deductible under Medicare Part A, it does not have to be met again under Part B.

After your $183 annual Medicare Part B deductible is met, Plan N will cover the coinsurance amount of Medicare approved medical services, which is generally 20% of the approved amount.

Coverage of cost sharing for all Part A Medicare eligible hospice care and respite care expense is included.

### *Additional Features*

Plan N includes the core Medigap coverage, plus four extra features and benefits.

- Your Medicare Part A in-patient hospital deductible ($1,340 per benefit period in 2018).
- You will have a co-payment of up to $20 per physician visit or $50 per Emergency Room visit under Part B. The ER co-pay will be waived if admitted.
- Your coinsurance amount for skilled nursing facility care for the 21st through the 100th day of your stay (the amount is $167.50 per day in 2018).
- Any emergency care you may require when you are in a foreign country after a $250 deductible. This benefit pays 80% of the cost of your care for the first 60 days of each trip, up to $50,000 in your lifetime.

If you feel that Plan N fits your needs, take a look at the two tables below to find out what price you should expect to be charged for this plan. The tables outline the typical annual premiums charged for Plan N depending on age and gender. These rates are based on our 2018 nationwide collection of insurance premiums.

## PLAN N

### *Female*

| Age | Average Premium | Lowest Premium | Highest Premium | Median Premium |
|---|---|---|---|---|
| 65 | $1,477 | $773 | $4,338 | $1,336 |
| 70 | $1,681 | $819 | $4,446 | $1,552 |
| 75 | $1,979 | $1,000 | $5,111 | $1,857 |
| 80 | $2,210 | $1,021 | $5,526 | $2,076 |
| 85 | $2,427 | $1,021 | $5,869 | $2,294 |
| 90 | $2,608 | $1,021 | $6,145 | $2,496 |
| 95 | $2,730 | $1,021 | $6,705 | $2,623 |

### *Male*

| Age | Average Premium | Lowest Premium | Highest Premium | Median Premium |
|---|---|---|---|---|
| 65 | $1,607 | $866 | $4,388 | $1,454 |
| 70 | $1,834 | $917 | $5,111 | $1,678 |
| 75 | $2,155 | $1,021 | $5,879 | $1,998 |
| 80 | $2,415 | $1,021 | $6,358 | $2,257 |
| 85 | $2,661 | $1,021 | $6,749 | $2,522 |
| 90 | $2,862 | $1,021 | $7,072 | $2,748 |
| 95 | $3,001 | $1,021 | $7,952 | $2,888 |

# Part IV: Index of Medigap Insurers

Following is a reference list of Medicare supplement insurers with their Weiss Safety Rating, corporate address, phone number, and the states in which they are licensed to do business.

| RATING | INSURANCE COMPANY NAME | ADDRESS | CITY | STATE | ZIP | PHONE |
|---|---|---|---|---|---|---|
| B+ | AETNA HEALTH & LIFE INS CO | 151 FARMINGTON AVENUE | HARTFORD | CT | 6156 | (860) 273-0123 |
| B | AETNA LIFE INS CO | 151 FARMINGTON AVENUE | HARTFORD | CT | 6156 | (860) 273-0123 |
| C | ALLIANCE HEALTH & LIFE INS CO | 2850 WEST GRAND BLVD | DETROIT | MI | 48202 | (313) 872-8100 |
| C | AMALGAMATED LIFE & HEALTH INS CO | 333 SOUTH ASHLAND AVENUE | CHICAGO | IL | 60607 | (914) 367-5000 |
| B- | AMERICAN CONTINENTAL INS CO | 800 CRESENT CENTRE DR STE 200 | FRANKLIN | TN | 37067 | (800) 264-4000 |
| B+ | AMERICAN FAMILY LIFE ASR CO OF COLUM | 10306 REGENCY PARKWAY DRIVE | OMAHA | NE | 68114 | (706) 323-3431 |
| B+ | AMERICAN FAMILY MUTL INS CO SI | 6000 AMERICAN PARKWAY | MADISON | WI | 53783 | (608) 249-2111 |
| B | AMERICAN GENERAL LIFE INS CO | 2727-A ALLEN PARKWAY 3-D1 | HOUSTON | TX | 77019 | (713) 522-1111 |
| B- | AMERICAN NATIONAL LIFE INS CO OF TX | ONE MOODY PLAZA | GALVESTON | TX | 77550 | (409) 763-4661 |
| C | AMERICAN PROGRESSIVE L&H I C OF NY | 44 SOUTH BROADWAY SUITE 1200 | WHITE PLAINS | NY | 10601 | (813) 290-6200 |
| B | AMERICAN REPUBLIC CORP INS CO | 601 SIXTH AVE | DES MOINES | NE | 50309 | (866) 705-9100 |
| A- | AMERICAN REPUBLIC INS CO | 601 SIXTH AVENUE | DES MOINES | IA | 50309 | (800) 247-2190 |
| C+ | AMERICAN RETIREMENT LIFE INS CO | 1300 EAST NINTH STREET | CLEVELAND | OH | 44114 | (512) 451-2224 |
| C- | AMERIHEALTH INSURANCE CO OF NJ | 8000 MIDLANTIC DR STE 333 | MOUNT LAUREL | NJ | 08054 | (609) 662-2400 |
| B- | ANTHEM HEALTH PLANS INC | 108 LEIGUS RD | WALLINGFORD | CT | 06492 | (203) 677-4000 |
| B+ | ANTHEM HEALTH PLANS OF KENTUCKY INC | 13550 TRITON PARK BLVD | LOUISVILLE | KY | 40223 | (800) 331-1476 |
| B+ | ANTHEM HEALTH PLANS OF MAINE INC | 2 GANNETT DR | SOUTH PORTLAND | ME | 04106 | (866) 583-6182 |
| B | ANTHEM HEALTH PLANS OF NEW | 1155 ELM ST | MANCHESTER | NH | 03101 | (603) 541-2000 |
| B- | ANTHEM HEALTH PLANS OF VIRGINIA | 2015 STAPLES MILL RD | RICHMOND | VA | 23230 | (804) 354-7000 |
| B- | ANTHEM INS COMPANIES INC | 120 MONUMENT CIRCLE | INDIANAPOLIS | IN | 46204 | (317) 488-6000 |
| B- | ASURIS NORTHWEST HEALTH | 1800 NINTH AVE | SEATTLE | WA | 98101 | (206) 464-3600 |
| C | AVALON INS CO | 2500 ELMERTON AVE | HARRISBURG | PA | 17177 | (717) 541-7000 |
| C | AVERA HEALTH PLANS INC | 3816 S ELMWOOD AVE SUITE 100 | SIOUX FALLS | SD | 57105 | (605) 322-4500 |
| D | BANKERS CONSECO LIFE INS CO | 350 JERICHO TURNPIKE SUITE 304 | JERICHO | NY | 11753 | (317) 817-6100 |
| B- | BANKERS FIDELITY ASR CO | 4370 PEACHTREE RD NE | ATLANTA | GA | 30319 | (800) 241-1439 |
| B | BANKERS FIDELITY LIFE INS CO | 4370 PEACHTREE ROAD NE | ATLANTA | GA | 30319 | (800) 241-1439 |
| D+ | BANKERS LIFE & CAS CO | 111 EAST WACKER DRIVE STE 2100 | CHICAGO | IL | 60601 | (312) 396-6000 |
| B+ | BLUE CARE NETWORK OF MICHIGAN | 20500 CIVIC CENTER DRIVE | SOUTHFIELD | MI | 48076 | (248) 799-6400 |
| B- | BLUE CROSS & BLUE SHIELD OF FLORIDA | 4800 DEERWOOD CAMPUS | JACKSONVILLE | FL | 32246 | (904) 791-6111 |
| B | BLUE CROSS BLUE SHIELD OF ALABAMA | 450 RIVERCHASE PARKWAY EAST | BIRMINGHAM | AL | 35244 | (205) 220-2100 |
| A+ | BLUE CROSS BLUE SHIELD OF ARIZONA | 2444 W LAS PALMARITAS DR | PHOENIX | AZ | 85021 | (602) 864-4100 |
| B- | BLUE CROSS BLUE SHIELD OF GEORGIA | 3350 PEACHTREE RD NE | ATLANTA | GA | 30326 | (404) 842-8000 |
| B | BLUE CROSS BLUE SHIELD OF KANSAS INC | 1133 SW TOPEKA BOULEVARD | TOPEKA | KS | 66629 | (785) 291-7000 |
| C+ | BLUE CROSS BLUE SHIELD OF KC | 2301 MAIN ST | KANSAS CITY | MO | 64108 | (816) 395-2222 |
| B- | BLUE CROSS BLUE SHIELD OF MA | 101 HUNTINGTON AVE | BOSTON | MA | 02199 | (617) 246-5000 |
| C | BLUE CROSS BLUE SHIELD OF MICHIGAN | 600 LAFAYETTE EAST | DETROIT | MI | 48226 | (313) 225-9000 |
| C | BLUE CROSS BLUE SHIELD OF MINNESOTA | 3535 BLUE CROSS RD | EAGAN | MN | 55122 | (651) 662-8000 |
| B | BLUE CROSS BLUE SHIELD OF MS, MUTUAL | 3545 LAKELAND DR | FLOWOOD | MS | 39232 | (601) 932-3704 |
| B | BLUE CROSS BLUE SHIELD OF NC | 4705 UNIVERSITY DR BLDG 700 | DURHAM | NC | 27707 | (919) 489-7431 |
| C | BLUE CROSS BLUE SHIELD OF NEBRASKA | 1919 AKSARBEN DR | OMAHA | NE | 68180 | (402) 982-7000 |
| C | BLUE CROSS BLUE SHIELD OF RI | 500 EXCHANGE ST | PROVIDENCE | RI | 02903 | (401) 459-1000 |
| A- | BLUE CROSS BLUE SHIELD OF SC INC | 2501 FARAWAY DR | COLUMBIA | SC | 29219 | (803) 788-3860 |
| B | BLUE CROSS BLUE SHIELD OF VERMONT | 445 INDUSTRIAL LANE | BERLIN | VT | 05602 | (802) 223-6131 |
| B- | BLUE CROSS BLUE SHIELD OF WISCONSIN | N17 W24340 RIVERWOOD DR | WAUKESHA | WI | 53188 | (262) 523-4020 |
| B- | BLUE CROSS BLUE SHIELD OF WYOMING | 4000 HOUSE AVE | CHEYENNE | WY | 82001 | (307) 634-1393 |
| B | BLUE CROSS OF IDAHO HEALTH SERVICE | 3000 E PINE AVE | MERIDIAN | ID | 83642 | (208) 345-4550 |
| B | BLUECROSS BLUESHIELD OF TENNESSEE | 1 CAMERON HILL CIRCLE | CHATTANOOGA | TN | 37402 | (423) 535-5600 |
| C | CAPITAL ADVANTAGE INS CO | 2500 ELMERTON AVE | HARRISBURG | PA | 17177 | (717) 541-7000 |
| B- | CAPITAL BLUE CROSS | 2500 ELMERTON AVE | HARRISBURG | PA | 17177 | (717) 541-7000 |
| C+ | CAREFIRST OF MARYLAND INC | 1501 S CLINTON ST | BALTIMORE | MD | 21224 | (410) 581-3000 |
| E+ | CDPHP UNIVERSAL BENEFITS INC | 500 PATROON CREEK BLVD | ALBANY | NY | 12206 | (518) 641-3000 |
| C+ | CELTIC INS CO | 77 W WACKER DR STE 1200 | CHICAGO | IL | 60601 | (800) 714-4658 |

| RATING | INSURANCE COMPANY NAME | ADDRESS | CITY | STATE | ZIP | PHONE |
|---|---|---|---|---|---|---|
| C+ | CENTRAL RESERVE LIFE INS CO | 1300 EAST NINTH STREET | CLEVELAND | OH | 44114 | (512) 451-2224 |
| A- | CENTRAL STATES H & L CO OF OMAHA | 1212 NORTH 96TH STREET | OMAHA | NE | 68114 | (402) 397-1111 |
| C+ | CENTRAL STATES INDEMNITY CO OF OMAHA | 1212 NORTH 96TH STREET | OMAHA | NE | 68114 | (402) 997-8000 |
| B | CHRISTIAN FIDELITY LIFE INS CO | 1999 BRYAN STREET SUITE 900 | DALLAS | TX | 75201 | (602) 263-6666 |
| B | CIGNA HEALTH & LIFE INS CO | 900 COTTAGE GROVE ROAD | BLOOMFIELD | CT | 6002 | (860) 226-6000 |
| D+ | COLONIAL PENN LIFE INS CO | 399 MARKET STREET | PHILADELPHIA | PA | 19181 | (215) 928-8000 |
| B | COLUMBIAN MUTUAL LIFE INS CO | 4704 VESTAL PKWY E PO BOX 1381 | BINGHAMTON | NY | 13902 | (607) 724-2472 |
| C+ | COMBINED INS CO OF AMERICA | 111 E WACKER DRIVE | CHICAGO | IL | 60601 | (800) 225-4500 |
| B+ | COMMUNITY INS CO (OH) | 4361 IRWIN SIMPSON RD | MASON | OH | 45040 | (513) 872-8100 |
| B- | COMMUNITYCARE L&H INS CO | 218 W 6TH ST | TULSA | OK | 74119 | (918) 594-5200 |
| B+ | COMPANION LIFE INS CO | 2501 FARAWAY DRIVE | COLUMBIA | SC | 29219 | (803) 735-1251 |
| B- | CONNECTICUT GENERAL LIFE INS CO | 900 COTTAGE GROVE ROAD | BLOOMFIELD | CT | 6002 | (860) 226-6000 |
| D | CONSTITUTION LIFE INS CO | 4888 LOOP CENTRAL DR STE 700 | HOUSTON | TX | 77081 | (407) 547-3800 |
| C+ | CONTINENTAL GENERAL INS CO | 11001 LAKELINE BLVD STE 120 | AUSTIN | TX | 78717 | (866) 830-0607 |
| C+ | CONTINENTAL LIFE INS CO OF BRENTWOOD | 800 CRESCENT CENTRE DR STE 200 | FRANKLIN | TN | 37067 | (800) 264-4000 |
| A+ | COUNTRY LIFE INS CO | 1701 N TOWANDA AVENUE | BLOOMINGTON | IL | 61701 | (309) 821-3000 |
| B | COVENTRY HEALTH & LIFE INS CO | 550 MARYVILLE CENTRE DR #300 | ST. LOUIS | MO | 63141 | (800) 843-7421 |
| B- | CSI LIFE INS CO | 1212 NORTH 96TH STREET | OMAHA | NE | 68114 | (402) 997-8000 |
| B+ | DEAN HEALTH PLAN INC | 1277 DEMING WAY | MADISON | WI | 53717 | (608) 836-1400 |
| A | EMI HEALTH | 852 EAST ARROWHEAD LANE | MURRAY | UT | 84107 | (801) 262-7476 |
| B- | EMPIRE HEALTHCHOICE ASSURANCE INC | 1 LIBERTY PLAZA 165 BROADWAY | NEW YORK | NY | 10006 | (212) 476-1000 |
| B- | EQUITABLE LIFE & CASUALTY INS CO | 3 TRIAD CENTER | SALT LAKE CITY | UT | 84180 | (801) 579-3400 |
| B+ | EXCELLUS HEALTH PLAN INC | 165 COURT ST | ROCHESTER | NY | 14647 | (585) 454-1700 |
| E | FALLON HEALTH & LIFE ASR CO | 10 CHESTNUT ST | WORCESTER | MA | 01608 | (508) 799-2100 |
| C | FAMILY LIFE INS CO | 10777 NORTHWEST FREEWAY | HOUSTON | TX | 77092 | (713) 529-0045 |
| B | FIRST COMMUNITY HEALTH PLAN INC | 699 GALLATIN ST SW STE A2 | HUNTSVILLE | AL | 35801 | (256) 532-2780 |
| B- | FIRST HEALTH LIFE & HEALTH INS CO | 3200 HIGHLAND AVENUE | DOWNERS GROVE | IL | 60515 | (630) 737-7900 |
| B | FORETHOUGHT LIFE INS CO | 10 W MARKET ST STE 2300 | INDIANAPOLIS | IN | 46204 | (317) 223-2700 |
| C+ | GEISINGER INDEMNITY INS CO | 100 N ACADEMY AVE MC 32-51 | DANVILLE | PA | 17822 | (570) 271-8777 |
| B- | GENWORTH LIFE & ANNUITY INS CO | 6610 WEST BROAD STREET | RICHMOND | VA | 23230 | (804) 662-2400 |
| C+ | GENWORTH LIFE INS CO | 251 LITTLE FALLS DR | WILMINGTON | DE | 19808 | (804) 662-2400 |
| B+ | GERBER LIFE INS CO | 1311 MAMARONECK AVENUE | WHITE PLAINS | NY | 10605 | (914) 272-4000 |
| B- | GLOBE LIFE & ACCIDENT INS CO | 10306 REGENCY PARKWAY DRIVE | OMAHA | NE | 68114 | (972) 569-3744 |
| B+ | GLOBE LIFE INSURANCE CO OF NY | 301 PLAINFIELD RD STE 150 | SYRACUSE | NY | 13212 | (315) 451-2544 |
| B | GOLDEN RULE INS CO | 7440 WOODLAND DRIVE | INDIANAPOLIS | IN | 46278 | (317) 290-8100 |
| B+ | GOVERNMENT PERSONNEL MUTUAL L I C | 2211 NE LOOP 410 | SAN ANTONIO | TX | 78217 | (210) 357-2222 |
| B- | GREAT AMERICAN LIFE INS CO | 301 EAST FOURTH STREET | CINCINNATI | OH | 45202 | (513) 357-3300 |
| D | GROUP HEALTH COOP OF S CENTRAL WI | 1265 JOHN Q HAMMONS DRIVE | MADISON | WI | 53717 | (608) 251-4156 |
| E | GROUP HEALTH INCORPORATED | 55 WATER ST | NEW YORK | NY | 10041 | (646) 447-5000 |
| B- | GROUP HOSP & MEDICAL SERVICES INC | 840 FIRST ST NE | WASHINGTON | DC | 20065 | (410) 581-3000 |
| B | GUARANTEE TRUST LIFE INS CO | 1275 MILWAUKEE AVENUE | GLENVIEW | IL | 60025 | (847) 699-0600 |
| C- | GUNDERSEN HEALTH PLAN INC | 1836 SOUTH AVENUE | LA CROSSE | WI | 54601 | (608) 881-8279 |
| B- | HARTFORD LIFE & ACCIDENT INS CO | ONE HARTFORD PLAZA | HARTFORD | CT | 06155 | (860) 547-5000 |
| C+ | HARTFORD LIFE INS CO | ONE HARTFORD PLAZA | HARTFORD | CT | 06155 | (860) 547-5000 |
| C | HEALTH ALLIANCE CONNECT INC | 301 S VINE ST | URBANA | IL | 61801 | (800) 851-3379 |
| B- | HEALTH ALLIANCE MEDICAL PLANS | 301 S VINE | URBANA | IL | 61801 | (800) 851-3379 |
| B | HEALTH CARE SVC CORP A MUT LEG RES | 300 EAST RANDOLPH ST | CHICAGO | IL | 60601 | (312) 653-6000 |
| E- | HEALTH NET HEALTH PLAN OF OREGON INC | 13221 SW 68TH PARKWAY SUITE 20 | TIGARD | OR | 97223 | (314) 724-4477 |
| C | HEALTH NET LIFE INS CO | 21281 BURBANK BOULEVARD B3 | WOODLAND HILLS | CA | 91367 | (314) 725-4477 |
| B | HEALTH TRADITION HEALTH PLAN | 1808 EAST MAIN STREET | ONALASKA | WI | 54650 | (507) 538-5212 |
| C+ | HEALTHNOW NY INC | 257 WEST GENESEE ST | BUFFALO | NY | 14202 | (716) 887-6900 |
| A- | HEALTHY ALLIANCE LIFE INS CO | 1831 CHESTNUT ST | ST. LOUIS | MO | 63103 | (314) 923-4444 |

| RATING | INSURANCE COMPANY NAME | ADDRESS | CITY | STATE | ZIP | PHONE |
|---|---|---|---|---|---|---|
| B- | HEARTLAND NATIONAL LIFE INS CO | 401 PENNSYLVANIA PKWY STE 300 | INDIANAPOLIS | IN | 46280 | (816) 478-0120 |
| B- | HIGHMARK BCBSD INC | 800 DELAWARE AVE | WILMINGTON | DE | 19801 | (302) 421-3000 |
| C | HIGHMARK INC | 1800 CENTER ST | CAMP HILL | PA | 17011 | (412) 544-7000 |
| B | HIGHMARK WEST VIRGINIA INC | 614 MARKET ST | PARKERSBURG | WV | 26101 | (304) 424-7700 |
| B- | HORIZON INS CO | 3 PENN PLAZA EAST PP-15D | NEWARK | NJ | 07105 | (973) 466-5607 |
| D- | HPHC INS CO | 93 WORCESTER ST | WELLESLEY | MA | 02481 | (781) 263-6000 |
| B | HUMANA HEALTH BENEFIT PLAN LA | ONE GALLERIA BLVD SUITE 1200 | METAIRIE | LA | 70001 | (504) 219-6600 |
| B- | HUMANA HEALTH INS CO OF FL INC | 3501 SW 160TH AVE | MIRAMAR | FL | 33027 | (305) 626-5616 |
| A- | HUMANA INS CO (WI) | 1100 EMPLOYERS BLVD | DEPERE | WI | 54115 | (920) 336-1100 |
| C | HUMANA INS CO OF KENTUCKY | 500 WEST MAIN STREET | LOUISVILLE | KY | 40202 | (502) 580-1000 |
| B- | HUMANA INS CO OF NY | 845 THIRD AVE 7TH FL | NEW YORK | NY | 10022 | (800) 201-3687 |
| C- | INDEPENDENCE BLUE CROSS | 1901 MARKET ST | PHILADELPHIA | PA | 19103 | (215) 241-2400 |
| D | INDIVIDUAL ASR CO LIFE HEALTH & ACC | 930 E 2ND ST STE 100 | EDMOND | OK | 73034 | (405) 285-0838 |
| U | INTER-COUNTY HOSPITALIZATION PLAN | 1900 MARKET ST STE 500 | PHILADELPHIA | PA | 19103 | (215) 657-8900 |
| C | JEFFERSON NATIONAL LIFE INS CO | 350 NORTH ST PAUL STREET | DALLAS | TX | 75201 | (866) 667-0561 |
| B | KAISER FNDTN HLTH PLAN WA OPTN | 320 WESTLAKE AVE N STE 100 | SEATTLE | WA | 98109 | (206) 448-5600 |
| B | LA HEALTH SERVICE & INDEMNITY CO | 5525 REITZ AVE | BATON ROUGE | LA | 70809 | (225) 295-3307 |
| B | LIBERTY NATIONAL LIFE INS CO | 10306 REGENCY PARKWAY DR | OMAHA | NE | 68114 | (972) 569-4000 |
| C | LIFEWISE HEALTH PLAN OF OREGON | 2020 SW 4TH ST STE 1000 | PORTLAND | OR | 97201 | (425) 918-4000 |
| B- | LINCOLN HERITAGE LIFE INS CO | 920 S SPRING ST | SPRINGFIELD | IL | 62704 | (602) 957-1650 |
| B- | LOYAL AMERICAN LIFE INS CO | 1300 EAST NINTH STREET | CLEVELAND | OH | 44114 | (512) 451-2224 |
| B | MANHATTAN LIFE INS CO | 225 COMMUNITY DRIVE SUITE 11 | GREAT NECK | NY | 11021 | (713) 529-0045 |
| B+ | MEDICAL HEALTH INS CORP OF OHIO | 2060 EAST NINTH STREET | CLEVELAND | OH | 44115 | (216) 687-7000 |
| A | MEDICAL MUTUAL OF OHIO | 2060 EAST NINTH ST | CLEVELAND | OH | 44115 | (216) 687-7000 |
| A- | MEDICO CORP LIFE INS CO | 601 SIXTH AVE | DES MOINES | IA | 50309 | (800) 822-9993 |
| B | MEDICO INS CO | 601 Sixth Ave | DES MOINES | IA | 50309 | (800) 228-6080 |
| C | MEMBERS HEALTH INS CO | 24 WEST CAMELBACK AVE STE A546 | PHOENIX | AZ | 85013 | (931) 560-0041 |
| C | MERCYCARE HMO | 580 N WASHINGTON | JANESVILLE | WI | 53545 | (608) 752-3431 |
| B+ | MUTUAL OF OMAHA INS CO | MUTUAL OF OMAHA PLAZA | OMAHA | NE | 68175 | (402) 342-7600 |
| B- | NATIONWIDE LIFE INS CO | ONE WEST NATIONWIDE BLVD | COLUMBUS | OH | 43215 | (614) 249-7111 |
| C | NEW ERA LIFE INS CO | 11720 KATY FREEWAY SUITE 1700 | HOUSTON | TX | 77079 | (281) 368-7200 |
| C+ | NEW ERA LIFE INS CO OF THE MIDWEST | 11720 KATY FREEWAY SUITE 1700 | HOUSTON | TX | 77079 | (281) 368-7200 |
| E- | NEW WEST HEALTH SERVICES | 130 NEILL AVENUE | HELENA | MT | 59601 | (406) 457-2200 |
| A- | NEW YORK LIFE INS CO | 51 MADISON AVENUE | NEW YORK | NY | 10010 | (212) 576-7000 |
| B | NORIDIAN MUTUAL INS CO | 4510 13TH AVE S | FARGO | ND | 58121 | (701) 282-1100 |
| B | NORTH AMERICAN INS CO | 575 DONOFRIO DRIVE SUITE 100 | MADISON | WI | 53719 | (877) 667-9368 |
| C | OLD SURETY LIFE INS CO | 5201 NORTH LINCOL BLVD | OKLAHOMA CITY | OK | 73105 | (405) 523-2112 |
| B- | OMAHA INS CO | MUTUAL OF OMAHA PLAZA | OMAHA | NE | 68175 | (402) 342-7600 |
| B | OXFORD LIFE INS CO | 2721 NORTH CENTRAL AVENUE | PHOENIX | AZ | 85004 | (602) 263-6666 |
| C+ | PACIFICARE LIFE & HEALTH INS CO | 7440 WOODLAND DRIVE | INDIANAPOLIS | IN | 46278 | (608) 783-8610 |
| A- | PARAMOUNT INS CO (OH) | 1901 INDIAN WOOD CIRCLE | MAUMEE | OH | 43537 | (419) 887-2500 |
| B | PEKIN LIFE INS CO | 2505 COURT STREET | PEKIN | IL | 61558 | (309) 346-1161 |
| U | PENNSYLVANIA LIFE INS CO | 27 N FRONT ST | HARRISBURG | PA | 17101 | (401) 770-9669 |
| B | PHILADELPHIA AMERICAN LIFE INS CO | 11720 KATY FREEWAY SUITE 1700 | HOUSTON | TX | 77079 | (281) 368-7200 |
| C | PHYSICIANS BENEFITS TRUST LIFE INS | 20 NORTH MICHIGAN AVE STE 700 | CHICAGO | IL | 60602 | (312) 782-2749 |
| A- | PHYSICIANS LIFE INS CO | 2600 DODGE STREET | OMAHA | NE | 68131 | (402) 633-1000 |
| A+ | PHYSICIANS MUTUAL INS CO | 2600 DODGE STREET | OMAHA | NE | 68131 | (402) 633-1000 |
| D+ | PHYSICIANS PLUS INS CORP | 2650 NOVATION PARKWAY | MADISON | WI | 53713 | (608) 282-8900 |
| B+ | PREMERA BLUE CROSS | 7001 220TH ST SW | MOUNTLAKE TERRACE | WA | 98043 | (425) 918-4000 |
| B+ | PRINCIPAL LIFE INS CO | 711 HIGH STREET | DES MOINES | IA | 50392 | (515) 247-5111 |
| A | PRIORITY HEALTH | 1231 EAST BELTLINE NE | GRAND RAPIDS | MI | 49525 | (616) 942-0954 |
| B | PROVIDENT AMER LIFE & HEALTH INS CO | 1300 EAST NINTH STREET | CLEVELAND | OH | 44114 | (512) 451-2224 |

| RATING | INSURANCE COMPANY NAME | ADDRESS | CITY | STATE | ZIP | PHONE |
|---|---|---|---|---|---|---|
| C- | PURITAN LIFE INS CO OF AMERICA | 701 BRAZOS STREET SUITE 720 | AUSTIN | TX | 78701 | (888) 474-9519 |
| D- | PYRAMID LIFE INS CO | 10851 MASTIN BLVD STE 1000 | OVERLAND PARK | KS | 66210 | (407) 547-3336 |
| D | QUALCHOICE L&H INS CO | 12615 CHENAL PARKWAY STE 300 | LITTLE ROCK | AR | 72211 | (501) 219-5109 |
| B+ | REGENCE BL CROSS BL SHIELD OREGON | 100 SW MARKET ST | PORTLAND | OR | 97201 | (503) 225-5221 |
| B- | REGENCE BLUE CROSS BLUE SHIELD OF UT | 2890 EAST COTTONWOOD PARKWAY | SALT LAKE CITY | UT | 84121 | (801) 333-2000 |
| B | REGENCE BLUESHIELD | 1800 NINTH AVE | SEATTLE | WA | 98101 | (206) 464-3600 |
| B | REGENCE BLUESHIELD OF IDAHO INC | 1602 21ST AVE | LEWISTON | ID | 83501 | (208) 746-2671 |
| B- | RESERVE NATIONAL INS CO | 601 EAST BRITTON ROAD | OKLAHOMA CITY | OK | 73114 | (405) 848-7931 |
| B | ROCKY MOUNTAIN HOSPITAL & MEDICAL | 700 BROADWAY | DENVER | CO | 80273 | (303) 831-2131 |
| C | SANFORD HEALTH PLAN | 300 CHERAPA PLACE SUITE 201 | SIOUX FALLS | SD | 57103 | (605) 328-6868 |
| A- | SECURITY HEALTH PLAN OF WI INC | 1515 ST JOSEPH AVE | MARSHFIELD | WI | 54449 | (715) 221-9555 |
| C- | SENTINEL SECURITY LIFE INS CO | 1405 WEST 2200 SOUTH | SALT LAKE CITY | UT | 84119 | (801) 484-8514 |
| B- | SHENANDOAH LIFE INS CO | 4415 PHEASANT RIDGE RD STE 300 | ROANOKE | VA | 24014 | (540) 985-4400 |
| B | SIERRA HEALTH AND LIFE INS CO INC | 2720 N TENAYA WAY | LAS VEGAS | NV | 89128 | (702) 242-7732 |
| A- | STANDARD LIFE & ACCIDENT INS CO | ONE MOODY PLAZA | GALVESTON | TX | 77550 | (409) 763-4661 |
| D | STANDARD LIFE & CAS INS CO | 420 E SOUTH TEMPLE SUITE 555 | SALT LAKE CITY | UT | 84111 | (801) 538-0376 |
| B+ | STATE FARM MUTUAL AUTOMOBILE INS CO | ONE STATE FARM PLAZA | BLOOMINGTON | IL | 61710 | (309) 766-2311 |
| C- | STATE MUTUAL INS CO | 210 E SECOND AVENUE SUITE 301 | ROME | GA | 30161 | (706) 291-1054 |
| D+ | STERLING INVESTORS LIFE INS CO | 10201 N ILLINOIS ST SUITE 280 | INDIANAPOLIS | IN | 46290 | (317) 208-2200 |
| B- | STERLING LIFE INS CO | 525 W MONROE ST | CHICAGO | IL | 60661 | (512) 451-2224 |
| D | THP INS CO | 52160 NATIONAL RD EAST E | ST. CLAIRSVILLE | OH | 43950 | (740) 695-3585 |
| B | TRANSAMERICA FINANCIAL LIFE INS CO | 440 MAMARONECK AVENUE | HARRISON | NY | 10528 | (914) 627-3630 |
| B | TRANSAMERICA LIFE INS CO | 4333 EDGEWOOD RD NE | CEDAR RAPIDS | IA | 52499 | (319) 355-8511 |
| C+ | TRANSAMERICA PREMIER LIFE INS CO | 4333 EDGEWOOD RD NE | CEDAR RAPIDS | IA | 52499 | (319) 355-8511 |
| C | TRH HEALTH INS CO | 147 BEAR CREEK PIKE | COLUMBIA | TN | 38401 | (931) 560-0041 |
| B- | TRIPLE-S SALUD INC | FD ROOSEVELT AVE 1441 | SAN JUAN | PR | 00920 | (787) 749-4949 |
| C- | TUFTS INS CO | 705 MOUNT AUBURN ST | WATERTOWN | MA | 02472 | (617) 972-9400 |
| B- | UNICARE LIFE & HEALTH INS CO | 120 MONUMENT CIRCLE | INDIANAPOLIS | IN | 46204 | (877) 864-2273 |
| B | UNIFIED LIFE INS CO | CSC-LAWYERS INC SERV 211 E 7TH | AUSTIN | TX | 78701 | (877) 492-4678 |
| B- | UNITED AMERICAN INS CO | 10306 REGENCY PARKWAY DR | OMAHA | NE | 68114 | (972) 529-5085 |
| C | UNITED HEALTHCARE INS CO | 185 ASYLUM STREET | HARTFORD | CT | 06103 | (877) 832-7734 |
| B- | UNITED HEALTHCARE INS CO OF NY | 2950 EXPRESSWAY DR S STE 240 | ISLANDIA | NY | 11749 | (877) 832-7734 |
| B- | UNITED HEALTHCARE OF ALABAMA INC | 33 INVERNESS CENTER PARKWAY | BIRMINGHAM | AL | 35242 | (205) 437-8500 |
| B | UNITED NATIONAL LIFE INS CO OF AM | 1275 MILWAUKEE AVENUE | GLENVIEW | IL | 60025 | (847) 803-5252 |
| B | UNITED OF OMAHA LIFE INS CO | MUTUAL OF OMAHA PLAZA | OMAHA | NE | 68175 | (402) 342-7600 |
| B+ | UNITED WORLD LIFE INS CO | MUTUAL OF OMAHA PLAZA | OMAHA | NE | 68175 | (402) 342-7600 |
| C | UNITY HEALTH PLANS INS CORP | 840 CAROLINA STREET | SAUK CITY | WI | 53583 | (608) 643-2491 |
| D | UNIVERSAL FIDELITY LIFE INS CO | 13931 QUAIL POINTE DRIVE | OKLAHOMA CITY | OK | 73134 | (800) 366-8354 |
| A | USAA LIFE INS CO | 9800 FREDERICKSBURG RD | SAN ANTONIO | TX | 78288 | (210) 498-1411 |
| A+ | USABLE MUTUAL INS CO | 601 S GAINES | LITTLE ROCK | AR | 72201 | (501) 378-2000 |
| C+ | VERMONT HEALTH PLAN LLC | 445 INDUSTRIAL LANE | BERLIN | VT | 05602 | (802) 223-6131 |
| D+ | WASHINGTON NATIONAL INS CO | 11825 NORTH PENNSYLVANIA STREE | CARMEL | IN | 46032 | (317) 817-6100 |
| B- | WELLMARK INC | 1331 GRAND AVE | DES MOINES | IA | 50309 | (515) 376-4500 |
| B+ | WELLMARK OF SOUTH DAKOTA INC | 1601 WEST MADISON ST | SIOUX FALLS | SD | 57104 | (605) 373-7200 |
| C | WILCO LIFE INS CO | 12821 E NEW MARKET ST STE 250 | CARMEL | IN | 46032 | (203) 762-4400 |
| C | WISCONSIN PHYSICIANS SERVICE INS | 1717 WEST BRDWAY | MADISON | WI | 53713 | (608) 977-5000 |

# Section VII

# Analysis of Medicare Managed Care Complaints

An analysis of complaints filed against

**U.S. Medicare Managed Care Plans**

Companies are listed in alphabetical order.

# Section VII Contents

As discussed in the previous section, no single measure is an end-all indicator of the quality of service provided by a health insurer. However, if you are a Medicare beneficiary, complaint information can give you a preliminary basis for informed shopping – especially for Medicare Managed Care plans. It will answer questions such as: Does the company have a high rate of enrollee complaints against it? Are most complaints upheld or overturned? Are many withdrawn before a decision is rendered?

The complaint information on the following pages will give you an indication of what beneficiaries, like yourself, have experienced with various Medicare insurers. This section is based on "reconsideration" data, reprinted from the Centers for Medicare and Medicaid Services (formerly known as Health Care Financing Administration) for providers with Medicare contracts.

"Reconsiderations" are complaints by members of Medicare Managed Care plans that have reached a federal review. Once they reach that stage, the complaints have already gone through at least two levels of internal appeals. Consequently, they are relatively serious and involve anywhere from several hundred dollars to many thousands of dollars of unpaid medical bills. In this section, all complaints cited are reconsiderations.

Complaints that were settled within the Plan's internal appeal process are not reflected. It is difficult to say what types of complaints these might be, but, in general, they are more likely to pertain to services of a lower dollar value.

We have made no attempt to render an opinion on the data contained in this section. Rather, we are reprinting the information strictly to help provide you with valuable information when shopping for a Medicare plan.

## The Drawbacks of Complaint Data

One problem with the data is the time lag due to the lengthy reconsideration process. A company that has a high complaint rate in this section may have already begun to make improvements in its system to handle the types of issues that were raised in the complaints. Therefore, because it takes so long for a complaint to make it through the federal process, the company may appear to have worse service quality than it currently has.

Conversely, numerous companies that have obtained Medicare contracts very recently (within the past year), may show few or no complaints. But this may reflect merely the fact that the complaints filed against these companies have not yet reached the federal level. So before you make a final decision to select a company with a low level of complaints, find out how long it has had its Medicare contract. We estimate that the contract should be in force for about two years before these data reflect the complaints.

If you are interested in a company with a seemingly high complaint level, do take the time to ask the company what improvements, if any, it has made to correct the problems reflected in the complaint data. If a high rate of complaints against it have been upheld at the federal level, it will be far more difficult to explain away.

The plans included here are those from whom reconsiderations were received during 2016 or companies that had members enrolled in a specific Medicare contract as of July of that year. Not included are: 1) updates for later appeals of cases that have been decided and 2) companies whose contracts are so new that they don't have any current enrollment.

The plan name in this table represents one or more contracts with the Centers for Medicare and Medicaid Services (CMS). You may find some plans listed more than once; this is because they have contracts in different CMS-designated regions (see Column 3). If a plan has more than one contract in a particular region, the reconsideration data have been combined so that the company is only listed once for each region.

Three types of Medicare contracts are included here: risk, cost, and Health Care Prepayment Plans (HCPPs). A Medicare risk contract is one in which the CMS pays the plan a capitalization rate equal to a percentage of the average fee-for-service expense, in a given geographic area. A Medicare cost contract is one in which the CMS reimburses the plan for retroactively determined Part A and B costs. And an HCPP contract is similar to a cost contract but only Part B costs are paid by the CMS.

The following **BOLD** headings are the column reference guides for the tables

1. **Insurance Company Name** — The legally-registered name, which sometimes can differ from the name that the plan uses for advertising. If you cannot find the plan you are interested in, or if you have any doubts regarding the precise name, verify the information before looking it up in this Guide. Also, determine the domicile state for confirmation.

2. **Domicile State** — The state which has primary regulatory responsibility for the company. It may differ from the location of the company's corporate headquarters. You do not have to be living in the domicile state to purchase insurance from this firm, provided it is licensed to do business in your state.

   Also use this column to confirm that you have located the correct company. It is possible for two unrelated companies to have the same name if they are domiciled in different states.

3. **Safety Rating** — Our rating is measured on a scale from A to F and considers a wide range of factors. Highly-rated companies are, in our opinion, less likely to experience financial difficulties than lower rated firms. See *About Weiss Safety Ratings* for more information.

**4. Region**

The CMS region in which the complaint data applies for a particular company. The regions are as follows:

**Boston: 1** (Connecticut, Maine, Massachusetts, New Hampshire, Rhode Island, Vermont), **New York: 2** (New Jersey, New York, Puerto Rico, Virgin Islands), **Philadelphia: 3** (Delaware, District of Columbia, Maryland, Pennsylvania, Virginia, West Virginia), **Atlanta: 4** (Alabama, Florida, Georgia, Kentucky, Mississippi, North Carolina, South Carolina, Tennessee), **Chicago: 5** (Illinois, Indiana, Michigan, Minnesota, Ohio, Wisconsin), **Dallas: 6** (Arkansas, Louisiana, Oklahoma, New Mexico, Texas), **Kansas City: 7** (Iowa, Kansas, Missouri, Nebraska), **Denver: 8** (Colorado, Montana, North Dakota, South Dakota, Utah, Wyoming), **San Francisco: 9** (Arizona, California, Guam, Hawaii, Nevada, Samoa), **Seattle: 10** (Alaska, Idaho, Oregon, Washington).

**5. Rate**

The rate of reconsiderations per 1,000 members, and is calculated as the sum of appeals received per year. Divided by the mid-year (July) enrollment, times 1,000.

"N/R" means that there were "no reconsiderations" for that particular plan's contract in that particular region. "N/E" means there was "no enrollment" during 2016. This happens when the complaints reflect prior enrollments in specific contracts, demonstrate the lag time between enrollment, and the complaint being represented in the reconsideration system.

**6. Reconsiderations Received 2016**

The number of reconsiderations received by the CMS from the health plan for the Medicare contract(s) only. Regardless of the number of complaints upheld or overturned (See columns 8 and 9), if this number is high relative to other Medicare plans, it signals that the plan has trouble satisfying its policyholders.

The health plan may have other business besides treating Medicare beneficiaries but this figure only pertains to enrollees that are served under a Medicare contract.

**7. Reconsiderations Not Yet Decided**

The number of reconsiderations received during 2016 that have not yet been settled.

**8. Reconsiderations Upheld**

The number of cases in which the CMS upheld the decision of the Medicare plan. This is the number of times CMS ruled against the policyholder in favor of the plan. If the number is high relative to the total number of reconsiderations received (Column 6), it is a sign that the firm's complaint process is somewhat ironclad and appeals beyond it are often futile. This, however, does not necessarily mean that the plan was not at fault.

**9. Reconsiderations Overturned**

The number of cases in which the CMS completely overturned the decision of the Medicare Managed Care plan. This is the number of times the CMS ruled in favor of the policyholder. If the number of complaints overturned is high, relative to the total number of reconsiderations received (Column 6), it is a sign that either the plan is falling short in meeting the needs of its policyholders; or, its complaint process is not streamlined enough to carry complaints to the appropriate conclusion.

**10. Reconsiderations Withdrawn**

The number of reconsiderations that were withdrawn from review.

The Regional CMS office will investigate the case and determine if the enrolee should revert back to fee-for-service (disenroll). If the CMS does not grant disenrollment, the case re-enters the reconsideration process and follows the same course as other complaints.

A high number of disenrollments may indicate that the plan has failed to clearly identify its coverage limitations at the time the policy is sold.

**11. Reconsiderations Dismissed**

The number of cases in which the CMS Regional Office decided the appeal is not valid or the CMS Regional Office does not have jurisdiction over the appeal.

| INSURANCE COMPANY NAME | DOM. STATE | RATING | REGION | RATE | RECONS REC'VD | RECONS NOT YET DECIDED | RECONS UPHELD | RECONS OVER-TURNED | RECONS WITH-DRAWN | RECONS DISMISSED |
|---|---|---|---|---|---|---|---|---|---|---|
| ABSOLUTE TOTAL CARE INC | SC | **C-** | 4 | 3.24 | 7 | 0 | 5 | 1 | 1 | 0 |
| ADVANTAGE HEALTH SOLUTIONS INC | IN | **F** | 5 | N/E | -- | -- | -- | -- | -- | -- |
| ADVICARE CORP | SC | **C+** | 4 | 0.28 | 1 | 0 | 0 | 0 | 0 | 1 |
| AETNA BETTER HEALTH OF MICHIGAN INC | MI | **B** | 5 | 0.54 | 4 | 0 | 0 | 1 | 0 | 3 |
| AETNA HEALTH INC (A CT CORP) | CT | **C** | 8 | 4.83 | 120 | 0 | 97 | 7 | 3 | 8 |
| AETNA HEALTH INC (A FLORIDA CORP) | FL | **B+** | 8 | 1.01 | 68 | 0 | 54 | 4 | 5 | 5 |
| AETNA HEALTH INC (A GEORGIA CORP) | GA | **B** | 8 | 13.33 | 11 | 0 | 11 | 0 | 0 | 0 |
| AETNA HEALTH INC (A MAINE CORP) | ME | **B-** | 8 | 3.19 | 21 | 0 | 20 | 1 | 0 | 0 |
| AETNA HEALTH INC (A NEW JERSEY CORP) | NJ | **B** | 8 | 2.81 | 113 | 0 | 98 | 6 | 0 | 7 |
| AETNA HEALTH INC (A NEW YORK CORP) | NY | **C+** | 8 | 3.21 | 50 | 0 | 44 | 2 | 1 | 3 |
| AETNA HEALTH INC (A PA CORP) | PA | **C+** | 8 | 2.29 | 148 | 0 | 121 | 12 | 7 | 8 |
| AETNA HEALTH INC (A TEXAS CORP) | TX | **C+** | 8 | 1.89 | 48 | 0 | 40 | 3 | 2 | 3 |
| AETNA HEALTH OF CALIFORNIA INC | CA | **C+** | 8 | 2.64 | 42 | 0 | 34 | 5 | 1 | 2 |
| AETNA HEALTH OF IOWA INC | IA | **C+** | 8 | 1.11 | 5 | 0 | 5 | 0 | 0 | 0 |
| AETNA HEALTH OF UTAH INC | UT | **C+** | 8 | 1.42 | 10 | 0 | 9 | 1 | 0 | 0 |
| AETNA LIFE INS CO | CT | **B** | 1 | N/E | -- | -- | -- | -- | -- | -- |
| AETNA LIFE INS CO | CT | **B** | 8 | 2.50 | 1743 | 0 | 1457 | 115 | 40 | 113 |
| AIDS HEALTHCARE FOUNDATION MCO OF FL | FL | **E-** | 9 | 1.50 | 2 | 0 | 2 | 0 | 0 | 0 |
| ALIGNMENT HEALTH PLAN | CA | **E** | 10 | 3.93 | 78 | 0 | 67 | 7 | 0 | 3 |
| ALLIANCE HEALTH & LIFE INS CO | MI | **C** | 5 | 3.95 | 13 | 0 | 8 | 3 | 1 | 1 |
| ALOHACARE | HI | **C+** | 9 | 1.21 | 1 | 0 | 1 | 0 | 0 | 0 |
| ALPHACARE OF NEW YORK INC | NY | **C-** | 2 | 5.79 | 6 | 0 | 4 | 1 | 0 | 1 |
| AMERICAN PROGRESSIVE L&H I C OF NY | NY | **C** | 6 | 9.49 | 203 | 0 | 136 | 32 | 4 | 30 |
| AMERICAS 1ST CHOICE HEALTH PLANS INC | SC | **E+** | 4 | 4.61 | 4 | 0 | 2 | 0 | 0 | 2 |
| AMERICAS 1ST CHOICE SOUTH CAROLINA | SC | **E-** | 4 | N/E | -- | -- | -- | -- | -- | -- |
| AMERIGROUP COMMUNITY CARE NM | NM | **B-** | 5 | 3.09 | 6 | 0 | 2 | 0 | 2 | 2 |
| AMERIGROUP NEW JERSEY INC | NJ | **B+** | 5 | 6.04 | 49 | 0 | 34 | 2 | 4 | 9 |
| AMERIGROUP TENNESSEE INC | TN | **B-** | 5 | 2.47 | 22 | 0 | 15 | 0 | 1 | 5 |
| AMERIGROUP TEXAS INC | TX | **A-** | 5 | 2.90 | 94 | 0 | 57 | 1 | 6 | 30 |
| AMERIGROUP TEXAS INC | TX | **A-** | 6 | 2.42 | 33 | 0 | 19 | 1 | 6 | 7 |
| AMERIGROUP WASHINGTON INC | WA | **A-** | 5 | 5.55 | 8 | 0 | 7 | 0 | 1 | 0 |
| AMERIHEALTH HMO INC | PA | **C** | 3 | 11.36 | 218 | 0 | 190 | 22 | 3 | 2 |
| AMERIHEALTH MICHIGAN INC | MI | **C-** | 5 | 4.38 | 17 | 0 | 8 | 1 | 0 | 7 |
| AMGP GEORGIA MANAGED CARE CO INC | GA | **A-** | 5 | N/E | -- | -- | -- | -- | -- | -- |
| ANTHEM BLUE CROSS LIFE & HEALTH INS | CA | **B-** | 5 | 6.96 | 53 | 0 | 40 | 1 | 6 | 6 |
| ANTHEM HEALTH PLANS INC | CT | **B-** | 5 | 6.94 | 121 | 0 | 87 | 6 | 6 | 19 |
| ANTHEM HEALTH PLANS OF KENTUCKY INC | KY | **B+** | 5 | 7.56 | 39 | 0 | 26 | 4 | 3 | 6 |
| ANTHEM HEALTH PLANS OF MAINE INC | ME | **B+** | 5 | 21.54 | 7 | 0 | 5 | 0 | 1 | 1 |
| ANTHEM HEALTH PLANS OF NEW HAMPSHIRE | NH | **B** | 5 | 2.86 | 5 | 0 | 3 | 1 | 1 | 0 |
| ANTHEM HEALTH PLANS OF VIRGINIA | VA | **B-** | 5 | 1.10 | 1 | 0 | 0 | 1 | 0 | 0 |
| ANTHEM INS COMPANIES INC | IN | **B-** | 5 | 18.70 | 342 | 0 | 254 | 27 | 35 | 22 |
| ARKANSAS SUPERIOR SELECT INC | AR | **E** | 6 | N/E | -- | -- | -- | -- | -- | -- |
| ASPIRE HEALTH PLAN | CA | **E-** | 9 | 6.71 | 10 | 0 | 7 | 3 | 0 | 0 |
| ASURIS NORTHWEST HEALTH | WA | **B-** | 10 | 2.22 | 3 | 0 | 3 | 0 | 0 | 0 |
| ATLANTIS HEALTH PLAN | NY | **U** | 4 | N/E | -- | -- | -- | -- | -- | -- |
| ATRIO HEALTH PLANS INC | OR | **C-** | 10 | 18.15 | 69 | 0 | 53 | 9 | 0 | 6 |
| AULTCARE INS CO | OH | **C+** | 5 | 2.38 | 51 | 0 | 47 | 0 | 0 | 4 |
| AVMED INC | FL | **C** | 4 | 1.54 | 47 | 0 | 44 | 0 | 1 | 2 |
| BEHEALTHY FLORIDA INC | FL | **D+** | 4 | 8.19 | 21 | 0 | 15 | 4 | 0 | 2 |
| BLUE CROSS & BLUE SHIELD MA HMO BLUE | MA | **A-** | 1 | 2.78 | 62 | 0 | 59 | 2 | 0 | 1 |
| BLUE CROSS & BLUE SHIELD OF FLORIDA | FL | **B-** | 4 | 12.56 | 318 | 0 | 237 | 26 | 2 | 50 |
| BLUE CROSS BLUE SHIELD HEALTHCARE GA | GA | **A-** | 5 | 6.54 | 13 | 0 | 13 | 0 | 0 | 0 |

| INSURANCE COMPANY NAME | DOM. STATE | RATING | REGION | RATE | RECONS REC'VD | RECONS NOT YET DECIDED | RECONS UPHELD | RECONS OVER-TURNED | RECONS WITH-DRAWN | RECONS DISMISSED |
|---|---|---|---|---|---|---|---|---|---|---|
| BLUE CROSS BLUE SHIELD OF ALABAMA | AL | **B** | 4 | 1.59 | 86 | 0 | 69 | 7 | 0 | 9 |
| BLUE CROSS BLUE SHIELD OF GEORGIA | GA | **B-** | 5 | 5.41 | 13 | 0 | 7 | 0 | 4 | 2 |
| BLUE CROSS BLUE SHIELD OF MICHIGAN | MI | **C** | 5 | 0.96 | 107 | 0 | 78 | 6 | 5 | 18 |
| BLUE CROSS BLUE SHIELD OF MINNESOTA | MN | **C** | 5 | 0.25 | 49 | 0 | 45 | 1 | 0 | 2 |
| BLUE CROSS BLUE SHIELD OF NC | NC | **B** | 4 | 4.69 | 259 | 0 | 216 | 26 | 6 | 8 |
| BLUE CROSS BLUE SHIELD OF RI | RI | **C** | 1 | 1.45 | 77 | 0 | 72 | 4 | 0 | 1 |
| BLUE CROSS OF CALIFORNIA | CA | **A+** | 5 | 1.21 | 26 | 0 | 18 | 3 | 3 | 2 |
| BLUE CROSS OF IDAHO HEALTH SERVICE | ID | **B** | 10 | 8.32 | 115 | 0 | 86 | 14 | 1 | 14 |
| BLUE SHIELD OF CALIFORNIA | CA | **A+** | 9 | 3.99 | 379 | 0 | 281 | 4 | 34 | 58 |
| BLUECROSS BLUESHIELD OF TENNESSEE | TN | **B** | 4 | 7.51 | 723 | 0 | 628 | 36 | 16 | 39 |
| BRAVO HEALTH MID-ATLANTIC INC | MD | **C+** | 6 | 10.07 | 200 | 0 | 66 | 25 | 92 | 15 |
| BRAVO HEALTH PENNSYLVANIA INC | PA | **B** | 6 | 5.67 | 286 | 0 | 154 | 60 | 58 | 13 |
| BUCKEYE COMMUNITY HEALTH PLAN INC | OH | **C+** | 5 | 3.12 | 32 | 0 | 18 | 5 | 2 | 7 |
| BUCKEYE COMMUNITY HEALTH PLAN INC | OH | **C+** | 10 | 15.38 | 12 | 0 | 10 | 0 | 0 | 2 |
| CAPITAL ADVANTAGE INS CO | PA | **C** | 3 | 3.91 | 55 | 0 | 46 | 7 | 0 | 1 |
| CAPITAL DISTRICT PHYSICIANS HEALTH P | NY | **B** | 2 | 7.08 | 263 | 0 | 212 | 41 | 2 | 5 |
| CAPITAL HEALTH PLAN INC | FL | **B** | 4 | 1.91 | 36 | 0 | 32 | 2 | 1 | 1 |
| CARE 1ST HEALTH PLAN INC | CA | **A+** | 9 | 14.28 | 453 | 0 | 341 | 29 | 5 | 77 |
| CARE IMPROVEMENT PLUS OF TEXAS INS | TX | **C** | 9 | 9.91 | 854 | 0 | 525 | 16 | 17 | 294 |
| CARE IMPROVEMENT PLUS SOUTH CENTRAL | AR | **C** | 9 | 20.63 | 1878 | 0 | 1186 | 42 | 29 | 621 |
| CARE IMPROVEMENT PLUS WI INS | WI | **C** | 9 | 14.36 | 29 | 0 | 19 | 0 | 0 | 10 |
| CARE N CARE INS CO | TX | **C** | 6 | 2.07 | 22 | 0 | 16 | 4 | 1 | 1 |
| CARE WISCONSIN HEALTH PLAN INC | WI | **B** | 5 | 0.80 | 1 | 0 | 0 | 0 | 0 | 1 |
| CAREMORE HEALTH PLAN | CA | **B+** | 5 | 3.08 | 161 | 0 | 139 | 10 | 0 | 9 |
| CAREMORE HEALTH PLAN OF ARIZONA INC | AZ | **B-** | 5 | 8.67 | 104 | 0 | 87 | 5 | 1 | 11 |
| CAREMORE HEALTH PLAN OF NEVADA | NV | **D** | 5 | 4.18 | 29 | 0 | 20 | 1 | 0 | 8 |
| CAREPLUS HEALTH PLANS INC | FL | **B-** | 7 | 2.52 | 279 | 0 | 260 | 7 | 0 | 12 |
| CARESOURCE | OH | **B-** | 5 | 15.44 | 252 | 0 | 182 | 20 | 8 | 39 |
| CARITEN HEALTH PLAN INC | TN | **B** | 7 | 1.20 | 131 | 0 | 41 | 6 | 27 | 57 |
| CATHOLIC SPECIAL NEEDS PLAN LLC | NY | **C** | 2 | N/E | -- | -- | -- | -- | -- | -- |
| CDPHP UNIVERSAL BENEFITS INC | NY | **E+** | 2 | 9.10 | 33 | 0 | 30 | 3 | 0 | 0 |
| CENTRAL HEALTH PLAN OF CALIFORNIA | CA | **E+** | 10 | 1.34 | 44 | 0 | 34 | 5 | 0 | 5 |
| CHA HMO INC | KY | **C+** | 7 | 1.25 | 19 | 0 | 10 | 1 | 1 | 7 |
| CHRISTUS HEALTH PLAN | TX | **C-** | 6 | N/E | -- | -- | -- | -- | -- | -- |
| CIGNA HEALTH & LIFE INS CO | CT | **B** | 6 | 4.67 | 10 | 0 | 4 | 3 | 2 | 1 |
| CIGNA HEALTHCARE OF ARIZONA INC | AZ | **E-** | 6 | 4.08 | 209 | 0 | 168 | 21 | 3 | 15 |
| CIGNA HEALTHCARE OF GEORGIA INC | GA | **E** | 6 | 4.86 | 192 | 0 | 103 | 29 | 40 | 20 |
| CIGNA HEALTHCARE OF NORTH CAROLINA | NC | **C** | 6 | 6.68 | 58 | 0 | 29 | 8 | 12 | 9 |
| CIGNA HEALTHCARE OF SOUTH CAROLINA | SC | **D-** | 6 | 4.50 | 45 | 0 | 22 | 5 | 4 | 4 |
| CLEARRIVER HEALTH | TN | **D** | 8 | 3.60 | 2 | 0 | 2 | 0 | 0 | 0 |
| CMNTY CARE HLTH PLAN INC (WI) | WI | **C** | 5 | 38.76 | 10 | 0 | 8 | 0 | 0 | 2 |
| COLORADO ACCESS | CO | **E** | 8 | N/E | -- | -- | -- | -- | -- | -- |
| COMMUNITY CARE ALLIANCE OF ILLINOIS | IL | **C-** | 5 | N/E | -- | -- | -- | -- | -- | -- |
| COMMUNITY HEALTH GROUP | CA | **B** | 9 | 0.21 | 1 | 0 | 1 | 0 | 0 | 0 |
| COMMUNITY HEALTH PLAN OF WASHINGTON | WA | **B** | 10 | 8.82 | 64 | 0 | 36 | 16 | 1 | 11 |
| COMMUNITY INS CO (OH) | OH | **B+** | 5 | 3.01 | 417 | 0 | 354 | 23 | 28 | 11 |
| COMMUNITYCARE HMO INC | OK | **B+** | 6 | 1.91 | 55 | 0 | 47 | 2 | 0 | 6 |
| COMPCARE HEALTH SERVICES INS CORP | WI | **A-** | 5 | 2.80 | 7 | 0 | 6 | 0 | 0 | 1 |
| CONNECTICARE INC | CT | **C** | 2 | 4.97 | 280 | 0 | 266 | 10 | 0 | 2 |
| CONSTELLATION HEALTH LLC | PR | **E-** | 2 | 2.08 | 17 | 0 | 12 | 4 | 0 | 0 |
| CONTRA COSTA COUNTY MED SVCS | CA | **C** | 9 | N/E | -- | -- | -- | -- | -- | -- |
| COVENTRY HEALTH & LIFE INS CO | MO | **B** | 8 | 0.95 | 160 | 0 | 133 | 11 | 7 | 8 |

| INSURANCE COMPANY NAME | DOM. STATE | RATING | REGION | RATE | RECONS REC'VD | RECONS NOT YET DECIDED | RECONS UPHELD | RECONS OVER-TURNED | RECONS WITH-DRAWN | RECONS DISMISSED |
|---|---|---|---|---|---|---|---|---|---|---|
| COVENTRY HEALTH CARE OF ILLINOIS INC | IL | **C** | 8 | 1.28 | 23 | 0 | 15 | 2 | 2 | 3 |
| COVENTRY HEALTH CARE OF KANSAS INC | KS | **C+** | 8 | 1.39 | 25 | 0 | 23 | 1 | 1 | 0 |
| COVENTRY HEALTH CARE OF MISSOURI INC | MO | **C+** | 8 | 1.88 | 73 | 0 | 60 | 6 | 1 | 5 |
| COVENTRY HEALTH CARE OF NEBRASKA INC | NE | **B** | 8 | 2.20 | 18 | 0 | 16 | 0 | 0 | 1 |
| COVENTRY HEALTH CARE OF VIRGINIA INC | VA | **C+** | 8 | N/E | -- | -- | -- | -- | -- | -- |
| COVENTRY HEALTH CARE OF WEST VA INC | WV | **B+** | 8 | 2.78 | 14 | 0 | 14 | 0 | 0 | 0 |
| COVENTRY HEALTH PLAN OF FLORIDA INC | FL | **U** | 8 | N/E | -- | -- | -- | -- | -- | -- |
| DEAN HEALTH PLAN INC | WI | **B+** | 5 | 1.21 | 29 | 0 | 19 | 4 | 0 | 6 |
| DENVER HEALTH MEDICAL PLAN INC | CO | **B** | 8 | 1.35 | 6 | 0 | 6 | 0 | 0 | 0 |
| EASY CHOICE HEALTH PLAN | CA | **C-** | 4 | 4.67 | 148 | 0 | 120 | 5 | 2 | 20 |
| ELDERPLAN INC | NY | **C** | 2 | 39.07 | 145 | 0 | 75 | 17 | 28 | 25 |
| EMPIRE HEALTHCHOICE ASSURANCE INC | NY | **B-** | 5 | 8.16 | 56 | 0 | 39 | 0 | 4 | 12 |
| EMPIRE HEALTHCHOICE HMO INC | NY | **C+** | 5 | 3.67 | 250 | 0 | 198 | 16 | 12 | 22 |
| ESSENCE HEALTHCARE INC | MO | **B+** | 7 | 5.38 | 324 | 0 | 256 | 46 | 6 | 16 |
| EXCELLUS HEALTH PLAN INC | NY | **B+** | 2 | 11.00 | 636 | 0 | 524 | 77 | 9 | 23 |
| FALLON COMMUNITY HEALTH PLAN | MA | **B-** | 1 | 13.69 | 252 | 0 | 205 | 28 | 3 | 13 |
| FAMILYCARE HEALTH PLANS INC | OR | **E-** | 10 | 4.07 | 18 | 0 | 7 | 0 | 0 | 11 |
| FIRST HEALTH LIFE & HEALTH INS CO | TX | **B-** | 8 | N/E | -- | -- | -- | -- | -- | -- |
| FIRST MEDICAL HEALTH PLAN INC | PR | **E** | 2 | N/E | -- | -- | -- | -- | -- | -- |
| FIRSTCAROLINACARE INS CO | NC | **D** | 4 | 6.26 | 20 | 0 | 17 | 3 | 0 | 0 |
| FREEDOM HEALTH INC | FL | **D-** | 4 | 2.51 | 175 | 0 | 141 | 0 | 2 | 30 |
| FRIDAY HEALTH PLANS OF CO INC | CO | **E-** | 8 | N/E | -- | -- | -- | -- | -- | -- |
| GATEWAY HEALTH PLAN INC | PA | **B-** | 3 | 6.15 | 317 | 0 | 287 | 8 | 6 | 15 |
| GATEWAY HEALTH PLAN OF OHIO INC | OH | **C** | 3 | 22.75 | 168 | 0 | 153 | 0 | 3 | 12 |
| GEISINGER HEALTH PLAN | PA | **B+** | 3 | 2.74 | 196 | 0 | 172 | 16 | 0 | 6 |
| GEISINGER INDEMNITY INS CO | PA | **C+** | 3 | 1.68 | 27 | 0 | 21 | 6 | 0 | 0 |
| GEISINGER INDEMNITY INS CO | PA | **C+** | 8 | N/E | -- | -- | -- | -- | -- | -- |
| GEISINGER QUALITY OPTIONS INC | PA | **C+** | 3 | 6.18 | 5 | 0 | 5 | 0 | 0 | 0 |
| GEISINGER QUALITY OPTIONS INC | PA | **C+** | 8 | N/E | -- | -- | -- | -- | -- | -- |
| GHS HEALTH MAINTENANCE ORGANIZATION | OK | **B-** | 6 | 7.34 | 35 | 0 | 13 | 6 | 2 | 12 |
| GHS INS CO | OK | **E-** | 6 | 5.33 | 17 | 0 | 6 | 3 | 4 | 4 |
| GHS MANAGED HEALTH CARE PLANS INC | OK | **E** | 6 | 11.97 | 55 | 0 | 21 | 10 | 1 | 21 |
| GLOBALHEALTH INC | OK | **D** | 6 | 0.76 | 1 | 0 | 1 | 0 | 0 | 0 |
| GOLDEN STATE MEDICARE HEALTH PLAN | CA | **E+** | 10 | 7.88 | 55 | 0 | 45 | 6 | 2 | 2 |
| GROUP HEALTH INCORPORATED | NY | **E** | 2 | 3.33 | 23 | 0 | 19 | 2 | 0 | 2 |
| GROUP HEALTH PLAN INC | MN | **A-** | 5 | 0.84 | 43 | 0 | 39 | 1 | 1 | 2 |
| GUNDERSEN HEALTH PLAN INC | WI | **C-** | 5 | 9.07 | 131 | 0 | 98 | 20 | 4 | 7 |
| GUNDERSEN HLTH PLAN MN INC | MN | **C** | 5 | 4.34 | 3 | 0 | 3 | 0 | 0 | 0 |
| HAP MIDWEST HEALTH PLAN INC | MI | **C** | 5 | 15.49 | 39 | 0 | 2 | 0 | 0 | 37 |
| HARBOR HEALTH PLAN INC | MI | **E** | 6 | 3.09 | 2 | 0 | 1 | 0 | 0 | 1 |
| HARMONY HEALTH PLAN INC | IL | **C** | 4 | 6.42 | 98 | 0 | 87 | 1 | 0 | 10 |
| HARVARD PILGRIM HEALTH CARE INC | MA | **C+** | 1 | 36.31 | 88 | 0 | 69 | 6 | 2 | 10 |
| HAWAII MEDICAL SERVICE ASSOCIATION | HI | **B-** | 9 | 0.57 | 21 | 0 | 15 | 3 | 1 | 2 |
| HCSC INS SERVICES CO | IL | **D-** | 6 | 8.22 | 94 | 0 | 52 | 19 | 1 | 21 |
| HEALTH ALLIANCE CONNECT INC | IL | **C** | 5 | 9.41 | 10 | 0 | 9 | 1 | 0 | 0 |
| HEALTH ALLIANCE MEDICAL PLANS | IL | **B-** | 5 | 18.80 | 172 | 0 | 123 | 45 | 1 | 3 |
| HEALTH ALLIANCE NORTHWEST HEALTH PL | WA | **B-** | 5 | 2.82 | 15 | 0 | 14 | 1 | 0 | 0 |
| HEALTH ALLIANCE PLAN OF MICHIGAN | MI | **C+** | 5 | 7.64 | 264 | 0 | 176 | 31 | 24 | 31 |
| HEALTH ALLIANCE-MIDWEST INC | IL | **E** | 5 | 8.80 | 3 | 0 | 3 | 0 | 0 | 0 |
| HEALTH CARE SVC CORP A MUT LEG RES | IL | **B** | 5 | 1.61 | 22 | 0 | 8 | 7 | 0 | 5 |
| HEALTH CARE SVC CORP A MUT LEG RES | IL | **B** | 6 | 15.50 | 383 | 0 | 210 | 74 | 20 | 76 |
| HEALTH INSURANCE PLAN OF GREATER NY | NY | **C-** | 2 | 12.23 | 308 | 0 | 252 | 21 | 4 | 27 |

| INSURANCE COMPANY NAME | DOM. STATE | RATING | REGION | RATE | RECONS REC'VD | RECONS NOT YET DECIDED | RECONS UPHELD | RECONS OVER-TURNED | RECONS WITH-DRAWN | RECONS DISMISSED |
|---|---|---|---|---|---|---|---|---|---|---|
| HEALTH NET COMMUNITY SOLUTIONS INC | CA | **B** | 9 | 2.95 | 54 | 0 | 42 | 4 | 2 | 6 |
| HEALTH NET HEALTH PLAN OF OREGON INC | OR | **E-** | 10 | 3.74 | 123 | 0 | 84 | 17 | 11 | 11 |
| HEALTH NET LIFE INS CO | CA | **C** | 10 | 20.90 | 14 | 0 | 9 | 1 | 3 | 1 |
| HEALTH NET OF ARIZONA INC | AZ | **C** | 10 | 5.47 | 140 | 0 | 80 | 18 | 29 | 11 |
| HEALTH NET OF CALIFORNIA INC | CA | **C** | 10 | 4.06 | 561 | 0 | 451 | 35 | 37 | 37 |
| HEALTH NEW ENGLAND INC | MA | **C-** | 1 | 8.52 | 78 | 0 | 58 | 16 | 1 | 3 |
| HEALTH OPTIONS INC | FL | **B+** | 4 | 5.98 | 370 | 0 | 304 | 16 | 1 | 47 |
| HEALTH PARTNERS PLANS INC | PA | **B-** | 3 | 10.09 | 162 | 0 | 136 | 25 | 0 | 1 |
| HEALTH PLAN OF CAREOREGON INC | OR | **C** | 10 | 1.76 | 23 | 0 | 21 | 0 | 0 | 2 |
| HEALTH PLAN OF NEVADA INC | NV | **B** | 9 | 1.80 | 91 | 0 | 82 | 1 | 0 | 8 |
| HEALTH PLAN OF WV INC | WV | **C** | 3 | N/E | -- | -- | -- | -- | -- | -- |
| HEALTHASSURANCE PENNSYLVANIA INC | PA | **B-** | 8 | 1.68 | 117 | 0 | 86 | 9 | 7 | 11 |
| HEALTHFIRST HEALTH PLAN INC | NY | **C+** | 2 | 3.94 | 537 | 0 | 166 | 3 | 213 | 154 |
| HEALTHKEEPERS INC | VA | **B+** | 3 | 3.16 | 38 | 0 | 21 | 1 | 3 | 13 |
| HEALTHKEEPERS INC | VA | **B+** | 5 | 6.51 | 25 | 0 | 19 | 2 | 0 | 4 |
| HEALTHNOW NY INC | NY | **C+** | 2 | 3.58 | 71 | 0 | 58 | 9 | 3 | 1 |
| HEALTHNOW NY INC | NY | **C+** | 8 | N/E | -- | -- | -- | -- | -- | -- |
| HEALTHPARTNERS | MN | **A+** | 5 | 0.63 | 2 | 0 | 2 | 0 | 0 | 0 |
| HEALTHPLUS INS CO TRUST | MI | **U** | 5 | N/E | -- | -- | -- | -- | -- | -- |
| HEALTHSPRING L&H INS CO | TX | **C+** | 6 | 38.71 | 538 | 0 | 372 | 54 | 70 | 36 |
| HEALTHSPRING OF ALABAMA INC | AL | **B** | 6 | 4.83 | 273 | 0 | 130 | 43 | 76 | 22 |
| HEALTHSPRING OF FLORIDA INC | FL | **B+** | 6 | 5.75 | 288 | 0 | 226 | 19 | 7 | 35 |
| HEALTHSPRING OF TENNESSEE INC | TN | **B+** | 5 | 2.04 | 13 | 0 | 9 | 2 | 0 | 2 |
| HEALTHSPRING OF TENNESSEE INC | TN | **B+** | 6 | 12.88 | 397 | 0 | 228 | 49 | 78 | 36 |
| HEARTLANDPLAINS HEALTH | NE | **E-** | 8 | 5.61 | 5 | 0 | 3 | 0 | 1 | 1 |
| HIGHMARK CHOICE CO | PA | **U** | 3 | 2.30 | 271 | 0 | 234 | 19 | 3 | 12 |
| HIGHMARK SENIOR HEALTH CO | PA | **U** | 3 | 1.92 | 366 | 0 | 304 | 40 | 2 | 13 |
| HM HEALTH INS CO | PA | **U** | 3 | 3.01 | 21 | 0 | 19 | 2 | 0 | 0 |
| HMO MINNESOTA | MN | **C** | 5 | 0.64 | 5 | 0 | 5 | 0 | 0 | 0 |
| HMO MISSOURI INC | MO | **B** | 5 | 2.23 | 10 | 0 | 10 | 0 | 0 | 0 |
| HMO PARTNERS INC | AR | **A+** | 6 | 0.42 | 1 | 0 | 0 | 0 | 0 | 1 |
| HOMETOWN HEALTH PLAN INC | NV | **C-** | 10 | 7.80 | 56 | 0 | 39 | 5 | 4 | 8 |
| HORIZON HEALTHCARE OF NEW JERSEY INC | NJ | **A-** | 2 | 8.51 | 2 | 0 | 1 | 0 | 0 | 1 |
| HORIZON INS CO | NJ | **B-** | 2 | 4.20 | 98 | 0 | 59 | 6 | 0 | 33 |
| HUMANA BENEFIT PLAN OF ILLINOIS | IL | **A-** | 7 | 2.66 | 113 | 0 | 43 | 2 | 21 | 47 |
| HUMANA EMPLOYERS HEALTH PLAN OF GA | GA | **C** | 7 | 1.33 | 60 | 0 | 22 | 3 | 10 | 25 |
| HUMANA HEALTH BENEFIT PLAN LA | LA | **B** | 7 | 1.19 | 164 | 0 | 61 | 14 | 37 | 52 |
| HUMANA HEALTH CO OF NEW YORK INC | NY | **D-** | 7 | 2.50 | 28 | 0 | 7 | 2 | 3 | 16 |
| HUMANA HEALTH INS CO OF FL INC | FL | **B-** | 7 | 1.34 | 15 | 0 | 7 | 1 | 2 | 5 |
| HUMANA HEALTH PLAN INC | KY | **B-** | 3 | 4.18 | 43 | 0 | 7 | 1 | 29 | 6 |
| HUMANA HEALTH PLAN INC | KY | **B-** | 5 | 3.35 | 22 | 0 | 4 | 1 | 16 | 1 |
| HUMANA HEALTH PLAN INC | KY | **B-** | 7 | 5.30 | 683 | 0 | 248 | 60 | 123 | 250 |
| HUMANA HEALTH PLAN OF CALIFORNIA INC | CA | **U** | 7 | N/E | -- | -- | -- | -- | -- | -- |
| HUMANA HEALTH PLAN OF OHIO INC | OH | **B-** | 7 | 1.91 | 92 | 0 | 28 | 7 | 13 | 43 |
| HUMANA HEALTH PLAN OF TEXAS INC | TX | **C** | 7 | N/E | -- | -- | -- | -- | -- | -- |
| HUMANA HEALTH PLANS OF PUERTO RICO | PR | **C+** | 7 | 1.22 | 45 | 0 | 29 | 1 | 2 | 13 |
| HUMANA INS CO (WI) | WI | **A-** | 7 | 13.95 | 2506 | 0 | 876 | 187 | 388 | 1042 |
| HUMANA INS CO OF NY | NY | **B-** | 7 | 1.87 | 22 | 0 | 9 | 1 | 6 | 6 |
| HUMANA INS CO OF PUERTO RICO INC | PR | **B-** | 7 | 13.72 | 15 | 0 | 11 | 3 | 0 | 1 |
| HUMANA MEDICAL PLAN INC | FL | **B** | 7 | 0.93 | 426 | 0 | 144 | 47 | 75 | 160 |
| HUMANA MEDICAL PLAN OF MICHIGAN INC | MI | **C+** | 7 | 2.66 | 11 | 0 | 4 | 0 | 0 | 7 |
| HUMANA MEDICAL PLAN OF PENNSYLVANIA | PA | **B** | 7 | 2.36 | 14 | 0 | 2 | 1 | 2 | 9 |

| INSURANCE COMPANY NAME | DOM. STATE | RATING | REGION | RATE | RECONS REC'VD | RECONS NOT YET DECIDED | RECONS UPHELD | RECONS OVER-TURNED | RECONS WITH-DRAWN | RECONS DISMISSED |
|---|---|---|---|---|---|---|---|---|---|---|
| HUMANA MEDICAL PLAN OF UTAH INC | UT | **C+** | 7 | 0.76 | 4 | 0 | 0 | 0 | 2 | 2 |
| HUMANA REGIONAL HEALTH PLAN INC | AR | **B-** | 7 | 1.40 | 4 | 0 | 2 | 0 | 0 | 2 |
| HUMANA WISCONSIN HEALTH ORGANIZATION | WI | **B-** | 7 | 1.39 | 64 | 0 | 28 | 2 | 11 | 23 |
| ILLINICARE HEALTH PLAN INC | IL | **C-** | 5 | 1.58 | 8 | 0 | 7 | 0 | 0 | 1 |
| INDEPENDENT CARE HEALTH PLAN | WI | **A-** | 5 | 3.26 | 21 | 0 | 14 | 5 | 0 | 1 |
| INDEPENDENT HEALTH ASSOC INC | NY | **B-** | 2 | 5.93 | 534 | 0 | 483 | 23 | 1 | 21 |
| INDEPENDENT HEALTH BENEFITS CORP | NY | **C** | 2 | 4.63 | 18 | 0 | 16 | 2 | 0 | 0 |
| INDIANA UNIVERSITY HEALTH PLANS INC | IN | **E-** | 5 | 1.35 | 22 | 0 | 18 | 2 | 0 | 2 |
| INS CO OF SCOTT & WHITE | TX | **E-** | 6 | 6.98 | 28 | 0 | 20 | 1 | 0 | 7 |
| INTERVALLEY HEALTH PLAN | CA | **D** | 10 | 1.79 | 41 | 0 | 32 | 0 | 0 | 8 |
| K S PLAN ADMINISTRATORS LLC | TX | **B+** | 6 | 1.87 | 57 | 0 | 54 | 2 | 0 | 1 |
| KAISER FNDTN HLTH PLAN OF WA | WA | **B+** | 10 | 7.32 | 661 | 0 | 569 | 54 | 5 | 30 |
| KAISER FOUNDATION HEALTH PLAN INC | CA | **A** | 9 | 8.88 | 1001 | 0 | 866 | 36 | 23 | 67 |
| KAISER FOUNDATION HP MID-ATL STATES | MD | **B** | 9 | 0.93 | 63 | 0 | 58 | 0 | 1 | 4 |
| KAISER FOUNDATION HP NORTHWEST | OR | **B** | 9 | 1.51 | 126 | 0 | 117 | 3 | 4 | 2 |
| KAISER FOUNDATION HP OF CO | CO | **B** | 9 | 0.89 | 92 | 0 | 86 | 4 | 0 | 2 |
| KEYSTONE HEALTH PLAN CENTRAL INC | PA | **C+** | 3 | 2.53 | 27 | 0 | 24 | 3 | 0 | 0 |
| KEYSTONE HEALTH PLAN EAST INC | PA | **C+** | 3 | 8.29 | 753 | 0 | 677 | 54 | 6 | 10 |
| LOCAL INITIATIVE HEALTH AUTH LA | CA | **C** | 9 | 2.82 | 36 | 0 | 29 | 4 | 1 | 1 |
| LOVELACE HEALTH SYSTEMS INC | NM | **U** | 6 | 5.86 | 96 | 0 | 51 | 19 | 6 | 18 |
| MARTINS POINT GENERATIONS LLC | ME | **U** | 1 | 3.02 | 52 | 0 | 39 | 5 | 1 | 7 |
| MATTHEW THORNTON HEALTH PLAN | NH | **B** | 5 | 2.30 | 2 | 0 | 2 | 0 | 0 | 0 |
| MCLAREN HEALTH PLAN INC | MI | **A-** | 5 | N/E | -- | -- | -- | -- | -- | -- |
| MCS ADVANTAGE INC | PR | **E+** | 2 | 1.58 | 326 | 0 | 265 | 3 | 7 | 51 |
| MEDICA HEALTH PLANS | MN | **C** | 5 | 0.56 | 6 | 0 | 5 | 1 | 0 | 0 |
| MEDICA HEALTHCARE PLANS INC | FL | **E** | 9 | 1.22 | 46 | 0 | 41 | 18 | 0 | 4 |
| MEDICA INS CO | MN | **B** | 5 | 0.31 | 58 | 0 | 47 | 8 | 0 | 3 |
| MEDICAL ASSOC CLINIC HEALTH PLAN | WI | **C+** | 7 | 0.30 | 1 | 0 | 1 | 0 | 0 | 0 |
| MEDICAL ASSOCIATES HEALTH PLAN INC | IA | **B-** | 7 | 0.09 | 1 | 0 | 1 | 0 | 0 | 0 |
| MEDISUN INC | AZ | **B-** | 9 | 9.82 | 603 | 0 | 486 | 66 | 3 | 43 |
| MEDSTAR FAMILY CHOICE INC | MD | **C** | 3 | 16.53 | 157 | 0 | 117 | 25 | 2 | 13 |
| MEMORIAL HERMANN HEALTH PLAN INC | TX | **D+** | 6 | 17.00 | 50 | 0 | 29 | 8 | 6 | 5 |
| MERCY MARICOPA INTEGRATED CARE | AZ | **U** | 9 | N/E | -- | -- | -- | -- | -- | -- |
| MERIDIAN HEALTH PLAN OF ILLINOIS INC | IL | **C+** | 5 | 11.75 | 37 | 0 | 23 | 5 | 0 | 9 |
| MERIDIAN HEALTH PLAN OF IOWA INC | IA | **E+** | 5 | N/E | -- | -- | -- | -- | -- | -- |
| MERIDIAN HEALTH PLAN OF MICHIGAN INC | MI | **B** | 5 | 19.97 | 72 | 0 | 58 | 8 | 0 | 5 |
| MHS HEALTH WISCONSIN | WI | **C+** | 10 | 3.01 | 3 | 0 | 2 | 0 | 0 | 1 |
| MICHIGAN COMPLETE HEALTH INC | MI | **C-** | 5 | 9.55 | 21 | 0 | 5 | 2 | 1 | 13 |
| MICHIGAN COMPLETE HEALTH INC | MI | **C-** | 10 | N/E | -- | -- | -- | -- | -- | -- |
| MMM HEALTHCARE LLC | PR | **E-** | 2 | 2.21 | 376 | 0 | 303 | 17 | 1 | 55 |
| MODA HEALTH PLAN INC | OR | **E** | 10 | 35.67 | 169 | 0 | 112 | 41 | 4 | 11 |
| MOLINA HEALTHCARE OF CALIFORNIA | CA | **C-** | 9 | 5.25 | 68 | 0 | 42 | 11 | 2 | 12 |
| MOLINA HEALTHCARE OF CALIFORNIA | CA | **C-** | 10 | 9.45 | 40 | 0 | 24 | 4 | 0 | 11 |
| MOLINA HEALTHCARE OF FLORIDA INC | FL | **E** | 10 | 13.05 | 28 | 0 | 19 | 4 | 0 | 5 |
| MOLINA HEALTHCARE OF ILLINOIS INC | IL | **E** | 5 | 12.47 | 52 | 0 | 27 | 9 | 5 | 9 |
| MOLINA HEALTHCARE OF MICHIGAN INC | MI | **B-** | 5 | 4.99 | 52 | 0 | 39 | 6 | 2 | 3 |
| MOLINA HEALTHCARE OF MICHIGAN INC | MI | **B-** | 10 | 7.22 | 72 | 0 | 50 | 13 | 3 | 5 |
| MOLINA HEALTHCARE OF NEW MEXICO | NM | **C** | 10 | 9.93 | 35 | 0 | 21 | 4 | 1 | 8 |
| MOLINA HEALTHCARE OF OHIO INC | OH | **B-** | 5 | 3.35 | 35 | 0 | 25 | 7 | 0 | 3 |
| MOLINA HEALTHCARE OF OHIO INC | OH | **B-** | 10 | N/E | -- | -- | -- | -- | -- | -- |
| MOLINA HEALTHCARE OF SOUTH CAROLINA | SC | **C** | 4 | 7.59 | 15 | 0 | 6 | 5 | 1 | 3 |
| MOLINA HEALTHCARE OF TEXAS INC | TX | **B-** | 6 | 6.94 | 87 | 0 | 30 | 15 | 3 | 37 |

| INSURANCE COMPANY NAME | DOM. STATE | RATING | REGION | RATE | RECONS REC'VD | RECONS NOT YET DECIDED | RECONS UPHELD | RECONS OVER-TURNED | RECONS WITH-DRAWN | RECONS DISMISSED |
|---|---|---|---|---|---|---|---|---|---|---|
| MOLINA HEALTHCARE OF TEXAS INC | TX | **B-** | 10 | 8.37 | 34 | 0 | 15 | 7 | 1 | 11 |
| MOLINA HEALTHCARE OF UTAH INC | UT | **C-** | 10 | 12.43 | 106 | 0 | 57 | 28 | 0 | 20 |
| MOLINA HEALTHCARE OF WASHINGTON INC | WA | **B** | 10 | 8.28 | 81 | 0 | 47 | 20 | 4 | 9 |
| MOLINA HEALTHCARE OF WISCONSIN INC | WI | **E+** | 10 | 6.38 | 6 | 0 | 4 | 1 | 0 | 1 |
| MOUNT CARMEL HEALTH INS CO | OH | **D** | 5 | 1.60 | 4 | 0 | 4 | 0 | 0 | 0 |
| MOUNT CARMEL HEALTH PLAN INC | OH | **C** | 5 | 1.20 | 65 | 0 | 58 | 4 | 0 | 2 |
| MVP HEALTH PLAN INC | NY | **B-** | 2 | 13.54 | 299 | 0 | 245 | 29 | 6 | 17 |
| NETWORK HEALTH INS CORP | WI | **C** | 8 | 1.69 | 3 | 0 | 3 | 0 | 0 | 0 |
| NEW WEST HEALTH SERVICES | MT | **E-** | 8 | 4.71 | 67 | 0 | 52 | 8 | 0 | 6 |
| OKLAHOMA SUPERIOR SELECT INC | OK | **E** | 6 | N/E | -- | -- | -- | -- | -- | -- |
| ON LOK SENIOR HEALTH SERVICES | CA | **B** | 9 | N/E | -- | -- | -- | -- | -- | -- |
| OPTIMA HEALTH PLAN | VA | **A-** | 3 | 4.61 | 9 | 0 | 7 | 1 | 0 | 1 |
| OPTIMUM HEALTHCARE INC | FL | **E** | 4 | 3.11 | 139 | 0 | 112 | 1 | 0 | 26 |
| ORANGE PREVENTION & TREATMENT INTEGR | CA | **A-** | 9 | 43.44 | 51 | 0 | 39 | 5 | 0 | 7 |
| OXFORD HEALTH PLANS (CT) INC | CT | **B-** | 9 | 3.11 | 134 | 0 | 92 | 2 | 4 | 35 |
| OXFORD HEALTH PLANS (NJ) INC | NJ | **B** | 9 | 5.66 | 225 | 0 | 130 | 5 | 3 | 87 |
| OXFORD HEALTH PLANS (NY) INC | NY | **B+** | 9 | 2.54 | 207 | 0 | 132 | 1 | 3 | 71 |
| PACIFICARE OF ARIZONA INC | AZ | **U** | 9 | N/E | -- | -- | -- | -- | -- | -- |
| PACIFICARE OF COLORADO INC | CO | **B** | 9 | 1.06 | 259 | 0 | 207 | 0 | 2 | 50 |
| PACIFICARE OF NEVADA INC | NV | **E** | 9 | N/E | -- | -- | -- | -- | -- | -- |
| PACIFICSOURCE COMMUNITY HEALTH PLANS | OR | **B-** | 10 | 10.25 | 233 | 0 | 191 | 26 | 1 | 15 |
| PARAMOUNT CARE INC | OH | **C+** | 5 | 0.74 | 12 | 0 | 3 | 1 | 0 | 8 |
| PEACH STATE HEALTH PLAN INC | GA | **C+** | 10 | 15.97 | 5 | 0 | 5 | 0 | 0 | 0 |
| PEOPLES HEALTH INC | LA | **D** | 6 | 7.94 | 433 | 0 | 415 | 12 | 1 | 5 |
| PHOENIX HEALTH PLANS INC | AZ | **E** | 6 | 19.14 | 264 | 0 | 93 | 27 | 37 | 106 |
| PIEDMONT COMMUNITY HEALTHCARE | VA | **D+** | 3 | 2.90 | 15 | 0 | 12 | 1 | 0 | 2 |
| PIEDMONT WELLSTAR HEALTHPLANS INC | GA | **E** | 4 | N/E | -- | -- | -- | -- | -- | -- |
| PMC MEDICARE CHOICE LLC | PR | **D** | 2 | 1.54 | 32 | 0 | 20 | 3 | 0 | 9 |
| PREFERRED CARE PARTNERS INC | FL | **E** | 9 | 1.37 | 170 | 0 | 139 | 3 | 1 | 27 |
| PREMERA BLUE CROSS | WA | **B+** | 10 | 6.36 | 163 | 0 | 134 | 13 | 3 | 12 |
| PREMIER HEALTH INSURING CORP | OH | **E** | 5 | 7.28 | 68 | 0 | 50 | 11 | 0 | 7 |
| PRESBYTERIAN INS CO | NM | **B-** | 6 | 6.23 | 50 | 0 | 29 | 12 | 2 | 6 |
| PRIORITY HEALTH | MI | **A** | 5 | 15.97 | 885 | 0 | 850 | 15 | 2 | 17 |
| PROMINENCE HEALTHFIRST OF TEXAS INC | TX | **D+** | 9 | 1.53 | 7 | 0 | 2 | 0 | 0 | 5 |
| PROVIDENCE HEALTH PLAN | OR | **A+** | 10 | 4.13 | 206 | 0 | 168 | 21 | 3 | 10 |
| PYRAMID LIFE INS CO | KS | **D-** | 6 | N/E | -- | -- | -- | -- | -- | -- |
| QCC INS CO | PA | **C** | 3 | 6.89 | 65 | 0 | 60 | 5 | 0 | 0 |
| REGENCE BL CROSS BL SHIELD OREGON | OR | **B+** | 10 | 4.66 | 114 | 0 | 101 | 8 | 2 | 3 |
| REGENCE BLUE CROSS BLUE SHIELD OF UT | UT | **B-** | 10 | 2.94 | 20 | 0 | 19 | 1 | 0 | 0 |
| REGENCE BLUESHIELD | WA | **B** | 10 | 8.85 | 68 | 0 | 60 | 2 | 2 | 4 |
| REGENCE BLUESHIELD OF IDAHO INC | ID | **B** | 10 | 1.71 | 7 | 0 | 5 | 2 | 0 | 0 |
| RIVERLINK HEALTH | OH | **E+** | 8 | 9.11 | 22 | 0 | 20 | 0 | 1 | 1 |
| ROCKY MOUNTAIN HEALTH MAINT ORG | CO | **C** | 8 | 2.32 | 56 | 0 | 52 | 1 | 0 | 3 |
| SAMARITAN HEALTH PLANS INC | OR | **B** | 10 | 5.07 | 26 | 0 | 20 | 3 | 0 | 3 |
| SAN MATEO HEALTH COMMISSION | CA | **B+** | 9 | 6.37 | 36 | 0 | 29 | 3 | 1 | 3 |
| SANFORD HEART OF AMERICA HEALTH PLAN | ND | **D+** | 8 | N/E | -- | -- | -- | -- | -- | -- |
| SANTA CLARA COUNTY HEALTH AUTHORITY | CA | **C** | 9 | 1.11 | 9 | 0 | 3 | 0 | 3 | 3 |
| SCAN HEALTH PLAN | CA | **C** | 9 | 29.58 | 1063 | 0 | 927 | 395 | 26 | 37 |
| SCOTT & WHITE HEALTH PLAN | TX | **C-** | 6 | 1.51 | 44 | 0 | 34 | 0 | 1 | 9 |
| SECURITY HEALTH PLAN OF WI INC | WI | **A-** | 5 | 2.85 | 124 | 0 | 98 | 19 | 1 | 5 |
| SECURITYCARE OF TENNESSEE INC | TN | **B** | 4 | 15.97 | 44 | 0 | 39 | 1 | 2 | 2 |
| SELECT HEALTH OF SOUTH CAROLINA INC | SC | **B-** | 4 | 2.32 | 9 | 0 | 5 | 0 | 0 | 4 |

| INSURANCE COMPANY NAME | DOM. STATE | RATING | REGION | RATE | RECONS REC'VD | RECONS NOT YET DECIDED | RECONS UPHELD | RECONS OVER-TURNED | RECONS WITH-DRAWN | RECONS DISMISSED |
|---|---|---|---|---|---|---|---|---|---|---|
| SELECTCARE HEALTH PLANS INC | TX | **C+** | 6 | 6.92 | 21 | 0 | 16 | 1 | 1 | 3 |
| SELECTCARE OF TEXAS INC | TX | **B** | 6 | 12.11 | 794 | 0 | 745 | 18 | 3 | 25 |
| SELECTHEALTH INC | UT | **C** | 8 | 5.94 | 225 | 0 | 203 | 14 | 1 | 7 |
| SENIOR WHOLE HEALTH OF NEW YORK INC | NY | **E** | 1 | N/E | -- | -- | -- | -- | -- | -- |
| SENIOR WHOLE HEALTH OF NEW YORK INC | NY | **E** | 2 | N/E | -- | -- | -- | -- | -- | -- |
| SHA LLC | TX | **E** | 6 | 1.65 | 5 | 0 | 5 | 0 | 0 | 0 |
| SHARP HEALTH PLAN | CA | **B** | 9 | 9.32 | 3 | 0 | 2 | 1 | 0 | 0 |
| SIERRA HEALTH AND LIFE INS CO INC | NV | **B** | 9 | 8.08 | 2666 | 0 | 1866 | 30 | 20 | 745 |
| SIMPLY HEALTHCARE PLANS INC | FL | **A-** | 5 | 6.66 | 226 | 0 | 179 | 9 | 5 | 32 |
| SOUNDPATH HEALTH | WA | **E-** | 8 | 4.75 | 128 | 0 | 105 | 4 | 2 | 17 |
| STABLEVIEW HEALTH INC | KY | **D+** | 8 | 15.15 | 3 | 0 | 2 | 0 | 0 | 1 |
| STANFORD HEALTH CARE ADVANTAGE | CA | **E-** | 9 | N/E | -- | -- | -- | -- | -- | -- |
| SUMMACARE INC | OH | **C+** | 5 | 5.60 | 134 | 0 | 120 | 11 | 0 | 3 |
| SUNSHINE HEALTH | FL | **E** | 10 | 3.10 | 3 | 0 | 1 | 0 | 0 | 2 |
| SUPERIOR HEALTHPLAN INC | TX | **C+** | 6 | 3.56 | 32 | 0 | 24 | 3 | 0 | 5 |
| SUPERIOR HEALTHPLAN INC | TX | **C+** | 10 | 8.26 | 7 | 0 | 6 | 0 | 0 | 1 |
| SUTTER HEALTH PLAN | CA | **D-** | 9 | N/E | -- | -- | -- | -- | -- | -- |
| THP INS CO | WV | **D** | 3 | 1.87 | 2 | 0 | 2 | 0 | 0 | 0 |
| TOUCHSTONE HEALTH HMO INC | NY | **E+** | 2 | N/E | -- | -- | -- | -- | -- | -- |
| TRILLIUM COMMUNITY HEALTH PLAN INC | OR | **C+** | 10 | 12.23 | 21 | 0 | 14 | 0 | 2 | 5 |
| TRIPLE-S ADVANTAGE INC | PR | **C** | 2 | 0.98 | 98 | 0 | 88 | 4 | 1 | 5 |
| TRIPLE-S SALUD INC | PR | **B-** | 2 | 1.53 | 28 | 0 | 23 | 3 | 0 | 2 |
| TUFTS ASSOCIATED HEALTH MAINT ORG | MA | **B** | 1 | 5.78 | 617 | 0 | 547 | 26 | 9 | 32 |
| TUFTS HEALTH PUBLIC PLANS INC | MA | **C+** | 1 | 11.32 | 33 | 0 | 23 | 8 | 0 | 2 |
| UCARE HEALTH INC | WI | **E** | 5 | N/E | -- | -- | -- | -- | -- | -- |
| UCARE MINNESOTA | MN | **B** | 5 | 3.51 | 240 | 0 | 216 | 17 | 2 | 5 |
| UHC OF CALIFORNIA INC | CA | **C** | 9 | 2.00 | 668 | 0 | 592 | 5 | 15 | 54 |
| ULTIMATE HEALTH PLANS INC | FL | **E** | 4 | 4.38 | 25 | 0 | 21 | 3 | 0 | 0 |
| UNION HEALTH SERVICE INC | IL | **B** | 5 | N/E | -- | -- | -- | -- | -- | -- |
| UNITED HEALTHCARE INS CO | CT | **C** | 9 | 56.20 | 2312 | 0 | 1569 | 18 | 17 | 706 |
| UNITED HEALTHCARE OF ALABAMA INC | AL | **B-** | 9 | 2.30 | 84 | 0 | 55 | 0 | 0 | 29 |
| UNITED HEALTHCARE OF ARIZONA INC | AZ | **C** | 9 | N/E | -- | -- | -- | -- | -- | -- |
| UNITED HEALTHCARE OF FLORIDA INC | FL | **D+** | 9 | N/E | -- | -- | -- | -- | -- | -- |
| UNITED HEALTHCARE OF GEORGIA INC | GA | **B** | 9 | 3.66 | 65 | 0 | 56 | 3 | 0 | 6 |
| UNITED HEALTHCARE OF NC INC | NC | **B** | 9 | N/E | -- | -- | -- | -- | -- | -- |
| UNITED HEALTHCARE OF NEW ENGLAND INC | RI | **B-** | 9 | 1.69 | 63 | 0 | 40 | 1 | 0 | 22 |
| UNITED HEALTHCARE OF NY INC | NY | **B+** | 9 | 6.26 | 194 | 0 | 136 | 0 | 2 | 56 |
| UNITED HEALTHCARE OF OHIO INC | OH | **C** | 9 | N/E | -- | -- | -- | -- | -- | -- |
| UNITED HEALTHCARE OF THE MIDLANDS | NE | **B** | 9 | 1.89 | 57 | 0 | 31 | 0 | 0 | 26 |
| UNITED HEALTHCARE OF THE MIDWEST INC | MO | **C+** | 9 | 1.78 | 170 | 0 | 105 | 1 | 1 | 63 |
| UNITED HEALTHCARE OF UTAH | UT | **B** | 9 | 0.88 | 48 | 0 | 28 | 0 | 3 | 17 |
| UNITED HEALTHCARE OF WISCONSIN INC | WI | **B** | 9 | 1.48 | 511 | 0 | 401 | 5 | 6 | 99 |
| UNITEDHEALTHCARE BENEFITS OF TEXAS | TX | **B-** | 9 | 1.29 | 273 | 0 | 213 | 0 | 3 | 56 |
| UNITEDHEALTHCARE COMMUNITY PLAN INC | MI | **B** | 9 | N/E | -- | -- | -- | -- | -- | -- |
| UNITEDHEALTHCARE COMMUNITY PLAN TX | TX | **B+** | 9 | 4.83 | 153 | 0 | 113 | 0 | 1 | 39 |
| UNITEDHEALTHCARE OF OKLAHOMA INC | OK | **B** | 9 | 1.28 | 34 | 0 | 25 | 1 | 1 | 7 |
| UNITEDHEALTHCARE OF OREGON | OR | **B** | 9 | 0.83 | 78 | 0 | 57 | 0 | 2 | 19 |
| UNITEDHEALTHCARE OF WASHINGTON INC | WA | **C** | 9 | N/E | -- | -- | -- | -- | -- | -- |
| UNITEDHEALTHCARE PLAN RIVER VALLEY | IL | **B** | 9 | 2.34 | 130 | 0 | 73 | 0 | 4 | 53 |
| UNIVERSAL CARE | CA | **E-** | 9 | 1.19 | 13 | 0 | 8 | 1 | 1 | 3 |
| UPMC FOR YOU INC | PA | **B+** | 3 | 11.86 | 255 | 0 | 230 | 18 | 0 | 6 |
| UPMC HEALTH NETWORK INC | PA | **C** | 3 | 10.78 | 95 | 0 | 88 | 4 | 0 | 2 |

| INSURANCE COMPANY NAME | DOM. STATE | RATING | REGION | RATE | RECONS REC'VD | RECONS NOT YET DECIDED | RECONS UPHELD | RECONS OVER-TURNED | RECONS WITH-DRAWN | RECONS DISMISSED |
|---|---|---|---|---|---|---|---|---|---|---|
| UPMC HEALTH PLAN INC | PA | **A-** | 3 | 11.66 | 1468 | 0 | 1389 | 43 | 12 | 22 |
| UPPER PENINSULA HEALTH PLAN INC | MI | **A** | 5 | 8.74 | 36 | 0 | 23 | 2 | 0 | 11 |
| USABLE MUTUAL INS CO | AR | **A+** | 6 | 0.06 | 1 | 0 | 0 | 0 | 0 | 1 |
| VANTAGE HEALTH PLAN INC | LA | **C-** | 6 | 3.92 | 64 | 0 | 42 | 2 | 1 | 19 |
| VIRGINIA PREMIER HEALTH PLAN INC | VA | **B+** | 3 | 1.52 | 9 | 0 | 6 | 1 | 1 | 1 |
| VISTA HEALTH PLAN INC | PA | **B-** | 3 | 4.10 | 19 | 0 | 14 | 3 | 0 | 2 |
| VIVA HEALTH INC | AL | **B+** | 4 | 2.97 | 129 | 0 | 110 | 8 | 4 | 7 |
| VOLUNTEER STATE HEALTH PLAN INC | TN | **A+** | 4 | 1.59 | 18 | 0 | 16 | 1 | 0 | 1 |
| WELLCARE HEALTH INS OF ARIZONA INC | AZ | **C** | 4 | 1.15 | 9 | 0 | 6 | 0 | 1 | 2 |
| WELLCARE HEALTH PLANS OF NEW JERSEY | NJ | **C** | 4 | N/E | -- | -- | -- | -- | -- | -- |
| WELLCARE OF CONNECTICUT INC | CT | **C+** | 4 | 3.51 | 24 | 0 | 19 | 2 | 0 | 2 |
| WELLCARE OF FLORIDA INC | FL | **E** | 4 | 3.29 | 304 | 0 | 249 | 7 | 1 | 47 |
| WELLCARE OF GEORGIA INC | GA | **C** | 4 | 2.69 | 102 | 0 | 81 | 3 | 1 | 17 |
| WELLCARE OF TEXAS INC | TX | **C** | 4 | 3.89 | 134 | 0 | 113 | 2 | 0 | 19 |

# Section VIII

# Rating Upgrades and Downgrades

A list of all

**U.S. Health Insurers**

receiving a rating upgrade or downgrade during the current quarter.

# Section VIII Contents

This section identifies those companies receiving a rating change since the previous edition of this publication, whether it is a new rating to this guide, withdrawn rating, rating upgrade, rating downgrade or a, newly rated company. A rating may be withdrawn due to a merger, dissolution, or liquidation. A rating upgrade or downgrade may entail a change from one letter grade to another, or it may mean the addition or deletion of a plus or minus sign within the same letter grade previously assigned to the company. Ratings are normally updated once each quarter of the year. In some instances, however, a company's rating may be downgraded outside of the normal updates due to overriding circumstances.

1. **Insurance Company Name** The legally-registered name, which can sometimes differ from the name that the company uses for advertising. An insurer's name can be very similar to that of another, so verify the company's exact name and state of domicile to make sure you are looking at the correct company.

2. **Domicile State** The state which has primary regulatory responsibility for the company. It may differ from the location of the company's corporate headquarters. You do not have to be living in the domicile state to purchase insurance from this firm, provided it is licensed to do business in your state.

3. **Total Assets** All assets admitted by state insurance regulators in millions of dollars as of the most recent year end. This includes investments and current business assets such as receivables from agents, reinsurers and subscribers.

4. **New or Current Safety Rating** The rating assigned to the company as of the date of this Guide's publication. Our rating is measured on a scale from A to F and considers a wide range of factors. Highly-rated companies are, in our opinion, less likely to experience financial difficulties than lower-rated firms. See *About Weiss Safety Ratings* for more information.

5. **Previous Safety Rating** The rating assigned to the company prior to its most recent change.

6. **Date of Change** The date on which the rating upgrade or downgrade officially occurred. Normally, all rating changes are put into effect on a single day each quarter of the year. In some instances, however, a rating may have been changed outside of this normal update.

## Appearing in this Edition for the First Time

None during this quarter

## Withdrawn Ratings

| INSURANCE COMPANY NAME | DOM. STATE | TOTAL ASSETS ($MIL) | RATING | PREVIOUS RATING | DATE |
|---|---|---|---|---|---|
| AMERIGROUP FLORIDA INC | FL | 243.6 | U | B | 10/19/17 |
| BETTER HEALTH INC | FL | 76.6 | U | A- | 10/19/17 |
| HERITAGE HEALTH SYS OF NY INC | NY | 0.0 | U | U | 10/19/17 |

## Rating Upgrades

**AETNA BETTER HEALTH (AN OHIO CORP) (OH)** was upgraded to B from B- in March 2018 based on development in the stability index and expansion in the profitability index.

**AETNA BETTER HEALTH OF TEXAS INC (TX)** was upgraded to B+ from B in March 2018 based on substantial development in the stability index and expansion in the profitability index.

**BLUE CROSS & BLUE SHIELD MA HMO BLUE** was upgraded to A- from B+ in March 2018 based on the overall strength of the index ratios

**CARE N CARE INS CO (TX)** was upgraded to C from C- in March 2018 based on substantial expansion in the profitability index and an increase in the capitalization index.

**CHESAPEAKE LIFE INS CO** was upgraded to B from B- in January 2018 based on a higher capitalization index and a higher five-year profitability index.

**COMMUNITY CARE ALLIANCE OF ILLINOIS (IL)** was upgraded to C- from D+ in March 2018 based on a substantial increase in the capitalization index, substantial development in the stability index, and expansion in the profitability index.

**DRISCOLL CHILDRENS HEALTH PLAN (TX)** was upgraded to C+ from C in March 2018 based on an increase in the capitalization index.

**FIRST MEDICAL HEALTH PLAN INC (PR)** was upgraded to E from E- in March 2018 based on an increase in the capitalization index and expansion in the profitability index.

**FREEDOM HEALTH INC (FL)** was upgraded to D- from E in March 2018 based on an increase in the capitalization index.

**FRESNO-KINGS-MADERA REGIONAL HEALTH (CA)** was upgraded to D+ from D in March 2018 based on an increase in the capitalization index.

**HARBOR HEALTH PLAN INC (MI)** was upgraded to E from E- in March 2018 based on substantial expansion in the profitability index, substantial development in the stability index, and an increase in the capitalization index.

**HEALTH ALLIANCE NORTHWEST HEALTH PL (WA)** was upgraded to B- from C+ in March 2018 based on substantial development in the stability index, expansion in the profitability index, and an increase in the capitalization index.

**HEALTH FIRST HEALTH PLANS INC (FL)** was upgraded to B from B- in March 2018 based on development in the stability index and an increase in the capitalization index.

**HEALTH FIRST INS INC (FL)** was upgraded to D from D- in March 2018 based on expansion in the profitability index.

**HEALTH OPTIONS INC** was upgraded to B+ from B in March 2018 based on the overall strength of the index ratios

**HOOSIER MOTOR MUTUAL INS CO (IN)** was upgraded to B from C+ in March 2018 based on expansion in the profitability index.

**KENTUCKY HOME LIFE INS CO** was upgraded to C- from D+ in January 2018 based on an improved capitalization index and an improved five-year profitability index. composite rating for affiliated Kentucky National Ins Group LLC rose to C- from D+.

**LIBERTY UNION LIFE ASR CO** was upgraded to C from C- in March 2018 based on the overall strength of the index ratios

**LOYAL AMERICAN LIFE INS CO** was upgraded to B- from C+ in January 2018 based on a markedly improved capitalization index and a higher stability index.

**MCLAREN HEALTH PLAN COMMUNITY (MI)** was upgraded to B- from C+ in March 2018 based on an increase in the capitalization index.

**MCLAREN HEALTH PLAN INC (MI)** was upgraded to A- from B in March 2018 based on an increase in the capitalization index.

**MISSOURI VALLEY LIFE AND HLTH INS CO** was upgraded to C+ from C in January 2018 based on a higher stability index. enhanced financial strength of affiliates in Blue Cross Blue Shield Kansas City Group.

## Rating Upgrades (Continued)

**NEW ERA LIFE INS CO OF THE MIDWEST** was upgraded to C+ from C in January 2018 based on an improved capitalization index, an improved investment safety index, an improved five-year profitability index and a markedly improved stability index.

**NORTH AMERICAN INS CO** was upgraded to B from B- in January 2018 based on a higher capitalization index and a markedly improved five-year profitability index.

**OPTIMA HEALTH PLAN (VA)** was upgraded to A- from B+ in March 2018 based on expansion in the profitability index and an increase in the capitalization index.

**OPTIMUM HEALTHCARE INC** was upgraded to E from E- in March 2018 based on the overall strength of the index ratios

**PARTNERRE LIFE RE CO OF AM** was upgraded to C from C- in January 2018 based on a markedly improved stability index. composite rating for affiliated Aurigen Capital Limited Group rose to C+ from E.

**PRIORITY HEALTH (MI)** was upgraded to A from A- in March 2018 based on an increase in the capitalization index.

**PRIORITY HEALTH INS CO (MI)** was upgraded to B from B- in March 2018 based on expansion in the profitability index and an increase in the capitalization index.

**PROSPECT HEALTH PLAN (CA)** was upgraded to E+ from E in March 2018 based on an increase in the capitalization index and development in the stability index.

**RYDER HEALTH PLAN INC (PR)** was upgraded to C from C- in March 2018 based on expansion in the profitability index.

**SELECTCARE HEALTH PLANS INC (TX)** was upgraded to C+ from C in March 2018 based on expansion in the profitability index.

**SUN LIFE ASR CO OF CANADA** was upgraded to D- from E+ in January 2018 based on a higher capitalization index, a higher investment safety index, an improved five-year profitability index and a higher stability index.

**TIMBER PRODUCTS MANUFACTURERS TRUST (WA)** was upgraded to D- from E+ in March 2018 based on a substantial increase in the capitalization index, progress in the liquidity index, and expansion in the profitability index.

**TRUSTED HEALTH PLAN INC (DC)** was upgraded to C+ from C in March 2018 based on an increase in the capitalization index and progress in the liquidity index.

**UNICARE HEALTH PLAN OF WEST VIRGINIA (WV)** was upgraded to A- from B+ in March 2018 based on development in the stability index, expansion in the profitability index, and an increase in the capitalization index.

**UNITED SECURITY ASR CO OF PA** was upgraded to E+ from E in January 2018 based on a higher capitalization index and a higher five-year profitability index.

**UPMC HEALTH PLAN INC (PA)** was upgraded to A- from B+ in March 2018 based on development in the stability index and an increase in the capitalization index.

**UPPER PENINSULA HEALTH PLAN INC (MI)** was upgraded to A from A- in March 2018 based on an increase in the capitalization index.

**WEST COAST LIFE INS CO** was upgraded to B- from C+ in January 2018 based on an improved five-year profitability index and a higher stability index.

## Rating Downgrades

**AEGIS SECURITY INS CO** was downgraded to C+ from B- in February 2018 based on a decrease in the profitability index from a 5.30(good) to 5.10(good) and capitalization index from a 3.80(fair) to 3.60(fair).

**AETNA HEALTH OF CALIFORNIA INC (CA)** was downgraded to C+ from B in March 2018 based on a substantial drop in the stability index, a diminishment in the profitability index, a decrease in the capitalization index, and contraction in the liquidity index.

**AETNA HEALTH OF UTAH INC (UT)** was downgraded to C+ from B- in March 2018 based on a substantial drop in the stability index, a diminishment in the profitability index, and contraction in the liquidity index.

**AETNA HEALTHASSURANCE PA INC (PA)** was downgraded to D from C+ in March 2018 based on a decrease in the capitalization index and a drop in the stability index.

**AMERICASHEALTH PLAN INC (CA)** was downgraded to E+ from D in March 2018 based on contraction in the liquidity index.

**ATLANTIC SPECIALTY INS CO** was downgraded to C+ from B- in February 2018 based on a decrease in the profitability index from a 3.00(fair) to 2.20(weak). Other factors: Capital and surplus decreased during the period by 21.9%, from $595.9 million to $488.7 million.

**CALIFORNIA HEALTH & WELLNESS PLAN (CA)** was downgraded to C from B- in March 2018 based on a substantial drop in the stability index, a diminishment in the profitability index, and a decrease in the capitalization index.

**CARESOURCE WEST VIRGINIA CO (WV)** was downgraded to C from B- in March 2018 based on a substantial diminishment in the profitability index.

**COLORADO BANKERS LIFE INS CO** was downgraded to B- from B in January 2018 due to a significant decline in its capitalization index and a declining investment safety index. In addition, the financial strength of affiliates in SNA Capital LLC is declining Group.

**COMMUNITY HEALTH CHOICE INC (TX)** was downgraded to D from C- in March 2018 based on a substantial decline in the capitalization index.

**COX HEALTH SYSTEMS INS CO (MO)** was downgraded to D+ from C- in March 2018 based on a substantial decline in the capitalization index, a drop in the stability index, and contraction in the liquidity index.

**EQUITABLE LIFE & CASUALTY INS CO** was downgraded to B- from B in January 2018 due to a significant decline in its capitalization index, a substantially lower investment safety index and a significant decline in its five-year profitability index.

**FIRST CARE INC (MD)** was downgraded to C+ from B- in March 2018 based on a substantial diminishment in the profitability index.

**GHS INS CO (OK)** was downgraded to E- from E in March 2018 based on a decrease in the capitalization index.

**HARVARD PILGRIM HEALTH CARE OF CT (CT)** was downgraded to D+ from C- in March 2018 based on a drop in the stability index and a diminishment in the profitability index.

**HEALTHSPRING L&H INS CO (TX)** was downgraded to C+ from B- in March 2018 based on a diminishment in the profitability index and a decrease in the capitalization index.

**KAISER FNDTN HLTH PLAN OF WA (WA)** was downgraded to B+ from A- in March 2018 based on a drop in the stability index.

**PARTNERSHIP HEALTHPLAN OF CALIFORNIA (CA)** was downgraded to A- from A in March 2018 based on a substantial diminishment in the profitability index and a substantial drop in the stability index.

**PREMIER HEALTH PLAN SERVICES INC (CA)** was downgraded to D from C- in March 2018 based on a substantial diminishment in the profitability index, a substantial decline in the capitalization index, a substantial drop in the stability index, and contraction in the liquidity index.

**SOUNDPATH HEALTH (WA)** was downgraded to E- from E in March 2018 based on a substantial decline in the capitalization index, a drop in the stability index, and contraction in the liquidity index.

## Rating Downgrades (Continued)

**TOTAL HEALTH CARE INC (MI)** was downgraded to C+ from B- in March 2018 based on a diminishment in the profitability index.

**TRH HEALTH INS CO (TN)** was downgraded to C from C+ in March 2018 based on a diminishment in the profitability index and a decrease in the capitalization index.

**TRIPLE-S SALUD INC (PR)** was downgraded to B- from B in March 2018 based on a substantial drop in the stability index, a decrease in the capitalization index, and a diminishment in the profitability index.

**UNITED HEALTHCARE OF ALABAMA INC (AL)** was downgraded to B- from B in March 2018 based on a substantial drop in the stability index, a decrease in the capitalization index, and a diminishment in the profitability index.

**UNITEDHEALTHCARE BENEFITS OF TEXAS (TX)** was downgraded to B- from B in March 2018 based on a substantial drop in the stability index and a decrease in the capitalization index.

# Appendix

# Risk-Adjusted Capital in Weiss Rating Models

There are three distinct rating models used to generate the ratings in this Guide. The first model is for companies that register with state insurance departments under the official classification of Life and Annuity Insurers. The second model is for companies that register under the official classification of Property and Casualty Insurers. The third is for health insurers that register as Health plans with the state insurance departments.

A key aspect of both models is the risk-adjusted capital calculations. Therefore, these are discussed in greater detail.

## Risk-Adjusted Capital for Life and Annuity Insurers in Weiss Rating Model

Among the most important indicators used in the analysis of an individual company are our two risk-adjusted capital ratios, which are useful tools in determining exposure to investment, liquidity and insurance risk in relation to the capital the company has to cover those risks.

The first risk-adjusted capital ratio evaluates the company's ability to withstand a moderate loss scenario. The second ratio evaluates the company's ability to withstand a severe loss scenario.

In order to calculate these risk-adjusted capital ratios, we follow these steps:

**1. Capital Resources** First, we add up all of the company's resources which could be used to cover losses. These include capital, surplus, the Asset Valuation Reserve (AVR), and a portion of the provision for future policyholders' dividends, where appropriate. Additional credit may also be given for the use of conservative reserving assumptions and other "hidden capital" when applicable.

**2. Target Capital** Next, we determine the company's target capital. This answers the question: Based upon the company's level of risk in both its insurance business and its investment portfolio, how much capital would it need to cover potential losses during a moderate loss scenario? In other words, we determine how much capital we believe this company *should* have.

**3. Risk-Adjusted Capital Ratio #1** We compare the results of step 1 with those of step 2. Specifically, we divide the "capital resources" by the "target capital" and express it in terms of a ratio. This ratio is called RACR #1. (See next page for more detail on methodology.)

If a company has a Risk-Adjusted Capital Ratio of 1.0 or more, it means the company has all of the capital we believe it requires to withstand potential losses which could be inflicted by a moderate loss scenario. If the company has less than 1.0, it does not currently have all of the basic capital resources we think it needs. During times of financial distress, companies often have access to additional capital through contributions from a parent company, current profits or reductions in policyholder dividends. Therefore, an allowance is made in our rating system for firms with somewhat less than 1.0 Risk-Adjusted Capital Ratios.

**4. Risk-Adjusted Capital Ratio #2** We repeat steps 2 and 3, but now assuming a severe loss scenario. This ratio is called RACR #2.

**5. Capitalization Index** We convert RACR #1 and #2 into an index. It is measured on a scale of zero to ten, with ten being the best and seven or better considered strong. A company whose capital, surplus and AVR equal its target capital will have a Risk-Adjusted Capital Ratio of 1.0 and a Risk-Adjusted Capital Index of 7.0.

## How We Determine Target Capital

The basic procedure for determining target capital is to ask these questions:

1. What is the breakdown of the company's investment portfolio and types of business?
2. For each category, what are the potential losses which could be incurred in the loss scenario?
3. In order to cover those potential losses, how much in capital resources does the company need? It stands to reason that more capital is needed as a cushion for losses on high-risk investments, such as junk bonds, than would be necessary for low-risk investments, such as AAA-rated utility bonds.

   Unfortunately, the same questions we have raised about Wall Street rating systems with respect to how they rate insurance companies can be asked about the way they rate bonds. However, we do not rate bonds ourselves. Therefore, we must rely upon the bond ratings of other rating agencies. This is another reason why we have stricter capital requirements for the insurance companies. It accounts for the fact that they may need some extra protection in case an AAA-rated bond may not be quite as good as it appears to be.

   Finally, target capital is adjusted for the company's spread of risk in the diversification of its investment portfolio, the size and number of the policies it writes and the diversification of its business.

**Table 1** on the next page shows target capital percentages used in Weiss Risk-Adjusted Capital Ratios #1 and #2 (RACR #1 and RACR #2).

The percentages shown in the table answer the question: How much should the firm hold in capital resources for every $100 it has committed to each category? Several of the items in Table 1 are expressed as ranges. The actual percentages used in the calculation of target capital for an individual company may vary due to the levels of risks in the operations, investments or policy obligations of that specific company.

**Table 1. Target Capital Percentages**

| | Weiss Ratings | |
|---|---|---|
| **Asset Risk** | **RACR#1 (%)** | **RACR#2 (%)** |
| Bonds | | |
| *Government guaranteed bonds* | 0 | 0 |
| *Class 1* | .5-.75 | 1-1.5 |
| *Class 2* | 2 | 5 |
| *Class 3* | 5 | 15 |
| *Class 4* | 10 | 30 |
| *Class 5* | 20 | 60 |
| *Class 6* | 20 | 60 |
| Mortgages | | |
| *In good standing* | 0.5 | 1 |
| *90 days overdue* | 1.7-20 | 3.8-25 |
| *In process of foreclosure* | 25-33 | 33-50 |
| Real Estate | | |
| *Class 1* | 20 | 50 |
| *Class 2* | 10 | 33 |
| Preferred Stock | | |
| *Class 1* | 3 | 5 |
| *Class 2* | 4 | 6 |
| *Class 3* | 7 | 9 |
| *Class 4* | 12 | 15 |
| *Class 5* | 22 | 29 |
| *Class 6* | 30 | 39 |
| *Class 7* | 3-30 | 5-39 |
| Common Stock | | |
| *Unaffiliated* | 25 | 33 |
| *Affiliated* | 25-100 | 33-100 |
| Short-term investment | 0.5 | 1 |
| Premium notes | 2 | 5 |
| Collateral loans | 2 | 5 |
| Separate account equity | 25 | 33 |
| Other invested assets | 5 | 10 |
| **Insurance Risk** | | |
| Individual life reserves* | .06-.15 | .08-.21 |
| Group life reserves* | .05-.12 | .06-.16 |
| Individual Health Premiums | | |
| *Class 1* | 12-20 | 15-25 |
| *Class 2* | 9.6 | 12 |
| *Class 3* | 6.4 | 8 |
| *Class 4* | 12-28 | 15-35 |
| *Class 5* | 12-20 | 15-25 |
| Group Health Premiums | | |
| *Class 1* | 5.6-12 | 7-15 |
| *Class 2* | 20 | 25 |
| *Class 3* | 9.6 | 12 |
| *Class 4* | 6.4 | 8 |
| *Class 5* | 12-20 | 15-25 |
| Managed care credit | 5-40 | 6-50 |
| Premiums subject to rate guarantees | 100-209 | 120-250 |
| Individual claim reserves | 4 | 5 |
| Group claim reserves | 4 | 5 |
| Reinsurance | 0-2 | 0-5 |
| **Interest Rate Risk** | | |
| Policy loans | 0-2 | 0-5 |
| Life reserves | 1-2 | 1-3 |
| Individual annuity reserves | 1-3 | 1-5 |
| Group annuity reserves | 1-2 | 1-3 |
| Guaranteed interest contract reserves | 1-2 | 1-3 |

All numbers are shown for illustrative purposes. Figures actually used in the formula vary annually based on industry experience.
*Based on net amount at risk.

| **Investment Class** | | **Descriptions** |
|---|---|---|
| Government guaranteed bonds | | Guaranteed bonds issued by U.S. and other governments which receive the top rating of state insurance commissioners. |
| Bonds | Class 1 | Investment grade bonds rated AAA, AA or A by Moody's or Standard & Poor's or deemed AAA - A equivalent by state insurance commissioners. |
| | Class 2 | Investment grade bonds with some speculative elements, rated BBB or equivalent. |
| | Class 3 | Noninvestment grade bonds, rated BB or equivalent. |
| | Class 4 | Noninvestment grade bonds, rated B or equivalent. |
| | Class 5 | Noninvestment grade bonds, rated CCC, CC or C or equivalent. |
| | Class 6 | Noninvestment grade bonds, in or near default. |
| Mortgages | | Mortgages in good standing |
| | | Mortgages 90 days past due |
| | | Mortgages in process of foreclosure |
| Real Estate | Class 1 | Properties acquired in satisfaction of debt. |
| | Class 2 | Company occupied and other investment properties. |
| Preferred stock | Class 1 | Highest quality unaffiliated preferred stock. |
| | Class 2 | High quality unaffiliated preferred stock. |
| | Class 3 | Medium quality unaffiliated preferred stock. |
| | Class 4 | Low quality unaffiliated preferred stock. |
| | Class 5 | Lowest quality unaffiliated preferred stock. |
| | Class 6 | Unaffiliated preferred stock, in or near default. |
| | Class 7 | Affiliated preferred stock. |
| Common stock | | Unaffiliated common stock. |
| | | Affiliated common stock. |
| Short-term investments | | All investments whose maturities at the time of acquisition were one year or less. |
| Premium Notes | | Loans for payment of premiums. |
| Collateral loans | | Loans made to a company or individual where the underlying security is in the form of bonds, stocks, or other marketable securities. |
| Separate account assets | | Investments held in an account segregated from the general assets of the company, generally used to provide variable annuity benefits. |
| Other invested assets | | Any invested assets that do not fit under the main categories above. |
| Individual life reserves | | Funds set aside for payment of life insurance benefits under an individual contract rather than a company or group, underwriting based on individual profile. |
| Group life reserves | | Funds set aside for payment of life insurance benefits under a contract with at least 10 people whereby all members have a common interest and are joined for a reason other than to obtain insurance. |
| Individual health premiums | Class 1 | Usual and customary hospital and medical premiums which include traditional medical reimbursement plans that are subject to annual rate increases based on the company's claims experience. |
| | Class 2 | Medicare supplement, dental, and other limited benefits anticipating rate increases. |
| | Class 3 | Hospital indemnity plans, accidental death and dismemberment policies, and other limited benefits not anticipating rate increases. |

| | | |
|---|---|---|
| | Class 4 | Noncancelable disability income. |
| | Class 5 | Guaranteed renewable disability income. |
| Group health premiums | Class 1 | Usual and customary hospital and medical premiums which include traditional medical reimbursement plans that are subject to annual rate increases based on the company's claims experience. |
| | Class 2 | Stop loss and minimum premium where a known claims liability is minimal or nonexistent. |
| | Class 3 | Medicare supplement, dental, and other limited benefits anticipating rate increases. |
| | Class 4 | Hospital indemnity plans, accidental death and dismemberment policies, and other limited benefits not anticipating rate increases. |
| | Class 5 | Disability Income. |
| Managed care credit | | Premiums for HMO and PPO business which carry less risk than traditional indemnity business. Included in this credit are provider compensation arrangements such as salary, capitation and fixed payment per service. |
| Premiums subject to rate guarantees | | Health insurance premiums from policies where the rate paid by the policyholder is guaranteed for a period of time, such as one year, 15 months, 27 months or 37 months. |
| Individual claim reserves | | Accident and health reserves for claims on individual policies. |
| Group claim reserves | | Accident and health reserves for claims on group policies. |
| Reinsurance | | Amounts recoverable on paid and unpaid losses for all reinsurance ceded; unearned premiums on accident and health reinsurance ceded; and funds held with unauthorized reinsurers. |
| Policy loans | | Loans against the cash value of a life insurance policy. |
| Life reserves | | Reserves for life insurance claims net of reinsurance and policy loans. |
| Individual annuity reserves | | Reserves held in order to pay off maturing individual annuities or those surrendered before maturity. |
| Group annuity reserves | | Reserves held in order to pay off maturing group annuities or those surrendered before maturity. |
| GIC reserves | | Reserves held to pay off maturing guaranteed interest contracts. |

**Table 2.** Bond Default Rates - potential losses as a percent of bond portfolio

| *Bond Rating* | *(1) Moody's 15 Yr Rate (%)* | *(2) Moody's 12 Yr Rate (%)* | *(3) Worst Year (%)* | *(4) 3 Cum. Recession Years (%)* | *(5) Weiss 15 Year Rate (%)* | *(6) Assumed Loss Rate (%)* | *(7) Losses as % of Holdings (%)* | *(8) RACR #2 Rate (%)* |
|---|---|---|---|---|---|---|---|---|
| Aaa | 0.73 | 0.55 | 0.08 | 0.24 | 0.79 | 50 | 0.95 | 1.00 |
| Aa | 1.39 | 1.04 | 0.13 | 0.39 | 1.43 | 50 | 1.09 | 1.00 |
| A | 4.05 | 2.96 | 0.35 | 1.05 | 4.02 | 55 | 2.02 | 1.00 |
| Baa | 7.27 | 5.29 | 0.67 | 2.02 | 7.31 | 60 | 5.15 | 5.00 |
| Ba | 23.93 | 19.57 | 2.04 | 6.11 | 25.68 | 65 | 23.71 | 15.00 |
| B | 43.37 | 39.30 | 4.99 | 14.96 | 54.26 | 70 | 43.57 | 30.00 |

## Comments On Target Capital Percentages

The factors that are chiefly responsible for the conservative results of our Risk-Adjusted Capital Ratios are the investment risks of bond Classes 2 - 6, mortgages, real estate and affiliate common stock as well as the interest rate risk for annuities and GICs. Comments on the basis of these figures are found below. Additional comments address factors that vary based on particular performance or risk characteristics of the individual company.

**Bonds** Target capital percentages for bonds are derived from a model that factors in historical cumulative bond default rates from the last 45 years and the additional loss potential during a prolonged economic decline. **Table 2** shows how this was done for each bond rating classification. A 15-year cumulative default rate is used (column 1), due to the 15-year average maturity at issue of bonds held by life insurance companies. These are historical default rates for 1970-2015 for each bond class, taken from *Annual Default Study.*

To factor in the additional loss potential of a severe three-year-long economic decline, we reduced the base to Moody's 12-year rate (column 2), determined the worst single year experience (column 3), extended that experience over three years (column 4), and added the historical 12-year rate to the 3-year projection to derive Weiss Ratings 15-year default rate (column 5). The next step was to determine the losses that could be expected from these defaults. This would be equivalent to the capital a company should have to cover those losses. Loss rates were assigned for each bond class (column 6), based on the fact that higher-rated issues generally carry less debt and the fact that the debt is also better secured, leading to higher recovery rates upon default. Column 7 shows losses as a percent of holdings for each bond class. Column 8 shows the target capital percentages that are used in RACR #2 (Table 1, RACR #2 column, Bonds – classes 1 to 6).

Regulations limiting junk bond holdings of insurers to a set percent of assets are a tacit acknowledgement that the reserve requirements used by State Insurance Commissioners are inadequate. If the figure adequately represented full loss potential, there would be no need to limit holdings through legislation since an adequate loss reserve would provide sufficient capital to absorb potential losses.

**Mortgages**

Mortgage default rates for the Risk-Adjusted Capital Ratios are derived from historical studies of mortgage and real estate losses in selected depressed markets. The rate for RACR #2 (Table 1, RACR #2 column, Mortgages – 90 days overdue) will vary between 3.8% and 25%, based on the performance of the company's mortgage portfolio in terms of mortgage loans 90 days or more past due, in process of foreclosure and foreclosed during the previous year.

**Real Estate**

The 33% rate (Table 1, RACR #2 column, Real Estate - Class 2) used for potential real estate losses in Weiss Ratings ratios is based on historical losses in depressed markets.

**Affiliate Common Stock**

The target capital rate on affiliate common stock for RACR #2 can vary between 33% and 100% (Table 1, RACR #2 column, Common stock – Affiliate), depending on the financial strength of the affiliate and the prospects for obtaining capital from the affiliate should the need arise.

**Insurance Risk**

Calculations of target capital for insurance risk vary according to categories. For individual and group life insurance, target capital is a percentage of net amount at risk (total amount of insurance in force less reserves). Individual and group health insurance risk is calculated as a percentage of premium. Categories vary from "usual and customary hospital and medical premiums" where risk is relatively low because losses from one year are recouped by annual rate increases, to "noncancellable disability income" where the risk of loss is greater because disability benefits are paid in future years without the possibility of recovery.

**Reinsurance**

This factor varies with the quality of the reinsuring companies and the type of reinsurance being used (e.g., co-insurance, modified co-insurance, yearly renewable term, etc.).

**Interest Rate Risk On Annuities**

The 1 - 5% rate on individual annuities as a percentage of reserves (Table 1, RACR #2 column 3, Individual annuity reserves), and the 1 - 3% rate for group annuities as a percentage of reserves (Table 1, RACR #2 column 3, Group annuity reserves and GICs), are derived from studies of potential losses that can occur when assets and liabilities are not properly matched.

Companies are especially prone to losses in this area for one of two reasons: (1) They promise high interest rates on their annuities and have not locked in corresponding yields on their investments. If interest rates fall, the company will have difficulties earning the promised rate. (2) They lock in high returns on their investments but allow policy surrenders without market value adjustments. If market values decline and surrenders increase, liquidity problems can result in substantial losses.

The target capital figure used for each company is based on the surrender characteristics of its policies, the interest rate used in calculating reserves and the actuarial analyses found in New York Regulation 126 filing, or similar studies where applicable.

## Risk-Adjusted Capital for Property and Casualty Insurers

Over 100 companies that are registered with state insurance departments as property and casualty insurers offer health insurance policies. Our ratings on these companies make use of the data in the Property and Casualty Statutory Statements that are required by state insurance departments. These financial statements employ a system of accounting that differs from that used by companies filing Life and Health Statutory Statements. Some of the chief distinguishing features of the Property and Casualty Statutory Accounting include:

- Life and health companies must hold reserves to protect specifically against investment losses. Property and casualty insurers keep no equivalent protection. One of the consequences of the lack of an investment loss reserve is that property and casualty companies, on the average, hold more nonaffiliated common stock than do life insurers. This factor is considered in our evaluation of capital adequacy.

- Policy reserves for life insurers are reduced to reflect investment income to be earned between the time premiums are received by the company, and the time when claims are to be paid. Property and casualty companies generally do not reduce or discount their reserves for the time value of money.

- Underwriting profits and losses for property and casualty insurers are calculated without reference to investment income.

Despite these factors, it is our goal to provide ratings that consumers can easily understand and to make technical differences as transparent to consumers as possible. The final ratings are intended to give the same message about our opinion of insurers financial strength.

As with the life and health companies, there are two risk-adjusted capital ratios, which measure whether the company has enough capital to cover unexpected losses.

However, unlike the life and health companies, the risks related to pricing and claims are more important, while the risks associated with investments are reduced because there is little exposure to risky investments such as junk bonds or mortgages.

**Pricing Risk** The risk that premium levels are not sufficient to establish adequate reserves and/or pay claims and related expenses. Individual target capital percentages are used for each line of business based on the riskiness of the line and the company's own experience with underwriting losses and reserve shortfalls. Target capital requirements are reduced to account for the time value of money.

**Risky Lines of Business and Catastrophic Losses** These include fire, earthquake, multiple peril (including storm damage), and similar personal and commercial property coverage. Even excluding Hurricane Andrew, the insured losses from natural disasters since 1989 have been far greater than in previous decades. Yet, too many insurance companies are basing their risk calculations on the assumption that losses will return to more normal levels. They are not ready for the possibility that the pattern of increasing disasters might be a real, continuing trend.

Also considered high-risk lines are medical malpractice, general liability, product liability, and other similar liability coverage. Court awards for damages often run into the millions. These settlement amounts can be very difficult to predict. This uncertainty hinders an insurer's ability to accurately assess how much to charge policyholders and how much to set aside to pay claims. Of special concern are large, unexpected liabilities related to environmental damages such as asbestos. Similar risk may lie hidden in coverage for medical equipment and procedures, industrial wastes, carcinogens, and other substances found in products previously viewed as benign. Companies that offer a variety of types of insurance in addition to health coverage can get into financial difficulties due to any of their lines of business. Accordingly, it is essential that the company's whole operation be strong. If the company is overrun with claims from an earthquake of hurricane, its ability to pay health claims will also be affected.

## Risk-Adjusted Capital for Health Insurers

As with the other rating systems, the health insurance system includes two risk-adjusted capital ratios to measure a company's ability to withstand unexpected losses during moderate and severe loss scenarios. Health insurers are more likely exposed to risk from pricing and claims than from investments. They have no interest rate risk, in terms of potential policy surrenders, the way life insurance companies do.

Capital resources include the company's net worth adjusted for surplus notes; credit or penalty for overstating or understating reserves; and credit or penalty for the company's ability to spread risk based on overall net worth of the company's affiliate group.

These health plans file yet another type of statutory statement, different from life and health or property and casualty insurers. Weiss Rating System for health insurers addresses the unique business and accounting factors relevant to these firms. Among the many differences are the following:

- Rather than setting up reserves as a liability the way life insurance companies do, health insurer claims reserves are part of net worth.

- Investments are carried at book value, but market value is shown on Schedule B of the statutory statement. Market values are considered in the capitalization and liquidity indexes.

- Health insurers do not hold reserves to protect specifically against investment losses. This factor is considered in our evaluation of capital adequacy.

- Health insurers do not have long-term obligations like life insurance and annuities. Accordingly, reserves are not discounted for the time value of money. Our analysis examines reserve adequacy by comparing one year's reserve estimates with claims and medical expenses actually paid during the subsequent year, without factoring in investment income.

# LONG-TERM CARE INSURANCE PLANNER

This planner is designed to help you decide what kind of long-term care insurance is best for you and help you shop for the policy that meets your needs. Many insurers charge a lot more – or less – for very similar policies. So there's a great benefit to shopping around. No policy is exactly alike. However, if you follow these steps, it will be easier to compare policies side by side:

**Step 1: Try to determine, ahead of time, what type of care you think you will need from others <u>beyond</u> the assistance your own family members may be able to provide:**

| | Yes | No |
|---|---|---|
| Custodial Care | [ ] | [ ] |
| Intermediate Care | [ ] | [ ] |
| Skilled Care | [ ] | [ ] |

This isn't easy, because it's often hard to anticipate your future needs, but try your best to decide if you're going to want access to one of the following. <u>Custodial care</u> is provided by someone without medical training who helps you with daily activities. <u>Intermediate care</u> includes occasional nursing and rehabilitative care supervised by skilled medical personnel. <u>Skilled care</u> includes 24-hour care provided by a skilled nurse or therapist.

**Step 2: Decide <u>where</u> you would most likely be receiving the care?**

| | Yes | No |
|---|---|---|
| In-Home Care* | [ ] | [ ] |
| Nursing Home* | [ ] | [ ] |
| Adult Day Care | [ ] | [ ] |
| Assisted Living Facility | [ ] | [ ] |
| Other _______________ | [ ] | [ ] |

*Typically available with all three levels of care – custodial, intermediate, and skilled.

Most people prefer in-home care. However, if you have no family members to help you at home, in-home care could be prohibitively expensive, especially if it requires skilled care. Nursing homes are designed for 24-hour care and are best utilized for short-term stays. Adult day care is an option, but will probably require someone, such as a family member, who can drop you off and pick you up daily. Assisted living facilities are increasingly popular, offering a good balance between independence and assistance. Other types of care could include hospice care (for the terminally ill) or respite care (temporary assistance to help relieve family members).

**Step 3: Check out the facilities in the area in which you plan to live, make sure you're comfortable with them, and find out much how they cost:**

| | Estimated Costs |
|---|---|
| In-Home Care | ____________________ |
| Nursing Home | ____________________ |
| Assisted Living Facility | ____________________ |
| Adult Day Care | ____________________ |
| Other | ____________________ |

The insurance company is going to pay you a daily benefit that will be applied toward the cost of your care. Most of the costs above that daily benefit will have to come out of your own pocket. Therefore, find a facility that you'd be comfortable with, and then try to get a general idea of how much it would cost. Each facility may offer a different rate schedule for each level of care it provides, so make sure you understand the differences. For care within your home, contact a home care agency and ask them about the going rates for home nurses and therapists. Also consider costs associated with any modifications that may be needed for your home, such as wheelchair accessibility, handicap rails, etc.

**Step 4: Try to estimate how much of the long-term care expenses you will be able to pay on your own: $________ per month.**

Your financial planner may be able to give you an estimate of your retirement income available for health care. However, even a good estimate can be off the mark, so make sure your policy covers enough to avoid being financially strapped by long-term care expenses. Later, make sure your agent takes this information into consideration when he works out the terms of your policy. He should limit your out-of-pocket expenses to what you have indicated here.

**Step 5: Try to arrive at a reasonable guess regarding when you might start using the benefits.**

________________

Again, it's hard to predict. But if you're in reasonably good health and you have a family history of longevity, that's something to consider. If you're already suffering from chronic health problems, you may need the benefits sooner rather than later. If it's more than 10 years from now, you can buy a long-term care policy with an optional inflation protection feature to help protect against the rising cost of health care. This can add significantly to the cost, but you get what you pay for. Typically, the insurance company will add an extra five percent to your daily benefit, compounded annually. Thus, if the policy provides a $100 daily benefit now, it would rise to $163 in 10 years.

**Step 6: Determine whether you prefer a "tax-qualified" policy or a "non-qualified" policy:**

| | Yes | No |
|---|---|---|
| Tax-Qualified Policy | [ ] | [ ] |
| Non-Qualified Policy | [ ] | [ ] |

If you buy a tax-qualified policy, you will be able to claim the policy premiums as itemized medical expenses on your tax return. Furthermore, the benefits you receive will not be subject to federal income taxation, up to a dollar cap. If you purchase a non-qualified policy, you will not be able to itemize the premiums. As to the benefits, the IRS has yet to clarify whether or not they will be subject to federal income taxation. Do not assume that a tax-qualified policy will automatically be more beneficial. Reason: Typically, a tax-qualified policy will have stricter guidelines as to when you can access the policy benefits. You also may not be able to take advantage of the tax benefits. You may want to consult with a tax advisor on this subject.

**Step 7: Find insurance agents in your area that specialize in long-term care policies:**

| Agent Name | Phone Number | Specialization in LTC? | Name of insurance company |
|---|---|---|---|
| ____________ | ____________ | (Y / N) | ____________________ |
| ____________ | ____________ | (Y / N) | ____________________ |
| ____________ | ____________ | (Y / N) | ____________________ |
| ____________ | ____________ | (Y / N) | ____________________ |

Long-term care insurance is very complex. Therefore, make sure you work with an agent who specializes in long-term care policies, and don't limit your choices to someone you know or who is associated with your broker. The agent should be able to help educate you and clarify any questions you have – not only on policies he or she sells, but on others as well. Try to avoid agents that work strictly with one insurance company. Complete the remaining steps with the direct assistance of the agent you choose.

**Step 8: Ask your agent for the names of at least three different policies, from different insurers, that you can compare.**

| | Policy A | Policy B | Policy C |
|---|---|---|---|
| Insurance Company Name | ____________ | ________________ | ________________ |
| Policy Name/Number | ____________ | ________________ | ________________ |

**Step 9: Have your agent check the safety rating for each company.**

| | Safety Rating |
|---|---|
| Policy A: | __________________ |
| Policy B: | __________________ |
| Policy C: | __________________ |

It may be a long time before you begin to submit claims. Therefore, you will want to make sure your insurance company will still be viable at that time. If you use the Safety Ratings, we recommend you favor companies with a rating of B+ (good) or higher, and we suggest you avoid companies with a rating of D+ (weak) or lower.

**Step 10: Favor companies that have more experience with long-term care insurance.**

| | Years of experience with long-term care | Have they ever raised rates for existing policyholders? |
|---|---|---|
| Policy A: | ______________________________ | (Y / N) |
| Policy B: | ______________________________ | (Y / N) |
| Policy C: | ______________________________ | (Y / N) |

This should not be a deal breaker. But you're better off with a company that has been offering long-term care policies for a while and has never raised rates for existing policyholders. In contrast, companies that are new in long-term care – or have a history of raising rates on existing policies – are more likely to raise your rates in the future.

**Step 11: If you're considering buying a policy with your spouse, check how you qualify for a spousal discount.**

Policy A: ____________________________________________________________

Policy B: ____________________________________________________________

Policy C: ____________________________________________________________

In some cases, you may need to be married to qualify; in others you don't have to be formally married. Some insurers require that the policies be exactly the same, while others do not.

**Step 12: Ask your agent for quotes on the monthly premiums. Make sure the quotes are based on the preferences and needs that you outlined in steps 1-6.**

| | Single Policy Premium | Combined Policy Premium | % Savings |
|---|---|---|---|
| Policy A: | ____________ | ____________ | ______ |
| Policy B: | ____________ | ____________ | ______ |
| Policy C: | ____________ | ____________ | ______ |

If you can buy your long-term care policy with a spouse or significant other, make sure you take advantage of spousal discounts, which can save you up to 20% on the combined premium.

**Step 13: Find out exactly what each policy covers in addition to the basics that you require:**

| | Policy A | Policy B | Policy C |
|---|---|---|---|
| Custodial | ( Y / N ) | ( Y / N ) | ( Y / N ) |
| Intermediate | ( Y / N ) | ( Y / N ) | ( Y / N ) |
| Skilled | ( Y / N ) | ( Y / N ) | ( Y / N ) |

The actual policies that your agent has suggested may differ somewhat from your wish list of benefits, including some that you did not ask for, or excluding others that you wanted. This may help explain some, but not all, of the price differences.

**Step 14: Ask your agent to give you a list of the types of facilities that are included and how they are defined.** Facilities may include nursing home care, in-home care, adult day care, hospice care, assisted living facilities, and other options.

Policy A

________________________________________

________________________________________

________________________________________

Policy B

________________________________________

________________________________________

________________________________________

Policy C

________________________________________

________________________________________

________________________________________

**Step 15: Find out the basic terms of coverage and reimbursement, as follows:**

**Policy A:** How the company calculates elimination period: ____________________

| Facility of Care | Elimination Periods | Benefit Periods | Daily Benefit |
|---|---|---|---|
| In-home care: | ____________ | __________ | __________ |
| Nursing home | ____________ | __________ | __________ |
| Assisted living: | ____________ | __________ | __________ |
| Adult day care: | ____________ | __________ | __________ |

**Policy B**: How the company calculates elimination period: ______________________________

| Facility of Care | Elimination Periods | Benefit Periods | Daily Benefit |
|---|---|---|---|
| In-home care: | ______________ | ___________ | ___________ |
| Nursing home | ______________ | ___________ | ___________ |
| Assisted living: | ______________ | ___________ | ___________ |
| Adult day care: | ______________ | ___________ | ___________ |

**Policy C**: How the company calculates elimination period: ______________________________

| Facility of Care | Elimination Periods | Benefit Periods | Daily Benefit |
|---|---|---|---|
| In-home care: | ______________ | ___________ | ___________ |
| Nursing home | ______________ | ___________ | ___________ |
| Assisted living: | ______________ | ___________ | ___________ |
| Adult day care: | ______________ | ___________ | ___________ |

**Elimination Period:** This is similar to a deductible. It is the amount of time you pay for services out of your own pocket before the insurance policy takes over. Typically, you can select elimination periods of 0, 30, 60, 90, or 180 days, depending on the policy and insurance company. But you must find out exactly how the elimination period is satisfied. Let's say, for example, you need care on days 1, 4 and 10. With some policies, that would be counted as only THREE days toward your elimination period. With other policies, it would be counted as TEN days, which would mean you'd start collecting the benefits much sooner.

**Benefit Period (or maximum):** Some companies tell you the length of time the policy will be paid; others just tell you the maximum value of benefits to be paid. The benefit period can typically range from 2 to 5 years, and some may even have an unlimited lifetime period.

**Daily Benefit:** The amount the policy will pay for each day of covered services. Some plans offer a daily benefit reimbursable on a weekly or monthly basis giving you more flexibility. For example, if you selected a daily benefit of $100 reimbursable on a weekly basis you would be reimbursed for up to $700 dollars per week in expenses no matter how much you incurred on any one day.

### Step 16: Determine if the policy is "a pool of money" contract.

| | Pool of money? |
|---|---|
| Policy A: | (Y / N) |
| Policy B: | (Y / N) |
| Policy C: | (Y / N) |

Most current policies will actually give you more time to collect the benefits than indicated by the benefit period. For example, in a four-year policy, if you need care on and off, you may not use up all your benefits in that four-year period. So you could continue to collect those unused benefits in subsequent years as well. These are called "pool of money" contracts. (To calculate your pool, just multiple the total numbers of days by the daily benefit.) Other policies will actually end at the end of the four years, no matter what.

### Step 17: Check into the requirements needed to activate the policy.

Policy A: ____________________________________________________________

____________________________________________________________________

Policy B: ____________________________________________________________

____________________________________________________________________

Policy C: ____________________________________________________________

____________________________________________________________________

You will need to meet what is referred to as "benefit triggers" before the policy can begin covering expenses and these can vary from policy to policy. Under most policies, you will be qualified for benefits when you meet certain conditions, such as: 1) The inability to perform activities of daily living ("ADLs"), which typically include bathing, dressing, transferring, toileting, eating, continence, and taking medication on your own; and 2) cognitive impairment. Some plans require you to satisfy either condition (1) or (2); some require that you satisfy both conditions. Still others also allow for a third trigger, often referred to as "medical necessity." This means that a doctor determines if you need care due to an injury or sickness. Make sure you find out the precise requirements of each policy.

**Step 18: Find out what other features are included (or can be added by a "rider") to the policy.**
Your agent should explain any additional features that may be included in the policies you are comparing including the following:

| | Policy A | Policy B | Policy C |
|---|---|---|---|
| Waiver of Premium | (Y / N) | (Y / N) | (Y / N) |
| Nonforfeiture | (Y / N) | (Y / N) | (Y / N) |
| Restoration of Benefits | (Y / N) | (Y / N) | (Y / N) |
| Alternate Care Plan | (Y / N) | (Y / N) | (Y / N) |
| Bed Reservation | (Y / N) | (Y / N) | (Y / N) |
| Guaranteed Renewable | (Y / N) | (Y / N) | (Y / N) |
| Inflation Protection | (Y / N) | (Y / N) | (Y / N) |

Your agent will explain the details. Just make sure that you actually need these additional benefits, because they can add substantially to your total costs.

# Medicare Prescription Drug Planner

**This planner is designed to help you compare the annual premium costs of a senior benefit package that includes prescription drug coverage. In conjunction with the worksheet attached, follow the steps for calculating the costs of prescription drug coverage options. Upon completion, you'll be able to compare the annual cost of each option. In addition to the cost, keep other out-of-pocket expenses, benefit coverage, and provider accessibility in mind, and then select the plan best suited to meet your needs.**

## STEP ONE: Review the cost of your current health care coverage.

Look up your current coverage and find the premium you pay, if any, for the coverage.

### Original Medicare – Part A and Part B coverage

Do you receive benefits directly through the Original Medicare program? ...................... Y / N

If yes, you may be paying the Part B premium (there is no premium for Part A) yourself or perhaps you have an employer plan or a Medicare Supplement insurance policy that pays the premium.

▶ Record the annual amount, if any, you pay: **Part A and B: $** ________________

Transfer this figure to the available lines under the Part A and B column on the worksheet.

### Employer Retirement Plan Coverage

Do you receive benefits through an Employer plan? ........................................................ Y / N

If yes, the coverage is most likely comprehensive and includes drug coverage.

▶ Record the annual amount, if any, you pay: **Employer Plan: $** ________________

Transfer this figure to the available lines under the Employer Plan column on the worksheet.

### Medicare Supplement Insurance Policy ("Medigap")

Do you own a Medigap Plan? ........................................................................................ Y / N

▶ If so, what do you pay in annual premiums? **Medigap Plan A thru N: $** ____________

Transfer this figure to the available line under the Medigap Plan column on the worksheet.

## Medicare Advantage Plan

Medicare Advantage policies are available through private insurers. You pay the insurer a premium and they provide coverage that is at least as good, if not better, than Medicare Part A and B. In turn, they receive reimbursement from the government. You are often restricted to a network of physicians with these plans.

Do you receive your benefits from a Medicare Advantage insurer? .................................. Y / N

▶ If so, what do you pay in annual premiums, if any? **Medicare Advantage Plan:** $ ________

Transfer this figure to the Annual Cost column in the Medicare Advantage row on the worksheet.

**STEP TWO: Find the cost of your preferred Part D Prescription Drug Provider/Plan.**

Part D is the new Prescription Drug component of the Medicare program. Under Part D you can obtain some coverage for your medications through a private provider. These plans will provide, at a minimum, the coverage mandated by the government. Otherwise each plan will vary depending on drugs covered, premiums, co-pays and participating pharmacies.

In this step we guide you through what you need to do in order to select a Part D provider. The average cost for Part D plans range from $39.32 to $63.65 per month. However, the range within each state can be significant. Your goal is to find the lowest cost plan that gives you the best price on the prescriptions you use and has convenient participating pharmacies.

Everything you need to do can be done on the Medicare website, however, you will need a computer and internet access. The site is loaded with information, so we recommend that you first spend a few hours browsing the site to learn more. The site and process of selecting a provider can be overwhelming so you may want to have a family member or someone else to work with you through this process.

**First:** Gather critical information. Make sure to have the following:

- ✓ Medicare Number ........................................................................ ____________
- ✓ Effective Date of Medicare Part A or B coverage ............................ ____________
- ✓ Birth Date ........................................................................ ____________
- ✓ Zip Code ........................................................................ ____________
- ✓ List of prescription drugs you use and their dosages.

| **Drug** | **Dosage** |
|---|---|
| ______________________ | __________ |
| ______________________ | __________ |
| ______________________ | __________ |
| ______________________ | __________ |
| ______________________ | __________ |
| ______________________ | __________ |

- ✓ Preferred pharmacies in your area.

**Pharmacy Name**

______________________

______________________

______________________

## Second: Visit www.Medicare.gov.

We can't list all of the website's steps here but to start out Click [*Compare Medicare Prescription Drug Plans*] and then Click [*Find a Medicare Prescription Drug Plan*]. You will then be asked to enter your personal information. The website will walk you through entering your prescription drugs and dosages so that you can get a list of Part D providers in your state that cover your drugs, the pharmacies and the contact information. You may select three plans to compare side by side at one time.

## Third: Narrow down your choices.

Don't overburden yourself trying to compare all 40+ plans available in your state. Narrow your list down to the five or seven plans that cover your prescriptions and contract with local pharmacies. The premium cost of a plan for the minimum coverage will run you between $57.60 to $1,756.80 per year in 2018, depending on where you live.

To narrow down your list further look for plans that reduce your out-of-pocket costs by covering the $405 deductible, the 25% co-payments and/or the $5,000 gap in coverage. After that, the government limits your co-payment to $3.35 for generic drugs and $8.35 all other drugs.

Use the lines below to enter the information to help you compare your choices. Enter the annual Premium charged by the plan and then under Deductible, Co-Pay and Gap enter the dollar amount <u>you would be responsible for</u> under each of the plan choices. Add these across to get an estimate of your total estimated costs under each plan.

| Provider/Plan Name: | Premium | | Annual Deductible (max $405) | | Co-Pay Max (max $836) | | Cost $1,250 Gap | | Total Estimate |
|---|---|---|---|---|---|---|---|---|---|
| ________ | ________ | + | ________ | + | ________ | + | ________ | = | ________ |
| ________ | ________ | + | ________ | + | ________ | + | ________ | = | ________ |
| ________ | ________ | + | ________ | + | ________ | + | ________ | = | ________ |
| ________ | ________ | + | ________ | + | ________ | + | ________ | = | ________ |
| ________ | ________ | + | ________ | + | ________ | + | ________ | = | ________ |

If you still need to narrow down your choices, then look for plans that either reduces your co-payment amount to less than $3.35 for generic drugs and $8.36 all other drugs and/or provide other benefits that you find attractive.

**<u>Final Part D Provider Selection</u>**

| **<u>Provider / Plan Name</u>** | **<u>Total Cost Estimate</u>** |
|---|---|
| ________________ | $ ________ |

Transfer the total cost estimate of your final selection (above) to the available lines under the Part D column on the worksheet.

## STEP THREE: Consider a Medicare Advantage Plan.

If you already have a Medicare Advantage plan that you are happy with, you may want to skip this step.

The Medicare Advantage program allows you to join a private plan that participates in the Medicare program. Medicare Advantage providers receive funds from the government for providing you benefits and often provides coverage beyond what Medicare offers.

Most of these plans provide prescription drug coverage at the same level or better than the requirements set by Medicare, either inclusive in their plan or in combination with a Medicare Part D provider. Either way you will only pay one premium to the Medicare Advantage insurer for all the coverage.

If you already belong to a Medicare Advantage plan they will send you information regarding their coverage for prescription drugs. Otherwise you can find information on the medicare.gov website or from the insurers through the mail, local kiosks or by calling their toll-free numbers. To narrow down your choices based on the prescription drug coverage use the following space to compare the different plans. Don't forget to check Weiss Safety Rating to find out if the insurer is in good financial health.

| Provider/Plan Name: | Premium | Annual Deductible (max $400) | Co-Pay Max (max $836) | Cost $1,250 Gap | Total Estimate |
|---|---|---|---|---|---|
| ______________ | __________ + | __________ + | __________ + | __________ = | __________ |
| ______________ | __________ + | __________ + | __________ + | __________ = | __________ |
| ______________ | __________ + | __________ + | __________ + | __________ = | __________ |
| ______________ | __________ + | __________ + | __________ + | __________ = | __________ |
| ______________ | __________ + | __________ + | __________ + | __________ = | __________ |

**Final Medicare Advantage Provider Selection**

| **Provider Plan Name** | **Total Cost Estimate** |
|---|---|
| ______________________________ | $ ______________ |

Once you have narrowed down your choices you will then want to consider other benefits that the Medicare Advantage plan offers.

When you have made a selection, transfer this figure to the Annual Cost column in the Medicare Advantage row on the worksheet.

## STEP FOUR: Find the cost of your preferred Medicare Supplement Insurance ("Medigap") policy.

If you have a Medigap policy you want to keep, then you may want to skip this step.

Medigap policies are available through private insurers. Prior to 2006 there were 10 standardized plans (referred to as A through J) that an insurer could offer. Starting in 2006, two additional plans, K and L, became available. Medigap policies help to pay the expenses not paid under Medicare Part A and B. You cannot get any prescription drug coverage from these plans as a new policyholder after 2005.

The price of Medigap policies can differ dramatically even within the same city. You can learn more about the various Medigap plans available and the premium rates you would be charged based on your age, gender, and zip code by going to our website at http://www.weissmedigap.com. Once you have educated yourself and are leaning towards the purchase of a supplemental policy, you will need to meet with an insurance agent to further refine your selection and purchase a policy.

Make sure to check the financial stability of any insurer by using Weiss Safety Rating.

Once you have selected a Medicare Supplement policy enter the annual cost under the Medigap Plan column on the worksheet. If you need an estimate to enter into the worksheet until an amount can be determined, use $2000 as a placeholder for the annual price.

## STEP FIVE: Complete the worksheet.

If you haven't done so already, use the figures from Steps 1 through 4 to fill in the dollar amounts in the relevant parts of the worksheet to determine your total annual cost for every option you want to consider. Re-use the worksheet if you need to make adjustments.

## STEP SIX: Narrow down your choices.

The worksheet helps you to narrow down your choices by providing a snapshot, based on cost, of the prescription drug benefit options available to you. Of course, premiums are only one of the components needed to make a final decision. You must also consider other out-of-pocket costs, completeness of coverage, accessibility, and insurer financial strength.

## STEP SEVEN: More Information.

Educate yourself. The www.Medicare.gov website, Medicare & You 2018 Handbook, local workshops, and Medicare benefit agents on hand at 1-800-MEDICARE are available to assist in answering your questions. Take advantage of these resources to make sure you fully understand your options.

# Medicare Prescription Drug Worksheet

| | | Part A and B | | Employer Plan | | Medigap Plan H, I or J | | Medigap Plan | | Part D | | Annual Cost |
|---|---|---|---|---|---|---|---|---|---|---|---|---|
| Medicare | Part A and B *plus* Employee Retirement Plan Coverage | $ ______ | + | $ ______ | | | | | | | = | $ ______ |
| Medicare | Part A and B *plus* existing Medigap H, I or J | $ ______ | | | + | $ ______ | | | | | = | $ ______ |
| Medicare | Part A, B and D | $ ______ | | | | | | | + | $ ______ | = | $ ______ |
| Medicare | Part A, B and D *plus* Medigap | $ ______ | | | | | + | $ ______ | + | $ ______ | = | $ ______ |
| | Medicare Advantage (Private Medicare-Sponsored Provider) including prescription drug coverage | | | | | | | | | | = | $ ______ |

# RECENT INDUSTRY FAILURES
## 2017

| Company Name | Headquarters | Industry | Date of Failure | At Date of Failure | |
|---|---|---|---|---|---|
| | | | | Total Assets ($Mil) | Safety Rating |
| IFA Insurance Co | New Jersey | P&C | 03/07/17 | 8.4 | E (Very Weak) |
| Public Service Ins Co | New York | P&C | 03/16/17 | 278.5 | E (Very Weak) |
| Zoom Health Plan Inc | Oregon | Health | 04/26/17 | 6. | U (Unrated) |
| Galen Insurance Co | Missouri | P&C | 05/31/17 | 103.0 | E- (Very Weak) |
| Fiduciary Ins. Co of America | New York | P&C | 07/25/17 | 90.7 | E- (Very Weak) |
| Evergreen Health Inc. | Maryland | Health | 07/27/17 | 37.2 | E- (Very Weak) |
| Minuteman Health Inc | Massachusetts | Health | 08/02/17 | 111.7 | E- (Very Weak) |
| Sawgrass Mutual Ins. Co | Florida | P&C | 08/22/17 | 32.3 | D+ (Weak) |
| Guarantee Ins. Co | Florida | P&C | 08/28/17 | 400.4 | E+ (Very Weak) |
| Oceanus Ins. Co A RRG | South Carolina | P&C | 09/04/17 | 52.9 | D- (Weak) |

# 2016

| Company Name | Headquarters | Industry | Date of Failure | At Date of Failure | |
|---|---|---|---|---|---|
| | | | | Total Assets ($Mil) | Safety Rating |
| Consumers Choice Health Ins Co | South Carolina | Health | 01/06/16 | 92.4 | D (Weak) |
| Moda Health Plan Inc | Oregon | Health | 01/28/16 | 445.5 | D+ (Weak) |
| Family Health Hawaii MBS | Hawaii | Health | 04/07/16 | 5.5 | D (Weak) |
| Health Republic Ins of NY Corp | New York | Health | 04/22/16 | 525.3 | D (Weak) |
| Coordinated Health Mutual Inc | Ohio | Health | 5/26/16 | 94.9 | E (Very Weak) |
| HealthyCT Inc | Connecticut | Health | 07/01/16 | 112.3 | D+ (Weak) |
| Oregons Health Co-Op | Oregon | Health | 07/11/16 | 46.6 | D (Weak) |
| Land of Lincoln Mut Health Ins Co | Illinois | Health | 07/14/16 | 107.8 | D+ (Weak) |
| Excalibur Reins Corp | Pennsylvania | P&C | 07/18/16 | 9.0 | U (Unrated) |
| Castlepoint Florida Ins | Florida | P&C | 07/28/16 | 100.00 | D (Weak) |
| Castlepoint Insurance Co | New York | P&C | 07/28/16 | 178.4 | E (Very Weak) |
| Castlepoint National Ins Co | California | P&C | 07/28/16 | 355.1 | C- (Fair) |
| Hermitage Insurance Co | New York | P&C | 07/28/16 | 167.6 | E+ (Very Weak) |
| Massachusetts Homeland Ins Co | Massachusetts | P&C | 07/28/16 | 8.9 | C (Fair) |
| North East Insurance Co | Maine | P&C | 07/28/16 | 35.9 | D (Weak) |
| York Ins Co of Maine | Maine | P&C | 07/28/16 | 47.0 | C (Fair) |
| Careconcepts Ins Inc A RRG | Montana | P&C | 08/08/16 | 3.8 | E+ (Very Weak) |
| Freelancers Consumer Operated | New Jersey | Health | 09/12/16 | 135.3 | D+ (Weak) |
| Doctors & Surgeons Natl RRG IC | Kentucky | P&C | 10/07/16 | 9.1 | E+ (Very Weak) |
| American Medical & Life Ins Co | New York | L&A | 12/28/16 | 4.4 | U (Unrated) |

# 2015

| Company Name | Headquarters | Industry | Date of Failure | At Date of Failure | |
|---|---|---|---|---|---|
| | | | | Total Assets ($Mil) | Safety Rating |
| Millers Classified Ins Co | Illinois | P&C | 01/20/15 | 2.7 | E (Very Weak) |
| Eveready Ins Co | New York | P&C | 01/29/15 | 10.6 | E- (Very Weak) |
| Jordan Funeral and Ins Co, Inc | Alabama | L&H | 02/17/15 | 1.1 | U (Unrated) |
| Drivers Insurance Co | New York | P&C | 03/12/15 | 3.0 | E- (Very Weak) |
| Lumbermens U/W Alliance | Missouri | P&C | 05/19/15 | 354.3 | E- (Very Weak) |
| Pinelands Ins Co RRG, Inc | D.C. | P&C | 08/25/15 | 4.9 | E (Very Weak) |
| Louisiana Hlth Cooperative, Inc | Louisiana | Health | 09/01/15 | 59.5 | E (Very Weak) |
| Affirmative Ins Co | Illinois | P&C | 09/16/15 | 181.2 | E (Very Weak) |
| Affirmative Casualty Ins Co | Louisiana | P&C | 10/05/15 | 32.6 | D+ (Weak) |
| Affirmative Direct Ins Co | New York | P&C | 10/05/15 | 5.3 | U (Unrated) |
| Nevada Health Co-op | Nevada | Health | 10/14/15 | 47.9 | E- (Very Weak) |
| WINHealth Partners | Wyoming | Health | 10/21/15 | 34.0 | D (Weak) |
| Kentucky Hlth Cooperative Inc | Kentucky | Health | 10/29/15 | 189.5 | D+ (Weak) |
| Regis Ins Co | Pennsylvania | P&C | 10/30/15 | 0.6 | E- (Very Weak) |
| Meritus Health Partners | Arizona | Health | 10/30/15 | 43.0 | D+ (Weak) |
| Meritus Mutual Health Partners | Arizona | Health | 10/30/15 | 45.8 | D (Weak) |
| Arches Mutual Ins Co | Utah | Health | 11/02/15 | 77.2 | D (Weak) |
| Lincoln General Ins Co | Pennsylvania | P&C | 11/05/15 | 65.6 | E- (Very Weak) |
| Advantage Health Solutions Inc | Indiana | Health | 11/06/15 | 64.2 | E (Very Weak) |
| Colorado Hlth Ins Coop Inc | Colorado | Health | 11/10/15 | 108.7 | D+ (Weak) |
| Consumer Mut Ins of Michigan | Michigan | Health | 11/13/15 | 60.4 | E- (Very Weak) |

# 2014

| Company Name | Headquarters | Industry | Date of Failure | At Date of Failure | |
|---|---|---|---|---|---|
| | | | | Total Assets ($Mil) | Safety Rating |
| Union Mutual Ins Co | Oklahoma | P&C | 01/24/14 | 5.1 | E+ (Very Weak) |
| Commonwealth Ins Co | Pennsylvania | P&C | 03/20/14 | 1.1 | E (Very Weak) |
| LEMIC Ins Co | Louisiana | P&C | 03/31/14 | 51.6 | D (Weak) |
| Interstate Bankers Casualty Co | Illinois | P&C | 04/16/14 | 16.2 | D+ (Weak) |
| Freestone Ins Co | Delaware | P&C | 04/28/14 | 421.2 | D- (Weak) |
| Alameda Alliance For Health | California | Health | 05/05/14 | 176.3 | D (Weak) |
| Sunshine State Ins Co | Florida | P&C | 06/03/14 | 22.9 | E+ (Very Weak) |
| Physicians United Plan Inc | Florida | Health | 06/09/14 | 110.7 | E (Very Weak) |
| Professional Aviation Ins Co | Nevada | P&C | 07/03/14 | N/A | N/A |
| Red Rock Ins Co | Oklahoma | P&C | 08/01/14 | 28.5 | E+ (Very Weak) |
| DLE Life Ins Co | Louisiana | L&H | 10/02/14 | 39.3 | D- (Weak) |
| Mothe Life Ins Co | Louisiana | L&H | 10/02/14 | 15.2 | E- (Very Weak) |
| First Keystone RRG Inc | S. Carolina | P&C | 10/21/14 | 13.6 | E+ (Very Weak) |
| PROAIR Risk Retention Grp Inc | Nevada | P&C | 11/12/14 | 0.5 | U (Unrated) |
| SeeChange Health Ins Co | California | Health | 11/19/14 | 23.4 | D- (Weak) |
| Florida Healthcare Plus, Inc | Florida | Health | 12/10/14 | 11.1 | U (Unrated) |
| CoOportunity Health, Inc | Iowa | Health | 12/23/14 | 195.7 | U (Unrated) |

# 2013

| Company Name | Headquarters | Industry | Date of Failure | At Date of Failure | |
|---|---|---|---|---|---|
| | | | | Total Assets ($Mil) | Safety Rating |
| Partnership Health Plan Inc | Wisconsin | Health | 01/18/13 | 27.1 | D (Weak) |
| Driver's Insurance Co | Oklahoma | P&C | 02/21/13 | 33.1 | D+ (Weak) |
| Lewis & Clark LTC RRG | Nevada | P&C | 02/28/13 | 16.4 | E (Very Weak) |
| Pride National Ins Co | Oklahoma | P&C | 03/08/13 | 17.1 | E+ (Very Weak) |
| Santa Fe Auto | Texas | P&C | 03/08/13 | 22.9 | E (Very Weak) |
| Ullico Casualty Co | Delaware | P&C | 03/11/13 | 327.7 | D (Weak) |
| Builders Ins Co Inc | Nevada | P&C | 03/15/13 | 15.0 | U (Unrated) |
| Nevada Contractors Ins Co Inc | Nevada | P&C | 03/15/13 | 49.0 | U (Unrated) |
| Universal Health Care Ins Co Inc | Florida | Health | 03/22/13 | 106.1 | C (Fair) |
| Universal Health Care Inc | Florida | Health | 03/25/13 | 109.0 | D (Weak) |
| Universal HMO of Texas | Texas | Health | 04/18/13 | 15.3 | C- (Fair) |
| Universal Health Care of NV Inc | Nevada | Health | 06/03/13 | 1.9 | D+ (Weak) |
| Liberty First RRG Ins Co | Utah | P&C | 08/06/13 | 2.5 | E (Very Weak) |
| United Contractors Ins Co Inc, RRG | Delaware | P&C | 08/22/13 | 17.0 | E (Very Weak) |
| Advance Phys. Ins RRG, Inc | Arizona | P&C | 08/29/13 | 1.9 | D (Weak) |
| Georgia Mutual Ins Co | Georgia | P&C | 09/10/13 | 3.3 | D (Weak) |
| Ocean Risk Retention Group | D. C. | P&C | 09/06/13 | 7.9 | E (Very Weak) |
| Gertrude Geddes Willis L I C | Louisiana | L&H | 10/24/13 | 4.9 | U (Unrated) |
| San Antonio Indemnity Co | Texas | P&C | 10/31/13 | 2.8 | E+ (Very Weak) |
| Higginbotham Burial Ins Co | Arkansas | L&H | 11/04/13 | 1.3 | U (Unrated) |
| Indemnity Ins Corp RRG | Delaware | P&C | 11/07/13 | 83.2 | D- (Weak) |
| Concert Health Plan Ins Co | Illinois | L&H | 12/10/13 | 1.8 | D- (Weak) |
| ICM Insurance Co | New York | P&C | 12/23/13 | 5.0 | E+ (Very Weak) |

# 2012

| Company Name | Headquarters | Industry | Date of Failure | At Date of Failure | |
|---|---|---|---|---|---|
| | | | | Total Assets ($Mil) | Safety Rating |
| Autoglass Ins Co | New York | P&C | 01/09/12 | 29.7 | U (Unrated) |
| Health Facilities of CA Mutual | Nevada | P&C | 01/10/12 | 1.9 | U (Unrated) |
| Republic Mortgage Ins Co | North Carolina | P&C | 01/19/12 | 1.4 | E (Very Weak) |
| CAGC Ins Co | North Carolina | P&C | 01/26/12 | 11.8 | U (Unrated) |
| First Sealord Surety Inc | Pennsylvania | P&C | 02/08/12 | 15.2 | U (Unrated) |
| Scaffold Industry Ins Co RRG | D.C. | P&C | 05/01/12 | 5.1 | E+ (Very Weak) |
| Financial Guaranty Ins Co | New York | P&C | 06/11/12 | 2,054.0 | E- (Very Weak) |
| Global Health Plan & Ins Co | Puerto Rico | Health | 06/13/12 | 1.1 | U (Unrated) |
| Garden State Indemnity Co, Inc | New Jersey | P&C | 06/22/12 | 2.93 | E- (Very Weak) |
| AvaHealth Inc | Florida | HMO | 06/27/12 | 3.3 | E (Very Weak) |
| American Manufacturers Mutual | Illinois | P&C | 07/02/12 | 10.3 | E+ (Very Weak) |
| Lumbermens Mutual Casualty | Illinois | P&C | 07/02/12 | 789.4 | E (Very Weak) |
| Millers First Ins Co | Illinois | P&C | 07/24/12 | 23.0 | E (Very Weak) |
| American Motorists Ins Co | Illinois | P&C | 08/16/12 | 19.7 | D (Weak) |
| Home Value Ins Co | Ohio | P&C | 08/31/12 | 3.5 | U (Unrated) |
| Northern Plains Ins Co | South Dakota | P&C | 09/18/12 | 1.4 | D (Weak) |
| Jamestown Ins Co RRG | South Carolina | P&C | 09/24/12 | 5.9 | E+ (Very Weak) |
| Interstate Auto Ins Co | Maryland | P&C | 10/11/12 | 4.6 | D (Weak) |
| Regional Health Ins Co, RRG | D.C. | P&C | 10/18/12 | 0.6 | U (Unrated) |
| DC Chartered Health Plan Inc | D.C. | HMO | 10/19/12 | 65.4 | E- (Very Weak) |
| American Fellowship Mut Ins Co | Michigan | P&C | 10/29/12 | 50.0 | D (Weak) |
| Gramercy Ins Co | Texas | P&C | 12/04/12 | 41.8 | D (Weak) |
| Triad Guaranty ASR Corp | Illinois | P&C | 12/11/12 | 16.1 | B (Good) |
| Triad Guaranty Ins Corp | Illinois | P&C | 12/11/12 | 766.7 | E (Very Weak) |

# State Insurance Commissioners'

## Website and Departmental Phone Numbers

| State | Official's Title | Website Address | Phone Number |
|---|---|---|---|
| **Alabama** | Commissioner | www.aldoi.org | (334) 269-3550 |
| **Alaska** | Director | www.dced.state.ak.us/insurance/ | (907) 465-2515 |
| **Arizona** | Director | www.id.state.az.us | (800) 325-2548 |
| **Arkansas** | Commissioner | www.insurance.arkansas.gov | (800) 282-9134 |
| **California** | Commissioner | www.insurance.ca.gov | (800) 927-4357 |
| **Colorado** | Commissioner | www.dora.state.co.us/insurance/ | (800) 930-3745 |
| **Connecticut** | Commissioner | www.ct.gov/cid/ | (860) 297-3800 |
| **Delaware** | Commissioner | www.state.de.us/inscom/ | (302) 674-7300 |
| **Dist. of Columbia** | Commissioner | disr.dc.gov/disr/ | (202) 727-8000 |
| **Florida** | Commissioner | www.fldfs.com | (800) 342-2762 |
| **Georgia** | Commissioner | www.gainsurance.org | (800) 656-2298 |
| **Hawaii** | Commissioner | www.hawaii.gov/dcca/areas/ins/ | (808) 586-2790 |
| **Idaho** | Director | www.doi.idaho.gov | (800) 721-3272 |
| **Illinois** | Director | www.idfpr.com/doi/ | (217) 782-4515 |
| **Indiana** | Commissioner | www.ia.org/idoi/ | (317) 232-2385 |
| **Iowa** | Commissioner | www.iid.state.ia.us | (877) 955-1212 |
| **Kansas** | Commissioner | www.ksinsurance.org | (800) 432-2484 |
| **Kentucky** | Executive Director | www.doi.ppr.ky.gov/kentucky/ | (800) 595-6053 |
| **Louisiana** | Commissioner | www.ldi.state.la.us | (800) 259-5300 |
| **Maine** | Superintendent | www.maine.gov/pfr/insurance/ | (800) 300-5000 |
| **Maryland** | Commissioner | www.mdinsurance.state.md.us | (800) 492-6116 |
| **Massachusetts** | Commissioner | www.mass.gov/doi/ | (617) 521-7794 |
| **Michigan** | Commissioner | www.michigan.gov/cis/ | (877) 999-6442 |
| **Minnesota** | Commissioner | www.commerce.state.mn.us | (651) 296-4026 |
| **Mississippi** | Commissioner | www.doi.state.ms.us | (800) 562-2957 |
| **Missouri** | Director | www.insurance.mo.gov/ | (800) 726-7390 |
| **Montana** | Commissioner | www.sao.state.mt.us | (800) 332-6148 |
| **Nebraska** | Director | www.nebraska.gov | (402) 471-2306 |
| **Nevada** | Commissioner | doi.state.nv.us | (775) 687-4270 |
| **New Hampshire** | Commissioner | www.nh.gov/insurance/ | (800) 852-3416 |
| **New Jersey** | Commissioner | www.state.nj.us/dobi/ | (800) 446-7467 |
| **New Mexico** | Superintendent | www.nmprc.state.nm.us/id.htm | (888) 427-5772 |
| **New York** | Superintendent | www.ins.state.ny.us | (800) 342-3736 |
| **North Carolina** | Commissioner | www.ncdoi.com | (800) 546-5664 |
| **North Dakota** | Commissioner | www.nd.gov/ndins/ | (800) 247-0560 |
| **Ohio** | Director | www.ohioinsurance.gov | (800) 686-1526 |
| **Oklahoma** | Commissioner | www.oid.state.ok.us | (800) 522-0071 |
| **Oregon** | Insurance Administrator | www.cbs.state.or.us/ins/ | (503) 947-7980 |
| **Pennsylvania** | Commissioner | www.ins.state.pa.us/ins/ | (877) 881-6388 |
| **Puerto Rico** | Commissioner | www.ocs.gobierno.pr | (787) 722-8686 |
| **Rhode Island** | Superintendent | www.dbr.state.ri.us | (401) 222-2223 |
| **South Carolina** | Director | www.doi..sc.gov | (800) 768-3467 |
| **South Dakota** | Director | www.state.sd.us/drr2/reg/insurance/ | (605) 773-3563 |
| **Tennessee** | Commissioner | www.state.tn.us/commerce/insurance/ | (800) 342-4029 |
| **Texas** | Commissioner | www.tdi.state.tx.us | (800) 252-3439 |
| **Utah** | Commissioner | www.insurance.utah.gov | (800) 439-3805 |
| **Vermont** | Commissioner | www.bishca.state.vt.us | (802) 828-3301 |
| **Virgin Islands** | Lieutenant Governor | www.ltg.gov.vi | (340) 774-7166 |
| **Virginia** | Commissioner | www.scc.virginia.gov/division/boi/ | (877) 310-6560 |
| **Washington** | Commissioner | www.insurance.wa.gov | (800) 562-6900 |
| **West Virginia** | Commissioner | www.wvinsurance.gov | (304) 558-3386 |
| **Wisconsin** | Commissioner | oci.wi.gov | (800) 236-8517 |
| **Wyoming** | Commissioner | insurance.state.wy.us | (800) 438-5768 |

# Glossary

This glossary contains the most important terms used in this publication.

**Admitted Assets** The total of all investments and business interests that are acceptable under statutory accounting rules.

**Asset/Liability Matching** The designation of particular investments (assets) to particular policy obligations (liabilities) so that investments mature at the appropriate times and with appropriate yields to meet policy obligations as they come due.

**Asset Valuation Reserve (AVR)** A liability established under statutory accounting rules whose purpose is to protect the company's surplus from the effects of defaults and market value fluctuation on stocks, bonds, mortgages, and real estate. This replaces the Mandatory Securities Valuation Reserve (MSVR) and is more comprehensive in that it includes a mortgage loss reserve, whereas the MSVR did not.

**Average Recession** A recession involving a decline in real GDP which is approximately equivalent to the average of the postwar recessions of 1957-58, 1960, 1970, 1974-75, 1980, 1981-82, 1990-1991, 2001, and 2007-2009. It is assumed, however, that in today's market, the financial losses suffered from a recession of that magnitude would be greater than those experienced in previous decades. (See also "Severe Recession.").

**Capital** Strictly speaking, capital refers to funds raised through the sale of common and preferred stock. Mutual companies have capital in the form of retained earnings. In a more general sense, the term capital is commonly used to refer to a company's equity or net worth, that is, the difference between assets and liabilities (i.e., capital and surplus as shown on the balance sheet).

**Capital Resources** The sum of various resources which serve as a capital cushion to losses, including capital, surplus, and Asset Valuation Reserve (AVR).

**Capitalization Index** An index, expressed on a scale of zero to ten, with seven or higher considered excellent, that measures the adequacy of the company's capital resources to deal with a variety of business and economic scenarios. It combines Risk-Adjusted Capital Ratios #1 and #2 as well as a leverage test that examines pricing risk.

| | |
|---|---|
| **Cash and Demand Deposits** | Includes cash on hand and on deposit. A negative figure indicates that the company has more checks outstanding than current funds to cover those checks. This is not an unusual situation for an insurance company. |
| **Collateralized Mortgage Obligation (CMO)** | Mortgage-backed bond that splits the payments from mortgage pools into different classes, called tranches. The investor may purchase a bond or tranche that passes through to him or her the principal and interest payments made by the mortgage holders in that specific maturity class (usually two, five, 10, or 20 years). The risk associated with a CMO is in the variation of the payment speed on the mortgage pool which, if different than originally assumed, can cause the total return to vary greatly. |
| **Common and Preferred Stocks** | See "Stocks". |
| **Deposit Funds** | Accumulated contributions of a group out of which immediate annuities are purchased as the individual members of the group retire. |
| **Direct Premiums Written** | Total gross premiums derived from policies issued directly by the company. This figure excludes the impact of reinsurance. |
| **Safety Rating** | Weiss Safety Ratings grade insurers on a scale from A (Excellent) to F (Failed). Ratings are based on five major factors: investment safety, policy leverage, capitalization, profitability, and stability of operations. |
| **Five-Year Profitability Index** | See "Profitability Index." |
| **Government Securities** | Securities issued and/or guaranteed by U.S. and foreign governments which are rated as highest quality (Class 1) by state insurance commissioners. Included in this category are bonds issued by governmental agencies and guaranteed with the full faith and credit of the government. Regardless of the issuing entity, they are viewed as being relatively safer than the other investment categories. See "Investment Grade Bonds" to determine which items are excluded from this category. |
| **Health Claims Reserve** | Funds set aside from premiums for the eventual payment of health benefits after the end of the statement year. |
| **Insurance Risk** | The risk that the level of claims and related expenses will exceed current premiums plus reserves allocated for their payment. |
| **Interest Rate Risk** | The risk that, due to changes in interest rates, investment income will not meet the needs of policy commitments. This risk can be reduced by effective asset/liability matching. |

**Invested Assets** The total size of the firm's investment portfolio.

**Investment Grade Bonds** This covers all investment grade bonds other than those listed in "Government Securities" (above). Specifically, this includes: (1) nonguaranteed obligations of governments, (2) obligations of governments rated as Class 2 by state insurance commissioners, (3) state and municipal bonds, plus (4) investment grade corporate bonds.

**Investment Safety Index** Measured on a scale of zero to ten, with ten being the best and seven or better considered strong. Each investment area is rated as to quality and vulnerability during an unfavorable economic environment (updated using quarterly data when available).

**Investments in Affiliates** Includes bonds, preferred stocks, and common stocks, as well as other vehicles which many insurance companies use to invest in, and establish a corporate link with affiliated companies.

**Life and Annuity Claims Reserve** Funds set aside from premiums for the eventual payment of life and annuity claims.

**Liquidity Index** An index, expressed on a scale from zero to ten, with seven or higher considered excellent, which measures the company's ability to raise the necessary cash to meet policyholder obligations. This index includes a stress test which considers the consequences of a spike in claims or a run on policy surrenders. Sometimes a company may appear to have the necessary resources, but may be unable to sell its investments at the prices at which they are valued in the company's financial statements.

**Mandatory Security Valuation Reserve (MSVR)** Reserve for investment losses and asset value fluctuation mandated by the state insurance commissioners for companies registered as life and health insurers. As of December 31, 1992, this was replaced by the Asset Valuation Reserve. HMDI companies are not required to establish such a reserve.

**Moderate Loss Scenario** An economic decline from current levels approximately equivalent to that of the average postwar recession.

**Mortgages in Good Standing** Mortgages which are current in their payments (excludes mortgage-backed securities).

**Net Premiums Written** The total dollar volume of premiums retained by the company. This figure is equal to direct premiums written, plus reinsurance assumed less reinsurance ceded.

**Noninvestment Grade Bonds** Low-rated issues, commonly known as "junk bonds," which carry a high risk as defined by the state insurance commissioners. These include bond Classes 3 - 6.

**Nonperforming Mortgages** Mortgages which are (a) 90 days or more past due or (b) in process of foreclosure.

**Other Investments** Items not included in any of the other categories such as contract loans (which include premium notes), receivables for securities, aggregate write-ins and other invested assets.

| | |
|---|---|
| **Other Structured Securities** | Nonresidential-mortgage-related and other securitized loan-backed or asset-backed securities. This category also includes CMOs with noninvestment grade ratings. |
| **Policy Leverage** | A measure of insurance risk based on the relationship of net premiums to capital resources. |
| **Policy Loans** | Loans to policyholders under insurance contracts. |
| **Profitability Index** | Measured on a scale of zero to ten, with ten being the best and seven or better considered strong. A composite of five factors: (1) gain or loss on operations, (2) consistency of operating results, (3) impact of operating results on surplus, (4) adequacy of investment income as compared to the needs of policy reserves, and (5) expenses in relation to industry averages. Thus, the overall index is an indicator of the health of a company's current and past operations. |
| **Purchase Money Mortgages** | Mortgages written by an insurance company to facilitate the sale of property owned by the company. |
| **Real Estate** | Direct real estate investments including property (a) occupied by the company, (b) acquired through foreclosure and (c) purchased as an investment. |
| **Reinsurance Assumed** | Insurance risk acquired by taking on partial or full responsibility for claims on policies written by other companies. (See "Reinsurance Ceded.") |
| **Reinsurance Ceded** | Insurance risk sold to another company. |
| **Risk-Adjusted Capital** | The capital resources that would be needed in a worsening economic environment (same as "Target Capital"). |
| **Risk-Adjusted Capital Ratio #1** | The capital resources which a company currently has, in relation to the resources that would be needed to deal with a moderate loss scenario. This scenario is based on historical experience during an average recession and adjusted to reflect current conditions and vulnerabilities (updated using quarterly data when available). |
| **Risk-Adjusted Capital Ratio #2** | The capital resources which a company currently has, in relation to the resources that would be needed to deal with a severe loss scenario. This scenario is based on historical experience of the postwar period and adjusted to reflect current conditions and the potential impact of a severe recession (updated using quarterly data when available). |
| **Separate Accounts** | Funds segregated from the general account and valued at market. Used to fund indexed products, such as variable life and variable annuity products. |
| **Severe Loss Scenario** | An economic decline from current levels in which the loss experience of the single worst year of the postwar period is extended for a period of three years. (See also "Moderate Loss Scenario" above.) |
| **Severe Recession** | A prolonged economic slowdown in which the single worst year of the postwar period is extended for a period of three years. (See also "Average Recession" above.) |

| | |
|---|---|
| **Stability Index** | Measured on a scale of zero to ten. This integrates a wide variety of factors that reflects the company's financial stability and diversification of risk. |
| **State of Domicile** | Although most insurance companies are licensed to do business in many states, they have only one state of domicile. This is the state that has primary regulatory responsibility for the company. Use the state of domicile to make absolutely sure that you have the correct company. Bear in mind, however, that this need not be the state where the company's main offices are located. |
| **State Guaranty Funds** | Funds that are designed to raise cash from existing insurance carriers to cover policy claims of bankrupt insurance companies. |
| **Stocks** | Common and preferred equities, including ownership in affiliates. |
| **Surplus** | The difference between assets and liabilities, including paid-in contributed surplus, plus the statutory equivalent of "retained earnings" in noninsurance business corporations. |
| **Target Capital** | See "Risk-Adjusted Capital." |
| **Total Assets** | Total admitted assets, including investments and other business assets. See "Admitted Assets." |